World Cars®

1980

ISBN 0-910714-12-6
LC 74-643381
Published in the English language
edition throughout the world in 1980
by
HERALD BOOKS
Pelham, New York

WORLD CARS® 1980

Published annually by
THE AUTOMOBILE CLUB OF ITALY

Edited by
L'EDITRICE DELL'AUTOMOBILE LEA

Management
ARNOLDO MONDADORI EDITORE
OFFICINE GRAFICHE

HERALD BOOKS, PELHAM, NEW YORK

Cover pictures

Clénet Cabriolet (front)
Lancia Delta, Mercedes-Benz S-class,
Bertone Tundra, Ital Design Isuzu Ace of Clubs (back)

Cover and layout

Ovidio Ricci
Francesco Ricciardi

Editor

Annamaria Lösch

Contributors and correspondents

Alberto Bellucci

Gianni Costa (China, India)
John Crawford (Australia)
Filippo Crispolti
Vittorio Della Rossa
Flora Di Giovanni
Alan Langley (Great Britain)
Antonio Lioy
Roberto Nobilio
Alberto Pasquarelli
Hilmar Schmitt (Germany)
Marshall Schuon
L.J.K. Setright
Bob Tripolsky (USA)
Jack K. Yamaguchi (Japan)

Language consultant

Jean Gribble

Editorial offices

L'Editrice dell'Automobile LEA
Viale Regina Margherita 279
00198 Rome, Italy

Composition and printing

OGAM, Verona, Italy

Illustrations

Riproduzioni-Lith, Rome, Italy

SUMMARY

Editor's note

The aim of *World Cars* is to present accurate information that is as complete as possible and to present it in a concise form. It is not always easy to reconcile the search for accuracy and completeness, for clarity and uniformity, and one or two preliminary remarks may help readers consulting this reference book.

The technical data is based on questionnaires completed by motor manufacturers throughout the world, and only when this information was incomplete or not made available has it been supplemented from other reliable sources.

Different cultures have always used different formulae to express maximum power and torque. DIN and SAE standards are familiar to most readers, while Japan alone uses the Japanese Industrial Standard (JIS). Expressed in DIN, power or torque is 20% lower than when expressed in SAE gross but about the same as or slightly higher than in SAE net, while JIS ratings roughly correspond to SAE gross ratings. Horsepower in Anglo-Saxon countries expresses slightly higher power than the horsepower used by other countries (1.0139:1).

The innovation that marks recent editions of *World Cars* stems from the new units of measurement established by the Système Internationale d'Unités (SI). These are the kilowatt (kW), which replaces horsepower (hp), and the Newton metre (Nm), which replaces lb/ft. The conversion ratios are:

1 hp = 0.736 kW or 1 kW = 1.360 hp
1 kg m = 7 lb ft = 9.807 Nm or 1 Nm = 0.714 lb ft = 0.012 kg m

Fuel consumption, indicated by figures that are inevitably only a rough calculation, is based on a medium load and a cruising speed of about 60% of the car's maximum speed on a varied run. By dry weight is meant the fully-equipped car ready for the road plus water, oil and petrol.

Since two valves per cylinder are now the norm and dual braking circuits are prevalent, only exceptions to the two have been indicated. Again, when in V8 engines the cylinders are slanted at 90°, this indication has been omitted. The turning circle should be taken as between walls unless otherwise specified.

Quite often a model is available with engines differing both in size and power. For the production of the United States, Canada, South Africa, and Australia, and some German, British and Japanese makes, each of these engines is described separately. In this case, whenever they are not given, the measurements and weight are the same as in the standard version. When the power-weight ratio is given, this usually refers to the 4-door sedan version. For other countries, the various engines have been listed under "Variations" at the foot of the basic description and — except when otherwise specifically indicated — should be taken as being available for all the models that refer back to the basic description. The "Optional Accessories" also apply to all the models that refer back to the basic description, except when otherwise specified. Some accessories may become "standard" or not be available, and others may be added, but this is always specified.

Editorial problems have prevented us from making certain corrections to the prices in the main body of the volume after the end of 1979 and so the reader is advised to refer to the price index for more recent prices of models, many of which may be raised in the course of the year. When prices are shown in the currency of the country of origin, these should be taken as ex-factory and therefore subject to revision if the car is imported into another country. Prices with a single asterisk include VAT (value added tax) or its equivalent in other European countries, and in Great Britain also SCT (special car tax). Prices with two asterisks are ex-showroom. The prices for American cars refer to models equipped with a standard engine of the lowest power listed (generally a four- or six-cylinder engine). Any surcharge for higher power standard engines is indicated at the foot of the list of models and prices. For cars imported into the United States, asterisked figures denote prices ex-showroom. In view of the requirements of Federal legislation, cars imported into the United States differ from the ones on sale in the respective countries of origin. Every attempt is made to quote accurate prices but both variations in what the companies include in the price quoted and frequent price modifications make our task a difficult one.

Technical and photographic coverage is given to over 1,500 models at present in production. It has sometimes been necessary to exclude models produced in very small numbers or visually almost identical to others illustrated, and also models that, even if built or assembled under another name outside the country of origin, are to all purposes a repetition of the model presented as part of the maker's standard range.

INTELLIGENCE AND RELIABILITY

by Filippo Crispolti

Forecasts for 1979 led us to expect that the Formula 1 season would be unsettled and variable but, as it turned out, the unexpected only rarely happened. Out of the fifteen races run, six were won by a Ferrari, five by a Williams and three by a Ligier. The only victory by an outsider was the single Renault win and this isolated phenomenon did in fact lead quite a few astray, tempting prophesies of a string of successes for supercharged cars. But the technique was challenged at once by the majority of the members of the Formula One Constructors Association.

But like so many other years of Grand Prix racing, 1979 failed us neither on the level of dramatic events and sensations, nor on the more down-to-earth one of technical experimentation. The two seasons that preceded it had seen the early experiments with and then the unchallenged supremacy of the aerodynamic principle known as ground effect. This wily expedient had given the Cosworth engine a new lease of life, allowing it to put off the day when it would only sporadically be able to hold the other power units at bay. Slowly but surely, however, Lotus's rival teams had managed to absorb the new aerodynamic principle and it was only to be expected that 1979 would see the clash between the various interpretations of ground effect.

But what seemed to be a fairly simple procedure proved to be full of pitfalls. Even the Lotus technicians, instead of exploring new ground, merely tried to find further de-

Jody Scheckter and, hard by, Alan Jones who was to be his most dangerous rival in the second part of the season.

velopments for the excellent basic idea, making it exaggeratedly complicated and thus losing their way in the meanders of infinite variables that were far from easy to perfect over the short term.

The solution to the problem was a different one and only partly hinged upon ground effect. Strange to say, only a very few people paid sufficient heed to the stress imposed on the tyres by the new aerodynamic principle. In fact, since ground effect at speed entails downforce that often tops 100 kilograms, ground effect cars need completely different calibration of the springs and dampers and bear down heavily on the tyres, due to the flattening effect of both side-pods and wings.

Thus the secret of the 1979 World Championship was to work out the maximum stress the tyres could take in their present state of development, bear this factor constantly in mind and aim at sparing the tyres, particularly on corners and in braking. This in fact was the goal — at any rate in the second half of the season — of the Williams team, and one they punctually attained. They staked everything on the lightness of the whole and on overall simplicity rather than increasing the already marked vacuum obtainable under the monocoque's hull by means of systems similar to the ones used by Lotus in 1979.

But the excellent results they obtained would surely have come to nothing if there had not been a supply of rather special engines, certainly the finest in circulation, hypertuned above all as far as the "life" of the most delicate parts is concerned. Let us suppose that a connecting rod on the Cosworth is statistically reliable for a running time of a hundred hours. In the engines destined for the Williams, that "lifetime" was halved and the consequent reduction of weight improved the reliability of the whole. This kind of operation needs not so much a shrewd brain as a well-stacked bank account. When the chips are down, only an extra touch of class can guarantee competitiveness, and the Saudi-Williams stable, even if somewhat late in the day, certainly managed to make the right choice.

It might seem less than correct to deal first with the team that runs on petrodollars and not with the one that won the World Championship. But the team captained by Frank Williams, who, until the British Grand Prix this year, had never seen one of his cars first past the chequered flag, was the novelty of last season and is confirming its form this year.

The Ferrari team, too, was successful partly because it followed, somewhat accidentally, a different line from the one that, on the cards, looked like the winning one. The flat 12 engine — which purists will insist on calling a 180° Vee — does not make for an ideal outlet of the side-pods which are the basic element of ground effect. Even though the outside of the boxer unit was streamlined in the T4, by the middle of the season this was not enough. So then they worked on the exhaust pipes, pointing them upwards, and on the side-pods which were wider and had a more pronounced rear outlet.

The Lotus team ran into a troubled patch with the "80". Above, Colin Chapman himself grapples with a damper together with his mechanics. Right, the "80" in action at Zolder. The total hull raised adjustment problems.

This only partially solved the roadholding problem. The renowned reliability — only one works engine fell by the way during the whole season — did the rest, together with the careful strategy played out by Villeneuve at least. As to the tyres, Michelin — even though lacking the ultra-soft qualifying tyres — was almost always able to give the driver what he wanted. For, having to equip only for Grand Prix cars, it could have a wider range of types available. If the choice at the start was right, the result was almost in the bag. On the other hand the radial tyres did not always warn the driver in good time of a dangerous loss of pressure. This happened to Villeneuve in the memorable Dutch Grand Prix when Gilles finally threw away his chance of taking the title.

But let us analyze the various stages of this thirtieth World Championship, the ninth won at the wheel of a Ferrari. Jody Scheckter had touched down at Maranello baldly asserting that he meant to become World Champion, and the Ferrari team backed him all the way. But Jody was no mere passenger in the 312/T4. The South African worked his way to the top of the table, constant, purposeful and above all intelligent, as well as highly skilled at the wheel. There was just that certain something that gave him the edge over Villeneuve, the runner-up, at the wheel of an identical car. The points that separate Gilles from Jody are a true reflection of the gap that built up between them over the course of the season. It is a gap that may alter in the future as Villeneuve's experience widens, for he has a will to win that is a motive power needing only to be properly harnessed.

Everything started off, as usual, in Argentina but at Buenos Aires on 21 January the Formula 1 panorama — and the general outlook — was very different from the scene today. We had just seen the close of a season dominated right to the end by Lotus thanks to a fairly revolutionary technical principle. Everyone knew that the rest of the field would surely follow suit but the practical results remained to be seen. The challenge launched by Colin Chapman was sure to be swiftly taken up by all those in the speed circus whose goals are not merely economic ones but who aim at an effective development of the "formula" ratified by its technical regulations.

Certainly no one in the Formula 1 circus expected that the Ligiers would dominate as they did, above all because the French car was powered for the first time by the 8-cylinder Cosworth. The Matra twelve had been abandoned because its Vélizy constructors had given ample proof in the two preceding years that they had no intention of developing it in a way that would guarantee a competitive level of power and reliability.

And so Ligier, estranged from Matra and newly espoused to Cosworth, was not expected to give trouble. However, the red light of danger was clearly to be seen during the Castellet practice days when the Anglo-French cars were going very fast

and in practice in Argentina the Ligier supremacy was strikingly obvious. Laffite took the pole position and his team-mate, Depailler (ex-Tyrrell) was alongside him. For the French team had doubled its strength, fielding two number ones, another worrying factor for the other teams.

Laffite, however, coasted home, followed by Reutemann who had moved over to Lotus from the Ferrari team, and by Watson in the M28 McLaren. In spite of a pit stop, Depailler was fourth. In the fearful mix-up at the first start, Watson tangled with Scheckter, sparking off a multiple accident in which the worst was avoided only because there is plenty of free space on the sides of the Argentinian track. The organizers refused to allow Scheckter to start the second time because it was considered that the South African's wrist had been damaged in the accident.

In Brazil, two weeks later, came the confirmation that the Ligier exploit was no isolated episode. This time the French make brought off a resounding one-two, outclassing the rest. In this early part of the season the two Ferrari drivers had to content themselves with the old T3 and just keeping in touch, for it was clear that their cars were outdated even though they managed to earn third-row places in the grid, behind the two Ligiers and two Lotuses. The Williams team, protagonist of the second part of the season, was not yet ready, for Jones started in the seventh row and Regazzoni in the ninth. The field had not yet settled down and a valid choice of tyres by Goodyear played an important part at this stage of the championship. Since Ligier would have liked to be Michelin-shod, it was in Goodyear's interest to show that the French cars could go like the wind on its tyres. For that matter the Ligier looked like the best-prepared car and it was therefore sound policy to give it the tyres to show off its paces. Later on the policy as far as tyres were concerned underwent marked changes.

There is exactly a month's interval between Buenos Aires and the South African Grand Prix, the third in the series, and great is the curiosity on 1 March when everybody is reunited at Kyalami for the first official practice session. It is clear at once that the balance of power has shifted. The debutante Ferrari T4 wing car, even though it has to cede the honour of the pole position to Jabouille's Renault (the turbo engine of the French car is less affected by the thin air of the South African plateau), shows at once that it is to be reckoned with by taking first and second places. The French cars take no points, partly due external circumstances including a second start because of a downpour that washed out the first one after three laps. The two Ligier drivers both spin out of the race while the two Williams start out in the tenth and eleventh rows. The Lotus cars do not appear to be too badly outclassed by the more recent machines but suffer from minor technical faults. Colin Chapman is absorbed in the preparation of his new car and perhaps the attention given to the '79 suffers from this.

All in all, the third Grand Prix of the season leaves a number of questions unanswered. Lauda looks all set to play an important part with the Brabham-Alfa Romeo fitted with the new 60° Vee engine, specially built to harmonize with ground effect. Niki, third at the start, was no better than sixth at the finish.

Another month's pause and it is the turn of Long Beach, California. The town circuit is exactly suited to Villeneuve's tastes and his radial tyres. So the Canadian, together with Scheckter, repeats the South African one-two finish and the T4 confirms that it is the car to beat. The Ligiers are already in trouble but Alan Jones's third place with the Williams shows that, in the race at least, they are aiming high. The Renault has trouble in adapting to the circuit and breaks too many engines. Jabouille's fears that two cars are too many this year, before reliability has been achieved, would seem to be confirmed.

At this point the championship is on the brink of the transfer to Europe. Normally this is when the championship begins to be decided and when the advertising men go to town. This time the honour of the European "opening" goes to Spain. At Jarama the clash is acted out on a fairly slow track and so no surprises are expected. Instead, partly because of the rather special asphalt, partly because of the ever-important tyres to which a good 30% of the merit is attributed for every success, it is the Ligier that unexpectedly asserts its superiority once more, monopolizing the front row of the grid and going on to win, this time with Depailler. It is a black day for the Ferraris that can only come fourth with Scheckter and seventh with Villeneuve. But the most interesting symptom — misleading as it was later to prove — is Andretti's third place with the new Lotus 80 with integral ground effect. It is apparently of little importance that it follows home Reutemann in the old 79, a fact that causes little surprise because the 80 is only at its debut. But its expected development fails to take place and this partial success was to lead Chapman astray, making him waste pre-

Marlboro
Marlboro

Right, Scheckter who took the title by forswearing much of his aggressiveness and driving in the "Lauda-style". Villeneuve (far right), on the other hand, was often spectacular but ran too many risks. Below, the start of the French Grand Prix demonstrates the dangers of this extremely delicate phase of Grands Prix. Left, Jabouille's Renault "Turbo" during the French Grand Prix where it marked up the first win for a supercharged car. Laffite at Monte Carlo (below left) had Depailler as his rival for the last time on his home ground.

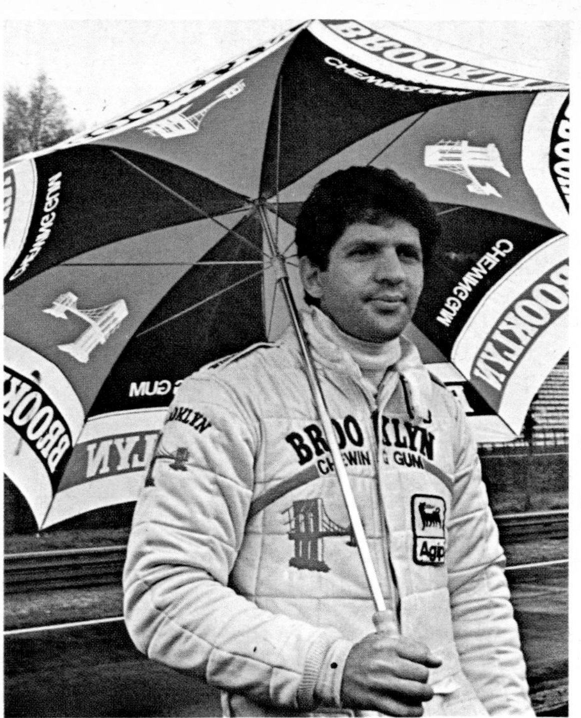

photos by Filippo Crispolti

cious time and compromise Andretti's chances of becoming champion. Another to fall into the trap was Southgate who was desiging the new Arrows to be presented at the French Grand Prix. It has some analogies with the youngest Lotus and unhappily (for Patrese and Mass) was to show it shared with the British car the inability to finish in the first three because of difficulties in preparation and replacing the springs, besides its weight and the poor cooling of the engine enclosed in the total hull.

In my opinion, this was the turning-point of the season. To match the false turning taken by the Lotus team — three more different exemplars of the 80 prove to be dogged by the same almost insoluble problems — there is the decline of the Ligiers whose showings are too irregular due to road holding problems, even if until Monza this remains the only make with any hopes of snatching the title from the Ferrari team. The Ligier team is also deprived of the services of Depailler after the Monte Carlo Grand Prix. He is replaced by Ickx after a hang-gliding accident.

The Belgian Grand Prix, usually a favourite Ferrari hunting ground, is no exception to the rule this year. It is a magnificent pursuit race for the two Ferrari men, only one of whom however takes the chequered flag. Scheckter in fact wins, but Villeneuve — after coming up through the field from twenty-fourth to third place — is brought to a halt within sniffing distance of the line by lack of petrol. The leadership of the race changes hands no less than six times and there is a family battle between the two Ligiers which ends up with Laffite in second place and Depailler off the track due to tyre trouble.

Monte Carlo, with its drawing room circuit, is once again favourable ground for the Ferraris and for the first time Scheckter and Villeneuve monopolize the front row of the grid which Laffite and Depailler had managed to hang on to in Belgium. Jody takes the lead from the start and stays there while Gilles gets too familiar with the pavements and retires with gearbox failure. Regazzoni drives a fine pursuit race and it is a debacle for the Ligiers with Laffite eliminated by his transmission and Depailler lagging badly. Lauda, who is driving a good race in second place, is rammed by Pironi. This is a pity, for the Brabham Alfa Romeo needs a good placing.

In the French Grand Prix, which this year is run on the Mickey Mouse circuit at Dijon, the Renault breaks the bank by getting its two drivers in the front row at the start. For the French firm, which has now spent exactly two years in F. 1 racing, there is an urgent need to get results if they are not to undergo heavy cuts in their racing programme. And they do get the result at long last after a race with a thrilling finish marked by a ruthless wheel-bashing duel between two "number twos", Arnoux and Villeneuve. The Canadian prevailed and torpedoed the chance of a one-two finish for the turbo-engined cars, which win with Jabouille. This success of the 1500 cc six-cylinder supercharged engine is undoubtedly an historic event for motor racing and probably marks a technical turning-point for F. 1 racing. Giacomelli's Alfa Romeo, which had made a very quiet debut at Zolder, is back on the track here, but stops for fresh tyres ruined its chances.

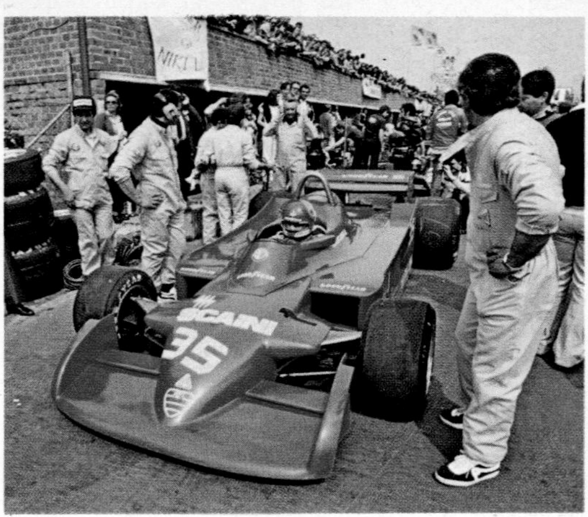

With the return of an all Alfa Romeo monocoque the F. 1 front of the real constructors is strengthened.

Another surprise was in store in the British Grand Prix and one that was to be repeated during the season. Formula 1 sees a new claimant to the throne in the Williams in a day packed with fuel feed problems for the Ferraris and roadholding headaches for the Ligiers. Jones has the impudence to snatch the pole position from Jabouille. From now on, a Williams alongside a Renault was the norm at the start.

With the British Grand Prix began the second part of the World Championship season and the series of ultra-fast circuits. These meant aerodynamic problems for the Ferrari team which pays for its ground effect with internal aerodynamic loads that limit the maximum speed. If in England Scheckter and Villeneuve started only in eleventh and thirteenth positions, even their third and fifth rows at Hockenheim in Germany are not much for a pretender to a title. Laffite, for instance, starts in the second row, behind Jabouille and Jones. The Williams here takes its revenge for its defeat at Silverstone due to trouble in the cooling system. Incredibly, Scheckter is fourth, pipped at the post by Watson. In Austria it is the Williams again followed home by the Renault. This time Arnoux takes the pole position with Jones alongside. In the race, after a fabulous (but risky) start by Villeneuve, Jones takes the lead and stays there till the finishing line. Scheckter is again naive (or correct) enough to let himself be overtaken on the last lap, this time by Laffite who sneaks into fourth place. The South African, rather mortified, looks to the future.

In Holland, too, it is Williams all the way. Arnoux is back in the pole position with the Renault but at the start the turbo car is slow in getting away because the driver has to match the turbo engine's revolutions with the clutch and the green light. Regazzoni makes a mess of things by tangling with Arnoux and so the way is open for Jones's team-mate. Scheckter, however, takes an excellent second place while Villeneuve, who had been in the lead from the eleventh to the forty-seventh lap, as usual clips the kerbs too close, wears down his tyres, spins round, and starts off again with a flat tyre, doing a whole lap on the suspension, a useless exploit that caused a good deal of criticism. Here the Canadian has to say farewell to any hopes of the championship.

The Italian Grand Prix, at a Monza renewed at last, promises to be extremely important for the assignment of the title. The Renault and the Williams again head the field at the start but the Ferrari team has a renovated T4 with external brakes and improved aerodynamics. The Ligiers are still struggling with their springs. It is a triumph for the Italian cars and the title passes from Andretti to Scheckter two races before the end of the season.

At Monza Jones has electrical trouble while the Renaults are afflicted with fragile brakes and a faulty trim. These are details on which work will be done for next season. Laffite breaks his engine and for the Ligiers it is goodbye to championship hopes.

The North American transfer is therefore merely an academic adventure. The Williams makes a comeback in Montreal, and Jones robs Villeneuve of victory on his home ground with an impudent overtaking manoeuvre on a corner. At the finish, the starting order in the front row of the grid is unchanged. Scheckter is fourth.

At Watkins Glen, the epilogue to the championship, Villeneuve upholds Ferrari's right to the championship by winning in great style a hecatomb of a race that sees only seven cars finish out of the 24 at the start. De Angelis is fourth with the Shadow. But the most startling news from America is the retirement of Niki Lauda who, unable to resign himself to driving less competitive cars than the one that gave him two titles, hangs up his helmet for the last time. Unless he changes his mind...

And thus the season comes to an end. It did not have many protagonists but was interesting on both the human and the technical level. And, what is important, there were no very serious accidents.

Special bodies

Illustrations and technical information

ARCADIPANE Bobcat AUSTRALIA

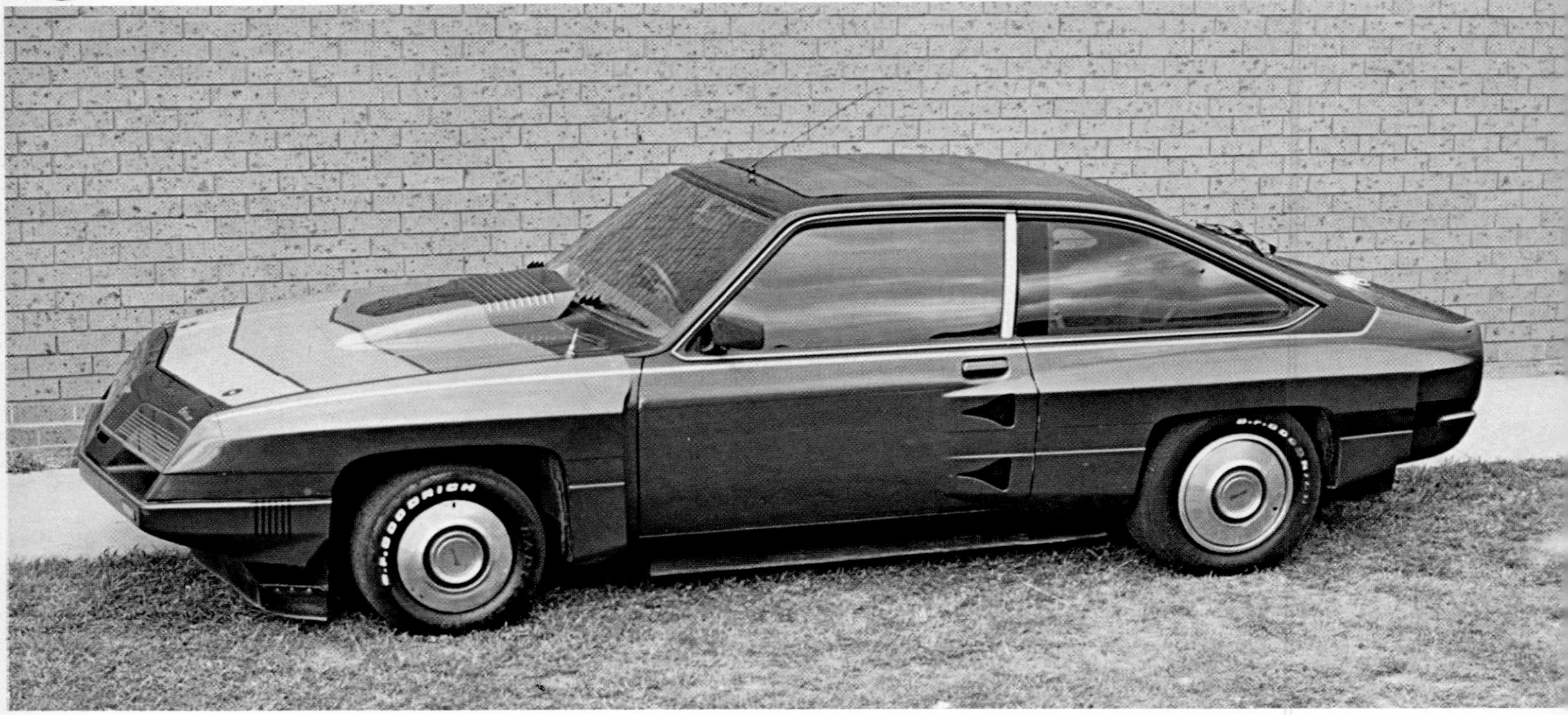

The latest version of the Mystere-Taipan series is again based on the Holden Torana hatchback. Its turbocharged 6-cylinder engine has water injection, waste gate and a fourteen pound boost, giving about 300 bhp. Top speed is about 240 km/h. There is a built-in telephone, dash-mounted 3 in TV, digital instrument panel and long-range tank. Price is about Australian $ 17,500.

ARCADIPANE Imitator AUSTRALIA

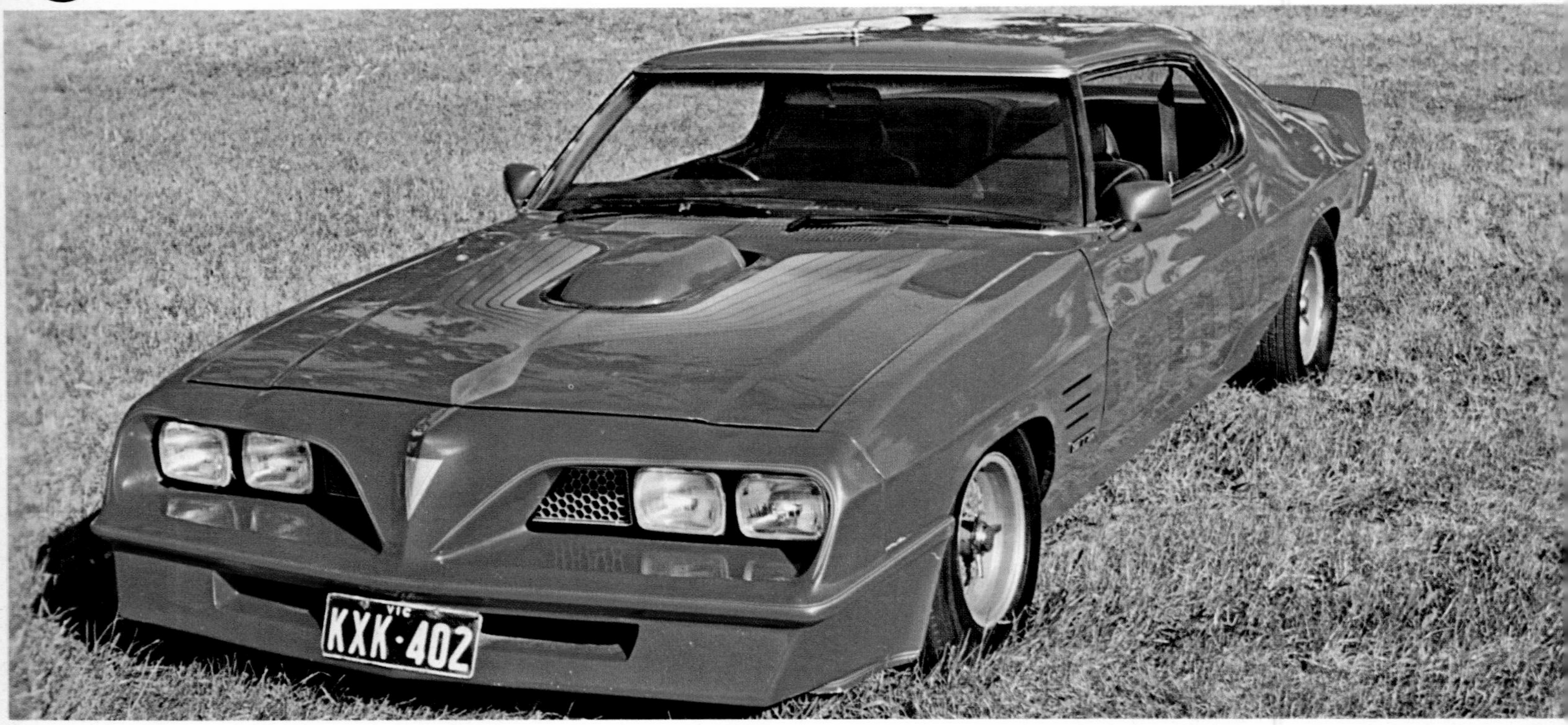

The Imitator, as its name suggests, is an Australian equivalent of the Pontiac Firebird. It has GM running gear, including a 400 cu in small block Chevrolet engine mounted to a turbo-hydro auto. The BBS 8 x 14 light alloy wheels mount high speed radials. The paint is a special candy apple red.

GERMANY FR

BMW Hardtop Cabriolet

BAUR 

Using the mechanics of the entire range of the BMW Series 3, the Stuttgart coachbuilder has designed this streamlined cabriolet, fitted with an ample rollbar to give the entire shell rigidity. For the front part of the roof there is a hardtop (which can be stowed in the boot) and a folding hood for the rear.

ITALY

Sibilo

BERTONE

The 'hiss' is based on the Lancia Stratos running gear and chassis but is 4 in (10 cm) longer. Taking his dream-car one step further, Bertone tries to integrate the glass area into the body. An original steering wheel fits the natural grip of the hand and also houses warning lights, switches and a loudspeaker.

BERTONE — Fiat Ritmo Cabriolet — ITALY

The purpose of Bertone's elegant and functional Ritmo Cabriolet is to complete the extensive Fiat series with a limited production of a four-seater cabriolet — a model that should enjoy renewed popularity with the lower speeds imposed by soaring fuel prices. When the hood is down, it disappears entirely and safety and rigidity are guaranteed by a solid roll-bar.

BERTONE — Fiat X1/9 1500 Five Speed — ITALY

A wedge-shaped convertible spider with lively performance from a 1500 cc 85 hp (DIN) engine centrally mounted is Bertone's version of the Fiat X1/9, distinguished by a 5-speed gearbox and modified front end and bumpers.

ITALY **Tundra** **BERTONE**

Presented at the 1979 Geneva Motor Show, the Tundra is the result of a new collaboration between Volvo and Bertone. This study for an elegant sporting four-seater saloon is based on the Volvo 343 with manual gearbox.
Though lower and wider in the central section, the dimensions are similar to the saloon's. It has impact-absorbing bumpers and a tailgate.

ITALY **Volvo 264 TE** **BERTONE**

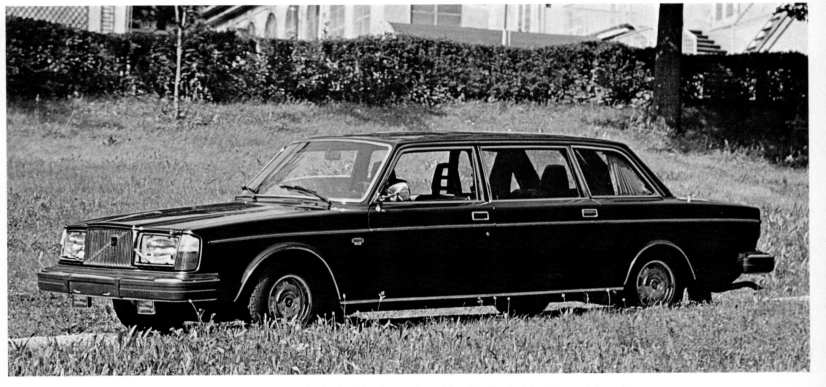

Derived from the Volvo 264 GL saloon, this elegant limousine is destined for diplomats and the like. The hull has been reinforced and lengthened by the insertion of new doors, windows, roof and various other elements. The sumptuous equipment includes a radio telephone and refrigerator. Overall length 220.47 in (560 cm), height 56.69 in (144 cm).

BERTONE Volvo 262C ITALY

Bertone is building the 262C to Volvo specifications aimed at providing maximum comfort and low noise levels in a 4-seater coupé for an exclusive clientèle. The spare tyre is stowed flat in the boot, to be blown up with a compressed air cylinder when needed.

BITTER SC GERMANY FR

Bitter's new four-seater GT coupé is based on the Opel Senator. A top speed of 137 mph with acceleration from 0 to 60 mph in 8 seconds is claimed for its 2,968 cc engine. The car is superbly finished with either velour upholstery and trim or Italian leather as an optional. Overall length 190.94 in (485 cm) and width 71.65 in (182 cm).

USA **Cabriolet** **CLENET**

Frenchman Alain Clénet handmounts an all-steel body with handlaid fiberglass fenders on Lincoln-Mercury components. His cabriolet has a 5.7 litre V8 engine and 3-speed automatic transmission. It is equipped with cruise control, air-conditioning, AM/FM stereo, leather upholstery and a solid walnut dashboard. It sells at about $ 65,000.

GREAT BRITAIN **Grosvenor Mk VI** **COLEMAN-MILNE**

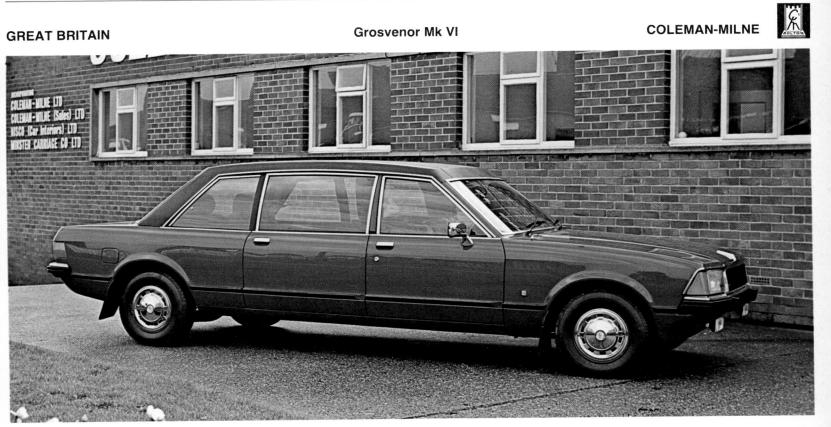

Coleman-Milne's imposing seven-seater limousine is based on the Ford Granada and mounts a 2.8 litre six-cylinder engine. Compared with the original model, it has been extended by 31 inches. The overall length is 211 in (536 cm), width 70.50 in (179 cm) and height 61 in (155 cm).

CRAYFORD **Ford Cortina MK IV** **GREAT BRITAIN**

Distributed worldwide by Bristol Street Motors, the new ' T ' Bar Convertible is a handsome car for the young at heart. An exclusive seat style provides virtually the same leg and head room for front and rear passengers as in the normal saloon model.

CRAYFORD **Mercedes-Benz 280 CE St. Tropez** **GREAT BRITAIN**

This sophisticated town car also offers open air four-seater luxury. The car's high standard of refinement plus outstanding roominess for passengers and luggage makes it a most luxurious four-seater convertible.

John Z. DeLorean's dream car is designed by Giugiaro. The elastic reservoir molding (ERM) process is used for the large body parts, while the front and rear fenders are stainless steel. Powered by a 120 hp Renault 6-cylinder engine, the DMC is 154 in long. The gull-wing doors extend less than 12 inches laterally.

JAPAN Dome-O P2 DOME

The striking midship-engined Dome-O has progressed to phase 2. The use of FRP for its outer body panels contributes to reducing the weight to a respectable 950 kg. The bumpers are now heavier to meet American standards. The power unit is unchanged — a carburettor version of Nissan's L 28 2.8 litre in line six.

 DUCHATELET | Mercedes-Benz 450 SEL | BELGIUM

Alterations to the original model include a personalized design, sunroof over the passenger seats and tinted glass. All chrome parts, including the US-version bumpers, are treated and tinted. The deluxe equipment features a central console with TV, four-speaker radio, cassette, refrigerator, telephone and dictaphone. The inside temperature can be regulated from a range of two kilometres.

FRUA | BMW GT Coupé | ITALY

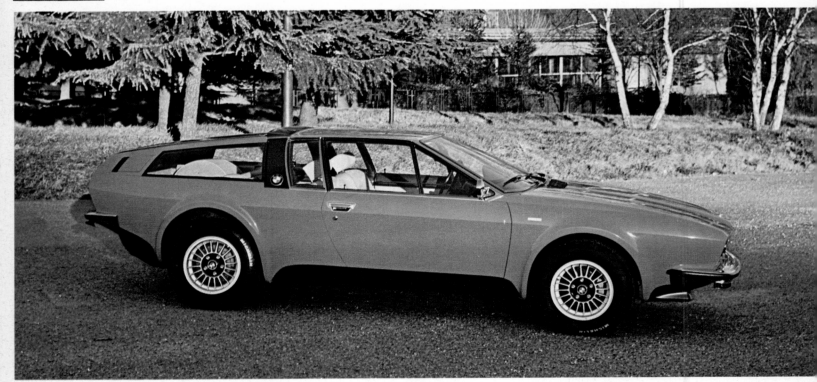

On the chassis of the Series 5, Frua has created this snappy coupé with wheelbase shortened to 94.49 in, (240 cm). BMW 520 I mechanics with a 1,990 cc injection engine and 5-speed gearbox are used. The belt line is low to increase lateral vision and a tailgate gives access to the luggage area. Overall length 167.32 in (425 cm) and width 69.68 in (177 cm).

Maserati Kyalami

FRUA

This 2+2 coupé is called Kyalami, after the famous South African Grand Prix track near Johannesburg. The mechanical parts are by Maserati, with the V8 4,136 cc 265 bhp engine developing a maximum speed in the region of 150 mph (240 km/h).

Ford Fiesta GTK

GHIA

At the 1979 Geneva Show, Ghia presented the longest — and the shortest — Fiesta in the world. The elegant aerodynamic GTK saloon with its three doors has a wheelbase 102 mm longer than the original and is a further development of the Megastars based on the Granada and Taunus. There is an on-board computer and electronic instrumentation.

GHIA

Mustang R.S.X.

ITALY

R.S.X. stands for Rallye Sport Experimental, and in fact Ghia's highly aerodynamic 2-seater is an entirely new concept of the 4-seater Mustang. It is shorter, lower, narrower and lighter. The R.S.X. is powered by a 2.3 litre 4-cylinder engine and a four-speed box. It has servo steering and air-conditioning. The wheelbase is 14.2 cm shorter than the original.

GHIA

Navarre

ITALY

In combining European design themes with the latest down-sized U.S. vehicle dimensions, Ghia has demonstrated in conjunction with the Ford Design Centre how the car of the future might be conceived internationally. This sporting 5-seater coupé has a unit construction steel body and a Ford 5-litre V8 engine. A four-headlamp system is supplemented by twin long-range lamps.

Coupé Royale Convertible

GRANDEUR MOTOR CAR

This personal luxury convertible starts out as a 4-door Lincoln Versailles. The back seat portion s cut 21 inches and the front extended by 21 inches, thus retaining the basic 110 in wheelbase and an overall length of 200.7 in. It is powered by a 5-litre Lincoln Versailles engine and costs $ 49,000.

USA

SJJ-1

GUANCI

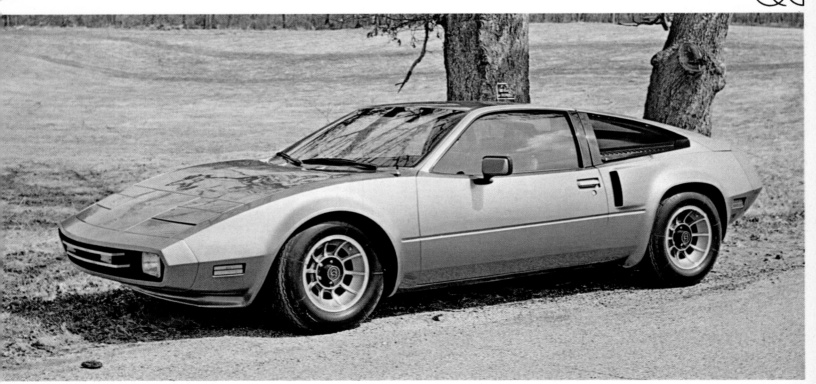

The GM V8 ohv engine transverse mounted amidships develops 220 bhp at 5,200 rpm and drives the rear wheels of the SJJ-1 through a 3-speed automatic transmission. The seating of this 2-seater offers exceptional comfort including lumbar, thigh and shoulder support adjustment. The wheelbase is 102 in (259 cm).

HEULIEZ — **Peugeot 604 HLZ** — **FRANCE**

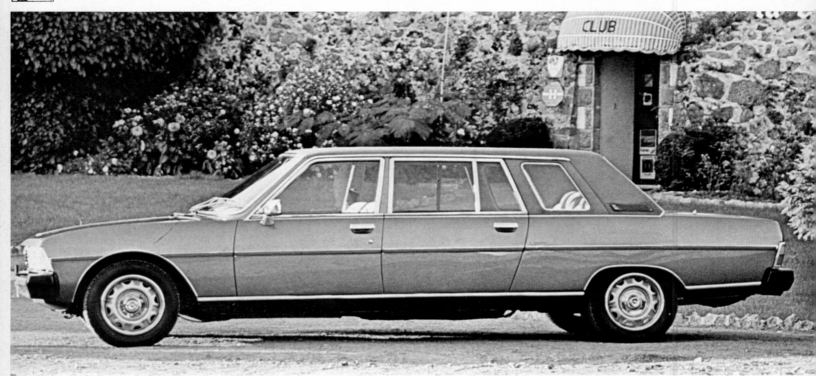

Heuliez's taxi and limousine version is 24.41 in (62 cm) longer than the standard 604. The taxi has two folding seats in the central part. At the rear, the large central armrest accommodates an ashtray, lighter and controls for the rear windows. This imposing car weighs 3,087 lb (1,400 kg).

HUMBERSTONE — **Range Rover Excelsior** — **GREAT BRITAIN**

This long wheelbase Range Rover converted to limousine design has a 4.4 litre Leyland Terrier V8 engine and automatic transmission. Its equipment includes electric division and windows, twin air-conditioning systems, refrigerator, power steering and in-car hi-fi and TV, plus a cocktail cabinet. Prices apparently start around £ 35,000.

TALY — Isuzu Ace of Clubs — ITAL DESIGN

'his 4-seater coupé design study on the Isuzu Gemini 1800 Saloon frame has a twin overhead camshaft injection engine. It is designed ɔ meet the requirements of production technology and the few modifications to the Gemini chassis include a revised radiator area ɔ improve aerodynamics and a new location for the fuel tank and spare wheel to obtain more rational luggage space.

TALY — Lancia Delta — ITAL DESIGN

Vith the Delta, Lancia returns to a section of the market where in the past it has held a leading position.
'he lines of the Giugiaro design are in fact classic and easy on the eye,
vhile the internal comfort is of the highest quality both in the choice of materials and in the equipment.

ITAL DESIGN — Maserati Quattroporte — ITALY

In close collaboration with Maserati, Ital Design has created a thoroughbred high-performance 4-seater beautifully finished throughout. The side lines are upswept with respect to the belt line and the rear quarter lights set well forward to give the rear seat passengers privacy. Overall length 192.13 in (488 cm), width 66.54 in (169 cm) and height 52.76 in (134 cm).

LE VICOMTE CLASSIC — Renaissance — CANADA

*A numbered series of 50 will be built of the 4-seater luxury touring car reminiscent of the '30s.
Based on a modified Ford van chassis with Ford running gear and 400 cu in V8 engine, it rides and handles well.
There is a choice of automatic or manual transmission, and power steering and electric windows are featured. The wheelbase is 144 in (366 cm).*

USA **Kanzler Coupé** **NEWPORT COACHWORKS**

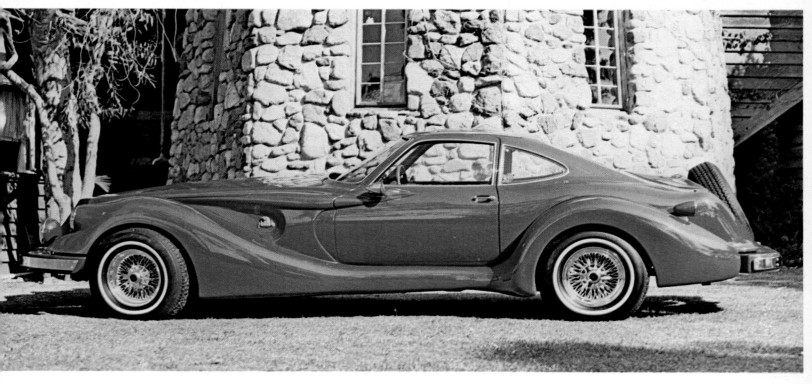

A limited edition luxury car, the aerodynamic Kanzler Coupé has fluid styling and interior elegance. It mounts a Mercury Cougar V8 351 cu in engine and also uses the complete chassis and drive train. Maximum speed is 125 mph (201 km/h). De luxe fittings are used in the all-steel passenger compartment. Price $ 64,633.

GREAT BRITAIN **10-20 Glassback** **OGLE**

The Leyland Princess, the first car to use a Triplex advanced safety windscreen, has been restyled as a one-off estate car to demonstrate the latest skills in automotive glass. It has a curved, all-glass rear door, Hyviz windscreen for demisting, de-icing and radio reception, flexing glass sunroof and glassed rear extension. There is an all-round protective buffer.

PACIFIC COACHWORKS — Di Napoli Coupé — USA

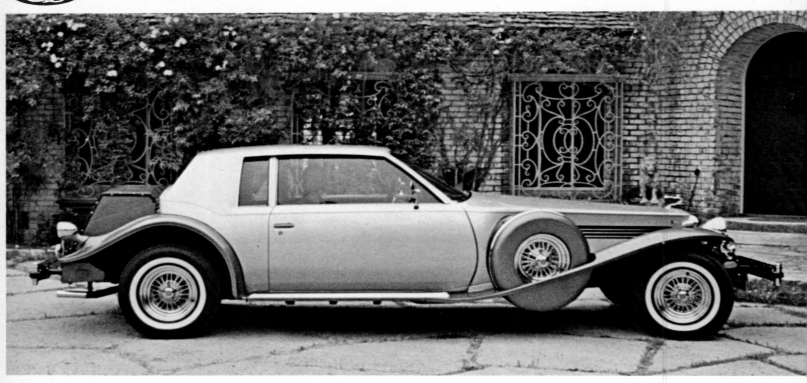

One hundred units are being built of this nostalgic de luxe coupé which has however its full compliment of safety equipment. A 3.8 turbocharged Buick V6 engine and Turbo-Hydramatic automatic transmission are standard. It also features automatic air-conditioning, electric windows and a power sunshine roof. Wheelbase 150 in (381 cm).

PHAETON — Mirage — USA

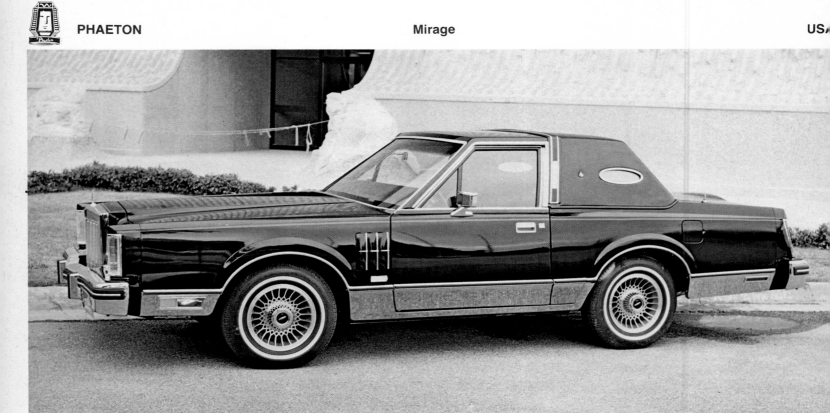

The Phaeton Mirage is a conversion of a 1980 four-door Lincoln Mark VI. The original is shortened 22 in (56 cm), giving a new overall length of 197.2 in (501 cm). The height is 56.3 in (143 cm) and the curb weight 3,520 lb (1,596 kg). The Mirage mounts a Lincoln 302 cu in V8 fuel-injected engine with a 351 cu in engine as an optional.

ITALY — **Alfa Romeo Duetto** — **PININFARINA**

In this version, destined for the United States only, the famous spider has been slightly modified, above all externally. American-type bumpers are fitted and light alloy wheels. The engine is the well-established 2-litre injection with twin overhead camshaft.

ITALY — **Ferrari Mondial 8** — **PININFARINA**

Launched at the 1980 Geneva Motor Show, the latest Ferrari is a 4-seater coupé capable of touching 230 km/h. The 2,925 cc engine, which is mounted transversally at the rear, is a V8 slanted at 90°. Bosch K-Jetronic electronic injection fuel feed is used.

PININFARINA — Ferrari 308 GTS — ITALY

Derived from the Ferrari 308 GTB berlinetta, this comfortable spider with modern lines and marked sporting characteristics does not fail to respect the contemporary demand for safety features and reliability. It is produced by Ferrari and the Carrozzeria Scaglietti.

PININFARINA — Ferrari 400 Automatic i — ITALY

This Ferrari, which is the evolution of the 365 GT4, whose lines it retains unchanged, is notable for the innovations in the mechanics and the interior. It is in fact the first Ferrari with automatic transmission but this has meant no loss in its traditional high performance characteristics. Space has been found in the interior for four comfortable seats.

TALY | Ferrari 512 B.B. | PININFARINA

The fascination of this car, typical of all the others of the marque of the rampant horse, does not lie merely in its high performance figures. The great attraction is the smooth, clean lines, studied specially to allow its powerful 12-cylinder engine developing 360 bhp (DIN) to top 300 km/h (186 mph).

ITALY | Fiat 124 Spider 2000 | PININFARINA

To date over 150 thousand of these cars, which are at present sold only in the United States, have been built. At present the 124 Spider has a 2-litre twin overhead camshaft engine. The body has been updated both internally and externally.

PININFARINA **Jaguar XJ Spider** ITALY

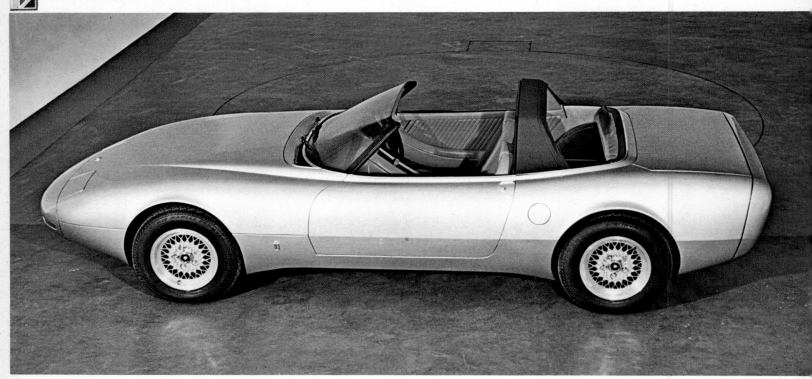

This aerodynamic prototype spider, based on the XJS coupé, harks back to the glorious models D and E, re-evoking their rounded lines and the oval front air intake. A soft back and soft nose have replaced the traditional bumpers. The interior, surprisingly simple, is dictated by safety principles. Luggage space is unusually ample.

PININFARINA **Lancia Montecarlo** ITALY

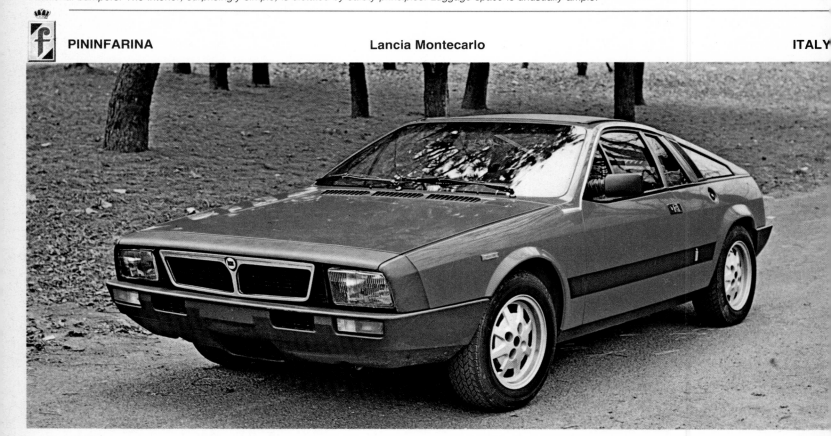

Low, wide and aggressive at the same time, this car has original lines and several stylistic innovations. The central-rear engine geometry, typical of modern sports cars, makes comfortable and safe seating possible. The arrangement of the various instruments is rational and they are in easy reach.

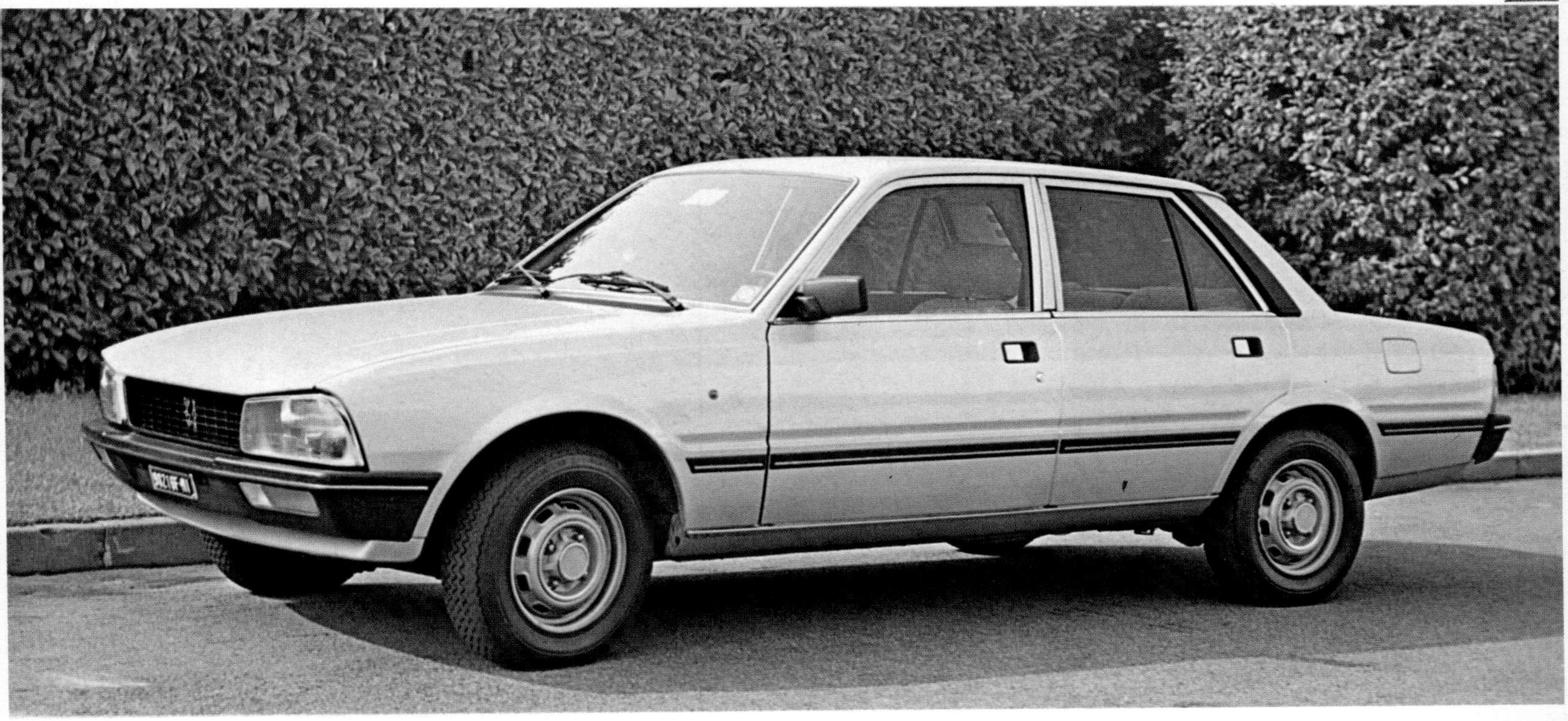

The new 505 shares a certain family air with the 504 and 305 also designed by Pininfarina, but has cleaner lines with a larger and more steeply raked windscreen and trapezoidal headlamps. The facia is new, its porthole frame recalling a television screen. A diesel version is planned.

SWITZERLAND Function Car SBARRO

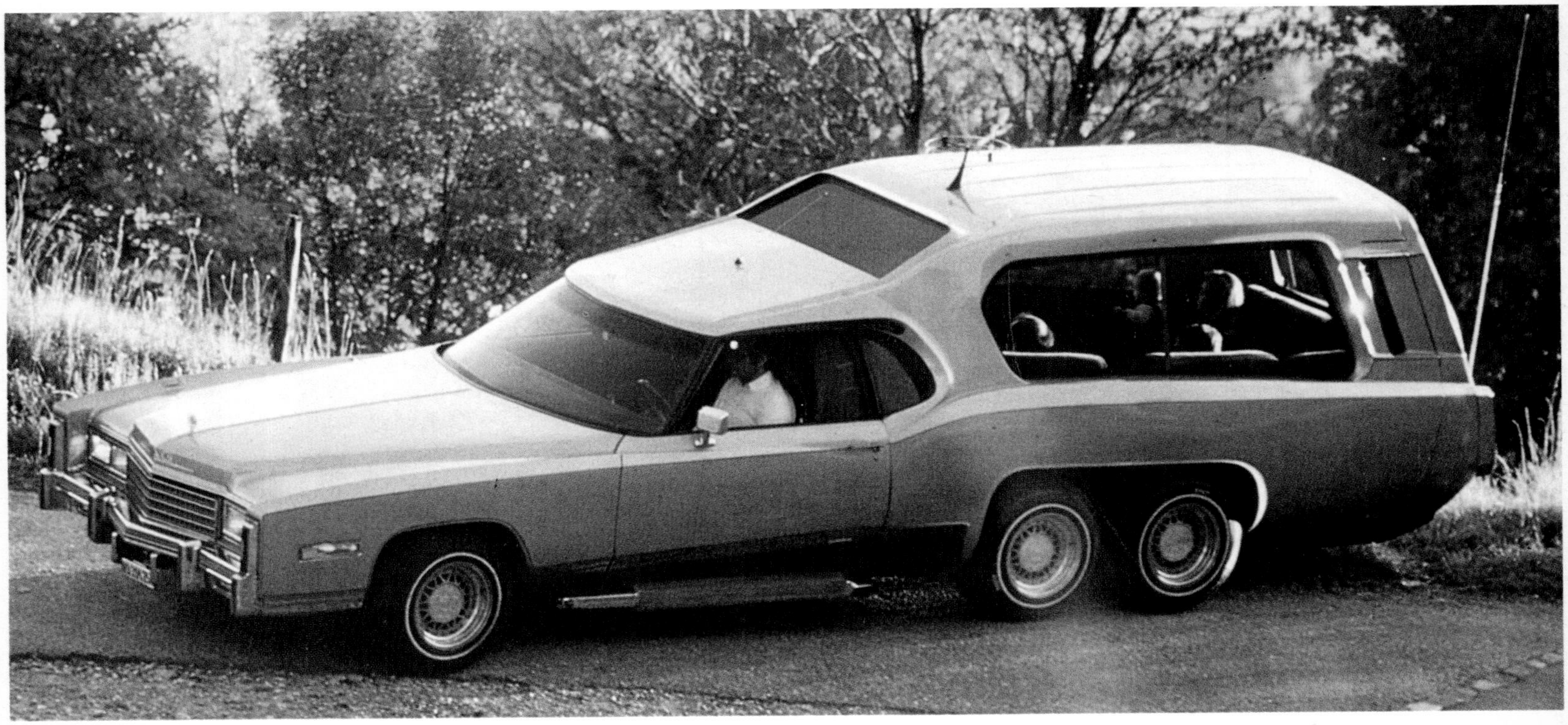

Sbarro's extremely unusual triple-axle function car is derived from a Cadillac Eldorado. It can seat six and, in addition to the two front doors, has a large tailgate and a small communicating door between the two interior sections.
Overall length is 276 in (700 cm) and weight about 6,174 lb (2,800 kg). It costs 250,000 Swiss francs.

SBARRO — Royale — SWITZERLAND

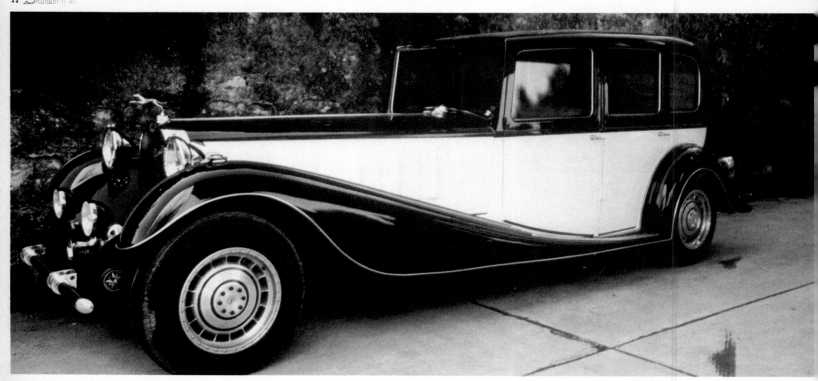

The customer has a choice of engines for this new 5/6 seater limousine interpretation of the Bugatti Royale which is extremely faithful in style to the original. Maximum speed is in the region of 180 km/h. Automatic transmission is used. Armoured plating is available.

SPARKS — Turbo Phaeton — USA

Gold-plate grille bars and chrome exhausts, 18k gold plating inside and out, white wall tyres and hand-etched glass windows. The makers understandably claim you will never see anything like it on the road. The 8-cylinder 90° V Cadillac engine has a Quadrojet turbocharger. Wheelbase 165 in (419 cm).

USA **Baronta** TAFCO

Revised GM mechanics allied with a design based on the ground effect principle allow the Baronta to top 150 mph (240 km/h). The body is handcrafted from a .035 steel over a tubular inner body. Wheelbase 92 in (234 cm). Accessories include full instrumentation, radio telephone, stereo and tapes, as well as air-conditioning and power brakes.

USA **Turbo Phantom** THE PHANTOM

Designed to be built on a custom basis only, this 3-wheeled luxury sports car has a tilt canopy door and is powered by a special turbocharged version of the Honda Gold Wing engine. Power is delivered through a 5-speed transmission to the shaft-driven rear wheel. Rigid urethane foam surrounds the passenger compartment for structural safety. Length 168 in (427 cm), top speed 130 mph (209 km/h).

VEHICLE DESIGN FORCE — Vector Twinturbo W 2 — USA

An advanced wedge design with the upper "greenhouse" area integrated into the lower body form. The 350 cu in Chevrolet V8 engine has two Rayjay turbochargers and Bosch K-Jetronic electronic fuel injection. Over 500 bhp is obtainable and speeds are hoped to reach 200 mph. Replicas obtained from the prototype would be aimed at the élite GT sports car market.

ZAGATO — Lancia Beta Spider — ITALY

For his Lancia Beta Spider destined for the American market, Zagato has replaced the canvas section around the rear window by a fibreglass hardtop which will stand up to the rigours of harsh winters or to razor blades and sharp knives.

ɪITSUBISHI — Pajero II — JAPAN

ɪn engineering and styling exercise ɪn a 4WD theme, the Pajero II has ɪdependent front suspension with ɔrsion bar springs. Instrumentation ɪcludes an attitude indicator ɦowing the angle of the vehicle.

ɪAPAN — SSW — MITSUBISHI

ʼhe compact Super Space Wagon ccommodates up to seven ccupants. The chassis is obviously ʼirectly derived from the FWD ɪirage sedan with its transverse ngine layout. Instrumentation is by ED display.

ɪAPAN — CX80 — TOYOTA

ɦe CX, a styling exercise, has ɔout the same floor space as ɔyota's smallest car, the Starlet ɹt will have a transverse engine ʼiving the front wheels. Door ɪnges are angled for easier gress-egress.

CALSPAN — RSV — USA

Derived from a 1976 Chrysler Simca, this 5-passenger hatchback sedan has a plastic foam front end. There is an air bag on the driver's side and an automatic air belt for the front-seat passenger.

MINICARS — Research Safety Vehicle — USA

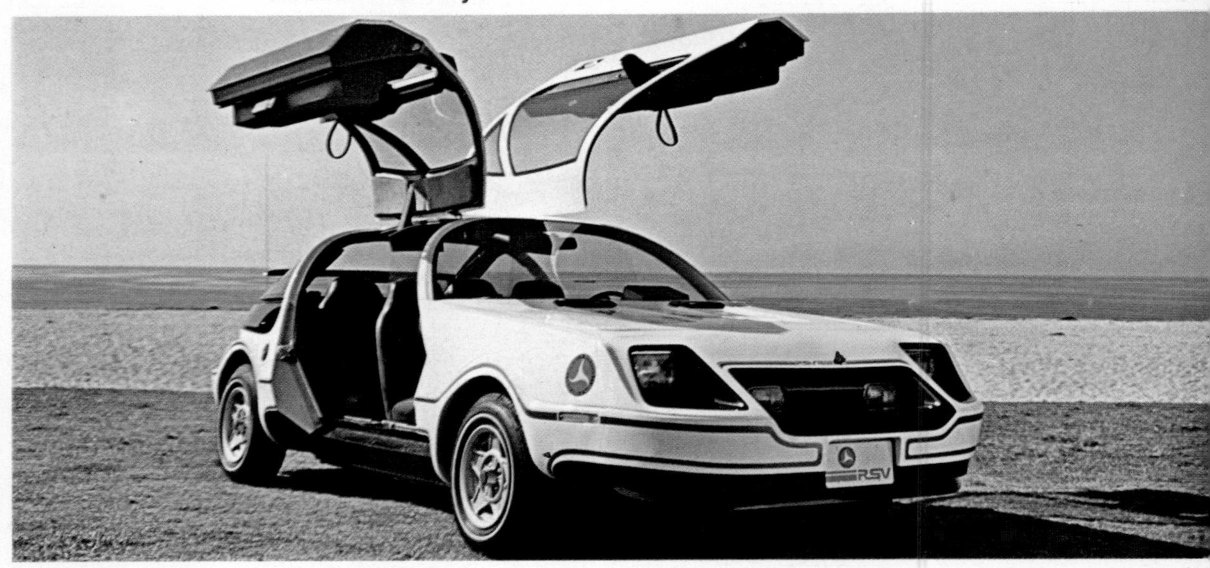

Dual-chambered air-cushion restraints at the front and force limiters combined with 3-point harnesses at the rear. Resilient plastic body panels cover the energy-abosorbent, foam-filled steel structure.

MINICARS — Large Research Safety Vehicle — USA

Based on a Chevrolet Impala with Volvo Lambda-Sond turbo-charged engine, this 6-seater has air-cushion restraints giving protection in 40 mph frontal crashes. Emissions and mileage are also improved.

Electric cars

Illustrations and technical information

USA

B & Z — Electra King PFS 125

This two-seater coupé designed by B & Z staff has a fiberglass-reinforced body with sliding glass windows. A series motor developing 6 hp at 1400 rpm and 2 hp at 2,800 rpm is regulated by the electromechanical switching of the series resistance. Six 6 V lead-acid batteries in a single pack under the seat give 190 Ah. Top speed, which is also cruising speed, is 20 mph (30 km/h) and the range is 22 miles (35 km). A larger motor and larger batteries, available as optionals, give increased speed and range. The length is 101 in (256 cm), width 45 in (114 cm) and height 60 in (152 cm), while the wheelbase is 65 in (165 cm). Curb weight with batteries is 1,100 lb (500 kg).

BRIGGS & STRATTON — Hybrid

An 18 hp Briggs & Stratton i.c. engine coupled by a Borg-Warner duo-cam clutch to a Baldor 28 hp series wound dc electric motor gives this 2+2 sports coupé prototype designed in collaboration with Brooks Stevens Design Associates Inc. a range of 30-300 miles (48-480 km). The separately suspended battery trailer carrier containing 12 6 V lead-acid batteries reduces rolling resistance for improved fuel economy and performance. There are drum brakes on the four rear wheels. Top speed is 55 mph (88 km/h). The overall length is 174 in (442 cm), the wheelbase 86 in and 112 in (218 cm and 284 cm) and the weight 3,200 lb (1,451 kg). The six-wheel design and dual rear axles make this a striking car.

FRANCE

C.E.D.R.E. — Midinette 1000

This little 3-wheeler has a steerable and driven front wheel thanks to a novel steering system. The aluminium and fiberglass body is described as having 1½ seats, with sliding doors used for ventilation. The series motor with electromagnetic variable voltage regulation develops 5 kW at 400 rpm and 1 kW at 5,000 rpm. The 6 V 240 Ah batteries are mounted 2 in front and 4 at the rear. The on-board, self-regulated high energy rate recharging system is original, without electronic charging. There are hydraulic Luchier brakes plus reverse voltage braking on the front wheel. Top speed is 28 mph (45 km/h) and range 75 miles (120 km). Length is 79 in (200 cm). Price 20,000 francs before tax.

USA

COMMUTER — 111-DW Comuta-Car

Commuter's little 2-door two-seater is, as its name suggests, built for short trips in town. Access is by two side doors and a rear hatchback door. Rally stripes, aerodynamic styling and high impact energy absorbing bumpers are featured. The series-wound dc motor develops 5.76 kW at 4,100 revs and has high current contacters for battery switching. 8 6 V 106 Ah lead-acid batteries in 3 packs are mounted front and rear. There is a built-in charger for overnight charging from a wall socket. At the top speed of 50 mph (80 km/h), range is 30 miles (48 km), but 40 miles (64 km) at cruising speed. Overall length is 120 in (285 cm), wheelbase 65 in (166 cm) and curb weight 1,480 lb (671 kg). Price $ 5,000.

USA

COPPER Runabout

The mass of the Runabout, CDA's latest prototype, is about two-thirds the Town Car's. Designed by them, but using many Renault R5 components, it has 3 doors and seats four, 2 facing rearwards. The height ensures good visibility and a tinted glass sunroof improves ventilation. The 28 kW Reliance motor is powered by twelve EV 4-19 Globe Union batteries mounted centrally under the car and sliding out lengthwise on teflon rails. They have common venting and a single-point water fill system. Top speed is 59 mph (95 km/h) and range 72 miles (116 km). The suspension has a large amount of front and rear antilift to minimize pitch altitude changes. Weight with batteries is only 2,152 lb (976 kg).

COPPER Town Car

This 2-seater hatchback prototype is built by the Copper Development Association Inc. using existing components and innovative technology. The streamlined car's range is 103 miles (165 km) at 40 mph (64 km/h) with a top speed of 59 mph (95 km/h). The 18 6 V batteries are housed in the central tunnel, sliding out from the rear. They power a separately excited 42 kW motor with a proprietary control system. The unusual doors swing outward until they clear the car's body and then travel rearward parallel to the body. The wheelbase is 80 in (203 cm), length 145 in (368 cm), width 60 in (152 cm), and height 54.5 in (138 cm). Weight with the batteries — which weigh 1,206 lb (547 kg) — is 3,036 lb (1,377 kg).

JAPAN

DAIHATSU Preet

Derived from the Max Cuore 550 cc sedan this 2-door prototype with two front seats is part of the *P*ublic *R*ent an *E*lectric *T*owncar project advocated by the Japanese Electric Vehicle Association. The relative software program identifies a registered user by means of a credit card-like magnetised card which also opens the Preet car door. The mileage is recorded and charged to the user. The 14 kW dc compound motor is powered by 8 12 V 100 Ah lead-acid batteries housed in a rear compartment. The range is 32 miles (52 km) at 25 mph (40 km/h) and top speed is 38 mph (62 km/h). Overall length is 124 in (316 cm), width 55 in (139 cm), height 50 in (127 cm) and weight 2,112 lb (958 kg).

DAIHATSU Charade Electric

Built to order for Daihatsu's Australian distributors and shown at the 24th Sydney Motor Show in August 1979, this 4-door hatchback sedan prototype derived from the Charade 1000 cc sedan has 2 front seats. The eight 12 V lead-acid batteries powering the 14 kW dc compound motor are housed in a rear compartment. Recharging takes eight hours from a 240 V source. The maximum speed is 47 mph (75 km/h) and the Charade has a range of 47 miles (75 km) at 32 mph (51 km/h). It has a 3-speed mechanical gearbox and disc brakes at the front and drum at the rear. Overall length is 136 in (346 cm), width 59 in (151 cm), height 51 in (130 cm) and the wheelbase is 90 in (230 cm).

JAPAN

DAIHATSU-MATSUSHITA BCX-M

Another electric derivation of the Charade sedan in the 2-door, 2-seater hatchback prototype jointly developed by Daihatsu and Matsushita Electric. The rear compartment has been converted to accommodate the eight 19 V iron-nickel Matsushita batteries, whose trade name is Panasonic. The 7.4 kW dc compound electric motor, SCR chopper and 5-speed gearbox give a maximum speed of 70 mph (113 km/h) and a range of 94 miles (151 km) at a cruising speed of 25 mph (40 km/h). Overall length is 153 in (389 cm), width 59 in (151 cm), height 51 in (129 cm) and wheelbase 90 in (230 cm). The weight with batteries is 2,380 lb (1,080 kg). There are disc brakes at the front and drum at the rear.

DAIHATSU Charmant Hybrid

Daihatsu's latest hybrid project is a 4-door sedan seating 2 at the front and 2 at the rear, derived from the Charmant sedan. It has 2 dc electric motors and a 550 cc SOHC 2-cylinder i.c. engine. An on-board central computer determines which power unit is suited for given driving conditions. The piston engine is normally used during cruising, while single or twin motors are used in acceleration. The lead-acid batteries are housed at the rear in the boot and are regenerated while the car is in motion by the i.c. engine. No performance figures are available. A thyrister chopper is used, and there are front disc and rear drum brakes. Wheelbase is 92 in (233 cm).

USA

DIE MESH Spider

The infinite speed traction transmission invented by Die Mesh's president, Domenic Borello, is being evaluated by the Federal Energy Research and Development Administration. The University of Michigan, too, is interested in a transmission that has no gears and does not work by friction, but combines parallel cone-shaped components with a power transfer wheel. Mounted on a Fiat 850 sport spider body, 16 6 V lead acid batteries in two packs power a 10 hp motor. Top speed in 50 mph (80 km/h) and range 35 miles (55 km). It weighs (batteries included) slightly more than the original model at 2,600 lb (1,179 kg) but length and height are unchanged. The wheelbase is 77.80 in (203 cm).

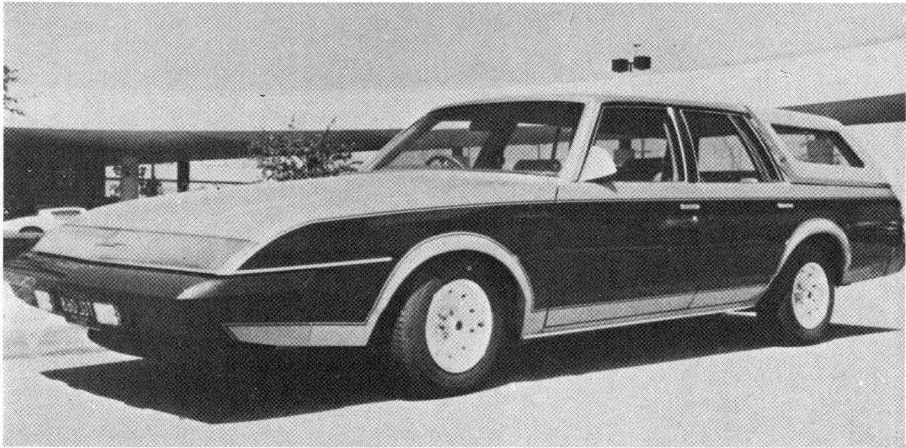

E.A.C. 1980 Silver Volt

Based on a GM Buick Century, this 5-seater wagon has aerodynamic bodywork and crash designed bumpers. Production of around 300 research vehicles is scheduled for 1980. It has a series motor with 80 kW peak and 25 kW continuous rating with regenerative braking down to 15 mph (24 km/h). 2 packs of EFP fast charge TPX4 batteries with single point watering giving 150 V and 250 Ah at the 2 hr rate are mounted, one forward and one rear. Top speed is 70 mph (112 km/h) and range 80-100 miles (129-160 km) per charge. The low-noise rotary i.c. engine will extend the range to 100 miles when required. Air conditioning, power brakes and steering, electric windows and power seats are standard.

USA

ELECTRICAR Lectric Leopard 952

Featuring a sunroof, tinted glass and a rear-window defogger/washer, Electricar's 3-door 4-seater hatchback sedan is already in production. It is designed for short haul driving and claims to be virtually maintenance free. The compound wound Prestolite 48 V dc motor is regulated by voltage switching control. 16 6 V lead-acid batteries developing 440 Ah are mounted in 2 packs at the front and rear. Maximum speed is 50 mph (80 km/h) and the range is from 60-70 miles (96-113 km), depending on the driving conditions. The overall length is 142 in (361 cm), width 60 in (152 cm), height 55 in (140 cm) and wheelbase 95 in (242 cm). Weight with batteries is 2,580 lb (1,172 kg). Price: from $ 7,495 to 8,995.

EVA Change of Pace

Based, like a previous EVA model, on the AMC Pacer, this station wagon seats 4 and has a fold-down rear seat for additional cargo space. It is supplied complete with every detail, including a gas heater. The series motor develops 26 kW at 3,000 revs with SCR speed control and is powered by 20 6 V lead-acid batteries housed front and rear in 2 packs. An on-board charger fits standard wall outlets. Transmission is automatic and there are disc brakes at the front and drum at the rear. Top speed is 55 mph (88 km/h) and range 40-50 miles (64-80 km) at cruising speed, or 30 miles (48 km) at maximum speed. Overall length is 216 in (549 cm), width 77 in (196 cm) and height 57 in (145 cm).

BELGIUM

EVELEC Electrotest

Production starts this year on the electric conversion of the little DAF 66 for two front seat passengers. The series type 6 kW motor is regulated by a 350 Amp transistorized chopper. Maximum power is 17 kW at 1,980 rpm. The 96 V 120 Ah lead-acid batteries are mounted in the rear compartment and recharged by a 40 A outboard charger. At the car's maximum speed of 31 mph (50 km/h) the range is only 28 miles (45 km) but this rises to 30 miles (50 km) at cruising speed. Overall length is 165 in (419 cm), width 65 in (166 cm) and height 57 in (144 cm). The wheelbase is 94 in (240 cm) and the Electrotest weighs 2,701 lb (1,225 kg), with the batteries accounting for 772 lb (350 kg).

ITALY

FIAT X 1/23

The Fiat X 1/23 is a little two-seater experimental car for town use. It was presented some years ago at the Turin Motor Show minus power unit and in 1976 it was fitted with a 14 kW electric motor with separate exciting field and lead-acid batteries. The traditional brakes are supplemented by a regenerating brake. Cooling is by a fan driven by an auxiliary electric motor. An electronic impulse traction regulator adjusts the speed of the vehicle continuously from zero to top speed, ensures that it functions in a regular manner at all speeds and provides for energy-recovery braking. The X 1/23 has front wheel drive while the batteries are housed at the rear. Top speed is 45 mph (75 km/h) and the range about 50 miles (80 km).

ITALY

FIAT 131 Ibrido

Hybrids seem to be a characteristic of 1980. The 131 based saloon prototype designed by the Fiat Research Centre is part of a project sponsored by the US Dept. of Energy. It is powered by the i.c. engine of the Fiat 127 with power reduced to 33 hp coupled to a 20 kW electric motor by means of a torque converter. They are mounted in line in the gearbox housing. The twelve 12 V batteries, with a 45 Ah capacity, are housed in the boot. Massive use is made of electronics in the passage of power from the i.c. engine to the electric motor, in maintaining the battery charge level and in keeping fuel consumption low. Hybrid systems require lighter, more aerodynamic vehicles to compensate for the weight of the batteries.

AUSTRALIA

FLINDERS Investigator Mk II

The Flinders University team has spent five years developing its twin-module motor electric version of a Fiat 127. A practical and viable propulsion system is linked to advanced battery developments to give exceptional acceleration and hill-climbing and a range of up to 50 miles (80 km) at 37-47 mph (60-75 km/h). The novelty is a printed circuit motor and a method of matching impedance with a series-pass transistor. The motor and control system is designed as a modular assembly and the Flinders linear current control system (FLCC) allows infinitely variable power control of both output and regenerative power. There are plans to add a third motor module to the two 5 kW motors.

USA

GARRETT DOE Electric

This all plastic prototype is part of a project sponsored by the US Department of Energy. Two 21 kW dc motors with field control are powered by 18 6 V lead-acid batteries mounted in the central tunnel. There is an on-board charger for a 110 V receptical. An experimental electromechanical fully automatic gearbox is controlled by a computer-micro processor. This 4-seater compact has a passing speed of 68 mph (109 km/h) and a range of 120 miles (193 km) at a cruising speed of 40 mph (64 km/h). A composite wound flywheel housed in a low-pressure aluminum chamber stores energy to provide high transient power capability for acceleration and recovery of kinetic energy during braking.

GE ETV-1

This experimental 4-passenger 2-door hatchback was developed for the U.S. Department of Energy by the General Electric Research and Development Center and Chrysler Corporation. It is powered by 18 6 V high energy density lead-acid batteries feeding a front-mounted separately excited d.c. motor with a peak rating of 31 kW. The batteries are mounted in a separate tunnel and removable as a unit. There is a transistorized armature chopper. The ETV-1 features low aerodynamic drag, computerized electronic controls, on-board charger and regenerative braking. Its range under certain driving conditions can be over 100 miles (160 km) and top speed is 60 mph (96 km/h). Length is 169 in (430 cm).

GLOBE UNION — Endura

This lightweight fiberglass prototype is designed as a test vehicle for Globe Union's technology in batteries. Using a four individual seat configuration, it has the flexibility of a combined sport sedan and station wagon thanks to the easy interchange of a rear quarter panel. The 20 Globe Union high energy density advanced lead-acid 12 V batteries are mounted on an aluminium frame and roller subassembly tray. A Monopanel electronic control board controls ignition, lights, wiper and other accessories. The 20 hp series wound motor allows a top speed of over 60 mph (96 km/h) and a range at cruising speed of 100 miles (161 km). Length is 184 in (467 cm), width 72 in (183 cm), wheelbase 108 in (277 cm).

GLOBE UNION — Maxima

This prototype developed from the Mercury Zephyr has the safety features of a 1978 model of that car, a steel and fiberglass body with 2 bucket front seats and rear bench seat. Both the 24 hp motor and regulation are by General Electric. The 20 prototype 12 V 70 Ah batteries are housed in 2 packs in the front engine compartment and under the rear cargo area. Recharging is by a current tape with a voltage limit. Top speed is 75 mph (120 km/h) and range is not declared. The car is capable of operating as a 240 or 120 V system for acceleration or economy. The Maxima has a mechanical gearbox, front disc and rear drum brakes and polyester radial tyres. Length is 198 in (503 cm), weight 4,350 lb (1,973 kg).

GM — Electrovette

GM are continuing development work on their series of experimental electric vehicles, confident in the future of this form of traction. The first prototype is a 2-seater coupé with a removable sunroof based on the Chevrolet Chevette. In the space once occupied by the engine is mounted an on-board computer that is a control signal processor and "brain" of the system; a chopper which is a motor-power controller; a "choke" or motor current smoothing reactor; a dc motor generator; a 110/220 V ac transformerless charger, a gearbox and an auxiliary battery. A 240 V battery system (150 zinc-nickel oxide cells) is located in the rear seat area. Top speed is 60 mph (96 km/h) and range 112 miles (180 km) at 30 mph.

GURGEL — Itaipu Mod. 1

Gurgel's little four-wheeled Itaipu Mod. 1 is a prototype mounting a 3 kW motor powered by ten 12 V batteries giving 68 Ah. The batteries are placed behind the seats. The wedge-nosed Mod. 12 has a maximum speed of 31 mph (50 km/h) and an autonomy of 37 miles (60 km) at that speed. It is designed to seat two persons and can carry a load of 66 lb (30 kg). The chief dimensions are: overall length 102 in (260 cm), overall width 61 in (155 cm), overall height 57 in (145 cm) and ground clearance 6 in (16 cm). It weighs 1,103 lb (500 kg) without the batteries which account for 706 lb (320 kg) of the total weight.

H-M-VEHICLES Free-Way

This year H-M-Vehicles 3-wheel commuter hatchback with tandem seating for two goes into mass production. The original design with small frontal profile and low air drag features a steel frame and fiberglass body. Regulation of the permanent magnet motor is by mechanical variation of variable speed belt drive with on/off contactor. 4 12 V deep cycle batteries in the rear motor compartment provide 8.5 kW at 2,600 rpm. Mounted in a fiberglass case, they slide out from the side. Regenerative braking is controlled through the accelerator pedal. Top speed is 55 mph (88 km/h) and range at cruising speed 75 miles (121 km). Length is 115 in (292 cm) and height 51 in (130 cm). Price $ 2,995.

HYBRICON Centaur II

The 2-door 4-seater body of the Centaur is designed for Hybricon by George Barris. Two double shuntfield electric motors drive the rear wheels through electric clutches and helical gears, while the 32 hp gasoline 2-cylinder engine driving the front wheels through a 4-speed transaxle can charge the batteries 80% in an hour at 50 mph (80 km/h). There is a common regenerative and hydraulic brake. Eight 6 V lead-acid batteries are placed behind the rear seat. Regulation is by a power transister chopper. Top speed is 35 mph (56 km/h) or 70 mph (112 km/h) with the i.c. engine. The electric motors provide one hour's range and with the hybrid system there are obvious advantages of range and economy.

JMJ ELECTRONICS ElectraCar

Five years' research have been devoted to combining JMJ technology with the proven Dodge Omni and Plymouth Horizon. Four passenger vehicles and 2 compact pickups are soon to go into production. They feature a 10-15 hp series wound motor and a JMJ controller. 3-cell 6 V lead-acid batteries are used with an optional on-board charger. The maximum speed is g–* mph (109 km/h) with a range of 50-70 miles (80-112 km) at the cruising speed of 55 mph (88 km/h). The overall length is 201 in (510 cm) and height 54 in (137 cm). Designed for commuting, shopping and trips around town, the ElectraCar has tinted glass, bumper protection, fiberglass radial tyres and front disc and rear brakes.

MARATHON C-300

This passenger/utility vehicle, with fabric top, accommodates driver and one passenger in bucket seats. The front-mounted 8 hp dc traction motor is powered by 12 6 V 130 Ah batteries. Top speed is 30 mph (49 km/h) and range 30 miles (49 km). The controller is a Marathon patent. 4-speed transmission, an inboard semi-automatic charger, a tubular steel frame, and a steering ratio of 5:1 are other features. The 13 inch wheels mount 13/145 tyres. Overall length 151 (383 cm), width 62 in (157 cm), and height 53 in (135 cm). Weight with batteries is 2,300 lb (1,058 kg), the batteries accounting for 1,000 lb (460 kg). A payload of 500 lb (230 kg) can be carried. Price $ 7,500.

JAPAN

MAZDA — Familia EV

Derived from the Familia 323/GLS sedan, Toyo Kogyo's 4-door hatchback prototype sedan retains the same seating arrangement. Developed for urban use, it has a simple two-pedal control system and the mechanical gearbox has only a forward and reverse change. Eight 12 V lead-acid batteries housed in the boot and at the front supply the power for the dc motor which has a maximum power of 11 kW. Regulation is by a thyristor chopper and recharging takes 12 hours from a separate 200 V charger. A maximum speed of 43 mph (70 km/h) is allied to a range of 40 miles (65 km) at a cruising speed of 25 mph (40 km/h). Length is 151 in (383 cm), the wheelbase is 91 in (231 cm) and weight 2,524 lb (1,145 kg).

USA

McKEE — Sundancer

McKee's two-seater commuter car has an upward opening top for easy access. The 12 6 V lead-acid batteries plus an auxiliary battery fit into a battery tray which can be rolled out and replaced in 5 minutes. The tray is housed in the backbone frame pioneered by McKee, because this battery location ensures a low centre of gravity and isolation from the car's occupants. The 8 hp motor allows a top speed of 60 mph (96 km/h) and a range of 120 miles (193 km) at 30 mph (48 km/h), or 75-85 miles (120-136 km) of city driving. Curb weight, complete with batteries, is 1,600 lb (725 kg), and the car has a wheelbase of 72 in (183 cm). It is only 40 in (102 cm) high.

ITALY

P.G.E. — 6 P

This snub-nosed little open runabout, built of light alloy flat panels riveted and framed with square section steel, can carry six passengers in addition to the driver. The motor, which weighs 99 lb (45 kg), develops a continuous power of 5 kW. The nominal tension of the batteries, which are housed in a central tray, is 72 V. The instruments provided include an ammeter for the armature current, a voltmeter for the tension of the batteries, a tachometer and an instrument indicating the state of charge of the batteries. The maximum speed that can be reached by the 6 P is about 37 mph (60 km/h) and it has a range between charges of about 62 miles (100 km) when driven in normal town conditions.

P.G.E. — Ambulanza

P.G.E.'s neat little ambulance carries 3 passengers. The 5 kW motor has a peak power of 10 kW and is fed by twelve 6 V batteries each with a capacity of 185 Ah. The top speed is only 28 mph (45 km/h) but at that speed there is a range of 65 miles (105 km). The ambulance can tackle a maximum gradient of 18% at 12 mph (20 km/h) or a continuous gradient of 6% at 15 mph (25 km/h). The vehicle is fitted with disc brakes at the front and drum brakes at the rear and has front-wheel drive. The main dimensions are: overall length 135 in (342 cm), overall width 58 in (147 cm), overall height 55 in (140 cm), and the curb weight is 2,646 lb (1,200 kg). With different finishings, a school bus is available.

ITALY

PININFARINA Ecos

Pininfarina is collaborating with Fiat on the development of electric cars on an experimental basis. Ease of entry, good visibility and comfort plus ample battery housing are ensured in the 4-seater Ecos by a forward motor, front-wheel drive and battery pouffs under the seats. Fiat, mostly Ritmo, components are used. An electronic regulator provides energy recovery during braking. 16 6 V high energy and high power density batteries are recharged on board by an automatic current rectifier. The rear seats fold independently for easy access to the batteries and to increase luggage space. Top speed is 50 mph (80 km/h) and range in town 37 miles (60 km). Length is 154 in (390 cm) and height 59 in (149 cm).

USA

QUINCY-LYNN Trimuter E

In production from the spring of this year, this 3-wheeler fiberglass sports coupé has a clamshell canopy for entry to the two side-by-side seats. The series-wound 7 hp motor has a pulse-width modulator and is powered by ten 6 V lead-acid batteries mounted in two packs, 5 down the centre and 5 behind the passenger compartment. There is an on-board charger. Steering is through the single front wheel, with rear-wheel drive. There is direct drive via an HTD timing belt to the differential. At the top speed of 55 mph (88 km/h), the range is 30 miles (50 km) but rises to 65 miles (105 km) at cruising speed. The overall length is 144 in (366 cm), width 66 in (168 cm) and height 46 in (117 cm). It costs $ 6,995.

QUINCY-LYNN Urba Electric

In an aim to avoid unnecessary energy loss, generally caused above all by the speed control system, Quincy-Lynn have patented a continuously variable transmission (CVT). It starts the compound wound Jack & Heinz motor at full voltage, putting the current directly to the 25 hp motor, which runs at constant voltage and speed. Vehicle speed is controlled through the transmission. The CVT shifts in response to a signal from a foot pedal, controlling the speed from 10 to 60 mph (16 to 96 km/h). Transmission efficiency is about 90%. Top speed is 55 mph (88 km/h) or 60 plus with field weakening circuit and range up to 65 miles (104 km). Length is 126 in (320 cm). The cost of this build-it-yourself project is about $ 2,500.

SWITZERLAND

SBARRO Carville

Sbarro's elegant little 3-door 2+2 seater features a polyester body. Derived from the Pilcar electric car and the fruit of seven year's research, it is already in production. The 84 V 22 hp dc motor has a maximum power of 8/16 kW. The rear-mounted 12 V batteries are easily accessible and rechargeable from a 220 V electric point. The Carville has 4-speed automatic transmission and hydraulic drum brakes all round. Top speed is 50 mph (80 km/h) and range 62 miles (100 km). The overall length is 126 in (321 cm), width 57 in (145 cm) and height 59 in (150 cm). The curb weight is 2,535 lb (1,150 kg) and it has a useful load of 661 lb (300 kg). Available in red, blue, white, black and silver it costs 16,000 francs.

USA

SEARS — XDH-1

Created to mark the 10th anniversary of the famous Die Hard Battery used in USAC races, Sears' 3-door hatchback prototype based on the Fiat 128 3P has front-wheel drive and 2 bucket seats. A compound-wound 40 hp motor with regulation by solid state field weakening is mounted transversely. 20 6 V batteries are mounted in 2 packs, 5 under the hood and 15 in the former rear-seat area. Top speed is a lively 75 mph (120 km/h) with a range of 90 miles (145 km) at a cruising speed of 47 mph (75 km/h). Sears steel belted radial tyres are fitted and the car's weight, with batteries, is 3,110 lb (1,410 kg). Overall length is 151 in (386 cm), width 61 in (155 cm), height 52 in (132 cm) and wheelbase 88 in (223 cm).

AUSTRALIA

SHERWOOD OVERSEAS — Phase II

Aerodynamic shape, rolling resistance and light weight are the criteria of this specially designed 3-seater with fiberglass and aluminium body and light-weight high tensile steel chassis. The dc shunt motor provides traction and regenerative braking and an alternator keeps the auxiliary batteries fully charged. Motor speed is controlled by series, parallel switching providing 8 acceleration speeds with negligible losses in switching circuits. Transmission is stepless variable through a light-weight differential driving the front wheel. The batteries are housed in a removable tray on roller tracks between the rear wheels. Top speed is 43 mph (70 km/h) and range 74 miles (120 km). Weight is 1,102 lb (500 kg).

S.C.T. — R-1

The US Department of Energy is testing several prototypes of the front motor/front wheel drive SCT R-1 while development testing continues on others. Based on the VW Rabbit (called Golf in Europe) and carrying two, this 3-door hatchback is suited to all urban uses. It features a 17 kW separately excited Siemens motor, transistorized chopper and 18 6 V lead-acid EV 130 batteries recharged by an on-board charger. Acceleration from 0-30 mph (48 km/h) takes 10 seconds and top speed is 65 mph (105 km/h). Range naturally varies with driving conditions but in the SAE J227a(c) cycle it is 57 miles (92 km), almost double the DOE's minimum requirement. Length is 153 in (388 cm) and curb weight 3,100 lb (1,410 kg).

JAPAN

SUZUKI — Alto EV

In this electric prototype version of the new little Suzuki Alto 550 cc, the 2-door hatchback sedan layout has been retained with two seats in the front. A dc electric motor with a maximum power of 11 kW and a thyristor chopper are combined with 8 12 V lead-acid 120 Ah batteries mounted at the rear. Recharging takes 8 hours from a 200-200 V point but a rapid charge is possible in one hour. A 4-speed mechanical gearbox, drum brakes and 5,00-10 tyres are featured. The top speed is 47 mph (75 km/h) and range at a cruising speed of 25 mph (40 km/h) is 56 miles (90 km). Overall length is 126 in (319 cm), width 55 in (139 cm), height 53 in (133 cm), wheelbase 84 in (215 cm) weight 1,962 lb (890 kg).

FRANCE

TEILHOL Handicar

This 4-wheeler is primarily intended for the disabled or invalids using a wheel-chair. By pressing a button the floor descends to ground level allowing simple access in a wheel-chair by the rear door. The floor is then raised again. The rear door can be opened from the driving seat by pressing a button. The 2-seater stratified polyester body is mounted on a steel frame and has lateral boxes for the eight 12 V Ah batteries. The Handicar has a 4 kW motor, independent wheels and hydraulic drum brakes on all 4 wheels. Length 95.28 in (242 cm), width 53.15 in (135 cm), height 61.02 in (155 cm), dry weight with batteries 1,389 lb (630 kg). Top speed is 30 mph (50 km/h) and range 25-38 miles (40-60 km). Price 33,640 francs.

TEILHOL Citadine/Messagette

Using the same 2-seater polyester body with welded steel tubing frame, Teilhol offers two types of Citadine for urban transport and five versions of the Messagette for leisure use. The beach buggy's top speed in only 15 mph (25 km/h) with a range of 50-62 miles (80-100 km) but this speed is doubled for the Citadine by using 12 V 105 Ah batteries instead of 6 V 220 Ah ones, so that the 96 V motor has 4 kW power as compared with the 2 kW 48 V Messagette. The motor drives the rear wheel through a 2-stage helicoid pinion reduction gear. Length is 91 in (230 cm), width 54 in (138 cm) height 61 in (155 cm), and dry weight with batteries 1,323 lb (600 kg). No driving license is needed in France. Price - 25,275 to 26,845 francs.

USA

TP LABORATORIES Kesling Yare

This bright yellow egg-shaped prototype is the brainchild of a 77-year-old dentist. The low-slung fiberglass body seats three adults and two children. Centre wheels front and back take care of the steering while the two drive wheels are at the sides, slightly rear of centre. The tricycle arrangement (two side and rear wheels) carrying the 12 6 V lead-acid batteries is easily detached for service. The single gull-wing door affords easy access and exit from the kerb side only. Regulation of the 2-speed dc gearless motor is by Borisoff Engineering controls. Top speed is over 55 mph (88 km/h) and range 35-40 miles (56-64 km). Dimensions are: overall length 168 in (427 cm), height 52 in (132 cm) and wheelbase 144 in (366 cm).

SWEDEN

VOLVO Prototype

To gain know-how about electric cars while waiting for developments in batteries, Volvo has built two prototypes which are narrower and higher than the smallest Volvo production model but weigh 2,205 lb (1,000 kg). Rear-wheel drive, button selection of forward or reverse and an electronically actuated transmission make for easy driving. Thyristors aid starting and slow running, making them jerk-free. The 4-seater passenger car has a 8 kW 11 hp motor and the 2-seater van with sliding door mounts a 9.5 kW 13 hp motor. The 12 traction batteries of the 4-seater provide 72 V and the 10 of the van 60 V. The battery containers allows swift replacement. Top speed is 43 mph (70 km/h) cruising speed 31 mph (50 km/h) and range 31 miles (50 km).

WESTERN RESEARCH Lektricar II

Developed from a Datsun 310, this 2-door hatchback is already in production at a price of $ 12,000. It features 2 front bucket seats plus a folding bench rear seat. The Prestolite series motor develops 22 hp at 4,200 rpm and is powered by 18 108 V lead-acid batteries housed in 2 packs, one in the front engine compartment and the other at the rear beneath the deck. An on-board charger is optional, as is the air conditioner. Top speed is 75 mph (120 km/h) and range at cruising speed 60-70 miles (96-112 km) under normal traffic conditions. Overall length is 162 in (411 cm) and height 53 in (135 cm) with a wheelbase of 94 in (239 cm). The batteries account for 1,260 lb (572 kg) of the curb weight of 3,100 lb (1,406 kg).

WITKOFF Henney Kilowatt

This Renault Dauphine based 4-door sedan is already in production. The compact unitized, laminated steel body has 2 front seats with cargo space or optional jump seats at the rear. 14 heavy-duty 6 V lead-acid batteries power a traction GE 7.1 hp series wound motor with GE EVI SCR controller. The transmission is automatic with forward and reverse control operated by a switch on the dashboard. The motor is connected directly to a single unitized gear housing. Top speed is 50 mph (80 km/h) with a range of 60 miles (96 km) at cruising speed. The weight is 2,545 lb (1,154 kg), with the batteries accounting for 1,129 lb (512 kg). The overall length is 89 in (226 cm).

ZAGATO Zele 1000 and 2000

Various versions of the Zele are produced, the 1000 and the 2000, and the Van and Golf, carrying two plus luggage, with bodywork in reinforced polyester. They are driven by accumulator traction in four 12 V groups of 160 Ah batteries. Suspension is independent at the front and drum brakes are used all round. Dimensions: overall length 76.77 in (195 cm), width 53.15 in (135 cm), height 63.39 in (161 cm), curb weight 1,091 lb (495 kg), wheelbase 51.18 in (130 cm), front track 43.31 in (110 cm), rear track 42.52 in (108 cm), turning circle about 11.5 ft (3.5 m). For the 1000 version top speed is 25 mph (40 km/h) and range about 43 miles (70 km), and for the 2000 34 mph (55 km/h) and 31 miles (50 km).

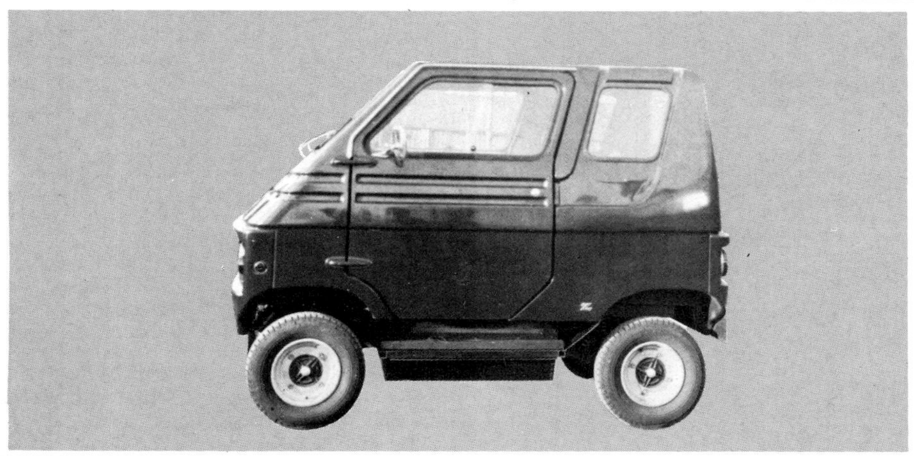

ZAGATO Zele Van

In view of the success of the Zeles, Zagato presented a new electric Van at the Chicago International Electric Vehicle Show. The range, top speed and battery recharging and replacement have been improved. Eight 6 V 215 Ah batteries power a 48 V dc motor which allows a top speed of over 30 mph (50 km/h) and a range about 37 miles (60 km). It is expected that a more powerful motor and improved batteries will shortly be adopted. The batteries are housed under the car's floor in an independent sliding tray. The chief dimensions are: overall length 81.89 in (208 cm), overall width 55.12 in (140 cm), height 60.63 in (154 cm) and wheelbase 53.15 in (135 cm). The compact reinforced glass fibre body is designed by the Zagato styling centre.

EVERYTHING UNKNOWN IS TAKEN AS MARVELLOUS...

by L.J.K. Setright

During the Hitler war, the British Broadcasting Corporation made much play with an old marching tune called Lillibulero, sounding it on their domestic and European services as a rallying-song for all the allies. They only played the tune; were they now to look back and consider the words, they might feel some embarrassment:

Ho, by my shoul, it is de Talbot
Lillibulero, bullen-a-la
And' a shall cut all the English throat
Lillibulero, bullen-a-la...

Talbot, once one of the most highly esteemed names in the motoring nomenclature, has been revived as a convenient and romantically attractive name for the cars which until lately had issued from a variety of English and French factories under the guise of Chrysler. As recorded in last year's edition of this book, the PSA constellation (of which the twin stars are Peugeot and Citroën) swallowed up the European properties that had been such an embarrassment to Chrysler; and there thus fell into one tenure all the firms whose names had once been associated with, or who had vested interests in, that of Talbot. It could simplify things no end, but if the naming of the first British car to emerge under the new banner is representative, it will not: for a quick car (which it is) the Talbot Sunbeam Lotus takes a long time to enunciate. While the erstwhile Simca factories make Horizons and a profit, maybe the English will do their own tracheotomies.

In the circumstances, PSA could have been pardoned for standing back to take stock of the situation, which must have involved vast outpourings of Peugeot's admittedly substantial capital resources. Instead they confidently went ahead with new launches, both Citroën and Peugeot improving their ranges. Citroën did so by attributes appear in a different order of priorities, Citroën brought the engine of the Diesel CX up to 2.5 litres and quite transformed what had been a nasty lumpen pudding of a car into one that was reasonably fuss-free, not unreasonably slow, and unquestionably abstemious, a car that is adopting the efficient 2-litre SFM engine (made at the Peugeot-Renault-Volvo 'club' factory at Douvrin) for the bodily efficient CX, the resulting Athena version being quite the sweetest CX yet, surely the most economical, and seemingly one of the more lively. For customers to whom these

Limited production is planned for the Renault 5 Turbo with 165 bhp rear engine.

quite the nicest of all diesels, though that may be to damn it with faint praise. In fact it was a good job well done, and the same may be said of Citroën's updating of the decade-old GS to keep it still one of the most competent cars in its class for the 1980s. Economy is hard to avoid in a car that needs only 30 bhp to sustain 75 mph, as the clean-lined GS does; but the new GSA version reinforces its scope for frugal driving with a 5-speed gearbox that does more to transform the car's character than the new tailgated luggage compartment, and perfectly complements the 1.3 litre engine that is the latest and torquiest of the flat-four series.

The use made by Peugeot of that 2-litre Douvrin engine is in the best examples of the new 505 range. Stylistically related to the 305 that was so extremely impressive a debutante a year earlier, the 505 is even sweeter and more forgiving in its behaviour, as well as being bigger. The significant difference is that it is a rear-drive machine, whereas the 305 is hauled along by its front wheels. If it would be mistaken to yield to the temptation to divide the generality of cars into Golfs and Cortinas (which is how it tends to look), there are few exceptions to a classification that sees only small front-drive and larger rear-drive cars; and there are evidently very few firms left who do not recognize the division as lying somewhere in the region of 1.6 litres. To make a 2 litre car of nice balance and elegant proproportions, Peugeot had everything to hand: to the front suspension and platform of the old 504 (which is not yet out of production) they added the independent rear suspension of the 604, drew a stretched 305-style body over them, dropped in any of a choice of engines (of which only the SFM deserves mention), and produced a car that does not fail by its orthodoxy to be utterly delightful.

A more adventurous approach to solving the latest motoring problems was displayed when PSA introduced the Visa. This small car, with its pert styling, inspiring manners and practical utility, is an amalgam of Peugeot and Citroën, though it is under the latter banner that it parades. The larger of two alternative engines is that of the Peugeot 104; the smaller is a new flat-twin Citroën engine that, while generally redolent of earlier air-cooled Citroën engines, is cleverly refined in many respects and is quite the most beautifully detailed engine to have been introduced by anybody for some years. Not the least of its virtues is the best electronic ignition system yet to grace a car; but it would be a shame to overlook the opportunity presented by the lightness and compactness of this engine for Citroën to modify the steering and front suspension geometry of the Visa in this form, giving it superior roadholding and handing responses. No less important to all Visa drivers is another Citroën achievement, which is a clustering of the minor controls in an ergonomically studied arrangement that perhaps beats even that paragon of switchbearers, the CX. More important still, as more people than ever buy a Visa, is that this little car is the harbinger of a new fashion, the precursor of other cars which will similarly span a wide range of categories from the artfully economical to the artlessly parsimonious, even from the sublime to the ridiculous, with the aid of a couple of alternative and very different engines.

The next in this line will be a Fiat, due to take its bow in 1980 with either the two-cylinder air-cooled 126 or the four-cylinder water-cooled 127 engine under its bonnet. Fiat have been busy with many things, meeting the demand for the Ritmo, making an alcohol-burning version of the 127 for Brazil, preparing what may be the final updating of the 132, and developing their diesel business; but most of all they can be seen to have been busy in restoring their erstwhile strength. It is just a pity that they have abjured the upper-class echelons of the market where the 130 saloon and coupé once lent an air of decorous but densely-engineered elegance, but in transferring the cure of that parish to their subsidiary Lancia they have probably done the

There are seven versions of the Renault Fuego coupé, sports version of the 18. The 1400, 1600 and 2000 cc engines have top speeds from 160 to 190 km/h.

The Audi Quattro which mounts a 200 bhp engine with turbocompressor is the only touring car with four-wheel drive.

commercially right thing. Certainly the new Lancia Delta, which takes the engine and drive-line and sundry other things from the Ritmo and dresses them in a first-class Ital Design body, has been so well and so deservedly well received that Lancia's function as the élitist of the Fiat group must be confirmed. To drive the Delta is to be convinced enough, but merely to stand it alongside a Ritmo is almost enough. That comparison may be more telling than we suppose, for it may reveal tastes and susceptibilities among the judges of the European International Car of the Year: in 1978 they voted the Ritmo a good second, but in 1979 they appointed the Delta first by a margin of surprising generosity, giving it more than 70% of all the votes cast. Directly or indirectly, Fiat should be pleased.

The diesel campaignings of Fiat must have reassured them too, for compression-ignition versions of the staple Fiat 131 have made good headway in the marketplace. At some cost in weight and balance, the 131 was allowed to retain some practicality as a car of tolerable performance despite a diesel engine: in place of the 1.6 litre engine in the Supermirafiori, there is a diesel of no less than 2.5 litres in the 131 Diesel Super — and it is an engine that is only rivalled in efficiency (using brake mean effective pressure as a yardstick) by the 2.5 litre Citroën in the same class. That a diesel could be effective on the road was publicly demonstrated when Fiat provided both versions of the 131 for contestants in the Italian 1979 Mobil Economy Run: run to very tight schedules which enforced energetic driving on twisting and hilly roads, this event produced some of the most interesting results in its history. While averaging a fraction over 44 mph, the petrol-engined 1.6 litre Supermirafiori cars returned an average fuel consumption of 39.39 mpg, while the Diesel Super 2500 managed 42.74, an improvement of 8.5%. It must be said that the conditions of the contest favoured the diesel, which is at its best in part-load operation; but the fact that it could match the required speed of the petrol-burners (which was as high as most ordinary drivers would have wanted to travel on such roads) while yet consuming less fuel was eloquent of how far the diesel has progressed.

The diesel engine has found protagonists elsewhere, too, including Alfa Romeo, Opel, Peugeot and most successfully VW whose diesel-engined Golf has enjoyed tremendous commercial favour. In a busy year, Renault added a diesel version of the

20 to their incessantly growing range; but that was only a part of the gap-plugging that they continued during 1979. At the base of their pyramid they found the venerable R4 losing friends because it was too feeble for some of the conditions in which it must nowadays work, so they updated it and uprated it with a bigger engine to make the 4GTL. Likewise they put some sparkle into the performance of the 14 in a bigger-engined TS, while adding two doors to the R5 to make it the only small 5-door car in the world that does not look like a model for a railway carriage.

An estate version of the R18 was another cunning move in a year which has shown the Régie's management of the market to be masterly.

A somewhat similar game has been played by Alfa Romeo, whose offer of larger engines in the Alfasud Sprint and Giulietta has made both those cars even more attractive than they already were. A bigger question mark hangs over the brand new "big" Alfa, the V6 with its engine curiously redolent in valvegear and carburation of forgotten racing cars; the scope for development of this motor is great, but its chances of enjoying such a fruitful life may depend on more circumstances than are within the firm's control.

Engines of V6 configuration have been very much to the fore in the past two or three years, but there is still a marked reluctance to abandon the V8 in some quarters, and prominent among its preservers are Daimler-Benz. Their new S-class cars arrived on the scene with tremendous impact, for while we all marvelled at the announcement of new light-alloy V8 engines of 3.8 and 5 litres coupled to four-speed automatic gearboxes, we had it impressed on us that the new Mercedes-Benz bodies that they propelled were aerodynamically so much improved as to allow the 380 to match the performance of the former 450, the 5.0 to match the 6.9 litre, and the fuel consumption in each case to be better than before. Drag coefficients

The Voyage, a family version of the new Kadett, is particularly well finished. The 1,300 cc 75 bhp engine allows a top speed of 100 mph (160 km/h).

The new Mercedes "S" coupé-roadsters mount the 8-cylinder light alloy propulsor of the "S" saloons. A four-speed automatic gearbox built by Daimler-Benz themselves is standard.

are falling almost everywhere, but the drop to 0.37 in these new Mercedes-Benz bodies is especially praiseworthy, bearing in mind from what unblushingly blunt predecessors they have descended.

The 5 litre V8 has been around for some time in a premium version of the 450 SLC which was supposed to be a competitor for the Porsche 928, the depredations of which into the Daimler-Benz market had been understandably painful. Porsche's even more painful answer in 1979 was the 928 S, with a bigger and much more powerful engine, some of the bib-and-tucker fanciwork beloved of present high-speed fashionmongers, and a degree of blatant vulgarity in the paintwork and general finish that confirms as endemic to Porsche a tastelessness that some earlier versions of the 911 (and more lately the Turbo 924) had revealed as merely acute rather than chronic. Still, if one wants a really fast 928 one can now have it, and with automatic transmission as standard. There need be no doubts about the suitability of such a transmission for the purpose; and if there were, they would be scotched by an even more staggering arrival on the luxury-hyperfast scene. Who would have thought that Bristol, who only late in 1979 had announced an LPG version of their 412 for the environmentally conscientious, would have revealed in the first days of 1980 a retyred, tweaked, tuned and turbocharged version of this 5.9 litre silent sports tourer, named the Beaufighter in loving and appropriate memory of that famous (and uncannily quiet) Bristol warplane? With a revised turret-top, more headlamps and tankage, and a host of refinements, the Beaufighter proves that even the best cars can be improved, and that in places there are still cars designed and specified by people who are real serious drivers. The Bristol was already in a class of its own; now the Beaufighter makes it the fastest-accelerating full four-seater available.

The upratings and improvements given to the Jaguar range early in 1979 pale by comparison, perhaps, but they too were encouraging in their intent and effect. One of the subtlest changes in the XJ saloons is to the roof line lifted at the rear to give more headroom and a bigger rear window; but the most important is the standardization of petrol injection for the 4.2 litre six-cylinder engine, restoring its performance to the level of 1969 when the car was new and emission controls had not yet emasculated it. It is an improvement in every way: emission regulations have made modern carburettors so full of self-defeating complications that injection is now simpler, and with the injection system able to share the control facilities becoming commonplace with the evolution of electronic ignition, the whole business of fuelling and sparking becomes cleaner, more reliable, and easier to understand, while the engine itself performs better and responds far better. This is a trend that will surely spread, and indeed Jaguar are not the only ones currently following it. They may be the only ones in the whole of the British Leyland group to be making visible design or development progress, however, for about the only other novelty to emerge from BL during the year was the expected soft-top Triumph TR7. The rest was all familiar stuff, strikes and disputes and doubts about the future; when it was announced that at some time in the future BL would be making in England a car designed by Honda, the immediate

The Triumph TR7 convertible has a 2-litre engine giving 105 bhp and a top speed of 176 km/h.

The classic Bristol 412/S3 Beaufighter with 5,900 cc engine and automatic gearbox. The long list of accessories includes air-conditioning.

Above, the Lotus Esprit Turbo emblazoned with the name of the petrol company sponsoring the F.1 Lotuses. The 2-litre engine develops 210 bhp at 6,000 rpm. Left, the Rover V8 S, a more luxurious 3,500 cc version of the saloon.

reaction of many people was to enquire about the possibility of buying the same car made in Japan. As the historian Tacitus observed in his *Agricola* "Everything unknown is taken as marvellous; but now the limits of Britain are laid bare".

Germany remains the only fully-developed country to offer roads with no limits, and deserves the utmost praise and respect for maintaining such an independent and rational attitude to speed, recognizing its value as well as its price. Germany is also apparently, and perhaps by way of reward, a nation which is without limits in the manufacturing sense too. The VW Golf has now passed the 3-million tally in production, and the range continues to proliferate. Latest addition is the Jetta, essentially a three-box or booted Golf, just as the Derby extended the Polo appeal; but there have been lots of other developments as well. The diesel Golf, as already mentioned, has prospered astonishingly, but the injection of petrol has as important a place in the VW scheme of things as the injection of oil: GLI versions of the Golf and Scirocco have brought new levels of performance to the class. At the same time, the ordinary 1.6 litre engine has been phased out as the 1.5 litre assumes wider-ranging duties to supplement the 1.3 which can be had in almost anything short of an Audi 100, where the temptation to turbocharge the biggest of their engines and make it into an Audi 200 proved irresistible. No less easy to resist is the temptation offered to Americans (and now others) of buying an open Golf, a drophead cabriolet.

It was known that Opel would be following the Golf course, and turning the Kadett around to be a front-wheel-drive car for youngish customers rather than a rear-driver for a clientele whom Opel discovered to be disappointingly elderly. When it turned out to have such impeccable handling and roadholding that hardly a trace of front-drive characteristics remained to corrupt it, the Kadett was seen to be more

Electronic injection and ignition for the 4-seater Ferrari Mondial 8 upholstered in Connolly leather and with a wealth of accessories. Top speed is 230 km/h.

The Fiat Panda in the 45 version with 903 cc engine and a top speed of 140 km/h. It seats five.

than merely imitative, and the quality of the engineering that has gone into it (notably in the rear suspension but also in the hull and the new overhead-camshaft engine) is impressively high. What came as a surprise was that Opel were not tempted to follow the VW line in styling: instead of offering a booted triple-box body as an alternative to the usual two-box hatchback, they have decided that the taste for such things will prove transitory. Instead, they have catalogued, an option that is more racy, not less, a body deliberately modelled on that of the Alfasud. There are all the variations of trim and specification that one would expect, and every one of them makes sense; but only the flared SR with Recaro seats and Pirelli P6 tyres is actually stimulating.

Tyres such as the P6 have made important contributions to the safety and pleasure of many 1979 cars. The Pirelli itself has been welcomed to the bosom of Alfa Romeo, Fiat, Opel, VW and several others; and the industry's familiar distaste for single-sourcing of components has been overcome by the introduction of a competitive tyre, the NCT, from Goodyear. These two between them promise to run riot throughout the whole list of cars from AC to somewhere west of Zlin, attracting imitation among the other tyre-makers just as the original Pirelli concept of the nylon-bandaged steel-belted tyre (first made as the CN36 and developed in the superb P7 and P6, and more modestly in the P3 and recently in the P5) is now being adopted by Avon, Dunlop, Firestone, and others. Michelin may have made a mistake in their TRX, a good and clever tyre that needed a special wheel and was still not as useful as the Pirelli, and it would do them no harm to admit it even though the possibility is as remote as their spokesmen always are.

Tyres of this new generation are already to be seen on the prototypes of cars that are past the possibility stage, and loom as probabilities for 1980. Vauxhall have a beautifully styled sports car, the Equus, nearly ready to go into production in the spring. Reliant have a new 8.8-litre drophead to cut a slice of market for which the old Scimitar has lost its edge. Renault have just brought out a dashing new Fuego coupé. Daimler-Benz, now they have put the finishing touches to their new S-class with SL and SLC versions of those brave new V8s, will doubtless ready their long-promised "small" car, the W201. Fiat are known to have more shots in their locker, as have Ford; Talbot surely have, BMW ought to have, and Volvo urgently need to have. The big question remains hanging over British Leyland — not whether they have any more ammunition, but whether they are still in the fight.

Volvo's experimental Concept Car derived from the 240 series can mount a 6-cylinder diesel with turbocompressor

Japan

CONSUMMATION OF THE TURBULENT DECADE

by Jack K. Yamaguchi

That the nineteen-seventies was a turbulent decade, as President Teizo Yamamoto of mighty Toyota Motor Sales Company affirmed in his New Year message, leaves no doubt or question. In retrospect, however, it is equally undeniable that it was an immensely lucrative and rewarding decade for the automobile industry of Japan.

The year 1979 followed the pattern with all the proper ingredients that marked the ten years. It was an intensive year packed with hopes, worries, uncertainties, a couple of megaton jolts and unprecedented wealth. To begin where we left off last year: the prospect for 1979 was no prospect at all. It would be a year of no growth. The industry hoped the domestic buyer who was seemingly recovering his autonomous buying habit would continue buying. The darker side of the picture was exports. The last two months of 1978 had shown a marked slide which might continue throughout 1979. The Big Two's production forecast was modest. Toyota expected no growth, while Nissan's volume would increase by a meager 2.2%.

The automobile industry was wary, apprehensive and sober, bracing itself for the worst. The strength of the Japanese yen did not encourage the exporting members. In January 1979, every dollar earned in the United States brought in only 201 yen. In the same month, the Shah left his country and the Ayatollah took over. Oil Crisis II was here, and our Ministry of International Trade and Industry quickly declared February a "month of energy saving", following up with a series of decrees and administrative guidances. Airconditioning thermostats in major government and private buildings would be set at 28 degrees Celsius or above, and the honorable minister advocated a "no necktie campaign", quickly donning a safari-jacket himself as an energy conservation suit in the coming summer. Of more immediate concern to the motorist were spiralling fuel prices, and the closing of filling stations on

The Corolla has many faces, for proliferation is Toyota's watchword. Here, the 4-door sedan.

Sundays and holidays, which must somehow have dampened his enthusiasm for new car purchase. There were other worrisome signs, like diesel pumps running dry nationwide in the early summer, chilling the diesel fever that had just been catching on, much to the consternation of a few manufacturers preparing to launch models powered by new compression ignition engines. These were, however, momentary symptoms and passing ailments and the domestic market held on strongly remaining active throughout the season.

As feared, exports did not fare well in the first half of the year, dropping by some 8% compared with the same period in 1978. But once again the mystical oriental goddess of Fortune smiled and endowed the Japanese with her blessings. To be fair, it wasn't her doing alone, for credit was largely due to the Goddess of Liberty whose country consumed more Japanese cars than expected. In July, for the first time in ten months, more vehicles were exported than the same month in 1978, and the surge continued and gathered momentum. By October, the industry's export performance had shown a growth rate of 1.1% over 1978. "Pleasantly, we were proven wrong!", exclaimed the marketing generalissimo of Toyota.

At mid-year, there were hurried changes of plans. Toyota upped its production plans from 2.93 million vehicles, to 3.08 million for the year. Number Two, Nissan, also stepped up production, its force of diligent workers putting in many hours of overtime to achieve this result. The 1979 performance surpassed the wildest expectations of the most optimistic. The Japanese industry turned out 10.1 million motor vehicles, 6.5 million of which were passenger cars. Domestic sales reached the magic 5 million mark, three million being passenger cars. In ten years, production had doubled and exports quadrupled. The Big Two, Toyota and Nissan, were busily rewriting chapters on production, home sales, export and profits in their record books. Toyo Kogyo, maker of Mazda vehicles, who only a few years ago was poring into the dark abyss, was given a clean bill of health by its main bank, the Sumitomo, who also arranged a minor capital participation by Ford of America. Mazda is now a million-vehicle-per-year producer. The logical development of this Toyo Kogyo-Ford marriage was the latter's divorce from Honda, who had marketed the smaller Ford cars in Japan through a subsidiary dealer network. Honda in turn extended its hand to Great Britain's BL, who will build a Honda designed and developed car called "Bounty" at its Cowley plant for release in 1981. Despite Chrysler Corporation's financial troubles, Mitsubishi stays put with its American partner in the joint venture Mitsubishi Motor Corporation. Mitsubishi's modern and efficient Kyoto plant is now geared to produce 200,000 four-cylinder engines for Chrysler's new FWD K-car series, and Mitsubishi has also undertaken the design and development of a mini pickup truck to be produced by Chrysler in the U.S.A. Likewise, Isuzu will supply its brand-new 1.8 litre 4-cylinder diesel engine to Chevrolet to be installed in the 1981 Chevette. Isuzu is also an important and integral part of the GM J-car project. It is also a known fact that Toyo Kogyo will supply its new partner with transaxle units for the new Ford Erica front wheel drive car.

Of the remaining three members who

Above, Japan's Car of the Year, the Cedric 430 Turbo S. Nissan's Cedric/Gloria twins offer a bewildering variety of power units and trims. Below, Japan's first 6-cylinder diesel engine, offered in the Cedric/Gloria range.

produce passenger cars, Daihatsu belongs to the Toyota group of companies, and Fuji Heavy Industries (Subaru) to the Nissan group. Suzuki remains alone but its forte is in the local light car sector, supported by the company's booming motorcycle business. Thus the Japanese have neatly set their house in order, with now more than a tinge of international color.

The automobile is still described as "a thorn in U.S.-Japanese relations", for Japanese imports accounted for 16.6% of 1979 U.S. new car sales, marking a whopping 30% increase over the previous season. One positive way to fend off criticism that the industry is too indigenous, con-

Subaru's new Swingback series includes the four-wheel drive sedan with dual speed range auxiliary gearbox.

fined within these far eastern isles, and to reduce trade friction would be the establishment of production bases in the U.S.A. A marketing chieftain remarked on the subject that it might be more a political necessity than economically feasible. Nissan's President Isihara is more cautious and would like first to watch the performance of a crop of new U.S. small cars, like GM's J-car and Ford's Erica, but admitted it might be necessary to consider producing Datsuns in the U.S. in the 'eighties. Toyota, a paragon of efficiency, cost saving and quality control, has always abhorred the thought of building cars in the new world, but it, too, is changing its tone. Mr. Eiji Toyoda, President of Toyota Motor Company, recently stated that his company would seriously study the possibility of U.S. production to meet any contingencies, adding emphatically that any decision would be based on sound commercial judgement, not under political pressure.

But it was Honda that shook the industry and observers by announcing its bold plans to establish a manufacturing base in the U.S.A., employing some 2,000 workers for a monthly production of 10,000 cars to commence in 1982. Honda's experience of super-bike production in Ohio must have encouraged the corporate planners to launch their ambitious new venture.

What accelerated the home market boom more than anything else was the industry's mid-year spate of new and revamped cars. Of these, two cars were most significant. One is Toyota's best-selling Corolla. In the thirteen years since the original 2-door sedan was announced, Toyota has produced over 8 million Corollas and its twin sister Sprinters. From 1974 through 1977, the Corolla was the best selling car in the world, in 1978 only beaten by VW's ubiquitous Golf-Rabbit (647,506 vs. 662,393). From the modest single body range, the family has grown to comprise no less than six basic body types with four sizes of engines. Of the 1966-1979 aggregate, three million were exported, not counting overseas production.

Sheer volume of production, the international nature of the operation with production abroad and a need for adequate servicing often in remote corners of the world, were all reasons why Toyota did not go FWD in the series 70 Corolla. By tradition and nature, Toyota people are a cautious lot who try anything new on a small scale before adopting it on a wholesale scale. "We know the conventional front-

To further improve fuel economy, Mazda has developed a "lean burn" rotary engine system using a 2-layer catalytic converter and claims a 20% improvement in fuel economy. Above, the Teutonic-looking Mazda Luce. Below, the Cosmo RX5 121 with the popular rectangular headlamps.

engined, rear wheel drive configuration best," insists Chief Engineer Agetsuma in charge of the Corolla-Sprinter project, "and we can offer the increasingly demanding and affluent Grand Public whom this car is aimed at better value". Conventional as it may be, the series 70 Corolla is no reskinned type 30. The car offers more interior space in a shell that isn't that much bigger than the old model, and the weight has actually been reduced, ranging from the basic 1300's 25 kg to a deluxe version's considerable 85 kg. Proliferation is the name of the game at Toyota, and, as mentioned, there are six basic body types and four engine options. The type 3A-U engine is the newest, and is a development of the type 1A-U originally used in the front wheel drive Tercel-Corsa twins, but without the 1A-U's tiny deadend auxiliary combustion chamber called TGP (turbulence generating pot). The 3A-U has very normal looking wedge-shaped combustion chambers, and in the domestic U (emission controlled) form, cleanses exhaust pollutants by means of an oxidizing catalyst, secondary air induction and exhaust gas recirculation. This 1500 cc engine is mated to a lighter type K gearbox, and the total saving in weight is 43 kg as compared with the old type T power unit. The three remaining engine options are from the existing Toyota engine families. The type 4K is the familiar pushrod slant four in 1290 cc capacity. Sporting Corollas and Sprinters are powered by the delightful Yamaha-built type 2T-GEU twin cam electronic fuel-injected 1.6 litre inline four rated at 115 hp JIS at 6,000 rpm (deduct about 15% to reach a comparable SAE net figure). For the U.S. market, Toyota decided on a bigger engine, a 1770 cc type T unit. This engine, with TGP head, was quickly added to the domestic lineup. In the chassis department, the Corolla has finally done away with the antique car springs in the rear suspension. A live axle is now properly located by trailing links, torque rods and Panhard rod, and sprung by coils. Another notable departure from the established Toyota practice, although on a limited scale, is seen in the steering. The 1300 Corolla is given a new rack-and-pinion steering. Chief Engineer Agetsuma had been subjected to criticism, especially from his European customers, on the vague recirculating ball steering, so he finally decided to adopt rack-and-pinion on the 1300. Like any Toyota car, the new Corolla will not exalt you with dynamic pleasure, but it is a vastly improved car with properly resilient suspension and a willing engine. And like any Toyota, it is extremely well-equipped and quality control is first class.

One of the most significant Japanese cars for the 'eighties is Honda's new Civic range. BL of Great Britain will build a Civic derivative at its Cowley plant.

Mitsubishi's Lancer EX follows the same evolutionary trend as the Corolla. "EX" stands for exceed, and exceed it does the old cart-sprung Lancer. Again the Lancer EX is a conventional car, and it, too, got a 4-link located, coil-sprung rear axle. Semi-elliptic leaf springs in the rear suspension are now almost extinct in this country, at long last! The Lancer's engine choices are Mitsubishi's MCA-Jet Orion 1400 and Saturn 1600, the latter with twin contrarotating omni-phase balancer shafts. At the 1979 Tokyo Motor Show, Mitsubishi showed an interesting "Reference model (not for production or sale, yet)" based on

GROWTH OVER THE DECADE

	1970	1978	1979 (estimate)	1980 (forecast)*
I. PRODUCTION				
Total motor vehicles (excluding motorcycles)	5,289,157	9,269,153	10,100,000	—
Passenger cars	3,178,708	5,975,968	6,445,000	—
II. DOMESTIC NEW CAR REGISTRATIONS				
Total motor vehicles (excluding motorcycles)	4,097,361	4,681,893	5,154,000	5,154,000
Passenger cars	2,373,054	2,856,799	3,046,000	3,039,000
III. EXPORT				
Total motor vehicles (excluding motorcycles)				
a) Complete vehicles	1,086,776	4,270,414	4,543,000	—
b) Units for assembly	—	330,321	403,000	—
Passenger cars				
a) Complete cars	725,587	2,819,074	3,115,000	—
b) Units for assembly	—	223,163	384,000	—

*** Forecast by Nissan Motor Co.**

Mitsubishi's Lancer EX sedan is one of the many converts to rectangular headlamps.

Suzuki, a motorcycle manufacturer, has launched this Alto hatchback selling at 470,000 yen (about $1,900, at Y250 to $1 conversion).

a Lancer EX sedan. This was an international rally version suitably attired in spoilers and airdam, equipped with an elaborate electronic route/time guidance system and more significantly a brand new engine called "Sirius 2000". Speculation was that this engine did not have MCA-Jet third valves that let in air to create swirls. Instead, the Sirius four would employ a sophisticated closed loop 3-way catalyst system complete with digital fuel injection of Mitsubishi's own design and manufacture. It would be no mean feat if the company could successfully avoid payment of royalties to a certain Herr Bosch...

Honda has finally converted to the catalyst school, albeit on a limited scale initially. The latest CVCC charge stratification engine in the 1500 cc size uses a small capacity catalyst to help relieve the engine, now tuned for higher performance and better fuel economy, of some of the exhaust cleaning chore. According to Honda's own data, the 1500 CVCC-catalyst Civic will travel 18 km on a litre of fuel on the Japanese emission city cycle mode while the pure CVCC 1300 will cover only 12 km! The 1300's reason for being in the Honda catalogue, they hasten to add, is a lower initial price. Honda is expected to convert an 1850 cc CVCC engine in the sporty Prelude coupé to the new catalyst specifications soon, followed eventually by other versions of the engine family.

Some years ago, a group of top engineers and designers got together under the direction of Tadashi Kume, president of Honda R&D Company, a wholly owned subsidiary of Honda, and conceived what they hoped would become a practical and ideal car for the 'eighties. The project was named "NA", short for new automobile. They reasoned that the 1973 oil crisis would linger on and be a chronic problem, so the NA should be an economy "world car". They decided upon an engine capacity of 1500 cc as it would be the most popular size in Japan and Europe, and the Americans would soon be accustomed to smaller cars. Body dimensions were based on providing sufficient space for five adults in comfort: it was to be 3.8 m long, 1.6 m wide on a 2.3 m wheelbase and 1.35 m tracks. Three prototype cars were built on the NA principle, which incorporated Honda's technologies for the new decade including a brand-new "fire breather" engine, which I suspect was a non-CVCC twin cam four. "Four to five years hence, the NA with minor refinements and modifications could be put on the market. Except for its smaller size, the NA could be equal to a Mercedes... If any car could benefit the national interests of the country it is exported to, it would be the NA", such was the confidence of Honda in this prototype. It wouldn't have been a cheap car, with its advanced technical features and innovations. A possible going price of US $ 7,000 was hinted at. The NA was never meant to be put into production as it stood, but it was to be the basis of a family of new Honda cars. The first to emerge was the Prelude coupé. Now this car bowed to need for compromise. For one thing, the production of that fire-breathing four was put off for several years, so it had to make do with a bulky 1850 cc version of the CVCC family, which transformed the car's character from a lively 2-seater sports coupé to a luxuriously appointed 2+2 cruiser.

The new Civic has kept more of the spirit of the NA. The car offers more performance, comfort and general amenities. Honda's sporting flair is represented by a CX version with a tuned 1500 cc engine and firmer suspension, that can outaccelerate a well-driven Mazda RX7 for the first 100 meters, run abreast with it for the next 100, after which the more powerful sports car will gradually pull away. The NA will give birth to more new models. A Wako-Delta (the location of an R&D-Lancia Delta-like 5-door hatchback) is to be given to Honda's second dealer network in Japan, which must now be content with the Prelude. Mid-year will see another variant, most likely a notchback sedan which may be the car to be built by BL.

The performance of Fuji Heavy Industries' FWD Leone range was disheartening in its homeland. Thriving exports to the United States must have sustained production. For some unexplicable reasons, the animal seemed to enjoy popularity in America. The Leone was clearly aged and its driving paws wanted more power in the competitive sector The new Leone range was initially available with two engine sizes and in two body styles, 4-door sedan and 2-door hardtop coupé, subsequently joined by a third body, a 2-door hatchback, and with it a smaller engine. The engine is the familiar watercooled aluminium flat four, in 1.3, 1.6 and 1.8 litre sizes. What is new for 1980 is Subaru's use of a catalyst in addition to the SEEC-T engine modifications which was really an add-on device system relying on the flat four's thermal and combustion characteristics to cleanse the exhaust. Like Honda's CVCC and Toyota's 3A-U, the Subaru found more power and consumes less fuel. Subaru's catalyst is the monolithic platinum-rodium variety and works as a partial 3-way system without the aid of an oxygen sensor or an onboard computer. By careful and elaborate tuning the 2-barrel carburetter adjusts air-fuel ratio to the ideal 14.7:1 on high load conditions thus reducing the three major pollutants in exhaust fumes. When running on lighter loads, the carburetter feeds leaner mixtures in the order of 15.5:1, thus conserving precious fuel. As before Subaru offers 4WD versions in three of the Leone body styles, 4-door sedan, wagon-van and new swing-back hatchback. The 1800 4WD is further improved in its climbing ability by a new dual-range transfer gearbox.

Another important catalyst convert is Mazda with its Wankel rotary engine which had hitherto been fitted with a thermal reactor system. The new two-layer partial 3-way catalyst helps improve the fuel consumption of the Wankel-powered Mazda by a remarkable 20% measured on Japan's city mode emission test cycle. With the catalyst and a clever deceleration control device called a shutter valve (which blocks off one bank, and directs all incoming charges to the other "active" bank, thus ensuring positive firing on deceleration), the engine is happier with leaner mixtures. Mazda does not advertise it but actually the engine puts out more power at the top end, and produces fatter torque at low and medium rpm ranges.

If you cannot offer entirely new ranges of cars, then you can always facelift your existing models. Rectangular headlamps and slant noses were fad items in 1979. Mazda's popular Familia-née-323-née-GLC got a pair of SAE proprietary rectangulars. Nissan's Sunny followed suit, and it would now take a pair of really keen eyes to tell if a car in your rear-view mirror is a Mazda or a Nissan. Isuzu's Gemini on the GM T-car (pre-Opel Kadett FWD) theme has undergone major nose and tail surgery, putting on a slant nose and rectangulars. Actually in Isuzu's case, it wasn't just the shape, for a larger engine bay and front end opening were needed for two new engines that must have more cooling air. More expensive cars gained custom-cut rectangular lenses, like Nissan's Skyline GT-240K GT, Mazda's Cosmo RX5/121 and Luce 929L. The Luce is unashamedly a Mercedes in its extended nose.

Isuzu's Gemini, which is now available with a 1.8 diesel or a twin cam four, is another convert to rectangular headlamps.

1979 saw an interesting phenomenon. Our K-class (kei means light in Japanese) had been stagnant for several years, annual sales touching 170,000 cars. The Hamamatsu-based motorcycle manufacturer Suzuki had always been a staunch protagonist of the K movement, and in spring launched a series of new FWD models, at considerable development and tooling expense. Mr. Suzuki saw an unexploited market niche with a stripped 3-door Fronte, renamed it Alto, put on a rock bottom 470,000 yen price tag (about $1900 at $1=Y250 conversion). This bargain price was made possible by several concessions for a commercial vehicle. First its 2-stroke 3-cylinder engine is exempt from the stringent emission control law. This would be a saving of about $230. Then there is the fact that commercial vehicles are exempt from the commodity tax levied on passenger cars. The Alto has only two doors, compared with its twin sister Fronte's four, thus saving another $135. The Alto was a micro sensation, and quickly imitated by

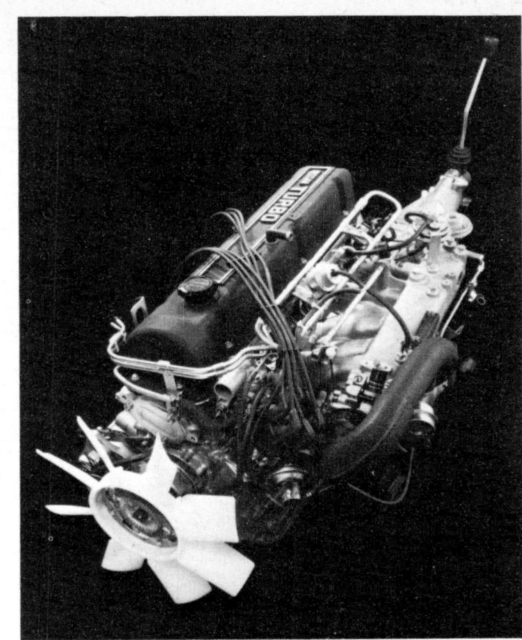

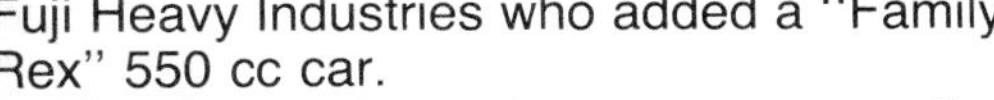

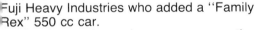

Above, Nissan's 2-litre turbocharged inline six, the first of its kind to be type-approved in Japan. Top left, Nissan's Silvia replacement has been joined by a Gazelle twin, in notchback and hatchback versions. Bottom left, the thoroughly up-to-date Bluebird sedan, the best Datsun ever.

Fuji Heavy Industries who added a "Family Rex" 550 cc car.

Another curious phenomenon was the increased popularity of forward control station wagons, which were really derivatives of commercial vans. For the first time in Japan's motoring history, the number of registrations of wagon-vans reached 120,000 in 1979. American influence must have been very strong, attracting younger buyers to this type of vehicle. The same may be true of 4WD vehicles. In addition to the vigorous push of 4WD cars, by Subaru, Toyota introduced a 4WD pickup and Isuzu launched a similar vehicle in Japan.

This is a country where innovations abound, but try to introduce any unprecedented innovative features in the automobile, and you face formidable and official walls of Jericho. The most effective weapon to bring them down nowadays is energy conservation, and that's how Nissan won mandatory type approval for Japan's first turbocharged car, the Cedric/Gloria twins. A single Garrett AiResearch TO3 turbocharger is used in conjunction with Nissan's electronic fuel injection and boosts the power output of the type L20 SOHC 2 litre engine to 145 bhp at 5,600 rpm. This is undoubtedly one of the best turbo applications anywhere. The engine in a big Cedric/Gloria shell is tractable and flexible at lower rpm, while turbo comes in strongly at 3,500 rpm, and rpm soars up. Nissan has done its homework very well indeed. The other twenty-one judges in our Car of the Year panel must have felt the same way as I did, and this late release of the season was promptly given the top honor. The 430 series Cedric/Gloria was a new car in the upper echelon. Like lesser models, the 430 got a coil-sprung rear axle which brought about considerable refinement of its road behavior. The non-turbo 280E version is also the first Japanese car to adopt digital fuel injection and an engine management system called ECCS. Nissan is a powerful advocate of electronics, and about 35% of Nissan-Datsun cars sold in Japan were fitted with electronic fuel injection, ranging from the small Pulsar/310/Cherry to the big President, and this year the number is rapidly increasing.

Another notable first in the 430 Cedric/Gloria is a 2.8 litre 6-cylinder diesel engine. The 91 hp six is undoubtedly the smoothest and most pleasant in the recent crop of diesels, among which are Toyota's 2.2 litre four now used in the Crown and Mark II ranges, and Isuzu's 1.8 litre four in the Gemini. Nissan won't hold its monopoly of the turbo for long, for Toyota is readying a turbo Crown, which also underwent a major change in 1979. Mitsubishi is tooling to produce its own turbo units, first to be put on an Astron silent shaft four-based diesel.

The last release of the season was also from Nissan, and should be a potent contender in the international middle class sector. It is the series 910 Bluebird, a conventional front-engined, rear wheel drive car that combines all the technical refinements Japan can offer: electronic fuel injection, twin sparking plugs, fast-burn low-emission engine, onboard computer display, fully independent suspension, four wheel disc brakes, rack-and-pinion steering across the board at long last and a kilometer-long list of comfort and convenience features. And the car is internationally good-looking. What more can you ask of this young industry which two decades ago was nowhere on the map of automobildom...

United States of America

SQUEEZING OUT THE MILEAGE

by Marshall Schuon

Pete Estes arranged a serious face below his shock of black hair and looked down at the audience. "I'm not sure that we want to build cars that get any more than maybe 30 miles to the gallon", he told the motoring press gathered for the introduction of General Motors' 1980 models at a restaurant in New York's Central Park. The tall, tanned and mustachioed president of GM then hastened to add that, in his opinion, 30 mpg was probably the point at which any additional cost might better be spent on development of synthetic fuels to relieve America's dependence on ever-scarcer and uncertain petroleum imports.

Pete Estes, known more formally as Elliot M., was addressing the key problem facing his industry in a year that is a kind of Jekyll and Hyde nightmare, a year that presents both a seller's market in small cars and an uncertain door to a decade of the most stringent mileage and pollution standards in history. This year, manufacturers' fleets must average 20 mpg, and that figure will rise to 27.5 by 1985.

American Motors has introduced six models of the 4WD Eagle with a new viscous coupling transfer case.

More to the point, though, the marketplace has overtaken government regulations in forcing better mileage. The American buyer, fearing a return of 1979's gasoline shortages and angry at skyrocketing costs at the pump, is demanding smaller and lighter cars. In addition, federal rules on exhaust emissions are growing tighter, while ongoing health studies leave some doubt about the future of the fuel-thrifty diesel.

Nineteen-eighty is thus an unsettling time for U.S. auto makers. Coming on top of last year's long gas lines and correspondingly short sales figures, it found Chrysler Corporation on the brink of bankruptcy and the rest of Detroit with vast numbers of unsold 1979 models, forcing cash rebates to customers and "dealer incentives" that in some cases totaled thousands of lost dollars on each car sold. Because of the glut of leftover '79 models, in fact, the manufacturers put back their introductions of the 1980 cars for several weeks to give dealers added time to clear their lots.

Nonetheless, the year holds its share of bright spots for the auto buff, with sophisticated under-the-skin engineering generally taking the place of the usual sheet-metal fancy. There are a few all-new models, too, as well as three new nameplates — AMC Eagle, Chevrolet Citation and Dodge Mirada, the first a smooth-riding four-wheel-drive sedan and station wagon, and the latter two replacing the Chevy Nova and the Dodge Magnum/Charger.

Cadillac's Seville was redesigned with a bustle that makes it look like a 1930s Rolls-Royce, and there are more and more turbochargers and diesels smoking up the roads, both with hot performance and in the truly sooty sense. General Motors'

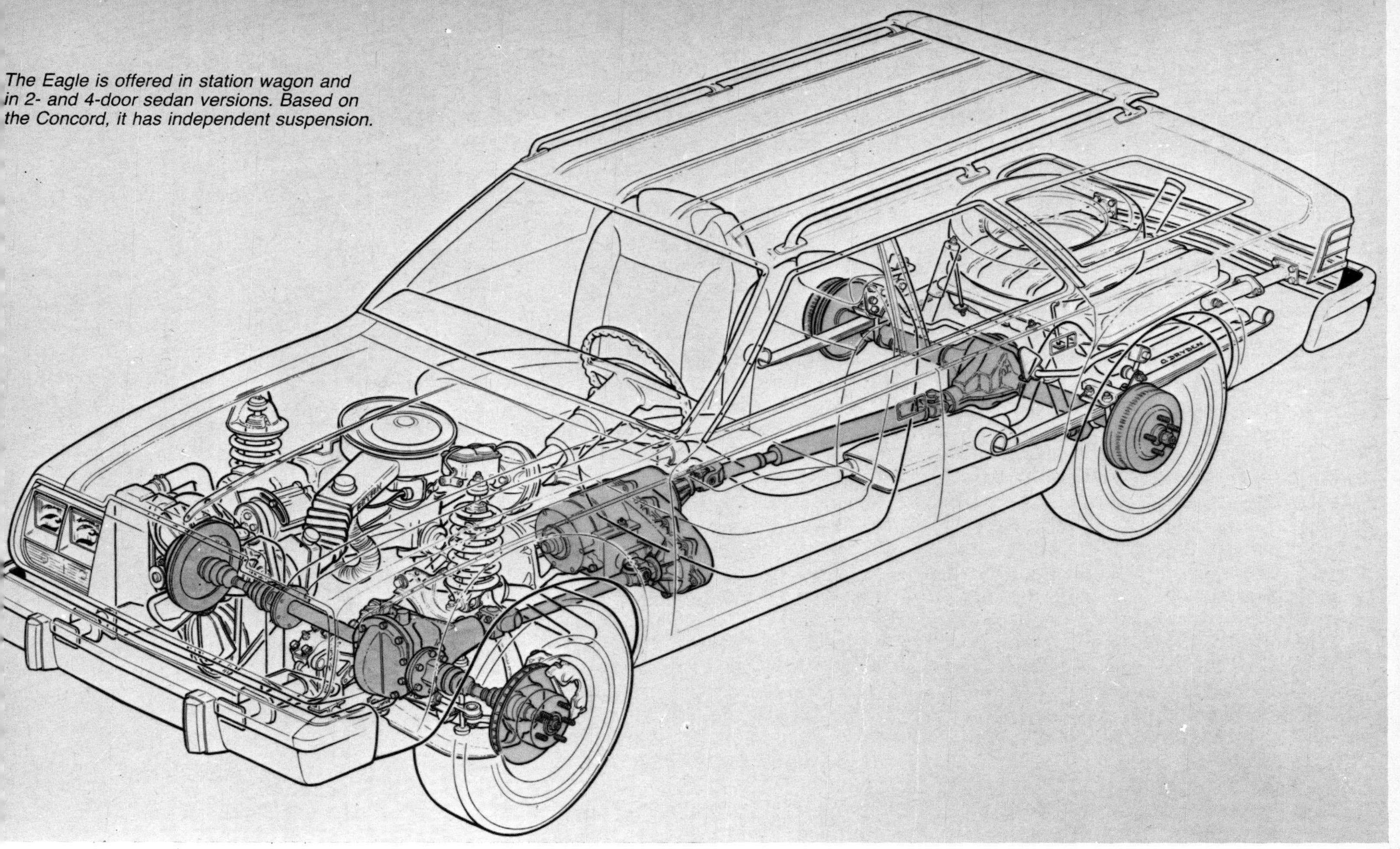

The Eagle is offered in station wagon and in 2- and 4-door sedan versions. Based on the Concord, it has independent suspension.

compact X-body cars, introduced as 1980 models in April '79 continue to make the accountants happy and to give the production people fits, lagging as much as five months behind customer demand. For Ford, 1980 is another step toward downsizing with a lighter Lincoln and a thriftier Thunderbird. And for Chrysler, well...

America's Number Three auto maker and tenth largest corporation entered the year teetering on the edge of financial disaster as a result of its 1979 loss of more than a billion dollars, the worst in U.S. corporate history. Actual bankruptcy, it was said, would cost hundreds of thousands of jobs and be a national calamity, affecting not only the company but its suppliers and dealers and the tax-bases of their various communities and states as well. Thus, the government in Washington voted to take up a position on the other end of the seesaw, balancing the threat with a bailout in the form of $1.5 billion in loan guarantees.

Earlier, the SOS from Chrysler had touched off widespread debate about the propriety of public aid to private enterprise, with calls in Congress for "sacrifices" on the part of both management and the United Automobile Workers union, which had just signed a three-year contract that guaranteed hefty wage increases. Chrysler, meanwhile, was forced to sell off some of its more profitable corporate entities to raise cash, and has tried to salvage what it can from its money-losing ventures around the world. Lee Iacocca, the corporation's chairman, said Chrysler had to remain a full-line producer, stressing that the company could not live on the profits from small cars and noting that they were "simply not sufficient to sustain the operation in and of themselves".

As if to underscore its intent, the company went into 1980 with 38 different models, compared with 29 last year. In addition to the new Mirada, other models were added to the Volare, Aspen, Diplomat and Le Baron lines, while the standard-size Gran Fury was brought back to give Plymouth dealers their first full-sized car in three years.

GM, on the other hand, cut the number of its entries from 152 last year to 122 for 1980, mostly thanks to the X-body cars, which replaced or consolidated various models of the Chevy Nova, Pontiac Phoenix, Oldsmobile Omega and Buick Skylark lines. Dropped from production were the Olds Starfire and Buick Skyhawk, both versions of GM's H-Special body.

Ford continued with 60 offerings, balancing additions with deletions. Eight models were added to the Pinto/Bobcat, LTD, Lincoln and Mark series, while the LTD II and base Cougar sedans were dropped. AMC introduced six new Eagle models and ended production of the Pacer and two Concord models. The only other "domestic" manufacturer, Volkswagen (in Westmoreland, Pennsylvania), made no changes.

General Motors, traditionally the most optimistic in industry forecasts, continued to expect sunny days, despite the slow start in 1980 sales. Thomas A. Murphy, the company's chairman, said Detroit would sell "something more than 11 million passenger cars" before his scheduled retirement at the end of this year. Ford's president, Philip Caldwell, was a bit more cautious, saying he believed production would be about 10.5 million, with sales reversing the 1979 pattern by building to a strong finish.

Total car sales in the United States last year were 10,641,099, with the domestics off 10% from 1978, while the more fuel-efficient imports soared to 21.5% of the market. GM suffered the least, although its sales fell to 4.9 million cars from 5.3 million a year earlier. AMC, helped by its new Eagle, also was hurt less than others, increasing its share of the market from 1.89% to 1.95%.

Even before the model year was two months old, though, Ford and GM were forced to add 30,000 more factory workers to those laid off earlier as a result of the whopping stocks of unsold 1979 cars. That meant a total of 120,000 idled workers and a slash in production to recession levels. Chrysler had already placed 29,000 auto workers on indefinite layoff status, and a company official said layoffs were certain to increase, a statement that brought unhappy agreement from Douglas A. Fraser, president of the auto workers' union.

During all this, the cars that were selling strongly were the gas sippers, in particular the GM X-bodies. On the drawing board since the Arab oil embargo of 1973, they poured forth at the rate of 205 an hour, 17 hours a day, six days a week. And because of the hunger for small cars, GM predicted that all 1980 cars, domestic and imported, would average 22.7 mpg, about 2.7 better than the required Corporate Average Fuel Economy (CAFE) for the year. GM's own projected average is 21.4 mpg.

Meanwhile, the specter of a gas-short nation was generating some very real energy of its own, primarily in new research on alcohol, batteries and other alternative forms of power for the country's 100 million automobiles. "The thing is, the urgency wasn't there before", said a Chrysler Corporation engineer. "Now everybody's paying attention, and reams of reports are coming in from all over the world".

Cadillac's controversial 1980 Seville has its roots in the British classics of the '30s and '40s, but front wheel drive and a 350 cu in diesel engine as standard are strictly 1980.

GM continued its search for a better battery to power future vehicles, having already revealed that it would be producing substantial numbers of electric cars and vans by the middle of the decade. Late last year, the company announced a breakthrough in zinc/nickel oxide technology, and said it meant that batteries could be much lighter while offering better range.

But the real replacement for gasoline, at least in the short term, appears to be diesel oil, and General Motors plunged ahead with diesel development, counting heavily on the engine to help in meeting CAFE requirements. In 1979, GM built 190,000 diesels — roughly 2.5% of its total production. But for 1980 that number will rise to 4%, and the engines are available in a wider variety of cars.

Previously, GM had concentrated diesel production on its luxury car lines, obviously working to create a better image for what traditionally had been a plebian mover of trucks. Now, though, all full-size 1980 Chevrolets, Pontiacs, Oldsmobiles, Buicks, and Cadillacs, can be ordered with 350 cu in diesel V-8s, and the engines are standard equipment on the drastically restyled Cadillac Seville, the first American car ever to have a diesel as its primary powerplant. Because of problems with government certification of the 260 cu in diesel, however, GM dropped it completely — no great loss, since it was far too weak to power most of the 1979 cars in which the company had installed it.

Ford, which has had a great deal of experience in making diesel trucks, was hesitant about following GM's lead in the passenger car field, although William O. Bourke, the company's executive vice president, said that would change if the ongoing studies gave the diesel a clean bill of health. Insiders have pointed out, too, that both Ford and Chrysler do plan to offer imported Japanese diesels in some small cars by 1982.

Nobody was neglecting the conventional gasoline engine, though, and the 1980 models have more new gadgets under the hood than ever before. Ford introduced its third generation of Electronic Engine Controls, and Cadillac's version of the system uses a digital computer to add a self-diagnosing ability, several backup measures in case of failure, and a system to let the mechanic know if he has correctly done the job of fixing the engine.

Turbochargers also have become more commonplace, with Ford's Fairmont and its twin, the Mercury Zephyr, adding the option. Pontiac's hot Trans Am has dropped its 400 cu in V-8 in favor a 301 cu in powerplant with a turbo option that boosts its 170 hp to 210, and the cars's "screaming chicken" hood decal now breathes a flash of decorative fire. Chevrolet, which last offered an exhaust-driven turbocharger on its long-gone Corvair, returns to the ranks with a Monte Carlo version, and Buick and the Ford Mustang carry over their turbos from last year.

The novelty of Lincoln's Mark VI series is a 4-door model. The smooth-riding Continentals and Marks bristle with electronic features that do everything from controlling engine functions to opening the rear deck lid.

Chrysler, which has often led the way in technological innovation, introduced its "lock-up" automatic transmission several years ago, and Ford and GM have followed suit to increase fuel economy of certain top-line models in 1980. The system uses an electronically activated clutch to lock the hydraulic clutch in place when the car is cruising above certain speeds, thereby eliminating gas-wasting slippage.

Ford also has brought out Detroit's first four-speed automatic transmission that helps economy by shifting into overdrive at about 40 mph. For the Lincoln, that change — and others — means a mileage increase of about 38%.

Those other changes, in fact, make the Lincoln quite a different car for 1980. Fresh from the reducing salon, the car weighs 800 lb less than last year's model, has a 302 cu in engine instead of the 1979's 400 cu in V-8, and new styling that cuts aerodynamic drag by as much as 22% for the Continental and 14% for the Mark. The latter also gets a new designation this year as a Mark VI.

Not content with computerized engine controls, the Lincoln and Thunderbird put electronics to work in the area of driver convenience as well, adding a version of Cadillac's Trip Computer that offers digital readouts of everything from fuel in the tank to an estimated time of arrival at any given destination. An electronic "Keyless Entry System" unlocks the doors and trunk through five illuminated buttons in the chrome windowsill of the driver's door. And, gimmicky as it might seem at first, the combination lock would be a convenience worth having, even if it only meant that a driver would never lock his keys inside the car again.

Pushing the right sequence of five numbers — for instance, 4-4-0-0-8, or whatever combination the owner programs into the system — unlocks all the doors. The first push also lights the numbered buttons and the interior of the car. Then, within five seconds, a push on the last button will unlock the trunk. And the really handy thing is that all doors can be locked by depressing the last two buttons in the row before walking away from the car. Conventional key locks act as a backup, in case the driver returns to find that the battery has called in sick.

Tires, which are pretty much taken for granted, have come in for attention this year, too, with pressure increased to more than 30 lb on some cars in order to reduce rolling resistance. But the biggest area for squeezing extra miles out of each gallon of gasoline remains the paring of pounds through use of plastics and other lightweight materials.

Some of those materials, such as aluminium, are household words. But others, such as the hybrid "exotics", have a nomenclature that is alien to most drivers — things such as polyester/glass-sheet molding compounds, thermoplastic polymerics, hot-chamber diecast magnesium and graphite-fiber composites. The materials are, or will be, used in nearly every part of the automobile.

The average General Motors car currently has about 190 lb of plastic, or 5% of its weight. But as the heavier metals are stripped away, the use of plastics substitutes is expected to rise to 225 lb by 1985. And it could reach 300 lb by then if engineers can find ways to use plastics in structural components such as driveshafts, leaf springs and transmission supports.

GM estimates that the use of iron will fall from the current average of about 600 lb to about 300 lb by 1987. And at Ford, Fred Bolling, executive engineer for vehicle materials development and planning, estimates that one-quarter to one-third of mileage gains will be achieved through downweighting.

Meanwhile, auto stylists have been pressed into service to do more than make last year's model obsolete. While there are few dazzling displays of new design for

1980, there are subtle changes that have helped gain fuel economy. The design studios have found that aerodynamics dictate gently sloping hoods at the front of the new cars and higher trunk lids at the back. "For the first time", said one stylist, "I feel like I'm doing something really important — not just changing sheetmetal for the sake of changing sheetmetal".

The Cadillac Seville, of course, is a startling exception, since it has both radical new design that smacks of a 1930s Rolls-Royce and engineering that has made it a front-wheel-drive vehicle for the first time. It also has a dramatically increased price, being tagged at $ 20,000 — $ 4,000 more than its 1979 counterpart.

As might be expected, the car is controversial and the standard wisdom is that you either love it or hate it. "Some people think it's the ugliest car they've ever seen", said the sales manager for one Cadillac dealer. Another, however, called the Seville "the best car we've had in several years" and added that he felt it looked "more like a Cadillac" than ever.

The design was fathered by William L. Mitchell, who retired in 1977 as GM's vice president for styling, and the idea goes back farther than that. Mitchell said he was fascinated by the big luxury cars of London when he was there 15 years ago, and he resolved to bring those elegant lines home to Detroit. And if the car does resemble a Rolls, that's not all bad, he says, adding: "I'll never forget what my father once told me — if you're going to steal, rob a bank, not a grocery store".

The other all-out change for Detroit comes in the form of the American Motors Eagle, and the success of the 4WD sedan seems to have surprised even AMC. The car — and its station wagon incarnation — seems at first glance to be wholly conventional. An AMC Concord, in other words, albeit a little gangly and awkward. But the sophisticated underpinnings make it a joy to drive, particularly where other cars wouldn't be moving at all.

A 258 cu in inline six is standard in the Eagle, with the full-time 4WD operating through a new transfer case that uses a viscous coupling of liquid silicone to achieve limited slip differentiation. Called Quadra-Trac, the new single-speed transfer case was pioneered by FF Developments in England and has been used in some competition cars and specialized vehicles. The Eagle is equipped with a three-speed automatic transmission and has power steering, power brakes and radial tires as standard items.

According to the company, the car looks different because it is "very much its own machine, sitting three inches higher off the ground (than a Concord), using 15-inch wheels and tires instead of 14s, and having a totally unique lower body side treatment".

That treatment includes injection-molded fender flares made of a styrene-butadiene rubber material, the same dent- and ding-proof material that is used for fender flares on the company's highly successful Jeep CJ. And, while passing traffic may see just a slightly sporty vehicle, the view over the steering wheel is much like that from a small pickup truck, giving the driver a smug smile of tall superiority.

As usual with 4WD, there is a loss of fuel economy, but the Eagle's relatively light weight gives it about 16 mpg, still far more economical than the truck-based vehicles, such as Chevy's Blazer and the Ford Bronco. The Eagle, in fact, may be the harbinger of things to come — and it proves again that good things can come in small packages. In this decade, that notion is going to become a very big one indeed.

The Gran Fury, Plymouth's first big car since 1976, mounts a 225 cu in slant six with a one-barrel carburetor. 318 and 360 cu in V8s are optional.

Above, Pontiac's Trans Am with turbocharged 301 cu in V8. Left for 1980 the Dodge Omni 024 offers a De Tomaso sport package in red or yellow with lower body accents in black

Europe

Models now in production

Illustrations and technical information

CUSTOCA AUSTRIA

Hurrycane

PRICE EX WORKS: 125,000 schillings

ENGINE Volkswagen, rear, 4 stroke; 4 cylinders, horizontally opposed; 96.7 cu in, 1,584 cc (3.37 x 2.72 in, 85.5 x 69 mm); max power (DIN): 50 hp (37 kW) at 4,000 rpm; max torque (DIN): 78 lb ft, 10.8 kg m (106 Nm) at 2,800 rpm; 31.6 hp/l (23.2 kW/l).

PERFORMANCE max speeds: (I) 22 mph, 35 km/h; (II) 47 mph, 75 km/h; (III) 68 mph, 110 km/h; (IV) 96 mph, 155 km/h; power-weight ratio: 30.9 lb/hp (41.9 lb/kW), 14 kg/hp (19 kg/kW); acceleration: standing ¼ mile 12.5 sec; consumption: 23.5 m/imp gal, 19.6 m/US gal, 12 l x 100 km.

STEERING turns lock to lock: 2.50.

ELECTRICAL EQUIPMENT 12 V; 4 headlamps.

DIMENSIONS AND WEIGHT wheel base: 94,49 in, 240 cm; tracks: 55.12 in, 140 cm front, 55.91 in, 142 cm rear; length: 171.26 in, 435 cm; width: 67.72 in, 172 cm; height: 44.09 in, 112 cm; ground clearance: 6.30 in, 16 cm; weight: 1,544 lb, 700 kg; weight distribution: 46% front, 54% rear; turning circle: 41 ft, 12.5 m; fuel tank: 9.2 Imp gal, 11.1 US gal, 42 l.

BODY coupé, in plastic material; 2 doors; 2+2 seats.

PRACTICAL INSTRUCTIONS tyre pressure: front 19 psi, 1.2 atm, rear 22 psi, 1.5 atm.

Strato ES

See Hurrycane, except for:

PRICE EX WORKS: 130,000 schillings

PERFORMANCE power-weight ratio: 30 lb/hp (40.7 lb/kW), 13.6 kg/hp (18.5 kg/kW).

DIMENSIONS AND WEIGHT length: 164.57 in, 418 cm; width: 62.99 in, 160 cm; weight: 1,499 lb, 680 kg.

LEDL AUSTRIA

Bugatti 35 B

PRICE EX WORKS: 89,060 schillings

ENGINE Volkswagen, rear, 4 stroke; 4 cylinders, horizontally opposed; 72.7 cu in, 1,192 cc (3.03 x 2.52 in, 77 x 64 mm); compression ratio: 7:1; max power (DIN): 34 hp (25 kW) at 3,600 rpm; max torque (DIN): 61 lb ft, 8.4 kg m (82 Nm); at 2,000 rpm; max engine rpm: 4.500; 28.5 hp/l (21 kW/l); cylinder block with cast iron liners and light alloy fins, light alloy head; 4 crankshaft bearings; valves: overhead, push-rods and rockers; camshafts: 1, central, lower; lubrication: gear pump, filter in sump, oil cooler, 4.4 imp pt, 5.3 US pt, 2.5 l; 1 Solex 28 PCCT-2 downdraught single barrel carburettor; fuel feed: mechanical pump; air-cooled.

CUSTOCA Strato Es

TRANSMISSION driving wheels: rear; clutch: single dry plate; gearbox: mechanical; gears: 4, fully synchronized; ratios: I 3.800, II 2.060, III 1.320, IV 0.890, rev 3.880; lever: central; final drive: spiral bevel; axle ratio: 4.375; width of rims: 5.5"; tyres: 185 185/70 x 15.

PERFORMANCE max speeds: (I) 19 mph, 31 km/h; (II) 35 mph, 57 km/h; (III) 58 mph, 94 km/h; (IV) 71 mph, 115 km/h; power-weight ratio: 51.2 lb/hp (69.7 lb/kW), 23.2 kg/hp (31.6 kg/kW); carrying capacity: 463 lb, 210 kg; acceleration: standing ¼ mile 23 sec, 0-50 mph (0-80 km/h) 18 sec; speed in top at 1.000 rpm: 18.3 mph, 29.5 km/h; consumption: 37.7 m/imp gal, 31,4 m/US gal, 7.5 l x 100 km.

CHASSIS backbone platform; front suspension: independent, twin swinging longitudinal trailing arms, transverse laminated torsion bars, anti-roll bar, telescopic dampers; rear: independent, swinging semi-axle, swinging longitudinal trailing arms, transverse torsion bars, telescopic dampers.

STEERING worm and roller; turns lock to lock: 2.60.

BRAKES drum; swept area: front 55.8 sq in, 360 sq cm, rear 40.3 sq in, 260 sq cm, total 96.1 sq in, 620 sq cm.

ELECTRICAL EQUIPMENT 6 V; 66 Ah battery; 200 W dynamo; Bosch distributor; 2 headlamps.

LEDL Bugatti 35 B

DIMENSIONS AND WEIGHT wheel base: 94.49 in, 240 cm; tracks: 53.54 in, 136 cm front, 57.09 in, 145 cm rear; length: 157.09 in, 399 cm; width: 65.35 in, 166 cm; height 53.94 in, 137 cm; weight: 1,742 lb, 790 kg.

BODY convertible, in plastic material; no doors; 2 seats, bench front seats.

PRACTICAL INSTRUCTIONS fuel: 87 oct petrol; oil: engine 4.4 imp pt, 5.3 US pt, 2.5 l, SAE 10W-20 (winter) 20W-30 (summer), change every 3,100 miles, 5,000 km - gearbox and final drive 5.3 imp pt, 6.3 US pt, 3 l, SAE 90, change every 31,000 miles, 50,000 km; greasing: every 6,200 miles, 10,000 km, 4 points; sparking plug: 145°; tappet clearances: inlet 0.004 in, 0,10 mm, exhaust 0.004 in, 0.010 mm; valve timing: 6° 35°5' 42°5' 3°; tyre pressure: front 16 psi, 1.1 atm, rear 24 psi, 1.7 atm.

VARIATIONS

ENGINE Volkswagen, 78.4 cu in, 1,285 cc (3.03 x 2.72 in, 77 x 69 mm).
ENGINE Volkswagen, 91.1 cu in, 1,493 cc (3.27 x 2.72 in, 83 x 69 mm).
ENGINE Volkswagen, 96.7 cu in, 1,584 cc (3.37 x 2.72 in, 85.5 x 69 mm).

Mercedes SS 29

PRICE EX WORKS: 94,840 schillings

ENGINE rear, 4 stroke; 4 cylinders, horizontally opposed; 91.1 cu in, 1,493 cc (3.27 x 2.72 in, 83 x 69 mm); compression ratio: 7.5:1; max power (DIN): 45 hp (33 kW) at 3,800 rpm: max torque (DIN): 78 lb ft, 10.8 kg m (106 Nm) at 2,000 rpm; max engine rpm: 4,200; 30.1 hp/l (22,2 kW/l); cylinder block with cast iron liners and light alloy fins, light alloy head; 4 crankshaft bearings; valves: overhead, push-rods and rockers; camshafts: 1, central, lower; lubrication: gear pump, filter in sump, oil cooler, 5.3 imp pt, 6.3 US pt, 3 l; 1 Solex 32 PHN 2 horizontal single barrel carburettor; fuel feed: mechanical pump; air-cooled.

TRANSMISSION driving wheels: rear; clutch: single dry plate; gearbox: mechanical; gears: 4, fully synchronized; ratios: I 3.800, II 2.060, III 1.260, IV 0.890, rev 3.880; lever: central; final drive: spiral bevel; axle ratio: 4.125; width of rims: 5.5"; tyres: 185/70 x 15.

PERFORMANCE max speeds: (I) 22 mph, 35 km/h; (II) 40 mph, 65 km/h; (III) 66 mph, 107 km/h; (IV) 78 mph, 125 km/h; power-weight ratio: 37.3 lb/hp (50.7 lb/kW), 16.9 kg/hp (23 kg/kW); carrying capacity: 750 lb, 340 kg; acceleration: standing ¼ mile 21.4 sec, 0-50 mph (0-80 km/h) 15 sec; speed in top at 1,000 rpm: 19.6 mph, 31,5 km/h; consumption: 32.5 m/imp gal, 27 m/US gal, 8.7 l x 100 km.

CHASSIS backbone platform, rear auxiliary frame; front suspension: independent, twin swinging longitudinal trailing arms, transverse torsion bars anti-roll bar, telescopic dampers; rear: independent, semi-trailing arms, transverse torsion bars, telescopic dampers.

STEERING worm and roller, telescopic damper; turns lock to lock: 2.80.

BRAKES front disc (diameter 10.91 in, 27,7 cm), rear drum.

ELECTRICAL EQUIPMENT 12 V; 36 Ah battery; 420 W dynamo; Bosch distributor; 2 headlamps.

DIMENSIONS AND WEIGHT wheel base: 94.49 in, 240 cm; tracks: 53.54 in, 136 cm front, 57.09 in, 145 cm rear; length 157.48 in, 400 cm; width: 66.93 in, 170 cm; height: 47.24 in, 120 cm; weight: 1,676 lb, 760 kg.

BODY convertible, in plastic material; 2 doors on request; 2-4 seats; separate front seats.

PRACTICAL INSTRUCTIONS fuel: 85 oct petrol; oil: engine 4.4 imp pt, 5.3 US pt, 2.5 l, SAE 20W-30, change every 3,100 miles, 5,000 km - gearbox and final drive oil 5.3 imp pt, 6.3 US pt, 3 l, SAE 90; greasing: every 6,200 miles, 10,000 km, 4 points; sparking plug: 145°; tappet clearances: inlet 0.004 in, 0.10 mm, exhaust 0.004 in, 0.10 mm: valve timing: 7°5' 37° 44°5' 4°; tyre pressure: front 17 psi, 1.2 atm, rear 28 psi, 1.6 atm.

VARIATIONS

ENGINE Volkswagen, 72.7 cu in, 1,192 cc (3.03 x 2.52 in, 77 x 64 mm).
ENGINE Volkswagen, 78.4 cu in, 1,285 cc (3.03 x 2.72 in, 77 x 69 mm).
ENGINE Volkswagen, 96.7 cu in, 1,584 cc (3.37 x 2.72 in, 85.5 x 69 mm).

LEDL Mercedes SS 29

Tanga

PRICE EX WORKS: about 185,000 schillings

ENGINE Ford, rear, transverse, 4 stroke; 4 cylinders, in line; 79.1 cu in, 1,297 cc (3.19 x 2.48 in, 81 x 63 mm); compression ratio: 9.2:1; max power (DIN): 66 hp (49 kW) at 5,600 rpm; max torque (DIN): 70 lb ft, 9.6 kg m (94 Nm) at 4,600 rpm; max engine rpm: 6,300; 50.9 hp/l (37.5 kW/l); light alloy block and head; 5 crankshaft bearings; valves: overhead; camshafts: 1, overhead; lubrication: rotary pump, full flow filter, 5.6 imp pt, 6.8 US pt, 3,2 l; 1 Weber Register carburettor; fuel feed: mechanical pump; water-cooled, 8.8 imp pt, 10.6 US pt, 5 l.

TRANSMISSION driving wheels: rear; clutch: single dry plate; gearbox: mechanical; gears: 4, fully synchronized; ratios: I 3.580, II 2.050, III 1.350, IV 0.960; lever: central; axle ratio: 3.840; width of rims: 5.5" front, 7" rear; tyres: 185/60 x 13 front, 205/60 x 13 rear.

PERFORMANCE max speeds: (I) 31 mph, 50 km/h; (II) 54 mph, 87 km/h; (III) 83 mph, 133 km/h; (IV) 111 mph, 178 km/h; power-weight ratio: 25.8 lb/hp, (34.8 lb/kW), 11.7 kg/hp (15.8 kg/kW); carrying capacity: 353 lb, 160 kg; speed in direct top at 1,000 rpm: mph, 27.3 km/h; consumption: 36.2 m/imp gal, 30.2 m/US gal, 7.8 l x 100 km.

CHASSIS front suspension: independent, coil springs, wishbones, trailing links, telescopic dampers; rear: indepent by McPherson, twin coil springs coaxial with telescopic dampers.

STEERING rack-and-pinion.

BRAKES disc.

ELECTRICAL EQUIPMENT 12 V; 45 Ah battery; alternator; Bosch or Lucas distributor; 2 headlamps.

DIMENSIONS AND WEIGHT wheel base: 94.49 in, 240 cm; tracks: 55.12 in, 140 cm front, 56.69 in, 144 cm rear; length: 169.29 in, 430 cm; width: 68.90 in, 175 cm; height: 40.94 in, 104 cm; ground clearance: 5.91 in, 15 cm; weight: 1,709 lb, 775 kg; weight distribution: 40% front, 60% rear; turning circle: 34.8 ft, 10.6 m.

LEDL Tanga

BODY coupé, in plastic material; 2 doors; 2 seats, separate front seats.

PRACTICAL INSTRUCTIONS fuel: 98 oct petrol; oil: engine 5.6 imp pt, 6.8 US pt, 3.2 l, change every 6,200 miles, 10,000 km - gearbox 4.4 imp pt, 5.3 US pt, 2.5 l, SAE 90, no change recommended; greasing: none; valve timing: 29° 63° 71° 21°.

ŠKODA 105 S

ŠKODA CZECHOSLOVAKIA

105 S

PRICE IN GB: £ 1,970*

ENGINE rear, 4 stroke; 4 cylinders slanted 30° to right, in line; 63.8 cu in, 1.046 cc (2.68 x 2.83 in, 68 x 72 mm); compression ratio: 8.5:1; max power (DIN): 46 hp (34 kW) at 4.800 rpm; max torque (DIN): 55 lb ft, 7.6 kg m (74 Nm) at 3,000 rpm; max engine rpm: 5,200; 43.2 hp/l (31.8 kW/l): light alloy block, cast iron head, wet liners; 3 crankshaft bearings; valves: overhead, in line, push-rods and rockers; camshafts: 1, side; lubrication: gear pump, cartridge on by-pass, 7 Imp pt, 8.5 US pt, 4 l; 1 Jikov EDS R downdraught carburettor; fuel feed: mechanical pump; water-cooled, front radiator, 22 imp pt, 26.4 US pt, 12.5 l.

105 S

TRANSMISSION driving wheels: rear; clutch: single dry plate, hydraulically controlled; gearbox: mechanical; gears: 4, fully synchronized; ratios: I 3.800, II 2.120, III 1.410, IV 0.960, rev 3.270; lever: central; final drive: spiral bevel; axle ratio: 4.444; width of rims: 4.5''; tyres: 165 SR x 13.

PERFORMANCE max speeds: (I) 20 mph, 32 km/h; (II) 34 mph, 55 km/h; (III) 53 mph, 85 km/h; (IV) 81 mph, 130 km/h; power-weight ratio: 41 lb/hp (55.6 lb/kW), 18.6 kg/hp (25.2 kg/kW); carrying capacity: 882 lb, 400 kg; speed in top at 1,000 rpm: 15.5 mph, 25 km/h; consumption: 40.4 m/imp gal, 33.6 m/US gal, 7 l x 100 km.

CHASSIS integral; front suspension: independent, wishbones, coil springs, anti-roll bar, telescopic dampers; rear: independent, swinging semi-axles, swinging longitudinal leading arms, coil springs, telescopic dampers.

STEERING screw and nut; turns lock to lock: 2.50.

BRAKES servo, front disc (diameter 9.92 in, 25.2 cm), rear drum; lining area: front 11.8 sq in, 76 sq cm, rear 59.7 sq in, 385 sq cm, total 71.5 sq in, 461 sq cm.

ELECTRICAL EQUIPMENT 12 V; 35 Ah battery; 490 W alternator; Pal distributor; 2 headlamps.

DIMENSIONS AND WEIGHT wheel base: 94,49 in, 240 cm; tracks: 50.39 in, 128 cm front, 49.21 in, 125 cm rear; length: 163.78 in, 416 cm; width: 62.60 in, 159 cm; height: 55.12 in, 140 cm; ground clearance: 6.69 in, 17 cm; weight: 1,885 lb, 855 kg; turning circle: 36.1 ft, 11 m; fuel tank: 8,4 imp gal, 10 US gal, 38 l.

BODY saloon/sedan; 4 doors; 5 seats, separate front seats.

PRACTICAL INSTRUCTIONS fuel: 90 oct petrol; oil: engine 7 imp pt, 8.5 US pt, 4 l, SAE 20W (winter) 40W (summer). change every 3.100 miles, 5,000 km - gearbox and final drive 4,4 imp pt, 5.3 US pt, 2.5 l, SAE 90, change every 12,400 miles, 20,000 km; greasing: every 6,200 miles, 10,000 km, 4 points; tyre pressure: front 21 psi, 1.4 atm, rear 23 psi, 1.6 atm.

VARIATIONS

(only for export)

ENGINE max power (DIN) 45 hp (33.1 kW) at 4.800 rpm, 43 hp/l (31.6 kW/l).
PERFORMANCE power-weight ratio 41.9 (56.9 lb/kW), 19 kg/hp (25.8 kg/kW).

OPTIONALS 4.666 axle ratio; 5.5'' light alloy wheels.

105 L

See 105 S, except for:

PRICE IN GB: £ 2,076*

PERFORMANCE power-weight ratio: 41.9 lb/hp (56.9 lb/kW), 19 kg/hp (25.8 kg/kW).

DIMENSIONS AND WEIGHT weight: 1,929 lb, 875 kg.

ŠKODA S 110 R Coupé

120 L

See 105 S, except for:

PRICE IN GB: £ 2,183*

ENGINE 71.6 cu in, 1,174 cc (2.83 x 2.83 in, 72 x 72 mm); max power (DIN): 52 hp (38 kW) at 5.000 rpm; max torque (DIN): 63 lb ft, 8.7 kg m (85 Nm) at 3,000 rpm; max engine rpm: 5,400; 44.3 hp/l (32.6 kW/l).

PERFORMANCE max speed: 87 mph, 140 km/h: power-weight ratio: 37.1 lb/hp (50.4 lb/kW). 16.8 kg/hp (22.8 kg/kW); consumption: 35.8 m/imp gal, 29.8 m/US gal, 7.9 l x 100 km.

DIMENSIONS AND WEIGHT weight: 1,929 lb, 875 kg.

VARIATIONS

None.

120 LS

See 120 L, except for:

PRICE IN GB: £ 2,448*

ENGINE compression ratio: 9.5:1; max power (DIN): 58 hp (43 kW) at 5.200 rpm; max torque (DIN): 67 lb ft, 9.2 kg m (90 Nm) at 3,250 rpm; max engine rpm: 5,500; 49.4 hp/l (36.2 kW/l); lubrication: oil cooler, 8.1 imp pt, 9.7 US pt, 4.6 l.

TRANSMISSION width of rims: 5.5''.

PERFORMANCE max speed: 93 mph, 150 km/h; power-weight ratio: 33.7 lb/hp (45.6 lb/kW), 15.3 kg/hp (20.7 kg/kW); consumption: 32.8 m/imp gal, 27.3 m/US gal, 8.6 l x 100 km.

ELECTRICAL EQUIPMENT 4 headlamps.

DIMENSIONS AND WEIGHT weight: 1,951 lb, 885 kg.

PRACTICAL INSTRUCTIONS fuel: 95 oct petrol; oil: engine 8.1 imp pt, 9.7 US pt, 4.6 l.

S 110 R Coupé

PRICE IN GB: £ 2,129*

ENGINE rear, 4 stroke; 4 cylinders slanted 30° to right, in line; 67.5 cu in, 1,107 cc (2.83 x 2.68 in, 72 x 68 mm); compression ratio: 9.5:1; max power (DIN): 52 hp (38 kW) at 4,650 rpm; max torque (DIN): 59 lb ft, 8.1 kg m (79 Nm) at 3,500 rpm; max engine rpm: 5,800; 47 hp/l (34.6 kW); light alloy block, cast iron head, wet liners; 3 crankshaft bearings; valves: overhead, in line, push-rods and rockers; camshafts: 1, side; lubrication: gear pump, cartridge on by-pass, oil cooler, 8.1 imp pt, 9.7 US pt, 4.6 l; 1 Jikov 32 DDS R downdraught twin barrel carburettor; fuel feed: mechanical pump; water-cooled, front radiator, 13 imp pt, 15,6 US pt, 7.4 l.

TRANSMISSION driving wheels: rear; clutch: single dry plate, hydraulically controlled; gearbox: mechanical; gears: 4, fully synchronized; ratios: I 3.800, II 2.120, III 1.410, IV 0.960, rev 3.270; lever: central; final drive: spiral bevel; axle ratio: 4.444; width of rims: 4.5''; tyres: 155 SR x 14.

PERFORMANCE max speeds: (I) 20 mph, 32 km/h; (II) 35 mph, 56 km/h; (III) 54 mph, 87 km/h; (IV) 90 mph, 145 km/h; power-weight ratio: 35.4 lb/hp (48.1 lb/kW), 16 kg/hp (21.8 kg/kW); carrying capacity: 805 lb, 365 kg; speed in top at 1,000 rpm: 15.5 mph, 25 km/h; consumption: 33.2 m/imp gal, 27.7 m/US gal, 8.5 l x 100 km.

CHASSIS integral; front suspension: independent, wishbones, coil springs, anti-roll bar, telescopic dampers; rear: independent, swinging semi-axles, swinging longitudinal leading arms, coil springs, telescopic dampers.

STEERING screw and nut; turns lock to lock: 2.50.

BRAKES servo, front disc (diameter 9.92 in, 25.2 cm), rear drum; lining area: front 11.8 sq in, 76 sq cm, rear 59.7 sq in, 385 sq cm, total 71.5 sq in, 461 sq cm.

ELECTRICAL EQUIPMENT 12 V; 35 Ah battery; 35 A alternator; Pal distributor; 4 headlamps (2 halogen).

DIMENSIONS AND WEIGHT wheel base: 94.49 in, 240 cm; tracks: 50.39 in, 128 cm front, 49.21 in, 125 cm rear; length: 163.39 in, 415 cm; width: 63.78 in, 162 cm; height: 52.76 in, 134 cm; ground clearance: 6.89 in, 17.5 cm; weight: 1,841 lb, 835 kg, turning circle: 33.5 ft, 10.2 m; fuel tank: 8.4 imp gal, 10 US gal, 38 l.

BODY coupé; 2 doors; 2+2 seats, built-in headrests.

PRACTICAL INSTRUCTIONS fuel: 95 oct petrol; oil: engine 8.1 imp pt, 9.7 US pt, 4.6 l, SAE 20W (winter) 40W (summer), change every 3,100 miles, 5,000 km - gearbox and final drive 4.4 imp pt, 5.3 US pt, 2.5 l, SEA 90, change every 12,400 miles, 20,000 km; greasing: every 6,200 miles, 10.000 km, 4 points; valve timing: 18° 49° 53° 14°; tyre pressure: front 21 psi. 1,4 atm, rear 23 psi, 1.6 atm.

OPTIONALS 4.666 axle ratio.

TATRA — CZECHOSLOVAKIA

T 613

ENGINE rear, 4 stroke; 8 cylinders, Vee-slanted; 213.3 cu in, 3,495 cc (3.35 x 3.03 in, 85 x 77 mm); compression ratio: 9.2:1; max power (DIN): 165 hp (121 kW) at 5,200 rpm; max torque (DIN): 196 lb ft, 27 kg m (265 Nm) at 2,500 rpm; max engine rpm: 5.600; 47.2 hp/l (34.7 kW/l); cast iron block, light alloy head; 5 crankshaft bearings; valves: overhead, Vee-slanted, rockers; camshafts: 2,1 per bank, overhead; lubrication: gear pump, full flow filter (cartridge), oil cooler, 16.7 imp pt, 20.1 US pt, 9.5 l; 2 Jikov EDSR 32/34 downdraught twin barrel carburettors; fuel feed: mechanical pump; air-cooled.

TRANSMISSION driving wheels: rear; clutch: single dry plate, hydraulically controlled; gearbox: mechanical; gears: 4. fully synchronized; ratios: I 3.394, II 1.889, III 1.165, IV 0.862, rev 3.243;ver: central; final drive: hypoid bevel; axle ratio: 3.909; width of rims: 6''; tyres: 215/70 HR x 14.

PERFORMANCE max speeds: (I) 29 mph, 47 km/h; (II) 53 mph, 85 km/h; (III) 86 mph, 138 km/h; (IV) 116 mph, 186 km/h; power-weight ratio: 21,4 lb/hp (29.1 lb/kW), 9.7 kg/hp (13.2 kg/kW); carrying capacity: 1,036 lb, 470 kg; speed in top at 1,000 rpm: 22.2 mph, 35.8 km/h; consumption: 15.7 m/imp gal, 13.1 m/US gal, 18 l x 100 km.

CHASSIS integral; front suspension: independent (by McPherson), wishbones, coil springs, anti-roll bar, telescopic dampers; rear: independent, swinging semi-axle, swinging longitudinal trailing arms, coil springs, telescopic dampers.

STEERING rack-and-pinion, damper; turns lock to lock: 4.25.

BRAKES disc, servo; lining area: frotn 30.7 sq in, 198 sq cm, rear 21.1 sq in, 136 sq cm, total 51.8 sq in, 334 sq cm.

ELECTRICAL EQUIPMENT 12 V; 75 Ah 2 x 6 V batteries; 55 A alternator; PAL Magneton distributor; electronic ignition; 4 headlamps, 2 iodine fog lamps.

DIMENSIONS AND WEIGHT wheel base: 117.32 in, 298 cm; front and rear track: 60 in, 152 cm; length: 198 in, 503 cm; width: 71 in, 180 cm; height: 59.25 in, 151 cm; ground clearance: 6.30 in, 16 cm; weight: 3,528 lb, 1,600 kg; weight distribution: 43% front, 57% rear; turning circle: 41 ft, 12.5 m; fuel tank: 15.8 imp gal, 19 US gal, 72 l.

BODY saloon/sedan; 4 doors; 5 seats, separate front seats, reclining backrests, built-in headrests.

PRACTICAL INSTRUCTIONS fuel: 96 oct petrol; oil: engine 16.7 imp pt, 20.1 US pt, 9.5 l, SAE 20W-50, change every 6,200 miles, 10,000 km - gearbox 3.5 imp pt, 4.2 US pt, 2 l, SAE 90, change every 18,600 miles, 30,000 km - final drive 1.8 imp pt, 2.1 US pt, 1 l, SAE 90, change every 6,200 miles, 10,000 km; greasing: none; sparking plug: 200°; tappet clearances: inlet 0.004 in, 0.10 mm, exhaust 0.004 in, 0.10 mm; valve timing: 0° 30° 30° 0°; tyre pressure (max load): front 24 psi, 1.7 atm, rear 33 psi, 2.3 atm.

TATRA T 613

ALPINE RENAULT FRANCE

A 310 V6

PRICE EX WORKS: 94,000 francs**

ENGINE Renault, rear, 4 stroke; 6 cylinders, Vee-slanted at 90°; 162.6 cu in, 2,664 cc (3.46 x 2.87 in, 88 x 73 mm); compression ratio: 10.1:1; max power (DIN): 150 hp (108 kW) at 6,000 rpm; max torque (DIN): 151 lb ft, 20.8 kg m (204 Nm) at 3,500 rpm; max engine rpm: 6,400; 56.3 hp/l 40.5 kW/l); light alloy block and head, wet liners, hemispherical combustion chambers; 4 crankshaft bearings; valves: overhead, Vee-slanted, rockers; camshafts: 2,1 per bank, overhead; lubrication: gear pump, full flow filter, 10.6 imp pt, 12.7 US pt, 6 l; 1 Solex 34 TBIA downdraught single barrel carburettor and 1 Solex 35 CEEI downdraught twin barrel carburettor; fuel feed: mechanical pump; sealed circuit cooling, expansion tank, 21.1 imp pt, 25.4 p US pt, 12 l, viscous coupling thermostatic fan.

TRANSMISSION driving wheels: rear; clutch: single dry plate (diaphragm), hydraulically controlled; gearbox: mechanical; gears: 4, fully synchronized; ratios: I 3.364, II 2.059, III 1.318, IV 0.931, rev 3.182; lever: central; final drive: hypoid bevel; axle ratio: 3.444; width of rims: 7''; tyres: 185/70 VR x 13 front, 205/70 VR x 13 rear.

PERFORMANCE max speeds: (I) 39 mph, 62 km/h; (II) 63 mph, 102 km/h; (III) 99 mph, 159 km/h; (IV) 137 mph, 220 km/h; power-weight ratio: 14.9 lb/hp (20.7 lb/kW), 6.8 kg/hp (9.4 kg/kW); carrying capacity: 794 lb, 360 kg; acceleration: standing ¼ mile 15.4 sec; speed in top at 1,000 rpm: 22 mph, 35.4 km/h; consumption: 30.7 m/imp gal, 25.6 m/US gal, 9.2 l x 100 km at 75 mph, 120 km/h.

CHASSIS integral, central steel backbone; front suspension: independent, wishbones, rubber elements, coil springs, anti-roll bar, telescopic dampers; rear: independent, wishbones, coil springs, anti-roll bar, telescopic dampers.

STEERING rack-and-pinion; turns lock to lock: 3.60.

BRAKES disc, front internal radial fins, dual circuit, servo; lining area: total 22.5 sq in, 145 sq cm.

ELECTRICAL EQUIPMENT 12 V; 50 Ah battery; 50 A alternator; Ducellier distributor; 4 headlamps.

DIMENSIONS AND WEIGHT wheel base: 89.37 in, 227 cm; tracks: 55.28 in, 140 cm front, 56.30 in, 143 cm rear; length: 164.57 in, 418 cm; width: 64.57 in, 164 cm; height: 45.28 in, 115 cm; ground clearance: 6.30 in, 16 cm; weight: 2,238 lb, 1,015 kg; turning circle: 34.8 ft, 10.6 m; fuel tank: 13.6 imp gal, 16.4 US gal, 62 l.

BODY coupé, in plastic material; 2 doors; 2+2 seats, separate front seats, reclining backrests; electric windows; heated rear window.

PRACTICAL INSTRUCTIONS fuel: 98-100 oct petrol; oil: engine 10.6 imp pt, 12.7 US pt, 6 l, SAE 10W-30, change every 4,650 miles, 7,500 km - gearbox and final drive 6.5 imp pt, 7.8 US pt, 3.7 l, SAE 80, change every 9,300 miles, 15,000 km; tappet clearances: inlet 0.004-0.006 in, 0.10-0.15 mm, exhaust 0.010-0.012 in, 0.25-0.30 mm; valve timing: 9° 45° 45° 9° (left), 7° 43° 43° 7° (right); tyre pressure: front 23 psi, 1.6 atm, rear 38 psi, 2.7 atm.

OPTIONALS tinted glass; leather upholstery; metallic spray.

ALPINE RENAULT A 310 V6

CITROËN 2 CV 6 Spécial

CITROËN FRANCE

2 CV 6 Spécial / Club

PRICES IN GB AND EX WORKS:	**£**	**francs**
Spécial	**2,072***	**17,300****
Club	—	**19,700****

ENGINE front, 4 stroke; 2 cylinders, horizontally opposed; 36.7 cu in, 602 cc (2.91 x 2.76 in, 74 x 70 mm); compression ratio: 8.5:1; max power (DIN): 29 hp (21 kW) at 5,750 rpm; max torque (DIN): 29 lb ft, 4 kg m (39 Nm) at 3,500 rpm; max engine rpm: 5,900; 48.2 hp/l (35.4 kW/l); cast iron block, light alloy head, dry liners, light alloy sump, hemispherical combustion chambers; 2 crankshaft bearings; valves: overhead, Vee-slanted at 70°, push-rods and rockers; camshafts: 1, central, lower; lubrication: rotary pump, filter in sump, oil cooler, 4 imp pt, 4.9 US pt, 2.3 l; 1 Solex 26 / 35 CSIC downdraught twin barrel carburettor; fuel feed: mechanical pump; air-cooled.

2 CV 6 SPÉCIAL / CLUB

TRANSMISSION driving wheels: front (double homokinetic joints); clutch: single dry plate; gearbox: mechanical; gears: 4, II, III and IV synchronized; ratios: I 5.203, II 2.656, III 1.786, IV 1.316, rev 5.203; lever: on facia; final drive: spiral bevel; axle ratio: 4.125; width of rims: 4"; tyres: 125 x 15.

PERFORMANCE max speeds: (I) 19 mph, 30 km/h; (II) 37 mph, 59 km/h; (III) 55 mph, 88 km/h; (IV) 68 mph, 110 km/h; power-weight ratio: 42.6 lb/hp, (58 lb/kW), 19.3 kg/hp (26.3 kg/kW); carrying capacity: 739 lb, 335 kg; acceleration: standing ¼ mile 22.7 sec; speed in top at 1,000 rpm: 12.7 mph, 20.4 km/h; consumption: 47.1 m/imp gal, 39.2 m/US gal, 6 l x 100 km at 56 mph, 90 km/h.

CHASSIS platform: front suspension: independent, swinging leading arms, 2 friction dampers, 2 inertia-type patter dampers; rear: independent, swinging longitudinal coil springs, 2 inertia-type patter dampers, 2 telescopic dampers.

STEERING rack-and-pinion; turns lock to lock: 3.25.

BRAKES drum, single circuit; lining area: front 30.4 sq in, 196 sq cm, rear 34.7 sq in, 224 sq cm, total 65.1 sq in, 420 sq cm.

ELECTRICAL EQUIPMENT 12V; 25 Ah battery; 390 W alternator; 2 headlamps, height adjustable from driving seat.

DIMENSIONS AND WEIGHT wheel base: 94.49 in, 240 cm; tracks: 49.61 in, 126 cm front, 49.61 in, 126 cm rear; length: 150.79 in, 383 cm; width: 58.27 in, 148 cm; height: 62.99 in, 160 cm; ground clearance: 5.91 in, 15 cm; weight: 1.235 lb, 560 kg; weight distribution: 58% front, 42% rear; turning circle: 36.7 ft, 11.2 m; fuel tank: 5.5 imp gal, 6.6 US gal, 25 l.

BODY saloon/sedan; 4 doors; 4 seats, separate front seats; folding rear seat; fully opening canvas sunshine roof.

PRACTICAL INSTRUCTIONS fuel: 98 oct petrol; oil: engine 6.2 imp pt, 7.4 US pt, 3.5 l, SAE 20W-50, change every 4,600 miles, 7,500 km - gearbox 1.6 imp pt, 1.9 US pt, 0.9 l, SAE 80, change every 14,000 miles, 22,500 km - final drive 0.9 imp pt, 1.1 US pt, 0.5 l; greasing: every 1,900 miles, 3,000 km, 4 points; sparking plug: 225°; tappet clearances: inlet 0.008 in, 0.20 mm, exhaust 0.008 in, 0.20 mm; valve timing: 0°5' 49°15' 35°55' 3°30'; tyre pressure: front 20 psi, 1.4 atm, rear 26 psi, 1.8 atm.

OPTIONALS centrifugal clutch.

Mehari 4 x 4 / 2 + 2

PRICES EX WORKS:	**francs**
4 x 4	—
2+2	**22,800****

ENGINE front, 4 stroke; 2 cylinders, horizontally opposed; 36.7 cu in, 602 cc (2.91 x 2.76 in, 74 x 70 mm); compression ratio: 8.5:1; max power (DIN): 29 hp (21 kW) at 5,750 rpm; max torque (DIN): 29 lb ft, 4 kg m (39 Nm) at 3,500 rpm; max engine rpm: 5,900; 48.2 hp/l (35.4 kW/l); cast iron block, light alloy head, dry liners , light alloy sump, hemispherical combustion chambers: 2 crankshaft bearings; valves: overhead, Vee-slanted at 70°, push-rods and rockers; camshafts: 1, central, lower; lubrication: rotary pump, filter in sump, oil cooler, 4 imp pt, 4.9 US pt, 2.3 l; 1 Solex 26/35 CSIC downdraught twin barrel carburettor; fuel feed: mechanical pump; air-cooled.

TRANSMISSION driving wheels: front or front and rear; clutch: single dry plate; gearbox: mechanical; gears: 4, fully synchronized; high ratios: I 6.060, II 3.125, III 1.923, IV 1.421, rev 6.060; low ratios: 16, 8.167 and 5.086; lever: on facia; final drive: spiral bevel; axle ratio: 3.875; width of rims: 4"; tyres: 135 x 15.

PERFORMANCE max speeds: (I) 15 mph, 24 km/h; (II) 29 mph, 46 km/h; (III) 47 mph, 75 km/h; (IV) 62 mph, 100 km/h; power-weight ratio: 54.8 lb/hp, (74.5 lb/kW), 24.8 kg/hp (33.8 kg/kW); carrying capacity: 882 lb, 400 kg; acceleration: standing ¼ mile 24.9 sec; speed in top at 1,000 rpm: 12.7 mph, 20.4 km/h; consumption: 37.2 m/imp gal, 30.9 m/US gal, 7.6 l x 100 km at 56 mph, 90 km/h.

CHASSIS platform; front suspension: independent, swinging leading arms, 2 friction dampers, 2 inertia-type patter dampers; rear: independent, swinging longitudinal trailing arms linked to front suspension by longitudinal coil springs, 2 inertia-type patter dampers, 2 telescopic dampers.

STEERING rack-and-pinion; turns lock to lock: 3.25.

BRAKES disc; lining area: front 13 sq in, 84 sq cm, rear 11.2 sq in, 72 sq cm, total 24.2 sq in, 156 sq cm.

ELECTRICAL EQUIPMENT 12 V; 25 Ah battery; 390 W alternator; 2 headlamps, height adjustable from driving seat.

DIMENSIONS AND WEIGHT wheel base: 93.31 in, 237 cm; tracks: 49.61 in, 126 cm front, 49.61 in, 126 cm rear; length: 146.46 in, 372 cm; width: 60.24 in, 153 cm; height: 64.57 in, 164 cm; ground clearance: 9.45 in, 24 cm; weight: 1,588 lb, 720 kg; weight distribution: (4 x 4) 69% front, 31% rear (2+2) 63% front, 37% rear; turning circle: (4 x 4) 36.7 ft, 11.2 m (2+2) 36.1 ft, 11 m; fuel tank: 5.5 imp gal, 6.6 US gal, 25 l.

BODY open, in plastic material; 2 doors; 4 seats, separate front seats.

PRACTICAL INSTRUCTIONS fuel: 98 oct petrol; oil: engine 4 imp pt, 4.9 US pt, 2.3 l, SAE 20W-50, change every 4,600 miles, 7.500 km - gearbox 2.3 imp pt, 2.7 US pt, 1.3 l, SAE 80, change every 14,000 miles, 22,500 km - final drive 0.5 imp pt, 0.6 US pt, 0.3 l; greasing: every 1,900 miles, 3,000 km, 8 point; sparking plug: 225°; tappet clearances: inlet 0.008 in, 0.20 mm, exhaust 0.008 in, 0.20 mm; valve timing: 2°5' 41°30' 35°55' 3°30'; tyre pressure: front 24 psi, 1.7 atm, rear 24 psi, 1.7 atm.

Dyane 6

PRICE IN GB: £ 2,290*
PRICE EX WORKS: 21,000 francs**

ENGINE front, 4 stroke; 2 cylinders, horizontally opposed; 36.7 cu in, 602 cc (2.91 x 2.76 in, 74 X 70 mm); compression ratio: 9:1; max power (DIN): 32 hp (24 kW) at 5,750 rpm; max torque (DIN): 30 lb ft, 4.2 kg m (41 Nm) at 4,000 rpm; max engine rmp: 5,900; 53.3 hp/l (39.2 kW/l); cast iron block, light alloy head, dry liners, light alloy sump, hemispherical combustion chambers; 2 crankshaft bearings; valves: overhead, Vee-slanted at 70°, push-rods and rockers; camshafts: 1, central, lower; lubrication: rotary pump, filter in sump, oil cooler, 4 imp pt, 4.9 US pt, 2.3 l; 1 Solex 26/35 CSIC downdraught twin barrel carburettor; fuel feed: mechanical pump; air-cooled.

TRANSMISSION driving wheels: front (double homokinetic joints); clutch: single dry plate; gearbox: mechanical; gears: 4, fully synchronized; ratios: I 5.749, II 2.935, III 1.923, IV 1.350, rev 5.749; lever: on facia; final drive: spiral bevel; axle ratio: 3.875; width of rims: 4"; tyres: 125 x 15.

PERFORMANCE max speeds: (I) 17 mph, 28 km/h; (II) 35 mph, 56 km/h; (III) 53 mph, 85 km/h; (IV) 75 mph, 120 km/h; power-weight ratio: 41.3 lb/hp (56.1 lb/kW), 18.7 kg/hp (25.4 kg/kW); carrying capacity: 728 lb, 330 kg; acceleration: standing ¼ mile 22 sec; speed in top at 1,000 rpm: 12.8 mph, 20.6 km/h; consumption: 49.6 m/imp gal, 41.3 m/US gal, 5.7 l x 100 km at 56 mph, 90 km/h.

CHASSIS platform; front suspension: independent, swinging leading arms, 2 friction dampers, 2 inertia-type patter dampers; rear: independent, swinging longitudinal trailing arms linked to front suspension by longitudinal coil springs, 2 inertia-type patter dampers, 2 telescopic dampers.

STEERING rack-and-pinion; turns lock to lock: 3.25.

BRAKES front disc (diameter 9.61 in, 24.4 cm), rear drum, single circuit; lining area: front 13 sq in, 84 sq cm, rear 34.7 sq in, 224 sq cm, total 47.7 sq in, 308 sq cm.

ELECTRICAL EQUIPMENT 12 V; 25 Ah battery; 390 W alternator; 2 headlamps, height adjustable from driving seat.

DIMENSIONS AND WEIGHT wheel base: 94.49 in, 240 cm; front and rear tracks: 49.16 in, 126 cm; length: 152,36 in, 387 cm; width: 59.06 in, 150 cm; height: 60.63 in, 154 cm; ground clearance: 5.91 in, 15 cm; weight: 1,323 lb, 600 kg; weight distribution: 61% front, 39% rear; turning circle: 36.4 ft, 11.1 m; fuel tank: 5.5 imp gal, 6.6 US gal, 25 l.

BODY saloon/sedan: 4+1 doors; 4 seats, bench front seats; fully opening canvas sunshine roof.

CITROËN Mehari 4x4

CITROËN Dyane 6

CITROËN LNA

PRACTICAL INSTRUCTIONS fuel: 80-85 oct petrol; oil: engine 4 imp pt, 4.9 US pt, 2.3 l, SAE 20W-50, change every 4,600 miles, 7,500 km - gearbox 1.6 imp pt, 1.9 US pt, 0.9 l, SAE 80, change every 14,000 miles, 22,500 km - final drive 0.9 imp pt, 1.1 US pt, 0.5 l; greasing: every 1,900 miles, 3,000 km, 4 points; sparking plug: 225°; tappet clearances: inlet 0.008 in, 0.20 mm, exhaust 0.008 in, 0.20 mm; valve timing: 0°5' 49°15' 35°55' 3°30'; tyre pressure: front 20 psi, 1.4 atm, rear 26 psi, 1.8 atm.

OPTIONALS centrifugal clutch; separate front seats; folding rear seat.

LNA

PRICE EX WORKS: 23,960 francs**

ENGINE front, 4 stroke; 2 cylinders, horizontally opposed; 39.8 cu in, 652 cc (3.03 x 2.76 in, 77 X 70 mm); compression ratio: 9:1; max power (DIN): 36 hp (26 kW) at 5,500 rpm; max torque (DIN): 38 lb ft, 5.3 kg m (52 Nm) at 3,500 rpm; max engine rpm: 5,850; 55.2 hp/l (40.6 kW/l); light alloy block and head; 3 crankshaft bearings; valves: overhead, Vee-slanted at 33°, push-rods and rockers; camshafts: 1, central, lower; lubrication: rotary pump, filter in sump, oil cooler, 5.8 imp pt, 7 US pt, 3.3 l; 1 Solex 26/35 CSIC downdraught twin barrel carburettor; fuel feed: mechanical pump; air-cooled.

TRANSMISSION driving wheels: front (double homokinetic joints); clutch: single dry plate (diaphragm); gearbox: mechanical; gears: 4, II, III and IV synchronized; ratios: I 4.545, II 2.500, III 1.463, IV 1.147, rev 4.184; lever: central; final drive: spiral bevel; axle ratio: 4.125; width of rims: 4"; tyres: 135 SR x 13.

PERFORMANCE max speeds: (I) 19 mph, 31 km/h; (II) 35 mph, 57 km/h; (III) 53 mph, 86 km/h; (IV) 77 mph, 125 km/h; power-weight ratio: 43.5 lb/hp, (59.1 lb/kW), 19.7 kg/hp (26.8 kg/kW); carrying capacity: 728 lb, 320 kg; acceleration: standing ¼ mile 21.5 sec; speed in top at 1,000 rpm: 13.2 mph, 21.2 km/h; consumption: 47.9 m/imp gal, 39.9 m/US gal, 5.9 l x 100 km at 56 mph, 90 km/h.

CHASSIS platform; front suspension: independent, swinging leading arms, 2 friction dampers, 2 inertia-type patter dampers; rear: independent, swinging longitudinal trailing arms linked to front suspension by longitudinal coil springs, 2 inertia-type patter dampers, 2 telescopic dampers.

STEERING rack-and-pinion; turns lock to lock: 3.33.

BRAKES front disc (diameter 9.49 in, 24.1 cm), rear drum, rear compensator; lining area: front 23.9 sq in, 154 sq cm, rear 24.5 sq in, 158 sq cm, total 48.4 sq in, 312 sq cm.

ELECTRICAL EQUIPMENT 12 V; 36 Ah battery; 460 W alternator; Thomson fully electronic ignition.

DIMENSIONS AND WEIGHT wheel base: 87.80 in, 223 cm; tracks: 50.79 in, 129 cm front, 48.82 in, 124 cm rear; length: 133.07 in, 338 cm; width: 59.84 in, 152 cm; height: 53.94 in, 137 cm; ground clearance: 4.72 in, 12 cm; weight: 1,566 lb, 710 kg; weight distribution: 66% front, 34% rear; turning circle: 9.4 m; fuel tank: 8.8 imp gal, 10.6 US gal, 40 l.

BODY coupé; luxury equipment; 2+1 doors; 4 seats, separate front and rear seats; reclining driving seat; folding rear seats.

PRACTICAL INSTRUCTIONS fuel: 98 oct petrol; oil: engine 5.3 imp pt, 6.3 US pt, 3 l, SAE 20W-50, change every 4,600 miles, 7,500 km - gearbox 2.5 imp pt, 3 US pt, 1.4 l, SAE 80, change every 14,000 miles, 22,500 km - final drive 0.9 imp pt, 1.1 US pt, 0.5 l; greasing: none; sparking plug: 225°; tappet clearances: inlet 0.008 in, 0.20 mm, exhaust 0.008 in, 0.20 mm; valve timing: 7° 42° 35° 6°; tyre pressure: front 24 psi, 1.7 atm, rear 27 psi, 1.9 atm.

OPTIONALS rear window wiper-washer; heated rear window; metallic spray; reclining backrests.

Visa Spécial / Club

PRICES EX WORKS:	**francs**
Spécial	**24,800****
Club	**26,000****

ENGINE front, longitudinal, slanted 7°13' to rear, 4 stroke; 2 cylinders, horizontally opposed; 39.8 cu in, 652 cc (3.03 x 2.76 in, 77 x 70 mm); compression ratio: 9:1; max power (DIN): 36 hp (26 kW) at 5,500 rpm; max torque (DIN): 38 lb ft, 5.3 kg m (52 Nm) at 3,500 rpm; max engine rpm: 5,850; 55.2 hp/l (40.6 kW/l); light alloy block and head; 3 crankshaft bearings; valves: overhead, Vee-slanted at 33°, push-rods and rockers; camshafts: 1, central; lubrication: rotary pump, filter in sump, oil cooler, 5.8 imp pt, 7 US pt, 3.3 l; 1 Solex 26/35 CSIC downdraught twin barrel carburettor; fuel feed: mechanical pump; air-cooled.

TRANSMISSION driving wheels: front (double homokinetic joints); clutch: single dry plate; gearbox: mechanical; gears: 4, fully synchronized; ratios: I 4,545, II 2.500, III 1.643, IV 1.147, rev 4.184; lever: central; final drive: spiral bevel; axle ratio: 4.125; width of rims: 4"; tyres: 135 SR x 13.

PERFORMANCE max speeds: (I) 19 mph, 31 km/h; (II) 35 mph, 57 km/h; (III) 53 mph, 86 km/h; (IV) 77 mph, 124 km/h; power-weight ratio: 45 lb/hp (61.2 lb/kW), 20.4 kg/h (27.7 kg/kW); carrying capacity: 728 lb, 330 kg; acceleration, standing ¼ mile 21.9 sec; speed in top at 1,000 rpm: 13.2 mph, 21.2 km/h consumption: 49.6 m/imp gal, 41.3 m/US gal, 5.7 l x 100 km at 56 mph, 90 km/h.

CHASSIS integral; front suspension: independent, by McPherson, coil springs/telescopic damper struts, lower wishbones (trailing links), anti-roll bar; rear: independent, swinging longitudinal trailing arms, coil springs, telescopic dampers.

STEERING rack-and-pinion; turns lock to lock: 3.33.

BRAKES front disc (diameter 9.49 in, 24.1 cm), rear drum; lining area: front 23.9 sq in, 154 sq cm. rear 24.5 sq in, 158 sq cm, total 48.4 sq in, 312 sq cm.

ELECTRICAL EQUIPMENT 12 V; 35 Ah battery; 460 W alternator; Thomson fully electronic ignition; 2 headlamps, height adjustable from driving seat.

DIMENSIONS AND WEIGHT wheel base: 95.67 in, 243 cm; tracks: 50.79 in, 129 cm front, 48.82 in, 124 cm rear; length: 145.28 in, 369 cm; width: 59.45 in, 151 cm; height: 55.51 in, 141 cm; ground clearance: 5.16 in, 13.1 cm; weight: 1.621 lb, 735 kg; weight distribution: 59% front, 41% rear; turning circle: 32.1 ft, 9.8 m; fuel tank: 8.8 imp gal, 10.6 US gal, 40 l.

BODY saloon/sedan; 4+1 doors; 4 seats, separate front seats; for Club only, luxury equipment and reclining backrests.

PRACTICAL INSTRUCTIONS fuel: 98 oct petrol; oil: engine 5.3 imp pt, 6.3 US pt, 3 l, SAE 15W-40 (summer) 10W-30 (winter), change every 4,600 miles, 7,500 km - gearbox 5.3 imp pt, 6.3 US pt, 3 l, SAE 80 EP, change every 14,000 miles, 22,500 km - final drive 0.4 imp pt, 0.4 US pt, 0.2 l; greasing: none: tappet clearances: inlet 0.008 in, 0.20 mm, exhaust 0.008 in, 0.20 mm; valve timing: 7° 42° 35° 6°; tyre pressure: front 24 psi, 1.7 atm, rear 28 psi, 2 atm.

OPTIONALS heated rear window; rear window wiper-washer; metallic spray; for Spécial only, reclining backrests; for Club only, headrests on front seats and tinted glass.

Visa Super

See Visa Spécial/Club, except for:

PRICE EX WORKS: 28,300 francs**

ENGINE Peugeot, transverse, slanted 72° to rear; 4 cylinders, in line; 68.6 cu in, 1,124 cc (2.83 x 2.72 in, 72 x 69 mm); compression ratio: 9.2:1; max power (DIN) 57 hp (42 kW) at 6,250 rpm; max torque (DIN): 59 lb ft, 8.2 kg m (80 Nm) at 3,000 rpm; max engine rpm: 6,500; 50,7 hp/l (37.4 kW/l); light alloy block and head, wet liners, bi-spherical combustion chambers; 5 crankshaft bearings; valves: overhead, Vee-slanted, rockers; camshafts: 1, overhead; lubrication: gear pump, full flow filter, 7.9 imp pt, 9.5 US pt, 4.5 l; Solex 32 PBISA 7 horizontal single barrel carburettor; sealed circuit cooling, liquid, expansion tank, 13.2 imp pt, 15.9 US pt, 7.5 l, electric thermostatic fan.

CITROËN Visa Club

VISA SUPER

TRANSMISSION gearbox ratios: I 3.882, II 2.297, III 1.500, IV 1.042, rev 3.569; axle ratio: 3.562; width of rims: 4.5"; tyres: 145 SR x 13.

PERFORMANCE max speeds: (I) 24 mph, 39 km/h; (II) 40 mph, 65 km/h; (III) 62 mph, 100 km/h; (IV) 89 mph, 144 km/h; power-weight ratio: 30.9 lb/hp (42 lb/kW), 14 kg/hp (19 kg/kW); carrying capacity: 904 lb, 410 kg; acceleration: standing ¼ mile 19.9 sec; speed in top at 1,000 rpm: 17.3 mph, 27.8 km/h; consumption: 45.6 m/imp gal, 37.9 m/US gal, 6.2 l x 100 km at 56 mph, 90 km/h - 33.6 m/imp gal, 28 m/US gal, 8.4 l x 100 km at 75 mph, 120 km/h.

CHASSIS rear suspension: anti-roll bar.

ELECTRICAL EQUIPMENT Ducellier or Paris-Rhône distributor.

DIMENSIONS AND WEIGHT wheel base: 95.28 in, 242 cm; width: 60.39 in, 153 cm; height: 55.71 in, 141 cm; ground clearance: 5.91 in, 15 cm; weight: 1,764 lb, 800 kg; weight distribution: 62% front, 38% rear; turning circle: 32.5 ft, 9.9 m.

BODY folding rear seat.

PRACTICAL INSTRUCTIONS oil: engine 7.9 imp pt, 9.5 US pt, 4.5 l - gearbox 7.9 imp pt, 9.5 US pt, 4.5 l; tappet clearances: inlet 0.006 in, 0.15 mm, exhaust 0.010 in, 0.25 mm; valve timing: 5°20' 36°50' 36°50' 5°20'; tyre pressure: front 24 psi, 1.7 atm, rear 27 psi, 1.9 atm.

OPTIONALS headrests on front seats; tinted glass.

GS Spécial Berline

PRICE IN GB: £ 3,279*
PRICE EX WORKS: 29,900 francs**

ENGINE front, 4 stroke; 4 cylinders, horizontally opposed; 68.9 cu in, 1,129 cc (2.91 x 2.58 in, 74 x 65.6 mm); compression ratio: 9:1; max power (DIN): 56 hp (41 kW) at 5,750 rpm; max torque (DIN): 59 lb ft, 8.1 kg m (79 Nm) at 3,500 rmp; max engine rpm: 6,000; 49,6 hp/l (36.5 kW/l); light alloy block, head with cast iron liners, light alloy fins, hemispherical combustion chambers; 3 crankshaft bearings; valves: overhead, Vee-slanted; camshafts: 2,1 per bank, overhead, cogged belt; lubrication: gear pump, full flow filter, oil cooler, 7 imp pt, 8.5 US pt, 4 l; 1 Solex 28 CIC 2 or Weber 30 DGS 14/250 downdraught twin barrel carburettor; fuel feed: mechanical pump; air-cooled.

TRANSMISSION driving wheels: front; clutch: single dry plate (diaphragm); gearbox: mechanical; gears: 4, fully synchronized; ratios: I 3.818, II 2.295, III 1.500, IV 1.031, rev 4.182; lever: central; final drive: spiral bevel; axle ratio: 4.125; width of rims: 4.5"; tyres: 145 SR x 15.

PERFORMANCE max speeds: (I) 28 mph, 45 km/h; (II) 45 mph, 73 km/h; (III) 71 mph, 114 km/h; (IV) 93 mph, 149 km/h; power-weight ratio: 36.4 lb/hp (49.5 lb/kW), 16.5 kg/hp (22.4 kg/kW); carrying capacity: 904 lb, 410 kg; acceleration: standing ¼ mile 20.7 sec; speed in top at 1,000 rpm: 16.4 mph, 26.4 km/h; consumption: 44.1 m/imp gal, 36,.8 m/US gal, 6.4 l x 100 km at 56 mph, 90 km/h - 33.6 m/imp gal, 28 m/US gal, 8.4 l x 100 km at 75 mph, 120 km/h.

CHASSIS integral; front suspension: independent, wishbones, hydropneumatic suspension, anti-roll bar, automatic levelling control; rear: independent, swinging trailing arms, hydropneumatic suspension, anti-roll bar, automatic levelling control.

STEERING rack-and-pinion; turns lock to lock: 3.80.

BRAKES disc (front diameter 10.63 in, 27 cm, rear diameter 7.01 in, 17.8 cm), servo; lining area: front 22.6 sq in, 146 sq cm, rear 11.2 sq in, 72 sq cm, total 33.8 sq in, 218 sq cm.

ELECTRICAL EQUIPMENT 12 V; 40 Ah battery; 490 W alternator; Sev distributor; 2 headlamps.

DIMENSIONS AND WEIGHT wheel base: 100.39 in, 255 cm; tracks: 54.33 in, 138 cm front, 52.36 in, 133 cm rear; length: 162.20 in, 412 cm; width: 63.39 in, 161 cm; constant height: 53.14 in, 135 cm; ground clearance (variable): 6.06 in, 15.4 cm; weight: 2,040 lb, 925 kg; weight distribution: 63% front, 37% rear; turning circle: 34.1 ft, 10.4 m; fuel tank: 9.5 imp gal, 11.4 US gal, 43 l.

BODY saloon/sedan; 4 doors; 5 seats, separate front seats, reclining backrests.

PRACTICAL INSTRUCTIONS fuel: 98 oct petrol; oil: engine 7 imp pt, 8.5 US pt, 4 l, SAE 20W-50, change every 4,600 miles, 7,500 km - gearbox and final drive 2.5 imp pt, 3 US pt, bì.4 l, SAE 90, change every 14,000 miles, 22,500 km - hydropneumatic suspension 7.4 imp pt, 8.9 US pt, 4.2 l; greasing: none; sparking plug: 200°; tappet clearances: inlet 0.008 in, 0.20 mm, exhaust 0.008 in, 0.20 mm; valve timing: 4°10' 31°50' 36°10' 0°20'; tyre pressure: front 26 psi, 1.8 atm, rear 27 psi, 1.9 atm.

OPTIONALS folding rear seat; heated rear window; tinted glass; sunshine roof; metallic spray.

GS Spécial Break

See GS Spécial Berline, except for:

PRICE IN GB: £ 3,569*
PRICE EX WORKS: 31,200 francs**

PERFORMANCE max speed: 91 mph, 146 146 km/h: power-weight ratio: 36.8 lb/hp (50 lb/kW), 16.7 kg/hp (22.7 kg/kW); carrying capacity: 893 lb, 405 kg; acceleration: standing ¼ mile 20.9 sec; consumption: 43.5 m/imp gal, 36.2 m/US gal, 6.5 l x '100 km at 56 mph, 90 km/l - 32.5 m/imp gal, 27 m/US gal, 8.7 l x 100 km at 75 mph, 120 km/h.

DIMENSIONS AND WEIGHT ground clearance (variable): 5.91 in, 15 cm; weight: 2,062 lb, 935 kg.

BODY estate car/st. wagon; 4+1 doors rear window wiper-washer; folding rear seat (standard).

OPTIONALS sunshine roof not available.

GSA Series

PRICES IN GB AND EX WORKS:	£	francs
Club	3,633*	33,600**
Pallas	4,049*	35,900**
Club C Matic	3,876*	35,300**
Pallas C Matic	4,292*	37,600**
X 3	—	35,500**

CITROËN GSA Pallas

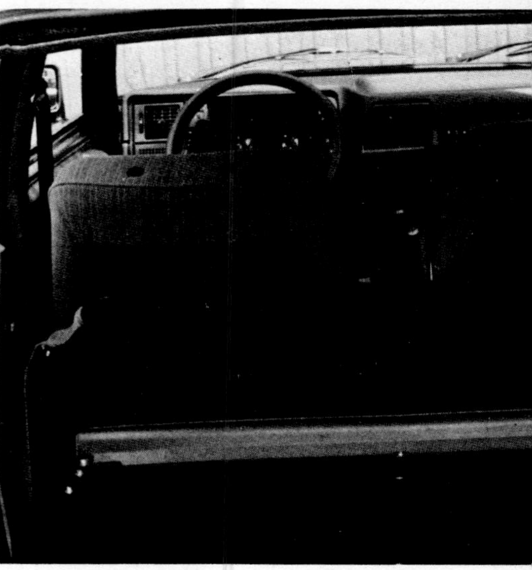

CITROËN GSA Club

ENGINE front, 4 stroke; 4 cylinders; horizontally opposed; 79.3 cu in, 1,299 cc (3.13 x 2.58 in, 79.4 x 65.6 mm); compression ratio: 8.7:1; max power (DIN): 65 hp (48 kW) at 5,500 rpm; max torque (DIN): 72 lb ft, 10 kg m (98 Nm) at 3,500 rpm; max engine rpm: 6,500; 50 hp/l (36.8 kW/l); light alloy block, head with cast iron liners, light alloy fins, hemispherical combustion chambers; 3 crankshaft bearings; valves: overhead, Vee-slanted; camshafts: 2,1 per bank, overhead, cogged belt; lubrication: rotary pump, full flow filter, oil cooler, 7 imp pt, 8.5 US pt, 4 l; 1 Solex CIC or Weber 30 DGS 13/250 downdraught twin barrel carburettor; fuel feed: mechanical; pump: air-cooled.

TRANSMISSION driving wheels: front; clutch: single dry plate (diaphragm); gearbox: mechanical - for C Matic models only semi-automatic transmission hydraulic torque converter and planetary gears with 3 ratios (I 2.730, II 1.700, III 1.030, rev 2.500), max ratio of converter at stall 2, possible manual selection; gears: 4 (5 for X 3 only), fully synchronized; ratios: I 3.810, II 2.290, III 1.500, IV 1.030 (for X 3 1.300, V 0.910), rev 4.180; lever: central; final drive: spiral bevel; axle ratio: 4.125; width of rims: 4.5"; tyres: 145 SR X 15.

PERFORMANCE max speeds: (I) 29 mph, 46 km/h; (II) 42 mph, 67 km/h; (III) 73 mph, 118 km/h; (IV) 98 mph, 158 km/h - C Matic models (I) 42 mph, 68 km/h; (II) 63 mph, 101 km/h; (III) 92 mph, 148 km/h; power-weight ratio: 32.4 lb/hp, (44.1 lb/kW), 14.7 kg/hp (20 kg/kW) - for X 3 only 31.9 lb/hp (43.4 lb/kW), 14.5 kg/hp (19.7 kg/kW); carrying capacity: 882 lb, 400 kg; acceleration: standing ¼ mile 19.1 sec - C Matic models 21 sec; speed in top at 1,000 rpm: 16.6 mph, 26.7 km/h - for X3 only 17.6 mph, 28.4 km/h; consumption: 31.4 m/imp gal, 26.1 m/US gal, 9 l x 100 km at 75 mph, 120 km/h - C Matic models 29.1 m/imp gal, 24.2 m/US gal, 9.7 l x 100 km at 75 mph, 120 km/h - (for X3 only) 41.5 m/imp gal, 34.6 m/US gal, 6.8 l x 100 km at 56 mph, 90 km/h, 29.1 m/imp gal, 24.2 m/US gal, 9.7 l x 100 km at 75 mph, 120 km/h.

CHASSIS integral; front suspension: independent, wishbones, hydropneumatic suspension, anti-roll bar, automatic levelling control; rear: independent, swinging trailing arms, hydropneumatic suspension, anti-roll bar, automatic levelling control.

STEERING rack-and-pinion; turns lock to lock: 3.80.

BRAKES disc (front diameter 10.63 in, 27 cm, rear diameter 7.01 in, 17.8 cm), servo; lining area: front 22.6 sq in, 146 sq cm, rear 11.2 sq in, 72 sq cm, total 33.8 sq in, 218 sq cm.

ELECTRICAL EQUIPMENT 12 V; 40 Ah battery - for X 3 only 45 Ah; 490 W alternator; Sev distributor; 2 headlamps.

DIMENSIONS AND WEIGHT wheel base: 100.39 in, 255 cm; tracks: 54.33 in, 138 cm front, 52.36 in, 133 cm rear; length: 164.96 in, 419 cm; width: 63.39 in, 161 cm; constant height: 53.15 in, 135 cm; ground clearance (variable): 6.06 in, 15,4 cm; weight: 2,106 lb, 955 kg - for X 3 2,073 lb, 940 kg; weight distribution: 57% front, 43% rear; turning circle: 34.1 ft, 10.4 m; fuel tank: 9.5 imp gal, 11.4 US gal, 43 l.

BODY saloon/sedan; 4+1 doors; 5 seats, separate front seats, reclining backrests; heated rear window.

PRACTICAL INSTRUCTIONS fuel: 98 oct petrol; oil: engine 7 imp pt, 8.5 US pt, 4 l, SAE 20W-50, change every 4,600 miles, 7500 km - gearbox 2.5 imp pt, 3 US pt, 1.4 l, SAE 80, change every 14,000 miles, 22,500 km - final drive 7.4 imp pt, 8.9 US pt, 4.2 l, change every 14,000 miles, 22,500 km; greasing: none; sparking plug: 200°; tappet clearances: inlet 0.008 in, 0.20 mm, exhaust 0.008 in, 0.20 mm; valve timing: 5°30' 34°30' 32° 4°30'; tyre pressure: front 26 psi, 1.8 atm, rear 27 psi, 1.9 atm.

PTIONALS for Pallas only, 5 - speed fully synchronized mechanical gearbox; folding rear seats; sunshine roof; metallic spray; rear window wiper-washer.

GSA Club Break

ee GSA Series, except for:

RICE IN GB: £ 3,888*
RICE EX WORKS: 34,800 francs**

ERFORMANCE max speed: 93 mph, 149 km/h; power-weight atio: 32.7 lb/hp (44.5 lb/kW), 14.8 kg/hp (20.2 kg/kW); carrying apacity: 882 lb, 400 kg; consumption: 41.5 m/imp gal, 34.6 n/US gal, 6.8 l x 100 km at 56 mph, 90 km/h - 28.8 m/imp gal, 4 m/US gal, 9.8 l x 100 km at 75 mph, 120 km/h.

IMENSIONS AND WEIGHT weight: 2,128 lb, 965 kg.

ODY estate car/st. wagon; 4+1 doors; rear window wiper-vasher.

PTIONALS Targa equipment; sunshine roof not available.

CX Reflex / Athena

RICES IN GB AND EX WORKS:	£	francs
eflex	5,697*	44,600**
thena	6,229*	51,200**

CITROËN CX Reflex

CITROËN CX Athena

ENGINE front, transverse, slanted 15° to front, 4 stroke; 4 cylinders, in line; 119.3 cu in, 1,955 cc (3.46 x 3.23 in, 88 x 82 mm); compression ratio: 9.2:1; max power (DIN): 106 hp (78 kW) at 5,500 rpm; max torque (DIN): 122 lb ft, 16.9 kg m (166 Nm) at 3,250 rpm; max engine rpm: 5,600; 54.2 hp/l (39.9 kW/l); cast iron block, light alloy head; 5 crankshaft bearings; valves: overhead, Vee-slanted at 33°, push-rods and rockers; camshafts: 1, side; lubrication: rotary pump, full flow filter, 9.1 mp pt, 9.7 US pt, 4.6 l; 1 Weber 34 DMTR 46/250 downdraught win barrel carburettor; fuel feed: mechanical pump; water-cooled, 16.9 imp pt, 20.3 US pt, 9.6 l, electric thermostatic fan.

TRANSMISSION driving wheels: front; clutch: single dry plate diaphragm); gearbox: mechanical; gears: 4, fully synchronized; atios: I 3.166, II 1.833, III 1.133, IV 0.800, rev 3.153; lever: central; final drive: spiral bevel; axle ratio: 4.769; width of rims: 5.5"; tyres: 185 SR x 14 front, 175 SR x 14 rear.

PERFORMANCE max speeds: (I) 29 mph, 47 km/h; (II) 50 mph, 81 km/h; (III) 81 mph, 131 km/h; (IV) 108 mph, 174 km/h; power-weight ratio: 25.6 lb/hp, (34.8 lb/kW), 11.6 kg/hp (15.8 kg/kW); carrying capacity: 1,058 lb, 480 kg; acceleration: standing ¼ mile 17.9 sec; speed in top at 1,000 rpm; 20.2 mph, 32.5 km/h; consumption: 35,8 m/imp gal, 29.8 m/US gal, 7.9 l x 100 km at 56 mph, 90 km/h - 29.1 m/imp gal, 24.2 m/US gal, 9.7 l x 100 km at 75 mph, 120 km/h.

CHASSIS integral with front and rear subframes; front suspension: independent, wishbones, hydropneumatic suspension, anti-roll bar, automatic levelling control; rear: independent, swinging trailing arms, hydropneumatic suspension, anti-roll bar, automatic levelling control.

STEERING rack-and-pinion; turns lock to lock: 4.50.

BRAKES disc (front diameter 10.24 in, 26 cm, rear diameter 8.82 in, 22.4 cm), internal radial fins, rear compensator, servo; lining area: front 40.3 sq in, 260 sq cm, rear 34.7 sq in, 224 sq cm, total 75 sq in, 484 sq cm.

ELECTRICAL EQUIPMENT 12 V; 45 Ah battery; 1,008 W alternator; Ducellier distributor; 2 halogen headlamps.

DIMENSIONS AND WEIGHT wheel base: 111.81 in, 284 cm; tracks: 57.87 in, 147 cm front, 53.54 in, 136 cm rear; length: 183,46 in, 466 cm; width: 68.11 in, 173 cm; height: 53.54 in, 136 cm; ground clearance: 6.10 in, 15.5 cm; weight: 2,712 lb, 1.230 kg; weight distribution: 66% front, 34% rear; turning circle 38.7 ft, 11.8 m; fuel tank: 15 imp gal, 18 US gal, 68 l.

BODY saloon/sedan; 4 doors; 5 seats, separate front seats, reclining backrests, built-in headrests; heated rear window.

PRACTICAL INSTRUCTIONS fuel: 95 oct petrol; oil: engine 8.1 imp pt, 9.7 US pt, 4.6 l, SAE 10W-50, change every 4,600 miles, 7,500 km - gearbox 2.8 imp pt, 3.4 US pt, 1.6 l, SAE 80, change every 14,000 miles, 22,500 km - final drive and hydraulic sospension 7.4 imp pt, 8.9 US pt, 4.2 l, change every 18,900 miles, 30,000 km; greasing: none; sparking plug: 225°; tappet clearances: inlet 0.004 in, 0.10 mm, exhaust 0.010 in, 0.25 mm; valve timing: 20° 60° 60° 20°; tyre pressure: front 27 psi, 1.9 atm, rear 30 psi, 2.1 atm.

OPTIONALS for Athena only, 5-speed fully synchronized mechanical gearbox; tinted glass; electric sunshine roof; metallic spray; electric windows.

CX Reflex Break

See CX Reflex/Athena, except for:

PRICE EX WORKS: 50,500 francs**

TRANSMISSION tyres: 185 SR x 14.

PERFORMANCE max speed: 104 mph, 168 km/h; power-weight ratio: 27,7 lb/hp, (37.6 lb/kW), 12.5 kg/hp (17 kg/kW); consumption: 27.7 m/imp gal, 23.1 m/US gal, 10.2 l x 100 km at 75 mph, 120 km//h.

DIMENSIONS AND WEIGHT wheel base: 121.85 in, 309 cm; rear track: 54.72 in, 139 cm; length: 195.28 in, 496 cm; height: 57.68 in, 146 cm; weight: 2,933 lb, 1,330 kg.

BODY estate car/st. wagon; 4+1 doors.

CX 2400 Series

See CX Reflex/Athena, except for:

PRICES IN GB AND EX WORKS:	£	francs
Break Super	—	57,700**
Familiale Super	6,779*	59,300**
Pallas Berline	7,131*	54,700**

ENGINE 143.2 cu in, 2,347 cc (3.68 x 3.37 in, 93.5 x 85.5 mm); compression ratio: 8.75:1; max power (DIN): 115 hp (85 kW) at 5,500 rpm; max torque (DIN): 133 lb ft, 18.3 kg m (179 Nm) at 2.750 rpm; max engine rpm: 5,750; 49 hp/l (36 kW/l); 1 Weber 34 DMTR 35/250 or Solex 34 CICF downdraught twin barrel carburettor.

TRANSMISSION tyres: 185 SR x 14.

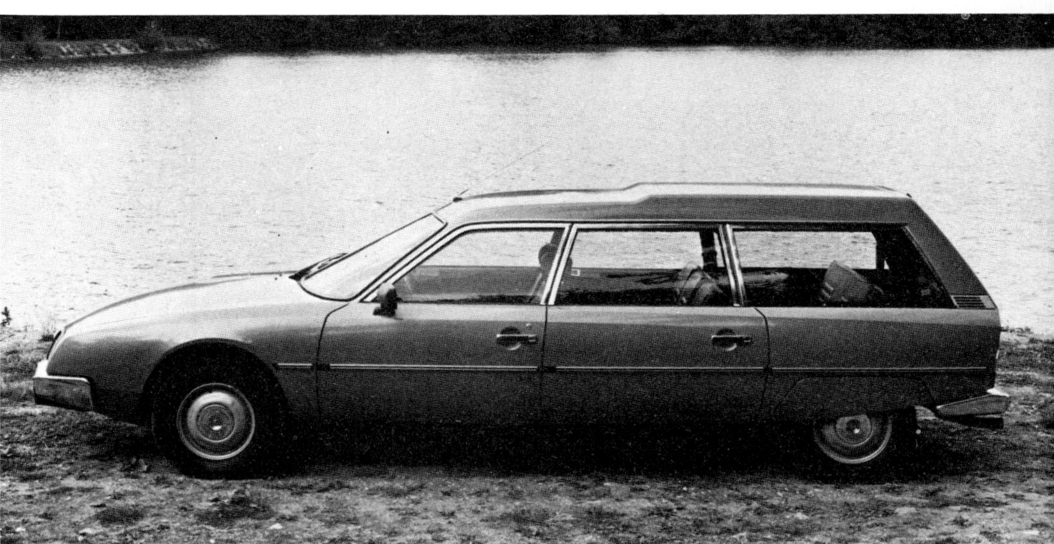

CITROËN CX 2400 Break Super

CX 2400 SERIES

PERFORMANCE max speed: 108 mph, 174 km/h; power-weight ratio: Break Super 26.9 ln/hp, (36.6 lb/kW), 12.2 kg/hp (16.6 kg/kW); carrying capacity: Break Super 1,521 lb, 690 kg - Familiale Super 1,488 lb, 675 kg - Pallas 2,900 lb, 1,315 kg; acceleration: standing ¼ mile 18 sec; consumption: 30.7 m/imp gal, 25.6 m/US gal, 9.2 l x 100 km at 56 mph, 90 km/h - 24.6 m/imp/gal, 20.5 m/US gal, 11.5 l x 100 km at 75 mph, 120 km/h.

CHASSIS reinforced suspension.

BRAKES lining area: front 34.1 sq in, 220 sq cm, rear 22.5 sq in, 145 sq cm, total 56.6 sq in, 365 sq cm.

ELECTRICAL EQUIPMENT 55 Ah battery.

DIMENSIONS AND WEIGHT wheel base: 121.65 in, 309 cm; length: 194.96 in, 495 cm; height: 57.48 in, 146 cm; weight: Break Super 3,098 lb, 1,405 kg - Familiale Super 3,120 lb, 1,415 kg - Pallas 2,900 lb, 1,315 kg; weight distribution: 64% front, 36% rear; turning circle 41.7 ft, 12.7 m.

BODY estate car/st. wagon; 4+1 doors; folding rear seat; Familiale Super 8 seats; Pallas saloon/sedan, 4 doors, luxury equipment and metallic spray; heated rear window with wiper-washer.

PRACTICAL INSTRUCTIONS sparking plug: 175°; valve timing: 0°30' 42°30' 38°30' 4°30'; tyre pressure: front 30 psi, 2.1 atm, rear 31 psi, 2.2 atm.

OPTIONALS metallic spray; 5-speed fully synchronized mechanical gearbox (I 3.166, II 1.833, III 1.250, IV 0.939, V 0.733, rev 3.153), 4.357 axle ratio, max speed 112 mph, 180 km/h.

CX 2400 GTI

See CX 2400 Series, except for:

PRICE IN GB: £ 7,777*
PRICE EX WORKS: 62,300 francs**

ENGINE max power (DIN): 128 hp (94 kW) at 4,800 rpm; max torque (DIN): 146 lb ft, 20.1 kg m (197 Nm) at 3,600 rpm; max engine rpm: 5,500; 54.5 hp/l (40.1 kW/l); Bosch L-Jetronic injection; fuel feed: electric pump; cooling: 21.6 imp pt, 26 US pt, 12.3 l.

TRANSMISSION gears: 5, fully synchronized; ratios: I 3.166, II 1.833, III 1.250, IV 0,939, V 0.733, rev 3.153; axle ratio: 4.769; width of rims: 6''; tyres: 185 HR x 14.

PERFORMANCE max speeds: (I) 27 mph, 44 km/h; (II) 47 mph, 76 km/h; (III) 69 mph, 111 km/h; (IV) 92 mph, 148 km/h; (V) 117 mph, 189 km/h; power-weight ratio: 23.7 lb/hp (32.2 lb/kW), 10.7 kg/hp (14.6 kg/kW); acceleration: standing ¼ mile 17.1 sec; speed in top at 1,000 rpm: 21 mph, 33.8 km/h; consumption: 34.9 m/imp gal, 29 m/US gal, 8.1 l x 100 km at 56 mph, 90 km/h - 28 m/imp gal, 23.3 m/US gal, 10.1 l x 100 km at 75 mph, 120 km/h.

STEERING servo, variable ratio (standard); turns lock to lock: 2.50.

ELECTRICAL EQUIPMENT 60 Ah battery; 1,120 W alternator.

CITROËN CX Prestige

DIMENSIONS AND WEIGHT weight: 3,032 lb, 1,375 kg; weight distribution: 68% front, 32% rear.

BODY saloon/sedan; 4 doors; metallic spray.

PRACTICAL INSTRUCTIONS tyre pressure: front 30 psi, 2.1 atm, rear 31 psi, 2.2 atm.

OPTIONALS leather upholstery.

CX 2400 Pallas Injection C Matic

See CX 2400 GTI, except for:

PRICE IN GB: £ 7,799*
PRICE EX WORKS: 63,200 francs**

TRANSMISSION gearbox: 'C Matic" semi-automatic transmission, hydraulic torque converter and planetary gears with 3 ratios, possible manual selection; ratios: I 2.176, II 1.133, III 0.750, rev 2.389; width of rims: 5.5''.

PERFORMANCE max speeds: (I) 39 mph, 62 km/h; (II) 73 mph, 118 km/h; (III) 112 mph, 180 km/h; power-weight ratio: 23.9 lb/hp (32.5 lb/kW), 10.8 kg/hp (14.7 kg/kW); carrying capacity: 1,021 lb, 463 kg; acceleration: standing ¼ mile 18.6 sec; speed in top at 1,000 rpm: 20.5 mph, 33 km/h; consumption: 31.4 m/imp gal, 26.1 m/US gal, 9 l x 100 km at 56 mph, 90 km/h - 24.1 m/imp gal, 20.1 m/US gal, 11.7 l x 100 km at 75 mph, 120 km/h.

CITROËN CX 2500 Diesel Super Berline

DIMENSIONS AND WEIGHT weight: 3,058 lb, 1,387 kg; weight distribution: 68.9% front, 31.1% rear.

PRACTICAL INSTRUCTIONS oil: semi-automatic transmission 7.9 imp pt, 9.5 US pt, 4.5 l.

CX Prestige

See CX 2400 GTI, except for:

PRICE IN GB: £ 10,416*
PRICE EX WORKS: 80,600 francs**

TRANSMISSION axle ratio: 4.357; width of rims: 5.5''.

PERFORMANCE max speeds: (I) 27 mph, 43 km/h; (II) 47 mph, 75 km/h; (III) 52 mph, 84 km/h; (IV) 91 mph, 147 km/h; (V) 11[illegible] mph, 190 km/h; power-weight ratio: 25.4 lb/hp (34.5 lb/kW), 11.5 kg/hp (15.7 kg/kW); carrying capacity: 992 lb, 450 kg; acceleration: standing ¼ mile 17.6 sec; speed in top at 1,000 rpm: 23 mph, 37 km/h; consumption: 37.2 m/imp gal, 30.9 m/US gal, 7.6 l x 100 km at 56 mph, 90 km/h - 29,.1 m/imp gal, 24.2 m/US gal, 9.7 l x 100 km at 75 mph, 120 km/H.

ELECTRICAL EQUIPMENT 70 Ah battery.

DIMENSIONS AND WEIGHT wheel base: 121.65 in, 309 cm; length: 193.70 in, 492 cm; height: 53.94 in, 137 cm; weight: 3,252 lb, 1,475 kg; weight distribution: 67,5% front, 32.5% rear.

BODY luxury equipment; metallic spray; air-conditioning.

PRACTICAL INSTRUCTIONS tyre pressure: front 31 psi, 2.2 atm, rear 31 psi, 2.2 atm.

OPTIONALS «C Matic» semi-automatic transmission with 3 ratios (I 2.176, II 1.133, III 0.750, rev 2.389), 4.769 axle ratio, max speed 112 mph, 180 km/h, acceleration standing ¼ mile 19.1 sec, speed in top at 1,000 rpm 20.5 mph, 33 km/h, consumption 31.4 m/imp gal, 26.1 m/US gal, 9 l x 100 km at 56 mph, 90 km/h - 24.1 m/imp gal, 20.1 m/US gal, 11.7 l x 100 km at 75 mph, 120 km/h; leather upholstery; tinted glass; vinyl roof.

CX 2500 Diesel Series

See CX Reflex/Athena, except for:

PRICES IN GB AND EX WORKS:	£	francs
Confort Berline	7,039*	52,100**
Break Confort	7,167*	58,000**
Super Berline	—	57,400**
Break Super	—	63,300**
Familiale Super	7,159*	64,900**
Pallas Berline	—	60,300**

ENGINE diesel, 4 stroke; 152.6 cu in, 2,500 cc (3.66 x 3.62 in, 93 x 92 mm); compression ratio: 22.25:1; max power (DIN): 75 hp (55 kW) at 4,250 rpm; max torque (DIN): 111 lb ft, 15.3 kg m (150 Nm) at 2,000 rpm; max engine rpm: 4,525; 30 hp/l (22.1 kW/l); lubrication: 8.3 imp pt, 9.9 US pt, 4.7 l; Roto-Diesel injection; cooling: 21.6 imp pt, 26 US pt, 12.3 l.

TRANSMISSION axle ratio: 4.538.

PERFORMANCE max speeds: (I) 23 mph, 37 km/h; (II) 40 mph, 64 km/h (III) 65 mph, 104 km/h; (IV) 91 mph, 147 km/h; power-weight ratio: Confort 39.1 lb/hp, (53.1 lb/kW), 17.7 kg/hp (24.1 kg/kW); carrying capacity: Confort 1,036 lb, 470 kg -

Break Confort 1,455 lb, 660 kg - Super and Pallas 1,003 lb, 455 kg - Break Super 1,422 lb, 645 kg - Familiale Super 1,411 lb, 640 kg; acceleration: standing ¼ mile 20.7 sec - estate cars 21.6 sec; speed in top at 1,000 rpm: 20.3 mph, 32.6 km/h; consumption: 43.5 m/imp gal, 36.2 m/US gal, 6.5 l x 100 km at 56 mph, 90 km/h - 32.5 m/imp gal, 27 m/US gal, 8.7 l x 100 km at 75 mph, 120 km/h.

ELECTRICAL EQUIPMENT 88 Ah battery.

DIMENSIONS AND WEIGHT wheel base: estate cars 121.65 in, 309 cm; length: estate cars 194.96 in, 495 cm; height; estate cars 57.48 in, 146 cm; weight: Confort 2,933 lb, 1,330 kg - Break Confort 3,197 lb, 1,450 kg - Super and Pallas 2,966 lb, 1,345 kg - Break Super 3,230 lb, 1,465 kg - Familiale Super 3,241 lb, 1,470 kg; weight distribution: saloons 68.4% front, 31.6% rear - estate cars 64.8% front, 35.2% rear; turning circle: estate cars 41.7 ft, 12.7 m.

BODY for estate cars/st.wagons only 4+1 doors, folding rear seat and heated rear window with wiper-washer; Familiale Super 8 seats; for Pallas only luxury equipment and metallic spray.

PRACTICAL INSTRUCTIONS fuel: diesel oil: engine 8.1 imp pt, 9.7 US pt, 4.6 l, SAE 80, change every 3,100 miles, 5,000 km; tappet clearances: inlet 0.006 in, 0.15 mm, exhaust 0.008 in, 0.20 mm; valve timing: 2°52' 33°08' 37°48' 4°12'; tyre pressure: saloons front 30 psi, 2.1 atm, rear 30 psi, 2.1 atm - estate cars front 27 psi, 2 atm, rear 31 psi, 2.2 atm.

OPTIONALS 5-speed fully synchronized mechanical gearbox (I 3.166, II 1.833, III 1.250, IV 0.939, V 0.733, rev 3.153), max speed 97 mph, 156 km/h acceleration standing ¼ mile 20.4 sec, speed in top at 1,000 rpm 22.1 mph, 35.5 km/h, consumption 46.3 m/imp gal, 38.6 m/US gal, 6.1 l x 100 km at 56 mph, 90 km/h - 34.9 m/imp gal, 29 m/US gal, 8.1 l x 100 km at 75 mph, 120 km/h; for estate cars only, metallic spray; for Pallas only, leather upholstery..

PEUGEOT FRANCE

104 Series

	PRICES IN GB AND EX WORKS:	£	francs
1	GL 4+1-dr Berline	2,981*	25,710**
2	ZA 2+1-dr Coupé	2,959*	—
3	GR 4+1-dr Berline	—	28,210**
4	ZR 2+1-dr Coupé	—	27,210**
5	ZR Grand Confort 2+1-dr Coupé	—	29,210**
6	SR 4+1-dr Berline	3,337*	29,732**
7	SR Grand Confort 4+1-dr Berline	—	32,410**
8	S 4+1-dr Berline	3,811*	32,054**
9	ZS 2+1-dr Coupé	3,504*	31,054**

Power team:	Standard for:	Optional for:
45 hp	1,2	—
57 hp	3 to 5	—
57 hp (1,219 cc)	6,7	—
72 hp	8,9	—

45 hp power team

ENGINE front, transverse, slanted 72° to rear, 4 stroke; 4 cylinders, in line; 58.2 cu in, 954 cc (2.76 x 2.44 in, 70 x 62 mm); compression ratio: 8.8:1; max power (DIN): 45 hp (33 kW) at 6,000 rpm; max torque (DIN): 45 lb ft, 6.2 kg m (61 Nm) at 3,000 rpm; max engine rpm: 6,250; 47.2 hp/l (35 kW/l); light alloy block and head, wet liners, bi-hemispherical combustion chambers; 5 crankshaft bearings; valves: overhead, Vee-slanted, rockers; camshafts: 1, overhead; lubrication: gear pump, full flow filter, 7.9 imp pt, 9.5 US pt, 4.5 l; Solex 32 HSA2 horizontal single barrel carburettor; fuel feed: mechanical pump; water-cooled, 9.9 imp pt, 11.8 US pt, 5.6 l, electric thermostatic fan.

TRANSMISSION driving wheels: front; clutch: single dry plate (diaphragm); gearbox: mechanical, in unit with engine and final drive; gears: 4, fully synchronized; ratios: I 3.882, II 2.296, III 1.501, IV 1.042, rev 3.568; lever: central; final drive: spiral bevel; axle ratio: 4.067; width of rims: 4"; tyres: 135SR x 13.

PERFORMANCE max speeds: (I) 28 mph, 45 km/h; (II) 47 mph, 76 km/h; (III) 72 mph, 116 km/h; (IV) 84 mph, 135 km/h; power-weight ratio: 38.6 lb/hp (52 lb/kW), 17.3 kg/hp (23.6 kg/kW); carrying capacity: 882 lb, 400 kg; acceleration: standing ¼ mile 20.5 sec; speed in top at 1,000 rpm: 14.7 mph, 23.6 km/h: consumption: 32.5 m/imp gal, 27 m/US gal, 8.7 l x 100 km.

CHASSIS integral; front suspension: independent, by McPherson, coil springs/telescopic damper struts, lower wishbones (trailing links), anti-roll bar; rear: independent, swinging longitudinal trailing arms, coil springs, telescopic dampers.

STEERING rack-and-pinion; turns lock to lock: 3.33.

BRAKES front disc (diameter 9.49 in, 24.1 cm), rear drum, dual circuit, rear compensator; swept area: front 176.1 sq in, 1,136 sq cm, rear 68.4 in, 441 sq cm, total 244.5 sq in, 1,577 sq cm.

ELECTRICAL EQUIPMENT 12 V; 28 Ah battery; 500 W alternator; Ducellier or Paris-Rhone distributor; 2 headlamps.

DIMENSIONS AND WEIGHT wheel base: 95.28 in, 242 cm; traks: 50.79 in, 129 cm front, 48.82 in, 124 cm rear; length:140.94 in, 358 cm; width: 59.84 in, 152 cm; 55.12 in, 140 cm; ground clearance: 5.04 in, 12.8 cm; weight: 1,720 lb, 780 kg; turning circle: 33.1 ft, 10.1 m; fuel tank: 8.8 imp gal, 10.6 US gal, 40 l.

BODY saloon/sedan, coupé; 5 seats, separate front seats; folding rear seat.

PRACTICAL INSTRUCTIONS fuel: 88 oct petrol; oil: engine, gearbox and final drive 7 imp pt, 8.5 US pt, 4 l, SAE 10W-50, change every 3,100 miles, 5,000 km; greasing: every 3,100 miles, 5,000 km, 1 point; valve timing: -2° 32° 33°30' -2°; tyre pressure: front 26 psi, 1.8 atm, rear 28 psi, 2 atm.

OPTIONALS heated rear window; sunshine roof; tinted glass; headrests; metallic spray (for ZA only).

57 hp power team

See 45 hp power team, except for:

ENGINE 68.6 cu in, 1,124 cc (2.83 x 2.72 in, 72 x 69 mm); compression ratio: 9.2:1; max power (DIN): 57 hp (41 kW) at 6,000 rpm; max torque (DIN): 59 lb ft, 8.2 kg m (80 Nm) at 3,000 rpm; max engine rpm: 6,500; 50.7 hp/l (36.5 kW/l); lubrication: 8.8 imp pt. 10.6 US pt, 5 l; 1 Solex 32 PBISA 7 downdraught single barrel carburettor.

TRANSMISSION axle ratio: 3.867.

PERFORMANCE max speed: 90 mph, 145 km/h; power-weight ratio: GR 30.6 lb/hp, (42.6 lb/kW), 13.9 kg/hp (19.3 kg/kW); carrying capacity: 706 lb, 320 kg; acceleration: standing ¼ mile 20 sec; speed in top at 1,000 rpm: 15.5 mph, 24.9 km/h; consumption: 34 m/imp gal, 28.3 m/US gal, 8.3 l x 100 km.

DIMENSIONS AND WEIGHT wheel base: ZR models 87.80 in, 223 cm; length: GR 142,36 in, 362 cm - ZR models 132.28 in, 336 cm; weight: GR 1,742 lb, 790 kg - ZR models 1,632 lb, 740 kg; turning circle: ZR models 30.8 ft, 9.4 m.

BODY luxury equipment (for ZR Grand Confort only).

PRACTICAL INSTRUCTIONS fuel: 95 oct petrol; oil: engine, gearbox and final drive 7.9 imp pt, 9.5 US pt, 4.5 l; valve timing: 5°20' 36°50' 36°50' 5°20'.

OPTIONALS tweed upholstery (standard for ZR Grand Confort); tinted glass with rear window wiper-washer; electric windows.

57 hp power team (1,219 cc)

See 45 hp power team, except for:

ENGINE 74.4 cu in, 1,219 cc (2.95 x 2.72 in, 75 x 69 mm); compression ratio: 9.3:1; max power (DIN): 57 hp (41 kW) at 5,500 rpm; max torque (DIN): 68 lb ft, 9.4 kg m (92 Nm) at 2,750 rpm; max engine rpm: 6,000; 21.4 hp/l (29.7 kW/l); 1 Solex 32 PBISA II downdraught single barrel carburettor.

PEUGEOT 104 SR Berline

PEUGEOT 104 SR Berline

TRANSMISSION axle ratio: 3.867; width of rims: 4.5"; tyres: 145 SR x 13.

PERFORMANCE max speed: 90 mph, 145 km/h; power-weight ratio: 30.9 lb/hp (43 lb/kW), 14 kg/hp (19.5 kg/kW); carrying capacity: 882 lb, 400 kg; acceleration: standing ¼ mile 20.1 sec; speed in top at 1,000 rpm: 16.7 mph, 26.9 km/h.

DIMENSIONS AND WEIGHT length: 142.36 in, 362 cm; weight: 1,764 lb, 800 kg.

BODY heated rear window; reclining backrests with headrests; sunshine roof; tweed upholstery and luxury equipment (for SR Grand Confort only).

PRACTICAL INSTRUCTIONS fuel: 95 oct petrol; oil: engine, gearbox and final drive 7.9 imp pt, 9.5 US pt, 4.5 l.

OPTIONALS metallic spray; electric windows.

72 hp power team

See 45 hp power team, except for:

ENGINE 83 cu in, 1,360 cc (2.95 x 3.03 in, 75 x 77 mm); compression ratio: 9.3:1; max power (DIN): 72 hp (53 kW) at 6,000 rpm; max torque (DIN): 79 lb ft, 10.9 kg m (107 Nm) at 3,000 rpm; max engine rpm: 6,500; 53 hp/l (39 kW/l); 1 Solex 32 TMNIA downdraught twin barrel carburettor.

TRANSMISSION axle ratio: 3.867; width of rims: 4.5"; tyres: 165/70 SR x 13.

PERFORMANCE max speed: 98 mph, 158 km/h; power-weight

72 HP POWER TEAM

ratio: S 25.3 lb/hp, (34.4 lb/kW), 11.5 kg/hp (15.6 kg/kW); speed in top at 1,000 rpm: 16.1 mph, 25.9 km/h; consumption: 30.7 m/imp gal, 25.6 m/US gal, 9.2 l x 100 km.

BRAKES servo.

DIMENSIONS AND WEIGHT length: S 142.36 in, 362 cm -ZS 132.28 in, 336 cm; weight: S 1,819 lb, 825 kg - ZS 1,764 lb, 800 kg.

BODY reclining backrests with headrests; heated rear window; electric windows.

PRACTICAL INSTRUCTIONS fuel: 95 oct petrol; oil: engine, gearbox and final drive 7.9 imp pt, 9.5 US pt, 4.5 l.

OPTIONALS light alloy wheels; metallic spray.

PEUGEOT 304 SL Break

304 Break Series

PRICES IN GB AND EX WORKS:	£	francs
1 GL	3,624*	30,854**
2 SL	3,911*	33,254**
3 GLD	—	36,132**

Power team:	Standard for:	Optional for:
65 hp	1,2	—
50 hp (diesel)	3	1

65 hp power team

ENGINE front, transverse, slanted 20° to front, 4 stroke; 4 cylinders, in line; 78,7 cu in, 1,290 cc (3.07 x 2.66 in, 78 x 67.5 mm); compression ratio: 8.8:1; max power (DIN): 65 hp (47 kW) at 6,000 rpm; max torque (DIN): 70 lb ft, 9.6 kg m (94 Nm) at 3,750 rpm; max engine rpm: 6,100; 50.4 hp/l (36.4 kW/l); light alloy block and head, wet liners, bi-hemispherical combustion chambers; 5 crankshaft bearings; valves: overhead, Vee-slanted, rockers; camshafts: 1 overhead; lubrication: rotary pump, cartridge on by-pass, 7 imp pt, 8.5 US pt, 4 l; Solex 34 PBISA-5 downdraught single barrel carburettor; fuel feed: mechanical pump; water-cooled, 10.2 imp pt, 12.3 US pt, 5.8 l, electromagnetically-operated fan.

TRANSMISSION driving wheels: front; clutch: single dry plate (diaphragm), hydraulically controlled; gearbox: mechanical; gears: 4, fully synchronized; ratios: I 3.647, II 2.213, III 1.451, IV 0.985, rev 3.942; lever: steering column; final drive: helical spur gears; axle ratio: 4.067; width of rims: 4.5''; tyres: 145 SR x 14.

PERFORMANCE max speeds: (I) 27 mph, 44 km/h; (II) 45 mph, 73 km/h; (III) 69 mph, 111 km/h; (IV) 93 mph, 150 km/h; power-weight ratio GL 31.7 lb/hp (43.9 lb/kW), 14.4 kg/hp (19.9 kg/kW); carrying capacity: 882 lb, 400 kg; acceleration: standing ¼ mile 20.1 sec; speed in top at 1,000 rpm: 16.7 mph, 26.9 km/h; consumption: 29.7 m/imp gal, 24.8 m/US gal, 9.5 l x 100 km.

CHASSIS integral; front suspension: independent, by McPherson, coil springs/telescopic dampers, lower wishbones, anti-roll bar; rear: independent, swinging longitudinal trailing arms, anti-roll bar, coil springs/telescopic dampers.

STEERING rack-and-pinion; turns lock to lock: 3.60.

BRAKES front disc (diameter 10.08 in, 25.6 cm), rear drum, dual circuit, rear compensator, servo; swept area: front 192.2 sq in, 1,240 sq cm, rear 89,1 sq in, 575 sq cm, total 281.3 sq in, 1,815 sq cm.

ELECTRICAL EQUIPMENT 12 V; 36 Ah battery; 500 W alternator; Ducellier distributor; 2 headlamps.

DIMENSIONS AND WEIGHT wheel base: 101.97 in, 259 cm; tracks: 53.94 in, 1.37 cm front, 50.79 in, 129 cm rear; length: 157.87 in, 401 cm; width: 61.81 in, 157 cm; height: 56.30 in, 143 cm; ground clearance: 4.72 in, 12 cm; weight: GL 2,062 lb, 935 kg - SL 2,095 lb, 950 kg; turning circle: 34.8 ft, 10.6 m; fuel tank: 9.2 imp gal, 11.1 US gal, 42 l.

BODY estate car/st. wagon; 4+1 doors; 5 seats, separate front seats, reclining backrests; heated rear window; folding rear seat.

PRACTICAL INSTRUCTIONS fuel: 95 oc t petrol; oil: engine, gearbox and final drive 7 imp pt, 8.5 US pt, 4 l, SAE 20W-40, change every 3,100 miles, 5,000 km; greasing: every 3,100 miles, 5,000 km, 5 points; tyre pressure: front 23 psi, 1.6 atm, rear 27 psi, 1.9 atm.

OPTIONALS sunshine roof; metallic spray.

50 hp power team

See 65 hp power team, except for:

ENGINE diesel; 94.5 cu in, 1,548 cc (3.15 x 3.03 in, 80 x 77 mm); compression 22.5:1; max power (DIN): 50 hp (37 kW) at 5,000 rpm; max torque (DIN): 64 lb ft, 8.8 kg m (86 Nm) at 2.500 rpm; max engine rpm: 5,500; 31 hp/l (42.1 kW/l); lubrication: 8.8 imp pt, 10.6 US pt, 5 l; heating plugs on head; Bosch injection pump; cooling : 11.4 imp pt, 13.7 US pt, 6.5 l.

TRANSMISSION gearbox ratios: I 3.733, II 2.264, III 1.485, IV 1.008, rev 4.034.

PERFORMANCE max speed: 84 mph, 135 km/h; power-weight ratio: 43.7 lb/hp, (59.3 lb/kW), 19.8 kg/hp (26.9 kg/kW); consumption: 45.6 m/imp gal, 37.9 m/US gal, 6.2 l x 100 km.

ELECTRICAL EQUIPMENT 60 Ah battery.

DIMENSIONS AND WEIGHT weight: 2,183 lb., 990 kg.

PRACTICAL INSTRUCTIONS fuel: diesel oct petrol; oil: engine gearbox and final drive 8.8 imp pt, 10.6 US pt, 5 l, change every 1,600 miles, 2,500 km; tyre pressure: front and rear 24 psi, 1.7 atm.

OPTIONALS rear window wiper-washer.

PEUGEOT 305 SR Berline

305 Berline Series

PRICES IN GB AND EX WORKS:	£	francs
1 GL	3,799*	32,654**
2 GR	4,125*	35,154**
3 SR	4,509*	38,356**
4 SR Grand Confort	—	41,156**
5 GRD	4,798*	40,432**
6 GRD Grand Confort	—	42,756**

Power team:	Standard for:	Optional for:
65 hp	1,2	—
74 hp	3,4	—
50 hp (diesel)	5,6	—

65 hp power team

ENGINE front, transverse, slanted 20° to front, 4 stroke; 4 cylinders, in line; 78.7 cu in, 1,290 cc (3.07 x 2.66 in, 78 x 67.5 mm); compression ratio: 8.8:1; max power (DIN): 65 hp (47 kW) at 6,000 rpm; max torque (DIN): 70 lb ft, 9.6 kg m (944 Nm) at 3,750 rpm; max engine rpm: 6,500; 50.4 hp/l (36.4 kW/l); light alloy block and head, wet liners, bi-hemispherical combustion chambers; 5 crankshaft bearings; valves: overhead, Vee-slanted, rockers; camshafts: 1, overhead; lubrication: rotary pump, cartridge on by-pass, 7 imp pt, 8.5 US pt, 4 l; 1 Solex 34 PBISA5 downdraught single barrel carburettor; fuel feed: mechanical pump; water-cooled, 10.2 imp pt, 12.3 US pt, 5.8 l, electromagnetically-operated fan.

TRANSMISSION driving wheels: front; clutch: single dry plate (diaphragm); gearbox: mechanical; gears: 4, fully synchronized; ratios: I 3.647, II 2.213, III 1.451, IV 0.985, rev 3.942; lever: central; final drive: helical spur gears; axle ratio: 4.065; width of rims: 4.5''; tyres: 165 SR x 13.

PERFORMANCE max speed: 91 mph, 147 km/h; power-weight ratio: 31.3 lb/hp (43.4 lb/kW), 14.2 kg/hp (19.7 kg/kW); carrying apacity: 915 lb, 415 kg; acceleration: standing ¼ mile 19.9 ec; speed in top at 1,000 rpm: 16.7 mph, 26.9 km/h; consump-on: 29.7 m/imp gal, 24.8 m/US gal, 9.5 l x 100 km.

:HASSIS integral; front suspension: independent, by Mc-'herson, coil springs/telescopic dampers, lower wishbones, nti-roll bar; rear: independent, coil springs, anti-roll bar, tele-copic dampers.

;TEERING rack-and-pinion; turns lock to lock: 3.60.

RAKES front disc (diameter 10.35 in, 26.3 cm), rear drum, ual circuit, rear compensator, servo; swept area: total 275.2 q in, 1,775 sq cm.

LECTRICAL EQUIPMENT 12 V; 45 Ah battery; 500 W alterna-or; Ducellier distributor; 2 headlamps.

IMENSIONS AND WEIGHT wheel base: 103.15 in, 262 cm; acks: 53.94 in, 137 cm front, 51.97 in, 132 cm rear; length: 66.93 in, 424 cm; width: 64.17 in, 163 cm; height: 55.12 in, 40 cm; ground clearance: 4.96 in, 12.6 cm; weight: 2,040 lb, 25 kg; turning circle: 35.4 ft, 10.8 m; fuel tank: 9.5 imp gal, 1.4 US gal, 43 l.

ODY saloon/sedan; 4 doors; 5 seats, separate front seats, eclining backrests; heated rear window.

RACTICAL INSTRUCTIONS fuel: 97 oct petrol; oil: engine, earbox and final drive 7 imp pt, 8.5 US pt, 4 l, SAE 10W-40, hange every 4,750 miles, 7,500 km; valve timing: 6° 38° 45° °; tyre pressure : front 26 psi, 1.8 atm, rear 30 psi, 2.1 atm.

PEUGEOT 504 Berline

PTIONALS sunshine roof (only for GR); metallic spray; luxury quipment.

74 hp power team

ee 65 hp power team, except for:

:NGINE 89.8 cu in, 1,472 cc (3.07 x 3.03 in, 78 x 77 mm); ompression ratio: 9.2:1; max power (DIN): 74 hp (53 kW) at ,000 rpm; max torque (DIN): 86 lb ft, 11.8 kg m (116 Nm) at ,000 rpm; 50.3 hp/l (36 kW/l); 1 Solex 35 PBISA9 downdraught ingle barrel carburettor.

'RANSMISSION gearbox ratios: I 3.334, II 1.929, III 1.312, IV .929, rev 3.436.

'ERFORMANCE max speed: 95 mph, 153 km/h: power-weight atio: 28 lb/hp (39.1 lb/kW) 12.7 kg/hp (17.7 kg/kW); accelera-on: standing ¼ mile 18.5 sec; speed in top at 1,000 rpm: 17.8 nph, 28.6 km/h; consumption: 31.7 m/imp gal, 26.4 m/US gal, .9 l x 100 km.

IMENSIONS AND WEIGHT ground clearance: 4.72 in, 12 cm; veight: 2,073 lb, 940 kg.

ODY SR Grand Confort luxury equipment.

'RACTICAL INSTRUCTIONS valve timing: 3° 41° 42° 2°.

PTIONALS tinted glass; sunshine roof (standard for SR Grand :onfort); luxury equipment; electric windows.

50 hp power team

See 65 hp power team, except for:

ENGINE diesel; 94.5 cu in, 1,548 cc (3.15 x 3.03 in, 80 x 77 mm); compression ratio: 22.5:1; max power (DIN): 50 hp (37 KW) at 5,000 rpm; max torque (DIN): 64 lb ft, 8.8 kg m (86 Nm) at 2,500 rpm; max engine rpm: 5,500; 31 hp/l (42.2 kW/l); lubrication: 8.8 imp pt, 10.6 US pt, 5 l; heating plugs on head; Bosch injection pump; cooling: 11.4 imp pt, 13.7 US pt, 6.5 l.

TRANSMISSION gearbox ratios: I 3.733, II 2.264, III 1.485, IV 1.008, rev 4.034.

PERFORMANCE max speed: 84 mph, 135 km/h; power-weight ratio: 43 lb/hp, (58.4 lb/kW), 19.5 kg/hp (26.5 kg/kW); consump-tion: 45.6 m/imp gal, 37.9 m/US gal, 6.2 l x 100 km.

ELECTRICAL EQUIPMENT 60 Ah battery.

DIMENSIONS AND WEIGHT weight: 2,150 lb, 975 kg.

PRACTICAL INSTRUCTIONS fuel: diesel; oil: engine gearbox and final drive, 8.8 imp pt, 10.6 US pt, 5 l, change every 1,600 miles, 2,500 km; tyre pressure: front and rear 24 psi, 1.7 atm.

OPTIONALS tinted glass.

504 Berline Series

PRICES EX WORKS:	francs
1 GR	37,600**
2 SR	40,600**
3 GRD Diesel	43,556**
4 SRD Diesel	46,556**

For GB and USA prices, see price index.

Power team:	Standard for:	Optional for:
79 hp	1,2	—
65 hp (diesel)	3,4	—

79 hp power team

ENGINE front, slanted 45° to right, 4 stroke; 4 cylinders, in line; 109.6 cu in, 1,796 cc (3.31 x 3.19 in, 84 x 81 mm); compression ratio: 7.5:1, max power (DIN): 79 hp (57 kW) at 5,100 rpm; max torque (DIN): 105 lb ft, 14.5 kg m (142 Nm) at 2,500 rpm; max engine rpm: 5,500; 44 hp/l (31.7 kW/l); cast iron block, wet liners, light alloy head, hemispherical combustion chambers; 5 crankshaft bearings; valves: overhead, Vee-slanted, push-rods and rockers; camshafts: 1, side; lubrication: gear pump, metal gauze filter, 7 imp pt, 8.5 US pt, 4 l; 1 Solex 34 BICSA 3 downdraught single barrel carburettor; fuel feed: mechanical pump; water-cooled, 13.7 imp pt, 16.5 US pt, 7.8 l, electro-magnetic thermostatic fan.

TRANSMISSION driving wheels: rear; clutch: single dry plate (diaphragm), hydraulically controlled; gearbox: mechanical; gears: 4, fully synchronized; ratios: I 3.704, II 2.170, III 1.409, IV 1, rev 3.747; lever: central; final drive: hypoid bevel; axle ratio: 3.889; width of rims: 5"; tyres GR 165 SR x 14 - SR 175 SR x 14.

PERFORMANCE max speeds: (I) 25 mph, 40 km/h; (II) 43 mph, 70 km/h; (III) 65 mph, 105 km/h; (IV) 96 mph, 154 km/h; power-weight ratio: 32.4 lb/hp (44.9 lb/kW), 14.7 kg/hp (20.3 kg/kW); carrying capacity: 1.169 lb, 530 kg; acceleration: stand-ing ¼ mile 19.6 sec, 0-50 mph (0-80 km/h) 10.6 sec; speed in direct drive at 1,000 rpm: 18.1 mph, 29.1 km/h; consumption: 26.9 m/imp gal, 22.4 m/US gal, 10.5 l x 100 km.

CHASSIS integral; front suspension: independent, by Mc-Pherson, coil springs/telescopic damper struts, lower wish-bones, anti-roll bar; rear: rigid axle, trailing lower radius arms, upper oblique torque arms, coil springs, anti-roll bar, telescopic dampers.

STEERING rack-and-pinion; turns lock to lock: 4.50.

BRAKES front disc (diameter 10.75 in, 27.3 cm), rear drum, dual circuit, rear compensator, servo; swept area: total 400.5 sq in, 2,583 sq cm.

ELECTRICAL EQUIPMENT 12 V; 44 Ah battery; 500 W alterna-tor; Ducellier distributor; 2 headlamps.

DIMENSIONS AND WEIGHT wheel base: 107.87 in, 274 cm; tracks: 55.91 in, 142 cm front, 53.54 in, 136 cm rear; length: 176.77 in, 449 cm; width: 66.54 in, 169 cm; height: 57.48 in, 146 cm; ground clearance: 6.30 in, 16 cm; weight: 2,558 lb, 1,160 kg; turning circle: 35.8 ft, 10.9 m; fuel tank: 12.3 imp gal, 14.8 US gal, 56 l.

BODY saloon/sedan; 4 doors; 5 seats, separate front seats, reclining backrests; heated rear window; electric windows, tinted glass, leather upholstery and sunshine roof (standard for SR).

PRACTICAL INSTRUCTIONS fuel: 85 oct petrol; oil: engine 7 imp pt, 8.5 US pt, 4 l, SAE 20W-40, change every 3,100 miles, 5,000 km - gearbox 1.9 imp pt, 2.3 US pt, 1.1 l, SAE 20W-40, change every 6,200 miles, 10,000 km - final drive 2.1 imp pt, 1.5 US pt, 1.2 l, GP 90, change every 6,200 miles, 10,000 km; greasing: every 3,100 miles, 5,000 km, 6 points; tappet clear-ances: inlet 0.004 in, 0.10 mm, exhaust 0.010 in, 0.25 mm; tyre pressure: front 21 psi, 1.5 atm, rear 26 psi, 1.8 atm.

OPTIONALS ZF automatic transmission, hydraulic torque con-verter and planetary gears with 3 ratios (I 2.564, II 1.520, III 1, rev 2), max ratio of converter at stall 2.3, max speed 91 mph, 146 km/h; leather upholstery; sunshine roof; tinted glass; elec-tric windows.

65 hp power team

See 79 hp power team, except for:

ENGINE diesel; 128.9 cu in, 2,112 cc (3.54 x 3.27 in, 90 x 83); compression ratio: 22.2:1; max power (DIN): 65 hp (45 kW) at 4,500 rpm; max torque (DIN): 88 lb ft, 12.1 kg/m (119 Nm) at 2,500 rpm; max engine rpm: 4,750; 30.8 hp/l (21.5 kW/l); Bosch injection pump.

TRANSMISSION axle ratio: 3.779; tyres: SRD 175 SR x 14.

PERFORMANCE max speed: 84 mph, 135 km/h; power-weight ratio: 41 lb/hp, (58.6 lb/kW), 18.6 kg/hp (26.6 kg/kW); accelera-tion: standing ¼ mile 21.8 sec; speed in direct drive at 1,000 rpm: 18.6 mph, 30 km/h; consumption: 33.6 m/imp gal, 28 m/US gal, 8.4 l x 100 km.

PEUGEOT 504 SR Berline

PEUGEOT 504 GR Break

65 HP POWER TEAM

ELECTRICAL EQUIPMENT 60 Ah battery.

DIMENSIONS AND WEIGHT weight: 2,668 lb, 1,210 kg.

BODY (standard for SRD) electric windows, tinted glass, leather upholstery and sunshine roof.

PRACTICAL INSTRUCTIONS fuel: diesel.

OPTIONALS ZF automatic transmission not available.

504 Break Series

PRICES IN GB AND EX WORKS:	£	francs
1 Break Essence	5,191*	39,800**
2 GR	5,798*	43,622**
3 Familial	5,837*	45,922**
4 Break Diesel	5,864*	45,756**
5 Familial Diesel	6,628*	52,378**

For USA prices, see price index.

Power team:	Standard for:	Optional for:
73 hp	1	—
96 hp	2,3	—
59 hp (diesel)	4	—
70 hp (diesel)	5	—

73 hp power team

ENGINE front, slanted 45° to right, 4 stroke; 4 cylinders, in line; 109.6 cu in, 1,796 cc (3.31 x 3.19 in, 84 x 81 mm); compression ratio: 7.5:1; max power (DIN): 73 hp (52 kW) at 5,000 rpm; max torque (DIN) 101 lb ft, 14 kg m (138 Nm) at 2,500 rpm; max engine rpm: 5,500; 40.6 hp/l (29.2 kW/l); cast iron block, wet liners, light alloy head, hemispherical combustion chambers; 5 crankshaft bearings; valves: overhead, Vee-slanted, push-rods and rockers; camshafts: 1, side; lubrication: gear pump, metal gauze filter, 7 imp pt, 8.5 US pt, 4 l; 1 Solex 34 BICSA 3 downdraught single barrel carburettor; fuel feed: mechanical pump; water-cooled, 13.7 imp pt, 16.5 US pt, 7.8 l, electromagnetic thermostatic fan.

TRANSMISSION driving wheels: rear; clutch: single dry plate (diaphragm), hydraulically controlled; gearbox: mechanical; gears: 4, fully synchronized; ratios: I 3.704, II 2.170, III 1409, IV 1, rev 3.747: lever: steering column; final drive: hypold bevel; axle ratio: 4,222; width of rims: 5''; tyres: 185 SR x 14.

PERFORMANCE max speeds: (I) 25 mph, 40 km/h; (II) 43 mph, 70 km/h; (III) 65 mph, 105 km/h; (IV) 91 mph, 146 km/h; power-weight ratio: 38,5 lb/hp (53.6 lb/kW), 17.5 kg/hp (24.3 kg/kW); carrying capacity: 1,477 lb, 670 kg; acceleration: standing ¼ mile 19.6 sec, 0-50 mph (0-80 km/h) 10.6 sec; speed in direct drive at 1,000 rpm: 17.4 mph, 28 km/h; consumption: 20.6 m/imp gal, 17.2 m/US gal, 13.7 l x 100 km.

CHASSIS integral; front suspension: independent, by McPherson, coil springs/telescopic damper struts, lower wishbones, anti roll-bar; rear: rigid axle, trailing lower radius arms, upper oblique torque arms, 4 coil springs, anti-roll bar, telescopic dampers.

STEERING rack-and-pinion; turns lock to lock: 4.50.

BRAKES front disc (diameter 10.75 in, 27.3 cm), rear drum dual circuit, rear compensator, servo; swept area: total 400.5 sq in, 2.583 sq cm.

ELECTRICAL EQUIPMENT 12 V; 44 Ah battery; 500 W alternator; Ducellier distributor; 2 headlamps.

DIMENSIONS AND WEIGHT wheel base: 114.17 in, 290 cm tracks: 55.91 in, 142 cm front , 53.54 in, 136 cm rear; length 118.98 in, 480 cm; width: 66.54 in, 169 cm; height: 61.02 in 155 cm; ground clearance: 6.50 in, 16.5 cm; weight: 2,811 lb 1,275 kg; turning circle: 37.4 ft, 11.4 m; fuel tank: 13.2 imp gal 15.8 US gal, 60 l.

BODY estate car/st. wagon; 4+1 doors; 5 seats, separate front seats, reclining backrests; heated rear window; folding rear seat.

PRACTICAL INSTRUCTIONS fuel: 85 oct petrol; oil: engine 7 imp pt, 8.5 US pt, 4 l, SAE 20W-40, change every 3,100 miles 5,000 km - gearbox 1.9 imp pt, 2.3 US pt, 1.1 l, SAE 20W-40 change every 6,200 miles, 10,000 km - final drive 2.1 imp pt 1.5 US pt, 1.2 l, GP 90, change every 6,200 miles, 10,000 km greasing: every 3,100 miles, 5,000 km, 6 points; tappet clearances: inlet 0.004 in, 0.10 mm, exhaust 0.010 in, 0.25 mm; tyre pressure: front 21 psi, 1.5 atm, rear 26 psi, 1.8 atm.

96 hp power team

See 73 hp power team, except for:

ENGINE 120.3 cu in, 1,971 cc (3.46 x 3.19 in, 88 x 81 mm) compression ratio: 8.8:1; max power (DIN): 96 hp (69 kW) at 5,200 rpm; max torque (DIN): 119 lb ft, 16.4 kg m (161 Nm) at 3,000 rpm; 48.7 hp/l; (35 kW/l); 1 Zenith 35-40 INAT or Solex 32-35 TMIMA downdraught twin barrel carburettor.

TRANSMISSION gearbox ratios: I 3.592, II 2.104, III 1.366, IV 1, rev 3.634.

PERFORMANCE max speed: 102 mph, 164 km/h; power-weight ratio: 30.5 lb/hp (42.6 lb/kW), 13.8 kg/hp (19.3 kg/kW); acceleration: standing ¼ mile 18.4 sec; consumption: 23.7 m/imp gal 19.8 m/US gal, 11.9 l x 100 km.

CHASSIS rear suspension: independent, oblique semi-trailing arms, coil springs/telescopic dampers, anti-roll bar.

BRAKES disc (diameter 10.75 in, 27.3 cm), dual circuit, rear compensator, servo; swept area: front 236.9 sq in, 1,528 sq cm rear 201.6 sq in, 1,300 sq cm, total 438.5 sq in, 2,828 sq cm

ELECTRICAL EQUIPMENT halogen headlamps.

DIMENSIONS AND WEIGHT weight: 2,933 lb, 1,330 kg.

BODY 7 seats; built-in adjustable headrests.

PRACTICAL INSTRUCTIONS fuel: 95 oct petrol.

OPTIONALS (only for GR) ZF automatic transmission, hydraulic torque converter and planetary gears with 3 ratios (I 2.564, II 1.520, III 1, rev 2), max ratio of converter at stall 2.3 , max speed 91 mph, 146 km/h; rear window wiper-washer.

59 hp power team

See 73 hp power team, except for:

ENGINE diesel; 128.9 cu in, 2,112 cc (3.54 x 3.27 in, 90 x 83 mm); compression ratio: 22.1:1; max power (DIN): 59 hp (43 kW) at 4,500 rpm; max torque (DIN): 80 lb ft, 11,1 kg/m (109 Nm) at 2,500 rpm; max engine rpm: 4,750; 35.8 hp/l (48.7 kW/l); Bosch injection pump.

PERFORMANCE max speed: 78 mph, 126 km/h; power-weight ratio: 50.4 lb/hp, (68,6 lb/kW), 23 kg/hp (31.1 kg/kW); acceleration: standing ¼ mile 23.1 sec; consumption: 31.7 m/imp gal 26.4 m/US gal, 8.9 l x 100 km.

ELECTRICAL EQUIPMENT 60 Ah battery.

DIMENSIONS AND WEIGHT weight: 2,977 lb, 1,350 kg.

BODY built-in adjustable headrests.

PRACTICAL INSTRUCTIONS fuel: diesel.

OPTIONALS ZF automatic transmission not available; rear window wiper-washer.

70 hp power team

See 73 hp power team, except for:

ENGINE diesel; slanted 20°; 140.6 cu in, 2,304 cc (3.70 x 3.27 in, 94 x 83 mm); compression ratio: 22.2:1; max power (DIN) 70 hp (50 kW) at 4,500 rpm; max torque (DIN): 97 lb ft, 13.4 kg m (131 Nm) at 2,200 rpm; 30.4 hp/l (21.9 kW/l); Bosch injection pump.

PEUGEOT 504 Cabriolet

PEUGEOT 504 Cabriolet / Coupé

ERFORMANCE max speed: 81 mph, 130 km/h; power-weight atio: 44.4 lb/hp (61.5 lb/kW), 20.1 kg/hp (27.9 kg/kW); consumption: 30.1 m/imp gal, 25 m/US gal, 9.4 l x 100 km.

LECTRICAL EQUIPMENT 60 Ah battery.

IMENSIONS AND WEIGHT weight: 3,109 lb, 1,410 kg.

ODY built-in adjustable headrests.

RACTICAL INSTRUCTIONS fuel: diesel.

PTIONALS ZF automatic transmission not available; rear indow wiper-washer.

504 Cabriolet / Coupé

RICES EX WORKS:	francs
04 Cabriolet	**65,522****
04 Coupé	**65,522****

NGINE front, slanted 45° to right, 4 stroke; 4 cylinders, in line; 20.3 cu in, 1,971 cc (3.46 x 3.19 in, 88 x 81 mm); compression atio: 8.8:1; max power (DIN): 106 hp (76 kW) at 5,200 rpm; nax torque (DIN): 125 lb ft, 17.2 kg m (169 Nm) at 3,000 rpm; nax engine rpm: 5,500; 53.8 hp/l (38.8 kW/l); cast iron block, et liners, light alloy head, hemispherical combustion chambers; 5 crankshaft bearings; valves: overhead, Vee-slanted, ush-rods and rockers; camshafts: 1, side; lubrication: gear ump, metal gauze filter, 7 imp pt, 8.5 US pt, 4 l; 4 cylinder njection pump in inlet pipes (Kugelfischer system); fuel feed: lectric pump; water-cooled, 13.7 imp pt, 16.5 US pt, 7.8 l, lectromagnetic thermostatic fan.

RANSMISSION driving wheels: rear; clutch: single dry plate diaphragm), hydraulically controlled; gearbox: mechanical; ears: 4, fully synchronized; ratios: I 3.592, II 2.104, III 1.366, V 1, rev 3.634; lever: central; final drive: hypoid bevel; axle atio: 3.700; width of rims: 5.5"; tyres: 175 HR x 14.

ERFORMANCE max speed: 111 mph, 179 km/h; power-weight atio: Cabriolet 25.6 lb/hp (35.5 lb/kW), 11.6 kg/hp (16.1 kg/ W); carrying capacity: 706 lb 320 kg; speed in direct drive at ,000 rpm: 19.4 mph, 31.3 km/h; consumption: 21.9 m/imp gal, 8.2 m/US gal, 12.9 l x 100 km.

HASSIS integral; front suspension: independent, by McPherson, coil springs/telescopic damper struts, lower wishbones, anti-roll bar; rear: independent, oblique semi-trailling rms, coil springs/telescopic damper struts, anti-roll bar.

TEERING rack-and pinion, servo; turns lock to lock: 3.50.

RAKES disc (diameter 10.75 in, 27.3 cm), front internal radial ns, dual circuit, rear compensator, servo; lining area: front 2.9 sq in, 148 sq cm, rear 16.7 sq in, 108 sq cm, total 39.6 sq , 256 sq cm.

LECTRICAL EQUIPMENT 12 V; 45 Ah battery; 750 W alternator; Ducellier distributor; 4 halogen headlamps.

IMENSIONS AND WEIGHT wheel base: 100.39 in, 255 cm; acks: 58.66 in, 149 cm front, 56.30 in, 143 cm rear; length: 71.65 in, 436 cm; width: 66.93 in, 170 cm; height: 53.34 in, 36 cm; ground clearance: 4.72 in, 12 cm; weight: Cabriolet ,723 lb, 1,235 kg - Coupé 2,756 lb, 1,250 kg; turning circle: 4.8 ft, 10.6 m; fuel tank: 12.3 imp gal, 14.8 US gal, 56 l.

ODY convertible, 2+2 seats - coupé, 4 seats; 2 doors; separate front seats, reclining backrests with built-in headrests; electric windows; heated rear window; tinted glass.

PRACTICAL INSTRUCTIONS fuel: 95 oct petrol; oil: engine 7 imp pt, 8.5 US pt, 4 l, SAE 20W-40, change every 3,100 miles, 5,000 km - gearbox 2.3 imp pt, 2.7 US pt, 1.3 l, SAE 20W-40, change every 6,200 miles, 10,000 km - final drive 2.6 imp pt, 3.2 US pt, 1.5 l, SAE 80, change every 6,200 miles, 10,000 km; greasing every 3,100 miles, 5,000 km, 6 points.

OPTIONALS metallic spray; ZF automatic transmission (for Coupé only).

504 V6 Coupé

See 504 Cabriolet/Coupé, except for:

PRICE EX WORKS: 78,170 francs**

ENGINE 6 cylinders, Vee-slanted at 90°; 162.6 cu in, 2,664 cc (3.46 x 2.87 in, 88 x 2.73 mm); compression ratio: 8.65:1; max power (DIN): 144 hp (104 kW) at 5,500 rpm; max torque (DIN): 160 lb ft, 22.1 kg m (217 Nm) at 3,000 rpm; max engine rpm: 6,000; 54 hp/l (39 kW/l); light alloy block and head, wet liners, bi-hemispherical combustion chambers; 4 crankshaft bearings; valves: overhead, Vee-slanted, rockers; camshafts: 2, 1 per bank, overhead; lubrication: gear pump, full flow filter, 10.6 imp pt, 12.7 US pt, 6 l; Bosch K-Jetronic injection; fuel feed: mechanical pump; water-cooled, expansion tank, 18.1 imp pt, 21.8 US pt, 10.3 l, viscous coupling thermostatic fan.

TRANSMISSION gears: 5, fully synchronized; gearbox ratios: I 3.862, II 2.183, III 1.445, IV 1, V 0.844, rev 3.587; tyres: 190/65 HR x 390.

PERFORMANCE max speed: 117 mph, 189 km/h; power-weight ratio: 19.8 lb/hp (27.4 lb/kW), 9 kg/hp (2.4 kg/kW); speed in direct drive at 1,000 rpm: 23 mph, 37.1 km/h; consumption: 17.5 m/imp gal, 14.6 m/US gal, 16.1 l x 100 km.

ELECTRICAL EQUIPMENT electronic ignition.

DIMENSIONS AND WEIGHT height 52.76 in, 134 cm; weight: 2,885 lb, 1,295 kg; fuel tank: 13.2 imp gal, 15.8 US gal, 60 l.

BODY coupé; 4 seats.

PRACTICAL INSTRUCTIONS oil: engine 10.6 imp pt, 12.7 US pt, 6 l, SAE 10W-50; tappet clearances: inlet 0.006 in, 0.15 mm, exhaust 0.012 in, 0.30 mm; valve timing: 32° 72° 20° 32°.

505 Berline Series

PRICES EX WORKS:	francs
1 GR	**45,000****
2 SR	**48,000****
3 TI	**50,322****
4 STI	**54,122****
5 GRD Diesel	**51,478****
6 SRD Diesel	**55,278****

Power team:	Standard for:	Optional for:
96 hp	1,2	—
110 hp	3,4	—
70 hp (diesel)	5,6	—

96 hp power team

ENGINE front, slanted 45° to right, 4 stroke; 4 cylinders, in line; 120.3 cu in, 1,971 cc (3.46 x 3.19 in, 88 x 81 mm); compression ratio: 8.8:1; max power (DIN): 96 hp (69 kW) at 5,200 rpm; max torque (DIN): 119 lb ft, 16.4 kg m (161 Nm) at 3,000 rpm; max engine rpm: 5,500; 20.5 hp/l (28.5 kW/l); cast iron block, wet liners, light alloy head, hemispherical combustion chambers; 5 crankshaft bearings; valves: overhead, Vee-slanted, push-rods and rockers; camshafts: 1, side; lubrication: gear pump, metal gauze filter, 7 imp pt, 8.5 US pt, 4 l; 1 Zenith 35-40 INAT or Solex 32-35 TMIMA downdraught twin barrel carburettor; fuel feed: mechanical pump; water-cooled, 13.7 imp pt, 16.5 US pt, 7.8 l, electromagnetic thermostatic fan.

TRANSMISSION driving wheels: rear; clutch: single dry plate (diaphragm), hydraulically controlled; gearbox: mechanical; gears: 4, fully synchronized; ratios: I 3.592, II 2.104, III 1.366, IV 1, rev 3.634; lever: central; final drive: hypoid bevel; axle ratio: 3.889; width of rims: 5"; tyres: 175 SR x 14.

PERFORMANCE max speed: 102 mph, 164 km/kh; power-weight ratio: 27.6 lb/hp, (38.4 lb/kW), 12.5 kg/hp (17.4 kg/kW); carrying capacity: 1,058 lb, 480 kg; acceleration: standing ¼ mile 18.4 sec; speed in direct drive at 1,000 rpm: 18.1 mph, 29.1 km/h; consumption: 23.7 m/imp gal, 19.8 m/US gal, 11.9 l x 100 km.

CHASSIS integral; front suspension: independent, by McPherson, coil springs/telescopic damper struts, lower wishbones, anti-roll bar; rear suspension: independent, oblique semi-trailing arms, coil springs/telescopic dampers, anti-roll bar.

STEERING rack-and-pinion, servo (for SR only); turns lock to lock: 4.50.

BRAKES front disc (diameter 10.75 in, 27.3 cm), rear drum, dual circuit, rear compensator, servo; swept area: total 400.5 sq in, 2,583 sq cm.

ELECTRICAL EQUIPMENT 12 V; 44 Ah battery; 500 W alternator; Ducellier distributor; 2 halogen headlamps.

DIMENSIONS AND WEIGHT wheel base: 107.87 in, 274 cm; tracks: 57.48 in, 146 cm front, 56.30 in, 143 cm rear; length: 180.31 in, 458 cm; width: 67.72 in, 172 cm; height: 57.09 in, 145 cm; ground clearance: 4.72 in, 12 cm; weight: 2,646 lb, 1,200 kg; weight distribution: 53% front, 47% rear; turning circle: 36.7 ft, 11.2 m; fuel tank: 12.3 imp gal, 14.8 US gal, 56 l.

BODY saloon/sedan; 4 doors; 5 seats, separate front seats, reclining backrests; heated rear window; (standard for SR electric windows) tinted glass and leather upholstery.

PRACTICAL INSTRUCTIONS fuel: 95 oct petrol; oil: engine 7 imp pt, 8.5 US pt, 4 l, SAE 20W-40, change every 3,100 miles, 5,000 km - gearbox 1.9 imp pt, 2.3 US pt, 1.1 l, SAE 20W-40, change every 6,200 miles, 10.000 km - final drive 2.1 imp pt, 1.5 US pt, 1.2 l, GP 90, change every 6,200 miles, 10,000 km; greasing: every 3,100 miles, 5,000 km, 6 points; tappet clearances: inlet 0.004 in, 0.10 mm, exhaust 0.010 in, 0.25 mm; tyre pressure: front 23 psi, 1.6 atm, rear 27 psi, 1.9 atm.

OPTIONALS ZF 3 HP22 automatic transmission, hydraulic torque converter and planetary gears with 3 ratios (I 2.480, II 1.480, III 1, rev 2.090), max ratio of converter at stall 2.3, max speed 98 mph, 158 km/h; leather upholstery; sunshine roof; tinted glass, electric windows; metallic spray.

PEUGEOT 505 SR - STI - SRD Diesel Berline

110 hp power team

See 96 hp power team, except for:

ENGINE slanted 12° to right; 121.7 cu in, 1,995 cc (3.46 x 3.23 in, 88 x 82 mm); compression ratio: 9.2:1; max power (DIN): 110 hp (81 kW) at 5,250 rpm; max torque (DIN): 126 lb ft, 17.4 kg m (171 Nm) at 4,000 rpm; max engine rpm: 5,500; 18.1 hp/l (24.6 kW/l); bi-hemispherical combustion chambers; lubrication: 7.9 imp pt, 9.5 US pt, 4.5 l; fuel feed: electric pump; Bosch K-Jetronic injection.

TRANSMISSION gears: 5, fully synchronized; ratios: I 3.460, II 2.060, III 1.410, IV 1, V 0.820, rev 3.490; axle ratio: 4.110.

PERFORMANCE max speed: 109 mph, 175 km/h; power-weight ratio: 24.2 lb/hp, (32.8 lb/kW), 11 kg/hp (14.9 kg/kW); acceleration: standing ¼ mile 17.5 sec, 0-62 mph (0-100 km/h) 10.8 sec; speed in direct drive at 1,000 rpm: 21.3 mph, 34.2 km/h; consumption: 21.6 m/imp gal, 18 m/US gal, 13.1 l x 100 km.

STEERING STI model servo.

BRAKES disc.

ELECTRICAL EQUIPMENT 750 W alternator.

DIMENSIONS AND WEIGHT weight: 2,668 lb, 1,210 kg.

BODY (standard for STI) electric windows, tinted glass and leather upholstery.

OPTIONALS ZF 3HP 22 automatic transmission , hydraulic torque converter and planetary gears with 3 ratios (I 2.560, II 1.520, III 1, rev 2), max ratio of converter at stall 2.3, max speed 105 mph, 169 km/h.

70 hp power team

See 96 hp power team, except for:

ENGINE diesel; slanted 20°; 140.6 cu in, 2.304 cc (3.70 x 3.27 in, 94 x 83 mm); compression ratio: 22.2:1; max power (DIN): 70 hp (50 kW) at 4,500 rpm; max torque (DIN): 97 lb ft, 13.4 kg m (131 Nm) at 2,000 rpm; max engine rpm: 5,000; 30.4 hp/l (21.9 kW/l); turbolence chambers; lubrication: 8.8 imp pt, 10.6 US pt, 5 l; Bosch EP/VAC injection pump.

TRANSMISSION gears: 4, fully synchronized; ratios: I 3.700, II 2.169, III 1.408, IV 1, rev 3.745; lever: steering column; axle ratio: 3.700.

PERFORMANCE max speed: 88 mph, 141 km/h; power-weight ratio: 40.5 lb/hp, (56 lb/kW), 18.3 kg/hp (25.4 kg/kW); speed in direct drive at 1,000 rpm: 19.4 mph, 31.3 km/h; consumption: 32.5 m/imp gal, 27 m/US gal, 8.7 l x 100 km.

STEERING SRD servo.

ELECTRICAL EQUIPMENT 60 Ah battery.

DIMENSIONS AND WEIGHT weight: 2,833 lb, 1,285 kg.

BODY (standard for SRD) electrical windows, tinted glass and leather upholstery.

PRACTICAL INSTRUCTIONS fuel: diesel.

OPTIONALS ZF 3HP 22 automatic transmission, max speed 82 mph, 132 km/h, central lever.

604 Berline Series

PRICES IN GB AND EX WORKS:	£	francs
1 SL	8,117*	57,570**
2 TI	9,258*	64,570**
3 TI Grand Confort	—	70,170**
4 D Turbo	—	65,756**
5 D Turbo Grand Confort	—	70,056**

For USA prices, see price index.

Power team:	Standard for:	Optional for:
136 hp	1	—
144 hp	2,3	—
80 hp (diesel)	4,5	—

136 hp power team

ENGINE front, 4 stroke; 6 cylinders, Vee-slanted at 90°; 162.6 cu in, 2,664 cc (3.46 x 2.87 in, 88 x 73 mm); compression ratio: 8.65:1; max power (DIN): 136 hp (98 kW) at 5,750 rpm; max torque (DIN): 153 lb ft, 21.1 kg m (207 Nm) at 3,500 rpm; max engine rpm: 6,000; 51 hp/l (36.8 kW/l); light alloy block and head, wet liners, bi-hemispherical combustion chambers; 4 crankshafts bearings; valves; overhead, Vee-slanted, rockers; camshafts: 2, 1 per bank, overhead; lubrication: gear pump, full flow filter, 10.6 imp pt, 12.7 US pt, 6 l; 1 Solex 34 TBIA downdraught single barrel carburettor and 1 Solex 35 CEEI downdraught twin barrel carburettor; fuel feed: mechanical pump; water-cooled, expansion tank, 18.1 imp pt, 21.8 US pt, 10.3 l, viscous coupling thermostatic fan.

PEUGEOT 604 TI Berline

TRANSMISSION driving wheels: rear; clutch: single dry plate (diaphragm), hydraulically controlled; gearbox: mechanical; gears: 4, fully synchronized; ratios: I 3.862, II 2.183, III 1.445, IV 1, rev 3.587: lever: central; final drive: hypoid bevel; axle ratio: 3.580; width of rims: 5.5"; tyres: 175 HR x 14.

PERFORMANCE max speeds: (I) 32 mph, 52 km/h; (II) 56 mph, 88 km/h; (III) 80 mph, 129 km/h; (IV) 113 mph, 182 km/h; power-weight ratio: 22.5 lb/hp (30.6 lb/kW), 10.2 kg/hp (3.9 kg/kW); carrying capacity: 1,257 lb, 570 kg; acceleration: standing ¼ mile 17.2 sec; speed in direct drive at 1,000 rpm: 20 mph, 32.3 km/h; consumption: 17.7 m/imp gal, 14.7 m/US gal, 16 l x 100 km.

CHASSIS integral; front suspension: independent, by McPherson, coil springs/telescopic damper struts, lower wishbones, anti-roll bar; rear: independent, oblique semi-trailing arms, coil springs, anti-roll bar, telescopic dampers.

STEERING rack-and-pinion, servo; turns lock to lock: 3.50.

BRAKES disc (diameter 10.75 in, 27.3 cm), front internal radial fins, dual circuit, rear compensator, servo; swept area: front 223 sq in, 1,438 sq cm, rear 192 sq in, 1,239 sq cm, total 415 sq in, 2,677 sq cm.

ELECTRICAL EQUIPMENT 12 V; 45 Ah battery; 750 W alternator; Ducellier distributor; 4 halogen headlamps.

DIMENSIONS AND WEIGHT wheel base: 110.24 in, 280 cm; tracks: 58.66 in, 149 cm front, 56.30 in, 143 cm rear; length: 185.83 in, 472 cm; width: 69.68 in, 177 cm; height: 56.30 in, 143 cm; ground clearance: 5.91 in, 15 cm; weight: 3.065 lb, 1,390 kg; turning circle: 37.7 ft, 11.5 m; fuel tank: 15.4 imp ga 18.5 US gal, 70 l.

BODY saloon/sedan; 4 doors; 5 seats, separate front seats reclining backrests with built-in headrests; electric windows heated rear window.

PRACTICAL INSTRUCTIONS fuel: 95 oct petrol; oil: engin 10.6 imp pt, 12.7 US pt, 6 l, SAE 10W-50, change every 3,10 miles, 5,000 km - gearbox 2.3 imp pt, 2.7 US pt, 1.3 l, SAE 20W-40, change every 6,200 miles, 10,000 km - final drive 2.6 imp pt, 3.2 US pt, 1.5 l, SAE 80, change every 6,200 miles 10,000 km; greasing: every 3,100 miles, 5,000 km; tappe clearances: inlet 0.006 in, 0.15 mm, exhaust 0.012 in, 0.30 mm valve timing: 32° 72° 20° 32°.

OPTIONALS automatic transmission with 3 ratios (I 2.400, I 1.480, III 1, rev 1.920), max ratio of converter at stall 2.3 possible manual selection, max speed 111 mph, 178 km/h acceleration standing ¼ mile 18.3 sec, consumption 21.7 m imp gal, 18.1 m/US gal, 13 l x 100 km; electric sunshine roof leather upholstery; metallic spray.

144 hp power team

See 136 hp power team, except for:

ENGINE max power (DIN): 144 hp (104 kW) at 5,500 rpm; max torque (DIN): 160 lb ft, 22.1 kg m (217 Nm) at 3,000 rpm; 54 hp/l (39 kW/l); Bosch K-Jetronic injection; fuel feed: electric pump.

PEUGEOT 604 D (turbo-diesel engine)

RANSMISSION gears: 5, fully synchronized; gearbox ratios: I .862, II 2.183, III 1.445, IV 1, V 0.844, rev 3.587; axle ratio: .700.

ERFORMANCE max speed: 115 mph, 185 km/h; power-weight atio: 21.6 lb/hp (29.9 lb/kW), 9.8 kg/hp (13.6 kg/kW); consump-on: 16.8 m/imp gal, 14 m/US gal, 16.8 l x 100 km.

ODY TI Grand Confort leather upholstery, sunshine roof and nted glass.

LECTRICAL EQUIPMENT electronic ignition.

IMENSIONS AND WEIGHT weight: 3,109 lb, 1,410 kg.

PTIONALS air-conditioning.

80 hp diesel power team

ee 136 hp power team, except for:

NGINE diesel; 4 cylinders, in line, slanted 20°; 104.6 cu in, ,304 cc (3.70 x 3.27 in, 94 x 83 mm); compression ratio: 21:1; ıax power (DIN): 80 hp (60 kW) at 4,150 rpm; max torque DIN): 136 lb ft, 18.8 kg m (184 Nm) at 2,000 rpm; max engine m: 4,500; 28.8 hp/l (38.4 kW/l); 5 crankshaft bearings; lubri-ation: 9.5 imp pt, 11.4 US pt, 5.4 l; Bosch injection; Garret iresearch T03 turbocharger.

RANSMISSION gears: 5, fully synchronized; ratios: I 3.862, II .183, III 1.445, IV 1, V 0.844, rev 3.587; axle ratio: 3.700.

ERFORMANCE max speed: 93 mph, 150 km/h; power-weight atio: 40.2 lb/hp, (53.6 lb/kW), 18.2 kg/hp (24.3 kg/kW); cceleration: standing ¼ mile 20.5 sec; speed in direct drive at ,000 rpm: 24 mph, 38 km/h; consumption: 31 m/imp gal, 25.8 /US gal, 9.1 l x 100 km.

LECTRICAL EQUIPMENT 60 Ah battery.

IMENSIONS AND WEIGHT weight: 3,219 lb, 1,460 kg; weight istribution: 53% front, 47% rear.

ODY D Turbo Grand Confort leather upholstery, tinted glass nd sunshine roof.

RACTICAL INSTRUCTIONS fuel: diesel.

PTIONALS 4-speed fully synchronized mechanical gearbox (I .862, II 2.183, III 1.445, IV 1, rev 3.587).

RENAULT FRANCE

4 Break Series

RICES IN GB AND EX WORKS:	£	francs
4	—	20,400**
4 Export	2,500*	—
TL	—	22,500**
TL Export	2,713*	—
GTL	—	24,300**

ower team:	Standard for:	Optional for:
7 hp	1,3	—
4 hp (845 cc)	2,4	—
4 hp	5	—

27 hp power team

NGINE front, 4 stroke; 4 cylinders, vertical, in line; 47.7 cu in, 82 cc (2.20 x 3.15 in, 55.8 x 80 mm); compression ratio: 8.5:1; ıax power (DIN): 27 hp (19 kW) at 5,000 rpm; max torque DIN): 38 lb ft, 5.2 kg m (51 Nm) at 2,500 rpm; max engine rpm: ,000; 34.5 hp/l (24.9 kW/l); cast iron block, wet liners, light lloy head; 3 crankshaft bearings; valves: overhead, in line, ush-rods and rockers; camshafts: 1, side; lubrication: gear ump, filter in sump, 8.4 imp pt, 10.1 US pt, 4.8 l; 1 Zenith 28 downdraught single barrel carburettor; fuel feed: mechanical ump; sealed circuit cooling, liquid, expansion tank, 10.4 imp t, 18.1 US pt, 5.9 l.

RANSMISSION driving wheels: front; clutch: single dry plate diaphragm); gearbox: mechanical; gears: 4, fully synchronized; atios: I 3.833, II 2.235, III 1.458, IV 1.026, rev 3.545; lever: on acia; final drive: spiral bevel; axle ratio: 4.125; width of rims: "; tyres: 135 SR x 13.

ERFORMANCE max speeds: (I) 21 mph, 33 km/h; (II) 34 mph, 4 km/h; (III) 52 mph, 83 km/h; (IV) 68 mph, 110 km/h; ower-weight ratio: 56.7 lb/hp (78.6 lb/kW), 25.7 kg/hp (35.6 g/kW); carrying capacity: 728 lb, 330 kg: acceleration: stand-ng ¼ mile 23.8 sec, 0-50 mph (0-80 km/h) 34.2 sec; speed in p at 1,000 rpm: 14.7 mph, 23.7 km/h; consumption: 34 m/imp al, 28.3 m/US gal, 8.3 l x 100 km.

HASSIS platform; front suspension: independent, wishbones, ngitudinal torsion bars, anti-roll bar, telescopic dampers; rear: dependent, swinging longitudinal trailing arms, transverse orsion bars, telescopic dampers.

STEERING rack-and-pinion; turns lock to lock: 3.

BRAKES drum (front diameter 7.87 in, 20 cm, rear 6.30 in, 16 cm), dual circuit, rear compensator; lining area: front 36.4 sq in, 235 sq cm, rear 17.4 sq in, 112 sq cm, total 53.8 sq in, 347 sq cm.

ELECTRICAL EQUIPMENT 12 V; 38 Ah battery; 35 A alternator; 2 headlamps.

DIMENSIONS AND WEIGHT wheel base: 96.46 in, 245 cm (right), 94.49 in, 240 cm (left); tracks: 50.39 in, 128 cm front, 48.82 in, 124 cm rear; length: 144.49 in, 367 cm; width: 58.27 in, 148 cm; height: 61.02 in, 155 cm; ground clearance: 6.89 in, 17.5 cm; weight: 1,532 lb, 695 kg; weight distribution: 56.1% front, 43.9% rear; turning circle: 33.1 ft, 10.1 m; fuel tank: imp gal, 9 US gal, 34 l.

BODY estate car/st. wagon; 4+1 doors; 4 seats, bench front seats - TL separate front seats; folding rear seat; heated rear window.

PRACTICAL INSTRUCTIONS fuel: 85 oct petrol; oil: engine 8.4 imp pt, 10.1 US pt, 4.8 l, SAE 10W-40, change every 4,650 miles, 7,500 km - gearbox and final drive 3.2 imp pt, 3.8 US pt, 1.8 l, SAE 80 EP, change every 9,300 miles, 15,000 km; greasing: none; tappet clearances: inlet 0.006-0.007 in, 0.15-0.18 mm, exhaust 0.007-0.009 in, 0.18-0.22 mm; valve timing: 10° 34° 9° 11°; tyre pressure: front 20 psi, 1.4 atm, rear 24 psi, 1.7 atm.

OPTIONALS luxury interior; (for TL only) metallic spray, reclining backrests and sunshine roof.

34 hp power team

(For export only)

See 27 hp power team, except for:

ENGINE 51.6 cu in, 845 cc (2.28 x 3.15 in, 58 x 80 mm); compression ratio: 8:1 ; max power (DIN): 34 hp (25 kW) at 5,000 rpm; max torque (DIN): 43 lb ft, 5.9 kg m (58 Nm) at 2,500 rpm; 40.2 hp/l (29.6 kW/l); water-cooled, 9.7 imp pt, 11.6 US pt, 5.5 l.

PERFORMANCE max speed: 78 mph, 125 km/h; powerweight ratio: 45 lb/hp (61.3 lb/kW), 20.4 kg/hp (27.8 kg/kW).

34 hp power team

See 27 hp power team, except for:

ENGINE 67.6 cu in, 1,108 cc (2.76 x 2.83 in, 70 x 72 mm); compression ratio: 9.5:1; max power (DIN): 34 hp (25 kW) at 4,000 rpm; max torque (DIN): 54.3 lb/ft, 7.5 kg m (74 Nm) at 2,500 rpm; 42.4 hp/l (22.6 kW/l); lubrication: 5.3 imp pt, 6.3 US pt, 3 l.

TRANSMISSION axle ratio: 3.100.

PERFORMANCE max speed: 75 mph, 120 km/h; power-weight ratio: 46.7 lb/hp (63.5 lb/kW), 21.2 kg/hp (28.8 kg/kW); acceleration: standing ¼ mile 22.9 sec; speed in top at 1,000 rpm: 19.6 mph., 31.5 km/h; consumption: 40.4 m/imp gal, 33.6 m/US gal, 7 l x 100 km.

RENAULT 4 GTL Break

RENAULT 4 TL Break

STEERING turns lock to lock: 3.75.

BRAKES drum (front diameter 8.9 in, 23 cm, rear 7.1 in, 18 cm); lining area: front 49.3 sq in, 318 sq cm, rear 24.8 sq in, 160 sq cm, total 74.1 sq in, 478 sq cm.

DIMENSIONS AND WEIGHT weight: 1,588 lb, 720 kg.

BODY separate front seats.

PRACTICAL INSTRUCTIONS fuel: 98-100 oct petrol; oil: engine 5.3 imp pt, 6.3 US pt, 3 l; tappet clearances: inlet 0.012 in, 0.30 mm, exhaust 0.012 in, 0.30 mm; valve timing: 12° 48° 52° 8°; tyre pressure: rear 21.3 psi, 1.5 atm.

OPTIONALS sunshine roof; metallic spray; reclining backrests.

Rodeo 4

PRICE EX WORKS: 24,402** francs

ENGINE front, 4 stroke; 4 cylinders, vertical, in line; 51.6 cu in, 845 cc (2.28 x 3.15 in, 58 x 80 mm); compression ratio: 8:1; max power (DIN): 34 hp (25 kW) at 5,000 rpm; max torque (DIN): 43 lb ft, 6 kg m (58 Nm): at 2,500 rpm; max engine rpm: 5,000; 40.2 hp/l (29.6 kW/l); cast iron block, wet liners, light alloy head; 3 crankshaft bearings; valves: overhead, in line, push-rods and rockers; camshafts: 1, side; lubrication: gear pump, filter in sump, 8.4 imp pt, 10.1 US pt, 4.8 l; 1 Zenith 28 IF downdraught single barrel carburettor; fuel feed: mechanical pump; water-cooled, 9.7 imp pt, 11.6 us pt, 5.5 l.

TRANSMISSION driving wheels: front; clutch: single dry plate

RODEO 4

(diaphragm); gearbox: mechanical; gears: 4, fully synchronized; ratios: I 3.833, II 2.235, III 1.458, IV 1.026, rev 3.545; lever: on facia; final drive: spiral bevel; axle ratio: 4.125; width of rims: 4"; tyres: 145 SR x 13.

PERFORMANCE max speeds: (I) 21 mph, 34 km/h; (II) 35 mph 56 km/h; (III) 53 mph, 86 km/h; (IV) 68 mph, 110 km/h; power-weight ratio: 43.4 lb/hp (59.1 lb/kW), 19.7 kg/hp (26.8 kg/kW); carrying capacity: 728 lb, 330 kg: acceleration: standing ¼ mile 23.8 sec, 0-50 mph (0-80 km/h) 34.2 sec; speed in top at 1,000 rpm: 15,2 mph, 24.4 km/h; consumption: 34 m/imp gal, 28.3 m/US gal, 8.3 l x 100 km.

CHASSIS reinforced platform; front suspension: independent, wishbones, longitudinal torsion bars, anti-roll bar, telescopic dampers; rear: independent, swinging longitudinal trailing arms, transverse torsion bars, anti-roll bar, telescopic dampers.

STEERING rack-and-pinion; turns lock to lock: 3.33.

BRAKES drum (front diameter 8.98 in, 22.8 cm, rear 6.30 in, 16 cm), dual circuit, rear compensator: lining area; front 44.8 sq in, 289 sq cm, rear 17.4 sq in, 112 sq cm, total 62.2 sq in, 401 sq cm.

ELECTRICAL EQUIPMENT 12 V; 28 Ah battery; 30/40 A alternator; 2 headlamps.

DIMENSIONS AND WEIGHT wheel base: 96.46 in, 245 cm (right), 94.49 in, 240 cm (left); tracks: 50.39 in, 128 cm front, 48.82 in, cm rear; length: 146.85 in, 373 cm; width: 60.79 in, 154 cm; height: 62.99 in, 160 cm; ground clearance: 5.51 in, 14 cm; weight: 1,477 lb, 670 kg; weight distribution: 56.1% front, 43.9% rear; turning circle: 33.1 ft, 10.1 m; fuel tank: 7.5 imp gal, 9 US gal, 34 l.

BODY open, in plastic material; 2 doors; 2 or 4 seats; folding rear seat.

PRACTICAL INSTRUCTIONS fuel: 85 oct petrol; oil: engine 8.4 imp pt, 10.1 US pt, 4.8 l, SAE 10W-40, change every 4,650 miles, 7,500 km - gearbox and final drive 3.2 imp pt, 3.8 US pt, 1.8 l, SAE 80 EP., change every 9,300 miles, 15,000 km; greasing: none; tappet clearances: inlet 0.006-0.007 in, 0.15-0.18 mm, exhaust 0.007-0.009 in, 0.18-0.22 mm; valve timing: 16° 52° 52° 16°; tyre pressure: front 18 psi, 1.3 atm, rear 24 psi, 1.7 atm.

OPTIONALS 4-wheel drive; "Evasion" version; "Quatre saisons" version; "Artisane" version.

Rodeo 6

See Rodeo 4, except for:

PRICE EX WORKS: 35,133 francs**

ENGINE 79.3 cu in, 1,300 cc (2.76 x 2.83 in, 70 x 72 mm); compression ratio: 9.5:1; max power (DIN): 48 hp (34 kW) at 5,300 rpm; max torque (DIN): 57 lb ft, 7.9 kg m (77 Nm) at 3,000 rpm; max engine rpm: 5,400; 43.3 hp/l (31.1 kW/l); 5.3 imp pt, 6.3 US pt, 3 l; 1 Zenith 32 IF 8 downdraught single barrel carburettor; water-cooled, 11.1 imp pt, 13.3 US pt, 6.3 l.

PERFORMANCE max speeds: (I) 23 mph, 37 km/h; (II) 37 mph, 60 km/h; (III) 58 mph, 93 km/h; (IV) 81 mph, 130 km/h; power-weight ratio: 34.2 lb/hp (47.6 lb/kW), 15.5 kg/hp (21.6 kg/kW).

STEERING turns lock to lock: 3.25.

BRAKES front disc (diameter 8.98 in, 22.8 cm), rear drum, rear compensator; lining area: front 19.8 sq in, 128 sq cm, rear 22.2 sq in, 143 sq cm, total 42 sq in, 271 sq cm.

DIMENSIONS AND WEIGHT tracks: 50.63 in, 129 cm front, 49.13 in, 125 cm rear; length: 148.62 in, 377 cm; height: 61.18 in, 155 cm; ground clearance: 5.71 in, 14.5 cm; weight: 1,643 lb, 745 kg; turning circle: 35.4 ft, 10.8 m; fuel tank: 8.8 imp gal, 10.6 US gal, 40 l.

BODY 2 seats.

PRACTICAL INSTRUCTIONS oil: engine 5.3 imp pt, 6.3 US pt, 3 l; tappet clearances: inlet 0.006 in, 0.15 mm, exhaust 0.008 in, 0.20 mm; valve timing: 18° 54° 53° 23°; tyre pressure: front 20 psi, 1.4 atm, rear 24 psi, 1.7 atm.

OPTIONALS "Bachée" version; "Hardtop" version.

5 Berline Series

PRICES IN GB AND EX WORKS:	£	francs
1 5 2+1-dr	2,965*	24,000**
2 5 4+1-dr	—	25,500**
3 TL 2+1-dr	3,065*	27,000**
4 TL 4+1-dr	—	28,500**
5 GTL 2+1-dr	3,240*	29,000**
6 GTL 4+1-dr	3,375*	30,500**
7 Automatic 2+1-dr	3,689*	32,500**
8 TS 2+1-dr	3,614*	32,000**
9 Alpine 2+1-dr	4,664*	42,800**

Power team:	Standard for:	Optional for:
36 hp	1,2	—
44 hp	3,4	—
42 hp	5,6	—
55 hp	7	—
64 hp	8	—
93 hp	9	—

36 hp power team

ENGINE front, 4 stroke; 4 cylinders, vertical, in line 51.6 cu in, 845 cc (2.28 x 3.15 in, 58 x 80 mm); compression ratio: 8:1; max power (DIN): 36 hp (26 kW) at 5,500 rpm; max torque (DIN): 42 lb ft, 5.8 kg m (57 Nm) at 2,500 rpm; max engine rpm: 6,000; 42.6 hp/l (31.4 kW/l); cast iron block, wet liners, light alloy head; 3 crankshaft bearings; valves: overhead, in line, push-rods and rockers; camshafts: 1, side; lubrication: gear pump, filter in sump (cartridge), 4.4 imp pt, 5.3 US pt, 2.5 l; 1 Solex 32 DIS downdraught single barrel carburettor; fuel feed: mechanical pump; sealed circuit cooling, liquid, expansion tank, 10.2 imp pt, 12.3 US pt, 5.8 l.

TRANSMISSION driving wheels: front; clutch: single dry plate (diaphragm); gearbox: mechanical; gears: 4, fully synchronized; ratios: I 3.833, II 2.235, III 1.458, IV 1.026, rev 3.545; lever: central; final drive: spiral bevel; axle ratio: 4.125; width of rims: 4"; tyres: 135 SR x 13.

RENAULT Rodeo 6

RENAULT 5 Alpine

PERFORMANCE max speeds: (I) 24 mph, 38 km/h; (II) 39 mph 63 km/h; (III) 60 mph, 97 km/h; (IV) 76 mph, 123 km/h power-weight ratio: 44.7 lb/hp (60.7 lb/kW), 20.3 kg/hp (27. kg/kW); carrying capacity: 728 lb, 330 kg; speed in top at 1,00 rpm: 14.7 mph, 23.7 km/h; consumption: 34.9 m/imp gal, 2 m/US gal, 8.1 l x 100 km.

CHASSIS integral; front suspension: independent, wishbones longitudinal torsion bar, anti-roll bar, telescopic dampers; rea independent, swinging longitudinal trailing arms, transvers torsion bars, telescopic dampers.

STEERING rack-and-pinion; turns lock to lock: 3.75.

BRAKES drum (diameter 7.87 in, 20 cm front, 6.30 in, 16 cr rear), dual circuit, rear compensator; lining area: front 68.2 s in, 440 sq cm, rear 38.9 sq in, 251 sq cm, total 107.1 sq in, 69 sq cm.

ELECTRICAL EQUIPMENT 12 V; 28 Ah battery; 35 A alterna tor; R 220 distributor; 2 headlamps.

DIMENSIONS AND WEIGHT wheel base: 94.49 in, 240 c (right), 95.67 in, 243 cm (left); tracks: 50.39 in, 128 cm fron 48.82 in, 124 cm rear; length: 138.19 in, 351 cm; width: 59.8 in, 152 cm; height: 55.12 in, 140 cm; ground clearance: 7.87 i 20 cm; weight: 1,610 lb, 730 kg; weight distribution: 58.2 front, 41.8% rear; turning circle: 33.1 ft, 10.1 m; fuel tank: 8. imp gal, 10 US gal, 38 l.

BODY saloon/sedan; 4 seats, separate front seats; heated rea window; folding rear seat.

PRACTICAL INSTRUCTIONS fuel: 98-100 oct petrol; oil: er gine 4.4 imp pt, 5.3 US pt, 2.5 l, SAE 20W-40, change ever 4,650 miles, 7,500 km - gearbox and final drive 3.2 imp pt, 3. US pt, 1.8 l, SAE 80 EP, change every 9,300 miles, 15,000 kn greasing: none; tappet clearances: inlet 0.006-0.007 in, 0.1 0.18 mm, exhaust 0.007-0.009 in, 0.18-0.22 mm; valve timin 20° 56° 53° 23°; tyre pressure: front 24 psi, 1.7 atm, rear 2 psi, 1.9 atm.

OPTIONALS luxury interior; metallic spray.

44 hp power team

See 36 hp power team, except for:

ENGINE 58.3 cu in, 956 cc (2.56 x 2.83 in, 65 x 72 mm); con pression ratio: 9.25:1; max power (DIN): 44 hp (32 kW) at 5,50 rpm; max torque (DIN): 48 lb ft, 6.5 kg m (64 Nm) at 3,500 rpn 46 hp/l (33.2 kW/l); 5 crankshaft bearings; lubrication: 5.3 im pt, 6.3 US pt, 3 l; sealed circuit cooling, liquid electric therm static fan, 11.1 imp pt, 13.3 US pt, 6.3 l.

PERFORMANCE max speeds: (I) 24 mph, 39 km/h; (II) 40 mp 64 km/h; (III) 62 mph, 100 km/h; (IV) 87 mph, 140 km/ power-weight ratio: 38.8 lb/hp (53.9 lb/kW), 17.6 kg/hp (24. kg/kW); carrying capacity: 882 lb, 400 kg; consumption: 31 m/imp gal, 26.1 m/US gal, 9 l x 100 km.

BRAKES front disc (diameter 8.98 in, 22.8 cm), rear drum, du circuit, rear compensator; swept area: front 157.2 sq in, 1,01 sq cm, rear 52.6 sq in, 339 sq cm, total 209.8 sq in, 1,353 s cm.

ELECTRICAL EQUIPMENT 30/40 A alternator; R 248 C 3 distributor.

DIMENSIONS AND WEIGHT front track: 50.71 in, 129 cr

eight: 1,709 lb, 775 kg: weight distribution: 60% front, 40% ear.

ODY 5 seats, reclining backrests.

RACTICAL INSTRUCTIONS oil: engine 5.3 imp pt, 6.3 US pt, l; tappet clearances: inlet 0.006 in, 0.15 mm, exhaust 0.008 , 0.20 mm; valve timing: 18° 54° 53° 23°.

PTIONALS tinted glass; sunshine roof; rear window wiper-asher.

42 hp power team

ee 44 hp power team, except for:

NGINE 68.2 cu in, 1,118 cc (2.76 x 2.83 in, 70 x 72 mm); ompression ratio: 9.5:1; max power (DIN): 42 hp (30 kW) at ,000 rpm; max torque (DIN): 61 lb ft, 8.4 kg m (82 Nm) at ,500 rpm; max engine rpm: 5,000; 26.6 hp/l (37 kW/l); 1 Zenith 2 IF7 downdraught carburettor.

RANSMISSION axle ratio: 3.100.

ERFORMANCE max speeds: (I) 26 mph, 42 km/h; (II) 45 mph, 2 km/h; (III) 68 mph, 110 km/h; (IV) 85 mph, 136 km/h; ower-weight ratio: 41.2 lb/hp (57.3 lb/kW), 18.7 kg/hp (26 g/kW); speed in top at 1,000 rpm: 19.6 mph, 31.5 km/h; onsumption: 32.5 m/imp gal, 27 m/US gal, 8.7 l x 100 km.

RAKES servo.

IMENSIONS AND WEIGHT width: 61.02 in, 155 cm; weight: ,731 lb, 785 kg.

RACTICAL INSTRUCTIONS valve timing: 22° 62° 65° 25°.

55 hp power team

ee 44 hp power team, except for:

NGINE 78.7 cu in, 1,289 cc (2.87 x 3.03 in, 73 x 77 mm); ompression ratio: 9.5:1 max power (DIN): 55 hp (40 kW) at ,750 rpm; max torque (DIN): 70 lb ft, 9.6 kg m (94 Nm) at ,500 rpm; max engine rpm: 5,750; 42.7 hp/l (31 kW/l); 1 Solex 2 SEIA downdraught.

RANSMISSION gearbox: automatic transmission, hydraulic orque converter and planetary gears with 3 ratios, max torque f converter at stall 2, possible manual selection; ratios: I ,266, II 1.403, III 0.971, rev 1.943; axle ratio: 3.555.

ERFORMANCE max speeds: (I) 32 mph, 52 km/h; (II) 62 mph, 00 km/h; (III) 89 mph, 144 km/h; power-weight ratio: 32.5 lb/hp 44.6 lb/kW), 14.7 kg/hp (20.2 kg/kW); speed in top at 1,000 om: 17.8 mph, 28.7 km/h; consumption: 34 m/imp gal, 28.3 /US gal, 8.3 l x 100 km.

RAKES servo.

IMENSIONS AND WEIGHT weight: 1,786 lb, 810 kg.

RACTICAL INSTRUCTIONS valve timing: 22° 62° 65° 25°.

64 hp power team

ee 44 hp power team, except for:

NGINE 78.7 cu in, 1,289 cc (2.87 x 3.03 in, 73 x 77 mm); ompression ratio: 9.5:1; max power (DIN): 64 hp (46 kW) at ,000 rpm; max torque (DIN): 70 lb ft, 9.6 kg m (94 Nm) at ,500 rpm; 49.6 hp/l (36 kW/l); 1 Weber 32 DIR 11 downdraught win barrel carburettor.

RANSMISSION ratios: I 3.833, II 2.375, III 1.522, IV 1.026, ev 3.545; axle ratio: 3.625; width of rims: 4.5"; tyres: 145 R x 13.

ERFORMANCE max speeds: (I) 29 mph, 47 km/h; (II) 45 mph, 3 km/h; (III) 70 mph, 113 km/h; (IV) 96 mph, 155 km/h; ower-weight ratio: 27.6 lb/hp (38 lb/kW), 12.5 kg/hp (17.2 g/kW); speed in top at 1,000 rpm: 17.2 mph, 27.7 km/h; onsumption: 31.7 m/imp gal, 26.4 m/US gal, 8.9 l x 100 km.

HASSIS rear suspension: anti-roll bar.

RAKES servo.

LECTRICAL EQUIPMENT 36 Ah battery; 50 A alternator; dine headlamps.

IMENSIONS AND WEIGHT weight: 1,764 lb, 800 kg.

ODY rear window wiper-washer (standard).

RACTICAL INSTRUCTIONS valve timing: 22° 62° 65° 25°; re pressure: front 23 psi, 1.6 atm, rear 27 psi, 1.9 atm.

93 hp power team

ee 44 hp power team, except for:

RENAULT 5 Berline

ENGINE 85.2 cu in, 1,397 cc (2.99 x 3.03 in, 76 x 77 mm); compression ratio: 10.2:1; max power (DIN): 93 hp (67 kW) at 6,400 rpm; max torque (DIN): 86 lb ft, 11.8 kg m (116. Nm) at 4,000 rpm; max engine rpm: 6,500; 66.6 hp/l (48 kW/l); 1 Weber 32 DIR 58 downdraught twin barrel carburettor.

TRANSMISSION gears: 5, fully synchronized; ratios: I 3.818, II 2.235, III 1.478, IV 1.036, V 0.861, rev 3.083; axle ratio: 3.875; width of rims: 4.5"; tyres: 155/70 HR x 13.

PERFORMANCE max speeds: (I) 27 mph, 44 km/h; (II) 46 mph, 74 km/h; (III) 70 mph, 113 km/h; (IV) 100 mph, 161 km/h; (V) 109 mph, 175 km/h; power-weight ratio: 20.1 lb/hp (28 lb/kW), 9.1 kg/hp (12.7 kg/kW); carrying capacity: 992 lb, 450 kg; speed in top at 1,000 rpm: 18.8 mph, 30.2 km/h; consumption: 26.4 m/imp gal, 22 m/US gal, 10.7 l x 100 km.

CHASSIS rear suspension: anti-roll bar.

STEERING turns lock to lock: 3.66.

BRAKES servo.

ELECTRICAL EQUIPMENT 36 Ah battery; 50 A alternator; iodine headlamps.

DIMENSIONS AND WEIGHT wheel base: 94.96 in, 241 cm (right), 96.14 in, 244 cm (left); tracks: 50.94 in, 129 cm front 49.21 in, 125 cm rear; length: 139.49 in, 354 cm; height: 52.76 in, 134 cm; ground clearance: 4.72 in, 12 cm; weight: 1,874 lb, 850 kg.

BODY tinted glass and rear window wiper-washer (standard).

PRACTICAL INSTRUCTIONS oil: gearbox and final drive, 3 imp pt, 3.6 US pt, 1.7 l; tappet clearances: inlet 0.008-0.009 in, 0.20-0.22 mm, exhaust 0.010-0.011 in, 0.25-0.27 mm; valve timing: 30° 72° 72° 30°; tyre pressure: front 23 psi, 1.6 atm, rear 28 psi, 2 atm.

6 TL

PRICE IN GB: £ 3,282*
PRICE EX WORKS: 27,400 francs**

ENGINE front, 4 stroke; 4 cylinders, vertical, in line; 67.6 cu in, 1,108 cc (2.76 x 2.83 in, 70 x 72 mm); compression ratio: 9.5:1; max power (DIN): 48 hp (34 kW) at 5,300 rpm; max torque (DIN): 57 lb ft, 7.9 kg m (77 Nm) at 3,000 rpm; max engine rpm: 5,700; 43.3 hp/l (31.2 kW/l); cast iron block, wet liners, light alloy head; 5 crankshaft bearings; valves: slanted, push-rods and rockers; camshafts: 1, side; lubrication: full flow filter, 5.3 imp pt, 6.3 US pt, 3 l; 1 Zenith 32 IF 8 or Solex 32 SEIA downdraught carburettor; fuel feed: mechanical pump; sealed circuit cooling, liquid, expansion tank, 11.1 imp pt, 13.3 US pt, 6.3 l, electric thermostatic fan.

TRANSMISSION driving wheels: front; clutch: single dry plate (diaphragm); gearbox: mechanical; gears: 4, fully synchronized; ratios: il 3.833, II 2.235, III 1.458, IV 1.026, rev 3.545; lever: on facia; final drive: spiral bevel; axle ratio: 4.125; width of rims: 4"; tyres: 145 SR x 13.

PERFORMANCE max speeds: (I) 22 mph, 35 km/h; (II) 39 mph, 63 km/h; (III) 60 mph, 97 km/h; (IV) 84 mph, 135 km/h; power-weight ratio: 37.7 lb/hp, (52.2 lb/kW), 17.1 kg/hp (23.7 kg/kW); carrying capacity: 882 lb, 400 kg; speed in top at 1,000 rpm: 15.2 mph, 24.4 km/h; consumption: 30.7 m/imp gal, 25.6 m/US gal, 9.2 l x 100 km.

RENAULT 6 TL

CHASSIS platform; front suspension: independent, wishbones, longitudinal torsion bars, anti-roll bar, telescopic dampers; rear: independent, swinging longitudinal trailing arms, transverse torsion bars, anti-roll bar, telescopic dampers.

STEERING rack-and-pinion; turns lock to lock: 3.75.

BRAKES front disc (diameter 8.98 in, 22.8 cm), rear drum, dual lining circuit, rear compensator; area: front 19.8 sq in, 128 sq cm, rear 52.6 sq in, 339 sq cm, total 72.4 sq in, 467 sq cm.

ELECTRICAL EQUIPMENT 12 V; 28 Ah battery; 30/40 A alternator; Lucas distributor; 2 headlamps.

DIMENSIONS AND WEIGHT wheel base: 96.46 in, 245 cm; (right), 94.49 in, 240 cm (left); tracks: 50.79 in, 129 cm front, 49.21 in, 125 cm rear; length: 151.97 in, 386 cm; width: 59.06 in, 150 cm; height: 57.87 in, 147 cm; ground clearance: 4.92 in, 12.5 cm; weight: 1,808 lb, 820 kg; weight distribution: 56.1% front, 43.9% rear; turning circle: 34.1 ft, 10.4 m; fuel tank: 8.6 imp gal, 10.3 US gal, 39 l.

BODY saloon/sedan; 4+1 doors; 5 seats, separate front seats; reclining backrests; folding rear seat; heated rear window.

PRACTICAL INSTRUCTIONS fuel: 90 oct petrol; oil: engine 5.3 imp pt, 6.3 US pt, 3 l, SAE 10/20W-40, change every 4,600 miles, 7,500 km - gearbox and final drive 3.2 imp pt, 3.8 US pt, 1.8 l, SAE 80 EP, change every 9,300 miles, 15,000 km; greasing: none; tappet clearances: inlet 0.006 in, 0.15 mm, exhaust 0.009 in, 0.22 mm; valve timing: 18° 54° 53° 23°; tyre pressure: front 20 psi, 1.4 atm, rear 24 psi, 1.7 atm.

OPTIONALS tinted glass; metallic spray; luxury interior.

RENAULT 14 GTL Berline

14 Berline Series

PRICES IN GB AND EX WORKS:	£	francs
1 TL	3,468*	30,900**
2 GTL	3,592*	32,900**
3 TS	4,044*	36,100**

Power team:	Standard for:	Optional for:
57 hp	1,2	—
69 hp	3	—

57 hp power team

ENGINE front, transverse, slanted 72° to rear, 4 stroke; 4 cylinders, vertical, in line; 74.3 cu in, 1,218 cc (2.95 x 2.72 in, 75 x 69 mm); compression ratio: 9.3:1; max power (DIN): 57 hp (41 kW) at 6,000 rpm; max torque (DIN): 67 lb ft, 9.3 kg m (91 Nm) at 3,000 rpm; max engine rpm: 5,500; 46.8 hp/l (33.7 kW/l); light alloy block and head, wet liners, hemispherical combustion chambers; 5 crankshaft bearings; valves: overhead, Vee-slanted, rockers; camshafts: 1, overhead; lubrication: gear pump, full flow filter, 7 imp pt, 8.3 US pt, 4 l; 1 Solex 32 PBISA horizontal single barrel carburettor; sealed circuit cooling, liquid, expansion tank, 10.6 imp pt, 12.7 US pt, 6 l, electric thermostatic fan.

TRANSMISSION driving wheels: front; clutch: single dry plate (diaphragm); gearbox: mechanical, in unit with engine and final drive; gears: 4, fully synchronized; ratios: I 3.883, II 2.296, III 1.501, IV 1.042, rev 3.568; lever: central; final drive: spiral bevel; axle ratio: 3.867; width of rims: 4.5"; tyres: 145 SR x 13.

PERFORMANCE max speeds: (I) 26 mph, 42 km/h; (II) 43 mph, 70 km/h; (III) 66 mph, 107 km/h; (IV) 89 mph, 143 km/h; power-weight ratio: 33.4 lb/hp (46.5 lb/kW), 15.2 kg/hp (21.1 kg/kW); carrying capacity: 882 lb, 400 kg; acceleration: standing ¼ mile 20 sec; speed in top at 1,000 rpm: 15.9 mph , 25.6 km/h; consumption: 31 m/imp gal, 25.8 m/US gal, 9.1 l x 100 km.

CHASSIS integral; front suspension: independent, by McPherson, coil springs/telescopic damper struts, lower wishbones, anti roll bar; rear: independent, swinging longitudinal trailing arms, transverse torsion bars, telescopic dampers.

STEERING rack-and-pinion; turns lock to lock: 4.

BRAKES front disc (diameter 9.49 in, 24.1 cm), rear drum, dual circuit, rear compensator, servo; lining area: front 22.2 sq in, 143 sq cm, rear 35.2 sq in, 227 sq cm, total 57,4 sq in, 378 sq cm.

ELECTRICAL EQUIPMENT 12 V; 32 Ah battery; 40 A alternator; 2 headlamps.

DIMENSIONS AND WEIGHT wheel base: 98.35 in, 250 cm (right)), 99.61 in, 253 cm (left); tracks: 53.23 in, 135 cm front, 54.25 in, 138 cm rear; length: 158.46 in, 402 cm; width: 63.94 in, 162 cm; height: 55.31 in 140 cm; ground clearance: 5.91 in, 15 cm; weight: 1,907 lb, 865 kg; turning circle: 34.8 ft, 10.6 m; fuel tank: 10.6 imp gal, 12.7 US gal, 48.

BODY saloon/sedan; 4+1 doors; 5 seats, separate front seats; folding rear seat; heated rear window.

PRACTICAL INSTRUCTIONS fuel: 98-100 oct petrol; oil: engine, gearbox and final drive 7 imp pt, 8.3 US pt, 4 l, change every 4,650 miles, 7,500 km; tappet clearances: inlet 0.004-0.006 in, 0.10-0.15 mm, exhaust 0.009-0.011 in, 0.23-0.28 mm; valve timing: 15° 45° 46° 15°; tyre pressure: front 24 psi, 1.7 atm, rear 27 psi, 1.9 atm.

OPTIONALS luxury interior; metallic spray; sunshine roof.

69 hp power team

See 57 hp power team, except for:

ENGINE 83 cu in, 1,360 cc (2.95 x 3.03 in, 75 x 77 mm); max power (DIN): 69 hp (50 kW) at 6,000 rpm; max torque (DIN): 71 lb/ft, 9.8 kg m (96 Nm) at 3,000 rpm; 50.7 hp/l (37.3 kW/l); 1 Solex 32 CICSA horizontal twin barrel carburettor.

PERFORMANCE max speed: 96 mph, 155 km/h; power-weight ratio: 28.1 lb/hp (38.4 lb/kW), 12.7 kg/hp (17.4 kg/kW); acceleration: standing ¼ mile 18.7 sec; consumption: 27.4 m/imp gal, 22.8 m/US gal, 10.3 l x 100 km.

CHASSIS rear suspension: anti-roll bar.

BRAKES lining area: front 19.8 sq in, 128.2 cm, rear 65.4 sq in, 422.2 sq cm, total 85.2 sq in, 550.4 sq cm.

ELECTRICAL EQUIPMENT 50 A alternator.

DIMENSIONS AND WEIGHT weight: 1,940 lb, 880 kg.

PRACTICAL INSTRUCTIONS valve timing: 19° 49° 49° 19°.

OPTIONALS tinted glass; rear window wiper-washer.

16 Berline Series

PRICES IN GB AND EX WORKS:	£	francs
1 TL	4,238*	36,800*
2 TX	5,165*	43,100*
3 TX Automatic	5,532*	45,600*

Power team:	Standard for:	Optional for:
55 hp	1	—
90 hp	2,3	—

55 hp power team

ENGINE front, 4 stroke; 4 cylinders, vertical, in line; 95.5 cu in, 1,565 cc (3.03 x 3.31 in, 77 x 84 mm); compression ratio: 8:1 max power (DIN): 55 hp (40 kW) at 5,000 rpm; max torque (DIN): 79 lb ft, 10.9 kg m (107 Nm) at 2,500 rpm; max engine rpm: 5,200; 35.1 hp/l (25.6 k/W/l); light alloy block and head wet liners; 5 crankshaft bearings; valves: overhead, in line slanted at 20°, push-rods and rockers; camshafts: 1, side lubrication: eccentric pump, filter in sump, 7 imp pt, 8.5 US pt 4 l; 1 Solex MIMAT downdraught carburettor; fuel feed: mechanical pump; sealed circuit cooling, liquid, expansion tank, 10.[illegible] imp pt, 13.1 US pt, 6.2 l, electric thermostatic fan.

TRANSMISSION driving wheels: front; clutch: single dry plate (diaphragm); gearbox: mechanical; gears: 4, fully synchronized ratios: I 3.818, II 2.235, III 1.478, IV 1.036, rev 3.083; lever steering column; final drive : hypoid bevel; axle ratio: 3.778 width of rims: 4.5"; tyres: 145 SR x 14.

PERFORMANCE max speeds: (I) 24 mph, 39 km/h; (II) 41 mph 66 km/l; (III) 63 mph, 101 km/h; (IV) 87 mph, 140 km/h power-weight ratio: 40.5 lb/hp (55.7 lb/kW), 18.4 kg/hp (25.[illegible] kg/kW); carrying capacity: 882 lb, 400 kg; speed in top at 1,000 rpm: 17.1 mph, 27.6 km/h; consumption: 27.4 m/imp gal, 22.[illegible] m/US gal, 10.3 l x 100 km.

CHASSIS platform; front suspension: independent, wishbones longitudinal torsion bars, anti-roll bar, telescopic dampers; rear independent, swinging longitudinal trailing arms, transverse torsion bar, anti-roll bar, telescopic dampers.

STEERING rack-and-pinion; turns lock to lock: 4.11.

BRAKES front disc, rear drum, rear compensator, dual circuit servo; lining area: front 22.2 sq in, 143 sq cm, rear 42.3 sq in 273 sq cm, total 64.5 sq in, 416 sq cm.

ELECTRICAL EQUIPMENT 12 V; 36 Ah battery; 30/40 A alternator; 4 headlamps.

DIMENSIONS AND WEIGHT wheel base: 104.33 in, 265 cm (right), 107.09 in, 272 cm (left); tracks: 52.76 in, 134 cm front 50.79 in, 129 cm rear; length: 166.93 in, 424 cm; width: 64.1 in, 163 cm; height: 57.09 in, 145 cm; ground clearance: 4.13 in 10.5 cm; weight: 2,227 lb, 1,010 kg; weight distribution: 55.9% front, 44.1% rear; turning circle: 36.1 ft, 11 m; fuel tank: 11 imp gal, 13.2 US gal, 50 l.

BODY saloon/sedan; 4+1 doors; 5 seats, separate front seats reclining backrests; folding rear seat; heated rear window.

PRACTICAL INSTRUCTIONS fuel: 85 oct petrol; oil: engine imp pt, 8.5 US pt, 4 l, SAE 10W-40, change every 4,600 miles 7,500 km - gearbox and final drive 2.8 imp pt, 3.4 US prt, 1.6

RENAULT 16 TX Berline

AE 80 EP, change every 9,300 miles, 15,000 km; greasing: one; tappet clearances: inlet 0.008 in, 0.20 mm, exhaust 0.010 ı, 0.25 mm; valve timing: 18° 54° 58° 18°; tyre pressure: front 3 psi, 1.6 atm, rear 28 psi, 2 atm.

PTIONALS luxury interior; metallic spray.

90 hp power team

ee 55 hp power team, except for:

NGINE 100.5 cu in, 1,647 cc (3.11 x 3.31 in, 79 x 84 mm); ompression ratio: 9.25:1; max power (DIN): 90 hp (65 kW) at ,000 rpm; max torque (DIN): TX 95 lb ft, 13.1 kg m (128 Nm) t 4,000 rpm - TX Automatic 96 lb ft, 13.2 kg m (129.5 Nm) at ,500 rpm; max engine rpm: 6,300; 54.6 hp/l (39.5 kW/l); alves: Vee-slanted; lubrication: eccentric pump, full flow filter; Weber 32 DAR 7 twin barrel carburettor; cooling: 12 imp pt, 4.4 US pt, 6.8 l.

RANSMISSION gears: TX 5, fully synchronized (TX Automatic ansmission, hydraulic torque converter and planetary gears ith 3 ratios, max ratio of converter at stall 2,3, possible ıanual selection ; ratios: I 2.459, II 1.523, III 1.054, rev 2.108); atios: I 3.818, II 2.235, III 1.478, IV 1.036, V 0.861, rev 3.083; xle ratio: TX 3.875 - TX Automatic 3.556; tyres: 155 SR x 14.

ERFORMANCE max speeds: TX (I) 28 mph, 45 km/h; (II) 48 ıph, 77 km/l; (III) 72 mph, 116 km/h; (IV) 103 mph, 166 km/h; V) 106 mph, 170 km/h; - TX Automatic (I) 47 mph, 76 km/h; (II) 6 mph, 123 km/h; (III) 103 mph, 165 km/l; power-weight ratio: X 26.1 lb/hp (36.1 lb/kW), 11.8 kg/hp (16.4 kg/kW); carrying apacity: 937 lb, 425 kg; acceleration: 0-50 mph (0-80 km/h) .1 sec; speed in top at 1,000 rpm: TX 20.7 mph, 33.3 km/h - X Automatic 18.5 mph, 29.7 km/h; consumption: TX 26.4 ı/imp gal, 22 m/US gal, 10.7 l x 100 km - TX Automatic 25.2 ı/imp gal, 21 m/US gal, 11,2 l x 100 km.

LECTRICAL EQUIPMENT 50 A alternator; 4 iodine head- amps.

IMENSIONS AND WEIGHT ground clearance: 4.13 in, 10.5 m; weight: TX 2,348 lb, 1,065 kg - TX Automatic 2,403 lb, ,090 kg; weight distribution: 56.6% front, 43.4% rear.

ODY reclining backrests with built-in headrests; electric win- ows; rear window wiper-washer.

RACTICAL INSTRUCTIONS fuel: 98-100 oct petrol; oil: TX earbox and final drive 3 imp pt, 3.6 US pt, 1.7 l - TX Automatic utomatic transmission and final drive 10.6 imp pt, 12.7 US pt, l, change every 18,600 miles, 30,000 km; valve timing: TX 24° 8° 68° 24° - TX Automatic 21° 59° 59° 21°; tyre pressure: front 4 psi, 1.7 atm.

PTIONALS luxury interior; metallic spray; leather upholstery; nted glass; electric sunshine roof; air-conditioning.

18 Series

RICES IN GB AND EX WORKS:	£	francs
1 4-dr Berline	—	32,200**
2 TL 4-dr Berline	3,723*	35,000**
3 GTL 4-dr Berline	4,287*	38,400**
4 4+1-dr Break	—	35,200**
5 TL 4+1-dr Break	4,040*	38,000**
6 TS 4-dr Berline	4,070*	38,700**
7 GTS 4-dr Berline	4,758*	42,200**
8 Automatic 4-dr Berline	4,870*	41,800**
9 TS 4+1-dr Break	4,440*	41,700**
0 TS 4+1-dr Break Automatic	—	45,100**

ower team:	**Standard for:**	**Optional for:**
4 hp	1 to 5	—
9 hp	6 to 10	—

64 hp power team

NGINE front, 4 stroke; 4 cylinders, vertical, in line; 85.2 cu in, ,397 cc (2.99 x 3.03 in, 76 x 77 mm); compression ratio: .25:1; max power (DIN): 64 hp (46 kW) at 5,500 rpm; max orque (DIN): 76.1 lb ft, 10.5 kg m (103 Nm) at 3,000 rpm; max ngine rpm: 6,000; 45.8 hp/l (32.9 kW/l); light alloy block and ead, wet liners; crankshaft bearings; valves: overhead, in line, ush-rods and rockers; camshafts: 1, in side; lubrication: gear ump, filter in sump, 5.3 imp pt, 6.3 US pt, 3 l; 1 Solex 32 SEIA owndraught single barrel carburettor; fuel feed: mechanical ump; sealed circuit cooling, liquid, expansion tank, 10.5 imp t, 12.7 US pt, 6 l.

RANSMISSION driving wheels: front; clutch: single dry plate diaphragm); gearbox: mechanical; gears: 4, fully synchronized; atios: I 3.818, II 2.235, III 1.478, IV 0.971, rev 3.083; lever: entral; final drive: hypoid bevel; axle ratio: 3.778; width of ims: 5"; tyres: 155 SR x 13.

ERFORMANCE max speeds: (I) 25 mph, 40 km/h; (II) 42 mph, 8 km/h; (III) 64 mph, 103 km/h; (IV) 95 mph, 153 km/h; ower-weight ratio: sedans 31.7 lb/hp (44.1 lb/kW), 14.4 kg/hp 20 kg/kW); carrying capacity: 904 lb, 410 kg; acceleration: tanding ¼ mile 19.3 sec; speed in top at 1,000 rpm: 17.9 mph, 8.8 km/h; consumption: 26.9 m/imp gal, 22.4 m/US gal, 10.5 x 100 km.

RENAULT 18 GTS Berline

CHASSIS integral; front suspension: independent, wishbones, anti-roll bar, coil springs/telescopic dampers; rear: rigid axle, trailing arms, A-bracket, anti-roll bar, coil springs/telescopic dampers.

STEERING rack-and-pinion; turns lock to lock: 3.55.

BRAKES front disc, rear drum, dual circuit, rear compensator, servo; lining area: front 22.2 sq in, 143.2 sq cm, rear 66.4–70.4 sq in, 428-454 sq cm, total 86.8–92.6 sq in, 571.2-597.2 sq cm.

ELECTRICAL EQUIPMENT 12 V; 36 Ah battery; 50 A alternator; 2 headlamps, halogen headlamps (for GTL only).

BODY saloon/sedan, 4 doors - estate car/st. wagon, 4+1 doors; 5 seats, separate front seats, reclining backrests; heated rear window; rear window wiper-washer and folding rear seat (for st. wagon only); luxury interior, electric windows and headrests (for GTL only).

DIMENSIONS AND WEIGHT wheel base: 96.1 in, 2,44 cm; tracks: 55.7 in, 142 cm front, 53.40 in, 136 cm rear; length: sedans 172 in, 437 cm - st. wagons 175.20 in, 445 cm; width: 66.20 in, 168 cm; height: 55.30 in, 140 cm; weight: sedans 2,028 lb, 920 kg - st. wagons 2,315 lb, 1,050 kg; weight distribution: 60,3% front, 39.7% rear; turning circle: 36.1 ft, 11 m; fuel tank: sedans 11.7 imp gal, 14 US gal, 53 l - st. wagons 12.5 imp gal, 15 US gal, 57 l.

PRACTICAL INSTRUCTIONS fuel: 98-100 oct petrol; oil: engine 5.3 imp pt, 6.3 US pt, 3 l, SAE 15W-40 change every 4,650 miles, 7,500 km - gearbox and final drive 3.5 imp pt, 4.2 US pt, 2 l, SAE 80 EP, change every 18,600 miles, 30,000 km; greasing: none; tappet clearences: inlet 0.006 in, 0.15 mm, exhaust 0.008 in, 0.20 mm; valve timing: 22° 62° 65° 25°; tyre pressure: front 26 psi, 1.8 atm, rear 28 psi, 2 atm.

OPTIONALS luxury interior; tinted glass; metallic spray; sunshine roof (for GTL only).

RENAULT 18 TS Break

79 hp power team

See 64 hp power team, except for:

ENGINE 100.5 cu in, 1,647 cc (3.11 x 3.31 in, 79 x 84 mm); compression ratio: 9.3:1; max power (DIN): 79 hp (57 kW) at 5,500 rpm; max torque (DIN): 90.6 lb ft, 12.5 kg m(123 Nm) at 3,000 rpm; max engine rpm: 6,000; 47.9 hp/l (34.8 kW/l); lubrication: 7 imp pt, 8.5 US pt, 4 l; 1 Solex 35 EITA; cooling: 11.1 imp pt, 13.3 US pt, 6.3 l.

TRANSMISSION (for automatic models only) automatic transmission, hydraulic torque converter and planetary gears with 3 ratios, max ratio of converter at stall 2.3, possible manual selection; ratios: I 2.396, II 1.484, III 1.027, rev 2.054; axle ratio: 3.556.

PERFORMANCE max speed: 101 mph, 163 km/h - automatic models 98 mph, 157 km/h; power-weight ratio: sedans 26.2 lb/hp, (36.1 lb/kW), 11.9 kg/hp (16.4 kg/kW); acceleration: standing ¼ mile 18.7 sec - automatic models 20.4 sec; consumption: 28.5 m/imp gal, 23.8 m/US gal, 9.9 l x 100 km - automatic models 26.6 m/imp gal, 22.2 m/US gal, 10.6 l x km.

ELECTRICAL EQUIPMENT iodine headlamps.

DIMENSIONS AND WEIGHT weight: sedans 2,072 lb, 940 kg - st. wagons 2,381 lb, 1,080 kg.

PRACTICAL INSTRUCTIONS oil: engine 7 imp pt, 8.5 US pt, 4 l; valve timing: 22° 70° 70° 22°.

20 TL / GTL

PRICES IN GB AND EX WORKS:	£	francs
TL	5,042*	43,200**
GTL	—	46,700**

ENGINE front, 4 stroke; 4 cylinders, vertical, in line; 100.5 cu in, 1,647 cc (3.11 x 3.31 in, 79 x 84 mm); compression ratio: 9.3:1; max power (DIN): 96 hp (69 KW) at 5,750 rpm; max torque (DIN): 99 lb ft, 13.6 kg m (133 Nm) at 3.500 rpm; max engine rpm: 6,000; 58.3 hp/l (41.9 kW/l); light alloy block and head, wet liners, hemispherical combustion chambers; 5 crankshaft bearings; valves: overhead, Vee-slanted, push-rods and rockers; camshafts: 1, side; lubrication: gear pump, full flow filter, 7 imp pt, 8.5 US pt, 4 l; 1 Weber 32 DARA downdraught twin barrel carburettor; sealed circuit cooling, liquid, expansion tank, 12.3 imp pt, 14.8 US pt, 7 l, electric thermostatic fan.

TRANSMISSION driving wheels: front; clutch: single dry plate (diaphragm), hydraulically controlled; gearbox: mechanical, in unit with engine and final drive; gears: 4, fully synchronized; ratios: I 3.818, II 2.235, III 1.478, IV 1.036, rev 3.083; lever: central; final drive: hypoid bevel; axle ratio: 3.778; width of rims: 5.5"; tyres: 165 SR x 13.

PERFORMANCE max speeds: (I) 28 mph, 45 km/h; (II) 48 mph, 77 km/h; (III) 73 mph, 117 km/h; (IV) 103 mph, 165 km/h; power-weight ratio: 27.2 lb/hp (37.9 lb/kW), 12.3 kg/hp (17.2

RENAULT 20 TS

20 TL / GTL

kg/kW); carrying capacity: 882 lb, 400 kg; speed in top at 1,000 rpm: 17.2 mph, 27.7 km/h; consumption: 25.7 m/imp gal, 21.4 m/US gal, 11 l x 100 km.

CHASSIS integral; front suspension: independent, by McPherson, coil springs/telescopic damper struts, lower wishbones, anti-roll bar; rear: independent, oblique semi-trailing arms, coil springs, anti-roll bar, telescopic dampers.

STEERING rack-and-pinion, servo (for GTL only); turns lock to lock: 4-3 (for GTL only).

BRAKES front disc, internal radial fins, rear drum, rear compensator, dual circuit, servo; lining area: front 22.2 sq in, 143 sq cm, rear 42.3 sq in, 273 sq cm, total 64.5 sq in, 416 sq cm.

ELECTRICAL EQUIPMENT 12 V; 40 Ah battery; 50 A alternator; 2 headlamps.

DIMENSIONS AND WEIGHT wheel base: 104.68 in, 266 cm; tracks: 56.85 in, 144 cm front, 56.61 in, 144 cm rear; length: 177.95 in, 452 cm; width: 67.95 in, 173 cm; height: 56.50 in, 143 cm; weight: 2,613 lb, 1,185 kg; turning circle: 36.7 ft, 11.2 m; fuel tank: 13.2 imp gal, 15.8 US gal, 60 l.

BODY saloon/sedan; 4+1 doors; 5 seats, separate front seats, reclining backrests; heated rear window; luxury equipment and electric windows (for GTL only).

PRACTICAL INSTRUCTIONS fuel: 98-100 oct petrol; oil: engine 7 imp pt, 8.5 US pt, 4 l, SAE 10W-50, change every 4,600 miles, 7,500 km - gearbox 3.5 imp pt, 4.2 US pt, 2 l, SAE 20W-40, change every 9,300 miles, 15,000 km - final drive 2.8 imp pt, 3.4 US pt, 1.6 l, SAE 80, change every 9,300 miles, 15,000 km; tappet clearances: inlet 0.008 in, 0.20 mm, exhaust 0.010 in, 0.25 mm; valve timing: 30° 72° 72° 30°; tyre pressure: front and rear 27 psi, 1.9 atm.

OPTIONALS luxury interior; metallic spray; tinted glass; electric sunshine roof.

20 TS

See 20 TL/GTL, except for:

PRICE IN GB: £ 6,167*
PRICE EX WORKS: 48,400 francs**

ENGINE 121.7 cu in, 1,995 cc (3.46 x 3.23 in, 88 x 82 mm); compression ratio: 9.2:1; max power (DIN): 109 hp (79 kW) at 5,550 rpm; max torque (DIN): 123 lb ft, 17.1 kg m (168 Nm) at 3,000 rpm; 54.6 hp/l (39.6 kW/l); camshafts: 1, overhead, cogged belt.

TRANSMISSION gearbox ratios: I 3.364, II 2.059, III 1.318, IV 0.931, rev 3.182; axle ratio: 4.125; tyres: 165 SR x 14.

PERFORMANCE max speed: 106 mph, 170 km/h; power-weight ratio: 25.9 lb/hp (35.7 lb/kW), 11.7 kg/hp (16.2 kg/kW); speed in top at 1,000 rpm: 13 mph, 20.9 km/h; consumption: 22.8 m/imp gal, 19 m/US gal, 12.4 l x 100 km.

STEERING servo; turns lock to lock: 3.25.

BRAKES lining area: front 27.3 sq in, 176 sq cm, rear 42.3 sq in, 273 sq cm, total 69.6 sq in, 449 sq cm.

DIMENSIONS AND WEIGHT weight: 2,822 lb, 1,280 kg; turning circle: 37.4 ft, 11.4 m; fuel tank: 14.7 imp gal, 17.7 US gal, 67 l.

BODY luxury equipment; electric windows.

PRACTICAL INSTRUCTIONS tappet clearances: inlet 0.010-0.012 in, 0.15-0.18 mm, exhaust 0.006-0.008 in, 0.25-0.30 mm; valve timing: 20° 60° 60° 20°; tyre pressure: front 27 psi, 1.9 atm, rear 28 psi, 2 atm.

OPTIONALS 5-speed mechanical gearbox (I 3.364, II 2.059, III 1.380, IV 1.060, V 0.820, rev 3.182); air-conditioning.

20 TS Automatic

See 20 TL/GTL, except for:

PRICE IN GB: £ 6,440*
PRICE EX WORKS: 51,800 francs**

ENGINE 121.7 cu in, 1,995 cc (3.46 x 3.23 in, 88 x 82 mm); compression ratio: 9.2:1; max power (DIN): 109 hp (79 kW) at 5,500 rpm; max torque (DIN): 123 lb ft, 17.1 kg m (168 Nm) at 3,000 rpm; 54.6 hp/l (39.6 kW/l); camshafts: 1, overhead, cogged belt.

TRANSMISSION gearbox: automatic transmission, hydraulic torque converter and planetary gears with 3 ratios, max ratio of converter at stall 2.3, possible manual selection; ratios: I 2.222, II 1.370, III 0.926, rev 1.777; axle ratio: 4.125; tyres: 165 SR x 14.

PERFORMANCE max speed: 103 mph, 165 km/h; power-weight ratio: 25.9 lb/hp (35.7 lb/kW), 11.7 kg/hp (16.2 kg/kW); speed in top at 1,000 rpm: 18.5 mph, 29.7 km/h; consumption: 24.8 m/imp gal, 20.6 m/US gal, 11.4 l x 100 km.

STEERING servo; turns lock to lock: 3.25.

BRAKES lining area: front 27.3 sq in, 176 sq cm, rear 42.3 sq in, 273 sq cm, total 69.6 sq in, 449 sq cm.

DIMENSIONS AND WEIGHT weight: 2,822 lb, 1,280 kg; turning circle: 37.4 ft, 11.4 m; fuel tank: 14.7 imp gal, 17.7 US gal, 67 l.

BODY luxury equipment; electric windows.

PRACTICAL INSTRUCTIONS oil: automatic transmission 10.6 imp pt, 12.7 US pt, 6 l, change every 18,600 miles, 30,000 km; tappet clearances: inlet 0.010-0.012 in, 0.15-0.18 mm, exhaust 0.006-0.008 in, 0.25-0.30 mm; valve timing: 20° 60° 60° 20°; tyre pressure: front and rear 28 psi, 2 atm.

OPTIONALS air-conditioning.

20 TD / GTD

See 20 TL/GTL, except for:

PRICES EX WORKS:	**francs**
TD	**49,700****
GTD	**53,800****

ENGINE diesel; 126.2 cu in, 2,068 cc (3.39 x 3.50 in, 86 x 89 mm); compression ratio: 21.5:1; max power (DIN): 64 hp (47 kW) at 4,500 rpm; max torque (DIN): 94 lb ft, 13 kg m (128 Nm) at 2,250 rpm; max engine rpm: 5,000; 31 hp/l (22.7 kW/l); camshafts: 1, overhead, cogged belt; lubrication: 11.4 imp pt, 13.7 US pt, 6.5 l; 4-cylinder Bosch indirect injection pump.

TRANSMISSION gears: 5, fully synchronized; ratios: I 3.818, II 2.235, III 1.478, IV 1.036, V 0.861, rev 3.083; axle ratio: 3.268.

PERFORMANCE max speed: 91 mph, 146 km/h; power-weight ratio: 43.4 lb/hp, (59.1 lb/kW), 19.7 kg/hp (26.8 kg/kW); acceleration: standing ¼ mile 21 sec, 0-50 mph (0-80 km/h) 7.9 sec; consumption: 32.5 m/imp gal, 27 m/US gal, 8.7 l x 100 km at 75 mph, 120 km/h.

STEERING servo (for GTD only); turns lock to lock: 3.

DIMENSIONS AND WEIGHT weight: 2,778 lb, 1,260 kg; weight distribution: 63% front, 37% rear; turning circle: 37.4 ft, 11.4 m.

PRACTICAL INSTRUCTIONS fuel: diesel oil; oil: engine 11.4 imp pt, 13.7 US pt, 6.5 l, change every 3,100 miles, 5,000 km; tyre pressure: front 31 psi, 2.2 atm, rear 28 psi, 2 atm.

30 TS

PRICE IN GB: £ 7,326*
PRICE EX WORKS: 53,800 francs**

ENGINE front, 4 stroke; 6 cylinders, Vee-slanted at 90°; 162.6 cu in, 2,664 cc (3.46 x 2.87 in, 88 x 73 mm); compression ratio 9.2:1; max power (DIN): 128 hp (92 kW) at 5,500 rpm; max torque (DIN): 149.3 lb ft, 20.6 kg m (202 Nm) at 2,500 rpm; max engine rpm: 6,000; 48 hp/l (34.7 kW/l); light alloy block and head, wet liners, hemispherical combustion chambers; 4 crankshaft bearings; valves: overhead; lubrication: gear pump, full flow filter, 9.7 imp pt, 11.6 US pt, 5.5 l; 1 Weber 38-38 DGAR downdraught twin barrel carburettor; fuel feed: mechanical pump; water-cooled, expansion tank, 17.2 imp pt, 20.7 US pt, 9.8 l, viscous coupling thermostatic fan.

TRANSMISSION driving wheels: front; clutch: single dry plate (diaphragm), hydraulically controlled; gearbox: mechanical; gears: 4, fully synchronized; ratios: I 3.364, II 2.059, III 1.318, IV 0.931, rev 3.182; lever: central; final drive: hypoid bevel; axle ratio: 3.889; width of rims: 5.5"; tyres: 175 HR x 14.

PERFORMANCE max speeds: (I) 31 mph, 50 km/h; (II) 50 mph, 81 km/h; (III) 79 mph, 127 km/h; (IV) 114 mph, 183 km/h; power-weight ratio: 22.7 lb/hp (31.5 lb/kW), 10.3 kg/hp (14.3 kg/kW); carrying capacity: 926 lb, 420 kg; acceleration: standing ¼ mile 17.4 sec, 0-50 mph (0-80 km/h) 6.8 sec; speed in top at 1,000 rpm: 19.9 mph, 32 km/h consumption: 16.3 m/imp gal, 13.6 m/US gal, 17.3 l x 100 km.

CHASSIS integral; front suspension: independent, by McPherson, coil springs/telescopic damper struts, lower wishbones, anti-roll bar; rear: independent, oblique semi-trailing arms, coil springs, anti-roll bar, telescopic dampers.

STEERING rack-and-pinion, servo; turns lock to lock: 3.50.

BRAKES disc (front diameter 9.92 in, 25.2 cm, rear 10 in, 25.4 cm), front internal radial fins, rear compensator, dual circuit, servo; lining area: front 29.8 sq in, 192 sq cm, rear 22.2 sq in, 143 sq cm, total 52 sq in, 335 sq cm.

ELECTRICAL EQUIPMENT 12 V; 50 Ah battery; 50 A alternator; dual ignition; 4 iodine headlamps, height adjustable from driving seat.

DIMENSIONS AND WEIGHT wheel base: 105.12 in, 267 cm; tracks: 56.89 in, 144.5 cm front, 56.69 in, 144 cm rear; length

RENAULT 20 TS

RENAULT 30 TS

177.95 in, 452 cm; width: 68.11 in, 173 cm; height: 56.30 in, 143 cm; weight: 2,911 lb, 1,320 kg; turning circle: 35.8 ft, 10.9 m; fuel tank: 14.7 imp gal, 17.7 US gal, 67 l.

BODY saloon/sedan; 4+1 doors; 5 seats, separate front seats, reclining backrests with adjustable built-in headrests; electric front windows; heated rear window; headlamps with wiper-washers; tinted glass.

PRACTICAL INSTRUCTIONS fuel: 98-100 oct petrol; oil: engine 9.7 imp pt, 11.6 US pt, 5.5 l, SAE 10W-50, change every 4,600 miles, 7,500 km - gearbox 6 imp pt, 7.2 US pt, 3.4 l, SAE 20W-40, change every 9,300 miles, 15,000 km - final drive 2.8 imp pt, 3.4 US pt, 1.6 l, SAE 80, change every 9,300 miles, 15,000 km; tappet clearances: inlet 0.004-0.006 in, 0.10-0.15 mm, exhaust 0.010-0.012 in, 0.25-0.30 mm; valve timing: 9° 45° 45° 9° (left), 7° 43° 43° 7° (right); tyre pressure: front 26 psi, 1.8 atm, rear 28 psi, 2 atm.

OPTIONALS metallic spray; electric sunshine roof; leather upholstery; air-conditioning.

30 TS Automatic

See 30 TS, except for:

PRICE IN GB: £ 7,737*
PRICE EX WORKS: 57,200 francs**

TRANSMISSION gearbox: automatic transmission, hydraulic torque converter and planetary gears with 3 ratios, max ratio of converter at stall 2.3, possible manual selection; ratios: I 2.307, II 1.423, III 0.961, rev 1.846.

PERFORMANCE max speeds: (I) 45 mph, 72 km/h; (II) 70 mph, 113 km/h; (III) 110 mph, 177 km/h; power-weight ratio: 23.1 lb/hp (31.9 lb/kW), 10.4 kg/hp (14.5 kg/kW); carrying capacity: 882 lb, 400 kg; speed in top at 1,000 rpm: 19.3 mph, 31 km/h; consumption: 17.1 m/imp gal, 14.3 m/US gal, 16.5 l x 100 km.

STEERING turns lock to lock: 3.25.

DIMENSIONS AND WEIGHT weight: 2,955 lb, 1,340 kg; turning circle: 37.4 ft, 11.4 m.

PRACTICAL INSTRUCTIONS oil: automatic transmission 13.4 imp pt, 16.1 US pt, 7.6 l; tyre pressure: front 27 psi, 1.9 atm.

30 TX

See 30 TS, except for:

PRICE IN GB: £ 8,712*
PRICE EX WORKS: 62,800 francs**

ENGINE max power (DIN): 142 hp (102 kW) at 5,500 rpm; max torque (DIN): 161.6 lb ft, 22.3 kg m (219 Nm) at 3,000 rpm; max engine rpm: 6,000; 53.3 hp/l (38.5 kW/l); Bosch K-Jetronic electronic injection.

TRANSMISSION gears: 5, fully synchronized; ratios: I 3.360, II 2.060, III 1.380, IV 1.060, V 0.820, rev 3.182; axle ratio: 3.150.

PERFORMANCE max speeds: (I) 33 mph, 53 km/h; (II) 53 mph, 86 km/h; (III) 80 mph, 129 km/h; (IV) 105 mph, 169 km/h; (V) 117 mph, 188 km/h; power-weight ratio: 20.8 lb/hp (28.8 lb/kW), 9.4 kg/hp (13.1 kg/kW); acceleration: standing ¼ mile 17.3 sec; speed in top at 1,000 rpm: 22.5 mph, 36.3 km/h; consumption: 17.1 m/imp gal, 14.3 m/US gal, 16.5 l x 100 km.

STEERING turns lock to lock: 3.25.

ELECTRICAL EQUIPMENT 70 A alternator.

DIMENSIONS AND WEIGHT weight: 2,955 lb, 1,340 kg; turning circle: 37.4 ft, 11.4 m.

OPTIONALS 150 TR x 390 or TRX 190/65 HR x 390 tyres.

30 TX Automatic

See 30 TS, except for:

PRICE IN GB: £ 8,985*
PRICE EX WORKS: 65,200 francs**

ENGINE max power (DIN): 142 hp (102 kW) at 5,500 rpm; max torque (DIN): 161.6 lb ft, 22.3 kg m (219 Nm) at 3,000 rpm; max engine rpm: 6,000; 53.3 hp/l (38.5 kW/l); Bosch K-Jetronic electronic injection.

TRANSMISSION gearbox: automatic transmission, hydraulic torque converter and planetary gears with 3 ratios, max ratio of converter at stall 2.3, possible manual selection; ratios: I 2.307, II 1.423, III 0.961, rev 1.846; axle ratio: 3.150.

PERFORMANCE max speeds: (I) 48 mph, 78 km/h; (II) 79 mph, 128 km/h; (III) 113 mph, 182 km/h; power-weight ratio: 21.1 lb/hp (29.2 lb/kW), 9.6 kg/hp (13.2 kg/kW); acceleration: standing ¼ mile 18.3 sec; speed in top at 1,000 rpm: 19.9 mph, 32.1 km/h; consumption: 18.5 m/imp gal, 15.4 m/US gal, 15.3 l x 100 km.

STEERING turns lock to lock: 3.25.

ELECTRICAL EQUIPMENT 70 A alternator.

DIMENSIONS AND WEIGHT weight: 2,999 lb, 1,360 kg; turning circle: 37.4 ft, 11.4 m.

PRACTICAL INSTRUCTIONS oil: automatic transmission 13.4 imp pt, 16.1 US pt, 7.6 l.

OPTIONALS 150 TR x 390 or TRX 190/65 HR x 39 tyres.

STIMULA FRANCE

Bugatti 55

PRICE EX WORKS: 138,000 francs

ENGINE Opel, front, 4 stroke; 6 cylinders, in line; 169.9 cu in, 2,784 cc (3.62 x 2.75 in, 92 x 69.8 mm); compression ratio: 9:1; max power (DIN): 155 hp (114 kW) at 5,.600 rpm; max torque (DIN): 160 lb ft, 22.1 kg m (216 Nm) at 4,200 rpm; max engine rpm: 6,000; 55.7 hp/l (41 kW/l); cast iron block and head; 7 crankshaft bearings; valves: overhead, in line, hydraulic tappets; camshafts: 1, overhead; lubrication: gear pump, full flow filter, 9.7 imp pt, 11.6 US pt, 5.5 l; Bosch electronic injection; fuel feed: electric pump.

TRANSMISSION driving wheels: rear; clutch: single dry plate (diaphragm); gearbox: mechanical; gears: 4, fully synchronized; ratios: I 3.428, II 2.156, III 1.366, IV 1, rev 3.317; lever: central; final drive: hypoid bevel; axle ratio: 3.450; tyres: 165 SR X 15.

PERFORMANCE max speed: 124 mph, 200 km/h; power-weight ratio: 13.4 lb/hp (18.3 lb/kW), 6.1 kg/hp (8.3 kg/kW).

CHASSIS tubular and box-type; front suspension: independent, wishbones, lower trailing links, coil springs, anti-roll bar, telescopic dampers; rear; rigid axle, twin trailing radius arms, upper torque arms, transverse linkage bar, coil springs, anti-roll bar, telescopic dampers.

STEERING recirculating ball; turns lock to lock: 4.5.

BRAKES front disc, rear drum, servo.

ELECTRICAL EQUIPMENT 12 V; 44 Ah battery; 55 A alternator; Bosch distributor; 2 halogen headlamps.

DIMENSIONS AND WEIGHT wheel base: 110.24 in, 280 cm; length: 161.42 in, 410 cm; width: 64.96 in, 165 cm; weight: 2,095 lb, 950 kg.

BODY roadster, in plastic material; no doors; 2 seats; light alloy wheels; leather upholstery.

PRACTICAL INSTRUCTIONS fuel: 98 oct petrol; oil: engine 8.8 imp pt, 10,6 US pt, 5 l, SAE 20W-30, change every 3,100 miles, 5,000 km - gearbox 1.9 imp pt, 2.3 US pt, 1.1 l, SAE 80, no change recommended - final drive 2.5 imp pt, 3 US pt, 1.4 l, SAE 90, no change recommended; greasing: none; sparking plug: 200°; valve timing: 30° 90° 70° 50°.

STIMULA Bugatti 55

TALBOT FRANCE

Matra Rancho

PRICE IN GB: £ 6,316*
PRICE EX WORKS: 46,456 francs**

ENGINE Simca, front, transverse, slanted 41° to rear, 4 stroke; 4 cylinders, in line; 88 cu in, 1,442 cc (3.02 x 3.07 in, 76.7 x 78 mm); compression ratio: 9.5:1; max power (DIN): 80 hp (59 kW) at 5,600 rpm; max torque (DIN): 87 lb ft, 12 kg m (118 Nm) at 3,000 rpm; max engine rpm; 6,000; 55.5 hp/l (40.8 kW/l); cast iron block, light alloy head; 5 crankshaft bearings; valves: overhead, in line, push-rods and rockers; camshafts: 1, side; lubrication: gear pump, full flow filter, 5.3 imp pt, 6.3 US pt, 3 l; 1 Weber 36 DCNVA downdraught twin barrel carburettor; fuel feed: mechanical pump; sealed circuit cooling, expansion tank, liquid, 10.6 imp pt, 12.7 US pt, 6 l, electric thermostatic fan.

TRANSMISSION driving wheels: front; clutch: single dry plate (diaphragm), hydraulically controlled; gearbox: mechanical; gears: 4, fully synchronized; ratios; I 3.900, II 2.312, III 1.524, IV 1.080, rev 3.769; lever: central; final drive: cylindrical gears; axle ratio: 3.706; width of rims: 5.5"; tyres: 185/70 SR x 14.

PERFORMANCE max speed: 90 mph, 145 km/h; power weight ratio: 31.1 lb/hp (42.3 lb/kW), 14.1 kg/hp (19.2 kg/kW); carrying capacity: 1,147 lb, 520 kg; speed in top at 1,000 rpm: 17.6 mph, 28.4 km/h; consumption: 24.6 m/imp gal, 20.5 m/US gal, 11.5 l x 100 km at 75 mph, 120 km/h.

CHASSIS integral, box-type reinforced platform; front suspension: independent, wishbones, longitudinal torsion bars, anti-roll bar, telescopic dampers; rear: independent, swinging longitudinal trailing arms, transverse torsion bars, anti-roll bar, telescopic dampers.

STEERING rack-and-pinion; turns lock to lock: 3.75.

BRAKES front disc (diameter 9.37 in, 23.8 cm) rear drum, rear compensator, servo; swept area: front 158.8 sq in, 1,024 sq cm, rear 90.2 sq in, 582 sq cm, total 249 sq in,1,606 sq cm.

ELECTRICAL EQUIPMENT 12 V; 40 Ah battery; 40 A alternator; Chrysler transistorized ignition; 4 iodine headlamps.

DIMENSIONS AND WEIGHT wheel base: 99.21 in, 252 cm; tracks: 55.51 in, 141 cm front, 53.15 in, 135 cm rear; length: 169.68 in, 431 cm; width: 65.35 in, 166 cm; height: 68.11 in, 173 cm; ground clearance: 6.57 in, 16.7 cm front, 6.69 in, 17 cm rear; weight: 2,492 lb, 1,130 kg; turning circle: 36.1 ft, 11 m; fuel tank: 13.2 imp gal, 15.8 US gal, 60 l.

BODY estate car/st. wagon in plastic material; 2 doors; 5 seats, separate front seats, reclining backrests with built-in headrests; folding rear seat; heated rear window with wiper-washer.

PRACTICAL INSTRUCTIONS fuel: 98-100 oct petrol; oil: engine 5.3 imp pt, 6.3 US pt, 3 l, SAE 20W-40, change every 3,100 miles, 5,000 km - gearbox and final drive 1.9 imp pt, 2.3 US pt, 1.1 l, SAE 90 EP, change every 6,200 miles, 10,000 km; greasing: none.

Matra Rancho Grand Raid

See Matra Rancho, except for:

PRICE EX WORKS: 55,456 francs**

ENGINE Simca, 8.8:1 compression ratio, max power (DIN) 78 hp (57 kW) at 5,600 rpm, max torque (DIN) 86 lb ft, 11.8 kg m (116 Nm) at 3,000 rpm, 54.1 hp/l (39.8 kW/l).

TRANSMISSION 3.937 axle ratio.

PERFORMANCE power-weight ratio 31.9 lb/hp (43.4 lb/kW), 14.5 kg/hp (19.7 kg/kW), consumption 23.5 m/imp gal, 19.6 m/US gal, 12 l x 100 km at 75 mph , 120 km/h.

PRACTICAL INSTRUCTIONS 85 oct petrol.

OPTIONALS light alloy wheels; metallic spray; tinted glass; electric winch.

Matra Bagheera

PRICE EX WORKS: 46,854 francs**

ENGINE Simca, central, transverse, slanted 41° to rear, 4 stroke; 4 cylinders, in line; 88 cu in, 1,442 cc (3.02 x 3.07 in, 76.7 x 78 mm); compression ratio: 9.5:1; max power (DIN): 84 hp (62 kW) at 5,600 rpm; max torque (DIN): 91 lb ft, 12.6 kg m (124 Nm)at 3,200 rpm; max engine rpm: 6,300; 58.3 hp/l (42.9 kW/l); cast iron block, light alloy head; 5 crankshafts: bearings; valves: overhead, push-rods and rockers; camshafts: 1, side; lubrication: gear pump, full flow filter, 5.3 imp pt, 6.3 US pt, 3 l; 1 Weber 36 DCNF downdraught twin barrel carburettor; fuel feed: mechanical pump; sealed circuit cooling, expansion tank, radiator on front, electric thermostatic fan, 17.6 imp pt, 21,.1 US pt, 10 l.

TALBOT Matra Rancho Grand Raid

TRANSMISSION driving wheels: rear; clutch: single dry plate (diaphragm), hydraulically controlled; gearbox: mechanical; gears: 4, fully synchronized; ratios: I 3.900, II 2.312, III 1.524, IV 1.080, rev 3.769; lever: central; final drive: cylindrical gears; axle ratio: 3.470; width of rims: 5.5" tyres: 155 HR x 13 front, 185 HR x 13 rear.

PERFORMANCE max speed: 115 mph, 185 km/h; power-weight ratio: 25.7 lb/hp (35 lb/kW), 11.7 kg/hp (15.9 kg/kW); consumption: 28.5 m/imp gal, 23.8 m/US gal, 9.9 l x 100 km.

CHASSIS integral, box-type reinforced platform; front suspension: independent, wishbones, longitudinal torsion bars, anti-roll bar, telescopic dampers; rear: independent, swinging longitudinal trailing arms, transverse torsion bars, anti-roll bar, telescopic dampers.

STEERING rack-and-pinion; turns lock to lock: 3.25.

BRAKES disc (front diameter 9.37 in, 23.8 cm, rear 9.21 in, 23.4 cm), rear compensator, servo; swept area: front 158.8 sq in, 1,024 sq cm, rear 161.6 sq in, 1,042 sq cm, total 320.4 sq in, 2,066 sq cm.

ELECTRICAL EQUIPMENT 12 V; 40 Ah battery; 40 A alternator; Ducellier distributor; 4 headlamps, 2 retractable iodine long-distance lights.

DIMENSIONS AND WEIGHT wheel base: 93.31 in, 237 cm; tracks: 55.12 in, 140 cm front, 57.48 in, 146 cm rear; length:157.87 in, 401 cm; width: 68.39 in, 174 cm; height: 48.03 in, 122 cm; ground clearance: 6.73 in, 17.1 cm front, 7.48 in, 19 cm rear; weight: 2,161 lb, 980 kg; weight distribution: 41% front, 59% rear; turning circle; 32.8 ft, 10 m; fuel tank: 12.3 imp gal, 14.8 US gal, 56 l.

BODY coupé, in plastic material; 2 doors; 3 front seats in a row, separate driving seat, built-in headrests; heated rear window.

PRACTICAL INSTRUCTIONS fuel: 98-100 oct petrol; oil: engine 5.3 imp pt, 6.3 US pt, 3 l, SAE 20W-40, change every 3,100 miles, 5,000 km - gearbox and final drive 1.9 imp pt, 2.3 US pt, 1.1 l, SAE 90 EP, change every 6,200 miles, 10,000 km; greasing: none; tyre pressure: front 20 psi, 1.4 atm, rear 28 psi, 2 atm.

OPTIONALS light alloy wheels; metallic spray; sunshine roof; tinted glass; electric windows.

Matra Bagheera X

See Matra Bagheera, except for:

PRICE EX WORKS: 54,354 francs**

ENGINE max power (DIN): 90 hp (66 kW) at 5,800 rpm; max torque (DIN): 88 lb ft, 12.2 kg m (120 Nm) at 3,200 rpm; 62.4 hp/l (45.9 kW/l); 2 Weber 36 DCNF downdraught twin barrel carburettors.

TRANSMISSION light alloy wheels.

TALBOT Matra Bagheera

PERFORMANCE max speed: 118 mph, 190 km/h; power-weight ratio: 24.9 lb/hp (33.8 lb/kW), 11.3 kg/hp (15.3 kg/kW); consumption: 28 m/imp gal, 23.3 m/US gal, 10.1 l x 100 km.

ELECTRICAL EQUIPMENT 48 Ah battery; 50 A alternator.

DIMENSIONS AND WEIGHT weight: 2,238 lb, 1,015 kg.

BODY electric tinted glass (standard); luxury equipment; heated rear window with wiper-washer.

Simca 1100 Series

PRICES EX WORKS:			francs
1	LE	2+1-dr Berline	**23,282****
2	LE	4+1-dr Berline	**25,282****
3	LE	4+1-dr Break	**28,032****
4	GLS	4+1-dr Berline	**28,632****
5	GLS	4+1-dr Break	**30,432****

Power team:	Standard for:	Optional for:
50 hp	1,2	3
58 hp	3 to 5	—

50 hp power team

ENGINE front, transverse, slanted 41° to rear, 4 stroke; 4 cylinders, in line; 68.2 cu in, 1,118 cc (2.91 x 2.56 in, 74 x 65 mm); compression ratio: 8.8:1; max power (DIN): 50 hp (37 kW) at 5,800 rpm; max torque (DIN): 57 lb ft, 7.8 kg m (76 Nm) at 3,000 rpm; max engine rpm: 6,000; 44.7 hp/l (32.9 kW/L); cast iron block, light alloy head; 5 crankshaft bearings; valves: overhead, in line, push-rods and rockers; camshafts: 1, side; lubrication: gear pump, full flow filter, 5.3 imp pt, 6.3 US pt, 3 l; 1 Bressel or Weber 32 IBSA downdraught single barrel carburettor; fuel feed: mechanical pump; sealed circuit cooling, liquid, expansion tank, 10.6 imp pt, 12.7 US pt, 6 l, electric thermostatic fan.

TRANSMISSION driving wheels: front; clutch: single dry plate (diaphragm), hydraulically controlled; gearbox: mechanical, in unit with final drive; gears: 4, fully synchronized; ratios: I 3.900, II 2.312, III 1.524, IV 1.080, rev 3.769; lever: central; final drive: cylindrical gears; axle ratio: 3.937; width of rims: 5"; tyres: 145 SR x 13 or 155 SR x 13.

PERFORMANCE max speeds: (I) 25 mph, 40 km/h (II) 42 mph, 68 km/h; (III) 64 mph, 103 km/h; (IV) 87 mph, 140 km/h; power-weight ratio: 4-dr 41 lb/hp (55.7 lb/kW), 18.6 kg/hp (25.3 kg/kW) - 2-dr 40.1 lb/hp (54.5 lb/kW), 18.2 kg/hp (24.7 kg/kW); carrying capacity: 882 lb, 400 kg; speed in top at 1,000 rpm: 15 mph, 24 km/h; consumption: 30.1 m/imp gal, 25 m/US gal, 9.4 l x 100 km.

CHASSIS integral; front suspension: independent, wishbones, longitudinal torsion bars, anti-roll bar, telescopic dampers; rear: independent, longitudinal trailing arms, transverse torsion bars, anti-roll bar, telescopic dampers.

STEERING rack-and-pinion; turns lock to lock: 3.25.

BRAKES front disc (diameter 9.21 in, 23.4 cm), rear drum, rear compensator, servo; swept area: front 146.2 sq in, 943 sq cm, rear 73.8 sq in, 476 sq cm, total 220 sq in, 1,419 sq cm.

ELECTRICAL EQUIPMENT 12 V; 36 Ah battery; 40 A alternator; Chrysler transistorized ignition; 2 headlamps.

DIMENSIONS AND WEIGHT wheel base: 99.21 in, 252 cm; front track: 53.94 in, 137 cm - 2-dr 54.33 in, 138 cm; rear track: 51.57 in, 131 cm - 2-dr 52.36 in, 133 cm; length: 155.12 in, 394 cm; width: 62.60 in, 159 cm; height: 57.48 in, 146 cm; ground clearance: 5.12 in, 13 cm; weight: 2,051 lb, 930 kg - 2-dr 2,007 lb, 910 kg; turning circle: 34.1 ft, 10.4 m; fuel tank: 9.2 imp gal, 11.1 US gal, 42 l.

BODY 5 seats, separate front seats; folding rear seat; heated rear window.

PRACTICAL INSTRUCTIONS fuel: 85 oct petrol; oil: engine 5.3 imp pt, 6.3 US pt, 3 l, SAE 20W-40, change every 4,650 miles, 7,500 km - gearbox and final drive 1,9 imp pt, 2.3 US pt, 1.1 l, SAE 90 EP, change every 9,300 miles, 15,000 km; greasing: none; tyre pressure: front 25 psi, 1.7 atm, rear 26 psi, 1.8 atm.

OPTIONALS sunshine roof; light alloy wheels; tinted glass; metallic spray.

58 hp power team

See 50 hp power team, except for:

ENGINE compression ratio: 9.6:1 ; max power (DIN): 58 hp (43 kW) at 6,000 rpm; max torque (DIN): 64 lb ft, 8.8 kg m (86 Nm) at 3,000 rpm; 51.9 hp/l (38.2 kW/l); 1 Solex 32 BISA or Weber or Bressel 32 IBSA downdraught single barrel carburettor.

PERFORMANCE max speed: 91 mph, 146 km/h - Break models 87 mph, 140 km/h; power-weight ratio: 35.4 lb/hp (48 lb/kW), 16 kg/hp (21.8 kg/kW); carrying capacity: Break models 992 lb, 450 kg; consumption: 29.1 m/imp gal, 24.2 m/US gal, 9.7 l x 100 km.

TALBOT Simca 1100 Berline

DIMENSIONS AND WEIGHT length: Break models 154.72 in, 393 cm; height: Break models 58.27 in, 148 cm; ground clearance: Break models 5.51 in, 14 cm; weight: 2,051 lb, 930 kg.

BODY built-in headrests on front seats (except for Break models).

PRACTICAL INSTRUCTIONS fuel: 98-100 oct petrol.

OPTIONALS Ferodo 3-speed semi-automatic transmission, hydraulic torque converter (I 2.469, II 1.650, III 1.080, rev 3.774), max ratio of converter at stall 2, possible manual selection, max speeds (I) 40 mph, 64 km/h, (II) 59 mph, 95 km/h, (III) 91 mph, 146 km/h (Break models 87 mph, 140 km/h), consumption 29.4 m/imp gal, 24.5 m/US gal, 9.6 l x 100 km.

Simca Horizon Series

PRICES IN GB AND EX WORKS:		£	francs
1	LS	**3,320***	**29,732****
2	GL	**3,958***	**32,304****
3	GLS	—	**35,154****
4	SX	—	**39,304****

Power team:	Standard for:	Optional for:
59 hp	1	—
68 hp	2	—
69 hp	3	—
83 hp	4	—

59 hp power team

ENGINE front, transverse, slanted 41° to rear, 4 stroke; 4 cylinders, in line; 68.2 cu in, 1,118 cc (2.91 x 2.56 in, 74 x 65 mm); compression ratio: 9.6:1; max power (DIN): 59 hp (43 kW) at 5,600 rpm; max torque (DIN): 66 lb ft, 9.1 kg m (89 Nm) at 3,000 rpm; max engine rpm: 6,300; 52.8 hp/l (38.8 kW/l); cast iron block, light alloy head; 5 crankshaft bearings; valves: overhead, push-rods and rockers, thimble tappets; camshafts: 1, side; lubrication: gear pump, full flow filter, 5.3 imp pt, 6.3 US pt, 3 l; 1 Solex 32 BISA 6 or Weber 32 IBSA single barrel carburettor; fuel feed: mechanical pump; sealed circuit cooling, expansion tank, liquid, 10.6 imp pt, 12.7 US pt, 6 l, electric thermostatic fan.

TRANSMISSION driving wheels: front; clutch: single dry plate (diaphragm), hydraulically controlled; gearbox: mechanical; gears: 4, fully syncronized; ratios: I 3.900, II 2.312, III 1.524, IV 1.080, rev 3.769; lever: central; final drive: cylindrical gears; axle ratio: 3.705; width of rims: 4.5"; tyres: 145 SR x 13.

PERFORMANCE max speed: 92 mph, 148 km/h; power-weight ratio: 35.3 lb/hp hp (48 lb/kW), 16 kg/hp (21.8 kg/kW); carrying capacity: 981 lb, 445 kg; acceleration: standing ¼ mile 20.7 sec; consumption: 29.4 m/imp gal, 24.5 m/US gal, 9.6 l x 100 km.

CHASSIS integral; front suspension: independent, longitudinal torsion bars, wishbones, anti-roll bar, telescopic dampers; rear: independent, swinging longitudinal trailing arms, coil springs, anti-roll bar, telescopic dampers.

TALBOT Simca Horizon GL

59 HP POWER TEAM

STEERING rack-and-pinion; turns lock to lock: 4.35.

BRAKES front disc (diameter 9.37 in, 23.8 cm), rear drum, rear compensator, servo; swept area: front 155 sq in, 1,000 sq cm, rear 89 sq in, 574 sq cm, total 244 sq in, 1,574 sq cm.

ELECTRICAL EQUIPMENT 12 V; 40 Ah battery; 40 A alternator; Chrysler transistorized ignition; 2 headlamps.

DIMENSIONS AND WEIGHT wheel base: 99.21 in, 252 cm; tracks: 55.91 in, 142 cm front, 53.94 in, 137 cm rear; length: 155.91 in,396 cm; width: 66.14 in, 168 cm; height: 55.51 in, 141 cm; ground clearance: 7.09 in, 18 cm; weight: 2,084 lb, 945 kg; weight distribution: 59.4% front, 40.6% rear; turning circle: 33.5 ft, 10.2 m; fuel tank: 10.3 imp gal, 12.4 US gal, 47 l.

BODY saloon/sedan; 4+1 doors; 5 seats, separate front seats, reclining backrests; heated rear window; folding rear seat.

PRACTICAL INSTRUCTIONS fuel: 98-100 oct petrol; oil: engine 5.3 imp pt, 6.3 US pt, 3 l, SAE 20W-40, change every 4,650 miles, 7,500 km - gearbox and final drive 1.9 imp pt, 2.3 US pt, 1.1 l, SAE 90 EP, change every 9,300 miles, 15,000 km; greasing: none.

OPTIONALS metallic spray; iodine headlamps; rear window wiper-washer; tinted glass; adjustable headrests on front seats; vinyl roof.

68 hp power team

See 59 hp power team, except for:

ENGINE 79 cu in, 1,294 cc (3.02 x 2.76 in, 76.7 x 70 mm); compression ratio: 9.5:1; max power (DIN): 68 hp (50 kW) at 5,600 rpm; max torque (DIN): 76 lb ft, 10.5 kg m (103 Nm) at 2,800 rpm; 52.6 hp/l (38.7 kW/l).

TRANSMISSION axle ratio: 3.588.

PERFORMANCE max speed: 96 mph, 155 km/h; power-weight ratio: 31.1 lb/hp (42.3 lb/kW), 14.1 kg/hp (19.2 kg/kW); carrying capacity: 948 lb, 430 kg; acceleration: standing ¼ mile 19.5 sec; consumption: 30.1 m/imp gal, 25 m/US gal, 9.4 l x 100 km.

DIMENSIONS AND WEIGHT weight: 2,117 lb, 960 kg.

69 hp power team

See 59 hp power team, except for:

ENGINE 88 cu in, 1,442 cc (3.02 x 3.07 in, 76.7 x 78 mm); compression ratio: 9.5:1; max power (DIN): 69 hp (51 kW) at 5,200 rpm; max torque (DIN): 85 lb ft, 11.7 kg m (115 Nm) at 3,000 rpm; 47.9 hp/l (35.2 kW/l); 1 Solex 32 BISA 7 or Weber 32 IBSA single barrel carburettor.

TRANSMISSION gearbox ratios: I 3.900, II 2.312, III 1.524, IV 1.040, rev 3.769; axle ratio: 3.471.

PERFORMANCE max speed: 96 mph, 155 km/h; power-weight ratio: 32.6 lb/hp (42.3 lb/kW), 14.1 kg/hp (19.2 kg/kW); carrying capacity: 915 lb, 415 kg; acceleration: standing ¼ mile 19.5 sec; consumption: 31.7 m/imp gal, 26.4 m/US gal, 8.9 l x 100 km.

ELECTRICAL EQUIPMENT iodine headlamps (standard).

DIMENSIONS AND WEIGHT weight: 2,150 lb, 975 kg.

BODY (standard) adjustable backrests on front seats, rear window wiper-washer.

OPTIONALS light alloy wheels; headlamps with wiper-washers.

83 hp power team

See 59 hp power team, except for:

ENGINE 88 cu in, 1,442 cc (3.02 x 3.07 in, 76.7 x 78 mm); compression ratio: 9.5:1; max power (DIN): 83 hp (61 kW) at 5,600 rpm; max torque (DIN): 89 lb ft, 12.3 kg m (121 Nm) at 3,000 rpm; 57.6 hp/l (42.4 kW/l); 1 Weber 36 DCA 2 downdraught twin barrel carburettor; liquid-cooled, 11.3 imp pt, 13.5 US pt, 6.4 l.

TRANSMISSION gearbox: Chrysler 415 automatic transmission, hydraulic torque converter and planetary gears with 3 ratios, max ratio of converter at stall 1,.224, possible manual selection; ratios: I 2.475, II 1.475, III 1, rev 2.103; axle ratio: 3,000; width of rims: 5''; tyres: 155 SR x 13.

PERFORMANCE max speed: 100 mph, 161 km/h; power-weight ratio: 27.2 lb/hp (37 lb/kW), 12.3 kg/hp (16.8 kg/kW); carrying capacity: 882 lb, 400 kg; consumption: 29.4 m/imp gal, 24.5 m/US gal, 9.6 l x 100 km.

TALBOT Simca Horizon GLS

TALBOT Simca 1510 SX

ELECTRICAL EQUIPMENT 50 A alternator; iodine headlamps (standard).

DIMENSIONS AND WEIGHT rear track: 54.33 in, 138 cm; weight: 2,260 lb, 1,025 kg.

BODY (standard) adjustable backrests on front seats, rear window wiper-washer, automatic speed control, trip computer.

PRACTICAL INSTRUCTIONS oil: automatic transmission 11.3 imp pt, 13.5 US pt, 6.4 l.

OPTIONALS light alloy wheels; headlamps with wiper-washers.

Simca 1510 Series

PRICES EX WORKS:	francs
1 LS	34,304**
2 GL	37,554**
3 GLS	40,954**
4 SX	46,856**

Power team:	Standard for:	Optional for:
68 hp	1	—
85 hp	2,3	—
88 hp	4	—

68 hp power team

ENGINE front, transverse, slanted 41° to rear, 4 stroke; 4 cylinders, in line; 79 cu in, 1,294 cc (3.02 x 2.76 in, 76.7 x 70 mm); compression ratio: 9.5:1; max power (DIN): 68 hp (50 kW) at 5,600 rpm; max torque (DIN): 78 lb ft, 10.7 kg m (105 Nm) at 2,800 rpm; max engine rpm 6,300; 52.6 hp/l (38.6 kW/l); cast iron block, light alloy head; 5 crankshaft bearings; valves: overhead, in line, push-rods and rockers; camshafts: 1, side; lubrication: gear pump, full flow filter, 5.3 imp pt, 6.3 US pt, 3 l; 1 Solex 32 BISA 5 A or Weber 32 IBSA 9 downdraught single barrel carburettor; fuel feed: mechanical pump; sealed circuit cooling, expansion tank, liquid, 10.7 imp pt, 12.9 US pt, 6.1 l, electric thermostatic fan.

TRANSMISSION driving wheels: front; clutch: single dry plate (diaphragm), hydraulically controlled; gearbox: mechanical; gears: 4, fully synchronized; ratios: I 3.900, II 2.312, III 1.524, IV 1.080, rev 3.769; lever: central; final drive: cylindrical gears; axle ratio: 3.706; width of rims: 5;''; tyres: 155 SR x 13.

PERFORMANCE max speed: 94 mph, 152 km/h; power-weight ratio: 34 lb/hp (46.3 lb/kW), 15.4 kg/hp (21 kg/kW); carrying capacity: 882 lb, 400 kg; acceleration: standing ¼ mile 19.8 sec, 0-50 mph (0-80 km/h) 10.7 sec; speed in top at 1,000 rpm: 16.4 mph, 26.4 km/h; consumption: 33.6 m/imp gal, 28 m/US gal, 8.4 l x 100 km.

CHASSIS integral; front suspension: independent, wishbones, longitudinal torsion bars, anti-roll bar, telescopic dampers; rear: independent, swinging longitudinal trailing arms, coil springs, anti-roll bar, telescopic dampers.

STEERING rack-and-pinion; turns lock to lock: 4.15.

BRAKES front disc (diameter 9.45 in, 24 cm), rear drum, rear compensator, servo; swept area: front 169.3 sq in, 1,092 sq cm, rear 90.2 sq in, 582 sq cm, total 259.5 sq in, 1,674 sq cm.

ELECTRICAL EQUIPMENT 12 V; 40 Ah battery; 40 A alternator; Chrysler transistorized ignition; 2 headlamps.

DIMENSIONS AND WEIGHT wheel base: 102.36 in, 260 cm; tracks: 55.51 in, 141 cm front, 54.72 in, 139 cm rear; length: 169,68 in, 431 cm; width: 66.14 in, 168 cm; height: 54.72 in, 139 cm; ground clearance: 5.12 in, 13 cm; weight: 2,315 lb, 1,050 kg; turning circle: 36.1 ft, 11 m; fuel tank: 12.8 imp gal, 15.3 US gal, 58 l.

BODY saloon/sedan; 4+1 doors; 5 seats, separate front seats, reclining backrests; heated rear window; folding rear seat.

PRACTICAL INSTRUCTIONS fuel: 98-100 oct petrol; oil: engine 5.3 imp pt, 6.3 US pt, 3 l, SAE 20W-40, change every 4,650 miles, 7,500 km - gearbox and final drive 1.9 imp pt, 2.3 US pt, 1.1 l, SAE 90 EP, change every 9,300 miles, 15,000 km; greasing: none.

OPTIONALS metallic spray; iodine headlamps; adjustable headrests on front seats; tinted glass; vinyl roof; sunshine roof; rear window wiper-washer.

85 hp power team

See 68 hp power team, except for:

ENGINE 88 cu in, 1,442 cc (3.02 x 3.07 in, 76.7 x 78 mm); max power (DIN): 85 hp (63 kW) at 5,600 rpm; max torque (DIN): 92 lb ft, 12.7 kg·m (124 Nm) at 3,000 rpm; 58.9 hp/l (43.4 kW/l); 1 Weber 36 DCNV A downdraught twin barrel carburettor.

TRANSMISSION axle ratio: 3.588.

PERFORMANCE max speed: 102 mph, 164 km/h; power-weight ratio: 27.9 lb/hp (37.9 lb/kW) 12.6 kg/hp (17.2 kg/kW); carrying capacity: 1,103 lb, 500 kg; acceleration: standing ¼ mile 19 sec, 0-50 mph (0-80 km/h) 8.9 sec; speed in top at 1,000 rpm: 17.6 mph, 28.3 km/h; consumption: 28.5 m/imp gal, 23.8 m/US gal, 9.9 l x 100 km.

ELECTRICAL EQUIPMENT GL iodine headlamps - GLS iodine headlamps with wiper-washers (standard).

DIMENSIONS AND WEIGHT weight: 2,370 lb, 1,075 kg.

BODY adjustable headrests on front seats (standard); for GLS only, electric windows (standard).

OPTIONALS light alloy wheels; for GL only, headlamps with wiper-washers; power steering; for GL only, electric windows.

88 hp power team

See 68 hp power team, except for:

ENGINE 97.1 cu in, 1,592 cc (3.17 x 3.07 in, 80.6 x 78 mm); compression ratio: 9.35:1; max power (DIN): 88 hp (65 kW) at 5,400 rpm; max torque (DIN): 99 lb ft, 13.7 kg m (134 Nm) at 3,000 rpm; 55.3 hp/l (40.7 kW/l); 1 Weber 36 DCA 100 downdraught twin barrel carburettor; liquid cooled, 11.1 imp pt, 13.3 US pt, 6.3 l.

TRANSMISSION gearbox: Chrysler 415 automatic transmission, hydraulic torque converter and planetary gears with 3 ratios, max ratio of converter at stall 1.224, possible manual selection; ratios: I 2.475, II 1.475, III 1, rev 2.103; axle ratio: 3.000.

PERFORMANCE max speed: 106 mph, 170 km/h; power-weight ratio: 27.8 lb/hp (37.7 lb/kW), 12.6 kg/hp (17.1 kg/kW); carrying capacity: 882 lb, 400 kg; speed in direct drive at 1,000 rpm: 17.8 mph, 28.7 km/h; consumption: 26.9 m/imp gal, 22.4 m/US gal, 10.5 l x 100 km.

STEERING servo; turns lock to lock: 2.80.

BRAKES front disc (diameter 9.45 in, 24 cm), rear drum, rear compensator, servo; swept area: front 169.3 sq in, 1,092 sq cm, rear 89 sq in, 574 sq cm, total 258.3 sq in, 1,666 sq cm.

ELECTRICAL EQUIPMENT 50 A alternator; iodine headlamps with wiper-washers (standard).

DIMENSIONS AND WEIGHT weight: 2,448 lb, 1,110 kg; turning circle: 34.1 ft, 10.4 m.

BODY (standard) adjustable backrests on front seats, rear window wiper-washer, automatic speed control.

PRACTICAL INSTRUCTIONS oil: automatic transmission 11.3 imp pt, 13.5 US pt, 6.4 l.

OPTIONALS light alloy wheels; leather upholstery.

TALBOT Simca 1510 SX

TALBOT Simca 2 L Automatique

Simca 1610

PRICES EX WORKS: 39,122 francs**

ENGINE front, slanted 15° to right, 4 stroke; 4 cylinders, in line; 120.9 cu in, 1,981 cc (3.61 x 2.95 in, 91.7 x 75 mm); compression ratio: 9.45:1; max power (DIN): 110 hp (81 kW) at 5,800 rpm; max torque (DIN): 117 lb ft, 16.2 kg m (159 Nm) at 3,400 rpm; max engine rpm: 5,800; 55.5 hp/l (40.9 kW/l); cast iron block, light alloy head; 5 crankshaft bearings; valves: overhead, rockers; camshafts: 1, overhead; lubrification: gear pump, full flow filter, 7 imp pt, 8.5 US pt, 4 l; 1 Weber 34 ADS-D downdraught twin barrel carburettor; fuel feed: mechanical pump ; water-cooled, 17.6 imp pt, 21.1 US pt, 10 l, electric thermostatic fan.

TRANSMISSION driving wheels: rear; clutch: single dry plate (diaphragm), hydraulically controlled; gearbox: mechanical; gears: 4, fully synchronized; ratios: I 3.546, II 2.175, III 1.418, IV 1, rev 3.226; lever: central; final drive: hypoid bevel; axle ratio: 3.727; width of rims: 5.5"; tyres: 175 SR x 14 or 175 HR x 14.

PERFORMANCE max speed: 109 mph, 175 km/h; power-weight ratio: 22.6 lb/hp (30.6 lb/kW), 10.2 kg/hp (13.9 kg/kW); carrying capacity: 882 lb, 400 kg; speed in direct drive at 1,000 rpm: 18.8 mph, 30.2 km/h; consumption: 25.9 m/imp gal, 21.6 m/US gal, 10.9 l x 100 km.

CHASSIS integral; front suspension: independent, by McPherson, coil springs/telescopic damper struts, lower wishbones, anti-roll bar; rear: rigid axle, lower longitudinal trailing arms, upper torque arms, transverse linkage bar, coil springs, telescopic dampers.

STEERING rack-and-pinion; turns lock to lock: 4.

BRAKES disc (front diameter 9.92 in, 25.2 cm, rear 9.02 in, 22.9 cm), rear compensator, servo; swept area: front 186 sq in, 1,200 sq cm, rear 140.8 sq in, 908 sq cm, total 326.8 sq in, 2,108 sq cm.

ELECTRICAL EQUIPMENT 12 V; 36 Ah battery; 35 A alternator; Chrysler transistorized ignition; 2 headlamps, iodine long-distance lights.

DIMENSIONS AND WEIGHT wheel base: 105.12 in, 267 cm; tracks: 55.12 in, 140 cm front, 55.12 in, 140 cm rear; length: 178.35 in, 453 cm; width: 68.11 in, 173 cm; height: 56.69 in, 144 cm; ground clearance: 5.71 in, 14.5 cm; weight: 2,481 lb, 1,125 kg; turning circle: 33.8 ft, 10.3 m; fuel tank: 14.3 imp gal, 17.2 US gal, 65 l.

BODY saloon/sedan; 4+1 doors; 5 seats, separate front seats; built-in headrests; heated rear window; tinted glass.

PRACTICAL INSTRUCTIONS fuel: 98-100 oct petrol; oil: engine 7 imp pt, 8.5 US pt, 4 l, SAE 10 W-50, change every 4,650 miles, 7,500 km - gearbox 2.6 imp pt, 3.2 US pt, 1.5 l, SAE 90 EP, change every 12,400 miles, 20,000 km - final drive 2.3 imp pt, 2.7 US pt, 1.3 l, SAE 90 EP, change every 12,400 miles, 20,000 km; greasing: none; sparking plug: 225° tappet clearances: inlet 0.010 in, 0.25 mm, exhaust 0.014 in, 0.35 mm; tyre pressure: front 24 psi, 1.7 atm, rear 27 psi, 1.9 atm.

OPTIONALS light alloy wheels; vinyl roof; metallic spray.

TRABANT 601 Limousine

Simca 2 L Automatique

See Simca 1610, except for:

PRICE IN GB: £ 5,305*
PRICE EX WORKS: 42,222 francs**

TRANSMISSION gearbox: Chrysler A904 automatic transmission, hydraulic torque converter and planetary gears with 3 ratios, max ratio of converter at stall 2.2, possible manual selection; ratios: I 2.450, II 1.450, III 1, rev 2.200.

PERFORMANCE max speed: 106 mph, 170 km/h; acceleration: standing ¼ mile 18.7 sec; speed in direct drive at 1,000 rpm: 18.3 mph, 29.5 km/h; consumption: 23.7 m/imp gal, 19.8 m/US gal, 11.9 l x 100 km.

STEERING turns lock to lock: 4.50.

BODY 4 doors.

PRACTICAL INSTRUCTIONS oil: automatic transmission 14.1 imp pt, 16.9 US pt, 8 l.

TRABANT GERMANY DR

601 Limousine

ENGINE front, transverse, 2 stroke: 2 cylinders, in line; 36.2 cu in, 594.5 cc (2.83 x 2.87 in, 72 x 73 mm); compression ratio: 7.6:1; max power (DIN): 26 hp (19 kW) at 4,200 rpm; max torque (DIN): 40 lb ft, 5.5 kg m (54 Nm) at 3.000 rpm; max engine rpm: 4,500; 43.7 hp/l (32.1 kW); light alloy block and head, dry liners; 3 crankshaft bearings; valves: 1, per cylinder, rotary; lubrication: mixture; 1 BVF type 28 HB 2-8 horizontal single barrel carburettor; fuel feed: gravity; air-cooled.

TRANSMISSION driving wheels: front; clutch: single dry plate: gearbox: mechanical; gears: 4, fully synchronized; ratios: I 4.080, II 2.320, III 1.520, IV 1.103, rev 3.830; lever: on facia; final drive: conic bevel; axle ratio: 3.950; width of rims: 4"; tyres: 5.20 or 145 SR x 13.

PERFORMANCE max speeds: (I) 16 mph, 25 km/h; (II) 28 mph, 45 km/h; (III) 43 mph, 70 km/h; (IV) 62 mph, 100 km/h; power-weight ratio: 52.1 lb/hp (71 lb/kW), 23.6 kg/hp (32.2 kg/kW): carrying capacity: 849 lb, 385 kg; acceleration: 0-50 mph (0-80 km/h) 22.5 sec; speed in top at 1,000 rpm; 14.6 mph, 23.5 km/h; consumption: 40.4 m/imp gal, 33.6 m/US gal, 7 l x 100 km.

CHASSIS integral; front suspension: independent, wishbones, trasverse leafspring upper arms, telescopic dampers; rear: independent, swinging semi-axle, transverse semi-elliptic leafspring, telescopic dampers.

STEERING rack-and-pinion; turns lock to lock: 2.60.

BRAKES drum, single circuit; swept area: front 38.9 sq in, 251 sq cm, rear 34.1 sq in, 220 sq cm, total 73 sq in, 471 sq cm.

ELECTRICAL EQUIPMENT 6 V; 56 Ah battery; 220 W dynamo; AKA distributor; 2 headlamps.

DIMENSIONS AND WEIGHT wheel base: 79.53 in, 202 cm; tracks: 47.64 in, 121 cm front, 49.21 in, 125 cm rear; length: 139.76 in, 355 cm; width: 59.06 in, 150 cm; height: 56.69 in, 144 cm; ground clearance: 6.10 in, 15.5 cm; weight: 1,356 lb, 615 kg; weight distribution: 45% front, 55% rear; turning circle: 32.8 ft, 10 m; fuel tank: 5.7 imp gal, 6.9 US gal, 26 l.

BODY saloon/sedan; 2 doors; 4 seats, separate front seats, reclining backrests.

PRACTICAL INSTRUCTIONS fuel: mixture 1:50, 88 oct petrol, SAE 20; oil: gearbox and final drive 2.6 imp pt, 3.2 US pt, 1.5 l, SAE 10W-30, change every 9,300 miles, 15,000 km; greasing: every 3,100 miles, 5,000 km, 9 points; sparking plug: 14 x 225°; valve timing: 45° 45° 72°5' 72°5': tyre pressure: front 20 psi, 1.4 atm, rear 20 psi, 1.4 atm.

OPTIONALS Hycomat automatic clutch.

601 Universal

See 601 Limousine, except for:

PERFORMANCE power-weight ratio: 55.1 lb/hp (75 lb/kW). 25 kg/hp (34 kg/kW); carrying capacity: 860 lb, 390 kg.

DIMENSIONS AND WEIGHT length: 140.16 in, 356 cm; width: 59.45 in, 151 cm; height: 57.87 in, 147 cm; weight: 1,433 lb, 650 kg; weight distribution: 44% front 56% rear.

BODY estate car/st. wagon; 2+1 doors; folding rear seat.

WARTBURG GERMANY DR

353 W

ENGINE front, 2 stroke; 3 cylinders, vertical, in line; 60.5 cu in, 992 cc (2.89 x 3.07 in, 73.5 x 78 mm); compression ratio: 7.5:1; max power (DIN): 50 hp (37 kW) at 4,250 rpm; max torque (DIN): 72 lb ft, 10 kg m (98 Nm) at 3,000 rpm; max engine rpm: 4,250; 50.4 hp/l (37.1 kW/l); cast iron block, light alloy head; 4 crankshaft bearings; lubrication: mixture 1:50; 1 BVF 40F1-11 single barrel carburettor; fuel feed: mechanical pump; sealed circuit cooling, liquid, 13.2 imp pt, 15.9 US pt, 7.5 l.

TRANSMISSION driving wheels: front; clutch: single dry plate; gearbox: mechanical; gears: 4, fully synchronized; ratios: I 3.769, II 2.160, III 1.347, IV 0.906, rev 3.385; lever: steering column; final drive: spiral bevel; axle ratio: 4.222; width of rims: 4,5"; tyres: 6.00 x 13 or 165 SR x 13.

PERFORMANCE max speeds: (I) 20 mph, 32 km/h; (II) 35 mph, 57 km/h; (III) 56 mph, 90 km/h; (IV) 81 mph, 130 km/h; power-weight ratio: 40.6 lb/hp (55.1 lb/kW), 18.4 kg/hp (25 kg/kW); carrying capacity: 882 lb, 400 kg; acceleration: 0-50 mph (0-80 km/h) 14.5 sec; speed in top at 1,000 rpm: 17.4 mph, 28 km/h; consumption: 28.8 m/imp gal, 24 m/US gal, 9.8 l x 100 km.

CHASSIS box-type ladder frame; front suspension: independent, wishbones, coil springs, rubber elements, telescopic dam-

TRABANT 601 Limousine

WARTBURG 353 W De Luxe

bers; rear: independent, semi-trailing arms, coil springs, rubber elements, anti-roll bar, telescopic dampers.

STEERING rack-and-pinion; turns lock to lock: 3.50.

BRAKES front disc, rear drum, rear compensator; lining area: front 20 sq in, 129 sq cm, rear 61.4 sq in, 396 sq cm, total 81.4 sq in, 525 sq cm.

ELECTRICAL EQUIPMENT 12 V; 42 Ah battery; 588 W alternator; FEK distributor; 2 headlamps.

DIMENSIONS AND WEIGHT wheel base: 96.46 in, 245 cm; tracks: 50.39 in, 128 cm front, 51.18 in, 130 cm rear; length: 166.14 in, 422 cm; width: 64.57 in, 164 cm; height: 58.66 in, 149 cm; ground clearance: 6.10 in, 15,5 cm; weight: 2.029 lb, 920 kg; weight distribution: 51.5% front, 48.5% rear; turning circle: 33.5 ft, 10,2 m; fuel tank: 9.7 imp gal, 11.6 US gal, 44 l.

BODY saloon/sedan; 4 doors; 5 seats, separate front seats, reclining backrests.

PRACTICAL INSTRUCTIONS fuel: mixture 1:50, SAE 20-40; oil: gearbox and final drive 3.2 imp pt, 3.8 US pt, 1.8 l, SAE 80 EP, change every 31.100 miles, 50,000 km; greasing: every 6,200 miles, 10,000 km, 3 points; sparking plug: 175°; opening timing: 62°17' 62°17' 78°2' 78°2'; tyre pressure: front 23 psi, 1.6 atm, rear 24 psi, 1.7 atm.

OPTIONALS central lever; halogen headlamps; sunshine roof; luxury version.

353 W Tourist / De Luxe

See 353 W, except for:

PERFORMANCE max speed: 78 mph, 125 km/h; power-weight ratio: 42.8 lb/hp (58.1 lb/kW), 19.4 kg/hp (26.4 kg/kW); carrying capacity: 970 lb, 440 kg; consumption: 28.2 m/imp gal, 23.5 m/US gal, 10 l x 100 km.

DIMENSIONS AND WEIGHT length: 172.44 in, 438 cm; weight: 2,139 lb, 970 kg.

BODY estate car/st. wagon; 4+1 doors; folding rear seat; for De Luxe only, luxury equipment and sunshine roof.

PRACTICAL INSTRUCTIONS tyre pressure: rear 27 psi, 1.9 atm.

AUDI GERMANY FR

Audi 80 Limousine Series

PRICES EX WORKS:	DM
1 2-dr	12,884*
2 4-dr	13,474*
3 L 2-dr	13,787*
4 L 4-dr	14,377*
5 S 2-dr	13,454*
6 S 4-dr	14,044*
7 LS 2-dr	14,357*
8 LS 4-dr	14,947*
9 GL 2-dr	14,745*
10 GL 4-dr	15,335*
11 GLS 2-dr	15,315*
12 GLS 4-dr	15,905*
13 LS 2-dr	14,685*
14 LS 4-dr	15,275*
15 GLS 2-dr	15,643*
16 GLS 4-dr	16,233*
17 GLE 2-dr	17,081*
18 GLE 4-dr	17,671*

For GB and USA prices, see price index.

Power team:	Standard for:	Optional for:
55 hp	1 to 4	—
75 hp	5 to 12	—
85 hp	13 to 16	—
110 hp	17,18	—

55 hp power team

ENGINE front, 4 stroke; 4 cylinders, in line; 77.6 cu in, 1,272 cc (2.95 x 2.83 in, 75 x 72 mm); compression ratio: 8.2:1; max power (DIN): 55 hp (40 kW) at 5,800 rpm; max torque (DIN): 66.7 lb ft, 9.2 kg m (90 Nm) at 3,400 rpm; max engine rpm: 6,200; 43.2 hp/l (31.8 kW); cast iron block, light alloy head; 5 crankshaft bearings; valves: overhead, in line, thimble tappets; camshafts: 1, overhead, cogged belt; lubrication: gear pump, full flow filter, 6.2 imp pt, 7.4 US pt, 3.5 l; 1 Solex 30-35 PDSIT downdraught single barrel carburettor; fuel feed: mechanical pump; water cooled, 11.4 imp pt, 13.7 US pt, 6.5 l, electric thermostatic fan.

AUDI 80 L Limousine

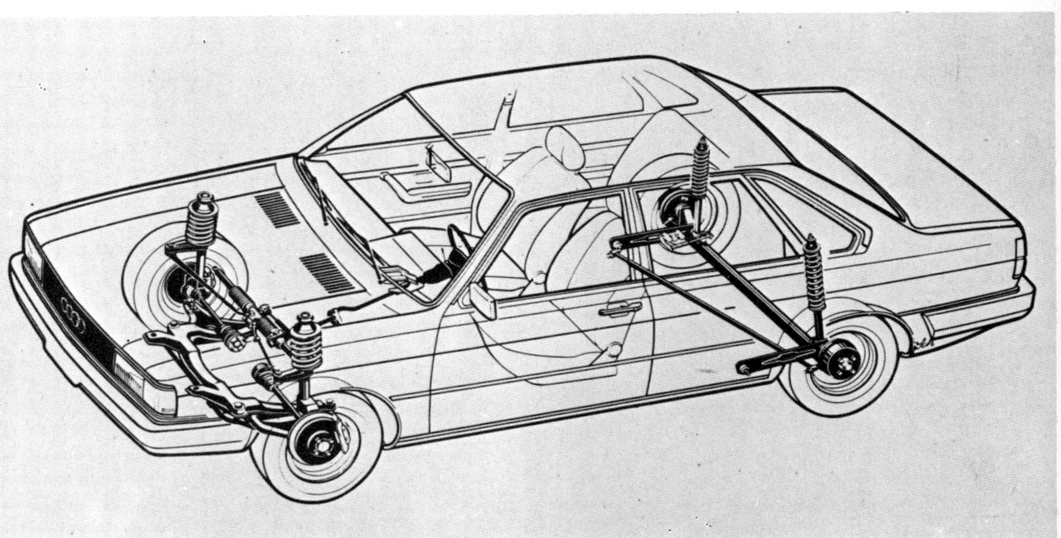

AUDI 80 Series

AUDI 80 GLS Limousine

TRANSMISSION driving wheels: front; clutch: single dry plate (diaphragm); gearbox: mechanical; gears: 4, fully synchronized; ratios: I 3.455, II 1.944, III 1.286, IV 0.969, rev 3.166; lever: central; final drive: hypoid bevel; axle ratio: 4.444; width of rims: 5"; tyres: 155 SR x 13.

PERFORMANCE max speeds: (I) 25 mph, 41 km/h; (II) 42 mph, 68 km/h; (III) 68 mph, 110 km/h; (IV) 90 mph, 145 km/h; power-weight ratio: 36.5 lb/hp (49.6 lb/kW), 16.5 kg/hp (22.5 kg/kW); carrying capacity: 1,014 lb, 460 kg; acceleration: 0-50 mph (0-80 km/h) 11 sec; speed in top at 1,000 rpm: 14.9 mph, 24 km/h; consumption 29.4 m/imp gal, 24.5 m/US gal, 9.6 l x 100 km at 75 mph, 120 km/h.

CHASSIS integral, front auxiliary subframe; front suspension: independent, by McPherson, lower wishbones, coil springs/telescopic damper struts; rear: rigid axle, trailing radius arms, Panhard rod, telescopic damper struts.

STEERING rack-and-pinion; turns lock to lock: 3.94.

BRAKES front disc (diameter 9.43 in, 23.9 cm), dual circuit, rear drum, servo.

ELECTRICAL EQUIPMENT 12 V; 36 Ah battery; 35 A alternator; Bosch distributor; 2 headlamps.

DIMENSIONS AND WEIGHT wheel base: 100 in, 254 cm; tracks: 55.1 in, 140 cm front, 55.9 in, 142 cm rear; length: 172.6 in, 438 cm; width: 66.2 in, 168 cm; height: 53.54 in, 136 cm; ground clearance: 4.21 in, 10.7 cm; weight: 2,007 lb, 910 kg; turning circle: 34.1 ft, 10.4 m; fuel tank: 15 imp gal, 18 US gal, 68 l.

55 HP POWER TEAM

BODY saloon/sedan; 5 seats, separate front seats.

PRACTICAL INSTRUCTIONS fuel: 91 oct petrol; oil: engine 5.3 imp pt, 6.3 US pt, 3 l, SAE 20W-30, change every 4,700 miles, 7,500 km - gearbox and final drive 3.2 imp pt, 3.8 US pt, 1.8 l, SAE 80 or 90; greasing: none: sparking plug: 175°; tappet clearances: inlet 0.008-0.012 in, 0.20-0.30 mm, exhaust 0.016-0.020 in, 0.40-0.50 mm; tyre pressure: front 26 psi, 1.8 atm, rear 26 psi, 1.8 atm.

OPTIONALS 175/70 SR x 13 tyres; halogen headlamps; sunshine roof; vinyl roof; metallic spray.

75 hp power team

See 55 hp power team, except for:

ENGINE 96.9 cu in, 1,588 cc (3.13 x 3.15 in, 79.5 x 80 mm); max power (DIN): 75 hp (55 kW) at 5,600 rpm; max torque (DIN): 88 lb ft, 12.1 kg m (119 Nm) at 3,200 rpm; max engine rpm: 6,000: 47.2 hp/l (34.8 kW/l); water-cooled, 12.3 imp pt, 14.8 US pt, 7 l.

TRANSMISSION gearbox ratios: IV 0.909; axle ratio: 4.111; tyres: 165 SR x 13.

PERFORMANCE max speeds: (I) 27 mph, 44 km/h; (II) 47 mph, 75 km/h; (III) 70 mph, 112 km/h (IV) 99 mph, 160 km/h; power-weight ratio: 27.9 lb/hp (37.9 lb/kW), 12.7 kg/hp (17.2 kg/kW); acceleration: 0-50 mph (0-80 km/h) 8.7 sec; speed in top at 1,000 rpm: 16.2 mph, 26 km/h; consumption: 30.6 m/imp gal, 25.5 m/US gal, 9.2 l x 100 km at 75 mph, 120 km/h.

CHASSIS front suspension: anti-roll bar.

DIMENSIONS AND WEIGHT weight: 2,095 lb, 950 kg.

PRACTICAL INSTRUCTIONS sparking plug: 200°; valve timing: 3° 47° 43° 7°.

OPTIONALS automatic transmission, hydraulic torque converter and planetary gears with 3 ratios (I 2.550, II 1.450, III 1, rev 2.460), max ratio of converter at stall 2.2, possible manual selection, 3.910 axle ratio, 5" wide rims, max speed 97 mph, 156 km/h, consumption 29.7 m/imp gal, 24.8 m/US gal, 9.5 l x 100 km.

85 hp power team

See 55 hp power team, except for:

ENGINE 96.9 cu in, 1,588 cc (3.13 x 3.15 in, 79.5 x 80 mm); max power (DIN): 85 hp (63 kW) at 5,600 rpm; max torque (DIN): 92 lb ft, 12.7 kg m (124 Nm) at 3,200 rpm; max engine rpm: 6,000; 53.5 hp/l (39.4 kW/l); 1 Solex 32-35 TDID downdraught carburettor; water-cooled, 12.3 imp pt, 14.8 US pt, 7 l.

TRANSMISSION gearbox ratios: IV 0.909; axle ratio: 4.111; tyres: 175/70 SR x 13.

PERFORMANCE max speeds: (I) 29 mph, 46 km/h; (II) 48 mph, 78 km/h; (III) 73 mph, 117 km/h; (IV) 102 mph, 165 km/h; power-weight ratio: 24.6 lb/hp (33.5 lb/kW), 11.2 kg/hp (15.2 kg/kW); acceleration: 0-50 mph (0-80 km/h) 7.9 sec; speed in top at 1,000 rpm: 17.4 mph, 28 km/h; consumption: 32.1 m/imp gal, 26.7 m/US gal, 8.8 l x 100 km.

CHASSIS front suspension: anti-roll bar.

ELECTRICAL EQUIPMENT 45 Ah battery; 55 A alternator; halogen headlamps.

DIMENSIONS AND WEIGHT weight: 2,095 lb, 950 kg.

PRACTICAL INSTRUCTIONS sparking plug: 225°; valve timing: 3° 47° 43° 7°

OPTIONALS automatic transmission with 3 ratios (I 2.550, II 1.450, III 1, rev 2.460), 3.909 axle ratio, 5" wide rims, max speed 100 mph, 161 km/h, consumption 30.7 m/imp gal, 25.6 m/US gal, 9.2 l x 100 km; air-conditioning.

AUDI 80 GLS Limousine

110 hp power team

See 55 hp power team, except for:

ENGINE 96.9 cu in, 1,588 cc (3.13 x 3.15 in, 79.5 x 80 mm); compression ratio: 9.5:1; max power (DIN): 110 hp (81 kW) at 6,100 rpm; max torque (DIN): 101 lb ft, 14 kg m (137 Nm) at 5,000 rpm; max engine rpm: 6,500; 59.3 hp/l (51 kW/l); lubrication 6.2 imp pt, 7.4 US pt, 3.5 l; Bosch K-Jetronic injection; fuel feed: electric pump.

TRANSMISSION gearbox ratios: IV 0.909; axle ratio: 3.890; tyres: 175/70 HR x 13.

PERFORMANCE max speeds: (I) 31 mph, 50 km/h; (II) 52 mph, 83 km/h; (III) 80 mph, 128 km/h; 128 h; (IV) 112 mph, 181 km/h; power-weight ratio: 19 lb/hp (25.9 lbkW), 8.6 kg/hp (11.7 kg/kW); acceleration: 0-50 mph (0-80 km/h) 6.8 sec; speed in top at 1,000 rpm: 17.5 mph, 28.2 km/h; consumption: 32.8 m/imp gal, 27.3 m/US gal, 8.6 l x 100 km at 75 mph, 120 km/h.

BRAKES lining area: front 16.3 sq in, 105 sq cm, rear 34.6 sq in, 223 sq cm, total 50.9 sq in, 328 sq cm.

CHASSIS front suspension: anti-roll bar.

ELECTRICAL EQUIPMENT 45 Ah battery; 55 A alternator; halogen headlamps.

DIMENSIONS AND WEIGHT weight: 2,095 lb, 950 kg.

BODY built-in headrests.

PRACTICAL INSTRUCTIONS fuel: 97 oct petrol; oil: engine 6.2 imp pt, 7.4 US pt, 3.5 l, SAE 20W-30, change every 4,700 miles, 7,500 km; sparking plug: 225°; valve timing: 4° 46° 44° 6°.

Audi 100 Limousine Series

PRICES EX WORKS:	DM
1 2-dr	16,435*
2 4-dr	17,065*
3 L 2-dr	17,375*
4 L 4-dr	18,005*
5 GL 4-dr	19,425*
6 5S 2-dr	17,475*
7 5S 4-dr	18,105*
8 L5S 2-dr	18,415*
9 L5S 4-dr	19,045*
10 GL5S 4-dr	20,465*
11 CD5S 4-dr	24,160*
12 5E 2-dr	18,617*
13 5E 4-dr	19,247*
14 L5E 2-dr	19,557*
15 L5E 4-dr	20,187*
16 GL5E 4-dr	21,390*
17 CD5E 4-dr	24,875*
18 5D 2-dr	19,010*
19 5D 4-dr	19,640*
20 L5D 2-dr	19,950*
21 L5D 4-dr	20,580*
22 GL5D 4-dr	22,000*
23 CD5D 4-dr	25,490*

For USA prices, see price index.

Power team:	Standard for:	Optional for:
85 hp	1 to 5	—
115 hp	6 to 11	—
136 hp	12 to 17	—
70 hp (diesel)	18 to 23	—

85 hp power team

ENGINE front, 4 stroke; 4 cylinders, in line; 96.9 cu in, 1,588 cc (3.13 x 3.15 in, 79.5 x 80 mm); compression ratio: 8.2:1; max power (DIN): 85 hp (63 kW) at 5,600 rpm; max torque (DIN): 90 lb ft, 12.4 kg m (122 Nm) at 3,200 rpm; max engine rpm: 6,200; 53.5 hp/l (39.4 kW/l); cast iron block, light alloy head; 5 crankshaft bearings; valves: overhead, in line, rockers; cam-

AUDI 100 L Limousine

AUDI 100 GL5E Limousine

hafts: 1, overhead, cogged belt; lubrication: gear pump, full ow filter, 6.2 imp pt, 7.4 US pt, 3.5 l; 1 Solex 2 B2 down-raught carburettor; fuel feed: mechanical pump; water-cooled, 2.3 imp pt, 14.8 US pt, 7 l, electric thermostatic fan.

RANSMISSION driving wheels: front; clutch: single dry plate diaphgram); gearbox: mechanical; gears: 4, fully synchronized; atios: I 3.454, II 1.944, III 1.286, IV 0.909, rev 3.166; lever: entral; final drive: hypoid bevel; axle ratio: 4.444; width of ims: 5.5"; tyres: 165 SR x 14.

ERFORMANCE max speed: (I) 29 mph, 46 km/h; (II) 52 mph, 3 km/h; (III) 77 mph, 124 km/h; (IV) 99 mph, 160 km/h; ower-weight ratio: 28.8 lb/hp (39.1 lb/kW), 13.1 kg/hp (17.7 g/kW); carrying capacity: 1,014 lb, 460 kg; acceleration: 0-50 nph (0-80 km/h) 8.6 sec; speed in top at 1,000 rpm: 17.6 mph, 8.3 km/h; consumption: 30.6 m/imp gal, 25.5 m/US gal, 9.2 x 100 km at 75 mph, 120 km/h.

HASSIS integral, front auxiliary subframe; front suspension: ndependent, by McPherson, lower wishbones, anti-roll bar, coil prings/telescopic damper struts; rear: rigid axle, swinging lon-itudinal trailing radius arms, Panhard rod, anti-roll bar, tele-copic dampers.

TEERING rack-and-pinion.

RAKES front disc (diameter 10.24 in, 26 cm), rear drum, dual ircuit, servo; lining area: front 20.2 sq in, 130 sq cm, rear 39.7 q in, 256 sq cm, total 59.9 sq in, 386 sq cm.

LECTRICAL EQUIPMENT 12 V; 45 Ah battery; 55 A alternator 65 A for GL only; Bosch distributor; 2 headlamps.

IMENSIONS AND WEIGHT wheel base: 105.40 in, 268 cm; racks: 57.90 in, 147 cm front, 56.90 in, 144 cm rear; length: 84.30 in, 468 cm - GL 185 in, 470 cm; width: 69.60 in, 177 cm; eight: 54.80 in, 139 cm; ground clearance: 5.10 in, 13 cm; veight: 2,448 lb, 1,110 kg; weight distribution: 49% front, 51% ear; turning circle: 37.1 ft, 11.3 m; fuel tank: 13.2 imp gal, 15.8 JS gal, 60 l.

ODY saloon/sedan; 5 seats, separate front seats, reclining ackrests; heated rear window.

RACTICAL INSTRUCTIONS fuel: 91 oct petrol; oil: engine 5.3 np pt, 6.3 US pt, 3 l, SAE 10W-30, change every 4,700 miles, ,500 km - gearbox and drive 3 imp pt, 3.6 US pt, 1.7 l, SAE 80; reasing: none; tyre pressure: front 28 psi, 2 atm, rear 28 psi, 2 tm.

PTIONALS automatic transmission, hydraulic torque conver-er and planetary gears with 3 ratios (I 2.552, II 1.448, III 1, rev .091), axle ratio, max speed 97 mph, 156 km/h, acceleration -50 mph (0-80 km/h) 11,5 sec, consumption 29.7 m/imp gal, 4.8 m/US gal, 9.5 l x 100 km, 54 Ah battery; 185/70 SR x 14 yres; sunshine roof; metallic spray; halogen headlamps (except or L and GL models).

115 hp power team

See 85 hp power team, except for:

NGINE 5 cylinders, in line; 130.8 cu in, 2,144 cc (3.13 x 3.40 n, 74.5 x 86.4 mm); compression ratio: 8.3:1; max power (DIN): 15 hp (85 kW) at 5,500 rpm; max torque (DIN): 120 lb ft, 16.6 g m (163 Nm) at 4,000 rpm; 53.6 hp/l (39.5 kW/l); 6 crankshaft earings; lubrication: 8.8 imp pt, 10.6 US pt, 5 l; water-cooled, 4.3 imp pt, 17.1 US pt, 8.1 l.

TRANSMISSION gearbox ratios: I 3.600, II 2.125, III 1.360, IV 0.967, rev 3.500; axle ratio: 3.889.

PERFORMANCE max speed: 111 mph, 179 mph, km/h; power-weight ratio: 22.4 lb/hp (30.5 lb/kW), 10.2 kg/hp (13.8 kg/kW); consumption: 26.9 m/imp gal, 22.4 m/US gal, 10.5 l x 100 km at 75 mph, 120 km/h.

BRAKES lining area: front 20.2 sq in, 130 sq cm, rear 44.5 sq in, 287 sq cm, total 64.7 sq in, 417 sq cm.

ELECTRICAL EQUIPMENT 63 Ah battery; electronic ignition.

DIMENSIONS AND WEIGHT weight: 2,580 lb, 1,170 kg.

PRACTICAL INSTRUCTIONS oil: engine 7.9 imp pt, 9.5 US pt, 4.5 l.

OPTIONALS with automatic transmission 3.727 axle ratio, max speed 107 mph, 172 km/h, consumption 25.4 m/imp gal, 21.2 m/US gal, 11.1 l x 100 km; power steering; air-conditioning.

136 hp power team

See 85 hp power team, except for:

ENGINE 5 cylinders, in line; 130.8 cu in, 2,144 cc (3.13 x 3.40 in, 79.5 x 86.4 mm); compression ratio: 9.3:1; max power (DIN): 136 hp (100 kW) at 5,700 rpm; max torque (DIN): 134 lb ft, 18.5 kg m (181 Nm) at 4,200 rpm; 63.4 hp/l (46.7 kW/l); 6 crankshaft bearings; lubrication: 8.8 imp pt, 10.6 US pt, 5 l; Bosch K-Jetronic injection; water-cooled, 14.3 imp pt, 17.1 US pt, 8.1 l.

TRANSMISSION gearbox ratios: I 3.600, II 2.125, III 1.360, IV 0.967, rev 3.500; axle ratio: 3.889; tyres: 185/70 HR x 14.

PERFORMANCE max speed: 118 mph, 190 km/h; power-weight ratio: 19 lb/hp (25.8 lb/kW), 8.6 kg/hp (11.7 kg/kW); consumption: 27.1 m/imp gal, 22.6 m/US gal, 10.4 l x 100 km at 75 mph, 120 km/h.

BRAKES lining area: front 20.2 sq in, 130 sq cm, rear 44.5 sq in, 287 sq cm, total 64.7 sq in, 417 sq cm.

ELECTRICAL EQUIPMENT 63 Ah battery; 75 A alternator; electronic ignition.

DIMENSIONS AND WEIGHT weight: 2,580 lb, 1,170 kg.

PRACTICAL INSTRUCTIONS fuel: 98 oct petrol; oil: engine 7.9 imp pt, 9.5 US pt. 4.5 l.

OPTIONALS with automatic transmission 3.727 axle ratio, max speed 115 mph, 185 km/h, consumption 25.4 m/imp gal, 21.2 m/US gal, 11.1 l x 100 km; power steering; air-conditioning.

70 hp (diesel) power team

See 85 hp power team, except for:

ENGINE diesel; 5 cylinders, in line; 121.2 cu in, 1,986 cc (3.01 x 3.40 in, 76.5 x 86.4 mm); compression ratio: 23:1; max power (DIN): 70 hp (51 kW) at 4,800 rpm; max torque (DIN): 91 lb ft, 12.5 kg m (123 Nm) at 3,000 rpm; max engine rpm: 5,000; 35.2 hp/l (25.9 kW/l); 6 crankshaft bearings; lubrication: 8.8

AUDI 100 GL5E Limousine

AUDI 100 CD5D Limousine

AUDI 100 Avant CD5S Limousine

gal, 24.8 m/US gal, 9.5 l x 100 km, 54 Ah battery; 185/70 SR x 14 tyres; sunshine roof; metallic spray; rear window wiper washer.

115 hp power team

See 85 hp power team, except for:

ENGINE 5 cylinders, in line; 130.8 cu in, 2,144 cc (3.13 x 3.40 in, 79.5 x 86.4 mm); compression ratio: 8.3:1; max power (DIN): 115 hp (85 kW) at 5,500 rpm; max torque (DIN): 120 lb ft, 16.6 kg m (163 Nm) at 4,000 rpm; 53.6 hp/l (39.5 kW/l); 6 crankshaft bearings; lubrication: 8.8 imp pt, 10.6 US pt, 5 l; water-cooled, 14.3 imp pt, 17.1 US pt, 8.1 l.

TRANSMISSION gearbox ratios: I 3.600, II 2.125, III 1.360, IV 0.967, rev 3.500; axle ratio: 3.889.

PERFORMANCE max speed: 111 mph, 179 km/h; power-weight ratio: 22.4 lb/hp (30.5 lb/kW), 10.2 kg/hp (13.8 kg/kW); consumption: 26.9 m/imp gal, 22.4 m/US gal, 10.5 l x 100 km at 75 mph, 120 km/h.

BRAKES lining area: front 20.2 sq in, 130 sq cm, rear 44.5 sq in, 287 sq cm, total 64.7 sq in, 417 sq cm.

ELECTRICAL EQUIPMENT 63 Ah battery; electronic ignition

DIMENSIONS AND WEIGHT weight: 2,580 lb, 1,770 kg.

PRACTICAL INSTRUCTIONS oil: engine 7.9 imp pt, 9.5 US pt 4.5 l.

70 HP (DIESEL) POWER TEAM

imp pt, 10.6 US pt, 5 l; Bosch injection; water-cooled, 14.3 imp pt, 17.1 US pt, 8.1 l.

TRANSMISSION gearbox ratios: I 3.600, II 1.941, III 1.231, IV 0.857, rev 3.500; axle ratio: 4.300; tyres: 185/70 SR x 14 (standard).

PERFORMANCE max speed: 93 mph, 150 km/h; power-weight ratio: 38.1 lb/hp (51.8 lb/kW), 17.3 kg/hp (23.5 kg/kW); speed in top at 1,000 rpm: 19.2 mph, 30.9 km/h; consumption: 33.2 m/imp gal, 27.7 m/US gal, 8.5 l x 100 km at 75 mph, 120 km/h.

ELECTRICAL EQUIPMENT 88 Ah battery; 55 A alternator.

DIMENSIONS AND WEIGHT weight: 2,668 lb, 1,210 kg.

OPTIONALS automatic transmission not available.

Audi 100 Avant Limousine Series

PRICES IN GB AND EX WORKS:	£	DM
1 L	5,839*	18,655*
2 GL	—	20,075*
3 L5S	6,313*	19,695*
4 GL5S	6,823*	21,115*
5 CD5S	—	24,810*
6 L5E	—	20,837*
7 GL5E	7,551*	22,040*
8 CD5E	9,303*	25,525*
9 L5D	7,089*	21,230*
10 GL5D	—	22,650*
11 CD5D	—	26,140*

Power team:	Standard for:	Optional for:
85 hp	1,2	—
115 hp	3 to 5	—
136 hp	6 to 8	—
70 hp (diesel)	9 to 11	—

85 hp power team

ENGINE front, 4 stroke; 4 cylinders, in line; 96.9 cu in, 1,588 cc (3.13 x 3.15 in, 79.5 x 80 mm); compression ratio: 8.2:1; max power (DIN): 85 hp (63 kW) at 5,600 rpm; max torque (DIN): 90 lb ft, 12.4 kg m (122 Nm) at 3,200 rpm; max engine rpm: 6,200; 53.5 hp/l (39.4 kW/l); cast iron block, light alloy head; 5 crankshaft bearings; valves: overhead, in line, rockers; camshafts: 1, overhead, cogged belt; lubrication: gear pump, full flow filter, 6.2 imp pt, 7.4 US pt, 3.5 l; 1 Solex 2 B2 downdraught carburettor; fuel feed: mechanical pump; water-cooled, 12.3 imp pt, 14.8 US pt, 7 l, electric thermostatic fan.

TRANSMISSION driving wheels: front; clutch: single dry plate (diaphragm); gearbox: mechanical; gears: 4, fully synchronized; ratios: I 3.454, II 1.944, III 1.286, IV 0.909, rev 3.166; lever: central; final drive: hypoid bevel; axle ratio: 4.444; width of rims: 5.5"; tyres: 165 SR x 14.

PERFORMANCE max speeds: (I) 29 mph, 46 km/h; (II) 52 mph, 83 km/h; (III) 77 mph, 124 km/h; (IV) 99 mph, 160 km/h; power-weight ratio: 28.8 lb/hp (39.1 lb/kW), 13.1 kg/hp (17.7 kg/kW); carrying capacity: 1,014 lb, 460 kg; acceleration: 0-50 mph (0-80 km/h) 8.6 sec; speed in top at 1,000 rpm: 17.6 mph, 28.3 km/h; consumption: 30.6 m/imp gal, 25.5 m/US gal, 9.2 l x 100 km at 75 mph, 120 km/h.

AUDI 100 Avant CD5S Limousine

CHASSIS integral, front auxiliary subframe; front suspension: independent, by McPherson, lower wishbones, anti-roll bar, coil springs/telescopic damper struts; rear: rigid axle, swinging longitudinal trailing radius arms, Panhard rod, anti-roll bar, telescopic dampers.

STEERING rack-and-pinion.

BRAKES front disc (diameter 10.24 in, 26 cm), rear drum, dual circuit, 2 X circuits, servo; lining area: front 20.2 sq in, 130 sq cm, rear 39.7 sq in, 256 sq cm, total 59.9 sq in, 386 sq cm.

ELECTRICAL EQUIPMENT 12 V; 45 Ah battery; 55 A alternator; Bosch distributor; 2 headlamps.

DIMENSIONS AND WEIGHT wheel base: 105.40 in, 268 cm; tracks: 57.90 in, 147 cm front, 56.90 in, 144 cm rear; length: L 180.59 in, 459 cm - GL 181.38 in, 461 cm; width: 69.60 in, 177 cm; height: 54.80 in, 139 cm; ground clearances: 5.10 in, 13 cm; weight: 2,448 lb, 1,110 kg; turning circle: 37.1 ft, 11.3 m; fuel tank: 13.2 imp gal, 15.8 US gal, 60 l.

BODY saloon/sedan; 4+1 doors; 5 seats, separate seats, reclining backrests; heated rear window; folding rear seat.

PRACTICAL INSTRUCTIONS fuel: 91 oct petrol; oil: engine 5.3 imp pt, 6.3 US pt, 3 l, SAE 10W-30, change every 4,700 miles, 7,500 km - gearbox and final drive 3 imp pt, 3.6 US pt, 1.7 l, SAE 80; greasing: none; tyre pressure: front 28 psi, 2 atm, rear 28 psi, 2 atm.

OPTIONALS automatic transmission, hydraulic torque converter and planetary gears with 3 ratios (I 2.552, II 1.448, III 1, rev 2.462), 4.091 axle ratio, max speed 97 mph, 156 km/h, acceleration 0-50 mph (0-80 km/h) 11.5 sec, consumption 29.7 m/imp

OPTIONALS with automatic transmission 3.727 axle ratio, max speed 107 mph, 172 km/h, consumption 25.4 m/imp gal, 21.2 m/US gal, 11.1 l x 100 km; power steering; air-conditioning.

136 hp power team

See 85 hp power team, except for:

ENGINE 5 cylinders, in line; 130.8 cu in, 2,144 cc (3.13 x 3.40 in, 79.5 x 86.4 mm); compression ratio: 9.3:1; max power (DIN): 136 hp (100 kW) at 5,700 rpm; max torque (DIN): 134 lb ft, 18.5 kg m (181 Nm) at 4,200 rpm; 63.4 hp/l (46.7 kW/l); 6 crankshaft bearings; lubrication: 8.8 imp pt, 10.6 US pt, 5 l; Bosch K Jetronic injection; water-cooled, 14.3 imp pt, 17.1 US pt, 8.1 l.

TRANSMISSION gearbox ratios: I 3.600, II 2.125, III 1.360, IV 0.967, rev 3.500; axle ratio: 3.889; tyres: 185/70 HR x 14.

PERFORMANCE max speed: 118 mph, 190 km/h; power-weight ratio: 19 lb/hp (2.58 lb/kW), 8.6 kg/hp (11.7 kg/kW); acceleration 0-50 mph (0-80 km/h) 6.3 sec; consumption: 27.1 m/imp gal, 22.6 m/US gal, 10.4 l x 100 km at 75 mph, 120 km/h.

BRAKES lining area: front 20.2 sq in, 130 sq cm, rear 44.5 sq in, 287 sq cm, total 64.7 sq in, 417 sq cm.

ELECTRICAL EQUIPMENT 63 Ah battery; 75 A alternator; electronic ignition.

DIMENSIONS AND WEIGHT weight: 2,580 lb, 1,170 kg.

PRACTICAL INSTRUCTIONS fuel: 98 oct petrol; oil: engine 7.9 imp pt, 9.5 US pt, 4.5 l.

AUDI 200 5T Limousine

OPTIONALS with automatic transmission 3.727 axle ratio, max speed 115 mph, 185 km/h, acceleration 0-50 mph (0-80 km/h) .8 sec, consumption 25.4 m/imp gal, 21.2 m/US gal, 11.1 x 100 km; power steering; air-conditioning.

70 hp (diesel) power team

See 85 hp power team, except for:

ENGINE diesel; 5 cylinders, in line; 121.2 cu in, 1,986 cc (3.01 x 3.40 in, 76.5 x 86.4 mm); compression ratio: 23.1; max power (DIN): 70 hp (51 kW) at 4,800 rpm; max torque (DIN): 91 lb ft, 12.5 kg m (123 Nm) at 3,000 rpm; max engine rpm: 5,000; 35.2 hp/l (25.9 kW/l); 6 crankshaft bearings; lubrication: 8.8 imp pt, 10.6 US pt, 5 l; Bosch injection; water-cooled, 14.3 imp pt, 17.1 US pt, 8.1 l.

TRANSMISSION gearbox ratios: I 3.600, II 1.941, III 1.231, IV 0.857, rev 3.500; axle ratio: 4.300; tyres: 185/70 SR x 14 (standard).

PERFORMANCE max speed: 93 mph, 150 km/h; power- weight ratio: 38.1 lb/hp (51.8 lb/kW), 17.3 kg/hp (23.5 kg/kW); speed in top at 1,000 rpm: 19.2 mph, 30.9 km/h; consumption: 33.2 m/imp gal, 27.7 m/US gal, 8.5 l x 100 km at 75 mph, 120 km/h.

ELECTRICAL EQUIPMENT 88 Ah battery; 55 A alternator.

DIMENSIONS AND WEIGHT weight: 2,668 lb, 1,210 kg.

OPTIONALS automatic transmission not available.

Audi 200 Limousine Series

PRICES EX WORKS:	DM
1 5E	27,875*
2 5T	30,550*

Power team:	Standard for:	Optional for:
136 hp	1	—
170 hp	2	—

136 hp power team

ENGINE front, 4 stroke; 5 cylinders, in line; 130.8 cu in, 2,144 cc (3.13 x 3.40 in, 79.5 x 86.4 mm); compression ratio: 9.3:1; max power (DIN): 136 hp (100 kW) at 5,700 rpm; max torque (DIN): 137 lb ft, 18.9 kg m (185 Nm) at 4,200 rpm; max engine rpm: 6,200; 63.4 hp/l (46.7 kW/l); cast iron block, light alloy head; 6 crankshaft bearings; valves: overhead, in line, rockers; camshafts: 1, overhead, cogged belt; lubrication: gear pump, full flow filter, 8.8 imp pt, 10.6 US pt, 5 l; Bosch K-Jetronic injection system; fuel feed: mechanical pump; water-cooled, 14.3 imp pt, 17.1 US pt, 8.1 l.

TRANSMISSION driving wheels: front; clutch: single dry plate (diaphragm); gearbox: mechanical; gears: 5, fully synchronized; ratios: I 3.600, II 1.941, III 1.231, IV 0.903, V 0.684, rev 3.500; lever: central; final drive: hypoid bevel; axle ratio: 3.888; width of rims: 6"; tyres: 205/60 HR x 15.

PERFORMANCE max speed: 117 mph, 188 km/h; power-weight ratio: 20.4 lb/hp, (27.7 lb/kW), 9.3 kg/hp (12.6 kg/kW); carrying capacity: 1,136 lb, 505 kg; speed in top at 1,000 rpm: 18.8 mph, 30.3 km/h; consumption: 30.3 m/imp gal, 25.3 m/US gal, 9.3 l x 100 km at 75 mph, 120 km/h.

CHASSIS integral, front auxiliary subframe; front suspension: independent, by McPherson, lower wishbones, anti-roll bar, coil springs/telescopic damper struts; rear: rigid axle, swinging longitudinal trailing radius arms, Panhard rod, anti-roll bar, telescopic dampers.

STEERING recirculating ball, servo.

BRAKES disc (front diameter 11 in, 28 cm, rear 9.6 in, 24.5 cm), front internal radial fins, 2 X circuits, rear compensator, servo.

ELECTRICAL EQUIPMENT 12 V; 63 Ah battery; 75 A alternator; electronic ignition; 4 halogen headlamps.

DIMENSIONS AND WEIGHT wheel base: 105.40 in, 268 cm; tracks: 57.90 in, 147 cm front, 57.08 in, 145 cm rear; length: 184.64 in, 469 cm; width: 69.60 in, 177 cm; height: 54.80 in, 139 cm; weight: 2,778 lb, 1,260 kg; turning circle: 37 ft, 11.3 m; fuel tank: 16.5 imp gal, 19.8 US gal, 75 l.

BODY saloon/sedan; 4 doors; 5 seats, separate front seats, reclining backrests, built-in adjustable headrests; heated rear window; light alloy wheels.

PRACTICAL INSTRUCTIONS fuel: 98 oct petrol; oil: engine 8.8 imp pt, 10.6 US pt, 5 l, SAE 10W-50, change every 4,700 miles, 7,500 km - gearbox and final drive 3 imp pt, 3.6 US pt, 1.7 l, SAE 80, change every 14,000 miles, 22,500 km; greasing: none; tyre pressure: front and rear 28 psi, 2 atm.

OPTIONALS automatic transmission; sunshine roof; air-conditioning; tinted glass.

170 hp power team

See 136 hp power team, except for:

ENGINE compression ratio: 7:1; max power (DIN): 170 hp (125 kW) at 5,300 rpm; max torque (DIN): 196 lb/ft, 27 kg m (265 Nm) at 3,300 rpm; 79.3 hp/l (58.3 kW/l); Bosch K-Jetronic injection with exhaust KKK turbocharger.

TRANSMISSION gearbox ratios: I 3.600, II 2.125, III 1.360, IV 0.966, V 0.829, rev 3.500.

PERFORMANCE max speed: 125 mph, 202 km/h; power-weight ratio: 16.3 lb/hp (22.2 lb/kW), 7.4 kg/hp (10 kg/kW).

BMW GERMANY FR

(For cars imported into the USA and Canada, exhaust system with thermal reactor and lower compression ratio).

316

PRICE IN GB: £ 5,100*
PRICE EX WORKS: DM 16,250*

ENGINE front, 4 stroke; 4 cylinders, slanted at 30°, in line; 96 cu in, 1,573 cc (3.31 x 2.80 in, 84 x 71 mm); compression ratio: 8.3:1; max power (DIN): 90 hp (66 kW) at 6,000 rpm; max torque (DIN): 91 lb ft, 12.5 kg m (123 Nm) at 4,000 rpm; max engine rpm: 6,000; 57.2 hp/l (42.1 kW/l); cast iron block, light alloy head, hemispherical combustion chambers; 5 crankshaft bearings; valves: overhead, Vee-slanted at 52°, rockers; camshafts: 1, overhead; lubrication: gear pump, full flow filter, 7.4 imp pt, 8.9 US pt, 4.2 l; 1 Solex DIDTA 32/32 downdraught twin barrel carburettor; fuel feed: mechanical pump; water-cooled, 12.3 imp pt, 14.8 US pt, 7 l.

TRANSMISSION driving wheels: rear; clutch: single dry plate (diaphragm), hydraulically controlled; gearbox: mechanical; gears: 4, fully synchronized; ratios: I 3.764, II 2.043, III 1.320, IV 1, rev 4.096; lever: central; final drive: hypoid bevel: axle ratio: 4.100; width of rims: 5"; tyres: 165 SR x 13.

PERFORMANCE max speeds: (I) 26 mph, 42 km/h; (II) 49 mph, 79 km/h; (III) 75 mph, 121 km//h; (IV) 99 mph, 160 km/h; power-weight ratio: 25 lb/hp (34 lb/kW), 11.3 kg/hp (15.4 kg/kW); carrying capacity: 926 lb, 420 kg; acceleration: standing ¼ mile 18.8 sec, 0-50 mph (0-80 km/h) 8.7 sec; speed in direct drive at 1,000 rpm: 16.3 mph, 26.3 km/h; consumption: 27.9 m/imp gal, 23.3 m/US gal, 10.1 l x 100 km at 75 mph, 120 km/h.

CHASSIS integral; front suspension: independent, by McPherson, coil springs/telescopic damper struts, auxiliary rubber springs, lower wishbones, lower trailings links, anti-roll bar; rear: independent, oblique semi-trailing arms, auxiliary rubber springs, coil springs, telescopic dampers.

BMW 316 - 318

316

STEERING ZF, räck-and-pinion; turns lock to lock: 4.05.

BRAKES front disc (diameter 10.04 in, 25.5 cm), rear drum, dual circuit, servo; lining area: front 23.9 sq in, 154 sq cm, rear 51.5 sq in, 332 sq cm, total 75.4 sq in, 486 sq cm.

ELECTRICAL EQUIPMENT 12 V; 36 Ah battery; 630 W alternator; Bosch distributor; 2 halogen headlamps.

DIMENSIONS AND WEIGHT wheel base: 100.79 in, 256 cm; tracks: 53.80 in, 137 cm front, 54.10 in, 137 cm rear; length: 171.26 in, 435 cm; width: 63.39 in, 161 cm; height: 54.33 in, 138 cm; ground clearance: 5.51 in, 14 cm; weight: 2,249 lb, 1,020 kg; turning circle: 33.5 ft, 10.2 m; fuel tank: 12.8 imp gal, 15.3 US gal, 58 l.

BODY saloon/sedan; 2 doors; 5 seats, separate front seats, reclining backrests, built-in adjustable headrests; heated rear window.

PRACTICAL INSTRUCTIONS fuel: 92 oct petrol; oil: engine 7.4 imp pt, 8.9 US pt, 4.2 l, SAE 20W-50, change every 3,700 miles, 6,000 km - gearbox 1.8 imp pt, 2.1 US pt, 1 l, SAE 80, change every 14,800 miles, 24,000 km - final drive 1.6 imp pt, 1.9 US pt, 0.9 l, SAE 90, no change recommended; greasing: none; sparking plug: 145°.

OPTIONALS 5 speed mechanical gearbox (I 3.682, II 2.002, III 1.330, IV 1, V 0.813, rev 3.705); limited slip differential; power steering; headlamps with wiper-washers; anti-roll bar on rear suspension; fog lamps; 55 Ah battery; 185/70 HR x 13 tyres; light alloy wheels; sunshine roof; metallic spray; tinted glass.

BMW 318

318

See 316, except for:

PRICE EX WORKS: DM 17,350*

ENGINE 107.8 cu in, 1,766 cc (3.50 x 2.80 in, 89 x 71 mm); max power (DIN): 98 hp (72 kW) at 5,800 rpm; max torque (DIN): 105 lb ft, 14.5 kg m (142 Nm) at 4,000 rpm; 55.5 hp/l (40.8 kW/l).

PERFORMANCE max speed: 103 mph, 165 km/h; power-weight ratio: 22.9 lb/hp (31.2 lb/kW), 10.4 kg/hp (14.1 kg/kW); acceleration: standing ¼ mile 17.9 sec, 0-50 mph (0-80 km/h) 7.6 sec; speed in direct drive at 1,000 rpm: 17.2 mph, 27.7 km/h; consumption: 29.1 m/imp gal, 24.2 m/US gal, 9.7 l x 100 km at 75 mph, 120 km/h.

OPTIONALS ZF HP 22 automatic transmission, hydraulic torque converter and planetary gears with 3 ratios (I 2.478, II 1.478, III 1, rev 2.090), max ratio of converter at stall 2, possible manual selection, max speed 99 mph, 160 km/h, consumption 26.4 m/imp gal, 22 m/US gal, 10.7 l x 100 km.

320

See 316, except for:

PRICE IN GB: £ 6,469*
PRICE EX WORKS: DM 19,850*

ENGINE 6 cylinders, in line; 121.4 cu in, 1,990 cc (3.15 x 2.60 in, 80 x 66 mm); compression ratio: 9.2:1; max power (DIN): 122 hp (90 kW) at 6,000 rpm; max torque (DIN): 118 lb ft, 16.3 kg m (160 Nm) at 4,000 rpm; max engine rpm: 6,000; 61.3 hp/l (45.1 kW/l); 7 crankshaft bearings; valves: overhead, Vee-slanted, rockers; lubrication: 10 imp pt, 12 US pt, 5.7 l; 1 Solex 4A1 downdraught 4-barrel carburettor; cooling: 21.1 imp pt, 25.4 US pt, 12 l.

TRANSMISSION axle ratio: 3.640; width of rims: 5.5"; tyres: 185/70 HR x 13.

PERFORMANCE max speed: 112 mph, 181 km/h; power-weight ratio: 20.1 lb/hp (27.4 lb/kW), 9.1 kg/hp (12.4 kg/kW); acceleration: standing ¼ mile 17.4 sec, 0-50 mph (0-80 km/h) 7.2 sec; speed in direct drive at 1,000 rpm: 18.8 mph, 30.2 km/h.

ELECTRICAL EQUIPMENT 44 Ah battery; 910 W alternator; 4 halogen headlamps.

DIMENSIONS AND WEIGHT tracks: 54.70 in, 139 cm front, 55 in, 140 cm rear; weight: 2,459 lb, 1,115 kg.

PRACTICAL INSTRUCTIONS fuel: 98 oct petrol; oil: engine 10 imp pt, 12 US pt, 5.7 l.

OPTIONALS ZF HP 22 automatic transmission, hydraulic torque converter and planetary gears with 3 ratios (I 2.478, II 1.478, III 1, rev 2.090), max ratio of converter at stall 2, possible manual selection, max speed 109 mph, 176 km/h, consumption 27.2 m/imp gal, 22.6 m/US gal, 10.4 l x 100 km.

BMW 323 i

323 i

See 316, except for:

PRICE IN GB: £ 7,550*
PRICE EX WORKS: DM 22,500*

ENGINE 6 cylinders, in line; 141 cu in, 2,315 cc (3.15 x 3.02 in, 80 x 76.8 mm); compression ratio: 9.5:1; max power (DIN): 143 hp (105 kW) at 6,000 rpm; max torque (DIN): 141 lb ft, 19.4 kg m (190 Nm) at 4,500 rpm; max engine rpm: 6,000; 61.8 hp/l (45.4 kW/l); 7 crankshaft bearings; valves: overhead, Vee-slanted, rockers; lubrication 10 imp pt, 12 US pt, 5.7 l; Bosch K-Jetronic injection; cooling: 21.1 imp pt, 25.4 US pt, 12 l.

TRANSMISSION axle ratio: 3.450; width of rims: 5.5"; tyres 185/70 HR x 13.

PERFORMANCE max speed: 118 mph, 190 km/h; power-weight ratio: 17.5 lb/hp (23.8 lb/kW), 7.9 kg/hp (10.8 kg/kW); acceleration: standing ¼ mile 16.7 sec, 0-50 mph (0-80 km/h) 6.4 sec; speed in direct drive at 1,000 rpm: 19.7 mph, 31.7 km/h consumption: 26.9 m/imp gal, 22.4 m/US gal, 10.5 l x 100 km at 75 mph, 120 km/h.

BRAKES disc, front internal radial fins.

ELECTRICAL EQUIPMENT 55 Ah battery; 910 W alternator transistorized ignition; 4 halogen headlamps.

DIMENSIONS AND WEIGHT tracks: 54.70 in, 139 cm front 55.20 in, 140 cm rear; weight: 2,503 lb, 1,135 kg.

PRACTICAL INSTRUCTIONS fuel: 98 oct petrol; oil: engine 10 imp pt, 12 US pt, 5.7 l.

OPTIONALS ZF HP 22 automatic transmission, hydraulic torque converter and planetary gears with 3 ratios (I 2.478, I 1.478, III 1, rev 2.090), max ratio of converter at stall 2 possible manual selection, max speed 115 mph, 185 km/h.

518

PRICE IN GB: £ 6,654*
PRICE EX WORKS: DM 19,550

ENGINE front, 4 stroke; 4 cylinders, in line; 107.8 cu in, 1,766 cc (2.80 x 3.50 in, 71 x 89 mm); compression ratio: 8.3:1; max power (DIN): 90 hp (66 kW) at 5,800 rpm; max torque (DIN) 104 lb ft, 14.3 kg m (140 Nm) at 3,500 rpm; max engine rpm 6,300; 51 hp/l (37.5 kW/l); cast iron block, light alloy head hemispherical combustion chambers; 5 crankshaft bearings valves: overhead, Vee-slanted at 52°, rockers; camshafts: 1 overhead; lubrication: rotary pump, full flow filter, 7.4 imp pt 8.9 US pt, 4.2 l; 1 Solex DIDTA 32/32 downdraught twin barrel carburettor; fuel feed: mechanical pump; water-cooled, 12.3 imp pt, 14.8 US pt, 7 l.

TRANSMISSION driving wheels: rear; clutch: single dry plate gearbox: mechanical; gears: 4, fully synchronized; ratios: I 3.764, II 2.043, III 1.320, IV 1, rev 4.096; lever: central; final drive: hypoid bevel; axle ratio: 4.270; width of rims: 5.5"; tyres 175 SR x 14.

PERFORMANCE max speeds: (I) 27 mph, 43 km/h; (II) 49 mph 79 km/h; (III) 76 mph, 122 km/h; (IV) 99 mph, 160 km/h power-weight ratio: 30.4 lb/hp (41.3 lb/kW), 13.8 kg/hp (18.7 kg/kW); carrying capacity: 1,014 lb, 460 kg; speed in direct drive at 1,000 rpm: 15.8 mph, 25.5 km/h; standard consumption 28.8 m/imp gal, 24 m/US gal, 9.8 l x 100 km

BMW 300 Series

BMW 520

ɪASSIS integral; front suspension: independent, by McPher-n, coil springs/telescopic damper struts, auxiliary rubber rings, lower wishbones, lower trailing links, anti-roll bar; rear dependent, oblique semi-trailing arms, auxiliary rubber rings, coil springs, telescopic dampers.

'EERING ZF, worm and roller.

ʀAKES front disc (diameter 11 in, 28 cm), internal radial fins, ar drum, dual circuit, rear compensator, servo.

.ECTRICAL EQUIPMENT 12 V; 36 Ah battery; 630 W alterna-; 4 halogen headlamps.

MENSIONS AND WEIGHT wheel base: 103.94 in, 264 cm; cks: 56 in, 142 cm front, 57.70 in, 147 cm rear; length: 1.89 in, 462 cm; width: 66.54 in, 169 cm; height: 55.91 in, 2 cm; ground clearance: 5.51 in, 14 cm; weight: 2,734 lb, 240 kg; turning circle: 34.4 ft, 10.5 m; fuel tank: 15.4 imp gal, .5 US gal, 70 l.

DDY saloon/sedan; 4 doors; 5 seats, separate front seats, clining backrests; heated rear window.

ACTICAL INSTRUCTIONS fuel: 92 oct petrol; oil: engine 7.4 p pt, 8.9 US pt, 4.2 l, SAE 20W-50, change every 3,700 les, 6,000 km - gearbox 1.8 imp pt, 2.1 US pt, 1 l, SAE 80, ange every 14,900 miles, 24,000 km - final drive 1.6 imp pt, 9 US pt, 0.9 l, SAE 90, no change recommended; greasing: ne.

PTIONALS limited slip differential; 195/70 HR x 14 tyres; light oy wheels; power steering; manual or electric sunshine roof; g lamps; metallic spray; 55 Ah battery; 770 W alternator; ZF 3 22 automatic transmission, hydraulic torque converter and anetary gears with 3 ratios (I 2.478, II 1.478, III 1, rev 2.090), ax ratio of converter at stall 2, possible manual selection, max eed 96 mph, 155 km/h, consumption 26.4 m/imp gal, 22 m/US l, 10.7 l x 100 km.

520

e 518, except for:

ICE IN GB: £ 7,772*
ICE EX WORKS: DM 22,300*

GINE 6 cylinders, in line; 121.4 cu in, 1,990 cc (3.15 x 2.60 80 x 66 mm); compression ratio: 9.2:1; max power (DIN): 2 hp (90 kW) at 6,000 rpm; max torque (DIN): 118 lb ft, 16.3 m (160 Nm); at 4,000 rpm; max engine rpm; 6,000; 61.3 hp/l 5.1 kW/l); 7 crankshaft bearings; valves: overhead, Vee-nted, rockers; lubrication: 10 imp pt, 12 US pt, 5.7 l; 1 Solex 1 downdraught 4-barrel carburettor; cooling: 21.1 imp pt, .4 US pt, 12 l.

ANSMISSION axle ratio: 3.900; tyres: 175 HR x 14.

ERFORMANCE max speed: 112 mph, 180 km/h; power-weight io: 23.7 lb/hp (32.2 lb/kW), 10.7 kg/hp (14.6 kg/kW); speed in ect drive at 1,000 rpm: 18.8 mph, 30.2 km/h; standard nsumption: 27.4 m/imp gal, 22.8 m/US gal, 10.3 l x 100 km.

.ECTRICAL EQUIPMENT 44 Ah battery; 770 W alternator.

MENSIONS AND WEIGHT weight: 2,889 lb, 1,310 kg.

ACTICAL INSTRUCTIONS fuel: 98 oct petrol; oil: engine 10 p pt, 12 US pt, 5.7 l.

BMW 728 i

OPTIONALS ZF 3 HP 22 automatic transmission, hydraulic torque converter and planetary gears with 3 ratios (I 2.478, II 1.478, III 1, rev 2.090), max ratio of converter at stall 2, possible manual selection, 3.900 axle ratio, max speed 108 mph, 174 km/h, consumption 25.2 m/imp gal, 21 m/US gal, 11.2 l x 100 km; 66 Ah battery.

525

See 518, except for:

PRICE IN GB: £ 8,890*
PRICE EX WORKS: DM 24,950*

ENGINE 6 cylinders, in line; 152.2 cu in, 2,494 cc (3.39 x 2.82 in, in, 86 x 71.6 mm); compression ratio: 9:1; max power (DIN): 150 hp (110 kW) at 6,000 rpm; max torque (DIN): 154 lb ft, 21.2 kg m (208 Nm) at 4,000 rpm; max engine rpm: 6,000; 60.1 hp/l (44.2 kW/l); 7 crankshaft bearings; valves: overhead, Vee-slanted, rockers; lubrication: 10 imp pt, 12 US pt, 5.7 l; 1 Solex 4A1 downdraught 4-barrel carburettor ; cooling: 21.1 imp pt, 25.4 US pt, 12 l.

TRANSMISSION gearbox ratios: I 3.855, II 2.203. III 1.402, IV 1, rev 4.300; axle ratio: 3.640; tyres: 175 HR x 14.

PERFORMANCE max speed: (I) 32 mph, 51 km/h; (II) 57 mph, 91 km/h; (III) 87 mph, 140 km/h; (IV) 120 mph, 193 km/h; power-weight ratio: 19.8 lb/hp (26.9 lb/kW), 9 kg/hp (12.2 kg/kW); carrying capacity: 1,014 lb, 460 kg; acceleration: standing ¼ mile 17.1 sec; standard consumption: 27.1 m/imp gal, 22.6 m/US gal, 10.4 l x 100 km.

CHASSIS front and rear suspension: anti-roll bar.

BRAKES rear disc (diameter 10.71 in, 27.2 cm).

ELECTRICAL EQUIPMENT 55 Ah battery; 770 W alternator.

DIMENSIONS AND WEIGHT weight: 2,977 lb, 1.350 kg.

PRACTICAL INSTRUCTIONS fuel: 98 oct petrol; oil: engine 10 imp pt, 12 US pt, 5.7 l.

OPTIONALS ZF 3 HP 22 automatic transmission, hydraulic torque converter and planetary gears with 3 ratios (I 2.478, II 1.478, III 1, rev 2.090), max ratio of converter at stall 2, possible manual selection, 3.900 axle ratio, max speed 115 mph, 185 km/h, consumption 24.8 m/imp gal, 20.6 m/US gal, 11.4 l x 100 km.

528 i

See 518, except for:

PRICE IN GB: £ 10,115*
PRICE EX WORKS: DM 29,150*

ENGINE 6 cylinders, in line; 170.1 cu in, 2.788 cc (3.39 x 3.15 in, 86 x 80 mm); compression ratio: 9.3:1; max power (DIN): 184 hp (135 kW) at 5.800 rpm; max torque (DIN): 177 lb ft, 24.5 kg m (240 Nm) at 4,200 rpm; max engine rpm: 6,500: 65.9 hp/l (48.4 kW/l); 7 crankshaft bearings; valves: overhead, Vee-slanted, rockers; lubrication: 10 imp pt, 12 US pt, 5.7 l; cooling: 21.1 imp pt, 25.4 US pt, 12 l. Bosch L-Jetronic injection.

TRANSMISSION axle ratio: 3.900; width of rims: 6"; tyres: 195/70 VR x 14.

PERFORMANCE max speed: 129 mph, 208 km/h; power-weight ratio: 16.9 lb/hp (23 lb/kW), 7.7 kg/hp (10.4 kg/kW); speed in direct drive at 1,000 rpm: 18.8 mph, 30.2 km/h; standard consumption: 26.6 m/imp gal, 22.2 m/US gal, 10.6 l x 100 km.

STEERING servo (standard).

ELECTRICAL EQUIPMENT 44 Ah battery; 910 W alternator.

DIMENSIONS AND WEIGHT weight: 3,109 lb, 1,410 kg.

PRACTICAL INSTRUCTIONS fuel: 98 oct petrol; oil: engine 10 imp pt, 12 US pt, 5.7 l.

OPTIONALS ZF 3 HP 22 automatic transmission, hydraulic torque converter and planetary gears with 3 ratios (I 2.478, II 1.478, III 1, rev 2.090), max ratio of converter at stall 2, possible manual selection, 3.900 axle ratio, max speed 124 mph, 200 km/h, consuption 24.4 m/imp gal, 20.3 m/US gal, 11.6 l x 100 km.

728 i

PRICE IN GB: £ 11,180*
PRICE EX WORKS: DM 33,700

ENGINE front, 4 stroke; 6 cylinders, in line; 170.1 cu in, 2,788 cc (3.39 x 3.15 in, 86 x 80 mm); compression ratio: 9.3:1; max power (DIN): 184 hp (135 kW) at 5,800 rpm; max torque (DIN): 177 lb ft, 24.5 kg m (240 Nm) at 4,200 rpm; max engine rpm:

728 i

6,500; 65.9 hp/l (48.4 kW/l); cast iron block, light alloy head, polispherical combustion chambers; 7 crankshaft bearings; valves: overhead, Vee-slanted, rockers; camshafts: 1, overhead; lubrication: rotary pump, full flow filter, 10 imp pt, 12 US pt, 5.7 l; Bosch L-Jetronic injection; fuel feed: electric pump; water-cooled, 21.1 imp pt, 25.4 US pt, 12 l.

TRANSMISSION driving wheels: rear; clutch: single dry plate (diaphragm), hydraulically controlled; gearbox: mechanical; gears: 4, fully synchronized; ratios: I 3.855, II 2.203, III 1.402, IV 1, rev 4.300; lever: central; final drive: hypoid bevel; axle ratio: 3.640; width of rims: 6''; tyres: 195/70 HR x 14.

PERFORMANCE max speed: 122 mph, 196 km/h; power-weight ratio 17.8 lb/hp (24 lb/kW), 8 kg/hp (11 kg/kW); carrying capacity: 1,036 lb, 470 kg; consumption: 25.2 m/imp gal, 21 m/US gal, 11.2 l x 100 km at 75 mph, 120 km/h.

CHASSIS integral; front suspension: independent, by McPherson, coil springs/telescopic damper struts, auxiliary rubber springs, lower wishbones (trailing links), anti-roll bar; rear: independent, semi-trailing arms, auxiliary rubber springs, coil springs, telescopic dampers.

STEERING ZF, recirculating ball, variable ratio servo; turns lock to lock: 3.80.

BRAKES disc (diameter 11 in, 28 cm), front internal radial fins, 2 X circuits, servo.

ELECTRICAL EQUIPMENT 12 V; 55 Ah battery; 65 A alternator; contactless fully electronic distributor; 4 halogen headlamps.

DIMENSIONS AND WEIGHT wheel base: 110 in, 279 cm; tracks: 59.45 in, 151 cm front, 59.84 in, 152 cm rear; length: 191.30 in, 486 cm; width: 70.90 in, 180 cm; height: 56.30 in, 143 cm; weight: 3,286 lb, 1,490 kg; turning circle: 37.4 ft, 11.4 m; fuel tank: 18.7 imp gal, 22.4 US gal, 85 l.

BODY saloon/sedan; 4 doors; 5 seats, separate front seats, reclining backrests, adjustable built-in headrests; heated rear window.

PRACTICAL INSTRUCTIONS fuel: 98 oct petrol; oil: engine 10 imp pt, 12 US pt, 5.7 l, SAE 20W-50, change every 3,700 miles, 6,000 km - gearbox 2.1 imp pt, 2.5 US pt, 1.2 l, SAE 20W-50, change every 14,800 miles, 24,000 km - final drive 2.6 imp pt, 3.2 US pt, 1.5 l, SAE 90, no change recommended; greasing: none.

OPTIONALS limited slip differential; ZF automatic transmission, hydraulic torque converter and planetary gears with 3 ratios (I 2.478, II 1.478, III 1, rev 2.090), max ratio of converter at stall 2, possible manual selection, max speed 119 mph, 191 km, consumption 22.6 m/imp gal, 18.8 m/US gal, 12.5 l x 100 km; anti-brake-locking system (ABS); light alloy wheels; sunshine roof; air-conditioning.

732 i

See 728 i, except for:

PRICE EX WORKS: DM 37,700*

ENGINE 195.81 cu in, 3,210 cc (3.50 x 3.39 in, 89 x 86 mm); max power (DIN): 197 hp (145 kW) at 5,500 rpm; max torque (DIN): 210 lb ft, 29.1 kg m (285 Nm) at 4,300 rpm; 61.4 hp/l (45.2 kW/l); Bosch L-Jetronic electronic injection.

TRANSMISSION axle ratio: 3.450; width of rims: 6.5''; tyres: 205/70 VR x 14.

PERFORMANCE max speed: 127 mph, 205 km/h; power-weight ratio: 17.1 lb/hp (23.3 lb/kW), 7.8 kg/hp (10.6 kg/kW); speed in direct drive at 1,000 rpm: 19.6 mph, 31.5 km/h; consumption: 24.6 m/imp gal, 20.5 m/US gal, 11.5 l x 100 km at 75 mph, 120 km/h.

ELECTRICAL EQUIPMENT 66 Ah battery; digital engine and electronic ignition.

DIMENSIONS AND WEIGHT weight: 3,374 lb, 1,530 kg.

OPTIONALS ZF automatic transmission, 3.450 axle ratio, max speed 123 mph, 198 km/h, consumption 22.1 m/imp gal, 18.4 m/US gal, 12.8 l x 100 km.

735 i

See 728 i, except for:

PRICE EX WORKS: DM 43,750*

ENGINE 210.7 cu in, 3,453 cc (3.68 x 3.31 in, 93.4 x 84 mm); max power (DIN): 218 hp (160 kW) at 5,200 rpm; max torque (DIN): 229 lb ft, 31.6 kg m (310 Nm) at 4,000 rpm; max engine rpm: 5,600; 63.1 hp/l (46.3 kW/l); lubrication: thermostatic oil cooler.

TRANSMISSION gears: 5, fully synchronized; ratios: I 3.822, II 2.202, III 1.398, IV 1, V 0.812, rev 3.705; axle ratio: 3.250; width of rims: 6.5''; tyres: 205/70 VR x 14.

BMW 745 i

PERFORMANCE max speed: 132 mph, 212 km/h; power-weight ratio: 15.5 lb/hp (21 lb/kW), 7 kg/hp (9.6 kg/kW); consumption: 26.1 m/imp gal, 21.8 m/US gal, 10.8 l x 100 km at 75 mph, 120 km/h.

ELECTRICAL EQUIPMENT 66 Ah battery.

DIMENSIONS AND WEIGHT weight: 3,374 lb, 1,530 kg.

745 i

See 728 i, except for:

PRICE EX WORKS: DM 52,000*

ENGINE 195.81 cu in, 3,210 cc (3.50 x 3.39 in, (3.50 x 3.39 in, 89 x 86 mm); compression ratio: 7:1; max power (DIN): 252 hp (185 kW) at 5,500 rpm; max torque (DIN): 265 lb ft, 36.6 kg m (360 Nm) at 4,200 rpm; 78.5 hp/l (57.6 kW/l); lubrication: thermostatic oil cooler; Bosch L-Jetronic injection with exhaust turbocharger.

TRANSMISSION gears: 5, fully synchronized; ratios: I 3.822, II 2.202, III 1.398, IV 1, V 0.813, rev 3.705; axle ratio: 3.380; width of rims: 6.5''; tyres: 205/70 VR x 14.

PERFORMANCE max speed: above 137 mph, 220 km/h; power-weight ratio: 14 lb/hp (18.9 lb/kW), 6.3 kg/hp (8.6 kg/kW).

BRAKES anti-brake-locking system (ABS) (standard).

ELECTRICAL EQUIPMENT 66 Ah battery.

DIMENSIONS AND WEIGHT weight: 3,528 lb, 1,600 kg.

OPTIONALS ZF automatic transmission, 3.250 or 3.150 ax ratio, max speed above 133 mph, 215 km/h.

628 CSi

PRICE EX WORKS: DM 46,000*

ENGINE front, 4 stroke; 6 cylinders, in line; 170.1 cu in, 2,78 cc (3.39 x 3.15 in, 86 x 80 mm); compression ratio: 9.3:1; ma power (DIN): 184 hp (135 kW) at 5,800 rpm; max torque (DIN 177 lb ft, 24.5 kg m (240 Nm) at 4,200 rpm; max engine rpm 6,500; 65.9 hp/l (48.4 kW/l); cast iron block, light alloy head polispherical combustion chambers; 7 crankshaft bearings valves: overhead, Vee-slanted at 52°, rockers; camshafts: overhead, chain-driven; lubrication: rotary pump, full flow filte 10 imp pt, 12 US pt, 5.7 l; Bosch L-Jetronic injection; fuel feed electric pump; water-cooled, 21.1 imp pt, 25.4 US pt, 12 l.

TRANSMISSION driving wheels: rear; clutch: single dry pla (diaphragm), hydraulically controlled; gearbox: mechanica gears: 4, fully synchronized; ratios: I 3.855, II 2.203, III 1.40 IV 1, rev 4.300; lever: central; final drive: hypoid bevel; ax ratio: 3.450; width of rims: 6''; tyres: 195/70 VR x 14.

PERFORMANCE max speeds: (I) 34 mph, 54 km/h; (II) 59 mp 95 km/h; (III) 93 mph, 150 km/h; (IV) 130 mph, 210 km/ power-weight ratio: 17.4 lb/hp (23.7 lb/kW), 7.9 kg/hp (10.

BMW 633 CSi

g/kW); carrying capacity: 838 lb, 380 kg; acceleration: standg ¼ mile 16.3 sec, 0-50 mph (0-80 km/h) 5.9 sec; speed in rect drive at 1,000 rpm: 20.9 mph, 33.7 km/h; consumption: 7.9 m/imp gal, 23.3 m/US gal, 10.1 l x 100 km at 75 mph, 120 m/h.

HASSIS integral; front suspension: independent, by Mcherson, coil springs/telescopic damper struts, auxiliary rubber prings, anti-roll bar, lower wishbones; rear: independent, semiailing arms, auxiliary rubber springs, coil springs, telescopic ampers.

TEERING ZF, recirculating ball, variable ratio servo; turns ck to lock: 3.50.

RAKES disc (diameter 11 in, 28 cm), internal radial fins, dual rcuit, servo, rear compensator.

LECTRICAL EQUIPMENT 12 V; 66 Ah battery; 770 W alternar; contactless fully electronic, 4 halogen headlamps.

IMENSIONS AND WEIGHT wheel base: 103.15 in, 262 cm; acks: 55.91 in, 142 cm front, 58.27 in, 148 cm rear; length: 87.01 in, 475 cm; width: 67.72 in, 172 cm; height: 53,54 in, 36 cm; ground clearance: 5.51 in, 14 cm; weight: 3.197 lb, 450 kg; turning circle: 36.7 ft, 11.2 m; fuel tank: 15.4 imp gal, 8.5 US gal, 70 l.

ODY coupé; 2 doors; 4 seats, separate front seats, reclining ackrests; tinted glass; heated rear window.

RACTICAL INSTRUCTIONS fuel: 98 oct petrol; oil: engine 10 np pt, 12 US pt, 5.7 l, change every 3,700 miles, 6,000 km - earbox 2.1 imp pt, 2.5 US pt, 1.2 l, SAE 20W-50, change very 14,800 miles, 24,000 km - final drive 2.6 imp pt, 3.2 US t, 1.5 l, SAE 90, no change recommended; greasing: none; parking plug: 175° T30; tappet clearances: inlet 0.010 in, 0.25 m, exhaust 0.012 in, 0.30 mm; valve timing: 6° 50° 50° 6°; re pressure: front 28 psi, 2 atm, rear 27 psi, 1.9 atm.

PTIONALS ZF 3 HP 22 automatic transmission, hydraulic rque converter and planetary gears with 3 ratios (I 2.478, II 478, III 1, rev 2.090), max ratio of converter at stall 2, ossible manual selection, max speed 126 mph, 202 km/h, onsumption 22.8 m/imp gal, 19 m/US gal, 12.4 l x 100 km; mited slip differential; tyres with 7" wide rims.

633 CSi

ee 628 CSi, except for:

RICE IN GB: £ 17,462* (automatic)
RICE IN USA: $ 31,870*

NGINE 195.81 cu in, 3,210 cc (3.50 x 3.39 in, 89 x 86 mm); ax power (DIN): 197 hp, (145 kW) at 5,500 rpm; max torque DIN): 210 lb ft, 29 kg m (284 Nm) at 4,300 rpm; max engine m: 6,000; 61.4 hp/l (45.2 kW/l).

RANSMISSION axle ratio: 3.250.

ERFORMANCE max speeds: (I) 35 mph, 56 km/h; (II) 61 mph, 8 km/h; (III) 95 mph, 153 km/h; (IV) 134 mph, 215 km/h; ower-weight ratio: 16.4 lb/hp (22.3 lb/kW), 7.5 kg/hp (10.1 g/kW); carrying capacity: 838 lb, 380 kg; acceleration: standg ¼ mile 15.8 sec 0-50 mph (0-80 km/h) 5.6 sec; speed in rect drive at 1,000 rpm: 22.2 mph, 35.8 km/h; consumption: 7.1 m/imp gal, 22.6 m/US gal, 10.4 l x 100 km at 75 mph, 120 m/h.

BMW 635 CSi

ELECTRICAL EQUIPMENT 910 W alternator.

DIMENSIONS AND WEIGHT weight: 3,241 lb, 1,470 kg.

OPTIONALS ZF 3 HP 22 automatic transmission, max speed 129 mph, 207 km/h.

635 CSi

See 628 CSi, except for:

PRICE IN GB: £ 18,740*
PRICE EX WORKS: DM 51,900*

ENGINE 210.7 cu in, 3,453 cc (3.68 x 3.31 in, 93.4 x 84 mm); compression ratio: 9.3:1; max power (DIN): 218 hp (160 kW) at 5,200 rpm; max torque (DIN): 229 lb ft, 31.6 kg m (310 Nm) at 4,000 rpm; max engine rpm: 5,600; 63.1 hp/l (46.3 kW/l); Bosch L-Jetronic intermittent injection pump in inlet pipes and automatic starting device.

TRANSMISSION gears 5, fully synchronized; ratios: I 3.717, II 2.403, III 1.766, IV 1.263, V 1, rev 4.234; axle ratio: 3.070; width of rims: 6.5".

PERFORMANCE max speeds: (I) 37 mph, 60 km/h; (II) 58 mph, 94 km/h; (III) 79 mph 127 km/h; (IV) 111 mph, 178 km/h; (V) 138 mph, 222 km/h; power-weight ratio: 15.2 lb/hp, (20.7 lb/kW), 6.9 kg/hp (9.4 kg/kW); speed in direct drive at 1,000 rpm: 25 mph, 40.2 km/h; consumption 27.4 m/imp gal, 22.8 m/US gal, 10.3 l x 100 km at 75 mph, 120 km/h.

BMW M 1

ELECTRICAL EQUIPMENT 910 W alternator.

DIMENSIONS AND WEIGHT weight: 3,307 lb, 1,500 kg.

M 1

ENGINE centre-rear, longitudinal, 4 stroke; 6 cylinders, in line, 210.7 cu in, 3,453 cc (3.68 x 3.31 in, 93.4 x 84 mm); compression ratio: 9:1; max power (DIN): 277 hp (204 kW); at 6,500 rpm; max torque (DIN): 239 lb ft, 32.9 kg m (330 Nm) at 5,000 rpm; max engine rpm: 7,000; 80,2 hp/l (59.1 kW/l); cast iron block, light alloy head, polispherical combustion chambers; 7 crankshaft bearings; valves: 4 per cylinder, overhead, Vee-slanted at 52°, rockers; camshafts: 2, overhead, chain-driven; lubrication: gear pump, full flow filter, dry sump, 14.1 imp pt, 16.9 US pt, 8 l; Kugelfiseher-Bosch mechanical injection, 3 double intake pipes with 6 throttles; fuel feed: 2 electric pumps; water-cooled, 21.1 imp pt, 25.4 US pt, 12 l.

TRANSMISSION driving wheels: rear; clutch: F & S, 2-disc dry, hydraulically controlled; gearbox: ZF, mechanical; gears: 5, fully synchronized; ratios: I 2.420, II 1.610, III 1.140, IV 0.846, V 0.704 rev 2.860; lever: central; final drive: hypoid bevel, limited slip differential; axle ratio: 4.220; width of rims: 7" front, 8" rear; tyres: 205/55 VR x 16 front, 225/50 VR x 16 rear.

PERFORMANCE max speed: 163 mph, 262 km/h; power-weight ratio: 10.3 lb/hp (14 lb/kW), 4.7 kg/hp (6.4 kg/kW); carrying capacity: 661 lb, 300 kg; speed in top at 1,000 rpm: 23.2 mph, 37.4 km/h; consumption: 14.4 m/imp gal, 12 m/US gal, 19.6 l x 100 km (ECE method A 70).

CHASSIS separate steel; front suspension: independent, wishbones, anti-roll bar, coil springs/telescopic dampers (adjustable for height); rear: independent, wishbones, anti-roll bar, coil springs/telescopic dampers (adjustable for height).

STEERING rack-and-pinion.

BRAKES disc (front diameter 11.8 in, 30 cm, rear 11.7 in, 29.7 cm), internal radial fins, dual circuit, servo, rear compensator.

ELECTRICAL EQUIPMENT 12 V; 55 Ah battery; 65 A alternator; Magneti-Marelli contactless fully electronic distributor; 2 halogen headlamps.

DIMENSIONS AND WEIGHT wheel base: 100.8 in, 256 cm; tracks: 61 in, 155 cm front, 62 in, 158 cm rear; length: 171.7 in, 436 cm; width: 71.8 in, 182 cm; height: 44.9 in, 114 cm; ground clearance: 4.90 in, 12 cm; weight: 2,867 lb, 1,300 kg; turning circle: 42.7 ft, 13 m; fuel tanks: 25.5 imp gal, 30.6 US gal, 116 l (2 separate tanks).

BODY coupé, in plastic material; 2 doors; 2 seats; light alloy wheels.

PRACTICAL INSTRUCTIONS fuel: 98 oct petrol; oil: engine 14.1 imp pt, 16.9 US pt, 8 l, SAE 10W-50, change every 3,700 miles, 6,000 km - gearbox and final drive 3 imp pt, 3.6 US pt, 1.7 l, SAE 90, change every 18,600 miles, 30,000 km; greasing: none; tyre pressure: front 34 psi, 2.4 atm, rear 37 psi, 2.6 atm.

VARIATIONS

(Competition version)

ENGINE 213.6 cu in, 3,500 cc (3.70 x 3.31 in, 94 x 84 mm). max power (DIN) 470 hp (345 kW) at 9,000 rpm, max torque (DIN) 282 lb ft, 38.9 kg m (390 Nm) at 7,000 rpm, 134.3 hp/l (98.6 kW/l), front-mounted oil cooler.

M 1

TRANSMISSION width of rims front 11", rear 12.5", 10/23.5 x 16 front, 12.5/25 x 16 rear ryres.
PERFORMANCE max speed 189 mph, 310 km/h, power-weight ratio 4.8 lb/hp (6.5 lb/kW), 2.2 kg/hp (2.9 kg/kW).
DIMENSIONS AND WEIGHT front track 62.8 in, 159 cm, rear track 61.4 in, 156 cm, width 75.7 in, 192 cm, height 43.7 in, 111 cm, weight 2,249 lb, 1,020 kg.

CLASSIC CAR GERMANY FR

Bugatti 35 B / 55

PRICES EX WORKS:	DM
Bugatti 35 B	21,500*
Bugatti 55	23,100*

ENGINE Volkswagen, rear, 4 stroke; 4 cylinders, horizontally opposed; 96.7 cu in, 1,584 cc (3.37 x 2.72 in, 85.5 x 69 mm); compression ratio: 7.5:1; max power (DIN): 50 hp (37 kW) at 4,000 rpm; max torque (DIN): 78 lb ft, 10.8 kg m (106 Nm) at 2,800 rpm; max engine rpm: 4,500; 31.6 hp/l (23.2 kW/l); block with cast iron liners and light alloy fins, light alloy head; 4 crankshaft bearings; valves: overhead, push-rods and rockers; camshafts: 1, central, lower; lubrication: gear pump, filter in sump, oil cooler, 5.3 imp pt, 6.3 US pt, 3 l; 1 Solex 34 PICT 2 downdraught carburettor; fuel feed: mechanical pump; air-cooled.

TRANSMISSION driving wheels: rear; clutch; single dry plate; gearbox: mechanical; gears: 4, fully synchronized; ratios: I 3.780, II 2.060, III 1.260, IV 0.930, rev 4.010; lever: central; final drive: spiral bevel; axle ratio: 4.375; width of rims: 4.5"; tyres: 155 x 15.

PERFORMANCE max speed: about 84 mph, 135 km/h; power-weight ratio: 33.5 lb/hp (45.2 lb/kW), 15.2 kg/hp (20.5 kg/kW); carrying capacity: 442 lb, 200 kg; speed in top at 1,000 rpm: 21.7 mph, 35 km/h; consumption: 30.7 m/imp gal, 25.6 m/US gal, 9.2 l x 100 km.

CHASSIS backbone platform; front suspension: independent, twin swinging longitudinal trailing arms, transverse laminated torsion bars, anti-roll bar, telescopic dampers; rear: independent, semi-trailing arms, transverse compensating torsion bar, telescopic dampers.

STEERING worm and roller, telescopic damper; turns lock to lock: 2.60.

BRAKES front disc (diameter 10.91 in, 27.7 cm), rear drum; lining area: front 12.4 sq in, 80 sq cm, rear 55.5 sq in, 358 sq cm, total 67.9 sq in, 438 sq cm.

ELECTRICAL EQUIPMENT 12 V; 36 Ah battery; 50 A alternator; Bosch distributor; 2 headlamps.

DIMENSIONS AND WEIGHT wheel base: 94.50 in, 240 cm; tracks: 56 in, 142 cm front, 57 in, 144 cm rear; length: 153.54 in, 390 cm; width: 64.96 in, 165 cm; height: 50.39 in, 128 cm; ground clerance: 9 in, 22.9 cm; weight: 1,676 lb, 760 kg; fuel tank: 8.8 imp gal, 10.6 US gal, 40 l.

BODY sports, in plastic material; no doors; 2 seats.

PRACTICAL INSTRUCTIONS fuel: 91 oct petrol; oil: engine 4.4 imp pt, 5.3 US pt, 2.5 l, SAE 10W-20 (winter) 20W-30 (summer), change every 3,100 miles, 5,000 km - gearbox and final drive 5.3 imp pt, 6.3 US pt, 3 l, SAE 90, change every 31,000 miles, 50,000 km; greasing: every 6,200 miles, 10,000 km, 4 points; sparking plug: 175°; tappet clearances: inlet 0.004 in, 0.10 mm, exhaust 0.004 in, 0.10 mm; valve timing: 7°30' 37° 44°30' 4°.

OPTIONALS 3-speed automatic transmission; 185/70 x 15 or F 78 x 15 tyres; tonneau cover; wire wheels.

Blower Phaeton

PRICE EX WORKS: DM 25,500*

ENGINE Volkswagen, rear, 4 stroke; 4 cylinders, horizontally opposed; 96.7 cu in, 1,584 cc (3.37 x 2.72 in, 85.5 x 69 mm); compression ratio: 7.5:1; max power (DIN): 50 hp (37 kW) at 4,00 rpm; max torque (DIN): 78 lb ft, 10.8 kg m (106 Nm) at 2,800 rpm; max engine rpm: 4,500; 31.6 hp/l (23.2 kW/l); block with cast iron liners and light alloy fins, light alloy head; 4 crankshaft bearings; valves; overhead, push-rods and rockers; camshafts: 1, central, lower; lubrication: gear pump, filter in sump, oil cooler, 5.3 imp pt, 6.3 US pt, 3 l; 1 Solex 34 PICT 2 downdraught carburettor; fuel feed: mechanical pump; air-cooled.

CLASSIC CAR Bugatti 35 B

TRANSMISSION driving wheels: rear; clutch: single dry plate; gearbox: mechanical; gears: 4, fully synchronized; ratios: I 3.780, II 2.060, III 1.260, IV 0.930, rev 4.010; lever; central; final drive: spiral bevel; axle ratio: 4.375; width of rims: 4.5"; tyres: 155 x 15.

PERFORMANCE max speed: about 79 mph, 127 km/h; power-weight ratio: 40.6 lb/hp (54.9 lb/kW), 18.4 kg/hp (24.9 kg/kW); carrying capacity: 706 lb, 320 kg; speed in top at 1.000 rpm: 21.7 mph, 35 km/h; consumption: 30.7 m/imp gal, 25.6 m/US gal, 9.2 l x 100 km.

CHASSIS backbone platform; front suspension: independent, twin swinging longitudinal trailing arms, transverse laminated torsion bars, anti-roll bar, telescopic dampers; rear: independent, semi-trailing arms, transverse compensating torsion bar, telescopic dampers.

STEERING worm and roller, telescopic damper; turns lock to lock: 2.60.

BRAKES front disc (diameter 10.91 in, 27.7 cm), rear drum; lining area: front 12.4 sq in, 80 sq cm, rear 55.5 sq in, 358 sq cm, total 67.9 sq in 438 sq cm.

ELECTRICAL EQUIPMENT 12 V; 36 Ah battery; 50 A alternator; Bosch distributor; 2 headlamps.

DIMENSIONS AND WEIGHT wheel base: 108.66 in, 276 cm; tracks: 56 in, 142 cm front, 57 in, 144 cm rear; length: 161.42 in, 410 cm; width: 60.24 in, 153 cm; height: 59.06 in, 150 cm; ground clearance: 9 in, 22.9 cm; weight: 2,029 lb, 920 kg; fue[l] tank 8.8 imp gal, 10.6 US gal, 40 l.

BODY sports, in plastic material; 4 doors; 4 seats.

PRACTICAL INSTRUCTIONS fuel: 91 oct petrol; oil: engine 4. imp pt, 5.3 US pt, 2.5 l, SAE 10W-20 (winter) 20W-30 (sum mer), change every 3,100 miles, 5,000 km - gearbox and fina drive 5.3 imp pt, 6.3 US pt, 3 l, SAE 90, change every 31,00 miles, 50,000 km; greasing: every 6,200 miles, 10,000 km, points; sparking plug: 175°; tappet clearances: inlet 0.004 ir 0.10 mm, exhaust 0.004 in, 0.10 mm; valve timing: 7°30' 37 44°30' 4°.

OPTIONALS 3-speed automatic transmission; 185/70 x 15 or 78 x 15 tyres; tonneau cover; wire wheels.

Gepard SS 100

PRICE EX WORKS: DM 25,000*

ENGINE Volkswagen, rear, 4 stroke; 4 cylinders, horizontall opposed; 96.7 cu in, 1,584 cc (3.37 x 2.72 in, 85.5 x 69 mm) compression ratio: 7.5:1; max power (DIN): 50 hp (37 kW) a 4,000 rpm; max torque (DIN): 78 lb ft, 10.8 kg m (106 Nm) a 2,800 rpm; max engine rpm: 4,500; 31.6 hp/l (23.2 kW/l); bloc with cast iron liners and light alloy fins, light alloy head; crankshaft bearings; valves: overhead, push-rods and rockers

CLASSIC CAR Blower Phaeton

camshafts: 1, central, lower; lubrication: gear pump, filter in sump, oil cooler, 5.3 imp pt, 6.3 US pt, 3 l; 1 Solex 34 PICT 2 downdraught carburettor; fuel feed: mechanical pump; air-cooled.

TRANSMISSION driving wheels: rear; clutch: single dry plate; gearbox: mechanical; gears: 4, fully synchronized; ratios: I 3.780, II 2.060, III 1.260, IV 0.930, rev 4.010; lever: central; final drive: spiral bevel; axle ratio: 4.375; width of rims: 4.5"; tyres 155 x 15.

PERFORMANCE max speed: 82 mph, 132 km/h; power-weight ratio: 37.9 lb/hp (51.2 lb/kW), 17.2 kg/hp (23.2 kg/kW); carrying capacity: 442 lb, 200 kg; speed in top at 1,000 rpm: 21.7 mph, 35 km/h; consumption: 30.7 m/imp gal, 25.6 m/US gal, 9.2 l x 100 km.

CHASSIS backbone platform; front suspension: independent, twin swinging longitudinal trailing arms, transverse laminated torsion bars, anti roll bar, telescopic dampers; rear: independent, semi-trailing arms, transverse compensating torsion bar, telescopic dampers.

STEERING worm and roller, telescopic damper; turns lock to lock: 2.60.

BRAKES front disc (diameter 10.91 in, 27.7 cm), rear drum; lining area: front 12.4 sq in, 80 sq cm, rear 55.5 sq in, 358 sq cm, total 67.9 sq in, 438 sq cm.

ELECTRICAL EQUIPMENT 12 V, 36 Ah battery; 50 A alternator: Bosch distributor; 2 headlamps.

DIMENSIONS AND WEIGHT wheel base: 108.66 in, 276 cm; tracks: 56 in, 142 cm front, 57 in, 144 cm rear; length: 159.45 in, 405 cm; width: 62.99 in, 160 cm; height: 48.82 in, 124 cm; ground clearance: 9 in, 22.9 cm; weight: 1,896 lb, 860 kg: fuel tank: 8.8 imp gal, 10.6 US gal, 40 l.

BODY sports, in plastic material; 2 doors; 2 seats.

PRACTICAL INSTRUCTIONS fuel: 91 oct petrol; oil: engine 4.4 imp pt, 5.3 US pt, 2.5 l, SAE 10W-20 (winter) 20W-30 (summer), change every 3,100 miles, 5,000 km - gearbox and final drive 5.3 imp pt, 6.3 US pt, 3 l, SAE 90, change every 31,000 miles, 50,000 km; greasing: every 6,200 miles, 10,000 km, 4 points; sparking plug: 175°; tappet clearances: inlet 0.004 in, 0.10 mm, exhaust 0.004 in, 0.10 mm; valve timing: 7°30' 37° 44°30' 4°.

OPTIONALS 3-speed automatic transmission; 185/70 x 15 or F 78 x 15 tyres; tonneau cover; wire wheels.

CLASSIC CAR Gepard SS 100

FIBERFAB GERMANY FR

Sherpa

PRICE EX WORKS: DM 13,400*

ENGINE Citroën, front 4 stroke; 2 cylinders, horizontally opposed: 36.4 cu in, 597 cc (2.91 x 2.76 in, 74 x 70 mm); compression ratio: 8.5:1; max power (DIN): 32 hp (24 kW) at 5,750 rpm; max torque (DIN): 30 lb ft, 4.2 kg m (41 Nm) at 4,000 rpm; max engine rpm: 6,750; 53.6 hp/l (39.4 kW/l); light alloy block and head, dry liners, light alloy sump, hemispherical combustion chambers; 2 crankshaft bearings; valves: overhead, Vee-slanted at 70°, push-rods and rockers; camshafts: 1, central, lower; lubrication: rotary pump, filter in sump, oil cooler, 4.4 imp pt, 5.3 US pt, 2.5 l; 1 Solex 34 PICS 6 downdraught carburettor; fuel feed: mechanical pump; air-cooled.

TRANSMISSION driving wheels: front (double) homokinetic joints; clutch: single dry plate; gearbox: mechanical; gears: 4, fully synchronized; tyres: Michelin X 135 x 15.

PERFORMANCE max speed: 73 mph, 118 km/h; power-weight ratio: 43 lb/hp, (57.3 lb/kW), 19.5 kg/hp (26 kg/kW); carrying capacity: 717 lb, 325 kg; consumption: 46.3 m/imp gal, 38.6 m/US gal, 6.1 l x 100 km.

CHASSIS platform; front suspension: independent, swinging leading arms, 2 friction dampers, 2 inertia-type patter dampers; rear: independent, swinging longitudinal trailing arms linked to front suspension by longitudinal coil springs, 2 inertia-type patter dampers, 2 telescopic dampers.

BRAKES front disc, rear drum.

ELECTRICAL EQUIPMENT 12 V; 33 Ah battery; 390 W alternator; 2 headlamps.

DIMENSIONS AND WEIGHT wheel base: 94.49 in, 240 cm; front and rear track: 49.61 in, 126 cm; length: 138.58 in, 352 cm; width: 59.84 in, 152 cm; height: 62.99 in, 160 cm; ground clearance: 11.81 in, 30 cm; weight: 1,378 lb, 625 kg; turning circle: 35.1 ft, 10.7 m; fuel tank: 44 imp gal, 52.9 US gal, 25 l.

BODY open, in plastic material; 2+1 doors; 4 seats, separate reclining front seats, adjustable height, built-in headrests on front seats; canvas roof; folding rear seat.

FIBERFAB Sherpa

FIBERFAB Sherpa

FORD GERMANY FR

Fiesta Series

PRICES EX WORKS:	DM
1 Limousine	9,605*
2 L Limousine	10,231*
3 S Limousine	11,582*
4 Ghia Limousine	12,369*

Power team:	Standard for:	Optional for:
40 hp	1,2,4	—
45 hp	—	1,2,4
53 hp	3	1,2,4
66 hp	—	3,4

40 hp power team

ENGINE front, transverse, 4 stroke; 4 cylinders, vertical, in line; 58.4 cu in, 957 cc (2.91 x 2.19 in, 74 x 55.7 mm); compression ratio: 8.3:1; max power (DIN): 40 hp (29 kW) at 5,500 rpm; max torque (DIN): 47 lb ft, 6.5 kg m (64 Nm) at 2,700 rpm; max engine rpm: 5,700; 41.8 hp/l (30.7 kW/l); cast iron block and head; 3 crankshaft bearings; valves: overhead, in line, push-rods and rockers; camshafts: 1, side, chain-driven; lubrication: gear pump, full flow filter (cartridge), 5.6 imp pt, 6.8 US pt, 3.2 l; 1 Ford downdraught single barrel carburettor; fuel feed: mechanical pump; semi-sealed circuit cooling, expansion tank, 8.8 imp pt, 10.6 US pt, 5 l, electric fan.

40 HP POWER TEAM

TRANSMISSION driving wheels: front; clutch: single dry plate (diaphragm); gearbox: mechanical, in unit with final drive; gears: 4, fully synchronized; ratios: I 3.583, II 2.050, III 1.346, IV 0.959, rev 3.769; lever: central; final drive: spiral bevel; axle ratio: 4.060; width of rims: 4" - Ghia 4.5"; tyres: 145 SR x 12.

PERFORMANCE max speed: 81 mph, 130 km/h; power-weight ratio: 40.2 lb/hp (54.7 lb/kW), 18.2 kg/hp (24.8 kg/kW); carrying capacity: 948 lb, 430 kg; acceleration: 0-50 mph (0-80 km/h) 14.2 sec; speed in top at 1,000 rpm: 15.8 mph, 25.4 km/h; consumption: 34.4 m/imp gal, 28.7 m/US gal, 8.2 l x 100 km at 75 mph, 120 km/h.

CHASSIS integral; front suspension: independent, by McPherson, coil springs/telescopic damper struts, lower wishbones (trailing links); rear: rigid axle, swinging longitudinal trailing arms, upper oblique torque arms, Panhard rod, coil springs, telescopic dampers.

STEERING rack-and-pinion; turns lock to lock: 3.40.

BRAKES front disc (diameter 8.71 in, 22.1 cm), rear drum, rear compensator, servo (standard for S and Ghia only); lining area: front 18.6 sq in, 120 sq cm, rear 26.4 sq in, 169.9 sq cm, total 45 sq in, 289.9 sq cm.

ELECTRICAL EQUIPMENT 12 V; 35 Ah battery; 45 A alternator; Motorcraft distributor; 2 headlamps (2 halogen headlamps standard for Ghia only).

DIMENSIONS AND WEIGHT wheel base: 90.16 in, 229 cm; tracks: 52.36 in, 133 cm front, 51.97 in, 132 cm rear; length: 140.16 in, 356 cm; width: 61.81 in, 157 cm; height: 53.54 in, 136 cm; weight: ground clearance: 5.51 in, 14 cm; weight: 1,610 lb, 730 kg; turning circle: 32.1 ft, 9.8 m; fuel tank: 7.5 imp gal, 9 US gal, 34 l.

BODY saloon/sedan; 2+1 doors; 5 seats, separate front seats; folding rear seat; light alloy wheels (standard for Ghia only).

PRACTICAL INSTRUCTIONS fuel: 90 oct petrol; oil: engine 4.8 imp pt, 5.7 US pt, 2.7 l, change every 6,200 miles, 10,000 km - gearbox and final drive 3.9 imp pt, 4.7 US pt, 2.2 l, change every 6,200 miles, 10,000 km; valve timing: 21° 55° 70° 22°.

OPTIONALS 155 SR x 12 tyres with 4.5" wide rims; servo brake; headrests on front seats; tinted glass; light alloy wheels; sunshine roof; rear window wiper-washer; headlamps with wiper-washers; halogen headlamps; fog lamps; metallic spray; Touring equipment (except for Ghia).

45 hp power team

See 40 hp power team, except for:

ENGINE compression ratio: 9:1; max power (DIN): 45 hp (33 kW) at 6,000 rpm; max torque (DIN): 48 lb ft, 6.6 kg m (65 Nm) at 3,300 rpm; max engine rpm: 6,500; 47 hp/l (34.6 kW/l).

TRANSMISSION axle ratio: 4.290.

PERFORMANCE max speed: 85 mph, 137 km/h; power-weight ratio: 35.8 lb/hp (48.6 lb/kW), 16.2 kg/hp (22 kg/kW); speed in top at 1,000 rpm: 14.9 mph, 24 km/h; consumption: 34 m/imp gal, 28.3 m/US gal, 8.3 l x 100 km at 75 mph, 120 km/h.

PRACTICAL INSTRUCTIONS fuel: 97 oct petrol.

53 hp power team

See 40 hp power team, except for:

ENGINE 68.2 cu in, 1,117 cc (2.91 x 2.56 in, 74 x 65 mm); compression ratio: 9:1; max power (DIN): 53 hp (39 kW) at 5,700 rpm; max torque (DIN): 59 lb ft, 8.2 kg m (80 Nm) at 3,000 rpm; max engine rpm: 6,000; 47.4 hp/l (34.9 kW/l); semi-sealed circuit cooling, expansion tank, 8.8 imp pt, 10.6 US pt, 5 l, electric thermostatic fan.

TRANSMISSION width of rims: 4.5".

PERFORMANCE max speed: 90 mph, 145 km/h; power-weight ratio: 30.4 lb/hp (41.3 lb/kW), 13.8 kg/hp (18.7 kg/kW); consumption: 33.6 m/imp gal, 28 m/US gal, 8.4 l x 100 km at 75 mph, 120 km/h.

CHASSIS rear suspension: anti-roll bar.

PRACTICAL INSTRUCTIONS fuel: 97 oct petrol.

66 hp power team

See 40 hp power team, except for:

ENGINE 79.2 cu in, 1,297 cc (3.19 x 2.48 in, 81 x 63 mm); compression ratio: 9.2:1; max power (DIN): 66 hp (49 kW) at

FORD Fiesta L Limousine

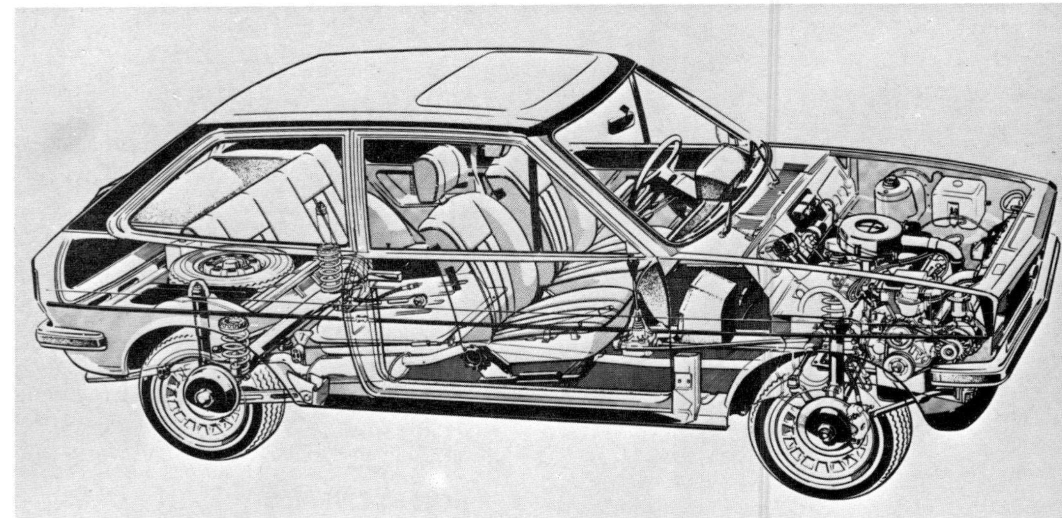

FORD Fiesta Ghia Limousine

FORD Escort Ghia Limousine

,600 rpm; max torque (DIN): 70 lb ft, 9.6 kg m (94 Nm) at ,250 rpm; max engine rpm: 6,000; 50.8 hp/l (37.9 kW/l); 1 Veber downdraught single barrel carburettor; semi-sealed cir- uit cooling, expansion tank, 10.9 imp pt, 13.1 US pt, 6.2 l, lectric thermostatic fan.

TRANSMISSION axle ratio: 3.840; width of rims: 4.5"; tyres: 55 SR x 12.

PERFORMANCE max speed: 98 mph, 158 km/h; power-weight atio: 25.9 lb/hp (35.2 lb/kW), 11.7 kg/hp (15.9 kg/kW); speed in op at 1,000 rpm: 16.3 mph, 26.3 km/h; consumption: 33.6 n/imp gal, 28 m/US gal, 8.4 l x 100 km at 75 mph, 120 km/h.

CHASSIS rear suspension: anti-roll bar.

DIMENSIONS AND WEIGHT weight: 1,709 lb, 775 kg.

PRACTICAL INSTRUCTIONS fuel: 97 oct petrol.

Escort Series

PRICES EX WORKS:	DM
1 2-dr Limousine	10,372*
2 4-dr Limousine	10,937*
3 2+1-dr Turnier	11,134*
4 L 2-dr Limousine	10,917*
5 L 4-dr Limousine	11,482*
6 L 2+1-dr Turnier	11,729*
7 GL 2-dr Limousine	12,047*
8 GL 4-dr Limousine	12,612*
9 GL 2+1-dr Turnier	12,849*
0 Ghia 2-dr Limousine	14,236*
1 Ghia 4-dr Limousine	14,801*
2 Sport 2-dr Limousine	12,440*
3 Sport 4-dr Limousine	13,005*
4 RS 2000 2-dr Limousine	15,931*

Power team:	Standard for:	Optional for:
46 hp	—	1,3,4
54 hp	1 to 9	10,11
60 hp	—	1,2,4,5,7,8
73 hp	10,11	4,5,7,8,12,13
86 hp	12,13	10,11
10 hp	14	—

46 hp power team

ENGINE front, 4 stroke; 4 cylinders, vertical, in line; 67 cu in, ,098 cc (3.19 x 2.10 in, 81 x 53.3 mm); compression ratio: 8:1; nax power (DIN): 46 hp (34 kW) at 5,750 rpm; max torque DIN): 52 lb ft, 7.2 kg m (71 Nm) at 3,000 rpm; max engine rpm: ,000; 41.9 hp/l (30.9 kW/l); cast iron block and head; 5 rankshaft bearings; valves: overhead, in line, push-rods and ockers; camshafts: 1, side; lubrication: gear pump, full flow ilter (cartridge), 5.6 imp pt, 6.8 US pt, 3.2 l; 1 Ford down- raught single barrel carburettor; fuel feed: mechanical pump; vater-cooled, 8.8 imp pt, 10.6 US pt, 5 l.

TRANSMISSION driving wheels: rear; clutch: single dry plate diaphragm); gearbox: mechanical; gears: 4, fully synchronized; atios: I 3.656, II 2.185, III 1.425, IV 1, rev 4.235; lever: central; inal drive: hypoid bevel; axle ratio: 4.110; width of rims: 4.5"; yres: 155 SR x 13.

PERFORMANCE max speeds: (I) 24 mph, 38 km/h; (II) 41 mph, 66 km/h; (III) 62 mph, 100 km/h; (IV) 81 mph, 130 km/h; power-weight ratio: L 2-dr limousines 42.2 hp/l (57 lb/kW), 19.1 kg/hp (25.9 kg/kW); carrying capacity: 970 lb, 440 kg; speed in direct drive at 1,000 rpm: 16 mph, 25.7 km/h; consumption: 25.7 m/imp gal, 21.4 m/US gal, 11 l x 100 km (Turnier 28.2 n/imp gal, 23.5 m/US gal, 10 l x 100 km) at 75 mph, 120 km/h.

CHASSIS integral; front suspension: independent, by Mc- Pherson, coil springs/telescopic damper struts, anti-roll bar; ear: rigid axle, semi-elliptic leafsprings, torque trailing arms, anti-roll bar, telescopic dampers.

STEERING rack-and-pinion; turns lock to lock: 3.50.

BRAKES front disc (diameter 9.72 in, 24.7 cm), rear drum, servo, lining area: front 23.4 sq in, 151.2 sq cm, rear 36.4 sq in, 235 sq cm, total 59.8 sq in, 386.2 sq cm.

ELECTRICAL EQUIPMENT 12 V; 35 Ah battery; 45 A alternator (Turnier 35 A); Motorcraft distributor; 2 headlamps.

DIMENSIONS AND WEIGHT wheel base: 94.88 in, 241 cm; tracks: 50.78 in, 129 cm front, 51.57 in, 131 cm rear; length: 156.69 in, 398 cm - Turnier 159.84 in, 406 cm; width: 62.99 in, 160 cm - Turnier 61.42 in, 156 cm; height: 55.12 in, 140 cm - Turnier 55.51 in, 141 cm; ground clearance: 4.72 in, 12 cm; weight: 2-dr Limousine 1,940 lb, 880 kg - L 2-dr Limousine 2,007 lb, 910 kg - Turnier 2,029 lb, 920 kg; turning circle: 31.2 ft, 9.5 m; fuel tank: 9 imp gal, 108 US gal, 41 l.

BODY 4-5 seats, separate front seats.

PRACTICAL INSTRUCTIONS fuel: 90 oct petrol; oil: engine 4.8 imp pt, 5.7 US pt, 2.7 l, SAE 10W-30, change every 6,200 miles, 10,000 km - gearbox 1.6 imp pt, 1.9 US pt, 0.9 l, SAE 80, no change recommended - final drive 2.6 imp pt, 3.2 US pt, 1.5 l, SAE 90, no change recommended; greasing: none; tappet

FORD Escort RS 2000 Limousine

clearances: inlet 0.010 in, 0.25 mm, exhaust 0.017 in, 0.43 mm; valve timing: 17° 51° 51° 17°; tyre pressure: front 24 psi, 1.7 atm, rear 24 psi, 1.7 atm.

OPTIONALS 5" wide rims; 55 Ah battery; halogen headlamps.

54 hp power team

See 46 hp power team, except for:

ENGINE 79.2 cu in, 1,298 cc (3.19 x 2.48 in, 81 x 63 mm); max power (Din): 54 hp (40 kW) at 5,750 rpm; max torque (DIN): 63 lb ft, 8.7 kg m (85 Nm) at 3,000 rpm; 41.6 hp/l (30.6 kW/l).

TRANSMISSION axle ratio: 3.890; width of rims: 5".

PERFORMANCE max speed: 87 mph, 140 km/h; power-weight ratio: 4-dr limousines 37.4 lb/hp (50.8 lb/kW), 16.9 kg/hp (23 kg/kW) - Ghia 4-dr Limousine 38.4 lb/hp (52.2 lb/kW), 17.4 kg/hp (23.7 kg/kW); carrying capacity: Ghia models 937 lb, 425 kg; speed in direct drive at 1,000 rpm: 16.9 mph, 27.2 km/h; consumption: 30.4 m/imp gal, 25.3 m/US gal, 9.3 l x 100 km at 75 mph, 120 km/h.

ELECTRICAL EQUIPMENT 45 A alternator and halogen head- lamps standard for GL Turnier and GL limousines.

DIMENSIONS AND WEIGHT weight: 2-dr limousines 1,951 lb, 885 kg - 4-dr limousines 2,018 lb, 915 kg - Turnier models 2,029 lb, 920 kg - Ghia 2-dr Limousine 2,007 lb, 910 kg - Ghia 4-dr Limousine 2,073 lb, 940 kg.

FORD Escort RS 2000 Limousine

60 hp power team

See 46 hp power team, except for:

ENGINE 79.2 cu in, 1,298 cc (3.19 x 2.48 in, 81 x 63 mm); compression ratio: 9.2:1; max power (DIN): 60 hp (44 kW) at 5,750 rpm; max torque (DIN): 68 lb ft, 9.4 kg m (92 Nm) at 3,000 rpm; 46.2 hp/l (33.9 kW/l); lubrication: oil cooler.

TRANSMISSION gearbox: Ford C3 automatic transmission, hydraulic torque converter and planetary gears with 3 ratios, max ratio of converter at stall 2, possible manual selection; ratios: I 2.474, II 1.474, III 1, rev 2.111; axle ratio: 3.890; width of rims: 5.5".

PERFORMANCE max speed: 88 mph, 141 km/h; power-weight ratio: 4-dr limousines 33.6 lb/hp (45.8 lb/kW), 15.2 kg/hp (20.8 kg/kW) - GL 4-dr Limousine 34.5 lb/hp (47.1 lb/kW), 15.7 kg/hp (21.4 kg/kW); speed in direct drive at 1,000 rpm: 15.3 mph, 24.6 km/h; consumption: 28.8 m/imp gal, 24 m/US gal, 9.8 l x 100 km at 75 mph, 120 km/h

ELECTRICAL EQUIPMENT 44 Ah battery.

DIMENSIONS AND WEIGHT weight: 2-dr limousines 1,951 lb, 885 kg - 4-dr limousines 2,018 lb, 915 kg.

PRACTICAL INSTRUCTIONS fuel: 97 oct petrol.

73 hp power team

See 46 hp power team, except for:

ENGINE 79.2 cu in, 1,298 cc (3.19 x 2.48 in, 81 x 63 mm); compression ratio: 9.2:1; max power (DIN): 73 hp (54 kW) at 5,750 rpm; max torque (DIN): 72 lb ft, 10 kg m (98 Nm) at 4,500 rpm; 56.2 hp/l (41.6 kW/l); 1 Weber downdraught twin barrel carburettor.

TRANSMISSION gearbox ratios: I 3.337, II 1.995, III 1.418, IV 1, rev 3.867; width of rims: 5.5"; tyres: Sport models 175/70 SR x 13.

PERFORMANCE max speed: 97 mph, 156 km/h; power-weight ratio: Ghia 4-dr limousine 28.8 lb/hp (39 lb/kW), 13 kg/hp (17.7 kg/kW) - Sport 4-dr Limousine 27.6 lb/hp (37.4 lb/kW), 12.5 kg/hp (16.9 kg/kW); carrying capacity: Ghia models 937 lb, 425 kg - Sport models 970 lb, 440 kg; consumption: 30.1 m/imp gal, 25 m/US gal, 9.4 x 100 km at 75 mph, 120 km/h.

BRAKES lining area: front 23.4 sq in, 151.2 sq cm, rear 47.3 sq in, 305.2 sq cm, total 70.7 sq in, 456.4 sq cm.

ELECTRICAL EQUIPMENT 2 halogen headlamps.

DIMENSIONS AND WEIGHT length: Sport models 160.63 in, 408 cm; height: Sport models 54.33 in, 138 cm; weight: Ghia 2-dr Limousine 2,040 lb, 925 kg - Ghia 4-dr Limousine 2,106 lb, 955 kg - Sport 2-dr Limousine 1,951 lb, 885 kg - Sport 4-dr Limousine 2,018 lb, 915 kg.

PRACTICAL INSTRUCTIONS fuel: 97 oct petrol.

86 hp power team

See 46 hp power team, except for:

ENGINE 97.6 cu in, 1,599 cc (3.19 x 3.06 in, 81 x 77.6 mm); compression ratio: 9:1; max power (DIN): 86 hp (63 kW) at

86 HP POWER TEAM

5,750 rpm; max torque (DIN): 92 lb/ft 12.7 kg m (124 Nm) at 3,600 rpm; 53.8 hp/l (39.4 kW/l); 1 Weber downdraught twin barrel carburettor; cooling: 9.5 imp pt, 11.4 US pt, 5.4 l.

TRANSMISSION gearbox ratios: I 3.337, II 1.995, III 1.418, IV 1, rev 3.867; axle ratio: 3.540; width of rims: 5.5"; tyres: Sport models 175/70 SR x 13.

PERFORMANCE max speed: 102 mph, 165 km/h; power-weight ratio: Sport 4-dr Limousine 23.8 lb/hp (32.5 lb/kW), 10.8 kg/hp (14.7 kg/kW) - Ghia 4-dr Limousine 24.5 lb/hp (33.4 lb/kW), 11.1 kg/hp (15.1 kg/kW); speed in direct drive at 1,000 rpm: 18.5 mph, 29.8 km/h; consumption: 32.1 m/imp gal, 26.7 m/US gal, 8.8 l x 100 km at 75 mph, 120 km/h.

BRAKES lining area: front 23.4 sq in, 151.2 sq cm, rear 47.3 sq in, 305.2 sq cm, total 70.7 sq in, 456.4 sq cm.

ELECTRICAL EQUIPMENT 2 halogen headlamps.

DIMENSIONS AND WEIGHT length: Sport models 160.63 in, 408 cm; height: Sport models 54.33 in, 138 cm; weight: Sport 2-dr Limousine 1,985 lb, 900 kg - Sport 4-dr Limousine 2,051 lb, 930 kg - Ghia 2-dr Limousine 2,040 lb, 925 kg - Ghia 4-dr Limousine 2,106 lb, 955 kg.

PRACTICAL INSTRUCTIONS fuel: 97 oct petrol.

OPTIONALS Ford C3 automatic transmission hydraulic torque converter and planetary gears with 3 ratios (I 2.474, II 1.474, III 1, rev 2.111), max ratio of converter at stall 2, possible manual selection, max speed 99 mph, 160 km/h, consumption 30.7 m/imp gal, 25.6 m/US gal, 9.2 l x 100 km at 75 mph, 120 km/h, oil cooler, 44 Ah battery.

110 hp power team

See 46 hp power team, except for:

ENGINE 121.6 cu in, 1,993 cc (3.57 x 3.03 in, 90.8 x 76.9 mm); compression ratio: 9.2:1; max power (DIN): 110 hp (81 kW) at 5,500 rpm; max torque (DIN): 119 lb ft, 16.4 kg m (161 Nm) at 3,750 rpm; max engine rpm: 6,500; 55.2 hp/l (40.6 kW/l); valves: overhead, Vee-slanted, rockers; camshafts: 1, overhead, cogged belt; lubrication: 6.7 imp pt, 8 US pt, 3.8 l; 1 Weber downdraught twin barrel carburettor; water-cooled, 10.7 imp pt, 12.9 US pt, 6.1 l, electric thermostatic fan.

TRANSMISSION gearbox ratios: I 3.656, II 1.970, III 1.370, IV 1, rev 3.660; axle ratio: 3.540; width of rims: 5.5"; tyres: 175/70 HR x 13.

PERFORMANCE max speed: 112 mph, 180 km/h; power-weight ratio: 18.6 lb/hp (25.2 lb/kW), 8.4 kg/hp (11.4 kg/kW); carrying capacity: 882 lb, 400 kg; consumption: 32.5 m/imp gal, 27 m/US gal, 8.7 l x 100 km.

BRAKES lining area: front 23.4 sq in, 151.2 sq cm, rear 47.3 sq in, 305.2 sq cm, total 70.07 sq in, 456.4 sq cm.

ELECTRICAL EQUIPMENT Ah battery (standard); 55 A alternator; 4 halogen headlamps.

DIMENSIONS AND WEIGHT length: 163.39 in, 415 cm; height: 55.51 in, 141 cm; ground clearance: 5.51 in, 14 cm; weight: 2,040 lb, 925 kg; turning circle: 32.1 ft 9.8 m.

FORD Taunus 2.3 Ghia Limousine

BODY built-in headrests; heated rear window.

PRACTICAL INSTRUCTIONS fuel: 97 oct petrol; oil: engine 5.8 imp pt, 7 US pt, 3.3 l.

Taunus Series

PRICES EX WORKS:	DM
1 2-dr Limousine	12,295*
2 4-dr Limousine	12,880*
3 4+1-dr Turnier	13,505*
4 L 2-dr Limousine	13,540*
5 L 4-dr Limousine	14,125*
6 L 4+1-dr Turnier	14,750*
7 GL 2-dr Limousine	14,605*
8 GL 4-dr Limousine	15,190*
9 GL 4+1-dr Turnier	15,815*
10 Ghia 2-dr Limousine	16,545*
11 Ghia 4-dr Limousine	17,130*

Power team:	Standard for:	Optional for:
59 hp	1 to 3	4 to 6
70 hp	—	1 to 9
73 hp	4 to 9	1,2,3,10,11
90 hp	10,11	4 to 9
101 hp	—	4 to 11
114 hp	—	4 to 11

FORD Taunus 2.3 Ghia Limousine

59 hp power team

ENGINE front, 4 stroke; 4 cylinders, vertical, in line; 78.9 cu in, 1,294 cc (3.11 x 2.60 in, 79 x 66 mm); compression ratio: 8:1 max power (DIN): 59 hp (43 kW) at 5,750 rpm; max torque (DIN): 68 lb ft, 9.4 kg m (92 Nm) at 3,500 rpm; max engine rpm 6,000; 45.6 hp/l (33.2 kW/l); cast iron block and head; crankshaft bearings; valves: overhead, Vee-slanted, rockers camshafts: 1, overhead, cogged belt; lubrication: gear pump full flow filter (cartridge), 6.5 imp pt, 7.8 US pt, 3.7 l; 1 Ford downdraught carburettor; fuel feed: mechanical pump; water cooled, 11.7 imp pt, 14.1 US pt, 6.6 l.

TRANSMISSION driving wheels: rear; clutch: single dry plate (diaphragm); gearbox: mechanical; gears: 4, fully synchronized ratios: I 3.660, II 2.180, III 1.430, IV 1, rev 4.240; lever: central final drive: hypoid bevel; axle ratio: 4.110 - Turnier models 4.440; width of rims: 4.5"; tyres: 165 SR x 13.

PERFORMANCE max speed: 86 mph, 138 km/h; power-weight ratio: 4-dr limousines 36.8 lb/hp (50.5 lb/kW), 16.7 kg/hp (22. kg/kW); carrying capacity: 2-dr limousines 1,136 lb, 515 kg 4-dr limousines 1,091 lb, 495 kg - Turnier models 1,389 lb, 63 kg (with heavy - duty suspension); speed in direct drive at 1,000 rpm: 14.2 mph, 22.8 km/h; consumption: 28.2 m/imp gal 23.5 m/US gal, 10 l x 100 km at 75 mph, 120 km/h.

CHASSIS integral; front suspension: independent, wishbones (lower trailing links), coil springs/telescopic dampers, anti-roll bar; rear: rigid axle, lower trailing arms, upper oblique torque arms, coil springs, anti-roll bar, telescopic dampers.

STEERING rack-and-pinion.

BRAKES front disc (diameter 9.72 in, 24.7 cm), rear drum, rea compensator, servo; lining area: front 23.4 sq in, 151.2 sq cm rear 40.9 sq in, 264.5 sq cm, total 64.3 sq in, 415.7 sq cm

ELECTRICAL EQUIPMENT 12 V; 44 Ah battery; 45 A alternator; Bosch distributor; 2 headlamps.

DIMENSIONS AND WEIGHT wheel base: 102.57 in, 258 cm tracks: 56.88 in, 144 cm front, 55.91 in, 142 cm rear; length 172.44 in, 438 cm - Turnier models 176.38 in, 448 cm; width 66.93 in, 170 cm; height: 53.54 in, 136 cm - Turnier models 53.94 in, 137 cm; ground clearance: 3.82 in, 9.7 cm; weight 2-dr limousine 2,128 lb, 965 kg - 4-dr limousines 2,172 lb, 98 kg - Turnier models 2,315 lb, 1,050 kg; turning circle: 34.8 ft 10.6 m; fuel tank: 11.9 imp gal, 14.3 US gal, 54 l.

BODY 5 seats, separate front seats; heated rear window.

PRACTICAL INSTRUCTIONS fuel: 90 oct petrol; oil: engine 5. imp pt, 6.8 US pt, 3.2 l, SAE 10W-40, change every 6,20 miles, 10,000 km - gearbox 1.4 imp pt, 1.7 US pt, 0.8 l, SAE 8 EP, change every 12,400 miles, 20,000 km - final drive 1.8 im pt, 2.1 US pt, 1 l, SAE 90, change every 12,400 miles, 20,00 km; greasing: every 31,100 miles, 50,000 km, 2 points; tyre pressure: front 24 psi, 1.7 atm, rear 24 psi, 1.7 atm.

OPTIONALS 4.440 axle ratio; 185/70 SR x 13 tyres with 5.5" wide rims; halogen headlamps; built-in headrests on fron seats; fog lamps; metallic spray; sunshine roof except fo Turnier models.

70 hp power team

See 59 hp power team, except for:

ENGINE 97.2 cu in, 1,593 cc (3.45 x 2.60 in, 87.6 x 66 mm) compression ratio: 8.2:1; max power (DIN): 70 hp (51 kW) a 5,300 rpm; max torque (DIN): 83 lb ft, 11.5 kg m (113 Nm) a 2,700 rpm; 43.9 hp/l (32 kW/l); cooling: 12.9 imp pt, 15.5 US pt 7.3 l.

TRANSMISSION gearbox ratios: I 3.650, II 1.970, III 1.370, I 1, rev 3.660; axle ratio: 3.890 - Turnier models 4.110; width o rims: GL models 5.5".

PERFORMANCE max speed: 92 mph, 148 km/h; power-weigh ratio: 4-dr limousines 31.2 lb/hp (42.8 lb/kW), 14.1 kg/hp (19. kg/kW); speed in direct drive at 1,000 rpm: 15.2 mph, 24. km/h; consumption: 29.1 m/imp gal, 24.2 m/US gal, 9.7 l x 10 km at 75 mph, 120 km/h.

DIMENSIONS AND WEIGHT weight: 2-dr limousines 2,139 lb 970 kg, 4-dr limousines 2,183 lb, 990 kg - Turnier models 2,326 lb, 1,055 kg.

OPTIONALS 4.110 axle ratio; Ford C3 automatic transmission hydraulic torque converter and planetary gears with 3 ratios (2.474, II 1.474, III 1, rev 2.111), max ratio of converter at sta 2, possible manual selection, 55 Ah battery, max speed 8 mph, 142 km/h, consumption 25 m/imp gal, 20.8 m/US gal, 11. l x 100 km at 75 mph, 120 km/h, oil cooler.

73 hp power team

See 59 hp power team, except for:

ENGINE 97.2 cu in, 1,593 cc (3.45 x 2.60 in, 87.6 x 66 mm) compression ratio: 9.2:1; max power (DIN): 73 hp (54 kW) a 5,300 rpm; max torque (DIN): 86 lb ft, 11.9 kg m (117 Nm) a 2,700 rpm; 45.8 hp/l (33.9 kW/l); cooling: 12.9 imp pt, 15.5 U pt, 7.3 l.

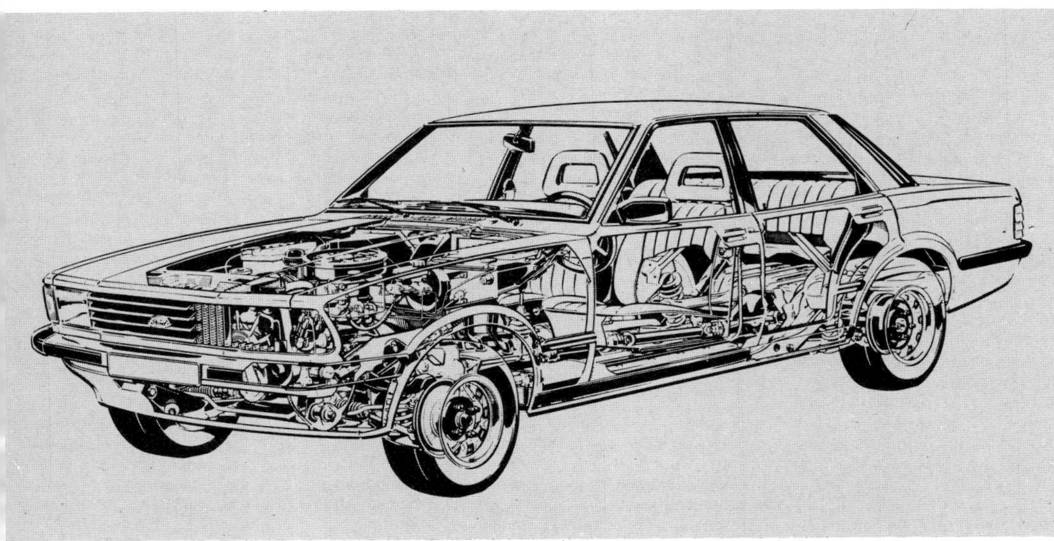

FORD Taunus Limousine Series

TRANSMISSION gearbox ratios: I 3.650, II 1.970, III 1.370, IV 1, rev 3.600; axle ratio: 3.890 - Turnier models 4.110; width of rims: GL and Ghia models 5.5"; tyres: Ghia models 185/70 SR x 13.

PERFORMANCE max speed: 94 mph, 152 km/h; power-weight ratio: 4-dr limousines 29.9 lb/hp (40.4 lb/kW), 13.6 kg/hp (18.3 kg/kW); speed in direct drive at 1,000 rpm: 15.7 mph, 25.3 km/h; consumption: 29.7 m/imp gal, 24.8 m/US gal, 9.5 l x 100 km at 75 mph, 120 km/h.

ELECTRICAL EQUIPMENT halogen headlamps (standard for GL and Ghia models only).

DIMENSIONS AND WEIGHT weight: 2-dr limousines 2,139 lb, 970 kg - 4-dr limousines 2,183 lb, 990 kg - Turnier models 2,326 lb, 1,055 kg.

PRACTICAL INSTRUCTIONS fuel: 97 oct petrol.

OPTIONALS 4.110 axle ratio; Ford C3 automatic transmission, hydraulic torque converter and planetary gears with 3 ratios (I 2.474, II 1.474, III 1, rev 2.111), max ratio of converter at stall 2, possible manual selection, 55 Ah battery, max speed 90 mph, 145 km/h, consumption: 27.2 m/imp gal, 22.6 m/US gal, 10.4 l x 100 km at 75 mph, 120 km/h.

90 hp power team

See 59 hp power team, except for:

ENGINE 6 cylinders, Vee-slanted at 60°; 121.9 cu in, 1,998 cc (3.31 x 2.37 in, 84 x 60.1 mm); compression ratio: 8.2:1; max power (DIN): 90 hp (66 kW) at 5,100 rpm; max torque (DIN): 104 lb ft, 14.4 kg m (141 Nm) at 3,000 rpm; 45 hp/l (33 kW/l); 4 crankshaft bearings; camshafts: 1, at centre of Vee; lubrication: 7.4 imp pt, 8.9 US pt, 4.2 l; 1 Solex 32/32 EEIT downdraught twin barrel carburettor; cooling: 12.5 imp pt, 15 US pt, 7.1 l.

TRANSMISSION gearbox ratios: I 3.650, II 1.970, III 1.370, IV 1, rev 3.660; axle ratio: 3.450; width of rims: 4.5" - GL and Ghia models 5.5"; tyres: Ghia models 185/70 SR x 13.

PERFORMANCE max speed: 101 mph: 163 km/h; power-weight ratio: 4-dr limousines 25.7 lb/hp (35.1 lb/kW), 11.7 kg/hp (15.9 kg/kW); speed in direct drive at 1,000 rpm: 16.9 mph, 27.2 km/h; consumption: 27.7 m/imp gal, 23.1 m/US gal, 10.2 l x 100 km at 75 mph, 120 km/h.

BRAKES lining area: front 23.4 sq in, 151.2 sq cm, rear 58.6 sq in, 377.6 sq cm total 82 sq in, 528.8 sq cm.

ELECTRICAL EQUIPMENT halogen headlamps (standard for GL and Ghia models only).

DIMENSIONS AND WEIGHT weight: 2-dr limousines 2,271 lb, 1,030 kg - 4-dr limousines 2,315 lb, 1,050 kg - Turnier models 2,459 lb, 1,115 kg.

PRACTICAL INSTRUCTIONS fuel: 97 oct petrol; oil: engine 7 imp pt, 8.5 US pt, 4 l.

OPTIONALS Ford C3 automatic transmission, hydraulic torque converter and planetary gears with 3 ratios (I 2.474 II 1.474, III 1, rev 2.111), max ratio of converter at stall 2, possible manual selection, 55 Ah battery, max speed 97 mph, 156 km/h, consumption 24.8 m/imp gal, 20.6 m/US gal, 11.4 l x 100 km at 75 mph, 120 km/h, oil cooler; power steering.

101 hp power team

See 59 hp power teram, except for:

ENGINE 121.6 cu in, 1,993 cc (3.89 x 3.03 in, 90.8 x 76.9 mm); compression ratio: 9.2:1; max power (DIN): 101 hp (74 kW) at 5,200 rpm; max torque (DIN): 113 lb ft, 15.6 kg m (153 Nm) at 4,000 rpm; max engine rpm: 6,500; 50.7 hp/l (37.8 kW/l); 1 Weber 32/36 DGAV downdraught twin barrel carburettor; cooling : 12.9 imp pt, 15.5 US pt, 7.3 l.

TRANSMISSION gearbox ratios: I 3.650, II 1.970, III 1.370, IV 1, rev 3.660; axle ratio: 3.450 - Turnier models 3.750; width of rims: 5.5"; tyres: 185/70 SR x 13.

PERFORMANCE max speed: 105 mph, 169 km/h; power-weight ratio: 4-dr limousines 22.3 lb/hp (30.4 lb/kW), 10.1 kg/hp (13.8 kg/kW); speed in direct drive at 1,000 rpm: 17.3 mph, 27.8 km/h; consumption: 28.8 m/imp gal, 24 m/US gal, 9.8 l x 100 km at 75 mph, 120 km/h.

BRAKES lining area: front 23.4 sq in, 151.2 sq cm, rear 58.6 sq in, 377.6 sq cm, total 82 sq in, 528.8 sq cm.

ELECTRICAL EQUIPMENT 4 halogen headlamps (standard).

DIMENSIONS AND WEIGHT weight: 2-dr limousines 2,205 lb, 1,000 kg - 4-dr limousines 2,249 lb, 1,020 kg - Turnier models 2,392 lb, 1,085 kg.

PRACTICAL INSTRUCTIONS fuel: 97 oct petrol.

OPTIONALS Ford C3 automatic transmission, hydraulic torque converter and planetary gears with 3 ratios (I 2.474, II 1.474, III 1, rev 2.111), max ratio of converter at stall 2, possible manual selection, 55 Ah battery, max speed 101 mph, 162 km/h, consumption 25.7 m/imp gal, 21.4 m/US gal, 11 l x 100 km at 75 mph, 120 km/h, oil cooler; power steering.

114 hp power team

See 59 hp power team, except for:

ENGINE 6 cylinders, Vee-slanted at 60°; 139.9 cu in, 2,294 cc (3.54 x 2.37 in, 90 x 60.1 mm); compression ratio: 9:1; max power (DIN): 114 hp (84 kW) at 5,300 rpm; max torque (DIN): 130 lb ft, 18 kg m (176 Nm) at 3,000 rpm; 49.6 hp/l (37 kW/l); 4 crankshaft bearings; camshafts: 1, at centre of Vee; lubrication: 7.4 imp pt, 8.9 US pt, 4.2 l; Solex 35/35 EEIT downdraught twin barrel carburettor; cooling: 12.5 imp pt, 15 US pt, 7.1 l.

TRANSMISSION gearbox ratios: I 3.650, II 1.970, III 1.370, IV 1, rev 3.660; axle ratio: 3.440; width of rims: 5.5"; tyres: 185/70 SR x 13.

PERFORMANCE max speed: 109 mph, 176 km/h; power-weight ratio: 4-dr limousines 20.4 lb/hp (27.7 lb/kW), 9.2 kg/hp (12.5 kg/kW); speed in direct drive at 1,000 rpm: 17.9 mph, 28.8 km/h; consumption: 24.1 m/imp gal, 22 m/US gal, 10.7 l x 100 km at 75 mph, 120 km/h.

BRAKES lining area: front 23.4 sq in, 151.2 sq cm, rear 58.6 sq in, 377.6 sq cm, total 82 sq in, 528.8 sq cm.

ELECTRICAL EQUIPMENT 4 headlamps (standard).

DIMENSIONS AND WEIGHT weight: 2-dr limousines 2,282 lb, 1,035 kg - 4-dr limousines 2,326 lb, 1,055 kg - Turnier models 2,469 lb, 1,120 kg.

PRACTICAL INSTRUCTIONS fuel: 97 oct petrol; oil: engine 7 imp pt, 8.5 US pt, 4 l.

OPTIONALS Ford C3 automatic transmission, hydraulic torque converter and planetary gears with 3 ratios (I 2.474, II 1.474, III 1, rev 2.111), max ratio of converter at stall 2, possible manual selection, 55 Ah battery, max speed 104 mph, 168 km/h, consumption 25.2 m/imp gal, 21 m/US gal, 11.2 l x 100 km at 75 mph, 120 km/h, oil cooler; power steering.

Capri II Series

PRICES EX WORKS:	DM
1 L Coupé	**13,691***
2 GL Coupé	**15,305***
3 S Coupé	**17,757***
4 Ghia Coupé	**20,814***

Power team	Standard for:	Optional for:
68 hp	—	1,2
72 hp	1,2	—
90 hp	3	1,2
114 hp	4	3
138 hp	—	3,4

FORD Capri II S Coupé

68 hp power team

ENGINE front, 4 stroke; 4 cylinders, vertical, in line; 97.2 cu in, 1,593 cc (3.45 x 2.60 in, 87.7 x 66 mm); compression ratio: 8.2:1; max power (DIN): 68 hp (50 kW) at 5.500 rpm; max torque (DIN): 85 lb ft, 11.7 kg m (115 Nm) at 2,700 rpm; max engine rpm: 6,000; 43.1 hp/l (31.7 kW/l); cast iron block and head; 5 crankshaft bearings; valves: overhead, Vee-slanted, rockers; camshaft: 1, overhead, cogged belt; lubrication: rotary pump, full flow filter (cartridge), 6.5 imp pt, 7.8 US pt, 3.7 l; 1 Ford downdraught carburettor; fuel feed: mechanical pump; water-cooled, 10.2 imp pt, 12.3 US pt, 5.8 l.

TRANSMISSION driving wheels: rear; clutch: single dry plate (diaphragm); gearbox: mechanical; gears: 4, fully synchronized; ratios: I 3.650, II 1.970, III 1.370, IV 1, rev 3.660; lever: central; final drive: hypoid bevel; axle ratio: 3.770; width of rims: 5"; tyres: 165 SR x 13.

PERFORMANCE max speeds: (I) 29 mph, 47 km/h; (II) 54 mph, 87 km/h; (III) 78 mph, 125 km/h; (IV) 96 mph, 155 km/h; power-weight ratio: 32.7 lb/hp (44.5 lb/kW), 14.8 kg/hp (20.2 kg/kW); carrying capacity: 816 lb, 370 kg; speed in direct drive at 1,000 rpm: 17.8 mph, 28.6 km/h; consumption: 29.1 m/imp gal, 24.2 m/US gal, 9.7 l x 100 km.

CHASSIS integral; front suspension: independent, by McPherson, coil springs/telescopic damper struts, lower transverse arms, anti-roll bar; rear: rigid axle, semi-elliptic leafsprings, rubber springs, anti-roll bar, telescopic dampers.

STEERING rack-and-pinion.

BRAKES front disc (diameter 9.61 in, 24.4 cm), rear drum, servo; lining area: front 17.4 sq in, 151.2 sq cm, rear 45.4 sq in, 293.4 sq cm, total 62.8 sq in, 444.6 sq cm.

ELECTRICAL EQUIPMENT 35 Ah battery; 55 A alternator.

DIMENSIONS AND WEIGHT wheel base: 100.79 in, 256 cm; tracks: 53.15 in, 135 cm front, 54.33 in, 138 cm rear; length: 174.80 in, 444 cm; width: 66.93 in, 170 cm; height: 51.97 in, 132 cm; ground clearance: 4.92 in, 12.5 cm; weight: 2,227 lb, 1,010 kg; turning circle: 35.4 ft, 10.8 m; fuel tank 12.8 imp gal, 15.3 US gal, 58 l.

BODY coupé; 2+1 doors; 5 seats, separate front seats, reclining backrests; folding rear seat.

PRACTICAL INSTRUCTIONS fuel: 90 oct petrol; oil: engine 5.6 imp pt, 6.8 US pt, 3.2 l, SAE 20W-40, change every 6,200 miles, 10,000 km - gearbox 2.3 imp pt, 2.7 US pt, 1.3 l, SAE 80, change every 12,400 miles, 20,000 km - final drive 1.9 imp pt, 2.3 US pt, 1.1 l, SAE 90, change every 12,400 miles, 20,000 km; greasing: none.

OPTIONALS servo brake; heated rear window; rear window wiper; headrests on front seats; sunshine roof; vinyl roof; halogen headlamps; metallic spray; 185/70 SR x 13 tyres; Ford C3 automatic transmission, hydraulic torque converter and planetary gears with 3 ratios (I 2.474, II 1.474, III 1, rev 2.111), max ratio of converter at stall 2, possible manual selection, oil cooler, 55 Ah battery, max speed 93 mph, 150 km/h, consumption 27.7 m/imp gal, 21.4 m/US gal, 10.2 l x 100 km.

72 hp power team

See 68 hp power team, except for:

ENGINE compression ratio: 9.2:1; max power (DIN): 72 hp (53 kW) at 5,200 rpm; max torque (DIN): 87 lb ft, 12 kg m (118 Nm) at 2,700 rpm; 45.7 hp/l (33.6 kW/l).

PERFORMANCE max speed: 98 mph, 158 km/h; power-weight ratio: 30.9 lb/hp (42 lb/kW), 14 kg/hp (19 kg/kW); consumption: 28.5 m/imp gal, 23.5 m/US, 9.9 l x 100 km at 75 mph, 120 km/h.

PRACTICAL INSTRUCTIONS fuel: 97 oct petrol.

OPTIONALS with Ford C-3 automatic transmission, max speed 95 mph, 153 km/h, consumption 25.4 m/imp gal, 21.2 m/US gal, 11.1 l x 100 km at 75 mph, 120 km/h.

90 hp power team

See 68 hp power team, except for:

ENGINE 6 cylinders, Vee-slanted at 60°; 121.9 cu in, 1,998 cc (3.31 x 2.37 in, 84 x 60.1 mm); max power (DIN): 90 hp (66 kW) at 5,100 rpm; max torque (DIN): 104 lb ft, 14.4 kg m (141 Nm) at 3,000 rpm; 45 hp/l (33 kW/l); 4 crankshaft bearings; valves: overhead, push-rods and rockers; camshafts: 1, at centre of Vee; lubrication: 7.4 imp pt, 8.9 US pt, 4.2 l; 1 Solex 32/32 EEIT downdraught twin barrel carburettor; cooling: 13.7 imp pt, 16.5 US pt, 7.8 l.

TRANSMISSION axle ratio: 3.440; width of rims: 5.5".

PERFORMANCE max speed: 106 mph, 170 km/h - S 107 mph, 173 km/h; power-weight ratio: 26.5 lb/hp (36.1 lb/kW), 12 kg/hp (16.4 kg/kW); consumption: 28.8 m/imp gal, 24 m/US gal, 9.8 l x 100 km at 75 mph, 120 km/h - S 29.7 m/imp gal, 24.8 m/US gal, 9.5 l x 100 km at 75 mph, 120 km/h.

FORD Capri II S Coupé

ELECTRICAL EQUIPMENT 44 Ah battery; 4 headlamps.

DIMENSIONS AND WEIGHT weight: 2,381 lb, 1,080 kg.

PRACTICAL INSTRUCTIONS fuel: 97 oct petrol.

OPTIONALS with Ford C-3 automatic transmission max speed 102 mph, 165 km/h (S 104 mph, 168 km/h), consumption: 27.7 m/imp gal, 21.8 m/US gal, 10.8 l x 100 km; S 26.9 m/imp gal, 22.4 m/US gal, 10.5 l x 100 km at 75 mph, 120 km/h; power steering.

114 hp power team

See 68 hp power team, except for:

ENGINE 6 cylinders, Vee-slanted at 60°; 139.9 cu in, 2,294 cc (3.54 x 2.37 in, 90 x 60.1 mm); compression ratio: 9:1; max power (DIN): 114 hp (84 kW) at 5,300 rpm; max torque (DIN): 130 lb ft, 18 kg m (176 Nm) at 3,000 rpm; max engine rpm: 5,600; 49.6 hp/l (37 kW/l); 4 crankshaft bearings; valves: overhead, push-rods and rockers; camshafts: 1, centre of Vee; lubrication: 7.4 imp pt, 8.9 US pt, 4.2 l; 1 Solex 35/35 EEIT downdraught twin barrel carburettor; cooling: 13.7 imp pt, 16.5 US pt, 7.8 l.

TRANSMISSION axle ratio: 3.220; width of rims: 5.5"; tyres: 185/70 HR x 13 standard.

PERFORMANCE max speed: 114 mph, 183 km/h - S 115 mph, 186 km/h; power-weight ratio: 21.5 lb/hp (29.1 lb/kW), 9.7 kg/hp (13.2 kg/kW); speed in direct drive at 1,000 rpm: 20.8 mph, 33.4 km/h; consumption: 28.2 m/imp gal, 23.5 m/US gal, 10 l x 100 km at 75 mph, 120 km/h - S 29.1 m/imp gal, 24.2 m/US gal, 9.7 l x 100 km at at 75 mph, 120 km/h.

ELECTRICAL EQUIPMENT 44 Ah battery; halogen headlamps and fog lamps.

DIMENSIONS AND WEIGHT weight: 2,447 lb, 1,110 kg.

BODY light alloy wheels; headrests on front seats; heated rear window.

PRACTICAL INSTRUCTIONS fuel: 97 oct petrol.

OPTIONALS with Ford C-3 automatic transmission max speed 111 mph, 178 km/h (S 112 mph, 181 km/h), consumption: 26.6 m/imp gal, 22.2 m/US gal, 10.6 l x 100 km (S 27.4 m/imp gal, 22.8 m/US gal, 10.3 l x 100 km) at 75 mph, 120 km/h; power steering.

138 hp power team

See 68 hp power team, except for:

ENGINE 6 cylinders, Vee-slanted at 60°; 182.7 cu in, 2,993 cc (3.69 x 2.85 in, 93.7 x 72.4 mm); compression ratio: 9:1; max power (DIN): 138 hp (102 kW) at 5,000 rpm; max torque (DIN): 174 lb ft, 24 kg m (235 Nm) at 3,000 rpm; 46.1 hp/l (33.9 kW/l); 4 crankshaft bearings; valves: overhead, push-rods and rockers; camshafts: 1, at centre of Vee; lubrication: 8.8 imp pt, 10.6

FORD Granada Limousine

US pt, 5 l; 1 Weber 38/38 EGAS downdraught twin barrel carburettor; cooling: 16.4 imp pt, 19.7 US pt, 9.3 l.

TRANSMISSION gearbox ratios: I 3.163, II 1.940, III 1.412, IV 1, rev 3.346; axle ratio: 3.090; width of rims: 5.5"; tyres: 185/70 HR x 13.

PERFORMANCE max speed: 122 mph, 197 km/h - S 124 mph, 200 km/h; power-weight ratio: 18.4 lb/hp (24.9 lb/kW), 8.3 kg/hp (11.3 kg/kW); speed in direct drive at 1,000 rpm: 21.8 mph, 35.1 km/h; consumption: 25.4 m/imp gal, 21.2 m/US gal, 11.1 l x 100 km at 75 mph, 120 km/h.

BRAKES front disc (diameter 9.72 in, 24.7 cm), rear drum; lining area: front 17.4 sq in, 151.2 sq cm, rear 59.5 sq in, 384.4 cm, total 76.9 sq in, 535.6 sq cm.

ELECTRICAL EQUIPMENT 44 Ah battery; halogen headlamps, fog lamps.

DIMENSIONS AND WEIGHT weight: 2,535 lb, 1,150 kg.

BODY light alloy wheels; tinted glass; headrests on front seats; heated rear window.

PRACTICAL INSTRUCTIONS fuel: 97 oct petrol.

OPTIONALS with Ford C-3 automatic transmission max speed 119 mph, 192 km/h (S 121 mph, 195 km/h), consumption: 24.4 m/imp gal, 20.3 m/US gal, 11.6 l x 100 km at 75 mph, 120 km/h; power steering.

FORD Granada GLS Turnier

Granada Series

PRICES EX WORKS:	DM
1 2-dr Limousine	15,265*
2 4-dr Limousine	15,865*
3 4+1-dr Turnier	16,556*
4 L 2-dr Limousine	16,032*
5 L 4-dr Limousine	16,562*
6 L 4+1-dr Turnier	17,601*
7 GL 4-dr Limousine	19,786*
8 GL 4+1-dr Turnier	21,057*
9 Ghia 4-dr Limousine	25,132*
10 Ghia 4+1-dr Turnier	26,608*

Power team:	Standard for:	Optional for:
71 hp	1 to 6	—
74 hp	—	1 to 6
90 hp	7,8	1 to 6
101 hp	—	1 to 6
114 hp	9,10	1 to 8
135 hp	—	all except 1,2,3,6
160 hp	—	all except 1,2,3,6
63 hp (diesel)	—	1,2,4,5,7

71 hp power team

ENGINE front, 4 stroke; 4 cylinders, Vee-slanted at 60°; 103.7 cu in, 1,700 cc (3.54 x 2.63 in, 90 x 66.8 mm); compression ratio: 7.75:1; max power (DIN): 71 hp (52 kW) at 5,000 rpm; max torque (DIN): 88 lb/ft, 12.2 kg m (120 Nm) at 3,000 rpm; max engine rpm: 5,500; 41.7 hp/l (30.6 kW/l); cast iron block and head; 3 crankshaft bearings; valves: overhead, in line, rockers; camshafts: 1, at centre of Vee; lubrication: gear pump, full flow filter, 6.5 imp pt, 7.8 US pt, 3.7 l; Solex 32 TDID downdraught carburettor; fuel feed: mechanical pump; water-cooled, 10.6 imp pt, 12.7 US pt, 6 l, electric thermostatic fan.

TRANSMISSION driving wheels: rear; clutch: single dry plate (diaphragm); gearbox: mechanical; gears: 4, fully synchronized; ratios: I 3.650, II 1.970, III 1.370, IV 1, rev 3.660; lever: central; final drive: hypoid bevel; axle ratio: 4.110 - Turnier models 4.440; width of rims: 6"; tyres 175 SR x 14 - Turnier models 185 SR x 14.

PERFORMANCE max speed: 91 mph, 147 km/h; power-weight ratio: 4-dr limousines 37.3 lb/hp (50.9 lb/kW), 16.9 kg/hp (23.1 kg/kW); speed in direct drive at 1,000 rpm: 16.8 mph, 27.1 km/h; consumption: 25.7 m/imp gal, 21.4 m/US gal, 11 l x 100 km at 75 mph, 120 km/h - Turnier models 23.3 m/imp gal, 19.4 m/US gal, 12.1 l x 100 km at 75 mph, 120 km/h.

CHASSIS integral, front and rear auxilliary frames; front suspension: independent, wishbones (lower trailing links), coil springs, anti-roll bar, telescopic dampers; rear: independent, semi-trailing arms, coil springs, telescopic dampers.

STEERING rack-and-pinion.

BRAKES front disc (diameter 10.31 in, 26.2 cm), rear drum, servo; lining area: front 23.4 sq in, 151.2 sq cm, rear 58 sq in, 374.6 sq cm, total 81.4 sq in, 528.5 sq cm - Turnier models front 23.4 sq in, 151.2 sq cm, rear 83.4 sq in, 538.5 sq cm, total 106.8 sq in, 689.7 sq cm.

ELECTRICAL EQUIPMENT 12 V; 35 Ah battery; 45 A (L limousines 55 A) alternator; Ford distributor; 2 headlamps.

DIMENSIONS AND WEIGHT wheel base: 109.05 in, 277 cm; tracks: 59.45 in, 151 cm front, 60.24 in, 153 cm rear; length: 185.83 in, 472 cm - Turnier models 189.76 in, 482 cm; width: 70.47 in, 179 cm; height: 55.91 in, 142 cm; weight: 2-dr limousines 2,613 lb, 1,185 kg - 4-dr limousines 2,646 lb, 1,200 kg - Turnier models 2,800 lb, 1,270 kg; turning circle: 36.7 ft, 11.2 m; fuel tank: 14.5 imp gal, 17.4 US gal, 66 l - Turnier models 13.6 imp gal, 16.4 US gal, 62 l.

BODY 5 seats, separate front seats, reclining backrests; heated rear window.

PRACTICAL INSTRUCTIONS fuel: 90 oct petrol; oil: engine 5.6 imp pt, 6.8 US pt, 3.2 l, SAE 10W-40, change every 6,200 miles, 10,000 km - gearbox 3 imp pt, 3.6 US pt, 1.8 l, SAE 80, no change recommended - final drive 3.2 imp pt, 3.8 US pt, 1.8 l, SAE 90, no change recommended; greasing: none; tappet clearances: inlet 0.014 in, 0.35 mm, exhaust 0.016 in, 0.40 mm; valve timing: 24° 84° 65° 42°; tyre pressure: front 20 psi, 1.4 atm, rear 23 psi, 1.6 atm.

OPTIONALS 4.440 axle ratio; 185 SR x 14 tyres with 6" wide rims; 66 Ah battery; 55 A alternator; halogen headlamps; power steering; built-in headrests; heated rear window; sunshine roof; metallic spray; S equipment with 190/65 HR 390 TRX tyres; rear window wiper-washer; headlamps with wiper-washers.

74 hp power team

See 71 hp power team, except for:

ENGINE compression ratio: 8.75:1; max power (DIN): 74 hp (54 kW) at 5,000 rpm; max torque (DIN): 93 lb ft, 12.8 kg m (125 Nm) at 3,000 rpm; 43.4 hp/l (32 kW/l).

PERFORMANCE max speed: 93 mph, 149 km/h; power-weight ratio: 4-dr limousines 35.7 lb/hp (49 lb/kW), 16.2 kg/hp (22.2 kg/kW); consumption: 27.7 m /imp gal, 23.1 m/US gal, 10.2 l x 100 km at 75 mph, 120 km/h.

PRACTICAL INSTRUCTIONS fuel: 97 oct petrol.

OPTIONALS Ford C-3 automatic transmission, hydraulic torque converter and planetary gears with 3 ratios (I 2.474, II 1.474, III 1, rev 2.111), max ratio of converter at stall 2, possible manual selection, oil cooler, max speed 87 mph, 140 km/h, consumption: 25.2 m/imp gal, 21 m/US gal, 11.2 l x 100 km at 75 mph, 120 km/h - Turnier models 23.3 m/imp gal, 19.4 m/US gal, 12.1 l x 100 km at 75 mph, 120 km/h, 55 Ah battery.

90 hp power team

See 71 hp power team, except for:

ENGINE 6 cylinders, Vee-slanted at 60°; 121.9 cu in, 1,998 cc (3.31 x 2.37 in, 84 x 60.1 mm); compression ratio: 8.2:1; max power (DIN): 90 hp (66 kW) at 5,100 rpm; max torque (DIN): 104 lb ft, 14.4 kg m (141 Nm) at 3,000 rpm; 45 hp/l (33 kW/l); 4 crankshaft bearings; lubrication: 7.4 imp pt, 8.9 US pt, 4.2 l; 1 Solex 32/32 EEIT downdraught twin barrel carburettor; cooling: 17.9 imp pt, 21.6 US pt, 10.2 l.

TRANSMISSION axle ratio: 3.890; width of rims: GL limousines 6"; tyres: 185 SR x 14.

PERFORMANCE max speed: 98 mph, 159 km/h; power-weight ratio: GL 4-dr Limousine 30.7 lb/hp (41.9 lb/kW), 13.9 kg/hp (19 kg/kW); speed in direct drive at 1,000 rpm: 17.3 mph, 27.9

FORD Granada Ghia Limousine

90 HP POWER TEAM

km/h; consumption: 24.8 m/imp gal, 20.6 m/US gal, 11.4 l x 100 km at 75 mph, 120 km/h.

STEERING servo (standard for GL models only).

BRAKES lining area (except for Turnier models): front 23.4 sq in, 151.2 sq cm, rear 75.3 sq in, 486 sq cm, total 98.7 sq in, 637.2 sq cm.

ELECTRICAL EQUIPMENT 44 Ah battery.

DIMENSIONS AND WEIGHT weight: GL 4-dr Limousine 2,767 lb, 1,255 kg - GL Turnier 2,922 lb, 1,325 kg.

PRACTICAL INSTRUCTIONS fuel: 97 oct petrol; oil: engine 7 imp pt, 8.5 US pt, 4 l.

OPTIONALS Ford C-3 automatic transmission, hydraulic torque converter and planetary gears with 3 ratios (I 2.474, II 1.474, III 1, rev 2.111), max ratio of converter at stall 2, possible manual selection, 3,890 axle ratio, max speed 94 mph, 152 km/h, consumption: 22.6 m/imp gal, 18.8 m/US gal, 12.5 l x 100 km at 75 mph, 120 km/h - Turnier 21.4 m/imp gal, 17.8 m/US gal, 13.2 l x 100 km at 75 mph, 120 km/h, 55 Ah battery.

114 hp power team

See 71 hp power team, except for:

ENGINE 6 cylinders, Vee-slanted at 60°; 139.9 cu in, 2,294 cc (3.54 x 2.37 in, 90 x 60.1 mm); compression ratio: 9:1; max power (DIN): 114 hp (85 kW) at 5,300 rpm; max torque (DIN): 130 lb ft, 18 kg m (176 Nm) at 3,000 rpm; max engine rpm: 5,600; 49.6 hp/l (37 kW/l); 4 crankshaft bearings; lubrication: 7.4 imp pt, 8.9 US pt, 4.2 l; 1 Solex 35/35 EEIT downdraught twin barrel carburettor; cooling: 17.9 imp pt, 21.6 US pt, 10.2 l.

TRANSMISSION gearbox ratios (for Turnier models only): I 3.360, II 1.810, III 1.260, IV 1, rev 3.370; axle ratio: 3.640; width of rims: Ghia and GL limousine 6"; tyres 185 SR x 14.

PERFORMANCE max speed: 107 mph, 172 km/h; power-weight ratio: 4-dr limousines 24.4 lb/hp (32.7 lb/kW), 11 kg/hp (14.8 kg/kW); speed in direct in drive at 1,000 rpm: 18.5 mph, 29.8 km/h; consumption: 25.7 m/imp gal, 21.4 m/US gal, 11 l x 100 km at 75 mph, 120 km/h.

STEERING servo (standard for GL and Ghia models only).

BRAKES lining area (except for Turnier models): front 23.4 sq in, 151.2 sq cm, rear 75.3 sq in, 486 sq cm, total 98.7 sq in, 637.2 sq cm.

ELECTRICAL EQUIPMENT 44 Ah battery.

DIMENSIONS AND WEIGHT weight: 2-dr limousines 2,745 lb, 1,245 kg - 4-dr limousines 2,778 lb, 1,260 kg - Turnier models 2,933 lb, 1,330 kg.

BODY heated rear window (standard).

PRACTICAL INSTRUCTIONS fuel: 97 oct petrol; oil: engine 7 imp pt, 8.5 US pt, 4 l.

OPTIONALS Ford C-3 automatic transmission, hydraulic torque converter and planetary gears with 3 ratios (I 2.474, II 1.474, III 1, rev 2.111), max ratio of converter at stall 2, possible manual selection, oil cooler, max speed 100 mph, 161 km/h, consumption: 23.7 m/imp gal, 19.8 m/US gal, 11.9 l x 100 km at 75 mph, 120 km/h; 55 Ah battery; air-conditioning.

101 hp power team

See 71 hp power team, except for:

ENGINE 4 cylinders, in line; 121.6 cu in, 1,993 cc (3.89 x 3.03 in, 90.8 x 76.9 mm); max power (DIN): 101 hp (74 kW) at 5,200 rpm; max torque (DIN): 130 lb ft, 18 kg m (176 Nm) at 3,000 rpm; max engine rpm: 6,000; 50.7 hp/l (37.8 kW/l); 5 crankshaft bearings; camshafts: 1, overhead; 1 Weber 32/36 DGAV downdraught twin barrel carburettor; water-cooled: 12.8 imp pt, 15.4 US pt, 7.3 l.

TRANSMISSION axle ratio: 3.890.

PERFORMANCE max speed: 102 mph, 165 km/h; power-weight ratio: 4-dr limousines 26.5 lb/hp (36.2 lb/kW), 12 kg/hp (16.4 kg/kW); consumption: 27.7 m/imp gal, 23.1 m/US gal, 10.2 l x 100 km at 75 mph, 120 km/h.

ELECTRICAL EQUIPMENT 44 Ah battery.

DIMENSIONS AND WEIGHT weight: 2-dr limousines 2,734 lb, 1,240 kg - 4-dr limousines 2,679 lb, 1,215 kg - Turnier models 2,833 lb, 1,285 kg.

PRACTICAL INSTRUCTIONS fuel: 97 oct petrol.

OPTIONALS Ford C-3 automatic transmission hydraulic torque converter and planetary gears with 3 ratios (I 2.474, II 1.474, III 1, rev 2.111), max ratio of converter at stall 2, possible manual

FORD Granada Limousine

selection, 3.890 axle ratio, max speed 98 mph, 158 km/h, consumption 25 m/imp gal, 20.8 m/US gal, 11.3 l x 100 km at 75 mph, 120 km/h.

135 hp power team

See 71 hp power team, except for:

ENGINE 6 cylinders, Vee-slanted at 60°; 170.4 cu in, 2,792 cc (3.66 x 2.70 in, 93 x 68.5 mm); compression ratio: 9.2:1; max power (DIN): 135 hp (99 kW) at 5,200 rpm; max torque (DIN): 159 lb ft, 22 kg m (216 Nm) at 3,000 rpm; 48.4 hp/l (35.6 kW/l); 4 crankshaft bearings; lubrication: 8.8 imp pt, 10.6 US pt, 5 l; 1 Solex downdraught twin barrel carburettor; cooling: 18 imp pt, 21.6 US pt, 10.2 l.

TRANSMISSION gearbox ratios: I 3.160, II 1.940, III 1.410, IV 1, rev 3.350; axle ratio: 3.450; width of rims: GL and Ghia limousines 6"; tyres: 185 HR x 14.

PERFORMANCE max speed: 114 mph, 183 km/h; power-weight ratio: 4-dr limousines 21.7 lb/hp (29.6 lb/kW), 9.8 kg/hp (13.4 kg/kW); speed in top at 1,000 rpm: 20.7 mph, 33.3 km/h; consumption: 24.6 m/imp gal, 20.5 m/US gal, 11.5 l x 100 km at 75 mph, 120 km/h.

STEERING servo (standard for GL and Ghia models).

BRAKES front disc with internal radial fins; lining area (except for Turnier models): front 29.3 sq in, 188.8 sq cm, rear 75.3 sq in, 486 sq cm, total 104.6 sq in, 674.8 sq cm.

ELECTRICAL EQUIPMENT 44 Ah battery.

DIMENSIONS AND WEIGHT weight: 2-dr limousines 2,900 lb, 1,315 kg - 4-dr limousines 2,933 lb, 1,330 kg - Turnier models 3,010 lb, 1,365 kg.

BODY heated rear window (standard).

PRACTICAL INSTRUCTIONS fuel: 97 oct petrol; oil: engine 7.4 imp pt, 8.9 US pt, 4.2 l.

OPTIONALS Ford C-3 automatic transmission, hydraulic torque converter and planetary gears with 3 ratios (I 2.474, II 1.474, III 1, rev 2.111), max ratio of converter at stall 2, possible manual selection, oil cooler, 3.450 axle ratio, max speed 109 mph, 176 km/h, consumption: 23.5 m/imp gal, 19.6 m/US gal, 12 l x 100 km at 75 mph, 120 km/h; 55 Ah battery; air-conditioning.

160 hp power team

See 71 hp power team, except for:

ENGINE 6 cylinders, Vee-slanted at 60°; 170.4 cu in, 2,792 cc (3.66 x 2.70 in, 93 x 68.5 mm); compression ratio: 9.2:1; max power (DIN): 160 hp (118 kW) at 5,700 rpm; max torque (DIN): 163 lb ft, 22.5 kg m (221 Nm) at 4,300 rpm; max engine rpm: 5,700; 57.3 hp/l (42.3 kW/l); lubrication: 8.8 imp pt, 10.6 US pt, 5 l; Bosch K-Jetronic injection; cooling: 18 imp pt, 21.6 US pt, 10.2 l.

TRANSMISSION gearbox ratios: I 3.160, II 1.940, III 1.410, IV 1, rev 3.350; axle ratio: 3.450; width of rims: GL and Ghia limousines 6"; tyres: 185 HR x 14.

PERFORMANCE max speed: 120 mph, 193 km/h; power-weight ratio: 2- and 4-dr limousines 18.4 lb/hp (24.9 lb/kW), 8.3 kg/hp (11.3 kg/kW); speed in direct drive at 1,000 rpm: 21,2 mph,

FORD Granada GL Series

33.9 km/h; consumption: 25.9 m/imp gal, 21.6 m/US gal, 10.9 l x 100 km at 75 mph, 120 km/h.

STEERING servo (standard for GL and Ghia models).

BRAKES front disc with internal radial fins; lining area (except for Turnier models): front 29.3 sq in, 188.8 sq cm, rear 75.3 sq in, 486 sq cm, total 104.6 sq in, 674.8 sq cm.

ELECTRICAL EQUIPMENT 44 Ah battery; 70 A alternator.

DIMENSIONS AND WEIGHT weight: 2-dr limousines 2,900 lb, 1,315 kg - 4-dr limousines 2,933 lb, 1,330 kg - GL Turnier 3,010 lb, 1,365 kg.

BODY heated rear window (standard).

PRACTICAL INSTRUCTIONS fuel: 97 oct petrol; oil: engine 7.4 imp pt, 8.9 US pt, 4.2 l.

OPTIONALS Ford C-3 automatic transmission, hydraulic torque converter and planetary gears with 3 ratios (I 2.474, II 1.474, III 1, rev 2.111), max ratio converter at stall 2, possible manual selection, oil cooler, 3.450 axle ratio, max speed 117 mph, 188 km/h, consumption 23.9 m/imp gal, 19.9 m/US gal, 11.8 l x 100 km at 75 mph, 120 km/h.

63 hp (diesel) power team

See 71 hp power team, except for:

ENGINE diesel; 4 cylinders, in line; 128.9 cu in, 2,112 cc (3.54 x 3.27 in, 90 x 83 mm); compression ratio: 22.8:1; max ɔwer (DIN): 63 hp (46 kW) at 4,500 rpm; max torque (DIN): ɜ.8 lb ft, 12.4 kg m (122 Nm) at 2,000 rpm; max engine rpm: 700; 30 hp/l (21.9 kW/l); 5 crankshaft bearings; camshafts: 1, ⁄verhead; lubrication: 9.3 imp pt, 11.2 US pt, 5.3 l; Roto-diesel jection; cooling: 17.6 imp pt, 21.1 US pt, 10 l.

RANSMISSION gearbox ratios: I 3.980, II 2.330, III 1.420, IV rev 3.990; axle ratio: 3.890.

ERFORMANCE max speed: 85 mph, 137 km/h; power-weight tio: Ghia Limousine 46 lb/hp (63 lb/kW), 20.9 kg/hp (28.6 ı/kW); consumption at 75 mph, 120 km/h: 28.5 m/imp gal, 23.5 /US gal, 9.9 l x 100 km.

LECTRICAL EQUIPMENT 88 Ah battery.

IMENSIONS AND WEIGHT weight: Ghia Limousine 2,900 lb, 315 kg.

RACTICAL INSTRUCTIONS fuel: diesel oil; oil: engine 9.3 ıp pt, 11.2 US pt, 5.3 l.

IERCEDES-BENZ GERMANY FR

200 Limousine Series

IICES IN GB AND EX WORKS:	£	DM
200 4-dr	7,823*	21,050*
D 4-dr	7,999*	22,159*

›wer team:	Standard for:	Optional for:
hp	1	—
hp diesel	2	—

94 hp power team

IGINE front, 4 stroke; 4 cylinders, vertical, in line; 121,3 cu 1,988 cc (3.43 x 3.29 in, 87 x 83.6 mm); compression ratio: ı; max power (DIN): 94 hp (69 kW) at 4,800 rpm; max torque IN): 117 lb ft, 16.1 kg m (158 Nm) at 3,000 rpm; max engine m: 6,000; 47.3 hp/l (34.6 kW/l); cast iron block, light alloy ad; 5 crankshaft bearings; valves: overhead, in line, finger ›ers; camshafts: 1, overhead; lubrication: gear pump, oil-ıter heat exchanger, full flow filter (cartridge), 9.7 imp pt, 11.6 S pt, 5.5 l; 1 Stromberg 175 CD horizontal carburettor; fuel ɘd: mechanical pump; water-cooled, 18.8 imp pt, 22.6 US pt, .7 l.

IANSMISSION driving wheels: rear; clutch: single dry plate, draulically controlled; gearbox: mechanical; gears: 4, fully nchronized; ratios: I 3.900, II 2.300, III 1.410, IV 1, rev 360; lever: steering column or central; final drive: hypoid vel; axle ratio: 3.920; width of rims: 5.5"; tyres: 175 SR x 14.

ERFORMANCE max speeds: (I) 28 mph, 45 km/h; (II) 47 ɔh, 75 km/h; (III) 78 mph, 125 km/h; (IV) 99 mph, 160 km/h; wer-weight ratio: 31.4 lb/hp (42.7 lb/kW), 14.3 kg/hp (19.4 /kW); carrying capacity: 1,145 lb, 520 kg; consumption: 25.4 imp gal, 21.2 m/US gal, 11.1 l x 100 km.

IASSIS integral, front auxiliary frame; front suspension: dependent, wishbones, coil springs, auxiliary rubber springs, ti-roll bar, telescopic dampers; rear: independent, oblique mi-trailing arms, coil springs, auxiliary rubber springs, anti-l bar, telescopic dampers.

EERING recirculating ball.

IAKES disc (front diameter 10.75 in, 27.3 cm, rear 10.98 in, .9 cm), dual circuit, servo; swept area: front 225.4 sq in, 454 sq cm, rear 195.8 sq in, 1,263 sq cm, total 421.2 sq in, 717 sq cm.

.ECTRICAL EQUIPMENT 12 V; 55 Ah battery; 770 W alterna-; Bosch distributor; 4 headlamps.

MENSIONS AND WEIGHT wheel base: 110.04 in, 279 cm; ıcks: 58.58 in, 149 cm front, 56.93 in, 145 cm rear; length: 6.02 in, 472 cm; width: 70.31 in, 179 cm; height: 56.69 in, 4 cm; ground clearance: 6.50 in, 16.5 cm; weight: 2,955 lb, 340 kg; turning circle: 37.1 ft, 11.3 m; fuel tank: 14.3 imp gal, .2 US gal, 65 l.

ODY saloon/sedan; 4 doors; 5 seats, separate front seats, clining backrests.

IACTICAL INSTRUCTIONS fuel: 98 oct petrol; oil: engine 9.7 p pt, 11.6 US pt, 5.5 l, SAE 20W-30, change every 4,600 les, 7,500 km - gearbox 2.8 imp pt, 3.4 US pt, 1.6 l, ATF, ange every 12,400 miles, 20,000 km - final drive 1.9 imp pt, 3 US pt, 1.1 l, SAE 90, change every 12,400 miles, 20,000 ı; greasing: none; tappet clearances: inlet 0.003 in, 0.08 mm, haust 0.008 in, 0.20 mm: valve timing: 11° 47° 48° 16°; tyre essure: front 21 psi, 1.5 atm, rear 26 psi, 1.8 atm.

PTIONALS MB automatic transmission, hydraulic torque con-rter and planetary gears with 4 ratios (I 3.980, II 2.390, III 460, IV 1, rev 5.480), possible manual selection, max speeds 23 mph, 38 km/h, (II) 47 mph, 75 km/h, (III) 78 mph, 125 ı/h, (IV) 96 mph, 155 km/h; automatic levelling control on rear suspension; power steering; halogen headlamps; fog lamps; electric or manual sunshine roof; heated rear window; heated seats; electric windows; tinted glass; air-conditioning: light alloy wheels; metallic spray.

60 hp power team

See 94 hp power team, except for:

ENGINE diesel; compression ratio: 21:1; max power (DIN): 60 hp (44 kW) at 4,400 rpm; max torque (DIN): 83 lb ft, 11.5 kg m (113 Nm) at 2,400 rpm; max engine rpm: 5,300; 33.1 hp/l (45 kW/l); cast iron block and head; lubrication: gear pump, full flow (cartridge) and by-pass filters, 11.4 imp pt, 13.7 US pt, 6.5 l; 4-cylinder Bosch indirect injection pump.

PERFORMANCE max speeds: (I) 21 mph, 33 km/h; (II) 35 mph, 56 km/h; (III) 57 mph, 92 km/h; (IV) 84 mph, 135 km/h; power-weight ratio: 50.5 lb/hp, (68.6 lb/kW), 22.9 kg/hp (31.1 kg/kW); consumption: 34 m/imp gal, 28.3 m/US gal, 8.3 l x 100 km.

ELECTRICAL EQUIPMENT 66 Ah battery.

DIMENSIONS AND WEIGHT weight: 3,032 lb, 1,375 kg.

PRACTICAL INSTRUCTIONS fuel: diesel oil; oil: engine 11.4 imp pt, 13.7 US pt, 6.5 l, change every 3,100 miles, 5,000 km; tappet clearances: inlet 0.008 in, 0.10 mm, exhaust 0.016 in, 0.40 mm; valve timing: 12°30' 41°30' 45° 9°.

OPTIONALS with MB automatic transmission, max speeds (I) 20 mph, 32 km/h, (II) 35 mph, 56 km/h, (III) 57 mph, 92 km/h, (IV) 81 mph, 130 km/h.

230 Series

PRICES IN GB AND EX WORKS:	£	DM
4-dr Limousine	8,965*	22,227*
C 2-dr Coupé	10,952*	27,751*
T 4+1-dr Limousine	—	26,465*

ENGINE front, 4 stroke; 4 cylinders, vertical, in line; 140.8 cu in, 2,307 cc (3.69 x 3.29 in, 93.7 x 83.6 mm); compression ratio: 9:1; max power (DIN): 109 hp (80 kW) at 4,800 rpm; max torque (DIN): 137 lb ft, 18.9 kg m (185 Nm) at 3,000 rpm; max engine rpm: 6,000; 21.2 hp/l (28.8 kW/l); cast iron block, light alloy head; 5 crankshaft bearings; valves: overhead, in line, finger levers; camshafts: 1, overhead; lubrication: gear pump, oil-water heat exchanger, full flow filter (cartridge), 9.7 imp pt, 11.6 US pt, 5.5 l; 1 Stromberg 175 CD horizontal carburettor; fuel feed: mechanical pump; water-cooled, 18.8 imp pt, 22.6 US pt, 10.7 l.

TRANSMISSION driving wheels: rear; clutch: single dry plate, hydraulically controlled; gearbox: mechanical; gears: 4, fully synchronized; ratios: I 3.900, II 2.300, III 1.410, IV 1, rev 3.660; lever: steering column or central; final drive: hypoid bevel; axle ratio: 3.690; width of rims: Coupé and T 6"; tyres: Coupé and T 195/70 SR x 14.

MERCEDES-BENZ 200 Limousine

MERCEDES-BENZ 230 C Coupé

230 SERIES

PERFORMANCE max speeds: (I) 30 mph, 48 km/h; (II) 50 mph, 80 km/h; (III) 83 mph, 134 km/h; (IV) 106 mph, 170 km/h; power-weight ratio: 4-dr Limousine 27.3 lb/hp, (37.1 lb/kW), 12.4 kg/hp (16.8 kg/kW); carrying capacity: T Limousine 1,235 lb, 560 kg; consumption: 24.1 m/imp gal, 20.1 m/US gal, 11.7 l x 100 km.

CHASSIS integral, front auxiliary frame; front suspension: independent, wishbones, coil springs, auxiliary rubber springs, anti-roll bar, telescopic dampers; rear: independent, oblique semi-trailing arms, coil springs, auxiliary rubber springs, anti-roll bar, telescopic dampers, (for T only) automatic levelling control.

STEERING recirculating ball, servo (standard for Coupé only).

BRAKES disc (front diameter 10.75 in, 27.3 cm, rear 10.98 in, 27.9 cm), dual circuit, servo; swept area: front 225.4 sq in, 1,454 sq cm, rear 195.8 sq in, 1,263 sq cm, total 421.2 sq in, 2,717 sq cm.

ELECTRICAL EQUIPMENT 12 V; 55 Ah battery; 770 W alternator; Bosch distributor; 4 headlamps.

DIMENSIONS AND WEIGHT wheel base: 110.04 in, 279 cm - Coupé 106.69 in, 271 cm; tracks: 58.58 in, 149 cm front, 56.93 in, 145 cm rear; length: 186.02 in, 472 cm - Coupé 182.68 in, 464 cm; width: 70.31 in, 179 cm; height: 56.69 in, 144 cm - Coupé 54.72 in, 139 cm - T 56.10 in, 142 cm; ground clearance: 6.50 in, 16.5 cm; weight: 4-dr Limousine 2,977 lb, 1,350 kg - Coupé 3,032 lb, 1,375 kg - T 3,241 lb, 1,470 kg; turning circle: 37.1 ft, 11.3 m - Coupé 36.1 ft, 11 m; fuel tank: 14.3 imp gal, 17.2 US gal, 65 l - T 15.4 imp gal, 18.5 US gal, 70 l.

BODY saloon/sedan, 7-8 seats - coupé, 5 seats - T Limousine estate car/st. wagon, 5-7 seats, folding rear seat, rear window wiper-washer; separate front seats, reclining backrests.

PRACTICAL INSTRUCTIONS fuel: 98 oct petrol; oil: engine 9.7 imp pt, 11.6 US pt, 5.5 l, SAE 20W-30, change every 4,600 miles, 7,500 km - gearbox 2.8 imp pt, 3.4 US pt, 1.6 l, ATF, change every 12,400 miles, 20,000 km - final drive 1.9 imp pt, 2.3 US pt, 1.1 l, SAE 90, change every 12,400 miles, 20,000 km; greasing: none; tappet clearances: inlet 0.003 in, 0.08 mm, exhaust 0.008 in, 0.20 mm; valve timing: 11° 47° 48° 16°; tyre pressure: front 21 psi, 1.5 atm, rear 26 psi, 1.8 atm.

OPTIONALS MB automatic transmission, hydraulic torque converter and planetary gears with 4 ratios (I 3.980, II 2.390, III 1.460, IV 1, rev 5.480), possible manual selection, max speeds (I) 25 mph, 40 km/h, (II) 50 mph, 80 km/h, (III) 83 mph, 134 km/h, (IV) 103 mph 165 km/h; automatic levelling control on rear suspension (for 4-dr Limousine and coupé); (for 4-dr Limousine and T Limousine); power steering; halogen headlamps; fog lamps; electric or manual sunshine roof; heated rear window; heated seats; electric windows; tinted glass; air-conditioning; light alloy wheels; (for T Limousine only) 185 HR x 15 tyres with 5.5" wide rims; metallic spray.

250 Limousine Series

PRICES IN GB AND EX WORKS:

	£	DM
4-dr	10,334*	26,024*
Long Wheelbase 4-dr	14,043*	38,669*
T 4+1-dr	—	30,261*

ENGINE front, 4 stroke; 6 cylinders, vertical, in line; 154.1 cu in, 2,525 cc (3.39 x 2.85 in, 86 x 72.4 mm); compression ratio: 9:1; max power (DIN): 140 hp (103 kW) at 5,500 rpm; max torque (DIN): 177 lb ft, 24.4 kg m (239 Nm) at 3,500 rpm; max engine rpm: 6,000; 18 hp/l (24.5 kW/l); cast iron block, light alloy head; 4 crankshaft bearings; valves: overhead, in line, finger levers; camshafts: 1, overhead; lubrication: gear pump, oil-water heat exchanger, full flow filter (cartridge), 11.4 imp pt, 13.7 US pt, 6.5 l; 1 Solex 4 A 1 downdraught twin barrel carburettor; fuel feed: mechanical pump; water-cooled, 18.8 imp pt, 22.6 US pt, 10.7 l.

TRANSMISSION driving wheels: rear; clutch: single dry plate, hydraulically controlled; gearbox: mechanical; gears: 4, fully synchronized; ratios: I 3.980, II 2.290, III 1.450, IV 1, rev 3.740; lever: steering column or central; final drive: hypoid bevel; axle ratio: 3.690; width of rims: 5.5" - T Limousine 6"; tyres: 175 SR x 14 - Long Wheelbase 185 SR x 15 - T Limousine 195/70 HR x 14.

PERFORMANCE max speeds: (I) 30 mph, 48 km/h; (II) 50 mph, 80 km/h; (III) 83 mph, 134 km/h; (IV) 112 mph, 180 km/h; power weight ratio: 4-dr Limousine 21.7 lb/hp, (29.4 lb/kW), 9.8 kg/hp (13.3 kg/kW) carrying capacity: 4-dr Limousine 1,145 lb, 520 kg - Long Wheelbase 1,466 lb, 665 kg - T Limousine 1,235 lb, 560 kg; consumption: 23.9 m/imp gal, 19.9 m/US gal, 11.8 l x 100 km.

CHASSIS integral, front auxiliary frame; front suspension; independent, wishbones, coil springs, auxiliary rubber springs, anti-roll bar, telescopic dampers; rear: independent, oblique semi-trailing arms, coil springs, auxiliary rubber springs, anti-roll bar, telescopic dampers, (for T Limousine only) automatic levelling control.

STEERING recirculating ball; servo.

MERCEDES-BENZ 250 Limousine

BRAKES disc (front diameter 10.75 in, 27.3 cm, rear 10.98 in, 27.9 cm), dual circuit, servo; swept area: front 225.4 sq in, 1,454 sq cm, rear 195.8 sq in, 1,263 sq cm, total 421.2 sq in, 2,717 sq cm.

ELECTRICAL EQUIPMENT 12 V; 55 Ah battery; 770 W alternator; Bosch distributor; 4 headlamps.

DIMENSIONS AND WEIGHT wheel base: 110.04 in, 279 cm - Long Wheelbase 134.65 in, 342 cm; tracks: 58.58 in, 149 cm - Long Wheelbase 58.27 in, 148 cm front, 56.93 in, 145 cm - Long Wheelbase 56.30 in, 143 cm rear; length: 186.02 in, 472 cm - Long Wheelbase 210.36 in, 535 cm; width: 70.31 in, 179 cm; height: 4-dr Limousine 56.69 in, 144 cm - Long Wheelbase 58.27 in, 148 cm - T Limousine 56.10 in, 142 cm; ground clearance: 6.50 in, 16.5 cm; weight: 4-dr Limousine 3,032 lb, 1,375 kg - Long Wheelbase 3,396 lb, 1,540 kg - T Limousine 3,241 lb, 1,470 kg; turning circle: 37.1 ft, 11.3 m - Long Wheelbase 43.6 ft, 13.3 m; fuel tank: 14.3 imp gal, 17.2 US gal, 65 l - T Limousine 15.4 imp gal, 18.5 US gal, 70 l.

BODY saloon/sedan, 5 seats - Long Wheelbase, saloon/sedan, 7-8 seats - T Limousine, estate car/st. wagon, 5-7 seats, folding rear seat, rear window wiper-washer; separate front seats, reclining backrests.

PRACTICAL INSTRUCTIONS fuel: 98 oct petrol; oil: engine 11.4 imp pt, 13.7 US pt, 6.5 l, SAE 20W-30, change every 4,600 miles, 7,500 km - gearbox 2.8 imp pt, 3.4 US pt, 1.6 l, ATF, change every 12,400 miles, 20,000 km - final drive 1.9 imp pt, 2.3 US pt, 1.1 l, SAE 90; change every 12,400 miles, 20,000 km; greasing: none; tappet clearances: inlet 0.003 in, 0.08 mm, exhaust 0.008 in, 0.20 mm; valve timing: 11° 47° 48° 16°; tyre pressure: front 21 psi, 1.5 atm, rear 26 psi, 1.8 atm.

OPTIONALS MB automatic transmission, hydraulic torque converter and planetary gears with 4 ratios (I 3.980, II 2.390, III 1.460, IV 1, rev 5.480), possible manual selection, max speeds (I) 25 mph, 40 km/h; (II) 50 mph, 80 km/h; (III) 83 mph, 134 km/h; (IV) 109 mph, 175 km/h; (for 4-dr Limousine and Long Wheelbase only) automatic levelling control on rear suspension; halogen headlamps; fog lamps; electric or manual sunshine roof; heated seats; electric windows; tinted glass; air conditioning; light alloy wheels; (for T Limousine only) 185 HR x 15 tyres 5.5" wide rims; metallic spray.

240 Limousine Series

PRICES IN GB, USA AND EX WORKS:

	£	$	DM
D 4-dr	8,981*	16,670*	23,674
D Long Wheelbase 4-dr	14,043*	—	37,154
TD 4+1-dr	10,430*	—	27,911

ENGINE diesel; front, 4 stroke; 4 cylinders, vertical, in line; 146.7 cu in, 2,404 cc (3.58 x 3.64 in, 91 x 92.4 mm); compression ratio: 21:1; max power (DIN): 72 hp (53 kW) at 4,400 rpm; max torque (DIN): 101 lb ft, 14 kg m (137 Nm) at 2,400 rpm; max engine rpm: 5,300; 33.4 hp/l (45.4 kW/l); cast iron block and head; 5 crankshaft bearings; valves: overhead, in line, finger levers; camshafts: 1, overhead; lubrication: gear pump, oil cooler, full flow (cartridge) and by-pass filters, 11.4 imp pt, 13.7 US pt, 6.5 l; 4-cylinder Bosch indirect injection pump; fuel feed: mechanical pump; cooling: 17.6 pt, 21.1 US pt, 10 l.

TRANSMISSION driving wheels: rear; clutch: single dry plate, hydraulically controlled; gearbox: mechanical; gears: 4, fully synchronized; ratios: I 3.900, II 2.300, III 1.410, IV 1, rev 3.660; lever: steering column or central; final drive: hypoid bevel; axle ratio: 3.690; width of rims: 5.5" - TD 6"; tyres: 175 SR x 14 - Long Wheelbase 185 SR x 15 - TD 195/70 SR x 14.

PERFORMANCE max speeds: (I) 22 mph, 35 km/h; (II) 37 mph, 60 km/h; (III) 61 mph, 98 km/h; (IV) 89 mph, 143 km/h; power-weight ratio: D 42.4 lb/hp, (57.6 lb/kW), 19.2 kg/hp (26. kg/kW); carrying capacity: D 1,145 lb, 520 kg - D Long Wheelbase 1,466 lb, 665 kg - TD 1,235 lb, 560 kg; consumption: 29.7 m/imp gal, 24.8 m/US gal, 9.5 l x 100 km.

CHASSIS integral, front auxiliary frame; front suspension: independent, wishbones, coil springs, auxiliary rubber springs, anti-roll bar, telescopic dampers; rear: independent, oblique semi-trailing arms, coil springs, auxiliary rubber springs, anti-roll bar, telescopic dampers, automatic levelling control (standard for TD only).

STEERING recirculating ball, servo (standard for Long Wheelbase only).

BRAKES disc (front diameter 10.75 in, 27.3 cm, rear 10.98 in, 27.9 cm), dual circuit, servo; swept area: front 225.4 sq in, 1,454 sq cm, rear 195.8 sq in, 1,263 sq cm, total 421.2 sq in, 2,717 sq cm.

ELECTRICAL EQUIPMENT 12 V; 88 Ah battery; 770 W alternator; Bosch distributor; 4 headlamps.

DIMENSIONS AND WEIGHT wheel base: 110.04 in, 279 cm Long Wheelbase 134.65 in, 342 cm; tracks: 58.58 in, 149 cm Long Wheelbase 58.27 in, 148 cm front, 56.93 in, 145 cm Long Wheelbase 56.30 in, 143 cm rear; length: 186.02 in, 47

MERCEDES-BENZ 240 D Limousine

m - Long Wheelbase 210.36 in, 535 cm; width: 70.31 in, 179 m; height: D 56.69 in, 144 cm - Long Wheelbase 58.27 in, 148 m - TD 56.10 in, 142 cm; ground clearance: 6.50 in, 16.5 cm; eight: D 3,054 lb, 1,385 kg - Long Wheelbase 3,451 lb, 1,565 g - TD 3,241 lb, 1,470 kg; turning circle: 37.1 ft, 11.3 m - ong Wheelbase 43.6 ft, 13.3 m; fuel tank: 14.3 imp gal, 17.2 S gal, 65 l - TD 15.4 imp gal, 18.5 US gal, 70 l.

ODY saloon/sedan, 5 seats - Long Wheelbase, saloon/sedan, -8 seats; TD Limousine estate car/st. wagon, 5-7 seats, olding rear seats, rear window wiper-washer; separate front eats, reclining backrests; heated rear window.

RACTICAL INSTRUCTIONS fuel: diesel oil; oil: engine 11.4 np pt, 13.7 US pt, 6.5 l, SAE 20W-30, change every 4,600 iles, 7,500 km - gearbox 2.8 imp pt, 3.4 US pt, 1.6 l, ATF, hange every 12,400 miles, 20,000 km - final drive 1.9 imp pt, .3 US pt, 1.1 l, SAE 90, change every 12,400 miles, 20,000 n; greasing: none; tappet clearances: inlet 0.003 in, 0.08 mm, xhaust 0.008 in, 0.20 mm; valve timing: 11° 47° 48° 16°; tyre ressure: front 21 psi, 1.5 atm, rear 26 psi, 1.8 atm.

PTIONALS MB automatic transmission, hydraulic torque conerter and planetary gears with 4 ratios (I 3.980, II 2.390, III .460, IV 1, rev 5.480), possible manual selection, max speeds) 21 mph, 34 km/h, (II) 37 mph, 60 km/h, (III) 61 mph, 98 n/h, (IV) 84 mph, 135 km/h; (for D and Long Wheelbase only) utomatic levelling control on rear suspension; halogen headmps; fog lamps; electric or manual sunshine roof; heated eats; electric windows; tinted glass; air-conditioning; light alloy heels; (for TD only) 185 HR x 15 tyres with 5.5" wide rims; etallic spray.

MERCEDES-BENZ 300 D Limousine

MERCEDES-BENZ 300 SD (turbodiesel engine)

300 Series

RICES IN USA AND EX WORKS:

	$	DM
D 4-dr Limousine	**23,638***	**26,150***
D Long Wheelbase 4-dr Limousine	—	**38,900***
TD 4+1 dr Limousine	**27,029***	**30,385***
SD Turbodiesel 4-dr Limousine	**29,511***	—

or GB prices, see price index.

ower team:	Standard for:	Optional for:
80 hp	1 to 3	—
10 hp	4	—

80 hp power team

NGINE diesel; front, 4 stroke; 5 cylinders, vertical, in line; 83.4 cu in, 3,005 cc (3.58 x 3.64 in, 91 x 92.4 mm); compreson ratio: 21:1; max power (DIN): 80 hp (59 kW) at 4,000 rpm; ax torque (DIN): 127 lb ft, 17.5 kg m (172 Nm) at 2,400 rpm; ax engine rpm: 5,100; 37.6 hp/l (51 kW/l); cast iron block and ead; 6 crankshaft bearings; valves: overhead, in line, finger vers; camshafts: 1, overhead; lubrication: gear pump, oil ooler, full flow (cartridge) and by-pass filter, 11.4 imp pt, 13.7 S pt, 6.5 l; 5-cylinders Bosch indirect injection pump; fuel ed: mechanical pump; cooling: 19 imp pt, 22.8 US pt, 108 l.

RANSMISSION driving wheels: rear; clutch: single dry plate, ydraulically controlled; gearbox: mechanical; gears: 4, fully ynchronized; ratios: I 3.900, II 2.300, III 1.410, IV 1, rev 3.660; lever: steering column or central; final drive: hypoid bevel; axle ratio: 3.690; width of rims: 5.5" - TD 6"; tyres: 175 SR x 14 - Long Wheelbase 185 SR x 15 - TD 195/70 SR x 14.

PERFORMANCE max speeds: (I) 24 mph, 38 km/h; (II) 40 mph, 64 km/h; (III) 65 mph, 104 km/h; (IV) 92 mph, 148 km/h; power weight ratio: D 39.8 lb/hp, (54 lb/kW), 18.1 kg/hp (24.5 kg/kW); carrying capacity: 1,445 lb, 520 kg - Long Wheelbase 1,466 lb, 665 kg - TD 1,235 lb, 560 kg; acceleration: 0-62 mph (0-100 km/h) 19.9 sec - TD 20.9 sec; consumption: 26.2 m/imp gal, 21.8 m/US gal, 10.8 l x 100 km.

CHASSIS integral, front auxiliary frame; front suspension: independent, wishbones, coil springs, auxiliary rubber springs, antiroll bar, telescopic dampers; rear: independent, oblique semitrailing arms, coil springs, auxiliary rubber springs, anti-roll bar, telescopic dampers, (for TD only) automatic levelling control.

STEERING recirculating ball, servo.

BRAKES disc (front diameter 10.75 in, 27.3 cm, rear 10.98 in, 27.9 cm), dual circuit servo; swept area: front 225.4 sq in, 1,454 sq cm, rear 195.8 sq in, 1,263 sq cm, total 421.2 sq in, 2,717 sq cm.

ELECTRICAL EQUIPMENT 12 V; 88 Ah battery; 770 W alternator; Bosch distributor; 4 headlamps.

DIMENSIONS AND WEIGHT wheel base: 110.04 in, 279 cm - Long Wheelbase 134.65 in, 342 cm; tracks: 58.58 in, 149 cm - Long Wheelbase 58.27 in, 148 cm front, 56.93 in, 145 cm - Long Wheelbase 56.30 in, 143 cm rear; length: 186.02 in, 472 cm - Long Wheelbase 210.36 in, 535 cm; width: 70.31 in, 179 cm; height: D 56.69 in, 144 cm - Long Wheelbase 58.27 in, 148 cm - TD 56.10 in, 142 cm; ground clearance: 6.50 in, 16.5 cm; weight: D 3,186 lb, 1,445 kg - Long Wheelbase 3,561 lb, 1,615 kg - TD 3,241 lb, 1,470 kg; turning circle: 37.1 ft, 11.3 m - Long Wheelbase 43.6 ft, 13.3 m; fuel tank: 14.3 imp gal, 17.2 US gal, 65 l - TD 15.4 imp gal, 18.5 US gal, 70 l.

BODY saloon/sedan, 5 seats - Long Wheelbase, saloon/sedan 7-8 seats - TD Limousine, estate car/st. wagon, 5-7 seats, folding rear seat, rear window wiper-washer; separate front seats, reclining backrests; heated rear window.

PRACTICAL INSTRUCTIONS fuel: diesel oil; oil: engine 11.4 imp pt, 13.7 US pt, 6.5 l, SAE 20W-30, change every 4,600 miles, 7,500 km - gearbox 2.8 imp pt, 3.4 US pt, 1.6 l, ATF, change every 12,400 miles, 20,000 km - final drive 1.9 imp pt, 2.3 US pt, 1.1 l, SAE 90, change every 12,400 miles, 20,000 km; greasing: none; tappet clearances: inlet 0.003 in, 0.008 mm, exhaust 0.008 in, 0.20 mm; valve timing: 11° 47° 48° 16°; tyre pressure: front 21 psi, 1.5 atm, rear 26 psi, 1.8 atm.

OPTIONALS MB automatic transmission, hydraulic torque converter and planetary gears with 4 ratios (I 3.980, II 2.390, III 1.460, IV 1, rev 5.480), possible manual selection, max speeds (I) 22 mph, 36 km/h, (II) 40 mph, 64 km/h, (III) 65 mph, 104 km/h, (IV) 89 mph, 143 km/h; (for D and Long Wheelbase only) automatic levelling control on rear suspension; halogen headlamps; fog lamps; electric or manual sunshine roof; heated seats; electric windows; tinted glass; air-conditioning; light alloy wheels; (for TD only) 185 HR x 15 tyres with 5.5" wide rims; metallic spray.

110 hp power team

(Only for USA)

See 80 hp power team, except for:

ENGINE turbocharged; compression ratio: 21.5:1; max power (SAE net): 110 hp (81 kW) at 4,200 rpm; max torque (SAE net): 168 lb ft, 23.2 kg m (227 Nm) at 2,400 rpm; 27.3 hp/l (37.1 kW/l); lubrication: full flow filter, 15.1 imp pt, 18.2 US pt, 8.6 l; 5-cylinder Bosch indirect injection pump and Garret turbocharger with exhaust gas recirculation.

TRANSMISSION axle ratio: 3.070.

PERFORMANCE max speed: 103 mph, 165 km/h; power-weight ratio: 35.4 lb/hp, (48 lb/kW), 16 kg/hp (21.8 kg/kW); carrying capacity: 1,147 lb, 520 kg; speed in direct drive at 1,000 rpm: 23.9 mph, 38.5 km/h.

CHASSIS front suspension: upper wishbones with single transverse rod, longitudinal leading arm in unit with anti-roll bar.

STEERING damper, servo.

BRAKES (front diameter 10.94 in, 27.8 cm); swept area: front 255.5 sq in, 1,648 sq cm, rear 195.8 sq in, 1,263 sq cm, total 451.3 sq in, 2,911 sq cm.

DIMENSIONS AND WEIGHT wheel base: 112.60 in, 286 cm; tracks: 59.84 in, 152 cm front, 59.05 in, 150 cm rear; length: 205.51 in, 522 cm; width: 73.62 in, 187 cm; height: 55.90 in, 142 cm; ground clearance: 5.91 in, 15 cm; weight: 3,892 lb, 1,765 kg; fuel tank: 21.1 imp gal, 25.3 US gal, 96 l.

BODY saloon/sedan; 5 seats.

PRACTICAL INSTRUCTIONS oil: engine 15.1 imp pt, 18.2 US pt, 8.6 l.

110 HP POWER TEAM

OPTIONALS with MB automatic transmission, max speed 99 mph, 160 km/h.

280 Series

PRICES IN GB, USA AND EX WORKS:

	£	$	DM
1 4-dr Limousine	—	—	28,894*
2 C 2-dr Coupé	—	—	33,007*
3 S 4-dr Limousine	—	—	34,160*
4 E 4-dr Limousine	12,351*	25,234*	31,075*
5 CE 2-dr Coupé	13,425*	28,217*	35,188*
6 TE 4+1-dr Limousine	13,837*	—	35,256*
7 SE 4-dr Limousine	14,458*	29,386*	36,533*
8 SEL 4-dr Limousine	—	—	38,895*
9 SL 2-dr Roadster	—	—	38,996*
10 SLC 2-dr Coupé	—	—	45,934*

Power team:	Standard for:	Optional for:
156 hp	1 to 3	—
185 hp	4 to 10	—

156 hp power team

ENGINE front, 4 stroke; 6 cylinders, vertical, in line; 167.6 cu in, 2,746 cc (3.39 x 3.10 in, 86 x 78.8 mm); compression ratio: 8.7:1; max power (DIN): 156 hp (115 kW) at 5,500 rpm; max torque (DIN): 164 lb ft, 22.7 kg m (223 Nm) at 4,000 rpm; max engine rpm: 6,500; 56.8 hp/l (41.8 kW/l); cast iron block, light alloy head; 7 crankshaft bearings; valves: overhead, Vee-slanted at 54°, finger levers; camshafts: 2, overhead; lubrication: gear pump, oil-water heat exchanger, filter (cartridge) on by-pass, oil cooler, 11.4 imp pt, 13.7 US pt, 6.5 l; 1 Solex 4 A 1 downdraught twin barrel carburettor; fuel feed: mechanical pump; water-cooled, 17.1 imp pt, 20.5 US pt, 9.7 l, - (S 19.4 imp pt, 23.3 US pt, 11 l), magnetically-controlled fan - (S thermostatic fan).

TRANSMISSION driving wheels: rear; clutch: single dry plate, hydraulically controlled; gearbox: mechanical; gears: 4, fully synchronized; ratios: I 3.980, II 2.290, III 1.450, IV 1, rev 3.740; lever: steering column or central - S central; final drive: hypoid bevel; axle ratio: 3.540 - S 3.690; width of rims: 6"; tyres: 195/70 HR x 14.

PERFORMANCE max speeds: (I) 34 mph, 55 km/h; (II) 55 mph, 88 km/h; (III) 90 mph, 145 km/h; (IV) 118 mph, 190 km/h; power-weight ratio: 4-dr Limousine 20.6 lb/hp (27.9 lb/kW), 9.3 kg/hp (12.7 kg/kW); carrying capacity: 1,147 lb, 520 kg; consumption: 22.6 m/imp gal, 18.8 m/US gal, 12.5 l x 100 km.

CHASSIS integral; front suspension: independent, upper wishbones with single transverse rod, longitudinal leading arm in unit with anti-roll bar, coil springs, telescopic dampers; rear: independent, oblique semi-trailing arms, coil springs, auxiliary rubber springs, anti-roll bar, telescopic dampers.

STEERING recirculating ball, damper, servo.

BRAKES disc (front diameter 10.94 in, 27.8 cm, rear 10.98 in, 27.9 cm), rear compensator, dual circuit, servo; swept area: front 255.5 sq in, 1,648 sq cm, rear 195 sq in, 1,263 sq cm, total 451.3 sq in, 2,911 sq cm.

ELECTRICAL EQUIPMENT 12 V; 55 Ah battery; 770 W alternator; Bosch distributor; 4 halogen headlamps.

DIMENSIONS AND WEIGHT wheel base: 4-dr Limousine 110.04 in, 279 cm - C 106.69 in, 271 cm - S 112.60 in, 286 cm; tracks: 58.58 in, 149 cm front, 56.93 in, 145 cm rear - S 59.84 in, 152 cm front, 59.05 in, 150 cm rear; length: 4-dr Limousine 186.02 in, 472 cm - C 182.68 in, 464 cm - S 195.28 in, 496 cm; width: 70.31 in, 179 cm - S 73.62 in, 187 cm; height: 4-dr Limousine 56.69 in, 144 cm - C 54.72 in, 139 cm - S 55.90 in, 142 cm; ground clearance: 6.50 in, 16.5 cm - S 5.91 in, 15 cm; weight: 4-dr Limousine 3,208 lb, 1,455 kg - C 3,186 lb, 1,445 kg - S 3,550 lb, 1,610 kg; turning circle: 37.1 ft, 11.3 m - C 36.1 ft, 11 m; fuel tank: 17.6 imp gal, 21.1 US gal, 80 l - S 21.1 imp gal, 25.3 US gal, 96 l.

BODY saloon/sedan - coupé; 5 seats, separate front seats, reclining backrests with built-in headrests.

PRACTICAL INSTRUCTIONS fuel: 98 oct petrol; oil: engine 11.4 imp pt, 13.7 US pt, 6.5 l, SAE 20W-30, change every 4,600 miles, 7,500 km - gearbox 3.2 imp pt, 3.8 US pt, 1.8 l, ATF, change every 12,400 miles, 20,000 km - final drive 4.4 imp pt, 5.3 US pt, 2.5 l, SAE 90, change every 12,400 miles, 20,000 km; greasing: every 3,100 miles, 5,000 km, 20 points; tyre pressure: front 22 psi, 1.6 atm, rear 28 psi, 1.9 atm.

OPTIONALS MB automatic transmission, hydraulic torque converter and planetary gears with 4 ratios (I 3.980, II 2.390, III 1.460, IV 1, rev 5.470), max ratio of converter at stall 2.2, possible manual selection, max speeds (I)26 mph, 42 km/h; (II) 55 mph, 88 km; (III) 90 mph, 145 km/h; (IV) 115 mph, 185 km/h; automatic levelling control on rear suspension; fog lamps; electric or manual sunshine roof; heated rear window; heated seats; electric windows; tinted glass; air-conditioning; light alloy wheels; metallic spray.

MERCEDES-BENZ 280 TE Limousine

185 hp power team

See 156 hp power team, except for:

ENGINE compression ratio: 9:1; max power (DIN): 185 hp (136 kW) at 5,800 rpm; max torque (DIN): 177 lb ft, 24.5 kg m (240 Nm) at 4,500 rpm; 67.4hp/l (49.6 kW/l); Bosch K-Jetronic injection; fuel feed: electric pump; cooling: (SE, SEL, SL and SLC) 19.4 imp pt, 23.3 US pt, 11 l, thermostatic fan.

TRANSMISSION width of rims: (for SL only) 6.5".

PERFORMANCE max speeds: (I) 34 mph, 55 km/h; (II) 55 mph, 88 km/h; (III) 90 mph, 145 km/h; (IV) 124 mph, 200 km/h; power-weight ratio: E 174 lb/hp, (23.7 lb/kW), 7.9 kg/hp (10.7 kg/kW); carrying capacity: TE 1,235 lb, 560 kg - SL 926 lb, 420 kg - SLC 1,080 lb, 490 kg.

CHASSIS rear suspension: (for TE only) automatic levelling control.

ELECTRICAL EQUIPMENT (for SE, SEL, SL and SLC) transistorized ignition.

MERCEDES-BENZ 280 CE Coupé

DIMENSIONS AND WEIGHT wheel base: SEL 116.73 ir 296 cm - SL 96.85 in, 246 cm - SLC 111.02 in, 282 cm tracks: SL 57.09 in, 145 cm front, 56.69 in, 144 cm rear - T 57.20 in, 145 cm front and rear; length: SEL 199.21 in, 50 cm - SL 172.83 in, 439 cm - SLC 187.01 in, 475 cm; heigh TE 56.10 in, 142 cm - SEL 56.30 in, 143 cm - SL 51.18 ir 130 cm - SLC 52.36 in, 133 cm; ground clearance: SL 5.3 in, 13.5 cm; weight: E 3,219 lb, 1,460 kg - CE 3,197 lt 1,450 kg - TE 3,407 lb, 1,545 kg - SE 3,550 lb, 1,610 kg SEL 3,627 lb, 1,645 kg - SL 3,308 lb, 1,500 kg - SLC 3,41 lb, 1,550 kg; turning circle: SEL 38.7 ft, 11.8 m - SL 33.8 f 10.3 m - SLC 37.7 ft, 11.5 m; fuel tank: TE 15.4 imp ga 18.5 US gal, 70 l - SL and SLC 19.8 imp gal, 23.8 US ga 90 l.

BODY saloon/sedan - coupé - SL, convertible, 2 seats - T Limousine estate car/st. wagon, 5-7 seats, folding rea seat, rear window wiper-washer.

OPTIONALS (for SL only) hardtop.

350 Series

PRICES IN GB AND EX WORKS:

	£	DM
1 SE 4-dr Limousine	16,840*	40,680
2 SEL 4-dr Limousine	—	43,042
3 SL 2-dr Roadster	16,669*	43,143
4 SLC 2-dr Coupé	—	50,082

Power team:	Standard for:	Optional for:
205 hp	1,2	—
195 hp	3,4	—

205 hp power team

ENGINE front, 4 stroke; 8 cylinders, Vee-slanted; 213.5 c in, 3,499 cc (3.62 x 2.59 in, 92 x 65.8 mm); compressic ratio: 9:1; max power (DIN): 205 hp (151 kW) at 5,750 rpn max torque (DIN): 210 lb ft, 29 kg m (285 Nm) at 4,000 rpn max engine rpm: 6,300; 58.6 hp/l (43.1 kW/l); cast irc block, light alloy head; 5 crankshaft bearings; valves: ove head, finger levers; camshafts: 2, 1 per bank, overhea lubrication: gear pump, full flow filter, oil cooler, 14.1 im pt, 16.9 US pt, 8 l; Bosch electronic injection, injectors inlet pipes; fuel feed: electric pump; cooling: 23.8 imp p 28.5 US pt, 13.5 l, thermostatic fan.

TRANSMISSION driving wheels: rear; clutch: single d plate, hydraulically controlled; gearbox: mechanical; gear 4, fully synchronized; ratios: I 3.960, II 2.340, III 1.430, I 1, rev 3.720; lever: central; final drive: hypoid bevel; ax ratio: 3.460; width of rims: 6.5"; tyres: 205/70 HR x 14.

PERFORMANCE max speeds: (I) 34 mph, 54 km/h; (II) 5 mph, 90 km/h; (III) 93 mph, 150 km/h; (IV) 127 mph, 20 km/h; power-weight ratio: 18 lb/hp, (24.5 lb/kW), 8.2 kg/h (11.1 kg/kW); carrying capacity: 1,147 lb, 520 kg; speed direct drive at 1,000 rpm: 21.1 mph, 33.9 km/h; consum tion: 21.7 m/imp gal, 18.1 m/US gal, 13 l x 100 km.

CHASSIS integral; front suspension: independent, upp wishbones with single transverse rod, longitudinal leadir arm in unit with anti-roll bar, coil springs, telescopic dar pers; rear: independent, oblique semi-trailing arms, cc springs, anti-roll bar, auxiliary rubber springs, telescop dampers.

STEERING recirculating ball, damper, servo.

BRAKES disc (front diameter 10.94 in, 27.8 cm, rear 10.98 in, 27.9 cm), rear compensator, dual circuit, servo; swept area: front 255.5 sq in, 1,648 sq cm, rear 195.8 sq in, 1,263 sq cm, total 451.3 sq in, 2,911 sq cm.

ELECTRICAL EQUIPMENT 12 V; 66 Ah battery; 770 W alternator; transistorized ignition; Bosch distributor; 4 headlamps.

DIMENSIONS AND WEIGHT wheel base: SE 112.60 in, 286 cm - SEL 116.73 in, 296 cm; tracks: 59.84 in, 152 cm front, 59.05 in 150 cm rear; length: SE 195.28 in, 496 cm - SEL 199.21 in, 506 cm; width: 73.62 in, 187 cm; height: SE 55.90 in, 142 cm - SEL 56.30 in, 143 cm; ground clearance: 5.91 in, 15 cm; weight: SE 3,693 lb, 1,675 kg - SEL 3,749 lb, 1,700 kg; turning circle: SE 37.4 ft, 11.4 m - SEL 38.7 ft, 11.8 m; fuel tank: 21.1 imp gal, 25.3 US gal, 96 l.

BODY saloon/sedan; 5 seats, separate front seats, reclining backrests.

PRACTICAL INSTRUCTIONS fuel: 98 oct petrol; oil: engine 14.1 imp pt, 16.9 US pt, 8 l, SAE 20W-30, change every 4,600 miles, 7,500 km - gearbox 3.2 imp pt, 3.8 US pt, 1.8 l, AFT, change every 12,400 miles, 20,000 km - final drive 4.4 imp pt, 5.3 US pt, 2.5 l, SAE 90, change every 12,400 miles, 20,000 km; greasing: every 3,100 miles, 5,000 km, 20 points; tyre pressure: front 22 psi, 1.6 atm, rear 28 psi, 1.9 atm.

OPTIONALS MB automatic transmission, hydraulic torque converter and planetary gears with 3 ratios (I 2.310, II 1.460, III 1, rev 1.840), max ratio of converter at stall 2.2, possible manual selection, steering column or central lever, max speeds (I) 56 mph, 90 km/h; (II) 93 mph, 150 km/h; (III) 124 mph, 200 km/h; rev counter; electric sunshine roof; heated rear window; electric windows; headrests; metallic spray; light alloy wheels; tinted glass; air-conditioning.

195 hp power team

See 205 hp power team, except for:

ENGINE max power (DIN): 195 hp (144 kW) at 5,500 rpm; max torque (DIN): 203 lb ft, 28 kg m (275 Nm) at 4,000 rpm; max engine rpm: 6,300; 55.7 hp/l (41 kW/l); water-cooled, fan with revolution limiting device (1.900 rpm), 25.2 imp pt, 30.2 US pt, 14.3 l.

TRANSMISSION tyres: 205/70 VR x 14.

PERFORMANCE max speed: SLC 130 mph, 210 km/h; power-weight ratio: SL 17.4 lb/hp, (23.7 lb/kW), 7.9 kg/hp (10.7 kg/kW); carrying capacity: SL 926 lb, 420 kg - SLC 1,080 lb, 490 kg; consumption: 21.7 m/imp gal, 18.1 m/US gal, 13 l x 100 km.

CHASSIS backbone platform with box-type ladder frame; front suspension: independent, wishbones, coil springs, auxiliary rubber springs, anti-roll bar, telescopic dampers; rear: independent, oblique semi-trailing arms, coil springs, auxiliary rubber springs, anti-roll, bar, telescopic dampers.

MERCEDES-BENZ 350 SL Roadster

BRAKES disc (front diameter 10.75 in, 27.3 cm, rear 10.98 in, 27.9 cm), front internal radial fins.

ELECTRICAL EQUIPMENT 2 iodine headlamps.

DIMENSIONS AND WEIGHT wheel base: SL 96.85 in, 246 cm - SLC 111.02 in, 282 cm; tracks: 57.08 in, 145 cm front, 56.69 in, 144 cm rear; length: SL 172.83 in, 439 cm - SLC 187.01 in, 475 cm; width: 70.47 in, 179 cm; height: SL 51.18 in, 130 cm - SLC 52.36 in, 133 cm; ground clearance: 5.12 in, 13 cm; weight: SL 3,396 lb, 1,540 kg - SLC 3,506 lb, 1,590 kg; turning circle: SL 33.8 ft, 10.3 m - SLC 37.7 ft, 11.5 m; fuel tank: 19.8 imp gal, 23.8 US gal, 90 l.

BODY convertible, 2 seats - coupé, 5 seats.

PRACTICAL INSTRUCTIONS fuel: 96 oct petrol; oil: gearbox 9.5 imp pt, 11.4 US pt, 5.4 l, SAE 20W-30; sparking plug: 215°; tyre pressure: front 30 psi, 2.1 atm, rear 34 psi, 2.4 atm.

OPTIONALS with MB automatic transmission, max speed (SL) 124 mph, 200 km/h - (SLC) 127 mph, 205 km/h; limited slip differential; hardtop.

380 Limousine Series

PRICES EX WORKS:	DM
SE	**46,669***
SEL	**49,042***

MERCEDES-BENZ 380 SE Limousine

ENGINE front, 4 stroke; 8 cylinders, Vee-slanted; 233 cu in, 3,818 cc (3.62 x 2.83 in, 92 x 71.8 mm); compression ratio: 9:1; max power (DIN): 218 hp (160 kW) at 5,500 rpm; max torque (DIN): 225 lb ft, 31.1 kg m (305 Nm) at 4,000 rpm; max engine rpm: 6,000; 57.1 hp/l (42 kW/l); cast iron block, light alloy head; 5 crankshaft bearings; valves: overhead, Vee-slanted at 54°, finger levers; camshafts: 2, 1 per bank, overhead; lubrication: gears pump, oil-water heat exchanger, filter (cartridge) on by-pass, oil cooler, 14.1 imp pt, 16.9 US pt, 8 l; Bosch K-Jetronic injection; fuel feed: electric pump; water-cooled, 26.4 imp pt, 31.7 US pt, 15 l, thermostatic fan.

TRANSMISSION driving wheels: rear; gearbox: MB automatic transmission, hydraulic torque converter and planetary gears with 4 ratios, max ratio of converter at stall 2.2, possible manual selection; ratios: I 3.680, II 2.410, III 1.440, IV 1, rev 5.140; lever: steering column or central; final drive: hypoid bevel; axle ratio: 3.270; width of rims: 6.5"; tyres: 205/70 VR x 14.

PERFORMANCE max speed: 134 mph, 215 km/h; power-weight ratio: SE 16.1 lb/hp, (22 lb/kW), 7.3 kg/hp (10 kg/kW); carrying capacity: 1,147 lb, 520 kg; speed in direct drive at 1,000 rpm: 23 mph, 37 km/h; consumption: 21.2 m/imp gal, 17.7 m/US gal, 13.3 l x 100 km.

CHASSIS integral; front suspension: independent, upper wishbones with single transverse rod, longitudinal leading arm in unit with anti-roll bar, coil springs, telescopic dampers; rear: independent, oblique semi-trailing arms, coil springs, auxiliary rubber springs, anti-roll bar, telescopic dampers.

STEERING recirculating ball, damper, servo.

BRAKES disc (front diameter 10.94 in, 27.8 cm, rear 10.98 in, 27.9 cm), rear compensator, dual circuit, servo; swept area: front 255.5 sq in, 1,648 sq cm, rear 195.8 sq in, 1,263 sq cm, total 451.3 sq in, 2,911 sq cm.

ELECTRICAL EQUIPMENT 12 V; 66 Ah battery; 980 W alternator; Bosch (transistorized) distributor; 4 halogen headlamps.

DIMENSIONS AND WEIGHT wheel base: SE 112.60 in, 286 cm - SEL 120.87 in, 307 cm; tracks: 59.84 in, 152 cm front, 59.05 in, 150 cm rear; length: SE 195.28 in, 496 cm - SEL 201.97 in, 513 cm; width: 73.62 in, 187 cm; height: SE 55.90 in, 142 cm - SEL 56.69 in, 144 cm; ground clearance: 5.91 in, 15 cm; weight: SE 3,517 lb, 1,595 kg - SEL 3,561 lb, 1,615 kg; turning circle: SE 37.1 ft, 11.3 m - SEL 40.3 ft, 12.3 m; fuel tank: 21.1 imp gal, 25.3 US gal, 96 l.

BODY saloon/sedan; 4 doors; 5 seats, separate front seats, reclining backrests with built-in headrests.

PRACTICAL INSTRUCTIONS fuel: 98 oct petrol; oil: engine 14.1 imp pt, 16.9 US pt, 8 l, SAE 20W-30, change every 4,600 miles, 7,500 km; greasing: every 3,100 miles, 5,000 km, 20 points; sparking plug: 215°; tyre pressure: front 30 psi, 2.1 atm, rear 34 psi, 2.4 atm.

OPTIONALS automatic levelling control on rear suspension; fog lamps; electric or manual sunshine roof; heated rear window; heated seats; electric windows; tinted glass; air-conditioning; light alloy wheels; metallic spray.

500 Limousine Series

PRICES EX WORKS: DM

	DM
SE	50,680*
SEL	56,161*

ENGINE front, 4 stroke; 8 cylinders, Vee-slanted; 303.5 cu in, 4,973 cc (3.82 x 3.35 in, 97 x 85 mm); compression ratio: 8.8:1; max power (DIN): 240 hp (177 kW) at 4,750 rpm; max torque (DIN): 297 lb ft, 41 kg m (402 Nm) at 3,200 rpm; max engine rpm: 5,800; 48.3 hp/l (35.5 kW/l); light alloy block and head; 5 crankshaft bearings; valves: overhead, Vee-slanted at 54°, finger levers; camshafts: 2, 1 per bank, overhead, lubrication: gear pump, oil-water heat exchanger, filter (cartridge) on by-pass, oil cooler, 14.1 imp pt, 16.9 US pt, 8 l; Bosch K-Jetronic injection; fuel feed: electric pump; water-cooled, 26.4 imp pt, 31.7 US pt, 15 l, thermostatic fan.

TRANSMISSION driving wheels: rear; gearbox: MB automatic transmission, hydraulic torque converter and planetary gears with 4 ratios, max ratio of converter at stall 2.2, possible manual selection; ratios: I 3.680, II 2.410, III 1.440, IV 1, rev 5.140; lever: steering column or central; final drive: hypoid bevel; axle ratio: 2.820; width of rims: 6.5"; tyres: 205/70 VR x 14.

PERFORMANCE max speed: 140 mph, 225 km/h; power-weight ratio: SE 14.9 lb/hp, (20.2 lb/kW), 6.8 kg/hp (9.2 kg/kW); carrying capacity: 1,147 lb, 520 kg; speed in direct drive at 1,000 rpm: 27 mph, 43 km/h; consumption: 20.9 m/imp gal, 17.4 m/US gal, 13.5 l x 100 km.

CHASSIS integral; front suspension: independent, upper wishbones with single transverse rod, longitudinal leading arm in unit with anti-roll bar, coil springs, telescopic dampers; rear: independent, oblique semi-trailing arms, coil springs, auxiliary rubber springs, anti-roll bar, telescopic dampers.

STEERING recirculating ball, damper, servo.

BRAKES disc (front diameter 10.94 in, 27.8 cm, rear 10.98 in, 27.9 cm), rear compensator, dual circuit, servo, swept area: front 255.5 sq in, 1,648 sq cm, rear 195.8 sq in, 1,263 sq cm, total 451,3 sq in, 2,911 sq cm.

ELECTRICAL EQUIPMENT 12 V; 66 Ah battery; 980 W alternator; Bosch (transistorized) distributor; 4 halogen headlamps.

DIMENSIONS AND WEIGHT wheel base: SE 115.35 in, 293 cm - SEL 120.87 in, 307 cm; tracks: 59.84 in, 152 cm front, 59.05 in, 150 cm rear; length: SE: 196.85 in, 500 cm - SEL 197.36 in, 513 cm; width: 73.62 in, 187 cm; height: 56.69 in, 144 cm; ground clearance: 5.91 in, 15 cm; weight: SE 3,572 lb, 1,620 kg - SEL 3,649 lb 1,655 kg; turning circle: SE 38.7 ft, 11.8 m - SEL 40.3 ft, 12.3 m; fuel tank: 21.1 imp gal, 25.3 US gal, 96 l.

BODY saloon/sedan; 4 doors 5 seats, separate front seats, reclining backrests with built-in headrests.

PRACTICAL INSTRUCTIONS fuel: 98 oct petrol; oil: engine 14.1 imp pt, 16.9 US pt, 8 l, SAE 20W-30, change every 4,600 miles, 7,500 km; greasing: every 3,100 miles, 5,000 km, 20 points; sparking plug: 215°; tyre pressure: front 30 psi, 2.1 atm, rear 34 psi, 2.4 atm.

OPTIONALS automatic levelling control on rear suspension; fog lamps; electric or manual sunshine roof; heated rear window; heated seats; electric windows; tinted glass; air-conditioning; light alloy wheels; metallic spray.

450 Series

PRICES IN GB, USA AND EX WORKS:

		£	$	DM
1	SE 4-dr Limousine	18,139*	—	45,629*
2	SEL 4-dr Limousine	19,161*	36,886*	51,087*
3	SL 2-dr Roadster	17,820*	34,527*	48,093*
4	SLC 2-dr Coupé	20,987*	41,033*	55,031*
5	SLC 5.0 2-dr Coupé	—	—	65,517*
6	SEL 6.9 4-dr Limousine	30,476*	—	81,247*

Power team:	Standard for:	Optional for:
225 hp	1,2	—
217 hp	3,4	—
240 hp	5	—
286 hp	6	—

225 hp power team

ENGINE front, 4 stroke; 8 cylinders, Vee-slanted; 275.8 cu in, 4,520 cc (3.62 x 3.35 in, 92 x 85 mm); compression ratio: 8.8:1; max power (DIN): 225 hp (165 kW) at 5,000 rpm; max torque (DIN): 272 lb ft, 37.5 kg m (370 Nm) at 3,250 rpm; max engine rpm: 5,800; 49.8 hp/l (36.5 kW/l); cast iron block, light alloy head; 5 crankshaft bearings; valves: overhead, finger levers; camshafts 2, 1 per bank, overhead; lubrication: gear pump, full flow filter, oil cooler, 14.1 imp pt, 16.9 US pt, 8 l; Bosch electronic injection; fuel feed: electric pump; water-cooled, viscous coupling thermostatic fan, 26.4 imp pt, 31.7 US pt, 15 l.

MERCEDES-BENZ 500 SE Limousine

TRANSMISSION driving wheels: rear; gearbox: MB automatic transmission, hydraulic torque converter and planetary gears with 3 ratios, max ratio of converter at stall 2.5, possible manual selection; ratios: I 2.310, II 1.460, III 1, rev 1.840; lever: central or steering column; final drive: hypoid bevel; axle ratio: 3.070; width of rims: 6.5"; tyres: 205/70 VR x 14.

PERFORMANCE max speeds: (I) 59 mph, 95 km/h; (II) 96 mph, 155 km/h; (III) 130 mph, 210 km/h; power-weight ratio: SE 16.9 lb/hp (23.1 lb/kW), 7.7 kg/hp (10.5 kg/kW); carrying capacity: 1,147 lb, 520 kg; speed in direct drive at 1,000 rpm: 21.9 mph, 35.3 km/h; consumption: 19.5 m/imp gal, 16.2 m/US gal, 14.5 l x 100 km.

CHASSIS integral, front auxiliary frame (welded to body); front suspension: independent, wishbones, coil springs, anti-roll bar, telescopic dampers; rear: independent, oblique semi-trailing arms, coil springs, anti-roll bar, auxiliary rubber springs, telescopic dampers.

STEERING recirculating ball, servo; turns lock to lock: 2.70.

BRAKES disc (front diameter 10.94 in, 27.8 cm, rear 10.98 in, 27.9 cm), rear compensator, dual circuit, servo; swept area: front 255.5 sq in, 1,648 sq cm, rear 195.8 sq in, 1,263 sq cm, total 451.3 sq in, 2,911 sq cm.

ELECTRICAL EQUIPMENT 12 V; 66 Ah battery; 770 W alternator; Bosch (transistorized) distributor; 2 iodine headlamps.

MERCEDES-BENZ 500 SE Limousine

DIMENSIONS AND WEIGHT wheel base: SE 112.60 in, 286 cm - SEL 116.54 in, 296 cm; tracks: 59.84 in, 152 cm front, 59.06 in, 150 cm rear; length: SE 195.28 in, 496 cm - SEL 199.21 in, 506 cm; width: 73.62 in, 187 cm; height: SE 55.91 in, 142 cm - SEL 56.30 in, 143 cm; ground clearance: 5.31 in, 13.5 cm; weight: SE 3,815 lb, 1,730 kg - SEL 3,892 lb, 1,765 kg; turning circle: SE 37.4 ft, 11.4 m - SEL 38.7 ft, 11.8 m; fuel tank: 21.1 imp gal, 25.3 US gal, 96 l.

BODY saloon/sedan; 5 seats, separate front seats, reclining backrests, headrests; automatic safety belts; (standard for SEL only) electric windows.

PRACTICAL INSTRUCTIONS fuel: 98 oct petrol; oil: engine 14.1 imp pt, 16.9 US pt, 8 l, SAE 20W-40, change every 4,600 miles, 7,500 km - automatic transmission 15.7 imp pt, 18.8 US pt, 8.9 l, ATF, change every 12,400 miles, 20,000 km - final drive 2.3 imp pt, 2.7 US pt, 1.3 l, SAE 90, change every 12,400 miles, 20,000 km; sparking plug: 200°; tappet clearances (cold): inlet 0.003 in, 0.08 mm, exhaust 0.008 in, 0.20 mm; valve timing: 5° 21° 25° 5°; tyre pressure: front 30 psi, 2.1 atm, rear 34 psi, 2.4 atm.

OPTIONALS electric sunshine roof; electric windows; rev counter; heated rear window; headrests; metallic spray; light alloy wheels; automatic levelling control; tinted glass; air-conditioning.

217 hp power team

See 225 hp power team, except for:

ENGINE max power (DIN): 217 hp (160 kW) at 5,000 rpm; max torque (DIN): 266 lb ft, 36.7 kg m (360 Nm) at 3,250 rpm; 48 hp/l (35.3 kW/l).

PERFORMANCE power-weight ratio: SL 16 lb/hp, (21.8 lb/kW), 7.3 kg/hp (9.9 kg/kW); carrying capacity: SL 926 lb, 420 kg - SLC 1,080 lb, 490 kg.

STEERING turns lock to lock: 3.

DIMENSIONS AND WEIGHT wheel base: SL 96.46 in, 245 cm - SLC 110.63 in, 281 cm; tracks: 57.09 in, 145 cm front, 56.69 in, 144 cm rear; length: SL 177.83 in, 439 cm - SLC 187.01 in, 475 cm; width: 70.47 in, 179 cm; height: SL 51.18 in, 130 cm - SLC 52.36 in, 133 cm; weight: SL 3,484 lb, 1,580 kg - SLC 3,954 lb, 1,630 kg; turning circle: SL 33.8 ft, 10.3 m - SLC 37.7 ft, 11.5 m; fuel tank: 19.8 imp gal, 23.8 US gal, 90 l.

BODY convertible, 2 seats - coupé, 4 seats.

OPTIONALS (for SL only) hardtop.

240 hp power team

See 225 hp power team, except for:

ENGINE 303.5 cu in, 4,973 cc (3.82 x 3.35 in, 97 x 85 mm); max power (DIN): 240 hp (177 kW) at 5,000 rpm; max torque (DIN): 297 lb ft, 41 kg m (402 Nm) at 3,200 rpm; 48.3 hp/l (35.5 kW/l); light alloy block and head.

PERFORMANCE max speed: 140 mph, 225 km/l; power-weight ratio: 13.9 lb/hp (18.9 lb/kW), 6.3 kg/hp (8.6 kg/kW); speed in direct drive at 1,000 rpm: 24.1 mph, 38.8 km/h.

STEERING turns lock to lock: 3.

MERCEDES-BENZ 450 SLC 5.0 Coupé

DIMENSIONS AND WEIGHT wheel base: 110.63 in, 281 cm; tracks: 57.09 in, 145 cm front, 56.69 in, 144 cm rear; length: 187.01 in, 475 cm; width: 70.47 in, 179 cm; height: 52.36 in, 133 cm; weight: 3,341 lb, 1,515 kg; turning circle: 37.7 ft, 11.5 m; fuel tank: 19.8 imp gal, 23.8 US gal, 90 l.

BODY coupé; 4 seats.

286 hp power team

See 225 hp power team, except for:

ENGINE 417 cu in, 6,834 cc (4.21 x 3.74 in, 107 x 95 mm); max power (DIN): 286 hp (210 kW) at 4,250 rpm; max torque (DIN): 406 lb ft, 56 kg m (549 Nm) at 3,000 rpm; max engine rpm: 5,300; 41.8 hp/l (30.8 kW/l); lubrication: gear pump, full flow filter, dry sump, oil cooler, 19.4 imp pt, 23.2 US pt, 11 l; Bosch K-Jetronic injection.

TRANSMISSION final drive: limited slip differential; axle ratio: 2.650; tyres: 215/70 VR x 14.

PERFORMANCE max speeds: (I) 59 mph, 95 km/h; (II) 96 mph, 155 km/h; (III) 140 mph, 225 km/h; power-weight ratio: 14.9 lb/hp (20.3 lb/kW), 6.8 kg/hp (9.2 kg/kW); carrying capacity: 1,069 lb, 485 kg; speed in direct drive at 1,000 rpm: 28.3 mph, 45.5 km/h; consumption: 17.7 m/imp gal, 14.7 m/US gal, 16 l x 100 km.

CHASSIS front suspension: independent, wishbones, hydropneumatic suspension, anti-roll bar, automatic levelling control, hydropneumatic telescopic dampers; rear: independent, oblique semi-trailing arms, hydropneumatic suspension, anti-roll bar, automatic levelling control, hydropneumatic telescopic dampers.

ELECTRICAL EQUIPMENT 88 Ah battery; 1,050 W alternator.

DIMENSIONS AND WEIGHT wheel base: 116.54 in, 296 cm; length: 199.21 in, 506 cm; height: 56.69 in, 144 cm; weight: 4,267 lb, 1,935 kg; turning circle: 39.7 ft, 12.1 m.

BODY headrests, tinted glass with air-conditioning, heated rear window, electric windows, headlamps with wiper-washers (standard).

PRACTICAL INSTRUCTIONS oil: engine 19.4 imp pt, 23.2 US pt, 11 l, change every 9,300 miles, 15,000 km.

OPTIONALS ABS antilock braking system.

230 G

PRICE EX WORKS: DM 30,000*

ENGINE front, 4 stroke; 4 cylinders, vertical, in line; 140.8 cu in, 2,307 cc (3.69 x 3.29 in, 93.7 x 83.6 mm); compression ratio: 9:1; max power (DIN): 102 hp (75 kW) at 5,250 rpm; max torque (DIN): 127 lb ft, 17.5 kg m (172 Nm) at 3,000 rpm; max engine rpm: 6,000; 22.6 hp/l (30.8 kW/l); cast iron block, light alloy head; 5 crankshaft bearings; valves: overhead, in line, finger levers; camshafts: 1, overhead; lubrication: gear pump, oil-water heat exchanger, full flow filter (cartridge); 9.7 imp pt, 11.6 US pt, 5.5 l; 1 Stromberg 175 CD horizontal carburettor; fuel feed: mechanical pump; water-cooled, 18.8 imp pt, 22.6 US pt, 10.7 l, thermostatic fan.

TRANSMISSION driving wheels: front (automatically engaged with transfer box low ratio) and rear; clutch: single dry plate; hydraulically controlled; gearbox: mechanical; gears: 4, fully synchronized; final drive: hypoid bevel; width of rims: 5.5"; tyres: 6.50 R x 16.

PERFORMANCE max speed: 81 mph, 131 km/h; power-weight ratio: 37.2 lb/hp, (50.6 lb/kW), 17 kg/hp (22.9 kg/kW); carrying capacity: 1,808 lb, 820 kg.

CHASSIS welded frame with box sections and tubular members; front suspension: rigid axle, longitudinal control arms, transverse control arm (Panhard rod), coil springs, helper springs, telescopic dampers, torsion anti-roll bar; rear: rigid axle, longitudinal control arms, transverse control arm (Panhard rod), (progressively acting) coil springs, helper springs, telescopic dampers.

STEERING recirculating ball, worm and nut.

BRAKES front disc, rear drum; dual circuit.

ELECTRICAL EQUIPMENT 12 V; 88 Ah battery; 55 A alternator; Bosch distributor; 2 headlamps.

DIMENSIONS AND WEIGHT wheel base: 94.49 in, 240 cm; front and rear track: 56.30 in, 143 cm; length: 155.51 in, 395 cm; width: 66.93 in, 170 cm; height: 77.95 in, 198 cm; ground clearance: 8.46 in, 21.5 cm; weight: 3,793 lb, 1,720 kg; turning circle: 37.4 ft, 11.4 m; fuel tank: 16.5 imp gal, 19.8 US gal, 75 l.

BODY open; 2 doors; 7 seats, separate front seats.

PRACTICAL INSTRUCTIONS fuel: 98 oct petrol; oil: engine 9.7 imp pt, 11.6 US pt, 5.5 l, SAE 20W-30, change every 4,600 miles, 7,500 km - gearbox 2.8 imp pt, 3.4 US pt, 1.6 l, ATF, change every 12,400 miles, 20,000 km - final drive 1.9 imp pt, 2.3 US pt, 1.1 l, SAE 90, change every 12,400 miles, 20,000 km; tappet clearances: inlet 0.003 in, 0.08 mm, exhaust 0.008 in, 0.20 mm; valve timing: 11° 47° 48° 16°.

OPTIONALS MB automatic transmission; long wheel base; limited slip differential; power steering.

280 GE

PRICE EX WORKS: DM 36,220*

See 230 G, except for:

ENGINE 6 cylinders; 167.6 cu in, 2,746 cc (3.39 x 3.10 in, 86 x 78.8 mm); compression ratio: 8:1; max power (DIN): 150 hp (110 kW) at 5,250 rpm; max torque (DIN): 162 lb ft, 22.4 kg m (220 Nm) at 4,280 rpm; max engine rpm: 6,000; 54.6 hp/l (40.2 kW/l); 7 crankshaft bearings; valves: overhead, Vee-slanted at 54°; camshafts: 2, overhead; lubrication: 11.4 imp pt, 13.7 US pt, 6.5 l; Bosch K-Jetronic injection; water-cooled, 17.1 imp pt, 20.5 US pt, 9.7 l.

PERFORMANCE max speed: 93 mph, 150 km/h; power-weight ratio: 26.1 lb/hp (35.6 lb/kW), 11.8 kg/hp (16.1 kg/kW); carrying capacity: 1,852 lb, 840 kg.

DIMENSIONS AND WEIGHT weighe: 3,914 lb, 1,775 kg.

PRACTICAL INSTRUCTIONS fuel: 98 oct petrol; oil: engine 11.4 imp pt, 13.7 US pt, 6.5 l, SAE 20W-30, change every 4,600 miles, 7.500 km - gearbox 3.2 imp pt, 3.8 US pt, 1.8 l, ATF, change every 12,400 miles, 20,000 km - final drive 4.4 imp pt, 5.3 US pt, 2.5 l, SAE 90, change every 12,400 miles, 20,000 km.

240 GD

PRICE EX WORKS: DM 31,470*

ENGINE diesel; front, 4 stroke; 4 cylinders, vertical, in line; 146.4 cu in, 2,399 cc (3.58 x 3.64 in, 91 x 92.4 mm); compression ratio: 21:1; max power (DIN): 72 hp (53 kW) at 4,400 rpm; max torque (DIN): 101 lb ft, 14 kg m (137 Nm) at 2,400 rpm; max engine rpm: 5,300; 30 hp/l (22.1 kW/l); cast iron block and head; 5 crankshaft bearings; valves: overhead, in line, finger levers; camshafts: 1, overhead; lubrication: gear pump, oil cooler, full flow (cartridge) and by-pass filters, 11.4 imp pt, 13.7 US pt, 6.5 l; 4-cylinder Bosch indirect injection pump; fuel feed: mechanical pump; cooling: 17.6 imp pt, 21.1 US pt, 10 l, thermostatic fan.

TRANSMISSION driving wheels: front (automatically engaged with transfer box low ratio) and rear; clutch: single dry plate, hydraulically controlled; gearbox: mechanical; gears: 4, fully synchronized; final drive: hypoid bevel; width of rims: 5.5"; tyres: 6.50 R x 16.

PERFORMANCE max speed: 75 mph, 120 km/h; power-weight ratio: 54.4 lb/hp (73.8 lb/kW), 24.6 kg/hp (33.5 kg/kW); carrying capacity: 1,918 lb, 860 kg.

MERCEDES-BENZ 230 G

240 GD

CHASSIS welded frame with box sections and tubular members; front suspension: rigid axle, longitudinal control arms, transverse control arm (Panhard rod) coil springs, helper springs, telescopic dampers, torsion anti-roll bar; rear; rigid axle, longitudinal control arms, transverse control arm (Panhard rod), (progressively acting) coil springs, helper springs, telescopic dampers.

STEERING recirculating ball, worm and net.

BRAKES front disc, rear drum; dual circuit.

ELECTRICAL EQUIPMENT 12 V; 88 Ah battery; 55 A alternator; Bosch distributor; 2 headlamps.

DIMENSIONS AND WEIGHT wheel base: 94.49 in, 240 cm; front and rear track: 56.30 in, 143 cm; length: 155.51 in, 395 cm; width: 66.93 in, 170 cm; height: 77.95 in, 198 cm; ground clearance: 8.46 in, 21.5 cm; weight: 3,914 lb, 1,775 kg; turning circle: 37.4 ft, 11,4 m; fuel tank: 16.5 imp gal, 19.8 US gal, 75 l.

BODY open; 2 doors; 7 seats, separate front seats.

PRACTICAL INSTRUCTIONS fuel: diesel oil; oil: engine 11.4 imp pt, 13.7 US pt, 6.5 l, SAE 20W-30, change every 4,600 miles, 7.500 km.

OPTIONALS MB automatic transmission; long wheel base; limited slip differential; power steering.

300 GD

PRICE EX WORKS: DM 33,278*

See 240 GD, except for:

ENGINE 5 cylinders, vertical, in line; 182.9 cu in, 2,998 cc (3.58 x 3.64 in, 91 x 92.4 mm); max power (DIN): 80 hp (59 kW) at 4,000 rpm; max torque (DIN): 127 lb ft, 17.5 kg m (172 Nm) at 2,400 rpm; max engine rpm: 5,100; 26.7 hp/l (19.7 kW/l); 6 crankshaft bearings; 5-cylinder Bosch indirect injection pump; cooling: 19 imp pt, 22.8 US pt, 10.8 l.

PERFORMANCE max speed: 76 mph, 123 km/h; power-weight ratio: 49.3 lb/hp, (66.9 lb/kW), 22.4 kg/hp (30.3 kg/kW); carrying capacity: 1,819 lb, 825 kg.

DIMENSIONS AND WEIGHT weight: 3,947 lb, 1,790 kg.

MERCEDES-BENZ G Series

OPEL GERMANY FR

Kadett Series

PRICES EX WORKS:		DM
1	2-dr Limousine	**10,745***
2	4-dr Limousine	**11,315***
3	2+1-dr Limousine	**10,980***
4	4+1-dr Limousine	**11,550***
5	Luxus 2-dr Limousine	**11,420***
6	Luxus 4-dr Limousine	**11,990***
7	Luxus 2+1-dr Limousine	**11,705***
8	Luxus 4+1-dr Limousine	**12,275***
9	Berlina 2-dr Limousine	**12,270***
10	Berlina 4-dr Limousine	**12,840***
11	Berlina 2+1-dr Limousine	**12,555***
12	Berlina 4+1-dr Limousine	**13,125***
13	2+1-dr Caravan	**11,945***
14	4+1-dr Caravan	**12,515***
15	Luxus 2+1-dr Caravan	**12,620***
16	Luxus 4+1-dr Caravan	**13,190***

For 60 hp engine add DM 395 (limousines) - DM 255 (caravan models); for 75 hp engine add DM 650 (limousines) - DM 510 (caravan models).

Power team:	Standard for:	Optional for:
53 hp	all	—
60 hp	—	all
75 hp	—	all

53 hp power team

ENGINE front, transverse, 4 stroke; 4 cylinders, in line; 73 cu in, 1,196 cc (3.11 x 2.40 in, 79 x 61 mm); compression ratio: 7.8:1; max power (DIN): 53 hp (39 kW) at 5,400 rpm; max torque (DIN): 61 lb ft, 8.4 kg m (82 Nm) at 3,600 rpm; max engine rpm: 6,000; 44.3 hp/l (32.6 kW/l); cast iron block and head; 3 crankshaft bearings; valves: overhead, push-rods and rockers; camshafts: 1, side, chain-driven; lubrication: gear pump, full flow filter, 4.8 imp pt, 5.7 US pt, 2.7 l; 1 Solex 35 PDSI downdraught single barrel carburettor; fuel feed: mechanical pump; anti-freeze liquid cooled, 8.1 imp pt, 9.7 US pt, 4.6 l, electric thermostatic fan.

TRANSMISSION driving wheels: front; clutch: single dry plate (diaphragm); gearbox: mechanical; gears: 4, fully synchronized; ratios: I 3.636, II 2.188, III 1.429, IV 0.969, rev 3.182; lever: central; final drive: helical spur gears; axle ratio: 4.290 - Caravan models; 4.530; width of rims: 4.5" - Luxus models 5" - Berlina and Caravan models 5.5"; tyres: 145 SR x 13 - Luxus and Berlina models 155 SR x 13.

PERFORMANCE max speed: 87 mph, 140 km/h; power-weight ratio: 4+1-dr limousines 34.7 lb/hp, (47.2 lb/kW), 15.7 kg/hp (20.9 kg/kW); carrying capacity: 882 lb, 410 kg; speed in top at 1,000 rpm: 14.5 mph, 23.3 km/h; consumption: limousines 30.4 m/imp gal, 25.3 m/US gal, 9.3 l x 100 km - Caravan models 29.1 m/imp gal, 24.2 m/US gal, 9.7 l x 100 km at 75 mph, 120 km/h.

CHASSIS integral; front suspension: independent, by McPherson, coil springs/telescopic damper struts, heavy-duty rubber bearings, direction-stabilizing swivelling radius arm; rear: crank compound, coil springs with progressive rate, auxiliary rubber springs, telescopic dampers.

STEERING rack-and-pinion; turns lock to lock: 3.90.

BRAKES front disc, rear drum, dual circuit; lining area: total 57.05 sq in, 368 sq cm.

ELECTRICAL EQUIPMENT 12 V; 36 Ah battery; 45 A alternator; Bosch distributor; 2 headlamps.

DIMENSIONS AND WEIGHT wheel base: 98.98 in, 251 cm; tracks: 55.12 in, 140 cm front, 55.35 in, 141 cm rear; length: 157.40 in, 399 cm - Caravan models 165.63 in, 421 cm; width: 64.41 in, 164 cm; height: 54.33 in, 138 cm - Caravan models 55.12 in, 140 cm; ground clearance: 5.12 in, 13 cm; weight: 2+1-dr limousines 1,797 lb, 815 kg - 4+1-dr limousines 1,841 lb, 835 kg - 2+1-dr Caravan models 1,929 lb, 875 kg - 4+1-dr Caravan models 1,973 lb, 895 kg; turning circle: 34.4 ft, 10.5 m; fuel tank: limousines 9.2 imp gal 11.1 US gal, 42 l - Caravan models 11 imp gal, 13.2 US gal, 50 l.

BODY saloon/sedan, estate car/st. wagon; 5 seats; separate front seats.

PRACTICAL INSTRUCTIONS fuel: 91 oct petrol; oil: engine 4.8 imp pt, 5.7 US pt, 2.7 l, SAE 20W-30, change every 6,200 miles, 10,000 km - gearbox and final drive 3.2 imp pt, 3.8 US pt, 1.8 l, SAE 90 EP, no change recommended; greasing: none; sparking plug: ACR42-6FS; tappet clearances: inlet 0.006 in, 0.15 mm, exhaust 0.009 in, 0.25 mm; valve timing: 46° 90° 70° 30°; tyre pressure: front 25 psi, 1.8 atm, rear 25 psi, 1.8 atm.

OPTIONALS 175/70 SR x 13 tyres with 5.5" wide rims; anti-roll bar on front and rear suspension (for limousines only); servo brake; 44 or 55 Ah battery; sunshine roof; metallic spray; rear window wiper-washer.

60 hp power team

See 53 hp power team, except for:

ENGINE 79.14 cu in, 1,297 cc (2.95 x 2.89 in, 75 x 73.4 mm); compression ratio: 8.2:1, max power (DIN): 60 hp (44 kW) at 5,800 rpm; max torque (DIN): 69 lb ft, 9.6 kg m (87 Nm) at 3,400-3,800 rpm; 46.3 hp/l (33.9 kW/l); light alloy head; 5 crankshaft bearings; valves: overhead, in line, rockers, hydraulic tappets; camshafts: 1, overhead, cogged belt; anti-freeze liquid cooled, 11.1 imp pt, 13.3 US pt, 6.3 l.

PERFORMANCE max speed: 91 mph, 147 km/h; power-weight ratio: 4+1-dr limousines 31.4 lb/hp (42.8 lb/kW), 14,2 kg/hp (19.4 kg/kW); consumption: 30.7 m/imp gal, 25.6 m/US gal, 9.2 l x 100 km at 75 mph, 120 km/h.

BRAKES servo (standard).

DIMENSIONS AND WEIGHT weight: 2+1-dr limousines 1,841 lb. 835 kg - 4+1-dr limousines 1,885 lb, 855 kg - 2+1-dr Caravan models 1,951 lb, 855 kg - 4+1-dr Caravan models 1,995 lb, 905 kg.

PRACTICAL INSTRUCTIONS sparking plug: AC R 42 XLS; valve timing: 24° 73° 66° 30°.

75 hp power team

See 53 hp power team, except for:

ENGINE 79.14 cu in, 1,297 cc (2.95 x 2.89 in, 75 x 73.4 mm); compression ratio: 9.2:1; max power (DIN): 75 hp (55 kW) at 5,800 rpm; max torque (DIN): 75 lb ft, 10.3 kg m (101 Nm) at 3,800-4,600 rpm; 57.8 hp/l (42.4 kW/l); light alloy head; 5 crankshaft bearings; valves: overhead, in line, rockers, hydraulic tappets; camshafts: 1, overhead, cogged belt; 1 GMF Varajet II downdraught single barrel carburettor; anti-freeze liquid cooled 11.1 imp pt, 13.3 US pt, 6.3 l.

TRANSMISSION axle ratio: 4.180.

OPEL Kadett Berlina Limousine

ERFORMANCE max speed: 98 mph, 158 km/h; power-weight atio: 4+1-dr limousines 25.1 lb/hp (35.3 lb/kW), 11.4 kg/hp 15.5 kg/kW); consumption: 34 m/imp gal, 28.3 m/US gal, 8.3 x 100 km at 75 mph, 120 km/h.

HASSIS front and rear suspension: anti-roll bar (standard).

RAKES servo (standard).

IMENSIONS AND WEIGHT weight: 2+1-dr limousines 1,841), 835 kg - 4+1-dr limousines 1,885 lb, 855 kg - 2+1-dr aravan models 1,951 lb, 885 kg - 4+1-dr Caravan models ,995 lb, 905 kg.

RACTICAL INSTRUCTIONS fuel: 98 oct petrol; sparking plug: C R 42 X LS; valve timing: 24° 78° 68° 36°.

Kadett SR Series

RICES EX WORKS:	DM
2-dr Limousine	14,220*
2+1-dr Limousine	14,560*

75 hp power team

NGINE front, transverse, 4 stroke; 4 cylinders, in line; 79.14 u in; 1,297 cc (2.95 x 2.89 in, 75 x 73.4 mm); compression atio: 9.2:1; max power (DIN): 75 hp (55 kW) at 5,800 rpm; max orque (DIN): 75 lb ft, 10.3 kg m (101 Nm) at 3,800-4,600 rpm; ax engine rpm: 6,200; 57.8 hp/l (42.4 kW/l); cast iron block, ght alloy head; 5 crankshaft bearings; valves: overhead, in ne, rockers, hydraulic tappets; camshafts: 1, overhead, cog- ed belt; lubrication: gear pump, full flow filter, 4.8 imp pt, 5.7 S pt, 2.7 l; 1 GMF Varajet II downdraught single barrel arburettor; fuel feed: mechanical pump; anti-freeze liquid ooled, 11.1 imp pt, 13.3 US pt, 6.3 l, electric thermostatic fan.

RANSMISSION driving wheels: front; clutch: single dry plate diaphragm); gearbox: mechanical; gears: 4, fully synchronized; atios: I 3.636, II 2.188, III 1.429, IV 0.969, rev 3.182; lever: entral; final drive: helical spur gears; axle ratio: 4.180; width f rims: 5.5"; tyres: 185/60 SR x 14.

ERFORMANCE max speed: 98 mph, 158 km/h; power-weight atio: 25.1 lb/hp (35.3 lb/kW), 11.4 kg/hp (15.5 kg/kW); carrying apacity: 937 lb, 425 kg; consumption: 34 m/imp gal, 28.3 m/US al, 8.3 l x 100 km at 75 mph, 120 km/h.

HASSIS integral; front suspension: independent, by McPher- on, coil springs/telescopic damper struts, anti-roll bar, heavy- uty rubber bearings, direction stabilizing radius arm; rear: rank compound, coil springs with progressive rate,anti-roll bar, uxiliary rubber springs, telescopic dampers.

TEERING rack-and-pinion; turns lock to lock: 3.90.

RAKES front disc, rear drum, dual circuit, servo; lining area: otal 57.05 sq in, 368 sq cm.

LECTRICAL EQUIPMENT 12 V; 36 Ah battery; 45 A alterna- r; Bosch distributor; 2 headlamps.

IMENSIONS AND WEIGHT wheel base: 98.98 in, 251 cm; acks: 55.12 in, 140 cm front, 55.35 in, 141 cm rear; length: 57.40 in, 399 cm; width: 65.19 in, 166 cm; height: 55.12 in, 40 cm; ground clearance: 5.12 in, 13 cm; weight: 1,885 lb, 855 g; turning circle: 34.4 ft, 10.5 m; fuel tank: 9.2 imp gal, 11.1 S gal, 42 l.

ODY saloon/sedan; 2 or 2+1 doors; light alloy wheels.

RACTICAL INSTRUCTIONS fuel: 98 oct petrol; oil: engine 4.8 np pt, 5.7 US pt, 2.7 l, SAE 20W-30, change every 6,200 iiles, 10,000 km - gearbox and final drive 3.5 imp pt, 4.2 US t, 2 l, SAE 90 EP, no change recommended; greasing: none; parking plug: AC R 42XLS; valve timing: 24° 78° 68° 36°; tyre ressure: front 25 psi, 1.8 atm, rear 25 psi, 1.8 atm.

PTIONALS metallic spray; rear window wiper-washer; 55 A lternator; 44 or 55 Ah battery; sunshine roof.

Ascona Series

RICES EX WORKS:	DM
2-dr Limousine	12,545*
4-dr Limousine	13,125*
Luxus 2-dr Limousine	13,465*
Luxus 4-dr Limousine	14,045*
Berlina 2-dr Limousine	14,241*
Berlina 4-dr Limousine	14,664*

or 60 hp 1.6 engine add DM 197; for 75 hp engine add DM 82; for 90 hp engine add DM 711; for 100 hp engine add DM 58; for 58 hp diesel engine add DM 3,335.

ower team:	Standard for:	Optional for:
60 hp	1 to 6	—
60 hp (1,584 cc)	—	1 to 6
75 hp	—	1 to 6
90 hp	—	1 to 6
00 hp	—	1 to 6
58 hp (diesel)	—	1 to 6

OPEL Kadett Luxus Caravan

60 hp power team

ENGINE front, 4 stroke; 4 cylinders, in line; 79.14 cu in, 1,297 cc (2.95 x 2.89 in, 75 x 73.4 mm); compression ratio: 8.2:1; max power (DIN) : 60 hp (44 kW) at 5,800 rpm; max torque (DIN); 71 lb ft, 9.8 kgm (96 Nm) at 3,800 rpm; max engine rpm: 6,200; 46.3 hp/l (33.9 kW/l); cast iron block, light alloy head; 5 crankshaft bearings; valves: overhead, rockers, hydraulic tappets; camshafts: 1, overhead, cogged belt; lubrication: gear pump, full flow filter, 4.8 imp pt, 5.7 US pt, 2.7 l; 1 Solex 35 PDSI downdraught single barrel carburettor; fuel feed: mechanical pump; anti-freeze liquid cooled, 10.2 imp pt, 12.3 US pt, 5.8 l.

TRANSMISSION driving wheels: rear; clutch: single dry plate (diaphragm); gearbox: mechanical; gears: 4, fully synchronized; ratios: I 3.640, II 2.120, III 1.336, IV 1, rev 3.522; lever: central; final drive: hypoid bevel; axle ratio: 4.375; width of rims: 5"; tyres: 165 SR x 13.

PERFORMANCE max speed: 90 mph, 145 km/h; power-weight ratio: 4-dr 33.5 lb/hp (45.6 lb/kW), 15.2 kg/hp (20.7 kg/kW); carrying capacity: 2-dr 937 lb, 425 kg - 4-dr 893 lb, 405 kg; acceleration: standing ¼ mile 21 sec, 0-50 mph (0-80 km/h) 12 sec; speed in direct drive at 1,000 rpm: 23.7 mph, 38.1 km/h; consumption: 31.4 m/imp gal, 26.1 m/US gal, 9 l x 100 km.

CHASSIS integral; front suspension: independent, wishbones, coil springs, anti-roll bar, telescopic dampers; rear: rigid axle (torque tube), trailing radius arms, transverse linkage bar, coil springs, anti-roll bar, telescopic dampers.

STEERING rack-and-pinion; turns lock to lock: 4.

BRAKES front disc, rear drum, dual circuit, servo; lining area: front 22.9 sq in, 148 sq cm, rear 47.1 sq in, 304 sq cm, total 70 sq in, 452 sq cm.

ELECTRICAL EQUIPMENT 12 V; 36 Ah battery; 45 A alternator; Bosch or Delco Remy distributor; 2 headlamps.

DIMENSIONS AND WEIGHT wheel base: 99.21 in, 252 cm; tracks: 54.33 in, 138 cm front, 54.13 in, 137 cm rear; length: 170.12 in, 432 cm; width: 65.75 in, 167 cm; height: 54.33 in, 138 cm; ground clearance: 5.12 in, 13 cm; weight: 2-dr 1,973 lb, 895 kg - 4-dr 2,018 lb, 915 kg; turning circle: 33.1 ft, 10.1 m; fuel tank: 11 imp gal, 13.2 US gal, 50 l.

BODY saloon/sedan; 5 seats, separate front seats, adjustable backrests.

PRACTICAL INSTRUCTIONS fuel: 91 oct petrol; oil: engine 4.8 imp pt, 5.7 US pt, 2.7 l, SAE 20W-30, change every 6,200 miles, 10,000 km - gearbox 1.1 imp pt, 1.3 US pt, 0.6 l, SAE 80, no change recommended - final drive 1.1 imp pt, 1.3 US pt, 0.6 l, SAE 90, no change recommended; greasing: none; sparking plug: 200°; valve timing: 24° 73° 66° 30°; tyre pressure: front 24 psi, 1.7 atm, rear 24 psi, 1.7 atm.

OPTIONALS 185/70 SR x 13 tyres with 5.5" wide rims; 44 or 55 Ah battery; sunshine roof; heated rear window; headrests; halogen headlamps; vinyl roof; headlamps with wiper-washers; metallic spray; SR equipment.

OPEL Kadett SR Limousine

60 hp (1,584 cc) power team

See 60 hp power team, except for:

ENGINE 96.7 cu in, 1,584 cc (3.35 x 2.75 in, 85 x 69.8 mm); compression ratio: 8:1; max power (DIN): 60 hp (44 kW) at 5,000 rpm; max torque (DIN): 76 lb ft, 10.5 kg m (103 Nm) at 3,000-3,400 rpm; max engine rpm: 6,000; 37.9 hp/l (27.9 kW/l); lubrication: 6.7 imp pt, 8 US pt, 3.8 l; cooling: 11.1 imp pt, 13.3 US pt, 6.3 l.

TRANSMISSION axle ratio: 3.700.

PERFORMANCE max speed: 90 mph, 145 km/h; power-weight ratio: 4-dr 35.6 lb/hp (48.3 lb/kW), 16.1 kg/hp (21.9 kg/kW); acceleration: standing ¼ mile 20 sec, 0-50 mph (0-80 km/h) 11 sec; speed in direct drive at 1,000 rpm: 21.3 mph, 34.3 km/h; consumption: 26.4 m/imp gal, 22 m/US gal, 10.7 l x 100 km.

DIMENSIONS AND WEIGHT weight: 2-dr 2,095 lb, 950 kg - 4-dr 2,139 lb, 970 kg.

PRACTICAL INSTRUCTIONS oil: engine 6.7 imp pt, 8 US pt, 3.8 l, SAE 20W-30, change every 6,200 miles, 10,000 km - gearbox 1.9 imp pt, 2.3 US pt, 1.1 l, SAE 80, no change recommended - final drive 1.9 imp pt, 2.3 US pt, 1.1 l, SAE 90, no change recommended; tappet clearances (hot): inlet 0.012 in, 0.30 mm, exhaust 0.012 in, 0.30 mm; valve timing: 44° 86° 84° 46°.

OPTIONALS Opel automatic transmission with 3 ratios (I 2.400, II 1.480, III 1, rev 1.920), max ratio of converter at stall 2.5, 3.670 axle ratio, max speed 87 mph, 140 km/h, consumption 24.6 m/imp gal, 20.5 m/US gal, 11.5 l x 100 km; 55 A alternator; air-conditioning.

75 hp power team

See 60 hp power team, except for:

ENGINE 115.8 cu in, 1,897 cc (3.66 x 2.75 in, 93 x 69.8 mm); compression ratio: 7.9:1; max power (DIN): 75 hp (55 kW) at 4,800 rpm; max torque (DIN): 98 lb ft, 13.5 kg m (132 Nm) at 2,200-3,400 rpm; max engine rpm: 5,200; 39.5 hp/l (29.1 kW/l); lubrication: 6.7 imp pt, 8 US pt, 3.8 l; cooling: 10.4 imp pt, 12.5 US pt, 5.9 l.

TRANSMISSION axle ratio: 3.670.

PERFORMANCE max speed: 98 mph, 157 km/h; power-weight ratio: 4-dr 29.4 lb/hp (39.9 lb/kW), 13.3 kg/hp (18.1 kg/kW); acceleration: standing ¼ mile 20 sec, 0-50 mph (0-80 km/h) 11 sec; speed in direct drive at 1,000 rpm: 21.3 mph, 34.3 km/h; consumption: 26.4 m/imp gal, 22 m/US gal, 10.7 l x 100 km.

ELECTRICAL EQUIPMENT 44 Ah battery.

DIMENSIONS AND WEIGHT weight: 2-dr 2,161 lb, 980 kg - 4-dr 2,205 lb, 1,000 kg.

PRACTICAL INSTRUCTIONS oil: engine 6.7 imp pt, 8 US pt, 3.8 l, SAE 20W-30, change every 6,200 miles, 10,000 km - gearbox 1.9 imp pt, 2.3 US pt, 1.1 l, SAE 80, no change recommended - final drive 1.9 imp pt, 2.3 US pt, 1.1 l, SAE 90, no change recommended; tappet clearances (hot): inlet 0.012 in, 0.30 mm, exhaust 0.012 in, 0.30 mm; valve timing: 44° 86° 84° 46°.

OPTIONALS Opel automatic transmission with 3 ratios (I 2.400, II 1.480, III 1, rev 1.920), max ratio of converter at stall 2.5, 3.670 axle ratio, max speed 95 mph, 152 km/h, consumption 24.6 m/imp gal, 20.5 m/US gal, 11.5 l x 100 km; air-conditioning.

90 hp power team

See 60 hp power team, except for:

ENGINE 120.8 cu in, 1,979 cc (3.74 x 2.75 in, 95 x 69.8 mm); compression ratio: 8:1; max e power (DIN): 90 hp (66 kW) at 5,200 rpm; max torque (DIN): 105 lb ft, 14.5 kg m (149 Nm) at 3,800 rpm; max engine rpm: 5,500; 45.4 hp/l (33.4 kW/l); 5 crankshaft bearings, valves: hydraulic tappets; lubrication: 6.7 imp pt, 8 US pt, 3.8 l; 1 GMF Varajet II downdraught single barrel carburettor; cooling: 10.9 imp pt, 13.1 US pt, 6.2 l.

TRANSMISSION axle ratio: 3.670.

PERFORMANCE max speed: 104 mph, 167 km/h; power-weight ratio: 4-dr 24.5 lb/hp (33.3 lb/kW), 11.1 kg/hp (15.1 kg/kW); carrying capacity: 2-dr 970 lb, 400 kg - 4-dr 926 lb, 420 kg; acceleration: standing ¼ mile 18 sec, 0-50 mph (0-80 km/h) 8 sec; speed in direct drive at 1,000 rpm: 21.1 mph, 34 km/h; consumption: 28.2 m/imp gal, 23.5 m/US gal, 10 l x 100 km.

BRAKES rear compensator; lining area: front 22.9 sq in, 148 sq cm, rear 62.8 sq in, 405 sq cm, total 85.7 sq in, 553 sq cm.

ELECTRICAL EQUIPMENT 44 Ah battery.

DIMENSIONS AND WEIGHT weight: 2-dr 2,161 lb, 980 kg - 4-dr 2,205 lb, 1,000 kg.

PRACTICAL INSTRUCTIONS oil: engine 6.7 imp pt, 8 US pt, 3.8 l, SAE 20W-30, change every 6,200 miles, 10,000 km - gearbox 1.9 imp pt, 2.3 US pt, 1.1 l, SAE 80, no change recommended - final drive 1,9 imp pt, 2.3 US pt, 1.1 l, SAE 90, no change recommended; tappet clearances (hot): inlet 0.012 in, 0.30 mm, exhaust 0.012 in, 0.30 mm; valve timing: 44° 86° 84° 46°.

OPTIONALS Opel automatic transmission with 3 ratios (I 2.400, II 1.480, III 1, rev 1.920), max ratio of converter at stall 2.5, 3.670 axle ratio, max speed 101 mph, 162 km/h, consumption 26.4 m/imp gal, 22 m/US gal, 10.7 l x 100 km; limited slip differential; air-conditioning.

100 hp power team

See 60 hp power team, except for:

ENGINE 120.8 cu in, 1,979 cc (3.74 x 2.75 in, 95 x 69.8 mm); compression ratio: 9:1; max power (DIN): 100 hp (74 kW) at 5,400 rpm: max torque (DIN): 111 lb ft, 15.3 kg m (150 Nm) at 3,800 rpm; max engine rpm: 6,000; 50.5 hp/l (37.2 kW/l); valves: hydraulic tappets; lubrication: 6.7 imp pt, 8 US pt, 3.8 l; 1 GMF Varajet II downdraught single barrel carburettor; cooling: 10.9 imp pt, 13.1 US pt, 6.2 l.

TRANSMISSION axle ratio: 3.440.

PERFORMANCE max speed: 109 mph, 175 km/h; power-weight ratio: 4-dr 22 lb/hp (29.9 lb/kW), 10 kg/hp (13.6 kg/kW); acceleration: standing ¼ mile 20 sec, 0-50 mph (0-80 km/h) 11 sec; speed in direct drive at 1,000 rpm: 18.1 mph, 29.2 km/h; consumption: 28.2 m/imp gal, 23.5 m/US gal, 10 l x 100 km.

BRAKES rear compensator; lining area: front 22.9 sq in, 148 sq cm, rear 62.8 sq in, 405 sq cm, total 85.7 sq in, 553 sq cm.

ELECTRICAL EQUIPMENT 44 Ah battery.

DIMENSIONS AND WEIGHT weight: 2-dr 2,161 lb, 980 kg - 4-dr 2,205 lb, 1,000 kg.

PRACTICAL INSTRUCTIONS fuel: 98 oct petrol; oil: engine 6.7 imp pt, 8 US pt, 3.8 l, SAE 20W-30, change every 6,200 miles, 10,000 km - gearbox 1.9 imp pt, 2.3 US pt, 1.1 l, SAE 80, no change recommended - final drive 1.9 imp pt, 2.3 US pt, 1.1 l, SAE 90, no change recommended: tappet clearances (hot) inlet 0.012 in, 0.30 mm, exhaust 0.012 in, 0.30 mm; valve timing: 32° 90° 72° 50°.

OPTIONALS Opel automatic transmission with 3 ratios (I 2.400, II 1.480, III 1, rev 1.920), max ratio of converter at stall 2.5, 3.670 axle ratio, max speed 106 mph, 170 km/h, consumption 26.4 m/imp gal, 22 m/US gal, 10.7 l x 100 km; air-conditioning.

58 hp (diesel) power team

See 60 hp power team, except for:

ENGINE diesel; 121.9 cu in, 1,998 cc (3.41 x 3.35 in, 86.5 x 85 mm); compression ratio: 22:1; max power (DIN): 58 hp (43 kW) at 4,200 rpm; max torque (DIN): 85 lb ft, 11.7 kg m (115 Nm) at 2,400 rpm; max engine rpm: 4,600; 29 hp/l (21.5 kW/l); lubrication: 9.7 imp pt, 11.6 US pt, 5.5 l; Bosch injection; cooling 19.7 imp pt, 23.7 US pt, 11.2 l.

TRANSMISSION axle ratio: 3.670.

PERFORMANCE max speed: 85 mph, 137 km/h; power-weight ratio: 40.6 lb/hp, (54.8 lb/kW), 18.4 kg/hp (24.6 kg/kW), acceleration: standing ¼ mile 20 sec, 0-50 mph (0-80 km/h) 11 sec; speed in direct drive at 1,000 rpm: 21.3 mph, 34.3 km/h

BRAKES lining area: total 85.7 sq in, 553 sq cm.

ELECTRICAL EQUIPMENT 44 Ah battery.

DIMENSIONS AND WEIGHT weight: 2,359 lb, 1,070 kg.

BODY heated rear window.

PRACTICAL INSTRUCTIONS fuel: diesel oil; oil: engine 9.7 imp pt, 11.6 US pt, 5.5 l, SAE 20W-30, change every 6,200 miles, 10,000 km - gearbox 1.9 imp pt, 2.3 US pt, 1.1 l, SAE 80 no change recommended - final drive 1,9 imp pt, 2.3 US pt, 1.1 l, SAE 90, no change recommended; tappet clearances (hot) inlet 0.008 in, 0.20 mm, exhaust 0.012 in, 0.30 mm; valve timing: 44° 86° 84° 46°.

OPTIONALS Opel automatic transmission with 3 ratios (I 2.400 II 1.480, III 1, rev 1.920), max ratio of converter at stall 2.5 3.670 axle ratio, max speed 82 mph, 132 km/h, consumption 2.82 m/imp gal, 23.5 m/US gal, 10 l x 100 km.

Manta Series

PRICES EX WORKS:		DM
1	2-dr Coupé	13,765*
2	Luxus 2-dr Coupé	14,685*
3	Berlinette 2-dr Coupé	15,461*
4	CC 2+1-dr Hatchback Coupé	14,180*
5	CC Luxus 2+1-dr Hatchback Coupé	15,100*
6	CC Berlinetta 2+1-dr Hatchback Coupé	15,876*
7	GT/E 2-dr Coupé	17,168*
8	E Luxus 2-dr Coupé	17,229*
9	E Berlinetta 2-dr Coupé	17,970*
10	CC GT/E 2+1-dr Hatchback Coupé	17,583*
11	CC E Luxus 2+1-dr Hatchback Coupé	17,644*
12	CC E Berlinetta 2+1-dr Hatchback Coupé	18,385*

For 60 hp (1,584 cc) engine add DM 197; for 75 hp engine add DM 482; for 90 hp engine add DM 711; for 100 hp engine add DM 858.

Power team:	Standard for:	Optional for:
60 hp	1 to 6	—
60 hp (1,584 cc)	—	1 to 6
75 hp	—	1 to 6
90 hp	—	1 to 6
100 hp	—	1 to 6
110 hp	7 to 12	—

60 hp power team

ENGINE front, 4 stroke; 4 cylinders, in line; 79.14 cu in, 1,297 cc (2.95 x 2.89 in, 75 x 73.4 mm); compression ratio: 8.2:1; max power (DIN): 60 hp (44 kW) at 5,800 rpm; max torque (DIN): 71 lb ft, 9.8 kg m (96 Nm) at 3,800 rpm; max engine rpm: 6,200 46.3 hp/l (33.9 kW/l); cast iron block, light alloy head; 5 crankshaft bearings; valves: overhead, rockers, hydraulic tappets; camshafts: 1, overhead, cogged belt; lubrication: gear pump, full flow filter, 4.8 imp pt, 5.7 US pt, 2.7 l; 1 Solex 35 PDSI downdraught single barrel carburettor; fuel feed: mechanical pump; anti-freeze liquid cooled, 10.2 imp 12.3 US pt, 5.8 l

TRANSMISSION driving wheels: rear; clutch: single dry plate (diaphragm); gearbox: mechanical; gears: 4, fully synchronized

OPEL Ascona Berlina Limousine

OPEL Manta GT/E Coupé

ratios: I 3.640, II 2.120, III 1.336, IV 1, rev 3.522; lever: central; final drive: hypoid bevel; axle ratio: 4.375; width of rims: 5"; tyres: 165 SR x 13.

PERFORMANCE max speed: 93 mph, 150 km/h; power-weight ratio: 34 lb/hp (46.4 lb/kW), 15.4 kg/hp (21 kg/kW); carrying capacity: 816 lb, 370 kg; acceleration: standing ¼ mile 21 sec, 0-50 mph (0-80 km/h) 12 sec; speed in direct drive at 1,000 rpm: 23.7 mph, 38.1 km/h; consumption: 32.5 m/imp gal, 27 m/US gal, 8.7 l x 100 km.

CHASSIS integral; front suspension: independent, wishbones (lower trailing links), coil springs, anti-roll bar, telescopic dampers; rear: rigid axle (torque tube), trailing radius arms, transverse linkage bar, coil springs, anti-roll bar, telescopic dampers.

STEERING rack-and-pinion; turns lock to lock: 4.

BRAKES front disc, rear drum, dual circuit, rear compensator, servo; lining area: front 22.9 sq in, 148 sq cm, rear 47.1 sq in, 304 sq cm, total 70 sq in, 452 sq cm.

ELECTRICAL EQUIPMENT 12 V; 36 Ah battery; 45 A alternator; Bosch or Delco Remy distributor; 2 headlamps.

DIMENSIONS AND WEIGHT wheel base: 99.13 in, 252 cm; tracks: 54.33 in, 138 cm front, 54.13 in, 137 cm rear; length: 175.39 in, 444 cm - CC models 172.28 in, 438 cm; width: 65.75 in, 167 cm; height: 52.36 in, 133 cm; ground clearance: 5.12 in, 13 cm; weight: 2,040 lb, 925 kg; turning circle: 33.8 ft, 10.3 m; fuel tank: 11 imp gal, 13.2 US gal, 50 l.

BODY coupé; 5 seats, separate front seats, adjustable backrests.

PRACTICAL INSTRUCTIONS fuel: 91 oct petrol; oil: engine 4.8 imp pt, 5.7 US pt, 2.7 l, SAE 20W-30, change every 6,200 miles, 10,000 km - gearbox 1.1 imp pt, 1.3 US pt, 0.6 l, SAE 80, no change recommended - final drive 1.1 imp pt, 1.3 US pt, 0.6 l, SAE 90, no change recommended; greasing: none; sparking plug: 200°; valve timing: 24° 73° 66° 30°; tyre pressure: front 24 psi, 1.7 atm, rear 24 psi, 1.7 atm.

OPTIONALS 185/70 SR x 13 tyres with 5.5" wide rims; 44 or 55 Ah battery; heated rear window; sunshine roof; headrests; metallic spray; halogen headlamps; vinyl roof; headlamps with wiper-washers; SR equipment.

60 hp (1,584 cc) power team

See 60 hp power team, except for:

ENGINE 96.7 cu in, 1,584 cc (3.35 x 2.75 in, 85 x 69.8 mm); compression ratio: 8:1; max power (DIN): 60 hp (44 kW) at 5,000 rpm; max torque (DIN): 76 lb ft, 10.5 kg m (103 Nm) at 3,000-3,400 rpm; max engine rpm: 6,000; 37.9 hp/l (27.9 kW/l); lubrication: 6.7 imp pt, 8 US pt, 3.8 l; cooling: 11.4 imp pt, 13.7 US pt, 6.5 l.

TRANSMISSION axle ratio: 3.700.

PERFORMANCE max speed: 93 mph, 150 km/h; power-weight ratio: 36 lb/hp (48.9 lb/kW), 16.3 kg/hp (22.2 kg/kW); acceleration: standing ¼ mile 20 sec, 0-50 mph (0-80 km/h) 11 sec; speed in direct drive at 1,000 rpm: 21.3 mph, 34.3 km/h; consumption: 28.2 m/imp gal, 23.5 m/US gal, 10 l x 100 km.

DIMENSIONS AND WEIGHT weight: 2,161 lb, 980 kg.

PRACTICAL INSTRUCTIONS oil: engine 6.7 imp pt, 8 US pt, 3.8 l, SAE 20W-30, change every 6,200 miles, 10,000 km - gearbox 1.9 imp pt, 2.3 US pt, 1.1 l, SAE 90, no change recommended; tappet clearances (hot): inlet 0.012 in, 0.30 mm, exhaust 0.012 in, 0.30 mm; valve timing: 44° 86° 84° 46°.

OPTIONALS Opel automatic transmission with 3 ratios (I 2.400, II 1.480, III 1, rev 1.920), max ratio of converter at stall 2.5, 3.670 axle ratio, max speed 90 mph, 145 km/h, consumption 26.4 m/imp gal, 22 m/US gal, 10.7 l x 100 km.

75 hp power team

See 60 hp power team, except for:

ENGINE 115.8 cu in, 1,897 cc (3.66 x 2.75 in, 93 x 69.8 mm); compression ratio: 7.9:1; max power (DIN): 75 hp (55 kW) at 4,800 rpm; max torque (DIN): 98 lb ft, 13.5 kg m (132.4 Nm) at 2,200-3,400 rpm; max engine rpm: 5,200; 39.5 hp/l (29.1 kW/l); lubrication: 6.7 imp pt, 8 US pt, 3.8 l; cooling: 10.4 imp pt, 12.5 US pt, 5.9 l.

TRANSMISSION axle ratio: 3.670.

PERFORMANCE max speed: 101 mph, 162 km/h; power-weight ratio: 29.4 lb/hp (39.9 lb/kW), 13.3 kg/hp (18.1 kg/kW); acceleration: standing ¼ mile 20 sec, 0-50 mph (0-80 km/h 11 sec; speed in direct drive at 1,000 rpm: 21.3 mph, 34.3 km/h; consumption: 27.7 m/imp gal, 23.1 m/US gal, 10.2 l x 100 km.

BRAKES lining area: front 22.9 sq in, 148 sq cm, rear 62.8 sq in, 405 sq cm, total 85.7 sq in, 553 sq cm.

ELECTRICAL EQUIPMENT 44 Ah battery.

DIMENSIONS AND WEIGHT weight: 2,205 lb, 1,000 kg.

PRACTICAL INSTRUCTIONS oil: engine 6.7 imp pt, 8 US pt, 3.8 l, SAE 20W-30, change every 6,200 miles, 10.000 km - gearbox 1.9 imp pt, 2.3 US pt, 1.1 l, SAE 90, no change recommended; tappet clearances (hot): inlet 0.012 in, 0.30 mm, exhaust 0.012 in, 0.30 mm; valve timing: 44° 86° 84° 46°.

OPTIONALS Opel automatic transmission with 3 ratios (I 2.400, II 1.480, III 1, rev 1.920), max ratio of converter at stall 2.5, 3.670 axle ratio, max speed 97 mph, 157 km/h, consumption 25.7 m/imp gal, 21.4 m/US gal, 11 l x 100 km; air-conditioning.

90 hp power team

See 60 hp power team, except for:

ENGINE 115.8 cu in, 1.897 cc (3.74 x 2.75 in, 95 x 69.8 mm); compression ratio: 8:1; max power (DIN): 90 hp (66 kW) at 5,200 rpm; max torque (DIN): 109 lb ft, 15 kg m (147 Nm) at 2,600-3,800 rpm; max engine rpm: 6,000; 47.7 hp/l (34.9 kW/l); lubrication: 6.7 imp pt, 8 US pt, 3.8 l; 1 GMF Varajet II downdraught carburettor; cooling: 11.3 imp pt, 13.5 US pt, 6.4 l.

TRANSMISSION axle ratio: 3.670.

PERFORMANCE max speed: 107 mph, 172 km/h; power-weight ratio: 24.5 lb/hp (33.3 lb/kW), 11.1 kg/hp (15.1 kg/kW); acceleration: standing ¼ mile 18 sec, 0-50 mph (0-80 km/h) 8 sec; speed in direct drive at 1,000 rpm: 21.1 mph, 34 km/h; consumption: 31.4 m/imp gal, 26.1 m/US gal, 9 l x 100 km.

BRAKES lining area: front 22.9 sq in, 148 sq cm, rear 62.8 sq in, 405 sq cm, total 85.7 85.7 sq in, 553 sq cm.

ELECTRICAL EQUIPMENT 44 Ah battery.

DIMENSIONS AND WEIGHT weight: 2,205 lb, 1,000 kg.

PRACTICAL INSTRUCTIONS oil: engine 6.7 imp pt, 8 US pt, 3.8 l, SAE 20W-30, change every 6,200 miles, 10,000 km - gearbox 1.9 imp pt, 2.3 US pt, 1.1 l, SAE 90, no change recommended; tappet clearances (hot): inlet 0.012 in, 030 mm, exhaust 0.012 in, 0.30 mm; valve timing: 44° 86° 84° 46°.

OPTIONALS Opel automatic transmission with 3 ratios (I 2.400, II 1.480, III 1, rev 1.920), max ratio of converter at stall 2.5, max speed 104 mph, 167 km/h, consumption 29.1 m/imp gal, 24.2 m/US gal, 9.7 l x 100 km; limited slip differential; air-conditioning.

100 hp power team

See 60 hp power team, except for:

ENGINE 120.8 cu in, 1,979 cc (3.74 x 2.75 in, 95 x 69.8 mm); compression ratio: 9:1; max power (DIN): 100 hp (74 kW) at 5,400 rpm; max torque (DIN): 111 lb ft, 15.3 kg m (150 Nm) at 3,800 rpm; max engine rpm: 6,000; 50.5 hp/l (37.2 kW/l); valves: hydraulic tappets; lubrication: 6.7 imp pt, 8 US pt, 3.8 l; 1 GMF Varjet II downdraught single barrel carburettor; cooling: 10.9 imp pt, 13.1 US pt, 6.2 l.

OPEL Manta CC E Berlinetta Hatchback Coupé

100 HP POWER TEAM

TRANSMISSION axle ratio: 3.440; tyres: 165 HR x 13.

PERFORMANCE max speed: 112 mph, 180 km/h; power-weight ratio: 22 lb/hp (29.9 lb/kW), 10 kg/hp (13.6 kg/kW); acceleration: standing ¼ mile 20 sec, 0-50 mph (0-80 km/h) 11 sec; speed in direct drive at 1,000 rpm: 20.7 mph, 33.3 km/h; consumption: 31.4 m/imp gal, 26.1 m/US gal, 9 l x 100 km.

BRAKES lining area: front 22.9 sq in, 148 sq cm, rear 62.8 sq in, 405 sq cm, total 85.7 sq in, 553 sq cm.

ELECTRICAL EQUIPMENT 44 Ah battery.

DIMENSIONS AND WEIGHT weight: 2,205 lb, 1,000 kg.

PRACTICAL INSTRUCTIONS fuel: 98 oct petrol; oil: engine 6.7 imp pt, 8 US pt, 3.8 l, SAE 20W-30, change every 6,200 miles, 10.000 km - gearbox 1.9 imp pt, 2.3 US pt, 1.1 l, SAE 90, no change recommended; tappet clearances (hot): inlet 0.012 in, 0,30 mm, exhaust 0.012 in, 0.30 mm; valve timing: 32° 90° 72° 50°.

OPTIONALS Opel automatic transmission with 3 ratios (I 2.400, II 1.480, III 1, rev 1.920), max ratio of converter at stall 2.5, 3.670 axle ratio, max speed 109 mph, 175 km/h, consumption 29.1 m/imp gal, 24.2 m/US gal, 9.7 l x 100 km; 185/70 HR x 13 tyres with 5.5" wide rims; air-conditioning.

110 hp power team

See 60 hp power team, except for:

ENGINE 120.8 cu in, 1,979 cc (3.74 x 2.75 in, 95 x 69.8 mm); compression ratio: 9.4:1; max power (DIN): 110 hp (81 kW) at 5,400 rpm; max torque (DIN): 117 lb ft, 16.2 kg m (159 Nm) at 3,400 rpm; max torque engine rpm: 6,000; 55.6 hp/l (40.9 kW/l); valves: hydraulic tappets; lubrication: 6.7 imp pt, 8 US pt, 3.8 l; Bosch L-Jetronic electronic injection; cooling, 10.9 imp pt, 13.1 US pt, 6.2 l.

TRANSMISSION axle ratio: 3.440; width of rims: E and CC E models 5.5" - GT/E models 6"; tyres: 185/70 HR x 13.

PERFORMANCE max speed: 116 mph, 187 km/h; power-weight ratio: E models 20 lb/hp (27.2 lb/kW) 9.1 kg/hp (12.3 kg/kW); acceleration: standing ¼ mile 20 sec, 0-50 mph (0-80 km/h) 11 sec; speed in direct drive at 1,000 rpm: 19.6 mph, 31.5 km/h; consumption: 31.4 m/imp gal, 26.1 m/US gal, 9 l x 100 km.

BRAKES lining area: front 22.9 sq in, 148 sq cm, rear 62.8 sq in, 405 sq cm, total 85.7 sq in, 553 sq cm.

ELECTRICAL EQUIPMENT 44 Ah battery.

DIMENSIONS AND WEIGHT weight: E models 2,205 lb, 1,000 kg - GT/E 2,227 lb, 1,010 kg - CC E and CC GTE models 2,293 lb, 1,040 kg.

PRACTICAL INSTRUCTIONS fuel: 98 oct petrol; oil: engine 6.7 imp pt, 8 US pt, 3.8 l, SAE 20W-30, change every 6,200 miles, 10,000 km - gearbox 1.9 imp pt, 2.3 US pt, 1.1 l, SAE 90 no change recommended; tappet clearances (hot): inlet 0.012 in, 0.30 mm, exhaust 0.012 in, 0.30 mm; valve timing: 34° 88° 74° 48°.

OPTIONALS Opel automatic transmission with 3 ratios (I 2.400, II 1.480, III 1, rev 1.920), max ratio of converter at stall 2.5, 3.670 axle ratio, max speed 113 mph, 182 km/h, consumption 29.1 m/imp gal, 24.2 m/US gal, 9.7 l x 100 km; 195/70 HR x 13 tyres; air conditioning.

Rekord Series

PRICES EX WORKS:		DM
1	2-dr Limousine	**14,935***
2	4-dr Limousine	**15,550***
3	Luxus 2-dr Limousine	**15,785***
4	Luxus 4-dr Limousine	**16,235***
5	Berlina 2-dr Limousine	**16,575***
6	Berlina 4-dr Limousine	**17,025***
7	2+1-dr Caravan	**15,540***
8	4+1-dr Caravan	**16,155***
9	Luxus 4+1-dr Caravan	**17,000***

For 90 hp engine add DM 515; for 100 hp engine add DM 660; for 110 hp engine add DM 2.235; for 65 hp diesel engine add DM 3,396.

Power team:	Standard for:	Optional for:
60 hp	—	all
75 hp	all	—
90 hp	—	all
100 hp	—	all
110 hp	—	all
65 hp (diesel)	—	all

60 hp power team

ENGINE front, 4 stroke; 4 cylinders, in line; 103.6 cu in, 1,698 cc (3.46 x 2.75 in), 88 x 69.8 mm); compression ratio: 8:1; max power (DIN): 60 hp (44 kW) at 4,800 rpm; max torque (DIN): 83 lb ft, 11.4 kg m (114 Nm) at 2,200-3,000 rpm; max engine rpm: 5,000; 35.3 hp/l (26 kW/l); cast iron block and head; 5 crankshaft bearings; valves: overhead, in line, rockers; camshafts: 1, overhead; lubrication: gear pump, full flow filter, 6.7 imp pt, 8 US pt, 3.8 l; 1 Solex 35 PDSI downdraught carburettor; fuel feed: mechanical pump; anti-freeze liquid cooled, 11.1 imp pt, 13.3 US pt, 6.3 l.

TRANSMISSION driving wheels: rear; clutch: single dry plate (diaphragm); gearbox: mechanical; gears: 4, fully synchronized; ratios: I 3.640, II 2.120, III 1.336, IV 1, rev 3.522; lever: central; final drive: hypoid bevel; axle ratio: 4.220; width of rims: 5.5"; tyres: 175 SR x 14.

PERFORMANCE max speed: 91 mph, 146 km/h - st. wagons 89 mph, 143 km/h; power-weight ratio: 4-dr limousines 41 lb/hp (55.6 lb/kW), 18.6 kg/hp (25.2 kg/kW); speed in direct drive at 1,000 rpm: 18.3 mph, 29.4 km/h; consumption: 26.9 m/imp gal, 22.4 m/US gal, 10.5 l x 100 km - st. wagons 24.6 m/imp gal, 20.5 m/US gal, 11.5 l x 100 km.

CHASSIS integral; front suspension: independent, wishbones, lower trailing links, coil springs, anti-roll bar, telescopic dampers; rear: rigid axle, trailing lower radius arms, upper torque arms, transverse linkage bar, coil springs, anti-roll bar, telescopic dampers.

STEERING recirculating ball; turns lock to lock: 4.

OPEL Rekord Series (diesel engine)

BRAKES front disc (diameter 9.37 in, 23.8 cm), rear drum, dual circuit, servo; lining area: total 85.7 sq in, 553 sq cm.

ELECTRICAL EQUIPMENT 12 V; 44 Ah battery; 45 A alternator; Bosch distributor; 2 headlamps.

DIMENSIONS AND WEIGHT wheel base: 105.04 in, 267 cm; tracks: 56.34 in, 143 cm front, 55.59 in, 141 cm rear; length: 108.75 in, 459 cm - st. wagons 181.81 in, 462 cm; width: 68.03 in, 173 cm; height: 55.71 in, 141 cm - st. wagons 56.69 in, 144 cm; ground clearance: 5.12 in, 13 cm; weight: 2-dr limousines 2,414 lb, 1,095 kg - 4-dr limousines 2,459 lb, 1,115 kg - 2+1-dr Caravan 2,514 lb, 1,140 kg - 4+1-dr Caravan 2,569 lb, 1,165 kg; turning circle: 37.4 ft, 11.4 m; fuel tank: 15.4 imp gal, 18.5 US gal, 70 l.

BODY saloon/sedan, estate car/st. wagon; 5 seats, separate front seats, reclining backrests; heated rear window.

PRACTICAL INSTRUCTIONS fuel: 91 oct petrol; oil: engine 6.7 imp pt, 8 US pt, 3.8 l, SAE 20W-30, change every 6,200 miles, 10,000 km - gearbox 1.9 imp pt, 2.3 US pt, 1.1 l, SAE 80, no change recommnded - final drive 1.9 imp pt, 2.3 US pt, 1.1 l, SAE 90, no change recommended; greasing: none; sparking plug: 200°; tappet clearances (hot): inlet 0.012 in, 0.30 mm, exhaust 0.012 in, 0.30 mm; valve timing: 44° 86° 84° 46°; tyre pressure: front 24 psi, 1.7 atm, rear 25 psi, 1.8 atm.

OPTIONALS 185/70 SR x 14 tyres with 5.5" wide rims; sunshine roof; headrests; 55 Ah battery; 55 A alternator; halogen headlamps; metallic spray; headlamps with wiper-washer; rear window wiper-washer (for st. wagons only).

OPEL Rekord Berlina Diesel Limousine

75 hp power team

See 60 hp power team, except for:

ENGINE 115.8 cu in, 1,897 cc (3.66 x 2.75 in, 93 x 69.8 mm); compression ratio: 7.9:1; max power (DIN): 75 hp (55 kW) at 4,800 rpm; max torque (DIN): 100 lb ft, 13.8 kg m (135 Nm) at 2,200-3,400 rpm; 39.5 hp/l (29.1 kW/l); cooling: 10.9 imp pt, 13.1 US pt, 6.2 l.

TRANSMISSION axle ratio: 3.890.

PERFORMANCE max speed: 96 mph, 155 km/h - st. wagons 94 mph, 152 km/h; power-weight ratio: 4-dr limousines 32.8 lb/hp (44.5 lb/kW), 14.9 kg/hp (20.2 kg/kW); speed in direct drive at 1,000 rpm: 19.4 mph, 31.2 km/h; consumption: 25.7 m/imp gal, 21.4 m/US gal, 11 l x 100 km - st. wagons 24.6 m/imp gal, 20.5 m/US gal, 11.5 l x 100 km.

OPTIONALS Opel automatic transmission with 3 ratios (I 2.400, II 1.480, III 1, rev 1.920), max ratio of converter at stall 2.5, possible manual selection, max speed 93 mph, 150 km/h - st. wagons 91 mph, 147 km/h, consumption 24.6 m/imp gal, 20.5 m/US gal, 11.5 l x 100 km - st. wagons 23.5 m/imp gal, 19.6 m/US gal, 12 l x 100 km.

90 hp power team

See 60 hp power team, except for:

ENGINE 120.8 cu in, 1,979 cc (3.74 x 2.75 in, 95 x 69.8 mm); max power (DIN): 90 hp (66 kW) at 5,200 rpm; max torque (DIN): 107 lb ft, 14.8 kg m (145 Nm) at 3,000-3,800 rpm; 45.4 hp/l (33.4 kW/l); valves: hydraulic tappets; 1 GMF Varajet II downdraught carburettor.

TRANSMISSION axle ratio: 3.890.

PERFORMANCE max speed: 103 mph, 165 km/h - st. wagons 101 mph, 162 km/h; power-weight ratio: 4-dr limousines 27.3 lb/hp (37 lb/kW), 12.4 kg/hp (16.8 kg/kW); speed in direct drive at 1,000 rpm: 20.4 mph, 32.8 km/h; consumption: 24.6 m/imp gal, 20.5 m/US gal, 11.5 l x 100 km - st. wagons 23.5 m/imp gal, 19.6 m/US gal, 12 l x 100 km.

BRAKES st. wagons, rear compensator.

PRACTICAL INSTRUCTIONS valve timing: 32° 90° 72° 50°.

OPTIONALS Opel automatic transmission with 3 ratios (I 2.400, II 1.480, III 1, rev 1.920), max ratio of converter at stall 2.5, possible manual selection, max speed 99 mph, 160 km/h - st. wagons 97 mph, 157 km/h, consumption 23.2 m/imp gal, 19.3 m/US gal, 12.2 l x 100 km - st. wagons 22.2 m/imp gal, 18.5 m/US gal, 12.7 l x 100 km; limited slip differential.

100 hp power team

See 60 hp power team, except for:

ENGINE 120.8 cu in, 1,979 cc (3.74 x 2.75 in, 95 x 69.8 mm); compression ratio: 9:1; max power (DIN): 100 hp (74 kW) at 5,200 rpm; max torque (DIN): 117 lb ft, 16.1 kg m (158 Nm) at 3,400-3,800 rpm; max engine rpm: 5,500; 50.5 hp/l (37.2 kW/l); valves: hydraulic tappets; 1 Zenith 35/40 INAT downdraught carburettor.

PERFORMANCE max speed: 107 mph, 173 km/h - st. wagons 106 mph, 170 km/h; power-weight ratio: 4-dr limousines 24.6 lb/hp (33.3 lb/kW), 11.1 kg/hp (15.1 kg/kW); speed in direct drive at 1,000 rpm: 19.8 mph, 31.8 km/h; consumption: 27.7 m/imp gal, 23.1 m/US gal, 10.2 l x 100 km - st. wagons 26.4 m/imp gal, 22 m/US gal, 10.7 l x 100 km.

BRAKES st. wagons rear compensator.

PRACTICAL INSTRUCTIONS fuel: 98 oct petrol; valve timing: 32° 90° 72° 50°.

OPTIONALS Opel automatic transmission with 3 ratios (I 2.400, II 1.480, III 1, rev 1.920), max ratio of converter at stall 2.5, possible manual selection, max speed 104 mph, 168 km/h - st. wagons 103 mph, 165 km/h, consumption 25.7 m/imp gal, 21.4 m/US gal, 11 l x 100 km - st. wagons 24.6 m/imp gal, 20.5 m/US gal, 11.5 l x 100 km; limited slip differential.

110 hp power team

See 60 hp power team, except for:

ENGINE 120.8 cu in, 1979 cc (3.74 x 2.75 in, 95 x 69.8 mm); compression ratio: 9.4:1; max power (DIN): 110 hp (81 kW) at 5,400 rpm; max torque (DIN): 120 lb ft, 16.5 kg m (162 Nm) at 3,000 rpm; max engine rpm: 6,000; 55.6 hp/l (40.9 kW/l); valves: hydraulic tappets; Bosch L-Jetronic electronic injecton; cooling, 16 imp pt, 19.2 US pt, 9.1 l.

PERFORMANCE max speed: 111 mph, 179 km/h - st. wagons 109 mph, 176 km/h; power-weight ratio: 4-dr limousines 22.3 lb/hp (30.3 lb/kW), 10.1 kg/hp (13.8 kg/kW); speed in direct drive at 1,000 rpm: 18.6 mph, 30 km/h; consumption: 27.7 m/imp gal, 23.1 m/US gal, 10.2 l x 100 km - st. wagons 26.4 m/imp gal, 22 m/US gal, 10.7 l x 100 km.

OPEL Rekord Luxus Caravan

BRAKES st. wagons rear compensator.

PRACTICAL INSTRUCTIONS fuel: 98 oct petrol; valve timing: 34° 88° 74° 48°.

OPTIONALS Opel automatic transmission with 3 ratios (I 2.400, II 1.480, III 1, rev 1.920), max ratio of converter at stall 2.5, possible manual selection, max speed 108 mph, 174 km/h - st. wagons 106 mph, 171 km/h, consumption 25.7 m/imp gal, 21.4 m/US gal, 11 l x 100 km - st. wagons 24.6 m/imp gal, 20.5 m/US gal, 11.5 l x 100 km; limited slip differential.

65 hp (diesel) power team

See 60 hp power team, except for:

ENGINE diesel; 137.9 cu in, 2,260 cc (3.62 x 3.35 in, 92 x 85 mm); compression ratio: 22:1; max power (DIN): 65 hp (48 kW) at 4,200 rpm; max torque (DIN): 12 lb ft, 12.9 kg m (126 Nm) at 2,500 rpm; max engine rpm: 4,600; 28.7 hp/l (21.2 kW/l)); lubrication: 9.7 imp pt, 11.6 US pt, 5.5 l; Bosch injection; cooling, 20.6 imp pt, 24.7 US pt, 11.7 l.

TRANSMISSION axle ratio: 3.670.

PERFORMANCE max speed: 84 mph, 135 km/h; power-weight ratio: 4-dr, limousines 42.4 lb/hp (57.4 lb/kW), 19.2 kg/hp (26 kg/kW); speed in direct drive at 1,000 rpm: 18 mph, 29 km/h; consumption: 31.4 m/imp gal, 26.1 m/US gal, 9 l x 100 km.

ELECTRICAL EQUIPMENT 2 x 44 Ah batteries; 55 A alternator.

DIMENSIONS AND WEIGHT height: 56.50 in, 143 cm; weight: 2-dr limousines 2,712 lb, 1,230 kg - 4-dr limousines 2,756 lb, 1,250 kg - 2+1-dr Caravan 2,789 lb, 1,265 kg - 4+1-dr Caravan 2,844 lb, 1,290 kg.

PRACTICAL INSTRUCTIONS fuel: diesel oil; oil: engine 9.7 imp pt, 11.6 US pt, 5.5 l; tappet clearances (hot): inlet 0.008 in, 0.20 mm, exhaust 0.008 in, 0.20 mm; valve timing: 24° 76° 48° 27°; tyre pressure: front 28 psi, 2 atm, rear 28 psi, 2 atm.

VARIATIONS

(For Italy only)

ENGINE 121.9 cu in, 1,998 cc (3.41 x 3.35 in, 86.5 x 85 mm), max power (DIN) 57 hp (42 kW) at 4,400 rpm, max torque (DIN) 83 lb ft, 11.5 kg m (113 Nm) at 2,200 rpm, 28.5 hp/l (21 kW/l). **PERFORMANCE** max speed 81 mph, 130 km/h, power-weight ratio 4-dr limousines 48.3 lb/hp (65.7 lb/kW), 21.9 kg/hp (29.8 kg/kW), consumption 37.7 m/imp gal, 31.4 m/US gal, 7.5 l x 100 km.

OPTIONALS Opel automatic transmission with 3 ratios (I 2,400, II 1.480, III 1, rev 1.920), max ratio of converter at stall 2.5, possible manual selection, max speed 81 mph, 130 km/h, consumption 29.1 m/imp gal, 24.2 m/US gal, 9.7 l x 100 km; power steering; sunshine roof; headrests; halogen headlamps; metallic spray; headlamps with wiper-washers; rear window wiper-washer (for st. wagons only).

Commodore Series

PRICES EX WORKS:	DM
1 2-dr Limousine	**17,895***
2 4-dr Limousine	**18,350***
3 Berlina 2-dr Limousine	**18,575***
4 Berlina 4-dr Limousine	**19,030***

115 hp power team

ENGINE front, 4 stroke; 6 cylinders, in line; 151.9 cu in, 2,490 cc (3.43 x 2.75 in, 87 x 69.8 mm); compression ratio: 9.2:1; max power (DIN): 115 hp (85 kW) at 5,200 rpm; max torque (DIN): 130 lb ft, 17.9 kg m (179 Nm) at 3,800-4200 rpm; max engine rpm: 6,000; 46.1 hp/l (34.1 kW/l); cast iron block and head; 7 crankshaft bearings; valves: overhead, in line, hydraulic tappets; camshafts: 1, overhead; lubrication: gear pump, full flow filter, 9.7 imp pt, 11.6 US pt, 5.5 l; 1 Zenith 35/40 INAT downdraught carburettor; fuel feed: mechanical pump; anti-freeze liquid cooled, 17.8 imp pt, 21.4 US pt, 10.1 l.

TRANSMISSION driving wheels: rear; clutch: single dry plate (diaphragm); gearbox: mechanical; gears: 4, fully synchronized; ratios: I 3.640, II 2.120, III 1.336, IV 1, rev 3.522; lever: central; final drive: hypoid bevel; axle ratio: 3.700; width of rims: 6"; tyres: 175 HR x 14.

PERFORMANCE max speed: 112 mph, 180 km/h; power-weight ratio: 23 lb/hp (31.1 lb/kW), 10.4 kg/hp (14.1 kg/kW); carrying capacity: 1,169 lb, 530 kg; speed in direct drive at 1,000 rpm: 20.8 mph, 33.5 km/h; consumption: 26.4 m/imp gal, 22 m/US gal, 10.7 l x 100 km.

CHASSIS integral; front suspension: independent, wishbones, lower trailing links, coil springs, anti-roll bar, telescopic dampers; rear: rigid axle, twin trailing radius arms, upper torque arms, transverse linkage bar, coil springs, anti-roll bar, telescopic dampers.

OPEL Commodore Berlina Limousine

115 HP POWER TEAM

STEERING recirculating ball; turns lock to lock: 4.50.

BRAKES front disc, rear drum, rear compensator, servo; lining area: total 87.4 sq in, 564 sq cm.

ELECTRICAL EQUIPMENT 12 V; 44 Ah battery; 55 A alternator; 2 halogen headlamps.

DIMENSIONS AND WEIGHT wheel base: 105.12 in, 267 cm; tracks: 56.85 in, 144 cm front, 56.77 in, 142 cm rear; length: 185.04 in, 470 cm; width: 67.79 in, 172 cm; height: 55.71 in, 141 cm; ground clearance: 55.71 in, 14 cm; weight: 2,645 lb, 1,200 kg; turning circle: 36.1 ft, 11.5 m; fuel tank: 14.3 imp gal, 17.2 US gal, 65 l.

BODY saloon/sedan; 5 seats, separate front seats, reclining backrests with headrests; heated rear window.

PRACTICAL INSTRUCTIONS fuel: 98 oct petrol; oil: engine 9.7 imp pt, 11.6 US pt, 5.5 l, SAE 20W-30, change every 3,100 miles, 5000 km - gearbox 1.9 imp pt, 2.3 US pt, 1.1 l, SAE 80, no change recommended - final drive 2.5 imp pt, 3 US pt, 1.4 l, SAE 90, no change recommended; greasing: none; sparking plug: 200°; valve timing: 40° 88° 80° 48°; tyre pressure: front 28 psi, 2 atm, rear 30 psi, 2.2 atm.

OPTIONALS Opel automatic transmission with 3 ratios (I 2.400, II 1.480, III 1, rev 1.920); limited slip differential; light alloy wheels; 195/70 HR x 14 tyres; power steering; 55 Ah battery; rear seat headrests; sunshine roof; metallic spray; headlight washer; vinyl roof.

Senator Series

PRICES EX WORKS:	DM
1 4-dr Limousine	**24,415***
2 C 4-dr Limousine	**26,454***
3 CD Automatic 4-dr Limousine	**38,925***

For 150 hp engine add DM 836; 180 hp engine add DM 4,188 (DM 3,949 for C model); for Opel Automatic transmission add DM 1,750.

Power team:	Standard for:	Optional for:
140 hp	1,2	—
150 hp	—	1,2
180 hp	3	1,2

140 hp power team

ENGINE front, 4 stroke; 6 cylinders, in line; 169.9 cu in, 2,784 cc (3.62 x 2.75 in 92 x 69.8 mm); compression ratio: 9:1; max power (DIN): 140 hp (103 kW) at 5,200 rpm; max torque (DIN): 158 lb ft, 21.8 kg m (218 Nm) at 3.400 rpm; max engine rpm: 6,000; 50.2 hp/l (36.9 kW/l); cast iron block and head; 7 crankshaft bearings; valves: overhead, in line hydraulic tappets; camshafts: 1, overhead, lubrication: gear pump, full flow filter, 9.7 imp pt, 11.6 US pt, 5.5 l; 1 DVG 4 A1 4-barrel downdraught carburettor; fuel feed: mechanical pump; anti-freeze liquid cooled, 17.2 imp pt, 20.7 US pt, 9.8 l.

TRANSMISSION driving wheels: rear; clutch: single dry plate (diaphragm); gearbox: mechanical; gears: 4, fully synchronized; ratios: I 3.504, II 2.017, III 1.410, IV 1, rev 3.569; lever: central; final drive: hypoid bevel; axle ratio: 3.450; width of rims: 6"; tyres: 175 HR x 14.

PERFORMANCE max speed: 118 mph, 190 km/h; power-weight ratio: 21.6 lb/hp (29.4 lb//kW), 9.8 kg/hp (13.3 kg/kW); carrying capacity: 1,158 lb, 525 kg; consumption: 26.4 m/imp gal, 22 m/US gal, 10.7 l x 100 km.

CHASSIS integral; front suspension: independent, by McPherson, wishbones, lower trailing links, coil springs, anti-roll bar, telescopic dampers; rear: independent, semitrailing arms, coil spring, anti-roll bar, telescopic dampers.

STEERING recirculating ball, servo; turns lock to lock: 4.

BRAKES disc; lining area: total 40.9 sq in, 264 sq cm.

ELECTRICAL EQUIPMENT 12 V; 44 Ah battery; 55 A alternator; 2 halogen headlamps, fog lamps.

DIMENSIONS AND WEIGHT wheel base: 105.12 in, 267 cm; tracks: 56.85 in, 144 cm front, 57.87 in, 147 cm rear; length: 189.37 in, 481 cm; width: 68.11 in, 173 cm; height: 55.51 in, 141 cm; ground clearance: 5.57 in, 14 cm; weight: 3,032 lb, 1,375 kg; turning circle: 35.4 ft, 10.8 m; fuel tank: 16.5 imp gal, 19.8 US gal, 75 l.

BODY saloon/sedan, 5 seats, separate front seats, reclining backrests, headrests.

PRACTICAL INSTRUCTIONS fuel: 98 oct petrol; oil: engine 9.7 imp pt, 11.6 US pt, 5.5 l, SAE 20W-30, change every 3,100 miles, 5,000 km - gearbox 1.9 imp pt, 2.3 US pt, 1.1 l, SAE 80, no change recommended- final drive 2.5 imp pt, 3 US pt, 1.4 l, SAE 90, no change recommended; greasing: none; sparking

OPEL Senator C Limousine

plug: AC 42-6 FS; valve timing: 32° 90° 72° 50°; tyre pressure: front 28 psi, 2 atm, rear 30 psi, 2.2 atm

OPTIONALS Opel automatic transmission with 3 ratios (I 2.400, II 1.480, III 1, rev 1.920); 195/70 HR x 14 tyres 215/60 VR x 15 tyres.

150 hp power team

See 140 hp power team, except for:

ENGINE 181.1 cu in, 2,968 cc (3.74 x 2.75 in, 95 x 69.8 mm); compression ratio: 9.2:1; max power (DIN): 150 hp (110 kW) at 5,200 rpm; max torque (DIN): 170 lb ft, 23.5 kg m (230 Nm) at 3,400 rpm; 50.3 hp/l (37 kW/l); cooling, 18 imp pt, 21.6 US pt, 10.2 l.

TRANSMISSION gearbox ratios: I 3.855, II 2.203, III 1.402, IV 1, rev 4.269.

PERFORMANCE max speed: 120 mph, 193 km/h; power-weight ratio: 20.2 lb/hp (27.5 lb/kW), 9.1 kg/hp (12.5 kg/kW); consumption: 24.6 m/imp gal, 20.5 m/US gal, 11.5 l x 100 km.

180 hp power team

See 140 hp power team, except for:

ENGINE compression ratio: 9.4:1; max power (DIN): 180 hp (132 kW) at 5,800 rpm; max torque (DIN): 180 lb ft, 24.8 kg m (248 Nm) at 4,500 rpm; 60.6 hp/l (44.4 kW/l); Bosch L-Jetron injection; cooling: 18 imp pt, 21.6 US pt, 10.2 l.

TRANSMISSION tyres: 195/70 VR x 14.

PERFORMANCE max speed: 130 mph, 210, km/h; power weight ratio: 17.4 lb/hp, (23.8 lb/kW), 7.9 kg/hp (10.7 kg/kW

DIMENSIONS AND WEIGHT weight: 3,142 lb, 1,425 kg.

Monza Series

PRICES EX WORKS:	DM
1 Hatchback Coupé	**26,430**
2 C Hatchback Coupé	**27,434**

For 150 hp engine add DM 836; for 180 hp engine add DM 4,188 (DM 3,949 for C model); for Opel Automatic transmissio add DM 1,750.

Power team:	Standard for:	Optional for:
140 hp	both	—
150 hp	—	both
180 hp	—	both

140 hp power team

ENGINE front, 4 stroke; 6 cylinders, in line; 169.9 cu in, 2,78 cc (3.62 x 2.75 in, 92 x 69.8 mm); compression ratio: 9:1; ma

OPEL Monza C Hatchback Coupé

ɔwer (DIN): 140 hp (103 KW) at 5,200 rpm; max torque (DIN): 58 lb ft, 21.8 kg m (218 Nm) at 3,400 rpm; max engine rpm: 000; 50.2 hp/l (36.9 kW/l); cast iron block and head; 7 ankshaft bearings; valves: overhead, in line, hydraulic tapets; camshafts: 1, overhead; lubrication: gear pump, full flow ter, 9.7 imp pt, 11.6 US pt, 5.5 l; 1 DVG 4 A1 4-barrel ɔwndraught carburettor; fuel feed: mechanical pump; antieeze liquid cooled, 17.2 imp pt, 20.7 US pt, 9.8 l.

RANSMISSION driving wheels: rear; clutch: single dry plate iaphragm); gearbox: mechanical; gears: 4, fully synchronized; atios: I 3.504, II 2.017, III 1.410, IV 1, rev 3.569; lever: central; nal drive: hypoid bevel; axle ratio: 3.450; width of rims: 6"; res: 175 HR x 14.

ERFORMANCE max speed: 121 mph, 195 km/h; power-weight atio: 21.6 lb/hp (29.4 lb/kW), 9.8 kg/hp (13.3 kg/kW); carrying apacity: 1,158 lb, 525 kg; consumption: 26.4 m/imp gal, 22 /US gal, 10.7 l x 100 km.

HASSIS integral; front suspension: independent, by McPherɔn, wishbones, lower trailing links, coil springs, anti-roll bar, elescopic dampers; rear: independent, semi-trailing arms, coil ɔrings, anti-roll bar, telescopic dampers.

TEERING recirculating ball, servo; turns lock to lock: 4.

RAKES disc; lining area: total 40.9 sq in, 264 sq cm.

LECTRICAL EQUIPMENT 12 V; 44 Ah battery; 55 A alternar; 2 halogen headlamps, fog lamps.

IMENSIONS AND WEIGHT wheel base: 105.12 in, 267 cm; acks: 56.85 in, 144 cm front, 57.87 in, 147 cm rear; length: 34.65 in, 469 cm; width: 68.11 in, 173 cm; height: 54.33 in, 38 cm; ground clearance: 55.71 in, 14 cm; weight: 3,032 lb, 375 kg; turning circle: 35.4 ft, 10.8 m; fuel tank: 15.4 imp gal, 3.5 US gal, 70 l.

ODY coupé; 2 doors; 4 seats, separate front seats, reclining ackrests, headrests.

RACTICAL INSTRUCTIONS fuel: 98 oct petrol; oil: engine 9.7 np pt, 11.6 US pt, 5.5 l, SAE 20W-30, change every 3,100 iles, 5,000 km - gearbox 1.9 imp pt, 2.3 US pt, 1.1 l, SAE 80, ɔ change recommended - final drive 2.5 imp pt, 3 US pt, 1.4 l, AE no change recommended; greasing: none; sparking plug: C42-6FS; valve timing: 32° 90° 72° 50°; tyre pressure: front 3 psi, 2 atm, rear 30 psi, 2.2 atm.

PTIONALS Opel automatic transmission with 3 ratios (I 2.400, 1.480, III 1, rev 1.920); 195/70 HR x 14 tyres; 215/60 VR x 15 res.

150 hp power team

ee 140 hp power team, except for:

NGINE 181.1 cu in, 2,968 cc (3.74 x 2.75 in, 95 x 69.8 mm); ɔmpression ratio: 9.2:1; max power (DIN): 150 hp (110 kW) at ,200 rpm; max torque (DIN): 170 lb ft, 23.5 kg m (230 Nm) at ,400 rpm; 50.3 hp/l (37 kW/l); cooling, 18 imp pt, 21.6 US pt, 0.2 l.

RANSMISSION gearbox ratios: I 3.855, II 2.203, III 1.402, IV , rev 4.269.

ERFORMANCE max speed: 123 mph, 198 km/h; power-weight atio: 20.2 lb/hp (27.5 lb/kW), 9.1 kg/hp (12.5 kg/kW); consumpon: 24.6 m/imp gal, 20.5 m/US gal, 11.5 l x 100 km.

180 hp power team

ee 140 hp power team, except for:

NGINE compression ratio: 9.4:1; max power (DIN): 180 hp 32 kW) at 5,800 rpm; max torque (DIN): 180 lb ft, 24.8 kg m 248 Nm) at 4.500 rpm; 60.6 hp/l (44.4 kW/l); Bosch L-Jetronic ijection; cooling, 18 imp pt, 21.6 US pt, 10.2 l.

RANSMISSION tyres: 195/70 VR x 14.

ERFORMANCE max speed: 134 mph, 215 km/h; power-weight atio: 16.8 lb/hp (23 lb/kW), 7.6 kg/hp (10.4 kg/kW).

ᑭORSCHE GERMANY FR

924

RICE IN GB: £ 9,103*
RICE EX WORKS: DM 27,980*

NGINE Audi, front, 4 stroke; 4 cylinders, vertical, in line; 21.1 cu in, 1,984 cc (3.41 x 3.32 in, 86.5 x 84.4 mm); comression ratio: 9.3:1; max power (DIN): 125 hp (92 kW) at 5,800 ɔm; max torque (DIN): 122 lb ft, 16.8 kg m (165 Nm) at 3,500 ɔm; max engine rpm: 6,500; 63 hp/l (46.3 kW/l); cast iron lock, light alloy head: 5 crankshaft bearings; valves: overhead, line, thimble tappets; camshsfts: 1, overhead, cogged belt;

OPEL Monza C Hatchback Coupé

lubrication: gear pump, full flow filter, 8.8 imp pt, 10.6 US pt, 5 l; Bosch K-Jetronic injection; fuel feed: electric pump; watercooled, 14.1 imp pt, 16.9 US pt, 8 l, electric thermostatic fan.

TRANSMISSION driving wheels: rear; clutch: single dry plate; gearbox: rear, mechanical, in unit with differential; gears: 5, fully synchronized; ratios: I 2.780, II 1.720, III 1.210, IV 0.930, V 0.700, rev 2.500; lever: central; final drive: hypoid bevel; axle ratio: 4.714; width of rims: 6"; tyres: 185/70 HR x 14.

PERFORMANCE max speeds: (I) 35 mph, 56 km/h; (II) 60 mph, 96 km/h; (III) 93 mph, 150 km/h; (IV) 124 mph, 200 km/h; power-weight ratio: 19 lb/hp (26 lb/kW), 8.6 kg/hp (11.7 kg/kW); carrying capacity: 706 lb, 320 kg; speed in top at 1,000 rpm: 19.5 mph, 31.4 km/h; consumption: 34.9 m/imp gal, 29 m/US gal, 8.1 l x 100 km at 75 mph, 120 km/h.

CHASSIS integral; front suspension: independent, by McPherson, lower wishbones, coil springs/telescopic damper struts; rear: independent, semi-trailing arms, transverse torsion bars, coil springs/telescopic damper struts.

STEERING rack-and-pinion.

BRAKES front disc, rear drum, 2 X circuits, servo; lining area: total 72.9 sq in, 470 sq cm.

ELECTRICAL EQUIPMENT 12 V; 45 Ah battery; 1,050 W alternator; Bosch electronic ignition; 4 headlamps, 2 retractable.

DIMENSIONS AND WEIGHT wheel base: 94.49 in, 240 cm;

PORSCHE 924 Turbo

tracks: 55.83 in, 142 cm front, 54.02 in, 137 cm rear; length: 165.35 in, 420 cm; width: 66.34 in, 168 cm; height: 50 in, 127 cm; weight: 2,381 lb, 1,080 kg; fuel tank: 13.6 imp gal, 16.4 US gal, 62 l.

BODY coupé; 2 doors; 2+2 seats, separate front seats, reclining backrests with built-in headrests; heated rear window; light alloy wheels.

PRACTICAL INSTRUCTIONS fuel: 98 oct petrol; oil: engine 8.8 imp pt, 10.6 US pt, 5 l, SAE 30W (summer), 20W (winter), change every 6,100 miles, 10,000 km - gearbox and final drive 4.6 imp pt, 5.5 US pt, 2.6 l, SAE 80; greasing none; sparking plug: 225°.

OPTIONALS automatic transmission, hydraulic torque converter and planetary gears with 3 ratios (I 2.551, II 1.448, III 1, rev 2.461), max ratio of converter at stall 2.1 possible manual selection, 3.454 axle ratio, max speed 121 mph, 195 km/h, consumption 29.7 m/imp gal, 24.8 M/US gal, 9.5 l x 100 km at 75 mph, 120 km/h; anti-roll bar on front and rear suspension; headlamps with wiper-washers; metallic spray; air-conditioning; sunshine roof; fog lamps; 63 Ah battery.

924 (USA)

See 924, except for:

PRICE IN USA: $ 15,970*

ENGINE compression ratio: 8.5:1; max power (DIN): 112 hp (82 kW) at 5,750 rpm; max torque (DIN): 115 lb ft, 15.9 kg m (156 Nm) at 3,500 rpm; 56.5 hp/l (41.5 kW/l).

PERFORMANCE max speed: 119 mph, 192 km/h; power-weight ratio: 23 lb/hp (31.3 lb/kW), 10.4 kg/hp (14.2 kg/kW); carrying capacity: 507 lb, 230 kg.

DIMENSIONS AND WEIGHT length: 170.08 in, 432 cm; weight: 2,580 lb, 1,170 kg.

PRACTICAL INSTRUCTIONS fuel: 91 oct petrol.

OPTIONALS automatic transmission with 3.727 axle ratio.

924 Turbo

See 924, except for:

PRICE IN GB: £ 13,629*
PRICE EX WORKS: DM 39,980*

ENGINE turbocharged; compression ratio: 7.5:1; max power (DIN): 170 hp (125 kW) at 5,500 rpm; max torque (DIN): 181 lb ft, 25 kg m (245 Nm) at 3,500 rpm; 85.7 hp/l (63.1 kW/l); lubrication: gear pump, full flow filter, dry sump, oil cooler, 9.7 imp pt, 11.6 US pt, 5.5 l; Bosch K-Jetronic injection with KKK exhaust turbocharger.

TRANSMISSION clutch: single dry plate, hydraulically controlled; ratios: I 3.617, II 1.778, III 1.217, IV 0.931, V 0.706, rev 3.167; tyres: 185/70 VR x 15.

PERFORMANCE max speed: 140 mph, 225 km/h; power-weight ratio: 15.3 lb/hp (20.8 lb/kW), 6.9 kg/hp (9.4 kg/kW); consumption: 26.9 m/imp gal, 22.4 m/US gal, 10.5 l x 100 km at 75 mph, 120 km/h.

CHASSIS (standard) anti-roll bar on front and rear suspension.

DIMENSIONS AND WEIGHT rear track: 54.80 in, 139 cm; length: 165.83 in, 421 cm; weight: 2,602 lb, 1,180 kg.

PRACTICAL INSTRUCTIONS oil: engine 9.7 imp pt, 11.6 US pt, 5.5 l.

OPTIONALS 205/55 VR x 16 tyres with aluminium wheels.

911 SC Coupé

PRICE IN GB: £ 16,109*
PRICE EX WORKS: DM 46,950*

ENGINE rear, 4 stroke; 6 cylinders, horizontally opposed; 182.7 cu in, 2,994 cc (3.74 x 2.77 in, 95 x 70.4 mm); compression ratio: 8.6:1; max power (DIN): 188 hp (138 kW) at 5,500 rpm; max torque (DIN): 196 lb ft, 27 kg m (26.5 Nm) at 4,200 rpm; max engine rpm: 7,000; 62.8 hp/l (46.1 kW/l); light alloy block with cast iron liners, light alloy head; 8 crankshaft bearings; valves: overhead, Vee-slanted, rockers; camshafts: 2, 1 per bank, overhead, double cogged belt; lubrication: gear pump, full flow filter, dry sump, thermostatic oil cooler, 22.9 imp pt, 27.5 US pt, 13 l; Bosch K-Jetronic injection; fuel feed: electronic pump; air-cooled.

TRANSMISSION driving wheels: rear; clutch: single dry plate; gearbox: mechanical; gears: 5, fully synchronized; ratios: I 3.181, II 1.833, III 1.261, IV 1, V 0.821, rev 3.325; lever: central; final drive: spiral bevel; axle ratio: 3.875; width of rims: 6" front, 7" rear; tyres: 185/70 VR x 15 front, 215/60 VR x 15 rear.

911 SC COUPÉ

PERFORMANCE max speed: over 140 mph, 225 km/h; power-weight ratio: 14.2 lb/hp (19.3 lb/kW), 6.4 kg/hp (8.7 kg/kW); carrying capacity: 750 lb, 340 kg: speed in top at 1,000 rpm: 25 mph, 40 km/h; consumption 24.8 m/imp gal, 20.6 m/US gal, 11.4 l x 100 km at 75 mph, 120 km/h.

CHASSIS integral; front suspension: independent, by McPherson, coil springs/telescopic damper struts, longitudinal torsion bars, lower wishbones, anti-roll bar; rear: independent, semi-trailing arms, transverse torsion bars, anti-roll bar, telescopic dampers.

STEERING ZF rack-and-pinion; turns lock to lock: 3.10.

BRAKES disc (front diameter 9.25 in, 23.5 cm, rear 9.61 in, 24.4 cm), internal radial fins; lining area: total 39.8 sq in, 257 sq cm.

ELECTRICAL EQUIPMENT 12 V; 66 Ah battery; 980 W alternator; Bosch electronic ignition; 2 iodine headlamps.

DIMENSIONS AND WEIGHT wheel base: 89.41 in, 227 cm; tracks: 54.02 in, 137 cm front, 54.33 in, 138 cm; length: 168.90 in, 429 cm; width: 64.96 in, 165 cm; height: 51.97 in, 132 cm; ground clearance: 4.72 in, 12 cm; weight: 2,558 lb, 1,160 kg; turning circle: 35.8 ft, 10.9 m; fuel tank: 17.6 imp gal, 21.1 US gal, 80 l.

BODY coupé; 2 doors; 2 + 2 seats, separate front seats, adjustable backrests, built-in headrests; heated rear window; light alloy wheels; automatic heating.

PRACTICAL INSTRUCTIONS fuel: 91 oct petrol; oil: engine 17.6 imp pt, 21.1 US pt, 10 l, SAE 30 (summer) 20 (winter), change every 6,200 miles, 10,000 km - gearbox and final drive 5.3 imp pt, 6.3 US pt, 3 l, SAE 90, change every 6,200 miles, 10,000 km; greasing: none; sparking plug: 225°; tappet clearances: inlet 0.004 in, 0.10 mm, exhaust 0.004 in, 0.10 mm; valve timing: 35° 50° 40° 20°; tyre pressure: front 29 psi, 2 atm, rear 34 psi, 2.4 atm.

OPTIONALS Sportomatic semi-automatic transmission with 3 ratios (I 2.400, II 1.429, III 0.926, rev 2.534), single dry plate clutch automatically operated by gear lever, hydraulic torque converter, max ratio of converter at stall 2.18, 3.375 axle ratio; Sportomatic transmission clutch; ZF limited slip differential (only with mechanical gearbox); air-conditioning; electric sunshine roof; electric windows; rear window wiper-washer; tinted glass; 88 Ah battery; 205/55 VR x 16 front tyres, 225/50 VR x 16 rear tyres; metallic spray; fog lamps.

911 SC Coupé (USA)

See 911 SC Coupé, except for:

PRICE IN USA: $ 25,900*

ENGINE max power (DIN): 172 hp (127 kW) at 5,500 rpm; max torque (DIN): 189 lb ft, 26.1 kg m (256 Nm) at 4,200 rpm; 57.4 hp/l (42.3 kW/l).

PERFORMANCE power-weight ratio: 14.9 lb/hp (20.2 lb/kW), 6.7 kg/hp (9.2 kg/kW).

PORSCHE 924

DIMENSIONS AND WEIGHT tracks: 53.60 in, 136 cm front, 53.80 in, 137 cm rear; height: 52.80 in, 134 cm; ground clearance: 5.60 in, 14.3 cm.

911 SC Targa

See 911 SC Coupé, except for:

PRICE IN GB: £ 16,109*
PRICE IN USA: $ 27,250*

BODY convertible; roll bar, detachable roof.

Turbo Coupé

See 911 SC Coupé, except for:

PRICE IN GB: £ 27,950*
PRICE EX WORKS: DM 82,950*

ENGINE turbocharged; 201.3 cu in, 3,299 cc (3.82 x 2.93 in, 97 x 74.4 mm); compression ratio: 7:1; max power (DIN): 300 hp (220 kW) at 5,500 rpm; max torque (DIN): 304 lb ft, 42 kg m (412 Nm) at 4,000 rpm; max engine rpm: 6,800; 90.9 hp/l (66.7 kW/l); Bosch K-Jetronic injection with KKK exhaust turbocharger; fuel feed: 2 electric pumps.

TRANSMISSION gears: 4, fully synchronized; ratios: I 2.250, II 1.304, III 0.893, IV 0.656, rev 3.325; axle ratio: 4.222; width of rims: 7" front, 8" rear; tyres: 205/55 VR x 16 front, 225/50 VR x 16 rear.

PORSCHE Turbo Coupé

PERFORMANCE max speed: over 162 mph, 260 km/h; power weight ratio: 9.6 lb/hp (13 lb/kW), 4.3 kg/hp (5.9 kg/kW) carrying capacity: 838 lb, 380 kg; speed in top at 1,000 rpm 29.3 mph, 47.2 km/h; consumption: 19.9 m/imp gal, 16.6 m/US gal, 14.2 l x 100 km at 75 mph, 120 km/h.

BRAKES lining area: total 58.3 sq in, 376 sq cm.

DIMENSIONS AND WEIGHT tracks: 56.30 in, 143 cm front 59.06 in, 150 cm rear; width: 69.68 in, 177 cm; height: 51.57 in 131 cm; weight: 2,867 lb, 1,300 kg; turning circle: 35.1 ft 10.7 m.

BODY rear window wiper-washer (standard).

PRACTICAL INSTRUCTIONS fuel: 98 oct petrol; oil: gearbo and final drive 6.5 imp pt, 7.8 US pt, 3.7 l; sparking plug: 280°

OPTIONALS only limited slip differential, electric sunshine roo and air-conditioning.

Turbo Coupé (USA)

See 911 SC Coupé, except for:

PRICE IN USA: $ 27,250*

ENGINE turbocharged; 201.3 cu in, 3,299 cc (3.82 x 2.93 in 97 x 74.4 mm); compression ratio: 7:1; max power (DIN): 26 hp (192 kW) at 5,500 rpm; max torque (DIN): 291 lb ft, 40.1 kg m (393 Nm) at 4,000 rpm; max engine rpm: 6,800; 79.1 hp/ (58.2 kW/l); Bosch K-Jetronic injection with KKK exhaust turbocharger; fuel feed: 2 electric pumps.

TRANSMISSION gears: 4, fully synchronized; ratios: I 2.250, 1.304, II 0.893, IV 0.656, rev 3.325; axle ratio: 4.222; width o rims: 7" front, 8" rear; tyres: 205/55 VR x 16 front, 225/5 VR x 16 rear.

PERFORMANCE max speed: 155 mph, 250 km/h; power-weigh ratio: 10.9 lb/hp (14.9 lb/kW), 5 kg/hp (6.7 kg/kW); carrying capacity: 453 lb, 205 kg; speed in top at 1,000 rpm: 29.3 mph 47.2 km/h; consumption: 19.9 m/imp gal, 16.6 m/US gal, 14. l x 100 km at 75 mph, 120 km/h.

BRAKES lining area: total 58.3 sq in, 376 sq cm.

DIMENSIONS AND WEIGHT tracks: 56.30 in, 143 cm front 59.06 in, 150 cm rear; width: 69.68 in, 177 cm; height: 52.30 in 133 cm; ground clearance: 5.50 in, 14 cm; weight: 2,855 lb 1,295 kg; turning circle: 34.8 ft, 10.6 m.

BODY rear window wiper-washer (standard).

PRACTICAL INSTRUCTIONS oil: gearbox and final drive 6. imp pt, 7.8 US pt, 3.7 l; sparking plug: 280°.

OPTIONALS only limited slip differential, electric sunshine roo and air-conditioning.

928

PRICE IN GB: £ 21,827*
PRICE IN USA: $ 35,450*

ENGINE front, 4 stroke; 8 cylinders, Vee-slanted; 273 cu in 4,474 cc (3.74 x 3.11 in, 95 x 78.9 mm); compression ratio 8.5:1; max power (DIN): 240 hp (176.7 kW) at 5.250 rpm; ma ɔrque (DIN): 280 lb ft, 38.7 kg m (380 Nm) at 3,600 rpm; 53.6 p/l (39.5 kW/l); light alloy block and head; 5 crankshaft bear-ıgs; valves: overhead, in line, hydraulic tappets; camshafts: 2, per bank, overhead, cogged belt; lubrication: gear pump, full ow filter, 11.4 imp pt, 13.7 US pt, 6.5 l; Bosch K-Jetronic lectronic injection; fuel feed: electric pump; water-cooled, 28.2 np pt, 33.8 US pt, 16 l.

RANSMISSION driving wheels: rear; clutch: single dry plate; earbox: mechanical, in unit with differential; gears: 5, fully ynchronized; ratios: I 3.601, II 2.466, III 1.819, IV 1.343, V 1, ev 3.162; lever: central; final drive: hypoid bevel; axle ratio: .750; width of rims: 7"; tyres: 215/60 VR x 15.

ERFORMANCE max speed: over 143 mph, 230 km/h; power-eight ratio: 13.3 lb/hp (18.1 lb/kW), 6 kg/hp (8.2 kg/kW); arrying capacity: 926 lb, 420 kg; speed in direct drive at 1,000 ɔm: 26.5 mph, 42.6 km/h; consumption: 23.7 m/imp gal, 19.8 ı/US gal, 11.9 l x 100 km at 75 mph, 120 km/h.

HASSIS integral; front suspension: independent, wishbones, oil springs/telescopic damper struts, anti-roll bar; rear: inde-endent, Weissach axle, wishbones, semi-trailing arms, trans-erse torsion bars, coil springs/telescopic damper struts.

TEERING rack-and-pinion, servo.

RAKES disc (front diameter 11.10 in, 28.2 cm, rear 11.38 in, 8.9 cm), internal radial fins, servo; lining area: total 49 sq in, 16 sq cm.

LECTRICAL EQUIPMENT 12 V; 66 Ah battery; 1,260 W lternator; electronic ignition; 2 retractable headlamps.

IMENSIONS AND WEIGHT wheel base: 98.43 in, 250 cm; racks: 60.98 in, 155 cm front, 59.88 in, 152 cm rear; length: 75.20 in, 445 cm; width: 72.44 in, 184 cm; height: 50.47 in, 28 cm; weight: 3,197 lb, 1,450 kg; turning circle: 37.7 ft, 11.5 ı; fuel tank: 18.9 imp gal, 22.7 US gal, 86 l.

ODY coupé; 2 doors; 2 + 2 seats, separate front seats, reclin-ıg backrests with built-in headrests; heated rear window with iper-washer.

RACTICAL INSTRUCTIONS fuel: 91 oct petrol; oil: engine 1.4 imp pt, 13.7 US pt, 6.5 l, SAE 15W-50/20W-50 - gearbox nd final drive 6.7 imp pt, 8 US pt, 3.8 l; sparking plug: 145°.

PTIONALS automatic transmission with 3 ratios (I 2.310, II .460, III 1, rev 1.840), max ratio of converter at stall 2, ossible manual selection; 225/50 VR x 16 tyres; limited slip ifferential; 88 Ah battery; air-conditioning; metallic spray; sun-hine roof.

928 S

ee 928, except for:

RICE IN GB: £ 25,251*
RICE EX WORKS: DM 72,900*

NGINE 284.6 cu in, 4,664 cc (3.82 x 3.11 in, 97 x 78.9 mm); ompression ratio: 10:1; max power (DIN): 300 hp (221 kW) at ,900 rpm; max torque (DIN): 284 lb ft, 39.2 kg m (380 Nm) at ,500 rpm; 64.3 hp/l (47.4 kW/l).

RANSMISSION tyres: 225/50 VR x 16 (standard).

ERFORMANCE max speed: over 155 mph, 250 km/h; power-eight ratio: 10.7 lb/hp (14.5 lb/kW), 4.8 kg/hp (6.6 kg/kW); onsumption: 22.6 m/imp gal, 18.8 m/US gal, 12.5 l x 100 km at 5 mph, 120 km/h.

RACTICAL INSTRUCTIONS fuel: 98 oct petrol.

OLKSWAGEN GERMANY FR

Polo Series

RICES IN GB AND EX WORKS:	£	DM
1 Limousine	2,944*	9,403*
2 L Limousine	3,245*	10,079*
3 GL Limousine	—	10,886*
4 S Limousine	—	9,736*
5 LS Limousine	—	10,412*
6 GLS Limousine	3,588*	11,219*
7 GT Limousine	—	—

or 60 hp engine add DM 646.

ower team:	Standard for:	Optional for:
40 hp	1 to 3	—
50 hp	4 to 6	—
60 hp	—	4 to 7

PORSCHE 928 S

40 hp power team

ENGINE front, transverse, slanted 15° to front, 4 stroke; 4 cylinders, in line; 54.6 cu in, 895 cc (2.74 x 2.32 in, 69.5 x 59 mm); compression ratio: 8:1; max power (DIN): 40 hp (29 kW) at 5,900 rpm; max torque (DIN): 45 lb ft, 6.2 kg m (61 Nm) at 3,500 rpm; max engine rpm: 6,000; 44.7 hp/l (32.8 kW/l); cast iron block, light alloy head; 5 crankshaft bearings; valves: overhead, in line, thimble tappets; camshafts: 1, overhead, cogged belt; lubrication: gear pump, full flow filter, 6.2 imp pt, 7.4 US pt, 3.5 l; 1 Solex 31 PICT-5 downdraught single barrel carburettor; fuel feed: mechanical pump; water-cooled, 8.8 imp pt, 10.6 US pt, 5 l, electric thermostatic fan.

TRANSMISSION driving wheels: front; clutch: single dry plate; gearbox: mechanical; gears: 4 fully synchronized; ratios: I 3.454, II 2.050, III 1.347, IV 0.963, rev 3.384; lever: central; final drive: spiral bevel; axle ratio: 4.571; width of rims: 4.5"; tyres: 135 SR x 13.

PERFORMANCE max speeds: (I) 27 mph, 43 km/h; (II) 46 mph, 74 km/h; (III) 62 mph, 110 km/h; (IV) 84 mph, 135 km/h; power-weight ratio: 37.7 lb/hp (51.4 lb/kW), 17.1 kg/hp (23.3 kg/kW); carrying capacity: 915 lb, 415 kg; acceleration: 0-50 mph (0-80 km/h) 12.7 sec; speed in top at 1,000 rpm: 14.2 mph, 22.8 km/h; consumption: 32.8 m/imp gal, 27.3 m/US gal, 8.6 l x 100 km at 75 mph, 120 km/h.

CHASSIS integral; front suspension: independent, by McPherson, lower wishbones, anti-roll bar, coil springs/telescopic damper struts; rear: independent, longitudinal trailing radius arms, coil springs/telescopic damper struts.

STEERING rack-and-pinion; turns lock to lock: 3.25.

BRAKES front disc, rear drum, 2 X circuits.

ELECTRICAL EQUIPMENT 12 V; 36 Ah battery; 35 A alternator; Bosch distributor; 2 headlamps.

DIMENSIONS AND WEIGHT wheel base: 91.93 in, 233 cm; tracks: 51.02 in, 130 cm front, 51.65 in, 131 cm rear; length: 141.93 in, 360 cm; width: 61.38 in, 156 cm; height: 52.91 in, 134 cm; ground clearance: 4.72 in, 12 cm; weight: 1,510 lb, 685 kg; turning circle: 31.5 ft, 9.6 m; fuel tank: 7.9 imp gal, 9.5 US gal, 36 l.

BODY saloon/sedan; 2+1 doors; 4-5 seats, separate front seats, reclining backrests with built-in headrests; heated rear window; folding rear seat.

PRACTICAL INSTRUCTIONS fuel: 91 oct petrol; oil: engine 5.3 imp pt, 6.3 US pt, 3 l, SAE 20W-30, change every 4,700 miles, 7,500 km - gearbox and final drive 4 imp pt, 4.9 US pt, 2.3 l, SAE 80 or 90; greasing: none; sparking plug: 175°; tyre pressure: front 26 psi, 1.8 atm, rear 28 psi, 2 atm.

OPTIONALS rear window wiper-washer; halogen headlamps; 155/70 SR x 13 tyres; sunshine roof; metallic spray (for L and GL models only).

VOLKSWAGEN Polo GLS Limousine

VOLKSWAGEN Derby GL Limousine

50 hp power team

See 40 hp power team, except for:

ENGINE 66.7 cu in, 1,093 cc (2.74 x 2.83 in, 69.5 x 72 mm); max power (DIN): 50 hp (37 kW) at 5,900 rpm; max torque (DIN): 56 lb ft, 7.7 kg m (75 Nm) at 3,500 rpm; 47.5 hp/l (33.7 kW/l); cooling: 10.9 imp pt, 13.1 US pt, 6.2 l.

TRANSMISSION tyres: 145 SR x 13.

PERFORMANCE max speed: 90 mph, 145 km/h; power-weight ratio: 30.2 lb/hp (41 lb/kW), 13.7 kg/hp (18.6 kg/kW); acceleration: 0-50 mph (0-80 km/h) 9.6 sec; consumption: 31.7 m/imp gal, 26.4 m/US gal, 8.9 l x 100 km at 75 mph, 120 km/h.

BRAKES servo.

60 hp power team

See 40 hp power team, except for:

ENGINE 77.6 cu in, 1,272 cc (2.95 x 2.83 in, 75 x 72 mm); compression ratio: 8.2:1; max power (DIN): 60 hp (44 kW) at 5,600 rpm; max torque (DIN): 70 lb ft, 9.7 kg m (95 Nm) at 3,500 rpm; 47.2 hp/l (34.7 kW/l); cooling: 10.9 imp pt, 13.1 US pt, 6.2 l.

TRANSMISSION axle ratio: 4.063; tyres: 145 SR x 13 - GT 155/70 SR x 13.

PERFORMANCE max speed: 96 mph, 154 km/h: power-weight ratio: 25.2 lb/hp (34.2 lb/kW), 11.4 kg/hp (15.5 kg/kW); acceleration: 0-50 mph (0-80 km/h) 8.3 sec; consumption: 31 m/imp gal, 25.8 m/US gal, 9.1 l x 100 km at 75 mph, 120 km/h.

CHASSIS rear suspension: anti-roll bar.

BRAKES rear compensator, servo.

Derby Series

PRICES IN GB AND EX WORKS:	£	DM
1 Limousine	—	9,797*
2 L Limousine	—	10,473*
3 GL Limousine	—	11,103*
4 S Limousine	3,100*	10,130*
5 LS Limousine	3,440*	10,809*
6 GLS Limousine	3,785*	11,436*
7 CL Limousine	—	—
8 CLS Limousine	—	—

For 60 hp engine add DM 646.

Power team:	Standard for:	Optional for:
40 hp	1,2,3	—
50 hp	4,5,6	—
60 hp	—	5,6,8

40 hp power team

ENGINE front, transverse, slanted 15° to front, 4 stroke; 4 cylinders, in line; 54.6 cu in, 895 cc (2.74 x 2.32 in, 69.5 x 59 mm); compression ratio: 8:1; max power (DIN): 40 hp (29 kW) at 5,900 rpm; max torque (DIN): 45 lb ft, 6.2 kg m (61 Nm) at 3,500 rpm; max engine rpm: 6,000; 44.7 hp/l (32.8 kW/l); cast iron block, light alloy head; 5 crankshaft bearings; valves: overhead, in line, thimble tappets; camshafts: 1, overhead, cogged belt; lubrication: gear pump, full flow filter, 6.2 imp pt, 7.4 US pt, 3.5 l; 1 Solex 35 PICT-5 downdraught single barrel carburettor; fuel feed: mechanical pump; water-cooled, 8.8 imp pt, 10.6 US pt, 5 l, electric thermostatic fan.

TRANSMISSION driving wheels: front; clutch: single dry plate; gearbox: mechanical; gears: 4, fully synchronized; ratios: I 3.454, II 2.050, III 1.347, IV 0.963, rev 3.384; lever: central; final drive: spiral bevel; axle ratio: 4.571; width of rims: 4.5''; tyres: 145 SR x 13.

PERFORMANCE max speeds: (I) 27 mph, 43 km/h; (II) 46 mph, 74 km/h; (III) 62 mph, 110 km/h; (IV) 84 mph, 135 km/h; power-weight ratio: 38.6 lb/hp (52.5 lb/kW), 17.5 kg/hp (23.8 kg/kW); carrying capacity: 948 lb, 430 kg; acceleration: 0-50 mph (0-80 km/h) 12.7 sec; speed in top at 1,000 rpm: 14.2 mph, 22.8 km/h; consumption: 32.8 m/imp gal, 27.3 m/US gal, 8.6 l x 100 km at 75 mph, 120 km/h.

CHASSIS integral; front suspension: independent, by McPherson, lower wishbones, anti-roll bar, coil springs/ telescopic damper struts; rear: independent, longitudinal trailing radius arms, coil springs/telescopic damper struts.

STEERING rack-and-pinion; turns lock to lock: 3.25.

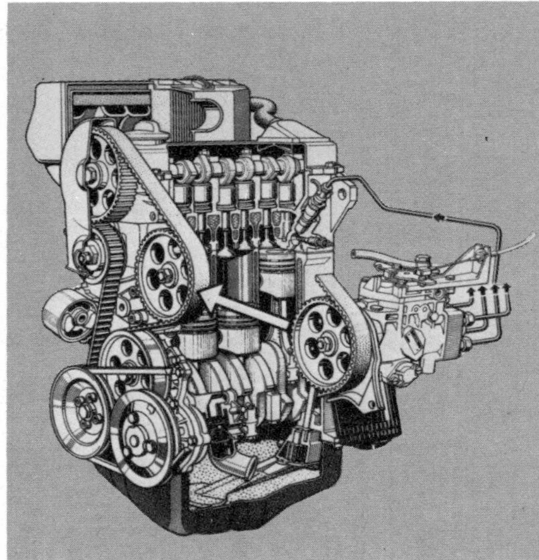

VOLKSWAGEN Golf Diesel Series

BRAKES front disc (diameter 9.41 in, 23.9 cm), rear drum 2 X circuits; lining area: front 16.3 sq in, 105 sq cm, rea 45.6 sq in, 189 sq cm, total 61.9 sq in, 294 sq cm.

ELECTRICAL EQUIPMENT 12 V; 36 Ah battery; 35 A alternator; Bosch distributor; 2 headlamps.

DIMENSIONS AND WEIGHT wheel base: 91.93 in, 233 cm tracks: 51.02 in, 130 cm front, 51.65 in, 131 cm rear length: 154.13 in, 391 cm; width: 61.38 in, 156 cm; height 53.23 in, 135 cm; ground clearance: 3.74 in, 9.5 cm; weight 1,544 lb, 700 kg; turning circle: 31.5 ft, 9.6 m; fuel tank: 7.9 imp gal, 9.5 US gal, 36 l.

BODY saloon/sedan; 2 doors; 4-5 seats, separate fron seats, reclining backrests with built-in headrests; heate rear window.

PRACTICAL INSTRUCTIONS fuel: 91 oct petrol; oil: engine 5.3 imp pt, 6.3 US pt, 3 l, SAE 20W-30, change every 4,700 miles, 7,500 km - gearbox and final drive 4 imp pt, 4.9 US pt, 2.3 l, SAE 80 or 90; greasing: none; sparking plug 175°; tyre pressure: front 26 psi, 1.8 atm, rear 28 psi, 2 atm.

OPTIONALS 155/70 SR x 13 tyres; sunshine roof; halogen headlamps; metallic spray (for L and GL models only).

50 hp power team

See 40 hp power team, except for:

ENGINE 66.7 cu in, 1,093 cc (2.74 x 2.83 in, 69.5 x 72 mm) max power (DIN): 50 hp (37 kW) at 5,800 rpm; max torque (DIN): 56 lb ft, 7.7 kg m (75 Nm) at 3,500 rpm; 47.5 hp/ (33.7 kW/l); cooling, 10.9 imp pt, 13.1 US pt, 6.2 l.

TRANSMISSION axle ratio: 4.267.

PERFORMANCE max speed: 90 mph, 145 km/h; power weight ratio: 30.9 lb/hp (41.9 lb/kW), 14 kg/hp (19 kg/kW) acceleration: 0-50 mph (0-80 km/h) 9.6 sec; speed in top a 1,000 rpm: 15.7 mph, 25.2 km/h; consumption: 31.7 m/imp gal, 26.4 m/US gal, 8.9 l x 100 km at 75 mph, 120 km/h

BRAKES servo.

60 hp power team

See 40 hp power team, except for:

ENGINE 77.6 cu in, 1,272 cc (2.95 x 2.83 in, 75 x 72 mm) compression ratio: 8.2:1; max power (DIN): 60 hp (44 kW at 5,600 rpm; max torque (DIN): 70 lb ft, 9.7 kg m (95 Nm at 3,500 rpm; 47.2 hp/l (34.7 kW/l); cooling, 10.9 imp pt 13.1 US pt, 6.2 l.

TRANSMISSION axle ratio: 4.063.

PERFORMANCE max speed: 96 mph, 154 km/h; power weight ratio: 25.7 lb/hp (34.9 lb/kW), 11.7 kg/hp (15.8 kg/kW); acceleration: 0-50 mph (0-80 km/h) 8.3 sec; speed in top at 1,000 rpm: 16.4 mph, 26.4 km/h; consumption: 31 m/imp gal, 25.8 m/US gal, 9.1 l x 100 km at 75 mph, 120 km/h.

CHASSIS rear suspension: anti-roll bar.

BRAKES rear compensator, servo.

Golf Series

PRICES IN GB AND EX WORKS:	£	DM
1 2+1-dr Limousine	3,258*	10,463*
2 4+1-dr Limousine	—	11,043
3 2+1-dr L Limousine	—	11,229
4 4+1-dr L Limousine	3,699*	11,809
5 2+1-dr GL Limousine	3,875*	12,082
6 4+1-dr GL Limousine	—	12,662
7 2+1-dr S Limousine	—	11,144*
8 4+1-dr S Limousine	—	11,724*
9 2+1-dr LS Limousine	—	11,910*
10 4+1-dr LS Limousine	—	12,490*
11 2+1-dr GLS Limousine	—	12,763*
12 4+1-dr GLS Limousine	4,312*	13,343
13 2+1-dr GTI Limousine	5,135*	16,133
14 2-dr GLS Cabriolet	—	17,389
15 2-dr GLI Cabriolet	—	20,052

Power team:	Standard for:	Optional for:
50 hp	1 to 6	—
60 hp	7 to 12	—
70 hp	14	—
110 hp	13,15	—

50 hp power team

ENGINE front, transverse, slanted 15° to front, 4 stroke; 4 cylinders, vertical, in line; 66.7 cu in, 1,093 cc (2.74 x 2.83 in, 69.5 x 72 mm); compression ratio: 8:1; max power (DIN) 50 hp (37 kW) at 6,000 rpm; max torque (DIN): 57 lb ft, 7.9 kg m (79 Nm) at 3,000 rpm; 45.7 hp/l (33.7 kW/l); cast iron

VOLKSWAGEN Golf GL Limousine

block, light alloy head; 5 crankshaft bearings; valves: overhead, in line, thimble tappets; camshafts: 1, overhead, cogged belt; lubrication: gear pump, full flow filter, 5.3 imp pt, 6.3 US pt, 3 l; 1 Solex 35 PCIT-5 downdraught single barrel carburettor; fuel feed: mechanical pump; liquid-cooled, expansion tank, 10.9 imp pt, 13.1 US pt, 6.2 l, electric thermostatic fan.

TRANSMISSION driving wheels: front; clutch: single dry plate, hydraulically controlled; gearbox: mechanical; gears: 4, fully synchronized; ratios: I 3.454, II 2.055, III 1.350, IV 0.960, rev 3.390; lever: central; final drive: spiral bevel; axle ratio: 4.570; width of rims: 4.5"; tyres: 145 SR x 13.

PERFORMANCE max speed: 87 mph, 140 km/h; power-weight ratio: 2+1-dr limousines 33 lb/hp (44.9 lb/kW), 15 kg/hp (20.4 kg/kW); carrying capacity: 2+1-dr limousines 992 lb, 450 kg - 4+1-dr limousines 937 lb, 425 kg; acceleration: 0-50 mph (0-80 km/h) 10 sec; speed in top at 1,000 rpm: 14.9 mph, 24 km/h; consumption: 30.7 m/imp gal, 25.6 m/US gal, 9.2 l x 100 km at 75 mph, 120 km/h.

CHASSIS integral; front suspension: independent, by McPherson, lower wishbones, coil springs/telescopic damper struts; rear: independent, swinging longitudinal trailing arms linked by a T-section cross-beam, coil springs/telescopic damper struts.

STEERING rack-and-pinion.

BRAKES front disc, rear drum, 2 X circuits.

ELECTRICAL EQUIPMENT 12 V; 36 Ah battery; 36 A alternator; Bosch distributor; 2 headlamps.

DIMENSIONS AND WEIGHT wheel base: 94.49 in, 240 cm; tracks: 54.72 in, 139 cm front, 53.46 in, 136 cm rear; length: 150.20 in, 381 cm; width: 63.39 in, 161 cm; height: 55.51 in, 141 cm; ground clearance: 4.92 in, 12.5 cm; weight: 2+1-dr limousines 1,654 lb, 750 kg - 4+1-dr limousines 1,709 lb, 775 kg; turning circle: 33.8 ft, 10.3 m; fuel tank: 8.8 imp gal, 10 US gal, 40 l.

BODY saloon/sedan; 5 seats, separate front seats; folding rear seat; heated rear window.

PRACTICAL INSTRUCTIONS fuel: 90 oct petrol; oil: engine 5.3 imp pt, 6.3 US pt, 3 l, SAE 20W-30, change every 4,700 miles, 7,500 km - gearbox and final drive 3.2 imp pt, 3.8 US pt, 1.8 l, SAE 80 or 90; sparking plug: 175°; tyre pressure: front 26 psi, 1.8 atm, rear 26 psi, 1.8 atm.

OPTIONALS 5" wide rim sports wheels: 175/70 SR x 13 tyres with 5" wide rims; 155 SR x 13 tyres with 4.5" wide rims; servo brake; halogen headlamps; sunshine roof; built-in headrests on front seats; rear window wiper-washer; metallic spray (for L and Gl models only).

60 hp power team

See 50 hp power team, except for:

ENGINE 77.6 cu in, 1,272 cc (2.95 x 2.83 in, 75 x 72 mm); compression ratio: 8.2:1; max power (DIN): 60 hp (44 kW) at 5,600 rpm; max torque (DIN): 70 lb ft, 9.7 kg m (95 Nm) at 3,500 rpm; 47.2 hp/l (34.7 kW/l).

TRANSMISSION axle ratio: 4.267; width of rims: 5"; tyres: 155 SR x 13.

PERFORMANCE max speed: 93 mph, 150 km/h; power-weight ratio: 2+1-dr limousines 27.6 lb/hp (37.6 lb/kW), 12.5 kg/hp (17 kg/kW); speed in top at 1,000 rpm: 15.9 mph, 25.6 km/h; consumption: 30.1 m/imp gal, 25 m/US gal, 9.4 l x 100 km at 75 mph, 120 km/h.

BRAKES servo (standard).

70 hp power team

See 50 hp power team, except for:

ENGINE front, transverse, slanted 15° to rear; 88.9 cu in, 1,457 cc (13.3 x 2.89 in, 79.5 x 73.4 mm); compression ratio: 8.2:1; max power (DIN): 70 hp (51 kW) at 5,600 rpm; max torque (DIN): 81 lb ft, 11.2 kg m (110 Nm) at 2,500 rpm; 48 hp/l (35.3 kW/l); 1 Solex 34 PICT-5 downdraught single barrel carburettor.

TRANSMISSION gearbox ratios: I 3.454, II 1.960, III 1.370, IV 0.970, rev 3.170; axle ratio: 3.900; width of rims: 5"; tyres: 155 SR x 13 (standard).

PERFORMANCE max speed: 98 mph, 158 km/h; power-weight ratio: 28.7 lb/hp (39.2 lb/kW), 13 kg/hp (17.8 kg/kW); acceleration: 0-50 mph (0-80 km/h) 8.2 sec; speed in top at 1,000 rpm: 17.3 mph, 27.8 km/h; consumption: 29.7 m/imp gal, 24.8 m/US gal, 9.5 l x 100 km at 75 mph, 120 km/h.

BRAKES servo (standard).

DIMENSIONS AND WEIGHT weight: 2,007 lb, 910 kg.

OPTIONALS automatic transmission, hydraulic torque converter and planetary gears with 3 ratios (I 2.550, II 1.450, III 1, rev 2.410), max ratio of converter at stall 2.44, possible manual selection, central lever, 3.760 axle ratio, max speed 95 mph, 153 km/h, acceleration 0-50 mph (0-80 km/h) 9.4 sec, consumption 30.7 m/imp gal, 25.6 m/US gal, 9.2 l x 100 km at 75 mph, 120 km/h.

110 hp power team

See 50 hp power team, except for:

ENGINE front, transverse, slanted 20° to rear; 96.9 cu in, 1,588 cc (3.13 x 3.15 in, 79.5 x 80 mm); compression ratio: 9.5:1; max power (DIN): 110 hp (81 kW) at 6,100 rpm; max torque (DIN): 101 lb ft, 14 kg m (137 Nm) at 5,000 rpm; max engine rpm: 6,900; 69.3 hp/l (51 kW/l); lubrication: oil cooler, 6.5 impt pt, 7.8 US pt, 3.7 l; Bosch K-Jetronic electronic injection; fuel feed: electric pump.

TRANSMISSION gear: 5, fully synchronized; gearbox ratios: I 3.450, II 2.118, III 1.444, IV 1.129, V 0.912, rev 3.170; axle ratio: 3.895; width of rims: 5.5"; tyres: 175/70 HR x 13.

PERFORMANCE max speed: Limousine 113 mph, 182 km/h - Cabriolet 107 mph, 172 km/h; power-weight ratio: Limousine 16.2 lb/hp (22 lb/kW), 7.4 kg/hp (10 kg/kW); carrying capacity: 926 lb, 420 kg; acceleration: 0-50 mph (0-80 km/h) 6.1 sec; speed in top at 1,000 rpm: 18.5 mph, 29.8 km/h; consumption: 33.2 m/imp gal, 27.7 m/US gal, 8.5 l x 100 km at 75 mph, 120 km/h.

BRAKES rear compensator, servo (standard).

ELECTRICAL EQUIPMENT 55 A alternator; 2 halogen headlamps (standard).

DIMENSIONS AND WEIGHT tracks: 55.28 in, 140 cm front, 54.02 in, 137 cm rear; width: 64.09 in, 163 cm; height: 54.72 in, 139 cm; weight: Limousine 1,786 lb, 810 kg - Cabriolet 2,073 lb, 940 kg.

BODY built-in headrests on front seats (standard).

PRACTICAL INSTRUCTIONS fuel: 98-100 oct petrol; oil: engine 5.6 imp pt, 6.8 US pt, 3.2 l.

Golf Diesel Series

PRICES IN GB AND EX WORKS:	£	DM
2+1-dr D Limousine	—	12,027*
4+1-dr D Limousine	—	12,607*
2+1-dr LD Limousine	—	12,793*
4+1-dr LD Limousine	4,470*	13,374*
2+1-dr GLD Limousine	—	13,646*
4+1-dr GLD Limousine	—	14,226*

50 hp power team

ENGINE diesel, front, transverse, 4 stroke; 4 cylinders, vertical, in line; 89.8 cu in, 1,471 cc (3.01 x 3.15 in, 76.5 x 80 mm); compression ratio: 23.5:1; max power (DIN):

VOLKSWAGEN Golf GTI Limousine

50 HP POWER TEAM

50 hp (37 kW) at 5,000 rpm; max torque (DIN): 59 lb ft, 8.2 kg m (80 Nm) at 3,000 rpm; max engine rpm: 5,000; 34 hp/l (25 kW/l); cast iron block, light alloy head; 5 crankshaft bearings; valves: overhead, in line, thimble tappets; camshafts: 1, overhead, cogged belt; lubrication: gear pump, full flow filter, 6.2 imp pt, 7.4 US pt, 3.5 l; Bosch injection pump; liquid-cooled, expansion tank, 10.9 imp pt, 13.1 US pt, 6.2 l, electric thermostatic fan.

TRANSMISSION driving wheels: front; clutch: single dry plate, hydraulically controlled; gearbox: mechanical; gears: 4, fully synchronized; ratios: I 3.454, II 2.055, III 1.350, IV 0.960, rev 3.390; lever: central; final drive: spiral bevel; axle ratio: 4.570; width of rims: 4.5"; tyres: 145 SR x 13.

PERFORMANCE max speed: 87 mph, 140 km/h; power-weight ratio: 2+1-dr limousines 35.5 lb/hp (48.2 lb/kW), 16.1 kg/hp (21.9 kg/kW); carrying capacity: 2+1-dr limousines 981 lb, 445 kg - 4+1-dr limousines 926 lb, 420 kg; acceleration: 0-50 mph (0-80 km/h) 11.5 sec; speed in top at 1,000 rpm: 17.4 mph, 28 km/h; consumption: 36.2 m/imp gal, 30.2 m/US gal, 7.8 l x 100 km at 75 mph, 120 km/h.

CHASSIS integral; front suspension: independent, by McPherson, lower wishbones, coil springs/telescopic damper struts; rear: independent, swinging longitudinal trailing arms linked by a T-section cross-beam, coil springs/telescopic damper struts.

STEERING rack-and-pinion.

BRAKES front disc, rear drum, 2 X circuits.

ELECTRICAL EQUIPMENT 12 V; 36 Ah battery; 35 A alternator; 2 headlamps.

DIMENSIONS AND WEIGHT wheel base: 94.49 in, 240 cm; tracks: 54.72 in, 139 cm front, 53.46 in, 136 cm rear; length: 150.20 in, 381 cm; width: 63.39 in, 161 cm; height: 55.51 in, 141 cm; ground clearance: 4.92 in, 12.5 cm; weight: 2+1-dr limousines 1,775 lb, 805 kg - 4+1-dr limousines 1,830 lb, 830 kg; turning circle: 33.8 ft, 10.3 m; fuel tank: 8.8 imp gal, 10.6 US gal, 40 l.

BODY saloon/sedan; 5 seats, separate front seats; built-in headrests: folding rear seat; heated rear window.

PRACTICAL INSTRUCTIONS fuel: diesel oil; oil: engine 5.3 imp pt, 6.3 US pt, 3 l - gearbox and final drive 3.2 imp pt, 3.8 US pt, 1.8 l, SAE 80; tyre pressure: front 26 psi, 1.8 atm, rear 26 psi, 1.8 atm.

OPTIONALS 175/70 SR x 13 or 155 SR x 13 tyres with 5" wide rims; servo brake; halogen headlamps; sunshine roof; metallic spray (for LD and GLD models only); rear window wiper-washer.

1200 L

PRICE EX WORKS: DM 8,505*

(For technical data, see Volkswagen Mexico)

Scirocco Series

PRICES IN GB, USA AND EX WORKS:

	£	$	DM
1 Coupé	—	—	**13,610***
2 L Coupé	—	—	**14,674***
3 S Coupé	—	—	**14,185***
4 LS Coupé	—	—	**15,249***
5 GT Coupé	—	—	**15,789***
6 GL Coupé	—	**7,745***	**16,566***
7 GTI Coupé	—	—	**18,690***
8 GLI Coupé	**6,304***	—	**19,467***

For 85 hp engine add DM 1,014 (for S and LS only); add DM 439 (for GT and GL only).

Power team:	Standard for:	Optional for:
60 hp	1,2	—
70 hp	3 to 6	—
85 hp	—	3 to 6
110 hp	7,8	—

60 hp power team

ENGINE front, transverse, slanted 15° to front, 4 stroke; 4 cylinders, vertical, in line; 77.6 cu in, 1,272 cc (2.95 x 2.83 in, 75 x 72 mm); compression ratio: 8.2:1; max power (DIN): 60 hp (44 kW) at 5,600 rpm; max torque (DIN): 70 lb/ft, 9.7 kg m (95 Nm) at 3,500 rpm; 47.2 hp/l (34.7 kW/l); cast iron block, light alloy head; 5 crankshaft bearings; valves: overhead, in line, thimble tappets; camshafts: 1, overhead, cogged belt; lubrication: gear pump, full flow filter, 6.2 imp pt, 7.4 US pt, 3.5 l; 1 Solex 35 PICT-5 downdraught single barrel carburettor; fuel feed: mechanical pump; liquid cooled, expansion tank, 10.9 imp pt, 13.1 US pt, 6.2 l, electric thermostatic fan.

TRANSMISSION driving wheels: front; clutch: single dry plate, hydraulically controlled; gearbox: mechanical; gears: 4, fully synchronized; ratios: I 3.454, II 2.055, III 1.370, IV 0.939, rev 3.166; lever: central: final drive: spiral bevel; axle ratio: 4.570; width of rims: 5"; tyres: 155 SR x 13.

PERFORMANCE max speed: 96 mph, 154 km/h; power-weight ratio: 28.6 lb/hp (39.1 lb/kW), 13 kg/hp (17.7 kg/kW); carrying capacity: 860 lb, 390 kg; acceleration: 0-50 mph (0-80 km/h) 8.5 sec; speed in top at 1,000 rpm: 15.9 mph, 25.7 km/h; consumption: 30.7 m/imp gal, 25.6 m/US gal, 9.2 l x 100 km at 75 mph, 120 km/h.

CHASSIS integral; front suspension: independent, by McPherson, lower wishbones, coil springs/telescopic damper struts; rear: independent, swinging longitudinal trailing arms linked by a T-section cross beam, coil springs/telescopic damper struts.

STEERING rack-and-pinion.

BRAKES front disc (diameter 9.41 in, 23.9 cm), rear drum, 2 X circuits, servo; swept area: front 160 sq in, 1,032 sq cm, rear 90.9 sq in, 586 sq cm, total 250.9 sq in, 1,618 sq cm.

ELECTRICAL EQUIPMENT 12 V; 36 Ah battery; 35 A alternator; Bosch distributor; 2 headlamps.

DIMENSIONS AND WEIGHT wheel base: 94.49 in, 240 cm; tracks: 54.72 in, 139 cm front, 53.46 in, 136 cm rear; length: 152.95 in, 388 cm; width: 63.78 in, 162 cm; height: 51.53 in, 131 cm; ground clearance: 4.92 in, 12.5 cm; weight: 1,720 lb, 780 kg; turning circle: 33.8 ft, 10.3 m; fuel tank: 8.8 imp pt, 10.6 US pt, 40 l.

BODY coupé; 2+1 doors; 4 seats, separate front seats heated rear window; folding rear seat; built-in headrests on front seats (for L only).

PRACTICAL INSTRUCTIONS fuel: 90 oct petrol; oil: engine 5.3 imp pt, 6.3 US pt, 3 l, SAE 20W-30, change every 4,700 miles, 7,500 km - gearbox and final drive 3.2 imp pt, 3.8 US pt, 1.8 l, SAE 80 or 90; sparking plug: 175°; tyre pressure front 26 psi, 1.8 atm, rear 26 psi, 1.8 atm.

OPTIONALS 5" wide rim sports wheels; 175/70 SR x 13 tyres; halogen headlamps; built-in headrests on front seats (for Coupé only); reclining front seats; rear window wiper-washer; metallic spray.

70 hp power team

See 60 hp power team, except for:

ENGINE front, transverse, slanted 20° to rear; 88.9 cu in 1,457 cc (3.13 x 2.89 in, 79.5 x 73.4 mm); max power (DIN) 70 hp (51 kW) at 5,600 rpm; max torque (DIN): 81 lb ft, 11.2 kg m (110 Nm) at 2,500 rpm; 48 hp/l (35.3 kW/l); 1 Solex 34 PICT-5 downdraught single barrel carburettor.

TRANSMISSION gearbox ratios: I 3.454, II 1.960, III 1.370, IV 0.970, rev 3.170; axle ratio: 3.900.

VOLKSWAGEN Golf GLS Cabriolet

VOLKSWAGEN Scirocco GLI Coupé

VOLKSWAGEN Jetta Limousine

ERFORMANCE max speed: 101 mph, 162 km/h; power-eight ratio: 25.2 lb/hp (34.2 lb/kW), 11.4 kg/hp (15.5 /kW); acceleration: 0-50 mph (0-80 km/h) 8.1 sec; speed top at 1,000 rpm: 17.3 mph, 27.9 km/h; consumption:).4 m/imp gal, 25.3 m/US gal, 9.3 l x 100 km at 75 mph, 20 km/h.

LECTRICAL EQUIPMENT 45 A alternator; 4 halogen eadlamps (standard).

IMENSIONS AND WEIGHT weight: 1,764 lb, 800 kg.

ODY built-in headrests on front seats (standard); tinted ass.

PTIONALS automatic transmission, hydraulic torque con-erter and planetary gears with 3 ratios (I 2.550, II 1.450, III rev 2.410), max ratio of converter at stall 2.44, possible anual selection, central lever, 3.760 axle ratio, max speed 3 mph, 157 km/h, acceleration 0-50 mph (0-80 km/h) 9.3 ec, carrying capacity 849 lb, 385 kg, consumption 28.5 /imp gal, 23.5 m/US gal, 9.9 l x 100 km at 75 mph, 120 n/h.

85 hp power team

ee 60 hp power team, except for:

NGINE front, transverse, slanted 20° to rear; 96.9 cu in, 588 cc (3.13 x 3.15 in, 79.5 x 80 mm); max power (DIN): 5 hp (63 kW) at 5,600 rpm; max torque (DIN): 92 lb ft, 12.8 g m (125 Nm) at 3,800 rpm; 53.5 hp/l (39.4 kW/l); 1 Solex 4 PICT-5 downdraught single barrel carburettor.

RANSMISSION gearbox ratios: (I 3.454, II 1,960, III 1.370, 0.970, rev 3.170; axle ratio: 3.900; tyres: 175/70 R x 13.

ERFORMANCE max speed: 107 mph, 172 km/h; power-eight ratio: 20.7 lb/hp (28.2 lb/kW), 9.4 kg /hp (12.8 /kW); acceleration: 0-50 mph (0-80 km/h) 7.5 sec; speed top at 1,000 rpm: 17.3 mph, 27.9 km/h; consumption: 31 /imp gal, 25.8 m/US gal, 9.1 l x 100 km at 75 mph, 120 n/h.

LECTRICAL EQUIPMENT 45 A alternator; 4 halogen eadlamps (standard).

IMENSIONS AND WEIGHT weight: 1,764 lb, 800 kg.

ODY built-in headrests on front seats (standard); tinted ass.

110 hp power team

ee 60 hp power team, except for:

NGINE front, transverse, slanted 20° to rear; 96.9 cu in, 588 cc (3.13 x 3.15 in, 79.5 x 80 mm); compression ratio: 5:1; max power (DIN): 110 hp (81 kW) at 6,100 rpm; max rque (DIN): 101 lb ft, 14 kg m (137 Nm) at 5,000 rpm; max ngine rpm: 6,900; 69.3 hp/l (51 kW/l); lubrication: oil oler, 6.5 imp pt, 7.8 US pt, 3.7 l; Bosch K-Jetronic ectronic injection; fuel feed: electric pump.

RANSMISSION gears: 5, fully synchronized, gearbox tios: I 3.450, II 2.118, III 1.444, IV 1.129, V 0.912, rev 170; axle ratio: 3.895; width of rims: 5.5"; tyres: 175/70 R x 13.

VOLKSWAGEN Jetta GL Limousine

PERFORMANCE max speed: 115 mph, 185 km/h; power-weight ratio: 16 lb/hp (21.8 lb/kW), 7.3 kg/hp (9.9 kg/kW); carrying capacity: 904 lb, 410 kg; acceleration: 0-50 mph (0-80 km/h) 5.8 sec; speed in top at 1,000 rpm: 18.8 mph, 30.3 km/h; consumption: 34 m/imp gal, 28.3 m/US gal, 8.3 l x 100 km at 75 mph, 120 km/h.

CHASSIS front and rear suspension: anti-roll bar.

ELECTRICAL EQUIPMENT 45 A alternator; 4 halogen headlamps.

DIMENSIONS AND WEIGHT tracks: 55.28 in, 140 cm front, 54.02 in, 137 cm rear; weight: 1,764 lb, 800 kg.

BODY built-in headrests on front seats (standard); tinted glass.

PRACTICAL INSTRUCTIONS fuel: 98-100 oct petrol; oil: engine 5.6 imp pt, 6.8 US pt, 3.2 l.

Jetta Series

PRICES EX WORKS:		DM
1	2-dr Limousine	**11,395***
2	4-dr Limousine	**11,975***
3	2-dr L Limousine	**12,190***
4	4-dr L Limousine	**12,770***
5	2-dr GL Limousine	**13,170***
6	4-dr GL Limousine	**13,750***
7	2-dr S Limousine	**12,070***
8	4-dr S Limousine	**12,650***
9	2-dr LS Limousine	**12,865***
10	4-dr LS Limousine	**13,445***
11	2-dr GLS Limousine	**13,845***
12	4-dr GLS Limousine	**14,425***
13	2-dr LI Limousine	**14,855***
14	4-dr LI Limousine	**15,435***
15	2-dr GLI Limousine	**15,835***
16	4-dr GLI Limousine	**16,415***

Power team:	Standard for:	Optional for:
60 hp	1 to 6	—
70 hp	7 to 12	—
110 hp	13 to 16	—

60 hp power team

ENGINE front, transverse, slanted 15° to front, 4 stroke; 4 cylinders, vertical, in line; 77.6 cu in, 1,272 cc (2.95 x 2.83 in, 75 x 72 mm); compression ratio: 8.2:1; max power (DIN): 60 hp (44 kW) at 5,600 rpm; max torque (DIN): 70 lb ft, 9.7 kg m (95 Nm) at 3,500 rpm; max engine rpm: 6,000; 47.2 hp/l (34.7 kW/l); cast iron block, light alloy head; 5 crank-shaft bearings; valves: overhead, in line, thimble tappets; camshafts: 1, overhead, cogged belt; lubrication: gear pump, full flow filter, 6.2 imp pt, 7.4 US pt, 3.5 l; 1 Solex 35 PICT-5 downdraught single barrel carburettor; fuel feed: mechanical pump; cooling, liquid expansion tank, 10.9 imp pt, 13.1 US pt, 6.2 l, electric thermostatic fan.

TRANSMISSION driving wheels: front; clutch: single dry plate, hydraulically controlled; gearbox: mechanical; gears: 4, fully synchronized; ratios: I 3.454, II 2.055, III 1.347, IV 0.963, rev 3.384; lever: central; final drive: spiral bevel; axle ratio: 4.570; width of rims: 5"; tyres: 155 SR x 13.

VOLKSWAGEN Jetta GLI Limousine

60 HP POWER TEAM

PERFORMANCE max speeds: (I) 26 mph, 42 kmh; (II) 43 mph, 70 km/h; (III) 66 mph, 107 km/h; (IV) 92 mph, 148 km/h; power-weight ratio: 4-dr limousines 29.8 lb/hp, (40.6 lb/kW), 13.5 kg/hp (18.4 kg/kW); carrying capacity: 948 lb, 430 kg; acceleration: 0-50 mph (0-80 km/h) 9 sec; speed in top at 1,000 rpm: 14.9 mph, 24 km/h; consumption: 29.7 m/imp gal, 24.8 m/US gal, 9.5 l x 100 km at 75 mph, 120 km/h.

CHASSIS integral; front suspension: independent, by McPherson, lower wishbones, coil springs/telescopic damper struts; rear: swinging longitudinal trailing arms linked by a T-section cross beam, anti-roll bar, coil springs/telescopic damper struts.

STEERING rack-and-pinion.

BRAKES front disc (diameter 9.41 in, 23.9 cm), rear drum, 2 X circuits, servo.

ELECTRICAL EQUIPMENT 12 V; 36 Ah battery; 35 A alternator; Bosch distributor; 2 headlamps.

DIMENSIONS AND WEIGHT wheel base: 94.49 in, 240 cm; tracks: 54.72 in, 139 cm front, 53.46 in, 136 cm rear; length: 164.98 in, 419 cm; width: 63.39 in, 161 cm; height: 55.51 in, 141 cm; ground clearance: 4.92 in, 12.5 cm; weight: 2-dr limousines 1,731 lb, 785 kg - 4-dr limousines 1,786 lb, 810 kg; turning circle: 33.8 ft, 10.3 m; fuel tank: 8.8 imp gal, 10.6 US gal, 40 l.

BODY saloon/sedan; 2 or 4 doors; 5 seats, separate front seats, reclining backrests with built-in headrests; heated rear window.

PRACTICAL INSTRUCTIONS fuel: 91 oct petrol; oil: engine 5.3 imp pt, 6.3 US pt, 3 l, SAE 20W-30, change every 4,700 miles, 7,500 km - gearbox and final drive 3.2 imp pt, 3.8 US pt, 1,8 l, SAE 80 or 90, change every 18,600 miles, 30,000 km; greasing: none; sparking plug: Bosch 200 T 30; tyre pressure: front 26 psi, 1.8 atm, rear 26 psi, 1.8 atm.

OPTIONALS 5.5'' wide rim sports wheels; 175/70 SR x 13 tyres; halogen headlamps; metallic spray; sunshine roof.

70 hp power team

See 60 hp power team, except for:

ENGINE front, transverse, slanted 20° to rear; 88.9 cu in, 1,457 cc (3.13 x 2.89 in, 79.5 x 73.4 mm); max power (DIN): 70 hp (51 kW) at 5,600 rpm; max torque (DIN): 81 lb ft, 11.2 kg m (110 Nm) at 2,500 rpm; 48 hp/l (35.3 kW/l); 1 Solex 34 PICT-5 downdraught single barrel carburettor.

TRANSMISSION gearbox ratios: I 3.454, II 1.940, III 1.290, IV 0.970, rev 3.170; axle ratio: 3.900; width of rims: 5.5''; tyres: 175/70 SR x 13 (standard).

PERFORMANCE max speed: 97 mph, 156 km/h; power-weight ratio: 4-dr limousines 26.5 lb/hp (36.3 lb/kW), 12 kg/hp (16.5 kg/kW); acceleration: 0-50 mph (0-80 km/h) 8.5 sec; speed in top at 1,000 rpm: 18.2 mph, 29.3 km/h; consumption: 29.4 m/imp gal, 24.5 m/US gal, 9.6 l x 100 km at 75 mph, 120 km/h.

ELECTRICAL EQUIPMENT 45 A alternator.

DIMENSIONS AND WEIGHT tracks: 55.27 in, 140 cm front, 54.02 in, 137 cm rear; width: 64.17 in, 163 cm; weight: 2-dr limousines 1,797 lb, 815 kg - 4-dr limousines 1,852 lb, 840 kg.

OPTIONALS automatic transmission, hydraulic torque converter and planetary gears with 3 ratios (I 2.550, II 1.450, III 1, rev 2.410), max ratio of converter at stall 2.44, possible manual selection, central lever, 3.760 axle ratio, max speed 94 mph, 151 km/h, acceleration 0-50 mph (0-80 km/h) 9.8 sec, consumption 27.7 m/imp gal, 23.1 m/US gal, 10.2 l x 100 km at 75 mph, 120 km/h.

110 hp power team

See 60 hp power team, except for:

ENGINE front, transverse, slanted 20° to rear; 96.9 cu in, 1,588 cc (3.13 x 3.15 in, 79.5 x 80 mm); compression ratio: 9.5:1; max power (DIN) 110 hp (81 kW) at 6,100 rpm; max torque (DIN): 101 lb ft, 14 kg m (140 Nm) at 5,000 rpm; max engine rpm: 6,900; 69.3 hp/l (51kW/l); lubrication: oil cooler, 6.5 imp pt, 7.8 US pt, 3.7 l; Bosch K-Jetronic electronic injection; fuel feed: electric pump.

TRANSMISSION gears: 5, fully synchronized; gearbox ratios: I 3.450, II 2.118, III 1.444, IV 1.129, V 0.912, rev 3.170; axle ratio: 3.895; width of rims: 5.5''; tyres: 175/70 HR x 13.

PERFORMANCE max speed: 111 mph, 178 km/h; power-weight ratio: 4-dr limousines 17.6 lb/hp (23.9 lb/kW), 8 kg/hp (10.9 kg/kW); acceleration: 0-50 mph (0-80 km/h) 6.4 sec; speed in top at 1,000 rpm: 18.2 mph, 29.3 km/h; consumption: 32.8 m/imp gal, 27.3 m/US gal, 8.6 l x 100 km at 75 mph, 120 km/h.

CHASSIS front and rear suspension: anti-roll bar.

BRAKES rear compensator.

ELECTRICAL EQUIPMENT 45 A alternator.

DIMENSIONS AND WEIGHT tracks: 55.27 in, 140 cm front, 54.02 in, 137 cm rear; width; 64.17 in, 163 cm; height: 54.92 in, 139 cm; weight: 2-dr limousines 1,885 lb, 855 kg - 4-dr limousines 1,940 lb, 880 kg.

PRACTICAL INSTRUCTIONS fuel: 98-100 oct petrol; oil: engine 5.6 imp pt, 6.8 US pt, 3.2 l.

Passat Series

PRICES IN GB, USA AND EX WORKS:

		£	$	DM
1	2+1-dr Limousine	—	—	**12,258***
2	4+1-dr Limousine	—	—	**12,849***
3	4+1-dr Variant	—	—	**13,247***
4	2+1-dr L Limousine	—	—	**13,076***
5	4+1-dr Limousine	—	—	**13,666***
6	4+1-dr Variant	—	—	**14,064***
7	2+1-dr GL Limousine	—	—	**14,064***
8	4+1-dr GL Limousine	—	—	**14,655***
9	4+1-dr GL Variant	—	—	**15,053***
10	2+1-dr S Limousine	—	—	**12,778***
11	4+1-dr S Limousine	—	—	**13,369***
12	4+1-dr S Variant	—	—	**13,767***
13	2+1-dr LS Limousine	—	**7,590***	**13,596***
14	4+1-dr LS Limousine	**4,783***	**7.790***	**14,186***
15	4+1-dr LS Variant	**5,068***	**8,070***	**14,584***
16	2+1-dr GLS Limousine	—	—	**14,584***
17	4+1-dr GLS Limousine	**5,191***	—	**15,175***
18	4+1-dr GLS Variant	**5,532***	—	**15,573***
19	2+1-dr GLI Limousine	—	—	**16,506***
20	4+1-dr GLI Limousine	—	—	**17,098***
21	4+1-dr GLI Variant	—	—	**17,495***

For 85 hp engine add DM 898.

Power team:	Standard for:	Optional for:
55 hp	1 to 9	—
75 hp	10 to 18	—
85 hp	—	13 to 18
110 hp	19 to 21	—

55 hp power team

ENGINE front, slanted 20° to right, 4 stroke; 4 cylinders, in line; 77.6 cu in, 1,272 cc (2.95 x 2.83 in, 75 x 72 mm); compression ratio: 8.2:1; max power (DIN): 55 hp (40 kW) at 5,800 rpm; max torque (DIN): 68 lb ft, 9.4 kg m (92 Nm) at 3,400 rpm; max engine rpm: 6,500; 42.4 hp/l (31.2 kW/l); cast iron block, light alloy head; 5 crankshaft bearings; valves: overhead, in line, thimble tappets; camshafts: 1, overhead, cogged belt: lubrication: gear pump, full flo[w] filter, 5.3 imp pt, 6.3 US pt, 3 l; 1 Solex 30-35 PDSI (T) downdraught single barrel carburettor; fuel feed: mechanic[al] pump; water-cooled, 10.9 imp pt, 13.1 US pt, 6.2 [l,] electric thermostatic fan.

TRANSMISSION driving wheels: front; clutch: single dr[y] plate (diaphragm); gearbox: mechanical; gears: 4, fully syn[-]chronized; ratios: I 3.454, II 2.055, III 1.370, IV 0.968, re[v] 3.166; central; final drive: spiral bevel; axle ratio: 4.55[5]; width of rims: 5''; tyres: 155 SR x 13.

PERFORMANCE max speeds: (I) 25 mph, 41 km/h; (II) 4[?] mph, 68 km/h; (III)) 68 mph, 110 km/h; (IV) 93 mph, 15[?] km/h; power-weight ratio: 2+1-dr limousines 34.4 lb/h[p] (46.8 lb/kW), 15.6 kg/hp (21.2 kg/kW); carrying capacit[y:] 2+1-dr limousines 1,036 lb, 470 kg - 4+1-dr limousines 98[?] lb, 445 kg; acceleration: 0-50 mph (0-80 km/h) 10.5 se[c;] speed in top at 1,000 rpm: 14.9 mph, 24 km/h; consumptio[n:] 29.7 m/imp gal, 24.8 m/US gal, 9.5 l x 100 km at 75 mp[h,] 120 km/h.

CHASSIS integral, front auxiliary subframe; front suspe[n]sion: independent, by McPherson, lower wishbones, ant[i-]roll bar, coil springs/telescopic damper struts; rear: rig[id] axle, trailing radius arms, transverse linkage bar, co[il] springs, anti-roll bar, telescopic dampers.

STEERING rack-and-pinion, damper.

BRAKES front disc (diameter 9.41 in, 23.9 cm), rear drum[,] 2 X circuits, servo.

ELECTRICAL EQUIPMENT 12 V; 36 Ah battery; 35 A alte[r]nator; Bosch distributor; 2 headlamps.

DIMENSIONS AND WEIGHT wheel base: 97.24 in, 247 cm; tracks: 52.76 in, 134 cm front, 53.15 in, 135 cm rea[r;] length: 168.90 in, 429 cm - Variant models 167.91 in, 42[?] cm; width: 63.58 in, 161 cm; height: 53.54 in, 136 cm; ground clearance: 7.09 in, 18 cm; weight: 2+1-[dr] limousines 1,896 lb, 860 kg - 4+1-dr limousines 1,951 l[b,] 885 kg - Variant models 2,029 lb, 920 kg; turning circl[e:] 33.8 ft, 10.3 m; fuel tank: 9.9 imp gal, 11.9 US gal, 45 [l.]

BODY 5 seats, separate front seats, reclining backres[ts] with headrests; heated rear window; folding rear seat (f[or] Variant models only).

PRACTICAL INSTRUCTIONS fuel: 86 oct petrol; oil: engi[ne] 4.4 imp pt, 5.3 US pt, 2.5 l, SAE 20W-30, change eve[ry] 9,000 miles, 15,000 km - gearbox and final drive 3.2 imp p[t,] 3.8 US pt, 1.8 l, SAE 80, no change recommended; grea[s]ing: none; sparking plug: 175°; tappet clearances: inl[et] 0.008-0.012 in, 0.20-0.30 mm, exhaust 0.016-0.020 i[n,] 0.40-0.50 mm; tyre pressure: front 24 psi, 1.7 atm, rear [2?] psi, 1.7 atm.

OPTIONALS 175/70 SR x 13 tyres; sport wheels; sunshi[ne] roof; halogen headlamps; metallic spray; tinted glass; ta[il]gate with folding rear seat (for limousines only); rear wi[n]dow wiper-washer (for Variant models only).

VOLKSWAGEN Passat GLI Limousine

75 hp power team

ee 55 hp power team, except for:

NGINE 96.9 cu in, 1,588 cc (3.13 x 3.15 in, 79.5 x 80 mm); ax power (DIN): 75 hp (55 kW) at 5,600 rpm; max torque DIN): 88 lb ft, 12.1 kg m (119 Nm) at 3,200 rpm; 47.2 hp/l 34.8 kW/l); 1 Solex PDSIT downdraught single barrel carurettor.

RANSMISSION axle ratio: 4.111.

ERFORMANCE max speed: 102 mph, 164 km/h; powereight ratio: 2+1-dr, limousines 25.4 lb/hp (34.3 lb/kW), 1.5 kg/hp (15.6 kg/kW); acceleration: 0-50 mph (0-80 km/) 8.4 sec; speed in top at 1,000 rpm: 16.3 mph, 26.3 km/h; onsumption: 30.7 m/imp pt, 25.6 m/US pt, 9.2 l x 100 km at 5 mph, 120 km/h.

LECTRICAL EQUIPMENT 45 A alternator; 4 halogen eadlamps (standard for GLS models only).

PTIONALS automatic transmission, hydraulic torque conerter and planetary gears with 3 ratios (I 2.650, II 1.580, III , rev 1.800), max ratio of converter at stall 2.2 , possible anual selection, 4.091 axle ratio, max speed 99 mph, 159 m/h, acceleration 0-50 mph (0-80 km/h) 9.6 sec, consumpon 28.8 m/imp gal, 24 m/US gal, 9.8 l x 100 km at 75 mph, 20 km/h.

85 hp power team

ee 55 hp power team, except for:

NGINE 96.9 cu in, 1,588 cc (3.13 x 3.15 in, 79.5 x 80 mm); ax power (DIN): 85 hp (63 kW) at 5,600 rpm; max torque DIN): 92 lb ft, 12.7 kg m (124 Nm) at 3,200 rpm; 53.5 hp/l 39.4 kW/l); 1 Solex 32/35 TDID downdraught twin barrel arburettor.

RANSMISSION axle ratio: 4.111; tyres: 175/70 SR x 13.

ERFORMANCE max speed: 107 mph, 173 km/h; powereight ratio: 2+1-dr, limousines 22.3 lb/hp (30.3 lb/kW), 0.1 kg/hp (13.7 kg/kW); acceleration: 0-50 mph (0-80 km/) 7.9 sec; speed in top at 1,000 rpm: 16.5 mph, 26.6 km/h; onsumption: 32.1 m/imp gal, 26.7 m/US gal, 8.8 l x 100 km t 75 mph, 120 km/h.

LECTRICAL EQUIPMENT 45 Ah battery; 45 A alternator; 4 alogen headlamps (standard for GLS models only).

PTIONALS automatic transmission, hydraulic torque conerter and planetary gears with 3 ratios (I 2.590, II 1.590, III , rev 1.800), max ratio of converter at stall 2.2, possible anual selection, 3.909 axle ratio, max speed 104 mph, 168 m/h, acceleration 0-50 mph (0-80 km) 9.1 sec, consumpon 30.1 m/imp gal, 25 m/US gal, 9.4 l x 100 km at 75 mph, 20 km/h.

110 hp power team

ee 55 hp power team, except for:

NGINE 96.9 cu in, 1,588 cc (3.13 x 3.15 in, 79.5 x 80 mm); ompression ratio: 9.5:1; max power (DIN): 110 hp (81 kW) t 6,100 rpm; max torque (DIN): 101 lb ft, 14 kg m (140 Nm) t 5,000 rpm; max engine rpm: 6,900; 69.3 hp/l (51 kW/l); ubrication: oil cooler, 6.5 imp pt, 7.8 US pt, 3.7 l; Bosch -Jetronic electronic injection; fuel feed: electric pump.

RANSMISSION axle ratio: 4.111; tyres: 175/70 HR x 13.

ERFORMANCE max speed: 114 mph, 184 km/h; powereight ratio: 2+1-dr limousines 17.2 lb/hp (23.4 lb/kW), 7.8 g/hp (10.6 kg/kW); acceleration: 0-50 mph (0-80 km/h) 6.5 ec; speed in top at 1,000 rpm: 16.5 mph, 26.6 km/h; onsumption: 32.8 m/imp gal, 27.3 m/US gal, 8.6 l x 100 km t 75 mph, 120 km/h.

RAKES rear compensator.

LECTRICAL EQUIPMENT 45 Ah battery; 45/A alternator; 4 alogen headlamps (standard).

RACTICAL INSTRUCTIONS fuel: 98-100 oct petrol; oil: ngine 5.6 imp pt, 6.8 US pt, 3.2 l.

PTIONALS automatic transmission, hydraulic torque conerter and planetary gears with 3 ratios (I 2.650, II 1.580, III , rev 1.800), max ratio of converter at stall 2.2, possible anual selection, 4.091 axle ratio, max speed 99 mph, 159 m/h, acceleration 0-50 mph (0-80 km/h) 9.6 sec, consumpon 28.8 m/imp gal, 24 m/US gal, 9.8 l x 100 km at 75 mph, 20 km/h.

Passat Diesel Series

RICES IN USA AND EX WORKS:	$	DM
+1-dr D Limousine	—	**13,918***
+1-dr D Limousine	—	**14,509***
4+1-dr D Variant	—	**14,907***
2+1-dr LD Limousine	**8,110***	**14,737***
4+1-dr LD Limousine	**8,310***	**15,326***
4+1-dr LD Variant	**8,590***	**15,724***
2+1-dr GLD Limousine	—	**15,724***
4+1-dr GLD Limousine	—	**16,315***
4+1-dr GLD Variant	—	**16,713***

50 hp power team

ENGINE diesel, front, 4 stroke; 4 cylinders, vertical, in line; 89.8 cu in, 1,471 cc (3.01 x 3.15 in, 76.5 x 80 mm); compression ratio: 23.5:1; max power (DIN): 50 hp (37 kW) at 5,000 rpm; max torque (DIN): 59 lb ft, 8.2 kg m (80 Nm) at 3,000 rpm; max engine rpm: 5,000; 34 hp/l (25 kW/l); cast iron block, light alloy head; 5 crankshaft bearings; valves: overhead, in line, thimble tappets; camshafts: 1, overhead, cogged belt; lubrication: gear pump, full flow filter, 6.2 imp pt, 7.4 US pt, 3.5 l; Bosch injection pump; cooling, liquid, expansion tank, 10.9 imp pt, 13.1 US pt, 6.2 l, electric thermostatic fan.

TRANSMISSION driving wheels: front; clutch: single dry plate (diaphragm); gearbox: mechanical; gears: 4, fully synchronized; ratios: I 3.454, II 1.944, III 1.286, IV 0.909, rev 3.167; lever: central; final drive: spiral bevel; axle ratio: 4.444; width of rims: 5''; tyres: 155 SR x 13.

PERFORMANCE max speed: (I) 24 mph, 38 km/h; (II) 42 mph, 67 km/h; (III) 63 mph, 102 km/h; (IV) 88 mph, 142 km; power-weight ratio: 3-dr limousines 39 lb/hp (53 lb/kW), 17.7 kg/hp (24 kg/kW); carrying capacity: 3-dr. Limousines 981 lb, 445 kg; acceleration: 0-50 mph (0-80 km/h) 13 sec; speed in top at 1,000 rpm: 16.2 mph, 26.1 km/h; consumption: 35.8 m/imp gal, 29.8 m/US gal, 7.9 l x 100 km at 75 mph, 120 km/h.

CHASSIS integral, front auxiliary subframe; front suspension: independent by McPherson, lower wishbones, anti-roll bar, coil springs/telescopic damper struts; rear: rigid axle, trailing radius arms, transverse linkage bar, coil springs, anti-roll bar, telescopic dampers.

STEERING rack-and-pinion, damper.

BRAKES front disc (diameter 9.41 in, 23.9 cm), rear drum, 2 X circuits, servo.

ELECTRICAL EQUIPMENT 12 V; 63 Ah battery; 45 A alternator; 4 headlamps.

DIMENSIONS AND WEIGHT wheel base: 97.24 in, 247 cm; tracks: 52.76 in, 134 cm front, 53.15 in, 135 cm rear; length: 168.90 in, 429 cm - Variant models 167.91 in, 426 cm; width: 63.58 in, 161 cm; height: 53.54 in, 136 cm; ground clearance: 7.09 in, 18 cm; weight: 2+1-dr limousines 1,951 lb, 885 kg - 4+1-dr limousines 2,007 lb, 910 kg - Variant models 2,084 lb, 945 kg; turning circle: 33.8 ft, 10.3 m; fuel tank: 9.9 imp gal, 11.9 US gal, 45 l.

BODY 5 seats, separate front seats, reclining backrests with headrests; heated rear window; folding rear seat (for Variant models only).

PRACTICAL INSTRUCTIONS fuel: diesel oil; oil: engine 5.3 imp pt, 6.3 US pt, 3 l - gearbox and final drive 3.2 imp pt, 3.8 US pt, 1.8 l, SAE 80, no change recommended; tyre pressure: front 24 psi, 1.7 atm, rear 24 psi, 1.7 atm.

OPTIONALS 175/70 SR x 13 tyres; sport wheels; sunshine roof; halogen headlamps; metallic spray; tinted glass; tailgate with folding rear seat (for limousines only); rear window wiper-washer (for Variant models only).

Iltis

ENGINE front, 4 stroke; 4 cylinders, vertical, in line; 104.6 cu in, 1,714 cc (3.13 x 3.40 in, 79.5 x 86.4 mm); compression ratio: 8.2:1; max power (DIN): 75 hp (55 kW) at 5,000 rpm; max torque (DIN): 100 lb ft, 13.8 kg m (135 Nm) at 2,800 rpm; max engine rpm: 5,500; 43.7 hp/l (32.1 kW/l); cast iron block, light alloy head; 5 crankshaft bearings; valves: overhead, in line, thimble tappets; camshafts:1, overhead, cogged belt; lubrication: gear pump, full flow filter, 6.2 imp pt, 7.4 US pt, 3.5 l; 1 Solex 1 B1 downdraught single barrel carburettor; fuel feed: mechanical pump; cooling, liquid expansion tank, 10.9 imp pt, 13.1 US pt, 6.2 l.

TRANSMISSION driving wheels: front (automatically - engaged with transfer box) and rear; clutch: single dry plate (diaphragm), hydraulically controlled; gearbox: mechanical; gears: 4, fully synchronized and 2-ratio transfer box; ratios: I 3.909, II 2.278, III 1.458, IV 1.086, rev 7.318; lever: central; final drive: hypoid bevel; axle ratio: 5.286; width of rims: 5.5'' or 6.5''; tyres: 6.50 R x 16 or 6.50 K x 15 H2 or Tracker A-T 9 x 15.

PERFORMANCE max speed: 81 mph, 130 km/h; power-weight ratio: 38.2 lb/hp (52.1 lb/kW), 17.3 kg/hp (23.6 kg/kW); carrying capacity: 1,543 lb, 700 kg; acceleration: 0-50 mph (0-80 km/h) 11.5 sec; speed in top at 1,000 rpm: 14.7 mph, 23.6 km/h; consumption: 26.9 m/imp gal, 22.4 m/US gal, 10.5 l x 100 km at 56 mph, 90 km/h.

CHASSIS box-type ladder frame; front suspension: rigid axle, longitudinal radius arms, transverse linkage bar, coil springs, telescopic dampers; rear: rigid axle, longitudinal radius arms, coil springs, telescopic dampers.

STEERING rack-and-pinion.

BRAKES drum, 2 X circuits, servo.

ELECTRICAL EQUIPMENT 12 V; 45 Ah battery; 55 A alternator; Bosch distributor; 2 headlamps.

DIMENSIONS AND WEIGHT wheel base: 79.41 in, 202 cm; tracks: 48.42 in, 123 cm front, 49.61 in, 126 cm rear; length: 153.03 in, 339 cm; width: 59.84 in, 152 cm; height: 72.32 in, 184 cm; ground clearance: 8.86 in, 22.5 cm; weight: 2,866 lb, 1,300 kg; turning circle: 36.1 ft, 11 m; fuel tank: 9.9 imp gal, 11.9 US gal, 45 l.

BODY estate car / st. wagon; 2+1 doors; 4 seats, separate front seats, reclining backrests, headrests.

PRACTICAL INSTRUCTIONS fuel: 91 oct petrol; oil: engine 6.2 imp pt, 7.4 US pt, 3.5 l, SAE 20W-30, change every 4,700 miles, 7,500 km; tyre pressure: front 25 psi, 1.7 atm, rear 25 psi, 1.7 atm.

VOLKSWAGEN Iltis

AC GREAT BRITAIN

3000 ME

PRICE EX WORKS: £ 13,238*

ENGINE Ford, centre-rear, transverse, 4 stroke; 6 cylinders, Vee-slanted at 60°; 182.7 cu in 2,994 cc (3.69 x 2.85 in, 93.7 x 72.4 mm); compression ratio: 9:1; max power (DIN): 138 hp (102 kW) at 5,000 rpm; max torque (DIN): 174 lb ft, 24 kg m (235 Nm) at 3,000 rpm; max engine rpm: 5,750; 46.1 hp/l (33.9 kW/l); cast iron block and head; 4 crankshaft bearings; valves: overhead, push-rods and rockers; camshafts: 1, at centre of Vee; lubrication: rotary pump, full flow filter, oil cooler, 10.9 imp pt, 13.1 US pt, 6.2 l; 1 Weber 38/38 EGAS downdraught twin barrel carburettor; fuel feed: mechanical pump; water-cooled, 18 imp pt, 21.6 US pt, 10.2 l, electric thermostatic fan.

TRANSMISSION driving wheels: rear; clutch: single dry plate; gearbox: mechanical; gears: 5, fully synchronized; ratios: I 3.242, II 1.947, III 1.403, IV 1, V 0.835, rev 2.901; lever: central; final drive: hypoid bevel; axle ratio: 3.167; width of rims: 7"; tyres: 205/60 HR x 14.

PERFORMANCE max speed: 125 mph, 201 km/h; power-weight ratio: 17.3 lb/hp (23.5 lb/kW), 7.9 kg/hp (10,.7 kg/kW); speed in top at 1,000 rpm: 25.3 mph, 40.7 km/h; consumption: 26.9 m/imp gal, 22.4 m/US gal, 10.5 l x 100 km.

CHASSIS perimeter box-type frame; front suspension: independent, wishbones, vertical links, coil springs/telescopic dampers; rear: independent, wishbones, vertical links, coil springs/telescopic dampers.

STEERING rack-and-pinion, adjustable steering wheel; turns lock to lock: 3.

BRAKES disc (front diameter 10 in, 25.4 cm, rear 9.41 in, 23.9 cm), dual circuit; swept area: front 200.8 sq in, 1,295 sq cm, rear 172.1 sq in, 1,110 sq cm, total 372.9 sq in, 2,405 sq cm.

ELECTRICAL EQUIPMENT 12 V; 55 Ah battery; 35 A alternator; Lucas distributor; 2 retractable headlamps.

DIMENSIONS AND WEIGHT wheel base: 90.50 in, 230 cm; tracks: 55 in, 140 cm front, 56 in, 142 cm rear; length: 157 in, 399 cm; width: 65 in, 165 cm; height: 45 in, 114 cm; ground clearance: 5.25 in, 13.3 cm; weight: 2,387 lb, 1,085 kg; weight distribution: 40% front, 60% rear; turning circle: 32 ft, 9.8 m; fuel tank: 14 imp gal, 16.8 US gal, 64 l.

BODY coupé, in plastic material; 2 doors; 2 seats with built-in headrests; detachable roof; electric windows; light alloy wheels.

PRACTICAL INSTRUCTIONS fuel: 97 oct petrol; oil: engine 9.7 imp pt, 11.6 US pt, 5.5 l, SAE 20W-50, change every 6,200 miles, 10,000 km; greasing: every 6,200 miles, 10,000 km, 4 points; tappet clearances: inlet 0.012 in, 0.30 mm, exhaust 0.012 in, 0.30 mm; valve timing: 20° 56° 62° 14°.

OPTIONALS servo brake.

AC 3000 ME

ARGYLL GREAT BRITAIN

Turbo GT

PRICES EX WORKS: £ **12,500** (V8 engine)
£ **10,700** (4-cylinder engine)

ENGINE Rover, turbocharged, central, transverse, 4 stroke; 8 cylinders, Vee-slanted; 215 cu in, 3,528 cc (3.50 x 2.80 in, 88.9 x 71.1 mm); compression ratio: 8.5:1; max power (DIN): 250 hp (184 kW) at 5,200-6,200 rpm; max torque (DIN): 310 lb ft, 42.8 kg m (420 Nm) at 3,500-4,500 rpm; max engine rpm: 6,200; 70.9 hp/l (52.2 kW/l); light alloy block and head, dry liners; 5 crankshaft bearings; valves: overhead, in line, push-rods and rockers, hydraulic tappets; camshaft: 1, at centre of Vee; lubrication: gear pump, full flow filter, oil cooler, 15 imp pt, 18 US pt, 8.5 l; 1 Minnow Fish TM7 carburettor; turbocharger; fuel feed: electric pump; water-cooled, 30 imp pt, 35.9 US pt, 17 l.

TRANSMISSION driving wheels: rear; clutch: single dry plate; gerarbox: ZF mechanical; gears: 5, fully synchronized; ratios: I 2.580, II 1.520, III 1.040, IV 0.850, V 0.740, rev 2.860; lever: central; final drive: hypoid bevel, limited slip differential; width of rims: 7" front, 8" rear; tyres: 205 x 15.

PERFORMANCE max speed: over 150 mph, 241 km/h; power-weight ratio: 9.3 lb/hp (12.6 lb kW), 4.2 kg/hp (5.7 kg/kW); carrying capacity: 353 lb, 160 kg; consumption: not declared.

CHASSIS box-section with integral roll cage; front suspension: independent, coil springs, telescopic dampers, double wishbone, anti-roll bar; rear: independent, semi-trailing arms, coil springs, telescopic dampers.

STEERING rack-and-pinion; turns lock to lock: 2.50.

BRAKES disc (diameter 10.30 in, 26 cm), servo.

ARGYLL Turbo GT

ARKLEY SS

ASTON MARTIN V8

ELECTRICAL EQUIPMENT 12 V; 60 Ah battery; alternator; Lucas distributor; 4 headlamps.

DIMENSIONS AND WEIGHT wheel base: 118 in, 300 cm; front and rear track: 59.50 in, 151 cm; length: 183 in, 465 cm; width: 72 in, 183 cm; height: 48 in, 122 cm; ground clearance: 6 in, 15 cm; weight: 2,300 lb, 1,043 kg; weight distribution: 48% front, 52% rear; fuel tank: 20 imp gal, 24 US gal, 91 l.

BODY coupé, in plastic material; 2 doors; 2 seats.

PRACTICAL INSTRUCTIONS fuel: 97 oct petrol; oil: engine 15 imp pt, 18 US pt, 8.5 l, SAE 20W-30, change every 3,100 miles, 5,000 km - gearbox and final drive 5.8 imp pt, 7 US pt, 3.3 l, SAE 90, change every 12,400 miles, 20,000 km; tyre pressure: front 22 psi, 1.5 atm, rear 24 psi, 1.7 atm.

VARIATIONS

ENGINE 4 cylinders, in line, 121.1 cu in, 1,985 cc (3.54 x 3.07 in, 90 x 78 mm), 7.5:1 compression ratio, max power (DIN) 175 hp (129 kW) at 5,500-6,500 rpm, max torque (DIN) 220 lb ft, 30.3 kg m (297 Nm) at 3,500-4,500 rpm, max engine rpm 6,500, 88.2 hp/l (64.9 kW/l), cast iron block, light alloy head, 1 overhead camshaft, 1 Minnow Fish TB7 carburettor.
TRANSMISSION 4-speed fully synchronized mechanical gearbox, 185 x 15 tyres.
PERFORMANCE max speed 130 mph, 209 km/h, power-weight ratio 13.2 lb/hp (17.9 lb/kW), 6 kg/hp (8.1 kg/kW), carrying capacity 706 lb, 320 kg.
ELECTRICAL EQUIPMENT Bosh distributor.
BODY 4 seats.

OPTIONALS power steering.

ARKLEY GREAT BRITAIN

SS

PRICE EX WORKS: £ 4,950*

ENGINE Triumph, front, 4 stroke; 4 cylinders, vertical, in line; 91.1 cu in, 1,493 cc (2.90 x 3.44 in, 73.7 x 87.5 mm); compression ratio: 9:1; max power (DIN): 65 hp (48 kW) at 5,500 rpm; max torque (DIN): 84 lb ft, 11.6 kg m (114 Nm) at 3,000 rpm; max engine rpm: 6,000; 43.5 hp/l (32 kW/l); cast iron block and head; 3 crankshaft bearings; valves: overhead, in line, push-rods and rockers; camshafts: 1, side; lubrication: eccentric pump, full flow filter, 7 imp pt, 8.5 US pt, 4 l; 2 SU type HS4 horizontal carburettors; fuel feed: electric pump; sealed circuit cooling, water, 6 imp pt, 7.2 US pt, 3.4 l.

TRANSMISSION driving wheels: rear; clutch: single dry plate (diaphragm); gearbox: mechanical; gears: 4, fully synchronized; ratios: I 3.412, II 2.112, III 1.433, IV 1, rev 3.753; lever: central; final drive: hypoid bevel; axle ratio: 3.900; width of rims: 7"; tyres: 195/70 x 13.

PERFORMANCE max speeds: (I) 35 mph, 57 km/h; (II) 59 mph, 96 km/h; (III) 85 mph, 137 km/h; (IV) 110 mph, 177 km/h; power-weight ratio: 19.8 lb/hp (26.9 lb/kW), 9 kg/hp (12.2 kg/kW); carrying capacity: 353 lb, 160 kg; acceleration: standing ¼ mile 17.5 sec, 0-50 mph (0-80 km/h) 8.2 sec; speed in direct drive at 1,000 rpm: 19.8 mph, 31.8 km/h; consumption: 38 m/imp gal, 31.8 m/US gal, 7.4 l x 100 km.

CHASSIS integral; front suspension: independent, wishbones, coil springs, anti-roll bar, telescopic dampers; rear: rigid axle, semi-elliptic leafsprings, telescopic dampers.

STEERING rack-and-pinion; turns lock to lock: 2.25.

BRAKES front disc (diameter 8.25 in, 21 cm), rear drum.

ELECTRICAL EQUIPMENT 12 V; 40 Ah battery; 34 A alternator; Lucas distributor; 2 headlamps.

DIMENSIONS AND WEIGHT wheel base: 79.92 in, 203 cm; tracks: 46.46 in, 118 cm front, 44.88 in, 114 cm rear; length: 123 in, 312 cm; width: 60 in, 152 cm; height: 47.50 in, 121 cm; ground clearance: 4.50 in, 10.3 cm; weight: 1,288 lb, 584 kg; weight distributor: 52.4% front, 47.6% rear; turning circle: 32 ft, 9.8 m; fuel tank: 7 imp gal, 8.4 US gal, 32 l.

BODY convertible; 2 doors; 2 seats, reclining backrests with built-in headrests.

PRACTICAL INSTRUCTIONS fuel: 98 oct petrol; oil: engine 6.5 imp pt, 7.8 US pt, 3.7 l, SAE 10W-30 (winter) 20W-50 (summer), change every 6,000 miles, 9,700 km - gearbox 2.3 imp pt, 2.7 US pt, 1.3 l, SAE 10W-30 (winter) 20W-50 (summer) - final drive 1.4 imp pt, 1.7 US pt, 0.8 l, SAE 90, change every 6,000 miles, 9,700 km; greasing: every 3,000 miles, 4,800 km, 8 points; tappet clearances: inlet 0.010 in, 0.25 mm, exhaust 0.010 in, 0.25 mm; valve timing: 18° 58° 58° 18°; tyre pressure: front 18 psi, 1.3 atm, rear 20 psi, 1.4 atm.

ASTON MARTIN GREAT BRITAIN

V8

PRICE IN USA: $ 65,000*
PRICE EX WORKS: £ 28,749*

ENGINE front, 4 stroke; 8 cylinders, Vee-slanted; 325.8 cu in, 5,340 cc (3.94 x 3.35 in, 100 x 85 mm); compression ratio: 9:1; max engine rpm: 6,000; light alloy block and head, wet liners, hemispherical combustion chambers; 5 crankshaft bearings; valves: overhead, Vee-slanted at 64°, thimble tappets; camshafts: 4, 2 per bank, overhead; lubrication: rotary pump, full flow filter, 2 oil coolers, 24 imp pt, 28.8 US pt, 13.6 l; 4 Weber 42 DCNF downdraught twin barrel carburettors; fuel feed: 2 electric pumps; water-cooled, 32 imp pt, 38.5 US pt, 18.2 l, viscous coupling fan drive.

TRANSMISSION driving wheels: rear; clutch: single dry plate (diaphragm), hydraulically controlled; gearbox: mechanical; gears: 5, fully synchronized; ratios: I 2.900, II 1.780, III 1.220, IV 1, V 0.845, rev 2.630; lever: central; final drive: hypoid bevel, limited slip differential; axle ratio: 3.310; width of rims: 7"; tyres: GR 70 VR x 15.

PERFORMANCE max speeds: (I) 47 mph, 75 km/h; (II) 77 mph, 124 km/h; (III) 112 mph, 180 km/h; (IV) 136 mph, 219 km/h; (V) 160 mph, 257 km/h; acceleration: standing ¼ mile 14 sec, 0-50 mph (0-80 km/h) 4.5 sec; speed in top at 1,000 rpm: 27 mph, 43.5 km/h; consumption: 15 m/imp gal, 12.5 m/US gal, 18.8 l x 100 km.

CHASSIS box-type platform; front suspension: independent, wishbones, coil springs, anti-roll bar, telescopic dampers; rear: de Dion rigid axle, parallel trailing arms, transverse Watt linkage, coil springs, telescopic dampers.

STEERING rack-and-pinion, adjustable height of steering wheel, servo; turns lock to lock: 2.90.

BRAKES disc (front diameter 11.50 in, 29.2 cm, rear 10.80 in, 27.4 cm), internal radial fins, rear compensator, dual circuit, dual servo; swept area: front 259 sq in, 1,670 sq cm, rear 209 sq in, 1,348 sq cm, total 468 sq in, 3,018 sq cm.

ELECTRICAL EQUIPMENT 12 V; 73 Ah battery; 75 A alternator; Lucas transistorized ignition; 2 halogen headlamps.

DIMENSIONS AND WEIGHT wheel base: 102.75 in, 261 cm; front and rear track: 59 in, 150 cm; length: 182 in, 462 cm; width: 72 in, 183 cm; height: 52.25 in, 133 cm; ground clearance: 5.50 in, 14 cm; weight: 3,900 lb, 1,769 kg; weight distribution: 52% front, 48% rear; turning circle: 43 ft, 13.1 m; fuel tank: 23 imp gal, 27.5 US gal, 104 l.

BODY coupé; 2 doors; 4 seats, separate front seats, reclining backrests; adjustable two-position clutch, brake and accelerator pedals; leather upholstery; heated rear window; electric windows; air-conditioning.

PRACTICAL INSTRUCTIONS fuel: 98 oct petrol; oil: engine 22 imp pt, 26.4 US pt, 12.5 l, SAE 10W-50, change every 5,000 miles, 8,000 km; greasing: every 5,000 miles, 8,000 km, 6 points; tappet clearances: inlet 0.010 in, 0.25 mm, exhaust 0.012 in, 0.30 mm; valve timing: 30° 66° 68° 28°; tyre pressure: front 35 psi, 2.4 atm, rear 35 psi, 2.4 atm.

OPTIONALS Chrysler-Torqueflite automatic transmission, hydraulic torque converter and planetary gears with 3 ratios (I 2.450, II 1.450, III 1, rev 2.200), max ratio of converter at stall 2.1, possible manual selection, 3.070 axle ratio; sunshine roof; headlamps with wiper-washers.

V8 Vantage

See V8, except for:

PRICE IN USA: $ 52,250*
PRICE EX WORKS: £ 30,878*

ENGINE compression ratio: 9.3:1; max engine rpm: 6,500; 4 Weber 48IDF downdraught twin barrel carburettors.

TRANSMISSION tyres: 255/60 VR x 15.

PERFORMANCE max speeds: (I) 46 mph, 74 km/h; (II) 75 mph, 120 km/h; (III) 109 mph, 175 km/h; (IV) 133 mph, 214 km/h; (V) 170 mph; 273 km/h; acceleration: 0-50 mph (0-80 km/h) 3.8 sec.

ELECTRICAL EQUIPMENT 4 headlamps.

V8 Volante

See V8, except for:

PRICE IN USA: $ 95,000*
PRICE EX WORKS: £ 36,059*

TRANSMISSION tyres: 235/70 HR x 15.

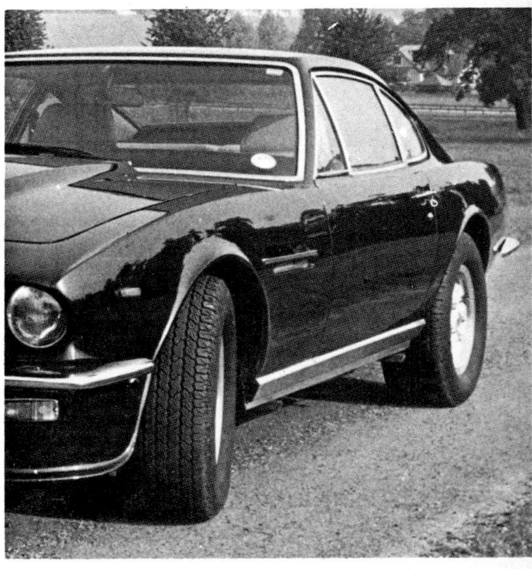

ASTON MARTIN V8 Vantage

V8 VOLANTE

PERFORMANCE max speeds: (I) 45 mph, 72 km/h; (II) 73 mph, 116 km/h; (III) 104 mph, 166 km/h; (IV) 120 mph, 192 km/h; (V) 130 mph, 209 km/h; acceleration: 0-50 mph (0-80 km/h) 4.8 sec.

DIMENSIONS AND WEIGHT fuel tank: 21.6 imp gal, 26 US gal, 98 l.

BODY convertible.

Lagonda

PRICE EX WORKS: £ 39,921*

ENGINE front, 4 stroke; 8 cylinders, Vee-slanted; 325.8 cu in, 5,340 cc (3.94 x 3.35 in, 100 x 85 mm); compression ratio: 9:1; max engine rpm: 6,000; light alloy block and head; 5 crankshaft bearings; valves: overhead, Vee slanted at 64°, thimble tappets; camshafts: 4, 2 per bank, overhead; lubrication: rotary pump, full flow filter, 2 oil coolers, 24 imp pt, 28.8 US pt, 13.6 l; 4 Weber 42 DCNF downdraught twin barrel carburettors; fuel feed: 2 electric pumps; water-cooled, 32 imp pt, 38.5 US pt, 18.2 l, hydrostatic fan drive.

TRANSMISSION driving wheels: rear; gearbox: Chrysler Torqueflite automatic transmission, hydraulic torque converter and planetary gears with 3 ratios, max ratio of converter at stall 2.1, possible manual selection; ratios: I 2.450, II 1.450, III 1, rev 2.200; lever: central; final drive: hypoid bevel, limited slip differential; axle ratio: 3.070; width of rims: 6"; tyres: 235/70 HR x 15.

PERFORMANCE max speed: 140 mph, 225 km/h; speed in direct drive at 1,000 rpm: 24.4 mph, 39.3 km/h; consumption: 15 m/imp gal, 12.5 m/US gal, 18.8 l x 100 km.

CHASSIS box-type platform; front suspension: independent, wishbones, coil springs, anti-roll bar, telescopic dampers; rear: de Dion rigid axle, parallel trailing arms, transverse Watt linkage, coil springs, telescopic dampers, self-levelling system.

STEERING rack-and-pinion, variable ratio servo; turns lock to lock: 2.30.

BRAKES disc, internal radial fins, rear compensator, dual circuit, dual servo.

ELECTRICAL EQUIPMENT 12 V; 73 Ah battery; 75A alternator; Lucas transistorized ignition; 4 halogen headlamps.

DIMENSIONS AND WEIGHT wheel base: 114.02 in, 290 cm; tracks: 58.27 in, 148 cm front, 59.06 in, 150 cm rear; length: 207.99 in,528 cm; width: 70 in, 178 cm; height: 50.98 in, 129 cm; ground clearance: 9.84 in, 25 cm; weight: 4,400 lb, 2,000 kg: weight distribution: 52% front, 48% rear; turning circle: 38 ft, 11.6 m; fuel tank: 28 imp gal, 33.8 US gal, 128 l.

BODY saloon/sedan; 4 doors; 4 seats, separate front seats, reclining backrests, headrests; adjustable two-position clutch, brake and accelerator pedals; leather upholstery; heated rear window; electric windows; air-conditioning; cruise control; laminated windscreen; glass panel in roof above rear compartment.

PRACTICAL INSTRUCTIONS fuel: 98 oct petrol; oil: engine 22 imp pt, 26.4 US pt, 12.5 l, SAE 10W-50, change every 5,000 miles, 8,000 km; greasing: every 5,000 miles, 8,000 km, 6 points; tappet clearances: inlet 0.010 in, 0.25 mm, exhaust 0.012 in, 0.30 mm; valve timing: 30° 66° 68° 28°; tyre pressure: front 35 psi, 2.4 atm, rear 35 psi, 2.4 atm.

ASTON MARTIN V8 Volante

ASTON MARTIN Lagonda

AUSTIN GREAT BRITAIN

Allegro 3 Series

PRICES EX WORKS:	£
1 1.1 2-dr Saloon	3,085*
2 1.3 2-dr Saloon	3,206*
3 1.3 4-dr Saloon	3,330*
4 1.3 2+1-dr Estate Car	3,568*
5 1.3 L 2-dr Saloon	3,470*
6 1.3 L 4-dr Saloon	3,594*
7 1.3 L 2+1-dr Estate Car	3,832*
8 1.3 HL 4-dr Saloon	4,014*
9 1.5 L 4-dr Saloon	3,760*
10 1.5 L 2+1-dr Estate Car	3,998*
11 1.5 HL 4-dr Saloon	4,180*
12 1.7 L 4-dr Saloon	4,182*
13 1.7 L 2+1-dr Estate Car	4,420*
14 1.7 HL 4-dr Saloon	4,377*

Power team:	Standard for:	Optional for:
45 hp	1	—
54 hp	2 to 8	—
77 hp	9 to 11	—
72 hp	12,13	—
90 hp	14	—

45 hp power team

ENGINE front, transverse, 4 stroke, in unit with gearbox and final drive; 4 cylinders, vertical, in line; 67 cu in, 1,098 cc (2.54 x 3.29 in, 64.4 x 83.5 mm); compression ratio: 8.5:1; max power (DIN): 45 hp (33 kW) at 5,250 rpm; max torque (DIN): 55 lb ft, 7.6 kg m (74 Nm) at 2,900 rpm; max engine rpm: 6,000; 41 hp/l (30.1 kW/l); cast iron block and head; 3 crankshaft bearings; valves: overhead, in line, push-rods and rockers; camshafts: 1, side; lubrication: rotary pump, full flow filter by cartridge, 8.5 imp pt, 10.1 US pt, 4.8 l; 1 SU type HS4 single barrel carburettor; fuel feed: mechanical pump; sealed circuit cooling, liquid, 7.2 imp pt, 8.7 US pt, 4.1 l, electric thermostatic fan.

TRANSMISSION driving wheels: front; clutch: single dry plate (diaphragm); gearbox: mechanical; gears: 4, fully synchronized; ratios: I 3.525, II 2.218, III 1.433, IV 1, rev 3.544; lever: central; final drive: helical spur gears; axle ratio: 4.133; width of rims: 4" or 4.5"; tyres: 145 x 13.

PERFORMANCE max speeds: (I) 26 mph, 42 km/h; (II) 41 mph, 66 km/h; (III) 64 mph, 103 km/h; (IV) 87 mph, 140 km/h; power-weight ratio: 41.4 lb/hp (54.5 lb/kW), 18.8 kg/hp (24.7 kg/kW); carrying capacity: 710 lb, 320 kg; acceleration: standing ¼ mile 22.1 sec; speed in direct drive at 1,000 rpm: 15.5 mph, 24.9 km/h; consumption: 32.4 m/imp gal, 27 m/US gal, 8.7 l x 100 km at 75 mph, 120 km/h.

CHASSIS integral; front suspension: independent, wishbones, hydragas (liquid and gas) rubber cone springs, hydraulic connecting pipes to rear wheels; rear: independent, swinging longitudinal trailing arms, hydragas (liquid and gas) rubber cone springs, hydraulic connecting pipes to front wheels.

STEERING rack-and-pinion; turns lock to lock: 3.50.

BRAKES front disc (diameter 9.68 in, 24.6 cm), rear drum, servo; swept area: front 178 sq in, 1,148 sq cm, rear 75.6 sq in, 487 sq cm, total 253.6 sq in, 1,635 sq cm.

ELECTRICAL EQUIPMENT 12 V; 40 Ah battery; 36 A alternator; Lucas distributor; 2 headlamps.

DIMENSIONS AND WEIGHT wheel base: 96.14 in, 244 cm; tracks: 54.33 in, 138 cm front, 54.41 in, 138 cm rear; length: 151.67 in, 385 cm; width: 63.52 in, 161 cm; height: 54.87 in, 139 cm; ground clearance: 7.48 in, 19 cm; weight: 1,795 lb, 814 kg; turning circle: 33.3 ft, 10.2 m; fuel tank: 10.5 imp gal, 12.7 US gal, 48 l.

BODY 4-5 seats, separate front seats, reclining backrests; heated rear window.

PRACTICAL INSTRUCTIONS fuel: 97 oct petrol; oil: engine, gearbox and final drive 8.5 imp pt, 10.1 US pt, 4.8 l, SAE 20W-50, change every 6,000 miles, 9,700 km; greasing: every 6,000 miles, 9,700 km, 4 points; tappet clearances (cold): inlet 0.012 in, 0.30 mm, exhaust 0.012 in, 0.30 mm; valve timing: 5° 45° 51° 21°; tyre pressure: front 26 psi, 1.8 atm, rear 24 psi, 1.7 atm.

OPTIONALS headrests; tinted glass; metallic spray; fog lamps.

54 hp power team

See 45 hp power team, except for:

ENGINE 77.8 cu in, 1,275 cc (2.78 x 3.20 in, 70.5 x 81.2 mm);

AUSTIN Allegro 3 1.5 L Estate Car

ompression ratio: 8.8:1; max power (DIN): 54 hp (40 kW) at ,250 rpm; max torque (DIN): 64 lb ft, 8.9 kg m (87 Nm) at ,000 rpm; 42.3 hp/l (31.1 kW/l).

RANSMISSION axle ratio: 3.938; tyres: 1.3 HL 4-dr Saloon 55 x 13.

ERFORMANCE max speeds: (I) 30 mph, 48 km/h; (II)48 mph, 7 km/h; (III) 74 mph, 119 km/h; (IV) 92 mph, 148 km/h; ower-weight ratio: 1.3 2-dr Saloon 33.5 lb/hp (45.2 lb/kW), 5.2 kg/hp (20.5 kg/kW); acceleration standing ¼mile 21.4 sec, -50 mph (0-80 km/h) 14 sec; speed in direct drive at 1,000 om: 16.4 mph, 26.4 km/h; consumption: 33.7 m/imp gal, 28 /US gal, 8.4 l x 100 km at 75 mph, 120 km/h.

LECTRICAL EQUIPMENT 1.3 HL 4-dr Saloon 4 headlamps, og lamps (standard).

IMENSIONS AND WEIGHT tracks: 1.3 HL 4-dr Saloon 53.62 , 136 cm front, 53.70 in, 136 cm rear; length: Estate Cars 55.22 in, 394 cm; height: estate cars 56.75 in, 144 cm; ground learance: 1.3 HL 4-dr Saloon 7.64 in, 19.4 cm estate cars - .30 in, 16 cm; weight: 1.3 2-dr Saloon 1,813 lb, 822 kg - 1.3 -dr Saloon 1,857 lb, 842 kg - 1.3 2+1-dr Estate Car 1,876 lb, 51 kg - 1.3 L 2-dr Saloon 1,869 lb, 847 kg - 1.3 L 4-dr Saloon ,918 lb, 870 kg - 1.3 L 2+1-dr Estate Car 1,984 lb, 900 kg - .3 HL 4-dr Saloon 1,936 lb, 878 kg.

ODY for 1.3 HL 4-dr Saloon only, headrests and tinted glass; or estate cars only, rear window wiper-washer.

PTIONALS automatic transmission; metallic spray; headrests nd tinted glass (except 1.3 HL 4-dr Saloon).

77 hp power team

ee 45 hp power team, except for:

NGINE 90.6 cu in, 1,485 cc (3 x 3.20 in, 76.1 x 81.2 mm); ompression ratio: 9:1; max power (DIN): 77 hp (57 kW) at ,750 rpm; max torque (DIN): 83 lb ft, 11.5 kg m (113 Nm) at ,250 rpm; max engine rpm: 6,500; 51.9 hp/l (38.2 kW/l); 5 rankshaft bearings; valves: overhead, Vee-slanted, thimble appets; camshafts: 1, overhead, chain-driven; lubrication: 9.7 np pt, 11.6 US pt, 5.5 l; 1 SU type HIF4 twin barrel carburet- or; cooling: 9.7 imp pt, 11.6 US pt, 5.5 l.

RANSMISSION gears: 5, fully synchronized; ratios: I 3.202, II .004, III 1.372, IV 1, V 0.869, rev 3.467; axle ratio: 3.647; yres: 155 x 13.

ERFORMANCE max speeds: (I) 33 mph, 53 km/h; (II) 54 nph, 87 km/h; (III) 78 mph, 125 km/h; (IV) 92 mph, 148 km/h; V) 90 mph, 145 km/h; power-weight ratio: 1.5 L 4-dr Saloon 5.8 lb/hp (34.8 lb/kW), 11.7 kg/hp (15.8 kg/kW); acceleration: tanding ¼ mile 20 sec, 0-50 mph (0-80 km/h) 10 sec; speed in op at 1,000 rpm: 19 mph, 30.5 km/h; consumption: 33.2 m/imp al, 27.7 m/US gal, 8.5 l x 100 km at 75 mph, 120 km/h.

LECTRICAL EQUIPMENT 1.5 HL 4-dr Saloon 4 headlamps, og lamps (standard).

IMENSIONS AND WEIGHT tracks: 1.5 HL 4-dr Saloon 53.62 , 136 cm front, 53.70 in, 136 cm rear; length: Estate Car 55.22 in, 394 cm; height: Estate Car 56.75 in, 144 cm; ground learance: 1.5 HL 4-dr Saloon 7.64 in, 19.4 cm - Estate Car .30 in, 16 cm; weight: 1.5 L 4-dr Saloon 1,980 lb, 898 kg - 1.5 2+1-dr Estate Car 2,046 lb, 928 kg - 1.5 HL 4-dr Saloon ,998 lb, 906 kg.

ODY rear window wiper-washer (for Estate Car only).

PRACTICAL INSTRUCTIONS oil: engine, gearbox and final drive 9.7 imp pt, 11.6 US pt, 5.5 l; tappet clearance: inlet 0.012-0.018 in, 0.30-0.45 mm, exhaust 0.012-0.022 in, 0.30-0.55 mm; valve timing: 9° 50° 48° 11°.

OPTIONALS automatic transmission with 4 ratios (I 2.612, II 1.807, III 1.446, IV 1, rev 3.467, max ratio of converter at stall 2, possible manual selection, 3.800 axle ratio, max speed 87 mph, 140 km/h; metallic spray; headrests; tinted glass; fog lamps.

72 hp power team

See 45 hp power team, except for:

ENGINE 106.7 cu in, 1,748 cc (3 x 3.77 in, 76.1 x 95.7 mm); compression ratio: 8.7:1; max power (DIN): 72 hp (53 kW) at 4,900 rpm; max torque (DIN): 97 lb ft, 13.4 kg m (131 max Nm) at 2,600 rpm; max engine rpm: 6,500; 41.2 hp/l (30.3 kW/l); 5 crankshaft bearings; valves: overhead, Vee-slanted, thimble tappets; camshafts: 1, overhead, chain-driven; lubrication: 9.7 imp ft, 11.6 US pt, 5.5 l; 1 SU type HS6 single barrel carburet-tor; cooling: 9.7 imp pt, 11.6 US pt, 5.5 l.

TRANSMISSION gearbox: automatic transmission, hydraulic torque converter and planetary gears with 4 ratios, max ratio of converter at stall 2, possible manual selection; ratios: I 2.612, II 1.807, III 1.446, IV 1, rev 3.467; axle ratio: 3,800.

PERFORMANCE max speeds: (I) 34 mph, 54 km/h; (II) 54 mph, 87 km/h; (III) 80 mph, 128 km/h; (IV) 90 mph, 145 km/h; power-weight ratio: Saloon 27.8 lb/hp (37.9 lb/kW), 12.6 kg/hp (17.2 kg/kW); acceleration: standing ¼ mile 19.1 sec, 0-50 mph (0-80 km/h) 9.2 sec; consumption: 25.7 m/imp gal, 21.4 m/US gal, 11 l x 100 km at 75 mph, 120 km/h.

DIMENSIONS AND WEIGHT length: Estate Car 155.22 in, 394 cm; height: Estate Car 56.75 in, 144 cm; ground clearance: Estate Car 6.30 in, 16 cm; weight: Saloon 2,004 lb, 909 kg - Estate Car 2,070 lb, 939 kg.

BODY rear window wiper-washer (for Estate Car only).

PRACTICAL INSTRUCTIONS oil: engine, gearbox and final drive 9.7 imp pt, 11.6 US pt, 5.5 l; tappet clearances: inlet 0.012-0.018 in, 0.30-0.45 mm, exhaust 0.012-0.022 in, 0.30-0.55 mm; valve timing: 9° 51° 49° 11°

OPTIONALS metallic spray; headrests; tinted glass; fog lamps.

90 hp power team

See 72 hp power team, except for:

ENGINE compression ratio: 9.5:1; max power (DIN): 90 hp (66 kW) at 5,500 rpm; max torque (DIN): 104 lb ft, 14.4 kg m (141 Nm) at 3,100 rpm; 51.5 hp/l (37.9 kW/l); 2 SU type HS6 twin barrel carburettors.

TRANSMISSION gearbox: mechanical; gears: 5, fully synchronized; ratios: I 3.202, II 2.004, III 1.372, IV 1, V 0.869, rev 3.467; axle ratio: 3.647.

PERFORMANCE max speed: 94 mph, 151 km/h; power-weight ratio: 22.3 lb/hp (30.2 lb/kW) 10.1 kg/hp (13.7 kg/kW); speed in top at 1,000 rpm: 19.4 mph, 31.2 km/h; consumption: 33.3 m/imp gal, 27.7 m/US gal, 8.5 l x 100 km at 75 mph, 120 km/h.

ELECTRICAL EQUIPMENT 4 headlamps, fog lamps (standard).

DIMENSIONS AND WEIGHT tracks: 53.62 in, 136 cm front, 53.70 in, 136 cm rear; weight: 1,998 lb, 906 kg.

Maxi Series

PRICES EX WORKS: £

1 1500 Saloon	**4,093***
2 1750 Saloon	**4,271***
3 1750 HL Saloon	**4,547***
4 1750 HLS Saloon	**4,676***

Power team:	Standard for:	Optional for:
68 hp	1	—
72 hp	2,3	—
91 hp	4	—

68 hp power team

ENGINE front, transverse, 4 stroke, in unit with gearbox and final drive; 4 cylinders, in line; 90.6 cu in, 1,485 cc (3 x 3.20 in, 76.2 x 81.3 mm); compression ratio: 9:1; max power (DIN): 68 hp (50 kW) at 5,500 rpm; max torque (DIN): 82 lb/ft, 11.3 kg m (111 Nm) at 3,200 rpm; max engine rpm: 6,000; 45.8 hp/l (33.7 kW/l); cast iron block and head; 5 crankshaft bearings; valves: overhead, Vee-slanted, thimble tappets; camshafts: 1, overhead, chaindriven; lubrication: rotary pump, full flow filter, 9.5 imp pt, 11.4 US pt, 5.4 l; 1 SU type HS6 horizontal carburettor; fuel feed: mechanical pump; water-cooled, 9.5 imp pt, 11.4 US pt, 5.4 l.

TRANSMISSION driving wheels: front; clutch: single dry plate (diaphragm), hydraulically controlled; gearbox: mechanical; gears: 5, fully synchronized; ratios: I 3.202, II 2.004; III 1.372, IV 1, V 0.795, rev 3.467; lever: central; final drive: helical spur gears; axle ratio: 3.938; width of rims: 4.5"; tyres: 155 x 13.

PERFORMANCE max speeds: (I) 30 mph, 48 km/h; (II) 50 mph, 80 km/h; (III) 70 mph, 112 km/h; (IV) 90 mph, 145 km/h; (V) 85 mph, 136 km/h; power-weight ratio: 32 lb/hp (43.4 lb/kW), 14.5 kg/hp (19.7 kg/kW); carrying capacity: 882 lb, 400 kg; speed in 4th gear at 1,000 rpm: 15.6 mph, 25.2 km/h; consumption: 29 m/imp gal, 24.2 m/US gal, 9.7 l x 100 km at 75 mph, 120 km/h.

CHASSIS integral; front suspension: independent, wishbones, hydragas (liquid and gas) rubber cone springs, hydraulic connecting pipes to rear wheels; rear: independent, swinging longitudinal trailing arms, hydragas (liquid and gas) rubber cone springs, hydraulic connecting pipes to front wheels.

STEERING rack-and-pinion; turns lock to lock: 3.90.

BRAKES front disc (diameter 9.68 in, 24.6 cm), rear drum, servo; swept area: front 182 sq in, 1,174 sq cm, rear 75.3 sq in, 486 sq cm, total 257.3 sq in, 1,660 sq cm.

ELECTRICAL EQUIPMENT 12 V; 40 Ah battery; 34 A alternator; Lucas distributor; 2 headlamps.

DIMENSIONS AND WEIGHT wheel base: 104.10 in, 264 cm; front and rear track: 53.80 in, 137 cm; length: 158.30 in, 402 cm; width: 64.10 in, 163 cm; height: 55.60 in, 141 cm; ground clearance: 5.50 in, 14 cm; weight: 2,170 lb, 984 kg; weight distribution: 62.3% front, 37.7% rear; turning circle: 33.9 ft, 10.3 m; fuel tank: 10.5 imp gal, 12.7 US gal, 48 l.

BODY 4+1 doors; 4-5 seats, separate front seats, reclining backrests; heated rear window.

AUSTIN Maxi 1750 Saloon

72 hp power team

See 68 hp power team, except for:

ENGINE 106.7 cu in, 1,748 cc (3 x 3.77 in, 76.2 x 95.7 mm); compression ratio: 8.75:1; max power (DIN): 72 hp (53 kW) at 4,900 rpm; max torque (DIN): 97 lb ft, 13.4 kg m (131 Nm) at 2,600 rpm; 41.2 hp/l (30.3 kW/l).

TRANSMISSION gearbox ratio: V 0.869; axle ratio: 3.647; tyres: 1750 HL 165 x 13.

PERFORMANCE max speeds: (I) 34 mph, 54 km/h; (II) 56 mph, 90 km/h; (III) 78 mph, 125 km/h; (IV) 92 mph, 148 km/h; (V) 86 mph, 138 km/h; power-weight ratio: 1750, 30.2 lb/hp (41 lb/kW), 13.7 kg/hp (18.6 kg/kW); speed in 4th gear at 1,000 rpm: 16,8 mph, 27 km/h.

DIMENSIONS AND WEIGHT weight: 1750 2,170 lb, 984 kg - 1750 HL 2,183 lb, 990 kg.

BODY 1750 HL tinted glass (standard).

PRACTICAL INSTRUCTIONS tappet clearance: inlet 0.012 in, 0.30 mm, exhaust 0.012 in, 0.30 mm; valve timing: 9° 51° 49° 11°.

91 hp power team

See 68 hp power team, except for:

ENGINE 106.7 cu in, 1,748 cc (3 x 3.77 in, 76.2 x 95.7 mm); compression ratio: 9.5:1; max power (DIN): 91 hp (67 kW) at 5,250 rpm; max torque (DIN): 104 lb ft, 14.4 kg m (141 Nm) at 3,400 rpm; 52.1 hp/l (38.3 kW/l); 2 SU type HS6 twin barrel carburettors.

TRANSMISSION gearbox ratio: V 0.869; axle ratio: 3.647; tyres: 165 x 13.

PERFORMANCE max speeds: (I) 35 mph, 56 km/h; (II) 56 mph, 90 km/h; (III) 82 mph, 132 km/h; (IV) 98 mph, 158 km/h; (V) 96 mph, 155 km/h; power-weight ratio: 24 lb/hp (32.8 lb/kW), 10.9 kg/hp (14.9 kg/kW)); speed in top at 1,000 rpm: 19.9 mph, 32 km/h; consumption: 29.3 m/imp gal, 24.5 m/US gal, 9.6 l x 100 km at 75 mph, 120 km/h.

STEERING turns lock to lock: 4.20.

DIMENSIONS AND WEIGHT weight: 2,194 lb, 995 kg.

BODY tinted glass (standard).

PRACTICAL INSTRUCTIONS tappet clearances: inlet 0.012 in, 0.30 mm, exhaust 0.012 in, 0.30 mm; valve timing: 9° 51° 49° 11°.

OPTIONALS metallic spray.

AUSTIN Maxi 1750 HL Saloon

BENTLEY T2 Saloon

BENTLEY — GREAT BRITAIN

T2 Saloon

PRICE IN USA: $ 77,150*
PRICE EX WORKS: £ 36,652*

ENGINE front, 4 stroke; 8 cylinders, Vee-slanted; 411.9 cu in, 6,750 cc (4.10 x 3.90 in, 104.1 x 99.1 mm); compression ratio: 8:1; aluminium alloy block and head, cast iron wet liners; 5 crankshaft bearings; valves: overhead, in line, slanted, push-rods and rockers, hydraulic tappets; camshafts: 1, at centre of Vee; lubrication: gear pump, full flow filter (cartridge), 14.7 imp pt, 17.5 US pt, 8.3 l; 2 SU type HIF7 horizontal carburettors; dual exhaust system; fuel feed: 2 electric pumps; sealed circuit cooling, expansion tank, 28.5 imp pt, 34.2 US pt, 16.2 l, viscous coupling thermostatic fan.

TRANSMISSION driving wheels: rear; gearbox: Turbo-Hydramatic 400 automatic transmission, hydraulic torque converter and planetary gears with 3 ratios, max ratio of converter at stall 2, possible manual selection; ratios: I 2.500, II 1.500, III 1, rev 2; lever: steering column; final drive: hypoid bevel; axle ratio: 3.080; width of rims: 6"; tyres: 235/70 HR x 15.

PERFORMANCE max speeds: (I) 47 mph, 76 km/h; (II) 79 mph, 126 km/h; (III) 118 mph, 190 km/h; carrying capacity: 1,014 lb, 460 kg; speed in direct drive at 1,000 rpm: 26.2 mph, 42.2 km/h; consumption: 11.1 m/imp gal, 9.3 m/US gal, 25.4 l x 100 km (town) - 19.5 m/imp gal, 16.2 m/US gal, 14.5 l x 100 km at 56 mph, 90 km/h - 15.9 m/imp gal, 13.2 m/US gal, 17.8 l x 100 km at 75 mph, 120 km/h.

CHASSIS integral, front and rear auxiliary frames; front suspension: independent, lower wishbones, coil springs, anti-roll bar, telescopic dampers; rear: independent, semitrailing arms, coil springs, anti-roll bar, automatic levelling control, telescopic dampers.

STEERING rack-and-pinion, servo, right or left-hand drive; turns lock to lock: 3.20.

BRAKES disc (diameter 11 in, 27.9 cm), front internal radial fins, servo; swept area: front 227 sq in, 1,464 sq cm, rear 286 sq in, 1,845 sq cm, total 513 sq in, 3,309 sq cm.

ELECTRICAL EQUIPMENT 12 V; 68 Ah battery; 75 A alternator; Lucas transistorized distributor; 4 headlamps, 2 front and 2 rear fog lamps.

DIMENSIONS AND WEIGHT wheel base: 120.10 in, 305 cm; tracks: 60 in, 152 cm front, 59.60 in, 151 cm rear; length: 204,55 in, 520 cm; width: 72 in, 183 cm; height: 59.75 in, 152 cm; ground clearance 6.50 in, 16.5 cm; weight: 4,928 lb, 2,235 kg; turning circle: 38.5 ft, 11.7 m; fuel tank: 23.5 imp gal, 28.2 US gal, 107 l.

BODY saloon/sedan; 4 doors; 5 seats, separate front seats, adjustable and reclining backrests; automatic air-conditioning; heated rear window; electric windows; seat adjustment and gear range selector.

PRACTICAL INSTRUCTIONS fuel: 98 oct petrol; oil: engine 14.7 imp pt, 17.5 US pt, 8.3 l, SAE 20W-50, change every 6,000 miles, 9,700 km - automatic transmission 18.6 imp pt, 22.4 US pt, 10.6 l, Dexron, change every 24,000 miles, 38,600 km - final drive 4.5 imp pt, 5.3 US pt, 2.5 l, SAE 90 EP, change every 24,000 miles, 38,600 km - power steering and automatic levelling control change every 20,000 miles, 32,000 km; greasing: every 12,000 miles, 19,300 km, 5 points; valve timing: 26° 60° 68° 18°; tyre pressure: front 24 psi, 1.7 atm, rear 28 psi, 2 atm.

OPTIONALS iodine headlamps; headrests; Everflex roof.

VARIATIONS

(For USA, Japan and Australia only)
ENGINE 7.3:1 compression ratio, catalytic converter; Pierbur fuel pump (except for Japan).

Corniche Saloon

See T2 Saloon, except for:

PRICE IN USA: $ 130,990*
PRICE EX WORKS: £ 53,322*

ENGINE 1 Solex 4A1 4-barrel carburettor; fuel feed: Pierburg pump.

CHASSIS rear suspension: independent, coil springs, semi-trailing arms, struts, anti-roll bar, automatic ride height control.

DIMENSIONS AND WEIGHT width: 71.65 in, 182 cm; height 58.75 in, 149 cm; ground clearance: 6 in, 15.2 cm; weight 5,045 lb, 2,288 kg.

ELECTRICAL EQUIPMENT 55 A alternator.

BODY 2 doors; 4 seats.

BRISTOL 603 S2

Corniche Convertible

See T2 Saloon, except for:

PRICE IN USA: $ 139,500*
PRICE EX WORKS: £ 56,636*

ENGINE 1 Solex 4A1 4-barrel carburettor; fuel feed: Pierburg pump.

CHASSIS rear suspension: independent, coil springs, semi-trailing arms, struts, anti-roll bar, automatic ride height control.

DIMENSIONS AND WEIGHT width: 71.65 in, 182 cm; ground clearance: 6 in, 15.2 cm; weight: 5,204 lb, 2,360 kg.

ELECTRICAL EQUIPMENT 55 A alternator.

BODY convertible; 2 doors; 4 seats.

BRISTOL GREAT BRITAIN

603 S2

PRICE EX WORKS: £ 34,481*

ENGINE Chrysler, front, 4 stroke; 8 cylinders, Vee-slanted; 360 cu in, 5,900 cc (4 x 3.58 in, 101.6 x 90.9 mm); compression ratio: 8:1; cast iron block and head; 5 crankshaft bearings; valves: overhead, hydraulic tappets, push-rods and rockers; camshafts: 1, at centre of Vee, chain driven; lubrication: rotary pump, full flow filter, 8.4 imp pt, 10.1 US pt, 4.8 l; 1 Carter downdraught 4-barrel carburettor; fuel feed: mechanical pump; water-cooled, 29 imp pt, 34.9 US pt, 16.5 l, 2 electric thermostatic fans.

TRANSMISSION driving wheels: rear; gearbox: Torqueflite automatic transmission, hydraulic torque converter and planetary gears with 3 ratios, max ratio of converter at stall 2.2, possible manual selection; ratios: I 2.450, II 1.450, III 1, rev 2.200; lever: central; final drive: hypoid bevel, limited slip differential; axle ratio: 2.880; width of rims: 6"; tyres: 205 VR X 15.

PERFORMANCE max speeds: (I) 54 mph, 87 km/h; (II) 92 mph, 148 km/h; (III) 132 mph, 212 km/h; speed in direct drive at 1,000 rpm: 28.4 mph, 45.7 km/h; consumption: 21 m/imp gal, 17.6 m/US gal, 13.4 l x 100 km at 56 mph, 90 km/h.

CHASSIS box-type ladder frame with cross members; front suspension: independent, wishbones, coil springs, anti-roll bar, adjustable telescopic dampers; rear: rigid axle, longitudinal torsion bars, trailing lower radius arms, upper torque link, transverse Watt linkage, automatic levelling control, adjustable telescopic dampers.

STEERING recirculating ball, servo; turns lock to lock: 3.

BRAKES disc (front diameter 10.91 in, 27.7 cm, rear 10.60 in, 26.9 cm), dual circuit, servo; swept area: front 224 sq in, 1,445 sq cm, rear 196 sq in, 1,264 sq cm, total 420 sq in, 2,709 sq cm.

ELECTRICAL EQUIPMENT 12 V; 71 Ah battery; 65 A alternator; Chrysler electronic ignition; 4 headlamps.

BRISTOL 412 S2

DIMENSIONS AND WEIGHT wheel base: 114 in, 290 cm; tracks: 54.50 in, 138 cm front, 55 in, 139 cm rear; length: 193 in, 491 cm; width: 69.50 in, 177 cm; height 56.65 in, 144 cm; ground clearance: 5 in, 13 cm; weight: 3,951 lb, 1,792 kg; weight distribution: 53% front, 47% rear; turning circle: 39.4 ft, 12 m; fuel tank: 18 imp gal, 21.6 US gal, 82 l.

BODY saloon/sedan; 2 doors; 4 seats, reclining backrests, detachable headrests front and rear; leather upholstery; electric windows; heated rear window; air-conditioning; electric seats; laminated windscreen.

PRACTICAL INSTRUCTIONS fuel: 91 oct petrol; oil: engine 8.4 imp pt, 10.1 US pt, 4.8 l, SAE 20W-50, change every 3,100 miles, 5,000 km - gearbox 13.9 imp pt, 16.7 US pt, 7.9 l, Dexron II, change every 20,000 miles, 32,000 km - final drive 3.5 imp pt, 4.2 US pt, 2 l, change every 20,000 miles, 32,000 km; greasing: every 20,000 miles, 32,000 km, 4 points; valve timing: 18° 54° 57° 15°; tyre pressure: front 28 psi, 2 atm, rear 28 psi, 2 atm.

OPTIONALS light alloy wheels; 3.070 axle ratio.

VARIATIONS

ENGINE Chrysler, 318 cu in, 5,211 cc (3.91 x 3.31 in, 99.3 x 84.1 mm), 8.5:1 compression ratio, 1 Carter downdraught twin barrel carburettor.
PERFORMANCE max speed about 118 mph, 190 km/h.

412 S2

See 603 S2, except for:

PRICE EX WORKS: £ 31,161*

ELECTRICAL EQUIPMENT 2 headlamps.

DIMENSIONS AND WEIGHT length: 192.50 in, 490 cm; weight: 3,859 lb, 1,750 kg.

BODY convertible.

OPTIONALS air-conditioning; electric seats.

CATERHAM CARS GREAT BRITAIN

Super 7

PRICE EX WORKS: £ 5,098*

ENGINE Lotus front, 4 stroke; 4 cylinders, vertical, in line; 97.6 cu in, 1,599 cc (3.19 x 3.06 in, 81 x 77.6 mm); compression ratio: 9.5:1; max power (DIN): 120 hp (88 kW) at 6,200 rpm; max torque (DIN): 106 lb ft, 14,6 kg m (143 Nm) at 5,500 rpm; max engine rpm: 6,500; 75 hp/l (55.2 kW/l); cast iron block, light alloy head; 5 crankshaft bearings; valves: overhead, Vee-slanted, thimble tappets; camshafts: 2, overhead; lubrication: rotary pump, full flow filter by cartridge, 7.5 imp pt, 8.9 US pt, 4.2 l; 2 Dell'Orto 40 DHLA twin barrel carburettors; fuel feed: mechanical pump; water-cooled, 12 imp pt, 14.4 US pt, 6.8 l.

CATERHAM CARS Super 7

SUPER 7

TRANSMISSION driving wheels: rear; clutch: single dry plate (diaphragm), hydraulically controlled; gearbox: mechanical; gears: 4, fully synchronized; ratios: I 2.972, II 2.010, III 1.400, IV 1, rev 3.325; lever: central; final drive: hypoid bevel; axle ratio: 3.540; width of rims: 5.5"; tyres: 165 SR x 13.

PERFORMANCE max speeds: (I) 42 mph, 68 km/h; (II) 62 mph, 100 km/h, 100 km/h; (III) 89 mph, 143 km/h; (IV) 112 mph, 180 km/h; power-weight ratio: 9.9 lb/hp (13.7 lb/kW), 4.5 kg/hp (6.2 kg/kW); carrying capacity: 450 lb, 204 kg; acceleration: standing ¼ mile 14.6 sec, 0-50 mph (0-80 km/h) 4.4 sec; speed in direct drive at 1,000 rpm: 19.1 mph, 30.7 km/h; consumption: 25 m/imp gal, 20.8 m/US gal, 11.3 l x 100 km.

CHASSIS tubular space-frame with aluminium panels; front suspension: independent, lower wishbones, anti-roll bar, coil springs/telescopic dampers units; rear: rigid axle, twin trailing radius arms, A-bracket, coil spring/telescopic dampers units.

STEERING rack-and-pinion; turns lock to lock: 2.75.

BRAKES front disc, rear drum; swept area: total 242 sq in, 1,561 sq cm.

ELECTRICAL EQUIPMENT 12 V; 39 Ah battery; dynamo; Lucas distributor; 2 headlamps.

DIMENSIONS AND WEIGHT wheel base: 88 in, 223 cm; tracks: 49 in, 124 cm front, 51.50 in, 131 cm rear; length: 133 in, 338 cm; width: 65.50 in, 159 cm; height: 43.50 in, 110 cm; ground clearance: 4 in, 10 cm; weight: 1,200 lb, 544 kg; turning circle: 29.6 ft, 9 m; fuel tank: 8 imp gal, 9.5 US gal, 36 l.

BODY sports; no doors; 2 seats.

PRACTICAL INSTRUCTIONS fuel: 97 oct petrol; oil: engine 6.5 imp pt, 7.8 US pt, 3.7 l, SAE 20W-50, change every 6,000 miles, 9,700 km - gearbox 2 imp pt, 2.3 US pt, 1.1 l, SAE 80 EP, no change recommended - final drive 2 imp pt, 2.3 US pt, 1.1 l, SAE 90 EP, no change recommended; greasing: every 6,000 miles, 9,700 km, 5 points; tappet clearances: inlet 0.005-0.007 in, 0.12-0.17 mm, exhaust 0.009-0.011 in , 0.22-0.27 mm; valve timing: 26° 66° 66° 26°; tyre pressure: front 20 psi, 1.4 atm, rear 20 psi, 1.4 atm.

DAIMLER GREAT BRITAIN

Sovereign 4.2

PRICE EX WORKS: £ 15,387*

ENGINE front, 4 stroke; 6 cylinders, vertical, in line; 258.4 cu in, 4,235 cc (3.63 x 4.17 in, 92 x 106 mm); compression ratio: 8.7:1; max power (DIN): 205 hp (151 kW) at 5,000 rpm; max torque (DIN): 232 lb ft, 32 kg m (314 Nm) at 1,500 rpm; max engine rpm: 5,500; 48.4 hp/l (35.6 kW/l); cast iron block dry liners, light alloy head, hemispherical combustion chambers; 7 crankshaft bearings; valves: overhead, Vee-slanted, thimble tappets; camshafts: 2, overhead; lubrication: rotary pump, full flow filter, oil cooler, 14.5 imp pt, 17.3 US pt, 8.2 l; Lucas electronic injection; fuel feed: electric pump; water-cooled, 32.5 imp pt, 38.9 US pt, 18.4 l, viscous coupling thermostatic fan.

TRANSMISSION driving wheels: rear; gearbox: Borg-Warner 66 automatic transmission, hydraulic torque converter and planetary gears with 3 ratios, max ratio of converter at stall 2, possible manual selection; ratios: I 2.390, II 1.450, III 1, rev 2.090; lever: central; final drive: hypoid bevel; axle ratio: 3.310; width of rims: 6"; tyres: E 70 VR x 15.

PERFORMANCE max speeds: (I) 49 mph, 79 km/h; (II) 81 mph, 130 km/h; (III) 118 mph, 190 km/h; power-weight ratio: 19.2 lb/hp (26.2 lb/kW), 8.7 kg/hp (11.9 kg/kW); carrying capacity: 904 lb, 410 kg; acceleration: standing ¼ mile 17.5 sec; speed in direct drive at 1,000 rpm: 22.9 mph, 36.8 km/h; consumption: 15.3 m/imp. gal, 12.7 m/US gal, 18.5 l x 100 km.

CHASSIS integral, front and rear auxiliary frames; front suspension: independent, wishbones, coil springs, anti-roll bar, telescopic dampers; rear: independent, lower wishbones, semi-axles as upper arms, trailing lower radius arms, 4 coil springs, 4 telescopic dampers.

STEERING rack-and-pinion, adjustable steering wheel, servo; turns lock to lock: 3.30.

BRAKES disc (front diameter 11.18 in, 28.4 cm, rear 10.38 in, 26.4 cm), front internal radial fins, servo; swept area: front 234.5 sq in, 1,512 sq cm, rear 213.7 sq in, 1,378 sq cm, total 448.2 sq in, 2,890 sq cm.

ELECTRICAL EQUIPMENT 12 V; 66 Ah battery: 45 A alternator; Lucas distributor; 4 headlamps, halogen and fog headlamps.

DIMENSIONS AND WEIGHT wheel base: 112.80 in, 286 cm; tracks: 57.99 in, 147 cm front, 58.58 in, 149 cm rear; length: 195.20 in, 496 cm; width: 69.68 in, 177 cm; height: 54 in, 137 cm; ground clearance: 7.09 in, 18 cm; weight 3,947 lb, 1,790 kg; turning circle: 40 ft, 12.2 m; fuel tank: 20 imp gal, 24 US gal, 91 l (2 separate tanks).

BODY saloon/sedan; 4 doors; 5 seats, separate front seats, reclining backrests, headrests; heated rear window; electric windows; tinted glass.

PRACTICAL INSTRUCTIONS fuel: 97 oct petrol; oil: engine 14.5 imp pt, 17.3 US pt, 8.2 l, SAE 20W-50, change every 6,000 miles, 9,700 km - gearbox 4.5 imp pt, 6.3 US pt, 2.5 l, SAE 90 EP, change every 12,000 miles, 19.400 km - final drive 2.7 imp pt, 3.2 US pt, 1.5 l, SAE 90 EP, change every 12,000 miles, 19,400 km; greasing: every 6,000 miles, 9,700 km, 17 points; tappet clearances: inlet 0.012-0.014 in, 0.30-0.35 mm, exhaust 0.012-0.014 in, 0.30-0.35 mm; tyre pressure: front 25 psi, 1.7 atm, rear 26 psi, 1.8 atm.

OPTIONALS 5-speed fully synchronized mechanical gearbox (I 3.321, II 2.087, III 1.396, IV 1, V 0.833, rev 3.428) max speed 121 mph, 195 km/h, acceleration standing ¼ mile 16.4 sec, consumption 16 m/imp gal, 13.4 gal, 13.4 m/US gal, 17.6 l x 100 km; limited slip differential; air-conditioning; light alloy wheels.

Vanden Plas 4.2

See Sovereign 4.2, except for:

PRICE EX WORKS: £ 20,394*

PERFORMANCE power-weight ratio: 23.1 lb/hp (31.5 lb/kW), 10.5 kg/hp (14.3 kg/kW).

DIMENSIONS AND WEIGHT weight: 4,763 lb, 2,160 kg.

BODY air-conditioning (standard).

Double-Six 5.3

PRICE EX WORKS: £ 18,417*

ENGINE front, 4 stroke; 12 cylinders, Vee-slanted at 60°; 326 cu in, 5,343 cc (3.54 x 2.76 in, 90 x 70 mm); compression ratio: 10:1; max power (DIN): 295 hp (217 kW) at 5,500 rpm; max torque (DIN): 294 lb ft, 40.7 kg m (399 Nm) at 3,500 rpm; max engine rpm: 6,500; 55.2 hp/l (40.6 kW/l); light alloy block and head, wet liners; 7 crankshaft bearings; valves: overhead, in line, thimble tappets; camshafts 2, 1 per bank, overhead; lubrication: rotary pump, full flow filter, oil cooler, 19 imp pt, 22.8 US pt, 10.8 l; Lucas-Bosch electronic injection; fuel feed electronic pump; water-cooled, 36 imp pt, 43.3 US pt, 20.5 l, 1 viscous coupling thermostatic and 1 electric thermostatic fans.

TRANSMISSION driving wheels: rear; gearbox: Turbo-Hydramatic 400 automatic transmission, hydraulic torque converter and planetary gears with 3 ratios, max ratio of converter at stall 2, possible manual selection; ratios: I 2.480, II 1.480, III 1, rev 2.070; lever: central; final drive: hypoid bevel, limited slip differential; axle ratio: 3.070; width of rims: 6"; tyres: 205/70 VR x 15.

PERFORMANCE max speeds: (I) 58 mph, 94 km/h; (II) 96 mph, 155 km/h; (III) 140 mph, 225 km/h; power-weight ratio: 14.1 lb/hp (19.2 lb/kW), 6.4 kg/hp (8.7 kg/kW); carrying capacity: 904 lb, 410 kg; acceleration: standing ¼ mile 15.7 sec, 0-50 mph (0-80 km/h) 6.1 sec; speed in direct drive at 1,000 rpm

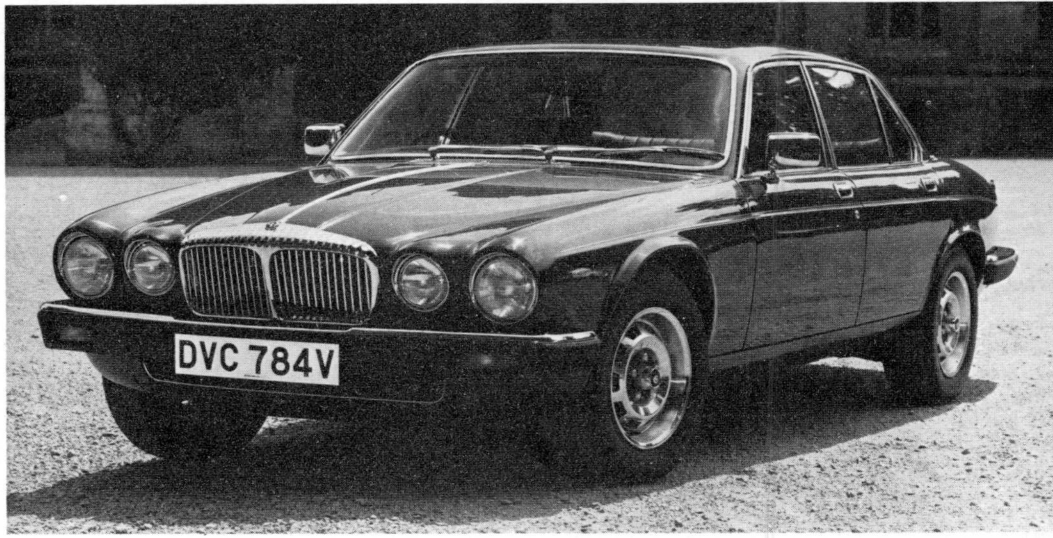

DAIMLER Sovereign 4.2

DAIMLER Double-Six 5.3

24.6 mph, 39.6 km/h; consumption: 14.1 m/imp gal, 11.8 m/US gal, 20 l x 100 km.

CHASSIS integral, front and rear auxiliary frames; front suspension: independent, wishbones, coil springs, anti-roll bar, telescopic dampers; rear: independent, wishbones, semi-axle as upper arms, trailing lower radius arms, 4 coil springs, 4 telescopic dampers.

STEERING rack-and-pinion, adjustable steering wheel, servo; turns lock to lock: 3.30.

BRAKES disc (front diameter 11.18 in, 28.4 cm rear 10.38 in, 26.4 cm), front internal radial fins, servo; swept area: front 234.5 sq in, 1,512 sq cm, rear 213.7 sq in, 1,378 sq cm, total 448.2 sq in, 2,890 sq cm.

ELECTRICAL EQUIPMENT 12 V; 68 Ah battery; 60 A alternator; Lucas electronic distributor; 4 headlamps, halogen and fog headlamps.

DIMENSIONS AND WEIGHT wheel base: 112.80 in, 286 cm; tracks: 57.99 in, 147 cm front, 58.58 in, 149 cm rear; length: 194.68 in, 494 cm; width: 69.68 in, 177 cm; height: 54.13 in, 137 cm; ground clearance: 7.09 in, 18 cm; weight: 4,156 lb, 1,885 kg; turning circle: 40 ft, 12.2 m; fuel tank: 20 imp gal, 24 US gal, 91 l (2 separate tanks).

BODY saloon/sedan; 4 doors; 5 seats, separate front seats, reclining backrests with built-in headrests; heated rear window; electric windows.

PRACTICAL INSTRUCTIONS fuel: 97 oct petrol; oil: engine 19 imp pt, 22.8 US pt, 10.8 l, SAE 10W-40 (winter) 20W-50 (summer), change every 6,000 miles, 9.700 km; final drive 2.7 imp pt, 3.2 US pt, 1.5 l, SAE 90 EP, change every 12,000 miles, 19.400 km; greasing: every 6,000 miles, 9,700 km, 17 points; tappet clearances: inlet 0.012-0.014 in, 0.30-0.35 mm, exhaust 0.012-0.014 in, 0.30-0.35 mm; tyre pressure: front 25 psi, 1.7 atm, rear 26 psi, 1.8 atm.

OPTIONALS air-conditioning; light alloy wheels.

Double-Six Vanden Plas 5.3

See Double-Six 5.3, except for:

PRICE EX WORKS: £ 23,805*

PERFORMANCE power-weight ratio: 13.9 lb/hp (19 lb/kW), 6.3 kg/hp (8.6 kg/kW).

DIMENSIONS AND WEIGHT weight: 4,116 lb, 1,866 kg.

BODY luxury equipment; air-conditioning (standard).

Limousine

PRICE EX WORKS: £ 22,213*

ENGINE front, 4 stroke; 6 cylinders, vertical, in line; 258.4 cu in, 4,235 cc (3.63 x 4.17 in, 92.1 x 106 mm); compression ratio: 7.5:1; max power (DIN): 162 hp (119 kW) at 4,250 rpm; max torque (DIN): 222 lb ft, 30.7 kg m (301 Nm) at 3,000 rpm; max engine rpm: 5,500; 38.2 hp/l (28.1 kW/l); cast iron block, dry liners, light alloy head, hemispherical combustion chambers; 7 crankshaft bearings; valves: overhead, Vee-slanted at 70°, thimble tappets; camshafts: 2, overhead; lubrication: mechanical pump, full flow filter, 12 imp pt, 14.4 US pt, 6.8 l; 2 SU type HIF 7 horizontal carburettors; fuel feed: 2 electric pumps; water-cooled, 25.5 imp pt, 30.7 US pt, 14.5 l, viscous coupling thermostatic fan.

DAIMLER Limousine

TRANSMISSION driving wheels: rear; gearbox: Borg-Warner automatic transmission, hydraulic torque converter and planetary gears with 3 ratios, max ratio of converter at stall 2, possible manual selection; ratios: I 2.401, II 1.458, III 1, rev 2; lever: steering column; final drive: hypoid bevel; axle ratio: 3.540; tyres: 205/70 HR x 15.

PERFORMANCE max speeds: (I) 48 mph, 78 km/h; (II) 79 mph, 127 km/h; (III) 115 mph, 185 km/h; power-weight ratio: 29 lb/hp (39.7 lb/kW), 13.2 kg/hp (17.9 kg/kW); carrying capacity: 1,235 lb, 560 kg; acceleration: standing ¼ mile 19.5 sec; speed in direct drive at 1,000 rpm: 20.9 mph, 33.6 km/h; consumption: 17.6 m/imp gal, 14.7 m/US gal, 16 l x 100 km.

CHASSIS integral, front and rear auxiliary frames; front suspension: independent, wishbones, coil springs, anti-roll bar, telescopic dampers; rear: independent, wishbones, semi-axle as upper arm, trailing lower radius arms, 4 coil springs, 4 telescopic dampers.

STEERING recirculating ball, adjustable steering wheel, variable ratio gearing, servo; turns lock to lock: 2.75.

BRAKES disc (front diameter 11.18 in, 28.4 cm, rear 10.38 in, 26.4 cm), internal radial fins, servo; swept area: front 234 sq in, 1,509 sq cm, rear 212 sq in, 1,367 sq cm, total 446 sq in, 2,876 sq cm.

ELECTRICAL EQUIPMENT 12 V; 60 Ah battery; 45 A alternator; Lucas distributor; 4 headlamps, halogen headlamps.

DIMENSIONS AND WEIGHT wheel base: 141 in, 358 cm; front and rear track: 58 in, 147 cm; length: 226 in, 574 cm; width: 77.56 in, 197 cm; height: 63.39 in, 161 cm; ground clearance: 7.09 in, 18 cm; weight: 4,705 lb, 2,134 kg; turning circle: 46 ft, 14 m; fuel tank: 20 imp gal, 24 US gal, 91 l (2 separate tanks).

BODY limousine; 4 doors; 8 seats, bench front seats; glass partition.

PRACTICAL INSTRUCTIONS fuel: 97 oct petrol; oil: engine 12 imp pt, 14.4 US pt, 6.8 l, multigrade, change every 3,000 miles, 5,000 km; tappet clearances: inlet 0.012-0.014 in, 0.31-0.36 mm, exhaust 0.012-0.014 in, 0.31-0.36 mm.

OPTIONALS air-conditioning; electric glass partition; electric windows; tinted glass; heated rear window.

DUTTON GREAT BRITAIN

Phaeton

ENGINE Ford Cortina 1600, front, 4 stroke; 4 cylinders, vertical, in line; 97.2 cu in, 1,593 cc (3.45 x 2.60 in, 87.6 x 66 mm); compression ratio: 9:1; max power (DIN): 72 hp (53 kW) at 5,500 rpm; max torque (DIN): 87 lb ft, 12 kg m (118 Nm) at 3,000 rpm; max engine rpm: 6,000; 45.2 hp/l (33.3 kW/l); cast iron block and head; 5 crankshaft bearings; valves: overhead; camshafts: 1, overhead; lubrication: rotary pump, full flow filter, 6 imp pt, 7.2 US pt, 3.4 l; 1 Weber downdraught twin barrel carburettor; fuel feed: mechanical pump; water-cooled, 11.4 imp pt, 13.7 US pt, 6.5 l.

TRANSMISSION driving wheels: rear; clutch: single dry plate (diaphragm); gearbox: mechanical; gears: 4, fully synchronized; ratios: I 3.580, II 2.010, III 1.400, IV 1, rev 3.320; lever: central; final drive: hypoid bevel; axle ratio: 3.700; width of rims: 5.5" or 6".

PERFORMANCE power-weight ratio: 15.6 lb/hp (21.2 lb/kW), 7.1 kg/hp (9.6 kg/kW); consumption: 31 m/imp gal, 25.8 m/US gal, 9.1 l x 100 km.

CHASSIS multi-tubular space frame; front suspension: independent, radius arm, Panhard rods, lower wishbones, coil springs/telescopic damper units, anti-roll bar; rear: rigid axle, twin trailing radius arms, A-bracket, coil springs/telescopic damper units.

STEERING rack-and-pinion; turns lock to lock: 3.50.

BRAKES front disc, rear drum.

ELECTRICAL EQUIPMENT 12 V; 2 headlamps.

DIMENSIONS AND WEIGHT wheel base: 86 in, 218 cm; front and rear track: 52 in, 132 cm; length: 139 in, 353 cm; width: 61 in, 155 cm; height: 42 in, 107 cm; ground clearance: 6 in, 15 cm; weight: about 1,125 lb, 510 kg.

BODY open, in plastic material; 2 bucket seats; 2 side screens; laminated windscreen; integral roll bar.

DUTTON Phaeton

PHAETON

VARIATIONS

ENGINE Ford Capri II 3000, 6 cylinders, Vee-slanted at 60°, 182.7 cu in, 2,994 cc (3.69 x 2.85 in, 93.7 x 72.4 mm), max power (DIN) 142 HP (104 kW) at 5,100 rpm, max torque (DIN) 174 lb ft, 24 kg m (235 Nm) at 3,000 rpm, 47.4 hp/l (34.9 kW/l).
PERFORMANCE power-weight ratio 7.9 lb/hp (10.8 lb/kW), 3.6 kg/hp (4.9 kg/kW).

OPTIONALS electric sunshine roof.

FAIRTHORPE GREAT BRITAIN

TX-S 1500

PRICE EX WORKS: £ 5,965*

ENGINE front, 4 stroke; 4 cylinders, in line; 91.1 cu in, 1,493 cc (2.90 x 3.44 in, 73.7 x 87.5 mm); compression ratio: 9.5:1; max power (SAE): 71 hp (52 kW) at 5,000 rpm; max torque (SAE): 82 lb ft, 11.3 kg m (111 Nm) at 3,000 rpm; max engine rpm: 6,000; 47.6 hp/l (35 kW/l); cast iron block and head; 5 crankshaft bearings; valves: overhead, in line, push-rods and rockers; camshafts: 1, side; lubrication: gear pump, full flow filter, 8 imp pt, 9.5 US pt, 4.5 l; 2 SU type HS 4 semi-downdraught carburettors; fuel feed: mechanical pump; water-cooled, 6 imp pt, 7.2 US pt, 3.4 l.

TRANSMISSION driving wheels: rear; clutch: single dry plate (diaphragm), hydraulically controlled; gearbox: mechanical; gears: 4, fully synchronized; ratios: I 3.500, II 2.160, III 1.390, IV 1, rev 3.990; lever: central; final drive: hypoid bevel; axle ratio: 3.890; width of rims: 5"; tyres: 165 SR x 13.

PERFORMANCE max speed: 105 mph, 169 km/h; power-weight ratio: 21.3 lb/hp (28.9 lb/kW), 9.6 kg/hp (13.1 kg/kW); carrying capacity: 672 lb, 304 kg; speed in direct drive at 1,000 rpm: 17.2 mph, 27.7 km/h; consumption: 33 m/imp gal, 27.7 m/US gal, 8.5 l x 100 km.

CHASSIS double backbone, box section with outriggers; front suspension: independent, wishbones, coil springs, telescopic dampers; rear: independent, wishbones, transverse leafspring as upper arms, lower trailing links, telescopic dampers.

STEERING rack-and-pinion; turns lock to lock: 3.50.

BRAKES front disc (diameter 9 in, 22.3 cm), rear drum; swept area: front 197 sq in, 1,270 sq cm, rear 63 sq in, 406 sq cm, total 260 sq in, 1,676 sq cm.

ELECTRICAL EQUIPMENT 12 V; 52 Ah battery; 17 A alternator; Lucas distributor; 2 headlamps.

DIMENSIONS AND WEIGHT wheel base: 83 in, 211 cm; front and rear track: 49.50 in, 126 cm; length: 146.46 in, 372 cm; width: 58 in, 147 cm; height: 44.49 in, 113 cm; ground clearance: 5 in, 12,7 cm; weight: 1,512 lb, 685 kg; turning circle: 25.3 ft, 7.7 m; fuel tank: 9.7 imp gal, 11.6 US gal, 44 l.

BODY coupé, in reinforced plastic material; 2 doors; 2 seats.

PRACTICAL INSTRUCTIONS fuel: 97 oct petrol; oil: engine 6.5 imp pt, 7.8 US pt, 3.7 l, SAE 20W-30, change every 6,000 miles, 9,700 km - gearbox 1.4 imp pt, 1.7 US pt, 0.8 l, SAE 90, no change recommended - final drive 1.6 imp pt, 1.9 US pt, 0.9 l, SAE 90, no change recommended; greasing: every 6,000 miles, 9,700 km, 3 points; tappet clearances: inlet 0.010 in, 0,25 mm, exhaust 0.010 in, 0.25 mm; valve timing: 18° 58° 58° 18°; tyre pressure: front 23 psi, 1.6 atm, rear 23 psi, 1.6 atm.

TX-S 2000

See TX-S 1500, except for:

ENGINE 121.9 cu in, 1,998 cc (3.56 x 3.07 in, 90.3 x 78 mm); maw power (SAE): 127 hp (93 kW) at 5,700 rpm; max torque (SAE): 122 lb ft, 16.8 kg m (165 Nm) at 4,500 rpm; 63.6 hp/l (46.8 kW/l); cast iron block, light alloy head; valves: overhead, in line, thimble tappets; camshafts: 1, overhead; 2 Stromberg 175 CD SEV horizontal carburettors; cooling: 12.8 imp pt, 15,4 US pt, 7.3 l.

PERFORMANCE max speed: 118 mph, 190 km/h; power-weight ratio: 12.8 lb/hp (17.4 lb/kW), 5.8 kg/hp (7.9 kg/kW); carrying capacity: 728 lb, 330 kg; speed in direct drive at 1,000 rpm: 19.7 mph, 31.7 km/h; consumption: 24 m/imp gal, 19.9 m/US gal, 11.8 l x 100 km.

DIMENSIONS AND WEIGHT weight: 1,624 lb, 736 kg.

PRACTICAL INSTRUCTIONS tappet clearances: inlet 0.008 in, 0.20 mm, exhaust 0.008 in, 0.20 mm; valve timing: 16° 56° 56° 16°

FAIRTHORPE TX-S 1500 - 2000

FORD GREAT BRITAIN

Fiesta Series

PRICES EX WORKS:	£
1 Saloon	**2,840***
2 L Saloon	**3,148***
3 S Saloon	**3,648***
4 Ghia Saloon	**3,971***

Power team:	Standard for:	Optional for:
40 hp	1	—
45 hp	2	—
53 hp	3,4	1,2
66 hp	—	3,4

40 hp power team

ENGINE front, transverse, 4 stroke; 4 cylinders, vertical, in line; 58.4 cu in, 957 cc (2.91 x 2.19 in, 74 x 55.7 mm); compression ratio: 8.3:1; max power (DIN): 40 hp (29 kW) at 5,500 rpm; max torque (DIN): 47 lb ft, 6.5 kg m (64 Nm) at 2,700 rpm; max engine rpm: 5,700; 41,8 hp/l (30.7 kW/l); cast iron block and head; 3 crankshaft bearings; valves: overhead, in line, push-rods and rockers; camshafts: 1, side, chain-driven; lubrication: gear pump, full flow filter (cartridge), 6.2 imp pt, 7.4 US pt, 3.5 l; 1 Ford downdraught single barrel carburettor; fuel feed: mechanical pump; semi-sealed circuit cooling, expansion tank, 8.8 imp pt, 10.6 US pt, 5 l, electric fan.

TRANSMISSION driving wheels: front; clutch: single dry plate (diaphragm); gearbox: mechanical, in unit with final drive; gears: 4, fully synchronized; ratios: I 3.583, II 2.050, III 1.346, IV 0.959, rev 3.769; lever: central; final drive: spiral bevel; axle ratio: 4.060; width of rims: 4", tyres: 135 SR x 12.

PERFORMANCE max speed: 81 mph, 130 km/h; power-weight ratio: 38.6 lb/hp (52.5 lb/kW), 17.5 kg/hp (23.8 kg/kW); carrying capacity: 948 lb, 430 kg; acceleration: 0-50 mph (0-80 km/h) 14.2 sec; speed in top at 1,000 rpm: 15.8 mph, 25.4 km/h; consumption: 35.8 m/imp gal, 29.8 m/US gal, 7,9 l x 100 km at 75 mph, 120 km/h .

CHASSIS integral; front suspension: independent, by McPherson, coil springs/telescopic damper struts, lower wishbones (trailing links); rear: rigid axle, swinging longitudinal trailing arms, upper oblique torque arms, Panhard rod, coil springs, telescopic dampers.

STEERING rack-and-pinion; turns lock to lock: 3.40.

BRAKES front disc (diameter 8.71 in, 22.1 cm), rear drum, dual circuit, rear compensator; lining area: front 18.6 sq in, 120 sq cm, rear 26.4 sq in, 169.9 sq cm, total 45 sq in, 289.9 sq cm.

ELECTRICAL EQUIPMENT 12 V; 35 Ah battery; 45 A alternator; Motorcraft distributor; 2 headlamps.

FORD Fiesta S Saloon

IMENSIONS AND WEIGHT wheel base: 90.16 in, 229 cm; acks: 52.36 in, 133 cm front, 51.97 in, 132 cm rear; length: 40.16 in, 356 cm; width: 61.81 in, 157 cm; height: 53.54 in, 36 cm; weight: ground clearance: 5.51 in, 14 cm; weight: 544 lb, 700 kg; turning circle: 32.1 ft, 9.8 m; fuel tank: 7.5 imp al, 9 US gal, 34 l.

ODY saloon/sedan; 2+1 doors; 5 seats, separate front seats; lding rear seat.

RACTICAL INSTRUCTIONS fuel: 90 oct petrol; oil: engine 4.8 np pt, 5.7 US pt, 2.7 l, change every 6,200 miles, 10.000 km - earbox and final drive 3.9 imp pt, 4.7 US pt, 2.2 l, change very 6,200 miles, 10.000 km; valve timing: 21° 55° 70° 22°.

PTIONALS 155 SR x 12 tyres with 4.5" wide rims; servo rake; headrests on front seats; tinted glass; light alloy wheels; unshine roof; rear window wiper-washer; headlamp washers; alogen headlamps; fog lamps; metallic spray; Touring equipment.

45 hp power team

ee 40 hp power team, except for:

NGINE compression ratio: 9:1; max power (DIN): 45 hp (33 V) at 6,000 rpm; max torque (DIN): 48 lb ft, 6.6 kg m (65 Nm) 3,300 rpm; max engine rpm: 6,500; 47 hp/l (34.6 kW/l).

RANSMISSION axle ratio: 4.290; tyres: 145 SR x 12.

ERFORMANCE max speed: 85 mph, 137 km/h; power-weight tio: 34.3 lb/hp (46.6 lb/kW), 15.6 kg/hp (21.1 kg/kW); speed in p at 1,000 rpm: 14.9 mph, 24 km/h; consumption: 34.4 m/imp al, 28.7 m/US gal, 8.2 l x 100 km at 75 mph, 120 km/h.

RACTICAL INSTRUCTIONS fuel: 97 oct petrol.

53 hp power team

ee 40 hp power team, except for:

NGINE 68.2 cu in, 1,117 cc (2,91 x 2.56 in, 74 x 65 mm); ompression ratio: 9:1; max power (DIN): 53 hp (39 kW) at 700 rpm; max torque (DIN): 59 lb ft, 8.2 kg m (80 Nm) at 000 rpm; max engine rpm: 6,000; 47.4 hp/l (34.9 kW/l); ectric thermostatic fan.

RANSMISSION width of rims: 4.5".

ERFORMANCE max speed: 90 mph, 145 km/h; power-weight tio: S 30.1 lb/hp (40.9 lb/kW), 13.6 kg/hp (18.5 kg/kW) - Ghia 0.4 lb/hp (41.2 lb/kW), 13.8 kg/hp (18.7 kg/kW); consumption: 2.1 m/imp gal, 26.7 m/US gal, 8.8 l x 100 km at 75 mph, 120 m/h.

HASSIS rear suspension: anti-roll bar.

RAKES servo (standard).

IMENSIONS AND WEIGHT weight: S 1,594 lb, 723 kg - Ghia ,610 lb, 730 kg.

ODY Ghia light alloy wheels.

RACTICAL INSTRUCTIONS fuel: 97 oct petrol.

FORD Fiesta S Saloon

FORD Fiesta L Saloon

66 hp power team

See 40 hp power team, except for:

ENGINE 79.2 cu in, 1,298 cc (3.19 x 2.48 in, 81 x 63 mm); compression ratio: 9.2:1; max power (DIN): 66 hp (49 kW) at 5,600 rpm; max torque (DIN): 68 lb ft, 9.4 kg m (92 Nm) at 3,250 rpm; max engine rpm: 6,000; 50.8 hp/l (37.9 kW/l); 1 Ford downdraught twin barrel carburettor.

TRANSMISSION axle ratio: 3.842; width or rims: 4.5": tyres: 155 SR x 12.

PERFORMANCE max speed: 98 mph, 158 km/h; power-weight ratio: 25.7 lb/hp (34.5 lb/kW), 11.7 kg/hp (15.6 kg/kW): consumption: 31.4 m/imp gal, 26.1 m//US gal, 9 l x 100 km at 75 mph, 120 km/h.

CHASSIS front and rear suspension: anti-roll bar and adjustable telescopic dampers.

BRAKES servo (standard).

DIMENSIONS AND WEIGHT weight: 1,698 lb, 770 kg.

Escort Series

PRICES EX WORKS:		£
1	Popular 1100 2-dr Saloon	2,876*
2	Popular 1100 Plus 2-dr Saloon	2,963*
3	Popular 1100 4-dr Saloon	3,088*
4	1100 2+1-dr Estate Car	3,174*
5	1100 L 2-dr Saloon	3,193*
6	1100 L 4-dr Saloon	3,318*
7	Popular 1300 2-dr Saloon	3,003*
8	Popular 1300 Plus 2-dr Saloon	3,091*
9	Popular 1300 Plus 4-dr Saloon	3,214*
10	1300 2+1-dr Estate Car	3,346*
11	1300 L 2-dr Saloon	3,286*
12	1300 L 4-dr Saloon	3,412*
13	1300 L 2+1-dr Estate Car	3,662*
14	1300 GL 2-dr Saloon	3,573*
15	1300 GL 4-dr Saloon	3,700*
16	1300 GL 2+1-dr Estate Car	4,023*
17	1300 Sport 2-dr Saloon	3,873*
18	1300 Ghia 2-dr Saloon	4,111*
19	1300 Ghia 4-dr Saloon	4,240*
20	1600 Sport 2-dr Saloon	3,985*
21	1600 Ghia 4-dr Saloon	4,353*
22	RS 2000 2-dr Saloon	4,716*
23	RS 2000 Custom 2-dr Saloon	5,335*

Power team:	Standard for:	Optional for:
41 hp (economy)	1 to 6	—
48 hp (standard)	1 to 6	—
57 hp	7 to 16	—
70 hp	17 to 19	—
84 hp	20,21	—
110 hp	22,23	—

41 hp power team (economy)

ENGINE front, 4 stroke; 4 cylinders, vertical, in line; 67 cu in, 1,098 cc (3.19 x 2.10 in, 81 x 53.3 mm); compression ratio: 9:1; max power (DIN): 41 hp (30 kW) at 5,300 rpm; max torque (DIN): 52 lb ft, 7.2 kg m (71 Nm) at 3,000 rpm; max engine rpm: 6,000: 37.3 hp/l (27.5 kW/l); cast iron block and head; 5 crankshaft bearings; valves: overhead, in line, push-rods and rockers; camshafts: 1, side, chain-driven; lubrication: rotary or vane-type pump, full flow filter, 5.7 imp pt, 6.8 US pt, 3.2 l; 1 Ford GPD downdraught single barrel carburettor; fuel feed: mechanical pump; water-cooled, 8.8 imp pt, 10.6 US pt, 5 l.

TRANSMISSION driving wheels: rear; clutch: single dry plate (diaphragm); gearbox: mechanical; gears: 4, fully synchronized; ratios: I 3.656, II 2.185, III 1.425, IV 1, rev 4.235; lever: central; final drive: hypoid bevel; axle ratio: 3.890; width of rims: 4.5"; tyres: 155 SR x 12.

PERFORMANCE max speed: 77 mph, 124 km/h; power-weight ratio: 43.9 lb/hp (59.6 lb/kW), 19.9 kg/hp (27 kg/kW); carrying capacity: 939 lb, 426 kg; speed in direct drive at 1,000 rpm: 16 mph, 25.8 km/h; consumption: 30.4 m/imp gal, 25.3 m/US gal, 9.3 l x 100 km at 75 mph, 120 km/h.

CHASSIS integral; front suspension: independent, by McPherson, coil springs/telescopic damper struts, anti-roll bar; rear: rigid axle, semi-elliptic leafsprings, telescopic dampers.

STEERING rack-and-pinion; turns lock to lock: 3.50.

BRAKES front disc (diameter 9.60 in, 24.4 cm), rear drum (drum front and rear on Popular models), dual circuit.

ELECTRICAL EQUIPMENT 12 V; 38 Ah battery; 35 A alternator; Motorcraft distributor; 2 headlamps.

DIMENSIONS AND WEIGHT wheel base: 94.50 in, 240 cm; tracks: 49.50 in, 126 cm front, 50.60 in, 128 cm rear; length:

FORD Escort 1600 Sport Saloon

41 HP POWER TEAM

156.80 in, 398 cm; width: 61.80 in, 157 cm; height: 54.50 in, 138 cm; ground clearance: 4.92 in, 12.5 cm; weight: 1,799 lb, 816 kg; turning circle: 29.2 ft, 8.9 m; fuel tank: 9 imp gal, 10.8 US gal, 41 l.

BODY 5 seats, separate front seats; reclining backrests and heated rear window (standard for L models only).

PRACTICAL INSTRUCTIONS fuel: 97 oct petrol; oil: engine 5.8 imp pt, 7 US pt, 3.3 l, SAE 10W-30, change every 6,000 miles, 9,700 km - gearbox 1.6 imp pt, 1.9 US pt, 0.9 l, SAE 80, no change recommended - final drive 1.7 imp pt, 2.1 US pt, 1 l, SAE 90, no change recommended; greasing: none; tappet clearances: inlet 0.010 in 0.25 mm, exhaust 0.017 in, 0.43 mm; valve timing: 21° 55° 70° 22°; tyre pressure: front 24 psi, 1.7 atm, rear 24 psi, 1.7 atm.

OPTIONALS laminated windscreen; heated rear window; halogen headlamps; rear fog lamps; headrests; metallic spray; servo brake (for Estate Car only); reclining backrests: 155 SR x 12 tyres (for L models only); tinted glass; vinyl roof; sports road wheels.

48 hp power team (standard)

See 41 hp power team, except for:

ENGINE max power (DIN): 48 hp (35 kW) at 5,500 rpm; max torque (DIN): 54 lb ft, 7.5 kg m (74 Nm) at 3,000 rpm; 43.7 hp/l (32.1 kW/l).

PERFORMANCE max speed: 82 mph, 132 km/h; power-weight ratio: 37.4 lb/hp (50.9 lb/kW), 17 kg/hp (23.1 kg/kW); consumption: 27.7 m/imp gal, 23.1 m/US gal, 10.2 l x 100 km at 75 mph, 120 km/h.

57 hp power team

See 41 hp power team, except for:

ENGINE 79.2 cu in, 1,298 cc (3.19 x 2.48 in, 81 x 63 mm); compression ratio: 9.2:1; max power (DIN): 57 hp (42 kW) at 5,500 rpm; max torque (DIN): 67 lb ft, 9.3 kg m (91 Nm) at 3,000 rpm; max engine rpm: 5,700; 43.9 hp/l (32.3 kW/l).

TRANSMISSION tyres: 155 SR x 13.

PERFORMANCE max speed: 88 mph, 141 km/h; power-weight ratio: 1300 Gl saloons 32.6 lb/hp (44.4 lb/kW), 14.8 kg/hp (20.1 kg/kW); acceleration: 0-50 mph (0-80 km/h) 16.5 sec; consumption: 38.2 m/imp gal, 31.8 m/US gal, 7.4 l x 100 km at 75 mph, 120 km/h.

CHASSIS rear suspension: anti-roll bar.

ELECTRICAL EQUIPMENT halogen headlamps (standard for GL models only).

DIMENSIONS AND WEIGHT length: 1300 GL saloons 159.50 in, 405 cm; weight: 1300 GL saloons 1,859 lb, 843 kg.

OPTIONALS Ford C3 automatic transmission, hydraulic torque converter and planetary gears with 3 ratios (I 2.474, II 1.474, III 1, rev 2.111), max ratio of converter at stall 2.3, possible manual selection, max speed 84 mph, 135 km/h.

70 hp power team

See 41 hp power team, except for:

ENGINE 79.2 cu in, 1,298 cc (3.19 x 2.48 in, 81 x 63 mm); compression ratio: 9.2:1; max power (DIN): 70 hp (51 kW) at 5,500 rpm; max torque (DIN): 68 lb ft, 9.4 kg m (92 Nm) at 4,000 rpm; max engine rpm; 6,500; 53.9 hp/l (39.7 kW/l); 1 Weber 32/32 DGV downdraught twin barrel carburettor.

TRANSMISSION gearbox ratios: I 3.337, II 1.995, III 1.418, IV 1, rev 3.876; axle ratio: 4.125; width of rims: 5''; tyres: 155 SR x 13 - 1300 Sport 175/70 SR x 13.

PERFORMANCE max speed: 94 mph, 151 km/h - 1300 Ghia saloons 95 mph, 153 km/h; power-weight ratio: 1300 Sport 27.1 lb/hp (36.8 lb/kW), 12,3 kg/hp (16.7 kg/kW) - 1300 Ghia saloons 27.7 lb/hp (37.7 lb/kW) 12.6 kg/hp (17.1 kg/kW); consumption: 29.1 m/imp gal, 24.2 m/US gal, 9.7 l x 100 km at 75 mph, 120 km/h.

CHASSIS rear suspension: anti-roll bar.

BRAKES servo (standard).

ELECTRICAL EQUIPMENT halogen headlamps (standard).

DIMENSIONS AND WEIGHT weight: 1300 Sport 1,896 lb. 860 kg - 1300 Ghia saloons 1,940 lb, 880 kg.

PRACTICAL INSTRUCTIONS valve timing: 29° 63° 71° 21°.

FORD Escort 1300 GL Saloon

84 hp power team

See 41 hp power team, except for:

ENGINE 97.6 cu in, 1,599 cc (3.19 x 3.06 in, 81 x 77.6 mm): max power (DIN): 84 hp (62 kW) at 5,500 rpm; max torque (DIN): 92 lb ft, 12.7 kg m (124 Nm) at 3,500 rpm: max engine rpm: 6,600; 52.5 hp/l (38.6 kW/l) 1 Weber 32/36 DGV downdraught twin barrel carburettor; cooling: 9.5 imp pt, 11,4 US pt, 5.4 l.

TRANSMISSION gearbox ratios: I 3.337, II 1.995, III 1.418, IV 1. rev 3.876; axle ratio: 3.540; width of rims: 5''; tyres: 155 SR x 13 - Sport 175/70 SR x 13.

PERFORMANCE max speed: 102 mph, 164 km/h; power-weight ratio: Sport 23.6 lb/hp (32 lb/kW), 10.7 kg/hp (14.5 kg/kW) - Ghia 24.2 lb/hp (32.9 lb/kW), 11 kg/hp (14.9 kg/kW): speed in direct drive at 1,000 rpm: 18.5 mph, 29.7 km/h: consumption: 25.7 m/imp gal, 21.4 m/US gal, 11 l x 100 km at 75 mph, 120 km/h.

CHASSIS rear suspension: anti-roll bar.

BRAKES servo (standard).

ELECTRICAL EQUIPMENT halogen headlamps (standard).

DIMENSIONS AND WEIGHT weight: Sport 1,980 lb, 898 kg - Ghia 2,035 lb, 923 kg.

BODY reclining backrests with built-in headrests, sports roa wheels and heated rear window (standard).

PRACTICAL INSTRUCTIONS valve timing: 29° 63° 71° 21°.

OPTIONALS (for Ghia only) Ford C3 automatic transmissior hydraulic torque converter and planetary gears with 3 ratios (2.474, II 1.474, III 1, rev 2.111) max ratio of converter at sta 2.3, possible manual selection; laminated windscreen; rear fo lamps; metallic spray; tinted glass; vinyl roof; sports roa wheels.

110 hp power team

See 41 hp power team, except for:

ENGINE 121.6 cu in, 1,993 cc (3.57 x 3.03 in, 90.8 x 76.9 mm) compression ratio: 9.2:1; max power (DIN): 110 hp (81 kW) a 5,500 rpm; max torque (DIN): 118 lb ft, 16.3 kg m (160 Nm) a 3,750 rpm; max engine rpm: 6,600; 55.2 hp/l (40.6 kW/l) valves: overhead, Vee-slanted, rockers; camshafts: 1, ove head, cogged belt; lubrication: gear or vane-type pump, full flo filter, oil cooler, 6.7 imp pt, 8 US pt, 3.8 l; 1 Weber 32/36 DGA downdraught twin barrel carburettor; cooling: 12.5 imp pt, 1 US pt, 7.1 l, electric thermostatic fan.

TRANSMISSION gearbox ratios: I 3.656, II 1.970, III 1.370, I 1, rev 3.660; axle ratio: 3.540; width of rims: 6''; tyres: 175/7 HR x 13.

FORD Escort 1600 Sport Saloon

FORD Escort RS 2000 Saloon

PERFORMANCE max speeds: (I) 32 mph, 53 km/h; (II) 60 mph, 96 km/h; (III) 86 mph, 138 km/h; (IV) 110 mph, 177 km/h; power-weight ratio: 18.7 lb/hp (25.5 lb/kW), 8.5 kg/hp (11.5 kg/kW); speed in direct drive at 1,000 rpm: 18.6 mph, 29.9 km/h; consumption: 27.6 m/imp gal, 23.1 m/US gal, 10.2 l x 100 km at 75 mph, 120 km/h.

CHASSIS rear suspension: trailing radius arms.

STEERING turns lock to lock: 3.30.

BRAKES front disc (diameter 9.60 in 24.4 cm), rear drum, servo (standard); swept area: front 195 sq in, 1,258 sq cm, rear 99 sq in, 639 sq cm, total 294 sq in, 1,897 sq cm.

ELECTRICAL EQUIPMENT 55 Ah battery; 45 A alternator; halogen headlamps (standard).

DIMENSIONS AND WEIGHT wheel base; 94 in, 239 cm; tracks: 50.30 in, 128 cm front, 51.10 in, 130 cm rear; length: 161.80 in, 411 cm; width: 61.60 in, 156 cm; height: 55 in, 140 cm; weight: 2,062 lb, 935 kg; weight distribution: 54% front, 46% rear.

BODY reclining backrests with built-in headrests and heated rear window (standard).

PRACTICAL INSTRUCTIONS oil: engine 6.7 imp pt, 8 US pt, 3.8 l, SAE 10W-30, change every 6,000 miles, 9,700 km - gearbox 2.4 imp pt, 2.7 US pt, 1.3 l - final drive 2 imp pt, 2.3 US pt, 1.1 l; tappet clearances: inlet 0.008 in, 0.20 mm, exhaust 0.010 in, 0.25 mm; valve timing: 18° 70° 64° 24°.

OPTIONALS competition equipment; sports road wheels; metallic spray; tinted glass with laminated windscreen; vinyl roof; rear fog lamps.

Cortina Series

PRICES EX WORKS:		£
1	1300 2-dr Saloon	3,503*
2	1300 4-dr Saloon	3,638*
3	1300 L 2-dr Saloon	3,849*
4	1300 L 4-dr Saloon	3,985*
5	1600 4-dr Saloon	4,195*
6	1600 4+1-dr Estate Car	4,274*
7	1600 L 4-dr Saloon	4,195*
8	1600 L 4+1-dr Estate Car	4,661*
9	1600 GL 4-dr Saloon	4,588*
10	1600 GL 4+1-dr Estate Car	5,054*
11	1600 Ghia 4-dr Saloon	5,422*
12	1600 Ghia 4+1-dr Estate Car	5,888*
13	2000 GL 4-dr Saloon	4,839*
14	2000 GL 4+1-dr Estate Car	5,305*
15	2000 GLS 4-dr Saloon	4,991*
16	2000 Ghia 4-dr Saloon	5,579*
17	2000 Ghia 4+1-dr Estate Car	6,045*
18	2300 GL 4-dr Saloon	5,474*
19	2300 GL 4+1-dr Estate Car	5,941*
20	2300 GLS 4-dr Saloon	5,627*
21	2300 Ghia 4-dr Saloon	6,215*
22	2300 Ghia 4+1-dr Estate Car	6,681*

Power team:	Standard for:	Optional for:
60 hp	1 to 4	—
74 hp	5 to 10	—
91 hp	11,12	—
101 hp	13 to 17	—
114 hp	18 to 22	—

60 hp power team

ENGINE front, 4 stroke; 4 cylinders, vertical, in line; 79.2 cu in, 1,298 cc (3.19 x 2.48 in, 81 x 63 mm); compression ratio: 9.2:1; max power (DIN): 60 hp (45 kW) at 6,000 rpm; max torque (DIN): 68 lb ft, 9.4 kg m (92 Nm) at 3,000 rpm; max engine rpm: 6,000; 46.2 hp/l (34.4 kW/l); cast iron block and head; 5 crankshaft bearings; valves: overhead, push-rods and rockers; camshafts: 1, side, chain-driven; lubrication: rotary pump, full flow filter, 6 imp pt, 7.2 US pt, 3.4 l; 1 Motorcraft VV downdraught single barrel carburettor; fuel feed: mechanical pump; water-cooled, 8.7 imp pt, 10.4 US pt, 4.9 l.

TRANSMISSION driving wheels: rear; clutch: single dry plate (diaphragm); gearbox: mechanical; gears: 4, fully synchronized; ratios: I 3.580, II 2.010, III 1.400, IV 1, rev 3.320; lever: central; final drive: hypoid bevel; axle ratio: 4.440; width of rims: 4.5"; tyres: 165 SR x 13.

PERFORMANCE max speeds: (I) 24 mph, 38 km/h; (II) 37 mph, 59 km/h; (III) 63 mph, 101 km/h; (IV) 87 mph, 140 km/h; power-weight ratio: 35.4 lb/hp (47.2 lb/kW), 16.1 kg/hp; (21.4 kg/kW); carrying capacity: 1,133 lb, 515 kg; speed in direct drive at 1,000 rpm: 15.2 mph, 24.3 km/h; consumption: 29.7 m/imp gal, 24.8 m/US gal, 9.5 l x 100 km at 75 mph, 120 km/h.

CHASSIS integral, front auxiliary frame; front suspension: independent, wishbones, anti-roll bar, coil springs/telescopic dampers; rear: rigid axle, lower longitudinal trailing arms, upper oblique torque arms, coil springs, anti-roll bar, telescopic dampers.

FORD Cortina Series

STEERING rack-and-pinion; turns lock to lock: 3.70.

BRAKES front disc (diameter 9.72 in, 24.7 cm), rear drum, dual circuit, servo.

ELECTRICAL EQUIPMENT 12 V; 38 Ah battery; 35 A alternator; Ford distributor; 2 headlamps.

DIMENSIONS AND WEIGHT wheel base: 101.50 in, 258 cm: tracks: 56.90 in, 144 cm front, 56 in, 142 cm rear; length: 170.87 in, 434 cm; width: 67.32 in, 171 cm; height: 53.54 in, 136 cm; ground clearance: 5.12 in, 13 cm; weight: 2,123 lb, 965 kg; weight distribution: 53% front, 47% rear; turning circle: 32 ft, 9.8 m; fuel tank: 12 imp gal. 14.3 US gal, 54 l.

BODY saloon/sedan; 5 seats, separate front seats.

PRACTICAL INSTRUCTIONS fuel: 97 oct petrol; oil: engine 6 imp pt, 7.2 US pt, 3.4 l, SAE 10W-30, change every 6.000 miles, 9.700 km - gearbox 1.6 imp pt, 1.9 US pt, 0.9 l, SAE 80 EP, no change recommended - final drive 1.8 imp pt, 2.1 US pt, 1 l, SAE 90 EP, no change recommended; greasing: none; tappet clearances: inlet 0.004 in, 0.10 mm, exhaust 0.007 in, 0.17 mm; valve timing: 21° 55° 70° 22°; tyre pressure: front 24 psi, 1.7 atm, rear 24 psi, 1.7 atm.

OPTIONALS metallic spray; headrests (for L models only); sunshine roof; tinted glass; vinyl roof; 185/70 SR x 13 tyres only with sports road wheels.

74 hp power team

See 60 hp power team, except for:

ENGINE 97.2 cu in, 1,593 cc (3.45 x 2.60 in, 87.6 x 66 mm); max power (DIN): 74 hp (55 kW) at 5,300 rpm; max torque (DIN): 86 lb ft, 11.9 kg m (117 Nm) at 2,700 rpm; max engine rpm: 5,500; 46.4 hp/l (34.5 kW/l); valves: overhead, Vee-slanted, rockers; camshafts: 1, overhead, cogged belt.

TRANSMISSION axle ratio: 3.890.

PERFORMANCE max speed: 94 mph, 151 km/h; power-weight ratio: 28.9 lb/hp (38.9 lb/kW), 13.1 kg/hp (17.6 kg/kW); carrying capacity: 1,166 lb, 530 kg; speed in direct drive at 1,000 rpm: 17.3 mph, 27.8 km/h; consumption: 30.4 m/imp gal 25.3 m/US gal, 9.3 l x 100 km at 75 mph, 120 km/h.

DIMENSIONS AND WEIGHT weight: 2,139 lb, 970 kg.

OPTIONALS Ford C3 automatic transmission, hydraulic torque converter and planetary gears with 3 ratios (I 2.474, II 1.474, III 1, rev 2.111), max ratio of converter at stall 2, possible manual selection, max speed 90 mph, 145 km/h.

91 hp power team

See 60 hp power team, except for:

ENGINE max power (DIN): 91 hp (67 kW) at 5,900 rpm; max torque (DIN): 92 lb ft, 12.7 m (124 Nm) at 4,000 rpm; max engine rpm: 6,000; 57.1 hp/l (43 kW/l).

TRANSMISSION axle ratio: 3.890.

PERFORMANCE max speed: 101 mph, 163 km/h; power-weight ratio: 23.9 lb/hp (32.6 lb/kW), 10.9 kg/hp (14.8 kg/kW); carrying capacity: 1,122 lb, 510 kg; speed in direct drive at 1,000 rpm: 17.3 mph, 27.8 km/h; consumption: 29.1 m/imp gal, 24.2 m/US gal, 9.7 l x 100 km at 75 mph, 120 km/h.

DIMENSIONS AND WEIGHT weight: 2,183 lb, 990 kg.

OPTIONALS Ford C3 automatic transmission, hydraulic torque converter and planetary gears with 3 ratios (I 2.474, II 1.474, III 1, rev 2.111), max ratio of converter at stall 2, possible manual selection, max speed 96 mph, 155 km/h.

101 hp power team

See 60 hp power team, except for:

ENGINE 121.6 cu in, 1,993 cc (3.89 x 3.03 in, 90.8 x 76.9 mm); max power (DIN): 101 hp (74 kW) at 5,200 rpm; max torque (DIN): 113 lb ft, 15.6 kg m (153 Nm) at 4,000 rpm; max engine rpm: 6,000; 50.7 hp/l (37.8 kW/l); 1 Weber 32/36 DGAV downdraught twin barrel carburettor; cooling: 13.7 imp pt, 16.5 US pt, 7.8 l.

TRANSMISSION gearbox ratios: I 3.650, II 1.970, III 1.370, IV 1, rev 3.660; axle ratio: 3,450; width of rims: 5.5".

PERFORMANCE max speed: 105 mph, 169 km/h; power-weight ratio: 22.2 lb/hp (30.3 lb/kW), 10.1 kg/hp (13.8 kg/kW); carrying capacity: 1,111 lb, 505 kg; speed in direct drive at 1,000 rpm: 19.6 mph, 31.6 km/h; consumption: 28.5 m/imp gal, 23.5 m/US gal, 9.9 l x 100 km at 75 mph, 120 km/h.

ELECTRICAL EQUIPMENT halogen headlamps.

DIMENSIONS AND WEIGHT weight: 2,244 lb, 1,020 kg.

BODY sports road wheels: light alloy wheels and headrests (except for GL models); tinted glass (for Ghia models only).

FORD Cortina Saloon

101 HP POWER TEAM

PRACTICAL INSTRUCTIONS tappet clearances: inlet 0.008 in, 0.20 mm, exhaust 0.010 in, 0.25 mm; valve timing: 18° 70° 64° 24°.

OPTIONALS Ford C3 automatic transmission, hydraulic torque converter and planetary gears with 3 ratios (I 2.474, II 1.474, III 1, rev 2.111), max ratio of converter at stall 2, possible manual selection, max speed 100 mph, 161 km/h; 66 Ah battery; sunshine roof; 185/70 SR x 13 tyres (for S and Ghia models only).

114 hp power team

See 60 hp power team, except for:

ENGINE 6 cylinders, Vee-slanted at 60°; 139.9 cu in, 2,293 cc (3.54 x 2.37 in, 90 x 60.1 mm); compression ratio: 9:1; max power (DIN): 114 hp (85 kW) at 5,300 rpm; max torque (DIN): 130 lb ft, 18 kg m (176 Nm) at 3,000 rpm; max engine rpm: 5,500; 49.6 hp/l (37 kW/l); 1 Solex 35/35 downdraught twin barrel carburettor; cooling: 13.7 imp pt, 16.5 US pt, 7.8 l.

TRANSMISSION gearbox ratios: I 3.650, II 1.970, III 1.370, IV 1, rev 3.660; axle ratio: 3.440; width of rims: 5.5''.

PERFORMANCE max speed: 109 mph, 176 km/h; power-weight ratio: 20.3 lb/hp (27.3 lb/kW), 9.2 kg/hp (12.4 kg/kW); carrying capacity: 1,122 lb, 510 kg; speed in direct drive at 1,000 rpm: 19.6 mph, 31.6 km/h; consumption: 25.2 m/imp gal, 21 m/US gal, 11.2 l x 100 km at 75 mph, 120 km/h.

DIMENSIONS AND WEIGHT weight: 2,321 lb, 1,053 kg.

BODY sports road wheels (standard); light alloy wheels and headrests (except for GL models); tinted glass (for Ghia models only).

PRACTICAL INSTRUCTIONS tappet clearances: inlet 0.014 in, 0.35 mm, exhaust 0.016 in, 0.40 mm; valve timing: 20° 56° 62° 14°.

OPTIONALS Ford C3 automatic transmission, hydraulic torque converter and planetary gears with 3 ratios (I 2.474, II 1.474, III 1, rev 2.111), max ratio of converter at stall 2, possible manual selection, max speed 105 mph, 169 km/h; 66 Ah battery; sunshine roof; 185/70 SR x 13 tyres (for S and Ghia models only).

FORD Cortina 2000 GLS Saloon

Capri II Coupé Series

PRICES EX WORKS:		£
1	1300 L	**3,867***
2	1600 L	**4,083***
3	1600 GL	**4,400***
4	1600 S	**4,970***
5	2000 GL	**4,673***
6	2000 S	**5,185***
7	2000 Ghia	**5,934***
8	3000 S	**5,574***
9	3000 Ghia	**6,704***

Power team:	Standard for:	Optional for:
57 hp	1	—
72 hp	2,3	—
91 hp	4	—
101 hp	5 to 7	—
138 hp	8,9	—

57 hp power team

ENGINE front, 4 stroke; 4 cylinders, vertical, in line; 79.2 cu in, 1,298 cc (3.19 x 2.48 in, 81 X 63 mm); compression ratio: 9.2:1; max power (DIN): 57 hp (42 kW) at 5,500 rpm; max torque (DIN): 67 lb/ft, 9.3 kg m (91 Nm) at 3,000 rpm; max engine rpm: 6,000; 43,9 hp/l (33.3 kW/l); cast iron block and head; 5 crankshaft bearings; valves: overhead, in line, push-rods and rockers; camshafts: 1, side, chain-driven; lubrication: rotary or vane-type pump, full flow filter, 5.7 imp pt, 6.8 US pt, 3.2 l; 1 Motorcraft GPD downdraught single barrel carburettor; fuel feed: mechanical pump; water-cooled, 8.2 imp pt, 9.7 US pt, 4.6 l.

TRANSMISSION driving wheels: rear; clutch: single dry plate (diaphragm); gearbox: mechanical; gears: 4, fully synchronized; ratios: I 3.580, II 2.010, III 1.400, IV 1, rev 3.320; lever: central; final drive: hypoid bevel; axle ratio: 3.890; width or rims: 5''; tyres: 165 SR x 13.

PERFORMANCE max speeds: (I) 27 mph, 43 km/h; (II) 33 mph, 53 km/h; (III) 69 mph, 111 km/h; (IV) 91 mph, 146 km/h; power-weight ratio: 39.1 lb/hp (53.1 lb/kW) 17.7 kg/hp (24.1 kg/kW); carrying capacity: 750 lb, 340 kg; speed in direct drive at 1,000 rpm: 17.3 mph, 27.9 km/h; consumption: 27.2 m/imp gal, 22.6 m/US gal, 10.4 l x 100 km at 75 mph, 120 km/h.

CHASSIS integral; front suspension: independent, by McPherson, coil springs/telescopic damper struts, lower wishbones (trailing arms), anti-roll bar; rear: rigid axle, semielliptic leafsprings, anti-roll bar (acting as torque radius arms), telescopic dampers.

STEERING rack-and-pinion.

BRAKES front disc (diameter 9.60 in, 24.4 cm), rear drum dual circuit, servo.

ELECTRICAL EQUIPMENT 12 V; 38 Ah battery; 45 A alternator; Motorcraft distributor; 4 headlamps.

DIMENSIONS AND WEIGHT wheel base: 100.80 in, 256 cm; tracks: 53.30 in, 135 cm front, 54.40 in, 138 cm rear; length: 168 in, 427 cm; width: 66.90 in, 170 cm; height: 51.10 in, 130 cm; ground clearance: 4.50 in, 11 cm; weight: 2,227 lb, 1,010 kg; weight distribution: 52.5% front, 47.5% rear; turning circle: 32 ft, 9.8 m; fuel tank: 12.7 imp gal, 15.3 US gal, 58 l.

BODY coupé; 2 doors; 4 seats, separate front seats, reclining backrests.

PRACTICAL INSTRUCTIONS fuel: 97 oct petrol; oil: engine 5.3 imp pt, 6.3 US pt, 3 l, SAE 10W-30, change every 6.000 miles, 9.700 km - gearbox 1.7 imp pt, 1.9 US pt, 0.9 l, SAE 80, no change recommended - final drive 2 imp pt, 2.3 US pt, 1.1 l, SAE 90, no change recommended; greasing: none; tappet clearances: inlet 0.010 in, 0.25 mm, exhaust 0.017 in, 0.44 mm; valve timing: 21° 55° 70° 22°; tyre pressure: front 24 psi, 1.7 atm, rear 27 psi, 1.9 atm.

OPTIONALS 4.444 axle ratio; sunshine roof; vinyl roof; sports road wheels; tinted glass with laminated windscreen; halogen headlamps; metallic spray; rear window wiper-washer.

72 hp power team

See 57 hp power team, except for:

ENGINE 97.2 cu in, 1,593 cc (3.45 x 2.60 in, 87.6 x 66 mm); max power (DIN): 72 hp (53 kW) at 5,200 rpm; max torque (DIN): 87 lb ft, 12 kg m (118 Nm) at 2,700 rpm; 45.2 hp/l (33.3 kW/l); valves: overhead, Vee-slanted, rockers; camshafts: 1, overhead, cogged belt; lubrication: 6.5 imp pt, 7.8 US pt, 3.7 l.

TRANSMISSION axle ratio: 3.770.

PERFORMANCE max speed: 98 mph, 157 km/h; power-weight ratio: 31.7 lb/hp (43.3 lb/kW), 14.4 kg/hp (19.6 kg/kW); acceleration: standing ¼ mile 18.9 sec, 0-50 mph (0-80 km/h) 9 sec; speed in direct drive at 1,000 rpm: 17.8 mph, 28.6 km/h; consumption: 25.4 m/imp gal, 21.2 m/US gal, 11.1 l x 100 km at 75 mph, 120 km/h.

DIMENSIONS AND WEIGHT weight: 2,293 lb, 1,040 kg; weight distribution: 52.6% front, 47.4% rear.

PRACTICAL INSTRUCTIONS oil: engine 6.5 imp pt, 7.8 US pt, 3.7 l.

OPTIONALS Ford C3 automatic transmission, hydraulic torque converter and planetary gears with 3 ratios (I 2.474, II 1.474, III 1, rev 2.111), max ratio of converter at stall 2.3, possible manual selection, max speed 95 mph, 153 km/h, 55 Ah battery.

91 hp power team

See 57 hp power team, except for:

ENGINE 97.2 cu in, 1.593 cc (3.45 x 2.60 in, 87.6 x 66 mm); max power (DIN): 91 hp (67 kW) at 5,900 rpm; max torque (DIN): 92 lb ft, 12.7 kg m (124 Nm) at 4,000 rpm; max engine rpm: 6,500; 57.1 hp/l (43 kW/l); valves: overhead, Vee-slanted, rockers; camshafts: 1, overhead, cogged belt; lubrication: 6.5 imp pt, 7.8 US pt, 3.7 l; 1 Weber 32/36 DGV downdraught twin barrel carburettor.

TRANSMISSION axle ratio: 3.750.

PERFORMANCE max speed: 109 mph, 175 km/h; power-weight ratio: 25.6 lb/hp (34.7 lb/kW), 11.6 kg/hp (15.7 kg/kW); speed in direct drive at 1,000 rpm: 18 mph, 28.9 km/h; consumption 32.1 m/imp gal, 26.7 m/US gal, 8.8 l x 100 km at 75 mph, 120 km/h.

ELECTRICAL EQUIPMENT 44 Ah battery.

DIMENSIONS AND WEIGHT weight: 2,326 lb, 1,055 kg; weight distribution: 52.6% front, 47.4% rear.

PRACTICAL INSTRUCTIONS oil: engine 6.5 imp pt, 7.8 US pt, 3.7 l; tappet clearances: inlet 0.008 in, 0.20 mm, exhaust 0.010 in, 0.25 mm; valve timing: 18° 70° 69° 24°.

OPTIONALS Ford C3 automatic transmission, hydraulic torque converter and planetary gears with 3 ratios (I 2.474, II 1.474, III 1, rev 2.111), max ratio of converter at stall 2.3, possible manual selection, max speed 102 mph, 164 km/h, 55 Ah battery; sports equipment.

101 hp power team

See 57 power team, except for:

ENGINE 121.6 cu in, 1,993 cc (3.89 x 3.03 in, 90.8 x 76.9 mm); max power (DIN): 101 hp (74 kW) at 5,200 rpm; max torque (DIN): 112 lb ft, 15.4 kg m (151 Nm) at 3,500 rpm; max engine rpm: 6,500; 50.7 hp/l (37.8 kW/l); valves: overhead, Vee-slanted, rockers; camshafts: 1, overhead, cogged belt; 1 Weber 32/36 DGAV downdraught twin barrel carburettor: cooling: 13.7 imp pt, 16.5 US pt, 7.8 l.

TRANSMISSION gearbox ratios: I 3.650, II 1.970, III 1.370, IV 1, rev 3.160; axle ratio: 3.440.

PERFORMANCE max speed: 111 mph, 179 km/h; power-weight ratio: 21.7 lb/hp (29.6 lb/kW), 9.8 kg/hp (13.4 kg/kW); acceleration: standing ¼ mile 18.2 sec, 0-50 mph (0-80 km/h) 7.5 sec; speed in direct drive at 1,000 rpm: 19.5 mph, 31.4 km/h; consumption: 29.7 m/imp gal, 24.8 m/US gal, 9.5 l x 100 km.

ELECTRICAL EQUIPMENT 44 Ah battery.

DIMENSIONS AND WEIGHT weight: 2,194 lb, 995 kg; weight distribution: 55.1% front, 44.9% rear.

PRACTICAL INSTRUCTIONS tappet clearances: inlet 0.008 in, 0.20 mm, exhaust 0.010 in, 0.25 mm; valve timing: 18° 70° 64° 24°.

OPTIONALS Ford C3 automatic transmission hydraulic torque converter and planetary gears with 3 ratios (I 2.474, II 1.474, III 1, rev 2.111), max ratio of converter at stall 2, possible manual selection, max speed 105 mph, 169 km/h, 55 Ah battery; sports equipment.

FORD Cortina L Estate Car

138 hp power team

See 57 hp power team, except for:

ENGINE 6 cylinders, Vee-slanted at 60°; 182.7 cu in, 2,994 cc (3.69 x 2.85 in, 93.7 x 72.4 mm); compression ratio: 9:1; max power (DIN): 138 hp (102 kW) at 5,000 rpm; max torque (DIN): 174 lb ft, 24 kg m (235 Nm) at 3,000 rpm; max engine rpm: 5,500; 46.1 hp/l (33.9 kW/l); 4 crankshaft bearings; camshafts: 1, at centre of Vee; lubrication: 7.6 imp pt, 9.1 US pt, 4.3 l; 1 Weber 38/38 EGAS downdraught twin barrel carburettor; cooling: 16.4 imp pt, 19.7 US pt, 9.3 l.

TRANSMISSION gearbox ratios: I 3.160, II 1.940, III 1.412, IV 1, rev 3.346; axle ratio: 3.090; tyres: 185/70 HR x 13.

PERFORMANCE max speed: 124 mph, 200 km/h; power-weight ratio: 18.7 lb/hp (25.4 lb/kW), 8.5 kg/hp (11.5 kg/kW); acceleration: standing ¼ mile 16.6 sec, 0-50 mph (0-80 km/h) 6 sec; speed in direct drive at 1,000 rpm: 21.9 mph, 35.2 km/h; consumption: 24.4 m/imp gal, 20.3 m/US gal, 11.6 l x 100 km at 75 mph, 120 km/h.

BRAKES front disc (diameter 9.72 in, 24.7 cm).

DIMENSIONS AND WEIGHT weight: 2,580 lb, 1,170 kg.

PRACTICAL INSTRUCTIONS oil: engine 6.7 imp pt, 8 US pt, 3.8 l - gearbox 3.2 imp pt, 3.8 US pt, 1.8 l; tappet clearances: inlet 0.012 in, 0.30 mm, exhaust 0.012 in, 0.30 mm; valve timing: 20° 56° 62° 14°.

OPTIONALS Ford C3 automatic transmission, hydraulic torque converter and planetary gears with 3 ratios (I 2.474, II 1.474, III 1, rev 2.111) max ratio of converter at stall 2.2, possible manual selection, max speed 118 mph, 190 km/h, 55 Ah battery.

FORD Capri II 2000 GL Coupé

FORD Capri II 3000 S Coupé

Granada Series

	PRICES EX WORKS:	£
1	2000 L Saloon	**5,499***
2	2000 L Estate Car	**6,086***
3	2100 Diesel Saloon	**5,943***
4	2300 L Saloon	**6,101***
5	2300 L Estate Car	**6,688***
6	2300 GL Saloon	**7,240***
7	2800 GL Saloon (Automatic)	**7,733***
8	2800 GL Estate Car (Automatic)	**8,057***
9	2800i GLS Saloon	**8,325***
10	2800i GLS Estate Car	**8,649***
11	2800 Ghia Saloon (Automatic)	**9,173***
12	2800 Ghia Estate Car (Automatic)	**9,510***
13	2800i Ghia Saloon	**9,595***
14	2800i Ghia Estate Car	**9,931***

Power team:	Standard for:	Optional for:
101 hp	1,2	—
63 hp (diesel)	3	—
114 hp	4 to 6	—
135 hp	7,8,11,12	—
160 hp	9,10,13,14	—

FORD Granada 2800i GLS Saloon

101 hp power team

ENGINE front, 4 stroke; 4 cylinders, vertical, in line; 121.6 cu in, 1,993 cc (3.89 x 3.03 in, 90.8 x 76.9 mm); compression ratio: 9.2:1; max power (DIN): 101 hp (74 kW) at 5,200 rpm; max torque (DIN): 111 lb ft, 15.3 kg m (150 Nm) at 3,500 rpm; max engine rpm: 6,500; 50.7 hp/l (37.8 kW/l); cast iron block and head; 5 crankshaft bearings; valves: overhead, Vee-slanted, rockers; camshafts: 1, overhead, cogged belt; lubrication: rotary pump, full flow filter, 6.6 imp pt, 7.8 US pt, 3.7 l; 1 Weber 32/36 DGAV downdraught carburettor; fuel feed: mechanical pump; water-cooled, 10.8 imp pt, 12.9 US pt, 6.1 l.

TRANSMISSION driving wheels: rear; clutch: single dry plate (diaphragm); gearbox: mechanical; gears: 4, fully synchronized; ratios: I 3.650, II 1.970, III 1.370, IV 1, rev 3.660; lever: central; final drive: hypoid bevel; axle ratio: 3.890; width of rims: 6"; tyres: 175 SR x 14.

PERFORMANCE max speeds: (I) 29 mph, 47 km/h; (II) 54 mph, 87 km/h; (III) 78 mph, 125 km/h; (IV) 103 mph, 165 km/h; power-weight ratio: 25.9 lb/hp (35.3 lb/kW), 11.7 kg/hp (16 kg/kW); speed in direct drive at 1,000 rpm: 18 mph, 29 km/h; consumption: 27.4 m/imp gal, 22.8 m/US gal, 10.3 l x 100 km at 75 mph, 120 km/h.

CHASSIS integral, front and rear auxiliary frames; front suspension: independent, wishbones (lower trailing links), coil springs, anti-roll bar, telescopic dampers; rear: independent, semi-trailing arms, coil springs, telescopic dampers.

STEERING rack-and-pinion; turns lock to lock: 4.39.

BRAKES front disc (diameter 10.31 in, 26.2 cm), rear drum, dual circuit, servo.

ELECTRICAL EQUIPMENT 12 V; 44 Ah battery; 45 A alternator; Motorcraft distributor; 2 halogen headlamps.

DIMENSIONS AND WEIGHT wheel base: 109.05 in, 277 cm; tracks: 59.45 in, 151 cm front, 60.63 in, 154 cm rear; length: 182.28 in, 463 cm; width: 70.47 in, 179 cm; height: 53.94 in, 137 cm; ground clearance: 5.12 in, 13 cm; weight: 2,613 lb, 1,185 kg; turning circle: 34.1 ft, 10.4 m; fuel tank: 14.3 imp gal, 17.2 US gal, 65 l.

BODY saloon/sedan, 4 doors - estate car/st. wagon, 4+1 doors; 5 seats, separate front seats, reclining backrests, headrests.

PRACTICAL INSTRUCTIONS fuel: 97 oct petrol; oil: engine 6 imp pt, 7.2 US pt, 3.4 l, SAE 20W-50, change every 6,200 miles, 10,000 km - gearbox 3 imp pt, 3.6 US pt, 1.7 l, SAE 80, no change recommended - final drive 3.2 imp pt, 3.8 US pt, 1.8 l, SAE 90, no change recommended; greasing: none; tappet clearances: inlet 0.008 in, 0.20 mm, exhaust 0.010 in, 0.25 mm; valve timing: 18° 70° 64° 24°; tyre pressure: front 24 psi, 1.7 atm, rear 26 psi, 1.8 atm.

OPTIONALS Ford C3 automatic transmission, hydraulic torque converter and planetary gears with 3 ratios (I 2.474, II 1.474, III 1, rev 2.111), max ratio of converter at stall 2.34, possible manual selection, max speed 95 mph, 153 km/h, consumption 25.7 m/imp gal, 21.4 m/US gal, 11 l x 100 km at 75 mph, 120 km/h; 185 SR x 14 tyres with 6" wide rims; power steering; sunshine roof; metallic spray; fog lamps.

63 hp (diesel) power team

See 101 hp power team, except for:

ENGINE diesel; 128.9 cu in, 2,112 cc (3.54 x 3.27 in, 90 x 83 mm); compression ratio: 22.2:1; max power (DIN): 63 hp (46 kW) at 4,500 rpm; max torque (DIN): 90 lb ft, 12.4 kg m (12.2 Nm) at 2,500 rpm; max engine rpm: 4,700; 29.8 hp/l (22 kW/l); lubrication: 8.8 imp pt, 10.6 US pt, 5 l; Bosch injection; water-cooled, 17.6 imp pt, 21.1 US pt, 10 l.

PERFORMANCE max speed: 84 mph, 135 km/h; power-weight ratio: 43.6 lb/hp (59.2 lb/kW), 19.8 kg/hp (26.8 kg/kW); consumption: 31 m/imp gal, 25.8 m/US gal, 9.1 l x 100 km at 75 mph, 120 km/h.

DIMENSIONS AND WEIGHT weight: 2,745 lb, 1,245 kg.

114 hp power team

See 101 hp power team, except for:

ENGINE 6 cylinders, Vee-slanted at 60°; 139.9 cu in, 2,293 cc (3.54 x 2.37 in, 90 x 60.1 mm); compression ratio: 9.2:1; max power (DIN): 114 hp (85 kW) at 5,300 rpm; max torque (DIN): 130 lb ft, 18 kg m (176 Nm) at 3,000 rpm; max engine rpm: 5,600; 49.6 hp/l (37 kW/l); 4 crankshaft bearings; lubrication: 7.4 imp pt, 8.9 US pt, 4.2 l; 1 Solex 35/35 EEIT downdraught twin barrel carburettor; cooling: 15.3 imp pt, 18.4 US pt, 8.7 l.

PERFORMANCE max speed: 107 mph, 171 km/h; power-weight ratio: 25 lb/hp (33.6 lb/kW), 11.4 kg/hp (15.2 kg/kW); speed in direct drive at 1,000 rpm: 19.6 mph, 31.6 km/h; consumption: 25.9 m/imp gal, 21.6 m/US gal, 10.9 l x 100 km at 75 mph, 120 km/h.

STEERING servo (standard for GL only).

BRAKES front disc, internal radial fins; lining area: front 23.3 sq in, 150 sq cm, rear 75 sq in, 484 sq cm, total 98.3 sq in, 634 sq cm.

ELECTRICAL EQUIPMENT 55 Ah battery; 55 A alternator.

DIMENSIONS AND WEIGHT weight: 2,855 lb, 1,295 kg.

PRACTICAL INSTRUCTIONS oil, engine 7 imp pt, 8.5 US pt, 4 l.

135 hp power team

See 101 hp power team, except for:

ENGINE 6 cylinders, Vee-slanted at 60°; 170.4 cu in, 2,792 cc (3.66 x 2.70 in, 93 x 68.5 mm); max power (DIN): 135 hp (99 kW) at 5,200 rpm; max torque (DIN): 159 lb ft, 22 kg m (21.6 Nm) at 3,000 rpm; max engine rpm: 5,600; 48.4 hp/l (35.6 kW/l); 4 crankshaft bearings; lubrication: 7.4 imp pt, 8.9 US pt, 4.2 l; 1 Solex 35/35 EEIT downdraught twin barrel carburettor; cooling: 15.3 imp pt, 18.4 US pt, 8.7 l.

TRANSMISSION gearbox ratios: I 3.160, II 1.950, III 1.410, IV 1, rev 3.350; axle ratio: 3.450; width of rims: Ghia models 6"; tyres: Ghia models 185 SR x 14.

PERFORMANCE max speed: 113 mph, 182 km/h; power-weight ratio: 21.2 lb/hp (28.7 lb/kW), 9.6 kg/hp (13 kg/kW); speed in

FORD Granada 2800 Ghia Estate Car

FORD Granada Ghia Series

LAND ROVER 88" Regular

K.M.B. GREAT BRITAIN

GTM Mk 1-3

ENGINE British Leyland, central, transverse, 4 stroke; 4 cylinders, vertical, in line; 77.8 cu in, 1,275 cc (2.78 x 3.20 in, 70.7 x 81.4 mm); compression ratio: 9.9:1; max power (SAE): 90 hp (66 kW) at 5,800 rpm; max torque (SAE): 83 lb ft, 11.4 kg m (112 Nm) at 3,200 rpm; max engine rpm: 7,600; 70.6 hp/l (51.9 kW/l); cast iron block and head; 3 crankshaft bearings; valves: overhead, in line, push-rods and rockers; camshafts: 1, side; lubrication; rotary pump, full flow filter, oil cooler, 8 imp pt, 9.5 US pt, 4.5 l; 2 SU carburettors; fuel feed: electric pump; water-cooled, 7 imp pt, 8.5 US pt, 4 l, rear mounted radiator.

TRANSMISSION driving wheels: rear; clutch: single dry plate (diaphragm); gearbox: mechanical; gears: 4, fully synchronized; ratios: I 3.203, II 1.919, III 1.358, IV 1, rev 3.350; lever: central; final drive: helical spur gears; axle ratios: from 2.900 to 4.300; width of rims: 5"; tyres: 145 x 10 or 165 x 10.

PERFORMANCE max speeds: (I) 39 mph, 62 km/h; (II) 61 mph, 98 km/h; (III) 90 mph, 145 km/h; (IV) 120 mph, 193 km/h; power-weight ratio: 13 lb/hp (17.9 lb/kW), 5.9 kg/hp (8.1 kg/hp); carrying capacity: 953 lb, 432 kg; acceleration: standing ¼ mile 17.5 sec, 0-50 mph (0-80 km/h) 7 sec; speed in direct drive at 1,000 rpm: 16 mph, 25.7 km/h; consumption: 38 m/imp gal, 31.8 m/US gal, 7.4 l x 100 km.

CHASSIS integral with front and rear tubular frame sections; front suspension: independent, wishbones, coil springs, telescopic dampers; rear: independent, wishbones, rubber elements, telescopic dampers.

STEERING rack-and-pinion; turns lock to lock: 3.20.

BRAKES front disc, rear drum, servo.

ELECTRICAL EQUIPMENT 12 V; 75 Ah battery; dynamo or alternator; Lucas distributor; 2 headlamps.

DIMENSIONS AND WEIGHT wheel base: 84 in, 213 cm; front and rear track: 48 in, 122 cm; length: 128 in, 325 cm; width: 56 in, 142 cm; height: 43 in, 109 cm; ground clearance: 5 in, 13 cm; weight: 1,175 lb, 533 kg; weight distribution: 45% front, 55% rear; fuel tank: 10 imp gal, 11,9 US gal, 45 l.

BODY coupé, in plastic material; 2 doors; 2 seats.

PRACTICAL INSTRUCTIONS oil: engine, gearbox and final drive 8 imp pt, 9.5 US pt, 4.5 l, SAE 20W-50, change every 6,000 miles, 9,600 km; greasing: every 6,000 miles, 9,600 km, 12 points; tyre pressure: front 20 psi, 1.3 atm, rear 30 psi, 2.1 atm.

VARIATIONS

ENGINE 51.7 cu in, 848 cc.

LAND ROVER 109" V8

LAND ROVER GREAT BRITAIN

88" Regular

(for export only)

ENGINE front, 4 stroke; 4 cylinders, vertical, in line; 139.5 cu in, 2,286 cc (3.56 x 3.50 in, 90.5 x 88.9 mm); compression ratio: 8:1; max power (DIN): 71 hp (52 kW) at 4,000 rpm; max torque (DIN): 120 lb ft, 16.5 kg m (162 Nm) at 1,500 rpm; max engine rpm: 5,000; 31.1 hp/l (22.9 kW/l); cast iron block and head; 3 crankshaft bearings; valves: overhead, in line, roller tappets, push-rods and rockers; camshafts: 1, side, chain-driven; lubrication: gear pump, full flow filter, 10.9 imp pt, 13.1 US pt, 6.2 l; 1 Zenith 36 IV downdraught single barrel carburettor; fuel feed: mechanical pump; water-cooled, 15.2 imp pt, 18.3 US pt, 8.7 l.

TRANSMISSION driving wheels: front (automatically engaged with transfer box low ratio) and rear; clutch: single dry plate (diaphragm), hydraulically controlled; gearbox: mechanical; gears: 4, fully synchronized and 2-ratio transfer box (high 1.148, low 2.350); ratios: I 3.680, II 2.220, III 1.500, IV 1, rev 4.020; gear and transfer levers: central; front and rear final drive; spiral bevel; front and rear axle ratio: 4.700; width of rims: 5"; tyres: 6.00 x 16.

PERFORMANCE max speeds: (I) 21 mph, 33 km/h; (II) 34 mph, 54 km/h; (III) 50 mph, 80 km/h; (IV) 66 mph, 106 km/h; power-weight ratio: 41.7 lb/hp (56.7 lb/kW), 18.9 kg/hp (25.7 kg/kW); carrying capacity: 1,499 lb, 680 kg; acceleration: 0-50 mph (0-80 km/h) 16.3 sec; speed in direct drive at 1,000 rpm: 15 mph, 24.1 km/h; consumption: 19.1 m/imp gal, 15.9 m/US gal, 14.8 x 100 km.

CHASSIS box-type ladder frame; front suspension: rigid axle, semi-elliptic leafsprings, telescopic dampers; rear: rigid axle, semi-elliptic leafsprings, telescopic dampers.

STEERING recirculating ball; turns lock to lock: 3.35.

BRAKES drum; lining area: total 105 sq in, 677 sq cm.

ELECTRICAL EQUIPMENT 12 V; 58 Ah battery; 34 A alternator; Lucas distributor; 2 headlamps.

DIMENSIONS AND WEIGHT wheel base: 88 in, 223 cm; front and rear track: 51.50 in, 131 cm; length: 142.35 in, 362 cm; width: 66.54 in, 169 cm; height: 77.56 in, 197 cm; ground clearance: 6.89 in, 17.5 cm; weight: 2,953 lb, 1,339 kg; weight distribution: 52.5% front, 47.5% rear; turning circle: 38 ft, 11.6 m; fuel tank: 10 imp gal, 12 US gal, 45 l.

BODY estate car/st. wagon; 2+1 doors; 7-8 seats, separate front seats.

PRACTICAL INSTRUCTIONS fuel: 90 oct petrol; oil: engine 10.9 imp pt, 13.1 US pt, 6.2 l, SAE 20W, change every 6,200 miles, 10,000 km - gearbox 2.5 imp pt, 3 US pt, 1.4 l - transfer box 4.4 imp pt, 5.3 US pt, 2.5 l, SAE 90 EP, change every 24,000 miles, 39,000 km - final drive 3 imp pt, 3.6 US pt, 1.7 l, SAE 90 EP, change every 24,000 miles, 39,000 km; greasing: every 6,200 miles, 10.000 km, 1 point; tappet clearances: inlet 0.010 in, 0.25 mm, exhaust 0.010 in, 0.25 mm; valve timing: 6° 52° 34° 24°; tyre pressure: front 25 psi, 1.7 atm, rear 25 psi, 1.7 atm.

VARIATIONS

ENGINE diesel, 23:1 compression ratio, max power (DIN) 63 hp (46 kW) at 4,000 rpm, max torque (DIN) 103 lb ft, 14.2 kg m (139 Nm) at 1,800 rpm, max engine rpm 4,000, 27.6 hp/l (20.3 kW) cast iron head with precombustion chambers, CAV injection; cooling, 14.8 imp pt, 17.8 US pt, 8.4 l.
PERFORMANCE power-weight ratio 48.3 lb/hp (66.1 lb/kW), 21.9 kg/hp (30 kg/kW); consumption: 26.9 m/imp gal, 22.4 m/US gal, 10.5 l x 100 km.
ELECTRICAL EQUIPMENT 95 Ah battery.
DIMENSIONS AND WEIGHT weight: 3,041 lb, 1,379 kg.

OPTIONALS overdrive, 0.790 ratio; oil cooler; front and rear power take-off; 7/7.50 x 16 tyres; servo brake; 45 A alternator; hardtop; special equipment.

109"

(for export only)

See 88" Regular, except for:

TRANSMISSION width of rims: 5.5"; tyres: 7.50 x 16.

PERFORMANCE power-weight ratio: 52.9 lb/hp (72.1 lb/kW), 24 kg/hp 32.7 kg/kW).

BRAKES swept area: total 171.9 sq in, 1,109 sq cm.

DIMENSIONS AND WEIGHT wheel base: 109 in, 277 cm; front and rear track: 52.36 in, 133 cm; length: 175 in, 444 cm; height: 79.13 in, 201 cm; ground clearance: 8.25 in, 21 cm; weight: 3,752 lb, 1,702 kg; weight distribution: 46.5% front, 53.5% rear; turning circle: 46.9 ft, 14.3 m; fuel tank: 15 imp gal, 18 US gal, 68 l.

109"

BODY estate car/st. wagon; 2+1 or 4+1 doors; 10-12 seats, separate front seats.

VARIATIONS

ENGINE diesel.
ENGINE 6 cylinders, 160.2 cu in, 2,625 cc (3.06 x 3.63 in, 77.8 x 92.1 mm), 7.8:1 compression ratio, max power (DIN) 87 hp (64 kW) at 4,500 rpm, max torque (DIN) 132 lb ft, 18.2 kg m (178 Nm) at 1,500 rpm, 33.1 hp/l (24.4 kW/l) cast iron block, light alloy head, 7 crankshaft bearings, lubrication 12.8 imp pt, 15.4 US pt, 7.3 l, 1 Zenith 175-CD2S horizontal carburettor, electric full pump, cooling 21.1 imp pt, 25.4 US pt, 12 l [or 7:1 compression ratio, max power (DIN) 82 hp (60 kW) at 4,500 rpm, max torque (DIN) 128 lb ft, 17.7 kg m (174 Nm) at 1,500 rpm, 31.2 hp/l (23 kW/l)].
PERFORMANCE max speed 72 mph, 116 km/, power-weight ratio 45 lb/hp (61.1 lb/kW), 20.4 kg/hp (27.7 kg/kW), speed in direct drive at 1,000 rpm 16.5 mph, 26.6 km/h, consumption 14.6 m/imp gal, 12.1 m/US gal, 19.4 l x 100 km.
DIMENSIONS AND WEIGHT weight 3,910 lb, 1,774 kg.

109" V8

(for export only)

See 88" Regular, except for:

ENGINE 8 cylinders, Vee-slanted at 90°; 215.5 cu in, 3,532 cc (3.42 x 2.80 in, 88.9 x 71.1 mm); max power (DIN): 92 hp (68 kW) at 3,500 rpm; max torque (DIN): 167 lb ft, 23 kg m (226 Nm) at 2,000 rpm; 26 hp/l (19.1 kW/l); light alloy block and head, dry liners; 5 crankshaft bearings; camshafts: 1, central, chain-driven; lubrication: 10 imp pt, 12 US pt, 5.7 l; 2 Zenith-Stromberg CDSE semi-downdraught carburettors; cooling 19.9 imp pt, 23.9 US pt, 11.3 l.

TRANSMISSION gears: 4, fully synchronized and 2-ratio transfer box (high 1.170, low 3.320); ratios: I 4.070, II 2.450, III 1.500, IV 1, rev 3.660; width of rims: 5.5"; tyres: 7.50 V x 16.

PERFORMANCE max speed: about 73 mph, 118 km/h; power-weight ratio: 43.2 lb/hp (58.4 lb/kW), 19.6 kg/hp (26.5 kg/kW); consumption: 17.1 m/imp gal, 14.3 m/US gal, 16.5 l x 100 km.

BRAKES swept area: total 171.9 sq in, 1,109 sq cm.

ELECTRICAL EQUIPMENT 60 Ah battery; 34 or 45 A alternator.

DIMENSIONS AND WEIGHT wheel base: 109 in, 277 cm; front and rear track: 52.36 in, 133 cm; length: 175 in, 444 cm; height: 79.13 in, 201 cm; ground clearance: 8.25 in, 21 cm; weight: 3,980 lb, 1,805 kg; turning circle: 46.9 ft, 14.3 m; fuel tank: 15 imp gal, 18 US gal, 68 l.

BODY estate car/st. wagon; 2+1 or 4+1 doors; 10-12 seats, separate front seats.

Range Rover

PRICE EX WORKS: £ 12,396*

ENGINE front, 4 stroke; 8 cylinders, Vee-slanted at 90°; 215 cu in, 3,528 cc (3.50 x 2.80 in, 88.9 x 71.1 mm); compression ratio: 8.13:1; max power (DIN): 132 hp (97 kW) at 5,000 rpm; max torque (DIN): 187 lb ft, 25.8 kg m (251 Nm) at 2,500 rpm; max engine rpm: 5,200; 37.4 hp/l (27.5 kW/l); light alloy block and head, dry liners; 5 crankshaft bearings; valves: overhead, in line, push-rods and rockers, hydraulic tappets; camshafts: 1, at centre of Vee; lubrication: gear pump, full flow filter, 10 imp pt, 12 US pt, 5.7 l; 2 Zenith-Stromberg CD2 semi-downdraught carburettors; fuel feed: electric pump; water-cooled, expansion tank, 20 imp pt, 23.9 US pt, 11.3 l.

TRANSMISSION driving wheels: 4, with lockable differential in transfer box; clutch: single dry plate (diaphragm), hydraulically controlled; gearbox: mechanical; gears: 4, fully synchronized, and 2-ratio transfer box (high 1.174, low 3.321); ratios: I 4,069, II 2.448, III 1,505, IV 1, rev 3.664; gear and transfer levers: central; front and rear final drive: spiral bevel; front and rear axle ratio: 3.540; width of rims: 6"; tyres: 205 x 16.

PERFORMANCE max speeds: (I) 24 mph, 39 km/h; (II) 41 mph, 66 km/h; (III) 68 mph, 109 km/h; (IV) 96 mph, 154 km/h; power-weight ratio: 28.8 lb/hp (39.1 lb/kW), 13.1 kg/hp (17.8 kg/kW); carrying capacity: 1,720 lb, 780 kg; acceleration: standing ¼ mile 19.3 sec, 0-50 mph (0-80 km/h) 11.1 sec; speed in direct drive at 1,000 rpm: 20 mph, 32.2 km/h; consumption: 18.2 m/imp gal, 15.1 m/US gal, 15.5 l x 100 km.

CHASSIS box-type ladder frame; front suspension: rigid axle, longitudinal radius arms, transverse linkage bar, coil springs/telescopic dampers units; rear: rigid axle, longitudinal radius arms, upper A-bracket, Boge Hydromat self-energizing levelling device, coil springs, telescopic dampers.

STEERING Burman, recirculating ball, worm and nut; turns lock to lock: 4.75.

LAND ROVER Range Rover

BRAKES disc (front diameter 11.75 in, 29.8 cm, rear 11.42 in, 29 cm), servo; swept area: front 261 sq in, 1,683 sq cm, rear 235 sq in, 1,516 sq cm, total 496 sq in, 3,199 sq cm.

ELECTRICAL EQUIPMENT 12 V; 60 Ah battery; 45 A alternator; Lucas distributor; 2 headlamps.

DIMENSIONS AND WEIGHT wheel base: 100 in, 254 cm; front and rear track: 58.50 in, 149 cm; length: 176 in, 447 cm; width: 70 in, 178 cm; height: 70 in, 178 cm; ground clearance: 7.50 in, 19 cm; weight: 3,800 lb, 1,724 kg; weight distribution: 50% front, 50% rear; turning circle: 37 ft, 11.3 m; fuel tank: 18 imp gal, 21.6 US gal, 82 l.

BODY estate car/st. wagon; 2+1 doors; 5 seats, separate front seats, reclining backrests; heated rear window with wiper-washer; laminated windscreen; folding rear seat.

PRACTICAL INSTRUCTIONS fuel: 91-93 oct petrol; oil: engine 10 imp pt, 12 US pt, 5.7 l, SAE 20W, change every 6,200 miles, 10,000 km - gearbox 4.5 imp pt, 5.5 US pt, 2.6 l, SAE 80 EP, change every 24,000 miles, 39,000 km - transfer box 5.5 imp pt, 6.6 US pt, 3.1 l, SAE 80 EP, change every 6,200 miles, 10,000 km - final drive rear 2.7 imp pt, 3.2 US pt, 1.5 l, SAE 80 EP, change every 24,000 miles, 39,000 km, front 3 imp pt, 3.6 US pt, 1.7 l, SAE 80 EP, change every 24,000 miles, 39,000 km; greasing: every 6,200 miles, 10,000 km, 6 points; valve timing: 30° 75° 68° 37°; tyre pressure: front 25 psi, 1.7 atm, rear 25 psi, 1.7 atm.

OPTIONALS power steering; headrests; tinted glass; 65 A alternator.

LENHAM — GREAT BRITAIN

Austin-Healey 3000

PRICE EX WORKS: £ 7,100*

ENGINE Austin-Healey, front, 4 stroke; 6 cylinders, in line, 178.1 cu in, 2,912 cc (3.28 x 3.50 in, 83.3 x 88.9 mm); compression ratio: 8.5:1; max power (DIN): 120 hp (88 kW) at 4,60[0] rpm; max torque (DIN): 167 lb ft, 23 kg m (226 Nm) at 2,70[0] rpm; max engine rpm: 5,000; 41.2 hp/l (30.3 kW/l); cast iro[n] block and head; 4 crankshaft bearings; valves: overhead, push rods and rockers; camshafts: 1, side; lubrication: rotary pump, full flow filter, 12 imp pt, 14.4 US pt, 6.8 l; 2 SU type HD6 [or] HS6 semi-downdraught carburettor; fuel feed: electric pump; water-cooled, 30 imp pt, 35.9 US pt, 17 l.

TRANSMISSION driving wheels: rear; clutch: single dry plate; gearbox: mechanical; gears: 4 + overdrive; ratios: I 2.930, [II] 2.053, III 1.309, IV 1; lever: central; final drive: hypoid bevel; axle ratio: 3.900; width of rims: 6"; tyres: 185 x 15.

PERFORMANCE max speeds: (I) 28 mph, 45 km/h; (II) 45 mph, 72 km/h; (III) 80 mph, 128 km/h; (IV) 100 mph, 161 km/h; (overdrive-top) 120 mph, 193 km/h; power-weight ratio: 16.[?] lb/hp (22 lb/kW), 7.3 kg/hp (10 kg/kW); carrying capacity: 35[?] lb, 160 kg; acceleration: 0-50 mph (0-80 km/h) 6 sec; speed in direct drive at 1,000 rpm: 20 mph, 32.2 km/h; consumption: 2[?] m/imp gal, 20.8 m/US gal, 11.3 l x 100 km.

LENHAM Austin-Healey 3000

HASSIS box section frame; front suspension: independent, ıequal length wishbones, coil springs, anti-roll bar, lever ımpers; rear: rigid axle, two longitudinal leafsprings, lever ımpers.

TEERING cam and peg; turns lock to lock: 2.75.

RAKES front disc (diameter 11.25 in, 28.6 cm), rear drum.

.ECTRICAL EQUIPMENT 12 V; 50 Ah battery; dynamo; Lucas stributor; 2 headlamps.

IMENSIONS AND WEIGHT wheel base: 92.13 in, 234 cm: acks: 50.50 in, 128 cm front, 52.50 in, 133 cm rear; length: 51 in, 383 cm; width: 63 in, 160 cm; height: 47 in, 119 cm; ound clearance: 6 in, 15 cm; weight: 1,940 lb, 880 kg; weight stribution: 60% front, 40% rear; turning circle: 36 ft, 11 m; fuel nk: 12 imp gal, 14.3 US gal, 54 l.

ODY open, in composite aluminum and fiberglass material; no ors: 2 seats: folding windscreen; outside handbrake: Connel- hide trim; stainless steel exhaust system; screen washers d wipers; tonneau cover; wood rim steering wheel.

RACTICAL INSTRUCTIONS fuel: 98 oct petrol; oil: engine 12 p pt, 14.4 US pt, 6.8 l, SAE 20/50, change every 3,000 miles, 800 km - gearbox 6 imp pt, 7.2 US pt, 3.4 l, SAE 20/50 - final ive 3 imp pt, 3.6 US pt, 1.7 l; greasing: every 2,000 miles, 200 km, 10 points; tappet clearances (hot): inlet and exhaust 012 in, 0.30 mm; valve timing: 5° 45° 40° 10°; tyre pressure: ont 24 psi, 1.7 atm, rear 20 psi, 1.4 atm.

PTIONALS 3.540 axle ratio without overdrive; side-mounted are wheel; hood; heater; centre hinged bonnet.

LOTUS Elite

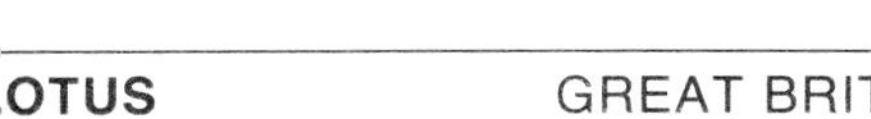

.OTUS GREAT BRITAIN

Elite

RICES IN USA AND EX WORKS:	$	£
)1	—	**14,676***
)2	—	**15,641***
3	**37,200***	**16,227***
4	**37,900***	**16,445***

NGINE front, 4 stroke; 4 cylinders, in line, slanted 45° to left; 20.4 cu in, 1,973 cc (3.75 x 2.72 in, 95.2 x 69.2 mm); com- ession ratio: 9.5:1; max power (DIN): 155 hp (114 kW) at 500 rpm; max torque (DIN): 135 lb ft, 18.6 kg m (182 Nm) at 000 rpm; max engine rpm: 7,000; 78.6 hp/l (57.8 kW/l); light loy block and head, wet liners; 5 crankshaft bearings; valves: per cylinder, overhead, slanted at 38°, thimble tappets; mshafts: 2, overhead, cogged belt; lubrication: rotary pump, ll flow filter, 10 imp pt, 12 US pt, 5.7 l; 2 Dell'Orto DHLA 45E orizontal twin barrel carburettors; fuel feed: electric pump; ater-cooled, 12 imp pt, 14.4 US pt, 6.8 l, electric thermostatic n.

RANSMISSION driving wheels: rear; clutch: single dry plate iaphragm); gearbox: mechanical (for 504 only automatic ansmission, hydraulic torque converter and planetary gears ith 3 ratios, max ratio of convert at stall 2, possible manual selection, ratios I 2.390, II 1.450, III 1, rev 2.090); gears: 5, fully synchronized; ratios: I 3.200, II 2.010, III 1.370, IV 1, V 0.800, rev 3.467; lever: central; final drive: hypoid bevel; axle ratio: 4.100 - for 504 3.730; width of rims: 7"; tyres: 205/60 VR x 14.

PERFORMANCE max speeds: (I) 40 mph, 64 km/h; (II) 64 mph, 103 km/h; (III) 93 mph, 149 km/h; (IV) 128 mph, 206 km/h; (V) 125 mph, 201 km/h; power-weight ratio: 15 lb/hp (20.5 lb/kW), 6.8 kg hp (9.3 kg/kW); carrying capacity: 860 lb, 390 kg; speed in top at 1,000 rpm: 20.7 mph, 33.3 km/h; consumption: 26.4 m/imp gal, 22 m/US gal, 10.7 l x 100 km.

CHASSIS box-type backbone; front suspension: independet, wishbones, coil springs, anti-roll bar, telescopic dampers; rear: independent, lower wide-based wishbones, semi-axles as upper arms, coil springs/telescopic struts.

STEERING rack-and-pinion - for 503 and 504 servo; turns lock to lock: 3.50.

BRAKES disc (diameter 10.40 in, 26.4 cm), rear drum, servo.

ELECTRICAL EQUIPMENT 12 V; 50 Ah battery; 60 A alterna- tor; Lucas distributor; 2 retractable headlamps - for 502, 503 and 504 halogen headlamps.

DIMENSIONS AND WEIGHT wheel base: 97.64 in, 248 cm; tracks: 58.50 in, 149 cm front, 58.50 in, 149 cm rear; length: 175.50 in, 446 cm; width: 71.50 in, 182 cm; height: 47.65 in, 121 cm; ground clearance: 5.50 in, 14 cm; weight: 2,338 lb, 1,060 kg; turning circle: 34.5 ft, 10.5 m; fuel tank: 14.7 imp gal, 17.7 US gal, 67 l.

BODY coupé, in reinforced plastic material; 2 doors; 4 seats, separate front seats, reclining backrests, built-in front and rear headrests; electric windows; heated rear window; light alloy wheels; rear window wiper-washer; for 502, 503 and 504 tinted glass and air-conditioning.

PRACTICAL INSTRUCTIONS fuel: 98-100 oct petrol; oil: en- gine 9.2 imp pt, 11 US pt, 5.2 l, SAE 20W-50, change every 3,000 miles, 4,800 km - gearbox 2 imp pt, 2.3 US pt, 1.1 l, SAE 80 EP, change every 6,000 miles, 9,700 km - final drive 2 imp pt, 2.3 US pt, 1.1 l, SAE 90 EP, change every 12,000 miles 20,000 km; greasing: every 3,000 miles, 4,800 km, 2 points; tappet clearances: inlet 0.010 in, 0.25 mm, exhaust 0,010 in, 0.25 mm; valve timing: 25° 65° 65° 25°; tyre pressure: front 22 psi, 1.6 atm, rear 22 psi, 1.6 atm.

VARIATIONS

(For USA only)
ENGINE 8.4:1 compression ratio, max power (DIN) 142 hp (104 kW) at 6,500 rpm, max torque (DIN) 130 lb ft, 18 kg m (176 Nm) at 5,000 rpm, 72 hp/l (53 kW/l), 2 Zenith-Stromberg 175 CD 2SE horizontal carburettors.
PERFORMANCE max speed 118 mph, 190 km/h, power-weight ratio 16.1 lb/hp (22.4 lb/kW), 7,3 kg/hp (10.1 kg/kW).
PRACTICAL INSTRUCTIONS valve timing 26° 66° 66° 26°.

OPTIONALS automatic transmission, hydraulic torque conver- ter and planetary gears with 3 ratios (I 2.390, II 1.450, III 1, rev 2.090), max ratio of converter at stall 2, possible manual selection, 3.730 axle ratio (for 501 only); power steering (for 501 only); metallic spray; vinyl roof.

LOTUS Eclat

Eclat

PRICES IN USA AND EX WORKS:	$	£
520	—	**12,974***
521	—	**14,002***
522	—	**14,999***
523	**36,100***	**15,559***
524	**36,650***	**15,808***

ENGINE front, 4 stroke; 4 cylinders, in line; 120.4 cu in, 1,973 cc (3.75 x 2.72 in, 95.2 x 69.2 mm); compression ratio: 9.5:1; max power (DIN): 160 hp (118 kW) at 6,200 rpm; max torque (DIN): 140 lb ft, 19.3 kg m (189 Nm) at 4,900 rpm; max engine rpm: 7,300; 81.1 hp/l (59.7 kW/l): light alloy block and head, wet liners; 5 crankshaft bearings; valves: 4 per cylinder, over- head, slanted at 38°, thimble tappets; camshafts: 2 overhead, cogged belt; lubrication: rotary pump, full flow filter, 10.5 imp pt, 12.5 US pt, 5.9 l; 2 Dell'Orto DHLA 45E horizontal twin barrel carburettors; fuel feed: electric pump; water-cooled, 12 imp pt, 14.4 US pt, 6.8 l, electric thermostatic fan.

TRANSMISSION driving wheels: rear; clutch: single dry plate (diaphragm); gearbox: mechanical (for 524 only, automatic transmission, hydraulic torque converter and planetary gears with 3 ratios, max ratio of converter at stall 2, possible manual selection, ratios I 2.390, II 1.450, III 1, rev 2.090); gears: 4 (5 for 521, 522 and 523), fully synchronized; ratios: I 3.160, II 1.950, III 1.410, IV 1, rev 3.350 (for 521, 522 and 523 I 3.200, II 2.010, III 1.370, IV 1, V 0.800, rev 3.467); lever: central; final drive: hypoid bevel; axle ratio: 3.730 (4.100 for 521, 522 and 523); width of rims: 5.5" (7" for 521, 522 and 523); tyres: 185/70 HR x 13 (for 521, 522 and 523 205/60 VR x 14).

ECLAT

PERFORMANCE max speeds: (I) 40 mph, 65 km/h; (II) 66 mph, 106 km/h; (III) 92 mph, 148 km/h: (IV) 130 mph, 209 km/h - for 521, 522, 523 and 524 (I) 42 mph, 67 km/h; (II) 66 mph, 106 km/h; (III) 97 mph, 156 km/h; (IV) 105 mph, 169 km/h; (V) 132 mph, 212 km/h; power-weight ratio: 13.5 lb/hp (18.3 lb/kW), 6.1 kg/hp (8.3 kg/kW); carrying capacity: 706 lb, 320 kg: acceleration: standing ¼ mile 15.8 (16 for 521, 522, 523 and 524) sec, 0-50 mph (0-80 km/h) 6 (6.1 for 521, 522, 523 and 524) sec; speed in direct drive at 1,000 rpm: 17.9 mph, 28.8 km/h; consumption: 28 m/imp gal, 23.3 m/US gal, 10.1 l x 100 km.

CHASSIS box-type backbone; front suspension: independent, wishbones, coil springs, anti-roll bar, telescopic dampers; rear: independent, lower wide-based wishbones, semi-axles as upper arms, coil springs, telescopic dampers.

STEERING rack-and-pionion, for 523 and 524 servo; turns lock to lock: 3.50.

BRAKES front disc, rear drum, servo.

ELECTRICAL EQUIPMENT 12 V; 48 Ah battery; 45 A alternator; Lucas distributor; 2 retractable headlamps - for 522, 523 and 524 halogen headlamps.

DIMENSIONS AND WEIGHT wheel base: 97.75 in, 248 cm; tracks: 58.50 in, 149 cm front, 59 in, 150 cm rear; length: 175.50 in, 446 cm; width: 71.50 in, 182 cm; height: 47.25 in, 120 cm; ground clearance: 5.40 in, 13.7 cm; weight: 2,160 lb, 979 kg; fuel tank: 14.7 imp gal, 17.7 US gal, 67 l.

BODY coupé, in reinforced plastic material; 2 doors; 2+2 seats, separate front seats, reclining backrests with built-in headrests; electric windows; heated rear window; for 521, 522, 523 and 524 light alloy wheels; for 522, 523 and 524 air-conditioning and tinted glass.

PRACTICAL INSTRUCTIONS fuel: 98 oct petrol; oil: engine 10.5 imp pt, 12.5 US pt, 5.9 l, SAE 20W-50, change every 3,000 miles, 4,800 km - gearbox 2 imp pt, 2.3 US pt, 1.1 l. SAE 80 EP, change every 6,000 miles, 9,700 km - final drive 2 imp pt, 2.3 US pt, 1.1 l, SAE 90 EP, change every 12,000 miles, 20,000 km; greasing: every 3,000 miles, 4,800 km, 4 points; tappet clearances: inlet 0.004-0.006 in, 0.11-0.14 mm, exhaust 0.008-0.010 in, 0.20-0.25 mm; valve timing: 30° 50° 50° 30°; tyre pressure: front 20 psi, 1.4 atm, rear 22 psi, 1.6 atm.

OPTIONALS (for 521 only) automatic transmission, hydraulic torque converter and planetary gears with 3 ratios (I 2.390, II 1.450, III 1, rev 2.090), max ratio of converter at stall 2, possible manual selection, 3.730 axle ratio; for 521 only, power steering.

Esprit S2

PRICE IN USA: $ 35,600*
PRICE EX WORKS: £ 14,870*

ENGINE central, rear, longitudinal, 4 stroke; 4 cylinders, in line; 120.4 cu in, 1,973 cc (3.75 x 2.72 in, 95.2 x 69.2 mm); compression ratio: 9.5:1; max power (DIN): 160 hp (118 kW) at 6,200 rpm; max torque (DIN): 140 lb ft, 19.3 kg m (189 Nm) at 4,900 rpm; max engine rpm: 7,300; 81.1 hp/l (59.7 kW/l); light alloy block and head, wet liners; 5 crankshaft bearings; valves: 4 per cylinder, overhead, slanted at 38°, thimble tappets; camshafts: 2 overhead, cogged belt; lubrication: rotary pump, full flow filter, 10.5 imp pt, 12.5 US pt, 5.9 l; 2 Dell'Orto DHLA 45 horizontal twin barrel carburettors; fuel feed: electric pump; water-cooled, 15.8 imp pt, 19 US pt, 9 l, front radiator, electric thermostatic fans.

TRANSMISSION driving wheels: rear; clutch: single dry plate (diaphragm), hydraulically controlled; gearbox: mechanical; gears: 5, fully synchronized; ratios: I 2.920, II 1.940, III 1.320, IV 0.970, V 0.760, rev 4.375; lever: central; final drive: hypoid bevel, in unit with gearbox; axle ratio: 4.375; width of rims: 6" front, 7" rear; tyres: 195/70 HR x 14 front, 205/70 HR x 14 rear.

PERFORMANCE max speeds: (I) 36 mph, 58 km/h; (II) 54 mph, 87 km/h; (III) 79 mph, 127 km/h; (IV) 108 mph, 174 km/h; (V) 138 mph, 222 km/h; power-weight ratio: 12,4 lb/hp (16.8 lb/kW), 5.6 kg/hp (7.6 kh/kW); carrying capacity: 500 lb, 227 kg: acceleration: standing ¼ mile 15 sec, 0-50 mph (0-80 km/h) 4.9 sec; speed in top at 1,000 rpm: 21.8 mph, 35.1 km/h; consumption: 28 m/imp gal, 23.3 m/US gal, 10.1 l x 100 km.

CHASSIS box-type backbone with space-frame section; front suspension: independent, wishbones, coil springs, anti-roll bar, telescopic dampers; rear: independent, wishbones, diagonal trailing arm and lateral link with fixed length driveshaft, coil springs, telescopic dampers.

STEERING rack-and-pinion.

BRAKES disc (front diameter 9.7 in, 24.6 cm, rear 10.6 in, 25.6 cm).

ELECTRICAL EQUIPMENT 12 V; 48 Ah battery; 45 A alternator; Lucas distributor; 4 retractable halogen headlamps.

DIMENSIONS AND WEIGHT wheel base: 96 in, 244 cm: front and rear track: 59.50 in, 151 cm; length: 165 in. 419 cm; width: 73.25 in, 186 cm; height: 43.70 in, 111 cm; ground clearance: 5.50 in, 14 cm; weight: 1,980 lb, 898 kg; fuel tank: 15 imp gal, 18 US gal, 68 l.

LOTUS Esprit S2

BODY coupé, in reinforced plastic material; 2 doors; 2 seats with built-in headrests; electric windows; light alloy wheels; heated rear window; tinted glass.

PRACTICAL INSTRUCTIONS fuel: 98 oct petrol; oil: engine 10.5 imp pt, 12.5 US pt, 5.9 l, SAE 20W-50, change every 3,000 miles, 4,800 km - gearbox and final drive 4.4 imp pt, 5.3 US pt, 2.5 l, SAE 80 EP, change every 12,000 miles, 20,000 km; greasing: every 3,000 miles, 4,800 km, 4 points; tappet clearances: inlet 0.004-0.006 in, 0.11-0.14 mm, exhaust 0.008-0.010 in, 0.20-0.25 mm; valve timing: 30° 50° 50° 30°; tyre pressure: front 18 psi, 1.3 atm, rear 28 psi 2 atm.

OPTIONALS metallic spray.

LYNX — GREAT BRITAIN

D Type

PRICE EX WORKS: £ 24,000*

ENGINE Jaguar XKE, front, 4 stroke; 6 cylinders, in line; 258.4 cu in, 4,235 cc (3.63 x 4.17 in, 92.1 x 106 mm); compression ratio: 9:1; max power (DIN): 171 hp (126 kW) at 4,500 rpm; ma torque (DIN): 230 lb ft, 31.8 kg m (312 Nm) at 2,500 rpm; ma engine rpm: 5,500; 40.4 hp/l (29.7 kW/l); block with chrome iro dry liners, head with aluminium alloy hemispherical combustic chambers; 7 crankshaft bearings; valves: overhead, Vee slanted at 70°, thimble tappets; camshafts: 2, overhead; lubr cation: rotary pump, full flow filter, 15 imp pt, 18 US pt, 8.5 l; Weber semi-downdraught carburettors; fuel feed: electric pump water-cooled, 32.9 imp pt, 39.5 US pt, 18.7 l, automatic thermo static fan.

TRANSMISSION driving wheels: rear; clutch: single dry plat (diaphragm), hydraulically controlled; gearbox: mechanica gears: 4, fully synchronized; ratios: I 2.933, II 1.905, III 1.38 IV 1, rev 3.378; lever: central; final drive: hypoid bevel, limite slip differential; axle ratio: 3.070; width of rims: 6"; tyres: E7 VR x 15.

PERFORMANCE max speeds: (I) 48 mph, 77 km/h: (II) 73 mp 117 km/h; (III) 108 mph, 174 km/h; (IV) 150 mph, 241 km/ power-weight ratio: 12.8 lb/hp (17.4 lb/kW), 5.8 kg/hp (7. kg/kW); carrying capacity: 408 lb, 185 kg; acceleration: stan ing ¼ mile 16 sec, 0-50 mph (0-80 km/h) 5.4 sec; consumptio 18.8 m/imp gal, 15.7 m/US gal, 15 l x 100 km.

CHASSIS integral, front and rear tubular auxiliary frames; fro suspension: independent, wishbones, swinging longitudinal to sion bars, anti-roll bar, telescopic dampers; rear: independen wide-based wishbones, semi-axles as upper arms, trailing low radius arms, 4 coil springs, 4 telescopic dampers.

STEERING rack-and-pinion.

LYNX D Type

RAKES disc (front diameter 11.18 in, 28.4 cm, rear 10.38 in, 5.4 cm), twin master cylinder; swept area: front 234.5 sq in, 512 sq cm, rear 213.7 sq in, 1,378 sq cm, total 448.2 sq in, 890 sq cm.

LECTRICAL EQUIPMENT 12 V; 68 A h battery; 60 A alternar; Lucas distributor; 2 headlamps.

IMENSIONS AND WEIGHT wheel base: 90.50 in, 230 cm; acks: 50.75 in, 129 cm front, 51.50 in, 131 cm rear; length: 59 in, 404 cm; width: 63 in, 160 cm; height: 45.50 in, 116 cm; ound clearance: 5 in, 12.7 cm; weight: 2,184 lb, 990 kg; eight distribution: 51% front, 49% rear; turning circle: 32 ft, 8 m; fuel tank: 20 imp gal, 24 US gal, 91 l.

ODY sports; 2 doors; 2 seats.

RACTICAL INSTRUCTIONS fuel: 97 oct petrol; oil: engine 15 np pt, 18 US pt, 8.5 l, SAE 20W-50, change every 6,000 miles, 700 km - gearbox 2.5 imp pt, 3 US pt, 1.4 l, SAE 90 EP, nange every 12,000 miles, 19,300 km - final drive 2.7 imp pt, 2 US pt, 1.5 l, SAE 90 EP, change every 12,000 miles,19,300 n; greasing: every 6,000-12,000 miles, 9,700-19,300 km; tapet clearances: inlet 0.012-0.014 in, 0.30-0.35 mm, exhaust 012-0.014 in, 0.30-0.35 mm; valve timing: 17° 59° 59° 17°; re pressure: front 24 psi, 1.7 atm, rear 28 psi, 2 atm.

VARIATIONS

NGINE Jaguar, tuned, max power (DIN) 285 hp (210 kW).
NGINE Jaguar, tuned, max power (DIN) 320 hp (235 kW).

PTIONALS 8:1 compression ratio: XKSS model; short ose body-work; dry sump lubrication with oil tank; oil ooler; light alloy peg-drive wheels; 6.50L x 15 tyres; side xit exhaust.

IG GREAT BRITAIN

Midget

RICE EX WORKS: £ 3,604*

NGINE front, 4 stroke; 4 cylinders, vertical, in line; 91.1 cu n, 1,493 cc (2.90 x 3.44 in, 73.7 x 87.4 mm); compression atio: 9:1; max power (DIN): 65 hp (48 kW) at 5,500 rpm; nax torque (DIN): 78 lb ft, 10.8 kg m (106 Nm) at 3,000 om; max engine rpm: 6,000; 43.5 hp/l (32 kW/l); cast iron lock and head; 3 crankshaft bearings; valves: overhead, ush-rods and rockers; camshafts: 1, side; lubrication: ccentric pump, full flow filter, 7 imp pt, 8.5 US pt, 4 l; 2 SU ype HS4 semi-downdraught carburettors; fuel feed: mechaical pump; water-cooled, 6 imp pt, 7.2 US pt, 3.4 l.

RANSMISSION driving wheels: rear; cluth: single dry plate diaphragm), hydraulically controlled; gearbox: mechanical; ears: 4, fully synchronized; ratios: I 3.411, II 2.113, III .433, IV 1, rev 3.753; lever: central; final drive: hypoid evel; axle ratio: 3.720; width of rims: 4"; tyres: 145 x 13.

MG Midget

PERFORMANCE max speeds: (I) 29 mph, 46 km/h; (II) 47 mph, 75 km/h; (III) 69 mph, 111 km/h; (IV) 95 mph, 153 km/h power-weight ratio: 27.3 lb/hp (36.8 lb/kW), 12.4 kg/hp (16.7 kg/kW); carrying capacity: 353 lb, 160 kg; speed in direct drive at 1,000 rpm: 16.4 mph, 26.4 km/h; consumption: 35.3 m/imp gal, 29.4 m/US gal, 8 l x 100 km.

CHASSIS integral; front suspension: independent, wishbones, coil springs, anti-roll bar, telescopic dampers; rear: rigid axle, semi-elliptic leafsprings, telescopic dampers.

STEERING rack-and-pinion; turns lock to lock: 2.25.

BRAKES front disc (diameter 8.25 in, 21 cm), rear drum.

ELECTRICAL EQUIPMENT 12 V; 40 Ah battery; 34 A alternator; Lucas distributor; 2 headlamps.

DIMENSIONS AND WEIGHT wheel base: 80 in, 206 cm; tracks: 46.31 in, 118 cm front, 44.75 in, 114 cm rear; length: 141 in, 358 cm; width: 60.25 in, 153 cm; height: 48.25 in, 123 cm; ground clearance: 3.25 in, 8.2 cm; weight: 1,774 lb, 804 kg; weight distribution: 52.4% front, 47.6% rear; turning circle: 30.2 ft, 9.2 m; fuel tank: 7 imp gal, 8.4 US gal, 32 l.

BODY convertible; 2 doors; 2 separate seats, built-in headrests; tonneau cover; polyurethane bumpers.

PRACTICAL INSTRUCTIONS fuel: 97 oct petrol; oil: engine 6.5 imp pt, 7.8 US pt, 3.7 l, SAE 20W-50, change every 6,000 miles, 9,700 km - gearbox 2 imp pt, 2.3 US pt, 1.1 l, SAE 90, change every 3,000 miles, 4,800 km - final drive 1.7 imp pt, 1.9 US pt, 0.9 l, SAE 90, change every 3,000 miles, 4,800 km; greasing: every 3,000 miles, 4,800 km, 8 points; tappet clearances: inlet 0.010 in, 0.25 mm, exhaust 0.010 in, 0.25 mm; valve timing: 18° 58° 58° 18°; tyre pressure: front 22 psi, 1.5 atm, rear 24 psi, 1.7 atm.

VARIATIONS

ENGINE 8:1 compression ratio.
TRANSMISSION (for export only) 5.20 x 13 tyres.

OPTIONALS oil cooler; wire wheels; hardtop.

MGB GT

PRICE EX WORKS: £ 5,533*

ENGINE front, 4 stroke; 4 cylinders, in line; 109.7 cu in, 1,798 cc (3.16 x 3.50 in, 80.3 x 88.9 mm); compression ratio: 9:1; max power (DIN): 97 hp (71 kW) at 5,500 rpm; max torque (DIN): 104 lb ft, 14.5 kg m (142 Nm) at 2,500 rpm; max engine rpm: 6,200; 53.9 hp/l (39.7 kW/l); cast iron block and head; 5 crankshaft bearings; valves: overhead, push-rods and rockers; camshafts: 1, side; lubrication: eccentric pump, full flow filter (cartridge), oil cooler, 6.5 imp pt, 7.8 US pt, 3.7 l; 2 SU type HIF 4 semi-downdraught carburettors; fuel feed: electric pump; sealed circuit cooling, liquid, expansion tank, 10 imp pt, 12 US pt, 5.7 l, thermostatic electric fan.

TRANSMISSION driving wheels: rear; clutch: single dry plate (diaphragm), hydraulically controlled; gearbox: mechanical; gears: 4, fully synchronized, and Laycock-de Normanville overdrive on III and IV; ratios: I 3.333, II 2.167 III 1.381 (overdrive 1.133), IV 1 (overdrive 0.820), rev 3.095; lever: central; final drive: hypoid bevel; axle ratio: 3.909; width of rims: 5"; tyres: 165 SR x 14.

PERFORMANCE max speeds: (I) 32 mph, 51 km/h; (II) 51 mph, 82 km/h; (III) 81 mph, 130 km/h; (IV) 107 mph, 172 km/h; power-weight ratio: 24.9 lb/hp (34 lb/kW), 11.3 kg/hp (15.4 kg/kW); carrying capacity: 529 lb, 240 kg; speed in direct drive at 1,000 rpm: 18 mph, 28.9 km/h; consumption: 25.4 m/imp gal, 21.2 m/US gal, 11.1 l x 100 km.

CHASSIS integral; front suspension: independent, wishbones, coil springs,anti-roll bar, lever dampers as upper arms; rear: rigid axle, semi-elliptic leafsprings, anti-roll bar, lever dampers.

STEERING rack-and-pinion; turns lock to lock: 3.57.

BRAKES front disc (diameter 10.75 in, 27.3 cm), rear drum servo; lining area: front 20 sq in, 129 sq cm, rear 67.3 sq in, 434 sq cm, total 87.3 sq in, 563 sq cm.

ELECTRICAL EQUIPMENT 12 V; 66 Ah battery; 45 A alternator; Lucas distributor; 2 halogen headlamps.

DIMENSIONS AND WEIGHT wheel base: 91 in, 231 cm; tracks: 49.50 in, 126 cm front, 49.75 in, 126 cm rear; length: 158.25 in, 402 cm; width: 61.75 in, 157 cm; height: 51 in, 129 cm; ground clearance: 4.19 in, 10.6 cm; weight: 2,409 lb, 1,092 kg; turning circle: 32 ft, 8.1 m; fuel tank: 11 imp gal, 13.2 US gal, 50 l.

BODY coupé; 2 doors; 2+2 seats, separate front seats, built-in headrests; tinted glass; heated rear window; impact

MG MGB GT

MGB GT

absorbing bumpers; laminated windscreen; folding rear seats.

PRACTICAL INSTRUCTIONS fuel: 98-100 oct petrol; oil: engine 6 imp pt, 7.2 US pt, 3.4 l, SAE 10W-30 (winter) 20W-50 (summer), change every 3,000 miles, 4,800 km - gearbox 4.6 imp pt, 5.5 US pt, 2.6 l, SAE 20W-50 - final drive 1.5 imp pt, 1.9 US pt, 0.9 l, SAE 90; greasing: every 3,000 miles, 4,800 km, 8 points; tappet clearances: inlet 0.015 in, 0.38 mm, exhaust 0.015 in, 0.38 mm; valve timing: 16° 56° 51° 21°; tyre pressure: front 21 psi, 1.5 atm, rear 24 psi, 1.7 atm.

OPTIONALS wire wheels; light alloy wheels with 185/70 x 14 tyres.

MGB Sports

See MGB GT, except for:

PRICE IN USA: $ 7,950*
PRICE EX WORKS: £ 4,849*

PERFORMANCE power-weight ratio: 24.3 lb/hp (33.1 lb/kW), 11 kg/hp (15 kg/kW).

DIMENSIONS AND WEIGHT weight: 2,348 lb, 1,065 kg.

BODY sports; 2 doors; 2 separate seats, built-in headrests; impact absorbing bumpers; laminated windscreen.

OPTIONALS wire wheels; light alloy wheels with 185/70 x 14 tyres; hardtop.

MG MGB Sports

MG MGB Sports

MINI GREAT BRITAIN

850 City / Super

PRICES EX WORKS: £

850 City	2,404*
850 Super	2,641*

ENGINE front, transverse, in unit with gearbox and final drive, 4 stroke; 4 cylinders, vertical, in line; 51.7 cu in, 848 cc (2.48 x 2.69 in, 62.9 x 68.2 mm); compression ratio: 8.3:1; max power (DIN): 33 hp (24 kW) at 5,300 rpm; max torque (DIN): 40 lb ft, 5.5 kg m (54 Nm) at 2,500 rpm; max engine rpm: 5,500; 38.9 hp/l (28.7 kW/l); cast iron block and head; 3 crankshaft bearings; valves: overhead, in line, push-rods and rockers; camshafts: 1, side; lubrication: rotary pump, full flow filter by cartridge, 8.4 imp pt, 10.1 US pt, 4.8 l; 1 SU type HS4 semi-downdraught carburettor; fuel feed: mechanical pump; water-cooled, 6.2 imp pt, 7.4 US pt, 3.5 l.

TRANSMISSION driving wheels: front; clutch: single dry plate (diaphragm), hydraulically controlled; gearbox: mechanical; gears: 4, fully synchronized; ratios: I 3.525, II 2.218, III 1.433, IV 1, rev 3.544; lever: central; final drive helical spur gears; axle ratio: 3.765; width of rims: 3.5"; tyres: 145 SR x 10 (5.20 x 10 only for export).

PERFORMANCE max speeds: (I) 22 mph, 35 km/h; (II) 35 mph, 56 km/h; (III) 54 mph, 87 km/h; (IV) 73 mph, 117 km/h; power-weight ratio: 39.9 lb/hp (54.9 lb/kW), 18.1 kg/hp (24.9 kg/kW); carrying capacity: 706 lb, 320 kg; acceleration: standing ¼ mile 23.6 sec, 0-50 mph (0-80 km/h) 18.3 sec; speed in direct drive at 1,000 rpm: 15.9 mph, 25.6 km/h; consumption: 48.7 m/imp gal, 40.6 m/US gal, 5.8 l x 100 km at 56 mph, 90 km/h.

CHASSIS integral, front and rear auxiliary frames; front suspension: independent, wishbones, rubber cone springs, telescopic dampers; rear: independent, swinging longitudinal trailing arms, rubber cone springs, telescopic dampers.

STEERING rack-and-pinion; turns lock to lock: 2.33.

BRAKES drum, single circuit , 2 front leading shoes; swept area: front 66 sq in, 426 sq cm, rear 55 sq in, 355 sq cm, total 121 sq in, 781 sq cm.

ELECTRICAL EQUIPMENT 12 V; 30 Ah battery; 34 A alternator; Lucas distributor; 4 headlamps.

DIMENSIONS AND WEIGHT wheel base: 80.16 in, 204 cm; tracks: 47.82 in, 121 cm front, 46.40 in, 118 cm rear; length: 120.25 in, 305 cm; width: 55.50 in, 141 cm; height 53 in, 135 cm; ground clearance: 5.75 in, 14.7 cm; weight 1,318 lb, 598 kg; weight distribution: 61% front, 39% rear; turning circle: 29.5 ft, 9 m; fuel tank: 7.5 imp gal, 9 US gal, 34 l.

BODY saloon/sedan; 2 doors; 4 seats, separate front seats; heated rear window.

PRACTICAL INSTRUCTIONS fuel: 94 oct petrol; oil: engine, gearbox and final drive 9 imp pt, 10.8 US pt, 5.1 l, SAE 20W-50, change every 6,000 miles, 9,700 km; greasing: every 6,000 miles, 9,700 km, 8 points; tappet clearances: inlet 0.012 in, 0.30 mm, exhaust 0.012 in, 0.30 mm; valve timing: 5° 45° 40° 10°; tyre pressure: front 24 psi, 1.7 atm, rear 21 psi, 1.5 atm.

MINI 850 Super

1000 Super

See 850 City/Super except for:

PRICE EX WORKS: £ 2,710*

ENGINE 60.9 cu in, 998 cc (2.54 x 3 in, 64.6 x 76.2 mm); max power (DIN): 39 hp (29 kW) at 4.750 rpm; max torque (DIN): 51 lb ft, 7.1 kg m (70 Nm) at 2,000 rpm: 39 hp/l (28.8 kW/l).

TRANSMISSION axle ratio: 3.444.

PERFORMANCE max speeds: (I) 26 mph, 42 km/h; (II) 49 mph, 79 km/h: (III) 62 mph, 100 km/h; (IV) 77 mph, 123 km/h; power-weight ratio: 33.8 lb/hp (45.9 lb/kW), 15.3 kg/hp (20.8 kg/kW); consumption: 33 m/imp gal, 27.3 m/US gal, 8.6 l x 100 km at 75 mph 120 km/h.

OPTIONALS AP automatic transmission, hydraulic torque converter with 2 conic bevel gears (twin concentric differential-like gear clusters) with 4 ratios (I 2.690, II 1.845, III

460, IV 1.269, rev 2.690), operated by 3 brake bands and multi-disc clutches, max ratio of converter at stall 2, ɔssible manual selection.

Clubman Saloon / Estate Car

ee 850 City/Super, except for:

RICES EX WORKS: £

ubman 2-dr Saloon	3,000*
ubman 2+2-dr Estate Car	3,267*

NGINE 67 cu in, 1,098 cc (2.54 x 3.29 in, 64.4 x 83.5 mm); ɔmpression ratio: 8.5:1; max power (DIN): 45 hp (33 kW) : 5,250 rpm; max torque (DIN): 56 lb ft, 7.7 kg m (75 Nm) : 2,700 rpm; 41 hp/l (30.1 kW/l).

RANSMISSION axle ratio: 3.444.

ERFORMANCE max speed: 81 mph, 130 km/h; power-eight ratio: Saloon 31.6 lb/hp (43 lb/kW), 14.4 kg/hp (19.5 g//kW); consumption: Saloon 32.1 m/imp gal, 26.7 m/US al, 8.8 l x 100 km at 75 mph, 120 km/h - Estate Car 33.7 /imp gal, 28 m/US gal, 8.4 l x 100 km at 75 mph, 120 km/h.

LECTRICAL EQUIPMENT 36 Ah battery.

IMENSIONS AND WEIGHT wheel base: Saloon 80.20 in,)4 cm - Estate Car 84.20 in, 214 cm; tracks: Saloon 48.77 , 124 cm front, 47.43 in, 120 cm rear - Estate Car 47.82 , 121 cm front, 46.40 in, 118 cm rear; length: Saloon 24.60 in, 316 cm - Estate Car 133.90 in, 340 cm; height: state Car 53.50 in, 136 cm; ground clearance: Saloon 6.55 , 16.6 cm - Estate Car 6.30 in, 16 cm; weight: Saloon 424 lb, 646 kg - Estate Car 1,458 lb, 661 kg; turning rcle: Saloon 30 ft, 9.2 m - Estate Car 30.5 ft, 9.3 m; fuel nk: Estate Car 6 imp gal, 7.1 US gal, 27 l.

ODY tinted glass; Saloon heated rear window; Estate Car lding rear seat.

RACTICAL INSTRUCTIONS fuel: 97 oct petrol: valve tim-g: 5° 45° 51° 21°

PTIONALS (only with 998 cc engine) AP automatic trans-ission, hydraulic torque converter with 2 conic bevel gears win concentric differential-like gear clusters) with 4 ratios 2.690, II 1.845, III 1.460, IV 1.269, rev 2.690), operated y 3 brake bands and 2 multi-disc clutches, max ratio of ɔnverter at stall 2, possible manual selection; metallic ɔray (for Saloon only).

1275 GT

ee 850 City/Super, except for:

RICE EX WORKS: £ 3,376*

NGINE 77.8 cu in, 1,275 cc (2.78 x 3.20 in, 70.6 x 81.3 m); compression ratio: 8.8:1; max power (DIN): 54 hp (40 V) at 5,250 max torque (DIN): 67 lb ft, 9.2 kg m (90 Nm) at 500 rpm; 42.4 hp/l (31.1 kW/l).

RANSMISSION ratios: I 3.330, II 2.094, III 1.353, IV 1, rev 347; axle ratio: 3.444; width of rims: 4.5"; tyres: 155/65 x 310.

MINI 1275 GT

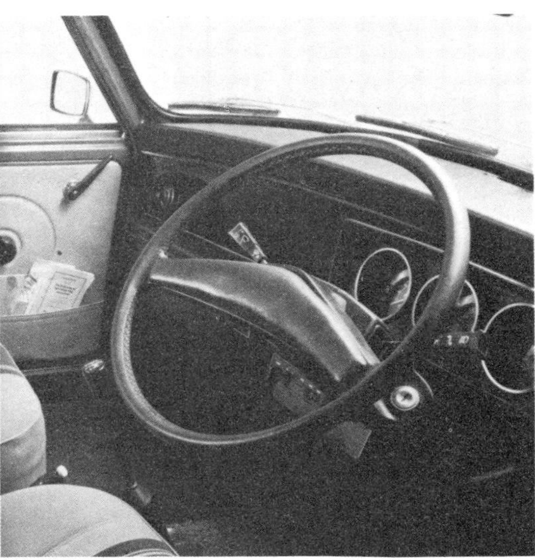

MINI 1275 GT

PERFORMANCE max speeds: (I) 28 mph, 45 km/h; (II) 44 mph, 71 km/h; (III) 68 mph, 110 km/h; (IV) 87 mph, 140 km/h; power-weight ratio: 26.4 lb/hp (35.9 lb/kW), 12 kg/hp (16.3 kg/kW); acceleration: 0-50 mph (0-80 km/h) 9.5 sec; speed in direct drive at 1,000 rpm: 16.8 mph, 27 km/h; consumption: 33.3 m/imp gal, 27.7 m/US gal, 8.5 l x 100 km at 75 mph, 120 km/h.

BRAKES front disc (diameter 8.50 in, 21.6 cm), rear drum, servo; swept area: front 134.5 sq in, 867 sq cm, rear 55 sq in, 355 sq cm, total 189.5 sq in, 1,222 sq cm.

ELECTRICAL EQUIPMENT 40 Ah battery.

DIMENSIONS AND WEIGHT wheel base: 80.20 in, 204 cm; tracks: 48.77 in, 124 cm front, 47.43 in, 120 cm rear; length: 124.60 in, 316 cm; height: 53.55 in, 136 cm; ground clearance: 6.55 in, 16.6 cm; weight: 1,424 lb, 646 kg; turning circle: 30 ft, 9.1 m; fuel tank : 7.5 imp gal, 9 US gal, 34 l.

PRACTICAL INSTRUCTIONS fuel: 97 oct petrol.

OPTIONALS metallic spray.

MORGAN GREAT BRITAIN

4/4 1600 2-seater

PRICE EX WORKS: £ 5,064*

ENGINE Ford, front, 4 stroke; 4 cylinders, vertical, in line; 97.6 cu in 1,599 cc (3.19 x 3.06 in, 81 x 77.6 mm); compression ratio: 9:1; max power (DIN): 84 hp (62 kW) at 5,500 rpm; max torque (DIN): 92 lb ft, 12.7 kg m (124 Nm) at 3,500 rpm; max engine rpm: 6,000; 52.5 hp/l (38.6 kW/l); cast iron block and head; 5 crankshaft bearings; valves: overhead, push-rods and rockers; camshafts: 1, side; lubrication: rotary pump, full flow filter, 7.5 imp pt, 8.9 US pt, 4.2 l; 1 Weber 32/36 downdraught twin barrel carburettor; fuel feed: mechanical pump; water-cooled, 12 imp pt, 14.4 US pt, 6.8 l.

TRANSMISSION driving wheels: rear; clutch: single dry plate, hydraulically controlled; gearbox: mechanical; gears: 4, fully synchronized; ratios: I 2.976, II 2.024, III 1.390, IV 1, rev 3.317; lever: central; final drive: hypoid bevel; axle ratio: 4.100; tyres: 165 x 15.

PERFORMANCE max speeds: (I) 37 mph, 59 km/h; (II) 55 mph, 88 km/h; (III) 80 mph, 128 km/h; (IV) 105 mph, 169 km/h; power-weight ratio: 19.3 lb/hp (26.3 lb/kW), 8.8 kg/hp (11.9 kg/kW); carrying capacity: 353 lb, 160 kg; speed in direct drive at 1,000 rpm: 18.5 mph, 29.7 km!h; consumption: 35.3 m/imp gal, 29.4 m/US gal, 8 l x 100 km.

CHASSIS ladder frame, Z-section long members, tubular and box-type cross members; front suspension: independent, vertical sliding pillars, coil springs, telescopic dampers; rear: rigid axle, semi-elliptic leafsprings, lever dampers.

STEERING cam and peg; turns lock to lock: 2.25.

BRAKES front disc (diameter 11 in, 27.9 cm), rear drum, dual circuit; swept area: total 325.1 sq in, 2,097 sq cm.

MORGAN 4/4 1600 4-seater

MORGAN Plus 8

4/4 1600 2-SEATER

ELECTRICAL EQUIPMENT 12 V; 38 Ah battery; alternator; 2 headlamps.

DIMENSIONS AND WEIGHT wheel base: 96 in, 244 cm; tracks: 47 in, 119 cm front, 49 in, 124 cm rear; length: 144 in, 366 cm; width: 56 in, 142 cm; height: 51 in, 129 cm; ground clearance: 7 in, 17.8 cm; weight: 1,624 lb, 736 kg; weight distribution: 48% front, 52% rear; turning circle: 32 ft, 9.8 m; fuel tank: 8.5 imp gal, 10.3 US gal, 39 l.

BODY roadster; 2 doors; 2 seats.

PRACTICAL INSTRUCTIONS fuel: 98 oct petrol; oil: engine 7 imp pt, 8.5 US pt, 4 l, SAE 10W-30, change every 6,000 miles, 9,700 km - gearbox 1.8 imp pt, 2.1 US pt, 1 l, SAE 80 - final drive 1.9 imp pt, 2.3 US pt, 1.1 l, SAE 90; greasing: every 3,000 and 9,000 miles, 4,800 and 14,500 km, 10 points; tyre pressure: front 17 psi, 1.2 atm, rear 17 psi, 1.2 atm.

OPTIONALS wire wheels; tonneau cover; reclining backrests; leather upholstery; headrests.

4/4 1600 4-seater

See 4/4 1600 2-seater, except for:

PRICE EX WORKS: £ 5,581*

PERFORMANCE power-weight ratio: 20 lb/hp (27.2 lb/kW), 9.1 kg/hp (12.3 kg/kW).

DIMENSIONS AND WEIGHT weight: 1,680 lb, 762 kg; fuel tank: 10 imp gal, 12.1 US gal, 46 l.

BODY 4 seats.

Plus 8

See 4/4 1600 2-seater except for:

PRICE EX WORKS: £ 7,444*

ENGINE Rover; 8 cylinders, Vee-slanted; 215.3 cu in, 3,528 cc (3.50 x 2.80 in, 89 x 71 mm); compression ratio: 9.35: 1; max power (DIN): 155 hp (114 kW) at 5,250 rpm; max torque (DIN): 199 lb, 27.5 kg m (270 Nm) at 2,500 rpm; max engine rpm: 5,800; 43.9 hp/l (32.3 kW/l); light alloy block and head; valves: hydraulic tappets; camshafts: 1, at centre of Vee; lubrication: gear pump, full flow filter, 9.5 imp pt, 11.4 US pt, 5.4 l; 2 SU type HIF6 semi-downdraught carburettors; water-cooled, 15 imp pt, 18 US pt, 8.5 l, electric thermostatic fan.

TRANSMISSION clutch: single dry plate (diaphragm), hydraulically controlled; gears: 5, fully synchronized; ratios: I 3.320, II 2.080, III 1.390, IV 1, V 0.860, rev 3.110; final drive: hypoid bevel, limited slip differential; axle ratio: 3.310; width of rims: 6"; tyres: 195 x 14.

PERFORMANCE max speeds: (I) 40 mph, 64 km/h; (II) 64 mph, 103 km/h; (III) 95 mph, 153 km/h; (IV) 132 mph, 212 km/h; (V) 150 mph, 241 km/h; power-weight ratio: 11.8 lb/hp (16 lb/kW), 5.3 kg/hp (7.3 kg/kW); acceleration: standing ¼ mile 14.5 sec, 0-50 mph (0-80 km/h) 5.1 sec; speed in direct drive at 1,000 rpm: 27.4 mph, 44.1 km/h; consumption: 24 m/imp gal, 20.1 m/US gal, 11.7 l x 100 km.

ELECTRICAL EQUIPMENT 58 Ah battery; 4 headlamps.

DIMENSIONS AND WEIGHT wheel base: 98 in, 249 cm; tracks: 52 in, 132 cm front, 53 in, 135 cm rear; length: 147 in, 373 cm; width: 62 in, 158 cm; height: 52 in, 132 cm; weight: 1,826 lb, 828 kg; turning circle: 38 ft, 11.5 m; fuel tank: 13.5 imp gal, 16.1 US gal, 61 l.

OPTIONALS 185 x 15 tyres.

MORRIS GREAT BRITAIN

Marina Series

PRICES EX WORKS: £

1	1300 2-dr Coupé	**3,323***
2	1300 4-dr Saloon	**3,457***
3	1300 4+1-dr Estate Car	**3,937***
4	1300 L 2-dr Coupé	**3,594***
5	1300 L 4-dr Saloon	**3,694***
6	1300 HL 4-dr Saloon	**4,088***
7	1700 4-dr Saloon	**3,757***
8	1700 4+1-dr Estate Car	**4,211***
9	1700 L 4-dr Saloon	**3,994***
10	1700 L 4+1-dr Estate Car	**4,448***
11	1700 HL 4-dr Saloon	**4,418***
12	1700 HL 4+1-dr Estate Car	**4,836***

Power team:	Standard for:	Optionals for:
57 hp	1 to 6	—
78 hp	7 to 12	—

57 hp power team

ENGINE front, 4 stroke; 4 cylinders, in line; 77.8 cu in, 1,275 cc (2.78 x 3.20 in, 70.6 x 81.3 mm); compression ratio: 8.8:1; max power (DIN): 57 hp (42 kW) at 5,500 rpm; max torque (DIN): 68 lb ft, 9.5 kg m (93 Nm) at 2,450 rpm; max engine rpm: 6,500; 44.7 hp/l (32.9 kW/l); cast iron block and head; 3 crankshaft bearings; valves: overhead, in line, push-rods and rockers; camshaft: 1, side chain-driven; lubrication: rotary pump, full flow filter, 7.6 imp pt, 9.1 US pt, 4.3 l; 1 SU type HS4 semi-downdraught carburettor; fuel feed: mechanical pump; water-cooled, 7.4 imp pt, 8.9 US pt, 4.2 l.

TRANSMISSION driving wheels: rear; clutch: single dry plate (diaphragm), hydraulically controlled; gearbox: mechanical; gears: 4, fully synchronized; ratios: I 3.412, II 2.112, III 1.433, IV 1, rev 3.753; lever: central; final drive: hypoid bevel; axle ratio: 4.111; width of rims: 4.5"; tyres: 145 x 13 - Estate Car and HL models 155 x 13.

PERFORMANCE max speeds: (I) 30 mph, 48 km/h; (II) 49 mph, 79 km/h; (III) 72 mph, 116 km/h; (IV) 86 mph, 138 km/h; power-weight ratio: 4-dr saloons 34.6 lb/hp (47.2 lb/kW), 15.7 kg/hp (21.4 kg/kW); carrying capacity: 882 lb, 400 kg; acceleration: standing ¼ mile 22 sec; speed in direct drive at 1,000 rpm: 15.7 mph, 25.2 km/h; consumption: 30.7 m/imp gal, 25.6 m/US gal, 9.2 l x 100 km at 75 mph, 120 km/h - Estate Car 30.1 m/imp gal, 25 m/US ga 9.4 l x 100 at 75 mph, 120 km/h.

CHASSIS integral; front suspension: independent, wisl bones, lower trailing links, longitudinal torsion bars, leve dampers as upper arms, telescopic dampers, anti-roll ba (except Estate Car); rear: rigid axle, semi-elliptic lea springs, telescopic dampers, anti-roll bar (except Esta Car).

STEERING rack-and-pinion; turns lock to lock: 4.

BRAKES front disc (diameter 9.78 in, 24.8 cm), rear drun servo; swept area: front 182.2 sq in, 1,175 sq cm, rear 7 sq in, 490 sq cm, total 258.1 sq in, 1,665 sq cm.

ELECTRICAL EQUIPMENT 12 V; 40 44 or 50 Ah battery; 3 A alternator; Lucas distributor; 4 headlamps, 2 fog lamps for HL model only 2 halogen headlamps.

DIMENSIONS AND WEIGHT wheel base: 96 in, 244 cn front and rear track: 52 in, 132 cm; length: 2-dr coupé 165.75 in, 421 cm - 4-dr saloons 169 in, 429 cm - Esta Car 170.09 in, 432 cm; width: 64.57 in, 164 cm; heigh 55.91 in, 142 cm - Estate Car 56.60 in, 144 cm; grour clearance: 6.10-6.30 in, 15.5-16 cm; weight: 2-dr coupé 1,951 lb 885 kg - 4-dr saloons 1,973 lb, 895 kg - Estate Ca 2,139 lb, 970 kg; turning circle: 33.1 ft, 10.1 m; fuel tan 11.5 imp gal, 13.7 US gal, 52 l.

BODY 5 seats, separate front seats, reclining backrest heated rear window; for HL model only headrests and tinte glass; for Estate Car only, rear window wiper-washer.

PRACTICAL INSTRUCTIONS fuel: 97 oct petrol; oil: engir 7.6 imp pt, 9.1 US pt, 4.3 l, SAE 20W-50, change eve 6,000 miles, 9,700 km - gearbox 2.2 imp pt, 2.5 US pt, 1.2 change every 6,000 miles, 9,700 km - final drive 1.2 imp p 1.5 US pt, 0.7 l, change every 6,000 miles, 9,700 kr greasing: every 3,000 miles, 4,800 km, 4 points; sparkir plug: 225°; tappet clearances: inlet 0.012 in, 0.30 mr exhaust 0.012 in, 0.30 mm; valve timing: 5° 45° 51° 21 tyre pressure: front 26 psi, 1.8 atm, rear 28 psi, 2 atm.

OPTIONALS 8:1 compression ratio; (only for L 4-dr and H models) Borg-Warner 65 automatic transmission, hydraul torque converter and planetary gears with 3 ratios (I) 2.39 II 1.450, III 1, rev 2.094), max ratio of converter at stall possible manual selection; 165/70 SR x 13 tyres; (for L ar HL models only) metallic spray; tinted glass; (for L 4- model only) vinyl roof; laminated windscreen.

78 hp power team

See 57 hp power team, except for:

ENGINE 103.6 cu in, 1,698 cc (3.33 x 2.98 in, 84.5 x 75 mm); compression ratio: 9:1; max power (DIN): 78 hp (5 kW) at 5,150 rpm; max torque (DIN): 93 lb ft, 12,9 kg m (12 Nm) at 3,400 rpm; max engine rpm: 5,600; 45.9 hp/l (33 kW/l); cast iron block, light alloy head; 5 crankshaft bea ings; camshafts: 1, overhead, chain-driven; lubrication: 9 imp pt, 9.7 US pt, 4.6 l; 1 SU type HIF6 semi-downdraug carburettor; cooling: 10 imp pt, 12 US pt, 5.7 l.

TRANSMISSION gearbox ratios: I 3.111, II 1.926, III 1.30 IV 1, rev 3.422; axle ratio: 3.636; tyres: 155 x 13.

MORRIS Marina 1700 Series

MORRIS Marina 1700 L Saloon

PRACTICAL INSTRUCTIONS fuel: 87 oct petrol; oil: engine 4.4 imp pt, 5.3 US pt, 2.5 l, SAE 10W-20 (winter) 20W-30 (summer), change every 3,100 miles, 5,000 km, gearbox and final drive 5.3 imp pt, 6.3 US pt, 3 l, SAE 90, change every 31,000 miles, 50,000 km; greasing: every 6,200 miles, 10,000 km, 4 points; sparking plug: 175°; tappet clearances: inlet 0.004 in, 0.10 mm, exhaust 0.004 in, 0.10 mm; valve timing: 7°30' 37° 43°30' 4°.

OPTIONALS electric roof; air-conditioning; tinted glass; sunshine roof; halogen headlamps.

PANTHER GREAT BRITAIN

Lima

PRICE EX WORKS: £ 8,250*

ENGINE Vauxhall, front, slanted at 45°, 4 stroke; 4 cylinders, in line; 139.2 cu in, 2,279 cc(3.84 x 3 in, 97.5 x 76.2 mm); compression ratio: 8.5:1; max power (DIN): 108 hp (79 KW) at 5,000 rpm; max torque (DIN): 138 lb ft, 19 kg m (186 Nm) at 3,000 rpm; max engine rpm: 5,500; 47.4 hp/l (34.9 kW/l); cast iron block and head; 5 crankshaft bearings; valves: overhead, in line, push-rods; camshafts: 1, overhead, cogged belt; lubrication: gear pump, full flow filter, 8.5 imp pt, 10.1 US pt, 4.8 l; 1 Zenith-Stromberg 175 CD2

ERFORMANCE max speeds: (I) 33 mph, 53 km/h; (II) 53 ıph, 85 km/h; (III) 78 mph, 125 km/h; (IV) 95 mph, 153 m/h; power-weight ratio: saloons 26.2 lb/hp (35.5 lb/kW), 1,9 kg/hp (16.1 kg/kW); speed in direct drive at 1,000 rpm: 8.1 mph, 29.2 km/h; consumption: saloons 28.9 m/imp gal, 4 m/US gal, 9.8 l x 100 km at 75 mph, 120 km/h - estate ars 28.4 m/imp gal, 23.5 m/US gal, 9.9 l x 100 km at 75 ıph, 120 km/h.

LECTRICAL EQUIPMENT 55 Ah battery.

IMENSIONS AND WEIGHT weight: saloons 2,040 lb, 925 g - estate cars 2,194 lb, 995 kg.

IOVA GREAT BRITAIN

Sports

RICE EX WORKS: £ 5,200*

NGINE Volkswagen, rear, 4 stroke; 4 cylinders, horizontal-y opposed; 96.7 cu in, 1,584 cc (3.37x2.72 in, 85.5 x 69 ım); compression ratio: 7.5:1; max power (DIN): 50 hp (37 W) at 4,000 rpm; max torque (DIN): 78 lb ft, 10.8 kg m (106 lm) at 2,800 rpm; max engine rpm: 4,500; 31.6 hp/l (23.2 W/l); block with cast iron liners and light alloy fins, light lloy head; 4 crankshaft bearings; valves: overhead, push-ods and rockers; camshafts: 1, central, lower; lubrication: ear pump, filter in sump, oil cooler, 4.4 imp pt, 5.3 US pt, .5 l; 1 Nikki downdraught carburettor; fuel feed: mechanic-l pump; air-cooled.

RANSMISSION driving wheels: rear; clutch: single dry late, heavy-duty; gearbox: mechanical; gears: 4, fully syn-hronized; ratios: I 3.780, II 2.060, III 1.260, IV 0.930, rev .010; lever: central; final drive: spiral bevel; axle ratio: .375; width of rims: 7"; tyres: 205 x 14.

ERFORMANCE max speed: 110 mph, 177 km/h; power-veight ratio: 31.3 lb/hp (42.6 lb/kW), 14.2 kg/hp (19.3 g/kW); carrying capacity: 353 lb, 160 kg; consumption: 35 ı/imp gal, 29 m/US gal, 8.1 x l x 100 km.

HASSIS backbone platform; front suspension: independent, twin swinging longitudinal trailing arms, transverse aminated torsion bars, anti-roll bar, lowered and uprated elescopic dampers; rear: independent, semi-trailing arms, ransverse compensating torsion bar, lowered telescopic ampers.

STEERING worm and roller, telescopic damper.

RAKES front disc, rear drum.

LECTRICAL EQUIPMENT 12 V; 12 V heavy-duty battery; ynamo; Bosch distributor; 2 headlamps.

IMENSIONS AND WEIGHT length: 174 in, 442 cm; width: 6 in, 168 cm; height: 45 in, 114 cm; ground clearance: 5 in, 3 cm; weight: 1,568 lb, 711 kg; weight distribution: 40% ront, 60% rear; fuel tank: 9 imp gal, 10.8 US gal, 41l.

ODY sports, in plastic material with lift up roof section; 1 oor; 2 seats.

NOVA Sports

PANTHER Lima

PANTHER J 72 4.2-litre

LIMA

downdraught single barrel carburettor; fuel feed: mechanical pump; water-cooled, 13.5 imp pt, 16.1 US pt, 7.6 i, viscous coupling thermostatic fan.

TRANSMISSION driving wheels: rear; clutch: single dry plate (diaphragm); gearbox: mechanical; gears: 4, fully synchronized; ratios: I 3.300, II 2.145, III 1.414, IV 1, rev 3.063; lever: central; final drive: hypoid bevel; axle ratio:3.730; width of rims: 5.5''; tyres: 185/70 HR x 13.

PERFORMANCE max speed: 110 mph, 177 km/h; power-weight ratio: 16.7 lb/hp (22.6 lb/kW), 7.6 kg/hp (10.3 kg/kW); carrying capacity: 353 lb, 160 kg; speed in direct drive at 1,000 rpm: 18.9 mph, 30.4 km/h; consumption: 25 m/imp gal, 20.8 m/US gal, 11.3 l x 100 km.

CHASSIS integral; front suspension: independent, wishbones,coil springs, anti-roll bar, telescopic dampers; rear: rigid axle, twin trailing radius arms, transverse linkage bar, coil springs, anti-roll bar, telescopic dampers.

STEERING rack-and-pinion; turns lock to lock: 3.16.

BRAKES disc (front diameter 10.03 in, 25.5 cm, rear 9 in, 22.9 cm), servo.

ELECTRICAL EQUIPMENT 12 V; 39 Ah battery; 28 A alternator; Lucas distributor; 2 headlamps.

DIMENSIONS AND WEIGHT wheel base: 97 in, 246 cm; tracks: 52.30 in, 133 cm front, 52 in, 132 cm rear; length: 142.13 in, 361 cm; width: 63.39 in, 161 cm; height: 48.03 in, 122 cm; ground clearance: 4.53 in, 11.5 cm; weight: 1,800 lb, 816 kg; weight distribution: 50% front, 50% rear; turning circle: 32.2 ft, 9.8 m; fuel tank: 10 imp gal, 12.1 US gal, 46 l.

BODY roadster, in plastic material; 2 doors; 2 seats; leather upholstery.

PRACTICAL INSTRUCTIONS fuel: 98 oct petrol; oil: engine 8.5 imp pt, 10.1 US pt, 4.8 l, SAE 20W-50, change every 6,000 miles, 9,700 km - gearbox and final drive 2.5 imp pt, 3 US pt, 1.4 l, SAE 90 EP; greasing: none; tappet clearances: inlet 0.007-0.010 in, 0.17-0.25 mm, exhaust 0.015-0.019 in, 0.37-0.45 mm; valve timing: 31°36' 63°36' 63°36' 31°36'; tyre pressure: front 24 psi, 1.7 atm, rear 24 psi, 1.7 atm.

OPTIONALS automatic transmission, hydraulic torque converter and planetary gears with 3 ratios (I 2.400, II 1.480, III 1, rev 1.920), max ratio of converter at stall 2.25, possible manual selection; wire wheels; laminated glass; metallic spray; tonneau cover; front spoiler; tuned engine with max speed 125 mph, 200 km/h; hardtop; luggage rack.

VARIATIONS

ENGINE 1 Holley-Weber carburettor with Airesearch turbocharger.
TRANSMISSION 6'' wide rims, 205/60 VR x 14 tyres.

J 72 4.2-litre

PRICE EX WORKS: £ 23,995*

ENGINE Jaguar, front, 4 stroke; 6 cylinders, vertical, in line; 258.4 cu in, 4,235 cc (3.63 x 4.17 in, 92 x 106 mm); compression ratio: 8:1; max power (DIN): 190 hp (140 kW) at 5,000 rpm; max torque (DIN): 200 lb ft, 27.6 kg m (271 Nm) at 2,000 rpm; max engine rpm: 6,000; 44.9 hp/l (33 kW/l); cast iron block, light alloy head, hemispherical combustion chambers; 7 crankshaft bearings; valves: overhead Vee-slanted at 70°, thimble tappets; camshafts: 2, overhead; lubrication: rotary pump, full flow filter, 14.5 imp pt 17.3 US pt, 8.2 l; 2 SU type AED horizontal carburettors fuel feed: 2 electric pumps; water-cooled, 20 imp pt, 23.9 US pt, 11.3 l.

TRANSMISSION driving wheels: rear; clutch: single dry plate (diaphragm); gearbox: mechanical; gears: 4, fully synchronized with overdrive/top; ratios: I 3.040, II 1.970, III 1.330, IV 1, overdrive 0.780, rev 3.490; lever: central; final drive: hypoid bevel, limited slip differential; axle ratio 3.540; width of rims: 6''; tyres: 225/70VR x 15.

PERFORMANCE max speeds: (I) 43 mph, 69 km/h; (II) 66 mph, 106 km/h; (III) 94 mph, 151 km/h; (IV) 114 mph, 183 km/h; power-weight ratio: 13.6 lb/hp (18.4 lb/kW), 6.2 kg/hp (8.3 kg/kW); carrying capacity: 420 lb, 190 kg; acceleration standing 1¼ mile 15.3 sec; speed in direct drive at 1,000 rpm: 20.2 mph, 32.5 km/h; consumption: 15 m/imp gal, 12.5 m/US gal, 18.8 x 100 km.

CHASSIS square section ladder frame; front suspension independent, wishbones, coil springs, anti-roll bar, telescopic dampers; rear; rigid axle, trailing arms, Panhard rod, adjustable coil springs/telescopic damper units.

STEERING recirculating ball; turns lock to lock: 2.80.

BRAKES front disc, rear drum, servo.

ELECTRICAL EQUIPMENT 12 V; 57 Ah battery; 45 A alternator; Lucas distributor; 2 headlamps.

DIMENSIONS AND WEIGHT wheel base: 111 in, 282 cm tracks: 58.50 in, 149 cm front, 58.50 in, 149 cm rear length: 165 in, 419 cm; width: 68.50 in, 174 cm; height: 49 in 124 cm; ground clearance: 5 in, 12.7 cm; weight: 2,57- lb, 1,166 kg; weight distribution: 53.5% front, 46.5% rear turning circle: 40 ft, 9.3 m; fuel tank: 26 imp gal, 31.2 US gal, 118 l.

BODY roadster in light alloy; 2 doors; 2 seats; leather upholstery; laminated windscreen.

PRACTICAL INSTRUCTIONS fuel: 98 oct petrol; oil: engine 13 imp pt, 15.6 US pt, 7.4 l, SAE 20W-50, change every 6,000 miles, 9,700 km - gearbox and overdrive 4 imp pt, 4.- US pt, 2.3 l, SAE 90 EP, change every 12,000 miles, 20,000 km - final drive 2.7 imp pt, 3.2 US pt, 1.6 l, SAE 90 change every 12,000 miles, 20,000 km; greasing: every 6,000 miles, 10,000 km, 4 points; tyre pressure: front 22 psi, 1.- atm, rear 19 psi, 1.3 atm.

OPTIONALS Borg-Warner 65 automatic transmission, hydraulic torque converter and planetary gears with 3 ratios (I 2.400, II 1.450, III 1, rev 2.100), max ratio of converter at stall 2. possible manual selection; headrests; air conditioning; metallic spray; tonneau cover; power steering hardtop.

PANTHER De Ville Saloon

De Ville Saloon

PRICE EX WORKS: £ 58,250*

ENGINE Jaguar, front, 4 stroke; 12 cylinders, Vee-slanted at 60°; 326 cu in, 5,343 cc (3.54 x 2.76 in, 90 x 70 mm); compression ratio: 9:1; cast iron block with light alloy wet liners, aluminium alloy head with hemisperical combustion chambers; 7 crankshaft bearings; valves: overhead, in line thimble tappets; camshafts: 2, 1 per bank, overhead; lubrication: rotary pump, full flow filter, 17.6 imp pt, 21.1 US pt, 10 electronic fuel injection; fuel feed: 2 electric pumps; water cooled, 36 imp pt, 43.3 US pt, 20.5 l.

TRANSMISSION driving wheels: rear; gearbox: GM 400 automatic transmission, hydraulic torque converter and planetary gears with 3 ratios, max ratio of converter at stall 2, possible manual selection; ratios: I 2.460, II 1.460, III 1 rev 2.090; lever: central; final drive: hypoid bevel, limited slip differential; axle ratio: 3.310; width of rims: 6''; tyres 235/70 HR x 15.

PERFORMANCE max speed: 128 mph, 206 km/h; carrying capacity: 925 lb, 419 kg; acceleration: speed in direct drive at 1,000 rpm: 21.1 mph, 31.7 km/h; consumption: not declared.

CHASSIS ladder tube; front suspension: independent, wishbones, coil springs, anti-roll bar, telescopic dampers; rear independent, wishbones (trailing links), 4 coil springs transverse linkage bar, 4 telescopic dampers.

STEERING rack-and-pinion, servo.

PANTHER 6

ɪAKES disc (front diameter 11.2 in, 28.4 cm, rear 10.4 in, .4 cm), front internal radial fins, servo; swept area: total 8 sq in, 2,890 sq cm.

.ECTRICAL EQUIPMENT 12 V; 68 Ah battery; 67 A alternator; Lucas distributor; 2 headlamps.

MENSIONS AND WEIGHT wheel base: 142 in, 361 cm; ont and rear track: 58 in, 147 cm; length: 204 in, 519 cm; dth: 71 in, 180 cm; height: 61 in, 155 cm; weight: 4,360 1,973 kg; fuel tank: 22 imp gal, 26.4 US gal, 100 l.

ODY saloon/sedan; 4 doors; 4 seats; separate front seats, clining backrests with built-in headrests; leather upholstery; tinted glass; heated rear window; electric windows; r-conditioning; laminated windscreen; chrome wire heels.

ACTICAL INSTRUCTIONS fuel: 97 oct petrol; oil: engine imp pt,19.2 US pt, 9.1 l, SAE 20W-50, change every 000 miles, 9,700 km - automatic transmission 16 imp pt, .2 US pt, 9.1 l, TOF no change recommended - final drive 7 imp pt, 3.4 US pt, 1.6 l, SAE 90, change every 12,000 les, 20,000 km; greasing: every 6,000 miles, 9,700 km, points tappet clearances: inlet 0.012-0.014 in, 0.30-0.35 n, exhaust 0.012-0.014 in, 0.30-0.35 mm; tyre pressure: ont 30 psi, 2.1 atm, rear 32 psi, 2.2 atm.

VARIATIONS

NGINE Jaguar, 6 cylinders, vertical, in line, 258.4 cu in, 235 cc (3.63 x 4.17 in, 92 x 106 mm), 8:1 compression tio, 7 crankshaft bearings, Vee-slanted valves, 2 overad camshafts, lubrication 14.5 imp pt, 17.3 US pt, 8.2 l, 2 J type AED horizontal carburettors, cooling 20 imp pt, .9 US pt, 11.3 l.
ANSMISSION Borg-Warner 65 automatic transmission, draulic torque converter and planetary gears with 3 ratios 2.390, II 1.450, III 1, rev 2.090).

PTIONALS 4-speed fully synchronized mechanical gearbox; ectric sunshine roof; metallic spray.

De Ville Convertible

RICE EX WORKS: £ 72,215*

ODY convertible; 2 doors; tonneau cover.

PTIONALS detachable hardtop; electric sunshine roof not ailable.

6

RICE EX WORKS: on application.

NGINE Cadillac, central rear, 4 stroke; 8 cylinders, Veeanted; 500 cu in, 8,194 cc (4.30 x 4.30 in, 109.1 x 109.1 m); compression ratio: 8.5:1; cast iron block and head; 5 ankshaft bearings; valves: overhead, in line, push-rods d rockers, hydraulic tappets; camshaftfs: 1, at centre of e; lubrication: gear pump, full flow filter, oil cooler, 10 p pt, 12 US pt, 5.7 l; 2 Airesearch TO4 turbochargers with Holley downdraught 4-barrel carburettor; water-cooled, .1 imp pt, 51.8 US pt, 24.5 l, 2 electric fans.

TRANSMISSION driving wheels: rear; gearbox: Turbo-Hydramatic 425 automatic transmission, hydraulic torque converter and planetary gears with 3 ratios, max ratio of converter at stall 2, possible manual selection; ratios: I 2.480, II 1.480, III 1, rev 2.090; lever: steering column; final drive: spiral bevel; axle ratio: 1.800; width of rims: 6" front, 9" rear; tyres: P7 205/40 VR x 13 front, P7 265/50 VR x 16 rear.

PERFORMANCE max speed: over 200 mph, 322 km/h.

CHASSIS tubular; front suspension: independent, wishbones, coil springs, anti-roll bar, telescopic dampers; rear: independent, wishbones, coil springs, anti-roll bar, telescopic dampers.

STEERING rack-and-pinion, servo; turns lock to lock: 2.80.

BRAKES disc (front diameter 10 in, 25.4 cm, rear 11 in, 27.9 cm), 3 circuits; swept area: front 400 sq in, 2,580 sq cm, rear 224 sq in, 1,445 sq cm, total 624 sq in, 4,025 sq cm.

ELECTRICAL EQUIPMENT 12 V; 66 Ah battery; 100 A alternator; 4 halogen headlamps.

DIMENSIONS AND WEIGHT wheel base: 105 in, 267 cm; tracks: 61.50 in, 156 cm front, 64.50 in,164 cm rear; length: 192 in, 487 cm; width: 80 in, 203 cm; height: 48 in, 122 cm; ground clearance: 7 in, 17.8 cm; weight: 2,870 lb, 1,302 kg; fuel tank: 30 imp gal, 36.2 US gal, 137 l (2 separate tanks).

BODY convertible; 2 doors; 3 seats; leather upholstery; air-conditioning; tinted glass.

PRACTICAL INSTRUCTIONS fuel: 98 oct petrol: oil: engine; 10 imp pt, 12 US pt, 5.7 l - automatic transmission 10.3 imp pt, 12.3 US pt, 5.8 l - final drive 3.3 imp pt, 4 US pt, 1.9 l.

OPTIONALS electric seats; hardtop; metallic spray.

PRINCESS GREAT BRITAIN

1700-2000-2200 Series

PRICES EX WORKS:	£
1 1700 L Saloon	4,319*
2 1700 HL Saloon	4,694*
3 1700 HLS Saloon	5,216*
4 2000 HL Saloon	4,956*
5 2000 HLS Saloon	5,475*
6 2200 HL Saloon	5,352*
7 2200 HLS Saloon	5,966*

Power team:	Standard for:	Optional for:
87 hp	1 to 3	—
93 hp	4,5	—
110 hp	5,6	—

87 hp power team

ENGINE front, transverse, in unit with gearbox and final drive, 4 stroke; 4 cylinders, vertical, in line; 103.7 cu in, 1,700 cc (3.35 x 2.99 in, 85 x 76 mm); compression ratio: 9:1; max power (DIN): 87 hp (64 kW) at 5,200 rpm; max torque (DIN): 98 lb ft, 13.5 kg m (132 Nm) at 3,800 rpm; max engine rpm: 5,600; 51.2 hp/l (37.7 kW/l); cast iron block, light alloy head; 5 crankshaft bearings; valves: overhead, push-rods and rockers; camshafts: 1, overhead, chain-driven; lubrication: rotary pump, magnetic metal gauze filter in sump and full flow, 10.2 imp pt, 12.3 US pt, 5.8 l; 1 SU type HIF6 semi-downdraught carburettor; fuel feed: electric pump; sealed circuit cooling, liquid, expansion tank, 10.6 imp pt, 12.7 US pt, 6 l, electric thermostatic fan.

TRANSMISSION driving wheels: front; clutch: single dry plate (diaphgram), hydraulically controlled; gearbox: mechanical, in unit with engine; gears: 4, fully synchronized; ratios: I 3.292, II 2.059, III 1.384, IV 1, rev 3.075; lever: central; final drive: spiral bevel; axle ratio: 3.720; width of rims: 4.5"; tyres: 185/70 SR x 14.

PERFORMANCE max speeds: (I) 35 mph, 56 km/h; (II) 55 mph, 88 km/h; (III) 82 mph, 132 km/h; (IV) 99 mph, 159 km/h; power-weight ratio: L model 28.9 lb/hp (39.2 lb/kW), 13.1 kg/hp (17.8 kg/kW); carrying capacity: 882 lb, 400 kg; speed in direct drive at 1,000 rpm: 18.8 mph, 30.3 km/h; consumption: 28.4 m/imp gal, 23.5 m/US gal, 9.9 l x 100 km at 75 mph, 120 km/h.

PRINCESS 1700 HLS Saloon

87 HP POWER TEAM

CHASSIS integral; front suspension: independent, wishbones, hydragas (liquid and gas) rubber cone springs, hydraulic connecting pipes to rear wheels; rear: independent, swinging longitudinal trailing arms, hydragas (liquid and gas) rubber cone springs, hydraulic connecting pipes to front wheels.

STEERING rack-and-pinion; turns lock to lock: 4.57.

BRAKES front disc (diameter 10.63 in, 27 cm), rear drum, dual circuit, servo; lining area: front 26.4 sq in, 170 sq cm, rear 47.9 sq in, 309 sq cm, total 74.3 sq in, 479 sq cm.

ELECTRICAL EQUIPMENT 12 V; 55 Ah battery; 45 A alternator; Lucas distributor; 2 headlamps - for HLS model only, halogen headlamps.

DIMENSIONS AND WEIGHT wheel base: 105.24 in, 267 cm; tracks: 58 in, 147 cm front, 57.36 in, 146 cm rear; length: 175.41 in, 445 cm - HLS model 176.37 in, 448 cm; width: 68.11 in, 173 cm; height: 55.48 in, 141 cm; ground clearance: 6.45 in, 16.4 cm; weight: L model 2,515 lb, 1,140 kg - HL model 2,523 lb, 1,144 kg - HLS model 2,543 lb, 1,153 kg; weight distribution: 63.5% front, 36.5% rear; turning circle: 37.1 ft, 11.3 m; fuel tank: 16 imp gal, 19.3 US gal, 73 l.

BODY saloon/sedan; 4 doors; 5 seats, separate front seats, reclining backrests; heated rear window; laminated windscreen; for HLS model only, headrests and tinted glass.

PRACTICAL INSTRUCTIONS fuel: 96-98 oct petrol; oil: engine, gearbox and final drive 10.2 imp pt, 12.3 US pt, 5.8 l, SAE 20W-50, change every 6,000 miles, 9,700 km; greasing: every 6,000 miles 9,700 km; tappet clearances: inlet 0.015 in, 0.38 mm, exhaust 0.015 in, 0.38 mm; valve timing: 5° 45° 40° 10°; tyre pressure: front 23 psi, 1.6 atm, rear, rear 21 psi 1.5 atm.

OPTIONALS Borg-Warner automatic transmission, hydraulic torque converter and planetary gears with 3 ratios (I 2.388, II 1.449, III 1, rev 2.090), max ratio of converter at stall 2, on facia lever, 3.830 axle ratio, max speed 96 mph, 155 km/h; power steering; tinted glass and headrests (except HLS model); 195/65 SR x 350 tyres: Denovo wheels and tyres; metallic spray; (for HL model only) vinyl roof.

93 hp power team

See 87 power team, except for:

ENGINE 121.7 cu in, 1,994 cc (3.35 x 3.50 in, 85 x 89 mm); max power (DIN): 93 hp (68 kW) at 4,900 rpm; max torque (DIN): 113 lb ft, 15.6 kg m (153 Nm) at 3,400 rpm; 46.6 hp/l (34.3 kW/l).

PERFORMANCE power-weight ratio: HL model 27.1 lb/hp (37 lb/kW), 12.3 kg/hp (16.8 kg/kW); acceleration: standing ¼ mile 19.4 sec; consumption: 27.7 m/imp gal, 23.1 m/US gal, 10.2 l x 100 km at 75 mph, 120 km/h.

DIMENSIONS AND WEIGHT weight: HL model 2,523 lb, 1,144 kg - HLS model 2,543 lb, 1,153 kg.

PRINCESS 2000 HL Saloon

PRACTICAL INSTRUCTIONS tappet clearances (cold): inlet 0.012 in, 0.30 mm, exhaust 0.012 in, 0.30 mm; tyre pressure: front 26 psi, 1.8 atm, rear 24 psi, 1.7 atm.

110 hp power team

See 87 hp power team, except for:

ENGINE 6 cylinders; 135.9 cu in, 2,227 cc (3 x 3.20 in, 76.2 x 81.3 mm); max power (DIN): 110 hp (81 kW) at 5,250 rpm; max torque (DIN): 125 lb ft, 17.2 kg m (169 Nm) at 3,500 rpm; 49.4 hp/l (36.4 kW/l); cast iron block and head; 7 crankshaft bearings; lubrication: 13 imp pt, 15.6 US pt, 7.4 l; 2 SU type HIF6 horizontal carburettors; fuel feed: mechanical pump; cooling: 15 imp pt, 18 US pt, 8.5 l.

PERFORMANCE max speed: 106 mph, 170 km/h; power-weight ratio: 24.3 lb/hp (33.1 lb/kW), 11 kg/hp (15 kg/kW); consumption: 27 m/imp gal, 22.4 m/US gal, 10.5 l x 100 km at 75 mph, 120 km/h.

STEERING servo (standard).

DIMENSIONS AND WEIGHT weight: 2,677 lb, 1,214 kg.

PRACTICAL INSTRUCTIONS oil: engine, gearbox and final drive 13 imp pt, 15.6 US pt, 7.4 l; tappet clearances: inlet 0.015-0.016 in, 0.38-0.40 mm, exhaust 0.015-0.016 in, 0.38-0.40 mm.

RAPPORT Quadraporte

RAPPORT — GREAT BRITAIN

Quadraporte

PRICE EX WORKS: £ 19,250*

ENGINE front, 4 stroke; 8 cylinders, Vee-slanted at 90°; 269.3 cu in, 4,414 cc (3.50 x 3.50 in, 88.9 x 88.9 mm); compression ratio: 8:1; max power (DIN): 131 hp (96 kW) at 3,000 rpm; max torque (DIN): 220 lb ft, 30.3 kg m (297 Nm) at 1,750 rpm; max engine rpm: 5,600; 29.7 hp/l (21.9 kW/l); light alloy block, aluminium alloy head; 5 crankshafts bearings; valves: overhead, hydraulic tappets; camshafts: 1 overhead; lubrication: gear pump; 1 Holley downdraught twin barrel carburettor; fuel feed: electric pump; cooling, 2[illegible] imp pt, 23.9 US pt, 11.3 l.

TRANSMISSION driving wheels: front and rear; clutch single dry plate (diaphragm); gearbox: mechanical; gears 5, fully synchronized; lever: central; axle ratio: 3.540; width of rims: 7''; tyres: 205/70 x 15.

PERFORMANCE max speed: 108 mph, 174 km/h; power-weight ratio: 32 lb/hp, (43.4 lb/kW), 14.5 kg/hp (19.7 kg/kW); carrying capacity: 1,720 lb, 780 kg; acceleration: standing ¼ mile 17.9 sec; consumption: 18.2 m/imp gal, 15.2 m/US gal, 15.5 l x 100 km.

CHASSIS ladder frame; front suspension: radius arms, Panhard rod, coil springs, hydraulic dampers; rear: radius arms, wishbone, coil springs.

STEERING turns lock to lock: 3.50.

BRAKES disc, servo.

ELECTRICAL EQUIPMENT 12 V; 65 Ah battery; alternator; Lucas distributor; 2 headlamps.

DIMENSIONS AND WEIGHT wheel base: 110 in, 279 cm; front and rear track: 58.50 in, 149 cm; length: 191 in, 48[illegible] cm; width: 70 in, 178 cm; height: 70 in, 178 cm; ground clearance: 7.50 in, 19 cm; weight: 4,180 lb, 1,896 kg; weight distribution: 50% front, 50% rear; turning circle: 3[illegible] ft, 11.6 m; fuel tank: 18 imp gal, 21.6 US gal, 82 l.

BODY estate car/st. wagon; 4 + 1 doors; 5 seats, separate front seats.

OPTIONALS automatic transmission with 3 ratios.

RELIANT — GREAT BRITAIN

Kitten DL Saloon / Estate Car

PRICES EX WORKS: £

Kitten DL 2-dr Saloon	3,091
Kitten DL 2+1-dr Estate Car	3,339

ENGINE front, 4 stroke; 4 cylinders, in line; 51.7 cu in, 84[illegible] cc (2.46 x 72 in, 62.5 x 69.1 mm); compression ratio: 9.5:1

RELIANT Kitten DL Saloon

ax power (DIN): 40 hp (29 kW) at 5,500 rpm; max torque)IN): 46 lb ft, 6.3 kg m (62 Nm) at 3,500 rpm; max engine m: 5,500; 47.2 hp/l (34.7 kW/l); light alloy block and head, et liners; 3 crankshaft bearings; valves: overhead, in line, ush-rods and rockers; camshafts: 1, side; lubrication: rotary pump, full flow filter, 5.5 imp pt, 6.6 US pt, 3.1 l; 1 SU S2 1¼ semi-downdraught single barrel carburettor; fuel ed: mechanical pump; sealed circuit cooling, anti-freeze quid, 6.5 imp pt, 7.8 US pt, 3.7 l.

RANSMISSION driving wheels: rear; clutch: single dry late; gearbox: mechanical; gears: 4, fully synchronized; atios: I 3.876, II 2.046, III 1.319, IV 1, rev 3.250; lever: entral; final drive: spiral bevel; axle ratio: 3.230; width of ms: 3.5"; tyres: 145 x 10.

ERFORMANCE max speeds: (I) 24 mph, 39 km/h; (II) 45 ph, 73 km/h; (III) 71 mph, 114 km/h; (IV) 80 mph, 128 n/h; power-weight ratio: Saloon 29.4 lb/hp (40 lb/kW), 3.3 kg/hp (18.1 kg/kW); carrying capacity: 700 lb, 317 kg; cceleration: standing ¼ mile 20.4 sec, 0-50 mph (0-80 n/h) 11.1 sec; speed in direct drive at 1,000 rpm: 17 mph, 7.3 km/h; consumption: 38.9 m/imp gal, 32.2 m/US gal, 7.3 x 100 km.

HASSIS box section side members and channel section iagonal reinforcements; front suspension: independent, ishbones, anti-roll bar, coil springs/telescopic damper units; rear: rigid axle, semi-elliptic leafsprings, telescopic ampers.

TEERING rack-and-pinion; turns lock to lock: 3.50.

BRAKES drum (diameter 7 in, 17.8 cm); swept area: front 66 sq in, 426 sq cm, rear 55 sq in, 355 sq cm, total 121 sq in, 781 sq cm.

ELECTRICAL EQUIPMENT 12 V; 30 Ah battery; 28 A alternator; Lucas distributor; 2 headlamps.

DIMENSIONS AND WEIGHT wheel base: 84.50 in, 215 cm; tracks: 48.50 in, 123 cm front, 49 in, 124 cm rear; length: Saloon 131 in, 133 cm - Estate Car 131.75 in, 335 cm; width: 56 in, 142 cm; height: 55 in, 140 cm; ground clearance: 5 in, 12.7 cm; weight: Saloon 1,175 lb, 533 kg - Estate Car 1,189 lb, 539 kg; turning circle: 24 ft, 7.3 m; fuel tank: 6 imp gal, 7.1 US gal, 27 l.

BODY saloon/sedan, estate car/st. wagon, in plastic material; 4 seats, separate front seats, reclining driving seat; heated rear window; folding rear seat.

PRACTICAL INSTRUCTIONS fuel: 97 oct petrol; oil: engine 5.5 imp pt, 6.6 US pt, 3.1 l, SAE 20W-50, change every 6,000 miles, 9,700 km - gearbox 1,1 imp pt, 1.3 US pt, 0.6 l, SAE 80 EP change every 12,000 miles, 19,400 km - final drive 2.2 imp pt, 2.5 US pt, 1.2 l, SAE 90 EP, change every 6,000 miles, 9,700 km; greasing: every 6,000 miles, 9,700 km, 7 points; tappet clearances: inlet 0.010 in, 0.25 mm, exhaust 0.010 in, 0.25 mm; valve timing: 13° 72° 54° 29°; tyre pressure: front 20 psi, 1.4 atm, rear 22 psi, 1.6 atm.

OPTIONALS light alloy wheels; laminated windscreen; (for Estate Car only) rear window wiper-washer.

Robin 850 / Super

PRICES EX WORKS:	£
Robin 850 2-dr Saloon	**2,444***
Robin 850 2+1-dr Estate Car	**2,681***
Robin 850 Super 2-dr Saloon	**2,836***
Robin 850 Super 2+1-dr Estate Car	**3,004***

ENGINE front, 4 stroke; 4 cylinders, in line; 51.7 cu in, 848 cc (2.46 x 2.72 in, 62.5 x 69.1 mm); compression ratio: 9.5:1; max power (DIN): 40 hp (29 kW) at 5,500 rpm; max torque (DIN): 46 lb ft, 6.3 kg m (62 Nm) at 3,500 rpm; max engine rpm: 5,500; 47.2 hp/l (34.7 kW/l); light alloy block and head; 3 crankshaft bearings; valves: overhead, push-rods and rockers; camshafts: 1, side; lubrication: rotary pump, full flow filter, 5.5 imp pt, 6.6 US pt, 3.1 l; 1 SU type HS2 1¼ semi-downdraught carburettor; fuel feed: mechanical pump; water-cooled, 5 imp pt, 5.9 US pt, 2.8 l.

TRANSMISSION driving wheels: rear; clutch: single dry plate; gearbox: mechanical; gears: 4, fully synchronized; ratios: I 3.880, II 2.050, III 1.320, IV 1, rev 3.250; lever: central; final drive: spiral bevel; axle ratio: 3.230; width of rims: 3.5"; tyres: 5.20 x 10.

PERFORMANCE max speeds: (I) 25 mph, 40 km/h; (II) 47 mph, 75 km/h; (III) 73 mph, 117 km/h; (IV) 80 mph, 128 km/h; power-weight ratio: 24 lb/hp (32.7 lb/kW), 10.9 kg/hp (14.8 kg/kW); carrying capacity: 788 lb, 357 kg; acceleration: standing ¼ mile 20.9 sec, 0-50 mph (0-80 km/h)11.4 sec; speed in direct drive at 1,000 rpm: 17 mph, 27.3 km/h; consumption: 60 m/imp gal, 50 m/US gal, 4.7 l x 100 km.

CHASSIS box-section ladder frame, tubular cross members; front suspension: single wheel, swinging leading arm, coil springs, telescopic dampers; rear: rigid axle, semi-elliptic leafsprings, anti-roll bar, telescopic dampers.

STEERING worm and peg; turns lock to lock: 2.25.

BRAKES drum, single circuit; swept area: front 33 sq in, 213 sq cm, rear 55 sq in, 355 sq cm, total 88 sq in, 568 sq cm.

ELECTRICAL EQUIPMENT 12 V; 30 Ah battery; 28 A alternator; Lucas distributor; 4 headlamps.

DIMENSIONS AND WEIGHT wheel base: 85 in, 216 cm; front and rear track 49 in, 124 cm; length: 131 in, 333 cm; width: 56 in, 142 cm; height: 54 in, 137 cm; ground clearance: 5 in, 12.7 cm; weight: 962 lb, 436 kg; weight distribution: 44% front, 56% rear; turning circle: 27 ft, 8.2 m; fuel tank: 6 imp gal, 7.1 US gal, 27 l.

BODY saloon/sedan, estate car/st. wagon, in plastic material; 4 seats, separate front seats; heated rear window.

PRACTICAL INSTRUCTIONS fuel: 97 oct petrol; oil: engine 5.5 imp pt, 6.6 US pt, 3.1 l, SAE 20W-50, change every 6,000 miles, 9,700 km - gearbox 1.1 imp pt, 1.3 US pt, 0.6 l, SAE 80 EP, change every 12,000 miles, 19,400 km - final drive 2.2 imp pt, 2.5 US pt, 1.2 l, SAE 90 EP, change every 6,000 miles 9,700 km; greasing: every 6,000 miles 9,700 km, 4 points; tappet clearances: inlet 0.010 in, 0.25 mm hot, exhaust 0.010 in, 0.25 mm hot; valve timing: 13° 72° 54° 29°; tyre pressure: front 30 psi, 2.1 atm, rear 24 psi, 1.7 atm.

OPTIONALS (for Super models only) light alloy wheels.

RELIANT Scimitar GTE

RELIANT 850 Robin Saloon

Scimitar GTE / GTC

PRICES EX WORKS:	£
Scimitar GTE	9,343*
Scimitar GTC	—

ENGINE Ford, front, 4 stroke; 6 cylinders, Vee-slanted at 60°; 170.4 cu in, 2,792 cc (3.66 x 2.70 in, 93 x 68.5 mm); compression ratio: 9.2:1, max power (DIN): 135 hp (99 kW) at 5,200 rpm; max torque (DIN): 152 lb ft, 21 kg m (206 Nm) at 3,000 rpm; max engine rpm: 6,000; 48.4 hp/l (35.6 kW/l) cast iron block and head; 4 crankshaft bearings; valves: overhead, push-rods and rockers; camshafts: 1, at centre of Vee; lubrication: rotary pump, full flow filter, 7.5 imp pt, 8.9 US/pt, 4.2 l; 1 Solex 78TF 9510 CA/DA downdraught twin barrel carburettor; fuel feed: mechanical pump; water-cooled, 21.5 imp pt, 26 US pt, 12.2 l, electric thermostatic fan.

TRANSMISSION driving wheels: rear; clutch: single dry plate (diaphragm); gearbox: mechanical; gears: 4 and overdrive on III and IV , fully synchronized; ratios: I 3.163, II 1.950, III 1.412 (overdrive 1.160), IV 1 (overdrive 0.780), rev 3.350; lever: central; final drive: hypoid bevel; axle ratio: 3.540; width of rims: GTE 5.5''-GTC 6'' tyres: 185 HR x 14.

PERFORMANCE power-weight ratio: 20.7 lb/hp (28.1 lb/kW) 9.4 kg/hp (12.8 kg/kW); carrying capacity: 990 lb, 449 kg; speed in direct drive at 1,000 rpm: 20.7 mph, 33.3 km/h; consumption: 35.6 m/imp gal, 29.8 m/US gal, 7.9 l x 100 km at 56 mph, 90 km/h.

CHASSIS box-type ladder frame, tubular cross members; front suspension: independent, wishbones, anti-roll bar, coil springs/telescopic damper units; rear: rigid axle, twin trailing arms, transverse Watt linkage, coil springs/telescopic damper units.

STEERING rack-and-pinion, servo; turns lock to lock: 2.50.

BRAKES front disc (diameter 10.51 in, 26.6 cm), rear drum, rear compensator, servo; swept area: front 237 sq in, 1,529 sq cm, rear 110 sq in, 710 sq cm, total 347 sq in, 2,239 sq cm.

ELECTRICAL EQUIPMENT 12 V; 55 Ah battery; 770 W alternator; Motorcraft distributor; 4 headlamps.

DIMENSIONS AND WEIGHT wheel base: 103.80 in, 264 cm; tracks: 58.10 in, 148 cm front, 56.10 in, 142 cm rear; length: 174.50 in, 443 cm; width: 67.80 in, 172 cm; height: 52 in, 132 cm; ground clearance: 5.50 in, 14 cm; weight: 2,790 lb, 1,265 kg; weight distribution: 54% front, 46% rear; turning circle: 38.5 ft, 1.7 m; fuel tank: 20 imp gal, 24 US gal, 91 l.

BODY coupé, convertible, in plastic material; 2 doors; 4 seats, separate front seats, reclining backrests with built-in headrests; folding rear seat; heated rear window; (for GTC only) sunshine roof, roll bar and (standard) light alloy wheels.

PRACTICAL INSTRUCTIONS fuel: 97 oct petrol; oil: engine 7.5 imp pt, 8.9 US pt, 4.2 l, SAE 10W-40 change every 6,000 miles, 9,700 km - gearbox 5 imp pt, 6 US pt, 2.8 l, SAE 80, change every 6,000 miles, 9,700 km - final drive 3.5 imp pt, 4.2 US pt, 2 l, SAE 90, change every 6,000 miles, 9,700 km; greasing: every 6,000 miles, 9,700 km, 4 points; tappet clearances: inlet 0.014 in, 0.35 mm, exhaust 0.016 in, 0.40 mm; valve timing: 20° 56° 62° 14°; tyre pressure: front 24 psi, 1.6 atm, rear 24 psi, 1.6 atm.

OPTIONALS Ford C3 automatic transmission, hydraulic torque converter and planetary gears with 3 ratios (I 2.474, II 1.474, III 1, rev 2.111), max ratio of converter at stall 2, possible manual selection; electric windows; (for GTE only) 6'' wide rims; tinted glass; fog lamps; leather upholstery.

ROLLS-ROYCE GREAT BRITAIN

Silver Shadow II

PRICE IN USA: $ 77,600*
PRICE EX WORKS: £ 36,652*

ENGINE front, 4 stroke; 8 cylinders, Vee-slanted; 411.9 cu in, 6,750 cc (4.10 x 3.90 in, 104.1 x 99.1 mm); compression ratio: 8:1; aluminium alloy block and head, cast iron wet liners; 5 crankshaft bearings; valves: overhead, in line, slanted, push-rods and rockers, hydraulic tappets; camshafts: 1, at centre of Vee; lubrication: gear pump, full flow filter (cartridge), 14.7 imp pt, 17.5 US pt, 8.3 l; 2 SU type HIF7 horizontal carburettors; dual exhaust system; fuel feed: 2 electric pumps; sealed circuit cooling, expansion tank, 28.5 imp pt, 34.2 US pt, 16.2 l, viscous coupling thermostatic fan.

TRANSMISSION driving wheels: rear; gearbox: Turbo-Hydramatic 400 automatic transmission, hydraulic torque converter and planetary gears with 3 ratios, max ratio of converter at stall 2, possible manual selection; ratios: I 2.500, II 1.500, III 1, rev 2; lever: steering column; final drive: hypoid bevel; axle ratio: 3.080; width of rims: 6''; tyres: 235/70 HR x 15.

PERFORMANCE max speeds: (I) 47 mph, 76 km/h; (II) 79 mph, 126 km/h; (III) 118 mph, 190 km/h; carrying capacity: 1,014 lb, 460 kg; speed in direct drive at 1,000 rpm: 26.2 mph, 42.2 km/h; consumption: 11.1 m/imp gal, 9.3 m/US gal, 25.4 l x 100 km (town) - 19.5 m/imp gal, 16.2 m/US gal, 14.5 l x 100 km at 56 mph, 90 km/h - 15.9 m/imp gal, 13.2 m/US gal, 17.8 l x 100 km at 75 mph, 120 km/h.

CHASSIS integral, front and rear auxilary frames; front suspension: independent, lower wishbones, coil springs, anti-roll bar, telescopic dampers; rear: independent, semitrailing arms, coil springs, anti-roll bar, automatic levelling control, telescopic dampers.

STEERING rack-and-pinion, servo, right or left-hand drive; turns lock to lock: 3.20.

BRAKES disc (diameter 11 in, 27.9 cm), front internal radial fins, servo; swept area: front 227 sq in, 1,464 sq cm, rear 286 sq in, 1,845 sq cm, total 513 sq in, 3,309 sq cm.

ELECTRICAL EQUIPMENT 12 V; 68 Ah battery; 75 A alternator; Lucas transistorized distributor; 4 headlamps, 2 front and 2 rear fog lamps.

ROLLS-ROYCE Silver Shadow II

DIMENSIONS AND WEIGHT wheel base: 120.10 in, 305 cr tracks: 60 in, 152 cm front, 59.60 in, 151 cm rear; lengt 204.55 in, 520 cm; width: 72 cm in, 183 cm; height: 59.75 i 152 cm; ground clearance: 6.50 in, 16.5 cm; weight: 4,928 l 2,235 kg; turning circle: 38.5 ft, 11.7 m; fuel tank: 23.5 imp ga 28.2 US gal, 107 l.

BODY saloon/sedan; 4 doors; 5 seats, separate front seat adjustable and reclining backrests; automatic air-conditionin heated rear window; electric windows; seat adjustment ar gear range selector.

PRACTICAL INSTRUCTIONS fuel: 98 oct petrol; oil: engin 14.7 imp pt, 17.5 US pt, 8.3 l, SAE 20W-50, change eve 6,000 miles, 9,700 km - automatic transmission 18.6 imp p 22.4 US pt, 10.6 l, Dexron, change every 24,000 miles, 38,60 km - final drive 4.5 imp pt, 5.3 US pt, 2.5 l, SAE 90 EP, chang every 24,000 miles, 38,600 km - power steering and automat levelling control change every 20,000 miles, 32,000 km; grea ing: every 12,000 miles 19,300 km, 5 points; valve timing: 2 60° 68° 18°; tyre pressure : front 24 psi, 1.7 atm , rear 28 psi, atm.

OPTIONALS iodine headlamps; headrests; Everflex roof.

VARIATIONS

(For USA, Japan and Australia only)
ENGINE 7.3:1 compression ratio, catalytic converter, Pierbu fuel pump (except for Japan).

ROLLS-ROYCE Silver Shadow II

ROLLS-ROYCE Silver Wraith II

ROLLS-ROYCE Corniche Convertible

Silver Wraith II

See Silver Shadow II, except for:

PRICE IN USA: $ 91,000*
PRICE EX WORKS: £ 43,181*

DIMENSIONS AND WEIGHT wheel base: 123 in, 312 cm; length: 208.50 in, 530 cm; weight: 5,020 lb, 2,277 kg; turning circle: 40 ft, 12.2 m.

Silver Wraith II with division

See Silver Shadow II, except for:

PRICE EX WORKS: £ 45,535*

DIMENSIONS AND WEIGHT wheel base: 123 in, 312 cm; length: 208.50 in, 530 cm; weight: 5,259 lb, 2,385 kg; turning circle: 40 ft, 12.2 m.

BODY glass partition.

PRACTICAL INSTRUCTIONS tyre pressure: rear 30 psi, 2.1 atm.

Corniche Saloon

See Silver Shadow II, except for:

PRICE IN USA: $ 131,300*
PRICE EX WORKS: £ 53,322*

ENGINE 1 Solex 4A1 4-barrel carburettor; fuel feed: Pierburg pump.

CHASSIS rear suspension: independent, coil springs, semi-trailing arms, struts, anti-roll bar, automatic ride height control.

DIMENSIONS AND WEIGHT width:71.65 in, 182 in, cm; height: 58.75 in, 149 cm; ground clearance: 6 in, 15.2 cm; weight: 5,045 lb, 2,285 kg.

ELECTRICAL EQUIPMENT 55 A alternator.

BODY 2 doors; 4 seats.

Corniche Convertible

See Silver Shadow II, except for:

PRICE IN USA: $ 140,000*
PRICE EX WORKS: £ 56,636*

ENGINE 1 Solex 4A1 4-barrel carburettor; fuel feed: Pierburg pump.

CHASSIS rear suspension: independent, coil springs, semi-trailing arms, struts, anti-roll bar, automatic ride height control.

DIMENSIONS AND WEIGHT width 71.65 in, 182 cm; ground clearance: 6 in, 15.2 cm; weight: 5,204 lb, 2,360 kg.

ELECTRICAL EQUIPMENT 55 A alternator.

BODY convertible; 2 doors; 4 seats.

ROLLS-ROYCE Corniche Convertible

Phantom VI

PRICE EX WORKS: quotation on request.

ENGINE front, 4 stroke; 8 cylinders, Vee-slanted; 411.9 cu in, 6,750 cc (4.10 x 3.90 in, 104.1 x 99.1 mm); compression ratio: 8:1; aluminium alloy block and head, cast iron wet liners; 5 crankshaft bearings; valves: overhead, in line, slanted, push-rods and rockers, hydraulic tappets; camshafts: 1, at centre of Vee; lubrication: gear pump, full flow filter (cartridge), 14.5 imp pt, 17.5 US pt, 8.3 l; 2 SU type HIF 7 horizontal carburettors; fuel feed: 2 electric pumps; sealed circuit cooling, expansion tank, 28.5 imp pt, 34.2 US pt, 16.2 l, viscous coupling thermostatic fan.

TRANSMISSION driving wheels: rear; gearbox: TurboHydramatic 400 automatic transmission, hydraulic torque converter and planetary gears with 3 ratios, max ratio of converter at stall 2, possible manual selection; ratios: I 2.500, II 1.500, III 1, rev 2; lever: steering column; final drive: hypoid bevel; axle ratio: 3.890; width of rims: 6''; tyres: 8.90S x 15.

PERFORMANCE max speeds: (I) 29 mph, 47 km/h; (II) 42 mph, 68 km/h; (III) 77 mph, 124 km/h; (IV) 112 mph, 180 km/h; carrying capacity: 1,235 lb, 560 kg; acceleration: standing ¼ mile 19.4 sec, 0-50 mph (0-80 km/h) 9.7 sec; speed in direct drive at 1,000 rpm 22.5 mph, 36.2 km/h; consumption: 9.9 m/imp gal, 8.3 m/US gal, 28.5 l x 100 km (town) - 15 m/imp gal, 12.5 m/US gal, 18.8 l x 100 km at 56 mph, 90 km/h - 12.4 m/imp gal, 10.3 m/US gal, 22.8 l x 100 km at 75 mph, 120 km/h.

CHASSIS box-type ladder frame; front suspension: independent, wishbones, coil springs, anti-roll bar, lever dampers; rear: rigid axle, asymmetrical semi-elliptic leafsprings, Z-type transverse linkage bar, electrically-adjustable lever dampers.

STEERING worm and roller, progressive servo (50%-80%); turns lock to lock: 4.25.

BRAKES drum, 2 independent power hydraulic circuits; swept area: front 211.9 sq in, 1,361 sq cm, rear 211.9 sq in, 1,361 sq cm, total 423.8 sq in, 2,722 sq cm.

ELECTRICAL EQUIPMENT 12 V; 68 Ah battery; 75 A alternator; Lucas Opus Mark II distributor; 4 headlamps.

DIMENSIONS AND WEIGHT wheel base: 145 in, in 368 cm; tracks: 60.87 in, 155 cm front, 64 in, 162 cm rear; length: 238 in, 604 cm; width: 79 in, 201 cm; height: 69 in, 175 cm; ground clearance: 7.25 in, 18.4 cm; weight: 6,045 lb, 2,742 kg; weight distribution: 48% front, 52% rear; turning circle: 52 ft, 15.9 m; fuel tank: 23 imp gal, 27.7 US gal, 105 l.

BODY limousine; 4 doors; 7 seats, separate front seats; glass partition; air-conditioning; electric windows; heated rear window.

PRACTICAL INSTRUCTIONS fuel: 98 oct petrol; oil: engine 14.1 imp pt, 16.9 US pt, 8 l, SAE 20W-50, change every 6,000 miles, 9,700 km - automatic transmission 21 imp pt, 25.2 US pt, 11.9 l, change every 24,000 miles, 38,600 km - final drive 1.8 imp pt, 2.1 US pt, 1 l, SAE 90 EP, change every 24,000 miles, 38,600 km; greasing: every 12,000 miles, 19,300 km, 21 points; valve timing: 20° 61° 62° 19°; tyre pressure: front 24 psi, 1.7 atm, rear 30 psi, 2.1 atm.

OPTIONALS Landaulette version.

ROLLS-ROYCE Phantom VI

ROLLS-ROYCE Camargue

Camargue

PRICE IN USA: $ 136,500*
PRICE EX WORKS: £ 64,970*

ENGINE front, 4 stroke; 8 cylinders, Vee-slanted; 411.9 cu in, 6,750 cc (4.10 x 3.90 in, 104.1 x 99.1 mm); compression ratio: 8:1; aluminium alloy block and head, cast iron wet liners; 5 crankshaft bearings; valves: overhead, in line, push-rods and rockers, hydraulic tappets; camshafts: 1, at centre of Vee; lubrication: gear pump, full flow filter (cartridge), 14.7 imp pt, 17.5 US pt, 8.3 l; 1 Solex 4A1 horizontal 4-barrel carburettor; dual exhaust system; fuel feed: Pierburg pump; sealed circuit cooling, expansion tank, 28.5 imp pt, 34.2 US pt, 16.2 l, viscous coupling thermostatic fan.

TRANSMISSION driving wheels: rear; gearbox: Turbo-Hydramatic 400 automatic transmission, hydraulic torque converter and planetary gears with 3 ratios, max ratio of converter at stall 2, possible manual selection; ratios: I 2.500, II 1.500, III 1, rev 2; lever: steering column; final drive: hypoid bevel; axle ratio: 3.080; width of rims: 6"; tyres HR70 x 15 or 235/70 HR x 15.

PERFORMANCE max speeds: (I) 47 mph, 76 km/h; (II) 79 mph, 127 km/h; (III) 118 mph, 190 km/h; carrying capacity: 882 lb, 400 kg; speed in direct drive at 1,000 rpm: 26.2 mph, 42.2 km/h; consumption: 10.1 m/imp gal, 8.4 m/US gal, 28 l x 100 km (town) - 17.6 m/imp gal, 14.6 m/US gal, 16.1 l x 100 km at 56 mph, 90 km/h - 14.5 m/imp gal, 12.1 m/US gal, 19.5 l x 100 km at 75 mph, 120 km/h.

CHASSIS integral, front and rear auxiliary frames; front suspension: independent, lower wishbones, coil springs, anti-roll bar, telescopic dampers; rear: independent, semitrailing arms, coil springs, anti-roll bar, automatic levelling control, telescopic dampers.

STEERING rack-and-pinion, servo; turns lock to lock: 3.20.

BRAKES disc [diameter (twin calipers) 11 in, 27.9 cm], front internal radial fins, servo; swept area: front 227 sq in, 1,464 sq cm, rear 286 sq in, 1,845 sq cm, total 513 sq in, 3,309 sq cm.

ELECTRICAL EQUIPMENT 12 V; 68 Ah battery; 75 A alternator; Lucas Opus electronic ignition; 4 headlamps, 2 front and 2 rear fog lamps.

DIMENSIONS AND WEIGHT wheel base: 120.10 in, 305 cm; tracks: 60 in, 152 cm front, 59.60 in, 151 cm rear; length: 203.50 in, 517 cm; width: 75.59 in, 192 cm; height: 57.87 in 147 cm; ground clearance: 6.50 in, 16.5 cm; weight: 5,138 lb, 2,330 kg; turning circle: 38.5 ft, 11.7 m; fuel tank: 23.5 imp gal, 28.2 US gal, 107 l.

BODY saloon/sedan; 2 doors; 5 seats, separate front seats, adjustable and reclining backrests; built-in headrests; leather upholstery; automatic air-conditioning; electric windows; seat adjustment and gear range selector; heated rear window.

PRACTICAL INSTRUCTIONS fuel: 98 oct petrol; oil: engine 14.7 imp pt, 17.5 US pt, 8.3 l, SAE 20W-50, change every 6,000 miles, 9,700 km - automatic transmission 18.6 imp pt, 22.4 US pt, 10.6 l, Dexron, change every 24,000 miles, 38,600 km - final drive 4.5 imp pt, 5.3 US pt, 2.5 l, SAE 90 EP, change every 24,000 miles, 38,600 km - automatic levelling control 4,5 imp pt, 5.3 US pt, 2.5 l - power steering 3 imp pt, 3.6 US pt, 1.7 l; greasing: every 12,000 miles, 19,300 km; tyre pressure: front 24 psi, 1,7 atm, rear 28 psi, 2 atm.

VARIATIONS

(For USA, Japan and Australia only)

ENGINE 7.3:1 compression ratio, 2 SU type HIF 7 horizontal carburettors, catalytic converter (except for Japan).

ROVER GREAT BRITAIN

3500

PRICE EX WORKS: £ 9,052*

ENGINE front, 4 stroke; 8 cylinders, Vee-slanted; 215 cu in, 3,528 cc (3.50 x 2.80 in, 88.9 x 71.1 mm); compression ratio: 9.35:1; max power (DIN): 155 hp (114 kW) at 5,250 rpm; max torque (DIN): 198 lb ft, 27.3 kg m (268 Nm) at 2,500 rpm; max engine rpm: 6,000; 43.9 hp/l (32.3 kW/l); light alloy block and head, dry liners; 5 crankshaft bearings; valves: overhead, in line, push-rods and rockers, hydraulic tappets; camshafts: 1, at centre of Vee; lubrication: gear pump, full flow filter, 9.5 imp pt, 11.4 US pt, 5.4 l; 2 SU type HIF6 semi-downdraught carburettors; fuel feed: electric pump; water-cooled, 19.5 imp pt, 23.5 US pt, 11.1 l, viscous-coupling thermostatic fan.

TRANSMISSION driving wheels: rear; clutch: single dry plate (diaphragm), hydraulic controlled; gearbox: mechanical; gears: 5, fully synchronized; ratios: I 3.321, II 2.087, III 1.396, IV 1, V 0.833, rev 3.428; lever: central; final drive: hypoid bevel; axle ratio: 3.080: width of rims: 6"; tyres: 185 HR x 14.

PERFORMANCE max speed: 126 mph, 203 km/h; power-weight ratio: 19.2 lb/hp (26.2 lb/kW), 8.7 kg/kp (11.9 kg/kW) carrying capacity: 1,235 lb, 560 kg; acceleration: 0-50 mph (0-80 km/h) 6.4 sec; speed in top at 1,000 rpm: 28.8 mph, 46.4 km/h; consumption: 28 m/imp gal, 23.3 m/US gal, 10.1 l x 100 km at 75 mph, 120 km/h.

CHASSIS integral, front cross members; front suspension: independent, by McPherson, wishbones (lower trailing links), coil springs/telescopic damper struts, anti-roll bar; rear: rigid axle (torque tube), coil springs with combined telescopic dampers and self-levelling struts, Watt linkage.

STEERING rack-and-pinion, adjustable steering column, servo, turns lock to lock: 2.70.

BRAKES front disc (diameter 10.15 in, 25.8 cm), rear drum, rear compensator, servo.

ELECTRICAL EQUIPMENT 12 V; 66 Ah battery; 55 A alternator; Lucas electronic ignition; 4 halogen headlamps, 2 fog lamps.

DIMENSIONS AND WEIGHT wheel base: 111 in, 282 cm; front and rear track: 59 in, 150 cm; length: 185 in, 469 cm; width 69.60 in, 177 cm; height: 54.33 in, 138 cm; weight: 2,990 lb, 1,356 kg; turning circle: 34.3 ft, 10.5 m; fuel tank: 14.5 imp gal, 17.4 US gal, 66 l.

BODY saloon/sedan; 4+1 doors; 5 seats, separate front seats, reclining backrests; adjustable built-in headrests; electric windows; laminated windscreen with tinted glass; heated rear window; metallic spray; folding rear seat.

PRACTICAL INSTRUCTIONS fuel: 97 oct petrol; oil: engine 9.5 imp pt, 11.4 US pt, 5.4 l, SAE 20W-30, change every 6,000 miles, 9,700 km - gearbox 2.7 imp pt, 3.2 US pt, 1.5 l, SAE 90 EP, change every 6,000 miles, 9,700 km - final drive 1.6 imp pt, 1.9 US pt, 0.9 l, SAE 90 EP, change every 6,000 miles, 9,700 km; valve timing: 30° 75° 68° 37°; tyre pressure: front 26 psi, 1.8 atm, rear 26 psi, 1.8 atm.

OPTIONALS Borg-Warner 65 automatic transmission, hydraulic torque converter and planetary gears with 3 ratios (I 2.390, II 1.450, III 1, rev 2.090), max ratio of converter at stall 2.08, possible manual selection, max speed 123 mph, 198 km/h, speed in direct drive at 1,000 rpm 23.9 mph, 38.4 km/h, consumption 23.5 m/imp gal, 19.6 m/US gal, 12 l x 100 km; Dunlop Denovo wheels and tyres; 195/70 HR x 14 tyres with light alloy wheels; sunshine roof; leather upholstery.

2600

See 3500, except for:

PRICE EX WORKS: £ 7,403*

ENGINE 6 cylinders, in line; 158.5 cu in, 2,597 cc (3.19 x 3.31 in, 81 x 84 mm); max power (DIN): 136 hp (100 kW) at 5,000 rpm; max torque (DIN): 152 lb ft, 21 kg m (206 Nm) at 3,750 rpm; 52.4 hp/l (38.5 kW/l); cast iron block, light alloy head; 4 crankshaft bearings; valves: overhead, Vee-slanted, thimble tappets; camshafts: 1, overhead, cogged belt; lubrication: rotary pump, full flow filter, 10.8 imp pt, 12.9 US pt, 6.1 l; 2 SU

ROVER 3500

ROVER 2600

type HS6 horizontal carburettors; cooling: 18.2 imp pt, 21.8 US pt, 10.3 l.

TRANSMISSION gears: 4, fully synchronized; ratios: I 3.321, II 2.087, III 1.396, IV 1, rev 3.428; axle ratio: 3.450; width of rims: 5.5"; tyres: 175 HR x 14.

PERFORMANCE max speed: 114 mph, 183 km/h; power-weight ratio: 23.6 lb/hp (32.2 lb/kW), 10.7 kg/hp (14.6 kg/kW); speed in direct drive at 1,000 rpm: 21 mph, 33.8 km/h; consumption: 27.4 m/imp gal, 22.8 m/US gal, 10.3 l x 100 km at 75 mph, 120 km/h.

STEERING rack-and-pinion; turns lock to lock: 2.75.

DIMENSIONS AND WEIGHT weight: 2,900 lb, 1,315 kg.

PRACTICAL INSTRUCTIONS fuel: 97 oct petrol; oil: engine 10.8 imp pt, 12.9 US pt, 6.1 l; tappet clearances: inlet 0.018 in, 0.46 mm, exhaust 0.018 in, 0.46 mm; valve timing: 10° 56° 56° 16°; tyre pressure: front 26 psi, 1.8 atm, rear 28 psi, 2 atm.

OPTIONALS 5-speed fully synchronized mechanical gearbox (I 3.321, II 2.087, III 1.396, IV 1, V 0.833, rev 3.428); Borg-Warner automatic gearbox; power steering; halogen headlamps; fog lamps; tinted glass; metallic spray; Dunlop Denovo wheels (for United Kingdom only).

type HS6 horizontal carburettors; cooling: 18.2 imp pt, 21.8 US pt, 10.3 l.

TRANSMISSION axle ratio: 3.450; width of rims: 5.5"; tyres: 175 HR x 14.

PERFORMANCE max speed: 119 mph, 191 km/h; power-weight ratio: 21.8 lb/hp (29.8 lb/kW), 9.9 kg/hp (13.5 kg/kW); speed in top at 1,000 rpm: 25 mph, 40.2 km/h; consumption: 30.1 m/imp gal, 25 m/US gal, 9.4 l x 100 km at 75 mph, 120 km/h.

STEERING rack-and-pinion; turns lock to lock: 2.75.

DIMENSIONS AND WEIGHT weight: 2,978 lb, 1,351 kg.

OPTIONALS Borg-Warner automatic gearbox; electric windows; fog lamps; tinted glass; metallic spray, light alloy wheels; 195/70 H x 14 tyres; Denovo wheels (for United Kingdom only).

2300

See 3500, except for:

PRICE EX WORKS: £ 6,384*

ENGINE 6 cylinders, in line; 143.5 cu in, 2,351 cc (3.19 x 2.99 in, 81 x 76 mm); max power (DIN): 123 hp (90 kW) at 5,500 rpm; max torque (DIN): 134 lb ft, 18.5 kg m (181 Nm) at 4,000 rpm; 52.3 hp/l (38.5 kW/l); cast iron block, light alloy head; 4 crankshaft bearings; valves: overhead, Vee-slanted, thimble tappets; camshafts: 1, overhead, cogged belt; lubrication: rotary pump, full flow filter, 10.8 imp pt, 12.9 US pt, 6.1 l; 2 SU

ROVER 2600

SPARTAN CARS 2-seater Sports

SPARTAN CARS GREAT BRITAIN

2-seater Sports

PRICE EX WORKS: £ 4,680*

ENGINE Ford, front, 4 stroke; 4 cylinders, vertical, in line; 97.5 cu in, 1,598 cc (3.19 x 3.06 in, 81 x 77.6 mm); compression ratio: 9:1 max power (DIN): 84 hp (62 kW) at 5,500 rpm; max torque (DIN): 92 lb ft, 12.7 kg m (124 Nm) at 3,500 rpm; max engine rpm: 6,600; 52.6 hp/l (38.7 kW/l); cast iron block and head; 5 crankshaft bearings; valves: overhead, in line, push-rods and rockers; camshafts: 1, side, chain-driven; lubrication: rotary or vane-type pump, full flow filter, 5.7 imp pt, 6.8 US pt, 3.2 l; 1 Weber 32/32 DGV downdraught twin barrel carburettor; fuel feed: mechanical pump; water-cooled, 9.5 imp pt, 11.4 US pt, 5.4 l.

TRANSMISSION driving wheels: rear; clutch: single dry plate (diaphragm); gearbox: mechanical; gears: 4, fully synchronized; ratios: I 3.337, II 1.995, III 1.418, IV 1, rev 3.876; lever: central; final drive: hypoid bevel; axle ratio: 3.770; width of rims: 5.5"; tyres: 175/70 SR x 13.

PERFORMANCE max speed: 108 mph, 174 km/h; power-weight ratio: 18.7 lb/hp (25.4 lb/kW), 8.5 kg/hp (11.5 kg/kW); carrying capacity: 353 lb, 160 kg; acceleration: standing ¼ mile 17.3 sec; consumption: 33 m/imp gal, 27.7 m/US gal, 8.5 l x 100 km.

CHASSIS tubular space-frame with aluminium panels; front suspension: independent, by McPherson, coil springs/telescopic damper struts, anti-roll bar; rear: rigid axle, trailing lower radius arms, upper oblique torque arms, coil springs, telescopic dampers.

STEERING rack-and-pinion, turns lock to lock: 3.50.

BRAKES front disc (diameter 9.60 in, 24.4 cm), rear drum.

ELECTRICAL EQUIPMENT 12 V; 38 Ah battery; 35 A alternator; Motorcraft distributor; 4 headlamps.

DIMENSIONS AND WEIGHT length: 150 in, 381 cm; width: 62.60 in, 159 cm; height: 49.61 in, 126 cm; weight: 1,568 lb, 711 kg; fuel tank: 9 imp gal, 10.8 US gal, 41 l.

BODY sports; 2 doors; 2 seats; built-in headrests.

PRACTICAL INSTRUCTIONS fuel: 97 oct petrol; oil: engine 5.8 imp pt, 7 US pt, 3.3 l, SAE 10W-30, change every 6,000 miles, 9,700 km - gearbox 1.6 imp pt, 1.9 US pt, 0.9 l, SAE 80, no change recommended - final drive 1.7 imp pt, 2.1 US pt, 1 l, SAE 90, no change recommended; greasing: every 6,000 miles, 9,700 km, 2 points; tappet clearances: inlet 0.010 in, 0.25 mm, exhaust 0.017 in, 0.43 mm; valve timing: 29° 63° 71° 21°; tyre pressure: front 24 psi, 1.7 atm, rear 24 psi, 1.7 atm.

OPTIONALS light alloy wheels; reclining backrests; leather upholstery; halogen headlamps; rear fog lamps; tonneau cover; metallic spray.

2+2-seater Sports

See 2-seater Sports, except for:

PRICE EX WORKS: £ 5,035*

PERFORMANCE power-weight ratio: 20.2 lb/hp (27.5 lb/kW), 9.2 kg/hp (12.5 kg/kW); carrying capacity: 706 lb, 320 kg.

DIMENSIONS AND WEIGHT length: 156 in, 396 cm; height: 52.11 in, 132 cm; weight: 1,700 lb, 771 kg.

BODY 2+2 seats.

TALBOT GREAT BRITAIN

Sunbeam Series

PRICES EX WORKS: £

1 1.0 LS	**3,041***
2 1.0 GL	**3,333***
3 1.3 LS	**3,289***
4 1.3 GL	**3,581***
5 1.6 GL	**3,732***
6 1.6 GLS	**4,261***
7 1.6 TI	**4,566***
8 Lotus	**7,205***

Power team:	Standard for:	Optional for:
42 hp	1,2	—
59 hp	3,4	—
69 hp	5	—
80 hp	6	—
100 hp	7	—
150 hp	8	—

42 hp power team

ENGINE front, 4 stroke; 4 cylinders, in line; 56.6 cu in, 928 cc (2.76 x 2.37 in, 70 x 60.3 mm); compression ratio: 9:1; max power (DIN): 42 hp (31 kW) at 5,000 rpm; max torque (DIN): 51 lb ft, 7 kg m (69 Nm) at 2,600 rpm; max engine rpm: 6,000; 45.3 hp/l (33.3 kW/l); light alloy block and head; 3 crankshaft bearings; valves: overhead; camshafts: 1, overhead; lubrication: rotary pump, full flow filter, 5.3 imp pt, 6.3 US pt, 3 l; 1 Zenith 150 DC3 downdraught single barrel carburettor; fuel feed: mechanical pump; water-cooled, 9 imp pt, 10.8 US pt, 5.1 l, electric thermostatic fan.

TRANSMISSION driving wheels: rear; clutch: single dry plate (diaphragm); gearbox: mechanical; gears: 4, fully synchronized; ratios: I 3.894, II 2,382, III 1.527, IV 1, rev 4.050; lever: central; final drive: hypoid bevel; axle ratio: 4.375; width of rims: 4.5"; tyres: 145 x 13.

PERFORMANCE max speeds: (I) 23 mph, 36 km/h; (II) 37 mph, 60 km/h; (III) 58 mph, 93 km/h; (IV) 80 mph, 128 km/h; power-weight ratio: LS 42.8 lb/hp (57.8 lb/kW), 19.4 kg/hp (26.2 kg/kW); carrying capacity: 980 lb, 445 kg; acceleration: 0-50 mph (0-80 km/h) 14.3 sec; speed in direct drive at 1,000 rpm: 14.7 mph, 23.6 km/h; consumption: 44.7 m/imp gal, 37.3 m/US gal, 63 l x 100 km at 56 mph, 90 km/h.

CHASSIS integral; front suspension: independent, by McPherson, coil springs/telescopic damper struts, wishbones, anti-roll bar; rear: rigid axle, swinging longitudinal trailing arms, upper oblique torque arms, coil springs, telescopic dampers.

STEERING rack-and-pinion; turns lock to lock: 3.66.

BRAKES front disc (diameter 9.50 in, 24.1 cm), rear drum, servo; swept area: front 177.8 sq in, 1,147 sq cm, rear 74 sq in, 477 sq cm, total 251.8 sq in, 1,624 sq cm.

ELECTRICAL EQUIPMENT 12 V; 40 Ah battery; 35 A alternator; Lucas distributor; electronic ignition; 2 headlamps.

DIMENSIONS AND WEIGHT wheel base: 95 in, 241 cm; tracks: 51.80 in, 132 cm front, 51.30 in, 130 cm rear; length: 150.70 in, 383 cm; width: 63.10 in, 160 cm; height: 54.90 in, 139 cm; ground clearance: 6.50 in, 16.6 cm; weight: LS 1,792 lb, 813 kg - GL 1,814 lb, 822 kg; weight distribution: 52% front, 48% rear; turning circle: 31.5 ft, 9.6 m; fuel tank: 9 imp gal, 10.8 US gal, 41 l.

BODY hatchback saloon; 2+1 doors; 4 seats, separate front seats, reclining backrests; folding rear seat; heated rear window; rear fog lamps; trip recorder; headrests (for GL only).

PRACTICAL INSTRUCTIONS fuel: 97 oct petrol; oil: engine 5.3 imp pt, 6.3 US pt, 3 l, SAE 20W-50, change every 5,000 miles, 8,000 km - gearbox 3 imp pt, 3.6 US pt, 1.7 l, SAE 20W-50, no change recommended; final drive 1.5 imp pt, 1.9 US pt, 0.9 l, SAE 90 EP, no change recommended; greasing: none; tappet clearances: inlet 0.007 in, 0.17 mm, exhaust 0.009 in, 0.22 mm; valve timing: 27° 61° 55° 9°; tyre pressure: front 21 psi, 1.5 atm, rear 26 psi, 1.8 atm.

OPTIONALS laminated windscreen; metallic spray; rear window wiper-washer; vinyl roof (for GL only).

59 hp power team

See 42 hp power team, except for:

ENGINE 79 cu in, 1,295 cc (3.09 x 2.62 in, 78.6 x 66.7 mm); compression ratio: 8.8:1; max power (DIN): 59 hp (43 kW) at 5,000 rpm; max torque (DIN): 69 lb ft, 9.5 kg m (93 Nm) at 2,600 rpm; max engine rpm: 5,900; 45.5 hp/l (33.5 kW/l); cast iron block and head; 5 crankshaft bearings; valves: overhead, push-rods and rockers; camshafts: 1, side; lubrication: 7 imp pt, 8.5 US pt, 4 l; cooling system: 13.9 imp pt, 16.7 US pt, 7.9 l.

TRANSMISSION axle ratio: 3.890; tyres: 155 x 13.

TALBOT Sunbeam 1.3 GL

PERFORMANCE max speeds: (I) 27 mph, 43 km/h; (II) 44 mph, 71 km/h; (III) 69 mph, 111 km/h; (IV) 89 mph, 143 km/h; power-weight ratio: LS 32.8 lb/hp (45 lb/kW), 14.9 kg/hp (20.4 kg/kW); carrying capacity: 960 lb, 435 kg; acceleration: 0-50 mph (0-80 km/h) 12.6 sec; speed in direct drive at 1,000 rpm: 16.8 mph, 27 km/h; consumption: 40.3 m/imp gal, 33.6 m/US gal, 7 l x 100 km at 56 mph, 90 km/h.

DIMENSIONS AND WEIGHT weight: LS 1,936 lb, 878 kg - GL 1,958 lb, 888 kg; weight distribution: 55.5% front, 44.5% rear.

PRACTICAL INSTRUCTIONS oil: engine 7 imp pt, 8.5 US pt, 4 l; tappet clearances: inlet 0.008 in, 0.20 mm, exhaust 0.016 in, 0.40 mm; valve timing: 38° 66° 72° 20°; tyre pressure: front 22 psi, 1.6 atm, rear 22 psi, 1.6 atm.

OPTIONALS Borg-Warner 45 automatic transmission, hydraulic torque converter and planetary gears with 4 ratios (I 3, II 1.937, III 1.351, IV 1, rev 4.692). max ratio of converter at stall 2.43, possible manual selection, acceleration 0-50 mph (0-80 km/h) 10 sec, consumption 37.6 m/imp gal, 31.6 m/US gal, 7.5 l x 100 km at 56 mph, 90 km/h; laminated windscreen; metallic spray; rear window wiper-washer; vinyl roof (for GL only).

69 hp power team

See 42 hp power team, except for:

ENGINE 97.5 cu in, 1,598 cc (3.44 x 2.62 in, 87.3 x 66.7 mm); compression ratio: 8.8:1; max power (DIN): 69 hp (51 kW) at 4,800 rpm; max torque (DIN): 91 lb ft, 12.5 kg m (123 Nm) at 2,900 rpm; max engine rpm: 5,700; 43.2 hp/l (31.8 kW/l); cast iron block and head; 5 crankshaft bearings; valves: overhead, push-rods and rockers; camshafts: 1, side; lubrication: 7 imp pt, 8.5 US pt, 4 l; cooling, 13.9 imp pt, 16.7 US pt, 7.9 l.

TRANSMISSION gearbox ratios: I 3.538, II 2.165, III 1.387, IV 1, rev 3.680; axle ratio: 3.540; tyres: 155 x 13.

PERFORMANCE max speeds: (I) 30 mph, 48 km/h; (II) 49 mph, 79 km/h; (III) 76 mph, 122 km/h; (IV) 95 mph, 153 km/h; power-weight ratio: 28.4 lb/hp (38.4 lb/kW), 12.9 kg/hp (17. kg/kW); carrying capacity: 920 lb, 416 kg; acceleration: 0-50 mph (0-80 km/h) 9.4 sec; speed in direct drive at 1,000 rpm: 18.4 mph, 29.6 km/h; consumption: 42.1 m/imp gal, 35.1 m/US gal, 6.7 l x 100 km at 56 mph, 90 km/h.

DIMENSIONS AND WEIGHT weight: 1,958 lb, 888 kg; weight distribution: 55% front, 45% rear.

BODY headrests (standard).

PRACTICAL INSTRUCTIONS oil: engine 7 imp pt, 8.5 US pt, 4 l; tappet clearances: inlet 0.008 in, 0.20 mm, exhaust 0.016 in, 0.40 mm; valve timing: 38° 66° 72° 20°; tyre pressure: front 22 psi, 1.6 atm, rear 22 psi, 1.6 atm.

OPTIONALS Borg-Warner 45 automatic transmission, hydraulic torque converter and planetary gears with 4 ratios (I 3, II 1.937, III 1.351, IV 1, rev 4.692), max ratio of converter at stall 2.43, possible manual selection, acceleration 0-50 mph (0-80 km/h) 10 sec, consumption 39.4 m/imp gal, 32.7 m/US gal, 7.2 l x 100 km at 56 mph, 90 km/h; laminated windscreen; metallic spray; rear window wiper-washer; vinyl roof.

TALBOT Sunbeam 1.6 GLS

80 hp power team

See 42 hp power team, except for:

ENGINE 97.5 cu in, 1,598 cc (3.44 x 2.62 in, 87.3 x 66.7 mm); compression ratio: 8.8:1; max power (DIN): 80 hp (59 kW) at 5,400 rpm; max torque (DIN): 86 lb ft, 11.9 kg m (117 Nm) at 4,400 rpm; max engine rpm: 6,500; 50 hp/l (36.9 kW/l); cast iron block and head; 5 cranckshaft bearings; valves: overhead, push-rods and rockers; camshafts: 1, side; lubrication: 7 imp pt, 8.5 US pt, 4 l; 1 Zenith-Stromberg 175 CD3 VX horizontal carburettor; cooling, 13.9 imp pt, 16.7 US pt, 7.9 l.

TRANSMISSION gearbox ratios: I 3.538, II 2.165, III 1.387, IV 1, rev 3.680; axle ratio: 3.700; tyres: 155 x 13.

PERFORMANCE max speeds: (I) 30 mph, 48 km/h; (II) 51 mph, 82 km/h; (III) 79 mph, 127 km/h; (IV) 100 mph, 161 km/h; power-weight ratio: 25.1 lb/hp (34.2 lb/kW), 11.4 kg/hp (15.5 kg/kW); carrying capacity: 920 lb, 416 kg; acceleration: 0-50 mph (0-80 km/h) 8.5 sec; speed in direct drive at 1,000 rpm: 17.7 mph, 28.5 km/h; consumption: 38.5 m/imp gal, 32.2 m/US gal, 7.3 l x 100 km at 56 mph, 90 km/h.

ELECTRICAL EQUIPMENT halogen headlamps.

DIMENSIONS AND WEIGHT weight: 2,013 lb, 913 kg; weight distribution: 55% front, 45% rear.

BODY laminated windscreen, rear window wiper-washer, vinyl roof and tinted glass (standard); rev counter.

TALBOT Sunbeam 1.6 TI

TALBOT Sunbeam Lotus

PRACTICAL INSTRUCTIONS oil: engine 7 imp pt, 8.5 US pt, 4 l; tappet clearances: inlet 0.010 in, 0.25 mm, exhaust 0.016 in, 0.40 mm; valve timing: 44° 78° 69° 23°; tyre pressure: front 22 psi, 1.6 atm, rear 22 psi, 1.6 atm.

OPTIONALS Borg-Warner 45 automatic transmission, hydraulic torque converter and planetary gears with 4 ratios (I 3, II 1.937, III 1.351, IV 1, rev 4.692), max ratio of converter at stall 2.43, possible manual selection, max speed 95 mph, 153 km/h, acceleration 0-50 mph (0-80 km/h) 10 sec, consumption 35.4 m/imp gal, 29.4 m/US gal, 8 l x 100 km at 56 mph, 90 km/h; metallic spray.

100 hp power team

See 42 hp power team, except for:

ENGINE 97.5 cu in, 1,598 cc (3.44 x 2.62 in, 87.3 x 66.7 mm); compression ratio: 9.4:1; max power (DIN): 100 hp (74 kW) at 6,000 rpm; max torque (DIN): 96 lb ft, 13.2 kg m (129 Nm) at 4,600 rpm; max engine rpm: 6,400; 62.6 hp/l (46.1 kW/l); cast iron block and head; 5 cranckshaft bearings; valves: overhead, push-rods and rockers; camshafts: 1, side; lubrication: 7 imp pt, 8.5 US pt, 4 l; 2 Weber downdraught twin barrel carburettors; electronic ignition; cooling, 13.9 imp pt, 16.7 US pt, 7.9 l.

TRANSMISSION gearbox ratios: I 3.538, II 2.165 III 1.387, IV 1, rev 3.680; axle ratio: 3.540; tyres: 175/70 x 13.

PERFORMANCE max speed: about 108 mph, 174 km/h; power-weight ratio: 20.1 lb/hp (27.1 lb/kW), 9.1 kg/hp (12.3 kg/kW); carrying capacity: 920 lb, 416 kg; consumption: 24.7 m/imp gal, 29 m/US gal, 8.1 l x 100 km at 56 mph, 90 km/h.

TALBOT Sunbeam Lotus

ELECTRICAL EQUIPMENT halogen headlamps; built-in fog lamps (standard).

DIMENSIONS AND WEIGHT weight: 2,008 lb, 910 kg; weight distribution: 55% front, 45% rear.

BODY rear spoiler; trip recorder; folding rear seat; heated rear window; rev counter; light alloy wheels; laminated winscreen, adjustable headrests and rear window wiper-washer (standard).

OPTIONALS metallic spray (only).

150 hp power team

See 42 hp power team, except for:

ENGINE 132.5 cu in, 2,172 cc (3.75 x 3 in, 95.2 x 76.2 mm); compression ratio: 9.44:1; max power (DIN): 150 hp (110 kW) at 5,600 rpm; max torque (DIN): 150 lb ft, 20.7 kg m (203 Nm) at 4,800 rpm; max engine rpm: 69.1 hp/l (50.9 kW/l); 5 crankshaft bearings; camshafts: 1, overhead, cogged belt; lubrication: 7 imp pt, 8.5 US pt, 4 l; 2 Dell'Orto DHLA 45E downdraught twin barrel carburettors; fuel feed: electric pump; cooling, 13.9 imp pt, 16.7 US pt, 7.9 l.

TRANSMISSION gears: 5, fully synchronized; ratios: I 3.420, II 1.940, III 1.390, IV 1, V 0.795, rev 3.670; axle ratio: 3.890; width of rims: 6"; tyres: 185/70 HR x 13, tubeless.

PERFORMANCE max speed: 120 mph, 193 km/h; power-weight ratio: 14.1 lb/hp (19.2 lb/kW), 6.4 kg/hp (8.7 kg/kW); speed in top at 1,000 rpm: 21.6 mph, 34.7 km/h.

BRAKES front disc (diameter 9.50 in, 24.1 cm), dual circuit, rear drum, vacuum servo.

ELECTRICAL EQUIPMENT 2 halogen headlamps.

DIMENSIONS AND WEIGHT length: 151.20 in, 384 cm; height: 55.30 in, 140 cm; weight: 2,116 lb, 960 kg; weight distribution: 55% front, 45% rear; turning circle: 32 ft, 9.8 m.

BODY light alloy wheels; bumpers; rev counter; laminated windscreen and rear window wiper-washer (standard).

PRACTICAL INSTRUCTIONS oil: engine 7 imp pt, 8.5 US pt, 4 l; tappet clearances: inlet 0.010 in, 0.25 mm, exhaust 0.016 in, 0.40 mm; valve timing: 44° 78° 69° 23°; tyre pressure: front 22 psi, 1.6 atm, rear 22 psi, 1.6 atm.

Avenger Series

PRICES EX WORKS:	£
1 1.3 LS Saloon	**3,416***
2 1.3 LS Estate Car	**3,817***
3 1.3 GL Saloon	**3,989***
4 1.3 GL Estate Car	**4,326***
5 1.6 LS Saloon	**3,568***
6 1.6 LS Estate Car	**3,969***
7 1.6 GL Saloon	**4,141***
8 1.6 GL Estate Car	**4,478***
9 1.6 GLS Saloon	**4,428***

Power team:	Standard for:	Optional for:
59 hp	1 to 4	—
69 hp	5 to 8	—
80 hp	9	—

59 hp power team

ENGINE front, 4 stroke; 4 cylinders, in line; 79 cu in, 1,295 cc (3.09 x 2.62 in, 78.6 x 66.7 mm); compression ratio: 8.8:1; max power (DIN): 59 hp (43 kW) at 5,000 rpm; max torque (DIN): 69 lb ft, 9.5 kg m (93 Nm) at 2,600 rpm; max engine rpm: 5,900; 45.6 hp/l (33.5 kW/l); cast iron block and head; 5 crankshaft bearings; valves; overhead, in line, push-rods and rockers; camshafts: 1, side, chain-driven; lubrication: rotary pump, full flow filter, 7 imp pt, 8.5 US pt, 4 l; 1 Zenith-Stromberg 150 CD3 horizontal carburettor; fuel feed: mechanical pump; water-cooled, 13.9 imp pt, 16.7 US pt, 7.9 l, electric thermostatic fan.

TRANSMISSION driving wheels: rear; clutch: single dry plate (diaphragm); gearbox: mechanical; gears: 4, fully synchronized; ratios: I 3.894, II 2.382, III 1.527, IV 1, rev 4.050; lever: central; final drive: hypoid bevel; axle ratio: saloons 3.890 - station wagons 4.110; width of rims: 4.5"; tyres: 155 SR x 13.

PERFORMANCE max speeds: (I) 27 mph, 43 km/h; (II) 43 mph, 69 km/h; (III) 68 mph, 109 km/h; (IV) 89 mph, 143 km/h; power-weight ratio: LS Saloon 33.3 lb/hp (45.6 lb/kW), 15.1 kg/hp (20.7 kg/kW); carrying capacity: 948 lb, 430 kg; acceleration: 0-50 mph (0-80 km/h) 12.2 sec; speed in direct drive at 1,000 rpm: 16.8 mph, 27 km/h; consumption: saloons 39.5 m/imp gal, 32.7 m/US gal, 7.2 l x 100 km at 56 mph, 90 km/h - estate cars 39.8 m/imp gal, 33.1 m/US gal, 7.1 l x 100 km at 56 mph, 90 km/h.

CHASSIS integral; front suspension: independent, by McPherson, coil springs/telescopic damper struts, wishbones, anti-roll bar; rear: rigid axle, swinging longitudinal trailing arms, upper oblique torque arms, coil springs, telescopic dampers (transverse linkage bar for st. wagons only).

STEERING rack-and-pinion; turns lock to lock: 3.66.

BRAKES front disc (diameter 9.50 in, 24.1 cm), dual circuit, rear drum vacuum servo; swept area: front 177.8 sq in, 1,147 sq cm, rear 74 sq in, 477 sq cm, total 251.8 sq in, 1,624 sq cm.

ELECTRICAL EQUIPMENT 12 V; 40 Ah battery; 34 A alternator; Lucas distributor; electronic ignition; 2 headlamps.

DIMENSIONS AND WEIGHT wheel base: 98 in, 248 cm; tracks: 51.80 in, 132 cm front, 51.30 in, 130 cm rear; length: LS Saloon 163 in, 414 cm - LS Estate Car 167 in, 424 cm - GL Saloon 164 in, 416 cm - GL Estate Car 168 in, 427 cm; width: 63.50 in, 161 cm; height: saloons 55.40 in, 141 cm - estate cars 55.70 in, 141 cm; ground clearance: saloons 5.60 in, 14.4 cm - estate cars 6.75 in, 17.2 cm; weight: LS Saloon 1,964 lb, 891 kg - LS Estate Car 2,061 lb, 935 kg - GL Saloon 1,997 lb, 905 kg - GL Estate Car 2,144 lb, 959 kg; turning circle: 31.7 ft, 9.6 m; fuel tank: 9.8 imp gal, 11.6 US gal, 44 l.

BODY saloon/sedan, 4 doors - estate car/st. wagon, 4+1 doors; 4-5 seats, separate front seats, reclining backrests; heated rear window; trip recorder; cloth upholstery; rear fog lamps; vinyl roof (for saloons only); headrests (for GL models only); rear window wiper-washer (for GL Estate car only).

PRACTICAL INSTRUCTIONS fuel: 97 oct petrol; oil: engine 7 imp pt, 8.5 US pt, 4 l, SAE 20W-50, change every 5,000 miles, 8,000 km - gearbox 3 imp pt, 3.6 US pt, 1.7 l, SAE 20W-50, no change recommended - final drive 1.5 imp pt, 1.9 US pt, 0.9 l, SAE 90 EP, no change recommended; greasing: none; tappet clearances: inlet 0.008 in, 0.20 mm, exhaust 0.016 in, 0.40 mm; valve timing: 38° 66° 72° 20°; tyre pressure: saloons front and rear 24 psi, 1.7 atm - estate cars, front and rear 22 psi, 1.5 atm.

TALBOT Avenger 1.6 GL Saloon

OPTIONALS Borg-Warner 45 automatic transmission, hydraulic torque converter and planetary gears with 4 ratios (I 3, II 1.937, III 1.351, IV 1, rev 4.692), max ratio of converter at stall 2.43, possible manual selection, max speed 90 mph, 145 km/h, acceleration 0-50 mph (0-80 km/h) 10.3 sec, consumption saloons 37 m/imp gal, 30.5 m/US gal, 7.7 l x 100 km at 56 mph, 90 km/h - estate cars 37.2 m/imp gal, 30.9 m/US gal, 7.6 l x 100 km at 56 mph, 90 km/h; metallic spray; laminated windscreen; rear window wiper-washer (for LS Estate Car only).

69 hp power team

See 59 hp power team, except for:

ENGINE 97.5 cu in, 1,598 cc (3.44 x 2.62 in, 87.3 x 66.6 mm); max power (DIN): 69 hp (51 kW) at 4,800 rpm; max torque (DIN): 91 lb ft, 12.6 kg m (124 Nm) at 2,900 rpm; 43.2 hp/l (31.8 kW/l).

TRANSMISSION gearbox ratios: I 3.538, II 2.165, III 1.387, IV 1, rev 3.680; axle ratio: 3.540.

PERFORMANCE max speeds: (I) 30 mph, 48 km/h; (II) 48 mph, 77 km/h; (III) 75 mph, 120 km/h; (IV) 95 mph, 153 km/h; power-weight ratio: LS Saloon 28.4 lb/hp (38.6 lb/kW), 12.9 kg/hp (17.5 kg/kW); acceleration: 0-50 mph (0-80 km/h) 9.4 sec; speed in direct drive at 1,000 rpm: 18.5 mph, 29.8 km/h; consumption: saloons 41.5 m/imp gal, 34.6 m/US gal, 6.8 l x 100 km at 56 mph, 90 km/h - estate cars 40.1 m/imp gal, 33.6 m/US gal, 7 l x 100 km at 56 mph, 90 km/h.

OPTIONALS Borg-Warner 45 automatic transmission, consumption saloons 38.8 m/imp gal, 32.2 m/US gal, 7.3 l x 100 km at 56 mph, 90 km/h - estate cars 39.2 m/imp gal, 32.7 m/US gal, 7.2 l x 100 km at 56 mph, 90 km/h.

80 hp power team

See 59 hp power team, except for:

ENGINE 97.5 cu in, 1,598 cc (3.44 x 2.62 in, 87.3 x 66.6 mm); max power (DIN): 80 hp (59 kW) at 5,400 rpm; max torque (DIN): 86 lb ft, 11.9 kg m (117 Nm) at 4,400 rpm; max engine rpm: 6,500; 50 hp/l (36.9 kW/l); 1 Zenith-Stromberg 175 CD3 VX horizontal carburettor.

TRANSMISSION axle ratio: 3.700.

PERFORMANCE max speeds: (I) 30 mph, 48 km/h; (II) 51 mph, 82 km/h; (III) 79 mph, 127 km/h; (IV) 100 mph, 161 km/h; power-weight ratio: 25.6 lb/hp (34.7 lb/kW), 11.6 kg/hp (15.7 kg/kW); acceleration: 0-50 mph (0-80 km/h) 8.5 sec; speed in direct drive at 1,000 rpm: 17.7 mph, 28.5 km/h; consumption: 36.2 m/imp gal, 30.2 m/US gal, 7.8 l x 100 km.

ELECTRICAL EQUIPMENT 2 halogen headlamps, fog lamps.

DIMENSIONS AND WEIGHT weight: 2,044 lb, 927 kg.

BODY saloon/sedan; 4 doors; 4-5 seats, separate front seats, reclining backrests, headrests; heated rear window; trip recorder; cloth upholstery; vinyl roof.

PRACTICAL INSTRUCTIONS tappet clearances: inlet 0.010 in, 0.25 mm; valve timing: 44° 78° 69° 23°.

OPTIONALS Borg-Warner 45 automatic transmission, max speed 95 mph, 153 km/h, acceleration 0-50 mph (0-80 km/h) 10 sec, consumption 33.5 m/imp gal, 28 m/US gal, 8.4 l x 100 km; laminated windscreen.

Horizon Series

PRICES EX WORKS:	£
1 1.1 LS	**3,420***
2 1.1 GL	**3,916***
3 1.3 LS	**3,582***
4 1.3 GL	**4,076***
5 1.3 GLS	**4,481***
6 1.5 SX Automatic	**5,098***

Power team:	Standard for:	Optional for:
58 hp	1,2	—
67 hp	3 to 5	—
82 hp	6	—

TALBOT Avenger 1.6 GLS Saloon

58 hp power team

ENGINE front, transverse, slanted 41° to rear, 4 stroke; 4 cylinders, in line; 68.2 cu in, 1,118 cc (2.91 x 2.56 in, 74 x 65 mm); compression ratio: 9.6:1; max power (DIN): 58 hp (43 kW) at 5,600 rpm; max torque (DIN): 67 lb ft, 9.2 kg m (90 Nm) at 3,000 rpm; max engine rpm: 6,300; 51.9 hp/l (38.2 kW/l); cast iron block, light alloy head; 5 crankshafts bearings; valves: overhead, push-rods and rockers, thimble tappets; camshafts: 1, side; lubrication: gear pump, full flow filter, 5.3 imp pt, 6.3 US pt, 3 l; 1 Solex 32 BISA 6 or Weber 32 IBSA single barrel carburettor; fuel feed: mechanical pump; sealed circuit cooling, water, expansion tank, 10.6 imp pt, 12.7 US pt, 6 l, electric thermostatic fan.

TRANSMISSION driving wheels: front; clutch: single dry plate (diaphragm), hydraulically controlled; gearbox: mechanical; gears: 4, fully synchronized; ratios: I 3.900, II 2.312, III 1.524, IV 1.080, rev 3.769; lever: central; final drive: cylindrical gears; axle ratio: 3.075; width of rims: 4.5"; tyres: 145 SR x 13.

PERFORMANCE max speed: 92 mph, 148 km/h; power-weight ratio: LS 35.9 lb/hp, (48.5 lb/kW), 16.3 kg/hp (22 kg/kW); consumption: 42.8 m/imp gal, 35.6 m/US gal, 6.6 l x 100 km at 56 mph, 90 km/h.

CHASSIS integral; front suspension: independent, longitudinal torsion bars, wishbones, anti-roll bar, telescopic dampers; rear: independent, swinging longitudinal trailing arms, coil springs, anti-roll bar, telescopic dampers.

STEERING rack-and-pinion; turns lock to lock: 4.35.

BRAKES front disc (diameter 9.40 in, 23.9 cm), dual circuit, rear drum, vacuum servo; swept area: front 155 sq in, 1,000 sq cm, rear 89 sq in, 574 sq cm, total 244 sq in, 1,574 sq cm.

ELECTRICAL EQUIPMENT 12 V; 40 Ah battery; 40 A alternator; electronic ignition; 2 headlamps; rear fog lamps; halogen headlamps (for GL only).

DIMENSIONS AND WEIGHT wheel base: 99.21 in, 252 cm; tracks: 55.91 in, 142 cm front, 53.94 in, 137 cm rear; length: 155.91 in, 396 cm; width: 66.14 in, 168 cm; height: 55.51 in,

TALBOT Horizon 1.5 SX Automatic

41 cm; ground clearance: 7.09 in, 18 cm; weight: LS 2,084 lb, 945 kg - GL 2,117 lb, 960 kg; weight distribution: 59.4% front, 40.6% rear; turning circle: 33.5 ft, 10.2 m; fuel tank: 10.3 imp gal, 12.4 US gal, 47 l.

BODY saloon/sedan; 4+1 doors; 5 seats, separate front seats, reclining backrests; folding rear seat; heated rear window; trip recorder; rear window wiper-washer (for GL only).

PRACTICAL INSTRUCTIONS fuel: 98-100 oct petrol; oil: engine 5.3 imp pt, 6.3 US pt, 3 l, SAE 20W-40, change every 4,700 miles, 7,500 km - gearbox and final drive 1.9 imp pt, 2.3 US pt, 1.1 l, SAE 90 EP, change every 9,300 miles, 15,000 km; greasing: none.

OPTIONALS laminated windscreen; adjustable headrests (for GL only); metallic spray; rear window wiper-washer (for LS only).

67 hp power team

See 58 hp power team, except for:

ENGINE 79 cu in, 1,294 cc (3.02 x 2.76 in, 76.7 x 70 mm); compression ratio: 9.5:1; max power (DIN): 67 hp (49 kW) at 5,600 rpm; max torque (DIN): 77 lb ft, 10.6 kg m (104 Nm) at 2,800 rpm; 51.8 hp/l (38.1 kW/l).

PERFORMANCE max speed: 96 mph, 155 km/h; power-weight ratio: GLS 32.2 lb/hp (43.9 lb/kW), 14.6 kg/hp (19.9 kg/kW); consumption: 44.1 m/imp gal, 36.8 m/US gal, 6.4 l x 100 km at 56 mph, 90 km/h.

ELECTRICAL EQUIPMENT halogen headlamps (except for LS).

DIMENSIONS AND WEIGHT weight: GLS 2,150 lb, 975 kg.

BODY saloon/sedan; 4+1 doors; 5 seats, separate front seats, reclining backrests; folding rear seat; heated rear window; trip recorder; rear windows wiper-washer (except for LS); adjustable headrests, laminated windscreen and velour upholstery (for GLS only).

OPTIONALS metallic spray; rear window wiper-washer (for LS only); adjustable headrests (for GL only); laminated windscreen (except for GLS); electronic trip computer, tinted glass and light alloy wheels with 155 SR x 13 tyres (for GLS only).

82 hp power team

See 58 hp power team, except for:

ENGINE 88 cu in, 1,442 cc (3.02 x 3.07 in, 76.7 x 78 mm); compression ratio: 9.5:1; max power (DIN): 82 hp (60 kW) at 5,600 rpm; max torque (DIN): 77 lb ft, 10.6 kg m (104 Nm) at 2,800 rpm; 56.9 hp/l (41.9 kW/l); 1 Weber 36 DCA 2 downdraught twin barrel carburettor; cooling, 11.3 imp pt, 13.5 US pt, 6.4 l.

TRANSMISSION gearbox: Torqueflite automatic transmission, hydraulic torque converter and planetary gears with 3 ratios, max ratio of converter at stall 1.2, possible manual selection; ratios: I 2.475, II 1.475, III 1, rev 2.103; axle ratio: 3.000; width of rims: 5"; tyres: 155 SR x 13.

PERFORMANCE max speed: 100 mph, 161 km/h; power-weight ratio: 26.7 lb/hp (36.6 lb/kW), 12.1 kg/hp (16.6 kg/kW); consumption: 38.7 m/imp gal, 32.2 m/US gal, 7.3 l x 100 km at 56 mph, 90 km/h.

TALBOT Horizon 1.5 SX Automatic

ELECTRICAL EQUIPMENT 50 A alternator; halogen headlamps (standard).

DIMENSIONS AND WEIGHT rear track: 54.33 in, 138 cm; weight: 2,194 lb 995 kg.

BODY saloon/sedan; 4+1doors; 5 seats, separate front seats, reclining backrests; folding rear seat; heated rear window; electronic trip computer; constant speed cruise control; (standard) adjustable headrests, tinted glass, rear window wiper-washer and laminated windscreen.

PRACTICAL INSTRUCTIONS oil: automatic transmission 11.3 imp pt, 13.5 US pt, 6.4 l.

OPTIONALS metallic spray; light alloy wheels.

Alpine Series

PRICES EX WORKS:	£
1 1.3 LS	**4,027***
2 1.3 GL	**4,288***
3 1.5 LS	**4,218***
4 1.5 GL	**4,740***
5 1.5 GLS	**5,442***
6 1.6 SX	**6,495***

Power team:	Standard for:	Optional for:
68 hp	1,2	—
85 hp	3 to 5	—
87 hp	6	—

68 hp power team

ENGINE front, transverse, slanted 41° to rear, 4 stroke, 4 cylinders, in line; 79 cu in, 1,294 cc (3.02 x 2.76 in, 76.7 x 70 mm); compression ratio: 9.5:1; max power (DIN): 68 hp (50 kW) at 5,600 rpm; max torque (DIN): 79 lb ft, 10.9 kg m (107 Nm) at 2,800 rpm; max engine rpm: 6,300; 52.6 hp/l (38.6 kW/l); cast iron block, light alloy head; 5 crankshaft bearings; valves: overhead, in line, pushrods and rockers; camshafts: 1, side; lubrication: gear pump, full flow filter, 5.3 imp pt, 6.3 US pt, 3 l; 1 Solex 32 BISA 5 A or Weber 32 IBSA 9 downdraught single barrel carburettor; fuel feed: mechanical pump; sealed circuit cooling, expansion tank, water, 10.7 imp pt, 12.9 US pt, 6.1 l, electric thermostatic fan.

TRANSMISSION driving wheels: front; clutch: single dry plate (diaphragm), hydraulically controlled; gearbox: mechanical; gears: 4, fully synchronized; ratios: I 3.900, II 2.312, III 1.524, IV 1.080, rev 3.769; lever: central; final drive: cilindrical gears; axle ratio: 3.706; width of rims: 5"; tyres: 155 SR x 13.

PERFORMANCE max speed: 94 mph, 152 km/h; power-weight ratio: LS 33.5 lb/hp (45.4 lb/kW), 15.2 kg/hp (20.6 kg/kW); carrying capacity: 882 lb, 400 kg; speed in top at 1,000 rpm: 16.3 mph, 26.2 km/h; consumption: 42.8 m/imp gal, 35.6 m/US gal, 6.6 l x 100 km at 56 mph, 90 km/h.

CHASSIS integral; front suspension: independent, wishbones, longitudinal torsion bars, anti-roll bar, telescopic dampers; rear: independent, swinging longitudinal trailing arms, coil springs, anti-roll bar, telescopic dampers.

STEERING rack-and-pinion; turns lock to lock: 4.15.

TALBOT Alpine 1.6 SX

68 HP POWER TEAM

BRAKES front disc (diameter 9.45 in, 24.1 cm), dual circuit, rear drum, rear compensator, vacuum servo; swept area: front 169.3 sq in, 1,092 sq cm, rear 90.2 sq in, 582 sq cm, total 259.5 sq in, 1,674 sq cm.

ELECTRICAL EQUIPMENT 12 V; 40 Ah battery; 40 A alternator; electronic ignition; 2 adjustable headlamps; rear fog lamps.

DIMENSIONS AND WEIGHT wheel base: 102.50 in, 260 cm; tracks: 55.51 in, 141 cm front, 54.72 in, 139 cm rear; length: 167.10 in, 424 cm; width: 66.10 in, 168 cm; height: 54.70 in, 139 cm; ground clearance: 5.12 in, 13 cm; weight: LS 2,275 lb 1,032 kg - GL 2,303 lb, 1,044 kg; turning circle: 34.1 ft, 10.4 m; fuel tank: 13.2 imp gal, 15.8 US gal, 60 l.

BODY saloon/sedan; 4+1 doors; 5 seats, separate front seats, reclining backrests; heated rear window; folding rear seat; bumpers; halogen headlamps (for GL only).

PRACTICAL INSTRUCTIONS fuel: 98-100 oct petrol; oil: engine 5.3 imp pt, 6.3 US pt, 3 l, SAE 20W-40, change every 4,700 miles, 7,500 km - gearbox and final drive 1.9 imp pt, 2.3 US pt, 1.1 l, SAE 90 EP, change every 9,300 miles, 15,000 km; greasing: none.

OPTIONALS laminated windscreen; rear window wiper-washer; adjustable headrests; metallic; sunshine roof (not available with winyl roof); electric door locks; (for GL only) headlamps with wiper-washer, tinted glass, light alloy wheel, vinyl roof and electric windows.

85 hp power team

See 68 hp power team, except for:

ENGINE 88 cu in, 1,442 cc (3.02 x 3.07 in, 76.7 x 78 mm); max power (DIN): 85 hp (63 kW) at 5,600 rpm; max torque (DIN): 94 lb ft, 13 kg m (127 Nm) at 3,000 rpm; max engine rpm: 6,000; 58.9 hp/l (43.4 kW/l); 1 Weber 36 DCNVA downdraught twin barrel carburettor.

TRANSMISSION axle ratio: 3.588; tyres: 165 SR x 13.

PERFORMANCE max speed: 102 mph, 164 km/h; power-weight ratio: LS 26.9 lb/hp (36.2 lb/kW), 12.2 kg/hp (16.4 kg/kW); speed in top at 1,000 rpm: 16.8 mph, 27.1 km/h; consumption: 42.2 m/imp gal, 35.1 m/US gal, 6.7 l x 100 km at 56 mph, 90 km/h.

ELECTRICAL EQUIPMENT halogen headlamps (except for LS).

DIMENSIONS AND WEIGHT weight: LS 2,282 lb, 1,035 kg - GL 2,315 lb, 1,050 kg - GLS 2,326 lb, 1,055 kg.

BODY saloon/sedan; 4+1 doors; 5 seats, separate front seats, reclining backrests; heated rear window; folding rear seat; bumpers; (for GLS only) rear window wiper-washer, headlamps with wiper-washer, tinted glass laminated windscreen, adjustable headrests, electric windows and vinyl roof.

OPTIONALS metallic spray; sunshine roof (not available with vinyl roof); electric door locks; (except GLS) adjustable headrests, laminated windscreen and rear window wiper-washer; (except LS) light alloy wheels; (for GL only) tinted glass, headlamps with wiper-washer, vinyl roof and electric windows.

87 hp power team

See 68 hp power team, except for:

ENGINE 97.1 cu in, 1,592 cc (3.17 x 3.07 in, 80.6 x 78 mm); compression ratio: 9.35:1; max power (DIN): 87 hp (64 kW) at 5,400 rpm; 54.6 hp/l (40.2 kW/l); 1 Weber 36 DCA 100 downdraught twin barrel carburettor; cooling, 11.1 imp pt, 13.3 US pt, 6.3 l.

TRANSMISSION gearbox: Torqueflite automatic transmission, hydraulic torque converter and planetary gears with 3 ratios, max ratio of converter at stall 1.2, possible manual selection; ratios: I 2.475, II 1.475, III 1, rev 2.103; axle ratio: 3.000; tyres: 165 SR x 13.

PERFORMANCE max speed: 106 mph, 170 km/h; consumption: 36.7 m/imp gal, 30.5 m/US gal, 7.7 l x 100 km at 56 mph, 90 km/h.

STEERING servo; turns lock to lock: 2.80.

ELECTRICAL EQUIPMENT 50 A alternator; halogen headlamps with wiper-washer (standard).

BODY saloon/sedan; 4+1 doors; 5 seats, separate front seats, reclining backrests; heated rear window; folding rear seat; electronic trip computer; constant speed cruise control; light alloy wheels; electric windows; rear window wiper-washer; tinted glass; laminated windscreen; velour upholstery.

PRACTICAL INSTRUCTIONS oil: automatic transmission 11.3 imp pt, 13.5 US pt, 6.4 l.

OPTIONALS adjustable headrests; metallic spray; sunshine roof; electric door locks.

TECHNICAL EXPONENTS TX Tripper 1500 - 2000 Sprint

TECHNICAL EXPONENTS
GREAT BRITAIN

TX Tripper 1500 / De Luxe

PRICES EX WORKS:	£
1500	4,243*
1500 De Luxe	—

ENGINE Triumph, front, 4 stroke; 4 cylinders, vertical, in line; 91.1 cu in, 1,493 cc (2.90 x 3.44 in, 73.7 x 87.5 mm); compression ratio: 9:1; max power (DIN): 71 hp (52 kW) at 5,500 rpm; max torque (DIN): 82 lb ft, 11.3 kg m (111 Nm) at 3,000 rpm; max engine rpm: 6,000; 47.6 hp/l (35 kW/l); cast iron block and head; 5 crankshaft bearings; valves: overhead, in line, pushrods and rockers; camshafts: 1, side; lubrication: gear pump, full flow filter, 8 imp pt, 9.5 US pt, 4,5 l; 2 SU type HS 4 semi-downdraught carburettors; fuel feed: mechanical pump; water-cooled, 6 imp pt, 7.2 US pt, 3.4 l.

TRANSMISSION driving wheels: rear; clutch: single dry plate (diaphragm); gearbox: mechanical; gears: 4, II, III and IV synchronized; ratios: I 3.750, II 2.160, III 1.390, IV 1, rev 3.750; lever: central; final drive: hypoid bevel; axle ratio: 3.690; width of rims: 5.5''; tyres: 165 x13.

PERFORMANCE max speeds: (I) 35 mph, 56 km/h; (II) 52 mph, 83 km/h; (III) 81 mph, 130 km/h; (IV) 108 mph, 174 km/h; power-weight ratio: 15 lb/hp (20.4 lb/kW), 6.8 kg/hp (9.3 kg/kW); carrying capacity: 784 lb, 356 kg; acceleration: standing ¼ mile 7.6 sec; speed in direct drive at 1,000 rpm: 18.5 mph, 29.7 km/h; consumption: 40 m/imp gal, 33.1 m/US gal, 7.1 l x 100 km.

CHASSIS box-type double backbone with outriggers; front suspension: independent, wishbones, coil springs, telescopic dampers; rear: independent, wishbones, transverse leafsprings as upper arms, telescopic dampers.

STEERING rack-and-pinion; turns lock to lock: 3.50.

BRAKES front disc (diameter 9 in, 22.9 cm), rear drum; swept area: total 197 sq in, 1,271 sq cm.

ELECTRICAL EQUIPMENT 12 V; 45 Ah battery; 15 W alternator; Lucas distributor; 2 headlamps.

DIMENSIONS AND WEIGHT wheel base: 83.07 in, 211 cm; tracks: 50.12 in, 127 cm front, 49.61 in, 126 cm rear; length: 145.08 in, 368 cm; width: 57.05 in 145 cm; height: 47.17 in, 120 cm; ground clearance: 6.50 in, 16.5 cm; weight: 1,067 lb, 484 kg; weight distribution: 52% front, 48% rear; turning circle: 25.3 ft, 7.7 m; fuel tank: 8.2 imp gal, 9.8 US gal, 37 l.

BODY open, in plastic material; no doors; 2 seats; De Luxe luxury equipment and folding rear seat.

TRIUMPH Dolomite 1300

RACTICAL INSTRUCTIONS fuel: 97-100 oct petrol; oil: en-ne 7 imp pt, 8.5 US pt, 4 l, SAE 20, change every 6,000 iles, 9,700 km - gearbox 1.5 imp pt, 1,9 US pt, 0.9 l, SAE 90 - nal drive 1.1 imp pt, 1.3 US pt, 0.6 l, SAE 90; greasing: every ,000 miles, 9,700 km, 3 points, every 12.000 miles, 19,300 m, 2 points; tappet clearances: inlet 0.010 in, 0.25 mm; valve ming: 18° 58° 58° 18°; tyre pressure: front 21 psi, 1.5 atm, ear 26 psi, 1.8 atm.

PTIONALS 3.270 or 4.110 axle ratio; overdrive, 0.797 ratio: il cooler; left-hand drive; servo brake; larger fuel tank; halogen eadlamps; laminated windscreen; hardtop with heated rear indow; tonneau cover; reclining backrests with built-in head-ests.

TX Tripper 2000 Sprint

ee TX Tripper 1500 / De Luxe, except for:

RICE EX WORKS: £ 4,895*

NGINE 121.9 cu in 1,998 cc (3.56 x 3.07 in, 90.3 x 78 mm); ompression ratio: 9.5:1; max power (DIN): 127 hp (93 kW) at ,700 rpm; max torque (DIN): 122 lb ft, 16.9 kg m (166 Nm) at ,500 rpm; max engine rpm: 6,500; 63.6 hp/l (46.8 kW/l); cast on block, light alloy head; valves: 4 per cylinder, overhead, in ne, thimble tappets; camshafts: 1, overhead; 2 US type HS 6 orizontal carburettors.

RANSMISSION gearbox ratios: I 2.995, II 2.100, III 1.386 overdrive 1.100), IV 1 (overdrive 0.797), rev 3.370; axle ratio: .450; width of rims: 5.5"; tyres: 175/70 HR x 13.

ERFORMANCE max speed: 125 mph, 201 km/h; power-weight atio: 8.4 lb/hp (11.4 lb/kW), 3.8 kg/hp (5.2 kg/kW); speed in irect drive at 1,000 rpm; 20.6 mph, 33.1 km/h; consumption: 0 m/imp gal, 25 m/US gal, 9.4 l x 100 km.

HASSIS anti-roll bar on front and rear suspension.

RAKES servo.

RACTICAL INSTRUCTIONS tappet clearances: inlet 0.018 , 0.45 mm, exhaust 0.018 in, 0.45 mm; valve timing: 10° 0° 50° 10°.

RIUMPH GREAT BRITAIN

Dolomite Series

RICES EX WORKS:

	£
1300	**3,832***
1500	**4,100***
1500 HL	**4,557***
1850 HL	**5,158***
Sprint	**6,288***

Power team:	Standard for:	Optional for:
58 hp	1	—
71 hp	2,3	—
91 hp	4	—
127 hp	5	—

58 hp power team

ENGINE front, 4 stroke; 4 cylinders, vertical, in line; 79.2 cu in, 1,296 cc (2.90 x 2.99 in, 73.7 x 76 mm); compression ratio: 8.5:1; max power (DIN): 58 hp (43 kW) at 5,500 rpm; max torque (DIN): 68 lb ft, 9.4 kg m (92 Nm) at 3,300 rpm; max engine rpm: 6,000; 44.8 hp/l (32.9 kW/l); cast iron block and head; 3 crankshaft bearings; valves: overhead, in line, push-rods and rockers; camshafts: 1, side; lubrication: rotary pump, full flow filter, 7.5 imp pt, 8.9 US pt, 4.2 l; 1 SU type HS4 E semi-downdraught carburettor; fuel feed: mechanical pump; water-cooled, 8.5 imp pt, 10.1 US pt, 4.8 l.

TRANSMISSION driving wheels: rear; clutch: single dry plate (diaphragm), hydraulically controlled; gearbox: mechanical; gears: 4, fully synchronized; ratios: I 3.504, II 2.158, III 1,394, IV 1, rev 3.988; lever: central; final drive: hypoid bevel; axle ratio: 4.110; width of rims: 4.5"; tyres: 155 SR x 13.

PERFORMANCE max speed: 85 mph, 136 km/h; power-weight ratio: 35.8 lb/hp (48.7 lb/kW), 16.3 kg/hp (22.1 kg/kW); carrying capacity: 831 lb, 377 kg; speed in direct drive at 1,000 rpm: 15.9 mph, 25.6 km/h; consumption: 27.2 m/imp gal, 22.6 m/US gal, 10.4 l x 100 km.

CHASSIS integral; front suspension: independent, wishbones, lower trailing links, coil springs, anti-roll bar, telescopic dampers; rear: rigid axle, lower trailing arms, upper oblique torque arms, coil springs, telescopic dampers.

STEERING rack-and-pinion; turns lock to lock: 3.50.

BRAKES front disc (diameter 8.75 in, 22.2 cm), rear drum, dual circuit, servo; swept area: total 240.6 sq in, 1,552 sq cm.

ELECTRICAL EQUIPMENT 12 V; 40 Ah battery; 34 A alternator; Lucas distributor; 2 headlamps.

DIMENSIONS AND WEIGHT wheel base: 96.61 in, 245 cm; tracks: 53 in, 135 cm front, 50 in, 127 cm rear; length: 162.40 in, 412 cm; width: 65.40 in, 166 cm; height: 54 in, 137 cm; ground clearance: 4.25 in, 10.8 cm; weight: 2,079 lb, 943 kg; weight distribution: 48% front, 52% rear; turning circle: 30.5 ft, 9.3 m; fuel tank: 12.5 imp gal, 15 US gal, 57 l.

BODY saloon/sedan; 4 doors; 4 seats, separate front seats, reclining backrests with headrests; laminated windscreen; heated rear window.

PRACTICAL INSTRUCTIONS fuel: 97 oct petrol; oil: engine 7.5 imp pt, 8.9 US pt, 4.2 l, SAE 20W-50, change every 6,000 miles, 9,700 km - gearbox 1.3 imp pt, 1.7 US pt, 0.8 l, SAE 90, change every 6,000 miles, 9,700 km - final drive 1.5 imp pt, 1.7 US pt, 0.8 l, SAE 90, change every 6,000 miles, 9,700 km; tappet clearances: inlet 0.010 in, 0.25 mm, exhaust 0.010 in,

TRIUMPH Dolomite 1500 HL

TRIUMPH Dolomite Sprint

0.25 mm; valve timing: 18° 58° 58° 18°; tyre pressure: front 26 psi, 1.8 atm, rear 30 psi, 2.1 atm.

OPTIONALS tinted glass.

71 hp power team

See 58 hp power team, except for:

ENGINE 91 cu in, 1,493 cc (2.90 x 3.44 in, 73.7 x 87.5 mm); compression ratio: 9:1; max power (DIN): 71 hp (52 kW) at 5,500 rpm; max torque (DIN): 82 lb ft, 11.3 kg m (111 Nm) at 3,000 rpm; 47.6 hp/l (35 kW/l); 2 SU type HS4 E semi-downdraught carburettors.

TRANSMISSION gearbox ratios: I 3.500, II 2.160, III 1.390, IV 1, rev 3.990; axle ratio: 3.630.

PERFORMANCE max speed: 94 mph, 151 km/h; power-weight ratio: 29.3 lb/hp (39.7 lb/kW), 13.3 kg/hp (18 kg/kW); speed in direct drive at 1,000 rpm: 18 mph, 29 km/h; consumption: 26.1 m/imp gal, 21.8 m/US gal, 10.8 l x 100 km at simulated urban driving.

ELECTRICAL EQUIPMENT 1500 HL 36 A alternator and 4 headlamps.

BODY 1500 HL luxury equipment.

OPTIONALS Borg-Warner automatic transmission with oil cooler, hydraulic torque converter and planetary gears with 3 ratios (I 2.390, II 1.450, III 1, rev 2.100), max ratio of converter at stall 2.26, possible manual selection; overdrive; tinted glass.

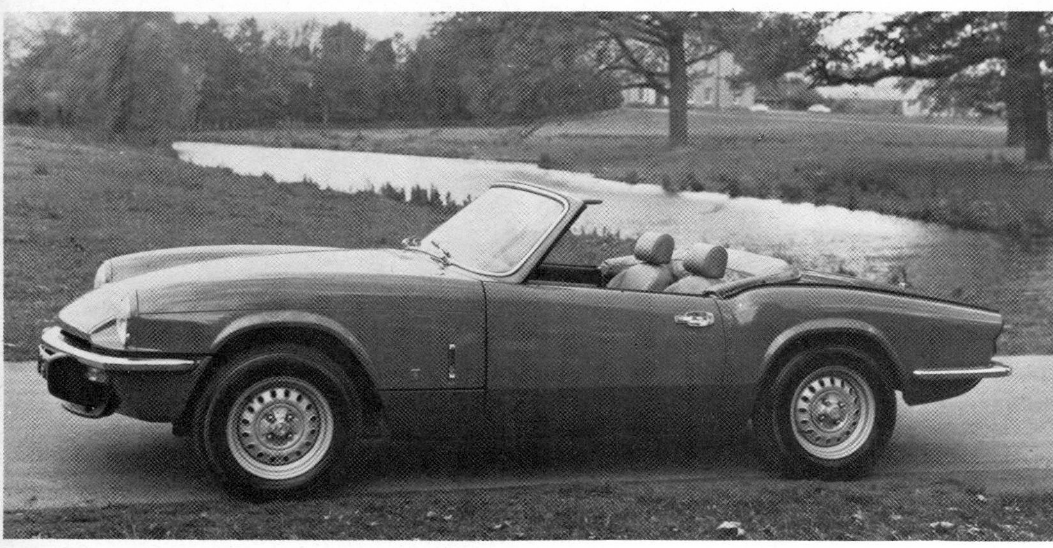

TRIUMPH Spitfire 1500

91 hp power team

See 58 hp power team, except for:

ENGINE 4 cylinders, slanted at 45°, in line; 113.2 cu in, 1,854 cc (3.42 x 3.07 in, 87 x 78 mm); compression ratio: 9:1; max power (DIN): 91 hp (67 kW) at 5,200 rpm; max torque (DIN): 105 lb ft, 14.5 kg m (142 Nm) at 3,500 rpm; 49.1 hp/l (36.1 kW/l); cast iron block, light alloy head; 5 crankshaft bearings; valves: overhead, in line, thimble tappets; camshafts: 1, overhead; lubrication: 8 imp pt, 9.5 US pt, 4.5 l; 2 SU type HS4 horizontal carburettors; water-cooled, 9.5 imp pt, 11.4 US pt, 5.4 l.

TRANSMISSION gearbox ratios: I 2.646, II 1.779, III 1.254, IV 1, rev 3.011; axle ratio: 3.630.

PERFORMANCE max speed: 102 mph, 164 km/h; power-weight ratio: 23.5 lb/hp (31.9 lb/kW), 10.6 kg/hp (14.5 kg/kW); speed in direct drive at 1,000 rpm: 18 mph, 29 km/h; consumption: 30.4 m/imp gal, 25.3 m/US gal, 9.3 l x 100 km.

CHASSIS integral, front subframe; rear suspension: anti-roll bar.

STEERING rack-and-pinion, adjustable steering wheel.

BRAKES lining area: front 17.4 sq in, 112 sq cm, rear 37.8 sq in, 245 sq cm, total 55.2 sq in, 357 sq cm.

ELECTRICAL EQUIPMENT 36 A alternator; AC Delco distributor; 4 headlamps.

DIMENSIONS AND WEIGHT tracks: 53.10 in, 135 cm front, 49.90 in, 127 cm rear; weight: 2,136 lb, 969 kg.

BODY tinted glass (standard).

PRACTICAL INSTRUCTIONS oil: engine 8 imp pt, 9.5 US pt, 4.5 l, SAE 20W-30, change every 6,000 miles 9,700 km - gearbox 1.8 imp pt, 2.1 US pt, 1 l, SAE 90, change every 6,000 miles, 9,700 km; greasing: every 6,000 miles, 9,700 km, 3 points; tappet clearances: inlet 0.008 in, 0.21 mm, exhaust 0.018 in, 0.45 mm; valve timing: 16° 56° 56° 16°.

OPTIONALS Borg-Warner automatic transmission with oil cooler, hydraulic torque converter and planetary gears with 3 ratios (I 2.390, II 1.450, III 1, rev 2.100), max ratio of converter at stall 2.26, possible manual selection; overdrive.

127 hp power team

See 58 hp power team, except for:

ENGINE 121.9 cu in, 1,998 cc (3.56 x 3.07 in, 90.3 x 78 mm); compression ratio: 9.5:1; max power (DIN): 127 hp (93 kW) at 5,700 rpm; max torque (DIN): 122 lb ft, 16.9 kg m (166 Nm) at 4,500 rpm; max engine rpm: 6,500; 63.6 hp/l (46.8 kW/l); valves: 4 per cylinder; 2 SU type HS6 horizontal carburettors; fuel feed: electric pump.

TRANSMISSION gearbox ratios: I 2.995, II 2.100 III 1.386 (overdrive 1.110), IV 1 (overdrive 0.797), rev 3.370; axle ratio: 3.450; width of rims: 5.5"; tyres: 175/70 HR x 13.

PERFORMANCE max speed: 116 mph, 186 km/h; power-weight ratio: 18.1 lb/hp (24.5 lb/kW), 8.2 kg/hp (11.1 kg/kW); consumption: 23.3 m/imp gal, 19.4 m/US gal, 12.1 l x 100 km.

STEERING steering wheel adjustable in height and distance.

BRAKES lining area: front 17.4 sq in, 112 sq cm, rear 49.5 sq in, 319 sq cm, total 66.9 sq in, 431 sq cm.

DIMENSIONS AND WEIGHT tracks: 53.40 in, 136 cm front 50.80 in, 129 cm rear; weight: 2,295 lb, 1,041 kg.

BODY vinyl roof; light alloy wheels.

PRACTICAL INSTRUCTIONS tappet clearances: inlet 0.018 in, 0.45 mm, exhaust 0.018 in, 0.45 mm; valve timing: 14° 50° 50° 14°; tyre pressure: front 22 psi, 1.5 atm, rear 24 psi, 1.7 atm.

OPTIONALS limited slip differential; Borg-Warner automatic transmission with oil cooler, hydraulic torque converter and planetary gears with 3 ratios (I 2.390, II 1.450, III 1, rev 2.100), max ratio of converter at stall 2.26, possible manual selection.

Spitfire 1500

PRICE IN USA: $ 7,365*
PRICE EX WORKS: £ 4,064*

ENGINE front, 4 stroke; 4 cylinders, vertical, in line; 91 cu in, 1,491 cc (2.90 x 3.44 in, 73.7 x 87.5 mm); compression ratio: 9:1; max power (DIN): 71 hp (52 kW) at 5,500 rpm; max torque (DIN): 82 lb ft, 11.3 kg m (111 Nm) at 3,000 rpm; max engine rpm: 6,000; 47.6 hp/l (35 kW/l); cast iron block and head; 3 crankshaft bearings; valves: overhead, in line, push-rods and rockers; camshaft: 1, side; lubrication: rotary pump, full flow filter, 8 imp pt, 9.5 US pt, 4.5 l; 2 SU type HS4 horizonta carburettors; fuel feed: mechanical pump; sealed circuit cooling, liquid, 8 imp pt, 9.5 US pt, 4.5 l, viscous coupling thermostatic fan.

TRIUMPH Spitfire 1500

TRANSMISSION driving wheels: rear; clutch: single dry plate (diaphragm), hydraulically controlled; gearbox: mechanical gears: 4, fully synchronized; ratios: I 3.500, II 2.160, III 1.390 IV 1, rev 3.990; lever: central; final drive: hypoid bevel; axle ratio: 3.630; width of rims: 5"; tyres: 155 SR x 13.

PERFORMANCE max speeds: (I) 31 mph, 50 km/h; (II) 50 mph 81 km/h; (III) 77 mph, 124 km/h; (IV) 100 mph, 161 km/h power-weight ratio: 24.6 lb/hp (33.5 lb/kW), 11.2 kg/hp (15.2 kg/kW); carrying capacity: 534 lb, 242 kg; speed in direct drive at 1,000 rpm: 18 mph, 29 km/h; consumption: 29.4 m/imp gal 24.5 m/US gal, 9.6 l x 100 km.

CHASSIS double backbone, channel section with outriggers front suspension: independent, wishbones, coil springs, anti roll bar, telescopic dampers; rear: independent, swinging axles, transverse leafspring, trailing arms, telescopic dampers.

STEERING rack-and-pinion; turns lock to lock: 3.75.

BRAKES front disc (diameter 9 in, 22.9 cm), rear drum, dual circuit; lining area: front 14.8 sq in, 95 sq cm, rear 34 sq in, 220 sq cm, total 48.8 sq in, 315 sq cm.

ELECTRICAL EQUIPMENT 12 V; 40 Ah battery; 34 A alternator; Lucas distributor; 2 headlamps.

DIMENSIONS AND WEIGHT wheel base: 83 in, 211 cm; tracks 49 in, 124 cm front, 50 in, 127 cm rear; length: 149 in, 378 cm width: 58.58 in, 149 cm; height: 45.80 in, 116 cm; ground clearance: 4.60 in, 11.8 cm; weight: 1,750 lb, 794 kg; weight distribution: 56% front, 44% rear; turning circle: 24 ft, 7.3 m fuel tank: 7.2 imp gal, 8.7 US gal, 33 l.

BODY convertible; 2 doors; 2 seats; headrests; laminated windscreen.

PRACTICAL INSTRUCTIONS fuel: 97 oct petrol; oil: engine 7 imp pt, 8.5 US pt, 4 l, SAE 20, change every 6,000 miles, 9,700 km - gearbox 1.5 imp pt, 1.7 US pt, 0.8 l, SAE 90 - final drive 1 imp pt, 1.1 US pt, 0.5 l, SAE 90; greasing: every 6,000 miles 9,700 km, 3 points, every 12.000 miles, 19,300 km, 2 points tappet clearances: inlet 0.010 in, 0.25 mm, exhaust 0.010 in 0.25 mm; valve timing: 18° 58° 58° 18°; tyre pressure: front 2 psi, 1.5 atm, rear 26 psi, 1.8 atm.

VARIATIONS

(For USA only)
ENGINE 7.5:1 compression ratio, max power (SAE) 52.5 hp (3 kW) at 5,000 rpm, max torque (SAE) 68.7 lb ft, 9.5 kg m (9 Nm) at 2,500 rpm, 35.2 hp/l (25.9 kW/l), 1 Stromberg 1.5 CD4T horizontal carburettor, water-cooled 9.3 imp pt, 11.2 US pt, 5.3 l.
TRANSMISSION 3.890 axle ratio.
PERFORMANCE max speeds (I) 29 mph, 47 km/h, (II) 47 mph 76 km/h, (III) 72 mph, 116 km/h, (IV) 92 mph, 148 km/h power-weight ratio 33.3 lb/hp (45.3 lb/kW), 15.1 kg/hp (20.6 kg/kW), speed in direct drive at 1,000 rpm 16.8 mph, 27 km/h consumption 40.9 m/imp gal, 34.1 m/US gal, 6.8 l x 100 km.
ELECTRICAL EQUIPMENT Lucas electronic ignition.
DIMENSIONS AND WEIGHT length 157.56 in, 400 cm.
PRACTICAL INSTRUCTIONS 91 oct petrol.

OPTIONALS Laycock-de Normanville overdrive on III and IV 0.797 ratio; hardtop.

TR 7

PRICE IN USA: $ 8,465*
PRICE EX WORKS: £ 5,533*

ENGINE front, 4 stroke; 4 cylinders, vertical, in line; 121.9 cu in, 1,998 cc (3.56 x 3.07 in, 90.3 x 78 mm); compression ratio 9.25:1; max power (DIN): 105 hp (77 kW) at 5,500 rpm; max torque (DIN): 119 lb ft, 16.4 kg m (160.1 Nm) at 3,500 rpm; max engine rpm: 6,500: 52.6 hp/l (38.7 kW/l); cast iron block, light alloy head; 5 crankshaft bearings; valves: overhead, in line, thimble tappets; camshafts: 1, overhead; lubrication: rotary pump, full flow filter, 8 imp pt, 9.5 US pt, 4.5 l; 2 SU type HS carburettors; fuel feed: mechanical pump; water-cooled, 13. imp pt, 16.1 US pt, 7.6 l.

TRANSMISSION driving wheels: rear; clutch: single dry plate (diaphragm), hydraulically controlled; gearbox: mechanical gears: 5, fully synchronized; ratios: I 3.332, II 2.090, III 1.400 IV 1, V 0.830, rev 3.430; lever: central; final drive: hypoid bevel; axle ratio: 3.900; width of rims: 5.5"; tyres: 185/7 HR x 13.

PERFORMANCE max speed: 114 mph, 183 km/h; power-weight ratio: 22 lb/hp (30.2 lb/kW), 10 kg/hp (13.7 kg/kW); consumption: 26.2 m/imp gal, 21.8 m/US gal, 10.8 l x 100 km.

CHASSIS integral, front subframe; front suspension: independent, by McPherson, coil springs/telescopic dampers struts lower wishbones (leading arm), anti-roll bar; rear: rigid axle lower trailing arms, upper oblique torque arms, coil springs anti-roll bar, telescopic dampers.

STEERING rack-and-pinion; turns lock to lock: 3.87.

BRAKES front disc (diameter 9.50 in, 24.1 cm), rear drum, dual ircuit, servo; swept area: front 183.5 sq in, 1,183 sq cm, rear 8.9 sq in, 638 sq cm, total 282.4 sq in, 1,821 sq cm.

ELECTRICAL EQUIPMENT 12 V; 40 Ah battery; 36 A alternaor; AC Delco distributor; 2 retractable headlamps.

DIMENSIONS AND WEIGHT wheel base: 85 in, 216 cm; racks: 55.50 in, 141 cm front, 55.30 in, 140 cm rear; length: 60 in, 406 cm; width: 66.20 in, 168 cm; height: 49.50 in, 126 m; ground clearance: 3.50 in, 9 cm; weight: 2,324 lb, 1,054 kg; veight distribution. 53% front, 47% rear; turning circle: 29 ft, .8 m; fuel tank: 12 imp gal, 14.3 US gal, 54 l.

BODY coupé, 2 doors; 2 seats; reclining backrests with headests; laminated windscreen; heated rear window.

PRACTICAL INSTRUCTIONS fuel: 97 oct petrol; oil: engine 8 mp pt, 9.5 US pt, 4.5 l, SAE 20W-30, change every 6,000 niles, 9,700 km - gearbox 2.7 imp pt, 3.2 US pt, 1.5 l, SAE 90, o change recommended - final drive 2 imp pt, 2.3 US pt, 1.1 l, SAE 90, no change recommended; greasing: none; tappet learances: inlet 0.008 in, 0.20 mm, exhaust: 0.018 in, 0.50 nm; valve timing: 16° 56° 56° 16°; tyre pressure: front 24 psi, .7 atm, rear 28 psi, 2 atm.

VARIATIONS

(For USA only)
ENGINE 8:1 compression ratio, max power (DIN) 88.5 hp (65 W) at 5,250 rpm, max torque (DIN) 100 lb ft, 13.8 kg m (135 Nm) at 2,500 rpm, max engine rpm 6,500, 44.3 hp/l (32.6 kW/l), 2 Stromberg 175 CDFVX horizontal carburettors.
TRANSMISSION 185/70SR x 13 tyres.
PERFORMANCE max speed 107 mph, 172 km/h, power-weight atio 26.2 lb/hp (35.9 lb/kW), 11.9 kg/hp (16.3 kg/kW), speed in direct drive at 1,000 rpm 17.3 mph, 27.8 km/h.
ELECTRICAL EQUIPMENT 50 Ah battery, Lucas electronic gnition.
DIMENSIONS AND WEIGHT length 164.29 in, 417 cm, weight 2,331 lb, 1,057 kg.
PRACTICAL INSTRUCTIONS 91 oct petrol.

OPTIONALS Borg-Warner automatic trasmission with oil cooler, hydraulic torque converter and planetary gears with 3 ratios I 2.390, II 1.450, III 1, rev 2.090), max ratio of converter at stall 1.91, possible manual selection, 3.270 axle ratio; sunshine oof; light alloy wheels; halogen headlamps; rear fog lamps; metallic spray; air-conditioning (for USA only).

TVR GREAT BRITAIN

Tasmin

PRICE EX WORKS: £ 12,800*

ENGINE front , 4 stroke; 6 cylinders, Vee-slanted at 60°; 170.4 cu in, 2,792 cc (3.66 x 2.07 in, 92.9 x 52.5 mm); compression atio: 9.2:1 max power (DIN): 160 hp (118 kW) at 5,700 rpm; max torque (DIN): 162 lb ft, 22.3 kg m (219 Nm) at 4,300 rpm; max engine rpm: 6,000; 57.3 hp/l (42.2 kW/l); cast iron block and head; 4 crankshaft bearings; valves: overhead, push-rods; camshafts: 1, at centre of Vee; lubrication: eccentric pump, ull flow filter, 8.3 imp pt, 9.9 US pt, 4.7 l; Bosch K-Jetronic njection; fuel feed: electric pump; water-cooled, 15.3 imp pt, 18.4 US pt, 8.7 l.

TRANSMISSION driving wheels: rear; clutch: single dry plate (diaphragm); gearbox: mechanical; gears; 4, fully synchronized; atios: I 3.160, II 1.940, III 1.410, IV 1, rev 3.350; lever: central; final drive: hypoid bevel; axle ratio: 3.070; width of ims: 7"; tyres: 205/60 VR x 14.

PERFORMANCE max speeds: (I) 42 mph, 67 km/h; (II 67 mph, 108 km; (III) 94 mph; 151 km/h; (IV) 133 mph, 214 km/h; power-weight ratio: 14.5 lb/hp, (19.6 lb/kW), 6.6 kg/hp (8.9 kg/kW); carrying capacity: 650 lb, 295 kg; acceleration: standing ¼ mile 16 sec, 0-50 mph (0-80 km/h) 5.6 sec; speed in direct drive at 1,000 rpm: 22.2 mph, 35.7 km/h; consumption: 24-30 m/imp gal, 20.3-25 m/US gal, 11.6-9.4 l x 100 km.

CHASSIS tubular, backbone with perimeter tubes; front suspension: independent, wishbones, lower transverse link, anti-roll bar, coil springs, telescopic dampers; rear: independent, lower transverse link, radius arm, coil springs, telescopic dampers.

STEERING rack-and-pinion; turns lock to lock: 3.70.

BRAKES disc servo; swept area: front 209.9 sq in, 1,354 sq cm, rear 189.1 sq in, 1,220 sq cm, total 399 sq in, 2,574 sq cm.

ELECTRICAL EQUIPMENT 12 V; 60 Ah battery; 55 A alternator; electronic Motorcraft ignition; 2 headlamps.

DIMENSIONS AND WEIGHT wheel base: 94 in, 239 cm; tracks: 56.50 in, 143 cm front, 56.70 in, 144 cm rear; length: 158 in, 401 cm; width: 68 in, 173 cm; height: 46.90 in, 119 cm; ground

TRIUMPH TR 7

TVR Tasmin

clearance: 5.40 in, 13.7 cm; weight: 2,315 lb, 1,050 kg; weight distribution: 51% front, 49% rear; turning circle: 31.5 ft, 9.6 m; fuel tank: 14 imp gal, 16.6 US gal, 63 l.

BODY coupé; 2 doors; 2 seats, separate front seats; electric windows; laminated windscreen.

PRACTICAL INSTRUCTIONS fuel: 97 oct petrol; oil: engine 8.3 imp pt, 9.9 US pt, 4.7 l, SAE 20W-50, change every 6,000 miles, 9,700 km - gearbox 3.6 imp pt, 4.2 US pt, 2 l, SAE 80, no change recommended - final drive 2 imp pt, 2.3 US pt, 1.1 l, SAE 90; greasing: every 6,000 miles, 9,700 km, 5 points; sparking plug: AGR 22 Motorcraft; tappet clearances: inlet 0.014 in, 0.35 mm, exhaust 0.016 in, 0.40 mm; valve timing: 24° 72° 73° 25°; tyre pressure: front 24 psi, 1.7 atm, rear 24 psi, 1.7 atm.

3000, Turbo and Taimar Series

PRICES IN USA AND EX WORKS:	$	£
1 3000 M Coupé	—	7,995*
2 Convertible 3000 S	16,000*	8,730*
3 Turbo Coupé	—	11,995*
4 Convertible Turbo	—	12,730*
5 Taimar Hatchback Coupé	16,000*	8,984*
6 Taimar Turbo Hatchback Coupé	—	12,984*

Power team:	Standard for:	Optional for:
142 hp	1,2,5	—
230 hp	3,4,6	—

TVR Tasmin

142 hp power team

ENGINE Ford, front, 4 stroke; 6 cylinders, Vee-slanted at 60°; 182.7 cu in, 2,994 cc (3.70 x 2.85 in, 94 x 72.4 mm); compression ratio: 8.9:1; max power (DIN): 142 hp (104 kW) at 5,000 rpm; max torque (DIN): 172 lb ft, 23.7 kg m (232 Nm) at 3,000 rpm; max engine rpm: 6,000; 47.4 hp/l (34.9 kW/l); cast iron block and head; 4 crankshaft bearings; valves: overhead, in line, push-rods and rockers; camshafts: 1, at centre of Vee; lubrication: eccentric pump, full flow filter, 9.8 imp pt, 11.6 US pt, 5.5 l; 1 Weber 40 DFA-1 downdraught twin barrel carburettor; fuel feed: mechanical pump; water-cooled, 19.9 imp pt, 23.9 US pt, 11.3 l, thermostatic electric fan.

TRANSMISSION driving wheels: rear; clutch: single dry plate (diaphragm), hydraulically controlled; gearbox: mechanical; gears: 4, fully synchronized; ratios: I 3.163, II 1.950, III 1.412, IV 1, rev 3.346; lever: central; final drive: hypoid bevel; axle ratio: 3.310; width of rims: 6"; tyres: 185 HR x 14.

PERFORMANCE max speeds: (I) 42 mph, 67 km/h; (II) 68 mph, 109 km/h; (III) 94 mph, 151 km/h; (IV) 133 mph, 214 km/h; power-weight ratio: 3000 M Coupé 15.5 lb/hp (21 lb/kW), 7 kg/hp (9.6 kg/kW); carrying capacity: 620 lb, 281 kg; acceleration: standing ¼ mile 16 sec, 0-50 mph (0-80 km/h) 5.6 sec; speed in direct drive at 1,000 rpm: 21.6 mph, 34.7 km/h; consumption: 22 m/imp gal, 18.4 m/US gal, 12.8 l x 100 km.

CHASSIS multi-tubular backbone with outriggers; front suspension: independent, wishbones, coil springs, anti-roll bar, telescopic dampers; rear: independent, wishbones, coil springs, anti-roll bar, coil springs, 4 telescopic dampers.

STEERING rack-and-pinion.

BRAKES front disc (diameter 10.87 in, 27.6 cm), rear drum, servo; swept area: front 233 sq in, 1,503 sq cm, rear 99 sq in, 639 sq cm, total 332 sq in, 2,142 sq cm.

ELECTRICAL EQUIPMENT 12 V; 58 Ah battery; 34 A alternator; 2 headlamps.

DIMENSIONS AND WEIGHT wheel base: 90 in, 229 cm; front and rear track: 53.75 in, 136 cm; length: 155.12 in, 394 cm; width: 63.78 in, 162 cm; height: coupés 44.88 in, 114 cm - convertible 44.09 in, 112 cm; ground clearance: coupés 5 in, 12.7 cm - convertible 5.51 in, 14 cm; weight: 3000 M Coupé 2,200 lb, 998 kg - Convertible 3000 S 2,137 lb, 969 kg - Taimar Hatchback Coupé 2,293 lb, 1,040 kg; turning circle: 35.7 ft, 10.9 m; fuel tank: 12 imp gal, 14.5 US gal, 55 l.

BODY 2 doors; 2 seats, reclining backrests with built-in headrests; laminated windscreen; heated rear window; aluminium alloy wheels; leather steering wheel; for convertible only, fully detachable hood.

PRACTICAL INSTRUCTIONS fuel: 98 oct petrol; oil: engine 9.8 imp pt, 11.6 US pt, 5.5 l, SAE 20W-50, change every 6,000 miles, 9,700 km - gearbox 2.5 imp pt, 3 US pt, 1.4 l, SAE 90, change every 6,000 miles, 9,700 km - final drive 2 imp pt, 2.5 US pt, 1.2 l, SAE 90, change every 6,000 miles, 9,700 km; greasing: every 6,000 miles, 9,700 km, 10 points; tappet clearances: inlet 0.013 in, 0.32 mm, exhaust 0.020 in, 0.50 mm; valve timing: 29° 67° 70° 14°; tyre pressure: front 22 psi, 1.6 atm, rear 24 psi, 1.7 atm.

OPTIONALS halogen headlamps; sunshine roof; vinyl roof; leather upholstery; light alloy wheels.

230 hp power team

See 142 hp power team, except for:

ENGINE Holset 3LD turbocharger; compression ratio: 8:1; max power (DIN): 230 hp (169 kW) at 5,500 rpm; max torque (DIN): 273 lb ft, 37.7 kg m (370 Nm) at 3,500 rpm max engine 76.8 hp/(56.5 kW/l).

TRANSMISSION final drive: limited slip differential; tyres: 195 VR x 14.

PERFORMANCE max speeds: (I) 45 mph, 72 km/h; (II) 72 mph, 116 km/h; (III) 105 mph, 169 km/h; (IV) 140 mph, 225 km/h; power-weight ratio: Turbo Coupé 10.1 lb/hp (13.8 lb/kW), 4.6 kg/hp (6.2 kg/kW); speed in direct drive at 1,000 rpm: 25 mph, 40.2 km/h.

DIMENSIONS AND WEIGHT weight: Turbo Coupé 2,333 lb, 1,058 kg - Convertible Turbo 2,270 lb, 1,030 kg - Taimar Turbo Hatchback Coupé 2,426 lb, 1,100 kg.

TVR Convertible 3000 S

VANDEN PLAS 1500

VANDEN PLAS GREAT BRITAIN

1500

PRICE EX WORKS: £ 4,860*

ENGINE front, transverse, in unit with gearbox and final drive, 4 stroke; 4 cylinders, vertical, in line; 90.6 cu in, 1,485 cc (3 x 3.20 in, 76.2 x 81.3 mm); compression ratio: 9:1; max power (DIN): 68 hp (50 kW) at 5,500 rpm; max torque (DIN): 80 lb ft, 11.1 kg m (109 Nm) at 2,900 rpm; max engine rpm; 5,900; 45.8 hp/l (33.7 kW/l); cast iron block and head; 5 crankshaft bearings; valves: overhead, Vee-slanted, thimble tappets; camshafts: 1, overhead, chain driven; lubrication: mechanical pump, full flow filter (cartridge), 9.7 imp pt, 11.6 US pt, 5.5 l; 1 SU type HS6 single barrel carburettor; fuel feed: mechanical pump; sealed circuit cooling, liquid, expansion tank, 11.5 imp pt, 13.7 US pt, 6.5 l, electric thermostatic fan.

TRANSMISSION driving wheels: front; clutch: single dry plate (diaphragm); gearbox: mechanical; gears: 5, fully synchronized ratios: I 3.202, II 2.004, III 1.372, IV 1, V 0.869, rev 3.467; lever: central; final drive: helical spur gears; axle ratio: 3.647; width of rims: 4"; tyres: 155 SR x 13.

PERFORMANCE max speeds: (I) 33 mph, 53 km/h; (II) 54 mph, 87 km/h; (III) 78 mph, 125 km/h; (IV) 92 mph, 148 km/h; (V) 90 mph, 145 km/h; power-weight ratio: 29.2 lb/hp (39.7 lb/kW), 13.2 kg/hp (18 kg/kW); carrying capacity: 710 lb, 320 kg acceleration: standing ¼ mile 20.2 sec, 0-50 mph (0-80 km/h) 10.4 sec; speed in top at 1,000 rpm: 20.1 mph, 32.3 km/h consumption: 30.3 m/imp gal, 25.3 m/US gal, 9.3 l x 100 km.

CHASSIS integral, front suspension: independent, wishbones hydragas (liquid and gas) rubber cone springs, hydraulic connecting pipes to rear wheels; rear: independent, swinging longitudinal trailing arms, hydragas (liquid and gas) rubber cone springs, hydraulic connecting pipes to front wheels.

STEERING rack-and-pinion; turns lock to lock: 3.50.

BRAKES front disc (diameter 9.68 in, 24.6 cm), rear drum vacuum servo; swept area: front 178 sq in, 1,148 sq cm, rear 75.6 sq in, 487 sq cm, total 253.6 sq in, 1,635 sq cm.

ELECTRICAL EQUIPMENT 12 V; 40 Ah battery; 34 A alternator; Lucas distributor; 2 headlamps, 2 fog lamps.

DIMENSIONS AND WEIGHT wheel base: 96.14 in, 244 cm tracks: 54.33 in, 138 cm front, 54.41 in, 138 cm rear; length 154.25 in, 392 cm; width: 63.52 in, 161 cm; height: 54.75 in 139 cm; ground clearance: 7.64 in, 19.4 cm; weight: 1,984 lb 900 kg; turning circle: 33.3 ft, 10.1 m; fuel tank: 10.5 imp gal 12.7 US gal, 48 l.

BODY saloon/sedan; 4 doors; 4 seats, separate front seats reclining backrests; picnic tables behind front seats; heated rear window; tinted glass.

PRACTICAL INSTRUCTIONS fuel: 97 oct petrol; oil: engine gearbox and final drive 9.7 imp pt, 11.6 US pt, 5.5 l, SAE 20W-50, change every 6,000 miles, 9,700 km; greasing: every 6,000 miles, 9,700 km, 4 points; tappet clearances: inlet 0.012 0.018 in, 0.030-0.45 mm, exhaust 0.012-0.022 in, 0.30-0.5 mm; valve timing: 9° 51° 49° 11°; tyre pressure front 26 psi 1.8 atm, rear 24 psi, 1.7 atm.

OPTIONALS headrests: automatic transmission with 4 ratios (I 2.612, II 1.807, III 1.446, IV 1, rev 2.612), 3.800 axle ratio metallic spray.

VAUXHALL GREAT BRITAIN

Chevette Series

RICES EX WORKS:	£
1 E 2-dr Saloon	2,921*
2 E 4-dr Saloon	3,047*
3 E 2+1-dr Hatchback	2,969*
4 L 2-dr Saloon	3,209*
5 L 4-dr Saloon	3,335*
6 L 2+1-dr Hatchback	3,257*
7 L 4+1-dr Estate Car	3,645*
8 GL 4-dr Saloon	3,705*
9 GL 2+1-dr Hatchback	3,627*
0 2300 HS 2+1-dr Hatchback	5,939*

ower team:	Standard for:	Optional for:
6.6 hp	1 to 9	—
35 hp	10	—

56.6 hp power team

NGINE front, 4 stroke; 4 cylinders, vertical, in line; 76.6 cu in, ,256 cc (3.19 x 2.40 in, 81 x 61 mm); compression ratio: 8.7:1; 7.3:1 for export only); max power (DIN): 56.6 hp (42 kW) at ,600 rpm; max torque (DIN): 66.4 lb ft, 9.2 kg m (90 Nm) at ,600 rpm; max engine rpm: 6,000; 45.1 hp/l (33.2 kW/l); hromium cast iron block and head; 3 crankshaft bearings; alves: overhead, in line, push-rods and rockers; camshafts: 1, ide; lubrication: gear pump, full flow filter, 5.5 imp pt, 6.6 US t, 3.1 l; 1 Zenith-Stromberg 150 CDS downdraught single arrel carburettor; fuel feed: mechanical pump; water-cooled, 0.2 imp pt, 12.3 US pt, 5.8 l, viscous coupling fan.

RANSMISSION driving wheels: rear; clutch: single dry plate diaphragm); gearbox mechanical; gears: 4, fully synchronized; atios: I 3.760, II 2.213, III 1.404, IV 1, rev 3.707; lever: central; nal drive: hypoid bevel; axle ratio: 4.111; width of rims: 5"; yres: 5.60 x 13 - L and GL models 155 SR x 13.

ERFORMANCE max speeds: (I) 31 mph, 50 km/h; (II) 49 mph, 9 km/h; (III) 77 mph, 124 km/h; (IV) 91 mph, 146 km/h; ower-weight ratio: E 4-dr Saloon 33.3 lb/hp (45 lb/kW), 15.1 g/hp (20.4 kg/kW); carrying capacity: 1,076 lb, 488 kg; cceleration: standing ¼ mile 19.6 sec, 0-50 mph (0-80 km/h) .6 sec; speed in direct drive at 1,000 rpm: 15.9 mph, 25.6 m/h; consumption: 29.7 m/imp gal, 24.8 m/US gal, 9.5 l x 100 m (town).

HASSIS integral; front suspension: independent, wishbones, oil springs, anti-roll bar, telescopic dampers; rear: rigid axle orque tube), longitudinal trailing radius arms, coil springs, anhard rod, anti-roll bar, telescopic dampers.

TEERING rack-and-pinion; turns lock to lock: 3.50.

RAKES front disc (diameter 9.37 in, 23.8 cm), self-adjusting ear drum, rear compensator, dual circuit, servo; swept area: ont 157.5 sq in, 1,016 sq cm, rear 73.8 sq in, 476 sq cm, total 31.3 sq in, 1,492 sq cm.

VAUXHALL Chevette GL Saloon

ELECTRICAL EQUIPMENT 12 V; 40 Ah battery; 630 W alternator; AC Delco distributor; 2 headlamps.

DIMENSIONS AND WEIGHT wheel base: 94.30 in, 239 cm; front and rear track: 51.20 in, 130 cm; length: 164.40 in, 417 cm - hatchbacks 155.20 in, 394 cm - Estate Car 164.90 in, 419 cm; width: 61.80 in, 157 cm; height: 2-dr saloons and hatchbacks 51.50 in, 131 cm - 4-dr saloons 51.30 in, 130 cm - Estate Car 52.10 in, 132 cm; ground clearance: 4.70 in, 11.9 cm; weight: E 2-dr Saloon 1,821 lb, 826 kg - E 4-dr Saloon 1,885 lb, 855 kg - E Hatchback 1,865 lb, 846 kg - L 2-dr Saloon 1,841 lb, 835 kg - L 4-dr Saloon 1,903 lb, 863 kg - Hatchback 1,885 lb, 855 kg - L Estate Car 1,951 lb, 885 kg - GL Hatchback 1,916 lb, 869 kg - GL 4-dr Saloon 1,929 lb, 875 kg; turning circle: 32.8 ft, 10 m; fuel tank: saloons 9.9 imp gal, 11.9 US gal, 45 l - Estate Car 9.5 imp gal, 11.4 US gal, 43 l - hatchbacks 8.4 imp gal, 10 US gal, 38 l.

BODY saloon/sedan, coupé, estate car/st. wagon; 5 seats, separate front seats.

PRACTICAL INSTRUCTIONS fuel: 98 oct petrol; oil: engine 5.5 imp pt, 6.6 US pt, 3.1 l, SAE 10W-30, change every 6,000 miles, 9,700 km - gearbox 1.1 imp pt, 1.3 US pt, 0.6 l, SAE 90, change every 6 months - final drive 1.2 imp pt, 1.5 US pt, 0.7 l, SAE 90, no change recommended; greasing: every 6 months, 4 points; tappet clearances: inlet 0.008 in, 0.20 mm, exhaust 0.008 in, 0.20 mm; valve timing: 37° 71° 69° 39°; tyre pressure: front 21 psi, 1.5 atm, rear 25 psi, 1.7 atm.

OPTIONALS automatic transmission (except for E models); 155 SR x 13 tyres; metallic spray (except for E models).

135 hp power team

See 56.6 hp engine, except for:

ENGINE 139.1 cu in, 2.279 cc (3.84 x 3.in, 97.5 x 76.2 mm); compression ratio: 8.2:1; max power (DIN): 135 hp (99 kW) at 5,500 rpm; 59.2 hp/l (43.6 kW/l); valves: 4 per cylinder; 2 Stromberg 175 CD carburettors.

TRANSMISSION gears: 5, fully synchronized; ratios: I 3.370, II 2.160, III 1.580, IV 1.240, V 1; axle ratio: 3.440; width of rims: 6"; tyres: 205/60 HR x 13.

PERFORMANCE max speed: 115 mph, 185 km/h; power-weight ratio: 14.5 lb/hp (19.7 lb/kW), 6.6 kg/hp (8.9 kg/kW).

DIMENSIONS AND WEIGHT weight: 1,960 lb, 889 kg.

Cavalier Series

PRICES EX WORKS:	£
1 1300 L 2-dr Saloon	3,657*
2 1300 L 4-dr Saloon	3,782*
3 1600 L 2-dr Saloon	3,863*
4 1600 L 4-dr Saloon	3,989*
5 1600 GL 4-dr Saloon	4,451*
6 1600 GL 2+1-dr Sports Hatchback	4,768*
7 1600 GLS 2+1-dr Sports Hatchback	5,230*
8 2000 GL 4-dr Saloon	4,694*
9 2000 GLS 4-dr Saloon	5,157*
10 2000 GLS 2+1-dr Sports Hatchback	5,473*

Power team:	Standard for:	Optional for:
56.6 hp	1,2	—
75 hp	3 to 7	—
100 hp	8 to 10	—

56.6 hp power team

ENGINE front, 4 stroke; 4 cylinders, vertical, in line; 76.6 cu in, 1,256 cc (3.19 x 2.40 in, 81 x 61 mm); compression ratio: 8.7:1; max power (DIN): 56.6 hp (42 kW) at 5.600 rpm; max torque (DIN): 66.4 lb ft, 9.2 kg m (90 Nm) at 2,600 rpm; max engine rpm: 6,000; 45.1 hp/l (33.2 kW/l); chromium cast iron block and head; 3 crankshaft bearings; valves: overhead, in line, push-rods and rockers; camshafts: 1, side ; lubrication: gear pump, full flow filter, 5.5 imp pt, 6.6 US pt, 3.1 l; 1 Zenith-Stromberg 150 CDS downdraught single barrel carburettor; fuel feed: mechanical pump; water-cooled, 10.2 imp pt, 12.3 US pt, 5.8 l, viscous coupling thermostatic fan.

TRANSMISSION driving wheels: rear; clutch: single dry plate (diaphragm): gearbox: mechanical; gears: 4, fully synchronized; ratios: I 3.760, II 2.213, III 1.404, IV 1, rev 3.707; lever: central; final drive: hypoid bevel; axle ratio: 4.111; width of rims: 5"; tyres 165 SR x 13.

PERFORMANCE max speed: (I) 30 mph, 48 km/h; (II) 46 mph, 74 km/h; (III) 73 mph, 117 km/h; (IV) 92 mph, 148 km/h; power-weight ratio: 4-dr Saloon 35.7 lb/hp (48.1 lb/kW), 16.2 kg/hp (21.8 kg/kW); carrying capacity: 893 lb, 405 kg; acceleration standing ¼ mile 20.9 sec, 0-50 mph (0-80 km/h) 12 sec; speed in direct drive at 1,000 rpm: 16.2 mph, 26 km/h; consumption: 30.7 m/imp gal, 25.6 m/US gal, 9.2 l x 100 km.

CHASSIS integral; front suspension: independent, wishbones, coil springs, anti-roll bar, telescopic dampers; rear: rigid axle

VAUXHALL Cavalier 2000 GLS Saloon

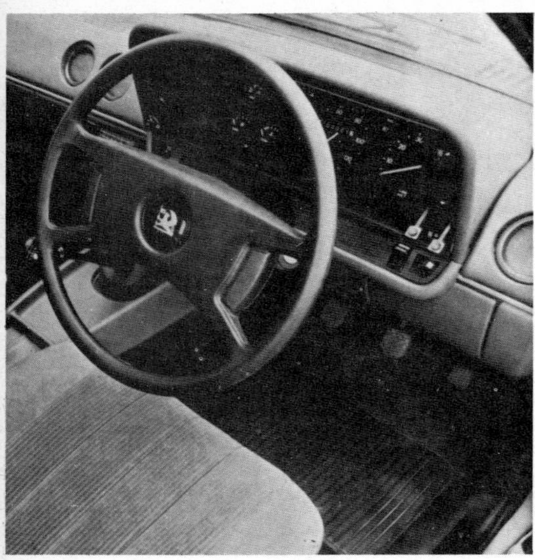

VAUXHALL Cavalier 2000 GLS Saloon

56.6 HP POWER TEAM

(torque tube), trailing radius arms, transverse linkage bar, coil springs, anti-roll bar, telescopic dampers.

STEERING rack-and-pinion; turns lock to lock: 4.

BRAKES front disc (diameter 9.70 in, 24.6 cm), rear drum, rear compensator, dual circuit, servo.

ELECTRICAL EQUIPMENT 12 V; 36 Ah battery; 45 A alternator; Delco-Remy distributor; 2 headlamps.

DIMENSIONS AND WEIGHT wheel base: 99.10 in, 252 cm; front and rear track: 54.10 in, 137 cm; length: 175.50 in, 446 cm; width: 64.70 in, 164 cm; height: 52 in, 132 cm; ground clearance: 5 in, 12.7 cm; weight: 2-dr Saloon 1,973 lb, 895 kg - 4-dr Saloon 2,018 lb, 915 kg; turning circle: 31.1 ft, 9.5 m; fuel tank: 11 imp gal, 13.2 US gal, 50 l.

BODY saloon/sedan; 5 seats, separate front seats, reclining backrests; heated rear window.

PRACTICAL INSTRUCTIONS fuel: 98 oct petrol; oil: engine 5.5 imp pt, 6.6 US pt, 3.1 l, SAE 10W-30, change every 6,000 miles, 9,700 km - gearbox 0.9 imp pt, 1.1 US pt, 0.5 l, SAE 90, change every 6 months - final drive 1.2 imp pt, 1.5 US pt, 0.7 l, SAE 90, no change recommended; greasing: none; tappet clearances: inlet: 0.008 in, 0.20 mm, exhaust 0.008 in, 0.20 mm; valve timing: 37° 71° 69° 39°; tyre pressure: front 28 psi, 2 atm, rear 28 psi, 2 atm.

75 hp power team

See 56.6 hp power team, except for:

ENGINE 96.7 cu in, 1,584 cc (3.35 x 2.75 in, 85 x 69.8 mm); compression ratio: 8.8:1; max power (DIN): 75 hp (55 kW) at 5,000 rpm; max torque (DIN): 81 lb ft, 11.2 kg m (110 Nm) at 3,800 rpm; 47.3 hp/l (34.8 kW/l); cast iron block, chromium cast iron head; 5 crankshaft bearings; camshafts: 1, overhead; lubrication: 8.7 imp pt, 10.4 US pt, 4.9 l; 1 Solex 32 DIDTA-4 downdraught single barrel carburettor; fuel feed: electric pump; cooling: 13.8 imp pt, 16.5 US pt, 7.8 l.

TRANSMISSION gearbox ratios: I 3.640, II 2.120, III 1,336, IV 1, rev 3.522; axle ratio: 3.670; width of rims: GLS Sports Hatchback 5.5"; tyres: GLS Sports Hatchback 185 SR x 13.

PERFORMANCE max speed: 98 mph, 158 km/h; power-weight ratio: 1600 L 4-dr Saloon 29.3 lb/hp (40.1 lb/kW), 13.3 kg/hp (18.2 kg/kW); carrying capacity: 937 lb, 425 kg; speed in direct drive at 1,000 rpm: 18.3 mph, 29.4 km/h; consumption: 25.7 m/imp gal, 21.4 m/US gal, 11 l x 100 km.

ELECTRICAL EQUIPMENT 44 Ah battery.

DIMENSIONS AND WEIGHT length: hatchbacks 171.80 in, 436 cm; weight: 1600 L 2-dr Saloon 2,161 lb, 980 kg - 1600 L and GL 4-dr Saloons 2,205 lb, 1,000 kg - 1600 GL and GLS Sports Hatchbacks 2,271 lb, 1,030 kg.

BODY saloon/sedan, coupé; 5 seats.

PRACTICAL INSTRUCTIONS oil: engine 6.7 imp pt, 8 US pt, 3.8 l, SAE 20W-30, change every 6,000 miles, 9,700 km - gearbox 2.3 imp pt, 2.7 US pt, 1.3 l, SAE 80, no change recommended - final drive 2.3 imp pt, 2.7 US pt, 1.3 l, SAE 90, no change recommended; tappet clearances: inlet 0.012 in, 0.30 mm, exhaust 0.012 in, 0.30 mm; valve timing: 44° 86° 84° 46°.

OPTIONALS G.M. automatic transmission, hydraulic torque converter and planetary gears with 3 ratios (I 2.400, II 1.480, III 1, rev 1.920), max ratio of converter at stall 2.5, possible manual selection, max speed 95 mph, 153 km/h, consumption 25.9 m/imp gal, 21.6 m/US gal, 10.9 l x 100 km; metallic spray.

100 hp power team

See 56.6 hp power team, except for:

ENGINE 120.8 cu in, 1,979 cc (3.74 x 2.75 in, 95 x 69.8 mm); compression ratio: 9:1; max power (DIN): 100 hp (74 kW) at 5,400 rpm; max torque (DIN): 113 lb/ft, 15.6 kg m (153 Nm) at 3,800 rpm; 50.5 hp/l (37.2 kW/l); cast iron block, chromium cast iron head; 5 crankshaft bearings; valves: hydraulic tappets; camshafts: 1, overhead; lubrication: 8.7 imp pt, 10.4 US pt, 4.9 l; 1 GMF Varajet II downdraught single barrel carburettor; fuel feed: electric pump; cooling: 13.8 imp pt, 16.5 US pt, 7.8 l.

TRANSMISSION gearbox ratios: I 3.640, II 2.120, III 1.336, IV 1, rev 3.552; axle ratio: 3.440; width of rims: GLS models 5.5"; tyres: Hatchback 185 HR x 13.

PERFORMANCE max speed: 109 mph, 175 km/h; power-weight ratio: saloons 22 lb/hp (29.8 lb/kW), 10 kg/hp (13.5 kg/kW); carrying capacity: 937 lb, 425 kg; speed in direct drive at 1,000 rpm GL 19.5 mph, 31.4 km/h GLS models 19.6 mph, 31.5 km/h; consumption: 23.7 m/imp gal, 19.8 m/US gal, 11.9 l x 100 km.

ELECTRICAL EQUIPMENT 44 Ah battery.

DIMENSIONS AND WEIGHT weight: saloons 2,205 lb, 1,000 kg - Hatchback 2,271 lb, 1,030 kg.

PRACTICAL INSTRUCTIONS oil: engine 6.7 imp pt, 8 US pt, 3.8 l, SAE 20W-30, change every 6,000 miles, 9,700 km - gearbox 2.3 imp pt, 2.7 US pt, 1.3 l, SAE 80, no change recommended - final drive 2.3 imp pt, 2.7 US pt, 1.3 l, SAE 90, no change recommended; tappet clearances: inlet 0.012 in, 0.30 mm, exhaust 0.012 in, 0.30 mm; valve timing: 44° 86° 84° 46°.

OPTIONALS G.M. automatic transmission, hydraulic torque converter and planetary gears with 3 ratios (I 2.400, II 1.480, III 1, rev 1.920), max ratio of converter at stall 2.5, possible manual selection; metallic spray.

Astra Series

PRICE EX WORKS:	£
GL Hatchback	4,60[illegible]
L Estate Car	4,37[illegible]

ENGINE front, transverse, 4 stroke; 4 cylinders, in line; 79.1[illegible] cu in, 1,297 cc (2.95 x 2.89 in, 75 x 73.4 mm); compression ratio: 9.2:1; max power (DIN): 75 hp (55 kW) at 5,800 rpm; max torque (DIN): 70 lb ft, 10.3 kg m (101 Nm) at 3,800 rpm; max engine rpm: 6,400; 57.8 hp/l (42.4 kW/l); cast iron block, light alloy head; 5 crankshaft bearings; valves: overhead, in line, rockers, hydraulic tappets; camshafts: 1, overhead, cogged belt; lubrication: gear pump, full flow filter, 4.8 imp pt, 5.7 US pt, 2.7 l; 1 GMF Varajet II downdraught single barrel carburettor; fuel feed: mechanical pump; anti-freeze cooling, liquid, 11.[illegible] imp pt, 13.3 US pt, 6.3 l, electric thermostatic fan.

VAUXHALL Astra L Estate Car

VAUXHALL Astra Series

TRANSMISSION driving wheels: front; clutch: single dry plate (diaphragm); gearbox: mechanical; gears: fully synchronized; ratios: I 3.636, II 2.188, III 1.429, IV 0.969, rev 3.182; lever: central; final drive: helical spur gears; axle ratio: 4.180; width of rims: Hatchback 5.5" - Estate Car 5"; tyres: 155 SR x 13.

PERFORMANCE max speeds: (I) 27 mph, 43 km/h; (II) 4[illegible] mph, 74 km/h; (III) 70 mph, 112 km/h; (IV) 98 mph, 157 km/h; power-weight ratio: Hatchback 25.1 lb/hp, (34.2 lb/kW), 11.[illegible] kg/hp (15.5 kg/kW); carrying capacity: 882 lb, 400 kg; speed in top at 1,000 rpm: 16.1 mph, 25.9 km/h; consumption: 34 m/imp gal, 28,3 m/US gal, 8.3 l x 100 km at 75 mph, 120 km/h.

CHASSIS integral; front suspension: independent, by McPherson coil springs/telescopic damper struts, anti-roll bar; rear: rigid axle, coil springs, trailing arms, anti-roll bar, telescopic dampers.

STEERING rack-and-pinion; turns lock to lock: 4.

BRAKES front disc (diameter 9.20 in, 23.4 cm), rear drum, dual circuit, vacuum servo; lining area: total 57.05 sq in, 368 sq cm.

ELECTRICAL EQUIPMENT 12 V; 36 Ah battery; 45 A alternator; Bosch distributor; 2 headlamps.

IMENSIONS AND WEIGHT wheel base: 99 in, 251 cm; tracks: 5.10 in, 140 cm front, 55.40 in, 141 cm rear; length: Hatchack 157.40 in, 400 cm - Estate Car 165.60 in, 421 cm; width: 4.50 in, 164 cm; height: Hatchback 52.20 in, 133 cm - Estate Car 1,996 lb, 905 kg; turning circle: 34.4 ft, 10.5 m; fuel tank: .2 imp gal, 11.1 US gal, 42 l.

ODY hatchback, estate car/st. wagon; 4+1 doors; 4-5 seats; ear folding seat; for L Estate Car only, reclining front seats vith built-in headrests, heated rear window and rear window viper-washer.

RACTICAL INSTRUCTIONS fuel: 98 oct petrol; oil: engine 4.8 mp pt, 5.7 US pt, 2.7 l, SAE 20W-30, change every 6,200 niles, 10,000 km - gearbox and final drive 3.5 imp pt, 4.2 US t, 2 l, SAE 90 EP, no change recommended; greasing: none; alve timing: 24° 78° 68° 36°; tyre pressure: front 25 psi, 1.8 tm, rear 25 psi, 1.8 atm.

PTIONALS sunshine roof and tinted glass (for GL Hatchback nly).

VAUXHALL Carlton 2000 Saloon

Carlton 2000 Saloon

RICE EX WORKS: £ 5,627*

NGINE front, 4 stroke; 4 cylinders, vertical, in line; 120.7 cu n, 1,979 cc (3.74 x 2.75 in, 95 x 69.8 mm); compression ratio: :1; max power (DIN): 100 hp (74 kW) at 5,200 rpm; max torque DIN): 116 lb ft, 16.1 kg m (158 Nm) at 3,600 rpm; max engine pm: 6,000; 50.5 hp/l (37.9 kW/l); cast iron block and head; 5 rankshaft bearings; valves: overhead, hydraulic tappets; camhafts: 1, overhead; lubrication: 6.7 imp pt, 8 US pt, 3.8 l; 1 GMF Varajet II carburettor; fuel feed: mechanical pump; waterooled, 11 imp pt, 13.1 US pt, 6.2 l.

RANSMISSION driving wheels: rear; clutch: single dry plate; earbox: mechanical; gears: 4, fully synchronized; ratios: I .640, II 2.120, III 1.336, IV 1, rev 3.522; lever: central; final rive: hypoid bevel; axle ratio: 3.670; width of rims: 5.5"; tyres: 75 SR x 14.

ERFORMANCE max speed: (I) 27 mph, 43 km/h; (II) 64 mph, 03 km/h; (III) 94 mph, 151 km/h; (IV) 107 mph, 172 km/h; ower-weight ratio: 24.9 lb/hp (33.7 lb/kW), 11.3 kg/hp (15.3 g/kW); carrying capacity: 1,036 lb, 470 kg; acceleration: tanding ¼ mile 18.2 sec, 0-50 mph, (0-80 km/h) 8.1 sec; peed in direct drive at 1,000 rpm: 19.5 mph, 31.4 km/h; onsumption: 24.4 m/imp gal, 20.3 m/US gal, 11.6 l x 100 km.

HASSIS integral; front suspension: independent, by McPheron, coil springs/telescopic damper struts, anti-roll bar; rear: igid axle, trailing lower radius arms, upper torque arms, transerse linkage bar, coil springs, anti-roll bar, telescopic damers.

STEERING recirculating ball; turns lock to lock: 4.

RAKES front disc (diameter 9.60 in, 24.4 cm), internal radial ins, self-adjusting rear drum, rear compensator, dual circuit, ervo; swept area: front 22.9 sq in, 148 sq cm, rear 62.8 sq in, 05 sq cm, total 85.7 sq in, 553 sq cm.

LECTRICAL EQUIPMENT 12 V; 44 Ah battery; 45 A alternaor; AC Delco distributor; 2 halogen headlamps.

IMENSIONS AND WEIGHT wheel base: 105 in, 267 cm; racks: 56.50 in, 144 cm front, 55.60 in, 141 cm rear; length: 186.70 in, 474 cm; width: 69.90 in, 173 cm; height: 53.60 in, 136 cm; ground clearance: 5.20 in, 13 cm; weight: 2,492 lb, 1,130 kg; weight distribution: 55.5% front, 44.5% rear; turning circle: 35.5 ft, 10.8 m; fuel tank: 14.3 imp gal, 17.2 US gal, 65 l.

BODY saloon/sedan; 4 doors; 5 seats, separate front seats, reclining backrests, headrests; heated rear window.

PRACTICAL INSTRUCTIONS fuel: 98.100 oct petrol; oil: engine 6.7 imp pt, 8 US pt, 3.8 l, SAE 10W-50 change every 6,000 miles, 9,700 km - gearbox 1.9 imp pt, 2.3 US pt, 1.1 l, SAE 80, change every 18,300 miles, 30,000 km - final drive 2.1 imp pt, 2.5 US pt, 1.2 l, SAE 90, no change recommended; greasing: none; valve timing: 32° 90° 72° 50°; tyre pressure: front 24 psi, 1.7 atm, rear 25 psi, 1.8 atm.

OPTIONALS automatic transmission; power steering; metallic spray; sports wheels.

Carlton 2000 Estate Car

See Carlton 2000 Saloon, except for:

PRICE EX WORKS: £ 6,197*

PERFORMANCE power-weight ratio: 26 lb/hp (35.1 lb/kW), 11.8 kg/hp (15.9 kg/kW); carrying capacity: 1,290 lb, 585 kg; consumption: 23.7 m/imp gal, 19.8 m/US gal, 11.9 l x 100 km.

DIMENSIONS AND WEIGHT length: 186.20 in, 473 cm; height: 56.20 in, 143 cm; ground clearance: 6.40 in, 16 cm; weight: 2,602 lb, 1,180 kg; weight distribution: 53% front, 47% rear; fuel tank: 15.4 imp gal, 18.5 US gal, 70 l.

BODY estate car/st. wagon; 4+1 doors.

VAUXHALL Royale Saloon

Royale Saloon

PRICE EX WORKS: £ 9,711*

ENGINE front, 4 stroke; 6 cylinders, vertical, in line; 169.9 cu in, 2,784 cc (3.62 x 2.75 in, 92 x 69.8 mm); compression ratio: 9:1; max power (DIN): 140 hp (103 kW) at 5,200 rpm; max torque (DIN): 161 lb ft, 22.2 kg m (218 Nm) at 3,400 rpm; max engine rpm: 6,150; 50.3 hp/l (37.4 kW/l); cast iron block and head; 7 crankshaft bearings; valves: overhead, hydraulic tappets; camshafts: 1, overhead; lubrication: 9.8 imp pt, 11.6 US pt, 5.5 l; 1 DVG 4A1 downdraught carburettor; fuel feed: mechanical pump; water-cooled, 17.2 imp pt, 20.7 US pt, 9.8 l.

TRANSMISSION driving wheels: rear; gearbox: automatic transmission, hydraulic torque converter and planetary gears with 3 ratios, max ratio of converter at stall 2, possible manual selection; ratios: I 2.400, II 1.480, III 1, rev 1.920; lever: central; final drive: hypoid bevel; axle ratio: 3.450; width of rims: 6"; tyres: 195/70 HR x 14.

PERFORMANCE max speed: 113 mph, 182 km/h; power-weight ratio: 21.8 lb/hp (29.5 lb/kW), 9.9 kg/hp (13.4 kg/kW); carrying capacity: 1,147 lb, 520 kg; acceleration: standing ¼ mile 18.3 sec, 0-50 mph (0-80 km/h) 8.5 sec; speed in direct drive at 1,000 rpm: 20.8 mph, 33.5 km/h; consumption: 19.3 m/imp gal, 16.1 m/US gal, 14.6 l x 100 km.

CHASSIS integral; front suspension: independent, by McPherson coil springs/telescopic damper struts, anti-roll bar; rear: independent, two semi-trailing arms, coil springs, anti-roll bar, telescopic dampers.

STEERING recirculating ball, servo; turns lock to lock: 4.

BRAKES disc (diameter front 10.60 in, 27.1 cm, rear 10.90 in, 27.7 cm), dual circuit, servo.

ELECTRICAL EQUIPMENT 12 V; 55 Ah battery; 55 A alternator; Bosch distributor; 2 halogen headlamps.

DIMENSIONS AND WEIGHT wheel base: 105.60 in, 268 cm; tracks: 56.80 in, 144 cm front, 57.70 in, 146 cm rear; length: 192 in, 488 cm; width: 68 in, 173 cm; ground clearance: 4.90 in, 12.4 cm; weight: 3,043 lb, 1,380 kg; weight distribution: 55% front, 45% rear; turning circle: 35.4 ft, 10.8 m; fuel tank: 16.5 imp gal, 19.8 US gal, 75 l.

BODY saloon/sedan; 4 doors; 4 seats, separate front seats, reclining backrests, headrests; tinted glass; electric windows; heated rear window.

PRACTICAL INSTRUCTIONS fuel: 98-100 oct petrol; oil: engine 9.8 imp pt, 11.6 US pt, 5.5 l, SAE 10W-50, change every 6,000 miles, 9,700 km - automatic transmission 10.6 imp pt, 12.7 US pt, 6 l, Dexron, change every 24,000 miles, 38,600 km - final drive 2.1 imp pt, 2.5 US pt, 1.2 l, SAE 90, no change recommended; greasing; none; valve timing: 32° 90° 72° 50°; tyre pressure: front 25 psi, 1.8 atm, rear 28 psi, 2 atm.

OPTIONALS mechanical gearbox; air-conditioning.

Royale Coupé

See Royale Saloon, except for:

PRICE EX WORKS: £ 10,069*

PERFORMANCE max speed: 115 mph, 185 km/h; power-weight ratio: 21.8 lb/hp (29.5 lb/kW), 9.9 kg/hp (13.4 kg/kW); carrying capacity: 1,136 lb, 515 kg; acceleration: 0-50 mph (0-80 km/h) 9 sec.

DIMENSIONS AND WEIGHT wheel base: 105 in, 267 cm; length: 187.30 in, 476 cm; width: 68.30 in, 173 cm; height 52.50 in, 134 cm; ground clearance: 4.60 in, 12 cm; weight: 3,054 lb, 1,385 kg; weight distribution: 53.5% front, 46.5% rear; fuel tank: 15.4 imp gal, 18.5 US gal, 70 l.

BODY coupé; 2+1 doors.

VOLVO HOLLAND

66 L / DL

PRICES EX WORKS:	florins
L	13,700*
DL	14,770*

ENGINE front, 4 stroke; 4 cylinders, vertical, in line; 67.6 cu in, 1,108 cc (2.76 x 2.83 in, 70 x 72 mm); compression ratio: 8.5:1; max power (DIN): 47 hp (35 kW) at 5,000 rpm; max torque (DIN): 54 lb ft, 7.6 kg m (74 Nm) at 2,700 rpm; max engine rpm: 6,200; 42.4 hp/l (31.2 kW/l); cast iron block, light alloy head; 5 crankshaft bearings; valves: overhead, in line, push-rods and rockers; camshafts: 1, side; lubrication: gear pump, full flow filter, 5.6 imp pt, 6.8 US pt, 3.2 l; 1 Solex 32 EHSAREN 577 carburettor; fuel feed: mechanical pump; water-cooled, 8.4 imp pt, 10.1 US pt, 4.8 l.

TRANSMISSION driving wheels: rear; clutch: automatic, centrifugal; transmission: C.V.T./transaxle automatic; gears: continuously variable ratio between 14.22 and 3.6; lever: central; width of rims: 4"; tyres: 135 SR x 14.

PERFORMANCE max speed: 85 mph, 136 km/h; power-weight ratio: 38.1 lb/hp (51.9 lb/kW), 17.3 kg/hp (23.6 kg/kW); carrying capacity: 849 lb, 385 kg; acceleration: 0-50 mph (0-80 km/h) 12.9 sec; consumption: 31.4 m/imp gal, 26.1 m/US gal, 9 l x 100 km.

CHASSIS integral; front suspension: independent, longitudinal torsion bars, telescopic damper struts, lower wishbones (trailing links), anti-roll bar; rear: de Dion rigid axle, semi-elliptic leafsprings, upper torque arms, telescopic dampers.

STEERING rack-and-pinion; turns lock to lock: 3.30.

BRAKES front disc, rear drum, servo; swept area: front 151.9 sq in, 980 sq cm, rear 74.4 sq in, 480 sq cm, total 226.3 sq in, 1,460 sq cm.

ELECTRICAL EQUIPMENT 12 V; 36 Ah battery; 500 W alternator; Ducellier distributor; 2 headlamps.

DIMENSIONS AND WEIGHT wheel base: 88.58 in, 225 cm; tracks: 51.57 in, 131 cm front, 48.82 in, 124 cm rear; length: 153.54 in, 390 cm; width: 59.84 in, 152 cm; height: 56.69 in, 144 cm; ground clearance: 4.72 in, 12 cm; weight: 1,797 lb, 815 kg; weight distribution: 56.2% front, 43.8% rear; turning circle: 32.1 ft, 9.8 m; fuel tank: 9.2 imp gal, 11.1 US gal, 42 l.

BODY saloon/sedan; 2 doors; 4-5 seats, separate front seats, reclining backrests, built-in headrests; tinted glass.

PRACTICAL INSTRUCTIONS fuel: 98 oct petrol; oil: engine 5.6 imp pt, 6.8 US pt, 3.2 l, SAE 10W-30 (summer) 20W-40 (winter), change every 3,100 miles, 5,000 km - C.V.T. automatic transmission 1.4 imp pt, 1.7 US pt, 0.8 l, SAE 80 EP, change every 12,400 miles, 20,000 km; greasing: none; tappet clearances: 0.006 in, 0.15 mm, exhaust 0.008 in, 0.20 mm; valve timing: 0°30' 36° 38°30'.5°; tyre pressure: front 22 psi, 1.6 atm, rear 26 psi, 1.8 atm.

OPTIONALS 155 SR x 13 tyres only with 4.5' wide rims; sunshine roof (for DL only).

66 GL

PRICE EX WORKS: 15,540 florins

See 66 L / DL, except for:

ENGINE 78.7 cu in, 1,289 cc (2.87 x 3.03 in, 73 x 77 mm); max power (DIN): 57 hp (42 kW) at 5,200 rpm; max torque (DIN): 61 lb ft, 9.6 kg m (94 Nm) at 2,800 rpm; 44.2 hp/l (32.5 kW/l); 1 Solex 32 EHSAREN 596 carburettor.

TRANSMISSION width of rims: 4.5"; tyres: 155 SR x 13.

PERFORMANCE max speed: 90 mph, 145 km/h; power-weight ratio: 32.5 lb/hp (44.1 lb/kW), 14.7 kg/hp (20 kg/kW); carrying capacity: 915 lb, 415 kg; acceleration: 0-50 mph (0-80 km/h) 10.8 sec; consumption: 28.2 m/imp gal, 23.5 m/US gal, 10 l x km.

ELECTRICAL EQUIPMENT 4 headlamps, 2 halogen.

DIMENSIONS AND WEIGHT width: 60.63 in, 154 cm; height: 54.33 in, cm; weight: 1,846 lb, 837 kg; weight distribution: 56.3% front, 43.7% rear; turning circle: 31.2 ft, 9.5 m.

PRACTICAL INSTRUCTIONS tyre pressure: front 20 psi, 1.4 atm, rear 23 psi, 1.6 atm.

OPTIONALS metallic spray.

340 Series

PRICES IN GB AND EX WORKS:	£	florins
343 L	—	16,690
343 DL (manual)	3,964*	17,890
343 DL (automatic)	4,131*	19,090
343 GL	—	19,090
345 L	—	17,590
345 DL	—	18,790
345 GL	—	19,990

ENGINE front, 4 stroke; 4 cylinders, vertical, in line; 85.2 cu ir 1,397 cc (2.99 x 3.03 in, 76 x 77 mm); compression ratio: 9.5:1 max power (DIN): 70 hp (51 kW) at 5,500 rpm; max torque (DIN): 80 lb ft, 11 kg m (108 Nm) at 3,500 rpm; max engin rpm: 6,000; 50.1 hp/l (36.9 kW/l); cast iron block, wet liners light alloy head; 5 crankshaft bearings; valves: overhead, i line, slanted, push-rods and rockers; camshafts: 1, side; lubri cation: gears pump, full flow filter, 6.2 imp pt, 7.4 US pt, 3.5 l; Weber 32 DIR 57-8400 downdraught carburettor; fuel feed mechanical pump; sealed circuit cooling, 10.6 imp pt, 12.7 US pt, 6 l, electric fan.

TRANSMISSION driving wheels: rear; clutch: single dry plate (diaphragm), or automatic, centrifugal; gearbox: mechanical, o C.V.T./transaxle automatic; gears: 4, fully synchronized; ratios I 3.705, II 2.159, III 1.369, IV 1 or, continuously variable between 14.22 and 3.86; lever: central; final drive: hypoi bevel; axle ratio: 3.680: width of rims: 5"; tyres: 155 SR x 13

PERFORMANCE max speed: 90 mph, 145 km/h; power weight ratio: 343 models 30.8 lb/hp (41.9 lb/kW), 14 kg/hp (1 kg/kW) - 345 models 32 lb/hp (43 lb/kW), 14.5 kg/hp (19. kg/kW); carrying capacity: 931 lb, 422 kg; acceleration: 0-5 mph (0-80 km/h) 10.5 sec; consumption: 31.4 m/imp gal, 26. m/US gal, 9 l x 100 km.

CHASSIS integral front suspension: independent, by Mc Pherson, lower wishbones, coil springs/telescopic dampe struts, anti-roll bar; rear: de Dion rigid axle, single leaf sem elliptic springs, swinging longitudinal trailing arm, telescopi dampers.

VOLVO 66 GL

VOLVO 345 DL

STEERING rack-and-pinion; turns lock to lock: 4.10.

BRAKES front disc, rear drum, servo; lining area: front 17.4 sq in, 112 sq cm, rear 37.7 sq in, 243 sq cm, total 55.1 sq in, 355 sq cm.

ELECTRICAL EQUIPMENT 12 V; 36 Ah battery; 700 W alternator; Ducellier distributor; 2 headlamps.

DIMENSIONS AND WEIGHT wheel base: 94.09 in, 239 cm; tracks: 53.15 in, 135 cm front, 54.33 in, 138 cm rear; length: 164.96 in, 419 cm; width: 65.35 in, 166 cm; height: 54.72 in, 139 cm; ground clearance: 5.31 in, 13.5 cm; weight: 343 models 2,156 lb, 978 kg - 345 models 2,236 lb, 1,014 kg; weight distribution: 53.7% front, 46.3% rear; turning circle: 30.2 ft, 9.2 m; fuel tank: 9.9 imp gal, 11.9 US gal, 45 l.

BODY saloon/sedan; 343 models 2+1 doors - 345 models 4+1 doors; 4-5 seats, separate front seats, reclining backrests with built-in headrests; detachable back seat; folding rear seat; heated rear window.

PRACTICAL INSTRUCTIONS fuel: 98 oct petrol; oil: engine 6.2 imp pt, 7.4 US pt, 3.5 l, SAE 10W-30 (summer) SAE 20W-40 (winter), change every 6,200 miles, 10,000 km - gearbox 3.7 imp pt, 4.4 US pt, 2.1 l, ATF - final drive 2.5 imp pt, 3 US pt, 1.4 l, API - GL - 5 - C.V.T. automatic transmission 1.4 imp pt, 1.7 US pt, 0.8 l, SAE 80 EP, change every 12,400 miles, 20,000 km; greasing: none; tappet clearances: inlet 0.006 in, 0.15 mm, exhaust 0.006 in, 0.15 mm; tyre pressure: front 24 psi, 1.7 atm, rear 28 psi, 2 atm.

OPTIONALS (for DL models only) 175/70 SR x 13 tyres; sunshine roof (except L models); tinted glass; metallic spray; halogen headlamps; headlamps with wiper-washer; vinyl upholstery.

ALFA ROMEO Alfasud 1.3 Super Berlina

ALFA ROMEO Alfasud 1.3 - 1.5 Sprint Veloce Coupé

ALFA ROMEO — ITALY

Alfasud Series

PRICES EX WORKS:	liras
1 1.2 4-dr Berlina (4 gears)	5,713,000*
2 1.2 4-dr Super Berlina (5 gears)	6,203,000*
3 1.3 4-dr Super Berlina	6,513,000*
4 1.3 2+1-dr Giardinetta	6,443,000*
5 1.3 ti 2-dr Berlina	6,396,000*
6 1.3 2-dr Sprint Veloce Coupé	7,835,000*
7 1.5 4-dr Super Berlina	6,823,000*
8 1.5 ti 2-dr Berlina	6,702,000*
9 1.5 2-dr Sprint Veloce Coupé	8,142,000*

Power team:	Standard for:	Optional for:
63 hp	1	—
68 hp	2	—
71 hp	4	—
79 hp	3,5	—
85 hp	7,8	—
86 hp	6	—
95 hp	9	—

63 hp power team

ENGINE front, 4 stroke; 4 cylinders, horizontally opposed; 72.4 cu in, 1,186 cc (3.15 x 2.32 in, 80 x 59 mm); compression ratio: 8.8:1; max power (DIN): 63 hp (46 kW) at 6,000 rpm; max torque (DIN): 65 lb ft, 9 kg m (88 Nm) at 3,200 rpm; max engine rpm: 6,000; 53.1 hp/l (39.1 kW/l); cast iron block, light alloy head; 3 crankshaft bearings; valves: overhead, in line, thimble tappets, new valve adjustment patented by Alfa Romeo; camshafts: 2, 1 per bank, overhead, cogged belt; lubrication: gear pump, full flow filter (cartridge), 7 imp pt, 8.5 US pt, 4 l; 1 Solex C32 DIS/40 or Dell'Orto FRDA 32F downdraught single barrel carburettor; fuel feed: mechanical pump; water-cooled, 12.8 imp pt, 15.4 US pt, 7.3 l, electric thermostatic fan.

TRANSMISSION driving wheels: front; clutch: single dry plate (diaphragm), hydraulically controlled; gearbox: mechanical; gears: 4, fully synchronized; ratios: I 3.545, II 1.941, III 1.292, IV 0.966, rev 3.091; lever: central; final drive: hypoid bevel; axle ratio: 4.111; width of rims: 5"; tyres: 165/70 SR x 13.

PERFORMANCE max speeds: (I) 26 mph, 42 km/h; (II) 48 mph, 77 km/h; (III) 71 mph, 115 km/h; (IV) over 93 mph, 150 km/h; power-weight ratio: 30.1 lb/hp (40.8 lb/kW), 13.6 kg/hp (18.5 kg/kW); carrying capacity: 882 lb, 400 kg; speed in top at 1,000 rpm: 16 mph, 25.7 km/h; consumption: 39.2 m/imp gal, 32.7 m/US gal, 7.2 l x 100 km at 62 mph, 100 km/h.

CHASSIS integral; front suspension: independent, by McPherson, coil springs/telescopic damper struts, lower trailing links, anti-roll bar; rear: rigid axle, longitudinal Watt linkage, Panhard transverse linkage bar, coil springs, telescopic dampers.

STEERING rack-and-pinion, adjustable height of steering wheel; turns lock to lock: 3.40.

BRAKES disc (front diameter 10.16 in, 25.8 cm, rear 9.17 in, 23.3 cm), dual circuit, rear compensator, servo; swept area: front 193 sq in, 1,245 sq cm, rear 155.5 sq in, 1,003 sq cm, total 348.5 sq in, 2,248 sq cm.

ELECTRICAL EQUIPMENT 12 V; 43 Ah battery; 600 W alternator; 2 headlamps.

DIMENSIONS AND WEIGHT wheel base: 96.65 in, 245 cm; tracks: 54.72 in, 139 cm front, 53.50 in, 136 cm rear; length: 157.28 in, 399 cm; width: 62,48 in, 159 cm; height: 53.15 in, 137 cm; ground clearance: 5.91 in, 15 cm; weight: 1,896 lb, 860 kg; turning circle: 30.8 ft, 9.4 m; fuel tank: 11 imp gal, 13.2 US gal, 50 l.

BODY saloon/sedan; 5 seats, separate front seats.

PRACTICAL INSTRUCTIONS fuel: 98-100 oct petrol; oil: engine 7 imp pt, 8.5 US pt, 4 l, SAE 20W-50, change every 6,200 miles, 10,000 km - gearbox and final drive 6 imp pt, 7.2 US pt, 3.4 l, SAE 90, change every 24,900 miles, 40,000 km; greasing: none; tappet clearance: inlet 0.014-0.016 in, 0.35-0.40 mm, exhaust 0.018-0.020 in, 0.45-0.50 mm; valve timing: 12° 48° 45° 7°; tyre pressure: front 28 psi, 1.9 atm, rear 21 psi, 1.5 atm.

OPTIONALS reclining backrests; heated rear window; antitheft.

68 hp power team

See 63 hp power team, except for:

ENGINE compression ratio: 9:1; max power (DIN): 68 hp (50 kW) at 6,000 rpm; max torque (DIN): 67 lb ft, 9.2 kg m (90 Nm) at 3,200 rpm; 57.3 hp/l (42.2 kW/l); 1 downdraught twin barrel carburettor.

TRANSMISSION gears: 5, fully synchronized; ratios: I 3.545, II 2.048, III 1.452, IV 1.114, V 0.921, rev 3.091; axle ratio: 4.111.

PERFORMANCE max speeds: (I) 28 mph, 45 km/h; (II) 45 mph, 73 km/h; (III) 65 mph, 105 km/h; (IV) 84 mph, 135 km/h; (V) 96 mph, 155 km/h; power-weight ratio: 28.2 lb/hp (38.4 lb/kW), 12.8 kg/hp (17.4 kg/kW); acceleration: standing ¼ mile 19.1 sec; speed in top at 1,000 rpm: 16.9 mph, 27.3 km/h; consumption: 40.9 m/imp gal, 34.1 m/US gal, 6.9 l x 100 km at 62 mph, 100 km/h.

DIMENSIONS AND WEIGHT weight: 1,918 lb, 870 kg.

OPTIONALS rev counter; light alloy wheels; headrests; metallic spray.

71 hp power team

See 63 hp power team, except for:

ENGINE 82.4 cu in, 1,350 cc (3.15 x 2.65 in, 80 x 67.2 mm); compression ratio: 9:1; max power (DIN): 71 hp (52 kW) at 5,800 rpm; max torque (DIN): 77 lb ft, 10.7 kg m (105 Nm) at 3,000 rpm; 52.6 hp/l (38.7 kW/l); 1 Solex C32 DIS/41 or Dell'Orto FRDA 32 G downdraught single barrel carburettor.

TRANSMISSION gears: 5, fully synchronized; ratios: I 3.545, II 2.048, III 1.452, IV 1.114, V 0.921, rev 3.091; axle ratio: 3.888.

71 HP POWER TEAM

PERFORMANCE max speed: over 96 mph, 155 km/h; power-weight ratio: 28.4 lb/hp (38.6 lb/kW), 12.9 kg/hp (17.6 kg/kW); consumption: 40,4 m/imp gal, 33.6 m/US gal, 7 l x 100 km at 62 mph, 100 km/h.

DIMENSIONS AND WEIGHT length: 156.69 in, 398 cm; weight: 2,018 lb, 915 kg.

BODY estate car/st. wagon; 2+1 doors.

OPTIONALS reclining backrests; heated rear window.

79 hp power team

See 63 hp power team, except for:

ENGINE 83.4 cu in, 1,350 cc (3.15 x 2.65 in, 80 x 67.2 mm); compression ratio: 9:1; max power (DIN): 79 hp (58 kW) at 6,000 rpm; max torque (DIN): 89 lb ft, 12.3 kg/m (111 Nm) at 3,500 rpm; 58.5 hp/l (43 kW/l); 1 Weber 32 DIR 81/250 downdraught twin barrel carburettor.

TRANSMISSION gears: 5, fully synchronized; ratios: I 3.545, II 2.048, III 1.452, IV 1.114, V 0.921, rev 3.091; axle ratio: 3.888.

PERFORMANCE max speed: 103 mph, 165 km/h; power-weight ratio: 24.3 lb/hp (33 lb/kW), 11 kg/hp (15 kg/kW); acceleration: standing ¼ mile 18.2 sec; speed in top at 1,000 rpm: 17.9 mph, 28.8 km/h; consumption: 40.4 m/imp gal, 33.6 m/US gal, 7 l x 100 km at 62 mph, 100 km/h.

ELECTRICAL EQUIPMENT 4 iodine headlamps (for ti only).

DIMENSIONS AND WEIGHT weight: 1,918 lb, 870 kg.

OPTIONALS light alloy wheels; metallic spray; adjustable head-rests.

85 hp power team

See 63 hp power team, except for:

ENGINE 90.9 cu in, 1,490 cc (3.31 x 2.65 in, 84 x 67.2 mm); compression ratio: 9:1; max power (DIN): 85 hp (63 kW) at 5,800 rpm; max torque (DIN): 89 lb ft, 12.3 kg/m (121 Nm) at 3,500 rpm; max engine rpm: 5,800; 57 hp/l (42.3 kW/l); 1 Weber 32 DIR 71/250 downdraught twin barrel carburettor.

TRANSMISSION gears: 5, fully synchronized; ratios: I 3.545, II 2.048, III 1.452, IV 1.114, V 0.921, rev 3.091; axle ratio: 3.888.

PERFORMANCE max speed: 105 mph, 170 km/h; power-weight ratio: 22.8 lb/hp (31 lb/kW), 10.3 kg/kW), 10.3 kg/hp (14.2 kg/kW); acceleration standing ¼ mile 17.8 sec; speed in top at 1,000 rpm: 17.9 mph, 28.8 km/h; consumption: 40.4 m/imp gal, 33.6 m/US gal, 7 l x 100 km at 62 mph, 100 km/h.

ELECTRICAL EQUIPMENT 4 iodine headlamps (for ti only).

DIMENSIONS AND WEIGHT weight: 1,940 lb, 880 kg.

OPTIONALS light alloy wheels; metallic spray.

86 hp power team

See 63 hp power team, except for:

ENGINE 82.4 cu in, 1,350 cc (3.15 x 2.65 in, 80 x 67.2 mm); compression ratio: 9.7:1; max power (DIN): 86 hp (63 kW) at 5,800 rpm; max torque (DIN): 88 lb ft, 12.1 kg m (119 Nm) at 4,000 rpm; 63.7 hp/l (46.7 kW/l); 2 downdraught twin barrel carburettors.

TRANSMISSION gears: 5, fully synchronized; ratios: I 3.545, II 2.048, III 1.452, IV 1.114, V 0.921, ref 3.091; axle ratio: 3.888.

PERFORMANCE max speed: over 105 mph, 170 km/h; power-weight ratio: 22.2 lb/hp (30.3 lb/kW), 10 kg/hp (13.7 kg/kW); consumption: 40.9 m/imp gal, 34.1 m/US gal, 6.9 l x 100 km at 75 mph, 120 km/h.

ELECTRICAL EQUIPMENT 4 iodine headlamps.

DIMENSIONS AND WEIGHT tracks: 54.99 in, 140 cm front, 53.70 in, 136 cm rear; length: 158.23 in, 402 cm; width: 63.38 in, 161 cm; height: 51.38 in, 130 cm; weight: 1,907 lb, 865 kg.

BODY coupé.

OPTIONALS light alloy wheels; metallic spray.

95 hp power team

See 63 hp power team, except for:

ENGINE 90.9 cu in, 1,490 cc (3.31 x 2.65 in, 84 x 67.2 mm); compression ratio: 9.5:1; max power (DIN): 95 hp (70 kW) at 5,800 rpm; max torque (DIN): 96 lb ft, 13.3 kg/m (131 Nm) at 4,000 rpm; 63.7 hp/l (46.9 kW/l); 2 downdraught twin barrel carburettors.

TRANSMISSION gears: 5, fully synchronized; ratios: I 3.545, II 2.048, III 1.452, IV 1.114, V 0.921, rev 3.091; axle ratio: 3.888.

PERFORMANCE max speed: over 109 mph, 175 km/h; power-weight ratio: 20.1 lb/hp (27.2 lb/kW), 9.1 kg/hp (12.3 kg/kW); consumption: 40.4 m/imp gal, 33.6 m/US gal, 7 l x 100 km at 75 mph, 120 km/h.

ELECTRICAL EQUIPMENT 4 iodine headlamps.

DIMENSIONS AND WEIGHT tracks: 54.99 in, 140 cm front, 53.70 in, 136 cm rear; length: 158.23 in, 402 cm; width: 63.38 in, 161 cm; height: 51.38 in, 130 cm; weight: 1,907 lb, 865 kg.

OPTIONALS light alloy wheels; metallic spray.

Giulietta 1.3

PRICE EX WORKS: 8,921,000* liras

ENGINE front, 4 stroke; 4 cylinders, vertical, in line; 82.8 cu in, 1,357 cc (3.15 x 2.66 in, 80 x 67.5 mm); compression ratio: 9:1; max power (DIN); 95 hp (70 kW) at 6,000 rpm; max torque (DIN): 89 lb ft, 12.3 kg m (121 Nm) at 4,500 rpm; max engine rpm: 6,100; 70 hp/l (51.5 kW/l); light alloy block and head, wet liners, hemispherical combustion chambers; 5 crankshaft bearings; valves: overhead, Vee-slanted at 80°, thimble tappets; camshafts: 2, overhead, chain-driven; lubrication: gear pump, full flow filter (cartridge), 11.4 imp pt, 13.7 US pt, 6.5 l; 2 Solex Cho ADDHE downdraught twin barrel carburettors; fuel feed: mechanical pump; water-cooled, 14.1 imp pt, 16.9 US pt, 8 l, electric thermostatic fan.

TRANSMISSION driving wheels: rear; clutch: single dry plate (diaphragm), hydraulically controlled; gearbox: mechanical, in unit with differential; gears: 5 fully synchronized; ratios: I 3.307, II 1.956, III 1.345, IV 1.026, V 0.833, rev 2.615; lever: central; final drive: hypoid bevel; axle ratio: 4.778; width of rims: 5"; tyres: 165 SR x 13 tubeless.

PERFORMANCE max speeds: (I) 25 mph, 41 km/h; (II) 43 mph, 70 km/h; (III) 63 mph, 101 km/h; (IV) 83 mph, 133 km/h; (V) 103 mph, 165 km/h; power-weight ratio: 24.9 lb/hp (33.7 lb/kW), 11.3 kg/hp (15.3 kg/kW); carrying capacity: 882 lb, 400 kg; acceleration: standing ¼ mile 18.8 sec; speed in top at 1,000 rpm: 16.9 mph, 27.2 km/h; consumption: 37.7 m/imp gal, 31.4 m/US gal, 7.5 l x 100 km.

CHASSIS integral; front suspension: independent, wishbones (upper trailing links), torsion bars, anti-roll bar, telescopic dampers; rear: de Dion rigid axle, oblique trailing arms, transverse Watt linkage, coil springs, anti-roll bar, telescopic dampers.

STEERING rack-and-pinion, adjustable height of steering wheel; turns lock to lock: 3.50.

BRAKES disc (diameter 9.84 in, 25 cm), dual circuit, rear compensator, servo; swept area: front 173.3 sq in, 1,118 sq cm, rear 156.6 sq in, 1,010 sq cm, total 329.9 sq in, 2,128 sq cm.

ELECTRICAL EQUIPMENT 12 V; 50 Ah battery; 540 W alternator; Bosch or Marelli distributor; 2 iodine headlamps.

DIMENSIONS AND WEIGHT wheel base: 98.82 in, 251 cm; front and rear track: 53.54 in, 136 cm; length: 165.75 in, 421 cm; width: 64.96 in, 165 cm; height: 55.12 in, 140 cm; ground clearance: 5.51 in, 14 cm; weight: 2,359 lb, 1,070 kg; weight distribution: 50% front, 50% rear; turning circle: 35.8 ft, 10.9 m; fuel tank: 11 imp gal, 13.2 US gal, 50 l.

BODY saloon/sedan; 4 doors; 5 seats, separate front seats, reclining backrests, adjustable headrests; heated rear window.

PRACTICAL INSTRUCTIONS fuel: 98 oct petrol; oil: engine 11.4 imp pt, 13.7 US pt, 6.5 l, SAE 10W-50, change every 6,200 miles, 10,000 km - gearbox 4.9 imp pt, 5.9 US pt, 2.8 l, SAE 90, change every 24,900 miles, 40,000 km; tappet clearances: inlet 0.019-0.020 in, 0.47-0.50 mm, exhaust 0.020-0.022 in, 0.52-0.55 mm; valve timing: 33°54' 57°54' 51°14' 21°14'; tyre pressure: front 26 psi, 1.8 atm, rear 28 psi, 2 atm.

OPTIONALS metallic spray; light alloy wheels.

Giulietta 1.6

See Giulietta 1.3, except for:

PRICE IN GB: £ 4,845*
PRICE EX WORKS: 9,499,000* liras

ENGINE 95.8 cu in, 1,570 cc (3.07 x 3.23 in, 78 x 82 mm); max power (DIN): 109 hp (80 kW) at 5,600 rpm; max torque (DIN) 105 lb ft, 14.5 kg m (142 Nm) at 4,300 rpm; max engine rpm 5,800; 69.4 hp/l (51.1 kW/l); 2 Dell'Orto DHLA 40H downdraught twin barrel carburettors.

TRANSMISSION axle ratio: 4.300.

PERFORMANCE max speeds: (I) 26 mph, 42 km/h; (II) 45 mph, 72 km/h; (III) 65 mph, 105 km/h; (IV) 86 mph, 138 km/h; (V) 109 mph, 175 km/h; power-weight ratio: 21.6 lb/hp (29.3 lb/kW), 9.8 kg/hp (13.3 kg/kW); acceleration: standing ¼ mile 17.6 sec; speed in top at 1,000 rpm: 18.8 mph, 30.2 km/h; consumption 36.2 m/imp gal, 30.2 m/US gal, 7.8 l x 100 km.

OPTIONALS air-conditioning.

Giulietta 1.8

See Giulietta 1.3, except for:

PRICE IN GB: £ 5,165*
PRICE EX WORKS: 10,030,000* liras

ENGINE 108.6 cu in, 1,779 cc (3.15 x 3.48 in, 80 x 88.5 mm) compression ratio: 9.5:1; max power (DIN): 122 hp (90 kW) at 5,300 rpm; max torque (DIN): 123 lb ft, 17 kg m (167 Nm) at 4,000 rpm; max engine rpm: 5,300; 68.6 hp/l (50.6 kW/l); 2 Dell'Orto DHLA 40 A or Solex C 40 ADDHE downdraught twin barrel carburettors with thermostatic filter.

TRANSMISSION axle ratio: 4.100; width of rims: 5,5"; tyres 185/70 SR x 13 tubeless.

PERFORMANCE max speed: 112 mph, 180 km/h; power-weight ratio: 19.9 lb/hp (26.9 lb/kW), 9 kg/hp (12.2 kg/kW); acceleration: standing ¼ mile 17.1 sec; speed in top at 1,000 rpm: 19.7 mph, 31.8 km/h; consumption: 29.4 m/imp gal, 24.5 m/US gal 9.6 l x 100 km at 75 mph, 120 km/h.

DIMENSIONS AND WEIGHT weight: 2,425 lb, 1,100 kg.

OPTIONALS air-conditioning.

ALFA ROMEO Giulietta 1.8

ALFA ROMEO Alfetta 1.6 - 1.8

Alfetta 1.6

RICE EX WORKS: 9,475,000* liras

NGINE front, 4 stroke; 4 cylinders, vertical, in line; 95.8 cu in, 570 cc (3.07 x 3.23 in, 78 x 82 mm); compression ratio: 9:1; ax power (DIN): 108 hp (79 kW) at 5,600 rpm; max torque)IN): 105 lb ft, 14.5 kg m (142 Nm) at 4,300 rpm; max engine m: 5,600; 68.8 hp/l (50.6 kW/l); light alloy block and head, et liners, hemispherical combustion chambers; 5 crankshaft earings; valves: overhead, Vee-slanted at 80°, thimble tapets; camshafts: 2, overhead; lubrication: gear pump, full flow ter (cartridge), 11.4 imp pt, 13.7 US pt, 6.5 l; 2 Dell'Orto HLA 40F horizontal twin barrel carburettors; fuel feed: mechacal pump; water-cooled, 14.1 imp pt, 16.9 US pt, 8 l, electric ermostatic fan.

RANSMISSION driving wheels: rear; clutch: single dry plate iaphragm), hydraulically controlled; gearbox: mechanical, in nit with differential; gears: 5, fully synchronized; ratios: I 300, II 2, III 1.370, IV 1.040, V 0.830, rev 2.620; lever: entral; final drive: hypoid bevel; axle ratio: 4.300; width of ms: 5.5"; tyres: 165 SR x 14.

ERFORMANCE max speeds: (I) 28 mph, 45 km/h; (II) 47 mph, 5 km/h; (III) 68 mph, 109 km/h; (IV) 90 mph, 145 km/h; (V) 109 ph, 175 km/h; power-weight ratio: 21.2 lb/hp (28.9 lb/kW), 9.6 g/hp (13.1 kg/kW); carrying capacity: 882 lb, 400 kg; acceleraon standing ¼ mile 18 sec; speed in top at 1,000 rpm: 19.4 ph, 31.2 km/h; consumption: 33.6 m/imp gal, 28 m/US gal, 8.4 x 100 km.

CHASSIS integral; front suspension: independent, wishbones (upper trailing links), torsion bars, anti-roll bar, telescopic dampers; rear: de Dion rigid axle, oblique trailing arms, transverse Watt linkage, coil springs, anti-roll bar, telescopic dampers.

STEERING rack-and-pinion, adjustable height of steering wheel; turns lock to lock: 3.50.

BRAKES disc, dual circuit, rear compensator, servo; swept area: front 182.3 sq in, 1,76 sq cm, rear 156.6 sq in, 1,010 sq cm, total 338.9 sq in, 2,186 sq cm.

ELECTRICAL EQUIPMENT 12 V; 50 Ah battery; 540 W alternator; Bosch or Marelli distributor; 4 iodine headlamps.

DIMENSIONS AND WEIGHT wheel base: 98.82 in, 251 cm; tracks: 53.54 in, 136 cm front, 53.15 in, 135 cm rear; length: 168.50 in, 428 cm; width: 63.78 in, 162 cm; height: 56.30 in, 143 cm; ground clearance: 4.92 in, 12.5 cm; weight: 2,293 lb, 1,040 kg; weight distribution: 50% front, 50% rear; turning circle: 33.1 ft, 10.1 m; fuel tank: 10.8 imp gal, 12.9 US gal, 49 l.

BODY saloon/sedan; 4 doors; 5 seats, separate front seats, reclining backrests; heated rear window.

PRACTICAL INSTRUCTIONS fuel: 98 oct petrol; oil: engine 10.4 imp pt, 12.5 US pt, 5.9 l, SAE 20W-50 change every 6,200 miles, 10,000 km - gearbox and final drive 4.9 imp pt, 5.9 US pt, 2.8 l, SAE 90, change every 18,600 miles, 30,000 km; greasing: none; tappet clearances: inlet 0.019-0.020 in, 0.47-0.50 mm, exhaust 0.020-0.022 in, 0.52-0.55 mm; valve timing: 41°20' 62°20' 62°40' 25°40'; tyre pressure: front 22 psi, 1.6 atm, rear 26 psi, 1.8 atm.

ALFA ROMEO Alfetta GTV 2000 L

OPTIONALS adjustable headrests; Texalfa interior; light alloy wheels; metallic spray; tinted glass; adjustable headrests.

Alfetta GT 1.6

See Alfetta 1.6, except for:

PRICE IN GB: £ 5,856*
PRICE EX WORKS: 10,006,000* liras

PERFORMANCE max speeds: 112 mphg, 180 km/h; power-weight ratio: 20.3 lb/hp (27.6 lb/kW), 9.2 kg/hp (12.5 kg/kW); consumption: 34 m/imp gal, 28.3 m/US gal, 8.3 l x 100 km.

DIMENSIONS AND WEIGHT wheel base: 94.49 in, 240 cm; rear track: 53.54 in, 136 cm; length: 164.96 in, 419 cm; width: 65.35 in, 166 cm; height: 52.36 in, 133 cm; ground clearance: 4.80 in, 12 cm; weight: 2,183 lb, 990 kg.

BODY coupé; 2 doors; 4 seats, separate front seats, reclining backrests.

OPTIONALS 185/70 HR x 14 tyres.

Alfetta 1.8

See Alfetta 1.6, except for:

PRICE EX WORKS: 10,006,000* liras

ENGINE 108.6 cu in, 1,779 cc (3.15 x 3.48 in, 80 x 88.5 mm); compression ratio: 9.5:1; max power (DIN): 118 hp (87 kW) at 5,300 rpm; max torque (DIN): 123 lb ft, 17 kg m (167 Nm) at 4,400 rpm; max engine rpm: 5,300; 66.3 hp/l (48.8 kW/l); 2 Dell'Orto DHLA 40 (or Solex C40 DDHE or Weber 40 DCOE 32) horizontal twin barrel carburettors.

TRANSMISSION axle ratio: 4.100.

PERFORMANCE max speeds: (I) 29 mph, 46 km/h; (II) 48 mph, 77 km/h; (III) 70 mph, 112 km/h; (IV) 92 mph, 148 km/h; (V) 112 mph, 180 km/h; power-weight ratio: 19.8 lb/hp (26.9 lb/kW), 9 kg/hp (12.2 kg/kW); acceleration standing ¼ mile 17.3 sec; speed in top at 1,000 rpm: 20.8 mph, 33.5 km/h; consumption: 32.1 m/imp gal, 26.7 m/US gal, 8.8 l x 100 km.

DIMENSIONS AND WEIGHT weight: 2,337 lb, 1,060 kg.

OPTIONALS air-conditioning with tinted glass.

Alfetta 2000 L

See Alfetta 1.6, except for:

PRICE IN GB: £ 5,749*
PRICE EX WORKS: 11,847,000* liras

ENGINE 119.7 cu in, 1,962 cc ((3.31 x 3.48 in, 84 x 88.5 mm); max power (DIN): 130 hp (96 kW) at 5,400 rpm; max torque (DIN): 131 lb ft, 18.1 kg m (177 Nm) at 4,000 rpm; max engine rpm: 5,400; 66.2 hp/l (48.7 kW/l); 2 Dell'Orto DHLA 40 horizontal twin barrel carburettors.

TRANSMISSION axle ratio: 4.100; tyres: 165 HR x 14.

PERFORMANCE max speeds: (I) 28 mph, 45 km/h; (II) 46 mph, 74 km/h; (III) 68 mph, 109 km/h; (IV) 89 mph, 143 km/h; (V) 115 mph, 185 km/h; power-weight ratio: 18.5 lb/hp (24.1 lb/kW), 8.4 kg/hp (11.4 kg/kW); acceleration: standing ¼ mile 16.4 sec; speed in top at 1,000 rpm: 20.6 mph, 33.2 km/h; consumption: 29.7 m/imp gal, 24.8 m/US gal, 9.5 l x 100 km.

ELECTRICAL EQUIPMENT 60 Ah battery.

DIMENSIONS AND WEIGHT rear track: 53.46 in, 136 cm; length: 172.64 in, 438 cm; width: 64.57 in, 164 cm; ground clearance: 5.51 in, 14 cm; weight: 2,403 lb, 1,090 kg.

PRACTICAL INSTRUCTIONS valve timing: 41°20' 60°20' 53°40' 34°40'; tyre pressure: front 26 psi, 1.8 atm, rear 26 psi, 1.8 atm.

OPTIONALS ZF automatic transmission; limited slip differential; automatic levelling system; 185/70 HR x 14 tyres; light alloy wheels; metallic spray; air-conditioning; sunshine roof.

Alfetta GTV 2000 L

See Alfetta 1.6, except for:

PRICE IN GB: £ 6,526*
PRICE IN USA: $ 10,995*

ENGINE 119.7 cu in, 1,962 cc (3.31 x 3.48 in, 84 x 88.5 mm); max power (DIN): 130 hp (96 kW) at 5,400 rpm; max torque (DIN): 131 lb ft, 18.1 kg m (177 Nm) at 4,000 rpm; max engine rpm: 5,400; 66.2 hp/l (48.7 kW/l); 2 twin barrel carburettors.

TRANSMISSION axle ratio: 4.100; tyres: 165 HR x 14.

PERFORMANCE max speed: 121 mph, 194 km/h; power-weight ratio: 16.8 lb/hp (22.8 lb/kW), 7.6 kg/hp (10.3 kg/kW); speed in

ALFETTA GTV 2000 L

top at 1,000 rpm: 20.8 mph, 33.5 km/h; consumption: 31.4 m/imp gal, 26.1 m/US gal, 9 l x 100 km.

ELECTRICAL EQUIPMENT 60 Ah battery.

DIMENSIONS AND WEIGHT wheel base: 94.49 in, 240 cm; rear track: 53.54 in, 136 cm; length: 165.35 in, 420 cm; width: 65.35 in, 166 cm; height: 52.36 in, 133 cm; ground clearance: 4.80 in, 12 cm; weight: 2,183 lb, 990 kg.

BODY coupé; 2 doors; 4 seats, separate front seats, reclining backests.

PRACTICAL INSTRUCTIONS valve timing: 41°20' 60°20' 53°40' 34°40'.

OPTIONALS 185/70 HR x 14 tyres; light alloy wheels; metallic spray; air-conditioning.

Alfetta GTV 2000 Turbodelta

See Alfetta 1.6, except for:

PRICE EX WORKS: 17,098,000* liras

ENGINE turbocharged; 119.7 cu in, 1,962 cc (3.31 x 3.48 in, 84 x 88.5 mm); compression ratio: 7.1:1; max power (DIN): 150 hp (110 kW) at 5,500 rpm; max torque (DIN): 170 lb ft, 23.5 kg m (231 Nm) at 4,000 rpm; max engine rpm: 5,500; 76.4 hp/l (56.1 kW/l); 2 twin barrel carburettors with exhaust turbochager; fuel feed: electric pump.

TRANSMISSION axle ratio: 4.100; tyres: 185/70 HR x 14 (standard).

PERFORMANCE max speed: 127 mph, 205 km/h; power-weight ratio: 14.5 lb/hp (19.8 lb/kW), 6.6 kg/hp (9 kg/kW); consumption: 23.2 m/imp gal, 19.3 m/US gal, 12.2 l x 100 km at 75 mph, 120 km/h.

ELECTRICAL EQUIPMENT 60 Ah battery.

DIMENSIONS AND WEIGHT wheel base: 94.49 in, 240 cm; rear track: 53.54 in, 136 cm; length: 165.35 in, 420 cm; width: 65.35 in, 166 cm; height: 52.36 in, 133 cm; ground clearance: 4.80 in, 12 cm; weight: 2,183 lb, 990 kg.

BODY coupé; 2 doors; 4 seats, separate front seats, reclining backrests.

PRACTICAL INSTRUCTIONS valve timing: 41°20' 60°20' 53°40' 34°40'.

OPTIONALS only metallic spray and light alloy wheels.

Alfetta 2000 Turbo D

ENGINE diesel VM system; front, 4 stroke; 4 cylinders, vertical, in line; 121.7 cu in, 1,995 cc (3.46 x 3.23 in, 88 x 82 mm); compression ratio: 22:1; max power (DIN): 82 hp (60 kW) at 4,300 rpm; max torque (DIN): 120 lb ft, 16.5 kg m (162 Nm) at 2,300 rpm; max engine rpm: 4,300; 41.1 hp/l (30.1 kW/l); cast iron block, light alloy head; 5 crankshaft bearings; valves: overhead, in line, push-rods and rockers; camshafts: 1, in side; lubrication: gear pump, full flow filter, 10.7 imp pt, 12.9 US pt, 6.1 l; injection pump with exhaust turbocharger; water-cooled, expansion tank, 17.6 imp pt, 21.1 US pt, 10 l, electric thermostatic fan.

TRANSMISSION driving wheels: rear; clutch: single dry plate (diaphragm), hydraulically controlled; gearbox: mechanical, in unit with differential; gears: 5, fully synchronized; ratios: I 3.500, II 2, III 1.370, IV 1.040, V 0.780, rev 3; lever: central; final drive: hypoid bevel; axle ratio: 4.100; width of rims: 5.5"; tyres: 165 SR x 14.

PERFORMANCE max speeds: (I) 21 mph, 34 km/h; (II) 37 mph, 59 km/h; (III) 53 mph, 86 km/h; (IV) 73 mph, 118 km/h; (V) over 96 mph, 155 km/h; power-weight ratio: 33.6 lb/hp (45.9 lb/kW), 15.2 kg/hp (20.8 kg/kW); carrying capacity: 882 lb, 400 kg; acceleration: standing ¼ mile 19.7 sec; speed in top at 1,000 rpm: 21.9 mph, 35.3 km/h; consumption: 31.7 m/imp gal, 26.4 m/US gal, 8.9 l x 100 km at 75 mph, 120 km/h.

CHASSIS integral; front suspension: independent, wishbones (upper trailing links), torsion bars, anti-roll bar, telescopic dampers; rear: de Dion rigid axle, oblique trailing arms, transverse Watt linkage, coil springs, anti-roll bar, telescopic dampers.

STEERING rack-and-pinion, adjustable height of steering wheel; turns lock to lock: 3.80.

BRAKES disc, dual circuit, rear compensator, servo; swept area: front 182.3 sq in, 1,176 sq cm, rear 156.6 sq in, 1,010 sq cm, total 338.9 sq in, 2,186 sq cm.

ELECTRICAL EQUIPMENT 12 V; 77 Ah battery; 770 W alternator; 2 iodine headlamps.

DIMENSIONS AND WEIGHT wheel base: 98.82 in, 251 cm; tracks: 53.54 in, 136 cm front, 54.13 in, 137 cm rear; length: 172.64 in, 438 cm; width: 64.57 in, 164 cm; height: 56.30 in, 143 cm; ground clearance: 5.51 in, 14 cm; weight: 2,756 lb, 1,250 kg; weight distribution: 50% front, 50% rear; turning circle: 33.1 ft, 10.1 m; fuel tank: 10.8 imp gal, 12.9 US gal, 49 l.

BODY saloon/sedan; 4 doors; 5 seats, separate front seats, reclining backrests; heated rear window.

PRACTICAL INSTRUCTIONS fuel: diesel oil; oil: engine 10.7 imp pt, 12.9 US pt, 6.1 l, change every 3,100 miles, 5,000 km - gearbox and final drive 4.9 imp pt, 5.9 US pt, 2.8 l, SAE 90, change every 24,800 miles, 40,000 km; greasing: none; tappets clearance: inlet 0.012 in, 0.30 mm, exhaust 0.018 in, 0.45 mm; valve timing: 30° 62° 76° 32°; tyre pressure: front 22 psi, 1.6 atm, rear 26 psi, 1.8 atm.

OPTIONALS light alloy wheels; metallic spray; air-conditioning; sunshine roof.

ALFA ROMEO Alfetta 2000 Turbo D

ALFA ROMEO Alfa 6

2000 Spider Veloce

PRICE IN USA: $ 12,415*
PRICE EX WORKS: 11,493,000* liras

ENGINE front, 4 stroke; 4 cylinders, vertical, in line; 119.7 cu in, 1,962 cc (3.31 x 3.48 in, 84 x 88.5 mm); compression ratio: 9:1; max power (SAE): 147 hp (108 kW) at 5,300 rpm; max torque (SAE): 151 lb ft, 20.9 kg m (205 Nm) at 4,400 rpm; max engine rpm: 5,300; 74.9 hp/l (55.1 kW/l); light alloy block and head, wet liners, hemispherical combustion chambers; 5 crankshaft bearings; valves: overhead, Vee-slanted at 80°, thimble tappets; camshafts: 2, overhead; lubrication: gear pump, full flow filter (cartridge), 12.7 imp pt, 15.2 US pt, 7.2 l; 2 Solex C 40 DDH5 or Dell'Orto DHLA 40 horizontal twin barrel carbure tors; fuel feed: mechanical pump; water-cooled, 17.1 imp p 20.5 US pt, 9.7 l.

TRANSMISSION driving wheels: rear; clutch: single dry plat hydraulically controlled; gearbox: mechanical; gears: 5, fu synchronized; ratios: I 3.300, II 1.990, III 1.350, IV 1, V 0.79 rev 3.010; lever: central; final drive: hypoid bevel, limited sl differential; axle ratio: 4.100; width of rims: 5.5"; tyres: 1 HR x 14.

PERFORMANCE max speeds: (I) 29 mph, 47 km/h; (II) 48 mp 77 km/h; (III) 71 mph, 114 km/h; (IV) 96 mph, 154 km/h; (over 121 mph, 195 km/h; power-weight ratio: 15.7 lb/hp (21 lb/kW), 7.1 kg/hp (9.6 kg/kW); carrying capacity: 772 lb, 350 k acceleration: standing ¼ mile 16.8 sec; speed in top at 1,0 rpm: 20.9 mph, 33.7 km/h; consumption: 23.7 m/imp gal, 19 m/US gal, 11.9 l x 100 km.

CHASSIS integral; front suspension: independent, wishbon (lower trailing links), coil springs, anti-roll bar, telescopic da pers; rear: rigid axle, trailing lower radius arms, upper tra verse Vee radius arm, coil springs, anti-roll bar, telescop dampers.

STEERING recirculating ball or worm and roller; turns lock lock: 3.70.

BRAKES disc, rear compensator, servo; swept area: fro 229.8 sq in, 1,482 sq cm, rear 167.1 sq in, 1,078 sq cm, to 396.9 sq in, 2,560 sq cm.

ELECTRICAL EQUIPMENT 12 V; 50 Ah battery; 540 W altern tor; Bosch or Marelli distribution; 4 iodine headlamps.

DIMENSIONS AND WEIGHT wheel base: 88.58 in, 225 cm; tracks: 52.13 in, 132 cm front, 50.16 in, 127 cm rear; length: 162.20 in, 412 cm; width: 64.17 in, 163 cm; height: 50.79 in, 129 cm; ground clearance: 4.72 in, 12 cm; weight: 2,293 lb, 1,040 kg; turning circle: 34.4 ft, 10.5 m; fuel tank: 11.2 imp gal, 13.5 US gal, 51 l.

BODY convertible; 2 doors; 2 + 2 seats, separate front seats, reclining backrests; heated rear window.

PRACTICAL INSTRUCTIONS fuel: 98-100 oct petrol; oil: engine 11.8 imp pt, 14.2 US pt, 6.7 l, SAE 20W-50, change every 6,200 miles, 10,000 km - gearbox 3.2 imp pt, 3.8 US pt, 1.8 l, SAE 90 EP, change every 11,200 miles, 18,000 km - final drive 2.5 imp pt, 3 US pt, 1.4 l, SAE 90 EP, change every 11,200 miles, 18,000 km; greasing: every 18,600 miles, 30,000 km, 1 point; tappet clearance: inlet 0.019-0.020 in, 0.47-0.50 mm, exhaust 0.020-0.022 in, 0.52-0.55 mm; valve timing: 41°20' 62°20' 53°40' 34°40'; tyre pressure: front 24 psi, 1.7 atm, rear 26 psi, 1.8 atm.

OPTIONALS hardtop; adjustable headrests; light alloy wheels; metallic spray.

Alfa 6

PRICE EX WORKS: 20,453,000* liras

ENGINE front, 4 stroke; 6 cylinders, Vee-slanted at 60°; 152.1 cu in, 2,492 cc (3.46 x 2.69 in, 88 x 68.3 mm); compression ratio: 9:1; max power (DIN): 160 hp (118 kW) at 5,800 rpm; max torque (DIN): 162 lb ft, 22.4 kg m (120 Nm) at 4,000 rpm; max engine rpm: 5,800; 64.2 hp/l (47.4 kW/l); light alloy block and head, wet liners, hemispherical combustion chambers; 4 crankshaft bearings; valves: overhead, Vee-slanted at 46°45', thimble tappets, push-rods and rockers; camshafts: 2, 1 per bank, overhead, cogged belt; lubrication: gear pump, full flow filter, 10.6 imp pt, 12.7 US pt, 6 l; 6 Dell'Orto FRPA 40 downdraught single barrel carburettors with thermostatic filter; fuel feed: electric pump; cooling liquid, 21.1 imp pt, 25.4 US pt, 12 l, electric thermostatic fan.

TRANSMISSION driving wheels: rear; clutch: single dry plate (diaphragm), hydraulically controlled; gearbox: mechanical; gears: 5, fully synchronized; ratios: I 3.420, II 1.940, III 1.390, IV 1, V 0.790, rev 3.670; lever: central; final drive: hypoid bevel, limited slip differential (25%); axle ratio: 4.540; width of rims: 6"; tyres: 195/70 HR x 14 tubeless.

PERFORMANCE max speeds: (I) 27 mph, 43 km/h; (II) 47 mph, 75 km/h; (III) 65 mph, 105 km/h; (IV) 91 mph, 146 km/h; (V) over 121 mph, 195 km/h; power-weight ratio: 19.7 lb/hp (26.7 lb/kW), 8.9 kg/hp (12.1 kg/kW); carrying capacity: 992 lb, 450 kg; acceleration standing ¼ mile 16.7 sec, 0-50 mph (0-80 km/h) 6.9 sec; speed in top at 1,000 rpm: 19.7 mph, 31.8 km/h; consumption: 28.2 m/imp gal, 23.5 m/US gal, 10 l x 100 km (CUNA).

CHASSIS integral; front suspension: independent, wishbones (upper trailing links), torsion bars, anti-roll bar, telescopic dampers; rear: de Dion rigid axle, oblique trailing arms, transverse Watt linkage, coil springs, anti-roll bar, telescopic dampers.

STEERING rack-and-pinion, adjustable height of steering wheel, servo; turns lock to lock: 3.70.

BRAKES disc (diameter 10.24, 26 cm), front internal radial fins, dual circuit, rear compensator, servo; swept area: front 222.8 sq in, 1,437 sq cm, rear 180.2 sq in, 1,162 sq cm, total 403 sq in, 2,599 sq cm.

ELECTRICAL EQUIPMENT 12 V; 77 Ah battery; 780 W alternator; Marelli or Bosch electric ignition; 4 iodine headlamps.

DIMENSIONS AND WEIGHT wheel base: 102.36 in, 260 cm; tracks: 55.43 in, 141 cm front, 53.74 in, 136 cm rear; length: 187.40 in, 476 cm; 476 cm; width: 66.30 in, 168 cm; height: 54.88 in, 139 cm; ground clearance: 5.51 in, 14 cm; weight: 3,153 lb, 1,430 kg; turning circle: 36.7 ft, 11.2 m; fuel tank: 16.9 imp gal, 20.3 US gal, 77 l.

BODY saloon/sedan; 4 doors, 5 seats, separate front seats, reclining backrests with built-in headrests; electric windows; heated rear window; tinted glass.

PRACTICAL INSTRUCTIONS fuel: 98 oct petrol; oil: engine 10.6 imp pt, 12.7 US pt, 6 l, SAE 10W-50, change every 6,200 miles, 10,000 km - gearbox 2,8 imp pt, 3.4 US pt, 1.6 l, SAE 30 W, change every 24,800 miles, 40,000 km - final drive 2.1 imp pt, 2.5 US pt, 1.2 l, SAE 80 W/90, change every 24,800 miles, 40,000 km; greasing: none; tappet clearances: inlet 0.018 in, 0.47 mm, exhaust 0.009 in, 0.25 mm (adjustable); valve timing: 36°50' 60°50' 59°55' 23°55'; tyre pressure: front 27 psi, 1.9 atm, rear 28 psi, 2 atm.

OPTIONALS ZF automatic transmission with 3 ratios (I 2.480, II 1.480, III 1, rev 2.090), 3.610 axle ratio; light alloy wheels; metallic spray; air-conditioning; leather upholstery.

AUTOBIANCHI ITALY

A 112 Junior

PRICE EX WORKS: 4,596,000 liras**

ENGINE front, transverse, 4 stroke; 4 cylinders, in line; 55.1 cu in, 903 cc (2.56 x 2.68 in, 65 x 68 mm); compression ratio: 9:1; max power (DIN): 42 hp (31 kW) at 5,400 rpm; max torque (DIN): 51 lb ft, 7 kg m (69 Nm) at 2,800 rpm; max engine rpm: 6,400; 46.5 hp/l (34.2 kW/l); cast iron cylinder block, light alloy head; 3 crankshaft bearings; valves: overhead, push-rods and rockers; camshafts: 1, side; lubrication: gear pump, cartridge filter, 7 imp pt, 8.5 US pt, 4 l; 1 Weber 32 IBA 23 downdraught single barrel carburettor; fuel feed: mechanical pump; water-cooled, 8.8 imp pt, 10.6 US pt, 5 l, electric thermostatic fan.

TRANSMISSION driving wheels: front; clutch: single dry plate; gearbox: mechanical; gears: 4, fully synchronized; ratios: I 3.909, II 2.055, III 1.348, IV 0.963, rev 3.615; lever: central; final drive: cylinders gears; axle ratio: 4.461; width of rims: 4"; tyres: 135 SR x 13.

PERFORMANCE max speeds: (I) 23 mph, 37 km/h; (II) 43 mph, 70 km/h; (III) 66 mph, 107 km/h; (IV) 84 mph, 135 km/h; power-weight ratio: 34.4 lb/hp (46.7 lb/kW), 15.6 kg/hp (21.2 kg/kW); carrying capacity: 882 lb, 400 kg; speed in top at 1,000 rpm: 14.5 mph, 23.3 km/h; consumption: 44.8 m/imp gal, 37.3 m/US gal, 6.3 l x 100 km (CUNA).

CHASSIS integral; front suspension independent, by McPherson, coil springs/telescopic damper struts, lower wishbones (trailing links), anti-roll bar; rear: independent, wishbones, transverse anti-roll leafspring lower arms, telescopic dampers.

STEERING rack-and-pinion; turns lock to lock: 3.40.

BRAKES front disc, rear drum, dual circuit, rear compensator; lining area: front 19.2 sq in, 124 sq cm, rear 33.5 sq in, 216 sq cm, total 52.7 sq in, 340 sq cm.

ELECTRICAL EQUIPMENT 12 V; 34 Ah battery; 400 W alternator; Marelli distributor; 2 headlamps.

DIMENSIONS AND WEIGHT wheel base: 80.24 in, 204 cm; tracks: 49.21 in, 125 cm front, 48.19 in, 122 cm rear; length: 127.09 in, 323 cm; width: 58.27 in, 148 cm; height: 53.54 in, 136 cm; ground clearance: 5.59 in, 14.2 cm; weight: 1,444 lb, 655 kg; weight distribution: 60% front, 40% rear; turning circle: 29.2 ft, 8.9 m; fuel tank: 6.6 imp gal, 7.9 US gal, 30 l.

BODY saloon/sedan; 2+1 doors; 5 seats, separate front seats, reclining backrests; folding rear seat.

PRACTICAL INSTRUCTIONS fuel: 98 oct petrol; oil: engine 7 imp pt, 8.5 US pt, 4 l, SAE 10W-20 (winter) 30W-40 (summer), change every 6,200 miles, 10,000 km - gearbox and final drive 4.2 imp pt, 5.1 US pt, 2.4 l, ZC 90, change every 18,600 miles, 30,000 km; greasing: none; tappet clearances: inlet 0.006 in, 0.15 mm, exhaust 0.006 in, 0.15 mm; valve timing: 11° 43° 43° 11°; tyre pressure: front 24 psi, 1.7 atm, rear 27 psi, 1.9 atm.

OPTIONALS light alloy wheels; heated rear window; reclining backrests; headrests; iodine headlamps; rear window wiper-washer; rev counter.

A 112 Elegant

See A 112 Junior, except for:

PRICE EX WORKS: 4,962,000 liras**

ENGINE 58.9 cu in, 965 cc (2.65 x 2.68 in, 67.2 x 68 mm); compression ratio: 9.2:1; max power (DIN): 48 hp (35 kW) at 5,600 rpm; max torque (DIN): 53 lb ft, 7.3 kg m (72 Nm) at 3,300 rpm; 49.7 hp/l (36.5 kW/l); 1 Weber 30 IBA 27 downdraught single barrel carburettor.

PERFORMANCE max speed: 87 mph, 140 km/h; power-weight ratio: 31 lb/hp (42.2 lb/kW), 14 kg/hp (19.1 kg/kW); consumption: 40.9 m/imp gal, 34.1 m/US gal, 6.9 l x 100 km (CUNA).

DIMENSIONS AND WEIGHT weight: 1,488 lb, 675 kg.

BODY special luxury interior.

PRACTICAL INSTRUCTIONS tappet clearances: inlet 0.006 in, 0.15 mm, exhaust 0.008 in, 0.20 mm; valve timing: 17° 43° 57° 3°.

A 112 Elite

See A 112 Junior, except for:

PRICE EX WORKS: 4,446,000 liras**

ENGINE 58.9 cu in, 965 cc (2.65 x 2.68 in, 67.2 x 68 mm); compression ratio: 9.2:1; max power (DIN): 48 hp (35 kW) at 5,600 rpm; max torque (DIN): 53 lb ft, 7.3 kg m (72 Nm) at 3,300 rpm; 49.7 hp/l (36.5 kW/l); 1 Weber 30 IBA 27 downdraught single barrel carburettor.

TRANSMISSION gears: 5, fully synchronized; ratios: I 3.909, II 2.055, III 1.348, IV 0.963, V 0.828, rev 3.615.

PERFORMANCE max speed: 87 mph, 140 km/h; power-weight ratio: 31 lb/hp (42,2 lb/kW), 14 kg/hp (19.1 kg/kW); speed in top at 1,000 rpm: 16.8 mph, 27.1 km/h; consumption: 42.8 m/imp gal, 35.6 m/US gal, 6.6 l x 100 km (CUNA).

ELECTRICAL EQUIPMENT electronic ignition with impulser unit.

DIMENSIONS AND WEIGHT weight: 1,488 lb, 675 kg.

BODY special luxury interior.

PRACTICAL INSTRUCTIONS oil: gearbox and final drive 4.6 imp pt, 5.5 US pt, 2.6 l; tappet clearances: inlet 0.006 in, 0.15 mm, exhaust 0.008 in, 0.20 mm; valve timing: 17° 43° 57° 3°.

A 112 Abarth

See A 112 Junior, except for:

PRICE EX WORKS: 5,717,000 liras**

ENGINE 64.1 cu in, 1,050 cc (2.65 x 2.91 in, 67.2 x 74 mm); compression ratio: 10.4:1; max power (DIN): 70 hp (51 kW) at 6,600 rpm; max torque (DIN): 63 lb ft, 8.7 kg m (85 Nm) at 4,200 rpm; max engine rpm: 7,000; 66.7 hp/l (49.1 kW/l); lubrication: 7.9 imp pt, 9.5 US pt, 4.5 l; Weber 32 DMTR 3 vertical twin barrel carburettor.

AUTOBIANCHI A 112 Elite

A 112 ABARTH

TRANSMISSION gears: 5, fully synchronized; ratios: I 3.909, II 2.055, III 1.348, IV 0.963, V 0.828, rev 3.615.

PERFORMANCE max speed: 99 mph, 160 km/h; power-weight ratio: 22.1 lb/hp (30 lb/kW), 10 kg/hp (13.6 kg/kW); speed in top at 1,000 rpm: 16.8 mph, 27.1 km/h; consumption: 38.2 m/imp gal, 31.8 m/US gal, 7.4 l x 100 km (CUNA).

BRAKES servo.

ELECTRICAL EQUIPMENT electronic ignition with impulser unit; 2 iodine headlamps (standard).

DIMENSIONS AND WEIGHT weight: 1,544 lb, 700 kg; weight distribution 62% front, 38% rear.

BODY built-in headrests (standard); rev counter (standard).

PRACTICAL INSTRUCTIONS oil: engine 7.9 imp pt, 9.5 US pt, 4.5 l - gearbox and final drive 4.6 imp pt, 5.5 US pt, 2.6 l; tappet clearances: inlet 0.010 in, 0.25 mm, exhaust 0.012 in, 0.30 mm; valve timing: 16° 56° 56° 16°.

DE TOMASO Pantera L

DE TOMASO ITALY

Pantera L

PRICE IN GB: £ 18,585*
PRICE EX WORKS: 26,850,000 liras**

ENGINE Ford, centre-rear, 4 stroke; 8 cylinders, Vee-slanted at 90°; 351.7 cu in, 5,763 cc (4 x 3.50 in, 101.6 x 89 mm); compression ratio: 8.5:1; max power (SAE): 330 hp (243 kW) at 5,400 rpm; max torque (SAE): 326 lb ft, 45 kg m (441 Nm) at 3,400 rpm; max engine rpm: 6,000; 53.8 hp/l (42.2 kW/l); cast iron block and head; 5 crankshaft bearings; valves: overhead, slanted, push-rods and rockers, hydraulic tappets; camshafts: 1, at centre of Vee; lubrication: rotary pump, full flow filter, 9.7 imp pt, 11.6 US pt, 5.5 l; 1 Motorcraft downdraught 4-barrel carburettor; fuel feed: mechanical pump; water-cooled, 42.2 imp pt, 50.7 US pt, 24 l, electric fan.

TRANSMISSION driving wheels: rear; clutch: single dry plate, hydraulically controlled; gearbox: ZF mechanical; gears: 5, fully synchronized; ratios: I 2.230, II 1.475, III 1.040, IV 0.846 V 0.705, rev 2.865; lever: central; final drive: spiral bevel, limited slip differential; axle ratio: 4.220; width of rims: 7" front, 8" rear; tyres: 185/70 VR x 15 front, 215/70 VR x 15 rear.

PERFORMANCE max speed: 158 mph, 254 km/h; power-weight ratio: 9.5 lb/hp (12.9 lb/kW), 4.3 kg/hp (5.8 kg/kW); speed in top at 1,000 rpm: 27 mph, 43.5 km/h; consumption: 14.1 m/imp gal, 11.8 m/US gal, 20 l x 100 km.

CHASSIS integral; front and rear suspension: independent, wishbones, coil springs, anti-roll bar, telescopic dampers.

STEERING rack-and-pinion; turns lock to lock: 3.40.

DE TOMASO Pantera GTS

BRAKES disc (front diameter 11.18 in, 28.4 cm, rear 11.10 i 28.2 cm), dual circuit, internal radial fins, servo.

ELECTRICAL EQUIPMENT 12 V; 72 Ah battery; 55 A altern tor; 4 retractable headlamps.

DIMENSIONS AND WEIGHT wheel base: 98.82 in, 251 cm tracks: 57.09 in, 145 cm front, 57.48 in, 146 cm rear; lengt 168.11 in, 427 cm; width: 72.05 in, 183 cm; height: 43.31 i 110 cm; ground clearance: 4.72 in, 12 cm; weight: 3,131 l 1,420 kg; turning circle: 39.4 ft, 12 m; fuel tank: 17.6 imp ga 21.1 US gal, 80 l.

BODY coupé; 2 doors; 2 seats, built-in headrests; electr windows; tinted glass; heated rear window; air-conditionin light alloy wheels.

PRACTICAL INSTRUCTIONS fuel: 98-100 oct petrol; oil: er gine 9.2 imp pt, 11 US pt, 5.2 l, SAE 10W-40 (winter) 20W-5 (summer), change every 3,100 miles, 5,000 km - gearbox an final drive 6 imp pt, 7.2 US pt, 3.4 l, SAE 90, change eve 3,700 miles, 6,000 km; greasing: every 3,700 miles, 6,000 km points; valve timing: 14° 72° 70° 20°.

OPTIONALS 225/50 VR x 15 P7 front and 285/50 VR x 15 P rear tyres with 10" wide rims; right hand drive; metallic spra leather interior.

Pantera GTS

See Pantera L, except for:

PRICE IN GB: £ 19,061*
PRICE EX WORKS: 27,900,000 liras**

ENGINE max power (SAE): 350 hp (258 kW) at 6,000 rpm; ma torque (SAE): 333 lb ft, 46 kg m (451 Nm) at 3,800 rpm; 60. hp/l (44.7 kW/l).

PERFORMANCE max speed: about 174 mph, 280 km/h; powe weight ratio: 9 lb/hp (12.2 lb/kW), 4.1 kg/hp (5.5 kg/kW).

BODY front and rear spoiler.

DE TOMASO Deauville

Deauville

See Pantera L, except for:

PRICE IN GB: £ 24,418*
PRICE EX WORKS: 34,600,000 liras**

ENGINE Ford, front, 4 stroke; cooling, 31.7 imp pt, 38.1 US p 18 l.

TRANSMISSION gearbox: Select-Shift Cruise-o-Matic automa tic transmission, hydraulic torque converter and planetary gea with 3 ratios, max ratio of converter at stall 2.05, possib manual selection; ratios: I 2.460, II 1.460, III 1, rev 2.100; ax ratio: 3.070; width of rims: 7"; tyres: 215/70 VR x 15.

PERFORMANCE max speed: over 143 mph, 230 km/h; powe weight ratio: 13 lb/hp (17.6 lb/kW), 5.9 kg/hp (8 kg/kW); ca rying capacity: 1,169 lb, 530 kg; acceleration: standing ¼ mil 16 sec; speed in direct drive at 1,000 rpm: 23.9 mph, 38. km/h; consumption: 16 m/imp gal, 13.4 m/US gal, 17.6 l x 10 km.

HASSIS rear suspension: trailing radius arms, 4 coil springs, telescopic dampers.

TEERING servo.

IMENSIONS AND WEIGHT wheel base: 109.05 in, 277 cm; ont and rear track: 59.84 in, 152 cm; length: 195.52 in, 489 n; width: 73.94 in, 188 cm; height: 53.86 in, 137 cm; ground earance: 5.12 in, 13 cm; weight: 4,278 lb, 1,940 kg; turning rcle: 42.6 ft, 13 m; fuel tank: 26.4 imp gal, 31.7 US gal, 120 l.

ODY saloon/sedan; 4 doors; 5 seats, separate front seats, clining backrests; air-conditioning; electric windows; tinted ass; electric rear view mirror; roll safety belts; adjustable eering wheel; halogen headlamps; light alloy wheels; head- sts; leather upholstery; heated rear window; front spoiler.

RACTICAL INSTRUCTIONS oil: engine 7 imp pt, 8.5 US pt, 4 - automatic transmission 17.6 imp pt, 21.1 US pt, 10 l - final ive 3.2 imp pt, 3.8 US pt, 1.8 l.

PTIONALS oil cooler; right hand drive; metallic spray.

Longchamp 2+2

ee Pantera L, except for:

RICE IN GB: £ 21,285*
RICE EX WORKS: 32,500,000 liras**

NGINE Ford, front, 4 stroke; cooling, 31.7 imp pt, 38.1 US pt, 8 l.

RANSMISSION gearbox: Select-Shift Cruise-o-Matic automa- c transmission, hydraulic torque converter and planetary gears ith 3 ratios, max ratio of converter at stall 2.05 possible anual selection; ratios: I 2.460, II 1.460, III 1, rev 2.100; axle tio: 3.070; width of rims: 7"; tyres: 215/70 VR x 15.

ERFORMANCE max speed: 149 mph, 240 km/h; power-weight tio: 11.6 lb/hp (16.3 lb/kW), 5.3 kg/hp (7.2 kg/kW); speed in rect at 1,000 rpm: 24.9 mph, 40 km/h; consumption: 16.6 /imp gal, 13.8 m/US gal, 17 l x 100 km.

HASSIS rear suspension: trailing radius arms, 4 coil springs, telescopic dampers.

TEERING servo.

LECTRICAL EQUIPMENT 61 A alternator; 2 headlamps.

IMENSIONS AND WEIGHT wheel base: 102.36 in, 260 cm ont and rear track: 59.84 in, 152 cm; length: 177.95 in, 452 n; width: 72.44 in, 184 cm; height: 50.79 in, 129 cm; ground earance: 5.91 in, 15 cm; weight: 3,858 lb, 1,750 kg; turning rcle: 37.7 ft, 11.5 m; fuel tank: 22 imp gal, 26.4 US gal, 100 l.

ODY coupé; 2 doors; 2 + 2 seats, separate front seats, reclin- g backrests; air-conditioning; electric windows; tinted glass; ectric rear view mirror; roll safety belts; adjustable steering heel; halogen headlamps; light alloy wheels; headrests; leath- upholstery; heated rear window; front spoiler.

RACTICAL INSTRUCTIONS oil: engine 7 imp pt, 8.5 US pt, 4 - automatic transmission 17.6 imp pt, 21.1 US pt, 10 l - final ive 3.2 imp pt, 3.8 US pt, 1.8 l.

PTIONALS oil cooler; right hand drive; metallic spray.

DE TOMASO Longchamp 2+2

FERRARI ITALY

Dino 208 GT 4

PRICE EX WORKS: 23,069,000* liras

ENGINE centre-rear, transverse, 4 stroke; 8 cylinders, Vee-slanted at 90°; 121.5 cu in, 1,991 cc (2.63 x 2.80 in, 66.8 x 71 mm); compression ratio: 9:1; max power (DIN): 160 hp (118 kW) at 6,600 rpm; max torque (DIN): 134 lb ft, 18.5 kg m (182 Nm) at 5,400 rpm; max engine rpm: 7,700; 80.4 hp/l (59.3 kW/l); light alloy block and head, wet liners; 5 crankshaft bearings; valves: overhead, Vee-slanted, thimble tappets: cam-shafts: 2,1 per bank, overhead, cogged belt; lubrication: gear pump, full flow filter, oil cooler; 4 Weber 34 DCNF downdraught twin barrel carburettors; fuel feed: electric pump; water-cooled, front radiator, 2 electric automatic fans.

TRANSMISSION driving wheels: rear; clutch: single dry plate; gearbox: mechanical; gears: 5, fully synchronized; ratios: I 3,419, II 2.353, III 1.693, IV 1.244, V 0.881, rev 3.200; lever: central; final drive: hypoid bevel, limited slip differential; axle ratio: 4.600; width of rims: 6.5"; tyres: 195/70 VR 14 XDX.

PERFORMANCE max speed: 132 mph, 213 km/h; max speeds at 7,000 rpm: (I) 32 mph, 52 km/h; (II) 47 mph, 76 km/h; (III) 65 mph, 105 km/h; (IV) 89 mph, 143 km/h; (V) 125 mph, 202 km/h; power-weight ratio: 17.5 lb/hp (23.7 lb/kW), 7.9 kg/hp (10.8 kg/kW); acceleration: standing ¼ mile 16 sec; speed in top at 1,000 rpm: 17.9 mph, 28.8 km/h; consumption: 18.8/16.6 m/imp gal, 15.7/13.8 m/US gal, 15/17 l x 100 km.

CHASSIS tubular; front suspension: independent, wishbones, anti-roll bar, coil springs/telescopic dampers; rear: independent, wishbones, anti-roll bar, coil springs/telescopic dampers.

STEERING rack-and-pinion.

BRAKES disc, internal radial fins, dual circuit, servo.

ELECTRICAL EQUIPMENT 12 V; Marelli alternator and distributor; 4 retractable iodine headlamps.

DIMENSIONS AND WEIGHT wheel base: 100.39 in, 255 cm; front and rear track: 57.48 in, 146 cm; length: 169.29 in, 430 cm; width: 70.47 in, 179 cm; height: 47.64 in, 121 cm; ground clearance: 4.72 in, 12 cm; weight: 2,793 lb, 1,267 kg; turning circle: 40.3 ft, 12.3 m; fuel tank: 17.6 imp gal, 21.1 US gal, 80 l (2 separate tanks).

BODY coupé; 2 doors; 2+2 seats, separate front seats, reclining backrests, built-in headrests; tinted glass; electric windows; heated rear window; light alloy wheels; quartz clock.

PRACTICAL INSTRUCTIONS fuel: 98-100 oct petrol.

OPTIONALS sunshine roof; air-conditioning.

FERRARI Dino 308 GT 4

Dino 308 GT 4

See Dino 208 GT 4, except for:

PRICE IN GB: £ 17,534*
PRICE IN USA: $ 38,460* (with air-conditioning)

ENGINE 178.5 cu in, 2,926 cc (3.19 x 2.80 in, 81 x 71 mm); compression ratio: 8.8:1; max power (DIN): 230 hp (169 kW) at 6,600 rpm; max torque (DIN): 203 lb/ft, 28.1 kg m (275 Nm) at 4,600 rpm; 78.6 hp/l (57.8 kW/l); 4 Weber 40 DCNF downdraught twin barrel carburettors.

TRANSMISSION gearbox ratios: V 0.952; axle ratio: 3.706; width of rims: 6.5" or 7.5"; tyres: 205/70 VR x 14 XWX.

PERFORMANCE max speed: 148 mph, 238 km/h; max speeds at 7,000 rpm: (I) 41 mph, 66 km/h; (II) 59 mph, 95 km/h; (III) 83 mph, 133 km/h; (IV) 112 mph, 180 km/h; (V) 147 mph, 236 km/h; power-weight ratio: 12.3 lb/hp (16.8 lb/kW), 5.6 kg/hp (7.6 kg/kW); acceleration: standing ¼ mile 14.8 sec; speed in top at 1,000 rpm: 20.9 mph, 33.6 km/h; consumption: 16.6/14.9 m/imp gal, 13.8/12.4 m/US gal, 17/19 l x 100 km.

ELECTRICAL EQUIPMENT electronic ignition.

DIMENSIONS AND WEIGHT weight: 2,840 lb, 1,288 kg.

OPTIONALS leather upholstery; metallic spray; sunshine roof; air-conditioning.

308 GTB

See Dino 208 GT 4, except for:

PRICE IN GB: £ 18,973*
PRICE IN USA: $ 39,015* (with air-conditioning)

ENGINE 178.5 cu in, 2,926 cc (3.19 x 2.80 in, 81 x 71 mm); compression ratio: 8.8:1; max power (DIN): 230 hp (169 kW) at

308 GTB

6,600 rpm; max torque (DIN): 203 lb ft, 28.1 kg m (275 Nm) at 4,600 rpm; 78.6 hp/l (57.8 kW/l); 4 Weber 40 DCNF downdraught twin barrel carburettors; lubrication: dry sump.

TRANSMISSION gearbox ratio: V 0.920; axle ratio: 3.706; width of rims: 6.5" or 7.5"; tyres: 205/70 VR x 14 XWX.

PERFORMANCE max speed: 152 mph, 245 km/h; power-weight ratio: 12.3 lb/hp (16.8 lb/kW), 5.6 kg/hp (7.6 kg/kW), speed in top at 1,000 rpm: 21.7 mph, 34.8 km/h; consumption: 16.6/14.9 m/imp gal, 13.8/12.4 m/US gal, 17/19 l x 100 km.

ELECTRICAL EQUIPMENT electronic ignition.

DIMENSIONS AND WEIGHT wheel base: 92.13 in, 234 cm; front and rear track: 57.48 in, 146 cm; length: 166.54 in, 423 cm; width: 67.72 in, 172 cm; height: 44.09 in, 112 cm; weight: 2,840 lb, 1,288 kg; turning circle: 39.4 ft, 12 m; fuel tank: 17.6 imp gal, 21.1 US gal, 80 l.

BODY in light alloy; 2 seats.

OPTIONALS leather upholstery; metallic spray; sunshine roof; air-conditioning.

308 GTS

See Dino 208 GT 4, except for:

PRICE IN GB: £ 19,901*
PRICE IN USA: $ 43,185* (with air-conditioning)

ENGINE 178.5 cu in, 2,926 cc (3.19 x 2.80 in, 81 x 71 mm); compression ratio: 8.8:1; max power (DIN): 230 hp (169 kW) at 6,600 rpm; max torque (DIN): 203 lb ft, 28.1 kg m (275 Nm) at 4,600 rpm; 78.6 hp/l (57.8 kW/l); 4 Weber 40 DCNF downdraught twin barrel carburettors; lubrication: wet sump.

TRANSMISSION gearbox ratio: V 0.952; axle ratio: 3.706; width of rims: 6.5" or 7.5"; tyres: 205/70 VR x 14 XWX.

PERFORMANCE max speed: 152 mph, 245 km/h; power-weight ratio: 12.4 lb/hp (16.9 lb/kW), 5.6 kg/hp (7.7 kg/kW); speed in top at 1,000 rpm: 20.9 mph, 33.6 km/h.

DIMENSIONS AND WEIGHT wheel base: 92.13 in, 234 cm; front and rear track: 57.48 in, 146 cm; length: 166.54 in, 423 cm; width: 67.72 in, 172 cm; height: 44.09 in, 112 cm; weight: 2,859 lb, 1,297 kg; turning circle: 39.4 ft, 12 m; fuel tank: 17.6 imp gal, 21.1 US gal, 80 l.

BODY spider, in light alloy; 2 seats.

OPTIONALS leather upholstery; metallic spray; sunshine roof; air-conditioning.

400 Automatic i

PRICE IN GB: £ 31,809*
PRICE EX WORKS: 49,410,000* liras

ENGINE front, 4 stroke; 12 cylinders, Vee-slanted at 60°; 294.3 cu in, 4,823 cc (3.19 x 3.07 in, 81 x 78 mm); compression ratio: 8.8:1; max power (DIN): 310 hp (228 kW) at 6,400 rpm; max torque (DIN): 347 lb ft, 48 kg m (471 Nm) at 3,600 rpm; max engine rpm: 6,500; 64.3 hp/l (47.3 kW/l); light alloy block and head, wet liners; 7 crankshaft bearings; valves: overhead, Vee-slanted at 46°, thimble tappets; camshafts: 2, 1 per bank, overhead; lubrication: gear pump, 31.7 imp pt, 38.1 US pt, 18 l; Bosch K-Jetronic double injection system; fuel feed: 2 electric pumps; water-cooled, 22.9 imp pt, 27.5 US pt, 13 l, 2 electric automatic fans.

TRANSMISSION driving wheels: rear; gearbox: GM automatic transmission, hydraulic torque converter and planetary gears with 3 ratios, max ratio of converter at stall 2.20, possible manual selection; ratios: I 2.520, II 1.520, III 1, rev 1.940; lever: central; final drive: spiral bevel, limited slip differential; axle ratio: 3.250; width of rims: 7.5"; tyres: 215/70 VR x 15.

PERFORMANCE max speeds: (I) 61 mph, 98 km/h; (II) 101 mph, 164 km/h; (III) 152 mph, 245 km/h; power-weight ratio: 13 lb/hp (17.7 lb/kW), (5.9 kg/hp); (8 kg/kW); speed in direct drive at 1,000 rpm: 23.4 mph, 37.6 km/h; consumption: 13.5 m/imp gal, 11.2 m/US gal, 21 l x 100 km.

CHASSIS tubular; front suspension: independent, wishbones, anti-roll bar, coil springs/telescopic dampers; rear: independent, wishbones, anti-roll bar, coil springs/telescopic dampers.

STEERING recirculating ball, ZF servo; turns lock to lock: 3.80.

BRAKES discs (front diameter 11.89 in, 30.2 cm, rear 11.69 in, 29.7 cm), internal radial fins, dual circuit, servo; lining area: front 28.8 sq in, 186 sq cm, rear 19.5 sq in, 126 sq cm, total 48.3 sq in, 312 sq cm.

ELECTRICAL EQUIPMENT 12 V; 77 Ah battery; 960 W alternator; 2 Marelli S 138 C distributors; 4 retractable iodine headlamps.

FERRARI 400 Automatic i

DIMENSIONS AND WEIGHT wheel base: 106.30 in, 270 cm; tracks: 57.87 in, 147 cm front, 59.06 in, 150 cm rear; length: 189.37 in, 481 cm; width: 70.87 in, 180 cm; height: 51.57 in, 131 cm; ground clearance: 5.12 in, 13 cm; weight: 4,035 lb, 1,830 kg; turning circle: 40 ft, 12.2 m; fuel tank: 26.4 imp gal, 31.7 US gal, 120 l.

BODY coupé; 2 doors; 2+2 seats, separate front seats, reclining backrests with built-in headrests; folding rear seat; air-conditioning; electric windows; heated rear window.

PRACTICAL INSTRUCTIONS fuel: 98-100 oct petrol; oil: engine 31.7 imp pt, 38.1 US pt, 18 l, SAE 20W-40, change every 6,200 miles, 10,000 km - gearbox 7.9 imp pt, 9.5 US pt, 4.5 l, SAE 80 EP, change every 6,200 miles, 10,000 km - final drive 4.4 imp pt, 5.3 US pt, 2.5 l, change every 6,200 miles, 10,000 km; greasing: every 6,200 miles, 10,000 km, 8 points; tappet clearances: inlet 0.004-0.006 in, 0.10-0.15 mm, exhaust 0.010-0.012 in, 0.25-0.30 mm; tyre pressure: front 34 psi, 2.4 atm, rear 38 psi, 2.7 atm.

OPTIONALS 5-speed mechanical gearbox, ratios (I 2.590, II 1.700, III 1.254, IV 1, V 0.795, rev 2.240), 4.300 axle ratio.

BB 512

PRICE IN GB: £ 33,081*
PRICE EX WORKS: 52,785,000* liras

ENGINE centre-rear, 4 stroke; 12 cylinders, horizontally opposed; 301.6 cu in, 4,942 cc (3.23 x 3.07 in, 82 x 78 mm); compression ratio: 9.2:1; max power (DIN): 340 hp (250 kW) 6,200 rpm; max engine rpm: 6,800; 68.8 hp/l (50.6 kW/l); lig alloy block and head, cast iron liners; 7 crankshaft bearing valves: overhead, Vee-slanted, thimble tappets; camshafts: 2, per bank, cogged belt; lubrication: gear pump, full flow filte dry sump, 17.6 imp pt, 2.1 US pt, 10 l; 4 Weber 40 IF3 three-barrel carburettors; fuel feed: 2 electric pumps; wate cooled, 24.6 imp pt, 29.6 US pt, 14 l, 3 electric automatic fans

TRANSMISSION driving wheels: rear; clutch: single dry plat gearbox: mechanical, in unit with final drive; gears: 5, ful synchronized; ratios: I 2.937, II 2.099, III 1.587, IV 1.200, 0.913, rev 2.620; lever: central; final drive: hypoid bevel, mited slip differential; axle ratio: 3.214; width of rims: 7.5 front, 9" rear; tyres: 215/70 VR x 15 front, 225/70 VR x 15 rea

PERFORMANCE max speed: 176 mph, 283 km/h; max speec at 6,200 rpm: (I) 53 mph, 85 km/h; (II) 73 mph, 118 km/h; (I 97 mph, 156 km/h; (IV) 129 mph, 207 km/h; (V) 169 mph, 27 km/hp; power-weight ratio: 9.8 lb/hp (13.4 lb/kW), 4.4 kg/hp kg/kW); speed in top at 1,000 rpm: 27.4 mph, 44 km/h; co sumption: 12.8 m/imp gal, 10.7 m/US gal, 22 l x 100 km.

CHASSIS tubular; front suspension: independent, wishbone anti-roll bar, coil springs/telescopic dampers; rear: indepe dent, wishbones, coil springs, anti-roll bar, 4 telescopic dan pers.

STEERING worm and roller.

BRAKES disc, internal radial fins, servo.

FERRARI 400 Automatic i

ECTRICAL EQUIPMENT 12 V; 74 Ah battery; 780 W alterna-; Marelli distributor; electronic ignition; 2 retractable head-nps.

MENSIONS AND WEIGHT wheel base: 98.43 in, 250 cm; cks: 59.06 in, 150 cm front, 61.42 in, 156 cm rear; length: 3.23 in, 440 cm; width: 72.05 in, 183 cm; height: 44.09 in, 2 cm; ground clearance: 4.92 in, 12.5 cm; weight: 3,340 lb, 515 kg; turning circle: 39 ft, 11.9 m; fuel tank: 24 imp gal, 29 gal, 110 l.

DY coupé; 2 doors; 2 seats; light alloy wheels; electric ndows; air-conditioning.

RACTICAL INSTRUCTIONS fuel: 98-100 oct petrol.

FERRARI BB 512

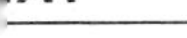

AT ITALY

126 Berlina Base

RICE IN GB: £ 2,008*
RICE EX WORKS: 2,932,000 liras**

IGINE rear, 4 stroke; 2 cylinders, vertical, in line; 39.8 cu in, 2 cc (3.03 x 2.76 in, 77 x 70 mm); compression ratio: 7.5:1; ax power (DIN): 24 hp (18 kW) at 4,500 rpm; max torque IN): 30 lb ft, 4.2 kg m (41 Nm) at 3,000 rpm; max engine rpm: 200; 36.8 hp/l (27.1 kW/l); light alloy block and head; 2 ankshaft bearings; valves: overhead, in line, push-rods and ckers; camshafts: 1, side; lubrication: gear pump, centrifugal er, 4.4 imp pt, 5.3 US pt, 2.5 l; 1 Weber 28 IMB downdraught rburettor; fuel feed: mechanical pump; air-cooled.

RANSMISSION driving wheels: rear; clutch: single dry plate; arbox: mechanical; gears: 4, II, III and IV silent claw cou-ng; ratios: I 3.250, II 2,067, III 1.300, IV 0.872, rev 4.024; ver: central; final drive: spiral bevel; axle ratio: 4.875; width rims: 4"; tyres: 135 SR x 12.

ERFORMANCE max speeds: (I) 19 mph, 30 km/h; (II) 31 mph, km/h; (III) 50 mph, 80 km/h; (IV) over 65 mph, 105 km/h; wer-weight ratio: 53.3 lb/hp (72.2 lb/hp (72.2 lb/kW), 24.2 /hp (33.4 kg/kW); carrying capacity: 706 lb, 320 kg; speed in p at 1,000 rpm: 14 mph, 22.6 km/h; consumption: 55.3 m/imp l, 46.1 m/US gal, 5.1 l x 100 km.

HASSIS integral; front suspension: independent, wishbones, ansverse leafspring lower arms, telescopic dampers; rear: dependent, oblique semi-trailing arms, coil springs, telescopic mpers.

TEERING screw and sector; turns lock to lock: 2.90.

RAKES drum; lining area: front 33.3 sq in, 215 sq cm, rear .3 sq in, 215 sq cm, total 66.6 sq in, 430 sq cm.

ECTRICAL EQUIPMENT 12 V; 34 Ah battery; 230 W dyna-o; Marelli distributor; 2 headlamps.

DIMENSIONS AND WEIGHT wheel base: 72.44 in, 184 cm; tracks: 44.96 in, 114 cm front, 47.36 in, 120 cm rear; length: 120.24 in, 305 cm; width: 54.21 in, 138 cm; height: 52.56 in, 133 cm; ground clearance: 4.92 in, 12.5 cm; weight: 1,279 lb, 580 kg; weight distribution: 40% front, 60% rear; turning circle: 28.2 ft, 8.6 m; fuel tank: 4.6 imp gal, 5.5 US gal, 21 l.

BODY saloon/sedan; 2 doors; 4 seats, separate front seats.

PRACTICAL INSTRUCTIONS fuel: 80-85 oct petrol; oil: engine 4.4 imp pt, 5.3 US pt, 2.5 l, SAE 30 W (summer) 20W (winter), change every 6,200 miles, 10,000 km - gearbox and final drive 1.9 imp pt, 2.3 US pt, 1.1 l, FIAT ZC 90, change every 18,600 miles, 30,000 km; greasing: every 3,100 miles, 5,000 km, 2 points; tappet clearances: inlet 0.008 in, 0.20 mm, exhaust 0.010 in, 0.25 mm; valve timing: 26° 57° 66° 17°; tyre pressure: front 22 psi, 1.4 atm, rear 28 psi, 2 atm.

OPTIONALS reclining backrests; luxury interior; opening rear windows; sunshine roof; folding rear seat; antitheft.

126 Personal

See 126 Berlina Base, except for:

PRICE IN GB: £ 2,199*
PRICE EX WORKS: 3,180,000 liras**

PERFORMANCE power-weight ratio: 53.7 lb/hp (72.8 lb/kW), 24.4 kg/hp (33 kg/kW).

ELECTRICAL EQUIPMENT 33 A alternator.

DIMENSIONS AND WEIGHT length: 123.19 in, 313 cm; width: 54.33 in, 138 cm; weight: 1,289 lb, 585 kg.

FIAT 126 Personal

Panda 30

PRICE EX WORKS: 3,970,000* liras

ENGINE front, 4 stroke; 2 cylinders, vertical, in line; 39.8 cu in, 652 cc (3.03 x 2.76 in, 77 x 70 mm); compression ratio: 8:1; max power (DIN): 30 hp (22 kW) at 5,500 rpm; max torque (DIN): 30 lb ft, 4.2 kg m (41 Nm) at 3,000 rpm; max engine rpm: 6,000; 46 hp/l (33.7 kW/l); light alloy block and head; 2 crankshaft bearings; valves: overhead, in line, push-rods and rockers; camshafts: 1, side; lubrication: gear pump, centrifugal filter, 4.9 imp pt, 5.9 US pt, 2.8 l; 1 Weber 30 DGF 1/250 or Solex C 30 DID/1 downdraught twin barrel carburettor; fuel feed: mechanical pump; air-cooled.

TRANSMISSION driving wheels: front; clutch: single dry plate (diaphragm); gearbox: mechanical; gears: 4, II, III and IV synchronized; ratios: I 3.500, II 2.067, III 1.300, IV 0.872, rev 4.237; lever: central; final drive: hypoid bevel; axle ratio: 5.125; width of rims: 4"; tyres: 135 SR x 13.

PERFORMANCE max speeds: (I) 20 mph, 33 km/h; (II) 35 mph, 57 km/h; (III) 56 mph, 90 km/h; (IV) 71 mph, 115 km/h; power-weight ratio: 47.8 lb/hp (65.1 lb/kW), 21.7 kg/hp (29.5 kg/kW); carrying capacity: 882 lb, 400 kg; acceleration: standing ¼ mile 23.8 sec; speed in top at 1,000 rpm: 13.9 mph, 22.4 km/h; consumption: 52.3 m/imp gal, 43.6 m/US gal, 5.4 l x 100 km at 56 mph, 90 km/h.

CHASSIS integral; front suspension: independent, by McPherson, coil springs/telescopic dampers struts, lower wishbones; rear: rigid axle, semi-elliptic leafsprings, telescopic dampers.

STEERING rack-and-pinion; turns lock to lock: 3.40.

BRAKES front disc (diameter 8.94 in, 22.7 cm), rear drum, dual circuit, rear compensator; lining area: front 19.2 sq in, 124 sq cm, rear 32.4 sq in, 209 sq cm, total 51.6 sq in, 333 sq cm.

ELECTRICAL EQUIPMENT 12 V; 34 Ah battery; 45 A alternator; contactless Marelli distributor; 2 headlamps.

DIMENSIONS AND WEIGHT wheel base: 85.04 in, 216 cm; tracks: 49.37 in, 125 cm front, 49.17 in, 125 cm rear; length: 133.07 in, 338 cm; width: 57.48 in, 146 cm; height: 56.89 in, 144 cm; weight: 1,433 lb, 650 kg; weight distribution: 61% front, 39% rear; turning circle: 30.2 ft, 9.2 m; fuel tank: 7.7 imp gal, 9.2 US gal, 35 l.

BODY saloon/sedan; 2+1 doors; 5 seats, separate front seats; folding rear seat.

PRACTICAL INSTRUCTIONS fuel: 98 oct petrol; oil: engine 4.9 imp pt, 5.9 US pt, 2.8 l, SAE 20W (winter) 30W (summer), change every 6,200 miles, 10,000 km - gearbox and final drive 2.6 imp pt, 3.2 US pt, 1.5 l, SAE 90, change every 18,600 miles, 30,000 km; greasing: every 18,600 miles, 30,000 km, homokinetic joints; sparking plug: Marelli CW 7 NP or Champion L 82 Y; tappet clearances: inlet 0.008 in, 0.20 mm, exhaust 0.010 in, 0.25 mm; valve timing: 21° 62° 61° 22°; tyre pressure: front 24 psi, 1.7 atm, rear 27 psi, 1.9 atm.

Panda 45

See Panda 30, except for:

PRICE EX WORKS: 4,702,000* liras

ENGINE front, transverse, 4 stroke; 4 cylinders, vertical, in line; 55.1 cu in, 903 cc (2.56 x 2.68 in, 65 x 68 mm); compression ratio: 9:1; max power (DIN): 45 hp (33 kW) at 5,600 rpm; max torque (DIN): 47 lb ft, 6.5 kg m (64 Nm) at 3,000 rpm; max engine rpm: 6,400; 49.8 hp/l (36.7 kW/l); cast iron block, light alloy head; 3 crankshaft bearings; lubrication: gear pump, full flow filter (cartridge), 6.7 imp pt, 8 US pt, 3.8 l; 1 Weber 32 ICEV 28/250 or Solex C32 DISA/7 downdraught single barrel carburettor; water-cooled, 9.2 imp pt, 11 US pt, 5.2 l.

TRANSMISSION gears: 4, fully synchronized; ratios: I 3.910, II 2.055, III 1.348, IV 0.963, rev 3.615; final drive: helical cylindrical; axle ratio: 4.462.

PERFORMANCE max speed: over 84 mph, 135 km/h; power-weight ratio: 33.3 lb/hp (45.4 lb/kW), 15.1 kg/hp (20.6 kg/kW); acceleration: standing ¼ mile 20.4 sec; speed in top at 1,000 rpm: 14.4 mph, 23.2 km/h; consumption: 48.7 m/imp gal, 40.6 m/US gal, 5.8 l 5.8 l x 100 km at 56 mph, 90 km/h.

DIMENSIONS AND WEIGHT weight: 1,499 lb, 680 kg; weight distribution: 49% front, 51% rear.

PRACTICAL INSTRUCTIONS oil: engine 6.7 imp pt, 8 US pt, 3.8 l, SAE 20W (winter) 30W (summer), change every 6,200 miles, 10,000 km - gearbox and final drive 4.2 imp pt, 5.1 US pt, 2.4 l, SAE 90, change every 18,600 miles, 30,000 km; sparking plug: Marelli CW 7 LPR or Champion RN 9 Y; valve timing: 17° 43° 57° 3°.

FIAT Panda 45

127 Series

PRICES IN GB AND EX WORKS:	£	liras
1 L 2-dr Berlina	**2,687***	**4,254,000****
2 L 2+1-dr Berlina	**2,821***	**4,366,000****
3 C 2-dr Berlina	—	**4,738,000****
4 C 2+1-dr Berlina	**2,944***	**4,850,000****
5 CL 2-dr Berlina	—	**4,962,000****
6 CL 2+1-dr Berlina	**3,065***	**5,074,000****
7 Sport 2+1-dr Berlina	**3,427***	**5,735,000****

Power team:	Standard for:	Optional for:
45 hp	1 to 4	—
50 hp	5,6	—
70 hp	7	—

45 hp power team

ENGINE front, transverse, 4 stroke; 4 cylinders, vertical, in line; 55.1 cu in, 903 cc (2.56 x 2.68 in, 65 x 68 mm); compression ratio: 9:1; max power (DIN): 45 hp (33 kW) at 5,600 rpm; max torque (DIN): 47 lb ft, 6.5 kg m (64 Nm) at 3,000 rpm; max engine rpm: 6,400; 49.8 hp/l (36.7 kW/l); cast iron block, light alloy head; 3 crankshaft bearings; valves: overhead, in line, push-rods and rockers; camshafts: 1, side; lubrication: gear pump, full flow filter (cartridge), 6.7 imp pt, 8 US pt, 3.8 l; 1 Weber 30 IBA 22 or Solex C 30 DI 40 downdraught single barrel carburettor; fuel feed: mechanical pump; water-cooled, 8.8 imp pt, 10.6 US pt, 5 l, electric thermostatic fan.

TRANSMISSION driving wheels: front; clutch: single dry plate; gearbox: mechanical; gears: 4, fully synchronized; ratios: I 3.910, II 2.055, III 1.348, IV 0.963, rev 3.615; lever: central; final drive: helical cylindrical; axle ratio: 4.071; width of rims: 4"; tyres: 135 SR x 13.

PERFORMANCE max speeds: (I) 25 mph, 40 km/h; (II) 43 mph, 70 km/h; (III) 65 mph, 105 km/h; (IV) over 84 mph, 135 km/h; power-weight ratio: 33.7 lb/hp (45.8 lb/kW), 15.3 kg/hp (20.8 kg/kW); carrying capacity: 882 lb, 400 kg; acceleration: standing ¼ mile 20.4 sec; speed in top at 1,000 rpm: 15.8 mph, 25.4 km/h; consumption: 40.9 m/imp gal, 34.1 m/US gal, 6.9 l x 100 km.

CHASSIS integral; front suspension: independent, by McPherson, coil springs/telescopic damper struts, lower wishbones, transverse anti-roll bar; rear: independent, single wide-based wishbones, transverse anti-roll leafspring, telescopic dampers.

STEERING rack-and-pinion; turns lock to lock: 3.50.

BRAKES front disc (diameter 8.94 in, 22.7 cm), rear drum, dual circuit, rear compensator; lining area: front 19.2 sq in, 124 sq cm, rear 33.3 sq in, 215 sq cm, total 52.6 sq in, 339 sq cm.

ELECTRICAL EQUIPMENT 12 V; 34 Ah battery; 33 A alternator; Marelli S 146 A distributor; 2 headlamps.

DIMENSIONS AND WEIGHT wheel base: 87.60 in, 222 cm; tracks: 50.39 in, 128 cm front, 50.79 in, 129 cm rear; length: 143.50 in, 364 cm; width: 60.12 in, 153 cm; height: 53.54 in, 136 cm; ground clearance: 5.12 in, 13 cm; weight: 1,517 lb, 688 kg; weight distribution: 62% front, 38% rear; turning circle: 31 ft, 9.6 m; fuel tank: 6.6 imp gal, 7.9 US gal, 30 l.

BODY saloon/sedan; 5 seats, separate front seats; folding re seat (for 2+1-dr models only).

PRACTICAL INSTRUCTIONS fuel: 98 oct petrol; oil: engine 6 imp pt, 7.6 US pt, 3.6 l, SAE 20W (winter) 30W (summe change every 6,200 miles, 10,000 km - gearbox and final dri 4.2 imp pt, 5.1 US pt, 2.4 l, SAE 90, change every 18,6 miles, 30,000 km; greasing: every 18,600 miles, 30, 000 k homokinetic joints; sparking plug: 260°; tappet clearances: in 0.006 in, 0.15 mm, exhaust 0.008 in, 0.20 mm; valve timing: 1 43° 57° 3°; tyre pressure: front 24 psi, 1.7 atm, rear 27 psi, 1 atm.

OPTIONALS headrests; reclining backrests; luxury interio opening rear windows; heated rear window; antitheft; metal spray.

50 hp power team

See 45 hp power team, except for:

ENGINE 64 cu in, 1,049 cc (2.99 x 2.27 in, 76 x 57.8 mm compression ratio: 9.3:1; max power (DIN): 50 hp (37 kW) 5,600 rpm; max torque (DIN): 57 lb ft, 7.9 kg m (77 Nm) 4,000 rpm; 55.4 hp/l (40.7 kW/l); 5 crankshaft bearings; ca shafts: 1, overhead; lubrication: four-lobe rotary pump, 6.2 i pt, 7.4 US pt, 3.5 l; 1 Weber 32 ICEV 16 or Solex C32 TDI downdraught carburettor; cooling, 9.7 imp pt, 11.6 US pt, 5.5

PERFORMANCE max speed: 87 mph, 140 km/h; power-weig ratio: 31.2 lb/hp (42.4 lb/kW), 14.2 kg/hp (19.2 kg/kW); accel ration: standing ¼ mile 19.9 sec; consumption: 36.2 m/imp g 30.2 m/US gal, 7.8 l x 100 km.

DIMENSIONS AND WEIGHT weight: 1,561 lb, 708 kg.

PRACTICAL INSTRUCTIONS oil: engine 5.5 imp pt, 6.6 US 3.1 l; valve timing: 2° 42° 42° 2°.

OPTIONALS sunshine roof (only for Top).

70 hp power team

See 50 hp power team, except for:

ENGINE 64 cu in, 1,049 cc (2.99 x 2.27 in, 76 x 57.8 mm compression ratio: 9.8:1; max power (DIN): 70 hp (51 kW) 6,500 rpm; max torque (DIN): 62 lb ft, 8.5 kg m (83 Nm) 4,500 rpm; 66.7 hp/l (49.1 kW/l) 5 crankshaft bearings; ca shafts: 1, overhead; lubrication: four-lobe rotary pump, 6.2 i pt, 7.4 US pt, 3.5 l; 1 Weber 34 DMTR downdraught twin bar carburettor; cooling, 9.7 imp pt, 11.6 US pt, 5.5 l.

TRANSMISSION axle ratio: 4,462; width of rims: 4.5".

PERFORMANCE max speed: about 99 mph, 160 km/h; pow weight ratio: 23.8 lb/hp (32.3 lb/kW), 10.8 kg/hp (14.6 kg/k acceleration: standing ¼ mile 18.5 sec; speed in top at 1,0 rpm: 14.3 mph, 23 km/h; consumption: 31.7 m/imp gal, 26 m/US gal, 8.9 l x 100 km.

ELECTRICAL EQUIPMENT 45 A alternator.

DIMENSIONS AND WEIGHT tracks: 50.78 in, 129 cm fro 51.18 in, 130 cm rear; weight: 1,665 lb, 755 kg.

FIAT 127 L Berlina

RACTICAL INSTRUCTIONS oil: engine 5.5 imp pt, 6.6 US pt, .1 l; valve timing: 6° 46° 47° 7°.

128 CL 1100

RICE EX WORKS: 5,782,000 liras**

NGINE front, transverse, 4 stroke; 4 cylinders, in line; 68.1 cu ı, 1,116 cc (3.15 x 2.19 in, 80 x 55.5 mm); compression ratio: .2:1; max power (DIN): 55 hp (40 kW) at 6,000 rpm max orque (DIN): 60 lb ft, 8.3 kg m (81 Nm) at 2,800 rpm; max ngine rpm: 6,500; 49.3 hp/l (36.2 kW/l); cast iron block, light lloy head; 5 crankshaft bearings; valves: overhead, thimble appets; camshafts: 1, overhead, cogged belt; lubrication: gear ump (cartridge) 8.8 imp pt, 10.6 US pt, 5 l; 1 Weber 32 ICEV 4 or Solex C 32 DISA 41 downdraught carburettor; fuel feed: echanical pump; water-cooled, expansion tank, 11.4 imp pt, 3.7 US pt, 6.5 l, electric thermostatic fan.

RANSMISSION driving wheels: front; clutch: single dry plate; earbox: mechanical; gears: 4, fully synchronized; ratios: I .583, II 2.235, III 1.454, IV 1.042, rev 3.714; lever: central; nal drive: helical cylindrical; axle ratio: 3.765; width of rims: .5"; tyres: 145 SR x 13.

ERFORMANCE max speeds: (I) 31 mph, 50 km/h; (II) 50 mph, 0 km/h; (III) 75 mph, 120 km/h; (IV) 87 mph, 140 km/h; ower-weight ratio: 30 lb/hp (40.9 lb/kW), 13.6 kg/hp (18.6 g/kW); carrying capacity: 882 lb, 400 kg; acceleration: standng ¼ mile 19.7 sec; speed in top at 1,000 rpm: 16.3 mph, 26.3 m/h; consumption: 35.3 m/imp gal, 29.4 m/US gal, 8 l x 100 m.

HASSIS integral; front suspension: independent, by McPheron, coil springs/telescopic damper struts, lower wishbones, nti-roll bar; rear: independent, single wide-based wishbones, ansverse anti-roll leafspring, telescopic dampers.

TEERING rack-and-pinion; turns lock to lock: 3.50.

RAKES front disc (diameter 8.94 in, 22.7 cm), rear drum, dual ircuit, rear compensator, servo; lining area: front 19.2 q in, 124 sq cm, rear 33.3 sq in, 215 sq cm, total 52.6 sq in, 39 sq cm.

LECTRICAL EQUIPMENT 12 V; 34 Ah battery; 33 A alternaor; Marelli distributor; 2 headlamps.

IMENSIONS AND WEIGHT wheel base: 96.38 in, 245 cm; racks: 51.50 in, 131 cm front, 51.69 in, 131 cm rear; length: 51.18 in, 384 cm; width: 62.60 in, 159 cm; height: 55.91 in, 42 cm; ground clearance: 5.71 in, 14.5 cm; weight: 1,698 lb, 70 kg; weight distribution: 64% front, 36% rear; turning circle: 3.8 ft, 10.3 m; fuel tank: 8.4 imp gal, 10 US gal, 38 l.

ODY saloon/sedan; 4 doors; 5 seats, separate front seats: eclining backrests.

RACTICAL INSTRUCTIONS fuel: 98 oct petrol; oil: engine 7.4 mp pt, 8.9 US pt, 4.2 l, SAE 20W (winter) 30W (summer), hange every 6,200 miles, 10,000 km - gearbox and final drive .5 imp pt, 6.6 US pt, 3.1 l, SAE 90, change every 18,600 niles, 30,000 km; greasing: every 18,600 miles, 30,000 km, omokinetic joints; sparking plug: 240°; tappet clearances: inlet).012 in, 0.30 mm, exhaust 0.016 in, 0.40 mm; valve timing: 12° 52° 52° 12°; tyre pressure: front 26 psi, 1.8 atm, rear 24 psi, .7 atm.

FIAT 128 CL 1100

OPTIONALS headrests; tinted glass with heated rear window; antitheft; light alloy wheels; heated rear window; metallic spray.

128 Panorama Base 1100

See 128 CL 1100, except for:

PRICE EX WORKS: 5,511,000 liras**

TRANSMISSION axle ratio: 4.077.

PERFORMANCE power-weight ratio: 31.7 lb/hp (43.1 lb/kW), 14.4 kg/hp (19.6 kg/kW); carrying capacity: 948 lb, 430 kg; speed in top at 1,000 rpm: 15.1 mph, 24.3 km/h.

DIMENSIONS AND WEIGHT weight: 1,742 lb, 790 kg.

BODY 2+1 doors; folding rear seat.

PRACTICAL INSTRUCTIONS tyre pressure: front 27 psi, 1.9 atm, rear 24 psi, 1.7 atm.

Ritmo Series

PRICES IN GB AND EX WORKS:	£	liras
1 60 L 2+1-dr Berlina	—	5,334,000**
2 60 L 4+1-dr Berlina	—	5,581,000**
3 60 CL 2+1-dr Berlina	—	5,876,000**
4 60 CL 4+1-dr Berlina	—	6,124,000**
5 65 L 4+1-dr Berlina	3,358*	5,717,000**

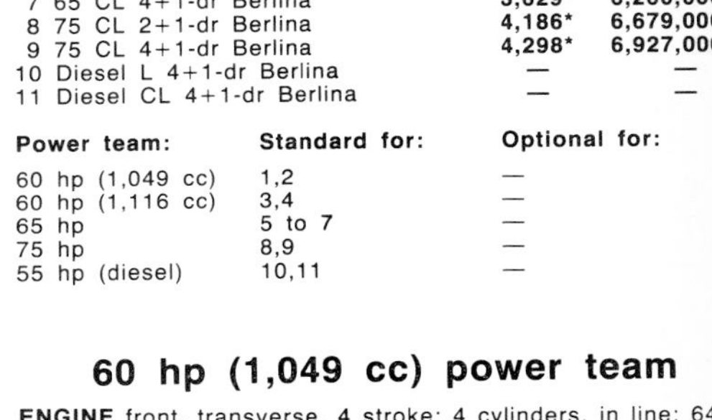

	£	liras
6 65 CL 2+1-dr Berlina	3,517*	6,012,000**
7 65 CL 4+1-dr Berlina	3,629*	6,260,000**
8 75 CL 2+1-dr Berlina	4,186*	6,679,000**
9 75 CL 4+1-dr Berlina	4,298*	6,927,000**
10 Diesel L 4+1-dr Berlina	—	—
11 Diesel CL 4+1-dr Berlina	—	—

Power team:	Standard for:	Optional for:
60 hp (1,049 cc)	1,2	—
60 hp (1,116 cc)	3,4	—
65 hp	5 to 7	—
75 hp	8,9	—
55 hp (diesel)	10,11	—

FIAT Ritmo 60 CL Berlina

60 hp (1,049 cc) power team

ENGINE front, transverse, 4 stroke; 4 cylinders, in line; 64 cu in, 1,049 cc (2.99 x 2.27 in, 76 x 57.8 mm); compression raio: 9.5:1; max power (DIN): 60 hp (44 kW) at 5,800 rpm; max torque (DIN): 60 lb ft, 8.3 kg m (81 Nm) at 3,500 rpm; 57.2 hp/l (42.1 kW/l); cast iron block light alloy head; 5 crankshaft bearings; valves: overhead, thimble tappets; camshafts: 1, overhead, cogged belt; lubrication: gear pump, cartridge filter, 8.3 imp pt, 9.9 US pt, 4.7 l; 1 Weber 32 ICEV 26/250 or Solex C32 DISA/5 downdraught single barrel carburettor; fuel feed: mechanical pump; water-cooled, expansion tank, 12.5 imp pt, 15 US pt, 7.1 l; electric thermostatic fan.

TRANSMISSION driving wheels: front; clutch: single dry plate; gearbox: mechanical; gears: 4, fully synchronized; ratios: I 3.583, II 2.235, III 1.454, IV 1.042, rev 3.714; lever: central; final drive: helical cylindrical; axle ratio: 4.077; width of rims: 4.5"; tyres: 145 SR x 13.

PERFORMANCE max speed: 90 mph, 145 km/h; power-weight ratio: L 2+1-dr 30.1 lb/hp (41 lb/kW), 13.7 kg/hp (18.6 kg/kW); carrying capacity: 882 lb, 400 kg; speed in top at 1,000 rpm: 15 mph, 24.2 km/h; consumption: 32.4 m/imp gal, 27 m/US gal, 8.7 l x 100 km.

CHASSIS integral; front suspension: independent, by McPherson, lower wishbones, trailing links, coil springs/telescopic damper struts; rear: independent, by McPherson, lower wishbones, transverse anti-roll leafspring, telescopic dampers.

STEERING rack-and-pinion; turns lock to lock: 3.50.

BRAKES front disc (diameter 8.94 in, 22.7 cm), rear drum, dual circuit, rear compensator; lining area: front 19.2 sq in, 124 sq cm, rear 33.3 sq in, 215 sq cm, total 52.5 sq in, 339 sq cm.

ELECTRICAL EQUIPMENT 12 V; 34 Ah battery; 45 A alternator; Marelli distributor; 2 headlamps.

DIMENSIONS AND WEIGHT wheel base: 96.38 in, 245 cm; tracks: 55.12 in, 140 cm front, 55.51 in, 141 cm rear; length: 155.12 in, 394 cm; width: 65 in, 165 cm; height: 55.12 in, 140 cm; weight: L 2+1-dr 1,808 lb, 820 kg - L 4+1-dr 1,852 lb, 840 kg; weight distribution: 62.5% front, 37.5% rear; turning circle: 33.8 ft, 10.3 m; fuel tank: 11.2 imp gal, 13.5 US gal, 51 l.

BODY saloon/sedan; 5 seats, separate front seats; folding rear seat.

PRACTICAL INSTRUCTIONS fuel: 98 oct petrol; oil: engine 7.7 imp pt, 9.3 US pt, 4.4 l, SAE 10W-40, change every 6,200 miles, 10,000 km - gearbox and final drive 5.3 imp pt, 6.3 US pt, 3 l, SAE 80W-90, chage every 18,600 miles, 30,000 km;

60 HP POWER TEAM

valve timing: 8° 36° 38° 6°; tyre pressure: front 27 psi, 1.9 atm, rear 26 psi, 1.8 atm.

OPTIONALS 5-speed fully synchronized mechanical gearbox (V 0.863); 165/70 SR x 13 tyres; sunshine roof; heated rear window; rear window with wiper-washer; headrests; metallic spray.

60 hp (1,116 cc) power team

See 60 hp (1,049 cc) power team, except for:

ENGINE 68.1 cu in, 1,116 cc (3.15 x 2.19 in, 80 x 55.5 mm); compression ratio: 9.2:1; 1 Weber 32 ICEV 21 or Solex C32 DISA/1 carburettor.

PERFORMANCE power-weight ratio: CL 2+1-dr 30.9 lb/hp (42 lb/kW), 14 kg/hp (19 kg/kW).

DIMENSIONS AND WEIGHT weight: CL 2+1-dr 1,852 lb, 840 kg - CL 4+1-dr 1,885 lb, 855 kg.

PRACTICAL INSTRUCTIONS valve timing: 12° 52° 52° 12°.

65 hp power team

See 60 hp (1,049 cc) power team, except for:

ENGINE 79.39 cu in, 1,301 cc (3.40 x 2.18 in, 86.4 x 55.5 mm); compression ratio: 9.1:1; max power (DIN): 65 hp (48 kW) at 5,800 rpm; max torque (DIN): 72 lb ft, 10 kg m (98 Nm) at 3,500 rpm; 49.9 hp/l (36.7 kW/l); 1 Weber 32 ICEV 22 or Solex C 32 DISA/2 downdraught single barrel carburettor; cooling, 13.9 imp pt, 16.7 US pt, 7.9.

TRANSMISSION axle ratio: 3.765.

PERFORMANCE max speed: 93 mph, 150 km/h; power-weight ratio: L 4+1-dr 28.4 lb/hp (38.6 lb/kW), 12.9 kg/hp (17.5 kg/kW); speed in top at 1,000 rpm: 16.3 mph, 26.2 km/h; consumption: 32.1 m/imp gal, 26.7 m/US gal, 8.8 l x 100 km.

ELECTRICAL EQUIPMENT 45 Ah battery.

OPTIONALS air-conditioning.

75 hp power team

See 60 hp (1,049 cc) power team, except for:

ENGINE 91.41 cu in, 1,498 cc (3.40 x 2.52 in, 86.4 x 63.9 mm); compression ratio: 9:1; max power (DIN): 75 hp (55 kW) at 5,800 rpm; max torque (DIN): 87 lb ft, 12 kg m (118 Nm) at 3,000 rpm; 1 Weber 34 ICEV 23/250 downdraught single barrel carburettor; cooling, 14.1 imp pt, 16.9 US pt, 8 l.

TRANSMISSION axle ratio: 3.588.

PERFORMANCE max speed: 99 mph, 160 km/h; power-weight ratio: CL 2+1-dr and L 5-dr 25 lb/hp (34.1 lb/kW), 11.3 kg/hp (15.4 kg/kW); speed in top at 1,000 rpm: 17.1 mph, 27.5 km/h; consumption: 33 m/imp gal, 27.7 m/US gal, 8.5 l x 100 km.

BRAKES servo.

DIMENSIONS AND WEIGHT weight: CL 2+1-dr 1,875 lb, 850 kg - CL 4+1-dr 1,907 lb, 865 kg.

OPTIONALS automatic transmission, hydraulic torque converter and planetary gears with 3 ratios (I 2.550, II 1.450, III 1, rev 2.460), max ratio of converter at stall 2.47, 3.565 axle ratio, anti-roll bar on front suspension, max speed 96 mph, 155 km/h, consumption 28.5 m/imp gal, 23.7 m/US gal, 9.9 l x 100 km; air-conditioning.

55 hp (diesel) power team

See 60 hp (1,049 cc) power team, except for:

ENGINE diesel; 104.59 cu in, 1,714 cc (3.27 x 3.12 in, 83 x 79.2 mm); compression ratio: 20:1; max power (DIN): 55 hp (40 kW) at 4,500 rpm; max torque (DIN): 72 lb ft, 10 kg m (98 Nm) at 3,000 rpm; 32.1 hp/l (23.3 kW/l); Bosch indirect injection pump; water-cooled, 15.7 imp pt, 18.8 US pt, 8.9 l, 2 electric thermostatic fans.

TRANSMISSION tyres: 155 SR x 13.

PERFORMANCE max speed: over 87 mph, 140 km/h; power-weight ratio: 39.9 lb/hp (54.8 lb/kW), 18.1 kg/hp (24.9 kg/kW); acceleration: standing ¼ mile 20.3 sec; consumption: 35.8 m/imp gal, 29.8 m/US gal, 7.9 l x 100 km at 75 mph, 120 km/h.

ELECTRICAL EQUIPMENT 65 Ah battery; 55 A alternator.

FIAT Strada Custom Sedan

DIMENSIONS AND WEIGHT weight: 2,194 lb, 995 kg.

PRACTICAL INSTRUCTIONS fuel: diesel oil; valve timing: 4° 40° 45° 5°.

Strada Series

(for USA only)

PRICES IN USA:

	$
2+1-dr Sedan	**4,496***
2+1-dr Custom Sedan	**4,952***
4+1-dr Custom Sedan	**5,102***

ENGINE front, transverse, 4 stroke; 4 cylinders, in line; 91.41 cu in, 1,498 cc (3.40 x 2.52 in, 86.4 x 63.9 mm); compression ratio: 8.5:1; max power (SAE net): 65 hp (48 kW) at 5,100 rpm; max engine rpm: 5,500; 43.4 hp/l (32 kW/l); cast iron block, light alloy head; 5 crankshaft bearings; valves: overhead, thimble tappets; camshafts: 1, overhead, cogged belt; lubrication: gear pump, full flow filter (cartridge), 8.3 imp pt, 9.9 US pt, 4.7 l; 1 Weber 28/30 DHTA 5/280 downdraught twin barrel carburettor, exhaust emission control system separate from CEC system; fuel feed: mechanical pump; water-cooled, expansion tank, 12.5 imp pt, 15 US pt, 7.1 l; electric thermostatic fan.

TRANSMISSION driving wheels: front; clutch: single dry plate; gearbox: mechanical; gears: 5, fully synchronized; ratios: I 3.583, II 2.235, III 1.454, IV 1.042, V 0.863, rev 3.714; lever: central; final drive: helical cylindrical; axle ratio: 3.588; width of rims: 4.5"; tyres: 145 SR x 13.

PERFORMANCE max speeds: (I) 30 mph, 48 km/h; (II) 48 mph, 77 km/h; (III) 73 mph, 118 km/h; (IV) 91 mph, 147 km/h; (V) 89 mph, 143; power-weight ratio: 2+1-dr Sedan 33.2 lb/hp (45 lb/kW), 15.1 kg/hp (20.4 kg/kW); carrying capacity: 882 lb, 400 kg; consumption: 32.1 m/imp gal, 26.7 m/US gal, 8.8 l x 100 km.

CHASSIS integral; front suspension: independent, by McPherson, lower wishbones, trailing links, coil springs/telescopic damper struts; rear: independent, by McPherson, lower wishbones, transverse anti-roll leafspring, telescopic dampers.

STEERING rack-and-pinion; turns lock to lock: 3.50.

BRAKES front disc (diameter 8.94 in, 22.7 cm), rear drum, dual circuit, rear compensator; lining area: front 19.2 sq in, 124 sq cm, rear 33.3 sq in, 215 sq cm, total 52.5 sq in, 33.9 sq cm.

ELECTRICAL EQUIPMENT 12 V; 60 Ah battery; 55 A alternator; Marelli distribution; 2 headlamps.

DIMENSIONS AND WEIGHT wheel base: 96.38 in, 245 cm; tracks: 55.12 in, 140 cm front, 55.51 in, 141 cm rear; length: 161.02 in, 409 cm; width: 65 in, 165 cm; height: 55.12 in, 140 cm; weight: 2+1-dr sedans 2,160 lb, 980 kg - 4+1-dr Sedan 2,195 lb, 996 kg; weight distribution: 62.5% front, 37.5% rear; turning circle: 33.8 ft, 10.3 m; fuel tank: 10.1 imp gal, 12.1 US gal, 46 l.

BODY saloon/sedan; 5 seats, separate front seats, headrests; folding rear seat; rear window wiper-washer.

PRACTICAL INSTRUCTIONS fuel: 100 oct petrol; oil: engine 7.7 imp pt, 9.3 US pt, 4.4 l, SAE 15W-40, change every 6,200 miles, 10,000 km - gearbox and final drive 5.3 imp pt, 6.3 US pt, 3 l, SAE 80W-90, change every 18,600 miles, 30,000 km; greasing: none; sparking plug: champion RN 9 Y or AC Delco R 42 XLS; valve timing: 10° 54° 54° 10°; tyre pressure: front 32 psi, 2.2 atm, rear 32 psi, 2.2 atm.

OPTIONALS automatic transmission, hydraulic torque converter and planetary gears with 3 ratios (I 2.550, II 1.450, III 1, rev 2.460), max ratio of converter at stall 2.47, 3.565 axle ratio, 1 Weber 28/30 DHTA 6/280 carburettor, anti-roll bar on front suspension, max speed 88 mph, 142 km/h, power-weight ratio 2+1-dr sedans 34.2 lb/hp (46.3 lb/kW), 15.5 kg/hp (21 kg/kW), weight 2+1-dr sedans 2,225 lb, 1,009 kg - 4+1-dr sedans 2,260 lb, 1,025 kg; 165/75 SR x 13 tyre; air-conditioning with 1 Weber 28/30 DHTA 5/180 carburettor.

FIAT X1/9 five speed

X1/9 five speed

PRICE IN GB: £ 5,323*
PRICE EX WORKS: 7,876,000 liras**

ENGINE central, rear, transverse, 4 stroke; 4 cylinders, vertical, in line; 91.4 cu in, 1,498 cc (3.40 x 2.52 in, 86.4 x 63.9 mm); compression ratio: 9.2:1; max power (DIN): 85 hp (62 kW) at 6,000 rpm; max torque (DIN): 87 lb ft, 12 kg m (118 Nm) at 3,200 rpm; max engine rpm: 6,500; 56.7 hp/l (41.7 kW/l); cast iron block, light alloy head; 5 crankshaft bearings; valves: overhead, in line, thimble tappets; camshafts: 1, overhead, cogged belt; lubrication: 7.9 imp pt, 9.5 US pt, 4.5 l; 1 Weber 34 DATR 7/250 downdraught twin barrel carburettor; fuel feed: mechanical pump; water-cooled, 20.4 imp pt, 24.5 US pt, 11.6 l, electric thermostatic fan.

TRANSMISSION driving wheels: rear; clutch: single dry plate (diaphragm), hydraulically controlled; gearbox: mechanical; gears: 5, fully synchronized; ratios: I 3.583, II 2.235, III 1.454, IV 1.042, V 0.863, rev 3.714; lever: central; final drive: helical cylindrical; axle ratio: 4.076; width of rims: 5"; tyres: 165/70 SR x 13.

ERFORMANCE max speeds: (I) 31 mph, 50 km/h; (II) 47 mph, 0 km/h; (III) 77 mph, 124 km/h; (IV) 102 mph, 165 km/h; (V) 12 mph, 180 km/h; power-weight ratio: 23.9 lb/hp (32.5 lb/kW), 0.8 kg/hp (14.7 kg/kW); carrying capacity: 441 lb, 200 kg; cceleration: standing ¼ mile 17.8 sec; speed in top at 1,000 pm: 17.2 mph, 27.7 km/h; consumption: 36.2 m/imp gal, 30.2 n/US gal, 7.8 l x 100 km.

HASSIS integral; front suspension: independent, by McPher-on (lower trailing links), coil springs/telescopic damper struts, ower wishbones; rear: independent, lower wishbones, each vith articulated transverse control bar, coil springs/telescopic lamper struts.

STEERING rack-and-pinion; turns lock to lock: 3.05.

BRAKES disc (diameter 8.94 in, 22.7 cm), dual circuit, servo; ning area: front 19.2 sq in, 124 sq cm, rear 19.2 sq in, 124 sq m, total 38.4 sq in, 284 sq cm.

LECTRICAL EQUIPMENT 12 V; 45 Ah battery; 45 A alterna-or; 2 retractable headlamps.

IMENSIONS AND WEIGHT wheel base: 86.69 in, 220 cm; racks: 53.35 in, 135 cm front, 53.15 in, 135 cm rear; length: 56.26 in, 397 cm; width: 61.81 in, 157 cm; height: 46.46 in, 18 cm; ground clearance: 4.92 in, 12.5 cm; weight: 2.029 lb, 20 kg; weight distribution: 40.2% front, 59.8% rear; turning ircle: 32.8 ft, 10 m; fuel tank: 10.8 imp gal, 12.9 US gal, 49 l.

ODY sports; 2 doors; 2 seats, built-in headrests; roll bar; etachable roof.

RACTICAL INSTRUCTIONS fuel: 98-100 oct petrol; oil: en-ine 7.9 imp pt, 9.5 US pt, 4.5 l, SAE 10W-50, change every ,200 miles, 10,000 km - gearbox and final drive 4.9 imp pt, 5.9 JS pt, 2.8 l, change every 18,600 miles, 30,000 km; greasing: one; valve timing: 24° 68° 64° 28°; tyre pressure: front 26 psi, .8 atm, rear 28 psi, 2 atm.

PTIONALS light alloy wheels; heated rear window; tinted lass with heated rear window.

VARIATIONS

for USA only)
ENGINE 8.5 compression ratio, max power (DIN) 67 hp (49 kW) at 5,250 rpm, 44.7 hp/l (32.9 kW/l).
ERFORMANCE max speed 106 mph, 170 km/h, power-weight atio 31.6 lb/hp (43 lb/kW), 14.4 kg/hp (19.5 kg/kW).
IMENSIONS AND WEIGHT weight 2,120 lb, 962 kg.

PTIONALS air-conditioning; metallic spray.

131 Series

RICES IN GB AND EX WORKS:	£	liras
1 Mirafiori 1300 L 4-dr Berlina	3,554*	6,230,000**
2 Mirafiori 1300 L 4+1-dr Panorama	—	6,738,000**
3 Mirafiori 1300 CL 2-dr Berlina	3,668*	6,803,000**
4 Mirafiori 1300 CL 4-dr Berlina	3,794*	7,127,000**
5 Mirafiori 1600 CL 4-dr Berlina	4,216*	7,281,000**
6 Mirafiori 1600 CL 4+1-dr Panorama	4,600*	7,788,000**
7 Supermirafiori 1300 4-dr Berlina	—	8,177,000**
8 Supermirafiori 1600 4-dr Berlina	4,874*	8,331,000**
9 Supermirafiori 1600 4+1-dr Panorama	—	8,962,000**
10 Racing 2000 2-dr Berlina	5,448*	8,897,000**
11 Diesel 2000 L 4-dr Berlina	—	8,201,000**
12 Diesel 2000 CL 4-dr Berlina	—	8,891,000**
13 Diesel 2000 CL 4+1-dr Panorama	—	9,393,000**
14 Diesel 2500 Super 4-dr Berlina	—	9,936,000**
15 Diesel 2500 4+1-dr Panorama Super	—	10,508,000**

Power team:	Standard for:	Optional for:
65 hp	1 to 4	—
75 hp	5,6	—
78 hp	7	—
96 hp	8,9	—
115 hp	10	—
60 hp (diesel)	11 to 13	—
72 hp (diesel)	14,15	—

65 hp power team

ENGINE front, 4 stroke; 4 cylinders, vertical, in line; 79.1 cu in, 1,297 cc (2.99 x 2.81 in, 76 x 71.5 mm); compression ratio: 9.2:1; max power (DIN): 65 hp (48 kW) at 5,200 rpm; max torque (DIN): 75 lb ft, 10.4 kg m (102 Nm) at 3,000 rpm; 50.2 hp/l (36.9 kW/l) cast iron block, light alloy head; 5 crankshaft bearings; valves: overhead, in line, slanted at 10°, push-rods and rockers; camshafts: 1, side, in crankcase, cogged belt; lubrication: gear pump, full flow filter (cartridge), 7.6 imp pt, 9.1 US pt, 4.3 l; 1 Weber 32 ADF/7 or Solex C32 TEIE/42 down-draught twin barrel carburettor; fuel feed: mechanical pump; water-cooled, expansion tank, 13.4 imp pt, 16.1 US pt, 7.6 l, electric thermostatic fan.

TRANSMISSION driving wheels: rear; clutch: single dry plate (diaphragm); gearbox: mechanical; gears: 4 fully synchronized; ratios: I 3.612, II 2.045, III 1.357, IV 1, rev 3.244; lever: central; final drive: hypoid bevel; axle ratio: 4.100; width of rims: 5"; tyres: L 4-dr 155 SR x 13 - L 4+1-dr and CL models 165 SR x 13.

FIAT 131 Mirafiori 1300 L Berlina

PERFORMANCE max speed: 93 mph, 150 km/h; power-weight ratio: CL 2-dr 32.2 lb/hp (43.8 lb/kW), 14.6 kg/hp (19.9 kg/kW); carrying capacity: 882 lb, 400 kg - Panorama 948 lb, 430 kg; acceleration: standing ¼ mile 19.3 sec; speed in direct drive at 1,000 rpm: 16.4 mph, 26.4 km/h; consumption: 31.7 m/imp gal, 26.4 m/US gal, 8.9 l x 100 km.

CHASSIS integral; front suspension: independent, by McPher-son, coil springs/telescopic damper struts, lower wishbones, anti-roll bar; rear: rigid axle, twin trailing lower radius arms, transverse linkage bar, coil springs, telescopic dampers.

STEERING rack-and-pinion, adjustable height of steering wheel (for CL models only); turns lock to lock: 3.50.

BRAKES front disc (diameter 8.94 in, 22.7 cm), rear drum dual circuit, rear compensator, servo; lining area: 19.2 sq in, 124 sq cm, rear 41.9 sq in, 270 sq cm, total 61.1 sq in, 394 sq cm.

ELECTRICAL EQUIPMENT 12 V; 45 Ah battery; 45 A alterna-tor; Marelli distributor; 2 headlamps.

DIMENSIONS AND WEIGHT wheel base: 98.03 in, 249 cm; tracks: 54.33 in, 138 cm front, 51.97 in, 132 cm rear; length: 167.72 in, 426 cm; width: 64.96 in, 165 cm; height: 54.33 in, 138 cm - Panorama 54.72 in, 139 cm; weight: GL 2-dr 2,095 lb, 950 kg - 4-dr models 2,138 lb, 965 kg - Panorama 2,172 lb, 985 kg; turning circle: 34 ft, 10.3 m; fuel tank: 11 imp gal, 13.2 US gal, 50 l.

BODY saloon/sedan, 2 or 4 doors - estate car/st. wagon, 4+1 doors; 5 seats, separate front seats, reclining backrests; folding rear seat (for Panorama only).

PRACTICAL INSTRUCTIONS fuel: 98-100 oct petrol; oil: en-gine 7 imp pt, 8.4 US pt, 4 l, SAE 10W-30 (winter) 20W-40 (summer), change every 6,200 miles, 10,000 km - gearbox 3.2 imp pt, 3.8 US pt, 1.8 l, SAE 90 EP, change every 18,600 miles, 30,000 km - final drive 1.8 imp pt, 2.1 US pt, 1 l, SAE 90 EP, change every 18,600 miles, 30,000 km; sparking plug: 200°; valve timing: 3° 45° 43° 5°; tyre pressure: front 26 psi, 1.8 atm, rear 26 psi, 1.8 atm (Panorama 31 psi, 2.2 atm).

OPTIONALS 5-speed fully synchronized mechanical gearbox (I 3.612, II 2.045, III 1.357, IV 1, V 0.870, rev 3.244), speed in top at 1,000 rpm 18 mph, 29 km/h (Panorama 18.9 mph, 30.4 km/h), consumption 32.8 m/imp gal, 27.3 m/US gal, 8.6 l x 100 km; light alloy wheels; heated rear window; tinted glass with heated rear window; reclining backrests with built-in headrests; antitheft; shock absorbing bumpers; opening rear window (for CL 2-dr only); metallic spray; vinyl roof; air-conditioning: 175/70 SR x 13 tyres; rear window wiper-washer (for Panorama only).

75 hp power team

See 65 hp power team, except for:

ENGINE 96.7 cu in, 1,585 cc (3.31 x 2.81 in, 84 x 71.5 mm); max power (DIN): 75 hp (55 kW) at 5,200 rpm; max torque (DIN): 91 lb ft, 12.6 kg m (124 Nm) at 3,000 rpm; 47.4 hp/l (34.8 kW/l); cooling, 13 imp pt, 15.6 US pt, 7.4 l.

FIAT 131 Racing 2000 Berlina

75 HP POWER TEAM

TRANSMISSION axle ratio: 3.900.

PERFORMANCE max speed: 99 mph, 160 km/h; power-weight ratio: CL 4-dr 28.4 lb/hp (38.6 lb/kW), 12.9 kg/hp (17.5 kg/kW); acceleration: standing ¼ mile 18.2 sec; speed in direct drive at 1,000 rpm: 16.8 mph, 27 km/h - Panorama 17.3 mph, 27.8 km/h; consumption: 30.7 m/imp gal, 25.6 m/US gal, 9.2 l x 100 km.

PRACTICAL INSTRUCTIONS valve timing: 10° 49° 50° 9°.

OPTIONALS limited slip differential; with 5-speed fully synchronized mechanical gearbox, 3.900 axle ratio, speed in top at 1,000 rpm 19 mph, 30.6 km/h (Panorama 19.9 mph, 32 km/h), consumption 31.7 m/imp gal, 26.4 m/US gal, 8.9 l x 100 km; GM automatic transmission, hydraulic torque converter and planetary gears with 3 ratios (I 2.400, II 1.480, III 1, rev 1.920), max ratio of converter at stall 2.4, possible manual selection, 3.900 axle ratio, acceleration standing ¼ mile 19 sec, consumption 28 m/imp gal, 23.3 m/US gal, 10.1 l x 100 km.

78 hp power team

See 65 hp power team, except for:

ENGINE compression ratio: 8.9:1; max power (DIN): 78 hp (57 kW) at 6,000 rpm; max torque (DIN): 76 lb ft, 10.5 kg m (103 Nm) at 4,000 rpm; 60.1 hp/l (44.2 kW/l); camshafts: 2, overhead; lubrication: 8.4 imp pt, 10.1 US pt, 4.8 l; 1 Weber 32 ADF13 downdraught twin barrel carburettor; cooling, 14.1 imp pt, 16.9 US pt, 8 l.

FIAT 131 Diesel 2500 Super Berlina

FIAT 131 Supermirafiori Series

TRANSMISSION gears: 5, fully synchronized; ratios: I 3.612, II 2.045, III 1.357, IV 1, V 0.870; tyres: 165 SR x 13.

PERFORMANCE max speed: 99 mph, 160 km/h; power-weight ratio: 28.3 lb/hp (38.4 lb/kW), 12.8 kg/hp (17.4 kg/kW); acceleration: standing ¼ mile 18.7 sec; consumption: 34 m/imp gal, 28.3 m/US gal, 8.3 l x 100 km.

ELECTRICAL EQUIPMENT 2 halogen headlamps.

DIMENSIONS AND WEIGHT length: 166.54 in, 423 cm; weight: 2,205 lb, 1,000 kg; weight distribution: 542.4% front, 47.6% rear.

BODY built-in headrests on front and rear seats.

PRACTICAL INSTRUCTIONS oil: engine 7.2 imp pt, 8.7 US pt, 4.1 l; valve timing: 17° 37° 48° 6°.

OPTIONALS GMS automatic transmission, hydraulic torque converter and planetary gears with 3 ratios (I 2.400, II 1.480, III 1, rev 1.920).

96 hp power team

See 65 hp power team, except for:

ENGINE 96.72 cu in, 1,585 cc (3.31 x 2.81 in, 84 x 71.5 mm); compression ratio: 9:1; max power (DIN): 96 hp (71 kW) at 6,000 rpm; max torque (DIN): 94 lb ft, 13 kg m (127 Nm) at 3,800 rpm; 60.1 hp/l (44.5 kW/l); camshafts: 2, overhead; lubrication: 8.4 imp pt, 10.1 US pt, 4.8 l; 1 Weber 32 ADF 14 downdraught twin barrel carburettor; cooling, 14.1 imp pt, 16.9 US pt, 8 l.

TRANSMISSION gears: 5, fully synchronized; ratios: I 3.612, II 2.045, III 1.357, IV 1, V 0.870; tyres: 165 SR x 13; axle ratio: 3.900.

PERFORMANCE max speed: 106 mph, 170 km/h; power-weight ratio: 22.9 lb/hp (31.2 lb/kW), 10.4 kg/hp (14.2 kg/kW); acceleration: standing ¼ mile 17.5 sec; speed in direct drive at 1,000 rpm: 17.3 mph, 27.8 km/h; consumption: 32.8 m/imp gal, 27.3 m/US gal, 8.6 l x 100 km.

ELECTRICAL EQUIPMENT 2 halogen headlamps.

DIMENSIONS AND WEIGHT length: 166.54 in, 423 cm; weight: 2.205 lb, 1,000 kg; weight distribution: 52.4% front, 47.6% rear.

BODY built-in headrests on front and rear seats.

PRACTICAL INSTRUCTIONS oil: engine 7.2 imp pt, 8.7 US pt, 4.1 l; valve timing: 12° 53° 54° 11°.

OPTIONALS GMS automatic transmission, hydraulic torque converter and planetary gears with 3 ratios (I 2.400, II 1.480, III 1, rev 1.920).

115 hp power team

See 65 hp power team, except for:

ENGINE 121.7 cu in, 1,995 cc (3.31 x 3.54 in, 84 x 90 mm); compression ratio: 8.9:1; max power (DIN): 115 hp (84 kW) at 5,800 rpm; max torque (DIN): 123 lb ft, 17 kg m (167 Nm) at 3,600 rpm; 57.6 hp/l (42.1 kW/l); camshafts: 2, overhead; lubrication: 8.4 imp pt, 10.1 US pt, 4.8 l; 1 Weber 34 ADF 15 downdraught twin barrel carburettor; cooling, 14.4 imp pt, 17.3 US pt, 8.2 l.

TRANSMISSION gears: 5, fully synchronized; ratios: I 3.612, II 2,045, III 1.357, IV 1, V 0.870; axle ratio: 3.900; width of rims: 5.5"; tyres: 185/70 SR x 13.

PERFORMANCE max speed: 112 mph, 180 km/h; power-weight ratio: 19.6 lb/hp (26.8 lb/kW), 8.9 kg/hp (12.1 kg/kW); acceleration: standing ¼ mile 16.5 sec; speed in direct drive at 1,000 rpm: 19.9 mph, 32.1 km/h; consumption: 28.8 m/imp gal, 24 m/US gal, 9.8 l x 100 km.

ELECTRICAL EQUIPMENT 4 headlamps.

DIMENSIONS AND WEIGHT rear track: 52.36 in, 133 cm; length: 166.54 in, 423 cm; width: 65.35 in, 166 cm; height: 55.12 in, 140 cm; weight: 2,250 lb, 1,020 kg; weight distribution: 54% front, 46% rear.

BODY built-in headrests on front and rear seats.

PRACTICAL INSTRUCTIONS oil: engine 7.2 imp pt, 8.7 US pt, 4.1 l; valve timing: 15° 55° 57° 13°.

60 hp (diesel) power team

See 65 hp power team, except for:

ENGINE diesel; 121.7 cu in, 1,995 cc (3.46 x 3.23 in, 88 x 82 mm); compression ratio: 22:1; max power (DIN): 60 hp (44 kW) at 4,400 rpm; max torque (DIN): 83 lb ft, 11.5 kg m (113 Nm) at 2,400 rpm; 30.1 hp/l (22.1 kW/l); camshafts: 1, overhead; lubrication: 11.6 imp pt, 13.9 US pt, 6.6 l; Bosch indirect injection pump; cooling, liquid, expansion tank, 19.4 imp pt, 23.3 US pt, 11 l, electromagnetic thermostatic fan.

TRANSMISSION gears: 5, fully synchronized; ratios: I 3.612, II 2.045, III 1.357, IV 1, V 0.870, rev 3.244; axle ratio: 3.900; tyres: 165 SR x 13.

PERFORMANCE max speed: 87 mph, 140 km/h; power-weight ratio: sedans 40.8 lb/hp (55.5 lb/kW), 18.5 kg/hp (25.2 kg/kW), Panorama 41.5 lb/hp (56.5 lb/kW), 18.8 kg/hp (25.6 kg/kW); acceleration: standing ¼ mile 22.8 sec; speed in direct drive at 1,000 rpm: 17.3 mph, 27.8 km/h; consumption: 35.7 m/imp gal, 29.8 m/US gal, 7.9 l x 100 km.

STEERING turns lock to lock: 4.08.

ELECTRICAL EQUIPMENT 77 Ah battery; 4 iodine headlamps.

DIMENSIONS AND WEIGHT height: 54.72 in, 139 cm; weight: sedans 2,477 lb, 1,110 kg - Panorama 2,492 lb, 1,130 kg; weight distribution: sedans 57.9% front, 42.1% rear - Panorama 56.4% front, 43.6% rear.

PRACTICAL INSTRUCTIONS fuel: diesel oil; oil: engine 9.7 imp pt, 11.6 US pt, 5.5 l; valve timing: 8° 48° 48° 8°; tyre pressure: front 30 psi, 2.1 atm, rear 28 psi, 2 atm.

72 hp (diesel) power team

See 65 hp power team, except for:

ENGINE diesel; 149.2 cu in, 2,445 cc (3.66 x 3.54 in, 93 x 90 mm); compression ratio: 22:1; max power (DIN): 72 hp (53 kW) at 4,200 rpm; max torque (DIN): 109 lb ft, 15 kg m (147 Nm) at 2,400 rpm; 29.4 hp/l (21.7 kW/l); camshafts: 1, overhead; lubrication: 11.6 imp pt, 13.9 US pt, 6.6 l; Bosch indirect injection pump; cooling, liquid, expansion tank, 19.4 imp pt, 23.3 US pt, 11 l, electromagnetic thermostatic fan.

TRANSMISSION gear: 5, fully synchronized; ratios: I 3.612, II 2.045, III 1.357, IV 1, V 0.870, rev 3,244; axle ratio: 3.900; tyres: 165 SR x 13.

PERFORMANCE max speed: over 93 mph, 150 km/h; power-weight ratio: 34 lb/hp (46.2 lb/kW), 15.4 kg/hp (20.9 kg/kW); acceleration: standing ¼ mile 20.5 sec; consumption: 34.4 m/imp gal, 28.7 m/US gal, 8.2 l x 100 km.

STEERING turns lock to lock: 4.08.

ELECTRICAL EQUIPMENT 77 Ah battery; 4 iodine headlamps.

DIMENSIONS AND WEIGHT height: 54.72 in, 139 cm; weight: Sedan 2,447 lb, 1,110 kg - Panorama 2,492 lb, 1,130 kg; weight distribution: Sedan 58.2% front, 41.8% rear - Panorama 56.4% front, 43.6% rear.

BODY built-in headrests on front and rear seats.

PRACTICAL INSTRUCTIONS fuel: diesel oil; oil: engine 9.7 imp pt, 11.6 US pt, 5.5 l; valve timing: 8° 48° 48° 8°; tyre pressure: front 30 psi, 2.1 atm, rear 28 psi, 2 atm.

Brava Series

or USA only)

RICES IN USA: $

2-dr Sedan	6,495*
4-dr Sedan	6,695*
4+1-dr St. Wagon	—

ower team:	Standard for:	Optional for:
80 hp	all	—
02 hp	—	all

80 hp power team

NGINE front, 4 stroke; 4 cylinders, vertical, in line; 121.7 cu , 1,995 cc (3.31 x 3.54 in, 84 x 90 mm); compression ratio: .1:1; max power (SAE net): 80 hp (59 kW) at 5,000 rpm; max ngine rpm: 5,500; 40.1 hp/l (29.6 kW/l); cast iron block, light lloy head; 5 crankshaft bearings; valves: overhead, Vee-lanted, thimble tappets; camshafts: 2, overhead, cogged belt; ubrication: gear pump, full flow filter (cartridge), 8.3 imp pt, 9.9 S pt, 4.7 l; 1 Weber 28/32 ADHA 5/280 downdraught twin arrel carburettor, exhaust emission control system separate om CEC system; fuel feed: mechanical pump; water-cooled, xpansion tank, 14.1 imp pt, 16.9 US pt, 8 l, electric thermosta-c fan.

RANSMISSION driving wheels: rear; clutch: single dry plate; earbox: mechanical; gears: 5, fully synchronized; ratios: I .612, II 2.045 , II 1.357, IV 1, V 0.830, rev 3.244; lever: entral; final drive: hypoid bevel; axle ratio: 3.583; width of ms: 5''; tyres: 160 SR x 13.

ERFORMANCE max speeds: (I) 31 mph, 50 km/h; (II) 55 mph, 9 km/h; (III) 83 mph, 134 km/h; (IV) 102 mph, 164 km/h; (V) 99 ph, 159 km/h; power-weight ratio: 2-dr Sedan 32.4 lb/hp (44 /kW), 14.7 kg/hp (19.9 kg/kW); carrying capacity: 882 lb, 400 g; speed in direct drive at 1,000 rpm: 18.5 mph, 29.9 km/h; onsumption: 30 m/imp gal, 25 m/US gal, 9.4 l x 100 km.

HASSIS integral; front suspension: independent, by Mc-herson, coil springs/telescopic damper struts, lower wish-ones, anti-roll bar; rear: rigid axle, twin trailing lower radius rms, transverse linkage bar, coil springs, telescopic dampers.

TEERING rack-and-pinion, servo, adjustable height of steer-g wheel; turns lock to lock: 3.50.

RAKES front disc (diameter 8.94 in, 22.7 cm), rear drum, dual rcuit, rear compensator, servo; lining area: front 19.2 sq in, 24 sq cm, rear 41.9 sq in, 270 sq cm. total 61.1 sq in, 394 sq m.

LECTRICAL EQUIPMENT 12 V; 60 Ah battery; 55 A alterna-or; Magneti distributor; 4 headlamps.

IMENSIONS AND WEIGHT wheel base: 98.03 in, 249 cm; acks: 54.17 in, 138 cm front, 51.93 in, 132 cm rear; length: 72.4 in, 438 cm; width: 65 in, 165 cm; height: 54.33 in, 138 m; weight: 2-dr Sedan 2,595 lb, 1,177 kg - 4 dr Sedan 2,630 , 1,193 kg - St. Wagon 2,675 lb, 1,213 kg; turning circle: 34.8 , 10.6 m; fuel tank: 10.1 imp gal, 12.1 US gal, 46 l.

FIAT Brava Sedan

BODY saloon/sedan, 2 or 4 doors - estate car / st. wagon, 4+1 doors; 5 seats, separate front seats, headrests reclining back-rests; folding rear seat and rear window wiper-washer (for St. Wagon only).

PRACTICAL INSTRUCTIONS fuel: 100 oct petrol; oil: engine 7.2 imp pt, 8.7 US pt, 4.1 l, SAE 15W-40, change every 6,200 miles, 10,000 km - gearbox 2.9 imp pt, 3.5 US pt, 1.6 l, SAE 90 EP, change every 18,600 miles, 30,000 km - final drive 2.3 imp pt, 2.7 US pt, 1.3 l, change every 18,600 miles, 30,000 km; greasing: none; sparking plug: Champion RN 9 Y or AC Delco R 42-XLS; valve timing: 5° 53° 53° 5°; tyre pressure: front 26 psi, 1.8 atm, rear 29 psi, 2 atm - St. Wagon 32 psi, 2.3 atm.

OPTIONALS GM automatic transmission with 3 ratios (I 2.400, II 1.480, III 1, rev 1.920), max ratio of converter at stall 2.4, 1 Weber 28/32 ADHA 6/280 carburettor, max speed 99 mph, 159 km/h; 175/75 x 13 tyres; air-conditioning with 1 Weber 28/32 ADHA 5/180 carburettor.

102 hp power team

See 80 hp power team, except for:

ENGINE compression ratio: 8.2:1; max power (SAE net): 102 hp (75 kW) at 5,500 rpm; max engine rpm: 6,000; 51.1 hp/l (37.6 kW/l); electronic injection.

PERFORMANCE max speed in IV 105 mph, 169 km/h; power-weight ratio: 2-dr Sedan 25.4 lb/hp (34.6 lb/kW), 11.5 kg/hp (15.7 kg/kW).

ELECTRICAL EQUIPMENT 65 A alternator; electronic ignition.

OPTIONALS with GM automatic transmission max speed 101 mph, 163 km/h.

124 Sport Spider 2000

(for USA only)

PRICE IN USA: $ 8,795

ENGINE front, 4 stroke; 4 cylinders, vertical, in line; 121.7 cu in, 1,995 cc (3.31 x 3.54 in, 84 x 90 mm); compression ratio: 8.1:1; max power (SAE net): 80 hp (59 kW) at 5,000 rpm; max engine rpm: 5,500; 40.1 hp/l (29.6 kW/l); cast iron block, light alloy head; 5 crankshaft bearings; valves: overhead, Vee-slanted at 63°30', thimble tappets; camshafts: 2, overhead, cogged belt; lubrication: gear pump, full flow filter (cartridge), 8.3 imp pt, 9.9 US pt, 4.7 l; 1 Weber 28/32 ADHA 7/180 downdraught twin barrel carburettor; fuel feed: electric pump; water-cooled, 14.1 imp pt, 16.9 US pt, 8 l.

TRANSMISSION driving wheels: rear; clutch: single dry plate; gearbox: mechanical; gears: 5, fully synchronized; ratios: I 3.612, II 2.045, III 1.357, IV 1, V 0.830, rev 3.244; lever: central; final drive: hypoid bevel; axle ratio: 3.900; width of rims: 5''; tyres: 165 SR x 13.

PERFORMANCE max speeds: (I) 28 mph, 45 km/h; (II) 50 mph, 80 km/h; (III) 76 mph, 122 km/h; (IV) 104 mph, 167 km/h; (V) over 105 mph, 169 km/h; power-weight ratio: 29.5 lb/hp (40 lb/kW), 13.4 kg/hp (18.1 kg/kW); carrying capacity: 706 lb, 320 kg; acceleration: standing ¼ mile 18 sec; speed in top at 1,000 rpm: 19.4 mph, 31.2 km/h; consumption: 32.8 m/imp gal, 27.3 m/US gal, 8.6 l x 100 km.

CHASSIS integral; front suspension: independent, wishbones, coil springs, anti-roll bar, telescopic dampers; rear: rigid axle, twin trailing radius arms, transverse linkage bar, coil springs, telescopic dampers.

STEERING worm and roller; turns lock to lock: 2.75.

BRAKES disc (diameter 8.94 in, 22.7 cm), dual circuit, servo; lining area: total 38.4 sq in, 248 sq cm.

ELECTRICAL EQUIPMENT 12 V; 35 Ah battery; 42 A alterna-tor; Marelli electronic ignition; 2 halogen headlamps.

DIMENSIONS AND WEIGHT wheel base; 89.76 in, 228 cm; tracks: 52.99 in, 135 cm front, 51.82 in, 132 cm rear; length: 163 in, 414 cm; width: 63.50 in, 161 cm; height: 48.20 in, 122 cm; ground clearance: 4.92 in, 12.5 cm; weight: 2,360 lb, 1,070 kg; weight distribution: 56% front, 44% rear; turning circle: 34.1 ft, 10.4 m; fuel tank: 9.9 imp gal, 11.9 US gal, 45 l.

BODY sports; 2 doors; 2+2 seats, separate front seats, reclin-ing backrests, headrests; tinted glass.

PRACTICAL INSTRUCTIONS fuel: 100 oct petrol; oil: engine 7.2 imp pt, 8.7 US pt, 4.1 l, SAE 30W (summer) 20W (winter), change every 6,200 miles, 10,000 km - gearbox 2.8 imp pt, 3.5 US pt, 1.6 l, FIAT ZC 90, change every 18,600 miles, 30,000 km - final drive 2.5 imp pt,3 US pt, 1.4 l, FIAT W90/W, change every 18,600 miles, 30,000 km; greasing: every 18,600 miles, 30,000 km, 4 points; tyre pressure: front 28 psi, 1.9 atm, rear 28 psi, 1.9 atm.

FIAT 124 Sport Spider 2000

OPTIONALS GM automatic transmission, hydraulic torque con-verter and planetary gears with 3 ratios (I 2.400, II 1.480, III 1,

FIAT 124 Sport Spider 2000

124 SPORT SPIDER 2000

rev 1.920), max ratio of converter at stall 2.4, possible manual selection, 3.583 axle ratio, max speed 103 mph, 166 km/h; electric windows; hardtop; light alloy wheels; metallic spray.

124 Sport Spider 2000 i

(for USA only)

See 124 Sport Spider 2000, except for:

ENGINE compression ratio: 8.2:1; max power (SAE net): 102 hp (75 kW) at 5,500 rpm; max engine rpm: 6,000; 51.1 hp/l (37.6 kW/l); electronic injection.

PERFORMANCE max speed: over 107 mph, 172 km/h; power-weight ratio: 23.1 lb/hp (31.5 lb/kW), 10.5 kg/hp (14.3 kg/kW).

ELECTRICAL EQUIPMENT 65 A alternator; electronic ignition.

OPTIONALS with GM automatic transmission max speed 104 mph, 167 km/h.

132 1600 Berlina

PRICE EX WORKS: 8,921,000 liras**

ENGINE front, 4 stroke; 4 cylinders, vertical, in line; 96.7 cu in, 1,585 cc (3.31 x 2.81 in, 84 x 71.5 mm); compression ratio: 9:1; max power (DIN): 98 hp (72 kW) at 5,600 rpm; max torque (DIN): 97 lb ft, 13.4 kg m (131 Nm) at 4,000 rpm; max engine rpm: 6,000; 61.8 hp/l (45.5 kW/l); cast iron block, light alloy head; 5 crankshaft bearings; valves: overhead, Vee-slanted, thimble tappets; camshafts: 2, overhead, cogged belt; lubrication: gear pump, full flow filter (cartridge), 8.3 imp pt, 9.9 US pt, 4.7 l; 1 Weber 32 ADF2 downdraught twin barrel carburettor; fuel feed: mechanical pump; water-cooled, expansion tank, 14.1 imp pt, 16.9 US pt, 8 l, electric thermostatic fan.

TRANSMISSION driving wheels: rear; clutch: single dry plate; gearbox: mechanical; gears: 5, fully synchronized; ratios: I 3.612, II 2.045, III 1.357, IV 1, V 0.870, rev 3.244; lever: central; final drive: hypoid bevel; axle ratio: 3.727; width of rims: 5.5"; tyres: 175/70 SR x 14.

PERFORMANCE max speeds: (I) 28 mph, 45 km/h; (II) 50 mph, 80 km/h; (III) 78 mph, 125 km/h; (IV) 103 mph, 165 km/h; (V) about 99 mph, 160 km/h; power-weight ratio: 23.9 lb/hp (32.5 lb/kW), 10.8 kg/hp (14.8 kg/kW); carrying capacity: 882 lb, 400 kg; acceleration: standing ¼ mile 18 sec; speed in direct drive at 1,000 rpm: 18.3 mph, 29.4 km/h; consumption: 30 m/imp gal, 25 m/US gal, 9.4 l x 100 km (DIN).

CHASSIS integral; front suspension: independent, wishbones (lower trailing links), coil springs, anti-roll bar, telescopic dampers; rear: rigid axle, lower longitudinal trailing radius arms, upper oblique torque arms, coil springs, telescopic dampers.

STEERING worm and roller; turns lock to lock: 3.05.

BRAKES front disc (diameter 9.88 in, 25.1 cm), rear drum, rear compensator, dual circuit, servo; lining area: front 19.2 sq in, 124 sq cm, rear 41.8 sq in, 270 sq cm, total 61.1 sq in, 394 sq cm.

ELECTRICAL EQUIPMENT 12 V; 45 Ah battery; 45 A alternator; Marelli distributor; 4 headlamps.

DIMENSIONS AND WEIGHT wheel base: 100.67 in, 256 cm; tracks: 51.97 in, 132 cm front, 52.36 in, 133 cm rear; length: 172.83 in, 436 cm; width: 64.57 in, 164 cm; height: 56.30 in, 143 cm; ground clearance: 4.92 in, 12.5 cm; weight: 2,348 lb, 1,065 kg; weight distribution: 53% front, 47% rear; turning circle: 35.4 ft, 10.8 m; fuel tank: 12.3 imp gal, 14.8 US gal, 56 l.

BODY saloon/sedan; 4 doors; 5 seats, separate front seats, reclining backrests.

PRACTICAL INSTRUCTIONS fuel: 98-100 oct petrol; oil: engine 7.2 imp pt, 8.7 US pt, 4.1 l, SAE 30W (summer) 20W (winter), change every 6,200 miles, 10,000 km - gearbox 3.2 imp pt, 3.8 US pt, 1.8 l, FIAT ZC 90, change every 18,600 miles, 30,000 km - final drive 2.3 imp pt, 2.7 US pt, 1.3 l, FIAT W90/M, change every 18,600 miles, 30,000 km; greasing: every 18,600 miles, 30,000 km, 4 points; tappet clearances: inlet 0.018 in, 0.45 mm, exhaust 0.024 in, 0.60 mm; valve timing: 12° 53° 54° 11°; tyre pressure: front 26 psi, 1.8 atm, rear 27 psi, 1.9 atm.

OPTIONALS GM automatic transmission, hydraulic torque converter and planetary gears with 3 ratios (I 2.400, II 1.480, III 1, rev 1.920), hydraulic torque converter, possible manual selection, max speeds (I) 43 mph, 70 km/h, (II) 71 mph, 115 km/h, (III) about 99 mph, 160 km/h, power-weight ratio 24.7 lb/hp (33.3 lb/kW), 11.2 kg/hp (15.1 kg/kW), acceleration standing ¼ mile 19.2 sec, consumption 25.4 m/imp gal, 21.2 m/US gal, 11.1 l x 100 km, weight 2,403 lb, 1,090 kg, gearbox oil 4.9 imp pt, 5.9 US pt, 2.8 l; limited slip differential; light alloy, wheels electronic ignition; headrests; heated rear window; tinted glass with heated rear window; rev counter; air-conditioning; metallic spray; antitheft.

132 2000 Berlina

See 132 1600 Berlina, except for:

PRICE IN GB: £ 5,742*
PRICE EX WORKS: 9,871,000 liras**

ENGINE 121.7 cu in, 1,995 cc (3.31 x 3.54 in, 84 x 90 mm) compression ratio: 8.9:1; max power (DIN): 112 hp (82 kW) at 5,600 rpm; max torque (DIN): 117 lb ft, 16.1 kg m (158 Nm) at 3,000 rpm; 56.1 hp/l (41.3 kW/l); 1 Weber 34 ADF downdraught twin barrel carburettor.

PERFORMANCE max speed: 105 mph, 169 km/h; power-weight ratio: 21.6 lb/hp (29.4 lb/kW), 9.8 kg/hp (13.3 kg/kW); acceleration: standing ¼ mile 17 sec; speed in top at 1,000 rpm: 20 mph, 32.2 km/h; consumption: 17.2 m/imp gal, 20.7 m/US gal 9.8 l x 100 km (DIN).

ELECTRICAL EQUIPMENT electronic ignition.

DIMENSIONS AND WEIGHT weight: 2,425 lb, 1,100 kg.

PRACTICAL INSTRUCTIONS valve timing: 15° 55° 57° 13°.

OPTIONALS with GM automatic transmission max speed about 102 mph, 165 km/h.

132 2000 i Berlina

See 132 2000 Berlina, except for:

PRICE EX WORKS: 10,655,000 liras**

ENGINE max power (DIN): 122 hp (90 kW) at 5,300 rpm; max torque (DIN): 127 lb ft, 17.5 kg m (172 Nm) at 3,500 rpm; max engine rpm: 5,800; 61.2 hp/l (45.1 kW/l), Bosch L-Jetronic injection pump in inlet pipes and automatic starting device; fuel feed: electric pump.

TRANSMISSION axle ratio: 4.100.

PERFORMANCE max speed: 109 mph, 175 km/h; power-weight ratio: 20.4 lb/hp (27.7 lb/kW), 9.3 kg/hp (12.6 kg/kW); acceleration: standing ¼ mile 16.8 sec; speed in direct drive at 1,000 rpm: 16.7 mph, 26.9 km/h; consumption: 28.2 m/imp gal, 23.5 m/US gal, 10 l x 100 km at 75 mph, 120 km/h.

ELECTRICAL EQUIPMENT 55 Ah battery; 55 A alternator.

DIMENSIONS AND WEIGHT weight: 2,492 lb, 1,130 kg.

OPTIONALS with GM automatic transmission max speed 106 mph, 170 km/h, acceleration standing ¼ mile 18.5 sec, consumption 25.9 m/imp gal, 21.6 m/US gal, 10.9 l x 100 km at 75 mph, 120 km/h.

FIAT 132 2000 i Berlina

132 Diesel 2000

See 132 1600 Berlina, except for:

PRICE EX WORKS: 10,767,000 liras**

ENGINE diesel; 121.7 cu in, 1,995 cc (3.46 x 3.23 in, 88 x 82 mm); compression ratio: 22:1; max power (DIN): 60 hp (44 kW) at 4,400 rpm; max torque (DIN): 83 lb ft, 11.5 kg m (113 Nm) at 2,400 rpm; 30.1 hp/l (22.1 kW/l); valves: overhead, in line; camshafts: 1, overhead; lubrication: 11.6 imp pt, 13.9 US pt, 6.6 l; Bosch indirect injection pump; cooling, liquid, expansion tank, 19.4 imp pt, 23.3 US pt, 11 l, electromagnetic thermostatic fan.

TRANSMISSION axle ratio: 4.100.

PERFORMANCE max speed: 84 mph, 135 km/h; power-weight ratio: 44.8 lb/hp (61 lb/kW), 20.3 kg/hp (27.7 kg/kW); acceleration: standing ¼ mile 23 sec; speed in direct drive at 1,000 rpm: 16.7 mph, 26.9 km/h; consumption: 33.2 m/imp gal, 27.7 m/US gal, 8.5 l x 100 km.

STEERING recirculating ball, servo; turns lock to lock: 2.90.

ELECTRICAL EQUIPMENT 77 Ah battery.

DIMENSIONS AND WEIGHT weight: 2,690 lb, 1,220 kg; weight distribution: 58% front, 42% rear.

PRACTICAL INSTRUCTIONS fuel: diesel oil; oil: engine 9.7 imp pt, 11.6 US pt, 5.5 l; valve timing: 8° 48° 48° 8°; tyre pressure: front 30 psi, 2.1 atm, rear 27 psi, 1.9 atm.

FIAT 132 Diesel 2500

132 Diesel 2500

See 132 1600 Berlina, except for:

PRICE EX WORKS: 11,281,000 liras**

ENGINE diesel; 149.2 cu in, 2,445 cc (3.66 x 3.54 in, 93 x 90 mm); compression ratio: 22:1; max power (DIN): 72 hp (53 kW) at 4,200 rpm; max torque (DIN): 109 lb ft, 15 kg m (147 Nm) at 2,400 rpm; 29.4 hp/l (21.7 kW/l); valves: overhead, in line; camshafts: 1, overhead; lubrication: 11.6 imp pt, 13.9 US pt, 6.6 l; Bosch indirect injection pump; cooling, liquid, expansion tank, 19.4 imp pt, 23.3 US pt, 11 l, electromagnetic thermostatic fan.

TRANSMISSION axle ratio: 3.727.

PERFORMANCE max speed: 93 mph, 150 km/h; power-weight ratio: 37.7 lb/hp (51.7 lb/kW), 17.1 kg/hp (23.2 kg/kW); acceleration: standing ¼ mile 20.8 sec; speed in direct drive at 1,000 rpm: 18.4 mph, 29.6 km/h; consumption: 31.7 m/imp gal, 26.4 m/US gal, 8.9 l x 100 km.

STEERING recirculating ball, servo; turns lock to lock: 2.90.

ELECTRICAL EQUIPMENT 77 Ah battery.

DIMENSIONS AND WEIGHT weight: 2,712 lb, 1,230 kg; weight distribution: 58% front, 42% rear.

PRACTICAL INSTRUCTIONS fuel: diesel oil; oil: engine 9.7 imp pt, 11.6 US pt, 5.5 l; valve timing: 8° 48° 48° 8°; tyre pressure: front 30 psi, 2.1 atm, rear 27 psi, 1.9 atm.

Campagnola

PRICE EX WORKS: 12,248,000* liras

ENGINE front, 4 stroke; 4 cylinders, vertical, in line; 121.7 cu in, 1,995 cc (3.31 x 3.54 in, 84 x 90 mm); compression ratio: 8.6:1; max power (DIN): 80 hp (59 kW) at 4,600 rpm; max torque (DIN): 112 lb ft, 15.4 kg m (151 Nm) at 2,800 rpm; 40.1 hp/l (29.5 kW/l); cast iron block, light alloy head; 5 crankshaft bearings; valves: overhead, slanted at 10°, push-rods and rockers; camshafts: 1, side, cogged belt; lubrication: gear pump, full flow filter (cartridge), 8.4 imp pt, 10.1 US pt, 4.8 l; 1 Solex C 32 PHHE 1 RM horizontal twin barrel carburettor; fuel feed: mechanical pump; water-cooled, 15.7 imp pt, 18.8 US pt, 8.9 l.

TRANSMISSION driving wheels: front and rear; clutch: single dry plate; gearbox: mechanical, in unit with engine; gears: 5, fully synchronized; high ratios: I 3.612, II 2.045, III 1.357, IV 1, V 0.870; 3.244; low ratios: 1.100 and 3.870; gear and transfer levers: central; final drive: hypoid bevel, rear limited slip differential; axle ratio (front and rear): 5.375; width of rims: 4.5" K; tyres: 7.00 x 16 C 6PR.

PERFORMANCE max speeds (high ratios): (I) 20 mph, 33 km/h; (II) 35 mph, 57 km/h; (III) 55 mph, 88 km/h (IV) 71 mph, 115 km/h; (V) over 75 mph, 120 km/h - (low ratios) (I) 7 mph, 11 km/h; (II) 12 mph, 19 km/h; (III) 18 mph, 29 km/h; (IV) 25 mph, 40 km/h; (V) 31 mph, 50 km/h; power-weight ratio: 44.3 lb/hp (60.2 lb/kW), 20.1 kg/hp (27.3 kg/kW); carrying capacity: 1,103 lb, 500 kg; speed in direct drive at 1,000 rpm: 14 mph, 22.5 km/h; consumption: 20.8 m/imp gal, 17.3 m/US gal, 13.6 l x 100 km (DIN).

CHASSIS integral; front suspension: independent, by McPherson, coil springs/telescopic damper struts, lower wishbones, torsion bars, anti-roll bar; rear: independent, by McPherson, coil springs, 4 telescopic dampers, lower wishbones, torsion bars, anti-roll bar.

STEERING worm and roller; turns lock to lock: 4.60.

BRAKES drum, dual circuit; swept area: front 91.5 sq in, 590 sq cm, rear 91.5 sq in, 590 sq cm, total 183 sq in, 1,180 sq cm.

ELECTRICAL EQUIPMENT 12 V; 55 Ah battery; 55 A alternator; Marelli distributor; 2 headlamps.

DIMENSIONS AND WEIGHT wheel base: 90.55 in, 230 cm; tracks: 53.54 in, 136 cm front, 55.91 in, 142 cm rear; length: 148.42 in, 377 cm; width: 62.20 in, 158 cm; height: 76.77 in, 195 cm; ground clearance: 10.16 in, 25.8 cm; weight: 3,550 lb, 1,610 kg; turning circle: 35.4 ft, 10.8 m; fuel tank: 12.5 imp gal, 15 US gal, 57 l.

BODY open; 2 doors; 7 seats, separate front seats.

PRACTICAL INSTRUCTIONS fuel: 99 oct petrol; oil: engine 7.4 imp pt, 8.9 US pt, 4.2 l, SAE 10W-40, change every 3,100 miles, 5,000 km - gearbox 2.5 imp pt, 3 US pt, 1.4 l, SAE 90 EP, change every 12,400 miles, 20,000 km - transfer box 3.9 imp pt, 4.7 US pt, 2.2 l, SAE 90 EP, change every 12,400 miles, 20,000 km - final drive 3.2 imp pt, 3.8 US pt, 1.8 l front, 3.2 imp pt, 3.8 US pt, 1.8 l rear, SAE 90 EP, change every 12,400 miles, 20,000 km; valve timing: 10° 49° 50° 9°; tyre pressure: front 26 psi, 1.8 atm, rear 36 psi, 2.5 atm.

OPTIONALS hardtop; front limited slip differential; 7.50 x 16 C 6 PR tyres; power steering.

Campagnola Lunga

See Campagnola, except for:

PRICE EX WORKS: 12,602,000* liras

TRANSMISSION axle ratio (front and rear): 5.625; width of rims: 5" K or 5" F.

PERFORMANCE max speeds (high ratios): (I) 19 mph, 31 km/h; (II) 34 mph, 54 km/h; (III) 52 mph, 84 km/h; (IV) 68 mph, 110 km/h; (V) 71 mph, 115 km/h - (low ratios) (I) 6 mph, 10 km/h; (II) 11 mph, 18 km/h; (III) 17 mph, 28 km/h; (IV) 24 mph, 38 km/h; (V) 28 mph, 45 km/h; power-weight ratio: 46.8 lb/hp (63.6 lb/kW), 21.3 kg/hp (28.9 kg/kW); carrying capacity: 1,433 lb, 650 kg.

DIMENSIONS AND WEIGHT length: 158.46 in, 403 cm; weight: 3,748 lb, 1,700 kg.

Campagnola Diesel

See Campagnola, except for:

PRICE EX WORKS: 14,018,000* liras

ENGINE diesel; 149.2 cu in, 2,445 cc (3.66 x 3.54 in, 93 x 90 mm); compression ratio: 22:1; max power (DIN): 72 hp (53 kW) at 4,200 rpm; max torque (DIN): 109 lb ft, 15 kg m (147 Nm) at 2,400 rpm; 29.4 hp/l (21.7 kW/l); valves: overhead, in line; camshafts: 1, overhead; lubrication: 11.6 imp pt, 13.9 US pt,

FIAT Campagnola Diesel

CAMPAGNOLA DIESEL

6.6 l; Bosch or CAV indirect injection pump; cooling liquid, expansion tank, 16.9 imp pt, 20.3 US pt, 9.6 l, electromagnetic thermostatic fan.

PERFORMANCE max speed: 71 mph, 115 km/h; power-weight ratio: 53.9 lb/hp (73.2 lb/kW), 24.4 kg/hp (33.2 kg/kW); carrying capacity: 1,654 lb, 750 kg; consumption: 22.4 m/imp gal, 18.7 m/US gal, 12.6 l x 100 km (DIN).

STEERING recirculating ball, servo (standard).

ELECTRICAL EQUIPMENT 88 Ah battery.

DIMENSIONS AND WEIGHT weight: 3,881 lb, 1,760 kg.

Campagnola Diesel Lunga

See Campagnola, except for:

PRICE EX WORKS: 14,372,000* liras

ENGINE diesel; 149.2 cu in, 2,445 cc (3.66 x 3.54 in, 93 x 90 mm); compression ratio: 22:1; max power (DIN): 72 hp (53 kW) at 4,200 rpm; max torque (DIN): 109 lb ft, 15 kg m (147 Nm) at 2,400 rpm; 29.4 hp/l (21.7 kW/l); valves: overhead, in line; camshafts: 1, overhead; lubrication: 11.6 imp pt, 13.9 US pt, 6.6 l; Bosch or CAV indirect injection pump; cooling, liquid, expansion tank, 16.9 imp pt, 20.3 US pt, 9.6 l, electromagnetic thermostatic fan.

TRANSMISSION axle ratio (front and rear): 5.625; width of rims: 5" k or 5" F.

PERFORMANCE max speed: 68 mph, 110 km/h; power-weight ratio. 56 lb/hp (76.1 lb/kW), 25.4 kg/hp (34.5 kg/kW).

STEERING recirculating ball, servo (standard).

ELECTRICAL EQUIPMENT 88 Ah battery.

DIMENSIONS AND WEIGHT height: 158.46 in, 403 cm; weight: 4,035 lb, 1,830 kg.

GIANNINI ITALY

Fiat Giannini 126 Series

PRICES EX WORKS:	liras
1 GP Base	3,135,000*
2 GP Personal	3,370,000*
3 GP Serie Speciale	3,685,000*
4 GPS Base	3,310,000*
5 GPS Personal	3,545,000*
6 GPS Serie Speciale	3,860,000*
7 Sport Base DC	3,505,000*
8 Sport Personal DC	3,765,000*
9 Sport Serie Speciale DC	4,060,000*
10 GPA Base	3,555,000*
11 GPA Personal	3,805,000*
12 GPA Serie Speciale	4,110,000*
13 Sport Base DC	3,805,000*
14 Sport Personal DC	4,035,000*
15 Sport Serie Speciale DC	4,350,000*

Power team:	Standard for:	Optional for:
29 hp	1 to 3	—
34 hp	4 to 6	—
37 hp	7 to 9	—
38 hp	10 to 12	—
41.4 hp	13 to 15	—

29 hp power team

ENGINE rear, 4 stroke; 2 cylinders, vertical, in line; 39.8 cu in, 652 cc (3.03 x 2.76 in, 77 x 70 mm); compression ratio: 8.7:1; max power (DIN): 29 hp (21 kW) at 5,000 rpm; max torque (DIN): 35 lb ft, 4.8 kg m at 3,500 rpm; max engine rpm: 5,300; 44.5 hp/l (52.8 kW/l); light alloy block and head; 2 crankshaft bearings; valves: overhead, in line, push-rods and rockers; camshafts: 1, side; lubrication: gear pump, centrifugal filter, 6.2 imp pt, 7.4 US pt, 3.5 l; 1 Weber 28 IMB downdraught carburettor; fuel feed: mechanical pump; air-cooled.

TRANSMISSION driving wheels: rear; clutch: single dry plate; gearbox: mechanical; gears: 4, II, III and IV silent claw coupling; ratios: I 3.250, II 2.067, III 1.300, IV 0.872, rev 4.024; lever: central; final drive: spiral bevel; axle ratio: 4.875; width of rims: 4"; tyres: 135 SR x 12.

PERFORMANCE max speed: 75 mph, 120 km/h; power-weight ratio: 44.5 lb/hp (61.5 lb/kW), 20.2 kg/hp (27.9 kg/kW); carrying capacity: 706 lb, 320 kg; speed in top at 1,000 rpm: 14.3 mph, 23 km/h; consumption: 56.5 m/imp gal, 47 m/US gal, 5 l x 100 km.

GIANNINI 126 GP Personal

CHASSIS integral; front suspension: independent, wishbones, transverse leafspring lower arms, telescopic dampers; rear: independent, oblique semi-trailing arms, coil springs, telescopic dampers.

STEERING screw and sector; turns lock to lock: 2.90.

BRAKES drum; lining area: front 33.5 sq in, 216 sq cm, rear 33.5 sq in, 216 sq cm, total 67 sq in, 432 sq cm.

ELECTRICAL EQUIPMENT 12 V; 34 Ah battery; 230 W alternator; Marelli distributor; 2 headlamps.

DIMENSIONS AND WEIGHT wheel base: 72.44 in, 184 cm; tracks: 44.96 in, 114 cm front, 47.36 in, 120 cm rear; length: 120.24 in, 305 cm; width: 54.21 in, 138 cm; height: 52.56 in, 133 cm; ground clearance: 5.51 in, 14 cm; weight: 1,290 lb, 585 kg; weight distribution: 40% front, 60% rear; turning circle: 28.2 ft, 8.6 m; fuel tank: 4.6 imp gal, 5.5 US gal, 21 l.

BODY saloon/sedan; 2 doors; 4 seats, separate front seats.

PRACTICAL INSTRUCTIONS fuel: 98-100 oct petrol; oil: engine 6.2 imp pt, 7.4 US pt, 3.5 l, SAE 20W-50, change every 3,700 miles, 6,000 km - gearbox and final drive 1.9 imp pt, 2.3 US pt, 1.1 l, Fiat ZC 90, change every 18,600 miles, 30,000 km; greasing: every 3,100 miles, 5,000 km, 2 points; sparking plug: 240°; tappet clearances: inlet 0.008 in, 0.20 mm, exhaust 0.010 in, 0.25 mm; valve timing: 28° 72° 66° 32°; tyre pressure: front 22 psi, 1.4 atm, rear 28 psi, 2 atm.

OPTIONALS light alloy wheels; electronic injection; roll-bar; twin barrel carburettor.

34 hp power team

See 29 hp power team, except for:

ENGINE 42.3 cu in, 694 cc (3.13 x 2.76 in, 79.5 x 70 mm); compression ratio: 8.5:1; max power (DIN): 34 hp (25 kW) at 5,400 rpm; max torque (DIN): 37 lb ft, 5.1 kg m (50 Nm) at 3,500 rpm; max engine rpm: 5,800; 49 hp/l (36.1 kW/l).

PERFORMANCE max speed: about 81 mph, 130 km/h; power-weight ratio: 42.8 lb/hp (58.2 lb/kW), 19.4 kg/hp (26.4 kg/kW); consumption: 52.3 m/imp gal, 43.6 m/US gal, 5.4 l x 100 km.

DIMENSIONS AND WEIGHT weight: 1,455 lb, 660 kg.

37 hp power team

See 29 hp power team, except for:

ENGINE 42.3 cu in, 694 cc (3.13 x 2.76 in, 79.5 x 70 mm); compression ratio: 8.8:1; max power (DIN): 37 hp (27 kW) at 5,700 rpm; max torque (DIN): 41 lb ft, 5.7 kg m (56 Nm) at 3,500 rpm; max engine rpm: 6,000; 53.3 hp/l (39.2 kW/l); 1 Weber DMIS 32 horizontal twin barrel carburettor.

PERFORMANCE max speed: 84 mph, 135 km/h; power-weight ratio: 35.7 lb/hp (48.9 lb/kW), 16.2 kg/hp (22.2 kg/kW); consumption: 51.4 m/imp gal, 42.8 m/US gal, 5.5 l x 100 km.

DIMENSIONS AND WEIGHT weight: 1,323 lb, 600 kg.

38 hp power team

See 29 hp power team, except for:

ENGINE 48.4 cu in, 794 cc (3.35 x 2.76 in, 85 x 70 mm); compression ratio: 8.5:1; max power (DIN): 38 hp (28 kW) at 5,000 rpm; max torque (DIN): 41 lb ft, 5.7 kg m (56 Nm) at 4,000 rpm; 47.9 hp/l (35.3 kW/l).

PERFORMANCE max speed: 84 mph, 135 km/h; power-weight ratio: 35.5 lb/hp (48.1 lb/kW), 16.1 kg/hp (21.8 kg/kW); consumption: 51.4 m/imp gal, 42.8 m/US gal, 5.5 l x 100 km.

DIMENSIONS AND WEIGHT weight: 1,345 lb, 610 kg.

41.4 hp power team

See 29 hp power team, except for:

ENGINE 48.4 cu in, 794 cc (3.35 x 2.76 in, 85 x 70 mm); compression ratio: 8.8:1; max power (DIN): 41.4 hp (30 kW) at 5,600 rpm; max torque (DIN): 41 lb ft, 5.7 kg m (56 Nm) at 3,800 rpm; 52.1 hp/l (38.3 kW/l); 1 Weber DHLB 32 horizontal twin barrel carburettor.

PERFORMANCE max speed: 87 mph, 140 km/h; power-weight ratio: 32.4 lb/hp (44.8 lb/kW), 14.7 kg/hp (20.3 kg/kW); consumption: 48.7 m/imp gal, 40.6 m/US gal, 5.8 l x 100 km.

DIMENSIONS AND WEIGHT weight: 1,345 lb, 610 kg.

Fiat Giannini 127 Series

PRICES EX WORKS:	liras
NP 2-dr Berlina Base	4,575,000*
NP 2+1-dr Berlina Base	4,695,000*
NP 2-dr Berlina Confort	5,075,000*
NP 2+1-dr Berlina Confort	5,195,000*

57 hp power team

ENGINE front, transverse, 4 stroke; 4 cylinders, vertical, in line; 55.1 cu in, 903 cc (2.56 x 2.56 in, 65 x 68 mm); compression ratio: 9.6:1; max power (DIN): 57 hp (42 kW) at 6,400 rpm; max torque (DIN): 50 lb ft, 6.9 kg m (68 Nm) at 4,600 rpm; max engine rpm: 7,000; 63.1 hp/l (46.4 kW/l); cast iron block, light alloy head; 3 crankshaft bearings; valves: overhead, in line, push-rods and rockers; camshafts: 1, side, chain-driven; lubrication: gear pump, full flow filter (cartridge), 5.6 imp pt, 6.8 US pt, 3.2 l; 1 Weber 32 IBA 20 downdraught twin barrel carburettor; fuel feed: mechanical pump; water-cooled, 8.8 imp pt, 10.6 US pt, 5 l, electric thermostatic fan.

TRANSMISSION driving wheels: front; clutch: single dry plate; gearbox: mechanical; gears: 4, fully synchronized; ratios: I 3.910, II 2.055, III 1.348, IV 0.963, rev 3.615; lever: central; final drive: hypoid bevel; axle ratio: 4.071; width of rims: 4"; tyres: 135 SR x 13.

PERFORMANCE max speed: 93 mph, 150 km/h; power-weight ratio: 27.6 lb/hp (37.3 lb/kW), 12.5 kg/hp (16.9 kg/kW); carrying capacity: 882 lb, 400 kg; speed in top at 1,000 rpm: 14 mph, 22 km/h; consumption: 40.4 m/imp gal, 33.6 m/US gal, 7 l x 100 km.

GIANNINI 127 NP Berlina

HASSIS integral; front suspension: independent, by Mc-herson, coil springs/telescopic damper struts, lower wish-ones, anti-roll bar; rear: independent, single wide-based wish-ones, transverse anti-roll leafsprings, telescopic dampers.

TEERING rack-and-pinion; turns lock to lock: 3.50.

RAKES front disc (diameter 8.94 in, 22.7 cm), rear drum, dual rcuit, rear compensator; lining area: front 19.2 sq in, 124 sq m, rear 33.5 sq in, 216 sq cm, total 52.7 sq in, 340 sq cm.

LECTRICAL EQUIPMENT 12 V; 34 Ah battery; 33 A altenator; arelli distributor; 2 headlamps.

IMENSIONS AND WEIGHT wheel base: 87.60 in, 222 cm; acks: 50.39 in, 128 cm front, 50.98 in, 129 cm rear; length: 43.31 in, 364 cm; width: 60.12 in, 153 cm; height: 52.76 in, 34 cm; ground clearance: 5.12 in, 13 cm; weight: 1,566 lb, 710 g; turning circle: 31.5 ft, 9.6 m; fuel tank: 6.6 imp gal, 7.9 US al, 30 l.

ODY saloon/sedan; 5 seats, separate front seat; folding rear eat (for 2+1-dr models only).

RACTICAL INSTRUCTIONS fuel: 98 oct petrol; oil: engine 5.6 np pt, 6.8 US pt, 3.2 l, SAE 20W (winter) 30 (summer), change very 6,200 miles, 10,000 km - gearbox and final drive 4.2 imp , 5.1 US pt, 2.4 l, SAE 90, change every 18,600 miles, 30,000 m; greasing: every 18,600 miles, 30,000 km; sparking plug: 60°; tappet clearances: inlet 0.006 in, 0.15 mm, exhaust 0.008 , 0.20 mm; valve timing: 25° 51° 64° 12°; tyre pressure: front 4 psi, 1.7 atm, rear 27 psi, 1.9 atm.

PTIONALS light alloy wheels; iodine fog lamps; electronic ijection; special instrument panel with rev counter.

Fiat Giannini Ritmo Series

RICES EX WORKS: **liras**

Veloce 2+1-dr Confort 60 CL	**6,220,000***
Veloce 4+1-dr Confort 60 CL	**6,520,000***
Autostrada 2+1-dr Confort 60 CL	**6,630,000***
Autostrada 4+1-dr Confort 60 CL	**6,920,000***

ower team:	Standard for:	Optional for:
2 hp	1,2	—
0 hp	3,4	—

72 hp power team

NGINE front, transverse, 4 stroke; 4 cylinders, vertical, in line; 3.1 cu in, 1,116 cc (3.15 x 2.19 in, 80 x 55.5 mm); compress-n ratio: 9.8:1; max power (DIN): 72 hp (53 kW) at 6,600 rpm; ax torque (DIN): 62 lb ft, 8.6 kg m (84 Nm) at 4,200 rpm; max ngine rpm: 6,500; 64.5 hp/l (47.5 kW/l); cast iron block, light loy head; 5 crankshaft bearings; valves: overhead, thimble ppets; camshafts: 1, overhead, cogged belt; lubrication: gear ump, full flow filter, cartridge, 5.8 imp pt, 7 US pt, 3.3 l; 1 eber 32 ICEV downdraught single barrel carburettor; fuel ed: mechanical pump; water-cooled, 11.4 imp pt, 13.7 US pt, .5 l, electric thermostatic fan.

RANSMISSION driving wheels: front; clutch: single dry plate; earbox: mechanical; gears: 4, fully synchronized; ratios: I 583, II 2.235, III 1.454, IV 1.047, rev 3.714; lever: central; nal drive: cylindrical gears; axle ratio: 4.077; width of rims: 5"; tyres: 145 SR x 13.

PERFORMANCE max speed: 96 mph, 155 km/h; power-weight ratio: 27.3 lb/hp (37.3 lb/kW), 12.4 kg/hp (16.9 kg/kW); carrying capacity: 882 lb, 400 kg; speed in top at 1,000 rpm: 15.1 mph, 24.3 km/h; consumption: 40.4 m/imp gal, 33.6 m/US gal, 7 l x 100 km.

CHASSIS integral; front suspension: independent, by McPherson, coil springs/telescopic damper struts, lower wishbones, anti-roll bar; rear: independent, single wide-based wishbones, transverse anti-roll leafsprings, telescopic dampers.

STEERING rack-and-pinion; turns lock to lock: 3.50.

BRAKES front disc (diameter 8.94 in, 22.7 cm), rear drum, dual circuit, rear compensator, servo; lining area: front 19.2 sq in, 124 sq cm, rear 33.5 sq in, 216 sq cm, total 52.7 sq in, 340 sq cm.

ELECTRICAL EQUIPMENT 12 V; 34 Ah battery; 230 W dynamo; Marelli distributor; 2 headlamps.

DIMENSIONS AND WEIGHT wheel base: 96.38 in, 245 cm; tracks: 55.12 in, 140 cm front, 55.51 in, 141 cm rear; lenght: 155.12 in, 394 cm; width: 64.96 in, 165 cm; height: 55.12 in, 140 cm; ground clearance: 5.71 in, 14.5 cm; weight: 1,973 lb, 895 kg; weight distribution: 61.5% front, 38.5% rear; turning circle: 33.8 ft, 10.3 m; fuel tank:11.2 imp gal, 13.5 US gal, 51 l.

BODY saloon/sedan; 5 seats, separate front seats, reclining backrests.

PRACTICAL INSTRUCTIONS fuel: 98 oct petrol; oil: engine 5.8 imp pt, 7 US pt, 3.3 l, SAE 20W (winter) 30 (summer), change every 6,200 miles, 10,000 km - gearbox and final drive 5.5 imp pt, 6.6 US pt, 3.1 l, SAE 90, change every 18,600 miles, 30,000 km; greasing: every 18,600 miles, 30,000 km; sparking plug: 240°; tappet clearance: inlet 0.012 in, 0.30 mm, exhaust 0.016 in, 0.40 mm; valve timing: 12° 52° 52° 12°; tyre pressure: front 26 psi, 1.8 atm, rear 24 psi, 1.7 atm.

OPTIONALS 5-speed fully synchronized mechanical gearbox (V 0.863 ratio); light alloy wheels; iodine fog lamps; electronic injection.

80 hp power team

See 72 hp power team, except for:

ENGINE max power (DIN): 80 hp (58 kW) at 7,000 rpm; max torque (DIN): 67 lb ft, 9.2 kg m (90 Nm) at 4,800 rpm; max engine rpm: 7,200; 71.7 hp/l (52.8 kW/l); electronic injection; 2 Weber 40 DCNF twin barrel carburettors.

TRANSMISSION gears: 5, fully synchronized; ratios I 3.583, II 2.235, III 1.454, IV 1.047, V 0.863, rev 3.714.

PERFORMANCE max speed: 109 mph, 175 km/h; power-weight ratio: 24.7 lb/hp (34 lb/kW), 11.2 kg/hp (15.4 kg/kW).

LAMBORGHINI ITALY

Urraco P 200

PRICE EX WORKS: 20,532,000* liras

ENGINE centre-rear, transverse, 4 stroke; 8 cylinders, Vee-slanted at 90°; 121.7 cu in, 1,994 cc (3.05 x 2.09 in, 77.4 x 53 mm); compression ratio: 9.8:1; max power (DIN): 182 hp (134 kW) at 7,500 rpm; max torque (DIN): 109 lb ft, 15 kg m (147 Nm) at 3,800 rpm; max engine rpm: 7,900; 91.3 hp/l (67.2 kW/l); light alloy block and head, wet liners; 5 crankshaft bearings; valves: overhead, in line, thimble tappets; camshafts: 2, 1 per bank, Vee-slanted at 70°, overhead, cogged belt; lubrication: gear pump, full flow filter, 13.2 imp pt, 15.9 US pt, 7.5 l; 4 Weber IDF 40 downdraught twin barrel carburettors: fuel feed: electric pump; water-cooled, 21.1 imp pt, 25.4 US pt, 12 l, 2 front fans, 1 electric and 1 thermostatic.

TRANSMISSION driving wheels: rear; clutch: single dry plate (diaphragm), hydraulically controlled; gearbox: mechanical; gears: 5, fully synchronized; ratios: I 2.935, II 2.105, III 1.565, IV 1.185, V 0.900, rev 2.540; lever: central; final drive: helical spur gears; axle ratio: 4.350; width of rims: 7.5"; tyres: 195/70 VR x 14 front, 205/70 VR x 14 rear.

PERFORMANCE max speed: 127 mph, 205 km/h; power-weight ratio: 15.1 lb/hp (20.6 lb/kW), 6.9 kg/hp (9.3 kg/kW); carrying capacity: 882 lb, 400 kg; speed in top at 1,000 rpm: 18.8 mph, 30.2 km/h; consumption: 20.5 m/imp gal, 17 m/US gal, 13.8 l x 100 km.

CHASSIS integral, rear auxiliary frame; front suspension: independent, by McPherson, coil springs/telescopic damper struts,

GIANNINI Ritmo Veloce Confort 60 CL

URRACO P 200

lower wishbones (trailing links), anti-roll bar; rear: independent, by McPherson, coil springs/telescopic damper struts, lower wishbones, anti-roll bar.

STEERING rack-and-pinion; turns lock to lock: 4.25.

BRAKES disc (diameter 10.94 in, 27.8 cm), internal radial fins, dual circuit, each with servo.

ELECTRICAL EQUIPMENT 12 V; 55 Ah battery; 770 W alternator; Marelli distributor; 4,2 iodine retractable headlamps.

DIMENSIONS AND WEIGHT wheel base: 96.46 in, 245 cm; front and rear track: 57.48 in, 146 cm; length: 168.50 in, 428 cm; width: 68.50 in, 174 cm; height: 44.88 in, 114 cm; ground clearance: 4.72 in, 12 cm; weight: 2,756 lb, 1,250 kg: turning circle: 35.1 ft, 10.7 m; fuel tank: 17.6 imp gal, 21.1 US gal, 80 l.

BODY coupé; 2 doors; 4 seats, separate front seats.

PRACTICAL INSTRUCTIONS fuel: 98-100 oct petrol; oil: engine 13.2 imp pt, 15.9 US pt, 7.5 l, SAE 20W-50, change every 2,500 miles, 4,000 km - gearbox and final drive 10.6 imp pt, 12.7 US pt, 6 l, SAE 90, change every 6,200 miles, 10,000 km; sparking plug: 235°; tappet clearances: inlet 0.018 in, 0.45 mm, exhaust 0.018 in, 0.45 mm; valve timing: 40° 60° 58° 38°; tyre pressure: front 28 psi, 2 atm, rear 31 psi, 2.2 atm.

OPTIONALS leather upholstery; metallic spray; electric tinted windows; air-conditioning.

Urraco P 250

See Urraco P 200, except for:

PRICE EX WORKS: 23,490,000* liras

ENGINE 150 cu in, 2,463 cc (3.39 x 2.09 in, 86 x 53 mm); compression ratio: 10.4:1; max power (DIN): 220 hp (162 kW) at 7,500 rpm; max torque (DIN): 167 lb ft, 23 kg m (226 Nm) at 5,600 rpm; 89.3 hp/l (65.7 kW/l).

PERFORMANCE max speed: over 149 mph, 240 km/h; power-weight ratio: 13.7 lb/hp (18.6 lb/kW), 6.2 kg/hp (8.5 kg/kW); speed in top at 1,000 rpm: 19.2 mph, 30.9 km/h; consumption: 18.8 m/imp gal, 15.7 m/US gal, 15 l x 100 km.

DIMENSIONS AND WEIGHT weight: 3,021 lb, 1,370 kg.

BODY (standard) leather upholstery, metallic spray and electric tinted windows.

Urraco P 300

See Urraco P 200, except for:

PRICE EX WORKS: 25,650,000* liras

ENGINE 128.8 cu in, 2,996 cc (3.39 x 2.54 in, 86 x 64.5 mm); compression ratio: 10.1:1; max power (DIN): 265 hp (195 kW) at 7,500 rpm; max torque (DIN): 203 lb ft, 28 kg m (275 Nm) at 3,500 rpm; 88.5 hp/l (65.1 kW/l); valves: Vee-slanted at 45°; camshafts: 4, 2 per bank, chain-driven; 4 Weber 40 DCNF downdraught twin barrel carburettors.

PERFORMANCE max speed: 165 mph, 265 km/h; power-weight ratio: 10.8 lb/hp (14.7 lb/kW), 4.9 kg/hp (67 kg/kW); speed in top at 1,000 rpm: 19.9 mph, 32 km/h; consumption: 17.7 m/imp gal, 14.7 m/US gal, 16 l x 100 km.

DIMENSIONS AND WEIGHT weight: 2,867 lb, 1,300 kg.

PRACTICAL INSTRUCTIONS valve timing: 32° 60° 60° 32°.

Silhouette

See Urraco P 200, except for:

PRICE EX WORKS: 31,050,000* liras

ENGINE 182.8 cu in, 2,996 cc (3.39 x 2.54 in, 86 x 64.5 mm); compression ratio: 10.1:1; max power (DIN): 265 hp (195 kW) at 7,500 rpm; max torque (DIN): 203 lb ft, 28 kg m (275 Nm) at 3,500 rpm; 88.5 hp/l (65.1 kW/l); valves: Vee-slanted at 45°; camshafts: 4, 2 per bank, chain-driven; 4 Weber 40 DCNF downdraught twin barrel carburettors.

TRANSMISSION axle ratio: 4; width of rims: 8" front, 11" rear; tyres: 195/50 VR x 15 P7 front, 285/40 VR x 15 P7 rear.

PERFORMANCE max speeds: (I) 47 mph, 75 km/h; (II) 62 mph, 100 km/h; (III) 89 mph, 143 km/h; (IV) 111 mph, 178 km/h; (V) over 155 mph, 250 km/h; power-weight ratio: 9.9 lb/hp (14.8 lb/kW), 4.5 kg/hp (6.7 kg/kW); speed in top at 1,000 rpm: 19.9 mph, 32 km/h; consumption: 17.7 m/imp gal, 14.7 m/US gal, 16 l x 100 km.

DIMENSIONS AND WEIGHT tracks: 58.66 in, 149 cm front, 61.02 in, 155 cm rear; length: 170.08 in, 432 cm; width: 74.02 in, 188 cm; height: 44.09 in, 112 cm; ground clearance: 5.51 in, 14 cm; weight: 2,867 lb, 1,300 kg.

BODY sports; 2 seats.

PRACTICAL INSTRUCTIONS oil: engine 21.1 imp pt, 25.4 US pt, 12 l - gearbox and final drive 6.7 imp pt, 8 US pt, 3.8 l; valve timing: 32° 60° 60° 32°; tyre pressure: front 36 psi, 2.5 atm, rear 40 psi, 2.8 atm.

LAMBORGHINI *Urraco P 300*

Espada 400 GT

PRICE EX WORKS: 41,175,000* liras

ENGINE front, 4 stroke; 12 cylinders, Vee-slanted at 60°; 239.7 cu in, 3,929 cc (3.23 x 2.44 in, 82 x 62 mm); compression ratio: 9.55:1; max power (DIN): 350 hp (258 kW) at 7,500 rpm; max torque (DIN): 290 lb ft, 40 kg m (392 Nm) at 5,500 rpm; max engine rpm: 7,900; 89.1 hp/l (65.6 kW/l); light alloy block and head, wet liners; 7 crankshaft bearings; valves: overhead, Vee-slanted at 70°, thimble tappets; camshafts: 4, 2 per bank, overhead, chain-driven; lubrication: gear pump, full flow filter, 25.2 imp pt, 30.2 US pt, 14.3 l; 6 Weber 40 DCOE 20/21 horizontal twin barrel carburettors; fuel feed: electric pump; water-cooled, 24.6 imp pt, 29.6 US pt, 14 l, 2 electric thermostatic fans.

TRANSMISSION driving wheels: rear; clutch: single dry plate (diaphragm), hydraulically controlled; gearbox: mechanical; gears: 5, fully synchronized; ratios: I 2.520, II 1.735, III 1.225, IV 1, V 0.815, rev 2.765; lever: central; final drive: hypoid bevel; axle ratio: 4.100; width of rims: 7"; tyres: 215/ VR x 15.

PERFORMANCE max speeds: (I) 47 mph, 75 km/h; (II) 68 mp 110 km/h; (III) 93 mph, 150 km/h; (IV) 124 mph, 200 km/h; (155 mph, 250 km/h; power-weight ratio: 10.3 lb/hp (13.1 lb/kW 4.7 kg/hp (6.3 kg/kW); carrying capacity: 937 lb, 425 k acceleration: standing ¼ mile 15.5 sec; speed in top at 1,0 rpm: 21.6 mph, 34.8 km/h; consumption: 14.9 m/imp gal, 12 m/US gal, 19 l x 100 km.

CHASSIS integral; front suspension: independent, wishbone coil springs, anti-roll bar, telescopic dampers; rear: indepe dent, wishbones, coil springs, anti-roll bar, telescopic damper

STEERING ZF screw and sector; turns lock to lock: 3.80.

BRAKES disc (front diameter 11.81 in, 30 cm, rear 11.02 in, cm), internal radial fins, dual circuit, each with servo; swe area: front 285.3 sq in, 1,840 sq cm, rear 206.2 sq in, 1,3 sq cm, total 491.5 sq in, 3,170 sq cm.

ELECTRICAL EQUIPMENT 12 V; 72 Ah battery; 2 x 770 alternators; Marelli distributor; 2 iodine headlamps, 2 iodine f lamps.

DIMENSIONS AND WEIGHT wheel base: 104.33 in, 265 c front and rear track: 58.66 in, 149 cm; length: 186.54 in, 4 cm; width: 73.23 in, 186 cm; height: 46.65 in, 118 cm; grou clearance: 4.92 in, 12.5 cm; weight: 3,605 lb, 1,635 kg; weig distribution: 49.5% front, 50.5% rear; turning circle: 39.4 ft, m; fuel tank: 20.9 imp gal, 25.1 US gal, 95 l (2 separate tanks

LAMBORGHINI *Silhouette*

ODY coupé; 2 doors; 4 seats, separate front seats, reclining ackrests; leather upholstery; air-conditioning; tinted glass; ectric windows; heated rear window.

RACTICAL INSTRUCTIONS fuel: 98-100 oct petrol; oil: enne 25.2 imp pt, 30.2 US pt, 14.3 l, SAE 20W-50, change every ,500 miles, 4,000 km - gearbox 7 imp pt, 8.5 US pt, 4 l, SAE 0, change every 6,200 miles, 10,000 km - final drive 2.6 imp t, 3.2 US pt, 1.5 l, SAE 90, change every 6,200 miles, 10,000 m; greasing: every 6,200 miles, 10,000 km, 2 points, every 2,400 miles, 20,000 km, 2 points; sparking plug: 235°; tappet earances: inlet 0.010 in, 0.25 mm, exhaust 0.010 in, 0.25 mm; alve timing: 32° 76° 64° 32°; tyre pressure: front 34 psi, 2.4 tm, rear 37 psi, 2.6 atm.

PTIONALS right hand drive; 4.090 axle ratio; power steering; etallic spray; special spray.

Countach "S"

RICE EX WORKS: 83,000,000* liras

NGINE centre-rear, longitudinal, 4 stroke; 12 cylinders, ee-slanted at 60°; 239.7 cu in, 3,929 cc (3.23 x 2.44 in, 2 x 62 mm); compression ratio: 10.5:1; max power (DIN): 375 p (276 kW) at 8,000 rpm; max torque (DIN): 267 lb ft, 36.8 kg (36 Nm) at 5,500 rpm; max engine rpm: 8,000; 95.4 hp/l 70.2 kW/l); light alloy block and head, wet liners; 7 crankshaft earings; valves: overhead, Vee-slanted at 70°, thimble tapets; camshafts: 4, 2 per bank, overhead, chain-driven; lubricaon: gear pump, full flow filter, oil cooler, 30.8 imp pt, 37 US pt,

LAMBORGHINI Espada 400 GT

LAMBORGHINI Espada 400 GT

7.5 l; 6 Weber 45 DCOE 104-105 horizontal twin barrel carurettors; fuel feed: 2 electric pumps; water-cooled, 29.9 imp t, 35.9 US pt, 17 l, 2 radiators, 2 electric fans (1 thermostatic).

RANSMISSION driving wheels: rear; clutch: single dry plate diaphragm), hydraulically controlled; gearbox: mounted ahead f engine, mechanical; gears: 5, fully synchronized; ratios: I .256, II 1.769, III 1.310, IV 0.990, V 0.755, rev 2.134; lever: entral; final drive: hypoid bevel, limited slip differential; axle atio: 4.090; width of rims: 8.5" front, 12" rear; tyres: 205/50 'R x 15 P7 front, 345/35 VR x 15 P7 rear.

ERFORMANCE max speeds: (I) 65 mph, 105 km/h; (II) 84 nph, 135 km/h; (III) 113 mph, 182 km/h; (IV) 150 mph, 241 m/h; (V) 196 mph, 315 km/h; power-weight ratio: 7.4 lb/hp (10 b/kW), 3.4 kg/hp (4.6 kg/kW); carrying capacity: 397 lb, 180 g; acceleration: 0-50 mph (0-80 km/h) 6, sec; speed in top at ,000 rpm: 23.2 mph, 37.3 km/h; consumption: 19.8 m/imp gal, 6.4 m/US gal, 14.3 l x 100 km.

HASSIS tubular; front suspension: independent, wishbones, oil springs, anti-roll bar, telescopic dampers; rear indepenent, wishbones (trailing links), coil springs, anti-roll bar, 4 elescopic dampers.

STEERING rack-and-pinion; turns lock to lock: 3.

BRAKES disc (diameter 11.81 in, 30 cm front, 11.02 in, 28 cm ear), internal radial fins, dual circuit rear compensator, servo; ning area: front 27.9 sq in, 180 sq cm, rear 26.5 sq in, 171 sq m, total 54.4 sq in, 351 sq cm.

ELECTRICAL EQUIPMENT 12 V; 72 Ah battery; 840 W alternaor; 2 Marelli distributors; 4 iodine retractable headlamps.

DIMENSIONS AND WEIGHT wheel base: 96.46 in, 245 cm; tracks: 58.66 in, 149 cm front, 63.39 in, 161 cm rear; length: 162.99 in, 414 cm; width: 78.74 in, 200 cm; height: 42.13 in, 107 cm; ground clearance: 4.92 in, 12.5 cm; weight: 2,778 lb, 1,260 kg; weight distribution: 42% front axle, 58% rear axle; turning circle: 42.6 ft, 13 m; fuel tank: 26.4 imp gal, 31.7 US gal, 120 l (2 separate tanks).

BODY coupé; 2 doors; 2 seats; leather upholstery; tinted glass; heated rear window; light alloy wheels.

PRACTICAL INSTRUCTIONS fuel: 98-100 oct petrol; oil: engine 30.8 imp pt, 37 US pt, 17.5 l, SAE 20W-50, change every 3,100 miles, 5,000 km - gearbox 5.6 imp pt, 6.8 US pt, 3.2 l, SAE 90, change every 9,300 miles, 15,000 km - final drive 11.3 imp pt, 13.5 US pt, 6.4 l, SAE 90, change every 9,300 miles, 15,000 km; greasing: none; sparking plug: 235°; tappet clearances: inlet 0.010 in, 0.25 mm, exhaust 0.010 in, 0.25 mm; valve timing: 42° 70° 64° 40°; tyre pressure: front 34 psi, 2.4 atm, rear 34 psi, 2.4 atm.

OPTIONALS right hand drive; air-conditioning.

LANCIA ITALY

Delta Berlina 1300 (4 gears)

PRICE EX WORKS: 7,534,000 liras**

ENGINE front, transverse, 4 stroke; 4 cylinders, in line; 79.39 cu in, 1,301 cc (3.40 x 2.18 in, 86.4 x 55.5 mm); compression ratio: 9.1:1; max power (DIN): 75 hp (55 kW) at 5,800 rpm; max torque (DIN): 77.5 lb ft, 10.7 kg m (105 Nm) at 3,500 rpm; max engine rpm: 6,200; 57.6 hp/l (42.3 kW/l); cast iron block, light alloy head; 5 crankshaft bearings; valves: overhead, thimble tappets; camshafts: 1, overhead, cogged belt; lubrication: gear pump, by cartridge, 6.5 imp pt, 7.8 US pt, 3.7 l; 1 Weber 32 DAT 7 downdraught twin barrel carburettors; air cleaner: dry, thimble type thermostatic intake; fuel feed: mechanical pump; cooling liquid, expansion tank, 14.1 imp pt, 16.9 US pt, 8 l, electric thermostatic fan.

TRANSMISSION driving wheels: front; clutch: single dry plate; gearbox: mechanical; gears: 4, fully synchronized; ratios: I 3.583, II 2.235, III 1.454, IV 1.042, rev 3.714; lever: central; final drive: helical spur gears; axle ratio: 3.765; width of rims: 5"; tyres: 145 SR x 13 tubeless.

PERFORMANCE max speeds: (I) 28 mph, 45 km/h; (II) 45 mph, 73 km/h; (III) 69 mph, 112 km/h; (IV) over 96 mph, 155 km/h; power-weight ratio: 28.1 lb/hp, (38.3 lb/kW), 12.7 kg/hp (17.4 kg/kW); carrying capacity: 1,049 lb, 475 kg; acceleration: standing ¼ mile 19.2 sec, 0-50 mph (0-80 km/h) 8.2 sec; speed in top at 1,000 rpm: 16.3 mph, 26.3 km/h; consumption: 31 m/imp gal, 25.8 m/US gal, 9.1 l x 100 km at 75 mph, 120 km/h.

CHASSIS integral; front suspension independent by McPherson, coil springs/telescopic damper struts, lower wishbones, anti-roll bar; rear: independent, transverse links, longitudinal reaction rods, coil springs/telescopic damper struts, anti-roll bar.

STEERING rack-and-pinion; turns lock to lock: 3.80.

LAMBORGHINI Countach "S"

DELTA BERLINA 1300 (4 GEARS)

BRAKES front disc (diameter 8.94 in, 22.7 cm), rear drum, 2X circuits, rear compensator, servo; lining area: front 21.4 sq in, 138 sq cm, rear 32.4 sq in, 209 sq cm, total 53.8 sq in, 347 sq cm.

ELECTRICAL EQUIPMENT 12 V; 45 Ah battery; 45 A alternator; Bosch or Marelli distributor; 2 iodine headlamps.

DIMENSIONS AND WEIGHT wheel base: 97.40 in, 247 cm; front and rear track: 55.10 in, 140 cm; length: 153 in, 388 cm; width: 63.80 in, 162 cm; height: 54.30 in, 138 cm; weight: 2,106 lb, 955 kg; turning circle: 34.4 ft, 10.5 m; fuel tank: 9.9 imp gal, 11.9 US gal, 45 l.

BODY saloon/sedan; 5 doors; 5 seats, separate front seats; heated rear window.

PRACTICAL INSTRUCTIONS fuel: 98-100 oct petrol; oil: engine 6.5 imp pt, 7.8 US pt, 3.7 l, SAE 10W-50, change every 6,200 miles, 10,000 km - gearbox and final drive 5.4 imp pt, 6.5 US pt, 3.1 l, SAE 90, change every 18,600 miles, 30,000 km; greasing: none; sparking plug: Champion RN 9Y; valve timing: 12° 52° 52° 12°; tyre pressure: front 26 psi, 1.8 atm, rear 26 psi, 1.8 atm.

OPTIONALS rear window with wiper-washer; light alloy wheels; 165/70 SR x 13 tyres; tinted glass; metallic spray.

Delta Berlina 1300 (5 gears)

See Delta Berlina 1300 (4 gears), except for:

PRICE EX WORKS: 7,947,000 liras**

TRANSMISSION gears: 5, fully synchronized; ratios: I 3.583, II 2.235, III 1.454, IV 1.042, V 0.863, rev 3.714; tyres: 165/70 SR x 13 tubeless (standard).

PERFORMANCE power-weight ratio: 28.5 lb/hp (38.9 lb/kW), 12.9 kg/hp (17.6 kg/kW); speed in top at 1,000 rpm: 19.8 mph, 31.8 km/h; consumption: 32.8 m/imp gal, 27.3 m/US gal, 8.9 l x 100 km at 75 mph, 120 km/h.

OPTIONAL electric windows.

Delta Berlina 1500

See Delta Berlina 1300 (4 gears), except for:

PRICE EX WORKS: 8,419,000 liras**

ENGINE 91.41 cu in, 1,498 cc (3.40 x 2.51 in, 86.4 x 63.9 mm); compression ratio: 9.2:1; max power (DIN): 85 hp (63 kW) at 5,800 rpm; max torque (DIN): 90 lb ft, 12.5 kg m (123 Nm) at 3,500 rpm; 1 Weber 34 DAT 8 downdraught twin barrel carburettor.

TRANSMISSION gears: 5, fully synchronized; ratios: I 3.583, II 2.235, III 1.454, IV 1.042, V 0.863, rev 3.714; tyres: 165/70 SR x 13 tubeless (standard).

PERFORMANCE max speed: over 99 mph, 160 km/h; power-weight ratio: 25.3 lb/hp (34.1 lb/kW), 11.5 kg/hp (15.5 kg/kW); acceleration: standing ¼ mile 18.2 sec, 0-50 mph (0-80 km/h) 7 sec; speed in top at 1,000 rpm: 17.8 mph, 28.6 km/h.

ELECTRICAL EQUIPMENT Bosch or Marelli electronic ignition.

PRACTICAL INSTRUCTIONS sparking plug: Champion RN 7 Y.

Beta Berlina 1600

PRICE EX WORKS: 9,658,300 liras**

ENGINE front, transverse, slanted 20° to rear, 4 stroke; 4 cylinders, in line; 96.7 cu in, 1,585 cc (3.31 x 2.81 in, 84 x 71.5 mm); compression ratio: 9.4:1; max power (DIN): 100 hp (74 kW) at 5,800 rpm; max torque (DIN): 99 lb ft, 13.7 kg m (134 Nm) at 3,000 rpm; max engine rpm: 6,400; 63.1 hp/l (46.4 kW/l); cast iron block, light alloy head, hemispherical combustion chambers; 5 crankshaft bearings; valves: overhead, Vee-slanted at 65°, thimble tappets; camshafts: 2, overhead, cogged belt; lubrication: gear pump, full flow filter, 6.7 imp pt, 8 US pt, 3.8 l; 1 Weber 34 DAT 1, or Solex C34TC1C2 downdraught twin barrel carburettor with power-valve and automatic starter; air cleaner: dry, thimble type thermostatic intake; fuel feed: mechanical pump; cooling, liquid, expansion tank, 13.4 imp pt, 16.1 US pt, 7.6 l, electric thermostatic fan.

TRANSMISSION driving wheels: front; clutch: single dry plate; gearbox: mechanical; gears: 5, fully synchronized; ratios: I 3.500, II 2.235, III 1.522, IV 1.152, V 0.925, rev 3.071; lever: central; final drive: cylindrical gears, in unit with gearbox; axle ratio: 4.071; width of rims: 5.5''; tyres: 175/70 SR x 14 tubeless.

PERFORMANCE max speeds: (I) 31 mph, 50 km/h; (II) 48 mph, 78 km/h; (III) 71 mph, 114 km/h; (IV) 94 mph, 151 km/h; (V) 106 mph, 170 km/h; power-weight ratio: 25.2 lb/hp (34.1 lb/kW), 11.4 kg/hp (15.5 kg/kW); carrying capacity: 1,102 lb, 500 kg; acceleration: standing ¼ mile 18.4 sec, 0-50 mph (0-80 km/h) 7.3 sec; speed in top at 1,000 rpm: 18.2 mph, 29.3 km/h; consumption: 29.4 m/imp gal, 24.5 m/US gal, 9.6 l x 100 km at 75 mph, 120 km/h.

LANCIA Delta Berlina 1300

LANCIA Beta Berlina 1600 - 2000

CHASSIS integral; front suspension: independent, lower wide-based wishbones, coil springs/telescopic damper struts, anti-roll bar; rear: independent, wishbones, coil springs/telescopic damper struts, anti-roll bar acting as longitudinal torque arm.

STEERING rack-and-pinion damper; turns lock to lock: 4.

BRAKES disc (diameter 9.88 in, 25.1 cm), rear compensator, Superduplex circuit, servo; lining area: front 24.8 sq in, 160 sq cm, rear 22 sq in, 142 sq cm, total 46.8 sq in, 302 sq cm.

ELECTRIC EQUIPMENT 12 V; 45 Ah battery; 750 W alternator; Bosch or Marelli electronic ignition; 4 iodine headlamps with automatically adjustable height.

DIMENSIONS AND WEIGHT wheel base: 100 in, 254 cm; tracks: 55.35 in, 141 cm front, 54.80 in, 139 cm rear; length: 170.27 in, 432 cm; width: 66.93 in, 171 cm; height: 55.12 in, 140 cm; ground clearance: 5.12 in, 13 cm; weight: 2,525 lb, 1,145 kg; turning circle: 35.7 ft, 10.9 m; fuel tank: 11.4 imp gal, 13.7 US gal, 52 l.

BODY saloon/sedan; 4 doors; 5 seats, separate front seats, reclining backrests; heated rear window.

PRACTICAL INSTRUCTIONS fuel: 98-100 oct petrol; oil: engine 6.7 imp pt, 8 US pt, 3.8 l, SAE 10W-50, change every 6,200 miles, 10,000 km - gearbox and final drive 3.2 imp pt, 3.8 US pt, 1.8 l, SAE 90, change every 18,600 miles, 30,000 km; greasing: none; sparking plug: Champion N 7 Y; tappet clearances: inlet 0.018-0.020 in, 0.39-0.45 mm, exhaust 0.016-0.01 in, 0.42-0.48 mm; valve timing: 17° 37° 48° 6°; tyre pressure front 24 psi, 1.7 atm, rear 24 psi, 1.7 atm.

OPTIONALS Lancia/AP automatic transmission, hydraulic torque converter and planetary gears with 3 ratios (I 2.346, II 1.402, III 1, rev 2.346), max ratio of converter at stall 2.05 possible manual selection, 4.384 axle ratio, max speed 10 mph, 165 km/h; air-conditioning; tinted glass; ZF progressive power steering; light alloy wheels; sunshine roof; rear window with wiper-washer; electric windows; tell-tale warning light metallic spray.

Beta Coupé 1300

See Beta Berlina 1600, except for:

PRICE IN GB: £ 5,051*
PRICE EX WORKS: 9,139,000 liras**

ENGINE 79.39 cu in, 1,301 cc (3 x 2.81 in, 76.1 x 71.5 mm) compression ratio: 8.9:1; max power (DIN): 82 hp (60 hp) a 5,800 rpm; max torque (DIN): 80 lb ft, 11 kg m (108 Nm) a 3,300 rpm; 63 hp/l (46.3 kW/l); 1 Weber 32 DAT 3 downdraugh twin barrel carburettor with power-valve.

TRANSMISSION axle ratio: 4.466; width of rims: 5''; tyres: 15 SR x 14.

PERFORMANCE max speed: 103 mph, 165 km/h; power-weigh ratio: 26.9 lb/hp (36.7 lb/kW), 12.2 kg/hp (16.7 kg/kW); carryin capacity: 882 lb, 400 kg; acceleration: standing ¼ mile 18 sec consumption: 36.2 m/imp gal, 30.2 m/US gal, 7.8 l x 100 kr (CUNA).

IMENSIONS AND WEIGHT wheel base: 92.52 in, 235 cm; ngth: 157.28 in, 399 cm; width: 64.96 in, 165 cm; height: 0.59 in, 128 cm; ground clearance: 5.31 in, 13.5 cm; weight: ,205 lb, 1,000 kg; turning circle: 33.5 ft, 10.2 m.

ODY coupé; 2 doors; 4 seats.

PTIONALS only 5.5" wide rims, 175/70 SR x 14 tyres, light lloy wheels, sunshine roof, tinted glass and metallic spray.

Beta Coupé 1600

ee Beta Berlina 1600, except for:

RICE IN GB: £ 5,766*
RICE EX WORKS: 10,036,000 liras**

ERFORMANCE max speed: 111 mph, 178 km/h; power-weight tio: 22 lb/hp (29.8 lb/kW), 10 kg/hp (13.5 kg/kW); carrying apacity: 882 lb, 400 kg; acceleration: standing ¼ mile 17.1 ec; consumption: 36.7 m/imp gal, 30.5 m/US gal, 7.7 l x 100 n (CUNA).

TEERING turns lock to lock: 3.75.

IMENSIONS AND WEIGHT wheel base: 92.52 in, 235 cm; ngth: 157.28 in, 399 cm; width: 64.96 in, 165 cm; height:).59 in, 128 cm; ground clearance: 5.31 in, 13.5 cm; weight: 205 lb, 1,000 kg; turning circle: 33.5 ft, 10.2 m.

ODY coupé; 2 doors; 4 seats.

Beta HPE 1600

ee Beta Berlina 1600, except for:

RICE IN GB: £ 6,514*
RICE EX WORKS: 10,036,000 liras**

ERFORMANCE max speed: 108 mph, 174 km/h; power-weight tio: 23.4 lb/hp (31.7 lb/kW), 10.6 kg/hp (14.4 kg/kW); carrying apacity: 1,102 lb, 500 kg; acceleration: standing ¼ mile 17.5 c; consumption: 32.5 m/imp gal, 27 m/US gal, 8.7 l x 100 km UNA).

TEERING turns lock to lock: 4.

IMENSIONS AND WEIGHT wheel base: 100 in, 254 cm; ngth: 168.70 in, 428 cm; width: 64.96 in, 165 cm; height: .57 in, 131 cm; ground clearance: 5.31 in, 13.5 cm; weight: 337 lb, 1,060 kg; turning circle: 33.5 ft, 10.2 m.

ODY coupé; 2 doors; 5 seats; rear window wiper-washer tandard).

Beta Berlina 2000

e Beta Berlina 1600, except for:

RICE IN USA: $ 8,551*
RICE EX WORKS: 10,685,000 liras**

NGINE 121.7 cu in, 1,995 cc (3.31 x 3.54 in, 84 x 90 mm); mpression ratio: 8.9:1; max power (DIN): 115 hp (85 kW) at 500 rpm; max torque (DIN): 130 lb ft, 17.9 kg m (176 Nm) at 2,800 rpm; 57.6 hp/l (42.4 kW/l); lubrication: 7.9 imp pt, 9.5 US pt, 4.5 l; 1 Weber 34 DAT 2 downdraught twin barrel carburettor with power-walve.

LANCIA Beta Berlina 1600 - 2000

TRANSMISSION axle ratio: 3.786.

PERFORMANCE max speeds: (I) 33 mph, 53 km/h; (II) 52 mph, 83 km/h; (III) 76 mph, 123 km/h; (IV) 101 mph, 162 km/h; (V) 112 mph, 180 km/h; power-weight ratio: 22.3 lb/hp (30.2 lb/kW), 10.1 kg/hp (13.7 kg/kW); acceleration: standing ¼ mile 17.5 sec; speed in top at 1,000 rpm: 19.6 mph, 31.5 km/h; consumption: 28.2 m/imp gal, 23.5 m/US gal, 10 l x 100 km at 75 mph, 120 km/h.

STEERING ZF progressive servo (standard).

DIMENSIONS AND WEIGHT weight: 2,569 lb, 1,165 kg.

BODY electric windows and control system (standard).

PRACTICAL INSTRUCTIONS valve timing: 13° 45° 49° 9°.

OPTIONALS with Lancia/AP automatic transmission max speed 109 mph, 175 km/h.

Beta Coupé 2000

See Beta Berlina 1600, except for:

PRICE IN GB: £ 6,242*
PRICE IN USA: $ 9,500*

ENGINE 121.7 cu in, 1,995 cc (3.31 x 3.54 in, 84 x 90 mm); compression ratio: 8.9:1; max power (DIN): 115 hp (85 kW) at 5,500 rpm; max torque (DIN): 130 lb ft, 17.9 kg m (176 Nm) at 2,800 rpm; 57.6 hp/l (42.4 kW/l); lubrication: 7.9 imp pt, 9.5 US pt, 4.5 l; 1 Weber 34 DAT 2 downdraught twin barrel carburettor with power-valve.

TRANSMISSION axle ratio: 3.786; tyres: 175/70 HR x 14.

PERFORMANCE max speed: 117 mph, 188 km/h; power-weight ratio: 19.2 lb/hp (25.9 lb/kW), 8.7 kg/hp (11.8 kg/kW); carrying capacity: 882 lb, 400 kg; acceleration: standing¼ mile 16.2 sec; consumption: 33.6 m/imp gal, 28.6 m/US gal, 8.4 l x 100 km (CUNA).

STEERING ZF progressive servo; turns lock to lock: 3.75.

DIMENSIONS AND WEIGHT wheel base: 92.52 in, 235 cm; length: 157.28 in, 399 cm; width: 64.96 in, 165 cm; height: 50.59 in, 128 cm; ground clearance: 5.31 in, 13.5 cm; weight: 2,205 lb, 1,000 kg; turning circle: 33.5 ft, 10.2 m.

BODY coupé; 2 doors; 4 seats; electric windows and control system (standard).

PRACTICAL INSTRUCTIONS valve timing: 13° 45° 49° 9°.

OPTIONALS with Lancia/AP automatic transmission max speed 109 mph, 175 km/h.

LANCIA Beta HPE 1600 - 2000

Beta HPE 2000

See Beta Berlina 1600, except for:

PRICE IN GB: £ 7,046*
PRICE IN USA: $ 9,985*

ENGINE 121.7 cu in, 1,995 cc (3.31 x 3.54 in, 84 x 90 mm); compression ratio: 8.9:1; max power (DIN): 115 hp (85 kW) at 5,500 rpm; max torque (DIN): 130 lb ft, 17.9 kg m (176 Nm) at 2,800 rpm; 57.6 hp/l (42.4 kW/l); lubrication: 7.9 imp pt, 9.5 US pt, 4.5 l; 1 Weber 34 DAT 2 downdraught twin barrel carburettor with power-valve.

TRANSMISSION axle ratio: 3.786; tyres: 175/70 SR x 14.

PERFORMANCE max speed: 112 mph, 180 km/h; power-weight ratio: 20.3 lb/hp (27.6 lb/kW), 9.2 kg/hp (12.5 kg/kW); carrying capacity: 1,102 lb, 500 kg; acceleration: standing ¼ mile 16.8 sec; consumption: 32.5 m/imp gal, 27 m/US gal, 8.7 l x 100 km (CUNA).

STEERING ZF progressive servo; turns lock to lock: 4.

DIMENSIONS AND WEIGHT wheel base: 100 in, 254 cm; length: 168.70 in, 428 cm; width: 64.96 in, 165 cm; height: 51.57 in, 131 cm; ground clearance: 5.31 in, 13.5 cm; weight: 2,337 lb, 1,060 kg; turning circle: 33.5 ft, 10.2 m.

BODY coupé; 2 doors; 5 seats; rear window wiper-washer electric windows and control system (standard).

PRACTICAL INSTRUCTIONS valve timing: 13° 45° 49° 9°.

OPTIONALS with Lancia/AP automatic transmission max speed 109 mph, 17.5 km/h.

LANCIA Montecarlo

Montecarlo

PRICE EX WORKS: 9,634,700 liras**

ENGINE centre-rear, transverse, in unit with gearbox and final drive, 4 stroke; 4 cylinders, in line; 121.7 cu in, 1,995 cc (3.31 x 3.54 in, 84 x 90 mm); compression ratio: 9.35:1; max power (DIN): 120 hp (88 kW) at 6,000 rpm; max torque (DIN): 126 lb ft, 17.4 kg m (171 Nm) at 3,400 rpm; max engine rpm: 6,400; 60.1 hp/l (44.3 kW/l); cast iron block, light alloy head, hemispherical combustion chambers; 5 crankshaft bearings; valves: overhead, Vee-slanted at 65°, thimble tappets; camshafts: 2, overhead, cogged belt; lubrication: gear pump, full flow filter (cartridge), 7.9 imp pt, 9.5 US pt, 4.5 l; 1 Weber 34 DATR 4/250 downdraught twin barrel carburettor; fuel feed: mechanical pump; cooling, liquid, 13.4 imp pt, 16.1 US pt, 7.6 l, electric thermostatic fan.

TRANSMISSION driving wheels: rear; clutch: single dry plate (diaphragm), hydraulically controlled; gearbox: mechanical; gears: 5, fully synchronized; ratios: I 3.750, II 2.235, III 1.522, IV 1.152, V 0.925, rev 3.071; lever: central; final drive: helical spur gears; axle ratio: 3.714; width of rims: 5.5''; tyres: 185/70 HR x 13.

PERFORMANCE max speeds: (I) 30 mph, 49 km/h; (II) 52 mph, 84 km/h; (III) 80 mph, 128 km/h; (IV) 101 mph, 162 km/h; (V) over 118 mph, 190 km/h; power-weight ratio: 19.1 lb/hp (25.9 lb/kW), 8.7 kg/hp (11.8 kg/kW); carrying capacity: 463 lb, 210 kg; acceleration: standing ¼ mile 16 sec; speed in top at 1,000 rpm: 19.6 mph, 31.6 km/h; consumption: 29.7 m/imp gal, 24.8 m/US gal, 9.5 l x 100 km.

CHASSIS integral; front suspension: independent, by McPherson, coil springs/telescopic damper struts, lower wishbones, anti-roll bar; rear: independent, by McPherson, coil springs/telescopic damper struts, lower wishbones, anti-roll bar.

STEERING rack-and-pinion.

BRAKES disc (diameter 8.94 in, 22.7 cm), dual circuit, servo.

ELECTRICAL EQUIPMENT 12 V; 45 Ah battery; 460 W alternator; Bosch or Marelli electronic ignition; 2 iodine headlamps.

DIMENSIONS AND WEIGHT wheel base: 90.55 in, 230 cm; tracks: 55.59 in, 141 cm front, 57.32 in, 146 cm rear; length: 150.12 in, 381 cm; width 66.77 in, 170 cm; height: 46.85 in, 119 cm; ground clearance: 5.20 in, 13.2 cm; weight: 2,293 lb, 1.040 kg; turning circle: 34.1 ft, 10.4 m; fuel tank: 13 imp gal, 15.6 US gal, 59 l.

BODY coupé; 2 doors; 2 seats; detachable roof; built-in headrests.

PRACTICAL INSTRUCTIONS fuel: 98 oct petrol; oil: engine 10.9 imp pt, 13.1 US pt, 6.2 l, SAE 10W-50, change every 3,100 miles, 5,000 km - gearbox and final drive 3 imp pt, 3,6 US pt, 1.7 l, SAE 90, change every 18,600 miles, 30,000 km; greasing: none; sparking plug: 200°; tappet clearance: inlet 0.016-0.020 in, 0.40-0.50 mm, exhaust 0.022-0.026 in, 0.55-0.65 mm; valve timing: 15° 55° 57° 13°; tyre pressure: front 24 psi, 1.7 atm, rear 27 psi, 1.9 atm.

OPTIONALS air-conditioning with tinted glass; metallic spray; leather upholstery; heated rear window; tinted glass with heated rear window; electric windows.

Gamma Berlina 2000

PRICE EX WORKS: 13,092,000 liras**

ENGINE front, 4 stroke; 4 cylinders, horizontally opposed; 122 cu in, 1,999 cc (3.60 x 2.99 in, 91.5 x 76 mm); compression ratio: 9:1; max power (DIN): 120 hp (88 kW) at 5,500 rpm; max torque (DIN): 127 lb ft, 17.5 kg m (172 Nm) at 3,500 rpm; max engine rpm: 6,200; 60 hp/l (44.2 kW/l); 3 crankshaft bearings; valves: overhead; camshafts: 2, 1 per bank, overhead; lubrication: rotary pump, full flow filter (cartridge), 10.7 imp pt, 12.9 US pt, 6.1 l; 1 Weber 36 ADL 1/250 twin barrel carburettor with power-valve and automatic starter; air cleaner: dry, thimble type thermostatic intake; fuel feed: mechanical pump; cooling, liquid, 15.8 imp pt, 19 US pt, 9 l.

TRANSMISSION driving wheels: front; clutch: single dry plate (diaphragm); gearbox: mechanical; gears: 5, fully synchronized; ratios: I 3.462, II 2.105, III 1.458, IV 1.129, V 0.897, rev 3.214; lever: central; final drive: hypoid bevel, in unit with gearbox; axle ratio: 4.100; width of rims: 6''; tyres: 185/70 HR x 14 tubeless.

PERFORMANCE max speeds: (I) 31 mph, 50 mph; (II) 51 mph, 82 km/h; (III) 73 mph, 118 km/h; (IV) 94 mph, 152 km/h; (V) 115 mph, 185 km/h; power-weight ratio: 24 lb/hp (32.9 lb/kW), 11 kg/hp (14.9 kg/kW); carrying capacity: 1,102 lb, 500 kg; acceleration: standing ¼ mile 17.4 sec; consumption: 29.7 m/imp gal, 24.8 m/US gal, 9.5 l x 100 km (CUNA).

CHASSIS integral; front and rear suspension: independent, wishbones, coil springs, telescopic damper struts, anti-roll bar.

STEERING rack-and-pinion, ZF progressive servo, adjustabl height and tilt; turns lock to lock: 3.

BRAKES ventilated disc, Superduplex circuit, servo.

ELECTRICAL EQUIPMENT 12 V; 60 Ah battery; 770 W alterna tor; Bosch or Marelli electronic ignition with impulser unit; iodine headlamps with automatically adjustable height.

DIMENSIONS AND WEIGHT wheel base: 105.12 in, 267 cm tracks: 57.09 in, 145 cm front, 56.69 in, 144 cm rear; length 180.31 in, 458 cm; width: 68.11 in, 173 cm; height: 55.51 in 141 cm; weight: 2,911 lb, 1,320 kg; fuel tank: 13.9 imp gal, 16. US gal, 63 l.

BODY saloon/sedan; 4 doors; 5 seats, separate front seats, built-in headrests, reclining backrests; front electric windows

PRACTICAL INSTRUCTIONS fuel: 98 oct petrol; oil: engin 10.7 imp pt, 12.9 US pt, 6.1 l, 15W-50, change every 6,20 miles, 10,000 km - gearbox and final drive 6.2 imp pt, 7.4 U pt, 3.5 l, 85W-90, change evey 18,600 miles, 30,000 km greasing: none; sparking plug: Bosch W200 T 30 OV Champio N 6 Y; tappet clearances: inlet 0.012 in, 0.30 mm, exhaus 0.014 in, 0.35 mm; valve timing: 15° 45° 53° 9°; front and rea tyre pressure: 26 psi, 1.8 atm.

OPTIONALS air-conditioning; metallic spray; tinted glass; rea electric windows; leather upholstery; light alloy wheels; fro and rear (wrap-round) belts; fog lamps and rear red fog lamp

Gamma Coupé 2000

See Gamma Berlina 2000, except for:

PRICE EX WORKS: 16,656,000 liras**

PERFORMANCE power-weight ratio: 23.3 lb/hp (31.7 lb/kW 10.6 kg/hp (14.4 kg/kW).

DIMENSIONS AND WEIGHT wheel base: 100.59 in, 255 cm length: 176.57 in, 448 cm; height: 52.36 in, 133 cm; weigh 2,800 lb, 1,270 kg.

BODY coupé; 2 doors; 4 seats.

Gamma Berlina 2500

See Gamma Berlina 2000, except for:

PRICE IN GB: £ 7,950*
PRICE EX WORKS: 15,721,000 liras**

ENGINE 151.6 cu in, 2,484 cc (4.02 x 2.99 in, 102 x 76 mm max power (DIN): 140 hp (103 kW) at 5,400 rpm; max torqu (DIN): 154 lb ft, 21.2 kg m (208 Nm) at 3,000 rpm; max engin rpm: 6,000; 56.4 hp/l (41.5 kW/l); 1 Weber 38 ADL/200 twi barrel carburettor.

TRANSMISSION axle ratio: 3.700.

PERFORMANCE max speeds: (I) 33 mph, 53 km/h; (II) 5 mph, 88 km/h; (III) 79 mph, 127 km/h; (IV) 101 mph, 163 km/h (V) 121 mph, 195 km/h; power-weight ratio: 20.7 lb/hp (28. lb/kW), 9.4 kg/hp (12.8 kg/hp (12.8 kg/kW); consumption: 29. m/imp gal, 24.5 m/US gal, 9.6 l x 100 km (CUNA).

BODY light alloy wheels (standard).

LANCIA Gamma Coupé 2000 - 2500

LAWIL S3 Varzina

Gamma Coupé 2500

›e Gamma Berlina 2000, except for:

ЯICE IN GB: £ 9,949*
ЯICE EX WORKS: 19,784,000* liras

ᴵGINE 151.6 cu in, 2,484 cc (4.02 x 2.99 in, 102 x 76 mm); ax power (DIN): 140 hp (103 kW) at 5,400 rpm; max torque ›N): 154 lb ft, 21.2 kg m (208 Nm) at 3,000 rpm; max engine ›n: 6,000; 56.4 hp/l (12.8 kg/kW); 1 Weber 38 ADL/200 twin rrel carburettor.

ЯANSMISSION axle ratio: 3.700.

:RFORMANCE max speed: over 121 mph, 195 km/h; power-›ight ratio: 20 lb/hp (27.2 lb/kW), 9.1 kg/hp (12.3 kg/kW); ›nsumption: 29.4 m/imp gal, 24.5 m/US gal, 9.6 l x 100 km ›UNA).

MENSIONS AND WEIGHT wheel base: 100.59 in, 255 cm; ›gth: 176.57 in, 448 cm; height: 52.36 in, 133 cm; weight: ›00 lb, 1,270 kg.

›DY coupé; 2 doors; 4 seats; light alloy wheels (standard).

AWIL ITALY

S3 Varzina

ЯICE EX WORKS: 2,596,000* liras

ᴵGINE front, 2 stroke; 2 cylinders, in line; 15 cu in, 246 cc 05 x 2.28 in, 52 x 58 mm); compression ratio: 7.5:1; max ›wer (SAE): 14 hp (10 kW) at 4,400 rpm; max torque (SAE): lb ft, 1.9 kg m (19 Nm) at 3,000 rpm; max engine rpm: 4,500; .9 hp/l (41.8 kW/l); cast iron block, light alloy head; 3 ›nkshaft bearings; lubrication: mixture; 1 Dell'Orto WHB hori-›ntal carburettor; fuel feed: gravity; air-cooled.

ЯANSMISSION driving wheels: rear; clutch: single dry plate; ›arbox: mechanical; gears: 4, silent claw coupling; ratios: I ›49, II 1.492, III 0.986, IV 0.674, rev 2.760; lever: central; ›al drive: spiral bevel; axle ratio: 3.083; width of rims: 3''; ›es: 4.000 x 10.

:RFORMANCE max speeds: (I) 12 mph, 20 km/h; (II) 19 mph, km/h; (III) 29 mph, 47 km/h; (IV) 39 mph, 63 km/h; power-›ight ratio: 50.5 lb/hp (68.6 lb/kW), 22.9 kg/hp (31.1 kg/kW); ›rrying capacity: 353 lb, 160 kg; consumption: 70.6 m/imp gal, .8 m/US gal, 4 l x 100 km.

ᴵASSIS tubular; front suspension: independent, wishbones, ›nsverse semi-elliptic leafsprings, telescopic dampers; rear: id axle, semi-elliptic leafsprings, telescopic dampers.

'EERING rack-and-pinion; turns lock to lock: 3.50.

ᴵAKES drum, single circuit.

.ECTRICAL EQUIPMENT 12 V; 35 Ah battery; 160 W alterna-›; Ducati (electronic) distributor; 2 headlamps.

DIMENSIONS AND WEIGHT wheel base: 46.06 in, 117 cm; tracks: 40.94 in, 104 cm front, 42.32 in, 107 cm rear; length: 81.50 in, 207 cm; width: 50 in, 127 cm; height: 53.54 in, 136 cm; ground clearance: 4.72 in, 12 cm; weight: 706 lb, 320 kg; weight distribution: 55% front, 45% rear; turning circle: 19.7 ft, 6 m; fuel tank: 2.4 imp gal, 2.9 US gal, 11 l.

BODY sport; 2 doors; 2 seats, bench front seats.

PRACTICAL INSTRUCTIONS fuel: mixture 1:50; oil: gearbox 1.8 imp pt, 2.1 US pt, 1 l, SAE 90 EP, change every 3,100 miles, 5,000 km - final drive 1.1 imp pt, 1.3 US pt, 0.6 l, SAE 90 EP, change every 6,200 miles, 10,000 km; greasing: every 3,100 miles, 5,000 km, 3 points; sparking plug: 240°; tyre pressure: front 18 psi, 1.3 atm, rear 20 psi, 1.4 atm.

OPTIONALS tonneau cover; roll-bar.

A4 City

See S3 Varzina, except for:

PRICE EX WORKS: 2,655,0000* liras

PERFORMANCE power-weight ratio: 55.1 lb/hp (75 lb/kW), 25 kg/hp (34 kg/kW).

DIMENSIONS AND WEIGHT length: 80.71 in, 205 cm; width: 50.39 in, 128 cm; height: 56.69 in, 144 cm; weight: 772 lb, 350 kg.

BODY saloon/sedan.

OPTIONALS none.

MASERATI ITALY

Merak

PRICE EX WORKS: 23,460,000* liras

ENGINE centre-rear, 4 stroke; 6 cylinders, Vee-slanted at 90°; 122 cu in, 1,999 cc (3.15 x 2.61 in, 80 x 66.3 mm); compression ratio: 9:1; max power (DIN): 159 hp (117 kW) at 7,000 rpm; max torque (DIN): 130 lb ft, 18 kg m (177 Nm) at 5,700 rpm; max engine rpm: 7,300 79.5 hp/l (58.5 kW/l); light alloy block and head, wet liners, hemispherical combustion chambers; 4 crank-shaft bearings; valves: overhead, Vee-slanted, thimble tappets; camshafts: 4, 2 per bank, overhead, chain-driven; lubrication: gear pump, full flow filter, oil cooler, 13 imp pt, 16 US pt, 7 l; 3 Weber 44 DCNF downdraught twin barrel carburettors; fuel feed: electric pump; water-cooled, 23 imp pt, 28 US pt, 14 l, front radiator, 2 electric fans.

TRANSMISSION driving wheels: rear; clutch: single dry plate (diaphragm), hydraulically controlled; gearbox: mechanical; gears: 5, fully synchronized; ratios: I 2.920, II 1.940, III 1.320, IV 0.970, V 0.750, rev 3.150; lever: central; final drive; hypoid bevel, limited slip differential; axle ratio: 5.444; width of rims: 7.5''; tyres 185/70 VR x 15 front, 205/70 VR x 15 rear.

PERFORMANCE max speed: 137 mph, 220 km/h; power-weight ratio: 18.7 lb/hp (25.4 lb/kW), 8.5 kg/hp (11.5 kg/kW); carrying capacity: 706 lb, 320 kg; speed in top at 1,000 rpm: 18.7 mph, 29.7 km/h; consumption: 30.7 m/imp gal, 25.6 m/US gal, 9.2 l x 100 km.

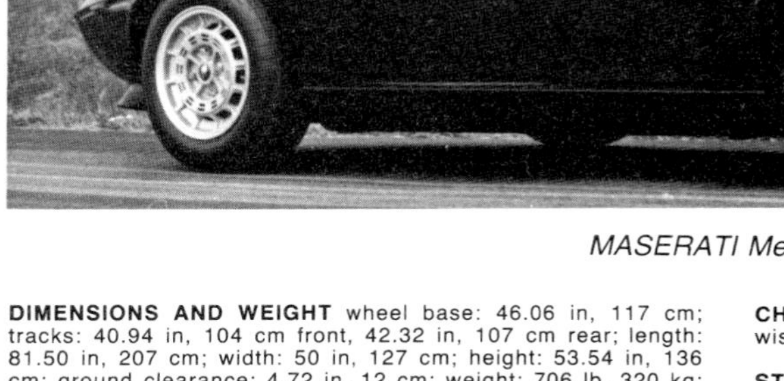

MASERATI Merak SS

CHASSIS integral; front and rear suspension: independent, wishbones, coil springs, anti-roll bar, telescopic dampers.

STEERING rack-and-pinion, adjustable tilt and height of steer-ing wheel; turns lock to lock: 3.

BRAKES ventilated discs, independent circuit for each axle, servo; swept area: front 244.2 sq in, 1,575 sq cm, rear 209 sq in, 1,348 sq cm, total 453.2 sq in, 2,923 sq cm.

ELECTRICAL EQUIPMENT 12 V; 60 Ah battery; 780 W alterna-tor; Bosch electronic ignition; 2 retractable iodine headlamps.

DIMENSIONS AND WEIGHT wheel base: 102.30 in, 260 cm; front and rear track: 58 in, 147 cm; length: 170 in, 433 cm; width: 69.60 in, 177 cm; height: 44.60 in, 113 cm; ground clearance: 5.12 in, 13 cm; weight: 2,977 lb, 1,350 kg; turning circle: 34.4 ft, 10.5 m; fuel tank: 18.6 imp gal, 22.4 US gal, 85 l.

BODY coupé; 2 doors; 2+2 seats, separate front seats, reclin-ing backrests, headrests; tinted glass; electric windows; heated rear window; air-conditioning; light alloy wheels.

PRACTICAL INSTRUCTIONS fuel: 98-100 oct petrol; oil: en-gine 12.3 imp pt, 14.8 US pt, 7 l, SAE 10W/50, change every 3,100 miles, 5,000 km - gearbox 4.4 imp pt, 5.3 US pt, 2.5 l, SAE 90, change every 12,400 miles, 20,000 km - final drive 2.5 imp pt, 3 US pt, 1.4 l, change every 12,400 miles, 20,000 km; greasing: 2 points, every 3,100 miles, 5000 km; sparking plug: Bosch 200 T 30; tappet clearances: inlet 0.011 in, 0.25 mm, exhaust 0.024 in, 0.50 mm; valve timing: 42° 80° 56° 20°; tyre pressure: front 33 psi, 2.3 atm, rear 36 psi, 2.5 atm.

OPTIONALS metallic spray.

MASERATI Quattroporte

Merak SS

See Merak, except for:

PRICE IN GB: £ 18,096*
PRICE IN USA: $ 35,120*

ENGINE 180.9 cu in, 2,965 cc (3.61 x 2.95 in, 91.6 x 75 mm); max power (DIN): 208 hp (153 kW) at 5,800 rpm; max torque (DIN): 188 lb ft, 26 kg m (255 Nm) at 5,000 rpm; max engine rpm: 6,500; 70.2 hp/l (51.7 kW/l).

TRANSMISSION axle ratio: 4.370; tyres: 195/70 VR x 15 front, 215/70 VR x 15 rear.

PERFORMANCE max speed: 155 mph, 250 km/h; power-weight ratio: 13.7 lb/hp (18.7 lb/kW), 6.2 kg/hp (8.5 kg/kW); speed in top at 1,000 rpm: 24 mph, 38.5 km/h; consumption: 26.6 m/imp gal, 22.2 M/US gal, 10.6 l x 100 km.

BRAKES swept area: front 244.2 sq in, 1,575 sq cm, rear 254.3 sq in, 1,640 sq cm, total 498.5 sq in, 3,215 sq cm.

DIMENSIONS AND WEIGHT weight: 2,867 lb, 1,300 kg.

OPTIONALS right hand drive; leather upholstery.

Quattroporte

PRICE IN GB: £ 28,900*
PRICE EX WORKS: 40,660,000* liras

ENGINE front, 4 stroke; 8 cylinders, Vee-slanted at 90°; 300.8 cu in, 4,930 cc (3.70 x 3.50 in, 93.9 x 89 mm); compression ratio 8.5:1; max power (DIN): 280 hp (206 kW) at 5,600 rpm; max torque (DIN): 289 lb ft, 40 kg m (39.2 Nm) at 3,000 rpm: max engine rpm: 6,000; 56.8 hp/l (41.8 kW/l); light alloy block and head, wet liners, hemispherical combustion chambers; 5 crankshaft bearings; valves: overhead; camshafts: 4, 2 per bank, overhead, chain-driven; lubrication: gear pump, full flow filter, 17 imp pt, 21 US pt, 9 l; 4 Weber 42 DCNF downdraught twin barrel carburettors; fuel feed: electric pump; water-cooled, 28 imp pt, 33.5 US pt, 16 l, 2 electric fans.

TRANSMISSION driving wheels: rear; clutch: single dry plate (diaphragm), hydraulically controlled; gearbox: ZF mechanical; gears: 5, fully synchronized; ratios: I 2.990, II 1.900, III 1.320, IV 1, V 0.890, rev 2.700; lever: central; final drive: hypoid bevel, limited slip differential; axle ratio: 3.310; width of rims: 7"; tyres: 215/70 VR x 15 XDX tubeless.

PERFORMANCE max speed: 143 mph, 230 km/h; power-weight ratio: 15 lb/hp (20.3 lb/kW), 6.8 kg/hp (9.2 kg/kW); carrying capacity: 1,103 lb, 500 kg; speed in top at 1,000 rpm: 24.2 mph, 39.5 km/h; consumption: 14.9 m/imp gal, 12.4 m/US gal, 19 l x 100 km.

CHASSIS integral; front and rear suspension: independent, wishbones, coil springs, anti-roll bar, telescopic dampers.

STEERING rack-and-pinion, adjustable height and distance, servo; turns lock to lock: 2.50.

BRAKES disc, ventilated, dual circuit, servo; swept area: front 245.4 sq in, 1,583 sq cm, rear 188.5 sq in, 1,216 sq cm, total 433.9 sq in, 2,799 sq cm.

ELECTRICAL EQUIPMENT 12 V; 72 Ah battery; 650 W alternator; Bosch electronic ignition; 4 iodine headlamps.

DIMENSIONS AND WEIGHT wheel base: 110.20 in, 280 cm; front and rear track: 60.03 in, 152 cm; length: 196 in, 498 cm; width: 70.47 in, 179 cm; height: 53.14 in, 135 cm; ground clearance: 5.55 in, 14 cm; weight: 4,190 lb, 1,900 kg; turning circle: 35 ft, 11.5 m; fuel tank: 22 imp gal, 26.4 US gal, 100 l.

BODY saloon/sedan; 4 doors; 5 seats, separate and reclining front seats; air-conditioning; tinted glass; electric windows; heated rear window; leather upholstery.

PRACTICAL INSTRUCTIONS fuel: 98-100 oct petrol; oil: engine 17 imp pt, 21 US pt, 9 l, SAE 10W/50, change every 3,000 miles, 5,000 km - gearbox 2.5 imp pt, 3 US pt,1.4 l - final drive 2.5 imp pt, 3 US pt, 1.4 l, SAE 90, change every 12,400 miles, 20,000 km; greasing: every 3,100 miles, 5,000 km; sparking plug: Bosch 200 T 30; tappet clearances: inlet 0.011 in, 0.25 mm, exhaust 0.024 in, 0.50 mm; valve timing: 40° 80° 55° 25°; tyre pressure: front 36 psi, 2.5 atm, rear 37 psi, 2.6 atm.

VARIATIONS

ENGINE 252.3 cu in, 4,136 cc (3.46 x 3.35 in, 88 x 85 mm), max power (DIN) 255 hp (188 kW) at 6,000 rpm, max torque (DIN) 261 lb ft, 36 kg m (353 Nm) at 3,200 rpm, 61.7 hp/l (45.4 kW/l).
PERFORMANCE power-weight ratio 16.5 lb/hp (22.3 lb/kW), 7.5 kg/hp (10.1 kg/kW).
OPTIONALS none.

OPTIONALS automatic transmission, hydraulic torque converter and planetary gears with 3 ratios (I 2.400, II 1.470, III 1, rev 2.700), max ratio of converter at stall 2.75, possible manual selection.

Kyalami

See Quattroporte, except for:

PRICE IN GB: £ 25,540*
PRICE EX WORKS: 39,053,000* liras

TRANSMISSION axle ratio: 3.540; width of rims: 7.5"; tyre 205/70 VR x 15, tubeless.

PERFORMANCE max speed: 152 mph, 245 km/h; power-weig ratio: 13.4 lb/hp (18.3 lb/kW), 6.1 kg/hp (8.3 kg/kW); speed top at 1,000 rpm: 24.5 mph, 39.7 km/h.

STEERING turns lock to lock: 2.

DIMENSIONS AND WEIGHT wheel base: 102.30 in, 260 c front and rear track: 60.20 in, 153 cm; length: 180 in, 458 c width: 72.80 in, 185 cm; height: 50 in, 127 cm; weight: 3,749 1,700 kg.

BODY coupé; 2 doors; 4 seats.

OPTIONALS right hand drive.

Khamsin

PRICE IN GB: £ 28,031*
PRICE IN USA: $ 44,990*

ENGINE front, 4 stroke; 8 cylinders, Vee-slanted at 90°; 30C cu in, 4,930 cc (3.70 x 3.50 in, 93.9 x 89 mm); compressi ratio: 8.5:1; max power (DIN): 280 hp (206 kW) at 5,500 rp max torque (DIN): 330 lb ft, 45.5 kg m (446 Nm) at 3,400 rp max engine rpm: 6,000; 56.8 hp/l (41.8 kW/l); light alloy cyl der block and head, wet liners, hemispherical combusti chambers; 5 crankshaft bearings; valves: overhead, Ve slanted at 30°, thimble tappets; camshafts: 4, 2 per bar overhead, chain-driven; lubrication: gear pump, full flow filt dry sump, separate oil tank, 21.1 imp pt, 25.4 US pt, 12 l Weber 42 DCNF 6 downdraught twin barrel carburettors; f feed: 2 electric pumps; water-cooled, 28.2 imp pt, 33.8 US 16 l, 2 electric fans.

TRANSMISSION driving wheels: rear; clutch: single dry pla hydraulically controlled; gearbox: Zf mechanical; ratios: I 2.9 II 1.900, III 1.320, IV 1, V 0.890, rev 2.700; lever: central; fi drive: hypoid bevel; axle ratio: 3.310; width of rims: 7.5"; tyr 215/70 VR x 15.

PERFORMANCE max speed: 171 mph, 275 km/h; power-wei ratio: 13.2 lb/hp (18.1 lb/kW), 6 kg/hp (8.2 kg/kW); carryi capacity: 706 lb, 320 kg; speed in top at 1,000 rpm: 26.1 m 42 km/h; consumption: 19.3 m/imp gal, 16.1 m/US gal, 1 l x 100 km.

CHASSIS tubular; front suspension: independent, wishbon coil springs, anti-roll bar, telescopic dampers; rear: indepe dent, wishbones, coil springs, anti-roll bar, 4 telescopic da pers.

STEERING rack-and-pinion, adjustable height and distance steering wheel, variable ratio, servo; turns lock to lock: 2.

BRAKES discs (front diameter 10.75 in, 27.3 cm, rear 10.28 26.1 cm), internal radial fins, dual circuit, servo: swept ar

MASERATI Kyalami

MASERATI Khamsin

MASERATI Bora

ont 245.4 sq in, 1,583 sq cm, rear 188.5 sq in, 1,216 sq cm, otal 423.9 sq in, 2,799 sq cm.

LECTRICAL EQUIPMENT 12 V; 72 Ah battery; 650 W alterna-r; Bosch electronic ignition; 4 retractable iodine headlamps.

IMENSIONS AND WEIGHT wheel base: 100.39 in, 255 cm; acks: 56.69 in, 144 cm front, 57.87 in, 147 cm rear; length: 73.23 in, 440 cm; width: 70.87 in, 180 cm; height: 44.88 in 114 m; ground clearance: 5.51 in, 14 cm; weight: 3,704 lb, 1,680 g; turning circle: 34.4 ft, 10.5 m; fuel tank: 19.8 imp gal, 23.8 S gal, 90 l.

ODY coupé; 2 doors; 2+2 seats, separate front seats, reclin-g backrests, built-in headrests; heated rear window; tinted ass; electric windows; leather upholstery; light alloy wheels; ir-conditioning.

RACTICAL INSTRUCTIONS fuel: 98-100 oct petrol; oil: en-ne 21.1 imp pt, 25.4 US pt, 12 l, SAE 10W-50, change every 100 miles, 5,000 km - gerbox 2.5 imp pt, 3 US pt, 1.4 l, SAE 0, change every 12,400 miles, 20,000 km - final drive 2.5 imp t, 3 US pt, 1.4 l, SAE 90, change every 12,400 miles, 20,000 m; greasing: every 3,100 miles, 5,000 km, 4 points; sparking lug: 240°; tappet clearances: inlet 0.010 in, 0.25 mm, exhaust .020 in, 0.50 mm; valve timing: 40° 80° 55° 25°; tyre pressure: ont 34 psi, 2.4 atm, rear 37 psi, 2.6 atm.

PTIONALS right hand drive; limited slip differential; Borg-Varner automatic transmission, hydraulic torque converter and lanetary gears with 3 ratios (I 2.400, II 1.470, III 1, rev 2.700), ax ratio of converter at stall 2.75, possible manual selection; etallic spray.

Bora

PRICE EX WORKS: 39,860,000* liras

ENGINE centre-rear, 4 stroke; 8 cylinders, Vee-slanted at 90°; 300.8 cu in, 4,930 cc (3.70 x 3.50 in, 93.9 x 89 mm); compression ratio: 8.5:1; max power (DIN): 320 hp (235 kW) at 5,500 rpm; max torque (DIN): 335 lb ft, 49 kg m (480 Nm) at 4,000 rpm; max engine rpm: 6,000; 64.9 hp/l (47.8 kW/l); light alloy block and head, wet liners, hemispherical combustion chambers; 5 crankshaft bearings; valves: overhead, Vee-slanted at 30°, thimble tappets; camshafts: 4, 2 per bank, overhead, chain-driven; lubrication: gear pump, full flow filter, dry sump, separate oil tank, 21 imp pt, 25.4 US pt, 12 l; 4 Weber 42 DCNF 6 downdraught twin barrel carburettors; fuel feed: 2 electrc pumps; water-cooled, 28.2 imp pt, 33.8 US pt, 16 l, 2 electric fans.

TRANSMISSION driving wheels: rear; clutch: single dry plate (diaphragm), hydraulically controlled; gearbox: mechnical; gears: 5, fully synchronized; ratios: I 2.580, II 1.520, III 1.040, IV 0.850, V 0.740, rev 2.860; lever: central; final drive: hypoid bevel, limited slip differential; axle ratio: 3.770; width of rims: 7.5"; tyres: 215/70 x 15.

PERFORMANCE max speeds: (I) 49 mph, 79 km/h; (II) 83 mph, 133 km/h; (III) 121 mph, 194 km/h; (IV) 148 mph, 238 km/h; (V) 174 mph, 280 km/h; power-weight ratio: 9.5 lb/hp (13.5 lb/kW), 4.4 kg/hp (6.1 kg/kW); carrying capacity: 662 lb, 300 kg; acceleration: standing ¼ mile 14.4 sec, 0-50 mph (0-80 km/h) 4.4 sec; speed in top at 1,000 rpm: 28.9 mph, 46.5 km/h; consumption: 17.8 m/imp gal, 14.8 m/US gal, 15.9 l x 100 km.

CHASSIS integral; front suspension: independent, wishbones, coil springs, anti-roll bar, telescopic dampers; rear: independent, wishbones, coil springs, anti-roll bar, telescopic dampers.

STEERING rack-and-pinion, adjustable height and distance of steering wheel; turns lock to lock: 3.

BRAKES disc (front diameter 9.45 in, 24 cm, rear 9.76 in, 24.8 cm), internal radial fins, rear compensator, dual circuit, servo; swept area: front 244.2 sq in, 1,575 sq cm, rear 209 sq in, 1,348 sq cm, total 453.2 sq in, 2,923 sq cm.

ELECTRICAL EQUIPMENT 12 V; 66 Ah battery; 650 W alternator; Bosch electronic ignition; 2 retractable iodine headlamps.

DIMENSIONS AND WEIGHT wheel base: 102.36 in, 260 cm; tracks: 58.03 in, 147 cm front, 53.03 in, 145 cm rear; length: 170.67 in, 433 cm; width: 69.61 in, 177 cm; height: 44.49 in, 113 cm; ground clearance: 5.12 in, 13 cm; weight: 3,087 lb, 1,400 kg; weight distribution: 42% front, 58% rear; turning circle: 36.1 ft, 11 m; fuel tank: 22 imp gal, 26.4 US gal, 100 l.

BODY coupé; 2 doors; 2 seats; adjustable pedals; air conditioning; tinted glass; electric windows; heated rear window; leather upholstery.

PRACTICAL INSTRUCTIONS fuel: 98-100 oct petrol; oil: engine 17.6 imp pt, 21.1 US pt, 10 l, SAE 20W-50, change every 3,100 miles, 5,000 km - gearbox and final drive 5.8 imp pt, 7 US pt, 3.3 l, SAE 90, change every 12,400 miles, 20,000 km; greasing: every 3,100 miles, 5,000 km, 5 points; sparking plug: 240°; tappet clearances: inlet 0.011-0.012 in, 0.28-0.30 mm, exhaust 0.019-0.020 in, 0.47-0.50 mm; valve timing: 40° 80° 54° 22°; tyre pressure: front 36 psi, 2.5 atm, rear 38 psi, 2.7 atm.

OPTIONALS right hand drive; metallic spray.

NUOVA INNOCENTI — ITALY

Mini 90 N / 90 SL

PRICES EX WORKS:	liras
Mini 90 N	**3,840,000***
Mini 90 SL	**4,400,000***

ENGINE front, transverse, 4 stroke; 4 cylinders, vertical, in line; 60.9 cu in, 998 cc (2.54 x 3 in, 64.6 x 76.2 mm); compression ratio: 9:1; max power (DIN): 49 hp (36 kW) at 5,600 rpm; max torque (DIN): 51 lb ft, 7 kg m (69 Nm) at 2,600 rpm; max engine rpm: 6,000; 49.1 hp/l (36.2 kW/l); cast iron block and head; 3 crankshaft bearings; valves: overhead, in line, push-rods and rockers; camshafts: 1, side; lubrication: eccentric pump, full flow filter (cartridge), 8.8 imp pt, 10.6 US pt, 5 l; 1 SU type HS 4 semi-downdraught carburettor; fuel feed: mechanical pump; water-cooled, 6.7 imp pt, 8 US pt, 3.8 l, electric thermostatic fan.

TRANSMISSION driving wheels: front; clutch: single dry plate (diaphragm), hydraulically controlled; gearbox: mechanical, in unit with engine; gears: 4, fully synchronized; ratios: I 3.525, II 2.217, III 1.433, IV 1, rev 3.544; lever: central; final drive: spiral bevel; axle ratio: 3.937; width of rims: 4.5"; tyres: 135 SR x 12.

PERFORMANCE max speeds: (I) 25 mph, 40 km/h; (II) 39 mph, 63 km/h; (III) 61 mph, 98 km/h; (IV) about 87 mph, 140 km/h; power-weight ratio: 32.4 lb/hp (44 lb/kW), 14.7 kg/hp (20 kg/kW); carrying capacity: 882 lb, 400 kg; speed in direct drive at 1,000 rpm: 14.6 mph, 23.5 km/h; consumption: 36.7 m/imp gal, 30.5 m/US gal, 7.7 l x 100 km.

CHASSIS integral, front and rear auxiliary frames; front suspension: independent, wishbones (lower trailing links), rubber cone springs, telescopic dampers; rear: independent, swinging longitudinal trailing arms, rubber cone springs, telescopic dampers.

STEERING rack-and-pinion; turns lock to lock: 2.75.

BRAKES front disc (diameter 8.38 in, 21.3 cm), rear drum, dual circuit; lining area: front 17.7 sq in, 114 sq cm, rear 33.8 sq in, 218 sq cm, total 51.5 sq in, 332 sq cm.

ELECTRICAL EQUIPMENT 12 V; 43 Ah battery; 385 W alternator; Lucas or Bosch distributor; 2 headlamps.

DIMENSIONS AND WEIGHT wheel base: 80.16 in, 204 cm; front and rear track: 49.21 in, 125 cm; length: 122.83 in, 312 cm; width: 59.06 in, 150 cm; height: 54.33 in, 138 cm; ground clearance: 4.92 in, 12.5 cm; weight: 1,588 lb, 720 kg; turning circle: 28.2 ft, 8.6 m; fuel tank: 8.4 imp gal, 10 US gal, 38 l.

BODY saloon/sedan; 2+1 doors; 5 seats, separate front seats, reclining backrests; heated rear window; folding rear seat; rear window wiper-washer, tinted glass and headrests (for 90 SL only).

PRACTICAL INSTRUCTIONS fuel: 98-100 oct petrol; oil: engine, gearbox and final drive 8.8 imp pt, 10.6 US pt, 5 l, SAE 20W-50, change every 3,100 miles, 5,000 km; greasing: every 3,100 miles, 5,000 km, 7 points; sparking plug: 175°; tappet

MINI 90 N / 90 SL

clearances: inlet 0.012 in, 0.30 mm, exhaust 0.012 in, 0.30 mm; valve timing: 5° 45° 51° 21°; tyre pressure: front 30 psi, 2.1 atm, rear 28 psi, 2 atm.

OPTIONALS headrests (for 90 N only); metallic spray (for 90 SL only).

Mini 120 SL

See Mini 90 N/90 SL, except for:

PRICE EX WORKS: 4,630,000* liras

ENGINE 77.8 cu in, 1,275 cc (2.78 x 3.20 in, 70.6 x 81.3 mm); compression ratio: 9.75:1; max power (DIN): 65 hp (48 kW) at 5,600 rpm; max torque (DIN): 72 lb ft, 10 kg m (98 Nm) at 2,600 rpm; 51 hp/l (37.5 kW/l); oil cooler; 1 SU type HS 6 semi-downdraught carburettor; fuel feed: electric pump.

TRANSMISSION gearbox ratios: I 3.329, II 2.094, III 1.353, IV 1, rev 3.347; axle ratio: 3.647; tyres: 155/70 SR x 12.

PERFORMANCE max speeds: (I) 29 mph, 46 km/h; (II) 45 mph, 73 km/h; (III) 70 mph, 113 km/h; (IV) about 96 mph, 155 km/h; power-weight ratio: 24.8 lb/hp (33.7 lb/kW), 11.2 kg/hp (15.3 kg/kW); speed in direct drive at 1,000 rpm: 16 mph, 25.7 km/h; consumption: 33.6 m/imp gal, 28 m/US gal, 8.4 l x 100 km.

ELECTRICAL EQUIPMENT iodine headlamps.

DIMENSIONS AND WEIGHT weight: 1,610 lb, 730 kg.

BODY rear window wiper-washer; tinted glass; headrests.

PRACTICAL INSTRUCTIONS tappet clearances: inlet 0.014 in, 0.35 mm, exhaust 0.014 in, 0.35 mm; valve timing: 10° 50° 51° 21°.

Mini De Tomaso

See Mini 90 N/90 SL, except for:

PRICE EX WORKS: 5,145,000* liras

ENGINE 77.8 cu in, 1,275 cc (2.78 x 3.20 in, 70.6 x 81.3 mm); compression ratio: 9.75:1; max power (SAE): 77 hp (57 kW) at 6,050 rpm; max torque (SAE): 77 lb ft, 10.6 kg m (104 Nm) at 3,200 rpm; max engine rpm: 6,100; 60.4 hp/l (44.5 kW/l); oil cooler; 1 SU type HS 6 semi-downdraught carburettor; fuel feed: electric pump.

TRANSMISSION gearbox ratios: I 3.329, II 2.094, III 1.353, IV 1, rev 3.347; axle ratio: 3.647; tyres: 155/70 SR x 12.

PERFORMANCE max speeds: (I) 30 mph, 48 km/h; (II) 47 mph, 76 km/h; (III) 73 mph, 118 km/h, (IV) over 99 mph, 160 km/h; power-weight ratio: 21.4 lb/hp (29.1 lb/kW), 9.7 kg/hp (13.2 kg/kW); consumption: 33.6 m/imp gal, 28 m/US gal, 8.4 l x 100 km.

ELECTRICAL EQUIPMENT iodine headlamps.

DIMENSIONS AND WEIGHT length: 123.23 in, 313 cm; width: 59.84 in, 152 cm; height: 54.33 in, 138 cm; ground clearance: 5.12 in, 12 cm; weight: 1,654 lb, 750 kg.

BODY headrests; tinted glass; halogen fog lamps; rear window wiper-washer; light alloy wheels.

PRACTICAL INSTRUCTIONS tappet clearances: inlet 0.014 in, 0.35 mm, exhaust 0.014 in, 0.35 mm; valve timing: 10° 50° 51° 21°.

OPTIONALS special version.

POLSKI-FIAT   POLAND

126 P / 650

ENGINE rear, 4 stroke; 2 cylinders, vertical, in line; 39.8 cu in, 652 cc (3 x 2.70 in, 77 x 70 mm); compression ratio: 7.5:1; max power (DIN): 24 hp (18 kW) at 4,500 rpm; max torque (DIN): 30 lb ft, 4.2 kg m (41 Nm) at 3,000 rpm; max engine rpm: 5,400; 36.8 hp/l (27 kW/l); light alloy block and head; 2 crankshaft bearings; valves: overhead, in line, push-rods and rockers; camshafts: 1, side, chain-driven; lubrication gear pump, centrifugal filter, 4.8 imp pt, 5.7 US pt, 2.7 l; 1 Fos 28 IMB 5/250 downdraught carburettor; fuel feed: mechanical pump; air-cooled.

TRANSMISSION driving wheels: rear; clutch: single dry plate (diaphragm); gearbox: mechanical; gears: 4 II, III and

NUOVA INNOCENTI Mini De Tomaso

IV silent claw coupling; ratios: I 3.250, II 2.067, III 1.300, IV 0.872, rev 4.024; lever: central; final drive: spiral bevel; axle ratio: 4.875; width of rims: 4''; tyres: 135 SR x 12.

PERFORMANCE max speeds: (I) 19 mph, 30 km/h; (II) 31 mph, 50 km/h; (III) 50 mph, 80 km/h; (IV) 65 mph, 105 km/h; power-weight ratio: 55.6 lb/hp (75.7 lb/kW), 25.2 kg/hp (34.3 kg/kW); carrying capacity: 750 lb, 340 kg; speed in direct drive at 1,000 rpm: 14.7 mph, 23.6 km/h; consumption: 49.5 m/imp gal, 41.3 m/US gal, 5.7 l x 100 km.

CHASSIS integral; front suspension: independent, wishbones, transverse leafspring lower arms, telescopic dampers; rear: independent, semi-trailing arms, coil springs, telescopic dampers.

STEERING screw and sector; turns lock to lock: 2.90.

BRAKES drum; swept area: front 32.4 sq in, 208 sq cm, rear 32.4 sq in, 208 sq cm, total 64.8 sq in, 416 sq cm.

ELECTRICAL EQUIPMENT 12 V; 34 Ah battery; 400 W alternator; Zelmot distributor; 2 headlamps.

DIMENSIONS AND WEIGHT wheel base: 72.44 in, 184 cm; tracks: 44.88 in, 114 cm front, 47.24 in, 120 cm rear; length: 120.08 in, 305 cm; width: 54.33 in, 138 cm; height: 51.18 in, 130 cm; ground clearance: 5.51 in, 14 cm; weight: 1.323 lb, 600 kg; weight distribution: 39.5% front, 60.5% rear; turning circle: 28.2 ft, 8.6 m; fuel tank: 4.6 imp gal, 5.5 US gal, 21 l.

BODY saloon/sedan; 2 doors; 4 seats, separate front seats.

PRACTICAL INSTRUCTIONS fuel: 94 oct petrol; oil: engin 4.4 imp pt, 5.3 US pt, 2.5 l, SAE 10W-30, change ever 6,200 miles, 10,000 km - gearbox and final drive 1.9 imp p 2.3 US pt, 1.1 l, SAE 90, change every 18,600 miles, 30,00 km; greasing: every 6,200 miles, 10,000 km, 2 points tappet clearances; inlet 0.008 in, 0.20 mm, exhaust 0.01 in, 0.25 mm; valve timing: 26° 56° 66° 16°; tyre pressure front 22 psi, 1.4 atm, rear 29 psi, 2 atm.

OPTIONALS (I version): manual clutch, brake and accelera tor controls, fastenings for folding wheel chair; grab handl over left hand door, heated rear window; (S version) reclin ing backrests, tinted windscreen, heated rear window; (version) retractable seat belts, rear side windows openin half way down, heavy-duty brakes.

125 P 1300

ENGINE front, 4 stroke; 4 cylinders, in line; 79 cu in, 1,29 cc (2.83 x 3.13 in, 72 x 79.5 mm); compression ratio: 9: max power (DIN): 65 hp (48 kW) at 5,200 rpm; max torqu (DIN): 69 lb ft, 9.5 kg m (93 Nm) at 4,000 rpm; max engin rpm: 6,000; 50.2 hp/l (36.9 kW/l); cast iron block, light allo head, polispherical combustion chambers; 3 cranksha bearings; valves: overhead, push-rods and rockers; car shafts: 1, side, in crankcase; lubrication: gear pump, centr fugal filter (cartridge), 6.2 imp pt, 7.4 US pt, 3.5 l; 1 Web 34 DCHD 1-17 downdraught twin barrel carburettor; fu feed: mechanical pump; water-cooled, 11.8 imp pt, 14.2 U pt, 6.7 l.

POLSKI-FIAT 125 P 1300 - 1500

RANSMISSION driving wheels: rear; clutch: single dry ate, hydraulically controlled; gearbox: mechanical; gears: fully synchronized; ratios: I 3.753, II 2.303, III 1.493, IV rev 3.867; lever: central; final drive: hypoid bevel; axle tio: 4.100; width of rims: 4.5"; tyres: 165 SR x 13.

ERFORMANCE max speeds: (I) 25 mph, 40 km/h; (II) 40 ph, 65 km/h; (III) 62 mph, 100 km/h; (IV) over 90 mph, 145 n/h; power-weight ratio: 32.9 lb/hp (44.7 lb/kW), 14.9 /hp (20.3 kg/kW); carrying capacity: 882 lb, 400 kg; celeration: 0-50 mph (0-80 km/h) 13 sec; speed in direct ive at 1,000 rpm: 15.8 mph, 25.9 km/h; consumption: 29.7 /imp gal, 24.8 m/US gal, 9.5 l x 100 km.

HASSIS integral; front suspension: independent, wish- ones, coil springs, anti-roll bar acting as lower trailing ms, telescopic dampers; rear: rigid axle, semi-elliptic afsprings, telescopic dampers.

TEERING worm and roller; turns lock to lock: 3.

RAKES disc (diameter 8.94 in, 22.7 mm), servo; lining ea: total 38.4 sq in, 248 sq cm.

LECTRICAL EQUIPMENT 12 V; 45 Ah battery; 1,500 W ternator; Marelli distributor; 4 headlamps.

MENSIONS AND WEIGHT wheel base: 98.62 in, 250 cm; acks: 51.10 in, 130 cm front, 50.39 in, 128 cm rear; ngth: 166.65 in, 423 cm; width: 64.17 in, 163 cm; height: .69 in, 144 cm; ground clearance: 5.51 in, 14 cm; weight: 139 lb, 970 kg; turning circle: 35.4 ft, 10.8 m; fuel tank: 9 imp gal, 11.9 US gal, 45 l.

ODY saloon/sedan; 4 doors; 5 seats, separate front seats, clining backrests, built-in headrests.

RACTICAL INSTRUCTIONS fuel: 92 oct petrol; oil: engine 2 imp pt, 7.4 US pt, 3.5 l, SAE 20W-30, change every 200 miles, 10,000 km - gearbox 2.3 imp pt, 2.7 US pt, 1.3 SAE 90 EP, change every 18,600 miles, 30,000 km - final ive 3.5 imp pt, 4.2 US pt, 2 l, SAE 90 EP, change every ,600 miles, 30,000 km; greasing: none; sparking plug: 0°; tappet clearances: inlet 0.008 in, 0.20 mm, exhaust 010 in, 0.25 mm; valve timing: 5° 44° 47° 2°; tyre pres- re: front 23 psi, 1.6 atm, rear 27 psi, 1.9 atm.

PTIONALS luxury interior; sunshine roof.

125 P 1300 Estate

e 125 P 1300, except for:

ERFORMANCE power-weight ratio: 36.1 lb/hp (49.1 lb/ V), 16.4 kg/hp (22.3 kg/kW); carrying capacity: 992 lb, 450 .

MENSIONS AND WEIGHT length: 166.92 in, 424 cm; dth: 64.17 in, 163 cm; height: 55.51 in, 141 cm; ground earance: 6.06 in, 15.4 cm; weight: 2,348 lb, 1,065 kg.

DY estate car/st. wagon; 4+1 doors; folding rear seat.

125 P 1500

e 125 P 1300, except for:

RICE IN GB: £ 2,373*

NGINE 90.4 cu in, 1,481 cc (3.03 x 3.13 in, 77 x 79.5 mm); ax power (DIN): 75 hp (55 kW) at 5,400 rpm; max torque IN): 83 lb ft, 11.5 kg m (113 Nm) at 3,800 rpm; max gine rpm: 6,000; 50.6 hp/l (37.2 kW/l); electric thermosta- fan.

ERFORMANCE max speed: 96 mph, 155 km/h; power- eight ratio: 28.4 lb/hp (38.8 lb/kW), 12.9 kg/hp (17.6 /kW); acceleration: 0-50 mph (0-80 km/h) 11 sec; con- mption: 26.9 m/imp gal, 22.4 m/US gal, 10.5 l x 100 km.

125 P 1500 Estate

e 125 P 1300, except for:

RICE IN GB: £ 2,736*

NGINE 90.4 cu in, 1,481 cc (3.03 x 3.13 in, 77 x 79.5 mm); ax power (DIN): 75 hp (55 kW) at 5,400 rpm; max torque IN): 83 lb ft, 11.5 kg m (113 Nm) at 3,800 rpm; max gine rpm: 6,000; 50.6 hp/l (37.2 kW/l); electric thermosta- fan.

ERFORMANCE max speed: 96 mph, 155 km/h; power- eight ratio: 31.3 lb/hp (42.6 lb/kW), 14.2 kg/hp (19.3 /kW); acceleration: 0-50 mph (0-80 km/h) 12 sec; con- mption: 26.9 m/imp gal, 22.4 m/US gal, 10.5 l x 100 km.

MENSIONS AND WEIGHT length: 166.92 in, 424 cm; dth: 64.17 in, 163 cm; height: 55.51 in, 141 cm; ground earance: 6.06 in, 15.4 cm; weight: 2,348 lb, 1,065 kg

DY estate car/st. wagon; 4+ 1 doors; folding rear seat.

POLSKI-FIAT Polonez

Polonez

PRICE IN GB: £ 3,194*

ENGINE front, 4 stroke; 4 cylinders, in line; 90.4 cu in, 1,481 cc (3.03 x 3.13 in, 77 x 79.5 mm); compression ratio: 9:1; max power (DIN): 75 hp (55 kW) at 5,200 rpm; max torque (DIN): 85 lb ft, 11.7 kg m (115 Nm) at 3,200 rpm; max engine rpm; 6,000; 50.6 hp/l (37.2 kW/l); cast iron block, light alloy head; 3 crankshaft bearings; valves: 2 per cylinder, overhead, push-rods and rockers camshafts: 1, side; lubrication: gear pump, full flow filter, 7 imp pt, 8.5 US pt, 4 l; 1 Weber 34 DCMPI/250 downdraught twin barrel carburettor; fuel feed: mechanical pump; water-cooled, 13.2 imp pt, 15.8 US pt, 7.5 l.

TRANSMISSION driving wheels: rear; clutch: single dry plate; gearbox: mechanical; gears: 4, fully synchronized; ratios: I 3.753, II 2.132, III 1.378, IV 1, rev 3.867; lever: central; final drive: hypoid bevel; axle ratio: 4.100; width of rims: 5"; tyres: 175 SR x 13.

PERFORMANCE max speeds: (I) 26 mph, 42 km/h; (II) 47 mph, 75 km/h; (III) 71 mph, 115 km/h; (IV) 93 mph, 150 km/h; power-weight ratio: 32 lb/hp (43.4 lb/kW), 14.5 kg/hp (19.7 kg/kW); carrying capacity: 882 lb, 400 kg; accelera- tion: standing ¼ mile 19.8 sec, 0-50 mph, (0-80 km/h) 12.5 sec; speed in direct drive at 1,000 rpm: 16.8 mph, 27 km/h; consumption: 34.4 m/imp gal, 28.7 m/US gal, 8.2 l x 100 km.

CHASSIS integral; front suspension: independent, wish- bones, coil springs, anti-roll bar acting as lower trailing arms, telescopic dampers, distance rods; rear: rigid axle, 2 semi-elliptic leafsprings, 2 telescopic dampers, 2 distance rods.

STEERING worm and roller; turns lock to lock: 3.05.

BRAKES disc, servo; swept area: front 19.2 sq in, 124 sq cm, rear 19.2 sq in, 124 sq cm, total 38.4 sq in, 248 sq cm.

ELECTRICAL EQUIPMENT 12 V; 45 Ah battery; 840 W alternator; Marelli distributor; 4 headlamps.

DIMENSIONS AND WEIGHT wheel base: 98.78 in, 251 cm; tracks: 51.73 in, 131 cm front, 50.87 in, 129 cm rear; length: 168.20 in, 427 cm; width: 64.96 in, 165 cm; height: 54.33 in, 138 cm; ground clearance: 5.51 in, 14 cm; weight: 2,403 lb, 1,090 kg; weight distribution: 45% front, 55% rear; turning circle: 35.4 ft, 10.8 m; fuel tank: 9.9 imp gal, 11.9 US gal, 45 l.

BODY saloon/sedan; 4+1 doors; 5 seats, separate front seats, reclining backrests with adjustable headrests.

PRACTICAL INSTRUCTIONS fuel: 94 oct petrol; oil: engine 7 imp pt, 8.5 US pt, 4 l, SAE 20W-30, change every 6,200 miles, 10,000 km - gearbox 2.7 imp pt, 3.3 US pt, 1.5 l, SAE 90 EP, change every 18,600 miles, 30,000 km - final drive 2.1 imp pt, 2.5 US pt, 1.2 l, change every 18,600 miles, 30,000 km.

SYRENA 105

SYRENA — POLAND

105

ENGINE front, 2 stroke; 3 cylinders, vertical, in line; 51.4 cu in, 842 cc (2.76 x 2.87 in, 70 x 73 mm); compression ratio: 7-7.2:1; max power (DIN): 40 hp (29 kW) at 4,300 rpm; max torque (DIN): 58 lb ft, 8 kg m (78 Nm) at 2,750 rpm; max engine rpm: 5,200; 47.5 hp/l (34.9 kW/l); cast iron block, dry liners, light alloy head; 4 crankshaft bearings on ball bearings; lubrication: mixture; 1 Jikov 35POH/048 horizon- tal carburettor; fuel feed: mechanical pump; water-cooled, 12.3 imp pt, 14.8 US pt, 7 l.

TRANSMISSION driving wheels: front; clutch: single dry plate; gearbox: mechanical; gears: 4, free wheel, fully syn- chronized; ratios: I 3.900, II 2.357, III 1.474, IV 0.958, rev 3.273; lever: steering column; final drive: spiral bevel; axle ratio: 4.875; width of rims: 4"; tyres: 5.60 x 15.

PERFORMANCE max speeds: (I) 19 mph, 31 km/h; (II) 32 mph, 51 km/h; (III) 50 mph, 81 km/h; (IV) 75 mph, 120 km/h; power-weight ratio: 47.8 lb/hp (65 lb/kW), 21.7 kg/hp (29.5 kg/kW); carrying capacity: 706 lb, 320 kg; acceleration: 0-50 mph (0-80 km/h) 21 sec; speed in top at 1,000 rpm: 14.9 mph, 24 km/h; consumption: 32.1 m/imp gal, 26.7 m/US gal, 8.8 l x 100 km.

CHASSIS box-type ladder frame; front suspension: inde- pendent, wishbones, transverse leafspring lower arms, tele- scopic dampers; rear: rigid axle, transverse upper leafspring, trailing radius arms, telescopic dampers.

105

STEERING worm and roller; turns lock to lock: 2.80.

BRAKES drum; swept area: front 76.3 sq in, 492 sq cm, rear 45 sq in, 290 sq cm, total 121.3 sq in, 782 sq cm.

ELECTRICAL EQUIPMENT 12 V; 42 Ah battery; 300 W dynamo; 2 headlamps.

DIMENSIONS AND WEIGHT wheel base: 90.55 in, 230 cm; tracks: 47.24 in, 120 cm front, 48.82 in, 124 cm rear; length: 159.05 in, 404 cm; width: 61.42 in, 156 cm; height: 59.65 in, 151 cm; ground clearance: 7.87 in, 20 cm; weight: 1,912 lb, 867 kg; weight distribution: 48% front, 52% rear; turning circle: 34.1 ft, 10.4 m; fuel tank: 7 imp gal, 9.2 US gal, 35 l.

BODY saloon/sedan; 2 doors; 5 seats, separate front seats.

PRACTICAL INSTRUCTIONS fuel: mixture 1:30; oil: gearbox and final drive 4 imp pt, 4.9 US pt, 2.3 l, SAE 90, change every 7,500 miles, 12,000 km; greasing: every 7,500 miles, 12,000 km, 29 points; sparking plug: 175° or 225°; tyre pressure: front 23 psi, 1.6 atm, rear 23 psi, 1.6 atm.

ARO 103

PORTARO — PORTUGAL

250

ENGINE front, Daihatsu diesel; 4 cylinders, in line; 154.4 cu in, 2,530 cc (3.46 x 4.09 in, 88 x 104 mm); compression ratio: 20:1; max power (DIN): 80 hp (59 kW) at 3,800 rpm; max torque (DIN): 127 lb ft, 17.5 kg m (172 Nm) at 2,200 rpm; max engine rpm: 4,200; 31.6 hp/l (23.2 kW/l); cast iron block and head; 4 crankshaft bearings; valves: 8, overhead; camshafts: 1, overhead; lubrication: rotary pump, 11.4 imp pt, 13.7 US pt, 6.5 l; 1 Nippon Denso injection pump; fuel feed: mechanical pump; water-cooled, 23.4 imp pt, 28.1 US pt, 13.3 l.

TRANSMISSION driving wheels: rear, or front and rear; clutch: single dry plate; gearbox: mechanical; gears: 4, fully synchronized and 2 ratios transfer box; ratios: I 4.921, II 2.781, III 1.654, IV 1, rev 5.080; transfer box ratios: high 1, low 2.18; lever: central; final drive: spiral bevel; axle ratio: 4.714.

PERFORMANCE max speed: 70 mph, 112 km/h; power-weight ratio: 46.1 lb/hp (62.6 lb/kW), 20.9 kg/hp (28.4 kg/kW); carrying capacity: 2,977 lb, 1,350 kg; speed in direct drive at 1,000 rpm: 17.4 mph, 28 km/h; consumption: 28.2 m/imp gal, 23.5 m/US gal, 10 l x 100 km.

CHASSIS ladder frame; front suspension: independent, swinging arms, coil springs, telescopic dampers; rear: rigid axle, semi-elliptic leafsprings with rubber elements, telescopic dampers.

STEERING worm and roller; turns lock to lock: 2.25.

BRAKES drum.

ELECTRICAL EQUIPMENT 12 V; 120 Ah battery; 35 A alternator; 2 headlamps.

DIMENSIONS AND WEIGHT wheel base: 92.51 in, 235 cm; front and rear track: 56.89 in, 144 cm; length: 156.81 in, 398 cm; width: 70.24 in, 178 cm; height: 75.98 in, 193 cm; ground clearance: 9.05 in, 23 cm; weight: 3,682 lb, 1,670 kg; weight distribution: 52% front, 48% rear; turning circle: 39.4 ft, 12 m; fuel tank: 19.8 imp gal, 23.8 US gal, 90 l.

BODY estate car/st. wagon; 2+1 doors; 9 seats.

PRACTICAL INSTRUCTIONS fuel: diesel oil; oil: engine 11.4 imp pt, 13.7 US pt, 6.5 l, SAE 90 EP - gearbox 3.5 imp pt, 4.2 US pt, 2 l, SAE 90 EP - final drive 2.1 imp pt, 2.5 US pt, 1.2 l, SAE 90 EP; greasing: every 3,100 miles, 5,000 km, 6 points; tappet clearances: inlet 0.010 in, 0.25 mm, exhaust 0.010 in, 0.25 mm; valve timing: 25° 55° 60° 20°; tyre pressure: front 54 psi, 3.8 atm, rear 54 psi, 3.8 atm.

OPTIONALS servo brake; power steering; air-conditioning.

PORTARO 250

ARO — ROMANI

100 / 101 / 103 / 104

ENGINE front, 4 stroke; 4 cylinders, vertical, in line; 78.7 c in, 1,289 cc (2.87 x 3.03 in, 73 x 77 mm); compression rati 8.5:1; max power (DIN): 54 hp (40 kW) at 5,250 rpm; ma torque (DIN): 68 lb ft, 9.4 kg m (92 Nm) at 3,000 rpm; ma engine rpm: 5,500; 41.8 hp/l (30.8 kW/l); cast iron bloc light alloy head; 5 crankshaft bearings; valves: overhea push-rods and rockers; camshafts: 1, side; lubrication: ge pump, 4.4 imp pt, 5.3 US pt, 2.5 l; 1 Solex 32 IRM dow draught carburettor; fuel feed: mechanical pump; seale circuit cooling, liquid, 11.4 imp pt, 13.7 US pt, 6.5 l

TRANSMISSION driving wheels: rear and front; clutc single dry plate (diaphragm); gearbox: mechanical; gear 4, fully synchronized; ratios: I 4.376, II 2.455, III 1.514, I 1, rev 3.660; lever: central; final drive: spiral bevel; ax ratio: 5.142; width of rims: 5''; tyres: 6.95 x 14.

PERFORMANCE max speed: (I) 16 mph, 25 km/h; (II) mph, 45 km/h; (III) 47 mph, 75 km/h; (IV) 68 mph, 110 km/ power-weight ratio: 100 model 43 lb/hp (58 lb/kW), 19 kg/hp (26.2 kg/kW); carrying capacity: 100 model 1,103 l 500 kg - 101 model 1,058 lb, 480 kg - 103 model 992 lb, 4 kg - 104 model 948 lb, 430 kg; acceleration: standing mile 30 sec; speed in direct drive at 1,000 rpm: 13.8 mp 22.2 km/h; consumption: 33.2 m/imp gal, 27.7 m/US gal, 8 l x 100 km at 37 mph, 60 km/h.

CHASSIS box-type ladder frame front and rear suspensio independent, swinging semi-axles, coil springs, telescop dampers.

STEERING worm and double roller; turns lock to lock: 3.5

BRAKES disc; swept area: front 11.3 sq in, 73 sq cm, re 11.3 sq in, 73 sq cm, total 22.6 sq in, 146 sq cm.

ELECTRICAL EQUIPMENT 12 V; 45 Ah battery; 500 alternator; 2 headlamps.

DIMENSIONS AND WEIGHT wheel base: 94.09 in, 239 c front and rear track: 50.79 in, 129 cm; length: 141.34 359 cm; width: 62.99 in, 160 cm; height: 68.50 in, 174 c ground clearance: 8.66 in, 22 cm; weight: 100 model 2,3 lb, 1,050 kg - 101 model 2,359 lb, 1,070 kg - 103 mo 2,426 lb, 1,100 kg - 104 model 2,470 lb, 1,120 kg; turni circle: 34.4 ft, 10.5 m; fuel tank: 11.7 imp gal, 14 US gal, 5

BODY (100 and 101 models) open with canvas top - (10 and 104 models) hardtop; 2 doors; (100 and 103 models) seats - (101 and 104 models) 5 seats, folding rear seat separate front seats.

PRACTICAL INSTRUCTIONS fuel: 98 oct petrol; oil: engi 4.4 imp pt, 5.3 US pt, 2.5 l, SAE 10W-40, change eve 1,900 miles, 3,000 km - gearbox: 1.8 imp pt, 2.1 US pt, 1 SAE 90, change every 7,800 miles, 12,000 km - final dri 1.6 imp pt, 1.9 US pt, 0.9 l, SAE 90, change every 7,8 miles, 12,000 km; greasing: every 1,900 miles, 3,000 k 14 points.

OPTIONALS fog lamps; servo brake.

ARO 241

240 / 241 / 242 / 243 / 244

83 hp power team

tandard)

NGINE front, 4 stroke; 4 cylinders, vertical in line; 152.2 in, 2,495 cc (3.82 x 3.32 in, 97 x 84,4 mm); compression tio: 8:1; max power (DIN): 83 hp (61 kW) at 4,200 rpm; ax torque (DIN): 125 lb ft, 17.3 kg m (170 Nm) at 2,800 m; max engine rpm: 4,200; 33.3 hp/l (24.5 kW/l); cast iron ock and head; 5 crankshaft bearings; valves: overhead, ee-slanted, push-rods and rockers; camshafts: 1, side; brication: gear pump, full flow filter, 10.8 imp pt, 12.7 US , 6 l; 1 Weber W 250 twin barrel carburettor; fuel feed: echanical pump; water-cooled, 22.9 imp pt, 27.5 US pt, 13 l.

ANSMISSION driving wheels: rear and front; clutch: ngle dry plate, hydraulically controlled; gearbox: mechacal; gears: 4, fully synchronized and 2 ratios transfer box; tios: I 4.920, II 2.682, III 1.654, IV 1, rev 5.080; lever: ntral; transfer box ratios: high 1, low 2.180; final drive: iral bevel; axle ratio: 4.714; width of rims: 4.5"; tyres: 50 x 16.

ERFORMANCE max speeds: (I) 16 mph, 25 km/h; ((II) 28 ph, 45 km/h; (III) 43 mph, 70 km/h; (IV) 71 mph, 115 km/h; wer-weight ratio: 240 model 41.2 lb/hp (56 lb/kW), 18.7 /hp (25.4 kg/kW); carrying capacity: 240 and 243 models 554 lb, 700 kg - 241 model 1,191 lb, 540 kg - 242 model 764 lb, 800 kg - 244 model 1,191 lb, 540 kg; acceleration: anding ¼ mile 23 sec; speed in direct drive at 1,000 rpm: 18.1 mph, 29.2 km/h; consumption: 18.2 m/imp gal, 15.2 m/US gal, 15.5 l x 100 km.

CHASSIS box-type ladder frame; front suspension: independent, swinging semi-axles, coil springs, telescopic dampers; rear: rigid axle, leafsprings with rubber elements, telescopic dampers.

STEERING warm and double roller; turns lock to lock: 3.40.

BRAKES drum; swept area: front 83.7 sq in, 540 sq cm, rear 83.7 sq in, 540 sq cm, total 167.4 sq in, 1,080 sq cm.

ELECTRICAL EQUIPMENT 12 V; 70 Ah battery; 500 W alternator; 2 headlamps.

DIMENSIONS AND WEIGHT wheel base: 92.52 in, 235 cm; front and rear track: 56.69 in, 145 cm; length: 158.66 in, 403 cm; width: 69.88 in, 178 cm; height: 240 - 241 and 242 models 78.27 in, 199 cm - 243 model 79.25 in, 201 cm - 244 model 74.02 in, 188 cm; ground clearance: 8.66 in, 22 cm; weight: 240 model 3,418 lb, 1,550 kg - 241 and 242 models 3,506 lb, 1,590 kg - 243 model 3,572 lb, 1,620 kg - 244 model 3,660 lb, 1,660 kg; weight distribution: 51.6% front, 48.4% rear; turning circle: 39.4 ft, 12 m; fuel tank: 20.9 imp gal, 25.1 US gal, 95 l.

BODY (240 and 241 models) open with canvas top - (243 and 244 models) hardtop; (240 model) 2 doors, 8 seats; (241 and 244 models) 4 doors, 5 seats; (242 model) 2 doors, 2 seats; (243 model) 2 + 1 doors, 8 seats; separate front seats.

DACIA 1300 Break

PRACTICAL INSTRUCTIONS fuel: 90 oct petrol; oil: engine 10.6 imp pt, 12.7 US pt, 6 l, SAE 10W-40, change every 1,900 miles, 3,000 km - gearbox 3.5 imp pt, 4.2 US pt, 2 l, SAE 90, change every 7,800 miles, 12,000 km - final drive 2.1 imp pt, 2.5 US pt, 1.2 l, SAE 90, change every 7,800 miles, 12,000 km; greasing: every 1,900 miles, 3,000 km, 16 points; sparking plug: M14 x 225 SINTEROM; tappet clearances: inlet 0.018 in, 0.45 mm, exhaust 0.018 in, 0.45 mm; valve timing: 12° 57° 58° 8°; tyre pressure: front 28 psi, 2 atm, rear 42 psi, 3 atm.

OPTIONALS fog lamps; servo brake.

68 hp (diesel) power team

(optional)

See 83 hp power team, except for:

ENGINE diesel; 194.4 cu in, 3,120 cc (3.74 x 4.33 in, 95 x 110 mm); compression ratio: 17:1; max power (DIN): 68 hp (50 kW) at 3,200 rpm; max torque (DIN): 134 lb ft, 18.5 kg m (181 Nm) at 1,600 rpm; max engine rpm: 3,200; 21.8 hp/l (16 kW/l); lubrication: 13.2 imp pt, 15.9 US pt, 7.5 l; 1 CAV-DPAM 3842010 injection; cooling: 26.4 imp pt, 31.7 US pt, 15 l.

TRANSMISSION gearbox ratios: I 4.920, II 2.622, III 1.654, IV 1, rev 5.080; axle ratio: 3.720.

PERFORMANCE max speeds: (I) 16 mph, 25 km/h; (II) 25 mph, 40 km/h; (III) 39 mph, 63 km/h; (IV) 65 mph, 105 km/h; power-weight ratio: 240 model 54.3 lb/hp, (73.9 lb/kW), 24.6 kg/hp (33.5 kg/kW) acceleration: standing ¼ mile 27 sec; speed in direct drive at 1,000 rpm: 23 mph, 37 km/h; consumption: 25.7 m/imp gal, 21.4 m/US gal, 11 l x 100 km.

ELECTRICAL EQUIPMENT 2 x 66 Ah batteries.

DIMENSIONS AND WEIGHT length: 190.16 in, 483 cm; weight: 240 model: 3,693 lb, 1,675 kg - 241 and 242 models 3,782 lb, 1,715 kg - 243 model 3,849 lb, 1,745 kg - 244 model 3,936 lb, 1,785 kg.

PRACTICAL INSTRUCTIONS fuel: diesel oil: engine 13.2 imp pt, 15.9 US pt, 7.5 l, SAE 10W-30; tappet clearances: inlet 0.010 in, 0.25 mm, exhaust 0.014 in, 0.35 mm; valve timing: 3° 43° 48°30' 6°.

DACIA ROMANIA

1300 / 1301 Saloon

ENGINE front, 4 stroke; 4 cylinders, vertical, in line; 78.7 cu in, 1,289 cc (2.87 x 3.03 in, 73 x 77 mm); compression ratio: 8.5:1; max power (DIN): 54 hp (40 kW) at 5,250 rpm; max torque (DIN): 65 lb ft, 9 kg m (88 Nm) at 3,500 rpm; max engine rpm: 5,500; 41.8 hp/l (30.8 kW/l); cast iron block, wet liners, light alloy head; 5 crankshaft bearings; valves: overhead, slanted, push-rods and rockers; camshafts: 1, side; lubrication: gear pump, filter in sump, 5.3 imp pt, 6.3 US pt, 3 l; 1 Solex 32 EISA downdraught carburettor; fuel feed: mechanical pump; sealed circuit cooling, liquid, 8.8 imp pt, 10.6 US pt, 5 l.

TRANSMISSION driving wheels: front; clutch: single dry plate (diaphragm); gearbox: mechanical; gears: 4, fully synchronized; ratios: I 3.615, II 2.263, III 1.480, IV 1.030, rev 3.080; lever: central; final drive: hypoid bevel; axle ratio: 3.780; width of rims: 4.5"; tyres: 155 SR x 13.

PERFORMANCE max speeds: (I) 30 mph, 48 km/h; (II) 45 mph, 73 km/h; (III) 68 mph, 110 km/h; (IV) 90 mph, 145 km/h; power-weight ratio: 36.8 lb/hp (50 lb/kW), 16.7 kg/hp (22.7 kg/kW); carrying capacity: 882 lb, 400 kg; speed in top at 1,000 rpm: 16.8 mph, 27 km/h; consumption: 33.2 m/imp gal, 27.7 m/US gal, 8.5 l x 100 km.

CHASSIS integral; front suspension: independent, wishbones, anti-roll bar, coil springs, telescopic dampers; rear: rigid axle, trailing arms, A-bracket, anti-roll bar, coil springs, telescopic dampers.

STEERING rack-and-pinion; turns lock to lock: 3.50.

BRAKES front disc (diameter 8.98 in, 22.8 cm), rear drum, rear compensator; swept area: front 157.2 sq in, 1,014 sq cm, rear 70.1 sq in, 452 sq cm, total 227.3 sq in, 1,466 sq cm.

ELECTRICAL EQUIPMENT 12 V; 36 Ah battery; 30-40 A alternator; 2 headlamps.

DIMENSIONS AND WEIGHT wheel base: 96.06 in, 244 cm; front and rear track: 51.57 in, 131 cm; length: 170.87 in, 434 cm; width: 64.57 in, 164 cm; height: 56.30 in, 143 cm; ground clearance: 4.33 in, 11 cm; weight: 1,985 lb, 900 kg; weight distribution: 58.3% front, 41.7% rear; turning circle: 35.4 ft, 10.8 m; fuel tank: 11 imp gal, 13.2 US gal, 50 l.

BODY saloon/sedan; 4 doors; 4-5 seats, separate front seats; (for 1301 only) luxury equipment.

1300 Break

See 1300 / 1301 Saloon, except for:

ENGINE 1 Zenith 32 IF8 downdraught carburettor.

PERFORMANCE power-weight ratio: 39.2 lb/hp (53.4 lb/kW), 17.8 kg/hp (24.2 kg/kW).

DIMENSIONS AND WEIGHT length: 173.23 in, 440 cm; height: 57.28 in, 145 cm; weight: 2,117 lb, 960 kg.

FASA-RENAULT SPAIN

4 / TL

PRICES EX WORKS:	pesetas
4	313,000
4 TL	353,000

ENGINE front, 4 stroke; 4 cylinders, vertical, in line; 52 cu in, 852 cc (2.42 x 2.83 in, 61.4 x 72 mm); compression ratio: 8:1; max power (DIN): 32 hp (23 kW) at 5,000 rpm max torque (DIN): 40.6 lb ft, 5.6 kg m (55 Nm) at 2,750 rpm; 37.5 hp/l (27.6 kW/l); 5 crankshaft bearings; valves: overhead, in line, push-rods and rockers; camshafts: 1, side; lubrication: gear pump, filter in sump, 5.3 imp pt, 6.3 US pt, 3 l; 1 Zenith 28 downdraught single barrel carburettor; fuel feed: mechanical pump; sealed circuit cooling, liquid, expansion tank, 10.2 imp pt, 12.2 US pt, 5.8 l.

TRANSMISSION driving wheels: front; clutch: single dry plate (diaphragm); gearbox: mechanical; gears: 4, fully synchronized; ratios: I 3.833, II 2.235, III 1.458, IV 1.026, rev 3.545; lever: on facia; final drive: spiral bevel; axle ratio: 4.125; width of rims: 4"; tyres: 135 SR x 13.

PERFORMANCE max speed: 71 mph, 115 km/h; power-weight ratio: 46.8 lb/hp (63.8 lb/kW), 21.2 kg/hp (28.9 kg/kW); carrying capacity: 860 lb, 390 kg; speed in top at 1,000 rpm: 14.7 mph, 23.7 km/h; consumption: 43.5 m/imp gal, 36.2 m/US gal, 6.5 l x 100 km.

CHASSIS platform; front suspension: independent, wishbones, longitudinal torsion bars, anti-roll bar, telescopic dampers; rear: independent, swinging longitudinal trailing arms, transverse torsion bars, telescopic dampers.

STEERING rack-and-pinion.

BRAKES drum, rear compensator; lining area: front 44.5 sq in, 287 sq cm, rear 19.4 sq in, 125 sq cm, total 63.9 sq in, 412 sq cm.

ELECTRICAL EQUIPMENT 12 V; 30 Ah battery; dynamo; 2 headlamps

DIMENSIONS AND WEIGHT wheel base: 94.46 in, 245 cm (right), 94.49 in, 240 cm (left); tracks: 50.39 in, 128 cm front, 48.82 in, 124 cm rear; length: 144.49 in, 367 cm; width: 58.27 in, 148 cm; height: 61.02 in, 155 cm; weight: 4 1,499 lb, 680 kg - 4 TL 1,543 lb, 700 kg; turning circle: 31.8 ft, 9.7 m; fuel tank: 5.7 imp gal, 6.8 US gal, 26 l.

BODY estate car/st. wagon; 4+1 doors; 4 seats, bench front seats; folding rear seat; luxury interior (for 4 TL only).

OPTIONALS metallic spray; luxury interior; heated rear window; sunshine roof and separate front seats with reclining backrests (for TL only).

5 Series

PRICES EX WORKS:	pesetas
1 GTL	448,000
2 Copa	682,000

Power team:	Standard for:	Optional for:
50 hp	1	—
93 hp	2	—

50 hp power team

ENGINE front, 4 stroke; 4 cylinders, vertical, in line; 63.27 cu in, 1,037 cc (2.66 x 2.83 in, 67.7 x 72 mm); compression ratio: 9.5:1; max power (DIN): 50 hp (37 kW) at 5,500 rpm; max torque (DIN): 54 lb ft, 7.4 kg m (72 Nm) at 3,000 rpm; max engine rpm: 6,000; 48.2 hp/l (35.4 kW/l); cast iron block, wet liners, light alloy head; 5 crankshaft bearings; valves: overhead, in line, push-rods and rockers; camshafts: 1, side; lubrication: gear pump, 5.3 imp pt, 6.3 US pt, 3 l; 1 Solex 32 SEIA downdrought single barrel carburettor; fuel feed: mechanical pump; sealed circuit cooling, liquid expansion tank, 11 imp pt, 13 US pt, 6.3 l.

TRANSMISSION driving wheels: front; clutch: single dry plate (diaphragm); gearbox: mechanical; gears: 4, fully synchronized; ratios: I 3.383, II 2.235, III 1.458, IV 1.026, rev 3.545; lever: central; final drive: spiral bevel; axle ratio: 4.125; width of rims: 4"; tyres: 135 SR x 13.

PERFORMANCE max speed: 86 mph, 138 km/h; power-weight ratio: 34.6 lb/hp, (47.1 lb/kW), 15.7 kg/hp (21.4 kg/kW); carrying capacity: 882 lb, 400 kg; speed in top at 1,000 rpm: 14.6 mph, 23.6 km/h; consumption: 31.4 m/imp gal, 26.1 m/US gal, 9 l x 100 km.

CHASSIS integral; front suspension: independent, wishbones, longitudinal torsion bar, anti-roll bar, telescopic dampers; rear: independent, swinging longitudinal trailing arms, transverse torsion bars, anti-roll bar, telescopic dampers.

STEERING rack-and-pinion.

BRAKES front disc, rear drum, rear compensator, servo; lining area: front 78.6 sq in, 507 sq cm, rear 26.2 sq in, 169 sq cm, total 104.8 sq in, 676 sq cm.

ELECTRICAL EQUIPMENT 12 V; 28 Ah battery; alternator; 2 headlamps.

DIMENSIONS AND WEIGHT wheel base: 94.49 in, 240 cm (right), 95.67 in, 243 cm (left); tracks: 50.71 in, 129 cm front, 48.82 in, 124 cm rear; length: 138.19 in, 351 cm; width: 59.84 in, 152 cm; height: 55.12 in, 140 cm; weight: 1,730 lb, 785 kg; turning circle: 32.1 ft, 9.8 m; fuel tank: 8.4 imp gal, 10 US gal, 38 l.

BODY saloon/sedan; 2+1 doors; 4 seats, separate front seats reclining front seats; built-in headrests.

93 hp power team

See 50 hp power team, except for:

ENGINE 85.2 cu in, 1,397 cc (2.99 x 3.03 in, 76 x 77 mm) compression ratio: 10:1 max power (DIN): 93 hp (68 kW) a 6,400 rpm; max torque (DIN): 84 lb ft, 11.6 kg m (114 Nm) a 4,000 rpm; max engine rpm: 6,400; 66.5 hp/l (48.9 kW/l); Weber 32 DIR 58 T twin barrel carburettor.

TRANSMISSION ratios: I 3.810, II 2.230, III 1.470, IV 1.030 rev 3.500; axle ratio: 4.125; width of rims: 5.5"; tyres: 17 SR x 13.

PERFORMANCE max speed: 106 mph, 170 km/h; power-weigh ratio: 20.1 lb/hp (27.4 lb/kW), 9.1 kg/hp (12.4 kg/kW); speed i top at 1,000 rpm: 17.5 mph, 28.2 km/h; consumption: 28. m/imp gal, 23.5 m/US gal, 10 l x 100 km.

CHASSIS rear suspension: anti-roll bar, telescopic dampers

ELECTRICAL EQUIPMENT 36 Ah battery; 55 A alternator; halogen headlamps.

DIMENSIONS AND WEIGHT length: 139.30 in, 354 cm; weigh 1,874 lb, 850 kg.

BODY heated rear window; rear window wiper-washer.

FASA-RENAULT 5 GTL

FASA-RENAULT 4

6 TL

PRICE EX WORKS: 430,000 pesetas

ENGINE front, 4 stroke; 4 cylinders, vertical, in line; 63.3 cu i 1,037 cc (2.66 x 2.83 in, 67.7 x 72 mm); compression rati 9.5:1; max power (DIN): 50 hp (37 kW) at 5,500 rpm; ma torque (DIN): 54 lb ft, 7.4 kg m (37 Nm) at 3,000 rpm; ma engine rpm: 6,000: 48.2 hp/l (35.4 kW/l); cast iron block, w liners, light alloy head; 5 crankshaft bearings; valves: ove head, push-rods and rockers; camshafts: 1, side, chain-drive lubrication: gear pump, 5.3 imp pt, 6.3 US pt, 3 l; 1 Zenith 32 or Solex 32 DIS downdraught carburettor; fuel feed: mechanic pump; sealed circuit cooling, liquid, 11.1 imp pt, 13.3 US pt, 6 l.

TRANSMISSION driving wheels: front; clutch: single dry plat gearbox: mechanical; gears: 4, fully synchronized; ratios: 3.830, II 2.230, III 1.450, IV 1.020, rev 3.540; lever: on faci final drive: spiral bevel; axle ratio: 4.125; width of rims: 4.5 tyres 145 SR x 13.

PERFORMANCE max speed: 83 mph, 133 km/h; power-weig ratio: 36.6 lb/hp (49.8 lb/kW), 16.6 kg/hp (22.6 kg/kW); carryi capacity: 860 lb, 390 kg; speed in top at 1,000 rpm: 14.1 mp 22.7 km/h; consumption: 43.4 m/imp gal, 36.2 m/US gal, 6 l x 100 km.

CHASSIS integral; front suspension: independent, swingi arms, longitudinal torsion bars, anti-roll bar, telescopic dar pers; rear: independent, swinging longitudinal leading arm transverse torsion bars, anti-roll bar, telescopic dampers.

STEERING rack-and-pinion.

FASA-RENAULT 7 TL

RAKES front disc, rear drum, rear compensator; lining area: ont 78.6 sq in, 507 sq cm, rear 26.3 sq in, 169 sq cm, total)4.9 sq in, 676 sq cm.

LECTRICAL EQUIPMENT 12 V; 28 Ah battery; 35 A alterna-r; 2 headlamps.

IMENSIONS AND WEIGHT wheel base: 96.46 in, 245 cm ight), 94,49 in, 240 cm (left); tracks: 50.39 in, 128 cm front, 3.82 in, 124 cm rear; length: 151.97 in, 386 cm; width: 59.06 , 150 cm; height: 56.69 in, 144 cm; ground clearance: 4.92 in, 2.5 cm; weight: 1,830 lb, 830 kg; turning circle: 32.5 ft, 9.9 m; el tank: 8.8 imp gal, 10.5 US gal, 40 l.

ODY saloon/sedan; 4+1 doors; 4 seats, separate front seats; lding rear seat.

PTIONALS metallic spray; luxury interior.

7 TL

ee 6 TL, except for:

RICE EX WORKS: 437,000 pesetas

ERFORMANCE power-weight ratio: 35.9 lb/hp (48.9 lb/kW), 6.3 kg/hp (22.2 kg/kW); speed in top at 1,000 rpm: 15.2 mph, 4.4 km/h; consumption: 40.3 m/imp gal, 33.5 m/US gal, 7 x 100 km.

LECTRICAL EQUIPMENT 38 A alternator.

IMENSIONS AND WEIGHT wheel base: 99.60 in, 253 cm ight), 98.40 in, 250 cm (left); tracks: 50.78 in, 129 cm front, 9.21 in, 125 cm rear; length: 153.15 in, 389 cm; width: 59.80 , 152 cm; height: 55 in, 140 cm; ground clearance: 5.50 in, 14 m; weight: 1,797 lb, 815 kg; turning circle: 32.8 ft, 10 m; fuel nk: 8.4 imp gal, 10 US gal, 38 l.

12 Series

RICES EX WORKS:	**pesetas**
TL	**513,000**
TL Familiar	**544,000**
TS	**569,000**
TS Familiar	**595,000**

ower team:	Standard for:	Optional for:
7 hp	1,2	—
0 hp	3,4	—

57 hp power team

NGINE front, 4 stroke; 4 cylinders, vertical, in line; 78.7 cu in, ,289 cc (2.87 x 3.03 in, 73 x 77 mm); compression ratio: 8.5; ax power (DIN): 57 hp (42 kW) at 5,300 rpm; max torque DIN): 69 lb ft, 9.5 kg m (93 Nm) at 3,000 rpm; max engine rpm: ,300; 44.2 hp/l (32.5 kW/l); cast iron block, wet liners, light lloy head; 5 crankshaft bearings; valves: overhead, slanted, ush-rods and rockers; camshafts: 1, side; lubrication: gear ump, filter in sump, 5.3 imp pt, 6.3 US pt, 3 l; 1 Solex 32 owndraught single barrel carburettor; fuel feed: mechanical ump; sealed circuit cooling, liquid, 3.5 imp pt, 4.2 US pt, 2 l.

TRANSMISSION driving wheels: front; clutch: single dry plate; gearbox: mechanical; gears: 4, fully synchronized; ratios: I 3.818, II 2.235, III 1.478, IV 1.036, rev 3.083; lever: central; final drive: hypoid bevel; axle ratio: 3.778; width of rims: 5"; tyres: 155 x 330.

PERFORMANCE max speed: 87 mph, 140 km/h; power-weight ratio: TL 35 lb/hp (47.6 lb/kW), 15.8 kg/hp (21.6 kg/kW); carrying capacity: TL 882 lb, 400 kg; speed in top at 1,000 16.6 mph, 26.7 m/h; consumption: 35.3 m/imp gal, 29.4 m/US gal, 8 l x 100 km.

CHASSIS integral; front suspension: independent, wishbones, anti-roll bar, coil springs/telescopic dampers; rear: rigid axle, trailing arms, A-bracket, anti-roll bar, coil springs/telescopic dampers.

STEERING rack-and-pinion.

BRAKES front disc, rear drum, rear compensator, 12 TL servo; lining area: front 78.6 sq in, 507 sq cm, rear 35 sq in, 226 sq cm, total 113.6 sq in, 733 sq cm.

ELECTRICAL EQUIPMENT 12 V; alternator; 36 Ah battery; 2 headlamps.

DIMENSIONS AND WEIGHT wheel base: 96.06 in, 244 cm; front and rear track: 51.96 in, 132 cm; length: TL 172.44 in, 438 cm - TL Familiar 173.23 in, 440 cm; width: 63.78 in, 162 cm; height: TL 55.90 in, 142 cm - TL Familiar 57.08 in, 145 cm; ground clearance: 5.12 in, 13 cm; weight: TL 1,995 lb, 905 kg - TL Familiar 2,117 lb 960 kg; turning circle: 33 ft, 10.1 m; fuel tank: 11 imp gal, 13.2 US gal, 50 l.

BODY saloon/sedan, 4 doors - estate car/st. wagon, 4+1 doors; TL 5 seats - TL Familiar 5/7 seats, separate front seats; heated rear window.

70 hp power team

See 57 hp power team, except for:

ENGINE 85.2 cu in, 1,397 cc (2.99 x 3.03 in, 76 x 77 mm); compression ratio: 9.2:1; max power (DIN): 70 hp (51 kW) at 5,500 rpm; max torque (DIN): 80 lb ft, 11 kg m (108 Nm) at 3,500 rpm; max engine rpm: 5,600; 50.1 hp/l (36.9 kW/l); 1 Weber 32 DIR 40 T downdraught twin barrel carburettor.

PERFORMANCE max speed: 92 mph, 148 km/h; power-weight ratio: TS 28.9 lb/hp (39.3 lb/kW), 13.1 kg/hp (17.8 kg/kW).

ELECTRICAL EQUIPMENT 4 headlamps, 2 iodine.

DIMENSIONS AND WEIGHT weight: TS 2,028 lb, 920 kg - TS Familiar 2,149 lb, 975 kg.

BODY built-in headrests.

SEAT SPAIN

133 Lujo

(only for export)

PRICE EX WORKS: 249,000* pesetas

ENGINE rear, longitudinal, 4 stroke; 4 cylinders, vertical, in line; 51.4 cu in, 843 cc (2.56 x 2.50 in, 65 x 63.5 mm); compression ratio: 8:1; max power (DIN): 34 hp (25 kW) at 4,800 rpm; max torque (DIN): 40 lb ft, 5.5 kg m (54 Nm) at 3,200 rpm; max engine rpm: 5,500; 40.3 hp/l (29.7 kW/l); cast iron block, light alloy head; 3 crankshaft bearings; valves: overhead, in line, push-rods and rockers; camshafts: 1, side; lubrication: gear pump, full flow filter, 6 imp pt, 7.2 US pt, 3.4 l; 1 Bressel 30 ICF-3 or Solex 30 PIB-5 downdraught single barrel carburettor; fuel feed: mechanical pump; sealed circuit cooling, liquid,13.2 imp pt, 15.9 US pt, 7.5 l.

TRANSMISSION driving wheels: rear; clutch: single dry plate; gearbox: mechanical; gears: 4, fully synchronized; ratios: I 3.636, II 2.055, III 1.409, IV 0.963, rev 3.615; lever: central; final drive: hypoid bevel; axle ratio: 4.625; width of rims: 4"; tyres: 5.50 x 12.

PERFORMANCE max speeds: (I) 20 mph, 32 km/h; (II) 35 mph, 56 km/h; (III) 52 mph, 83 km/h; (IV) about 75 mph, 120 km/h; power-weight ratio: 44.7 lb/hp (60.8 lb/kW), 20.3 kg/hp (27.6 kg/kW); carrying capacity: 706 lb, 320 kg; speed in top at 1,000 rpm: 13.7 mph, 22.1 km/h; consumption: 40.9 m/imp gal, 34.1 m/US gal, 6.9 l x 100 km.

SEAT 133 Lujo

133 LUJO

CHASSIS integral; front suspension: independent, wishbones, transverse leafspring lower arms, transverse torsion bar, telescopic dampers; rear: independent, semi-trailing arms, coil springs, torsion bar, telescopic dampers.

STEERING rack-and-pinion; turns lock to lock: 2.80.

BRAKES drum, dual circuit; lining area: front 33.5 sq in, 216 sq cm, rear 33.5 sq in, 216 sq cm, total 67 sq in, 432 sq cm.

ELECTRICAL EQUIPMENT 12 V; 34 Ah battery; 230 W dynamo; Femsa DI 4-7 distributor; 2 headlamps.

DIMENSIONS AND WEIGHT wheel base: 79.92 in, 203 cm; tracks: 45.28 in, 115 cm front, 48.03 in, 122 cm rear; length: 135.83 in, 345 cm; width: 55.91 in, 142 cm; height: 52.36 in, 133 cm; ground clearance: 5.30 in, 13 cm; weight: 1,521 lb, 690 kg; weight distribution: 39% front, 61% rear; turning circle: 31.5 ft, 9.6 m; fuel tank: 6.6 imp gal, 7.9 US gal, 30 l.

BODY saloon/sedan; 2 doors; 4-5 seats, separate front seats; luxury equipment.

PRACTICAL INSTRUCTIONS fuel: 85 oct petrol; oil: engine 5.8 imp pt, 7 US pt, 3.3 l, SAE 40W (winter) 30 (summer), change every 6,200 miles, 10,000 km - gearbox and final drive 3.7 imp pt, 4.4 US pt, 2.1 l, SAE 90 EP, change every 18,600 miles, 30,000 km; greasing: every 1,600 miles, 2,500 km, 2 points; sparking plug: 175°; tappet clearances: inlet 0.006 in, 0.15 mm, exhaust 0.006 in, 0.15 mm; valve timing: 16° 56° 56° 16°; tyre pressure: front 20 psi, 1.4 atm, rear 28 psi, 2 atm.

SEAT 127 1000 Especial Confort Lujo

127 Series

PRICES EX WORKS:	pesetas
1 900 2 Puertas	**285,000***
2 900 2+1 Puertas	**296,000***
3 900 4 Puertas	**299,000***
4 900 2 Puertas Confort Lujo	**315,000***
5 900 2+1 Puertas Confort Lujo	**328,000***
6 900 4 Puertas Confort Lujo	**332,000***
7 1000 2 Puertas Especial Confort Lujo	**323,000***
8 1000 2+1 Puertas Especial Confort Lujo	**335,000***
9 1000 4 Puertas Especial Confort Lujo	**338,000***

Power team:	Standard for:	Optional for:
43 hp	1 to 6	—
52 hp	7 to 9	—

43 hp power team

ENGINE front, transverse, 4 stroke; 4 cylinders, vertical, in line; 55.1 cu in, 903 cc (2.56 x 2.68 in, 65 x 68 mm); compression ratio: 8.7:1; max power (DIN): 43 hp (32 kW) at 5,600 rpm; max torque (DIN): 44.2 lb ft, 6.1 kg m (60 Nm) at 3,000 rpm; max engine rpm: 6,200; 47.6 hp/l (35 kW/l); cast iron block, light alloy head; 3 crankshaft bearings; valves: overhead, in line, push-rods and rockers; camshafts: 1, side; lubrication: gear pump, full flow filter (cartridge), 6 imp pt, 7.2 US pt, 3.4 l; 1 Bressel 30 IBA-22/350 downdraught single barrel carburettor; fuel feed: mechanical pump; sealed circuit cooling, 8.8 imp pt, 10.6 US pt, 5 l.

TRANSMISSION driving wheels: front; clutch: single dry plate; gearbox: mechanical; gears: 4, fully synchronized; ratios: I 3.909, II 2.055, III 1.348, IV 0.963, rev 3.615; lever: central; final drive: cylindrical gears; axle ratio: 4.692; width of rims: 4"; tyres: 135 SR x 13.

PERFORMANCE max speeds: (I) 21 mph, 35 km/h; (II) 40 mph, 65 km/h; (III) 62 mph, 100 km/h; (IV) over 84 mph, 135 km/h; power-weight ratio: 36.4 lb/hp (49.5 lb/kW), 16.5 kg/hp (22.4 kg/kW); carrying capacity: 882 lb, 400 kg; acceleration: standing ¼ mile 20.9 sec; consumption: 43.4 m/imp gal, 36.2 m/US gal, 6.5 l x 100 km.

CHASSIS integral; front suspension: independent, by McPherson, coil springs/telescopic damper struts, lower swinging arms, anti-roll bar; rear: independent, lower swinging arms, transverse anti-roll leafsprings, telescopic dampers.

STEERING rack-and-pinion; turns lock to lock: 3.40.

BRAKES front disc (diameter 8.94 in, 22.7 cm), rear drum, rear compensator, dual circuit; lining area: front 19.2 sq in, 124 sq cm, rear 33.5 sq in, 216 sq cm, total 52.7 sq in, 340 sq cm.

ELECTRICAL EQUIPMENT 12 V; 45 Ah battery; 33 A alternator; Femsa distributor; 2 headlamps.

DIMENSIONS AND WEIGHT wheel base: 87.40 in, 222 cm; tracks: 50.39 in, 128 cm front, 50.79 in, 129 cm rear; length:142.90 in, 364 cm; width: 60.24 in, 153 cm; height: 53.50 in, 136 cm; ground clearance: 5.12 in, 13 cm; weight: 1,565 lb, 710 kg; weight distribution: 48% front, 52% rear; turning circle: 31.5 ft, 9.6 m; fuel tank: 6.6 imp gal, 7.9 US gal, 30 l.

SEAT Ritmo 65 CL

BODY saloon/sedan; 2 doors; 4 seats, separate front seats, (for Confort Lujo models only) luxury equipment.

PRACTICAL INSTRUCTIONS fuel: 90 oct petrol; oil: engine 6 imp pt, 7.2 US pt, 3.4 l, SAE 30W-40, change every 6,200 miles, 10,000 km - gearbox and final drive 4.2 imp pt, 5.1 US pt, 2.4 l, SAE 50, change every 18,600 miles, 30,000 km; greasing: none; tappet clearances: inlet 0.006 in, 0.15 mm, exhaust 0.008 in, 0.20 mm; valve timing: 17° 43° 57° 3°; tyre pressure: front 24 psi, 1.7 atm, rear 27 psi, 1.9 atm.

52 hp power team

See 43 hp power team, except for:

ENGINE 61.6 cu in, 1,010 cc (2.62 x 2.86 in, 66.5 x 72.7 mm); compression ratio: 9.4:1; max power (DIN): 52 hp (38 kW) at 5,800 rpm; max torque (DIN): 55 lb ft, 7.6 kg m (74 Nm) at 3,100 rpm; 51.5 hp/l (37.9 kW/l); 1 Bressel 32 DMTR-45/250 downdraught twin barrel carburettor.

TRANSMISSION axle ratio: 4.461.

PERFORMANCE max speeds: (I) 21 mph, 35 km/h; (II) 43 mph, 70 km/h; (III) 65 mph, 105 km/h; (IV) 90 mph, 145 km/; power-weight ratio: 30.1 lb/hp (40.9 lb/kW), 13.6 kg/hp (18.5 kg/kW); acceleration: standing ¼ mile 19.7 sec.

ELECTRICAL EQUIPMENT 22 A alternator.

PRACTICAL INSTRUCTIONS fuel: 96 oct petrol; valve timing: 7° 48° 45° 10°.

Ritmo Series

1 65 CL
2 75 CL

Power team:	Standard for:	Optional for:
64 hp	1	—
77 hp	2	—

64 hp power team

ENGINE front, transverse, 4 stroke; 4 cylinders, in line; 73 c in, 1,197 cc (2.87 x 2.81 in, 73 x 71.5 mm); compression ratio 8.4:1; max power (DIN): 64 hp (47 kW) at 5,800 rpm; ma torque (DIN): 68 lb ft, 9.4 kg m (92 Nm) at 3,000 rpm; ma engine rpm: 6,000; 53.5 hp/l (39.3 kW/l); cast iron block, ligh alloy head; 3 crankshaft bearings; valves: overhead, thimbl tappets; camshafts: 1, side, in crankcase, cogged belt; lubrica tion: gear pump full, flow filter (cartridge), 7.7 imp pt, 9.3 US p 4.4 l; 1 Bressel 32 DMTR 50/250 semi-downdraught twin barre carburettor; fuel feed: mechanical pump; water-cooled, expan sion tank, 13.2 imp pt, 15.9 US pt, 7.5 l, electric thermostati fan.

TRANSMISSION driving wheels: front; clutch single dry plate gearbox: mechanical; gears: 4, fully synchronized; ratios: 3.583, II 2.235, III 1.454, IV 1.042, rev 3.714; lever: centra final drive: spiral bevel; axle ratio: 4.077; width of rims: 4.5' tyres: 145 SR x 13.

PERFORMANCE max speeds: (I) 28 mph, 45 km/h; (II) 43 mph 70 km/h; (III) 68 mph, 110 km/h; (IV) 93 mph, 150 km/h power-weight ratio: 30.3 lb/hp (41.3 lb/kW), 13.7 kg/hp (18.7 kg/kW); carrying capacity: 882 lb, 400 kg; acceleration: standing ¼ mile 19.9 sec; speed in top at 1,000 rpm: 16.3 mph, 26.2 km/h; consumption: 32.1 m/imp gal, 26.7 m/US gal, 8.8 l x 100 km.

CHASSIS integral; front suspension: independent, by McPherson, lower wishbones, trailing links, coil springs/telescopic damper struts; rear: independent, by McPherson, lower wishbones, transverse anti-roll leafspring, telescopic dampers.

STEERING rack-and-pinion; turns lock to lock: 3.50.

BRAKES front disc (diameter 8.94 in, 22.7 cm), rear drum, dual circuit, rear compensator; lining area: front 19.2 sq in, 124 sq cm, rear 32.4 sq in, 209 sq cm, total 51.6 sq in, 333 sq cm.

ELECTRICAL EQUIPMENT 12 V; 45 Ah battery; 33 A alternator; 2 headlamps.

DIMENSIONS AND WEIGHT wheel base: 96.38 in, 245 cm; tracks: 55.12 in, 140 cm front, 55.51 in, 141 cm rear; length: 155.12 in, 394 cm; width: 65 in, 165 cm; height: 55.12 in, 140 cm; weight: 1,940 lb, 880 kg; weight distribution: 62.5% front, 37.5% rear; turning circle: 33.8 ft, 10.3 m; fuel tank: 11.2 imp gal, 13.5 US gal, 51 l.

BODY saloon/sedan; 4+1 doors; 5 seats, separate front seats; folding rear seat.

PRACTICAL INSTRUCTIONS fuel: 90 oct petrol; oil: engine 7.7 imp pt, 9.3 US pt, 4.4 l, SAE 30W-40, change every 3,100 miles, 5,000 km - gearbox and final drive 5.3 imp pt, 6.3 US pt, 3 l, SAE 90 EP, change every 18,600 miles, 30,000 km; greasing: none; sparking plug: Champion N9Y-Marelli CW7LP-Bosch W 7 D; tappet clearances: inlet 0.010 in, 0.25 mm, exhaust 0.010 in, 0.25 mm; valve timing: 9° 40° 49° 0°; tyre pressure: front 28 psi, 2 atm, rear 31 psi, 2.2 atm.

77 hp power team

See 64 hp power team, except for:

ENGINE 87.74 cu in, 1,438 cc (3.15 x 2.81 in, 80 x 71.5 mm); compression ratio: 9:1; max power (DIN): 77 hp (57 kW) at 5,600 rpm; max torque (DIN): 83 lb ft, 11.5 kg m (113 Nm) at 2,800 rpm; 53.5 hp/l (39.3 kW/l).

TRANSMISSION gears: 5, fully synchronized; ratios: I 3.583, II 2.235, III 1.454, IV 1.042, V 0.863, rev 3.714; axle ratio: 3.588; tyres: 165/70 SR x 13.

PERFORMANCE max speeds: (I) 25 mph, 40 km/h; (II) 40 mph, 65 km/h (III) 65 mph, 105 km/h; (IV) 90 mph, 145 km/h; (V) 99 mph, 160 km/h; power-weight ratio: 25.2 lb/hp, (34 lb/kW), 11.4 kg/hp (15.4 kg/kW); acceleration: standing ¼ mile 18.5 sec; speed in top at 1,000 rpm: 17.1 mph, 27.5 km/h; consumption: 33 m/imp gal, 27.7 m/US gal, 8.5 l x 100 km.

BRAKES servo.

PRACTICAL INSTRUCTIONS fuel: 96 oct petrol; valve timing: 10° 49° 50° 9°.

124-D / 124-D LS

PRICES EX WORKS:	**pesetas**
124-D	**378,000***
124-D LS	**417,000***

ENGINE front, 4 stroke; 4 cylinders, in line 73 cu in, 1,197 cc (2.87 x 2.81 in, 73 x 71.5 mm); compression ratio: 8.8:1; max power (DIN): 65 hp (48 kW) at 5,600 rpm; max torque (DIN): 65 lb ft, 9 kg m (88 Nm) at 3,400 rpm; max engine rpm: 5,600; 54.3 hp/l (39.9 kW/l); cast iron block, light alloy head; 5 crankshaft bearings; valves: overhead, push-rods and rockers; camshafts: 1, side, in crankcase; lubrication: gear pump, full flow filter (cartridge), 7.7 imp pt, 9.3 US pt, 4.4 l; 1 Bressel 32 DHS-20 downdraught twin barrel carburettor; fuel feed: mechanical pump; water-cooled, 13.2 imp pt, 15.9 US pt, 7.5 l.

TRANSMISSION driving wheels: rear; clutch: single dry plate; gearbox: mechanical; gears: 4, fully synchronized; ratios: I 3.750, II 2.300, III 1.490, IV 1, rev 3.870; lever: central; final drive: hypoid bevel; axle ratio: 4.300; width of rims: 4.5"; tyres: 150 SR x 13 or 155 SR x 13.

PERFORMANCE max speeds: (I) 22 mph, 35 km/h; (II) 37 mph, 60 km/h; (III) 59 mph, 95 km/h; (IV) about 93 mph, 150 km/h; power-weight ratio: 29.7 lb/hp (40.3 lb/kW), 13.4 kg/hp (18.3 kg/kW); carrying capacity: 882 lb, 400 kg; speed in direct drive at 1,000 rpm: 16.7 mph, 26.8 km/h; consumption: 35.3 m/imp gal, 29.4 m/US gal, 8 l x 100 km.

CHASSIS integral; front suspension: independent, wishbones, coil springs, anti-roll bar, telescopic dampers; rear: rigid axle, twin trailing radius arms, transverse linkage bar, coil springs, telescopic dampers.

STEERING worm and roller; turns lock to lock: 2.75.

BRAKES disc (diameter 8.94 in, 22.7 cm), rear compensator, servo; lining area: front 19.2 sq in, 124 sq cm, rear 19.2 sq in, 124 sq cm, total 38.4 sq in, 248 sq cm.

ELECTRICAL EQUIPMENT 12 V; 45 Ah battery; 540 W alternator; Femsa DI 4-8 distributor; 2 headlamps.

DIMENSIONS AND WEIGHT wheel base: 95.28 in, 242 cm; tracks: 52.36 in, 133 cm front, 51.18 in, 130 cm rear; length: 159.05 in, 404 cm; width: 63.39 in, 161 cm; height: 55.91 in, 142 cm; ground clearance: 5.12 in, 13 cm; weight: 1,929 lb, 875 kg; weight distribution: 43% front, 57% rear; turning circle: 35.1 ft, 10.7 m; fuel tank: 8.6 imp gal, 10.3 US gal, 39 l.

BODY saloon/sedan; 4 doors; 5 seats, separate front seats; heated rear window; (for 124-D LS only) tinted glass, built-in headrests and luxury equipment.

PRACTICAL INSTRUCTIONS fuel: 96 oct petrol; oil: engine 6.5 imp pt, 7.8 US pt, 3.7 l, SAE 30W (summer) 40 (winter), change every 6,200 miles, 10,000 km - gearbox 2.3 imp pt, 2.7 US pt, 1.3 l, ZC 90, change every 12,400 miles, 20,000 km - final drive 2.3 imp pt, 2.7 US pt, 1.3 l, SAE 90, change every 12,400 miles, 20,000 km; greasing: every 3,100 miles, 5,000 km, 4 points; sparking plug: 145°, tappet clearances: inlet and exhaust 0.010-0.012 in, 0.25-0.30 mm; valve timing: 10° 49° 50° 9°; tyre pressure: front 24 psi, 1.7 atm, rear 26 psi, 1.8 atm.

124-D Especial

See 124-D / 124-D LS, except for:

PRICE EX WORKS: 435,000* pesetas

ENGINE 87.7 cu in, 1,438 cc (3.15 x 2.81 in, 80 x 71.5 mm); compression ratio: 9:1; max power (DIN): 75 hp (55 kW) at 5,400 rpm; max torque (DIN): 82 lb ft, 11.3 kg m (111 Nm) at 3,400 rpm; max engine rpm: 6,000; 52.2 hp/l (38.4 kW/l); 1 Bressel 32 DHS-21 downdraught twin barrel carburettor.

TRANSMISSION gearbox ratios: I 3.797, II 2.175, III 1.410, IV 1, rev 3.655.

PERFORMANCE max speeds: (I) 25 mph, 40 km/h; (II) 43 mph, 70 km/h; (III) 68 mph, 110 km/h; (IV) about 96 mph, 155 km/h; power-weight ratio: 26.8 lb/hp (36.4 lb/kW), 12.1 kg/hp (16.5 kg/kW); speed in direct drive at 1,000 rpm: 16 mph, 25.8 km/h; consumption: 32.1 m/imp gal, 26.7 m/US gal, 8.8 l x 100 km.

DIMENSIONS AND WEIGHT weight: 2,007 lb, 910 kg; weight distribution: 44% front, 56% rear.

PRACTICAL INSTRUCTIONS sparking plug: 175°.

OPTIONALS 5-speed mechanical gearbox (I 3.667, II 2.100, III 1.361, IV 1, V 0.881).

124 Especial 2000

See 124-D / 124-D LS, except for:

PRICE EX WORKS: 465,000* pesetas

ENGINE 117.1 cu in, 1,919 cc (3.31 x 3.41 in, 84 x 86.6 mm); compression ratio: 9.3:1; max power (DIN): 114 hp (84 kW) at 6,000 rpm; max torque (DIN): 116 lb ft, 16 kg m (157 Nm) at 3,500 rpm; max engine rpm: 6,000; 59.4 hp/l (43.8 kW/l); camshafts: 2, overhead, cogged belt; 1 Weber 34 DMS-4/251 downdraught twin barrel carburettor; electric thermostatic fan.

SEAT 124-D Especial

TRANSMISSION gears: 5, fully synchronized; ratios: I 3.667, II 2.100, II 1.361, IV 1, V 0.881, rev 3.526; axle ratio: 4.100; width of rims: 5.5"; tyres: 175/70 SR x 13.

PERFORMANCE max speeds: (I) 28 mph, 45 km/h; (II) 50 mph, 80 km/h; (III) 75 mph, 120 km/h; (IV) 103 mph, 165 km/h; (V) 112 mph, 180 km/h; power-weight ratio: 18.8 lb/hp (25.5 lb/kW), 8.5 kg/hp (11.5 kg/kW); acceleration: standing ¼ mile 16.7 sec; consumption: 33.2 m/imp gal, 27.7 m/US gal, 8.5 l x 100 km.

STEERING rack-and-pinion.

ELECTRICAL EQUIPMENT 2 halogen headlamps.

DIMENSIONS AND WEIGHT weight: 2,139 lb, 970 kg.

131 1430 / Supermirafiori

PRICES EX WORKS:	**pesetas**
131 1430	**469,000***
131 Supermirafiori	**511,000***

ENGINE front, 4 stroke; 4 cylinders, vertical, in line; 87.7 cu in, 1,438 cc (3.15 x 2.81 in, 80 x 71.5 mm); compression ratio: 9:1; max power (DIN): 75 hp (55 kW) at 5,400 rpm; max torque (DIN): 82 lb ft, 11.3 kg m (111 Nm) at 3,400 rpm; max engine rpm: 6,300; 52.2 hp/l (38.4 kW/l); cast iron block, light alloy head; 5 crankshaft bearings; valves: overhead, push-rods and rockers; camshafts: 1, side, in crankcase; lubrication: gear

SEAT 131 CL 1430 5 Puertas

131 1430 / SUPERMIRAFIORI

pump, full flow filter (cartridge), 7.7 imp pt, 9.3 US pt, 4.4 l; 1 Bressel 32 DHS-26 or Solex 32EIES-4 downdraught twin barrel carburettor; fuel feed: mechanical pump; sealed circuit cooling, antifreeze liquid, 13.2 imp pt, 15.9 US pt, 7.5 l.

TRANSMISSION driving wheels: rear; clutch: single dry plate; gearbox: mechanical; gears: 4, fully synchronized; ratios: I 3.667, II 2.100, III 1.361, IV 1, rev 3.526; lever: central; final drive: hypoid bevel; axle ratio: 3.900; width of rims: 4.5"; tyres: 155 SR x 13.

PERFORMANCE max speeds: (I) 28 mph, 45 km/h; (II) 47 mph, 75 km/h; (III) 75 mph, 120 km/h; (IV) about 96 mph, 155 km/h; power-weight ratio: 28.5 lb/hp (38.7 lb/kW), 12.9 kg/hp (17.6 kg/kW); carrying capacity: 882 lb, 400 kg; acceleration: standing ¼ mile 19 sec; speed in direct drive at 1,000 rpm: 16.8 mph, 27.1 km/h; consumption: 36 m/imp gal, 30 m/US gal, 7.8 l x 100 km.

CHASSIS integral; front suspension: independent, by McPherson, coil springs/telescopic damper struts, lower wishbones, anti-roll bar; rear: rigid axle, twin trailing lower radius arms, transverse linkage bar, coil springs, telescopic dampers.

STEERING rack-and-pinion; turns lock to lock: 3.40.

BRAKES front disc (diameter 8.94 in, 22.7 cm), rear drum, rear compensator, dual circuit, vacuum servo; lining area: front 19.2 sq in, 124 sq cm, rear 41.7 sq in, 269 sq cm, total 60.9 sq in, 393 sq cm.

ELECTRICAL EQUIPMENT 12 V; 45 Ah battery; 540 W alternator; Femsa distributor; 2 headlamps.

DIMENSIONS AND WEIGHT wheel base: 98.03 in, 249 cm; tracks: 53.94 in, 137 cm front, 51.57 in, 131 cm rear; length: 166.93 in, 424 cm; width: 64.17 in, 163 cm; height: 53.54 in, 136 cm; weight: 2,139 lb, 970 kg; weight distribution: 44.4% front, 55.6% rear; turning circle: 34.8 ft, 10.6 m; fuel tank: 11 imp gal, 13.2 US gal, 50 l.

BODY saloon/sedan; 4 doors; 5 seats, separate front seats, reclining backrests; (for Supermirafiori only) tinted glass, heated rear window, front and rear headrests and halogen headlamps.

PRACTICAL INSTRUCTIONS fuel: 96 oct petrol; oil: engine 6.7 imp pt, 8 US pt, 3.8 l, SAE 30W (winter) 40 (summer), change every 6,200 miles, 10,000 km - gearbox and final drive 1.6 imp pt, 1.9 US pt, 0.9 l, SAE 50 VS type ZC; greasing: none; sparking plug: 175°; tappet clearances: inlet and exhaust 0.010-0.012 in, 0.25-0.30 mm; valve timing: 10° 49° 50° 9°; tyre pressure: front 24 psi, 1.7 atm, rear 26 psi, 1.8 atm.

131 CL 1430 5 Puertas

See 131 1430 / Supermirafiori, except for:

PRICE EX WORKS: 534,000* pesetas

TRANSMISSION axle ratio: 4.100; tyres: 165 SR x 13.

PERFORMANCE max speeds: (I) 25 mph, 40 km/h; (II) 43 mph, 70 km/h; (III) 71 mph, 115 km/h; (IV) about 93 mph, 150 km/h; power weight ratio: 29.5 lb/hp (40.1 lb/kW), 13.4 kg/hp (18.2 kg/kW); carrying capacity: 1,058 lb, 480 kg; acceleration: standing ¼ mile 19.1 sec.

DIMENSIONS AND WEIGHT tracks: 54.17 in, 138 cm front, 51.93 in, 132 cm rear; height: 55.12 in, 140 cm; weight: 2,216 lb, 1,005 kg.

BODY estate car/st. wagon; 4+1 doors; 5 seats, separate front seats, reclining backrests; folding rear seat.

PRACTICAL INSTRUCTIONS tyre pressure: front 26 psi, 1.8 atm, rear 31 psi, 2.2 atm.

131 Supermirafiori 1600

See 131 1430 / Supermirafiori, except for:

PRICE EX WORKS: 550,000* pesetas

ENGINE 97.1 cu in, 1,592 cc (3.15 x 3.12 in, 80 x 79.2 mm); compression ratio: 8.98:1; max power (DIN): 95 hp (70 kW) at 6,000 rpm; max torque (DIN): 93 lb ft, 12.8 kg m (125 Nm) at 4,000 rpm; max engine rpm: 6,700; 59.7 hp/l (43.9 kW/l); valves: overhead, Vee-slanted at 65°15', thimble tappets; camshafts: 2, overhead, cogged belt; 1 Bressel 34 BMS-1 downdraught twin barrel carburettor; sealed circuit cooling, antifreeze liquid, 13.4 imp pt, 16.1 US pt, 7.6 l, electric thermostatic fan.

TRANSMISSION gears: 5, fully synchronized; ratios: I 3.667, II 2.100, III 1.361, IV 1, V 0.881, rev 3.526; tyres: 160 SR x 13.

PERFORMANCE max speeds: (I) 31 mph, 50 km/h; (II) 56 mph, 90 km/h; (III) 84 mph, 135 km/h; (IV) 106 mph, 170 km/h; (V) 103 mph, 165 km/h; power-weight ratio: 23.2 lb/hp (31.5 lb/kW), 10.5 kg/hp (14.3 kg/kW); acceleration: standing ¼ mile 17.4 sec; speed in top at 1,000 rpm: 19.1 mph, 30.8 km/h; consumption: 31.7 m/imp gal, 26.4 m/US gal, 8.9 l x 100 km.

STEERING adjustable height of steering wheel.

ELECTRICAL EQUIPMENT 4 halogen headlamps.

DIMENSIONS AND WEIGHT length: 167.72 in, 426 cm; width: 64.57 in, 164 cm; weight: 2,205 lb, 1,000 kg; weight distribution: 44% front, 55.4% rear.

BODY front and rear headrests; tinted glass; heated rear window; bumper.

PRACTICAL INSTRUCTIONS sparking plug: 215°; tappet clearances: inlet 0.018-0.020 in, 0.45-0.50 mm, exhaust 0.024-0.026 in, 0.60-0.65 mm; valve timing: 12° 53° 52° 13°; front tyre pressure: 23 psi, 1.6 atm.

OPTIONALS GMS. ZM automatic transmission, hydraulic torque converter and planetary gears with 3 ratios (I 2.400, II 1.480, III 1, rev 1.920), max ratio of converter at stall 2.4, possible manual selection, 3.700 axle ratio; air-conditioning.

SEAT 131 Supermirafiori

131 CL 1600 5 Puertas

See 131 1430 / Supermirafiori, except for:

PRICE EX WORKS: 574,000* pesetas

ENGINE 97.1 cu in, 1,592 cc (3.15 x 3.12 in, 80 x 79.2 mm); compression ratio: 8.98:1; max power (DIN): 95 hp (70 kW) at 6,000 rpm; max torque (DIN): 93 lb ft, 12.8 kg m (125 Nm) at 4,000 rpm; max engine rpm: 6,700; 59.7 hp/l (43.9 kW/l) valves: overhead, Vee-slanted at 65°15', thimble tappets, camshafts: 2, overhead, cogged belt; 1 Bressel 34 BMS-1 downdraught twin barrel carburettor; sealed circuit cooling, antifreeze liquid, 13.4 imp pt, 16.1 US pt, 7.6 l, electric thermostatic fan.

TRANSMISSION gears: 5, fully synchronized; ratios: I 3.667, II 2.100, III 1.361, IV 1, V 0.881, rev 3.526; tyres: 165 SR x 13.

PERFORMANCE max speeds: (I) 31 mph, 50 km/h; (II) 56 mph 90 km/h; (III) 84 mph, 135 km/h; (IV) about 103 mph, 165 km/h (V) about 99 mph, 160 km/h; power-weight ratio: 24 lb/hp (32.6 lb/kW), 10.9 kg/hp (14.8 kg/kW); carrying capacity: 1,058 lb 480 kg; acceleration: standing ¼ mile 17.7 sec; speed in top at 1,000 rpm: 19.1 mph, 30.8 km/h; consumption: 31.7 m/imp gal 26.4 m/US gal, 8.9 l x 100 km.

STEERING adjustable height of steering wheel.

ELECTRICAL EQUIPMENT 4 halogen headlamps.

DIMENSIONS AND WEIGHT tracks: 54.17 in, 138 cm front 51.93 in, 132 cm rear; length: 167.72 in, 426; width: 64.57 in 164 cm; height: 55.12 in, 140 cm; weight: 2,282 lb, 1,035 kg weight distribution: 44.6% front, 55.4% rear.

BODY estate car/st. wagon; 4+1 doors; 5 seats, separate front seats, front and rear headrests; tinted glass; heated rear window; bumper.

PRACTICAL INSTRUCTIONS sparking plug: 215°; tappet clearances: inlet 0.018-0.020 in, 0.45-0.50 mm, exhaust 0.024-0.026 in, 0.060-0.65 mm; valve timing: 12° 53° 54° 11°; tyre pressure front 26 psi, 1.8 atm, rear 31 psi, 2.2 atm.

OPTIONALS G.M.S. ZM automatic transmission, hydraulic torque converter and planetary gears with 3 ratios (I 2.400, II 1.480, III 1, rev 1.920), max ratio of converter at stall 2.4 possible manual selection, 3.700 axle ratio; air-conditioning.

131 Supermirafiori 2000

See 131 1430 / Supermirafiori, except for:

PRICE EX WORKS: 637,000* pesetas

ENGINE 119.1 cu in, 1,952 cc (3.31 x 3.41 in, 84 x 86.6 mm) max power (DIN): 114 hp (84 kW) at 5,800 rpm; max torque (DIN): 116 lb ft, 16 kg m (157 Nm) at 3,000 rpm; max engine rpm: 6,000; 58.4 hp/l (43 kW/l); valves: overhead, Vee-slanted at 65°15', thimble tappets; camshafts: 2, overhead, cogged belt; 1 Bressel 34 BMS-1 downdraught twin barrel carburettor electric thermostatic fan.

TRANSMISSION: gears: 5, fully synchronized; ratios: I 3.667, II 2.100, II 1.361, IV 1, V 0.881, rev 3.526; axle ratio: 4.100; width of rims: 5.5"; tyres: 185/70 SR x 13.

PERFORMANCE max speeds: (I) 28 mph, 45 km/h; (II) 47 mph 75 km/h; (III) 71 mph, 115 km/h; (IV) 99 mph, 160 km/h; (V) 11[illegible] mph, 180 km/h; power-weight ratio: 18.8 lb/hp (25.5 lb/kW), 8.[illegible] kg/hp (11.5 kg/kW); acceleration: standing ¼ mile 17.3 sec consumption: 31.7 m/imp gal, 26.4 m/US gal, 8.9 l x 100 km

STEERING adjustable height of steering wheel.

SEAT 131 Supermirafiori

ELECTRICAL EQUIPMENT 2 halogen headlamps.

DIMENSIONS AND WEIGHT weight: 2,139 lb, 970 kg.

131 Diesel Perkins / Supermirafiori

See 131 1430 / Supermirafiori, except for:

PRICES EX WORKS:	pesetas
131 Diesel Perkins	607,000*
131 Diesel Perkins Supermirafiori	662,000*

ENGINE diesel Perkins; 107.4 cu in, 1,760 cc (3.13 x 3.50 in, 79.4 x 88.9 mm); compression ratio: 22:1; max power (DIN): 49 hp (36 kW) at 4,000 rpm; max torque (DIN): 77 lb ft, 10.6 kg m (104 Nm) at 2,200 rpm; 27.8 hp/l (20.5 kW/l); 3 crankshaft bearings.

TRANSMISSION gears: 5, fully synchronized; ratios: I 3.667, II 2.100, III 1.361, IV 1, V 0.881, rev 3.526; axle ratio: 3.700; tyres: 165 SR x 13.

PERFORMANCE max speed: 93 mph, 150 km/h; power-weight ratio: 48.1 lb/hp (65.3 lb/kW), 21.8 kg/hp (29.6 kg/kW); consumption: 34.4 m/imp gal, 28.7 m/US gal, 8.2 l x 100 km.

ELECTRICAL EQUIPMENT 68 Ah battery; halogen headlamps.

DIMENSIONS AND WEIGHT weight 2,359 lb, 1,070 kg.

BODY (for Supermirafiori only) luxury equipment.

131 Diesel Perkins 5 Puertas

See 131 1430 / Supermirafiori, except for:

PRICE EX WORKS: 625,000* pesetas

ENGINE diesel Perkins; 107.4 cu in, 1760 cc (3.13 x 3.50 in, 79.4 x 88.9 mm); compression ratio: 22:1; max power (DIN): 49 hp (36 kW) at 4,000 rpm; max torque (DIN): 77 lb ft, 10.6 kg m (104 Nm) at 2,200 rpm; 27.8 hp/l (20.5 kW/l); 3 crankshaft bearings.

TRANSMISSION gears: 5, fully synchronized; ratios: I 3.667, II 2.100, III 1.361, IV 1, V 0.881, rev 3.526; axle ratio: 3.700; tyres: 165 SR x 13.

PERFORMANCE max speed: 78 mph, 125 km/h; power-weight ratio: 49.8 lb/hp (67.5 (67.5 lb/kW), 22.6 kg/hp (30.6 kg/kW); carrying capacity: 1,058 lb, 480 kg; consumption: 34.4 m/imp gal, 28.7 m/US gal, 8.2 l x 100 km.

ELECTRICAL EQUIPMENT 68 Ah battery; halogen headlamps.

DIMENSIONS AND WEIGHT tracks: 54.17 in, 138 cm front, 51.93 in, 132 cm rear; height: 55.12 in, 140 cm; weight: 2,437 lb, 1,105 kg.

BODY estate car/st. wagon; 4+1 doors; 5 seats, separate front seats, reclining backrests; folding rear seat.

PRACTICAL INSTRUCTIONS tyre pressure: front 26 psi, 1.8 atm, rear 31 psi, 2.2 atm.

STEERING screw and sector, recirculating ball, servo, adjustable height of steering wheel; turns lock to lock: 3.05.

BRAKES front disc, rear drum, rear compensator, dual circuit, servo; lining area: front 19.2 sq in, 124 sq cm, rear 41.7 sq in, 269 sq cm, total 60.9 sq in, 393 sq cm.

ELECTRICAL EQUIPMENT 12 V; 55 Ah battery: 770 W alternator; Marelli distributor; transistorized ignition; 4 halogen headlamps.

DIMENSIONS AND WEIGHT wheel base: 100.67 in, 256 cm; tracks: 51.97 in, 132 cm front, 52.36 in, 133 cm rear; length: 172.83 in, 439 cm; width: 64.57 in, 164 cm; height: 56.29 in, 143 cm; ground clearance: 4.72 in, 12 cm; weight: 2,514 lb, 1,140 kg; turning circle: 36.1 ft, 11 m; fuel tank: 12.3 imp gal, 14.8 US gal, 56 l.

BODY saloon/sedan; 4 doors; 5 seats, separate front seats, reclining backrests with built-in headrests; heated rear window; electric windows.

PRACTICAL INSTRUCTIONS fuel: 96 oct petrol; oil: engine 7 imp pt, 8.5 US pt, 4 l, SAE 30W (summer) 40 (winter), change every 6,200 miles, 10,000 km - gearbox 2.3 imp pt, 2.7 US pt, 1.3 l, ZC 90, change every 18,600 miles, 30,000 km - final drive 2.8 imp pt, 3.4 US pt, 1.6 l, SAE 90 EP, change every 18,600 miles, 30,000 km; greasing: none; tappet clearances: inlet 0.018 in, 0.45 mm, exhaust 0.024 in, 0.60 mm; valve timing: 15° 55° 53° 17°; tyre pressure: front 27 psi, 1.9 atm, rear 28 psi, 2 atm.

OPTIONALS air-conditioning; metallic spray; GMS type ZR-T2 automatic transmission, hydraulic torque converter and planetary gears with 3 ratios (I 2.400, II 1.480, III 1, rev 1,920), max ratio of converter at stall 2.4, possible manual selection, max speed 103 mph, 165 km/h.

SEAT 132 2000 Lujo

132 Diesel 2200 / Lujo

See 132 2000 Lujo, except for:

PRICES EX WORKS:	pesetas
132 Diesel 2200	715,000*
132 Diesel 2200 Lujo	765,000*

ENGINE Mercedes-Benz, diesel, front, 4 stroke; 134.1 cu in, 2,197 cc (3.43 x 3.63 in, 87 x 92.4 mm); compression ratio: 21:1; max power (DIN): 60 hp (44 kW) at 4,200 rpm; max torque (DIN): 93 lb ft, 12.8 kg m (125 Nm) at 2,200 rpm; max engine rpm: 4,350; 27.3 hp/l (20.1 kW/l); valves: overhead, in line, finger levers; camshafts: 1, overhead; lubrication: gear pump, oil-water heat exchanger, full flow filter, 9.7 imp pt, 11.6 US pt, 5.5 l; Bosch injection pump.

TRANSMISSION width of rims: 5".

PERFORMANCE max speeds: (I) 22 mph, 35 km/h; (II) 37 mph, 60 km/h; (III) 59 mph, 95 m/h; (IV) 81 mph, 130 km/h; (V) 84 mph, 135 km/h; power-weight ratio: 44.6 lb/hp (60.7 lb/kW), 20.2 kg/hp (27.5 kg/kW); acceleration: standing ¼ mile 22.8 sec; speed in top at 1,000 rpm: 19.3 mph, 30 km/h; consumption: 34.9 m/imp gal, 29 m/US gal, 8.1 l x 100 km.

ELECTRICAL EQUIPMENT 66 Ah battery.

DIMENSIONS AND WEIGHT weight: 2,679 lb, 1,215 kg.

PRACTICAL INSTRUCTIONS fuel: diesel oil; oil: engine 7.9 imp pt, 9.5 US pt, 4.5 l, SAE 30W-40, change every 6,200 miles, 10,000 km; tappet clearances: inlet 0.008 in, 0.10 mm, exhaust 0.012 in, 0.30 mm; valve timing: 12°30' 41°30' 45° 9°.

SEAT Lancia Beta Coupé 2000

132 2000 Lujo

PRICE EX WORKS: 684,000* pesetas

ENGINE front, 4 stroke; 4 cylinders, vertical, in line; 117.1 cu in, 1,919 cc (3.31 x 3.41 in, 84 x 86.6 mm); compression ratio: 8.9:1; max power (DIN): 109 hp (80 kW) at 5,800 rpm; max torque (DIN): 112 lb ft, 15.4 kg m (151 Nm) at 3,000 rpm; max engine rpm: 6,300; 56.8 hp/l (41.8 kW/l); cast iron block, light alloy head; 5 crankshaft bearings; valves: overhead, Vee-slanted at 65°, thimble tappets; camshafts: 2, overhead, cogged belt; lubrication: gear pump, full flow filter (cartridge), 7.7 imp pt, 9.3 US pt, 4.4 l; 1 Weber 34 DMS/4 or Bressel 34 DMS 4-250 downdraught twin barrel carburettor; fuel feed: mechanical pump; sealed circuit cooling, anti-freeze liquid, 14.1 imp pt, 16.9 US pt, 8 l, electric thermostatic fan.

TRANSMISSION driving wheels: rear; clutch: single dry plate; gearbox: mechanical; gears: 5, fully synchronized; ratios: I 3.667, II 2.100, III 1.361, IV 1, V 0.881, rev 3.526; lever: central; final drive: hypoid bevel; axle ratio: 4.100; width of rims: 5.5"; tyres: 175 SR x 14.

PERFORMANCE max speeds: (I) 28 mph, 45 km/h; (II) 47 mph, 75 km/h; (III) 71 mph, 115 km/h; (IV) 99 mph, 160 km/h; (V) 106 mph, 170 km/h; power-weight ratio: 23.1 lb/hp (31.3 lb/kW), 10.5 kg/hp (14.2 kg/kW); carrying capacity: 882 lb, 400 kg; consumption: 33.2 m/imp gal 27.7 m/US gal, 8.5 l x 100 km.

CHASSIS integral; front suspension: independent, wishbones (lower trailing links), coil springs, anti-roll bar, telescopic dampers; rear: rigid axle, lower longitudinal trailing radius arms, upper oblique torque arms, coil springs, telescopic dampers.

Lancia Beta Coupé 2000

ENGINE front, transverse, slanted 20° to rear, 4 stroke; 4 cylinders, in line; 117.1 cu in, 1,919 cc (3.31 x 3.41 in, 84 x 86.6 mm); compression ratio: 8.9:1; max power (DIN): 111 hp (82 kW) at 5,500 rpm; max torque (DIN): 125 lb ft, 17.2 kg m (169 Nm) at 2,800 rpm; max engine rpm: 6,000; 57.8 hp/l (42.7 kW/l); cast iron block, light alloy head, hemispherical combustion chambers; 5 crankshafts bearings; valves: overhead, Vee-slanted at 65°, thimble tappets; camshafts: 2, overhead, cogged belt; lubrication: gear pump, full flow filter, 7.9 imp pt, 9.5 US pt, 4.5 l; 1 Weber 34 DAT-2/250 downdraught twin barrel carburettor with power valve and thermostatic filter; fuel feed: electric pump; cooling liquid, 13.4 imp pt, 16.1 US pt, 7.6 l, electric thermostatic fan.

TRANSMISSION driving wheels: front; clutch: single dry plate; gearbox: mechanical; gears: 5, fully synchronized; ratios: I 3.500, II 2.235, III 1.522, IV 1.152, V 0.925, rev 3.071; lever: central; final drive: hypoid bevel; axle ratio: 3.785; width of rims: 5"; tyres: 175/70 HR x 14.

PERFORMANCE max speeds: (I) 34 mph, 54 km/h; (II) 52 mph, 84 km/h; (III) 76 mph, 123 km/h; (IV) 101 mph, 163 km/h; (V) 114 mph, 183 km/h; power-weight ratio: 19.6 lb/hp (26.6 lb/kW), 8.9 kg/hp (12 kg/kW); carrying capacity: 794 lb, 360 kg; acceleration: standing ¼ mile 16.4 sec; consumption: 33.6 m/imp gal, 28.6 m/US gal, 8.4 l x 100 km.

CHASSIS integral; front suspension: independent, lower wide-based wishbones, coil springs, telescopic damper struts, anti-

LANCIA BETA COUPÉ 2000

roll bar; rear: independent, wishbones, coil springs, telescopic damper struts, anti-roll bar acting as longitudinal torque arm.

STEERING rack-and-pinion; ZF progressive servo; turns lock to lock: 3.10.

BRAKES disc (diameter 9.88 in, 25.1 cm), rear compensator, Superduplex circuit, servo; lining area: front 24.8 sq in, 160 sq cm, rear 22 sq in, 142 sq cm, total 46.8 sq in, 302 sq cm.

ELECTRICAL EQUIPMENT 12 V; 45 Ah battery; 55 A alternator; 4 iodine headlamps.

DIMENSIONS AND WEIGHT wheel base: 92.52 in, 235 cm; tracks: 55.35 in, 141 cm front, 54.80 in, 139 cm rear; length: 157.09 in, 399 cm; width: 64.96 in, 165 cm; height: 50.39 in, 128 cm; ground clearance: 5.31 in, 13.5 cm; weight: 2,180 lb, 988 kg; weight distribution: 61% front, 39% rear; turning circle: 33.5 ft, 10.2 m; fuel tank: 10.8 imp gal, 12.9 US gal, 49 l.

BODY coupé; 2 doors; 4 seats, separate front seats; reclining backrests; heated rear window.

PRACTICAL INSTRUCTIONS fuel: 96 oct petrol; oil: engine 7.9 imp pt, 9.5 US pt, 4.5 l, SAE 10W-50, change every 3,100 miles, 5,000 km - gearbox and final drive 3 imp pt, 3.6 US pt, 1.7 l, SAE 90, change every 18,600 miles, 30,000 km; greasing: none; sparking plug: Champion N7Y-Marelli CW78 LP; tappet clearances: inlet 0.017 in, 0.42 mm, exhaust 0.019 in, 0.48 mm; valve timing: 13° 45° 49° 9°; tyre pressure: front and rear 27 psi, 1.9 atm.

Lancia Beta HPE 2000

See Lancia Beta Coupé 2000, except for:

PERFORMANCE max speed: 109 mph, 175 km/h; power-weight ratio: 21 lb/hp (28.5 lb/kW), 9.5 kg/hp (12.9 kg/kW); carrying capacity: 992 lb, 450 kg; acceleration: standing ¼ mile 16.9 sec.

DIMENSIONS AND WEIGHT wheel base: 100 in, 254 cm; length: 168.50 in, 428 cm; height: 51.57 in, 131 cm; weight: 2,337 lb, 1,060 kg; turning circle: 34.8 ft, 10.6 m.

BODY 2+1 doors; rear window wiper-washer.

SEAT Lancia Beta HPE 2000

TALBOT SPAIN

Simca 1200 Series

PRICES EX WORKS:	pesetas
1 L 2+1-dr Sedan	339,600*
2 LS 4+1-dr Sedan	356,700*
3 LX 2+1-dr Sedan	371,600*
4 GLS 4+1-dr Sedan	383,300*
5 GLS Confort 4+1-dr Sedan	399,800*
6 GLS 4+1-dr Break	394,900*
7 GLS Confort 4+1-dr Break	411,300*

Power team:	Standard for:	Optional for:
50 hp	1,2	—
62 hp	3 to 7	—
83 hp	—	3

50 hp power team

ENGINE front, transverse, 4 stroke; 4 cylinders, in line; 68.2 cu in, 1,118 cc (2.91 x 2.56 in, 74 x 65 mm); compression ratio: 8.2:1; max power (DIN): 50 hp (37 kW) at 5,900 rpm; max torque (DIN): 55 lb ft, 7.6 kg m (75 Nm) at 3,000 rpm; max engine rpm: 6,000; 44.7 hp/l (32.9 kW/l); 5 crankshaft bearings; valves: overhead, in line, push-rods and rockers; camshafts: 1, side; lubrication: gear pump, full flow filter, 5.3 imp pt, 6.3 US pt, 3 l; 1 Bressel 32 IBS 7 downdraught single barrel carburettor; fuel feed: mechanical pump; sealed circuit cooling, liquid, expansion tank, 10.6 imp pt, 12.7 US pt, 6 l, electric thermostatic fan.

TRANSMISSION driving wheels: front; clutch: single dry plate (diaphragm), hydraulically controlled; gearbox: mechanical; gears: 4, fully synchronized; ratios: I 3.900, II 2.312, III 1.524, IV 1.080, rev 3.769; lever: central; final drive: cylindrical gears; axle ratio: 3.937; width of rims: 4.5"; tyres: 145 SR x 13 - LS 155 SR x 13.

PERFORMANCE max speed: 86 mph, 138 km/h; power-weight ratio: 40 lb/hp (54.2 lb/kW), 18.2 kg/hp ((24.6 kg/kW); carrying capacity: 882 lb, 400 kg; speed in top at 1,000 rpm: 15 mph, 24 km/h; consumption: 37.6 m/imp gal, 31.3 m/US gal, 7.5 l x 100 km.

CHASSIS integral; front suspension: independent, wishbones, longitudinal torsion bars, anti-roll bar, telescopic dampers; rear: independent, longitudinal trailing arms, transverse torsion bars, anti-roll bar, telescopic dampers.

STEERING rack-and-pinion; turns lock to lock: 3.25.

BRAKES front disc (diameter 9.21 in, 23.4 cm), rear drum, dual circuit, rear compensator, servo; swept area: front 146.2 sq in, 943 sq cm, rear 73.8 sq in, 476 sq cm, total 220 sq in, 1,419 sq cm.

ELECTRICAL EQUIPMENT 12 V; 36 Ah battery; 35 A alternator; 2 headlamps.

DIMENSIONS AND WEIGHT wheel base: 99.21 in, 252 cm; tracks: 54.33 in, 138 cm front, 52.36 in, 133 cm rear; length: 155.12 in, 394 cm; width: 62.60 in, 159 cm; height: 57.48 in, 146 cm; ground clearance: 5.50 in, 14 cm; weight: L 2,007 lb, 910 kg - LS 2,029 lb, 920 kg; turning circle: 34.1 ft, 10.4 m; fuel tank: 9.2 imp gal, 11.1 US gal, 42 l.

BODY saloon/sedan; 5 seats, separate front seats; folding rear seat.

62 hp power team

See 50 hp power team, except for:

ENGINE 79 cu in, 1,294 cc (3.02 x 2.76 in, 76.7 x 70 mm); compression ratio: 8.8:1; max power (DIN): 62 hp (46 kW) at 6,000 rpm; max torque (DIN): 71 lb ft, 9.8 kg m (96 Nm) at 2,800 rpm; max engine rpm: 6,300; 47.9 hp/l (35.5 kW/l); 1 Bressel 32/IBS 6 downdraught single barrel carburettor.

TRANSMISSION width of rims: LX 5.5".

PERFORMANCE max speed: 93 mph, 150 km/h; power-weight ratio: 32.7 lb/hp, (44.1 lb/kW), 14.8 kg/hp (20 kg/kW) carrying capacity: GLS models 904 lb, 410 kg; - LX 926 lb, 420 kg consumption: 35.3 m/imp gal, 29.4 m/US gal, 8 l x 100 km.

DIMENSIONS AND WEIGHT length: GLS Break models 54.33 in, 392 cm; height: GLS Break models 58.27 in, 148 cm; weight LX 2,029 lb, 920 kg; - GLS sedans 2,051 lb, 930 kg - GLS st. wagons 2,117 lb, 960 kg.

BODY GLS Confort and GLS Confort Break, heated rear window.

83 hp power team

See 50 hp power team, except for:

ENGINE 88 cu in, 1,442 cc (3.02 x 3.07 in, 76.7 x 78 mm) compression ratio: 9.5:1; max power (DIN): 83 hp (61 kW) at 5,600 rpm; max torque (DIN): 92 lb ft, 12.7 kg m (124 Nm) at 3,000 rpm; max engine rpm: 7,200 ; 57.5 hp/l (42.3 kW/l); 1 Weber DCNVA downdraught twin barrel carburettor.

TRANSMISSION axle ratio: 3,588; width of rims: 5".

TALBOT Simca 1200 L Sedan

PERFORMANCE max speed: 106 mph, 170 km/h; power-weight ratio: 26.4 lb/hp, (34 lb/kW), 11 kg/hp (15 kg/kW); consumption: 24.6 m/imp gal, 20.5 m/US gal, 11.5 l x 100 km.

ELECTRICAL EQUIPMENT 2 halogen headlamps.

DIMENSIONS AND WEIGHT length: 154.70 in, 393 cm; height: 57.09 in, 145 cm; weight: 2,029 lb, 920 kg.

BODY heated rear window.

150 Series

PRICES EX WORKS:	pesetas
1 LS	479,200*
2 S	509,600*
3 GT	543,000*
4 SX	645,500*

Power team:	Standard for:	Optional for:
75 hp	1	—
85 hp	2,3	—
88 hp	4	—

75 hp power team

ENGINE front, transverse, slanted 41° to rear, 4 stroke; 4 cylinders, in line; 88 cu in, 1,442 cc (3.02 x 3.07 in, 76.7 x 78 mm); compression ratio: 8.5:1; max power (DIN): 75 hp (55 kW)

TALBOT 150 GT

at 5,500 rpm; max torque (DIN): 80 lb ft, 11.1 kg m (109 Nm) at 3,500 rpm; max engine rpm: 6,000; 52 hp/l (38 kW/l); cast iron block, light alloy head; 5 crankshaft bearings; valves: overhead, in line, push-rods and rockers; camshafts: 1, side; lubrication: gear pump, full flow filter, 5.3 imp pt, 6.3 US pt, 3 l; 1 Weber 36 DCNVA downdraught twin barrel carburettor; fuel feed: mechanical pump; sealed circuit cooling, liquid, expansion tank, 11.4 imp pt, 13.7 US pt, 6.5 l, electric thermostatic fan.

TRANSMISSION driving wheels: front; clutch: single dry plate (diaphragm), hydraulically controlled; gearbox: mechanical; gears: 4, fully synchronized; ratios: I 3.900, II 2.312, III 1.524, IV 1.080, rev 3,769; lever: central; final drive: cylindrical gears; axle ratio: 3.588; width of rims: 5"; tyres: 155 SR x 13.

PERFORMANCE max speed: 102 mph, 164 km/h; power-weight ratio: 31.1 lb/hp, (42.5 lb/kW), 14.2 kg/hp (19.4 kg/kW); carrying capacity: 882 lb, 400 kg; acceleration: standing ¼ mile 19 sec, 0-50 mph (0-80 km/h) 8.9 sec; speed in top at 1,000 rpm: 16.8 mph, 27.1 km/h; consumption: 26.2 m/imp gal, 21.8 m/US gal, 10.8 l x 100 km.

CHASSIS integral; front suspension: independent, wishbones, longitudinal torsion bars, anti-roll bar, telescopic dampers; rear: independent, swinging longitudinal trailing arms, coil springs, anti-roll bar, telescopic dampers.

STEERING rack-and-pinion; turns lock to lock: 4.15.

BRAKES front disc (diameter 9.45 in, 24 cm), rear drum, rear compensator, servo; swept area: front 169.3 sq in, 1,092 sq cm, rear 90.2 sq in, 582 sq cm, total 259.5 sq in, 1,674 sq cm.

ELECTRICAL EQUIPMENT 12 V; 40 Ah battery; 40 A alternator; Chrysler transistorized ignition; 2 headlamps.

DIMENSIONS AND WEIGHT wheel base: 102.36 in, 260 cm; tracks: 55.51 in, 141 cm front, 54.72 in, 139 cm rear; length: 166.93 in, 424 cm; width: 66.14 in, 168 cm; height: 54.72 in, 139 cm; ground clearance: 5.12 in, 13 cm; weight: 2,339 lb, 1,070 kg; turning circle: 36.1 ft, 11 m; fuel tank: 13.2 imp gal, 15.8 US gal, 60 l.

BODY saloon/sedan; 4+1 doors; 5 seats, separate front seats, reclining backrests; heated rear window; folding rear seat.

PRACTICAL INSTRUCTIONS fuel: 98-100 oct petrol; oil: engine 5.3 imp pt, 6.3 US pt, 3 l, SAE 20W-40, change every 4,600 miles, 7,500 km - gearbox and final drive 1.9 imp pt, 2.3 US pt, 1.1 l, SAE 90 EP, change every 9,300 miles, 15,000 km; greasing: none.

OPTIONALS iodine long-distance lights; headrests on front seats; tinted glass; headlamps with wiper-washers; rear window wiper-washer; electric windows; vinyl roof; sunshine roof; power steering; tinted glass; metallic spray; light alloy wheels.

85 hp power team

See 75 hp power team, except for:

ENGINE max power (DIN): 85 hp (63 kW) at 5,600 rpm; max torque (DIN): 92 lb ft, 12.7 kg m (124 Nm) at 3,000 rpm; max engine rpm: 6,000; 58.9 hp/l (43.4 kW/l).

PERFORMANCE power-weight ratio: 27.9 lb/hp (37.9 lb/kW), 12.6 kg/hp (17.2 kg/kW).

ELECTRICAL EQUIPMENT iodine long-distance lights (standard).

DIMENSIONS AND WEIGHT weight: 2,370 lb, 1,075 kg.

BODY (standard) tinted glass, headlamps with wiper-washers, electric windows.

OPTIONALS headrests on front seats; rear window wiper washer; vinyl roof; sunshine roof; power steering; tinted glass; metallic spray; light alloy wheels.

88 hp power team

See 75 hp power team, except for:

ENGINE 97.1 cu in, 1,592 cc (3.17 x 3.07 in, 80.6 x 78 mm); compression ratio: 9.3:1; max power (DIN): 88 hp (65 kW) at 5,400 rpm; max torque (DIN): 99 lb ft, 13.7 kg m (134 Nm) at 3,000 rpm; max engine rpm: 6,000; 55.3 hp/l (40.8 kW/l); 1 Weber 36 DCA 100 downdraught twin barrel carburettor.

TRANSMISSION gearbox: automatic transmission, hydraulic torque converter and planetary gears with 3 ratios, possible manual selection; ratios: I 2.475, II 1.475, III 1, rev 2.103; tyres: 165 SR x 13.

PERFORMANCE max speed: 103 mph, 165 km/h; power-weight ratio: 27.4 lb/hp (37.1 lb/kW), 12.4 kg/hp (16.8 kg/kW); speed in direct drive at 1,000 rpm: 18.3 mph, 29.4 km/h; consumption: 26.6 m/imp gal, 22.2 m/US gal, 10.6 l x 100 km.

STEERING turns lock to lock: 2.80.

TALBOT 150 Series

ELECTRICAL EQUIPMENT 50 Ah battery; 50 A alternator.

DIMENSIONS AND WEIGHT height: 54.72 in, 139 cm; weight: 2,414 lb, 1,095 kg; weight distribution: 60.3% front, 39.7% rear; turning circle: 34.1 ft, 10.4 m.

180 Series

PRICES EX WORKS:	pesetas
1 180	604,700*
2 Automatico	654,300*
3 Diesel	668,900*
4 Diesel De Luxe	705,100*

Power team:	Standard for:	Optional for:
100 hp	1,2	—
60 hp (diesel)	3,4	—

100 hp power team

ENGINE front, slanted 15° to right, 4 stroke; 4 cylinders, in line; 110.6 cu in, 1,812 cc (3.45 x 2.95 in, 87.7 x 75 mm); compression ratio: 9.4:1; max power (DIN): 100 hp (74 kW) at 5,800 rpm; max torque (DIN): 107 lb ft, 14.7 kg m (144 Nm) at 3,800 rpm; max engine rpm: 5,800; 55.2 hp/l (40.6 kW/l); cast iron block, light alloy head; 5 crankshaft bearings; valves: overhead, rockers; camshafts: 1, overhead; lubrication: gear pump, full flow filter, 7 imp pt, 8.5 US pt, 4 l; 1 Weber 34 ADS-D downdraught twin barrel carburettor; fuel feed: mechanical pump; water-cooled, 17.6 imp pt, 21.1 US pt, 10 l, electric thermostatic fan.

TRANSMISSION driving wheels: rear; clutch: single dry plate (diaphragm), hydraulically controlled; gearbox: mechanical [Automatico, automatic transmission, hydraulic torque converter and planetary gears with 3 ratios (I 2.450, II 1.450, III 1, rev 2.200)]; gears: 4, fully synchronized; ratios: I 3.546, II 2.175, III 1.418, IV 1, rev 3.226; lever: central; final drive: hypoid bevel; axle ratio: 3.909 - Automatico 3.727; width of rims: 5.5"; tyres: 175 SR x 14.

PERFORMANCE max speeds: (I) 27 mph, 44 km/h; (II) 45 mph, 73 km/h; (III) 70 mph, 113 km/h; (IV) 106 mph, 170 km/h; power-weight ratio: 24.3 lb/hp (33 lb/kW), 11 kg/hp (14.9 kg/kW); carrying capacity: 915 lb, 415 kg; acceleration: standing ¼ mile 18.1 sec; speed in direct drive at 1,000 rpm: 18 mph, 29 km/h; consumption: 25.7 m/imp gal, 21.4 m/US gal, 11 l x 100 km.

CHASSIS integral; front suspension: independent, by McPherson, coil springs/telescopic damper struts, lower wishbones, anti-roll bar; rear: rigid axle, lower longitudinal trailing arms, upper torque arms, transverse linkage bar, coil springs, anti-roll bar, telescopic dampers.

STEERING rack-and-pinion; turns lock to lock: 4.

BRAKES disc (front diameter 9.80 in, 24.9 cm, rear 9.02 in, 22.3 cm), rear compensator, servo; swept area: front 186 sq in, 1,200 sq cm, rear 145.1 sq in, 936 sq cm, total 331 sq in, 2,136 sq cm.

ELECTRICAL EQUIPMENT 12 V; 40 Ah battery; 490 W alternator; Chrysler transistorized ignition; 2 headlamps, iodine long-distance lights.

DIMENSIONS AND WEIGHT wheel base: 105.12 in, 267 cm; front and rear track: 55.12 in, 140 cm; length: 178.35 in, 453

TALBOT 180 Diesel De Luxe

100 hp power team

ENGINE front, 4 stroke; 4 cylinders, slanted at 45°, in line; 121.1 cu in, 1,985 cc (3.54 x 3.07 in, 90 x 78 mm); compression ratio: 9.2:1; max power (DIN): 100 hp (74 kW) at 5,200 rpm; max torque (DIN): 120 lb ft, 16.5 kg m (162 Nm) at 3,500 rpm; max engine rpm: 6,000; 50.4 hp/l (37.1 kW/l); cast iron block, light alloy head; 5 crankshaft bearings; valves: overhead, thimble tappets; camshafts: 1, overhead, driven by double chain; lubrication: rotary pump, full flow filter, 6.2 imp pt, 7.4 US pt, 3.5 l; 1 Zenith-Stromberg 175 CDSEVX horizontal carburettor; fuel feed: mechanical pump; cooling, liquid, expansion tank, 14.1 imp pt, 16.9 US pt, 8 l, thermostatic fan.

TRANSMISSION driving wheels: front; clutch: single dry plate, hydraulically controlled; gearbox: mechanical, in unit with differential and engine (transfer chain in front of engine, ratio 0.968:1); gears: 4, fully synchronized; ratios: I 3.327, II 2.006, III 1.346, IV 0.968, rev 3.659; lever: central; final drive: spiral bevel; axle ratio: 3.889; width of rims: 5"; tyres: 165 SR x 15.

PERFORMANCE max speeds: (I) 34 mph, 55 km/h; (II) 57 mph, 91 km/h; (III) 84 mph, 135 km/h; (IV) 102 mph, 164 km/h; power-weight ratio: 2-dr 24.9 lb/hp (34 lb/kW), 11.3 kg/hp (15.4 kg/kW); carrying capacity: 948 lb, 430 kg; speed in top at 1,000 rpm: 19.3 mph, 31 km/h; consumption: 26.6 m/imp gal, 22.2 m/US gal, 10.6 l x 100 km.

CHASSIS integral; front suspension: independent, double wishbones, progressive action coil springs, telescopic dampers; rear: rigid axle, twin longitudinal leading arms, twin swinging

100 HP POWER TEAM

cm; width: 68.11 in, 173 cm; height: 57.09 in, 145 cm; ground clearance: 4.72 in, 12 cm; weight: 2,426 lb, 1,100 kg; weight distribution: 53.8% front, 46.2% rear; turning circle: 33.8 ft, 10.3 m; fuel tank: 14.3 imp gal, 17.2 US gal, 65 l.

BODY saloon/sedan; 4 doors; 5 seats, separate front seats, built-in headrests; vinyl roof; heated rear window.

PRACTICAL INSTRUCTIONS fuel: 98-100 oct petrol; oil: engine 7 imp pt, 8.5 US pt, 4 l, SAE 10W-50, change every 3,100 miles, 5,000 km - gearbox 2.6 imp pt, 3.2 US pt, 1.5 l, SAE 90 EP, change every 12,400 miles, 20,000 km - final drive 2.3 imp pt, 2.7 US pt, 1.3 l, SAE 90 EP, change every 12,400 miles, 20,000 km; greasing: none.

OPTIONALS tinted glass; metallic spray.

60 hp (diesel) power team

See 100 hp power team, except for:

ENGINE diesel, front; 117 cu in, 1,918 cc (3.23 x 3.57 in, 82 x 90.8 mm); compression ratio: 20:1; max power (DIN): 60 hp (44 kW) at 4,000 rpm; max torque (DIN): 93 lb ft, 12.8 kg m (125 Nm) at 2,100 rpm; max engine rpm: 4,000; 31.3 hp/l (23 kW/l).

PERFORMANCE max speed: 81 mph, 130 km/h; power-weight ratio: 45 lb/hp (61.1 lb/kW), 20.4 kg/hp (25.4 kg/kW); consumption: 35.3 m/imp gal, 29.4 m/US gal, 8 l x 100 km.

BRAKES front disc, rear drum.

ELECTRICAL EQUIPMENT 90 Ah battery; 700 W alternator

DIMENSIONS AND WEIGHT weight: 2,701 lb, 1,225 kg.

BODY De Luxe, luxury equipment.

SAAB SWEDEN

99 Series

PRICES IN GB AND USA:

	£	$
1 GL 2-dr Sedan	5,165*	7,995*
2 GL 4-dr Sedan	5,365*	—
3 Turbo 2-dr Sport Sedan	7,750*	—

Power team:	Standard for:	Optional for
100 hp	1,2	—
108 hp	—	1,2
115 hp	1	—
118 hp	—	2
145 hp	3	—

SAAB 99 GL Sedan

SAAB 99 GL Sedan

SAAB 900 GL Hatchback Sedan

'ailing radius arms, transverse linkage bar, coil springs, telecopic dampers.

TEERING rack-and-pinion; turns lock to lock: 4.10.

RAKES disc (front diameter 11.02 in, 28 cm, rear 10.61 in, 27 m), 2 separate X hydraulic circuits, servo; swept area: total 88.2 sq in, 2,504 sq cm.

LECTRICAL EQUIPMENT 12 V; 60 Ah battery; 790 W alterna-or; Bosch distributor; 2 halogen headlamps with wiper-washers.

IMENSIONS AND WEIGHT wheel base: 97.36 in, 247 cm; racks: 55.12 in, 140 cm front, 56.30 in, 143 cm rear; length: 76.38 in, 448 cm; width: 66.54 in, 169 cm; height: 57 in, 144 m; ground clearance: 6.90 in, 17.5 cm; weight: 2-dr 2,492 lb, ,130 kg - 4-dr 2,558 lb, 1,160 kg; weight distribution: 61.1% ont, 38,9% rear; turning circle: 34.4 ft, 10.5 m; fuel tank: 12.8 np gal, 15.3 US gal, 58 l.

ODY saloon/sedan; 5 seats, separate front seats, adjustable ackrests; heated driving seat; folding rear seat; impact-bsorbing bumpers; hazard lights; heated rear window.

RACTICAL INSTRUCTIONS fuel: 97 oct petrol; oil: engine 6.2 np pt, 7.4 US pt, 3.5 l, SAE 10W-40, change every 9,300 niles, 15,000 km - gearbox 4.4 imp pt, 5.3 US pt, 2.5 l, SAE 0W-30/40, change every 18,600 miles, 30.000 km; greasing: very 6,200 miles, 10,000 km; tappet clearances: inlet 0.006-.012 in, 0.15-0.30 mm, exhaust 0.014-020 in, 0.35-0.50 mm; alve timing: 10° 54° 54° 10°; tyre pressure: front 31 psi, 2.2 tm, rear 34 psi, 2.4 atm.

108 hp power team

2-dr available only for Finland; 4-dr available only for certain narkets excluding central Europe)

See 100 hp power team, except for:

NGINE max power (DIN): 108 hp (79 kW) at 5,200 rpm; max orque (DIN): 121 lb ft, 16.7 kg m (164 Nm) at 3,300 rpm; 54.4 p/l (40 kW/l); 2 Zenith-Stromberg 150 CDSEVX carburettors.

ERFORMANCE max speed: 105 mph, 169 km/h; power-weight atio: 4-dr 23.7 lb/hp (32.4 lb/kW), 10.7 kg/hp (14.7 kg/kW); onsumption: 28.2 m/imp gal, 23.5 m/US gal, 10 l x 100 km.

PTIONALS Borg-Warner 35 automatic transmission, hydraulic orque converter and planetary gears with 3 ratios (I 2.390, II .450, III 1, rev 2.090), max ratio of converter at stall 1.91, max peed 102 mph, 164 km/h, consumption 26.2 m/imp gal, 21.8 n/US gal, 10.8 l x 100 km.

115 hp power team

available only for Canada and USA)

See 100 hp power team, except for:

NGINE max power (DIN): 115 hp (85 kW) at 5,500 rpm; max orque (DIN) 123 lb ft, 17 kg m (167 Nm) at 3,700 rpm; 57.9 hp/l 42.8 kW/l); Bosch CI injection; fuel feed: electric pump.

RANSMISSION tyres: 175/70 HR x 15.

PERFORMANCE max speed: 105 mph, 169 km/h; power-weight ratio: 21.7 lb/hp (29.3 lb/kW), 9.8 kg/hp (13.3 kg/kW); consumption: 25.2 m/imp gal, 21 m/US gal, 11.2 l x 100 km.

BODY 5 seats, separate front seats, adjustable backrests; heated driving seat; folding rear seat; impact-absorbing bumpers; hazard lights; heated rear window; rev counter.

118 hp power team

(available only for central Europe)

See 100 hp power team, except for:

ENGINE max power (DIN): 118 hp (87 kW) at 5,500 rpm; max torque (DIN): 123 lb ft, 17 kg m (167 Nm) at 3,700 rpm; 59.4 hp/l (43.7 kW/l); Bosch CI injection; fuel feed: electric pump.

TRANSMISSION gearbox: Borg-Warner 35 automatic transmission, hydraulic torque converter and planetary; gears with 3 ratios, max ratio of converter at stall 1.91, possible manual selection; ratios: I 2.390, II 1.450, III 1, rev 2.090; tyres: 175/70 HR x 15.

PERFORMANCE max speed: 105 mph, 169 km/h; power-weight ratio: 22 lb/hp (29.7 lb/kW), 10 kg/hp (13.5 kg/kW); consumption: 25.2 m/imp gal, 21 m/US gal, 11.2 l x 100 km.

DIMENSIONS AND WEIGHT weight: 2,591 lb, 1,175 kg; weight distribution: 61.6% front, 38.4% rear.

BODY 5 seats, separate front seats, adjustable backrests; heated driving seat; folding rear seat; impact-absorbing bumpers; hazard lights; heated rear window; rev counter.

145 hp power team

See 100 hp power team, except for:

ENGINE turbocharged: compression ratio: 7.2:1; max power (DIN): 145 hp (107 kW) at 5,000 rpm; max torque (DIN): 174 lb ft, 24 kg m (235 Nm) at 3,000 rpm: 73 hp/l (53.8 kW/l); Bosch CI injection; centrifugal compressor, mounted coaxially with exhaust driven Garret Airresearch turbine; fuel feed: electric pump; water-cooled.

TRANSMISSION transfer chain in front of engine, ratio 0.839; gearbox ratios: I 3.053, II 1.841, III 1.235, IV 0.839, rev 3.358; width of rims: 5.5"; tyres: 175/70 HR x 15.

PERFORMANCE max speeds: (I) 36 mph, 58 km/h; (II) 59 mph, 95 km/h; (III) 88 mph, 142 km/h; (IV) 121 mph, 195 km/h; power-weight ratio: 17 lb/hp (23.8 lb/kW), 8.16 kg/hp (10.8 kg/kW); speed in top at 1,000 rpm: 21.9 mph, 35.3 km/h; consumption: 24.6 m/imp gal, 20.5 m/US gal, 11.5 l x 100 km.

ELECTRICAL EQUIPMENT 840 W alternator.

DIMENSIONS AND WEIGHT tracks: 55.51 in, 141 cm front, 56.69 in, 144 cm rear; weight: 2,558 lb, 1,160 kg; weight distribution: 61.8% front, 38.2 rear.

BODY 5 seats, separate front seats, adjustable backrests; heated driving seat; front spoiler; sport steering wheel; tinted glass; folding rear seat; impact-absorbing bumpers; hazard lights; heated rear window; light alloy wheels.

PRACTICAL INSTRUCTIONS oil engine: change every 4,700 miles, 7,500 km; valve timing: 12° 40° 62° 2°.

OPTIONALS 5-speed fully synchronized mechanical gearbox (I 3.320, II 2.002, III 1.343, IV 0.966, V 0.781, rev 3.652).

900 Series

PRICES IN GB AND USA:	£	$
1 GL 2+1-dr Hatchback Sedan	6,350*	—
2 GL 4+1-dr Hatchback Sedan	—	—
3 GLS 2+1-dr Hatchback Sedan	6,640*	—
4 GLS 4+1-dr Hatchback Sedan	6,920*	—
5 GLi 2+1-dr Hatchback Sedan	—	9,295*
6 GLi 4+1-dr Hatchback Sedan	—	—
7 EMS 2+1-dr Hatchback Sedan	7,720*	—
8 GLE 4+1-dr Hatchback Sedan	8,555*	10,295*
9 Turbo 2+1-dr Hatchback Sedan	9,910*	12,595*
10 Turbo 4+1-dr Hatchback Sedan	10,310	13,695*

Power team:	Standard for:	Optional for:
100 hp	1,2	—
108 hp	3 to 6	—
115 hp	5, 7, 8	—
118 hp	7, 8	—
145 hp	9, 10	—

100 hp power team

ENGINE front, 4 stroke; 4 cylinders, slanted at 45°, in line; 121.1 cu in, 1,985 cc (3.54 x 3.07 in, 90 x 78 mm); compression ratio: 9.2:1; max power (DIN): 100 hp (74 kW) at 5,200 rpm; max torque (DIN): 120 lb ft, 16.5 kg m (162 Nm) at 3,500 rpm; max engine rpm: 5,500; 50.4 hp/l (37.1 kW/l); cast iron block, light alloy head; 5 crankshaft bearings; valves: overhead, thimble tappets; camshafts: 1, overhead, driven by double chain; lubrication: rotary pump, full flow filter, 6.2 imp pt, 7.4 US pt, 3.5 l; 1 Zenith-Stromberg 175 CDSEVX horizontal carburettor; fuel feed: mechanical pump; cooling, liquid, expansion tank, 17.6 imp pt, 21.1 US pt, 10 l, thermostatic fan.

TRANSMISSION driving wheels: front; clutch: single dry plate, hydraulically controlled; gearbox: mechanical, in unit with differential and engine, transfer chain in front of engine, ratio 0.968; gears: 4, fully synchronized; ratios: I 3.327, II 2.006, III 1.346, IV 0.968, rev 3.659; lever: central; final drive: spiral bevel; axle ratio: 3.890; width of rims: 5"; tyres: 165 SR x 15.

PERFORMANCE max speeds: (I) 34 mph, 54 km/h; (II) 56 mph, 90 km/h; (III) 84 mph, 135 km/h; (IV) 102 mph, 164 km/h; power weight ratio: 26.1 lb/hp (35.7 lb/kW), 11.9 kg/hp (16.3 kg/kW); carrying capacity: 1,050 lb, 470 kg; speed in top at 1,000 rpm: 19.4 mph, 31.3 km/h; consumption: 26.6 m/imp gal, 22.2 m/US gal, 10.6 l x 100 km.

CHASSIS integral; front suspension: independent, double wishbones, progressive action coil springs, telescopic dampers; rear: rigid axle, twin longitudinal leading arms, twin swinging trailing radius arms, transverse linkage bar, coil springs, telescopic dampers.

STEERING rack-and-pinion; turns lock to lock: 4.20.

BRAKES disc (front diameter 11.02 in, 28 cm, rear 10.61 in, 27 cm), 2 separate X hydraulic circuits, servo; swept area: total 388.2 sq in, 2,504 sq cm.

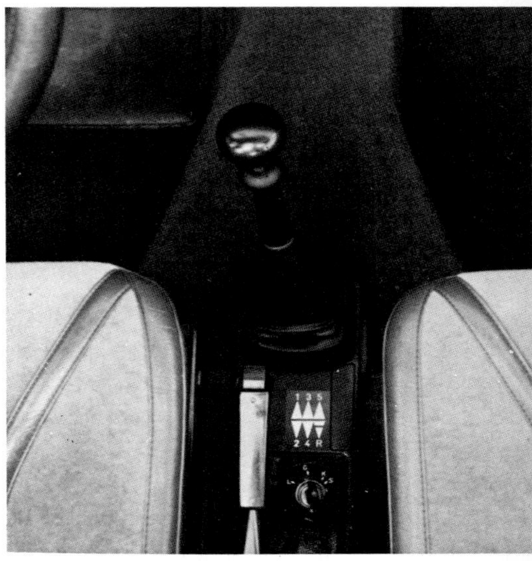

SAAB 900 5-speed gearbox

SAAB 900 EMS Hatchback Sedan

100 HP POWER TEAM

ELECTRICAL EQUIPMENT 12 V; 60 Ah battery; 790 W alternator; Bosch distributor; 2 halogen headlamps with wiper-washers.

DIMENSIONS AND WEIGHT wheel base: 99.21 in, 252 cm; tracks: 55.91 in, 142 cm front, 56.30 in, 143 cm rear; length: 186.61 in, 474 cm; width: 66.54 in, 169 cm; height: 55.91 in, 142 cm; ground clearance: 5.91 in, 15 cm; weight: 2,613 lb, 1,185 kg; turning circle: 33.8 ft, 10.3 m; fuel tank: 12.8 imp gal, 15.3 US gal, 58 l.

BODY hatchback; 5 seats, separate front seats, adjustable backrests; folding rear seat; impact-absorbing bumpers; hazard lights; heated rear window; front spoiler.

PRACTICAL INSTRUCTIONS fuel: 97 oct petrol; oil: engine 6.2 imp pt, 7.4 US pt, 3.5 l, SAE 10W-40, change every 9,300 miles, 15,000 km - gearbox 4.4 imp pt, 5.3 US pt, 2.5 l, SAE 10W-30/40, change every 18,600 miles, 30,000 km; greasing: every 6,200 miles, 10,000 km; tappet clearances: inlet 0.006-0.012 in, 0.15-0.30 mm, exhaust 0.014-0.020 in, 0.35-0.50 mm; valve timing: 10° 54° 54° 10°; tyre pressure: front 31 psi, 2.2 atm, rear 34 psi, 2.4 atm.

108 hp power team

See 100 hp power team, except for:

ENGINE max power (DIN): 108 hp (79 kW) at 5,200 rpm; max torque (DIN): 121 lb ft, 16.7 kg m (164 Nm) at 3,300 rpm; 54.4 hp/l (40.1 kW/l); 2 Zenith-Stromberg 150 CDSEVX horizontal carburettors - GLi models Bosch CI injection.

PERFORMANCE max speed: 105 mph, 169 km/h; power-weight ratio: 2+1-dr models 24.3 lb/hp (33.1 lb/kW), 11 kg/hp (15 kg/kW); consumption: 28.2 m/imp gal, 23.5 m/US gal, 10 l x 100 km.

DIMENSIONS AND WEIGHT weight: 2+1-dr models 2,613 lb, 1,185 kg - 4+1-dr models 2,690 lb, 1,220 kg.

OPTIONALS sunshine roof; power steering (for Great Britain only); Borg-Warner 35 automatic transmission, hydraulic torque converter and planetary gears with 3 ratios (I 2.390, II 1.450, III 1, rev 2.090), max ratio of converter at stall 2.37, max speed 102 mph, 164 km/h, consumption 26.2 m/imp gal, 21.8 m/US gal, 10.8 l x 100 km.

115 hp power team

(available only for Australia, Canada and USA)

See 100 hp power team, except for:

ENGINE max power (DIN): 115 hp (85 kW) at 5,500 rpm; max torque (DIN): 123 lb ft, 17 kg m (167 Nm) at 3,700 rpm; 57.9 hp/l (42.8 kW/l); Bosch CI injection; fuel feed: electric pump.

TRANSMISSION tyres: 175/70 HR x 15.

SAAB 900 Turbo Hatchback Sedan

PERFORMANCE max speed: 105 mph, 169 km/h; power-weight ratio: GLi 22.7 lb/hp (30.7 lb/kW), 10.3 kg/hp (13.9 kg/kW); consumption: 25.2 m/imp gal, 21 m/US gal, 11.2 l x 100 km.

STEERING (for EMS only) servo; turns lock to lock: 3.65.

BODY 5 seats, separate front seats, adjustable backrests; impact-absorbing bumpers; hazard lights; heated rear window; front spoiler; tinted glass; heated front seats; sunshine roof.

OPTIONALS (for EMS only) Borg-Warner 35 automatic transmission, hydraulic torque converter and planetary gears with 3 ratios (I 2.390, II 1.450, III 1, rev 2.090), max ratio of converter at stall 2.37, max speed 102 mph, 164 km/h, consumption 26.2 m/imp gal, 21.8 m/US gal, 10.8 l x 100 km.

118 hp power team

See 100 hp power team, except for:

ENGINE max power (DIN): 118 hp (87 kW) at 5,500 rpm; max torque (DIN): 123 lb ft, 17 kg m (167 Nm) at 3,700 rpm; 59.4 hp/l (43.7 kW/l); Bosch CI injection; fuel feed: electric pump.

TRANSMISSION tyres: EMS 175/70 HR x 15.

PERFORMANCE max speed: 108 mph, 174 km/h; power-weight ratio: EMS 22.1 lb/hp (30 lb/kW), 10 kg/hp (13.6 kg/kW) - GLE 23.4 lb/hp (31.7 lb/kW), 10.6 kg/hp (14.4 kg/kW); consumption: 25.2 m/imp gal, 21 m/US gal, 11.2 l x 100 km.

STEERING (for GLE only) servo; turns lock to lock: 3.65.

ELECTRICAL EQUIPMENT 840 W alternator.

DIMENSIONS AND WEIGHT weight: EMS 2,613 lb, 1,185 kg GLE 2,756 lb, 1,250 kg.

BODY 5 seats separate front seats, adjustable backrests; impact-absorbing bumpers; hazard lights; heated rear window front spoiler; tinted glass; heated front seats; sunshine roo (for EMS only) aluminium alloy wheels.

OPTIONALS (for EMS only) 5-speed fully synchronized mechanical gearbox (I 3.320, II 2.002, III 1.343, IV 0.966, V 0.781, re 3.652); (for GLE only) Borg-Warner 35 automatic transmissior hydraulic torque converter and planetary gears with 3 ratios 2.390, II 1.450, III 1, rev 2.090), max ratio of converter at sta 2.37, max speed 105 mph, 169 km/h, consumption 26.1 m/im gal, 21.8 m/US gal, 10.8 l x 100 km.

145 hp power team

See 100 hp power team, except for:

ENGINE compression ratio: 7.2:1; max power (DIN): 145 h (107 kW) at 5,500 rpm; max torque (DIN): 174 lb ft, 24 kg (235 Nm) at 3,000 rpm; 73 hp/l (53.8 kW/l); Bosch CI injectior centrifugal compressor, mounted coaxially with exhaust drive Garrett Airresearch turbine; fuel feed: electric pump.

TRANSMISSION transfer chain in front of engine, ratio 0.83 gearbox ratios: I 3.053, II 1.841, III 1.235, IV 0.839, rev 3.35 width of rims: 5.5"; tyres: 2+1-dr 195/60 HR x 15 - 4+1- 180/65 HR x 390.

PERFORMANCE max speeds: (I) 35 mph, 56 km/h; (II) 58 mp 93 km/h; (III) 86 mph, 139 km/h; (IV) 121 mph, 195 km power-weight ratio: 2+1-dr 18.5-19 lb/hp (25.1-25.6 lb/kW 8.4-8.6 kg/hp (11.4-11.6 kg/kW); speed in top at 1,000 rpr 21.2 mph, 34.1 km/h; consumption: 24.6 m/imp gal, 20.5 m/U gal, 11.5 l x 1200 km.

STEERING servo.

ELECTRICAL EQUIPMENT 950 W alternator; electronic ign tion.

DIMENSIONS AND WEIGHT tracks: 2+1-dr 56.30 in, 143 c front, 56.69 in, 144 cm rear; weight: 2+1-dr 2,679-2,734 l 1,215-1,240 kg - 4+1-dr 2,778-2,811 lb, 1,260-1,275 kg; fu tank: 2+1-dr 12.1 imp gal, 14.5 US gal, 55 l.

BODY 5 seats, separate front seats, adjustable backrest heated driving seat; front and rear spoiler; sport steering whee impact-absorbing bumpers; hazard lights; heated rear windo tinted glass; light alloy wheels.

PRACTICAL INSTRUCTIONS oil: engine, change every 4,70 miles, 7,500 km; valve timing: 12° 40° 62° 2°.

OPTIONALS 5-speed fully synchronized mechanical gearbox 3.320, II 2.002, III 1.343, IV 0.966, V 0.781, rev 3.652), transf chain 0.781 ratio; sunshine roof.

VOLVO 244 GL Sedan

/OLVO SWEDEN

240 Series

'RICES IN GB AND USA:

	£	$
244 DL 4-dr Sedan	5,995*	7,970*
244 GL 4-dr Sedan	7,379*	—
244 GL"S"4-dr Sedan	—	—
244 GLE 4-dr Sedan	7,996*	—
244 GLT 4-dr Sedan	—	—
245 DL 4+1-dr St. Wagon	6,736*	8,565*
245 GL 4+1-dr St. Wagon	7,450*	—
245 GLE 4+1-dr St. Wagon	8,110*	—
242 GT 2-dr Sedan	—	9,800*

'ower team:	Standard for:	Optional for:
7 hp	1, 2, 3, 6, 7	—
17 hp	4,8	1, 2, 3, 6, 7
40 hp	5,9	—

97 hp power team

NGINE front, 4 stroke; 4 cylinders, in line; 121 cu in, 1,986 cc 3.50 x 3.15 in, 88.9 x 80 mm); compression ratio: 8.5:1; max ower (DIN): 97 hp (71 kW) at 5,400 rpm; max torque (DIN): 16 lb ft, 16 kg m (157 Nm) at 3,200 rpm; max engine rpm: ,000; 48.8 hp/l (35.9 kW/l); cast iron block, light alloy head; 5 rankshaft bearings; valves: overhead, push-rods and rockers; amshafts: 1, side: lubrication: gear pump, full flow filter, 6.5 np pt, 7.8 US pt, 3.7 l; 1 SU type HIF 6 horizontal carburettor; uel feed: mechanical pump; sealed circuit cooling, liquid, 16.7 np pt, 20.1 US pt, 9.5 l.

RANSMISSION driving wheels: rear; clutch: single dry plate diaphragm); gearbox: mechanical; gears: 4, fully synchronized; atios: I 3.790, II 2.160, III 1.370, IV 1, rev 3.680; lever: central; nal drive: hypoid bevel; axle ratio: 3.910; width of rims: edans 5" - st. wagons 5.5"; tyres: 244 DL Sedan 165 SR x 14 244 GL Sedan 175 SR x 14 - 245 DL and GL st. wagons 185 R x 14.

'ERFORMANCE max speed: 103 mph, 165 km/h; power weight atio: 244 DL Sedan 28.8 lb/hp (39.1 lb/kW), 13.1 kg/hp (17.8 g/kW); carrying capacity: 1,191 lb, 540 kg; consumption: 28.2 n/imp gal, 23.5 m/US gal, 10 l x 100 km.

:HASSIS integral; front suspension: independent, by McPher-on, lower wishbones, coil springs, damper struts, anti-roll bar; ear: de Dion rigid axle, twin trailing radius arms, transverse nkage bar, coil springs, anti-roll bar, telescopic dampers.

;TEERING rack-and-pinion; turns lock to lock: 4,30.

RAKES disc (front diameter 10.71 in, 27.2 cm, rear 11.61 in, 9.5 cm), dual circuit, rear compensator, servo.

:LECTRICAL EQUIPMENT 12 V; 60 Ah battery; 55 A alterna-or; Bosch distributor; 2 halogen headlamps.

)IMENSIONS AND WEIGHT wheel base: 103.94 in, 264 cm; racks: 55.91 in, 142 cm front, 53.15 in, 135 cm rear; length: 92.91 in, 490 cm; width: 67.32 in, 171 cm; height: 56.30 in, 43 cm; ground clearance: 5.51 in, 14 cm; weight: 244 DL edan 2,794 lb, 1,270 kg - 244 GL and GL "S" sedans 2,833 , 1,285 kg - 245 DL St. Wagon 2,911 lb, 1,320 kg - 245 GL St. Vagon 2,944 lb, 1,335 kg; turning circle: 32.1 ft, 9.8 m; fuel ank: 13.2 imp gal, 15.8 US gal, 60 l.

BODY saloon/sedan, estate car/st. wagon; 5 seats, separate front seats, reclining backrests, built-in adjustable headrests; heated rear window.

PRACTICAL INSTRUCTIONS fuel: 93 oct petrol; oil: engine 5.6 imp pt, 6.8 US pt, 3.2 l, SAE 10W-40, change every 6,200 miles, 10,000 km - gearbox 1.2 imp pt, 1,5 US pt, 0.7 l, SAE 80-90, change every 24,900 miles, 40,000 km - final drive 2.3 imp pt, 2.7 US pt, 1.3 l, SAE 90; greasing: none; sparking plug: 175°; tappet clearances: inlet and exhaust 0.016-0.018 in, 0.40-0.45 mm; tyre pressure: front 26 psi, 1.8 atm, rear 28 psi, 1.9 atm.

OPTIONALS limited slip differential; Borg-Warner 35 automatic transmission, hydraulic torque converter and planetary gears with 3 ratios (I 2.390, II 1.450, III 1, rev 2.090), max ratio of converter at stall 2; 100 hp engine.

117 hp power team

See 97 hp power team, except for:

ENGINE compression ratio: 8.8:1; max power (DIN) 117 hp (86 kW) at 6,000 rpm; 58.9 hp/l (43.3 kW/l); camshafts: 1, overhead; Bosch CI injection.

TRANSMISSION gears: 4 and overdrive; ratios: I 3.710, II 2.160, III 1.370, IV 1, overdrive 0.798, rev 3.680; width of rims: 5.5"; tyres: 185/70 SR x 14.

PERFORMANCE max speeds: (I) 35 mph, 56 km/h; (II) 55 mph, 88 km/h; (III) 80 mph, 128 km/h; (IV) 109 mph, 175 km/h; power-weight ratio: 244 GLE 25.2 lb/hp (34.3 lb/kW), 11.4 kg/hp (15.6 kg/kW).

STEERING servo.

ELECTRICAL EQUIPMENT transistorized Bosch ignition.

DIMENSIONS AND WEIGHT weight: 244 GLE 2,950 lb, 1,338 kg - 245 GLE 3,043 lb, 1,385 kg.

PRACTICAL INSTRUCTIONS oil: engine 5.8 imp pt, 7 US pt, 3.3 l; tappet clearances: inlet and exhaust 0.012-0.020 in, 0.30-0.50 mm; front tyre pressure: 28 psi, 1.9 atm.

140 hp power team

See 97 hp power team, except for:

ENGINE 141.3 cu in, 2,316 cc (3.78 x 3.15 in, 96 x 80 mm); compression ratio: 10:1; max power (DIN): 140 hp (103 kW) at 5,750 rpm; max torque (DIN): 141 lb ft, 19.5 kg m (191 Nm) at 4,500 rpm; 60.4 hp/l (44.5 kW/l); camshafts: 1, overhead; Bosch CI injection.

TRANSMISSION gears: 4 and overdrive; ratios: I 3.710, II 2.160, III 1.370, IV 1, overdrive 0.798, rev 3.680; axle ratio: 3.730; width of rims: 5.5": tyres: 185/70 HR x 14.

PERFORMANCE max speed: 115 mph, 185 km/h; power-weight ratio: 20.7 lb/hp (28.1 lb/kW), 9.4 kg/hp (12.8 kg/kW); consumption: 25.9 m/imp gal, 21.6 m/US gal, 10.9 l x 100 km.

STEERING servo.

DIMENSIONS AND WEIGHT weight: 2,911 lb, 1,320 kg.

BODY saloon/sedan.

244 GL D6 / 245 GL D6

ENGINE Volkswagen, diesel; 6 cylinders, in line; 145.4 cu in, 2,383 cc (3.01 x 3.40 in, 76.5 x 86.4 mm); compression ratio: 23.5:1; max power (DIN): 82 hp (60 kW) at 4,800 rpm; max torque (DIN): 104 lb ft, 14.3 kg m (140 Nm) at 2,800 rpm; 34.4 hp/l (25.4 kW/l); cast iron block, light alloy head; 7 crankshaft bearings; valves: overhead; camshafts: 1, overhead, cogged belt; lubrication: full flow filter, 10.6 imp pt, 12.7 US pt, 6 l; Bosch VE injection; water-cooled, 16.7 imp pt, 20.1 US pt, 9.5 l.

TRANSMISSION driving wheels: rear; clutch: single dry plate (diaphragm); gearbox: mechanical; gears: 4, fully synchronized and overdrive; ratios: I 4.030, II 2.160, III 1.370, IV 1, overdrive 0.798, rev 3.680; lever: central; final drive: hypoid bevel; axle ratio: 3.730; width of rims: 244, 5" - 245, 5.5"; tyres: 244, 175 SR x 14 - 245, 185 SR x 14.

PERFORMANCE max speed: 92 mph, 148 km/h; power-weight ratio: 244, 36.6 lb/hp (49.6 lb/kW), 16.6 kg/hp (22.5 kg/kW); max speed in overdrive/top at 1,000 rpm: 24 mph, 38.7 km/h; consumption: 33.2 m/imp gal, 27.7 m/US gal, 8.5 l x 100 km.

CHASSIS integral; front suspension: independent, McPherson lower wishbones, coil springs, damper struts, anti-roll bar; rear: rigid axle, twin trailing radius arms, transverse linkage bar, coil springs, anti-roll bar, telescopic dampers.

VOLVO 244 GLT Sedan

244 GL D6 / 245 GL D6

STEERING rack-and-pinion, servo; turns lock to lock: 3.50.

BRAKES disc, dual circuit, rear compensator, servo.

ELECTRICAL EQUIPMENT 12 V; 90 Ah battery; 55 A alternator; 2 halogen headlamps.

DIMENSIONS AND WEIGHT wheel base: 104.33 in, 265 cm; tracks: 244, 55.91 in, 142 cm front, 53.15 in, 135 cm rear - 245, 56.30 in, 143 cm front, 53.54 in, 136 cm rear; length: 192.13 in, 488 cm; width: 67.32 in, 171 cm; height: 244, 56.30 in, 143 cm - 245, 57.09 in, 145 cm; ground clearance: 5.51 in, 14 cm; weight: 244, 2,999 lb, 1,360 kg - 245, 3,131 lb, 1,420 kg; turning circle: 32.1 ft, 9.8 m; fuel tank: 13.2 imp gal, 15.8 US gal, 60 l.

BODY 244, saloon/sedan, 4 doors - 245, estate car/st. wagon, 4+1 doors; 5 seats, separate front seats, reclining backrests, built-in adjustable headrests; heated rear window; heated driving seat; (for 245 only) folding rear seat.

PRACTICAL INSTRUCTIONS fuel: diesel oil; oil: engine 10.6 imp pt, 12.7 US pt, 6 l.

OPTIONALS Borg-Warner automatic transmission, hydraulic torque converter and planetary gears with 3 ratios (I 2.450, II 1.450, III 1, rev 2.210), 3.540 axle ratio, max speed 90 mph, 145 km/h.

VOLVO 245 GL Station Wagon

260 Series

PRICES IN GB AND USA:	£	$
1 264 GL 4-dr Sedan	**8,556***	**11,385***
2 264 GLE 4-dr Sedan	**9,706***	**12,985***
3 265 GL 4+1-dr St. Wagon	**8,713***	—
4 265 GLE 4+1-dr St. Wagon	**9,509***	**12,985***
5 262 C 2-dr Coupé	**14,287***	**17,345***

Power team:	Standard for:	Optional for:
125 hp	1.3	—
148 hp	2,4,5	—

125 hp power team

ENGINE front, 4 stroke; 6 cylinders, Vee-slanted at 90°; 162.6 cu in, 2,664 cc (3.46 x 2.87 in, 88 x 73 mm); compression ratio: 8.7:1; max power (DIN): 125 hp (92 kW) at 5,250 rpm; max torque (DIN): 145 lb ft, 20 kg m (196 Nm) at 3,500 rpm; max engine rpm: 6,000; 46.9 hp/l (34.5 kW/l); light alloy block and head; 4 crankshaft bearings; valves: overhead, Vee-slanted, rockers; camshafts: 2, 1 per bank, overhead; lubrication: gear pump, full flow filter, oil cooler, 11.4 imp pt, 13.7 US pt, 6.5 l; 1 SU type HIF 6 horizontal carburettor; fuel feed: electric pump; sealed circuit cooling, liquid, 19.2 imp pt, 23 US pt, 10.9 l.

TRANSMISSION driving wheels: rear; clutch: single dry plate (diaphragm); gearbox: mechanical; gears: 4, fully synchronized; ratios: I 3.710, II 2.160, III 1.370, IV 1, rev 3.680; lever: central; final drive: hypoid bevel; axle ratio: 3.730; width of rims: 5"; tyres: 175 HR x 14.

PERFORMANCE max speed: 106 mph, 170 km/h; weight ratio: Sedan 24.2 lb/hp (32.9 lb/kW), 11 kg/hp (14.9 kg/kW); carrying capacity: 1,103 lb, 500 kg; consumption: 25.7 m/imp gal, 21,4 m/US gal, 11 l x 100 km.

CHASSIS integral; front suspension: independent, lower wishbones, coil springs, telescopic damper struts, anti-roll bar; rear: rigid axle, twin trailing radius arms, transverse linkage bar, coil springs, telescopic dampers, anti-roll bar.

STEERING rack-and-pinion, servo; turns lock to lock: 4,30.

BRAKES disc, servo.

ELECTRICAL EQUIPMENT 12 V; 70 Ah battery; 770 W alternator; Bosch transistorized ignition; 2 halogen headlamps.

DIMENSIONS AND WEIGHT wheel base: 103.94 in, 264 cm; tracks: 56.30 in, 143 cm front, 53.54 in, 136 cm rear; length: 192.91 in, 490 cm; width: 67.32 in, 171 cm; height: 56.30 in, 143 cm; ground clearance: Sedan 5.51 in, 14 cm - St. Wagon 4.09 in, 10.4 cm; weight: Sedan 3,032 lb, 1,375 kg - St. Wagon 3,164 lb, 1,435 kg; turning circle: 32.1 ft, 9.8 m; fuel tank: 13.2 imp gal, 15.8 US gal, 60 l.

BODY saloon/sedan, 4 doors - estate car/st. wagon, 4+1 doors; 5 seats, separate front seats, reclining backrests, built-in adjustable headrests; heated rear window; heated driving seat.

PRACTICAL INSTRUCTIONS fuel: 93 oct petrol; oil: engine 10.6 imp pt, 12.7 US pt, 6 l, SAE 10W-40, change every 6,200 miles, 10,000 km - gearbox 1,9 imp pt, 2.3 US pt, 1.1 l, SAE 90, change every 24,900 miles, 40,000 km - final drive 2.8 imp pt, 3.4 US pt, 1.6 l, SAE 90 EP, change every 24,900 miles, 40,000 km; greasing: none; tappet clearances: inlet 0.006 in, 0.15 mm, exhaust 0.012 in, 0.30 mm; valve timing: 32° 72° 20° 32°; tyre pressure: front 26 psi, 1.8 atm, rear 27 psi, 1.9 atm.

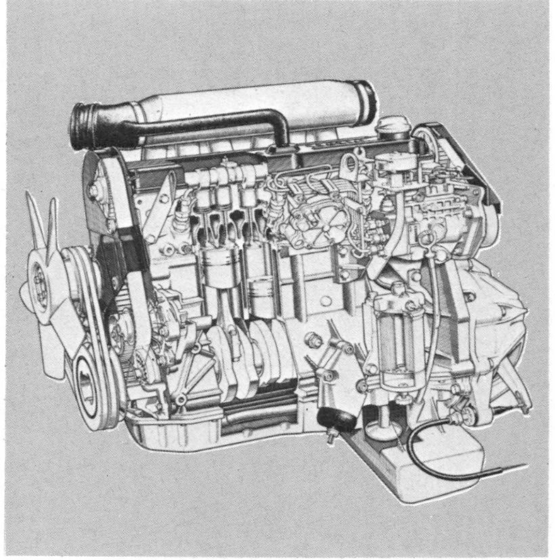

VOLVO 244 - 245 GL D6

OPTIONALS limited slip differential; 5-speed mechanical gea box; Borg-Warner 55 automatic transmission, hydraulic torqu converter and planetary gears with 3 ratios (I 2.390, II 1.450, I 1, rev 2.090), max ratio of converter at stall 2, 3.540 axle ratic air-conditioning.

148 hp power team

See 125 hp power team, except for:

ENGINE max power (DIN): 148 hp (109 kW) at 5,700 rpm; ma torque (DIN): 161 lb ft, 22.2 kg m (218 Nm) at 3,000 rpm; 55. hp/l (40.9 kW/l) Bosch CI injection.

TRANSMISSION gears: 4 and overdrive, fully synchronizec ratios: I 3.710, II 2.160, III 1.370, IV 1, overdrive 0.797, re 3.680; width of rims: 5.5"; tyres: 185/70 HR x 14.

PERFORMANCE max speed: 109 mph, 175 km/h; power-weigh ratio: 264, 20.5 lb/hp (27.8 lb/kW), 9.3 kg/hp (12.6 kg/kW).

DIMENSIONS AND WEIGHT length: 262, 192.12 in, 488 cm height: 262, 53.54 in, 136 cm; weight: 262, 3,197 lb, 1,450 kg

BODY coupé, 2 doors; air-conditioning; electric windows.

OPTIONALS Borg-Warner automatic transmission, hydrauli torque converter and planetary gears with 3 ratios (I 2.450, I 1.450, III 1, rev 2.810), 3.540 axle ratio.

VOLVO 262 C Coupé

'ELBER SWITZERLAND

Excellence Coupé / Roadster

RICES EX WORKS: francs

xcellence Coupé	53,000
xcellence Roadster	57,000

NGINE Pontiac, front, 4 stroke; 8 cylinders, Vee-slanted at)°; 400 cu in, 6,555 cc (4.12 x 3.75 in, 104.6 x 95.2 mm); ompression ratio: 8:1; max power (DIN): 225 hp (162 kW) at 000 rpm; max torque (DIN): 320 lb ft, 44.1 kg m (432 Nm) at 800 rpm; max engine rpm: 4,400; 34.3 hp/l (24.7 kW/l); cast on block and head; 5 crankshaft bearings; valves: overhead, line, push-rods and rockers, hydraulic tappets; camshafts: 1, centre of Vee; lubrication: gear pump, full flow filter, 10 imp , 12 US pt, 5.7 l; 1 Rochester downdraught 4-barrel carburet-r; air cleaner; exhaust system with catalytic converter; fuel ed: mechanical pump; water-cooled, 30.6 imp pt, 36.8 US pt, ′.4 l.

RANSMISSION driving wheels: rear; Turbo-Hydramatic auto-atic transmission, hydraulic torque converter and planetary ears with 3 ratios, max ratio of converter at stall 2.5, possible anual selection; ratios: I 2.520, II 1.520, III 1, rev 1.920; ver: central; final drive: hypoid bevel, limited slip differential; le ratio: 3.230; width of rims: 7"; tyres: GR70 x 15.

FELBER Excellence Coupé

FELBER Oasis

:RFORMANCE max speed: about 118 mph, 190 km/h; power-ight ratio 17.1 lb/hp (23.9 lb/kW), 7.8 kg/hp (10.8 kg/kW); rrying capacity: 926 lb, 420 kg; consumption: 15.7 m/imp gal, .1 m/US gal, 18 l x 100 km.

IASSIS integral with separate partial frame; front suspension: dependent, wishbones (lower trailing links), coil springs, anti-l bar, telescopic dampers; rear: rigid axle, semi-elliptic leafs-ngs, anti-roll bar, telescopic dampers.

'EERING recirculating ball, variable ratio servo; turns lock to :k: 2.41.

IAKES front disc, internal radial fins, rear drum, dual circuit, rvo.

.ECTRICAL EQUIPMENT 12 V; 3,200 W battery; 42 A alter-tor; Delco-Remy transistorized ignition; 4 headlamps.

MENSIONS AND WEIGHT wheel base: 108.20 in, 275 cm; .cks: 61.30 in, 156 cm front, 60 in, 152 cm rear; length: 6.80 in, 500 cm; width: 73.40 in, 186 cm; height: 49.30 in, 5 cm; ground clearance: 5.20 in, 13.2 cm; weight: 3,859 lb, 750 kg; turning circle: 41.3 ft, 12.6 m; fuel tank: 17.6 imp gal, US gal, 80 l.

)DY coupé or roadster; 2 doors; 2+2 seats; electric windows; ted glass; air-conditioning; sport wheels.

IACTICAL INSTRUCTIONS fuel: 100 oct petrol.

'TIONALS electric sunshine roof; leather upholstery; metallic ray.

Oasis

PRICE EX WORKS: 46,500 francs

ENGINE International, front, 4 stroke; 8 cylinders, Vee-slanted at 90°; 345 cu in, 5,654 cc (3.88 x 3.66 in, 98.5 x 92.9 mm); compression ratio: 8.05:1; max power (DIN): 165 hp (121 kW) at 3,600 rpm; max torque (DIN): 293 lb ft, 40.4 kg m (396 Nm) at 2,000 rpm; max engine rpm: 3,800; 29.2 hp/l (21.5 kW/l); cast iron block and head; 5 crankshaft bearings; valves: overhead, in line, push-rods and rockers, hydraulic tappets; camshafts: 1, at centre of Vee; lubrication: rotary pump, full flow filter, 13.2 imp pt, 15.9 US pt, 7.5 l; 1 downdraught twin barrel carburettor; dual exhaust system; fuel feed: mechanical pump; water-cooled, 34.3 imp pt, 41.2 US pt, 19.5 l.

TRANSMISSION driving wheels: front and rear with lockable front differential in transfer box; Torqueflite automatic transmission, hydraulic torque converter and planetary gears with 3 ratios, max ratio of converter at stall 2.16, possible manual selection; ratios: I 2.450, II 1.450, III 1, rev 2.200; lever: central; final drive: hypoid bevel, limited slip differential; axle ratio: 3.070; width of rims: 8.5"; tyres: LR78 x 15.

PERFORMANCE max speed: about 106 mph, 170 km/h; power-weight ratio: 21.8 lb/hp (29.6 lb/kW), 9.9 kg/hp (13.4 kg/kW); carrying capacity: 1,632 lb, 740 kg; consumption: 17.7 m/imp gal, 14.7 m/US gal, 16 l x 100 km.

CHASSIS box-type perimeter frame; front and rear suspension: rigid axle, semi-elliptic leafsprings, telescopic dampers.

STEERING worm and roller, servo.

BRAKES front disc (diameter 11.81 in, 30 cm), rear drum, dual circuit, servo.

ELECTRICAL EQUIPMENT 12 V; 65 Ah battery; 65 A alternator; 2 headlamps.

DIMENSIONS AND WEIGHT wheel base: 100 in, 254 cm; front and rear track: 57 in, 145 cm; length: 166.20 in, 422 cm; width: 70 in, 178 cm; height: 65.70 in, 167 cm; ground clearance: 7.60 in, 19.5 cm; weight: 3,598 lb, 1,632 kg; turning circle: 36.4 ft, 11.1 m; fuel tank: 15.8 imp gal, 19 US gal, 72 l.

BODY estate car/st. wagon; 2+1 doors; 5 seats, separate front seats, reclining backrests; built-in headrests; tinted glass; rear window wiper-washer; heated rear window.

PRACTICAL INSTRUCTIONS fuel: 91 oct petrol.

OPTIONALS air-conditioning; sunshine roof; leather upholstery; sport wheels; hydropneumatic suspension; metallic spray.

MONTEVERDI SWITZERLAND

Sierra

PRICE EX WORKS: 62,900 francs

ENGINE Chrysler, front, 4 stroke; 8 cylinders, Vee-slanted at 90°; 317.9 cu in, 5,210 cc (3.91 x 3.31 in, 99.3 x 84.1 mm); compression ratio: 8.5:1; max power (SAE net): 168 hp (124 kW) at 4,000 rpm; max torque (SAE net): 246 lb ft, 33.9 kg m (388 Nm) at 1,600 rpm; 32.2 hp/l (23.8 kW/l); 5 crankshaft bearings; valves: overhead, in line, hydraulic tappets; camshafts: 1, at centre of Vee; lubrication: rotary pump, full flow filter, 13.2 imp pt, 15.8 US pt, 7.5 l; 1 Carter downdraught 4-barrel carburettor; fuel feed: mechanical pump; water-cooled, 28.2 imp pt, 33.8 US pt, 16 l.

TRANSMISSION driving wheels: rear; gearbox: Torqueflite automatic transmission, hydraulic torque converter and planetary gears with 3 ratios, max ratio of converter at stall 2.3, possible manual selection; ratios: I 2.450, II 1,450, III 1, rev 2.200; lever: central; final drive: hypoid bevel, limited slip differential; axle ratio: 2.710; width of rims: 6"; tyres: 215/70 VR x 14.

PERFORMANCE max speed: about 124 mph, 200 km/h; power-weight ratio: 20.9 lb/hp (28.4 lb/kW), 9.5 kg/hp (12.9 kg/kW); carrying capacity: 1,554 lb, 750 kg; speed in direct drive at 1,000 rpm: 28.6 mph, 46 km/h; consumption: 20.2 m/imp gal, 16.8 m/US gal, 14 l x 100 km.

CHASSIS integral; front suspension: upper wishbones and lower horizontal arms combined with trailing radius rods, coil springs, anti-roll bar, adjustable telescopic dampers; rear: de Dion rigid axle, semi-elliptic leafsprings, adjustable telescopic dampers.

STEERING worm and roller, servo.

BRAKES front disc (diameter 11.8 in, 30 cm), internal radial fins, rear drum, dual circuit, servo; lining area: total 139.5 sq in, 900 sq cm.

ELECTRICAL EQUIPMENT 12 V; 65 Ah battery; 55 A alternator; 4 halogen headlamps.

DIMENSIONS AND WEIGHT wheel base: 112.20 in, 285 cm; tracks: 59.44 in, 151 cm front, 58.66 in, 149 cm rear; length: 192.12 in, 488 cm; width: 71.65 in, 182 cm; height: 55.12 in, 140 cm; ground clearance: 5.90 in, 15 cm; weight: 3,258 lb, 1,600 kg; turning circle: 41.9 ft, 12.8 m; fuel tank: 18 imp gal, 21.6 US gal, 82 l.

BODY saloon/sedan; 4 doors; 5 seats, separate front seats; air-conditioning; automatic speed control.

VARIATIONS

ENGINE 359.9 cu in, 5,898 cc (4 x 3.58 in, 101.6 x 90.9 mm), 8.4:1 compression ratio, max power (SAE net) 180 hp (132 kW) at 4,000 rpm, max torque (SAE net) 288 lb ft, 39.8 kg m (390 Nm) at 1,600 rpm, 30.5 hp/l (22.5 kW/l).
PERFORMANCE power-weight ratio 19.6 lb/hp (26.6 lb/kW), 8.9 kg/hp (12 kg/kW).

OPTIONALS 2,450 axle ratio.

Sierra Cabriolet

See Sierra, except for:

PRICE EX WORKS: 89,000 francs

TRANSMISSION axle ratio: 2.450 (standard).

PERFORMANCE max speed: 130 mph, 210 km/h; power-weight ratio: 17.2 lb/hp (23.3 lb/kW), 7.8 kg/hp (10.6 kg/kW).

manual selection; ratios: I 2.450, II 1.450, III 1 (transfer bo 2.030 ratio), rev 2.200; lever: central; final drive: hypoid beve limited slip differential; axle ratio: 3.070; width of rims: 8.5" tyres: LR 78 x 15.

PERFORMANCE max speed: about 106 mph, 170 km/h; powe weight ratio: 26.7 lb/hp (36.3 lb/kW), 12.1 kg/hp (16.5 kg/kW carrying capacity: 1,632 lb, 740 kg; acceleration: 0-50 mp (0-80 km/h) 9.8 sec; consumption: 17.7 m/imp gal, 14.7 m/U gal, 16 l x 100 km.

CHASSIS box-type perimeter frame; front and rear suspensio rigid axle, semi-elliptic leafsprings, telescopic dampers.

STEERING worm and roller, tilt of steering wheel, servo.

BRAKES front disc (diameter 11.81 in, 30 cm), rear drum, du circuit, servo.

ELECTRICAL EQUIPMENT 12 V; 65 Ah battery; 65 A altern tor; 4 headlamps.

DIMENSIONS AND WEIGHT wheel base: 100 in, 254 cm; fro and rear track: 58.27 in, 148 cm; length: 170.87 in, 434 cr width: 70.47 in, 179 cm; height: 68.11 in, 173 cm; grour clearance: 7.48 in, 19 cm; weight: 4,410 lb, 2,000 kg; turnir circle: 36.4 ft, 11.1 m; fuel tank: 18 imp gal, 21.6 US gal, 82

BODY estate car/st. wagon; 2+1 doors; 5 seats, separate fro seats, reclining backrests; built-in headrests on front and re seats; folding rear seat; tinted gass; air-conditioning.

MONTEVERDI Sierra

SIERRA CABRIOLET

DIMENSIONS AND WEIGHT wheel base: 107.87 in, 274 cm; length: 184.25 in, 468 cm; height: 50.39 in, 128 cm; weight: 3,087 lb, 1,400 kg; turning circle: 39.7 ft, 12.1 m.

BODY convertible; 2 doors.

Sahara

PRICE EX WORKS: 39,700 francs

ENGINE International, front, 4 stroke; 8 cylinders, Vee-slanted at 90°; 345 cu in, 5,654 cc (3.88 x 3.66 in, 98.5 x 92.9 mm); compression ratio: 8.05:1; max power (DIN): 165 hp (121 kW) at 3,600 rpm; max torque (DIN): 293 lb ft, 40.4 kg m (396 Nm) at 2,000 rpm; max engine rpm: 3,800; 29.2 hp/l (21.5 kW/l); cast iron block and head; 5 crankshaft bearings; valves: overhead, in line, push-rods and rockers, hydraulic tappets; camshafts: 1, at centre of Vee; lubrication: rotary pump, full flow filter, 13.2 imp pt, 15.9 US pt, 7.5 l; 1 downdraught twin barrel carburettor; dual exhaust system; fuel feed: mechanical pump; water-cooled, 34.3 imp pt, 41.2 US pt, 19.5 l.

TRANSMISSION driving wheels: front and rear with lockable front differential in transfer box; gearbox: Torqueflite automatic transmission, hydraulic torque converter and planetary gears with 3 ratios, max ratio of converter at stall 2.16, possible

MONTEVERDI Sahara

VARIATIONS

ENGINE Nissan, diesel, 6 cylinders vertical in line, 198 cu 3,245 cc (3.27 x 3.94 in, 83 x 100 mm), 22:1 compression rat max power (DIN) 82 hp (60 kW) at 3,800 rpm, max torque (DI 138 lb ft, 19.1 kg m (187 Nm) at 1,200-1,600 rpm, 25.3 h (18.7 kW/l), 7 crankshaft bearings, indirect injection.
TRANSMISSION 3.540 axle ratio.
PERFORMANCE max speed 90 mph, 145 km/h, power-weig ratio 53.8 lb/hp (72.9 lb/kW), 24.4 kg/hp (33.1 kg/kW), co sumption 28.2 m/imp gal, 23.5 m/US gal, 10 l x 100 km.
ELECTRICAL EQUIPMENT 85 Ah battery.
PRACTICAL INSTRUCTIONS fuel diesel oil.

OPTIONALS 4-speed mechanical gearbox; oil cooler.

MONTEVERDI Safari

Safari

PRICE EX WORKS: 59,500 francs

ENGINE International, front, 4 stroke; 8 cylinders, Vee-slant at 90°; 345 cu in, 5,654 cc (3.88 x 3.66 in, 98.5 x 92.9 mr compression ratio: 8.05:1; max power (DIN): 165 hp (121 k at 3,600 rpm; max torque (DIN): 293 lb ft, 40.4 kg m (396 N at 2,000 rpm; max engine rpm: 3,800; 29.2 hp/l (21.5 kW cast iron block and head; 5 crankshaft bearings; valves: ov head, in line, push-rods and rockers, hydraulic tappets; ca shafts: 1, at centre of Vee; lubrication: rotary pump, full fl filter, 13.2 imp pt, 15.9 US pt, 7.5 l; 1 downdraught twin bar carburettor; fuel feed: mechanical pump; water-cooled, 34 imp pt, 41.2 US pt, 19.5 l.

SBARRO Replica BMW 328 Standard

ANSMISSION driving wheels: front and rear with lockable nt differential in transfer box; gearbox: Torqueflite automatic nsmission, hydraulic torque converter and planetary gears th 3 ratios, max ratio of converter at stall 2.16, possible anual selection; ratios: I 2.450, II 1.450, III 1 (transfer box 030 ratio), rev 2.200; lever: central; final drive: hypoid bevel, nited slip differential; axle ratio: 3.070; width of rims: 7"; es: 225/235 x 15.

ERFORMANCE max speed: about 93 mph, 150 km/h; power- eight ratio: 25.4 lb/hp (34.5 lb/kW), 11.5 kg/hp (15.6 kg/kW); rrying capacity: 1,632 lb, 740 kg; consumption: 17.7 m/imp l, 14.7 m/US gal, 16 l x 100 km.

HASSIS box-type perimeter frame; front and rear suspension: id axle, semi-elliptic leafsprings, anti-roll bar; adjustable escopic dampers.

TEERING ZF, recirculating ball, servo.

RAKES front disc (diameter 11.81 in, 30 cm), internal radial s, rear drum, dual circuit, servo.

LECTRICAL EQUIPMENT 12 V; 65 Ah battery; 55 A alterna- r; 4 headlamps.

IMENSIONS AND WEIGHT wheel base: 100 in, 254 cm; front d rear track: 58.27 in, 148 cm; length: 179.50 in, 456 cm; dth: 70.87 in, 180 cm; height: 68.50 in, 174 cm; ground earance: 7.48 in, 19 cm; weight: 4,189 lb, 1,900 kg; turning rcle: 35.8 ft, 10.9 m; fuel tank: 18 imp gal, 21.6 US gal, 82 l.

ODY estate car/st. wagon; 2+1 doors; 5 seats, separate front eats, reclining backrests; built-in headrests on front and rear eats; folding rear seat; air-conditioning.

RACTICAL INSTRUCTIONS fuel: 91 oct petrol.

VARIATIONS

NGINE Chrysler, 439.7 cu in, 7,206 cc (4.32 x 3.75 in, 09.7 x 95.2 mm), 9.7:1 compression ratio, max power (DIN) 05 hp (224 kW) at 4,200 rpm, max torque (DIN) 450 lb ft, 62.1 m (609 Nm) at 3,300 rpm, 42.3 hp/l (31.2 kW/l).
ERFORMANCE max speed 124 mph, 200 km/h, power-weight tio 13.7 lb/hp (18.6 lb/kW), 6.2 kg/hp (8.5 kg/kW), consump- on 11.3 m/imp gal, 9.4 m/US gal, 25 l x 100 km.

PTIONALS 3.310 3.730 4.270 axle ratios; 4-speed mechanic- gearbox.

BARRO SWITZERLAND

Replica BMW 328 Standard

RICE EX WORKS: 35,000 francs

NGINE BMW, front, 4 stroke; 4 cylinders, slanted at 30°, in e; 96 cu in, 1,573 cc (3.31 x 2.80 in, 84 x 71 mm); compres- on ratio: 8.3:1; max power (DIN): 90 hp (66 kW) at 6,000 rpm; ax torque (DIN): 91 lb ft, 12.5 kg m (123 Nm) at 4,000 rpm; ax engine rpm: 6,200; 57.2 hp/l (42.1 kW/l); cast iron block, ht alloy head, hemispherical combustion chambers; 5 crank- shaft bearings; valves: overhead, Vee-slanted at 52°, rockers; camshafts: 1, overhead; lubrication: gear pump, full flow filter, 7.4 imp pt, 8.9 US pt, 4.2 l; 1 Solex DIDTA 32/32 downdraught twin barrel carburettor; fuel feed: mechanical pump; water-cooled, 12.3 imp pt, 14.8 US pt, 7 l.

TRANSMISSION driving wheels: rear; clutch: single dry plate (diaphragm), hydraulically controlled; gearbox: mechanical; gears: 4, fully synchronized; ratios: I 3.764, II 2.022, III 1.320, IV 1, rev 4.096; lever: central; final drive: hypoid bevel; axle ratio: 4.100; width of rims: 6".

PERFORMANCE max speeds: (I) 30 mph, 48 km/h; (II) 55 mph, 89 km/h; (III) 85 mph, 136 km/h; (IV) 112 mph, 180 km/h; power-weight ratio: 18.3 lb/hp (24.9 lb/kW), 8.3 kg/hp (11.3 kg/kW); carrying capacity: 353 lb, 160 kg; speed in direct drive at 1,000 rpm: 18 mph, 29 km/h; consumption: 29.4 m/imp gal, 24.5 m/US gal, 9.6 l x 100 km.

CHASSIS integral, box-type reinforced platform; front suspension: independent, coil springs/telescopic damper struts, auxiliary rubber springs, lower wishbones, lower links; rear: independent, oblique semi-trailing arms, auxiliary rubber springs, coil springs, telescopic dampers.

STEERING rack-and-pinion.

BRAKES front disc (diameter 10.71 in, 27.2 cm), dual circuit, rear drum, servo.

ELECTRICAL EQUIPMENT 12 V; 36 Ah battery; 630 W alternator; Bosch distributor; 2 headlamps.

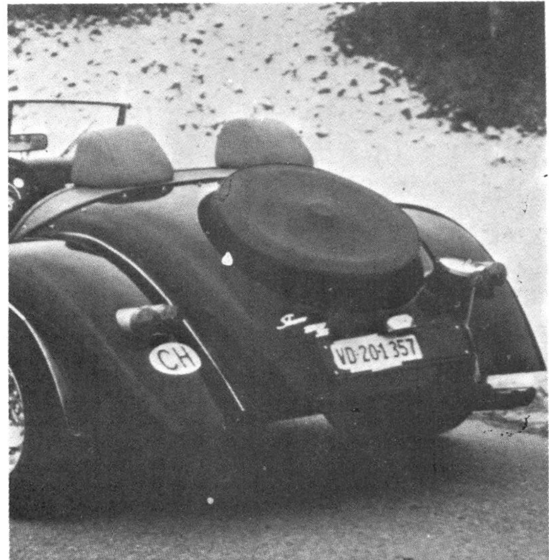

SBARRO Replica BMW 328

DIMENSIONS AND WEIGHT wheel base: 94.49 in, 240 cm; front and rear track: 57.09 in, 145 cm; length: 145.67 in, 370 cm; width: 61.42 in, 156 cm; ground clearance: 7.90 in, 18 cm; weight: 1,654 lb, 750 kg; turning circle: 29.5 ft, 9 m; fuel tank: 8.8 imp gal, 10.6 US gal, 40 l.

BODY roadster, in plastic material; 2 doors; 2 seats.

PRACTICAL INSTRUCTIONS fuel: 92 oct petrol; oil: engine 7.4 imp pt, 8.9 US pt, 4.2 l, SAE 20W-50, change every 3,700 miles, 6,000 km - gearbox 1.8 imp pt, 2.1 US pt, 1 l, SAE 80, change every 14,800 miles, 24,000 km - final drive 1.6 imp pt, 1.9 US pt, 0.9 l, SAE 90, no change recommended; greasing: none; sparking plug: 145°.

VARIATIONS

ENGINE BMW, 107.8 cu in, 1,766 cc (3.50 x 2.80 in, 89 x 71 mm), max power (DIN) 98 hp (72 kW) at 5,800 rpm, max torque (DIN) 105 lb ft, 14.5 kg m (142 Nm) at 4,000 rpm, 55.5 hp/l (40.8 kW/l).
TRANSMISSION 3.900 axle ratio.
PERFORMANCE power-weight ratio 17 lb/hp (22.9 lb/kW), 7.7 kg/hp (10.4 kg/kW), consumption 28.5 m/imp gal, 23.8 m/US gal, 9.9 l x 100 km.

ENGINE BMW, 121.4 cu in, 1,990 cc (3.50 x 3.15 in, 89 x 80 mm), 8.1:1 compression ratio, max power (DIN) 109 hp (80 kW) at 5,800 rpm, max torque (DIN) 116 lb ft, 16 kg m (157 Nm) at 3,700 rpm, 54.8 hp/l (40.3 kW/l).
TRANSMISSION 3.900 axle ratio.
PERFORMANCE power-weight ratio 15.2 lb/hp (20.7 lb/kW), 6.9 kg/hp (9.4 kg/kW), consumption 28.2 m/imp gal, 23.5 m/US gal, 10 l x 100 km.

ENGINE BMW, 121.4 cu in, 1,990 cc (3.50 x 3.15 in, 89 x 80 mm), 9.3:1 compression ratio, max power (DIN) 125 hp (92 kW) at 5,700 rpm, max torque (DIN) 127 lb ft, 17.5 kg m (172 Nm) at 4,350 rpm, 62.8 hp/l (46.2 kW/l), Bosch K-Jetronic injection, electric pump.
TRANSMISSION 3.640 axle ratio.
PERFORMANCE max speed 137 mph, 220 km/h, power-weight ratio 13.2 lb/hp (18.1 lb/kW), 6 kg/hp (8.2 kg/kW), consumption 32.1 m/imp gal, 26.7 m/US gal, 8.8 l x 100 km.

OPTIONALS 5-speed fully sunchronized mechanical gearbox (I 3.368, II 2.160, III 1.579, IV 1.241, V 1, rev 4); 3.640 or 3.450 axle ratio; 7" or 8" wide rims; disc brakes.

Replica BMW 328 America

See Replica BMW 328 Standard, except for:

PRICE EX WORKS: 44,000 francs

ENGINE 6 cylinders, in line; 152.2 cu in, 2,494 cc (3.39 x 2.82 in, 86 x 71.6 mm); compression ratio: 9:1; max power (DIN): 150 hp (110 kW) at 6,000 rpm; max torque (DIN): 154 lb ft, 21.2 kg m (208 Nm) at 4,000 rpm; 60.1 hp/l (44.2 kW/l); polispherical combustion chambers; 7 crankshaft bearings; lubrication: 10 imp pt, 12 US pt, 5.7 l; 1 Solex 4A1 downdraught twin barrel carburettor; cooling, 21.1 imp pt, 25.4 US pt, 12 l.

PERFORMANCE max speed: 132 mph, 212 km/h; power-weight ratio: 13.3 lb/hp (18 lb/kW), 6 kg/hp (8.2 kg/kW); speed in direct drive at 1,000 rpm: 21.3 mph, 34.2 km/h; consumption: 25.9 m/imp gal, 21.6 m/US gal, 10.9 l x 100 km.

BRAKES disc.

ELECTRICAL EQUIPMENT 55 Ah battery; 770 W alternator.

DIMENSIONS AND WEIGHT wheel base: 100.39 in, 255 cm; front and rear track: 64.17 in, 163 cm; length: 149.61 in, 380 cm; width: 67.32 in, 171 cm; weight: 1,989 lb, 902 kg.

BODY 2+1 seats, separate reclining front seats.

PRACTICAL INSTRUCTIONS oil: engine 10 imp pt, 12 US pt, 5.7 l; tappet clearances: inlet 0.010 in, 0.25 mm, exhaust 0.012 in, 0.30 mm; valve timing: 6° 50° 50° 6°.

VARIATIONS

ENGINE 170.1 cu in, 2,788 cc (3.39 x 3.15 in, 86 x 80 mm); 8.3:1 compression ratio, max power (DIN) 170 hp (125 kW) at 5,800 rpm, max torque (DIN) 172 lb ft, 23.8 kg m (233 Nm) at 4,000 rpm, 6,500 max engine rpm, 61 hp/l (44.9 kW/l).
PERFORMANCE power-weight ratio 11.7 lb/hp (15.9 lb/kW), 5.3 kg/hp (7.2 kg/kW), consumption 25.7 m/imp gal, 21.4 m/US gal, 11 l x 100 km.

ENGINE 182 cu in, 2,982 cc (3.50 x 3.15 in, 89 x 80 mm), 8:1 compression ratio, max power (DIN) 175 hp (129 kW) at 5,500 rpm, max torque (DIN) 185 lb ft, 25.5 kg m (250 Nm) at 4,500 rpm, 6,500 max engine rpm, 58.7 hp/l (43.2 kW/l), Bosch electronic injection, exhaust thermal reactor, electric thermostatic fan.
PERFORMANCE power-weight ratio 11.5 lb/hp (15.4 lb/kW), 5.2 kg/hp (7 kg/kW), consumption 24.8 m/imp gal, 20.6 m/US gal, 11.4 l x 100 km.
PRACTICAL INSTRUCTIONS valve timing 14° 54° 54° 14°.

ENGINE 195.6 cu in, 3,205 cc (3.50 x 3.39 in, 89 x 86 mm), max power (DIN) 200 hp (147 kW) at 5,500 rpm, max torque (DIN)

SBARRO Stash HS Cabriolet

REPLICA BMW 328 AMERICA

210 lb ft, 29 kg m (284 Nm) at 4,250 rpm, 62.4 hp/l (45.9 kW/l), Bosch L-Jetronic electronic injection, electric pump.
PERFORMANCE power-weight ratio 9.9 lb/hp (13.4 lb/kW), 4.5 kg/hp (6.1 kg/kW).

Stash HS Cabriolet

PRICE EX WORKS: 100,000 francs

ENGINE Mercedes-Benz, centre-rear, 4 stroke; 8 cylinders, Vee-slanted ar 90°; 417 cu in, 6,384 cc (4.21 x 3.74 in, 107 x 95 mm); compression ratio: 8.8:1; max power (DIN): 286 hp (210 kW) at 4,250 rpm; max torque (DIN): 406 lb ft, 56 kg m (549 Nm) at 3,000 rpm; max engine rpm: 5,300; 41.8 hp/l (30.8 kW/l); cast iron block, light alloy head; 5 crankshaft bearings; valves: overhead, finger levers; camshafts: 2, 1 per bank, overhead; lubrication: gear pump, full flow filter, dry sump, oil cooler, 21.1 imp pt, 25.4 US pt, 12 l; Bosch K-Jetronic injection; air cleaner; fuel feed: electric pump; water-cooled, viscous coupling thermostatic fan, 26.4 imp pt, 31.7 US pt, 15 l.

TRANSMISSION driving wheels: rear; clutch: MB automatic transmission, hydraulic torque converter and planetary gears with 3 ratios, max ratio of converter at stall 2.5, possible manual selection; ratios: I 2.310, II 1.460, III 1, rev 1.840; lever: central or steering column; final drive: hypoid bevel; axle ratio: 2.650; width of rims: 9" front, 13" rear; tyres: 9" x 15 front, 13" x 15 rear.

PERFORMANCE max speed: about 149 mph, 240 km/h; power-weight ratio: 10.8 lb/hp (14.7 lb/kW), 4.9 kg/hp (6.6 kg/kW)); carrying capacity: 926 lb, 420 kg; speed in direct drive at 1,000 rpm: 28.3 mph, 45.5 km/h; consumption: 17.7 m/imp gal, 14.7 m/US gal, 16 l x 100 km.

CHASSIS integral, box-type reinforced platform; front suspension: independent, wishbones, coil springs/telescopic dampers struts; rear: independent, wishbones, coil springs, telescopic dampers, anti-roll bar.

STEERING recirculating ball.

BRAKES disc, dual circuit, rear compensator, servo.

ELECTRICAL EQUIPMENT 12 V; 88 Ah battery; 1,050 W alternator; Bosch (transistorized) distributor; 2 iodine headlamps.

DIMENSIONS AND WEIGHT wheel base: 104.33 in, 265 cm; tracks: 55.90 in, 142 cm front, 62.99 in, 160 cm rear; length: 181.10 in, 460 cm; width: 74.80 in, 190 cm; height: 45.67 in, 116 cm; ground clearance: 5.91 in, 15 cm; weight: 3,087 lb, 1,400 kg; fuel tank: 11 imp gal, 13.2 US gal, 50 l.

BODY convertible, in plastic material; 2 doors; 2+2 seats; detachable roof.

PRACTICAL INSTRUCTIONS fuel: 98 oct petrol.

OPTIONALS limited slip differential.

Windhound 4 x 4

PRICE EX WORKS: 65,000 francs

ENGINE BMW, front, 4 stroke; 6 cylinders, in line; 182 cu in 2,982 cc (3.58 x 3.15 in, 89 x 80 mm), compression ratio: 8:1 max power (DIN): 175 hp (129 kW) at 5,500 rpm; max torqu (DIN): 185 lb ft, 25.5 kg m (250 Nm) at 4,500 rpm; max engin rpm: 6,500; 58.7 hp/l (43.2 kW/l); cast iron block, light allo head, polispherical combustion chambers; 7 crankshaft bearings; valves: overhead, Vee-slanted, rockers; camshafts: 1 overhead; lubrication: rotary pump, full flow filter, 10 imp pt, 1 US pt, 5.7 l; Bosch electronic injection, exhaust thermal reac tor; fuel feed: mechanical pump; water-cooled, 21.1 imp pt 25.4 US pt, 12 l.

TRANSMISSION driving wheels: front and rear; clutch: singl dry plate; gearbox: mechanical; gears: 4, fully synchronized ratios: I 3.855, II 2.203, III 1.402, IV 1, rev 4.030; gear an transfer levers: central; final drive: hypoid bevel; axle rati (front and rear): 3.640; tyres: 9 x 15 front, 11 x 15 rear.

PERFORMANCE max speeds: (I) 118 mph, 190 km/h; power weight ratio: 23.3 lb/hp (31.7 lb/kW), 10.6 kg/hp (14.4 kg/kW) consumption: 15.4 m/imp gal, 18.5 m/US gal, 14.4 l x 100 km

CHASSIS integral, box-type reinforced platform; front suspen sion: independent, by McPherson, coil springs/telescopic dam per struts, lower wishbones, torsion bar, automatic levellin control; rear: independent, oblique semi-trailing arms, co springs, torsion bar, automatic levelling control.

STEERING rack-and-pinion.

BRAKES drum, dual circuit, servo.

ELECTRICAL EQUIPMENT 12 V; 65 Ah battery; 55 A alterna tor; 4 headlamps.

DIMENSIONS AND WEIGHT wheel base: 106.30 in, 270 cm tracks: 58.66 in, 149 cm front, 59.45 in, 151 cm rear; length 177.16 in, 450 cm; width: 71.26 in, 181 cm; height: 66.93 ir 170 cm; ground clearance: 10.6-19.3 in, 27-49 cm; weigh 4,079 lb, 1,850 kg; fuel tank: 15.4 imp gal, 18.5 US gal, 70

BODY estate car/st. wagon, in plastic material; 2+1 doors; 4- seats.

PRACTICAL INSTRUCTIONS fuel: 98 oct petrol; oil: engine 1 imp pt, 12 US pt, 5.7 l, SAE 20W-50, change every 3,700 miles 6,000 km - gearbox 1.8 imp pt, 2.1 US pt, 1 l, SAE 80, chang every 14,900 miles, 24,000 km - final drive (front and rear) 1. imp pt, 1.9 US pt, 0.9 l, SAE 90, no change recommended greasing: none; tyre pressure: front 36 psi, 2.5 atm, rear 36 ps 2.5 atm.

VARIATIONS

ENGINE 4 cylinders - 6 cylinders - 8 cylinders - 12 cylinders

OPTIONALS 5-speed mechanical gearbox; ZF automatic trans mission; front disc brakes.

SBARRO Windhound 4 x 4

AZLK USSF

Moskvich 2138

ENGINE front, 4 stroke; 4 cylinders, in line; 82.8 cu in, 1,357 c (2.99 x 2.95 in, 76 x 75 mm); compression ratio: 7:1; max powe (DIN): 50 hp (37 kW) at 4,750 rpm; max torque (DIN): 67 lb f 9.3 kg m (91 Nm) at 2,750 rpm; max engine rpm: 4,750; 36. hp/l (27.1 kW/l); cast iron block, light alloy head; 3 crankshaf bearings; valves: overhead; camshafts: 1, side; lubrication gear pump, filter on by-pass, 7.9 imp pt, 9.5 US pt, 4.5 l; downdraught twin barrel carburettor; fuel feed: mechanica pump; water-cooled, 12.3 imp pt, 14.8 US pt, 7 l.

TRANSMISSION driving wheels: rear; clutch: single dry plate hydraulically controlled; gearbox: mechanical; gears: 4, II, I and IV synchronized; ratios: I 3.810, III 2.242, III 1.450, IV 1 rev 4.170; lever: central; final drive: hypoid bevel; axle ratio 4.220; width of rims: 4"; tyres: 5.90/6.00 x 13.

PERFORMANCE max speed: 75 mph, 120 km/h; power-weigh ratio: 46.7 lb/hp (63.5 lb/kW), 21.2 kg/hp (28.8 kg/kW); carryin capacity: 882 lb, 400 kg; speed in direct drive at 1,000 rpm 16.2 mph, 26 km/h; consumption: 26.9 m/imp gal, 22.4 m/U gal, 10.5 l x 100 km.

CHASSIS integral; front suspension: independent, wishbones coil springs, anti-roll bar, telescopic dampers; rear: rigid axle semi-elliptic leafsprings, telescopic dampers.

STEERING worm and roller.

BRAKES drum; lining area: front 59.5 sq in, 384 sq cm, rea 59.5 sq in, 384 sq cm, total 119 sq in, 768 sq cm.

AZLK Moskvich 2140 Combi IZh

ELECTRICAL EQUIPMENT 12 V; 42 or 55 Ah battery; 250 W dynamo; R 107 distributor; 2 headlamps.

DIMENSIONS AND WEIGHT wheel base: 94.49 in, 240 cm; tracks: 48.82 in, 124 cm front, 48.43 in, 123 cm rear; length: 167.32 in, 425 cm; width: 61.02 in, 155 cm; height: 58.48 in, 146 cm; ground clearance: 7.09 in, 18 cm; weight: 2,337 lb, 1,060 kg; turning circle: 37.7 ft, 11.5 m; fuel tank: 10.1 imp gal, 12.1 US gal, 46 l.

BODY saloon/sedan; 4 doors; 5 seats.

PRACTICAL INSTRUCTIONS fuel: 85 oct petrol; sparking plug: 175°.

VARIATIONS

(for export only)
ENGINE Perkins, diesel, 4 cylinders, in line with pre-combustion chamber, 107.4 cu in, 1,760 cc (3.13 x 3.50 in, 79.4 x 88.9 mm), 22:1 compression ratio, max power (DIN) 50 hp (37 kW) at 4,000 rpm, max torque (DIN) 80 lb ft, 11 kg m (108 Nm) at 2,200 rpm, 28.4 hp/l (20.9 kW/l), 1 camshaft in crankcase, lubrication 10.6 imp pt, 12.7 US pt, 6 l, sealed circuit cooling, water, 17.6 imp pt, 21.1 US pt, 10 l.
TRANSMISSION 4-speed mechanical fully synchronized gearbox, ratios (I 3.490, II 2.040, III 1.330, IV 1, rev 3.390), central lever, 4.5" wide rims, 165/175 SR x 13 tyres.
PERFORMANCE max speed 75 mph, 120 km/h, power-weight ratio 46.7 lb/hp (63.5 lb/kW), 21.2 kg/hp (28.8 kg/kW), consumption 33.6 m/imp gal, 28 m/US gal, 8.4 l x 100 km.
BRAKES front disc, rear drum, servo.
ELECTRICAL EQUIPMENT 66 Ah battery, 480 W alternator.

OPTIONALS 4.5" wide rims; front disc brakes; front and rear track 50 in, 127 cm.

AZLK Moskvich 2138

Moskvich 2136

See Moskvich 2138, except for:

TRANSMISSION tyres: 175 x 13.

PERFORMANCE power-weight ratio: 50.5 lb/hp (68.6 lb/kW), 22.9 kg/hp (31.1 kg/kW).

DIMENSIONS AND WEIGHT height: 59.45 in, 151 cm; weight: 2,525 lb, 1,145 kg.

BODY estate car/st. wagon; 4+1 doors.

Moskvich 2140 / Moskvich 2140 IZh

ENGINE front, slanted at 20°, 4 stroke; 4 cylinders, in line; 90.2 cu in, 1,479 cc (3.23 x 2.76 in, 82 x 70 mm); compression ratio: 8.8:1; max power (DIN): 75 hp (55 kW) at 5,800 rpm; max torque (DIN): 83 lb ft, 11.4 kg m (112 Nm) at 3,400 rpm; max engine rpm: 6,500; 50.7 hp/l (37.3 kW/l); light alloy block and head, wet liners; 5 crankshaft bearings; valves: overhead, Vee-slanted at 52°, rockers; camshafts: 1, overhead, chain-driven; lubrication: gear pump, full flow filter, 8.8 imp pt, 10.6 US pt, 5 l; 1 K-126 H downdraught twin barrel carburettor; fuel feed: mechanical pump; sealed circuit cooling, liquid, 13.2 imp pt, 15.9 US pt, 7.5 l.

TRANSMISSION driving wheels: rear; clutch: single dry plate (diaphragm), hydraulically controlled; gearbox: mechanical; gears: 4, fully sinchronized; ratios: I 3.490, II 2.040, III 1.330, IV 1, rev 3.390; lever: central; final drive: hypoid bevel; axle ratio: 4.220; width of rims: 4.5"; tyres: 6.45/6.95 x 13.

PERFORMANCE max speeds: (I) 27 mph, 43 km/h; (II) 45 mph, 73 km/h; (III) 70 mph, 113 km/h; (IV) 93 mph, 150 km/h; power-weight ratio: 31.7 lb/hp (43.2 lb/kW), 14.4 kg/hp (19.6 kg/kW); carrying capacity: 882 lb, 400 kg; speed in direct drive at 1,000 rpm: 16.9 mph, 27.2 km/h; consumption: 32.1 m/imp gal, 26.7 m/US gal, 8.8 l x 100 km.

CHASSIS integral; front suspension: independent, wishbones, coil springs, anti-roll bar, telescopic dampers; rear: rigid axle, semi-elliptic leafsprings, telescopic dampers.

STEERING worm and double roller; turns lock to lock: 3.50.

BRAKES front disc, rear drum, servo.

ELECTRICAL EQUIPMENT 12 V; 42 Ah battery; 40 A alternator; R 107 distributor; 2 headlamps.

DIMENSIONS AND WEIGHT wheel base: 94.49 in, 240 cm; tracks: 48.82 in, 124 cm front, 48.43 in, 123 cm rear; length: 167.32 in, 425 cm; width: 61.02 in, 155 cm; height: 58.27 in, 148 cm; ground clearance: 7.87 in, 20 cm; weight: 2,381 lb, 1,080 kg; turning circle: 37.7 ft, 11.5 m; fuel tank: 10.1 imp gal, 12.1 US gal, 46 l.

BODY saloon/sedan; 4 doors; 5 seats, separate front seats, reclining backrests with adjustable headrests; headlamps with wiper-washer.

OPTIONALS 165/175 SR x 13 tyres; cooling 17.6 imp pt, 21.1 US pt, 10 l; front and rear track 50 in, 127 cm.

Moskvich 2137 / Moskvich 2140 Combi IZh

See Moskvich 2140 / Moskvich 2140 IZh, except for:

TRANSMISSION axle ratio: 4.550; tyres: 6.40 x 13.

PERFORMANCE max speed: 84 mph, 135 km/h; power-weight ratio: 32.8 lb/hp (44.8 lb/kW), 14.9 kg/hp (20.3 kg/kW).

DIMENSIONS AND WEIGHT height: 59.45 in, 151 cm; weight: 2,470 lb, 1,120 kg.

BODY estate car/st. wagon; 4+1 doors.

GAZ USSR

Volga 24

ENGINE front, 4 stroke; 4 cylinders, in line; 149.3 cu in, 2,446 cc (3.62 x 3.62 in, 92 x 92 mm); compression ratio: 8.2:1; max power (SAE): 110 hp (81 kW) at 4,500 rpm; max torque (SAE): 152 lb ft, 21 kg m (206 Nm) at 2,400 rpm; max engine rpm: 4,500; 45 hp/l (33 kW/l); light alloy block and head, wet liners; 5 crankshaft bearings; valves: overhead, in line, push-rods and

GAZ Volga 24

rockers; camshafts: 1, side; lubrication: gear pump, filter on by-pass, 10.4 imp pt, 12.5 US pt, 5.9 l; 1 K-126 G downdraught twin barrel carburettor; fuel feed: mechanical pump; water-cooled, 20.2 imp pt, 24.3 US pt, 11.5 l.

TRANSMISSION driving wheels: rear; clutch: single dry plate, hydraulically controlled; gearbox: mechanical; gears: 4, fully synchronized; ratios: I 3.500, II 2.260, III 1.450, IV 1, rev 3.540; lever: central final drive: hypoid bevel; axle ratio: 4.100; width of rims: 5"; tyres: 7.35/185 x 14.

PERFORMANCE max speeds: (I) 25 mph, 41 km/h; (II) 40 mph, 64 km/h; (III) 62 mph, 100 km/h; (IV) 90 mph, 145 km/h; power-weight ratio: 29.1 lb/hp (39.7 lb/kW), 13.2 kg/hp (18 kg/kW); carrying capacity: 1,058 lb, 480 kg; speed in direct drive at 1,000 rpm: 18 mph, 29 km/h; consumption: 22.6 m/imp gal, 18.8 m/US gal, 12.5 l x 100 km.

CHASSIS integral; front suspension: independent, wishbones, coil springs, anti-roll bar, telescopic dampers; rear: rigid axle, semi-elliptic leafsprings, telescopic dampers.

STEERING worm and roller; turns lock to lock: 3.50.

BRAKES drum, servo; swept area: front 87.6 sq in, 565 sq cm, rear 87.6 sq in, 565 sq cm, total 175.2 sq in, 1,130 sq cm.

ELECTRICAL EQUIPMENT 12 V; 54 Ah battery; 40 A alternator; R 119-B distributor; 2 headlamps.

DIMENSIONS AND WEIGHT wheel base: 110.24 in, 280 cm; tracks: 57.87 in, 147 cm front, 55.91 in, 142 cm rear; length: 186.22 in, 473 cm; width: 70.87 in, 180 cm; height: 58.66 in, 149 cm; ground clearance: 7.09 in, 18 cm; weight: 3,208 lb, 1,455 kg; turning circle: 40.7 ft, 12.4 m; fuel tank: 12.1 imp gal, 14.5 US gal, 55 l.

BODY saloon/sedan; 4 doors; 5-6 seats, separate front seats, reclining backrests.

PRACTICAL INSTRUCTIONS fuel: 94 oct petrol; oil: engine 10.4 imp pt, 12.5 US pt, 5.9 l - gearbox 1.6 imp pt, 1.9 US pt, 0.9 l - final drive 0.2 imp pt, 0.2 US pt, 0.1 l; greasing: 9 points; sparking plug: 175°; tappet clearances: inlet 0.014 in, 0.35 mm, exhaust 0.014 in, 0.35 mm; tyre pressure: front 24 psi, 1.7 atm, rear 24 psi, 1.7 atm.

VARIATIONS

ENGINE 6.7:1; compression ratio, max power (SAE) 95 hp (70 kW) at 4,700 rpm, max torque (SAE) 141 lb ft, 19.5 kg m (191 Nm) at 2,400 rpm, 38.8 hp/l (28.5 kW/l).
PERFORMANCE power-weight ratio 33.7 lb/hp (45.9 lb/kW), 15.3 kg/hp (20.8 kg/kW).

ENGINE 7.8:1 compression ratio, max power (SAE) 105 hp (77 kW) at 4,700 rpm, max torque (SAE) 145 lb ft, 20 kg m (196 Nm) at 2,400 rpm, 43 hp/l (31.6 kW/l).
PERFORMANCE power-weight ratio 30.6 lb/hp (41.4 lb/kW), 13.9 kg/hp (18.8 kg/kW).

Volga 24-02

See Volga 24, except for:

PERFORMANCE power-weight ratio: 31.5 lb/hp (43 lb/kW), 14.3 kg/hp (19.5 kg/kW); carrying capacity: 1,235 lb, 550 kg.

DIMENSIONS AND WEIGHT height: 60.63 in, 154 cm; weight: 3,473 lb, 1,575 kg.

BODY estate car/st. wagon; 4+1 doors; 7 seats; folding rear seat.

Volga 24 Indenor Diesel

(for export only)

See Volga 24, except for:

ENGINE diesel; 4 cylinders, in line, slanted at 20° to right; 128.9 cu in, 2,112 cc (3.54 x 3.27 in, 90 x 83 mm); compression ratio: 22.2:1; max power (DIN): 59 hp (43 kW) at 4,500 rpm; max torque (DIN): 86 lb ft, 11.9 kg m (117 Nm) at 2,500 rpm; 27.9 hp/l (20.5 kW/l); injection pump.

PERFORMANCE max speed: 84 mph, 135 km/h; power-weight ratio: 54.5 lb/hp (73.9 lb/kW), 24.7 kg/hp (33.5 kg/kW); consumption: 35.3 m/imp gal, 29.4 m/US gal, 8 l x 100 km.

ELECTRICAL EQUIPMENT 65 Ah battery.

PRACTICAL INSTRUCTIONS fuel: diesel oil.

VARIATIONS

ENGINE 118.9 cu in, 1,948 cc (3.46 x 3.15 in, 88 x 80 mm); 21.8:1 compression ratio, max power (DIN) 50 hp (37 kW) at 4,500 rpm, max torque (DIN) 79 lb ft, 10.9 kg m (107 Nm) at 2,250 rpm, 25.7 hp/l (18.9 kW/l).

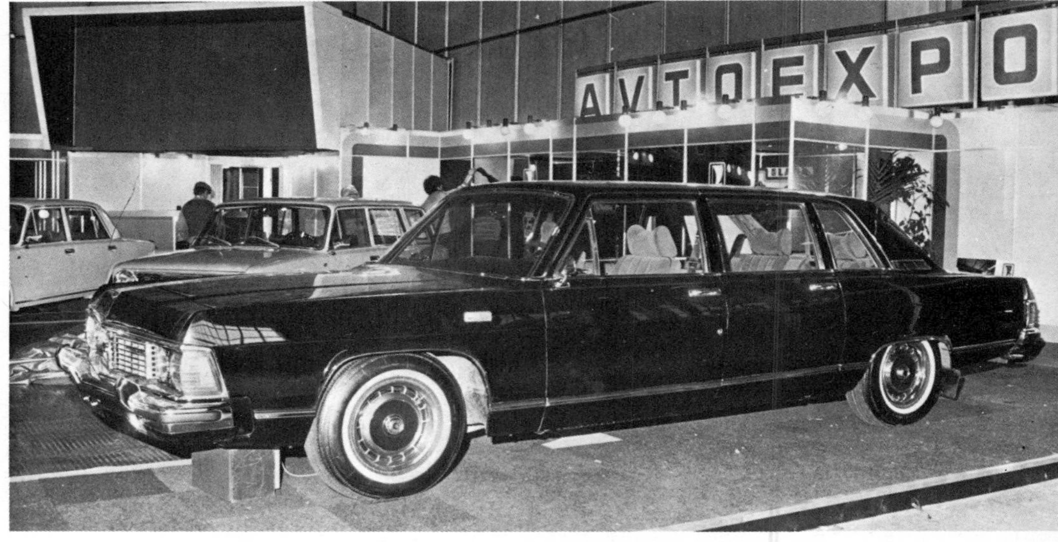

GAZ Chaika

PERFORMANCE power-weight ratio 64.2 lb/hp (87.1 lb/kW), 29.1 kg/hp (39.5 kg/kW).

Chaika

ENGINE front, 4 stroke; 8 cylinders, Vee-slanted; 337 cu in, 5,522 cc (3.94 x 3.46 in, 100 x 88 mm); compression ratio: 8.5:1; max power (DIN): 207 hp (152 kW) at 4,000 rpm; max torque (DIN): 297 lb ft, 41 kg m (402 Nm) at 2,300 rpm; max engine rpm: 4,400; 37.5 hp/l (27.6 kW/l); cast iron block, light alloy head; 5 crankshaft bearings; valves: overhead, in line; camshafts: 1, side; lubrication: gear pump, full flow filter, 11.4 imp pt, 13.7 US pt, 6.5 l; 2 LK3 type K113 downdraught 4-barrel carburettors; fuel feed: mechanical pump; water-cooled, thermostatic fan.

TRANSMISSION driving wheels: rear; gearbox: automatic transmission, hydraulic torque converter and planetary gears with 3 ratios; ratios: I 2.840, II 1.680, III 1; lever: push-button control; final drive: hypoid bevel; axle ratio: 3.540; tyres: 8.20 x 15.

PERFORMANCE max speed: about 112 mph, 180 km/h; power-weight ratio: 27.6 lb/hp (37.5 lb/kW), 12.5 kg/hp (17 kg/kW); carrying capacity: 1,235 lb, 560 kg; consumption: about 14.1 m/imp gal, 11.8 m/US gal, 20 l x 100 km.

CHASSIS integral; front suspension: independent, wishbones, coil springs, anti-roll bar, telescopic dampers; rear: rigid axle semi-elliptic springs, telescopic dampers.

STEERING roller and sector, servo.

BRAKES front disc, rear drum, servo.

ELECTRICAL EQUIPMENT 12 V; 68 Ah battery; 300 W dynamo; P13 distributor; 4 headlamps.

DIMENSIONS AND WEIGHT wheel base: 135.80 in, 345 cm tracks: 60.65 in, 154 cm front, 60.25 in, 153 cm rear; length 240.70 in, 611 cm; width: 79.50 in, 202 cm; height: 60 in, 152 cm; ground clearance: 7.10 in, 18 cm; weight: 5,698 lb, 2,584 kg; turning circle: 26.2 ft, 8 m; fuel tank: 17.6 imp gal, 21.1 US gal, 80 l.

BODY saloon/sedan; 4 doors; 7 seats; folding rear seat; headlamps with wiper-washers.

UAZ USSR

469 B

ENGINE front, 4 stroke; 4 cylinders, vertical, in line; 149.2 cu in, 2,445 cc (3.62 x 3.62 in, 92 x 92 mm); compression ratio: 6.7:1; max power (SAE): 78 hp (57 kW) at 4,000 rpm; max torque (SAE): 125 lb ft, 17.2 kg m (169 Nm) at 2,200-2,500 rpm; max engine rpm: 4,500; 31.9 hp/l (23.4 kW/l); cast iron

UAZ 469 B

ock and head; 4 crankshaft bearings; valves: overhead, in ne, push-rods and rockers; camshafts: 1, side; lubrication: ear pump, full flow filter, oil cooler, 10.6 imp pt, 12.7 US pt, 6 1 downdraught 4-barrel carburettor; fuel feed: mechanical ump; water-cooled, 22.9 imp pt, 27.5 US pt, 13 l.

RANSMISSION driving wheels: front (automatically engaged ith transfer box low ratio) and rear; clutch: single dry plate; earbox: mechanical; gears: 4, III and IV synchronized; ratios: I .120, II 2.640, III 1.580, IV 1, rev 3.738; lever: central; final rive: spiral bevel; axle ratio: 5.125; tyres: 8.40 x 15.

ERFORMANCE max speed: about 71 mph, 115 km/h; power-eight ratio: 43.5 lb/hp (59.2 lb/kW), 19.7 kg/hp (26.8 kg/kW); arrying capacity: 1,654 lb, 750 kg; speed in direct drive at ,000 rpm: 15.9 mph, 25.6 km/h; consumption: 23.5 m/imp gal, 9.6 m/US gal, 12 l x 100 km.

HASSIS box-type ladder frame; front rear suspension: rigid xle, semi-elliptic leafsprings, telescopic dampers.

TEERING worm and double roller.

RAKES drum; lining area: total 153.5 sq in, 990 sq cm.

LECTRICAL EQUIPMENT 12 V; 54 Ah battery; 350 W alterna-r; 2 headlamps.

IMENSIONS AND WEIGHT wheel base: 93.70 in, 238 cm; ont and rear track: 56.69 in, 144 cm; length 158.27 in, 402 m; width: 70.08 in, 178 cm; height: 79.13 in, 201 cm; ground earance: 8.66 in, 22 cm; weight: 3,396 lb, 1,540 kg; turning ircle: 39.4 ft, 12 m; fuel tank: 15.8 imp gal, 19 US gal, 72 l (2 eparate tanks).

ODY open; 4 doors; 7 seats, separate front seats.

RACTICAL INSTRUCTIONS fuel: 72 oct petrol.

VARIATIONS

NGINE Peugeot diesel, 128.9 cu in, 2,112 cc (3.54 x 3.27 in, 0 x 83 mm) 22.8:1; compression ratio, max power (DIN) 65 hp 48 kW) at 4,500 rpm, max torque (DIN) 89 lb ft, 12.3 kg m (121 m) at 2,200 rpm, max engine rpm 4,750, 30.8 hp/l (22.6 kW/l).
ERFORMANCE max speed 62 mph, 100 km/h, power-weight atio 55.2 lb/hp (71 lb/kW), 23.7 kg/hp (32.2 kg/kW), consump-on 31.7 m/imp gal, 26.4 m/US gal, 8.9 l x 100 km.

PTIONALS independent heating; hardtop: fabric top.

VAZ Lada 1200 Sedan

VAZ Lada 1200 - 1500 Combi

VAZ USSR

Lada Series

RICES IN GB:

		£
	1200 4-dr Sedan	2,280*
	1200 4+1-dr Combi	2,591*
3	1300 ES 4-dr Sedan	2,678*
4	1500 4-dr Sedan	—
5	1500 4+1-dr Combi	2,735*
6	1500 ES 4+1-dr Combi	3,099*
7	1600 4-dr Sedan	2,950*
8	1600 ES 4-dr Sedan	3,350*

Power team:	Standard for:	Optional for:
60 hp	1,2	—
68 hp	3	—
75 hp	4 to 6	—
78 hp	7,8	—

60 hp power team

ENGINE front, 4 stroke; 4 cylinders, in line; 73.1 cu in, 1,198 cc (2.99 x 2.60 in, 76 x 66 mm); compression ratio: 8.8:1; max power (DIN): 60 hp (44 kW) at 5,600 rpm; max torque (DIN): 64 lb ft, 8.9 kg m (87 Nm) at 3,400 rpm; max engine rpm: 6,000; 50.1 hp/l (36.9 kW/l); cast iron block, light alloy head; 5 crankshaft bearings; valves: overhead, in line, rockers; camshafts: 1, overhead, chain-driven; lubrication: gear pump, full flow filter, 6.5 imp pt, 7.8 pt, 3.7 l; 1 Weber 32 DCR downdraught twin barrel carburettor; fuel feed: mechanical pump; sealed circuit cooling, liquid, 15 imp pt, 18 US pt, 8.5 l.

TRANSMISSION driving wheels: rear; clutch: single dry plate (diaphragm), hydraulically controlled; gearbox: mechanical; gears: 4, fully synchronized; ratios: I 3.753, II 2.303, III 1.493, IV 1, rev 3.867; lever: central; final drive: hypoid bevel; axle ratio: Sedan 4.300, Combi 4.440; width of rims: 4.5"; tyres: Sedan 155 SR/6.15 x 13 - Combi 165 SR/6.45 x 13.

PERFORMANCE max speeds: (I) 25 mph, 40 km/h; (II) 40 mph, 65 km/h; (III) 62 mph, 100 km/h; (IV) 87 mph, 140 km/h; power-weight ratio: Sedan 35.7 lb/hp (48.3 lb/kW), 16.2 kg/hp (21.9 kg/kW) - Combi 37 lb/hp (50.5 lb/kW), 16.8 kg/hp (22.9 kg/kW); carrying capacity: 882 lb, 400 kg; acceleration: 0-50 mph (0-80 km/h) 12 sec; speed in direct drive at 1,000 rpm: 15.2 mph, 24.5 km/h; consumption: 31.4 m/imp gal, 26.1 m/US gal, 9 l x 100 km.

CHASSIS integral; front suspension: independent, wishbones, coil springs, anti-roll bar, telescopic dampers; rear: rigid axle, twin trailing radius arms, transverse linkage bar, coil springs, telescopic dampers.

STEERING worm and roller; turns lock to lock: 3.

BRAKES front disc (diameter 9.96 in, 25.3 cm), dual circuit, rear drum, rear compensator; lining area: front 20.9 sq in, 135 sq cm, rear 76.9 sq in, 496 sq cm, total 97.8 sq in, 631 sq cm.

ELECTRICAL EQUIPMENT 12 V; 55 Ah heavy-duty battery; 40 A alternator; R 125 distributor; 2 headlamps.

DIMENSIONS AND WEIGHT wheel base: 95.47 in, 242 cm; tracks: 52.76 in, 134 cm front, 51.38 in, 130 cm rear; length: Sedan 160.43 in, 407 cm - Combi 159.84 in, 406 cm; width: 63.43 in, 161 cm; height: Sedan 54.33 in, 138 cm - Combi 57.48 in, 146 cm; ground clearance: 6.69 in, 17 cm weight: Sedan 2,139 lb, 970 kg - Combi 2,227 lb, 1,010 kg; turning circle: 34.1 ft, 10.4 m; fuel tank: Sedan 8.6 imp gal, 10.3 US gal, 39 l - Combi 9.9 imp gal, 11.9 US gal, 45 l.

BODY saloon/sedan, estate car/st. wagon; 5 seats, separate front seats, reclining backrests, adjustable headrests.

68 hp power team

See 60 hp power team, except for:

ENGINE 79 cu in, 1,294 cc (3.11 x 2.60 in, 79 x 66 mm); max power (SAE): 68 hp (50 kW) at 5,400 rpm: max torque (SAE): 78 lb ft, 10.8 kg m (106 Nm) at 3,500 rpm; 52.6 hp/l (38.6 kW/l).

TRANSMISSION tyres: 155 x 13.

PERFORMANCE max speed: 92 mph, 148 km/h; power-weight ratio: 31.5 lb/hp (42.8 lb/kW), 14.3 kg/hp (19.4 kg/kW).

BODY vinyl roof; heated rear window; hazard lights.

75 hp power team

See 60 hp power team, except for:

ENGINE 88.6 cu in, 1,452 cc (2.99 x 3.15 in, 76 x 80 mm); max power (DIN): 75 hp (55 kW) at 5,600 rpm; max torque (DIN): 78 lb ft, 10.8 kg m (106 Nm) at 3,500 rpm; max engine rpm: 6,500; 51.6 hp/l (38 kW/l).

TRANSMISSION axle ratio: 4.100; width of rims: 5"; tyres: 165 SR x 13.

PERFORMANCE max speed: 93 mph, 150 km/h; power-weight ratio: 30.2 lb/hp (41.2 lb/kW), 13.7 kg/hp (18.7 kg/kW); acceleration: 0-50 mph (0-80 km/h) 10.7 sec.

BRAKES servo.

ELECTRICAL EQUIPMENT 53 A alternator; 4 headlamps.

75 HP POWER TEAM

DIMENSIONS AND WEIGHT wheel base: 94.88 in, 241 cm; tracks: 52.95 in, 135 cm front, 50.79 in, 129 cm rear; length: Sedan 162.20 in, 412 cm - st. wagon 159.84 in, 406 cm; height: st. wagon 55.12 in, 140 cm; ground clearance: 6.89 in, 17.5 cm; weight: 2,271 lb, 1,030 kg.

BODY (for 1500 ES 4+1-dr Combi only) heated rear window wiper-washer, vinyl roof and hazard lights.

78 hp power team

See 60 hp power team, except for:

ENGINE 95.7 cu in, 1,568 cc (3.11 x 3.15 in, 79 x 80 mm); max power (DIN): 78 hp (57 kW) at 5,200 rpm; max torque (DIN): 91 lb ft, 12.5 kg m (123 Nm) at 3,400 rpm; max engine rpm: 6,500 49.7 hp/l (36.6 kW/l).

TRANSMISSION axle ratio: 4.100; width of rims: 5''; tyres: 165 SR x 13.

PERFORMANCE max speed: 96 mph, 155 km/h; power-weight ratio: 29.1 lb/hp (39.5 lb/kW), 13.2 kg/hp (17.9 kg/kW).

BRAKES servo.

ELECTRICAL EQUIPMENT 53 A alternator; 4 headlamps.

DIMENSIONS AND WEIGHT tracks: 53.54 in, 136 cm front, 51.97 in, 132 cm rear; length: 161.81 in, 411 cm; ground clearance: 6.88 in, 17.5 cm; weight: 2,271 lb, 1,030 kg.

BODY (for 1600 ES 4-dr Sedan only) alloy sports wheels, vinyl roof and cloth upholstery.

Lada Niva 2121 4 x 4

PRICE IN GB: £ 4,273*

ENGINE front, 4 stroke; 4 cylinders, in line; 95.7 cu in, 1,568 cc (3.11 x 3.15 in, 79 x 80 mm); compression ratio: 8.5:1; max power (DIN): 78 hp (57 kW) at 5,400 rpm; max torque (DIN): 8 lb ft, 12.1 kg m (119 Nm) at 3,000 rpm; max engine rpm: 6,000; 49.7 hp/l (38.6 kW/l); cast iron block, light alloy head; 5 crankshaft bearings; valves: overhead, in line, rockers; camshafts: 1, overhead, chain-driven; lubrication: gear pump, full flow filter, 6.5 imp pt, 7.8 US pt, 3.7 l; 1 double Venturi multijet twin barrel carburettor; fuel feed: mechanical pump; sealed circuit cooling, water, 18.8 imp pt, 22.6 US pt, 10.7 l.

TRANSMISSION driving wheels: front and rear; clutch: single dry plate (diaphragm), hydraulically controlled; gearbox: mechanical; gears: 4 fully synchronized and 2-ratio transfer box; ratios: I 3.242, II 1.989, III 1.289, IV 1, rev 3.340; transfer box ratios: I 1.200, II 2.135; lever: central; final drive: hypoid bevel; axle ratio: 4.300; width of rims: 5''; tyres: 6.95/175 x 16.

PERFORMANCE max speeds: (I) 25 mph, 40 km/h; (II) 41 mph, 66 km/h; (III) 63 mph, 101 km/h; (IV) 82 mph, 132 km/h; power-weight ratio: 33.5 lb/hp (45.4 lb/kW), 15.2 kg/hp (20.6 kg/kW); carrying capacity: 882 lb, 400 kg; acceleration: standing ¼ mile 22.2 sec; consumption: about 25.9 m/imp gal, 21.6 m/US gal, 10.9 l x 100 km.

CHASSIS integral; front suspension: independent, wishbones, coil springs, anti-roll bar, telescopic double action dampers; rear: rigid axle, coil springs, transverse (Panhard) arm, 4 longitudinal arms, telescopic double action dampers.

STEERING worm and roller; turns lock to lock: 3.

BRAKES front disc (diameter 10.75 in, 27.3 cm), dual circuit, rear drum vacuum servo.

ELECTRICAL EQUIPMENT 12 V; 55 Ah heavy-duty battery; 42 A alternator; 2 headlamps.

DIMENSIONS AND WEIGHT wheel base: 86.61 in, 220 cm; tracks: 55.91 in, 142 cm front, 55.12 in, 140 cm rear; length: 146.06 in, 371 cm; width: 66.14 in, 168 cm; height: 64.57 in, 164 cm; ground clearance: 9.05 in, 23 cm; weight: 2,611 lb, 1,184 kg; weight distribution: 60% front, 40% rear; turning circle: 36 ft, 11 m; fuel tank: 9.9 imp gal, 11.9 US gal, 45 l.

BODY estate car/st. wagon; 2+1 doors; 5 seats, separate front seats, reclining backrests, adjustable headrests; heated rear window wiper-washer; impact absorbing bumpers.

PRACTICAL INSTRUCTIONS fuel: 93 oct petrol; oil: engine 6.5 imp pt, 7.8 US pt, 3.7 l, change every 6,000 miles, 9,700 km - gearbox 2.3 imp pt, 2.7 US pt, 1.3 l, change every 6,000 miles, 9,700 km - final drive 2.3 imp pt, 2.7 US pt, 1.3 l; tyre pressure: front 24 psi, 1.7 atm, rear 24 psi, 1.7 atm.

VAZ Lada 1600 ES Sedan

VAZ Lada Niva 2121 4 x 4

968-A

ENGINE rear, 4 stroke; 4 cylinders, Vee-slanted at 90°; 73 cu in, 1,196 cc (2.99 x 2.60 in, 76 x 66 mm); compression ratio 8.4:1; max power (DIN): 45 hp (33 kW) at 4,500 rpm; max torque (DIN): 59 lb ft, 8.2 kg m (80 Nm) at 3,200 rpm; max engine rpm: 4,600; 37.6 hp/l (27.6 kW/l); cast iron block, light alloy head; 3 crankshaft bearings; valves: overhead, push-rods and rockers; camshafts: 1, at centre of Vee; lubrication: gear pump, full flow filter, 5.8 imp pt, 7 US pt, 3.3 l; 1 K 12 downdraught carburettor; fuel feed: mechanical pump; air cooled.

TRANSMISSION driving wheels: rear; clutch: single dry plate hydraulically controlled; gearbox: mechanical; gears: 4, fully synchronized; ratios: I 3.800, II 2.120, III 1.410, IV 0.964, rev lever: 4.165; lever: central; final drive: hypoid bevel; axle ratio 4.125; tyres: 6.15 x 13 or 5.20/5.60 x 13 or 145 SR x 13.

PERFORMANCE max speed: 78 mph, 125 km/h; power-weight ratio: 38.7 lb/hp (52.6 lb/kW), 17.5 kg/hp (23.9 kg/kW); carrying capacity: 882 l, 400 kg; speed in top at 1,000 rpm: 16.5 mph 26.5 km/h; consumption: 35.3 m/imp gal, 29.4 m/US gal, l x 100 km.

CHASSIS integral; front suspension; independent, swinging longitudinal trailing arms, transverse torsion bars, telescopic dampers; rear: independent, semi-trailing arms, coil springs telescopic dampers.

STEERING worm and double roller.

BRAKES drum, dual circuit; lining area: total 78.9 sq in, 509 sq cm.

ELECTRICAL EQUIPMENT 12 V; 42 Ah battery; 250 W alternator; 2 headlamps.

DIMENSIONS AND WEIGHT wheel base: 85.04 in, 216 cm tracks: 48.03 in, 122 cm front, 47.24 in, 120 cm rear; length 146.85 in, 373 cm; width: 61.81 in, 157 cm; height: 55.12 in 140 cm; ground clearance: 7.48 in, 19 cm; weight: 1,742 lb, 79 kg; turning circle: 36.1 ft, 11 m; fuel tank: 6.6 imp gal, 7.9 US gal, 30 l.

BODY saloon/sedan; 2 doors; 5 seats, separate front seats front and rear reclining backrests; independent heating; anti theft; hazard lights.

OPTIONALS 155 SR x 13 tyres.

969-A 4 x 4

See 968-A, except for:

ENGINE front, 4 stroke; compression ratio: 7.2:1; max power (DIN): 38 hp (28 kW) at 4,400 rpm; 31.8 hp/l (23.4 kW/l).

TRANSMISSION driving wheels: front and rear; gears: 4, fully synchronized and low ratio; tyres: 5.90 x 13.

PERFORMANCE max speed: 56 mph, 90 km/h; power-weight ratio: 55.8 lb/hp (75.6 lb/kW), 25.3 kg/hp (34.3 kg/kW).

ZAZ 969-A 4 x 4

DIMENSIONS AND WEIGHT wheel base: 128.35 in, 326 cm; length: 227.56 in, 578 cm; weight: 6,395 lb, 2,900 kg; turning circle: 45.9 ft, 14 m.

BODY 5 seats.

ZCZ YUGOSLAVIA

Zastava 750 LC / M

ENGINE rear, 4 stroke; 4 cylinders, vertical, in line; 46.8 cu in, 767 cc (2.44 x 2.50 in, 62 x 63.5 mm); compression ratio: 7.5:1; max power (DIN): 25 hp (18 kW) at 4,600 rpm; max torque (DIN): 37 lb ft, 5.1 kg m (50 Nm) at 2,500 rpm; max engine rpm: 4,800; 32.6 hp /l (23.9 kW/l); cast iron block, light alloy head; 3 crankshaft bearings; valves: overhead, in line, push-rods and rockers; camshafts: 1, side; lubrication: gear pump, centrifugal filter, 6.5 imp pt, 7.8 US pt, 3.7 l; 1 IPM 28 MGV-10 downdraught single barrel carburettor; fuel feed: mechanical pump; water-cooled, 7.9 imp pt, 9.5 US pt, 4.5 l.

TRANSMISSION driving wheels: rear; clutch: single dry plate; gearbox: mechanical; gears: 4, II, III and IV synchronized; ratios: I 3,384, II 2.055, III 1.333, IV 0.869, rev 4.275; lever: central; final drive: spiral bevel; axle ratio: 4.875; width of rims: 3.5"; tyres: 5.20 x 12.

DIMENSIONS AND WEIGHT wheel base: 70.87 in, 180 cm; front and rear track: 51.97 in, 132 cm; length: 132.68 in, 337 cm; width: 63.39 in, 161 cm; height: 69.68 in, 177 cm; weight: ,117 lb, 960 kg.

BODY open.

ZIL USSR

114 Limousine

ENGINE front, 4 stroke; 8 cylinders, Vee-slanted; 424.8 cu in, ,962 cc (4.25 x 3.74 in, 108 x 95 mm); compression ratio: 9:1; max power (SAE): 300 hp (221 kW) at 4,400 rpm; max torque (SAE): 420 lb ft, 58 kg m (569 Nm) at 2,900 rpm; max engine rpm: 4,500; 43.1 hp/l (31.7 kW/l); cast iron block, light alloy head; 5 crankshaft bearings; valves: overhead, push-rods and rockers; camshafts: 1, at centre of Vee; lubrication: gear pump, full flow filter, 12.3 imp pt, 14.8 US pt, 7 l; 1 K 85 downdraught -barrel carburettor; fuel feed: electric pump; water-cooled, 9.9 imp pt, 48 US pt, 22.7 l.

TRANSMISSION driving: rear; gearbox: automatic transmission, hydraulic torque converter and planetary gears with 2 ratios, max ratio of converter at stall 2.5; ratios: I 1.720, II 1, rev 2.930; lever: push button control; final drive: hypoid bevel; axle ratio: 3.540; width of rims: 6.5"; tyres: 8.90 x 15 or .35 x 15.

PERFORMANCE max speed: 124 mph, 200 km/h; power-weight ratio: 23.4 lb/hp (31.7 lb/kW), 10.6 kg/hp (14.4 kg/kW); carrying capacity: 1,411 lb, 640 kg; consumption: 9.4 m/imp gal, 7.8 m/US gal, 30 l x 100 km.

CHASSIS box-type ladder frame and X cross members; front suspension: independent, wishbones, coil springs, anti-roll bar, lever dampers; rear: rigid axle, semi-elliptic laefsprings, telescopic dampers.

STEERING recirculating ball, servo; turns lock to lock: 4.30.

BRAKES disc, servo.

ELECTRICAL EQUIPMENT 12 V; 2 x 54 Ah batteries; 500 W dynamo; R-4 distributor; 4 headlamps; 2 fog lamps.

DIMENSIONS AND WEIGHT wheel base: 148.03 in, 376 cm; tracks: 61.81 in, 157 cm front, 63.78 in, 162 cm rear; length: 247.44 in, 628 cm; width: 81.50 in, 207 cm; height: 59.45 in, 151 cm; ground clearance: 7.09 in, 18 cm; weight: 7,001 lb, ,175 lg; turning circle: 52.4 ft, 16 m; fuel tank: 26.4 imp gal, 1.7 US gal, 120 l.

BODY limousine; 4 doors; 7 seats, separate front seats; air-conditioning; electric windows.

117 Limousine

See 114 Limuosine, except for:

PERFORMANCE power-weight ratio: 21.4 lb/hp (28.9 lb/kW), .7 kg/hp (13.1 kg/kW).

ZIL 114 Limousine

ZCZ Zastava 750 SC

ZASTAVA 750 LC / M

PERFORMANCE max speeds: (I) 19 mph, 30 km/h; (II) 28 mph, 45 km/h; (III) 43 mph, 70 km/h; (IV) 68 mph, 110 km/h; power-weight ratio: 54.2 lb/hp (73.7 lb/kW), 24.6 kg/hp (33.4 kg/kW); carrying capacity: 794 lb, 360 kg; acceleration: standing ¼ mile 26.7 sec, 0-50 mph (0-80 km/h) 24 sec; speed in top at 1,000 rpm: 14.1 mph, 22.7 km/h; consumption: 40.4 m/imp gal, 33.6 m/US gal, 7 l x 100 km.

CHASSIS integral; front suspension: independent, wishbones, transverse leafspring lower arms, telescopic dampers; rear: independent, oblique semi-trailing arms, coil springs, telescopic dampers.

STEERING screw and sector; turns lock to lock: 2.12.

BRAKES drum, single circuit; lining area: front 33.5 sq in, 216 sq cm, rear 33.5 sq in, 216 sq cm, total 67 sq in, 432 sq cm.

ELECTRICAL EQUIPMENT 12 V; 34 Ah battery; 230 W dynamo; Marelli distributor: 2 headlamps.

DIMENSIONS AND WEIGHT wheel base: 78.74 in, 200 cm; tracks: 45.28 in, 115 cm front, 45.67 in, 116 cm rear: length: 129.72 in, 329 cm; width: 54.25 in, 138 cm; height: 55.12 in, 140 cm; ground clearance: 5.71 in, 14.5 cm; weight: 1,334 lb, 605 kg; weight distribution: 46% front, 54% rear; turning circle: 28.5 ft, 8.7 m; fuel tank: 6.6 imp gal, 7.9 US gal, 30 l.

BODY saloon/sedan: 2 doors; 4 seats, separate front seats; folding rear seat; (for LC only) reclining backrests and luxury interior; (for M only) rear-hinged doors.

PRACTICAL INSTRUCTIONS fuel: 86 oct petrol; oil: engine 5.3 imp pt, 6.3 US pt, 3 l, SAE 10W-30 - change every 3,100 miles, 5,000 km - gearbox and final drive 2.6 imp pt, 3.2 US pt, 1.5 l, SAE 90, change every 12,400 miles, 20,000 km; tappet clearances (cold): inlet and exhaust 0.006 in, 0.15 mm valve timing: 4° 34° 29° 1°; tyre pressure: front 14 psi, 1 atm, rear 22 psi, 1.6 atm.

Zastava 750 SC

See Zastava 750 LC / M, except for:

ENGINE compression ratio: 8.5:1; max power (DIN): 30 hp (22 kW) at 5,400 rpm; max torque (DIN): 37 lb ft, 5.2 kg m (51 Nm) at 3,600 rpm; max engine rpm: 5,400; 39.1 hp/l (28.8 kW/l) 1 IMP 30 MGV-1 single barrel carburettor.

TRANSMISSION tyres: 145 SR x 12.

PERFORMANCE max speeds: (I) 20 mph, 32 km/h; (II) 33 mph, 53 km/h; (III) 51 mph, 82 km/h; (IV) 75 mph, 120 km/h; power-weight ratio: 47 lb/hp (63.8 lb/kW), 21.3 kg/hp (29 kg/kW).

DIMENSIONS AND WEIGHT weight: 1,411 lb, 640 kg.

PRACTICAL INSTRUCTIONS fuel: 98 oct petrol; tyre pressure: front 17 psi, 1.2 atm, rear 22 psi, 1.6 atm.

Zastava 101 B / Confort

ENGINE front, transverse, slanted 20° to front, 4 stroke; 4 cylinders, in line; 68.1 cu in, 1,116 cc (3.15 x 2.19 in, 80 x 55.5 mm); compression ratio: 9.2:1; max power (DIN): 55 hp (40 kW) at 6,000 rpm; max torque (DIN): 57 lb ft, 7.9 kg m (77 Nm) at 3,000 rpm; max engine rpm: 6,000; 49.3 hp/l (36.2 kW/l); cast iron block, light alloy head; 5 crankshaft bearings; valves overhead, thimble tappets; camshafts: 1, overhead; lubrication: gear pump (cartridge) 8.8 imp pt, 10.6 US pt, 5 l; 1 Weber 32 ICEV 14/250 or Solex C 32 DISA-41 or IMP 32 MGV-10 carburettor; fuel feed: mechanical pump; water-cooled, 11.4 imp pt, 13.7 US pt, 6.5 l, electric thermostatic fan.

TRANSMISSION driving wheels: front; clutch: single dry plate; gearbox: mechanical; gears: 4, fully synchronized; ratios: I 3.583, II 2,235, III 1.454, IV 1.042, rev 3.714; lever: central; final drive: cylindrical gears; axle ratio: 4.077; width of rims: 4.5"; tyres: 145 SR x 13.

PERFORMANCE max speeds: (I) 29 mph, 47 km/h; (II) 47 mph, 75 km/h; (III) 71 mph, 115 km/h; (IV) 84 mph, 135 km/h; power-weight ratio: 33.5 lb/hp (45.5 lb/kW), 15.2 kg/hp (20.7 kg/kW); carrying capacity: 992 lb, 450 kg; acceleration: standing ¼ mile 21 sec, 0-50 mph (0-80 km/h) 12.7 sec; speed in top at 1,000 rpm: 15.2 mph, 24.4 km/h; consumption: 33.2 ml/imp gal, 27.7 m/US gal, 8.5 l x 100 km.

CHASSIS integral; front suspension: independent, by McPherson, coil springs/telescopic dampers struts, lower wishbones, anti-roll bar; rear: independent, single widebased wishbones, transverse leafspring, telescopic dampers.

STEERING rack-and-pinion; turns lock to lock: 3.40.

BRAKES front disc (diameter 8.94 in, 22.7 cm) rear drum, rear compensator; lining area: front 19.2 sq in, 124 sq cm, rear 33.5 sq in, 216 sq cm, total 52.7 sq in, 340 sq cm.

ELECTRICAL EQUIPMENT 12 V; 34 Ah battery; 400 W alternator; Marelli distributor; 2 headlamps.

DIMENSIONS AND WEIGHT wheel base: 96.42 in, 245 cm tracks: 51.18 in, 130 cm front, 51.97 in, 132 cm rear; length: 151.18 in, 384 cm - Comfort 150.39 in, 382 cm; width: 62.60 in 159 cm; height: 53.94 in, 137 cm; ground clearance: 5.71 in 14.5 cm; weight: 1,841 lb, 835 kg; weight distribution: 61.5% front, 38.5% rear; turning circle: 33.8 ft, 10.3 m; fuel tank: 8.4 imp gal, 10 US gal, 38 l.

BODY saloon/sedan; 4+1 doors; 5 seats, separate front seats (for Comfort only) luxury equipment.

PRACTICAL INSTRUCTIONS fuel: 98 oct petrol; oil: engine 7.5 imp pt, 9 US pt, 4.2 l, SAE 10W-30 / SAE 20W-40, change every 3,100 miles, 5,000 km - gearbox and final drive 5.5 imp pt, 6.6 US pt, 3.1 l, HIP 90 CZ or UMOL 90 CZ (SAE 90) change every 12,400 miles, 20,000 km; tappet clearances (cold): inlet 0.015 in, 0.40 mm, exhaust 0.020 in, 0.50 mm; tyre pressure: front 26 psi, 1.8 atm, rear 24 psi, 1.7 atm.

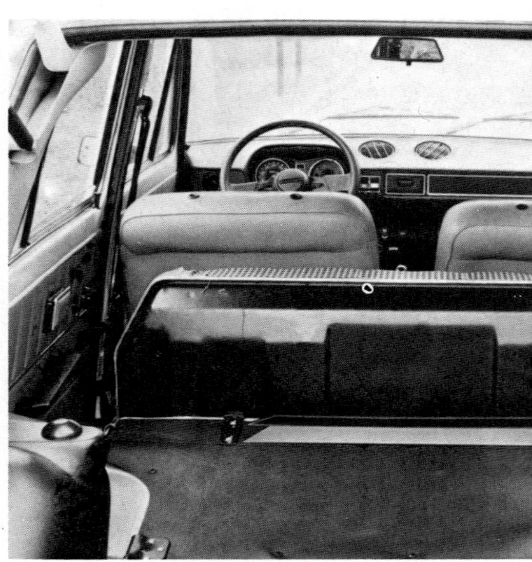

ZCZ Zastava 101 Confort

Zastava 101 SC

See Zastava 101 B / Confort, except for:

ENGINE max power (DIN): 64 hp (47 kW) at 6,000 rpm; max torque (DIN): 61 lb ft, 8.4 kg m (82 Nm) at 3,800 rpm; 57.3 hp/l (42.1 kW/l); 1 Weber 32 DMTR 32/250 carburettor.

PERFORMANCE max speed: 90 mph, 145 km/h; power-weight ratio: 29.5 lb/hp (40.1 lb/kW), 13.4 kg/hp (18.2 kg/kW); consumption: 29.4 m/imp gal, 24.7 m/US gal, 9.5 l x 100 km.

DIMENSIONS AND WEIGHT wheel base: 96.46 in, 245 cm; length: 149.21 in, 379 cm; weight: 1,887 lb, 856 kg

Zastava 101 Mediteran

See Zastava 101 B / Confort, except for:

DIMENSIONS AND WEIGHT length: 149.21 in, 379 cm.

VARIATIONS

ENGINE 78.7 cu in, 1,290 cc (3.39 x 2.19 in, 86 x 55.5 mm) max power (DIN) 73 hp (54 kW) at 6,000 rpm, 56.6 hp/l (41.7 kW/l), 1 Weber 32 DMTR 32/250 or Solex C 32 CIC 4 carburettor.
TRANSMISSION 165/70 SR x 13 tyres.
PERFORMANCE max speed 97 mph, 156 km/h, power-weight ratio 25.6 lb/hp (34.6 lb/kW), 11.6 kg/hp (15.7 kg/kW).
ELECTRICAL EQUIPMENT 45 Ah battery.
DIMENSIONS AND WEIGHT weight 1,874 lb, 850 kg.

Zastava 101 Special

See Zastava 101 B / Confort, except for:

ENGINE 78.7 cu in, 1,290 cc (3.39 x 2.19 in, 86 x 55.5 mm) max power (DIN): 73 (54 kW) at 6,000 rpm: 56.6 hp/l (41.7 kW/l); 1 Weber 32 DMTR 32/250 or Solex C 32 CIC 4 carburettor.

TRANSMISSION tyres: 165/70 SR x 13.

PERFORMANCE max speed: 97 mph, 156 km/h; power-weight ratio: 25.6 lb/hp (34.6 lb/kW), 11.6 kg/hp (15.7 kg/kW).

ELECTRICAL EQUIPMENT 45 Ah battery.

DIMENSIONS AND WEIGHT tracks: 52.36 in, 133 cm front 53.15 in, 135 cm rear; length: 149.21 in, 379 cm; weight: 1,87[illegible] lb, 850 kg.

ZCZ Zastava 101 Mediteran

The Americas

Models now in production

Illustrations and technical information

DODGE ARGENTINA

1500

PRICE EX WORKS: 14,100 pesos

ENGINE front, 4 stroke; 4 cylinders, vertical, in line; 91.4 cu in, 1,498 cc (3.39 x 2.53 in, 86.1 x 64.3 mm); compression ratio: 8:1; max power (SAE): 72 hp (54 kW) at 5,400 rpm; max torque (SAE): 88 lb ft, 12.2 kg m (119 Nm) at 3,200 rpm; max engine rpm: 5,400; 48 hp/l (35.3 kW/l); cast iron block and head; 5 crankshaft bearings; valves: overhead, in line, push-rods and rockers; camshafts: 1, side; lubrication: rotary pump, full flow filter, 7 imp pt, 8.5 US pt, 4 l; 1 Holley A-RX-7034A single barrel carburettor; fuel feed: mechanical pump; water-cooled, 13 imp pt, 15.6 US pt, 7.4 l.

TRANSMISSION driving wheels: rear; clutch: single dry plate (diaphragm); gearbox: mechanical; gears: 4, fully synchronized; ratios: I 3.317, II 2.029, III 1.366, IV 1, rev 3.450; lever: central; final drive: hypoid bevel; axle ratio: 3.890; width of rims: 5"; tyres: 5.60 x 13.

PERFORMANCE max speeds: (I) 29 mph, 46 km/h; (II) 48 mph, 77 km/h; (III) 71 mph, 114 km/h; (IV) 90 mph, 145 km/h; power-weight ratio: 28.2 lb/hp (38.3 lb/kW), 12.8 kg/hp (17.4 kg/kW); carrying capacity: 882 lb, 400 kg; acceleration: 0-50 mph (0-80 km/h) 9.5 sec; speed in direct drive at 1,000 rpm: 18.6 mph, 30 km/h; consumption: 25.7 m/imp gal, 21.4 m/US gal, 11 l x 100 km.

CHASSIS integral; front suspension: independent, by McPherson, lower trailing links, coil springs, anti-roll bar, telescopic dampers; rear: rigid axle, lower trailing radius arms, upper oblique torque arms, coil springs, telescopic dampers.

STEERING rack-and-pinion; turns lock to lock: 3.66

BRAKES front disc, rear drum; lining area: front 15.7 sq in, 101 sq cm, rear 53.5 sq in, 345 sq cm, total 69.2 sq in, 446 sq cm.

ELECTRICAL EQUIPMENT 12 V; 48 Ah battery; 32 A alternator; Chrysler-TRIA distributor; 2 headlamps.

DIMENSIONS AND WEIGHT wheel base: 97.99 in, 249 cm; tracks: 50.98 in, 129 cm front, 51.26 in, 130 cm rear; length: 162.99 in, 414 cm; width: 62.52 in, 159 cm; height: 53.15 in, 135 cm; ground clearance: 5.59 in, 14 cm; weight: 2,029 lb, 920 kg; weight distribution: 54.2% front, 45.8% rear; turning circle: 31.8 ft, 9.7 m; fuel tank: 9.9 imp gal, 11.9 US gal, 45 l.

BODY saloon/sedan; 4 doors; 5 seats, separate front seats, reclining backrests.

PRACTICAL INSTRUCTIONS fuel: 89-100 oct petrol; oil: engine 7 imp pt, 8.5 US pt, 4 l, change every 3,700 miles, 6,000 km - gearbox 3 imp pt, 3.6 US pt, 1.7 l - final drive 2.3 imp pt, 2.7 US pt, 1.3 l; greasing: 2 points; tyre pressure: front 24 psi, 1.7 atm, rear 26 psi, 1.8 atm.

OPTIONALS servo brake, dual circuit.

1500 M 1.8

PRICE EX WORKS: 16,000 pesos

ENGINE front, 4 stroke; 4 cylinders, vertical, in line; 109.7 cu in, 1,798 cc (3.39 x 3.04 in, 86.1 x 77.2 mm); compression ratio: 8.6:1; max power (SAE): 92 hp (69 kW) at 4,900 rpm; max torque (SAE): 116 lb ft, 16 kg m (157 Nm) at 3,400 rpm; max engine rpm: 5,800; 51.2 hp/l (37.7 kW/l); cast iron block and head; 5 crankshaft bearings; valves: overhead, in line, push-rods and rockers; camshafts: 1, side; lubrication: rotary pump, full flow filter, 7 imp pt, 8.5 US pt, 4 l; 1 Holley A-RX-7035A single barrel carburettor; fuel feed: mechanical pump; water-cooled, 13 imp pt, 15.6 US pt, 7.4 l.

TRANSMISSION driving wheels: rear; clutch: single dry plate (diaphragm); gearbox: mechanical; gears: 4, fully synchronized; ratios: I 3.317, II 2.029, III 1.366, IV 1, rev 3.450; lever: central; final drive: hypoid bevel; axle ratio: 3.890; width of rims: 5"; tyres: 5.60 x 13.

PERFORMANCE max speeds: (I) 31 mph, 50 km/h; (II) 47 mph, 75 km/h; (III) 78 mph, 125 km/h; (IV) 93 mph, 149 km/h; power-weight ratio: 22.9 lb/hp (31.1 lb/kW), 10.4 kg/hp (14.1 kg/kW); carrying capacity: 882 lb, 400 kg; acceleration: 0-50 mph (0-80 km/h) 9.5 sec; speed in direct drive at 1,000 rpm: 21.7 mph, 35 km/h; consumption: 31.4 m/imp gal, 26.1 m/US gal, 9 l x 100 km.

CHASSIS integral; front suspension: independent, by McPherson, lower trailing links, coil springs, anti-roll bar, telescopic dampers; rear: rigid axle, lower trailing radius arms, upper oblique torque arms, coil springs, telescopic dampers.

STEERING rack-and-pinion; turns lock to lock: 3.66.

BRAKES front disc, rear drum, servo, dual circuit; lining area: front 15.7 sq in, 101 sq cm, rear 53.5 sq in, 345 sq cm, total 69.2 sq in, 446 sq cm.

DODGE 1500

ELECTRICAL EQUIPMENT 12 V; 48 Ah battery; 32 A alternator; Chrysler-TRIA distributor; 2 iodine headlamps.

DIMENSIONS AND WEIGHT wheel base: 97.99 in, 249 cm; tracks: 50.98 in, 129 cm front, 51.26 in, 130 cm rear; length: 162.99 in, 414 cm; width: 62.52 in, 159 cm; height: 53.15 in, 135 cm; ground clearance: 5.59 in, 14 cm; weight: 2,110 lb, 957 kg; weight distribution 54.2% front, 45.8% rear; turning circle: 31.8 ft, 9.7 m; fuel tank: 9.9 imp gal, 11.9 US gal, 45 l.

BODY saloon/sedan; 4 doors; 5 seats, separate front seats, reclining backrests with built-in headrests.

PRACTICAL INSTRUCTIONS fuel: 89-100 oct petrol; oil: engine 7 imp pt, 8.5 US pt, 4 l, change every 3,700 miles, 6,000 km - gearbox 3 imp pt, 3.6 US pt, 1.7 l - final drive 2.3 imp pt, 2.7 US pt, 1.3 l; greasing: 2 points; tyre pressure: front 24 psi, 1.7 atm, rear 26 psi, 1.8 atm.

OPTIONALS Borg-Warner 45 automatic transmission: 155 x 13 tyres: heated rear window.

1500 M 1.8 Rural

See 1500 M 1.8, except for:

PRICE EX WORKS: 17,500 pesos

PERFORMANCE power-weight ratio: 24.4 lb/hp (32.6 lb/kW) 11.1 kg/hp (14.8 kg/kW).

CHASSIS rear suspension: 4 swinging links.

DIMENSIONS AND WEIGHT length: 165.35 in, 420 cm height: 53.54 in, 136 cm; weight: 2,250 lb, 1,021 kg; weight distribution: 45.8% front, 54.2% rear.

BODY estate car/st. wagon; 4+1 doors.

FIAT ARGENTINA

600 S

ENGINE rear, 4 stroke; 4 cylinders, vertical, in line; 51.4 cu in, 843 cc (2.56 x 2.50 in, 65 x 63.5 mm); compression ratio: 7.4:1; max power (DIN): 32 hp (24 kW) at 4,800 rpm; max torque (DIN): 38 lb ft, 5.2 kg m (51 Nm) at 3,000 rpm; max engine rpm: 5,000; 37.9 hp/l (28.5 kW/l); cast iron block, light alloy head; 3 crankshaft bearings; valves: overhead, in line, pushrods and rockers; camshafts: 1, side; lubrication: gear pump, full flow filter (cartridge), 6.5 imp pt, 7.8 US pt, 3.7 l; 1 Galileo 281 CP 10 or Bressel 28 IGP 10 downdraught single barrel carburettor; fuel feed: mechanical pump; sealed circuit cooling, liquid, 10.8 imp pt, 12.7 US pt, 6 l.

TRANSMISSION driving wheels: rear; clutch: single dry plate; gearbox: mechanical; gears: 4, fully synchronized; ratios: I 3.385, II 2.055, III 1.333, IV 0.896, rev 4.275; lever: central; final drive: spiral bevel; axle ratio: 4.875; width of rims: 4"; tyres: 5.20 x 12.

DODGE 1500 M 1.8 Rural

ERFORMANCE max speeds: (I) 19 mph, 30 km/h; (II) 28 mph, 5 km/h; (III) 43 mph, 70 km/h; (IV) 68 mph, 110 km/h; ower-weight ratio: 43 lb/hp (57.4 lb/kW), 19.5 kg/hp (26 kg/ W); carrying capacity: 706 lb, 320 kg; acceleration: standing 4 mile 26.7 sec, 0-50 mph (0-80 km/h) 26 sec; speed in top at ,000 rpm: 14.1 mph, 22.7 km/h; consumption: 48.7 m/imp gal, 0.6 m/US gal, 5.8 l x 100 km.

HASSIS integral; front suspension: independent, upper swing- ng arms, anti-roll bar, telescopic dampers; rear: independent, winging arms, coil springs, telescopic dampers.

TEERING screw and sector; turns lock to lock: 2.26.

RAKES drum; lining area: front 33.5 sq in, 216 sq cm, rear 3.5 sq in, 216 sq cm, total 67 sq in, 432 sq cm.

LECTRICAL EQUIPMENT 12 V; 32 Ah battery; 475 W alterna- or; Garef-Marelli distributor; 2 headlamps.

IMENSIONS AND WEIGHT wheel base: 78.74 in, 200 cm; acks: 45.28 in, 115 cm front, 45.67 in, 116 cm rear; length: 31.89 in, 335 cm; width: 54.33 in, 138 cm; height: 55.12 in, 40 cm; ground clearance: 5.71 in, 14.5 cm; weight: 1,378 lb, 25 kg; weight distribution: 46% front, 54% rear; turning circle: 9.5 ft, 9 m; fuel tank: 5.9 imp gal, 7.1 US gal, 27 l.

ODY saloon/sedan; 2 doors; 4 seats, separate front seats.

RACTICAL INSTRUCTIONS fuel: 90 oct petrol; oil: engine 5.3 np pt, 6.3 US pt, 3 l, SAE 20W-40, change every 3,100 miles, 000 km - gearbox 2.6 imp pt, 3.2 US pt, 1.5 l, SAE 90 EP, hange every 18,600 miles, 30,000 km; tappet clearances: inlet 006 in, 0.15 mm, exhaust 0.006 in, 0.15 mm; valve timing: 4° 5° 29° 1°; tyre pressure: front 14 psi, 1 atm, rear 23 psi, 1.6 m.

FIAT 600 S

FIAT 133 B

133 B

NGINE rear, longitudinal, 4 stroke; 4 cylinders, vertical, in ne; 55.1 cu in, 903 cc (2.56 x 2.68 in, 65 x 68 mm); compress- n ratio: 7.8:1; max power (DIN): 37 hp (27 kW) at 5,600 rpm; ax torque (DIN): 42 lb ft, 5.8 kg m (57 Nm) at 3,400 rpm; 41 p/l (30 k/l); cast iron block, light alloy head; 3 crankshaft earings; valves: overhead, in line, push-rods and rockers; amshafts: 1, side; lubrication: gear pump, full flow filter (car- idge) 6.5 imp pt, 7.8 US pt, 3.7 l; 1 Weber 30 ICF 19 vertical ngle barrel carburettor; exhaust gas recirculation; fuel feed: echanical pump; water-cooled, 13.2 imp pt, 15.9 US pt, 7.5 l.

RANSMISSION driving wheels: rear; clutch: single dry plate iaphragm); gearbox: mechanical; gears: 4, fully synchronized; tios: I 3.636, II 2.055, III 1.409, IV 0.963, rev 3.165; lever: entral; final drive: hypoid bevel; axle ratio: 4.625; width of ms: 4.5"; tyres: 145 x 13.

ERFORMANCE max speeds: (I) 22 mph, 35 km/h; (II) 39 mph, 2 km/h; (III) 57 mph, 91 km/h; (IV) 76 mph, 123 km/h; ower-weight ratio: 42.3 lb/hp (58 lb/kW), 19.18 kg/hp (26.2 /kW); carrying capacity: 706 lb, 320 kg; consumption: 40.9 /imp gal, 34.1 m/US gal, 6.9 l x 100 km.

HASSIS integral; front suspension: independent, wishbones, ansverse leafsprings lower arms, transverse torsion bar, anti- ll bar, telescopic dampers; rear: independent, semi-trailing arms, coil springs, torsion bar, anti-roll bar, telescopic dampers.

STEERING screw and sector; turns lock to lock: 2.26.

BRAKES front disc, rear drum.

ELECTRICAL EQUIPMENT 12 V; 34 Ah battery; 475 W alternator; 2 headlamps.

DIMENSIONS AND WEIGHT wheel base: 79.53 in, 202 cm; tracks: 45.28 in, 115 cm front, 47.64 in, 121 cm rear; length: 137.40 in, 349 cm; width: 55.91 in, 142 cm; height: 52.36 in, 133 cm; ground clearance: 5.51 in, 14 cm; weight: 1,566 lb, 710 kg; weight distribution: 46% front, 54% rear; turning circle: 31.5 ft, 9.6 m; fuel tank: 6.6 imp gal, 7.9 US gal, 30 l.

BODY saloon/sedan; 2 doors; 4 seats, separate front seats.

PRACTICAL INSTRUCTIONS fuel: 90 oct petrol; oil: engine 5.8 imp pt, 6.9 US pt, 3.3 l, SAE 20W-40, change every 3,100 miles, 5,000 km - gearbox: 3.7 imp pt, 4.4 US pt, 2.1 l, SAE 90 EP, change every 18,600 miles, 30,000 km; greasing: none; tappet clearances: inlet 0.006 in, 0.15 mm, exhaust 0.008 in, 0.20 mm; valve timing: 25° 51° 64° 12°; tyre pressure: front 20 psi, 1.4 atm, rear 28 psi, 2 atm.

133 L

See 133 B, except for:

ENGINE compression ratio: 8.4:1; max power (DIN): 40 hp (29 kW) at 5,600 rpm; max torque (DIN): 43 lb ft, 6 kg m (59 Nm) at 3,600 rpm 44.3 hp/l (32.6 kW/l).

PERFORMANCE max speeds: (I) 22 mph, 36 km/h; (II) 40 mph, 65 km/h; (III) 59 mph, 95 km/h; (IV) 81 mph, 130 km/h; power-weight ratio: 39 lb/hp (54 lb/kW), 17.7 kg/hp (24.5 kg/kW).

133 T

See 133 B, except for:

ENGINE compression ratio: 9.39:1; max power (DIN): 50 hp (37 kW) at 6,500 rpm; max torque (DIN): 51 lb ft, 7 kg m (68 Nm) at 3,500 rpm; 55.4 hp/l (41 kW/l).

TRANSMISSION width of rims: 5.5".

PERFORMANCE max speeds: (I) 28 mph, 45 km/h; (II) 48 mph, 78 km/h; (III) 70 mph, 112 km/h; (IV) 84 mph, 135 km/h; power-weight ratio: 31.5 lb/hp (43.8 lb/kW), 14.3 kg/hp (19.8 kg/kW).

ELECTRICAL EQUIPMENT 4 headlamps.

DIMENSIONS AND WEIGHT tracks: 46.46 in, 118 cm front, 48.82 in, 124 cm rear; weight: 1,577 lb, 715 kg.

PRACTICAL INSTRUCTIONS fuel: 92 oct petrol; tappet clearances: inlet 0.008 in, 0.20 mm, exhaust 0.010 in, 0.25 mm; valve timing: 20° 46° 60° 6°.

128 C

ENGINE front, transverse, 4 stroke; 4 cylinders, in line; 68.1 cu in, 1,116 cc (3.15 x 2.19 in, 80 x 55.5 mm); compression ratio: 8.8:1; max power (DIN): 62 hp (46 kW) at 6,000 rpm; max torque (DIN): 59 lb ft, 8.1 kg m (79 Nm) at 3,000 rpm; max engine rpm: 6,000; 49.2 hp/l (41.2 kW/l); cast iron block, light alloy head; 5 crankshaft bearings; valves: overhead, thimble tappets; camshafts: 1, overhead, cogged belt; lubrication: gear pump, full flow filter (cartridge) 7.9 imp pt, 9.5 US pt, 5 l; 1 Weber 32 ICEV 14 or Solex C 32 DISA 24 downdraught single barrel carburettor; fuel feed: mechanical pump; water-cooled, 11.4 imp pt, 13.7 US pt, 6.5 l, electric thermostatic fan.

TRANSMISSION driving wheels: front; clutch: single dry plate; gearbox: mechanical; gears: 4, fully synchronized; ratios: I 3.583, II 2.235, III 1.454, IV 1.042, rev 3.714; lever: central; final drive: cylindrical gears; axle ratio: 4.077; width of rims: 4.5"; tyres: 145 SR x 13.

PERFORMANCE max speeds: (I) 28 mph, 45 km/h; (II) 47 mph, 75 km/h; (III) 71 mph, 115 km/h; (IV) 87 mph, 140 km/h; power-weight ratio: 28.7 lb/hp (38.6 lb/kW), 13 kg/hp (17.5 kg/kW); carrying capacity: 882 lb, 400 kg; acceleration: standing 1/4 mile 19.7 sec, 0-50 mph (0-80 km/h) 11.6 sec; speed in top at 1,000 rpm: 15.2 mph, 24.4 km/h; consumption: 35.3 m/imp gal, 29.4 m/US gal, 8 l x 100 km.

CHASSIS integral; front suspension: independent, by McPherson, coil springs/telescopic damper struts, lower wishbones, anti-roll bar; rear: independent, single widebased wishbones, transverse anti-roll leafsprings, telescopic dampers.

STEERING rack-and-pinion; turns lock to lock: 3.40.

BRAKES front disc (diameter 8.94 in, 22.7 cm), rear drum, rear compensator, servo; lining area: front 19.2 sq in, 124 sq cm, rear 33.5 sq in, 216 sq cm, total 52.7 sq in, 340 sq cm.

ELECTRICAL EQUIPMENT 12 V; 34 Ah battery; 38 A alternator; Garef-Marelli distributor; 2 headlamps.

128 C

DIMENSIONS AND WEIGHT wheel base: 96.06 in, 244 cm; front and rear track: 51.57 in, 131 cm; length: 152.76 in, 388 cm; width: 62.60 in, 159 cm; height: 55.91 in, 142 cm; ground clearance: 7.60 in, 19.3 cm; weight: 1,775 lb, 805 kg; weight distribution: 61.5% front, 38.5% rear; turning circle: 33.8 ft, 10.3 m; fuel tank: 8.4 imp gal, 10 US gal, 38 l.

BODY saloon/sedan; 4 doors; 5 seats, separate front seats.

PRACTICAL INSTRUCTIONS fuel: 92 oct petrol; oil: engine 7 imp pt, 8.4 US pt, 4 l, SAE 20W-40, change every 3,100 miles, 5,000 km - gearbox 5.6 imp pt, 6.7 US pt, 3.2 l, SAE 90 EP, change every 18,600 miles, 30,000 km; valve timing: 12° 52° 52° 12°; tyre pressure: front 25 psi, 1.8 atm, rear 24 psi, 1.7 atm.

128 CL

See 128 C, except for:

ENGINE 78.7 cu in, 1,290 cc (3.39 x 2.19 in, 86 x 55.5 mm); compression ratio: 8.9:1; max power (DIN): 70 hp (51 kW) at 6,000 rpm; max torque (DIN): 72 lb ft, 10 kg m (98 Nm) at 3,000 rpm; 54.3 hp/l (39.5 kW/l); 1 Weber 32 ICEV 10 downdraught single barrel carburettor.

TRANSMISSION tyres: 155 SR x 13.

PERFORMANCE max speeds: (I) 28 mph, 45 km/h; (II) 47 mph, 75 km/h; (III) 73 mph, 118 km/h; (IV) over 90 mph, 145 km/h; power-weight ratio: 26.1 lb/hp, (36.1 lb/kW), 11.9 kg/hp (16.4 kg/kW); speed in top at 1,000 rpm: 15.5 mph, 25 km/h; consumption: 33.2 m/imp gal, gal, 27.7 m/US gal, 8.5 l x 100 km.

STEERING turns lock to lock: 3.50.

DIMENSIONS AND WEIGHT weight: 1,841 lb, 835 kg; turning circle: 35.8 ft, 10.9 m.

BODY luxury equipment; reclining front seats.

128 1300 TV lava

See 128 C, except for:

ENGINE 78.7 cu in, 1,290 cc (3.39 x 2.19 in, 86 x 55.5 mm); compression ratio: 9.3:1; max power (DIN): 90 hp (66 kW) at 6,750 rpm; max torque (DIN): 72 lb ft, 10 kg m (98 Nm) at 3,000 rpm; max engine rpm: 7,000; 69.8 hp/l (51.2 kW/l); 1 Solex C 34 EIES downdraught twin barrel carburettor; exhaust gas recirculation.

TRANSMISSION width of rims: 5"; tyres: 155 SR x 13.

PERFORMANCE max speed: over 99 mph, 160 km/h; power-weight ratio: 20.5 lb/hp (28 lb/kW), 9.3 kg/hp (12.7 kg/kW); speed in top at 1,000 rpm: 15.5 mph, 25 km/h; consumption: 33.2 m/imp gal, 27.7 m/US gal, 8.5 l x 100 km.

STEERING turns lock to lock: 3.50.

DIMENSIONS AND WEIGHT tracks: 52.76 in, 134 cm front, 53.15 in, 135 cm rear; weight: 1,841 lb, 835 kg; turning circle: 35.8 ft, 10.9 m.

BODY luxury equipment; reclining front seats.

FIAT 128 C

128 CLF

See 128 C, except for:

ENGINE 78.7 cu in, 1,290 cc (3.39 x 2.19 in, 86 x 55.5 mm); compression ratio: 8.9:1; max power (DIN): 70 hp (51 kW) at 6,000 rpm; max torque (DIN): 72 lb ft, 10 kg m (98 Nm) at 3,000 rpm; 54.3 hp/l (39.5 kW/l); 1 Weber 32 ICEV 10 downdraught single barrel carburettor.

TRANSMISSION tyres: 155 SR x 13.

PEFORMANCE max speed: over 90 mph, 145 km/h; power-weight ratio: 26.9 lb/hp (36.9 lb/kW), 12.2 kg/hp (16.8 kg/kW); acceleration: standing ¼ mile 20 sec. 0-50 mph (0-80 km/h) 12 sec.

STEERING turns lock to lock: 3.50.

DIMENSIONS AND WEIGHT length: 153.15 in, 389 cm; weight: 1,885 lb, 855 kg; weight distribution: 60% front, 40% rear; turning circle: 35.8 ft, 10.9 m.

BODY estate car/st. wagon; 4+1 doors; 5 seats, separate front seats, reclining backrests; folding rear seats; luxury equipment.

FIAT 125 S

125 BN / T

ENGINE front, 4 stroke; 4 cylinders, vertical, in line; 98.1 cu i 1,608 cc (3.15 x 3.15 in, 80 x 80 mm); compression ratio: 7.7: max power (DIN): 100 hp (74 kW) at 6,200 rpm; max torqu (DIN): 96 lb ft, 13.3 kg m (130 Nm) at 4,000 rpm; max engin rpm: 6,200; 62 hp/l (46 kW/l); cast iron block, light alloy head; crankshaft bearings; valves: ovehead; camshafts: 2, overhea cogged belt; lubrication: gear pump, full flow filter, 8.6 imp p 10.4 US pt, 4.9 l; 1 Weber 34 DCHE 21 or Solex C34 PAIA/3 downdraught twin barrel carburettor; exhaust gas recirculatio fuel feed: mechanical pump; water-cooled, 13.2 imp pt, 15. US pt, 7.5 l, electric thermostatic fan.

TRANSMISSION driving wheels: rear; clutch: single dry plat gearbox: mechanical; gears: 4, fully synchronized; ratios: 3.670, II 2.110, III 1.360, IV 1, rev 3.570; lever: central; fin drive: hypoid bevel; axle ratio: 3.900; width of rims: 5"; tyre 175 S x 13.

PERFORMANCE max speeds: (I) 28 mph, 45 km/h; (II) 50 mp 80 km/h; (III) 78 mph, 125 km/h; (IV) 106 mph, 170 km/ power-weight ratio: 23.1 lb/hp (31.4 lb/kW), 10.5 kg/hp (14. kg/kW); carrying capacity: 882 lb, 400 kg; acceleration: stan ing ¼ mile 18.6 sec, 0-50 mph (0-80 km/h) 9 sec; speed direct drive at 1,000 rpm: 17.5 mph, 28.2 km/h; consumptio 28.5 m/imp gal, 23.8 m/US gal, 9.9 l x 100 km.

CHASSIS integral; front suspension: independent, wishbone coil springs, anti-roll bar, telescopic dampers; rear: rigid axl upper torque arms, semi-elliptic leafsprings, telescopic dam pers.

STEERING worm and roller.

BRAKES front disc, rear drum, servo.

ELECTRICAL EQUIPMENT 12 V; 48 Ah battery; 550 W altern tor; Garef-Marelli distributor; 2 headlamps.

DIMENSIONS AND WEIGHT wheel base: 98.82 in, 251 cr tracks: 51.57 in, 131 cm front, 50.79 in, 129 cm rear; lengt 167.32 in, 144 cm; width: 63.39 in, 161 cm; height: 56.69 i 144 cm; ground clearance: 7.28 in, 18.5 cm; weight: 2,326 l 1,055 kg; weight distribution: 58% frnt, 42% rear; turning circl 35.4 ft, 10.8 m; fuel tank: 9.9 imp gal, 11.9 US gal, 45 l.

BODY saloon/sedan; 4 doors; 5 seats, separate front seat reclining backrests.

PRACTICAL INSTRUCTIONS fuel: 90 oct petrol; oil: engine 6 imp pt, 7.4 US pt, 3.5 l, SAE 20W-40, change every 3,1 miles, 5,000 km - gearbox 2.5 imp pt, 2.9 US pt, 1.4 l, SAE EP, change every 18,600 miles, 30,000 km - final drive 2.6 in pt, 3.2 US pt, 1.5 l, SAE 90 EP, change every 18,600 mile 30,000 km; greasing: none; tappet clearances: inlet 0.018 i 0.45 mm, exhaust 0.020 in, 0.50 mm; valve timing: 26° 66° 6 26°; tyre pressure: front 21 psi, 1.5 atm, rear 24 psi, 1.7 atn

OPTIONALS 175 SR x 13 tyres with 5.5" wide rims.

125 S

See 125 BN / T, except for:

ENGINE compression ratio: 8.8:1; valves: side; camshafts: side; 1 Solex C 34 EIES downdraught twin barrel carburetto

BRAKES servo.

ELECTRICAL EQUIPMENT 4 headlamps.

125 SL

ȷee 125 BN / T, except for:

:NGINE compression ratio: 9:1; max power (DIN): 110 hp (81 W) at 6,200 rpm; 68.4 hp/l (50.3 kW/l); valves: side; camhafts: 2, side; 1 Solex C 34 EIES downdraught twin barrel arburettor.

RANSMISSION tyres: 185/70 HR x 13.

'ERFORMANCE power-weight ratio: 21.1 lb/hp (28.7 lb/kW), .6 kg/hp (13 kg/kW).

RAKES servo.

LECTRICAL EQUIPMENT 4 headlamps.

RACTICAL INSTRUCTIONS tappet clearances: inlet 0.018 in, .45 mm, exhaust 0.024 in, 0.60 mm; valve timing: 24° 66° 64° 6°.

125 SF

ee 125 BN / T, except for:

NGINE compression ratio: 8.8:1; valves: side; camshafts: 2, de; 1 Solex C 34 EIES downdraught twin barrel carburettor.

ERFORMANCE power-weight ratio: 24 lb/hp (27.6 lb/kW), 0.9 kg/hp (14.7 kg/kW); acceleration: standing ¼ mile 19 sec, -50 mph (0-80 km/h) 9.5 sec.

RAKES servo.

LECTRICAL EQUIPMENT 4 headlamps.

IMENSIONS AND WEIGHT length: 168.11 in, 427 cm; weight: ,043 lb, 1,090 kg; weight distribution: 50% front, 50% rear.

ODY estate car/st. wagon; 4+1 doors; 5 seats, separate front eats, reclining backrests; folding rear seat.

'ORD ARGENTINA

Taunus L 2000 Sedan / GXL Sedan

RICES EX WORKS:	pesos
aunus L 2000 Sedan	14,100
aunus GXL Sedan	—

NGINE front, 4 stroke; 4 cylinders, in line; 121.4 cu in, ,990 cc (3.52 x 3.13 in, 89.3 x 79.4 mm); compression atio: 8:1; max power (SAE): 92 hp (68 kW) at 5,500 rpm; ax torque (SAE): 109 lb ft, 15.1 kg m (148 Nm) at 3,000 om; max engine rpm: 6,000 46.2 hp/l (34 kW/l); cast iron lock and head; 5 crankshaft bearings; valves: overhead, ush-rods and rockers; camshafts: 1, overhead, cogged elt; lubrication: gear pump, full flow filter, 7.9 imp pt, 9.5 S pt, 4.5 l; 1 Galileo Argentina downdraught single barrel arburettor; fuel feed: mechanical pump; water-cooled, 13.9 np pt, 16.7 US pt, 7.9 l.

FORD Taunus L 2000 Sedan

TRANSMISSION driving wheels: rear; clutch: single dry plate; gearbox: mechanical; gears: 4, fully synchronized; ratios: I 3.360, II 1.810, III 1.260, IV 1, rev 3.360; lever: central; final drive: hypoid bevel; axle ratio: 3.540; width of rims: 5.5''; tyres: 6.95 S x 13.

PERFORMANCE max speed: 95 mph, 153 km/h; power-weight ratio: 27.1 lb/hp (36.8 lb/kW), 12.3 kg/hp (16.7 kg/kW); speed in direct drive at 1,000 rpm: 18.5 mph, 29.7 km/h; consumption: 26.6 m/imp gal, 22.2 m/US gal, 10.6 l x 100 km.

CHASSIS integral; front suspension: independent, wishbones, coil springs/telescopic dampers, anti-roll bar; rear: rigid axle lower trailing arms, upper oblique trailing arms, coil springs, telescopic dampers.

STEERING rack-and-pinion.

BRAKES front disc (diameter 9.75 in, 24.8 cm), rear drum; lining area: front 28.5 sq in, 184 sq cm, rear 59.8 sq in, 386 sq cm, total 88.3 sq in, 570 sq cm.

ELECTRICAL EQUIPMENT 12 V; 45 Ah battery; 540 W alternator; 2 headlamps.

DIMENSIONS AND WEIGHT wheel base: 101.57 in, 258 cm; front and rear track: 55.91 in, 142 cm; length: 171.26 in, 435 cm; width: 66.93 in, 170 cm; height: 52.76 in, 134 cm; ground clearance: 4.61 in, 11.7 cm; weight: 2,496 lb, 1,132 kg; turning circle: 35.1 ft, 10.7 m; fuel tank: 11.9 imp gal, 14.3 US gal, 54 l.

FORD Taunus GT Coupé

BODY saloon/sedan; 4 doors; 5 seats; (for GXL only) luxury equipment.

OPTIONALS servo brake; 175 SR x 13 tyres; anti-roll bar on rear suspension.

Taunus GXL 2300 Sedan / GT Coupé

See Taunus L 2000 Sedan / GXL Sedan, except for:

PRICES EX WORKS:	pesos
Taunus GXL 2300 Sedan	17,600
Taunus GT Coupé	20,100

ENGINE 140.3 cu in, 2,299 cc (3.78 x 3.13 in, 96 x 79.4 mm); compression ratio: 9:1; max power (SAE): 122 hp (90 kW) at 5,000 rpm; max torque (SAE): 142 lb ft, 19.6 kg m 192 Nm) at 3,500 rpm; max engine rpm: 5,500; 53 hp/l (39 kW/l); 1 Argelite downdraught twin barrel carburettor; cooling: 13.7 imp pt, 16.5 US pt, 7.8 l.

PERFORMANCE max speed: 106 mph, 170 km/h; power-weight ratio: 20.5 lb/hp (27.8 lb/kW), 9.3 kg/hp (12.6 kg/kW); consumption: 28.5 m/imp gal, 23.8 m/US gal, 9.9 l x 100 km.

ELECTRICAL EQUIPMENT 38 A alternator.

DIMENSIONS AND WEIGHT height: Coupé 51.97 in, 132 cm

BODY saloon/sedan, 4 doors - coupé, 2 doors; 5 seats; (for GXL only) luxury equipment.

OPTIONALS automatic transmission with 3 ratios (I 2.470, II 1.470, III 1); 3.310 axle ratio; air-conditioning.

Taunus GT Coupé SP

See Taunus L 2000 Sedan / GXL Sedan, except for:

ENGINE 140.3 cu in, 2,999 cc (3.78 x 3.13 in, 96 x 79.4 mm); compression ratio: 9:1; max power (SAE): 132 hp (97 kW) at 5,500 rpm; max torque (SAE): 147 lb ft, 20.3 kg m (199 Nm) at 3,500 rpm; max engine rpm: 6,000; 44 hp/l (32.3 kW/l); 1 Argelite downdraught twin barrel carburettor; cooling: 13.7 imp pt, 16.5 US pt, 7.8 l.

PERFORMANCE max speed: 106 mph, 170 km/h; power-weight ratio: 18.9 lb/hp, (25.7 lb/kW), 8.6 kg/hp (11.7 kg/kW); consumption: 28.5 m/imp gal, 23.8 m/US gal, 9.9 l x 100 km.

ELECTRICAL EQUIPMENT 38 A alternator.

DIMENSIONS AND WEIGHT height: 51.97 in, 132 cm.

BODY coupé; 2 doors.

OPTIONALS automatic transmission with 3 ratios (I 2.470, II 1.470, III 1), 3.310 axle ratio; air-conditioning.

Fairlane LTD 3600 Sedan

ENGINE front, 4 stroke; 6 cylinders, in line; 221 cu in, 3,620 cc (3.68 x 3.46 in, 93.5 x 87.9 mm); compression ratio: 8.2:1; max power (SAE): 132 hp (97 kW) at 4,000 rpm; max torque (SAE): 201 lb ft, 27.8 kg m (273 Nm) at 1,800 rpm; 36.6 hp/l (26.9 kW/l); cast iron block and head; 7 crankshaft

FORD Fairlane LTD-V8 Sedan

FAIRLANE LTD 3600 SEDAN

bearings; valves: overhead, push-rods and rockers; camshafts: 1, side, timing chain; lubrication: gear pump, full flow filter, 7.9 imp pt, 9.5 US pt, 4.5 l; 1 Argelite downdraught twin barrel carburettor; fuel feed: mechanical pump; water-cooled, 14.7 imp pt, 17.6 US pt, 8.3 l.

TRANSMISSION driving wheels: rear; clutch: single dry plate; gearbox: mechanical; gears: 3, fully synchronized; ratios: I 2.990, II 1.750, III 1, rev 3.170; lever: steering column; axle ratio: 3.310; tyres: 7.35 x 14.

PERFORMANCE max speed: 96 mph, 154 km/h; power-weight ratio: 25.9 lb/hp (35.2 lb/kW), 11.7 kg/hp (15.9 kg/kW); acceleration: standing ¼ mile 20 sec, 0-50 mph (0-80 km/h) 10.5 sec; consumption: 19.4 m/imp gal, 16.2 m/US gal, 14.5 l x 100 km.

CHASSIS integral; front suspension: independent, coil springs, anti-roll bar; telescopic dampers; rear: rigid axle, long leafsprings, telescopic dampers.

STEERING recirculating ball; servo.

BRAKES front disc (diameter 10.90 in, 27.7 cm), rear drum, servo; lining area: front 28 sq in, 181 sq cm, rear 85 sq in, 548 sq cm, total 113 sq in, 729 sq cm.

ELECTRICAL EQUIPMENT 12 V; 55 Ah battery; 725 W alternator; 4 headlamps.

DIMENSIONS AND WEIGHT wheel base: 116 in, 295 cm; front and rear track: 58.50 in, 149 cm length: 205 in, 520 cm; width: 74.80 in, 190 cm; height: 55 in, 140 cm; ground clearance: 6.70 in, 17 cm; weight: 3,418 lb, 1,550 kg; fuel tank: 16.5 imp gal, 19.8 US gal, 75 l.

BODY saloon/sedan; 4 doors; 5 seats.

OPTIONALS air-conditioning; twin drive rear axle; "Elite" luxury equipment.

Fairlane LTD-V8 Sedan

See Fairlane LTD 3600 Sedan, except for:

PRICE EX WORKS: 24,300 pesos

ENGINE 8 cylinders, Vee-slanted; 292 cu in, 4,785 cc (3.75 x 3.30 in, 95.2 x 83.8 mm); compression ratio: 8:1; max power (SAE): 180 hp (132 kW) at 4,500 rpm; max torque (SAE): 270 lb ft, 37.3 kg m (367 Nm) at 2,500 rpm; 37.6 hp/l (27.7 kW/l); cast iron block and head; 5 crankshafts bearings; valves: overhead, push-rods and rockers; camshaft: 1; lubrication: full flow filter, 9.7 imp pt, 11.6 US pt, 5.5 l; water-cooled, 28.2 imp pt, 33.8 US pt, 16 l.

TRANSMISSION tyres: 7.75 x 14.

PERFORMANCE max speed: 109 mph, 175 km/h; power-weight ratio: 20.4 lb/hp (27.7 lb/kW), 9.6 kg/hp (12.6 kg/kW); acceleration: standing ¼ mile 19.5 sec, 0-50 mph (0-80 km/h) 9.8 sec; consumption: 18.4 m/imp gal, 15.4 m/US gal, 15.3 l x 100 km.

BRAKES front disc (diameter 11.30 in, 28.7 km), rear drum; lining area: front 38.5 sq in, 248 sq cm, rear 84.8 sq in, 547 sq cm; total 123.3 sq in, 795 sq cm.

DIMENSIONS AND WEIGHT weight: 3,667 lb, 1,663 kg.

Falcon Sedan Standard / De Luxe

PRICES EX WORKS:	pesos
Falcon Sedan Standard	15,700
Falcon Sedan De Luxe	18,100

ENGINE front, 4 stroke; 6 cylinders, in line; 188 cu in, 3,080 cc (3.68 x 2.94 in, 93.5 x 74.7 mm); compression ratio: 7.4:1; max power (SAE): 116 hp (85 kW) at 4,000 rpm; max torque (SAE): 176 lb ft, 24.3 kg m (238 Nm) at 2,300 rpm; 37.7 hp/l (27.7 kW/l); 7 crankshaft bearings; valves: overhead, push-rods and rockers; camshafts: 1, side, timing chain; lubrication: gear pump, full flow filter, 7.9 imp pt, 9.5 US pt, 4.5 l; 1 Galileo or Argelite downdraught single barrel carburettor; fuel feed: mechanical pump; water-cooled, 15.2 imp pt, 18.3 US pt, 8.6 l.

TRANSMISSION driving wheels: rear; clutch: single dry plate; gearbox: mechanical; gears: 3, fully synchronized; ratios: I 2.990, II 1.750, III 1, rev 3.170; lever: steering column; axle ratio: 3.310; tyres: 6.95 x 14.

PERFORMANCE max speed: 95 mph, 153 km/h; power-weight ratio: 23.6 lb/hp (32 lb/kW), 10.7 kg/hp (14.5 kg/kW); acceleration: standing ¼ mile 20.9 sec, 0-50 mph (0-80 km/h) 11.5 sec; consumption: 23.7 m/imp gal, 19.7 m/US gal, 11.9 l x 100 km.

CHASSIS integral; front suspension: independent, coil springs, suspension arms mounted on silent blocks, anti-roll bar, telescopic dampers; rear: rigid axle, leafsprings, telescopic dampers.

STEERING recculating ball.

BRAKES front disc (diameter 10.96 in, 27.7 cm), rear drum lining area: front 28 sq in, 180 sq cm, rear 67.3 sq in, 43 sq cm, total 95.3 sq in, 614 sq cm.

ELECTRICAL EQUIPMENT 12 V; 45 Ah battery; 540 W alternator; 2 headlamps.

DIMENSIONS AND WEIGHT wheel base: 109.50, 278 cm tracks: 55.60 in, 141 cm front, 54.50 in, 138 cm rea length: 186.30 in, 473 cm; width: 70.60 in, 179 cm; heigh 55.20 in, 140 cm; ground clearance: 7.04 in, 18 cm; weigh 2.740 lb, 1,243 kg; fuel tank: 11.6 imp gal, 14 US gal, 53

BODY saloon/sedan; 4 doors; 5 seats; (for De Luxe onl luxury equipment.

OPTIONALS 3.6 cc engine; 4-speed mechanical gearbo power steering; twin drive rear axle; (for De Luxe onl air-conditioning; halogen headlamps.

Falcon St. Wagon Standard / De Luxe

See Falcon Sedan Standard / De Luxe, except for:

PRICES EX WORKS:	pesc
Falcon St. Wagon Standard	17,9(
Falcon St. Wagon De Luxe	22,3(

TRANSMISSION axle ratio: 3.540.

PERFORMANCE power-weight ratio: 26 lb/hp (35.3 kg/kW 11.8 kg/hp (16 kg/kW).

DIMENSIONS AND WEIGHT weight: 3.013 lb, 1,367 kg; fu tank: 14.4 imp gal, 17.3 US gal, 65.5 l.

BODY estate car/st. wagon; 4+1 doors.

Falcon Sedan Futura

See Falcon Sedan Standard / De Luxe, except for:

PRICE EX WORKS: 21,600 pesos

ENGINE 221 cu in, 3,621 cc (3.68 x 3.46 in, 93.5 x 87 mm); compression ratio: 8.2:1; max power (SAE): 132 h (97 kW) at 4,000 rpm; max torque (SAE): 201 lb ft, 27.8 kg (273 Nm) at 1,800 rpm; 36.6 hp/l (26.9 kW/l).

TRANSMISSION gears: 4, fully synchronized; ratios: 2.850, II 2.020, III 1.260, IV 1, rev 2.850; lever: centra

PERFORMANCE max speed: 97 mph, 156 km/h; powe weight ratio: 21.3 lb/hp (28.9 lb/kW), 9.7 lb/kW (13.2 k kW); acceleration: standing ¼ mile 19 sec, 0-50 mph (0-8 km/h) 13.8 sec; consumption: 21.5 m/imp gal, 17.9 m/U gal, 13.1 l x 100 km.

DIMENSIONS AND WEIGHT weight: 2,811 lb, 1,275 kg.

BODY luxury equipment.

Falcon Sedan Sprint

See Falcon Sedan Standard / De Luxe, except for:

FORD Falcon Sedan De Luxe

FORD Falcon Station Wagon De Luxe

RICE EX WORKS: 23,100 pesos

NGINE 221 cu in, 3,621 cc (3.68 x 3.46 in, 93.5 x 87.9 m); compression ratio: 8.1:1; max power (SAE): 166 hp 22 kW) at 4,500 rpm; max torque (SAE): 225 lb ft, 31 kg m 304 Nm) at 3,000 rpm; 46.1 hp/l (33.9 kW/l); 1 Argelite owndraught twin barrel carburettor.

ERFORMANCE max speed: 112 mph, 180 km/h; power-eight ratio: 17.3 lb/hp (23.5 lb/kW), 7.8 kg/hp (10.6 kg/W); acceleration: standing ¼ mile 16.6 sec, 0-50 mph -80 km/h) 6.5 sec; consumption: 21.4 m/imp gal, 17.8 /US gal, 13.2 l x 100 km.

RANSMISSION axle ratio: 3.070; tyres: 175 R x 14.

RENAULT ARGENTINA

4 S

NGINE front, 4 stroke; 4 cylinders, vertical, in line; 62.24 u in, 1,020 cc (2.56 x 2.64 in, 65 x 77 mm); compression atio: 8.2:1; max power (SAE): 48 hp (35 kW) at 5,200 rpm; ax torque (SAE): 60 lb ft, 8 kg m (79 Nm) at 3,000 rpm; 47 p/l (34.6 kW/l); cast iron block, wet liners, light alloy ead; 5 crankshaft bearings; valves: overhead, in line, push-rods and rockers; camshafts: 1, side; Weber 28 ICP downdraught single barrel carburettor; fuel feed: mechanical pump; water-cooled.

TRANSMISSION driving wheels: front; clutch: single dry plate (diaphragm); gearbox: mechanical; gears: 4, fully synchronized; lever: on facia; final drive: hypoid bevel; axle ratio: 3.875; width of rims: 4''; tyres: 145 x 13.

PERFORMANCE max speed: over 75 mph, 120 km/h; power-weight ratio: 34.1 lb/hp (46.3 lb/kW), 15.4 kg/hp (21 kg/kW); consumption: 40.9 m/imp gal, 34.1 m/US gal, 6.9 l x 100 km.

CHASSIS platform; front suspension: independent, wishbones, longitudinal torsion bars, anti-roll bar, telescopic dampers; rear: independent, swinging longitudinal trailing arms, transverse torsion bars, telescopic dampers.

STEERING rack-and-pinion; turns lock to lock: 3.10.

BRAKES drum, rear compensator.

ELECTRICAL EQUIPMENT 12 V; 40 Ah battery; 28 A alternator; 2 headlamps.

DIMENSIONS AND WEIGHT wheel base: 96.06 in, 244 cm (right), 94.09 in, 239 cm (left); tracks: 50.39 in, 128 cm front, 49.21 in, 125 cm rear; length: 149.21 in, 379 cm; width: 58.27 in, 148 cm; height: 60.23 in, 153 cm; ground clearance: 8.07 in, 20.5 cm; weight: 1,636 lb, 742 kg; turning circle: 33 ft, 10 m; fuel tank: 5.7 imp gal, 6.9 US gal, 26 l.

RENAULT 6 GTL

BODY estate car/st. wagon; 4+1 doors; 4 seats, separate front seats; folding rear seat.

PRACTICAL INSTRUCTIONS fuel: 85 oct petrol.

6 / GTL

ENGINE front, 4 stroke; 4 cylinders, vertical, in line; 85.43 cu in, 1,397 cc (2.99 x 3.03 in, 76 x 77 mm); compression ratio: 9:1; max power (SAE): 60 hp (44 kW) at 4,500 rpm; max torque (SAE): 80 lb ft, 11 kg m (108 Nm) at 2,000 rpm; 42.8 hp/l (31.5 kW/l); cast iron block, wet liners, light alloy head; 5 crankshaft bearings: valves: overhead, in line, push-rods and rockers; camshafts: 1, side; 1 Weber 30 ICF downdraught single barrel carburettor; fuel feed: mechanical pump; water-cooled, electric fan.

TRANSMISSION driving wheels: front; clutch: single dry plate (diaphragm); gearbox: mechanical; gears: 4 fully synchronized; lever: on facia; final drive: hypoid bevel; axle ratio: 3.180; width of rims: 4''; tyres: 145 x 13.

PERFORMANCE max speed: 78 mph , 125 km/h; power-weight ratio: 31.2 lb/hp (42.5 lb/kW), 14.2 kg/hp (19.3 kg/kW); consumption: 45.6 m/imp gal, 37.9 m/US gal, 6.2 l x 100 km.

CHASSIS platform; front suspension: independent, wishbones, longitudinal torsion bars, anti-roll bar, telescopic dampers; rear: independent, swinging longitudinal trailing arms, transverse torsion bars, anti-roll bar, telescopic dampers.

STEERING rack-and-pinion; turns lock to lock: 3.10.

BRAKES drum, rear compensator.

ELECTRICAL EQUIPMENT 12 V; 40 Ah battery; 28 A alternator; 2 headlamps.

DIMENSIONS AND WEIGHT wheel base: 96.06 in, 244 cm (right), 94.09 in, 239 cm (left); tracks: 50.39 in, 128 cm front, 49.21 in, 125 cm rear; length: 157.08 in, 399 cm; width: 59.05 in, 150 cm; height: 59.05 in, 150 cm; ground clearance: 7.90 in, 20 cm; weight: 1,874 lb, 850 kg; fuel tank: 7.9 imp gal, 9.5 US gal, 36 l.

BODY saloon/sedan; 4+1 doors; 4-5 seats, separate front seats; folding rear seat.

PRACTICAL INSTRUCTIONS fuel: 92 oct petrol.

12 TL

ENGINE front, 4 stroke; 4 cylinders, vertical, in line; 85.24 cu in, 1,377 cc (2.99 x 3.03 in, 76 x 77 mm); compression ratio: 8:1; max power (SAE): 72 hp (53 kW) at 5,500 rpm; max torque (SAE): 80 lb ft, 11 kg m (108 Nm) at 3,000 rpm; 51.5 hp/l (38 kW/l); cast iron block, wet liners, light alloy head; 5 crankshaft bearings; valves: overhead; 1 Solex 32 EISA-3 downdraught carburettor; fuel feed: mechanical pump; water-cooled.

TRANSMISSION driving wheels: front; clutch: single dry plate (diaphragm); gearbox: mechanical; gears: 4, fully synchronized; lever: central; final drive: hypoid bevel; axle ratio: 3.770; width of rims: 4.5''; tyres: 175 S x 13.

PERFORMANCE max speed: 87 mph, 140 km/h; power-weight ratio: 28.2 lb/hp (38.3 lb/kW), 12.8 kg/hp (17.4 kg/kW); consumption: 27.4 m/imp gal, 22.8 m/US gal, 10.3 l x 100 km.

CHASSIS integral; front suspension: independent, wishbones, anti-roll bar, coil springs, telescopic dampers; rear: rigid axle, trailing arms, A-bracket, anti-roll bar, coil springs, telescopic dampers.

STEERING rack-and-pinion.

BRAKES front disc, rear drum.

ELECTRICAL EQUIPMENT 12 V; 40 Ah battery; 28 A alternator; 2 headlamps.

DIMENSIONS AND WEIGHT wheel base: 96.06 in, 244 cm; front and rear track: 51.57 in, 131 cm; length: 172.05 in, 473 cm; width: 64.56 in, 164 cm; height: 56.69 in, 144 cm; ground clearance: 6.70 in, 17 cm; weight: 2,033 lb 922 kg; turning circle: 33 ft, 10 m; fuel tank: 9.9 imp gal, 11.9 US gal, 45 l.

BODY saloon/sedan; 4 doors; 5 seats, separate front seats.

PRACTICAL INSTRUCTIONS fuel: 92 oct petrol.

12 TS

See 12 TL, except for:

ENGINE compression ratio: 9.5:1; max power (SAE): 90 hp (66 kW) at 5,500 rpm; max torque (SAE): 92 lb ft, 12.7 kg m (124 Nm) at 3,500 rpm; 64.4 hp/l (47.4 kW/l); 1 Solex C 34 EIES2 downdraught twin barrel carburettor.

12 TS

TRANSMISSION tyres: 155 SR x 13.

PERFORMANCE max speed: 96 mph, 155 km/h; power-weight ratio: 22.6 lb/hp (30.7 lb/kW), 10.2 kg/hp (13.9 kg/kW).

BRAKES dual circuit, servo.

BODY built-in headrests; air-conditioning.

12 TS Break

See 12 TL, except for:

ENGINE compression ratio: 9.5:1; max power (SAE): 90 hp (66 kW) at 5,500 rpm; max torque (SAE): 92 lb ft, 12.7 kg m (124 Nm) at 3,500 rpm; 64.4 hp/l (47.4 kW/l); 1 Solex C 34 EIES2 downdraught twin barrel carburettor.

TRANSMISSION tyres: 165 SR x 13.

PERFORMANCE max speed: 94 mph, 151 km/h; power-weight ratio: 23.9 lb/hp (32.6 lb/kW), 10.9 kg/hp (14.8 kg/kW).

BRAKES dual circuit, servo.

DIMENSIONS AND WEIGHT length: 174.80 in, 444 cm; height: 59.45 in, 151 cm; ground clearance: 7.50 in, 19 cm; weight: 2,158 lb, 979 kg.

BODY 4+1 doors; built-in headrests; folding rear seat; air-conditioning.

12 Alpine

See 12 TL, except for:

ENGINE compression ratio: 9.5:1; max power (SAE): 110 hp (81 kW) at 6,200 rpm; max torque (SAE): 99 lb ft, 13.7 kg m (134 Nm) at 5,000 rpm; 78.7 hp/l (57.9 kW/l); 1 Solex C 34 EIES2 downdraught twin barrel carburettor.

TRANSMISSION gearbox ratios: I 3.615, II 2.263, III 1.480, IV 1.032, rev 3.076; tyres: 155 SR x 13.

PERFORMANCE max speed: over 109 mph, 175 km/h; power-weight ratio: 19.2 lb/hp (26.1 lb/kW), 8.7 kg/hp (11.8 kg/kW); consumption: 23.5 m/imp gal, 19.6 m/US gal, 12 l x 100 km.

STEERING turns lock to lock: 3.50.

BRAKES dual circuit, servo.

ELECTRICAL EQUIPMENT 38 A alternator; 4 headlamps.

DIMENSIONS AND WEIGHT length: 171.26 in, 435 cm; height: 56.30 in, 143 cm; weight: 2,108 lb, 956 kg.

BODY built-in headrests; air-conditioning.

RENAULT 12 TS

Torino Grand Routier GR

ENGINE front, 4 stroke; 6 cylinders, in line; 230 cu in, 3,770 cc (3.34 x 4.37 in, 84.9 x 111.1 mm); compression ratio: 8.3:1; max power (SAE): 180 hp (132 kW) at 4,700 rpm; max torque (SAE): 225 lb ft, 31 kg m (304 Nm) at 2,500 rpm; max engine rpm: 5,000; 47.7 hp/l (35.1 kW/l); 7 crankshaft bearings; valves: overhead; camshafts: 1, overhead; lubrication: gear pump, full flow filter, 7.9 imp pt, 9.5 US pt, 4.5 l; 1 Carter ABD 2060-S downdraught twin barrel carburettor; fuel feed: mechanical pulp; water-cooled, 20.4 imp pt, 24.5 US pt, 11.6 l.

TRANSMISSION driving wheels: rear; clutch: single dry plate; gearbox: mechanical; gears: 4, fully synchronized; ratios: I 2.830, II 1,850, III 1.380, IV 1, rev 3.150; lever: central; final drive: hypoid bevel: axle ratio: 3.310; width of rims: 5''; tyres: 185 HR x 14.

PERFORMANCE max speed: 115 mph, 185 km/h; power-weight ratio: 17.4 lb/hp (23.8 lb/kW), 7.9 kg/hp (10.8 kg/kW); consumption: 21.7 m/imp gal, 18.1 m/US gal, 13 l x 100 km.

CHASSIS integral; front suspension: independent, wishbones, anti-roll bar, coil springs, telescopic dampers; rear: rigid axle, 4 linkage bars, coil springs, telescopic dampers.

STEERING recirculating ball.

BRAKES front disc, rear drum, dual circuit, servo; swept area: total 202.8 sq in, 1,308 sq cm.

ELECTRICAL EQUIPMENT 12 V; 55 Ah battery; 42 A alternator; 4 headlamps.

DIMENSIONS AND WEIGHT wheel base: 107.09 in, 272 cm tracks: 57.48 in, 146 cm front, 55.51 in, 141 cm rea length: 185.83 in, 472 cm; width: 70.08 in, 178 cm; heigh 56 69 in, 144 cm; ground clearance: 6.69 in, 17 cm; weigh 3,138 lb, 1,423 kg; turning circle: 41 ft, 12.5 m; fuel tank 14.1 imp gal, 16.9 US gal, 64 l.

BODY saloon/sedan; 4 doors; 5-6 seats.

PRACTICAL INSTRUCTIONS fuel: 90 oct petrol; oil: engin 7.9 imp pt, 9.5 US pt, 4.5 l, SAE 30 HD, change every 3,10 miles, 5,000 km - gearbox 2.1 imp pt, 2.5 US pt, 1.2 l, SA 90, change every 18,600 miles, 30,000 km - final drive 2. imp pt, 2.7 US pt, 1.3 l, SAE 90; greasing: every 6,20 miles, 10,000 km, 12 points; valve timing: 18° 26° 13° 21 tyre pressure: front 28 psi, 2 atm, rear 28 psi, 2 atm.

Torino ZX Coupé

See Torino Grand Routier GR, except for:

ENGINE compression ratio: 8.2:1; max power (SAE): 200 h (147 kW) at 4,500 rpm; max torque (SAE): 239 lb ft, 33 kg (324 Nm) at 3,000 rpm; 53 hp/l (39 kW/l); 1 Carter AB 2053-S downdraught twin barrel carburettor; cooling: 21 imp pt, 26 US pt, 12.3 l.

TRANSMISSION gearbox ratios: I 3.540, II 2.310, III 1.50 IV 1, rev 3.150; width of rims: 6''.

PERFORMANCE max speed: 124 mph, 200 km/h; powe weight ratio: 15.3 lb/hp (20.9 kW), 6.9 kg/hp (9.5 kg/kW consumption: 18.8 m/imp gal, 15.7 m/US gal, 15 l x 100 km

DIMENSIONS AND WEIGHT height: 55.91 in, 142 cm ground clearance: 6.30 in, 16 cm; weight: 3,076 lb, 1,39 kg.

BODY hardtop; 2 doors; 5 seats.

RENAULT Torino Grand Routier GR

AVALLONE BRAZI

A 11

ENGINE front, 4 stroke; 4 cylinders, in line; 85.3 cu in, 1,398 (3.23 x 2.61 in, 82 x 66.2 mm); compression ratio; 7.8:1; ma power (DIN): 60 hp (44 kW) at 5,400 rpm; max torque (DIN): lb ft, 9.2 kg m (90 Nm) at 3,600 rpm; max engine rpm: 6,00 42.9 hp/l (31.6 kW/l); cast iron block, light alloy head; crankshaft bearings; valves: overhead, rockers; camshafts: overhead, cogged belt; lubrication: gear pump, full flow filte 6.2 imp pt, 7.4 US pt, 3.5 l; 1 Solex H 32/34 PSDI downdraug carburettor; fuel feed: mechanical pump; water-cooled, 12 imp pt, 14.8 US pt, 7 l.

TRANSMISSION driving wheels: rear; clutch: single dry pla (diaphragm); gearbox: mechanical; gears: 4, fully synchronize ratios: I 3.746, II 2.157, III 1.378, IV 1, rev 3.815; lever: centra final drive: hypoid bevel; axle ratio: 4.100; width of rims: 5 tyres: 165 x 13.

ERFORMANCE max speed: 90 mph, 145 km/h; power-weight tio: 28.7 lb/hp (38.9 lb/kW), 13 kg/hp (17.6 kg/kW); speed in ect drive at 1,000 rpm: 16 mph, 25.7 km/h; consumption: .7 m/imp gal, 31.4 m/US gal, 7.5 l x 100 km.

HASSIS integral; front suspension: independent, wishbones, il springs, anti-roll bar, telescopic dampers; rear: rigid axle, in trailing radius arms, transverse linkage bar, coil springs, ti-roll bar, telescopic dampers.

TEERING rack-and-pinion; turns lock to lock: 3.25.

RAKES front disc (diameter 9.37 in, 23.8 cm), rear drum, dual cuit; lining area: front 17.1 sq in, 110 sq cm, rear 46.8 sq in, 2 sq cm, total 63.9 sq in, 412 sq cm.

LECTRICAL EQUIPMENT 12 V; 36 Ah battery; 32 A alterna-r; Arno distributor; 4 headlamps.

MENSIONS AND WEIGHT wheel base: 94.09 in, 239 cm; ont and rear track: 51.18 in, 130 cm; length: 151.97 in, 386 n; width: 61.42 in, 156 cm; height: 49.21 in, 125 cm; ground earance: 5.51 in, 14 cm; weight: 1,720 lb, 780 kg; turning cle: 32.1 ft, 9.8 m; fuel tank: 9.9 imp gal, 11.9 US gal, 45 l.

ODY sports, in plastic material; 2 doors; 2 seats.

VARIATIONS

GINE 151 cu in, 2,474 cc (4 x 3 in, 101.6 x 76.2 mm), 7.5:1; mpression ratio, max power (DIN) 80 hp (59 kW) at 4,400 m, max torque (DIN) 120 lb ft, 16.5 kg m (162 Nm) at 2,500 m, 5,000 max engine rpm, 32.3 hp/l (23.8 kW/l), 1, side, mshafts 1 Zenith DFV 228/S downdraught carburettor, cool-g 15 imp pt, 18 US pt, 8.5 l.
RANSMISSION mechanical gearbox with 4 ratios (I 3.070, II 020, III 1.390, IV 1, rev 3.570), 3.080 axle ratio, 185/70 R x 13 tyres with 6" wide rims.
ERFORMANCE max speed over 99 mph, 160 km/h, power-eight ratio 22.8 lb/hp (31 lb/kW), 10.4 kg/hp (14.1 kg/kW), eed in top at 1,000 rpm 21 mph, 34 km/h, consumption 20.2 imp gal, 11.6 m/US gal, 14 l x 100 km.
LECTRICAL EQUIPMENT 45 Ah battery, 32 A alternator.
MENSIONS AND WEIGHT weight 1,830 lb, 830 kg.

PTIONALS 185/70 SR x 13 tyres; servo brake; 1.6-litre engine th 2 Weber carburettors; 2.5-litre engine, max power (DIN) 88 (64 kW) at 4,600 rpm, max torque (DIN) 135 lb ft, 18.6 kg m 83 Nm) at 2,600 rpm, 35.6 hp/l (26 kW/l), 1 Zenith DVF 228/S wndraught twin barrel carburettor, power-weight ratio 20.8 hp (28.6 lb/kW), 9.4 kg/hp (12.9 kg/kW); turbochanger; Tri-atic automatic transmission, hydraulic torque converter and anetary gears with 3 ratios (I 2.310, II 1.460, III 1, rev 1.850), ssible manual selection, 3.540 axle ratio; limited slip dif-ential.

HEVROLET BRAZIL

Chevette Series

RICES EX WORKS:	cruzeiros
D 2-dr Sedan	**147,000**
2-dr Sedan	**152,000**
. 2-dr Sedan	**166,000**
D 4-dr Sedan	**165,000**
. 4-dr Sedan	**184,000**
D 2+1-dr Hatchback	**164,000**
. 2+1-dr Hatchback	**185,000**

NGINE front, 4 stroke; 4 cylinders, in line; 85.3 cu in, 1,398 cc .23 x 2.61 in, 82 x 66.2 mm); compression ratio: 7.8:1; max wer (SAE): 64 hp (48 kW) at 5,800 rpm; max torque (SAE): lb ft, 11.1 kg m (109 Nm) at 3.000 rpm; max engine rpm: 400; 46 hp/l (34.3 kW/l); cast iron block and head; 5 crank-aft bearings; valves: overhead, rockers; camshafts: 1, over-ad, cogged belt; lubrication: gear pump, full flow filter, 6.2 p pt, 7.4 US pt, 3.5 l; 1 Solex or Wecarbras downdraught rburettor; fuel feed: mechanical pump; water-cooled, 12.3 p pt, 14.8 US pt, 7 l.

RANSMISSION driving wheels: rear; clutch: single dry plate aphragm); gearbox: mechanical; gears: 4, fully synchronized; tios: I 3.746, II 2.157, II 1.378, IV 1, rev 3.815; lever: central; al drive: hypoid bevel; axle ratio: 4.100; width of rims: 5"; es: 165 x 13.

ERFORMANCE max speed: 88 mph, 140 km/h; power-weight tio: 2-dr models 28.8 lb/hp (38.4 lb/kW), 13.1 kg/hp (17.4 /kW); carrying capacity: 915 lb, 415 kg; speed in direct drive 1,000 rpm: 16 mph, 25.7 km/h; consumption: 37.7 m/imp gal, .4 m/US gal, 7.5 l x 100 km.

HASSIS integral; front suspension: independent, wishbones, il springs, anti-roll bar, telescopic dampers; rear: rigid axle, in trailing radius arms, transverse linkage bar, coil springs, escopic dampers.

TEERING rack-and-pinion; turns lock to lock: 3.50

RAKES front disc (diameter 9.21 in, 23.4 cm), rear drum, rvo; swept area: total 248 sq in, 1,600 sq cm.

AVALLONE A 11

ELECTRICAL EQUIPMENT 12 V; 36 Ah battery; 28 A alternator; Arno Bosch distributor; 2 headlamps.

DIMENSIONS AND WEIGHT wheel base: 94.09 in, 239 cm; front and rear track: 51.18 in, 130 cm; length: 165.35 in, 420 cm; width: 61.81 in, 157 cm; height: 51.97 in, 132 cm; ground clearance: 5.51 in, 14 cm; weight: 2-dr models 1,843 lb, 836 kg - 4-dr models 1,881 lb, 855 kg - Hatchback models 1,912 lb, 865 kg; turning circle: 32.1 ft, 9.8 m; fuel tank: 9,9 imp gal, 11.9 US gal, 45 l.

BODY 5 seats, separate front seats; luxury equipment; reclining backrests with built-in headrests; folding rear seat (for Hatchback models only).

PRACTICAL INSTRUCTIONS fuel: 73 oct petrol; oil: engine 6.2 imp pt, 7.4 US pt, 3.5 l, SAE 20W-40 change every 3,100 miles, 5,000 km - gearbox 2.5 imp pt, 3 US pt, 1.4 l, SAE 90, change every 15,500 miles, 25,000 km - final drive 1.4 imp pt, 1.7 US pt, 0.8 l, SAE 90, change every 31,000 miles, 50,000 km; greasing: none; tappet clearances: inlet 0.010 in, 0.25 mm, exhaust 0.010 in, 0.25 mm; valve timing: 34° 86° 66° 54°; tyre pressure: front 20 psi, 1.4 atm, rear 24 psi, 1.7 atm.

OPTIONALS tinted glass; servo brake.

Opala Sedan / Coupé

PRICES EX WORKS:	cruzeiros
Opala 4-dr Sedan	**207,000**
Opala 2-dr Coupé	**208,000**

ENGINE front, 4 stroke; 4 cylinders, in line; 151 cu in, 2,470 cc (4 x 3 in, 101.6 x 76.2 mm); compression ratio: 7.5:1; max power (SAE): 88 hp (65 kW) at 4,800 rpm; max torque (SAE): 125 lb ft, 17.2 kg m (169 Nm) at 2,600 rpm; max engine rpm: 5,200; 35.6 hp/l (26.3 kW/l); cast iron block and head; 5 crankshaft bearings; valves: overhead, push-rods and rockers, hydramatic tappets; camshafts: 1, side; lubrication: gear pump, full flow filter, 6.2 imp pt, 7.4 US pt, 3.5 l; 1 Wecarbras downdraught single barrel carburettor; fuel feed: mechanical pump; water-cooled, 15.1 imp pt, 18.2 US pt, 8.6 l.

TRANSMISSION driving wheels: rear; clutch: single dry plate; gearbox: mechanical; gears: 3, fully synchronized; ratios: I 3.070, II 1.680, III 1, rev 3.570; lever: steering column; final drive: hypoid bevel; axle ratio: 3.540; width of rims: 5"; tyres: 6.45 x 14.

PERFORMANCE max speed: 93 mph, 150 km/h; power-weight ratio: 27.3 lb/hp (37 lb/kW), 12.4 kg/hp (16.8 kg/kW); carrying capacity: 1,091 lb, 495 kg; speed in direct drive at 1,200 rpm: 24.1 mph, 38.8 km/h; consumption: 22.6 m/imp gal, 18.8 m/US gal, 12.5 l x 100 km.

CHASSIS integral; front suspension: independent, wishbones, coil springs, anti-roll bar, telescopic dampers; rear: rigid axle, longitudinal torsion bars, transverse linkage bar, coil springs, anti-roll bar, telescopic dampers.

STEERING worm and roller; turns lock to lock: 3.75.

BRAKES front disc, rear drum, servo.

CHEVROLET Chevette STD Sedan

OPALA SEDAN / COUPÉ

ELECTRICAL EQUIPMENT 12 V; 45 Ah battery; 32 A alternator; Arno/Bosch distributor; 2 headlamps.

DIMENSIONS AND WEIGHT wheel base: 105.12 in, 267 cm; tracks: 55.91 in, 142 cm front, 55.51 in, 141 cm rear; length: 184.25 in, 468 cm; width: 68.90 in, 175 cm; height: Sedan 54.72 in, 139 cm - Coupé 53.54 in, 136 cm; ground clearance: 7.09 in, 18 cm; weight: Sedan 2,406 lb, 1,094 kg - Coupé 2,395 lb, 1,089 kg; turning circle: 37.1 ft, 11.3 m; fuel tank: 14.3 imp gal, 17.2 US gal, 65 l.

BODY saloon/sedan, 4 doors - coupé, 2 doors; 6 seats, bench front seats.

PRACTICAL INSTRUCTIONS fuel: 73 oct petrol; oil: engine 6.2 imp pt, 7.4 US pt, 3.5 l, SAE 20W-40, change every 3,100 miles, 5,000 km - gearbox 2.1 imp pt, 2.5 US pt, 1.2 l, SAE 90, change every 15,500 miles, 25,000 km - final drive 1.3 imp pt, 2.1 US pt, 0.9 l, change every 31,000 miles, 50,000 km; greasing: none; valve timing: 33° 81° 76° 38°; tyre pressure: front 20 psi, 1.4 atm, rear 22 psi, 1.6 atm.

VARIATIONS

ENGINE 6 cylinders in line, 250 cu in, 4,093 cc (3.87 x 3.53 in, 98.4 x 89.7 mm), max power (SAE) 134 hp (99 kW) at 4,200 rpm), max torque (SAE) 203 lb ft, 28.1 kg m (276 Nm) at 2,400 rpm), 32.7 hp/l (24.2 kW/l), 7 crankshaft bearings, lubrication 8.8 imp pt, 10.6 US pt, 5 l, 1 Wecarbras downdraught twin barrel carburettor, cooling 18 imp pt, 21.6 US pt, 10.2 l.
TRANSMISSION 3.080 axle ratio, 6.95 S x 14 tyres.
PERFORMANCE max speed about 106 mph, 170 km/h, power-weight ratio 19 lb/hp (25.5 lb/kW), 8.6 kg/hp (11.6 kg/kW), speed in direct drive at 1,000 rpm 21.4 mph, 34 km/h, consumption 18.2 m/imp gal, 15.2 m/US gal, 15.5 l x 100 km.
DIMENSIONS AND WEIGHT Sedan 2,550 lb, 1,159 kg - Coupé 2,539 lb, 1,154 kg.

OPTIONALS 4-speed fully synchronized mechanical gearbox (I 3.070, II 2.020, III 1.390, IV 1, rev 3.570), 3.080 axle ratio, central lever; "Automatic" automatic transmission, hydraulic torque converter and planetary gears with 3 ratios (I 2.310, II 1.460, III 1, rev 1.850), max ratio of converter at stall 2.1; power steering; separate front seats with reclining backrests; air-conditioning; tinted glass; metallic spray; heater; electric rear window; 175/70 SR x 14 tyres; rev counter.

Opala Caravan

See Opala Sedan / Coupé, except for:

PRICE EX WORKS: 231,000 cruzeiros

TRANSMISSION tyres: 6.95 x 14.

PERFORMANCE max speed: 87 mph, 140 km/h; power-weight ratio: 28.3 lb/hp (38.3 lb/kW), 12.9 kg/hp (17.4 kg/kW).

DIMENSIONS AND WEIGHT length: 182.28 in, 463 cm; height: 54.72 in, 139 cm; weight: 2,491 lb, 1,132 kg.

BODY estate car/st.wagon; 2+1 doors; folding rear seat.

OPTIONALS 175 SR x 14 tyres.

CHEVROLET Opala Sedan

Opala SS-4 Coupé

See Opala Sedan / Coupé, except for:

PRICE EX WORKS: 253,000 cruzeiros

ENGINE max power (SAE): 95 hp (70 kW) at 4,800 rpm; max torque (SAE): 134 lb ft, 18.5 kg m (181 Nm) at 2,600 rpm; 38.5 hp/l (28.3 kW/l); 1 Wecarbras downdraught twin barrel carburettor.

TRANSMISSION gears: 4, fully synchronized; ratios: I 3.400 II 2.160, III 1.390, IV 1, rev 3.810; lever: central; tyres: 195/70 SR x 14.

PERFORMANCE power-weight ratio: 25.8 lb/hp (35 lb/kW), 11.9 kg/hp (16.2 kg/kW); speed in direct drive at 1,000 rpm: 23.7 mph, 38.2 km/h.

DIMENSIONS AND WEIGHT tracks: 56.30 in, 143 cm front, 55.91 in, 142 cm rear; length: 185.43 in, 471 cm; height: 53.54 in, 136 cm; weight: 2,450 lb, 1,132 kg.

BODY coupé; 2 doors; 5 seats, separate front seats, reclining backrests.

Opala SS-4 Caravan

See Opala Sedan / Coupé, except for:

PRICE EX WORKS: 274,000 cruzeiros

ENGINE max power (SAE): 95 hp (70 kW) at 4,800 rpm; ma torque (SAE): 134 lb ft, 18.5 kg m (181 Nm) at 2,600 rpm; 38. hp/l (28.3 kW/l). 1 Wecarbras downdraught twin barrel car burettor.

TRANSMISSION gears: 4, fully synchronized; ratios: I 3.400, 2.160, III 1.390, IV 1, rev 3.810; lever: central; tyres: 17 SR x 14.

PERFORMANCE power-weight ratio: 26.7 lb/hp (36.2 lb/kW) 12.2 kg/kp (16.5 kg/kW); speed in direct drive at 1,000 rpm 23.7 mph, 38.2 km/h.

DIMENSIONS AND WEIGHT tracks: 56.30 in, 143 cm front 55.91 in, 142 cm rear; length: 183.86 in, 467 cm; height: 54.7 in, 139 cm; weight: 2,541 lb, 1,155 kg.

BODY estate car/st. wagon; 2+1 doors; 5 seats, separate fro seats, reclining backrests.

Opala SS-6 Coupé

See Opala Sedan / Coupé, except for:

PRICE EX WORKS: 276,000 cruzeiros

ENGINE 6 cylinders; 250 cu in, 4,097 cc (3.87 x 3.53 in 98.4 x 89.7 mm); compression ratio: 7.8:1; max power (SAE) 143 hp (105 kW) at 4,600 rpm; max torque (SAE): 206 lb ft 28.5 kg m (279 Nm) at 3,000 rpm; 34.9 hp/l (25.6 kW/l); crankshaft bearings; lubrication: 8.8 imp pt, 10.6 US pt, 5 l; Wecarbras downdraught twin barrel carburettor; cooling, 18 im pt, 21.5 US pt, 10.2 l.

TRANSMISSION gears: 4 fully synchronized; ratios: I 3.400, I 2.160, III 1.390, IV 1, rev 3.810; lever: central; axle ratio 3.080; tyres: 175/70 SR x 14.

PERFORMANCE max speed: about 109 mph, 174 km/h; power-weight ratio: 18 lb/hp (24.5 lb/kW), 8.2 kg/hp (11.1 kg/kW) speed in direct drive at 1,000 rpm: 23.7 mph, 38.2 km/h consumption: 18.2 m/imp gal, 15.2 m/US gal, 15.5 l x 100 km

DIMENSIONS AND WEIGHT tracks: 56.30 in, 143 cm front 55.91 in, 142 cm rear; length: 185.43 in, 471 cm; height: 53.5 in, 136 cm; weight: 2,570 lb, 1,168 kg.

BODY coupé; 2 doors; 5 seats, separate front seats, reclinin backrests.

Opala SS-6 Caravan

See Opala Sedan / Coupé, except for:

PRICE EX WORKS: 299,000 cruzeiros

ENGINE 6 cylinders; 250 cu in, 4,097 cc (3.87 x 3.53 in 98.4 x 89.7 mm); compression ratio: 7.8:1; max power (SAE) 143 hp (105 kW) at 4,600 rpm; max torque (SAE): 206 lb ft 28.5 kg m (279 Nm) at 3,000 rpm; 34.9 hp/l (25.6 kW/l); crankshaft bearings; lubrication: 8.8 imp pt, 10.6 US pt, 5 l; Wecarbras downdraught twin barrel carburettor; cooling, 18 im pt, 21.5 US pt, 10.2 l.

TRANSMISSION gears: 4, fully synchronized; ratios: I 3.400, 2.160, III 1.390, IV 1, rev 3.810; lever: central; axle ratio 3.080; tyres: 175/70 SR x 14.

PERFORMANCE max speed: about 109 mph, 174 km/h; power weight ratio: 19.1 lb/hp (26 lb/kW), 8.5 kg/hp (11.6 kg/kW)

CHEVROLET Opala SS-4 Caravan

peed in direct drive at 1,000 rpm: 23.7 mph, 38.2 km/h; onsumption: 18.2 m/imp gal, 15.2 m/US gal, 15.5 l x 100 km.

Diplomata Sedan / Coupé

RICES EX WORKS:	cruzeiros
iplomata 4-dr Sedan	343,000
iplomata 2-dr Coupé	342,000

NGINE front, 4 stroke; 4 cylinders, in line; 151 cu in, 2,470 cc x 3 in, 101.6 x 76.2 mm); compression ratio: 7.5:1; max pow- (SAE): 95 hp (70 kW) at 4,800 rpm; max torque (SAE): 134 lb , 18.5 kg m (181 Nm) at 2,600 rpm; max engine rpm: 5,200; 8.5 hp/l (28.3 kW/l); cast iron block and head; 5 crankshaft earings; valves: overhead, push-rods and rockers, hydraulic appets; camshafts: 1, side; lubrication: gear pump, full flow ter, 6.2 imp pt, 7.4 US pt, 3.5 l; 1 Wecarbras downdraught vin barrel carburettor; fuel feed: mechanical pump; water-ooled, 15.1 imp pt, 18.2 US pt, 8.6 l.

RANSMISSION driving wheels: rear; clutch: single dry plate; earbox: mechanical; gears: 4, fully synchronized; ratios: I .400, II 2.160, III 1.380, IV 1, rev 3.810; lever: central; final rive: hypoid bevel; axle ratio: 3.540; width of rims: 5"; tyres: .35 s x 14.

ERFORMANCE max speed: 93 mph, 150 km/h; power-weight atio: sedan 27.6 lb/hp (37.5 lb/kW), 12.6 kg/hp (17.1 kg/kW); arrying capacity: 1,091 lb, 495 kg; speed in direct drive at ,000 rpm: 25.7 mph, 41.3 km/h; consumption: 22.6 m/imp gal, 8.8 m/US gal, 12.5 l x 100 km.

CHEVROLET Diplomata Coupé

HASSIS integral; front suspension: independent, wishbones, oil springs, anti-roll bar, telescopic dampers; rear: rigid axle, ongitudinal torsion bars, transverse linkage bar, coil springs, nti-roll bar, telescopic dampers.

STEERING worm and roller; turns lock to lock: 3.75.

RAKES front disc, rear drum, servo.

LECTRICAL EQUIPMENT 12 V; 45 Ah battery; 55 A alterna- or; Arno/Bosch distributor; 2 headlamps.

IMENSIONS AND WEIGHT wheel base: 105.12 in, 267 cm; racks: 56.30 in, 143 cm front, 55.91 in, 142 cm rear; length: 86.61 in, 474 cm; width: 69.29 in, 176 cm; height: sedan 54.72 n, 139 cm - Coupé 53.54 in, 136 cm; ground clearance: 7.09 in, 8 cm; weight: Sedan 2,627 lb, 1,194 kg - Coupé 2,601 lb, ,182 kg; turning circle: 37.1 ft, 11.3 m; fuel tank: 14.3 imp gal, 7.2 US gal, 65 l.

BODY saloon/sedan, 4 doors - coupé, 2 doors; 6 seats, bench ront seats.

PRACTICAL INSTRUCTIONS fuel: 73 oct petrol; oil: engine 6.2 mp pt, 7.4 US pt, 3.5 l, SAE 20W-40, change every 3,100 miles, 5,000 km - gearbox 2.1 imp pt, 2.5 US pt, 1.2 l, SAE 90, change every 15,500 miles, 25,000 km - final drive 1.3 imp pt, 2.1 US pt, 0.9 l, change every 31,000 miles, 50,000 km; greasing: none; valve timing: 33° 81° 76° 38°; tyre pressure: ront 20 psi, 1.4 atm, rear 22 psi, 1.6 atm.

VARIATIONS

ENGINE 6 cylinders, in line, 250 cu in, 4,093 cc (3.87 x 3.53 in, 98.4 x 89.7 mm), max power (SAE) 134 hp (99 kW) at 4,200 rpm, max torque (SAE) 203 lb ft, 28.1 kg m (276 Nm) at 2,400 rpm, 32.7 hp/l (24.2 kW/l), 7 crankshaft bearings, lubrication 8.8 imp pt, 10.6 US pt, 5 l, cooling 19.4 imp pt, 23.3 US pt, 11 l.
TRANSMISSION 4-speed fully synchronized mechanical gear- box (I 3.070, II 2.020, III 1.390, IV 1, rev 3.570), 3.080 axle ratio, 7.35 s x 14 tyres.
PERFORMANCE max speed about 106 mph, 170 km/h, power- weight ratio Sedan 20.5 lb/hp (27.7 lb/kW), 9.3 kg/hp (12.6 kg/kW), speed in direct drive at 1,000 rpm 21.4 mph, 34 km/h, consumption 18.2 m/imp gal, 15.2 m/US gal, 15.5 l x 100 km.
DIMENSIONS AND WEIGHT Sedan 2,746 lb, 1,248 kg - Coupé 2,720 lb, 1,236 kg.

OPTIONALS 4-speed fully synchronized mechanical gearbox (I 3.070, II 2.020, III 1.390, IV 1, rev 3.570), 3.080 axle ratio; "Automatic" automatic transmission, hydraulic torque conver- ter and planetary gears with 3 ratios (I 2.310, II 1.460, III 1, rev 1.850), max ratio of converter at stall 2.1; power steering; separate front seats with reclining backrests; air-conditioning; tinted glass; metallic spray; vinyl roof; heater; electric rear window; 175/70 SR x 14 tyres; rev counter.

Comodoro Sedan / Coupé

PRICES EX WORKS:	cruzeiros
Comodoro 4-dr Sedan	230,000
Comodoro 2-dr Coupé	228,000

ENGINE front, 4 stroke; 4 cylinders, in line; 151 cu in, 2,740 cc (4 x 3 in, 101.6 x 76.2 mm); compression ratio: 7.5:1; max pow- er (SAE): 88 hp (65 kW) at 4,800 rpm; max torque (SAE): 125 lb ft, 17.2 kg m (169 Nm) at 2,600 rpm; max engine rpm: 5,200; 35.2 hp/l (26.4 kW/l); cast iron block and head; 5 crankshaft bearings; valves: overhead, in line, push-rods and rockers, hydraulic tappets; camshafts: 1, side; lubrication: gear pump, full flow filter, 6.2 imp pt, 7.4 US pt, 3.5 l; 1 Wecarbras downdraught single barrel carburettor; fuel feed: mechanical pump; water-cooled, 15 imp pt, 18 US pt, 8.5 l.

TRANSMISSION driving wheels: rear; clutch: single dry plate; gearbox: mechanical; gears: 3, fully synchronized; ratios: I 3.070, II 1.680, III 1, rev 3.570; lever: steering column; final drive: hypoid bevel; axle ratio: 3.540; width of rims: 5"; tyres: 6.95 x 14.

PERFORMANCE max speed: 96 mph, 154 km/h; power-weight ratio: Sedan 27.7 lb/hp (37.6 lb/kW), 12.6 kg/hp (17.1 kg/kW); carrying capacity: 1,091 lb, 495 kg; speed in direct drive at 1,000 rpm: 24.2 mph, 38.8 km/h; consumption: 22.6 m/imp gal, 18.8 m/US gal, 12.5 l x 100 km/h.

CHASSIS integral; front suspension: independent, wishbones, coil springs, anti-roll bar, telescopic dampers; rear: rigid axle, longitudinal torsion bars, transverse linkage bar, coil springs, anti-roll bar, telescopic dampers.

STEERING worm and roller.

BRAKES front disc, rear drum, servo.

ELECTRICAL EQUIPMENT 12 V; 45 Ah battery; 32 A alterna- tor; Arno distributor; 2 headlamps.

DIMENSIONS AND WEIGHT wheel base: 105.12 in, 267 cm; tracks: 55.91 in, 142 cm front, 55.51 in, 141 cm rear; length: 185.12 in, 470 cm; width: 69.29 in, 176 cm; height: Sedan 54.72 in, 139 cm - Coupé 53.54 in, 136 cm; ground clearance: 7.09 in, 18 cm; weight: Sedan 2,442 lb, 1,110 kg - Coupé 2,416 lb, 1,098 kg; turning circle: 37.1 ft, 11.3 m; fuel tank: 14.3 imp gal, 17.2 US gal, 65 l.

BODY saloon/sedan, 4 doors - coupé, 2 doors; 5 seats, bench front seats.

PRACTICAL INSTRUCTIONS fuel: 73 oct petrol; oil: engine 6.2 imp pt, 7.4 US pt, 3.5 l, SAE 20W-40, change every 3,100 miles, 5,000 km - gearbox 2.1 imp pt, 2.5 US pt, 1.2 l, SAE 90, change every 15,500 miles, 25,000 km - final drive 1.3 imp pt, 2.1 US pt, 1 l, change every 31,000 miles 50,000 km; greasing: none; valve timing: 33° 81° 76° 38°; tyre pressure: front 19 psi, 1.3 atm, rear 21 psi, 1.5 atm.

VARIATIONS

ENGINE 6 cylinders, in line, 250 cu in, 4,093 cc (3.87 x 3.53 in, 98.4 x 89.7 mm), max power (SAE) 134 hp (99 kW) at 4,200 rpm, max torque (SAE) 203 lb ft, 28.1 kg m (276 Nm) at 2,400 rpm, 32.7 hp/l (24.2 kW/l), 7 crankshaft bearings, lubrication 8.8 imp pt, 10.6 US pt, 5 l; 1 Wecarbras downdraught twin barrel carburettor, cooling 19.4 imp pt, 23.3 US pt, 11 l.
TRANSMISSION 3.080 axle ratio, 7.35 SR x 14 tyres.
PERFORMANCE max speed about 106 mph, 170 km/h, power- weight ratio Sedan 19 lb/hp (25.5 lb/kW), 8.6 kg/hp (11.6

CHEVROLET Comodoro Caravan

COMODORO SEDAN / COUPÉ

kg/kW), speed in direct drive at 1,000 rpm 21.4 mph, 34 km/h, consumption 18.2 m/imp gal, 15.2 m/US gal, 15.5 l x 100 km. **DIMENSIONS AND WEIGHT** Sedan 2,563 lb, 1,166 kg - Coupé 2,539 lb, 1,154 kg.

OPTIONALS "Automatic" automatic transmission, hydraulic torque converter and planetary gears with 3 ratios (I 2.310, II 1.460, III 1, rev 1.850), max ratio of converter at stall 2.1; power steering; separate front seats with reclining backrests; air-conditioning; tinted glass; metallic spray; vinyl roof; heater; electric rear window; 175/70 SR x 14 tyres; rev counter.

Comodoro Caravan

See Comodoro Sedan / Coupé, except for:

PRICE EX WORKS: 249,000 cruzeiros

PERFORMANCE max speed: 87 mph, 140 km/h; power-weight ratio: 28.3 lb/hp (38 lb/kW), 12.9 kg/hp (17.3 kg/kW).

DIMENSIONS AND WEIGHT length: 183.86 in, 467 cm; height: 54.72 in, 139 cm; weight: 2,510 lb, 1,441 kg.

BODY estate car/st. wagon; 2+1 doors; folding rear seat.

CHEVROLET Veraneio De Luxo Station Wagon

Veraneio Series

PRICES EX WORKS:	cruzeiros
Standard 4+1-dr St. Wagon	**281,000**
De Luxo 4+1-dr St. Wagon	**294,000**
Super Luxo 4+1-dr St. Wagon	**342,000**

ENGINE front, 4 stroke; 6 cylinders, vertical in line; 261.2 cu in, 4,280 cc (3.75 x 3.94 in, 95.2 x 100.1 mm); compression ratio: 7.8:1; max power (SAE): 151 hp (111 kW) at 3,800 rpm; max torque (SAE): 233 lb ft, 32.1 kg m (315 Nm) at 2,400 rpm; max engine rpm: 4,200; 35.3 hp/l (25.9 kW/l); cast iron block and head; 3 crankshaft bearings; valves: overhead, in line, push-rods and rockers; camshafts: 1, side; lubrication: gear pump, full flow filter, 8.3 imp pt, 9.9 US pt, 4.7 l; 1 Wecarbras-Zenith 228 downdraught single barrel carburettor; fuel feed: mechanical pump; water-cooled, 28.2 imp pt, 33.8 US pt 16 l.

TRANSMISSION driving wheels: rear; clutch: single dry plate (diaphragm); gearbox: mechanical; gears: 3, fully synchronized; ratios: I 3.617, II 1.753, III 1, rev 3.761; lever: steering column; final drive: hypoid bevel, limited slip differential; axle ratio: 3.900; width of rims: 5.5"; tyres; 7.10 x 15.

PERFORMANCE max speed: 90 mph, 145 km/h; power-weight ratio: 28.7 lb/hp (39.4 lb/kW), 13 kg/hp (17.7 kg/kW); carrying capacity: 1,191 lb, 540 kg; speed in direct drive at 1,000 rpm: 20.9 mph, 33.6 km/h; consumption: 17.7 m/imp gal, 14.7 m/US gal, 16 l x 100 km.

CHASSIS box-type ladder frame; front suspension: independent, wishbones, coil springs, telescopic dampers; rear: rigid axle, longitudinal trailing arms, coil springs, anti-roll bar, telescopic dampers.

STEERING worm and roller.

BRAKES drum; lining area: total 100.4 sq in, 648 sq cm.

ELECTRICAL EQUIPMENT 12 V; 45 Ah battery; 37 A alternator; Arno distributor; 2 headlamps.

DIMENSIONS AND WEIGHT wheel base: 114.96 in, 292 cm; tracks: 64.56 in, 164 cm front, 61.02 in, 155 cm rear; length: 203.15 in, 516 cm - De Luxo 207.87 in, 528 cm; width: 77.95 in, 198 cm; height: 68.11 in, 173 cm; ground clearance: 7.87 in, 20 cm; weight: 4,344 lb, 1,970 kg; turning circle: 42.6 ft, 13 m; fuel tank: 15.4 imp gal, 18.5 US gal, 70 l.

BODY estate car/st. wagon; 4+1 doors; 6 seats, bench front seats; folding rear seat; (for De Luxo only) luxury equipment.

PRACTICAL INSTRUCTIONS fuel: 73 oct petrol; oil: engine 8.3 imp pt, 9.9 US pt, 4.7 l, SAE 10W-50, change every 1,900 miles, 3,000 km - gearbox 2.1 imp pt, 2.5 US pt, 1.3 l, SAE 90, change every 15,500 miles, 25,000 km - final drive 3.5 imp pt, 4.2 US pt, 2 l, change every 31,000 miles, 50,000 km; greasing: none; valve timing: 11°30' 52°30' 51° 13°; tyre pressure: front 30 psi, 2.1 atm, rear 30 psi, 2.1 atm.

OPTIONALS power steering.

DODGE Polara Gran Luxo

DODGE BRAZIL

Polara / Gran Luxo

ENGINE front, 4 stroke; 4 cylinders, vertical, in line; 109.8 cu in, 1,799 cc (3.39 x 3.04 in, 86 x 77.1 mm); compression ratio: 7.7:1; max power (SAE): 85 hp (63 kW) at 5,000 rpm; max torque (SAE): 103 lb ft, 14.2 kg m (139 Nm) at 3,500 rpm; max engine rpm: 6,400; 47.2 hp/l (34.8 kW/l); cast iron block and head; 5 crankshaft bearings; valves: overhead, in line, push-rods and rockers; camshafts: 1, side; lubrication: rotary pump, full flow filter, 7.2 imp pt, 8.7 US pt, 4 l; 1 SU HS-6 horizontal single barrel carburettor; fuel feed: mechanical pump; water-cooled, 10.6 imp pt, 12.7 US pt, 6 l.

TRANSMISSION driving wheels: rear; clutch: single dry plate (diaphragm); gearbox: mechanical; gears: 4, fully synchronized; ratios: I 3.538, II 2.165, III 1.387, IV 1, rev 3.680; lever: central; final drive: hypoid bevel; axle ratio: 3.890; width of rims: 5"; tyres: 6.45 x 13.

PERFORMANCE max speeds: (I) 30 mph, 49 km/h; (II) 50 mph, 81 km/h; (III) 78 mph, 120 km/h; (IV) 95 mph, 153 km/h; power-weight ratio: 24 lb/hp (32.8 lb/kW), 10.9 kg/hp (14.9 kg/kW) - Gran Luxo 24.9 lb/hp (34 lb/kW), 11.3 kg/hp (15.4 kg/kW); carrying capcity: 882 lb, 400 kg; acceleration: standing ¼ mile 18.2 sec, 0-50 mph (0-80 km/h) 8.2 sec; speed in direct drive at 1,000 rpm: 17.4 mph, 28 km/h; consumption: 30.1 m/imp gal, 25 m/US gal, 9.4 l x 100 km.

CHASSIS integral; front suspension: independent, by McPherson, coil springs/telescopic damper struts, wishbones (lower trailing links), anti-roll bar; rear: rigid axle, swinging longitudinal trailing arms, upper oblique torque arms, coil springs, telescopic dampers.

STEERING rack-and-pinion; turns lock to lock: 3.60.

BRAKES front disc, rear drum, servo: swept area: front 22 sq in, 142 s cm, rear 60.1 sq in, 387 sq cm, total 82.1 sq in, 529 sq cm.

ELECTRICAL EQUIPMENT 12 V; 40 Ah battery; 360: W alternator; Bosch or Wapsa distributor; 2 headlamps.

DIMENSIONS AND WEIGHT wheel base: 98 in, 249 cm; tracks: 52.76 in, 134 cm front, 52 in, 132 cm rear; length: 165.75 in, 421 cm; width: 62.50 in, 159 cm; height: 54.20 in, 138 cm; ground clearance: 5.50 in, 14 cm; weight: 2.051 lb, 930 kg - Gran Luxo 2,126 lb, 964 kg; turning circle: 30.8 ft, 9.4 m; fuel tank: 9.2 imp gal, 11.1 US gal, 42 l.

BODY coupé; 2 doors; 5 seats, separate front seats.

PRACTICAL INSTRUCTIONS fuel: 73 oct petrol; oil: engine 7.2 imp pt, 8.7 US pt, 4 l, SAE 90 or SAE 20W-40, change every 3,100 miles, 5,000 km - gearbox 3 imp pt, 3.6 US pt, 1.7 l, SAE 90, change every 3,100 miles, 5,000 km - final drive 1.5 imp pt, 1.8 US pt, 0.8 l, change every 3,100 miles, 5,000 km; sparking plug: NGK-BP 7E; tappet clearances: inlet 0.008 in, 0.20 mm, exhaust 0.016 in, 0.40 mm; valve timing: 28° 64° 72° 20°; tyre pressure: front 20 psi, 1.4 atm, rear 20 psi, 1.4 atm.

OPTIONALS 165 SR x 13 tyres.

Dart Series

De Luxo 4-dr Sedan
De Luxo 2-dr Coupé
Gran 4-dr Sedan

ENGINE front, 4 stroke; 8 cylinders, Vee-slanted; 318 cu in, 5,212 cc (3.91 x 3.31 in, 99.3 x 84.1 mm); compression ratio: 7.5:1; max power (SAE): 149 hp (110 kW) at 4,400 rpm; max torque (SAE): 248 lb ft, 34.2 kg m (335 Nm) at 2,400 rpm; max engine rpm: 4,800 28.6 hp/l (21.2 kW/l); cast iron block and head; 5 crankshaft bearings; valves: overhead, in line, push-rods and rockers, hydraulic tappets; camshafts: 1, at centre of Vee; lubrication: rotary pump, full flow filter, 8.3 imp pt, 9.9 US pt, 4.7 l; 1 DFV downdraught twin barrel carburettor; fuel feed: mechanical pump; water-cooled, 33.4 imp pt, 40.2 US pt, 19 l.

TRANSMISSION driving wheels: rear; clutch: single dry plate; gearbox: mechanical; gears: 3, fully synchronized; ratios: I 2.670, II 1.600, III 1, rev 3.440; lever: steering column; final drive: hypoid bevel; axle ratio: 3.150; width of rims: 5.5"; tyres 185 SR x 14.

PERFORMANCE max speeds: (I) 48 mph, 78 km/h; (II) 71 mph, 115 km/h; (III) 102 mph, 164 km/h; power-weight ratio: De Luxo Sedan 22.1 lb/hp (30.1 lb/kW), 10.1 kg/hp (13.6 kg/kW) carrying capacity: 882 lb, 400 kg; acceleration: standing ¼ mile 19 sec, 0-50 mph (0-80 km/h) 9.8 sec; speed in direct drive at 1,000 rpm: 23 mph, 37 km/h; consumption: 17.7 m/imp gal, 14.3 m/US gal, 16.5 l x 100 km.

CHASSIS integral; front suspension: independent, wishbones (lower trailing links), longitudinal torsion bars, anti-roll bar, telescopic dampers; rear: rigid axle, semi-elliptic leafsprings, telescopic dampers.

STEERING recirculating ball, servo; turns lock to lock 6.50.

BRAKES front disc, rear drum, servo; swept area: total 354.3 sq in, 2,285 sq cm.

ELECTRICAL EQUIPMENT 12 V; 54 Ah battery; 480 W alternator; Chrysler electronic distributor; 2 headlamps.

DIMENSIONS AND WEIGHT wheels base: 111 in, 282 cm; tracks: 58.27 in, 148 cm front, 56.30 in, 143 cm rear; length: 202.36 in, 514 cm; width: 71.30 in, 181 cm; height: 54.70 in, 139 cm; ground clearance: 6.30 in, 16 cm; weight: De Luxo Sedan 3,301 lb, 1,497 kg - De Luxo Coupé 3,285 lb, 1,490 kg - Gran Sedan 3,285 lb, 1,490 kg; turning circle: 40.3 ft, 12.3 m; fuel tank: 23.5 imp gal, 28.2 US gal, 107 l.

BODY saloon/sedan, 4 doors - coupé, 2 doors; 6 seats, bench front seats.

PRACTICAL INSTRUCTIONS fuel: 73 oct petrol; oil: engine 8.3 imp pt, 9.9 US pt, 4.7 l, SAE 30 or 20W-40, change every 3,100 miles, 5,000 km - gearbox 3.5 imp pt, 4.2 US pt, 2 l, SAE 90, change every 9,300 miles, 15,000 km - final drive 4.2 imp pt, 5.1 US pt, 2.4 l, SAE 90, change every 6,200 miles, 10,000 km; sparking plug: NGK-AP6F; valve timing: 10° 50° 52° 16°; tyre pressure: front 18 psi, 26 atm, rear 1.8 psi, 26 atm.

OPTIONALS Torqueflite automatic transmission with 3 ratios (I 2.540, II 1.450, III 1, rev 2.200), max ratio of converter at stall 2.4, possible manual selection; 4-speed fully synchronized mechanical gearbox (I 2.670, II 1.860, III 1.300, IV 1, rev 3.140); central lever; 3.070 axle ratio; dual exhaust system; metallic spray; air-conditioning.

DODGE Dart De Luxo Coupé

DODGE Le Baron

Le Baron

ENGINE front, 4 stroke; 8 cylinders, Vee-slanted 318 cu in, 5,212 cc (3.91 x 3.31 in, 99.3 x 84.1 mm); compression ratio: 7.5:1; max power (SAE): 149 hp (110 kW) at 4,400 rpm; max torque (SAE): 248 lb ft, 34.2 kg m (335 Nm) at 2,400 rpm; max engine rpm: 4,800; 28.6 hp/l (21 kW/l); cast iron block and head: 5 crankshaft bearings; valves: overhead, in line, push-rods and rockers, hydraulic tappets; camshafts: 1 at centre of Vee; lubrication: rotary pump, full flow filter, 8.3 imp pt, 9.9 US pt, 4.7 l; 1 DFV downdraught twin barrel carburettor; dual exhaust system; fuel feed: mechanical pump: water-cooled, 33.4 imp pt, 40.2 US pt, 19 l.

TRANSMISSION driving wheels: rear; clutch: single dry plate; gearbox: mechanical; gears: 3, fully synchronized; ratios: I 2.670, II 1.600, III 1, rev 3.440 lever: steering column axle ratio: 3.150; width of rims: 5.5"; tyres: 7.35 S x 14.

PERFORMANCE max speeds: (I) 39 mph, 62 km/h; (II) 56 mph, 90 km/h; (III) 81 mph, 130 km/h; (IV) 112 mph, 180 km/h; power-weight ratio: 22.5 lb/hp (30.4 lb/kW), 10.2 kg/hp (13.8 kg/kW); carrying capacity: 882 lb, 400 kg; consumption: 20.2 m/imp gal, 16.8 m/US gal, 14 x 100 km.

CHASSIS integral; front suspension: independent, wishbones (lower trailing links), longitudinal torsion bars, anti-roll bar, telescopic dampers; rear: rigid axle, semi-elliptic leafsprings, telescopic dampers.

STEERING ricirculating ball, servo: turns lock to lock 6.50.

BRAKES front disc, rear drum, servo; swept area: total 354.3 sq in, 2,285 sq cm.

ELECTRICAL EQUIPMENT 12 V; 50 Ah battery; 480 W alternator; Chrysler electronic distributor: 4 headlamps.

DIMENSIONS AND WEIGHT wheel base: 111 in, 282 cm; tracks: 58,27 in, 148 cm front, 56.30 in, 143 cm rear; length: 202.36 in, 514 cm; width: 71.30 in, 181 cm; height: 54.70 in, 139 cm; ground clearance: 6.30 in, 16 cm; weight: 3,341 lb, 1,515 kg; turning circle: 40.3 ft, 12.3 m; fuel tank: 23.5 imp gal, 28.2 US gal, 107 l.

BODY saloon/sedan; 4 doors; 6 seats, bench front seats.

PRACTICAL INSTRUCTIONS fuel: 73 oct petrol; oil: engine 8.3 imp pt, 9.9 US pt, 4.7 l, SAE 30 or 20W-40, change every 3,100 miles, 5,000 km - gearbox 3.5 imp pt, 4.2 US pt, 2 l, SAE 90, change every 9,300 miles, 15,000 km - final drive 4.2 imp pt, 5.1 US pt, 2.4 l, SAE 90, change every 6,200 miles, 10,000 km; sparking plug: NGK-AP6F; valve timing: 10° 50° 52° 16°; tyre pressure: front 1.8 psi, 26 atm, rear 1.8 psi, 26 atm.

OPTIONALS Torqueflite automatic transmission, hydraulic torque converter and planetary gears with 3 ratios (I 2.540, II 1.450, III 1, rev 2.200), max ratio of converter at stall 2.4, possible manual selection, 3.070 axle ratio; air-conditioning.

Charger R/T - Magnum

See Le Baron, except for:

ENGINE max power (SAE): 165 hp (121 kW) at 4,400 rpm; max torque (SAE): 263 lb ft, 36.3 kg m (356 Nm) at 2,400 rpm; 31.7 hp/l (23.3 kW/l).

TRANSMISSION gears; 4, fully synchronized; ratios: I 2.670, II 1.860, III 1.300, IV 1, rev 3.140; lever: central; width of rims: Charger 6" - Magnum 5.5".

PERFORMANCE power-weight ratio: 20.3 lb/hp (27.6 lb/kW), 9.2 kg/hp (12.5 kg/kW).

BODY coupé; 2 doors; 5 seats, separate front seats.

DODGE Charger R/T

ENVEMO BRAZIL

90 Super Coupé / Cabriolet

ENGINE rear, 4 stroke; 4 cylinders, vertical, in line; 96.7 cu in, 1,584 cc (3.37 x 2.72 in, 85.5 x 69 mm); compression ratio: 7.2:1; max power (DIN): 65 hp (48 kW) at 4,600 rpm; max torque (DIN): 94 lb ft, 13 kg m (128 Nm) at 2,600 rpm; max engine rpm: 5,400; 41 hp/l (30.3 kW/l); light alloy block and head; 4 crankshaft bearings; valves: overhead, push-rods and rockers; camshafts: 1, central; lubrication: gear pump, 4.4 imp pt, 5.3 US pt, 2.5 l; 2 Solex 32 PDSIT downdraught twin barrel carburettors; fuel feed: mechanical pump; air-cooled.

TRANSMISSION driving wheels: rear; clutch: single dry plate; gearbox: mechanical; gears: 4, fully synchronized; ratios: I 3.800, II 2.060, III 1.320, IV 0.890, rev 3.700; lever: central; final drive: spiral bevel; axle ratio: 4.125; width of rims: 5.5''; tyres: 165 SR x 15.

PERFORMANCE max speed: 103 mph, 165 km/h; power-weight ratio: 29.2 lb/hp (39.7 lb/kW), 13.2 kg/hp (17.9 kg/kW); carrying capacity: 772 lb, 350 kg; speed in top at 1,000 rpm: 22 mph, 35 km/h; consumption: 32.5 m/imp gal, 27 m/US gal, 8.7 l x 100 km.

CHASSIS platform, reinforced side members; front suspension; independent, twin trailing links, anti-roll bar, transverse laminated torsion bars, telescopic dampers; rear: independent, swinging semi-axles, transverse laminated torsion bars, anti-roll bar, telescopic dampers.

STEERING worm and roller.

BRAKES front disc, rear drum; lining area: front 12.4 sq in, 80 sq cm, rear 69.8 sq in, 450 sq cm, total 82.2 sq in, 530 sq cm.

ELECTRICAL EQUIPMENT 12 V; 36 Ah battery; 25 A alternator; Bosch distributor; 2 headlamps.

DIMENSIONS AND WEIGHT wheel base: 82.68 in, 210 cm; tracks: 51.97 in, 132 cm front, 53.54 in, 136 cm rear; length: 157.87 in, 401 cm; width: 65.75 in, 167 cm; height: 52.36 in, 133 cm; ground clearance: 5.51 in, 14 cm; weight: 1,896 lb, 860 kg; turning circle: 36.1 ft, 11 m; fuel tank: 10.1 imp gal, 12.1 US gal, 46 l.

BODY coupé, convertible, in fiberglass material; 2 doors; 2+2 seats, separate front seats.

PRACTICAL INSTRUCTIONS fuel: 82 oct petrol; oil: engine 4.4 imp pt, 5.3 US pt, 2.5 l, SAE 20W-40, change every 3,100 miles, 5,000 km; tyre pressure: front 26 psi, 1.8 atm, rear 28 psi, 2.3 atm.

OPTIONALS leather upholstery; fog lamps; headrests; (for convertible only) detachable roof, hardtop and tonneau cover.

ENVEMO 90 Super Coupé

FIAT BRAZIL

147 Series

PRICES EX WORKS:	cruzeiro
1 147 2+1-dr Sedan	131,00
2 L 2+1-dr Sedan	136,10
3 GL 2+1-dr Sedan	147,70
4 GLS 2+1-dr Sedan	157,40
5 Rallye 2+1-dr Sedan	163,20

Power team:	Standard for:	Optional for:
57 hp	1 to 3	—
61 hp	4	—
72 hp	5	—

57 hp power team

ENGINE front, 4 stroke; 4 cylinders, transverse; 64 cu in 1,049 cc (2.99 x 2.23 in, 76 x 57.8 mm); compression ratio 7.2:1; max power (SAE): 57 hp (42 kW) at 5,800 rpm; max torque (SAE): 57 lb ft, 7.9 kg m (77 Nm) at 3,600 rpm; max engine rpm: 6,000; 54.3 hp/l (40 kW/l); light alloy block an head; 5 crankshaft bearings; valves: overhead; camshafts 1, overhead, cogged belt; lubrication: gear pump, full flo filter (cartridge), 7 imp pt, 8.5 US pt, 4 l; 1 downdraugh carburettor; fuel feed: mechanical pump; water-cooled, 10. imp pt, 12.3 US pt, 5.8 l.

TRANSMISSION driving wheels: front; clutch: single dr plate (diaphragm); gearbox: mechanical; gears: 4, fully syn chronized; ratios: I 4.091, II 2.235, III 1.455, IV 0.959, re 3.714; lever: central; final drive: cylindrical gears; ax ratio: 4.417; width of rims: 4''; tyres: 145 SR x 13.

PERFORMANCE max speeds: (I) 22 mph, 36 km/h; (II) 4 mph, 65 km/h; (III) 63 mph, 101 km/h; (IV) 85 mph, 13 km/h; power-weight ratio: 30.9 lb/hp (42 lb/kW), 14 kg/h (19.1 kg/kW); carrying capacity: 882 lb, 400 kg; accelera tion: standing ¼ mile 20.4 sec; consumption: 45 m/imp ga 38 m/US gal, 6.3 l x 100 km.

CHASSIS integral; front suspension: independent, b McPherson, coil springs/telescopic damper struts, lowe wishbones, anti-roll bar; rear: independent, single wide based wishbone, transverse anti-roll leafspring, telescopi dampers.

STEERING rack-and-pinion; turns lock to lock: 3.40.

BRAKES front disc, rear drum; lining area: front 12 sq in 77 sq cm, rear 16.7 sq in, 108 sq cm, total 28.7 sq in, 18 sq cm.

ELECTRICAL EQUIPMENT 12 V; 36 Ah battery; 35 A alter nator; 2 headlamps.

DIMENSIONS AND WEIGHT wheel base: 87.60 in, 223 cm tracks: 50 in, 127 cm front, 50.79 in, 129 cm rear; length 142.91 in, 363 cm; width: 60.83 in, 154 cm; height: 53.15 in 135 cm; ground clearance: 5.10 in, 14 cm; weight: 1,764 lb 800 kg; weight distribution: 49.6% front, 50.4% rear; turnin circle: 39 ft, 9.1 m; fuel tank: 8.4 imp gal, 10 US gal, 38

BODY saloon/sedan; 2+1 doors; 5 seats, separate fron seats; folding rear seat; headrests (for GL only).

PRACTICAL INSTRUCTIONS fuel: 72 oct petrol; oil: engin 7 imp pt, 8.3 US pt, 4 l, SAE 20W-40 change every 6,20 miles, 10,000 km - gearbox and final drive 5.3 imp pt, 6. US pt, 3.2 l, SAE 90, change every 18,600 miles, 30,00 km; greasing: none; sparking plug: Bosch NI 75 T 30 c NGK BP-7E; tappet clearances: inlet 0.016 in, 0.40 mm exhaust 0.020 in 0.50 mm); valve timing: 6° 46° 47° 7°; tyr pressure: front 27 psi, 1.9 atm, rear 31 psi, 2.2 atm.

OPTIONALS reclining backrests; headrests (for L only) metallic spray and heated rear window (for L and GL only)

61 hp power team

See 57 hp power team, except for:

ENGINE 79 cu in, 1,297 cc (2.99 x 2.81 in, 76 x 71.5 mm) compression ratio: 7.5:1; max power (SAE): 61 hp (45 kW at 5,400 rpm; max torque (SAE): 72 lb ft, 9.9 kg m (97 Nm at 3,000 rpm; 47 hp/l (34.6 kW/l).

TRANSMISSION axle ratio: 4.080.

PERFORMANCE max speeds: (I) 22 mph, 36 km/h; (II) 4 mph, 65 km/h; (III) 62 mph, 99 km/h; (IV) 87 mph, 140 km/h power-weight ratio: 29.3 lb/hp (39.8 lb/kW), 13.3 kg/hp (1 kg/kW).

DIMENSIONS AND WEIGHT weight: 1,786 lb, 810 kg.

72 hp power team

See 57 hp power team, except for:

FIAT 147 GLS Sedan

ENGINE 79 cu in, 1,297 cc (2.99 x 2.81 in, 76 x 71.5 mm); compression ratio: 7.5:1; max power (SAE): 72 hp (53 kW) at 5,800 rpm; max torque (SAE): 78 lb ft, 10.8 kg m (106 Nm) at 4,000 rpm; 55.5 hp/l (40.8 kW/l); downdraught twin barrel carburettor.

TRASMISSION axle ratio: 4.080.

PERFORMANCE max speeds: (I) 22 mph, 36 km/h; (II) 42 mph, 67 km/h; (III) 65 mph, 104 km/h; (IV) 93 mph, 150 km/h; power-weight ratio: 24.8 lb/hp (33.7 lb/kW), 11.2 kg/hp (15.2 kg/kW).

DIMENSIONS AND WEIGHT weight: 1,786 lb, 810 kg.

Alfa Romeo 2300 B

PRICE EX WORKS: 367,500 cruzeiros

ENGINE front, 4 stroke; 4 cylinders, vertical, in line; 141 cu in, 2,310 cc (3.46 x 3.74 in, 88 x 95 mm); compression ratio: 7.5:1; max power (SAE): 141 hp (104 kW) at 5,700 rpm; max torque (SAE): 156 lb ft, 21.5 kg m (211 Nm) at 3,500 rpm; max engine rpm: 5,700; 61 hp/l (44.9 kW/l); light alloy block and head; 5 crankshaft bearings; valves: overhead, Vee-slanted at 90°, thimble tappets; camshafts: 2, overhead; lubrication: gear pump, by-pass filter, 12.3 imp pt, 14.8 US pt, 7 l; 1 Solex C-34 EIES downdraught twin barrel carburettor; fuel feed: mechanical pump; watercooled, 16 imp pt, 19.2 US pt, 9.1 l, electric thermostatic fan.

TRANSMISSION driving wheels: rear; clutch: single dry plate (diaphragm), hydraulically controlled; gearbox: mechanical; gears: 5, fully synchronized; ratios: I 3.303, II 1.985, III 1.353, IV 1, V 0.790, rev 3.008; lever: central; final drive: hypoid bevel; axle ratio: 4.778; width of rims: 6"; tyres: 185 SR x 14.

PERFORMANCE max speeds: (I) 25 mph, 41 km/h; (II) 42 mph, 68 km/h; (III) 62 mph, 100 km/h; (IV) 84 mph, 135 km/h; (V) 106 mph, 170 km/h; power-weight ratio: 18.9 lb/hp (25.7 lb/kW), 8.6 kg/hp (11.7 kg/kW); carrying capacity: 1,180 lb, 535 kg; speed in top at 1,000 rpm: 19.3 mph, 31 km/h; consumption: 27.6 m/imp gal, 23 m/US gal, 10.2 l x 100 km.

CHASSIS integral; front suspension: independent, wishbones (lower trailing links), coil springs, anti-roll bar, telescopic dampers; rear: rigid axle, trailing lower radius arms, upper transverse Vee radius arms, twin transverse linkage bar, coil springs/telescopic damper struts.

STEERING worm and roller; turns lock to lock: 4.50.

BRAKES disc (front diameter 11.02 in, 28 cm, rear 11.06 in, 28.1 cm), dual circuit, rear compensator, servo; swept area: front 207.1 sq in, 1,336 sq cm, rear 207.1 sq in, 1,336 sq cm, total 414.2 sq in, 2,672 sq cm.

ELECTRICAL EQUIPMENT 12 V; 54 Ah battery; 420 W alternator; Bosch distributor; 4 iodine headlamps.

DIMENSIONS AND WEIGHT wheel base: 107.48 in, 273 cm; front and rear track: 55.12 in, 140 cm; length: 185.82 in, 472 cm; width: 66.54 in, 169 cm; height: 59.69 in, 144 cm; ground clearance: 5.91 in, 15 cm; weight: 2,668 lb, 1,210 kg; turning circle: 41 ft, 12.6 m; fuel tank: 22 imp gal, 26.4 US gal, 100 l.

BODY saloon/sedan; 4 doors; 5 seats, separate front seats, reclining backrests.

PRACTICAL INSTRUCTIONS fuel: 72 oct petrol; oil: engine 12.3 imp pt, 14.8 US pt, 7 l, SAE 20W-50, change every 6,200 miles, 10,000 km - gearbox 3.2 imp pt, 3.8 US pt, 1.8 l, SAE 90 EP, change every 6,200 miles, 10,000 km - final drive 5.1 imp pt, 6.1 US pt, 2.9 l, SAE 90 EP, change every 18,600 miles, 30,000 km; greasing: none; sparking plug: NGK-BP7E; tappet clearances: inlet 0.015 in, 0.37 mm, exhaust 0.017 in, 0.42 mm; valve timing: 13°20' 48°28' 48°28' 13°20'; tyre pressure: front 26 psi, 1.8 atm, rear 27 psi, 1.9 atm.

OPTIONALS air-conditioning; tinted glass; metallic spray.

Alfa Romeo 2300 TI

See Alfa Romeo 2300 B, except for:

PRICE EX WORKS: 469,200 cruzeiros

ENGINE max power (SAE): 149 hp (110 kW) at 5,700 rpm; max torque (SAE): 167 lb ft, 23 kg m (226 Nm) at 3,500 rpm; 64.5 hp/l; 2 Solex C-40 ADD HE-12 downdraught twin barrel carburettors.

PERFORMANCE max speed 109 mph, 175 km/h; power-weight ratio: 18.2 lb/hp, 8.2 kg/hp; consumption: 25.4 m/imp gal, 21 m/US gal, 11.1 l x 100 km.

ELECTRICAL EQUIPMENT 540 W alternator; 4 iodine headlamps.

FIAT 147 Rallye Sedan

FIAT Alfa Romeo 2300 TI

ALFA ROMEO 2300 TI

DIMENSIONS AND WEIGHT length: 185.82 in, 472 cm; height: 59.69 in, 144 cm; weight: 2,712 lb, 1,230 kg.

BODY luxury equipment; built-in headrests on rear seats; air-conditioning; tinted glass.

OPTIONALS only metallic spray.

FORD BRAZIL

Corcel II Base / L / LDO

PRICES EX WORKS:	**cruzeiros**
Corcel II Base 2-dr Sedan	**157,300**
Corcel II L 2-dr Sedan	**175,100**
Corcel II LDO 2-dr Sedan	**209,000**

ENGINE front, 4 stroke; 4 cylinders, vertical, in line; 83.7 cu in, 1,372 cc (2.96 x 3.03 in, 75.3 x 77 mm); compression ratio: 8:1; max power (SAE):72 hp (53 kW) at 5,400 rpm; max torque (SAE): 83 lb ft, 11.5 kg m (156 Nm) at 3,600 rpm; max engine rpm: 5,800; 52.5 hp/l (38.6 kW/l); cast iron block, light alloy head; 5 crankshaft bearings; valves: overhead, push-rods and rockers; camshafts: 1, in crankcase; lubrication: gear pump, full flow filter, 5.3 imp pt, 6.3 US pt, 3 l; 1 DFV 228 downdraught carburettor; fuel feed: mechanical pump; sealed circuit cooling, water, 7.6 imp pt, 9.1 US pt, 4.3 l.

TRANSMISSION driving wheels: front; clutch: single dry plate; gearbox: mechanical; gears: 4, fully synchronized; ratios: I 3.460, II 2.210, III 1.420, IV 0.970, rev 3.080; lever: central; final drive: hypoid bevel; axle ratio: 3.875; width of rims: 4.5"; tyres: 6.45 x 13.

PERFORMANCE max speeds: (I) 27 mph, 44 km/h; (II) 43 mph, 69 km/h; (III) 66 mph, 107 km/h; (IV) 88 mph, 141 km/h; power-weight ratio: Base 26.7 lb/hp (36.4 lb/kW), 12.1 kg/hp (16.5 kg/kW); carrying capacity: 873 lb, 396 kg; speed in top at 1,000 rpm: 17 mph, 27 km/h; consumption: 32.8 m/imp gal, 27.3 m/US gal, 8.6 l x 100 km.

CHASSIS integral; front suspension: independent, wishbones, upper trailing arms, coil springs, anti-roll bar, telescopic dampers; rear: rigid axle, upper and lower trailing arms, coil springs, telescopic dampers.

STEERING rack-and-pinion; turns lock to lock: 3.39.

BRAKES front disc, rear drum; lining area: total 150 sq in, 968 sq cm.

ELECTRICAL EQUIPMENT 12 v; 36 Ah battery; alternator; Bosch distributor; 2 headlamps.

DIMENSIONS AND WEIGHT wheel base: 96.06 in, 244 cm; tracks: 53.50 in, 136 cm front, 53.14 in, 135 cm rear; length: 175.98 in, 447 cm - LDO 177.16 in, 450 cm; width: 65.35 in, 166 cm; height: 53.14 in, 135 cm; ground clearance: 5.50 in, 14 cm; weight: Base 2,013 lb, 913 kg - L 2.033 lb, 922 kg - LDO 2,115 lb, 959 kg; weight distribution: 59% front, 41% rear; turning circle: 36.7 ft, 11.2 m; fuel tank: 12.5 imp gal, 15 US gal, 57 l.

BODY saloon/sedan; 2 doors; 5 seats, separate front seats.

VARIATIONS

ENGINE 94.9 cu in, 1,555 cc (3.03 x 3.29 in, 77 x 83.5 mm), max power (SAE) 90 hp (66 kW) at 5,600 rpm, max torque (SAE) 94 lb ft, 13 kg m (128 Nm) at 4,000 rpm, 1 Solex 2 V downdraught carburettor.

OPTIONALS 5-speed mechanical gearbox; servo brake; 5" wide rims; 185/70 SR x 13.

FORD Corcel II L Sedan

Corcel II Belina Base / L / LDO

See Corcel II Base / L / LDO, except for:

PRICES EX WORKS:	**cruzeiros**
Corcel II Belina Base 2+1-dr St. Wagon	**182,500**
Corcel II Belina L 2+1-dr St. Wagon	**195,900**
Corcel II Belina LDO 2+1-dr St. Wagon	**218,400**

PERFORMANCE power-weight ratio: Belina Base 27.8 lb/hp (37.7 lb/kW), 12.6 kg/hp (17.1 kg/kW); carrying capacity: 1,005 lb, 456 kg; acceleration: 0-50 mph (0-80 km/h) 20.6 sec; consumption: 30 m/imp gal, 25.1 m/US gal, 9.4 l x 100 km.

DIMENSIONS AND WEIGHT lenght: 176.77 in, 449 cm - Belina LDO 177.95 in, 452 cm; height: 53.54 in, 136 cm; weight: Belina Base 1,967 lb, 892 kg - Belina L 1,986 lb, 901 kg - Belina LDO 2,022 lb, 917 kg; fuel tank: 13.8 imp gal, 16.6 US gal, 63 l.

BODY estate car/st. wagon; 2+1 doors.

Corcel II GT

See Corcel II Base / L / LDO, except for:

PRICE EX WORKS: 202,300 cruzeiros

ENGINE max power (SAE): 90 hp (66 kW) at 5,600 rpm; max torque (SAE): 94 lb ft, 13 kg m (128 Nm) at 4,000 rpm; 65.6 hp/l (48 kW/l); 1 Solex 34 SIE-2V downdraught carburettor.

PERFORMANCE power-weight ratio: 21.7 lb/hp (29.7 lb/kW), 10 kg/hp (13.4 kg/kW).

ELECTRICAL EQUIPMENT 42 Ah battery.

DIMENSIONS AND WEIGHT weight: 1,958 lb, 888 kg.

VARIATIONS

ENGINE 94.9 cu in, 1,555 cc (3.03 x 3.29 in, 77 x 83.5 mm), 12:1 compression ratio, max power (SAE) 56 hp (41 kW) at 4,600 rpm, max torque (SAE) 83 lb, 11.5 kg m (113 Nm) a

FORD Corcel II Belina

FORD Corcel II Berlina LDO Station Wagon

,200 rpm; 36 hp/l (26.5 kW), 1 Solex 1 V downdraught car-urettor, hydrated alcohol fuel feed.

PTIONALS GPS70 steel belt tyres.

Galaxie 500 / LTD / Landau

RICES EX WORKS:	**cruzeiros**
alaxie 500 4-dr Sedan	**399,300**
alaxie LTD 4-dr Sedan	**447,500**
alaxie Landau 4-dr Sedan	**510,800**

NGINE front, 4 stroke; 8 cylinders, Vee-slanted at 90°; 302 cu n, 4,950 cc (4 x 3 in, 101.6 x 76.2 mm); compression ratio: .8:1; max power (SAE): 197 hp (145 kW) at 4,600 rpm; max orque (SAE): 288 lb ft, 39.8 kg m (390 Nm) at 2,400 rpm; max ngine rpm: 4,800; 40.2 hp/l (29.3 kW/l); cast iron block and ead; 5 crankshaft bearings; valves: overhead, push-rods and ockers; camshaft: 1, at centre of Vee; lubrication: gear pump, ull flow filter, 8.3 imp pt, 9.9 US pt, 4.7 l; 1 Motorcraft owndraught twin barrel carburettor; fuel feed: mechanical ump; water-cooled, 19.4 imp pt, 23.3 US pt, 11 l.

RANSMISSION driving wheels: rear; clutch: single dry plate; earbox: mechanical; gears: 3, fully synchronized; ratios: I .920, II 1.750, III 1, rev 3.760; lever: steering column; final rive: hypoid bevel; axle ratio: 3.540; width of rims: 5"; tyres: 15/70 HR x 15.

ERFORMANCE max speeds: (I) 37 mph, 59 km/h; (II) 61 mph,

FORD Corcel II GT

FORD Galaxie Landau Sedan

8 km/h; (III) 103 mph, 165 km/h; power-weight ratio: 19.4 lb/hp 26.7 lb/kW), 8.6 kg/hp (12.1 kg/kW); carrying capacity: 1,069 , 485 kg; speed in direct drive at 1,000 rpm: 22.2 mph, 35.7 m/h; consumption: 19.6 m/imp gal, 16.3 m/US gal, 14.4 l x 100 m.

HASSIS box-type ladder frame; front suspension: indepen-ent, wishbones, lower trailing arms, coil springs, antiroll bar, elescopic dampers; rear: rigid axle, lower trailing arms, upper orque arms, coil springs, telescopic dampers.

TEERING recirculating ball, servo; turns lock to lock: 4.

RAKES front disc, internal radial fins, rear drum, servo; lining rea: total 103.7 sq in, 669 sq cm.

LECTRICAL EQUIPMENT 12 V; 54 Ah battery; 55 A alterna-or; 4 headlamps.

IMENSIONS AND WEIGHT wheel base: 119.02 in, 302 cm; ront and rear track: 62.42 in, 158 cm; length: 212.99 in, 541 m; width: 78.74 in, 200 cm; height: 55.51 in, 141 cm; ground learance: 5.51 in, 14 cm; weight: 3,859 lb, 1,750 kg; turning ircle: 44 ft, 13.4 m; fuel tank: 16.7 imp gal, 20.1 US gal, 76 l.

ODY saloon/sedan; 4 doors; 6 seats; bench front seats; (for TD only) luxury equipment.

VARIATIONS

NGINE 11:1 compression ratio, max power (SAE) 154 hp (113 W) at 4,200 rpm, max torque (SAE) 236 lb ft, 32,6 kg m (320 m) at 2,800 rpm, 31.1 hp/l (22.8 kW/l).
LECTRICAL EQUIPMENT 12 V, 60 Ah battery.

OPTIONALS Ford-o-Matic automatic transmission, hydraulic torque converter and planetary gears with 3 ratios (I 2.460, II 1.460, III 1, rev 2.200), max ratio of converter at stall 2.1, possible manual selection, 3.310 axle ratio; air-conditioning.

Cavalo de Ferro

ENGINE front, 4 stroke; 4 cylinders, in line; 140.3 cu in, 2,300 cc (3.78 x 3.11 in, 96 x 79 mm); compression ratio: 7.8:1; max power (SAE): 91 hp (67 kW) at 5,000 rpm; max torque (SAE): 123 lb ft, 17 kg m (167 Nm) at 3,000 rpm; max engine rpm: 5,500; 39.6 hp/l (29.1 kW/l); 1 downdraught carburettor; lubrication: 8.3 imp pt, 18.4 US pt, 4.7 l; water-cooled.

TRANSMISSION driving wheels: front and rear; clutch: single dry plate; gearbox: mechanical; gears: 4, fully synchronized with transfer box; ratios: I 3.570, II 2.380, III 1.530, IV 1; rev 4.230; transfer box ratios: high 2.460, low 1; axle ratio: 4.890; width of rims: 4"; tyres: 6.00 x 16.

PERFORMANCE power-weight ratio: 26.5 lb/hp (36.2 lb/kW), 12 kg/hp (16.4 kg/kW); carrying capacity: 1,334 lb, 605 kg.

CHASSIS U box-type; front suspension: semi-elliptic leaf-springs, double effect telescopic dampers.

STEERING worm and wheel.

BRAKES drum; swept area: total 159.4 sq in, 1,028 sq cm.

ELECTRICAL EQUIPMENT 12 V; 40 Ah battery; 30 A alternator; 2 headlamps.

FORD Galaxie Landau Sedan

FORD Cavalo de Ferro

GURGEL X-12 TR

DIMENSIONS AND WEIGHT wheel base: 81.10 in, 206 cm; front and rear track: 48.43 in, 123 cm; length: 135.43 in, 344 cm; width: 80.31 in, 170 cm; height: 68.11 in, 173 cm; ground clearance: 8.03 in, 20.4 cm; weight: 2,417 lb, 1,096 kg; fuel tank: 8.8 imp gal, 10.6 US gal, 40 l.

BODY open; no doors; 5 seats, separate front seats.

OPTIONALS canvas top.

GURGEL BRAZIL

X-12 / X-12 TR

PRICE EX WORKS: 196,000 cruzeiros

ENGINE Volkswagen, rear, 4 stroke; 4 cylinders, horizontally opposed; 96.7 cu in, 1,584 cc (3.37 x 2.72 in, 85.5 x 69 mm); compression ratio: 7.2:1; max power (DIN): 50 hp (37 kW) at 4,200 rpm; max torque (DIN): 80 lb ft, 11 kg m (108 Nm) at 2,200 rpm; max engine rpm: 4,600; 31.6 hp/l (23.2 kW/l); block with cast iron liners and light alloy fins, light alloy head; 4 crankshaft bearings; valves: overhead, push-rods and rockers; camshafts: 1, central, lower; lubrication: gear pump, oil cooler, 4.4 imp pt, 5.3 US pt, 2.5 l; 1 Solex H 30 Pic downdraught single barrel carburettor; fuel feed: mechanical pump; air-cooled.

TRANSMISSION driving wheels: rear; clutch: single dry plate gearbox: mechanical; gears: 4, fully synchronized; ratios: 3.800, II 2.060, III 1.320, IV 0.890, rev 3.880; lever: centra final drive: spiral bevel; axle ratio: 4.375; width of rims: 5.5' tyres: 5.60 x 15.

PERFORMANCE max speed: (I) 17 mph, 27 km/h; (II) 32 mph 51 km/h; (III) 50 mph, 80 km/h; (IV) 73 mph, 118 km/h power-weight ratio: X-12 32.6 lb/hp (47.6 lb/kW), 14.8 kg/h (21.6 kg/kW); carrying capacity: 772 lb, 350 kg; acceleration 0-50 mph (0-80 km/h) 10.1 sec; speed in top at 1,000 rpm: 18. mph, 30 km/h; consumption: 28.2 m/imp gal, 23.5 m/US gal, 1 l x 100 km.

CHASSIS backbone platform; front suspension: independent twin swinging longitudinal trailing arms, transverse laminate torsion bars, telescopic dampers; rear: independent, swingin semi-axle, swinging longitudinal trailing arms, transverse tor sion bars, telescopic dampers.

STEERING worm and roller; turns lock to lock: 2.50.

BRAKES drum; lining area: front 20.5 sq in, 132 sq cm, rea 20.8 sq in, 134 sq cm, total 41.2 sq in, 266 sq cm.

ELECTRICAL EQUIPMENT 12 V; 36 Ah battery; 350 W dyna mo; Bosch distributor; 2 headlamps.

DIMENSIONS AND WEIGHT wheel base: 80.31 in, 204 cm tracks: 53.15 in, 135 cm front, 55.12 in, 140 cm rear; length 51.57 in, 331 cm; width: 64.57 in, 164 cm; height: 59.06 in, 15 cm; ground clearance: 13.11 in, 33 cm; weight: X-12 1,632 lb 740 kg - X-12 TR 1,764 lb, 800 kg; weight distribution: 60% front, 40% rear; turning circle: 36.1 ft, 11 m; fuel tank: 8.1 im gal, 9.8 US gal, 37 l.

BODY estate car/st. wagon, in plastic material; 2 doors; seats, separate front seats.

PRACTICAL INSTRUCTIONS fuel: 73 oct petrol; oil: engine 4. imp pt, 5.3 US pt, 2.5 l, SAE 20W-40, change every 3,10 miles, 5,000 km - gearbox 4.4 imp pt, 5.3 US pt, 2.5 l, SAE 9 EP, change every 9,300 miles, 15,000 km; greasing: ever 6,200 miles, 10,000 km, 4 points; valve timing: 9°48' 35°02 44°28' 4°14'; tyre pressure: front 16 psi, 1.1 atm, rear 20 ps 1.4 atm.

OPTIONALS limited slip differential; anti-roll bar on front an rear suspension.

LAFER BRAZIL

MP / TI

PRICES EX WORKS:	cruzeiro
MP	277,90
TI	300,40

ENGINE Volkswagen, rear, 4 stroke; 4 cylinders, horizontall opposed; 96.7 cu in, 1,584 cc (3.37 x 2.72 in, 85.5 x 69 mm) compression ratio: 7.2:1; max power (SAE): 65 hp (48 kW) a

LAFER TI

LAFER LL

,600 rpm; max torque (SAE): 87 lb ft, 12 kg m (118 Nm) at ,200 rpm; max engine rpm: 4,800; 41 hp/l (30.2 kW/l); block ith cast iron liners and light alloy fins, light alloy head; 4 rankshaft bearings; valves: overhead, in line, push-rods and ockers; camshafts: 1, central, lower; lubrication: gear pump, lter in sump, oil cooler, 4.4 imp pt, 5.3 US pt, 2.5 l; 2 Solex H 2 twin barrel carburettors; fuel feed: mechanical pump; air ooled.

RANSMISSION driving wheels: rear; clutch: single dry plate; earbox: mechanical; gears: 4, fully synchronized; ratios: I .800, II 2.060, III 1,320, IV 0.890, rev 3.880; lever: central; nal drive: spiral bevel; axle ratio: 4.125; width of rims: 4.5"; res: 5.60 x 15.

ERFORMANCE max speeds: (I) 25 mph, 41 km/h; (II) 48 mph, 7 km/h; (III) 71 mph, 115 km/h; (IV) 86 mph, 138 km/h; ower-weight ratio: 25.8 lb/hp (35.1 lb/kW), 11.7 kg/hp (15.9 g/kW); acceleration: standing ¼ mile 22.5 sec, 0-50 mph)-80 km/h) 9.9 sec; speed in direct drive at 1,000 rpm: 19.6 ph, 31.6 km/h; consumption: 32.8 m/imp gal, 27.3 m/US gal, .6 l x 100 km.

HASSIS backbone platform, rear auxiliary frame; front sus-ension: independent, twin swinging longitudinal trailing arms, ansverse laminated torsion bars, anti-roll bar, telescopic dam-ers; rear: independent, semi-trailing arms, transverse compen-ating torsion bars, anti-roll bar, telescopic dampers.

TEERING worm and roller; turns lock to lock: 2.60.

RAKES front disc (diameter 10.94 in, 27.8 cm), rear drum; ning area: front 11.7 sq in, 76 sq cm, rear 56.4 sq in, 364 sq m, total 68.2 sq in, 440 sq cm.

LECTRICAL EQUIPMENT 12 V; 36 Ah battery; 350 W alterna-r; Bosch distributor; 2 headlamps.

IMENSIONS AND WEIGHT wheel base: 94.49 in, 240 cm; acks: 51.57 in, 131 cm front, 53.15 in, 135 cm rear; length 53.94 in, 391 cm; width: 61.81 in, 157 cm; height: 53.15 in, 35 cm; ground clearance: 5.90 in, 15 cm; weight: 1,676 lb, 760 g; weight distribution: 40% front, 60% rear; turning circle: 36.1 , 11 m; fuel tank: 10.1 imp gal, 12.1 US gal, 46 l.

ODY roadster; 2 doors; 2 seats; TI luxury equipment.

RACTICAL INSTRUCTIONS fuel: 70-75 oct petrol; oil: engine .4 imp pt, 5.3 US pt, 2.5 l, change every 3,100 miles, 5,000 km gearbox 4.4 imp pt, 5.3 US pt, 2.5 l; greasing: every 6,200 iles, 10,000 km; tyre pressure: front 15 psi, 1.1 atm, rear 18 si, 1.3 atm.

PTIONALS 175 SR x 14 tyres with light alloy wheels; hardtop; auxiliary halogen headlamps; leather upholstery; tinted glass.

LL

RICE EX WORKS: 567,900 cruzeiros

NGINE front, 4 stroke; 6 cylinders, in line; 250 cu in, 4,097 cc 3.87 x 3.53 in, 98.4 x 89.6 mm); compression ratio: 8:1; max ower (SAE): 169 hp (124 kW) at 4,800 rpm; max torque (SAE): 61 lb ft, 36 kg m (353 Nm) at 2,400 rpm; max engine rpm: ,200; 42.2 hp/l (30.3 kW/l); cast iron block and head; 7 rankshaft bearings; valves: overhead, in line, push-rods and ockers; camshaft: 1, side; lubrication: gear pump, full flow lter, 7 imp pt, 8.5 US pt, 4 l; 1 Solex H 40 EIS downdraught ingle barrel carburettor; fuel feed: mechanical pump; water-ooled, 33.4 imp pt, 40.2 US pt, 19 l.

TRANSMISSION driving wheels: rear; clutch: single dry plate; gearbox: mechanical; gears: 4, fully synchronized; ratios: I 2.790, II 2.020, III 1.390, IV 1, rev 3.570; lever: central; final drive: hypoid bevel; axle ratio: 3.080; width of rims: 8"; tyres: 70 HR x 14.

PERFORMANCE max speeds: (I) 45 mph, 73 km/h; (II) 63 mph, 101 km/h; (III) 91 mph, 147 km/h; (IV) 137 mph, 220 km/h; power-weight ratio: 17.6 lb/hp (24 lb/kW), 7.9 kg/hp (10.9 kg/kW); carrying capacity: 706 lb, 320 kg; acceleration standing ¼ mile 18.3 sec, 0-50 mph (0-80 km/h) 7.5 sec; speed in direct drive at 1,000 rpm: 25 mph, 41 km/h; consumption: 19.5 m/imp gal, 16.2 m/US gal, 14.5 l x 100 km.

CHASSIS integral; front suspension: independent, wishbones, coil springs, anti-roll bar, telescopic dampers; rear: rigid axle, longitudinal trailing arms, coil springs, telescopic dampers.

STEERING recirculating ball, servo; turns lock to lock: 3.75.

BRAKES front disc, rear drum, servo; swept area: front 114.4 sq in, 738 sq cm, rear 58.9 sq in, 380 sq cm, total 173.3 sq in, 1,118 sq cm.

ELECTRICAL EQUIPMENT 12 V; 60 Ah battery, 55 A alterna-tor; Bosch distributor; 4 headlamps.

DIMENSIONS AND WEIGHT wheel base: 105.12 in, 267 cm; tracks: 57.09 in, 145 cm front, 58.66 in, 149 cm rear; length: 177.95 in, 452 cm; width: 69.68 in, 177 cm; height: 50.79 in, 129 cm; ground clearance: 7.09 in, 18 cm; weight: 2,977 lb, 1,350 kg; weight distribution: 53% front, 47% rear; turning circle: 41 ft, 12.5 m; fuel tank: 18.9 imp gal, 22.7 US gal, 86 l.

BODY coupé; 2 doors; 2 + 2 seats, separate front seats; elec-tric windows; tinted glass; leather upholstery; air-conditioning.

PRACTICAL INSTRUCTIONS fuel: 80 oct petrol; oil: engine 8,3 imp pt, 9.9 US pt, 4.7 l, change every 7,500 miles, 12,000 km - gearbox 6.2 imp pt, 7.4 US pt, 3.5 l, change every 3,100 miles, 5,000 km - final drive 2.1 imp pt, 2.5 US pt, 1.2 l, SAE 90, change every 5,000 miles, 8,000 km; tyre pressure: front 24 psi, 1.7 atm, rear 22 psi, 1.6 atm.

OPTIONALS 0.930 gearbox ratio in IV; automatic transmission.

MARQUEZ BRAZIL

GTM

ENGINE front, 4 stroke; 4 cylinders, horizontally opposed; 96.7 cu in, 1,585 cc (3.37 x 2.72 in, 85.5 x 69 mm); compression ratio: 7.2:1; max power (DIN): 54 hp (40 kW) at 4,200 rpm; max torque (DIN): 78 lb ft, 10.8 kg m (106 Nm) at 3,000 rpm; max engine rpm: 4,700; 34.1 hp/l (25.2 kW/l); light alloy block and head; 4 crankshaft bearings; valves: overhead; camshafts: 1, side; lubrication: gear pump, full flow filter, oil cooler, 4.4 imp pt, 5.3 US pt, 2.5 l; 2 Solex/Brosol 32 PDSIT downdraught carburettors; fuel feed: electric pump; air-cooled.

TRANSMISSION driving wheels: rear; clutch: single dry plate; gearbox: mechanical; gears: 4, fully synchronized; ratios: I 3.800, II 2.060, III 1.320, IV 0.890, rev 3.880; lever: central; final drive: hypoid bevel; axle ratio: 3.870; width of rims: 6" front, 8" rear; tyres: 175 SR x 14 front, 185 SR x 14 rear.

PERFORMANCE max speed: 93 mph, 150 km/h; power-weight ratio: 30 lb/hp (22.1 lb/kW), 13.6 kg/hp (18.5 kg/kW); consump-tion: 23.5 m/imp gal, 19.6 m/US gal, 12 l x 100 km.

CHASSIS backbone platform; front suspension: independent, upper torque arms, transverse torsion bars, telescopic dam-pers; rear: independent, swinging longitudinal leading arms, swinging leading arms, transverse torsion bar, anti-roll bar, telescopic dampers.

STEERING rack-and-pinion.

BRAKES front disc (diameter 10.94 in, 27.8 cm), rear drum.

ELECTRICAL EQUIPMENT 12 V; 36 Ah battery; 25 A alterna-tor; 2 retractable headlamps.

DIMENSIONS AND WEIGHT wheel base: 88.58 in, 225 cm; tracks: 54.72 in, 139 cm front, 55.12 in, 140 cm rear; length: 155.91 in, 396 cm; width: 66.14 in, 168 cm; height: 43.31 in, 110 cm; ground clearance: 5.12 in, 13 cm; weight: 1,621 lb, 735 kg; fuel tank: 8.8 imp gal, 10.6 US gal, 40 l.

BODY coupé, convertible; 2 doors; 2 seats.

PRACTICAL INSTRUCTIONS fuel: 70 oct petrol; oil: engine 4.4 imp pt, 5.3 US pt, 2.5 l, 20W-40, change every 3,100 miles, 5,000 km; greasing: every 6,200 miles, 10,000 km, 4 points; sparking plug: Bosch 175 NGKA 6; tyre pressure: front 26 psi, 1.8 atm, rear 27 psi, 1.9 atm.

MARQUEZ GTM

PUMA BRAZIL

GTE 1600 Coupé - GTS 1600 Sport

ENGINE Volkswagen, rear, 4 stroke; 4 cylinders, horizontally opposed; 96.7 cu in, 1.584 cc (3.37 x 2.72 in, 85.5 x 69 mm); compression ratio: 9:1; max power (SAE): 90 hp (66 kW) at 5,800 rpm; max torque (SAE): 96 lb ft, 13.2 kg m (129 Nm) at 3,000 rpm; max engine rpm: 6,000; 56.8 hp/l (41.8 kW/l); block with cast iron liners and light alloy fins, light alloy head; 4 crankshaft bearings; valves: overhead, push-rods and rockers; camshaft: 1, central, lower; lubrication: gear pump, filter in sump, oil cooler, 4.4 imp pt, 5.3 US pt, 2.5 l; 2 Solex-Brosol H40 EIS downdraught single barrel carburettors; fuel feed: mechanical pump; air-cooled.

TRANSMISSION driving wheels: rear; clutch: single dry plate; gearbox: mechanical; gears: 4, fully synchronized; ratios: I 3.800, II 2.060, III 1.320, IV 0.890, rev 3.880; lever: central; final drive: spiral bevel; axle ratio: 4.125; width of rims: 6''; tyres: front 185/70 HR x 14, rear 195/70 HR x 14.

PERFORMANCE max speeds: (I) 26 mph, 42 km/h; (II) 47 mph, 76 km/h; (III) 75 mph, 120 km/h; (IV) 113 mph, 182 km/h; power-weight ratio: 18.4 lb/hp (25 lb/kW), 8.3 kg/hp (11.3 kg/kW); carrying capacity: 507 lb, 230 kg; acceleration: 0-50 mph (0-80 km/h) 12.5 sec; speed in top at 1,000 rpm: 19.9 mph, 32 km/h; consumption: 35.3 m/imp gal, 29.4 m/US gal, 8 l x 100 km.

CHASSIS backbone, rear auxiliary frame; front suspension: independent, twin swinging longitudinal trailing arms, transverse torsion bars, anti-roll bar, telescopic dampers; rear: independent, semi-trailing arms, transverse linkage by oblique swinging trailing arms, transverse torsion bars, telescopic dampers.

STEERING worm and roller; turns lock to lock: 2.70.

BRAKES front disc (diameter 10.94 in, 27.8 cm), rear drum; lining area: front 11.2 sq in, 72 sq cm, rear 52.6 sq in, 339 sq cm, total 63.8 sq in, 441 sq cm.

ELECTRICAL EQUIPMENT 12 V; 36 Ah battery; 350 W alternator; Bosch distributor; 2 headlamps.

DIMENSIONS AND WEIGHT wheel base: 84.65 in, 215 cm; tracks: 54.33 in, 138 cm front, 55.11 in, 140 cm rear; length: 157.48 in, 400 cm; width: 65.55 in, 166 cm; height: 47.24 in, 120 cm; ground clearance: 5.98 in, 15.2 cm; weight: 1,654 lb, 750 kg; weight distribution: 40% front, 60% rear; turning circle: 32.5 ft, 9.9 m; fuel tank: 8.8 imp gal, 10.6 US gal, 40 l.

BODY coupé in reinforced fiber glass material; 2 doors; 2 seats, reclining backrests, built-in headrests; light alloy wheels.

VARIATIONS

ENGINE 103.7 cu in, 1,700 cc.
ENGINE 109.8 cu in, 1,800 cc.

OPTIONALS 4-speed fully synchronized mechanical gearbox (I 2.570, II 1.610, III 1.240, IV 0.960, rev 3.880), 4.375 axle ratio; 4-speed fully synchronized mechanical gearbox (I 1.740, II 1.320, III 1.120, IV 0.960, rev 3.880), 3.880 axle ratio; ZF limited slip differential; anti-roll bar on rear suspension; (for GTS 1600 Sport only) hardtop.

GTB S2

ENGINE front, 4 stroke; 6 cylinders, in line; 250 cu in, 4,097 cc (3.87 x 3.52 in, 98.4 x 89.5 mm); compression ratio: 7.8:1; max power (SAE): 171 hp (126 kW) at 4,800 rpm; max torque (SAE): 236 lb ft, 32.5 kg m ((319 Nm) at 2,600 rpm; max engine rpm: 5,000; 41.7 hp/l (30.7 kW/l); cast iron block and head; 7 crankshaft bearings; valves: overhead, in line, push-rods and rockers, hydraulic tappets; camshafts: 1, side; lubrication: gear pump, full flow filter, 7 imp pt, 8.5 US pt, 4 l; 1 DFV or Solex-Brosol 40 downdraught single barrel carburettor; fuel feed: mechanical pump; water-cooled, 18 imp pt, 21.6 US pt, 10.2 l.

TRANSMISSION driving wheels: rear; clutch: single dry plate (diaphragm), hydraulically controlled; gearbox: mechanical; gears: 4, fully synchronized; ratios: I 3.070, II 2.020, III 1.390, IV 1, rev 3.570; lever: central; final drive: hypoid bevel; axle ratio: 3.080; width of rims: front 7'', rear 8''; tyres: front 205/70 HR x 14, rear 215/70 HR x 14.

PERFORMANCE max speeds: (I) 40 mph, 64 km/h; (II) 61 mph, 98 km/h; (III) 88 mph, 142 km/h; (IVB) 123 mph, 198 km/h; power-weight ratio: 12.6 lb/hp (17.2 lb/kW), 5.7 kg/hp (7.8 kg/kW); carrying capacity: 617 lb, 280 kg; speed in direct drive at 1,000 rpm: 24.6 mph, 39.6 km/h; consumption: 21.4 m/imp gal, 17.8 m/US gal, 13.2 l x 100 km.

CHASSIS box-type perimeter frame with cross members; front suspension: independent, wishbones (lower trailing links), coil springs, telescopic dampers; rear: rigid axle, twin upper longitudinal leading arms, lower transverse arms, telescopic dampers.

STEERING worm and roller.

PUMA GTB S2

Sta MATILDE SM 4.1

BRAKES front disc, rear drum, servo.

ELECTRICAL EQUIPMENT 12 V; 44 Ah battery; 32 A alternator; Bosch distributor; 2 iodine headlamps.

DIMENSIONS AND WEIGHT wheel base: 95.28 in, 242 cm; front and rear track: 55.51 in, 141 cm; length: 169.29 in, 430 cm; width: 72.44 in, 184 cm; height: 50.39 in, 128 cm; ground clearance: 5.91 in. 15 cm; weight: 2,161 lb, 980 kg; turning circle: 33.8 ft, 10.3 m; fuel tank: 15,4 imp gal, 18.5 US gal, 70 l.

BODY coupé; 2 doors; 2+2 seats, separate front seats, reclining backrests; light alloy wheels; tinted glass; air-conditioning; power steering.

Sta MATILDE BRAZIL

SM 4.1

ENGINE front, 4 stroke; 6 cylinders, in line; 249.8 cu in, 4,093 cc (3.87 x 3.53 in, 98.4 x 89.6 mm); compression ratio: 7.8:1; max power (SAE): 171 hp (126 kW) at 4,800 rpm; max torque (SAE): 236 lb ft, 32.5 kg m (319 Nm) at 2,600 rpm; max engine rpm: 5,300; 41.8 hp/l (30.8 kW/l); cast iron block and head; 7 crankshaft bearings; valves: overhead, hydraulic tappets; camshafts: 1, side, chain-driven; lubrication: gear pump, full flow filter, 7 imp pt , 8.3 US pt, 4 l; 1 Brosel - Solex H 40 EIS downdraught twin barrel carburettor; air cleaner; fuel feed: mechanical pump; water-cooled, 18 imp pt, 21.6 US pt, 10.2 l.

TRANSMISSION driving wheels: rear; clutch: single dry plate gearbox: mechanical; gears: 4, fully synchronized; ratios: 3.070, II 2.020, III 1.390, IV 1, rev 3.570; lever central, final drive: hypoid bevel; axle ratio: 3.080; width of rims: 7''; tyres 205/70 HR x 14.

PERFORMANCE max speed: 124 mph, 200 km/h; power-weight ratio: 15.5 lb/hp (21 lb/kW), 7 kg/hp (9.5 kg/kW); speed in direct drive at 1,000 rpm: 24 mph, 39 km/h; consumption: 15.7 m/imp gal, 13.1 m/US gal, 18 l x 100 km at 75 mph, 120 km/h.

CHASSIS integral; front suspension: independent, upper wishbones (lower central arms), longitudinal torsion bars, Panhard cross bar, anti-roll bar, coil springs, telescopic dampers; rear rigid axle, swinging longitudinal leading arms, transverse leafsprings, telescopic dampers.

STEERING worm and roller, servo.

BRAKES disc, dual circuit, servo.

ELECTRICAL EQUIPMENT 12 V; 44 Ah battery; 32 A alternator; 4 headlamps.

DIMENSIONS AND WEIGHT wheel base: 93.31 in, 237 cm front and rear track: 55.51 in, 141 cm; length: 64.57 in, 418 cm width: 67.72 in, 172 cm; height: 51.97 in, 132 cm; ground clearance: 5.91 in, 15 cm; weight: 2,646 lb, 1,200 kg; turning circle: 34.4 ft, 10.5 m; fuel tank: 15.4 imp gal, 18.5 US gal, 70 l.

BODY coupé; 2 doors; 2+2 seats, separate front seats.

PRACTICAL INSTRUCTIONS fuel: 80 oct petrol; oil: engine imp pt, 8.3 US pt, 4 l, SAE 20W-40, change every 3,100 miles 5,000 km; greasing: none; sparking plug: AC 46 N.

VOLKSWAGEN Passat TS Limousine

OLKSWAGEN BRAZIL

1300 / 1300 L

RICES EX WORKS: cruzeiros

300	**102,000**
300 L	**106,000**

NGINE rear, 4 stroke; 4 cylinders, horizontally opposed; 78.4 in, 1,285 cc (3.03 x 2.72 in, 77 x 69 mm); compression ratio: 8:1; max power (DIN): 38 hp (28 kW) at 4,000 rpm; max rque (DIN): 62 lb ft, 8.5 kg m (83 Nm) at 2,200 rpm; max gine rpm: 4,600; 29.6 hp/l (21.8 kW/l); block with cast iron ers and light alloy fins, light alloy head; 4 crankshaft bear-gs; valves: overhead, push-rods and rockers; camshafts: 1, ntral, lower; lubrication: gear pump, filter in sump, oil cooler, 4 imp pt, 5.3 US pt, 2.5 l; 1 Solex H 30 PIC downdraught ngle barrel carburettor; fuel feed: mechanical pump; air-oled.

RANSMISSION driving wheels: rear; clutch: single dry plate; arbox: mechanical; gears: 4, fully synchronized; ratios: I 800, II 2.060, III 1.320, IV 0.880, rev 3.880; lever: central; al drive: spiral bevel; axle ratio: 4.375; width of rims: 4.5"; res: 5.60 x 15.

ERFORMANCE max speeds: (I) 17 mph, 28 km/h; (II) 32 mph, km/h; (III) 50 mph, 80 km/h; (IV) 75 mph, 120 km/h; wer-weight ratio: 45.2 lb/hp (61.4 lb/kW), 20.5 kg/hp (27.8 /kW); carrying capacity: 838 lb, 380 kg; acceleration: 0-50 ph (0-80 km/h) 14.3 sec; speed in top at 1,000 rpm: 18.6 mph, km/h; consumption: 39.8 m/imp gal, 33.1 m/US gal, 7.1 100 km.

HASSIS backbone platform; front suspension: independent, in swinging longitudinal trailing arms, transverse laminated rsion bars, anti-roll bar, telescopic dampers; rear: indepen-ent, swinging semi-axles, swinging longitudinal trailing arms, ansverse torsion bars, telescopic dampers.

TEERING worm and roller, telescopic dampers; turns lock to ck: 2.60.

RAKES drum; lining area: front 56.43 sq in, 364 sq cm, rear .43 sq in, 364 sq cm, total 112.87 sq in, 728 sq cm.

LECTRICAL EQUIPMENT 12 V; 36 Ah battery; 350 W dyna-o; Bosch distributor; 2 headlamps.

IMENSIONS AND WEIGHT wheel base: 94.49 in, 240 cm; acks: 51.18 in, 130 cm front, 53.15 in, 135 cm rear; length: 58.66 in, 403 cm; width: 60.63 in, 154 cm; height: 59.06 in, 50 cm; ground clearance: 5.91 in, 15 cm; weight: 1,720 lb, 780 ; turning circle: 36.1 ft, 11 m; fuel tank: 9 imp gal, 10.8 US al, 41 l.

ODY saloon/sedan; 2 doors; 5 seats, separate front seats, djustable backrests; (for 1300 L only) luxury equipment.

RACTICAL INSTRUCTIONS fuel: 73 oct petrol; oil: engine 4.4 p pt, 5.3 US pt, 2.5 l, SAE 20W-40, change every 3,100 les, 5,000 km - gearbox and final drive 5.5 imp pt, 6.3 US pt, l, SAE 90 EP, change every 9,300 miles, 15,000 km; greas-g: every 6,200 miles, 10,000 km, 8 points; valve timing: 9°48' 5°02' 44°28' 4°14'; tyre pressure: front 16 psi, 1.1 atm, rear) psi, 1.4 atm.

PTIONALS heating; built-in headrests.

1600 Limousine

See 1300 / 1300 L, except for:

PRICE EX WORKS: 110,000 cruzeiros

ENGINE 96.7 cu in, 1,584 cc (3.37 x 2.72 in, 85.5 x 69 mm); compression ratio: 7.2:1; max power (DIN): 56 hp (41 kW) at 4,200 rpm; max torque (DIN): 80 lb ft, 11 kg m (108 Nm) at 3,000 rpm; 35.3 hp/l (26 kW/l); 2 Solex 32 PDSIT downdraught single barrel carburettors.

TRANSMISSION axle ratio: 4.125; width of rims: 5"; tyres: 5.90 x 14.

PERFORMANCE max speed: 86 mph, 138 km/h; power-weight ratio: 31.4 lb/hp (42.7 lb/kW), 14.3 kg/hp (19.4 kg/kW); acceleration: 0-50 mph (0-80 km/h) 10.2 sec; consumption: 32.1 m/imp gal, 26.7 m/US gal, 8.8 l x 100 km.

BRAKES front disc (diameter 10.94 in, 27.8 cm), rear drum; lining area: front 11.8 sq in, 76 sq cm, rear 56.4 sq in, 364 sq cm, total 68.2 sq in, 440 sq cm.

DIMENSIONS AND WEIGHT tracks: 51.97 in, 132 cm front, 53.15 in, 135 cm rear.

BODY luxury equipment.

Passat Limousine Series

PRICES EX WORKS: cruzeiros

1 Surf 2-dr	**164,000**
2 LS 2-dr	**178,000**
3 LS 2+1-dr	**184,000**
4 LS 4-dr	**184,000**
5 TS 2-dr	**199,000**
6 LSE 4-dr	**214,000**

Power team:	Standard for:	Optional for:
65 hp	1 to 4	—
80 hp	5,6	—

65 hp power team

ENGINE front, slanted 20° to right, 4 stroke; 4 cylinders, in line; 89.8 cu in, 1,471 cc (3.01 x 3.15 in, 76.5 x 80 mm); compression ratio: 7.4:1; max power (DIN): 65 hp (48 kW) at 5,600 rpm; max torque (DIN): 75 lb ft, 10.3 kg m (101 Nm) at 3,000 rpm; max engine rpm: 6,500; 44.2 hp/l (32.5 kW/l); cast iron block, light alloy head; 5 crankshaft bearings; valves: overhead, in line, thimble tappets; camshafts: 1, overhead, cogged belt; lubrication: gear pump, full flow filter, 5.3 imp pt, 6.3 US pt, 3 l; 1 Solex H 35 PSDI (T) downdraught single barrel carburettor; fuel feed: mechanical pump; water-cooled, 9 imp pt, 10.8 US pt, 5.1 l, electric thermostatic fan.

TRANSMISSION driving wheels: front; clutch: single dry plate (diaphragm); gearbox: mechanical; gears: 4, fully synchronized; ratios: I 3.454, II 1.940, III 1.290, IV 0.910, rev 3.170; lever: central; final drive: spiral bevel; axle ratio: 4.111; width of rims: 4.5"; tyres: 155 SR x 13.

PERFORMANCE max speed: 90 mph, 145 km/h; power-weight ratio: 29.2 lb/hp (39.7 lb/kW), 13.2 kg/hp (17.9 kg/kW) - LS 4-dr 30 lb/hp (40.8 lb/kW), 13.6 kg/hp (18.5 kg/kW); carrying capacity: 992 lb, 450 kg - LS 4-dr 937 lb, 425 kg; speed in top at 1,000 rpm: 16.5 mph, 26.6 km/h; consumption: 34 m/imp gal, 28.3 m/US gal, 8.3 l x 100 km.

CHASSIS integral, front auxiliary subframe; front suspension: independent, by McPherson, lower wishbones, anti-roll bar, coil springs/telescopic dampers struts; rear: rigid axle, trailing radius arms, transverse linkage bar, coil springs, anti-roll bar, telescopic dampers.

STEERING rack-and-pinion, telescopic damper.

BRAKES front disc (diameter 9.41 in, 23.9 cm), rear drum, servo.

ELECTRICAL EQUIPMENT 12 V; 36 Ah battery; 35 A alternator; Bosch distributor; 2 headlamps.

DIMENSIONS AND WEIGHT wheel base: 97.24 in, 247 cm; tracks: 52.76 in, 134 cm front, 52.36 in, 133 cm rear; length: 168.50 in, 428 cm; width: 62.99 in, 160 cm; height: 53.35 in, 135 cm; ground clearance: 5.12 in, 13 cm; weight: 1,896 lb, 860 kg - LS 4-dr 1,951 lb, 885 kg; turning circle: 33.8 ft, 10.3 m; fuel tank: 9.9 imp gal, 11.9 US gal, 45 l.

BODY saloon/sedan; 5 seats, separate front seats, reclining backrests; (for LS models only) luxury equipment.

PRACTICAL INSTRUCTIONS fuel: 73 pct petrol; oil engine 5.3 imp pt, 6.3 US pt, 3 l, SAE 20W-40, change every 4,600 miles, 7,500 km - gearbox and final drive 2.6 imp pt, 3.2 US pt, 1.5 l, SAE 80, change every 28,000 miles, 45,000 km; valve timing:

VOLKSWAGEN Passat TS Limousine

4° 46° 44° 6°; tyre pressure: front 26 psi, 1.8 atm, rear 26 psi, 1.8 atm.

OPTIONALS (for LS models only) metallic spray, heating, built-in headrests, heated rear window, tinted glass, air-conditioning and halogen headlamps.

80 hp power team

See 65 hp power team, except for:

ENGINE 96.9 cu in, 1,588 cc (3.13 x 3.15 in, 79.5 x 80 mm); compression ratio: 7.5:1; max power (DIN): 80 hp (59 kW) at 5,600 rpm; max torque (DIN): 87 lb ft, 12 kg m (118 Nm) at 3,000 rpm; 50.4 hp/l (37.1 kW/l); 1 Solex H 32/35 DIDTA downdraught twin barrel carburettor.

TRANSMISSION gearbox ratios: I 3.454, II 1.950, III 1.290 IV 0.910, rev 3.170; width of rims: 5"; tyres: 175 SR x 13 or 175 HR x 13.

PERFORMANCE max speed: 99 mph, 160 km/h; power-weight ratio: TS 23.7 lb/hp (32.2 lb/kW), 10.7 kg/hp (14.5 kg/kW) - LSE 24.4 lb/hp (33.1 lb/kW), 11.1 kg/hp (15.1 kg/kW); carrying capacity: LSE 937 lb, 425 kg; consumption: 34.9 m/imp gal, 28 m/US gal, 8.1 l x 100 km.

ELECTRICAL EQUIPMENT 42 Ah battery.

DIMENSIONS AND WEIGHT length: 165.75 in, 421 cm; weight: LSE 1,951 lb, 885 kg.

BODY built-in headrests; (for LSE only) executive equipment.

VOLKSWAGEN Brasilia Limousine

Brasilia Limousine Series

PRICES EX WORKS:	cruzeiros
2-dr	**133,000**
4-dr	**134,000**
LS	**144,000**

ENGINE rear, 4 stroke; 4 cylinders, horizontally opposed; 96.7 cu in, 1;584 cc (3.37 x 2.72 in, 85.5 x 69 mm); compression ratio: 7.2:1; max power (DIN): 54 hp (40 kW) at 4,200 rpm; max torque (DIN): 78 lb ft, 10.8 kg m (106 Nm) - at 3,000 rpm; max engine rpm: 4,600; 34.1 hp/l (25.1 kW/l); cylinder block with cast liners and light alloy fins, light alloy head; 4 crankshaft bearings; valves: overhead, push-rods and rockers; camshafts: 1, central, lower; lubrication: gear pump, filter in sump, oil cooler, 4.4 imp pt, 5.3 US pt, 2.5 l; 2 Solex H 32 PDSI downdraught single barrel carburettors; fuel feed: mechanical pump; air-cooled.

TRANSMISSION driving wheels: rear; clutch: single dry plate; gearbox: mechanical; gears: 4, fully synchronized; ratios: I 3.800, II 2.060, III 1.320, IV 0.880, rev 3.880; lever: central; final drive: spiral bevel; axle ratio: 4.125; width of rims: 5"; tyres: 5.90 x 14.

PERFORMANCE max speeds: (I) 20 mph, 32 km/h; (II) 36 mph, 58 km/h; (III) 57 mph, 92 km/h; (IV) 86 mph, 138 km/h; power-weight ratio: 36.3 lb/hp (49.3 lb/kW), 16.5 kg/hp (22.4 kg/kW); carrying capacity: 926 lb, 420 kg; speed in top at 1,000 rpm: 19.3 mph, 31 km/h; consumption: 32.5 m/imp gal, 27 m/US gal, 8.7 l x 100 km.

CHASSIS backbone platform, rear auxiliary frame; front suspension: independent, twin swinging longitudinal trailing arms, transverse torsion bars, anti-roll bar, telescopic dampers; rear: independent, semi-trailing arms, transverse compensating torsion bar, anti-roll bar, telescopic dampers.

STEERING worm and roller, telescopic dampers; turns lock to lock: 2.70.

BRAKES front disc (diameter 10.94 in, 27.8 cm), rear drum; lining area: total 38.4 sq in, 248 sq cm.

ELECTRICAL EQUIPMENT 12 V; 36 Ah battery; 35 A alternator; Bosch distributor; 4 headlamps.

DIMENSIONS AND WEIGHT wheel base: 94.49 in, 240 cm; tracks: 51.97 in, 132 cm front, 53.54 in, 136 cm rear; length: 157.87 in, 401 cm; width 63.39 in, 161 cm; height: 56.30 in, 143 cm; weight: 1,962 lb, 890 kg; turning circle: 36.1 ft, 11 m; fuel tank: 10.1 imp gal, 12.1 US gal, 46 l.

BODY saloon/sedan; 2 or 4 doors; 5 seats, separate front seats, adjustable backrests; (for LS only) luxury equipment.

PRACTICAL INSTRUCTIONS fuel: 73 oct petrol; oil: engine 4.4 imp pt, 5.3 US pt, 2.5 l, SAE 20W-40, change every 3,100 miles, 5,000 km; gearbox and final drive 5.3 imp pt, 6.3 US pt, 3 l, SAE 90, change every 9,300 miles, 15,000 km; greasing: every 6,200 miles, 10,000 km, 4 points; sparking plug: 145°; tappet clearances: inlet 0.004 in, 0.10 mm, exhaust 0.004 in, 0.10 mm; valve timing: 9°48' 35°02' 44°28' 4°14'; tyre pressure: front 17 psi, 1.2 atm, rear 26 psi, 1.8 atm.

OPTIONALS heating; heated rear window; metallic spray; tinted glass.

VOLKSWAGEN Variant II

Variant II

PRICE EX WORKS: 169,000 cruzeiros

ENGINE rear, 4 stroke; 4 cylinders, horizontally opposed; 196.7 cu in, 1,584 cc (3.36 x 2.71 in, 85.5 x 69 mm); compression ratio: 7.2:1; max power (DIN): 56 hp (41 kW) at 4,200 rpm; max torque (DIN): 80 lb ft, 11 kg m (108 Nm) at 2,800 rpm; max engine rpm: 4,600; 35.3 hp/l (26 kW/l); block with cast iron liners and light alloy fins, light alloy head; 4 crankshaft bearings; valves: overhead, push-rods and rockers; camshafts: 1, central, lower; lubrication: gear pump, filter in sump, oil cooler, 4.4 imp pt, 5.3 US pt, 2.5 l; 2 Solex 32 PDSIT carburettors; fuel feed: mechanical pump; air-cooled.

TRANSMISSION driving wheels: rear; clutch: single dry plate; gearbox: mechanical; gears: 4, fully synchronized; ratios: I 3.800, II 2.060, III 1.320, IV 0.880, rev 3.880; lever: central; final drive: spiral bevel; axle ratio: 4.375; width of rims: 5"; tyres: 175 x 14.

PERFORMANCE max speeds: (I) 19 mph, 31 km/h; (II) 36 mph, 58 km/h; (III) 59 mph, 95 km/h; (IV) 86 mph, 138 km/h; power-weight ratio: 38.2 lb/hp (51.9 lb/kW), 17.3 kg/hp (23.5 kg/kW); carrying capacity: 1,102 lb, 500 kg; acceleration: 0-50 mph (0-80 km/h) 12.5 sec; speed in top at 1,000 rpm: 19.9 mph, 32 km/h; consumption: 30.4 m/imp gal, 25.3 m/US gal, 9.3 l x 100 km.

CHASSIS backbone platform, rear auxiliary frame; front suspension: independent, by McPherson, lower wishbones, anti-roll bar, coil springs/telescopic damper struts; rear: independent, transverse torsion bars, semi-axles with homokinetic joints, telescopic dampers.

STEERING rack-and-pinion; turns lock to lock: 3.94.

BRAKES front disc, rear drum; lining area: front 16.3 sq in, 105 sq cm, rear 70.1 sq in, 452 sq cm, total 86.4 sq in, 557 sq cm.

ELECTRICAL EQUIPMENT 12 V; 36 Ah battery; 490 W dynamo; Bosch distributor; 4 headlamps.

DIMENSIONS AND WEIGHT wheel base: 98.20 in, 249 cm; tracks: 53.74 in, 136 cm front, 55.20 in, 140 cm rear; length 170.31 in, 433 cm; width: 64.17 in, 163 cm; height: 56.29 in, 143 cm; ground clearance: 5.90 in, 15 cm; weight: 2,138 lb, 970 kg; weight distribution: 36.4% front, 63.6% rear; turning circle 34.4 ft, 10.5 m; fuel tank: 11 imp gal, 13.2 US gal, 50 l.

BODY estate car/st. wagon; 2+1 doors; 5 seats, separate front seats, adjustable backrests; folding rear seat.

PRACTICAL INSTRUCTIONS fuel: 73 oct petrol; oil: engine 4.4 imp pt, 5.3 US pt, 2.5 l, SAE 20W-30, change every 3,100 miles, 5,000 km - gearbox and final drive 4.4 imp pt, 5.3 US pt, 2.5 l, SAE 90, change every 9,300 miles, 15,000 km; tappet clearances: inlet and exhaust 0.006 in, 0.15 mm; valve timing 9°18' 35°02' 51°18' 11°; tyre pressure: front 17 psi, 1.2 atm, rear 26 psi, 1.8 atm.

OPTIONALS metallic spray; heating; built-in headrests; heated rear window; rear window wiper-washer.

CHEVROLET CANADA

Bel Air Series

PRICES EX WORKS:		Canadian $
1	4-dr Sedan	**7,384**
2	2-dr Coupé	**7,335**
3	4+1-dr 6-pass. St. Wagon	**8,083**
4	4+1-dr 9-pass. St. Wagon	**8,253**

Power team:	Standard for:	Optional for:
115 hp	1,2	—
120 hp	3,4	1,2
155 hp	—	all
105 hp (diesel)	—	3,4

115 hp power team

ENGINE front, 4 stroke; 6 cylinders, Vee-slanted at 90° 229 cu in, 3,752 cc (3.73 x 3.48 in, 94.9 x 88.4 mm); compression ratio: 8.6:1; max power (SAE net): 115 hp (84 kW) at 4,000 rpm; max torque (SAE net): 175 lb ft, 24.1 kg m (236 Nm) at 2,000 rpm; max engine rpm: 4,500; 30.1 hp/l (22.6 kW/l); cast iron block and head; 4 crankshaft bearings; valves: overhead, in line, push-rods and rockers hydraulic tappets; camshafts: 1, at centre of Vee; lubrication: gear pump, full flow filter, 7.4 imp pt, 8.4 US pt, 4 l; Rochester 2ME downdraught twin barrel carburettor; thermostatic air cleaner; exhaust system with catalytic converter; fuel feed: electric pump; water-cooled, 26.3 imp pt, 31.4 US pt, 15 l.

TRANSMISSION driving wheels: rear; gearbox: Turbo Hydramatic 350 automatic transmission, hydraulic torque converter and planetary gears with 3 ratios, max ratio of converter at stall 2, possible manual selection; ratios: I 2.520, II 1.520, III 1, rev 1.930; lever: steering column; final drive: hypoid bevel; axle ratio: 2.730; width of rims: 6"; tyres: P205/75 R x 15.

PERFORMANCE max speed: 99 mph, 159 km/h; power-weight ratio: Sedan 29.3 lb/hp (40.1 lb/kW), 13.3 kg/hp (18.2 kg/kW); speed in direct drive at 1,000 rpm: 28.6 mph, 45.7 km/h; consumption: 21.2 m/imp gal, 18 m/US gal, 13.1 l x 100 km.

CHASSIS perimeter box-type with 2 cross members; front suspension: independent, wishbones, coil springs, anti-roll bar, telescopic dampers; rear: rigid axle, lower trailing radius arms, upper oblique torque arms, coil springs, anti-roll bar, telescopic dampers.

STEERING recirculating ball, servo; turns lock to lock: 3.30.

BRAKES front disc (diameter 11 in, 27.9 cm), front internal radial fins, rear drum, servo; swept area: total 329.8 sq in, 2,127 sq cm.

ELECTRICAL EQUIPMENT 12 V; 2,500 W battery; 42 A alternator; Delco-Remy high energy ignition; 4 headlamps.

DIMENSIONS AND WEIGHT wheel base: 116 in, 294 cm; tracks: 62 in, 157 cm front, 61 in, 154 cm rear; length 212.10 in, 538 cm, width: 75.30 in, 191 cm; height: Sedan 55.90 in, 142 cm - Coupé 55.30 in, 140 cm; ground clearance: 11.10 in, 28 cm; weight: Sedan 3,364 lb, 1,526 kg - Coupé 3,348 lb, 1,518 kg - weight distribution: 55% front, 45% rear; turning circle: 44.5 ft, 13.6 m; fuel tank: 17.6 imp gal, 21 US gal, 80 l.

CHEVROLET Bel Air Coupé

CHEVROLET Bel Air Station Wagon

ODY saloon/sedan, coupé; 6 seats, bench front seats with uilt-in headrests.

PTIONALS central lever; limited slip differential; electric indows; heavy-duty suspension; P215/70R x 15 or P225/ OR x 15 tyres; automatic speed control; heated rear win- ow with electric blower; tilt of steering wheel; electric unshine roof; vinyl roof; air-conditioning; heavy-duty cool- g; 70A alternator; high intensity headlamps.

120 hp power team

ee 115 hp power team, except for:

NGINE 8 cylinders; 267 cu in, 4,376 cc (3.50 x 3.48 in, 3.9 x 88.4 mm); compression ratio: 8.3:1; max power (SAE et): 120 hp (88 kW) at 3,600 rpm; max torque (SAE net): 5 lb ft, 29.6 kg m (290 Nm) at 2,000 rpm; max engine m: 4,000; 27.5 hp/l (20.2 kW/l); 5 crankshaft bearings; 1 ochester 17080108 downdraught twin barrel carburettor; el feed: mechanical pump; cooling, 38.3 imp pt, 45.6 US , 21.9 l.

RANSMISSION axle ratio: 2.560 - Sedan and Coupé 410; width of rims: 7'' - Sedan and Coupé 6''; tyres: P 25/75 R x 15 - Sedan and Coupé P 205/75 R x 15.

ERFORMANCE max speed: st. wagons 104 mph, 167 km/h Sedan and Coupé 106 mph, 170 km/h; power-weight ratio: . wagons 32.4 lb/hp, (44.3 lb/kW), 14.7 kg/hp (20.1 kg/ V); speed in direct drive at 1,000 rpm: 32.4 mph, 51.8 n/h; consumption: 20.1 m/imp gal, 17 m/US gal, 13.9 100 km.

STEERING turns lock to lock: 3,30 - Sedan and Coupé 3.16.

ELECTRICAL EQUIPMENT 37 A alternator.

DIMENSIONS AND WEIGHT (for st. wagons only) length: 215 in, 546 cm; width: 79.30 in, 201 cm; height: 57.70 in, 147 cm; ground clearance: 11.60 in, 29 cm; weight: 3,893 lb, 1,766 kg; turning circle: 45.1 ft, 13.8 m.

OPTIONALS (for st. wagons only) estate equipment; roof carrier.

155 hp power team

See 115 hp power team, except for:

ENGINE 8 cylinders; 305 cu in, 4,999 cc (3.74 x 3.48 in, 94.9 x 88.4 mm); compression ratio: 8.6:1; max power (SAE net): 155 hp (113 kW) at 4,000 rpm; max torque (SAE net): 240 lb ft, 33.1 kg m (324 Nm) at 1,600 rpm; max engine rpm: 4,400; 32 hp/l (24 kW/l); 5 crankshaft bearings: 1 Rochester 17080202 downdraught 4-barrel carburettor; fuel feed: mecanical pump; cooling, 34.3 imp pt, 40.8 US pt, 19.6 l.

TRANSMISSION axle ratio: 2.410 - st. wagons 2.560.

PERFORMANCE max speed: 108 mph, 173 km/h - st. wagons 106 mph, 170 km/h; power-weight ratio: Sedan 20.1 lb/hp, (30 lb/kW), 10 kg/hp (13.6 kg/kW); speed in direct drive at 1,000 rpm: 32.4 mph, 51.8 km/h; consumption: 20.1 m/imp gal, 17 m/US gal, 13.9 l x 100 km.

STEERING turns lock to lock: 3.16 - st. wagons 3.30.

ELECTRICAL EQUIPMENT 37 A alternator.

DIMENSIONS AND WEIGHT weight: plus 119 lb, 54 kg - st. wagons 3,902 lb, 1,770 kg.

OPTIONALS 3.080 axle ratio.

105 hp (diesel) power team

See 115 hp power team, except for:

ENGINE diesel; 8 cylinders; 350 cu in, 5,736 cc (4.06 x 3.38 in, 103.9 x 86 mm); compression ratio: 22.5:1; max power (SAE net): 105 hp (78 kW) at 3,200 rpm; max torque (SAE net): 205 lb ft, 28.4 kg m (278 Nm) at 1,600 rpm; max engine rpm: 3,500; 18.4 hp/l (13.6 kW/l); 5 crankshaft bearings; lubrication: 12.4 imp pt, 14.8 US pt, 7.1 l; mechanical fuel injection pump; cooling, 28.7 imp pt, 33.9 US pt, 16.4 l.

PERFORMANCE max speed: 91 mph, 146 km/h; power-weight ratio: 39.5 lb/hp (53.1 lb/kW), 17.9 kg/hp (24.1 kg/kW); speed in direct drive at 1,000 rpm: 28.6 mph, 45.7 km/h; consumption: 23.8 m/imp gal, 20 m/US gal, 11.7 l x 100 km.

ELECTRICAL EQUIPMENT 55 A alternator.

DIMENSIONS AND WEIGHT weight: 4,146 lbb, 1,881 kg.

FORD CANADA

LTD 2-dr Sedan

PRICE EX WORKS: Canadian $ 7.797

ENGINE front, 4 stroke; 8 cylinders; 302 cu in, 4,950 cc (4 x 3 in, 101.6 x 76.2 mm; compression ratio: 8.4:1; max power (SAE net): 130 hp (97 kW) at 3,600 rpm; max torque (SAE net): 230 lb ft, 31.8 kg m (312 Nm) at 1,600 rpm; max engine rpm: 4,000; 26.3 hp/l (19.6 kW/l); cast iron block and head; 5 crankshaft bearings; valves: overhead, in line, push-rods and rockers, hydraulic tappets; camshafts: 1, at centre of Vee; lubrication: rotary pump, full flow filter, 6.7 imp pt, 8 US pt, 3.8 l; 1 Ford 2150 downdraught twin barrel carburettor; fuel feed: mechanical pump; water-cooled, 22.2 imp pt, 26.6 US pt, 12.6 l.

TRANSMISSION driving wheels: rear; gearbox: Select-Shift FMX automatic transmission, hydraulic torque converter and planetary gears with 3 ratios, max ratio of converter at stall 1.97, possible manual selection; ratios: I 2.400, II 1.470, III 1, rev 2; lever: steering column; final drive: hypoid bevel; axle ratio: 2.260; width of rims: 5.5''; tyres: P205/75 R x 14 BSW.

PERFORMANCE max speed: 100 mph, 160 km/h; power-weight ratio: 27.6 lb/hp, (36.9 lb/kW), 12.5 kg/hp (16.8

FORD LTD Sedan

LTD 2-DR SEDAN

kg/kW); carrying capacity: 1,257 lb, 570 kg; speed in direct drive at 1,000 rpm: 26.3 mph, 42.2 km/h; consumption: 20.5 m/imp gal, 17 m/US gal, 13.8 l x 100 km.

CHASSIS front and rear subframe; front suspension: independent, coil springs, wishbones, anti-roll bar, telescopic dampers; rear: rigid axle, lower trailing radius arms, upper oblique torque arms, coil springs, telescopic dampers.

STEERING recirculating ball, servo; turns lock to lock: 3.40.

BRAKES front disc (diameter 11.08 in, 28.1 cm), front internal radial fins, rear compensator, servo, rear drum; swept area: front 228.7 sq in, 1,475 sq cm, rear 157.1 sq in, 1,013 sq cm, total 385.8 sq in, 2,488 sq cm.

ELECTRICAL EQUIPMENT 12 V; 36 Ah battery; 60 A alternator; Motorcraft transistorized ignition; 4 headlamps.

DIMENSIONS AND WEIGHT wheel base: 114.30 in, 290 cm; tracks: 62.20 in, 158 cm front, 62 in, 157 cm rear; length: 209.30 in, 532 cm; width: 77.50 in, 197 cm; height: 54.70 in, 139 cm; ground clearance: 5.17 in, 13.1 cm; weight: 3,595 lb, 1,631 kg; turning circle: 39.2 ft, 11.9 m; fuel tank: 15.8 imp gal, 19 US gal, 72 l.

BODY saloon/sedan; 6 seats, separate front seats with built-in headrests.

OPTIONALS "Automatic" overdrive transmission, hydraulic torque converter and planetary gears with 4 ratios (I 2.400, II 1.470, III 1, IV 0.670, rev 2), max ratio of converter at stall 2.29, 3.080 axle ratio; P205/75R x 14 WSW, P225/75R x 14 WSW tyres with 6.5" wide rims; limited slip differential; light alloy wheels; digital electronic clock; tilt of steering wheel; tinted glass; electric windows; vinyl roof; sunshine roof; manual air-conditioning; automatic air-conditioning; 71 Ah heavy-duty battery; automatic speed control.

MERCURY CANADA

Bobcat Series

PRICES EX WORKS:	Canadian $
1 2-dr Special Sedan	5,039
2 2+1-dr Special Runabout	5,196
3 2+1-dr Special St. Wagon	5,611

ENGINE front, 4 stroke; 4 cylinders, in line, 140 cu in, 2,300 cc (3.78 x 3.13 in, 95.9 x 79.5 mm); compression ratio: 9:1; max power (SAE net): 88 hp (66 kW) at 4,600 rqm; max torque (SAE net): 119 lb/ft, 16.5 kg m (161 Nm) at 2,600 rpm; max engine rpm: 5,000; 38.3 hp/l (28.7 kW/l); cast iron block and head; 5 crankshaft bearings; valves: overhead, Vee-slanted, rockers, hydraulic tappets; camshafts: 1, overhead, cogged belt; lubrication: gear pump, full flow filter, 6.7 imp pt, 8 US pt, 3.8 l; 1 Holley-Weber EOEE-RA/GA downdraught twin barrel carburettor; air cleaner; exhaust system with catalytic converter; fuel feed: mechanical pump; water-cooled, 14.4 imp pt, 17.3 US pt, 8.2 l.

TRANSMISSION driving wheels: rear; clutch: single dry plate; gearbox: mechanical; gerars: 4, fully synchronized; ratios: I 3.980, II 2.140, III 1.420, IV 1, rev 3.990; lever: central; final drive: hypoid bevel; axle ratio: 2.730 St. Wagon 3.080; width of rims: 5"; tyres: BR78 x 13.

PERFORMANCE max speed: about 96 mph, 154 km/h; power-weight ratio: Runabout 28.8 lb/hp (38.4 lb/kW), 13.1 kg/hp (17.4 kg/kW); speed in direct drive at 1,000 rpm: 19.3 mph, 31 km/h; consumption: 28.8 m/imp gal, 24 m/US gal, 9.8 l x 100 km.

CHASSIS integral; front suspension: independent, wishbones, coil springs, telescopic dampers; rear: rigid axle, semi-elliptic leafsprings, telescopic dampers.

STEERING rack-and-pinion; turns lock to lock: 4.15.

BRAKES front disc (diameter 9.30 in, 23.6 cm), front internal radial fins, rear drum, rear compensator; swept area: front 145.5 sq in, 939 sq cm, rear 99 sq in, 639 sq cm, total 244.5 sq in, 1,578 sq cm.

ELECTRICAL EQUIPMENT 12 V; 45 Ah battery; 60 A alternator; Motorcraft transistorized ignition; 2 headlamps.

DIMENSIONS AND WEIGHT wheel base: 94.50 sq in, 240 cm - St. Wagon 94.80 in, 241 cm; tracks: 55 in, 140 cm front, 55.80 in, 142 cm rear; length: Runabout 170.80 in, 434 cm. St. Wagon 180.60 in, 459 cm; width: 69.40 in, 176 cm - St. Wagon 69.70 in, 177 cm; height: 50.50 in, 128 cm - St. Wagon 52 in, 132 cm; ground clearance: Runabout 4.63 in, 11.8 cm - St. Wagon 5.14 in, 13 cm; weight: Runabout 2,535 lb, 1,150 kg - St. Wagon 2,677 lb, 1,214 kg; turning circle: 35.9 ft, 10.9 m; fuel tank: 10.8 imp gal, 13 US gal, 49 l - St. Wagon 11.7 imp gal, 14 US gal, 53 l.

BODY saloon/sedan, coupé, estate car/st. wagon; 4 seats, separate front seats; folding rear seat.

OPTIONALS heavy-duty cooling; 3.080 axle ratio (except for St. Wagon); Select-Shift C-3 automatic transmission with 3 ratios (I 2.470, II 1.470, III 1, rev 2.110), max ratio of converter at stall 2.9, possible manual selection, central lever; Select-Shift C-4 automatic transmission with 3 ratios (I 2.460, II 1.460, III 1, rev 2.190), max ratio of converter at stall 2.3 possible manual selection, central lever, 3.080 or 3 axle ratio; aluminium wheels; BR 70 x 13 or BR 78 x 13 tyres with 5" wide rims; power steering; servo brake; 54 Ah heavy-duty battery; sunshine roof (except for St. Wagon); air-conditioning; luxury interior; sport equipment; anti-roll bar on front suspension; tilt of steering wheel; heated rear window; tilted glass.

Marquis Meteor Series

PRICES EX WORKS:	Canadian $
2-dr Sedan	7,836
4-dr Sedan	7,886

ENGINE front, 4 stroke; 8 cylinders; 302 cu in, 4,950 cc (4 x 3 in, 101.6 x 76.2 mm); compression ratio: 8.4:1; max power (SAE net): 130 hp (97 kW) at 3,600 rpm; max torque (SAE net): 230 lb ft, 31.8 kg/m (312 Nm) at 1,600 rpm; max engine rpm: 4,000; 26.3 hp/l (19.6 kW/l); cast iron block and head; 5 crankshaft bearings; valves: overhead, in line, push-rods and rockers, hydraulic tappets; camshafts: 1, a centre of Vee; lubrication: rotary pump, full flow filter, 6.7 imp pt, 8 US pt, 3.8 l; 1 Ford 2700 downdraught carburettor with variable Venturi; air cleaner; exhaust system with 2 catalytic converter; fuel feed: mechanical pump; water-cooled, 22.2 imp pt, 26.6 US pt, 12.6 l.

TRANSMISSION driving wheels: rear; gearbox: Select-Shift C-4 automatic transmission, hydraulic torque converter and planetary gears with 3 ratios, max ratio of converter at stal 1.97, possible manual selection; ratios; I 2.460, II 1.460, II 1, rev 2.200; lever: steering column; final drive: hypoid bevel; axle ratio: 2.260; - width of rims: 5.5"; tyres: P205 75 R x 14 BSW.

PERFORMANCE max speed: 96 mph, 154 km/h; power-weight ratio: 4-dr 28 lb/hp (37.5 lb/kW), 12.7 kg/hp (17 kg/kW); speed in direct drive at 1,000 rpm: 26.7 mph, 42.7 km/h; consumption: 20.5 m/imp gal, 17 m/US gal, 13.8 l x 100 km.

CHASSIS perimeter box-type frame; front suspension: independent, wishbones, coil springs, anti-roll bar, telescopic dampers; rear: rigid axle, lower trailing radius arms, upper oblique torque arms, coil springs, telescopic dampers.

STEERING recirculating ball, servo; turns lock to lock: 3.40

BRAKES front disc (diameter 11.08 in, 28.1 cm), front internal radial fins, rear compensator, rear drum, servo swept area: front 228.7 sq in, 1,475 sq cm, rear 157.1 sq in 1,013 sq cm, total 385.8 sq in, 2.488 sq cm.

MERCURY Bobcat Special Sport Runabout

MERCURY Marquis Meteor Sedan

PONTIAC Acadian Hatchback Coupé

ELECTRICAL EQUIPMENT 12 V; 36 Ah battery; 60 A alternator; Motorcraft transistorized ignition; 4 headlamps.

DIMENSIONS AND WEIGHT wheel base: 114.30 in, 290 cm; tracks: 62.20 in, 158 cm front, 62 in, 157 cm rear; length: 212.30 in, 539 cm; width: 77.50 in, 197 cm; height: 54.70 in, 139 cm; ground clearance: 5.17 in, 13 cm; weight: 3,636 lb, 1,649 kg; fuel tank: 15.8 imp gal, 19 US gal, 72 l.

BODY saloon/sedan; 6 seats, bench front seats with built-in headrests.

OPTIONALS heavy-duty cooling; P205/75R x 14 WSW tyres with 5.5" wide rims; P215/75 R x 14 BSW, P205/75R x 15 WSW, P225/75R x 14 WSW, T 125/90D x 16 BSW tyres with 5.5" wide rims; heavy-duty suspension with rear and front anti-roll bar; tilt of steering wheel; 71 Ah heavy-duty battery; electric window; heated rear window; automatic air-conditioning; manual air-conditioning; tinted glass; automatic speed control; metallic spray; limited slip differential; digital clock; light alloy wheels; wire wheels; vinyl roof; leather upholstery; reclining backrests; Select-Shift C-6 automatic transmission with 3 ratios (I 2.460, II 1.460, III 1, rev 2.180), max ratio of converter at stall 1.98, possible manual selection, steering column; luxury equipment; decor equipment.

PONTIAC CANADA

Acadian Series

PRICES EX WORKS:	Canadian $
4+1-dr Hatchback Sedan	5,081
2+1-dr S Hatchback Coupé	4,345
2+1-dr Hatchback Coupé	4,929

Power team:	Standard for:	Optional for:
70 hp	all	—
74 hp	—	all

70 hp power team

ENGINE front, 4 stroke; 4 cylinders, vertical, in line; 97.6 cu in, 1.599 cc (3.23 x 2.98 in, 82 x 75.6 mm); compression ratio: 8.6:1; max power (SAE net): 70 hp (51 kW) at 5,200 rpm; max torque (SAE net): 82 lb ft, 11.3 kg m (111 Nm) at 2,400 rpm; max engine rpm: 5,600; 43.8 hp/l (32.2 kW/l); cast iron block and head; 5 crankshaft bearings; valves: overhead, hydraulic tappets; camshafts: 1, overhead, cogged belt; lubrication: gear pump, full flow filter, 8.3 imp pt, 9.9 US pt, 4.7 l; 1 Holley 14004464 (14004472 for California only) downdraught twin barrel carburettor; air cleaner; exhaust system with catalytic converter; fuel feed: mechanical pump; water-cooled, 15.3 imp pt, 18.4 US pt, 8.7 l.

TRANSMISSION driving wheels: rear; clutch: single dry plate (diaphragm); gearbox: mechanical; gears: 4, fully synchronized; ratios: I 3.750, II 2.1260, III 1.380, IV 1, rev 3.820; lever: central; final drive: hypoid bevel; axle ratio: 3.700; width of rims: 5"; tyres: P155/80 R x 13.

PERFORMANCE max speed: 90 mph, 145 km/h; power-weight ratio: Hatchback Sedan 29.4 lb/hp (40 lb/kW), 13.3 kg/hp (18.1 kg/kW); speed in direct drive at 1,000 rpm: 17.9 mph, 28.8 km/h; consumption: 34.9 m/imp gal, 29 m/US gal, 8.1 l x 100 km.

CHASSIS integral with cross member reinforcement; front suspension: independent, wishbones, coil springs, anti-roll bar, telescopic dampers; rear: rigid axle (torque tube), longitudinal trailing radius arms, coil springs, transverse linkage bar, anti-roll bar, telescopic dampers.

STEERING rack-and-pinion; turns lock to clock: 3.60.

BRAKES front disc (diameter 9.68 in, 24.6 cm), rear drum; swept area: total 279.8 cq in, 1,804 sq cm.

ELECTRICAL EQUIPMENT 12 V; 2,500 W battery; 32 A alternator; Delco-Remy high energy ignition; 2 headlamps.

DIMENSIONS AND WEIGHT wheel base: 94.30 in, 239 cm - Hatchback Sedan 97.30 in, 247 cm; front and rear track: 51.20 in, 130 cm; length: Sedan 164.90 in, 419 cm - coupés 161.90 in, 411 cm; width: 61.80 in, 157 cm; height: 52.30 in, 133 cm; ground clearance: 5.30 in, 13.5 cm; weight: S Hatchback Coupé 1,943 lb, 881 kg - Hatchback Coupé 1,996 lb, 906 kg - Hatchback Sedan 2,056 lb, 933 kg; turning circle: 34.3 ft, 10.5 m - Hatchback Sedan 34.9 ft, 10.6 m; fuel tank: 10.3 imp gal, 12.5 US gal, 47 l.

BODY saloon/sedan, coupé; 4 seats, separate front seats with built-in headrests.

OPTIONALS Turbo-Hydramatic 180 automatic transmission, hydraulic torque converter and planetary gears with 3 ratios (I 2.400, II 1.480, III 1, rev 1.920), max ratio of converter at stall 2.20, possible manual selection, central lever; heavy-duty battery; servo brake: vinyl roof; heavy-duty radiator; tilt of steering wheel; heated rear window; air-conditioning; De Luxe equipment; Custom two-tone paint equipment.

74 hp power team

(not available in California)

See 70 hp power team, except for:

ENGINE max power (SAE net): 74 hp (54 kW) at 5,200 rpm; max torque (SAE net): 88 lb ft, 12.1 kg m (119 Nm) at 2,800 rpm;; 46.3 hp/l (34.1 kW/l); 1 Holley 14004468 downdraught twin barrel carburettor.

PERFORMANCE max speed: 93 mph, 150 km/h; power-weight ratio: Hatchback Sedan 27.7 lb/hp (37.6 lb/kW), 12.6 kg/hp (17.1 kg/kW).

Le Mans Series

1 4-dr Sedan
2 2-dr Coupé
3 4+1-dr St. Wagon

Power team:	Standard for:	Optional for:
115 hp	all	—
120 hp	—	all
155 hp	—	all

115 hp power team

ENGINE front, 4 stroke; 6 cylinders, Vee-slanted at 90°; 229 cu in, 3,752 cc (3.73 x 3.48 in, 94.9 x 88.4 mm); compression ratio: 8.6:1; max power (SAE net): 115 hp (84 kW) at 4,000 rpm; max torque (SAE net): 175 lb ft, 24.1 kg m (236 Nm) at 2,000 rpm; max engine rpm: 4,500; 34.1 hp/l (25.1 kW/l); cast iron block and head; 4 crankshaft bearings; valves: overhead, in line, push-rods and rockers, hydraulic tappets; camshafts: 1, at centre of Vee; lubrication: gear pump, full flow filter, 7.4 imp pt, 8.4 US pt, 4 l; 1 Rochester 17080131 downdraught twin barrel carburettor; thermostatic air cleaner; exhaust system with catalytic converter; fuel feed: mechanical pump; water-cooled, 26.3 imp pt, 31.4 US pt, 15 l.

TRANSMISSION driving wheels: rear clutch: single dry plate (diaphragm); gearbox: mechanical; gears: 3, fully synchronized; ratios: I 3.500, II 1.890, III 1 rev 3.620; lever: central; final drive: hypoid bevel; axle ratio: 2.410 - st. wagon 2.730; width of rims: 6"; tyres: P185/75 R x 14 - st. wagon P 195/75 R x 14.

PERFORMANCE max speed: 93 mph, 149 km/h; power-weight ratio: Sedan 26.4 lb/hp, (36 lb/kW), 12 kg/hp (16.3 kg/kW); speed in direct drive at 1,000 rpm: 27.4 mph, 44.1 km/h; consumption: 22.8 m/imp gal, 19 m/US gal, 13.1 l x 100 km.

CHASSIS perimeter box-type with front and rear cross members; front suspension: independent, wishbones, coil springs, anti-roll bar, telescopic dampers; rear: rigid axle, lower trailing radius arms, upper oblique torque arms, coil springs, telescopic dampers.

STEERING recirculating ball - St. Wagon variable ratio servo; turns lock to lock: 5.60 - St. Wagon 3.30.

BRAKES front disc (diameter 11 in, 27.9 cm.), front internal radial fins, rear drum, servo; swept area: total 307,8 sq in, 1,985 sq cm.

ELECTRICAL EQUIPMENT 12 V; 2,500 W battery; 42 A alternator; Delco-Remy high energy ignition; 2 headlamps.

DIMENSIONS AND WEIGHT wheel base: 108,10 in, 274 cm; tracks: 58.50 in, 149 cm front, 57.80 in, 147 cm rear; length: 198.70 in, 504 cm - St. Wagon 197.80 in, 502 cm; width: 72.30 in, 184 cm; height: Sedan 54.20 in, 138 cm - Coupé 53.30 in, 135 cm - St. Wagon 54.50 in 138 cm; ground clearance: 10.60 in, 27 cm; weight: Sedan 3,001 lb, 1,361 kg - Coupé 2,996 lb, 1,359 kg - St Wagon 3,141 lb, 1,425 kg; weight distribution: 54% front, 46% rear; turning circle: 40.1 ft, 12.2 m; fuel tank: 15.2 imp gal, 17.9 US gal, 68 l.

BODY saloon/sedan, coupé, estate car/st.wagon; 6 seats, front bench front seats with built-in headrests.

OPTIONALS Turbo-Hydraumatic 200 C automatic transmission, hydraulic torque converter and planetary gears with 3 ratios (I 2.740, II 1.570, III 1, rev 2.070), max ratio of converter at stall 2.35, possible manual selection, steering column or central lever; limited slip differential; heavy-duty suspension; power steering; heavy-duty battery; 63 A alternator; heavy-duty cooling; electric windows; tilt of steering wheels; trip computer; heated rear window; electric door lock.

PONTIAC Acadian Hatchback Coupé

120 hp power team

See 115 hp power team, except for:

ENGINE 8 cylinders; 267 cu in, 4,376 cc (3.50 x 3,48 in, 88.9 x 88.4 mm); compression ratio: 8.3:1; max power (SAE net): 120 hp (88 kW) at 3,600 rpm; max torque (SAE net): 215 lb ft, 29.6 kg m (290 Nm) at 2,000 rpm; max engine rpm: 4,000; 36,5 hp/l (26.8 kW/l); 5 crankshaft bearings; 1 Rochester 17080108 downdraught twin barrel carburettor; cooling, 27.5 imp pt, 32.7 US pt, 15.6 l.

TRANSMISSION axle ratio: 2.290 - St. Wagon 2.410.

PERFORMANCE max speed: 96 mph, 154 km/h; power-weight ratio: Sedan 26 lb/hp, (35.3 lb/kW), 11.8 kg/hp (16.1 kg/kW); speed in direct drive at 1,000 rpm: 31.4 mph, 50.2 km/h; consumption: 21.2 m/imp gal, 18 m/US gal, 13.1 l x 100 km.

ELECTRICAL EQUIPMENT 37 A alternator.

DIMENSIONS AND WEIGHT weight: plus 80 lb, 36 kg - St. Wagon plus 127 lb, 58 kg.

155 hp power team

See 110 hp power team, except for:

ENGINE 8 cylinders; 305 cu in, 4,999 cc (3.74 x 3.48 in, 94.9 x 88.4 mm); max power (SAE net): 155 hp (113 kW) at 4,000 rpm; max torque (SAE net): 240 lb ft, 33.1 kg m (324 Nm) at 1,600 rpm; max engine rpm: 4,500; 32 hp/l (24 kW/l); 5 crankshaft bearings; 1 Rochester 17080207 downdraught 4 - barrel carburettor; cooling, 27.6 imp pt, 32.8 US pt, 15.7 l.

TRANSMISSION gearbox: mechanical; gears: 4, fully synchronized; ratios: I 2.850, II 2.020, III 1.350, IV 1 rev 2.850; lever: central; axle ratio: 3.080.

PERFORMANCE max speed: 105 mph, 170 km/h; power-weight ratio: Sedan 20.2 lb/hp, (27.4 lb/kW), 9.1 kg/hp (12.4 kg/kW); speed in direct drive at 1,000 rpm: 22.9 mph, 36.9 km/h; consumption: 20.1 m/imp gal, 17 m/US gal, 13.9 l x 100 km.

ELECTRICAL EQUIPMENT 37 A alternator.

DIMENSIONS AND WEIGHT weight: plus 174 lb, 79 kg.

OPTIONALS Turbo-Hydramatic 250 C or 350 C automatic transmission, hydraulic torque converter and planetary gears with 3 ratios (I 2.520, II 1.520, III 1, rev 1.930), max ratio of converter at stall 2, possible manual selection steering column or central lever, (for Sedan and Coupé only) 2.290 or 2.730 - (for St. Wagon only) 2.410 or 2.730 axle ratio.

Catalina - Laurentian - Parisienne Series

PRICES EX WORKS:	Canadian $
1 Catalina 4-dr Sedan	—
2 Catalina 2-dr Coupé	—
3 Catalina 4+1-dr Safari St. Wagon	—
4 Laurentian 4-dr Sedan	**7,531**
5 Laurentian 2-dr Coupé	**7,482**
6 Laurentian 4+1-dr Safari St. Wagon	**8,208**
7 Parisienne 4-dr Sedan	**8,250**
8 Parisienne 2-dr Coupé	**8,116**
9 Parisienne 4+1-dr Safari St. Wagon	**9,207**

Power team:	Standard for:	Optional for:
115 hp	1,2,4,5	—
120 hp	3,6 to 9	1,2,4,5
155 hp	—	all
105 hp (diesel)	—	all

115 hp power team

ENGINE front, 4 stroke; 6 cylinders, Vee-slanted at 90°; 229 cu in, 3,752 cc (3.73 x 3.48 in, 94.9 x 88.4 mm); compression ratio: 8.6:1; max power (SAE net): 115 hp (84 kW) at 4,000 rpm; max torque (SAE net): 175 lb ft, 24.1 kg m (236 Nm) at 2,000 rpm; max engine rpm: 4,500; 30.2 hp/l (22.3 kW/l); cast iron block and head; 4 crankshaft bearings; valves: overhead, in line, push-rods and rockers, hydraulic tappets; camshafts: 1, at centre of Vee; lubrication: gear pump, full flow filter, 7.4 imp pt, 8.4 US pt, 4 l; 1 Rochester 17080130 downdraught twin barrel carburettor; thermostatic air cleaner; exhaust system with catalytic converter; fuel feed: electric pump; water-cooled, 26.3 imp pt, 31.4 US pt, 15 l.

TRANSMISSION driving wheels: rear gearbox: Turbo-Hydramatic 350 automatic transmission, hydraulic torque converter and planetary gears with 3 ratios, max ratio of converter at stall 2, possible manual selection; ratios: I 2.520, II 1.520, III 1, rev 1.930; lever: steering column; final drive: hypoid bevel; axle ratio: 2.730; width of rims: 6"; tyres: P 205/75 R x 15.

PONTIAC Laurentian Sedan

PERFORMANCE max speed: 93 mph, 149 km/h; power-weight ratio: Catalina Sedan 29.7 lb/hp, (40.4 lb/kW), 13.5 kg/hp (18.3 kg/kW); speed in direct drive at 1,000 rpm: 23.3 mph, 37.5 km/h; consumption: 21.6 m/imp gal, 18 m/US gal, 13.1 l x 100 km.

CHASSIS perimeter box-type with 2 cross members; front suspension: independent, wishbones, coil springs, anti-roll bar, telescopic dampers; rear: rigid axle, lower trailing radius arms, upper oblique torque arms, coil springs, anti-roll bar, telescopic dampers.

STEERING recirculating ball, variable ratio servo; turns lock to lock: 3.30.

BRAKES front disc (diameter 11 in, 27.9 cm), front internal radial fins, rear drum, servo; swept area: total 337.3 sq in, 2,176 sq cm.

ELECTRICAL EQUIPMENT 12 V; 2,500 W battery; 42 A alternator; Delco-Remy high energy ignition; 4 headlamps.

DIMENSIONS AND WEIGHT wheel base: 116 in, 294 cm; tracks: 61.70 in, 157 cm front, 60.70 in, 154 cm rear; length: 214.10 in, 544 cm; width: 76.40 in, 194 cm; height: 54.20 in, 138 cm; ground clearance: 5.46 in, 14.2 cm; weight: Catalina Sedan 3,419 lb, 1,551 kg - Catalina Coupé 3,394 lb, 1,539 kg - Laurentian Sedan 3,478 lb, 1,577 kg - Laurentian Coupé 3,430 lb, 1,556; turning circle: 41.6 ft, 12.7 m; fuel tank: 17.2 imp gal, 20.6 US gal, 78 l.

BODY 6 seats; separate front seats with built-in headrests.

OPTIONALS central lever; limited slip differential; electri windows; heavy-duty suspension; P 215 / 70R x 15 or 225/70 R x 15 tyres; automatic speed control; heated rea window; tilt of steering wheel; electric sunshine roof; viny roof; air-conditioning; heavy-duty cooling; 70 A alternato high intensity headlamps.

120 hp power team

See 115 hp power team, except for:

ENGINE 8 cylinders; 267 cu in, 4,376 cc (3.50 x 3.48 i 88.9 x 88.4 mm); compression ratio: 8.3:1; max power (SA net): 120 hp (88 kW) at 3,600 rpm; max torque (SAE net 215 lb ft, 29.6 kg m (290 Nm) at 2,000 rpm; max engin rpm: 4,000; 27.5 hp/l (20.2 kW/l); 5 crankshaft bearings; Rochester 17080108 downdraught twin-barrel carburetto fuel feed: mechanical pump; cooling, 38.3 imp pt, 45.6 U pt, 21.9 l.

TRANSMISSION gearbox: Turbo-Hydramatic 250 C automa tic transmission, hydraulic torque converter and planeta gears with 3 ratios, max ratio of converter at stall 2; poss ble manual selection; ratios: I 2.520, II 1.520, III 1, re 1.930; lever: steering column; axle ratio: 2.410 - st. wagon 2.560; width of rims: st. wagons 7"; tyres: st. wagons 225/75R x 155.

PERFORMANCE max speed: 96 mph, 154 km/h; powe weight ratio: Parisienne Sedan 30.4 lb/hp, (41.4 lb/kW 13.8 kg/hp (18.8 kg/kW); speed in direct drive at 1,000 rpm

PONTIAC Parisienne Coupé

2.4 mph, 51.8 km/h; consumption: 20.1 m/imp gal, 17 /US gal, 13.9 l x 100 km.

TEERING turns lock to lock: 3.16.

LECTRICAL EQUIPMENT 37 A alternator.

IMENSIONS AND WEIGHT length: st. wagons 215 in, 546 m; width: st. wagons 79.30 in, 201 cm; height: st. wagons 7.70 in, 147 cm; ground clearance: st. wagons 11.60 in, 29 m; weight: Parisienne Sedan 3,639 lb, 1,651 kg - Parisiene Coupé 3,571 lb, 1,620 kg - Catalina and Laurentian edans and coupés plus 109 lb, 52 kg - Catalina Safari St. Vagon 3,929 lb, 1,782 kg - Laurentian Safari St. Wagon ,949 lb, 1,791 kg; Parisienne Safari St. Wagon 3,976 lb, 1,806 g; turning circle: st. wagons 45.1 ft, 13.8 m.

PTIONALS (for Parisienne Sedan and Coupé only) leather quipment and Brougham equipment; (for st. wagons only) state equipment, roof carrier and 3.080 axle ratio.

155 hp power team

ee 115 hp power team, except for:

NGINE 8 cylinders; 305 cu in, 4,999 cc (3.74x3.48 in, 4.9 x 88.4 mm); compression ratio: 8.6:1; max power (SAE et): 155 hp (113 kW) at 4,000 rpm; max torque (SAE net): 40 lb ft, 33.1 kg m (324 Nm) at 1,600 rpm; max engine pm: 4,400; 32 hp/l (24 kW/l); 5 crankshaft bearings; 1 ochester 17080202 downdraught 4-barrel carburettor; fuel eed: mechanical pump; cooling, 34.3 imp pt, 40.8 US pt, 9.6 l.

RANSMISSION axle ratio: 2.410 - st. wagons 2.560.

ERFORMANCE max speed: 108 mph, 174 km/h; powereight ratio: Catalina Sedan 20.2 lb/hp, (27.4 lb/kW), 9.1 g/hp (12.4 kg/kW); speed in direct drive at 1,000 rpm: 31.4 nph, 50.2 km/h; consumption: 20.1 m/imp gal, 17 m/US gal, 3.9 l x 100 km.

LECTRICAL EQUIPMENT 37 A alternator.

IMENSIONS AND WEIGHT weight: Catalina and Laurenan sedans and coupés plus 174 lb, 79 kg Parisienne edan and Coupé and st. wagons plus 65 lb, 27 kg.

105 hp (diesel) power team

ee 115 hp power team, except for:

NGINE diesel; 8 cylinders; 350 cu in, 5,736 cc (4.06 x 3.38 , 103.9 x 86 mm); compression ratio: 22.5:1; max power AE net): 105 hp (78 kW) at 3,200 rpm; max torque (SAE et): 205 lb ft, 28.4 kg m (278 Nm) at 1,600 rpm; max ngine rpm: 3,500; 18.4 hp/l (13.6 kW/l); 5 crankshaft earings; lubrication: 12.4 imp pt, 14.8 US pt, 7.1 l; mechaical fuel injection pump; cooling, 28.7 imp pt, 33.9 US pt, 6.4 l.

RANSMISSION axle ratio: 2.730.

ERFORMANCE max speed: 85 mph, 136 km/h; powereight ratio: Catalina Sedan 35.1 lb/hp, (47.2 lb/kW), 15.9 g/hp (21.4 kg/kW); speed in direct drive at 1,000 rpm: 28.6 ph, 45.7 km/h; consumption: 23.8 m/imp gal, 20 m/US gal, 1.8 l x 100 km.

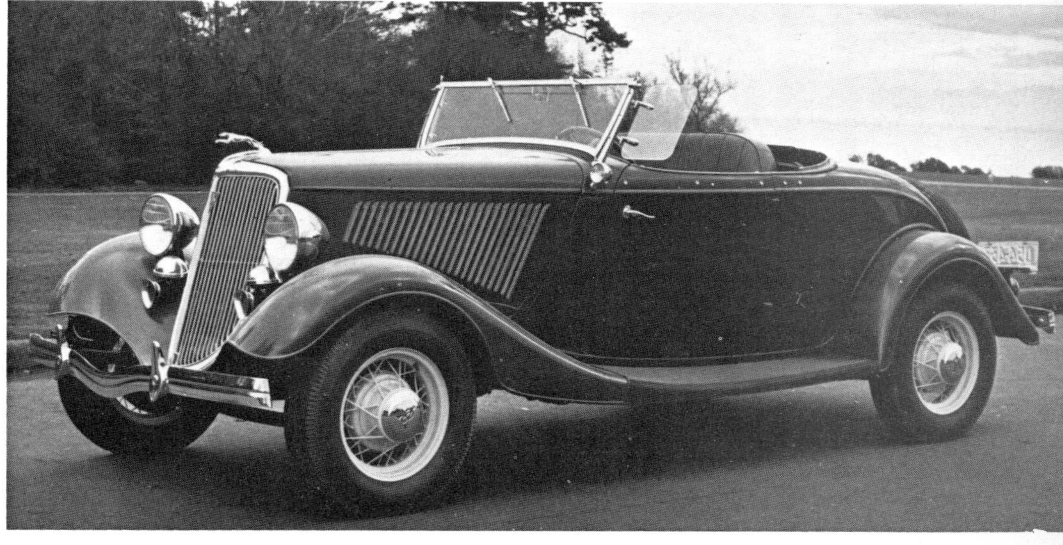

TIMMIS Ford V8 Roadster

ELECTRICAL EQUIPMENT 55 A alternator.

DIMENSIONS AND WEIGHT weight: sedans and coupés plus 253 lb, 115 kg - st. wagons plus 134 lb, 61 kg.

TIMMIS — CANADA

Ford V8 Roadster

PRICE EX WORKS: Canadian $ 30,000

ENGINE Ford, front, 4 stroke; 8 cylinders; 239.4 cu in, 3,923 cc (3.19 x 3.75 in, 80.9 x 95.2 mm); compression ratio: 8:1; max power (DIN): 125 hp (92 kW) at 3,800 rpm; max torque (DIN): 200 lb ft, 27.6 kg/m (271 Nm) at 1,850 rpm; max engine rpm: 4,200; 31.9 hp/l (23.5 kW/l); cast iron block and head; 3 crankshaft bearings; valves: overhead; camshafts: 1, at centre of Vee; lubrication: gear pump, 8 imp pt, 9.5 US pt, 4.5 l; 1 Ford downdraught twin barrel carburettor; fuel feed: mechanical pump; water-cooled, 44 imp pt, 52.9 US pt, 25 l.

TRANSMISSION driving wheels: rear; clutch: single dry plate; gearbox: mechanical; gears: 3, II and III synchronized; lever: central; final drive: hypoid bevel; axle ratio: 3.300, 3.540 or 3.550; tyres: Firestone 6.00 x 16.

PERFORMANCE max speed: 100 mph, 161 km/h; power-weight ratio: 18.7 lb/hp, (25.6 lb/kW); 8.5 kg/hp (11.6 kg/kW); carrying capacity: 700 lb, 317 kg; consumption: 20 m/imp gal, 16.7 m/US gal, 14.1 l x 100 km.

CHASSIS separate X frame; front suspension: independent, transverse leafsprings, anti-roll bar, telescopic dampers; rear: rigid axle, twin semi-elliptic leafsprings, anti-roll bar, telescopic dampers.

STEERING worm and roller; turns lock to lock: 5.

BRAKES drum; swept area: front 186 sq in, 1,200 sq cm, rear 186 sq in, 1,200 sq cm, total 372 sq in, 2,400 sq cm.

ELECTRICAL EQUIPMENT 6 V; 90 Ah battery; dynamo; Ford distributor; 2 headlamps.

DIMENSIONS AND WEIGHT wheel base: 112 in, 284 cm; tracks: 55,20 in, 140 cm front, 56.68 in, 144 cm rear; length: 175.90 in, 447 cm; width: 67.38 in, 171 cm; height: 65.50 in, 166 cm; ground clearance: 9 in, 22.9 cm; weight: 2,350 lb, 1,066 kg; weight distribution: 55% front, 45% rear; turning circle: 40 ft, 12,2 m; fuel tank: 11.7 imp gal, 14 US gal, 53 l.

BODY roadster, in fiberglass material; 2 doors; 2 seats, bench front seat; bucket seats; canvas top; wire wheels.

PRACTICAL INSTRUCTIONS fuel: 98 oct petrol; oil: engine 8 imp pt, 9.5 US pt, 4.5 l, SAE 30, change every 2,000 miles, 3,200 km - gearbox 2.1 imp pt, 2.5 US pt, 1.2 l, SAE 90, change every 6 months; final drive 1.6 imp pt, 2 US pt, 0.9 l, SAE 90, change every 6 months; greasing: every 3,200 km, 15 points; sparking plug: Champion H-10; tappet clearances: inlet 0.012 in, 0.30 mm, exhaust 0.014 in, 0.35 mm; valve timing: 0° 44° 48° 6°; tyre pressure: front and rear 26 psi, 1.8 atm.

VOLKSWAGEN 1200 L

VOLKSWAGEN — MEXICO

1200 L

ENGINE rear, 4 stroke; 4 cylinders, horizontally opposed; 72.7 cu in, 1,192 cc (3.03 x 2.52 in, 77 x 64 mm); compression ratio: 7.3:1 max power (DIN): 34 hp (25 kW) at 3,800 rpm; max torque (DIN): 55 lb ft, 7.6 kg m (75 Nm) at 1,700 rpm; max engine rpm: 4,500; 28.5 hp/l (21 kW/l); block with cast iron liners and light alloy fins, light alloy head; 4 crankshaft bearings; valves: overhead, push-rods and rockers; camshafts: 1, central, lower; lubrication: gear pump, filter in sump, oil cooler, 4.4 imp pt, 5.3 US pt, 2.5 l; 1 Solex 30 PICT downdraught single barrel carburettor; fuel feed: mechanical pump; air-cooled.

TRANSMISSION driving wheels: rear; clutch: single dry plate; gearbox: mechanical; gears: 4, fully synchronized; ratios: I 3.780, II 2.060, III 1.260, IV 0.890, rev 4.010; lever: central; final drive: spiral bevel; axle ratio: 4.375; width of rims: 4.5"; tyres: 155 SR x 15.

PERFORMANCE max speeds: (I) 18 mph, 31 km/h; (II) 35 mph, 57 km/h: (III) 58 mph, 94 km/h; (IV) 71 mph, 115 km/h; power-weight ratio: 50.6 lb/hp (68.8 lb/kW), 22.9 kg/hp (31.2 kg/kW); carrying capacity: 838 lb, 380 kg; acceleration: stand-

1200 L

ing ¼ mile 23 sec, 0-50 mph (0-80 km/h) 18 sec; speed in top at 1,000 rpm: 18.6 mph, 30 km/h; consumption: 39.2 m/imp gal, 32.7 m/US gal, 7.2 l x 100 km at 56 mph, 90 km/h.

CHASSIS backbone platform; front suspension: independent, twin swinging longitudinal trailing arms, transverse laminated torsion bars, anti-roll bar, telescopic dampers; rear: independent, swinging semi-axles, swinging longitudinal trailing arms, transverse torsion bars, telescopic dampers.

STEERING worm and roller, telescopic damper; turns lock to lock: 2.60.

BRAKES drum, dual circuit; lining area: total 111 sq in, 716 sq cm.

ELECTRICAL EQUIPMENT 12 V; 36 Ah battery; 270 W dynamo; Bosch distributor; 2 headlamps.

DIMENSIONS AND WEIGHT wheel base: 94.49 in, 240 cm; tracks: 51.57 in, 131 cm front, 53.15 in, 135 cm rear; length: 159.84 in, 406 cm; width: 61.02 in, 155 cm; height: 59.06 in, 150 cm; ground clearance: 5.90 in, 15 cm; weight: 1,720 lb, 780 kg; weight distribution: 43% front, 57% rear; turning circle: 36.1 ft, 11 m; fuel tank: 8.8 imp gal, 10.6 US gal, 40 l.

BODY saloon/sedan; 2 doors; 5 seats, separate front seats, adjustable backrests.

PRACTICAL INSTRUCTIONS fuel: 87 oct petrol; oil: engine 4.4 imp pt, 5.3 US pt, 2.5 l, SAE 10W-20 (winter) 20W-30 (summer), change every 3,100 miles, 5,000 km - gearbox and final drive 5.3 imp pt, 6.3 US pt, 3 l, SAE 90, change every 31,000 miles, 50,000 km; greasing: every 6,200 miles, 10,000 km, 4 points; sparking plug: 175°; tappet clearances: inlet 0.004 in, 0.10 mm, exhaust 0.004 in, 0.10 mm; valve timing: 6° 35°5' 42°5' 3°; tyre pressure: front 16 psi, 1.1 atm, rear 24 psi, 1.7 atm.

181

ENGINE rear, 4 stroke; 4 cylinders, horizontally opposed; 96.7 cu in, 1,584 cc (3.37 x 2.72 in, 85.5 x 69 mm); compression ratio: 7.5:1; max power (DIN): 48 hp (35 kW) at 4,000 rpm; max torque (DIN): 74 lb ft, 10.2 kg m (100 Nm) at 2,000 rpm; max engine rpm: 4,600; 30.3 hp/l (22.3 kW/l); block with cast iron liners and light alloy fins, light alloy head; 4 crankshaft bearings; valves: overhead, push-rods and rockers; camshafts: 1, central, lower; lubrication: gear pump, filter in sump, oil cooler, 4.4 imp pt, 5.3 US pt, 2.5 l; 1 Solex 30 PICT 2 downdraught carburettor; fuel feed: mechanical pump; air-cooled.

TRANSMISSION driving wheels: rear; clutch: single dry plate; gearbox: mechanical; gears: 4 and transfer box, fully synchronized; ratios: I 3.800, II 2.060, III 1.220, IV 0.820, rev 3.610; lever: central; final drive: spiral bevel; axle ratio: 4.880; width of rims: 5''; tyres: 185 SR x 14.

PERFORMANCE max speeds: (I) 15 mph, 24 km/h; (II) 28 mph, 45 km/h; (III) 47 mph, 76 km/h; (IV) 71 mph, 115 km/h; power-weight ratio: 41.3 lb/hp (56.2 lb/kW), 18.7 kg/hp (25.5 kg/kW), carrying capacity: 970 lb, 440 kg; acceleration: 0-50 mph (0-80 km/h) 14.5 sec; speed in top at 1,000 rpm: 18.3 mph, 29.5 Km/h; consumption: 29.7 m/imp gal, 24.8 m/US gal, 9.5 l x 100 km.

CHASSIS backbone platform; front suspension: independent, by McPherson, coil springs/telescopic damper struts, anti-roll bar, lower swinging trailing arms, rubber cone springs; rear: independent, semi-trailing arms, transverse compensating torsion bar, telescopic dampers.

STEERING worm and roller.

BRAKES drum, dual circuit; lining area: total 125.3 sq in, 808 sq cm.

ELECTRICAL EQUIPMENT 12 V; 36 Ah battery; 30 A alternator; Bosch distributor; 2 headlamps.

DIMENSIONS AND WEIGHT wheel base: 94.49 in, 240 cm; tracks: 53.35 in, 135 cm front, 54.53 in, 138 cm rear; length: 148.82 in, 378 cm; width: 64.57 in, 164 cm; height: 63.78 in, 162 cm; ground clearance: 8.07 in, 20.5 cm; weight: 1,985 lb, 900 kg; turning circle: 36.1 ft, 11 m; fuel tank: 8.8 imp gal, 10.6 US gal, 40 l.

BODY convertible; 4 doors; 5 seats, separate front seats.

PRACTICAL INSTRUCTIONS fuel: 87 oct petrol; oil: engine 4.4 imp pt, 5.3 US pt, 2.5 l, SAE 10W-30 (winter) 20W-30 (summer), change every 3,100 miles, 5,000 km - gearbox and final drive 4.4 imp pt, 5.3 US pt, 2.5 l, SAE 90, change every 31,000 miles, 50,000 km; greasing: every 6,200 miles, 10,000 km, 4 points; sparking plug: 175°; tappet clearances: inlet 0.004 in, 0.10 mm, exhaust 0.004 in, 0.10 mm; valve timing: 7°30' 37° 44°30' 4°; tyre pressure: front 16 psi, 1.1 atm, rear 24 psi, 1.7 atm.

OPTIONALS limited slip differential; 6.00 x 15 or 155 SR X 15 tyres.

VOLKSWAGEN 181

FIAT — URUGUAY

600 S

PRICE EX WORKS: 47,500 pesos

ENGINE rear, 4 stroke; 4 cylinders, vertical, in line; 51.4 cu in, 843 cc (2.56 x 2.50 in, 65 x 63.5 mm); compression ratio: 7.4:1; max power (DIN): 32 hp (24 kW) at 4,800 rpm; 37.9 hp/l (28.5 kW/l); cast iron block, light alloy head; 3 crankshaft bearings; valves: overhead, in line, push-rods and rockers; camshafts: 1, side; lubrication: gear pump, full flow filter (cartridge), 6.5 imp pt, 7.8 US pt, 3.7 l; 1 Galileo 285 CP 10 or Bressel 285 CP 10 downdraught single barrel carburettor; fuel feed: mechanical pump; sealed circuit liquid cooling, 7.9 imp pt, 9.5 US pt, 4.5 l.

TRANSMISSION driving wheels: rear; clutch: single dry plate; gearbox: mechanical; gears: 4, fully synchronized; ratios: I 3.385, II 2.055, III 1.333, IV 0.896, rev 4.275; lever: central; final drive: spiral bevel; axle ratio: 4.875; width of rims: 4''; tyres: 5.20 x 12.

PERFORMANCE max speeds: (I) 19 mph, 30 km/h; (II) 28 mph, 45 km/h; (III) 43 mph, 70 km/h; (IV) 68 mph, 110 km/h; power-weight ratio: 43 lb/hp (57.4 lb/kW), 19.5 kg/hp (26 kg/kW); carrying capacity: 706 lb, 320 kg; acceleration: standing ¼ mile 26.7 sec, 0-50 mph (0-80 km/h) 26 sec; speed in top at 1,000 rpm: 14.1 mph, 22.7 km/h; consumption: 48.7 m/imp ga 40.6 m/US gal, 5.8 l x 100 km.

CHASSIS integral; front suspension: independent, upper swing ing arms, anti-roll bar, telescopic dampers; rear: independent swinging arms, coil springs, telescopic dampers.

STEERING screw and sector; turns lock to lock: 2.12.

BRAKES drum; lining area: front 33.5 sq in, 216 sq cm, re 33.5 sq in, 216 sq cm, total 67 sq in, 432 sq cm.

ELECTRICAL EQUIPMENT 12 V; 32 Ah battery; 475 W alterna tor; Garef-Marelli distributor; 2 headlamps.

DIMENSIONS AND WEIGHT wheel base: 78.74 in, 200 cm tracks: 45.28 in, 115 cm front, 45.67 in, 116 cm rear; length 131.89 in, 335 cm; width: 54.33 in, 138 cm; height: 55.12 ir 140 cm; ground clearance: 5.71 in, 14.5 cm; weight: 1,378 l 625 kg; weight distribution: 46% front, 54% rear; turning circl 29.5 ft, 9 m; fuel tank: 5.9 imp gal, 7.1 US gal, 27 l.

BODY saloon/sedan; 2 doors; 4 seats, separate front seats

PRACTICAL INSTRUCTIONS fuel: 90 oct petrol; oil: engine 5. imp pt, 6.3 US pt, 3 l, SAE 20W-40, change every 3,100 miles 5,000 km - gearbox 2.6 imp pt, 3.2 US pt, 1.5 l, SAE 90 EI change every 18,600 miles, 30,000 km; tappet clearances: inle 0.006 in, 0.15 mm, exhaust 0.006 in, 0.15 mm; valve timing: 4 26° 29° 1°; tyre pressure: front 14 psi, 1 atm, rear 23 psi, 1. atm.

FIAT 600 S

\MERICAN CUSTOM INDUSTRIES
USA

American Turbo

'RICE EX WORKS: $ 32,000

.NGINE Chevrolet Corvette, turbocharged, front, 4 stroke; 8 ylinders; 350 cu in, 5,736 cc (4 x 3.48 in, 101.6 x 88.3 mm); ompression ratio: 8.5:1; cast iron block and head; 5 crankshaft earings; valves: overhead, in line, push-rods and rockers, ydraulic tappets; camshafts: 1, at centre of Vee; lubrication: ear pump, full flow filter, 8.3 imp pt, 9.9 US pt, 4.7 l; 1 owndraught 4-barrel carburettor with turbocharger; air cleaner; xhaust system with catalytic converter; fuel feed: mechanical ump; water-cooled, 34.5 imp pt, 41.4 US pt, 19.6 l.

RANSMISSION driving wheels: rear; gearbox: Turbo-Iydramatic automatic transmission, hydraulic torque converter nd planetary gears with 3 ratios; lever: central; final drive: ypoid bevel, limited slip differential; axle ratio: 3.550; width of ims: 8"; tyres: HR60 x 15 front, LR60 x 15 rear.

'ERFORMANCE max speed: 130 mph, 209 km/h; speed in irect drive at 1,000 rpm: 28 mph, 45 km/h; consumption: not eclared.

:HASSIS ladder frame with cross members; front suspension: ndependent, wishbones, coil springs, anti-roll bar, adjustable elescopic dampers; rear: independent, wishbones, coil springs, nti-roll bar, adjustable telescopic dampers.

;TEERING recirculating ball, servo.

BRAKES disc (diameter 11.75 in, 30 cm), internal radial fins, ervo.

:LECTRICAL EQUIPMENT 12 V; 3500 W battery; 42 A alterna-or; Delco-Remy high energy ignition; 2 retractable headlamps.

)IMENSIONS AND WEIGHT wheel base: 98 in, 249 cm; tracks: i1 in, 155 cm front, 62 in, 157 cm rear; length: 185.20 in, 470 m; width: 72 in, 183 cm front, 75 in, 190 cm rear; height: 48 in, 22 cm; weight: 3,320 lb, 1,505 kg; fuel tank: 20 imp gal, 24 US jal, 91 l.

BODY coupé or convertible, in fiberglass material; 2 doors; 2 eats.

)PTIONALS 3.360 axle ratio; special spray; De Luxe uphol-stery; digital (LED) read-out gauges; front and rear remote adar detectors.

AMERICAN CUSTOM INDUSTRIES American Turbo

AMERICAN MOTORS USA

Spirit Series

'RICES EX WORKS:

	$
Sedan	4,193
Liftback	4,293

'ower team:	Standard for:	Optional for:
82 hp	both	—
08 hp	—	both

AMERICAN MOTORS Spirit Liftback

82 hp power team

:NGINE front, 4 stroke; 4 cylinders, in line; 151 cu in, 2,475 cc 4 x 3 in, 101.6 x 76.2 mm); compression ratio: 8.3:1; max pow-er (SAE net): 82 hp (60 kW) at 4,000 rpm; max torque (SAE net): 125 lb ft, 17.3 kg m (170 Nm) at 2,600 rpm; max engine pm: 4,600; 33.1 hp/l (24.2 kW/l); cast iron block and head; 5 crankshaft bearings; valves: overhead, in line, push-rods and ockers, hydraulic tappets; camshafts: 1, side; lubrication: gear pump, full flow filter, 4.9 imp pt, 5.9 US pt, 2.8 l; 1 Rochester win barrel carburettor; air cleaner; exhaust system with cataly-ic converter; fuel feed: mechanical pump; water-cooled, 10.7 mp pt, 12.9 US pt, 6.1 l.

TRANSMISSION driving wheels: rear; clutch: single dry plate; gearbox: mechanical; gears: 4, fully synchronized; ratios: I 3.500, II 2.210, III 1.430, IV 1, rev 3.390; lever: central; final drive: hypoid bevel; axle ratio: 3.080; width of rims: 4.5"; tyres: C 78 x 14.

'ERFORMANCE max speed: 85 mph, 136 km/h; power-weight atio: Sedan 30.7 lb/hp (42 lb/kW), 13.9 kg/hp (19 kg/kW); speed in direct drive at 1,000 rpm: 20 mph, 32.8 km/h; con-sumption: 26.4 m/imp gal, 22 m/US gal, 10.7 l x 100 km.

:HASSIS integral; front suspension: independent, wishbones, coil springs, anti-roll bar (except for Sedan), telescopic dam-pers; rear: rigid axle, torque tube, semi-elliptic leafsprings, elescopic dampers.

STEERING recirculating ball; turns lock to lock: 5.

BRAKES front disc (diameter 10.27 in, 26.1 cm), front internal adial fins, rear drum; swept area: total 265.78 sq in, 1,714 sq cm.

ELECTRICAL EQUIPMENT 12 V; 45 Ah battery; 42 A alterna-tor; 4 headlamps.

DIMENSIONS AND WEIGHT wheel base: 96 in, 244 cm; tracks: 58.08 in, 147 cm front, 57.04 in, 145 cm rear; length: Sedan 166.82 in, 424 cm - Liftback 167.24 in, 425 cm; width: Sedan 71.96 in, 183 cm - Liftback 71.88 in, 183 cm; height: Sedan 51.66 in, 131 cm - Liftback 51.55 in, 131 cm; ground clearance: Sedan 4.16 in, 10.6 cm - Liftback 4.17 in, 10.6 cm; weight: Sedan 2,519 lb, 1,143 kg - Liftback 2,615 lb, 1,186 kg; turning circle: 35.3 ft, 10.8 m; fuel tank: 17.6 imp gal, 21 US gal, 80 l.

BODY saloon/sedan, liftback; 2 doors; 4 seats, separate front seats, reclining backrests; folding rear seat.

OPTIONALS Torque-Command automatic transmission, hyd-raulic torque converter and planetary gears with 3 ratios (I 2.450, II 1.450, III 1, rev 2.200), max ratio of converter at stall 2, possible manual selection, steering column or central lever, limited slip differential; D78 x 14 or P195/75R x 14 tyres with 5" wide rims; DR70 x 14 tyres with 6" wide rims; light alloy wheels; anti-roll bar on front suspension (for Sedan only); anti-roll bar on rear suspension; heavy-duty cooling; heavy-duty battery; power steering; servo brake; heated rear window; tinted glass; sunshine roof; air-conditioning; DL equipment; Limited equip-ment.

108 hp power team

See 82 hp power team, except for:

ENGINE 6 cylinders, in line; 258 cu in, 4,228 cc (3.75 x 3.90 in, 95.2 x 99 mm); compression ratio: 8.3:1; max power (SAE net): 108 hp (79 kW) at 3,000 rpm; max torque (SAE net): 200 lb ft, 27.6 kg m (271 Nm) at 2,600 rpm; max engine rpm: 3,600; 25 hp/l (18.7 kW/l); cast iron block and head; 7 crankshaft bear-ings; valves: push-rods and rockers, hydraulic tappets; cam-shafts: 1, side; lubrication: gear pump, full flow filter, 8.3 imp pt, 9.9 US pt, 4.7 l; 1 Carter BBD downdraught twin barrel carburettor; cooling: 10.9 imp pt, 13.1 US pt, 6.2 l.

TRANSMISSION gearbox ratios: I 4.070, II 2.570, III 1.660, IV 1, rev 3.950.

PERFORMANCE max speed: 90 mph, 144 km/h; power-weight ratio: Sedan 23.3 lb/hp (31.9 lb/kW), 10.6 kg/hp (14.5 kg/kW); speed in direct drive at 1,000 rpm: 23 mph, 36.8 km/h; con-sumption: 21.6 m/imp gal, 18 m/US gal, 13.1 l x 100 km.

BRAKES swept area: total 326.8 sq in, 2,108 sq cm.

AMX

PRICE EX WORKS: $ 5,653

ENGINE front, 4 stroke; 6 cylinders, in line; 258 cu in, 4,228 cc (3.75 x 3.90 in, 95.2 x 99 mm); compression ratio: 8.3:1; max power (SAE net): 108 hp (79 kW) at 3,000 rpm; max torque (SAE net): 200 lb ft, 27.6 kg m (271 Nm) at 1,800 rpm; max engine rpm: 3,500; 25 hp/l (18.7 kW/l); cast iron block and head; 7 crankshaft bearings; valves: overhead, in line, push-rods and rockers, hydraulic tappets; camshafts: 1, side; lubrica-tion: gear pump, full flow filter, 8.3 imp pt, 9.9 US pt, 4.7 l; 1 Carter BBD downdraught twin barrel carburettor; air cleaner; exhaust system with catalytic converter; fuel feed: mechanical pump; water-cooled, 10.9 imp pt, 13.1 US pt, 6.2 l.

AMERICAN MOTORS AMX

AMX

TRANSMISSION driving wheels: rear; clutch: single dry plate; gearbox: mechanical; gears: 4, fully synchronized; ratios: I 4.070, II 2.570, III 1.660, IV 1, rev 3.950; lever: central; final drive: hypoid bevel; axle ratio: 2.530; width of rims: 7"; tyres: C 78 x 14.

PERFORMANCE max speed: 90 mph, 144 km/h; power-weight ratio: 27.2 lb/hp (37.1 lb/kW), 12.3 kg/hp (16.8 kg/kW); speed in direct drive at 1,000 rpm: 23 mph, 36.8 km/h; consumption: 21.6 m/imp gal, 18 m/US gal, 13.1 l x 100 km.

CHASSIS integral; front suspension: independent, wishbones, coil springs, anti-roll bar, telescopic dampers; rear: rigid axle, torque tube, semi-elliptic leafsprings, telescopic dampers.

STEERING recirculating ball; turns lock to lock: 5.

BRAKES front disc (diameter 10.80 in, 27.4 cm), front internal radial fins, rear drum; swept area: total 323.70 sq in, 2,088 sq cm.

ELECTRICAL EQUIPMENT 12 V; 50 Ah battery; 42 A alternator; Motorcraft electronic distributor; 4 headlamps.

DIMENSIONS AND WEIGHT wheel base: 96 in, 244 cm; tracks: 58.08 in, 147 cm front, 57.04 in, 145 cm rear; length: 167.24 in, 425 cm; width: 71.88 in, 183 cm; height: 51.49 in, 131 cm; ground clearance: 4.20 in, 10.6 cm; weight: 2,934 lb, 1,330 kg; turning circle: 35.3 ft, 10.8 m; fuel tank: 17.6 imp gal, 21 US gal, 80 l.

BODY liftback; 2 doors; 4 seats, separate front seats, reclining backrests; folding rear seat; light alloy wheels.

OPTIONALS Torque-Command automatic transmission, hydraulic torque converter and planetary gears with 3 ratios (I 2.450, II 1.450, III 1, rev 2.200), max ratio of converter at stall 2, possible manual selection, steering column or central lever, 2.730 axle ratio; limited slip differential; anti-roll bar on rear suspension; heavy-duty cooling; heavy-duty battery; power steering; tilt of steering wheel; servo brake; tinted glass; sunshine roof; heated rear window; air-conditioning.

Concord Series

PRICES EX WORKS:	$
1 2-dr Sedan	4,753
2 4-dr Sedan	4,878
3 4+1-dr St. Wagon	5,078

Power team:	Standard for:	Optional for:
82 hp	1,2	—
108 hp	3	1,2

82 hp power team

ENGINE front, 4 stroke; 4 cylinders, in line; 151 cu in, 2,475 cc (4 x 3 in, 101.6 x 76.2 mm); compression ratio: 8.3:1; max power (SAE net): 82 hp (60 kW) at 4,000 rpm; max torque (SAE net): 125 lb ft, 17.3 kg m (170 Nm) at 2,600 rpm; max engine rpm: 4,600; 33.1 hp/l (24.2 kW/l); cast iron block and head; 5 crankshaft bearings; valves: overhead, in line, push-rods and rockers, hydraulic tappets; camshafts: 1, side; lubrication: gear pump, full flow filter, 4.9 imp pt, 5.9 US pt, 2.8 l; 1 Rochester twin barrel carburettor; air cleaner; exhaust system with catalytic converter; fuel feed: mechanical pump; water-cooled, 10.7 imp pt, 12.9 US pt, 6.1 l.

TRANSMISSION driving wheels: rear; clutch: single dry plate; gearbox: mechanical; gears: 4, fully synchronized; ratios: I 3.500, II 2.210, III 1.430, IV 1, rev 3.390; lever: central; final drive: hypoid bevel; axle ratio: 3.080; width of rims: 5"; tyres: D 78 x 14.

PERFORMANCE max speed: 85 mph, 136 km/h; power-weight ratio: 4-dr Sedan 33.7 lb/hp (46.1 lb/kW), 15.3 kg/hp (20.9 kg/kW); speed in direct drive at 1,000 rpm: 20 mph, 32.8 km/h; consumption: 26.4 m/imp gal, 22 m/US gal, 10.7 l x 100 km.

CHASSIS integral; front suspension: independent, wishbones, coil springs, anti-roll bar, telescopic dampers; rear: rigid axle, torque tube, semi-elliptic leafsprings, telescopic dampers.

STEERING recirculating ball; turns lock to lock: 6.

BRAKES front disc (diameter 10.80 in, 27.4 cm), front internal radial fins, rear drum; swept area: total 265.7 sq in, 1,714 sq cm.

ELECTRICAL EQUIPMENT 12 V; 50 Ah battery; 42 A alternator; 4 headlamps.

DIMENSIONS AND WEIGHT wheel base: 108 in, 274 cm; tracks: 57.64 in, 146 cm front, 57.06 in, 145 cm rear; length: 185 in, 470 cm; width: 71 in, 181 cm; height: 2-dr Sedan 51.87 in, 132 cm - 4-dr Sedan 51.31 in, 130 cm; ground clearance: 2-dr Sedan 4.22 in, 10.7 cm - 4-dr Sedan 3.69 in, 9.4 cm; weight: 2-dr Sedan 2,710 lb, 1,229 kg - 4-dr Sedan 2,767 lb, 1,255 kg; turning circle: 38.6 ft, 11.8 m; fuel tank: 18.3 imp gal, 22 US gal, 83 l.

BODY saloon/sedan; 2-dr model, 4 seats - 4-dr model, 5 seats; separate front seats.

OPTIONALS Torque-Command automatic transmission, hydraulic torque converter and planetary gears with 3 ratios (I 2.450, II 1.450, III 1, rev 2.200), max ratio of converter at stall 2, possible manual selection, steering column lever; limited slip differential; P195/75R x 14 tyres; DR70 x 14 tyres with 6" wide rims; anti-roll bar on rear suspension; heavy-duty suspension; heavy-duty cooling; heavy-duty battery; power steering; tilt of steering wheel; servo brake; reclining backrests; tinted glass; heated rear window; sunshine roof; light alloy wheels; air conditioning; DL equipment; Limited equipment.

108 hp power team

See 82 hp power team, except for:

ENGINE front, 4 stroke; 6 cylinders, in line; 258 cu in, 4,228 cc (3.75 x 3.90 in, 95.2 x 99 mm); compression ratio: 8.3:1; max power (SAE net): 108 hp (79 kW) at 3,000 rpm; max torque (SAE net): 200 lb ft, 27.6 kg m (271 Nm) at 2,600 rpm; max engine rpm: 3,600; 25 hp/l (18.7 kW/l); cast iron block and head; 7 crankshaft bearings; valves: overhead, in line, push-rods and rockers, hydraulic tappets; camshafts: 1, side; lubrication: gear pump, full flow filter, 8.3 imp pt, 9.9 US pt, 4.7 l; 1 Carter BBD downdraught twin barrel carburettor; cooling: 10.9 imp pt, 13.1 US pt, 6.2 l.

TRANSMISSION gearbox ratios: I 4.070, II 2.570, III 1.660, IV 1, rev 3.950.

PERFORMANCE max speed: 90 mph, 144 km/h; power-weight ratio: 4+1-dr St. Wagon 26 lb/hp (35.7 lb/kW), 11.8 kg/hp (16.2 kg/kW); speed in direct drive at 1,000 rpm: 23 mph, 36.8 km/h; consumption: 20.5 m/imp gal, 17 m/US gal, 13.8 l x 100 km.

BRAKES swept area: total 326.8 sq in, 2,108 sq cm.

DIMENSIONS AND WEIGHT height: 4+1-dr St. Wagon 51.55 in, 131 cm; ground clearance: 4+1-dr St. Wagon 3.95 in, 10 cm; weight: 4+1-dr St. Wagon 2,816 lb, 1,277 kg.

BODY estate car/st. wagon; 4+1 doors; 5 seats, separate front seats.

Pacer Series

PRICES EX WORKS:	$
2-dr Hatchback	5,407
2+1-dr St. Wagon	5,558

ENGINE front, 4 stroke; 6 cylinders, in line; 258 cu in, 4,228 cc (3.75 x 3.90 in, 95.2 x 99 mm); compression ratio: 8.3:1; max power (SAE net): 108 hp (79 kW) at 3,000 rpm; max torque (SAE net): 200 lb ft, 27.6 kg m (271 Nm) at 1,800 rpm; max engine rpm: 3,500; 25 hp/l (18.7 kW/l); cast iron block and head; 7 crankshaft bearings; valves: overhead, in line, push-rods and rockers, hydraulic tappets; camshafts: 1, side; lubrication: gear pump, full flow filter, 8.3 imp pt, 9.9 US pt, 4.7 l; 1

AMERICAN MOTORS Concord DL Sedan

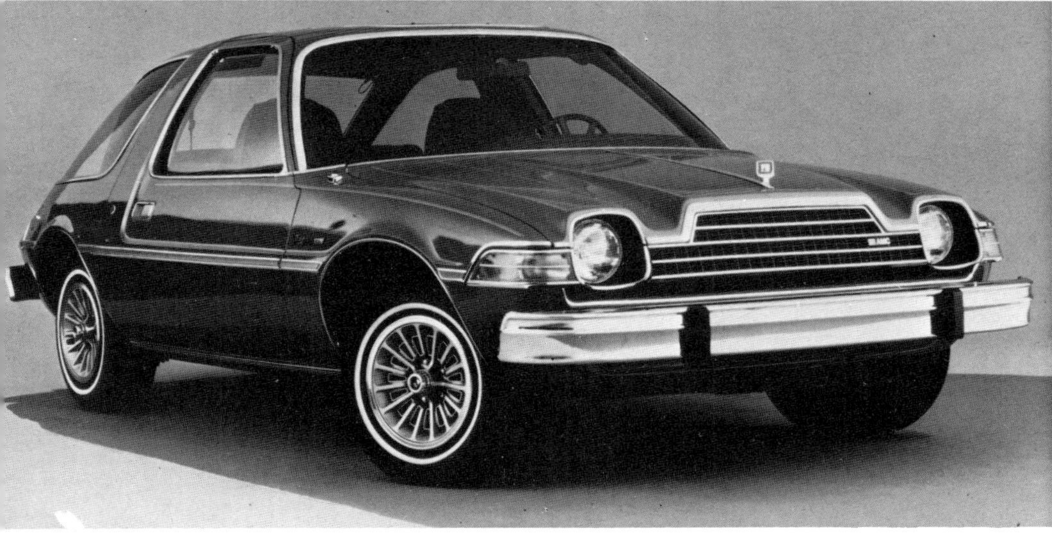

AMERICAN MOTORS Pacer DL Hatchback

Carter BBD downdraught twin barrel carburettor; air cleaner; exhaust system with catalytic converter; fuel feed: mechanical pump; water-cooled.

TRANSMISSION driving wheels: rear; clutch: single dry plate; gearbox: mechanical; gears: 4, fully synchronized; ratios: I 3.980, II 2.140, III 1.420, IV 1, rev 3.990; lever: central; final drive: hypoid bevel; axle ratio: 2.530; width of rims: 6"; tyres: P195/75 x 14.

PERFORMANCE max speed: 90 mph, 144 km/h; power-weight ratio: Hatchback 29.6 lb/hp (40.5 lb/kW), 13.4 kg/hp (18.3 kg/kW); speed in direct drive at 1,000 rpm: 25 mph, 40.1 km/h; consumption: 20.5 m/imp gal, 17 m/US gal, 13.8 l x 100 km.

CHASSIS integral; front suspension: independent, wishbones, coil springs, anti-roll bar, telescopic dampers; rear: rigid axle, semi-elliptic leafsprings, telescopic dampers.

STEERING rack-and-pinion; turns lock to lock: 5.80.

BRAKES front disc (diameter 10.80 in, 27.4 cm), front internal radial fins, rear drum; swept area: total 323.7 sq in, 2,088 sq cm.

ELECTRICAL EQUIPMENT 12 V; 45 Ah battery; 42 A alternator; 2 headlamps.

DIMENSIONS AND WEIGHT wheel base: 100 in, 254 cm; tracks: 61.08 in, 155 cm front, 60 in, 152 cm rear; length: Hatchback 173.91 in, 442 cm - St. Wagon 178.82 in, 454 cm; width: 77 in, 196 cm; height: Hatchback 52.80 in, 134 cm - St. Wagon 53.13 in, 135 cm; ground clearance: Hatchback 4.67 in, 11.8 cm - St. Wagon 4.90 in, 12.5 cm; weight: Hatchback 3,197 lb, 1,450 kg - St. Wagon 3,235 lb, 1,467 kg; turning circle: 39 ft, 11.9 m; fuel tank: 17.6 imp gal, 21 US gal, 80 l.

BODY coupé, estate car/st. wagon; 4 seats, separate front seats.

OPTIONALS Torque-Command automatic transmission, hydraulic torque converter and planetary gears with 3 ratios (I 2.450, II 1.450, III 1, rev 2.200), max ratio of converter at stall 2, possible manual selection, steering column or central lever; limited slip differential; light alloy wheels; heavy-duty cooling; heavy-duty battery; power steering; tilt of steering wheel; servo brake; electric windows; tinted glass; sunshine roof; heated rear window; rear window wiper-washer; reclining backrests; air-conditioning; Limited equipment; DL equipment.

Eagle Series

PRICES EX WORKS:	$
2-dr Sedan	**6,999**
4-dr Sedan	**7,249**
4+1-dr St. Wagon	**7,549**

ENGINE front, 4 stroke; 6 cylinders, in line; 258 cu in, 4,228 cc (3.75 x 3.90 in, 95.2 x 99 mm); compression ratio: 8.3:1; max power (SAE net): 115 hp (84 kW) at 3,200 rpm; max torque (SAE net): 205 lb ft, 28.3 kg m (278 Nm) at 1,800 rpm; max engine rpm: 3,800; 27.2 hp/l (19.9 kW/l): cast iron block and head; 7 crankshaft bearings; valves: overhead, in line, hydraulic tappets; camshafts: 1, side; lubrication: gear pump, 7 imp pt, 8.5 US pt, 4 l; 1 Carter BBD downdraught twin barrel carburettor; air cleaner; exhaust system with catalytic converter; fuel feed: mechanical pump; water-cooled, 23.2 imp pt, 27.9 US pt, 13.2 l.

TRANSMISSION driving wheels: front and rear; gearbox: Torque-Command automatic transmission, hydraulic torque converter and planetary gears with 3 ratios, max ratio of converter at stall 2, possible manual selection; ratios: I 2.450, II 1.450, III 1, rev 2.200; lever: central; axle ratio: 3.080; width of rims: 6"; tyres: P195/75 x 15.

PERFORMANCE max speed: 79 mph, 127 km/h; power-weight ratio: 4-dr Sedan 29.2 lb/hp (40 lb/kW), 13.2 kg/hp (18.1 kg/kW); speed in direct drive at 1,000 rpm: 24 mph, 38.5 km/h; consumption: 19.2 m/imp gal, 16 m/US gal, 14.7 l x 100 km.

CHASSIS integral; front suspension: independent, wishbones, telescopic dampers, coil springs, anti-roll bar; rear: rigid axle, semi-elliptic leafsprings, telescopic dampers.

STEERING recirculating ball, servo; turns lock to lock: 3.10.

BRAKES front disc (diameter 10.98 in, 27.9 cm), front internal radial fins, rear drum, servo; swept area: total 329 sq in, 2,123 sq cm.

ELECTRICAL EQUIPMENT 12 V; 50 Ah battery; 42 A alternator; Motorcraft electronic ignition; 4 headlamps.

DIMENSIONS AND WEIGHT wheel base: 109.27 in, 277 cm; tracks: 59.64 in, 151 cm front, 57.56 in, 146 cm rear; length: 184 in, 467 cm; width: 71 in, 180 cm; height: 2-dr Sedan 55.59 in, 141 cm - 4-dr Sedan 55.14 in, 140 cm - St. Wagon 55.05 in, 139 cm; ground clearance: 2-dr Sedan 6.95 in, 17.7 cm - 4-dr Sedan and St. Wagon 6.94 in, 17.6 cm; weight: 2-dr Sedan 3,306 lb, 1,500 kg - 4-dr Sedan 3,361 lb, 1,524 kg - St. Wagon 3,407 lb, 1,545 kg; turning circle: 38.09 ft, 11.6 m; fuel tank: 18.1 imp gal, 22 US gal, 82 l.

BODY saloon/sedan, estate car/st. wagon; 4 seats, separate front seats.

OPTIONALS 3.540 axle ratio; electric windows; digital clock; air-conditioning; electric door locks; heated rear window; fog lamps; halogen headlamps; heavy-duty battery; tilt of steering wheel; anti-roll bar on rear suspension; Limited equipment.

AMERICAN MOTORS Eagle Station Wagon

ANTIQUE & CLASSIC AUTOMOTIVE
USA

1927 Bugatti 37 B

PRICES EX WORKS: $ 7,500 (complete car)
$ 2,450 (kit only)

ENGINE Volkswagen, rear, 4 stroke; 4 cylinders, horizontally opposed; 96.7 cu in, 1,584 cc (3.37 x 2.72 in, 85.5 x 69 mm); compression ratio: 8.5:1; max power (DIN): 50 hp (37 kW) at 4,000 rpm; max torque (DIN): 78 lb ft, 10.8 kg m (106 Nm) at 2,800 rpm; max engine rpm: 4,600; 31.6 hp/l (23.2 kW/l); block with cast iron liners and light alloy fins, light alloy head; 4 crankshaft bearings; valves: overhead, push-rods and rockers; camshafts: 1, central, lower; lubrication: gear pump, filter in sump, oil cooler, 4.4 imp pt, 5.3 US pt, 2.5 l; 1 Solex 34 PICT 2 downdraught carburettor; fuel feed: mechanical pump; air-cooled.

TRANSMISSION driving wheels: rear; clutch: single dry plate; gearbox: mechanical; gears: 4, fully synchronized; ratios: I 3.780, II 2.060, III 1.260, IV 0.930, rev 4.010; lever: central; final drive: spiral bevel; axle ratio: 3.875; width of rims: 4"; tyres: 5.60 x 15.

PERFORMANCE max speed: 90 mph, 145 km/h; power-weight ratio: 32.6 lb/hp (44.3 lb/kW), 14.8 kg/hp (20.1 kg/kW); consumption: 30.7 m/imp gal, 25.6 m/US gal, 9.2 l x 100 km.

CHASSIS backbone platform; front suspension: independent, twin swinging longitudinal trailing arms, transverse laminated torsion bars, anti-roll bar, telescopic dampers; rear: independent, swinging semi-axles, swinging longitudinal trailing arms, transverse torsion bars, telescopic dampers.

STEERING worm and roller.

BRAKES drum; lining area: total 111 sq in, 716 sq cm.

ELECTRICAL EQUIPMENT 12 V; 36 Ah battery; alternator; Bosch distributor; 2 headlamps.

DIMENSIONS AND WEIGHT wheel base: 94,50 in, 240 cm; tracks: 51.50 in, 131 cm front, 53.10 in, 135 cm rear; length: 145 in, 368 cm; width: 60 in, 152 cm; height: 48 in, 122 cm; ground clearance: 7.20 in, 18.3 cm; weight: 1,580 lb, 716 kg; weight distribution: 40% front, 60% rear; fuel tank: 9.7 imp gal, 11.6 US gal, 44 l.

BODY roadster, in fiberglass material; no doors; 2 seats, bench front seats.

ANTIQUE & CLASSIC AUTOMOTIVE
1927 Bugatti 37 B

ANTIQUE & CLASSIC AUTOMOTIVE
1931 Alfa Romeo

1931 Alfa Romeo

PRICES EX WORKS: **$ 7,500** (complete car)
$ 2,450 (kit only)

ENGINE Volkswagen, rear, 4 stroke; 4 cylinders, horizontally opposed; 96.7 cu in, 1,584 cc (3.37 x 2.72 in, 85.5 x 69 mm); compression ratio: 8.5:1; max power (DIN): 50 hp (37 kW) at 4,000 rpm; max torque (DIN): 78 lb ft, 10.8 kg m (106 Nm) at 2,800 rpm; max engine rpm: 4,600; 31.6 hp/l (23.2 kW/l); block with cast iron liners and light alloy fins, light alloy head; 4 crankshaft bearings; valves: overhead, push-rods and rockers; camshafts: 1, central, lower; lubrication: gear pump, filter in sump, oil cooler, 4.4 imp pt, 5.3 US pt, 2.5 l; 1 Solex 34 PICT 2 downdraught carburettor; fuel feed: mechanical pump; air-cooled.

TRANSMISSION driving wheels: rear; clutch: single dry plate; gearbox: mechanical; gears: 4, fully synchronized; ratios: I 3.780, II 2.060, III 1.260, IV 0.930, rev 4.010; lever: central; final drive: spiral bevel; axle ratio: 3.875; width of rims: 4"; tyres: 5.60 x 15.

PERFORMANCE max speed: 90 mph, 145 km/h; power-weight ratio: 32.6 lb/hp (44.3 lb/kW), 14.8 kg/hp (20.1 hg/kW); consumption: 30.7 m/imp gal, 25.6 m/US gal, 9.2 l x 100 km.

CHASSIS backbone platform; front suspension: independent, twin swinging longitudinal trailing arms, transverse laminated torsion bars, anti-roll bar, telescopic dampers; rear: independent, swinging semi-axles, swinging longitudinal trailing arms, transverse torsion bars, telescopic dampers.

STEERING worm and roller.

BRAKES drum; lining area: total 111 sq in, 716 sq cm.

ELECTRICAL EQUIPMENT 12 V; 36 Ah battery; alternator; Bosch distributor; 2 headlamps.

DIMENSIONS AND WEIGHT wheel base: 94.50 in, 240 cm; tracks: 51.50 in, 131 cm front, 53.10 in, 135 cm rear; length: 145 in, 368 cm; width: 60 in, 152 cm; height: 50.50 in, 128 cm; ground clearance: 7.20 in, 18.3 cm; weight: 1,590 lb, 720 kg; weight distribution: 40% front, 60% rear; fuel tank: 2.7 imp gal, 11.6 US gal, 44 l.

BODY roadster, in fiberglass material; no doors; 2 seats, bench front seats.

Frazer Nash TT Interceptor

PRICES EX WORKS: **$ 10,550** (complete car)
$ 4,470 (kit only)

ENGINE Volkswagen, rear, 4 stroke; 4 cylinders, horizontally opposed; 96.7 cu in, 1,584 cc (3.37 x 2.72 in, 85.5 x 69 mm); compression ratio: 8.5:1; max power (DIN): 50 hp (37 kW) at 4,000 rpm; max torque (DIN): 78 lb ft, 10.8 kg m (106 Nm) at 2,800 rpm; engine rpm: 4,600; 31.6 hp/l (23.2 kW/l); block with cast iron liners and light alloy fins, light alloy head; 4 crankshaft bearings; valves: overhead, push-rods and rockers; camshafts: 1, central, lower; lubrication: gear pump, filter in sump, oil cooler, 4.4 imp pt, 5.3 US pt, 2.5 l; 1 Solex 34 PICT 2 downdraught carburettor; fuel feed: mechanical pump; air-cooled.

TRANSMISSION driving wheels: rear; clutch: single dry plate; gearbox: mechanical; gears: 4, fully synchronized; ratios: I 3.780, II 2.060, III 1.260, IV 0.930, rev 4.010; lever: central; final drive: spiral bevel; axle ratio: 3.875 width of rims: 4"; tyres: 5.60 x 15.

PERFORMANCE max speed: 90 mph, 145 km/h; power-weight ratio: 32.6 lb/hp (44.3 lb/kW), 14.8 kg/hp (20.1 kg/kW); consumption: 30.7 m/imp gal, 25.6 m/US gal, 9.2 l x 100 km.

CHASSIS backbone platform; front suspension: independent, twin swinging indepedent, twin swinging longitudinal trailing arms, transverse laminated torsion bars, anti-roll bar, telescopic dampers; rear: independent, swinging semi-axles, swinging longitudinal trailing arms, transverse torsion bars, telescopic dampers.

STEERING worm and roller.

BRAKES drum; lining area: total 111 sq in, 716 sq cm.

ELECTRICAL EQUIPMENT 12 V; 36 Ah battery; alternator; Bosch distributor; 4 headlamps.

DIMENSIONS AND WEIGHT wheel base: 108.50 in, 276 cm; tracks: 51.50 in, 131 cm front, 53.10 in, 135 cm rear; length: 159.50 in, 405 cm; height: 52 in, 132 cm; ground clearance: 7.20 in, 18.3 cm; weight: 1,630 lb, 739 kg; weight distribution: 35% front, 65% rear; fuel tank: 9.7 imp gal, 11.6 US gal, 44 l.

BODY roadster, in fiberglass material; 2 doors; 2 seats.

ANTIQUE & CLASSIC AUTOMOTIVE
1930 Blower Phaeton

ANTIQUE & CLASSIC AUTOMOTIVE Frazer Nash TT Interceptor

Jaguar SS 100

PRICES EX WORKS: **$ 12,995** (complete car)
$ 4,995 (kit only)

ENGINE Volkswagen, rear, 4 stroke; 4 cylinders, horizontally opposed; 96.7 cu in, 1,584 cc (3.37 x 2.72 in, 85.5 x 69 mm); compression ratio: 8.5:1; max power (DIN): 50 hp (37 kW) at 4,000 rpm; max torque (DIN): 78 lb ft, 10.8 kg m (106 Nm) at 2,800 rpm; max engine rpm: 4,600; 31.6 hp/l (23.2 kW/l); block with cast iron liners and light alloy fins, light alloy head; 4 crankshafts bearings; valves: overhead, push-rods and rockers; camshafts: 1, central, lower; lubrication: gear pump, filter in sump, oil cooler, 4.4 imp pt, 5.3 US pt, 2.5 l; 1 Solex 34 PICT 2 downdraught carburettor; fuel feed: mechanical pump; air-cooled.

TRANSMISSION driving wheels: rear; clutch: single dry plate; gearbox: mechanical; gears: 4, fully synchronized; ratios: I 3.780, II 2.060, III 1.260, IV 0.930, rev 4.010; lever: central; final drive: spiral bevel; axle ratio: 3.875; width of rims: 4"; tyres: 5.60 x 15.

PERFORMANCE max speed: 90 mph, 145 km/h; power-weight ratio: 32.6 lb/hp (44.3 lb/kW), 14.8 kg/hp (20.1 hg/kW); consumption: 30.7 m/imp gal, 25.6 m/US gal, 9.2 l x 100 km.

CHASSIS backbone platform; front suspension: independent, twin swinging longitudinal trailing arms, transverse laminated torsion bars, anti-roll bar, telescopic dampers; rear: independent, swinging semi-axles, swinging longitudinal trailing arms, transverse torsion bars, telescopic dampers.

STEERING worm and roller.

BRAKES drum; lining area: total 111 sq in, 716 sq cm.

ANTIQUE & CLASSIC AUTOMOTIVE Jaguar SS 100

LECTRICAL EQUIPMENT 12 V; 36 Ah battery; alternator; osch distributor; 2 headlamps.

MENSIONS AND WEIGHT wheel base: 108.50 in, 276 cm; acks: 51.50 in, 131 cm front, 53.10 in, 135 cm rear; length: 59.50 in, 405 cm; height: 52 in, 132 cm; ground clearance: 20 in, 18.3 cm; weight: 1,630 lb, 739 kg; weight distribution: 5% front, 65% rear; fuel tank: 9.7 imp gal, 11.6 US gal, 44 l.

ODY roadster, in fiberglass material; 2 doors; 2 seats.

1930 Blower Phaeton

RICES EX WORKS: $ 11,500 (complete car)
$ 4,625 (kit only)

NGINE Volkswagen, rear, 4 stroke; 4 cylinders, horizontally pposed; 96.7 cu in, 1,584 cc (3.37 x 2.72 in, 85.5 x 69 mm); ompression ratio: 8.5:1; max power (DIN): 50 hp (37 kW) at 000 rpm; max torque (DIN): 78 lb ft, 10.8 kg m (106 Nm) at 800 rpm; max engine rpm: 4,600; 31.6 hp/l (23.2 kW/l); block ith cast iron liners and light alloy fins, light alloy head; 4 ankshaft bearings; valves: overhead, push-rods and rockers; amshafts: 1, central, lower; lubrication: gear pump, filter in ump, oil cooler, 4.4 imp pt, 5.3 US pt, 2.5 l; 1 Solex 34 PICT 2 owndraught carburettor; fuel feed: mechanical pump; air-ooled.

TRANSMISSION driving wheels: rear; clutch: single dry plate; gearbox: mechanical; gears: 4, fully synchronized; ratios: I 3.780, II 2.060, III 1.260, IV 0.930, rev 4.010; lever: central; final drive: spiral bevel; axle ratio: 3.875; width of rims: 4"; tyres: 5.60 x 15.

PERFORMANCE max speed: 90 mph, 145 km/h; power-weight ratio: 32.6 lb/hp (44.3 lb/kW), 14.8 kg/hp (20.1 kg/kW); consumption: 30.7 m/imp gal, 25.6 m/US gal, 9.2 l x 100 km.

CHASSIS backbone platform; front suspension: independent, twin swinging longitudinal trailing arms, transverse laminated torsion bars, anti-roll bar, telescopic dampers; rear: independent, swinging semi-axles, swinging longitudinal trailing arms, transverse torsion bars, telescopic dampers.

STEERING worm and roller.

BRAKES drum; lining area: total 111 sq in, 716 sq cm.

ELECTRICAL EQUIPMENT 12 V; 36 Ah battery; alternator; Bosch distributor; 2 headlamps.

DIMENSIONS AND WEIGHT wheel base: 108.50 in, 276 cm; tracks: 51.50 in, 131 cm front, 53.10 in, 135 cm rear; length:161 in, 409 cm; width: 60 in, 152 cm; height: 59 in, 150 cm; ground clearance: 7.20 in, 18.3 cm; weight: 1,715 lb, 777 kg; weight distribution: 40% front, 60% rear; fuel tank: 9.7 imp gal, 11.6 US gal, 4.4 l.

BODY convertible, in fiberglass material; 2 doors, one front and one rear; 5 seats, bench front seats.

AUBURN Dual Cowl Phaeton

AUBURN USA

Speedster

PRICE EX WORKS: $ 28,650

ENGINE Lincoln Continental, front, 4 stroke; 8 cylinders; 460 cu in, 7,539 cc (4.36 x 3.85 in, 110.7 x 97.8 mm); compression ratio: 8:1; max power (DIN): 208 (153 kW) at 4,000 rpm; max torque (DIN): 356 lb ft, 49.1 kg m (481 Nm) at 2,000 rpm; max engine rpm: 4,400; 27.6 hp/l (20.3 kW/l); cast iron block and head; 5 crankshaft bearings; valves: overhead, in line, push-rods and rockers, hydraulic tappets; camshafts: 1, at centre of Vee; lubrication: rotary pump, full flow filter 8.3 imp pt, 9.9 US pt, 4.7 l; 1 Motorcraft 9510 D7VE-AA downdraught 4-barrel carburettor; air cleaner; dual exhaust system with catalytic converter; fuel feed: mechanical pump; water-cooled, 30.8 imp pt, 37 US pt, 17.5 l.

TRANSMISSION driving wheels: rear; gearbox: Select-Shift Merc-o-Matic automatic transmission, hydraulic torque converter and planetary gears with 3 ratios, max ratio of converter at stall 2.03, possible manual selection; ratios: I 2.460, II 1.460, III 1, rev 2.180; lever: central; final drive: hypoid bevel, limited slip differential; axle ratio: 2.750; width of rims: 6"; tyres JR78 x 15.

PERFORMANCE not declared; power-weight ratio: 15.4 lb/hp (20.9 lb/kW), 7 kg/hp (9.5 kg/kW); carrying capacity: 353 lb, 160 kg.

CHASSIS box type ladder frame; front suspension: independent, wishbones, lower trailing arms, coil springs, anti-roll bar, telescopic dampers; rear: rigid axle, lower trailing radius arms, upper torque arms, transverse linkage bar, coil springs, telescopic dampers.

STEERING recirculating ball, tilt of steering wheel, servo.

BRAKES front disc, front internal radial fins, rear drum.

ELECTRICAL EQUIPMENT 12 V; 68 Ah battery; 60 A alternator; Motorcraft transistorized ignition; 2 headlamps.

DIMENSIONS AND WEIGHT wheel base: 127 in, 323 cm; tracks: 63 in, 160 cm front, 65 in, 165 cm rear; length: 191 in, 485 cm; height: 58 in, 147 cm; ground clearance: 7 in, 17.8 cm; weight: 3,200 lb, 1,451 kg; weight distribution: 50% front, 50% rear; fuel tank: 15 imp gal, 18 US gal, 68 l.

BODY convertible, in plastic material; 2 doors; 2 seats; leather interior.

OPTIONALS tonneau cover; wire wheels; air-conditioning.

Dual Cowl Phaeton

PRICE EX WORKS: $ 60,000

ENGINE Lincoln Continental, front, 4 stroke; 8 cylinders; 460 cu in, 7,539 cc (4.36 x 3.85 in, 110.7 x 97.8 mm); compression ratio: 8:1; max power (DIN): 208 hp (153 kW) at 4,000 rpm; max torque (DIN): 356 lb ft, 49.1 kg m (481 Nm) at 2,000 rpm; max engine rpm: 4,400; 27.6 hp/l (20.3 kW/l); cast iron block and head; 5 crankshaft bearings; valves: overhead, in line, push-rods and rockers, hydraulic tappets; camshafts: 1, at centre of Vee; lubrication: rotary pump, full flow filter, 8.3 imp pt, 9.9 US pt, 4.7 l; 1 Motorcraft 9510 D7VE-AA downdraught 4-barrel carburettor; air cleaner; dual exhaust system with catalytic converter; fuel feed: mechanical pump; water-cooled, 30.8 imp pt, 37 US pt, 17.5 l.

TRANSMISSION driving wheels: rear; gearbox: Select-Shift Merc-o-Matic automatic transmission, hydraulic torque converter and planetary gears with 3 ratios, max ratio of converter at stall 2.03, possible manual selection; ratios: I 2.460, II 1.460, III 1, rev 2.180; lever: central; final drive: hypoid bevel, limited slip differential; axle ratio: 2.750; width of rims: 6"; tyres: JR78 x 15.

PERFORMANCE not declared; power-weight ratio: 19.6 lb/hp (26.7 lb/kW), 8.9 kg/hp (12.1 kg/kW); carrying capacity: 706 lb, 320 kg.

CHASSIS box-type ladder frame; front suspension: independent, wishbones, lower trailing arms, coil springs, anti-roll bar, telescopic dampers; rear: rigid axle, lower trailing radius arms, upper torque arms, transverse linkage bar, coil springs, telescopic dampers.

STEERING recirculating ball, tilt of steering wheel, servo.

BRAKES front disc, front internal radial fins, rear drum.

ELECTRICAL EQUIPMENT 12 V; 68 Ah battery; 60 A alternator; Motorcraft transistorized ignition; 2 headlamps.

DIMENSIONS AND WEIGHT wheel base: 140 in, 356 cm; tracks: 63 in, 160 cm front, 65 in, 165 cm rear; length: 204 in, 518 cm; height: 58 in, 147 cm; ground clearance: 7 in, 17.8 cm; weight: 4,100 lb, 1,860 kg; weight distributioon: 50% front, 50% rear; fuel tank: 20.9 imp gal, 25 US gal, 95 l.

DUAL COWL PHAETON

BODY convertible, in plastic material; 4 doors; 4 seats, bench front seats; leather interior; tonneau cover; air-conditioning.

OPTIONALS wire wheels.

AUTOMOBILI INTERMECCANICA USA

Speedster

PRICE EX WORKS: $ 17,900

ENGINE Volkswagen, rear, 4 stroke; 4 cylinders, horizontally opposed; 100 cu in, 1,640 cc (3.43 x 2.72 in, 87.1 x 69 mm); compression ratio: 8.5:1; max power (DIN): 90 hp (66 kW) at 5,000 rpm; max torque (DIN): 94 lb ft, 13 kg m (127 Nm) at 2,600 rpm; max engine rpm: 5,200; 56.9 hp/l (41.9 kW/l); block with cast iron liners and light alloy fins, light alloy head; 4 crankshaft bearings; valves: overhead, push-rods and rockers; camshafts: 1, central, lower; lubrication: gear pump, filter in sump, oil cooler, 4.4 imp pt, 5.3 US pt, 2.5 l; 2 Solex downdraught single barrel carburettors; fuel feed: mechanical pump; air-cooled.

TRANSMISSION driving wheels: rear; clutch: single dry plate; gearbox: mechanical; gears: 4, fully synchronized; ratios: I 3.780, II 2.060, III 1.260, IV 0.930, rev 4.010; lever: central; final drive: spiral bevel; axle ratio: 3.875; width of rims: 4"; tyres: P 165/SR x 15.

PERFORMANCE max speed: 105 mph, 170 km/h; power-weight ratio: 17.6 lb/hp (23.9 lb/kW), 7.9 kg/hp (10.8 kg/kW); carrying capacity: 353 lb, 160 kg; acceleration: standing ¼ mile 17.1 sec; consumption: 33.6 m/imp gal, 28 m/US gal, 8.4 l x 100 km.

CHASSIS box-section perimeter frame; front suspension: independent, twin swinging longitudinal trailing arms, transverse laminated torsion bars, anti-roll bar, telescopic dampers; rear: independent, swinging semi-axles, swinging longitudinal trailing arms, transverse torsion bars, telescopic dampers.

STEERING worm and roller.

BRAKES drum; lining area: total 111 sq in, 716 sq cm.

ELECTRICAL EQUIPMENT 12 V; 36 Ah battery; alternator; Bosch distributor; 2 headlamps.

DIMENSIONS AND WEIGHT wheel base: 82.70 in, 210 cm; tracks: 51.57 in, 131 cm front, 53.15 in, 135 cm rear; weight: 1,580 lb, 716 kg; weight distribution: 48% front, 52% rear; fuel tank: 11.5 imp gal, 13.7 US gal, 52 l.

BODY roadster, in plastic material; 2 doors; 2 seats; tonneau cover.

OPTIONALS turbocharger.

AUTOMOBILI INTERMECCANICA La Crosse

La Crosse

PRICE EX WORKS: $ 44,900

ENGINE Ford, front, 4 stroke; 8 cylinders; 351 cu in, 5,732 cc (4 x 3.50 in, 101.6 x 88.8 mm); compression ratio: 8:1; max power (SAE net): 149 hp (110 kW) at 3,800 rpm; max torque (SAE net): 258 lb ft, 35.6 kg m (349 Nm) at 2,200 rpm; max engine rpm: 4,400; 26 hp/l (19.1 kW/l); cast iron block and head; 5 crankshaft bearings; valves: overhead, in line, push-rods and rockers, hydraulic tappets; camshafts: 1, at centre of Vee; lubrication: rotary pump, full flow filter, 8.3 imp pt, 9.9 US pt, 4.7 l; 1 Ford 2150 A D9AE-AHA downdraught twin barrel carburettor; air cleaner; exhaust system with 2 cathalytic converters; fuel feed: mechanical pump; water-cooled, 23.8 imp pt, 28.5 US pt, 13.5 l.

TRANSMISSION driving wheels: rear gearbox: Select Shift automatic transmission, hydraulic torque converter and planetary gears with 3 ratios, max ratio of converter at stall 2.04 possible manual selection; ratios: I 2.460, II 1.460, III 1, rev 2.180; lever: steering column; final drive: hypoid bevel; axle ratio: 2.750; tyres: 225 x 15.

PERFORMANCE max speed: 106 mph, 170 km/h; power-weight ratio: 28.2 lb/hp (38.3 lb/kW), 12.8 kg/hp (17.3 kg/kW); speed in direct drive at 1,000 rpm: 26.1 mph, 42 km/h; consumption: 13.2 m/imp gal, 11 m/US gal, 21.4 l x 100 km.

CHASSIS perimeter box-type frame; front suspension: independent, wishbones, coil springs, anti-roll bar, telescopic dampers; rear: rigid axle, lower trailing radius arms, upper oblique torque arms, coil springs, telescopic dampers.

STEERING recirculating ball, servo; turns lock to lock: 4.10.

BRAKES front disc (diameter 11.08 in, 28.1 cm), front interna radial fins, rear compensator, rear drum, servo; swept area front 228.7 sq in, 1,475 sq cm, rear 157.1 sq in, 1,013 sq cm total 385.8 sq in, 2,488 sq cm.

ELECTRICAL EQUIPMENT 12 V; 45 Ah battery; 60 A alternator; Motorcraft transistorized ignition; 2 headlamps, anti-fog lamps.

DIMENSIONS AND WEIGHT wheel base: 132 in, 335 cm tracks: 62.90 in, 160 cm front, 62.60 in, 159 cm rear; length 210 in, 533 cm; width: 77 in, 196 cm; height: 52 in, 132 cm weight: 4,200 lb, 1,902 kg; turning circle: 42.4 ft, 12.9 m; fuel tank: 17.6 imp gal, 21 US gal, 80 l.

BODY roadster; 2 doors; 4 seats, separate front seats with built-in headrests; Connally leather upholstery; Wilton carpeting; air-conditioning; electric windows.

AVANTI USA

Avanti II

PRICE EX WORKS: $ 19,500

ENGINE Chevrolet Corvette, front, 4 stroke; 8 cylinders; 350 cu in, 5,736 cc (4 x 3.48 in, 101.6 x 88.3 mm); compression ratio 8.2:1; max power (SAE net): 190 hp (140 kW) at 4,400 rpm max torque (SAE net): 280 lb ft, 38.6 kg m (378 Nm) at 2,400 rpm; max engine rpm: 5,000; 33.1 hp/l (24.4 kW/l); cast iron block and head; 5 crankshaft bearings; valves: overhead, in line, push-rods and rockers, hydraulic tappets; camshafts: 1, at centre of Vee; lubrication: gear pump, full flow filter, 8.3 imp pt 9.9 US pt, 4.7 l; 1 Rochester 17059207 downdraught 4-barrel carburettor; thermostatic air cleaner; dual exhaust system with catalytic converter; fuel feed: mechanical pump; water-cooled 34.5 imp pt, 41.4 US pt, 19.6 l, viscous coupling thermostatic fan.

TRANSMISSION driving wheels: rear; gearbox: Turbo Hydramatic 400 automatic transmission, hydraulic torque converter and planetary gears with 3 ratios, max ratio of converter at stall 2, possible manual selection; ratios: I 2.480, II 1.480, III 1, rev 2.070; lever: central; final drive: hypoid bevel, limited slip differential; axle ratio: 3.070; width of rims: 8"; tyres: P225 70R x 15.

PERFORMANCE max speed: 124 mph, 198 km/h; power-weight ratio: 18.8 lb/hp (25.5 lb/kW), 8.5 kg/hp (11.6 kg/kW); speed in direct drive at 1,000 rpm: 30.6 mph, 49.3 km/h; consumption 19.2 m/imp gal, 16 m/US gal, 14.7 l x 100 km.

CHASSIS box-type ladder frame, X cross members; front suspension: independent, wishbones, coil springs, anti-roll bar telescopic dampers; rear: rigid axle, semi-elliptic leafsprings upper torque arms, anti-roll bar, telescopic dampers.

STEERING cam and lever, tilt of steering wheel, servo; turns lock to lock: 2.92.

BRAKES front disc, rear drum, servo.

AVANTI Avanti II

ELECTRICAL EQUIPMENT 12 V; 61 Ah battery; 37 A alternator; Delco-Remy high energy ignition; 2 headlamps.

DIMENSIONS AND WEIGHT wheel base: 109 in, 277 cm; tracks: 57.37 in, 146 cm front, 56.56 in, 144 cm rear; length: 197.80 in, 502 cm; width: 70.40 in, 179 cm; height: 54.40 in, 138 cm; ground clearance: 6.19 in, 15.7 cm; weight: 3.570 lb, 1619 kg; turning circle: 37.5 ft, 11.4 m; fuel tank: 15.8 imp gal, 19 US gal, 72 l.

BODY coupé, in fiberglass material; 2 doors; 4 seats, separate front seats, built-in headrests; heated rear window; tinted glass; air-conditioning.

OPTIONALS electric moonroof; electric windows; all leather interior fog lamps; automatic speed control; reclining front seats; genuine wood veneer dash and console panels; Recaro front seats; wire wheels; Magnum "500" wheels.

BLAKELY USA

Bearcat 'S'

PRICE EX WORKS: $ 9,250 (complete car)

ENGINE Ford Pinto, front, 4 stroke; 4 cylinders, in line; 140 cu in, 2,300 cc (3.78 x 3.13 in, 95.9 x 79.5 mm); compression ratio: 9.5:1; max power (DIN): 125 hp (92 kW) at 4,800 rpm; max torque (DIN): 134 lb ft, 18.5 kg m (181 Nm) at 3,200 rpm; max engine rpm: 5,200; 54.3 hp/l (40 kW/l); cast iron block and head; 5 crankshaft bearings; valves: overhead, Vee-slanted, rockers, hydraulic tappets; camshafts: 1, overhead, cogged belt; lubrication: gear pump, full flow filter, 8.3 imp pt, 9.9 US pt, 4.7 l; 1 Holley 390 C.F.M. downdraught 4-barrel carburettor; air cleaner; exhaust system with catalytic converter; fuel feed: mechanical pump; water-cooled, 15.8 imp pt, 19 US pt, 9 l.

TRANSMISSION driving wheels: rear; clutch: single dry plate; gearbox: mechanical; gears: 4, fully synchronized; ratios: I 3.460, II 1.460, III 1.240, IV 1, rev 2.460; lever: central; final drive: hypoid bevel; axle ratio: 2.730; width of rims: 5.5"; tyres: 5 R x 13.

PERFORMANCE max speed: 100 mph, 161 km/h; power-weight ratio: 14.4 lb/hp, (19.6 lb/kW), 6.5 kg/hp (8.9 kg/kW); consumption: 31.4 m/imp gal, 26 m/US gal, 9 l x 100 km.

CHASSIS tubular; front suspension: independent, unequal-length upper A arms, coil springs, telescopic dampers; rear: rigid axle, three-link cantilever leafspring with central trailing arm, telescopic dampers.

STEERING rack-and-pinion; turns lock to lock: 4.

BRAKES front disc (diameter 9.30 in, 23.6 cm), front internal radial fins, rear drum; swept area: front 145.5 sq in, 938 sq cm, rear 99 sq in, 639 sq cm, total 244.5 sq in, 1,577 sq cm.

ELECTRICAL EQUIPMENT 12 V; 70 Ah battery; 42 A alternator; Ford distributor; 2 headlamps.

DIMENSIONS AND WEIGHT wheel base: 93 in, 236 cm; tracks: 56 in, 142 cm front, 56.80 in, 144 cm rear; length: 145 in, 368 cm; width: 65 in, 165 cm; height: 46 in, 117 cm; ground clearance: 7 in, 17.8 cm; weight: 1,800 lb, 816 kg; turning circle: 30.6 ft, 9.3 m; fuel tank: 9.9 imp gal, 12 US gal, 45 l.

BODY roadster, in plastic material; 2 doors; 2 seats.

OPTIONALS Cruise-o-Matic automatic transmission with 3 ratios (I 2.470, II 1.470, III 1, rev 2.110), max ratio of converter at stall 2.9, possible manual selection, central lever; 61 A alternator; hardtop; sunshine roof installed in hardtop; wire wheels.

BUICK USA

Skyhawk Series

PRICES EX WORKS:

	$
Hatchback Coupé	4,993
Hatchback Coupé	5,211

ENGINE front, 4 stroke; 6 cylinders, Vee-slanted at 90°; 231 cu in, 3,785 cc (3.80x3.40 in, 96.4x86.3 mm); compression ratio: 8:1; max power (SAE net): 110 hp (81 kW) at 3,800 rpm; max torque (SAE net): 190 lb ft, 26.2 kg m (257 Nm) at 2,000 rpm; max engine rpm: 4,200; 29.1 hp/l (21.4 kW/l; cast iron block and head; 4 crankshaft bearings; valves: overhead, in line, push-rods and rockers, hydraulic tappets; camshafts: 1, at centre of Vee; lubrication: gear pump, full flow filter, 6.7 imp pt, 8 US pt, 3.8 l; 1 Rochester 2 ME downdraught twin barrel carburettor; thermostatic air cleaner; fuel feed: electric pump; water-cooled, 21.6 imp pt, 26 US pt, 12.3 l.

TRANSMISSION driving wheels: rear; clutch: single dry plate;

BLAKELY Bearcat 'S'

BUICK Skyhawk Road Hawk Hatchback Coupé

BUICK Skyhawk Hatchback Coupé

SKYHAWK SERIES

gearbox: mechanical; gears: 4, fully synchronized; ratios: I 3.500, II 2.480, III 1.660, IV 1, rev 3.500; lever: central; final drive: hypoid bevel; axle ratio: 2.930; width of rims: 6''; tyres: B78 x 13.

PERFORMANCE max speed: 99 mph, 159 km/h; power-weight ratio: 26 lb/hp (35.3 lb/kW), 11.8 kg/hp (16 kg/kW); consumption: 18 m/imp gal, 15 m/US gal, 15.7 l x 100 km.

CHASSIS integral; front suspension: independent, wishbones, coil springs, telscopic dampers; rear; rigid axle, coil springs, torque arms, transverse linkage bar, telescopic dampers.

STEERING recirculating ball; turns lock to lock: 4.40.

BRAKES front disc (diameter 9.74 in, 24.7 cm), front internal radial fins, rear drum; swept area: total 264.7 sq in, 1,707 sq cm.

ELECTRICAL EQUIPMENT 12 V; 275 Ah battery; 37 A alternator; Delco transistorized ignition; 2 headlamps.

DIMENSIONS AND WEIGHT wheel base: 97 in, 246 cm; tracks: 54.70 in, 139 cm front, 53.60 in, 136 cm rear; length: 179.30 in, 455 cm; width: 65.40 in, 166 cm; height: 50.80 in, 129 cm; ground clearance: 4.80 in, 12.4 cm; 'S' Hatchback Coupé 2,851 lb, 1,293 kg - weight: Hatchback Coupè 2,868 lb, 1,301 kg; turning circle: 38.5 ft, 11.7 m; fuel tank: 15.4 imp gal, 18.5 US gal, 70 l.

BODY 2 doors; 4 seats, separate front seats; folding rear seat.

OPTIONALS automatic transmission; 2.560 axle ratio (for California only); power steering; servo brake; heavy-duty battery; reclining backrests; air-conditioning; Road Hawk equipment.

Skylark Series

PRICES EX WORKS:		$
1	4-dr Sedan	**5,306**
2	2-dr Coupé	**5,160**
3	Limited 4-dr Sedan	**5,725**
4	Limited 2-dr Coupé	**5,579**
5	Sport 4-dr Sedan	**5,920**
6	Sport 2-dr Coupé	**5,774**

For 115 hp engine (with servo brake, power steering and automatic transmission) add $ 225.

Power team:	Standard for:	Optional for:
90 hp	all	—
115 hp	—	all

90 hp power team

ENGINE front, 4 stroke; 4 cylinders, in line; 151 cu in, 2,474 cc (4 x 3 in, 101.6 x 76.2 mm); compression ratio: 8.2:1; max power (SAE net): 90 hp (66 kW) at 4,000 rpm; max torque (SAE net): 134 lb ft, 13.7 kg m (187 Nm) at 2,400 rpm; max engine rpm: 4,400; 36 hp/l (26.5 kW/l); cast iron block and head; 3 crankshaft bearings; valves: push-rods and rockers, hydraulic tappets; camshafts: 1; lubrication: gear pump, full flow filter, 4.9 imp pt, 5.9 US pt, 2.8 l; 1 Rochester 17059619 downdraught twin barrel carburettor; air cleaner; fuel feed: mechanical pump; water-cooled, coupés 13.7 imp pt, 16.5 US pt, 7.8 l - sedans 17.6 imp pt. 21.1 US pt. 10 l.

TRANSMISSION driving wheels: front; clutch: single plate; gearbox: mechanical; gears: 4, fully synchronized; ratios: I 3.530, II 1.950, III 1.240, IV 0.810, rev 3.420; lever: central; final drive: hypoid bevel; axle ratio: 3.340; width of rims: 5.5''; tyres: T125 / 70 X 14.

PERFORMANCE max speeds: 93 mph, 150 km/h; 4-dr Sedan 27.8 lb/hp, (37.9 lb/kW), 12.6 kg/hp (17.2 kg/kW); carrying capacity: 882 lb, 400 kg; consumption: 28.8 m/imp gal, 24 m/US gal, 9.8 l x 100 km.

CHASSIS integral; front suspension; independent, by McPherson, coil springs, wishbones (lower trailing links), telescopic dampers; rear: trailing arm twist axle with track bar, telescopic dampers.

STEERING rack-and-pinion; turns lock to lock: 3.50.

BRAKES front disc (diameter 9.74 in, 24.7 cm), rear drum; front internal radial fins; swept area: total 272.7 sq in, 1,759 sq cm.

ELECTRICAL EQUIPMENT 12 V; 3,200 W battery: 25 A alternator; Delco transistorized ignition; 2 headlamps.

DIMENSIONS AND WEIGHT wheel base: 104.90 in, 266 cm; tracks: 58.70 in, 149 cm front, 57 in, 145 cm rear; length: 181.90 in, 462 cm; width: 67.70 in, 172 cm; height: 53.50 in 136 cm; ground clearance: 6.10 in, 15.6 cm; weight: Sedan l 2.502, 1.135 kg - Coupé lb 2,475, 1,123 kg - Limited Sedan l 2,535, 1,150 kg - Limited Coupé lb 2,506, 1,137 kg - Spo Sedan lb 2,537, 1.151 kg - Sport Coupé lb 2,511, 1,139 kg turning circle: 38.3 pt, 11.7 m; fuel tank: 11.7 imp gal, 14 U gal, 53 l.

BODY saloon/sedan, coupé; 4 seats, separate front seats.

OPTIONALS automatic transmission, 2.530 axle ratio, con sumption 26.4 m/imp gal, 22 m/US gal, 10.7 l x 100 km; powe steering; servo brake; heavy-duty battery; reclining backrests air-conditioning; heated rear window; electric windows.

115 hp power team

See 90 hp power team, except for:

ENGINE 6 cylinders, Vee-slanted at 90°; 173 cu in, 2,835 cc compression ratio: 8.5:1; max power (SAE net): 115 hp (84 kW at 4,800 rpm; max torque (SAE net): 145 lb ft, 20 kg/m (19 Nm) at 2,400 rpm; max engine rpm: 5,200; 41.1 hp/l (30. kW/l).

PERFORMANCE max speed: 110 mph, 177 km/h; power-weigh ratio: 4-dr Sedan 21.8 lb/hp (29.8 lb/kW), 9.9 kg/hp (13. kg/kW); consumption; 24.1 m/imp gal, 20 m/US gal, 11.7 l x 10 km.

OPTIONALS automatic transmission, 2.840 axle ratio.

BUICK Skylark Sedan

BUICK Skylark Sport Sedan

BUICK Skylark Sport Coupé

Century Series

RICES EX WORKS:	$
Notch 4-dr Sedan	5,646
Aero 2-dr Coupé	5,546
Limited Notch 4-dr Sedan	6,132
4+1-dr St. Wagon	5,922
4+1-dr Estate Wagon	6,220
Sport Turbo 2-dr Coupé	6,063

or 120 hp engine add $ 204 (for st. wagons only add $ 180); r 140 and 155 hp engines add $ 319 (for Sport Coupé and st. agons add $ 295).

ower team:	Standard for:	Optional for:
10 hp	1 to 5	—
20 hp	—	1 to 5
40 hp	—	1 to 5
55 hp	—	1 to 5
70 hp	6	—

110 hp power team

NGINE front, 4 stroke; 6 cylinders, Vee-slanted at 90°; 231 cu , 3,875 cc (3.80 x 3.40 in, 96.4 x 86.3 mm); compression ratio: 1; max power (SAE net): 110 hp (81 kW) at 3,800 rpm; max rque (SAE net): 190 lb ft, 26.2 kg m (257 Nm) at 2,000 rpm; ax engine rpm: 4,200; 29.1 hp/l (21.4 kW/l); cast iron block nd head; 4 crankshaft bearings; valves: overhead, in line, ush-rods and rockers, hydraulic tappets; camshafts: 1, at

BUICK Century Limited Notch Sedan

BUICK Century Aero Coupé

entre of Vee; lubrication: gear pump, full flow filter, 6.7 imp pt, US pt, 3.8 l; 1 Rochester 2 ME downdraught twin-barrel arburettor; thermostatic air cleaner; fuel feed: mechanical ump; water-cooled, 21.6 imp pt, 26 US pt, 12.3 l.

RANSMISSION driving wheels: rear; clutch: single dry plate; earbox: mechanical; gears: 3, fully synchronized; ratios: I .500, II 1.810, III 1 rev 3,620; lever: central; final drive: hypoid evel; axle ratio: 3.080 (except California) - st. wagons 2.730; idth of rims: 6"; tyres: P185/75 x 14 - st. wagons P 195/ 5 x 14.

ERFORMANCE max speed: 98 mph, 157 km/h - st. wagons 13 mph, 182 km/h; power-weight ratio: Notch Sedan 29.1 /hp, (39.5 lb/kW), 13.2 kg/hp (17.9 kg/kW); consumption: 26.4 /imp gal, 22 m/US gal, 10.7 l x 100 km.

HASSIS perimeter box-type frame; front suspension: independent, wishbones, coil springs, telescopic dampers; rear: rigid xle, coil springs, torque arms, transverse linkage bar, telescoc dampers.

TEERING recirculating ball; turns lock to lock: 6.14.

RAKES front disc (diameter 10.50 in, 22.7 cm), rear drum ont internal radial fins, servo; total 312.7 sq in, 2,017 sq cm.

LECTRICAL EQUIPMENT 12 V; 275 A battery; 25 A alternator; Delco transistorized ignition; 2 headlamps.

IMENSIONS AND WEIGHT wheel base: 108.10 in, 274 cm; acks: 58.50 in, 149 cm front, 57.80 in, 146 cm rear; length: 95.90 in, 498 cm; width: 71.10 in, 181 cm; height: 54.60 in, 39 cm; ground clearance: 6.10 in, 15.4 cm; weight: Notch Sedan 3,201 lb, 1,452 kg - Aero Coupé 3,181 lb, 1,443 kg - Limited Notch Sedan 3,245 lb, 1,472 kg - St. Wagon 3,331 lb, 1,511 kg - Estate Wagon 3,342 lb, 1,516 kg - Sport Coupé 3,243 lb, 1,471 kg; turning circle: 41.5 ft, 12.6 m; fuel tank: 15 imp gal, 18.1 US gal, 68 l - st. wagons 15.2 imp gal, 18.2 US gal, 69 l.

BODY saloon/sedan, coupé, estate car/st. wagon; 6 seats, separate front seats.

OPTIONALS 2.410 axle ratio; automatic transmission; power steering; tilt of steering wheel; heavy-duty cooling; heavy-duty battery; heated rear window; reclining backrests; electric windows; air-conditioning; automatic air-conditioning; electric sunshine roof; P195/75x14 or P205/75 x 14 tyres.

120 hp power team

(not available in California)

See 110 hp power team, except for:

ENGINE 8 cylinders; 265 cu in, 4,343 cc; max power (SAE net): 120 hp (88 kW) at 3,600 rpm; max torque (SAE net): 210 lb ft, 29 kg m (294 Nm) at 2,000 rpm; max engine rpm: 4,000; 27.9 hp/l (20.5 kW/l).

TRANSMISSION gearbox: Turbo-Hydramatic THM 350 automatic transmission, hydraulic torque converter and planetary gears with 3 ratios, max ratio of converter at stall 2, possible manual selection; ratios: I 2.520, II 1.520, III 1, rev 1.930; lever: steering column; axle ratio: 2.410.

PERFORMANCE max speed: 119 mph, 191 km/h - st. wagons 122 mph, 196 km/h; power-weight ratio: Notch Sedan 26.7 lb/hp (36.4 lb/kW), 12.1 kg/hp (16.5 kg/kW); consumption: 21.6 m/imp gal, 18 m/US gal, 13.1 l x 100 km.

140 hp power team

(not available in California)

See 110 hp power team, except for:

ENGINE 8 cylinders; 301 cu in, 4,933 cc; compression ratio: 8.2:1; max power (SAE net): 140 hp (103 kW) at 4,000 rpm, max torque (SAE net): 240 lb ft, 33.1 kg m (336 Nm) at 2,200 rpm; max engine rpm: 4,400; 28.6 hp/l (21 kW/).

TRANSMISSION gearbox: Turbo Hydramatic THM 350 automatic transmission, hydraulic torque converter and planetary gears with 3 ratios, max ratio of converter at stall 2, possible manual selection; ratios: I 2.520, II 1.520, III 1, rev 1.930; lever: steering column; axle ratio: 2.140 or 2.410 - st. wagons 2.290 or 2.560.

PERFORMANCE max speed: 148 mph, 238 km/h - st. wagons 141 mph, 227 km/h; power-weight ratio: Notch Sedan 22.9 lb/hp (31.1 lb/kW), 10.4 kg/hp (14.1 kg/kW); consumption: 20.5 m/imp gal, 17 /US gal, 13.8 l x 100 km.

155 hp power team

(for California only)

See 110 hp power team, except for:

ENGINE 8 cylinders; 305 cu in, 4,999 cc; compression ratio: 8.6:1; max power (SAE net): 155 hp (114 kW) at 4,000 rpm; max torque (SAE net): 240 lb ft, 33.1 kg m (336 Nm) at 2,000 rpm; max engine rpm: 4,400; 27.2 hp/l (20 kW/l).

TRANSMISSION gearbox: Turbo-Hydramatic THM 350 automatic transmission, hydraulic torque converter and planetary gears with 3 ratios, max ratio of converter at stall, possible manual selection; ratios: I 2.520, II 1.520, III 1, rev 1.930; lever: steering column; axle ratio: 2.290 or 2.730 - st. wagons 2.410.

PERFORMANCE max speed: 138 mph, 222 km/h - st. wagons 134 mph, 215 km/h; power-weight ratio: Notch Sedan 20.7 lb/hp (28 lb/kW), 9.4 kg/hp (12.7 kg/kW); consumption: 18 m/imp gal, 15 m/US gal, 15.7 l x 100 km.

170 hp power team

See 110 hp power team, except for:

ENGINE turbocharged; max power (SAE net): 170 hp (125 kW) at 4,000 rpm; max torque (SAE net): 265 lb ft, 36.5 kg m (371 Nm) at 2,800 rpm; max engine rpm: 4,400; 44.7 hp/l (32.9 kW/l).

TRANSMISSION gearbox: Turbo-Hydramatic THM 350 automatic transmission, hydraulic torque converter and planetary gears with 3 ratios, max ratio of converter at stall 2, possible manual selection; ratios: I 2.520, II 1.520, III 1, rev 1.930; lever: steering column; axle ratio: 2.730 or 3.080.

BUICK Regal Sport Coupé

170 HP POWER TEAM

PERFORMANCE max speed: 116 mph, 186 km/h; power-weight ratio: 19.2 lb/hp (26 lb kW), 8.7 kg/hp (11.8 kg/kW); consumption: 21.6 m/imp gal, 18 m/US gal 13.1 l x 100 km.

DIMENSIONS AND WEIGHT weight: 3,243 lb, 1,471 kg.

Regal Series

PRICES EX WORKS:

		$
1	Coupé	**6,305**
2	Limited Coupé	**6,724**
3	Sport Coupé	**6,952**

For 120 hp engine add $ 180; for 140 and 155 hp engines add $ 295.

Power team:	Standard for:	Optional for:
110 hp	1,2	—
120 hp	—	1,2
140 hp	—	1,2
155 hp	—	1,2
170 hp	3	—

110 hp power team

ENGINE front, 4 stroke; 6 cylinders, Vee-slanted at 90°; 231 cu in, 3,785 cc (3.80 x 3.40 in, 96.4 x 86.3 mm); compression ratio: 8:1; max power (SAE net): 110 hp (81 kW) at 3,800 rpm; max torque (SAE net): 190 lb ft, 26.2 kg m (257 Nm) at 2,000 rpm; max engine rpm: 4,200; 29.1 hp/l (21.4 kW/l); cast iron block and head; 4 crankshaft bearings; valves: overhead, in line, push-rods and rockers, hydraulic tappets; camshafts: 1, at centre of Vee; lubrication: gear pump, full flow filter, 6.7 imp pt, 8 US pt, 3.8 l; 1 Rochester 2 ME downdraught twin-barrel carburettor; thermostatic air cleaner; fuel feed: mechanical pump; water-cooled, 21.6 imp pt, 26 US pt, 12.3 l.

TRANSMISSION driving wheels: rear; clutch: single dry plate; gearbox: Turbo-Hydramatic THM 350 automatic transmission, hydraulic torque converter and planetary gears with 3 ratios, max ratio of converter at stall 2, possible manual selection; ratios: I 2.520, II 1.520, III 1, rev 1.930; lever: steering column; final drive: hypoid bevel; axle ratio: 3.080; width of rims: 6"; tyres: P 185/75 x 14.

PERFORMANCE max speed: 98 mph, 157 km/h; power-weight ratio: Coupé 29.5 lb/hp, (40 lb/kW), 13.4 kg/hp (18.1 kg/kW); consumption: 24.1 m/imp gal, 20 m/US gal, 11.7 l x 100 km.

CHASSIS perimeter box-type frame; front suspension: independent, wishbones, coil springs, telescopic dampers; rear: rigid axle, coil springs, torque arms, transverse linkage bar, telescopic dampers.

STEERING recirculating ball, variable ratio servo; turns lock to lock: 3.64.

BRAKES front disc (diameter 10.50 in, 22.7 cm), rear drum, front internal radial fins, servo; swept area: total 312.7 sq in, 2,017 sq cm.

ELECTRICAL EQUIPMENT 12 V; 275 Ah battery; 25 A alternator; Delco transistorized ignition; 4 headlamps.

DIMENSIONS AND WEIGHT wheel base: 108.10 in, 274 cm; tracks: 58.50 in, 149 cm front, 57.80 in, 146 cm rear; length: 200.30 in, 509 cm; width: 71.10 in, 181 cm; height: 54.60 in, 139 cm; ground clearance: 6.10 in, 15.4 cm; weight: Coupé 3,232 lb, 1,469 kg - Limited Coupé 3,269 lb, 1,486 kg; turning circle: 41.5 ft, 12.6 m; fuel tank: 15 imp gal, 18.1 US gal, 68 l.

BODY 2 doors; 6 seats, separate front seats.

OPTIONALS 2.410 axle ratio; tilt of steering wheel; heavy-duty cooling; heavy-duty battery; heated rear window; reclining backrests; electric windows; air-conditioning; automatic air-conditioning; electric sunshine roof; P 195/75 x 14 or P 205/75 x 14 tyres.

120 hp power team

(not available in California)

See 110 hp power team, except for:

ENGINE 8 cylinders; 265 cu in, 4,343 cc; max power (SAE net): 120 hp (88 kW) at 3,600 rpm; max torque (SAE net): 210 lb ft 29 kg m (294 Nm) at 2,000 rpm; max engine rpm: 4,000; 27.9 hp/l (20.5 kW/l).

TRANSMISSION axle ratio: 2.410.

PERFORMANCE max speed: 119 mph, 191 km/h; power-weight ratio: Coupé 26.5 lb/hp (36.1 lb/kW), 12 kg/hp (16.4 kg/kW); consumption: 21.6 m/imp gal, 18 m/US gal, 13.1 l x 100 km.

140 hp power team

(not available in California)

See 110 hp power team, except for:

ENGINE 8 cylinders; 301 cu in, 4,933 cc; compression ratio 8.2:1; max power (SAE net): 140 hp (103 kW) at 4,000 rpm; max torque (SAE net): 240 lb ft, 33.1 kg m (336 Nm) at 2,200 rpm; max engine rpm: 4,400; 28.6 hp/l (21 kW/l).

TRANSMISSION axle ratio: 2.140 or 2.410.

PERFORMANCE max speed: 148 mph, 238 km/h; power-weigh ratio: Coupé 22.7 lb/hp (30.9 lb/kW), 10.3 kg/hp (14 kg/kW) consumption: 20.5 m/imp gal, 17 m/US gal, 13.8 l x 100 km.

155 hp power team

(for California only)

See 110 hp power team, except for:

ENGINE 8 cylinders; 305 cu in, 4,999 cc; compression ratio 8.6:1; max power (SAE net): 155 hp (114 kW) at 4,000 rpm max torque (SAE net): 240 lb ft, 33.1 kg/m (336 Nm) at 2,000 rpm; max engine rpm: 4,400; 27.2 hp/l (20 kW/l).

TRANSMISSION axle ratio: 2.290 or 2.730.

PERFORMANCE max speed: 138 mph, 222 km/h; power-weigh ratio: Coupé 20.9 lb/hp (28.4 lb/kW), 9.5 kg/hp (12.9 kg/kW) consumption: 18 m/imp gal, 15 m/US gal, 15.7 l x 100 km.

170 hp power team

See 110 hp power team, except for:

ENGINE turbocharged; max power (SAE net): 170 hp (125 kW at 4,000 rpm; max torque (SAE net): 265 lb ft, 36.5 kg m (37 Nm) at 2,800 rpm; max engine rpm: 4,400; 44.7 hp/l (32. kW/l).

TRANSMISSION axle ratio: 2.730 or 3.080.

PERFORMANCE max speed: 116 mph, 186 km/h; power-weigh ratio: 20.3 lb/hp (27.8 lb kW), 9.2 kg/hp (12.5 kg/kW); consump tion 21.6 m/imp gal, 18 m/US gal 13.1 l x 100 km.

DIMENSIONS AND WEIGHT weight: 3,453 lb, 1,566 kg.

Le Sabre Series

PRICES EX WORKS:

		$
1	Thin Pillar 4-dr Sedan	**6,76**
2	2-dr Hardtop Coupé	**6,674**
3	Limited Thin Pillar 4-dr Sedan	**7,07**
4	Limited 2-dr Hardtop Coupé	**6,92**
5	Sport 2-dr Coupé	**7,78**
6	4+1-dr Estate Wagon	**7,67**

Coupés and sedans for 125 hp engine add $ 9, for 140 h engine add $ 295, for 160 hp engine add $ 425. Estate Wago for 160 hp engine add $ 130, for 105 hp engine add $ 860

BUICK Le Sabre Thin Pillar Sedan

BUICK Le Sabre Limited Hardtop Coupé

wer team:	Standard for:	Optional for:
0 hp	1 to 4	—
5 hp	—	1 to 4
0 hp	6	1 to 4
5 hp	—	1 to 4,6
0 hp	—	1 to 4,6
0 hp	5	—
5 hp (diesel)	6	—

110 hp power team

NGINE front, 4 stroke; 6 cylinders, Vee-slanted at 90°; 231 cu , 3,785 cc (3.80 x 3.40 in, 96.5 x 86.4 mm); compression ratio: 1; max power (SAE net): 110 hp (81 kW) at 3,800 rpm; max rque (SAE net): 190 lb ft, 26.2 kg m (257 Nm) at 2,000 rpm; ax engine rpm: 4,200; 28.9 hp/l (21.3 kW/l); cast iron block d head; 4 crankshaft bearings; valves: overhead, in line, sh-rods and rockers, hydraulic tappets; camshafts: 1, at ntre of Vee; lubrication: gear pump, full flow filter, 6.7 imp l, 8 US pt, 3.8 l; 1 Rochester 2 ME downdraught twin-barrel rburettor; thermostatic air cleaner; catalytic converter; fuel ed: mechanical pump; water-cooled, 20.8 imp pt, 24.9 US pt, .8 l.

RANSMISSION driving wheels: rear; clutch: automatic; gear-x: Turbo-Hydramatic THM 350 automatic transmission, hyd-ulic torque converter and planetary gears with 3 ratios, max tio of converter at stall 2.5, possible manual selection; ratios: 2.520, II 1.520, III 1, rev 1.930; lever: steering column; final ive: hypoid bevel; axle ratio: 2.730 or 3.230; width of rims: 6"; res: P 205/75 x 15.

PERFORMANCE max speed: 120 mph, 193 km/h; power-weight ratio: Thin Pillar Sedan 31.7 lb/hp (43 lb/kW), 14.4 kg/hp (19.5 kg/kW); consumption: 21.6 m/imp gal, 18 m/US gal, 13.1 l x 100 km.

CHASSIS perimeter box-type frame; front suspension: independent, wishbones, coil springs, anti roll bar, telescopic dampers; rear: rigid axle, coil springs, control arms, transverse linkage bar, telescopic dampers.

STEERING recirculating ball, variable ratio servo; turns lock to lock: 3.370.

BRAKES front disc (diameter 11 in, 279 cm), internal radial fins, rear drum, servo; swept area: total 344 sq in, 2,219 sq cm.

ELECTRICAL EQUIPMENT 12 V; 275 Ah battery; 42 A alternator; Delco transistorized ignition; 4 headlamps.

DIMENSIONS AND WEIGHT wheel base: 116 in, 294 cm; tracks: 61.80 in, 157 cm front, 60.70 in, 154 cm rear; length: 217.40 in, 552 cm; width: 78 in, 198 cm; height: 55 in, 140 cm; weight: Thin Pillar Sedan 3,485 lb, 1,581 kg - Hardtop Coupé 3,459 lb, 1,569 kg - Limited Thin Pillar Sedan 3,514 lb - 1,594 kg - Limited Coupé 3,466 lb, 1,572 kg; turning circle: 43.3 ft, 13.2 m; fuel tank: 20.9 imp gal, 25 US gal, 95 l.

BODY saloon/sedan, coupé; 6 seats, separate front seats.

OPTIONALS heavy-duty battery; heavy-duty cooling; automatic levelling control; P 215/75 x 15 tyres; 6" or 7" wide rims; speed control; electric windows; reclining backrests; air-conditioning; automatic air-conditioning.

BUICK Le Sabre Estate Wagon

125 hp power team

(not available in California)

See 110 hp power team, except for:

ENGINE 250 cu in, 4,097 cc; max power (SAE net): 125 hp (92 kW) at 4,000 rpm; max torque (SAE net): 205 lb ft, 28.3 kg/m (287 Nm) at 2,000 rpm; max engine rpm: 4,400; 30.5 hp/l (22.4 kW/l); 1 Rochester M4MC downdraught 4-barrel carburettor.

TRANSMISSION axle ratio: 2.930.

PERFORMANCE max speed: 117 mph, 188 km/h; power-weight ratio: Thin Pillar Sedan 27.8 lb/hp (37.9 lb/kW), 12.6 kg/hp (17.2 kg/kW); consumption: 20.5 m/imp gal, 17 m/US gal, 13.8 l x 100 km.

140 hp power team

(not available in California)

See 110 hp power team, except for:

ENGINE 8 cylinders; 301 cu in, 4,933 cc; compression ratio 8.2:1; max power (SAE net): 140 hp (103 kW) at 4,000 rpm; max torque (SAE net): 240 lb/ft, 33.1 kg m (336 Nm) at 1,800 rpm; max engine rpm; 4,400; 28.6 hp/l (21 kW/l); 1 Rochester M4ME downdraught 4-barrel carburettor; water-cooled, 34.8 imp pt, 41.9 US pt, 19.8 l.

TRANSMISSION axle ratio: 2.560 - coupés and sedans 2.410; width of rims: 7"; tyres: P 225/75 15.

PERFORMANCE max speed: 140 mph, 225 km/h - coupés and sedans 149 mph, 239 km/h; power-weight ratio: Estate Wagon 28.7 lb/hp (39 lb/kW), 13 kg/hp (17.7 kg kW); consumption: 19 m/imp gal, 16 m/US gal, 14.9 l x 100 km.

ELECTRICAL EQUIPMENT 350 Ah battery.

DIMENSIONS AND WEIGHT weight: Estate Wagon 4,017 lb, 1,822 kg.

155 hp power team

(not available in California)

See 110 hp power team, except for:

ENGINE 8 cylinders; 350 cu in, 5,736 cc; max power (SAE net): 155 hp (114 kW) at 3,400 rpm; max torque (SAE net): 280 lb ft, 38.6 kg m (392 Nm) at 1,600 rpm; max engine rpm: 3,800; 27.2 hp/l (20 kW/l).

TRANSMISSION axle ratio: 2.410 or 3.230 - Estate Wagon 2.730 or 3.080.

PERFORMANCE max speed: 123 mph, 198 km/h - Estate Wagon 113 mph, 182 km/h; power-weight ratio: Thin Pillar Sedan 22.5 lb/hp (30.6 lb/kW), 10.2 kg/hp (13.9 kg/kW).

BRAKES front disc (diameter 11.90 in, 301 cm), internal radial fins, rear drum; swept area: total 396.6 sq m, 2,559 sq cm.

DIMENSIONS AND WEIGHT fuel tank: 18 imp gal, 22 US gal, 82 l.

160 hp power team

(for California only)

See 110 hp power team, except for:

ENGINE 8 cylinders; 350 cu in, 5,736 cc; max power (SAE net):160 hp (118 kW) at 3,600 rpm; max torque (SAE net): 270 lb/ft, 37.2 kg m (378 Nm) at 1,600 rpm; max engine rpm: 4,000; 28.1 hp/l (20.7 kW/l); 1 Rochester M4MC downdraught 4-barrel carburettor.

TRANSMISSION axle ratio: 2.410 - Estate Wagon 2.560 or 2.730.

PERFORMANCE max speed: 130 mph, 209 km/h - Estate Wagon 127 mph, 204 km/h; power-weight ratio: Thin Pillar Sedan 21.8 lb/hp (29.5 lb/kW), 9.9 kg/hp (13.4 kg/kW); consumption: 18 m/imp gal, 15 m/US gal, 15.7 l x 100 km.

BRAKES front disc (diameter 11.90 in, 30.1 cm) internal radial fins, rear drum; swept area: total 396.6 sq in, 2,559 sq cm.

DIMENSIONS AND WEIGHT fuel tank: 18 imp gal, 22 US gal, 82 l.

170 hp power team

See 110 hp power team, except for:

ENGINE turbocharged; max power (SAE net): 170 hp (125 kW) at 4,000 rpm; max torque (SAE net): 265 lb ft, 36.6 kg m (359 Nm) at 2,400 rpm; max engine rpm: 4,400; 44.9 hp/l (33.1 kW/l).

170 HP POWER TEAM

TRANSMISSION axle ratio: 2.730 or 3.080.

PERFORMANCE max speed: 126 mph, 202 kmh; power-weight ratio: 20.9 lb/hp (28.7 lb/kW), 9.5 kg/hp (13 kg/kW); consumption: 20.5 m/imp gal, 17 m/US gal, 13.8 l x 100 km.

DIMENSIONS AND WEIGHT weight: 3,569 lb, 1,619 kg.

105 hp (diesel) power team

See 110 hp power team, except for:

ENGINE diesel; 8 cylinders; compression ratio: 22.5:1; max power (SAE net): 105 hp (77 kW) at 3,200 rpm; max torque (SAE net): 205 lb ft, 28.3 kg m (287 Nm) at 1,600 rpm; max engine rpm: 3,600; 18.4 hp/l (13.5 kW/l); 1 Rochester M4MC downdraught 4-barrel carburettor.

TRANSMISSION axle ratio: 2.730.

PERFORMANCE max speed: 107 mph, 172 km/h; power-weight ratio: 38.4 lb/hp (52.2 lb/kW), 17.4 kg/hp (23.7 kg/kW).

DIMENSIONS AND WEIGHT weight: 4,017 lb, 1,822 kg.

Electra Series

PRICES EX WORKS:	**$**
1 Limited 4-dr Sedan	9,287
2 Limited 2-dr Coupé	9,132
3 Park Avenue 4-dr Sedan	10,383
4 Park Avenue 2-dr Coupé	10,244
5 4+1-dr Estate Wagon	10,513

For 155 and 160 hp engines add $ 335 ($ 130 for Estate Wagon only); for 105 hp diesel engine add $ 930 ($ 860 for Estate Wagon).

Power team:	**Standard for:**	**Optional for:**
125 hp	1 to 4	—
140 hp	5	—
155 hp	—	all
160 hp	—	all
105 hp (diesel)	—	all

125 hp power team

(not available in California)

ENGINE front, 4 stroke; 6 cylinders, Vee-slanted at 90°; 252 cu in, 4,130 cc (4 x 3.40 in, 100.7 x 86.4 mm); compression ratio: 8:1; max power (SAE net): 125 hp (92 kW) at 4,000 rpm; max torque (SAE net): 205 lb ft, 28.3 kg m (287 Nm) at 2,000 rpm; max engine rpm: 4,400; 30.5 hp/l (22.4 kW/l); cast iron block and head; 4 crankshaft bearings; valves: overhead, in line, push-rods and rockers, hydraulic tappets; camshafts: 1, at centre of Vee; lubrication: gear pump, full flow filter, 6.7 imp pt, 8 US pt, 3.8 l; 1 Rochester M4ME downdraught 4-barrel carburettor; thermostatic air cleaner; fuel feed: mechanical pump; water-cooled, 20.8 imp pt, 24.9 US pt, 11.8 l.

BUICK Le Sabre Series (3.8-litre engine)

TRANSMISSION driving wheels: rear; gearbox: Turbo Hydramatic 400 automatic transmission, hydraulic torque cor verter and planetary gear: with, 3 ratios, max ratio of converte at stall 2, possible manual selection; ratios: I 2.480, II 1.480, I 1, rev 2.080; lever: steering column; final drive: hypoid beve axle ratio: 2.930; width of rims: 6"; tyres: P 215/75 x 15.

PERFORMANCE max speed: 120 mph, 193 km/h; power-weigh ratio: Limited Sedan 29.7 lb/hp, (40.3 lb/kW), 13.5 kg/hp (18. kg/kW); consumption: 20.5 m/imp gal, 17 m/US gal, 13.8 l x 10 km.

CHASSIS perimeter box-type frame; front suspension: indeper dent, wishbones, coil springs, anti-roll bar, telescopic dampers rear: independent, coil springs, control arms, transverse linkag bar, telescopic dampers.

STEERING recirculating ball, variable ratio servo; turns lock t lock: 3.37.

BRAKES front disc (diameter 11.86 in, 301 cm), front interna radial fins, rear drum, rear compensator, servo; swept area total 384.2 sq in, 2,479 sq cm.

ELECTRICAL EQUIPMENT 12 V; 275 Ah battery; 42 A alterna tor; Delco transistorized ignition; 4 headlamps.

DIMENSIONS AND WEIGHT wheel base: 118.90 in, 302 cm tracks: 61.80 in, 157 cm front, 61 in, 154 cm rear; length 220.30 in, 560 cm; width: 78 in, 198 cm; height; sedans 55.6 in, 138 cm - coupés 54.20 in, 141 cm; weight: Limited Coup 3,710 lb, 1,683 kg - Limited Sedan 3,717 lb, 1,686 kg - Par

BUICK Electra Park Avenue Sedan

BUICK Electra Limited Coupé

Avenue Coupé 3,736 lb, 1,695 kg - Park Avenue Sedan 3,74 lb, 1,698 kg; turning circle: 43.3-44.9 ft, 13.2-13.7 m; fuel tan 20.9 imp gal, 25 US gal, 95 l.

BODY saloon/sedan, coupé; 6 seats, separate front seats.

OPTIONALS reclining backrests; heated rear window; electr windows; speed control; P 225/75 x 15 tyres; heavy-duty ba tery; antitheft; automatic air-conditioning; tilt and telescop steering column.

140 hp power team

(not available in California)

See 125 hp power team, except for:

ENGINE 8 cylinders; 301 cu in, 4,933 cc; compression rati 8.2:1; max power (SAE net): 140 hp (103 kW) at 4,000 rpm max torque (SAE net): 240 lb ft, 33.1 kg m (336 Nm) at 1,8C rpm; max engine rpm: 4,400; 28.6 hp/l (21 kW/l); cooling, 37 imp gal, 44.4 US pt, 20.9 l.

TRANSMISSION axle ratio: 2.560.

PERFORMANCE max speed: 137 mph, 220 km/h; power-weig ratio: 30.2 lb/hp (40.9 lb/kW), 13.7 kg/hp (18.6 kg/kW).

BRAKES swept area: total 39.6 sq in, 2,559 sq cm.

DIMENSIONS AND WEIGHT wheel base: 116 in, 294 c tracks: 62.20 in, 158 cm front, 64.10 in, 163 cm rear; lengt 218.80 in, 556 cm; width: 80.10 in, 204 cm; height: 57.10

45 cm; weight: 4,215 lb, 1,912 kg; turning circle: 43.4-45.1 ft, 3.2-13.7 l; fuet tank: 18.3 imp gal, 22 US gal, 83 l.

ODY estate car/st. wagon.

155 hp power team

not available in California)

ee 125 hp power team, except for:

NGINE 8 cylinders; 350 cu in, 5,736 cc (4.05 x 3.40 in, 03 x 86 mm); max power (SAE net): 155 hp (114 kW) at 3,400 om; max torque (SAE net): 280 lb ft, 38.6 kg m (392 Nm) at ,600 rpm; max engine rpm: 3,800; 27.2 hp/l (20 kW/l); 5 rankshaft bearings; lubrication: 10.8 imp pt, 12.7 US pt, 6 l; 1 ochester M4MC downdraught 4-barrel carburettor.

RANSMISSION axle ratio: 2.410 or 3.230 - Estate Wagon .730 or 3.080.

ERFORMANCE max speed: 126 mph, 202 km/h - Estate Vagon 111 mph, 178 km/h; power-weight ratio: Limited Sedan 4 lb/hp (32.6 lb/kW), 10.9 kg/hp (14.8 kg/kW); consumption: 8 m/imp gal, 15 m/US gal, 15.7 l x 100 km.

160 hp power team

or California only)

ee 125 hp power team, except for:

NGINE 8 cylinders; 350 cu in, 5,736 cc (4.05 x 3.40 in, 03 x 86 mm); max power (SAE net): 160 hp (118 kW) at 3,600 om; max torque (SAE net): 270 lb/ft, 37.2 kg m (378 Nm) at ,600 rpm; max engine rpm: 4,000; 28.1 hp/l (20.7 kW/l); 5 rankshaft bearings; lubrication: 10.8 imp pt, 12.7 US pt, 6 l; 1 ochester M4MC downdraught 4-barrel carburettor.

RANSMISSION axle ratio: 2.410 - Estate Wagon 2.560 or .730.

ERFORMANCE max speed: 132 mph, 212 km/h - Estate Vagon 125 mph, 201 km/h; power-weight ratio: 23.1 lb/hp (31.4 /kW), 10.5 kg/hp (14.3 kg/kW); consumption: 18 m/imp gal, 15 /US gal, 15.7 l x 100 km.

105 hp (diesel) power team

ee 125 hp power team, except for:

NGINE diesel; 8 cylinders; compression ratio: 22.5:1; max ower (SAE net): 105 hp (77 kW) at 3,200 rpm; max torque SAE net): 205 lb ft, 28.3 kg m (287 Nm) at 1,600 rpm; max ngine rpm: 3,600; 18.4 hp/l (13.5 kW/l); 5 crankshaft bearings; ubrication: 10.8 imp pt, 12.7 US pt, 6 l; 1 Rochester M4MC owndraught 4-barrel carburettor.

RANSMISSION axle ratio: 2.410 - Estate wagon 2.730.

ERFORMANCE max speed: 119 mph, 191 km/h - Estate Vagon 105 mph, 169 km/h; power-weight ratio: 35.5 lb/hp (48.3 /kW), 16.1 kg/hp (21.9 kg/kW).

Riviera Series

RICES EX WORKS: $

Coupé	**11,492**
Sport Coupé	**11,823**

ower team:	Standard for:	Optional for:
60 hp	1	—
70 hp	2	—

160 hp power team

NGINE front, 4 stroke; 8 cylinders; 350 cu in, 5,736 cc 4.05 x 3.40 in, 103 x 86 mm); compression ratio: 8:1; max ower (SAE net: 160 hp (118 kW) at 3,600 rpm; max torque SAE net): 270 lb ft, 37.9 kg m (378 Nm) at 1,600 rpm; max ngine rpm: 4,000; 28.1 hp/l (20.7 kW/l); cast iron block and ead; 5 crankshaft bearings; valves: overhead, in line, push-ods and rockers, hydraulic tappets; camshafts: 1, at centre of ee; lubrication: gear pump, full flow filter, 10.8 imp pt, 12.7 US t, 6 l; 1 Rochester M4MC downdraught 4-barrel carburettor; hermostatic air cleaner; fuel feed: mechanical pump; water-ooled, 29.9 imp pt, 35.9 US pt, 17 l.

RANSMISSION driving wheels: front; gearbox: Turbo-Hydramatic 325 automatic transmission, hydraulic torque con-erter and planetary gears with 3 ratios, max ratio of converter t stall 2, possible manual selection; ratios: I 2.740, II 1.570, III , rev 2.070; lever: steering column; final drive: hypoid bevel; xle ratio: 2.410; width of rims: 6"; tyres: P 205/75 x 15.

ERFORMANCE max speed: 130 mph, 209 km/h; power-weight atio: 24.1 lb/hp, (32.6 lb/kW), 10.9 kg/hp (14.8 kg/kW); con-umption: 18 m/imp gal, 15 m/US gal, 15.7 l x 100 km.

HASSIS perimeter box-type frame; front suspension: indepen-ent, wishbones, torsion bar, anti-roll bar, telescopic dampers;

BUICK Electra Estate Wagon

BUICK Riviera "S" Coupé

rear: independent, coil springs, control arms, transverse linkage bar, telescopic dampers, automatic levelling control.

STEERING recirculating ball, variable ratio servo; turns lock to lock: 2.99.

BRAKES front disc (diameter 10.50 in, 26.7 mm), front internal radial fins, rear drum, rear compensator, servo; swept area: total 307.7 sq in, 1,985 sq cm.

ELECTRICAL EQUIPMENT 12 V; 250 Ah battery; 42 a alterna-tor; Delco-Remy transistorized ignitipn; 4 headlamps.

DIMENSIONS AND WEIGHT wheel base: 114 in, 289 cm; tracks: 59.30 in, 151 cm front, 60 in, 152 cm rear; length: 206.60 in, 525 cm; width: 72.70 in, 185 cm; height: 54.10 in, 138 cm; weight: 3,849 lb, 1,746 kg; turning circle: 42.7-44.1 ft, 13-13.4 m; fuel tank: 17.6 imp gal, 21 US gal, 80 l.

BODY coupé; 2 doors; 4 seats, separate front seats.

OPTIONALS reclining backrests; heated rear window; speed control; CR70 x 15 tyres; heavy-duty battery; heavy-duty cool-ing; electric windows; antitheft; automatic air-conditioning; tilt of steering column; London top; "S" equipment.

170 hp power team

See 160 hp power team, except for:

ENGINE turbocharged; 6 cylinders, Vee-slanted at 90°; 231 cu in, 3,785 cc (3.80 x 3.40 in, 96.5 x 86.4 mm); max power (SAE net): 170 hp (125 kW) at 4,000 rpm; max torque (SAE net): 265 lb ft, 36.5 kg m (358 Nm) at 2,400 rpm; max engine rpm: 4,400; 44.7 hp/l (32.9 kW/l); 4 crankshaft bearings; cooling, 22.2 imp pt, 26.6 US pt, 12.6 l.

TRANSMISSION axle ratio: 2.930.

PERFORMANCE max speed: 117 mph, 188 km/h; power-weight ratio: 22.1 lb/hp (30 lb kW), 10 kg/hp (13.6 kg/kW); consump-tion: 19.2 m/imp gal, 16 m/US gal, 14.7 l x 100 km.

DIMENSIONS AND WEIGHT weight: 3,751 lb, 1,705 kg.

CADILLAC USA

Seville

PRICE IN GB: £ 15,859*
PRICE EX WORKS: $ 19,662

105 hp (diesel) power team

(standard)

ENGINE front, 4 stroke; 8 cylinders; 350 cu in, 5,736 cc (4.06 x 3.38 in, 103 x 86 mm); compression ratio: 21.5:1; max power (SAE net): 105 hp (78 kW) at 3,200 rpm; max torque (SAE net): 205 lb ft, 28.3 kg m (278 Nm) at 1,600 rpm; max

105 HP (DIESEL) POWER TEAM

engine rpm: 3,500; 18.3 hp/l (13.6 kW/l); cast iron block and head; 5 crankshaft bearings; valves: overhead, in line, push-rods and rockers, hydraulic tappets; camshafts: 1, at centre of Vee; lubrication: gear pump, full flow filter, 11.6 imp pt, 14 US pt, 6.6 l; air cleaner; exhaust system with catalytic converter; fuel feed: mechanical pump; water-cooled, 30.6 imp pt, 36.8 US pt, 17.4 l.

TRANSMISSION driving wheels: front; gearbox: Turbo-Hydramatic 325 automatic transmission, hydraulic torque converter and planetary gears with 3 ratios, max ratio of converter at stall 2, possible manual selection; ratios: I 2.740, II 1.570, III 1, rev 2.070; lever: steering column; final drive: hypoid bevel; axle ratio: 2.410; width of rims: 6"; tyres: 75 R x 15.

PERFORMANCE max speed: 93 mph, 155 km/h; power-weight ratio: 39.9 lb/hp, (53.7 lb/kW), 18 kg/hp (24.3 kg/kW); carrying capacity: 1,040 lb, 470 kg: speed in direct drive at 1,000 rpm: 28 mph, 45 km/h; consumption: 16.6 m/imp gal, 14 m/US gal, 16.8 l x 100 km.

CHASSIS ladder frame cross members; front suspension: independent, wishbones, torsion bar, anti-roll bar, telescopic dampers; rear: independent, swinging longitudinal trailing arms, coil springs, automatic levelling control, telescopic dampers.

STEERING recirculating ball, tilt and telescopic adjustable steering wheel, variable ratio servo; turns lock to lock: 3.

BRAKES disc (diameter 10.40 in, 26.5 cm), internal radial fins, rear compensator, servo; swept area: front 198 sq in, 1,277 sq cm, rear 198 sq in, 1,277 sq cm, total 396 sq in, 2,554 sq cm.

ELECTRICAL EQUIPMENT 12 V; 2 batteries; 100 A alternator; 4 iodine headlamps.

DIMENSIONS AND WEIGHT wheel base: 114 in, 289 cm; tracks: 59.30 in, 150 cm front, 60.60 in, 153 cm rear; length: 204.80 in, 520 cm; width: 71.40 in, 181 cm; height: 54.30 in, 138 cm; ground clearance: 14 in, 35.6 cm; weight: 4,195 lb, 1,898 kg; weight distribution: 60% front, 40% rear; turning circle: 42.1 ft, 12.8 m; fuel tank: 19 imp gal, 23 US gal, 87 l.

BODY saloon/sedan; 4 doors; 5 seats, separate front seats, built-in headrests; electric windows; electronic air-conditioning; heated rear and side windows.

OPTIONALS heavy-duty cooling; sunshine roof; convertible roof; trip computer; automatic door locks; electric reclining seats; opera lamps.

145 hp power team

(optional, not available in California)

See 105 hp (diesel) power team, except for:

ENGINE front, 4 stroke; 8 cylinders; 368 cu in, 6,030 cc (4.06 x 3.38 in, 103 x 85.8 mm); compression ratio: 8.2:1; max power (SAE net): 145 hp (108 kW) at 3,600 rpm; max torque (SAE net): 270 lb ft, 37.3 kg m (366 Nm) at 2,000 rpm; max engine rpm: 4,000; 24.2 hp/l (18 kW/l); lubrication: gear pump, full flow filter, 8.3 imp pt, 9.9 US pt, 4.7 l; digital electronic injection; fuel feed: electric pump; water-cooled, 37.4 imp pt, 44.8 US pt, 21.2 l.

TRANSMISSION driving wheels: axle ratio: 2.190.

PERFORMANCE max speed: 115 mph, 185 km/h; power-weight ratio: 27.9 lb/hp, (37.4 lb/kW), 12.6 kg/hp (16.9 kg/kW); carrying capacity: 1,040 lb, 470 kg; speed in direct drive at 1,000 rpm: 32 mph, 51 km/h.

ELECTRICAL EQUIPMENT 1 battery; 80 A alternator.

DIMENSIONS AND WEIGHT weight: 4,020 lb, 1,823 kg; weight distribution: 59% front, 41% rear; fuel tank: 17 imp gal, 20.6 US gal, 78 l.

OPTIONALS 2.410 axle ratio.

160 hp power team

(optional, for California only)

See 105 hp (diesel) power team, except for:

ENGINE compression ratio: 8:1; max power (SAE net): 160 hp (119 kW) at 4,400 rpm; max torque (SAE net): 265 lb ft, 36.6 kg m (359 Nm) at 1,600 rpm; max engine rpm: 4,800; 28 hp/l (20.8 kW/l); lubrication: 6.7 imp pt, 8 US pt, 3.8 l; electronic injection; fuel feed: 2 electric pumps; water-cooled, 25.3 imp pt, 30.4 US pt, 14.4 l.

TRANSMISSION axle ratio: 2.190.

PERFORMANCE max speed: 125 mph, 200 km/h; power-weight ratio: 25.2 lb/hp (33.9 lb/kW), 11.3 kg/hp (15.3 kg/kW); speed in direct drive at 1,000 rpm: 26 mph, 41.6 km/h.

DIMENSIONS AND WEIGHT weight: 4,036 lb, 1,816 kg: weight distribution: 59% front, 41% rear.

CADILLAC Seville

CADILLAC Fleetwood Eldorado

OPTIONALS 2.410 axle ratio.

Fleetwood Eldorado

PRICE IN GB: £ 15,739*
PRICE EX WORKS: $ 15,509

145 hp power team

(standard, not available in California)

ENGINE front, 4 stroke; 8 cylinders; 368 cu in, 6,030 cc (4.06 x 3.38 in, 103 x 85.8 mm); compression ratio: 8.2:1; max power (SAE net): 145 hp (108 kW) at 3,600 rpm; max torque (SAE net): 270 lb ft, 37.3 kg m (366 Nm) at 2,000 rpm; max engine rpm: 4,000; 24.2 hp/l (18 kW/l); cast iron block and head; 5 crankshaft bearings; valves: overhead, in line, push-rods and rockers, hydraulic tappets; camshafts: 1, at centre of Vee; lubrication: gear pump, full flow filter, 8.3 imp pt, 9.9 US pt, 4.7 l; digital electronic injection; air cleaner; exhaust system with catalytic converter; fuel feed: electric pump; water-cooled, 37.4 imp pt, 44.8 US pt, 21.2 l.

TRANSMISSION driving wheels: front; gearbox: Turbo-Hydramatic 325 automatic transmission, hydraulic torque converter and planetary gears with 3 ratios, max ratio of converter at stall 2, possible manual selection; ratios: I 2.740, II 1.570, III 1, rev 2.070; lever: steering column; final drive: hypoid bevel; axle ratio: 2.190; width of rims: 6"; tyres: 75 R x 15.

PERFORMANCE max speed: 115 mph, 185 km/h; power-weight ratio: 27.2 lb/hp, (36.5 lb/kW), 12.2 kg/hp (16.4 kg/kW); carrying capacity: 1,045 lb, 470 kg; speed in direct drive at 1,00 rpm: 32 mph, 51 km/h; consumption: 16,6 m/imp gal, 14 m/U gal, 16.8 l x 100 km.

CHASSIS ladder frame with cross members; front suspension independent, wishbones, longitudinal torsion bar, anti-roll ba telescopic dampers; rear: independent, swinging longitudina trailing arms, coil springs, automatic levelling control, telesco pic dampers.

STEERING recirculating ball, tilt and telescopic adjustabl steering wheel, variable ratio servo; turns lock to lock: 3.

BRAKES disc (diameter 10.40 in, 26.5 cm), internal radial fins rear compensator, servo; swept area: front 198 sq in, 1,277 s cm, rear 198 sq in, 1,277 sq cm, total 396 sq in, 2,554 sq cm

ELECTRICAL EQUIPMENT 12 V; 80 A alternator; electroni ignition; 4 iodine headlamps.

DIMENSIONS AND WEIGHT wheel base: 114 in, 289 cm tracks: 59.30 in, 150 cm front, 60.60 in, 154 cm rear; length 204 in, 519 cm; width: 71.50 in, 182 cm; height: 54.20 in, 13 cm; ground clearance: 13 in, 33 cm; weight: 3,944 lb, 1,775 kg weight distribution: 61% front, 39% rear; turning circle: 42.2 f 12.8 m; fuel tank: 17 imp gal, 20.6 US gal, 78 l.

BODY hardtop coupé; 2 doors; 4 seats, separate front seat built-in headrests; electric windows; electronic air-conditionin heated rear and side windows.

OPTIONALS heavy-duty cooling; 2.410 axle ratio; light allo wheels; electric reclining seats; leather seats; electric sunshir roof with Biarritz equipment; 100 A alternator; trip compute

CADILLAC De Ville Sedan

160 hp power team

(standard, for California only)

See 145 hp power team, except for:

ENGINE 350 cu in, 5,736 cc (4.06 x 3.38 in, 103 x 85 mm); compression ratio: 8:1; max power (SAE net): 160 hp (119 kW) at 4,400 rpm; max torque (SAE net): 265 lb ft, 36.6 kg m (359 Nm) at 1,600 rpm; max engine rpm: 4,800; 28 hp/l (20.8 kW/l); lubrication: 6.7 imp pt, 8 US pt, 3.8 l; electronic injection; fuel feed: 2 electric pumps; water-cooled, 25.3 imp pt, 30.4 US pt, 14.4 l.

PERFORMANCE max speed: 125 mph, 200 km/h; power-weight ratio: 24,5 lb/hp, (33 lb/kW), 11 kg/hp (14.8 kg/kW).

DIMENSIONS AND WEIGHT weight: 3,928 lb, 1,768 kg; weight distribution: 60% front, 40% rear.

105 hp (diesel) power team

(optional)

See 145 hp power team, except for:

ENGINE front, 4 stroke; 8 cylinders; 350 cu in, 5,736 cc (4.06 x 3.38 in, 103 x 86 mm); compression ratio: 21.5:1; max power (SAE net): 105 hp (78 kW) at 3,200 rpm; max torque (SAE net): 205 lb ft, 28.3 kg m (278 Nm) at 1,600 rpm; max engine rpm: 3,500; 18.3 hp/l (13.6 kW/l); lubrication: gear pump, full flow filter, 11.6 imp pt, 14 US pt, 6.6 l; diesel injection pump; fuel feed: mechanical pump; water-cooled, 30.6 imp pt, 36.8 US pt, 17.4 l.

TRANSMISSION axle ratio: 2.410.

PERFORMANCE max speed: 93 mph, 155 km/h; power-weight ratio: 39.1 lb/hp, (52.7 lb/kW), 17.6 kg/hp ((23.7 kg/kW); speed in direct drive at 1,000 rpm: 28 mph, 45 km/h.

ELECTRICAL EQUIPMENT 12 V; 2 batteries.

DIMENSIONS AND WEIGHT weight: 4,111 lb, 1,850 kg; weight distribution: 62% front, 38% rear; fuel tank: 19 imp gal, 23 US gal, 87 l.

OPTIONALS 2.190 axle ratio not available.

De Ville - Fleetwood Series

PRICES EX WORKS:		$
1	De Ville 2-dr Coupé	**12,401**
2	De Ville 4-dr Sedan	**12,770**
3	Fleetwood 4-dr Brougham	**14,927**
4	Fleetwood 4-dr Limousine	**22,586**
5	Fleetwood 4-dr Formal Limousine	**23,388**

Power team:	Standard for:	Optional for:
150 hp	all	—
105 hp (diesel)	—	1,2,3

CADILLAC Fleetwood Brougham

150 hp power team

ENGINE front, 4 stroke; 8 cylinders; 368 cu in, 6,030 cc (4.06 x 3.38 in, 103 x 85.8 mm); compression ratio: 8.2:1; max power (SAE net): 150 hp (112 kW) at 3,800 rpm; max torque (SAE net): 265 lb ft, 36.5 kg m (359 Nm) at 1,600 rpm; max engine rpm: 4,200; 25 hp/l (18.7 kW/l); cast iron block and head; 5 crankshaft bearings; valves: overhead, in line, push-rods and rockers, hydraulic tappets; camshafts: 1, at centre of Vee; lubrication: gear pump, full flow filter, 6.7 imp pt, 8 US pt, 3.8 l; 1 Rochester M4ME 4-barrel downdraught carburettor (in California 1 Rochester E4ME 4-barrel downdraught carburettor air cleaner only for Brougham and De Ville models); exhaust system with catalytic converter; fuel feed: mechanical pump; water-cooled, 35.7 imp pt, 42.9 US pt, 20.3 l.

TRANSMISSION driving wheels: rear; gearbox: Turbo-Hydramatic 400 automatic transmission, hydraulic torque converter and planetary gears with 3 ratios, max ratio of converter at stall 2, possible manual selection; ratios: I 2.480, II 1.480, III 1, rev 2.070; lever: steering column; final drive: hypoid bevel; axle ratios: Brougham and De Ville models 2.280 - in California 2.560 - limousines 3.080; width of rims: 6"; tyres: 75 R x 15.

PERFORMANCE max speed: Brougham and De Ville models 118 mph, 190 km/h - in California 105 mph, 170 km/h - limousines 92 mph, 148 km/h; power-weight ratio: Brougham and De Ville Sedan 28.4 lb/hp (38.6 lb/kW), 12.8 kg/hp (17.4 kg/kW) - De Ville Coupé 28 lb/hp (38 lb/kW), 12.6 kg/hp (17.1 kg/kW) - Limousine 32 lb/hp (43.5 lb/kW), 14.4 kg/hp (19.6 kg/kW) - Formal Limousine 32.6 lb/hp (44.3 lb/kW), 14.7 kg/hp (20.1 kg/kW); carrying capacity: Brougham and De Ville models 1,270 lb, 570 kg - Limousine 1,620 lb, 730 kg - Formal Limousine 1,440 lb, 650 kg; speed in direct drive at 1,000 rpm: Brougham and De Ville models 31 mph, 50 km/h - limousines 28 mph, 45 km/h; consumption: 18 m/imp gal, 15 m/US gal, 15.7 l x 100 km.

CHASSIS ladder frame with cross members; front suspension: independent, wishbones, coil springs, automatic levelling control (except for De Ville models), anti-roll bar, telescopic dampers; rear: rigid axle, lower trailing radius arms, upper oblique torque arms, coil springs, automatic levelling control (except for De Ville models), anti-roll bar, telescopic dampers.

STEERING recirculating ball, variable ratio servo; turns lock to lock: Brougham and De Ville models 3.20 - limousines 3.90.

BRAKES front disc (diameter 11.7 in, 298 mm), internal radial fins, rear drum, servo; swept area: Brougham and De Ville models front 236 sq in, 1,528 sq cm, rear 138 sq in, 892 sq cm, total 374 sq in, 2,420 sq cm - Limousines front 236 sq in, 1,528 sq cm, rear 188 sq in, 1,216 sq cm, total 424 sq in, 2,736 sq cm.

ELECTRICAL EQUIPMENT 12 V; 63 A alternator; Delco-Remy electronic high energy ignition; 4 iodine headlamps.

DIMENSIONS AND WEIGHT wheel base: 121.50 in, 308 cm - Limousine and Formal Limousine 144.50 in, 367 cm; tracks: 61.70 in, 157 cm front, 60.70 in, 154 cm rear, length: 221.20 in, 562 cm - Limousine and Formal Limousine 244.20 in, 620 cm; width: 76.40 in, 194 cm; height: Brougham 56.70 in, 144 cm - De Ville Coupé 54.40 in, 138 cm - De Ville Sedan 55.30 in, 140 cm - Limousine and Formal Limousine 56.90 in, 145 cm; ground clearance: Brougham 5.50 in, 14 cm - De Ville 5.70 in, 14.5 cm - Limousine and Formal Limousine 6.10 in, 15.6 cm; weight: De Ville Coupé 4,143 lb, 1,879 kg - De Ville Sedan 4,212 lb, 1,913 kg - Brougham 4,250 lb, 1,928 kg - Limousine 4,782 lb, 2,169 kg - Formal Limousine 4,866 lb, 2,207 kg; turning circle: De Ville models 44.1 ft, 13.4 m - Brougham 51.2 ft, 15.6 m - Limousine and Formal Limousine 57.2 ft, 17.4 m; fuel tank: Brougham and De Ville models 17.3 imp gal, 20.7 US gal, 78 l - limousines 20.9 imp gal, 25 US gal, 95 l.

BODY Brougham and De Ville models 6 seats - Limousine 8 seats - Formal Limousine 7 seats; electric windows, electronic air-conditioning.

OPTIONALS heavy-duty cooling; limited slip differential; 2.730 axle ratio (except for limousines); H78 x 15 tyres; 478 x 15 tyres with 5" wide rims (for De Ville models only); wire wheels; automatic levelling control (for De Ville models only); speed control device; 80 A alternator (except for limousines); heated rear window; reclining backrests; vinyl roof, electric sunshine roof; leather upholstery; Cabriolet equipment (for Coupé only); d'Elegance equipment; Custom Phaeton equipment (for De Ville models only).

105 hp (diesel) power team

See 150 hp power team, except for:

ENGINE 8 cylinders; 350 cu in, 5,736 cc (4.06 x 3.38 in, 103 x 86 mm); compression ratio: 22.5:1; max power (SAE net): 105 hp (78 kW) at 3,200 rpm; max torque (SAE net): 205 lb ft, 28.3 kg m (278 Nm) at 1,600 rpm; max engine rpm; 3,500; 18.3 hp/l (13.6 kW/l); lubrication: 11.6 imp pt, 14 US pt, 6.6 l; diesel injection pump cooling: 30.6 imp pt, 36.8 US pt, 17.4 l.

TRANSMISSION gearbox: Turbo-Hydramatic 200 automatic transmission, hydraulic torque converter and planetary gears with 3 ratios, max ratio of converter at stall 2.2, possible manual selection; ratios: I 2.740, II 1.570, III 1, rev 2.070; axle ratio: 2.560.

105 HP (DIESEL) POWER TEAM

PERFORMANCE max speed: 92 mph, 150 km/h; power-weight ratio: Brougham 41.8 lb/hp (56.9 lb/kW), 18.8 kg/hp (25.6 kg/kW) - De Ville Sedan 41.6 lb/hp (56.6 lb/kW), 18,7 kg/hp (25.5 kg/kW) - De Ville Coupé 41.1 lb/hp (56.0 lb/kW), 18.5 kg/hp (25.2 kg/kW); speed in direct drive at 1,000 rpm: 26.6 mph, 42,8 km/h; consumption: 16.6 m/imp gal, 14 m/US gal, 16.8 l x 100 km.

ELECTRICAL EQUIPMENT 2 batteries; 80 A alternator.

DIMENSIONS AND WEIGHT weight: Brougham 4,390 lb, 1,975 kg - De Ville Sedan 4,360 lb, 1,962 kg - De Ville Coupé 4,322 lb, 1,945 kg; weight distribution: Brougham front 55%, rear 45% - De Ville models front 56%, rear 44%, fuel tank: 22.7 imp gal, 27 US gal, 102 l.

OPTIONALS 2.280 or 2.730 axle ratio not available.

CHECKER USA

Marathon Series

PRICES EX WORKS:	$
1 A12	7,986
2 A12 E De Luxe	9,060

Power team:	Standard for:	Optional for:
115 hp	1	—
120 hp	2	1
155 hp	—	both
125 hp (diesel)	—	both

115 hp power team

(not available in California)

ENGINE front, 4 stroke; 6 cylinders, Vee-slanted at 90°; 229 cu in, 3,752 cc (3.73 x 3.48 in, 94.9 x 88.4 mm); compression ratio: 8.6 :1; max power (SAE net): 115 hp (86 kW) at 4,000 rpm; max torque (SAE net): 175 lb ft, 24.1 kg m (236 Nm) at 2,000 rpm; max engine rpm: 4,400; 34.1 hp/l (25.1 kW/l); cast iron block and head; 4 crankshaft bearings; valves: overhead, in line, push-rods and rockers, hydraulic tappets; camshafts: 1, at centre of Vee; lubrication: gear pump, full flow filter, 12.4 imp pt, 14.7 US pt, 7.1 l; 1 Rochester 1780130 downdraught twin barrel carburettor; thermostatic air cleaner; exhaust system with catalytic converter; fuel feed: mechanical pump; water-cooled, 20 imp pt, 23.5 US pt, 11.4 l.

TRANSMISSION driving wheels: rear; gearbox: Turbo-Hydramatic 400 automatic transmission, hydraulic torque converter and planetary gears with 3 ratios, max ratio of converter at stall 2.2, possible manual selection; ratios: I 2.480, II 1.480, III 1, rev 2.070; lever: steering column; final drive: hypoid bevel; axle ratio: 2.720; width of rims: 6"; tyres: P 215/75 R x 15.

PERFORMANCE max speed: about 90 mph, 145 km/h; power-weight ratio: 31.4 lb/hp (42.6 lb/kW), 14.2 kg/hp (19.3 kg/kW); speed in direct drive at 1,000 rpm: 24.2 mph, 38.9 km/h; consumption: 22.8 m/imp gal, 19 m/US gal, 12.4 l x 100 km.

CHASSIS box-type ladder frame with X reinforcements; front suspension: independent, wishbones, coil springs, anti-roll bar, telescopic dampers; rear: rigid axle, semielliptic leafsprings, telescopic dampers.

STEERING recirculating ball, variable ratio servo; turns lock to lock: 3.46.

BRAKES front disc (diameter 11.86 in, 30.1 cm), front internal radial fins, rear drum, servo; swept area: total 375.1 sq in, 2.419 sq cm.

ELECTRICAL EQUIPMENT 12 V; 80 Ah battery; 63 A alternator; Delco-Remy high energy ignition; 4 headlamps.

DIMENSIONS AND WEIGHT wheel base: 120 in, 305 cm; tracks: 64.45 in, 164 cm front, 63.31 in, 161 cm rear; length: 204.75 in, 520 cm; width: 76 in, 193 cm; height: 62.75 in, 159 cm; ground clearance: 7.50 in, 19 cm; weight: 3,680 lb, 1,669 kg; weight distribution: 52% front, 48% rear; turning circle: 43.3 ft, 13.2 m; fuel tank: 17,9 imp gal, 21.6 US gal, 82 l.

BODY saloon/sedan; 4 doors; 6 seats.

OPTIONALS limited slip differential; HR78 x 15 tyres; auxiliary rear seats; air-conditioning; heavy-duty telescopic dampers; tinted glass.

120 hp power team

(not available in California)

See 115 hp power team, except for:

ENGINE 8 cylinders; 267 cu in, 4,376 cc (3.50 x 3.48 in, 88.9 x 88.4 mm); compression ratio: 8.3:1; max power (SAE net): 120 hp (88 kW) at 3,600 rpm; max torque (SAE net): 215 lb ft, 29.6 kg m (290 Nm) at 2,000 rpm; max engine rpm: 4,000; 27.5 hp/l (20.2 kW/l); 5 crankshaft bearings; 1 Rochester 17080138 downdraught twin barrel carburettor; fuel feed: mechanical pump; cooling, 28.2 imp pt, 33.2 US pt, 16.1 l.

TRANSMISSION tyres: A12 E De Luxe P 225/75R x 15.

PERFORMANCE max speed: 95 mph, 153 km/h; power-weight ratio: A 12 E De Luxe 33.3 lb/hp (45.3 lb/kW), 15.1 kg/hp (20.5 kg/kW); consumption: 21.4 m/imp gal, 18 m/US gal, 13.1 l x 100 km.

DIMENSIONS AND WEIGHT A 12E De Luxe wheel base: 129 in, 328 cm; length: 213.75 in, 543 cm; weight: 3,999 lb, 1,814 kg; weight distribution: 55% front, 45% rear.

BODY (for A 12 E De Luxe only) 9 seats.

CHECKER Marathon A12

155 hp power team

(for California only)

See 115 hp power team, except for:

ENGINE 8 cylinders; 305 cu in, 4,999 cc (3.74 x 3.48 in, 94.9 x 88.4 mm); compression ratio: 8.6:1; max power (SAE net): 155 hp (113 kW) at 4,000 rpm; max torque (SAE net): 23[illegible] lb ft, 31.7 kg m (312 Nm) at 2,400 rpm; max engine rpm: 4,400; 32 hp/l (24 kW/l); 5 crankshaft bearings; 1 Rochester 1708050[illegible] downdraught 4-barrel carburettor; fuel feed: mechanical pump; cooling, 28.2 imp pt, 33.2 US pt, 16.1 l.

TRANSMISSION tyres: A 12E De Luxe P 225/75 R x 15.

PERFORMANCE max speed: 106 mph, 170 km/h; power-weigh[t] ratio: A12 25.4 lb/hp (34.5 lb/kW), 11.5 kg/hp (15.6 kg/kW); consumption: 19.2 m/imp gal, 16 m/US gal, 14.7 l x 100 km.

DIMENSIONS AND WEIGHT weight: A12 3,940 lb, 1,787 kg - A12E De Luxe 4,100 lb, 1,860 kg.

125 hp (diesel) power team

(not available in California)

See 115 hp power team, except for:

ENGINE diesel; compression ratio: 22.5:1; max power (DIN): 125 hp (92 kW) at 3,600 rpm; max torque (DIN): 225 lb ft, 31 kg m (304 Nm) at 1,600 rpm; 21.8 hp/l (16 kW/l); lubrication: 15 imp pt, 18 US pt, 8.5 l; diesel injection pump: cooling, 30.6 imp pt, 36.8 US pt, 17.4 l.

PERFORMANCE max speed: about 96 mph, 155 km/h; power-weight ratio: A12 33.3 lb/hp (45.2 lb/kW), 15.1 kg/hp (20.5 kg/kW); speed in direct drive at 1,000 rpm: 28.5 mph, 45.8 km/h; consumption: 25.2 m/imp gal, 21 m/US gal, 11.2 l x 100 km.

DIMENSIONS AND WEIGHT weight: A12 4,162 lb, 1,888 kg - A12E De Luxe 4,322 lb, 1,960 kg; weight distribution: 54% front, 46% rear.

CHEVROLET USA

Chevette Series

PRICES EX WORKS:	$
1 4+1-dr Hatchback Sedan	4,417
2 2+1-dr Scooter Hatchback Coupé	3,781
3 2+1-dr Hatchback Coupé	4,288

For 74 hp engine add $ 60.

Power team:	Standard for:	Optional for:
70 hp	all	—
74 hp	—	all

70 hp power team

ENGINE front, 4 stroke; 4 cylinders, vertical, in line; 97.6 cu in, 1,599 cc (3.23 x 2.98 in, 82 x 75.6 mm); compression ratio: 8.6:1; max power (SAE net): 70 hp (51 kW) at 5,200 rpm; max torque (SAE net): 82 lb ft, 11.3 kg m (111 Nm) at 2,400 rpm; max engine rpm: 5,600; 43.8 hp/l (32.2 kW/l); cast iron block and head: 5 crankshaft bearings; valves: overhead, hydraulic tappets; camshafts: 1, overhead, cogged belt; lubrication: gear pump, full flow filter, 8.3 imp pt, 9.9 US pt, 4.7 l; 1 Holley 14004464 (14004472 for California only) downdraught twin barrel carburettor; air cleaner; exhaust system with catalytic converter; fuel feed: mechanical pump; water-cooled, 15.3 imp pt, 18.4 US pt, 8.7 l.

TRANSMISSION driving wheels: rear; clutch: single dry plate (diaphragm); gearbox: mechanical; gears: 4, fully synchronized; ratios: I 3.750, II 2.160, III 1.380, IV 1, rev 3.820; lever: central; final drive: hypoid bevel; axle ratio: 3.700; width of rims: 5"; tyres: P155/80 R x 13.

PERFORMANCE max speed: 90 mph, 145 km/h; power-weight ratio: Hatchback Sedan 29.4 lb/hp (40 lb/kW), 13.3 kg/hp (18.1 kg/kW); speed in direct drive at 1,000 rpm: 17.9 mph, 28.8 km/h; consumption: 34.9 m/imp gal, 29 m/US gal, 8.1 l x 100 km.

CHASSIS integral with cross member reinforcement; front suspension: independent, wishbones, coil springs, anti-roll bar, telescopic dampers; rear: rigid axle (torque tube), longitudinal trailing radius arms, coil springs, transverse linkage bar, anti-roll bar, telescopic dampers.

STEERING rack-and-pinion; turns lock to lock: 3.60.

CHEVROLET Chevette Hatchback Sedan

RAKES front disc (diameter 9.68 in, 24.6 cm), rear drum; wept area: total 279.8 sq in, 1,804 sq cm.

LECTRICAL EQUIPMENT 12 V; 2,500 W battery; 32 A alter-ator; Delco-Remy high energy ignition; 2 headlamps.

IMENSIONS AND WEIGHT wheel base: 94.30 in, 239 cm - atchback Sedan 97.30 in, 247 cm; front and rear track: 51.20 , 130 cm length: Sedan 164.90 in, 419 cm - coupés 161.90 in, 11 cm; width: 61.80 in, 157 cm; height: 52.30 in, 133 cm; ound clearance: 5.30 in, 13.5 cm; weight: Scooter hatchback oupé 1,943 lb, 881 kg - Hatchback coupé 1,996 lb, 906 kg - atchback Sedan 2,056 lb, 933 kg; turning circle: 34.3 ft, 10.5 - Hatchback Sedan 34.9 ft, 10.6 m; fuel tank: 10.3 imp gal, 2.5 US gal, 47 l.

ODY 4 seats, separate front seats with built-in headrests.

PTIONALS Turbo-Hydramatic 180 automatic transmission, ydraulic torque converter and planetary gears with 3 ratios (I .400, II 1.480, III 1, rev 1.920), max ratio of converter at stall .2, possible manual selection, central lever; heavy-duty bat-ery; servo brake; vinyl roof; heavy-duty radiator; tilt of steering heel; heated rear window; air-conditioning; de Luxe equip-ent; Custom two-tone paint equipment.

74 hp power team

not available in California)

ee 70 hp power team, except for:

NGINE max power (SAE net): 74 hp (54 kW) at 5,200 rpm; ax torque (SAE net): 88 lb ft, 12.1 kg m (119 Nm) at 2,800 om; 46.3 hp/l (34.1 kW/l); 1 Holley 14004468 downdraught twin arrel carburettor.

ERFORMANCE max speed: 93 mph, 150 km/h; power-weight atio: Hatchback Sedan 27.7 lb/hp (37.6 lb/kW), 12.6 kg/hp 17.1 kg/kW).

Monza Series

RICES EX WORKS:	$
2-dr Coupé	**4,184**
2+1-dr Hatchback Coupé	**4,497**
2+1-dr Sport Hatchback Coupé	**4,921**

or 110 hp engine add $ 225.

ower team:	Standard for:	Optional for:
86 hp	all	—
10 hp	—	all

86 hp power team

NGINE front, 4 stroke; 4 cylinders, vertical, in line; 151 cu in, ,474 cc (4 x 3 in, 101.5 x 76.1 mm); compression ratio: 8.2:1, ax power (SAE net): 86 hp (63 kW) at 4,000 rpm; max torque SAE net): 128 lb ft, 17.6 kg m (172 Nm) at 2,400 rpm; max ngine rpm: 4,800; 34.8 hp/l (25.6 kW/l); cast iron block and ead; 5 crankshaft bearings; valves: overhead, in line, push-ods and rockers, hydraulic tappets; camshafts: 1, side; lubrica-on: gear pump, full flow filter 5.2 imp pt, 6.2 US pt, 3 l; 1 ochester 17059675 downdraught twin barrel carburettor; air leaner; exhaust system with catalytic converter; fuel feed: echanical pump; water-cooled, 20.1 imp pt, 23.9 US pt, 11.5 l.

TRANSMISSION driving wheels: rear; clutch: single dry plate (diaphragm); gearbox: mechanical; gears: 4, fully synchronized; ratios: I 3.500, II 2.480, III 1.660, IV 1, rev 3.500; lever: central; final drive: hypoid bevel; axle ratio: 2,730- - California 2,930; width of rims: 5"; tyres: A78 x 13.

PERFORMANCE max speed: 96 mph, 154 km/h; power weight ratio: Coupè 30.4 lb/hp (41.4 lb/kW), 13.8 kg/hp (18.7 kg/kW); speed in direct drive at 1,000 rpm: 24 mph, 38.7 km/h; con-sumption: 28.8 m/imp gal, 24 m/US gal, 9.8 l x 100 km.

CHASSIS integral; front suspension: independent, wishbones, coil springs, anti-roll bar, telescopic dampers; rear: rigid axle, lower trailing radius arms, upper oblique torque arms, coil springs, telescopic dampers.

STEERING recirculating ball; turns lock to lock: 4.40.

BRAKES front disc (diameter 9.74 in, 24.7 cm), rear drum; swept area: total 264.8 sq in, 1,708 sq cm.

ELECTRICAL EQUIPMENT 12 V; 3,200 W battery; 37 A alter-nator; Delco-Remy high energy ignition; 2 headlamps - Sport Hatchback Coupé 4 headlamps.

DIMENSIONS AND WEIGHT wheel base: 97 in, 246 cm; tracks: 54.80 in, 139 cm front, 53.60 in, 136 cm rear; length: 179.90 in, 457 cm - Sport Hatchback Coupé 179.30 in, 455 cm; width: 65.40 in,166 cm; height: 50.20 in, 127 cm - Coupé 49.80 in, 126 cm; ground clearance: 4.80 in, 12.2 cm; weight: Coupé 2,617 lb, 1,187 kg - Hatchback Coupé 2,672 lb, 1,212 kg - Sport Hatchback Coupé 2,729 lb, 1,238 kg; turning circle: 38.4 ft, 11.7 m; fuel tank: 15.4 imp gal, 18.5 US gal, 70 l.

BODY 4 seats, separate front seats with built-in headrests.

OPTIONALS limited slip differential; 2.930 axle ratio; Turbo-Hydramatic 200 automatic transmission with 3 ratios (I 2.740, II 1.570, III 1, rev 2.070), max ratio of converter at stall 2, possible manual selection, central lever; BR 70 x 13 tyres with 6" wide rims; power steering; tilt of steering wheel; servo brake; heavy-duty radiator; heavy-duty battery; reclining back-rests; folding rear seat (for Coupé only); heated rear window; sunshine roof (for Coupé only); anti-roll bar on rear suspension; "Spyder" equipment (for Sport Hatchback Coupé only); air-conditioning.

110 hp power team

See 86 hp power team, except for:

ENGINE 6 cylinders, Vee-slanted at 90°; 231 cu in, 3,785 cc (3.80 x 3.40 in, 96.5 x 86.4 mm); max power (SAE net): 110 hp (81 kW) at 3,800 rpm; max torque (SAE net): 190 lb ft, 26.2 kg m (257 Nm) at 2,000 rpm; max engine rpm: 4,200; 29.1 hp/l (21.4 kW/l); 4 crankshaft bearings; camshafts: 1, at centre of Vee; lubrication: 8.3 imp pt, 9.9 US pt, 4.7 l; 1 Rochester 17080191 downdraught twin barrel carburettor; fuel feed: elec-tric pump; cooling: 20.4 imp pt, 24.5 US pt, 11.6 l.

TRANSMISSION axle ratio: 2.930; width of rims: 6"; tyres: B78 x 13.

CHEVROLET Monza "Spyder" Hatchback Coupé

CHEVROLET Monza Hatchback Coupé

110 HP POWER TEAM

PERFORMANCE max speed: 103 mph, 165 km/h; power-weight ratio: Coupé 26 lb/hp (35.3 lb/kW), 11.8 kg/hp (16 kg/kW); speed in direct drive at 1,000 rpm: 27 mph, 43.4 km/h; consumption: 24.1 m/imp gal, 20 m/US gal, 11.7 l x 100 km.

ELECTRICAL EQUIPMENT 2,500 W battery.

DIMENSIONS AND WEIGHT weight: plus 249 lb, 113 kg.

OPTIONALS Turbo-Hydramatic 350 automatic transmission with 3 ratios (I 2.520, II 1.520, III 1, rev 1.930), max ratio of converter at stall 2.35, possible manual selection, 2.560 or 2.930 axle ratio.

Citation Series

PRICES EX WORKS:	$
1 4+1-dr Hatchback Sedan	5,153
2 2-dr Coupé	4,491
3 2-dr Club Coupé	4,905
4 2+1-dr Hatchback Coupé	5,032

For V6 engine add $ 225.

Power team:	Standard for:	Optional for:
90 hp	all	—
90 hp (California)	all	—
110 hp	—	all
115 hp	—	all

90 hp power team

(not available in California)

ENGINE front, transverse, 4 stroke; 4 cylinders, in line; 151 cu in, 2,475 cc (4 x 3 in, 101.6 x 76.2 mm); compression ratio: 8.2:1; max power (SAE net): 90 hp (66 kW) at 4,000 rpm; max torque (SAE net): 134 lb ft, 18.6 kg m (182 Nm) at 2,400 rpm; max engine rpm: 4,400; 20,5 hp/l (15.1 kW/l); cast iron block and head; 5 crasnkshaft bearings; valves: overhead, in line, push-rods and rockers, hydraulic tappets; camshaft: 1, side; lubrication: gear pump, full flow filter, 6.7 imp pt, 8 US pt, 3.8 l; 1 Rochester 17059619 downdraught twin barrel carburettor; air cleaner; exhaust system with catalytic converter; fuel feed: mechanical pump; water-cooled, 17.8 imp pt, 21.4 US pt, 10.1 l.

TRANSMISSION driving wheels: front; clutch: self-adjusting single dry plate (diaphragm); gearbox: mechanical; gears: 4, fully synchronized; ratios: I 3.530, II 1.960, III 1.240, IV 0.810, rev 3.420; lever: central; final drive: spiral bevel; axle ratio: 3.320; width of rims: 5''; tyres: P 185/80 R x 13.

PERFORMANCE max speed: 87 mph, 140 km/h; power-weight ratio: 27.1 lb/hp, (36.6 lb/kW), 12.2 kg/hp (16.6 kg/kW); speed in top at 1,000 rpm: 19.8 mph, 31.8 km/h consumption: 28,4 m/imp gal, 24 m/US gal, 9.9 l x 100 km.

CHASSIS integral; front suspension: independent, by McPherson, coil springs, lower control arms, telescopic dampers; rear: rigid axle, trailing arm, control arms, coil springs, telescopic dampers.

STEERING rack-and-pinion; turns lock to lock: 3.50.

BRAKES front disc (diameter 9.72 in, 24.7 cm), internal radial fins) rear drum; swept area: total 261.6 sq in, 1,687 sq cm.

ELECTRICAL EQUIPMENT 12 V; 3,200 W battery: 42 A alternator; Delco-Remy high energy ignition; 2 headlamps.

DIMENSIONS AND WEIGHT wheel base: 104.90 in, 267 cm; tracks: 58.70 in, 149 cm front, 57 in, 145 cm rear; length: 176.70 in, 449 cm; width: 68.30 in, 174 cm; height: 53.10 in, 135 cm; ground clearance: 7.60 in, 19.2 cm; weight: sedan 2,438 lb, 1,105 kg - Coupé 2,393 lb, 1,085 kg - Club Coupé 2,398 lb, 1,088 kg - Hatchback Coupé 2,418 lb, 1,097 kg; weight distribution: 63% front, 37% rear; turning circle: 41 ft, 12.5 m; fuel tank: 12 imp gal, 14 US gal, 53 l.

BODY 5 seats, separate front seats with built-in headrests.

OPTIONALS automatic transmission with 3 ratios (I 2.840, II 1.600, III 1, rev 2.070), max ratio of converter at stall 1.9, possible manual selection, steering column lever, 2.530 axle ratio; tilt of steering wheel; sunshine roof; reclining seats; Custom upholstery; heated rear window; air-conditioning; servo brake; power steering; electric windows; electric door lock; de luxe equipment; sport equipment; P 205/70 R x 13 tyres; heavy-duty battery; 70 A alternator; heavy-duty cooling.

90 hp power team

(for California only)

See 90 hp power team, except for:

CHEVROLET Citation Coupé

ENGINE max power (SAE net): 90 hp (66 kW) at 4,400 rpm; max torque (SAE net): 128 lb ft, 17.7 kg m (173 Nm) at 2,400 rpm; max engine rpm: 5,000; 1 Rochester 17059715 downdraught twin barrel carburettor.

PERFORMANCE max speed: 93 mph, 150 km/h.

110 hp power team

(for California only)

See 90 hp power team, except for:

ENGINE 6 cylinders, Vee-slanted at 60°; 173 cu in, 2,835 cc (3.50 x 3 in, 89 x 76.2 mm); compression ratio: 8.5:1; max power (SAE net): 110 hp (82 kW) at 4,800 rpm; max torque (SAE net): 140 lb ft, 19.4 kg m (190 Nm) at 2,400 rpm; max engine rpm: 5,300; 38.6 hp/l (28.4 kW/l); 4 crankshaft bearings; camshafts: 1, at centre of Vee; lubrication: 6.7 imp pt, 7.9 US pt, 3.8 l; 1 Rochester 17059763 downdraught twin barrel carburettor; cooling: 16.9 imp pt, 20.2 US pt, 9.7 l.

PERFORMANCE max speed: 106 mph, 170 km/h; power-weight ratio: sedan 21.8 lb/hp, (29.3 lb/kW), 9.9 kg/hp (13.3 kg/kW); speed in top at 1,000 rpm: 23.1 mph, 37.3 km/h; consumption: 23.7 m/imp gal, 20 m/US gal, 11.8 l x 100 km.

DIMENSIONS AND WEIGHT weight: less 25 lb, 12 kg.

OPTIONALS automatic transmission with 2.840 axle ratio.

CHEVROLET Citation Custom Coupé

115 hp power team

(not available in California)

See 90 hp power team, except for:

ENGINE 6 cylinders, Vee-slanted at 60°; 173 cu in, 2,835 c (3.50 x 3 in, 89 x 76.2 mm); compression ratio: 8.5:1; max pow er (SAE net): 115 hp (85 kW) at 4,800 rpm; max torque (SA net): 145 lb ft, 20.1 kg m (197 Nm) at 2,400 rpm; max engin rpm: 5,300; 40.6 hp/l (29.9 kW/l); 4 crankshaft bearings; can shafts: 1, at centre of Vee; lubrication: 6.7 imp pt, 7.9 US p 3.8 l; 1 Rochester 17059651 downdraught twin barrel carbure tor; cooling: 16.9 imp pt, 20.2 US pt, 9.7 l.

PERFORMANCE max speed: 106 mph, 170 km/h; power-weig ratio: sedan 21.1 lb/hp, (28.7 lb/kW), 9.6 kg/hp (13 kg/kW speed in top at 1,000 rpm: 23.1 mph, 37.3 km/h; consumptio 23.7 gal, 20 m/US gal, 11.8 l x 100 km.

DIMENSIONS AND WEIGHT weight: less 25 lb, 12 kg.

OPTIONALS automatic transmission with 2.840 axle ratio.

Camaro Series

PRICES EX WORKS:	$
1 Sport Coupé	5,49
2 Rally Sport Coupé	5,91
3 Berlinetta Coupé	6,26
4 Z28 Sport Coupé	7,12

For 120 hp engine add $ 180; for 155 hp engine add $ 295; fo 165 hp engine $ 50.

Power team:	Standard for:	Optional for:
110 hp	1 to 3	—
115 hp	1 to 3	—
120 hp	—	1 to 3
155 hp	—	1 to 3
155 hp (California)	—	1 to 3
165 hp	4	—
190 hp	4	—

110 hp power team

(for California only)

ENGINE front, 4 stroke; 6 cylinders, Vee-slanted at 90°; 231 c in, 3,785 cc (3.80 x 3.40 in, 96.5 x 86.5 mm); compression rati 8:1; max power (SAE net): 110 hp (81 kW) at 3,800 rpm; ma torque (SAE net): 190 lb ft, 26.1 kg m (256 Nm) at 1,600 rpn max engine rpm: 4,200; 29.3 hp/l (21.5 kW/l); cast iron bloc and head; 4 crankshaft bearings; valves: overhead, in lin push-rods and rockers, hydraulic tappets; camshafts: 1, centre of Vee; lubrication: gear pump, full flow filter, 7.4 imp p 8.4 US pt, 4 l; 1 Rochester 17080490 downdraught twin barr carburettor; thermostatic air cleaner; exhaust system with cata lytic converter; fuel feed: mechanical pump; water-cooled, 21. imp pt, 25.6 US pt, 12.2 l.

TRANSMISSION driving wheels: rear; gearbox: Turbo Hydramatic 350 automatic transmission, hydraulic torque co verter and planetary gears with 3 ratios, max ratio of convert at stall 2, possible manual selection; ratios: I 2.520, II 1.520, I 1, rev 1.930; lever: steering column; final drive: hypoid beve ıxle ratio: 2.730; width of rims: 6" - Berlinetta 7"; tyres: P '05/75 R x 14.

'ERFORMANCE max speed: 106 mph, 171 km/h; power-weight atio: Sport Coupé 29.2 lb/hp (39.7 lb/kW), 13.3 kg/hp (18 .g/kW); speed in direct drive at 1,000 rpm: 25.9 mph, 41.7 :m/h; consumption: 22.6 m/imp gal, 19 m/US gal, 12.4 l x 100 :m.

:HASSIS integral with separate partial front box-type frame; ront suspension: independent, wishbones, coil springs, anti-roll ar, telescopic dampers; rear: rigid axle, semi-elliptic leafsprings, anti-roll bar, telescopic dampers.

;TEERING recirculating ball, servo; turns lock to lock: 2.41.

3RAKES front disc (diameter 11 in, 27.9 cm), front internal adial fins, rear drum; swept area: total 326.4 sq in, 2,105 sq m.

:LECTRICAL EQUIPMENT 12 V; 3,200 W battery; 42 A alternator; Delco-Remy high energy ignition; 4 headlamps.

)IMENSIONS AND WEIGHT wheel base: 108 in, 274 cm; racks: Sport Coupé 61.30 in, 155 cm front, 60 in, 152 cm rear - 3erlinetta 61.60 in, 156 cm front, 60.30 in, 153 cm rear; length: 97.60 in, 502 cm; width: 74.50 in, 191 cm; height: 49.20 in, 25 cm; ground clearance: 5.80 in, 14.7 cm; weight: Sport Coupé 3,218 lb, 1,459 kg - Berlinetta 3,260 lb, 1,479 kg; weight listribution: 54.7% front, 43.3% rear; turning circle: 41.1 ft, 2.5 m; fuel tank: 17.6 imp gal, 21 US gal, 80 l.

3ODY coupé; 2 doors; 4 seats, separate front seats.

)PTIONALS limited slip differential; central lever; E78 x 14 yres with 6" or 7" wide rims; tilt of steering wheel; servo brake; electric windows; heavy-duty battery; heavy-duty radiator; reclining front seats; removable glass roof panels; tinted glass; ir-conditioning; trip computer; heated rear window; rear spoiler.

115 hp power team

not available in California)

See 110 power team, except for:

:NGINE 229 cu in, 2,752 cc (3.73 x 3.48 in, 94.9 x 88.4 mm); ompression ratio: 8.6:1; max power (SAE net): 115 hp (84 kW) t 4,000 rpm; max torque (SAE net): 175 lb ft, 24.1 kg m (236 Nm) at 2,000 rpm; max engine rpm: 4,400; 34.1 hp/l (25.1 :W/l); 1 Rochester 17080131 downdraught twin barrel carburetor; cooling: 26.3 imp pt, 31.4 US pt, 15 l.

'RANSMISSION clutch: single dry plate (diaphragm); gearbox: nechanical; gears: 3, fully synchronized; ratios: I 3.500, II .890, III 1, rev 3.620; lever: central.

'ERFORMANCE max speed: 108 mph, 175 km/h; power-weight atio: Sport 28 lb/hp, (38.1 lb/kW), 12.7 kg/hp (17.3 kg/kW); consumption: 23.7 m/imp gal, 20 m/US gal, 11.8 l x 100 km.

:LECTRICAL EQUIPMENT 37 A alternator.

)PTIONALS Turbo-Hydramatic 200 c automatic transmission with 3 ratios (I 2.740, II 1.570, III 1, rev 2.070), max ratio of converter at stall 2.35, possible manual selection, steering column or central lever.

120 hp power team

(not available in California)

See 110 hp power team, except for:

ENGINE 8 cylinders; 267 cu in, 4,376 cc (3.50 x 3.48 in, 88.9 x 88.4 mm); compression ratio: 8.3:1; max power (SAE net): 120 hp (88 kW) at 3,600 rpm; max torque (SAE net): 215 lb ft, 29.6 kg m (290 Nm) at 2,000 rpm; max engine rpm: 4,000; 36.5 hp/l (26.8 kW/l); 5 crankshaft bearings; 1 Rochester 17080108 downdraught twin barrel carburettor; cooling: 27.5 imp pt, 32.7 US pt, 15.7 l.

TRANSMISSION axle ratio: 2,560.

PERFORMANCE max speed: 110 mph, 178 km/h; power-weight ratio: Sport Coupé 27.7 lb/hp, (37.7 lb/kW), 12.5 kg/hp (17.1 kg/kW); speed in direct drive at 1,000 rpm: 27.6 mph, 44.5 km/h; consumption: 21.3 m/imp gal, 18 m/US gal, 13.1 l x 100 km.

BRAKES servo (standard).

ELECTRICAL EQUIPMENT 37 A alternator.

DIMENSIONS AND WEIGHT weight: plus 126 lb, 57 kg.

155 hp power team

(not available in California)

CHEVROLET Camaro Z28 Sport Coupé

CHEVROLET Camaro Rally Sport Coupé

See 110 hp power team, except for:

ENGINE 8 cylinders; 305 cu in, 4,999 cc (3.74 x 3.48 in, 94.9 x 88.4 mm); max power (SAE net): 155 hp (113 kW) at 4,000 rpm; max torque (SAE net): 240 lb ft, 33.1 kg m (324 Nm) at 1,600 rpm; max engine rpm: 4,500; 32 hp/l (24 kW/l); 5 crankshaft bearings; 1 Rochester 17080207 downdraught 4-barrel carburettor; cooling: 27.6 imp pt, 32.8 US pt, 15.7 l.

TRANSMISSION clutch: single dry plate (diaphragm); gearbox: mechanical; gears: 4, fully synchronized; ratios: I 2.850, II 2.020, III 1.350, IV 1, rev 2.850; lever: central; axle ratio: 3.080.

PERFORMANCE max speed: 105 mph, 170 km/h; power-weight ratio: Sport Coupé 21.4 lb/hp, (29.2 lb/kW), 9.7 kg/hp (13.2 kg/kW); speed in direct drive at 1,000 rpm: 22.9 mph, 36.9 km/h; consumption: 20.1 m/imp gal, 17 m/US gal, 13.9 l x 100 km.

BRAKES servo (standard).

ELECTRICAL EQUIPMENT 37 A alternator.

DIMENSIONS AND WEIGHT weight: plus 121 lb, 55 kg.

OPTIONALS Turbo-Hydramatic 350 automatic transmission with 3 ratios (I 2.520, II 1.520, III 1, rev 1.930), max ratio of converter at stall 2, possible manual selection, steering column or central lever, 2.560 or 3.080 axle ratio.

155 hp power team

(for California only)

See 110 hp power team, except for:

ENGINE 8 cylinders; 305 cu in, 4,999 cc (3.74 x 3.48 in, 94.9 x 88.4 mm); max power (SAE net): 155 hp (113 kW) at 4,000 rpm; max torque (SAE net): 230 lb ft, 31.7 kg m (312 Nm) at 2,400 rpm; max engine rpm: 4,400; 32 hp/l (24 kW/l); 5 crankshaft bearings; 1 Rochester 17080502 downdraught 4-barrel carburettor; cooling: 27.6 imp pt, 32.8 US pt, 15.7 l.

TRANSMISSION axle ratio: 2.560.

PERFORMANCE max speed: 115 mph, 186 km/h; power-weight ratio: Sport Coupé 21.4 lb/hp, (29.2 lb/kW), 9.7 kg/hp (13.2 kg/kW); speed in direct drive at 1,000 rpm: 27.6 mph, 44.5 km/h; consumption: 20.1 m/imp gal, 17 m/US gal, 13.9 l x 100 km.

BRAKES servo (standard).

ELECTRICAL EQUIPMENT 37 A alternator.

DIMENSIONS AND WEIGHT weight: plus 121 lb, 55 kg.

165 hp power team

(for California only)

See 110 hp power team, except for:

ENGINE 8 cylinders; 305 cu in, 4,999 cc (3.74 x 3.48 in, 94.9 x 88.4 mm); max power (SAE net): 165 hp (121 kW) at 4,000 rpm; max torque (SAE net): 245 lb ft, 33.7 kg m (331 Nm) at 2,400 rpm; max engine rpm: 4,500; 33 hp/l (24.3 kW/l); 5 crankshaft bearings; 1 Rochester 17080502 downdraught 4-barrel carburettor; cooling: 27.6 imp pt, 32.8 US pt, 15.7 l.

TRANSMISSION axle ratio: 3,420.

PERFORMANCE max speed: 100 mph, 161 km/h; power-weight ratio: 20.1 lb/hp, (27.3 lb/kW), 9.1 kg/hp (12.4 kg/kW); speed in direct drive at 1,000 rpm: 20.7 mph, 33.3 km/h; consumption: 20,1 m/imp gal, 17 m/US gal, 13.9 l x 100 km.

BRAKES servo (standard).

ELECTRICAL EQUIPMENT 37 A alternator.

DIMENSIONS AND WEIGHT weight: plus 121 lb, 55 kg.

190 hp power team

(not available in California)

See 110 hp power team, except for:

ENGINE 8 cylinders; 350 cu in, 5,736 cc (4 x 3.48 in, 101.6 x 88.4 mm); compression ratio: 8.2:1; max power (SAE net): 190 hp (140 kW) at 4,200 rpm; max torque (SAE net): 280 lb ft, 38.5 kg m (378 Nm) at 2,400 rpm; max engine rpm: 4,600; 33.1 hp/l (24.3 kW/l); 5 crankshaft bearings; 1 Rochester 17080207 downdraught 4-barrel carburettor; double exhaust system with catalytic converter; cooling: 29 imp pt, 34.5 US pt, 16.4 l.

TRANSMISSION clutch: single dry plate (diaphragm); gearbox: mechanical; gears: 4, fully synchronized; ratios: I 3.420, II 2.280, III 1.450, IV 1, rev 3.510; lever: central; axle ratio: 3.080; tyres: P 225/70 R x 15.

190 HP POWER TEAM

PERFORMANCE max speed: 109 mph, 175 km/h; power-weight ratio: 17.6 lb/hp, (23.9 lb/kW), 7.9 kg/hp (10.8 kg/kW); speed in direct drive at 1,000 rpm: 22.9 mph, 36.9 km/h; consumption: 16.6 m/imp gal, 14 m/US gal, 16.9 l x 100 km.

BRAKES servo (standard).

ELECTRICAL EQUIPMENT 37 A alternator.

DIMENSIONS AND WEIGHT weight: 3,348 lb, 1,517 kg.

OPTIONALS Turbo-Hydramatic 350 automatic transmission with 3 ratios (I 2.520, II 1.520, III 1, rev 1.930), max ratio of converter at stall 2, possible manual selection; steering column or central lever; 3,420 axle ratio.

Malibu Series

PRICES EX WORKS:	$
1 4-dr Sedan	5,246
2 2-dr Sport Coupé	5,133
3 4+1-dr St. Wagon	5,401
4 Classic 4-dr Sedan	5,567
5 Classic 2-dr Sport Coupé	5,439
6 Classic 2-dr Landau Coupé	5,688
7 Classic 4+1-dr St. Wagon	5,653

For 120 hp engine add $ 180; for 155 hp engine add $ 295.

Power team:	Standard for:	Optional for:
110 hp	all	—
115 hp	all	—
120 hp	—	all
155 hp	—	all
155 hp (California)	—	all

110 hp power team

(for California only)

ENGINE front, 4 stroke; 6 cylinders, Vee-slanted at 90°; 231 cu in, 3,785 cc (3.80 x 3.40 in, 96.5 x 86.5 mm); compression ratio: 8:1; max power (SAE net): 110 hp (81 kW) at 3,800 rpm; max torque (SAE net): 190 lb ft, 26.1 kg m (256 Nm) at 1,600 rpm; max engine rpm: 4,200; 29.3 hp/l (21.5 kW/l); cast iron block and head; 4 crankshaft bearings; valves: overhead, in line, push-rods and rockers, hydraulic tappets; camshafts: 1, at centre of Vee; lubrication: gear pump, full flow filter, 7.4 imp pt, 8.4 US pt, 4 l; 1 Rochester 17080490 downdraught twin barrel carburettor; thermostatic air cleaner; exhaust system with catalytic converter; fuel feed: mechanical pump; water-cooled, 21.5 imp pt, 25.6 US pt, 12.2 l.

TRANSMISSION driving wheels: rear; gearbox: Turbo-Hydramatic 350 automatic trasmission, hydraulic torque converter and planetary gears with 3 ratios, max ratio of converter at stall 2, possible manual selection; ratios: I 2.520, II 1.520, III 1, rev 1,930; lever: steering column; final drive: hypoid bevel; axle ratio: 2.410 - St. Wagon 2.730; width of rims: 6"; tyres: P 185/75 R x 14 - St. Wagon P 195/75 R x 14.

PERFORMANCE max speed: 100 mph, 161 km/h; power-weight ratio: Sedan 27.3 lb/hp, (37.1 lb/kW), 12.3 kg/hp (16.8 kg/kW); speed in direct drive at 1,000 rpm: 29.8 mph, 47.7 km/h; consumption: 23.7 m/imp gal, 20 m/US gal, 11.8 l x 100 km.

CHASSIS perimeter box-type with front and rear cross members; front suspension: independent, wishbones, coil springs, anti-roll bar, telescopic dampers; rear: rigid axle, lower trailing radius arms, upper oblique torque arms, coil springs, telescopic dampers.

STEERING recirculating ball; turns lock to lock: 5.30.

BRAKES front disc (diameter 10.50 in, 26.7 cm), front internal radial fins, rear drum, servo; swept area: total 307.8 sq in, 1,985 sq cm.

ELECTRICAL EQUIPMENT 12 V; 2,500 W battery; 42 A alternator; Delco-Remy high energy ignition; 2 headlamps.

DIMENSIONS AND WEIGHT wheel base: 108.10 in, 274 cm; tracks: 58.50 in, 149 cm front, 57.80 in, 147 cm rear; length: 192.70 in, 489 cm - St. Wagon 193.40 in, 491 cm; width: 71.30 in, 181 cm; height: sedans 54.20 in, 138 cm - Coupés 53.30 in, 135 cm - st. wagons 54.50 in, 138 cm; ground clearance: 10.60 in, 27 cm; weight: sedan 3,001 lb, 1,361 kg - Coupé 2,996 lb, 1,359 kg - St. Wagon 3,141 lb, 1,425 kg - Classic Sedan 3,031 lb, 1,375 kg - Classic coupés 3,027 lb, 1,374 kg - Classic St. Wagon 3,167 lb, 1,436 kg; weight distribution: 54% front, 46% rear; turning circle: 40.1 ft, 12.2 m; fuel tank: 15.2 imp gal, 17.9 US gal, 68 l.

BODY 6 seats; (for coupés and Classic models only) separate front seats; built-in headrests.

OPTIONALS limited slip differential; heavy-suspension; power steering; heavy-duty battery; 63 A alternator; heavy cooling; electric windows; tilt of steering wheel; trip computer; heated rear window; electric door lock.

CHEVROLET Malibu Classic Station Wagon

115 hp power team

(not available in California)

See 110 hp power team, except for:

ENGINE 229 cu in, 3,752 cc (3.73 x 3.48 in, 94.9 x 88.4 mm); compression ratio: 8.6:1; max power (SAE net): 115 hp (84 kW) at 4,000 rpm; max torque (SAE net): 175 lb ft, 24.1 kg m (236 Nm) at 2,000 rpm; max engine rpm: 4,400; 34.1 hp/l (28.1 kW/l); 1 Rochester 17080131 downdraught twin barrel carburettor; cooling: 26.3 imp pt, 31.4 US pt, 15 l.

TRANSMISSION clutch: single dry plate (diaphragm); gearbox: mechanical; gears: 3, fully synchronized; ratios: I 3.500, II 1.890, III 1, rev 3.620; lever: central; axle ratio: 2.730.

PERFORMANCE power-weight ratio: Sedan 26.2 lb/hp, (35.5 lb/kW), 11.8 kg/hp (16.1 kg/kW.

ELECTRICAL EQUIPMENT 37 A alternator.

OPTIONALS Turbo-Hydramatic 200 C automatic transmission hydraulic torque converter and planetary gears with 3 ratios (I 2.740, II 1.570, III 1, rev 2.070) max ratio of converter at stall 2.35, possible manual selection, steering column or central lever, (sedan and coupés) 2.410 axle ratio.

120 hp power team

(not available in California)

See 110 hp power team, except for:

ENGINE 8 cylinders; 267 cu in, 4,376 cc (3.50 x 3.48 in, 88.9 x 88.4 mm); compression ratio: 8.3:1; max power (SAE net): 120 hp (88 kW) at 3,600 rpm; max torque (SAE net): 215 lb ft, 29.6 kg m (290 Nm) at 2,000 rpm; max engine rpm: 4,000; 36.5 hp/l (26.8 kW/l); 5 crankshaft bearings; 1 Rochester 17080108 downdraught twin barrel carburettor; cooling: 27.5 imp pt, 32.7 US pt, 15.6 l.

TRANSMISSION axle ratio: 2.290 - st. wagons 2.560.

PERFORMANCE max speed: 108 mph, 174 km/h; power-weight ratio: Sedan 26.1 lb/hp, (35.4 lb/kW), 11.8 kg/hp (16.1 kg/kW); speed in direct drive at 1,000 rpm: 31.4 mph, 50.2 km/h; consumption: 20.1 m/imp gal, 17 m/US gal, 13.9 l x 1200 km.

ELECTRICAL EQUIPMENT 37 A alternator.

DIMENSIONS AND WEIGHT weight: plus 126 lb, 57 kg.

155 hp power team

(not available in California)

See 110 hp power team, except for:

ENGINE 8 cylinders; 305 cu in, 4,999 cc (3.74 x 3.48 in, 94.9 x 88.4 mm); max power (SAE net): 155 hp (113 kW) at 4,000 rpm; max torque (SAE net): 240 lb ft, 33.1 kg m (324 Nm) at 1,600 rpm; max engine rpm: 4,500; 32 hp/l (24 kW/l); 5 crankshaft bearings; 1 Rochester 17080207 downdraught 4-barrel carburettor; cooling: 27.6 imp pt, 32.8 US pt, 15.7 l.

TRANSMISSION clutch: single dry plate (diaphragm); gearbox: mechanical; gears: 4, fully synchronized; ratios: I 2.850, II 2.020, III 1.350, IV 1, rev 2.850; lever: central; axle ratio 3.080.

PERFORMANCE max speed: 105 mph, 170 km/h; power-weight ratio: Sedan 20.2 lb/hp, (27.4 lb/kW), 9.1 kg/hp (12. kg/kW); speed direct drive at 1,000 rpm: 22.9 mph, 36.9 km/h consumption: 20.1 m/imp gal, 17 m/US gal, 13.9 l x 100 km.

ELECTRICAL EQUIPMENT 37 A alternator.

DIMENSIONS AND WEIGHT weight: plus 174 lb, 79 kg.

OPTIONALS Turbo-Hydramatic 250 C or 350 C automati transmission with 3 ratios (I 2.520, II 1.520, III 1, rev 1.930) max ratio of converter at stall 2, possible manual selection steering column or central lever, 2.290 or 2.730 - 2.410 or 2.730 axle ratio (for st. wagons only).

155 hp power team

(for California only)

See 110 hp power team, except for:

ENGINE 8 cylinders; 305 cu in, 4,999 cc (3.74 x 3.48 in 94.9 x 88.4 mm); max power (SAE net): 155 hp (113 kW) a 4,000 rpm; max torque (SAE net): 230 lb ft, 31.7 kg m (312 Nm at 2,400 rpm; max engine rpm: 4,400; 32 hp/l (24 kW/l); crankshaft bearings; 1 Rochester 17080502 downdraught 4 barrel carburettor; cooling: 27.6 imp pt, 32.8 US pt, 15.7 l.

TRANSMISSION axle ratio: 2.290 - st. wagons 2.410.

PERFORMANCE max speed: 108 mph, 174 km/h; power-weigh ratio: Sedan 20.2 lb/hp, (27.4 lb/kW), 9.1 kg/hp (12.4 kg/kW) speed in direct drive at 1,000 rpm: 31.4 mph, 50.2 km/h; con sumption: 20.1 m/imp gal, 17 m/US gal, 13.9 l x 100 km.

ELECTRICAL EQUIPMENT 37 A alternator.

DIMENSIONS AND WEIGHT weight: plus 174 lb, 79 kg.

Monte Carlo Series

PRICES EX WORKS:	$
1 Sport Coupé	6,12
2 Landau Coupé	6,41

For 120 hp engine add $ 180; for 155 hp engine add $ 295; fo 170 hp turbo engine add $ 500.

Power team:	Standard for:	Optional for:
110 hp	both	—
115 hp	both	—
120 hp	—	both
155 hp	—	both
155 hp (California)	—	both
170 hp	—	both

110 hp power team

(for California only)

ENGINE front, 4 stroke; 6 cylinders, Vee-slanted at 90°; 231 c in, 3,785 cc (3.80 x 3.40 in, 96.5 x 86.5 mm); compression ratic 8:1; max power (SAE net): 110 hp (81 kW) at 3,800 rpm; ma orque (SAE net): 190 lb ft, 26.1 kg m (256 Nm) at 1,600 rpm; nax engine rpm: 4,200; 29.3 hp/l (21.5 kW/l); cast iron block and head; 4 crankshaft bearings; valves: overhead, in line, push-rods and rockers, hydraulic tappets; camshafts: 1, at centre of Vee; lubrication: gear pump, full flow filter, 7.4 imp pt, 8.4 JS pt, 4 l; 1 Rochester 17080490 downdraught twin barrel carburettor; thermostatic air cleaner; exhaust system with catalytic converter; fuel feed: mechanical pump; water-cooled, 21.5 imp pt, 25.6 US pt, 12.2 l.

TRANSMISSION driving wheels: rear; gearbox: Turbo-Hydramatic 350 automatic transmission, hydraulic torque converter and planetary gears with 3 ratios, max ratio of converter at stall 2, possible manual selection; ratios: I 2.520, II 1.520, III 1, rev 1.930; lever: steering column; final drive: hypoid bevel; axle ratio: 2.410; width of rims: 6"; tyres: P 205/70 R x 14.

PERFORMANCE max speed: 100 mph, 161 km/h; power-weight ratio: 28.2 lb/hp, (38.3 lb/kW), 12.8 kg/hp (17.4 kg/kW); speed in direct drive at 1,000 rpm: 29.8 mph, 47.7 km/h; consumption: 23.7 m/imp gal, 20 m/US gal, 11.8 l x 100 km.

CHASSIS perimeter box-type with front and rear cross members; front suspension: independent, wishbones, coil springs, anti-roll bar, telescopic dampers; rear: rigid axle, lower trailing radius arms, upper oblique torque arms, coil springs, anti-roll bar, telescopic dampers.

STEERING recirculating ball, servo; turns lock to lock: 3.30.

BRAKES front disc (diameter 10.50 in, 26.7 cm), front internal radial fins, rear drum, servo; swept area: total 307.8 sq in, 1,985 sq cm.

ELECTRICAL EQUIPMENT 12 V; 2,500 W battery; 42 A alternator; Delco-Remy high energy ignition; 4 headlamps.

DIMENSIONS AND WEIGHT wheel base: 108.10 in, 274 cm; tracks: 58.50 in, 149 cm front, 57.80 in, 147 cm rear; length: 200,40 in, 509 cm; width: 71.50 in, 182 cm; height: 53.90 in, 137 cm; ground clearance: 8.20 in, 21 cm; weight: 3,104 lb, 1,408 kg; weight distribution: 57% front, 43% rear; turning circle: 40.5 ft, 12.4 m; fuel tank: 15.3 imp gal, 18.1 US gal, 68 l.

BODY coupé; 2 doors; 6 seats, bench front seats with built-in headrests.

OPTIONALS heavy-duty cooling; limited slip differential; heavy-duty battery; 70 A alternator; heavy-duty front and rear suspension; air-conditioning; heated rear window; electric windows; electric sunshine roof; removable glass roof panels; electric door lock; Appearance Group equipment; separate front seats.

115 hp power team

(not available in California)

See 110 hp power team, except for:

ENGINE 229 cu in, 3,752 cc (3.73 x 3.48 in, 94.9 x 88.4 mm); compression ratio: 8.6:1; max power (SAE net): 115 hp (84 kW) at 4,000 rpm; max torque (SAE net): 175 lb ft, 24.1 kg m (236 Nm) at 2,000 rpm; max engine rpm: 4,400; 34.1 hp/l (25.1 kW/l); 1 Rochester 17080130 downdraught twin barrel carburettor; cooling: 26.3 imp pt, 31.4 US pt, 15 l.

TRANSMISSION gearbox: Turbo-Hydramatic 200 C automatic transmission, hydraulic torque converter and planetary gears with 3 ratios, max ratio of converter at stall 2.35; possible manual selection; ratios: I 2.740, II 1.570, III 1, rev 2.070; lever: steering column.

PERFORMANCE power-weight ratio: 27 lb/hp, (36.7 lb/kW), 12.2 kg/hp (16.6 kg/kW).

ELECTRICAL EQUIPMENT 37 A alternator.

120 hp power team

(not available in California)

See 110 hp power team, except for:

ENGINE 8 cylinders; 267 cu in, 4,376 cc (3.50 x 3.48 in, 88.9 x 88.4 mm); compression ratio: 8.3:1; max power (SAE net): 120 hp (88 kW) at 3,600 rpm; max torque (SAE net): 215 lb ft, 29.6 kg m (290 Nm) at 2,000 rpm; max engine rpm: 4,000; 26.5 hp/l (26.8 kW/l); 5 crankshaft hearings; 1 Rochester 17080108 downdraught twin barrel carburettor; cooling: 38.3 imp pt, 45.6 US pt, 21.9 l.

TRANSMISSION gearbox: Turbo-Hydramatic 250 C automatic transmission, hydraulic torque converter and planetary gears with 3 ratios, max ratio of converter at stall 2, possible manual selection; ratios: I 2.520, II 1.520, III 1, rev 1.930; lever: steering column; axle ratio: 2.290.

PERFORMANCE max speed: 108 mph, 174 km/h; power-weight ratio: 26.8 lb/hp, (36.5 lb/kW), 12.1 kg/hp (16.5 kg/kW); speed in direct drive at 1,000 rpm: 31.4 mph, 50.2 km/h; consumption: 20.1 m/imp gal, 17 m/US gal, 13.9 l x 100 km.

ELECTRICAL EQUIPMENT 37 A alternator.

DIMENSIONS AND WEIGHT weight: plus 115 lb, 52 kg.

CHEVROLET Monte Carlo Sport Coupé Turbo

155 hp power team

(not available in California)

See 110 hp power team, except for:

ENGINE 8 cylinders; 305 cu in, 4,999 cc (3.74 x 3.48 in, 94.9 x 88.4 mm); compression ratio: 8.6:1; max power (SAE net): 155 hp (113 kW) at 4,000 rpm; max torque (SAE net): 240 lb ft, 33.1 kg m (324 Nm) at 1,600 rpm; max engine rpm: 4,400; 32 hp/l (24 kW/l); 5 crankshaft bearings; 1 Rochester 17080202 downdraught 4-barrel carburettor; cooling: 34.3 imp pt, 40.8 US pt, 19.6 l.

TRANSMISSION axle ratio: 2.290.

PERFORMANCE max speed: 105 mph, 170 km/h; power-weight ratio: 20.8 lb/hp, (28.3 lb/kW), 9.4 kg/hp (12.8 kg/kW); speed in direct drive at 1,000 rpm: 31.4 mph, 50.2 km/h; consumption: 20.1 m/imp gal, 17 m/US gal, 13.9 l x 100 km.

ELECTRICAL EQUIPMENT 37 A alternator.

DIMENSIONS AND WEIGHT weight: plus 124 lb, 56 kg.

OPTIONALS 2.730 axle ratio.

155 hp power team

(for California only)

CHEVROLET Monte Carlo Series (3.8-litre turbocharged engine)

See 110 hp power team, except for:

ENGINE 8 cylinders; 305 cu in, 4,999 cc (3.74 x 3.48 in, 94.9 x 88.4 mm); compression ratio: 8.6:1; max power (SAE net): 155 hp (113 kW) at 4,000 rpm; max torque (SAE net): 230 lb ft, 31.7 kg m (312 Nm) at 2,400 rpm; max engine rpm: 4,400; 31, hp/l (22.8 kW/l); 5 crankshaft bearings; 1 Rochester 17080502 downdraught 4-barrel carburettor; cooling: 34.3 imp pt, 40.8 US pt, 19.6 l.

TRANSMISSION axle ratio: 2.290.

PERFORMANCE max speed: 105 mph, 170 km/h; power-weight ratio: 20.8 lb/hp, (28.3 lb/kW), 9.4 kg/hp (12.8 kg/kW); speed in direct drive at 1,000 rpm: 31.4 mph, 50.2 km/h; consumption: 20.1 m/imp gal, 17 m/US gal, 13.9 l x 100 km.

ELECTRICAL EQUIPMENT 37 A alternator.

DIMENSIONS AND WEIGHT weight: plus 124 lb, 56 kg.

OPTIONALS 2.730 axle ratio.

170 hp power team

See 110 hp power team, except for:

ENGINE turbocharged; max power (SAE net): 170 hp (127 kW) at 4,000 rpm; max torque (SAE net): 265 lb ft, 36.6 kg m (359 Nm) at 2,400 rpm; max engine rpm: 4,500; 44.7 hp/l (44.3 kW/l); 1 Rochester 17080243 downdraught 4-barrel carburettor; turbo compressor coupled with exhaust system; cooling: 27 imp pt, 32.à US pt, 15.4 l.

TRANSMISSION axle ratio: 2.410 - California 2.730.

PERFORMANCE max speed: 113 mph, 181 km/h; power-weight ratio: 18.6 lb/hp, (25.2 lb/kW), 8.4 kg/hp (11.4 kg/kW); speed in direct drive at 1,000 rpm: 29.8 mph, 47.7 km/h; consumption: 21.3 m/imp gal, 18 m/US gal, 13.1 l x 100 km.

ELECTRICAL EQUIPMENT 55 A alternator.

DIMENSIONS AND WEIGHT weight: plus 56 lb, 25 kg.

Impala - Caprice Classic Series

PRICES EX WORKS:	$
1 Impala 4-dr Sedan	**6,289**
2 Impala 2-dr Coupé	**6,180**
3 Impala 4+1-dr 6-pass. St. Wagon	**6,780**
4 Impala 4+1-dr 9-pass St. Wagon	**6,925**
5 Caprice Classic 4-dr Sedan	**6,710**
6 Caprice Classic 2-dr Sport Coupé	**6,579**
7 Caprice Classic 2-dr Landau Coupé	**7,029**
8 Caprice Classic 4+1-dr 6-pass St. Wagon	**7,099**
9 Caprice Classic 4+1-dr 9-pass St. Wagon	**7,266**

For 120 hp engine add $ 180; for 155 hp engine add $ 295; for 105 hp diesel engine add $ 915.

Power team:	Standard for:	Optional for:
110 hp	1,2,5,6,7	—
115 hp	1,2,5,6,7	—
120 hp	3,4,8,9	1,2,5,6,7
155 hp	—	all
155 hp (California)	—	all
105 hp (diesel)	—	3,4,8,9

CHEVROLET Caprice Classic Sedan

110 hp power team

(for California only)

ENGINE front, 4 stroke; 6 cylinders, Vee-slanted at 90°; 231 cu in, 3,785 cc (3.80 x 3.40 in, 96.5 x 86.5 mm); compression ratio: 8:1; max power (SAE net): 110 hp (81 kW) at 3,800 rpm; max torque (SAE net): 190 lb ft, 26.1 kg m (256 Nm) at 1,600 rpm; max engine rpm: 4,200; 29.3 hp/l (21.5 kW/l); cast iron block and head; 4 crankshaft bearings; valves: overhead, in line, push-rods and rockers, hydraulic tappets; camshafts: 1, at centre of Vee; lubrication: gear pump, full flow filter, 7.4 imp pt, 8.4 US pt, 4 l; 1 Rochester 17080490 downdraught twin barrel carburettor; thermostatic air cleaner; exhaust system with catalytic converter; fuel feed: electric pump; water-cooled, 21.5 imp pt, 25.6 US pt, 12.2 l.

TRANSMISSION driving wheels: rear; gearbox: Turbo-Hydramatic 350 automatic transmission, hydraulic torque converter and planetary gears with 3 ratios, max ratio of converter at stall 2, possible manual selection; ratios: I 2.520, II 1.520, III 1, rev 1.930; lever: steering column; final drive: hypoid bevel; axle ratio: 2.730; width of rims: 6''; tyres: P 205/75 R x 15.

PERFORMANCE max speed: 99 mph, 159 km/h; power-weight ratio: Impala Sedan 30.6 lb/hp (41.5 lb/kW), 13.8 kg/hp (18.8 kg/kW); speed in direct drive at 1,000 rpm: 28.6 mph, 45.7 km/h; consumption: 21.2 m/imp gal, 18 m/US gal, 13.1 l x 100 km.

CHASSIS perimetral box-type with 2 cross members; front suspension: independent, wishbones, coil springs, anti-roll bar, telescopic dampers; rear: rigid axle, lower trailing radius arms, upper oblique torque arms, coil springs, anti-roll bar, telescopic dampers.

CHEVROLET Impala - Caprice Classic Series (5.7-litre diesel engine)

STEERING recirculating ball, servo; turns lock to lock: 3.30.

BRAKES front disc (diameter 11 in, 27.9 cm); front internal radial fins, rear drum, servo; swept area: total 329.8 sq in, 2,127 sq cm.

ELECTRICAL EQUIPMENT 12 V; 2,500 W battery; 42 A alternator; Delco-Remy high energy ignition; 4 headlamps.

DIMENSIONS AND WEIGHT wheel base: 116 in, 294 cm; tracks: 62 in, 157 cm front, 61 in, 154 cm rear; length: 212.10 in, 538 cm; width: 75.30 in, 191 cm; height: sedans 55.90 in, 142 cm - coupés 55.30 in, 140 cm; ground clearance: 11.10 in, 28 cm; weight: Impala Sedan 3,364 lb, 1,526 kg - Impala Coupé 3,348 lb, 1,518 kg - Caprice Classic Sedan 3,414 lb, 1,548 kg - Caprice Classic coupés 3,380 lb, 1,533 kg; weight distribution: 55% front, 45% rear; turning circle: 44.5 ft, 13.6 m; fuel tank: 17.6 imp gal, 21 US gal, 80 l.

BODY saloon/sedan, coupé, estate car/st. wagon; 6 seats, bench front seats with built-in headrests.

OPTIONALS central lever; limited slip differential; electric windows; heavy-duty suspension; P 215/70 R x 15 or P 225/70 R x 15 tyres; automatic speed control; heated rear window; tilt of steering wheel; electric sunshine roof; vinyl roof; air-conditioning; heavy-duty cooling; 70 A alternator.

115 hp power team

(not available in California)

See 110 hp power team, except for:

ENGINE 229 cu in, 3,752 cc (3.73 x 3.48 in, 94.9 x 88.4 mm); compression ratio: 8.6:1; max power (SAE net): 115 hp (84 kW) at 4,000 rpm; max torque (SAE net): 175 lb ft, 24.1 kg m (236 Nm) at 2,000 rpm ; max engine rpm: 4,400; 34.1 hp/l (25.1 kW/l); 1 Rochester 17080130 downdraught twin barrel carburettor; cooling: 26.3 imp pt, 31.4 US pt, 15 l.

TRANSMISSION gearbox: Turbo-Hydramatic 200 C automatic transmission, hydraulic torque converter and planetary gears with 3 ratios, max ratio of converter at stall 2.35, possible manual selection; ratios: I 2.740, II 1.570, III 1, rev 2.070; lever: steering column.

PERFORMANCE power-weight ratio: Impala Sedan 29.2 lb/hp, (39.7 lb/kW), 13.2 kg/hp (18 kg/kW).

ELECTRICAL EQUIPMENT 37 A alternator.

OPTIONALS Turbo-Hydramatic 250 C automatic transmission with 3 ratios (I 2.520, II 1.520, III 1, rev 1.930), hydralic torque converter and planetary gears, max ratio of converter at stall 2, central or steering column lever, possible manual selection.

120 hp power team

(not available in California)

See 110 hp power team, except for:

ENGINE 8 cylinders; 267 cu in, 4,376 cc (3.50 x 3.48 in, 88.9 x 88.4 mm); compression ratio: 8.3:1; max power (SAE net): 120 hp (88 kW) at 3,600 rpm; max torque (SAE net): 215 lb ft, 29.6 kg m (290 Nm) at 2,000 rpm; max engine rpm: 4,000; 36.5 hp/l (26.8 kW/l); 5 crankshaft bearings; 1 Rochester 17080108 downdraught twin barrel carburettor; fuel feed: mechanical pump; cooling: 38.3 imp pt, 45.6 US pt, 21.9 l.

TRANSMISSION gearbox: Turbo-Hydramatic 250 C automatic transmission, hydraulic torque converter and planetary gears with 3 ratios, max ratio of converter at stall 2, possible manual selection; ratios: I 2.520, II 1.520, III 1, rev 1.930; lever: steering column; axle ratio: 2.410 st. wagons 2.560; width of rims: st. wagons 7''; tyres: st. wagons P 225/75 R x 15.

PERFORMANCE max speed: 106 mph, 170 km/h; power-weight ratio: Impala Sedan 28,5 lb/hp, (38,7 lb/kW), 12,9 hp (17.5 kg/kW); speed in direct drive at 1,000 rpm: 32.4 mph, 51.8 km/h; consumption: 20.1 m/imp gal, 17 m/US gal, 13.9 l x 100 km.

STEERING turns lock to lock: 3.16 - st. wagons 3,30.

ELECTRICAL EQUIPMENT 37 A alternator.

DIMENSIONS AND WEIGHT (for st. wagons only) length: 215 in, 546 cm; width: 79.30 in, 201 cm; height: 57.70 in, 147 cm; ground clearance: 11.60 in, 29 cm; weight: Impala 3,893 lb, 1,766 kg - Caprice Classic 3,932 lb, 1,783 kg; turning circle: 45.1 ft, 13.8 m.

OPTIONALS (for st. wagons only) estate equipment.

155 hp power team

(not available in California)

See 110 hp power team, except for:

ENGINE 8 cylinders; 305 cu in, 4,999 cc (3.74 x 3.48 in, 94.9 x 88.4 mm); compression ratio: 8.6:1; max power (SAE net): 155 hp (113 kW) at 4,000 rpm; max torque (SAE net): 240 lb ft, 33.1 kg m (324 Nm) at 1,600 rpm; max engine rpm: 4,400; 32 hp/l (24 kW/l); 5 crankshaft bearings; 1 Rochester 17080202 downdraught 4-barrel carburettor; fuel feed: mechanical pump; cooling: 34.3 imp pt, 40.8 US pt, 19.6 l.

TRANSMISSION axle ratio: 2.410 - st. wagons 2.560.

PERFORMANCE max speed: 108 mph, 173 km/h; power-weight ratio: Impala Sedan 20.1 lb/hp, (30 lb/kW), 10 kg/hp (13.6 kg/kW); speed in direct drive at 1,000 rpm: 32.4 mph, 51.8 km/h; consumption: 20.1 m/imp gal, 17 m/US gal, 13.9 l x 100 km.

STEERING turns lock to lock: 3.16 - st. wagons 3.30.

ELECTRICAL EQUIPMENT 37 A alternator.

DIMENSIONS AND WEIGHT weight: plus 119 lb, 54 kg - st. wagons plus 9 lb, 4 kg.

OPTIONALS 3.080 axle ratio.

155 hp power team

(for California only)

See 110 hp power team, except for:

ENGINE 8 cylinders; 305 cu in, 4,999 cc (3.74 x 3.48 in, 94.9 x 88.4 mm); compression ratio: 8.6:1; max power (SAE net): 155 hp (113 kW) at 4,000 rpm; max torque (SAE net): 230 lb ft, 31.7 kg m (312 Nm) at 2,400 rpm; max engine rpm: 4,400; 32 hp/l (24 kW/l); 5 crankshaft bearings; valves: 1 Rochester 17080502 downdraught 4-barrel carburettor; fuel feed: mechanical pump; cooling: 34.3 imp pt, 40.8 US pt, 19.6 l.

TRANSMISSION axle ratio: 2.410 - st. wagons 2.560.

PERFORMANCE max speed: 108 mph, 173 km/h; power-weight ratio: Impala Sedan 20.1 lb/hp, (30 lb/kW), 10 kg/hp (13.6 kg/kW); speed in direct drive at 1,000 rpm: 32.4 mph, 51.8 km/h; consumption: 20.1 m/imp gal, 17 m/US gal, 13.9 l x 100 km.

STEERING turns lock to lock: 3.16 - st. wagons 3.30.

ELECTRICAL EQUIPMENT 37 A alternator.

DIMENSIONS AND WEIGHT weight: plus 119 lb, 54 kg - st. wagons plus 9 lb, 4 kg.

OPTIONALS 3.080 axle ratio.

105 hp (diesel) power team

See 110 hp power team, except for:

ENGINE 8 cylinders; 350 cu in, 5,736 cc (4.06 x 3.38 in, 103,9 x 86 mm); compression ratio: 22.5:1; max power (SAE net): 105 hp (78 kW) at 3,200 rpm; max torque (SAE net): 205 lb ft, 28.4 kg m (278 Nm) at 1,600 rpm; max engine rpm: 3,500; 18.4 hp/l (13.6 kW/l); 5 crankshaft bearings; lubrication: 12.4 imp pt, 14.8 US pt, 7,1 l; fuel feed: mechanical injection pump cooling: 28.7 imp pt, 33.9 US pt, 16.4 l.

CHEVROLET Corvette Coupé

:RFORMANCE max speed: 85 mph, 136 km/h; power-weight tio: Impala 39.51 lb/hp (53.1 lb/kW), 17.9 kg/hp (24.1 kg/kW); eed in direct drive at 1,000 rpm: 28,6 mph, 45.7 km/h; con-mption: 16.5 m/imp gal, 14 m/US gal, 16.9 l x 100 km.

.ECTRICAL EQUIPMENT 55 A alternator.

MENSIONS AND WEIGHT weight: Impala 4,148 lb, 1,881 kg - price Classic 4,185 lb, 1,898 kg.

BODY coupé, in plastic material; 2 doors; 2 seats, built-in headrests; electric windows; air-conditioning.

OPTIONALS Turbo-Hydramatic 350 automatic transmission with 3 ratios (I 2.520, II 1.520, III 1, rev 1.930), max ratio of converter at stall 2, possible manual selection, central lever, 3.550 axle ratio; Gymkhana suspension; heavy-duty battery; heated rear window; tinted glass; removable tinted glass roof panels; automatic speed control; aluminium wheels.

Corvette Coupé

ICE EX WORKS: $ 13,140

r 180 hp engine add $ 50; for 230 hp engine add $ 595.

190 hp power team

andard, not available in California)

NGINE front, 4 stroke; 8 cylinders; 350 cu in, 5,736 cc x 3.48 in, 101.6 x 88.4 mm); compression ratio: 8.2:1; max wer (SAE net): 190 hp (140 kW) at 4,400 rpm; max torque AE net): 280 lb ft, 38.6 kg m (378 Nm) at 2,400 rpm; max gine rpm: 5.000; 33.1 hp/l (24.4 kW/l); cast iron block and ad; 5 crankshaft bearings; valves: overhead, in line, push-ds and rockers, hydraulic tappets; camshafts: 1, at centre of e; lubrication: gear pump, full flow filter, 8.3 imp pt, 9.9 US 4.7 l, 1 Rochester 17059207 downdraught 4-barrel carburet-; thermostatic air cleaner; dual exhaust system with catalytic nverter; fuel feed: mechanical pump; water-cooled, 34.5 imp 41.4 US pt, 19.6 l, viscous coupling thermostatic fan.

ANSMISSION driving wheels: rear; clutch: single dry plate, mi-centrifugal; gearbox: mechanical gears: 4, fully synchro-zed; ratios: I 2.880, II 1.910, III 1.330, IV 1, rev 2.780; lever: ntral; final drive: hypoid bevel, limited slip differential; axle tio: 3.070; width of rims: 8"; tyres: P 225/70 R x 15.

:RFORMANCE max speed: 124 mph, 198 km/h; power-weight tio: 17 lb/hp (22.9 lb/kW), 7.7 kg/hp (10.4 kg/kW); speed in ect drive at 1,000 rpm: 30.6 mph, 49.3 km/h; consumption: .2 m/imp gal, 16 m/US gal, 14.7 l x 100 km.

IASSIS ladder frame with cross members; front suspension: dependent, wishbones, coil springs, anti-roll bar, telescopic mpers; rear: independent, wishbones, semi-axle as upper ms, transverse semi-elliptic leafspring, trailing radius arms, escopic dampers.

EERING recirculating ball, servo, tilt of steering wheel; turns k to lock: 2.92.

AKES disc (diameter 11.75 in, 30 cm), internal radial fins, rvo; swept area: total 498.30 sq in, 3,214 sq cm.

.ECTRICAL EQUIPMENT 12 V; 3,500 W battery; 63 A alter-tor; Delco-Remy high energy ignition; 4 retractable head-nps.

MENSIONS AND WEIGHT wheel base: 98 in, 249 cm; tracks: .70 in, 149 cm front, 59.50 in, 151 cm rear; length: 185.20 in, 0 cm; width: 69 in, 175 cm; height: 48 in, 122 cm; ground arance: 4.30 in, 10.9 cm; weight: 3,205 lb, 1,454 kg; turning cle: 38.6 ft, 11.8 m; fuel tank: 20 imp gal, 24 US gal, 91 l.

230 hp power team

(not available in California)

See 190 hp power team, except for:

ENGINE compression ratio: 8.9:1; max power (SAE net): 230 hp (169 kW) at 5,200 rpm; max torque (SAE net): 275 lb ft, 37.9 kg m (371 Nm) at 3,600 rpm; max engine rpm: 5,600; 40.1 hp/l (29.7 kW/l); 1 Rochester 17080228 downdraught 4-barrel car-burettor.

TRANSMISSION gearbox: Turbo-Hydramatic 350 automatic transmission (standard), hydraulic torque converter and planet-ary gears with 3 ratios, max ratio of converter at stall 2.35, possible manual selection; ratios: I 2.520, II 1.520, III 1, rev 1.930.

PERFORMANCE max speed: 131 mph, 211 km/h; power-weight ratio: 13.9 lb/hp (19 lb/kW), 6.3 kg/hp (8.6 kg/kW).

180 hp power team

(for California only)

See 190 hp power team, except for:

ENGINE 305 cu in, 4,999 cc (3.74 x 3.48 in, 94.9 x 88.4 mm); compression ratio: 8.6:1; max power (SAE net): 180 hp (132 kW) at 4,200 rpm; max torque (SAE net): 255 lb ft, 35.1 kg m (344 Nm) at 2,000 rpm; max engine rpm: 4,600; 36 hp/l (26 kW/l); 1 Rochester 18080504 downdraught 4-barrel carburettor; cooling: 35.8 imp pt, 42.2 US pt, 20.4 l.

TRANSMISSION gearbox: Turbo-Hydramatic 350 automatic transmission, hydraulic torque converter and planetary gears with 3 ratios, max ratios of converter at stall 2, possible manual selection; ratios: I 2.520, II 1.520, III 1, rev 1.930; lever: cen-tral.

PERFORMANCE max speed: 118 mph, 190 km/h; power-weight ratio: 17.8 lb/hp, (24.2 lb/kW), 8.1 kg/hp (10.9 kg/kW).

CHRYSLER USA

Le Baron Series

PRICES EX WORKS:	$
1 4-dr Sedan	**6,103**
2 2-dr Coupé	**5,948**
3 4+1-dr Town and Country St. Wagon	**6,894**
4 4-dr Salon Sedan	**6,348**
5 2-dr Salon Coupé	**6,229**
6 4+1-dr Salon St. Wagon	**6,305**
7 4-dr Medallion Sedan	**6,888**
8 2-dr Medallion Coupé	**6,783**

Power team:	Standard for:	Optional for:
90 hp	all	—
120 hp	—	all
155 hp	—	all

90 hp power team

ENGINE front, 4 stroke; 6 cylinders, vertical, in line; 225 cu in, 3,687 cc (3.40 x 4.12 in, 86.4 x 104.6 mm); compression ratio: 8.4:1; max power (SAE net): 90 hp (67 kW) at 3,600 rpm; max torque (SAE net): 160 lb ft, 22.1 kg m (217 Nm) at 1,600 rpm; max engine rpm: 4,400; 24.4 hp/l (18 kW/l); cast iron block and head; 4 crankshaft bearings; valves: overhead, in line, push-rods and rockers; camshafts: 1, side: lubrication: rotary pump, full flow filter, 6.7 imp pt, 8 US pt, 3.8 l; 1 Holley R-8831 A (California R-8719 A) downdraught single barrel carburettor; air cleaner; exhaust system with catalytic converter; fuel feed: mechanical pump; water-cooled, 19.2 imp pt, 23 US pt, 10.9 l.

TRANSMISSION driving wheels: rear; gearbox: Torqueflite automatic transmission, hydraulic torque converter and planet-ary gears with 3 ratios, max ratio of converter at stall 2.01, possible manual selection; ratios: I 2.740, II 1.540, III 1, rev 2.220; lever: steering column; axle ratio: 2.760 - for California

CHRYSLER Le Baron Medallion Sedan

90 HP POWER TEAM

and st. wagons 2.940; width of rims: 5.5"; tyres: P 195/75 R x 15.

PERFORMANCE max speed: 90 mph, 145 km/h; power-weight ratio: Sedan 37.7 lb/hp (50 lb/kW), 17.1 kg/hp (23 kg/kW); speed in direct drive at 1,000 rpm: 25.5 mph, 41 km/h: consumption: 20.2 m/imp gal, 17 m/US gal, 13.6 l x 100 km.

CHASSIS integral with isolated front cross member: front suspension: independent, wishbones, transverse torsion bars, anti-roll bar, telescopic dampers; rear: rigid axle, semi-elliptic leafsprings, telescopic dampers.

STEERING recirculating ball, servo; turns lock to lock: 3.50.

BRAKES front disc (diameter 10.82 in, 27.5 cm), front internal radial fins, rear drum, rear compensator, servo; swept area: total 355.24 sq in, 2,292 sq cm.

ELECTRICAL EQUIPMENT 12 V; 430 A battery; 60 A alternator; Essex or Prestolite transistorized ignition with electronic spark control; 4 headlamps.

DIMENSIONS AND WEIGHT wheel base: 112.70 in, 286 cm - coupés 108.70 in, 276 cm; tracks: 60 in, 152 cm front, 59.50 in, 151 cm rear; length: coupés 201.20 in, 511 cm - sedans 205.20 in, 521 cm - st. wagons 205.50 in, 522 cm; width: 74.20 in, 188 cm; height: coupés 53 in, 135 cm - sedans 55.30 in, 140 cm - st. wagons 55.70 in, 141 cm; ground clearance: 5.90 in, 15 cm - st. wagons 5.80 in, 14.7 cm; weight: Coupé 3,309 lb, 1,501 kg - Sedan 3,393 lb, 1,539 kg - St. Wagon 3,545 lb, 1,608 kg - Salon Coupé 3,320 lb, 1,506 kg - Salon Sedan 3,414 lb, 1,549 kg - Salon St. Wagon 3,585 lb, 1,622 kg - Medallion Coupé 3,375 lb, 1,531 kg - Medallion Sedan 3,493 lb, 1,584 kg; turning circle: 43.6 ft, 13.3 m - coupés 42.4 ft, 12.9 m; fuel tank: 15 imp gal, 18 US gal, 68 l.

BODY saloon/sedan, coupé, estate car/st. wagon; 6 seats, built-in headrests on front seats; separate front seats - sedans bench front seats.

OPTIONALS heavy-duty suspension (standard for st. wagon only); tilt of steering column; automatic speed control; electric windows; electric sunshine roof; halogen headlamps; vinyl roof; air-conditioning; T-bar roof; "LS" equipment.

120 hp power team

(not available in California)

See 90 hp power team, except for:

ENGINE 8 cylinders; 318 cu in, 5,211 cc (3.91 x 3.31 in, 99.2 x 84 mm); compression ratio: 8.5:1; max power (SAE net): 120 hp (89 kW) at 3,600 rpm; max torque (SAE net): 245 lb ft, 33.8 kg m (331 Nm) at 1,600 rpm; 23 hp/l (17 kW/l); 5 crankshaft bearings; valves: hydraulic tappets; camshafts: 1, at centre of Vee; 1 Carter BBD-82335 twin barrel carburettor; cooling; 25 imp pt, 30 US pt, 14.2 l.

TRANSMISSION axle ratio: 2.470 - st. wagons 2.450.

CHRYSLER Le Baron Town and Country Station Wagon

PERFORMANCE max speed: 102 mph, 164 km/h; power-weight ratio: Sedan 28.9 lb/hp (39.1 lb/kW), 13.1 kg/hp (17.7 kg/kW), speed in direct drive at 1,000 rpm: 25.5 mph, 41 km/h; consumption: 17.8 m/imp gal, 15 US gal, 15.4 l x 100 km.

ELECTRICAL EQUIPMENT 325 A battery.

DIMENSIONS AND WEIGHT weight: Coupé 3,389 lb, 1,537 kg - Sedan 3,476 lb, 1,577 kg - St. Wagon 3,627 lb, 1,645 kg - Salon Coupé 3,400 lb, 1,542 kg - Salon Sedan 3,497 lb, 1,586 kg - Salon St. Wagon 3,657 lb, 1,659 kg - Medallion Coupé 3,451 lb, 1,565 kg - Medallion Sedan 3,576 lb, 1,622 kg.

155 hp power team

See 90 hp power team, except for:

ENGINE max power (SAE net): 155 hp (115 kW) at 4,000 rpm; max torque (SAE net): 245 lb/ft, 33.8 kg m (325 Nm) at 2,000 rpm; 29.8 hp/l (22.1 kW/l); 1 Carter TQ-9295S 4-barrel carburettor (for California 1 Carter TQ-9234S 4-barrel carburettor); cooling: 25 imp pt, 30 US pt, 14.2 l.

TRANSMISSION axle ratio: 2.940 (2.47 - St. Wagon 2.45 for California).

PERFORMANCE max speed: 104 mph, 166 km/h; power weight ratio: Sedan 22.4 lb/hp (30.2 lb/kW), 10.2 kg/hp (13.7 kg/kW); consumption: 16.7 m/imp gal, 14 m/US gal, 16.8 l x 100 km.

ELECTRICAL EQUIPMENT 325 A battery.

DIMENSIONS AND WEIGHT weight: Coupé 3,389 lb, 1,537 kg Sedan 3,476 lb, 1,577 kg - St. Wagon 3,627 lb, 1,645 kg Salon Coupé 3,400 lb, 1,542 kg - Salon Sedan 3,497 lb, 1,58 kg - Salon St. Wagon 3,657 lb, 1,659 kg - Medallion Coup 3,451 lb, 1,565 kg - Medallion Sedan 3,576 lb, 1,622 kg.

Cordoba

PRICE EX WORKS: $ 6,601

90 hp power team

(not available in California)

ENGINE front, 4 stroke; 6 cylinders, vertical, in line; 225 cu i 3,687 cc (3.40 x 4.12 in, 86.4 x 104.6 mm); compression rati 8.4:1; max power (SAE net): 90 hp (67 kW) at 3,600 rpm; ma torque (SAE net): 160 lb ft, 22 kg m (217 Nm) at 1,600 rp max engine rpm: 4,400; 24.4 hp/l (17.9 kW/l); cast iron bloc and head; 4 crankshaft bearings; valves; overhead, in lin push-rods and rockers; camshaft: 1, side; lubrication: rota pump, full flow filter, 8.3 imp pt, 9.9 US pt, 4.7 l; 1 Holle R8831 A downdraught single barrel carburettor; air cleane exhaust system with catalytic converter; fuel feed: mechanic pump; water-cooled, 19.2 imp pt, 23 US pt, 10.9 l.

TRANSMISSION driving wheels: rear; gearbox: Torquefli automatic transmission, hydraulic torque converter and plane ary gears with 3 ratios, max ratio of converter at stall 1,9 possible manual selection; ratios: I 2.740, II 1.550, III 1, re 2.220; lever: steering column or central; axle ratio: 2.760; wid of rims: 5.5"; tyres: FR78 x 15.

PERFORMANCE max speed: 90 mph, 145 km/h; power-weig ratio: 37.5 lb/hp (51 lb/kW), 17 kg/hp (23.1 kg/kW); speed direct drive at 1,000 rpm: 25.5 mph, 41 km/m; consumptio 21.6 m/imp gal, 18 m/US gal, 13.1 l x 100 km.

CHASSIS integral with isolated front cross members: fro suspension: independent, wishbones, transverse torsion bar anti-roll bar, telescopic dampers; rear: rigid axle, semi-ellipt leafsprings, telescopic dampers.

STEERING recirculating ball, servo; turns lock to lock: 3.5

BRAKES front disc (diameter 11.58 in, 29.4 cm), front intern radial fins, rear drum, rear compensator, servo; swept are total 375.3 sq in, 2,421 sq cm.

ELECTRICAL EQUIPMENT 12 V; 430 A battery; 60 A altern tor; Essex or Prestolite or Mopar transistorized ignition wi electronic spark control; 2 headlamps.

DIMENSIONS AND WEIGHT wheel base: 112.70 in, 286 c tracks: 60 in, 152 cm front, 59.50 in, 151 cm rear; length: 2 in, 532 cm; width: 72.70 in, 185 cm; height: 53.30 in, 135 c ground clearance: 10.20 in, 26 cm; weight: 3,362 lb, 1,525 k weight distribution: 57% front, 43% rear; turning circle: 43.6 13.3 m; fuel tank: 15.1 imp gal, 18 US gal, 68 l.

BODY hardtop coupé; 2 doors, 6 seats, separate front sea with built-in headrests.

OPTIONALS 2.710 axle ratio; electronic air-conditioning; t computer; long life battery; heavy-duty cooling; heated re window with 65 A alternator; iodine headlamps; electric do

CHRYSLER Cordoba Crown

ıcks; electric windows; heavy-duty suspension; sunshine roof; -bar roof; Basic Group equipment; Light equipment; Sport ppearance equipment; Roadability equipment; Protection quipment; "300" equipment; convertible roof; Crown equip- ent.

120 hp power team

ɔptional, not available in California)

ee 90 hp power team, except for:

NGINE 8 cylinders; 318 cu in, 5,211 cc (3.91 x 3.31 in, 9.2 x 84 mm); compression ratio: 8.5:1; max power (SAE net): 20 hp (89 kW) at 3,600 rpm; max torque (SAE net): 245 lb ft, 3.8 kg m (332 Nm) at 1,600 rpm; max engine rpm: 4,000; 23 p/l (16.9 kW/l); 5 crankshaft bearings: valves: hydraulic tap- ets; camshafts: 1, at centre of Vee; Carter BBD-8233S owndraught twin barrel carburettor; water-cooled, 25 imp pt, 0 US pt, 14.2 l.

RANSMISSION gearbox ratios: I 2.450, II 1.450, III 1, rev .220; axle ratio: 2.470.

ERFORMANCE max speed: 106 mph, 170 km/h; power-weight atio: 28.8 lb/hp (39.2 lb/kW), 13 kg/hp (17.8 kg/kW); speed in rect drive at 1,000 rpm: 29.3 mph, 47.2 km/h; consumption: 6.8 m/imp gal, 14 m/US gal, 16.8 l x 100 km.

LECTRICAL EQUIPMENT 325 A battery.

IMENSIONS AND WEIGHT weight: 3,444 lb, 1,562 kg; weight istribution: 58% front, 42% rear.

PTIONALS 2.450 axle ratio.

155 hp power team

ɔptional, standard for California only)

ee 90 hp power team, except for:

NGINE 8 cylinders; 318 cu in, 5,211 cc (3.91 x 3.31 in, 9.2 x 84 mm); compression ratio: 8.5:1; max power (SAE net): 55 hp (114 kW) at 4,000 rpm; max torque (SAE net): 240 lb ft, 3.2 kg m (Nm) 29.7 hp/l (21.9 kW/l); 5 crankshaft bearings; alves: hydraulic tappets; camshafts: 1, at centre of Vee; 1 arter TQ 9295S downdraught 4-barrel carburettor; cooling: 25 np pt, 30 US pt, 14.2 l.

RANSMISSION gearbox ratios: I 2.450, II 1.450, III 1, rev 220; axle ratio: 2.940 - California 2.450.

ERFORMANCE max speed: 110 mph, 177 km/h; power-weight ratio: 22.3 lb/hp (30.3 lb/kW), 10.1 kg/hp (13.7 kg/kW); speed direct drive at 1,000 rpm: 31 mph, 49.7 km/h; consumption: 6.8 m/imp gal, 14 m/US gal, 16.8 l x 100 km.

LECTRICAL EQUIPMENT 325 A battery.

IMENSIONS AND WEIGHT weight: 3,444 lb, 1,562 kg; weight stribution: 58% front, 42% rear.

185 hp power team

ɔptional with "300" equipment only, not available in California)

ee 90 hp power team, except for:

NGINE 8 cylinders; 360 cu in, 5,900 cc (4 x 3.58 in, 01.6 x 89.6 mm); compression ratio: 8:1; max power (SAE et): 185 hp (138 kW) at 4,000 rpm; max torque (SAE net): 275 ft, 38.1 kg m (373 Nm) at 2,000 rpm; 31.9 hp/l (23.4 kW/l); 5 rankshaft bearings; valves: hydraulic tappets; camshafts: 1, at entre of Vee; 1 Carter TQ 9244S downdraught 4-barrel car- urettor; dual exhaust system with catalytic converter; cooling: 5 imp pt, 30 US pt, 14.2 l.

RANSMISSION gearbox ratios: I 2.450, II 1.450, III 1, rev .220; axle ratio: 2.940.

ERFORMANCE max speed: 115 mph, 185 km/h; power-weight atio: 19.6 lb/hp, (26.6 lb/kW), 8.8 kg/hp (12 kg/kW); speed in irect drive at 1,000 rpm: 28.7 mph, 46.2 km/h; consumption: 6.8 m/imp gal, 14 m/US gal, 16.8 l x 100 km.

LECTRICAL EQUIPMENT 430 A battery.

IMENSIONS AND WEIGHT weight: 3,621 lb, 1,642 kg; weight istribution: 58% front, 42% rear.

Newport - New Yorker

RICES EX WORKS:	$
Newport Pillared Hardtop	6,849
New Yorker Pillared Hardtop	10,459

ower team:	**Standard for:**	**Optional for:**
90 hp	1	—
20 hp	2	1
130 hp	—	both
155 hp	—	both

CHRYSLER Newport Pillared Hardtop

90 hp power team

(not available in California)

ENGINE front, 4 stroke; 6 cylinders, vertical, in line; 225 cu in, 3,687 cc (3.40 x 4.12 in, 86.4 x 104.6 mm); compression ratio: 8.4:1; max power (SAE net): 90 hp (67 kW) at 3,600 rpm; max torque (SAE net): 160 lb ft, 22 kg m (217 Nm) at 1,600 rpm; max engine rpm: 4,000; 24.4 hp/l (17.9 kW/l); cast iron block and head; 4 crankshaft bearings; valves: overhead, in line, push-rods and rockers: camshafts: 1, side: lubrication: rotary pump, full flow filter, 8.3 imp pt, 9.9 US pt, 4.7 l; 1 Holley R-8831A downdraught carburettor; air cleaner; exhaust system with catalytic converter; fuel feed: mechanical pump; water-cooled, 19.2 imp pt, 23 US pt, 10.9 l.

TRANSMISSION driving wheels: rear; gearbox: Torqueflite automatic transmission, hydraulic torque converter and planetary gears with 3 ratios, max ratio of converter at stall 1.9, possible manual selection; ratios: I 2.740, II 1,540, III 1, rev 2.220; lever: steering column; final drive: hypoid bevel; axle ratio: 2.940; width of rims: 5.5"; tyres: P195/75R x 15.

PERFORMANCE max speed: 93 mph, 149 km/h; power-weight ratio: 40.6 lb/hp (55.2 lb/kW), 13.8 kg/hp (18.8 kg/kW); speed in direct drive at 1,000: 25.9 mph, 41.7 km/h; consumption: 20.5 m/imp gal, 17 m/US gal, 13.8 l x 100 km.

CHASSIS integral with isolated front cross members; front suspension: independent, wishbones lower trailing links, longitudinal torsion bars, anti-roll bar telescopic dampers; rear: rigid axle, semi-elliptic leafsprings, telescopic dampers.

STEERING recirculating ball, servo; turns lock to lock: 3.50.

BRAKES front disc (diameter 11.58 in, 29.4 cm), front internal radial fins, rear drum, rear compensator, servo; swept area: total 375.3 sq in, 2,421 sq cm.

ELECTRICAL EQUIPMENT 12 V; 430 A battery; 65 A alternator; Essex or Prestolite or Mopar transistorized ignition with electronic spark control; 4 headlamps.

DIMENSIONS AND WEIGHT wheel base: 118.50 in, 301 cm; tracks: 61.90 in, 157 cm front, 62 in, 157 cm rear; length: 220.20 in, 559 cm; width: 77.10 in, 196 cm; height: 54.50 in, 138 cm; ground clearance: 5.30 in, 13.5 cm; weight: 3,654 lb, 1,657 kg; turning circle: 45.8 ft, 13.9 m; fuel tank: 17.4 imp gal, 20.9 US gal, 79 l.

BODY hardtop; 4 doors; 6 seats, separate front seats with built-in headrests.

OPTIONALS heavy-duty cooling; limited slip differential; light alloy wheels; P205/75R x 15 tyres; P225/70R x 15, FR70 x 15 or GR70 x 15 tyres with 7" wide rims; heavy-duty suspension; tilt of steering wheel; automatic speed control; reclining backrests; anti-roll bar on rear suspension; electric windows; tinted glass; heated rear window with 100 A alternator; electric sunshine roof; vinyl roof; halogen headlamps; air-conditioning; light equipment; heavy-duty equipment.

CHRYSLER New Yorker Fifth Avenue Pillared Hardtop

120 hp power team

(not available in California)

See 90 hp power team, except for:

ENGINE 8 cylinders; 318 cu in, 5,211 cc (3.91 x 3.31 in, 99.2 x 84 mm); compression ratio: 8.5:1; max power (SAE net): 120 hp (89 kW) at 4,000 rpm; max torque (SAE net): 245 lb ft, 33.8 kg m (332 Nm) at 1,600 rpm; 23 hp/l (16.9 kW/l); 5 crankshaft bearings; valves: hydraulic tappets; camshafts: 1, at centre of Vee; 1 Carter BBD 8233S downdraught twin barrel carburettor; cooling: 25 imp pt 30 US pt, 14.2 l.

TRANSMISSION gearbox ratios: I 2.450, II 2.450, III 1; axle ratio: 2.450; tyres; (for New Yorker only) P205/75 R x 15.

PERFORMANCE max speed: 96 mph, 155 km/h; power-weight ratio: Newport 31.2 lb/hp (42.4 lb/kW) 14.1 kg/hp (19.2 kg/kW); consumption: 19.2 m/imp gal, 16 m/US gal, 14.7 l x 100 km.

ELECTRICAL EQUIPMENT 325 A battery.

DIMENSIONS AND WEIGHT weight: Newport 3,740 lb, 1,696 kg - New Yorker 3,920 lb, 1,778 kg.

OPTIONALS electronic air-conditioning; trip computer; (for New Yorker only) Fifth Avenue Edition equipment.

130 hp power team

(optional, not available in California)

See 90 hp power team, except for:

ENGINE 8 cylinders; 360 cu in, 5,900 cc (4 x 3.58 in, 101.6 x 89.6 mm); max power (SAE net): 130 hp (97 kW) at 3,200 rpm; max torque (SAE net): 255 lb ft, 35.9 kg m (345 Nm) at 2,000 rpm; 22 hp/l (16.2 kW/l); 5 crankshaft bearings; valves: hydraulic tappets; camshafts: 1, at centre of Vee; 1 Carter BBD 8237S downdraught twin barrel carburettor; cooling: 26.6 imp pt, 31.9 US pt, 15.1 l.

TRANSMISSION gearbox ratios: I 2.450, II 1.450, III 1; axle ratio: 2.450.

PERFORMANCE max speed: 99 mph, 160 km/h; power-weight ratio: Newport 29.3 lb/hp (39.8 lb/kW), 13.3 kg/hp (18 kg/kW); speed in direct drive at 1,000 rpm: 27.6 mph, 44.4 km/h; consumption: 16.8 m/imp gal, 14 m/US gal, 16.8 l x 100 km.

ELECTRICAL EQUIPMENT 430 A battery.

DIMENSIONS AND WEIGHT weight: Newport 3,806 lb, 1,726 kg - New Yorker 3,960 lb, 1,796 kg.

OPTIONALS 3.210 axle ratio; electronic air-conditioning; trip computer; (for New Yorker only) Fifth Avenue Edition equipment.

155 hp power team

(optional, standard for California only)

See 90 hp power team, except for:

ENGINE 8 cylinders; 318 cu in, 5,211 cc (3.91 x 3.31 in, 99.2 x 84 mm); compression ratio: 8.5:1; max power (SAE net): 155 hp (114 kW) at 4,000 rpm; max torque (SAE net): 245 lb ft, 33.8 kg m (331 Nm) at 1,600 rpm; 29.7 hp/l (21.9 kW/l); 5 crankshaft bearings; valves: hydraulic tappets; camshafts: 1, at centre of Vee; 1 Carter TQ 9295S (California TQ 9234S) downdraught 4-barrel carburettor; cooling: 25 imp pt, 30 US pt, 14.2 l.

TRANSMISSION gearbox ratios: I 2.450, II 1.450, III 1, axle ratio: 2.940 - California 2.450.

PERFORMANCE max speed: 103 mph, 165 km/h - for California 114 mph, 182 km/h; power-weight ratio: Newport 241 lb/hp (32.8 lb/kW), 10.9 kg/kW (14.9 kg/kW); speed in direct drive at 1,000 rpm: 25.6 mph, 41.2 km/h - for California 28.8 mph, 37.9 km/h; consumption: 15.6 m/imp gal, 13 m/US gal, 18.1 l x 100 km.

ELECTRICAL EQUIPMENT 325 A battery.

DIMENSIONS AND WEIGHT weight: Newport 3,740 lb, 1,696 kg - New Yorker 3,920 lb, 1,778 kg.

OPTIONALS electronic air-conditioning; trip computer; (for New Yorker only) Fifth Avenue Edition equipment.

DAYTONA USA

Migi

PRICE EX WORKS: $ 8,500

ENGINE Volkswagen, rear, 4 stroke; 4 cylinders, horizontally opposed; 96.7 cu in, 1,584 cc (3.37 x 2.72 in, 85.5 x 69 mm); compression ratio: 7.2:1; max power (DIN): 56 hp (41 kW) at 4,200 rpm; max torque (DIN): 80 lb ft, 11 kg m (108 Nm) at 3,000 rpm; max engine rpm: 4,600; 35.4 hp/l (26 kW/l); block with cast iron liners and light alloy fins, light alloy head; 4 crankshaft bearings; valves: overhead, push-rods and rockers; camshafts: 1, central, lower; lubrication: gear pump, filter in sump, oil cooler, 4.4 imp pt, 5.3 US pt, 2.5 l; 2 Solex H 32 twin barrel carburettors; fuel feed: mechanical pump; air-cooled.

TRANSMISSION driving wheels: rear; clutch: single dry plate; gearbox: mechanical; gears: 4, fully synchronized; ratios: I 3.800, II 2.060, III 1.320, IV 0.880, rev 3.880; lever: central; final drive: spiral bevel; axle ratio: 4.125; width of rims: 5"; tyres: 5.60 x 15.

PERFORMANCE max speed: about 90 mph, 145 km/h; power-weight ratio: 24.6 lb/hp (33.4 lb/kW), 11.1 kg/hp (15.1 kg/kW); speed in top at 1,000 rpm: 21.2 mph, 34.2 km/h; consumption: 37.2 m/imp gal, 31 m/US gal, 7.6 l x 100 km.

CHASSIS backbone platform; front suspension: independent, twin swinging longitudinal trailing arms, transverse laminated torsion bars, anti-roll bar, telescopic dampers; rear: independent, swinging semi-axles, swinging longitudinal trailing arms, transverse torsion bars, telescopic dampers.

STEERING worm and roller; turns lock to lock: 2.60.

BRAKES front disc (diameter 10.94 in, 27.8 cm), rear drum; lining area: front 11.8 sq in, 76 sq cm, rear 56.4 sq in, 364 sq cm, total 68.2 sq in, 440 sq cm.

ELECTRICAL EQUIPMENT 12 V; 36 Ah battery; 350 W dynamo; Bosch distributor; 4 headlamps.

DIMENSIONS AND WEIGHT wheel base: 94.50 in, 240 cm; tracks: 51.50 in, 131 cm front, 53 in, 134 cm rear; length: 137 in, 348 cm; width: 60 in, 152 cm; ground clearance: 5.91 in, 15 cm; weight: 1,375 lb, 624 kg; turning circle: 36.1 ft, 11 m; fuel tank: 9 imp gal, 10.8 US gal, 41 l.

BODY roadster, in fiberglass material; 2 doors; 2 seats; tonneau cover.

OPTIONALS luxury interior; wire wheels; wooden steering wheel.

DAYTONA Migi

DODGE USA

Omni Series

PRICES EX WORKS: £

4+1-dr Hatchback	4,925
O24 2+1-dr Hatchback	5,271

ENGINE front, transverse, slanted 15° to front, 4 stroke; 4 cylinders, in line; 104.7 cu in, 1,714 cc (3.13 x 3.40 in, 79.5 x 86.4 mm); compression ratio: 8.2:1; max power (SAE net): 65 hp (48 kW) at 5,200 rpm; max torque (SAE net): 85 lb ft, 11.7 kg m (115 Nm) at 2,400 rpm; max engine rpm: 6,500; 37.9 hp/l (28 kW/l); cast iron block, light alloy head; 5 crankshaft bearings; valves: overhead, in line, thimble tappets; camshafts: 1, overhead, cogged belt; lubrication: gear pump, full flow filter, 6.7 imp pt, 8 US pt, 3.8 l; 1 Holley R-9108A (R-8676A for California only) downdraught twin barrel carburettor; air cleaner; exhaust system with catalytic converter; fuel feed: mechanical pump; watercooled, 10 imp pt, 12 US pt, 5.7 l.

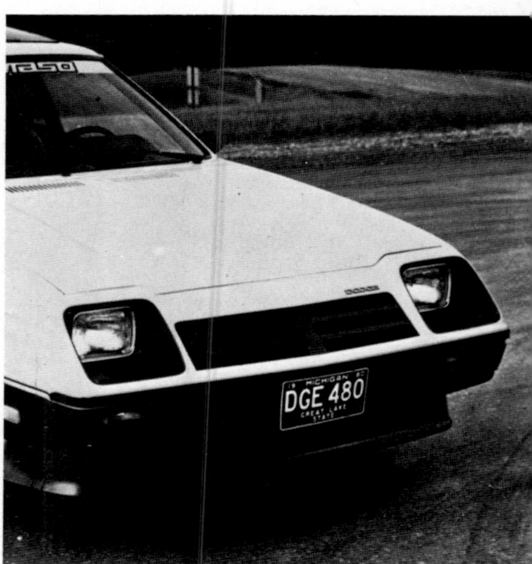

DODGE Omni De Tomaso

TRANSMISSION driving wheels: front; clutch: single dry plate (diaphragm); gearbox: mechanical; gears: 4, fully synchronized; ratios: I 3.450, II 1.940, III 1.290, IV 0.970, rev 3.170; lever: central; final drive: spiral bevel; axle ratio: 3.370; width rims 2-dr 5"-4-dr 4.5"; tyres: 2-dr P175/75R x 13. - 4-dr P155/80R x 13.

PERFORMANCE max speed: 91 mph, 146 km/h; power-weight ratio: 2-dr 33.8 lb/hp (45.7 lb/kW), 15.3 kg/hp (20.7 kg/W) - 4-dr 31.3 lb/hp (44.8 lb/kW), 15 kg/hp (20.3 kg/kW); speed in top at 1,000 rpm: 16.7 mph, 26.9 km/h; consumption: 28.8 m/imp gal, 24 m/US gal, 9.8 l x 100 km.

CHASSIS integral; front suspension: independent, by McPherson, lower wishbones, anti-roll bar, coil springs/telescopic damper struts; rear: independent, semi-trailing arms, coil springs, telescopic dampers.

STEERING rack-and-pinion; turns lock to lock: 4.

BRAKES front disc (diameter 8.98 in, 22.8 cm), front internal radial fins, rear drum; swept area: total 197.5 sq in, 1,274 sq cm.

DODGE Omni 024 Hatchback

LECTRICAL EQUIPMENT 12 V; 310 A battery; 65 A alterna-r; Essex or Prestolite transistorized ignition with electronic ɔark control; 2 headlamps.

IMENSIONS AND WEIGHT wheel base: 2-dr 96.70 in, 246 cm 4-dr 99.20 in, 252 cm; tracks: 56 in, 142 cm front, 55.60 in, 41 cm rear; length: 2-dr 173.30 in, 440 cm - 4-dr 164.80 in, 19 cm; width: 2-dr 66.70 in, 159 cm - 4-dr 65.80 in, 167 cm; eight: 2-dr 51.40 in, 131 cm - 4-dr 53.70 in, 136 cm; ground earance: 5 in, 12.7 cm; weight: 2-dr 2,196 lb, 996 kg - 4-dr ,154 lb, 977 kg; turning circle: 36.1 ft, 11 m; fuel tank: 10.8 ηp gal, 13 US pt, 49 l.

ODY 4 seats, separate front seats with built-in headrests; ɘated rear window.

PTIONALS Torquelite automatic transmission, hydraulic tor-ue converter and planetary gears with 3 ratios (I 2.470, II ,470, III 1, rev 2.100) max ratio of converter at stall 1.97, ossible manual selection, central lever, 3.480 axle ratio; P165/ 5R x 13 tyres (for 2-dr only); P175/75R x 13 tyres with 5" wide ms; P185/70R x 13 tyres with 5" wide rims (for 2-dr only); 185/70 R x 13 tyres with 5.5" wide rims (for 2-dr only); heavy-uty suspension; power steering; servo brake; reclining back-ests; rear window wiper-washer; vinyl roof; sunshine roof; r-conditioning; Custom or Premium Woodgrain equipment (for -dr only); Sport or De Tomaso equipment (for 2-dr only).

Aspen Series

RICES EX WORKS:	$
4-dr Sedan	4,859
2-dr Coupé	4,742
4-dr Sedan Special	4,994
2-dr Coupé Special	4,977
4+1-dr St. Wagon	5,101

ower team:	Standard for:	Optional for:
90 hp	all	—
90 hp (California)	all	—
20 hp	—	all
55 hp	—	all

90 hp power team

(not available in California)

NGINE front, 4 stroke; 6 cylinders, vertical, in line; 225 cu in, 687 cc (3.40 x 4.12 in, 86.4 x 104.6 mm); compression ratio: 4:1; max power (SAE net): 90 hp (66 kW) at 3,600 rpm; max rque (SAE net): 160 lb ft, 22.1 kgm (217 Nm) at 1,600 rpm; ax engine rpm: 4,400; 24.4 hp/l (18 kW/l); cast iron block and ead; 4 crankshaft bearings; valves: overhead, in line; push-ods and rockers; camshafts: 1, side; lubrication: rotary pump, ll flow filter, 8.3 imp pt, 9.9 US pt, 4.7 l; 1 Holley R-8718A Special models R8831A) downdraught single barrel carburet-r; thermostatic air cleaner; exhaust system with catalytic onverter; fuel feed: mechanical pump; water-cooled, 19.2 imp , 23 US pt, 10.9 l.

RANSMISSION driving wheels: rear; clutch: single dry plate; earbox: mechanical (Special models, Torqueflite automatic ansmission hydraulic torque converter and planetary gears ith 3 ratios, max ratio of converter at stall 2.01, possible anual selection; ratios: I 2.450, II 1.450, III 1, rev 2.220); ears: 3, fully synchronized; ratios: I 3.080, II 1.700, III 1, rev 900; lever: central - Special models steering column or cen-al; final drive: hypoid bevel; axle ratio: 3.230 - Special models 2.760 - St. Wagon 3.210; width of rims: 5" - St. Wagon 5.5"; tyres: P195/75 R x 14.

PERFORMANCE max speed: 90 mph, 145 km/h - Special models 105 mph, 165 km/h; power-weight ratio: sedans 34.6 lb/hp (47.2 lb/kW), 15.7 kg/hp (21.4 kg/kW); speed in direct drive at 1,000 rpm: 20.4 mph, 32.9 km/h; consumption: 20.5 m/imp gal, 17 m/US gal, 13.8 l x 100 km.

CHASSIS integral with front cross members; front suspension: independent, wishbones, transverse torsion bars, anti-roll bar, telescopic dampers; rear: rigid axle, semielliptic leafsprings, anti-roll bar, telescopic dampers.

STEERING recirculating ball; turns lock to lock: 5.30.

BRAKES front disc (diameter 10.82 in, 27.5 cm), front internal radial fins, rear drum, rear compensator; swept area: total 355.24 sq in, 2,292 sq cm.

ELECTRICAL EQUIPMENT 12 V; 325 A battery; 60 A alterna-tor; Essex or Prestolite or Mopar transistorized ignition with electronic spark control; 2 headlamps.

BODY sedans and st. wagon 6 seats - coupés 5 seats, separate front seats with built-in headrests.

DIMENSIONS AND WEIGHT wheel base: 112.70 in, 286 cm - coupés 108.70 in, 276 cm; tracks: 60 in, 152 cm front, 58.50 in, 149 cm rear; length: 201.20 in, 511 cm - coupés 197.20 in, 501 cm; width: 72.80 in, 185 cm; height: coupés 53.30 in, 135 cm - sedans 55.30 in, 140 cm - St. Wagon 55.70 in, 141 cm; ground clearance: 5.90 in, 15 cm - St. Wagon 6.20 in, 15.7 cm; weight: coupés 3,050 lb, 1,383 kg - sedans 3,114 lb, 1,413 kg - St. Wagon 3,323 lb, 1,507 kg; turning circle: 43.5 ft, 13.2 m - coupés 42.1 ft, 12.8 m; fuel tank: 15 imp gal, 18 US gal, 68 l - St. Wagon 16.3 imp gal, 19.5 US gal, 74 l.

OPTIONALS limited slip differential; 3.210 axle ratio; Torqueflite automatic transmission with 3 ratios (I 2.450, II 1.450, III 1, rev 2.220), max ratio of converter at stall 2.01, possible manual selection, steering column or central lever, 2.760 or 2.710 axle ratio (except Special models); 4-speed fully synchronized mechanical gearbox with overdrive/top (I 3.090, II 1.670, III 1, IV 0.710, rev 3), central lever, 3.230 or 3.210 axle ratio; heavy-duty cooling; P195/75 R x 14 or P205/75 R x 14 tyres with 5.5" wide rims; FR70 x 14 tyres with 6" wide rims; light alloy wheels; heavy-duty suspension; power steering; tilt of steering wheel; servo brake; heavy-duty battery; tinted glass; electric windows; heated rear window; automatic speed control; vinyl roof; luxury equipment; air-conditioning; Custom equipment; Special Edition equipment; R/T equipment (for coupés only); Sunrise equipment (for coupés only); Sport equipment (for St. Wagon only); value equipment (sedans and coupés only); T-Bar roof (for coupés only).

90 hp power team

(for California only)

See 90 hp power team, except for:

ENGINE 1 Holley R 8719A downdraught single barrel carburettor.

TRANSMISSION gearbox: Torqueflite automatic transmission (standard), hydraulic torque converter and planetary gears with 3 ratios, max ratio of converter at stall 2.01, possible manual selection; ratios: I 2.450, II 1.450, III 1, rev 2.220; lever: steering column or central; axle ratio: 2.940.

PERFORMANCE consumption: 19.2 m/imp gal, 16 m/US gal, 14.7 l x 100 km.

OPTIONALS 4-speed fully synchronized mechanical gearbox with overdrive/top not available.

120 hp power team

(not available in California)

See 90 hp power team, except for:

ENGINE 8 cylinders; 318 cu in, 5,211 cc (3.91 x 3.31 in, 99.2 x 84 mm); compression ratio: 8.5:1; max power (SAE net): 120 hp (89 kW) at 3600 rpm; max torque (SAE net): 245 lb ft, 33.9 kgm (332 Nm) at 1,600 rpm; 23.1 hp/l (16.9 kW/l); 5 crankshaft bearings; valves: hydraulic tappets; camshafts: 1 at centre of Vee; 1 Carter BBD 8233S downdrought twin barrel carburettor; cooling: 25 imp pt, 30 US pt, 14.2 l.

TRANSMISSION gearbox: Torqueflite automatic transmission (standard), hydraulic torque converter and planetary gears with 3 ratios, max ratio of converter at stall 1.90, possible manual selection; ratios: I 2.450, II 1.450, III 1, rev 2.220; lever: steering column or central; axle ratio: 2.470 - St. Wagon 2.450.

PERFORMANCE max speed: 102 mph, 164 km/h; power-weight ratio: sedans 26.9 lb/hp (36,6 lb/kW), 12.2 kg/hp (16.6 kg/kW);

DODGE Aspen Sunrise Coupé

120 HP POWER TEAM

speed in direct drive at 1,000 rpm: 25.5 mph, 41 km/h; consumption: 18 m/imp gal, 15 m/US gal, 15.7 l x 100 km.

DIMENSIONS AND WEIGHT weight: coupés 3,258 lb, 1,478 kg - sedans 3,318 lb, 1,505 kg - St. Wagon 3,481 lb, 1,579 kg; fuel tank: 16.3 imp gal, 19.5 US gal, 74 l.

OPTIONALS 4-speed fully synchronized mechanical gearbox with overdrive/top not available.

155 hp power team

(for California only)

See 90 hp power team, except for:

ENGINE 8 cylinders; 318 cu in, 5,211 cc (3.91 x 3.31 in, 99.2 x 84 mm); compression ratio: 8.5:1; max power (SAE net): 155 hp (114 kW) at 4,000 rpm; max torque (SAE net): 245 lb ft, 33.8 kg m (331 Nm) at 1,600 rpm; 29.7 hp/l (21.9 kW/l); 5 crankshaft bearings; valves: hydraulic tappets; camshafts: 1, at centre of Vee; 1 Carter TQ9234 downdraught 4-barrel carburettor; cooling: 25 imp pt, 30 US pt, 14.2 l.

TRANSMISSION gearbox: Torqueflite automatic transmission (standard), hydraulic torque converter and planetary gears with 3 ratios, max ratio of converter at stall 1.90, possible manual selection; ratios: I 2.450, II 1.450, III 1, rev 2.220; lever: steering column or central; axle ratio: 2.470 - St. Wagon 2.450.

PERFORMANCE max speed: 103 mph, 165 km/h; power-weight ratio: sedans 21.4 lb/hp (29.1 lb/kW), 9.7 kg/hp (13.2 kg/km); speed in direct drive at 1,000 rpm: 25.6 mph, 41.2 km/h; consumption: 18 m/imp gal, 15 m/US gal, 15.7 l x 100 km.

DIMENSIONS AND WEIGHT weight: coupés 3,258 lb, 1,478 kg - sedans 3,318 lb, 1,505 kg - St. Wagon 3,481 lb, 1,579 kg; fuel tank: 16.3 imp gal, 19.5 US gal, 74 l.

OPTIONALS 4-speed fully synchronized mechanical gearbox with overdrive/top not available.

Diplomat Series

PRICES EX WORKS:		$
1	4-dr Sedan	5,832
2	2-dr Coupé	5,681
3	4+1-dr St. Wagon	5,971
4	Salon 4-dr Sedan	6,119
5	Salon 2-dr Coupé	5,997
6	Salon 4+1-dr St. Wagon	6,661
7	Medallion 4-dr Sedan	6,698
8	Medallion 2-dr Coupé	6,551

Power team:	Standard for:	Optional for:
90 hp	all	—
120 hp	—	all
155 hp	—	all

90 hp power team

ENGINE front, 4 stroke; 6 cylinders, vertical, in line; 225 cu in, 3,687 cc (3.40 x 4.12 in, 86.4 x 104.6 mm); compression ratio: 8.4:1; max power (SAE net): 90 hp (67 kW) at 3,600 rpm; max torque (SAE net): 160 lb ft, 22.1 kg m(217 Nm) at 1,600 rpm; max engine rpm: 4,400; 24.4 hp/l (18 kW/l); cast iron block and head; 4 crankshaft bearings; valves: overhead, in line, push-rods and rockers; camshafts: 1, side; lubrication: rotary pump, full flow filter, 6.7 imp pt, 8 US pt, 3.8 l; 1 Holley R-8831A (California R-8719A) downdraught single barrel carburettor; air cleaner; exhaust system with catalytic converter; fuel feed: mechanical pump; water-cooled, 19.2 imp pt, 23 US pt, 10.9 l.

TRANSMISSION driving wheels: rear; gearbox: Torqueflite automatic transmission, hydraulic torque converter and planetary gears with 3 ratios, max ratio of converter at stall 2.01, possible manual selection; ratios: I 2.740, II 1.540, III 1, rev 2.220; lever: steering column; axle ratio: 2.760 - California 2.940 - St. Wagon 2.940; width of rims: 5.5"; tyres: P195/75 R x 15.

PERFORMANCE max speed: 90 mph, 145 km/h; power-weight ratio: Sedan 37.7 lb/hp (50 lb/kW), 17.1 kg/hp (23 kg/kW); speed in direct drive 1,000 rpm: 25.5 mph, 41 km/h; consumption: 20.2 m/imp gal, 17 m/US gal, 13.6 l x 100 km.

CHASSIS integral with isolated front cross member; front suspension: independent, wishbones, transverse torsion bars, anti-roll bar, telescopic dampers; rear: rigid axle, semi-elliptic leafsprings, telescopic dampers.

STEERING recirculating ball, servo; turns lock to lock: 3.50.

BRAKES front disc (diameter 10.82 in, 27.5 cm), front internal radial fins, rear drum, rear compensator, servo; swept area: total 355.24 sq in, 2,292 sq cm.

ELECTRICAL EQUIPMENT 12 V; 430 A battery; 60 A alternator; Essex or Prestolite transistorized ignition with electronic spark control; 4 headlamps.

DODGE Aspen Station Wagon

DIMENSIONS AND WEIGHT wheel base: 112.70 in, 286 cm - coupés 108.7 in, 276 cm; tracks: 60 in, 152 cm front, 59.50 in, 151 cm rear; length: coupés 201.20 in, 511 cm - sedans 205.20 in, 521 cm - St. Wagon 205.50 in, 522 cm; width: 74.20 in, 188 cm; height: coupés 53 in, 135 cm - sedans 55.30 in, 140 cm - St. Wagon 55.70 in, 141 cm; ground clearance: 5.90 in, 15 cm - St. Wagon 5.80 in, 14.7 cm; weight: Coupé 3,309 lb, 1,501 kg - Sedan 3,393 lb, 1,539 kg - St. Wagon 3,545 lb, 1,608 kg - Salon Coupé 3,320 lb, 1,506 kg - Salon Sedan 3,414 lb, 1,549 kg - Salon St. Wagon 3,585 lb, 1,622 kg - Medallion Coupé 3,375 lb, 1,531 kg - Medallion Sedan 3,493 lb, 1,584 kg; turning circle: 43.6 ft, 13.3 in - coupés 42.4 ft, 12.9 m; fuel tank: 15 imp gal, 18 US gal, 68 l.

BODY 6 seats, separate front seats - Sedan bench front seats; built-in headrests.

OPTIONALS heavy-duty suspension (standard for St. Wagon); tilt of steering wheel; automatic speed control; electric windows; electric sunshine roof; halogen lamps; vinyl roof; air-conditioning; T-bar roof; electronic digital clock.

120 hp power team

(not available in California)

See 90 hp power team, except for:

ENGINE 8 cylinders; 318 cu in, 5,211 cc (3.91 x 3.31 in, 99.2 x 84 mm); compression ratio: 8.5:1; max power (SAE net): 120 hp (89 kW) at 3,600 rpm; max torque (SAE net): 245 lb ft, 33.8 kg m (331 Nm) at 1,600 rpm; 23 hp/l (17 kW/l); crankshaft bearings; valves: hydraulic tappets; camshafts: 1, a centre of Vee; 1 Carter BBD-8233S downdraught twin barre carburettor; cooling: 25 imp pt, 30 US pt, 14.2 l.

TRANSMISSION axle ratio: 2.470 - St. Wagon 2.450.

PERFORMANCE max speed: 102 mph, 164 km/h; power-weigh ratio: Sedan 28.9 lb/hp (39.1 lb/kW), 13.1 kg/hp (17.7 kg/kW) speed in direct drive at 1,000 rpm: 25.5 mph, 41 km/h; con sumption: 17.8 m/imp gal, 15 m/US gal, 15.4 l x 100 km.

ELECTRICAL EQUIPMENT 325 A battery.

DIMENSIONS AND WEIGHT weight: Coupé 3,389 lb, 1,537 kg Sedan 3,476 lb, 1,577 kg - St. Wagon 3,627 lb, 1,645 kg Salon Coupé 3,400 lb, 1,542 kg - Salon Sedan 3,497 lb, 1,58 kg - Salon St. Wagon 3,657 lb, 1,659 kg - Medallion Coup 3,451 lb, 1,659 kg - Medallion Sedan 3,576 lb, 1,622 kg.

155 hp power team

See 90 hp power team, except for:

ENGINE 8 cylinders; 318 cu in, 5,211 cc (3.91 x 3.31 ir 99.2 x 84 mm); compression ratio: 8.5:1; max power (SAE net 155 hp (115 kW) at 4,000 rpm; max torque (SAE net): 240 lb/f 33.1 kg m (325 Nm) at 2,000 rpm; 29.8 hp/l (22.1 kW/l); crankshaft bearings; valves; hydraulic tappets; camshafts: 1, a centre of Vee; 1 Carter TQ-9295S (California TQ-9234S) down draught 4-barrel carburettor; cooling: 25 imp pt, 30 US pt, 14. l.

TRANSMISSION axle ratio: 2.940 - St. Wagon 2.470 - Califor nia 2.450.

PERFORMANCE max speed: 104 mph, 166 km/h; power-weigh ratio: sedan 22.4 lb/hp (30.2 lb/kW), 10.2 kg/hp (13.7 kg/kW speed in direct drive at 1,000 rpm: 25.5 mph, 41 km/h; cor sumption: 17.8 m/imp gal, 15 m/US gal, 15.4 l x 100 km.

ELECTRICAL EQUIPMENT 325 A battery.

DIMENSIONS AND WEIGHT weight: Coupé 3,389 lb, 1,537 kg Sedan 3,476 lb, 1,577 kg - St. Wagon 3,627 lb, 1,645 kg Salon Coupé 3,400 lb, 1,542 kg - Salon Sedan 3,497 lb, 1,58 kg - Salon St. Wagon 3,657 lb, 1,659 kg - Medallion Coup 3,451 lb, 1,565 kg - Medallion Sedan 3,576 lb, 1,622 kg.

Mirada

PRICE EX WORKS: $ 6,364

90 hp power team

(not available in California)

ENGINE front, 4 stroke; 6 cylinders, vertical, in line; 225 cu i 3,687 cc (3.40 x 4.12 in, 86.4 x 104.6 mm); compression rati 8.4:1; max power (SAE net): 90 hp (67 kW) at 3,600 rpm; ma torque (SAE net): 160 lb ft, 22 kg m (217 Nm) at 1,600 rpm max engine rpm: 4,400; 24.4 hp/l (17.9 kW/l); cast iron bloc and head; 4 crankshaft bearings; valves: overhead, in lin push-rods and rockers; camshafts: 1, side; lubrication: rota pump, full flow filter, 8.3 imp pt, 9.9 US pt, 4.7 l; 1 Holle

DODGE Diplomat Station Wagon

DODGE Mirada

8831A downdraught single barrel carburettor; air cleaner exaust system with catalytic converter; fuel feed: mechanical ump; water-cooled, 19.2 imp pt, 23 US pt, 10.9 l.

RANSMISSION driving wheels: rear; gearbox: Torqueflite utomatic transmission, hydraulic torque converter and planetry gears with 3 ratios, max ratio of converter at stall 1.90, ossible manual selection; ratios: I 2.740, II 1.550, III 1, rev .220; lever: steering column or central; axle ratio: 2.760; width f rims: 5.5"; tyres: FR78 x 15.

ERFORMANCE max speed: 90 mph, 145 km/h; power-weight atio: 37.5 lb/hp (51 lb/kW) 17 kg/hp (23.1 kg/kW); speed in irect drive at 1,000 rpm: 25.5 mph, 41 km/h; consumption: 0.5 m/imp gal, 17 m/US gal, 13.8 l x 100 km.

HASSIS integral with isolated front cross member; front susension: independent, wishbones, transverse torsion bars, anti-oll bar, telescopic dampers; rear: rigid axle, semi-elliptic leafsrings, telescopic dampers.

TEERING recirculating ball, servo; turns lock to lock: 3.50.

RAKES front disc (diameter 11.58 in 29.4 cm) front internal adial fins, rear drum, rear compensator, servo; swept area: otal 375,29 sq in, 2,421 sq cm.

LECTRICAL EQUIPMENT 12 V; 430 A battery; 60 A alternaor; Essex or Prestolite or Mopar transistorized ignition with lectronic spark control, combustion computer with feedback arburettor controller; 4 headlamps.

IMENSIONS AND WEIGHT wheel base: 112.70 in, 286 cm; acks: 60 in, 152 cm front, 59.50 in, 151 cm rear; length: 209 , 532 cm; width: 72.70 in, 185 cm; height: 53.30 in, 135 cm; ound clearance: 10.20 in, 26 cm; weight: 3,373 lb, 1,530 kg; eight distribution: 57% front, 43% rear; turning circle: 43,6 ft, 3.3 m; fuel tank: 15.1 imp gal, 18 US gal, 68 l.

ODY coupé; 2 doors; 6 seats, separate front seats with uilt-in headerests.

PTIONALS 2.710 axle ratio; electronic air-conditioning; trip omputer; longlife battery; heavy-duty cooling; rear window efroster with 65 A alternator; iodine headlamps; electric door ocks; electric windows; heavy-duty suspension; sunshine roof; -bar roof; Sport handling equipment; CMX equipment.

120 hp power team

optional, not available in California)

ee 90 hp power team, except for:

NGINE 8 cylinders; 318 cu in, 5,211 (3.91 x 3.31 in, 99.2 x 84 m); compression ratio: 8.5:1; max power (SAE net): 120 hp 39 kW) at 3,600 rpm; max torque (SAE net): 245 lb ft, 33.8 kg (332 Nm) at 1,600 rpm; max engine rpm: 4,000; 23 hp/l (16.9 W/l); 5 crankshaft bearings; valves: overhead, in line, push-ods and rockers, hydraulic tappets; camshafts: 1, at centre of ee; 1 Carter BBD-8233S downdraught twin barrel carburettor; ooling: 25 imp pt, 30 US pt, 14.2 l.

RANSMISSION gearbox ratios: I 2.450, II 1.450, III 1, rev .220; axle ratio: 2.470.

ERFORMANCE max speed: 106 mph, 170 km/h; power-weight atio: 28.8 lb/hp (39.2 lb/kW), 13 kg/hp (17.8 kg/kW); speed in irect drive at 1,000 rpm: 29.3 mph, 47.2 km/h; consumption: 8 m/imp gal, 15 m/US gal, 15.7 l x 100 km.

ELECTRICAL EQUIPMENT 325 A battery.

DIMENSIONS AND WEIGHT weight: 3,453 lb, 1,566 kg; weight distribution: 58% front, 42% rear.

OPTIONALS 2.450 axle ratio.

155 hp power team

(optional, standard for California only)

See 90 hp power team, except for:

ENGINE 8 cylinders; 318 cu in, 5,211 cc (3.91 x 3.31 in, 99.2 x 84 mm); compression ratio: 8.5:1; max power (SAE ret): 155 hp (114 kW) at 4,000 rpm; max torque (SAE net): 240 lb ft, 33.2 kg m (325 Nm) at 1,600 rpm; 29.7 hp/l (21.9 kW/l); 5 crankshaft bearings; valves: hydraulic tappets; camshafts: 1, at centre of Vee; 1 Carter TQ9295S downdraught 4-barrel carburettor; cooling: 25 imp pt, 30 US pt, 14.2 l.

TRANSMISSION gearbox ratios; I 2.450, II 1.450, III 1, rev 2.220; axle ratio: 2.940 - California 2.450.

PERFORMANCE max speed: 110 mph, 177 km/h; power-weight ratio: 22.3 lb/hp (30.3 lb/kW), 10.1 kg/hp (13.7 kg/kW); speed in direct drive at 1,000 rpm: 31 mph, 49.7 km/h; consumption: 19.2 m/imp gal, 16 m/US gal, 14.7 l x 100 km.

ELECTRICAL EQUIPMENT 325 A battery.

DIMENSIONS AND WEIGHT weight: 3,453 lb, 1,566 kg; weight distribution: 58% front, 42% rear.

185 hp power team

(optional for CMX equipment only, not available in California)

See 90 hp power team, except for:

ENGINE 8 cylinders; 360 cu in, 5,900 cc (4 x 3.58 in, 101.6 x 89.6 mm); compression rato: 8:1; max power (SAE net): 185 hp (138 kW) at 4,000 rpm; max torque (SAE net): 275 lb ft, 38.1 kg m (373 Nm) at 2,000 rpm; 31.9 hp/l (23.4 kW/l); 5 crankshaft bearings; valves hydraulic tappets; camshafts: 1, at centre of Vee; 1 Carter TQ 9244S downdraught 4-barrel carburettor; dual exhaust system with catalytic converter; cooling: 25 imp pt, 30 US pt, 14.2 l.

TRANSMISSION gearbox ratios: I 2.450, II 1.450, III 1, rev 2.220; axle ratio: 2.940.

PERFORMANCE max speed: 115 mph, 185 km/h; power-weight ratio: 19.6 lb/hp, (26.6 lb/kW), 8.8 kg/hp (121 kg/kW); speed in direct drive at 1,000 rpm: 28.7 mph, 46.2 km/h; consumption: 16.8 m/imp gal, 14 m/US gal, 16.8 l x 100 km.

DIMENSIONS AND WEIGHT weight: 3,622 lb, 1,643 kg; weight distribution: 58% front, 42% rear.

St. Regis

PRICE EX WORKS: $ 6,724

90 hp power team

(standard, not available in California)

ENGINE front, 4 stroke; 6 cylinders, vertical, in line; 225 cu in, 3,687 cc (3.40 x 4.12 in, 86.4 x 104.6 mm); compression ratio: 8.4:1; max power (SAE net): 90 hp (67 kW) at 3,600 rpm; max torque (SAE net): 160 lb ft, 22 kg m (217 Nm) at 2,000 rpm; max engine rpm: 4,400; 24.4 hp/l (17.9 kW/l); cast iron block and head; 4 crankshaft bearings; valves: overhead, in line, push-rods and rockers; camshafts: 1, side; lubrication: rotary pump, full flow filter, 8.3 imp pt, 9.9 US pt, 4.7 l; 1 Holley R-8831A downdraught single barrel carburettor; air cleaner; exhaust system with catalytic converter; fuel feed: mechanical pump; water-cooled, 19.2 imp pt, 23 US pt, 10.9 l.

TRANSMISSION driving wheels: rear; gearbox: Torqueflite automatic transmission, hydraulic torque converter and planetary gears with 3 ratios, max ratio of converter at stall 1.90, possible manual selection; ratios: I 2.740, II 1.540, III 1, rev 2.220; lever: steering column; final drive: hypoid bevel; axle ratio: 2.940; width of rims: 5.5"; tyres: P195/75R x 15.

PERFORMANCE max speed: 93 mph, 149 km/h; power-weight ratio: 39.8 lb/hp (54.2 lb/kW), 17.9 kg/hp (24.4 kg/kW); carrying capacity: 1,270 lb, 570 kg; speed in direct drive at 1,000 rpm: 25.9 mph, 41.7 km/h; consumption: 19.2 m/imp gal, 16 m/US gal, 14.7 l x 100 km

CHASSIS integral with isolated front cross member; front suspension: independent, wishbones (lower trailing links), longitudinal torsion bars, anti-roll bar, telescopic dampers; rear: rigid axle, semi-elliptic leafsprings, telescopic dampers.

DODGE St. Regis

90 HP POWER TEAM

STEERING recirculating ball, servo; turns lock to lock: 3.50.

BRAKES front disc (diameter 11.58 in, 29.4 cm), front internal radial fins, rear drum, rear compensator, servo; swept area: total 375.3 sq in, 2,421 sq cm.

ELECTRICAL EQUIPMENT 12 V; 430 A battery; 65 A alternator; Essex or Prestolite or Mopar transistorized ignition with electronic spark control; 4 headlamps.

DIMENSIONS AND WEIGHT wheel base: 118.50 in, 301 cm; tracks: 61.90 in, 157 cm front, 62 in, 157 cm rear; length: 220.20 in, 559 cm; width: 77.10 in, 196 cm; height: 54.50 in, 138 cm; ground clearance: 5.30 in, 13.5 cm; weight: 3,557 lb, 1,613 kg; turning circle: 45.8 ft, 13.9 m; fuel tank: 17.6 imp gal, 21 US gal, 80 l.

BODY hardtop; 4 doors; 6 seats, separate front seats with built-in headrests.

OPTIONALS heavy-duty cooling; limited slip differential; light alloy wheels; P205/75R x 15 tyres; P225/70 R x 15, FR70 x 15 or GR70 x 15 tyres with 7" wide rims; heavy-duty suspension; tilt of steering wheel; automatic speed control; reclining backrests; anti-roll bar on rear suspension; electric windows; tinted glass; heated rear window with 100 A alternator; electric sunshine roof; vinyl roof; halogen headlamps; air-conditioning.

120 hp power team

(optional, not available in California)

See 90 hp power team, except for:

ENGINE 8 cylinders; 318 cu in, 5,211 cc (3.91 x 3.31 in, 99.2 x 84 mm); compression ratio: 8.5:1; max power (SAE net): 120 hp (89 kW) at 4,000 rpm; max torque (SAE net): 245 lb ft, 33,8 kg m (332 Nm) at 1,600 rpm; 23 hp/l (16.9 kW/l); 5 crankshaft bearings; valves: hydraulic tappets; camshafts: 1, at centre of Vee; 1 Carter BBD 8233S downdraught twin barrel carburettor; cooling 25 imp pt, 30 US pt, 14.2 l.

TRANSMISSION gearbox ratios: I 2.450, II 1,450; III 1, rev 2.220; axle ratio: 2.450.

PERFORMANCE max speed: 96 mph, 155 km/h; power-weight ratio: 26.9 lb/hp (36.5 lb/kW), 12.2 kg/hp (16.6 kg/kW); consumption: 18 m/imp gal, 15 m/US gal, 15.7 l x 100 km.

ELECTRICAL EQUIPMENT 325 A battery.

DIMENSIONS AND WEIGHT weight: 3,628 lb, 1,646 kg.

155 hp power team

(standard for California only)

See 90 hp power team, except for:

ENGINE 8 cylinders; 318 cu in, 5,211 cc (3.91 x 3.31 in, 99.2 x 84 mm); compression ratio: 8.5:1; max power (SAE net): 155 hp (114 kW); max torque (SAE net): 245 lb ft, 33.8 kg m (331 Nm) at 1,600 rpm; 29.7 hp/l (21.9 kW/l); 5 crankshaft bearings; valves: hydraulic tappets; camshafts: 1, at centre of Vee; 1 carter TQ9234S downdraught 4-barrel carburettor; cooling 25 imp pt, 30 US pt, 14.2 l.

TRANSMISSION gearbox ratios: I 2.450, II 1.450, III 1, rev 2.220; axle ratio: 2.450.

PERFORMANCE max speed: 114 mph, 182 km/h; power-weight ratio: 23.4 lb/hp (31.8 lb/kW), 10.6 kg/hp (14.4 kg/kW); speed in direct drive at 1,000 rpm: 28,8 mph 46.3 km/h; consumption: 19.2 m/imp gal, 16 m/US gal, 14.7 l x 100 km.

ELECTRICAL EQUIPMENT 325 A battery.

DIMENSIONS AND WEIGHT weight: 3,628 lb, 1,646 kg.

130 hp power team

(optional, not available in California)

See 90 hp power team, except for:

ENGINE 8 cylinders; 360 cu in, 5,900 cc (4 x 3.58 in, 101.6 x 89.6 mm); max power (SAE net): 130 hp (97 kW) at 3,200 rpm; max torque (SAE net): 255 lb ft, 35.9 kg m (345 Nm) at 2,000 rpm; 220 hp/l (16.2 kW/l); 5 crankshaft bearings; valves: hydraulic tappets; camshafts: 1, at centre of Vee; 1 Carter BBD8237S downdraught twin barrel carburettor; cooling: 26.6 imp pt, 31.9 US pt, 15.1 l.

TRANSMISSION gearbox ratios: I 2.450, II 1.450, III 1, rev 2.220; axle ratio: 2.450.

PERFORMANCE max speed: 99 mph, 160 km/h; power-weight ratio: 28.4 lb/hp (38.7 lb/kW), 12.9 kg/hp (17.5 kg/kW); speed in direct drive at 1,000 rpm: 27.6 mph, 44.4 km/h; consumption: 16.8 m/imp gal, 14 m/US gal, 16.8 l x 100 km.

DIMENSIONS AND WEIGHT weight: 3,691 lb, 1,674 kg.

OPTIONALS 3,210 axle ratio.

ELEGANT MOTORS USA

898 Elegante

PRICE EX WORKS: $ 60,000

ENGINE Jaguar, front, 4 stroke; 12 cylinders, Vee-slanted at 60°; 326 cu in, 5,343 cc (3.54 x 2.76 in, 90 x 70 mm); compression ratio: 8:1; max power (DIN): 288 hp (212 kW) at 5,750 rpm; max torque (DIN): 295 lb ft, 40.7 kg m (399 Nm) at 3,500 rpm; max engine rpm: 6,500; 53.9 hp/l (39.7 kg m (399 Nm) at kW/l); light alloy block and head, wet liners, hemispherical combustion chambers; 7 crankshaft bearings; valves: overhead, in line, thimble tappets; camshafts: 2, 1 per bank, overhead; lubrication: rotary pump, full flow filter, oil cooler, 19 imp pt, 22.8 US pt, 10.8 l; Lucas-Bosch electronic injection; fuel feed: electric pump; water-cooled, 36 imp pt, 43.3 US pt, 20.5 l, 1 viscous coupling thermostatic fan and 1 electric thermostatic fan.

TRANSMISSION driving wheels: rear; clutch: single dry plate (diaphragm), hydraulically controlled; gearbox: mechanical; gears: 4, fully synchronized; ratios: I 3.238, II 1.905, III 1.389, IV 1, rev 3.428; lever: central; final drive: hypoid bevel, limited slip differential; axle ratio: 3.070; width of rims: 6"; tyres: 205/70VR x 15.

PERFORMANCE max speed: about 150 mph, 241 km/h; power-weight ratio: 10.4 lb/hp (14.1 lb/kW), 4.7 kg/hp (6.4 kg/kW); speed in direct drive at 1,000 rpm: 24.8 mph, 39.9 km/h; consumption: 14 m/imp gal, 11.6 m/US gal, 20.2 l x 100 km.

CHASSIS box-type ladder frame with cross members; front suspension: independent, wishbones, coil springs, anti-roll bar, telescopic dampers; rear: independent, wishbones, semiaxles as upper arms, transverse semi-elliptic leafsprings, trailing radius arms, telescopic dampers.

STEERING recirculating ball, servo; turns lock to lock: 4.10.

BRAKES front disc, rear drum.

ELECTRICAL EQUIPMENT 12 V; 2 headlamps.

DIMENSIONS AND WEIGHT wheel base: 128 in, 325 cm; length: 203.94 in, 518 cm; height: 57.09 in, 145 cm; ground clearance: 10 in, 25.4 cm; weight: 3,000 lb, 1,360 kg; fuel tank: 16.7 imp gal, 20 US gal, 76 l.

BODY phaeton, in plastic material; 2 doors; 4 seats, separate front seats.

OPTIONALS leather upholstery; tonneau cover; electric windows; dual exhaust system; supercharger; air-conditioning.

898 Phaeton

See 898 Elegante, except for:

PRICE EX WORKS: $ 50,000

BODY 2+2 seats.

856 Speedster

See 898 Elegante, except for:

PRICE EX WORKS: $ 40,000

BODY roadster; 2 seats.

Elegante Sports Brougham

See 898 Elegante, except for:

PRICE EX WORKS: $ 60,000

TRANSMISSION width of rims: front 7".

DIMENSIONS AND WEIGHT length: 207.13 in, 526 cm; width 78 in, 198 cm; height: 56 in, 142 cm; ground clearance: 7 in 17.8 cm.

ELITE USA

Laser 917

PRICES EX WORKS:	$
(body only)	7,50
(kit only)	4,59

ENGINE Volkswagen, rear, 4 stroke; 4 cylinders, horizontall opposed; 96.7 cu in, 1,584 cc (3.37 x 2.72 in, 85.5 x 69 mm) compression ratio: 8.5:1; max power (DIN): 50 hp (37 kW) a 4,000 rpm; max torque (DIN): 78 lb ft, 10.8 kg m (106 Nm) a 2,800 rpm; max engine rpm: 4,600; 31.6 hp/l (23.3 kW/l); bloc with cast iron liners and light alloy fins, light alloy head; crankshaft bearings; valves: overhead, push-rods and rockers camshafts: 1, central, lower; lubrication: gear pump, filter i sump, oil cooler, 4.4 imp pt, 5.3 US pt, 2.5 l; 1 Solex 34 PICT downdraught carburettor; fuel feed: mechanical pump; air cooled.

TRANSMISSION driving wheels: rear; clutch: single dry plate gearbox: mechanical; gears: 4, fully synchronized; ratios: 3.780, II 2.060, III 1.260, IV 0.930, rev 4010; lever: centra final drive: spiral bevel; axle ratio: 3.875; width of rims: 4' tyres: 5.60 x 15.

ELEGANT MOTORS Elegante Sports Brougham

ELITE Laser 917

PERFORMANCE max speed: about 100 mph, 161 km/h; power-weight ratio: 39 lb/hp (52.9 lb/kW), 17.6 kg/hp (24 kg/kW); carrying capacity: 353 lb, 160 kg; consumption: 30.7 m/imp gal, 25.6 m/US gal, 9.2 l x 100 km.

CHASSIS backbone platform; front suspension: independent, twin swinging longitudinal trailing arms, transverse laminated torsion bars, anti-roll bar, telescopic dampers; rear: independent, swinging semi-axles, swinging longitudinal trailing arms, transverse torsion bars, telescopic dampers.

STEERING worm and roller.

BRAKES front disc (diameter 10.91 in, 27.7 cm), rear drum; lining area: front 12.4 sq in, 80 sq cm, rear 55.5 sq in, 358 sq cm, total 67.9 sq in, 438 sq cm.

ELECTRICAL EQUIPMENT 12 V; 36 Ah battery; 50 A alternator; Bosch distributor; 4 headlamps.

DIMENSIONS AND WEIGHT wheel base: 94.50 in, 240 cm; tracks: 58 in, 147 cm front, 59 in, 150 cm rear; length: 174 in, 442 cm; height: 43.50 in, 110 cm; ground clearance: 6.50 in, 16.5 cm; weight: 1,950 lb, 884 kg; weight distribution: 40% front, 60% rear; fuel tank: 12.5 imp gal, 15 US gal. 57 l.

BODY sports, in plastic material; 2 doors; 2 seats.

EXCALIBUR USA

Series III

PRICES EX WORKS: $

SS Roadster	**28,800**
SS Phaeton	**28,800**

215 hp power team

(not available in California)

ENGINE Chevrolet, front, 4 stroke; 8 cylinders; 454 cu in, 7,440 cc (4.25 x 4 in, 107.9 x 101.6 mm); compression ratio: 7.9:1; max power (DIN): 215 hp (158 kW) at 4,000 rpm; max torque (DIN): 350lb ft, 48.3 kg m (474 Nm) at 2,400 rpm; max engine rpm: 4,400; 28.9 hp/l (21.3 kW/l); cast iron block and head; 5 crankshaft bearings; valves: overhead, in line, push-rods and rockers, hydraulic tappets; camshafts: 1, at centre of Vee; lubrication: gear pump, full flow filter, 8.3 imp pt, 9.9 US pt, 4.7 l; 1 Rochester 7045200 downdraught 4-barrel carburettor; air cleaner; dual exhaust system; water-cooled, 52.8 imp pt, 63.4 US pt, 30 l.

TRANSMISSION driving wheels: rear; gearbox: Turbo-Hydramatic 400 automatic transmission, hydraulic torque converter and planetary gears with 3 ratios, max ratio of converter at stall 2.2, possible manual selection; ratios: I 2.480, II 1.480, III 1, rev 2.080; lever: steering column or central; final drive: hypoid bevel, limited slip differential; axle ratio: 2.730; width of rims: 7.5''; tyres: GR78 x 15.

PERFORMANCE max speed: 110 mph, 177 km/h; power-weight ratio: 20.2 lb/hp (27.6 lb/kW), 9.2 kg/hp (12.5 kg/kW); speed in direct drive at 1,000 rpm: 25 mph, 40.2 km/h; consumption: 12.3 m/imp gal, 10.2 m/US gal, 23 l x 100 km.

CHASSIS box-type ladder frame; front suspension: independent, wishbones, coil springs, anti-roll bar, telescopic dampers; rear: independent, semi-axle as upper pivoting arm and angular strut rod as lower pivoting arm, transverse semi-elliptic leafspring, trailing radius arms, anti-roll bar, telescopic dampers adjustable while running.

STEERING recirculating ball, variable ratio, tilt and telescopic, servo; turns lock to lock: 3.

BRAKES disc, internal radial fins, servo; swept area: total 461 sq in, 2,973 sq cm.

ELECTRICAL EQUIPMENT 12 V; 73 Ah battery; 61 A alternator; Delco-Remy high energy ignition; 4 headlamps.

DIMENSIONS AND WEIGHT wheel base: 112 in, 284 cm; front and rear track: 62.50 in, 159 cm; length: 175 in, 444 cm; width: 72 in, 183 cm; height: 58 in, 147 cm; ground clearance: 5.70 in, 14.4 cm; weight: 4,350 lb, 1,973 kg; weight distribution: 48% front, 52% rear; turning circle: 35 ft, 10.7 m; fuel tank: 20.9 imp gal, 25 US gal, 95 l.

BODY roadster, 2 seats - phaeton, 4 seats; 2 doors; separate front seats; leather upholstery; wire wheels; all-weather removable hardtop; tonneau cover; air-conditioning; heating and defrosting system; luggage rack; two side-mounted spare wheels.

EXCALIBUR Series III SS Phaeton

FORD USA

Pinto Series

PRICES EX WORKS: $

2-dr Sedan	**4,999**
2+1-dr Runabout	**5,156**
2+1-dr St. Wagon	**5,570**

ENGINE front, 4 stroke; 4 cylinders, in line; 140 cu in, 2,300 cc (3.78 x 3.13 in, 95.9 x 79.5 mm); compression ratio: 9:1; max power (SAE net): 88 hp (66 kW) at 4,600 rpm; max torque (SAE net): 119 lb ft, 16.4 kg m (161 Nm) at 2,600 rpm; max engine rpm: 5,000; 38.3 hp/l (28.7 kW/l); cast iron block and head; 5 crankshaft bearings; valves: overhead, Vee-slanted, rockers, hydraulic tappets; camshafts: 1, overhead, cogged belt; lubrication: gear pump, full flow filter, 6.7 imp pt, 8 US pt, 3.8 l; 1 Holley-Weber EOEE-RA/GA (EOEE-VA/NA for California only) downdraught twin barrel carburettor; air cleaner; exhaust system with catalytic converter; fuel feed: mechanical pump; water-cooled, 14.4 imp pt, 17.3 US pt, 8.2 l.

TRANSMISSION driving wheels: rear; clutch: single dry plate; gearbox: mechanical; gears: 4, fully synchronized; ratios: I 3.980, II 2.140, III 1.420, IV 1, rev 3.990; lever: central; final drive: hypoid bevel; axle ratio; 2.730 - St. Wagon 3.080; width of rims: 5''; tyres: BR 78 x 13B BSW.

PERFORMANCE max speed: about 96 mph, 154 km/h; power-weight ratio: Sedan 28.3 lb/hp (37.7 lb/kW), 12.8 kg/hp (17.1 kg/kW); speed in direct drive at 1,000 rpm: 19.3 mph, 31 km/h; consumption: 28.8 m/imp gal, 24 m/US gal, 9.8 l.

CHASSIS integral; front suspension: independent, wishbones, coil springs, telescopic dampers; rear: rigid axle, semi-elliptic leafsprings, telescopic dampers.

STEERING rack-and-pinion; turns lock to lock: 4.16.

BRAKES front disc (diameter 9.30 in, 23.6 cm), front internal radial fins, rear drum, rear compensator; swept area: front 145.5 sq in, 939 sq cm, rear 99 sq in, 639 sq cm, total 244.5 sq in, 1,578 sq cm.

ELECTRICAL EQUIPMENT 12 V; 45 Ah battery; 60 A alternator; Motorcraft transistorized ignition; 2 headlamps.

DIMENSIONS AND WEIGHT wheel base: 94.50 in, 240 cm - St. Wagon 94.80 in, 241 cm; tracks: 55 in, 140 cm front, 55.80 in, 142 cm rear; length: 170.80 in, 434 cm - St. Wagon 180.60 in, 459 cm; width: 69.40 in, 176 cm - St. Wagon 69.70 in, 177 cm; height: 50.60 in, 128 cm - St. Wagon 52.10 in, 132 cm; ground clearance: 4.63 in, 11.8 cm - St. Wagon 5.14 in, 13 cm; weight: Sedan 2,488 lb, 1,129 kg - Runabout 2,529 lb, 1,147 kg - St. Wagon 2,662 lb, 1,207 kg; turning circle: 33.6 ft, 10.2 m; fuel tank: 10.8 imp gal, 13 US gal, 49 l - St. Wagon 11.7 imp gal, 14 US gal, 53 l.

BODY saloon/sedan, coupé, estate car/st. wagon; 4 seats, separate front seats; folding rear seat (for Runabout and St. Wagon only).

OPTIONALS 2.790 or 3.080 axle ratio (not available for St. Wagon); Select-Shift C-3 automatic transmission with 3 ratios (I 2.470, II 1.470, III 1, rev 2.110), max ratio of converter at stall

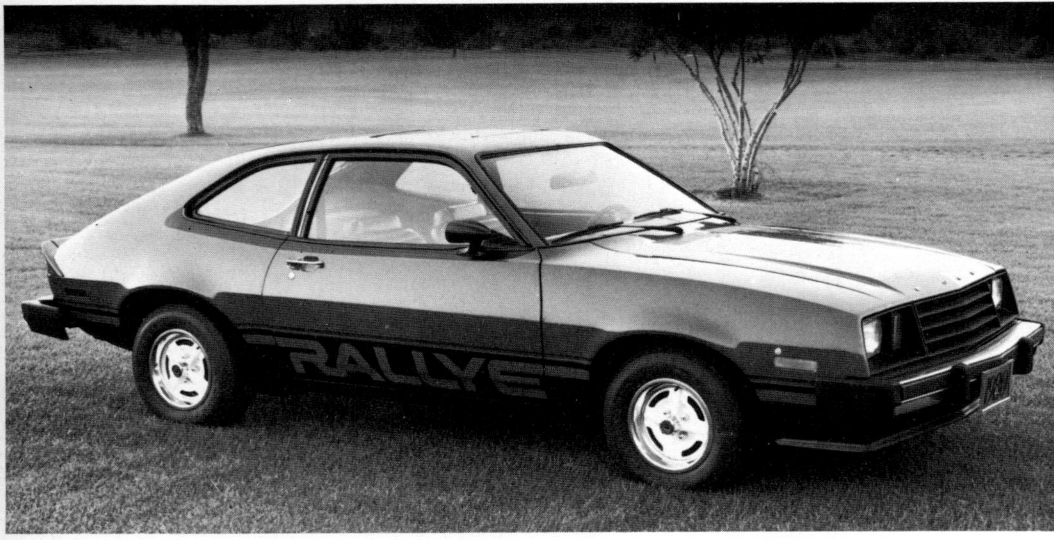

DIMENSIONS AND WEIGHT weight plus 19 lb, 8.6 kg.

OPTIONALS Select-Shift C-3 automatic transmission, hydraulic torque converter and planetary gears with 3 ratios (I 2.470, II 1.470, III 1, rev 2.110), max ratio of converter at stall 2.49 possible manual selection, 3.450 axle ratio; Select-Shift C-4 automatic transmission, hydraulic torque converter and planetary gears with 3 ratios (I 2.460, II 1.460, III 1, rev 2.190) max ratio of converter at stall 2, possible manual selection 3.450 axle ratio; light alloy wheels; wire wheels; heavy-duty suspension; power steering; tilt of steering wheel; servo brake; metallic spray; tinted glass; heated rear window; vinyl roof; sunshine roof; manual air-conditioning; leather upholstery; Recaro seats (for Ghia models only); carriage roof; 54 Ah heavy-duty battery; automatic speed control; rear window wiper-washer (for 2-dr models only); Cobra equipment (for 2+1-dr Sedan only); Sport equipment.

89 hp power team

(for California only)

See 88 hp power team, except for:

ENGINE max power (SAE net): 89 hp (66 kW) at 4,800 rpm; max torque (SAE net):122 lb ft, 16.9 kg m (165 Nm) at 2,600 rpm; max engine rpm: 5,200; 38.7 hp/l (28.7 kW/l); 1 Holley-Weber EOEE-VA/NA downdraught twin barrel carburettor.

TRANSMISSION axle ratio: 3.080.

FORD Pinto Runabout Rallye

PINTO SERIES

2.9, possible manual selection, central lever, 3 or 3.080 axle ratio; Select-Shift C-4 automatic transmission with 3 ratios (I 2.460, II 1.460, III 1, rev 2.190), max ratio of converter at stall 2.3, possible manual selection, central lever, 3 or 3.080 axle ratio; light alloy wheels; wire wheels; BR 78 x 13B WSW or BR70 x 13B tyres; power steering; servo brake; tinted glass; air - conditioning; metallic spray; heated rear window; sunshine roof; Pony equipment (except for Runabout); Cruising equipment (except for Sedan); ESS equipment (for Runabout only); Rallye equipment (except for Sedan); Squire equipment (for St. Wagon only).

Mustang Series

PRICES EX WORKS:	$
1 2-dr Sedan	**5,961**
2 2+1-dr Sedan	**6,151**
3 Ghia 2-dr Sedan	**6,446**
4 Ghia 2+1-dr Sedan	**6,514**

For 150 hp turbocharged engine add $ 633; for 118 hp engine add $ 505.

Power team:	Standard for:	Optional for:
88 hp	all	—
89 hp	all	—
118 hp	—	all
150 hp	—	all

FORD Mustang Sedan (carriage roof)

88 hp power team

(not available in California)

ENGINE front, 4 stroke; 4 cylinders, in line; 140 cu in, 2,300 cc (3.78 x 3.13 in, 95.9 x 79.5 mm); compression ratio: (SAE net): 88 hp (66 kW) at 4,600 rpm; max torque (SAE net): 119 lb ft, 16.4 kg m (161 Nm) at 2,600 rpm; max engine rpm: 5,000; 38.3 hp/l (28.7 kW/l); cast iron block and head; 5 crankshaft bearings; valves: overhead, Vee-slanted, rockers, hydraulic tappets; camshafts: 1, over-head, cogged belt; lubrication: rotary pump, full flow filter, 6.7 imp pt, 8 US pt, 3.8 l; 1 Holley-Weber EOEE-RA/GA downdraught twin barrel carburettor; air cleaner; exhaust system with catalytic converter; fuel feed: mechanical pump; water-cooled, 17.1 imp pt, 20.5 US pt, 9.7 l.

TRANSMISSION driving wheels: rear; clutch: single dry plate; gearbox: mechanical; gears: 4, fully synchronized; ratios: I 3.980, II 2.140, III 1.420, IV 1, rev 3.990; lever: central; final drive: hypoid bevel; axle ratio: 3.080; width of rims: 5"; tyres: P185/80R x 13 BSW.

PERFORMANCE max speed: 96 mph, 154 km/h; power-weight ratio: 2-dr Sedan 29.6 lb/hp (39.4 lb/kW), 13.4 kg/hp (17.9 kg/kW); speed in direct drive at 1,000 rpm: 20.9 mph, 33.5 km/h; consumption: 27.7 m/imp gal, 23 m/US gal, 10.2 l x 100 km.

CHASSIS platform with front subframe; front suspension: independent, by McPherson, wishbones (lower control arms), coil springs/telescopic damper struts, anti-roll bar; rear: rigid axle, lower trailing radius arms, upper oblique torque arms, transverse linkage bar, coil springs, telescopic dampers.

STEERING rack-and-pinion; turns lock to lock: 4.08.

BRAKES front disc (diameter 9.31 in, 23.6 cm), front internal radial fins, rear compensator, rear drum; swept area: front 150.8 sq in, 973 sq cm, rear 99 sq in, 639 sq cm, total 249.8 sq in, 1,612 sq cm.

ELECTRICAL EQUIPMENT 12 V; 45 Ah battery; 40 A alternator; Motorcraft transistorized ignition; 4 headlamps.

DIMENSIONS AND WEIGHT wheel base: 100.40 in, 255 cm; tracks: 56.60 in, 144 cm front, 57 in, 145 cm rear; length: 179.10 in, 455 cm; width: 69.10 in, 176 cm; height: 51.50 in, 131 cm; ground clearance: 5.67 in, 14.5 cm; weight: 2-dr Sedan, 2,601 lb, 1,180 kg - Ghia 2-dr Sedan 2,665 lb, 1,208 kg - 2+1-dr Sedan 2,635 lb, 1,195 kg - Ghia 2+1-dr Sedan 2,692 lb, 1,222 kg; turning circle: 37.2 ft, 11.3 m; fuel tank: 9.5 imp pt, 11.5 US pt, 43 l.

BODY saloon/sedan; 4 seats; separate front seats, reclining backrests with built-in headrests.

VARIATIONS

ENGINE 6 cylinders, in line, 200 cu in, 3,300 cc (3.68 x 3.13 in, 93.5 x 79.4 mm), compression ratio 8.6:1, 7 crankshaft bearings, 1 Holley-Weber EOZE-GA downdraught single barrel carburettor, cooling 15 imp pt, 18 US pt, 8.5 l.
TRANSMISSION gearbox ratios I 3.290, II 1.840, III 1, IV 0.810, rev 3.290.
PERFORMANCE max speed 100 mph, 160 km/h, speed in direct drive at 1,000 rpm 20.8 mph, 33.4 km/h.

VARIATIONS

ENGINE 6 cylinders, in line, 200 cu in, 3,300 cc (3.68 x 3.13 in, 93.5 x 79.4 mm), 8.6:1 compression ratio, 7 crankshaft bearings, 1 Holley 1946 EOBE-AAA downdraught twin barrel carburettor cooling 15 imp pt, 18 US pt, 8.5 l.
TRANSMISSION select-Shift C-4 automatic transmission, hydraulic torque converter and planetary gears with 3 ratios I 2.460, II 1.460, III 1, rev 2.110), max ratio of converter at stall 2.09, possible manual selection, central lever, 2.730 axle ratio.
PERFORMANCE max speed 100 mph, 160 km/h, speed in direct drive at 1,000 rpm 20.8 mph, 33.4 km/h.
DIMENSIONS AND WEIGHT weight plus 32 lb, 14.5 kg.

118 hp power team

See 88 hp power team, except for:

ENGINE 8 cylinders; 255 cu in, 4,179 cc (3.68 x 3 in, 93.5 x 76.2 mm); compression ratio: 8.8:1; max power (SAE net): 118 hp (88 kW) at 3,800 rpm; max torque (SAE net): 193 lb ft, 26.7 kgm(262 Nm) at 2,200 rpm; max engine rpm: 4,200; 28.2 hp/l (21.1 kW/l); valves: overhead, Vee-slanted, push-rods and rockers; camshafts 1, at centre of Vee, chain; 1 Ford 2150 EOKE-HA (EO4E-FA for California only) twin barrel carburettor; water-cooled, 23.6 imp pt, 28.3 US pt, 13.4 l.

TRANSMISSION gearbox: Select-Shift C-4 automatic transmission, hydraulic torque converter and planetary gears with 3 ratios, max ratio of converter at stall 2.09, possible manual selection; ratios: I 2.460, II 1.460, III 1, rev 2.190; lever: steering column; axle ratio: 2.260.

FORD Fairmont Series (2.3-litre engine)

ERFORMANCE max speed: 100 mph, 160 km/h; power weight atio: 2-dr Sedan 23.7 lb/hp (31.8 lb/kW), 10.8 kg/hp (14.4 g/kW); speed in direct drive at 1,000 rpm: 23.8 mph, 38.2 m/h; consumption: 21.6 m/imp gal, 18 m/US gal, 13.1 l x 100 m.

LECTRICAL EQUIPMENT 36 Ah battery; 60 A alternator.

IMENSIONS AND WEIGHT weight: plus 196 lb, 89 kg.

150 hp power team

ee 88 hp power team, except for:

NGINE turbocharged; max power (SAE net): 150 hp (110 kW) t 4,800 rpm; 65.2 hp/l (48 kW/l); lubrication: 9.2 imp pt, 11 US t, 5.2 l; 1 Holley-Weber EOZE-AMA downdraught twin barrel arburettor; exhaust system with turbo-charger.

RANSMISSION gearbox ratios: I 4.070, II 2.570, III 1.660, IV , rev 3.950; lever: central; axle ratio: 3.450.

ERFORMANCE max speed: about 109 mph, 175 km/h; power-eight ratio: 2-dr Sedan 17.8 lb/hp (24.1 lb/kW), 8.1 kg/hp 10.9 kg/kW); speed in direct drive at 1,000 rpm: 22.7 mph, 6.5 km/h; consumption: 26.4 m/imp gal, 22 m/US gal, 10.7 x 100 km.

IMENSIONS AND WEIGHT weight: plus 62 lb, 28.1 kg; fuel ank: 10.3 imp gal, 12.5 US ga, 47 l.

Fairmont Series

RICES EX WORKS:	$
2-dr Sedan	**5,467**
4-dr Sedan	**5,634**
4+1-dr St. Wagon	**5,828**
Futura 2-dr Coupé	**5,784**
Ghia 2-dr Sedan	**5,953**
Ghia 4-dr Sedan	**6,120**
Ghia Futura 2-dr Coupé	**6,012**

'or 150 hp turbocharged engine add $ 633; for 119 hp engine dd $ 505.

ower team:	**Standard for:**	**Optional for:**
88 hp	all	—
89 hp	all	—
19 hp	—	all
50 hp	—	all except 3

88 hp power team

not available in California)

NGINE front, 4 stroke; 4 cylinders, in line; 140 cu in, 2,300 cc 3.78 x 3.13 in, 95.9 x 79.5 mm); compression ratio: 9:1; max ower (SAE net): 88 hp (66 kW) at 4,600 rpm; max torque (SAE et): 119 lb ft, 16.4 kg m (161 Nm) at 2,600 rpm; max engine pm: 5,000; 38.3 hp/l (28.7 kW/l); cast iron block and head; 5 rankshft bearings; valves: overhead, Vee-slanted, rockers; amshafts: 1, overhead, cogged belt; lubrication: gear pump, ull flow filter, downdraught twin barrel carburettor; air cleaner; xhaust system with catalytic converter; fuel feed: mechanical ump; water-cooled,17.1 imp pt, 20.5 US pt, 9.7 l.

TRANSMISSION driving wheels: rear; clutch: single dry plate; gearbox: mechanical; gears: 4, fully synchronized; ratios: I 3.980, II 2.140, III 1.420, IV 1, rev 3.990; lever: central; final drive: hypoid bevel: axle ratio: 3.080; width of rims: 5" - St. Wagon 5.5"; tyres P175/75R x 14 BSW.

PERFORMANCE max speed: 96 mph, 154 km/h; power-weight ratio: 4-dr Sedan 30.5 lb/hp (40.7 lb/kW), 13.9 kg/hp (18.5 kg/kW); speed in direct drive at 1,000 rpm: 19.3 mph, 31 km/h; consumption: 27.7 m/imp gal, 23 m/US gal, 10.2 l x 100 km.

CHASSIS integral with 2 cross members; front suspension: independent, by McPherson, wishbones (lower control arms), coil springs/telescopic damper struts, anti-roll bar; rear: rigid axle, lower trailing radius arms, upper oblique torque arms, coil springs, telescopic dampers.

STEERING rack-and-pinion: turns lock to lock: 4.27.

BRAKES front disc (diameter 10.06 in, 25.4 cm), front internal radial fins, rear compensator, rear drum; swept area: front 176.6 sq in, 1,140 sq cm, rear 98.9 sq in, 638 sq cm - St. Wagon 110 sq in, 710 sq cm, total 275.5 sq in, 1,778 sq cm - St. Wagon 286.6 sq in, 1,850 sq cm.

ELECTRICAL EQUIPMENT 12 V; 45 Ah battery; 40 A alternator; Motorcraft transistorized ignition; 4 headlamps.

DIMENSIONS AND WEIGHT wheel base: 105,50 in, 268 cm; tracks: 56.60 in, 144 cm front, 57 in, 145 cm rear; length: 195.50 in, 496 cm - Futura 197.40 in, 501 cm; width: 71 in, 180 cm; height 52.90 in, 134 cm - Futura 51.70 in, 131 cm - St.

FORD Fairmont Turbo Sedan

Wagon 54.20 in, 138 cm; ground clearance: 4.38 in, 11.1 cm; weight: 2-dr Sedan 2,660 lb, 1,207 kg - 4-dr Sedan 2,688 lb, 1,219 kg - Futura 2,701 lb, 1,226 kg - St. Wagon 2,826 lb, 1,282 kg; turning circle: 39 ft, 11.9 m; fuel tank: 11.7 imp gal, 14 US gal, 53 l.

VARIATIONS

ENGINE 6 cylinders, in line, 200 cu in, 3,300 cc (3.68 x 3.13 in, 93.5 x 79.4 mm), 8.6:1, compression ratio; 7 crankshaft bearings, 1 Holley-Weber EOZE-GA downdraught single barrel carburettor, cooling 15 imp pt, 18 US pt, 8.5 l.
TRANSMISSION gearbox ratios I 3.290, II 1.840, III 1, IV 0.810, rev 3.290.
PERFORMANCE max speed 100 mph, 160 km/h, speed in top at 1,000 rpm 20.8 mph, 33.4 km/h.
DIMENSIONS AND WEIGHT weight plus 29 lb, 13.1 kg.

OPTIONALS Select-Shift C-3 automatic transmission, hydraulic torque converter and planetary gears with 3 ratios I 2.470, II 1.470, III 1, rev 2.110, max ratio of converter at stall 2.49, possible manual selection, 3.450 axle ratio; Select-Shift C-4 automatic transmission, hydraulic torque converter and planetary gears with 3 ratios (I 2.460, II 1.460, III 1, rev 2.190), max ratio of converter at stall 2.3, possible manual selection, 3.450 axle ratio; light alloy wheels; wire wheels; heavy-duty suspension; power steering; tilt of steering wheel; servo brake; metallic spray; tinted glass; heated rear window; electric windows; vinyl roof; sunshine roof; manual air-conditioning; electric clock; electric door locks; speed control; rear window wiper-washer (for St. Wagon only).

89 hp power team

(for California only)

See 88 hp power team, except for:

ENGINE max power (SAE net): 89 hp (66 kW) at 4,800 rpm; max torque (SAE net): 122 lb ft, 16.9 kgm (165 Nm) at 2,600 rpm; max engine rpm: 5,200; 38.7 hp/l (28.7 kW/l); 1 Holley-Weber EOEE-VA/NA downdraught twin barrel carburettor.

TRANSMISSION axle ratio: 3.080.

VARIATIONS

ENGINE 6 cylinders, in line, 200 cu in, 3,300 cc (3.68 x 3.13 in, 93.5 x 79.4 mm), 8.6:1 compression ratio, 7 crankshaft bearings, 1 Holley 1946 EOBE-AAA downdraught barrel carburettor, cooling 15 imp pt, 18 US pt, 8.5 l.
TRANSMISSION Select-Shift C-3 automatic transmission, hydraulic torque converter and planetary gears with 3 ratios (I 2.470, II 1.470, III 1, rev 2.190), max ratio of converter at stall 2.30, steering column lever, 2.730 axle ratio.
PERFORMANCE max speed 100 mph, 160 km/h, speed in direct drive at 1,000 rpm 20.8 mph, 33.4 km/h.
DIMENSIONS AND WEIGHT weight plus 31 lb, 14.1 kg.

119 hp power team

See 88 hp power team, except for:

ENGINE 8 cylinders; 255 cu in, 4,179 cc (3.68 x 3 in, 93.5 x 76.2 mm); compression ratio: 8.8:1; max power (SAE net): 119 hp (89 kW) at 3,800 rpm; max torque (SAE net): 194 lb ft, 26.8 kg m (263 Nm) at 2,200 rpm; max engine rpm: 4,200; 28.5 hp/l (21.3 kW/l); valves: overhead, Vee-slanted, push-rods and rockers; camshafts: 1, at centre of Vee, chain-driven; 1 Ford 2150 EOKE-HA (EO4E-FA with variable Venturi for California only) downdraught twin barrel carburettor, water-cooled, 23.6 imp pt, 28.3 US pt, 13.4 l.

TRANSMISSION gearbox: Select-Shift C-4 automatic transmission, hydraulic torque converter and planetary gears with 3 ratios, max ratio of converter at stall 2.09, possible manual selection; ratios: I 2.460, II 1.460, III 1, rev 2.190; lever: steering column; axle ratio: 2.260.

PERFORMANCE max speed: 100 mph, 160 km/h; power-weight ratio: 4-dr sedan 24.4 lb/hp (32.6 lb/kW), 11.1 kg/hp (14.8 kg/kW).

ELECTRICAL EQUIPMENT 36 Ah battery.

DIMENSIONS AND WEIGHT weight: plus 212 lb, 96 kg.

150 hp power team

See 88 hp power team, except for:

ENGINE turbocharged; max power (SAE net): 150 hp (110 kW) at 4,800 rpm; 65.2 hp/l (48 kW/l); lubrication: 9.2 imp pt, 11 US pt, 5.2 l; 1 Holley-Weber EOZE-AMA downdraught twin barrel carburettor; exhaust system with turbocharger.

150 HP POWER TEAM

TRANSMISSION gearbox: Select-Shift C-3 automatic transmission, hydraulic torque converter with planetary gears with 3 ratios, max ratio of converter at stall 2.49, possible manual selection; ratios: I 2.470, II 1.470, III 1, rev 2.110; lever: steering column; axle ratio: 3.450

PERFORMANCE max speed: 109 mph, 175 km/h; power weight ratio: 4-dr Sedan 18.5 lb/hp (25.1 lb/kW), 8.4 kg/hp (11.4 kg/kW); speed in direct at 1,000 rpm: 22.7 mph, 36.5 km/h; consumption: 26.4 m/imp gal, 22 m/US gal, 10.7 l x 100 km.

DIMENSIONS AND WEIGHT weight: plus 83 lb, 38 kg; fuel tank: 10.6 imp gal, 12.7 US gal, 48 l.

Granada Series

PRICES EX WORKS:	$
1 2-dr Sedan	**6,001**
2 4-dr Sedan	**6,155**
3 Ghia 2-dr Sedan	**6,452**
4 Ghia 4-dr Sedan	**6,606**
5 ESS 2-dr Sedan	**6,597**
6 ESS 4-dr Sedan	**6,750**

For 117 hp and 134 hp engines add $ 245.

Power team:	Standard for:	Optional for:
97 hp	all	—
117 hp	all	—
134 hp	—	all

97 hp power team

ENGINE front, 4 stroke; 6 cylinders, in line; 250 cu in, 4,097 cc (3.68 x 3.91 in, 93.5 x 99.3 mm); compression ratio: 8.6:1; max power (SAE net): 97 hp (71 kW) at 3,200 rpm; max torque (SAE net): 210 lb ft, 29 kg m (284 Nm) at 1,400 rpm; max engine rpm: 3,800; 23.7 hp/l (17.4 kW/l); cast iron block and head; 7 crankshaft bearings; valves: overhead, in line, push-rods and rockers, hydraulic tappets; camshafts: 1, side; lubrication: rotary pump, full flow filter, 6.7 imp pt, 8 US pt, 3.8 l; 1 Carter - YFA EODE-NA downdraught single barrel carburettor; air cleaner; exhaust system with catalytic converter; fuel feed: mechanical pump; water-cooled, 17.4 imp pt, 21 US pt, 9.9 l.

TRANSMISSION driving wheels: rear; clutch: single dry plate, semi-centrifugal; gearbox: mechanical; gears: 4, fully synchronized with overdrive/top; ratios: I 3.290, II 1.840, III 1, IV 0.810, rev 3.290: lever: central; final drive: hypoid bevel; axle ratio: 3; width of rims: 6"; tyres: DR78 x 14.

PERFORMANCE max speed: 93 mph, 149 km/h; power-weight ratio: 2-dr sedans 33.1 lb/hp (44.9 lb/kW), 15 kg/hp (20.4 kg/kW); speed in direct drive at 1,000 rpm: 29.1 mph, 46.6 km/h; consumption: 22.8 m/imp gal, 19 m/US gal, 12.4 l x 100 km.

CHASSIS integral; front suspension: independent, wishbones, coil springs, anti-roll bar, telescopic dampers; rear: rigid axle, semi-elliptic leafsprings, telescopic dampers.

FORD Granada ESS Sedan

FORD Granada Ghia Sedan

STEERING recirculating ball; turns lock to lock: 5.18.

BRAKES front disc (diameter 11.03 in, 28 cm), front internal radial fins, rear compensator, rear drum; swept area: total 348.2 sq in, 2,247 sq cm.

ELECTRICAL EQUIPMENT 12 V; 36 Ah battery; 60 A alternator; Motorcraft transistorized ignition; 2 headlamps.

DIMENSIONS AND WEIGHT wheel base: 109.90 in, 279 cm; tracks: 59 in, 150 cm front, 57.70 in, 147 cm rear; length: 199.70 in, 507 cm; width: 74.50 in, 189 cm; height: 53.20 in, 135 cm - 4-dr 53.30 in, 135 cm; ground clearance: 4.62 in, 11.7 cm; weight: 2-dr sedans 3,207 lb, 1,454 kg - 4-dr sedans 3,250 lb, 1,474 kg; turning circle: 39 ft, 11.9 m; fuel tank: 15 imp gal, 18 US gal, 68 l.

BODY saloon/sedan; 5 seats, separate front seats, reclining backrests.

OPTIONALS Select-Shift C-4 automatic transmission with 3 ratios (I 2.460, II 1.460, III 1, rev 2.190), max ratio of converter at stall 2.3, possible manual selection, central or steering column lever, 2.790 axle ratio; ER 78 x 14/B BSW or FR x 14/B BSW tyres with 6" wide rims; light alloy wheels; wire wheels; heavy-duty suspension; power steering; tilt of steering wheel; servo brake; metallic spray; tinted glass; heated rear window; electric window; electric door locks; electric sunshine roof; vinyl roof; 54 Ah heavy-duty battery.

117 power team

(for California only)

See 97 hp power team, except for:

ENGINE 8 cylinders; 255 cu in, 4,200 cc (3.68 x 3 in, 93.5 x 76.2 mm); compression ratio: 8.4:1; max power (SAE net): 117 hp (87 kW) at 3,800 rpm; max torque (SAE net): 193 lb ft, 26.7 kg m (262 Nm) at 2,000 rpm; max engine rpm: 4,200; 27.9 hp/l (20.7 kW/l); cast iron block and head; 5 crankshaft bearings; camshafts: 1, at centre of Vee; 1 Ford 2150 EO4E-FA with variable Venturi downdraught carburettor; cooling, 23.6 imp pt, 28.3 US pt, 13.4 l.

TRANSMISSION gearbox: Select-Shit automatic transmission, hydraulic torque converter and planetary gears with 3 ratios, possible manual selection; ratios: I 2.460, II 1.460, III 1, rev 2.190; lever: steering column; final drive: hypoid bevel; axle ratio: 2.790; width of rims: 6"; tyres: DR 78 x 14 BSW.

PERFORMANCE max speed: 96 mph, 154 km/h; power-weight ratio: 2-dr sedans 27.4 lb/hp (36.9 lb/kW), 12.4 kg/hp (16.7 kg/kW); carrying capacity: 992 lb, 450 kg; speed in direct drive at 1,000 rpm: 25.3 mph, 40.5 km/h; consumption: 19.2 m/imp gal, 16 m/US gal, 14.7 l x 100 km.

DIMENSIONS AND WEIGHT weight: plus 79 lb, 36 kg.

134 hp power team

(not available in California)

See 97 hp power team, except for:

ENGINE 8 cylinders; 302 cu in, 4,950 cc (4 x 3 in, 101.6 x 76.2 mm); compression ratio: 8.4:1; max power (SAE net): 134 hp (100 kW) at 3,600 rpm; max torque (SAE net): 232 lb ft, 32.1 k m (315 Nm) at 1,600 rpm; max engine rpm: 4,000; 27.1 hp (20.2 kW/l); 5 crankshaft bearings; camshafts: 1, at centre o Vee; 1 Ford 2150 EOSE-HA downdraught twin barrel carburettor; cooling, 23.6 imp pt, 28.3 US pt, 13.4 l.

PERFORMANCE max speed: about 103 mph, 165 km/h; power weight ratio: 2-dr sedans 24.7 lb/hp (33.1 lb/kW), 11.2 kg/h (15 kg/kW); consumption: 20.5 m/imp gal, 13.8 l x 100 km.

DIMENSIONS AND WEIGHT weight: plus 106 lb, 48 kg.

OPTIONALS Select-Shift C-4 automatic transmission with ma ratio of converter at stall 2.

Thunderbird Sedan

PRICE EX WORKS: $ 8,069

For 131 hp engine add $ 266.

115 hp power team

ENGINE front; 4 stroke; 8 cylinders; 255 cu in, 4,200 c (3.68 x 3 in, 93.5 x 76.2 mm); compression ratio: 8.8:1; ma power (SAE net): 115 hp (86 kW) at 3,800 rpm; max torqu (SAE net): 191 lb ft, 26.4 kg m (259 Nm) at 2,000 rpm; ma engine rpm: 4,200; 27.4 hp/l (20.5 kW/l); cast iron block an head; 5 crankshaft bearings; valves: overhead, in line, push rods and rockers, hydraulic tappets; camshafts: 1, at centre o Vee; lubrication: rotary pump, full flow filter, 7 imp pt, 8.5 U pt, 4l; 1 Ford 2150 EOKE-HA (EO4E-FA with variable Ventu for California only) downdraught twin barrel carburettor; a cleaner; exhaust system with catalytic converter; fuel feed mechanical pump; water-cooled, 23.6 imp pt, 28.3 US pt, 13.4 l

TRANSMISSION driving wheels: rear; gearbox: Select-Shift C- automatic transmission, hydraulic torque converter and planet ary gears with 3 ratios, max ratio of converter at stall 2.09 (2.2 for California only), possible manual selection; ratios: I 2.460, 1.460, III 1, rev 2.190; lever: steering column; final drive hypoid bevel; axle ratio: 2.260; width of rims: 5.5"; tyres: 185/75 x 14 BSW.

PERFORMANCE max speed: 97 MPH, 155 km/h; power-weigh ratio: 28.4 lb/hp (37.9 lb/kW), 12.9 kg/hp (17.2 kg/kW); carryin capacity: 816 lb, 370 kg; speed in direct drive at 1,000 rpm 25.5 mph, 40.9 km/h; consumption: 21.6 m/imp gal, 18 m/U gal, 13.1 l x 100 km.

CHASSIS integral with two cross members; front suspension independent by McPherson, wishbones (lower control arm), co springs, telescopic dampers; rear: rigid axle, lower trailin radius arms, upper oblique torque arms, coil springs, telescopi dampers.

STEERING rack-and-pinion, variable ratio, servo; turns lock t lock: 3.40.

BRAKES front disc (diameter 10.06 in, 25.5 cm), front interna radial fins, rear compensator, rear drum, servo; swept area front 176.6 sq in, 1,140 sq cm, rear 99 sq in, 638 sq cm, tota 275.6 sq in, 1,778 sq cm.

ELECTRICAL EQUIPMENT 12 V; 36 Ah battery; 60 A alterna tor; Motorcraft transistorized ignition; 4 headlamps.

DIMENSIONS AND WEIGHT wheel base: 108.40 in, 27.5 cm tracks: 58.10 in, 148 cm front, 57 in, 145 cm rear; length

200.40 in, 509 cm; width: 74.10 in, 188 cm; height: 53 in, 135 cm; ground clearance: 4.89 in, 124 cm; weight: 3,262 lb, 1,480 kg; weight distribution: 57% front, 43% rear; turning circle: 40.1ft, 12.2 m; fuel tank: 14.5 imp gal, 17.4 US gal, 66 l.

BODY saloon/sedan; 2 doors; 4 seats, bench front seats, built-in headrests.

OPTIONALS light alloy wheels; limited slip differential; 45 Ah heavy-duty battery; manual air-conditioning; automatic air-conditioning; tinted glass; electric door locks; keyless entry system; electric windows; speed control; vinyl roof; sunshine roof.

131 hp power team

See 115 hp power team, except for:

ENGINE 302 cu in, 4,950 cc (4 x 3 in, 101.6 x 76.2 mm); compression ratio: 8.4:1; max power (SAE net): 131 hp (98 kW) at 3,600 rpm; max torque (SAE net): 231 lb ft, 31.9 kg m (313 Nm) at 1,600 rpm; max engine rpm: 4,000; 26.5 hp/l (19.8 kW/l); 1 Ford 2150 EOSE-HA (EO4E-FA for California only) downdraught twin barrel carburettor.

PERFORMANCE max speed: 100 mph, 160 km/h; power-weight ratio: 25.3 lb/hp, (33.8 lb/kW), 11.5 kg/hp (15.3 kg/kW); speed in direct drive at 1,000 rpm: 27.7 mph, 44.5 km/h; consumption: 20.5 m/imp gal, 17 m/US gal, 13.8 l x 100 km.

DIMENSIONS AND WEIGHT weight: plus 50 lb, 22.7 kg.

OPTIONALS Overdrive automatic transmission with 4 ratios (I 2.470, II 1.470, III 1, IV 0.670, rev 2) , max ratio of converter at stall 2.29, possible manual selection, 3.080 axle ratio.

FORD Thunderbird Sedan

LTD Series

PRICES EX WORKS:

		$
1	S 2-dr Sedan	**7,797**
2	S 4-dr Sedan	**7,846**
3	2-dr Sedan	**7,998**
4	4-dr Sedan	**8,107**
5	Crown Victoria 2-dr Sedan	**8,659**
6	Crown Victoria 4-dr Sedan	**8,794**
7	S 4+1-dr St. Wagon	**8,322**
8	4+1-dr St. Wagon	**8,487**
9	Country Squire 4+1-dr St. Wagon	**9,169**

For 140 hp engine add $ 266.

Power team:	Standard for:	Optional for:
130 hp	all	—
140 hp	—	all

130 hp power team

ENGINE front, 4 stroke; 8 cylinders; 302 cu in, 4,950 cc (4 x 3 in, 101.6 x 76.2); compression ratio: 8.4:1; max power (SAE net): 130 hp (97 kW) at 3,600 rpm; max torque (SAE net): 230 lb ft, 31.8 kg m (312 Nm) at 1,600 rpm; max engine rpm: 4,000; 26.3 hp/l (19.6 kW/l); cast iron block and head; 5 crankshaft bearings; valves: overhead, in line, push-rods and rockers, hydraulic tappets; camshafts: 1, at centre of Vee; lubrication: rotary pump, full flow filter, 6.7 imp pt, 8 US pt, 3.8 l; 1 Ford 2700 with variable Venturi (7200 for California only) downdraught carburettor; fuel feed: mechanical pump; water-cooled, 22.2 imp pt, 26.6 US pt, 12.6 l.

FORD Thunderbird Sedan (4.2-litre engine)

TRANSMISSION driving wheels: rear; gearbox: Select-Shift FMX automatic transmission, hydraulic torque converter and planetary gears with 3 ratios, max ratio of converter at stall 1.97, possible manual selection; ratios: I 2.400, II 1.470, III 1, rev 2; lever: steering column; final drive: hypoid bevel; axle ratio: 2.260 (2.730 for st. wagons only); width of rims: 5.5" - st. wagons 6.5"; tyres: P205/75R x 14 BSW.

PERFORMANCE max speed: 100 mph, 160 km/h; power-weight ratio: 2-dr sedans 27.6 lb/hp (36.9 lb/kW), 12.5 kg/hp (16.8 kg/kW); carrying capacity: 1,257 lb, 570 kg; speed in direct drive at 1,000 rpm: 26.3 mph, 42.2 km/h; consumption: 20.5 m/imp gal, 17 m/US gal,13.8 l x 100 km.

CHASSIS front and rear subframe; front suspension: independent, coil springs, wishbones, telescopic damper, anti-roll bar; rear: rigid axle, lower trailing radius arms, upper oblique torque arms, coil springs, telescopic dampers.

STEERING recirculating ball, servo; turns lock to lock: 3.40.

BRAKES front disc (diameter 11.08 in, 28.1 cm), front internal radial fins, rear compensator, rear drum servo; swept area: front 228.7 sq in, 1,475 sq cm, rear 157.1 sq in, 1,013 sq cm, - st. wagons 156 sq in, 1,006 sq cm, total 385.8 sq in, 2,488 sq cm - st. wagons 384.7 sq in, 2,481 sq cm.

ELECTRICAL EQUIPMENT 12 V; 36 Ah battery; 60 A alternator; Motorcraft transistorized ignition; 4 headlamps.

DIMENSIONS AND WEIGHT wheel base: 114.30 in, 290 cm; tracks: 62.20 in, 158 cm front, 62 in, 157 cm rear; length: 209.30 in, 532 cm; width: 77.50 in, 197 cm; height: 54.70 in, 139 cm - st. wagons 57.40 in, 146 cm; ground clearance: 5.17 in, 13.1 cm - st. wagons 5.63 in, 14.3 cm; weight: 2-dr sedans 3,595 lb, 1,631 kg - 4-dr sedans 3,623 lb, 1,643 kg - st. wagons 3,871 lb, 1,756 kg; turning circle: 39.2 ft, 11.9 m; fuel tank: 15.8 imp gal, 19 US gal, 72 l - st. wagons 16.7 imp gal, 20.1 US gal, 76 l.

BODY saloon/sedan, estate car/st. wagon; 6 seats, separate front seats with built-in headrests.

OPTIONALS Automatic overdrive transmission with 4 ratios (I 2.400, II 1.470, III 1, IV 0.670, rev 2), max ratio of converter at stall 2.29, possible manual selection, 3.080 axle ratio; P205/75R x 14 WSW or P225/ 75R x 14 WSW tyres with 6.5" wide rims; limited slip differential; light alloy wheels; digital electronic clock; tilt of steering wheel; tinted glass; electric windows; vinyl roof; sunshine roof; manual air-conditioning; automatic air-conditioning; 71 Ah heavy-duty battery; automatic speed control.

FORD LTD Country Squire Station Wagon

140 hp power team

See 130 hp power team, except for:

ENGINE 351 cu in, 5,753 cc (4x3.50 in, 101.6 x 88.9 mm); compression ratio: 8.3:1; max power (SAE net): 140 hp (104 kW) at 3,400 rpm; max torque (SAE net): 265 lb ft, 36.6 kg m (359 Nm) at 2,000 rpm; max engine rpm: 3,800; 24.3 hp/l (18.1 kW/l); 1 Ford 7200 downdraught with variable Venturi carburettor; cooling, 23.9 imp pt, 28.8 US pt, 13.6 l.

140 HP POWER TEAM

PERFORMANCE max speed: 106 mph, 170 km/h; power-weight ratio: 2-dr sedans 26.2 lb/hp (35.5 lb/kW), 11.9 kg/hp (16.1 kg/kW); sped in direct drive at 1,000 rpm: 31.2 mph, 49.9 km/h; consumption: 19.2 m/imp gal, 16 m/US gal, 14.7 l x 100 km.

ELECTRICAL EQUIPMENT 45 Ah battery.

DIMENSIONS AND WEIGHT weight: plus 91 lb, 41 kg.

OPTIONALS 3.080 axle ratio.

INTERNATIONAL HARVESTER USA

Scout Series

PRICES EX WORKS:

		$
1	II 4 x 4	**7,748**
2	II 4 x 4 Diesel	**9,861**
3	Traveler 4 x 4	**8,783**
4	Traveler 4 x 4 Diesel	**10,378**

For 122.3 hp V8 engine add $ 368; for 148 hp V8 engine add $ 499 - Traveler $ 131.

Power team:	Standard for:	Optional for:
76.5 hp	1	—
122.3 hp	3	—
148 hp	—	1.3
101 hp (diesel)	2,4	—

76.5 hp power team

ENGINE front, 4 stroke; 4 cylinders, in line; 196 cu in, 3,212 cc (4.13 x 3.66 in, 104.8 x 92.9 mm); compression ratio: 8.02:1; max power (DIN): 76.5 hp (56 kW) at 3,600 rpm, max torque (DIN): 153 lb ft, 21.2 kg m (208 Nm) at 2,000 rpm; max engine rpm: 4,000; 23.9 hp/l (17.6 kW/l); cast iron block and head; 5 crankshaft bearings; valves: overhead, in line, push-rods and rockers, hydraulic tappets; camshafts: 1, side; lubrication: gear pump, full flow filter, 11.6 imp pt, 14 US pt, 6.6 l; 1 Holley 1940 downdraught single barrel carburettor; air cleaner; fuel feed: mechanical pump; water-cooled, 23.2 imp pt, 27.9 US pt, 13.2 l.

TRANSMISSION driving wheels: front and rear; clutch: single dry plate; gearbox: mechanical; gears: 3, fully synchronized; ratios: I 2.997, II 1.550, III 1, rev 2.997; lever: central; final drive: hypoid bevel; axle ratio: 3.730; width of rims: 5.5''; tyres H78 x 15.

PERFORMANCE max speed: 80 mph, 128 km/h; power-weight ratio: 50.3 lb/hp (68.6 lb/kW), 22.8 kg/hp (31.1 kg/kW); speed in direct drive at 1,000 rpm: 20.1 mph, 32.3 km/h; consumption: 18 m/imp gal, 15 m/US gal, 15.7 l x 100 km.

CHASSIS perimeter box-type frame; front and rear suspension: rigid axle, semi-elliptic leafsprings, telescopic dampers.

STEERING worm and roller, servo.

BRAKES front disc (diameter 11.75 in, 29.8 cm), rear drum; swept area: front 226 sq in, 1,458 sq cm, rear 101.8 sq in, 656 sq cm, total 327.8 sq in, 2,114 sq cm.

ELECTRICAL EQUIPMENT 12 V; 62 Ah battery; 37 A alternator; Prestolite electronic ignition; 2 headlamps.

DIMENSIONS AND WEIGHT wheel base: 100 in, 254 cm; tracks: 58.50 in, 149 cm front, 57.62 in, 146 cm rear; length: 166.20 in, 422 cm; width: 70 in, 178 cm; height: 65.70 in, 167 cm; ground clearance: 7.60 in, 19.3 cm; weight: 3,840 lb, 1,741 kg; turning circle: 36.4 ft, 11.1 m; fuel tank: 15.8 imp gal, 19 US gal, 72 l.

BODY estate car/st. wagon; 2+1 doors; 5 seats, separate front seats.

OPTIONALS 4-speed fully synchronized mechanical gearbox (I 4.020, II 2.410, III 1.410, IV 1, rev 4.730 or I 6.320, II 3.090, III 1.680, IV 1, rev 6.960); gearbox with transfer box; 3-speed automatic transmission; 3.450 axle ratio; HR78 x 15 tyres; limited slip differential; tilt of steering wheel; bucket front seats with console; folding rear seat; 61 A alternator; 72 Ah battery; heavy-duty front and rear suspension; air-conditioning; Rallye equipment.

122.3 hp power team

See 76.5 hp power team, except for:

ENGINE 8 cylinders; 304 cu in, 4,982 cc (3.88 x 3.22 in, 98.5 x 81.7 mm); compression ratio: 8.19:1; max power (DIN): 122.3 hp (90 kW) at 3,400 rpm; max torque (DIN): 226 lb ft, 31 kg m (304 Nm) at 2,000 rpm; 24.5 hp/l (18 kW/l); camshafts: 1, at centre of Vee; dual exhaust system.

INTERNATIONAL HARVESTER Scout Traveler 4 x 4

TRANSMISSION axle ratio: 3.310.

PERFORMANCE max speed: 90 mph, 145 km/h; power-weight ratio: Traveler 34.4 lb/hp (46.7 lb/kW), 15.6 kg/hp (21.2 kg/kW); speed in direct drive at 1,000 rpm: 20.3 mph, 36.2 km/h; consumption: 16.8 m/imp gal, 14 m/US gal, 16.8 l x 100 km.

DIMENSIONS AND WEIGHT weight: II 4 x 4 3,995 lb, 1,812 kg - Traveler 4 x 4 4,201 lb, 1,905 kg.

148 hp power team

See 76.5 hp power team, except for:

ENGINE 8 cylinders; 345 cu in, 5,654 cc (3.88 x 3.66 in, 98.5 x 92.9 mm); compression ratio: 8.05:1; max power (DIN): 148 hp (109 kW kW) at 3,600 rpm; max torque (DIN): 265 lb ft, 35.9 kg m (352 Nm) at 2,000 rpm; max engine rpm: 3,800; 26.1 hp/l (19.2 kW/l); camshafts: 1, at centre of Vee; dual exhaust system; cooling, 33.3 imp pt. 40 US pt, 18.9 l.

TRANSMISSION axle ratio: 3.540.

PERFORMANCE max speed: 90 mph, 145 km/h; power-weight ratio II 4 x 4 24.9 lb/hp (33.8 lb/kW), 11.3 kg/hp (15.3 kg/kW); speed in direct drive at 1,000 rpm: 25 mph, 40.3 km/h; consumption: 15.6 m/imp gal, 13 m/US gal, 18.1 l x 100 km.

JEEP CJ-7 Laredo Roadster

DIMENSIONS AND WEIGHT weight: II 4 x 4 3,686 lb, 1,672 kg - Traveler 4 x 4 3,891 lb, 1,765 kg.

101 hp (diesel) power team

See 76.5 hp power team, except for:

ENGINE diesel, turbocharged, 4 stroke; 6 cylinders, vertical, in line; 198 cu in, 3.245 cc (3.27 x 3.94 in, 83 x 100 mm); compression ratio: 22:1; max power (DIN): 101 hp (74 kW) at 3,800 rpm; max torque (DIN): 175 lb ft, 24.1 kg m (236 Nm) at 2,200 rpm; max engine rpm: 4.000; 31.1 hp/l (22.9 kW/l); 7 crankshaft bearings.

PERFORMANCE power-weight ratio: II 4 x 4 37.9 lb/hp (51.8 lb/kW), 17.2 kg/hp (23.5 kg/kW).

JEEP CORPORATION USA

Jeep Series

PRICES EX WORKS:

		$
1	CJ-5 Roadster	**6,095**
2	CJ-7 Roadster	**6,295**

Power team:	Standard for:	Optional for:
90 hp	both	—
98 hp	—	both
126 hp	—	both

90 hp power team

ENGINE front, 4 stroke; 4 cylinders, in line; 151 cu in, 2,475 cc (4 x 3 in, 101.6 x 76.2 mm); compression ratio: 8.2:1; max power (DIN): 90 hp (66 kW) at 4,400 rpm; max torque (DIN): 128 lb ft, 17.6 kg m (173 Nm) at 2,400 rpm; max engine rpm: 5,200; 36.4 hp/l (26.7 kW/l); cast iron block and head; 5 crankshaft bearings; valves: overhead, in line, push-rods and rockers, hydraulic tappets; camshafts: 1, side; lubrication: gear pump, full flow filter, 6.7 imp pt. 8 US pt, 3.8 l; 1 Holley 5210 downdraught twin barrel carburettor; air cleaner; exhaust system with catalytic converter; fuel feed: mechanical pump; water-cooled 17.8 imp pt, 21.4 US pt, 10.1 l.

TRANSMISSION driving wheels: front (automatically-engaged with transfer box low ratio) and rear; clutch: single dry plate; gearbox: mechanical; gears: 4, fully synchronized; ratios: I 3.500, II 2.480, III 1.660, IV 1, rev 3.500; lever: central; final drive: hypoid bevel; axle ratio: 3.540; width of rims: 5.5''; tyres: H 78 x 15 B.

PERFORMANCE max speed: 78 mph, 125 km/h; power-weight ratio: CJ-5 27.6 lb/hp (37.5 lb/kW), 12.5 kg/hp (17 kg/kW); speed in direct drive at 1,000 rpm: 15 mph, 25 km/h; consumption: 25.2 m/imp gal, 21 m/US gal, 11.2 l x 100 km.

CHASSIS perimeter box-type with cross members; front and rear suspension: rigid axle, semi-elliptic leafsprings, telescopic dampers.

STEERING recirculating ball.

RAKES front disc (diameter 11.75 in, 29.8 cm); internal radial ns, rear drum.

LECTRICAL EQUIPMENT 12 V; 50 Ah battery; 37 A alternar; electronic ignition; 2 headlamps.

IMENSIONS AND WEIGHT wheel base: CJ-5 83.50 in, 212 cm CJ-7 93.50 in, 237 cm; tracks: 51.50 in, 131 cm front, 50 in, 27 cm rear; length: CJ-5 144.30 in, 366 cm - CJ-7 153.20 in, 89 cm; width: 68.60 in, 174 cm; height: 67.60 in, 172 cm; round clearance: 6.90 in, 17.5 cm; weight: CJ-5 2,484 lb, 125 kg - CJ-7 2,544 lb, 1,152 kg; turning circle: CJ-5 36.7 ft, 1.2 m - CJ-7 40.9 ft, 12.5 m; fuel tank: 12.5 imp gal, 15 US al, 57 l.

ODY roadster; no doors; 4 seats, separate front seats.

PTIONALS 4.090 axle ratio; rear limited slip differential; ports steering wheel; power steering; servo brake; all or half etal top; rear bench seats; heavy-duty suspension; light alloy heels; Levi's interior; Renegade equipment with luxury interior, racing style roll bar, heavy-duty cooling and L78 x 15 res; Golden Eagle equipment with luxury interior, styled steel heels, roll bar, rear bench seats and H78 x 15 G or 9 x 15 res; Laredo equipment; (for CJ-7 only) Turbo-Hydramatic utomatic transmission with 4-wheel drive Quadra-Trac system; ll plastic top.

98 hp power team

ee 90 hp power team, except for:

NGINE front, 4 stroke; 6 cylinders, in line; 258 cu in, 4,228 cc .75 x 3.90 in, 95.2 x 99 mm); compression ratio: 8:1; max ower (DIN): 98 hp (72 kW) at 3,200 rpm; max torque (DIN): 93 lb ft, 26.6 kg m (261 Nm) at 1,600 rpm; max engine rpm: ,000; 23.2 hp/l (17.1 kW/l); cast iron block and head; 7 rankshaft bearings; valves: overhead, in line, push-rods and ockers, hydraulic tappets; camshafts: 1, side; lubrication: gear ump, full flow filter, 10 imp pt, 12 US pt, 5.7 l; 1 downdraught vin barrel carburettor; fuel feed: mechanical pump; waterooled, 17.4 imp pt, 21 US pt, 9.9 l.

RANSMISSION axle ratio: 3.070.

ERFORMANCE max speed: 78 mph, 125 km/h; power-weight atio: CJ-5 25.4 lb/hp (34.4 lb/kW), 11.5 kg/hp (15.6 kg/kW); peed in direct drive at 1,000 rpm: 23.6 mph, 38 km/h; conumption: 21.6 m/imp gal, 18 m/US gal, 13.1 l x 100 km.

PTIONALS 3.540 axle ratio.

126 hp power team

ee 90 hp power team, except for:

NGINE 8 cylinders; 304 cu in, 4,982 cc (3.75 x 3.44 in, 5.2 x 87.3 mm); compression ratio: 8.4:1; max power (DIN): 26 hp (93 kW) at 3,600 rpm; max torque (DIN): 219 lb ft, 30.2 g m (296 Nm) at 2,000 rpm; 25.3 hp/l (18.6 kW/l); 5 crankshaft earings; camshafts: 1, at centre of Vee; lubrication: 8.3 imp pt, .9 US pt, 4.7 l; 1 downdraught twin barrel carburettor; exhaust ystem with catalytic converter; cooling, 23.2 imp pt, 28 US pt, 3.2 l.

RANSMISSION axle ratio: 3.070.

JEEP Cherokee Laredo Station Wagon

PERFORMANCE max speed: 84 mph, 135 km/h; power-weight ratio: CJ-5 19.6 lb/hp (26.7 lb/kW), 8.9 kg/hp (12.1 kg/kW); consumption: 19.2 m/imp gal, 16 m/US gal, 14.7 l x 100 km.

STEERING for California only, servo.

OPTIONALS 3.540 axle ratio.

Cherokee Series

PRICES EX WORKS:	$
1 2+1-dr Wagon	7,730
2 Wide Wheel 2+1-dr Wagon	8,298
3 4+1-dr Wagon	7,842

Power team:	Standard for:	Optional for:
114 hp	all	—
129 hp	—	all

114 hp power team

(not available in California)

ENGINE front, 4 stroke; 6 cylinders, in line; 258 cu in, 4,228 cc (3.75 x 3.90 in, 95.2 x 99 mm); compression ratio: 8:1; max power (DIN): 114 hp (84 kW) at 3,600 rpm; max torque (DIN): 192 lb ft, 26.5 kg m (260 Nm) at 2,000 rpm; max engine rpm: 4,000; 27 hp/l (19.9 kW/l); cast iron block and head; 7 crankshaft bearings; valves: ovrhead, in line, push-rods and rockers, hydraulic tappets; camshafts: 1, side; lubrication: gear pump, full flow filter, 10 imp pt, 12 US pt, 5.7 l; 1 Carter downdraught twin barrel carburettor; fuel feed: mechanical pump; water-cooled, 17.4 imp pt, 21 US pt, 9.9 l.

TRANSMISSION driving wheels: front and rear (Quadra - Trac system with central limited slip differential); clutch: single dry plate; gearbox: mechanical; gears: 4, fully synchronized, ratios: I 3.500, II 2.480, III 1.660, IV 1, rev 3.500; lever: central; final drive: hypoid bevel; axle ratio: 3.310; width of rims: 5.5"; tyres: H78 x 15 - Wide Wheel 10 x 15.

PERFORMANCE max speed: 90 mph, 145 km/h; power-weight ratio: 2+1-dr 33.5 lb/hp (45.4 lb/kW), 15.2 kg/hp (20.6 kg/kW); speed in direct drive at 1,000 rpm: 22.5 mph, 36.2 km/h; consumption: 21.6 m/imp gal, 18 m/US gal, 13.1 l x 100 km.

CHASSIS perimeter box-type with cross members; front and rear suspension: rigid axle, semi-elliptic leafsprings, telescopic dampers.

STEERING recirculating ball, variable ratio servo.

BRAKES front disc (diameter 12 in, 30.5 cm), rear drum, servo.

ELECTRICAL EQUIPMENT 12 V; 50 Ah battery; 37 A alternator; electronic ignition; 2 headlamps.

DIMENSIONS AND WEIGHT wheel base: 108.70 in, 276 cm; front track: 59.40 in, 151 cm - Wide Wheel 65.40 in, 166 cm; rear track: 57.80 in, 147 cm - Wide Wheel 62.30 in, 158 cm; length: 183.50 in, 466 cm; width: 75.60 in, 192 cm - Wide Wheel 78.90 in, 200 cm; height: 66.90 in, 170 cm - Wide Wheel 67.60 in, 172 cm; ground clearance: 7.70 in, 19.6 cm - Wide Wheel 8.60 in, 21.8 cm; weight: 2-dr 3,822 lb, 1,731 kg - Wide Wheel 3,911 lb, 1,772 kg - 4-dr 3,883 lb, 1,759 kg; turning circle: 37.7 ft, 11.5 m - Wide Wheel 39.4 ft, 12 m; fuel tank: 17.8 imp gal, 21.5 US gal, 81 l.

BODY estate car/st. wagon; 5 seats, separate front seats.

OPTIONALS Turbo-Hydramatic automatic transmission with 4-wheel drive Quadra-Trac system and 2.730 (for wide Wheel only 3.310) axle ratio; rear limited slip differential; light alloy wheels; sports steering wheel; tilt of steering wheel; De Luxe interior; heavy-duty cooling; 70 Ah battery; 63 A alternator; anti-roll bar on front suspension; heavy-duty suspension; tinted glass; heated rear window; air-cônditioning; S equipment, Chief equipment and Golden Eagle equipment (for Wide Wheel only); Laredo equipment.

JEEP Wagoneer Limited

129 hp power team

(standard in California)

See 114 hp power team, except for:

ENGINE 8 cylinders; 360 cu in, 5,899 cc (4.08 x 3.44 in, 103.6 x 87.3 mm); compression ratio: 8.25:1; max power (DIN): 129 hp (95 kW) at 3,700 rpm; max torque (DIN): 245 lb ft, 33.8 kg m (331 Nm) at 1,600 rpm; max engine rpm: 4,200; 21.9 hp/l (16.1 kW/l); 5 crankshaft bearings; camshafts: 1, at centre of Vee; lubrication: 8.3 imp pt, 9.9 US pt, 4.7 l; 1 downdraught twin barrel carburettor; air cleaner; cooling, 21.6 imp pt, 26 US pt, 12.3 l.

PERFORMANCE max speed 99 mph, 160 km/h; power weight ratio: 2-dr 29.5 lb/hp (40.1 lb/kW), 13.4 kg/hp (18.2 kg/kW); speed in direct drive at 1,000 rpm: 24.9 mph, 40 km/h; consumption: 16.8 m/imp gal, 14 m/US gal, 16.8 l x 100 km.

129 HP POWER TEAM

ELECTRICAL EQUIPMENT 60 Ah battery; 40 A alternator.

OPTIONALS Turbo-Hydramatic automatic transmission with 4-wheel drive Quadra-Trac system and 2.730 axle ratio.

Wagoneer Series

PRICES EX WORKS:

		$
1	Standard	9,356
2	Limited	13,240

Power team:	Standard for:	Optional for:
114 hp	—	both
129 hp	both	—

114 hp power team

(not available in California)

ENGINE front, 4 stroke; 6 cylinders, in line; 258 cu in, 4,228 cc (3.75 x 3.90 in, 95.2 x 99 mm); compression ratio: 8:1; max power (DIN): 114 hp (84 kW) at 3,600 rpm; max torque (DIN): 192 lb ft, 26.5 kg m (260 Nm) at 2,000 rpm; max engine rpm: 4,000; 27 hp/l (19.9 kW/l); cast iron block and head; 7 crankshaft bearings; valves: overhead, in line, push-rods and rockers, hydraulic tappets; camshafts: 1, side; lubrication: gear pump, full flow filter, 10 imp pt, 12 US pt, 5.7 l; 1 Carter downdraught twin barrel carburettor; fuel feed: mechanical pump; water-cooled, 17.4 imp pt, 21 US pt, 9.9 l.

TRANSMISSION driving wheels: front and rear (Quadra-Trac system with central limited slip differential); gearbox: Turbo-Hydramatic automatic transmission, hydraulic torque converter and planetary gears with 3 ratios, max ratio of converter at stall 2.3, possible manual selection; ratios: I 2.480, II 1.480, III 1, rev 2.080; lever: central; final drive: hypoid bevel; axle ratio: 2.730; width of rims: 5.5"; tyres: H78 x 15.

PERFORMANCE max speed: 90 mph, 145 km/h; power-weight ratio: 36 lb/hp (48.9 lb/kW), 16.3 kg/hp (22.1 kg/kW); speed in direct drive at 1,000 rpm: 22.5 mph, 36.2 km/h; consumption: 21.6 m/imp gal, 18 m/US gal, 13.1 l x 100 km.

CHASSIS perimeter box-type cross members; front and rear suspension: rigid axle, semi-elliptic leafsprings, telescopic dampers.

STEERING recirculating ball, variable ratio servo.

BRAKES front disc (diameter 12 in, 30 cm), rear drum, servo.

ELECTRICAL EQUIPMENT 12 V; 50 Ah battery; 37 A alternator; electronic ignition; 2 headlamps.

DIMENSIONS AND WEIGHT wheel base: 108.70 in, 276 cm; tracks: 59.40 in, 151 cm front, 57.80 in, 147 cm rear; length: 183.50 in, 466 cm; width: 75.60 in, 192 cm; height: 66.70 in, 169 cm; ground clearance: 7.70 in, 19.6 cm; weight: 4,149 lb, 1,879 kg; turning circle: 37.7 ft, 11.5 m; fuel tank: 17.8 imp gal, 21.5 US gal, 81 l.

BODY estate car/st. wagon; 4+1 doors; 6 seats, bench front seats; folding rear seat; (for Limited only) luxury equipment, light alloy wheels and HR 78 x 15 tyres.

OPTIONALS 3.310 axle ratio; anti-roll bar on front suspension; light alloy wheels; tilt of steering wheel; 70 Ah battery; 63 A alternator; heavy-duty cooling; heavy-duty suspension; tinted glass; heated rear window; air-conditioning.

129 hp power team

(standard in California)

See 114 hp power team, except for:

ENGINE 8 cylinders; 360 cu in, 5,899 cc (4.08 x 3.44 in, 103.6 x 87.3 mm); compression ratio: 8.25:1; max power (DIN): 129 hp (95 kW) at 3,700 rpm; max torque (DIN): 245 lb ft, 33.8 kg m (331 Nm) at 1,600 rpm; max engine rpm: 4,200; 21.9 hp/l (16.1 kW/l); 5 crankshaft bearings; camshafts: 1, at centre of Vee; lubrication: 8.3 imp pt, 9.9 US pt, 4.7 l; air cleaner; cooling, 21.6 imp pt, 26 US pt, 12.3 l.

PERFORMANCE max speed: 99 mph, 159 km/h; power-weight ratio: 32.2 lb/hp (43.7 lb/kW), 14.6 kg/hp (19.8 kg/kW); speed in direct drive at 1,000 rpm: 26.4 mph, 42.5 km/h; consumption: 16.8 m/imp gal, 14 m/US gal, 16.8 l x 100 km.

ELECTRICAL EQUIPMENT 50 Ah battery; 37 A alternator.

KELMARK USA

GT

PRICE EX WORKS: $ 11,400

ENGINE Volkswagen-Porsche, rear, 4 stroke; 4 cylinders, horizontally opposed; 102.4 cu in, 1,679 cc (3.54 x 2.60 in, 90 x 66 mm); compression ratio: 8.5:1; max power (DIN): 100 hp (74 kW) at 5,000 rpm; max torque (DIN): 110 lb ft, 13.8 kg m (135 Nm) at 3,500 rpm; max engine rpm: 5,500; 59.6 hp/l (43.8 kW/l); light alloy block and head, separate cylinders with Ferral chromium walls; 4 crankshaft bearings; valves: overhead, in line, push-rods and rockers; camshafts: 1, central, lower; lubrication: gear pump, filter in sump, oil cooler, 6.2 imp pt, 7.4 US pt, 3.5 l; 2 Weber downdraught carburettors; fuel feed: electric pump; air-cooled.

TRANSMISSION driving wheels: rear; clutch: single dry plate (diaphragm), hydraulically controlled; gearbox: mechanical; gears: 4, fully synchronized; ratios: I 3.560, II 2.060, III 1.250, IV 0.890; lever: central; final drive: hypoid bevel; width of rims: front 7", rear 8.5"; tyres: ER60 x 14 front, GR50 x 15 rear.

PERFORMANCE max speed: 125 mph, 201 km/h; power-weight ratio: 17 lb/hp (23.1 lb/kW), 7.7 kg/hp (10.5 kg/kW); speed in top at 1,000 rpm: 24.9 mph, 40 km/h; consumption: 42.2 m/imp gal, 35 m/US gal, 6.7 l x 100 km.

CHASSIS backbone platform; front suspension: independent, twin swinging longitudinal trailing arms, transverse laminated torsion bars, anti-roll bar, telescopic dampers; rear: independent, swinging semi-axles, swinging longitudinal trailing arms, transverse torsion bars, telescopic dampers.

STEERING rack-and-pinion.

BRAKES front disc, rear drum.

ELECTRICAL EQUIPMENT 12 V; 43 Ah battery; alternator; Bosch distributor; 2 headlamps.

DIMENSIONS AND WEIGHT wheel base: 95 in, 241 cm; tracks: 58 in, 147 cm front, 60 in, 152 cm rear; length: 174 in, 442 cm; width: 73 in, 185 cm; height: 45 in, 114 cm; ground clearance: 7 in, 17.8 cm; weight: 1,700 lb, 771 kg; weight distribution: 40% front, 60% rear; fuel tank: 8.4 imp gal, 10 US gal, 38 l.

BODY coupé, in plastic material; 2 doors; 2 seats.

OPTIONALS light alloy wheels; air-conditioning; sunshine roof; leather upholstery; fog lamps.

LINCOLN USA

Versailles

PRICE EX WORKS: $ 14,674

ENGINE front, 4 stroke; 8 cylinders; 302 cu in, 4,950 cc (4 x 3 in, 101.6 x 76.2 mm); compression ratio: 8.4:1; max power (SAE net): 132 hp (98 kW) at 3,600 rpm; max torque (SAE net): 232 lb ft, 32.1 kg m (315 Nm) at 1,400 rpm; max engine rpm: 4,000; 26.6 hp/l (19.8 kW/l); cast iron block and head; 5 crankshaft bearings; valves: overhead, in line, push-rods and rockers, hydraulic tappets; camshafts: 1, at centre of Vee; lubrication: rotary pump, full flow filter, 6.7 imp pt, 8 US pt, 3.8 l; 1 Ford 2700 D94E-KA downdraught carburettor with variable Venturi; air cleaner; exhaust system with catalytic converter; fuel feed: mechanical pump; water-cooled, 23.9 imp pt, 28.8 US pt, 13.6 l.

TRANSMISSION driving wheels: rear; gearbox: Select-Shift automatic transmission, hydraulic torque converter and planetary gears with 3 ratios, max ratio of converter at stall 2, possible manual selection; ratios: I 2.460, II 1.460, III 1, rev 2.190; lever: steering column; final drive: hypoid bevel; axle ratio: 2.470; width of rims: 6"; tyres: FR78 x 14.

PERFORMANCE max speed: 109 mph, 175 km/h; power-weight ratio: 28.9 lb/hp (38.9 lb/kW), 13.1 kg/hp (17.6 kg/kW); speed in direct drive at 1,000 rpm: 30 mph, 48.3 km/h; consumption: 21.6 m/imp gal, 18 m/US gal, 13.1 l x 100 km.

CHASSIS integral; front suspension: independent, wish-bones, coil springs, anti-roll bar, telescopic dampers; rear: rigid axle, semi-elliptic leafsprings, telescopic dampers.

STEERING recirculating ball, servo; turns lock to lock: 3.70.

BRAKES disc (front diameter 11.03 in, 28 cm, rear 10.66 in, 27.1 cm), internal radial fins, rear compensator, servo; swept area: front 222.5 sq in, 1,435 sq cm, rear 232.3 sq in, 1,499 sq cm, total 454.8 sq in, 2,934 sq cm.

ELECTRICAL EQUIPMENT 12 V; 53 Ah battery; 60 A alternator; Motorcraft transistorized ignition; 4 halogen headlamps.

DIMENSIONS AND WEIGHT wheel base: 109.90 in, 279 cm; tracks: 59 in, 150 cm front, 57.70 in, 147 cm rear; length: 201

KELMARK GT

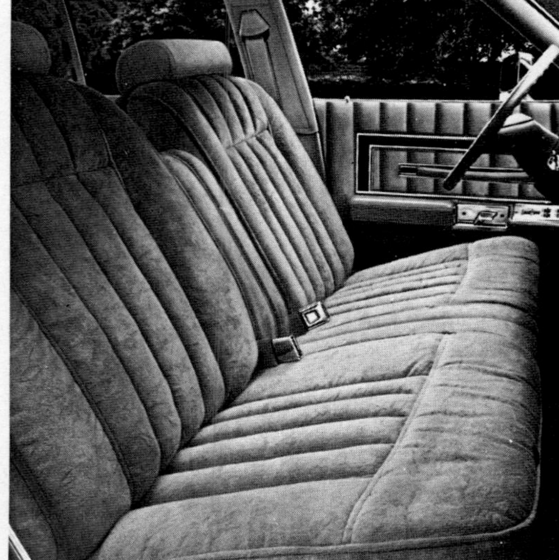

LINCOLN Versailles

, 510 cm; width: 74.50 in, 189 cm; height: 54.30 in, 138 cm; ound clearance: 5.14 in, 13 cm; weight: 3,814 lb, 1,730 kg; el tank: 16.1 imp gal, 19.2 US gal, 73 l.

ODY saloon/sedan; 4 doors; 5 seats, bench front seats with ilt-in headrests; electric windows; tinted glass; speed control vice; air-conditioning; vinyl roof.

PTIONALS central lever; tilt of steering wheel; heated rear ndow; separate front seats with reclining backrests; sunshine of; 70 A alternator.

Continental Series

ICES EX WORKS:	$
4-dr Sedan	**12,884**
2-dr Coupé	**12,555**

r 140 hp engine add $ 160.

wer team:	Standard for:	Optional for:
9 hp	both	—
0 hp	—	both

129 hp power team

IGINE front, 4 stroke; 8 cylinders; 302 cu in, 4,950 cc (4 x 3 101.6 x 76.2 mm); compression ratio: 8.4:1; max power (SAE t): 129 hp (96 kW) at 3,600 rpm; max torque (SAE net): 231 lb ft, 31.9 kg m (313 Nm) at 2,000 rpm; max engine rpm: 4,000; 26 hp/l (19.4 kW/l); cast iron block and head; 5 crankshaft bearings; valves: overhead, in line, push-rods and rockers, hydraulic tappets; camshafts: 1, at centre of Vee; lubrication: rotary pump, full flow filter, 6.7 imp pt, 8 US pt, 3.8 l; electronic injection; air cleaner; exhaust system with catalytic converter; fuel feed: electric pump; water-cooled, 22.2 imp pt, 26.6 US pt, 12.6 l.

TRANSMISSION driving wheels: rear; gearbox: automatic overdrive transmission, hydraulic torque converter and planetary gears with 4 ratios, max ratio of converter at stall 2.29, possible manual selection; ratios: I 2.400, II 1.470, III 1, overdrive 0.670, rev 2.000; lever: steering column; final drive: hypoid bevel, limited slip differential; axle ratio: 3.080; width of rims: 6"; tyres: P205/75 x 15.

PERFORMANCE max speed: 92 mph, 147 km/h; power-weight ratio: Sedan 31.7 lb/hp (42.4 lb/kW), 14.4 kg/hp (19.3 kg/kW); speed in direct drive at 1,000 rpm: 25 mph, 41 km/h; consumption: 21.6 m/imp gal, 18 m/US gal, 13.1 l x 100 km.

CHASSIS box-type ladder frame, front suspension: independent, wishbones, coil springs, anti-roll bar, telescopic dampers; rear: rigid axle, lower trailing radius arms, upper oblique torque arms, coil springs, telescopic dampers.

STEERING recirculating ball, servo; turns lock to lock: 3.40.

BRAKES front disc (diameter 11.08 in, 28.1 cm), front internal radial fins, rear compensator, rear drum, servo; swept area: front 229 sq in, 1,475 sq cm, rear 157 sq in, 1,013 sq cm, total 386 sq in, 2,488 sq cm.

LINCOLN Versailles

LINCOLN Continental Coupé

ELECTRICAL EQUIPMENT 12 V; 54 Ah battery; 60 A alternator; Motorcraft transistorized ignition; 4 headlamps.

DIMENSIONS AND WEIGHT wheel base: 117.30 in, 298 cm; tracks: 62.20 in, 158 cm front, 62 in, 157 cm rear; length: 219 in, 556 cm; width: 78.10 in, 198 cm; height: Sedan 56.10 in, 143 cm - Coupé 55.40 in, 141 cm; ground clearance: 5.68 in, 14.5 cm; weight: Sedan 4,090 lb, 1,855 kg - Coupé 4,010 lb, 1,819 kg; fuel tank: 15 imp gal, 18 US gal, 68.1 l.

BODY saloon/sedan, coupé; 6 seats, bench front seats with built-in headrests; tinted glass; electric windows; air-conditioning.

OPTIONALS electronic instrument panel; heated rear window; electric door locks; keyless entry; automatic garage door opening; sunshine roof; Town equipment.

140 hp power team

See 129 hp power team, except for:

ENGINE 351 cu in, 5,753 cc (4 x 3.50 in, 101.6 x 88.9 mm); compression ratio: 8.3:1; max power (SAE net): 140 hp (104 kW) at 3,400 rpm; max torque (SAE net): 265 lb ft, 36.6 kg m (359 Nm) at 2,000 rpm; max engine rpm: 3,800; 24.3 hp/l (18.1 kW/l); 1 Ford 7200 carburettor downdraught with variable Venturi; fuel feed: mechanical pump; cooling, 23.9 imp pt, 28.8 US pt, 13.6 l.

TRANSMISSION axle ratio: 2.730.

PERFORMANCE max speed: 98 mph, 156 km/h; power-weight ratio: Sedan 29.2 lb/hp (39.2 lb/kW), 13.2 kg/hp (17.8 kg/kW); speed in direct drive at 1,000 rpm: 29 mph, 46 km/h; consumption: 18 m/imp gal, 15 m/US gal, 15.7 l x 100 km.

BRAKES swept area: front 229 sq in, 1,475 sq cm, rear 156 sq in, 1,006 sq cm, total 385 sq in, 2,481 sq cm.

ELECTRICAL EQUIPMENT 45 Ah battery.

OPTIONALS 3.080 axle ratio; 54 Ah battery.

Continental Mark VI

PRICES EX WORKS:	$
1 4-dr Sedan	**15,824**
2 2-dr Coupé	**15,424**

For 140 hp engine add $ 160.

Power team:	Standard for:	Optional for:
129 hp	both	—
140 hp	—	both

129 hp power team

ENGINE front, 4 stroke; 8 cylinders; 302 cu in, 4,950 cc (4 x 3 in, 101.6 x 76.2 mm); compression ratio: 8.4:1; max power (SAE net): 129 hp (96 kW) at 3,600 rpm; max torque (SAE net): 231 lb ft, 31.9 kg m (313 Nm) at 2,000 rpm; max engine rpm: 4,000; 26 hp/l (19.4 kW/l); cast iron block and head; 5 crankshaft bearings; valves: overhead, in line, push-rods and rockers, hydraulic tappets; camshafts: 1, at centre of Vee; lubrication: rotary pump, full flow filter, 6.7 imp pt, 8 US pt, 3.8 l; electronic injection; air cleaner; exhaust system with catalytic converter; fuel feed: electric pump; water-cooled, 22.2 imp pt, 26.6 US pt, 12.6 l.

TRANSMISSION driving wheels: rear; gearbox: automatic overdrive transmission, hydraulic torque converter and planetary gears with 4 ratios, max ratio of converter at stall 2.29, possible manual selection; ratios: I 2.400, II 1.470, III 1, overdrive 0.670, rev 2; lever: steering column; final drive: hypoid bevel, limited slip differential; axle ratio: 3.080; width of rims: 6"; tyres: P205/75 x 15.

PERFORMANCE max speed: 92 mph, 147 km/h; power-weight ratio: Sedan 31.1 lb/hp (43 lb/kW), 14.6 kg/hp (19.5 kg/kW); speed in direct drive at 1,000 rpm: 25 mph, 41 km/h; consumption: 21.6 m/imp gal, 18 m/US gal, 13.1 l x 100 km.

CHASSIS box-type ladder frame; front suspension: independent, wishbones, coil springs, anti-roll bar, telescopic dampers; rear: rigid axle, lower trailing radius arms, upper oblique torque arms, coil springs, telescopic dampers.

STEERING recirculating ball, servo; turns lock to lock: 3.40.

BRAKES front disc (diameter 11.08 in, 28.1 cm), front internal radial fins, rear compensator, rear drum, servo; swept area: front 229 sq in, 1,475 sq cm, rear 157 sq in, 1,013 sq cm, total 386 sq in, 2,488 sq cm.

ELECTRICAL EQUIPMENT 12 V; 54 Ah battery; 60 A alternator; Motorcraft transistorized ignition; 4 headlamps.

DIMENSIONS AND WEIGHT wheel base: Sedan 117.30 in, 298 cm - Coupé 114.30 in, 290 cm; tracks: 62.20 in, 158 cm front, 62 in, 157 cm rear; length: Sedan 219.10 in, 556 cm - Coupé 216 in, 549 cm; width: 78.10 in, 198 cm; height: Sedan 56.30

129 HP POWER TEAM

in, 143 cm - Coupé 55.40 in, 141 cm; ground clearance: 5.68 in, 14.4 cm; weight: Sedan 4,146 lb, 1,881 kg - Coupé 4,046 lb, 1,835 kg; fuel tank: 15 imp gal, 18 US gal, 68.1 l.

BODY saloon/sedan, coupé; 6 seats, bench front seats with built-in headrests; tinted glass; electric windows; air-conditioning.

OPTIONALS electric door locks; keyless entry; automatic garage door opening; sunshine roof; carriage roof; Signature equipment; Pucci equipment; Bill Blass equipment; Givenchy equipment; Cartier equipment.

140 hp power team

See 129 hp power team, except for:

ENGINE 351 cu in, 5,753 cc (4 x 3.50 in, 101.6 x 88.9 mm); compression ratio: 8.3:1; max power (SAE net): 140 hp (104 kW) at 3,400 rpm; max torque (SAE net): 265 lb ft, 36.6 kg m (359 Nm) at 2,000 rpm; max engine rpm: 3,800; 24.3 hp/l (18.1 kW/l); 1 Ford 7200 carburettor downdraught with variable Venturi; fuel feed: mechanical pump; cooling, 23.9 imp pt, 28.8 US pt, 13.6 l.

TRANSMISSION axle ratio: 2.730.

PERFORMANCE max speed: 98 mph, 156 km/h; power-weight ratio: Sedan 29.6 lb/hp (39.7 lb/kW), 13.4 kg/hp (18 kg/kW); speed in direct drive at 1,000 rpm: 29 mph, 46 km/h; consumption: 18 m/imp gal, 15 m/US gal, 15.7 l x 100 km.

BRAKES swept area: front 229 sq in, 1,475 sq cm, rear 156 sq in, 1,006 sq cm, total 385 sq in, 2,481 sq cm.

ELECTRICAL EQUIPMENT 45 Ah battery.

OPTIONALS 3.080 axle ratio; 54 Ah battery.

MERCURY USA

Bobcat Series

PRICES EX WORKS:

		$
1	2+1-dr Runabout	**5,196**
2	2+1-dr St. Wagon	**5,611**
3	Villager 2+1-dr St. Wagon	**5,911**

Power team:	Standard for:	Optional for:
88 hp	all	—
89 hp	all	—

88 hp power team

ENGINE front, 4 stroke; 4 cylinders, in line; 140 cu in, 2,300 cc (3.78 x 3.13 in, 95.9 x 79.5 mm); compression ratio: 9:1; max power (SAE net): 88 hp (66 kW) at 4,600 rpm; max torque (SAE net): 119 lb ft, 16.5 kg m (161 Nm) at 2,600 rpm; max engine rpm; 5,000; 38.3 hp/l (28.7 kW/l); cast iron block and head; 5 crankshaft bearings; valves: overhead, Vee-slanted, rockers, hydraulic tappets; camshafts: 1, overhead, cogged belt; lubrication: gear pump, full flow filter, 6.7 imp pt, 8 US pt, 3.8 l; 1 Holley-Weber EOEE-RA/GA downdraught twin barrel carburettor; air cleaner; exhaust system with catalytic converter; fuel feed: mechanical pump; water-cooled, 14.4 imp pt, 17.3 US pt, 8.2 l.

TRANSMISSION driving wheels: rear; clutch: single dry plate; gearbox: mechanical; gears: 4, fully synchronized; ratios: I 3.980, II 2.140, III 1.420, IV 1, rev 3.990; lever: central; final drive: hypoid bevel; axle ratio: 2.730 - st. wagons 3.080; width of rims: 5"; tyres: BR78 x 13.

PERFORMANCE max speed: about 96 mph, 154 km/h; power-weight ratio: Runabout 28.8 lb/hp (38.4 lb/kW), 13.1 kg/hp (17.4 kg/kW); speed in direct drive at 1,000 rpm: 19.3 mph, 31 km/h; consumption 28.8 m/imp gal, 24 m/US gal, 9.8 l x 100 km.

CHASSIS integral; front suspension: independent, wishbones, coil springs, telescopic dampers; rear: rigid axle, semi-elliptic leafsprings, telescopic dampers.

STEERING rack-and-pinion; turns lock to lock: 4.15.

BRAKES front disc (diameter 9.30 in, 23.6 cm), front internal radial fins, rear drum, rear compensator; swept area: front 145.5 sq in, 939 sq cm, rear 99 sq in, 639 sq cm, total 244.5 sq in, 1,578 sq cm.

ELECTRICAL EQUIPMENT 12 V; 45 Ah battery; 60 A alternator; Motorcraft transistorized ignition; 2 headlamps.

DIMENSIONS AND WEIGHT wheel base: Runabout 94.50 in,

LINCOLN Continental Mark VI Sedan

240 cm - st. wagons 94.80 in, 241 cm; tracks: 55 in, 140 cm front, 55.80 in, 142 cm rear; length: Runabout 170.80 in, 434 cm - st. wagons 180.60 in, 459 cm; width: Runabout 69.40 in, 176 cm - st. wagons 69.70 in, 177 cm; height: Runabout 50.50 in, 128 cm - st. wagons 52 in, 132 cm; ground clearance: Runabout 4.63 in, 11.8 cm - st. wagons 5.14 in, 13 cm; weight: Runabout 2,535 lb, 1,150 kg - st. wagons 2,677 lb, 1,214 kg; turning circle: 35.9 ft, 10.9 m; fuel tank: Runabout 10.8 imp gal, 13 US gal, 49 l - st. wagons 11.7 imp gal, 14 US gal, 53 l.

BODY coupé, estate car/st. wagon; 4 seats, separate front seats; folding rear seat.

OPTIONALS 3.080 axle ratio (for Runabout only); Select-Shift C-3 automatic transmission with 3 ratios (I 2.470, II 1.470, III 1, rev 2.110), max ratio of converter at stall 2.9, possible manual selection, central lever; Select-Shift C-4 automatic transmission with 3 ratios (I 2.460, II 1,460, III 1, rev 2.190), max ratio of converter at stall 2.3 , possible manual selection, central lever, 3.080 or 3 axle ratio; aluminium wheels; BR70 x 13 or BR78 x 13 tyres with 5" wide rims; power steering; servo brake; 54 Ah heavy-duty battery; sunshine roof (for Runabout only); air-conditioning; luxury interior; Sports equipment.

89 hp power team

(for California only)

See 88 hp power team, except for:

ENGINE max power (SAE net): 89 hp (66 kW) at 4,800 rpm; max torque (SAE net): 122 lb ft, 16.9 kg m (165 Nm) at 2,60 rpm; max engine rpm: 5,200; 38.7 hp/l (28.7 kW/l); 1 Holley Weber EOEE-VA/NA downdraught twin barrel carburettor.

TRANSMISSION axle ratio: 3 - st. wagons 3.080.

Zephyr Series

PRICES EX WORKS:

		$
1	2-dr Sedan	**5,67**
2	4-dr Sedan	**5,84**
3	4+1-dr St. Wagon	**6,03**
4	Z-7 2-dr Sports Coupé	**5,81**

For 119 hp V8 engine add $ 505.

Power team:	Standard for:	Optional for:
88 hp	all	—
119 hp	—	all

88 hp power team

ENGINE 4 stroke; 4 cylinders, in line; 140 cu in, 2,300 c (3.78 x 3.13 in, 95.9 x 79.5 mm); compression ratio: 9:1; ma power (SAE net): 88 hp (66 kW) at 4,600 rpm; max torque (SA net): 119 lb ft, 16.5 kg m (161 Nm) at 2,600 rpm; max engin rpm: 5,000; 38.3 hp/l (28.7 kW/l); cast iron block and head; crankshaft bearings; valves: overhead, Vee-slanted, rocker hydraulic tappets; camshafts: 1, overhead, cogged belt; lubrica

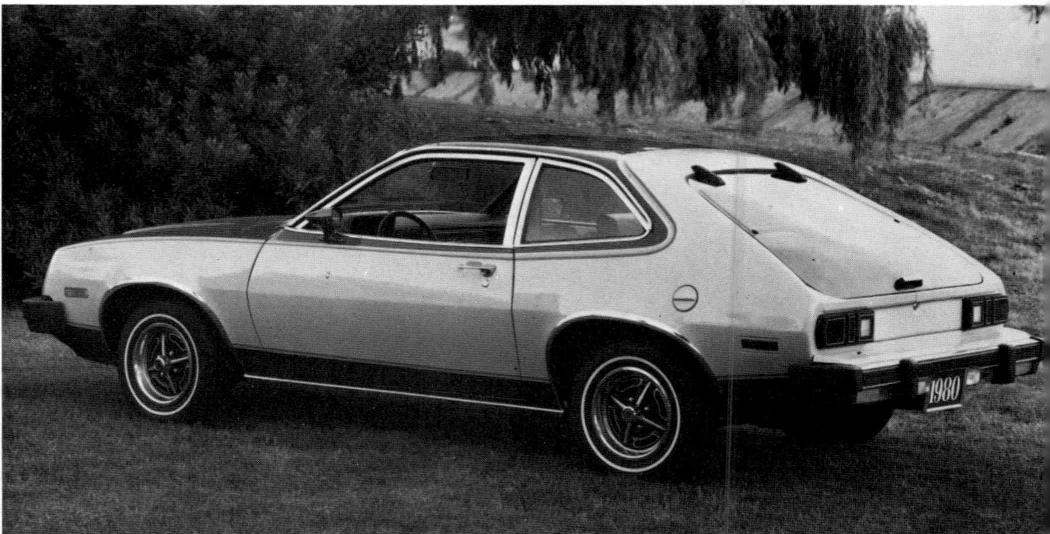

MERCURY Bobcat Runabout

on: gear pump, full flow filter, 6.7 imp pt, 8 US pt, 3.8 l; 1 Holley-Weber EOEE-RA/GA (EOEE-VA/NA for California only) downdraught twin barrel carburettor; air cleaner; exhaust system with catalytic converter; fuel feed: mechanical pump; water-cooled, 17.1 imp pt, 20.5 US pt, 9.7 l.

TRANSMISSION driving wheels: rear; clutch: single dry plate; gearbox: mechanical; gears: 4, fully synchronized; ratios: I 3.980, II 2.140, III 1.420, IV 1, rev 3.990; lever: central; final drive: hypoid bevel; axle ratio: 3.080; width of rims: 5"; tyres: 175/75 x 14.

PERFORMANCE max speed: 96 mph, 154 km/h; power-weight ratio: 2-dr Sedan 30.4 lb/hp (40.5 lb/kW), 13.8 kg/hp (18.4 kg/kW); speed in direct drive at 1,000 rpm: 20.9 mph, 33.5 km/h; consumption: 27.7 m/imp gal, 23 m/US gal, 10.2 l x 100 km.

CHASSIS integral with two cross members; front suspension: independent, by McPherson, wishbones (lower control arms), coil springs/telescopic damper struts, anti-roll bar; rear: rigid axle, upper and lower control arms, coil springs, telescopic dampers.

STEERING rack-and-pinion; turns lock to lock: 4.27.

BRAKES front disc (diameter 10.06 in, 25.5 cm), front internal radial fins, rear drum, rear compensator; swept area: front 176.6 sq in, 1,140 sq cm, rear 99 sq in, 638 sq cm, total 275.6 sq in, 1,178 sq cm - St. Wagon front 176.6 sq in, 1,140 sq cm, rear 110 sq in, 710 sq cm, total 286.6 sq in, 1,850 sq cm.

ELECTRICAL EQUIPMENT 12 V; 45 Ah battery; 40 A alternator; Motorcraft transistorized ignition; 4 headlamps.

DIMENSIONS AND WEIGHT wheel base: 105.50 in, 268 cm; tracks: 56.60 in, 144 cm front, 57 in, 145 cm rear; length: 195.50 in, 496 cm - Z7 Sports Coupé 197.40 in, 501 cm; width: 71 in, 180 cm; height: 52.90 in, 134 cm - Z7 Sports Coupé 51.70 in, 131 cm - St. Wagon 50 in, 127 cm; ground clearance: 4.38 in, 11.1 cm; weight: 2-dr Sedan 2,673 lb, 1,212 kg - 4-dr Sedan 2,703 lb, 1,226 kg - Z-7 Sports Coupé 2,700 lb, 1,224 kg - St. Wagon 2,835 lb, 1,286 kg; turning circle: 39 ft, 11.9 m; fuel tank: 11.7 imp gal, 14 US gal, 53 l.

BODY saloon/sedan, coupé, estate car/st. wagon; 5 seats, bench front seats with built-in headrests.

VARIATIONS

ENGINE turbocharged, 1 Holley-Weber EOZE-AMA downdraught twin barrel carburettor, electric fuel pump.
TRANSMISSION gearbox Select-Shift C-4 automatic transmission, hydraulic torque converter and planetary gears with 3 ratios (I 2.460, II 1.460, III 1, rev 2.190), max ratio of converter at stall 2.3, possible manual selection, steering column lever, 3.450 axle ratio.
DIMENSIONS AND WEIGHT fuel tank 9.5 imp pt, 11.4 US pt, 5.3 l, weight plus 83 lb, 38 kg.

ENGINE 6 cylinders, in line, 200 cu in, 3,300 cc (3.68 x 3.13 in, 93.5 x 79.4 mm), 8.6:1 compression ratio, 7 crankshaft bearings, 1 Holley 1946 EOZE-GA (EOBE-AAA for California only) downdraught single barrel carburettor, water-cooled 15 imp pt, 18 US pt, 8.5 l.
TRANSMISSION 4-speed, fully synchronized, mechanical gearbox (I 3.290, II 1.840, III 1, IV 0.810, rev 3.290), central lever.

MERCURY Zephyr Z-7 Sports Turbo Coupé

PERFORMANCE consumption 25.2 m/imp gal, 21 m/US gal, 11.2 l x 100 km.
DIMENSIONS AND WEIGHT weight plus 31 lb, 14 kg.

OPTIONALS aluminium wheels; heavy-duty suspension; power steering; tilt of steering wheel; servo brake; P175/75R x 14 WSW, P185/75R x 14 BSW, P185/75R x 14 WSW or P185/75R x 14 RWL tyres; 54 Ah heavy-duty battery; heated rear window; tinted glass; electric windows; metallic spray; vinyl roof; sunshine roof (except St. Wagon); luxury interior; speed control device; air-conditioning; electric analogic clock; electric door locks; Ghia equipment; Villager equipment (for St. Wagon only); separate front seats with reclining backrests; Select-Shift C-3 automatic transmission with 3 ratios (I 2.470, II 1.470, III 1, rev 2.110), max ratio of converter at stall 2.49, possible manual selection, 3.080 axle ratio

119 hp power team

See 88 hp power team, except for:

ENGINE 8 cylinders; 255 cu in, 4,200 cc (3.68 x 3 in, 93.5 x 76.2 mm); compression ratio: 8.8:1; max power (SAE net): 119 hp (89 kW) at 3,800 rpm; max torque (SAE net): 194 lb ft, 26.8 kg m (263 Nm) at 2,200 rpm; max engine rpm: 4,200; 28.3 hp/l (21.2 kW/l); valves: overhead, in line, push-rods and rockers; camshafts: 1, at centre of Vee, chain-driven; 1 Ford 2150 EOKE-HA downdraught twin barrel carburettor (EO4E-FA with variable Venturi for California only); water-cooled, 23.6 imp pt, 28.3 US pt, 13.4 l.

TRANSMISSION gearbox: Select-Shift C-4 automatic transmission, hydraulic torque converter and planetary gears with 3 ratios, max ratio of converter at stall 2.09, possible manual selection; ratios: I 2.460, II 1.460, III 1, rev 2.190; lever: steering column; axle ratio: 2.260.

PERFORMANCE max speed: 100 mph, 160 km/h; power-weight ratio: 2-dr Sedan 24.2 lb/hp (32.4 lb/kW), 11 kg/hp (14.7 kg/kW); speed in direct drive at 1,000 rpm: 23.8 mph, 38.2 km/h; consumption: 21.6 m/imp gal, 18 m/US gal, 13.1 l x 100 km.

ELECTRICAL EQUIPMENT 36 Ah battery.

DIMENSIONS AND WEIGHT weight: plus 212 lb, 96 kg.

Capri Series

PRICES EX WORKS:	$
1 2+1-dr Coupé	6,220
2 Ghia 2+1-dr Coupé	6,577

For 118 hp V8 engine add $ 505.

Power team:	Standard for:	Optional for:
88 hp	both	—
89 hp	both	—
118 hp	—	both

88 hp power team

(not available in California)

ENGINE front, 4 stroke; 4 cylinders, in line; 140 cu in, 2,300 cc (3.78 x 3.13 in, 95.9 x 79.5 mm); compression ratio: 9:1; max power (SAE net): 88 hp (66 kW) at 4,600 rpm; max torque (SAE net): 119 lb ft, 16.5 kg m (161 Nm) at 2,600 rpm; max engine rpm: 5,000; 38.3 hp/l (28.7 kW/l); cast iron block and head; 5 crankshaft bearings; valves: overhead, Vee-slanted, rockers, hydraulic tappets; camshafts: 1, overhead, cogged belt; lubrication: gear pump, full flow filter, 6.7 imp pt, 8 US pt, 3.8 l; 1 Holley-Weber EOEE-RA/GA downdraught twin barrel carburettor; air cleaner; exhaust system with catalytic converter; fuel feed: mechanical pump; water-cooled, 17.1 imp pt, 20.5 US pt, 9.7 l.

TRANSMISSION driving wheels: rear; clutch: single dry plate; gearbox: mechanical; gears: 4, fully synchronized; ratios: I 3.980, II 2.140, III 1.420, IV 1, rev 3.990; lever: central; final drive: hypoid bevel; axle ratio: 3.080; width of rims: 5"; tyres: P185/80R x 13 BSW (P175/75R x 14 BSW for Ghia Coupé only).

PERFORMANCE max speed: 96 mph, 154 km/h; power-weight ratio: Coupé 30 lb/hp (40 lb/kW), 13.6 kg/hp (18.1 kg/kW); speed in direct drive at 1,000 rpm: 19.3 mph, 31 km/h; consumption: 27.7 m/imp gal, 23 m/US gal, 10.2 l x 100 km.

CHASSIS platform with front subframe; front suspension: independent, by McPherson, wishbones (lower control arms), coil springs/telescopic damper struts, anti-roll bar; rear: rigid axle, lower trailing radius arms, upper oblique torque arms, transverse linkage bar, coil springs, telescopic dampers.

STEERING rack-and-pinion; turns lock to lock: 4.08.

BRAKES front disc (diameter 9.31 in, 23.6 cm), front internal radial fins, rear compensator, rear drum; swept area: front

MERCURY Capri Turbo RS Coupé

88 HP POWER TEAM

150.8 sq in, 973 sq cm, rear 99 sq in, 639 sq cm, total 249.8 sq in, 1,612 sq cm.

ELECTRICAL EQUIPMENT 12 V; 45 Ah battery; 40 A alternator; Motorcraft transistorized ignition; 4 halogen headlamps.

DIMENSIONS AND WEIGHT wheel base: 100.40 in, 255 cm; tracks: 56.60 in, 144 cm front, 57 in, 145 cm rear; length: 179.10 in, 455 cm; width: 69.10 in, 176 cm; height: 51.50 in, 131 cm; ground clearance: 5.67 in, 14.5 cm; weight: Coupé 2,637 lb, 1,196 kg - Ghia Coupé 2,697 lb, 1,223 kg; turning circle: 37.2 ft, 11.3 m; fuel tank: 9.5 imp gal, 11.5 US gal, 43 l.

BODY coupé; 2+1 doors; 4 seats, separate front seats, reclining backrests with built-in headrests.

VARIATIONS

ENGINE turbocharged, 1 Holley-Weber EOZE-AMA downdraught twin barrel carburettor.
TRANSMISSION gearbox ratios I 4.070, II 2.570, III 1.660, IV 1, rev 3.950, 3.450 axle ratio.
DIMENSIONS AND WEIGHT weight plus 62 lb, 28 kg, fuel tank 10.3 imp gal, 12.5 US gal, 47 l.

ENGINE 6 cylinders, 200 cu in, 3,300 cc (3.68 x 3.13 in, 93.5 x 79.4 mm), 8.6:1 compression ratio, 7 crankshaft bearings, 1 Holley 1946 EOZE-GA downdraught single barrel carburettor, water-cooled 15 imp pt, 18 US pt, 8.5 l.
TRANSMISSION gearbox ratios I 3.290, II 1.840, III 1, IV 0.810, rev 3.290.
PERFORMANCE consumption 25.2 m/imp gal, 21 m/US gal, 11.2 l x 100 km.
DIMENSIONS AND WEIGHT weight plus 19 lb, 8.6 kg.

OPTIONALS heavy-duty cooling; Select-Shift C-3 automatic transmission with 3 ratios (I 2.470, II 1.470, III 1, rev 2.110), max ratio of converter at stall 2.490, possible manual selection, central lever, 3.450 axle ratio; aluminium wheels; P175/75R x 14 WSW, P185/75R x 14 WSW or P185/75R x 14 RWL tyres with 5.5" wide rims; 190/65R x 390 BSW tyres with 5.9" wide rims and TRX forged aluminium wheels; heavy-duty suspension with rear anti-roll bar; power steering; tilt of steering wheel; servo brake; 54 Ah heavy-duty battery; heated rear window; tinted glass; air-conditioning; sunshine roof; vinyl roof; speed control device; metallic spray; rear window wiper-washer; leather upholstery (for Ghia Coupé only); RS equipment.

89 hp power team

(for California only)

See 88 hp power team, except for:

ENGINE max power (SAE net): 89 hp (66 kW) at 4,800 rpm; max torque (SAE net): 122 lb ft, 16.8 kg m (165 Nm) at 2,600 rpm; max engine rpm: 5,300; 38.7 hp/l (28.7 kW/l); 1 Holley-Weber EOEE-VA/NA downdraught twin barrel carburettor.

118 hp power team

See 88 hp power team, except for:

ENGINE 8 cylinders; 255 cu in, 4,200 cc (3.68 x 3 in, 93.5 x 76.2 mm); compression ratio: 8.8:1; max power (SAE net): 118 hp (88 kW) at 3,800 rpm; max torque (SAE net): 193 lb ft, 26.7 kg m (262 Nm) at 2,200 rpm; max engine rpm: 4,200; 28.1 hp/l (21 kW/l); valves: overhead, in line, push-rods and rockers; camshafts: 1, at centre of Vee, chain-driven; 1 Ford 2150 EOKE-HA twin barrel carburettor (EO4E-FA for California only); water-cooled, 23.6 imp pt, 28.3 US pt, 13.4 l.

TRANSMISSION gearbox: Select-Shift C-4 automatic transmission, hydraulic torque converter and planetary gears with 3 ratios, max ratio of converter at stall 2.09, possible manual selection; ratios: I 2.460, II 1.460, III 1, rev 2.190; lever: steering column; axle ratio: 2.260.

PERFORMANCE max speed: 100 mph, 160 km/h; power-weight ratio: Coupé 24.1 lb/hp (32.4 lb/kW), 11 kg/hp (14.7 kg/kW); speed in direct drive at 1,000 rpm: 23.8 mph, 38.2 km/h; consumption: 21.6 m/imp gal, 18 m/US gal, 13.1 l x 100 km.

ELECTRICAL EQUIPMENT 36 Ah battery; 60 A alternator.

DIMENSIONS AND WEIGHT weight: plus 212 lb, 96 kg.

Monarch Series

PRICES EX WORKS:	$
1 2-dr Sedan	**6,071**
2 4-dr Sedan	**6,224**

For V8 engines add $ 245.

MERCURY Capri Coupé

MERCURY Monarch ESS Sedan

MERCURY Monarch Sedan

Power team:	Standard for:	Optional for:
97 hp	both	—
117 hp	both	—
134 hp	—	both

97 hp power team

(not available in California)

ENGINE front, 4 stroke; 6 cylinders, in line; 250 cu in, 4,097 cc (3.68 x 3.91 in, 93.5 x 99.3 mm); compression ratio: 8.6:1; max power (SAE net): 97 hp (71 kW) at 3,200 rpm; max torque (SAE net): 210 lb ft, 29 kg m (284 Nm) at 1,400 rpm; max engine rpm: 3,800; 23.7 hp/l (17.4 kW/l); cast iron block and head; 7 crankshaft bearings; valves: overhead, in line, push-rods and rockers, hydraulic tappets; camshafts: 1, side; lubrication: rotary pump, full flow filter, 6.7 imp pt, 8 US pt, 3.8 l; 1 Carter YFA 9510 EODE-NA downdraught single barrel carburettor; air cleaner; exhaust system with catalytic converter; fuel feed: mechanical pump; water-cooled, 17.4 imp pt, 21 US pt, 9.9 l.

TRANSMISSION driving wheels: rear; clutch: single dry plate, semi-centrifugal; gearbox: mechanical; gears: 4, fully synchronized with overdrive/top; ratios: I 3.290, II 1.840, III 1, IV 0.810, rev 3.290; lever: central; final drive: hypoid bevel; axle ratio: 3; width of rims: 6"; tyres: DR78 x 14.

PERFORMANCE max speed: about 93 mph, 149 km/h; power-weight ratio: 4-dr 33.5 lb/hp (45.5 lb/kW), 15.2 kg/hp (20.7 kg/kW); speed in top at 1,000 rpm: 25.5 mph, 41 km/h; consumption: 21.6 m/imp gal, 18 m/US gal, 13.1 l x 100 km.

CHASSIS integral; front suspension: independent, wishbones, coil springs, anti-roll bar, telescopic dampers; rear: rigid axle, semi-elliptic leafsprings, telescopic dampers.

STEERING recirculating ball and nut; turns lock to lock: 5.18.

BRAKES front disc (diameter 11.03 in, 28 cm), front internal fins, rear compensator, rear drum; swept area: total 348.2 sq in, 2,247 sq cm.

ELECTRICAL EQUIPMENT 12 V; 36 Ah battery; 60 A alternator; Motorcraft transistorized ignition; 4 headlamps.

DIMENSIONS AND WEIGHT wheel base: 109.90 in, 279 cm; tracks: 59 in, 150 cm front, 57.70 in, 147 cm rear; length: 199.70 in, 507 cm; width: 74 in, 188 cm; height: 2-dr 53.20 in, 135 cm - 4-dr 53.30 in, 135 cm; ground clearance: 4.62 in, 11.7 cm; weight: 2-dr 3,205 lb, 1,454 kg - 4-dr 3,250 lb, 1,474 kg; turning circle: 39 ft, 11.9 m; fuel tank: 15 imp gal, 18 US gal, 68 l.

BODY saloon/sedan; 5 seats, bench front seats with built-in headrests.

OPTIONALS heavy-duty cooling; Select-Shift Cruise-o-Matic automatic transmission with 3 ratios (I 2.460, II 1.460, III 1, rev 2.190), max ratio of converter at stall 2.3, possible manual selection, steering column or central lever, 2.790 axle ratio; aluminium wheels; ER78 x 14 or FR78 x 14 tyres with 6" wide rims; heavy-duty suspension; power steering; tilt of steering wheel; servo brake; automatic speed control; electric windows; tinted glass; 54 Ah heavy-duty battery; metallic spray; vinyl roof; separate front seats with reclining backrests; electric sunshine roof; air-conditioning; ESS equipment; Ghia equipment; heated rear window.

MERCURY Cougar XR-7

117 power team

(for California only)

See 97 hp power team, except for:

ENGINE 8 cylinders; 255 cu in, 4,200 cc (3.68 x 3 in, 93.5 x 76.2 mm); compression ratio: 8.8:1; max power (SAE net): 117 hp (87 kW) at 3,800 rpm; max torque (SAE net): 193 lb ft, 26.7 kg m (262 Nm) at 2,000 rpm; max engine rpm: 4,200; 27.8 hp/l (20.7 kW/l); 5 crankshaft bearings; camshafts: 1, at centre of Vee; 1 Ford 2150 EO4E-FA with variable Venturi downdraught carburettor; water-cooled, 23.6 imp pt, 28.3 US pt, 13.4 l.

TRANSMISSION gearbox: Select-Shift C-4 automatic transmission, hydraulic torque converter and planetary gears with 3 ratios, max ratio of converter at stall 2, possible manual selection; ratios: I 2.460, II 1.460, III 1, rev 2.190; lever: steering column or central; axle ratio: 2.470.

PERFORMANCE max speed: 95 mph, 152 km/h; power-weight ratio: 4-dr 28.4 lb/hp (38.3 lb/kW), 12.9 kg/hp (17.3 kg/kW); speed in direct drive at 1,000 rpm: 25 mph, 40 km/h.

DIMENSIONS AND WEIGHT weight: plus 79 lb, 36 kg.

134 hp power team

(not available in California)

See 97 hp power team, except for:

ENGINE 8 cylinders; 302 cu in, 4,950 cc (4 x 3 in, 101.6 x 76.2 mm); compression ratio: 8.4:1; max power (SAE net): 134 hp (100 kW) at 3,600 rpm; max torque (SAE net): 232 lb ft, 32.1 kg m (315 Nm) at 1,600 rpm; max engine rpm: 4,000; 27.1 hp/l (20.2 kW/l); 5 crankshaft bearings; camshafts: 1, at centre of Vee; 1 Ford 2150 EOSE-HA downdraught twin barrel carburettor; cooling, 23.6 imp pt, 28.3 US pt, 13.4 l.

PERFORMANCE max speed: 103 mph, 165 km/h; power-weight ratio: lb/hp (33.6 lb/kW), 11.3 kg/hp (15.2 kg/kW); consumption: 20.5 m/imp gal, 17 m/!US gal, 13.8 l x 100 km.

DIMENSIONS AND WEIGHT weight: plus 106 lb, 48 kg.

Cougar XR-7

PRICE EX WORKS: $ 8,089

For 131 hp engine add $ 265.

115 hp power team

ENGINE front, 4 stroke; 8 cylinders; 255 cu in, 4,200 cc (3.68 x 3 in, 93.5 x 76.2 mm); compression ratio: 8.8:1; max power (SAE net): 115 hp (86 kW) at 3,800 rpm; max torque (SAE net): 191 lb ft, 26.4 kg m (259 Nm) at 2,000 rpm; max engine rpm: 4,200; 27.4 hp/l (20.5 kW/l); cast iron block and head; 5 crankshaft bearings; valves: overhead, in line, push-rods and rockers, hydraulic tappets; camshafts: 1, at centre of Vee, chain-driven; lubrication: rotary pump, full flow filter, 7 imp pt, 8.5 US pt, 4 l; 1 Ford 2150 EOKE-HA downdraught twin barrel carburettor; air cleaner; exhaust system with 2 catalytic converters; fuel feed: mechanical pump; water-cooled, 23.6 imp pt, 28.3 US pt, 13.4 l.

MERCURY Cougar XR-7

TRANSMISSION driving wheels: rear; gearbox: Select-Shift C-4 automatic transmission, hydraulic torque converter and planetary gears with 3 ratios, max ratio of converter at stall 2.09, possible manual selection; ratios: I 2.460, II 1.460, III 1, rev 2.190; lever: steering column; final drive: hypoid bevel; axle ratio: 2.260; width of rims: 5.5"; tyres: P185/75R x 14 BSW.

PERFORMANCE max speed: 118 mph, 190 km/h; power-weight ratio: 28.1 lb/hp (37.5 lb/kW), 12.7 kg/hp (17 kg/kW); speed in direct drive at 1,000 rpm: 31 mph, 49.8 km/h; consumption: 21.6 m/imp gal, 18 m/US gal, 13.1 l x 100 km.

CHASSIS integral with 2 cross members; front suspension: independent, by McPherson, wishbones (lower control arms), coil springs/telescopic damper struts, anti-roll bar; rear: coil springs, upper and lower control arms, telescopic dampers.

STEERING rack-and-pinion, servo; turns lock to lock: 3.40.

BRAKES front disc (diameter 10.06 in, 25.5 cm), front internal radial fins, rear drum, rear compensator, servo; swept area: front 176.6 sq in, 1,140 sq cm, rear 99 sq in, 638 sq cm, total 275.6 sq in, 1,778 sq cm.

ELECTRICAL EQUIPMENT 12 V; 36 Ah battery; 60 A alternator; Motorcraft transistorized ignition; 4 headlamps.

DIMENSIONS AND WEIGHT wheel base: 108.40 in, 275 cm; tracks: 58.10 in, 148 cm front, 57 in, 145 cm rear; length: 200.40 in, 509 cm; width: 74.10 in, 188 cm; height: 53 in, 135 cm; ground clearance: 4.89 in, 12.4 cm; weight: 3,228 lb, 1,464 kg; weight distribution: 57% front, 43% rear; turning circle: 40 ft, 12.2 m; fuel tank: 14.5 imp gal, 17.4 US gal, 66 l.

BODY coupé; 2 doors; 4 seats, bench front seats with built-in headrests.

OPTIONALS heavy-duty cooling; P195/75R x 14 BSW, P195/75R X 14 WSW, 220/55R x 390 WSW or P205/60R x 390 WSW tyres; heavy-duty suspension; central lever; tilt of steering wheel; 45 Ah heavy-duty battery; heated rear window; electric windows; tinted glass; air-conditioning; separate front seats with reclining backrests; automatic speed control; sunshine roof; vinyl roof; leather upholstery; Decor equipment; Sport equipment; Luxury equipment; digital instrument panel.

131 hp power team

(not available in California)

See 115 hp power team, except for:

ENGINE 302 cu in, 5,000 cc (4 x 3 in, 101.6 x 76.2 mm); compression ratio: 8.4:1; max power (SAE net): 131 hp (98 Kw) at 3,800 rpm; max torque (SAE net): 231 lb ft, 31.9 kg m (313 Nm) at 1,600 rpm; max engine rpm: 4,000; 26.2 hp/l (19.6 kW/l); 1 Ford 2150 EOSE-HA downdraught twin barrel carburettor.

PERFORMANCE max speed: 121 mph: 121 mph, 194 km/h; power-weight ratio: 24.6 lb/hp (32.9 lb/kW), 11.2 kg/hp (14.9 kg/kW); speed in direct drive at 1,000 rpm: 31.8 mph, 51 km/h; consumption: 20.5 m/imp gal, 17 m/US gal, 13.8 l x 100 km.

DIMENSIONS AND WEIGHT weight: plus 9 lb, 4 kg.

OPTIONALS Overdrive automatic transmission with 4 ratios (I 2.470, II 1.470, III 1, IV 0.670, rev 2), max ratio of converter at stall 2.29, possible manual selection, 3.080 axle ratio.

132 hp power team

(for California only)

See 115 hp power team, except for:

ENGINE 302 cu in, 5,000 cc (4 x 3 in, 101.6 x 76.2 mm); compression ratio: 8.4:1; max power (SAE net): 132 hp (98 kW) at 3,600 rpm; max torque (SAE net): 232 lb ft, 32.1 kg m (315 Nm) at 1,400 rpm; max engine rpm: 4,000; 26.4 hp/l (19.6 kW/l); 1 Ford 2150 EO4E-FA downdraught carburettor with variable Venturi.

PERFORMANCE max speed: 121 mph, 194 km/h; power-weight ratio: 24.4 lb/hp (32.9 lb/kW), 11.1 kg/hp (14.9 kg/kW); speed in direct drive at 1,000 rpm: 33.6 mph, 53.9 km/h; consumption: 20.5 m/imp gal, 17 m/US gal, 13.8 l x 100 km.

DIMENSIONS AND WEIGHT weight: plus 9 lb, 4 kg.

OPTIONALS Overdrive automatic transmission with 4 ratios (I 2.470, II 1.470, III 1, IV 0.670, rev 2), max ratio of converter at stall 2.29, possible manual selection, 3.080 axle ratio.

Marquis - Grand Marquis Series

PRICES EX WORKS:		$
1	Marquis 2-dr Sedan	**8,171**
2	Marquis 4-dr Sedan	**8,307**
3	Marquis Meteor 2-dr Sedan	**7,836**
4	Marquis Meteor 4-dr Sedan	**7,886**
5	Marquis Brougham 2-dr Sedan	**8,984**
6	Marquis Brougham 4-dr Sedan	**9,189**
7	Marquis 4+1-dr St. Wagon	**8,712**
8	Marquis Meteor 4+1-dr St. Wagon	**8,444**
9	Marquis Colony Park 4+1-dr St. Wagon	**9,754**
10	Grand Marquis 2-dr Sedan	**9,746**
11	Grand Marquis 4-dr Sedan	**9,934**

For 140 hp engine add $ 269.

Power team:	Standard for:	Optional for:
130 hp	all	—
140 hp	—	all

130 hp power team

ENGINE front, 4 stroke; 8 cylinders; 302 cu in, 4,950 cc (4 x 3 in, 101.6 x 76.2 mm); compression ratio: 8.4:1; max power (SAE net): 130 hp (97 kW) at 3,600 rpm; max torque (SAE net): 230 lb ft, 31.8 kg m (312 Nm) at 1,600 rpm; max engine rpm: 4,000; 26.3 hp/l (19.6 kW/l); cast iron block and head; 5 crankshaft bearings; valves: overhead, in line, push-rods and rockers, hydraulic tappets; camshafts: 1, at centre of Vee; lubrication: rotary pump, full flow filter, 6.7 imp pt, 8 US pt, 3.8 l; 1 Ford 2700 (Ford 7200 for California only) downdraught carburettor with variable Venturi; air cleaner; exhaust system with 2 catalytic converters; fuel feed: mechanical pump; water-cooled, 22.2 imp pt, 26.6 US pt, 12.6 l.

TRANSMISSION driving wheels: rear; gearbox: Select-Shift C-4 automatic transmission, hydraulic torque converter and planetary gears with 3 ratios, max ratio of converter at stall 1.97, possible manual selection; ratios: I 2.460, II 1.460, III 1, rev 2.200; lever: steering column; final drive: hypoid bevel; axle ratio: 2.260 - st. wagons 2.730; width of rims: 5.5" - st. wagons 6.5"; tyres: P205/75R x 14 BSW - st. wagons P215/75R x 14 BSW.

130 HP POWER TEAM

PERFORMANCE max speed: 96 mph, 154 km/h; power-weight ratio: Marquis 4-dr Sedan 28 lb/hp (37.5 lb/kW), 12.7 kg/hp (17 kg/kW); speed in direct drive at 1,000 rpm: 26.7 mph, 42.7 km/h; consumption: 20.5 m/imp gal, 17 m/US gal, 13.8 l x 100 km.

CHASSIS perimeter box-type frame; front suspension: independent, wishbones, coil springs, anti-roll bar, telescopic dampers; rear: rigid axle, lower trailing radius arms, upper oblique torque arms, coil springs, telescopic dampers.

STEERING recirculating ball, servo; turns lock to lock: 3.40.

BRAKES front disc (diameter 11.08 in, 28.1 cm), front internal radial fins, rear drum, rear compensator, servo; swept area: front 228.7 sq in, 1,475 sq cm, rear 157.1 sq in, 1,013 sq cm - st. wagons 155.9 sq in, 1,006 sq cm, total 385.8 sq in, 2,488 sq cm - st. wagons 384.6 sq in, 2,481 sq cm.

ELECTRICAL EQUIPMENT 12 V; 36 Ah battery; 60 A alternator; Motorcraft transistorized ignition; 4 headlamps.

DIMENSIONS AND WEIGHT wheel base: 114.30 in, 290 cm; tracks: 62.20 in, 158 cm front, 62 in, 157 cm rear; length: sedans 212.30 in, 539 cm - st. wagons 218 in, 554 cm; width: sedans 77.50 in, 197 cm - st. wagons 79.30 in, 201 cm; height: sedans 54.70 in, 139 cm - st. wagons 57.40 in, 146 cm cm; ground clearance: sedans 5.17 in, 13 cm - st. wagons 5.63 in, 14 cm; weight: Marquis 4-dr Sedan 3.636 lb, 1,649 kg - Marquis Brougham 4-dr Sedan 3,676 lb, 1,667 kg - Grand Marquis 4-dr Sedan 3,667 lb, 1,663 kg - Marquis 4+1 St. Wagon 3,854 lb, 1,748 kg; fuel tank: sedans 15.8 imp gal, 19 US gal, 72 l - st. wagons 16.7 imp gal, 20 US gal, 76 l.

BODY saloon/sedan, estate car/st. wagon; 6 seats, bench front seats with built-in headrests.

OPTIONALS heavy-duty cooling; P205/75R x 14 WSW tyres with 5.5" wide rims (for sedans only); P215/75R x 14 BSW, P205/75R x 15 WSW, P225/75R x 14 WSW or T125/90D x 16 BSW tyres with 6.5" wide rims; P225/75R x 14 WSW tyres with 6.5" wide rims (for st. wagons only); heavy-duty suspension with rear and front anti-roll bar; tilt of steering wheel; 71 Ah heavy-duty battery; electric windows; heated rear window; automatic air-conditioning; manual air-conditioning; tinted glass; automatic speed control; metallic spray; limited slip differential; light alloy wheels; wire wheels; vinyl roof; leather upholstery; reclining backrests; Select-Shift C-6 automatic transmission with 3 ratios (I 2.460, II 1.460, III 1, rev 2.180), max ratio of converter at stall 1.98, possible manual selection, steering column; luxury equipment; decor equipment.

140 hp power team

See 130 hp power team, except for:

ENGINE 351 cu in, 5,753 cc (4 x 3.50 in, 101.6 x 88.9 mm); compression ratio: 8.3:1; max power (SAE net): 140 hp (104 kW) at 3,400 rpm; max torque (SAE net): 265 lb ft, 36.6 kg m (359 Nm) at 2,000 rpm; max engine rpm: 3,800; 24.3 hp/l (18.1 kW/l); 1 Ford 7200 downdraught carburettor with variable Venturi; water-cooled, 23.9 imp pt, 28.8 US pt, 13.6 l.

MERCURY Grand Marquis Sedan

MERCURY Grand Marquis Sedan

TRANSMISSION gearbox: Select-Shift FMX automatic transmission hydraulic torque converter and planetary gears with 3 ratios, max ratio of converter at stall 1.97, possible manual selection; ratios: I 2.400, II 1.470, III 1, rev 2).

PERFORMANCE max speed: 103 mph, 165 km/h; power-weight ratio: Marquis 4-dr Sedan 28.7 lb/hp (35.8 lb/kW), 12.9 kg/hp (16.1 kg/kW); speed in direct drive at 1,000 rpm: 30.3 mph, 48.6 km/h; consumption: 19.2 m/imp gal, 16 m/US gal, 14.7 l x 100 km.

DIMENSIONS AND WEIGHT weight: plus 91 lb, 41 kg.

MERCURY Marquis Station Wagon

OLDSMOBILE USA

Starfire Series

PRICES EX WORKS:	$
1 Coupé	**4,750**
2 SX Coupé	**4,950**

For 110 hp engine add $ 225.

Power team:	Standard for:	Optional for:
86 hp	both	—
110 hp	—	both

86 hp power team

ENGINE front, 4 stroke; 4 cylinders, vertical, in line; 151 cu in, 2,474 cc (4 x 3 in, 101.5 x 76.1 mm); compression ratio: 8.2:1; max power (SAE ret): 86 hp (63 kW) at 4,000 rpm; max torque (SAE net): 128 lb ft, 17.6 kg m (172 Nm) at 2,400 rpm; max engine rpm: 4,800; 34.8 hp/l (25.6 kW/l); cast iron block and head; 5 crankshaft bearings; valves: overhead, in line, push-rods and rockers, hydraulic tappets; camshafts: 1, side; lubrication: gear pump, full flow filter, 5.2 imp pt, 6.2 US pt, 3 l; 1 Rochester 2 ME downdraught twin barrel carburettor; air cleaner; exhaust system with catalytic converter; fuel feed: mechanical pump; water-cooled, 20.1 imp pt, 23.9 US pt, 11.5 l.

TRANSMISSION driving wheels: rear; clutch: single dry plate (diaphragm); gearbox: mechanical; gears: 4, fully synchronized; ratios: I 3.500, II 2.480, III 1.660, IV 1, rev 3.500; lever: central; final drive: hypoid bevel; axle ratio: 2.730 - 2.930 (for California only) width of rims: 6"; tyres: A78 x 13.

PERFORMANCE max speed: 96 mph, 154 km/h; power-weight ratio: Coupé 30.7 lb/hp (41.7 lb/kW), 13.9 kg/hp (18.9 kg/kW); speed in direct drive at 1,000 rpm: 24 mph, 38.7 km/h; consumption: 28/8 m/imp gal, 24 m/US gal, 9.8 l x 100 km.

CHASSIS integral; front suspension: independent, wishbones, coil springs, anti-roll bar, telescopic dampers; rear: rigid axle, lower trailing radius arms, upper oblique torque arms, coil springs, telescopic dampers.

STEERING recirculating ball; turns lock to lock: 4.40.

BRAKES front disc (diameter 9.74 in, 24.7 cm), rear drum; swept area; total 264.8 sq in, 1,708 sq cm.

ELECTRICAL EQUIPMENT 12 V; 3,200 W battery; 37 A alternator; Delco-Remy high energy ignition; 2 headlamps - SX Coupé 4 headlamps.

DIMENSIONS AND WEIGHT wheel base: 97 in, 246 cm; tracks: 54.80 in, 139 cm; front, 53.60 in, 136 cm rear; length: 179.80 in, 455 cm; width: 65.40 in, 166 cm; height: 50.20 in, 127 cm; ground clearance: 4.80 in, 12.2 cm; weight: Coupé 2,637 lb, 1,196 kg - SX Coupé 2,654 lb, 1,204 kg; turning circle: 38.4 ft, 11.7 m; fuel tank: 15.4 imp gal, 18.5 US gal, 70 l.

BODY hatchback coupé; 2+1 doors; 4 seats, separate front seats with built-in headrests.

OPTIONALS limited slip differential; 2.930 axle ratio; Turbo-Hydramatic 200 automatic transmission with 3 ratios (I 2.740, II 1.570, III 1, rev 2.070), max ratio of converter at stall 2, possible manual selection, central lever, 2.730 axle ratio; BR 70 x 13 tyres; power steering; tilt of steering wheel; servo brake; heavy-duty radiator; heavy-duty battery; reclining backrests; folding rear seat (for Coupé only); heated rear window; sunshine roof (for Coupé only); anti-roll bar on rear suspension; Firenza equipment; air-conditioning; halogen headlamps.

110 hp power team

See 86 hp power team, except for:

ENGINE 6 cylinders, Vee-slanted at 90°; 231 cu in, 3,785 cc (3.80 x 3.40 in, 96.5 x 86.4 mm); max power (SAE net): 110 hp (81 kW) at 3,800 rpm; max torque (SAE net): 190 lb ft, 26.2 kg m (257 Nm) at 2,000 rpm; max engine rpm: 4,200; 29.1 hp/l (21.4 kW/l); 4 crankshaft bearings; camshafts: 1, at centre of Vee; lubrication: 8.3 imp pt, 9.9 US pt, 4.7 l; fuel feed: electrical pump; cooling, 20.4 imp pt, 24.5 US pt, 11.6 l.

TRANSMISSION axle ratio: 2.930; tyres: B78 x 13.

PERFORMANCE max speed: 103 mph, 165 km/h; power-weight ratio: Coupé 26.2 lb/hp (35.6 lb/kW), 11.9 kg/hp (16.1 kg/kW); speed in direct drive at 1,000 rpm: 27 mph, 43.4 km/h; consumption: 24.1 m/imp gal, 20 m/US gal, 11.7 l x 100 km.

ELECTRICAL EQUIPMENT 2,500 W battery.

DIMENSIONS AND WEIGHT weight: plus 249 lb, 113 kg.

OPTIONALS Turbo-Hydramatic 350 automatic transmission with 3 ratios (I 2.520, II 1.520, III 1, rev 1.930), max ratio of converter at stall 2.35, possible manual selection, 2.560 or 2.930 axle ratio.

Omega Series

PRICES EX WORKS:	$
1 4-dr Sedan	**5,266**
2 2-dr Coupé	**5,100**
3 4-dr Brougham Sedan	**5,530**
4 2-dr Brougham Coupé	**5,380**

For 110 and 115 hp V6 engines add $ 225.

Power team:	Standard for:	Optional for:
90 hp	all	—
90 hp (California)	all	—
110 hp	—	all
115 hp	—	all

90 hp power team

(not available in California)

ENGINE front, transverse 4 stroke; 4 cylinders, in line; 151 cu in, 2,475 cc (4 x 3 in, 101.6 x 76.2 mm); compression ratio: 8.2:1; max power (SAE net): 90 hp (66 kW) at 4,000 rpm; max torque (SAE net): 134 lb ft, 18.6 kg m (182 Nm) at 2,400 rpm; max engine rpm: 4,400; 20.5 hp/l (15.1 kW/l); cast iron block and head; 5 crankshaft bearings; valves: overhead, in line, push-rods and rockers, hydraulic tappets; camshafts: 1, side; lubrication: gear pump, full flow filter, 5.2 imp pt, 6.2 US pt, 3 l; 1 Rochester 17059614 downdraught twin barrel carburettor; air cleaner; exhaust system with catalytic converter; fuel feed: mechanical pump; water-cooled, 13.8 imp pt, 16.3 US pt, 7.9 l.

TRANSMISSION driving wheels: front; clutch: self-adjusting single dry plate (diaphragm); gearbox: mechanical; gears: 4, fully synchronized; ratios: I 3.530, II 1.960, III 1.240, IV 0.810, rev 3.420; lever: central; final drive: spiral bevel; axle ratio: 3.320; width of rims: 5"; tyres: P185/80R x 13.

PERFORMANCE max speed: 87 mph, 140 km/h; power-weight ratio: Sedan 27 lb/hp, (36.5 lb/kW), 12.1 kg/hp (16.5 kg/kW); speed in top at 1,000 rpm: 19.8 mph, 31.8 km/h; consumption: 28.4 m/imp gal, 24 m/US gal, 9.9 l x 100 km.

CHASSIS integral; front suspension: independent, by McPherson, coil springs, stamped lower control arms, telescopic dampers; rear: rigid axle, trailing arm, stamped control arms, coil springs, telescopic dampers.

OLDSMOBILE Starfire Firenza Coupé

OLDSMOBILE Omega Brougham Sedan

STEERING rack-and-pinion; turns lock to lock: 3.50.

BRAKES front disc (diameter 9.72 in, 24.7 cm); internal radial fins, rear drum; swept area: total 272.7 sq in, 1,759 sq cm.

ELECTRICAL EQUIPMENT 12 V; 3,200 W battery; 42 A alternator; Delco-Remy high energy ignition; 2 headlamps.

DIMENSIONS AND WEIGHT wheel base: 105 in, 266 cm; tracks: 58.70 in, 149 cm front, 57 in, 145 cm rear; length:181.80 in, 462 cm; width: 69.80 in, 177 cm; height: 51.90 in, 132 cm; ground clearance: 6 in, 15.3 cm; weight: Sedan 2,430 lb, 1,102 kg - Coupé 2,403 lb, 1,090 kg - Brougham Sedan 2,462 lb, 1,116 kg - Brougham Coupé 2,433 lb, 1,104 kg; weight distribution: 63% front, 37% rear; turning circle: 40.3 ft, 12.3 m; fuel tank: 12 imp gal, 14 US gal, 53 l.

BODY saloon/sedan, coupé; 5 seats, separate front seats with built-in headrests.

OPTIONALS automatic transmission with 3 ratios (I 2.840, II 1.600, III 1, rev 2.070), max ratio of converter at stall 1.9, possible manual selection, steering column lever, 2.530 axle ratio; tilt of steering wheel; intermittent wiper; sunshine roof; reclining seats; custom interior; heated rear window; air-conditioning servo brake; power steering; electric windows; electric door locks; P205/70R x 13 tyres; heavy-duty battery; 70A alternator; heavy-duty cooling; SX equipment.

90 hp power team

(for California only)

See 90 hp power team, except for:

ENGINE max power (SAE net): 90 hp (66 kW) at 4,000 rpm; max torque (SAE net): 128 lb ft, 17.7 kg m (173 Nm) at 2,400 rpm; max engine rpm: 4,500.

110 hp power team

(for California only)

See 90 hp power team, except for:

ENGINE 6 cylinders, Vee-slanted at 60°; 173 cu in, 2,835 cc (3.50 x 3 in, 89 x 76.2 mm); compression ratio: 8.5:1; max power (SAE net): 110 hp (82 kW) at 4,800 rpm; max torque (SAE net): 140 lb ft, 19.4 kg m (190 Nm) at 2,400 rpm; max engine rpm: 5,300; 38.6 hp/l (28.4 kW/l); 4 crankshaft bearings; camshafts: 1, at centre of Vee; lubrication: 6.7 imp pt, 7.9 US pt, 3.8 l; 1 Rochester 17059761 downdraught twin barrel carburettor; cooling, 16.9 imp pt, 20.2 US pt, 9.7 l.

PERFORMANCE max speed: 106 mph, 170 km/h; power-weight ratio: Sedan 22.4 lb/hp, (30.5 lb/kW), 10.1 kg/hp (13.8 kg/kW); speed in top at 1,000 rpm: 23.1 mph, 37.3 km/h; consumption: 23.7 m/imp gal, 20 m/US gal, 11.8 l x 100 km.

DIMENSIONS AND WEIGHT weight: plus 39 lb, 18 kg.

OPTIONALS 2.840 axle ratio with automatic transmission.

115 hp power team

(not available in California)

See 90 hp power team, except for:

OLDSMOBILE Omega Brougham Coupé

transmission); width of rims: 6"; tyres: P185/75R x 14 - st. wagons P195/75R x 14.

PERFORMANCE max speed: 99 mph, 159 km/h; power-weight ratio: Salon Sedan 28 lb/hp (38 lb/kW), 12.7 kg/hp (17.2 kg/kW); speed in direct drive at 1,000 rpm: 24.2 mph, 38.9 km/h; consumption: 23.8 m/imp gal, 20 m/US gal, 11.8 l x 100 km.

CHASSIS channel section perimeter type frame; front suspension: independent, wishbones, coil springs, anti-roll bar, telescopic dampers; rear: rigid axle, lower trailing radius arms, upper oblique torque arms, coil springs, telescopic dampers.

STEERING recirculating ball servo (for st. wagons only); turns lock to lock: 6.60 - st. wagons 4.13.

BRAKES front disc (diameter 10.50 in, 26.7 cm), front internal radial fins, rear drum, rear compensator, servo; swept area: total 312.7 sq in, 2,017 sq cm.

ELECTRICAL EQUIMPENT 2,500 W battery; 42 A alternator; Delco-Remy transistorized ignition; 2 headlamps.

DIMENSIONS AND WEIGHT wheel base: 108.10 in, 274 cm; tracks: 58.50 in, 149 cm front, 57.80 in, 147 cm rear; length: 197.70 in, 502 cm - Supreme Coupé, Calais Coupé and Supreme Brougham Coupé 200.10 in, 508 cm - st. wagons 197.60 in, 502 cm; width: 71.90 in, 183 cm - Supreme Coupé, Calais Coupé and Supreme Brougham Coupé 71.30 in, 181 cm - st. wagons 71.70 in, 182 cm; height: 53.50 in, 136 cm - sedans 54.50 in, 138 cm - in, 138 cm - Salon Coupé 53.70 in, 136 cm - st. wagons 54.90 in, 139 cm; ground clearance: 5.20 in, 13.1 cm - st. wagons 7.42 in, 18.8 cm; weight: Salon Sedan 3,077 lb, 1,396 kg - Coupé 3,057 lb, 1,387 kg - Salon Brougham Coupé 3,098 lb, 1,405 kg - Supreme Sedan 3,188 lb, 1,446 kg - Supreme Coupé 3,088 lb, 1,401 kg - Calais Coupé 3,210 lb, 1,452 kg - Supreme Brougham Sedan 3,213 lb, 1,457 kg - Supreme Brougham Coupé 3,192 lb, 1,450 kg - Cruiser St. Wagon 3,267 lb, 1,482 kg - Cruiser Brougham St. Wagon 3,315 lb, 1,504 kg; turning circle: coupés 40.2 ft, 12.2 m - sedans 40.6 ft, 12.5 m - st. wagons 40.5 ft, 12.3 m; fuel tank: 15.2 imp gal, 18.2 US gal, 69 l.

OPTIONALS limited slip differential; Turbo-Hydramatic automatic transmission with 3 ratios (I 2.740, II 1.567, III 1, rev 2.006), max ratio of converter at stall 2.10, possible manual selection, steering column or central lever, 2.730 or 3.230 axle ratio; P195/75R x 14 tyres; automatic levelling control; heavy-duty suspension; heavy-duty cooling system; power steering; tilt of steering wheel; heavy-duty battery; heavy-duty alternator; heated rear window; electric windows; automatic speed control; electric sunshine roof; air-conditioning.

115 HP POWER TEAM

ENGINE 6 cylinders, Vee-slanted at 60°; 173 cu in, 2,835 cc (3.50 x 3 in, 89 x 76.2 mm); compression ratio: 8.5:1; max power (SAE net): 115 hp (85 kW) at 4,800 rpm; max torque (SAE net): 145 lb ft, 20.1 kg m (197 Nm) at 2,400 rpm; max engine rpm: 5,300; 40.6 hp/l (29.9 kW/l); 4 crankshaft bearings; camshafts: 1, at centre of Vee; lubrication: 6.7 imp pt, 7.9 US pt, 3.8 l; 1 Rochester 17059751 downdraught twin barrel carburettor; cooling, 16.9 imp pt, 20.2 US pt, 9.7 l.

PERFORMANCE max speed: 106 mph, 170 km/h; power-weight ratio: Sedan 21.5 lb/hp (29.3 lb/kW), 9.8 kg/hp (13.3 kg/kW); speed in top at 1,000 rpm: 23.1 mph, 37.3 km/h; consumption: 23.7 m/imp gal, 20 m/US gal, 11.8 l x 100 km.

DIMENSIONS AND WEIGHT weight: plus 39 lb, 18 kg.

OPTIONALS 2.840 axle ratio with automatic transmission.

Cutlass Series

PRICES EX WORKS:	$
1 4-dr Sedan	**5,532**
2 2-dr Salon Coupé	**5,372**
3 2-dr Salon Brougham Coupé	**5,662**
4 4-dr Luxury Supreme Sedan	**6,353**
5 2-dr Supreme Coupé	**6,252**
6 4-dr Brougham Sedan	**6,776**
7 2-dr Supreme Brougham Coupé	**6,691**
8 2-dr Calais Coupé	**6,716**
9 4+1-dr Cruiser St. Wagon	**5,978**
10 4+1-dr Cruiser Brougham St. Wagon	**6,377**

For 105 hp engine add $ 180; for 155 hp engine add $ 295; for 105 hp diesel add $ 960.

Power team:	Standard for:	Optional for:
110 hp	all	—
105 hp	—	all
155 hp	—	all
155 hp (California)	—	all
105 hp (diesel)	—	all

OLDSMOBILE Cutlass Sedan

110 hp power team

ENGINE front, 4 stroke; 6 cylinders, Vee-slanted at 90°; 231 cu in, 3,785 cc (3.80 x 3.40 in, 96.5 x 86.4 mm); compression ratio: 8:1; max power (SAE net): 110 hp (81 kW) at 3,800 rpm; max torque (SAE net): 190 lb ft, 26.1 kg m (256 Nm); max engine rpm: 4,200; 29.3 hp/l (21.5 kW/l); cast iron block and head; 4 crankshaft bearings; valves: overhead, in line, push-rods and rockers, hydraulic tappets; camshafts: 1, at centre of Vee; lubrication: gear pump, full flow filter, 8.3 imp pt, 9.9 US pt, 4.7 l; 1 Rochester 2ME downdraught twin barrel carburettor; air-cleaner; exhaust system with catalytic converter; fuel feed: mechanical pump; water-cooled, 22.2 imp pt, 26.6 US pt, 12.6 l.

TRANSMISSION driving wheels: rear; clutch: single dry plate (diaphragm), centrifugal; gearbox: mechanical (Turbo-Hydramatic automatic transmission standard for Cruiser, Supreme and Supreme Brougham only); gears: 3 fully synchronized; ratios: I 3.500, II 1.895, III 1, rev 3.620; lever: central; final drive: hypoid bevel; axle ratio 3.080 (2.410 with automatic transmission); width of rims: 6"; tyres: P185/75R x 14 - st. wagons P195/75R x 14.

OLDSMOBILE Cutlass Series (diesel engine)

105 hp power team

See 110 hp power team, except for:

ENGINE 8 cylinders; 260 cu in, 4,261 cc (3.50 x 3.38 in, 88.8 x 85.8 mm); compression ratio: 7.5:1; max power (SAE net): 105 hp (77.3 kW) at 3,600 rpm; max torque (SAE net): 205 lb ft, 28.3 kg m (277.5 Nm) at 1,800 rpm; 24.6 hp/l (18.1 kW/l); 5 crankshaft bearings; 1 Rochester 2MC downdraught twin barrel carburettor; cooling system: 26.9 imp pt, 32.3 US pt, 15.3 l.

OLDSMOBILE Cutlass Cruiser Brougham Station Wagon

TRANSMISSION gearbox: Turbo-Hydramatic automatic transmission (standard), hydraulic torque converter and planetary gears with 3 ratios, max torque of converter at stall 2.10, possible manual selection; ratios: I 2.470, II 1.570, III 1, rev 2.070; lever: steering column or central; axle ratio: 2.290 - Cruiser St. Wagon 2.410.

PERFORMANCE max speed: 96 mph, 155 km/h; power-weight ratio: Salon Sedan 30.6 lb/hp (41.5 lb/kW), 13.9 kg/hp (18.8 kg/kW) - Salon Brougham Sedan 30.9 lb/hp (42 lb/kW), 14 kg/hp (19.1 kg/kW); consumption: 22.8 m/imp gal, 19 m/US gal, 12.4 l x 100 km.

STEERING servo (standard); turns lock to lock: 3.60.

ELECTRICAL EQUIPMENT 63 A alternator.

DIMENSIONS AND WEIGHT weight: plus 131 lb, 59 kg - st. wagons 177 lb, 80 kg.

OPTIONALS 2.930 axle ratio.

155 hp power team

(not available in California)

See 110 hp power team, except for:

ENGINE 8 cylinders; 305 cu in, 4,999 cc (3.74 x 3.48 in, 94.9 x 88.4 mm); max power (SAE net): 155 hp (113 kW) at 4,000 rpm; max torque (SAE net): 240 lb ft, 33.1 kg m (324 Nm) at 1,600 rpm; max engine rpm: 4,500; 32. hp/l (24 kW/l); 5 crankshaft bearings; 1 Rochester M4 downdraught 4-barrel carburettor; cooling 27.6 imp pt, 32.8 US pt, 15.7 l.

TRANSMISSION clutch: single dry plate (diaphragm) gearbox: mechanical; gears: 4, fully syncronized ratios: I 2.850, II 2.020, III 1.350, IV 1, rev, 2.850; lever: central axle ratio: 2.29 - St. Wagon 2.410.

PERFORMANCE max speed: 105 mph, 170 km/h; power-weight ratio: 20.8 lb/hp, (28.4 lb/kW), 9.4 kg/hp (12.8 kg/kW) speed in direct drive at 1,000 rpm: 22.9 mph, 36.9 km/h; consumption: 20.1 m/imp gal, 17 m/US gal, 13.9 l x 100 km.

ELECTRICAL EQUIPMENT 63 A alternator.

DIMENSIONS AND WEIGHT weight: plus 150 lb, 68 kg - st. wagons 181 lb, 82 kg.

OPTIONALS 2.930 axle ratio.

155 hp power team

(California only)

See 110 hp power team, except for:

ENGINE 8 cylinders; 305 cu in, 4,999 cc (3.74 x 3.48 in, 94.9 x 88.4 mm); max power (SAE net): 155 hp (113 kW) at 4,000 rpm; max torque (SAE net): 230 lb ft, 31.7 kg m (312 Nm) at 2,400 rpm; max engine rpm: 4,400; 32 hp/l (24 kW/l); 5 crankshaft bearings; 1 Rochester M4 downdraught 4-barrel carburettor; cooling 27.6 imp pt, 32.8 US pt, 15.7 l.

TRANSMISSION axle ratio: 2.29 - st. wagons 2.410.

PERFORMANCE max speed: 108 mph, 174 km/h; power-weight ratio: Salon Sedan 20.8 lb/hp, (28.4 lb/kW), 9.4 kg/hp (12.8 kg/kW); speed in direct drive at 1,000 rpm: 31.4 mph, 50.2 km/h; consumption: 20.1 m/imp gal, 17 m/US gal, 13.9 l x 100 km.

ELECTRICAL EQUIPMENT 63 A alternator.

DIMENSIONS AND WEIGHT weight: plus, 150 lb, 68 kg - St. Wagons 181 lb, 82 kg.

OPTIONALS 2.930 axle ratio.

105 hp (diesel) power team

See 110 hp power team except for

ENGINE diesel; 8 cylinders; 350 cu in, 5,736 cc (4.057 x 3.385 in, 103.9 x 86 mm) compression ratio: 22.5:1; max power (SAE net): 105 hp (78 kW) at 3,200 rpm; max torque (SAE net): 205 lb ft, 28.4 kg m (278 Nm) at 1,600 rpm; max engine rpm: 3,500; 18.4 hp/l (13.6 kW/l); 5 crankshaft bearings; lubrication: 12.4 imp pt, 14.8 US pt, 7,1 l; mechanical injection pump; cooling: 28.7 imp pt, 33.9 US pt, 16.4 l.

TRANSMISSION axle ratio: 2.290.

PERFORMANCE max speed: 94 mph, 151 km/h; power-weight ratio: 34.5 lb/hp, (44.1 lb/kW), 14.7 kg/hp (20 kg/kW); speed in direct drive at 1,000 rpm: 28.6 mph, 45.7 km/h; consumption: 17.7 m/imp gal, 15 m/US gal, 15.8 l x 100 km.

ELECTRICAL EQUIPMENT 55 A alternator.

DIMENSIONS AND WEIGHT weight: plus 332 lb, 151 kg - st. wagons, 368 lb, 167 kg.

Delta 88 - Ninety Eight - Custom Cruiser Series

PRICES EX WORKS:	$
1 Delta 88 4-dr Sedan	**6,552**
2 Delta 88 2-dr Coupé	**6,457**
3 Delta 88 Royale 4-dr Sedan	**6,864**
4 Delta 88 Royale 2-dr Coupé	**6,716**
5 Delta 88 Royale Brougham 4-dr Sedan	**7,160**
6 Delta 88 Royale Brougham 2-dr Coupé	**7,080**
7 Ninety Eight 4-dr Luxury Sedan	**9,112**
8 Ninety Eight 4-dr Regency Sedan	**9,741**
9 Ninety Eight 2-dr Regency Coupé	**9,619**
10 Custom Cruiser 4+1-dr St. Wagon	**7,443**

For 120 hp V8 engine add $ 180; for 150 hp V8 engine add $ 295; for 160 hp V8 engine add $ 425 (Custom Cruiser and Ninety Eight models add $ 130); for 105 hp (diesel) engine add $ 960 (Custom Cruiser and Ninety Eight models add $ 860).

Power team:	Standard for:	Optional for:
110 hp	1 to 6	—
120 hp	—	1 to 6
150 hp	7 to 10	1 to 6
160 hp	—	all
105 hp (diesel)	—	all

110 hp power team

ENGINE front, 4 stroke; 6 cylinders, Vee-slanted at 90°; 231 cu in, 3,785 cc (3.80 x 3.40 in, 96.5 x 86.5 mm); compression ratio: 8:1; max power (SAE net): 110 hp (81 kW) at 3,800 rpm; max torque (SAE net): 190 lb ft, 26.1 kg m (256 Nm) at 1,600 rpm; max engine rpm: 4,200; 29.3 hp/l (21.5 kW/l); cast iron block and head; 4 crankshaft bearings; valves: overhead, in line, push-rods and rockers, hydraulic tappets; camshafts: 1, at centre of Vee; lubrication: gear pump, full flow filter, 7.4 imp pt, 8.4 US pt, 4 l; 1 Rochester 17080490 downdraught twin barrel carburettor; thermostatic air cleaner; exhaust system with catalytic converter; fuel feed: mechanical pump; water-cooled, 21.5 imp pt, 25.6 US pt, 12.2 l.

TRANSMISSION driving wheels: rear; gearbox: Turbo-Hydramatic 350 automatic transmission, hydraulic torque converter and planetary gears with 3 ratios, max ratio of converter at stall 2, possible manual selection; ratios: I 2.520, II 1.520, III 1, rev 1,930; lever: steering column; final drive: hypoid bevel; axle ratio: 2.730; width of rims: 6"; tyres: P205/75 R x 15.

PERFORMANCE max speed: 95 mph, 152 km/h; power-weight ratio: Sedan 30.9 lb/hp, (42 lb/kW), 14 kg/hp (19 kg/kW); speed in direct drive at 1,000 rpm: 29.8 mph, 47.7 km/h; consumption: 21.4 m/imp gal, 18 m/US gal, 13.1 l x 100 km.

CHASSIS perimeter box-type with front and rear cross members; front suspension: independent, wishbones, coil springs, anti-roll bar, telescopic dampers; rear: rigid axle, lower trailing radius arms, upper oblique torque arms, coil springs, telescopic dampers.

OLDSMOBILE Delta 88 Sedan

110 HP POWER TEAM

STEERING recirculating ball, servo; turns lock to lock: 4.10.

BRAKES front disc (diameter 11 in, 27.9 cm), front internal radial fins, rear drum, servo; swept area: total 384.2 sq in, 2,478 sq cm.

ELECTRICAL EQUIPMENT 12 V; 2,500 W battery; 42 A alternator; Delco-Remy transistorized ignition; 4 headlamps.

DIMENSIONS AND WEIGHT wheel base: 116 in, 294 cm; tracks: 61.70 in, 157 cm front, 60.70 in, 154 cm rear; length: 218 in, 555 cm; width: 76.30 in, 194 cm; height: sedans 54.70 in, 139 cm - coupés 54.10 in, 137 cm; ground clearance: 7 in, 18 cm; weight: Sedan 3,397 lb, 1,541 kg - Coupé 3,371 lb, 1,529 kg - Royale Sedan 3,364 lb, 1,526 kg - Royale Coupé 3,375 lb, 1,531 kg - Royale Brougham Sedan 3,397 lb, 1,541 kg - Royale Brougham Coupé 3,404 lb, 1,544 kg; weight distribution: 54% front, 46% rear; turning circle: 42.8 ft, 13 m; fuel tank: 17.4 imp gal, 20.7 US gal, 78 l.

BODY saloon/sedan, coupé; 6 seats, separate front seats (for Royale and Royale Brougham only), built-in headrests.

OPTIONALS limited slip differential; 3.230 axle ratio; heavy-duty cooling; heavy-duty suspension; heavy-duty battery; halogen headlamps; engine block heater; heated rear window; trip computer; anti-theft; electric sunshine roof; electric back-rests; tilt and telescopic steering wheel; P215/75 R x 15 tyres; tinted glass.

OLDSMOBILE Ninety Eight Regency Sedan

120 hp power team

See 110 hp power team, except for:

ENGINE 8 cylinders; 267 cu in, 4,376 cc (3.50 x 3.48 in, 88.9 x 88.4 mm); compression ratio: 8.3:1; max power (SAE net): 120 hp (88 kW) at 3,600 rpm; max torque (SAE net): 215 lb ft, 29.6 kg m (290 Nm) at 2,000 rpm; max engine rpm: 4,000; 36.5 hp/l (26.8 kW/l); 5 crankshaft bearings; 1 Rochester 17080108 downdraught twin barrel carburettor; cooling, 27.5 imp pt, 32.7 US pt, 15.6 l.

TRANSMISSION axle ratio: 2.410.

PERFORMANCE max speed: 108 mph, 174 km/h; power-weight ratio: Sedan 29.4 lb/hp (40 lb/kW), 13.3 kg/hp (18.1 kg/kW); speed in direct drive at 1,000 rpm: 29.8 mph, 48 km/h; consumption: 20.1 m/imp gal, 17 m/US gal, 13.9 l x 100 km.

ELECTRICAL EQUIPMENT 37 A alternator.

DIMENSIONS AND WEIGHT weight: plus 126 lb, 57 kg; fuel tank: 21 imp gal, 25 US gal, 95 l.

OPTIONALS 2.730 or 3.080 axle ratio.

150 hp power team

See 110 hp power team, except for:

ENGINE 8 cylinders; 307 cu in, 5,032 cc (3.80 x 3.38 in, 96.5 x 86 mm); max power (SAE net): 150 hp (110 kW) at 3,600 rpm; max torque (SAE net): 245 lb ft, 33.8 kg m (331 Nm) at 1,600 rpm; max engine rpm: 4,000; 30 hp/l (22 kW/l); 5 crankshaft bearings; water-cooled, 23.4 imp pt, 30 US pt, 14,5 l.

TRANSMISSION axle ratio: 2.410 - Custom Cruiser 2.560; tyres: Ninety Eight models 215/75R x 15 - Custom Cruiser 225/75R x 15.

PERFORMANCE max speed: 105 mph, 168 km/h - Delta 88 models 108 mph, 174 km/h; power-weight ratio: Ninety Eight Luxury Sedan 25.1 lb/hp, (34.2 lb/kW), 11.4 kg/hp (15.5 kg/kW); speed in direct drive at 1,000 rpm: 29.8 mph, 48 km/h; consumption: 20.1 m/imp gal, 17 m/US gal, 13.9 l x 100 km.

STEERING turns lock to lock: Ninety Eight models 3.50 - Custom Cruiser 4.

BRAKES (for Ninety Eight models and Custom Cruiser only) front disc (diameter 11.88 in, 30.2 cm), rear drum; swept area: total 396.6 sq in, 2,559 sq cm.

DIMENSIONS AND WEIGHT (for Ninety Eight models and Custom Cruiser only) wheel base: 119 in, 302 cm - Custom Cruiser 116 in, 294 cm; tracks: 61.70 in, 157 cm front, 60.70 in, 154 cm rear - Custom Cruiser 62.10 in, 158 cm front, 64.10 in, 163 cm rear; length: 221.40 in, 562 cm - Custom Cruiser 220 in, 560 cm; width: 76.30 in, 194 cm - Custom Cruiser 79.80 in, 203 cm; height: 55.30 in, 140 cm - Custom Cruiser 56.60 in, 144 cm; ground clearance: 12.20 in, 31 cm; weight: Ninety Eight Luxury Sedan 3,770 lb, 1,710 kg - Ninety Eight Regency Sedan 3,818 lb, 1,732 kg - Ninety Eight Regency Coupé 3,801 lb, 1,724 kg - Custom Cruiser 3,964 lb, 1,798 kg; weight distribution: Ninety Eight Luxury Sedan 56% front, 44% rear; turning circle: 43.5 ft, 13.2 m - Custom Cruiser 42.8 ft, 13 m; fuel tank: 21 imp gal, 25 US gal, 95 l - Custom Cruiser 18.6 imp gal, 22 US gal, 83 l.

OPTIONALS 2.730 or 3.080 axle ratio.

160 hp power team

See 110 hp power team, except for:

ENGINE 8 cylinders; 350 cu in, 5,736 cc (4.06 x 3.38 in, 103 x 85.8 mm); max power (SAE net): 160 hp (118 kW) at 3,600 rpm; max torque (SAE net): 270 lb ft, 37.2 kg m (365 Nm) at 2,000 rpm; 27.9 hp/l (20.5 kW/l); 5 crankshaft bearings; 1 Rochester downdraught 4-barrel carburettor; cooling, 24.3 imp pt, 29.2 US pt, 13.8 l.

TRANSMISSION axle ratio: 2.410.

PERFORMANCE max speed 110 mph, 178 km/h - Ninety Eight and Custom Cruiser 108 mph, 174 km/h; power-weight ratio: Delta 88 Sedan 22.4 lb/hp (30.4 lb/kW), 10.1 kg/hp (13.8 kg/kW); speed in direct drive at 1,000 rpm: 28.5 mph, 45.8 km/h; consumption: 18 m/imp gal, 15 m/US gal, 15.7 l x 100 km.

DIMENSIONS AND WEIGHT weight: Delta 88 models plus 185 lb, 84 kg - Ninety Eight Luxury Sedan 3,778 lb, 1,714 kg - Ninety Eight Regency Sedan 3,826 lb, 1,802 kg - Ninety Eight Regency Coupé 3,809 lb, 1,732 kg - Custom Cruiser 3,972 lb, 1,806 kg; fuel tank: 21 imp gal, 25 US gal, 95 l - Custom Cruiser 18.6 imp gal, 22 US gal, 83 l.

OPTIONALS 2.730 or 3.080 axle ratio.

OLDSMOBILE Custom Cruiser Station Wagon

105 hp (diesel) power team

See 110 hp power team, except for:

ENGINE diesel; 8 cylinders; 350 cu in, 5,736 cc (4.06 x 3.38 in, 103.9 x 86 mm); compression ratio: 22.5:1; max power (SAE net): 105 hp (78 kW) at 3,200 rpm; max torque (SAE net): 205 lb ft, 28.4 kg m (278 Nm) at 1,600 rpm; max engine rpm: 3,500; 18.4 hp/l (13.6 kW/l); 5 crankshaft bearings; lubrication: 12.4 imp pt, 14.8 US pt, 7.1 l; fuel feed: mechanical injection pump; cooling, 28.7 imp pt, 33.9 US pt, 16.4 l.

TRANSMISSION axle ratio: 2.410 - Custom Cruiser 2.730.

PERFORMANCE max speed: 85 mph, 136 km/h; power-weight ratio: Delta 88 Sedan 35.9 lb/hp, (48.3 lb/kW), 16.3 kg/hp (21.9 kg/kW); speed in direct drive at 1,000 rpm: 28.6 mph, 45.7 km/h; consumption: 16.5 m/imp gal, 14 m/US gal, 16.9 l x 100 km.

ELECTRICAL EQUIPMENT 55 A alternator.

DIMENSIONS AND WEIGHT weight: Delta 88 models plus 378 lb, 171 kg - Ninety Eight Luxury Sedan 3,954 lb, 1,789 kg - Ninety Eight Regency Sedan 3,992 lb, 1,811 kg - Ninety Eight Regency Coupé 3,975 lb, 1,803 kg - Custom Cruiser 4,138 lb, 1,877 kg; fuel tank: 22.7 imp gal,27 US gal, 102 l.

Toronado

PRICE EX WORKS: $ 11,361

For 160 hp engine add $ 130; for 105 hp (diesel) engine add $ 860.

150 hp power team

standard)

ENGINE front, 4 stroke; 8 cylinders; 307 cu in, 5,032 cc 3.80 x 3.38 in, 96.5 x 86 mm); compression ratio: 8:1; max power (SAE net): 150 hp (110 kW) at 3,600 rpm; max torque SAE net): 245 lb ft, 33.8 kg m (331 Nm) at 1,600 rpm; max engine rpm: 4,000; 30 hp/l (22 kW/l); cast iron block and head; crankshaft bearings; valves: overhead, in line, push-rods and ockers, hydraulic tappets; camshafts: 1, at centre of Vee; ubrication: gear pump, full flow filter, 6.6 imp pt, 7.8 US pt, 3.8 ; 1 Rochester M4MC downdraught 4-barrel carburettor; Thermostatic air cleaner; fuel feed: mechanical pump; water cooled, 23.4 imp pt, 30 US pt, 14.5 l.

TRANSMISSION driving wheels: front, gearbox: Torque-Hydramatic 200 C automatic transmission, hydraulic torque onverter and planetary gears with 3 ratios, max ratio of converter at stall 2.2, possible manual selection; ratios: I 2.740, II 1.570, III 1, rev 2.070; lever: steering column; final drive: hypoid bevel; axle ratio: 2.410; width of rims: 6"; tyres: P205/75R x 15.

PERFORMANCE max speed: 112 mph, 180 km/h; power-weight atio: 24.2 lb/hp (32.9 lb/kW), 10.9 kg/hp (14.9 kg/kW); speed in direct drive at 1,000 rpm: 31.1 mph, 50 km/h; consumption: 0.1 m/imp gal, 17 m/US gal, 13.9 l x 100 km.

CHASSIS channel section perimeter type frame; front suspension: independent, wishbones, longitudinal torsion bars, anti-roll bar, telescopic dampers; rear: independent, swinging longitudinal trailing arms, coil springs, automatic levelling control, telescopic dampers.

STEERING recirculating ball, servo; turns lock to lock: 3.

BRAKES front disc (diameter 10.50 in, 26.7 cm), front internal radial fins, rear drum, rear compensator, servo; swept area: total 307.8 sq in, 1,985 sq cm.

ELECTRICAL EQUIPMENT 12 V; 80 Ah battery; 63 A alternator; Delco-Remy transistorized ignition; 4 headlamps.

DIMENSIONS AND WEIGHT wheel base: 114 in, 289 cm; tracks: 59.30 in, 151 cm front, 60 in, 152 cm rear; length: 205.60 in, 522 cm; width: 80 in, 203 cm; height: 54.20 in, 138 cm; ground clearance: 5.11 in, 13 cm; weight: 3,629 lb, 1,644 kg; turning circle: 44.2 ft, 13.5 m; fuel tank: 17.8 imp gal, 21 US gal, 79 l.

BODY coupé; 2 doors; 4 seats, separate front seats with built-in headrests; electric tinted windows; air-conditioning.

OPTIONALS heavy-duty cooling; heavy-duty battery; heavy-duty alternator; tilt of steering wheel; speed control; heated rear window; electric sunshine roof; heavy-duty suspension; Reminder equipment; XSC equipment; reclining backrests.

160 hp power team

See 150 hp power team, except for:

ENGINE 350 cu in, 5,736 cc (4.06 x 3.38 in, 103 x 85.8 mm); max power (DIN): 160 hp (118 kW) at 3,600 rpm; max torque (DIN): 270 lb ft, 37.2 kg m (365 Nm) at 2,000 rpm; 27.9 hp/l (20.5 kW/l); 5 crankshaft bearings; 1 Rochester downdraught 4-barrel carburettor; cooling, 24.3 imp pt, 29.2 US pt, 13.8 l.

PERFORMANCE max speed: 116 mph, 187 km/h; power-weight ratio: 22.8 lb/hp (30.9 lb/kW), 10.3 kg/hp (14 kg/kW); consumption: 17.7 m/imp gal, 15 m/US gal, 15.8 l x 100 km.

DIMENSIONS AND WEIGHT weight: 3,637 lb, 1,650 kg.

105 hp (diesel) power team

See 150 hp power team, except for:

ENGINE 350 cu in, 5,736 cc (4.06 x 3.38 in, 103.9 x 86 mm); compression ratio: 22.5:1; max power (SAE net): 105 hp (78 kW) at 3,200 rpm; max torque (SAE net): 205 lb ft, 28.4 kg m (278 Nm) at 1,600 rpm; max engine rpm: 3,500; 18.4 hp/l (13.6 kW/l); 5 crankshaft bearings; lubrication: 12.4 imp pt, 14.8 US pt, 7.1 l; fuel feed: mechanical injection pump; cooling' 28.7 imp pt, 33.9 US pt, 16.4 l.

TRANSMISSION axle ratio: 2.410.

PERFORMANCE max speed: 94 mph, 151 km/h; power-weight ratio: 35.6 lb/hp (48.4 lb/kW), 16.1 kg/hp (21.9 kg/kW); speed in direct drive at 1,000 rpm: 28.6 mph, 45.7 km/h; consumption: 17.7 m/imp gal, 15 m/US gal, 15.8 l x 100 km.

DIMENSIONS AND WEIGHT weight: 3,737 lb, 1,695 kg.

OLDSMOBILE Toronado

PLYMOUTH USA

Horizon Series

PRICES EX WORKS: $

4-dr Hatchback	**4,925**
TC3 2-dr Hatchback	**5,271**

ENGINE front, transverse, slanted 15° to front, 4 stroke; 4 cylinders, in line; 104.7 cu in, 1,714 cc (3.13 x 3.40 in, 79.5 x 86.4 mm); compression ratio: 8.2:1; max power (SAE net): 65 hp (48 kW) at 5,200 rpm; max torque (SAE net): 85 lb ft, 11.7 kg m (115 Nm) at 2,400 rpm; max engine rpm: 6,500; 37.9 hp/l (27.9 kW/l); cast iron block, light alloy head; 5 crankshaft bearings; valves: overhead, in line, thimble tappets; camshafts: 1, overhead, cogged belt; lubrication: gear pump, full flow filter, 6.7 imp pt, 8 US pt, 3.8 l; 1 Holley R-9108A (California R-8676A) twin barrel carburettor; air cleaner; exhaust system with catalytic converter; fuel feed: mechanical pump; water-cooled, 10 imp pt, 12 US pt, 5.7 l.

TRANSMISSION driving wheels: front; clutch: single dry plate (diaphragm); gearbox: mechanical; gears: 4, fully synchronized; ratios: I 3.450, II 1.940, III 1.290, IV 0.970, rev 3.170; lever: central; final drive: spiral bevel; axle ratio: 3.370: width of rims: 2-dr 5", 4-dr 4.5"; tyres: 2-dr P175/75R x 13 - 4-dr P155/80R x 13.

PERFORMANCE max speed: 91 mph, 146 km/h; power-weight ratio; 2-dr 33.8 lb/hp (45.7 lb/kW), 15.3 kg/hp (20.7 kg/kW) - 4-dr 31.3 lb/hp (44.8 lb/kW), 15 kg/hp (20.3 kg/kW); speed in top at 1,000 rpm: 16.7 mph, 26.9 km/h; consumption: 28.8 m/imp gal, 24 m/US gal, 9.8 l x 100 km.

CHASSIS integral; front suspension: independent, by McPherson, lower wishbones, anti-roll bar, coil springs/telescopic damper struts; rear: independent, semi-trailing arms, coil springs, telescopic dampers.

STEERING rack-and-pinion; turns lock to lock: 4.

BRAKES front disc (diameter 8.98 in, 22.8 cm), front internal radial fins, rear drum; swept area: total 197.5 sq in, 1,274 sq cm.

ELECTRICAL EQUIPMENT 12 V; 310 A battery: 65 A alternator; Essex or Prestolite transistorized ignition with electronic spark control; 2 headlamps.

DIMENSIONS AND WEIGHT wheel base: 2-dr 96.70 in, 246 cm - 4-dr 99.20 in, 252 cm; tracks: 56 in, 142 cm front, 55.60 in, 141 cm rear; length: 2-dr 173.30 in, 440 cm - 4-dr 164.80 in, 419 cm; width: 2-dr 66.70 in, 169 cm - 4-dr 65.80 in, 167 cm; height: 2-dr 51.40 in, 131 cm - 4-dr 53-70 in, 136 cm; ground clearance: 5 in, 12.7 cm; weight: 2-dr 2,196 lb, 996 kg - 4-dr 2,154 lb, 977 kg: turning circle: 36.1 ft, 11 m; fuel tank: 10.8 imp gal, 13 US pt, 49 l.

BODY 4 seats, separate front seats with bullt-in headrests; heated rear window.

OPTIONALS Torqueflite automatic transmission, hydraulic torque converter and planetary gears with 3 ratios (I 2.470, II 1.470, III 1, rev 2.100), max ratio of converter at stall 1.97, possible manual selection, central lever, 3.480 axle ratio:

PLYMOUTH Horizon Hatchback

PLYMOUTH Horizon Hatchback

HORIZON SERIES

P165/75R x 13 tyres (for 2-dr only); P175/75R x 13 tyres with 5" wide rims; P185/70R x 13 tyres with 5" wide rims (for 2-dr only); P185/70R x 13 tyres with 5.5" wide rims (for 2-dr only); - heavy-duty suspension; power steering; servo brake; reclining backrests; rear window wiper-washer; vinyl roof; sunshine roof; air-conditioning; Custom or Premium Woodgrain equipment (for 4-dr only); Premium equipment; Sport or Turismo equipment (for 2-dr only).

Volaré Series

PRICES EX WORKS:

		$
1	4-dr Sedan	**4,847**
2	2-dr Coupé	**4,730**
3	4-dr Sedan Special	**4,994**
4	2-dr Coupé Special	**4,977**
5	4+1-dr St. Wagon	**5,089**

Power team:	Standard for:	Optional for:
90 hp	all	—
90 hp (California)	all	—
120 hp	—	all
155 hp	—	all

90 hp power team

(not available in California)

ENGINE front, 4 stroke; 6 cylinders, vertical, in line; 225 cu in, 3,687 cc (3.40 x 4.12 in, 86.4 x 104.6 mm); compression ratio: 8.4:1; max power (SAE net): 90 hp (66 kW) at 3,600 rpm; max torque (SAE net): 160 lb ft, 22.1 kgm (217 Nm) at 1,600 rpm; max engine rpm: 4,400; 24.4 hp/l (18 kW/l); cast iron block and head; 4 crankshaft bearings; valves: overhead, in line, push-rods and rockers; camshafts: 1, side; lubrication: rotary pump, full flow filter, 8.3 imp pt, 9.9 US pt, 4.7 l; 1 Holley R-8718A (Special models R8831A) downdraught single barrel carburettor; thermostatic air cleaner; exhaust system with catalytic converter; fuel feed: mechanical pump; water-cooled, 19.2 imp pt, 23 US pt, 10.9 l.

TRANSMISSION driving wheels: rear; clutch: single dry plate; gearbox: mechanical (Special models Torqueflite automatic transmission with hydraulic torque converter and planetary gears 3 ratios, max ratio of converter at stall 2,01, possible manual selection; ratios: I 2.450, II 1.450, III 1, rev 2.220; gears: 3, fully synchronized; ratios: I 3.080, II 1.700, III 1, rev 2.900; lever: central - Special models steering column or central; final drive: hypoid bevel; axle ratio: 3.230, 2.760 Special models - 3,210 St. Wagon; width of rims: 5" - St. Wagon 5.5"; tyres: P 195/75R x 14.

PERFORMANCE max speed: 90 mph, 145 km/h - Special models 105 mph, 165 km/h; power-weight ratio: sedans 32.5 lb/hp (44.3 lb/kW), 15.2 kg/hp (20.3 kg/kW); speed in direct drive at 1,000 rpm: 20.4 mph, 32.9 km/h; consumption: 20.5 m/imp gal, 17 m/US gal, 13.8 l x 100 km.

CHASSIS integral with front cross members; front suspension: independent, wishbones, transverse torsion bars, anti-roll bar, telescopic dampers; rear: rigid axle, semi-elliptic leafsprings, anti-roll bar, telescopic dampers.

STEERING recirculating ball; turns lock to lock: 5.30.

BRAKES front disc (diameter 10.82 in, 27.5 cm), front internal radial fins, rear drum, rear compensator; swept area: total 355.24 sq in, 2,292 sq cm.

ELECTRICAL EQUIPMENT 12 V; 325 A battery; 60 A alternator; Essex or Prestolite or Mopar transistorized ignition with electronic spark control; 4 headlamps.

BODY Sedan and St. Wagon 6 seats - Coupé 5 seats, separate front seats; built-in headrests.

DIMENSIONS AND WEIGHT wheel base: 112.70 in, 286 cm - coupés 108.70 in, 276 cm; tracks: 60 in, 152 cm front, 58.50 in, 149 cm rear; length: 201.20 in, 511 cm - coupés 197.20 in, 501 cm; width: 72.80 in, 185 cm; height: coupés 53.30 in, 135 cm - sedans 55.30 in, 140 cm - St. Wagon 55.70 in, 141 cm; ground clearance: 5.90 in, 15 cm - St. Wagon 6.20 in, 15.7 cm; weight: coupés 3,200 lb, 1,452 kg - sedans 3,258 lb, 1,478 kg - St. Wagon 3,432 lb, 1,557 kg; turning circle: 43.5 ft, 13.2 m - coupés 42.1 ft, 12.6 m; fuel tank: 15 imp gal, 18 US gal, 68 l - St. Wagon 16.3 imp gal, 19.5 US gal, 74 l.

OPTIONALS limited slip differential; 3.210 axle ratio; Torqueflite automatic transmission with 3 ratios (I 2.450, II 1.450, III 1, rev 2.220), max ratio of converter at stall 2.01, possible manual selection, steering column or central lever, 2.760 or 2.710 axle ratio; 4-speed fully synchronized mechanical gearbox with overdrive/top (I 3.090, II 1.670, III 1, IV 0.710, rev 3), central lever, 3.230 or 3.210 axle ratio; heavy-duty cooling; P195/75R x 14 or P205/75R x 14 tyres with 5.5" wide rims; FR70 x 14 tyres with 6" wide rims light alloy wheels; heavy-duty suspension; power steering; tilt of steering wheel; servo brake; heavy-duty battery; tinted glass; electric window; heated rear window; automatic speed control; vinyl roof; luxury equipment; air-conditioning; Custom equipment; Premier equipment; De Luxe equipment; Sport equipment; Volaré Road Runner equipment (for coupés only).

90 hp power team

(for California only)

See 90 hp power team, except for:

ENGINE 1 Holley R 8719 A downdraught single barrel carburettor.

TRANSMISSION gearbox: Torqueflite automatic transmission (standard), hydraulic torque converter and planetary gears with 3 ratios, max ratio of converter at stall 2.01, possible manual selection; ratios: I 2.450, II 1.450, III 1, rev 2.220; lever: steering column or central; axle ratio: 2.940.

PERFORMANCE power-weight ratio: sedans 34.6 lb/hp (47.5 lb/kW), 15.7 kg/hp (21.3 kg/kW).

OPTIONALS 4-speed fully synchronized mechanical gearbox with overdrive/top not available.

120 hp power team

(not available in California)

See 90 hp power team, except for:

ENGINE 8 cylinders: 318 cu in, 5.211 cc (3.91 x x 3.31 in, 99.2 x 84 mm); compression ratio: 8.5:1; max power (SAE net): 120 hp (89 kW) at 3,600 rpm; max torque (SAE net): 245 lb ft, 33.9 kg m (332 Nm) at 1,600 rpm; 23.1 hp/l (16.9 kW/l); crankshaft bearings; valves: hydraulic tappets; camshafts: 1, at centre of Vee; 1 Carter BBD 8233S downdraught twin barrel carburettor; cooling: 25 imp pt, 30 US pt, 14.2 l.

TRANSMISSION gearbox: Torqueflite automatic transmission (standard), hydraulic torque converter planetary gears with 3 ratios, max ratio of converter at stall 1.90, possible manual selection; ratios: I 2.450, II 1.450, III 1, rev 2.220; lever: steering column or central; axle ratio: 2.470 - St. Wagon 2.450.

PERFORMANCE max speed: 102 mph, 164 km/h; power-weight ratio: sedans 26.9 lb/hp (36.6 lb/kW), 12.2 kg/hp (16.6 kg/kW); speed in direct drive at 1,000 rpm: 25.5 mph, 41 km/h; consumption: 18 m/imp gal, 5 m/US gal, 15.7 l x 100 km.

DIMENSIONS AND WEIGHT weight: coupés 3,258 lb, 1,478 kg - sedans 3,318 lb, 1,505 kg - St. Wagon 3,481 lb, 1,579 kg; fuel tank: 16.3 imp gal, 19.5 US gal, 74 l.

OPTIONALS 4-speed fully synchronized mechanical gearbox with overdrive/top not available.

155 hp power team

(for California only)

See 90 hp power team, except for:

ENGINE 8 cylinders; 318 cu in, 5,211 cc (3.91 x 3.31 in, 99.2 x 84 mm); compression ratio: 8.5:1; max power (SAE net): 155 hp (114 kW) at 4,000 rpm; max torque (SAE net): 245 lb ft, 33.8 kg m (331 Nm) at 1,600 rpm; 29.7 hp/l (21.9 kW/l); crankshaft bearings; valves: hydraulic tappets; camshafts: 1, at centre of Vee: 1 Carter TQ 9234 downdraught 4-barrel carburettor; cooling: 25 imp pt, 30 US pt, 14.2 l.

TRANSMISSION gearbox: Torqueflite automatic transmission (standard), hydraulic torque converter planetary gears with 3 ratios, max ratio of converter at stall 1.90, possible manual selection; ratios: I 2.450, II 1,450, III 1, rev 2.220; lever: steering column or central; axle ratio: 2.470 - St. Wagon 2.450.

PERFORMANCE max speed: 103 mph, 165 km/h; power-weight ratio: sedans 21.4 lb/hp (29.1 lb/kW), 9.7 kg/hp (13.2 kg/kW); speed in direct drive at 1,000 rpm: 25.6 mph, 41.2 km/h; consumption: 18 m/imp gal, 15 m/US gal, 15.7 l x 100 km.

DIMENSIONS AND WEIGHT weight: coupés 3,258 lb, 1,478 kg - sedans 3,318 lb, 1,505 kg - St. Wagon 3,481 lb, 1,579 kg; fuel tank: 16.3 imp gal, 19.5 US gal, 74 l.

OPTIONALS 4-speed fully synchronized mechanical gearbox with overdrive/top not available.

Gran Fury Series

PRICES EX WORKS:

	$
Pillared Hardtop	**6,28**
Salon Pillared Hardtop	**6,71**

PLYMOUTH Volaré Sedan

PLYMOUTH Volaré Premier Coupé

PLYMOUTH Volaré Premier Station Wagon

90 hp power team

(not available in California)

ENGINE front, 4 stroke; 6 cylinders, vertical, in line: 225 cu in, 3,687 cc (3.40 x 4.12 in, 86.4 x 104.6 mm); compression ratio: 8.4:1; max power (SAE net): 90 hp (67 kW) at 3,600 rpm; max torque (SAE net): 160 lb ft, 22 kg m (217 Nm) at 1,600 rpm; max engine rpm: 4,000; 24.4 hp/l (17.9 kW/l); 4 crankshaft bearings; valves: overhead, in line, push-rods and rockers; camshafts: 1, side; lubrication: rotary pump, full flow filter, 8.3 imp pt, 9.9 US pt, 4.7 l; 1 Holley R 8831 A downdraught twin barrel carburettor; air cleaner; exhaust system with catalytic converter; fuel feed: mechanical pump; water-cooled, 19.2 imp pt, 23 US pt, 10.9 l.

TRANSMISSION driving wheels: rear; gearbox: Torqueflite automatic transmission, hydraulic torque converter and planetary gears with 3 ratios; max ratio of converter at stall 1,90, possible manual selection; ratios: I 2.740, II 1.540, III 1, rev 2.220; lever: steering column; final drive: hypoid bevel; axle ratio: 2.940; width of rims: 5.5"; tyres: P195/75R x 15.

PERFORMANCE max speed: 93 mph, 149 km/h; power-weight ratio: 39.1 lb/hp (53.2 lb/kW), 17.6 kg/hp (23.9 kg/kW) - Salon 39.4 lb/hp (53.6 lb/kW), 17.7 kg/hp (24.1 kg/kW); speed in direct drive at 1,000 rpm: 25.9 mph, 41.7 km/h; consumption: 19.2 m/imp gal, 16 m/US gal, 14.7 l x 100 km.

CHASSIS integral with isolated front cross member; front suspension: independent, wishbones, longitudinal torsion bars, anti-roll bar, telescopic dampers; rear: rigid axle, semi-elliptic leafsprings, telescopic dampers.

STEERING recirculating ball, servo; turns lock to lock: 3.50.

BRAKES front disc (diameter 11.58 in, 29.4 cm), front internal radial fins, rear drum, rear compensator, servo; swept area: total 375.3 sq in, 2,421 sq cm.

ELECTRICAL EQUIPMENT 12 V; 430 A battery; 65 A alternator; Essex or Prestolite or Mopar transistorized ignition with electronic spark control; 4 headlamps.

DIMENSIONS AND WEIGHT wheel base: 118.50 in, 301 cm; tracks: 61.90 in, 157 cm front, 62 in, 157 cm rear; length: 220.20 in, 559 cm; width: 77.10 in, 196 cm; height 54.50 in, 138 cm; ground clearance: 5.30 in, 13.5 cm; weight: 3,520 lb, 1,597 kg - Salon 3,546 lb 1,608 kg; turning circle: 45.8 ft, 13.9 m; fuel tank 17.6 imp gal, 21 US gal, 80 l.

BODY hardtop; 4 doors; 6 seats, bench front seats with built-in headrests.

OPTIONALS heavy-duty cooling; limited slip differential; P205/75R x 15 tyres; P225/70R x 15; heavy-duty suspension; tilt of steering wheel; heavy-duty battery; halogen headlamps; heated rear window with 100 A alternator; electric windows; electric sunshine roof; speed control device; reclining backrests; Landau vinyl roof; air-conditioning; heavy-duty equipment.

120 hp power team

(not available in California)

See 90 hp power team, except for:

ENGINE 8 cylinders; 318 cu in, 5,211 cc (3.91 x 3.31 in, 99.2 x 84 mm); compression ratio: 8.5:1; max power (SAE net): 120 hp (89 kW) at 3,600 rpm; max torque (SAE net): 245 lb ft, 33.8 kg m (332 Nm) at 1,600 rpm; 23 hp/l (16.9 kW/l); 5 crankshaft bearings valves: hydraulic tappets; camshafts: 1, at centre of Vee; 1 Carter 8233 S downdraught twin barrel carburettor; cooling: 25 imp pt, 30 US pt, 14.2 l.

TRANSMISSION gearbox: Torqueflite automatic transmission, hydraulic torque converter and planetary gears with 3 ratios, max ratio of converter at stall 1.90, possible manual selection; ratios: I 2.450, II 1.450, III 1, rev 2.200; lever: steering column or central; axle ratio: 2.450.

PERFORMANCE max speed: 102 mph, 164 km/h; power-weight ratio: 30 lb/hp (40.9 lb/kW), 13.6 kg/hp (18.5 kg/kW) - Salon 30.3 lb/hp (41.2 lb/kW), 13.7 kg/hp (18.7 kg/kW); speed in direct drive at 1,000 rpm: 25.5 mph, 41 km/h; consumption: 18 m/imp gal, 15 m/US gal, 15.7 l x 100 km.

ELECTRICAL EQUIPMENT 325 A battery.

DIMENSIONS AND WEIGHT weight: 3,606 lb, 1,636 kg - Salon 3,632 lb, 1,647 kg.

OPTIONALS electronic air-conditioning; trip computer.

155 hp power team

(optional, standard for California only)

See 90 hp power team, except for:

ENGINE 8 cylinders; 318 cu in, 5,211 cc (3.91 x 3.31 in,

PLYMOUTH Gran Fury Pillared Hardtop

155 HP POWER TEAM

99.2 x 84 mm); compression ratio: 8.5:1; max power (SAE net): 155 hp (114 kW) at 4,000 rpm; max torque (SAE net): 245 lb ft, 33.8 kg m (331 Nm) at 1,600 rpm; 29.7 hp/l (21.9 kW/l); 5 crankshaft bearings; valves: hydraulic tappets; camshafts: 1, at centre of Vee; 1 Carter TQ92955 (California 9234S) downdraught 4-barrel carburettor; cooling: 25 imp pt, 30 US pt, 14.2 l.

TRANSMISSION gearbox ratios: I 2.450, II 1.450, III 1, rev 2.220; lever: steering column or central; axle ratio: in California 2.450.

PERFORMANCE max speed: 106 mph, 170 km/h - in California 112 mph, 180 km/h; power-weight ratio: 23.3 lb/hp (31.6 lb/kW), 10.5 kg/hp (14.3 kg/kW) - Salon 23.4 lb/hp (31.9 lb/kW), 10,6 kg/hp (14.4 kg/kW); speed in direct drive at 1,000 rpm: 29.3 mph, 47.2 km/h - California 35.1 mph, 55.4 km/h; consumption: 18 m/imp gal; 15 m/US gal, 15.7 l x 100 km.

ELECTRICAL EQUIPMENT 325 A battery.

DIMENSIONS AND WEIGHT weight: 3,606 lb, 1,636 kg - Salon 3,632 lb, 1,647 kg.

OPTIONALS electronic air-conditioning; trip computer.

130 hp power team

(not available in California)

See 90 hp power team, except for:

ENGINE 8 cylinders; 360 cu in, 5,900 cc (4 x 3.58 in, 101.6 x 89.6 mm); max power (SAE net): 130 hp (97 kW) at 3,200 rpm; max torque (SAE net): 255 lb ft, 35.9 kgm (345 Nm) at 2,000 rpm; 22 hp/l (16.2 kW/l); 5 crankshaft bearings; valves: hydraulic tappets; camshafts: 1, at centre of Vee; 1 Carter BBD 8237S downdraught twin-barrel carburettor; cooling: 25 imp pt, 30 US pt, 14.2 l.

TRANSMISSION gearbox ratios: I 2.450, II 1.450, III 1, rev 2.220; lever: steering column or central; axle ratio: 2.450.

PERFORMANCE max speed: 109 mph, 175 km/h; power-weight ratio: 28.1 lb/hp (38.3 lb/kW) 12.7 kg/hp (17.3 kg/kW) - Salon 28.3 lb/hp (38.4 lb/kW), 12.8 kg/hp (17.4 kg/kW); speed in direct drive at 1,000 rpm: 27.2 mph, 43.7 km/h; consumption: 16.8 m/imp gal, 14 m/US gal, 16.8 l x 100 km.

DIMENSIONS AND WEIGHT weight: 3,652 lb, 1,657 kg - Salon 3,678 lb, 1,668 kg.

OPTIONALS electronic air-conditioning; trip computer.

PONTIAC USA

Sunbird Series

PRICES EX WORKS:	**$**
1 2-dr Coupé	**4,371**
2 2-dr Sport Coupé	**4,620**
3 2+1-dr Sport Hatchback Coupé	**4,731**

For 110 hp V6 engine add $ 225.

Power team:	Standard for:	Optional for:
86 hp	all	—
110 hp	—	all

86 hp power team

ENGINE front, 4 stroke; 4 cylinders, vertical, in line; 151 cu in, 2,474 cc (4 x 3 in, 101.5 x 76.1 mm); compression ratio: 8.2:1; max power (SAE net): 86 hp (63 kW) at 4,000 rpm; max torque (SAE net): 128 lb ft, 17.6 kg m (172 Nm) at 2,400 rpm; max engine rpm: 4,800; 34.8 hp/l (25.6 kW/l); cast iron block and head; 5 crankshaft bearings; valves: overhead: in line, push-rods and rockers, hydraulic tappets; camshafts: 1, side; lubrication: gear pump, full flow filter 5.2 imp pt, 6.2 US pt, 3 l; 1 Rochester 17059675 2SE downdraught twin barrel carburettor; air cleaner; exhaust system with catalytic converter; fuel feed: mechanical pump; water-cooled, 20.1 imp pt, 23.9 US pt, 11.5 l.

TRANSMISSION driving wheels: rear; clutch: single dry plate (diaphragm); gearbox: mechanical; gears: 4, fully synchronized; ratios: I 3.500, II 2.480, III 1.660, IV 1, rev 3.500; lever: central; final drive: hypoid bevel; axle ratio: 2.730-2.930 (for California only); width of rims: 5"; tyres: A78 x 13.

PERFORMANCE max speed: 96 mph, 154 km/h; power-weight ratio: Coupé 30.2 lb/hp (41.2 lb/kW), 13.7 kg/hp (18.7 kg/kW); speed in direct drive at 1,000 rpm: 24 mph, 38.7 km/h; consumption: 28.8 m/imp gal, 24 m/US gal, 9.8 l x 100 km.

CHASSIS integral; front suspension: independent, wishbones, coil springs, anti-roll bar, telescopic dampers; rear: rigid axle, lower trailing radius arms, upper oblique torque arms, coil springs, telescopic dampers.

STEERING recirculating ball; turns lock to lock: 4.40.

BRAKES front disc (diameter 9.74 in, 24.7 cm), rear drum; swept area: total 264.8 sq in, 1,708 sq cm.

ELECTRICAL EQUIPMENT 12 V; 3,200 W battery; 37 A alternator; Delco-Remy high energy ignition; 2 headlamps - Sport Coupé 4 headlamps.

DIMENSIONS AND WEIGHT wheel base: 97 in, 246 cm; tracks: 55.30 in, 140 cm front, 54.10 in, 137 cm rear; length: 179.30 in, 455 cm; width: 65.40 in, 166 cm; height: 49.60 in, 126 cm - Sport Hatchback Coupé 49.90 in, 127 cm; ground clearance: 4.80 in, 12.2 cm; weight: Coupé 2,603 lb, 1,180 kg - Sport Coupé 2,608 lb, 1,183 kg - Sport Hatchback Coupé 2,657 lb, 1,205 kg; turning circle: 38.4 ft, 11.7 m; fuel tank: 15.4 imp gal, 18.5 US gal, 70 l.

BODY coupé; 4 seats, separate front seats with built-in headrests.

OPTIONALS limited slip differential; 2.930 axle ratio; Turbo-Hydramatic 200 automatic transmission with 3 ratios (I 2.740, II 1.570, III 1, rev 2.070), max ratio of converter at stall 2, possible manual selection, central lever, 2.730 axle ratio; BR 70 x 13 tyres with 6" wide rims; power steering; tilt of steering wheel; servo brake; heavy-duty radiator; heavy-duty battery, reclining backrests; folding rear seat; heated rear windo sunshine roof; anti-roll bar on rear suspension; Formula equi ment (for Sport Hatchback Coupé only); air-conditioning.

110 hp power team

See 86 hp power team, except for:

ENGINE 6 cylinders, Vee-slanted at 90°; 231 cu in, 3,785 (3.80 x 3.40 in, 96.5 x 86.4 mm); max power (SAE net): 110 (81 kW) at 3,800 rpm; max torque (SAE net): 190 lb ft, 26.2 m (257 Nm) at 2,000 rpm; max engine rpm: 4,200; 30.4 h (22.3 kW/l); 4 crankshaft bearings; camshafts: 1, at centre Vee; lubrication 8.3 imp pt, 9.9 US pt, 4.7 l; 1 Rochest 17080191 downdraught twin barrel carburettor; fuel feed: ele tric pump; cooling, 20.4 imp pt, 24.5 US pt, 11.6 l.

TRANSMISSION axle ratio: 2.930; tyres: B78 x 13.

PERFORMANCE max speed: 103 mph, 165 km/h; power-weig ratio: Coupé 23.9 lb/hp (32.4 lb/kW), 10.8 kg/hp (14.7 kg/kW speed in direct drive at 1,000 rpm: 27 mph, 43.4 km/h; co sumption: 24.1 m/imp gal, 20 m/US gal, 11.7 l x 100 km.

ELECTRICAL EQUIPMENT 2,500 W battery.

DIMENSIONS AND WEIGHT weight: plus 152 lb, 69 kg.

OPTIONALS 2,560 axle ratio with automatic transmission.

PONTIAC Sunbird Coupé

PONTIAC Sunbird Formula Sport Hatchback Coupé

PONTIAC Phoenix SJ Hatchback Sedan

Phoenix Series

ICES EX WORKS:	$
.4+1-dr Hatchback Sedan	5,250
2-dr Coupé	5,067
LJ 4+1-dr Hatchback Sedan	5,704
LJ 2-dr Coupé	5,520

r 110 and 115 hp V6 engines add $ 225.

wer team:	Standard for:	Optional for:
0 hp	all	—
0 hp (California)	all	—
0 hp	—	all
5 hp	—	all

90 hp power team

ot available in California)

GINE front, transverse, 4 stroke; 4 cylinders, in line; 151 cu 2,475 cc (4 x 3 in, 101.6 x 76.2 mm); compression ratio: :1; max power (SAE net): 90 hp (66 kW) at 4,000 rpm; max que (SAE net): 134 lb ft, 18.6 kg m (182 Nm) at 2,400 rpm; ax engine rpm: 4,400; 20.5 hp/l (15.1 kW/l); cast iron block d head; 5 crankshaft bearings; valves: overhead, in line, sh-rods and rockers, hydraulic tappets; camshafts: 1, side; orication: gear pump, full flow filter, 6.7 imp pt, 8 US pt, 3.8 l; Rochester 17059619 downdraught twin barrel carburettor; air eaner; exhaust system with catalytic converter; fuel feed: echanical pump; water-cooled, 17.8 imp pt, 21.4 US pt, 10.1 l.

ANSMISSION driving wheels: front; clutch: self-adjusting ngle dry plate (diaphragm); gearbox: mechanical; gears: 4, ly synchronized; ratios: I 3.530, II 1.960, III 1.240, IV 0.810, / 3.420; lever: steering column; final drive: spiral bevel; axle io: 3.340; width of rims: 5"; tyres: P185/80 R x 13.

RFORMANCE max speed: 87 mph, 140 km/h; power-weight tio: Hatchback Sedan 27.8 lb/hp, (37.9 lb/kW), 12.6 kg/hp 7.2 kg/kW); speed in top at 1,000 rpm: 19.8 mph, 31.8 km/h; nsumption: 28,4 m/imp gal, 24 m/US gal, 9.9 l x 100 km.

HASSIS integral; front suspension: independent, by McPher- n, coil springs, stamped lower control arms, telescopic dam- rs; rear: rigid axle, trailing arm, stamped control arms, coil rings, telescopic dampers.

TEERING rack-and-pinion; turns lock to lock: 3.50.

RAKES front disc (diameter 9.72 in, 24.7 cm), internal radial s, rear drum; swept area: total 261.6 sq in, 1,687 sq cm.

ECTRICAL EQUIPMENT 12 V; 3,200 W battery; 42 A alter- tor; Delco-Remy high energy ignition; 2 headlamps.

MENSIONS AND WEIGHT wheel base: 104.90 in, 266 cm; cks: 58.70 in, 149 cm front, 57 in, 145 cm rear; length: tchback sedans 179 in, 455 cm - coupés 182 in 463 cm; dth: hatchback sedans 69.60 in, 177 cm - coupés 69.10 in, 5 cm; weight: Hatchback Sedan 2,501 lb, 1,135 kg - Coupé 459 lb, 1,116 kg - LJ Hatchback Sedan 2,552 lb, 1,157 kg - LJ oupé 2,491 lb, 1,130 kg; weight distribution: 63% front, 37% ar; turning circle: 41 ft, 12.5 m; fuel tank: 12 imp gal, 14 US l, 53 l.

DDY saloon/sedan, coupé; 5 seats, separate front seats with ilt-in headrests.

OPTIONALS automatic transmission with 3 ratios (I 2.840, II 1.600, III 1, rev 2.070), max ratio of converter at stall 1.9, possible manual selection, steering column lever, 2.530 axle ratio; tilt of steering wheel; intermittent wiper; roof carrier; sunshine roof, reclining seats; custom interior; heated rear window; air-conditioning; servo brake; power steering; electric windows; electric door locks; P205/70R x 13 tyres; heavy-duty battery; 70 A alternator; heavy-duty cooling.

90 hp power team

(for California only)

See 90 hp power team, except for:

ENGINE max power (SAE net): 90 hp (66 kW) at 4,400 rpm; max torque (SAE net): 128 lb ft, 17.7 kg Mm (173 Nm) at 2,400 rpm; max engine rpm: 5,000; 1 Rochester 17059715 downdraught twin barrel carburettor.

PERFORMANCE max speed: 93 mph, 150 km/h.

110 hp power team

(for California only)

See 90 hp power team, except for:

ENGINE 6 cylinders, Vee-slanted at 60°; 173 cu in, 2,835 cc (3.50 x 3 in, 89 x 76.2 mm); compression ratio: 8.5:1; max power (SAE net): 110 hp (82 kW) at 4,800 rpm; max torque (SAE net): 140 lb ft, 19.4 kg m (190 Nm) at 2,400 rpm; max engine rpm: 5,300; 38.6 hp/l (28.4 kW/l); 4 crankshaft bearings; camshafts: 1, at centre of Vee; lubrication: 6.7 imp pt, 7.9 US pt, 3.8 l; 1 Rochester 17059761 downdraught twin barrel carburettor; cooling, 16.9 imp pt, 20.2 US pt, 9.7 l.

PONTIAC Phoenix LJ Hatchback Sedan

PERFORMANCE max speed: 106 mph, 170 km/h; power-weight ratio: Hatchback Sedan 23.1 lb/hp, (31.1 lb/kW), 10.5 kg/hp (14.1 kg/kW); speed in top at 1,000 rpm: 23.1 mph, 37.3 km/h; consumption: 23.7 m/imp gal, 20 m/US gal, 11.8 l x 100 km.

DIMENSIONS AND WEIGHT weight: plus 35 lb, 18 kg.

OPTIONALS 2.840 axle ratio with automatic transmission.

115 hp power team

(not available in California)

See 90 hp power team, except for:

ENGINE 6 cylinders, Vee-slanted at 60°; 173 cu in, 2,835 cc (3.50 x 3 in, 89 x 76.2 mm); compression ratio: 8.5:1; max power (SAE net): 115 hp (85 kW) at 4,800 rpm; max torque (SAE net): 145 lb ft, 20.1 kg m (197 Nm) at 2,400 rpm; max engine rpm: 5,300; 40.6 hp/l (29.9 kW/l); 4 crankshaft bearings; camshafts: 1, at centre of Vee; lubrication: 6.7 imp pt, 7.9 US pt, 3.8 l; 1 Rochester 17059651 downdraught twin barrel carburettor; cooling, 16.9 imp pt, 20.2 US pt, 9.7 l.

PONTIAC Phoenix Series

PERFORMANCE max speed: 106 mph, 170 km/h; power-weight ratio: Hatchback Sedan 22.1 lb/hp (29.9 lb/kW), 10 kg/hp (13.6

115 HP POWER TEAM

kg/kW); speed in top at 1,000 rpm: 23.1 mph, 37.3 km/h; consumption: 23.7 m/imp gal, 20 m/US gal, 11.8 l x 100 km.

DIMENSIONS AND WEIGHT weight: plus 35 lb, 18 kg.

OPTIONALS 2.840 axle ratio with automatic transmission.

Le Mans - Grand Le Mans - Grand Am Series

PRICES EX WORKS:	$
1 Le Mans 4-dr Sedan	5,377
2 Le Mans 2-dr Coupé	5,274
3 Le Mans 4+1-dr Safari St. Wagon	5,861
4 Grand Le Mans 4-dr Sedan	5,728
5 Grand Le Mans 2-dr Coupé	5,560
6 Grand Le Mans 4+1-dr Safari St. Wagon	6,273
7 Grand Am 2-dr Coupé	7,299

For 120 hp engine add $ 180; for 140 hp engine add $ 295; for 150 hp engine add $ 295 - Grand Am deduct $ 150.

Power team:	Standard for:	Optional for:
115 hp	1 to 6	—
120 hp	—	1 to 6
140 hp	—	1 to 6
150 hp	—	all
155 hp	7	—

115 hp power team

ENGINE front, 4 stroke; 6 cylinders, Vee-slanted at 90°; 231 cu in, 3,785 cc (3.80 x 3.40 in, 96.5 x 86.4 mm); compression ratio: 8:1; max power (SAE net): 115 hp (84 kW) at 3,800 rpm; max torque (SAE net): 190 lb ft, 26.2 kg m (257 Nm) at 2,000 rpm; max engine rpm: 4,400; 30.4 hp/l (22.4 kW/l); cast iron block and head; 4 crankshaft bearings; valves: overhead, in line, push-rods and rockers, hydraulic tappets; camshafts: 1, at centre of Vee; lubrication: gear pump, full flow filter, 8.3 imp pt, 9.9 US pt, 4.7 l; 1 Rochester 2ME downdraught twin barrel carburettor; air cleaner; exhaust system with catalytic converter; fuel feed: mechanical pump; water-cooled, 27.6 imp pt, 33.2 US pt, 15.7 l.

TRANSMISSION driving wheels: rear; clutch: single dry plate; gearbox: mechanical (Turbo-Hydramatic transmission standard for st. wagons); gears: 3, fully synchronized; ratios: I 3.500, II 1.890, III 1, rev 3.500; lever: steering column; final drive: hypoid bevel; axle ratio: 2.930 - st. wagons 2.730; width of rims: 6"; tyres: P185/75R x 14 - st. wagons P195/75R x 14.

PERFORMANCE max speed: 93 mph, 149 km/h; power-weight ratio: Le Mans Sedan 26.4 lb/hp (36 lb/kW), 12 kg/hp (16.3 kg/kW); speed in direct drive at 1,000 rpm: 27.4 mph, 44.1 km/h; consumption: 22.8 m/imp gal, 19 m/US gal, 12.4 l x 100 km.

CHASSIS perimeter; front suspension: independent, wishbones (lower trailing links), coil springs, anti-roll bar, telescopic dampers; rear: rigid axle, lower trailing radius arms, upper oblique torque arms, coil springs, telescopic dampers.

PONTIAC Grand Le Mans Sedan

STEERING recirculating ball (variable ratio servo standard for st. wagons); turns lock to lock: 5.60 - st. wagons 3.30.

BRAKES front disc (diameter 11 in, 27.9 cm), front internal radial fins, rear drum, rear compensator (servo standard for st. wagons); swept area: total 307.7 sq in, 1,984 sq cm.

ELECTRICAL EQUIPMENT 12 V; 2,500 W battery; 42 A alternator; Delco-Remy transistorized ignition; 2 headlamps.

DIMENSIONS AND WEIGHT wheel base: 108.10 in, 274 cm; tracks: 58.50 in, 149 cm front, 57.80 in, 147 cm - st. wagons 58 in, 147 cm rear; length: 198.60 in, 504 cm - st. wagons 197.80 in, 502 cm; width: 72.40 in, 184 cm - st. wagons 72.60 in, 184 cm; height: coupés 53.50 in, 136 cm - sedans 54.40 in, 138 cm - st. wagons 5.54.80 in, 139 cm; ground clearance: 5.60 in, 14.2 cm - st. wagons 5.90 in, 15 cm; weight: Le Mans Sedan 3,042 lb, 1,379 kg - Le Mans Coupé 3,024 lb, 1,371 kg - Le Mans Safari St. Wagon 3,231 lb, 1,464 kg - Grand Le Mans Sedan 3,088 lb, 1,400 kg - Grand Le Mans Coupé 3,050 lb, 1,383 kg - Grand Le Mans Safari St. Wagon 3,265 lb, 1,481 kg; fuel tank: 15.2 imp gal, 18.2 US gal, 69 l.

OPTIONALS limited slip differential Turbo-Hydramatic automatic transmission with 3 ratios (I 2.740, II 1.570, III 1, rev 2.070), max ratio of converter at stall 2, possible manual selection, steering column lever, 2.410 or 2.730 axle ratio: P205/70R x 14 tyres; tilt of steering wheel; power steering (except for st. wagons); servo brake (except for st. wagons); electric windows; speed control; heated rear window; electric sunshine roo air-conditioning; heavy-duty battery; heavy-duty cooling.

120 hp power team

(not available in California)

See 115 hp power team, except for:

ENGINE 8 cylinders; 265 cu in, 4,336 cc (3.75 x 3 in 95.2 x 76.2 mm); compression ratio: 8.3:1; max power (SA net): 120 hp (88 kW) at 3,600 rpm; max torque (SAE net): 21 lb ft, 28.9 kg m (283 Nm) at 1,600 rpm; max engine rpm: 4,00 36.5 hp/l (26.8 kW/l); 5 crankshaft bearings; cooling, 34.6 im pt, 40.9 US pt, 19.8 l.

TRANSMISSION gearbox: Turbo-Hydramatic 200 automati transmission, hydraulic torque converter and planetary gear with 3 ratios, max ratio of converter at stall 2.1, possib manual selection; ratios: I 2.740, II 1.570, III 1, rev 2.07 lever: steering column; axle ratio: 2.290 - st. wagons 2.410

PERFORMANCE max speed: 96 mph, 154 km/h; power-weigh ratio: Le Mans Sedan 26 lb/hp, (35.3 lb/kW), 11.8 kg/hp (16. kg/kW); speed in direct drive at 1,000 rpm: 35.1 mph, 56. km/h; consumption: 21.2 m/imp gal, 18 m/US gal, 13.1 l x 10 km.

DIMENSIONS AND WEIGHT weight: plus 80 lb, 36 kg - s wagons plus 127 lb, 58 kg.

140 hp power team

(not available in California)

See 115 hp power team, except for:

ENGINE 8 cylinders; 301 cu in, 4,932 cc (4 x 3 in, 101.6 x 76. mm); compression ratio: 8.1:1; max power (SAE net): 140 h (103 kW) at 4,000 rpm; max torque (SAE net): 240 lb ft, 33.1 k m (325 Nm) at 1,800 rpm; 28.4 hp/l (20.9 kW/L); 5 cranksha bearings; 1 Rochester M4ME downdraught 4-barrel carburetto cooling, 34.8 imp pt, 41.9 US pt, 19.8 l.

TRANSMISSION gearbox: Turbo-Hydramatic 200 automati transmission (standard), hydraulic torque converter and plane ary gears with 3 ratios, max ratio of converter at stall 2 possible manual selection; ratios: I 2.740, II 1.570, III 1, re 2.070; lever: steering column; axle ratio: 2.140 - st. wagon 2.290.

PERFORMANCE max speed: 103 mph, 165 km/h; power-weigh ratio: Le Mans Sedan 22.3 lb/hp (30.4 lb/kW), 10.1 kg/hp (13. kg/kW); speed in direct drive at 1,000 rpm: 27 mph, 43.4 km/h consumption: 21.6 m/imp gal, 18 m/US gal, 13.1 l x 100 km

ELECTRICAL EQUIPMENT 3,200 W battery; 63 A alternator

DIMENSIONS AND WEIGHT weight: plus 86 lb, 39 kg - s wagons plus 136 lb, 62 kg.

OPTIONALS 2.410 - st. wagons 2.560 axle ratio.

150 hp power team

See 115 hp power team, except for:

ENGINE 8 cylinders; 305 cu in, 4,999 cc (3.74 x 3.48 ir

PONTIAC Grand Am Coupé

PONTIAC Firebird Turbo Trans Am Hardtop Coupé

x 88.4 mm); compression ratio: 8.4:1; max power (SAE net): 0 hp (110 kW) at 3,800 rpm; max torque (SAE net): 230 lb ft, kg m (310 Nm) at 2,400 rpm; 30.4 hp/l (22.4 kW/l); 5 ankshaft bearings; 1 Rochester M4MC downdraught 4-barrel rburettor; cooling, 29.9 imp pt, 35.9 US pt, 17 l.

ANSMISSION gearbox: Turbo-Hydramatic 200 automatic nsmission (standard), hydraulic torque converter and planet-y gears with 3 ratios, max ratio of converter at stall 2, ssible manual selection; ratios: I 2.740, II 1.570, III 1, rev)70; lever: steering column; axle ratio: 2.290 - st. wagons 410.

RFORMANCE max speed: 109 mph, 175 km/h; power-weight io: Le Mans Sedan 20.8 lb/hp (28.7 lb/kW), 9.6 kg/hp (13.2 kW); speed in direct drive at 1,000 rpm: 27.2 mph, 43.7 n/h; consumption: 19.2 m/imp gal, 16 m/US gal, 14.7 l x 100 .

ECTRICAL EQUIPMENT 3,200 W battery; 63 A alternator.

MENSIONS AND WEIGHT weight: plus 108 lb, 49 kg - st. gons plus 157, lb, 71 kg - Grand Am Coupé 3,280 lb, 1,488

TIONALS 2.730 axle ratio.

155 hp power team

ot available in California)

e 115 hp power team, except for:

IGINE 8 cylinders; 301 cu in, 4,392 cc (4 x 3 in, 101.6 x 76.2 n); compression ratio: 8.1:1; max power (SAE net): 155 hp 14 kW) at 4,400 rpm; max torque (SAE net): 240 lb ft, 33.1 kg (324 Nm) at 2,200 rpm; max engine rpm: 5,000; 31 hp/l (22.8 V/l); 5 crankshaft bearings; 1 Rochester 17080270 down-aught 4-barrel carburettor; cooling, 34.8 imp pt, 41.9 US pt, .8 l.

ANSMISSION gearbox: Turbo-Hydramatic 200 automatic nsmission (standard), hydraulic torque converter and planet-y gears with 3 ratios, max ratio of converter at stall 2, ssible manual selection; ratios: I 2,740, II 1.570, III 1, rev)70; lever: steering column; axle ratio: 2.930; tyres: P205/ R x 14.

RFORMANCE max speed: 106 mph, 170 km/h; power-weight io: 21.3 lb/hp (28.9 lb/kW), 9.6 kg/hp (13.1 kg/kW); speed in ect drive: 23 mph, 37 km/h. consumption: 19.2 m/imp gal, 16 US gal, 14.8 l x 100 km.

ECTRICAL EQUIPMENT 3,200 W battery; 63 A alternator.

MENSIONS AND WEIGHT weight: 3,299 lb, 1,497 kg.

Firebird Series

ICES EX WORKS:	$
Firebird 2-dr Hardtop Coupé	**5,604**
Esprit 2-dr Hardtop Coupé	**5,967**
Formula 2-dr Hardtop Coupé	**6,954**
Trans Am 2-dr Hardtop Coupé	**7,178**

r 120 hp engine add $ 180; for 140 hp engine add $ 325 and Esprit; for 150 hp engine add $ 295 for Firebird Esprit - duct $ 180 for Trans Am; for 155 hp add $ 180 for Formula;

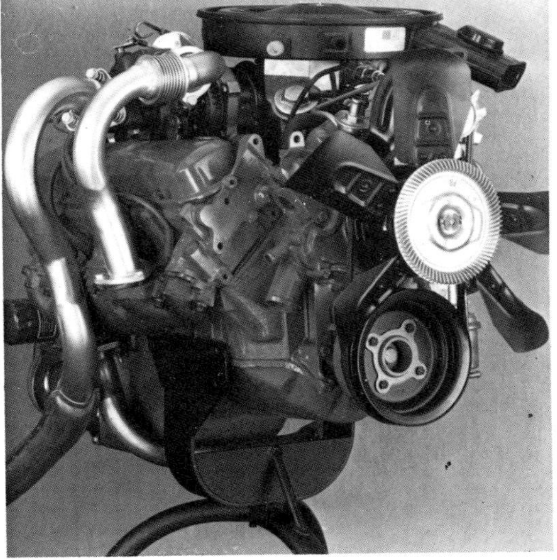

PONTIAC Firebird Series (turbocharged engine)

for 210 hp turbo engine add $ 530 for Formula - $ 350 for Trans Am.

Power team:	Standard for:	Optional for:
115 hp	1,2	—
120 hp	—	1,2
140 hp	3	1,2
150 hp	—	all
155 hp	4	1,2,3
210 hp (turbo)	—	3,4

115 hp power team

ENGINE front, 4 stroke; 6 cylinders, Vee-slanted at 90°; 231 cu in, 3,785 cc (3.80 x 3.40 in, 96.5 x 86.4 mm); compression ratio: 8:1; max power (SAE net): 115 hp (85 kW) at 3,800 rpm; max torque (SAE net): 188 lb ft, 25.8 kg m (254 Nm) at 2,000 rpm; max engine rpm: 4,400; 30.4 hp/l (22.4 kW/l); cast iron block and head; 4 crankshaft bearings; valves: overhead, in line, push-rods and rockers, hydraulic tappets; camshafts: 1, at centre of Vee; lubrication: gear pump, full flow filter, 8.3 imp pt, 9.9 US pt, 4.7 l; 1 Rochester 2ME downdraught twin barrel carburettor; Thermostatic air cleaner; exhaust system with catalytic converter; fuel feed: mechanical pump; water-cooled, 22.2 imp pt, 26.6 US pt, 12.6 l.

TRANSMISSION driving wheels: rear; clutch: single dry plate; gearbox: mechanical; gears: 3, fully synchronized; ratios: I 3.110, II 1.840, III 1, rev 3.220; lever: central; final drive: hypoid bevel; axle ratio: 3.080; width of rims: 6"; tyres: P205/ 75R x 15.

PERFORMANCE max speed: 93 mph, 149 km/h; power-weight ratio: Firebird 28.3 lb/hp (38.5 lb/kW), 12.8 kg/hp (17.5 kg/kW); speed in direct drive at 1,000 rpm; 27.4 mph, 44.1 km/h; consumption: 21.6 m/imp gal, 18 m/US gal, 13.1 l x 100 km.

CHASSIS integral with separate partial frame; front suspension: independent, wishbones (lower trailing links), coil springs, anti-roll bar, telescopic dampers; rear: rigid axle, semi-elliptic leaf-springs, anti-roll bar, telescopic dampers.

STEERING recirculating ball, variable ratio servo; turns lock to lock: 2.41.

BRAKES front disc (diameter 11 in, 27.9 cm), front internal radial fins, rear drum; swept area: total 326.49 sq in, 2,106 sq cm.

ELECTRICAL EQUIPMENT 12 V; 2,500 W battery; 42 A alternator; Delco-Remy transistorized ignition; 4 headlamps.

DIMENSIONS AND WEIGHT wheel base: 108.20 in, 275 cm; tracks: 61.30 in, 156 cm front, 60 in, 152 cm rear; length: 198.10 in, 503 cm; width: 73 in, 185 cm; height: 49.30 in, 125 cm; ground clearance: 4.60 in, 11.7 cm; weight: Firebird 3,269 lb, 1,483 kg - Esprit 3,304 lb, 1,499 kg; turning circle: 41.3 ft, 12.6 m; fuel tank: 17.6 imp gal, 21 US gal, 80 l.

BODY hardtop coupé; 2 doors; 4 seats, separate front seats, built-in headrests.

OPTIONALS limited slip differential; Turbo-Hydramatic automatic transmission with 3 ratios (I 2.520, II 1,520, III 1, rev 1.920), max ratio of converter at stall 2.25, possible manual selection, steering column or central lever; 2.560, 2.730 or 3.230 axle ratio; P225/70R x 15 tyres with 7" wide rims; heavy-duty radiator; tilt of steering wheel; disc brakes; servo brake; heavy-duty battery; heavy-duty alternator; electric windows; heated rear windows; removable roof panels; air-conditioning; Yellow Bird equipment (for Esprit only).

PONTIAC Firebird Trans Am Hardtop Coupé

120 hp power team

(not available in California)

See 115 hp power team, except for:

ENGINE 8 cylinders; 267 cu in, 4,375 cc (3.50 x 3.48 in, 88.9 x 88.4 mm); compression ratio: 8.3:1; (SAE net): 120 hp (88 kW) at 3,600 rpm; max torque (SAE net): 210 lb ft, 29 kg m (283 Nm) at 1,600 rpm; max engine rpm: 4,000; 27.5 hp/l (20 kW/l); 5 crankshaft bearings; 1 Rochester M2ME downdraught twin barrel carburettor; cooling, 34.3 imp pt, 41.2 US pt, 19.5 l.

TRANSMISSION gearbox: Turbo-Hydramatic 350 automatic transmission (standard), hydraulic torque converter and planetary gears with 3 ratios, max ratio of converter at stall 2, possible manual selection; ratios: I 2.520, II 1.520, III 1, rev 1.930; axle ratio: 2.410.

PERFORMANCE max speed: 98 mph, 158 km/h; power-weight ratio: Firebird 27.8 lb/hp (37.8 lb/kW), 12.6 kg/hp (17.1 kg/kW); speed in direct drive at 1,000 rpm: 25.6 mph, 41.2 km/h; consumption: 21.6 m/imp gal, 18 m/US gal, 13.1 l x 100 km.

BRAKES servo (standard).

120 HP POWER TEAM

ELECTRICAL EQUIPMENT 3,200 W battery.

DIMENSIONS AND WEIGHT weight: plus 73 lb, 33 kg.

140 hp power team

(not available in California)

See 115 hp power team, except for:

ENGINE 8 cylinders; 301 cu in, 4,932 cc (4 x 3 in, 101.6 x 76.2 mm); compression ratio: 8.1:1; max power (SAE net): 140 hp (103 kW) at 4,000 rpm; max torque (SAE net): 240 lb ft, 33.1 kg m (324 Nm) at 2,400 rpm; 28.4 hp/l (21 kW/l); 5 crankshaft bearings; 1 Rochester M4ME downdraught 4-barrel carburettor; cooling, 34.3 imp pt, 41.2 US pt, 19.5 l.

TRANSMISSION gearbox: Turbo-Hydramatic 350 automatic transmission (standard), hydraulic torque converter and planetary gears with 3 ratios, max ratio of converter at stall 2, possible manual selection; ratios: I 2.520, II 1.520, III 1, rev 1.920; lever: steering column or central; axle ratio: 2,410; width of rims: Formula 7"; tyres: Formula P225/70R x 15.

PERFORMANCE max speed: about 103 mph, 165 km/h; power-weight ratio: Formula 24.4 lb/hp (33.1 lb/kW), 11 kg/hp (15 kg/kW); speed in direct drive at 1,000 rpm: 25.6 mph, 41.2 km/h; consumption: 19.2 m/imp gal, 16 m/US gal, 14.4 l x 100 km.

BRAKES servo (standard).

ELECTRICAL EQUIPMENT 3,200 W battery.

DIMENSIONS AND WEIGHT weight: Formula 3,410 lb, 1.574 kg - Firebird and Esprit plus 84 lb, 38 kg.

150 hp power team

(for California only)

See 115 hp power team, except for:

ENGINE 8 cylinders; 305 cu in, 4,999 cc (3.74 x 3.48 in, 95 x 88.4 mm); compression ratio: 8.4:1; max power (SAE net): 150 hp (110 kW) at 3,800 rpm; max torque (SAE net): 230 lb ft, 31.8 kg m (311 Nm) at 2,400 rpm; 30 hp/l (22 kW/l); 5 crankshaft bearings; 1 Rochester M4MC downdraught 4-barrel carburettor; cooling, 34.8 imp pt, 41.9 US pt, 19.8 l.

TRANSMISSION gearbox: Turbo-Hydramatic automatic transmission (standard), hydraulic torque converter and planetary gears with 3 ratios, max ratio of converter at stall 2, possible manual selection; ratios: I 2.520, II 1.520, III 1, rev 1.920; lever: steering column or central; axle ratio 2.560 - Trans Am 3.080; width of rims: Formula and Trans Am 7"; tyres: Formula and Trans Am P225/70R x 15.

PERFORMANCE max speed: 99 mph, 160 km/h; power weight ratio: Firebird 22.5 lb/hp (30.5 lb/kW), 10.2 kg/hp (13.8 kg/kW).

BRAKES servo (standard).

ELECTRICAL EQUIPMENT 3,200 W battery.

DIMENSIONS AND WEIGHT weight: Trans Am 3,399 lb, 1,542 kg - Firebird and Esprit plus 104 lb, 47 kg.

155 hp power team

(not available in California)

See 115 hp power team, except for:

ENGINE 8 cylinders; 301 cu in, 4,932 cc (4 x 3 in, 101.6 x 76.2 mm); compression ratio: 8.1:1; max power (SAE net): 155 hp (114 kW) at 4,400 rpm; max torque (SAE net): 240 lb ft, 33.1 kg m (324 Nm) at 2,200 rpm; max engine rpm: 5,000; 31.4 hp/l (23 kW/l); 5 crankshaft bearings; 1 Rochester M4MC downdraught 4-barrel carburettor; cooling, 34.8 imp pt, 41.9 US pt, 19.8 l.

TRANSMISSION gearbox: Turbo-Hydramatic automatic transmission (standard), hydraulic torque converter and planetary gears with 3 ratios, max ratio of converter at stall 2, possible manual selection; ratios: I 2.740, II 1.570, III 1, rev 2.070; lever: central; axle ratio: 3.080; width of rims: 7"; tyres: P225/70R x 15.

PERFORMANCE max speed: 103 mph, 165 km/h; power-weight ratio: Trans Am 22.1 lb/hp (30 lb/kW), 10 kg/hp (13.6 kg/kW); speed in direct drive at 1,000 rpm: 25.6 mph, 41.2 km/h; consumption: 18 m/imp gal, 15 m/US gal, 15.7 l x 100 km.

BRAKES servo (standard).

ELECTRICAL EQUIPMENT 3,200 W battery.

DIMENSIONS AND WEIGHT weight: Trans Am, 3,429 lb, 1,555 kg.

210 hp power team

(not available in California)

See 115 hp power team, except for:

ENGINE turbocharged, 8 cylinders; 301 cu in, 4,932 cc (4 x 3 in, 101.6 x 76.2 mm); compression ratio: 7.6:1; max power (SAE net): 210 hp (155 kW) at 4,000 rpm; max torque (SAE net): 345 lb ft, 47.5 kg m (466 Nm) at 2,000 rpm; 42.6 hp/l (31.3 kW/l); 5 crankshaft bearings; 1 Rochester M4MC downdraught 4-barrel carburettor; turbo compressor coupled with exhaust system; cooling, 34.8 imp pt, 41.9 US pt, 19.8 l.

TRANSMISSION gearbox: Turbo-Hydramatic automatic transmission (standard), hydraulic torque converter and planetary gears with 3 ratios, max ratio of converter at stall 2, possible manual selection; ratios: I 2.520, II 1.520, III 1, rev 1.920; lever: steering column or central; axle ratio: 3.080; width of rims: 7"; tyres: P225/70 x 15.

PERFORMANCE max speed: about 118 mph, 190 km/h; power-weight ratio: 16.9 lb/hp (22.9 lb/kW), 7.6 kg/hp (10.4 kg/kW); speed in direct drive at 1,000 rpm: 25.6 mph, 41.2 km/h; consumption: 16.8 m/imp gal, 14 m/US gal, 17 l x 100 km.

BRAKES servo (standard).

ELECTRICAL EQUIPMENT 3,500 W battery.

DIMENSIONS AND WEIGHT weight: Trans Am 3,560 lb, 1,616 kg - Formula 3,544 lb, 1,607 kg.

Grand Prix Series

PRICES EX WORKS:	$
1 2-dr Hardtop Coupé	**6,219**
2 2-dr LJ Hardtop Coupé	**6,598**
3 2-dr SJ Hardtop Coupé	**7,044**

For 120 hp engine add $ 180; for 140 hp engine add $ 295; for 150 hp engine add $ 295 - SJ Hardtop Coupé deduct $ 150.

Power team:	Standard for:	Optional for:
115 hp	1,2	—
120 hp	—	1,2
140 hp	—	1,2
150 hp	—	all
155 hp	3	—

115 hp power team

ENGINE front, 4 stroke; 6 cylinders, Vee-slanted at 90°; 231 cu in, 3,785 cc (3.80 x 3.40 in, 96.5 x 86.4 mm); compression ratio: 8:1; max power (SAE net): 115 hp (85 kW) at 3,000 rpm; max torque (SAE net): 190 lb ft, 26.2 kg m (257 Nm) at 2,000 rpm; max engine rpm: 4,200; 30.4 hp/l (22.4 kW/l); cast iron block and head; 4 crankshaft bearings; valves: overhead, in line, push-rods and rockers, hydraulic tappets; camshafts: 1, at centre of Vee; lubrication: gear pump, full flow filter, 8.3 imp pt, 9.9 US pt, 4.7 l; 1 Rochester 2ME downdraught twin barrel carburettor; Thermostatic air cleaner; exhaust system with catalytic converter; fuel feed;; mechanical pump; water-cooled, 21.3 imp pt, 25.6 US pt, 12.1 l.

TRANSMISSION driving wheels: rear; gear box: Turbo-Hydramatic 200 automatic transmission, hydraulic torque converter and planetary gears with 3 ratios, max ratio of converter at stall 2.15, possible manual selection; ratios: I 2.740, II 1.570, III 1, rev 2.070; lever: steering column; final drive: hypoid bevel; axle ratio: 2.410; width of rims: 6"; tyres: P195/75R x 14.

PERFORMANCE max speed: about 96 mph, 154 km/h; power-weight ratio: Hardtop Coupé 27.4 lb/hp (37.3 lb/kW), 12.4 kg/hp (16.9 kg/kW); speed in direct drive at 1,000 rpm: 28.3 mph, 45.6 km/h; consumption: 22.8 m/imp gal, 19 m/US gal, 12.4 l x 100 km.

CHASSIS perimeter; front suspension: independent, wishbones, coil springs, anti-roll bar, telescopic dampers; rear: rigid axle, lower trailing radius arms, upper oblique torque arms, coil springs, telescopic dampers.

STEERING recirculating ball - LJ Hardtop Coupé variable ratio servo; turns lock to lock: 5.60 - LJ Hardtop Coupé 3.30.

BRAKES front disc (diameter 10.50 in, 26.7 cm), front internal radial fins, rear drum, rear compensator.

ELECTRICAL EQUIPMENT 12 V; 2,500 W battery; 42 A alternator; Delco-Remy transistorized ignition; 4 headlamps.

DIMENSIONS AND WEIGHT wheel base: 108.10 in, 275 cm tracks: 58.50 in, 149 cm front, 57.80 in, 147 cm rear; length 201.40 in, 512 cm; width: 72.70 in, 185 cm; height: 53.30 in 135 cm; ground clearance: 5.30 in, 13.5 cm; weight: Hardtop Coupé 3,189 lb, 1,424 kg - LJ Hardtop Coupé 3,279 lb, 1,487 kg; fuel tank: 15.2 imp gal, 18.2 US gal, 69 l.

BODY hardtop coupé; 2 doors; 6 seats, separate front seats with built-in headrests.

OPTIONALS limited slip differential; 2.730 axle ratio; P205/70R x 14 or P205/75R x 14 tyres; power steering; tilt of steering wheel; servo brake; heavy-duty battery; heavy-duty alternator heavy-duty radiator; electric windows; automatic levelling and speed controls; heated rear window; electric sunshine roof reclining backrests; air-conditioning; leather upholstery.

120 hp power team

(not available in California)

See 110 hp power team, except for:

ENGINE 8 cylinders; 265 cu in, 4,336 cc (3.50 x 3.48 in 88.9 x 88.4 mm); compression ratio: 8.3:1; max power (SAE net): 120 hp (88 kW) at 3,600 rpm; max torque (SAE net): 210 lb ft, 29.6 kg m (290 Nm) at 1,600 rpm; max engine rpm: 4,000 36.5 hp/l (26.8 kW/l); 5 crankshaft bearings; 1 Rochester 17080160 downdraught twin barrel carburettor; cooling, 27.5 imp pt, 32.7 US pt, 15.6 l.

TRANSMISSION axle ratio: 2.290.

PERFORMANCE max speed: 99 mph, 160 km/h; power-weight ratio: Hardtop Coupé 27.1 lb/hp, (37 lb/kW), 12.3 kg/hp (16.8 kg/kW); speed in direct drive at 1,000 rpm: 29.8 mph, 48.3 km/h; consumption: 21.4 m/imp gal, 18 m/US gal, 13.1 l x 100 km.

BRAKES servo (standard).

PONTIAC Grand Prix SJ Hardtop Coupé

PONTIAC Catalina Sedan

PONTIAC Bonneville Brougham Sedan

DIMENSIONS AND WEIGHT weight: plus 118 lb, 54 kg.

140 hp power team

(not available in California)

See 115 hp power team, except for:

ENGINE 8 cylinders; 301 cu in, 4,932 cc (4 x 3 in, 101.6 x 76.2 mm); compression ratio: 8.1:1; max power (SAE net): 140 hp (103 kW) at 4,000 rpm; max torque (SAE net): 240 lb ft, 33.1 kg m (324 Nm) at 1,800 rpm; max engine rpm: 4,500; 28.4 hp/l (21 kW/l); 5 crankshaft bearings; 1 Rochester M4ME downdraught 4-barrel carburettor; cooling, 34.3 imp pt, 41.2 US pt, 19.5 l.

TRANSMISSION axle ratio: 2.140.

PERFORMANCE max speed: 106 mph, 170 km/h; power-weight ratio: Hardtop Coupé 23.3 lb/hp, (31.7 lb/kW), 10.6 kg/hp (14.3 kg/kW); speed in direct drive at 1,000 rpm: 31 mph, 49.6 km/h; consumption: 20.2 m/imp gal, 17 m/US gal, 13.9 l x 100 km.

BRAKES servo (standard).

DIMENSIONS AND WEIGHT weight: plus 125 lb, 57 kg.

150 hp power team

(for California only)

See 115 hp power team, except for:

ENGINE 8 cylinders; 305 cu in, 4,999 cc (3.74 x 3.48 in, 95 x 88.4 mm); compression ratio: 8.4:1; max power (SAE net): 150 hp (110 kW) at 3,800 rpm; max torque (SAE net): 230 lb ft, 31.8 kg m (311 Nm) at 2,400 rpm; max engine rpm: 4,200; 30 hp/l (22 kW/l); 5 crankshaft bearings; 1 Rochester M4ME downdraught 4-barrel carburettor; cooling, 34.8 imp pt, 41.9 US pt, 19.8 l.

TRANSMISSION axle ratio: 2.290 - SJ Hardtop Coupé 2.730.

PERFORMANCE max speed: 103 mph, 165 km/h; power-weight ratio: Hardtop Coupé 22.7 lb/hp, (30.9 lb/kW), 9.9 kg/hp (13.4 kg/kW); speed in direct drive at 1,000 rpm: 29.8 mph, 48.3 km/h; consumption: 19.2 m/imp gal, 16 m/US gal, 14.8 l x 100 km.

STEERING SJ Hardtop Coupé variable ratio servo; turns lock to lock 3.30.

BRAKES servo (standard).

DIMENSIONS AND WEIGHT weight: plus 120 lb, 54 kg - SJ Hardtop Coupé 3,408 lb, 1,546 kg.

OPTIONALS Rally RTS equipment (for SJ Hardtop Coupé only).

155 hp power team

(not available in California)

See 115 hp power team, except for:

ENGINE 8 cylinders; 301 cu in, 4,932 cc (4 x 3 in, 101.6 x 76.2 mm); compression ratio: 8.1; max power (SAE net): 155 hp (114 kW) at 4,400 rpm; max torque (SAE net): 240 lb ft, 33.1 kg m (324 Nm) at 2,200 rpm; max engine rpm: 5,000; 31.4 hp/l (23 kW/l); 5 crankshaft bearings; 1 Rochester M4ME downdraught 4-barrel carburettor; cooling, 34.8 imp pt, 41.9 US pt, 19.8 l.

TRANSMISSION axle ratio: 2.930; width of rims.

PERFORMANCE max speed: 99 mph, 160 km/h; power-weight ratio: 22 lb/hp, (29.9 lb/kW), 9.9 kg/hp (13.5 kg/kW); speed in direct drive at 1,000 rpm: 23.8 mph, 38.1 km/h; consumption: 18 m/imp gal, 15 m/US gal, 15.7 l x 100 km.

BRAKES servo (standard).

DIMENSIONS AND WEIGHT weight: 3,411 lb, 1,548 kg.

OPTIONALS Rally RTS equipment.

Catalina - Bonneville Series

PRICES EX WORKS:		$
1	Catalina 4-dr Sedan	**6,397**
2	Catalina 2-dr Coupé	**6,341**
3	Catalina 4+1-dr Safari St. Wagon	**7,044**
4	Bonneville 4-dr Sedan	**6,792**
5	Bonneville 2-dr Coupé	**6,666**
6	Bonneville Brougham 4-dr Sedan	**7,885**
7	Bonneville Brougham 2-dr Coupé	**7,696**
8	Bonneville 4+1-dr Safari St. Wagon	**7,625**

For 120 hp engine add $ 180 except for Bonneville Brougham models; for 140 hp engine add $ 295 - $ 115 for Bonneville Brougham models; for 160 hp engine add $ 425 for Catalina and Bonneville models - $ 245 for Bonneville Brougham models - $ 130 for st. wagons; for 125 hp (diesel) engine add $ 915 for Bonneville Brougham models - $ 860 for st. wagons.

Power team:	Standard for:	Optional for:
115 hp	1,2,4,5	—
120 hp	6,7	1,2,4,5
140 hp	3,8	1,2,4 to 7
160 hp	—	all
125 hp (diesel)	—	3,6 to 8

115 hp power team

(not available in California)

ENGINE front, 4 stroke; 6 cylinders, Vee-slanted at 90°; 231 cu in, 3,785 cc (3.80 x 3.40 in, 96.5 x 86.4 mm); compression ratio: 8:1; max power (SAE net): 115 hp (85 kW) at 3,800 rpm; max torque (SAE net): 190 lb ft, 26.2 kg m (257 Nm) at 2,000 rpm; max engine rpm: 4,400; 30.4 hp/l (22.4 kW/l); cast iron block and head; 4 crankshaft bearings; valves: overhead, in line, push-rods and rockers, hydraulic tappets; camshafts: 1, at centre of Vee; lubrication: gear pump, full flow filter, 8.3 imp pt, 9.9 US pt, 4.7 l; 1 Rochester 17080160 downdraught twin barrel carburettor; air cleaner; exhaust system with catalytic converter; fuel feed: mechanical pump; water-cooled, 22.2 imp pt, 26.6 US pt, 12.6 l.

TRANSMISSION driving wheels: rear; gearbox: Turbo-Hydramatic 350 automatic transmission, hydraulic torque converter and planetary gears with 3 ratios, max ratio of converter at stall 2, possible manual selection; ratios: I 2.520, II 1.520, III 1, rev 1.940; lever: steering column; final drive: hypoid bevel; axle ratio: 2.730; width of rims: 6"; tyres: P205/75R x 15.

PERFORMANCE max speed: 93 mph, 149 km/h; power-weight ratio: Catalina Sedan: 29.7 lb/hp (40.4 lb/kW), 13.5 kg/hp (18.3 kg/kW); speed in direct drive at 1,000 rpm: 23.3 mph, 37.5 km/h; consumption: 21.6 m/imp gal, 18 m/US gal, 13.1 l x 100 km.

CHASSIS perimeter; front suspension: independent, wishbones, coil springs, anti-roll bar, telescopic dampers; rear: rigid axle, lower trailing radius arms, upper oblique torque arms, coil springs, telescopic dampers.

STEERING recirculating ball, variable ratio servo; turns lock to lock: 3.30.

BRAKES front disc (diameter 11 in, 27.9 cm), front internal radial fins, rear drum, servo; swept area: total 337.3 sq in, 2,176 sq cm.

ELECTRICAL EQUIPMENT 12 V; 2,500 W battery; 42 A alternator; Delco-Remy transistorized ignition; 4 headlamps.

DIMENSIONS AND WEIGHT wheel base: 116 in, 295 cm; tracks: 61.70 in, 157 cm front, 60.70 in, 154 cm rear; length: 214.30 in, 544 cm; width: 76.40 in, 194 cm; height: sedans 54.90 in, 139 cm - coupés 54.20 in, 138 cm; ground clearance: 5.60 in, 14.2 cm; weight: Catalina Sedan 3,419 lb, 1,551 kg - Catalina Coupé 3,394 lb, 1,539 kg - Bonneville Sedan 3,478 lb, 1,577 kg - Bonneville Coupé 3,430 lb, 1,556 kg; turning circle: 41.6 ft, 12.7 m; fuel tank: 17.2 imp gal, 20.6 US gal, 78 l.

BODY saloon/sedan, coupé; 6 seats, separate front seats with built-in headrests.

OPTIONALS limited slip differential; 3.230 axle ratio; GR78 x 15 or HR78 x 15 tyres with 6" wide rims; GR70 x 15

115 HP POWER TEAM

tyres with 7" wide rims; tilt of steering wheel; automatic levelling control; electric windows; reclining backrests; speed control; heated rear window; heavy-duty battery; heavy-duty alternator; air conditioning.

120 hp power team

(not available in California)

See 115 hp power team; except for:

ENGINE 8 cylinders; 267 cu in, 4,376 cc (3.50 x 3.48 in, 88.9 x 88.4 mm); compression ratio: 8.3:1; max power (SAE net): 120 hp (88 kW) at 3,600 rpm; max torque (SAE net): 215 lb ft, 29.6 kg m (290 Nm) at 2,000 rpm; max engine rpm: 4,000; 36.5 hp/l (26.8 kW/l); 5 crankshaft bearings; 1 Rochester 17080160 downdraught twin barrel carburettor; fuel feed: mechanical pump; cooling, 38.3 imp pt, 45.6 US pt, 21.9 l.

TRANSMISSION Turbo-Hydramatic 200 C automatic transmission, hydraulic torque converter and planetary gears with 3 ratios, max ratio of converter at stall 2, possible manual selection; ratios: I 2.740, II 1.570, III 1, rev 2.070; lever: steering column; axle ratio: 2.560.

PERFORMANCE max speed: 96 mph, 154 km/h; power-weight ratio: Catalina Sedan 29.4 lb/hp, (39.9 lb/kW), 13.3 kg/hp (18.1 kg/kW); speed in direct drive at 1,000 rpm: 24.8 mph, 40 km/h.

ELECTRICAL EQUIPMENT 3,200 W battery.

DIMENSIONS AND WEIGHT weight: plus 109 lb, 52 kg - Bonneville Brougham Sedan 3,639 lb, 1,651 kg - Bonneville Brougham Coupé 3,571 lb, 1,620 kg.

OPTIONALS leather upholstery (for Bonneville Brougham models only).

140 hp power team

(not available in California)

See 115 hp power team, except for:

ENGINE 8 cylinders; 301 cu in, 4,932 cc (4 x 3 in, 101.6 x 76.2 mm); compression ratio: 8.1:1; max power (SAE net): 140 hp (103 kW) at 4,000 rpm; max torque (SAE net): 240 lb ft, 33.1 kg m (324 Nm) at 1,600 rpm; 28.4 hp/l (20.9 kW/l); 5 crankshaft bearings; lubrication: 10 imp pt, 12 US pt, 5.7 l; 1 Rochester 17080272 downdraught 4-barrel carburettor; cooling, 34.8 imp pt, 41.9 US pt, 19.8 l.

TRANSMISSION axle ratio: 2.410 - st. wagons 2.560; tyres: st. wagons P225/75R x 15.

PERFORMANCE max speed: 99 mph, 160 km/h; power-weight ratio: Catalina Safari St. Wagon 28.1 lb/hp (38.1 lb/kW), 12.7 kg/hp (17.3 kg/kW) speed in direct drive at 1,000 rpm: 25 mph, 40 km/h; consumption: 18 m/imp gal, 15 m/US gal, 15.7 l x 100 km.

BRAKES swept area: total 362.6 sq in, 2,339 sq cm.

ELECTRICAL EQUIPMENT 3,200 W battery.

DIMENSIONS AND WEIGHT tracks: 62 in, 158 cm front, 64.10 in, 163 cm rear; length: 215.10 in, 546 cm; width: 79.90 in, 203 cm; height: 57.30 in, 146 cm; ground clearance: 6 in, 15.2 cm; weight: plus 121 lb, 55 kg - Catalina Safari St. Wagon 3,929 lb, 1,782 kg - Bonneville Safari St. Wagon 3,949 lb, 1,791 kg; turning circle: 42.3 ft, 12.9 m; fuel tank: 18.3 imp gal, 22 US gal, 83 l.

BODY saloon/sedan, coupé, estate car/st. wagon; 6 seats, separate front seats with built-in headrests; folding rear seat.

160 hp power team

(for California only)

See 115 hp power team, except for:

ENGINE 8 cylinders; 350 cu in, 5,736 cc (4.06 x 3.38 in, 103.8 x 86 mm); compression ratio: 7.9:1; max power (SAE net): 160 hp (118 kW) at 3,600 rpm; max torque (SAE net): 270 lb ft, 37.2 kg m (365 Nm) at 2,000 rpm; 27.9 hp/l (20.5 kW/l); 5 crankshaft bearings; 1 Rochester M4MC downdraught 4-barrel carburettor; cooling, 25.2 imp pt, 30.2 US pt, 14.3 l.

TRANSMISSION axle ratio: 2.410 - st. wagons 2.730; tyres: st. wagons 225/75R x 15.

PERFORMANCE max speed: 106 mph, 170 km/h; power-weight ratio: Catalina Sedan 22.7 lb/hp (30.8 lb/kW), 10.3 kg/hp (13.9 kg/kW); speed in direct drive at 1,000 rpm: 25.2 mph, 40.5 km/h; consumption: 16.8 m/imp gal, 14 m/US gal, 16.8 l x 100 km.

BRAKES swept area: st. wagons total 362.6 sq in, 2,339 sq cm.

ELECTRICAL EQUIPMENT 3,200 W battery.

DIMENSIONS AND WEIGHT weight: plus 213 lb, 96 kg - st. wagons plus 87 lb, 39 kg.

125 hp (diesel) power team

(optional)

See 115 hp power team, except for:

ENGINE diesel; compression ratio: 22.5:1; max power (SAE net): 125 hp (92 kW) at 3,600 rpm; max torque (SAE net): 225 lb ft, 31 kg m (304 Nm) at 1,600 rpm; 21.8 hp/l (16 kW/l); lubrication: 15 imp pt, 18 US pt, 8.5 l; diesel injection pump; cooling, 30.6 imp pt, 36.8 US pt, 17.4 l.

PERFORMANCE max speed: 96 mph, 155 km/h; power-weight ratio: Catalina Safari St. Wagon 33.1 lb/hp (45 lb/kW), 15 kg/hp (20.4 kg/kW); speed in direct drive at 1,000 rpm: 28.5 mph, 45.8 km/h; consumption: 25.2 m/imp gal, 21 m/US gal, 11.2 l x 100 km.

DIMENSIONS AND WEIGHT weight: plus 359 lb, 158 kg - st. wagons plus 220 lb, 98 kg; fuel tank: 18.9 imp gal, 22.8 US gal, 86 l.

QUINCY-LYNN USA

Trimuter G

PRICE EX WORKS: $ 4,995

ENGINE Briggs and Stratton, rear, 4 stroke; 2 cylinders, horizontally opposed; 40 cu in, 656 cc (3.44 x 2.16 in, 87.4 x 54.9 mm); max power (DIN): 16 hp (12 kW) at 3,600 rpm; max torque (DIN): 26 lb ft, 3.6 kg m (35 Nm) at 2,700 rpm; max engine rpm: 4,000; 25.2 hp/l (18.5 kW/l); light alloy block and head; valves: side; camshafts: 1, central; lubrication: 3.4 imp pt, 4 US pt, 1.9 l; 1 downdraught single barrel carburettor; fuel feed: mechanical pump; air-cooled.

TRANSMISSION driving wheels: rear; clutch: centrifugal; gearbox: centrifugal torque converter with continuosly variable ratio; ratios range: 3.950 to 1.

PERFORMANCE max speed: 60 mph, 96 km/h; power-weight ratio: 56.1 lb/hp (76.4 lb/kW), 25.5 kg/hp (34.6 kg/kW); carrying capacity: 353 lb, 160 kg; consumption: 71 m/imp gal, 60 m/US gal, 3.9 l x 100 km.

CHASSIS front suspension: leading fork-fold arm, coil springs, telescopic dampers; rear: independent, trailing A-fold arms, coil springs, telescopic dampers.

ELECTRICAL EQUIPMENT 12 V; 55 Ah battery; alternator; 2 headlamps.

DIMENSIONS AND WEIGHT wheel base: 88 in, 223 cm; rear track: 54.50 in, 138 cm; length: 144 in, 366 cm; width: 66 in, 168 cm; height: 46 in, 117 cm; ground clearance: 6 in, 15 cm; weight: 900 lb, 408 kg; weight distribution: 30% front, 70% rear; fuel tank: 14.3 imp gal, 17 US gal, 64 l.

BODY coupé in fiberglass material; one clam-shell door; 2 separate seats.

OPTIONALS LED instrument equipment; electric power team.

REPLICARS USA

Phaeton / Roadster / Hardtop

PRICES EX WORKS:	$
Phaeton	15,95[illegible]
Roadster	16,45[illegible]
Hardtop	18,45[illegible]

ENGINE Ford, front, 4 stroke; 8 cylinders; 302 cu in, 4,950 cc (4 x 3 in, 101.6 x 76.2 mm); compression ratio: 8.4:1; max power (DIN): 135 hp (99 kW) at 3,600 rpm; max torque (DIN): 24[illegible] lb ft, 33.1 kg m (325 Nm) at 2,000 rpm; max engine rpm: 4,000; 27.3 hp/l (20.1 kW/l); cast iron block and head; 5 crankshaft bearings; valves: overhead, in line, push-rods and rockers, hydraulic tappets; camshafts: 1, at centre of Vee; lubrication: 8.3 imp pt, 9.9 US pt, 4.7 l; 1 Ford 2150 D9BE-YB downdraught twin barrel carburettor; air cleaner; exhaust system with catalytic converter; fuel feed: mechanical pump; water-cooled, 23. imp pt, 27.7 US pt, 13.1 l.

TRANSMISSION driving wheels: rear; gearbox: Select-Shift automatic transmission, hydraulic torque converter and planetary gears with 3 ratios, max ratio of converter at stall 2, possible manual selection; ratios: I 2.460, II 1.460, III 1, rev 2.180; lever: steering column; final drive: hypoid bevel; axle ratio: 2.260; width of rims: 5"; tyres: E78 x 14.

PERFORMANCE max speed: about 106 mph, 170 km/h; power-weight ratio: 18.5 lb/hp (25.1 lb/kW), 8.4 kg/hp (11.4 kg/kW); speed in direct drive at 1,000 rpm: 29.3 mph, 47.2 km/h; consumption: 18 m/imp gal, 15 m/US gal, 15.7 l x 100 km.

CHASSIS box-type ladder frame with cross members; front suspension: independent, by McPherson, wishbones (lower control arms), coil springs/telescopic damper struts, anti-roll bar; rear: rigid axle, lower trailing radius arms, upper oblique torque arms, coil springs, telescopic dampers.

STEERING rack-and-pinion, tilt of steering wheel, variable ratio servo; turns lock to lock: 3.05.

BRAKES front disc (diameter 10.06 in, 25.4 cm), front internal radial fins, rear compensator, rear drum, servo; swept area: front 176.6 sq in, 1,140 sq cm, rear 98.9 sq in, 638 sq cm, total 275.5 sq in, 1,778 sq cm.

ELECTRICAL EQUIPMENT 12 V; 36 Ah battery; 40 A alternator; Motorcraft transistorized ignition; 2 headlamps.

DIMENSIONS AND WEIGHT wheel base: 102 in, 259 cm; front and rear track: 65.50 in, 166 cm; length: 160 in, 406 cm; width

QUINCY-LYNN Trimuter G

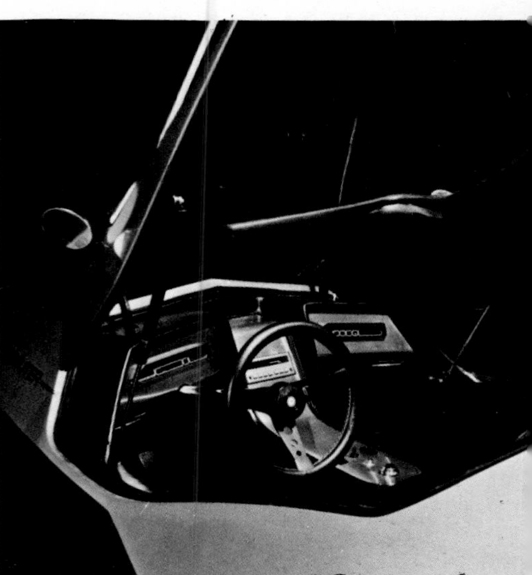

QUINCY-LYNN Trimuter G

REPLICARS Roadster

65 in, 165 cm; height: 54.50 in, 138 cm; ground clearance: 7 in, 17.8 cm; weight: 2,500 lb, 1,134 kg; weight distribution: 60% front, 40% rear; fuel tank: 10.6 imp gal, 12.6 US gal, 48 l.

BODY phaeton, roadster, hardtop, in plastic material; 2 doors; 4 seats, separate front seats; tinted glass; air-conditioning, wire wheels.

OPTIONALS metallic spray.

SCEPTRE USA

6.6 S

PRICE EX WORKS: $ 50,000

ENGINE Lincoln-Mercury, front, 4 stroke; 8 cylinders; 400 cu in, 6,555 cc (4 x 4 in, 101.6 x 101.6 mm); compression ratio: 8:1; max power (DIN): 168 HP (124 KW) at 4,000 rpm; max engine rpm: 4,400; 25.6 hp/l (18.9 kW/l); cast iron block and head; 5 crankshaft bearings; valves: overhead, in line, push-rods and rockers, hydraulic tappets; camshafts: 1, at centre of Vee; lubrication: rotary pump, full flow filter, 8.3 imp pt, 9.9 US pt, 4.7 l; 1 downdraught 4-barrel carburettor; fuel feed: mechanical pump; water-cooled, 34.1 imp pt, 41 US pt, 19.4 l, electric thermostatic fan.

TRANSMISSION driving wheels: rear; gearbox: Select-Shift automatic transmission, hydraulic torque converter and planetary gears with 3 ratios, max ratio of converter at stall 2, possible manual selection; ratios: I 2.460, II 1.460, III 1, rev 2.180; lever: central; final drive: hypoid bevel; axle ratio: 3 width of rims: 6"; tyres: GR70 x 15.

PERFORMANCE max speed: about 125 mph, 201 km/h; power-weight ratio: 18.1 lb/hp (24.6 lb/kW), 8.2 kg/hp (11.2 kg/kW); acceleration: 0-50 mph (0-80 km/h) 7.2 sec; speed in direct drive at 1,000 rpm: 31.1 mph, 50 km/h; consumption: 19.2 m/imp gal, 16 m/US gal, 14.7 l x 100 km.

CHASSIS box-type ladder frame; front suspension: independent, wishbones, coil springs, anti-roll bar, 4 telescopic dampers; rear: rigid axle, lower trailing radius arms, upper oblique torque arms, coil springs, 4 telescopic dampers.

STEERING recirculating ball, servo; turns lock to lock: 3.90.

BRAKES front disc, rear drum, servo.

ELECTRICAL EQUIPMENT 12 V; 77 Ah battery; 770 W alternator; Motorcraft transistorized ignition; 2 headlamps.

DIMENSIONS AND WEIGHT wheel base: 118.40 in, 301 cm; front and rear track: 65 in, 165 cm; length: 188.50 in, 479 cm; width: 74.50 in, 189 cm; height: 54 in, 137 cm; ground clearance: 6 in, 15.2 cm; weight: 3,045 lb, 1,381 kg; turning circle: 31.2 ft, 9.5 m; fuel tank: 16.3 imp gal, 19.5 US gal, 74 l.

BODY roadster, in plastic material; 2 separate front seats; leather upholstery; automatic speed control; wire wheels; air-conditioning.

OPTIONALS mouton lambswool overlay; halogen headlamps; tonneau cover; hardtop.

SCEPTRE 6.6 S

STUTZ USA

IV Porte Sedan

PRICE EX WORKS: $ 74,765

ENGINE front, 4 stroke; 8 cylinders; 350 cu in, 5,736 cc (4.06 x 3.38 in, 103.8 x 86 mm); compression ratio: 7.9:1; max power (DIN): 160 hp (118 kW) at 3,600 rpm; max torque (DIN): 270 lb ft, 37.2 kg m (365 Nm) at 2,000 rpm; max engine rpm: 4,000; 27.9 hp/l (20.5 kW/l); cast iron block and head, 5 crankshaft bearings; valves: overhead, in line, push-rods and rockers, hydraulic tappets; camshafts: 1, at centre of Vee; lubrication: gear pump, full flow filter, 10 imp pt, 12 US pt, 5.7 l; 1 Rochester M4MC downdraught 4-barrel carburettor; fuel feed: mechanical pump; water-cooled, 25.2 imp pt, 30.2 US pt, 14.4 l.

TRANSMISSION driving wheels: rear; gearbox: Turbo-Hydramatic 350 automatic transmission, hydraulic torque converter and planetary gears with 3 ratios, max ratio of converter at stall 2, possible manual selection; ratios: I 2.520, II 1.520, III 1, rev 1.930; final drive: hypoid bevel.

PERFORMANCE max speed: 106 mph, 170 km/h; power-weight ratio: 28.1 lb/hp (38.2 lb/kW), 12.7 kg/hp (17.3 kg/kW); consumption: 16.5 m/imp gal, 14 m/US gal, 16.9 l x 100 km.

CHASSIS box-perimeter frame; front suspension: independent, wishbones, coil springs, anti-roll bar, adjustable telescopic dampers; rear: rigid axle, lower trailing radius arms, upper oblique torque arms, coil springs, anti-roll bar, automatic telescopic dampers.

STEERING recirculating ball, variable ratio servo, tilt of steering wheel; turns lock to lock: 3.30.

BRAKES front disc (diameter 11 in, 27.9 cm), front internal radial fins, rear drum, servo; swept area: total 337.3 sq in, 2,175 sq cm.

ELECTRICAL EQUIPMENT 12 V; 3,200 W battery; alternator; Delco-Remy transistorized ignition; 2 headlamps.

DIMENSIONS AND WEIGHT wheel base: 116 in, 295 cm; tracks: 61.70 in, 157 cm front, 60.70 in, 154 cm rear; length: 224 in, 569 cm; width: 79 in 201 cm; height: 54 in, 137 cm; ground clearance: 5.60 in, 14.2 cm; weight: 4,500 lb, 2,041 kg; fuel tank: 17.2 imp gal, 20.6 US gal, 78 l.

BODY saloon/sedan; 4 doors; 6 seats, bench front seats with built-in headrests.

OPTIONALS board computer.

Blackhawk VI - Bearcat

PRICES EX WORKS:	$
Blackhawk VI 2-dr Coupé	69,500
Bearcat 2-dr Convertible	129,000

STUTZ IV Porte Sedan

BLACKHAWK VI / BEARCAT

ENGINE front, 4 stroke; 8 cylinders; 403 cu in, 6,605 cc (4.35 x 3.38 in, 110.5 x 85.8 mm); compression ratio: 7.9:1; max power (DIN): 185 hp (136 kW) at 3,600 rpm; max torque (DIN): 320 lb ft, 44.1 kg m (432 Nm) at 2,000 rpm; max engine rpm: 3,800; 28 hp/l (20.6 kW/l); cast iron block and head; 5 crankshaft bearings; valves: overhead, in line, push-rods and rockers, hydraulic tappets; camshafts: 1, at centre of Vee; lubrication: gear pump, 8.3 imp pt, 9.9 US pt, 4.7 l; 1 4-barrel carburettor; fuel feed: mechanical pump; water-cooled, 31.7 imp pt, 38.1 US pt, 18 l.

TRANSMISSION driving wheels: rear; gearbox: Turbo-Hydramatic automatic transmission, hydraulic torque converter and planetary gears with 3 ratios, possible manual selection; ratios: I 2.520, II 1.820, III 1, rev 1.930.

PERFORMANCE max speed: 118 mph, 190 km/h; power-weight ratio: 24 lb/hp (32.6 lb/kW), 10.9 kg/hp (14.8 kg/kW).

CHASSIS box-type perimeter frame; front suspension: independent, wishbones, coil springs, anti-roll bar, adjustable telescopic dampers; rear: rigid axle, lower trailing radius arms, upper oblique arms, coil springs, adjustable telescopic dampers.

STEERING recirculating ball, adjustable steering wheel, servo, tilt of steering wheel; turns lock to lock: 3.50.

BRAKES front disc (diameter II in, 27.9 cm), front internal radial fins, rear drum, servo; swept area: total 362.6 sq in, 2,339 sq cm.

ELECTRICAL EQUIPMENT 12 V; 3,500 W battery; alternator; Delco-Remy distributor; electronic ignition; 2 headlamps.

DIMENSIONS AND WEIGHT wheel base: 116 in, 295 cm; tracks: 61.60 in, 156 front, 61.10 in, 155 cm rear; length: 227 in, 577 cm; width: 79 in, 201 cm; height: 54 in, 137 cm; weight: Coupé 4,450 lb, 2,018 kg - Convertible 4,550 lb, 2,063 kg; fuel tank: 20.9 imp gal, 25 US gal, 95 l.

BODY coupé, convertible; 5-6 seats, bench or separate front seats - Convertible separate front seats.

OPTIONALS air-conditioning; tinted glass; electric sunshine roof (for Convertible only); electric windows; electric seats; leather upholstery.

STUTZ Blackhawk VI Coupé

STUTZ Bearcat Convertible

Royale Limousine

PRICE EX WORKS: $ 235,000

ENGINE front, 4 stroke; 8 cylinders; 425 cu in, 6,964 cc (4.08 x 4.06 in, 104 x 103 mm); compression ratio: 8.2:1; max power (DIN): 180 hp (132 kW) at 4,000 rpm; max torque (DIN): 320 lb ft, 44.2 kg m (433 Nm) at 2,000 rpm; max engine rpm: 4,500; 25.7 hp/l (18.9 kW/l); cast iron block and head; 5 crankshaft bearings; valves: overhead, in line, push-rods and rockers, hydraulic tappets; camshafts: 1, at centre of Vee; lubrication: gear pump, full flow filter, 8.3 imp pt, 9.9 US pt, 4.7 l; 1 Rochester M4ME downdraught 4-barrel carburettor; fuel feed: mechanical pump; water-coled, 34.7 imp pt, 41.6 US pt, 19.8 l.

TRANSMISSION driving wheels: rear; gearbox: Turbo - Hydramatic 400 automatic transmission, hydraulic torque converter and planetary gears with 3 ratios, max ratio of converter at stall 2, possible manual seelction; ratios: I 2.480, II 1.480, III 1, rev 2.070; lever: steering column; final drive: hypoid bevel.

PERFORMANCE max speed: 112 mph, 180 km/h.

CHASSIS ladder frame with cross members; front suspension: independent, wishbones, coil springs, anti-roll bar, telescopic dampers; rear: rigid axle lower trailing radius arms, upper oblique torque arms, coil springs, automatic telescopic dampers.

STEERING recirculating ball, variable ratio servo, tilt of steering wheel; turns lock to lock: 3.50.

BRAKES front disc (diameter 11.74 in, 29.8 cm), front internal radial fins, rear drum, servo; swept area: total 425.3 sq in, 2,743 sq cm.

ELECTRICAL EQUIPMENT 12 V; 365 A battery; alternator; Delco-Remy transistorized ignition; 2 headlamps.

DIMENSIONS AND WEIGHT wheel base: 171.86 in, 436 cm; tracks: 61.70 in, 157 cm front, 60.70 in, 154 cm rear; length: 295.27 in, 750 cm; width: 80 in, 203 cm; height: 56 in, 142 cm; ground clearance: 6.10 in, 15.6 cm; fuel tank: 20.9 imp gal, 25 US gal, 95 l.

BODY limousine; 4 doors; 7 seats, separate front seats with built-in headrests.

OPTIONALS electric sunshine roof at centre of car; throne seat for 2 hydraulically raised above roof line; 136.81 in, 347 cm or 144.50 in 367 cm wheel base.

STUTZ Royale Limousine

TOTAL REPLICA USA

Hi Boy

PRICE EX WORKS: $ 15,500

ENGINE Chevrolet, front, 4 stroke; 8 cylinders; 350 cu in, 5,736 cc (4 x 3.48 in,101.6 x 88.3 mm); compression ratio: 8:1; max power (DIN): 250 hp (184 kW); 43.6 hp/l (32.1 kW/l); cast iron block and head; 5 crankshaft bearings; valves: overhead, in line, push-rods and rockers, hydraulic tappets; camshafts: 1, at centre of Vee; lubrication: gear pump, full flow filter, 8.3 imp pt, 10 US pt, 4.7 l; 1 Holley 450 CFM 4-barrel carburettor; fuel feed: mechanical pump; water-cooled, 19.9 imp pt, 24 US pt, 11.3 l.

TRANSMISSION driving wheels: rear; gearbox: Turbo-Hydramatic automatic transmission, hydraulic torque converter and planetary gears with 3 ratios; lever: central; final drive: hypoid bevel.

PERFORMANCE max speed: about 100 mph, 161 km/h; power-weight ratio: 11.5 lb/hp (15.4 lb/kW), 5.2 kg/hp (7 kg/kW); consumption: 23.9 m/imp gal, 20 m/US gal, 11.8 l x 100 km.

CHASSIS perimeter box-type with front and rear cross members; front suspension: rigid axle, semi-elliptic leafsprings, telescopic dampers; rear: rigid axle, lower trailing radius arms, upper oblique torque arms, coil springs, telescopic dampers.

STEERING recirculating ball.

BRAKES front disc, rear drum, twin master cylinder.

ELECTRICAL EQUIPMENT 12 V; alternator; Delco-Remy high energy ignition; 2 headlamps.

DIMENSIONS AND WEIGHT wheel base: 106 in, 269 cm; length: 186 in, 472 cm; width: 68 in, 173 cm; height: 64.50 in, 164 cm; ground clearance: 5.50 in, 14 cm; weight: 2,850 lb, 1,292 kg; fuel tank: 9.9 imp gal, 12 US gal, 45 l.

BODY roadster, in fiberglass material; 2 doors; 2+2 seats, in rumble seat, bench front seats; chrome windshield frame with tinted glass and stainless posts; heater; luggage rack with matching chrome bumpers; wire wheels; sunshine roof.

OPTIONALS rear mounted spare tyre without luggage rack; side curtains.

Ford "B" Phaeton

PRICE EX WORKS: $ 22,500

ENGINE Chevrolet, front, 4 stroke; 8 cylinders; 350 cu in, 5,736 cc (4 x 3.48 in, 101.6 x 88.3 mm); compression ratio: 8:1; max power (DIN): 250 hp (184 kW); 43.6 hp/l (32.1 kW/l); cast iron block and head; 5 crankshaft bearings; valves: overhead, in line, push-rods and rockers, hydraulic tappets; camshafts: 1, at centre of Vee; lubrication: gear pump, full flow filter, 8.3 imp pt, 10 US pt, 4.7 l; 1 Holley 450 CFM 4-barrel carburettor; fuel feed: mechanical pump; water-cooled, 19.9 imp pt, 24 US pt, 11.3 l.

TRANSMISSION driving wheels: rear; gearbox: Turbo-Hydramatic automatic transmission, hydraulic torque converter and planetary gears with 3 ratios; lever: central; final drive: hypoid bevel.

PERFORMANCE max speed: about 100 mph, 161 km/h; power-weight ratio: 11.5 lb/hp (15.4 lb/kW), 5.2 kg/hp (7 kg/kW); consumption: 23.9 m/imp gal, 20 m/US gal, 11.8 l x 100 km.

CHASSIS perimeter box-type with front and rear cross members; front suspension: rigid axle, semi-elliptic leafsprings, telescopic dampers; rear: rigid axle, lower trailing radius arms, upper oblique torque arms, coil springs, telescopic dampers.

STEERING recirculating ball.

BRAKES front disc, rear drum, twin master cylinder.

ELECTRICAL EQUIPMENT 12 V; alternator; Delco-Remy high energy ignition; 2 headlamps.

DIMENSIONS AND WEIGHT wheel base: 106 in, 269 cm; length: 186 in, 472 cm; width: 68 in, 173 cm; height: 64.50 in, 164 cm; ground clearance: 5.50 in, 14 cm; weight: 2,850 lb, 1,292 kg; fuel tank: 9.9 imp gal, 12 US gal, 45 l.

BODY phaeton, in fiberglass material; 4 doors; 4 seats, bench front seats; chrome windshield frame with tinted glass and stainless posts; heater; luggage rack with matching chrome bumpers; wire wheels.

OPTIONALS rear mounted spare tyre without luggage rack; side curtains.

TOTAL REPLICA Ford "B" Phaeton

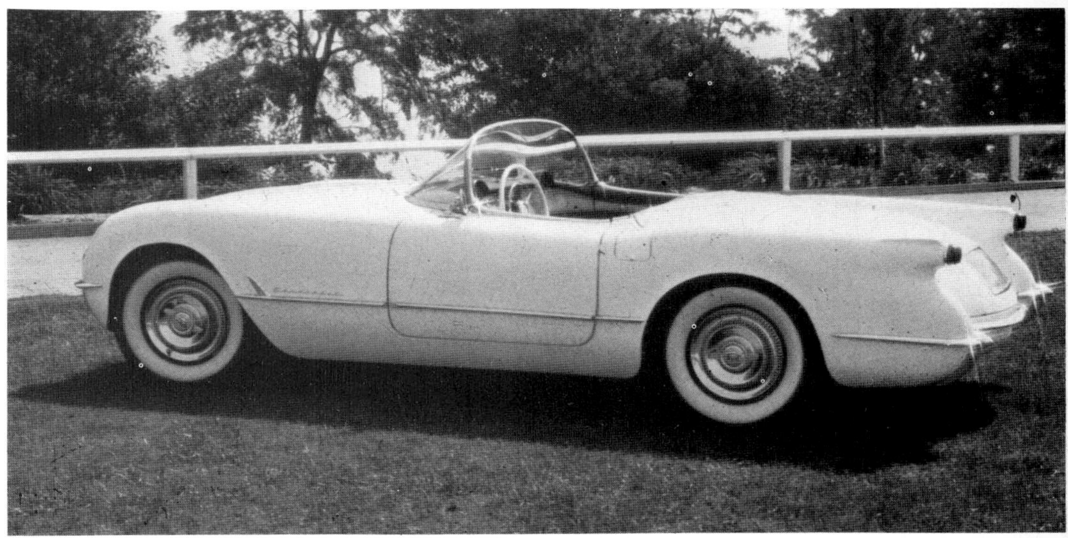

TOMORROWS CLASSIC 1953 Corvette Roadster Replica

TOMORROWS CLASSIC USA

1953 Corvette Roadster Replica

PRICE EX WORKS: $ 14,500

110 hp power team

(standard)

ENGINE front, 4 stroke; 6 cylinders, Vee-slanted at 90° 231 cu in, 3,785 cc (3.80 x 3.40 in, 96.5 x 86.5 mm); compression ratio: 8:1; max power (SAE net): 110 hp (81 kW) at 3,800 rpm; max torque (SAE net): 190 lb ft, 26.1 kg m (256 Nm) at 1,600 rpm; max engine rpm: 4,200; 29.3 hp/l (21.5 kW/l); cast iron block and head; 4 crankshaft bearings; valves: overhead, in line, push-rods and rockers, hydraulic tappets; camshafts: 1, at centre of Vee; lubrication: gear pump, full flow filter, 7.4 imp pt, 8.4 US pt, 4 l; 1 Rochester 2 ME downdraught twin barrel carburettor; thermostatic air cleaner; exhaust system with catalytic converter; fuel feed: mechanical pump; water-cooled, 21.5 imp pt, 25.6 US pt, 12.2 l.

TRANSMISSION driving wheels: rear; gearbox: Turbo-Hydramatic 350 automatic transmission, hydraulic torque converter and planetary gears with 3 ratios, max ratio of converter at stall 2, possible manual selection; ratios: I 2.520, II 1.520, III 1, rev 1.930; lever: steering column; final drive: hypoid bevel; axle ratio: 2.730.

PERFORMANCE power-weight ratio: 29.1 lb/hp (39.5 lb/kW), 13.2 kg/hp (17.9 kg/kW).

CHASSIS integral with separate partial front box-type frame; front suspension: independent, wishbones, coil springs, anti-roll bar, telescopic dampers; rear: rigid axle, coil springs, anti-roll bar, telescopic dampers.

STEERING recirculating ball, servo.

BRAKES front disc internal radial fins, rear drum.

ELECTRICAL EQUIPMENT 12 V; Delco-Remy high energy ignition, 2 headlamps.

DIMENSIONS AND WEIGHT wheel base: 102 in, 259 cm; tracks: 58.50 in, 149 cm front, 57.80 in, 147 cm rear; length: 167 in, 424 cm; with: 70 in, 178 cm; height: 33 in, 84 cm; weight: 3,200 lb, 1,449 kg.

BODY roadster, in fiberglass and plastic material; 2 doors; 2 seats.

155 hp power team

(optional)

See 110 hp power team, except for:

ENGINE 8 cylinders; 305 cu in, 4,999 cc (3.74 x 3.48 in, 94.9 x 88.4 mm); max power (SAE net): 155 hp (113 kW) at 4,000 rpm; max torque (SAE net): 230 lb ft, 31.7 kg m (312 Nm) at 2,400 rpm; max engine rpm: 4,400; 32 hp/l (24 kW/l); 5

155 HP POWER TEAM

crankshaft bearings; 1 Rochester M4 downdraught 4-barrel carburettor; cooling, 27.6 imp pt, 32.8 US pt, 15.7 l.

PERFORMANCE power-weight ratio: 21.4 lb/hp (29.1 lb/kW), 9.7 Kg/hp (13.2 Kg/kW).

DIMENSIONS AND WEIGHT weight: 3,321 lb, 1,504 kg.

Auburn Phaeton

PRICE EX WORKS: $ 35,000

ENGINE front, 4 stroke; 8 cylinders; 305 cu in, 4,999 cc (3.74 x 3.48 in, 94.9 x 88.4 mm); compression ratio: 8:1; max power (SAE net): 155 hp (113 kW) at 4,000 rpm; max torque (SAE net): 230 lb ft, 31.7 kg m (312 Nm) at 2,400 rpm; max engine rpm: 4,400; 32 hp/l (24 kW/l); cast iron block and head; 5 crankshaft bearings; valves: overhead, in line, push-rods and rockers, hydraulic tappets; camshafts: 1, at centre of Vee; lubrication: gear pump, full flow filter, 7.4 imp pt, 8.4 US pt, 4 l; 1 Rochester M4 downdraught 4-barrel carburettor; thermostatic air cleaner; exhaust system with catalytic converter; fuel feed: mechanical pump; water-cooled, 21.5 imp pt, 25.6 US pt, 12.2 l.

TRANSMISSION driving wheels: rear; gearbox: Turbo-Hydramatic 350 automatic transmission, hydraulic torque converter and planetary gears with 3 ratios, max ratio of converter at stall 2, possible manual selection; ratios: I 2.540, II 1.540, III 1, rev 1.930; lever: steering column.

PERFORMANCE power-weight ratio: 22.6 lb/hp (30.1 lb/kW), 10.2 kg/hp (13.9 kg/kW).

DIMENSIONS AND WEIGHT wheel base: 132 in, 335 cm; tracks: 58.50 in, 149 cm front, 57.80 in, 147 cm rear; length: 204 in, 518 cm; width: 78 in, 198 cm; height: 65 in, 165 cm; ground clearance: 10 in, 25 cm; weight: 3,500 lb, 1,585 kg; fuel tank: 18.6 imp gal, 22 US gal, 83 l.

BODY convertible, in fiberglass and plastic material; 2 doors; 4 seats, separate front seats.

TOMORROWS CLASSIC Auburn Phaeton

VOLKSWAGEN USA

Rabbit Series

PRICES EX WORKS:	$
1 2+1-dr Hatchback	**4,995**
2 2+1-dr Custom Hatchback	**5,475**
3 4+1-dr Custom Hatchback	**5,650**
4 2+1-dr De Luxe Hatchback	**5,875**
5 4+1-dr De Luxe Hatchback	**6,050**

For 48 hp (diesel) engine add $ 430.

Power team:	Standard for:	Optional for:
62 hp	all	—
76 hp	—	all
48 hp (diesel)	—	all

62 hp power team

(not available in California)

ENGINE front, transverse, slanted 15° to front, 4 stroke; 4 cylinders, vertical, in line; 88.9 cu in, 1,457 cc (3.13 x 2.89 in, 79.5 x 73.4 mm); compression ratio: 8:1; max power (SAE net): 62 hp (46 kW) at 5,400 rpm; max torque (SAE net): 77 lb ft, 10.6 kg m (104 Nm) at 3,000 rpm; max engine rpm: 6,000; 42.6 hp/l (31.4 kW/l); cast iron block, light alloy head; 5 crankshaft bearings; valves: overhead in line, thimble tappets; camshafts: 1, overhead, cogged belt; lubrication: gear pump, full flow filter, 5.3 imp pt, 6.3 US pt, 3 l; 1 downdraught single barrel carburettor; water-cooled, expansion tank, 10.9 imp pt, 13.1 US pt, 6.2 l; electric thermostatic fan.

TRANSMISSION driving wheels: front; clutch: single dry plate, hydraulically controlled; gearbox: mechanical; gears: 4, fully synchronized; ratios: I 3.450, II 1.940, III 1.290, IV 0.970, rev 3.170; lever: central; final drive: spiral bevel; axle ratio: 3.900; width of rims: 4.5"; tyres: 155 SR x 13-Hatchback 155 x 13.

PERFORMANCE max speed: 93 mph, 149 km/h; power-weight ratio: 2+1-dr models 29.1 lb/hp (39.2 lb/kW), 13.2 kg/hp (17.8 kg/kW); carrying capacity: 2+1-dr models 992 lb, 450 kg; consumption: 28.8 m/imp gal, 24 m/US gal, 9.8 l x 100 km at town speed.

CHASSIS integral; front suspension: independent, by McPherson, lower wishbones, coil springs/telescopic damper struts; rear: independent, swinging longitudinal trailing arms linked by a T-section cross-beam, coil springs/telescopic damper struts.

STEERING rack-and-pinion; turns lock to lock: 3.85.

BRAKES front disc (diameter 9.40 in, 23.9 cm), rear drum, 2 X circuits, servo.

ELECTRICAL EQUIPMENT 12 V; 45 Ah battery; 36 A alternator: Bosch distributor; electronic ignition; 2 headlamps.

DIMENSIONS AND WEIGHT wheel base: 94.50 in, 240 cm; tracks: 54.7 in, 139 cm front, 53.10 in, 135 cm rear; length: 155.30 in, 394 cm; width: 63.40 in, 161 cm; height: 55.50 in, 141 cm; ground clearance: 4.90 in, 12.5 cm; weight: 2+1-dr models 1,810 lb, 821 kg; turning circle : 31.2 ft, 9.5 m; fuel tank: 8.8 imp gal, 10.6 US gal, 40 l.

BODY hatchback; 5 seats, separate front seats, built-in headrests; folding rear seat; heated rear window.

OPTIONALS 5-speed mechanical gearbox (V 0.760), 4.170 axle ratio, consumption 30.1 m/imp gal, 25 m/US gal, 9.4 l x 100 km at town speed; automatic transmission, hydraulic torque converter and planetary gears with 3 ratios (I 2.550, II 1.450, III 1, rev 2.460), max ratio of converter at stall 2.44, possible manual selection, 3.760 axle ratio, consumption 27.7 m/imp gal, 23 m/US gal, 10.2 l x 100 km at town speed.

76 hp power team

See 62 hp power team, except for:

ENGINE 97 cu in, 1,588 cc (3.13 x 3.16 in, 79.5 x 80 mm); compression ratio: 8.2:1; max power (SAE net): 76 hp (56 kW) at 5,500 rpm; max torque (SAE net): 83 lb ft, 11.4 kg m (112 Nm) at 3.200 rpm; 47.9 hp/l (35.3 kW/l); CIS injection.

PERFORMANCE consumption: 21.6 m/imp gal, 26 m/US gal 10.9 l x 100 km at town speed.

OPTIONALS with automatic transmission, consumption 19.9 m/imp gal, 24 m/US gal, 11.8 l x 100 km at town speed.

48 hp (diesel) power team

See 62 hp power team, except for:

ENGINE diesel, front, transverse, slanted 15° to front, 4 stroke 89.8 cu in, 1,471 cc (3.01 x 3.15 in, 76.5 x 80 mm); compression ratio: 23:1; max power (SAE net): 48 hp (35 kW) at 5,000 rpm; max torque (SAE net): 56 lb ft, 7.7 kg m (76 Nm) at 3,000 rpm; 32.6 hp/l (24 kW/l); Bosch injection.

PERFORMANCE max speed: 87 mph, 140 km/h; power-weight ratio: 2+1-dr models 39 lb/hp (53.6 lb/kW) 17.7 kg/hp (24.3 kg/kW); consumption: 47.9 m/imp gal, 40 m/US gal, 5.9 l x 100 km at town speed.

STEERING turns lock to lock: 3.90.

ELECTRICAL EQUIPMENT 63 Ah battery.

DIMENSIONS AND WEIGHT weight: 2+1-dr models 1,878 lb 852 kg.

OPTIONALS 5-speed mechanical gearbox (V 0.760), 4.170 axle ratio, consumption 50.4 m/imp gal, 42 m/US gal, 5.6 l x 100 km at town speed.

VOLKSWAGEN Rabbit Custom Hatchback

Middle East
Africa
Asia
Australasia

Models now in production

Illustrations and technical information

OTOSAN TURKEY

Anadol SL

ENGINE Ford, front, 4 stroke; 4 cylinders, vertical in line; 79.1 cu in, 1,298 cc (3.19 x 2.48 in, 81 x 63 mm); compression ratio: 8:1; max power (DIN): 54 hp (40 kW) at 5,500 rpm; max torque (DIN): 63 lb ft, 8.7 kg m (85 Nm) at 3,000 rpm; max engine rpm: 5,700; 41.6 hp/l (30.6 kW/l); cast iron block and head; 5 crankshaft bearings; valves: overhead, in line, push-rods and rockers; camshafts: 1, side; lubrication: rotary or vanetype pump, full flow filter, 6.3 imp pt, 7.6 US pt, 3.6 l; 1 Ford GPD downdraught single barrel carburettor; fuel feed: mechanical pump; water-cooled, 10 imp pt, 12 US pt, 5.7 l.

TRANSMISSION driving wheels: rear; clutch: single dry plate (diaphragm); gearbox: mechanical; gears: 4, fully synchronized; ratios: I 3.580, II 2.010, III 1.397, IV 1, rev 3.963; lever: central; final drive: hypoid bevel; axle ratio: 4.125; width of rims: 4.5"; tyres: 5.60/5.90 x 13.

PERFORMANCE max speeds: (I) 22 mph, 35 km/h; (II) 36 mph, 58 km/h; (II) 56 mph, 90 km/h; (IV) 87 mph, 140 km/h; power-weight ratio: 37.6 lb/hp (51.8 kg/kW) 17 kg/hp (23.5 kg/kW); carrying capacity: 1,102 lb, 500 kg; speed in direct drive at 1,000 rpm: 16.3 mph, 26.3 km/h; consumption: 33.2 m/imp gal, 27.7 m/US gal, 8.5 l x 100 km.

CHASSIS box-type perimeter frame with cross members; front suspension: independent, wishbones, coil springs, anti-roll bar, telescopic dampers; rear: rigid axle, semi-elliptic leafsprings, telescopic dampers.

STEERING rack-and-pinion; turns lock to lock: 3.90.

BRAKES front disc (diameter 9.13 in, 23.2 cm), rear drum; lining area: front 15.7 sq in, 101 sq cm, rear 46 sq in, 297 sq cm, total 61.7 sq in, 398 sq cm.

ELECTRICAL EQUIPMENT 12 V; 45 Ah battery; 42 A alternator; Ford distributor; 2 headlamps.

DIMENSIONS AND WEIGHT wheel base: 100.98 in, 256 cm; tracks: 51.97 in, 132 cm front, 50.39 in, 128 cm rear; length: 174.80 in, 444 cm; width: 64.76 in, 164 cm; height: 55.91 in, 142 cm; ground clearance: 6.30 in, 16 cm; weight: 2,073 lb, 940 kg; weight distribution: 52% front, 48% rear; turning circle: 31.5 ft, 9.6 m; fuel tank: 8.6 imp gal, 10.3 US gal, 39 l.

BODY saloon/sedan, in reinforced plastic material; 4 doors; 5 seats, bench front seats; vinyl roof.

Anadol SV-1600

ENGINE front, 4 stroke; 4 cylinders, in line; 97.6 cu in, 1,599 cc (3.18 x 3.05 in, 81 x 77.6 mm); compression ratio: 8:1; max power (DIN): 65 hp (48 kW) at 5,200 rpm; max torque (DIN): 82 lb ft, 11.2 kg m (110 Nm) at 2,600 rpm; max engine rpm: 5,700; 40 hp/l (29.4 kW/l); 5 crankshaft bearings; valves: overhead, in line, push-rods and rockers; camshafts: 1, side; lubrication: rotary or vane pump type, full flow filter, 7.2 imp pt, 8.7 US pt, 4.1 l; 1 Ford GPD downdraught single barrel carburettor; fuel feed: mechanical pump; water-cooled, 13.7 imp pt, 16.5 US pt, 7.8 l.

TRANSMISSION driving wheels: rear; clutch: single dry plate (diaphragm); gearbox: mechanical; gears: 4, fully synchronized; ratios: I 2.972, II 2.010, III 1.397, IV 1, rev 3.324; lever: central; final drive: hypoid; axle ratio: 4.125; width of rims: 5.5"; tyres: 165 SR x 13.

PERFORMANCE max speed: 90 mph, 145 km/h; power-weight ratio: 30.4 lb/hp (43.2 lb/kW), 13.8 kg/hp (19.6 kg/kW); carrying capacity: 1,433 lb, 650 kg; consumption: 21.6 m/imp gal, 18 m/US gal, 13.1 l x 100 km.

CHASSIS box-type perimeter frame with cross members; front suspension: independent, wishbones, coil springs, anti-roll bar, telescopic dampers; rear: rigid axle, semi-elliptic leafsprings, telescopic dampers.

STEERING rack-and-pinion; turns lock to lock: 3.34.

BRAKES front disc, rear drum, servo; lining area: front 15.7 sq in, 101 sq cm, rear 46 sq in, 297 sq cm, total 61.7 sq in, 398 sq cm.

ELECTRICAL EQUIPMENT 12 V; 45 Ah battery; 42 A alternator; Autolite distributor; 2 headlamps.

DIMENSIONS AND WEIGHT wheel base: 100.79 in, 256 cm; tracks: 51.97 in, 132 cm front, 50.39 in, 128 cm rear; length: 174.80 in, 444 cm; width: 64.57 in, 164 cm; height: 55.51 in, 141 cm; ground clearance: 6.69 in, 17 cm; weight: 2,073 lb, 940 kg; turning circle: 35.1 ft, 10.7 m; fuel tank: 8.6 imp gal, 10.3 US gal, 39 l.

BODY estate car/st. wagon, in plastic material; 4+1 doors; 5 seats, separate front seats.

OTOSAN Anadol SV-1600

TOFAS TURKEY

Murat 131

ENGINE Fiat, front, 4 stroke; 4 cylinders, vertical, in line; 79.1 cu in, 1,297 cc (2.99 x 2.81 in, 76 x 71.5 mm); compression ratio: 7.8:1; max power (SAE): 70 hp (52 kW) at 5,250 rpm; max torque (SAE): 72 lb ft, 10 kg m (98 Nm) at 3,400 rpm; max engine rpm: 5,750; 54 hp/l (39.7 kW/l); cast iron block, light alloy head; 5 crankshaft bearings; valves: overhead, in line, slanted at 10°, push-rods and rockers; camshafts: 1, side, in crankcase, cogged belt; lubrication: gear pump, full flow filter (cartridge), 7.4 imp pt, 8.9 US pt, 4.2 l; 1 Solex 32 TEIE 42 downdraught twin barrel carburettor; fuel feed: mechanical pump; water-cooled, 13.4 imp pt, 16.1 US pt, 7.6 l, electric thermostatic fan.

TOFAS Murat 131

TRANSMISSION driving wheels: rear; clutch: single dry plate (diaphragm); gearbox: mechanical; gears: 4, fully synchronized; ratios: I 3.667, II 2.100, III 1.361, IV 1, rev 3.526; lever: central; final drive: hypoid bevel; axle ratio: 4.100; width of rims: 4.5"; tyres: 165 SR x 13.

PERFORMANCE max speed: 93 mph, 150 km/h; power-weight ratio: 31.1 lb/hp (41.7 lb/kW), 14.1 kg/hp (18.9 kg/kW); carrying capacity: 882 lb, 400 kg; acceleration: standing ¼ mile 19.2 sec; speed in direct drive at 1,000 rpm: 15.7 mph, 25.3 km/h; consumption: 31.7 m/imp gal, 26.4 m/US gal, 8.9 l x 100 km.

CHASSIS integral; front suspension: independent, by McPherson, coil springs/telescopic damper struts, lower wishbones, anti-roll bar; rear: rigid axle, twin trailing lower radius arms, transverse linkage bar, coil springs, telescopic dampers.

STEERING rack-and-pinion; turns lock to lock: 3.40.

BRAKES front disc (diameter 8.94 in, 22.7 cm), rear drum, rear compensator, servo; lining area: front 19.2 sq in, 124 sq cm, rear 36.9 sq in, 238 sq cm, total 56.1 sq in, 362 sq cm.

ELECTRICAL EQUIPMENT 12 V; 45 Ah 45 Ah battery; 44 A alternator; Marelli distributor; 2 headlamps.

DIMENSIONS AND WEIGHT wheel base: 98.03 in, 249 cm; tracks: 53.94 in, 137 cm front, 51.57 in, 131 cm rear; length: 166.93 in, 424 cm; width: 64.17 in, 163 cm; height: 55.12 in, 140 cm; ground clearance: 5.51 in, 14 cm; weight: 2,172 lb, 985 kg; weight distribution: 53% front, 47% rear; turning circle: 34.8 ft, 10.6 m; fuel tank: 11 imp gal, 13.2 US gal, 50 l.

BODY saloon/sedan; 4 doors; 5 seats, separate front seats.

ROM CARMEL ISRAEL

Rom 1301

NGINE front, 4 stroke; 4 cylinders, in line; 79 cu in, 1,295 cc .09 x 2.63 in, 78.6 x 66.7 mm); compression ratio: 7.8:1; max ower (DIN): 54 hp (40 kW) at 5,000 rpm; max torque (DIN): 66 ft, 9.1 kg m (92 Nm) at 2,500 rpm; max engine rpm: 6,000; .5 hp/l (30.8 kW/l); cast iron block and head; 5 crankshaft earings; valves: overhead, roller chain; camshafts: 1, overead; lubrication: rotary pump, full flow filter, 6.1 imp pt, 7.3 US , 3.4 l; 1 Zenith downdraught carburettor; fuel feed: mechacal pump; water-cooled, 8.8 imp pt, 10.6 US pt, 5 l.

RANSMISSION driving wheels: rear; clutch: single dry plate iaphragm); gearbox: mechanical; gears: 4, fully synchronized; tios: I 3.538, II 2.165, III 1.387, IV 1, rev 3.680; lever: central; nal drive: hypoid bevel; axle ratio: 4.110; width of rims: 4.5"; res: 5.60 x 13 or 155 SR x 13.

ERFORMANCE max speeds: (I) 26 mph, 41 km/h; (II) 42 mph, 7 km/h; (III) 65 mph, 105 km/h; (IV) 90 mph, 145 km/h; ower-weight ratio: 37 lb/hp (49.6 lb/kW), 16.7 kg/hp (22.5 g/kW); carrying capacity 992 lb, 450 kg; speed in direct drive 1,000 rpm: 15 mph, 24.2 km/h; consumption: 35.3 m/imp gal, 9.4 m/US gal, 8 l x 100 km.

HASSIS separate steel frame, boxed side-members, arc elded; front suspension: independent, wishbones, coil springs, nti-roll bar, telescopic dampers; rear: rigid axle, semi-elliptic afsprings, telescopic dampers.

TEERING rack-and-pinion; turns lock to lock: 3.

RAKES front disc, rear drum, servo; swept area: front 142.2 in, 917 sq cm, rear 62.8 sq in, 405 sq cm, total 205 sq in, 322 sq cm.

LECTRICAL EQUIPMENT 12 V; 40 Ah battery; 420 W alternar; Ducellier distributor; 2 headlamps.

IMENSIONS AND WEIGHT wheel base: 98.43 in, 250 cm; ont and rear track: 49.21 in, 125 cm; length: 162.99 in, 414 n; width: 61.42 in, 156 cm; height: 59.06 in, 150 cm; ground earance: 6.50 in, 16.5 cm; weight: 1,985 lb, 900 kg; turning rcle: 31.8 ft, 9.7 m; fuel tank: 9.2 imp gal, 11.1 US gal, 42 l.

ODY saloon/sedan, in plastic material; 4 doors; 5 seats, eparate front seats.

ROM CARMEL Rom 1301

EL NASR EGYPT

Nasr 133

RICE EX WORKS: 1,950 liras

NGINE rear, longitudinal, 4 stroke; 4 cylinders, vertical, in e; 51.4 cu in, 843 cc (2.56 x 2.50 in, 65 x 63.5 mm); comession ratio: 8:1; max power (DIN): 34 hp (25 kW) at 4,800 m; max torque (DIN): 40 lb ft, 5.5 kg m (54 Nm) at 3,200 rpm; ax engine rpm: 5,500; 40.3 hp/l (29.7 kW/l); cast iron block, ght alloy head; 3 crankshaft bearings; valves: overhead, in e, push-rods and rockers; camshafts: 1, side; lubrication: ear pump, full flow filter, 6 imp pt, 7.2 US pt, 3.4 l; 1 Bressel) ICF-3 or Solex 30 PIB-5 downdraught single barrel carburetr; fuel feed: mechanical pump; water-cooled, 13.2 imp pt, 5.9 US pt, 7.5 l.

RANSMISSION driving wheels: rear; clutch: single dry plate; earbox: mechanical; gears: 4, fully synchronized; ratios: I .636, II 2.055, III 1.409, IV 0.963, rev 3.615; lever: central; nal drive: hypoid bevel; axle ratio: 4.625; width of rims: 4"; res: 5.50 x 12.

ERFORMANCE max speeds: (I) 20 mph, 32 km/h; (II) 35 mph, 6 km/h; (III) 52 mph, 83 km/h; (IV) 75 mph, 120 km/h; ower-weight ratio: 44.7 lb/hp (60.8 lb/kW), 20.3 kg/hp (27.6 g/kW); carrying capacity: 706 lb, 320 kg; speed in top at 1,000 m: 13.7 mph, 22.1 km/h; consumption: 40.9 m/imp gal, 34.1 /US gal, 6.9 l x 100 km.

HASSIS integral; front suspension: independent, wishbones, ansverse leafspring lower arms, transverse torsion bar, teleopic dampers; rear: independent, semi-trailing arms, coil orings, torsion bar, telescopic dampers.

TEERING rack-and-pinion; turns lock to lock: 2.80.

RAKES drum, dual circuit, servo; lining area: front 33.5 sq in, 16 sq cm, rear 33.5 sq in, 216 sq cm, total 67 sq in, 432 q cm.

LECTRICAL EQUIPMENT 12 V; 34 Ah battery; 230 W dynao; DI 4-5 distributor; 2 headlamps.

IMENSIONS AND WEIGHT wheel base: 79.92 in, 203 cm; acks: 42.28 in, 115 cm front, 48.03 in, 122 cm rear; length: 35.83 in, 345 cm; width: 55.91 in, 142 cm; height: 52.36 in, 133 cm; ground clearance: 5.30 in, 13 cm; weight: 1,521 lb, 690 kg; weight distribution: 39% front, 61% rear; turning circle: 31.5 ft, 9.6 m; fuel tank: 6.6 imp gal, 7.9 US gal, 30 l.

BODY saloon/sedan; 2 doors; 4 seats, separate front seats.

PRACTICAL INSTRUCTIONS fuel: 85 oct petrol; oil: engine 5.8 imp pt, 7 US pt, 3.3 l, SAE 40W-30, change every 6,200 miles, 10,000 km - gearbox and final drive 3.7 imp pt, 4.4 US pt, 2.1 l, SAE 90 EP, change every 18,600 miles, 30,000 km; greasing: every 1,600 miles, 2,500 km, 2 points; sparking plug: 175°; tappet clearances: inlet 0.006 in, 0.15 mm, exhaust 0.006 in, 0.15 mm; valve timing: 16° 56° 56° 16°; tyre pressure: front 20 psi, 1.4 atm, rear 28 psi, 2 atm.

Nasr 128

PRICE EX WORKS: 3,603 liras

ENGINE front, transverse, slanted 20° to front, 4 stroke; 4 cylinders, in line; 68.1 cu in, 1,116 cc (3.15 x 2.19 in, 80 x 55.5 mm); compression ratio: 9.2:1; max power (DIN): 55 hp (40 kW) at 6,000 rpm; max torque (DIN): 57 lb ft, 7.9 kg m (77 Nm) at 3,000 rpm; max engine rpm: 6,000; 49.3 hp/l (36.2 kW/l); cast iron block, light alloy head; 5 crankshaft bearings; valves: overhead, thimble tappets; camshafts: 1, overhead, cogged belt; lubrication: gear pump (cartridge) 8.8 imp pt, 10.6 US pt, 5 l; 1 Weber 32 ICEV 14 or Solex C 32 DISA 41 downdraught single barrel carburettor; fuel feed: mechanical pump; water-cooled, expansion tank, 11.4 imp pt, 13.7 US pt, 6.5 l, electric thermostatic fan.

TRANSMISSION driving wheels: front; clutch: single dry plate (diaphragm); gearbox: mechanical; gears: 4, fully synchronized; ratios: I 3.583, II 2.235, III 1.454, IV 1.042, rev 3.714; lever: central; final drive: cylindrical gears; axle ratio: 3.765; width of rims: 4.5"; tyres: 145 SR x 13.

PERFORMANCE max speeds: (I) 30 mph, 48 km/h; (II) 50 mph, 80 km/h; (III) 75 mph, 120 km/h; (IV) 87 mph, 140 km/h; power-weight ratio: 32.3 lb/hp (44.4 lb/kW), 14.6 kg/hp (20.1 kg/kW); carrying capacity: 882 lb, 400 kg; acceleration: standing ¼ mile 19.7 sec, 0-50 mph (0-80 km/h) 15.8 sec; speed in top at 1,000 rpm: 16.3 mph, 26.3 km/h; consumption: 35.3 m/imp gal, 29.4 m/US gal, 8 l x 100 km.

CHASSIS integral; front suspension: independent, by McPherson, coil springs, telescopic damper struts, lower wishbones, anti-roll bar; rear: independent, single wide-based wishbones, transverse leafsprings, telescopic dampers.

STEERING rack-and-pinion; turns lock to lock: 3.50.

BRAKES front disc (diameter 8.94 in, 22.7 cm), rear drum, rear compensator, servo; lining area: front 19.2 sq in, 124 sq cm, rear 33.5 sq in, 216 sq cm, total 52.7 sq in, 340 sq cm.

ELECTRICAL EQUIPMENT 12 V; 34 Ah battery; 33 A alternator; Marelli distributor; 2 headlamps.

DIMENSIONS AND WEIGHT wheel base: 96.38 in, 245 cm; tracks: 51.50 in, 131 cm front, 51.69 in, 131 cm rear; length: 151.18 in, 384 cm; width: 62.60 in, 159 cm; height: 55.91 in, 142 cm; ground clearance: 5.71 in, 14.5 cm; weight: 1,775 lb,

EL NASR Nasr 133

NASR 128

805 kg; weight distribution: 61.5% front, 38.5% rear; turning circle: 35.8 ft, 10.9 m; fuel tank: 8.4 imp gal, 10 US gal, 38 l.

BODY saloon/sedan; 4 doors; 5 seats, separate front seats.

PRACTICAL INSTRUCTIONS fuel: 85 oct petrol; oil: engine 7.4 imp pt, 8.9 US pt, 4.2 l, SAE 20W-30, change every 6,200 miles, 10,000 km - gearbox and final drive 5.5 imp pt, 6.6 US pt, 3.1 l, SAE 90, change every 18,600 miles, 30,000 km; greasing: every 18,600 miles, 30,000 km; sparking plug: 240°; tappet clearances: inlet 0.012 in, 0.30 mm, exhaust 0.016 in, 0.40 mm; valve timing: 12° 52° 52° 12°; tyre pressure: front 26 psi, 1.8 atm, rear 24 psi, 1.7 atm.

Nasr 125

PRICE EX WORKS: 3,995 liras

ENGINE front, 4 stroke; 4 cylinders, vertical, in line; 90.4 cu in, 1,481 cc (3.03 x 3.13 in, 77 x 79.5 mm); compression ratio: 9:1; max power (DIN): 70 hp (51 kW) at 5,400 rpm; max torque (DIN): 83 lb ft, 11.5 kg m (113 Nm) at 3,200 rpm; max engine rpm; 5,500; 45.2 hp/l (34.4 kW/l); cast iron block, light alloy head; 3 crankshaft bearings; valves: overhead, in line, push-rods and rockers; camshafts: 1, side; lubrication: gear pump, centrifugal filter, cartridge on by-pass, 7.5 imp pt, 9 US pt, 4.3 l; 1 Weber 34 DCHD 1 downdraught twin barrel carburettor; fuel feed: mechanical pump; water-cooled, 11.8 imp pt, 14.2 US pt, 6.7 l.

TRANSMISSION driving wheels: rear; clutch: single dry plate, hydraulically controlled; gearbox: mechanical; gears: 4, fully synchronized; ratios: I 3.750, II 2.300, III 1.490, IV 1, rev 3.870; lever: central; final drive: hypoid bevel; axle ratio: 4.100; width of rims: 4.5"; tyres: 5.60 S x 13.

PERFORMANCE max speeds: (I) 25 mph, 40 km/h; (II) 40 mph, 65 km/h; (III) 62 mph, 100 km/h; (IV) 93 mph, 150 km/h; power-weight ratio: 31.1 lb/hp (42.8 lb/kW), 14.1 kg/hp (19.4 kg/kW); carrying capacity: 882 lb, 400 kg; acceleration: 0-50 mph (0-80 km/h) 13 sec; speed in direct drive at 1,000 rpm: 16.1 mph, 25.9 km/h; consumption: 29.7 m/imp gal, 24.8 m/US gal, 9.5 l x 100 km.

CHASSIS integral; front suspension: independent, wishbones, lower trailing links, coil springs, anti-roll bar, telescopic dampers; rear: rigid axle, semi-elliptic leafsprings, telescopic dampers.

STEERING worm and roller; turns lock to lock: 3.

BRAKES disc, servo.

ELECTRICAL EQUIPMENT 12 V; 53 Ah battery; 770 W alternator; Marelli distributor; 4 headlamps.

DIMENSIONS AND WEIGHT wheel base: 98.43 in, 250 cm; front and rear track: 51.18 in, 130 cm; length: 166.65 in, 423 cm; width: 63.98 in, 162 cm; height: 56.69 in, 144 cm; ground clearance: 5.51 in, 14 cm; weight: 2,183 lb, 990 kg; turning circle: 36.1 ft, 11 m; fuel tank: 9.9 imp gal, 11.9 US gal, 45 l.

BODY saloon/sedan; 4 doors; 5 seats, separate front seats, reclining backrests.

PRACTICAL INSTRUCTIONS fuel: 85 oct petrol; oil: engine 6.2 imp pt, 7.4 US pt, 3.5 l, SAE 20W-30, change every 6,200 miles, 10,000 km - gearbox 2.3 imp pt, 2.7 US pt, 1.3 l, SAE 90 EP, change every 18,600 miles, 30,000 km - final drive 3.5 imp pt, 4.2 US pt, 2 l, change every 18,600 miles, 30,000 km; sparking plug: 200°; valve timing: 25° 51° 64° 12°; tyre pressure: front 23 psi, 1.6 atm, rear 21 psi, 1.5 atm.

Nasr 131 CL

PRICE EX WORKS: 5,069 liras

ENGINE front, 4 stroke; 4 cylinders, vertical, in line; 79.1 cu in, 1,297 cc (2.99 x 2.81 in, 76 x 71.5 mm); compression ratio: 9.2:1; max power (DIN): 65 hp (48 kW) at 5,200 rpm; max torque (DIN): 75 lb ft, 10.4 kg m (102 Nm) at 3,000 rpm; max engine rpm: 5,200; 50.2 hp/l (36.9 kW/l); cast iron block, light alloy head; 5 crankshaft bearings; valves: overhead, in line, slanted at 10°, push-rods and rockers; camshafts: 1, side, in crankcase, cogged belt; lubrication: gear pump, full flow filter (cartridge), 7.6 imp pt, 9.1 US pt, 4.3 l; 1 Weber 32 ADF/7 or Solex C 32 TEIE/42 donwdraught twin barrel carburettor; fuel feed: mechanical pump; water-cooled, 13.4 imp pt, 16.1 US pt, 7.6 l, electric thermostatic fan.

TRANSMISSION driving wheels: rear; clutch: single dry plate (diaphragm); gearbox: mechanical; gears: 4, fully synchronized; ratios: I 3.612, II 2.045, III 1.357, IV 1, rev 3.244; lever: central; final drive: hypoid bevel; axle ratio: 4.100; width of rims: 5"; tyres: 155 SR x 13 or 175/70 SR x 13.

PERFORMANCE max speeds: (I) 28 mph, 45 km/h; (II) 47 mph, 75 km/h; (III) 71 mph, 115 km/h; (IV) 93 mph, 150 km/h; power-weight ratio: 32.7 lb/hp (44.3 lb/kW), 14.8 kg/hp (20.1 kg/kW); carrying capacity: 882 lb, 400 kg; acceleration: standing ¼ mile 19.3 sec; speed in direct drive at 1,000 rpm: 16.4 mph, 26.4 km/h; consumption: 31.7 m/imp gal, 26.4 m/US gal, 8.9 l x 100 km.

EL NASR Nasr 131 CL

CHASSIS integral; front suspension: independent, by McPherson, coil springs/telescopic damper struts, lower wishbones, anti-roll bar; rear: rigid axle, twin trailing lower radius arms, transverse linkage bar, coil springs, telescopic dampers.

STEERING rack-and-pinion; turns lock to lock: 3.50.

BRAKES front disc (diameter 8.94 in, 22.7 cm), rear drum, dual circuit rear compensator, servo; lining area: front 19.2 sq in, 124 sq cm, rear 41.9 sq in, 270 sq cm, total 61.1 sq in, 394 sq cm.

ELECTRICAL EQUIPMENT 12 V; 45 Ah battery; 45 A alternator; 4 headlamps.

DIMENSIONS AND WEIGHT wheel base: 98.03 in, 249 cm; tracks: 54.33 in, 138 cm front, 51.97 in, 132 cm rear; length: 167.72 in, 426 cm; width: 64.96 in, 165 cm; height: 54.33 in, 138 cm; ground clearance: 4.72 in, 12 cm; weight: 2,128 lb, 965 kg; turning circle: 34 ft, 10.3 m; fuel tank: 11 imp gal, 13.2 US gal, 50 l.

BODY saloon/sedan; 4 doors; 5 seats, separate front seats, reclining backrests.

PRACTICAL INSTRUCTIONS fuel: 85 oct petrol; oil: engine 7 imp pt, 8.4 US pt, 4 l, SAE 10W-30 / 20W-40, change every 6,200 miles, 10,000 km - gearbox 3.2 imp pt, 3.8 US pt, 1.8 l, SAE 90 EP, change every 18,600 miles, 30,000 km - final drive 1.8 imp pt, 2.1 US pt, 1 l, SAE 90 EP, change every 18,600 miles, 30,000 km; sparking plug: 200°; valve timing: 17° 37° 48° 6°; tyre pressure: front 26 psi, 1.8 atm, rear 26 psi, 1.8 atm.

VOLKSWAGEN NIGERIA

1200

ENGINE rear, 4 stroke; 4 cylinders, horizontally opposed; 72.7 cu in, 1,192 cc (3.03 x 2.52 in, 77 x 64 mm); compression ratio: 7.3:1; max power (DIN): 34 hp (25 kW) at 3,800 rpm: max torque (DIN): 55 lb ft, 7.6 kg m (74 Nm) at 1,700 rpm; max engine rpm: 4,500; 28.5 hp/l (20.9 kW/l); block with cast iron liners and light alloy fins, light alloy head; 4 crankshaft bearings; valves: overhead, push-rods and rockers; camshafts: 1, central, lower; lubrication: gear pump, filter in sump, oil cooler, 4.4 imp pt, 5.3 US pt, 2.5 l; 1 Solex 30 PICT downdraught single barrel carburettor; fuel feed: mechanical pump; air-cooled.

TRANSMISSION driving wheels: rear; clutch: single dry plate; gearbox: mechanical; gears: 4, fully synchronized; ratios: I 3.780, II 2.060, III 1.260, IV 0.890, rev 4.010; lever: central; final drive: spiral bevel; axle ratio: 4.375; width of rims: 4.5"; tyres: 155 SR x 15.

VOLKSWAGEN 1200

PERFORMANCE max speeds: (I) 19 mph, 31 km/h; (II) 35 mph, 57 km/h; (III) 58 mph, 94 km/h; (IV) 71 mph, 115 km/h; power-weight ratio: 50.6 lb/hp (68.8 lb/kW), 22.9 kg/hp (31.2 kg/kW); carrying capacity: 838 lb, 380 kg; acceleration: standing ¼ mile 23 sec, 0-50 mph (0-80 km/h) 18 sec; speed in top at 1,000 rpm: 18.6 mph, 30 km/h; consumption: 37.7 m/imp gal, 31.4 m/US gal, 7.5 l x 100 km.

CHASSIS backbone platform; front suspension: independent, twin swinging longitudinal trailing arms, transverse laminated torsion bars, anti-roll bar, telescopic dampers; rear: independent, swinging semi-axles, swinging longitudinal trailing arms, transverse torsion bars, telescopic dampers.

STEERING worm and roller, telescopic damper; turns lock to lock: 2.60.

BRAKES drum, dual circuit; lining area: total 111 sq in, 716 sq cm.

ELECTRICAL EQUIPMENT 12 V; 36 Ah battery; 270 W dynamo; Bosch distributor; 2 headlamps.

DIMENSIONS AND WEIGHT wheel base: 94.49 in, 240 cm; tracks: 51.57 in, 131 cm front, 53.15 in, 135 cm rear; length: 159.84 in, 406 cm; width: 61.02 in, 155 cm; height: 59.06 in, 150 cm; ground clearance: 5.90 in, 15 cm; weight: 1,720 lb, 780 kg; weight distribution: 43% front, 57% rear; turning circle: 36.1 ft, 11 m; fuel tank: 8.8 imp gal, 10.6 US gal, 40 l.

BODY saloon/sedan; 2 doors; 5 seats, separate front seats, adjustable backrests.

Igala

ENGINE rear, 4 stroke; 4 cylinders, horizontally opposed; 96.7 cu in, 1,584 cc (3.37 x 2.72 in, 85.5 x 69 mm); compression ratio: 7.2:1; max power (DIN): 54 hp (40 kW) at 4,200 rpm; max torque (DIN): 78 lb ft, 10.8 kg m (106 Nm) at 3,000 rpm; max engine rpm: 4,600; 34.1 hp/l (25.1 kW/l); block with cast iron liners and light alloy fins, light alloy head; 4 crankshaft bearings; valves: overhead, push-rods and rockers; camshafts: 1, central, lower; lubrication: gear pump, filter in sump, oil cooler, 4.4 imp pt, 5.3 US pt, 2.5 l; 2 Solex H 32 PDSI downdraught single barrel carburettors; fuel feed: mechanical pump; air-cooled.

TRANSMISSION driving wheels: rear; clutch: single dry plate; gearbox: mechanical; gears: 4 fully synchronized; ratios: I 3.800, II 2.060, III 1.320, IV 0.890, rev 3.880; lever: central; final drive: spiral bevel; axle ratio: 4.125; width of rims: 5"; tyres: 5.90 x 14.

PERFORMANCE max speeds: (I) 20 mph, 32 km/h; (II) 36 mph, 58 km/h; (III) 57 mph, 92 km/h; (IV) 86 mph, 138 km/h; power-weight ratio: 36.7 lb/hp (49.6 lb/kW), 16.6 kg/hp (22.5 kg/kW); carrying capacity: 926 lb, 420 kg; speed in top at 1,000 rpm: 19.3 mph, 31 km/h; consumption: 31 m/imp gal, 25.8 m/US gal, 9.1 l x 100 km.

CHASSIS backbone platform, rear auxiliary frame; front suspension: independent, twin swinging longitudinal trailing arms, transverse torsion bars, anti-roll bar, telescopic dampers; rear: independent, semi-trailing arms, transverse compensating torsion bar, anti-roll, telescopic dampers.

STEERING worm and roller, telescopic damper; turns lock to lock: 2.70.

BRAKES front disc (diameter 10.94 in, 27.8 cm), rear drum; lining area: front 12.4 sq in, 80 sq cm, rear 69.8 sq in, 450 sq cm, total 82.2 sq in, 530 sq cm.

ELECTRICAL EQUIPMENT 12 V; 36 Ah battery; 25 A alternator; Bosch distributor; 4 headlamps.

DIMENSIONS AND WEIGHT wheel base: 94.49 in, 240 cm; tracks: 51.97 in, 132 cm front, 53.54 in, 136 cm rear; length: 157.87 in, 401 cm; width: 63.39 in, 161 cm; height: 56.30 in, 143 cm; ground clearance: 5.91 in, 15 cm; weight: 1,985 lb, 900 kg; turning circle: 36.1 ft, 11 m; fuel tank: 10.1 imp gal, 12.1 US gal, 46 l.

BODY saloon/sedan; 5 doors; 5 seats, separate front seats, reclining backrests; folding rear seat.

PRACTICAL INSTRUCTIONS fuel: 70-75 oct petrol; oil: engine 4.4 imp pt, 5.3 US pt, 2.5 l, SAE 20W-40, change every 3,100 miles, 5,000 km - gearbox and final drive 5.3 imp pt, 6.3 US pt, 3 l, SAE 90, change every 9,300 miles, 15,000 km; greasing: every 6,200 miles, 10,000 km, 4 points; sparking plug: Bosch NGK-Champion; tappet clearances: inlet 0.004 in, 0.10 mm, exhaust 0.004 in, 0.10 mm; valve timing: 9°48' 35°02' 44°28' 4°14'; tyre pressure: front 17 psi, 1.2 atm, rear 26 psi, 1.8 atm.

OPTIONALS heated rear window; metallic spray.

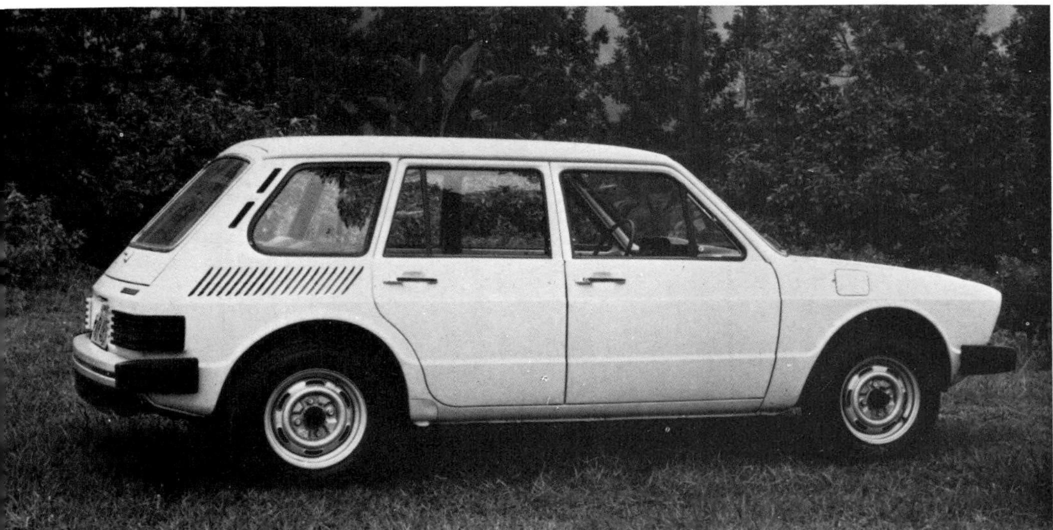

VOLKSWAGEN Igala

BMW 528

BMW SOUTH AFRICA

518

PRICE EX WORKS: 8,890 rand

ENGINE front, 4 stroke; 4 cylinders, in line; 107.8 cu in, 1,766 cc (3.50 x 2.80 in, 89 x 71 mm); compression ratio: 8.3:1; max power (DIN): 90 hp (66 kW) at 5,500 rpm; max torque (DIN): 107 lb ft, 14.8 kg m (145 Nm) at 3,500 rpm; max engine rpm: 6,300; 51 hp/l (37.5 kW/l); cast iron block, light alloy head, hemispherical combustion chambers; 5 crankshaft bearings; valves: overhead, Vee-slanted at 52°, rockers; camshafts: 1, overhead; lubrication: rotary pump, full flow filter, 7.4 imp pt, 8.9 US pt, 4.2 l; 1 Solex DIDTA 32/32 downdraught twin barrel carburettor; fuel feed: mechanical pump; water-cooled, 12.3 imp pt, 14.8 US pt, 7 l.

TRANSMISSION driving wheels: rear; clutch: single plate (diaphragm), hydraulically controlled; gearbox: mechanical; gears: 4, fully synchronized; ratios: I 3.764, II 2.022, III 1.320, IV 1, rev 4.096; lever: central; final drive: hypoid bevel; axle ratio: 4.440; width of rims: 5.5"; tyres: 175 SR x 14.

PERFORMANCE max speeds: (I) 27 mph, 43 km/h; (II) 49 mph, 79 km/h; (III) 76 mph, 122 km/h; (IV) 99 mph, 160 km/h; power-weight ratio: 30.4 lb/hp (41.3 lb/kW), 13.8 kg/hp (18.7 kg/kW); carrying capacity: 1,036 lb, 470 kg; speed in direct drive at 1,000 rpm: 15.8 mph, 25.5 km/h; consumption: 28.8 m/imp gal, 24 m/US gal, 9.8 l x 100 km.

CHASSIS integral; front suspension: independent, by McPherson, coil springs/telescopic damper struts, auxiliary rubber springs, lower wishbones, lower trailing links, anti-roll bar; rear: independent, oblique semi-trailing arms, auxiliary rubber springs, coil springs, telescopic dampers.

STEERING ZF, worm and roller.

BRAKES front disc (diameter 11 in, 28 cm), rear drum, dual circuit, rear compensator, servo.

ELECTRICAL EQUIPMENT 12 V; 45 Ah battery; 630 W alternator; 4 halogen headlamps.

DIMENSIONS AND WEIGHT wheel base: 103.94 in, 264 cm; tracks: 55.35 in, 141 cm front, 56.76 in, 144 cm rear; length: 181.89 in, 462 cm; width: 66.54 in, 169 cm; height: 55.91 in, 142 cm; ground clearance: 5.51 in, 14 cm; weight: 2,734 lb, 1,240 kg; turning circle: 34.4 ft, 10.5 m; fuel tank: 14.5 imp gal, 17.4 US gal, 66 l.

BODY saloon/sedan; 4 doors; 5 seats, separate front seats, reclining backrests.

PRACTICAL INSTRUCTIONS fuel: 90 oct petrol; oil: engine 7.4 imp pt, 8.9 US pt, 4.2 l, SAE 20W-50, change every 3,700 miles, 6,000 km - gearbox 1.8 imp pt, 2.1 US pt, 1 l, SAE 80, change every 14,900 miles, 24,000 km - final drive 1.6 imp pt, 1.9 US pt, 0.9 l, SAE 90, no change recommended; greasing: none.

OPTIONALS ZF3 HP 22 automatic transmission, hydraulic torque converter and planetary gears with 3 ratios (I 2.478, II 1.478, III 1, rev 2.090), max ratio of converter at stall 2.1, possible manual selection, 4.100 axle ratio, max speed 106 mph, 170 km/h, weight 2,778 lb, 1,260 kg.

BMW 528i

valves: overhead, Vee-slanted, rockers; camshafts: 1, overhead; lubrication: rotary pump, full flow filter, 10 imp pt, 12 US pt, 5.7 l; 1 Solex 4A1 downdraught 4-barrel carburettor; fuel feed: mechanical pump; water-cooled, 21.1 imp pt, 25.4 US pt, 12 l.

TRANSMISSION driving wheels: rear; clutch: single dry plate (diaphragm), hydraulically controlled; gearbox: mechanical; gears: 4, fully synchronized; ratios: I 3.855, II 2.203, III 1.402, IV 1, rev 4.300; lever: central; final drive: hypoid bevel; axle ratio: 3.640; width of rims: 6"; tyres 195/70 HR x 14.

PERFORMANCE max speed: 119 mph, 192 km/h; power-weight ratio: 19.8 lb/hp (27 lb/kW), 9 kg/hp (12.2 kg/kW); carrying capacity: 1,036 lb, 470 kg; speed in direct drive at 1,000 rpm: 18.4 mph, 29.6 km/h; consumption: 24.6 m/imp gal, 20.5 m/US gal, 11.5 l x 100 km.

CHASSIS integral; front suspension: independent, by McPherson, coil springs/telescopic damper struts, auxiliary rubber springs, lower wishbones (trailing links), anti-roll bar; rear: independent, semi-trailing arms, auxiliary rubber springs, coil springs, telescopic dampers.

STEERING ZF, recirculating ball, variable ratio servo; turns lock to lock: 3.80.

BRAKES disc (diameter 11 in, 28 cm), front internal radial fins, 2 X circuits, servo.

ELECTRICAL EQUIPMENT 12 V; 55 Ah battery; 55 A alternator; Bosch distributor; 4 halogen headlamps.

520

See 518, except for:

PRICE EX WORKS: 10,850 rand.

ENGINE 121.4 cu in, 1,990 cc (3.50 x 3.15 in, 89 x 80 mm); compression ratio: 9:1; max power (DIN): 115 hp (85 kW) at 5,800 rpm; max torque (DIN): 12 lb ft, 16.8 kg m (165 Nm) at 3,700 rpm; max engine rpm: 5,800; 57.8 hp/l (42.7 kW/l); 2 Stromberg 175 CDET downdraught carburettors.

TRANSMISSION axle ratio: 4.100; tyres: 185 SR x 14.

PERFORMANCE max speed: 109 mph, 175 km/h; power-weight ratio: 23.7 lb/hp (32.2 lb/kW), 10.8 kg/hp (14.6 kg/kW); acceleration: standing ¼ mile 17.4 sec, 0-50 mph (0-80 km/h) 7.3 sec; speed in direct drive at 1,00 rpm: 17.1 mph, 27.5 km/h; consumption: 26.4 m/imp gal, 22 m/US gal, 10.7 l x 100 km.

528i

See 518, except for:

PRICE EX WORKS: 13,390 rand

ENGINE 6 cylinders, in line; 170.1 cu in, 2,788 cc (3.39 x 3.15 in, 86 x 80 mm); compression ratio: 9:1; max power (DIN): 170 hp (125 kW) at 5,800 rpm; max torque (DIN): 176 lb ft, 24.3 kg m (238 Nm) at 4,000 rpm; 61.2 hp/l (44.8 kW/l); 7 crankshaft bearings; lubrication: 10.1 imp pt, 12.1 US pt, 5.7 l; Bosch L-Jetronic injection; water-cooled, 20.6 imp pt, 25.4 US pt, 12 l.

TRANSMISSION gearbox ratios: I 3.855, II 2.202, III 1.401, IV 1, rev 4.300; axle ratio: 3.640; width of rims: 6"; tyres: 195/70 HR x 14.

PERFORMANCE max speed: 118 mph, 190 km/h; power-weight ratio: 18.5 lb/hp (25.1 lb/kW), 8.4 kg/hp (11.4 kg/kW); carrying capacity: 915 lb, 415 kg; consumption: 26.3 m/imp gal, 21.9 m/US gal, 10.7 l x 100 km.

CHASSIS anti-roll bar on rear suspension.

BRAKES disc (front diameter 11 in, 28 cm, rear 10.7 in, 27.2 cm).

ELECTRICAL EQUIPMENT 55 Ah battery; 60 A alternator.

DIMENSIONS AND WEIGHT tracks: 55.90 in, 142 cm front, 57.48 in, 146 cm rear; weight: 3,142 lb, 1,425 kg; fuel tank: 15 imp gal, 17.9 US gal, 68 l.

530

See 518, except for:

PRICE EX WORKS: 15,350 rand

ENGINE 6 cylinders, in line; 182 cu in, 2,986 cc (3.50 x 3.15 in, 89 x 80 mm); compression ratio: 9:1; max power (DIN): 177 hp (130 kW) at 5,800 rpm; max torque (DIN): 188 lb ft, 26 kg m (255 Nm) at 3,500 rpm; 59.1 hp/l (43.5 kW/l); 7 crankshaft bearings; lubrication: 10.1 imp pt, 12.1 US pt, 5.7 l; 1 Solex 4A1 4-barrel downdraught carburettor; water-cooled, 20.6 imp pt, 25.4 US pt, 12 l.

BMW 530

TRANSMISSION gearbox ratios: I 3.855, II 2.202, III 1.401, IV 1, rev 4.300; axle ratio: 3.450; width of rims: 7"; tyres: 195 HR x 14.

PERFORMANCE max speed: 124 mph, 200 km/h; power-weight ratio: 17,8 lb/hp (24.2 lb/KW), 8.1 kg/hp (11 kg/kW); speed in direct drive at 1,000 rpm: 21.7 mph, 35 km/h; consumption: 26.1 m/imp gal, 21.8 m/US gal, 10.8 l x 100 km.

CHASSIS anti-roll bar on rear suspension.

STEERING servo.

BRAKES disc (front and rear diameter 11 in, 28 cm).

ELECTRICAL EQUIPMENT 55 Ah battery; 60 A alternator.

DIMENSIONS AND WEIGHT tracks: 55.90 in, 142 cm front, 57.48 in, 146 cm rear; weight: 3,142 lb, 1,425 kg; fuel tank: 15 imp gal, 17.9 US gal, 68 l.

OPTIONALS ZF3 HP 22 automatic transmission not available.

728

PRICE EX WORKS: 15,900 rand

ENGINE front, 4 stroke; 6 cylinders, in line; 170.1 cu in, 2,788 cc (3.39 x 3.15 in, 86 x 80 mm); compression ratio: 9:1; max power (DIN): 170 hp (125 kW) at 5,800 rpm: max torque (DIN): 172 lb ft, 23.8 kg m (233 Nm) at 4,000 rpm; max engine rpm: 6,500; 61 hp/l (44.9 kW/l); cast iron block, light alloy head, polispherical combustion chambers; 7 crankshaft bearings;

DIMENSIONS AND WEIGHT wheel base: 110 in, 279 cm; tracks: 59.45 in, 151 cm front, 59.84 in, 152 cm rear; length: 191.30 in, 486 cm; width: 70.90 in, 180 cm; height: 56.30 in, 143 cm; weight: 3,374 lb, 1,530 kg; turning circle: 37.4 ft, 11.4 m; fuel tank: 18.7 imp gal, 22.4 US gal, 85 l.

BODY saloon/sedan; 4 doors; 5 seats, separate front seats, reclining backrests, adjustable built-in headrests; heated rear window.

PRACTICAL INSTRUCTIONS fuel: 98 oct petrol; oil: engine 10 imp pt, 12 US pt, 5.7 l, SAE 20W-50, change every 3,700 miles, 6,000 km - gearbox 2.1 imp pt, 2.5 US pt, 1.2 l. SAE 20W-50, change every 14,800 miles, 24,000 km - final drive 2.6 imp pt, 3.2 US pt, 1.5 l, SAE 90, no change recommended; greasing: none.

OPTIONALS limited slip differential; ZF automatic transmission, hydraulic torque converter and planetary gears with 3 ratios (I 2.478, II 1.478, III 1, rev 2.090), max ratio of converter at stall 2, possible manual selection, 3.640 axle ratio,max speed 116 mph, 186 km, consumption 22.6 m/imp gal, 18.8 m/US gal, 12.5 l x 100 km; antibrake-locking system (ABS); light alloy wheels; sunshine roof; air-conditioning.

730

See 728, except for:

PRICE EX WORKS: 19,690 rand

ENGINE 182 cu in, 2,986 cc (3.50 x 3.15 in, 89 x 80 mm); max power (DIN): 184 hp (135 kW) at 5,800 rpm; max torque (DIN): 188 lb ft, 26 kg m (255 Nm) at 3,500 rpm; 61.6 hp/l (45.4 kW/l).

BMW 733i

TRANSMISSION ZF automatic transmission, hydraulic torque converter and planetary gears with 3 ratios, max ratio of converter at stall 2, possible manual selection; ratios: I 2.478, II 1.478, III 1, rev 2.090; axle ratio: 3.640; width of rims: 6.5"; tyres: 205/70 HR x 14.

PERFORMANCE max speed: 121 mph, 194 km/h; power-weight ratio: 18.9 lb/hp (25.7 lb/kW), 8.6 kg/hp (11.6 kg/kW); speed in direct drive at 1,000 rpm: 19.1 mph, 30.8 km/h; consumption: 21.9 m/imp gal, 18.2 m/US gal, 12.9 l x 100 km.

DIMENSIONS AND WEIGHT weight: 3,484 lb, 1,580 kg.

733i

See 728, except for:

PRICE EX WORKS: 23,500 rand

ENGINE 195.8 cu in, 3,210 cc (3.50 x 3.39 in, 89 x 86 mm); max power (DIN): 197 hp (145 kW) at 5,500 rpm; max torque (DIN): 207 lb ft, 28.5 kg m (279 Nm) at 4,300 rpm; 61.4 hp/l (45.2 kW/l); Bosch l-Jetronic electronic injection.

TRANSMISSION ZF automatic transmission, hydraulic torque converter and planetary gears with 3 ratios, max ratio of converter at stall 2, possible manual selection; ratios: I 2.478, II 1.478, III 1, rev 2.090; axle ratio: 3.450; width of rims: 6.5"; tyres: 205/70 VR 14.

PERFORMANCE max speed: 123 mph, 198 km/h; power-weight ratio: 17.9 lb/hp (24.3 lb/kW), 8.1 kg/hp (11 kg/kW); speed in direct drive at 1,000 rpm: 19.6 mph, 31.5 km/h; consumption: 22.1 m/imp gal, 18.4 m/US gal, 12.8 l x 100 km.

ELECTRICAL EQUIPMENT 65 A alternator.

DIMENSIONS AND WEIGHT weight: 3,528 lb, 1,600 kg.

CHEVROLET SOUTH AFRICA

Ascona Series

PRICES EX WORKS:	**rand**
1 4-dr Sedan	**4,760**
2 "S" 4-dr Sedan	**5,145**

Power team:	**Standard for:**	**Optional for:**
54 hp	1	—
57 hp	2	—

54 hp power team

ENGINE front, 4 stroke; 4 cylinders, vertical, in line; 76.6 cu in, 1,256 cc (3.18 x 2.40 in, 81 x 61 mm); compression ratio: 9.2:1; max power (DIN): 54 hp (40 kW) at 5,400 rpm; max torque (DIN): 61 lb ft, 8.4 kg m (82 Nm) at 2,400 rpm; max engine rpm: 5,800; 43 hp/l (31.8 kW/l); cast iron block and head; 3 crankshaft bearings; valves: overhead, in line, push-rods and rockers; camshafts: 1, side; lubrication: gear pump, full flow filter, 5.1 imp pt, 6.1 US pt, 2.9 l; 1 Stromberg CDS 1.50 downdraught carburettor; fuel feed: mechanical pump; water-cooled, 10.2 imp pt, 12.3 US pt, 5.8 l.

TRANSMISSION driving wheels: rear; clutch: single dry plate (diaphragm); gearbox: mechanical gears: 4, fully synchronized; ratios: I 3.760, II 2.213, III 1.404, IV 1, rev 3.707; lever: central; final drive: hypoid bevel; axle ratio: 4.440; width of rims: 5" tyres: 155 SR x 13.

PERFORMANCE max speed: 86 mph, 138 km/h; power-weight ratio: 37.4 lb/hp (50.4 lb/kW), 17 kg/hp (22.9 kg/kW); carrying capacity: 937 lb, 425 kg; acceleration: standing ¼ mile 21 sec, 0-50 mph (0-80 km/h) 12 sec; speed in direct drive at 1,000 rpm: 23.7 mph, 38.1 km/h; consumption: 31.4 m/imp gal, 26.1 m/US gal, 9 l x 100 km.

CHASSIS integral; front suspension: independent, wishbones, coil springs, anti-roll bar, telescopic dampers; rear: rigid axle (torque tube), trailing radius arms, transverse linkage bar, coil springs, anti-roll bar, telescopic dampers.

STEERING rack-and-pinion; turns lock to lock: 4.

BRAKES front disc, rear drum, servo; lining area: front 22.9 sq in, 148 sq cm, rear 47.1 sq in, 304 sq cm, total 70 sq in, 452 sq cm.

ELECTRICAL EQUIPMENT 12 V; 32 Ah battery; 45 A alternator; 2 headlamps.

DIMENSIONS AND WEIGHT wheel base: 99.21 in, 252 cm; front and rear track: 54.13 in, 137 cm; length: 170.12 in, 432 cm; width: 65.75 in, 167 cm; height: 54.33 in, 138 cm; ground clearance: 5.12 in, 13 cm; weight: 2,018 lb, 915 kg; turning circle: 31.2 ft, 9.5 m; fuel tank: 12.3 imp gal, 14.8 US gal, 56 l.

BODY saloon/sedan; 4 doors; 5 seats, separate front seats, headrests, reclining backrests.

OPTIONALS metallic spray.

57 hp power team

See 54 hp power team, except for:

ENGINE max power (DIN): 57 hp (42 kW) at 5,400 rpm; 45.4 hp/l (33.5 kW/l).

PERFORMANCE max speed: about 87 mph, 140 km/h; power-weight ratio: 35.4 lb/hp, (48 lb/kW), 16 kg/hp (21.7 kg/kW).

Chevair Series

PRICES EX WORKS:	**rand**
De Luxe 4-dr Sedan	**5,665**
GL 4-dr Sedan	**6,165**
Automatic Berlina 4-dr Sedan	**6,925**

ENGINE front, 4 stroke; 4 cylinders, vertical, in line; 141.6 cu in, 2,320 cc (3.87 x 3 in, 98.4 x 76.2 mm); compression ratio: 8.8:1; max power (DIN): 90 hp (66 kW) at 4,800 rpm; max torque (DIN): 124 lb ft, 17.1 kg m (168 Nm) at 2,800 rpm; max engine rpm: 5,500; 38.8 hp/l (28.4 kW/l); cast iron block and head; 5 crankshaft bearings; valves: overhead, hydraulic tappets; camshafts: 1, side; lubrication: gear pump, full flow filter, 5.8 imp pt, 7 US pt, 3.3 l; 1 Rochester Monojet downdraught carburettor; fuel feed: mechanical pump; water-cooled, 14.8 imp pt, 17.8 US pt, 8.4 l.

TRANSMISSION driving wheels: rear; clutch: single dry plate; gearbox: mechanical: gears: 4, fully synchronized; ratios: I 3.428, II 2.156, III 1.366, IV 1, rev 3.317; lever: central; final drive: hypoid bevel; axle ratio: 3.420; width of rims: 5.5"; tyres: 165 SR x 13.

PERFORMANCE max speed: 103 mph, 165 km/h; power-weight ratio: 24.7 lb/hp (33.7 lb/kW), 11.2 kg/hp (15.3 kg/kW); acceleration: 0-50 mph (0-80 km/h) 8.4 sec; speed in direct drive at 1,000 rpm: 20 mph, 32 km/h; consumption: 37.2 m/imp gal, 30.9 m/US gal, 7.6 l x 100 km.

CHASSIS integral; front suspension: independent, wishbones, coil springs, telescopic dampers; rear: rigid axle, trailing lower radius arms, coil springs, telescopic dampers.

STEERING rack-and-pinion; turns lock to lock: 4.

BRAKES front disc, rear drum.

ELECTRICAL EQUIPMENT 12 V; 32 Ah battery; 37 A alternator; 2 headlamps.

DIMENSIONS AND WEIGHT wheel base: 99.13 in, 252 cm; front and rear track: 54.13 in, 137 cm; length: 177.17 in, 450 cm; width: 64.96 in, 165 cm; height: 51.97 in, 132 cm; ground clearance: 5 in, 12.7 cm; weight: 2,227 lb, 1,010 kg; turning circle: 31.2 ft, 9.5 m; fuel tank: 12.3 imp gal, 14.8 US gal, 56 l.

CHEVROLET Ascona "S" Sedan

CHEVAIR SERIES

BODY saloon/sedan; 4 doors; 5 seats, separate front seats, reclining backrests, headrests.

OPTIONALS (standard for Berlina) Tri-Matic automatic transmission, hydraulic torque converter and planetary gears with 3 ratios (I 2.310, II 1.460, III 1, rev 1.860), max ratio of converter at stall 2.33, possible manual selection; metallic spray; vinyl roof; tinted glass.

Rekord Series

PRICES EX WORKS:	rand
1 4-dr Sedan	**6,585**
2 Automatic 4-dr Sedan	**6,895**
3 GL 4-dr Sedan	**6,925**
4 Automatic GL 4-dr Sedan	**7,170**
5 4+1-dr St. Wagon	**6,950**
6 4+1-dr Automatic St. Wagon	**7,165**

ENGINE front, 4 stroke; 4 cylinders, vertical, in line; 141.5 cu in, 2,319 cc (3.87 x 3 in, 98.4 x 76.2 mm); compression ratio: 9:1 max power (DIN): 90 hp (66 kW) at 4,800 rpm; max torque (DIN): 123 lb ft, 17 kg m (167 Nm) at 2,800 rpm; max engine rpm: 5,000; 39 hp/l (28.5 kW/l); cast iron block and head; 5 crankshaft bearings; valves: overhead, hydraulic tappets; camshafts: 1, overhead; lubrication: gear pump, full flow filter, 6.7 imp pt, 8 US pt, 3.8 l; 1 Rochester Monojet carburettor; fuel feed: mechanical pump; cooling, 11.1 imp pt, 13.3 US pt, 6.3 l.

TRANSMISSION driving wheels: rear; clutch: single dry plate; gearbox: mechanical; gears: 4, fully synchronized; ratios: I 3.640, II 2.120, III 1.336, IV 1, rev 3.317; lever: central; final drive hypoid bevel; axle ratio: 3.500; width of rims: 5.5"; tyres: 175 SR x 14.

PERFORMANCE max speed: sedans 103 mph, 165 km/h - st. wagons 101 mph, 162 km/h; power-weight ratio: sedans 27.3 lb/hp (37.3 lb/kW), 12.4 kg/hp (16.9 kg/kW); speed in direct drive at 1,000 rpm: 20.4 mph, 32.8 km/h; consumption: sedans 24.6 m/imp gal, 20.5 m/US gal, 11.5 l x 100 km - st. wagons 23.5 m/imp gal, 19.6 m/US gal, 12 l x 100 km.

CHASSIS integral; front suspension: independent, wishbones lower trailing links, coil springs, anti-roll bar, telescopic dampers; rear: rigid axle, trailing lower radius arms, upper torque arms, transverse linkage bar, coil springs, anti-roll bar, telescopic dampers.

STEERING recirculating ball; turns lock to lock: 4.

BRAKES front disc (diameter 9.37 in, 23.8 cm), rear drum, servo; lining area: total 85.7 sq in, 553 sq cm.

ELECTRICAL EQUIPMENT 12 V; 32 Ah battery; 37 A alternator; 2 headlamps.

DIMENSIONS AND WEIGHT wheel base: 105.40 in, 267 cm; tracks: 56.34 in, 143 cm front, 55.59 in, 141 cm rear; length: sedans 108.75 in, 459 cm - st. wagons 181.81 in, 462 cm; width: 68.03 in, 173 cm; height: sedans 55.71 in, 141 cm - st. wagons 56.69 in, 144 cm; ground clearance: 5.12 in, 13 cm; weight: sedans 2,459 lb, 1,115 kg - st. wagons 2,569 lb, 1,165 kg; turning circle: 32.6 ft, 9.9 m; fuel tank: 15.4 imp gal, 18.5 US gal, 70 l.

BODY saloon/sedan, 4 doors - estate car/st. wagon, 4+1 doors; 5 seats, separate front seats, reclining backrests, headrests.

OPTIONALS Opel automatic transmission with 3 ratios (I 2.400, II 1.480, III 1, rev 1.920), max ratio of converter at stall 2.5, possible manual selection, max speed sedans 99 mph, 160 km/h - st. wagons 97 mph, 157 km/h, consumption sedans 23.2 m/imp gal, 19.3 m/US gal, 12.2 l x 100 km - st. wagons 22.2 m/imp gal, 18.5 m/US gal, 12.7 l x 100 km; limited slip differential.

CHEVROLET Rekord Sedan

Commodore Series

PRICES EX WORKS:	rand
1 4-dr Sedan	**6,985**
2 Automatic 4-dr Sedan	**7,395**
3 GL 4-dr Sedan	**7,750**
4 GL Automatic 4+1-dr St. Wagon	**8,470**
5 GL Automatic 4-dr Sedan	**8,695**

Power team:	Standard for:	Optional for:
120 hp	1 to 4	—
132 hp	5	—

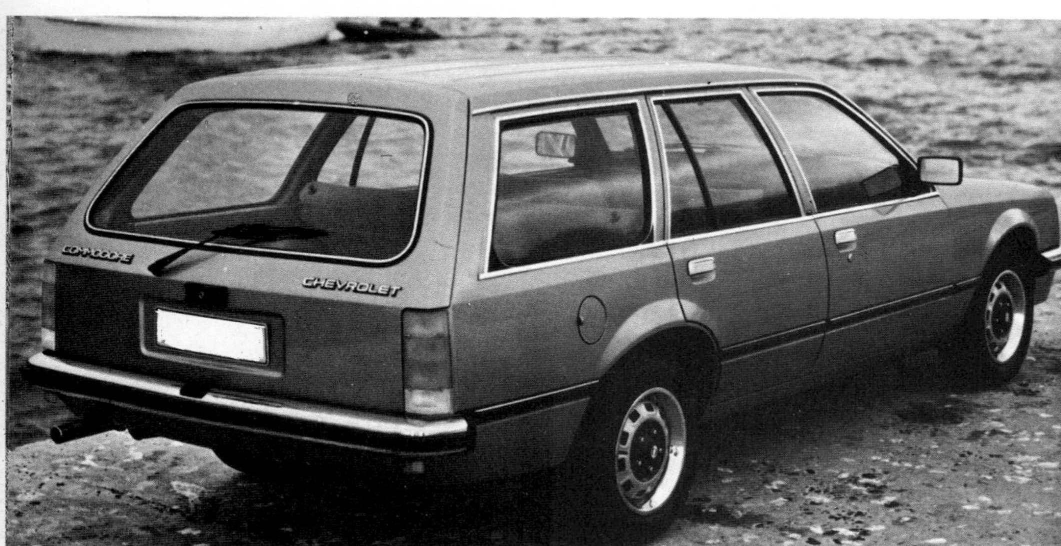

CHEVROLET Commodore GL Automatic Station Wagon

120 hp power team

ENGINE front, 4 stroke; 6 cylinders, vertical, in line; 230 cu in 3,769 cc (3.87 x 3.26 in, 98.4 x 82.5 mm); compression ratio 8.8:1; max power (DIN): 120 hp (88 kW) at 4,300 rpm; ma torque (DIN): 189 lb ft, 26.1 kg m (256 Nm) at 2,200 rpm; ma engine rpm: 4,600; 31.8 hp/l (23.3 kW/l); cast iron block an head; 7 crankshaft bearings; valves: overhead, in line, push rods and rockers, hydraulic tappets; camshafts: 1, side; lubrication: 7.6 imp pt, 9.1 US pt, 4.3 l; 1 Rochester Monojet carburettor; fuel feed: mechanical pump; cooling, 21.6 imp pt, 26 US pt 12.3 l.

TRANSMISSION driving wheels: rear; clutch: single dry plat (diaphragm), hydraulically controlled; gearbox: mechanical gears: 4, fully synchronized; ratios: I 3.500, II 2.480, III 1.660 IV 1, rev 3.500; lever: central; final drive: hypoid bevel; axl ratio: 2.920; width of rims: 6"; tyres: 175 SR x 14.

PERFORMANCE max speed: 103 mph, 165 km/h; power-weigh ratio: sedans 22.3 lb/hp (30.5 lb/kW), 10 kg/hp (13.8 kg/kW) st. wagons 22.8 lb/hp (31.1 lb/kW), 10.4 kg/hp (14.1 kg/kW)

CHASSIS integral; front suspension: independent, wishbones lower trailing links, coil springs, anti-roll bar, telescopic dam pers; rear: rigid axle, trailing lower radius arms, upper torqu arms, transverse linkage bar, coil springs, anti-roll bar, telesco pic dampers.

STEERING recirculating ball; turns lock to lock: 4.

BRAKES front disc (diameter 9.37 in, 23.8 cm), rear drum servo; lining area: total 85.7 sq in, 553 sq cm.

ELECTRICAL EQUIPMENT 12 V; 32 Ah battery; 37 A alterna tor; 2 headlamps.

DIMENSIONS AND WEIGHT wheel base: 105.40 in, 267 cm tracks: 56.34 in, 143 cm front, 55.59 in, 141 cm rear; length sedans 184.88 in, 469 cm - st. wagons 185.83 in, 472 cm width: 68.03 in, 173 cm; height: sedans 56.69 in, 144 cm - st wagons 58.66 in, 149 cm; ground clearance: 5.12 in, 13 cm weight: sedans 2,683 lb, 1,217 kg - st. wagons 2,741 lb, 1,24 kg; turning circle: 32.6 ft, 9.9 m; fuel tank: 15.4 imp gal, 18. US gal, 70 l.

BODY saloon/sedan, 4 doors - estate car/st. wagon, 4+ doors; 5 seats, separate front seats, reclining backrests, head rests.

OPTIONALS (standard for st. wagons) Tri-Matic automati transmission with 3 ratios (I 2.520, II 1.520, III 1, rev 1.940) max ratio of converter at stall 2, possible manual selection power steering; metallic spray; tinted glass.

132 hp power team

See 120 hp power team, except for:

ENGINE 249.7 cu in, 4,093 cc (3.87 x 3.53 in, 98.4 x 89.7 mm) max power (DIN): 132 hp (97 kW) at 4,400 rpm; max torqu (DIN): 198 lb ft, 27.3 kg m (268 Nm) at 1,500 rpm; max engin rpm: 4,800; 32.2 hp/l (23.7 kW/l); lubrication: 7.6 imp pt, 9.1 U pt, 4.3 l; cooling, 21.6 imp pt, 26 US pt, 12.3 l.

TRANSMISSION gearbox: Tri-Matic automatic transmissio with 3 ratios, max ratio of converter at stall 2, possible manua selection; ratios: I 2.520, II 1.520, III 1, rev 1.940.

ERFORMANCE max speeds: (I) 21 mph, 33 km/h; (II) 34 mph, 4 km/h; (III) 51 mph, 81 km/h; (IV) 80 mph, 128 km/h; ower-weight ratio: 42 lb/hp (56.4 lb/kW), 19 kg/hp (25.6 kg/ W).

LECTRICAL EQUIPMENT 330 W alternator.

ODY separate front seats; safety belts.

TANDARD INDIA

Gazel

NGINE front, 4 stroke; 4 cylinders, vertical, in line; 57.85 cu , 948 cc (2.48 x 2.99 in, 63 x 76 mm); compression ratio: .2:1; max power (DIN): 32 hp (24 kW) at 4,500 rpm; max rque (DIN): 43 lb ft, 6 kg m (60 Nm) at 3,000 rpm; max engine m: 4,500; 33.7 hp/l (25.3 kW/l); cast iron block and head; 3 rankshaft bearings; valves: overhead, push-rods and rockers; amshafts: 1, side; lubrication: full flow filter, 7 imp pt, 8.4 US , 4 l; 1 Solex M 32 BIC downdraught single barrel carburettor; el feed: mechanical pump; water-cooled, 8.4 imp pt, 10.1 US , 4.8 l.

RANSMISSION driving wheels: rear; clutch: single dry plate; earbox: mechanical; gears: 4, fully synchronized; ratios: I .271, II 2.460, III 1.454, IV 1, rev 4.271; lever: central; final rive: hypoid bevel; axle ratio: 4.550; width of rims: 3.5"; tyres; .60 x 13.

ERFORMANCE max speeds: (I) 19 mph, 30 km/h; (II) 31 mph, 0 km/h; (III) 53 mph, 85 km/h; (IV) 60 mph, 96 km/h; power-eight ratio: 62 lb/hp (82.7 lb/kW), 28.1 kg/hp (37.5 kg/kW); arrying capacity: 882 lb, 400 kg; acceleration: 0-50 mph (0-80 m/h) 31 sec; speed in direct drive at 1,000 rpm: 14.8 mph, 3.8 km/h; consumption: 23.5 to 20.2 m/imp gal, 19.6 to 16.8 /US gal, 12 to 14 l x 100 km.

HASSIS integral front, suspension: independent, wishbones, nti-roll bar, coil springs, telescopic double acting dampers; ar: rigid axle, 4 trailing links, Panhard rod, coaxial coil rings, anti-roll bar, telescopic double acting dampers.

TEERING rack-and-pinion.

RAKES drum; lining area: front 38.5 sq in, 250 sq cm, rear 8.5 sq in, 250 sq cm, total 76.9 sq in, 500 sq cm.

LECTRICAL EQUIPMENT 12 V; 45 Ah battery; 22 A dynamo; 5 D ignition distribution; 2 headlamps.

IMENSIONS AND WEIGHT wheel base: 93.98 in, 239 cm; acks: 47.99 in, 122 cm front, 48.50 in, 123 cm rear; length: 52.99 in, 389 cm; width: 59.68 in, 152 cm; height: 57.99 in, 47 cm; ground clearance: 6.22 in, 15.8 cm; weight: 1,985 lb, 00 kg; weight distribution: 40% front, 60% rear; turning circle: 7.9 ft, 8.5 m; fuel tank: 6.5 imp gal, 7.9 US gal, 30 l.

ODY saloon/sedan; 4 doors; 5 seats. bench front seats.

UNRISE INDIA

Badal

RICE EX WORKS: 21,100* rupias

NGINE rear, 2 stroke; 1 cylinder, horizontal; 12.1 cu in, 198 cc .63 x 2.28 in, 68 x 58 mm); compression ratio: 7.25:1; max ower (DIN): 9.8 hp (7 kW) at 4,800 rpm; max torque (DIN): 7 lb , 1 kg m (10 Nm) at 3,500 rpm; max engine rpm: 4,800; 4.9 p/l (3.6 kW/l); cast iron block, light alloy head; 2 crankshaft earings; lubrication: oil-petrol mixture; 1 Dell'Orto Clark down-raught single barrel carburettor; fuel feed: by gravity; air-ooled.

RANSMISSION driving wheels: rear; clutch: multi-disc; gear-ox: mechanical; gears: 4; ratios: I 3.390, II 1.752, III 1.102, IV .667, rev 3.624; lever: central, (two separate levers for for-ard and reverse); axle ratio: 3.700; tyres: 4.50 x 10.

ERFORMANCE max speed: 47 mph, 75 km/h; power-weight atio: 90 lb/hp (125.9 lb/kW), 40.8 kg/hp (57.1 kg/kW); carrying apacity: 794 lb, 360 kg; consumption: 70.6 m/imp gal, 58.8 /US gal, 4 l x 100 km.

HASSIS integral; front suspension: coil springs, telescopic ampers; rear: longitudinal arms, semi-elliptic leafsprings, tele-copic dampers.

TEERING rack-and-pinion; turns lock to lock: 7.30.

RAKES drum.

LECTRICAL EQUIPMENT 12 V; 30 Ah battery; Magneto distri-utor; 2 headlamps.

IMENSIONS AND WEIGHT wheel base: 66.93 in, 170 cm; ont and rear track: 40.94 in, 104 cm; length: 121.26 in, 308 cm; width: 53.15 in, 135 cm; height: 53.15 in, 135 cm; ground clearance: 47.24 in, 120 cm; weight: 882 lb, 400 kg; weight distribution: 21% front, 79% rear; turning circle: 23.9 ft, 7.3 m; fuel tank: 2.1 imp gal, 2.5 US gal, 9.5 l.

BODY 2+1 doors; 4 seats, separate front seats.

STANDARD Gazel

SUNRISE Badal

HONGQI CHINA (People's Republic)

6-pass. or 9-pass. Limousine

ENGINE front, 4 stroke; 8 cylinders, Vee-slanted at 90°; 344.9 cu in, 5,652 cc (3.94 x 3.54 in, 100 x 90 mm); compression ratio: 8.5:1; max power (SAE): 220 hp (162 kW) at 4,400 rpm; max torque (SAE): 304 lb ft, 42 kg m (412 Nm) at 2,800-3,000 rpm; max engine rpm: 4,400; 38.9 hp/l (28.6 kW/l); cast iron block and head; 5 crankshaft bearings; valves: overhead, in line, push-rods and rockers; camshafts: 1, at centre of Vee; lubrication: gear pump, full flow filter, 9.7 imp pt, 11.6 US pt, 5.5 l; 1 type 241 downdraught twin barrel carburettor; fuel feed: mechanical pump; water-cooled, 9-pass, 52.8 imp pt, 63.4 US pt, 30 l - 6-pass. 44 imp pt, 52.9 US pt, 25 l.

TRANSMISSION driving wheels: rear; gearbox: automatic transmission, hydraulic torque converter and planetary gears with 2 ratios, max ratio of converter at stall 2.5; ratios: I 1.720, II 1, rev 2.390; lever: steering column; final drive: hypoid bevel; axle ratio: 9-pass, 3.900 - 6-pass. 3.540; width of rims: 6"; tyres: 9-pass. 8.90 x 15 - 6-pass. 8.20 x 15.

PERFORMANCE max speed: 9-pass. 99 mph, 160 km/h - 6-pass. 112 mph, 180 km/h; power-weight ratios: 9-pass. 27.3 lb/hp (37.3 lb/kW), 12.4 kg/hp (16.9 kg/kW) - 6-pass. 22.7 lb/hp (30.9 lb/kW), 10.3 kg/hp (14 kg/kW); carrying capacity: 9-pass. 1,588 lb, 720 kg - 6-pass, 1,058 lb, 480 kg; consumption: 9-pass. 14.1 m/imp gal, 11.8 m/US gal, 20 l x 100 km - 6-pass. 15.7 m/imp gal, 13.1 m/US gal, 18 l x 100 km.

CHASSIS box-type ladder frame; front suspension: independent, wishbones, coil springs, horizontal torsion bars, telescopic dampers; rear: rigid axle, semi-elliptic leafsprings, telescopic dampers.

STEERING recirculating ball, servo.

BRAKES drum.

ELECTRICAL EQUIPMENT 12 V; 68 Ah battery (2 for 9-pass.); 36 Ah dynamo; 2 headlamps.

DIMENSIONS AND WEIGHT wheel base: 9-pass. 146.46 in, 372 cm - 6-pass. 120.87 in, 307 cm; tracks: 62.20 in, 158 cm front, 61.02 in, 155 cm rear; length: 9-pass. 235.43 in, 598 cm - 6-pass. 209.84 in, 533 cm; width: 78.35 in, 199 cm; height: 64.57 in, 164 cm; ground clearance: 7.09 in, 18 cm; weight: 9-pass. 6,020 lb, 2,730 kg - 6-pass. 5,005 lb, 2,270 kg; weight distribution: 9-pass. 52.2% front, 47.8% rear - 6-pass. 54% front, 46% rear; turning circle: 9-pass. 49.2 ft, 15 m - 6-pass. 42 ft, 12.8 m; fuel tank: 17.6 imp gal, 21.1 US gal, 80 l.

BODY limousine; 4 doors; 9 seats in three rows or 6 seats, bench front seats; electric rear seat; electric windows; air-conditioning.

HONGQI 9-passenger Limousine

CHASSIS box-type ladder frame; front and rear suspension rigid axle, semi-elliptic leafsprings, telescopic dampers.

STEERING worm and double roller.

BRAKES drum; lining area: total 153.5 sq in, 990 sq cm.

ELECTRICAL EQUIPMENT 12 V; 54 Ah battery; 250 W dynamo; 2 headlamps.

DIMENSIONS AND WEIGHT wheel base: 90.55 in, 230 cm front and rear track: 56.69 in, 144 cm; length: 153.54 in, 39 cm; width: 68.90 in, 175 cm; height: 73.62 in, 187 cm; ground clearance: 8.66 in, 22 cm; weight: 3,374 lb, 1,530 kg; weight distribution: 52% front, 48% rear; turning circle: 39.4 ft, 12 m fuel tank: 13.2 imp gal, 15.8 US gal, 60 l - (separate tank) 5. imp gal, 6.6 US gal, 25 l.

BODY open; 4 doors; 5 seats, separate front seats; canvas roof.

PEKING CHINA (People's Republic)

BJ 212

ENGINE front, 4 stroke; 4 cylinders, vertical, in line; 149.2 cu in, 2,445 cc (3.62 x 3.62 in, 92 x 92 mm); compression ratio: 6.6:1; max power (SAE): 75 hp (55 kW) at 3,500-4,000 rpm; max torque (SAE): 127 lb ft, 17.5 kg m (172 Nm) at 2,000-2,500 rpm; max engine rpm: 4,000; 30.7 hp/l (22.6 kW/l); cast iron block, light alloy head; 5 crankshaft bearings; valves: overhead, Vee-slanted, push-rods and rockers; camshafts: 1, side; lubrication: gear pump, full flow filter, 10.9 imp pt, 13.1 US pt 6.2 l; 1 type K-22D downdraught single barrel carburettor; fuel feed: mechanical pump; water-cooled, 18.5 imp pt, 22.2 US pt, 10.5 l.

TRANSMISSION driving wheels: front (automatically engaged with transfer box low ratio) and rear; clutch: single dry plate, hydraulically controlled; gearbox: mechanical; gears: 3, II and III synchronized; ratios: I 3.115, II 1.772, III 1, rev 3.738; transfer box ratios: high 1.200, low 2.648; lever: central; final drive: spiral bevel; axle ratio: 4.550: width of rims: 4.5"; tyres: 6.50 x 16.

PERFORMANCE max speeds: (I) 20 mph, 32 km/h; (II) 35 mph, 56 km/h; (III) 61 mph, 98 km/h; power-weight ratio: 45 lb/hp (61.3 lb/kW), 20.4 kg/hp (27.8 kg/kW); carrying capacity: 882 lb, 400 kg; consumption: 16.6 m/imp gal, 13.8 m/US gal, 17 l x 100 km.

PEKING BJ 212

SHANGHAI CHINA (People's Republic)

Sedan

ENGINE front, 4 stroke; 6 cylinders, in line; 136.2 cu in, 2,23 cc (3.15 x 2.91 in, 80 x 74 mm); compression ratio: 7.7:1; max

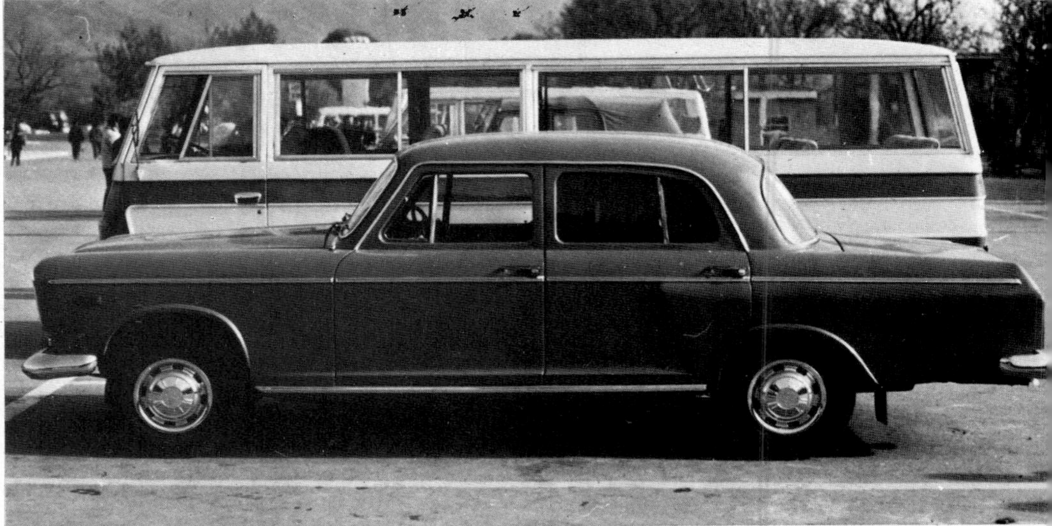
SHANGHAI Sedan

power (SAE): 90 hp (73 kW) at 4,800 rpm; max torque (SAE 109 lb ft, 15 kg m (147 Nm) at 3,500 rpm; max engine rpm 5,000; 40.3 hp/l (73.8 kW/l) cast iron block, light alloy head; crankshaft bearings; valves: overhead, in line: camshafts: side; lubrication: gear pump, full flow filter, 10.8 imp pt, 12 US pt, 6 l; 1 Shangfu 593 downdraught twin barrel carburetto fuel feed: mechanical pump; water-cooled, 19.4 imp pt, 23.3 U pt, 11 l.

TRANSMISSION driving wheels: rear; clutch: single dry plat gearbox: mechanical; gears: 4, fully synchronized; ratios: 3.520, II 2.320, III 1.520, IV 1, rev 3.290; lever: steerin column; final drive: hypoid bevel; axle ratio: 4.110; width rims: 5"; tyres: 6.70 x 13.

PERFORMANCE max speed: 81 mph, 130 km/h; power-weig ratio: 35.3 lb/hp (43.4 lb/kW), 16 kg/hp (19.7 kg/kW); carryi capacity: 882 lb, 400 kg.

CHASSIS integral; front and rear suspension: independent, c springs, telescopic dampers.

STEERING recirculating ball.

BRAKES drum.

ELECTRICAL EQUIPMENT 12 V; 54 Ah battery; 220 W dyn mo; 2 headlamps.

DIMENSIONS AND WEIGHT wheel base: 11.42 in, 283 c tracks: 56.69 in, 144 cm front, 58.27 in, 148 cm rear; leng 188.19 in, 478 cm; width: 69.68 in, 177 cm; height: 62.20 158 cm; ground clearance: 5.12 in, 13 cm; weight: 3,175

HYUNDAI Pony Station Wagon

,440 kg; turning circle: 36.7 ft, 11.2 m; fuel tank: 14.1 imp gal, ;.9 US gal, 64 l.

ODY saloon/sedan; 4 doors; 5 seats, bench front seats.

IYUNDAI KOREA

Pony Sedan

ony 2+1-dr Sedan
ony 4-dr Sedan

NGINE front, 4 stroke; 4 cylinders, vertical, in line; 75.5 cu in, ,238 cc (2.87 x 2.91 in, 73 x 74 mm); compression ratio: 9:1; ıax power (DIN): 55 hp (40 kW) at 5,000 rpm; max torque ϽIN): 62.3 lb ft, 8.6 kg m (84 Nm) at 4,000 rpm; max engine ɔm: 6,300; 44.4 hp/l (32.3 kW/l); 5 crankshaft bearings; valves: verhead, rockers; camshafts: 1, overhead; lubrication: trochoid ump (cartridge), 7 imp pt, 8.4 US pt, 4 l; 1 Mikuni Kogyo Stromberg type) downdraught twin barrel carburettor; fuel ɜed: mechanical pump; water-cooled, 10.5 imp pt, 12.7 US pt, l.

RANSMISSION driving wheels: rear; clutch: single dry plate diaphragm); gearbox: mechanical; gears: 4, fully synchronized, atios: I 3.525, II 2.193, III 1.442, IV 1, rev 3.867; lever: central; nal drive: hypoid bevel; axle ratio: 4.222; width of rims: 4.5"; res: 155 SR x 13.

ERFORMANCE max speeds: (I) 28 mph, 45 km/h; (II) 45 mph, 3 km/h; (III) 69 mph, 111 km/h; (IV) 96 mph, 155 km/h; ower-weight ratio: 36.5 lb/hp (50.2 lb/kW), 16.5 kg/hp (22.7 g/kW); carrying capacity: 714 lb, 324 kg; speed in direct drive 1,000 rpm: 15.8 mph, 25.4 km/h; consumption: 37.4 m/imp al, 31.2 m/US gal, 7.5 l x 100 km.

HASSIS integral; front suspension: independent, by McPheron, coil springs/telescopic damper struts, lower wishbones railing links), anti-roll bar; rear: rigid axle, semi-elliptic leafprings, telescopic dampers.

TEERING recirculating ball; turns lock to lock: 4.20.

RAKES front disc (diameter 8 in, 20.2 cm), rear drum; lining rea: front 9.6 sq in, 62 sq cm, rear 19.2 sq in, 124 sq cm, total 8.8 sq in, 186 sq cm.

LECTRICAL EQUIPMENT 12 V; 40 Ah battery; 480 W alternaɔr; Mitsubishi distributor; 4 headlamps.

IMENSIONS AND WEIGHT wheel base: 92.13 in, 234 cm; acks: 50.39 in, 128 cm front, 49.21 in, 125 cm rear; length: 56.30 in, 397 cm; width: 61.42 in, 156 cm; height: 53.54 in, 36 cm; ground clearance: 6.50 in, 16.5 cm; weight: 2,007 lb, 10 kg; weight distribution: 53% front, 47% rear; turning circle: 9.5 ft, 9 m; fuel tank: 9.9 imp gal, 11.9 US gal, 45 l.

ODY saloon/sedan; 4 seats, separate front seats, reclining ackrests.

RACTICAL INSTRUCTIONS fuel: 88 oct petrol; oil: engine 7 np pt, 8.4 US pt, 4 l, SAE 10W-30, change every 3,100 miles, ,000 km - gearbox 3 imp pt, 3.6 US pt, 1.7 l, SAE 80, change every 24,900 miles, 40,000 km - final drive 1.9 imp pt, 2.3 US pt, 1.1 l, SAE 80-90, change every 24,900 miles, 40,000 km; greasing: none; tappet clearances: inlet 0.006 in, 0.15 mm, exhaust 0.010 in, 0.25 mm; valve timing: 18° 50° 48° 20°; tyre pressure: front 24 psi, 1.7 atm, rear 24 psi, 1.7 atm.

VARIATIONS

ENGINE 87.8 cu in, 1,439 cc (2.87 x 3.38 in, 73 x 86 mm), max power (DIN) 68 hp (50 kW) at 5,000 rpm, max torque (DIN) 77 lb ft, 10.6 kg m (104 Nm) at 3,000 rpm, max engine rpm 6,300, 47.3 hp/l (34.7 kW/l).

OPTIONALS automatic transmission, hydraulic torque converter and planetary gears with 3 ratios, possible manual selection; luxury equipment.

Pony Station Wagon

See Pony Sedan, except for:

ENGINE 87.8 cu in, 1,439 cc (2.87 x 3.38 in, 73 x 86 mm); max power (DIN): 68 hp (50 kW) at 5,000 rpm; max torque (DIN): 77 lb ft, 10.6 kg m (104 Nm) at 3,000 rpm; max engine rpm: 6,300; 47.3 hp/l (34.7 kW/l).

TRANSMISSION axle ratio: 3.909.

PERFORMANCE max speeds: (I) 30 mph, 49 km/h; (II) 49 mph, 79 km/h; (III) 75 mph, 120 km/h; (IV) 99 mph, 160 km/h; power-weight ratio: 29.9 lb/hp (40.7 lb/kW), 13.6 kg/hp (18.4 kg/kW); carrying capacity: 772 lb, 350 kg; speed in direct drive at 1,000 rpm: 17.1 mph, 27.5 km/h.

DIMENSIONS AND WEIGHT length: 156.69 in, 398 cm; weight: 2,033 lb, 922 kg; weight distribution: 51% front, 49% rear.

BODY estate car/st. wagon; 4+1 doors; 4 seats, separate front seats, reclining backrests; folding rear seat.

KIA KOREA

Brisa 1000

ENGINE front, 4 stroke; 4 cylinders, in line; 60.1 cu in, 985 cc (2.76 x 2.52 in, 70 x 64 mm); compression ratio: 8.8:1; max power (DIN): 55 hp (40 kW) at 6,000 rpm; max torque (DIN): 51 lb ft, 7 kg m (69 Nm) at 3,500 rpm; max engine rpm: 6,000; 55.8 hp/l (40.6 kW/l); cast iron block, light alloy head; 5 crankshaft bearings; valves: overhead, rockers; camshafts: 1, overhead; lubrication: rotary pump, full flow filter, 5.3 imp pt, 6.3 US pt, 3 l; 1 Nikki downdraught twin barrel carburettor; fuel feed: mechanical pump; water-cooled, 8.8 imp pt, 10.6 US pt, 5 l.

TRANSMISSION driving wheels: rear; clutch: single dry plate (diaphragm); gearbox: mechanical; gears: 4, fully synchronized; ratios: I 3.655, II 2.185, III 1.425, IV 1, rev 3.655; lever: central; final drive: hypoid bevel; axle ratio: 4.300; width of rims: 4.5"; tyres: 6.15 x 13.

PERFORMANCE max speeds: (I) 25 mph, 40 km/h; (II) 40 mph, 65 km/h; (III) 65 mph, 105 km/h; (IV) 87 mph, 140 km/h; power-weight ratio: 31.7 lb/hp (43.5 lb/kW), 14.4 kg/hp (19.7 kg/kW); carrying capacity: 882 lb, 400 kg; acceleration: standing ¼ mile 21 sec, 0-50 mph (0-80 km/h) 14 sec; speed in direct drive at 1,000 rpm: 14.9 mph, 24 km/h; consumption: 35.3 m/imp gal, 29.4 m/US gal, 8 l x 100 km.

CHASSIS integral; front suspension: independent, by McPherson, coil springs/telescopic damper struts, lower wishbones (trailing links), anti-roll bar; rear: rigid axle, semielliptic leafsprings, telescopic dampers.

STEERING recirculating ball; turns lock to lock: 3.40.

BRAKES drum, dual circuit; lining area: front 39.7 sq in, 256 sq cm, rear 39.7 sq in, 256 sq cm, total 79.4 sq in, 512 sq cm.

ELECTRICAL EQUIPMENT 12 V; 45 Ah battery; 420 W alternator; Mitsubishi distributor; 4 headlamps.

DIMENSIONS AND WEIGHT wheel base: 88.98 in, 226 cm; tracks: 49.61 in, 126 cm front, 48.82 in, 124 cm rear; length: 151.57 in, 385 cm; width: 60.63 in, 154 cm; height: 54.72 in, 139 cm; ground clearance: 6.70 in, 17 cm; weight: 1,742 lb, 790 kg; weight distribution: 54% front, 46% rear; turning circle: 27.6 ft, 8.4 m; fuel tank: 8.8 imp gal, 10.6 US gal, 40 l.

BODY saloon/sedan; 4 doors; 5 seats, separate front seats.

PRACTICAL INSTRUCTIONS fuel: 86 oct petrol; oil: engine 5.3 imp pt, 6.3 US pt, 3 l, SAE 10W-30, change every 3,100 miles,

KIA Brisa 1300

BRISA 1000

5,000 km - gearbox 2.3 imp pt, 2.7 US pt, 1.3 l, SAE 80-90, change every 24,900 miles, 40,000 km - final drive 1.8 imp pt, 2.1 US pt, 1 l, SAE 80-90, change every 24,900 miles, 40,000 km; greasing: none; sparking plug: BP6ES; tappet clearances: inlet 0.010 in, 0.25 mm, exhaust 0.012 in, 0.30 mm; valve timing: 13° 50° 57° 6°; front and rear tyre pressure 27 psi, 1.9 atm.

Brisa 1300

See Brisa 1000, except for:

ENGINE 77.6 cu in, 1,272 cc (2.87 x 2.99 in, 73 x 76 mm); compression ratio: 9.2:1; max power (DIN): 65 hp (48 kW) at 6,000 rpm; max torque (DIN): 68 lb ft, 9.4 kg m (92 Nm) at 3,500 rpm; 51.1 hp/l (37.7 kW/l).

TRANSMISSION axle ratio: 4.100.

PERFORMANCE max speed: 93 mph, 150 km/h; power-weight ratio: 28.7 lb/hp (38.8 lb/kW), 13 kg/hp (17.6 kg/kW); acceleration: standing ¼ mile 18.1 sec; speed in direct drive at 1,000 rpm: 15.8 mph, 25.5 km/h.

DIMENSIONS AND WEIGHT weight: 1,863 lb, 845 kg.

PRACTICAL INSTRUCTIONS valve timing: 15° 55° 57° 12°.

YLN — TAIWAN

902 SD

ENGINE front, 4 stroke; 6 cylinders, in line; 121.9 cu in, 1,998 cc (3.07 x 2.74 in, 78 x 69.7 mm); compression ratio: 8.6:1; max power (SAE): 115 hp (85 kW) at 5,600 rpm; max torque (SAE): 120 lb ft, 16.6 kg m (163 Nm) at 4,000 rpm; max engine rpm: 5,600; 57.6 hp/l (42.4 kW/l); cast iron block and light alloy head; 7 crankshaft bearings; valves: 2 per cylinders, overhead, rockers; camshafts: 1, overhead; lubrication: trochoid pump (cartridge), 8.8 imp pt, 10.6 US pt, 5 l; 1 Hitachi DAF 342-22 downdraught twin barrel carburettor; fuel feed: mechanical pump; water-cooled, 15.6 imp pt, 18.8 US pt, 8.9 l.

TRANSMISSION driving wheels: rear; clutch: single dry plate (diaphragm); gearbox: mechanical; gears: 4, fully synchronized; ratios: I 3.592, II 2.246, III 1.415, IV 1, rev 3.657; lever: central; final drive: hypoid bevel; axle ratio: 3.910; width of rims: 5"; tyres: 175 SR x 14.

PERFORMANCE max speeds: (I) 28 mph, 45 km/h; (II) 47 mph, 75 km/h; (III) 71 mph, 115 km/h; (IV) 103 mph, 165 km/h; power-weight ratio: 23 lb/hp (31.1 lb/kW), 10.4 kg/hp (14.1 kg/kW); speed in direct drive at 1,000 rpm: 17.4 mph, 28 km/h; consumption: 35.3 m/imp gal, 29.4 m/US gal, 8 l x 100 km.

CHASSIS integral; front suspension: independent, coil springs/telescopic damper struts, stabilizer torsion bar; rear: rigid axle, 4 link coil springs, telescopic dampers.

STEERING recirculating ball.

BRAKES front disc, rear drum, vacuum booster servo; lining area: front 22.9 sq in, 148 sq cm, rear 53.9 sq in, 348 sq cm, total 76.8 sq in, 496 sq cm.

ELECTRICAL EQUIPMENT 12 V; 50 Ah battery; 600 W alternator; Shih-Lin distributor; 4 headlamps.

DIMENSIONS AND WEIGHT wheel base: 105.11 in, 267 cm; tracks: 54.33 in, 138 cm front, 53.93 in, 137 cm rear; length: 178.14 in, 452 cm; width: 66.33 in, 168 cm; height: 55.31 in, 140 cm; ground clearance: 6.69 in, 17 cm; weight: 2,646 lb, 1,200 kg; turning circle: 36 ft, 11 m; fuel tank: 13.2 imp gal, 15.8 US gal, 60 l.

BODY saloon/sedan; 4 doors; 5 seats, separate front seats, reclining backrests, built-in headrests.

803 DL

ENGINE diesel, front, 4 stroke; 4 cylinders, vertical, in line; 132 cu in, 2,164 cc (3.26 x 3.93 in, 83 x 100 mm); compression ratio: 20:1; max power (SAE): 66 hp (49 kW) at 4,000 rpm; max torque (SAE): 104 lb ft, 14.4 kg m (141 Nm) at 1,800 rpm; max engine rpm: 4,200; 30.5 hp/l (22.4 kW/l); cast iron block and head; 3 crankshaft bearings; valves: overhead, push-rods and rockers; camshafts: 1, side; lubrication: gear pump, full flow filter, 10.4 imp pt, 12.5 US pt, 5.9 l; fuel injection; fuel feed: mechanical pump; water-cooled, 14.1 imp pt, 16.9 US pt, 8 l.

TRANSMISSION driving wheels: rear; clutch: single dry plate (diaphragm); gearbox: mechanical; gears: 4, fully synchronized; ratios: I 3.592, II 2.246, III 1.415, IV 1, rev 3.657; lever: steering column; final drive: hypoid bevel; axle ratio: 4.100; width of rims: 5"; tyres: 175 SR x 14.

PERFORMANCE max speed: 78 mph, 125 km/h; power-weight ratio: 46.5 lb/hp (62.8 lb/kW), 21.1 kg/hp (28.5 kg/kW).

CHASSIS integral; front suspension: independent, double wishbones, coil springs, anti-roll bar, telescopic double acting dampers; rear: rigid axle, semi-elliptic leafsprings, telescopic double acting dampers.

STEERING recirculating ball.

BRAKES front disc, rear drum; swept area: front 227 sq in, 1,464 sq cm, rear 117.4 sq in, 757 sq cm, total 344.4 sq in, 2,221 sq cm.

ELECTRICAL EQUIPMENT 12 V; 70 Ah battery; 40 A alternator; 4 headlamps.

DIMENSIONS AND WEIGHT wheel base: 105.90 in, 269 cm; tracks: 54.53 in, 139 cm front, 54.33 in, 138 cm rear; length: 184.64 in, 469 cm; width: 66.53 in, 169 cm; height: 56.89 in, 144 cm; ground clearance: 7.48 in, 19 cm; weight: 3,076 lb, 1,395 kg; turning circle: 36.1 ft, 11 m; fuel tank: 14.7 imp gal, 17.7 US gal, 67 l.

BODY saloon/sedan; 4 doors; 6 seats, bench front seats.

YLN 902 SD

YLN 805 SD

302 DX

ENGINE front, 4 stroke; 4 cylinders, in line; 71.5 cu in, 1,171 cc (2.87 x 2.76 in, 73 x 70 mm); compression ratio: 9:1; max power (SAE): 69 hp (51 kW) at 6,000 rpm; max torque (SAE): 70 lb ft, 9.7 kg m (98 Nm) at 3,600 rpm; max engine rpm: 6,000; 58.9 hp/l (43.6 kW/l); cast iron block, light alloy head; 5 crankshaft bearings; valves: overhead; push-rods and rockers; camshafts: 1, side; lubrication: trochoid pump (cartridge), 6 imp pt, 7.2 US pt, 3.4 l; 1 Hitachi DCG 306-57 downdraught twin barrel carburettor; fuel feed: mechanical pump; water-cooled, 7.1 imp pt, 8.5 US pt, 4 l.

TRANSMISSION driving wheels: rear; clutch: single dry plate (diaphragm); gearbox: mechanical; gears: 4, fully synchronized; ratios: I 3.757, II 2.169, III 1.404, IV 1, rev 3.640; lever: central; final drive: hypoid bevel; axle ratio: 3.889; width of rims: 4"; tyres: 6.00 x 12.

PERFORMANCE max speed: (I) 24 mph, 38 km/h; (II) 41 mph, 66 km/h; (III) 64 mph, 103 km/h; (IV) 90 mph, 145 km/h; power-weight ratio: 25.6 lb/hp (34.5 lb/kW), 11.6 kg/hp (15.7 kg/kW); consumption: 56 m/imp gal, 47 m/US gal, 5 l x 100 km.

CHASSIS integral; front suspension: independent, coil springs, telescopic dampers; rear: rigid axle, 4 link coil springs, telescopic damper struts.

STEERING recirculating ball.

BRAKES drum; lining area: front 21.1 sq in, 136 sq cm, rear 21.1 sq in, 136 sq cm, total 42.2 sq in, 272 sq cm.

ELECTRICAL EQUIPMENT 12 V; 50 Ah battery; 420 W alternator; Shih Lin distributor; 2 headlamps.

DIMENSIONS AND WEIGHT wheel base: 92.13 in, 234 cm; tracks: 51.40 in, 130 cm front, 51.20 in, 130 cm rear; length: 115.80 in, 294 cm; width: 62.20 in, 158 cm; height: 53.50 in, 136 cm; ground clearance: 6.70 in, 17 cm; weight: 1,760 lb, 800 kg; turning circle: 33.5 ft, 10.2 m; fuel tank: 11 imp gal, 13.2 US gal, 50 l.

BODY saloon/sedan; 4 doors; 5 seats, separate front seats.

805 SD

ENGINE front, 4 stroke; 6 cylinders, in line; 146 cu in, 2,393 cc (3.27 x 2.90 in, 83 x 73.7 mm); compression ratio: 8.6:1; max power (SAE): 130 hp (97 kW) at 5,600 rpm; max torque (SAE): 145 lb ft, 20 kg m (203 Nm) at 3,600 rpm; max engine rpm: 5,600; 54.3 hp/l (40.4 kW/l); cast iron block, light alloy head; 7 crankshaft bearings; valves: overhead, rockers; camshafts: 1, overhead; lubrication: trochoid pump (cartridge), 7.2 imp pt, 8.7 US pt, 4.1 l; 1 Hitachi DAF 342-14B downdraught twin barrel carburettor; fuel feed: electric pump; water-cooled, 16.7 imp pt, 20.1 US pt, 9.5 l.

TRANSMISSION driving wheels: rear; clutch: single dry plate (diaphragm); gearbox: mechanical; gears: 4, fully synchronized; ratios: I 3.592, II 2.246, III 1.415, IV 1, rev 3.657; lever: central; final drive: hypoid bevel; axle ratio: 4.100; width of rims: 5"; tyres: 175 SR x 14.

PERFORMANCE max speeds: (I) 25 mph, 40 km/h; (II) 40 mph, 65 km/h; (III) 65 mph, 105 km/h; (IV) 106 mph, 170 km/h; power-weight ratio: 23.7 lb/hp (31.7 lb/kW), 10.7 kg/hp (14.4 kg/kW); speed in direct drive at 1,000 rpm: 17.4 mph, 28 km/h; consumption: 31.3 m/imp gal, 26.1 m/US gal, 9 l x 100 km.

CHASSIS integral; front suspension: independent, coil springs, telescopic dampers, stabilizer torsion bar; rear: rigid axle, semi-elliptic leafsprings, telescopic dampers, stabilizer torsion bar.

STEERING servo.

BRAKES front disc, rear drum, vacuum booster servo; lining area: front 24.8 sq in, 160 sq cm, rear 71.9 sq in, 464 sq cm, total 96.7 sq in, 624 sq cm.

ELECTRICAL EQUIPMENT 12 V; 60 Ah battery; 600 W alternator; Shih Lin distributor; 4 headlamps.

DIMENSIONS AND WEIGHT wheel base: 105.90 in, 269 cm; tracks: 54.53 in, 138 cm front, 54.33 in, 138 cm rear; length: 188.38 in, 478 cm; width: 66.53 in, 169 cm; height: 56.70 in, 144 cm; ground clearance: 7.08 in, 18 cm; weight: 3,076 lb, 1,395 kg; turning circle: 42.6 ft, 13 m; fuel tank: 14.7 imp gal, 17.7 US gal, 67 l.

BODY saloon/sedan; 4 doors; 5 seats, separate front seats.

DAIHATSU JAPAN

Max Cuore Series

PRICES (Tokyo):	yen
Standard 2-dr Sedan	572,000
DX 2-dr Sedan	628,000
Hi Custom 2-dr Sedan	681,000
DX 4-dr Sedan	648,000
Custom 4-dr Sedan	675,000
Hi Custom 4-dr Sedan	699,000
Hi Custom EX 4-dr Sedan	727,000

ENGINE front, transverse, 4 stroke; 2 cylinders, in line; 33.4 cu in, 547 cc (2.82 x 2.68 in, 71.6 x 68 mm); compression ratio: 8.7:1; max power (JIS): 31 hp (23 kW) at 6,000 rpm; max torque (JIS): 30 lb ft, 4.2 kg m (41 Nm) at 3,500 rpm; max engine rpm: 7,800; 51.2 hp/l (37.7 kW/l); cast iron block, light alloy head; 3 crankshaft bearings; valves: overhead, rockers; camshafts: 1 overhead, cogged belt; lubrication: rotary pump, full flow filter, 5.1 imp pt, 6.1 US pt, 2.9 l; 1 Aisan downdraught twin barrel carburettor; fuel feed: mechanical pump; emission control by Daihatsu lean-burn system with turbulence generating pot in each combustion chamber and catalytic converter; water-cooled, 5.3 imp pt, 6.3 US pt, 3 l.

TRANSMISSION driving wheels: front; clutch: single plate (diaphragm); gearbox: mechanical; gears: 4, fully synchronized; ratios I 3.666, II 2.150, III 1.464, IV 0.971, rev 3.529; lever: central; final drive: hypoid bevel; axle ratio: 5.470; width of rims: 3.5"; tyres: 5.20 x 10.

PERFORMANCE max speeds: (I) 18 mph, 29 km/h; (II) 31 mph, 50 km/h; (III) 45 mph, 73 km/h; (IV) 68 mph, 110 km/h; power-weight ratio: 2-dr 38.8 lb hp (52.7 lb/kW), 17.6 kg/hp (23.9 kg/kW) - 4-dr 40.2 lb/hp (54.7 lb/kW), 18.2 kg/hp (24.8 kg/kW); carrying capacity: 706 lb, 320 kg; acceleration: standing ¼ mile 21.8 sec; speed in top at 1,000 rpm: 8.8 mph, 14.2 km/h; consumption: 52.3 m/imp gal, 43.6 m/US gal, 5.4 l x 100 km at 37 mph, 60 km/h.

DAIHATSU Max Cuore Hi Custom EX Sedan

CHASSIS integral; front suspension: independent, by McPherson, coil springs/telescopic damper struts, lower wishbones (trailing links); rear: independent, semi-trailing arms, coil springs, telescopic dampers.

STEERING rack-and-pinion; turns lock to lock: 3.30.

BRAKES drum, single circuit; lining area: front 18.6 sq in, 120 sq cm, rear 18.6 sq in, 120 sq cm, total 37.2 sq in, 240 sq cm.

ELECTRICAL EQUIPMENT 12 V; 26 Ah battery; 35 A alternator; 2 headlamps.

DIMENSIONS AND WEIGHT wheel base: 82.28 in, 209 cm; front rear track: 48.03 in, 122 cm; length: 124.40 in, 316 cm; width: 54.72 in, 139 cm; height: 51.97 in, 132 cm; ground clearance: 7.09 in, 18 cm; weight: 2-dr 1,203 lb, 545 kg-4-dr 1,247 lb, 565 kg; weight distribution: 64% front, 36% rear; turning circle: 30.2 ft, 9.2 m; fuel tank: 5.7 imp gal, 6.9 US gal, 26 l.

BODY saloon/sedan; 4 seats, separate front seats.

OPTIONALS 145 SR x 10 tyres.

Charade Series

PRICES (Tokyo):	yen
1 XO 4+1-dr Sedan	653,000
2 XG 4+1-dr Sedan	698,000
3 XT 4+1-dr Sedan	748,000
4 XGE 4+1-dr Sedan	777,000
5 XTE 4+1-dr Sedan	815,000
6 XG 2+1-dr Coupé	704,000
7 XT 2+1-dr Coupé	764,000
8 XTE 2+1-dr Coupé	830,000

For GB prices, see price index.

Power team:	Standard for:	Optional for:
55 hp	1 to 4	—
60 hp	5 to 8	—

55 hp power team

ENGINE front, transverse, 4 stroke; 3 cylinders, in line; 60.6 cu in, 993 cc (2.99 x 2.87 in, 76 x 73 mm); compression ratio: 8.7:1; max power (JIS): 55 hp (40 kW) at 5,500 rpm; max torque (JIS): 57 lb ft, 7.8 kg m (76 Nm) at 2,800 rpm; max engine rpm: 6,000; 55.4 hp/l (40.8 kW/l); cast iron block, light alloy head; 4 crankshaft bearings, valves: overhead, push-rods and rockers; camshafts: 1, overhead; lubrication rotary pump, full flow filter, 5.1 imp pt, 6.1 US pt, 2.9 l; 1 Aisan-Stromberg downdraught twin barrel carburettor; fuel feed: mechanical pump; emission control by Daihatsu lean-burn system with turbulence generating pot in each combustion chamber and cylinder, catalitic converter; water-cooled, 7 imp pt, 8.5 US pt, 4 l.

TRANSMISSION driving wheels: front; clutch: single dry plate (diaphragm); gearbox: mechanical; gears: 4, fully synchronized; ratios: I 3.666, II 2.150, III 1.464, IV 0.971, rev 3.529; lever:

DAIHATSU Charade XTE Coupé

55 HP POWER TEAM

central; final drive: helical spur gears; axle ratio: 4.588; width of rims: 5"; tyres: 6.00 x 12 - XT models 155 SR x 12.

PERFORMANCE max speeds: (I) 25 mph, 40 km/h; (II) 40 mph, 64 km/h; (III) 58 mph, 94 km/h; (IV) 84 mph, 135 km/h; power-weight ratio: XO 25.4 lb/hp (34.6 lb/kW), 11.5 kg/hp (15.7 kg/kX); carrying capacity: 882 lb, 400 kg; consumption: 53.3 m/imp gal, 44.4 m/US gal, 5.3 l x 100 km at 37 mph, 60 km/h.

CHASSIS integral; front suspension: independent, by McPherson, coil springs/telescopic damper struts; rear: independent, upper and lower trailing links, Panhard rod, coil spring, telescopic dampers.

STEERING rack-and-pinion; turns lock to lock: 3.40.

BRAKES drum - front disc on XGE and XT only; lining area: front 47.1 sq in, 304 sq cm - disc 16.7 sq in, 108 sq cm, rear 37.2 sq in, 240 sq cm, total, 84.3 sq in, 544 sq cm 53.9 sq in, 412 sq cm.

ELECTRICAL EQUIPMENT 12 V; 30 Ah battery; 40 A alternator; 2 headlamps.

DIMENSIONS AND WEIGHT wheel base: 90.55 in, 230 cm; tracks: 51.18 in, 130 cm front, 50.39 in, 128 cm rear; length: 136.22 in, 346 cm; width: 59.45 in, 151 cm; height: 53.54 in, 136 cm; ground clearance: 7.09 in, 18 cm; weight: XO 1,389 lb, 630 kg - XG 1,411 lb, 640 kg - XT 1,433 lb, 650 kg - XGE 1,444 lb, 655 kg - XTE 1,455 lb, 660 kg; weight distribution: 63% front, 37% rear; turning circle: 32.8 ft, 10 m; fuel tank: 7.5 imp gal, 9 US gal, 34 l.

BODY saloon/sedan; 4+1 doors; 5 seats, separate front seats, reclining backrests, headrests.

OPTIONALS 5-speed mechanical gearbox, V 0.795, max speed 87 mph, 140 km/h.

60 hp power team

See 55 hp power team, except for:

ENGINE compression ratio: 9.1:1; max power (JIS): 60 hp (44 kW) at 5,600 rpm; max torque (JIS): 60 lb ft, 8.2 kg m (80 Nm) at 3,200 rpm; max engine rpm: 6,200; 60.4 hp/l (44.5 kW/l).

TRANSMISSION gears: 5, fully synchronized; ratios: I 3.666, II 2.150, III 1.464, IV 0.971, V 0.795, rev 3.529; axle ratio: 4.277; tyres: 155 SR x 12.

PERFORMANCE max speeds: (I) 25 mph, 40 km/h; (II) 42 mph, 67 km/h; (III) 62 mph, 100 km/h; (IV) 87 mph, 140 km/h; (V) 87 mph, 140 km/h; power-weight ratio: XG 23.5 lb/hp (32 lb/kW), 10.7 kg/hp (14.5 kg/kW).

BRAKES front disc, servo.

DIMENSIONS AND WEIGHT length: 138.98 in, 353 cm; weight: XTE Sedan 1,468 lb, 665 kg - XG Coupé 1,413 lb, 640 kg - XT Coupé 1,435 lb, 650 kg - XTE Coupé 1,468 lb, 665 kg.

Charmant Series

PRICES (Tokyo):	**yen**
1 1300 De Luxe 4-dr Sedan	**819,000**
2 1300 Custom 4-dr Sedan	**857,000**
3 1300 Hi Custom 4-dr Sedan	**891,000**
4 1300 LC 4-dr Sedan	**921,000**
5 1600 Custom 4-dr Sedan	**927,000**
6 1600 Hi Custom 4-dr Sedan	**961,000**
7 1600 SC 4-dr Sedan	**977,000**
8 1600 GC 4-dr Sedan	**1,011,000**

Power team:	**Standard for:**	**Optional for:**
72 hp	1 to 4	—
88 hp	5 to 8	—

72 hp power team

ENGINE front, 4 stroke; 4 cylinders, in line; 78.7 cu in, 1,290 cc (2.95 x 2.87 in, 75 x 73 mm); compression ratio: 9:1; max power (JIS): 72 hp (53 kW) at 5,600 rpm; max torque (JIS): 76 lb ft, 10.5 kg m (103 Nm) at 3,600 rpm; max engine rpm: 6,000; 55.8 hp/l (41.1 kW/l); cast iron block, light alloy head; 5 crankshaft bearings; valves: overhead, push-rods and rockers; camshafts: 1, side; lubrication: trochoid pump, full flow filter, 6.2 imp pt, 7.4 US pt, 3.5 l; 1 Aisan 4 K-U downdraught twin barrel carburettor; secondary air induction, EGR, catalytic converter; fuel feed: mechanical pump; water-cooled, 10.8 imp pt, 12.7 US pt, 6 l.

TRANSMISSION driving wheels: rear; clutch: single dry plate (diaphragm); gearbox: mechanical; gears: 4, fully synchronized; ratios: I 3.789, II 2.220, III 1.435, IV 1, rev 4.316; lever: central; final drive: hypoid bevel; axle ratio: 3.909; width of rims: 4.5"; tyres: 6.00 x 12.

PERFORMANCE max speed: (I) 25 mph, 40 km/h; (II) 43 mph, 70 km/h; (III) 75 mph, 110 km/h; (IV) 93 mph, 150 km/h; power-weight ratio: De Luxe 24.5 lb/hp (33.3 lb/kW), 11.1 kg/hp (15.1 kg/kW); carrying capacity: 882 lb, 400 kg; consumption: 40.7 m/imp gal, 34.2 m/US gal, 6.9 l x 100 km.

CHASSIS integral; front suspension: independent, by McPherson, coil springs/telescopic damper struts, lower transverse arms, trailing locating rods, anti-roll bar, rear: rigid axle, semi-elliptic leafsprings, telescopic dampers.

STEERING recirculating ball; turns lock to lock: 3.40.

BRAKES drum, dual circuit, servo; lining area: front 47.1 sq in, 304 sq cm, rear 41.6 sq in, 268 sq cm, total 88.7 sq in, 672 sq cm.

ELECTRICAL EQUIPMENT 12 V; 32 Ah battery; 30 A alternator; contactless fully transistorized distributor; 2 headlamps.

DIMENSIONS AND WEIGHT wheel base: 91.93 in, 233 cm; tracks: 49.21 in, 125 cm front, 49.02 in, 124 cm rear; length: 161.81 in, 411 cm; width: 60.24 in, 153 cm; height: 54.33 in, 138 cm; ground clearance 6.69 in, 17 cm; weight: De Luxe 1,764 lb, 800 kg - Custom 1,786 lb, 810 kg - Hi Custom and LC 1,797 lb, 815 kg; weight distribution: 56% front, 44% rear; turning circle: 33.5 ft, 10.2 m; fuel tank: 9.5 imp gal, 11.4 US gal, 43 l.

BODY saloon/sedan; 4 doors; 5 seats, separate front seats.

OPTIONALS 5-speed fully synchronized mechanical gearbox, V 0.865 (for Hi Custom and LC only).

DAIHATSU Charmant 1300 LC Sedan

88 hp power team

See 72 hp power team, except for:

ENGINE 96.9 cu in, 1,588 cc (3.35 x 2.76 in, 85 x 70 mm); max power (JIS): 88 hp (65 kW) at 5,600 rpm; max torque (JIS): 96 lb ft, 13.3 kg m (130 Nm) at 3,400 rpm: 55.4 hp/l (40.8 kW/l); lubrication: 7.4 imp pt, 8.9 US pt, 4.2 l; 1 12T-U downdraught twin barrel carburettor; 12T-U low emission engine with TGP high turbulence cylinder head; cooling 12.7 imp pt, 15.2 US pt, 7.2 l.

TRANSMISSION gearbox ratios: I 3.587, II 2.022, III 1.384, IV 1, rev 3.484; axle ratio: 3.727; tyres: 6.15 x 13 - SC 155 SR x 13.

PERFORMANCE max speeds: (I) 31 mph, 50 km/h; (II) 53 mph, 85 km/h; (III) 78 mph, 125 km/h; (IV) 99 mph, 160 km/h; power-weight ratio: Custom 22.3 lb/hp (30.2 lb/kW), 10.1 kg/hp (13.7 kg/kW); consumption: 35.3 m/imp gal, 29.4 m/US gal, 8 l x 100 km.

ELECTRICAL EQUIPMENT 35 Ah battery; 40 A alternator; 4 headlamps.

DIMENSIONS AND WEIGHT front track: 49.61 in, 126 cm; weight: Custom 1,962 lb, 890 kg - Hi Custom and SC 1,973 lb, 895 kg - GC 1,984 lb, 900 kg.

OPTIONALS 5-speed fully synchronized mechanical gearbox, V 0.861, 3.909 axle ratio (for Hi Custom, SC and GC only); automatic transmission with 3 ratios (I 2.450, II 1.450, III 1, rev 2.222), 3.909 axle ratio (for Hi Custom and GC only).

Delta Series

Standard Wagon
De Luxe Wagon
Custom Wagon
Custom EX Wagon

ENGINE front, 4 stroke; 4 cylinders, in line; 108 cu in, 1,770 cc (3.35 x 3.07 in, 85 x 78 mm); compression ratio: 8.5:1; max power (JIS): 92 hp (68 kW) at 5,000 rpm; max torque (JIS): 109 lb ft, 15 kg m (147 Nm) at 3,400 rpm; max engine rpm: 5,400; 52 hp/l (38.3 kW/l); cast iron block, light alloy head; 5 crankshaft bearings; valves: overhead, push-rods and rockers; camshafts: 1, side; lubrication: rotary pump, full flow filter, 7.4 imp pt, 8.9 US pt, 4.2 l; 1 Aisan 13T downdraught twin barrel carburettor; TGP high turbulence cylinder head, secondary air induction, exhaust gas recirculation and catalytic converter; fuel feed: mechanical pump; water-cooled, 14.1 imp pt, 16.9 US pt, 8 l.

TRANSMISSION driving wheels: rear; clutch: single dry plate (diaphragm); gearbox: mechanical; gears: 4, fully synchronized; ratios: I 3.674, II 2.114, III 1.403, IV 1, rev 4.183; lever: steering column; final drive: hypoid bevel; axle ratio: 4.100; width of rims: 4" - Custom models 4.5"; tyres: 5.50 x 13 - Custom models 165 SR x 14.

PERFORMANCE max speeds: (I) 23 mph, 37 km/h; (II) 40 mph, 65 km/h; (III) 61 mph, 98 km/h; (IV) 87 mph, 140 km/h; power-weight ratio: Standard 26 lb/hp (35.3 lb/kW) 11.8 kg/hp (16 kg/kW); consumption: 29.7 m/imp gal, 24.8 m/US gal, 9.5 l x 100 km.

DAIHATSU Delta Custom EX Wagon

DAIHATSU Taft Diesel F50S

CHASSIS integral; front suspension: independent, double wishbones, coil springs, telescopic dampers; rear rigid axle, semi-elliptic leafsprings, telescopic dampers.

STEERING recirculating ball.

BRAKES drum - Custom models front disc, dual circuit, servo; lining area: front 67.6 sq in, 436 sq cm. rear 54.6 sq in, 353 sq cm, total 122.2 sq in, 788 sq cm.

ELECTRICAL EQUIPMENT 12 V; 33 Ah battery; 40 A alternator; Denso distributor; 2 headlamps.

DIMENSIONS AND WEIGHT wheel base: 86.42 in, 219 cm; tracks: 56.30 in, 143 cm front, 52.95 in, 134 cm rear; length: 157.09 in, 399 cm; width: 64.96 in, 165 cm; height: 68.70 in, 174 cm - Custom EX 78.35 in, 199 cm; ground clearance: 6.89 in, 17.5 cm; weight: Standard and De Luxe 2.392 lb, 1,085 kg - Custom 2,414 lb, 1,095 kg - Custom EX 2,503 lb, 1,135 kg; weight distribution: 57.8% front, 42.2% rear; fuel tank: 12.1 imp gal, 14.5 US gal, 55 l.

BODY estate car/st. wagon; 2+1 doors; 8 seats, separate front seats.

Taft Series

1 Gran 1600 H-F20S (canvas doors)
2 Gran 1600 H-F20SK (steel doors)
3 Gran 1600 H-F20J (6-pass., canvas doors)
4 Gran 1600 H-F20JK (6-pass., steel doors)
5 Gran 1600 H-F20V (4-pass., steel body)
6 Diesel F50S (canvas doors)
7 Diesel F50SK (steel doors)
8 Diesel F50J (6-pass., canvas doors)
9 Diesel F50JK (6-pass., steel doors)
10 Diesel F50V (4-pass., steel body)

Power team:	Standard for:	Optional for:
80 hp	1 to 5	—
75 hp (diesel)	6 to 10	—

80 hp power team

ENGINE front, 4 stroke; 4 cylinders, in line; 96.8 cu in, 1,587 cc (3.17 x 3.07 in, 80.5 x 78 mm); compression ratio; 8.5:1; max power (JIS): 80 hp (59 kW) at 5,200 rpm; max torque (JIS): 91 lb ft, 12.5 kg m (122 Nm) at 3,000 rpm; max engine rpm: 5,700; 50.4 hp/l (37.1 kW/l); cast iron block, light alloy head; 3 crankshaft bearings; valves: overhead, push-rods and rockers; camshafts: 1, side; lubrication: trochoid pump, full flow filter, 7.4 imp pt, 8.9 US pt, 4.2 l; 1 Aisan 12 R-J downdraught twin barrel carburettor; fuel feed: mechanical pump; water-cooled, 12.3 imp pt, 14.8 US pt, 7 l.

TRANSMISSION driving wheels: rear, or front and rear; clutch: single dry plate (diaphragm); gearbox: mechanical; gears: 4, fully synchronized and 2-ratio transfer box; ratios: I 3.717, II 2.177, III 1.513, IV 1, rev 4.434; transfer box ratios: high 1.300, low 2.407; lever: central; final drive: hypoid bevel; front and rear axle ratio: 4.777; width of rims: 4.5"; tyres: 6.00 x 16.

PERFORMANCE max speeds (rear drive only): (I) 20 mph, 33 km/h; (II) 35 mph, 57 km/h; (III) 50 mph, 80 km/h; (IV) 71 mph, 115 km/h; power-weight ratio: H-F20S 29.2 lb/hp (39.7 lb/kW), 13.2 kg/hp (18 kg/hp); carrying capacity: 882 lb, 400 kg; consumption: 28.2 m/imp gal, 23.5 m/US gal, 10 l x 100 km at 37 mph, 60 km/h.

CHASSIS box-section ladder frame; front and rear suspension: rigid axle, semi-elliptic leafsprings, telescopic dampers.

STEERING recirculating ball; turns lock to lock: 2.70.

BRAKES drum; lining area: front 72.6 sq in, 468 sq cm, rear 72.6 sq in, 468 sq cm, total 145.2 sq in, 936 sq cm.

ELECTRICAL EQUIPMENT 12 V; 35 Ah battery; 35 A alternator; Denso distributor; 2 headlamps.

DIMENSIONS AND WEIGHT wheel base: 79.53 in, 202 cm; front and rear track: 47.24 in, 120 cm; length: H-F20S and H-F20SK 130.71 in, 332 cm - H-F20J, H-F20JK and H-F20V 137.20 in, 348 cm; width: 57.48 in, 146 in, 146 cm; height: H-F20S and H-F20SK 73.20 in, 186 cm - H-F20J and H-F20JK 73.03 in, 185 cm - H-F20V 73.42 in, 186 cm; ground clearance: 8.46 in, 21.5 cm; weight: H-T20S 2,337 lb, 1,060 kg - H-F20SK 2,370 lb, 1,075 kg - H-F20J 2,381 lb, 1,080 kg - H-F20JK 2,414 lb, 1,095 kg - H-F20V 2,492 lb, 1,130 kg; weight distribution: 56% front, 44% rear; turning circle: 35.4 ft, 10.8 m; fuel tank: 8.8 imp gal, 10.6 US gal, 40 l.

BODY open, canvas top, canvas or steel doors, steel hardtop; 4 or 6 seats, separate front seats, built-in headrests.

75 hp (diesel) power team

See 80 hp power team, except for:

ENGINE diesel; 154.4 cu in, 2,530 cc (3.46 x 4.94 in, 88 x 104 mm); max power (JIS): 75 hp (55 kW) at 3,600 rpm; max torque (JIS): 127 lb ft, 17.5 kg m (171 Nm) at 2,200 rpm; max engine rpm; 3,600; 29.6 hp/l (21.8 kW/l); Ricardo Comet swirl chamber type; lubrication: 9.7 imp pt, 11.6 US pt, 5.5 l; Denso plunger type mechanical injection; water-cooled, 17.6 imp pt, 21.1 US pt, 10 l.

TRANSMISSION gearbox ratios: I 3.717, II 2.276, III 1.513, IV 1, rev 4.434; axle ratio: 3.545.

PERFORMANCE max speeds (rear drive only): (I) 16 mph, 26 km/h; (II) 29 mph, 46 km/h; (III) 43 mph, 70 km/h; (IV) 65 mph, 105 km/h; power-weight ratio: F50S 34.8 lb/hp (47.4 lb/kW), 15.8 kg/hp (21.5 kg/kW); consumption: 42.2 m/imp gal, 35.1 m/US gal, 6.7 l x 100 km at 37 mph, 60 km/h.

DIMENSIONS AND WEIGHT length: F50S and F50SK 130.71 in, 332 cm - F50J, F50JK and F50V 137.20 in, 348 cm; height: F50S and F50SK 73.20 in, 186 cm - F50J and F50JK 73.03 in, 185 cm - F50V 73.42 in, 186 cm; weight: F50S 2,612 lb, 1,185 kg - F50SK 2,646 lb, 1,200 kg - F50J 2,657 lb, 1,205 kg - F50JK 2,690 lb, 1,220 kg - F50V 2,767 lb, 1,255 kg.

OPTIONALS power take-off; front wheel freewheeling hub.

HONDA JAPAN

Civic CVCC Series

PRICES (Tokyo):	yen
1 1300 SE 2+1-dr Sedan	**721,000**
2 1300 GL 2+1-dr Sedan	**807,000**
3 1300 LX 2+1-dr Sedan	**855,000**
4 1300 SE 4+1-dr Sedan	**764,000**
5 1300 GF 4+1-dr Sedan	**845,000**
6 1300 LX 4+1-dr Sedan	**885,000**
7 1500 SE 2+1-dr Sedan	**781,000**
8 1500 CE 2+1-dr Sedan	**877,000**
9 1500 SE 4+1-dr Sedan	**816,000**
10 1500 CF 4+1-dr Sedan	**912,000**
11 1500 CX 4+1-dr Sedan	**957,000**

Power team:	Standard for:	Optional for:
68 hp	1 to 6	—
80 hp	7 to 10	—
85 hp	11	—

68 hp power team

ENGINE front, transverse, 4 stroke, stratified charge; 4 cylinders, vertical, in line; 81.5 cu in, 1,335 cc (2.83 x 3.23 in, in, 72 x 82 mm); compression ratio: 7.9:1; max power (JIS): 68 hp (50 kW) at 5,500 rpm; max torque (JIS): 73 lb ft, 10 kg m (98 Nm) at 3,500 rpm; max engine rpm: 6,000; 50.9 hp/l (37.5 kW/l); light alloy block with cast iron liners, light alloy head; 5 crankshaft bearings; valves: 3 per cylinder (one intake and one exhaust in main combustion chamber, one intake in auxiliary chamber), overhead, Vee-slanted, rockers; camshafts: 1, overhead, cogged belt; lubrication: rotary pump, full flow filter, 5.3

HONDA Civic CVCC 1300 GL Sedan

68 HP POWER TEAM

imp pt, 6.3 US pt, 3 l; 1 Keihin-Honda downdraught 3-barrel CVCC carburettor; fuel feed: mechanical pump; water-cooled, 7 imp pt, 8.5 US pt, 4 l.

TRANSMISSION driving wheels: front; clutch: single dry plate (diaphragm); gearbox: mechanical; gears: 4 (5 for LX models), fully synchronized; ratios: I 2.916, II 1.764, III 1.181, IV 0.807, (for LX models V 0.655), rev 2.916; lever: central; final drive: helical spur gears; axle ratio: 4.933; width of rims: 4''; tyres: 6.00 x 12 - GL 155 SR x 12.

PERFORMANCE max speeds: (I) 26 mph, 42 km/h; (II) 45 mph, 72 km/h; (III) 70 mph, 112 km/h; (IV) 93 mph, 150 km/h; power-weight ratio: SE 2+1-dr 21.8 lb/hp (29.5 lb/kW), 9.9 kg/hp (13.4 kg/kW); carrying capacity: 882 lb, 400 kg; consumption: 33.7 m/imp gal, 28.4 m/US gal, 8.3 l x 100 km.

CHASSIS integral, front auxiliary frame; front suspension: independent, by McPherson, coil springs/telescopic damper struts, lower wishbones (trailing links), anti-roll bar; rear: independent, by McPherson, coil springs/telescopic damper struts, lower wishbones (torque arms).

STEERING rack-and-pinion; turns lock to lock: 3.20.

BRAKES front disc, rear drum, dual circuit servo; lining area: front 18 sq in, 116 cm, rear 24.8 sq in, 160 sq cm, total 42.8 sq in, 276 sq cm.

ELECTRICAL EQUIPMENT 12 V; 30 Ah battery; 35 A alternator; Mitsubishi distributor; 2 headlamps.

DIMENSIONS AND WEIGHT wheel base: 2+1-dr models 86.61 in, 220 cm, 4+1-dr models 89.76 in, 228 cm; tracks: 51.18 in, 130 cm front, 50.39 in, 128 cm rear; length: SE and GL 2+1-dr 140.16 in, 356 cm, LX 2+1-dr 143.50 in, 364 cm - SE and GF 4+1-dr 143.90 in, 366 cm, LX 4+1-dr 147.24 in, 374 cm; width: 59.25 in, 150 cm; height: 52.17 in, 132 cm; ground clearance: 6.69 in, 17 cm; weight: SE 2+1-dr 1,477 lb, 670 kg - GL 2+1-dr 1,521 lb, 690 kg - LX 2+1-dr 1,532 lb, 695 kg - SE 4+1-dr 1,621 lb, 735 kg - GF 4+1-dr 1,643 lb, 745 kg - LX 4+1-dr 1,654 lb, 750 kg; weight distribution: 63% front, 37% rear; turning circle: 2+1-dr models 33.8 ft, 10.3 m - 4+1-dr models 35.1 ft, 10.7 m; fuel tank: 2+1-dr models 8.4 imp gal, 10 US gal, 38 l - 4+1-dr models 8.8 imp gal, 10.6 US gal, 40 l.

OPTIONALS semi-automatic transmission with 2 ratios (I 1.565, II 0.903, rev 2.045), 4.117 axle ratio; air-conditioning.

80 hp power team

See 68 hp power team, except for:

ENGINE 90.8 cu in, 1,488 cc (2.91 x 3.41 in, 74 x 86.5 mm); compression ratio: 8.8:1; max power (JIS): 88 hp (65 kW) at 5,500 rpm; max torque (JIS): 89 lb ft, 12.3 kg m (120 Nm) at 3,500 rpm; 59.1 hp/l (43.5 kW/l); Honda CVCC stratified charge cylinder head, with catalytic converter and exhaust gas recirculation.

TRANSMISSION gears: SE models 4 - CE and CF 5; axle ratio: 3.875.

PERFORMANCE max speeds: (I) 33 mph, 53 km/h; (II) 53 mph, 85 km/h; (III) 81 mph, 130 km/h; (IV) 95 mph, 153 km/h; power-weight ratio: SE 2+1-dr 20.4 lb/hp (27.7 lb/kW), 9.2 kg/hp (12.6 kg/kW); consumption: 50.3 m/imp gal, 42.3 m/US gal, 5.6 l x 100 km.

STEERING turns lock to lock: 3.30.

DIMENSIONS AND WEIGHT length: 2+1-dr models 148 in, 376 cm - 4+1-dr models 150.79 in, 383 cm; height: 59.06 in, 150 cm; weight: SE 2+1-dr 1,633 lb, 740 kg - CE 2+1-dr 1,678 lb, 760 kg - SE 4+1-dr 1,689 lb, 765 kg - CF 4+1-dr 1,722 lb, 780 kg; fuel tank: 8.8 imp gal, 10.6 US gal, 40 l.

OPTIONALS semi-automatic transmission with 2 ratios (I 1.565, II 0.903, rev 2.045), 4.117 axle ratio, max speed 90 mph, 145 km/h (for SE 4+1-dr and CF only).

85 hp power team

See 68 hp power team, except for:

ENGINE 90.8 cu in, 1,488 cc (2.91 x 3.41 in, 74 x 86.5 mm); compression ratio: 8.8:1; max power (JIS): 85 hp (63 kW) at 5,500 rpm; max torque (JIS): 89 lb ft, 12.3 kg m (120 Nm) at 3,500 RPM: MAX ENGINE RPM: 6,000; 57.1 hp/l (42 kW/l).

TRANSMISSION gears: 5, fully synchronized; ratios: I 2.916, II 1.764, III 1.181, IV 0.807, V 0.655, rev 2.916; axle ratio: 4.642; width of rims: 4.5''; tyres: 155 SR x 13.

HONDA Civic CVCC 1500 CF Sedan

PERFORMANCE max speeds: (I) 27 mph, 43 km/h; (II) 46 mph, 74 km/h; (III) 71 mph, 115 km/h; (IV) 99 mph, 160 km/h; power-weight ratio: 20.3 lb/hp (27.5 lb/kW), 9.2 kg/hp (12.5 kg/kW).

CHASSIS anti-roll bar on rear suspension.

DIMENSIONS AND WEIGHT wheel base: 88.58 in, 225 cm; length: 152.36 in, 387 cm; weight: 1,722 lb, 780 kg; fuel tank: 8.8 imp gal, 10,6 US gal, 40 l.

OPTIONALS semi-automatic transmission not available.

Accord 1800 Series

PRICES (Tokyo):	yen
GL 2+1-dr Hatchback	**1,033,000**
LX 2+1-dr Hatchback	**1,093,000**
EX 2+1-dr Hatchback	**1,200,000**
EX-L 2+1-dr Hatchback	**1,340,000**
SL 4-dr Sedan	**998,000**
GF 4-dr Sedan	**1,108,000**
EX 4-dr Sedan	**1,225,000**
EX-L 4-dr Sedan	**1,385,000**

ENGINE front, transverse, 4 stroke, stratified charge; 4 cylinders, in line; 106.8 cu in, 1,750 cc (3.03 x 3.70 in, 77 x 94 mm); compression ratio: 8:1; max power (JIS): 90 hp (66 kW) at 5,300 rpm; max torque (JIS): 98 lb ft, 13.5 kg m (132 Nm) at 3,000 rpm; max engine rpm: 5,700; 51.4 hp/l (37.8 kW/l); cast iron block, light alloy head; 5 crankshaft bearings; valves: 3 per cylinders (one intake and one exhaust in main combustion chamber, one intake in auxiliary chamber), overhead, rockers, camshafts: 1, overhead, cogged belt; lubrication: trochoid pump, full flow filter, 7 imp pt, 8.5 US pt, 4 l; 1 Keihin downdraught 3-barrel CVCC carburettor; fuel feed: electric pump; water-cooled, 10.6 imp pt, 12.7 US pt, 6 l.

TRANSMISSION driving wheels: front; clutch: single dry plate (diaphragm), hydraulically controlled; gearbox: mechanical, gears: 5, fully synchronized; ratios: I 3.181, II 1.842, III 1.200, IV 0.896, V 0.718, rev 3; lever central; final drive: helical spur gears; axle ratio: 4.615; width of rims: 5''; tyres: 6.45 x 13 - EX and EX-L models 165 SR x 13.

PERFORMANCE max speeds: (I) 27 mph, 43 km/h; (II) 45 mph, 73 km/h; (III) 71 mph, 115 km/h; (IV) 93 mph, 150 km/h; (V) 93 mph, 150 km/h; power-weight ratio: GL 22 lb/hp (30 lb/kW), 10 kg/hp (13.6 kg/kW); consumption: 29.7 m/imp gal, 24.8 m/US gal, 9.5 l x 100 km.

CHASSIS integral, front auxiliary frame; front suspension: independent, by McPherson, coil springs/telescopic damper struts, lower transverse arms, diagonal links, anti-roll bar; rear: independent, by McPherson, coil springs/telescopic damper struts lower transverse arms, radius rods.

STEERING rack-and-pinion, EX and EX-L models servo; turns lock to lock: 3.50 - EX and EX-L models 2.90.

HONDA Accord EX-L Sedan

HONDA Prelude XR Coupé

BRAKES front disc, rear drum, dual circuit, rear compensator, servo; lining area: front 19.4 sq in, 125 sq cm, rear 34.7 sq in, 224 sq cm, total 54.1 sq in, 349 sq cm.

ELECTRICAL EQUIPMENT 12 V; 35 Ah battery; 50 A alternator; transistorized ignition; 4 headlamps.

DIMENSIONS AND WEIGHT wheel base: 93.70 in, 238 cm; tracks: 55.51 in, 141 cm front, 55.12 in, 140 cm rear; length: GL, LX and EX 2+1-dr 162.40 in, 412 cm - EX-L 2+1-dr 166.54 in, 423 cm - SL 170.28 in, 432 cm - GF and EX 4-dr 171.06 in, 434 cm - EX-L 4-dr 175.20 in, 445 cm; width: 63.78 in, 162 cm; height: 2+1-dr models 52.76 in, 134 cm - 4-dr models 53.54 in, 136 cm; ground clearance: 6.50 in, 16.5 cm; weight: GL 1,984 lb, 900 kg - LX 2,007 lb, 910 kg - EX 2+1-dr 2,040 lb, 925 kg - EX-L 2+1-dr 2,062 lb, 935 kg - SL 2,051 lb, 930 kg - GF 2,062 lb, 935 kg - EX 4-dr 2,117 lb, 960 kg - EX-L 4-dr 2,128 lb 965 kg; weight distribution: 61% front, 39% rear; turning circle: 36.1 ft, 11 m; fuel tank: 11 imp gal, 13.2 US gal, 50 l.

BODY hatchback, 2+1 doors - saloon/sedan, 4 doors.

OPTIONALS Hondamatic semi-automatic transmission, hydraulic torque converter and constant mesh with 3 ratios (I 2.047, II 1.370, III 0.969, rev 1.954), possible manual selection, 3.105 axle ratio, only with 85 hp (63 kW) power team.

Prelude Series

PRICES (Tokyo):	yen
XT 2-dr Coupé	1,160,000
E 2-dr Coupé	1,260,000
XE 2-dr Coupé	1,400,000
XR 2-dr Coupé	1,380,000

90 hp power team

ENGINE front, transverse, 4 stroke, stratified charge; 4 cylinders, in line; 106.8 cu in, 1,750 cc (3.03 x 3.70 in, 77 x 94 mm); compression ratio: 8:1; max power (JIS): 90 hp (66 kW) at 5,300 rpm; max torque (JIS): 98 lb ft, 13.5 kg m (132 Nm) at 3,000 rpm; max engine rpm: 5,700; 51.4 hp/l (37.8 kW/l); cast iron block, light alloy head; 5 crankshaft bearings; valves: 3 per cylinders (one intake and one exhaust in main combustion chamber, one intake in auxiliary chamber), overhead, rockers; camshaft: 1, overhead, cogged belt; lubrication: trochoid pump, full flow filter, 7 imp pt, 8.5 US pt, 4 l; 1 Keihin downdraught 3-barrel CVCC carburettor; fuel feed: electric pump; water-cooled, 9.8 imp pt, 11.8 US pt, 5.6 l.

TRANSMISSION driving wheels: front; clutch: single dry plate (diaphragm), hydraulically controlled; gearbox: mechanical; gears: 5, fully synchronized; ratios: I 3.181, II 1.842, III 1.200, IV 0.896, V 0.718, rev 3; lever: central; final drive: helical spur gears; axle ratio: 4.615; width of rims: 4.5" - XR 5"; tyres: 155 SR x 13 - XR 175/70 SR x 13.

PERFORMANCE max speeds: (I) 27 mph, 43 km/h; (II) 45 mph, 73 km/h; (III) 63 mph, 102 km/h; (IV) 93 mph, 150 km/h; (V) 106 mph, 170 km/h; power-weight ratio: XT 21.8 lb/hp (29.8 lb/kW), 9.9 kg/hp (13.5 kg/kW); consumption: 29.7 m/imp gal, 24.8 m/US gal, 9.5 l x 100 km.

CHASSIS integral; front suspension: independent, by McPherson, coil springs/telescopic damper struts, lower transverse I arms, anti-roll bar; rear: independent, by McPherson, coil springs/telescopic damper struts, trailing arms and transverse arms, anti-roll bar.

STEERING rack-and-pinion; turns lock to lock: 3.20.

BRAKES front disc (diameter 7.36 in, 187 mm), rear drum, dual circuit, servo.

ELECTRICAL EQUIPMENT 12 V; 35 Ah battery; 50 A alternator; transistorized ignition; 2 headlamps.

DIMENSIONS AND WEIGHT wheel base: 91.34 in, 232 cm; tracks: 55.12 in, 140 cm front, 55.51 in, 141 cm rear; length: 161.02 in, 409 cm; width: 64.35 in, 163 cm; height: 51.97 in, 132 cm; ground clearance: 6.30 in, 16 cm; weight: XT 1,962 lb, 890 kg - E 1,973 lb, 895 kg - XE 2,017 lb, 915 kg - XR 1,984 lb, 900 kg; weight distribution: 63.5% front, 36.5% rear; turning circle: 36.1 ft, 11 m; fuel tank: 11 imp gal, 13.2 US gal, 50 l.

BODY coupé; 2 doors; 2+2 seats, separate front seats.

OPTIONALS Hondamatic semi-automatic transmission, hydraulic torque converter and constant mesh with 3 ratios (I 2.047, II 1.370, III 0.969, rev 1.954), possible manual selection, 3.105 axle ratio, only with 85 hp (63 kW) power team; air-conditioning.

ISUZU JAPAN

Gemini Series

PRICES (Tokyo):	yen
1 1600 LD 4-dr Sedan	924,000
2 1600 LD 2-dr Coupé	954,000
3 1600 LT 4-dr Sedan	968,000
4 1600 LT 2-dr Coupé	998,000
5 1600 LS 4-dr Sedan	1,048,000
6 1600 LS 2-dr Coupé	1,105,000
7 1600 Minx 4-dr Sedan	1,040,000
8 1600 Minx 2-dr Coupé	1,070,000
9 1800 LT 4-dr Sedan	1,023,000
10 1800 LT 2-dr Coupé	1,053,000
11 1800 LS 4-dr Sedan	1,088,000
12 1800 LS 2-dr Coupé	1,135,000
13 1800 Minx 4-dr Sedan	1,095,000
14 1800 LS/G 2-dr Coupé	1,210,000
15 LD 4-dr Sedan	1,045,000
16 LT 4-dr Sedan	1,129,000
17 Minx 4-dr Sedan	1,201,000
18 LT Coupé	1,159,000
19 Minx 2-dr Coupé	1,231,000
20 ZZR 4-dr Sedan	1,482,000
21 ZZT 4-dr Sedan	1,612,000
22 ZZR 2-dr Coupé	1,512,000
23 ZZT 2-dr Coupé	1,652,000

ISUZU Gemini 1800 LS/G Coupé

Power team:	Standard for:	Optional for:
100 hp	1 to 8	—
110 hp	9 to 14	—
130 hp	20 to 23	—
61 hp (diesel)	15 to 19	—

100 hp power team

ENGINE front, 4 stroke; 4 cylinders, in line; 97.6 cu in, 1,584 cc (3.23 x 2.95 in, 82 x 75 mm); compression ratio: 8.7:1; max power (JIS): 100 hp (74 kW) at 6,000 rpm; max torque (JIS): 101 lb ft, 14 kg m (136 Nm) at 4,000 rpm; max engine rpm: 6,500; 63.1 hp/l (46.4 kW/l); cast iron block, light alloy head; 5 crankshaft bearings; valves: overhead, rockers; camshafts: 1, overhead; lubrication: rotary pump, full flow filter, 8.8 imp pt, 10.6 US pt, 5 l; 1 Nikki-Stromberg downdraught twin barrel carburettor, catalytic converter secondary air injection and exhaust gas recirculation; fuel feed: electric pump; water-cooled, 10.8 imp pt, 12.7 US pt, 6 l.

TRANSMISSION driving wheels: rear; clutch: single dry plate (diaphragm); gearbox: mechanical; gears: 4, fully synchronized; ratios: I 3.506, II 2.174, III 1.417, IV 1, rev 3.826; lever: central; final drive: hypoid bevel; axle ratio: 3.909; width of rims: 5"; tyres: 6.15 x 13 - 1600 LS 4-dr Sedan Z78 x 13 - 1600 LS 2-dr Coupé 155 SR x 13.

PERFORMANCE max speeds: (I) 29 mph, 47 km/h; (II) 48 mph, 78 km/h; (III) 73 mph, 117 km/h; (IV) 103 mph, 165 km/h; power-weight ratio: 1600 LD 4-dr Sedan 20.7 lb/hp (28.2 lb/kW), 9.4 kg/hp (12.7 kg/kW); carrying capacity: 882 lb, 400 kg; speed in direct drive at 1,000 rpm: 16.2 mph, 26.1 km/h; consumption: 39.8 m/imp gal, 33.1 m/US gal, 7.1 l x 100 km.

100 HP POWER TEAM

CHASSIS integral; front suspension: independent, wishbones, coil springs, anti-roll bar, telescopic dampers; rear: rigid axle, lower radius arms, torque tube, Panhard rod, coil springs, telescopic dampers.

STEERING rack-and-pinion; turns lock to lock: 4.20.

BRAKES front disc, rear drum, servo; lining area: front 17.4 sq in, 112 sq cm, rear 49 sq in, 316 sq cm, total 66.4 sq in, 428 sq cm.

ELECTRICAL EQUIPMENT 12 V; 35 Ah battery; alternator; Hitachi distributor; 2 headlamps.

DIMENSIONS AND WEIGHT wheel base: 94.49 in, 240 cm; tracks: 51.18 in, 130 cm front, 51.38 in, 130 cm rear; length: 165.75 in, 421 cm; width: 61.81 in, 157 cm; height: sedans 53.54 in, 136 cm - coupés 52.36 in, 133 cm; ground clearance: 6.30 in, 16 cm; weight: LD sedan 2,075 lb, 940 kg - LT and Minx sedans 2,086 lb, 945 kg - LS sedan 2,097 lb, 950 kg - LD Coupé 2,031 lb, 920 kg - LT Coupé 2,042 lb, 925 kg - LS Coupé 2,053 lb, 930 kg; weight distribution: 55% front, 45% rear; turning circle: 32.8 ft, 10 m; fuel tank: 11.4 imp gal, 13.7 US gal, 52 l.

BODY saloon/sedan, 4 doors - coupés, 2 doors; 4 seats, separate front seats.

OPTIONALS 5-speed mechanical gearbox (V 0.855); Borg-Warner automatic transmission, hydraulic torque converter and planetary gears with 3 ratios (I 2.450, II 1.450, III 1, rev 2.222), with max power (DIN) 94 hp (69 kW) at 5,400 rpm, max torque (DIN) 99 lb ft, 13.6 kg m (133 Nm) at 3,800 rpm, 59.3 hp/l (43.6 kW/l), power-weight ratio 22.5 lb/hp (30 lb/kW), 10.2 kg/hp (13.6 kg/kW), max speed 99 mph, 160 km/h; (for 1600 LS 2-dr Coupé only air-conditioning.

110 hp power team

See 100 hp power team, except for:

ENGINE 110.9 cu in, 1,817 cc (3.31 x 2.23 in, 84 x 82 mm); compression ratio: 8.5:1; max power (JIS): 110 hp (81 kW) at 5,600 rpm; max torque (JIS): 112 lb ft, 15.5 kg m (152 Nm) at 4,000 rpm; 60.5 hp/l (44.5 kW/l).

TRANSMISSION gears: 4, fully synchronized; ratios: I 3.207, II 1.989, III 1.356, IV 1, V 0.855, rev 3.438; axle ratio: 3.909, tyres: LS models 155 SR x 13 - 1800 LS/G Coupé 175/70 SR x 13.

PERFORMANCE max speed: 106 mph, 170 km/h; power-weight ratio: sedans 19.2 lb/hp (26.2 lb/kW), 8.7 kg/hp (11.9 kg/kW).

DIMENSIONS AND WEIGHT weight: sedans 2,019 lb, 960 kg - coupés 2,075 lb, 940 kg - LS/G Coupé 2,086 lb, 945 kg.

OPTIONALS with 3-speed automatic transmission engine max power (JIS) 105 hp (77 kW) at 5,400 rpm, 57.8 hp/l (42.5 kW/l), power-weight ratio sedans 20.1 lb/hp (27.6 lb/kW), 9.1 kg/hp (12.5 kg/kW).

130 hp power team

See 100 hp power team, except for:

ENGINE 110.9 cu in, 1,817 cc (3.31 x 3.23 in, 84 x 82 mm); compression ratio: 9:1; max power (JIS): 130 hp (96 kW) at 6,400 rpm; max torque (JIS): 120 lb ft, 16.5 kg m (162 Nm) at 5,000 rpm; max engine rpm: 6,800; 71.5 hp/l (52.7 kW/l); valves: overhead, thimble tappets; camshafts: 2, overhead, cogged belt; electronic injection; 3-way catalytic converter with oxygen sensor.

TRANSMISSION gears: 5, fully synchronized; ratios: I 3.207, II 1.989, III 1.356, IV 1, V 0.855, rev 3.438; width of rims: ZZT models 5" - ZZR models 5.5"; tyres: 175 HR x 13.

PERFORMANCE max speeds: (I) 35 mph, 56 km/h; (II) 57 mph, 92 km/h; (III) 91 mph, 146 km/h; (IV) 112 mph, 180 km/h; (V) 112 mph, 180 km/h; power-weight ratio: ZZR Sedan 16.9 lb/hp (22.9 lb/kW), 7.6 kg/hp (10.4 kg/kW); speed in direct drive at 1,000 rpm: 16.5 mph, 26.5 km/h; consumption: 31 m/imp gal, 26 m/US gal, 9.1 l x 100 km.

CHASSIS anti-roll bar on rear suspension.

BRAKES disc, servo; lining area: front 17.4 sq in, 112 sq cm, rear 17.4 sq in, 112 sq cm, total 34.8 sq in, 224 sq cm.

ELECTRICAL EQUIPMENT 50 A alternator; electronic ignition.

DIMENSIONS AND WEIGHT tracks: 51.57 in, 131 cm front, 51.97 in, 132 cm rear; length: 166.53 in, 423 cm; width: 61.81 in, 157 cm; height: sedans 53.54 in, 136 cm - Coupés 52.76 in, 134 cm; ground clearance: 6.30 in, 16 cm; weight: ZZR Sedan 2,196 lb, 995 kg - ZZT Sedan 2,218 lb, 1,005 kg; weight distribution: 57% front, 43% rear.

OPTIONALS limited slip differential; close-ratio gearbox ratios (I 3.507, II 2.175, III 1.418, IV 1, V 0.855, rev 3.759).

ISUZU Gemini 1800 Minx Sedan

61 hp (diesel) power team

See 100 hp power team, except for:

ENGINE diesel; 110, 9 cu in, 1,817 cc (3.31 x 3.23 in, 84 x 82 mm); compression ratio: 21:1; max power (JIS): 61 hp (46 kW) at 5,000 rpm; max torque (JIS): 81 lb ft, 11.2 kg m (110 Nm) at 2,000 rpm; max engine rpm: 5,200; 33.5 hp/l (25 kW/l); cast iron block and head; lubrication: 9.7 imp pt, 11.7 US pt, 5.5 l; Bosch VE diesel injection; cooling, 12.2 imp pt, 14.4 US pt, 7 l.

TRANSMISSION gears: 4 - LT and Minx models 5; ratios: I 3.467, II 1.989, III 1.356, IV 1, rev 3.500 - LT and Minx models V 0.782; axle ratio: 3.583; tyres: 6.15 x 13 - LT and Minx models 155 SR x 13.

PERFORMANCE max speeds: (I) 26 mph, 42 km/h; (II) 46 mph, 74 km/h; (III) 68 mph, 110 km/h; (IV) 90 mph, 145 km/h; power-weight ratio: LD Sedan 35.8 lb/hp (48.7 lb/kW), 16.2 kg/hp (22 kg/kW); speed in direct drive at 1,000 rpm: 17.4 mph, 27.9 km/h; consumption: 80 m/imp gal, 67 m/US gal, 3.4 l x 100 km at 37 mph, 60 km/h.

ELECTRICAL EQUIPMENT 65 Ah battery; 50 A alternator.

DIMENSIONS AND WEIGHT weight: LD Sedan 2,185 lb, 990 kg - LT and Minx sedans 2,207 lb 1,000 kg - LT and Minx coupés 2,163, 980 kg; weight distribution: 58% front, 42% rear.

OPTIONALS automatic transmission (for LT and Minx models only).

Florian SII Series

PRICES (Tokyo):	yen
1 1800 De Luxe 4-dr Sedan	1,252,000
2 1800 Super De Luxe 4-dr Sedan	1,424,000
3 Diesel 2000 Semi-De Luxe 4-dr Sedan	1,263,000
4 Diesel 2000 De Luxe 4-dr Sedan	1,308,000
5 Diesel 2000 Super De Luxe 4-dr Sedan	1,480,000

Power team:	Standard for:	Optional for:
110 hp	1,2	—
62 hp (diesel)	3 to 5	—

110 hp power team

ENGINE front, 4 stroke; 4 cylinders, vertical, in line; 110.9 cu in, 1,817 cc (3.31 x 3.23 in, 84 x 82 mm); compression ratio 8.8:1; max power (JIS): 110 hp (81 kW) at 5,600 rpm; max torque (JIS): 112 lb ft, 15.5 kg m (152 Nm) at 4,000 rpm; max engine rpm: 6,300; 60.4 hp/l (44.5 kW/l); cast iron block, light alloy head; 5 crankshaft bearings; valves: overhead, Vee slanted, rockers; camshafts: 1, overhead; lubrication: rotary pump, full flow filter, 6.3 imp pt, 7.6 US pt, 3.6 l; 1 Stromberg downdraught twin barrel carburettor, catalytic converter, secondary air injection and exhaust gas recirculation; fuel feed mechanical pump; water-cooled, 10.6 imp pt, 12.7 US pt, 6 l.

TRANSMISSION driving wheels: rear; clutch: single dry plate (diaphragm); gearbox: mechanical; gears: 5, fully synchronized ratios: I 3.207, II 1.989, III 1.356, IV 1, V 0.855, rev 3.438

ISUZU Florian SII 1800 De Luxe Sedan

lever: central; final drive: hypoid bevel; axle ratio: 3.727; width of rims: 4.5"; tyres: 6.45 x 13.

PERFORMANCE max speed: 99 mph, 160 km/h; power-weight ratio: De Luxe 22.8 lb/hp (31 lb/kW), 10.3 kg/hp (14.1 kg/kW); consumption: not declared.

CHASSIS integral; front suspension: independent, wishbones, coil springs, anti-roll bar, telescopic dampers; rear: rigid axle, semi-elliptic leafsprings, telescopic dampers.

STEERING worm and roller; turns lock to lock: 3.50.

BRAKES front disc, rear drum, servo; lining area: front 16.7 sq in, 108 sq cm, rear 57.5 sq in, 371 sq cm, total 74.2 sq in, 479 sq cm.

ELECTRICAL EQUIPMENT 12 V; 35 Ah battery; 40 A alternator; Hitachi distributor; 4 headlamps.

DIMENSIONS AND WEIGHT wheel base: 98.43 in, 250 cm; tracks: 52.56 in, 133 cm front, 51.77 in, 131 cm rear; length: 174.41 in, 443 cm; width: 63.78 in, 162 cm; height: 56.89 in, 144 cm; ground clearance: 6.69 in, 17 cm; weight: De Luxe 2,285 lb, 1,035 kg - Super De Luxe 2,296 lb, 1,040 kg; weight distribution: 55% front, 45% rear; turning circle: 34.1 ft, 10.4 m; fuel tank: 9.7 imp gal, 11.6 US gal, 44 l.

BODY saloon/sedan; 4 doors; 5 seats, separate front seats.

62 hp (diesel) power team

See 110 hp power team, except for:

ENGINE diesel; 119.1 cu in, 1,951 cc (3.39 x 3.31 in, 86 x 84 mm); compression ratio: 20:1; max power (JIS): 62 hp (46 kW) at 4,400 rpm; max torque (JIS): 91 lb ft, 12.5 kg m (123 Nm) at 2,200 rpm; valves: overhead, Vee-slanted, push-rods and rockers; lubrication: 11.4 imp pt, 13.7 US pt, 6.5 l; Bosch injection; cooling, 13.2 imp pt, 15.9 US pt, 7.5 l.

TRANSMISSION gears: 5 Semi-De Luxe 4, fully synchronized; ratios: I 3.467, II 1.989, III 1.356, IV 1, V 0.855, rev 3.483 - Semi-De Luxe I 3.467, II 1.989, III 1.356, IV 1, rev 3.499; axle ratio 4.100.

PERFORMANCE max speeds: (I) 22 mph, 35 km/h, (II) 39 mph, 62 km/h; (III) 59 mph, 95 km/h; (IV) 75 mph, 120 km/h; (V) 81 mph, 131 km/h; power-weight ratio: Semi-De Luxe 39 lb/hp (52.7 lb/kW), 17.7 kg/hp (23.9 kg/kW); consumption: 58.8 m/imp gal, 49 m/US gal, 4.8 l x 100 km at 37 mph, 60 km/h.

DIMENSIONS AND WEIGHT weight: Semi-De Luxe 2,426 lb, 1,100 kg - De Luxe and Super De Luxe 2,492 lb, 1,130 kg.

117 Series

PRICES (Tokyo):	yen
1 XT 1800 2-dr Coupé	1,527,000
2 XT 1950 2-dr Coupé	—
3 XTL 1950 2-dr Coupé	—
4 XC 1950 2-dr Coupé	1,765,000
5 XCJ 1950 2-dr Coupé	—
6 Giugiaro 2-dr Coupé	1,983,000
7 XG 2-dr Coupé	2,096,000
8 XE 2-dr Coupé	—
9 XD 2-dr Coupé	1,855,000
10 XDL 2-dr Coupé	1,990,000

Power team:	Standard for:	Optional for:
110 hp	1	—
115 hp	2,3	—
120 hp	4 to 6	—
135 hp	7,8	—
73 hp (diesel)	9,10	—

110 hp power team

ENGINE front, 4 stroke; 4 cylinders, vertical, in line; 110.9 cu in, 1,817 cc (3.31 x 3.23 in, 84 x 82 mm); compression ratio: 8.8:1; max power (JIS): 110 hp (81 kW) at 5,600 rpm; max torque (JIS): 112 lb ft, 15.5 kg m (152 Nm) at 4,000 rpm; max engine rpm: 6,600 60.4 hp/l (44.5 kW/l); cast iron block, light alloy head; 5 crankshaft bearings; valves: overhead, rockers; camshafts: 1, overhead; lubrication: rotary pump, full flow filter, 14.1 imp pt, 16.9 US pt, 8 l; 1 Stromberg downdraught twin barrel carburettor; fuel feed: mechanical pump, emission control with secondary air injection, catalytic converter; water-cooled, 15.8 imp pt, 19 US pt, 9 l.

TRANSMISSION driving wheels: rear; clutch: single dry plate (diaphragm); gearbox: mechanical; gears: 5, fully synchronized; ratios: I 3.207, II 1.989, III 1.355, IV 1, V 0.855, rev 3.438; lever: central; final drive: hypoid bevel; axle ratio: 3.727; tyres: 6.45 x 13.

PERFORMANCE max speed: 109 mph, 175 km/h; power-weight ratio: 21.2 lb/hp (28.9 lb/kW), 9.6 kg/hp (13.1 kg/kW); consumption: 30 m/imp gal, 25 m/US gal, 9.5 l x 100 km.

CHASSIS integral with platform; front suspension: independent, wishbones, coil springs, anti-roll bar, telescopic dampers; rear: rigid axle, semi-elliptic leafsprings, telescopic dampers.

ISUZU 117 XE Coupé

ISUZU 117 XE Coupé

STEERING recirculating ball; turns lock to lock: 3.50.

BRAKES front disc, rear drum, servo; lining area: front 16.7 sq in, 108 sq cm, rear 57.5 sq in, 371 sq cm, total 74.2 sq in, 479 sq cm.

ELECTRICAL EQUIPMENT 12 V; 35 Ah battery; 55 A alternator; Hitachi D408-53 alternator; 4 headlamps.

DIMENSIONS AND WEIGHT wheel base: 98.43 in, 250 cm; tracks: 53.15 in, 135 cm front, 51.57 in, 131 cm rear; length: 170.08 in, 432 cm; width: 62.99 in, 160 cm; height: 51.97 in, 132 cm; ground clearance: 70.87 in, 18 cm; weight: 2,337 lb, 1,060 kg; weight distribution: 55% front, 45% rear; turning circle: 37.4 ft, 11.4 m; fuel tank: 12.3 imp gal, 14.8 US gal, 56 l.

BODY coupé; 2 doors; 4 seats, separate front seats, reclining backrests, built-in headrests.

115 hp power team

See 110 hp power team, except for:

ENGINE 118.9 cu in, 1,949 cc (3.43 x 3.23 in, 87 x 82 mm); max power (JIS): 115 hp (85 kW) at 5,600 rpm; max torque (JIS): 115 lb ft, 16 kg m (157 Nm) at 3,800 rpm; 58.9 hp/l (43.4 kW/l).

TRANSMISSION tyres: XTL 165 SR x 13.

PERFORMANCE power-weight ratio: XT 20.5 lb/hp (27.9 lb/kW), 9.3 kg/hp (12.6 kg/kW).

DIMENSIONS AND WEIGHT weight: XT 2,359 lb, 1,070 kg - XTL 2,370 lb, 1,075 kg.

OPTIONALS Aishin Warner automatic transmission, hydraulic torque converter and planetary gears with 3 ratios (I 2.450, II 1.450, III 1, rev 2.222).

120 hp power team

See 110 hp power team, except for:

ENGINE 118.9 cu in, 1,949 cc (3.43 x 3.23 in, 87 x 82 mm); max power (JIS): 120 hp (79 kW) at 5,800 rpm; max torque (JIS): 119 lb ft, 16.5 kg m (162 Nm) at 4,000 rpm; max engine rpm: 6,800; 61.5 hp/l (45.3 kW/l); electronic injection.

TRANSMISSION axle ratio: 3.909; tyres: 165 SR x 13.

PERFORMANCE max speed: 109 mph, 175 km/h; power-weight ratio: XC 20 lb/hp (27.2 lb/kW), 9.1 kg/hp (12.3 kg/kW).

BRAKES rear disc.

OPTIONALS Aishin Warner automatic transmission, hydraulic torque converter and planetary gears with 3 ratios (I 2.450, II 1.450, III 1, rev 2.222); 3.727 axle ratio.

135 hp power team

See 110 hp power team, except for:

ENGINE 118.9 cu in, 1,949 cc (3.43 x 3.23 in, 87 x 82 mm); compression ratio: 9:1; max power (JIS): 135 (99 kW) at 6,200 rpm; max torque (JIS): 123 lb ft, 17 kg m (167 Nm) at 5,000 rpm; max engine rpm: 6,800; 69.3 hp/l (51 kW/l); valves: overhead, thimble tappets; camshafts: 2, 1 per bank, overhead; lubrication: rotary pump, full flow filter, 8.8 imp pt, 10.6 US pt, 5 l; Bosch electronic injection, emission control 3-way catalyst with oxygen sensor, exhaust gas recirculation.

TRANSMISSION axle ratio: 3.909.

PERFORMANCE max speeds: (I) 35 mph, 57 km/h; (II) 58 mph, 93 km/h; (III) 72 mph, 116 km/h; (IV) 112 mph, 180 km/h; power-weight ratio: XG 18.3 lb/hp (24.9 lb/kW), 8.3 kg/hp (11.3 kg/kW); consumption: 26.9 m/imp gal, 22.4 m/US gal, 10.5 l x 100 km.

CHASSIS rear suspension; rigid axle, semi-elliptic leafsprings, torque arms, anti-roll bar, telescopic dampers.

STEERING XG, recirculating ball, variable ratio - XE, servo.

BRAKES disc.

DIMENSIONS AND WEIGHT weight: XG 2,459 lb, 1,115 kg - XE 2,525 lb, 1,145 kg.

OPTIONALS Aishin Warner automatic transmission, hydraulic torque converter and planetary gears with 3 ratios (I 2.450, II 1.450, III 1,rev 2.222); air-conditioning.

73 hp (diesel) power team

See 110 hp power team, except for:

ENGINE diesel; 136 cu in, 2,238 cc (3.46 x 3.62 in, 88 x 92 mm); compression ratio: 21:1; max power (JIS): 73 hp (54 kW) at 4,300 rpm; max torque (JIS): 108 lb ft, 14.2 kg m (139 Nm) at

73 HP (DIESEL) POWER TEAM

2,400 rpm; max engine rpm: 4,700; 32.6 hp/l (24 kW/l); valves: overhead, push-rods and rockers; Ricardo Commet swirl combustion chamber; camshafts: 1, side; lubrication: 11.4 imp pt, 13.4 US pt, 6.5 l; Bosch injection; cooling, 12.3 imp pt, 14.4 US pt, 7 l.

TRANSMISSION gearbox ratio: V 0.782; axle ratio: 3.909; tyres: XD, 165 SR x 13 - XDL, 185/70 HR x 13.

PERFORMANCE max speed: 81 mph, 130 km/h; power-weight ratio: XD 35.3 lb/hp (47.9 lb/kW), 16 kg/hp (21.7 kg/kW); consumption: 53 m/imp gal, 44 m/US gal, 5.3 l x 100 km at 37 mph, 60 km/h.

CHASSIS torque rods and anti-roll bar on rear suspension.

STEERING XD variable ratio - XDL, servo.

BRAKES disc, servo.

ELECTRICAL EQUIPMENT 70 Ah battery; 50 A alternator.

DIMENSIONS AND WEIGHT weight: XD 2,572 lb, 1,165 kg - XDL 2,616 lb, 1185 kg.

OPTIONALS Aishin Warner automatic transmission, hydraulic torque converter and planetary gears with 3 ratios (I 2.450, II 1.450, III 1, rev 2.222).

MAZDA Familia GLC De Luxe Station Wagon

MAZDA — JAPAN

Familia AP Series

PRICES (Tokyo):		yen
1	1300 Standard 2+1-dr Sedan	**645,000**
2	1300 XC 2+1-dr Sedan	**685,000**
3	1300 XT 2+1-dr Sedan	**790,000**
4	1300 XL 2+1-dr Sedan	**830,000**
5	1300 XC 4+1-dr Sedan	**720,000**
6	1300 XT 4+1-dr Sedan	**825,000**
7	1300 XL 4+1-dr Sedan	**865,000**
8	1400 XG 2+1-dr Sedan	**898,000**
9	1400 XE 4+1-dr Sedan	**948,000**

Power team:	Standard for:	Optional for:
70 hp	1 to 7	—
80 hp	8,9	—

70 hp power team

ENGINE front, 4 stroke (1978 emission models, Mazda stabilized combustion engine with secondary air induction exhaust gas recirculation and 3-way catalyst); 4 cylinders, in line; 77.6 cu in, 1,272 cc (2.87 x 2.99 in, 73 x 76 mm); compression ratio: 9.2:1; max power (JIS): 70 hp (51 kW) at 5,500 rpm; max torque (JIS): 75 lb ft, 10,4 kg m (102 Nm) at 3,500 rpm; max engine rpm: 6,000; 55 hp/l (40.5 kW/l); cast iron block, light alloy head; 5 crankshaft bearings; valves: overhead, rockers; camshafts: 1, overhead; lubrication: rotary pump, full flow filter, 6,5 imp pt, 7.8 US pt, 3.7 l; 1 2-stage downdraught twin barrel carburettor; fuel feed: mechanical pump; water-cooled, 9.7 imp pt, 11.6 US pt, 5.5 l.

TRANSMISSION driving wheels: rear; clutch: single dry plate (diaphragm); gearbox: mechanical; gears: 4, fully synchronized; ratios: I 3.655, II 2.185, III 1.425, IV 1, rev 3.655); lever: central; final drive: hypoid bevel; axle ratio: 3.727; width of rims: 4.5"; tyres: 6.00 x 12.

PERFORMANCE max speeds: (I) 25 mph, 40 km/h; (II) 43 mph, 70 km/h; (III) 66 mph, 107 km/h; (IV) 90 mph, 145 km/h; power-weight ratio: Standard 24.5 lb/hp (33.7 lb/kW), 11.1 kg/hp (15.3 kg/kW); acceleration: standing ¼ mile 20.2 sec, 0-50 mph (0-80 km/h) 11 sec; speed in direct drive at 1,000 rpm: 15.3 mph, 24.6 km/h; consumption: 42 m/imp gal, 35 m/US gal, 6.7 l x 100 km.

CHASSIS integral; front suspension: independent, by McPherson, coil springs/telescopic damper struts, lower wishbones (trailing links), anti-roll bar; rear: rigid axle, lower trailing arms, upper torque rods, coil springs, telescopic dampers.

STEERING recirculating ball; turns lock to lock: 3.50.

BRAKES drum, dual circuit - XC, XT and XL models front disc, servo; lining area: front 39.7 sq in, 256 sq cm, rear 39.7 sq in, 256 sq cm, total 79.4 sq in, 512 sq cm.

ELECTRICAL EQUIPMENT 12 V; 32 Ah battery; 35 A alternator; 2 headlamps.

DIMENSIONS AND WEIGHT wheel base: 91.14 in, 231 cm; tracks: 50.98 in, 129 cm front, 51.57 in, 131 cm rear; length: Standard and XC models 153.35 in, 389 cm - XT and XL models 153.94 in, 391 cm; width: 63.19 in, 160 cm; height: 53.94 in, 137 cm; ground clearance: 6.30 in, 16 cm; weight: Standard 2+1-dr Sedan 1,720 lb, 780 kg - XC 2+1-dr Sedan 1,742 lb, 790 kg - XT 2+1-dr Sedan 1,753 lb, 795 kg - XL 2+1-dr Sedan 1,775 lb, 805 kg - XC 4+1-dr Sedan 1,775 lb, 805 kg - XT 4+1-dr Sedan 1,797 lb, 815 kg - XL 4+1-dr Sedan 1,808 lb, 820 kg; weight distribution: 56% front, 44% rear; fuel tank: 8.8 imp gal, 10.6 US gal, 40 l.

BODY saloon/sedan; 2+1 or 4+1 doors; 4 seats, separate front seats, built-in headrests, reclining front and rear seats.

80 hp power team

See 70 hp power team, except for:

ENGINE 86.3 cu in, 1,415 cc (3.03 x 2.99 in, 77 x 76 mm); compression ratio: 9:1; max power (JIS): 80 hp (59 kW) at 5,500 rpm; max torque (JIS): 88 lb ft, 11.6 kg m (114 Nm) at 3,500 rpm; 56.5 hp/l (41.6 kW/l).

TRANSMISSION gears: XG, 5, fully synchronized (V ratio 0.827); axle ratio: 3.636; tyres: 155 SR x 13.

PERFORMANCE max speeds: (I) 27 mph, 43 km/h; (II) 43 mph, 70 km/h; (III) 68 mph, 110 km/h; (IV) 93 mph, 150 km/h; power-weight ratio: XG 22.6 lb/hp (30.7 lb/kW), 10.2 kg/hp (13.9 kg/kW); consumption: 41 m/imp gal, 34 m/US gal, 6.9 l x 100 km.

BRAKES front disc.

DIMENSIONS AND WEIGHT length: 153.94 in, 391 cm; weight: XG 2+1-dr Sedan 1,808 lb, 820 kg - XE 4+1-dr Sedan 1,819 lb, 825 kg.

OPTIONALS (for XE only) 5-speed mechanical gearbox, V ratio 0.827; JATCO 3N 71B automatic transmission, hydraulic torque converter and planetary gears with 3 ratios (I 2.458, II 1.458, III 1, rev 2.181), 3.909 axle ratio only with 82 hp (60 kW) at 5,700 rpm engine.

Familia (USA) Series

PRICES IN USA:		$
1	GLC Regular 2+1-dr Sedan	**3,695**
2	GLC De Luxe 2+1-dr Sedan	**3,995**
3	GLC De Luxe 4+1-dr Sedan	**4,145**
4	GLC De Luxe 4+1-dr St. Wagon	**4,445**

Power team:	Standard for:	Optional for:
52 hp	1 to 3	—
65 hp	4	—

52 hp power team

ENGINE front, 4 stroke; catalytic converter air induction, EGR (catalytic converter air injection, EGR for California only); 4 cylinders, in line; 77.6 cu in, 1,272 cc (2.87 x 2.99 in, 73 x 76 mm); compression ratio: 9.2:1; max power (DIN): 52 hp (38 kW) [49 hp (36 kW) for California only] at 5,000 rpm; max torque (DIN): 64 lb ft, 8.8 kg m (86 Nm) [63 lb ft, 8.7 kg m (85 Nm) for California only] at 3,000 rpm; max engine rpm: 6,000; 40.9 hp/l (30.1 kW/l) [38.5 hp/l (28.3 kW/l) for California only]; cast iron block, light alloy head: 5 crankshaft bearings; valves: overhead, rockers; camshafts: 1, overhead; lubrication: rotary pump, full flow filter, 6.5 imp pt, 7.8 US pt, 3.7 l; 1 2-stage downdraught twin barrel carburettor; fuel feed: mechanical pump; water-cooled, 9.7 imp pt, 11.6 US pt, 5.5 l.

TRANSMISSION driving wheels: rear; clutch: single dry plate (diaphragm); gearbox: mechanical; gears: 4, fully synchronized; ratios: I 3.655, II 2.185, III 1.425, IV 1, rev 3.655; lever: central; final drive: hypoid bevel; axle ratio: 3.727; width of rims: 4.5"; tyres: 6.15 x 13.

PERFORMANCE max speeds: (I) 25 mph, 40 km/h; (II) 43 mph, 70 km/h; (III) 66 mph, 107 km/h; (IV) 86 mph, 138 km/h; power-weight ratio: 37.8 lb/hp (51.4 lb/kW), 17.1 kg/hp (23.2 kg/kW) [40.4 lb/hp (54.9 lb/kW), 17.3 kg/hp (23.5 kg/kW) for California only]: acceleration: standing ¼ mile 20.2 sec, 0-50 mph (0-80 km/h) 11 sec; speed in direct drive at 1,000 rpm: 15.3 mph, 24.6 km/h; consumption: 42 m/imp gal, 35 m/US gal 6.7 l x 100 km.

CHASSIS integral; front suspension: independent, by McPherson, coil springs/telescopic damper struts, lower wishbones (trailing links), anti-roll bar; rear: rigid axle, lower trailing arms, upper torque rods, coil springs, telescopic dampers.

STEERING recirculating ball; turns lock to lock: 3.50.

BRAKES front disc, rear drum; lining area: front 39.7 sq in, 256 sq cm, rear 39.7 sq in, 256 sq cm, total 79.4 sq in, 512 sq cm.

ELECTRICAL EQUIPMENT 12 V; 45 Ah battery (35 Ah battery for California only); 35 A alternator; 2 headlamps.

DIMENSIONS AND WEIGHT wheel base: 91.14 in, 231 cm; tracks: 50.98 in, 129 cm front, 51.57 in, 131 cm rear; length

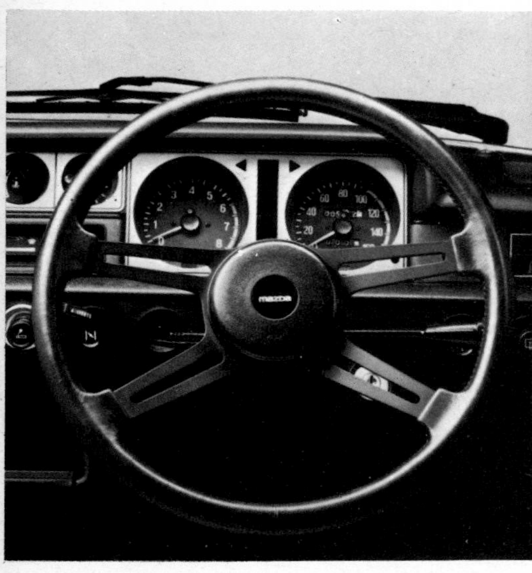

MAZDA Familia AP 1400 XG Sedan

54.33 in, 392 cm; width: 63.19 in, 160 cm; height: 53.94 in, 37 cm; ground clearance: 6.30 in, 16 cm; weight: 1,965 lb, 891 g (1,980 lb, 898 kg for California only); weight distribution: 6% front, 44% rear; fuel tank: 8.8 imp gal, 10.6 US gal, 40 l.

ODY saloon/sedan; 2+1 or 4+1 doors; 4 seats, separate front eats, built-in headrests, reclining front and rear seats.

PTIONALS 5-speed fully synchronized mechanical gearbox (I 655, II 2.185, III 1.425, IV 1, V 0.827); JATCO 3N 71B utomatic transmission, hydraulic torque converter and planet- ry gears with 3 ratios (I 2.458, II 1.458, III 1, rev 2.181), 4.100 xle ratio; 155 SR x 13 tyres; air-conditioning.

65 hp power team

ee 52 hp power team, except for:

NGINE 86.3 cu in, 1,415 cc (3.03 x 2.99 in, 77 x 76 mm); ompression ratio: 9:1; max power (DIN): 65 hp (48 kW) at 000 rpm; max torque (DIN): 76 lb ft, 10.5 kg m (103 Nm) at 000 rpm; 45.9 hp/l (33.8 kW/l).

RANSMISSION gears: 5; ratio: V 0.831; axle ratio: 3.636; res: 155 SR x 13 (standard).

ERFORMANCE max speeds: (I) 27 mph, 43 km/h; (II) 43 mph,) km/h; (III) 68 mph, 110 km/h; (IV) 96 mph, 155 km/h; ower-weight ratio: 32.6 lb/hp (44.3 lb/kW), 14.8 kg/hp (20.1 g/kW); consumption: 41 m/imp gal, 34 m/US gal, 6,9 l x 100 n.

HASSIS rear suspension: rigid axle, semi-elliptic leafsprings, lescopic dampers.

RAKES front disc.

IMENSIONS AND WEIGHT length: 163.19 in, 414 cm; height: 6.10 in, 142 cm; weight: 2,117 lb, 960 kg.

ODY estate car/st. wagon; 4+1 doors.

PTIONALS 5-speed mechanical gearbox, V ratio 0.831; JAT- O 3N 71B automatic transmission, with 3 ratios, 4.100 axle tio; air-conditioning.

Capella Series

RICES (Tokyo):	yen
1 1600 Standard Sedan	**850,000**
2 1600 De Luxe Sedan	**910,000**
3 1600 GL Sedan	**960,000**
4 1600 Super Custom Sedan	**1,030,000**
5 1600 De Luxe Hardtop	**945,000**
6 1600 GL Hardtop	**995,000**
7 1600 Super Custom Hardtop	**1,080,000**
8 1800 GL Sedan	**1,040,000**
9 1800 GL Hardtop	**1,100,000**
0 1800 Super Custom Sedan	**1,110,000**
1 1800 Super Custom Hardtop	**1,170,000**
2 2000 Limited Sedan	**1,295,000**
3 2000 Limited Hardtop	**1,330,000**

ower team:	Standard for:	Optional for:
0 hp	1 to 7	—
0 hp	8 to 11	—
0 hp	12, 13	—

90 hp power team

NGINE front, 4 stroke; 4 cylinders, in line; 96.8 cu in, 1,586 cc .07 x 3.27 in, 78 x 83 mm); compression ratio: 8.6:1; max ower (JIS): 90 hp (66 kW) at 5,700 rpm; max torque (JIS): 94 ft, 13 kg m (127 Nm) at 3,500 rpm; max engine rpm: 6,000; .7 hp/l (41.7 kW/l); cast iron block, light alloy head; 5 ankshaft bearings; valves: overhead, rockers; camshafts: 1, erhead; lubrication: rotary pump, full flow filter, 7.2 imp pt, 7 US pt, 4.1 l; 1 Nikki 242302 downdraught twin barrel rburettor with automatic air-fuel ratio adjustment; Mazda sta- ized combustion system, secondary air induction, EGR, 3- ay catalytic; fuel feed: electric pump; water-cooled, 12.3 imp , 14.8 US pt, 7 l.

RANSMISSION driving wheels: rear; clutch: single dry plate iaphragm); gearbox: mechanical; gears: 4, fully synchronized; tios: I 3.403, II 1.925, III 1.373, IV 1, rev 3.665; lever: central; al drive: hypoid bevel; axle ratio: 3.909; width of rims: 4.5" uper Custom models 5"); tyres: 6.45 x 13 (Super Custom odels 165 SR x 13).

ERFORMANCE max speeds: (I) 30 mph, 48 km/h; (II) 50 mph, km/h; (III) 73 mph, 117 km/h; (IV) 99 mph, 160 km/h; wer-weight ratio: Standard Sedan 24 lb/hp (32.6 lb/kW), 10.9 /hp (14.8 kg/kW); consumption: 40.9 m/imp gal, 34.1 m/US l, 6.9 l x 100 km.

HASSIS integral; front suspension: independent by Mc- erson, coil springs/telescopic damper struts, transverse l ms, trailing locating rods, anti-roll bar; rear: rigid axle, lower ailing arms, upper torque rods, Panhard rod, coil springs, lescopic dampers.

TEERING recirculating ball; turns lock to lock: 4.50.

MAZDA Capella 1800 Super Custom Sedan

MAZDA 626 Hardtop Coupé

BRAKES front disc, rear drum, dual circuit, servo; lining area: front 22.9 sq in, 148 sq cm, rear 39.7 sq in, 256 sq cm, total 62.6 sq in, 404 sq cm.

ELECTRICAL EQUIPMENT 12 V; 33 Ah battery; 50 A alterna- tor; IC high energy ignition; 2 headlamps.

DIMENSIONS AND WEIGHT wheel base: 98.82 in, 251 cm; tracks: 53.94 in, 137 cm front, 54.33 in, 138 cm rear; length: 169.49 in, 430 cm; width: 65.35 in, 166 cm; height: sedans 54.33 in, 138 cm - hardtops 53.35 in, 135 cm; ground clear- ance: 6.10 in, 15.5 cm; weight: Standard Sedan 2,161 lb, 980 kg - De Luxe models 2,172 lb, 985 kg - GL models 2,183 lb, 990 kg - Super Custom Sedan 2,205 lb, 1,000 kg - Super Custom Hardtop 2,194 lb, 995 kg; weight distribution: 53.5% front, 46.5% rear; turning circle: 34.7 ft, 10.6 m; fuel tank: 12.1 imp gal, 14.5 US gal, 55 l.

BODY saloon/sedan, hardtop; 5 seats, separate front seats, reclining backrests, built-in headrests.

100 hp power team

See 90 hp power team, except for:

ENGINE 107.9 cu in, 1,769 cc (3.15 x 3.46 in, 80 x 88 mm); max power (JIS): 100 hp (74 kW) at 5,500 rpm; max torque (JIS): 100 lb ft, 15.2 kg m (149 Nm) at 3,300 rpm; 56.5 hp/l (41.6 kW/l).

TRANSMISSION gears: Super Custom models and GL Hardtop 5; ratio: V 0.854; axle ratio: 3.727.

PERFORMANCE max speed: 103 mph, 165 km/h; power-weight ratio: GL Sedan 21.9 lb/hp (29.7 lb/kW), 9.9 kg/hp (13.4 kg/kW); consumption: 35.3 m/imp gal, 29.4 m/US gal, 8 l x 100 km.

DIMENSIONS AND WEIGHT weight: GL Sedan 2,194 lb, 995 kg - GL Hardtop 2,205 lb, 1,000 kg - Super Custom Sedan 2,227 lb, 1,010 kg - Super Custom Hardtop 2,238 lb, 1,015 kg.

OPTIONALS (for Super Custom Sedan only) JATCO automatic transmission with 3 ratios (I 2.458, II 1.458, III 1, rev 2.181); light alloy wheels with 5.5" wide rims; 185/70 SR x 13 tyres; air-conditioning.

110 hp power team

See 90 hp power team, except for:

ENGINE 120.2 cu in, 1,970 cc (3.15 x 3.86 in, 80 x 98 mm); max power (JIS): 110 hp (81 kW) at 5,300 rpm; max torque (JIS): 124 lb ft, 17 kg m (167 Nm) at 3,000 rpm; max engine rpm: 5,800; 55.8 hp/l (41.1 kW/l).

TRANSMISSION axle ratio: 3.636; tyres: 165 SR x 13.

PERFORMANCE max speeds: (I) 27 mph, 43 km/h; (II) 50 mph, 80 km/h; (III) 70 mph, 113 km/h; (IV) 99 mph, 160 km/h; power-weight ratio: 21.5 lb/hp (29.2 lb/kW), 9.7 kg/hp (13.2 kg/kW); speed in direct drive at 1,000 rpm: 18.7 mph, 30.2 km/h; consumption: 35 m/imp gal, 29 m/US gal, 8 l x 100 km.

CHASSIS anti-roll bar on rear suspension.

DIMENSIONS AND WEIGHT length: 173.82 in, 441 cm; weight: 2,362 lb, 1,070 kg.

110 HP POWER TEAM

OPTIONALS JATCO automatic transmission with 3 ratios (I 2.458, II 1.458, III 1, rev 2.181).

626 Series

PRICES IN USA:	**$**
4-dr Sedan	**5,495***
2-dr Hardtop Coupé	**5,795***

ENGINE front, 4 stroke; 4 cylinders, in line: 120.2 cu in, 1,970 cc (3.15 x 3.86 in, 80 x 98 mm); compression ratio: 8.6:1; max power (DIN) 90 hp (66 kW) at 4,800 rpm; max torque (DIN): 115 lb ft, 15.9 kg m (156 Nm) at 2,500 rpm; max engine rpm: 6,000; 45.7 hp/l (33.6 kW/l); cast iron block, light alloy head; 5 crankshaft bearings; valves: overhead, rockers; camshafts: 1, overhead; lubrication: rotary pump, full flow filter, 7.7 imp pt, 9.3 US pt, 4.4 l; 1 Nikki 242302 downdraught twin barrel carburettor with automatic air-fuel ratio adjustment; Mazda stabilized combustion system, secondary air induction, EGR, 3-way catalytic; fuel feed: electric pump; water-cooled, 13.2 imp pt, 15.8 US pt, 7.5 l.

TRANSMISSION driving wheels: rear; clutch: single dry plate (diaphragm); gearbox: mechanical; gears: 4, fully synchronized; ratios: I 3.214, II 1.818, III 1,296, IV 1, rev 3.461; lever: central; final drive: hypoid bevel; axle ratio: 3.636; width of rims: 4.5"; tyres: 165 SR x 13.

PERFORMANCE max speed: sedans 106 mph, 170 km/h - hardtops 109 mph, 175 km/h; power-weight ratio: sedans 26 lb/hp (35.3 lb/kW), 11.8 kg/hp (16 kg/kW); consumption: 31 m/imp gal, 25.8 m/US gal, 9.1 l x 100 km.

CHASSIS integral; front suspension: independent by McPherson, coil springs/telescopic damper struts, transverse I arms, trailing locating rods, anti-roll bar; rear: rigid axle, lower trailing arms, upper torque rods, Panhard rod, coil springs, telescopic dampers.

STEERING recirculating ball; turns lock to lock: 4.50.

BRAKES front disc, rear drum, dual circuit, servo; lining area: front 22.9 sq in, 148 sq cm, rear 39.7 sq in, 256 sq cm, total 62.6 sq in, 404 sq cm.

ELECTRICAL EQUIPMENT 12 V; 45 Ah battery; 50 A alternator; IC high energy ignition; 2 headlamps.

DIMENSIONS AND WEIGHT wheel base: 98.82 in, 251 cm; tracks: 53.94 in, 137 cm front, 54.33 in, 138 cm rear; length: 169.49 in, 430 cm; width: 65.35 in, 166 cm; height: sedans 54.33 in, 138 cm - hardtops 53.35 in, 135 cm; ground clearance: 6.10 in, 15.5 cm; weight: sedans 2,337 lb, 1,060 kg - hardtops 2,348 lb, 1,065 kg; weight distribution: 53.5% front, 46.5% rear; turning circle: 34.7 ft, 10.6 m; fuel tank: 12.1 imp gal, 14.5 US gal, 55 l.

BODY saloon/sedan, 4 doors - hardtop coupé, 2 doors; 5 seats, separate front seats, reclining backrests, built-in headrests.

OPTIONALS 5-speed mechanical gearbox, V ratio 0.860; JATCO automatic transmission with 3 ratios (I 2,458, II 1.458, III 1, rev 2.181); light alloy wheels with 5.5" wide rims; 185/70 SR x 13 tyres; air-conditioning.

Luce Series

	PRICES (Tokyo):	**yen**
1	1800 DX Sedan	**1,023,000**
2	1800 GL Sedan	**1,138,000**
3	1800 SG Sedan	**1,258,000**
4	2000 ST Sedan	**1,203,000**
5	2000 SG Sedan	**1,323,000**
6	2000 SGX Sedan	**1,428,000**
7	2000 ST Hardtop	**1,268,000**
8	2000 SG Hardtop	**1,388,000**
9	2000 SGX Hardtop	**1,493,000**
10	RE GT Hardtop	**1,493,000**
11	RE SE-GT Hardtop	**1,703,000**
12	RE Limited Hardtop	**2,058,000**

Power team:	**Standard for:**	**Optional for:**
100 hp	1 to 3	—
110 hp	4 to 9	—
140 hp	10 to 12	—

100 hp power team

ENGINE front, 4 stroke; 4 cylinders, in line; 107.9 cu in, 1,769 cc (3.15 x 3.46 in, 80 x 88 mm); compression ratio: 8.6:1; max power (JIS):100 hp (74 kW) at 5,500 rpm; max torque (JIS):110 lb ft, 15.2 kg m (149 Nm) at 3,300 rpm; max engine rpm: 6,000; 56.5 hp/l (41.6 kW/l); cast iron block, light alloy head; 5 crankshaft bearings; valves: overhead, rockers; camshafts: 1, overhead; lubrication: rotary pump, full flow filter, 7.2 imp pt, 8.7 US pt, 4.1 l; 1 downdraught twin barrel carburettor with automatic air-fuel ratio adjustment; Mazda stabilized combustion system, secondary air induction, EGR, 3-way catalyst; fuel feed: electric pump; water-cooled, 12.3 imp pt, 14.8 US pt, 7 l.

TRANSMISSION driving wheels: rear; clutch: single dry plate (diaphragm); gearbox: mechanical; gears: 4, fully synchronized; ratios: I 3.403, II 2.005, III 1.373, IV 1, rev 3.900; lever: central; final drive: hypoid bevel; axle ratio: 4.100; width of rims: 5"; tyres: 6.45 x 13.

PERFORMANCE max speeds: (I) 29 mph, 46 km/h; (II) 50 mph, 80 km/h; (III) 68 mph, 110 km/h; (IV) 96 mph, 155 km/h; power-weight ratio: DX 24 lb/hp (32.6 lb/kW), 10.9 kg/hp (14.8 kg/kW); carrying capacity: 882 lb, 400 kg; acceleration: standing ¼ mile 17.1 sec; speed in direct drive at 1,000 rpm: 19.5 mph, 31.4 km/h; consumption: 32 m/imp gal, 27 m/US gal, 8.7 l x 100 km.

CHASSIS integral; front suspension: independent, by McPherson, coil springs/telescopic damper struts, lower wishbones, anti-roll bar; rear: rigid axle, lower trailing arms, upper torque rods, Panhard rod, coil springs, telescopic dampers.

STEERING recirculating ball; turns lock to lock: 4.70.

BRAKES front disc, rear drum, dual circuit, servo; lining area: front 26.7 sq in, 172 sq cm, rear 59.5 sq in, 384 sq cm, total 86.2 sq in, 556 sq cm.

ELECTRICAL EQUIPMENT 12 V; 35 Ah battery; 55 A alternator; fully transistorized ignition with pointless contact breaker; 4 headlamps.

DIMENSIONS AND WEIGHT wheel base: 102.76 in, 261 cm; tracks: 56.30 in, 143 cm front, 55.12 in, 140 cm rear; length: 183.66 in, 466 cm; width: 66.54 in, 169 cm; height: 55.71 in, 141 cm; ground clearance: 6.89 in, 17.5 cm; weight: DX 2,406 lb, 1,090 kg - GL 2,417 lb, 1,095 kg - SG 2,472 lb, 1,120 kg; turning circle: 36.7 ft, 11.2 m; fuel tank: 14.3 imp gal, 17.2 US gal 65 l.

BODY saloon/sedan; 4 doors; 5 seats, separate front seats, reclining backrests, built-in headrests.

110 hp power team

See 100 hp power team, except for:

ENGINE 120.2 cu in, 1,970 cc (3.15 x 3.86 in, 80 x 98 mm); max power (JIS): 110 hp (81 kW) at 5,300 rpm; max torque (JIS): 123 lb ft, 17 kg m (167 Nm) at 3.000 rpm; max engine rpm: 5,600; 55.8 hp/l (41.1 kW/l); lubrication: 7.7 imp pt, 9.3 US pt, 4.4 l.

TRANSMISSION gears: 5, fully synchronized; ratios: I 3.403, II 1.925, III 1.373, IV 1, V 0.854, rev 3.665; axle ratio: 3.909; tyres: ST models 6.45 x 14 - SG and SGX models 175 SR x 14 with 5.5" wide rims.

PERFORMANCE max speed: 99 mph, 160 km/h; power-weight ratio: ST Sedan 22.4 lb/hp (30.4 lb/kW), 10.1 kg/hp (13.8 kg/kW); consumption: 29.7 m/imp gal, 24.7 m/US gal, 9.5 l x 100 km.

DIMENSIONS AND WEIGHT length: 183.66 in, 466 cm; weight: ST Sedan 2,464 lb, 1,115 kg - ST Hardtop 2,475 lb, 1,120 kg - SG Sedan 2,508 lb, 1,135 kg - SG Hardtop 2,519 lb, 1,140 lg - SGX models 2,530 lb, 1,145 kg.

BODY saloon/sedan, hardtop; 4 doors; 5 seats, separate front seats, reclining backrests, built-in, adjustable headrests.

OPTIONALS JATCO automatic transmission, hydraulic torque converter and planetary gears with 3 ratios (I 2.458, II 1.458, III 1, rev 2.181); power/steering.

140 hp power team

See 100 hp power team, except for:

ENGINE front, 4 stroke, Wankel rotary type with Mazda emission control system (oxidizing partially 3-way catalytic converter and secondary air injection); 2 co-axial 3-lobe rotors 39.9 x 2 cu in, 654 x 2 cc; max power (JIS): 140 hp (103 kW) at 6,500 rpm; max torque (JIS): 138 lb ft, 19 kg m (186 Nm) at 4,000 rpm; lubrication: trochoid pump, full flow filter, forced lubrication/cooling of rotors, 11 imp pt, 13.3 US pt, 6.3 l; downdraught 4-barrel carburettor; water-cooled housings, 17.[illegible] imp pt, 21.1 US pt, 10 l, oil-cooled rotors.

TRANSMISSION gearbox: mechanical with hydraulic fluid coupling; gears: 5, fully synchronized; ratios: I 3.380, II 2.077, III 1.390, IV 1, V 0.841, rev 3.389; axle ratio: 3.727; width of rims 5.5"; tyres: Limited 175 SR x 14 - GT and SE-GT 195/7[illegible] HR x 14.

PERFORMANCE max speeds: (I) 36 mph, 58 km/h; (II) 59 mph 95 km/h; (III) 90 mph, 145 km/h; (IV) 109 mph, 175 km/h; (V) 109 mph, 175 km/h; power-weight ratio: GT 18.5 lb/hp (25.[illegible] lb/kW), 8.4 kg/hp (11.4 kg/kW); consumption: 22 m/imp ga[illegible] 18.4 m/US gal, 12.8 l x 100 km.

STEERING servo; turns lock to lock: 4.

DIMENSIONS AND WEIGHT weight: 54.53 in, 138 cm; ground clearance: 6.10 in, 155 cm; weight: GT 2,596 lb, 1,175 kg SE-GT 2,651 lb, 1,200 kg - Limited 2,726 lb, 1,235 kg.

BODY hardtop.

OPTIONALS JATCO automatic transmission, hydraulic torque converter and planetary gears with 3 ratios (I 2.458, II 1.458, III 1, rev 2.181), max speed 106 mph, 170 km/h.

Cosmo Series

	PRICES (Tokyo):	**yen**
1	2000 ST Coupé	**1,218,00[illegible]**
2	2000 SG Coupé	**1,353,00[illegible]**
3	2000 SGX Coupé	**1,533,00[illegible]**
4	L 2000 SG Coupé	**1,413,00[illegible]**
5	L 2000 SGX Coupé	**1,648,00[illegible]**
6	RE GT Coupé	**1,498,00[illegible]**
7	RE SE-GT Coupé	**1,648,00[illegible]**
8	RE SE-Limited Coupé	**1,848,00[illegible]**
9	L RE SE-GT Coupé	**1,763,00[illegible]**
10	L RE SE-Limited Coupé	**1,908,00[illegible]**

Power team:	**Standard for:**	**Optional for:**
110 hp	1 to 5	—
140 hp	6 to 10	—

MAZDA Luce RE Limited Hardtop

MAZDA Cosmo L RE SE-Limited Coupé

110 hp power team

:NGINE front, 4 stroke, Mazda stabilized combustion engine vith secondary air induction, exhaust gas recirculation and artial 3-way catalytic converter; 4 cylinders, vertical, in line; 20.2 cu in, 1,970 cc (3.15 x 3.86 in, 80 x 98 mm); compression atio: 8.6:1; max power (JIS): 110 hp (81 kW) at 5,300 rpm; nax torque (JIS): 124 lb/ft, 17 kg m (167 Nm) at 3,000 rpm; nax engine rpm: 6,000; 55.8 hp/l (41.1 kW/l); cast iron block, ght alloy head; 5 crankshaft bearings; valves: overhead, rock-rs; camshafts: 1, overhead; lubrication: rotary pump, full flow lter, 6.3 imp pt, 7.6 US pt, 3.6 l; 1 Nikki downdraught twin arrel carburettor; fuel feed: electric pump; water-cooled, 12.3 mp pt, 14.8 US pt, 7 l.

'RANSMISSION driving wheels: rear; clutch: single dry plate diaphragm); gearbox: mechanical; gears: 5, fully synchronized; atios: I 3.403, II 1.925, III 1.373, IV 1, V 0.854, rev 3.665; ever: central; final drive: hypoid bevel; axle ratio: 3.909; width f rims: 5.5"; tyres: 185/70 SR x 14 - ST Coupé 6.45 x 14

'ERFORMANCE max speeds: (I) 27 mph, 45 km/h; (II) 52 mph, 3 km/h; (III) 71 mph, 113 km/h; (IV) 98 mph, 158 km/h; (V) 110 nph, 175 km/h; power-weight ratio: L 2000 SG 22,3 lb/hp (30.3 o/kW), 10.1 kg/hp (13.7 kg/kW); carrying capacity: 882 lb, 400 g; acceleration: standing ¼ mile 18.8 sec, 0-50 mph (0-80 m/h) 9.2 sec; speed in direct drive at 1,000 rpm: 18 mph, 28.9 m/h; consumption: 31 m/imp gal, 25.8 m/US gal, 9.1 l x 100 m.

:HASSIS integral with front and rear auxiliary frames; front uspension: independent, by Mc-Pherson, coil springs/ telesco-ic damper struts, lower wishbones (trailing links), anti-roll bar; ear: rigid axle, lower trailing arms, upper oblique torque arms, 'anhard rod, coil springs, telescopic dampers.

;TEERING recirculating ball, variable ratio; turns lock to lock: .30.

RAKES front disc, rear drum, dual circuit, servo; lining area: ont 26.7 sq in, 172 sq cm, rear 18.6 sq in, 120 sq cm, total 5.3 sq in, 292 sq cm.

:LECTRICAL EQUIPMENT 12 V; 35 Ah battery; 50 A alterna-or; Mitsubishi distributor; 4 headlamps.

IMENSIONS AND WEIGHT wheel base: 98.82 in, 251 cm; acks: 54.33 in, 138 cm front, 53.94 in, 137 cm rear; length: L 000 SG 178.93 in, 454 cm - SG models and ST 179.13 in, 455 m - L 2000 SGX 181.89 in, 462 cm - SGX 182.28 in, 463 cm; vidth: 66.34 in, 168 cm; height: 52.76 in, 134 cm; ground learance: 6.50 in, 16.5 cm; weight: L 2000 SG 2,450 lb, 1,110 g - ST 2,428 lb,1,100 kg - SG models 2,439 lb, 1,105 kg - SGX nd L SGX 2,472 lb, 1,120 kg; weight distribution: 56.7% front, 3.3% rear; turning circle: 36.7 ft, 11.2 m; fuel tank: 14.3 imp al, 17.2 US gal, 65 l.

ODY coupé; 2 doors; 5 seats, separate front seats.

PTIONALS JATCO automatic transmission, hydraulic torque onverter and planetary gears with 3 ratios (I 2.458, II 1.458, III , rev 2.181), max ratio of converter at stall 2, max speed 99 nph, 160 km/h.

140 hp power team

;ee 110 hp power team, except for:

:NGINE front, 4-stroke, Wankel type with Mazda emission ontrol system (cayalytic converter and secondary air injection); 2 co-axial 3-lobe rotors; 39.9 2 cu in, 654 x 2 cc; compression ratio: 9.4:1; max power (JIS): 140 hp (103 kW) at 6,000 rpm; max torque (JIS): 138 lb ft, 19 kg m (186 Nm) at 4,000 rpm; max engine rpm: 7,000; 107 hp/l (79 kW/l); light alloy trochoid chamber, cast iron side housings, cast iron rotors; 2 eccentric crankshaft bearings; lubrication: rotary pump, full flow filter, 11.1 imp pt, 13.3 US pt, 6.3 l; 1 Hitachi KCH 348 downdraught 4-barrel carburettor; cooling, 15.7 imp pt, 18.6 US pt, 9 l.

TRANSMISSION gearbox: mechanical with hydraulic fluid coupling; gears: 5, fully synchronized; ratios: I 3.380, II 2.077, III 1.390, IV 1, V 0.841, rev 3.389; axle ratio: 3.727; tyres: 190/70 HR x 14.

PERFORMANCE max speeds: (I) 39 mph, 63 km/h; (II) 65 mph, 104 km/h; (III) 96 mph, 155 km/h; (IV) 112 mph, 180 km/h; (V) 112 mph, 180 km/h; power-weight ratio: RE GT 18.2 lb/hp (24.7 lb/kW), 8.2 kg/hp (11.2 kg/kW); acceleration: standing ¼ mile 15.9 sec, 0-50 mph (0-80 km/h) 6.2 sec; speed in top at 1,000 rpm: 16.9 mph, 27.2 km/h; consumption: 21.9 m/imp gal, 18.4 m/US gal, 12.8 l x 100 km.

CHASSIS anti-roll bar on rear suspension.

STEERING servo; turns lock to lock: 3.50.

ELECTRICAL EQUIPMENT 45 Ah battery.

DIMENSIONS AND WEIGHT length: RE GT 179.13 in, 455 cm - L RE SE-GT and L RE SE-Limited 181.89 in, 462 cm - RE SE-Limited 182.28 in, 463 cm; weight: RE GT and RE SE-GT 2,549 lb, 1,155 kg - L RE SE-GT 2,561 lb, 1,160 kg - RE SE-Limited 2,572 lb, 1,165 kg - L RE SE-Limited 2,583 lb, 1,170 kg; weight distribution: 58% front, 42% rear.

OPTIONALS JATCO 3-speed automatic transmission, max speeds (I) 53 mph, 85 km/h, (II) 90 mph, 145 km/h, (III) 118 mph, 190 km/h, acceleration standing ¼ mile 17,7 sec, consumption 20 m/imp gal, 16.9 m/US gal, 13.9 l x 100 km; air-conditioning.

Savanna RX7 Series

PRICES (Tokyo):	yen
Custom 2+1 dr Coupé	**1,250,000**
Super Custom 2+1 dr Coupé	**1,380,000**
GT 2+1 dr Coupé	**1,420,000**
Limited 2+1 dr Coupé	**1,730,000**
SE GT 2+1 dr Coupé	**1,590,000**
SE Limited 2+1 dr Coupé	**2,130,000**

ENGINE front, 4 stroke, Wankel rotary type with Mazda REAPS emission control system (catalytic converter and secondary air injection); 2 co-axial 3-lobe rotors; 35 x 2 cu in, 573 x 2 cc; compression ratio: 9.4:1; max power (JIS): 130 hp (96 kW) at 7,000 rpm; max torque (JIS): 120 lb ft, 16.5 kg m (162 Nm) at 4,000 rpm; max engine rpm: 7,000; cast iron side-housings, light alloy trochoid housings, cast iron rotors; 2 crankshaft bearings; lubrication: trochoid pump, full flow filter, forced lubrication/cooling of rotors, 9.2 imp pt, 11 US pt, 5.2 l; 1 Nikki downdraught 4-barrel carburettor; fuel feed: electric pump; water-cooled housings, 15.8 imp pt, 19 US pt, 9 l, oil-cooled rotors.

TRANSMISSION driving wheels: rear; clutch: single dry plate (diaphragm), hydraulically controlled; gearbox: mechanical; gears: 5, fully synchronized; ratios: I 3.674, II 2.217, III 1,432, IV 1, V 0.825, rev 3.542; lever: central; final drive: hypoid bevel; axle ratio: 3.909; width of rims: 5" - Limited 5.5"; tyres: 165 SR x 13 - GT and Limited 185/70 SR x 13.

PERFORMANCE max speeds: (I) 32 mph, 52 km/h; (II) 54 mph, 87 km/h; (III) 82 mph, 132 km/h; (IV) 112 mph, 180 km/h; (V) 112 mph, 180 km/h; power-weight ratio: Custom 16.8 lb/hp (22.8 lb/kW), 7.6 kg/hp (10.3 kg/kW); acceleration: standing ¼ mile 15.8 sec; consumption: 23.5 m/imp gal, 19.8 m/US gal, 11.9 l x 100 km.

CHASSIS integral; front suspension: independent, by Mc-Pherson, coil springs/telescopic damper struts, transverse l arms, trailing locating rods, anti-roll bar; rear: rigid axle, lower trailing links, upper torque rods, Watts linkage, coil springs, telescopic dampers - GT and Limited anti-roll bar.

STEERING recirculating ball; turns lock to lock: 3.70.

BRAKES front disc, internal radial fins, rear drum, dual circuit, servo; lining area: front 24.8 sq in, 160 sq cm, rear 39.7 sq in, 256 sq cm, total 64.5 sq in, 416 sq cm.

ELECTRICAL EQUIPMENT 12 V; 35 Ah battery; 63 A alternator; 2 retractable headlamps.

DIMENSIONS AND WEIGHT wheel base: 94.88 in, 241 cm; tracks: 55.90 in, 142 cm front, 55.12 in, 140 cm rear; length: 168.70 in, 428 cm; width: 65.94 in, 167 cm; height: 49.60 in, 126 cm; ground clearance: 6.10 in, 15.5 cm; weight: Custom

MAZDA Savanna RX7 GT Coupé

SAVANNA RX7 SERIES

2,185 lb, 990 kg - Super Custom 2,194 lb, 995 kg - GT and Limited 2,216 lb, 1,005 kg - SE GT 2,229 lb, 1,010 kg - SE Limited 2,295 lb, 1,040 kg; weight distribution: 54% front, 46% rear; turning circle: 34.8 ft, 10.6 m; fuel tank: 12.1 imp gal, 14.5 US gal, 55 l.

BODY coupé; 2+1 doors; 2+2 seats, separate front seats; detachable sunshine roof (for SE models only).

OPTIONALS JATCO automatic transmission with 3 ratios (I 2.458, II 1.458, III 1, rev 2.181), max speed 112 mph, 180 km/h, acceleration standing ¼ mile 17.4 sec; air-conditioning.

MITSUBISHI JAPAN

Minica Ami 55 Series

PRICES (Tokyo):	yen
Hi De Luxe 2-dr Sedan	**563,000**
Super De Luxe 2-dr Sedan	**629,000**
GI 2-dr Sedan	**653,000**
XL 2-dr Sedan	**681,000**

ENGINE front, 4 stroke; 2 cylinders, in line; 33.3 cu in, 546 cc (2.75 x 2.79 in, 70 x 71 mm); compression ratio: 9:1; max power (JIS): 31 hp (23 kW) at 6,000 rpm; max torque (JIS): 30 lb ft, 4.1 kg m (40 Nm) at 3,000 rpm; max engine rpm: 6,500; 56.7 hp/l (41.7 kW/l); cast iron block, light alloy head; 3 crankshaft bearings; valves: overhead, rockers; camshafts: 1, overhead; lubrication: rotary pump, full flow filter, 5.1 imp pt, 6.1 US pt, 2.9 l; 1 Mikuni 24-30 DIDS downdraught twin barrel carburettor; fuel feed: electric pump; emission control catalytic converter, secondary air injection, exhaust gas recirculation; water-cooled, 5.3 imp pt, 6.3 US pt, 3 l.

TRANSMISSION driving wheels: rear; clutch: single dry plate (diaphragm); gearbox: mechanical; gears: 4, fully synchronized; ratios: I 3.882, II 2.265, III 1.473, IV 1, rev 4.271; lever: central; final drive: hypoid bevel; axle ratio: 4.625; width of rims: 3.5"; tyres: 5.20 x 10.

PERFORMANCE max speeds: (I) 20 mph, 32 km/h; (II) 34 mph, 55 km/h; (III) 53 mph, 85 km/h; (IV) 68 mph, 110 km/h; power-weight ratio: Hi De Luxe 40.2 lb/hp (54.2 lb/kW), 18.2 kg/hp (24.6 kg/kW); consumption: 62.8 m/imp gal, 52.3 m/US gal, 4.5 l x 100 km on Japanese emission test cycle.

CHASSIS integral; front suspension: independent, by McPherson, coil springs/telescopic damper struts, anti-roll bar, lower wishbones (trailing links); rear: rigid axle, twin longitudinal trailing radius arms, torque tube, transverse linkage bar, coil springs, telescopic dampers.

STEERING recirculating ball.

BRAKES drum, dual circuit; lining area: total 67 sq in, 432 sq cm.

ELECTRICAL EQUIPMENT 12 V; 24 Ah battery; 25 A alternator; Mitsubishi distributor; 2 headlamps.

DIMENSIONS AND WEIGHT wheel base: 78.84 in, 200 cm; tracks: 48.03 in, 122 cm front, 46.85 in, 119 cm rear; length: 124.41 in, 316 cm - Xl 125.19 in, 318 cm; width: 55.12 in 140 cm; height: 51.96 in, 132 cm; ground clearance: 5.51 in, 14 cm; weight: 1,245 lb, 565 kg - XL 1,257 lb, 570 kg; fuel tank: 6.6 imp gal, 7.9 US gal, 30 l.

BODY saloon/sedan; 2 doors; 4 seats, separate front seats, reclining backrests, built-in headrests; folding rear seat.

Mirage Series

PRICES EX WORKS:		yen
1	1200 EL 2-dr Sedan	**728,000**
2	1200 EL 4-dr Sedan	**766,000**
3	1200 TL 4-dr Sedan	**826,000**
4	1200 GL 2-dr Sedan	**828,000**
5	1200 GL 4-dr Sedan	**871,000**
6	1400 GL 2-dr Sedan	**865,000**
7	1400 GL 4-dr Sedan	**913,000**
8	1400 GLX 2-dr Sedan	**922,000**
9	1400 GLX 4-dr Sedan	**965,000**
10	1400 GLS 2-dr Sedan	**1,030,000**
11	1600 GT 2-dr Sedan	**982,000**
12	1600 GT 4-dr Sedan	**1,025,000**

Power team:	Standard for:	Optional for:
72 hp	1 to 5	—
82 hp	6 to 10	—
88 hp	11,12	—

MITSUBISHI Minica Ami 55 XL Sedan

MITSUBISHI Mirage 1600 GT Sedan

72 hp power team

ENGINE front, transverse, 4 stroke; 4 cylinders, in line; 75.9 cu in, 1,244 cc (2.74 x 3.23 in, 69.5 x 82 mm); compression ratio: 9:1; max power (JIS): 72 hp (53 kW) at 5,500 rpm; max torque (JIS): 77 lb ft, 10.7 kg m (105 Nm) at 3,000 rpm; max engine rpm: 6,000; 56.3 hp/l (41.4 kW/l); cast iron block, light alloy head; 5 crankshaft bearings; valves: 3 per cylinder, overhead, Vee-slanted, rockers; camshafts: 1, overhead; lubrication: gear pump, full flow filter, 6.2 imp pt, 7.4 US pt, 3.5 l; 1 Stromberg 26-30 DIDTA-11 downdraught twin barrel carburettor; Mitsubishi MCA-Jet super lean-burn low emission engine with third air inlet valve, exhaust gas recirculation and oxidizing catalyst; fuel feed: mechanical pump; water-cooled, 8.8 imp pt, 10.6 US pt, 5 l.

TRANSMISSION driving wheels: rear; clutch: single dry plate (diaphragm); gearbox: mechanical; gears: EL models 4, fully synchronized - TL and GL models 4 and Super-Shift 2-speed transfer box; ratios: I 4.225, II 2.365, III 1.466, IV 1.163, rev 4.108; TL and GL models transfer box: high 0.774, low 1; lever: central - TL and GL models two levers; final drive: spiral bevel; axle ratio: EL models 3.166 - TL and GL models 3.687; width of rims: 4.5"; tyres: 6.00 x 12.

PERFORMANCE max speeds: EL models (I) 27 mph, 43 km/h; (II) 47 mph, 75 km/h; (III) 75 mph, 120 km/h; (IV) 93 mph, 150 km/h; power-weight ratio: EL 2-dr Sedan 23.3 lb/hp (31.5 lb/kW), 10.6 kg/hp (14.3 kg/kW); carrying capacity: 882 lb, 400 kg; consumption: EL models 43.7 m/imp gal, 36.4 m/US gal, 6.4 l x 100 km.

CHASSIS integral; front suspension: independent, by McPherson, coil springs/telescopic damper struts, lower wishbones (trailing links), anti-roll bar; rear: independent, co springs, telescopic dampers, trailing radius arms.

STEERING rack-and-pinion; turns lock to lock: 3.90.

BRAKES front disc, rear drum, servo.

ELECTRICAL EQUIPMENT 12 V; 45 A alternator; Mitsubisl distributor; 2 headlamps.

DIMENSIONS AND WEIGHT wheel base: 2-dr models 90.55 in 230 cm - 4-dr models 93.70 in, 238 cm; tracks: 53.94 in, 13 cm front, 52.75 in, 134 cm rear; length: 2-dr models 149.21 in 379 cm - 4-dr models 153.35 in, 389 cm; width: 2-dr model 62.40 in, 158 cm - 4-dr models 62.60 in, 159 cm; height: 53.1 in, 135 cm; ground clearance: 6.69 in, 17 cm; weight: EL 2-c Sedan 1,676 lb, 760 kg - EL 4-dr Sedan 1,742 lb, 790 kg - T 4-dr Sedan 1,764 lb, 800 kg - GL 2-dr Sedan 1,709 lb, 775 kg GL 4-dr Sedan 1,775 lb, 805 kg; weight distribution: 62% fron 38% rear; turning circle: 4-dr models 35.4 ft, 10.8 m; fuel tank 8.8 imp gal, 10.6 US gal, 40 l.

BODY saloon/sedan; 2 or 4 doors; 5 seats, separate fron seats.

82 hp power team

See 72 hp power team, except for:

ENGINE 86 cu in, 1,410 cc (2.91 x 3.23 in, 74 x 82 mm); ma power (JIS): 82 hp (60 kW) at 5,500 rpm; max torque (JIS): 8 lb ft, 12.1 kg m (119 Nm) at 3,500 rpm; 58.1 hp/l (42.8 kW/l)

MITSUBISHI Lancer EX 1600 GT Sedan

ANSMISSION gears: 4, fully synchronized and Super-Shift speed transfer box; axle ratio: 3.470; tyres: 155 SR x 13.

:RFORMANCE max speed: 96 mph, 155 km/h; power-weight tio: GL 2-dr Sedan 20.8 lb/hp (28.4 lb/kW), 9.4 kg/hp (12.9 /kW); consumption: 42.3 m/imp gal, 35.3 m/US gal, 6.7 100 km.

MENSIONS AND WEIGHT weight: GL 2-dr Sedan 1,709 lb, 5 kg - GLX 2-dr Sedan 1,753 lb, 795 kg - GLS 2-dr Sedan 764 lb, 800 kg - GL 4-dr Sedan 1,786 lb, 810 kg - GLX 4-dr dan 1,830 lb, 830 kg.

PTIONALS automatic transmission with 3 ratios (I 2.551, II 488, III 1, rev 2.176), 3.943 axle ratio (except GLS).

88 hp power team

e 72 hp power team, except for:

IGINE 97.4 cu in, 1,597 cc (3.03 x 3.39 in, 76.9 x 86 mm); mpression ratio: 8.5:1; max power (JIS): 88 hp (65 KW) at 00 rpm; max torque (JIS): 98 lb ft, 13.5 kg m (132 Nm), at 00 rpm; 55.1 hp/l (40.6 kW/l).

ANSMISSION gears: 4, fully synchronized and Super-Shift speed transfer box; axle ratio: 3.470; tyres: 155 SR x 13.

:RFORMANCE max speed: 99 mph, 160 km/h; power-weight io: GT 2-dr Sedan 20.8 lb/hp (28.2 lb/kW), 9.4 kg/hp (12.8 kW); consumption: 42.8 m/imp gal, 35.6 m/US gal, 6.6 100 km on Japanese test cycle.

ASSIS anti-roll bar on rear suspension.

MENSIONS AND WEIGHT weight: GT 2-dr Sedan, 1,830 lb, 0 kg - GT 4-dr Sedan 1,896 lb, 860 kg.

PTIONALS automatic transmission with 3 ratios (I 2.551, II 488, III 1, rev 2.176), 3.943 axle ratio.

Lancer EX Series

ICES (Tokyo):	yen
1400 EL 4-dr Sedan	**858,000**
1400 GL 4-dr Sedan	**930,000**
1400 SL 4-dr Sedan	**995,000**
1600 GL 4-dr Sedan	**985,000**
1600 XL 4-dr Sedan	**1,041,000**
1600 XL-5 4-dr Sedan	**1,066,000**
1600 GT 4-dr Sedan	**1,080,000**

wer team:	Standard for:	Optional for:
hp	1 to 3	—
hp	4 to 7	—

80 hp power team

IGINE front, 4 stroke; 4 cylinders, vertical, in line; 86 cu in, 10 cc (2.91 x 3.23 in, 74 x 82 mm); compression ratio: 9:1; x power (JIS): 80 hp (59 kW) at 5,500 rpm; max torque (JIS): lb ft, 12.1 kg m (119 Nm) at 3,500 rpm; max engine rpm: 00; 58.1 hp/l (42.8 kW/l); cast iron block, light alloy head; 5 nkshaft bearings; valves: overhead, Vee-slanted, 3 per cylin- (two inlet, one, which is air inlet valve, for high swirl effect), kers; camshafts: 1, overhead; lubrication: rotary pump, full flow filter, 7 imp pt, 8.4 US pt, 4 l; 1 Stromberg 28-32 DIDSA downdraught twin barrel carburettor; fuel feed: mechanical pump; water-cooled, 10.6 imp pt, 12.7 US pt, 6 l.

TRANSMISSION driving wheels: rear; clutch: single dry plate (diaphragm); gearbox: mechanical; gears: 4 - SL 5, fully synchronized; ratios: I 3.525, II 2.112, III 1.442, IV 1, rev 3.867 - SL I 3.444, II 2, III 1.316, IV 1, V 0.853, rev 3.667; lever: central; final drive: hypoid bevel; axle ratio: 3.909 - SL 4.222; width of rims: 4"; tyres: 6.15 x 13 - SL 155 SR x 13.

PERFORMANCE max speeds: (I) 28 mph, 45 km/h; (II) 47 mph, 76 km/h; (III) 68 mph, 110 km/h; (IV) 93 mph, 150 km/h; power-weight ratio: EL 24.7 lb/hp (33.5 lb/kW), 11.2 kg/hp (15.2 kW/l); consumption: 40.9 m/imp gal, 34.1 m/US gal, 6.9 l x 100 km on Japanese emission test cycle.

CHASSIS integral; front suspension: independent, by McPherson, coil springs/telescopic damper struts, lower wishbones (trailing links), anti-roll bar; rear: rigid axle, lower trailing arms with diagonal reinforcing links, upper diagonal torque rods, coil springs, telescopic dampers.

STEERING recirculating ball, variable ratio; turns lock to lock: 3.80.

BRAKES front disc, rear drum; lining area: front 24.8 sq in, 160 sq cm, rear 47.8 sq in, 308 sq cm, total 72.6 sq in, 468 sq cm.

ELECTRICAL EQUIPMENT 12 V; 60 Ah battery; 40 A alternator; Mitsubishi distributor; 2 headlamps.

DIMENSIONS AND WEIGHT wheel base: 96.06 in, 244 cm; tracks: 52.56 in, 133 cm front, 52.17 in, 132 cm rear; length: 166.34 in, 422 cm; width: 63.78 in, 162 cm; height: 54.33 in, 138 cm; ground clearance: 6.30 in, 16 cm; weight: EL and GL 1,973 lb, 895 kg - SL 1,996 lb, 905 kg; weight distribution: 53% front, 47% rear; turning circle: 34.1 ft, 10.4 m; fuel tank: 11 imp gal, 13.2 US gal, 50 l.

BODY saloon/sedan; 4 doors; 5 seats, separate front seats, reclining backrests, built-in headrests.

86 hp power team

See 80 hp power team, except for:

ENGINE 97.4 cu in, 1,597 cc (3.03 x 3.39 in, 76.9 x 86 mm); compression ratio: 8.5:1; max power (JIS): 86 hp (63 kW) at 5,000 rpm; max torque (JIS): 98 lb ft, 13.5 kg m (132 Nm) at 3,000 rpm; max engine rpm: 6,000; 53.8 hp/l (39.6 kW/l); 1 Stromberg 28-72 DIDTA downdraught twin barrel carburettor.

TRANSMISSION gears: 4 - XL-5 and GT 5; width of rims: 5"; tyres: 6.45 x 13 - GT 165 SR x 13.

PERFORMANCE max speed: 96 mph, 155 km/h; power-weight ratio: GL 23.8 lb/hp (32.6 lb/kW), 10.8 kg/hp (14.8 kg/kW); consumption: 42.2 m/imp gal, 35.1 m/US gal, 6.7 l x 100 km on Japanese emission test cycle.

BRAKES GT disc.

DIMENSIONS AND WEIGHT height: 54,92 in, 139 cm - GT 54.72 in, 139 cm; weight: GL 2,051 lb, 930 kg - XL 2,062 lb, 935 kg - GT 2,095 lb, 950 kg.

OPTIONALS (for GL and XL only) automatic transmission with 3 ratios (I 2.450, II 1.450, III 1, rev 2.222), 3.909 axle ratio.

MITSUBISHI Celeste 2000 GT Coupé

Celeste Series

PRICES (Tokyo):		yen
1	1400 SR 2+1-dr Coupé	**935,000**
2	1400 GL 2+1-dr Coupé	**975,000**
3	1400 GSL 2+1-dr Coupé	**1,031,000**
4	1600 GL 2+1-dr Coupé	**1,117,000**
5	1600 XL 2+1-dr Coupé	**1,115,000**
6	1600 GT 2+1-dr Coupé	**1,117,000**
7	2000 GT 2+1-dr Coupé	**1,355,000**

Power team:	Standard for:	Optional for:
80 hp	1 to 3	—
86 hp	4 to 6	—
105 hp	7	—

80 hp power team

ENGINE front, 4 stroke; 4 cylinders, vertical, in line; 86 cu in, 1,410 cc (2.91 x 3.23 in, 74 x 82 mm); compression ratio: 9:1; max power (JIS): 80 hp (59 kW) at 5,400 rpm; max torque (JIS): 88 lb ft, 12.1 kg m (119 Nm) at 3,000 rpm; max engine rpm: 6,000; 56.7 hp/l (41.7 kW/l); cast iron block, light alloy head; 5 crankshaft bearings; valves: overhead, Vee-slanted, rockers; camshafts: 1, overhead; lubrication: rotary pump, full flow filter, 7 imp pt, 8.5 US pt, 4 l; 1 Stromberg 28-32 DIDTA downdraught

80 HP POWER TEAM

twin barrel carburettor; Mitsubishi MCA-Jet super lean-burn low emission engine with third air inlet valve, exhaust gas recirculation and small capacity catalyst in exhaust manifold; fuel feed: mechanical pump; water-cooled, 10.6 imp pt, 12.7 US pt, 6 l.

TRANSMISSION driving wheels: rear; clutch: single dry plate (diaphragm); gearbox: mechanical; gears: 4 - GSL 5, fully synchronized; ratios: I 3.525, II 2.193, III 1.442, IV 1, rev 3.867 - GSL I 3.215, II 2, III, 1.316, IV 1, V 0.853, rev 3.667; lever: central; final drive: hypoid bevel; axle ratio: 3.909 - GSL 4.222; width of rims: 4.5"; tyres 155 SR x 13.

PERFORMANCE max speeds: (I) 28 mph, 45 km/h; (II) 45 mph, 72 km/h; (III) 67 mph, 108 km/h; (IV) 96 mph, 155 km/h; power-weight ratio: SR 25.1 lb/hp (34 lb/kW), 11.4 kg/hp (15.4 kg/kW); carrying capacity: 882 lb, 400 kg; consumption: 39.8 m/imp gal, 33.1 m/US gal, 7.1 l x 100 km.

CHASSIS integral; front suspension: independent, by McPherson, coil springs/telescopic damper struts, lower wishbones (trailing links), anti-roll bar; rear: rigid axle, semi-elliptic leafsprings, telescopic dampers.

STEERING recirculating ball, variable ratio.

BRAKES front disc, rear drum, rear compensator.

ELECTRICAL EQUIPMENT 12 V; 32 Ah battery; 35 A alternator; Mitsubishi distributor; 2 headlamps.

DIMENSIONS AND WEIGHT wheel base: 92.13 in, 234 cm; tracks: 52.17 in, 132 cm front, 50.98 in, 129 cm rear; length: 163.58 in, 415 cm; width: 63.39 in, 161 cm; height: 52.17 in, 132 cm; ground clearance: 6.30 in, 16 cm; weight: SR and GL 2,007 lb, 910 kg - GSL 2,018 lb, 915 kg; weight distribution: 55.4% front, 44.6% rear; fuel tank: 11 imp gal, 13.2 US gal, 50 l.

BODY coupé; 2+1 doors; 5 seats, separate front seats.

86 hp power team

See 80 hp power team, except for:

ENGINE 97.4 cu in, 1,597 cc (3.03 x 3.39 in, 76.9 x 86 mm); compression ratio: 8.5:1; max power (JIS)) 86 hp (63 kW) at 5,000 rpm; max torque (JIS): 98 lb ft, 13.5 kg m (132 Nm) at 3,000 rpm; 57.6 hp/l (42.4 kW/l); Mitsubishi twin contra-rotating balancing shafts incorporated with crankshaft; camshafts: cogged belt.

TRANSMISSION gearbox: GL, automatic transmission, hydraulic torque converter and planetary gears with 3 ratios - XL and GT, 5-speed fully synchronized mechanical gearbox; ratios: GL I 2.680, II 1.508, III 1, rev 2.310 - XL and GT I 3.215, II 2, III 1.316, IV 1, V 0.853, rev 3.667; axle ratio: 3.909; tyres: GT 175/70 HR x 13.

PERFORMANCE max speed: GL 93 mph, 150 km/h - XL and GT 99 mph, 160 km/h; power-weight ratio: GL 24.5 lb/hp (33.5 lb/kW), 11.1 kg/hp (15.2 kg/kW); consumption: 38.2 m/imp gal, 31.8 m/US gal, 7.4 l x 100 km.

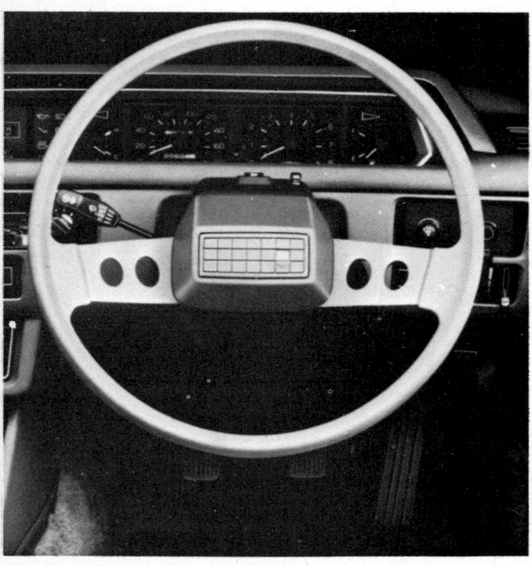

MITSUBISHI Galant Sigma 2000 Super Saloon Sedan

MITSUBISHI Galant Lambda 2600 Super Touring Coupé

DIMENSIONS AND WEIGHT weight: XL 2.073 lb, 940 kg - GT 2,084 lb, 945 kg - GL 2,106 lb, 955 kg.

105 hp power team

See 80 hp power team, except for:

ENGINE 121.7 cu in, 1,995 cc (3.31 x 3.54 in, 84 x 90 mm); max power (JIS): 105 hp (77 kW) at 5,400 rpm; max torque (JIS): 119 lb ft, 16.5 kg m (162 Nm) at 3,500 rpm; 52.6 hp/l (38.7 kW/l); Mitsubishi Astron 80 twin contrarotating balancing shafts incorporated with crankshaft; lubrication: gear pump, full flow filter, 7.6 imp pt, 9.1 US pt, 4.3 l; 1 Stromberg 30-32 DIDTA downdraught twin barrel carburettor; cooling, 13.6 imp pt, 16.3 US pt, 7.7 l.

TRANSMISSION gears: 5, fully synchronized; ratios: I 3.369, II 2.035, III 1.360, IV 1, V 0.836, rev 3.635; width of rims: 5"; tyres: 165 SR x 13.

PERFORMANCE max speed: 102 mph, 165 km/h; power-weight ratio: 20.9 lb/hp (28.4 lb/kW), 9.5 kg/hp (12.9 kg/kW); consumption: 31 m/imp gal, 25.8 m/US gal, 9.1 l x 100 km.

BRAKES disc.

DIMENSIONS AND WEIGHT height: 52.95 in, 134 cm; weight: 2,194 lb, 995 kg.

Galant Sigma Series

PRICES (Tokyo):		yen
1	1600 L 4-dr Sedan	**1,012,000**
2	1600 GL 4-dr Sedan	**1,087,000**
3	1600 SL 4-dr Sedan	**1,132,000**
4	1600 SL Super 4-dr Sedan	**1,222,000**
5	Eterna 1600 GL 4-dr Sedan	**1,077,000**
6	Eterna 1600 SL Super 4-dr Sedan	**1,202,000**
7	2000 GL 4-dr Sedan	**1,210,000**
8	2000 GLS 4-dr Sedan	**1,329,000**
9	2000 GSL Super 4-dr Sedan	**1,415,000**
10	Eterna 2000 GSL 4-dr Sedan	**1,309,000**
11	Eterna 2000 GSL Super 4-dr Sedan	**1,395,000**
12	2000 Super Saloon 4-dr Sedan	**1,540,000**

Power team:	Standard for:	Optional for:
86 hp	1 to 6	—
105 hp	7 to 12	—

86 hp power team

ENGINE front, 4 stroke; 4 cylinders, in line; 97.4 cu in, 1,597 cc (3.03 x 3.39 in, 76.9 x 86 mm); compression ratio: 8.5:1; max power (JIS): 86 hp (63 kW) at 5,000 rpm; max torque (JIS): 98 lb ft, 13.5 kg m (132 Nm) at 3,000 rpm; max engine rpm: 5,700; 53.8 hp/l (39.6 kW/l); cast iron block, light alloy head; 5 crankshaft bearings; Mitsubishi Saturn 80 omni-phase balancing shafts; valves: overhead, Vee-slanted, rockers; camshafts: 1, overhead; lubrication: rotary pump, full flow filter, 7 imp pt, 8.5 US pt, 4 l; 1 Stromberg 28-32 DIDTA downdraught twin barrel carburettor; Mitsubishi MCA-Jet super lean-burn low emission engine, with third air inlet valve, exhaust gas recirculation and catalyst in exhaust manifold; fuel feed: mechanical pump; water-cooled, 10.6 imp pt, 12.7 US pt, 6 l.

TRANSMISSION driving wheels: rear; clutch: single dry pla (diaphragm); gearbox: mechanical; gears: 4 - (SL, 5, SL onl fully synchronized; ratios: I 3.525, II 2.193, III 1.442, IV 1, r 3.867 - SL I 3.215, II 2, III 1.316, IV 1, V 0.853, rev 3.66 lever: central; final drive: hypoid bevel; axle ratio: 3.909 - 4.222; width of rims: 4.5" - SL, 4.5"; tyres: 6.45 x 13 - SL 1 SR x 13.

PERFORMANCE max speeds: (I) 28 mph, 45 km/h; (II) 45 mp 72 km/h; (III) 68 mph, 110 km/h; (IV) 96 mph, 155 km/h - SL (96 mph, 155 km/h; power-weight ratio: L, 22.4 lb/hp (3 lb/kW), 10.1 kg/hp (15.6 kg/kW); carrying capacity: 882 lb, 4 kg; consumption: 59.3 m/imp gal, 49.4 m/US gal, 4.8 l x 100 at 37 mph, 60 km/h.

CHASSIS integral; front suspension: independent, by M Pherson, coil springs/telescopic damper struts, lower wis bones (trailing links), anti-roll bar; rear: rigid axle, lower traili links with diagonal locating members, upper diagonal torq rods, coil springs, telescopic dampers.

STEERING recirculating ball, variable ratio.

BRAKES front disc, rear drum, servo; lining area: front 19.2 in, 124 sq cm, rear 47.8 sq in, 308 sq cm, total 67 sq in, 4 sq cm.

ELECTRICAL EQUIPMENT 12 V; 35 Ah battery; 40 A altern tor; Mitsubishi distributor; 4 headlamps - Eterna models 2.

DIMENSIONS AND WEIGHT wheel base: 99.02 in, 251 c tracks: 53.15 in, 135 cm front, 52.76 in, 134 cm rear; leng 172.44 in, 438 cm - SL Super 175.20 in, 445 cm; width: 65. in, 165 cm - SL Super 65.75 in, 167 cm; height: 53.54 in, 1 cm; ground clearance: 6.30 in, 16 cm; weight: L and GL mode 2,172 lb, 985 kg - SL 2,194 lb, 995 kg - SL Super models 2,2 lb, 1,010 kg; turning circle: 36.1 ft, 11 m; fuel tank: 13.2 in gal, 15.8 US gal, 60 l.

BODY saloon/sedan; 4 doors; 5 seats, separate front seat

OPTIONALS (for GL only) Borg-Warner 35 automatic transm sion with 3 ratios (I 2.450, II 1.450, III 1, rev 2.222).

105 hp power team

See 86 hp power team, except for:

ENGINE 121.7 cu in, 1,995 cc (3.31 x 3.54 in, 84 x 90 mm); m power (JIS): 105 hp (77 kW) at 5,400 rpm; max torque (JIS 119 lb ft, 16.5 kg m (162 Nm) at 3,500 rpm; 52.6 hp/l (38 kW/l); Mitsubishi Astron 80 twin contrarotating balancing sha incorporated with crankshaft; lubrication: gear pump, full fl filter, 7.6 imp pt, 9.1 US pt, 4.3 l; 1 Stromberg 30-32 DID downdraught twin barrel carburettor; cooling, 13.6 imp pt, 16 US pt, 7.7 l.

TRANSMISSION gears: 5, fully synchronized; ratios: I 3.369, 2.035, III 1.360, IV 1, V 0.856, rev 3.635; width of rims: 5 tyres: GL 6.45 x 13 - GSL models 165 SR x 14 - GSL Sup models and Super Saloon 185/70 HR x 13.

PERFORMANCE max speeds: (I) 28 mph, 45 km/h; (II) 45 mp 73 km/h; (III) 68 mph, 110 km/h; (IV) 92 mph, 148 km/h; (V) 1 mph, 165 km/h; power-weight ratio: GL 22.5 lb/hp (30.6 lb/k 10.2 kg/hp (13.9 kg/kW); consumption: 32.4 m/imp gal, m/US gal, 8.7 l x 100 km.

BRAKES GSL Super models and Super Saloon, disc.

MENSIONS AND WEIGHT length: 175.20 in, 445 cm - Eterna odels 172.83 in, 439 cm; weight: GL and GSL models 2,359 1,070 kg - GSL Super 2,425 lb, 1,100 kg - Eterna GSL Super 414 lb, 1,095 kg - Super Saloon 2,503 lb, 1,135 kg.

TIONALS (for GSL Super and Super Saloon only) Borg-arner 35 automatic transmission with 3 ratios (I 2.450, II 450, III 1, rev 2.222), 3.545 axle ratio; (for Super Saloon and SL Super only) power steering.

Galant Lambda Series

ICES (Tokyo):	**yen**
1600 SL 2-dr Coupé	**1,195,000**
1600 SL Super 2-dr Coupé	**1,275,000**
Eterna 1600 SR 2-dr Coupé	**1,225,000**
2000 GL 2-dr Coupé	**1,277,000**
2000 GSL 2-dr Coupé	**1,376,000**
2000 GSL Super 2-dr Coupé	**1,475,000**
2000 Super Touring 2-dr Coupé	**1,641,000**
Eterna 2000 XL 2-dr Coupé	**1,460,000**
2600 Super Touring 2-dr Coupé	**1,839,000**

wer team:	**Standard for:**	**Optional for:**
6 hp	1 to 3	—
5 hp	4 to 8	—
0 hp	9	—

86 hp power team

IGINE front, 4 stroke; 4 cylinders, in line; 97.45 cu in, 1,597 (3.03 x 3.38 in, 77 x 86 mm); compression ratio: 8.5:1; max wer (JIS) 86 hp (63 kW) at 5,000 rpm; max torque (JIS): 98 lb 13.5 kg m (132 Nm) at 3,000 rpm; max engine rpm: 5,700; .9 hp/l (39.7 kW/l); cast iron block, light alloy head; Mitsu-hi twin contrarotating balancing shafts incorporated with nkshaft; valves: overhead, rockers; camshafts: 1, overhead; rication: rotary pump, full flow filter, 7 imp pt, 8.4 US pt, 4 l; Stromberg 28-32 DIDTA downdraught twin barrel carburettor; subishi MCA-Jet super leanburn low emission engine with rd air inlet valve, exhaust gas recirculation and small capac-catalyst in exhaust manifold; fuel feed: mechanical pump; ter-cooled, 10.6 imp pt, 12.7 US pt, 6 l.

ANSMISSION driving wheels: rear; clutch: single dry plate aphragm); gearbox: mechanical; gears: 5, fully synchronized; ios: I 3.215, II 2, III 1,316, IV 1, V 0.853, rev 3.667; lever: ntral; final drive: hypoid bevel; axle ratio: 4.222; width of s: 5"; tyres: 165 SR x 13.

RFORMANCE max speed: 96 mph, 155 km/h; power-weight o: SL 26.5 lb/hp (36.2 lb/kW), 12.6 kg/hp (16.4 kg/kW); nsumption: 32.4 m/imp gal, 27 m/US gal, 8.7 l x 100 km.

ASSIS integral; front suspension: independent, by Mc-erson, coil springs/telescopic damper struts, anti-roll bar, ver wishbones; rear: rigid axle, lower trailing links with dia-nal locating members, upper torque rods, coil springs, tele-opic dampers.

EERING recirculating ball, variable ratio.

AKES front disc, rear drum.

ECTRICAL EQUIPMENT 12 V; 35 Ah battery; 45 A alterna-; Mitsubishi distributor; 4 headlamps.

DIMENSIONS AND WEIGHT wheel base: 99.02 in, 251 cm; tracks: 53.94 in, 137 cm front, 53.54 in, 136 cm rear; length: 174.41 in, 443 cm; width: 65.94 in, 167 cm; height: 52.36 in, 133 cm; ground clearance: 6.30 in, 16 cm; weight: SL and SL Super 2,282 lb, 1,035 kg, - Eterna SR 2,293 lb, 1,040 kg; turning circle: 36.1 ft, 11 m; fuel tank: 13.2 imp gal, 15.8 US gal, 60 l.

BODY coupé; 2 doors; 5 seats, separate front seats.

OPTIONALS Borg-Warner 35 automatic transmission with 3 ratios (I 2.450, II 1.450, III 1, rev 2.222).

105 hp power team

See 86 hp power team, except for:

ENGINE 121.7 cu in, 1,995 cc (3.31 x 3.54 in, 84 x 90 mm); max power (JIS): 105 hp (77 kW) at 5,400 rpm; max torque (JIS): 120 lb ft, 16.5 kg m (162 Nm) at 3,500 rpm; 52.6 hp/l (38.7 kW/l); lubrication: 7.6 imp pt, 9.1 US pt, 4.3 l; cooling, 12.3 imp pt, 14.8 US pt, 7 l.

TRANSMISSION gearbox ratios: I 3.369, II 2.035, III 1.360, IV, 1, V 0.856, rev 3.650; axle ratio: 3.889; tyres: 165 SR x 14 - Super Touring 195/70 HR x 14.

PERFORMANCE max speeds: (I) 30 mph, 48 km/h; (II) 48 mph, 77 km/h; (III) 73 mph, 117 km/h; (IV) 98 mph, 158 km/h; (V) 103 mph, 165 km/h; power-weight ratio: GL 22.9 lb/hp (31.3 lb/kW), 10.4 kg/hp (14.2 kg/kW).

BRAKES disc, servo; lining area: front 32.9 sq in, 219 sq cm, rear 19.8 sq in, 128 sq cm, total 52.7 sq in, 340 sq cm.

DIMENSIONS AND WEIGHT length: GL, GSL and GSL Super 177.56 in, 451 cm - Super Touring and Eterna XL 177.16 in, 450 cm; weight: GL 2,403 lb, 1,090 kg - GSL 2,447 lb, 1,110 kg - GSL Super 2,481 lb, 1,125 kg - Eterna XL 2,492 lb, 1,130 kg - Super Touring 2,580 lb, 1,170 kg.

OPTIONALS (for GSL, Eterna XL and Super Touring only) Borg-Warner 35 automatic transmission, hydraulic torque converter with 3 ratios (I 2.450, II 1.450, III 1, rev 2.222), 3.545 axle ratio.

120 hp power team

See 86 hp power team, except for:

ENGINE 155.9 cu in, 2,555 cc (3.59 x 3.86 in, 91.1 x 98 mm); compression ratio: 8.2:1; max power (JIS): 120 hp (88 kW) at 5,000 rpm; max torque (JIS): 152 lb ft, 21 kg m (206 Nm) at 3,000 rpm; max engine rpm: 5,500; 47 hp/l (34.6 kW/l); lubrication: 8.8 imp pt, 10.6 US pt, 5 l; 1 Stromberg 30-32 downdraught twin barrel carburettor; cooling, 13.2 imp pt, 15.9 US pt, 7.5 l.

TRANSMISSION gearbox ratios: I 3.369, II 2.035, III 1,360, IV 1, V 0.856, rev 3.650; axle ratio: 3.545; tyres: 195/70 HR x 14.

PERFORMANCE max speeds: (I) 30 mph, 48 km/h; (II) 48 mph, 77 km/h; (III) 73 mph, 117 km/h; (IV) 98 mph, 158 km/h; (V) 103 mph, 165 km/h; power-weight ratio: 22.4 lb/hp (30.6 lb/kW), 10.2 kg/hp (13.9 kg/kW); consumption: 25.9 m/imp gal, 21.6 m/US gal, 10.9 l x 100 km.

MITSUBISHI Debonair Executive SE Sedan

BRAKES disc, servo; lining area: front 32.9 sq in, 219 sq cm, rear 19.8 sq in, 128 sq cm, total 52.7 sq in, 340 sq cm.

DIMENSIONS AND WEIGHT length: 181.69 in, 461 cm; weight: 2,690 lb, 1,220 kg.

OPTIONALS (for GLS, Eterna XL and Super Touring only) Borg-Warner 35 automatic transmission, hydraulic torque converter with 3 ratios (I 2.450, II 1.450, III 1, rev 2.222), 3.545 axle ratio.

Debonair Series

PRICES (Tokyo):	**yen**
De Luxe 4-dr Sedan	**2,280,000**
Super De Luxe 4-dr Sedan	**2,440,000**
Executive SE 5-pass. 4-dr Sedan	**2,500,000**

ENGINE front, 4 stroke; 4 cylinders, in line; 155.9 cu in, 2,555 cc (3.59 x 3.86 in, 91.1 x 98 mm); compression ratio: 8.2:1; max power (JIS): 120 hp (88 kW) at 5,000 rpm; max torque (JIS): 152 lb ft, 21 kg m (206 Nm) at 3,000 rpm; max engine rpm: 5,500; 47 hp/l (34.6 kW/l); cast iron block, light alloy head; Mitsubishi twin contrarotating balancing shafts; 5 crankshafts bearings; valves: overhead, rockers; camshafts: 1, overhead; lubrication: rotary pump, full flow filter, 8.8 imp pt, 10.6 US pt, 5 l; 1 Stromberg 30-32 DIDTA downdraught twin barrel carburettor; emission control with thermal reactor and exhaust gas recirculation; fuel feed: mechanical pump; water-cooled, 13.2 imp pt, 15.9 US pt, 7.5 l.

TRANSMISSION driving wheels: rear; gearbox: automatic transmission, hydraulic torque converter and planetary gears with 3 ratios; ratios: I 2.680, II 1.508, III 1, rev 2.310; lever: steering column; final drive: hypoid bevel; axle ratio: 3.889; tyres: 175 SR x 14.

PERFORMANCE max speeds: (I) 35 mph, 57 km/h; (II) 65 mph, 105 km/h; (III) 96 mph, 155 km/h; power-weight ratio: 25.4 lb/hp (34.6 lb/kW), 11.5 kg/hp (15.7 kg/kW); consumption: 22.6 m/imp gal, 18.8 m/US gal, 12.5 l x 100 km on Japanese emission test cycle.

CHASSIS integral; front suspension: independent, double wishbones, coil springs/telescopic dampers, anti-roll bar; rear: rigid axle, semi-elliptic leafsprings, telescopic dampers.

STEERING recirculating ball, servo.

BRAKES front disc, rear drum, servo.

ELECTRICAL EQUIPMENT 12 V; 60 Ah battery; 55 A alternator; Mitsubishi distributor; 4 headlamps.

DIMENSIONS AND WEIGHT wheel base: 105.91 in, 269 cm; front and rear track: 54.72 in, 139 cm; length: 183.86 in, 467 cm; width: 66.54 in, 169 cm; height: 57.48 in, 146 cm; ground clearance: 6.69 in, 17 cm; weight: 3,043 lb, 1,380 kg; weight distribution: 56% front, 44% rear; fuel tank: 15.4 imp gal, 18.5 US gal, 70 l.

BODY saloon/sedan; 4 doors; 5 seats, separate front seats.

Jeep Series

PRICES (Tokyo):		**yen**
1	H-J58 (canvas top, 4-pass.)	**1,285,000**
2	H-J56 (canvas top, 4-pass.)	**1,325,000**
3	H-J26H (metal top, 5-pass.)	**1,460,000**
4	H-J46 (canvas top, 9-pass.)	**1,410,000**
5	J38 Wagon (6-pass.)	**1,630,000**
6	J54 Diesel (canvas top, 4-pass.)	**1,470,000**
7	J24 Diesel (canvas top, 7-pass.)	**1,530,000**
8	J24H Diesel (metal top, 5-pass.)	**1,625,000**
9	J44 Diesel (canvas top, 9-pass.)	**1,578,000**
10	J36 Diesel Wagon (6-pass.)	**1,795,000**

Power team:	**Standard for:**	**Optional for:**
100 hp	1	—
110 hp	2 to 5	—
80 hp (diesel)	6 to 10	—

100 hp power team

ENGINE front, 4 stroke; 4 cylinders, vertical, in line; 121.7 cu in, 1,995 cc (3.31 x 3.54 in, 84 x 90 mm); compression ratio: 8.5:1; max power (JIS): 100 hp (74 kW) at 5,000 rpm; max torque (JIS): 123 lb ft, 17 kg m (167 Nm) at 3,000 rpm; max engine rpm: 5,400; 50.1 hp/l (36.9 kW/l); cast iron block, light alloy head; 5 crankshaft bearings; valves: overhead, Vee-slanted, rockers; camshafts: 1, overhead; lubrication: rotary pump, full flow filter, 7.6 imp pt, 9.1 US pt, 4.3 l; 1 Stromberg 30-32 DIDTA downdraught twin barrel carburettor; fuel feed: mechanical pump; water-cooled, 14 imp pt, 17 US pt, 8 l.

TRANSMISSION driving wheels: front (automatically-engaged with transfer box) and rear; clutch: single dry plate (diaphragm), hydraulically controlled; gearbox: mechanical; gears: 4, fully synchronized; ratios: I 2.971, II 1.795, III 1.345, IV 1, rev 3.157; transfer box: high 1, low 2.465; lever: central; final drive: hypoid bevel; axle ratio: 5.375; width of rims: 4.5"; tyres: 6.00 x 16.

100 HP POWER TEAM

PERFORMANCE max speeds: (I) 27 mph, 43 km/h; (II) 47 mph, 75 km/h; (III) 58 mph, 94 km/h; (IV) 75 mph, 120 km/h; power-weight ratio: 23.8 lb/hp (32.2 lb/kW), 10.8 kg/hp (14.6 kg/kW); carrying capacity: 551 lb, 250 kg; speed in direct drive at 1,000 rpm: 13.8 mph, 22.2 km/h; consumption: not declared.

CHASSIS ladder frame; front and rear suspension: rigid axle, semi-elliptic leafsprings, telescopic dampers.

STEERING cam and lever, variable ratio.

BRAKES drum.

ELECTRICAL EQUIPMENT 12 V; 35 Ah battery; 35 A alternator; Mitsubishi distributor; 2 headlamps.

DIMENSIONS AND WEIGHT wheel base: 79.92 in, 203 cm; front and rear track: 48.62 in, 123 cm; length: 133.46 in, 339 cm; width: 65.55 in, 166 cm; height: 75 in, 190 cm; ground clearance: 8.27 in, 21 cm; weight: 2,381 lb, 1,080 kg; weight distribution: 55% front, 45% rear; turning circle: 40 ft, 12.2 m; fuel tank: 9.7 imp gal, 11.6 US gal, 44 l.

BODY open, 3 detachable doors; 4 seats, separate front seats; estate car/st. wagon, 5 doors, 7/9 seats.

110 hp power team

See 100 hp power team, except for:

ENGINE 145.5 cu in, 2,384 cc (3.46 x 3.86 in, 88 x 98 mm); compression ratio: 8:1; max power (JIS): 110 hp (81 kW) at 5,000 rpm; max torque (JIS): 145 lb ft, 20 kg m (196 Nm) at 3,000 rpm; 46.1 hp/l (33.9 kW/l).

TRANSMISSION H-J26H lever: steering column.

PERFORMANCE power-weight ratio: H-J56 22.7 lb/hp 10.3 kg/hp (14 kg/kW).

STEERING H-J26H recirculating ball.

ELECTRICAL EQUIPMENT 50 Ah battery.

DIMENSIONS AND WEIGHT wheel base: H-J46 and J38 103.94 in, 264 cm; length: H-J46 161.42 in, 410 cm - J38 168.90 in, 429 cm; width: J38 63.78 in, 162 cm; weight: H-J56 2,492 lb, 1,130 kg - H-J26H 2,855 lb, 1,295 kg - H-J46 2,988 lb, 1,355 kg - J38 3,330 lb, 1,510 kg.

80 hp power team

See 100 hp power team, except for:

ENGINE diesel; 162.3 cu in, 2,659 cc (3.62 x 3.94 in, 92 x 100 mm); compression ratio: 20:1; max power (JIS): 80 hp (59 kW) at 3,700 rpm; max torque (JIS): 130 lb ft, 18 kg m (177 Nm) 2,200 rpm; 30.1 hp/l (22.2 kW/l).

TRANSMISSION transfer box ratios: high 0.933, low 2.38 lever: J24 steering column.

PERFORMANCE power-weight ratio: J54 35.1 lb/hp (47.6 kW), 15.9 kg/hp (21.6 kg/kW).

STEERING J24 recirculating ball.

ELECTRICAL EQUIPMENT 24 V; 70 Ah x 2 batteries.

DIMENSIONS AND WEIGHT wheel base: J54 79.92 in, 203 c - J24 87.60 in, 222 cm - J44 and J36 103.94 in, 264 cm; leng J54 137.40 in, 346 cm - J24 145.08 in, 368 cm - J44 161.42 410 cm - J36 168.90 in, 429 cm; width: 65.75 in, 167 cm - J 63.78 in, 162 cm; weight: J54 2,811 lb, 1,275 kg - J24 3,164 1,435 kg - J44 3,296 lb, 1,495 kg - J36 3,649 lb, 1,655 k

MITSUBISHI Jeep J36 Diesel Wagon

NISSAN-DATSUN Pulsar 1200 TS Sedan

NISSAN-DATSUN JAPA

Pulsar Series

PRICES (Tokyo):	yen
1 1200 Custom 4+1-dr Sedan	774,0
2 1200 Custom D 4+1-dr Sedan	804,0
3 1200 TS 4+1-dr Sedan	870,0
4 1200 TS Coupé	918,0
5 1200 Standard Hatchback	740,0
6 1200 Custom Hatchback	766,0
7 1200 Custom D Hatchback	796,0
8 1200 TS Hatchback	860,0
9 1400 TS 4+1-dr Sedan	945,0
10 1400 TS-G 4+1-dr Sedan	1,013,0
11 1400 TS Coupé	993,0
12 1400 TS Hatchback	925,0
13 1400 TS-X Hatchback	1,010,0
14 1400 TS-GE 4+1-dr Sedan	1,108,0
15 1400 TS-XE 4+1-dr Sedan	1,090,0
16 1400 TS-XE Coupé	1,106,0
17 1400 TS-XE Hatchback	1,080,0

Power team:	Standard for:	Optional for:
70 hp	1 to 8	—
80 hp	9 to 13	—
92 hp	14 to 17	—

70 hp power team

ENGINE front, transverse, 4 stroke; 4 cylinders, in line; 75.5 in, 1,237 cc (2.95 x 2.75 in, 75 x 70 mm); compression rat 9:1; max power (JIS): 70 hp (51 kW) at 6,000 rpm; max torc (JIS): 74 lb ft, 10.2 kg m (100 Nm) at 3,600 rpm; max eng rpm: 6,000; 56.6 hp/l (41.7 kW/l); cast iron block, light al head; 5 crankshaft bearings; valves: overhead, push-rods a rockers; camshafts: 1, side; lubrication: rotary pump, full fl filter, 5.8 imp pt, 7 US pt, 3.3 l; 1 Hitachi DCH 306- downdraught twin barrel carburettor; emission control with ca lytic converter, secondary air induction and exhaust gas rec culation; fuel feed: mechanical pump; water-cooled, 8.8 imp 10.6 US pt, 5 l.

TRANSMISSION driving wheels: front; clutch: single dry pla (diaphragm); gearbox: mechanical; gears: 4, fully synchronize ratios: I 3.673, II 2.217, III 1.433, IV 1, rev 4.093; lever: centr final drive: helical spur gears; axle ratio: 3,933 - Standa 3.471; width of rims: 4''; tyres: 6.00 x 12.

PERFORMANCE max speeds: (I) 27 mph, 43 km/h; (II) 43 mp 70 km/h; (III) 68 mph, 110 km/h; (IV) 90 mph, 145 km power-weight ratio: Custom 4+1-dr 24.9 lb/hp (33.8 lb/kW 11.3 kg/hp (15.1 kg/kW); carrying capacity: 882 lb, 400 consumption: 42.1 m/imp gal, 35.1 m/US gal, 6.7 l x 100 k

CHASSIS integral; front suspension: independent, by McPh son, coil springs/telescopic damper struts, lower wishbon rear: independent, trailing arms, coil springs, telescopic da pers.

STEERING rack-and-pinion; turns lock to lock: 3.30.

BRAKES drum - TS models front disc, servo: lining area: fr 42.2 sq in, 272 sq cm, rear 42.2 sq in, 272 sq cm, total 84.4 in, 544 sq cm - TS models front 14.3 sq in, 92 sq cm, rear 42 sq in, 272 sq cm, total 56.5 sq in, 364 sq cm.

ELECTRICAL EQUIPMENT 12 V; 40 Ah battery; 35 A alterr tor; Hitachi distributor; 2 headlamps.

DIMENSIONS AND WEIGHT wheel base: 94.29 in, 239 c tracks: 54.13 in, 137 cm - TS and Custom D models 53.74 136 cm front, 52.86 in, 133 cm rear; length: 153.15 in, 389 c width: 62.99 in, 160 cm; height: sedans 53.54 in, 136 cm hatchbacks 53.54 in, 136 cm - Coupé 52.16 in, 132 cm; grou clearance: 6.69 in, 17 cm; weight: Custom models 1,742 lb, 790 kg - TS and Custom D sedans 1,764 lb, 800 kg - TS Coupé 1,175 lb, 805 kg - Standard Hatchback 1,720 lb, 780 kg; weight distribution: 63% front, 37% rear; turning circle: 36.6 ft, 10.8 m; fuel tank: 11 imp gal, 13.2 US gal, 50 l.

BODY saloon/sedan, hardtop, coupé; 5 seats separate front seats.

OPTIONALS (for hatchbacks and coupés only) 5-speed fully synchronized mechanical gearbox (I 4.018, II 2.475, III 1.720, III 1.720, IV 1.254, V 1, rev 4,093), 3.471 axle ratio.

80 hp power team

See 70 hp power team, except for:

ENGINE 85.2 cu in, 1,397 cc (2.99 x 3.03 in, 76 x 77 mm); max power (JIS): 80 hp (59 kW) at 6,000 rpm; max torque (JIS): 83 lb ft, 11.3 kg m (113 Nm) at 3,600 rpm; 57.3 hp/l (42.2 kW/l); 1 Hitachi DCH 306-53 downdraught twin barrel carburettor.

TRANSMISSION gearbox ratios: I 3.275, II 1.977, III 1.383, IV 1, rev 3.649 (Coupé gears: 5; ratios: I 4.018, II 2.475, III 1.720, IV 1.254, V 1, rev 4.093); axle ratio: 3.933 - Coupé 3.471; width of rims: 4.5'; tyres: 155 SR x 13 - Coupé and TS-X Hatchback 165/70 SR x 13.

CHASSIS front suspension: anti-roll bar.

NISSAN-DATSUN Sunny 1400 SGL Sedan

PERFORMANCE max speeds: (I) 27 mph, 43 km/h; (II) 50 mph, 80 km/h; (III) 73 mph, 117 km/h; (IV) 93 mph, 150 km/h - Coupé (I) 29 mph, 47 km/h; (II) 46 mph, 74 km/h; (III) 71 mph, 114 km/h; (IV) 89 mph, 143 km/h; (V) 93 mph, 150 km/h; power-weight ratio: TS Sedan 23 lb/hp (31.3 lb/kW), 10.4 kg/hp (14.1 kg/kW); consumption: 38.1 m/imp gal, 31.7 m/US gal, 7.4 l x 100 km.

DIMENSIONS AND WEIGHT track: 54.13 in, 137 cm front, 52.95 in, 134 cm rear; length: 155.11 in, 394 cm; width: 63.78 in, 162 cm; weight: TS models 1,841 lb, 835 kg - TS-G 1,863 lb, 845 kg.

OPTIONALS 5-speed fully synchronized mechanical gearbox (except for Coupé); Nissan Sportsmatic semi-automatic transmission, hydraulic torque converter with 3 ratios (I 1.603, II 1, III 0.726, rev 1.846), solenoid-operated clutch, 4.629 axle ratio; 5" wide rims with light alloy wheels.

92 hp power team

See 70 hp power team, except for:

ENGINE max power (JIS): 92 hp (68 kW) at 6,400 rpm; max torque (JIS): 85 lb ft, 11.7 kg m (115 Nm) at 3,600 rpm; max engine rpm: 6,800; 65.8 hp/l; Nissan EGI (Bosch L-Jetronic) electronic injection; fuel feed: electric pump.

TRANSMISSION gearbox ratios: I 3.275, II 1.977, III 1.383, IV 1, rev 3.649; axle ratio: 3.933; width of rims: 4.5"; tyres: 165/70 SR x 13.

CHASSIS front suspension: anti-roll bar.

NISSAN-DATSUN Sunny 1400 SGL Sedan

PERFORMANCE max speed: 99 mph, 160 km/h; power-weight ratio: TS-XE Sedan 20.4 lb/hp (27.7 lb/kW), 9.2 kg/hp (12.6 kg/kW); consumption: 36.7 m/imp gal, 30.6 m/US gal, 7.7 l x 100 km.

DIMENSIONS AND WEIGHT tracks: 54.13 in, 137 cm front, 52.95 in, 134 cm rear; length: 155.11 in, 394 cm; width: 63.78 in, 162 cm; weight: TS-GE 1,885 lb, 855 kg - TS-XE models 1.874 lb, 850 kg.

OPTIONALS 5-speed fully synchronized mechanical gearbox (except for Coupé); Nissan Sportsmatic semi-automatic transmission, hydraulic torque converter with 3 ratios (I 1.603, II 1, III 0.726, rev 1.846) solenoid operated clutch, 4,629 axle ratio; 5" wide rims with light alloy wheels.

Sunny Series

PRICES (Tokyo):		yen
1	1200 CT 2-dr Sedan	**737,000**
2	1200 CT 4-dr Sedan	**757,000**
3	1200 City De Luxe 2-dr Sedan	**760,000**
4	1200 City De Luxe 4-dr Sedan	**780,000**
5	1200 S Coupé	**838,000**
6	1200 GL 2-dr Sedan	**850,000**
7	1200 GL 4-dr Sedan	**870,000**
8	1200 GS Coupé	**910,000**
9	1400 De Luxe 2-dr Sedan	**833,000**
10	1400 De Luxe 4-dr Sedan	**853,000**
11	1400 ES Coupé	**883,000**
12	1400 GL 2-dr Sedan	**902,000**
13	1400 GL 4-dr Sedan	**917,000**
14	1400 GS Coupé	**947,000**
15	1400 SGL 4-dr Sedan	**975,000**
16	1400 GX 4-dr Sedan	**962,000**
17	1400 GX Coupé	**1,001,000**
18	1400 SGX 4-dr Sedan	**1,020,000**
19	1400 SGX Coupé	**1,089,000**
20	1400 California 4+1-dr DX Sedan	**934,000**
21	1400 California 4+1-dr GL Sedan	**982,000**
22	1400 California 4+1-dr SGL Sedan	**1,058,000**
23	1400 California 4+1-dr GX Sedan	**1,035,000**
24	1400 GX-E 4-dr Sedan	**1,032,000**
25	1400 RS-E Coupé	**999,000**
26	1400 SGX-E 4-dr Sedan	**1,090,000**
27	1400 SGX-E Coupé	**1,134,000**

For USA prices, see price index.

Power team:	Standard for:	Optional for:
70 hp	1 to 8	—
80 hp	9 to 23	—
92 hp	24 to 27	—

70 hp power team

ENGINE front, 4 stroke; 4 cylinders, vertical, in line; 75.48 cu in, 1,237 cc (2.95 x 2.76 in, 75 x 70 mm); compression ratio: 9:1; max power (JIS): 70 hp (51 kW) at 6,000 rpm; max torque (JIS): 74 lb ft, 10.2 kg m (100 Nm) at 3,600 rpm; max engine rpm; 6,250; 56.6 hp/l (41.7 kW/l) cast iron block, light alloy head: 5 crankshaft bearings; valves: overhead, push-rods full flow filter, 6 imp pt, 7.2 US pt, 3.4 l; 1 Hitachi DCH 306.41 downdraught twin barrel carburettor; emission control with catalytic converter secondary air injection and exhaust gas recirculation; fuel feed: mechanical pump; water-cooled, 7 imp pt, 8.4 US pt, 4 l.

TRANSMISSION driving wheels: rear: clutch: single dry plate (diaphragm); gearbox: mechanical; gears: 4, fully synchronized; ratios: I 3.757, II 2.169, III 1.404, IV 1, rev 3.640; lever: central; final drive: hypoid bevel; axle ratio: 3.889; width of rims: 4"; tyres: 6.00 x 12.

PERFORMANCE max speeds: (I) 25 mph, 40 km/h; (II) 44 mph, 70 km/h; (III) 70 mph, 112 km/h; (IV) 90 mph, 145 km/h; power-weight ratio: CT 2-dr Sedan 25.1 lb/hp (34.4 lb/kW), 11.4 kg/hp (15.6 kg/kW); speed in direct drive at 1,000 rpm: 16.4 mph, 26.4 km/h; consumption: 43.4 m/imp gal, 36 m/US gal, 6.5 l x 100 km.

CHASSIS integral; front suspension: independent by McPherson, coil springs/telescopic damper struts, lower wishbones (trailing links); rear: rigid axle, lower trailing rods, upper torque rods, coil springs, telescopic dampers.

STEERING recirculating ball; turns lock to lock: 3.50.

BRAKES drum - GS Coupé front disc; lining area: front 42.2 sq in, 272 sq cm, rear 42.2 sq in, 272 sq cm, total 84.4 sq in, 544 sq cm - GS Coupé front 13.3 sq in, 86 sq cm, total 55.5 sq in, 358 sq cm.

ELECTRICAL EQUIPMENT 12 V; 32 Ah battery; alternator; Hitachi distributor; 2 headlamps.

DIMENSIONS AND WEIGHT wheel base: 92.13 in, 234 cm; front and rear track: 51.18 in, length: CT models and S Coupé 157.08 in, 399 cm - GL models and GS Coupé 160.14 in, 4.06 cm; width: CT and City models and S Coupé 62.20 in 158 cm - GL models and GS Coupé 63 in, 160 cm; height: sedans 53.94 in, 137 cm - coupés 52.76 in 134 cm; ground clearance: 6.50 in, 16 cm; weight: CT 2-dr Sedan 1,753 lb, 795 kg - City 2-dr Sedan 1,764 lb, 800 kg - GL 2-dr Sedan and CT 4-dr Sedan 1,775 lb, 805 kg - City 4-dr Sedan and S Coupé 1,786 lb, 810 kg - GL 4-dr Sedan and GS Coupé 1,797 lb, 815 kg; turning circle: 31.5 ft, 9.6 m; fuel tank: 11 imp gal, 13.2 US gal, 50 l.

OPTIONALS 5-speed fully synchronized mechanical gearbox (I 3.513, II 2.170, III 1.378, IV 1, V 0.821, rev 3.764).

80 hp power team

See 70 hp power team, except for:

ENGINE 85.2 cu in, 1,397 cc (2.99 x 3.03 in, 76 x 77 mm); max power (JIS): 80 hp (59 kW) at 6,000 rpm; max torque (JIS): 83 lb ft, 11.5 kg m (133 Nm) at 3,600 rpm; max engine rpm: 6,600; 57.3 hp/l (42.2 kW/l); 1 Hitachi DCH 306-51 or 52 downdraught twin barrel carburettor.

TRANSMISSION gearbox ratios: I 3.513, II 2.170, III 1.378, IV 1, rev 3.764; tyres: SGX Sedan and GL and GX and SGX coupés 165/70 HR x 13 - ES Coupé 6.15 x 13 - GX Sedan 145 SR x 13 - GL and SGL sedans and GS Coupé 155 SR x 13.

PERFORMANCE max speeds: (I) 27 mph, 44 km/h; (II) 45 mph, 72 km/h; (III) 70 mph, 112 km/h; (IV) 93 mph 150 km/h; power-weight ratio: De Luxe 2-dr Sedan 22.6 lb/hp (30.6 lb/kW), 10.2 kg/hp (13.9 kg/kW); consumption: 38.1 m/imp gal, 31.8 m/US gal, 7.4 l x 100 km.

80 HP POWER TEAM

BRAKES front disc, rear drum; lining area: front 13.3 sq in, 86 sq cm, rear 42.2 sq in, 272 sq cm, total 55.5 sq in, 358 sq cm.

DIMENSIONS AND WEIGHT front track: 52.36 in, 133 cm; length: California models 165.94 in, 421 cm; width: 62.99 in, 160 cm - De Luxe models 62.20 in, 158 cm; weight: De Luxe 2-dr Sedan 1,808 lb, 820 kg - De Luxe 4-dr Sedan 1,830 lb, 830 kg - GL 2-dr Sedan 1,852 lb, 840 kg - GL and SGL 4-dr sedans 1,874 lb, 850 kg - GX and SGX 4-dr sedans 1,896 lb, 860 kg - ES and GS coupés 1,874 lb, 850 kg - GX and SGX coupés 1,896 lb, 860 kg - California DX 1,929 lb, 875 kg - California SGL 1,973 lb, 895 kg - California GX 1,995 lb, 905 kg.

OPTIONALS 5-speed fully synchronized mechanical gearbox (I 3.513, II 2.170, III 1.378, IV 1, V 0,831, rev 3.764); JATCO automatic transmission with 3 ratios (I 2.458, II 1.458, III 1, rev 2.182).

92 hp power team

See 70 hp power team, except for:

ENGINE 85.2 cu in, 1,397 cc (2.99 x 3.03 in, 76 x 77 mm); max power (JIS): 92 hp (68 kW) at 6,400 rpm; max torque (JIS): 85 lb ft, 11.7 kg m (115 Nm) at 3,600 rpm; max engine rpm: 6,800; 65.8 hp/l (48.4 kW/l); Nissan EGI (Bosh L-injection) electronic injection; fuel feed: electric pump.

TRANSMISSION gearbox ratios: I 3.513, II 2.170, III 1.378, IV 1, rev 3.764: tyres: 165/70 HR x 13.

PERFORMANCE max speed: 99 mph, 160 km/h consumption: 38.1 m/imp gal, 31.8 m/US gal, 7.4 l x 100 km.

BRAKES front disc, rear drum; lining area: front 13.3 sq in, 86 sq cm, rear 42.2 sq in, 272 sq cm, total 55.5 sq in, 358 sq cm.

DIMENSIONS AND WEIGHT front track: 52.36 in, 133 cm; width: 62.99 in, 160 cm.

OPTIONALS 5-speed fully synchronized mechanical gearbox (I 3.513, II 2.170, III 1.378, IV 1, V 0.821, rev 3.764); JATCO automatic transmission with 3 ratios (I 2.458, II 1.458, III 1, rev 2.182).

Violet - Auster - Stanza Series

	PRICES (Tokyo):	yen
1	Violet 1400 Standard Sedan	858,000
2	Violet 1400 De Luxe Sedan	926,000
3	Violet 1400 De Luxe Hatchback Coupé	956,000
4	Violet 1400 GL Sedan	969,000
5	Violet GL Hatchback Coupé	999,000
6	Violet 1600 De Luxe Sedan	951,000
7	Auster 1600 Custom Sedan	981,000
8	Violet 1600 GL Sedan	999,000
9	Violet 1600 GL Hatchback Coupé	1,029,000
10	Violet 1600 GL-L Sedan	1,063,000
11	Auster 1600 CS Sedan	1,042,000
12	Auster 1600 CS Hatchback Coupé	1,072,000
13	Violet 1600 GX Sedan	1,055,000
14	Violet 1600 GX Hatchback Coupé	1,085,000
15	Auster 1600 CS-L Sedan	1,105,000
16	Auster 1600 CS-L Hatchback Coupé	1,150,000
17	Stanza 1600 Luxury Sedan	976,000
18	Stanza 1600 Extra Sedan	1,032,000
19	Stanza 1600 Maxima Sedan	1,130,000
20	Stanza 1600 Resort 4+1-dr Sedan	1,026,000
21	Stanza 1600 Resort 4+1-dr L Sedan	1,082,000
22	Stanza 1600 Resort 4+1-dr G Sedan	1,192,000
23	Violet 1600 SGX-E Sedan	1,255,000
24	Violet 1600 SGX-E Hatchback Coupé	1,300,000
25	Auster 1600 CS-EL Sedan	1,179,000
26	Auster 1600 CS-EL Hatchback Coupé	1,224,000
27	Stanza 1600 GT-E Sedan	1,172,000
28	Stanza 1600 Maxima GT-E Sedan	1,230,000
29	Stanza 1800 Extra Sedan	1,080,000
30	Stanza 1800 Maxima Sedan	1,161,000
31	Stanza 1800 Resort 4+1-dr Sedan	1,140,000
32	Stanza 1800 Resort 4+1-dr G Sedan	1,226,000
33	Stanza 1800 Maxima X-E Sedan	1,353,000
34	Stanza 1800 Maxima GT-E Sedan	1,301,000
35	Stanza 1800 Resort 4+1-dr X-E Sedan	1,341,000
36	Auster 1800 GT Sedan	1,196,000
37	Auster 1800 GT Hatchback Coupé	1,226,000

Power team:	Standard for:	Optional for:
80 hp	1 to 5	—
95 hp	6 to 22	—
105 hp	23 to 28	—
105 hp (1,770 cc)	29 to 32,36,37	—
115 hp	33 to 35	—

80 hp power team

ENGINE front, 4 stroke; 4 cylinders, vertical, in line; 85.2 cu in, 1,397 cc (2.99 x 3.03 in, 76 x 77 mm); compression ratio: 9:1; max power (JIS): 80 hp (59 kW) at 6,000 rpm; max torque (JIS): 83 lb ft, 11.5 kg m (113 Nm) at 3,600 rpm) max engine rpm: 6,250; 57.3 hp/l (42.2 kW/l); cast iron block, light alloy head; 5 crankshaft bearings; valves: overhead, in line, push-rods and rockers; camshafts: 1, side; lubrication: rotary pump, full flow filter, 6 imp pt, 7.2 US pt, 3.4 l; 1 Hitachi DCH 306-32 downdraught twin barrel carburettor; emission control with catalytic converter, secondary air induction and exhaust gas recirculation; fuel feed: mechanical pump; water-cooled, 7 imp pt, 8.4 US pt, 4 l.

NISSAN-DATSUN Auster 1800 GT Hatchback Coupé

TRANSMISSION driving wheels: rear; clutch: single dry plate (diaphragm); gearbox: mechanical; gears: 4, fully synchronized; ratios: I 3.513, II 2.170, III 1.378, IV 1, rev 3.764; lever: central; final drive: hypoid bevel; axle ratio: 3.889; width of rims: 4.5"; tyres: standard 5.60 x 13 - De luxe Sedan and GL models 6.45 x 13 - De Luxe Coupé 165 SR x 13.

PERFORMANCE max speeds: (I) 28 mph, 45 km/h; (II) 47 mph, 75 km/h; (III) 75 mph, 120 km/h; (IV) 93 mph, 150 km/h; power-weight ratio: standard 23.9 lb/hp (32.5 lb/kW), 10.9 kg/hp (14.8 kg/kW); consumption: 39.2 m/imp gal, 32.9 m/US gal, 7.1 l x 100 km.

CHASSIS integral; front suspension: independent, by McPherson, coil springs/telescopic damper struts, lower wishbones (trailing links), anti-roll bar; rear: rigid axle, lower trailing rods, upper torque rods, coil springs, telescopic dampers.

STEERING recirculating ball; turns lock to lock: 3.70.

BRAKES front disc, rear drum, servo; lining area: front 17.4 sq in, 112 sq cm, rear 54 sq in, 348 sq cm, total 71.4 sq in, 460 sq cm.

ELECTRICAL EQUIPMENT 12 V; 32 Ah battery; 50 A alternator; Hitachi distributor; 4 headlamps.

DIMENSIONS AND WEIGHT wheel base: 94.49 in, 240 cm; front and rear track: 52.36 in, 133 cm; length: 166 in, 422 cm; width: 62.99 in, 160 cm; height: sedans 54.72 in, 139 cm - coupés 53.15 in, 135 cm; ground clearance: 6.30 in, 16 cm; weight: Standard 1,918 lb, 870 kg - De Luxe Sedan 1,929 lb, 875 kg - GL Sedan 1,940 lb, 880 kg - De Luxe and GL coupés 1,984 lb, 900 kg; weight distribution: 55% front, 45% rear; turning circle: 32.8 ft, 10 m; fuel tank: 11 imp gal, 13.2 US gal, 50 l.

OPTIONALS 5-speed mechanical gearbox (I 3.513, II 2.170, III 1.378, IV 1, V 0.821) (for GL models only).

95 hp power team

See 80 hp power team, except for:

ENGINE 97.3 cu in, 1,595 cc (3.27 x 2.90 in, 83 x 73.7 mm); compression ratio: 8.5:1; max power (JIS): 95 hp (70 kW) at 6,000 rpm; max torque (JIS): 98 lb ft, 13.5 kg m (132 Nm) at 3,600 rpm; 59.6 hp/l (43.9 kW/l); Nissan NAPS-Z fast burn cylinder head with 2 spark plugs per cylinder; valves: overhead, Vee-slanted, rockers; camshafts: 1, overhead; lubrication: 8.1 imp pt, 9.7 US pt, 4.6 l; 1 Hitachi 21A 304-201 downdraught twin barrel carburettor; cooling, 10.6 imp pt, 12.7 US pt, 6 l.

TRANSMISSION gearbox ratios: I 3.657, II 2.177, III 1.419, IV 1, rev 3.638; axle ratio: 3.700; tyres: 6.45 x 13 - GX, CS and CS-L models 165 SR x 13.

PERFORMANCE max speeds: (I) 27 mph, 43 km/h; (II) 60 mph, 80 km/h; (III) 78 mph, 126 km/h; (IV) 99 mph, 160 km/h; power-weight ratio: Violet De Luxe 21.5 lb/hp (29.2 lb/kW), 9.7 kg/hp (13.2 kg/kW); consumption: 39.2 m/imp gal, 32.9 m/US gal, 7.1 l x 100 km.

CHASSIS rear suspension: anti-roll bar.

DIMENSIONS AND WEIGHT length: Stanza models 168.31 in, 427 cm; weight: Violet De Luxe 2,039 lb, 925 kg - Violet GL and GL-L sedans 2,050 lb, 930 kg - Violet GL Coupé 2,094 lb, 950 kg - Violet GX Coupé 2,105 lb, 960 kg - Auster Custom 2,039 lb, 925 kg - Auster CS and CS-L sedans 2,072 lb, 940 kg - Auster CS and CS-L coupés 2,105 lb, 960 kg - Stanza Luxury Sedan 2,061 lb, 935 kg - Stanza Extra Sedan 2,072 lb, 940 kg - Stanza Resort S 2,105 lb, 960 kg - Stanza Resort L 2,116 lb, 965 kg - Stanza Resort G 2,127 lb, 970 kg.

OPTIONALS 5-speed fully synchronized mechanical gearbox (I 3.657, II 2.177, III 1.419, IV 1, V 0.852, rev 3.860); automatic transmission with 3 ratios (I 2.458, II 1.458, III 1, rev 2.182), 3.889 axle ratio, max speed 93 mph, 150 km/h.

105 hp power team

See 80 hp power team, except for:

ENGINE 97.3 cu in, 1,595 cc (3.27 x 2.90 in, 83 x 73.7 mm); max power (JIS): 105 hp (78 kW) at 6,000 rpm; max torque (JIS): 100 lb ft, 13.8 kg m (135 Nm) at 4,000 rpm; 65.8 hp/l (48.4 kW/l); Nissan NAPS-Z fast burn cylinder head with two spark plugs per cylinder; valves: overhead, Vee-slanted, rockers; camshafts: 1, overhead; lubrication: 8.1 imp pt, 9.7 US pt, 4.6 l; Bosch electronic injection; fuel feed: electric pump; cooling, 10.6 imp pt, 12.7 US pt, 6 l.

TRANSMISSION gearbox ratio: I 3.657, II 2.177, III 1.419, IV 1, rev 3.638; axle ratio: 3.700; tyres: 165 SR x 13.

PERFORMANCE max speed: 103 mph, 165 km/h; power-weight ratio: Violet SGX-E Sedan 20.8 lb/hp (28.2 lb/kW), 9.4 kg/hp (12.8 kg/kW).

CHASSIS rear suspension: anti-roll bar.

DIMENSIONS AND WEIGHT length: Stanza models 168.31 in, 427 cm; weight: Violet SGX-E Sedan 2,182 lb, 990 kg - Auster CS-EL Sedan 2,127 lb, 970 kg - Stanza Maxima GT-E Sedan 2,160 lb, 980 kg - Violet SGX-E Coupé 2,238 lb, 1,015 kg - Auster CS-EL Coupé 2,194 lb, 995 kg.

OPTIONALS 5-speed fully synchronized mechanical gearbox (I 3.657, II 2.117, III 1.419, IV 1, V 0.852, rev 3.860); automatic transmission with 3 ratios (I 2.458, II 1.458, III 1, rev 2.182), 3.889 axle ratio.

105 hp (1,770 cc) power team

See 80 hp power team, except for:

ENGINE 108 cu in, 1,770 cc (3.35 x 3.07 in, 85 x 78 mm); max power (JIS): 105 hp (78 kW) at 6,000 rpm; max torque (JIS): 109 lb ft, 15 kg m (147 Nm) at 3,600 rpm; 59.3 hp/l (43.7 kW/l); Nissan NAPS-Z fast burn head with 2 spark plugs per cylinder; valves: overhead, Vee-slanted, rockers; camshafts: 1, overhead; lubrication: 8.1 imp pt, 9.7 US pt, 4.6 l; 1 Hitachi 21A 304-20 downdraught twin barrel carburettor; cooling, 10.6 imp pt, 12.7 US pt, 6 l.

TRANSMISSION gearbox ratios: I 3.382, II 2.013, III 1.312, IV 1, rev 3.665; axle ratio: 3.700; tyres: 165 SR x 13 - Extra and Resort L 6.45 x 13.

ERFORMANCE max speeds: (I) 29 mph, 46 km/h; (II) 54 mph, 7 km/h; (III) 81 mph, 130 km/h; (IV) 106 mph, 170 km/h; ower-weight ratio: Auster GT Sedan 20.1 lb/hp (27.1 lb/kW), .1 kg/hp (12.3 kg/kW); consumption: 36.7 m/imp gal, 30.6 /US gal, 7.7 l x 100 km.

IMENSIONS AND WEIGHT length: Stanza models 168.31 in, 27 cm; weight: Auster GT Sedan 2,116 lb, 960 kg - Stanza xtra and Maxima sedans 2,105 lb, 955 kg - Auster GT Coupé, tanza Resort models 2,160 lb, 980 kg.

PTIONALS 5-speed fully synchronized mechanical gearbox (I .382, II 2.013, III 1.312, IV 1, V 0.854, rev 3.570); automatic ansmission with 3 ratios (I 2.458, II 1.458, III 1, rev 2.182), .889 axle ratio, max speed 102 mph, 165 km/h.

115 hp power team

ee 80 hp power team, except for:

NGINE 108 cu in, 1,770 cc (3.35 x 3.07 in, 85 x 78 mm); max ower (JIS): 115 hp (85 kW) at 6,000 rpm; max torque (JIS): 12 lb ft, 15.5 kg m (152 Nm) at 3,600 rpm; 65 hp/l (47.8 kW/l); issan NAPS-Z fast burn head with two spark plugs per cylin- er; valves: overhead, Vee-slanted, rockers; camshafts: 1, verhead, lubrication: 8.1 imp pt, 9.7 US pt, 4.6 l; Bosch lectronic injection; fuel feed: electric pump cooling, 10.6 imp t, 12.7 US pt, 6 l.

RANSMISSION gearbox ratios: I 3.382, II 2.013, III 1.312, IV , rev 3.665; axle ratio: 3.700; tyres: 165 SR x 13.

ERFORMANCE max speed: 109 mph, 175 km/h; power-weight atio: Stanza Maxima X-E 19.2 lb/hp (26 lb/kW), 8.7 kg/hp (11.8 g/kW); consumption: 35.3 m/imp gal, 29.4 m/US gal, 8 l x 100 m.

HASSIS rear suspension: anti-roll bar.

IMENSIONS AND WEIGHT length: 168.31 in, 427 cm; weight: tanza Maxima GT-E 2,183 lb, 990 kg - Stanza Maxima X-E ,216 lb, 1,005 kg - Stanza Resort X-E 2,260 lb, 1,025 kg.

PTIONALS 5-speed fully synchronized mechanical gearbox (I .382, II 2.013, III 1.312, IV 1, V 0.854, rev 3.570); automatic ansmission with 3 ratios (I 2.458, II 1.458, III 1, rev 2.182), .889 axle ratio, max speed 102 mph, 165 km/h.

Bluebird Series

RICES (Tokyo):	yen
1 1600 4-dr CT Sedan	949,000
2 1600 4-dr DX Sedan	989,000
3 1600 4-dr GL Sedan	1,046,000
4 1600 4-dr GF Sedan	1,203,000
5 1600 2-dr GL Hardtop	1,081,000
6 1600 2-dr GF Hardtop	1,238,000
7 1800 4-dr GL Sedan	1,127,000
8 1800 4-dr GF Sedan	1,294,000
9 1800 4-dr SSS Sedan	1,208,000
0 1800 2-dr GF Hardtop	1,329,000
1 1800 2-dr SSS Hardtop	1,243,000
2 1800 4-dr SSS-E Sedan	1,326,000
3 1800 2-dr SSS-E Hardtop	1,361,000
4 2000 4-dr SSS-EL Sedan	1,412,000
5 2000 4-dr SSS-EX Sedan	1,603,000
6 2000 4-dr SSS-EXG Sedan	1,698,000
7 2000 4-dr SSS-ES Sedan	1,473,000
8 2000 2-dr SSS-EL Hardtop	1,447,000
9 2000 2-dr SSS-EX Hardtop	1,638,000
0 2000 2-dr SSS-EXG Hardtop	1,733,000
1 2000 2-dr SSS-ES Hardtop	1,508,000

ower team:	Standard for:	Optional for:
95 hp	1 to 6	—
05 hp	7 to 11	—
15 hp	12,13	—
20 hp	14 to 21	—

95 hp power team

NGINE front, 4 stroke; 4 cylinders, in line; 97.3 cu in, 1,595 cc 3.27 x 2.90 in, 83 x 73.7 mm); compression ratio: 8.5:1; max ower (JIS): 95 hp (70 kW) at 6,000 rpm; max torque (JIS): 98 ɔ ft, 13.5 kg m (132 Nm) at 3,600 rpm; 59.6 hp/l (43.9 kW/l); ast iron block, light alloy head; 5 crankshaft bearings; valves: verhead, Vee-slanted, rockers; camshafts: 1, overhead; lubri- ation: rotary pump, full flow filter, 7.2 imp pt, 8.5 US pt, 4.1 l; issan NAPS-Z 1 Nikki 21A 304-32 fast burn engine with two park plugs per cylinder; downdraught twin barrel carburettor; mission control with catalytic converter, secondary air injec- on and exhaust gas recirculation; fuel feed: mechanical pump; vater-cooled, 13.5 imp pt, 15.9 US pt, 7.7 l.

RANSMISSION driving wheels: rear; clutch: single dry plate diaphragm); gearbox: mechanical; gears: 4, fully synchronized; atios: I 3.657, II 2.177, III 1.419, IV 1, rev 3.638; lever: central; nal drive: hypoid bevel; axle ratio: 3.889; width of rims: 4.5''; yres: 6.45 x 14 - GF 165 SR x 13.

ERFORMANCE max speeds: (I) 33 mph, 50 km/h; (II) 45 mph, 2 km/h; (III) 72 mph, 116 km/h; (IV) 99 mph, 160 km/h; ower-weight ratio: CT 22.7 lb/hp (28.9 lb/kW), 10.3 kg/hp (13.1 kg/kW); carrying capacity: 882 lb, 400 kg; consumption: 39.5 m/imp gal, 32.9 m/US gal, 7.1 l x 100 km.

CHASSIS integral; front suspension: independent, by McPher- son, coil springs/telescopic damper struts, lower wishbones (trailing links), anti-roll bar; rear: rigid axle, lower trailing arms, upper torque rods, coil springs, telescopic dampers.

STEERING recirculating ball; turns lock to lock: 4.

BRAKES front disc, rear drum, servo; lining area: front 15.5 sq in, 100 sq cm, rear 54 sq in, 348 sq cm, total 69.5 sq in, 448 sq cm.

ELECTRICAL EQUIPMENT 12 V; 33 Ah battery; 50 A alterna- tor; Hitachi distributor; 2 headlamps.

DIMENSIONS AND WEIGHT wheel base: 99.21 in, 252 cm; tracks: 53.94 in, 137 cm front, 53.54 in, 136 cm rear; length: sedans 171.26 in, 435 cm - hardtops 171.65 in, 436 cm; width: 64.96 in, 165 cm - CT and DX sedans 64.57 in, 164 cm; height: 54.33 in, 135 cm; ground clearance: 6.29 in, 16 cm; weight: CT 2,160 lb, 980 kg - DX 2,171 lb, 985 kg - GL models 2,182 lb, 990 kg - GF models 2,205 lb, 1,000 kg; weight distribution: 54% front, 46% rear; turning circle: 36 ft, 11 m; fuel tank: 13.8 imp gal, 16.4 US gal, 62 l.

BODY saloon/sedan, 4 doors - hardtop, 2 doors; 5 seats, separate front seats, reclining backrests, built-in headrests.

105 hp power team

See 95 hp power team, except for:

ENGINE 108 cu in, 1,770 cc (3.35 x 3.07 in, 85 x 78 mm); max power (JIS): 105 hp (78 kW) at 6,000 rpm; max torque (JIS): 109 lb ft, 15 kg m (147 Nm)) at 3,600 rpm; 59.3 hp/l, (43.7 kW/l); 1 Hitachi DCR 340-4 downdraught twin barrel car- burettor.

TRANSMISSION gearbox ratios: I 3.382, II 2.013, III 1.312, IV 1, rev 3.365 (SSS models I 3.321, II 2.077, III 1.308, IV 1); axle ratio: 3.889 - SSS models 4.111; tyres: GL and GF models 165 SR x 13 - SSS models 165 SR x 14.

PERFORMANCE power-weight ratio: GL 20.9 lb/hp (28.4 lb/ kW), 9.5 kg/hp (12.9 kg/kW); consumption: 35 m/imp gal, 29.4 m/US gal, 8 l x 100 km.

CHASSIS (for SSS models only) rear suspension: independent, semi-trailing arms, coil springs, telescopic dampers, anti-roll bar.

DIMENSIONS AND WEIGHT rear track: SSS models 53.15 in, 135 cm; weight: GL 2,194 lb, 995 kg - GF models 2,260 lb, 1,025 kg - SSS models 2,349 lb, 1,050 kg.

OPTIONALS 3-speed automatic transmission; (for SSS models only) 5-speed fully synchronized mechanical gearbox (I 3.382, II 2.013, III 1.312, IV 1, V 0.854, rev 3.570); power steering with 3-speed automatic transmission (for GL only).

115 hp power team

See 95 hp power team, except for:

ENGINE 108 cu in, 1,770 cc (3.35 x 3.07 in, 85 x 78 mm); max

NISSAN-DATSUN Bluebird 2000 SSS-ES Hardtop

power (JIS): 115 hp (85 kW) at 6,200 rpm; max torque (JIS): 112 lb ft, 15.5 kg m (152 Nm) at 3,600 rpm; 65 hp/l (47.8 kW/l); lubrication: Bosch electronic injection; fuel feed: electric pump.

TRANSMISSION gears: 5, fully synchronized; ratios: I 3.321, II 2.077, III 1.308, IV 1, V 0.833, rev 3.382; axle ratio: 4.111; width of rims: 5''; tyres: 185/70 HR x 14.

PERFORMANCE max speed: 106 mph, 170 km/h; power-weight ratio: 20.9 lb/hp (28.4 lb/kW), 9.5 kg/hp (12.9 kg/kW); consump- tion: 33.6 m/imp gal, 28.2 m/US gal, 8.3 l x 100 km.

CHASSIS rear suspension: independent, semi-trailing arms, coil springs, telescopic dampers, anti-roll bar.

BRAKES rear disc; lining area: front 15.5 sq in, 100 sq cm, rear 14.3 sq in, 92 sq cm, total 29.8 sq in, 192 sq cm.

DIMENSIONS AND WEIGHT length: 177.56 in, 451 cm; weight: 2,403 lb, 1,090 kg.

OPTIONALS JATCO automatic transmission, hydraulic torque converter and planetary gears with 3 ratios (I 2.458, II 1.458, III 1, rev 2.182).

120 hp power team

See 95 hp power team, except for:

ENGINE 119.1 cu in, 1,952 cc (3.35 x 3.39 in, 85 x 86 mm); compression ratio: 8.5:1; max power (JIS): 120 hp (88 kW) at 5,600 rpm; max torque (JIS): 123 lb ft, 17 kg m (167 Nm) at

NISSAN-DATSUN Bluebird 2000 SSS-ES Hardtop

NISSAN-DATSUN Skyline 1800 TI-L Sedan

120 HP POWER TEAM

3,600 rpm; max engine rpm: 6,000; 61.5 hp/l (45.2 kW/l); lubrication: 7.3 imp pt, 8.7 US pt, 4.2 l; Bosch L-Jetronic injection; fuel feed: electric pump; cooling, 14 imp pt, 16.5 US pt, 8 l.

TRANSMISSION gears: 5, fully synchronized; ratios: I 3.592, II 2.246, III 1.415, IV 1, V 0.813, rev 3.657; axle ratio: 4.111; tyres: 185/70 SR x 14 or 185/70 HR x 14.

PERFORMANCE max speeds: (I) 27 mph, 43 km/h; (II) 43 mph, 70 km/h; (III) 68 mph, 110 km/h; (IV) 106 mph, 170 km/h; (V) 106 mph, 170 km/h; power-weight ratio: SSS-EL models 20.3 lb/hp (27.6 lb/kW), 9.2 kg/hp (12.5 kg/kW); carrying capacity: 882 lb, 400 kg; speed in top at 1,000 rpm: 21.7 mph, 34.8 km/h; consumption: 29.5 m/imp gal, 24.8 m/US gal, 9.5 l x 100 km.

CHASSIS rear suspension: independent, semi-trailing arms, coil springs, telescopic dampers, anti-roll bar.

STEERING servo.

BRAKES rear disc.

DIMENSIONS AND WEIGHT rear track: 53.50 in, 136 cm; length: 177.56 in, 451 cm; weight: SSS-EL models 2,436 lb, 1,105 kg - SSS-EX models 2,524 lb, 1,145 kg - SSS-EXG models 2,524 lb, 1,145 kg - SSS-ES 2,447 lb, 1,110 kg.

OPTIONALS JATCO automatic transmission, hydraulic torque converter and planetary gears with 3 ratios (I 2.458, II 1.458, III 1, rev 2.182), max speed 103 mph, 165 km/h.

Skyline Series

PRICES (Tokyo):	yen
1 1600 TI Sedan	**1,021,000**
2 1600 TI-L Sedan	**1,110,000**
3 1600 TI-L Hardtop	**1,145,000**
4 1800 TI Sedan	**1,076,000**
5 1800 TI-L Sedan	**1,199,000**
6 1800 TI-L Hardtop	**1,234,000**
7 1800 TI-EL Sedan	**1,301,000**
8 1800 TI-EL Hardtop	**1,332,000**
9 1800 TI-EX Sedan	**1,396,000**
10 1800 TI-EX Hardtop	**1,428,000**
11 1800 TI-ES Sedan	**1,414,000**
12 1800 TI-ES Hardtop	**1,449,000**
13 2000 GT Sedan	**1,289,000**
14 2000 GT Hardtop	**1,334,000**
15 2000 GT-L Sedan	**1,360,000**
16 2000 GT-L Hardtop	**1,405,000**
17 2000 GT-E Sedan	**1,408,000**
18 2000 GT-E Hardtop	**1,451,000**
19 2000 GT-EL Sedan	**1,465,000**
20 2000 GT-EL Hardtop	**1,508,000**
21 2000 GT-EX Sedan	**1,654,000**
22 2000 GT-EX Hardtop	**1,698,000**
23 2000 GT-ES Sedan	**1,657,000**
24 2000 GT-ES Hardtop	**1,702,000**

Power team:	Standard for:	Optional for:
95 hp	1 to 3	—
105 hp	4 to 6	—
115 hp	7 to 12	—
115 hp (1,998 cc)	13 to 16	—
130 hp	17 to 24	—

95 hp power team

ENGINE front, 4 stroke; 4 cylinders, in line; 97.3 cu in, 1,595 cc (3.27 x 2.90 in, 83 x 73.7 mm); compression ratio: 8.5:1; max power (JIS): 95 hp (70 kW) at 6,000 rpm; max torque (JIS): 98 lb ft, 13.5 kg m (132 Nm) at 3,6000 rpm; max engine rpm: 6,300; 62.7 hp/l (46.1 kW/l); cast iron block, light alloy head; 5 crankshaft bearings; valves: overhead, Vee-slanted, rockers; camshafts: 1, overhead; lubrication: rotary pump, full flow filter, 7.7 imp pt, 9,1 US pt, 4.4 l; Nissan NAPS-Z fast burn engine with two spark plugs per cylinder; 1 Nikki 21A 304-20 downdraught twin barrel carburettor; emission control with catalytic converter, secondary air induction and exhaust gas recirculation; fuel feed: mechanical pump; water-cooled, 12.2 imp pt, 14.4 US pt, 7 l.

TRANSMISSION driving wheels: rear; clutch: single dry plate (diaphragm); gearbox: mechanical; gears: 4, fully synchronized; ratios: I 3.382, II 2.013, III 1.312, IV 1, rev 3.365; lever: central; final drive: hypoid bevel; axle ratio: 4.111; width of rims: 4.5"; tyres: 6.45 x 13.

PERFORMANCE max speeds: (I) 27 mph, 44 km/h; (II) 47 mph, 75 km/h; (III) 68 mph, 110 km/h; (IV) 96 mph, 155 km/h; power-weight ratio: TI 24.2 lb/hp (32.9 lb/kW), 11 kg/hp (14.9 kg/kW); consumption: 35.3 m/imp gal, 29.4 m/US gal, 8 l x 100 km.

CHASSIS integral; front suspension: independent, by McPherson, coil springs/telescopic damper struts, lower wishbones (trailing links), anti-roll bar: rigid axle, lower trailing links, upper torque rods, coil springs, telescopic dampers.

NISSAN-DATSUN Skyline 1800 TI-L Sedan

STEERING recirculating ball; turns lock to lock: 3.60.

BRAKES front disc, rear drum, servo; lining area: front 15.5 sq in, 100 sq cm, rear 54 sq in, 348 sq cm, total 69.5 sq in, 448 sq cm.

ELECTRICAL EQUIPMENT 12 V; 35 Ah battery; 50 A alternator; Hitachi distributor; 4 headlamps.

DIMENSIONS AND WEIGHT wheel base: 98.82 in, 251 cm; tracks: 53.54 in, 136 cm front, 53.15 in, 135 cm rear; length: 173.23 in, 440 cm; width: 63.78 in, 162 cm; height: sedan 54.72 in, 139 cm - Hardtop 54.13 in, 137 cm; ground clearance 6.30 in, 16 cm; weight: TI 2,304 lb, 1,045 kg - TI-L Sedan 2,33[illegible] lb, 1,060 kg - TI-L Hardtop 2,348 lb, 1,065 kg; turning circle 36.1 ft, 11 m; fuel tank: 13.2 imp gal, 15.8 US gal, 60 l.

105 hp power team

See 95 hp power team, except for:

ENGINE 108 cu in, 1,770 cc (3.35 x 3.07 in, 85 x 78 mm); max power (JIS): 105 hp (78 kW) at 6,000 rpm; max torque (JIS) 109 lb ft, 15 kg m (147 Nm) at 3,600 rpm; 59.3 hp/l (43.6 kW/l).

TRANSMISSION gearbox ratio: I 3.382, II 2.013, III 1.312, IV 1 rev 3.365; axle ratio: 3.889; tyres: TI-L models 165 SR x 13

PERFORMANCE max speeds: (I) 27 mph, 44 km/h; (II) 45 mph 73 km/h; (III) 68 mph, 110 km/h; (IV) 103 mph, 165 km/h power-weight ratio: TI 22.3 lb/hp (30.3 lb/kW), 10.1 kg/hp (13.7 kg/kW); consumption: 36.7 m/imp gal, 30.6 m/US gal, 7.7 l x 100 km.

DIMENSIONS AND WEIGHT weight: TI 2,337 lb, 1,060 kg - TI-L Sedan 2,359 lb, 1,070 kg - TI-L Hardtop 2,370 lb, 1,075 kg.

OPTIONALS 5-speed mechanical gearbox (I 3.382, II 2.013, III 1.312, IV 1, V 0.854, rev 3.570); automatic transmission with 3 ratios (I 2.458, II 1.458, III 1, rev 2.182).

115 hp power team

See 95 hp power team, except for:

ENGINE 108 cu in, 1,770 cc (3.35 x 3.07 in, 85 x 78 mm); max power (JIS): 115 hp (85 kW) at 6,200 rpm; max torque (JIS) 112 lb ft, 15.5 kg m (152 Nm) at 3,600 rpm; 65 hp/l (47.8 kW/l) Bosch L-Jetronic electronic injection.

TRANSMISSION gearbox ratios: I 3.382, II 2.013, III 1.312, IV 1, rev 3.365; axle ratio: 4.111; tyres: TI-EL and TI-EX models 165 SR x 14 - TI-ES models 185/70 HR x 14.

PERFORMANCE max speed: 103 mph, 165 km/h; power-weight ratio: TI-ES Sedan 20.8 lb/hp (28.3 lb/kW), 9.4 kg/hp (12.8 kg/kW); consumption: 33.9 m/imp gal, 28.2 m/US gal, 8.3 l x 100 km.

CHASSIS TI-ES models anti-roll bar on rear suspension.

BRAKES TI-ES models disc.

DIMENSIONS AND WEIGHT height: TI-EL and TI-ES sedans 55.31 in, 140 cm - TI-EL and TI-ES hardtops 54.92 in, 139 cm weight: TI-EL Sedan 2,392 lb, 1,085 kg - TI-EL Hardtop 2,403 lb, 1,090 kg - TI-EX Sedan 2,425 lb, 1,100 kg - TI-EX Hardtop 2,436 lb, 1,105 kg - TI-ES Sedan 2,447 lb, 1,110 kg - TI-ES Hardtop 2,458 lb, 1,115 kg.

115 hp power team (1,998 cc)

See 95 hp power team, except for:

ENGINE 6 cylinders, in line; 121.9 cu in, 1,998 cc (3.07 x 2.74 in, 78 x 69.7 mm); compression ratio: 8.6:1; max power (JIS): 115 hp (85 kW) at 5,600 rpm; max torque (JIS): 120 lb ft, 16.5 kg m (162 Nm) at 3,600 rpm; 57.6 hp/l (42.4 kW/l); 7 crankshaft bearings; valves: in line; lubrication: rotary pump, full flow filter, 10 imp pt, 12 US pt, 5.7 l; 1 Hitachi ECC air-fuel ratio adjusting downdraught barrel carburettor; emission control with 3-way catalytic converter; water-cooled, 15.8 imp pt, 19 US pt, 9 l.

TRANSMISSION gearbox ratios: I 3.592, II 2.246, III 1.415, IV 1, rev 3.657; tyres: 185/70 HR x 14.

PERFORMANCE max speeds: (I) 26 mph, 42 km/h; (II) 43 mph, 70 km/h; (III) 58 mph, 110 km/h; (IV) 99 mph, 160 km/h; power-weight ratio: GT Sedan 22.7 lb/hp, (30.8 lb/kW), 10.3 kg/hp (14 kg/kW); consumption: 26.5 m/imp gal, 22.1 m/US gal, 10.6 l x 100 km.

CHASSIS rear suspension: independent, semi-trailing arms, coil springs, telescopic dampers.

STEERING recirculating ball, variable ratio; turns lock to lock: 4.

BRAKES rear compensator; lining area: front 22.3 sq in, 144 sq cm, rear 54 sq in, 348 sq cm, total 89.3 sq in, 576 sq cm.

DIMENSIONS AND WEIGHT wheel base: 102.76 in, 261 cm; front track: 53.94 in, 137 cm; length: 181.10 in, 460 cm; weight: GT Sedan 2,613 lb, 1,185 kg - GT Hardtop and GT-L Sedan

2,624 lb, 1,190 kg - GT-L Hardtop 2,635 lb, 1,195 kg; turning circle: 38 ft, 11.6 m.

OPTIONALS 5-speed fully synchronized mechanical gearbox (I 3.321, II 2.077, III 1.308, IV 1, V 0.864, rev 3.382), 4.111 axle ratio, max speed 106 mph, 170 km/h; automatic transmission with 3 ratios (I 2.458, II 1.458, III 1, rev 2.182); power steering, 3.60 turns lock to lock.

130 hp power team

See 95 hp power team, except for:

ENGINE 6 cylinders, in line; 121.9 cu in, 1,998 cc (3.07 x 2.74 in, 78 x 69.7 mm); compression ratio: 8.6:1; max power (JIS): 130 hp (96 kW) at 6,000 rpm; max torque (JIS): 123 lb ft, 17 kg m (167 Nm) at 4,000 rpm; 65.1 hp/l (47.9 kW/l); 7 crankshaft bearings; lubrication: 10 imp pt, 12 US pt, 5.7 l; Bosch L-Jetronic electronic injection; emission control with 3-way catalytic converter, exhaust gas recirculation; fuel feed: electric pump; water-cooled, 15.8 imp pt, 19 US pt, 9 l.

TRANSMISSION gears: 5, fully synchronized; ratios: I 3.592, II 2.246, III 1.415, IV 1, V 0.882, rev 3.657; axle ratio: 4.111; width of rims: 5"; tyres: 185/70 HR x 14.

PERFORMANCE max speeds: (I) 28 mph, 45 km/h; (II) 47 mph, 76 km/h; (III) 71 mph, 115 km/h; (IV) and (V) 109 mph, 175 km/h; power-weight ratio: GT-EL Sedan 20.2 lb/hp (27.4 lb/kW), 9.1 kg/hp (12.4 kg/kW); consumption: 26.5 m/imp gal, 22.1 m/US gal, 10.6 l x 100 km.

NISSAN-DATSUN Laurel 2800 Medalist models

NISSAN-DATSUN Laurel 2000 GL 6 Hardtop

CHASSIS rear suspension: independent, semi-trailing arms, coil springs, telescopic dampers - GT-EX and GT-ES models anti-roll bar.

STEERING recirculating ball, variable ratios; turns lock to lock: 4.

BRAKES rear compensator, GT-EX and GT-ES models rear disc; lining area: front 22.3 sq in, 144 sq cm, rear 54 sq in, 348 sq cm, total 89.3 sq in, 576 sq cm - GT-EX and GT-ES models rear lining area 14.3 sq in, 92 sq cm.

DIMENSIONS AND WEIGHT wheel base: 102.76 in, 261 cm; tracks: 53.94 in, 137 cm front, 53.15 in, 135 cm rear; length: 181.10 in, 460 cm; width: GT-EX models 64.37 in, 163 cm; weight: GT-EL Sedan 2,624 lb, 1,190 kg - GT-EL Hardtop 2,635 lb, 1,195 kg - GT-EX Sedan 2,690 lb, 1,220 kg - GT-EX Hardtop 2,701 lb, 1,225 kg - GT-ES Sedan 2,668 lb, 1,210 kg - GT-ES Hardtop 2,679 lb, 1,215 kg; turning circle: 38 ft, 11.6 m.

OPTIONALS automatic transmission with 3 ratios (I 2.458, II 1.458, III 1, rev 2.182), 4.111 axle ratio, max speed 106 mph, 170 km/h; power steering, 3.60 turns lock to lock; 5.5" cast alloy wheels.

Laurel Series

PRICES (Tokyo):		yen
1	1800 Standard 4-dr Sedan	**1,098,000**
2	1800 Custom 4-dr Sedan	**1,138,000**
3	1800 GL 4-dr Sedan	**1,212,000**
4	1800 GL 2-dr Hardtop	**1,241,000**
5	1800 GL 4-dr Hardtop	**1,289,000**
6	1800 SGL 4-dr Sedan	**1,344,000**
7	2000 Diesel Standard 4-dr Sedan	**1,190,000**
8	2000 Diesel De Luxe 4-dr Sedan	**1,284,000**
9	2000 Diesel GL 4-dr Sedan	**1,406,000**
10	2000 Custom 6 4-dr Sedan	**1,263,000**
11	2000 GL 6 4-dr Sedan	**1,390,000**
12	2000 GL 6 2-dr Hardtop	**1,448,000**
13	2000 GL 6 4-dr Hardtop	**1,512,000**
14	2000 SGL 4-dr Sedan	**1,498,000**
15	2000 SGL-E 4-dr Sedan	**1,603,000**
16	2000 SGL-E 2-dr Hardtop	**1,659,000**
17	2000 SGL-E 4-dr Hadrtop	**1,717,000**
18	2000 GL6-E 4-dr Hardtop	**1,617,000**
19	2000 Medalist 4-dr Sedan	**1,888,000**
20	2000 Medalist 2-dr Hardtop	**1,965,000**
21	2000 Medalist 4-dr Hardtop	**2,032,000**
22	2800 Medalist 4-dr Sedan	**2,011,000**
23	2800 Medalist 2-dr Hardtop	**2,063,000**
24	2800 Medalist 4-dr Hardtop	**2,138,000**

Power team:	Standard for:	Optional for:
105 hp	1 to 6	—
60 hp (diesel)	7 to 9	—
115 hp	10 to 14	—
130 hp	15 to 21	—
140 hp	22 to 24	—

105 hp power team

ENGINE front, 4 stroke; 4 cylinders, in line; 108 cu in, 1,770 cc (3.35 x 3.07 in, 85 x 78 mm); compression ratio: 8.5:1; max power (JIS): 105 hp (78 kW) at 6,000 rpm; max torque (JIS): 109 lb ft, 15 kg m (147 Nm) at 3,600 rpm; max engine rpm: 6,400; 59.3 hp/l (43.6 kW/l); cast iron block, light alloy head; 5 crankshaft bearings; valves: overhead, Vee-slanted, rockers; camshafts: 1, overhead; lubrication: rotary pump, full flow filter, 8.1 imp pt, 9.7 US pt, 4.6 l; Nissan NAPS-Z fast burn engine with 2 spark plugs per cylinder; 1 Hitachi DCR 340-1 downdraught twin barrel carburettor; emission control with catalytic converter, secondary air induction and exhaust gas recirculation; fuel feed: mechanical pump; water-cooled, 14 imp pt, 16.9 US pt, 8 l.

TRANSMISSION driving wheels: rear; clutch: single dry plate (diaphragm); gearbox: mechanical; gears: 4, fully synchronized; ratios: I 3.382, II 2.013, III 1.312, IV 1, rev 3.365; lever: central; final drive: hypoid bevel; axle ratio: 4.111; width of rims: 5"; tyres: 6.45 x 14.

PERFORMANCE max speed: (I) 30 mph, 48 km/h; (II) 52 mph, 83 km/h; (III) 77 mph, 124 km/h; (IV) 99 mph, 160 km/h; power-weight ratio: Custom 23.6 lb/hp (32.1 lb/kW), 10.7 kg/hp (14.5 kg/kW); consumption: 28.2 m/imp gal, 23.5 m/US gal, 10 l x 100 km.

CHASSIS integral; front suspension: independent, by McPherson, coil springs/telescopic damper struts, lower wishbones (trailing links), anti-roll bar; rear: rigid axle, lower trailing links, upper torque rods, coil springs, telescopic dampers.

STEERING recirculating ball - SGL, servo; turns lock to lock: 4 - SGL, 3.20.

BRAKES front disc, rear drum, servo; lining area: front 22.3 sq in, 144 sq cm, rear 54 sq in, 348 sq cm, total 76.3 sq in, 492 sq cm.

ELECTRICAL EQUIPMENT 12 V; 35 Ah battery; 50 A alternator; Hitachi distributor; 4 headlamps.

DIMENSIONS AND WEIGHT wheel base: 105.12 in, 267 cm; tracks: 54.33 in, 138 cm front, 53.94 in, 137 cm rear; length: 182.09 in, 462 cm; width: 66.53 in, 169 cm; height: sedans 55.31 in, 140 cm - hardtops 54.92 in, 139 cm; ground clearance: 6.69 in, 17 cm; weight: Custom 2,481 lb, 1,125 kg - GL 4-dr Sedan 2,514 lb, 1,140 kg - GL 2-dr Hardtop 2,536 lb, 1,150 kg - GL 4-dr Hardtop 2,602 lb, 1,180 kg - SGL 2,569 lb, 1,165 kg; turning circle: 38 ft, 11.6 m; fuel tank: 13.2 imp gal, 15.8 US gal, 60 l.

BODY saloon/sedan, 4 doors, hardtop, 2 or 4 doors.

OPTIONALS 5-speed mechanical gearbox (V 0.854); automatic transmission with 3 ratios (I 2.458, II 1.458, III 1, rev 2.182), central lever; 5.5" light alloy wheels with 185/70 HR x 14 tyres.

60 hp (diesel) power team

See 105 hp power team, except for:

ENGINE diesel, Ricardo Comet swirl chamber type; 121.5 cu in, 1,991 cc (3.27 x 3.62 in, 83 x 92 mm); compression ratio: 20:1; max power (JIS): 60 hp (44 kW) at 4,000 rpm; max torque (JIS): 94 lb ft, 13 kg m (127 Nm) at 3,600 rpm; valves: overhead, Vee-slanted, push-rods and rockers; camshafts: 1, side; lubrication: gears pump, 11.4 imp pt, 13.7 US pt, 6.5 l; plunger type in line injection pump; water-cooled, 17.6 imp pt, 21.1 US pt, 10 l.

TRANSMISSION gears: 5, fully synchronized; ratios: I 3.592, II 2.246, III 1.415, IV 1, V 0.882, rev 3.657; lever: central; axle ratio: 3.889.

PERFORMANCE max speed: 81 mph, 130 km/h; power-weight ratio: De Luxe 44.1 lb/hp (59.9 lb/kW), 20 kg/hp (27.2 kg/kW); consumption: 59.3 m/imp gal, 49.4 m/US gal, 4.8 l x 100 km at 37 mph, 60 km/h.

DIMENSIONS AND WEIGHT weight: De Luxe 2,646 lb, 1,200 kg - GL 2,679 lb, 1,215 kg.

115 hp power team

See 105 hp power team, except for:

ENGINE 6 cylinders, in line; 121.9 cu in, 1,998 cc (3.07 x 2.74 in, 78 x 69.7 mm); compression ratio: 8.6:1; max power (JIS): 115 hp (85 kW) at 5,600 rpm; max torque (JIS): 120 lb ft, 16.5 kg m (162 Nm) at 3,600 rpm; max engine rpm: 6,000; 60 hp/l (44.2 kW/l); 7 crankshaft bearings; lubrication: 10 imp pt, 12 US pt, 5.7 l; 1 Hitachi DCR 340-11 with ECC air-fuel ratio adjusting system downdraught twin barrel carburettor; emission control with 3-way catalytic converter; water-cooled, 15.8 imp pt, 19 US pt, 9 l.

TRANSMISSION gearbox ratios: I 3.592, II 2.246, III 1.415, IV 1, rev 3.657; axle ratio: 4.100; tyres: SGL 185/70 SR x 14.

PERFORMANCE max speed: 102 mph, 165 km/h; power-weight ratio: Custom 6 22.9 lb/hp (31.1 lb/kW), 10.4 kg/hp (14.1 kg/kW); consumption: 24 m/imp gal, 20 m/US gal, 11.8 l x 100 km.

CHASSIS GL 6 hardtops, rear suspension: independent, semi-trailing arms, coil springs, telescopic dampers.

115 HP POWER TEAM

STEERING servo (except for Custom 6); turns lock to lock: 3.20 - Custom 6, 4.

BRAKES rear compensator.

DIMENSIONS AND WEIGHT rear track: hardtops 53.54 in, 136 cm; length: 182.09 in, 426 cm; weight: Custom 6 2,635 lb,1,195 kg - GL 6 4-dr Sedan 2,701 lb 1,225 kg - GL 6 2-dr Hardtop 2,756 lb, 1,250 kg - GL 6 4-dr Hardtop 2,789 lb, 1,265 kg - SGL 2,712 lb, 1,230 kg; weight distribution: 55.7% front, 44.3% rear.

OPTIONALS 5-speed mechanical gearbox (V 0.882).

130 hp power team

See 105 hp power team, except for:

ENGINE 6 cylinders, in line: 121.9 cu in, 1,998 cc (3.07 x 2.74 in, 78 x 69.7 mm); compression ratio: 8.6:1; max power (JIS): 130 hp (96 kW) at 6,000 rpm; max torque (JIS): 126 lb ft, 17 kg m (167 Nm) at 4,000 rpm; max engine rpm: 6,000; 65.1 hp/l (47.9 kW/l); 7 crankshaft bearings; lubrication: 10 imp pt, 12 US pt, 5.7 l; Bosch electronic fuel injection; emission control with 3-way catalytic converter; fuel feed: electric pump; water-cooled, 15.8 impo pt, 19 US pt, 9 l.

TRANSMISSION gearbox ratios: I 3.592, II 2.246, III 1.415, IV 1, rev 3.657; axle ratio: 4.100; tyres: 185/70 SR x 14 - Medalist models 185/70 HR x 14.

PERFORMANCE max speed: 109 mph, 175 km/h; power-weight ratio: SGL-E 4-dr Sedan 20.9 lb/hp (28.4 lb/kW), 9.5 kg/hp (12.9 kg/kW); consumption: 24 m/imp gal, 20 m/US gal, 11.8 l x 100 km.

CHASSIS hardtops, rear suspension: independent, semi-trailing arms, coil springs, telescopic dampers.

STEERING servo; turns lock to lock: 3.20.

BRAKES rear compensator - Medalist hardtops rear disc.

DIMENSIONS AND WEIGHT rear track: hardtops 53.54 in, 136 cm; length: 182.09 in, 426 cm; width: 66.53 in, 169 cm; weight: SGL-E 4-dr Sedan 2,712 lb, 1,230 kg - SGL-E 2-dr Hardtop 2,778 lb, 1,260 kg - SGL-E 4-dr Hardtop 2,811 lb, 1,275 kg - Medalist 4-dr Sedan 2,800 lb, 1,270 kg - Medalist 2-dr Hardtop 2,889 lb, 1,310 kg - Medalist 4-dr Hardtop 2,922 lb, 1,325 kg.

OPTIONALS 5-speed mechanical gearbox (V 0.882); 3-speed automatic transmission; 5.5" light alloy wheels with 185/70 HR x 14 tyres.

140 hp power team

See 105 hp power team, except for:

ENGINE 6 cylinders, in line; 168 cu in, 2,753 cc (3.39 x 3.11 in, 86 x 79 mm); compression ratio: 8.6:1; max power (JIS): 140 hp (103 kW) at 5,200 rpm; max torque (JIS): 163 lb ft, 22.5 kg m (221 Nm) at 3,600 rpm; max engine rpm: 6,200; 50.1 hp/l (36.9 kW/l); 7 crankshaft bearings; lubrication: 10 imp pt, 12 US pt, 5.7 l; 1 Hitachi DCR 360-1 downdraught twin barrel carburettor with electronic air-fuel ratio adjustment system; water-cooled, 17.6 imp pt, 21.1 US pt, 10 l.

TRANSMISSION gears: 5, fully synchronized; ratios: I 3.321, II 2.077, III 1.308, IV 1, V 0.864, rev 3.382; axle ratio: 3.700; tyres: 185/70 HR x 14.

PERFORMANCE max speeds: (I) 36 mph, 58 km/h; (II) 52 mph, 83 km/h; (7III) 89 mph, 144 km/h; (IV) 104 mph, 168 km/h; (V) 112 mph, 180 km/h; power-weight ratio: Medalist 4-dr Sedan 20.3 lb/hp (27.6 lb/kW), 9.2 kg/hp (12.5 kg/kW); consumption: 23.1 m/imp gal, 19.3 m/US gal, 12.2 l x 100 km.

CHASSIS hardtops, rear suspension: independent, semi-trailing arms, coil springs, telescopic dampers.

STEERING servo; turns lock to lock: 3.60.

BRAKES front disc, rear drum, rear compensator, servo; lining area: front 20.5 sq in, 132 sq cm.

DIMENSIONS AND WEIGHT rear track: hardtops 53.54 in, 136 cm; length: 182.09 in, 462 cm; width: 66.34 in, 168 cm; weight: Medalist 4-dr Sedan 2,844 lb, 1,290 kg - Medalist 2-dr Hardtop 2,944 lb, 1,335 kg - Medalist 4-dr Hardtop 2,977 lb, 1,350 kg.

OPTIONALS 3-speed automatic transmission.

Fairlady Series

PRICES (Tokyo):	yen
1 Z Sports	1,460,000
2 ZL Sports	1,625,000
3 ZT Sports	1,795,000
4 Z 2+2 Sports	1,598,000
5 ZL 2+2 Sports	1,793,000
6 ZT 2+2 Sports	1,988,000
7 280 ZL Sports	1,800,000
8 280 ZT Sports	2,155,000
9 280 ZL 2+2 Sports	1,965,000
10 280 ZT 2+2 Sports	2,373,000

Power team:	Standard for:	Optional for:
130 hp	1 to 6	—
145 hp	7 to 10	—

130 hp power team

ENGINE front, 4 stroke; 6 cylinders, in line; 121.9 cu in, 1,998 cc (3.07 x 2.74 in, 78 x 69.7 mm); compression ratio: 8.8:1; max power (JIS): 130 hp (96 kW) at 6,000 rpm; max torque (JIS): 123 lb ft, 17 kg m (167 Nm) at 4,000 rpm; max engine rpm: 6,400; 65.1 hp/l (47.9 kW/l); cast iron block, light alloy head; 7 crankshaft bearings; valves: overhead, in line, rockers; camshafts: 1, overhead; lubrication: rotary pump, full flow filter, 8.3 imp pt, 9.9 US pt, 4.7 l; Bosch electronic injection; emission control with 3-way catalytic converter and exhaust gas recirculation; fuel feed: electric pump; water-cooled, 17.6 imp pt, 21.1 US pt, 10 l.

TRANSMISSION driving wheels: rear; clutch: single dry plate, hydraulically controlled; gearbox: mechanical; gears: 5, fully synchronized; ratios: I 3.592, II 2.246, III 1.415, IV 1, V 0.822, rev 3.657; lever: central; final drive: hypoid bevel; axle ratio: 4.375; width of rims: 5.5"; tyres: 175 SR x 14 - ZL and ZT models 195/70 HR x 14.

PERFORMANCE max speeds: (I) 27 mph, 44 km/h; (II) 43 mph, 70 km/h; (III) 68 mph, 110 km/h; (IV) 99 mph, 160 km/h; (V) 112 mph, 180 km/h; power-weight ratio: Z 19.9 lb/hp (27 lb/kW), 9 kg/hp (12.2 kg/kW); carrying capacity: 397 lb, 180 kg; consumption: 25.7 m/imp gal, 21.4 m/US gal, 11 l x 100 km - 2+2 models 24 m/imp gal, 20 m/US gal, 11.8 l x 100 km.

CHASSIS integral; front suspension: independent, by McPherson, coil springs/telescopic damper struts, lower wishbones (trailing links), anti-roll bar; rear: independent, semi-trailing arms, coil springs, telescopic dampers, anti-roll bar.

STEERING rack-and-pinion; turns lock to lock: 3.50.

BRAKES disc, servo; lining area: front 28.5 sq in, 184 sq cm, rear 14.3 sq in, 92 sq cm, total 42.8 sq in, 276 sq cm.

ELECTRICAL EQUIPMENT 12 V; 35 Ah battery; 50 A alternator; contactless distributor; 2 headlamps.

DIMENSIONS AND WEIGHT wheel base: 91.34 in, 232 cm - 2+2 models 99.21 in, 252 cm; front and rear track: 54.52 in, 138 cm, 54.52 in, 138 cm length: 170.86 in, 434 cm - 2+2 models 178.74 in, 454 cm; width: 66.53 in, 169 cm; height: 50.98 in, 129 cm - 2+2 models 51.38 in, 130 cm; ground clearance: 5.90 in, 15 cm; weight: Z 2,591 lb, 1,175 kg - ZL 2,624 lb, 1,190 kg - ZT 2,635 lb, 1,195 kg - Z 2+2 2,657 lb, 1,205 kg - ZL 2+2 2,701 lb, 1,225 kg - ZT 2+2 2,712 lb, 1,230 kg; turning circle: 34.1 ft, 10.4 m - 2+2 models 38 ft, 11.6 m; fuel tank: 17.6 imp gal, 21.1 US gal, 80 l.

BODY coupé; 2+1 doors; 2 seats - 2+2 models 4, separate front seats.

OPTIONALS recirculating ball steering wheel, servo, 2.70 turns lock to lock; 3-speed automatic transmission (I 2.458, II 1.458, III 1, rev 2.182), 4.111 axle ratio; 6" light alloy wheels; air-conditioning.

145 hp power team

See 130 hp power team, except for:

ENGINE 168 cu in, 2,754 cc (3.39 x 3.11 in, 86 x 79 mm); compression ratio: 8.3:1; max power (JIS): 145 hp (107 kW) at 5,200 rpm; max torque (JIS): 167 lb ft, 23 kg m (225 Nm) at 4,000 rpm; 52.7 hp/l (38.8 kW/l).

TRANSMISSION gearbox ratios: I 3.321, II 2.077, III 1.308, IV 1, V 0.864, rev 3.382; axle ratio: 3.700; tyres: 195/70 HR x 14.

PERFORMANCE max speeds: (I) 31 mph, 50 km/h; (II) 48 mph, 78 km/h; (III) 73 mph, 118 km/h; (IV) 102 mph, 165 km/h; (V) 112 mph, 180 km/h; power-weight ratio: ZL 18.6 lb/hp (25.3 lb/kW), 8.4 kg/hp (11.4 kg/kW); consumption: 2-seater models 38.1 m/imp gal, 31.7 m/US gal, 7.4 l x 100 km.

ELECTRICAL EQUIPMENT 60 Ah battery; 60 A alternator.

DIMENSIONS AND WEIGHT length; 2-seater models 174.01 in, 442 cm - 2+2 models 181.89 in, 462 cm; weight: ZL 2,701 lb, 1,225 kg - ZT 2,800 lb, 1,270 kg - ZL 2+2 2,778 lb, 1,260 kg - ZT 2+2 2,877 lb, 1,305 kg.

NISSAN-DATSUN Fairlady 280 ZT 2+2 Sports

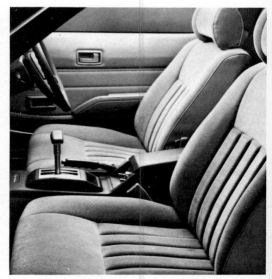

NISSAN-DATSUN Fairlady 280 ZT 2+2 Sports

NISSAN-DATSUN President Sovereign Sedan

barrel carburettor; fast-burn low emission with 2 spark plugs per cylinder, catalytic converter, exhaust gas recirculation and secondary air injection; fuel feed: mechanical pump; water-cooled, 12.2 imp pt, 14.4 US pt, 7 l.

TRANSMISSION driving wheels: rear; clutch: single dry plate (diaphragm); gearbox: mechanical; gears: 4, fully synchronized; ratios: I 3.382, II 2.013, III 1.312, IV, IV 1, rev 3.365; lever: central; final drive: hypoid bevel; axle ratio: 3.889; width of rims: 4.5"; tyres: 165 SR x 14 - LS 6.45 x 14.

PERFORMANCE max speeds: (I) 33 mph, 53 km/h; (II) 53 mph, 86 km/h; (III) 83 mph, 133 km/h; (IV) 106 mph, 170 km/h; power-weight ratio: LS 21.1 lb/hp (28.7 lb/kW), 9.6 kg/hp (13 kg/kW); carrying capacity: 822 lb, 400 kg; speed in dirct drive at 1,000 rpm: 16.8 mph, 27 km/h; consumption: 36.4 m/imp gal, 30.6 m/US gal, 7.7 l x 100 km.

CHASSIS integral; front suspension: independent by McPherson, coil springs/telescopic damper struts, transverse arm, trailing links, anti-roll bar; rear: rigid axle, lower trailing links, upper diagonal torque rods, coil springs, anti-roll bar (except LS), telescopic dampers.

STEERING recirculating ball; turns lock to lock: 3.90.

BRAKES front disc, rear drum, servo; lining area: front 15.3 sq in, 100 sq cm, rear 53.2 sq in, 348 sq cm, total 58.5 sq in, 448 sq cm.

ELECTRICAL EQUIPMENT 12 V; 35 Ah battery; 50 A alternator; 4 headlamps.

President Series

PRICES (Tokyo):	yen
C 4-dr Sedan	**3,846,000**
D 4-dr Sedan	**4,238,000**
Sovereign 4-dr Sedan	**4,627,000**

ENGINE front, 4 stroke; 8 cylinders, Vee-slanted; 269.3 cu in, 4,414 cc (3.62 x 3.27 in, 92 x 83 mm); compression ratio: 8.6:1; max power (JIS): 200 hp (147 kW) at 4,800 rpm; max torque (JIS): 250 lb ft, 34.5 kg m (338 Nm) at 3,200 rpm; max engine rpm: 5,200; 45.1 hp/l (33.2 kW/l); cast iron block, light alloy head; 5 crankshaft bearings; valves: overhead, Vee-slanted, push-rods and rockers, hydraulic tappets; camshafts: 1, at centre of Vee; lubrication: gear pump, full flow filter, 8.3 imp pt, 9.9 US pt, 4.7 l; Bosch L-Jetronic injection; emission control with 2 catalytic converters and exhaust gas recirculation; fuel feed: electric pump; water-cooled, 28.2 imp pt, 33.8 US pt, 16 l.

TRANSMISSION driving wheels: rear; gearbox: automatic transmission, hydraulic torque converter and planetary gears with 3 ratios; ratios: I 2.458, II 1.458, III 1, rev 2.182; lever: steering column; final drive: hypoid bevel; axle ratio: 3.364; width of rims: 5"; tyres: 7.75 S x 14.

PERFORMANCE max speed: (I) 42 mph, 68 km/h; (II) 65 mph, 115 km/h; (III) 112 mph, 180 km/h; power-weight ratio: C 20.3 lb/hp (27.6 lb/kW), 9.2 kg/hp (12.5 kg/kW); consumption: 14.7 m/imp gal, 12.2 m/US gal, 19.2 l x 100 km.

CHASSIS integral; front suspension: independent, wishbones, coil springs, anti-roll bar, telescopic dampers; rear: rigid axle, semi-elliptic leafsprings, telescopic dampers.

STEERING recirculating ball, servo; turns lock to lock: 4.10.

BRAKES front disc, rear drum, servo; lining area: front 26.7 sq in, 172 sq cm, rear 71.9 sq in, 464 sq cm, total 98.6 sq in, 636 sq cm.

ELECTRICAL EQUIPMENT 12 V; 60 Ah battery; 600 W alternator; Hitachi distributor; 4 headlamps.

DIMENSIONS AND WEIGHT wheel base: 112.20 in, 285 cm; front and rear track: 58.66 in, 149 cm; length: C 206.69 in, 525 cm - D and Sovereign 207.87 in, 528 cm; width: 72.05 in, 183 cm; height: 58.27 in, 148 cm; ground clearance: 7.28 in, 18 cm; weight: C 4,057 lb, 1,850 kg - D 4,123 lb, 1,870 kg - Sovereign 4,134 lb, 1,875 kg; weight distribution: 54% front, 46% rear; turning circle: 42 ft, 12.8 m; fuel tank: 16.5 imp gal, 19.8 US gal, 7.5 l.

BODY saloon/sedan; 4 doors; 6 seats, bench front seats, reclining backerests, built-in headrests; electric windows.

OPTIONALS air-conditioning; separate front seats.

NISSAN-DATSUN Gazelle 2000 Hatchback XE-II

Silvia - Gazelle Series

PRICES (Tokyo):	yen
1 Silvia 1800 LS 2-dr Coupé	**1,085,000**
2 Silvia 1800 LS-L 2-dr Coupé	**1,160,000**
3 Silvia 1800 LS-X 2-dr Coupé	**1,260,000**
4 Silvia 1800 2+1-dr Hatchback LS-L	**1,240,000**
5 Silvia 1800 2+2-dr Hatchback LS-X	**1,340,000**
6 Gazelle 1800 2-dr T-I Coupé	**1,165,000**
7 Gazelle 1800 2-dr T-II Coupé	**1,265,000**
8 Gazelle 1800 2+1-dr Hatchback T-I	**1,245,000**
9 Gazelle 1800 2+1-dr Hatchback T-II	**1,345,000**
10 Silvia 1800 LSE-L 2-dr Coupé	**1,255,000**
11 Silvia 1800 LSE-X 2-dr Coupé	**1,370,000**
12 Silvia 1800 LSE-L 2+1-dr Hatchback	**1,335,000**
13 Silvia 1800 LSE-X 2+1-dr Hatchback	**1,450,000**
14 Gazelle 1800 TE-I 2-dr Coupé	**1,260,000**
15 Gazelle 1800 TE-II 2-dr Coupé	**1,375,000**
16 Gazelle 2+1-dr Hatchback TE-I	**1,390,000**
17 Gazelle 2+1-dr Hatchback TE-II	**1,595,000**
18 Silvia 2000 ZSE-L 2-dr Coupé	**1,385,000**
19 Silvia 2000 ZSE-X 2-dr Coupé	**1,585,000**
20 Silvia 2000 2+1-dr Hatchback ZSE-L	**1,465,000**
21 Silvia 2000 2+1-dr Hatchback ZSE-X	**1,665,000**
22 Gazelle 2000 XE-I 2-dr Coupé	**1,390,000**
23 Gazelle 2000 XE-II 2-dr Coupé	**1,595,000**
24 Gazelle 2000 2+1-dr Hatchback XE-I	**1,470,000**
25 Gazelle 2000 2+1-dr Hatchback XE-II	**1,675,000**

Power team:	Standard for:	Optional for:
105 hp	1 to 9	—
115 hp	10 to 17	—
120 hp	18 to 25	—

105 hp power team

ENGINE front, 4 stroke; 4 cylinders, in line; 108 cu in, 1,770 cc (3.35 x 3.07 in, 85 x 78 mm); compression ratio: 8.8:1; max power (JIS): 105 hp (77 kW) at 6,000 rpm; max torque (JIS): 109 lb ft, 15 kg m (147 Nm) at 3,600 rpm; max engine rpm: 6,300; 59.3 hp/l (43.7 kW/l); cast iron block, light alloy head; 5 crankshaft bearings; valves: overhead, in line, rockers; camshafts: 1, overhead; lubrication: rotary pump, full flow filter, 7.9 imp pt, 9.3 US pt, 4.5 l; 1 Hitachi DCR 340 downdraught twin

DIMENSIONS AND WEIGHT wheel base: 94.49 in, 240 cm; front and rear tracks: 52.76 in, 134 cm; length: 173.23 in, 440 cm - hatchbacks 175.98 in, 447 cm; width: 66.14 in, 168 cm; height: 55.57 in, 131 cm; ground clearance: 6.69 in, 17 cm; weight: LS 2,216 lb, 1,005 kg - LS-L Coupé and T-I Hatchback 2,249 lb, 1,020 kg - LS-X Coupé and T-II Hatchback 2,293 lb, 1,040 kg - LS-L Hatchback 2,326 lb, 1055 kg - LS-X Hatchback 2,370 lb, 1,075 kg; weight distribution: 56% front, 44% rear; turning circle: 36.2 ft, 11 m; fuel tank: 11.8 imp gal, 14 US gal, 53 l - hatchbacks 13.4 imp gal, 15.9 US gal, 60 l.

BODY coupé, 2 doors - hatchback, 2+1 doors; 5 seats, separate front seats, built-in headrests.

OPTIONALS 5-speed fully synchronized mechanical gearbox (I 3.382, II 2.013, III 1.312, IV 1, V 0.854, rev 3.365); JATCO automatic transmission, hydraulic torque converter and planetary gears with 3 ratios (I 2.458, II 1.458, III 1, rev 2.182), possible manual selection.

115 hp power team

See 105 hp power team, except for:

ENGINE max power (JIS): 115 hp (85 kW) at 6,000 rpm; max torque (JIS): 113 lb ft, 15.5 kg m (152 Nm) at 3,600 rpm; max engine rpm: 6,500; 64.9 hp/l (47.8 kW/l); Bosch L-Jetronic injection; fuel feed: electric pump;

TRANSMISSION gears: 5, fully synchronized; ratios: I 3.382, II 2.013, III 1.312, IV 1, V 0.854, rev 3.365.

PERFORMANCE max speeds: 109 mph, 175 km/h; power-weight ratio: LSE-L 19.8 lb/hp (26.9 lb/kW), 9 kg/hp (12.2

115 HP POWER TEAM

kg/kW); consumption: 33.6 m/imp gal, 28.2 m/US gal, 8.3 l x 100 km.

DIMENSIONS AND WEIGHT weight: LSE-L and TE-I coupés 2,282 lb, 1,035 kg - LSE-X and TE-II coupés 2,326 lb, 1,055 kg - LSE-L and TE-I hatchbacks 2,359 lb, 1,070 kg - LSE-X and TE-II hatchbacks 2,403 lb, 1,090 kg.

OPTIONALS power steering.

120 hp power team

See 105 hp power team, except for:

ENGINE 119.1 cu in, 1,952 cc (3.35 x 3.39 in, 85 x 86 mm); compression ratio: 8.5:1; max power (JIS): 120 hp (88 kW) at 5,600 rpm; max torque (JIS): 123 lb ft, 17 kg m (167 Nm) at 3,600 rpm; max engine rpm: 6,000; 61.5 hp/l (45.2 kW/l); lubrication, 7.3 imp pt, 8.7 US pt, 4.2 l; Bosch L-Jetronic injection; fuel feed: electric pump; cooling, 14 imp pt, 16.5 US pt, 8 l.

TRANSMISSION gears: 5, fully synchronized; ratios: 3.321, II 2.077, III 1.308, IV 1, V 0.864, rev 3.382; axle ratio: 3.700; tyres: ZSE-L and XE-I models 165 SR x 14 - ZSE-X and XE-II models 185/70 SR x 14.

PERFORMANCE max speeds: (I) 33 mph, 53 km/h; (II) 52 mph, 83 km/h; (III) 81 mph, 130 km/h; (IV) 106 mph, 170 km/h; (V) 112 mph, 180 km/h; power-weight ratio: ZSE-L 19.9 lb/hp (27.1 lb/kW), 9 kg/hp (12.3 kg/kW); speed in direct top at 1,000 rpm: 18.7 mph, 30 km/h; consumption: 30.8 m/imp gal, 25.9 m/US gal, 9.1 l x 100 km.

STEERING servo; turns lock to lock: 3.10.

BRAKES rear disc; rear lining area: 14.1 sq in, 92 sq cm.

DIMENSIONS AND WEIGHT weight: ZSE-L and XE-I coupés 2,392 lb, 1,085 kg - ZSE-X Coupé 2,436 lb, 1,105 kg - ZSE-L and XE-I hatchbacks 2,469 lb, 1,120 kg - ZSE-X and XE-II hatchbacks 2,513 lb, 1,140 kg.

Cedric - Gloria Series

PRICES (Tokyo):	yen
1 Cedric 200 Standard Sedan	**1,324,000**
2 Cedric 200 De Luxe Sedan	**1,457,000**
3 Cedric 200 Custom De Luxe Sedan	**1,583,000**
4 Cedric 200 GL Sedan	**1,789,000**
5 Cedric 200 Custom S Hardtop	**1,730,000**
6 Cedric 200 GL Hardtop	**1,958,000**
7 Cedric 200 E De Luxe Sedan	**1,567,000**
8 Cedric 200 E Custom De Luxe Sedan	**1,723,000**
9 Cedric 200 E GL Sedan	**1,869,000**
10 Cedric 200 E SGL Sedan	**2,231,000**
11 Cedric 200 E SGL Extra Sedan	**2,315,000**
12 Cedric 200 E Custom S Hardtop	**1,810,000**
13 Cedric 200 E GL Hardtop	**2,038,000**
14 Cedric 200 E SGL Hardtop	**2,408,000**
15 Cedric 200 E SGL Extra Hardtop	**2,492,000**
16 Gloria 280 E Brougham Sedan.	**2,721,000**
17 Gloria 280 E Brougham Hardtop	**2,850,000**
18 Cedric 2000 Turbo SGL Extra Sedan	**2,465,000**
19 Cedric 2000 Turbo S Hardtop	**2,263,000**
20 Cedric 2000 Turbo SGL Extra Hardtop	**2,642,000**
21 Gloria 200 D Standard Sedan	**1,359,000**
22 Gloria 220 D Standard Sedan	**1,304,000**
23 Gloria 220 D DX Sedan	**1,562,000**
24 Gloria 220 D GL Sedan	**1,852,000**
25 Gloria 2800 D VO-6 Sedan	**1,635,000**
26 Gloria 2800 D VL-6 Sedan	**1,962,000**
27 Gloria 2800 D VX-6 Sedan	**2,405,000**
28 Gloria 2800 D VS-6 Hardtop	**1,903,000**
29 Gloria 2800 D VL-6 Hardtop	**2,131,000**
30 Gloria 2800 D VX-6 Hardtop	**2,582,000**

Power team	Standard for:	Optional for:
115 hp	1 to 6	—
130 hp	7 to 15	—
145 hp	16,17	—
145 hp (turbo)	18 to 20	—
60 hp (diesel)	21	—
65 hp (diesel)	22 to 24	—
91 hp (diesel)	25 to 30	—

115 hp power team

ENGINE front, 4 stroke; 6 cylinders, in line; 121.9 cu in, 1,998 cc (3.07 x 2.74 in, 78 x 69.7 mm); compression ratio: 8.8:1; max power (JIS): 115 hp (85 kW) at 5,600 rpm; max torque (JIS): 120 lb ft, 16.5 kg m (162 Nm) at 3,600 rpm; max engine rpm: 6,000; 57.6 hp/l (42.4 kW/l); cast iron block, light alloy head; 7 crankshaft bearings; valves: overhead, in line, rockers; camshafts: 1, overhead; lubrication: rotary pump, full flow filter, 8.3 imp pt, 9.9 US pt, 4.7 l; 1 Hitachi DCR 340 downdraught twin barrel carburettor with air-fuel ratio adjusting system; emission control with 3-way catalytic converter, secondary air induction and exhaust gas recirculation; fuel feed: mechanical pump; water-cooled, 17.6 imp pt, 21.1 US pt, 10 l.

NISSAN-DATSUN Cedric 200 E Custom S Hardtop

NISSAN-DATSUN Gloria 280 E Brougham Sedan

TRANSMISSION driving wheels: rear; clutch: single dry plate (diaphragm); gearbox: mechanical; gears: 5, fully synchronized; ratios: I 3.592, II 2.246, III 1.415, IV 1, V 0.882, rev 3.657; lever: central; final drive: hypoid bevel; axle ratio: 4.625; width of rims: 4.5"; tyres: sedans 6.95 x 14 - hardtops 185 SR x 14.

PERFORMANCE max speeds: (I) 25 mph, 40 km/h; (II) 37 mph, 60 km/h; (III) 62 mph, 100 km/h; (IV) 88 mph, 140 km/h; (V) 103 mph, 165 km/h; power-weight ratio: 200 De Luxe 25.2 lb/hp (34.2 lb/kW), 11.4 kg/hp (15.5 kg/kW); carrying capacity: 882 lb, 400 kg; speed in top at 1,000 rpm: 18.2 mph, 29.5 km/h; consumption: 23.3 m/imp gal, 19.6 m/US gal, 12 l x 100 km.

CHASSIS integral; front suspension: independent, wishbones, coil springs, anti-roll bar, telescopic dampers; rear: rigid axle lower trailing links, upper torque rods, Panhard rod, coil springs, telescopic dampers, anti-roll bar.

STEERING recirculating ball - GL models servo, turns lock to lock: 4.50 - GL models 3.20.

BRAKES front disc, rear drum, servo, lining area: front 20 sq in, 144 sq cm, rear 75.8 sq in, 496 sq cm, total 95.8 sq in, 640 sq cm.

ELECTRICAL EQUIPMENT 12 V; 35 Ah battery; 50 A alternator; 4 headlamps.

DIMENSIONS AND WEIGHT wheel base: 105.91 in, 269 cm; tracks: 55.50 in, 141 cm - GL Sedan and hardtops 55.90 in, 142 cm front, 53.93 in, 138 cm - GL Sedan and hardtops 54.73 in, 139 cm rear; length: 184.65 in, 469 cm; width: 66.54 in, 169 cm; height: sedans 56.30 in, 143 cm - hardtops 55.50 in, 141 cm; ground clearance: 7.09 in, 18 cm; weight: 200 De Luxe 2,899 lb, 1,315 kg - 200 GL Sedan 2,976 lb, 1,350 kg - 200 Custom S 2,965 lb, 1,345 kg - 200 GL Hardtop 3,031 lb, 1,375 kg; turning circle: 39.4 ft, 12 m; fuel tank: 16 imp gal, 19 US gal, 72 l.

BODY saloon/sedan, hardtop; 5 seats, separate front seats, reclining backrests, built-in headrests.

OPTIONALS 4-speed fully synchronized mechanical gearbox (I 3.143, II 1.641, III 1, IV 0.784, rev 3.657), steering column or central lever, 4.625 axle ratio; Nissan automatic transmission with 3 ratios (I 2.458, II 1.458, III 1, rev 2.182), steering column lever; 4.625 axle ratio.

130 hp power team

See 115 hp power team, except for:

ENGINE max power (JIS): 130 hp (96 kW) at 6,000 rpm; max torque (JIS): 123 lb ft, 17 kg m (167 Nm) at 4,400 rpm; 65.1 hp/l (47.9 kW/l); Bosch electronic injection; emission control with 3-way catalytic converter; fuel feed: electric pump.

TRANSMISSION 200 E De Luxe and Custom De Luxe automatic transmission, hydraulic torque converter and planetary gears with 3 ratios (I 2.458, II 1.458, III 1, rev 2.182).

PERFORMANCE max speed: 106 mph, 170 km/h; power-weight ratio: 200 E De Luxe 22.4 lb/hp (30.4 lb/kW), 10.1 kg/hp (13.8 kg/kW); consumption: 23.4 m/imp gal, 19.5 m/US gal, 12 l x 100 km.

TEERING servo; turns lock to lock: 3.20.

IMENSIONS AND WEIGHT weight: 200 E De Luxe 2,910 lb, ,320 kg - 200 E Custom De Luxe 2,921 lb, 1,325 kg - 200 E GL edan 2,976 lb 1,350 kg - 200 E SGL Sedan 3,086 lb, 1,400 kg 200 E Custom S 2,965 lb, 1,345 kg - 200 E GL Hardtop 3,031 , 1,375 kg - 200 E SGL Hardtop 3,152 lb, 1,430 kg.

145 hp power team

ee 115 hp power team, except for:

NGINE 168 cu in, 2,753 cc (3.39 x 3.11 in, 86 x 79 mm); ompression ratio: 8.3:1; max power (JIS): 145 hp (107 kW) at ,200 rpm; max torque (JIS): 167 lb ft, 23 kg m (206 Nm) at ,000 rpm; 52.7 hp/l (38.8 kW/l); Bosch L-Jetronic injection; el feed: electric pump.

RANSMISSION JATCO automatic transmission, hydraulic torue converter and planetary gears with 3 ratios; ratios: I 2.458, 1.458, III 1, rev 2.182; lever: steering column or central; axle atio: 4.111; tyres: 185 SR x 14.

ERFORMANCE max speed: 96 mph, 155 km/h; power-weight atio: 280 E Brougham Sedan 23.1 lb/hp (31.4 lb/kW), 10.5 g/hp (14.3 kg/kW); consumption: 21.9 m/imp gal, 18.4 m/US al, 12.8 l x 100 km.

TEERING servo; turns lock to lock: 3.20.

RAKES rear disc.

IMENSIONS AND WEIGHT length: 189.76 in, 482 cm; weight: 80 E Brougham Sedan 3,241 lb, 1,470 kg - 280 E Brougham ardtop 3,296 lb, 1,495 kg.

145 hp (turbo) power team

ee 115 hp power team, except for:

NGINE turbocharged; compression ratio: 7.3:1; max power JIS): 145 hp (107 kW) at 5,600 rpm; max torque (JIS): 152 lb , 21 kg m (206 Nm) at 3,200 rpm; max engine rpm: 6,000; 72.5 p/l (33.4 kW/l); Bosch L-Jetronic electronic injection, iresearch T 03 exhaust turbocharger with intake by-pass and xhaust wastegate; 3-way catalytic converter with oxygen senor and exhaust gas recirculation; fuel feed: electric pump.

RANSMISSION gears: 5, fully synchronized; ratios: I 3.592, II .246, III 1.415, IV 1, V 0.813, rev 3.657; axle ratio: 4.375; yres: SGL Extra models 185 SR x 14 - S 195/70 HR x 14.

ERFORMANCE max speeds: (I) 25 mph, 40 km/h; (II) 40 mph, 7 km/h; (III) 66 mph, 107 km/h; (IV) 93 mph, 150 km/h; (V) 112 nph, 180 km/h; power-weight ratio: SGL Extra Sedan 21.4 lb/hp 29.1 lb/kW), 9.7 kg/hp (13.2 kg/kW).

TEERING servo; turns lock to lock: 3.20.

RAKES disc, front internal radial fins, servo.

IMENSIONS AND WEIGHT tracks: SGL Extra models 55.71 , 141 cm front, 54.33 in, 138 cm rear - S 56.10 in, 142 cm ont, 54.72 in, 139 cm rear; weight: SGL Extra Sedan 3,110 lb, ,410 kg - SGL Extra Hardtop 3,174 lb, 1,440 kg - S 3,064 lb, ,390 kg.

60 hp (diesel) power team

See 115 hp power team, except for:

ENGINE diesel; 4 cylinders, in line; 121.5 cu in, 1,991 cc (3.27 x 3.62 in, 83 x 92 mm); compression ratio: 20:1; max power (JIS): 60 hp (44.2 kW) at 4,000 rpm: max torque (JIS): 94 lb ft, 13 kg m (127 Nm) at 1,800 rpm; 30.1 hp/l (22 kW/l); 3 crankshaft bearings; valves: overhead, in line, push-rods and rockers; camshafts: 1, side; lubrication: 9.9 imp pt, 11.8 US pt, 5.6 l; 1 245304 LPG carburettor; plunger type in line injection pump; Ricardo Comet swirl chamber type.

TRANSMISSION gears: 4, fully synchronized; ratios: I 3.143, II 1.641, III 1, IV 0.784, rev 3.657; lever: steering column; tyres: 6.40 x 14.

PERFORMANCE max speed: 68 mph, 110 km/h; power-weight ratio: 48.5 lb/hp (65.9 lb/kW), 22 kg/hp (29.9 kg/kW); consumption: 54.6 m/imp gal, 45.9 m/US gal, 5.1 l x 100 km at 37 mph, 60 km/h.

BRAKES drum, servo.

DIMENSIONS AND WEIGHT weight: 2,910 lb, 1,320 kg.

OPTIONALS 5-speed fully synchronized mechanical gearbox (I 3.592, II 2.246, III 1.415, IV 1, V 0.882, rev 3.657); central lever, 4.111 axle ratio.

65 hp (diesel) power team

See 60 hp power team, except for:

ENGINE diesel; 4 cylinders, in line; 132 cu in, 2,164 cc (3.27 x 3.94 in, 83 x 100 mm); compression ratio: 20.8:1; max power (JIS): 65 hp (48 kW) at 4,000 rpm; max torque (JIS): 105 lb ft, 14.5 kg m (142 Nm) at 1,800 rpm; 30 hp/l (22.1 kW/l); 3 crankshaft bearings; valves: overhead, in line, push-rods and rockers; camshafts: 1, side; lubrication: 9.9 imp pt, 11.8 US pt, 5.6 l; 1 245304 LPG carburettor; plunger type in line injection pump; Ricardo Comet swirl chamber type.

TRANSMISSION gears: 4, fully synchronized; ratios: I 3.143, II 1.641, III 1, IV 0.784, rev 3.657; lever: steering column; tyres: Standard 6.40 x 14 - DX and GL 6.95 x 14.

PERFORMANCE max speed: 81 mph, 130 km/h; power-weight ratio: Standard 44.8 lb/hp (60.8 lb/kW), 20.3 kg/hp (27.6 kg/kW).

STEERING GL, servo; turns lock to lock: 3.20.

BRAKES Standard drum - GL and DX front disc, servo.

DIMENSIONS AND WEIGHT weight: Standard 2,910 lb, 1,320 kg - DX 2,954 lb, 1,340 kg - GLS 3,055 lb, 1,385 kg.

OPTIONALS 5-speed fully synchronized mechanical gearbox (I 3.592, II 2.246, III 1.415, IV 1, V 0.882, rev 3.657), central lever, 4.111 axle ratio.

91 hp (diesel) power team

See 115 hp power team, except for:

NISSAN-DATSUN Patrol 4WD

NISSAN-DATSUN Cedric 200 E Custom S Hardtop

ENGINE diesel; 170.3 cu in, 2,792 cc (3.33 x 3.27 in, 84.5 x 83 mm); compression ratio: 22:1; max power (JIS): 91 hp (67 kW) at 4,600 rpm; max torque (JIS): 126 lb ft, 17.3 kg m (170 Nm) at 2,400 rpm; max engine rpm: 4,800; 32.5 hp/l (23.9 kW/l); lubrication: 10 imp pt, 11.8 US pt, 5.7 l; Bosch diesel injection pump; Ricardo Comet swirl combustion chambers; cooling, 17.5 imp pt, 20.6 US pt, 10 l.

TRANSMISSION gearbox: JATCO automatic transmission, hydraulic torque converter and planetary gears with 3 ratios, possible manual selection; ratios: I 2.458, II 1.458, III 1, rev 2.182; axle ratio: 4.111; tyres: 6.95 x 14 or 185 SR x 14.

PERFORMANCE max speeds: (I) 25 mph, 40 km/h; (II) 44 mph, 70 km/h; (III) 84 mph, 135 km/h; power-weight ratio: VO-6 33.7 lb/hp (45.6 lb/kW), 15.3 kg/hp (20.7 kg/kW); consumption: 41.8 m/imp gal, 35.1 m/US gal, 6.7 l x 100 km at 37 mph, 60 km/h.

STEERING servo; turns lock to lock: 3.20.

DIMENSIONS AND WEIGHT weight: VO-6 3,064 lb, 1,390 kg - VL - 6 Sedan 3,141 lb, 1,425 kg - VX-6 Sedan 3,252 lb, 1,475 kg - VS-6 Hardtop 3,130 lb, 1,420 kg - VL-6 Hardtop 3,197 lb, 1,450 kg - VX-6 Hardtop 3.318 lb, 1,505 kg.

Patrol 4WD

PRICE (Tokyo): 1,337,000 yen

ENGINE front, 4 stroke; 6 cylinders, vertical, in line; 241.4 cu in, 3,956 cc (3.37 x 4.50 in, 85.7 x 114.3 mm); compression ratio: 7.6:1; max power (JIS): 130 hp (96 kW) at 3,600 rpm; max torque (JIS): 217 lb ft, 30 kg m (294 Nm) at 1,600 rpm; max engine rpm: 3,600; 32.9 hp/l (24.2 kW/l); cast iron block and head; 7 crankshaft bearings; valves: overhead, in line, push-rods and rockers; camshafts: 1, side; lubrication: gear pump, full flow filter, oil cooler, 9.3 imp pt, 11.2 US pt, 5.3 l; 1 Hitachi VC 42-4A downdraught carburettor; fuel feed: mechanical pump; water-cooled, 32.2 imp pt, 38.7 US pt, 18.3 l.

TRANSMISSION driving wheels: front (automatically engaged with transfer box low ratio) and rear; clutch: single dry plate; gearbox: mechanical; gears: 3, with high and low ratios, II and III synchronized; ratios: I 2.900, II 1.562, III 1, rev 4.015; low ratios: I 6.565, II 3.536, III 2.264, rev 9.089; levers: 3, central; final drive: hypoid bevel; axle ratio: 4.100; tyres: 6.50 x 16.

PERFORMANCE max speed: 78 mph, 125 km/h; power-weight ratio: 28.2 lb/hp (38.3 lb/kW), 12.8 kg/hp (17.4 kg/kW), carrying capacity: 1,654 lb, 750 kg; speed in direct drive at 1,000 rpm: 21.6 mph, 34.7 km/h; consumption: not declared.

CHASSIS ladder frame; front and rear suspension: rigid axle, semi-elliptic leafsprings, telescopic dampers.

STEERING worm and roller.

BRAKES drum, servo.

ELECTRICAL EQUIPMENT 12 V; 60 Ah battery; 35 A alternator; Hitachi distributor; 2 headlamps.

DIMENSIONS AND WEIGHT wheel base: 98.43 in, 250 cm; tracks: 54.57 in, 139 cm front, 55.28 in, 140 cm rear; length: 160.24 in, 407 cm; width: 67.52 in, 171 cm; height: 79.33 in, 201 cm; ground clearance: 7.68 in, 19.5 cm; weight: 3,660 lb, 1,660 kg; turning circle: 38.7 ft, 11.9 m; fuel tank: 14.3 imp gal, 17.2 US gal, 65 l.

BODY open; 2 doors; 3 seats, bench front seats.

SUBARU JAPAN

Rex 550 SEEC-T Series

PRICES (Tokyo):	yen
1 B 2 dr Sedan	**561,000**
2 AI 2-dr Sedan	**618,000**
3 AI 4-dr Sedan	**643,000**
4 AII 4-dr Sedan	**682,000**
5 AIIG 4-dr Sedan	**709,000**
6 Swingback AI	**638,000**
7 Swingback AII	**677,000**
8 Swingback AIIG	**704,000**
9 Family Rex	**480,000**

Power team:	Standard for:	Optional for:
31 hp	1 to 8	—
28 hp	9	—

31 hp power team

ENGINE rear, low emission SEEC-T type, transverse, 4 stroke; 2 cylinders, in line; 33.2 cu in, 544 cc (2.99 x 2.36 in, 76 x 60 mm); compression ratio: 8.5:1; max power (JIS): 31 hp (23 kW) at 6,200 rpm; max torque (JIS): 30 lb ft, 4.2 kg m (41 Nm) at 3,500 rpm; max engine rpm: 7,000; 56.9 hp/l (41.9 kW/l); cast iron block, light alloy head; 3 crankshaft bearings; valves: overhead; Vee-slanted, rockers; camshafts: 1, overhead; lubrication: rotary pump, full flow filter, 4.4 imp pt, 5.3 US pt, 2.5 l; 1 Hitachi DCG306 downdraught twin barrel carburettor; fuel feed: mechanical pump; water-cooled, 10.6 imp pt, 12.7 US pt, 6 l.

TRANSMISSION driving wheels: rear; clutch: single dry plate (diaphragm); gearbox: mechanical; gears: 4, fully synchronized; ratios: I 4.363, II 2.625, III 1.809, IV 1.269, rev 4.272; lever: central; final drive: helical spur gears; axle ratio: 4.315; width of rims: 3.5"; tyres: 5.20 x 10.

PERFORMANCE max speeds: (I) 21 mph, 34 km/h; (II) 34 mph, 55 km/h; (III) 50 mph, 80 km/h; (IV) 65 mph, 105 km/h; power-weight ratio: B 2-dr 38 lb/hp (51.6 lb/kW), 17.3 kg/hp (23.5 kg/kW); carrying capacity: 706 lb, 320 kg; consumption: 58.8 m/imp gal, 48 m/US gal, 4.8 l x 100 km.

CHASSIS integral; front and rear suspension: independent, semi-trailing arms, torsion bars, telescopic dampers.

STEERING rack-and-pinion; turns lock to lock: 3.20.

BRAKES drum - AII and AIIG front disc brakes; lining area: front 37.2 sq in, 240 sq cm, rear 33.5 sq in, 216 sq cm, total 70.7 sq in, 456 sq cm.

ELECTRICAL EQUIPMENT 12 V; 30 Ah battery; 35 A alternator; Hitachi distributor; 2 headlamps.

DIMENSIONS AND WEIGHT wheel base: 75.59 in, 192 cm; tracks: 48.43 in, 123 cm front, 47.83 in, 121 cm rear; length: B and AI models 125.39 in, 318 cm AII and AIIG 125.79 in, 319 cm; height: 52.17 in, 132 cm; width: 54.92 in, 139 cm; ground clearance: 6.89 in, 17.5 cm; weight: B 2-dr 1,180 lb, 535 kg - AI 2-dr 1,202 lb, 545 kg - AI 4-dr 1,246 lb, 565 kg - AI 4-dr 1,235 lb 560 kg - AII 4-dr 1,257 lb, 570 kg - AIIG 4-dr 1,257 lb, 570 kg; weight distribution: 37% front, 63% rear; turning circle: 30.2 ft, 9.2 m; fuel tank: 5.5 imp gal, 6.6 US gal, 25 l.

BODY saloon/sedan; 4 seats, separate front seats, reclining backrests, built-in headrests; (for Swingback models) opening rear window.

28 hp power team

See 31 hp power team, except for:

ENGINE compression ratio: 9:1; max power (JIS): 28 hp (21 kW) at 6,000 rpm; max torque (JIS): 30 lb ft, 4.2 kg m (41 Nm) at 3,500 rpm; max engine rpm: 7,000; 51.5 hp/l (37.9 kW/l).

PERFORMANCE power-weight ratio: 44 lb/hp (60 lb/kW), 20 kg/hp (27.2 kg/kW).

DIMENSIONS AND WEIGHT weight: 1,236 lb, 560 kg.

BODY 2+1 doors; 2+2 seats.

Leone Series

PRICES (Tokyo):	yen
1 1300 E Swingback	**730,000**
2 1300 LE Swingback	**825,000**
3 1600 GLF Swingback	**954,000**
4 1600 GLS Swingback	**1,045,000**
5 1600 SRX Swingback	**1,198,000**
6 1600 L 4-dr Sedan	**880,000**
7 1600 LF 4-dr Sedan	**935,000**
8 1600 GLF 4-dr Sedan	**1,010,000**
9 1600 GLS 4-dr Sedan	**1,120,000**
10 1600 GLF Hardtop	**1,042,000**
11 1600 Swingback 4WD	**1,210,000**
12 1600 Estate 4WD	**1,102,000**
13 1800 GTL 4-dr Sedan	**1,195,000**
14 1800 GTS 4-dr Sedan	**1,355,000**
15 1800 GTL Hardtop	**1,245,000**
16 1800 GTS Hardtop	**1,380,000**
17 1800 4-dr Sedan 4WD	**1,446,000**
18 1800 Swingback 4WD	**1,336,000**
19 1800 Estate 4WD	**1,247,000**

SUBARU Rex 550 SEEC-T AIIG Sedan

Power team:	Standard for:	Optional for:
72 hp	1,2	—
87 hp	3,4,6 to 10	—
87 hp (4WD)	11,12	—
95 hp	19	—
100 hp	5	—
100 hp (1,800 cc)	11 to 14	—
100 hp (1,800 cc, 4WD)	17,18	—

72 hp power team

ENGINE front, SEEC-T low emission system with secondary air induction, EGR and 3-way catalytic converter (open loop system), 4 stroke; 4 cylinders, horizontally opposed; 79.2 cu in, 1,298 cc (3.27 x 2.36 in, 83 x 60 mm); compression ratio: 9:1; max power (JIS): 72 hp (53 kW) at 5,600 rpm; max torque (JIS): 76 lb ft, 10 kg m (98 Nm) at 3,600 rpm; max engine rpm: 6,000; 55.4 hp/l (40.7 kW/l); light alloy block with cast iron liners, light alloy head; 3 crankshaft bearings; valves: overhead, push-rods and rockers; camshafts: 1, under crankshaft; lubrication: rotary pump, full flow filter, 6.1 imp pt, 7.2 US pt, 3.5 l; 1 Hitachi - Zenith DCG 306 twin barrel carburettor; fuel feed: electric pump; water-cooled, 8.9 imp pt, 10.5 US pt, 5 l, electric fan.

TRANSMISSION driving wheels: front; clutch: single dry pla (diaphragm); gearbox: mechanical; gears: 4, fully synchronize ratios: I 3.666, II 2.157, III 1.379, IV 0.971, rev 4.100; leve central; final drive: hypoid bevel; axle ratio: 3.889; width rims: 4.5"; tyres: 6.15 x 13.

PERFORMANCE max speeds: (I) 27 mph, 44 km/h; (II) 46 mp 75 km/h; (III) 71 mph, 115 km/h; (IV) 93 mph, 150 km/ power-weight ratio: 25.1 lb/hp (34.1 lb/kW), 11.4 kg/hp (15. kg/kW); carrying capacity: 882 lb, 400 kg; speed in top at 1,00 rpm: 15.5 mph, 25 km/h; consumption: 45 m/imp gal, 38 m/U gal, 6.2 l x 100 km.

CHASSIS integral; front suspension: independent by McPhe son, coil springs/telescopic damper struts, lower wishbone (trailing links), anti-roll bar; rear: independent, semi-trailir arms, torsion bars, telescopic dampers.

STEERING rack-and-pinion; turns lock to lock: 3.80.

BRAKES drum; lining area: front 66.5 sq in, 429 sq cm, re 26.1 sq in, 168 sq cm, total 82.6 sq in, 597 sq cm.

ELECTRICAL EQUIPMENT 12 V; 35 Ah battery; 50 A altern tor; Hitachi distributor; 2 headlamps.

DIMENSIONS AND WEIGHT wheel base: 93.70 in, 238 cr tracks: 52.80 in, 134 cm front, 53.54 in, 136 cm rear; lengt 151.97 in, 386 cm; width: 63.39 in, 161 cm; height: 53.54 i 136 cm; ground clearance: 6.89 in, 17.5 cm; weight: 1,810 l 820 kg; weight distribution: 62% front, 38% rear; turning circl 34.2 ft, 10.4 m; fuel tank: 15.7 imp gal, 13.2 US gal, 50 l

SUBARU Leone 1600 SRX Swingback

BODY hatchback; 2+1 doors; 5 seats, separate front seats, built-in headrests.

87 hp power team

See 72 hp power team, except for:

ENGINE 97.3 cu in, 1,595 cc (3.62 xx 2.36 in, 92 x 60 mm); max power (JIS): 87 hp (64 kW) at 5,600 rpm; max torque (JIS): 89 lb ft, 12.3 kg m (120 Nm) at 3,600 rpm; max engine rpm: 6,000; 54.5 hp/l (40.1 kW/l); 1 Hitachi-Zenith-Stromberg DCG 306 downdraught twin barrel carburettor.

TRANSMISSION gears: 4 - GLS models, 5 fully synchronized; ratios: I 3.307, II 1.944, III 1.344, IV 0.942 - GLS models V 0.725, rev 4.100; lever: central.

PERFORMANCE max speeds: (I) 30 mph, 48 km/h; (II) 51 mph, 82 km/h; (III) 74 mph, 120 km/h; (IV) 99 mph, 160 km/h; power-weight ratio: L 21.8 lb/hp (29.7 lb/kW), 9.9 kg/hp (13.4 kg/kW); speed in top at 1,000 rpm: 16.6 mph, 26.7 km/h; consumption: 42 m/imp gal, 35 m/US gal, 6.7 l x 100 km.

BRAKES GLF and GLS models front disc, servo; lining area: front 24.2 sq in, 156 sq cm, total 50.2 sq in, 324 sq cm.

DIMENSIONS AND WEIGHT wheel base: sedans 96.85 in, 246 cm; tracks: 52.36 in,133 cm front, 52.76 in, 134 cm rear; length: LF, L and GFL models 162.60 in, 413 cm - GLS models 163.58 in, 415 cm; width: 63.79 in, 162 cm - LF and L 63.39 in, 161 cm; height: sedans 53.54 in, 136 cm - swingback models 53.14 in, 135 cm; weight: L and LF 1,898 lb, 860 kg - GLF Sedan and Hardtop 1,920 lb, 870 kg - GLS Sedan 1,942 lb, 880 kg - GLF Swingback 1,865 lb, 845 kg - GLS Swingback 1,887 lb, 855 kg.

87 hp (4WD) power team

See 72 hp power team, except for:

ENGINE 97.3 cu in, 1,595 cc (3.62 x 2.36 in, 92 x 60 mm); max power (JIS): 87 hp (64 kW) at 5,600 rpm; max torque (JIS): 89 lb ft, 12.3 kg m (120 Nm) at 3,600 rpm; max engine rpm: 6,000; 54.5 hp/l (40.1 kW/l); 1 Hitachi-Zenith-Stromberg DCG 306 downdraught twin barrel carburettor.

TRANSMISSION driving wheels: front or front and rear; gearbox: mechanical and transfer box; gears: 4, fully synchronized; ratios: I 4.090, II 2.157, III 1.379, IV 0.971, rev 4.100; lever: central with auxiliary transfer lever; axle ratio: 3.889 front, 3.900 rear; tyres: 155 SR x 13.

PERFORMANCE max speeds: (I) 25 mph, 40 km/h; (II) 47 mph, 72 km/h; (III) 71 mph, 115 km/h; (IV) 90 mph, 145 km/h; power-weight ratio: 23 lb/hp (31.6 lb/kW), 10.5 kg/hp (14.3 kg/kW); speed in top at 1,000 rpm: 15 mph, 24.2 km/h; consumption: 36 m/imp gal, 30 m/US gal, 7.7 l x 100 km.

BRAKES front disc, servo; lining area: front 24.2 sq in, 156 sq cm, total 50.2 sq in, 324 sq cm.

DIMENSIONS AND WEIGHT wheel base: 93.40 in, 237 cm; tracks: 51.81 in, 131 cm front, 52.99 in, 134 cm rear; length: 156.81 in, 398 cm; width: 63.83 in, 162 cm; height: 55.75 in, 141 cm; ground clearance: 8.07 in, 20.5 cm; weight: 2,020 lb, 915 kg; weight distribution: 60% front, 40% rear.

SUBARU Leone 1800 GTS models

95 hp power team

See 72 hp power team, except for:

ENGINE 108.7 cu in, 1,781 cc (3.62 x 2.64 in, 92 x 67 mm); compression ratio: 8.7:1; max power (JIS): 95 hp (70 kW) at 5,200 rpm; max torque (JIS): 111 lb ft, 15.3 kg m (150 Nm) at 3,200 rpm; max engine rpm: 5,600; 53.4 hp/l (39.3 kW/l); lubrication: 7 imp pt, 8.3 US pt, 4 l; 1 Hitachi DCM 306 downdraught twin barrel carburettor; without catalytic converter and SEEC-T low emission system.

TRANSMISSION driving wheels: front or front and rear; gears: 4, fully synchronized and 2-ratio transfer box; ratios: I 3.636, II 2.157, III 1.266, IV 0.885, rev 3.583; transfer box ratios: high 1, low 1.462; axle ratio: 3.889 front, 3.900 rear; tyres: 155 SR x 13.

PERFORMANCE max speeds: (I) 26 mph, 42 km/h; (II) 44 mph, 71 km/h; (III) 76 mph, 121 km/h; (IV) 84 mph, 135 km/h; power-weight ratio: 21.3 lb/hp (28.9 lb/kW), 9.6 kg/hp (13.1 kg/kW).

DIMENSIONS AND WEIGHT wheel base: 96.26 in, 244 cm; tracks: 51.77 in, 131 cm front, 52.56 in, 134 cm rear; length: 168.31 in, 427 cm; height: 56.89 in, 144 cm; ground clearance: 8.27 in, 21 cm; weight: 2,019 lb, 915 kg.

SUBARU Leone 1800 Sedan 4WD

BODY estate car/st. wagon; 4+1 doors.

100 hp power team

See 72 hp power team, except for:

ENGINE 97.3 cu in, 1,595 cc (3.62 x 2.36 in, 92 x 60 mm); compression ratio: 9.5:1; max power (JIS): 100 hp (74 kW) at 6,000 rpm; max torque (JIS): 83 lb ft, 12.5 kg m (122 Nm) at 4,000 rpm; max engine rpm: 6,500; 62.7 hp/l (46.1 kW/l); 2 Hitachi-Zenith-Stromberg DCG 306 downdraught twin barrel carburettors.

TRANSMISSION gears: 5, fully synchronized; ratios: I 3.666, II 2.157, III 1.518, IV 1.156, V 0.942, rev 4.100; axle ratio: 3.700; width of rims: 5"; tyres: 175/70 HR x 13.

PERFORMANCE max speeds: (I) 31 mph, 50 km//h; (II) 52 mph, 83 km/h; (III) 75 mph, 120 km/h; (IV) 98 mph, 158 km/h; (V) 106 mph, 170 km/h; power-weight ratio: 19.2 lb/hp (26 lb/kW), 8.7 kg/hp (11.8 kg/kW); speed in top at 1,000 rpm: 16.2 mph, 26.1 km/h; consumption: 34 m/imp gal, 28 m/US gal, 8.3 l x 100 km.

CHASSIS anti-roll bar on rear suspension.

BRAKES disc, servo; lining area: front 24.2 sq in, 156 sq cm, rear 11.8 sq in, 76 sq cm, total 36 sq in, 232 sq cm.

DIMENSIONS AND WEIGHT tracks: 52.36 in, 133 cm front, 52.76 in, 134 cm; weight: 1,920 lb, 870 kg.

100 hp (1,800 cc) power team

See 72 hp power team, except for:

ENGINE 108.7 cu in, 1,781 cc (3.62 x 2.64 in, 92 x 67 mm); compression ratio: 8.7:1; max power (JIS): 100 hp (74 kW) at 5,600 rpm; max torque (JIS): 109 lb ft, 15 kg m (147 Nm) at 3,600 rpm; max engine rpm: 6,000; 56.1 hp/l (41.3 kW/l); lubrication: 7 imp pt, 8.3 US pt, 4 l; 1 Hitachi DCM 306 downdraught twin barrel carburettor.

TRANSMISSION gears: 5, fully synchronized; ratios: I 3.307, II 1.950, III 1.344, IV 0.942, V 0.725, rev 3.583; axle ratio: 3.700; tyres: 155 SR x 13 - GTS models 175/70 HR x 13.

PERFORMANCE max speeds: (I) 31 mph, 50 km/h; (II) 54 mph, 87 km/h; (III) 79 mph, 128 km/h; (IV) 106 mph, 170 km/h; (V) 106 mph, 170 km/h; power-weight ratio: GTL Sedan 19.8 lb/hp (26.9 lb/kW), 9 kg/hp (12.2 kg/kW); speed in top at 1,000 rpm: 17.6 mph, 28.3 km/h; consumption: 35 m/imp gal, 29 m/US gal, 8 l x 100 km.

CHASSIS GTS models anti-roll bar on rear suspension.

BRAKES front disc - GTS models rear disc, servo; lining area: front 24.2 sq in, 156 sq cm, total 50.2 sq in, 324 sq cm.

DIMENSIONS AND WEIGHT length: GTL models 163.58 in, 415 cm - GTS models 168 in, 427 cm; width: 63.40 in, 161 cm; weight: GTL Sedan 1,986 lb, 900 kg - GTS Sedan 2,064 lb, 935 kg - GTL Hardtop 1,965 lb, 890 kg - GTS Hardtop 2,041 lb, 925 kg.

OPTIONALS (for GTL models only) automatic transmission, hydraulic torque converter and planetary gears with 3 ratios (I 2.600, II 1.505, III 1, rev 2.167), 3.589 axle ratio.

100 hp (1,800 cc, 4WD) power team

See 72 hp power team, except for:

ENGINE 108.7 cu in, 1,781 cc (3.62 x 2.64 in, 92 x 67 mm); compression ratio: 8.7:1; max power (JIS): 100 hp (74 kW) at 5,600 rpm; max torque (JIS): 109 lb ft, 15 kg m (147 Nm) at 3,600 rpm; max engine rpm: 6,000; 56.1 hp/l (41.3 kW/l); lubrication: 7 imp pt, 8.3 US pt, 4 l; 1 Hitachi DCM 306 downdraught twin barrel carburettor.

TRANSMISSION driving wheels: front or front and rear; gears: 4, fully synchronized and 2-ratio transfer box; ratios: I 3.636, II 2.157, III 1.266, IV 0.885, rev 3.583; transfer box ratios: high 1, low 1.462; axle ratio: 3.889 front, 3.900 rear; tyres: 155 SR x 13.

PERFORMANCE max speeds: (I) 28 mph, 45 km/h; (II) 47 mph, 76 km/h; (III) 81 mph, 130 km/h; (IV) 90 mph, 145 km/h; power-weight ratio: Sedan 21.3 lb/hp (28.9 lb/kW), 9.6 kg/hp (13.1 kg/kW); consumption: 34 m/imp gal, 28 m/US gal, 8.3 l x 100 km.

DIMENSIONS AND WEIGHT wheel base: Sedan 96.46 in, 245 cm - Swingback 93.30 in, 237 cm; tracks: 51.77 in, 131 cm front, 52.76 in, 134 cm rear; width: 63.78 in, 162 cm; height: Sedan 55.51 in, 141 cm - Swingback 55.91 in, 142 cm; weight: Sedan 2,130 lb, 965 kg - Swingback 2,052 lb, 930 kg.

SUZUKI JAPAN

Fronte Series

PRICES (Tokyo):	yen
1 FX 4+1-dr Hatchback	**568,000**
2 FXL 4+1-dr Hatchback	**638,000**
3 FXC 4+1-dr Hatchback	**678,000**
4 FXG 4+1-dr Hatchback	**718,000**
5 FS 4+1-dr Hatchback	**589,000**
6 FSL 4+1-dr Hatchback	**638,000**
7 FSC 4+1-dr Hatchback	**678,000**
8 FSG 4+1-dr Hatchback	**718,000**

Power team:	Standard for:	Optional for:
28 hp (2-stroke)	1 to 4	—
31 hp (4-stroke)	5 to 8	—

28 hp power team

(2-stroke engine)

ENGINE front, transverse, 2 stroke; 3 cylinders, in line; 32.9 cu in, 539 cc (2.40 x 2.42 in, 61 x 61.5 mm); compression ratio: 7:1; max power (JIS): 28 hp (21 kW) at 5,500 rpm; max torque (JIS): 38 lb ft, 5.3 kg m (52 Nm) at 3,000 rpm; max engine rpm: 7,000; 51.9 hp/l (38.2 kW/l); cast iron block, light alloy head; 4 crankshaft bearings on ball bearings; lubrication: mechanical pump, injection to cylinders and crankshaft bearings, total loss system, 8.9 imp pt, 10.5 US pt, 5 l; 1 Mikuni-Solex 30 PCB1 downdraught carburettor; fuel feed: mechanical pump; secondary air injection pump, 2-stage catalytic converters (one exhaust manifold and one exhaust system); water-cooled, 6.1 imp pt, 7.2 US pt, 3.5 l, electric fan.

TRANSMISSION driving wheels: front; clutch: single dry plate (diaphragm); gearbox: mechanical, gears: 4, fully synchronized; ratios: I 3.583, II 2.166, III 1.375, IV 0.933, rev 3.363; lever: central; final drive: helical spur gears; axle ratio: 5.687; width of rims: 3.5"; tyres: 5.20 x 10.

PERFORMANCE max speeds: (I) 19 mph, 30 km/h; (II) 31 mph, 50 km/h; (III) 50 mph, 80 km/h; (IV) 68 mph, 110 km/h; power-weight ratio: FX 43.8 lb/hp (59.4 lb/kW), 19.8 kg/hp (26.9 kg/kW); speed in top at 1,000 rpm: 9.8 mph, 15.7 km/h; consumption: 56 m/imp gal, 47 m/US gal, 5 l x 100 km.

CHASSIS integral; front suspension: independent, by McPherson, coil sprinès/telescopic damper struts, anti-roll bar; rear: rigid axle, semi-elliptic leafsprings, telescopic dampers.

STEERING rack-and-pinion; turns lock to lock: 2.75.

BRAKES drum; lining area: front 31.6 sq in, 204 sq cm, rear 31.6 sq in, 204 sq cm, total 63.2 sq in, 408 sq cm.

ELECTRICAL EQUIPMENT 12 V; 24 Ah battery; 35 A alternator; 2 headlamps.

DIMENSIONS AND WEIGHT wheel base: 84.65 in, 215 cm; tracks: 47.64 in, 121 cm front, 46.06 in, 117 cm rear; length: 125.59 in, 319 cm; width: 54.70 in, 139 cm; height: 52.36 in, 133 cm; ground clearance: 6.69 in, 17 cm; weight: FX and FXL 1,225 lb, 555 kg - FXC and FXG 1,236 lb, 560 kg; weight distribution: 63% front, 37% rear; turning circle: 28.9 ft, 8.8 m; fuel tank: 6 imp gal, 7.1 US gal, 27 l.

BODY hatchback; 4+1 doors; 4 seats, separate front seats, built-in headrests.

31 hp power team

(4-stroke engine)

See 28 hp power team, except for:

ENGINE front, transverse, 4 stroke; 33.1 cu in, 543 cc (2.36 x 2.44 in, 60 x 62 mm); compression ratio: 9.2:1; max power (JIS): 31 hp (23 kW) at 6,000 rpm; max torque (JIS): 30 lb ft, 4.2 kg m (41 Nm) at 4,000 rpm; max engine rpm: 7,000; 57.1 hp/l (42 kW/l); 4 crankshaft bearings; valves: overhead, in line, rockers; camshafts: 1, overhead; lubrication: gear pump, full flow filter, 5.1 imp pt 6 US pt, 2.9 l; 1 Mikuni-Solex downdraught twin barrel carburettor; fuel feed: mechanical pump; water-cooled, 6.1 imp pt, 7.2 US pt, 3.5 l, electric fan.

PERFORMANCE power-weight ratio: FS 40.2 lb/hp (54.6 lb/kW), 18.2 kg/hp (24.8 kg/kW); consumption: 59 m/imp gal, 49 m/US gal, 4.8 l x 100 km.

DIMENSIONS AND WEIGHT weight: FS and FSL 1,247 lb, 565 kg - FSC and FSG 1,258 lb, 570 kg.

Cervo Series

PRICES (Tokyo):	yen
1 CX Coupé	**608,000**
2 CXB Coupé	**608,000**
3 CXL Coupé	**639,000**
4 CXG Coupé	**698,000**
5 SC 100 Coupé	—

For GB prices, see price index.

Power team:	Standard for:	Optional for:
28 hp (2-stroke)	1 to 4	—
47 hp (4-stroke)	5	—

28 hp power team

(2-stroke engine)

ENGINE rear, transverse, 2 stroke; 3 cylinders, in line; 32.9 cu in, 539 cc (2.40 x 2.42 in, 61 x 61.5 mm); compression ratio: 7:1; max power (JIS): 28 hp (21 kW) at 5,000 rpm; max torque (JIS): 38 lb ft, 5.3 kg m (52 Nm) at 3,000 rpm; max engine rpm: 6,400; 51.9 hp/l (38.2 kW/l); cast iron block, light alloy head; 4 crankshaft bearings on ball bearings; lubrication: mechanical pump, injection to cylinders and crankshaft bearings, total loss system, 7 imp pt, 8.5 US pt, 4 l; 1 Mikuni-Solex downdraught carburettor; fuel feed: mechanical pump, emission control 2-3 stage catalyst; water-cooled, 9.5 imp pt, 11.4 US pt, 5.4 l.

TRANSMISSION driving wheels: rear; clutch: single dry plate (diaphragm); gearbox: mechanical; engine-gearbox ratio: 1.471; gears: 4, fully synchronized; ratios: I 3.182, II 1.875, III 1.238, IV 0.880, rev 2.727; lever: central; final drive: helical spur gears; axle ratio: 4.385; width of rims: 3.5"; tyres: 5.20 x 10 - CXG 145 SR x 10.

PERFORMANCE max speeds: (I) 18 mph, 30 km/h; (II) 32 mph, 52 km/h; (III) 49 mph, 79 km/h; (IV) 65 mph, 105 km/h; power-weight ratio: CX 42.1 lb/hp (56.2 lb/kW), 19.1 kg/hp (25.5 kg/kW); consumption: 49.5 m/imp gal, 41.3 m/US gal, 5.7 l x 100 km.

SUZUKI Fronte models

CHASSIS integral; front suspension: independent, wishbones, coil springs, anti-roll bar, telescopic dampers; rear: independent, semi-trailing arms, coil springs, telescopic dampers.

STEERING rack-and-pinion; turns lock to lock: 2.75.

BRAKES drum - CXG front disc; lining area: front 31.6 sq in, 204 sq cm, rear 31.6 sq in, 204 sq cm, total 63.2 sq in, 408 sq cm.

ELECTRICAL EQUIPMENT 12 V; 24 Ah battery; 35 A alternator; 2 headlamps.

DIMENSIONS AND WEIGHT wheel base: 79.92 in, 203 cm; tracks: 48.03 in, 122 cm front, 46.85 in, 119 cm rear; length: 125.59 in, 319 cm; width: 54.92 in, 139 cm; height: 47.64 in, 121 cm; weight: CX 1,180 lb, 535 kg - CXB 1,191 lb, 540 kg - CXL 1,202 lb, 545 kg - CXG 1,212 lb, 550 kg; turning circle: 26.9 ft, 8.2 m; fuel tank: 5.7 imp gal, 6.9 US gal, 26 l.

BODY coupé; 2+2 seats, separate front seats, reclining backrests, built-in headrests.

47 hp power team

(4-stroke engine, for Europe only)

See 28 hp power team, except for:

ENGINE rear, transverse, 4 stroke; 4 cylinders, in line; 59.2 cu in, 970 cc (2.58 x 2.83 in, 65.5 x 72 mm); compression ratio: 8.7:1; max power (JIS): 47 hp (35 kW) at 5,000 rpm; max torque (JIS): 61 lb ft, 8.4 kg m (82 Nm) at 2,500 rpm; 48.4 hp/l (35.6 kW/l); valves: overhead, rockers; camshafts: 1, overhead; lubrication gear pump, full flow filter; 1 Mikuni-Solex downdraught carburettor.

TRANSMISSION tyres: 145/70 SR x 12.

PERFORMANCE power-weight ratio: 29.3 lb/hp (39.5 lb/kW) 13.3 kg/hp (17.9 kg/kW).

BRAKES front disc, rear drum.

DIMENSIONS AND WEIGHT tracks: 48.03 in, 122 cm front, 46.85 in, 119 cm rear: height: 48.42 in, 123 cm; weight: 1,378 lb, 625 kg.

Alto Hatchback

PRICE (Tokyo): 470,000 yen

ENGINE front, transverse, 2 stroke; 3 cylinders, in line; 32.9 cu in, 539 cc (2.40 x 2.42 in, 61 x 61.5 mm); compression ratio: 7:1; max power (JIS): 28 hp (21 kW) at 5,500 rpm; max torque (JIS): 38 lb ft, 5.3 kg m (52 Nm) at 3,000 rpm; max engine rpm: 7,000; 51.9 hp/l (38.2 kW/l); cast iron block, light alloy head; 4 crankshaft bearings; lubrication: mechanical pump, injection to cylinders and crankshaft bearings, total loss system, 8.9 imp pt, 10.5 US pt, 5 l; 1 Mikuni-Solex 30 PCB1 downdraught carburettor; fuel feed: mechanical pump; water-cooled, 6.1 imp pt, 7.2 US pt, 3.5 l, electric fan.

TRANSMISSION driving wheels: front; clutch: single dry plate

SUZUKI Cervo CXG Coupé

ıaphragm); gearbox: mechanical; gears: 4, fully synchronized; ıtios: I 3.583, II 2.166, III 1.375, IV 0.933, rev 3.363; lever: ntral; final drive: helical spur gears; axle ratio: 5.687; width rims: 3.5''; tyres: 5.00 x 10.

:RFORMANCE max speeds: (I) 19 mph, 30 km/h; (II) 31 mph, km/h; (III) 50 mph, 80 km/h; (IV) 68 mph, 110 km/h; ›wer-weight ratio: 42.2 lb/hp (58.4 lb/kW), 19.5 kg/hp (26.4 /kW); speed in top at 1,000 rpm: 9.8 mph, 15.7 km/h; nsumption: 53 m/imp gal, 45 m/US gal, 5.3 l x 100 km.

HASSIS integral; front suspension: independent, by McPher- n, coil springs/telescopic damper struts, anti-roll bar, rear: ıid axle, semi-elliptic leafsprings, telescopic dampers.

TEERING rack-and-pinion; turns lock to lock: 2.75.

RAKES drum; lining area: front 31.6 sq in, 204 sq cm, rear .6 sq in, 204 sq cm, total 63.2 sq in, 408 sq cm.

.ECTRICAL EQUIPMENT 12 V; 24 Ah battery; 35 A alterna- r; 2 headlamps.

MENSIONS AND WEIGHT wheel base: 84.65 in, 215 cm; ıcks: 47.64 in, 121 cm front, 46.06 in, 117 cm rear; length: 5.59 in, 319 cm; width: 54.70 in, 139 cm; height: 52.36 in, 3 cm; ground clearance: 6.69 in, 17 cm; weight: 1,203 lb, 545 ; weight distribution: 61% front, 39 % rear; turning circle: .9 ft, 8.8 m; fuel tank: 6 imp gal, 7.1 US gal, 27 l.

ODY hatchback; 4+1 doors; 4 seats, separate front seats, ıilt-in headrests.

Jimny 55 - Jimny 8 Series

RICES (Tokyo):	yen
55 SJ10F	**748,000**
55 SJ10FM	**768,000**
55 SJ10V	**787,000**
55 SJ10VM	**797,000**
8 SJ20F	**889,000**
8 SJ20VM	**908,000**
8 SJ20FM	**879,000**

›wer team:	Standard for:	Optional for:
hp (2-stroke)	1 to 4	—
hp (4-stroke)	5 to 7	—

26 hp power team

-stroke engine)

IGINE front, 2 stroke; 3 cylinders, in line; 32.8 cu in, 539 cc .40 x 2.42 in, 61 x 61.5 mm); compression ratio: 6.2:1; max ›wer (JIS): 26 hp (19 kW) at 4,500 rpm; max torque (JIS): 38 ft, 5.3 kg m (52 Nm) at 3,000 rpm; max engine rpm: 6,000; .2 hp/l (35.5 kW/l); cast iron block, light alloy head; 4 ankshaft bearings, on ball bearings; lubrication: mechanical mp, injection to cylinders and crankshaft bearings, total stem, 4.9 imp pt, 5.9 US pt, 2.8 l; 1 Solex downdraught rburettor; fuel feed: mechanical pump; water-cooled, 7.2 imp , 8.7 US pt, 4.1 l.

RANSMISSION driving wheels: front and rear; clutch: single y plate; gearbox: mechanical; gears: 4, fully synchronized d 2-ratio transfer box; ratios: I 3.855, II 2.359, III 1.543, IV 1, v 4.026; transfer box ratios: I 3.012, II 1.714 or I 2.571, II 562; levers: central; final drive: hypoid bevel; axle ratio: 875; width of rims: 4.5''; tyres: 6.000 x 16.

ERFORMANCE max speeds: (I) 15 mph, 24 km/h; (II) 20 mph, km/h; (III) 37 mph, 60 km/h; (IV) 55 mph, 88 km/h; power- ›ight: 57.3 lb/hp (78.3 lb/kW), 26 kg/hp (35.5 kg/kW); carrying pacity: 551 lb, 250 kg; consumption: 47.9 m/imp gal, 39.9 'US gal, 5.9 l x 100 km at 37 mph, 60 km/h.

HASSIS box-type ladder frame; front suspension: rigid axle, ›mi-elliptic leafsprings, telescopic dampers; rear: rigid axle, ›mi-elliptic leafsprings, telescopic dampers.

TEERING recirculating ball; turns lock to lock: 3.20.

RAKES drum.

.ECTRICAL EQUIPMENT 12 V; 24 Ah battery; 35 A alterna- r; Nihon Denso distributor; 2 headlamps.

MENSIONS AND WEIGHT wheel base: 75.98 in, 193 cm; ıcks: 42.91 in, 109 cm front, 43.31 in, 110 cm rear; length: 4.80 in, 317 cm; width: 50.98 in, 129 cm; height: 72.64 in, 4 cm; ground clearance: 9.45 in, 24 cm; weight: 1,488 lb, 675 ; turning circle: 28.9 ft, 8.8 m; fuel tank: 5.7 imp gal, 6.9 US l, 26 l.

PTIONALS 2-ratio transfer box (I 1.714 II 3.012).

41 hp power team

-stroke engine)

ee 26 hp power team, except for:

IGINE front, 4 stroke; 4 cylinders, in line; 48.6 cu in, 797 cc (2.44 x 2.60 in, 62 x 66 mm); compression ratio: 8.7:1; max power (JIS): 41 hp (30 kW) at 5,500 rpm; max torque (JIS): 44 lb ft, 6.1 kg m (60 Nm) at 3,500 rpm; 51.4 hp/l (37.8 kW/l); valves: 2, overhead, rocker arms; camshafts: 1, overhead; lubrication: gear pump full flow filter, 6.2 imp pt, 7.4 US pt, 3.5 l; 1 Mikuni-Solex sidedraught carburettor; water-cooled, 6.7 imp pt, 8 US pt, 3.8 l.

TRANSMISSION axle ratio: 4.556.

PERFORMANCE max speeds: (I) 17 mph, 28 km/h; (II) 26 mph, 42 km/h; (III) 26 mph, 64 km/h; (IV) 60 mph, 97 km/h; power-weight ratio: 38.4 lb/hp (52.5 lb/kW), 17.4 kg/hp (23.8 kg/kW); consumption: 45.5 m/imp gal, 37.9 m/US gal, 6.2 l x 100 km at 37 mph, 60 km/h.

DIMENSIONS AND WEIGHT weight: 1,576 lb, 715 kg.

SUZUKI Alto Hatchback

SUZUKI Jimny 55 SJ10FM

TOYOTA JAPAN

Starlet Series

PRICES (Tokyo):	yen
DX 2+1-dr Sedan	**710,000**
DX 4+1-dr Sedan	**735,000**
XL 2+1-dr Sedan	**755,000**
XL 4+1-dr Sedan	**780,000**
S 2+1-dr Sedan	**808,000**
S 4+1-dr Sedan	**833,000**
SE 2+1-dr Sedan	**828,000**
SE 4+1-dr Sedan	**853,000**

ENGINE front, 4 stroke; 4 cylinders, in line; 78.7 cu in, 1,290 cc (2.95 x 2.87 in, 75 x 73 mm); max power (JIS): 72 hp (53 kW) at 5,600 rpm; max torque (JIS): 76 lb ft, 10.5 kg m (103 Nm) at 3,600 rpm; max engine rpm: 6,000; 58.9 hp/l, 41 kW/l; cast iron block, light alloy head; 5 crankshaft bearings; valves: overhead, push-rods and rockers; camshafts: 1, side; lubrication: rotary pump, full flow filter, 6.2 imp pt, 7.4 US pt, 3.5 l; 1 Aisan 4K-U downdraught twin barrel carburettor; emission control with oxidizing catalyst, secondary air induction and exhaust gas recirculation; fuel feed: mechanical pump; water-cooled, 8.8 imp pt, 10.6 US pt, 5 l.

TRANSMISSION driving wheels: rear; clutch: single dry plate (diaphragm); gearbox: mechanical; gears: 4, fully synchronized; ratios: I 3.789, II 2.220, III 1.435, IV 1, rev 4.316; lever: central; final drive: hypoid bevel; axle ratio: 3.417 - S models 3.583; width of rims: 4'' - S models 4.5''; tyres: 6.00 x 12 - S models 145 SR x 13 - SE models 155 SR x 12.

PERFORMANCE max speeds: (I) 29 mph, 46 km/h; (II) 51 mph, 82 km/h; (III) 79 mph, 127 km/h; (IV) 103 mph, 165 km/h; power-weight ratio: DX 2+1-dr 21.3 lb/hp (29 lb/kW), 9.6 kg/hp (13.1 kg/kW); carrying capacity: 882 lb, 400 kg; consumption: 46.6 m/imp gal, 38.8 m/US ga, 6.1 l x 100 km.

CHASSIS integral; front suspension: independent, by Mc-Pherson, coil springs/telescopic dampers, lower wishbones, anti-roll bar; rear: rigid axle, coil springs/telescopic dampers, trailing lower radius arms, upper torque arms.

STARLET SERIES

STEERING rack-and-pinion; turns lock to lock: 3.10.

BRAKES front disc, rear drum, servo; lining area: front 19.8 sq in, 128 sq cm, rear 31.6 sq in, 204 sq cm, total 51.4 sq in, 332 sq cm.

ELECTRICAL EQUIPMENT 12 V; 32 Ah battery; 45 A alternator; Denso distributor; 2 headlamps.

DIMENSIONS AND WEIGHT wheel base: 90.55 in, 230 cm; tracks: 50.79 in, 129 cm front, 50.19 in, 127 cm rear; length: DX and XL models 144.88 in, 368 cm - S models 146.65 in, 372 cm - SE models 147.44 in, 374 cm; width: 60.04 in, 152 cm - SE models 60.43 in, 154 cm; height: 54.33 in, 138 cm - S models 53.94 in, 137 cm; ground clearance: 6.50 in, 16.5 cm - S models 6.30 in, 16 cm; weight: DX 2+1-dr 1,532 lb, 695 kg - DX 4+1-dr and S 2+-dr sedans 1,565 lb, 710 kg - XL 2+1-dr 1,543 lb, 700 kg - XL 4+1-dr and SE 2+1-dr sedans 1,576 lb, 715 kg - S 4+1-dr 1,599 lb, 725 kg - SE 4+1-dr 1,609 lb, 730 kg; weight distribution: 55% front, 45% rear; turning circle: 32.1 ft, 9.8 m; fuel tank: 8.8 imp gal, 10.6 US gal, 40 l.

BODY saloon/sedan; 5 seats, separate front seats.

OPTIONALS 5-speed mechanical gearbox, V ratio 0.865, max speed 103 mph, 165 km/h; Toyoglide automatic transmission, hydraulic torque converter and planetary gears with 2 ratios (I 1.820, II 1, rev 1.820), 3.583 axle ratio.

Corsa - Tercel Series

PRICES (Tokyo):

		yen
1	Tercel 1300 2-dr Standard Sedan	**694,000**
2	Tercel 1300 2-dr De Luxe Sedan	**753,000**
3	Tercel 1300 2+1-dr De Luxe Sedan	**773,000**
4	Tercel 1300 2+1-dr Hi De Luxe Sedan	**819,000**
5	Tercel 1300 4-dr De Luxe Sedan	**778,000**
6	Tercel 1300 4-dr Hi De Luxe Sedan	**824,000**
7	Corsa 1300 2-dr Standard Sedan	**700,000**
8	Corsa 1300 2-dr De Luxe Sedan	**759,000**
9	Corsa 1300 2+1-dr De Luxe Sedan	**779,000**
10	Corsa 1300 4-dr De Luxe Sedan	**784,000**
11	Corsa 1300 4-dr GL Sedan	**836,000**
12	Tercel 1500 2+1-dr De Luxe Sedan	**808,000**
13	Tercel 1500 2+1-dr Hi De Luxe Sedan	**854,000**
14	Tercel 1500 S 2+1-dr Sedan	**928,000**
15	Tercel 1500 SE 2+1-dr Sedan	**942,000**
16	Tercel 1500 De Luxe 4-dr Sedan	**819,000**
17	Tercel 1500 Hi De Luxe 4-dr Sedan	**859,000**
18	Tercel 1500 SE 4-dr Sedan	**947,000**
19	Corsa 1500 2+1-dr De Luxe Sedan	**814,000**
20	Corsa 1500 2+1-dr GL Sedan	**869,000**
21	Corsa 1500 2+1-dr S Sedan	**936,000**
22	Corsa 1500 GSL 2+1-dr Sedan	**950,000**
23	Corsa 1500 De Luxe 4-dr Sedan	**819,000**
24	Corsa 1500 GL 4-dr Sedan	**871,000**
25	Corsa 1500 GSL 4-dr Sedan	**955,000**

Power team:	Standard for:	Optional for:
74 hp	1 to 11	—
83 hp	12 to 25	—

74 hp power team

ENGINE front, 4 stroke; 4 cylinders, in line; 79 cu in, 1,295 cc (3 x 2.80 in, 76 x 71.4 mm); compression ratio: 9:1; max power (JIS): 74 hp (54 kW) at 5,600 rpm; max torque (JIS): 78 lb ft, 10.7 kg m (105 Nm) at 3,600 rpm; max engine rpm: 6,000; 57.1 hp/l (42 kW/l); cast iron block, light alloy head; 5 crankshaft bearings; valves: overhead, rockers; camshafts: 1, overhead; lubrication: gear pump, full flow filter, 6.5 imp pt, 7.8 US pt, 3.7 l; 1 Aisan 2A-U twin barrel downdraught carburettor; emission control with catalytic converter, secondary air induction and exhaust gas recirculation; fuel feed: mechanical pump; water-cooled, 8.8 imp pt, 10.6 US pt, 5 l.

TRANSMISSION driving wheels: front; clutch: syngle dry plate (diaphragm); gearbox: mechanical; gears: 4, fully synchronized; ratios: I 3.457, II 2.070, III 1.376, IV 1, rev 3.408; lever: central; final drive: hypoid bevel; axle ratio: 3.909 - 2-dr models and 4-dr De Luxe 3.727; tyres: 6.15 x 13 - 2-dr models and 4-dr De Luxe 6.00 x 12.

PERFORMANCE max speeds: (I) 29 mph, 46 km/h; (II) 49 mph, 79 km/h; (III) 74 mph, 120 km/h; (IV) 99 mph, 160 km/h; power-weight ratio: De Luxe 2+1-dr 23.4 lb/hp (31.8 lb/kW), 10.6 kg/hp (14.4 kg/kW); consumption: 43.5 m/imp gal, 36.2 m/US gal, 6.5 l x 100 km.

CHASSIS integral; front suspension: independent, by McPherson, coil springs/telescopic damper struts, transverse trailing arms, trailing links, anti-roll bar; rear: independent, coil springs, telescopic dampers, trailing arms.

TOYOTA Tercel 1500 S Sedan

TOYOTA Starlet S Sedan

STEERING rack-and-pinion; turns lock to lock: 3.60.

BRAKES front disc, rear drum, servo; lining area: front 19.8 s in, 128 sq cm, rear 31.6 sq in, 204 sq cm, total 51.4 sq in, 33 sq cm.

ELECTRICAL EQUIPMENT 12 V; 33 Ah battery; 40 A alterna tor; Denso distributor; 2 headlamps.

DIMENSIONS AND WEIGHT wheel base: 98.42 in, 250 cm tracks: 52.36 in, 133 cm front, 51.77 in, 131 cm rear; lengt 155.90 in, 396 cm; width: 61.22 in, 17 cm; height: 54.13 in, 13 cm; ground clearance: 6.89 in, 17 cm; weight: 2-dr Standar 1,698 lb, 770 kg - 4-dr De Luxe 1,742 lb, 790 kg - 4-dr GL an Hi De Luxe 1,764 lb, 800 kg - 2+1-dr De Luxe 1,731 lb, 785 k - 2+1-dr Hi De Luxe 1,753 lb, 795 kg; weight distribution: 61 front, 39% rear; turning circle: 34.8 ft, 10.6 m; fuel tank: 9.9 im gal, 11.9 US gal, 45 l.

BODY saloon/sedan; 5 seats, separate front seats.

OPTIONALS 5-speed mechanical gearbox, V ratio 0.827, 3.58 axle ratio, max speeds (I) 31 mph, 50 km/h, (II) 52 mph; 8 km/h, (III) 79 mph, 127 km/h, (IV) and (V) 102 mph, 165 km/h

83 hp power team

See 74 hp power team, except for:

ENGINE 88.6 cu in, 1,452 cc (3.05 x 3.03 in, 77.5 x 77 mm max power (JIS): 83 hp (61 kW) at 5,600 rpm; max torque (JIS 87 lb ft, 12 kg m (118 Nm) at 3,600 rpm; 57.2 hp/l (42 kW/l); Aisan 3A-U downdraught twin barrel carburettor.

TRANSMISSION axle ratio: 3.727; tyres: De Luxe mode 6.00 x 12 - Hi De Luxe and GL models 6.15 x 13 - GSL and S models 145 SR x 13 - S models 165/70 SR x 13.

PERFORMANCE power-weight: De Luxe 4-dr models 20.9 lb/h (28.7 lb/kW), 9.5 kg/hp (13 kg/kW); consumption: 42.2 m/im gal, 35.1 m/US gal, 6.7 l x 100 km.

DIMENSIONS AND WEIGHT length: S and SE models 157.1 in, 399 cm; weight: De Luxe 4-dr models 1,742 lb, 790 kg - H De Luxe and GL 2+1-dr models 1,720 lb, 780 kg - Hi De Lux and GL 4-dr models 1,764 lb, 800 kg - GSL and SE 4-dr mode 1,797 lb, 815 kg - De Luxe 2+1-dr models 1,731 lb, 785 kg - H De Luxe and GL 2+1-dr models 1,753 lb, 795 kg - S mode 1,786 lb, 810 kg.

OPTIONALS automatic transmission, hydraulic torque conve ter and planetary gear with 3 ratios (I 2.737, II 1.565, III 1.03 rev 2.307), max speed 93 mph, 150 km/h, consumption 3 m/imp gal, 28.3 m/US gal, 8.3 l x 100 km.

Corolla Series

PRICES (Tokyo):

		yen
1	1300 2-dr Standard Sedan	**718,00**
2	1300 2-dr DX Sedan	**773,00**
3	1300 2-dr GL Sedan	**829,00**
4	1300 4-dr Standard Sedan	**743,00**
5	1300 4-dr Custom De Luxe Sedan	**771,00**
6	1300 4-dr DX Sedan	**798,00**
7	1300 4-dr GL Sedan	**854,00**
8	1300 Hardtop DX	**834,00**
9	1300 Hardtop GL	**882,00**
10	1300 Coupé DX	**844,00**

TOYOTA Corsa 1500 GSL Sedan

1	1300 Coupé GL	**904,000**
2	1300 Liftback DX	**854,000**
3	1300 Liftback GL	**914,000**
4	1500 4-dr DX Sedan	**844,000**
5	1500 4-dr GL Sedan	**899,000**
6	1500 4-dr SE Sedan	**977,000**
7	1500 Hardtop GL	**927,000**
8	1500 Hardtop SE	**1,008,000**
9	1500 Coupé SL	**949,000**
0	1500 Coupé SR	**1,043,000**
1	1500 Liftback GL	**959,000**
2	1500 Liftback SE	**1,045,000**
3	1600 4-dr GT Sedan	**1,285,000**
4	1600 Hardtop GT	**1,326,000**
5	1600 Coupé Levin	**1,343,000**
6	1600 Liftback GT	**1,360,000**
7	1800 4-dr GL Sedan	**970,000**
8	1800 4-dr SE Sedan	**1,051,000**
9	1800 Hardtop GL	**998,000**
0	1800 Hardtop SE	**1,082,000**
1	1800 Coupé SL	**1,020,000**
2	1800 Coupé SR	**1,152,000**
3	1800 Liftback GL	**1,030,000**
4	1800 Liftback SE	**1,119,000**

or GB prices, see price index.

ower team:	Standard for:	Optional for:
72 hp	1 to 13	—
30 hp	14 to 22	—
95 hp	27 to 34	—
15 hp	23 to 26	—

72 hp power team

NGINE front, 4 stroke; 4 cylinders, in line; 78.72 cu in, 1,290 : (2.95 x 2.87 in, 75 x 73 mm); compression ratio: 9:1; max ower (JIS): 72 hp (53 kW) at 5,600 rpm; max torque (JIS): 76 ft, 10.5 kg m (103 Nm) at 3,600 rpm; max engine rpm: 6,000; 5.8 hp/l (41 kW/l); cast iron block, light alloy head; 5 crankhaft bearings; valves: overhead, push-rods and rockers; camhafts: 1, side; lubrication: rotary pump, full flow filter, 6.2 imp , 7.4 US pt, 3.5 l; 1 Aisan 4 K-U downdraught twin barrel arburettor; emission control with catalytic converter, secondy air induction and exhaust gas recirculation; fuel feed: echanical pump; water-cooled, 8.8 imp pt, 10.6 US pt, 5 l.

RANSMISSION driving wheels: rear; clutch: single dry plate iaphragm); gearbox: mechanical; gears: 4, fully synchronized; tios: I 3.789, II 2.220, III 1.435, IV 1, rev 4.316; lever: central; nal drive: hypoid bevel; axle ratio: 3.909; width of rims: 4"; res: 6.00 x 12 - GL sedans 6.15 x 13.

ERFORMANCE max speeds: (I) 25 mph, 40 km/h; (II) 45 mph, 2 km/h; (III) 67 mph, 108 km/h; (IV) 97 mph, 155; powereight ratio: 2-dr Standard Sedan 24.2 lb/hp (32.9 lb/kW), 11 g/hp (14.9 kg/kW); consumption: 40.9 m/imp gal, 34.1 m/US al, 6.9 l x 100 km.

HASSIS integral; front suspension: independent by Mcherson, coil springs/telescopic dampers struts, lower wishones (trailing links), anti-roll bar; rear: rigid axle, lower trailing nks, upper torque rods, Panhard rod, coil springs, telescopic ampers.

TEERING rack-and-pinion; turns lock to lock: 3.30.

BRAKES front disc, rear drum, servo; lining area: front 19.8 sq in, 128 sq cm, rear 41.6 sq in, 268 sq cm, total 61.4 sq in, 396 sq cm.

ELECTRICAL EQUIPMENT 12 V; 32 Ah battery; 40 A alternator; Nihon-Denso distributor; 2 headlamps.

DIMENSIONS AND WEIGHT wheel base: 94.48 in, 240 cm; tracks: 51.96 in, 132 cm front, 52.40 in, 133 cm rear; length: sedans 159.05 in, 404 cm - coupés, hardtops and liftbacks 161.61 in, 410 cm; width: sedans 63.38 in, 161 cm - coupés, hardtops and liftbacks 63.98 in, 162 cm; height: sedans 54.53 in, 138 cm - hardtops and liftbacks 52.36 in, 133 cm - coupés 52.16 in, 132 cm; weight: 2-dr Standard Sedan and 2-dr DX Sedan 1,741 lb, 790 kg - 2-dr GL Sedan and Hardtop DX 1,785 lb, 810 kg - 4-dr Standard Sedan and 4-dr DX Sedan 1,774 lb, 805 kg - 4-dr GL Sedan, Coupé DX and Hardtop GL 1,818 lb, 825 kg; fuel tank: 11 imp gal, 13.2 US gal, 50 l.

BODY 5 seats, separate front seats, reclining backrests, built-in headrests.

OPTIONALS (for sedans and hardtops only) Toyoglide automatic transmission with 2 ratios (I 1.820, II 1, rev 1.820), 4.100 axle ratio.

80 hp power team

See 72 hp power team, except for:

ENGINE 88.97 cu in, 1,452 cc (3.05 x 3.03 in, 77.5 x 77 mm); max power (JIS): 80 hp (59 kW) at 5,600 rpm; max torque (JIS): 86 lb ft, 11.8 kg m (116 Nm) at 3,600 rpm; 55.1 hp/l (40.5 kW/l); valves: overhead, rockers; camshafts: 1, overhead, cogged belt; lubrication: gear pump, 6.5 imp pt, 7.8 US pt, 3.7 l; 1 Aisan 3A-U downdraught twin barrel carburettor, secondary air induction, catalytic converter, exhaust gas recirculation.

TRANSMISSION axle ratio: 3.727; tyres: SL 6.15 x 13 - SR 155 SR x 13.

PERFORMANCE max speeds: (I) 26 mph, 42 km/h; (II) 45 mph, 72 km/h; (III) 70 mph, 113 km/h; (IV) 97 mph, 155 km/h; power-weight ratio: 4-dr DX 23 lb/hp (31.3 lb/kW), 10.4 kg/hp (14.2 kg/kW); consumption: 42.2 m/imp gal, 35.1 m/US gal, 6.7 l x 100 km.

CHASSIS SR, anti-roll bar on rear suspension.

STEERING recirculating ball, variable ratio - SR constant ratio recirculating ball; turns lock to lock: 3.30 - SR, 2.80.

DIMENSIONS AND WEIGHT weight: 4-dr DX 1,840 lb, 835 kg - 4-dr GL Sedan and Hardtop GL 1,851 lb, 840 kg - 4-dr SE Sedan, Hardtop SE and Liftback GL 1,885 lb, 855 kg - Coupé SL 1,896 lb, 860 kg - Coupé SR 1,940 lb, 880 kg - Liftback SE 1,929 lb, 875 kg.

OPTIONALS 3.909 axle ratio; Toyoglide automatic transmission with 3 ratios (I 2.450, II 1.450, III 1, rev 2.222), 3.909 axle ratio; (for SL and SR coupés only) 5-speed fully synchronized mechanical gearbox (I 3.789, II 2.220, III 1.435, IV 1, V 0.865, rev 4.136).

95 hp power team

See 72 hp power team, except for:

ENGINE 108.4 cu in, 1,770 cc (3.30 x 3.10 in, 85 x 78 mm); compression ratio: 8.6:1; max power (JIS): 95 hp (70 kW) at 5,400 rpm; max torque (JIS): 109 lb ft, 15 kg m (147 Nm) at 3,400 rpm; max engine rpm: 5,800; 53.7 hp/ (39.4 kW/l); valves: Vee-slanted, push-rods and rockers; camshafts: 1, side; lubrication: 7.4 imp pt, 8.9 US pt, 4.2 l; 1 Aisan 13T-U twin barrel downdraught carburettor; Toyota turbulence generating pot low emission cylinder head, secondary air induction, catalytic converter; cooling, 14.1 imp pt, 16.9 US pt, 8 l.

TRANSMISSION gearbox: mechanical; gears: 4, fully synchronized; ratios: I 3.587, II 2.022, III 1.384, IV 1, rev 3.484; axle ratio: 3.727; tyres: 6.45 x 13 - SE models 165 S x 13 - SR 175/70 x 13.

PERFORMANCE max speeds: (I) 28 mph, 45 km/h; (II) 50 mph, 80 km/h; (III) 75 mph, 120 km/h; (IV) 103 mph, 165 ; power-weight ratio: 4-dr GL Sedan 21.2 lb/hp (28.9 lb/kW), 9.6 kg/hp (13.1 kg/kW); consumption: 35.3 m/imp gal, 29.4 m/US gal, 8 l x 100 km.

CHASSIS SR, anti-roll bar on rear suspension.

STEERING recirculating ball, variable ratio - SR, constant ratio; turns lock to lock: 3.30.

DIMENSIONS AND WEIGHT weight: GL Sedan and Hardtop 2,017 lb, 915 kg - SE Sedan and Hardtop 2,039 lb, 925 kg - SL 2,061 lb, 935 kg - SR 2,105 lb, 955 kg - Liftback GL 2,050 lb, 930 kg - Liftback SE 2,083 lb, 945 kg.

OPTIONALS 5-speed fully synchronized mechanical gearbox (I 3.789, II 2.220, III 1.435, IV 1, V 0.861, rev 4.136), 3.909 axle ratio; Toyoglide automatic transmission with 3 ratios (I 2.450, II 1.450, III 1, rev 2.222), 3.909 axle ratio.

115 hp power team

See 72 hp power team, except for:

ENGINE 96.9 cu in, 1,588 cc (3.35 x 2.76 in, 85 x 70 mm); compression ratio: 8.4:1; max power (JIS): 115 hp (84 kW) at 6,000 rpm; max torque (JIS): 109 lb ft, 15 kg m (147 Nm) at 4,800 rpm; max engine rpm: 6,400; 72.4 hp/l (53.2 kW/l); camshafts: 2, overhead; Bosch-Denso L-Jetronic electronic injection.

TRANSMISSION gears: 5, fully synchronized; ratios: I 3.587, II 2.022, III 1.384, IV 1, V 0.861, rev 3.484; axle ratio: 4.100; width of rims: 5"; tyres: GT Sedan 175/70 HR x 13 - other models 185/70 HR x 13.

PERFORMANCE max speeds: (I) 28 mph, 45 km/h; (II) 50 mph, 80 km/h; (III) 76 mph, 122 km/h; (IV) 104 mph, 167 km/h, (V) 110 mph, 175 km/h; power-weight ratio: GT Sedan 18.3 lb/hp (24.9 lb/kW), 8.3 kg/hp (11.3 kg/kW); consumption: 35.3 m/imp gal, 29.4 m/US gal, 8 l x 100 km.

CHASSIS anti-roll bar on rear suspension.

BRAKES rear disc.

DIMENSIONS AND WEIGHT tracks: 52.70 in, 134 cm front, 52.90 in, 134 cm rear; length: GT Sedan 166.30 in, 422 cm - other models 166.90 in, 424 cm; weight: GT Sedan 2,105 lb, 955 kg - Coupé Levin and Liftback GT 2,149 lb, 975 kg.

OPTIONALS 4.300 axle ratio.

TOYOTA Corolla 1600 Coupé Levin (injection engine)

TOYOTA Corolla 1600 Coupé Levin

Sprinter Series

PRICES (Tokyo):

		yen
1	1300 4-dr Sedan DX	**813,000**
2	1300 4-dr Sedan XL	**869,000**
3	1300 Hardtop DX	**849,000**
4	1300 Hardtop XL	**897,000**
5	1300 Coupé DX	**859,000**
6	1300 Coupé ST	**919,000**
7	1300 Liftback DX	**869,000**
8	1300 Liftback XL	**929,000**
9	1500 4-dr Sedan DX	**859,000**
10	1500 4-dr Sedan XL	**914,000**
11	1500 4-dr Sedan SE	**992,000**
12	1500 Hardtop XL	**942,000**
13	1500 Hardtop SE	**1,023,000**
14	1500 Coupé ST	**964,000**
15	1500 Coupé SR	**1,058,000**
16	1500 Liftback XL	**974,000**
17	1500 Liftback SE	**1,060,000**
18	1600 GT 4-dr Sedan	**1,300,000**
19	1600 GT Hardtop	**1,341,000**
20	1600 Coupé Trueno	**1,358,000**
21	1600 GT Liftback	**1,375,000**
22	1800 4-dr Sedan XL	**985,000**
23	1800 4-dr Sedan SE	**1,066,000**
24	1800 Hardtop XL	**1,013,000**
25	1800 Hardtop SE	**1,097,000**
26	1800 Coupé ST	**1,035,000**
27	1800 Coupé SR	**1,167,000**
28	1800 Liftback XL	**1,045,000**
29	1800 Liftback SE	**1,134,000**

Power team:	Standard for:	Optional for:
72 hp	1 to 8	—
80 hp	9 to 17	—
95 hp	22 to 29	—
115 hp	18 to 21	—

72 hp power team

ENGINE front, 4 stroke; 4 cylinders, in line; 78.7 cu in, 1,290 cc (2.95 x 2.87 in, 75 x 73 mm); compression ratio: 9:1; max power (JIS): 72 hp (53 kW) at 5,600 rpm; max torque (JIS): 76 lb ft, 10.5 kg m (103 Nm) at 3,600 rpm; max engine rpm: 6,000; 55.8 hp/l (41 kW/l); cast iron block, light alloy head; 5 crankshaft bearings; valves: overhead, push-rods and rockers; camshafts: 1, side; lubrication: rotary pump, full flow filter, 6.2 imp pt, 7.4 US pt, 3.5 l; 1 Aisan 4K-U downdraught twin barrel carburettor; emission control with catalytic converter, secondary air induction and exhaust gas recirculation; fuel feed: mechanical pump; water-cooled, 8.8 imp pt, 10.6 US pt, 5 l.

TRANSMISSION driving wheels: rear; clutch: single dry plate (diaphragm); gearbox: mechanical; gears: 4, fully synchronized; ratios: I 3.789, II 2.220, III 1.435, IV 1, rev 4.316; lever: central; final drive: hypoid bevel; axle ratio: 3.909; width of rims: 4" - ST 4.5"; tyres: 6.00 x 12.

PERFORMANCE max speeds: (I) 25 mph, 40 km/h; (II) 45 mph, 72 km/h; (III) 67 mph, 108 km/h; (IV) 97 mph, 155 km/h; power-weight ratio: Sedan DX 24.6 lb/hp (33.5 lb/kW), 11.2 kg/hp (15.2 kg/kW); consumption: 40.9 m/imp gal, 34.1 m/US gal, 6.9 l x 100 km.

TOYOTA Corolla (1,300 cc engine)

CHASSIS integral; front suspension: independent, by McPherson, coil springs/telescopic damper struts, lower wishbones (trailing links), anti-roll bar; rear: rigid axle, lower trailing links, upper torque rod, Panhard rod, coil springs, telescopic dampers.

STEERING rack-and-pinion; turns lock to lock: 3.30.

BRAKES front disc, rear drum, servo; lining area: 19.8 sq in, 128 sq cm front, 41.6 sq in, 268 sq cm rear, total 61.4 sq in, 396 sq cm.

ELECTRICAL EQUIPMENT 12 V; 40 Ah battery; 50 A alternator; Nihon-Denso distributor; 2 headlamps - sedans 4 headlamps.

DIMENSIONS AND WEIGHT wheel base: 94.50 in, 240 cm; tracks: 52 in, 132 cm front, 52.60 in, 133 cm rear; length: sedans 159.40 in, 405 cm - other models 162.20 in, 412 cm; width: sedans 63.40 in, 161 cm - other models 64 in, 162 cm; height: sedans 54.50 in, 138 cm - hardtops and liftbacks 52.40 in, 133 cm - coupés 52.20 in, 132 cm; weight: Sedan DX 1,774 lb, 805 kg - Sedan XL, Coupé DX and Hardtop XL 1,819 lb, 825 kg - coupé ST 1,874 lb, 850 kg - Hardtop DX 1,786 lb, 810 kg - Liftback DX 1,830 lb, 830 kg - Liftback XL 1,863 lb, 845 kg.

BODY 5 seats, separate front seats, reclining backrests, built-in headrests.

OPTIONALS 5-speed fully synchronized mechanical gearbox (I 3.789, II 2.220, III 1.453, IV 1, V 0.865, rev 4.316), 3.909 axle ratio; (for sedans and hardtops only) Toyoglide automatic transmission, hydraulic torque converter with 2 ratios (I 1.820, II 1, rev 1.820), 4.100 axle ratio.

80 hp power team

See 72 hp power team, except for:

ENGINE 89 cu in, 1,452 cc (3 x 3 in, 77.5 x 77 mm); compress ion ratio: 9:1; max power (JIS): 80 hp (59 kW) at 5,600 rpm max torque (JIS): 86 lb ft, 11.8 kg m (116 Nm) at 3,600 rpm max engine rpm: 6,000; 55 hp/l (40.5 kW/l); valves: overhea rockers; camshafts: 1, overhead, cogged belt; lubrication: ge pump, 6.5 imp pt, 7.8 US pt, 3.7 l; 1 Aisan 3A-U downdraug twin barrel carburettor.

TRANSMISSION axle ratio: 3.727; tyres: 6.15 x 13 - SR, 15 SR x 13.

PERFORMANCE max speeds: (I) 26 mph, 42 km/h; (II) 45 mp 72 km/h; (III) 70 mph, 113 km/h; (IV) 97 mph, 155 km/ power-weight ratio: Sedan DX 23 lb/hp (31.3 lb/kW), 10.4 kg/h (14.2 kg/kW); consumption: 42.2 m/imp gal, 35.1 m/US gal, 6. l x 100 km.

CHASSIS SR, anti-roll bar on rear suspension.

STEERING recirculating ball, variable ratio servo; turns lock lock: 3.30.

DIMENSIONS AND WEIGHT weight: Sedan DX 1,841 lb, 835 k - XL Sedan and Hardtop 1,852 lb, 840 kg - SE Sedan, Hardto SE and Liftback XL 1,885 lb, 855 kg - Coupé ST 1,896 lb, 86 kg - Coupé SR 1,940 lb, 880 kg - Liftback SE 1,929 lb, 875 k

OPTIONALS Toyoglide automatic transmission, hydraulic to que converter and planetary gears with 3 ratios (I 2.450, 1.450, III 1, rev 2.222), 3.909 axle ratio.

95 hp power team

See 72 hp power team, except for:

ENGINE 108 cu in, 1,770 cc (3.40 x 3.10 in, 85 x 78 mm compression ratio: 8.6:1; max power (JIS): 95 hp (70 kW) 5,400 rpm; max torque (JIS) 109 lb ft, 15 kg m (147 Nm) 3,400 rpm; max engine rpm: 5,800; 53.7 hp/l (39.4 kW/ valves: overhead, Vee-slanted, push-rods and rockers; car shafts: 1, side; lubrication: rotary pump, 7.4 imp pt, 8.9 US p 4.2 l; 1 Aisan 13 T-2 downdraught twin barrel carburetto Toyota turbulence generating pot low emission cylinder hea secondary air induction; cooling, 14.1 imp pt, 16.9 US pt, 8

TRANSMISSION gearbox: mechanical; gears: 4, fully synchr nized; ratios: I 3.587, II 2.022, III 1.384, IV 1, rev 3.484; ax ratio: 3.727; tyres: 6.45 x 13 - SR and SE models 165 S x 13 ST, 175/70 HR x 13.

PERFORMANCE max speeds: (I) 28.1 mph, 45 km/h; (II) 5 mph, 80 km/h; (III) 75 mph, 120 km/h; (IV) 103 mph, 165 km/ power-weight ratio: Sedan XL 21.2 lb/hp (28.9 lb/kW), 9.6 kg/ (13.1 kg/kW); consumption: 35.2 m/imp gal, 29.4 m/US gal, l x 100 km.

CHASSIS SR, anti-roll bar on rear suspension.

STEERING recirculating ball, variable ratio servo; turns lock lock: 3.30.

DIMENSIONS AND WEIGHT weight: XL Sedan and Hardto 2,017 lb, 915 kg - SE Sedan and Hardtop 2,039 lb, 925 kg - S

TOYOTA Sprinter 1500 SE models

2,061 lb, 935 kg - SR 2,105 lb, 955 kg - Liftback XL 2,050 lb, 930 kg - Liftback SE 2,083 lb, 945 kg.

OPTIONALS 5-speed fully synchronized mechanical gearbox (I 3.789, II 2.220, III 1.453, IV 1, V 0.861, rev 4.316), 3.909 axle ratio; Toyoglide automatic transmission, hydraulic torque converter with 3 ratios (I 2.450, II 1.450, III 1, rev 2.222), 3.909 axle ratio.

115 hp power team

See 72 hp power team, except for:

ENGINE 96.9 cu in, 1,588 cc (3.35 x 2.76 in, 85 x 70 mm); compression ratio: 8.4:1; max power (JIS): 115 hp (84 kW) at 6,000 rpm; max torque (JIS): 109 lb ft 15 kg m (147 Nm) at 4,800 rpm; max engine rpm: 6,400; 72.4 hp/l (53.2 kW/l); valves: overhead, Vee-slanted; camshafts: 2, overhead; lubrication: 7.4 imp pt, 8.9 US pt, 4.2 l; Bosch-Denso L-Jetronic electronic injection.

TRANSMISSION gears: 5, fully synchronized; ratios: I 3.587, II 2.022, III 1.384, IV 1, V 0.861, rev 3.484; axle ratio: 4.100; width of rims: 5"; tyres Sedan 175/70 HR x 13 other models 185/70 HR x 13.

PERFORMANCE max speeds: (I) 28 mph, 45 km/h; (II) 50 mph, 80 km/h; (III) 76 mph, 122 km/h; (IV) 104 mph, 167 km/h; (V) 109 mph, 175 km/h; power-weight ratio: GT Sedan 18.3 lb/hp (24.9 lb/kW), 8.3 kg/hp (11.3 kg/kW); consumption: 35.3 m/imp gal, 29.4 m/US gal, 8 l x 100 km.

DIMENSIONS AND WEIGHT tracks: 52.75 in, 134 cm front, 52.95 in, 134 cm rear; length: Sedan 164.56 in, 418 cm - other models 166.33 in, 425 cm; weight: GT Sedan and Hardtop 2,105 lb, 955 kg - Coupé Trueno and GT Liftback 2,149 lb, 975 kg.

OPTIONALS 4.300 axle ratio.

TOYOTA Sprinter 1500 Sedan SE

TOYOTA Sprinter 1500 Hardtop SE

Carina Series

PRICES (Tokyo):		yen
1	1600 Standard 2-dr Sedan	855,000
2	1600 Standard 4-dr Sedan	875,000
3	1600 De Luxe 2-dr Sedan	922,000
4	1600 De Luxe 4-dr Sedan	942,000
5	1600 De Luxe Hardtop	977,000
6	1600 Super De Luxe 4-dr Sedan	971,000
7	1600 Super De Luxe Hardtop	1,006,000
8	1600 ST 4-dr Sedan	1,046,000
9	1600 ST Hardtop	1,096,000
10	1600 SR Hardtop	1,091,000
11	1600 GT 4-dr Sedan	1,391,000
12	1600 GT Hardtop	1,426,000
13	1800 De Luxe 4-dr Sedan	999,000
14	1800 De Luxe Hardtop	1,097,000
15	1800 Super De Luxe 4-dr Sedan	1,133,000
16	1800 Super De Luxe Hardtop	1,183,000
17	1800 ST 4-dr Sedan	1,194,000
18	1800 ST Hardtop	1,238,000
19	1800 SE 4-dr Sedan	1,182,000
20	1800 SE Hardtop	1,193,000
21	1800 SR Hardtop	1,243,000
22	1800 EFI ST 4-dr Sedan	1,232,000
23	1800 EFI ST Hardtop	1,212,000
24	1800 EFI SR Hardtop	1,252,000
25	2000 SE 4-dr Sedan	1,296,000
26	2000 SE Hardtop	1,259,000
27	2000 GT 4-dr Sedan	1,501,000
28	2000 GT Hardtop	1,536,000

For GB prices, see price index.

Power team:	Standard for:	Optional for:
88 hp	1 to 10	—
115 hp	11,12	—
95 hp	13 to 21	—
105 hp	22 to 24	—
105 hp (1,972 cc)	25,26	—
135 hp	27,28	—

88 hp power team

ENGINE TTC-L lean-burn low emission type with turbulence generating pot auxiliary combustion chambers; front, 4 stroke; 4 cylinders, in line; 96.9 cu in, 1,588 cc (3.35 x 2.76 in, 85 x 70 mm); compression ratio: 9:1; max power (JIS): 88 hp (65 kW) at 5,600 rpm; max torque (JIS): 96 lb ft, 13.3 kg m (130 Nm) at 3,400 rpm; max engine rpm: 6,000; 55.4 hp/l (40.7 kW/l); cast iron block, light alloy head; 5 crankshaft bearings; valves: overhead, Vee-slanted, push-rods and rockers; camshafts: 1, side; lubrication: rotary pump, full flow filter, 7.4 imp pt, 8.9 US pt, 4.2 l; 1 Aisan 12T-U downdraught twin barrel carburettor; emission control with catalytic converter, secondary air induction and exhaust gas recirculation; fuel feed: mechanical pump; water-cooled, 14.1 imp pt, 16.9 US pt, 8 l.

TRANSMISSION driving wheels: rear; clutch: single dry plate (diaphragm); gearbox: mechanical; gears: 4 - SR and ST models 5, fully synchronized; ratios: I 3.587, II 2.022, III 1.384, IV 1, rev 3.484 - SR and ST models V 0.861; lever: central; final drive: hypoid bevel; axle ratio: 4.100 - SR 4.300; width of rims: Standard sedans 4" - other models 4.5"; tyres: Standard sedans 5.60 x 13 - De Luxe and Super De Luxe models 6.45 x 13 - ST models and SR 165 SR x 13.

PERFORMANCE max speeds: (I) 29 mph, 46 km/h; (II) 52 mph, 83 km/h; (III) 75 mph, 120 km/h; (IV) 103 mph, 165 km/h; power-weight ratio: Standard 2-dr Sedan 23.4 lb/hp (32.7 lb/kW), 10.6 kg/hp (14.8 kg/kW); consumption: 34 m/imp gal, 28 m/US gal, 8.3 l x 100 km.

CHASSIS integral; front suspension: independent, by McPherson, coil springs/telescopic damper struts, lower wishbones (trailing links), anti-roll bar; rear: rigid axle, twin trailing radius arms, transverse linkage bar, coil springs, telescopic dampers.

STEERING recirculating ball; turns lock to lock: 3.80 - SR, 3.50.

BRAKES Standard sedans drum - other models front disc; lining area: front 60.8 sq in, 392 sq cm, rear 54 sq in, 384 sq cm, total 114.8 sq in, 740 sq cm.

ELECTRICAL EQUIPMENT 12 V; 35 Ah Battery; 45 A alternator; Nihon-Denso distributor; 4 headlamps.

DIMENSIONS AND WEIGHT wheel base: 98.42 in, 250 cm; tracks: 52.56 in, 133 cm front, 53.15 in, 135 cm rear; length: Standard and De Luxe models 170.47 in, 435 cm - Super De Luxe models and ST Sedan 171.65 in, 436 cm - SR and ST hardtops 174.60 in, 443 cm; width: 64.17 in, 163 cm; height: sedans 54.72 in, 139 cm - De Luxe, Super De Luxe and ST hardtops 52.76 in, 134 cm - SR 52.36 in, 133 cm; ground clearance: 6.30 in, 16 cm; weight: Standard 2-dr Sedan, 2,116 lb, 960 kg - De Luxe 2-dr Sedan 2,127 lb, 965 kg - Standard 4-dr Sedan 2,138 lb, 970 kg - De Luxe 4-dr Sedan 2,149 lb, 975 kg - Super De Luxe 4-dr Sedan, ST 4-dr Sedan and De Luxe Hardtop 2,160 lb, 980 kg - Super De Luxe Hardtop 2,171 lb, 985 kg - ST Hardtop 2,204 lb, 1,000 kg - ST 2,216 lb, 1,005 kg; weight distribution: 57.3% front, 42.7% rear; turning circle: 35.4 ft, 10.8 m; fuel tank: 13.4 imp gal, 16.1 US gal, 61 l.

BODY 5 seats, separate front seats, reclining backrests, built-in headrests.

OPTIONALS 5-speed fully synchronized mechanical gearbox (I 3.587, II 2.022, III 1.384, IV 1, V 0.861, rev 3.484), 4.100 axle ratio.

115 hp power team

See 88 hp power team, except for:

ENGINE compression ratio: 8.4:1; max power (JIS): 115 hp (84 kW) at 6,000 rpm; max torque (JIS): 109 lb ft, 15 kg m (147 Nm) at 4,800 rpm; max engine rpm: 6,400; 72.4 hp/l (53.3 kW/l); camshafts: 2, overhead; Bosch-Denso L-Jetronic electronic injection.

TRANSMISSION gears: 5, fully synchronized; ratios: I 3.587, II 2.022, III 1.384, IV 1, V 0.861, rev 3.484; axle ratio: 4.100; width of rims: 5"; tyres: 185/70 HR x 13.

PERFORMANCE max speeds: (I) 29 mph, 47 km/h; (II) 52 mph, 83 km/h; (III) 76 mph, 122 km/h; (IV) 106 mph, 170 km/h; (V) 106 mph, 170 km/h; power-weight ratio: Sedan 19.6 lb/hp (26.7

115 HP POWER TEAM

lb/kW), 8.9 kg/hp (12.1 kg/kW); consumption: 33.6 m/imp gal, 28 m/US gal, 8.4 l x 100 km.

STEERING turns lock to lock: 3.50.

BRAKES rear disc.

CHASSIS anti-roll bar on rear suspension.

DIMENSIONS AND WEIGHT height: Sedan 54.33 in, 138 cm - Hardtop 52.36 in, 133 cm; tracks: 53.15 in, 135 cm front, 53.54 in, 136 cm rear; ground clearance: 6.10 in, 15.5 cm; weight: Sedan 2,249 lb, 1,020 kg - Hardtop 2,260 lb, 1,025 kg.

95 hp power team

See 88 hp power team, except for:

ENGINE 108 cu in, 1,770 cc (3.35 x 3.01 in, 85 x 78 mm); max power (JIS): 95 hp (70 kW) at 5,400 rpm; max torque (JIS): 109 lb ft, 15 kg m (147 Nm) at 3,400 rpm; 53.7 hp/l (39.4 kW/l); 1 13T-U downdraught twin barrel carburettor.

TRANSMISSION (ST models and SR gears: 5, fully synchronized; ratios: I 3.587, II 2.022, III 1.384, IV 1, V 0.861, rev 3.484; axle ratio: 4.100); axle ratio: 3.909; width of rims: SR, 5''; tyres: De Luxe and Super De Luxe models 6.45 x 13 - SE and ST models 165 SR x 13 - SR, 185/70 HR x 13.

PERFORMANCE max speeds: 106 mph, 170 km/h; power-weight ratio: De Luxe Sedan 22.8 lb/hp (31.1 lb/kW), 10.4 kg/hp (14.1 kg/kW); consumption: 33.6 m/imp gal, 28 m/US gal, 8.4 l x 100 km.

DIMENSIONS AND WEIGHT tracks: 52.95 in, 134 cm front, 53.14 in, 135 cm rear; length: De Luxe Sedan 170.47 in, 433 cm - sedans 171.65 in, 436 cm - hardtops 174.61 in, 443 cm; weight: De Luxe Sedan 2,171 lb, 985 kg - Super De Luxe Sedan and ST Sedan 2,182 lb, 990 kg - SE Sedan and Super De Luxe Hardtop 2,193 lb, 995 kg - ST Hardtop 2,227 lb, 1,010 kg - SR 2,249 lb, 1,020 kg - SE Hardtop 2,238 lb, 1,015 kg.

OPTIONALS 5-speed mechanical gearbox (except ST models and SR), 3.909 axle ratio; Toyoglide automatic transmission with 3 ratios (I 2.450, II 1.450, III 1, rev 2.222).

105 hp power team

See 88 hp power team, except for:

ENGINE cu in, 1,770 cc (3.35 x 3.01 in, 85 x 78 mm); max power (JIS): 105 hp (77 kW) at 5,400 rpm; max torque (JIS): 119 lb ft, 16.5 kg m (162 Nm) at 3,600 rpm; 59.3 hp/l (43.6 kW/l); Bosch-Denso L-Jetronic electronic injection; emission control without TTC-L and TGP cylinder head, 3-way catalytic converter.

TRANSMISSION gears: 5, fully synchronized; ratios: I 3.587, II 2.022, III 1.384, IV 1, V 0.861, rev 3.484; axle ratio: ST models 3.909 - SR 4.100; tyres: ST models 165 SR x 13 - SR, 185/70 HR x 13.

PERFORMANCE max speeds (with 3.909 axle ratio): (I) 29 mph, 46 km/h; (II) 48 mph, 78 km/h; (III) 71 mph, 114 km/h; (IV) 99 mph, 160 km/h; (V) 106 mph, 170 km/h; power-weight ratio: ST Sedan 21.2 lb/hp (28.8 lb/kW), 9.6 kg/hp (13.1 kg/kW); consumption: 33.9 m/imp gal, 28.2 m/US gal, 8.3 l x 100 km.

BRAKES front disc, rear drum, servo.

STEERING recirculating ball, variable ratio; turns lock to lock: 3.50.

DIMENSIONS AND WEIGHT tracks: 52.56 in, 133 cm front, 53.15 in, 135 cm rear; length: Sedan 171.65 in, 436 cm - hardtops 174.61 in, 443 cm; weight: ST Sedan 2,226 lb, 1,010 kg - ST Hardtop 2,271 lb, 1,030 kg - SR 2,293 lb, 1,040 kg.

OPTIONALS Toyoglide automatic transmission with 4 ratios (I 2.450, II 1.450, III 1, IV 0.689, rev 2.222).

105 hp (1,972 cc) power team

See 88 hp power team, except for:

ENGINE 120.3 cu in, 1,972 cc (3.30 x 3.50 in, 84 x 89 mm); compression ratio: 8.5:1; max power (JIS): 105 hp (77 kW) at 5,200 rpm; max torque (JIS): 120 lb ft, 16.5 kg m (162 Nm) at 3,600 rpm; max engine rpm: 5,600; 53.2 hp/l (39.2 kW/l); valves: overhead, rockers; camshafts: 1, overhead; lubrication: 8.8 imp pt, 10.6 US pt, 5 l; 1 Aisan 21R-U downdraught twin barrel carburettor; emission control without TGP cylinder head, 3-way catalytic converter, secondary air induction, exhaust gas recirculation.

TRANSMISSION gears: 5, fully synchronized; ratios: I 3.287, II 2.043, III 1.394, IV 1, V 0.853, rev 4.039; axle ratio: 3.909; width of rims: 4.5''; tyres: 165 SR x 13.

TOYOTA Carina 1800 EFI ST Hardtop

TOYOTA Carina 2000 SE models

PERFORMANCE max speeds: (I) 29 mph, 46 km/h; (II) 46 mph, 74 km/h; (III) 71 mph, 114 km/h; (IV) 96 mph, 155 km/h; (V) 109 mph, 175 km/h; power-weight ratio: SE Sedan 22 lb/hp (30.2 lb/kW), 10 kg/hp (13.7 kg/kW); consumption: 28 m/imp gal, 23 m/US gal, 10 l x 100 km.

STEERING variable ratio.

BRAKES front disc, rear drum, servo.

DIMENSIONS AND WEIGHT length: Sedan 136.22 in, 346 cm - Hardtop 174.61 in, 443 cm; weight: Sedan 2,326 lb, 1,055 kg - Hardtop 2,370 lb, 1,075 kg.

OPTIONALS Toyoglide automatic transmission, hydraulic torque converter and planetary gears with 3 ratios (I 2.450, II 1.450, III 1, rev 2.222); power steering, 3.40 turns lock to lock.

135 hp power team

See 88 hp power team, except for:

ENGINE 120.1 cu in, 1,968 cc (3.48 x 3.15 in, 88 x 80 mm); compression ratio: 8.3:1; max power (JIS): 135 hp (99 kW) at 5,800 rpm; max torque (JIS): 127 lb ft, 17.5 kg m (172 Nm) at 4,400 rpm; max engine rpm: 6,300; 66 hp/l (48.6 kW/l); valves: overhead, Vee-slanted, thimble tappets; camshafts: 2, overhead; lubrication: 8.2 imp pt, 9.9 US pt, 4.7 l; Bosch-Denso L-Jetronic electronic injection; emission control with 3-way catalytic converter; cooling, 16 imp pt, 19.2 US pt, 9.1 l.

TRANSMISSION gears: 5, fully synchronized; ratios: I 3.525, II 2.054, III 1.396, IV 1, V 0.858, rev 3.755; axle ratio: 3.909; width of rims: 5''; tyres: 185/70 HR x 13.

PERFORMANCE max speed: 112 mph, 180 km/h; power-weight ratio: Sedan 17.6 lb/hp (24 lb/kW), 8 kg/hp (10.9 kg/kW); consumption: 28 m/imp gal, 23 m/US gal, 10 l x 100 km.

CHASSIS anti-roll bar on rear suspension.

STEERING variable ratio, servo; turns lock to lock: 3.50.

BRAKES disc, servo.

ELECTRICAL EQUIPMENT transistorized ignition.

DIMENSIONS AND WEIGHT tracks: 53.15 in, 135 cm front, 53.54 in, 136 cm rear; height: Sedan 54.33 in, 138 cm - Hardtop 52.36 in, 133 cm; ground clearance: 5.91 in, 15 cm; weight: Sedan 2,381 lb, 1,080 kg - Hardtop 2,392 lb, 1,085 kg.

Celica Series

PRICES EX WORKS:		yen
1	1600 ET Coupé	**985,000**
2	1600 LT Coupé	**1,045,000**
3	1600 LT Liftback	**1,125,000**
4	1600 ST Coupé	**1,095,000**
5	1600 ST Liftback	**1,175,000**
6	1600 XT Coupé	**1,130,000**
7	1600 XT Liftback	**1,226,000**
8	1600 GT Coupé	**1,467,000**
9	1600 GT Liftback	**1,563,000**
10	1800 ST Coupé	**1,125,000**
11	1800 ST Liftback	**1,205,000**
12	1800 XT Coupé	**1,160,000**
13	1800 XT Liftback	**1,256,000**

TOYOTA Celica 2000 GT Liftback

4	1800 SE Coupé	**1,284,000**
5	1800 SE Liftback	**1,380,000**
6	1800 EFI ST Coupé	**1,208,000**
7	1800 EFI ST Liftback	**1,288,000**
8	2000 XT Coupé	**1,213,000**
9	2000 XT Liftback	**1,309,000**
0	2000 SE Coupé	**1,314,000**
1	2000 SE Liftback	**1,410,000**
2	2000 XX-L Liftback	**1,466,000**
3	2000 XX-S Liftback	**1,576,000**
4	2000 XX-G Liftback	**1,696,000**
5	2000 GT Rally Coupé	**1,440,000**
6	2000 GT Rally Liftback	**1,536,000**
7	2000 GT Coupé	**1,577,000**
8	2000 GT Liftback	**1,673,000**
9	2600 XX-S Liftback	**1,713,000**
0	2600 XX-G Liftback	**1,839,000**

or GB prices, see price index.

ower team:	Standard for:	Optional for:
88 hp	1 to 7	—
15 hp	8,9	—
95 hp	10 to 15	—
05 hp	16,17	—
35 hp	25 to 28	—
05 hp (1,972 cc)	18 to 21	—
25 hp	22 to 24	—
40 hp	29,30	—

88 hp power team

NGINE Toyota TTC-L lean-burn low emission engine with rbulence generating pot auxiliary combustion chamber; front, stroke; 4 cylinders, in line; 96.9 cu in, 1,588 cc (3.35 x 2.76 ı, 85 x 70 mm); compression ratio: 9:1; max power (JIS): 88 hp 65 kW) at 5,600 rpm; max torque (JIS): 96 lb ft, 13.3 kg m (130 m) at 3,400 rpm; max engine rpm: 6,000; 55 hp/l (40.7 kW/l); ast iron block, light alloy head; 5 crankshaft bearings; valves: verhead, Vee-slanted, push-rods and rockers; camshafts: 1, de; lubrication: rotary pump, full flow filter, 7.4 imp pt, 8.9 US t, 4.2 l; 1 Aisan 12T-U downdraught twin barrel carburettor; mission control with catalytic converter, secondary air injec-on and exhaust gas recirculation; fuel feed: mechanical pump; ater-cooled, 14.1 imp pt, 16.9 US pt, 8 l.

RANSMISSION driving wheels: rear; clutch: single dry plate diaphragm); gearbox: mechanical; gears: 4, fully synchronized; atios: I 3.587, II 2.022, III 1.384, IV 1, rev 3.484; lever: central; nal drive: hypoid bevel; axle ratio: 4.100; width of rims: 4.5"; yres: 6.45 x 13 - ST models and XT 165 SR x 13.

ERFORMANCE max speeds: (I) 29 mph, 46 km/h; (II) 52 mph, 3 km/h; (III) 75 mph, 120 km/h; (IV) 103 mph, 165 km/h; ower-weight ratio: ET and LT coupés 24.4 lb/hp (33.2 lb/kW), 1.1 kg/hp (15.1 kg/kW); consumption: 34 m/imp gal, 28.3 ı/US gal, 8.3 l x 100 km.

HASSIS integral; front suspension: independent, by Mc-herson, coil springs/telescopic damper struts, lower wish-ones (trailing links), anti-roll bar; rear: rigid axle, twin trailing adius arms, transverse linkage bar, coil springs, telescopic ampers.

TEERING recirculating ball; turns lock to lock: 3.80.

RAKES front disc, rear drum; lining area: front 24.2 sq in, 156 q cm, rear 54 sq in, 348 sq cm, total 78.2 sq in, 504 sq cm.

ELECTRICAL EQUIPMENT 12 V; 35 Ah battery; 45 A alterna-tor; Nihon-Denso distributor; 4 headlamps.

DIMENSIONS AND WEIGHT wheel base: 98.43 in, 250 cm; tracks: 52.56 in, 133 cm front, 53.15 in, 135 cm rear; length: LT models and ET 171.25 in, 435 cm - ST models 175.59 in, 446 cm; width: 64.17 in, 163 cm; height: 51.57 in, 131 cm; ground clearance: ET and LT models 6.30 in, 16 cm - ST models and XT 5.90 in, 15 cm; weight: ET and LT coupés 2,149 lb, 975 kg - LT Liftback 2,160 lb, 980 kg - ST and XT coupés 2,171 lb, 985 kg - XT Liftback 2,182 lb, 990 kg - 1600 ST Liftback 2,205 lb, 1,000 kg; weight distribution: 56.7% front, 43.3% rear; turning circle: 36.1 ft, 11 m; fuel tank: 13.4 imp gal, 16.1 US gal, 61 l.

BODY coupé, liftback; 5 seats, separate front seats, reclining backrests, built-in headrests.

OPTIONALS 5-speed fully synchronized mechanical gearbox (I 3.587, II 2.022, III 1.384, IV 1, V 0.861, rev 3.484), 4.100 axle ratio, max speed 106 mph, 170 km/h; Toyoglide automatic transmission, hydraulic torque converter with 3 ratios (I 2.450, II 1.450, III 1, rev 2.222).

115 hp power team

See 88 hp power team, except for:

ENGINE (without TTC-L engine); compression ratio: 8.4:1; max power (JIS): 115 hp (84 kW) at 6,000 rpm; max torque (JIS): 109 lb ft, 15 kg m (147 Nm) at 4,800 rpm; max engine rpm: 6,400; 69 hp/l (53.2 kW/l); camshafts: 2, overhead; lubrication:

TOYOTA Celica 2000 GT (injection engine)

6.7 imp pt, 8 US pt, 3.8 l; Bosch-Denso L-Jetronic electronic injection.

TRANSMISSION gears: 5, fully synchronized; ratios: I 3.587, II 2.022, III 1.384, IV 1, V 0.861, rev 3.484; axle ratio: 4.100; width of rims: 5"; tyres: 185/70 HR x 13.

PERFORMANCE max speeds: (I) 29 mph, 47 km/h; (II) 51 mph, 83 km/h; (III) 76 mph, 122 km/h; (IV) 106 mph, 170 km/h; (V) 109 mph, 175 km/h; power-weight ratio: XT Coupé (19.1 lb/hp (25.9 lb/kW), 8.6 kg/hp (11.8 kg/kW).

CHASSIS anti-roll bar on rear suspension.

STEERING turns lock to lock: 3.50.

BRAKES rear disc.

DIMENSIONS AND WEIGHT tracks: 53.15 in, 135 cm front, 53.54 in, 136 cm rear; length: 175.59 in, 446 cm; width 64.57 in, 164 cm; height: Coupé 51.38 in, 130 cm - Liftback 51.18 in, 130 cm; weight: Coupé 2,271 lb, 1,030 kg - Liftback 2.282 lb, 1,035 kg.

OPTIONALS Toyoglide automatic transmission, hydraulic tor-que converter with 3 ratios (I 2.450, II 1.450, III 1, rev 2.222).

95 hp power team

See 88 hp power team, except for:

ENGINE 108 cu in, 1,770 cc (3.35 x 3.07 in, 85 x 78 mm); max power (JIS): 95 hp (70 kW) at 5,400 rpm; max torque (JIS): 109 lb ft, 15 kg m (147 Nm) at 3,400 rpm; 54 hp/l (39.4 kW/l); 1 Aisan 13T-U downdraught twin barrel carburettor.

TRANSMISSION axle ratio: 3.909; tyres: 165 SR x 13.

PERFORMANCE max speed: 106 mph, 170 km/h; power-weight ratio: ST Coupé 23.3 lb/hp (31.7 lb/kW), 10.6 kg/hp (14.4 kg/kW); consumption: 32.4 m/imp gal, 27 m/US gal, 8.7 l x 100 km.,

DIMENSIONS AND WEIGHT width: SE models 64.57 in, 164 cm; weight: XT Coupé 2,193 lb, 995 kg - ST Coupé and SE Liftback 2,216 lb, 1,005 kg - SE Coupé and XT Liftback 2,205 lb, 1,000 kg - ST Liftback 2,227 lb, 1,010 kg.

105 hp power team

See 88 hp power team, except for:

ENGINE (without TTC-L engine); 108 cu in, 1,770 cc (3.35 x 3.07 in, 85 x 78 mm); max power (JIS): 105 hp (77 kW) at 5,400 rpm; max torque (JIS): 120 lb ft, 16.5 kg m (162 Nm) at 3,600 rpm; 59.3 hp/l (43.6 kW/l); Bosch-Denso L-Jetronic elec-tronic injection; emission control 3-way catalytic converter.

TRANSMISSION gears: 5, fully synchronized; ratios: I 3.287, II 2.043, III 1.394, IV 1, V 0.853, rev 4.039; axle ratio: 3.909; tyres: 165 SR x 13.

PERFORMANCE max speeds: (I) 29 mph, 47 km/h; (II) 47 mph, 76 km/h; (III) 71 mph, 114 km/h; (IV) 99 mph, 160 km/h; (V) 109 mph, 175 km/h; power-weight ratio: ST Coupé 21.5 lb/hp (29.3 lb/kW), 9.8 kg/hp (13.3 kg/kW); consumption: 33.9 m/imp gal, 28.2 m/US gal, 8.3 l x 100 km.

STEERING turns lock to lock: 3.50.

DIMENSIONS AND WEIGHT weight: ST Coupé 2,260 lb, 1,025 kg - ST Liftback 2,270 lb, 1,030 kg.

135 hp power team

See 88 hp power team, except for:

ENGINE 120.1 cu in, 1,968 cc (3.48 x 3.15 in, 88.5 x 80 mm); compression ratio: 8.3:1; max power (JIS): 135 hp (99 kW) at 5,800 rpm; max torque (JIS): 127 lb ft, 17.5 kg m (172 Nm) at 4,800 rpm; 68.6 hp/l (50.4 kW/l); cast iron block and head; valves: thimble tappets; camshafts: 2, overhead; Bosch-Denso L-Jetronic electronic injection.

TRANSMISSION gears: 5, fully synchronized; ratios: I 3.287, II 2.043, III 1.394, IV 1, V 0.853, rev 4.039; axle ratio: 3.909; width of rims: 5"; tyres: 185/70 HR x 13.

PERFORMANCE max speeds: (I) 37 mph, 60 km/h; (II) 55 mph, 88 km/h; (III) 79 mph, 127 km/h; (IV) and (V) 112 mph, 180 km/h; power-weight ratio: GT Coupé 17.6 lb/hp (24 lb/kW), 8 kg/hp (10.9 kg/kW); consumption: 28.2 m/imp gal, 23.5 m/US gal, 10 l x 100 km.

CHASSIS anti-roll bar on rear suspension.

STEERING variable ratio, servo; turns lock to lock: 3.50.

BRAKES rear disc, servo.

DIMENSIONS AND WEIGHT tracks: 53.13 in, 135 cm front, 53.54 in, 136 cm rear; length: 175.59 in, 446 cm; width: Rally models 64.37 in, 163 cm - GT models 64.57 in, 164 cm; weight: GT Coupé 2,381 lb, 1,080 kg - GT Liftbacks 2,414 lb, 1,095 kg.

OPTIONALS 185/70 HR x 14 tyres.

105 hp power team (1,972 cc)

See 88 hp power team, except for:

ENGINE (without TTC-L engine); 120.3 cu in, 1,972 cc (3.31 x 3.50 in, 84 x 89 mm); compression ratio: 8.5:1; max power (JIS): 105 hp (77 kW) at 5,200 rpm; max torque (JIS): 120 lb ft, 16.5 kg m (162 Nm) at 3,600 rpm; 53.2 hp/l (39.1 kW/l); cast iron block and light alloy head; valves: overhead, in line, rockers; camshafts: 1, overhead; 1 Aisan 21R-U downdraught twin barrel carburettor; emission control 3-way catalytic converter.

TRANSMISSION gears: 5, fully synchronized: ratios: I 3.287, II 2.043, III 1.394, IV 1, V 0.853, rev 4.039; axle ratio: 3.909; tyres: 165 SR x 13.

PERFORMANCE max speeds: (I) 29 mph, 46 km/h; (II) 47 mph, 75 km/h; (III) 70 mph, 112 km/h; (IV) 97 mph, 157 km/h; (V) 109 mph, 175 km/h; power-weight ratio: XT Coupé 22.1 lb/hp (30.1 lb/kW), 10 kg/hp (13.7 kg/kW); consumption: 28.2 m/imp gal, 23.5 m/US gal, 10 l x 100 km.

STEERING variable ratio.

BRAKES servo.

DIMENSIONS AND WEIGHT width: SE models 64.57 in, 164 cm; weight: XT Coupé 2,326 lb, 1,055 kg - XT Liftback and SE Coupé 2,337 lb, 1,060 kg - SE liftback 2,348 lb, 1,065 kg.

OPTIONALS Toyoglide automatic transmission, hydraulic torque converter with 3 ratios (I 2.400, II 1.479, III 1, rev 1.920), max speed 103 mph, 165 km/h.

125 hp power team

ENGINE front, 4 stroke; 6 cylinders, in line; 121.3 cu in, 1,988 cc (2.95 x 2.95 in, 75 x 75 mm); compression ratio: 8.6:1; max power (JIS): 125 hp (92 KkW) at 6,000 rpm; max torque (JIS): 123 lb ft, 17 kg m (167 Nm) at 4,400 rpm; max engine rpm: 6,200; 62.9 hp/l (46.2 kW/l); cast iron block and light alloy head; 7 crankshaft bearings; valves: overhead, rockers; camshafts: 1, overhead; lubrication: gear pump, full flow filter, 9.1 imp pt, 11 US pt, 5.2 l; Bosch-Denso electronic injection; emission control 3-way catalytic converter, exhaust gas recirculation; fuel feed: electric pump; water-cooled, 19.3 imp pt, 23.2 US pt, 11 l.

TRANSMISSION driving wheels: rear; clutch: single dry plate (diaphragm); gearbox: mechanical; gears: 5, fully synchronized; ratios: I 3.287, II 2.043, III 1.394, IV 1, V 0.853, rev 4.039; lever: central; final drive: hypoid bevel; axle ratio: 3.909; width of rims: 5.5"; tyres: L and S 185/70 HR x 14 - G 195/70 HR x 14.

PERFORMANCE max speeds: (I) 33 mph, 54 km/h; (II) 54 mph, 87 km/h; (III) 85 mph, 137 km/h; (IV) and (V) 112 mph, 180 km/h; power-weight ratio: L 20.3 lb/hp (27.6 lb/kW), 9.2 kg/hp (12.5 kg/kW); carrying capacity: 882 lb, 400 kg; consumption: 26.2 m/imp gal, 21.9 m/US gal, 10.7 l x 100 km.

CHASSIS integral; front suspension: independent, by McPherson, coil springs/telescopic damper struts, lower wishbones (trailing links), anti-roll bar; rear: rigid axle, twin trailing radius arms, transverse linkage bar, coil springs, telescopic dampers, anti-roll bar.

STEERING recirculating ball; turns lock to lock: 4.30.

BRAKES disc, servo.

ELECTRICAL EQUIPMENT 12 V; 35 Ah battery; 55 A alternator; Denso distributor; 4 headlamps.

DIMENSIONS AND WEIGHT wheel base: 103.54 in, 263 cm; front and rear track: 53.74 in, 136 cm; length: 181.10 in, 460 cm; width: 64.96 in, 165 cm; height: 51.57 in, 131 cm; ground clearance: 6.30 in, 16 cm; weight: L 2,536 lb, 1,150 kg - S and G 2,580 lb, 1,170 kg; weight distribution: 54% front, 46% rear; turning circle: 38 ft, 11.6 m; fuel tank: 13.4 imp gal, 16.1 US gal, 61 l.

BODY liftback; 2+1 doors; 5 seats, separate front seats.

OPTIONALS Toyoglide automatic transmission, hydraulic torque converter with 4 ratios (I 2.450, II 1.450, III 1, IV 0.689, rev 2.222), 4.300 axle ratio, max speed 109 mph, 175 km/h, consumption 23.1 m/imp gal, 19.3 m/US gal, 12.2 l x 100 km; automatic speed control; power steering, 3.30 turns lock to lock; air-conditioning; sunshine roof.

140 hp power team

See 125 hp power team, except for:

ENGINE 156.4 cu in, 2,563 cc (3.15 x 3.35 in, 80 x 85 mm); max power (JIS): 140 hp (103 kW) at 5,400 rpm; max torque (JIS): 156 lb ft, 21.5 kg m (211 Nm) at 3,600 rpm; max engine rpm: 5,600; 54.6 hp/l (40.1 kW/l).

TRANSMISSION tyres: S 185/70 HR x 14 - G 195/70 HR x 14.

TOYOTA Celica Supra ST Hardtop

PERFORMANCE max speeds: (I) 33 mph, 54 km/h; (II) 53 mph, 85 km/h; (III) 73 mph, 117 km/h; (IV) 107 mph, 173 km/h; (V) 112 mph, 180 km/h; power-weight ratio: 18.6 lb/hp (25.3 lb/kW), 8.4 kg/hp (11.5 kg/kW); consumption: 23.1 m/imp gal, 19.3 m/US gal, 12.2 l x 100 km.

STEERING servo; turns lock to lock: 3.30.

DIMENSIONS AND WEIGHT weight: 2,602 lb, 1,180 kg.

OPTIONALS Toyoglide automatic transmission, hydraulic torque converter with 4 ratios (I 2.450, II 1.450, III 1, IV 0.689, rev 2.222), 3.909 axle ratio, max speed 109 mph, 175 km/h, consumption 23.1 m/imp gal, 19.3 m/US gal, 12.2 l x 100 km; automatic speed control; air-conditioning; sunshine roof.

Celica Supra (USA) Series

PRICES IN USA:	$
ST Hardtop	**5,899***
GT Hardtop	**6,329***
GT Liftback	**6,559***

ENGINE front, 4 stroke; 4 cylinders, vertical, in line; 139.7 cu in, 2,289 cc; compression ratio: 8.4:1; max power (SAE net): 96 hp (71 kW) at 4,800 rpm; max torque (SAE net): 120 lb ft, 16.5 kg m (162 Nm) at 2,800 rpm; max engine rpm: 5,600; 41.9 hp/l (30.8 kW/l); cast iron block, light alloy head; 5 crankshaft bearings; valves: overhead, Vee-slanted, rockers; camshafts: 1, overhead; lubrication: rotary pump, full flow filter, 6.5 imp pt, 7.8 US pt, 3.7 l; 1 Aisan downdraught twin barrel carburettor; fuel feed: mechanical pump; water-cooled, 11.4 imp pt, 13.7 US pt, 6.5 l.

TRANSMISSION driving wheels: rear; clutch: single dry plate (diaphragm); gearbox: mechanical; gears: 4 - GT models 5, fully synchronized; ratios: I 3.579, II 2.081, III 1.397, IV 1, rev 4.399 - GT models I 3.287, II 2.043, III 1.394, IV 1, V 0.853, rev 4.039; lever: central; final drive: hypoid bevel; axle ratio: 3.727 - GT models 3.909; width of rims: 5"; tyres: ST 175 SR x 14 - GT models 185/70 HR x 14.

PERFORMANCE max speed: 109 mph, 175 km/h; consumption: not declared.

CHASSIS integral; front suspension: independent, by McPherson, coil springs/telescopic damper struts, lower wishbones (trailing links), anti-roll bar; rear: rigid axle, twin trailing radius arms, transverse linkage bar, coil springs, telescopic dampers.

STEERING recirculating ball; turns lock to lock: 3.50.

BRAKES front disc, rear drum, servo; lining area: front 24.2 sq in, 156 sq cm, rear 54 sq in, 348 sq cm, total 78.2 sq in, 504 sq cm.

ELECTRICAL EQUIPMENT 12 V; 35 Ah battery; 40 A alternator; Nihon-Denso distributor; 4 headlamps.

BODY hardtop, liftback; 5 seats, separate front seats, reclining backrests, built-in headrests.

OPTIONALS Toyoglide automatic transmission, hydraulic torque converter with 3 ratios (I 2.400, II 1.479, III 1, rev 1.920), 3.900 axle ratio, max speed 103 mph, 165 km/h, acceleration standing ¼ mile 19 sec.

Corona Series

	PRICES (Tokyo):	yen
1	1600 Standard 4-dr Sedan	**897,00**
2	1600 De Luxe 4-dr Sedan	**989,00**
3	1600 De Luxe Hardtop	**1,024,00**
4	1600 De Luxe Liftback	**1,039,00**
5	1600 GL 4-dr Sedan	**1,046,00**
6	1600 GL Hardtop	**1,081,00**
7	1600 GL Liftback	**1,096,00**
8	1600 SL 4-dr Sedan	**1,107,00**
9	1600 SL Hardtop	**1,145,00**
10	1600 SL Liftback	**1,157,00**
11	1800 De Luxe 4-dr Sedan	**1,022,00**
12	1800 De Luxe Hardtop	**1,057,00**
13	1800 De Luxe Liftback	**1,072,00**
14	1800 GL 4-dr Sedan	**1,107,00**
15	1800 GL Hardtop	**1,142,00**
16	1800 GL Liftback	**1,169,00**
17	1800 SL 4-dr Sedan	**1,169,00**
18	1800 SL Hardtop	**1,207,00**
19	1800 SL Liftback	**1,231,00**
20	1800 SL Touring 4-dr Sedan	**1,291,00**
21	1800 SL Touring Hardtop	**1,329,00**
22	1800 SL Touring Liftback	**1,355,00**
23	2000 GL 4-dr Sedan	**1,162,00**
24	2000 GL Hardtop	**1,197,00**
25	2000 GL Liftback	**1,224,00**
26	2000 SL 4-dr Sedan	**1,219,00**
27	2000 SL Hardtop	**1,257,00**
28	2000 SL Liftback	**1,281,00**
29	2000 CX 4-dr Sedan	**1,307,00**
30	2000 CX Hardtop	**1,342,00**
31	2000 CX Liftback	**1,371,00**
32	2000 GT 4-dr Sedan	**1,528,00**
33	2000 GT Hardtop	**1,571,00**
34	2000 GT Liftback	**1,592,00**

For GB prices, see price index:

Power team:	Standard for:	Optional for:
88 hp	1 to 10	—
95 hp	11 to 19	—
105 hp	20 to 22	—
135 hp	32 to 34	—
105 hp (1,972 cc)	23 to 31	—

88 hp power team

ENGINE TTC-L lean-burn system with turbulence generatin pot combustion chambers; front, 4 stroke; 4 cylinders, vertica in line; 96.9 cu in, 1,588 cc (3.35 x 2.76 in, 85 x 70 mm compression ratio: 9.3:1; max power (JIS): 88 hp (65 kW) a 5,600 rpm; max torque (JIS): 96 lb ft, 13.3 kg m (130 Nm) a 3,400 rpm; max engine rpm: 6,000; 55 hp/l (40.7 kW/l); cas iron block, light alloy head; 5 crankshaft bearings; valves overhead, push-rods and rockers; camshafts: 1, side; lubrica tion: rotary pump, full flow filter, 7.4 imp pt, 8.9 US pt, 4.2 l; Aisan 12T-U downdraught twin barrel carburettor; emissio control with catalytic converter, secondary air induction an exhaust gas recirculation; fuel feed: mechanical pump; wate cooled, 14.1 imp pt, 16.9 US pt, 8 l.

TRANSMISSION driving wheels: rear; clutch: single dry plat (diaphragm); gearbox: mechanical; gears: 4 - Standard 3 - S models 5, fully synchronized; ratios: I 3.587, II 2.022, III 1.384 IV 1, rev 3.484 - Standard I 3.368, II 1.644, III 1, rev 4.079 - S models V 0.861; lever: central - Standard steering column; fin drive: hypoid bevel; axle ratio: 3.909 - SL models 4.100; width of rims: 4.5"; tyres: 6.45 x 13 - SL models 165 SR x 13.

PERFORMANCE max speeds: (I) 29 mph, 46 km/h; (II) 52 mph, 83 km/h; (III) 75 mph, 120 km/h; (IV) 103 mph, 165 km/h; power-weight ratio: De Luxe Sedan 24.3 lb/hp (33.1 lb/kW), 11 kg/hp (15 kg/kW); carrying capacity: 882 lb, 400 kg; consumption: 31 m/imp gal, 25.8 m/US gal, 9.1 l x 100 km.

CHASSIS integral; front suspension: independent, by McPherson, coil springs/telescopic damper struts, lower wishbones (trailing links), anti-roll bar; rear: rigid axle, twin trailing radius arms, transverse linkage bar, coil springs, telescopic dampers.

STEERING recirculating ball, variable ratio; turns lock to to lock: 3.80.

BRAKES front disc, rear drum, servo; lining area: front 22.3 sq in, 144 sq cm, rear 53.9 sq in, 348 sq cm, total 76.2 sq in, 492 sq cm.

ELECTRICAL EQUIPMENT 12 V; 33 Ah battery; 55 A alternator; 4 headlamps.

DIMENSIONS AND WEIGHT wheel base: 99.41 in, 252 cm; front and rear track: 53.15 in, 135 cm - SL models 53.74 in, 136 cm; length: 167.72 in, 426 cm - GL and SL models 168.90 in, 429 cm; width: 64.76 in, 164 cm; height: sedans 55.12 in, 140 cm - hardtops 53.94 in, 137 cm - liftbacks 54.14 in, 138 cm; ground clearance: 6.50 in, 16.5 cm; weight: De Luxe Sedan 2,139 lb, 970 kg - GL Sedan 2,183 lb, 990 kg - De Luxe Hardtop 2,172 lb, 985 kg - De Luxe Liftback, GL Hardtop and SL Sedan 2,194 lb, 995 kg - GL Liftback and SL Hardtop 2,216 lb, 1,005 kg - SL Liftback 2,227 lb, 1,010 kg; weight distribution: 55% front, 45% rear; turning circle: 35.4 ft, 10.8 m; fuel tank: 13.4 imp gal, 16.1 US gal, 61 l.

BODY saloon/sedan, hardtop, liftback; 5 seats, separate front seats, reclining backrests, built-in headrests.

OPTIONALS (except SL models) 5-speed mechanical gearbox (V 0.861); Toyoglide automatic transmission, hydraulic torque converter with 3 ratios (I 2.450, II 1.450, III 1, rev 2.222).

95 hp power team

See 88 hp power team, except for:

ENGINE 108 cu in, 1,770 cc (3.35 x 3.07 in, 85 x 78 mm); compression ratio 8.6:1; max power (JIS): 95 hp (70 kW) at 5,400 rpm; max torque (JIS): 109 lb ft, 15 kg m (147 Nm) at 3,400 rpm; 54 hp/l (39.4 kW/l); 1 Aisan 13T-U downdraught twin barrel carburettor.

TRANSMISSION gears: SL models 5, fully synchronized; ratios: I 3.587, III 2.022, III 1.384, IV 1, V 0.861, rev 0.861; tyres: SL models 165 SR x 14.

PERFORMANCE max speeds: (I) 28 mph, 45 km/h; (II) 50 mph, 80 km/h; (III) 75 mph, 120 km/h; (IV) 102 mph 165 km/h; power-weight ratio: De Luxe Sedan 22.9 lb/hp (31.1 lb/kW), 10.4 kg/hp (14.2 kg/kW); consumption: 33.9 m/imp gal, 28.2 m/US gal, 8.3 l x 100 km.

DIMENSIONS AND WEIGHT length: SL models 175 in, 444 cm; weight: De Luxe Sedan 2,172 lb, 985 kg - De Luxe Hardtop 2,183 lb, 990 kg - GL Sedan 2,194 lb, 995 kg - GL Hardtop 2,205 lb, 1,000 kg - De Luxe Liftback 2,227 lb, 1,010 kg - GL Liftback 2,249 lb, 1,020 kg - SL Sedan 2,293 lb, 1,040 kg - SL Hardtop 2,315 lb, 1,050 kg - SL Liftback 2,337 lb, 1,060 kg.

OPTIONALS Toyoglide automatic transmission, hydraulic torque converter with 3 ratios (I 2.450, II 1.450, III 1, rev 2.222) (for SL and GL models only).

TOYOTA Corona 1800 SL Sedan

105 hp power team

See 88 hp power team, except for:

ENGINE (without TTC-L engine); 108 cu in, 1,770 cc (3.35 x 3.07 in, 85 x 78 mm); max power (JIS): 105 hp (77 kW) at 5,400 rpm; max torque (JIS): 120 lb ft, 16.5 kg m (162 Nm) at 3,600 rpm; max engine rpm: 5,800; 59.3 hp/l (43.6 kW/l); Bosch-Denso electronic injection; emission control with 3-way catalytic converter; fuel feed: electronic pump.

TRANSMISSION gears: 5, fully synchronized; ratios: I 3.287, II 2.043, III 1.394, IV 1, V 0.853, rev 4.039; axle ratio: 3.909; width of rims: 5"; tyres: 185/70 HR x 14.

PERFORMANCE max speeds: (I) 33 mph, 53 km/h; (II) 51 mph, 83 km/h; (III) 75 mph, 120 km/h; (IV) and (V) 109 mph, 175 km/h; power-weight ratio: Sedan 22.7 lb/hp (30.8 lb/kW), 10.3 kg/hp (14 kg/kW); consumption: 28.2 m/imp gal, 23.5 m/US gal, 10 l x 100 km.

CHASSIS anti-roll bar on rear suspension.

BRAKES rear disc; lining area: front 22.3 sq in, 144 cm, rear 18 sq in, 116 sq cm, total 40.3 sq in, 260 sq cm.

DIMENSIONS AND WEIGHT front and rear track: 53.54 in, 136 cm; length: 175 in, 444 cm; height: Sedan 55.31 in, 140 cm - Hardtop 54.13 in, 137 cm - Liftback 54.33 in, 138 cm; weight: Sedan 2,381 lb, 1,080 kg - Hardtop and Liftback 2,403 lb, 1,090 kg.

OPTIONALS 4.100 axle ratio.

135 hp power team

See 88 hp power team, except for:

ENGINE hemispherical combustion chambers without TTC-L lean-burn system; 120.1 cu in, 1,968 cc (3.48 x 3.15 in, 88.5 x 80 mm); compression ratio: 8.3:1; max power (JIS): 135 hp (99 kW) at 5,800 rpm; max torque (JIS): 127 lb ft, 17.5 kg m (172 Nm) at 4,800 rpm; max engine rpm 6,600; 68.6 hp/l (50.4 kW/l); valves: overhead, Vee-slanted, thimble tappets; camshafts: 2, overhead; lubrication: 8.3 imp pt, 9.9 US pt, 4.7 l; Bosch-Denso electronic injection; emission control with 3-way catalytic converter; cooling, 14.4 imp pt, 17.3 US pt, 8.2 l.

TRANSMISSION gears: 5, fully synchronized; ratios: I 3.287, II 2.043, III 1.394, IV 1, V 0.853; axle ratio: 4.100; width of rims: 5"; tyres: 195/70 HR x 14.

TOYOTA Corona 2000 SL Hardtop

TOYOTA Corona (2-litre engine)

135 HP POWER TEAM

PERFORMANCE max speed: 112 mph, 180 km/h; power-weight ratio: Sedan 18.3 lb/hp (24.9 lb/kW), 8.3 kg/hp (11.3 kg/kW); consumption: 28.2 m/imp gal, 23.5 m/US gal, 10 l x 100 km.

CHASSIS anti-roll bar on rear suspension.

STEERING turns lock to lock: 3.90.

BRAKES rear disc, servo.

DIMENSIONS AND WEIGHT length: 175 in, 444 cm; height: Sedan 55.11 in, 140 cm - Hardtop 53.94 in, 137 cm - Liftback 54.33 in, 138 cm; weight: Sedan 2,470 lb, 1,120 kg - Hardtop 2,492 lb, 1,130 kg - Liftback 2,514 lb, 1,140 kg.

OPTIONALS power steering, 3.60 turns lock to lock; limited slip differential.

105 hp (1,972 cc) power team

See 88 hp power team, except for:

ENGINE (without TTC-L engine); 120 cu in, 1,972 cc (3.31 x 3.50 in, 84 x 89 mm); compression ratio: 8.5:1; max power (JIS): 105 hp (77 kW) at 5,200 rpm; max torque (JIS): 120 lb ft, 16.5 kg m (162 Nm) at 3,600 rpm; 53.2 hp/l (39.1 kW/l); camshafts: 1, overhead; lubrication: 8.8 imp pt, 10.6 US pt, 5 l; emission control with 3-way catalytic converter, secondary air induction, exhaust gas recirculation.

TRANSMISSION gears: 5, fully synchronized; ratios: I 3.287, II 2.043, III 1.394, IV 1, V 0.853, rev 4.039; axle ratio: GL and CX models 3.727 - SL models 4.100; tyres: GL models 6.45 x 13 - SL models 165 SR x 14 - CX models 165 SR x 13.

PERFORMANCE max speeds: (I) 30 mph, 48 km/h; (II) 50 mph, 80 km/h; (III) 71 mph, 115 km/h; (IV) 102 mph, 164 km/h; (V) 109 mph, 175 km/h; power-weight ratio: GL Sedan 22.1 lb/hp (30.1 lb/kW), 10 kg/hp (13.7 kg/kW); consumption: 29.6 m/imp gal, 24.7 m/US gal, 9.5 l x 100 km.

BRAKES SL models rear disc.

DIMENSIONS AND WEIGHT length: GL and CX models 168.90 in, 429 cm - SL models 175 in, 444 cm; height: GL and CX sedans 55.11 in, 140 cm - SL Sedan 55.31 in, 141 cm - GL and CX hardtops 53.94 in, 137 cm - SL Hardtop, GL, CX and SL liftbacks 54.33 in, 138 cm; width: CX models 65.16 in, 165 cm; weight: GL Sedan 2,326 lb, 1,055 kg - SL Sedan 2,414 lb, 1,095 kg - CX Sedan 2,392 lb, 1,085 kg - GL Hardtop 2,337 lb, 1,060 kg - SL Hardtop and CX Liftback 2,436 lb, 1,105 kg - CX Hardtop 2,403 lb, 1,090 kg - GL Liftback 2,370 lb, 1,075 kg - SL Liftback 2,447 lb, 1,110 kg.

OPTIONALS Toyoglide automatic transmission, hydraulic torque converter with 3 ratios (I 2.450, II 1.450, III 1, rev 2.222); for CX models only) Toyoglide automatic transmission, hydraulic torque converter with 4 ratios (I 2.450, II 1.450, III 1, IV 0.689), 3.909 axle ratio.

Mark II - Chaser Series

PRICES (Tokyo):		yen
1	Mark II 1800 Standard 4-dr Sedan	**990,000**
2	Mark II 1800 De Luxe 4-dr Sedan	**1,066,000**
3	Mark II 1800 De Luxe 2-dr Hardtop	**1,107,000**
4	Chaser 1800 De Luxe 4-dr Sedan	**1,072,000**
5	Chaser 1800 De Luxe 2-dr Hardtop	**1,113,000**
6	Mark II 1800 GL 4-dr Sedan	**1,127,000**
7	Mark II 1800 GL 2-dr Hardtop	**1,169,000**
8	Chaser 1800 XL 4-dr Sedan	**1,133,000**
9	Chaser 1800 XL 2-dr Hardtop	**1,174,000**
10	Mark II 2000 De Luxe 4-dr Sedan	**1,096,000**
11	Mark II 2000 De Luxe 2-dr Hardtop	**1,137,000**
12	Chaser 2000 De Luxe 4-dr Sedan	**1,102,000**
13	Chaser 2000 De Luxe 4-dr Hardtop	**1,143,000**
14	Mark II 2000 GL 4-dr Sedan	**1,157,000**
15	Mark II 2000 GL 2-dr Hardtop	**1,198,000**
16	Chaser 2000 XL 4-dr Sedan	**1,163,000**
17	Chaser 2000 XL 4-dr Hardtop	**1,204,000**
18	Chaser 2000 GS 4-dr Sedan	**1,284,000**
19	Chaser 2000 GS 4-dr Hardtop	**1,362,000**
20	Mark II 2000 GSL 4-dr Sedan	**1,278,000**
21	Mark II 2000 GSL 2-dr Hardtop	**1,354,000**
22	Chaser 2000 SXL 4-dr Sedan	**1,366,000**
23	Chaser 2000 SXL 2-dr Hardtop	**1,438,000**
24	Mark II 2000 LG 4-dr Sedan	**1,459,000**
25	Mark II 2000 LG 2-dr Hardtop	**1,531,000**
26	Chaser 2000 SGS 4-dr Sedan	**1,482,000**
27	Chaser 2000 SGS 2-dr Hardtop	**1,554,000**
28	Mark II 2000 LG Touring 4-dr Sedan	**1,516,000**
29	Mark II 2000 LG Touring 2-dr Hardtop	**1,588,000**
30	Chaser 2000 SG Touring 4-dr Sedan	**1,608,000**
31	Chaser 2000 SG Touring 2-dr Hardtop	**1,645,000**
32	Mark II 2000 Grande 4-dr Sedan	**1,835,000**
33	Mark II 2000 Grande 2-dr Hardtop	**1,872,000**
34	Mark II 2600 Grande 4-dr Sedan	—
35	Mark II 2600 Grande 2-dr Hardtop	**2,092,000**
36	Mark II Diesel DX 4-dr Sedan	**1,243,000**
37	Mark II Diesel GL 4-dr Sedan	**1,304,000**
38	Mark II Diesel GL-Extra 4-dr Sedan	**1,404,000**

TOYOTA Corona (injection engine)

TOYOTA Chaser 2000 SGS models

Power team:	Standard for:	Optional for:
95 hp	1 to 9	—
72 hp (diesel)	36 to 38	—
105 hp	10 to 21	—
125 hp	22 to 33	—
140 hp	34,35	—

95 hp power team

ENGINE TTC-L lean-burn low emission engine with turbulence generating pot auxiliary combustion chamber; front, 4 stroke; 4 cylinders, in line; 108 cu in, 1,770 cc (3.35 x 3.07 in, 85 x 78 mm); compression ratio: 8.6:1; max power (JIS): 95 hp (70 kW) at 5,400 rpm; max torque (JIS): 109 lb ft, 15 kg m (147 Nm) at 3,400 rpm; max engine rpm: 6,000; 53.7 hp/l (39.4 kW/l); cast iron block, light alloy head; 5 crankshaft bearings; valves: overhead, rockers; camshafts: 1, overhead; lubrication: rotary pump, full flow filter, 7.4 imp pt, 8.9 US pt, 4.2 l; 1 Aisan 13T-U downdraught twin barrel carburettor; emission control with catalytic converter, secondary air injection and exhaust gas recirculation; fuel feed: mechanical pump; water-cooled, 14.1 imp pt, 16.9 US pt, 8 l.

TRANSMISSION driving wheels: rear; clutch: single dry plate (diaphragm); gearbox: mechanical; gears: 4, fully synchronized; ratios: I 3.579, II 2.081, III 1.397, IV 1, rev 4.399; lever: central; final drive: hypoid bevel; axle ratio: 3.909; width of rims: 5"; tyres: 6.45 x 14.

PERFORMANCE max speeds: (I) 29 mph, 47 km/h; (II) 52 mph, 83 km/h; (III) 76 mph, 123 km/h; (IV) 103 mph, 165 km/h; power-weight ratio: De Luxe sedans 24.5 lb/hp (33.3 lb/kW), 11.1 kg/hp (15.1 kg/kW); consumption: 32.5 m/imp gal, 27 m/US gal, 8.7 l x 100 km.

CHASSIS integral; front suspension: independent, by McPherson, lower transverse arms, diagonal trailing locating rods, anti-roll bar, coil springs, telescopic damper struts; rear: rigid axle, lower trailing links, upper torque rods, coil springs, telescopic dampers.

STEERING recirculating ball, variable ratio; turns lock to lock: 4.30.

BRAKES front disc, rear drum, servo; lining area: front 22.3 sq in, 144 sq cm, rear 54.6 sq in, 352 sq cm, total 76.9 sq in, 496 sq cm.

ELECTRICAL EQUIPMENT 12 V; 35 Ah battery; 55 A alternator; Nihon Denso distributor; 2 headlamps.

DIMENSIONS AND WEIGHT wheel base: 103.94 in, 264 cm; tracks: 53.94 in, 137 cm front, 53.15 in, 135 cm rear; length: De Luxe models 177.17 in, 450 cm - GL and XL models 178.35 in, 453 cm; width: 65.75 in, 167 cm; height: sedans 55.51 in, 141 cm - hardtops 54.72 in, 139 cm; ground clearance: 6.69 in, 17 cm; weight: Standard and De Luxe 4-dr sedans 2,326 lb, 1,055 kg - De Luxe hardtops 2,337 lb, 1,060 kg - GL and XL sedans

TOYOTA Chaser 2000 SGS Hardtop

2,359 lb, 1,070 kg - GL and XL hardtops 2,370 lb, 1,075 kg; weight distribution: 54% front, 46% rear; turning circle: 37 ft, 11.4 m.

BODY saloon/sedan, hardtop; 2 or 4 doors; 5 seats, separate front seats, reclining backrests, built-in headrests.

OPTIONALS 5-speed fully synchronized mechanical gearbox (I 3.287, II 2.043, III 1.394, IV 1, V 0.853); Toyoglide automatic transmission with 3 ratios (I 2.450, II 1.450, III 1, rev 2.222), 4.100 axle ratio.

72 hp (diesel) power team

See 95 hp power team, except for:

ENGINE front, diesel, Ricardo Comet swirl combustion chambers, 4 stroke; 4 cylinders, in line; 134 cu in, 2,188 cc (3.50 x 3.40 in, 90 x 86 mm); compression ratio: 21.5:1; max power (JIS): 72 hp (53 kW) at 4,200 rpm; max torque (JIS): 105 lb ft, 14.5 kg m (142 Nm) at 2,400 rpm; max engine rpm: 4,500; 32.9 hp/l (24.2 kW/l); lubrication: gear pump, full flow filter, 11.4 imp pt, 13.7 US pt, 6.5 l; Bosch distributor type, injection pump; cooling, 17.6 imp pt, 21.1 US pt, 10 l.

TRANSMISSION gearbox: mechanical; gears: 5, fully synchronized; ratios: I 3.287, II 2,043, III 1.394, IV 1, V 0.853, rev 4.039; axle ratio: 3.909.

PERFORMANCE max speeds: (I) 24 mph, 38 km/h; (II) 39 mph, 63 km/h; (III) 58 mph, 93 km/h; (IV) 81 mph, 130 km/h; (V) 87 mph, 140 km/h; power-weight ratio: DX 35.4 lb/hp (48.1 lb/kW), 16 kg/hp (21.8 kg/kW); consumption: 62.8 m/imp gal, 52.3 m/US gal, 4.5 l x 100 km.

CHASSIS rear suspension: rigid axle, lower trailing arms, upper torque arms, upper torque rods, Panhard rod, coil springs, telescopic dampers.

STEERING recirculating ball, GL-Extra servo.

DIMENSIONS AND WEIGHT length: 178.35 in, 453 cm; weight: DX 2,546 lb, 1,155 kg - GL and GL-Extra models 2,579 lb, 1,170 kg.

BODY saloon/sedan; 4 doors; 5 seats, separate front seats, reclining backrests, built-in headrests.

OPTIONALS 5-speed fully synchronized mechanical gearbox (I 3.287, II 2.043, III 1.394, IV 1, V 0.853); Toyoglide automatic transmission with 4 ratios (I 2.450, II 1.450, III 1, IV 0.689, rev 2.222), 4.100 axle ratio.

105 hp power team

See 95 hp power team, except for:

ENGINE (without TTC-L engine); 120.3 cu in, 1,972 cc (3.30 x 3.50 in, 84 x 89 mm); compression ratio: 8.5:1; max power (JIS): 105 hp (77 kW) at 5,200 rpm; max torque (JIS): 120 lb ft, 16.5 kg m (162 Nm) at 3,600 rpm; 53.2 hp/l (39.1 kW/l); cast iron block, light alloy head; lubrication: gear pump, 8.8 imp pt, 10.6 US pt, 5 l; 1 Aisan 21R-U downdraught twin barrel carburettor; emission control with 3-way catalytic converter.

TRANSMISSION gears: 4 - GSL and GS models 5, fully synchronized; ratios: I 3.579, II 2.081, III 1.397, IV 1, rev 4.399 - GSL and GS models I 3.287, II 2.043, III 1.394, IV 1, V 0.853, rev 4.039; axle ratio: 3.909 - GSL and GS models 4.100; tyres: 6.45 x 14 - GSL and GS models 175 SR x 14.

PERFORMANCE max speeds: (I) 31 mph, 50 km/h; (II) 53 mph, 86 km/h; (III) 78 mph, 126 km/h; (IV) 103 mph, 165 km/h; power-weight ratio: Mark II De Luxe Sedan 22.5 lb/hp (30.7 lb/kW), 10.2 kg/hp (13.9 kg/kW); consumption: 28.2 m/imp gal, 23.5 m/US gal, 10 l x 100 km.

BRAKES GSL and GS models disc; lining area: front 22.3 sq in, 144 sq cm, rear 18 sq in, 116 sq cm, total 40.3 sq in, 260 sq cm.

ELECTRICAL EQUIPMENT 50 A alternator.

DIMENSIONS AND WEIGHT rear track: GSL and GS models 54.33 in, 138 cm; length: De Luxe models 177.17 in, 450 cm - GL, GSL and GS models 178.35 in, 453 cm; height: sedans 55.71 in, 141 cm - hardtops 54.72 in, 139 cm; weight: Mark II De Luxe Sedan 2,370 lb, 1,075 kg - Chaser De Luxe Sedan 2,381 lb, 1,080 kg - De Luxe hardtops 2,392 lb, 1,085 kg - Mark II GL Sedan 2,403 lb, 1,090 kg - Chaser XL Sedan 2,414 lb, 1,095 kg - Chaser XL Hardtop 2,425 lb, 1,100 kg - Mark II GSL and Chaser GS sedans 2,525 lb, 1,145 kg - GSL and GS hardtops 2,536 lb, 1,150 kg.

OPTIONALS steering column lever; Toyoglide automatic transmission, hydraulic torque converter and planetary gears with 3 ratios (I 2.450, II 1.450, III 1, rev 2.222).

125 hp power team

See 95 hp power team, except for:

ENGINE (without TTC-L engine); 6 cylinders, in line; 121.3 cu in, 1,988 cc (2.95 x 2.95 in, 75 x 75 mm); compression ratio: 8.5:1; max power (JIS): 125 hp (92 kW) at 6,000 rpm; max torque (JIS): 123 lb ft, 17 kg m (167 Nm) at 4,400 rpm; 62.9 hp/l (46.2 kW/l); cast iron block, light alloy head; 7 crankshaft bearings; valves: overhead, Vee-slanted, rockers; lubrication: gear pump, 9.2 imp pt, 11 US pt, 5.2 l; Bosch-Denso L-Jetronic electronic injection; 3-way catalytic converter with oxygen sensor; cooling, 19.4 imp pt, 23.3 US pt, 11 l.

TRANSMISSION gears: 5, fully synchronized; ratios: I 3.287, II 2.043, III 1.394, IV 1, V 0.853, rev 4.039; tyres: 175 SR x 14 - SXL models 6.45 x 14 - SGS, SG Touring and Grande models 185/70 HR x 14.

PERFORMANCE max speeds: (I) 32 mph, 52 km/h; (II) 52 mph, 83 km/h; (III) 76 mph, 123 km/h; (IV) 109 mph, 175 km/h; (V) 109 mph, 175 km/h; power-weight ratio: SXL Sedan 20 lb/hp (27.2 lb/kW), 9.1 kg/hp (12.3 kg/kW); consumption: 25.4 m/imp gal, 21.2 m/US gal, 11.1 l x 100 km.

CHASSIS (except SXL models) rear suspension: independent, semi-trailing arms, coil springs, telescopic dampers, anti-roll bar.

TOYOTA Mark II 2600 Grande Sedan

TOYOTA Mark II 2600 Grande Sedan

TOYOTA Mark II 2600 Grande Hardtop

125 HP POWER TEAM

STEERING (except SXL and SGS models) servo; turns lock to lock: 3.40.

BRAKES (except SXL and LG models) rear disc.

DIMENSIONS AND WEIGHT tracks: Grande and SG Touring 54.72 in, 139 cm front and rear - SGS models 54.33 in, 138 cm; width: 66.14 in, 168 cm; weight: Chaser SXL Sedan 2,503 lb, 1,135 kg - Chaser SXL Hardtop 2,514 lb, 1,140 kg - Mark II LG Sedan 2,536 lb, 1,150 kg - Mark II LG Hardtop 2,547 lb, 1,155 kg - Chaser SGS Sedan, 2,580 lb, 1,170 kg - Chaser SGS Hardtop 2,591 lb, 1,175 kg - Mark II LG and Chaser SG Touring sedans 2,613 lb, 1,185 kg - Mark II LG and Chaser SG Touring hardtops 2,624 lb, 1,190 kg - Grande Sedan 2,767 lb, 1,255 kg - Grande Hardtop 2,712 lb, 1,230 kg.

OPTIONALS automatic transmission with 3 ratios (I 2.400, II 1.479, III 1, rev 1.920), 3.909 axle ratio; (for Grande, LG Touring and SG Touring models only) Toyoglide automatic transmission with 4 ratios (I 2.450, II 1.450, III 1, IV 0.689).

140 hp power team

See 95 hp power team, except for:

ENGINE (without TTC-L engine); 6 cylinders, in line; 156.4 cu in, 2,563 cc (3.15 x 3.35 in, 80 x 85 mm); compression ratio: 8.5:1; max power (JIS): 140 hp (103 kW) at 5,400 rpm; max torque (JIS): 156 lb ft, 21.5 kg m (211 Nm) at 3,600 rpm; 54.6 hp/l (40.1 kW/l); cast iron block, light alloy head; 7 crankshaft bearings; valves: overhead, Vee-slanted, rockers; lubrication: gear pump, 9.2 imp pt, 11 US pt, 5.2 l; Bosch-Denso electronic injection; emission control with 3-way catalytic converter and oxygen sensor; cooling 19.4 imp pt, 23.3 US pt, 11 l.

TRANSMISSION automatic transmission, hydraulic torque converter and planetary gears; ratios: I 2.450, II 1.450, III 1, IV 0.689, rev 2.222; axle ratio: 3.909; tyres: 185/70 HR x 14.

PERFORMANCE power-weight ratio: Grande Sedan 19.4 lb/hp (26 lb/kW), 8.8 kg/hp (12 kg/kW); consumption: 22 m/imp gal, 18.3 m/US gal, 12.8 l x 100 km.

CHASSIS rear suspension: independent, semi-trailing arms, coil springs, telescopic dampers, anti-roll bar.

STEERING servo.

BRAKES rear disc.

DIMENSIONS AND WEIGHT front and rear track: 54.72 in, 139 cm; length: 181.69 in, 461 cm; width: 66.14 in, 168 cm; weight: Grande Sedan 2,679 lb, 1,235 kg - Grande Hardtop 2,734 lb, 1,240 kg.

Century Series

PRICES EX WORKS:	yen
D 4-dr Sedan	4,276,000
C 4-dr Sedan	3,876,000

ENGINE front, 4 stroke; 8 cylinders, Vee-slanted at 90°; 206 cu in, 3,376 cc (3.27 x 3.07 in, 83 x 78 mm); compression ratio: 8.5:1; max power (JIS): 180 hp (132 kW) at 5,200 rpm; max torque (JIS): 199 lb ft, 27.5 kg m (270 Nm) at 4,400 rpm; max engine rpm: 6,000; 53.3 hp/l (39.2 kW/l); light alloy block and head; 5 crankshaft bearings; valves: overhead, push-rods and rockers; camshafts: 1, at centre of Vee; lubrication: gear pump, full flow filter, 8.8 imp pt, 10.6 US pt, 5 l; Bosch-Denso L-Jetronic electronic injection; emission control with 3-way catalytic converter and oxygen sensor, secondary air injection and exhaust gas recirculation; fuel feed: electric pump; water-cooled, 23.6 imp pt, 28.3 US pt, 13.4 l.

TOYOTA Century D Sedan

TOYOTA Landcruiser

TRANSMISSION driving wheels: rear; gearbox: Toyoglide automatic transmission, hydraulic torque converter and planetary gears with 3 ratios, max ratio of converter at stall 2; ratios: I 2.400, II 1.479, III 1, rev 1.920; lever: steering column; final drive: hypoid bevel; axle ratio: 3.727; tyres: F78 x 14.

PERFORMANCE max speed: 112 mph, 180 km/h; power-weight ratio: D 22.6 lb/hp (30.7 lb/kW), 10.2 kg/hp (13.9 kg/kW) - C 22.1 lb/hp (30.1 lb/kW), 10 kg/hp (13.6 kg/kW); carrying capacity: 1,058 lb, 480 kg; consumption: 15.5 m/imp gal, 12.9 m/US gal, 18.2 l x 100 km.

CHASSIS integral; front suspension: independent, by McPherson, air bellows/telescopic damper struts, lower wishbones (trailing links), anti-roll bar; rear: rigid axle, lower radius arms, upper torque arm, transverse linkage bar, coil springs, telescopic dampers.

STEERING recirculating ball, servo; turns lock to lock: 3.90.

BRAKES front disc, rear drum, servo; swept area: front 92.7 sq in, 598 sq cm, rear 75 sq in, 484 sq cm, total 167.7 sq in, 1,082 sq cm.

ELECTRICAL EQUIPMENT 12 V; 45 Ah battery; 780 W alternator; Nihon-Denso distributor; 2 iodine headlamps.

DIMENSIONS AND WEIGHT wheel base: 112.60 in, 286 cm; tracks: 60.24 in, 153 cm front, 60.63 in, 154 cm rear; length: 196.06 in, 498 cm; width: 74.41 in, 189 cm; height: 57.48 in, 146 cm; ground clearance: 6.89 in, 17 cm; weight: D Sedan 4,068 lb, 1,845 kg - C Sedan 3,980 lb, 1,805 kg; weight distribution: 53.9% front, 46.1% rear; turning circle: 37.4 ft, 11.4 m; fuel tank: 19.8 imp gal, 23.6 US gal, 90 l.

BODY saloon/sedan; 4 doors; 6 seats, bench front seats.

OPTIONALS limited slip differential; separate front seats; semi-separate front seats.

TOYOTA Landcruiser K-BJ41V-KCY

Landcruiser FJ56V-K

PRICE IN USA: $ 8,998*

ENGINE front, 4 stroke; 6 cylinders, vertical, in line; 258.1 cu in, 4,230 cc (3.70 x 4 in, 94 x 101.6 mm); compression ratio: 7.8:1; max power (SAE net): 140 hp (103 kW) at 3,600 rpm; max torque (SAE net): 217 lb ft, 30 kg m (294 Nm) at 1,800 rpm; max engine rpm: 4,000; 33.1 hp/l (24.3 kW/l); cast iron block and head; 7 crankshaft bearings; valves: overhead, in line, push-rods and rockers; camshafts: 1, side; lubrication: rotary pump, filter on by-pass, oil cooler, 15 imp pt, 18 US pt, 8.5 l; 1 Aisan downdraught twin barrel carburettor; fuel feed: mechanical pump; water-cooled, 26.8 imp pt, 32.1 US pt, 15.2 l.

TRANSMISSION driving wheels: front (automatically engaged with transfer box low ratio) and rear; clutch: single dry plate (diaphragm); gearbox: mechanical; gears: 4, with high and low ratios, fully synchronized; ratios: I 4.925, II 2.643, III 1.519, IV

, rev 4.925; low ratios: high 1, low 1.992; lever: central; final ·ive: hypoid bevel; axle ratio: 3.700; tyrs: 7.00 x 15.

ERFORMANCE max speed: 87 mph, 140 km/h; power-weight ıtio: 30.4 lb/hp (41.4 lb/kW), 13.8 kg/hp (18.7 kg/kW); carrying apacity: 1,103 lb, 500 kg; speed in direct drive at 1,000 rpm: 1.7 mph, 35 km/h; consumption: not declared.

HASSIS ladder frame; front and rear suspension: rigid axle, emi-elliptic leafsprings, telescopic dampers.

TEERING recirculating ball and nut.

RAKES drum.

LECTRICAL EQUIPMENT 12 V; 50 Ah battery; 40 A alterna-ır; Nihon-Denso distributor; 2 headlamps.

IMENSIONS AND WEIGHT wheel base: 106.30 in, 270 cm; acks: 55.71 in, 141 cm front, 55.12 in, 140 cm rear; length: 34.05 in, 467 cm; width: 68.31 in, 173 cm; height: 73.43 in, 36 cm; ground clearance: 8.27 in, 21 cm; weight: 4,256 lb, 930 kg; turning circle: 40.7 ft, 12.4 m; fuel tank: 18 imp gal, 1.6 US gal, 82 l.

ODY estate car/st. wagon; 4+1 doors; 6 or 9 seats.

Landcruiser K-BJ41V-KCY

ee Landcruiser FJ56V-K, except for:

RICE IN USA: $ 7,768*

NGINE diesel, 4 stroke; 4 cylinders, vertical, in line; 181.7 cu , 2,977 cc (3.74 x 4.13 in, 95 x 105 mm); compression ratio:):1; max power (SAE net): 85 hp (62 kW) at 3,600 rpm; max rque (SAE net): 145 lb ft, 20 kg m (196 Nm) at 2,200 rpm; 3.6 hp/l (21 kW/l); 5 crankshaft bearings; injection pump.

RANSMISSION axle ratio: 4.111.

ERFORMANCE max speed: 75 mph, 120 km/h; power-weight ıtio: 42.1 lb/hp (57.3 lb/kW), 19.1 kg/hp (26 kg/kW); speed in rect drive at 1,000 rpm: 18.6 mph, 30 km/h.

IMENSIONS AND WEIGHT wheel base: 89.96 in, 228 cm; ngth: 152.36 in, 387 cm; width: 65.55 in, 166 cm; height: 7.17 in, 196 cm; weight: 3,583 lb, 1,625 kg.

ODY open, 2+1 doors, 2 or 7 seats, fully opening canvas ınshine roof; estate car/st. wagon, 2+1 doors, 6 or 7 seats, ardtop.

Crown Series

RICES (Tokyo):	**yen**
2000 Standard Sedan	**1,313,000**
2000 De Luxe A Sedan	**1,423,000**
2000 De Luxe Sedan	**1,554,000**
2000 Super De Luxe Sedan	**1,740,000**
2000 De Luxe 4-dr Hardtop	**1,544,000**
2000 EFI Super De Luxe Sedan	**1,833,000**
2000 EFI Super Saloon Sedan	**2,080,000**
2000 EFI Super ED 2-dr Hardtop	**1,961,000**
2000 EFI Super Saloon 2-dr Hardtop	**2,197,000**
2000 EFI Custom ED 4-dr Hardtop	**1,808,000**

TOYOTA Crown Hardtop

11	2000 EFI Super ED 4-dr Hardtop	**1,998,000**
12	2000 EFI Super Saloon 4-dr Hardtop	**2,224,000**
13	2800 Super Saloon Sedan	**2,360,000**
14	2800 Royal Saloon Sedan	**2,702,000**
15	2800 Super Saloon 4-dr Hardtop	**2,489,000**
16	2800 Royal Saloon 4-dr Hardtop	**2,724,000**
17	2800 Royal Saloon 2-dr Hardtop	**2,745,000**
18	2200 Diesel Standard Sedan	**1,407,000**
19	2200 Diesel De Luxe A Sedan	**1,521,000**
20	2200 Diesel De Luxe Sedan	**1,651,000**
21	2200 Diesel Super De Luxe Sedan	**1,833,000**
22	2200 Diesel Custom ED 4-dr Hardtop	**1,760,000**

Power team:	**Standard for:**	**Optional for:**
110 hp	1 to 5	—
125 hp	6 to 12	—
145 hp	13 to 17	—
72 hp (diesel)	18 to 22	—

110 hp power team

ENGINE front, 4 stroke; 6 cylinders, vertical, in line; 121.3 cu in, 1,988 cc (2.95 x 2.95 in, 75 x 75 mm); compression ratio: 8.6:1; max power (JIS): 110 hp (81 kW) at 5,600 rpm; max torque (JIS): 116 lb ft, 16 kg m (157 Nm)) at 3,800 rpm; max engine rpm: 6,200; 55.3 hp/l (40.6 kW/l); cast iron block, light alloy head; 7 crankshaft bearings; valves: overhead; lubrication: rotary pump, full flow filter, 9.5 imp pt, 11.4 US pt, 5.4 l; 1 Aisan M-U type downdraught twin barrel carburettor; emission control with catalytic converter, secondary air injection and exhaust gas recirculation; fuel feed: mechanical pump; water-cooled, 17.6 imp pt, 21.1 US pt, 10 l.

TRANSMISSION driving wheels: rear; clutch: single dry plate (diaphragm) hydraulically controlled; gearbox: mechanical; gears: 4, fully synchronized; ratios: I 3.579, II 2.081, III 1.397, IV 1, rev 4.399; lever: central; final drive: hypoid bevel; axle ratio: 4.556; width of rims: 5"; tyres: 6.95 x 14.

PERFORMANCE max speeds: (I) 27 mph, 44 km/h; (II) 47 mph, 76 km/h; (III) 70 mph, 112 km/h; (IV) 99 mph, 160 km/h; power-weight ratio: De Luxe A Sedan 27 lb/hp (36.8 lb/kW), 12.3 kg/hp (16.7 kg/kW); carrying capacity: 882 lb, 400 kg; speed in direct drive at 1,000 rpm: 15.5 mph, 25 km/h; consumption: 23 m/imp gal, 19.1 m/US gal, 12.3 l x 100 km.

CHASSIS box-type perimeter frame; front suspension: independent, double wishbones, coil springs, anti-roll bar, telescopic dampers; rear: rigid axle, lower radius arms, upper torque arm, coil springs, telescopic dampers.

STEERING recirculating ball; turns lock to lock: 4.60.

BRAKES front disc, rear drum, servo; lining area: front 22.8 sq in, 148 sq cm, rear 75.7 sq in, 488 sq cm, total 98.5 sq in, 636 sq cm.

ELECTRICAL EQUIPMENT 12 V; 45 Ah battery; 50 A alternator; Denso distributor; 4 headlamps.

DIMENSIONS AND WEIGHT wheel base: 105.91 in, 269 cm; tracks: 55.51 in, 141 cm front, 54.33 in, 138 cm rear; length: 184.65 in, 469 cm; width: 66.49 in, 169 cm; height: sedans 56.49 in, 143 cm - Hardtop 55.51 in, 141 cm; weight: Standard Sedan 2,943 lb, 1,335 kg - De Luxe A Sedan 2,976 lb, 1,350 kg - Super De Luxe Sedan 3,031 lb, 1,375 kg - De Luxe Hardtop 3,009 lb, 1,365 kg; weight distribution: 63% front, 37% rear; turning circle: 39.4 ft, 12 m; fuel tank: 15.8 imp gal, 19 US gal, 72 l.

BODY saloon/sedan, hardtop; 5 seats, separate front seats, reclining backrests, built-in headrests.

OPTIONALS 4-speed fully synchronized mechanical gearbox (I 3.368, II 1.644, III 1, IV 0.813, rev 4.079), 4.778 axle ratio (except Super De Luxe Hardtop); automatic transmission with 3 ratios (I 2.400, II 1.479, III 1, rev 1.920), 4.556 axle ratio; power steering with 3.90 turns lock to lock; air-conditioning.

125 hp power team

See 110 hp power team, except for:

ENGINE max power (JIS): 125 hp (92 kW) at 6,000 rpm; max torque (JIS): 123 lb ft, 17 kg m (167 Nm) at 4,400 rpm; 62.9 hp/l (46.2 kW/l); Bosch-Denso electronic injection; emission control with 3-way catalytic converter with oxygen sensor and exhaust gas recirculation; fuel feed: electric pump.

TRANSMISSION gears: 5, fully synchronized; ratios: I 3.287, II 2.043, III 1.394, IV 1, V 0.853, rev 4.039; axle ratio: 4.778; tyres: sedans 6.95 x 14 - hardtops 185 SR x 14.

PERFORMANCE max speed: 106 mph, 170 km/h; power-weight ratio: Super De Luxe Sedan 24.3 lb/hp (33.1 lb/kW), 11.1 kg/hp (15 kg/kW); 23 m/imp gal, 19.1 m/US gal, 12.3 l x 100 km.

BRAKES Super Saloon models rear disc.

TOYOTA Crown Hardtop

125 HP POWER TEAM

STEERING servo; turns lock to lock: 3.90.

DIMENSIONS AND WEIGHT weight: Super De Luxe Sedan 3,042 lb, 1,380 kg - Super Saloon Sedan, Custom ED 4-dr Hardtop and Super ED 2-dr Hardtop 3,064 lb, 1,390 kg - Super ED 4-dr Hardtop 3,097 lb, 1,405 kg - Super Saloon 4-dr Hardtop 3,119 lb, 1,415 kg - Super Saloon 2-dr Hardtop 3,086 lb, 1,400 kg.

OPTIONALS automatic transmission with 4 ratios (I 2.400, II 1.450, III 1, IV 0.689, rev 2.222), 4.778 axle ratio; (for Super Saloon models only) 4-speed mechanical gearbox (I 3.360, II 1.644, III 1, IV 0.813, rev 4.079).

145 hp power team

See 110 hp power team, except for:

ENGINE 169 cu in, 2,759 cc (3.27 x 3.35 in, 83 x 85 mm); compression ratio: 8.8:1; max power (JIS): 145 hp (107 kW) at 5,000 rpm; max torque (JIS): 192 lb ft, 23.5 kg m (230 Nm) at 4,000 rpm; 52.5 hp/l (38.6 kW/l); Bosch-Denso electronic injection.

TRANSMISSION gearbox: mechanical; gears: 5, 5 - Royal Saloon and Super Saloon sedans automatic transmission, hydraulic torque converter and planetary gears with 4 ratios; fully synchronized ratios: I 3.287, II 2.043, III 1.394, IV 1, V 0.853, rev 4.039 - Royal Saloon and Super Saloon sedans I 2.450, II 1.450, III 1, IV 0.689, rev 2.222; axle ratio: 3.909; width of rims: 5.5''; tyres: 185 SR x 14.

PERFORMANCE max speed: 109 mph, 175 km/h; power-weight ratio: Super Saloon Sedan 21.7 lb/hp (29.6 lb/kW), 9.9 kg/hp (13.4 kg/kW).

STEERING servo; turns lock to lock: 3.90.

BRAKES disc, front internal radial fins, servo; lining area: front 28.2 sq in, 182 sq cm, rear 18.1 sq in, 117 sq cm, total 46.3 sq in, 299 sq cm.

DIMENSIONS AND WEIGHT tracks: 56.30 in, 143 cm front, 55.12 in, 140 cm rear; length: 191.34 in, 486 cm; width: 67.52 in, 171 cm; ground clearance: 7.09 in, 18 cm; weight: Super Saloon Sedan 3,153 lb, 1,430 kg - Royal Saloon Sedan and Royal Saloon 4-dr Hardtop 3,285 lb, 1,490 kg - Super Saloon 4-dr Hardtop 3,208 lb, 1,455 kg - Royal Saloon 2-dr Hardtop 3,252 lb, 1,475 kg.

OPTIONALS 4-speed automatic transmission, hydraulic torque converter and planetary gears with 3 ratios (I 2.450, II 1.450, III 1, IV 0.689, rev 2.222); (except for Royal Saloon and Super Saloon sedans); electronic skid control brakes.

TOYOTA Crown 2800 Royal Saloon Sedan

TORO 1300

72 hp (diesel) power team

See 110 hp power team, except for:

ENGINE front, diesel, 4 stroke; 4 cylinders, vertical, in lin 133.5 cu in, 2,188 cc (3.54 x 3.39 in, 90 x 86 mm); compressio ratio: 21.5:1; max power (JIS): 72 hp (53 kW) at 4,200 rpm max torque (JIS): 105 lb ft, 14.5 kg m (142 Nm) at 2,000 rpm max engine rpm: 4,500; 32.9 hp/l (24.2 kW/l); Ricardo Come precombustion chamber; camshafts: 1, overhead, cogged bel Bosch-Denso VE distributor type injection pump; lubricatior 11.4 imp pt, 13.7 US pt, 6.5 l; cooling, 15.8 imp pt, 19 US p 9 l.

TRANSMISSION gears: 5 Standard Sedan 4, fully synchro nized; ratios: I 3.287, II 2.043, III 1.394, IV 1, V 0.853, re 4.039 - Standard Sedan I 3.579, II 2.081, III 1.397, IV 1, re 4.399; axle ratio: 4.300 - Standard Sedan 3.909; width of rim 4.5''; tyres: 6.95 x 14 - Standard Sedan 6.40 x 14.

PERFORMANCE max speed: 81 mph, 130 km/h; power-weig ratio: Standard Sedan 40.9 lb/HP (55.6 lb/kW), 18.5 kg/hp (25 kg/kW); consumption: 55.4 m/imp gal, 46.1 m/US gal, 5. l x 100 km at 37 mph, 60 km/h.

BRAKES Standard Sedan drum.

DIMENSIONS AND WEIGHT length: 184.65 in, 469 cm - Star dard Sedan 183.86 in, 467 cm; weight: Standard Sedan 2,94 lb, 1,335 kg - De Luxe A Sedan, De Luxe Sedan 2,977 lb, 1,35 kg - Super De Luxe Sedan 3,031 lb, 1,375 kg - Custom E Hardtop 3,086 3,086 lb, 1,400 kg.

OPTIONALS Toyoglide automatic transmission with 4 ratios 2.450, II 1.450, III 1, IV 0.689, rev 2.222).

TORO PHILIPPINES

1300

ENGINE Volkswagen, rear, 4 stroke; 4 cylinders, horizontal opposed; 74.8 cu in, 1,285 cc (3.03 x 2.72 in, 77 x 69 mm compression ratio: 7.5:1; max power (DIN): 44 hp (32 kW) 4,100 rpm; max torque (DIN): 64 lb ft, 8.8 kg m (86 Nm) 3,000 rpm; max engine rpm: 4,600; 34.2 hp/l (25.2 kW/l); bloc with cast iron liners and light alloy fins, light alloy head; crankshaft bearings; valves: overhead, push-rods and rocker camshafts: 1, central, lower; lubrication: gear pump, filter sump, oil cooler, 4.4 imp pt, 5.3 US pt, 2.5 l; 1 Solex 31 PIC downdraught single barrel carburettor; fuel feed: mechanic pump; air-cooled.

TRANSMISSION driving wheels: rear; clutch: single dry plat gearbox: mechanical; gears: 4, fully synchronized; ratios: 3.780, II 2.060, III 1.260, IV 0.890, rev 4.010; lever: centra final drive: spiral bevel; axle ratio: 4.375; width of rims: 4 tyres: 5.60 x 15.

PERFORMANCE max speeds: (I) 25 mph, 41 km/h; (II) 47 mp 75 km/h; (III) 76 mph, 123 km/h; (IV) 96 mph, 155 km/ power-weight ratio: 44.6 lb/hp (61.3 lb/kW), 20.2 kg/hp (27. kg/kW); carrying capacity: 882 lb, 400 kg; speed in top at 1,00 rpm: 18.6 mph, 29.9 km/h; consumption: 32.1 m/imp gal, 26. m/US gal, 8.8 l x 100 km.

CHASSIS backbone platform; front suspension: independen twin swinging longitudinal trailing arms, transverse laminate torsion bars, anti-roll bar, telescopic dampers; rear: indepe dent, swinging semi-axles, swinging longitudinal trailing arm transverse torsion bars, telescopic dampers.

STEERING worm and roller, telescopic damper.

BRAKES drum; lining area: total 125.3 sq in, 808 sq cm.

ELECTRICAL EQUIPMENT 12 V; 36 Ah battery; 260 W dyna mo; Bosch distributor; 2 headlamps.

DIMENSIONS AND WEIGHT wheel base: 94.49 in, 240 cr tracks: 51.97 in, 132 cm front, 53.15 in, 135 cm rear; lengt 169.29 in, 430 cm; width: 64.37 in, 163 cm; height: 52.95 i 134 cm; weight: 1,962 lb, 890 kg; turning circle: 37.1 ft, 11.3 r fuel tank: 9 imp gal, 10.8 US gal, 41 l.

BODY coupé, in plastic material; 2 doors; 2+2 seats, separa front seats.

CHRYSLER AUSTRALIA

Sigma GE Series

PRICES EX WORKS:	Australian $
1 Galant 4-dr Sedan	**5,762**
2 Galant 4+1-dr Wagon	**6,419**
3 GL 4-dr Sedan	**6,314**
4 GL 4+1-dr Wagon	**6,862**
5 SE 4-dr Sedan	**7,113**
6 SE 4+1-dr Wagon	**7,663**

Power team:	Standard for:	Optional for:
74 hp	1,2	—
86 hp	3 to 6	—
98 hp	—	3 to 6

74 hp power team

ENGINE front, 4 stroke; 4 cylinders, in line; 97.4 cu in, 1,576 cc (3.03 x 3.39 in, 76.9 x 86 mm); compression ratio: 8.5:1; max power (SAE): 74 hp (55 kW) at 4,800 rpm; max torque (SAE): 83 lb ft, 11.5 kg m (117 Nm) at 3,200 rpm; max engine rpm: 5,700; 18.5 hp/l (13.7 kW/l); cast iron block and head; 5 crankshaft bearings; valves: overhead, Vee-slanted, rockers; camshafts: 1, overhead; lubrication: rotary pump, full flow filter, 7 imp pt, 8.5 US pt, 4 l; 1 Stromberg downdraught twin barrel carburettor; air cleaner; fuel feed: mechanical pump; water-cooled, 10.6 imp pt, 12.7 US pt, 6 l.

TRANSMISSION driving wheels: rear; clutch: single dry plate (diaphragm); gearbox: mechanical; gears: 4, fully synchronized; ratios: I 3.525, II 2.193, III 1.452, IV 1, rev 3.867; lever: central; final drive: hypoid bevel; axle ratio: 3.909; width of rims: 5"; tyres: A 78 SR x 13.

PERFORMANCE max speed: about 92 mph, 148 km/h; power-weight ratio: Sedan 30.6 lb/hp (41.2 lb/kW), 13.9 kg/hp (18.7 kg/kW); carrying capacity: 838 lb, 380 kg; speed in direct drive at 1,000 rpm: 16 mph, 26 km/h; consumption: 32 m/imp gal, 26.7 m/US gal, 8.8 l x 100 km.

CHASSIS integral; front suspension: independent, by McPherson, coil springs/telescopic damper struts, lower wishbones (trailing links), anti-roll bar; rear: rigid axle, semi-elliptic leafsprings, telescopic dampers.

STEERING recirculating ball.

BRAKES front disc (diameter 9.02 in, 22.9 cm), front internal radial fins, rear drum, servo; lining area: total 67 sq in, 432 sq cm.

ELECTRICAL EQUIPMENT 12 V; 40 Ah battery; 40 A alternator; Mitsubishi distributor; 4 headlamps.

DIMENSIONS AND WEIGHT wheel base: 99.10 in, 251 cm; tracks: 53.20 in, 135 cm front, 52.80 in, 134 cm rear; length: 169.40 in, 430 cm; width: 65.20 in, 165 cm; height: 53.60 in, 136 cm; ground clearance: 6.30 in, 16 cm; weight: Sedan 2,257 lb, 1,026 kg - Wagon 2,525 lb, 1,145 kg; turning circle: 16.4 ft, 5 m; fuel tank: 13.2 imp gal, 15.8 US gal, 60 l.

BODY saloon/sedan, 4 doors - estate car/st. wagon, 4+1 doors; 5 seats, separate front seats.

86 hp power team

See 74 hp power team, except for:

ENGINE 121.7 cu in, 1,995 cc (3.31 x 3.54 in, 84 x 90 mm); compression ratio: 9.5:1; max power (SAE): 86 hp (64 kW) at 5,200 rpm; max torque (SAE): 103 lb ft, 14.3 kg m (145 Nm) at 2,400 rpm; lubrication: gear pump, full flow filter, 7.6 imp pt, 9.1 US pt, 4.3 l; 1 Stromberg 30-32 DIDTA donwdraught twin barrel carburettor; water-cooled, 13.6 imp pt, 16.3 US pt, 7.7 l.

TRANSMISSION gears: 5, fully synchronized; ratio: I 3.369, II 2.035, III 1.360, IV 1, V 0.856, rev. 3.635; width of rims: 5"; tyres: 165 S x 13.

PERFORMANCE max speed: 99 mph, 160 km/h; power-weight ratio: GL Sedan 26.2 lb/hp (35.3 lb/kW), 11.9 kg/hp (16 kg/kW); consumption: 34 m/imp gal, 28.3 m/US gal, 8.3 l x 100 km.

OPTIONALS automatic transmission, hydraulic torque and planetary gears with 3 ratios (I 2.393, II 1.450, III 1, rev 2.090, 3.545 axle ratio; 5.5" wide rims; AR78 S x 13 tyres.

98 power team

See 74 hp power team, except for:

ENGINE 156 cu in, 2,555 cc (3.62 x 3.36 in, 91.9 x 98 mm); compression ratio: 8.2:1; max power (SAE): 98 hp (73 kW) at 4,500 rpm; max torque (SAE): 131 lb ft, 18.1 kg m (184 Nm) at 2,500 rpm; lubrication: gear pump, full flow filter, 7.6 imp pt, 9.1 US pt, 4.3 l; 1 Stromberg downdraught twin barrel carburettor; water-cooled, 14 imp pt, 16.7 US pt, 8 l.

TRANSMISSION axle ratio: 3.308.

CHRYSLER Sigma GE GL Sedan

CHRYSLER Sigma GE GL Wagon

Valiant CM Series

PRICES EX WORKS:	Australian $
1 4-dr Sedan	**7,021**
2 4+1-dr St. Wagon	**7,389**
3 Regal 4-dr Sedan	**8,751**
4 Regal 4+1-dr St. Wagon	**9,069**
5 Regal SE 4-dr Sedan	**12,302**
6 GLX Special 4-dr Sedan	**8,067**

Power team:	Standard for:	Optional for:
155 hp	1,2	—
143 hp	5	all
163 hp	3,4,6	1,2

155 hp power team

ENGINE front, 4 stroke; 6 cylinders, in line; 245 cu in, 4,015 cc (3.76 x 3.68 in, 95.4 x 93.4 mm); compression ratio: 9:1; max power (SAE): 155 hp (114 kW) at 4,400 rpm; max torque (SAE): 208 lb ft, 28.7 kg m (282 Nm) at 1,600 rpm; max engine rpm: 4,800; 38.6 hp/l (28.4 kW/l); cast iron block and head, hemispherical combustion chambers; 7 crankshaft bearings; valves: overhead, in line, push-rods and rockers, hydraulic tappets; camshafts: 1, side; lubrication: gear pump, full flow filter, 8.3 imp pt, 9.9 US pt, 4.7 l; 1 downdraught single barrel carburettor, electronic lean-burn fuel metering; air cleaner; fuel feed: mechanical pump; water-cooled, 23.2 imp pt, 27.9 US pt, 13.2 l.

TRANSMISSION driving wheels: rear; clutch: single dry plate (diaphragm); gearbox: mechanical; gears: 3, fully synchronized; ratios: I 2.950, II 1.690, III 1, rev 3,670; lever: central; final drive: hypoid bevel; axle ratio: 2.920; width of rims: 6"; tyres: ER78 x 13.

PERFORMANCE max speed: about 109 mph, 175 km/h; power-weight ratio: Sedan 21.8 lb/hp (29.6 lb/kW), 9.9 kg/hp (13.4 kg/kW); carrying capacity: 1,058 lb, 480 kg; speed in direct drive at 1,000 rpm: 23 mph, 37 km/h; consumption: not declared.

CHASSIS integral; front suspension: independent, wishbones, longitudinal torsion bars, telescopic dampers, anti-roll bar; rear: rigid axle, semi-elliptic leafsprings, telescopic dampers.

STEERING recirculating ball; turns lock to lock: 4.50.

BRAKES front disc (diameter 11 in, 27.9 cm), front integral radial fins, rear drum, servo; swept area: total 327 sq in, 2,113 sq cm.

ELECTRICAL EQUIPMENT 12 V; 45 Ah battery; 35 A alternator; Chrysler electronic ignition; 4 headlamps.

DIMENSIONS AND WEIGHT wheel base: 111 in, 282 cm; tracks: 59 in, 149 cm front, 59.30 in, 150 cm rear; length: 196 in, 501 cm; width: 75 in, 189 cm; height: 55 in, 140 cm; weight: Sedan 3,375 lb, 1,531 kg - St. Wagon 3,505 lb, 1,590 kg; turning circle: 38.6 ft, 11.8 m; fuel tank: 17.5 imp gal, 20.9 US gal, 79 l.

BODY saloon/sedan, 4 doors - estate car/st. wagon, 4+1 doors; 5 seats, separate front seats, reclining backrests.

OPTIONALS Torqueflite automatic transmission, hydraulic torque converter and planetary gears with 3 ratios (I 2.390, II

155 HP POWER TEAM

1,450, III 1, rev 2,090), max ratio of converter at stall 2, possible manual selection, steering column lever, power steering; limited slip differential; 7" wide rims, 7 R78 S x 14 tyres; heavy-duty suspension; vinyl roof; heated rear window.

143 hp power team

See 155 hp power team, except for:

ENGINE 8 cylinders, Vee-slanted at 90°; 318 cu in, 5,205 cc (3.91 x 3.31 in, 99.2 x 84 mm); compression ratio: 8.2:1; max power (SAE): 143 hp (105 kW) at 4,000 rpm; max torque (SAE): 245 lb ft, 33.8 kg m (332 Nm) at 2,000 rpm; 27.5 hp/l (20.2 kW/l); 5 crankshaft bearings; camshafts: 1, at centre of Vee; 1 downdraught twin barrel carburettor; water-cooled, 26 imp pt, 31.3 US pt, 14.8 l.

TRANSMISSION gearbox: Torqueflite automatic transmission, hydraulic torque converter and planetary gears with 3 ratios, max ratio of converter at stall 2, possible manual selection; ratios: I 2.450, II 1.450, III 1, rev 2.200; axle ratio: 2.920.

PERFORMANCE max speed: 108 mph, 173 km/h; power-weight ratio: Regal SE Sedan 25.6 lb/hp (34.6 lb/kW), 11.6 kg/hp (15.7 kg/kW); speed in direct drive at 1,000 rpm: 26.7 mph, 43 km/h.

ELECTRICAL EQUIPMENT 50 Ah battery.

DIMENSIONS AND WEIGHT weight: Regal SE Sedan 3,642 lb, 1,652 kg.

163 hp power team

See 155 hp power team, except for:

ENGINE 265.1 cu in, 4,345 cc (3.91 x 3.68 in, 99.2 x 93.4 mm); compression ratio: 9.1:1; max power (SAE): 163 hp (120 kW) at 4,400 rpm; max torque (SAE): 225 lb ft, 31 kg m (305 Nm) at 1,200 rpm; max engine rpm: 5,200; 37.5 hp/l (27.6 kW/l), 1 downdraught twin barrel carburettor.

PERFORMANCE max speed: 106 mph, 170 km/h; power-weight ratio: Regal Sedan 20.9 lb/hp (28.2 lb/kW), 9.5 kg/hp (12.8 kg/kW).

DIMENSIONS AND WEIGHT weight: Regal Sedan 3,397 lb, 1,541 kg - Regal St. Wagon 3,547 lb, 1,606 kg.

OPTIONALS 3.230 axle ratio; (for GLX only) 4-speed mechanical gearbox.

FORD AUSTRALIA

Escort Series

PRICES EX WORKS:	Australian $
1 L 2-dr Sedan	5,143
2 L 4-dr Sedan	5,284
3 GL 2-dr Sedan	5,471
4 GL 4-dr Sedan	5,613
5 Ghia 4-dr Sedan	6,543
6 RS 2000 2-dr Sedan	6,568
7 RS 2000 4-dr Sedan	6,709

Power team:	Standard for:	Optional for:
98 hp	1 to 4	—
112 hp	5 to 7	3,4

98 hp power team

ENGINE front, 4 stroke; 4 cylinders, vertical, in line; 97.5 cu in, 1,598 cc (3.19 x 3.06 in, 87 x 77.6 mm); compression ratio: 9:1; max power (SAE): 98 hp (72 kW) at 6,000 rpm; max torque (SAE): 101 lb ft, 14 kg m (141 Nm) at 4,000 rpm; max engine rpm: 6,500; 61.3 hp/l (45 kW/l); cast iron block and head; 5 crankshaft bearings; valves: overhead, in line, push-rods and rockers; camshafts: 1, side, chain-driven; lubrication: rotary or vane type pump, full flow filter, 5.7 imp pt, 6.8 US pt, 3.2 l; 1 Weber 32/32 DGV downdraught twin barrel carburettor; fuel feed: mechanical pump; water-cooled, 9.5 imp pt, 11.4 US pt, 5.4 l.

TRANSMISSION driving wheels: rear; clutch: single dry plate (diaphragm); gearbox: mechanical; gears: 4, fully synchronized; ratios: I 3.337, II 1.995, III 1.418, IV 1, rev 3.876; lever: central; final drive: hypoid bevel; axle ratio: 4.125; width of rims: 4.5"; tyres: 155 SR x 13.

PERFORMANCE max speed: 101 mph, 162 km/h; power-weight ratio: L 2-dr 19.7 lb/hp (26.9 lb/kW), 8.9 kg/hp (12.2 kg/kW); carrying capacity: 939 lb, 426 kg; acceleration: 50 mph (0-80 km/h) 16.5 sec; speed in direct drive at 1,000 rpm: 16 mph, 25.8 km/h; consumption: 37.8 m/imp gal, 31.4 m/US gal, 7.5 l x 100 km.

CHRYSLER Valiant CM Regal Sedan

CHASSIS integral; front suspension: independent, by McPherson, coil springs/telescopic damper struts, anti-roll bar; rear: rigid axle, semi-elliptic leafsprings, anti-roll bar, telescopic dampers.

STEERING rack-and-pinion; turns lock to lock: 3.50.

BRAKES front disc (diameter 9.60 in, 24.4 cm), rear drum, servo.

ELECTRICAL EQUIPMENT 12 V; 38 Ah battery; 35 A alternator; Motorcraft distributor; 2 headlamps.

DIMENSIONS AND WEIGHT wheel base: 94.50 in, 240 cm; tracks: 49.50 in, 126 cm front, 50.60 in, 128 cm rear; length: 156.80 in, 398 cm; width: 62.80 in, 159 cm; height: 54.50 in, 138 cm; ground clearance: 4.92 in, 12.5 cm; weight: L 2-dr 1,936 lb, 878 kg - GL 2-dr 1.959 lb, 884 kg - GL 4-dr 2,004 lb, 909 kg; turning circle: 29.5 ft, 9 m; fuel tank: 9 imp gal, 10.8 US gal, 41 l.

BODY saloon/sedan; 2 or 4 doors; 5 seats, separate front seats.

OPTIONALS Ford C3 automatic transmission, hydraulic torque converter and planetary gears with 3 ratios (I 2.474, II 1.474, III 1, rev 2.111), max ratio of converter at stall 2.3, possible manual selection.

112 hp power team

See 98 hp power team, except for:

ENGINE 121.9 cu in, 1,998 cc (3.56 x 3.02 in, 90.4 x 76.7 mm); compression ratio: 9.2:1; max power (SAE): 112 hp (82 kW) at 6,000 rpm; max torque (SAE): 122 lb ft, 16.8 kg m (171 Nm) at 3,500 rpm; 56 hp/l (41 kW/l); valves: overhead, Vee-slanted, rockers; camshafts: 1, overhead, cogged belt; lubrication: 6.2 imp pt, 7.4 US pt, 3.5 l; 1 Autolite downdraught twin barrel carburettor; cooling, 12.5 imp pt, 15 US pt, 7.1 l.

TRANSMISSION axle ratio: 3.540; width of rims: 5"; tyres: YR 78S x 13.

PERFORMANCE max speed: about 110 mph, 177 km/h; power-weight ratio: 18.5 lb/hp (29.1 lb/kW), 8.5 kg/hp (13.2 kg/kW); speed in direct drive at 1,000 rpm: 18.5 mph, 29.7 km/h; consumption: 36.7 m/imp gal, 30.5 m/US gal, 7.7 l x 100 km.

ELECTRICAL EQUIPMENT 4 headlamps.

DIMENSIONS AND WEIGHT weight: 2,095 lb, 950 kg.

FORD Escort L Sedan

Cortina TE Series

PRICES EX WORKS:	Australian $
1 L 4-dr Sedan	5,984
2 L 4+1-dr St. Wagon	6,616
3 GL 4-dr Sedan	6,454
4 GL 4+1-dr St. Wagon	7,136
5 Ghia 4-dr Sedan	7,139
6 Ghia 4+1-dr St. Wagon	7,821

Power team:	Standard for:	Optional for:
109 hp	all	—
110 hp	—	1 to 4
126 hp	5,6	all

109 hp power team

ENGINE front, 4 stroke; 4 cylinders, vertical, in line: 121.9 cu in, 1,998 cc (3.56 x 3.02 in, 90.4 x 76.7 mm); compression ratio: 9.2:1; max power (SAE): 109 hp (80 kW) at 6,000 rpm; max torque (SAE): 122 lb ft, 16.8 kg m (171 Nm) at 3,500 rpm; max engine rpm: 6,500; 54.5 hp/l (40 kW/l); cast iron block and head; 5 crankshaft bearings; valves: overhead, Vee-slanted, rockers; camshafts: 1, overhead, cogged belt; lubrication: rotary pump, full flow filter, 6.2 imp pt, 7.4 US pt, 3.5 l; 1 Autolite downdraught twin barrel carburettor; fuel feed: mechanical pump; water-cooled, 12.5 imp pt, 15 US pt, 7.1 l.

TRANSMISSION driving wheels: rear; clutch: single dry plate (diaphragm); gearbox: mechanical; gears: 4, fully synchronized; ratios: I 3.650, II 1.970, III 1.370, IV 1, rev 3.660; lever: central; final drive: hypoid bevel; axle ratio: 3.700; width of rims: 4.5" - Ghia Sedan 5.5"; tyres: 165 SR x 13 - Ghia Sedan 175 SR x 13.

PERFORMANCE max speed: about 103 mph, 165 km/h; power-weight ratio: sedans 23 lb/hp (31 lb/kW), 10 kg/hp (14 kg/kW); carrying capacity: 882 lb. 400 kg; speed in direct drive at 1,000 rpm: 18.3 mph, 29.5 km/h; consumption: 29.7 m/imp gal, 24.8 m/US gal, 9.5 l x 100 km.

CHASSIS integral, front auxiliary frame; front suspension: independent, wishbones, coil springs, anti-roll bar, telescopic damper; rear: rigid axle, lower longitudinal trailing radius arms, upper oblique torque arms, coil springs, anti-roll bar, telescopic dampers.

STEERING rack-and-pinion; turns lock to lock: 3.70.

BRAKES front disc (diameter 9.80 in, 24.9 cm), rear drum, servo.

ELECTRICAL EQUIPMENT 12 V; 55 Ah battery; 22 A alternator; Autolite distributor; 4 headlamps.

DIMENSIONS AND WEIGHT wheel base: 101.50 in, 258 cm; front and rear track: 56 in, 142 cm; length: sedans 167.70 in, 426 cm - st. wagons 171.70 in, 436 cm; width: 67.20 in, 171 cm; height: sedans 51.80 in, 131 cm - St. wagons 52.60 in, 134 cm; ground clearance: sedans 5.80 in, 14.7 cm - st. wagons 5.90 in, 14.8 cm; weight: sedans 2,510 lb, 1,138 kg - st. wagons 2,640 lb, 1,197 kg; turning circle: 31.8 ft, 9.7 m; fuel tank: 12 imp gal, 14.3 US gal, 54 l.

BODY saloon/sedan, 4 doors - estate car/st. wagon, 4+1 doors; 5 seats, separate front seats, reclining backrests; heated rear window (for Ghia Sedan only).

OPTIONALS automatic transmission, hydraulic torque converter and planetary gears with 3 ratios (I 2.393, II 1.450, III 1, rev 2.094), 3.500 axle ratio; 75 SR x 13 tyre with 5.5" wide rims (except Ghia Sedan); BR 704 x 13 tyres.

110 hp power team

See 109 hp power team, except for:

ENGINE 6 cylinders, vertical, in line; 200 cu in, 3,277 cc (3.68 x 3.13 in, 93.4 x 79.4 mm); compression ratio: 8.8:1; max power (SAE): 110 hp (81 kW) at 4,000 rpm; max torque (SAE): 168 lb ft, 23.2 kg m (235 Nm) at 2,400 rpm; max engine rpm: 4,800; 33.6 hp/l (24.8 kW/l); 7 crankshaft bearings; valves: overhead, in line, push-rods and rockers, hydraulic tappets; camshafts: 1, side; lubrication: 7 imp pt, 8.5 US pt, 4 l; 1 Autolite downdraught single barrel carburettor; cooling, 15.5 imp pt, 18.6 US pt, 8.8 l.

TRANSMISSION gears: 3, fully synchronized; ratios: I 2.950, II 1.690, III 1, rev 3.670; axle ratio: 2.920.

PERFORMANCE max speed: about 98 mph, 158 km/h; power-weight ratio: sedans 22.8 lb/hp (31 lb/kW), 10.3 kg/hp (14 kg/kW); speed in direct drive at 1,000 rpm: 22 mph, 35.4 km/h; consumption: 20 m/imp gal, 16.8 m/US gal, 14 l x 100 km.

ELECTRICAL EQUIPMENT 38 A alternator.

OPTIONALS 4-speed fully synchronized mechanical gearbox (I 2.820, II 1.840, III 1.320, IV 1, rev 2.560); automatic transmission, hydraulic torque converter and planetary gears with 3 ratios (I 2.393, II 1.450, III 1, rev 2.094): 175 SR x 13 tyres with 5.5" wide rims; BR 704 x 13 tyres.

126 hp power team

See 109 hp power team, except for:

ENGINE 6 cylinders, vertical, in line; 250 cu in, 4,097 cc (3.68 x 3.91 in, 93.4 x 99.2 mm); compression ratio: 9.3:1; max power (SAE): 126 hp (93 kW) at 3,600 rpm; max torque (SAE): 218 lb ft, 30.1 kg m (305 Nm) at 1,800 rpm; max engine rpm: 4,600; 31.5 hp/l (23.2 kW/l); 7 crankshaft bearings; valves: overhead, in line, push-rods and rockers, hydraulic tappets; camshafts: 1, side; lubrication: 7 imp pt, 8.5 US pt, 4 l; 1 Autolite downdraught single barrel carburettor; cooling, 15.5 imp pt, 18.6 US pt, 8.8 l.

TRANSMISSION gears: 3, fully synchronized; ratios: I 2.950, II 1.690, III 1, rev 3.670; axle ratio: 2.770.

PERFORMANCE max speed: about 101 mph, 162 km/h; power-weight ratio: sedans 19.9 lb/hp (27 lb/kW), 9 kg/hp (12.2 kg/kW); speed in direct drive at 1,000 rpm: 23.6 mph, 38 km/h; consumption: 18 m/imp gal, 15.1 m/US gal, 15.7 l x 100 km.

OPTIONALS 4-speed fully synchronized mechanical gearbox (I 2.820, II 1.840, III 1.320, IV 1, rev 2.560); automatic transmission, hydraulic torque converter and planetary gears with 3 ratios (I 2.393, II 1.450, III 1, rev 2.094).

FORD Escort RS 2000 Sedan

XD Falcon - Fairmont Series

PRICES EX WORKS:	Australian $
1 Falcon GL 4-dr Sedan	7,116
2 Falcon GL 4+1-dr St. Wagon	7,565
3 Fairmont 4-dr Sedan	8,964
4 Fairmont 4+1-dr St. Wagon	9,607
5 Fairmont 4-dr Ghia Sedan	10,307

Power team:	Standard for:	Optional for:
110 hp	1,2	—
126 hp	3 to 5	1,2
188 hp	—	all
200 hp	—	all

110 hp power team

ENGINE front, 4 stroke; 6 cylinders, in line; 200 cu in, 3,277 cc (3.68 x 3.13 in, 93.4 x 79.4 mm); compression ratio: 8.8:1; max power (SAE): 110 hp (81 kW) at 4,000 rpm; max torque (SAE): 168 lb ft, 23.2 kg m (235 Nm) at 2,000 rpm; max engine rpm: 4,800; 33.5 hp/l (24.8 kW/l); cast iron block and head; 7 crankshaft bearings; valves: overhead, push-rods and rockers, hydraulic tappets; camshafts: 1, side; lubrication: gear pump, full flow filter, 7 imp pt, 8.5 US pt, 4 l; 1 Bendix downdraught single barrel carburettor; fuel feed: mechanical pump; water-cooled, 15.5 imp pt, 18.6 US pt, 8.8 l.

FORD Cortina TE GL Sedan

110 HP POWER TEAM

TRANSMISSION driving wheels: rear; clutch: single dry plate (diaphragm), hydraulic controlled; gearbox: mechanical; gears: 3, fully synchronized; ratios: I 2.950, II 1.690, III 1, rev 3.670; lever: steering column; final drive: hypoid bevel; axle ratio: 2.920; width of rims: 5.5''; tyres: ER78S x 14.

PERFORMANCE max speed: about 96 mph, 154 km/h; power-weight ratio: Sedan 27.4 lb/hp (37.2 lb/kW), 12.4 kg/hp (16.9 kg/kW); speed in direct drive at 1,000 rpm: 20.5 mph, 33 km/h; consumption: 18 m/imp gal, 15.1 m/US gal, 15.7 l x 100 km.

CHASSIS integral; front suspension: independent, wishbones, lower trailing links, coil springs, anti-roll bar, telescopic dampers; rear: rigid axle, semi-elliptic leafsprings, telescopic dampers - Sedan anti-roll bar.

STEERING recirculating ball; turns lock to lock: 5.

BRAKES front disc (diameter 11.25 in, 28.6 cm), rear drum; swept area: total 297.2 sq in, 1,917 sq cm.

ELECTRICAL EQUIPMENT 12 V; 45 Ah battery; 38 A alternator; Autolite distributor; 2 headlamps.

DIMENSIONS AND WEIGHT wheel base: Sedan 110 in, 279 cm - St. Wagon 116 in, 295 cm; tracks: 61.40 in, 154 cm front, 60 in, 152 cm rear; length: Sedan 186.50 in, 474 cm - St. Wagon 196.10 in, 498 cm; width: 73.20 in, 186 cm; height: Sedan 54 in, 137 cm - St. Wagon 55 in, 139 cm; ground clearance: Sedan 5.40 in, 13.7 cm - St. Wagon 6.40 in, 16.2 cm; weight Sedan 3,014 lb, 1,367 kg - St. Wagon 3,314 lb, 1,503 kg; turning circle: Sedan 37.7 ft, 11.5 m - St. Wagon 40.7 ft, 12.4 m; fuel tank: Sedan 17 imp gal, 20.1 US gal, 76 l - St. Wagon 15.9 imp gal, 19.2 US gal, 73 l.

BODY saloon/sedan, 4 doors - estate car/st. wagon, 4+1 doors; 5 seats, separate front seats.

OPTIONALS Borg-Warner 35 automatic transmission hydraulic torque converter and planetary gears with 3 ratios (I 2.390, II 1.450, III 1, rev 2.090), max ratio of converter at stall 2, possible manual selection; ER70H x 14 tyres; power steering; rear disc brake; tinted glass; vinyl roof; GS Rally equipment; reclining backrests; sunshine roof (for Sedan only).

126 hp power team

See 110 hp power team, except for:

ENGINE 250 cu in, 4,097 cc (3.68 x 3.91 in, 93.4 x 99.2 mm); compression ratio: 9:1; max power (SAE): 126 hp (93 kW) at 3,600 rpm; max torque (SAE): 218 lb ft, 30 kg m (305 Nm) at 1,800 rpm; max engine rpm: 4,600; 30.7 hp/l (23.2 kW/l).

PERFORMANCE max speed: about 99 mph, 159 km/h; power-weight ratio: sedans 23.8 lb/hp (32.4 lb/kW), 10.8 kg/hp (14.7 kg/kW); speed in direct drive at 1,000 rpm: 22 mph, 35.4 km/h; consumption: 17.5 m/imp gal, 14.7 m/US gal, 16.1 l x 100 km.

CHASSIS sedans, anti-roll bar on rear suspension.

BRAKES front disc, internal radial fins, servo.

OPTIONALS Borg-Warner 35 automatic transmission, steering column or central lever, 2.920 axle ratio; 4-speed fully synchronized mechanical gearbox (I 3.060, II 1.840, III 1.320, IV 1, rev 3.040), central lever, 3.230 axle ratio; air-conditioning; electric windows.

188 hp power team

See 110 hp power team, except for:

ENGINE 8 cylinders Vee-slanted at 90°; 302 cu in, 4,950 cc (4 x 3 in, 101.6 x 76.1 mm); compression ratio: 9.4:1; max power (SAE): 188 hp (138 kW) at 4,500 rpm; max torque (SAE): 254 lb ft, 35 kg m (356 Nm) at 3,200 rpm; max engine rpm: 5,200; 37.9 hp/l (28.2 kW/l); 5 crankshaft bearings; camshafts: 1, at centre of Vee; 1 Autolite downdraught twin barrel carburettor; cooling, 22.5 imp pt, 27.1 US pt, 12.8 l.

TRANSMISSION gearbox Ford C4 automatic gearbox, hydraulic torque converter and planetary gears with 3 ratios; ratios: I 2.460, II 1.460, III 1, rev 2.200; lever: steering column; axle ratio: 2.920; width of rims: 6''; tyres: ER70H x 14.

PERFORMANCE max speed: about 112 mph, 180 km/h; power-weight ratio: sedans 16.1 lb/hp (21.8 lb/kW), 7.3 kg/hp (9.9 kg/kW); speed in direct drive at 1,000 rpm: 25 mph, 40 km/h; consumption: 14 m/imp gal, 11.7 m/US gal, 20.1 l x 100 km.

BRAKES front disc, internal radial fins, servo.

FORD XD Falcon GL Sedan

FORD Fairmont Ghia Sedan

DIMENSIONS AND WEIGHT (for Fairmont models only) wheel base: 111 in, 282 cm; rear track: 60.50 in, 154 cm; width: 77.50 in, 197 cm; height: 51.90 in, 132 cm; fuel tank: 17.5 imp gal, 20.9 US gal, 79 l.

OPTIONALS 4-speed fully synchronized mechanical gearbox (I 3.060, II 1.840, III 1.320, IV 1), central lever; air-conditioning; electric windows.

200 hp power team

See 110 hp power team, except for:

ENGINE 8 cylinders, Vee-slanted at 90°; 351 cu in, 5,752 cc (4 x 3.50 in, 101.6 x 88.8 mm); compression ratio: 9.1:1; max power (SAE): 200 hp (147 kW) at 4,300 rpm; max torque (SAE): 306 lb ft, 42 kg m (428 Nm) at 3,000 rpm; max engine rpm: 4,900; 35.1 hp/l (25.8 kW/l); 5 crankshaft bearings; camshafts: 1, at centre of Vee; 1 Autolite downdraught twin barrel carburettor; cooling, 24.6 imp pt, 29.6 US pt, 14 l.

TRANSMISSION clutch: 2 dry plate (diaphragm), hydraulically controlled; gears: 4, fully synchronized; ratios: I 2.460, II 1.780, III 1.270, IV 1, rev 2.470; lever: central; axle ratio: 2.920; width of rims: 6''; tyres: ER70H x 14.

PERFORMANCE max speed: about 118 mph, 190 km/h; power-weight sedans 15 lb/hp (20.5 lb/kW), 6.8 kg/hp (9.3 kg/kW); speed in direct drive at 1,000 rpm: 25 mph, 40 km/h; consumption: 13 m/imp gal, 10.9 m/US gal, 21.7 l x 100 km.

BRAKES front disc, internal radial fins, servo.

DIMENSIONS AND WEIGHT (for Fairmont models only) wheel base: 111 in, 282 cm; rear track: 60.50 in, 154 cm; width: 77.50 in, 197 cm; height: 51.90 in, 132 cm; fuel tank: 17.5 imp gal, 20.9 US gal, 79 l.

OPTIONALS Ford FMX automatic transmission, hydraulic torque converter and planetary gears with 3 ratios (I 2.460, II 1.460, III 1, rev 2.200), max ratio of converter at stall 2, steering column or central lever, 2.750 axle ratio; limited slip differential; dual exhaust; air-conditioning; electric windows.

ZJ Fairlane Sedan

PRICE EX WORKS: Australian $ 11,831

For 188 hp engine add $ 386; for 200 hp engine add $ 660.

126 hp power team

(standard)

ENGINE front, 4 stroke; 6 cylinders, in line; 250 cu in, 4,097 cc (3.68 x 3.91 in, 93.4 x 99.2 mm); compression ratio: 9:1; max power (SAE): 126 hp (93 kW) at 3,600 rpm; max torque (SAE): 218 lb ft, 30 kg m (305 Nm) at 1,800 rpm; max engine rpm: 4,900; 31 hp/l (22.7 kW/l); cast iron block and head; 7 crankshaft bearings; valves: overhead, push-rods and rockers, hydraulic tappets; camshafts: 1, side; lubrication: gear pump, full flow filter, 7 imp pt, 8.5 US pt, 4 l; 1 Bendix downdraught single barrel carburettor; fuel feed: mechanical pump; water-cooled, 15.5 imp pt, 18.6 US pt, 8.8 l.

TRANSMISSION driving wheels: rear; gearbox: Borg-Warner 35 automatic transmission, hydraulic torque converter and planetary gears with 3 ratios; ratios: I 2.390, II 1.450, III 1; lever: steering column or central; final drive: hypoid bevel; axle ratio: 2.920; width of rims: 6"; tyres: ER70H x 14.

PERFORMANCE max speed: 99 mph, 159 km/h; power-weight ratio: 28.5 lb/hp (38.6 lb/kW), 12.5 kg/hp (17.4 kg/kW); speed in direct drive at 1,000 rpm: 22 mph, 35.4 km/h; consumption: 17.5 m/imp gal, 14.7 m/US gal, 16.1 l x 100 km.

CHASSIS integral; front suspension: independent, wishbones, lower trailing links, coil springs, anti-roll bar, telescopic dampers; rear: rigid axle, semi-elliptic leafsprings, anti-roll bar, telescopic dampers.

STEERING recirculating ball, servo; turns lock to lock: 2.60.

BRAKES front disc (diameter 11.25 in, 28.6 cm), front internal radial fins, rear drum, servo; swept area: total 296.9 sq in, 1,191 sq cm.

ELECTRICAL EQUIPMENT 12 V; 45 Ah battery; 40 A alternator; Autolite distributor; 4 headlamps.

DIMENSIONS AND WEIGHT wheel base: 116 in, 294 cm; tracks: 61.40 in, 156 cm front, 61.10 in, 153 cm rear; length: 197.80 in, 502 cm; width: 73.50 in, 187 cm; height: 54.90 in, 139 cm; weight: 3,588 lb, 1,620 kg; fuel tank: 17.6 imp gal, 21 US gal, 80 l.

BODY saloon/sedan; 4 doors; 5 or 6 seats, separate front seats.

OPTIONALS sunshine roof; air-conditioning.

188 hp power team

(optional)

See 126 hp power team, except for:

ENGINE 8 cylinders, Vee-slanted at 90°; 302 cu in, 4,950 cc (4 x 3 in, 101.6 x 76.1 mm); compression ratio: 9.2:1; max power (SAE): 188 hp (138 kW) at 4,500 rpm; max torque (SAE): 254 lb ft, 35 kg m (356 Nm) at 3,200 rpm; max engine rpm: 5,200; 37.9 hp/l (28.2 kW/l); cast iron block and head; 5 crankshaft bearings; valves: overhead, push-rods and rockers, hydraulic tappets; camshafts: 1, at centre of Vee; lubrication: gear pump, full flow filter, 7.6 imp pt, 9.1 US pt, 4.3 l; 1 Carter Thermoquad downdraught 4-barrel carburettor; fuel feed: mechanical pump; water-cooled, 22.5 imp pt, 27.1 US pt, 12.8 l.

TRANSMISSION gearbox: Ford C4 automatic transmission hydraulic torque converter and planetary gears with 3 ratios, possible manual selection; ratios: I 2.460, II 1.460, III 1, rev 2.200; lever: steering column or central; axle ratio: 2.920.

200 hp power team

(optional)

See 126 hp power team, except for:

ENGINE 8 cylinders, Vee-slanted at 90°; 351 cu in, 5,752 cc (4 x 3.50 in, 101.6 x 88.8 mm); compression ratio: 9.2:1; max power (SAE): 200 hp (147 kW) at 4,300 rpm; max torque (SAE): 306 lb ft, 42 kg m (428 Nm) at 3,000 rpm; max engine rpm: 4,900; 34.7 hp/l (25.5 kW/l); cast iron block and head; 5 crankshaft bearings; valves: overhead, push-rods and rockers, hydraulic tappets; camshafts: 1, at centre of Vee; lubrication: gear pump, full flow filter, 7.6 imp pt, 9.1 US pt, 4.3 l; 1 Carter Thermoquad downdraught 4-barrel carburettor; fuel feed: mechanical pump; water-cooled, 24.6 imp pt, 29.6 US pt, 14 l.

TRANSMISSION gearbox: Ford FMX automatic transmission hydraulic torque converter and planetary gears with 3 ratios, possible manual selection; ratios: I 2.400, II 1.470, III 1, rev 2; lever: central; axle ratio: 2.770.

FC LTD Series

PRICES EX WORKS:	Australian $
1 4-dr Sedan	17,093
2 Cartier 4-dr Sedan	19,093

For 200 hp engine add $ 779.

Power team:	Standard for:	Optional for:
126 hp	1,2	—
200 hp	—	1,2

126 hp power team

ENGINE front, 4 stroke; 6 cylinders, in line; 250 cu in, 4,097 cc (3.68 x 3.91 in, 93.4 x 99.2 mm); compression ratio: 9:1; max power (SAE): 126 hp (93 kW) at 3,600 rpm; max torque (SAE): 218 lb ft, 30 kg m (305 Nm) at 1,800 rpm; max engine rpm: 4,900; 31 hp/l (22.7 kW/l); cast iron block and head; 7 crankshaft bearings; valves: overhead, push-rods and rockers, hydraulic tappets; camshafts: 1, side; lubrication: gear pump, full flow filter, 7 imp pt, 8.5 US pt, 4 l; 1 Bendix downdraught single barrel carburettor; fuel feed: mechanical pump; water-cooled, 15.5 imp pt, 18.6 US pt, 8.8 l.

TRANSMISSION driving wheels: rear; gearbox: Borg-Warner 35 automatic transmission, hydraulic torque converter and planetary gears with 3 ratios, possible manual selection; ratios: I 2.390, II 1.450, III 1; lever: central; final drive: hypoid bevel; axle ratio: 2.920; width of rims: 6"; tyres: ER70H x 14.

PERFORMANCE max speed: 99 mph, 159 km/h; power-weight ratio: 31.5 lb/hp (42.6 lb/kW), 14.3 kg/hp (19.3 kg/kW); speed in direct drive at 1,000 rpm: 22 mph, 35.4 km/h; consumption: 17.5 m/imp gal, 14.7 m/US gal, 16.1 l x 100 km.

CHASSIS integral; front suspension: independent, wishbones, lower trailing links, coil springs, anti-roll bar, telescopic dampers; rear: rigid axle, semi-elliptic leafsprings, anti-roll bar, telescopic dampers.

STEERING recirculating ball, servo; turns lock to lock: 2.60.

BRAKES front disc (diameter 11.25 in, 28.6 cm), front internal radial fins, rear drum, servo; swept area: total 296.9 sq in, 1,191 sq cm.

ELECTRICAL EQUIPMENT 12 V; 45 Ah battery; 40 A alternator; Autolite distributor; 4 headlamps.

FORD ZJ Fairlane Sedan

FORD FC LTD Sedan

FORD FC LTD Sedan

126 HP POWER TEAM

DIMENSIONS AND WEIGHT wheel base: 116 in, 294 cm; tracks: 61.40 in, 156 cm front, 60.10 in, 153 cm rear; length: 197.80 in, 502 cm; width: 73.50 in, 187 cm; height: 54.90 in, 139 cm; weight: 3,966 lb, 1,799 kg; fuel tank: 17.6 imp gal, 21 US gal, 80 l.

BODY saloon/sedan; 4 doors; 5 or 6 seats, separate front seats.

OPTIONALS sunshine roof; air-conditioning.

200 hp power team

See 126 hp power team, except for:

ENGINE 8 cylinders, Vee-slanted at 90°; 351 cu in, 5,752 cc (4 x 3.50 in, 101.6 x 88.8 mm); compression ratio: 8.9:1; max power (SAE): 200 hp (147 kW) at 4,300 rpm; max torque (SAE): 306 lb ft, 42 kg m (428 Nm) at 3,000 rpm; max engine rpm: 4,900; 34.7 hp/l (25.5 kW/l); cast iron block and head; 5 crankshaft bearings; valves: overhead, in line, push-rods and rockers, hydraulic tappets; camshafts: 1, at centre of Vee; lubrication: gear pump, full flow filter, 8.3 imp pt, 9.9 US pt, 4.7 l; 1 Carter Thermoquad 4-barrel carburettor; fuel feed: mechanical pump; water-cooled, 24.6 imp pt, 29.6 US pt, 14 l.

TRANSMISSION gearbox: Ford FMX automatic transmission hydraulic torque converter and planetary gears with 3 ratios, possible manual selection; ratios: I 2.400, II 1.147, III 1, rev 2; lever: central; axle ratio: 2.770.

HOLDEN AUSTRALIA

Gemini TD Series

PRICES EX WORKS:	Australian $
4-dr Sedan	**5,324**
SL 4-dr Sedan	**5,574**
SL/X 4-dr Sedan	**5,943**
4+1-dr St. Wagon	**6,118**

ENGINE front, 4 stroke; 4 cylinders, in line; 97.6 cu in, 1,584 cc (3.23 x 2.95 in, 82 x 75 mm); compression ratio: 8.3:1; max power (DIN): 67 hp (49 kW) at 5,200 rpm; max torque (DIN): 81 lb ft, 11.2 kg m (113 Nm) at 3,600 rpm; max engine rpm: 6,500; 52.4 hp/l (37.7 kW/l); cast iron block, light alloy head; 5 crankshaft bearings; valves: overhead, rockers; camshafts: 1, overhead; lubrication: rotary pump, full flow filter, 8.8 imp pt, 10.6 US pt, 5 l; 1 Nikki-Stromberg downdraught twin barrel carburettor; fuel feed: electric pump; water-cooled, 10.8 imp pt, 12.7 US pt, 6 l.

TRANSMISSION driving wheels: rear; clutch: single dry plate (diaphragm); gearbox: mechanical; gears: 4, fully synchronized; ratios: I 3.467, II 1.989, III 1.355, IV 1, rev 3.500; lever: central; final drive: hypoid bevel; axle ratio: 3.900; width of rims: 5"; tyres: YR78S X 13.

PERFORMANCE max speeds: (I) 31 mph, 50 km/h; (II) 50 mph, 81 km/h; (III) 76 mph, 123 km/h; (IV) 96 mph, 154 km/h; power-weight ratio: Sedan 31 lb/hp (42.5 lb/kW), 14.1 kg/hp (19.3 kg/kW); carrying capacity: 882 lb, 400 kg; acceleration: standing ¼ mile 19.4 sec; speed in direct drive at 1,000 rpm: 16.2 mph, 26.1 km/h; consumption: 30.1 m/imp gal, 25 m/US gal, 9.4 l x 100 km.

CHASSIS integral; front suspension: independent, wishbones, coil springs, anti-roll bar, telescopic dampers; rear: rigid axle, lower radius arms, torque tube, Panhard rod, coil springs, telescopic dampers, anti-roll bar.

STEERING rack-and-pinion; turns lock to lock: 4.20.

BRAKES front disc (diameter 9.41 in, 23.9 cm), rear drum; swept area: total 266.5 sq in, 1,719 sq cm.

ELECTRICAL EQUIPMENT 12 V; 40 Ah battery; Sedan 35 A alternator - other models 50 A alternator; 2 headlamps.

DIMENSIONS AND WEIGHT wheel base: 94.49 in, 240 cm; front and rear track: 51.18 in, 130 cm; length: 166.50 in, 423 cm; width: 61.81 in, 157 cm; height: 52.40 in, 133 cm; ground clearance: 5.71 in, 14.5; weight: Sedan 2,085 lb, 946 kg - SL Sedan 2,103 lb, 954 kg - SL/X Sedan 2,107 lb, 956 kg - St. Wagon 2,130 lb, 966 kg; turning circle: 31.1 ft, 9.5 m; fuel tank: 11.4 imp gal, 13.7 US gal, 52 l.

BODY saloon/sedan, 4 doors - estate car/st. wagon, 4+1 doors; 5 seats, separate front seats.

OPTIONALS 5-speed fully synchronized mechanical gearbox (I 3.467, II 1.989, III 1.355, IV 1, V 0.855, rev 3.438); Trimatic automatic transmission, hydraulic torque couverter and planetary gears with 3 ratios (I 2.310, II 1.460, III 1), central lever; air-conditioning.

Sunbird Series

PRICES EX WORKS:	Australian $
4-dr Sedan	**5,995**
De Luxe 4-dr Sedan	**6,161**
SL 4-dr Sedan	**6,439**
SL/E 4-dr Sedan	**7,096**

ENGINE front, 4 stroke; 4 cylinders, vertical, in line; 115.4 cu in, 1,892 cc (3.50 in, 88.9 x 76.2 mm); compression ratio: 8.7:1; max power (DIN): 81 hp (60 kW) at 4,800 rpm; max torque (DIN): 104 lb ft, 14.3 kg m (146 Nm) at 2,600 rpm; max engine rpm: 5,200; 43 hp/l (31.6 kW/l); cast iron block and head; 5 crankshaft bearings; valves: overhead, push-rods and rockers, hydraulic tappets; camshafts: 1, side; lubrication: gear pump; 1 Varajet twin barrel carburettor; fuel feed: mechanical pump; water-cooled, 15 imp pt, 18 US pt, 8.5 l.

TRANSMISSION driving wheels: rear; clutch: single dry plate (diaphragm); gearbox: mechanical; gears: 4, fully synchronized; ratios: I 3.050, II 2.020, III 1.410, IV 1, rev 1.850; lever: central; final drive: hypoid bevel; axle ratio: 3.900; width of rims: 6"; tyres: BR78 S x 13.

PERFORMANCE max speed: 99 mph, 159 km/h; power-weight ratio: 31.5 lb/hp (42.5 lb/kW), 14.3 kg/hp (19.3 kg/kW); carrying capacity: 1,091 lb, 495 kg; speed in direct drive at 1,000 rpm: 15.5 mph, 25 km/h; consumption: 28.2 m/imp gal, 23.5 m/US gal, 10 l x 100 km.

CHASSIS integral; front suspension: independent, wishbones, coil springs, anti-roll bar, telescopic dampers; rear: rigid axle, trailing lower radius arms, upper oblique radius arms, coi[l] springs, anti-roll bar, telescopic dampers.

STEERING rack-and-pinion; turns lock to lock: 3.80.

BRAKES front disc (diameter 10 in, 25.4 cm), rear drum, servo.

ELECTRICAL EQUIPMENT 12 V; 48 Ah battery; 250 W or 40 A alternator; AC Delco or Bosch distributor; 2 headlamps.

DIMENSIONS AND WEIGHT wheel base: 101.97 in, 259 cm; tracks: 55.71 in, 141 cm front, 54.40 in, 138 cm rear; length: 177.76 in, 451 cm; width: 66.93 in, 170 cm; height: 52.76 in, 134 cm; ground clearance: 4.80 in, 12.2 cm; weight: 2,551 lb, 1,157 kg; turning circle: 36 ft, 11 m; fuel tank: 12.1 imp gal, 14.5 US gal, 55 l.

BODY saloon/sedan; 4 doors; 4 seats, separate front seats, reclining backrests.

OPTIONALS Trimatic automatic transmission, hydraulic torque converter and planetary gears with 3 ratios (I 2.310, II 1.460, III 1, rev 1.850); heated rear window.

VB Commodore Series

PRICES EX WORKS:	Australian $
1 4-dr Sedan	**7,192**
2 S 4+1-dr St. Wagon	**7,558**
3 SL 4-dr Sedan	**8,623**
4 SL 4+1-dr St. Wagon	**9,227**
5 SL/E 4-dr Sedan	**11,717**

HOLDEN Gemini TD SL Sedan

HOLDEN Sunbird SL/E Sedan

HOLDEN VB Commodore SL Station Wagon

Power team:	Standard for:	Optional for:
85 hp	1,2	—
88 hp	3,4	1,2,5
117 hp	5	1 to 4
152 hp	—	1 to 5

85 hp power team

ENGINE front, 4 stroke; 6 cylinders, vertical, in line; 173 cu in, 2,838 cc (3.50 x 3 in, 88.9 x 76.2 mm); compression ratio: 9.2:1; max power (DIN): 85 hp (62 kW) at 4,000 rpm; max torque (DIN): 146 lb ft, 20.1 kg m (204 Nm) at 2,200 rpm; max engine rpm: 5,000; 29.9 hp/l (22.1 kW/l); cast iron block and head; 7 crankshaft bearings; valves: overhead, in line, push-rods and rockers, hydraulic tappets; camshafts: 1, side; lubrication: gear pump, full flow filter, 7.5 imp pt, 8.9 US pt, 4.2 l; 1 Bendix-Stromberg downdraught single barrel carburettor; fuel feed: mechanical pump; water-cooled, 14 imp pt, 16.7 US pt, 7.9 l.

TRANSMISSION driving wheels: rear; clutch: single dry plate (diaphragm); gearbox: mechanical; gears: 4, fully synchronized; ratios: I 3.500, II 2.020, III 1.410, IV 1, rev 3.570; lever: central; final drive: hypoid bevel; axle ratio: 3.360; width of rims: 6"; tyres: CR78 S x 14.

PERFORMANCE max speed: 94 mph, 151 km/h; power-weight ratio: 31.6 lb/hp (43.4 lb/kW), 14.3 kg/hp (19.7 kg/kW); carrying capacity: 882 lb, 400 kg; speed in direct drive at 1,000 rpm: 20 mph, 32.2 km/h; consumption: 19 m/imp gal, 15.9 m/US gal, 14.8 l x 100 km.

CHASSIS integral; front suspension: independent, wishbones, coil springs, anti-roll bar, telescopic dampers; rear: rigid axle, trailing lower radius arms, upper oblique radius arms, coil springs, telescopic dampers.

STEERING rack-and-pinion; turns lock to lock: 4.10.

BRAKES front disc, rear drum, servo; lining area: front 17.7 sq in, 114 sq cm, rear 11.1 sq in, 72 sq cm, total 28.8 sq in, 186 sq cm.

ELECTRICAL EQUIPMENT 12 V; 48 Ah battery; 40 A alternator; Bosch or Lucas distributor; 2 halogen headlamps.

DIMENSIONS AND WEIGHT wheel base: 105.04 in, 267 cm; tracks: 57.09 in, 145 cm front, 55.91 in, 142 cm rear; length: 185.24 in, 470 cm; width: 67.72 in, 172 cm; height: 53.94 in, 137 cm; weight: 2,690 lb, 1,220 kg; turning circle: 33.5 ft, 10.2 m; fuel tank: 13.9 imp gal, 16.6 US gal, 63 l.

BODY saloon/sedan, 4 doors - estate car/st. wagon, 4+1 doors; 5 seats, separate front seats, reclining backrests.

OPTIONALS Trimatic automatic transmission, hydraulic torque converter and planetary gears with 3 ratios (I 2.310, II 1.460, III 1, rev 1.850), 3.360 axle ratio; limited slip differential; power steering; electric windows; tinted glass; sunshine roof; air-conditioning.

88 hp power team

See 85 hp power team, except for:

ENGINE 201.2 cu in, 3,298 cc (3.62 x 3.25 in, 91.9 x 82.5 mm); max power (SAE): 88 hp (65 kW) at 3,600 rpm; max torque (SAE): 163 lb ft, 22.5 kg m (228 Nm) at 2,100 rpm; 26.6 hp/l (19.7 kW/l).

TRANSMISSION gearbox ratios: I 3.050, II 2.190, III 1.150, IV 1, rev 3.050.

PERFORMANCE max speed: 101 mph, 162 km/h; power-weight ratio: SL models 31.5 lb/hp (42.6 lb/kW), 14.3 kg/hp (19.3 kg/kW); consumption: 18 m/imp gal, 15 m/US gal, 15.7 l x 100 km.

DIMENSIONS AND WEIGHT weight: SL models 2,767 lb, 1,255 kg.

117 hp power team

See 85 hp power team, except for:

ENGINE 8 cylinders, Vee-slanted at 90°; 253 cu in, 4,142 cc (3.62 x 3.06 in, 91.9 x 77.6 mm); max power (SAE): 117 hp (86 kW) at 4,000 rpm; max torque (SAE): 199 lb ft, 27.6 kg m (279 Nm) at 2,000 rpm; 28.2 hp/l (21 kW/l); 5 crankshaft bearings; camshafts: 1, at centre of Vee; lubrication: 8.5 imp pt, 10.1 US pt, 4.8 l; 1 Bendix-Stromberg BXV-2 downdraught twin barrel carburettor; cooling, 21 imp pt, 25.2 US pt, 11.9 l.

PERFORMANCE max speed: about 109 mph, 175 km/h; power-weight ratios: SL/E 25.7 lb/hp (35 lb/kW), 11.7 kg/hp (15.9 kg/kW).

DIMENSIONS AND WEIGHT weight: SL/E 3,010 lb, 1,365 kg.

152 hp power team

See 85 hp power team, except for:

ENGINE 8 cylinders, Vee-slanted at 90°; 307.8 cu in, 5,044 cc (4 x 3.06 in, 101.6 x 77.7 mm); compression ratio: 9.7:1; max power (SAE): 152 hp (112 kW) at 4,800 rpm; max torque (SAE): 253 lb ft, 35 kg m (354 Nm) at 3,100 rpm; max engine rpm: 5,400; 30.1 hp/l (22 kW/l); 5 crankshaft bearings; camshafts: 1, at centre of Vee; lubrication: 8.5 imp pt, 10.1 US pt, 4.8 l; 1 Rochester 4MV downdraught 4-barrel carburettor; cooling, 20 imp pt, 23.9 US pt, 11.3 l.

TRANSMISSION gearbox: Turbo-Hydramatic automatic transmission; hydraulic torque converter and planetary with 3 ratios; ratios: I 2.480, II 1.480, III 1, rev 2.080; tyres: BR60 H x 15.

PERFORMANCE max speed: about 115 mph, 185 km/h; power-weight ratio: 20 lb/hp (27.1 lb/kW), 9.1 kg/hp (12.3 kg/kW).

STEERING servo.

ELECTRICAL EQUIPMENT 55 A alternator.

DIMENSIONS AND WEIGHT weight: 3,043 lb, 1,380 kg.

HZ Series

PRICES EX WORKS:	Australian $
1 Kingswood SL 4-dr Sedan	**7,219**
2 Kingswood SL 4+1-dr St. Wagon	**7,544**
3 Premier 4-dr Sedan	**9,412**
4 Premier 4+1-dr St. Wagon	**9,734**
5 Statesman De Ville 4-dr Sedan	**12,372**
6 Statesman Caprice 4-dr Sedan	**17,768**
7 Statesman SL/E 4-dr Sedan	**14,205**

Power team:	Standard for:	Optional for:
110 hp	1 to 4	—
161 hp	—	1 to 4
216 hp	5 to 7	1 to 4

110 hp power team

ENGINE front, 4 stroke; 6 cylinders, vertical, in line; 201.2 cu in, 3,298 cc (3.62 x 3.25 in, 91.9 x 82.5 mm); compression ratio: 9.4:1; max power (SAE): 110 hp (81 kW) at 4,000 rpm; max torque (SAE): 190 lb ft, 26.2 kg m (266 Nm) at 1,600 rpm; max engine rpm: 5,000; 33.3 hp/l (24.5 kW/l); cast iron block and head; 7 crankshaft bearings; valves: overhead, in line, push-rods and rockers, hydraulic tappets; camshafts: 1, side; lubrication: gear pump, full flow filter, 7.5 imp pt, 8.9 US pt, 4.2 l; 1 Bendix-Stromberg BXV-2 downdraught single barrel carburettor; fuel feed: mechanical pump; water-cooled, 14 imp pt, 16.7 US pt, 7.9 l.

TRANSMISSION driving wheels: rear; clutch: single dry plate (diaphragm); gearbox: mechanical - Premier models Trimatic automatic transmission; gears: 3, fully synchronized; ratios: I 3.070, II 1.680, III 1, rev 3.590 - Premier models I 2.310, II 1.460, III 1, rev 1.850; lever: steering column; final drive: hypoid bevel; axle ratio: 3.550 - Premier models 3.080 or 3.360; width of rims: 5"; tyres: Kingswood models C78L x 14 - Premier models E78L x 14.

PERFORMANCE max speed: about 96 mph, 154 km/h; power-weight ratio: Kingswood SL Sedan 26.9 lb/hp (36.5 lb/kW), 12.2 kg/hp (16.6 kg/kW); carrying capacity: 882 lb, 400 kg; speed in direct drive at 1,000 rpm: 20 mph, 32.2 km/h.

CHASSIS integral, front auxiliary box-type frame; front suspen-

HOLDEN HZ Kingswood SL Sedan

HOLDEN HZ Statesman SL/E Sedan

110 HP POWER TEAM

sion: independent, wishbones, coil springs, anti-roll bar, telescopic dampers; rear: rigid axle, trailing lower radius arms, upper oblique radius arms, coil springs, telescopic dampers.

STEERING recirculating ball; turns lock to lock: 3.68.

BRAKES front disc (diameter 10.8 in, 27.6 cm), internal radial fins, rear drum.

ELECTRICAL EQUIPMENT 12 V; 48 Ah battery; 35 A alternator; Bosch or Lucas distributor; 2 headlamps.

DIMENSIONS AND WEIGHT wheel base: sedans 111 in, 282 cm - St. wagons 114 in, 289 cm; tracks: 59.50 in, 151 cm front, 60.20 in, 153 cm rear; length: Kingswood SL Sedan 90.30 in, 483 cm - Kingswood SL St. Wagon 192.30 in, 488 cm - Premier Sedan 190.80 in, 485 cm - Premier St. Wagon 192.80 in, 490 cm; width: 74.30 in, 189 cm; height: Kingswood SL Sedan 54.10 in, 137 cm - Kingswood SL St. Wagon 55.30 in, 140 cm - Premier Sedan 54.40 in, 138 cm - Premier St. Wagon 55.10 in, 140 cm; ground clearance: 5.60 in, 14.2 cm; weight: Kingswood SL Sedan 2,960 lb, 1,342 - Kingswood SL St. Wagon 3,145 lb, 1,426 kg - Premier Sedan 3,062 lb, 1,389 kg - Premier St. Wagon 3,242 lb, 1,470 kg; turning circle: sedans 39.7 ft, 12.1 m - St. wagons 40.5 ft, 12.3 m; fuel tank: 16.5 imp gal, 19.8 US gal, 75 l.

BODY saloon/sedan, 4 doors - estate car/st. wagon, 4+1 doors; 5 seats, separate front seats.

OPTIONALS (for Kingswood models only) Trimatic automatic transmission, hydraulic torque converter and planetary gears with 3 ratios (I 2.310, II 1.460, III 1, rev 1.850), 3.360 axle ratio; 4-speed fully synchronized mechanical gearbox (I 3.740, II 2.190, III 1.510, IV 1, rev 3.050; limited slip differential; 3.900 or 3.360 axle ratio; central lever; power steering; servo brake; electric windows; tinted glass; sunshine roof; vinyl roof; air-conditioning.

161 hp power team

See 110 hp power team, except for:

ENGINE 8 cylinders, Vee-slanted at 90°; 253 cu in, 4,146 cc (3.62 x 3.06 in, 91.9 x 77.6 mm); max power (SAE): 161 hp (120 kW) at 4,500 rpm; max torque (SAE): 240 lb ft, 33.1 kg m (336 Nm) at 2,600 rpm; 38.8 hp/l (29.3 kW/l); 5 crankshaft bearings; camshafts: 1, at centre of Vee; lubrication: 8.5 imp pt, 10.1 US pt, 4.8 l; 1 Bendix-Stromberg BXV-2 downdraught twin barrel carburettor; cooling, 21 imp pt, 25.2 US pt, 11.9 l.

TRANSMISSION gears: 4, fully synchronized; ratios: I 3.050, II 2.190, III 1.510, IV 1, rev 3.050; width of rims: 6"; tyres: ER70H x 14.

PERFORMANCE max speed: about 109 mph, 175 km/h; power-weight ratio: 20.2 lb/hp (27.1 lb/kW), 9.2 kg/hp (12.3 kg/kW).

STEERING turns lock to lock: 3.07.

ELECTRICAL EQUIPMENT Bosch distributor.

DIMENSIONS AND WEIGHT tracks: 59.80 in, 152 cm front, 60.50 in, 154 cm rear; length: 190.30 in, 483 cm; width: 73.90 in, 188 cm; height: 53.70 in, 136 cm; weight: 3,253 lb, 1,475 kg.

OPTIONALS Trimatic automatic transmission, 2.780 axle ratio; 4-speed fully synchronized mechanical gearbox (I 2.540, II 1.830, III 1.380, IV 1, rev 2.540), central lever, 3.360 axle ratio.

216 hp power team

See 110 hp power team, except for:

ENGINE 8 cylinders, Vee-slanted at 90°; 307.8 cu in, 5,044 cc (4 x 3.06 in, 101.6 x 77.7 mm); compression ratio: 9.7:1; max power (SAE): 216 hp (159 kW) at 4,800 rpm; max torque (SAE): 295 lb ft, 40.7 kg m (413 Nm) at 3,100 rpm; max engine rpm: 5,400; 42.8 hp/l (31.2 kW/l); 5 crankshaft bearings; camshafts: 1, at centre of Vee; lubrication: 8.5 imp pt, 10.1 US pt, 4.8 l; 1 Rochester 4MV downdraught 4-barrel carburettor; cooling 20 imp pt, 23.9 US pt, 11.3 l.

TRANSMISSION gearbox: Turbo-Hydramatic automatic transmission, hydraulic torque converter and planetary gears with 3 ratios; ratios: I 2.480, II 1.480, III 1, rev 2.080; lever: central; axle ratio: 3.360; width of rims: 6"; tyres: De Ville E78 S x 14 - Caprice FR78 S x 14.

PERFORMANCE max speed: about 115 mph, 185 km/h; power-weight ratio: De Ville 15.7 lb/hp (21.4 lb/kW), 7.1 kg/hp (9.7 kg/kW).

STEERING servo; turns lock to lock: 3.07.

BRAKES servo.

ELECTRICAL EQUIPMENT 55 A alternator; Bosch distributor.

DIMENSIONS AND WEIGHT length: De Ville 203.10 in, 516 cm - Caprice 904.10 in, 518 cm; width: 74.30 in, 189 cm; height: De Ville 54.60 in, 139 cm - Caprice 54.80 in, 139 cm; weight: De Ville 3,406 lb, 1,545 kg - Caprice 3,635 lb, 1,649 kg.

OPTIONALS 4-speed fully synchronized mechanical gearbox (I 2.540, III 1.830, III 1.380, IV 1, rev 2.540).

LEYLAND AUSTRALIA

Mini-Moke Californian

PRICE EX WORKS: Australian $ 3,775

ENGINE front, transverse, 4 stroke; 4 cylinders, in line; 60.9 cu in, 998 cc (2.54 x 2.86 in, 64.5 x 72.6 mm); compression ratio: 8.3:1; max power (DIN): 39 hp (29 kW) at 5,200 rpm; max torque (DIN): 51 lb ft, 7 kg m (71 Nm) at 2,500 rpm; max engine rpm: 6,000; 39.1 hp/l (29.1 kW/l); cast iron block and head; 3 crankshaft bearings; valves: overhead, push-rods and rockers, camshafts: 1, overhead; lubrication: gear pump, full flow filter, 8.8 imp pt, 10.6 US pt, 5 l; 1 SU type HS4 carburettor; fuel feed: mechanical pump; water-cooled, 6.2 imp pt, 7.4 US pt, 3.5 l.

TRANSMISSION driving wheels: front; clutch: single dry plate gearbox: mechanical; gears: 4, fully synchronized; ratios: I 3.530, II 2.200, III 1.030, IV 1, rev 3.540; lever: central; final drive: hypoid bevel; axle ratio: 3.440; width of rims: 5.5"; tyres: 175R x 13.

PERFORMANCE max speed: 81 mph, 130 km/h; power-weight ratio: 35.7 lb/hp (48.1 lb/kW), 16.2 kg/hp (21.8 kg/kW); carrying capacity: 353 lb, 160 kg; speed in direct drive at 1,000 rpm: 13.5 mph, 21.7 km/h; consumption: 42 m/imp gal, 35.1 m/US gal, 6.7 l x 100 km.

CHASSIS integral, front and rear auxiliary frames; front suspension: independent, wishbones, rubber springs, telescopic dampers; rear: independent, swinging longitudinal trailing arms, rubber springs, telescopic dampers.

STEERING rack-and-pinion; turns lock to lock: 2.30.

BRAKES drum.

ELECTRICAL EQUIPMENT 12 V; 40 Ah battery; 40 W alternator; 2 headlamps.

DIMENSIONS AND WEIGHT wheel base: 82.48 in, 209 cm; tracks: 49.02 in, 124 cm front, 49.76 in, 126 cm rear; length: 127.17 in, 323 cm; width: 57.09 in, 145 cm; height: 62.99 in, 160 cm; ground clearance: 7.99 in, 20 cm; weight: 1,394 lb, 632 kg; turning circle: 32.1 ft, 9.8 m; fuel tank: 5.9 imp gal, 7.1 US gal, 27 l.

BODY open; no doors; 2 seats, separate front seats.

OPTIONALS 77.8 cu in, 1,275 cc engine, front disc brakes.

LEYLAND Mini-Moke Californian

Car manufacturers and coachbuilders

An outline of their history, structure and activities

CAR MANUFACTURERS

A.C. CARS Ltd **Great Britain**

Founded in 1900 by Portwine & Weller, assumed title Autocarriers (A.C.) Ltd in 1907, moved from London to Thames Ditton in 1911. Present title since 1930. Chairman: W.D. Hurlock. Managing Director: A.D. Turner. Works Director: R. Alsop. Secretary/Financial Director: A. Wilson. Head office, press office and works: The High Street, Thames Ditton, Surrey KT7 0SG. 170 employees. 100 cars produced in 1979. Models: ACE Bristol 2 l Le Mans (1959); ACE Cobra Le Mans (1963). Entries and wins in numerous competitions (Monte Carlo Rally, Le Mans, etc.).

ADAM OPEL AG **Germany (Federal Republic)**

Founded in 1862. Owned by General Motors Corp. USA since 1929. Chairman: J.F. Waters jr. Members of the board: W. Schlotfeldt, H. Zincke, K. Kartzke, C.J. Vaughan jr, E. Rohde, F. Schwenger, J.E. Rhame, J.O. Grettemberger. Head office and press office: 6090 Rüsselsheim/Main. Works: Bochum, Kaiserslautern, Rüsselsheim, Berlin. 64,844 employees. 956,455 cars produced 1978. Car production begun in 1898. Most important models: 10/18 (1908); 4/8 (1909); 6/16 (1910); 8/25 (1920); 4/12 (1924); 4/14 (1925-29); Olympia (1935); Super Six, Admiral (1938); Kapitän (1939); Rekord (1961); Kadett (1962); Admiral, Diplomat, Commodore (1968); GT (1969); Ascona, Manta (1970); Senator, Monza (1978).

ASSEMBLY IN OTHER COUNTRIES — **Australia:** GM Motors Holden's Pty Ltd, 241 Salmon St, Fishermens Bend, Melbourne, Victoria 3207, G.P.O. 1714, Melbourne 3001 (assem. Rekord). **Belgium:** GM Continental S.A. (associated company), Noorderlaan 75, Antwerp (assem. Kadett, Ascona, Manta, Rekord, Commodore). **Indonesia:** P.T. Garmak Motor Ltd, Jalan Cikini Raya 48, Djakarta (assem. Rekord). **Korea:** Saehan Motor Company, Hanshin Bldg, 62-10, 2GA Chung Mu-Ro, Jung-Gu, Seoul (assem. Rekord). **Malaysia:** Capital Motor Assembly Corp. Sdn, P.O.B. 204, Yohore Bahru (assem. Rekord). **Morocco:** Société Marocaine de Mécanique Industrielle et Automobile, Blod Moulay Ismael 22, Casablanca (assem. Rekord). **Philippines:** GM Philippinas Inc., Barrio Almanza, Las Pinas, Metro Manila (assem. Ascona, Manta, Rekord). **Portugal:** GM de Portugal Ltda, (associated company), Av. Marechal Gomes da Costa 33, Lisbon 6 (assem. Kadett, Rekord). **South Africa:** GM South African, Kempston Rd, P.O.B. 1137, Port Elizabeth (assem. Kadett, Senator). **Thailand:** Asoki Motors, 211-213 Asoki Rd, Sukhumwit, Bangkok 11 (assem. Rekord). **Uruguay:** GM Uruguay S.A. (associated company), Casilla de Correo 234, Montevideo (assem. Ascona, Rekord). **Zaire:** GM Zaire S.A.R.L. (associated company), Boulevard Patrice Lumumba, Masina 1, Kinshasa (assem. Ascona).

ALFA ROMEO S.p.A. **Italy**

Founded in 1910 as Anonima Lombarda Fabbrica Automobili, became Accomandita Semplice Ing. Nicola Romeo in 1915, Società Anonima Italiana Ing. Nicola Romeo & C. in 1918, S.A. Alfa Romeo in 1930. Became part of IRI group in 1933 and assumed name of S.A. Alfa Romeo Milano-Napoli in 1939. Present title since 1946. For volume of production it holds second place in Italian motor industry. President: E. Massacesi. Vice-President: E. Peracchi. Vice-President and Managing Director: C. Innocenti. Managing Director and General Manager: A. Lingiardi. Head office and press office: Arese (Milan), Works: Arese (Milan), Pomigliano d'Arco (Naples). 44,000 employees. 220,000 vehicles produced in 1979. Most important models: 24 hp (1910); 40-60 hp (1913); RL Targa Florio (1923); P2 (1924); 6C-1500 (1926); 6C-1750 (1929); 8C-2300 (1930); P3 (1932); 8C-2600 (1933); 8C-2900 (1935); 158 (1938); 6C-2500 SS (1939); 2500 Freccia d'Oro (1947); 1900 (1950); Giulietta Sprint (1954); Giulietta Berlina (1955); Giulietta Spider (1956); Giulietta TI (1957); 2000 (1958); Giulia TI, Giulia Sprint, Giulia Spider, 2600 (1962); Giulia Sprint GT, Giulia TZ (1963); Giulia 1300, Giulia Spider Veloce (1964); Giulia 1300 TI, Giulia Super, GTA (1965); Junior (1966); 1750, 1300 Spider Junior, GTA, 1300 Junior, "33" Coupé (1968); Giulia 1600 S, 1300 Junior Z (1969); Giulia 1300 Super, Montreal (1970); 2000 Berlina, 2000 GT Veloce, 2000 Spider Veloce (1970); 2000 Berlina, 2000 GT Veloce, 2000 Spider Veloce (1971); 2000 Spider Veloce (1971); Alfasud (1972); Alfetta (1973), Giulietta (1977). Entries and wins in numerous competitions. European Mountain Championship and European Touring Challenge Cup in 1967, in 1968 the 33/2 l was classified first at Daytona, in Targa Florio and Nürburgring 1000 km. In 1969 Alfa Romeo won European Touring Challenge Cup, National Championship for Makes in Brazil, three American National Drivers Championships and numerous national championships. In 1970, first place in European Championship for Touring Cars and many national championships. In 1971, in Makers' International Championship, a 33-3 was placed outright first in Brands Hatch 1000 km, in Targa Florio and Watkins Glen 6 Hour. It won European Touring Car Makers' Championship, coming first and second in final classification. In 1971 it also won a series of international championships, including Austrian Mountain Championship and Belgian Touring Drivers' Championship, Dutch Touring Championship for Touring Cars up to 1300 cc, Italian Absolute Championship for Special Touring Cars, American National Championship for SCCA Drivers, class C Sedan and Class C Sports Racing, and finally Venezuelan National Championship outright. In 1973 2000 GTV won Coupe du Roi and in 1974 2000 GTV won Coupe du Roi and 33 TT 12 finished 1, 2 and 3 in Monza 1000 km. 1975 holders of World Championship for Makes and 1977 of World Sports Car Championship.

ASSEMBLY IN OTHER COUNTRIES - **Indonesia:** Alfa Delta Motors (concessionaire), Jalon P. Arena; Pekan Raya IKt P.O.B. 2126, Djakarta (assem. Alfasud 1.3, 1.5, Alfetta 1.8, 2.0). **Malaysia:** City Motors SDN BHD (concessionaire), Foo yet Ka Building 270, Hugh how Street, Ipoh Perak (assem. Alfasud 1.3, 1.5, Alfetta 1.8, 2.0); Swedish Motor Assemblies (concessionaire), Kuala Lumpur (assem. Alfasud 1.3, 1.5, Alfetta 1.8, 2.0). **South Africa:** Alfa Romeo Sudafrica (Pty) Ltd (associated company), P.O.B. 78438, Johannesburg (assem. Alfasud 1.3, 1.5, Giulietta 1.8, Alfetta 1.8, 2.0, Alfetta GTV). **Thailand:** Siam Europe Motors (concessionaire), 404 Phayatha Rd, Bangkok (assem. Alfasud 1.3, Giulietta 1.6, Alfetta 2.0). **Uruguay:** Alfa Automotors SA (concessionaire) Av. 18 de Julio 1077, P.2 Montevideo (assem. Alfasud 1.3). 6,380 cars assembled outside Italy in 1979.

ALPINE RENAULT - see RÉGIE NATIONALE DES USINES RENAULT

AMERICAN CUSTOM INDUSTRIES Inc. **USA**

Coachworks division specializes in building special edition American Turbo, GT and Sportwagon Corvettes. Fiberglass manifacturing division specializes in the finest quality Corvette fiberglass. President: R. Schuller. Vice-President: M. Lavine. World headquarters: 5035 Alexis Rd, Sylvania, Ohio 43560.

AMERICAN MOTORS CORPORATION **USA**

(Makes: Spirit, Pacer, Concord, Jeep vehicles)

Established in 1954 as result of merger between Nash-Kelvinator Corp. and Hudson Motor Car Co; acquired Jeep Corp., Feb. 1970. Chairman: G.C. Meyers. President: W.P. Tippett, Jr. Central office and press office: American Center Building, P.O. Box 442, Southfield, Mich. 48034. Technical Center: 14250 Plymouth Rd., Detroit, Mich. 48232. Passenger car works: 5626, 25th Ave, Kenosha, Wisc. 53140; 3880 N Richards, Milwaukee, Wisc. 53201, Jeep plant: Toledo, Ohio. Plastics operations: Windsor Plastics, Inc., 601 N. Congress Ave, Evansville, Ind., 47711; Mercury Plastics Co., Inc., 34501 Harper, Mt Clemens, Mich. 48043; Evart Products Co., Evart Mich. 49631 (subsidiaries-injection moulding); AM General Corp., 32500 Van Born Rd, Wayne, Mich. 48184 (subsidiary). Works: 701 W. Chippewa Ave, South Bend, Ind., 46623; 13200 E. McKinley Hwy, Mishawaka, Ind., 46544; 1428 West Henry St Indianapolis, Ind. 46221 (military trucks, post-office delivery trucks and transit buses). 28,500 employees. 170,739 cars and 161,912 Jeep vehicles produced in 1978.

MANUFACTURE AND ASSEMBLY IN OTHER COUNTRIES — **Argentina:** Renault S.A., Sarmiento 1230, Buenos Aires (assem. Classic, Torino, Jeep CJ-5 and trucks). **Australia:** Australian Motor Industries Ltd (associated company), G.P.O. 2006S, 155 Bertie St., Port Melbourne (Matador). **Canada:** American Motors (Canada) Ltd (subsidiary), Brampton, Ont (Concord, Gremlin). **Costa Rica:** Motorizada de Costa Rica S.A., San José (assem. Jeep CJ-5, Wagoneer). **India:** Mahindra & Mahindra Ltd, Gateway Bldg, Apollo Bunder, Bombay (assem. Jeep CJ-4 and Wagoneer). **Indonesia:** N.V. Indonesian Service Co. Ltd, P.O.B. 121, Djakarta-Kota (assem. Jeep CJ-5). **Iran:** Sherkate Sahami Jeep, Ekbatan Ave, Jeep Bldg Teheran (assem. Arya, Shahin, Jeep CJ-5 and Wagoneer). **Israel:** Matmar Industries Ltd, P.O.B. 1007, Haifa (assem. Jeep CJ-5). **Japan:** Mitsubishi Heavy-Industries Ltd, No. 10, 2-chome, Marunouchi, Chiyoda-ku, Tokyo (manuf. Jeep CJ-5). **Korea:** Shinjin Jeep Co., 62-7 Ika Choong Mu-Ro Choong Ku Seoul (assem. Jeep CJ-5). **Mexico:** Vehiculos Automotores Mexicanos S.A., Poniente 150, num. 837, Industrial Vallejo Mexico City 16, D.F. (assem. American, Pacer, Jeep CJ-5 and Wagoneer). **Morocco:** Société d'Importation & Distribution Automobile, 84 av. Lalla Yacoute, Casablanca (assem. Jeep CJ-5). **Pakistan:** Naya Daur Motors Ltd., State Life Building Dr. Ziauddin Ahmed Rd, Karachi 3 (assem. Jeep trucks, Jeep station wagons and CJ-5). **Philippines:** Jeep Philippines, Guevent Bldg, 49 Libertad St., Mandaluyong, Rizal (assem. Jeep CJ-5, CJ-6). **South Africa:** Jeep South Africa, P.O.B. 80 Uitenhage (assem. Jeep CJ-5, CJ-7). **Spain:** Construcciones y Auxiliar de Ferrocarriles S.A., V.I.A.S.A. Division, Apdo 279 Zaragoza (manuf. Jeep CJ-5). **Taiwan:** Yue Loong Motor Co Ltd, 150 Nanking East Rd, Sec. II, Taipel (assem. Jeep CJ-5). **Thailand:** Thai Yarnyon Co. Ltd, 388/3 Petchburi Rd, Bangkok (assem. Jeep CJ-5). **Turkey:** Genoto General Otomotive Sanyi ve Ticaret AS, Takisim la Martin Cad. No. 8/1, Istanbul (assem. CJ-6, trucks). **Venezuela:** Constructora Venezolana de Vehiculos C.A., P.O.B. 61033, Caracas (assem. Hornet); Jeep de Venezuela S.A., Apdo 41-42, Tejerias, Edo Uragua (assem. Jeep CJ-5 and Wagoneer). 20,700 passengers cars and 28,300 Jeep vehicles produced outside USA in 1978.

ANTIQUE & CLASSIC AUTOMOTIVE Inc. **USA**

Established in 1973 as Antique & Classic Cars, Inc. Present

• *The information given in these discriptions refers specifically to cars and therefore does not cover the activities in which any of the car manufacturers are engaged in other fields of industry.*

title since 1977. Chairman: S.J. Wilson. General Manager: C.C. Holmberg. Head office, showroom: 100 Sonwil Industrial Park, Buffalo, N.Y. 14225. Works: Buffalo, N.Y. 14225. 28 employees. 600 cars in kit form produced in 1978. Most important models: 1937 Jaguar SS-100, 1930 Bentley Phaeton, 1934 Frazer Nash, 1927 Bugatti 35B, 1930 Alfa Romeo.

ARGYLL TURBO CARS Ltd — **Great Britain**

Founded in 1977. Directors: R.M. Henderson, A. Smith, H. Crow, J. Hughes. Head office and works: Minnow House, Lochgilphaed, Argyll, Scotland.

ARKLEY - see JOHN BRITTEN GARAGES Ltd

ARO INTREPRINDEREA MECANICA MUSCEL — **Romania**

General Manager: V. Naghi. Head office, press office and works: Str. Vasile Roaità 173. Cimpulung Muscel Jud. Arges.

ASTON MARTIN LAGONDA (1975) Ltd — **Great Britain**

Founded in 1913 as Bamford & Martin, it is one of the greatest names in the world of touring and competition cars. The name "Aston Martin" recalls the many successes in the Aston Clinton Hill Climb. In 1947, when it was taken over by David Brown, the title was changed to Aston Martin Lagonda Ltd. In January 1975 the company went into voluntary liquidation and since June 1975 has been owned by a consortium headed by P. Sprague and G. Minden, with the title Aston Martin Lagonda (1975) Ltd. Directors: P. Sprague (USA), A.G. Curtis, D.G. Flather (U.K.). Works: Tickford St., Newport Pagnell, Bucks MK 16 9AN. 420 employees. 280 cars produced in 1978. Most important models: Lionel Martin series (1921-25); first 1.5 l series (1927-32); second 1.5 l series (1932-34); third 1.5 l series (1934-36); 2 l series with single overhead camshaft (1936-40); 2 l DB1 series (1948-50); 2.6 l DB2 series (1950-1953); 2.6 and 2.9 l DB3 series (1952-1953); 2.6 and 2.9 l DB2/4 series (1953-55); 2.9 l DB3S series (1955-56); 2.9 l DB2/4 Mk II series (1955-57); 2.6 , 2.9 l Lagonda Saloon, Convertible (1949-1956); 2.9 l DB Mk II series (1957-59); 3.7 l DB4 series (1959-63); 3.7 l DB4 GT series (1959-63); 4 l Lagonda Rapide (1961-63); 4 l DB5 series (1963-65); 4 l DB6 Saloon and Volante Convertible (1965-69); DB6 Mk 2 Saloon with electronic fuel injection or carburettor induction (1969-70); DBS 4 l Saloon (1967); DBS V8 Saloon 5.35 l 4 O.H.C. fuel injection engine (1969); V8 (1973); Lagonda 4-door (1974); Lagonda 4-door (1976); V8 Vantage (1977); Volante (1978). Entries in numerous competitions (Le Mans, Spa, Tourist Trophy, Nürburgring, Aintree). Won Le Mans and World Sports Car Championship in 1959.

AUBURN-CORD-DUESENBERG Co. — **USA**

Founded by G.A. Pray in 1960. Purchased original name and inventory of original company at Auburn, Indiana. President: G.A. Pray. Head office, press office and works: 122 South Elm Place, Broken Arrow, Oklahoma 74012. 14 employees, 14 cars produced in 1978.

AUDI NSU AUTO UNION AG — **Germany (Federal Republic)**

Established in 1969 as result of merger between Auto Union GmbH (founded in Zwickau in 1932 and transferred to Ingolstadt in 1949 when Zwickau company was nationalized) and NSU Motorenwerke AG (founded in 1873 at Riedlingen, moved to Neckarsulm in 1880; changed its name to Neckarsulmer Fahrzeugwerke AG in 1919 and became NSU Motorenwerke AG in 1960). Board of Directors: W. Habbel, F. Piëch, H. Kialka, W. Neuwald, R. Gerech, M. Posth. Head office and press office: Postfach 220, D-8070 Ingolstadt. Works: as above, Neckarsulm. 29,662 employees. 340,000 cars produced in 1979. Most important models: NSU Ro 80 (1967); Audi 100 and 100 LS (1969); Audi 100 Coupé S (1970); Audi 100 GL (1971); Audi 80, 80 L. 80 S, 80 LS, 80 GL (1972).

ASSEMBLY IN OTHER COUNTRIES — **South Africa:** VW of South Africa Ltd (associated company), P.O.B. 80, Uitenhage (assem. Audi 100 range). 116.249 cars produced outside Federal Republic in 1976.

AUSTIN - see BL Ltd

AUTOBIANCHI — **Italy**

Created in 1955 in collaboration between Edoardo Bianchi firm and Fiat and Pirelli. Incorporated into Fiat in 1968 as Autobianchi, retaining, however, own maker's marks but incorporating sales organisation and maintenance services into Lancia. Office: Lancia, v. V. Lancia 27, 10141 Turin. About 4,000 employees. 88,800 cars produced in 1979.

AUTOMOBILES MONTEVERDI Ltd — **Switzerland**

Founded in 1967. Chairman and Managing Director: P. Monteverdi. Vice-Chairman: R. Jenzer. General Manager: P. Berer. Head office, press office and works: Oberwilerstr. 14-20, 4102 Binningen/Basel. 170 employees. 1300 cars produced in 1976. Most important models: 2-seater (1968); High Speed 375 L 2+2 (1969); Hai 450 SS (1970); High Speed 375/4 Limousine (1971); Berlinetta (1972); Hai 450 GTS (1973); Palm Beach (1975); Sierra (1977).

AUTOMOBILES PEUGEOT S.A. — **France**

Founded in 1890 as Les Fils Peugeot Fres. Present title since 1966. In December 1974 it acquired 38.2% of Citroën stock and in May 1976 take over full control of Citroën. In 1978 it acquired a controlling interest in the three Chrysler European companies, in the U.K. France and Spain, and full control of Chrysler Europe on 1 January 1979. Directorate: M. Parayre (President). P. Peugeot, J. Baratte (General Managers). Head office and press office: 75 av. de la Grande-Armée, Paris. Works: Dijon, Lille, Sochaux-Montbeliard, St. Etienne, Vesoul. About 70,000 employees. 861,000 cars produced in 1978. Most important models: Bebé Peugeot (1911); 201, 301, 302, 402, 203 (1948); 403 (1955); 404 (1960); 204 (1965); 504 (1968); 304 (1969); 604 (1975). First place in ACF (1912-13, 1923-24).

MANUFACTURE AND ASSEMBLY IN OTHER COUNTRIES — **Argentina:** Safrar (subsidiary), Buenos Aires (manuf. 404, 504). **Chile:** Automotores San Cristobal S.A.I.C., Santiago (assem. 404). **Madagascar:** Somocoa, Tananarive (assem. 304, 404). **Malaysia:** Asia Automobiles Industries, Petaling-Jaya (assem. 204, 504). **Nigeria:** Scoa, Lagos (assem. 404). **Paraguay:** Automotores y Maquinaria, C.C. 1160, Asuncion (assem. 404, 504). **Portugal:** Movauto, Setubal (assem. 204, 304, 404, 504). **South Africa:** SIGMA (subsidiary), Johannesburg (assem. 404, 504). **Uruguay:** S.A.D.A.R., Montevideo (assem. 404).

AUTOMOBILES STIMULA S.a.r.l. — **France**

Manufacturer of replicars in small series. Head office, press office and works: 23, quai Joseph Gillet, 69004 Lyon. Production of Bugatti 55 began in 1978.

AUTOMOBILES TALBOT — **France**

(Makes: Matra, Simca)

Founded in 1934 as Sté Industrielle de Mécanique et de Carrosserie Automobile. Assumed title Societé Simca Automobiles in 1960. In 1971 controlling interest passed to Chrysler Corp. and then in 1978 to PSA Peugeot-Citroën. Present title since 1980. Watch Committee: F. Gautier (President). P. Perrin (Vice-President). Management Board: F. Perrin-Pelletier (President). J. Peronnin (General Manager). D. Savey. Head office and presss office: 136 av. des Champs Elysées, 75008 Paris. Works: Poissy; La Rochelle-Perigny; Sully-sur-Loire; Sept Fons; Vieux Condé; Bondy; Valenciennes. 37,379 employees. 580,452 cars produced in 1978. Most important models: Simca 5 (1936); Simca 8-1100 (1938); Simca 6, 8-1100 (1948); Simca 8-1200, 8 Sport (1949); 9 Aronde (1951); Aronde, Coupé de Ville (1953); Aronde Week-End, Vedette (1955); Aronde 1300, Ocean, Plein Ciel (1956); Ariane 4 (1957); Aronde Montlhéry, Ariane 8, Vedette (1958); Aronde 6, 7, P.60 (1959); Aronde Etoile 6 and 7, P.60, Ocean, Plein Ciel (1960); Ariane (1961); Aronde Montlhéry and Monaco Spécial, Simca 1000 (1962); Simca 900, 1300, 1500 (1963); Simca 1000 and 1500 A (1966); Simca 1301, 1501, 1200 S (1967); Simca 1100 (1968); Simca 4 CV, 1000 Spécial, 1100 5 CV, 1501 Spécial (1969); Simca 1301 Spécial, 1000 Rallye (1970); Chrysler 160, 160 GT, 180, Simca 1100 Spécial (1971); Simca 1000, 1000 Rallye 1 (1972); Simca 1000 Rallye 2, 1100 VF2, Chrysler 2-litres (1973); Simca 1100 S, 1501 S, 1100 TI, 1100 LX (1974); Simca 1100 GLX, 1000 SR, 1307 GLS, 1307 S, 1308 GT (1975); Simca 1000 Extra, 1005 GLS, 1100 AS (1976); Simca 1005 LS, 1006 GLS, 1100 LE, 1100 GLX, 1100 ES, Rallye, 1307 GLS, 1308 GT, Chrysler Simca 1610, 2-litres (1977); Horizon (1978); Simca 1510 (1979).

AUTOMOBILI FERRUCCIO LAMBORGHINI S.p.A. — **Italy**

Founded in 1962 as Automobili Ferruccio Lamborghini Sas. Present title since 1965. President: G. Alfieri. Head office, press office and works: v. Modena 1b, 40019 S. Agata Bolognese (Bologna). About 180 employees. 180 cars produced in 1978. Models: 350 GT (1963); 400 GT (1966); Miura (1967); Espada, Islero (1968); Jarama (1970); Urraco (1971); Countach (1974); Countach S (1978).

AUTOMOBILI INTERMECCANICA — **USA**

President: A.E. Baumgartner. Vice-President: D.R. Bigham. Engineering Director: F.R. Reisner. Head office, press office and works: 2421 S. Susan St, Santa Ana, California. 45 employees. 325 cars produced in 1978.

AUTOMOVILES TALBOT — **Spain**

(Make: Simca)

Founded in 1951 as Barreiros Diesel S.A., 40% of shares were brought in 1963 by Chrysler Motor Corporation which became majority shareholder in 1967 eventually owing 99% of shares. Became Chrysler España in 1970. In 1978 a controlling interest was acquired by PSA Peugeot-Citroën. Present title since 1979. President: F. Perrin-Pelletier. Managing Director: G. Roy. Head office and press office: Apdo 140, Madrid 21. Works: Villaverde, Madrid. 16,500 employees. 98,000 cars produced in 1978.

AVALLONE - ACIEI Ltda — **Brazil**

Specializes in the production of sports cars. Head office, press office and works: Av. Friburgo 61, 04781 São Paulo. 70 cars produced in 1978.

AVANTI MOTOR CORPORATION — **USA**

Founded in 1965. Chairman: L. Newman. President: A.D. Altman. Vice-Presidents: F. Baer, E. Harding. Secretary and Treasurer: F. Baer. Head office and works: P.O.B. 1916, South Bend, Ind. 46634. 100 employees, 190 cars produced in 1978.

AZLK - AVTOMOBILNY ZAVOD IMENI LENINSKOGO KOMSOLA — **USSR**

(Make: Moskvich)

Press office: Avtoexport, Ul. Volkhonka 14, Moscow 119902. Works: Moscow, Izhevsk. 27,000 employees. About 314,000 cars produced in 1977.

BAYERISCHE MOTOREN WERKE AG — **Germany (Federal Republic)**

Established in 1916 as Bayerische Flugzeugwerke AG. Present title since 1918. Chairman: E. von Kuenheim. Members of the Board: H. Koch, H. Schäfer, K. Radermacher, H.E. Schönbeck, E. Sarfert, E. Haiber. Head office and press office: P.O.B. 400240, 8 Munich 40. Works: Munich, Landshut, Dingolfing. 35,171 employees. 320,853 cars produced in 1978. Most important models: 3/15 hp Saloon (1928); 326, 327, 328 (1936); 501 6 cyl. (1951); V8 (1954); 503 and 507 Sport (1955); 700 (1959); 1500 (1962); 1800 (1963); 2000 (1966); 2002, 2500, 2800 (1968); 3,0, CS (1971); 520, 520 i (1972); 2002 Turbo (1973); 518 (1974); 320 (1975); 633 CSi (1976); 323i (1977). Entries and wins in numerous competitions (Mille Miglia, Monza 12 hour, Hockenheim, Nürburgring, Friburg Mountain Record, Brands Hatch, European Mountain Championship, Salzburgring, Rally TAP; winner 1968, 1969, 1973, 1976 and 1978 European Touring Cars Championship; 1973, 1974, 1975 and 1978 European F2 Championship; 1977, 1978 World Championship for Makes (under 2000 cc).

ASSEMBLY IN OTHER COUNTRIES — **South Africa:** BMW (South Africa) (Pty) Ltd, 6 Frans de Toit St, Rosslyn, Pretoria (assem. 518, 520, 530, 528i, 728, 730, 733i). 7,027 cars assembled outside Federal Republic in 1978.

BENTLEY MOTORS Limited — **Great Britain**

Founded in 1920, taken over by Rolls-Royce Ltd in 1931, specializing in high-class vehicles. Head office and works: Crewe, Ches. Press office: 14-15 Conduit St, London W1. Most important models: first Bentley 3.5 l manufactured by Rolls-Royce (1933); 4.5 l (1936); 4.5 l MK VI (1946); Continental (1951); "R" Type (1952); S1 (1955); S2 (1959); S3 (1962) "T" series (1965); Corniche (1971); T2 (1977).

BL Ltd — **Great Britain**

(Makes: Austin, Daimler, Jaguar, Land Rover, MG, Mini, Morris, Princess, Rover, Triumph, Vanden Plas)

BL Ltd, 99% of whose shares are now held by British Government, is Britain's largest producer of motor vehicles. Formed in May 1968, following merger between British Motor Holdings (BMC and Jaguar) and Leyland Motor Corporation (Leyland Motors, Rover and Triumph). It employs 170,000 throughout the world and current annual sales exceed £ 3,000 million. The major subsidiaries are Austin Morris Ltd, Austin Morris House, Bickenhill, Birmingham (Austin, Princess); Jaguar Cars, Browns Lane Plant, Allesley, Coventry (Daimler, Jaguar); Rover Triumph Ltd, Canley Plant, Canley, Coventry (MG, Rover, Triumph); Land Rover Ltd, P.O.B. 2, Meteor Works, Lode Lane, Solihull (Land Rover, Range Rover). Head office: 35-38 Portman Sq., London W1H OHQ. Chairman and Chief Executive: M. Edwardes. 771,000 vehicles produced in 1978.

MANUFACTURE AND ASSEMBLY IN OTHER COUNTRIES — The Company sells its vehicles in 175 countries. The major manufacturing and assembly plants are at Seneffe in Belgium (cars), Madras in India (commercial vehicles). Sydney in Australia (mainly commercial vehicles but also Mini-Mokes), and Cape Town and Hong Kong. For specific details apply to BL Ltd, 35-38 Portman Sq., London W1H OHQ.

BLAKELY AUTO WORKS Ltd **USA**

Founded by D. Blakely in 1972. Chief Marketing Director: A. Herschberger. Head office and press office: 124 B Fulton St, Princeton, WI 54968. Works: 203 Pacific St, Davis Junction, Illinois 61020. 36 employees. 126 cars produced in 1977. Most important models: Bantam (1972); Bearcat (1973); Bearcat 'S' (1976).

BMW (South Africa) (Pty) Ltd **South Africa**

A privatly owned company began assembly of Glas bodies, BMW 1800 and 2000 version in 1968. In 1974 BMW AG, West Germany, took control and Series 5 was introduced that year and Series 7 in 1978. BMW 530 model raced in Group 2 FORM in 1976/77/78 in 40 races, 38 wins and 2 Championship wins. Managing Director: E. von Koerber. Directors: W. Jones, U.M. Doolan, D. Balfour, H. Doeg. Head office, press office and works: 6 Frans du Toit St, Rosslyn. 1,300 employees. 7,027 cars produced in 1978.

BRISTOL CARS Partnership **Great Britain**

Established in 1946 as Car Division of Bristol Aeroplane Co., became affiliated company of Bristol Aeroplane Co. in 1955, and subsidiary of Bristol Siddeley Engines In 1959. Became privately owned company in 1960 and owned by partnership from 1966. Partners: Bristol Cars Ltd, T.A.D. Crook, F.S. Derham. Head office, press office: 368-370 Kensington High St, London. Works: Filton, Bristol BS 997AR. Most important models: 400 (1947); 401 and 402 (1949); 403 and 404 (1953-55); 405 (1954-58); 406 (1958); 407 (1961); 408 (1963); 409 (1965); 410 (1967); 411 (1969); 412 (1975); 603 (1976). Entries and first places in numerous competitions with Bristol cars or Bristol-engined cars (Monte Carlo Rally, Targa Florio, Mille Miglia) with F1 and F2 (British GP, GP of Europe, Sebring, Reims, Montlhéry, Le Mans, etc.), from 1946 until 1955.

BUICK - see GENERAL MOTORS CORPORATION

CADILLAC - see GENERAL MOTORS CORPORATION

CATERHAM CAR Sales Ltd **Great Britain**

(Make: Seven)

In 1973 took over manufacture of Lotus Seven introduced by Lotus Cars Ltd in 1957. Managing Director: G.B. Nearn. Director: D.S. Wakefield. Head office, press office and works: 36/40 Town End, Caterham Hill, Surrey CR3 5UG. 18 employees. 160 cars produced in 1978. Model: Super Seven Series III powered by Lotus big valve twin cam engine.

CHECKER MOTORS CORPORATION **USA**

Founded in 1922. Chairman and President: D. Markin. Vice-President: R.E. Oakland. Vice-President Marketing: J.J. Love. Head office, press office and works: 2016 N. Pitcher St. Kalamazoo, Mich. 49007. 1,000 employees. 4,226 cars produced in 1978.

CHEVROLET - see GENERAL MOTORS CORPORATION GENERAL MOTORS OF CANADA Ltd and GENERAL MOTORS SOUTH AFRICA Ltd

CHRYSLER AUSTRALIA Ltd **Australia**

Founded in 1951. Affiliated with Chrysler Corporation USA. Chairman: T.D. Anderson. Directors: I. Webber, R. Smith, D.B. Coleman, J.M. Hill, J.W. Wiley. Head office, press office and works: South Rd, Clovelly Park, South Australia. 5,032 employees. 46,336 cars produced in 1978.

CHRYSLER CORPORATION **USA**

(Makes: Chrysler, Dodge, Plymouth)

Founded in 1925 as successor to Maxwell Motors Corp. it holds third place in U.S. motor industry. Chrysler Corp. American operations are made up of a U.S. Automotive Sales selling Chrysler, Dodge, Plymouth cars and trucks. Chairman and Chief Executive Officer: L.A. Iacocca. President and Chief Operating Officer: J.P. Bergmoser. Group Vice-President - International: E.H. Doyle. Head office and press office Chrysler Corp.: 12000 Lynn Townsend Dr., Highland Park Mich. Mailing address: Chrysler Corp., Chrysler Center, P.O. Box 1919, Detroit, Mich. 48288. Works: eight vehicle assembly plants and 32 supporting manufacturing plants throughout the U.S. and Canada. Over 131,700 employees. 1,129,933 (U.S.), 177,365 (Canada) cars produced in 1978. Most important models: Chrysler (1924); Plymouth and Dodge (1928).

MANUFACTURE AND ASSEMBLY IN OTHER COUNTRIES — **Australia:** Chrysler Australia Ltd (subsidiary), South Rd, Clovelly Park, South Australia (manuf. Chrysler Valiant, Regal, Sigma. **Mexico:** Chrysler de Mexico, S.A. (subsidiary), P.O. Box 53-951, Mexico 17, D.F. Mexico (manuf. Chrysler Le Baron, Dodge Dart, Valiant, Volare). **Peru:** Chrysler Perù S.A. (subsidiary), Apdo 5037, Lima (assem. Dodge Coronet. Hillman Hunter). 333,100 cars produced outside USA and Canada in 1978.

CHRYSLER FEVRE ARGENTINA S.A.I.C. **Argentina**

(Make: Dodge)

Founded in 1959 as Fevre y Basset Ltda. Present title since 1965. Chairman: C.M. Hollis. Head office and press office: Florencio Varela 1903, San Justo, Buenos Aires. Works: as above; Charcas 4200, Monte Chingolo, Lanús, Buenos Aires. 5,000 employees. 16,979 cars produced in 1978. Most important models: Valiant I (1962); Valiant II (1963); Valiant III (1964-65); Valiant IV (1966); Valiant V (1967-68); Dodge Polara, Coronado, GT (1969); Dodge Polara, Coronado, GT, GTX (1970); Polara, Coronado, GTX, Polara Coupé, 1500 (1971-72); Polara, Coronado, GTX, Polara Coupé, 1500, GT90 (1972-73); GTX, Polara, Polara RT, Coronado, 1500, GT90 (1974); Polara, Coronado, Polara RT, GTX, 1500, 1500 1.8 engine, 1500 Automatic (1975); Polara, Coronado, Polara RT, GTX, 1500, 1500 Automatic, 1500 1.8 engine (1977-78).

CHRYSLER MOTORS DO BRASIL Ltda **Brazil**

(Make: Dodge)

Founded in 1967 as Chrysler do Brasil S.A. Ind. e Comércio, it began producing Dodge trucks and Dodge Dart in May 1969. In 1971 it became Chrysler Corporation do Brasil and started production of Dodge 1800 in November 1972. Present title since 1979. Managing Director: D.W. Dancey. Head office, press office and works: Av. Dr. José Fornari 715, B. Ferrazopolis, São Bernardo do Campo, São Paulo. 3,666 employees. 16,312 cars produced in 1978. At present it produces Dodge trucks and Dodge Polara, Dart, Charger, Magnum and Le Baron models.

CITROËN - see S.A. AUTOMOBILES CITROËN

CLASSIC-CAR WITTEK GmbH **Germany (Federal Republic)**

Manufacturer of replicars in small series. Head office, press office and works: Feldhauser Weg 39, 4018 Langenfeld/Solingen.

COMPANHIA INDUSTRIAL SANTA MATILDE Inc. Co. **Brazil**

Chairman: H.J. Pimentel Duarte da Fonseca. Vice-Chairman: C.A. da Silveira. C.A. da Silveira. Directors: A.L. Pimentel Duarte da Fonseca, J.C. Pimentel Duarte, J.F. Capistrano Do Amaral. Head office: Rua Buenos Aires 100, Rio de Janeiro 20070. Press office: Rua Buenos Aires, 100 sala 78, Rio de Janeiro 20070. Works: Rua Isaltino Silveira 768, 25800 Tres Rios, Rio de Janeiro. 16 employees.

CUSTOCA **Austria**

Proprietor: G. Höller. Head office and works: 8714 Kraubath/Mur 55.

DACIA - UZINA DE AUTOTURISME PITESTI **Romania**

Foreign Trade Company: Auto-Dacia, 42, Mircea Voda St., Pitesti. Works: Colibasi - Pitesti. 68,055 cars produced in 1978.

DAIHATSU KOGYO COMPANY Ltd **Japan**

Established in 1907 as Hatsudoki Seizo Kabushiki Laisha, assumed title of Daihatsu Kogyo Co. Ltd in 1951. Now consists of Daihatsu Motor Co. Ltd and Daihatsu Motor Sales Co. Ltd, and belongs to Toyota Group. Chairman: M. Yamamoto. President: S. Ohhara. Senior Managing Directors: T. Eguchi, A. Makino, J. Ono. Head office and works: 1-1 Daihatsu-cho, Ikeda-shi, Osaka. Press office: Daihatsu Motor Sales Co. Ltd, 2-7 Ninonbashi-Honcho, Chuoku, Tokyo. 8,500 employees. 157,320 vehicles produced in 1978. Production of 4-wheeled vehicles begun in 1958. Most important models: Compagno Station Wagon (1963); Compagno 800 Sedan (1964); Compagno Spider and Sedan (1965); Fellow 360 (1966); Consorte Berlina (1969); Fellow Max (1970): Charmant (1974); Charade (1977); Charade Runabout (1978).

MANUFACTURE IN OTHER COUNTRIES — **Indonesia:** P.T. Gaya Motor, V1 Sulawasi 2 Pandiung Priok, Djakarta (manuf. Charade). **Ireland:** Irish Motor Body Build. Ltd., Long Mile Rd, Dublin 12 (manuf. Charade). **Thailand:** Bangchan Genera Assembly Co., Ltd, 99 Moo 4 Sukhapiba Rd, Tambol (manuf Charade).

DAIMLER - see BL Ltd

DAIMLER-BENZ AG **Germany (Federal Republic)**

(Make: Mercedes-Benz)

Established in 1926 as a result of merger between Daimler-Motorengellschaft and Benz & Cie; it is the best-known German manufacturer of highclass cars. Board of Directors: G. Prinz (Chairman); W. Ulsamer, W. Breitschwerdt, H. Schmidt, W Niefer, R. Osswald, H.C. Hoppe, E. Reuter (members). Head office and press office Mercedes-Strasse 136, 7 Stuttgart Works: as above, Sindelfingen, Mannheim, Gaggenau, Berlin-Marienfelde, Düsseldorf, Bad Homburg, Wörth/Rhein. 173,201 employees. 393,203 cars produced in 1977. Most important models: Stuttgart 200, Mannheim (1926); Stuttgart 260, Mannheim 350 and Sport-Wagen SSK (1928); Grosser Mercedes (1930); Nürburg 500 (1931); 170 V (1935); 260 D, first Diese car (1935); Grosser Mercedes (1938); 170 V (1946); 300 SL (1954); 190 SL (1955); 180 b/Db and 220 Sb (1959); 190 c/Dc and 300 SE (1961); 230 SL and 600 (1963); 250 (1966); 200, 220, 230, 250, 280 S, 280 SE, 300 SEL 6.3, 250 C, 250 SE (1968); 280 SE 3.5, 300 SEL 3.5 (1969); 350 SL, 450 SL (1971); 280 SE, 350 SE, 450 SE (1972); 240 D, 230/4 (1973) 240 D 3.0 (1974); 450 SEL 6.9 (1975); 200 D, 280 E (1976) 230-280 C, 280 CE (1977); 300 SD, 450 SLC, 240 - 300 TD 230-250 T, 280 TE (1978). First places in numerous international competitions (1894-1955).

DAYTONA AUTOMOTIVE FIBERGLASS Inc. **USA**

Established in 1976. President: LaVerne Martincic. Vice-President: M. Zimmerman. Production Manager and Secretary E. Kuhel. Head office, press office and works: 819 Carswel Ave, Holly Hill, Fla. 32017. 18 employees. 300 cars produced in 1978.

DE TOMASO MODENA S.p.A. AUTOMOBILI **Italy**

Founded in 1959. President: A. de Tomaso. General Manager A. Bertocchi. Head office, press office and works: v. Emilia Ovest 1250, Modena. 60 employees. 150 cars produced in 1978. Most important models: Berlinetta Vallelunga with Ford Cortina 1500 engine (two-seater); Sport Prototype 5-litre (1965); Mangusta with V8 4700 engine (1966); Pantera with V8 5700 engine, 310 hp (1970); Deauville 4-door with 5700 engine (1971); Longchamp 2+2 with V8 5700 engine (1973).

DODGE - see CHRYSLER CORPORATION, CHRYSLER MOTORS DO BRASIL, CHRYSLER FEVRE ARGENTINA S.A.I.C.

Dr. Ing. h.c. F. PORSCHE A.G. **Germany (Federal Republic)**

Founded in 1948. Owned by Porsche Holding Co. (Co-Chairmen: F. Porsche, L. Piëch). Managing Directors: E. Fuhrmann, H. Branitzki, L.R. Schmidt, H. Bott, K. Kalkbrenner, H. Kurtz. Head office and press office: Porschestr. 42, 7 Stuttgart-Zuffenhausen. Works: Schwieberdingestr., 7 Stuttgart-Zuffenhausen. 5,150 employees. 36,780 cars produced in 1978. Most important models: type 356/1100, 1300, 1300 S, 1500 S (1950-1955); 356 A/1300, 1300 S, 1600, 1600 S, Carrera (1955-1959); 356 B/1600, 1600 S, 1600 S-90, Carrera (1959-1963); 356 C/1600 C, 1600 SC (1963-1965); 911, 912 (1965-1966); 911, 911 S, 912 (1967); 911 T, S, 912 (1968); 911 T, E, S, Carrera (1969-1976); 924, Turbo (1975); 928 (1977). First places in numerous international competitions: Le Mans 24 hour with 1100 Coupé (1951), Sebring (1958-59), European Mountain Championship (1960-68), Targa Florio and Nürburgring (1959-1967-68-69-70-73), Constructors' Cup for F2 cars (1960), European Rally Championship with Carrera (1961), GT World Championship up to 2000 cc (1962-63-64-65), World Cup for speed and endurance, European Touring Car Trophy, 32 national championships. Overall wins in Le Mans 24 hours (1970-71-76-77), Rallye Monte Carlo winners (1968-69-70), International Rallye Championship (1968-69-70), Grand Touring Car Championship and International Manufacturers Championship (1969-70-71-76-77).

DUTTON SPORTS Ltd **Great Britain**

First Dutton built in 1968. Chairman and Managing Director: T. Dutton-Wolley. Head office, press office and works: Unit 10, Hambridge Industrial Estate, East Worthing, West Sussex, BN 14 8NA. 8 employees. 201 cars produced in 1977. Most important models: B Type (1971); B plus (1974); Malaga and Cantera (1975).

ELEGANT MOTORS Inc. USA

Founded in 1971. Owner: D.O. Amy. Head office press office and works: P.O. Box 13155, Airgate Branch, Sarasota, Fl. 33578. 8 employees.

ELITE ENTERPRISES Inc. USA

Established in 1969. President: G.W. Knapp. Head office, press office and works: 690 E 3rd St., Cokato, Minn. 55321. 8 employees. 175 cars produced in 1978.

EL-NASR AUTOMOTIVE MANUFACTURING Co. Egypt

Founded in 1959. Chairman: A. I. Gazarin. Vice-Chairman: O. M. Amin. Head office, press office and works: Wadi-Hof, Helwan. 10,500 employees. 14,000 cars produced in 1978

ENVEMO - ENGENHARIA DE VEICULOS E MOTORES Brazil

Founded in 1965. Manufacturer of cars, off-road vehicles, and racing accessories. Specializing in engineering and developing high output engines for road and race, and also in restoration of classic cars. Directors: L.F. Goncalves, A.M. Goncalves, J.G. Whitaker Ribeiro. Head office, press office and works: Rua Olimpiadas, 237 Vila Olimpia, SP. 150 employees. 200 cars produced in 1978.

EXCALIBUR AUTOMOBILE CORPORATION USA

Founded in 1964 as SS Automobiles Inc. Present title since 1976. President: D.B. Stevens. Executive Vice-President: W.C. Stevens. Head office and works: 1735 South 106th St, Milwaukee, Wisc. 53214. 98 employees. 295 cars produced in 1978. Models: Roadster SS, Phaeton SS.

FABRYKA SAMOCHODOW MALOLITRAZOWYCH Poland

(Makes: Fiat 126, Syrena)

Founded in 1972. State-owned company. Director: R. Dziopak. Works: Bielsko-Biala. About 200,000 Fiat 126 and 38.000 Syrena cars produced in 1979. Head office and press office: ul. R. Luksenburg 51, 43-300 Bielsko-Biala.

FABRYKA SAMOCHODOW OSOBOWYCH Poland

(Make: Polski-Fiat)

Founded in 1949. State-owned Company. Chairman: J. Bielecki. Vice-Presidents: M. Karwas, S. Tyminski, W. Komendarek, J. Burchard, Z. Chorazy, L. Fronczyk, J. Salamokczyk. Head office, press office and works: ul. Stalingradzka 50, Warsaw. 25,000 employees. About 125,000 cars produced in 1978. Most important models: Warzawa 223, 224 (1964-1973); Syrena 104 (1958-1973); Polski-Fiat 125 P (1968); Polonez (1978). Entries in Rallies (Monte Carlo, Acropolis, 1000 Lakes, etc.).

FAIRTHORPE Ltd Great Britain

Founded in 1957. Proprieor: D.C.T. Bennett. General Manager: T. Bennett. Head office: Deepwood House, Farnham Royal, Bucks. Press office and works: Denham Green Lane, Denham, Bucks. Most important models: Electron, Zeta, Mk VI EM, TXI, TX-GT, TX-S, TX-SS.

FASA-RENAULT Spain

Founded in 1951. President: M. Guasch Molins. Vice-President: B. Hanon. Managing Director: M.H. Bougler. Head office: p. Arco de Ladrillo 58, Valladolid. Press office: Carretera de Alcobendas, km 5.5, Apdo. 262, Madrid 34. Works: Valladolid, Sevilla. About 18,000 employees. 235,476 cars produced in 1978.

FELBER - see HAUTE PERFORMANCE MORGES

FERRARI S.p.A. Italy
Esercizio Fabbriche Automobili e Corse

Founded in 1929 as Scuderia Ferrari, became Società Autoavio Costruzioni Ferrari in 1940 and Ferrari S.p.A.-SEFAC in 1960. Since 1-7-1969, Fiat has been associated on joint venture basis and company has used its present title. Its name is bound up with superb technical achievements in field of racing and GT cars. Hon. President: E. Ferrari. President: N. Tufarelli. Managing Director: G. Sguazzini. General Manager: F. Alzati. Directors: L. Montezeolo, C. Pelloni, S. Pininfarina, P. Lardi. Head office: vl. Trento Trieste 31, 41100 Modena. Press office and works: v. Abetone Inferiore 2, 41053 Maranello (Modena). 1,576 employees (including Scaglietti, Modena). Over 2,200 cars produced in 1979. Most important GT models: 125 (1947); 166 Inter (1949); 340 America (1952); 250 GT, V12 250 GT, Superfast (1961); 275 GTB 4 Berlinetta (1963); Dino 206 GT Berlinetta, 365 Coupé GT 2+2 (1967): 365 GTB 4 Berlinetta, 246 GT Dino (1969); 308 GTB (1975). Entries and wins in various world competitions and championships. 23 times world champion.

FIAT (Uruguay) - see FIAT AUTO S.p.A.

FIAT AUTO S.p.A. Italy

Founded in July 1899 as Società Anonima Fabbrica Italiana di Automobili Torino. With the statutary modification of the shareholders' meeting in 1918, it assumed the title Fiat written either with capital or small letters. In 1968, FIAT incorporated Autobianchi which is still produced as separate make. In 1969 it took over Lancia and acquired 50% of Ferrari shares and in 1971 took over Abarth. In 1976, the reorganisation of the Fiat Group was practically completed. The new Fiat Holding is a structure in which all the sectors are now organized with their own design, production and marketing responsibilities, some of them as individual legal entities and other with Fiat S.p.A. but with similar management autonomy. Among these is Fiat Auto S.p.A. (incorporating Lancia-Autobianchi). Head office: c.so Agnelli 200, Turin. Press office: c.so Matteotti 26, 10121 Turin. Works: Mirafiori, Rivalta, Lingotto (Turin), Vado Ligure, Termini Imerese, Villar Perosa, Cassino, Florence, Bari. President: B. Beccaria. Vice-Presidents: U. Agnelli, C. Romiti. Managing Director: V. Ghidella. 169,680 employees. 1,322,000 vehicles produced in 1979. Most important models: Fiat 3½ HP (1899-1900); 6 HP and 8 HP, 12 HP, 24-32 HP (1900-04); 16-24 HP (1903-04); Brevetti and 60 HP (1905-09); 18-24 (1908); Fiacre mod. 1 (1908-10); Fiat 1,2,3,4,5 (1910-18); Zero and 3 ter (1912-15); 2B and 3A (1912-21); 70 (1915-20); 501 (1919-26); 505 and 510 (1919-25); Superfiat (1921-22); 519 (1922-24); 502 (1923-26); 509 (1925-27); 503 and 507 (1926-27); 512 (1926-28); 520 (1927-29); 521 (1928-31); 525 (1928-29); 525 S (1929-31); 514 and 514 MM (1929-32); 515, 522 C and 524 C (1931-34); 508 Balilla and 508 S Balilla Sport (1932-37); 518 Ardita (1933-38); 527 Ardita 2500 (1934-36); 1500 (1935-48); 500 (1936-48); 508 C Balilla 1100 (1937-39); 2800 (1938-44); 1100 (1939-48); 500 B and Giardiniera (1948-49); 1100 B and 1500 D (1948-49); 1500 E (1949-50); 1100 E (1949-53); 500 C (1949-54); 500 C Giardiniera (1949-52); 1100 ES (1950-51); 1400, 1400 A and 1400 B (1950-58); 500 C Belvedere (1951-55); 1900 A and 1900 B (1952-58); 8V (1952-54); Nuova 1100 and Nuova 1100 Familiare (1953-56); 1100 TV (1953-56); 600 (1955-60); 1100/103 E (1956-57); Nuova 500 Trasformabile (1957-60); 1100/103 D (1957-60); Nuova 500 Sport (1958-60); 1200 Gran Luce (1957-60); 1200 Trasformabile (1958-59); 1100/103 H (1959-60); 1800 and 1800 Familiare (1959-61); 1100 Special (1960-62); 500 D (1960-65); 600 D Multipla, 500 Giardiniera (1960-68); 1300, 1500, 1300 Familiare, 2300 Coupé, 2300 S Coupé (1961-68); 1600 S Cabriolet (1962-66); 850 (1964-71); 124 and 124 Sport Spider (1966); Dino Spider (1966); 125, Dino Coupé, 124 Sport Coupé, 850 Idroconvert (1967); 850 Special Sport Coupé, Sport Spider, 500 L, 124 Special, 125 Special (1968); 128, 128 Familiare, 124 Sport Coupé 1600, 124 Sport Spider 1600, Dino Coupé 2400, Dino Spider 2400, 130 (1969); 124 Special T (1970); 127, 128 Rally, 128 Coupé, 130 3200, 130 Coupé (1971); 126, 127 3 Porte, X 1/9, 124 Spider Rally, 124 Coupé and Spider 1600 and 1800, 132 (1972); 126 Tetto Apribile, 132 GLS, 128 Special, 127 Special, 131 Mirafiori (1974); 128 3P (1975); 126 Personal (1976); 132 1600-2000, 127 900-1050 CL (1972). It has been entering competitions since 1900, when true racing car was not yet born. First national wins, followed by many others. In Automobile Tour of Italy with 6-8 HP, a car with two horizontal rear cylinders. Since 1904 numerous first places in international field. In 1927 officially retired from motor racing. Since 1970 works competition in rallies. In 1977 and 1978 World Rally Championship with Fiat 131 Abarth.

MANUFACTURE AND ASSEMBLY IN OTHER COUNTRIES — **Argentina:** Fiat Automoviles S.A.I.C. (affiliated company), Cerrito 740, Buenos Aires (manuf. 600, 128, 125). **Brazil:** Fiat Automoveis Co. (affiliated company), Avda Sao Luiz 50, 28° Andar, São Paulo (manuf. 147). **Chile:** Fiat Chile S.A. (affiliated company), Carmen 8, Santiago (assem. 600, 125). **Colombia:** Compania Colombiana Automotriz S.A. (associated company), Calle 13 n. 38-54, Bogotà (assem. 128, 125). **Costa Rica:** S.A.V.A. (licensee company), Apdo 10042, San José (assem. 131, 127). **Egypt:** El-Nasr Automotive Mfg Co. Ltd (licensee company), Wadi-Hof, Helwan, Cairo (assem. 128, 131, Polmot 125). **Eire:** Fiat Ireland Ltd (affiliated company), Industrial Garden Estate, Chapelizod, Dublin (assem. 127, 128). **Indonesia:** Daha Motors (licensee company), Medan Merkeda Selatan 2, Djakarta (assem. 131, 127, 132 S). **Malaysia:** Sharikat Fiat Distributors (licensee company), Tanglin Rd 99/101, Singapore (assem. 127, 128, 131, 132). **Morocco:** Somaca (associated company), km 12 Autoroute de Rabat, Casablanca (assem. 127, 131, 132). **New Zealand:** Torino Motors Ltd (licensee company), 19/29 Nelson St, Auckland (assem. 128). **Poland:** Pol-Mot (licensee company), Stalingradzka 23, Warszawa (manuf. 126, 125 P). **Portugal:** Fiat Portuguesa Sarl (affiliated company), Av. Eng. Duarte Pacheco 15, Lisbon (assem. 127, 128, 131). **South Africa:** Fiat South Africa Pty Ltd, 2 Bosworth St, Alrode Extension, Alberton (assem. 128, 131, 132). **Spain:** Seat (associated company), av. del Generalisimo 146, Madrid (manuf. 133, 127, 128 3P, 1200/1400 Sport, 124, 131, 132). **Thailand:** Karnasuta General Assembly Co. (licensee company), P.O.B. 1421, Bangkok (assem. 128, 131, 132 S). **Turkey:** Tofas (associated company), K. 57 Mecidiyekoy, Istanbul (manuf. 131). **Uruguay:** Ayax S.A. (licensee company), Av. Rondeau 1751, Montevideo (assem. 125, 600, 128); Mar y Sierra (concessionaire), 8 de Octubre 3381, Montevideo (assem. 125). **Venezuela:** Fiav (associated company), Alcabala de Candelaria à Urapal 8, Caracas (assem. 131, 132). **Yugoslavia:** Zavodi Crvena Zastava (associated company), Span, Boraca 2, Kragujevac (manuf. Zastava 750, 128, 1300, 1500, 125 PZ, 126 P, 132 GLS). **Zambia:** Livingstone Motor Assemblers Ltd (associated company), P.O.B. 2718, Lusaka (assem. 127, 128, 131, 132 S). 900,000 cars produced outside Italy in 1978.

FIAT AUTOMOVEIS S.A. Brazil

(Makes: Fiat, Alfa Romeo)

Founded in March 1973, started production in June 1976. Chairman: M.A. Gonçalves De Souza. Vice-Chairman: A. De Vito. Manging Director: S. Valentino. Head office and press office: Rodovia Fernao Dias, km 9, Betim, Minas Gerais. 97,302 cars produced in 1978. Models: 147 (1976); 147 L, 147 GL, 147 GLS, 147 Rallye (1978); Alfa Romeo (1978). Entries in numerous Brasilian local rallies.

FIAT AUTOMOVILES S.A. Argentina

President: P. Sabatini. Vice-President: A. De Vito. Managing Director: R. Sanchea. Head office: Cerrito 740, Buenos Aires. Press office: as above; Division Automoviles, Juramento 750, Buenos Aires. Works: Humberto I - 1001, Palomar - Pcia Buenos Aires. About 12,000 employees. 23,200 cars produced in 1978.

FIBERFAB - KAROSSERIE Germany (Federal Republic)

Proprietor: J. Kuhnle. Head office, press office and works: D-7129 Ilsfeld-Auenstein b. Heilbronn. About 120 cars produced in 1976.

FORD BRASIL S.A. Brazil

Established in 1919. Ford-Willys merge in 1967. President and General Manager: R.C. Graham. Directors: R.C. Graham, E.T. Laumberg, J.P. Dias, N. Chiaparini, M. Borghetti. Head office and press office: Av. Rudge Ramos 1501, São Paulo. Works; Av. Henry Ford 1787, São Paulo; Av. do Taboão 899, São Bernardo do Campo; Parque das Industrias, Tambaté, SP; Av. Henry Ford 17, Osasco, SP. 21,000 employees. About 165,000 vehicles produced in 1978. Most important models: Ford T (1924); Willys Jeep (1954); Rural Jeep (1958); Renault Dauphine (1959); Aero Willys (1960); Itamaraty (1965); Ford Galaxie 500 (1967); Corcel Sedan and Ford LTD Landau (1968); Corcel Coupé (1969); Corcel Sedan and Ford LTD Landau (1968); Corcel Coupé (1969); Corcel Belina Station Wagon (1970); Maverick (1973); Corcel II, Corcel II Belina (1977). Entries in numerous competitions from 1962 to 1968. Brazilian Makers Championship in 1972-73 with Corcel. Brazilian Touring Car Championiship (Group 1) in 1973-74 with Maverick. Brazilian Makers Championship with Avallone-Ford in 1974 and with Hollywood-Berta-Ford in 1975. Formula Ford-Corcel promoter in 1972-73-74-75-76-77-78.

FORD MOTOR ARGENTINA S.A. Argentina

Incorporated 1959. President: J.M. Courard. Head office and press office: cc Central 696, Buenos Aires. Works: Pacheco. 8,132 employees. 34,951 cars produced in 1978.

FORD MOTOR COMPANY USA

(Makes: Ford, Lincoln, Mercury)

Founded in 1903, is the second largest of the American motor manufacturers. Chairman: Henry Ford II. Vice-Chairman, President and Chief Executive Officer: P. Caldwell. Executive Vice-President International Automotive Operations: D.E. Petersen. Executive Vice-President North American Automotive Operations: W.O. Bourke. Components include Ford Division (300 Renaissance Center, P.O.B. 43303, Detroit, Mich. 48423. Vice-President and General Manager W.S. Walla) and Lincoln-Mercury Division (300 Renaissance Center, P.O.B. 43322, Detroit, Mich. 48243. Vice-President and General Manager W.G. Oben). World headquarters: The American Rd, Dearborn, Mich. Assembly plants: Atlanta, Ga.; Chicago, Ill.; Dearborn, Wayne (2) and Wixom, Mich.; Kansas City and St. Louis, Mo.; Lorain and Avon Lake, Ohio; Los Angeles and San José, Calif.; Louisville, Ky. (2); Mahwah and Metuchen, N.J.; Norfolk, Va.; Twin Cities, Minn. 289,080 employees. 2,557,197 cars produced in 1978.

MANUFACTURE AND ASSEMBLY IN OTHER COUNTRIES (excluding models of Ford Motor Company Ltd, Great Britain, of Ford Motor Company of Canada Ltd, Canada, Ford Werke AG,

Germany, of Ford Brasil S.A., Brazil and of Ford Motor Company of Australia Ltd, (Australia) — **Argentina:** Ford Motor Argentina S.A. (subsidiary), C.C. Central 696, Buenos Aires 32/1 (manuf. and assem. Fairlane, Falcon, Taunus). **Ireland:** Henry Ford & Sons Ltd (subsidiary). Marina Cork (assem. Cortina, Escort, Capri, Granada, Fiesta). **Mexico:** Ford Motor Co. Branch S.A. (subsidiary), Apdo 39 bis, Mexico City (manuf. and assem. Fairmont, LTD, Mustang). **New Zealand:** Ford Motor Co. of New Zealand Ltd (subsidiary), P.O.B. 30012, Lower Hutt (assem. Falcon, Escort, Cortina, Fairlane, LTD). **Portugal:** Ford Lusitana S.A.R.L. (subsidiary), Apdo 2248 R. Rosa Aranjo 2, Lisbon (assem. Cortina, Escort). **Singapore:** Ford Motor Co. Private Ltd (subsidiary), P.O.B. 4047, Bukit Timah, Singapore (assem. Granada, Cortina, Escort). **Spain:** Ford España S.A. (subsidiary), Edificio Cuzco III/Avda Generalisimo 59, Madrid 15 (manuf. and assem. Fiesta). **South Africa:** Ford Motor Co. of South Africa (Pty) Ltd (subsidiary), P.O.B. 788, Port Elizabeth (assem. Granada, Cortina, Fairlane, Escort). **Taiwan:** Ford Lio Ho Motor Co. Ltd (subsidiary), Taipel (assem. Escort, Cortina, Granada). **Uruguay:** Ford (Uruguay) S.A. (subsidiary), C.C. 296, Montevideo (assem. Falcon, Escort). **Venezuela:** Ford Motor de Venezuela S.A. (subsidiary), Apdo 61131 del Este, Caracas (assem. Zephyr, Fairmont). 1,695,000 sold outside USA in 1978.

FORD MOTOR COMPANY Ltd — Great Britain

Founded in 1911, owned by Ford Motor Company USA, it had its first head office at Trafford Park (Manchester). In 1925, construction of Dagenham works was begun where production was started in 1931. Chairman and Managing Director: Sir Terence Beckett. Head office and press office: Eagle Way, Warley Brentwood, Essex. Works: Dagenham, Essex; Halewood, nr. Liverpool, and others, About 70,000 employees. 251,268 cars produced in 1978. Most important models: 8 hp "Y", 10 hp "C", 14.9 hp "B.F.", 24 hp "B", 30 hp "V8" (all prior to 2nd World War); Prefect (1938); Anglia (1939); Pilot (1947); Consul, Zephyr (1951); Anglia 100E, Popular, Zodiac (1953); Mk II Consul, Zephyr, Zodiac (1956); Anglia 105E (1959); Consul Classic 315, Capri (1961); Mk III Zephyr, Zodiac, Cortina (1962); Corsair (1963); Mk IV Zephyr, Zodiac (1966); Mk II Cortina (1966); Escort (1968); Capri (1969); Mk III Cortina (1970); Granada (1972); Fiesta (1977). Entries and wins in numerous competitions.

ASSEMBLY IN OTHER COUNTRIES — **Costa Rica:** Anglofores Ltda (concessionaire), Apdo 1768, San José (assem. Escort). **Eire:** Henry Ford and Son Ltd (associated company), Cork (assem. Cortina). **Holland:** N.V. Nederlandsche Ford Automobiel Fabriek (associated company), P.O.B. 795, Amsterdam (assem. Cortina). **Israel:** Palestina Automobile Corp. Ltd (concessionaire), P.O.B. 975, Tel Aviv (assem. Escort). **Korea:** Hyundai Motor Co. (concessionaire), 55 Chrongro 3KA, Seoul (assem. Cortina). **Malaysia:** Associated Motor Industries, Malaysian Sdn Bhd (concessionaire), 109 Jelan Pudu, Kuala Lumpur (assem. Cortina, Escort). **New Zealand:** Ford Motor Co. of New Zealand Ltd (associated company), P.O.B. 30012, Lower Hutt (assem. Escort, Cortina, Zephyr, Zodiac). **Pakistan:** All Autos Ltd (concessionaire), P.O.B. 4206, Karachi (assem. Cortina). **Peru:** Ford Motor Co. Perú S.A. (associated company), Apdo 4130, Lima (assem. Escort). **Philippines:** Ford Philipp. Inc. (associated company), P.O.B. 415, Makati Commercial Centre, Makati Rizal (assem. Cortina, Escort). **Portugal:** Ford Lusitana (associated company), Apdo 2248, R. Rosa Arajo 2, Lisbon (assem. Escort, Cortina). **Singapore:** Ford Motor Co. Private Ltd (associated company), P.O.B. 4047, Bukit Timah, Singapore (assem. Cortina, Escort, Capri). **South Africa:** Ford Motor Co. of South Africa (Pty) Ltd (associated company), P.O.B. 788, Port Elizabeth (assem. Escort, Cortina, Capri). **Venezuela:** Ford Motor Co. Venezuela S.A. (associated company), Apdo 61131 Del Este, Caracas (assem. Cortina). 59,230 cars produced outside U.K. in 1977.

FORD MOTOR COMPANY OF AUSTRALIA Ltd — Australia

Founded in 1925. Managing Director: B.S. Inglis. Directors: H. Ford II, F.Z. Herr, E.T. Gardner, B.L. Burton, M.F. Gransden, S.I. Gilman, E.A. Witts, D.C. Jacobi, J.A. Supina. Head office and press office: Private Bag, 6 Campbellfield, Victoria 3061 Works: Broadmeadows, Campbellfield, Geelong, Victoria. 14,287 employees. 100,574 cars produced in 1978.

FORD MOTOR COMPANY OF CANADA Ltd — Canada

(Makes: Ford, Mercury)

Founded in 1904 in Windsor, Ont. Has always built a large percentage of all cars and trucks produced by Canadian automotive industry. President and Chief Executive Officer: R.F. Bennett. Vice-Presidents: S. J. Surma, W. Mitchell, K.W. Harrigan, C.J. Roberts. Head office and press office: The Canadian Road, Oakville, Ont. 16J 5E4. Works: Oakville, St. Thomas, Windsor, Niagara Falls, Ont. 20,000 employees. 335,797 cars produced in 1978.

FORD MOTOR COMPANY OF SOUTH AFRICA — South Africa

Established in 1923. Now among the leaders in South African motor industry. Managing Director: D.B. Pitt. Directors: T.D. Bucknall, N.G. Cohen, J.C. Dill, F.H. Ferreira, S.D. Lockwood, D.M. Morris, W.F. Rautenbach, G. Simpson, W.H. Smith. Head office and press office: 55 Albany Rd, Port Elizabeth, 6001. Works: Neave Township, Struandale, Deal Party (Port Elizabeth). 5,236 employees. 35,976 cars produced in 1978. Company competes in rallying and the "works" Escorts were champions in 1977 and 1978.

FORD WERKE AG — Germany (Federal Republic)

Founded in 1925. Owned by Ford Motor Company USA. Chairman and Managing Director; P. Weiher. Directors: P.A. Guckel, H. Dederichs, H.W. Gäb, H.J. Lehmann, W. Inden, W. Ebers, A. Langer, D. Uilsperger. Head office and press office: Ottoplaz 2 Köln-Deutz. Works: Henry Ford-Strasse 1, Köln-Niehl, Saarlouis. 58,247 employees. 847,275 cars produced in 1978. Most important models: Köln 1 l, Rheinland 3 l (1933); Eifel 1.2 l (1935); Taunus (1938); Taunus (since 1948); 12M (1952); 15M (1955); 17M (1960); 12M (1962); 17M and 20M (1964); 12M and 15M (1966); 17M, 20M and 20M and 20M 2.3 l (1967); Escort (1968); Capri (1969); Taunus (1970); Consul, Granada (1972); Capri II (1974); Escort (1975); Fiesta (1976); Granada (1978). Winner of East African Safari in 1969. European Saloon Car Championship 1971, 1972, 1974.

MANUFACTURE AND ASSEMBLY IN OTHER COUNTRIES — **Belgium:** Ford Werke AG Fabrieken (subsidiary), Genk, **South Africa:** Ford Motor Co. of South Africa Pty (associated company), P.O.B. 788, Port Elizabeth (assem. Granada). **Taiwan:** Ford Lio Ho Motors Co. Ltd, Taipel (assem. Granada). 3,975 cars assembled outside F.R. in 1977 (South Africa and Taiwan).

FUJI HEAVY INDUSTRIES Ltd — Japan

(Make: Subaru)

A part of former Nakajima Aircraft Co. Reorganized after the end of World War II and named Fuji Sangyo Co. In August 1945. Disbanded and divided into 12 smaller companies by order of occupying Allied Forces in 1950. Five of smaller companies reunited as Fuji Heavy Industries Ltd in 1953. Manufacturer of cars and commercial vehicles, aircraft and industrial power units. Joined Nissan Group in 1968. Member of Nissan Group. Chairman: E. Ohhara. President: S. Sasaki. Executive Vice President: N. Sakata. Senior Managing Directors: S. Nagashima, S. Irie. Managing Directors: K. Kawabata, K. Ogawa. I. Shibuya. Y. Suzuki, H. Yamamoto. Head office and press office: 1-7-2 Subaru Bldg, Nishi-Shinjuku, Shinjuku-ku, Tokyo. Works: Gumma, 10-1 Higashi Hon-cho, Ohta City; Mitaka, 3-9-6 Oshawa, Mitakashi. 13,219 employees. 242,236 vehicles produced in 1978. Most important models: 360 Sedan (1958); 1000 (1966); 1000 Sport (1967); 1300 G, R2 (1970); Leone (1971).

GAZ - GORKOVSKI AVTOMOBILNY ZAVOD — USSR

(Make: Volga)

Press office: Avtoexport, Ul. Volkhonka 14, Moscow 119902. Works: Gorki. About 94,000 cars produced in 1978.

GENERAL MOTORS CORPORATION — USA

(Makes: Buick, Cadillac, Chevrolet, Oldsmobile, Pontiac)

Founded in 1908, is largest motor manufacturer in world with production range extending from the most economical and popular cars to the most costly. Chairman: T.A. Murphy. President: E.M. Estes. Executive Vice-Presidents: J.F. McDonald, R.R. Jensen, H.H. Kehrl, R.B. Smith. GM has brought together five American motor manufacting factories, transforming them into following divisions: Buick Motor Division (902 East Hamilton Ave, Flint, Mich. 48550), General Manager D.H. McPherson, 20,300 employees, 811,837 cars produced in 1978; Cadillac Motor Car Division (2860 Clark Ave, Detroit, Mich. 48232), General Manager E.C. Kennard, 12,000 employees, 351,122 cars produced in 1978; Chevrolet Motor Division (3044 West Grand Blvd, Detroit, Mich. 48202), General Manager R.D. Lund, 105,000 employees, 2,348,320 cars produced in 1978; Oldsmobile Division (920 Townsend St, Lansing, Mich. 48921), General Manager R.J. Cook, 19,000 employees, 911,138 cars produced in 1978; Pontiac Motor Division (One Pontiac Plaza, Pontiac, Mich. 48053), General Manager R.C. Stempel, 18,850 employees, 869,263 cars produced in 1978. GM also owns General Motors - Holden's Pty Ltd (Australia), Adam Opel AG (Germany) and Vauxhall Motors Ltd (Great Britain). Head office: 3044 West Grand Blvd, Detroit, Mich. 48202.

MANUFACTURE AND ASSEMBLY IN OTHER COUNTRIES (excluding: non-American GM makes) — **Belgium:** GM Continental (subsidiary), 75 Norderlaan, Antwerp (assem. imported vehicles). **Brazil:** GM do Brasil S.A. (subsidiary), Avda Golas 1805, Rio de Janeiro (manuf. Chevrolet Chevette, Opala). **Chile:** GM Chile S.A. (subsidiary), Piloto Lazo 99, P.O.B. 14370, Santiago (assem. imported vehicles). **Iran:** GM Joran Ltd (associated company), P.O. Box 8-6173, Teheran (manuf. Chevrolet Royale). **Kenya:** GM Kenya Ltd (associated company), P.O.B. 30527, Nairobi (assem. imported vehicles). **Malaysia:** GM Malaysia SDN.BHD (subsidiary), Batu Dua, Jalan Tampoi. P.O. Box 204, Johone Bahru (manuf. Harimau). **Mexico:** G.M. de Mexico S.A. de C.V. (subsidiary), Av. Ejercito Nacional 843, Mexico 59F (manuf. Chevrolet). **New Zealand:** GM New Zealand Ltd, (subsidiary), Trentham Assembly Plant,Alexander Rd Upper Hutt (assem. imported vehicles). **Philippines:** GM Philippines Inc. (subsidiary), P.O. Box 1497 MCC, Makati, Rizal 311 (manuf. BTV vehicles). **Portugal:** GM de Portugal Ltda (subsidiary), Av. Marechal Gomes da Costa 3, Lisbon 6 (assem imported vehicles). **South Africa:** GM South African (Pty) Lt (subsidiary), Kempston Rd, P.O.B. 1137,Port Elizabeth (manuf Chevrolet; assem. imported vehicles). **Thailand:** Bangchar General Assembly Co. Ltd (associated company), 4th Floor Cathay Trust Bldg, 1016 Rama IV Rd, Bangkok (assem. imported vehicles). **Uruguay:** GM Uruguaya S.A. (subsidiary), Av Sayago 1385, Montevideo (assem. imported vehicles). **Venezuela:** GM de Venezuela C.A. (subsidiary), Carapa, Carretera de Antimano, Caracas (assem. imported vehicles). **Zaire:** GM Zaire S.E.R.L. (subsidiary), Blvd Patrice Lumumba, Kinshas (assem. imported vehicles). 1,751,260 cars produced outside USA in 1978.

GENERAL MOTORS DO BRASIL — Brazi

(Make: Chevrolet)

Subsidiary of GM Corporation. Manging Director: J.J. Sanchez Head office, press office and works: Avda Goiás 1805, São Caetano do Sul, São Paulo. 18,488 employees. 165,000 car produced in 1978.

GENERAL MOTORS - HOLDENS Pty Ltd — Australi

Established in 1931 as result of merger between Genera Motors (Australia) Pty Ltd and Holden's Motor Body Builder Ltd Affiliate of GM Corp. USA. Managing Director: C. Chapman Head office and press office: 241 Salmon St, Fishermans Bend Melbourne, Victoria. Works: as above; Dandenong, Victoria Woodville, Elizabeth, S. Australia; Pagewood, N.S.W., Acaci Ridge, Queensland. 21,234 employees. 157,333 cars produce in 1978.

ASSEMBLY IN OTHER COUNTRIES — **New Zealand:** GM New Zealand Ltd, Trentham Plant No. 1, 1, Private Bag, Upper Hu (assem. Sedan, Premier). **South Africa:** GM South Africa (Pty) Ltd, Kempston Rd, Port Elizabeth (assem. Sedan).

GENERAL MOTORS OF CANADA Ltd — Canad

(Makes: Chevrolet, Pontiac)

Established in 1918 as result of merger between McLaughli Motor Car Company and Chevrolet Motor Car Company. It is wholly owned subsidiary of General Motors Corp. President an General Manager: F.A. Smith. Vice-President and Genera Manufacturing Manager: R.C. Walter. Vice-President and General Sales Manager: R.M. Colcomb. Vice-President and Finance Manager: W.R. Waugh. Vice-President and Genera Manager, Diesel Division: A. Grant Warner. Head office an press office: 215 William St, Oshawa, Ontario L1G IKZ. Works as above; Ste. Therese, P.Q., St. Catharines, London, Windso and Scarborough. 43,441 employees. 500,014 cars produced i 1978.

GENERAL MOTORS SOUTH AFRICAN (Pty) Ltd — South Afric

(Make: Chevrolet)

Founded in 1926. Managing Director: L.H. Wilking. Directors D.B. Sneesby, J.L. Fry, W.F. Kohl, H.D. Carr, J.B. Watson, R.J Ironside, D. Martin, Jr. Head office and press office: Kempsto Rd, Port Elizabeth. Works: as above; Aloes (Engine Plant), n Port Elizabeth, 3,583 employees. 17,920 cars produced i 1978.

GIANNINI AUTOMOBILI S.p.A. — Ital

Founded in 1920 as F.lli Giannini A. & D., it later becam Giannini Automobili S.p.A. President and Managing Director: V Polverelli. Head office, press office and works: v. Idrovore dell Magliana 57, Rome. 35 employees. About 1,500 cars produce in 1978. Most important models: 750 Berlinetta San Rem (1949); Fiat 750 TV and 850 GT (1963); 850 Coupé Gazzella Fiat 500 TV and 850 GT (1963); 850 Coupé Gazzella, Fiat 50 TV and TVS, 590 GT and GTS (1964); Fiat Berlina 850 S, 85 SL and 950, Fiat Coupé 850 and 1000, Fiat 1300 Super an 1500 GL, Fiat 500 TVS Montecarlo (1965); Fiat 650 NP, 12 NPS (1970); 650 NPL, 650 NP Modena, 128 NP-S, 128 N Rally (1971). It is engaged above all in producing variations c Fiat cars. Entries in various competitions and first places i category in various Italian championships.

GINETTA CARS Ltd — Great Britai

Founded in 1958. Chairman and Managing Director: K.R. Walklett. Directors: T.G. Walklett, D.J. Walklett, I.A. Walklett. Hea office, press office and works: West End Works, Witham, Esse GMB 1BE. 22 employees. 54 cars produced in 1978. Mos important model: G 21.

G.P. CONCESSIONAIRES Ltd — Great Britain

Head office, press office and works: Worton Hall, Worton Rd, Isleworth, Middlesex.

GROUP LOTUS CARS COMPANIES Ltd — Great Britain

Founded in 1952. Chairman: A.C.B. Chapman. Group Board: A.C.B. Chapman, F.R. Bushell, P.R. Kirwan-Taylor. Managing Director: M.J. Kimberley. Sales Director: R.G. Putnam. Head office, press office and works: Norwich, NR14 8EZ. 550 employees. 1,200 cars produced in 1978. Most important models: Mk Six (1952); Mk Eight, Mk Nine, Mk Ten, Elite (1957); Eleven (1960); Elan (1962); Cortina (1963); Elan + 2 (1967); Europa (1968); Elan Sprint, Elan + 2 'S' 130, Europa Twin Cam (1971); Europa Special (1972). Entries and first places in numerous international competitions with F1, F2, F3, F5 cars; seven F1 World Champion Constructors victories in last 10 years (Indianapolis, Le Mans, Monte Carlo GP, Pacific GP at Laguna Seca, etc.). May 1975 Elite design won European Don Safety Trophy.

GURGEL S.A. INDÚSTRIA E COMÉRCIO DE VEICULOS — Brazil

Chairman and President Director: J.A.C. do Amaral Gurgel. Head office and works: Rod. Washington Luiz, km 171, 13500 Rio Claro, S.P. Press office: Avda do Cursino 2400 Jardim de Saude, 04132 São Paulo. 300 employees. 1,708 cars produced in 1978.

HAUTE PERFORMANCE MORGES — Switzerland

(Make: Felber)

Founded in 1975. Proprietor: W.H. Felber. Special versions of high-class cars in small series. 42 cars produced in 1978. Head office, press office and works: route Suisse, Morges.

HINDUSTAN MOTORS Ltd — India

Founded in 1942. Chairman: B.M. Birla. Vice-Chairman: G.P. Birla. Directors: R.N. Mafatlal, B.P. Khaitan, G.D. Kothari, M.R. Damle, N.L. Hingorani, A.F. Couto, M.V. Arunchalam. Head office and press office: Birla Bldg, 9/1 R.N. Mukherjee Rd, Calcutta 1. Works: P.O. Hind Motor, Hooghly, West Bengal. Car production begun in 1951. About 16,000 employees. 28,000 cars produced in 1979. Most important models: Hindustan 10, Hindustan 14, Baby Hindustan, Landmaster (1954); Ambassador (1957); Ambassador Mk II (1963); Ambassador Mark III (1975); Ambassador MK IV (1979).

HOLDEN - see GENERAL MOTORS - HOLDEN'S Pty Ltd

HONDA MOTOR COMPANY Ltd — Japan

Founded in 1949 as Honda Giytsu Kenkunjo. Present title since 1948. Manufacturer and exporter of motorcycles from 50 to 750 cc, automobiles, trucks, portable generators, general-purpose engines, power tillers, water pumps and outbord motors. President: K. Kawashima. Executive Vice-Presidents: H. Sugiura, S. Shinomiya, M. Nishida. Senior Managing Directors: T. Kume, K. Yoshizawa, N. Okamura, M. Suzuki. Directors and advisors: S. Honda (founder), T. Fujisawa (cofounder). Head office and press office: 6-27-8 Jingumae, Shibuyaku, Tokyo, Japan 150. Works: Saitama, 8-1 Honcho, Wako-shi, Saitama-ken; Suzuka, 1907 Mirata-cho, Suzuka-shi, Mie-ken; Hamamatsu, 34 Oi-machi, Hamamatsushi, Shizuoka-ken; Sayama, 1-10 Shin-sayama, Sayama-shi, Saltama-ken. 20,949 employees. 659,131 vehicles produced in 1978. Models: Sports 500 (1962); Sports 800 (1964); L 700, L 800 (1966); N360, LN360 (1967); N600 (1968); 1300 (1969); 1300 Coupé, NIII Sedan, Z Coupé (1970); Life (1971); Civic (1972); Civic CVCC 4-dr. Sedan (1973); Accord (1976). Wins in F1 racings: Mexican GP (1965), Italian GP (1967). French GP and GP USA (1968) and entries in F1, F2, GP racings.

MANUFACTURE AND ASSEMBLY IN OTHER COUNTRIES — **Costa Rica:** FACO (affiliated company), Anexo Aeroplierto, Jan St. Maria, Acajufla. **Indonesia:** P.T. Prospect Motor (associated company), Jt. Jossubarso, P.O.B. TPK 31, Djakarta. **Malaysia:** Kah Motor (associated company), 24-C Farqumar St, Penang. **New Zealand:** N.Z.M.C. (associated company), 89 Courtney Place, Wellington. **Portugal:** Santomar S.A. (associated company). Av. Casal Ribeiro, 46-C, Lisbon. **Taiwan:** San Yang Industries Co. Ltd (joint venture), No. 124 Hsing-Ning Rd, Peelhu, Taipei. 14,060 cars produced outside Japan in 1977.

HONGQI — China (People's Republic)

Public Relations Office: China National Machinery Import & Export Corp., P.O.B. 49, Peking. Works: Chang-Chun, Kirin.

HYUNDAI MOTOR COMPANY — Korea

Founded in 1967. President: Jung. Se Young. Vice-President: Yun, Joo Won/Lee, Yang Sup. Managing Director: Chon Song Won. Director: Shin Hang Soo. Head office and press office: 140-2, Ke-Dong, Jongro-Ku, Seoul. Works: 700, Yangjung-Dong Ulsan. 12,000 employees. 103,000 cars produced in 1979. Most important models: Ford Cortina (1969); Pony Sedan (1976).

INTERNATIONAL HARVESTER INTERNATIONAL TRUCKS — USA

Founded in 1902. Principal products trucks, agricultural equipment, construction equipment and gas turbine engines sold in 168 countries. Chairman Executive Commettee: B. McCormik. Chairman and Chief Executive Officer: A.R. McCardell. President and Chief Operating Officer: W.J. Hayford. World Headquarters: 401 North Michigan Ave., Chicago, Illinois 60611. 95,450 employees worldwide. 150,823 vehicles produced in 1978.

MANUFACTURE IN OTHER COUNTRIES - **Philippines:** International Harvester MacLeod, Inc. (subsidiary), Manila. **United Kingdom:** Seddon Atkinson Vehicles Ltd (subsidiary), Oldham.

ISUZU MOTORS Ltd — Japan

Established in 1937 as result of merger between Ishika-Wajima motor manufacturing factory, which held Wolseley manufacturing licence from 1918 to 1927, and Tokyo Gas & Electric, which began the manufacture of military trucks in 1916. Present title since 1949. In 1971, it became a joint venture company with G.M. Corp. with capital participation of 34.2% by the latter. Chairman: T. Aramaki. President: T. Okamoto. Executive Vice-Presidents: I. Uesugi, Y. Shimuzu, H.V. Leonard Jr., T. Tsunoka. Senior Managing Directors: I. Iseki, K. Okumura, T. Ohishi, S. Hirose, T. Konishi, K. Sano. Head office and press office: 22-10 Minami-oi, 6-chome, Shinagawa-ku, Tokyo. Works: Kawasaki, 25-1 Tonomachi 3-chome, Kawasaki City; Fujisawa, 8 Tsuchitana, Fujisawa City. 12,856 employees. 101,123 cars produced in 1978. Most important models: Bellett (1962); Bellett, Bellett Standard (1963); Florian (1967); 117 Coupé (1968); Bellett Gemini (1974).

JAGUAR - see BL Ltd

JEEP - see AMERICAN MOTORS CORPORATION

JOHN BRITTEN GARAGES Ltd — Great Britain

(Make: Arkley)

Founded in 1971. Proprietor: J. Britten. Head office, press office and works: Barnet Rd, Arkley, Barnet, Herts. 8 employees. 20 cars produced in 1978.

JOHNARD VINTAGE CAR REPAIRS Ltd — Great Britain

Specializes in the repair of vintage cars. Car production on limited scale started in January 1976. Directors: J.R. Guppy, D.S. Beck, A.C.A. Head office, press office and works: Blandford Heights, Shaftesbury Lane, Blandford Forum, Dorset. 8 employees. 7 cars produced in 1978.

KELMARK ENGINEERING Inc. — USA

Established in 1969. President: R. Markham. Vice-President: R. Holmes. General Manager: J. Morrison. Head office: 2209 Jolly Rd. Okemos, Mich. 48864. Press office: Kelmark Promotions, P.O. Box K, Okemos, Mich. 48864. Works: Holt, Mich. 27 employees. 250 cars produced in 1978. First GT produced in 1974.

KIA INDUSTRIAL COMPANY Ltd — Korea

Founded in 1944 as bicycle manufacturer, it became a public company in 1973 and production of passenger cars began in 1974. Chairman: Kim, Sang Moon. President: Kim, Myung Kee. Executive Managing Director: Kim, Joon Whan Hong, Bok Ryul. Head office: 8, Yang-dong, Choong-ku, Seoul. Press office: C.P.O.B. 833, Planning and Controlling Division, Seoul. Works: 781-1, Soha-ri, Soha-eup, Shiheung-kun, Kyung Kee-do. 5,000 employees. 16,539 cars produced in 1978. Models: Brisa 1000 (1974); Brisa 1300 (1976).

K.M.B. AUTOSPORTS Ltd — Great Britain

Directors: M.R. Smith, M.A. Fenton, P.W. Jelley. Head office: Finedon, Northants. Press office and works: 228-230 Mill Rd, Wellingborough, Northants.

LAFER S.A. INDUSTRIA E COMERCIO — Brazil

Lafer S.A. Industria e Comercio is a Brazilian corporation controlled by the Lafer brothers, Samuel, Oscar and Percival. In October of 1972 entered the replicar field with the classic 1952 MG TD. A prototype appeared at the 1972 Brazilian Auto Show. Head office and press office: 01519 Rua Lavapés 6, São Paulo. Works: Rua Garcia Lorca 301, Vila Paulicéia, 09700 - São Bernardo do Campo, São Paulo. 152 employees. 650 cars produced in 1978.

LAMBORGHINI - see AUTOMOBILI FERRUCCIO LAMBORGHINI S.p.A.

LANCIA — Italy

Founded in 1906, noted for production of extremely well-finished prestige cars. In 1969 taken over by the Fiat Group and in 1978 incorporated into Fiat Auto S.p.A. Head office and press office: v. Vincenzo Lancia 27, Turin. Works: as above; v. Caluso 50, Chivasso (Turin); Strada comunale, Verone (Vercelli). About 13,000 employees. 52,400 cars produced in 1979. Most important models: first car 14 hp (1907); Alfa, Dialfa (1908); Beta (1909); Gamma (1910); Delta, Didelta, Epsilon, Eta (1911); Theta (1913); Kappa (1919); Dikappa (1921); Trikappa (1922); Lambda (1923); Dilambda (1928); Artena, Astura (1931); Augusta (1933); Aprilia (1937); Ardea (1939); Aurelia (1950); Aurelia B20 (1951); Appia (1953); Flaminia (1957); Flavia (1960); Flavia Coupé and Convertible (1962); Flavia Sport, Fulvia (1963); Fulvia Coupé, Fulvia Sport (1965); Fulvia Coupé 1.3 HF (1966); Flavia 819 (1967); Fulvia Coupé 1.6 HF (1968); Flavia 2000 (1970); 2000 Berlina, 2000 Coupé (1971); Beta Berlina (1972); Beta Coupé (1973); Stratos (1974); Beta Spider, Beta HPE, Beta Monte Carlo (1975); Gamma Berlina, Gamma Coupé (1976).

ASSEMBLY IN OTHER COUNTRIES — **South Africa:** Trans-African Continental Motors Co. Pty Ltd (concessionaire), 174 Anderson St, Johannesburg (assem. Beta Coupé). **Thailand:** Yontrakit Motor Co., 12-14 Rong Huand Soi 5 Rd, Bangkok (assem. Beta Berlina, Beta Coupé).

LAWIL S.p.A. — Italy

Founded in 1969. President: C. Lavezzari. Director: M. Calvi. Head office, press office and works: v. Maretti 29, Varzi (Pavia). 50 employees. About 1200 cars produced in 1978.

LEDL GmbH — Austria

Founded in 1973. Proprietor: G. Ledl. Head office, press office and works: Pottendorfer Str. 73, A-2523 Tattendorf. 36 employees. 152 cars produced in 1978. Most important models: Europa 2001 (1974); Tanga (1978).

LENHAM MOTOR COMPANY — Great Britain

Founded in 1962. Incorporating Lenham Sports Car Ltd and The Vintage & Sports Cars Ltd. Directors: J.K. Booty, P.J. Rix, G. Allfrey. Head office, press office and works: 47 West St, Harrietsham 570, Kent ME17 1HX. 15 employees. 10 cars produced in 1978. Championship 1600 cc GT cars in 1968.

LEYLAND MOTOR CORPORATION OF AUSTRALIA — Australia

Founded in 1946 as Nuffield (Australia) Pty Ltd, in 1954 it became British Motor Corporation (BMC). In 1972 it launched fully-manufactured P. 76 but manufacture ended in December 1974. Corporation now assembles Mini-Moke for worldwide markets, also assembling trucks, Land Rover, Range Rover, buses and coaches. Managing Director: R.J. Hancock. Directors: J. Heaven, J. Lamb, J. Wallis, K. Myles. Head office: Church & Heathcote Rds, Moorebank, NSW. Press office: 332 Oxford Street, Bondi Junction, NSW. Works: 142 Cosgrove Rd, Enfield, NSW. 2,700 employees. 2,150 cars produced in 1978.

LINCOLN - see FORD MOTOR COMPANY

LOTUS - see GROUP LOTUS CARS COMPANIES Ltd

(THE) LYNX COMPANY — Great Britain

It is a company formed to produce prototypes and low volume specialist performance cars. It offers a unique service since it has a direct involvment in all aspects of motor car design and development by working alongside its associated company. Lynx Engineering, which specializes in the restoration and development of performance cars concentrating mainly on Jaguars. Head office and works: Stantion Rd, Northiam, Nr. Rye, Sussex TN31 6QT. Press office and sales: Lynx Motor

Sales Ltd, 21, Lexham News, London WS. 15 employees. 30 kits and 20 complete cars produced in 1978.

MARQUEZ INDUSTRIA E COMERCIO DE VEICULOS Ltda — **Brazil**

Head office, press office and works: rua Dr. Fernando Costa, 1048 Cubatão, SP.

MASERATI - see OFFICINE ALFIERI MASERATI S.p.A.

MAZDA - see TOYO KOGYO COMPANY Ltd

MERCEDES-BENZ - see DAIMLER-BENZ AG

MERCURY - see FORD MOTOR COMPANY and FORD MOTOR COMPANY OF CANADA Ltd

MG - see BL Ltd

MINI - see BL Ltd

MITSUBISHI MOTOR CORPORATION — **Japan**

Established in October 1917 as Mitsubishi Shipbuilding & Engineering Co. Ltd, later changed its name to Mitsubishi Heavy Industries Ltd. After the Second World War it split into three companies under Enterprise Reorganization Law, but these again reunited in June 1964 as Mitsubishi Heavy Industries Ltd. Products include ships and other vessels, railway vehicles, aircraft, space equipment, missiles, atomic equipment, heavy machinery. The Automobile Division became an independent company in June 1970 under name of Mitsubushi Motor Corp. In May 1971 it became a joint venture company with Chrysler Corp. (USA), with Mitsubishi holding 65% and Chrysler 35% of shares. Chairman: T. Kubo. President: Y. Sone. Executive Vice Presidents: K. Sugiura, Y. Mochida. Senior Managing Directors: H. Iwasaki, N. Ichikawa, S. Arai, M. Mizuno, K. Kobayashi, S. Kobayashi, I. Nishina, K. Samema. Head office and press office: No. 33-8 Shiba 5-chome, Minatoku, Tokyo. Works: Mizushima, No. 1, 1-chome, Mizushima, Kalgandori, Kurashiki, Okoyama-Pref.; Nagaya, No. 2, Oyecho, Minato-ku, Nagoya. 22,000 employees. 677,275 cars produced in 1978.

MONTEVERDI - see AUTOMOBILES MONTEVERDI Ltd

MORGAN MOTOR COMPANY Ltd — **Great Britain**

Founded in 1910. Managing Director: P.H.G. Morgan. Head office, press office and works: Pickersleigh Rd, Malvern Link, Worcs. WR14 2LL. Production of 4-wheeled vehicles begun in 1936. 110 employees. 432 cars produced in 1978. Most important models: Morgan 4/4, Morgan Plus 8. Entries and wins in numerous competitions since 1911.

MORRIS - see BL Ltd

NISSAN MOTOR COMPANY Ltd — **Japan**

(Makes: Datsun, Nissan)

Founded in 1933 under the name of Jidosha Seizo Co. Ltd. Present title since 1934. In 1966 it took over Price Motors Ltd. Chairman: K. Kawamata. Vice-Chairman: T. Iwakoshi. President: T. Ishihara. Executive Vice-Presidents: M. Ohkuma, H. Takahashi. Senior Managing Directors: R. Yamazaki, K. Tanaka, T. Hara, Y. Yokoyama, S. Utsuno, K. Kanao. Head office and press office: Ginza, Chuo-ku, Tokyo. Works: Mitaka, 8-1, 5-chome, Shimo-Renjaku, Mitaka, Tokyo; Murayama, 6000 Nakafuji, Musashi-Murayama, Kitatama-gun, Tokyo; Agikubo, 5-1, 3-chome, Momoi, Suginami-ku, Tokyo; Oppama, 1, Natsushima-Cho, Yokosuka; Tochigi, 2500, Kaminokawa, Tochigi-ken; Yokohama 2, Takara-cho, Kanagawaku, Yokohama; Yoshiwara, 1-1, Takara-cho, Yoshiwara Fuji, Shizuoka-ken; Zama, 5070, Nagakubo, Zama, Kanagawa-Ken. 56,400 employees. 1,935,868 cars produced in 1978. Most important models: Cedric (1960); Sunny, Gloria (1962); President (1965); Datsun, Nissan Prince Royal (1966); Datsun Bluebird 510 (1967); Laurel (1968); Datsun 240-Z, Nissan Skyline (1969); Cherry (1970); Datsun Bluebird U (1972); Violet Auster, Stanza, Pulsar, Fairlady (1977). First places in Round Australia Rally (1958); East African Safari Rally and Kenya Rally (1966); Shell 4000 Canada Rally (1967-68); South Africa's Moonlight Rally and Beira Rally (1967); Zacateca Race, Malaysian Race, Aussie Race, Southern Cross Rally (1968); South African Castrol 2000 Rally, East African Safari Rally (1969-71).

MANUFACTURE AND ASSEMBLY IN OTHER COUNTRIES — **Australia:** Nissan Motor Manufacturing Co. (Australia) Ltd (subsidiary), Center Rd, Clayton, Victoria 3168. **Costa Rica:** Agencia Datsun S.A. (associated company), Apdo Postal 3219, San José; Motorcentro S.A. (associated company), Apdo 10046, San José. **Ghana:** Japan Motor Trading Co. Ltd (associated company), P.O.B. 5216, Accra. **Indonesia:** P.T. Indokaya Nissan Motors (associated company), 37-38 Jalan Ir. H. Huanda, Djakarta. **Ireland:** Datsun Ltd (associated company), Datsun House, P.O.B. 910, Naas Rd, Dublin 12. **Malaysia:** Tan Chong Motor Assemblies Sdn Bhd (affiliated company), Jalan Segambut, Kuala Lumpur. **Mexico:** Nissan Mexicana S.A. de C.V. (joint venture), Avda. Insurgentes Sur No. 1457, Piso del 1° al 5°, Mexico City 19. **New Zealand:** Nissan Motor Distributors (N.Z.) 1975 Ltd (joint venture), P.O.B. 61133, Otara, Auckland. **Nicaragua:** Distribudora Datsun S.A. (associated company), P.O.B. 3680, Managua. **Peru:** Nissan Motor del Perú S.A. (joint venture), P.O.B. 4265, Lima. **Philippines:** Universal Motor Corp. (associated company) 2232-34, Pason Tamo Ave., Makati, Rizal. **Portugal:** Entreposto Commercial de Automoveis S.a.r.l. (associated company), Av. Eng. Duarte Pacheco, 21-A, Lisbon. **Singapore:** Singapore Nissan Motor (Private) Ltd (affiliated company), 9 Jalan Pesawat, Jurong Town, Singapore-22. **South-Africa:** Datsun-Nissan Investment Co. Ltd (associated company), P.O.B. 10, Rosslyn, Pretoria, Transvaal. **Taiwan:** Yue Loong Motor Co. Ltd (associated company), 9th floor, 150 Nanking East Rd, Section 2, Taipel. **Thailand:** Siam Motors & Nissan Co. Ltd (associated company) 865, Rama I Rd, Bangkok. **Trinidad Tobago:** Neal & Massy Ltd (associated company), P.O.B. 1298, Port-of-Spain. **Venezuela:** Ensambladora Carabobo C.A. (associated company), Apdo 754, Valencia, E.do Carabobo. 224,020 vehicles produced outside Japan in 1977.

NOVA CARS Ltd — **Great Britain**

Original company founded in 1971, assumed present title in 1978. Chairman and Managing Director. V. Elam. Director: A. Elam. Head office and press office: Hill Top Garage Brighouse and Denholme Road Mountain, Queensbury, Bradford, W Yorks. Works: Nova House, Huddersfield Rd, Ravensthorpe Dawsbury, Yorks. BD.13.INA. 14 employees. 50 cars produced in 1978.

NUOVA INNOCENTI S.p.A. — **Italy**

Founded in 1933 as Società Anonima Fratelli Innocenti became Innocenti Anonima per Applicazioni Tubolari Acciaio and Innocenti Società Generale per l'Industria Metallurgica e Meccanica S.p.A. and Innocenti S.p.A. in 1961. Taken over by BLMC in 1972 and in 1976 by GEPI and de Tomaso assuming present title. BL Ltd holds 5% of Nuova Innocenti. Production begun in May 1976. President: R. Spera. Managing Director: A. de Tomaso. General Manager: T. Pirondini. Head office and press office: v. Rubattino 37, Milan. Works: v. Pitteri 84, Milan. 2,322 employees. About 38,000 cars produced in 1978. Most important models: Innocenti Austin A40 (1960); Innocenti Morris IM-3S (1963); Innocenti Austin J4 (1964); Innocenti Mini Minor (1965); Innocenti S. Spider (1966); Innocenti Mini Cooper Mk 2 (1968); Innocenti Mini Minor Mk 3, Mini Cooper Mk 3 and J5 (1970); Innocenti Mini 1000, Mini Cooper 1300 Mk 3, Austin J5 (1972); Innocenti Mini 90, Mini 120 and Regent (1974); Innocenti Mini De Tomaso (1977).

OFFICINE ALFIERI MASERATI S.p.A. — **Italy**

Founded in 1926, it is famous for its GT and racing cars. Managing Director: A. de Tomaso. Head office, press office and works: v. Ciro Menotti 322, Modena. About 450 employees. About 400 cars produced in 1978. Most important models: A 6/1500 (1948); A6G/2000 (1954); 3500 GT (1956); 5000 GT (1958); 3500 GTI, 5000 GTI (1960); Mistral, Quattroporte (1964); Mexico, Ghibli (1966); Indy (1969); Bora (1971); Merak (1972); Khamsin (1974); Merak SS (1975); Kyalami, Merak 2000, Quattroporte (1976). Victories up to 1957 in all types of motor racing: Targa Florio (1926), Indianapolis 500 Miles (1939-40), European Mountain Championship (1956-57), World Drivers' Championship with J.M. Fangio.

OLDSMOBILE - see GENERAL MOTORS CORPORATION

OPEL - see ADAM OPEL AG

OTOSAN A.S. — **Turkey**

Founded in 1959. It is part of Koç Group-Koç Holding and produces cars with fibreglass bodywork and Ford engines. General Manager: E. Gönül. Head office, press office and works: P.K. 102, Kadikoy, Istanbul. 2,630 employees. 3,040 cars produced in 1978.

PANTHER WESTWINDS Ltd — **Great Britai**

Founded in 1971. Managing Director: R. Jankel. Deputy Managing Director: L. Jankel. Head office, press office and works Canada Rd, Byfleet, Surrey. 211 employees. 550 cars produce in 1978. Most important models: J 724 2-litre (1972); Lazer, F (1973); De Ville Saloon (1974); Rio (1975); Lima, De Vill Convertible (1976); Turbo Lima (1978).

PEKING — **China (People's Republic**

Works: Dong Fang Hong, Peking. Public Relations Office: China National Machinery Import & Export Corp., P.O.B. 49 Peking.

PEUGEOT - see AUTOMOBILES PEUGEOT S.A

PLYMOUTH - see CHRYSLER CORPORATION

POLSKI-FIAT - see FABRYKA SAMOCHODOV OSOBOWYC

PONTIAC - see GENERAL MOTORS CORPORATION an GENERAL MOTORS OF CANADA Ltd

PORSCHE - see Dr. Ing. h.c. F. PORSCHE A.G.

PORTARO - see SEMAL - SOCIEDADE ELECTRO MECANICA DE AUTOMOVEIS Lda

(THE) PREMIER AUTOMOBILES Ltd — **Indi**

Founded in 1944. Chairman: L. Hirachand. Managing Director P.N. Vencatesan. Head office and press office: Constructio House, Walchand Hirachand Marg, Ballard Estate, Bombay 400 038. Works: L.B. Shastri Marg, Kurla, Bombay - 400 070 9,090 employees. 13,500 cars produced in 1978.

PRINCESS - see BL Ltd

PUMA INDUSTRIA DE VEICULOS S.A. — **Braz**

Founded in 1964 under name of Sociedade de Automòvel Luminari Ltda. Present title since 1975. Directors: L.R. Alves d Costa, M. Mastenguim. J.M. Hellmeister. Head office, pres office and works: Av. Presidente Wilson 4385, C.P. 42649, Sã Paulo. 630 employees. 1,911 cars produced in 1978. Models Malzoni GT with DKW engine (1964-65); Puma GT with DKW engine (1966-67); Puma 1500 GT with VW engine (1968-69) Puma 1600 GTE with VW engine (1970); Puma 1600 GTE an GTS with VW engine (1971); Puma GTB 4100 with GM engin (1974); Puma GTE, GTS (1978).

QUINCY-LYNN ENTERPRISES Inc. — **US**

Head office, press office and works: 2231 West Shangri-La Rd Unit W, Phoenix, AZ 85029.

RAPPORT INTERNATIONAL Ltd — **Great Britai**

Rapport merged with Humberstone Design early in 1979. Bot companies had been successfully producing specialist vehicle and have engineered many popular vehicles based on Rang Rover. First fruit of merger is a new sports car to be launche in 1980. Chairman: I.A. Leaf. Vice-Chairman: J.C.D. Brydon Managing Director: W.G.N. Manning. General Manager: J.P Leaf. Head office: Rapport House, 1 Great Eastern St, Londo EC2A 3EJ. Press office: Blake Communications. Works: Monu ment Rd, Woking, Surrey. 40 employees. 127 cars produced i 1978.

RÉGIE NATIONALE DES USINES RENAULT — **Franc**

Founded in 1898 under the name of Société Anonyme de Usines Renault. Present title since 1945 when it was nationa ized. Acquired Automobiles Alpine S.A. in 1977. It is today th largest and most important motor manufacturer in France President and General Manager: B. Vernier-Palliez. Head offic and press office: 34 quai du Point du Jour, Boulogne Billancou 92200. Works: Pierre-Lefaucheux, Flins; Usine de Cléon Cléon: Usine du Mans, Pierre-Piffault; Usine de Choisy, Choisy le-Roy; Usine d'Orléans, St. Jean-de-la-Ruelle; Usine d Havre, Sandouville; Usine de Dreux, Dreux; Usine de Doua Douai. 108,492 employees. 1,715,430 cars produced in 197

Most important models: 1.75 CV (1898); 2 cylinder (1904); 35 CV (1912); Marne Taxi, Type AG, Type TT (1923); 45 hp (1923-27); Celtaquatre (1934); Viva Grand Sport (1938); 4 CV (1947); Fregate (1951); Dauphine (1957); Floride (1959); Floride S, Caravelle, 8 (1962); Caravelle 1100 (1963); 8 Major (1964); 16 (1965); 4 Parisienne (1966); 16 TE, 6 (1968); 12 (1969); R 5, R 15, R 17 (1971); R 16 TX (1973); R 30, R 20 (1975); R 14 (1976); R 18 (1978). Entries and wins in numerous competitions (Monte Carlo Rally, Alpine Rally, Tour de Corse, Liège-Rome-Liège, Sebring, Reims, Nürburgring, Mobil Economy Run, 24 hours of Le Mans 1978, etc.).

MANUFACTURE AND ASSEMBLY IN OTHER COUNTRIES — **Argentina:** Renault Argentine S.A. (subsidiary), Avda, Santa Maria, C.C. 8, Cordoba (manuf. 4, 6, 12). **Australia:** Renault Australia Pty Ltd (subsidiary), Dougharty Road, P.O. Box 60, West Heidelberg, Victoria (assem. 8, 10, 12, 16, 16 TS). **Belgium:** Rnur (subsidiary), 499 Schaarbeeklei, Vilvoorde 1 (assem. 4, 6, 8, 10). **Chile:** Automotores Franco Chilena (subsidiary), Casilla 10173, Los Andes (assem. 4); Corme Canica (concessionaire), Casilla 10173, Los Andes (assem. 4). **Colombia:** Sofasa (associated company), Apartado Aereo 4529, Medellin (assem. 4, 6); Socofam (associated company), Duitama, Boyaca (assem. 4, 6). **Eire:** Smith Engineering Ltd (subsidiary), Trinity Street, Wexford (assem. 4, 6, 8, 10, 12, 16). **Greece:** Soheca (concessionaire), Athens 126. **Indonesia:** Gaya Motors (concessionaire), Jalan c Aphd, P.O Box 2126 DKT, Djakarta Fair, Djakarta. **Iran:** Saipa (concessionaire), 553 av. Eisenhower, Teheran. **Ivory Coast:** Safar (subsidiary), B.P. 2764, Abidjan (assem. 4, 5, 6, 10, 12, 16, 16 TS). **Madagascar:** Somacoa (associated company), Route de Majunga, B.P. 796, Tananarive (assem. 4, 6, 12, 16, 16 TS). **Malaysia:** Champion Motors Sdn Bhd, Jalan Usaha, Shah Alam Selangor, P.O Box 814, Kuala Lumpur (assem. 10, 16). **Mexico:** Diesel Association (concessionaire), Ciudad Sahagun, Hidalgo (assem. 4, 5, 10). **Morocco:** Somaca, km 12 Autoroute de Rabat, Casablanca (assem. 4, 6, 8, 12, 16, 16 TS). **New Zealand:** Campbell Industries Ltd (concessionaire), Jellicoe Crescent, P.O. Box 84, Thames (assem. 10, 12). **Philippines:** Renault Philippines (subsidiary), P.O. Box 1011, Makati, Rizal (assem. 4, 6, 8, 10, 12, 16, 16 TS). **Portugal:** Industrias Lusitanas Renault (associated company), Fabrica de Guarda, Guarda Gare (assem. 4, 6, 8, 10, 12, 16, 16 TS). **Romania:** Intreprinderea de Autoturisme de Pitesti (concessionaire), Casuta Postala I.A.P., Ju de tul Argès, Colibasi (assem. 8, Dacia 1300). **Singapore:** Associated Motors Industries (concessionaire), Taman Jurong, P.O.B. 19, Singapore 22 (assem. 10, 12). **South Africa:** Motors Assemblies Ltd (associated company), P.O. Box 12030, Jacobs, Durban (assem. 4, 6, 10, 12, 16 TS). **Spain:** Fasa-Renault S.A. (subsidiary), Apartado 262, Autopista de Francia, Madrid (assem. 4, 6, 8, 12). **Trinidad:** Amalgamated Industries Ltd, Tumpuna Road, Arima Trinidad, Port of Spain (assem. 10, 12, 16). **Tunisia:** Stia (associated company), Route de Monastir, Sousse (assem. 4). **Turkey:** Oyak Renault (associated company), Zone Industrielle, P.K. 255, Bursa (assem. 12). **Uruguay:** Automotores, Cerro Largo 888, Santa Rosa, Montevideo (assem. 10, 12, 16). **Venezuela:** Cvvca (associated company), Edificio Gran Avenida Piso 4, Apartado del Este 61033, Caracas (assem. 10, 12, 16); Cvvca (associated company), Edo Carabobo, Mariara (assem. 10, 12, 16). **Yugoslavia:** Industrija Motornih Vozil (concessionaire), B.P. 60, Novo Mesto (assem. 4, 6, 8, 10, 12, 16).

(THE) RELIANT MOTOR COMPANY Ltd — Great Britain

Founded in 1934 under the name of Reliant Engineering Co. (Tamworth) Ltd. Present title since 1962. Acquired Bond Cars Ltd in 1969. Chairman: J.F. Nash. Managing Director: R.L. Spencer. Directors: C. Burton, I. J. Jardine, M.E. Smith. Head office and works: Two Gates, Tamworth, Staffs. Public Relations Agents: W. Laing, Halton House, 20/23 Holborn, London, EC19 2JD. 1.000 employees. About 8,000 vehicles produced in 1978. Most important models: firts sports car Sabre (1960); Sabre 6 (1961); Regal 3/25 (1962); Scimitar GT, Rebel 700 (1964); Rebel 700 Estate (1967); Scimitar GTE (1968); Scimitar GTE Automatic, Kitten Saloon/Estate (1975); New Scimitar GTE Overdrive/Automatic (1976), Bond Bug (1970); Robin Saloon/Estate and Van (1973), all with glass fibre bodywork. Entries from 1962-64 in numerous competitions (Tulip Rally, RAC Rally of Great Britain, Monte Carlo Rally, Circuit of Ireland, Alpine Rally, Spa-Sofia-Liége Rally; winners of class in Total Economy Run in 1976 and 1977 with 55.5 mpg and 57.5 mpg respectively.

MANUFACTURE IN OTHER COUNTRIES — **Greece:** Mebea SA, 58-60 Aristotelous St, Athens 103 (manuf. TW9, Robin). **Turkey:** Otosan A.S., P.O.B. 102, Kadikoy, Istanbul (manuf. Anadol).

RENAULT (France) - see RÉGIE NATIONALE DES USINES RENAULT

RENAULT ARGENTINA S.A. — Argentina

Founded in 1955 under the name of Industrias Kaiser Argentina assumed title of Ika-Renault in 1968. Present title since 1975. Head office and press office: Sarmiento 1230, Buenos Aires. Works: Camino a Pajas Blancas, km 4, Cordoba. 7,471 employees. 28,886 cars produced in 1978. Most important models: 4 (1963); Torino (1966); R6 (1970); R12 (1971); Torino GR, Torino ZX (1979).

REPLICARS Inc. — USA

Established in 1975. President: J. W. Faircloth. Head office, press office and works: 3175 Belvedere Rd, West Palm Beach, Flo. 33406. 32 employees. 134 cars produced in 1977.

ROLLS-ROYCE MOTORS Limited — Great Britain

Rolls-Royce Motors Ltd was formed in April 1971 to take over the assets of the original Rolls-Royce Ltd in the automotive field. The first Rolls-Royce car ran in 1904 and they have always specialised in the production of high class cars of great quality. Chairman: I.J. Fraser, CBE, MC. Group Managing Director: D.A.S. Plastow. Directors: L.W. Harris, G.R. Fenn, T. Neville, C.S. Aston, H. Wuttke, H.P.N. Benson. Head office and works: Crewe, Ches. Press office: 14-15 Conduit St, London W1. 9,500 employees. 3,347 cars produced in 1978. Most important models: first Rolls-Royce in 1904; Silver Ghost (1906-25); Twenty (1911); Phantom I (1925-29); Phantom II (1929-36); Phantom III (1936); Silver Wraith (1946); Phantom IV (1950); Silver Cloud I (1955); Silver Cloud II, Phantom V (1959); Silver Cloud III (1962); Silver Shadow (1965); Phantom VI (1968); Corniche (1971); Camargue (1975); Silver Shadow II (1977).

ROM CARMEL - see URDAN INDUSTRIES Ltd

ROVER - see BL Ltd

R.V. ALFONSO DMG Inc. — Philippines

(Make: Toro)

Head office, press office and works: Guevent Bldg., P.O. Box 1263, Manila.

S.A. AUTOMOBILES CITROËN — France

Founded in 1919 by André Citroën, became S.A. André Citroën in 1927 and Citroën S.A. in 1968. Present title since 1975. December 1974 38.2% of stock acquired by Automobiles Peugeot S.A. Since May 1976 Citroën S.A. is owned by the Peugeot S.A. group (to which Automobiles Peugeot S.A. belongs also). The first car launched since the merger of the two firms is the Citroën LN, presented in the summer of 1976. Directorate: X. Karcher, R. Ravenel, J. Lombard. Head office and press office: 133 quai André Citroën, Paris 15e. Works: as above; Levallois, Aulnay, Clichy, Saint-Ouen, Asnières, Gutenberg, Nanterre, Rennes-La-Barre-Thomas, Rennes-La-Janais, Caen, Froncle, Saint-Etienne, Mulhouse, Reims, Metz. About 55,500 employees. 734,400 cars produced in 1978. Most important models: Torpedo A Type (1919); B2 10 CV (1921); 5 CV (1922); B12 10 CV (1925); B14 (1926); C6 (1928); 7A, 7 and 11 CV (1934); 15 Six (1938); 2 CV (1948); 2 CV 425 cc (1954); DS 19 (1955); ID 19 (1957); 2 CV 4 x 4 (1958); Ami 6 3 CV (1961); Ami 6 Break DS Pallas (1964); DS 21 (1965); Dyane (1967); Mehari (1968); Ami 8 (1969); SM and GS (1970); CX (1974); LN (1976); Visa, LNA (1978); Mehari 4 x 4 (1978). Entries and first places in numerous competitions: World Distance and Speed Record at Montlhéry (1932-33), 28th Monte Carlo Rally and Constructors' Cup (1959), Liège-Sofia-Liège Road Marathon (1961), Norwegian Snow and Ice Winter Rally, Lyon-Charbonnière-Solitude, Alpine Trophy, Thousand Lakes Rally, Constructors' Cup, Trophy of Nations (1962), Finnish Snow Rally, Northern Roads, Lyon-Charbonnière-Solitude, Norwegian Winter Rally, International Alpine Criterium, Constructors' Cup in Monte Carlo Rally and Liège-Sofia-Liège Marathon, Tour of Corsica (1963), Spa-Sofia-Liège Marathon (1964), Rallye Neige et Glace, Mobil Economy Run, Coupe des Alpes, Monte Carlo (1966), Constructors' Cup in Morocco Rally 1969-1977); Morocco Rally, TAP Portugal (1969); Chamonix Winter Run (1970); Morocco Rally (1970-71); World Cup Wembley-Munich (1974); Senegal Car Tour and Constructors' Cup London-Sydney (1977), Morocco Rally (1969, 1970 and 1971).

MANUFACTURE AND ASSEMBLY IN OTHER COUNTRIES — **Belgium:** Société Belge des Automobiles Citroën SA (subsidiary), 7 place de l'Yser, Brussels (assem. 2CV, Mehari, LN). **Chile:** Sociedad Importadora e Industrial J. Lhorente y Cia Ltda (subsidiary), Arica lote 26, Chinthorre (2CV, Ami). **Iran:** Teheran (assem. Dyane). **Madagascar:** Société Industrielle et Commerciale des Automobiles Malgaches (concessionnaire), route de Majunga, Tananarive (assem. 2CV, Mehari). **Portugal:** Sociedad Citroën Lusitania SARL (subsidiary), estrada de Nelas, Beira Alto, Mangualde (Dyane, GS, CX). **Spain:** Citroën Hispania (subsidiary), free zone of Vigo (manuf. 2CV, Ami 8, Dyane, Mehari, GS, CX). **Yugoslavia:** Tovarna Motornich Vozil (Tomos) (concessionnaire), Koper (manuf. Dyane, GS, CX). 159,400 cars produced outside France in 1978.

SAAB-SCANIA AB — Sweden

The first Saab car was made in 1950 by the former Svenska Aeroplan Aktiebolaget. Saab cars are currently manufactured by the Saab Car Division of Saab-Scania AB which was formed in 1969 through the merger of Saab Aktiebolag and Scania-Vabis. Other Saab-Scania products include Scania commercial vehicles, Saab aircraft, missiles, avionics, electronic equipment, computers, electromedical equipment, industrial valves, measuring systems, etc. Chairman: M. Wallenberg. President: H.S. Gustafsson. Chief Executive Saab Car Division: S. Wennio. Group head office: S-581 88 Linköping. Head office and press office: Saab Car Division: S-611 81 Nyköping. Works: Trollhättan, Nyköping, Kristineham, Arlöv. 14,000 employees. 72,600 cars produced in 1978. Most important models: 92, 93 (1950-60); 95 Estate (1959-78); 96 (1960); 96 V4 (1966); 99 (1968); Sonett III (1969); 99 Combi Coupé (1973), 900 (1979). Numerous wins in international rallies including Monte Carlo (twice), RAC (5 times), Tulip Rally, Baja 1000, Swedish KAK, arctic and 1000 Lakes in Finland, etc.

MANUFACTURE IN OTHER COUNTRIES — **Finland:** Oy Saab-Valmet Ab Uusikaupunki (manuf. 99, 900). About 26,000 cars produced outside Sweden in 1978.

SBARRO - see SOCIETÉ DE FABRICATION D'AUTOMOBILES SBARRO S.a.r.l.

SCEPTRE MOTOR CAR COMPANY — USA

Founded in 1978. Associated with Liberty Manufacturing in Santa Barbara. Chairman: T.W. McBurnie. President: M. Broggie. Director: S. Fields. Head office, press office and works: 7242 Hollister Ave., Goleta Valley, Cal. 93017. 30 employees.

SEAT - SOCIEDAD ESPAÑOLA DE AUTOMOVILES DE TURISMO S.A. — Spain

Founded in 1950. President: J.M. Antoñanzas. Vice-Presidents: F. Urquijo, F. Soria. Directors: P. Vidal, J. Pañella, D. de Bernardinis. Managing Director: P. Fusaro. Head office and press office: Avda. Generalisimo 146, Madrid 16. Works: Zona Franca, Martorell, Barcellona, Landaben, Pamplona. 32.000 employees. 248,103 cars produced in 1978. Most important models: 600 (1957); 1500 (1963); 850 (1966); 124 (1968); 1430 (1969); 127 (1971); 132 (1973); 133 (1974); 131 (1975); 1200 Sport (1976); 124 Berlina, 128 3P (1977); 132 Mercedes Diesel (1978); Ritmo, Lancia Beta Coupé, HPE (1979).

SEMAL - SOCIEDADE ELECTRO MECANICA DE AUTOMOVEIS Lda — Portugal

(Make: Portaro)

Founded in 1944. Director: H.M. Pires. Head office and press office: Rua Nova de S. Mamede, 7-2°, DTO, 1296 Lisboa. Works: En 249/4, km 4,6 Trajouce-Oeiras. 331 employees. 919 cars produced in 1978. Production of Portaro began in 1974.

SHANGHAI — China (People's Republic)

Public Relation Office: China National Machinery Import & Export Corp., P.O.B. 49, Peking. Works: Shanghai.

SIMCA - see AUTOMOBILES TALBOT S.A. and AUTOMOVILES TALBOT

ŠKODA - AUTOMOBILOVÉ ZÁVODY NÁRODNI PODNIK — Czechoslovakia

Founded in 1894 by Laurin and Klement for the construction of velocipedes, assumed title of Laurin & Klement Co. Ltd in 1907, Škoda in 1925, and in 1945 became national corporation (AZNP). Director: M. Zapadlo. Commercial Deputy Director: Z. Rubin. Head office, press office and works: Trida Rudé armady, Mladá Boleslav. 15,000 employees. 157,987 cars produced in 1978. Car production begun in 1905 (2-cylinder cars). Most important models: Laurin & Klement (1905); E 4-cyl. (1907); "S"Type (1911); 100, 105, 110, 120 Type (1923); 4R, 6R (1924); 420, 422 (1934); Popular, Rapid (1935-39); 1101, 1102 (1945-51); 440 (1956); Octavia, Felicia (1958); Octavia Combi, 1202 (1962); 1000 MB (1964); 100 L, 110 L, 1203 (1969); 110 R Coupé (1970), 105, 120 (1977).

SOCIETÉ DE FABRICATION D'AUTOMOBILES SBARRO S.a.r.l. — Switzerland

Founded in 1973. Proprietor: F. Sbarro. Head office, press office and works: ACA Atelier, 1411 Les Tuileries de Grandson, Yverdon, Lausanne. 15 employees. 35 cars produced in 1978.

SPARTAN CAR COMPANY — Great Britain

First Spartan built in 1973. Designer: J. McIntyre. Head office and press office: Kirkby Lane. Works: Pinxton, Nottinghamshire, NG16 6JA. 10 employees. 250 cars produced in 1978.

Sta. MATILDE - see COMPANHIA INDUSTRIAL SANTA MATILDE Inc. Co.

STANDARD MOTOR PRODUCTS OF INDIA Ltd — **India**

The company started with the assembly of the world-famous Standard Vanguard car in collaboration with Standard Motor Co. Ltd of Coventry, England. In 1960, the company left the Vanguard field and concentrated on small cars, the Standard Ten and Herald, the modified version of which is currently being produced by the company, known as the Standard Gazel. Managing Director: C.V. Karthik Narayanan. Head office: 134 Mount Rd, Madras 600 063. Works: Perungalathur, Madras 600063. 2,000 employees. 2,143 cars produced in 1978.

STIMULA - see AUTOMOBILES STIMULA S.a.r.l.

STUTZ MOTOR CAR OF AMERICA Inc. — **USA**

Established in 1968. President and Chairman: J.D. O'Donnell. Secretary Treasurer and Director: R.L. Curotto. Head office and press office: 336 Fifth Ave., New York, N.Y. 10001. Works: Torino, Italy. 50 employees. 50 cars produced in 1978.

SUBARU - see FUJI HEAVY INDUSTRIES Ltd

SUNRISE AUTO INDUSTRIES Ltd — **India**

(Make: Badal)

Founded in 1974. Chairman: S.M.D. Shivananjappa IAS. Managing Director: S.R.K. Sipani. Technical Director: S.C. Arunachalam. Head office, press office and works: 25/26 Industrial Suburb, Second Stage, Tumkur Rd, P.O.B. 2224, Bangalore 560022. 184 employees. 325 cars produced in 1978.

SUZUKI MOTOR COMPANY Ltd — **Japan**

Founded in 1909 under the name of Suzuki Shokkuki Selkakusho. Present title since 1954. Chairman: J. Suzuki. President: O. Suzuki. Managing Directors: A. Kinoshita, S. Inagawa. Head office and press office: 300 Kamimura, Hamagun, Shizuokaken. Works: Kosai, Shirasuka 4520, Kosaishi, Suzuoka-ken; Iwata, Iwai 500; Iwata-shi, Shizouka-ken; Ohsuka, Ombuchi 6333, Omsuka-cho, Ogasagun, Shizouka-ken. 8,900 employees. 102,147 cars produced in 1978. Most important models: Suzulight 360 (1955); Suzuki Fronte 360 LC10 (1967); Fronte 500 (1968); Fronte Coupé (1971).

SYRENA - see FABRYKA SAMOCHODÓW MALOLITRAZOWYCH

TALBOT MOTOR COMPANY Ltd — **Great Britain**

Founded in 1917 as Rootes Motors Ltd. In 1967 became a member of Chrysler Group but in 1978 a controlling interest was acquired by PSA Peugeot-Citroën. Present title since January 1980. Chairman and Managing Director: G. Turnbull. Deputy Managing Director: P. Griffiths. Head office: Administrative Offices, P.O.B. 122A, Whitley, Coventry. Works: Ryton On Dunsmore and Stoke, Coventry; Talbot Scotland Ltd, Linwood, Nr. Paisley, Renfrewshire, Scotland. 21,500 employees. 230,135 cars produced in 1978.

MANUFACTURE AND ASSEMBLY IN OTHER COUNTRIES — **Iran:** I.N.I.M., P.O.B. 14/1637, km 18, Industrial Manufacturing Co. Ltd (associated company), Karadj Rd, Teheran (manuf. and assem. Hunter/Paykan). **Ireland:** Talbot Ireland Ltd (subsidiary), Shanowen Rd, Whitehall, Dublin 9 (assem. Avenger). **New Zealand:** Todd Motors Ltd LMVD (concessionaire), P.O.B. 50-349, Todd Park, Heriot Drive, Porirua (assem. Avenger, Sunbeam).

TATRA NÁRODNI PODNIK — **Czechoslovakia**

Tatra is one of oldest European motor manufacturers. In second half of 19th century de luxe coaches were begun in 1882 in Nesselsdorf. Production of railway carriages was begun in 1882 and first motor-car, called the "President", was produced in 1897. General Director: M. Kopec. Head office and press office: Koprivnice. Works: Tatra Koprivnice okres Novy Jičin. 1,500 cars produced in 1977. Most important models: President (1897); B Type (1902); E Type 12 hp (1905); K Type (1906); T 14/15 (1914); Tatra 4/12, Tatra 11 (1923); 17/31 (1926-30); Tatra 30 (1927-29); Tatra 24/30 (1930-34); Tatra 52 (1930-38); Tatra 57 (1932); Tatra 75 (1933-37); Tatra 77 (1934); Tatra 87 (1936-38); Tatraplan (1949); Tatra 603 (1957); Tatra 2-603 (1964); Tatra 613 (1975). Has been entering competitions since 1900 (Targa Florio, Leningrad-Moscow-Tbilisi-Moscow, Alpine Rally, Polsky Rally, Vltava Rally, Marathon de la Route, etc.).

TECHNICAL EXPONENTS Ltd — **Great Britain**

Founded in 1965. Proprietor and General Manager: T.P. Bennett. Head office and press office: 74 Waterford Rd, London SW6. Works: Denham Green Lane, Denham, Bucks. Most important models: TX Tripper, 1500 and 2000 Dolomite Sprint.

TIMMIS MOTOR Co. Ltd — **Canada**

Founded in 1968. Producing current model since that time. Only Canadian-owned assembly operation and only car plant in Western Canada. One of first companies in North America to build replicas. President: A.J. Timmis. Head office: 4351 Blekinsop Rd, Victoria B.C. V8X2C3. Press office and works: 409 Swift St, Victoria. 6 employees. 10 cars produced in 1978.

TOFAS - see FIAT AUTO S.p.A.

TOMORROWS CLASSIC Inc. — **USA**

President: J.T. Richey. Vice-President: W.H. Richey. Treasurer: J.D. Richey. Head office, press office and works: Route 11, Hattiesburg Municipal Airport, Hattiesburg, MS 39401.

TORO - see R.V. ALFONSO DMG Inc.

TOTAL PERFORMANCE Inc. — **USA**

Established in 1971. President: M.V. Lauria. Vice-President: G.C. Gallicchio. Head office, press office and works: 406 S. Orchard St, Rt, 5, Wallingford, CT 06492. 20 employees. 40 cars produced in 1978.

TOYO KOGYO COMPANY Ltd — **Japan**

(Make: Mazda)

Founded in 1920 under the name of Toyo Cork Kogyo Co. Ltd. Present title since 1927. Chairman: K. Matsuda. President: Y. Yamasaki. Executive Vice-Presidents: M. Kono, T. Mural. Senior Managing Directors: K. Hoshino, T. Wakabayashi, K. Roppyakuda. Managing Directors: H. Mineoka, S. Inomata, T. Hasegawa, K. Yamamoto, M. Watanabe, H. Nakashima, A. Niira, A. Fuji. Head office, press office and works: 3-1 Shinchi, Fuchuco, Aki-gun, Hiroshima. 27,139 employees. 516,498 vehicles produced in 1978. Car production begun in 1930 with Mazda (3-speed). Most important models: R360 Coupé (1960); 360 and 600 (1962); 800 Sedan (1964); 1000 (1965); 1500 Sedan (1966); 1500 SS, 110 S (1967); R110 Coupé, R100 Coupé, 1800 Sedan (1968). RX-2, 616 Coupé and Sedan (1970); RX3 (1971); Cosmo RX5 (1975); 323/GLC (1977); RX7, 626 (1978). Entries in numerous competitions: Singapore GP (1966); Macao GP (1966-67); 84 hour Marathon (1968); Singapore GP, Francorchamps (1969); Francorchamps and Shell Springbok Series (1970).

TOYOTA MOTOR COMPANY Ltd — **Japan**

Founded in 1937. Chairman: M. Hanai. President: E. Toyoda. Executive Vice-Presidents: S. Toyoda, H. Mori, S. Yamamoto. Senior Managing Directors: S. Yamaoto, T. Hasegawa, M. Morita, T. Morita. Managing Directors: M. Nemoto, H. Ono, G. Tsuji, K. Matsumoto, K. Kusunoki, H. Fuse. Head office and press office: 1, Toyota-cho, Toyota City. Works: Housha, 1, Toyota-cho, Toyota City; Motomachi, 1 Motomachi, Toyota City; Tokaoka, 1 Honda, Toyota City; Tsutsumi, 1 Tsutsumi-cho, Toyota City; Hiyoshi, 1 Miyoshimachi, Nishikamo-gun. 44,889 employees. 2,301,464 cars produced in 1978. Most important models: Toyo Ace (1954); Toyopet Crown (1955); Toyopet Corona (1957); Toyopet Crown Deluxe (1958); Toyopet Crown Diesel (1959); Toyopet New Corona and Publica (1960); Toyopet New Crown (1962); Crown Eight (1963); Toyota Corolla 1100 (1966); Toyota Century (1967); Toyota Corona Mk II, Toyota 1000 (1968); Celica, Carina (1970); Sprinter (1971); Corsa/Tercel (1978).

MANUFACTURE AND ASSEMBLY IN OTHER COUNTRIES — **Australia:** Australian Motor Industries Ltd, 155 Bertie St, Port Melbourne, Victoria 3207; Thiess Toyota Pty Ltd, 7-28 Alexander Ave., Taren Point, N.S.W. 7229. **Benin:** CICA-Benin, Place du Marché Central Cotonou, B.P. 27, Cotonou. **Bolivia:** Toyota Bolivia Ltda, Av. Montes Nos 424-444, La Paz. **Cameroon:** Cameroon Motors Industries (CAMI), B.P. 1217, Rue Pau, Duala. **Canada:** Canadian Motor Sales Corporation Ltd, 1791 Bellamy Rd, North Scarborough, Ontario. **Canary Islands:** Blandy Brothers y Cia. S.A., Carretteria Del Rosario km 5. Taco Santa Cruz, Tenerifa. **Chad:** C.F.A.O. Chad, Rue Beck Ceccaldi, N'Djamena. **Congo:** C.F.A.O. Congo, Ave. du Camp, B.P. 247, Brazzaville. **El Salvador:** Distribudoira de Automoviles S.A., Colle Ruben Dario 1117, San Salvador. **Empire of Central Africa:** C.F.A.O. Autos Bangui, B.P. 837, Bangui. **Fiji:** Automotive Supplies Co. Ltd, P.O.B. 5177, Raiwaga Suva. **Ghana:** Fattal Brothers Ltd, Ring Rd, West Industrial Area, Accra. **Honduras:** Valentin Flores & Compania, S de R.L., Prolongacion Pasaje Ville 18, San Pedro Sula. **Indonesia:** P.T. Toyota-Astra Motor, Jalan Jenderal Sudirman 5, Djakarta. **Ireland:** Toyota (Ireland) Ltd, Toyota House, Naas Rd, Clondalkin, Dublin. **Kenia:** Westlands Motors Ltd, Koinange St, Nairobi. **Liberia:** Elias Brothers Co. Ltd, Tubman Ave, Sinkor Rd, Monrovia. **Malawi:** Moble Motors Ltd, P.O.B. 430, Blantyre. **Malaysia:** Borneo Motors (Malaysia) Sdn Bhd, 76 Jalan Ampang, Kuala Lumpur. **New Zealand:** Consolidated Motor Distributors Ltd, 125-137 Johnsonville Rd, Wellington. **Nicaragua:** Auto Centro S.A., Apdo 1595, Managua D.N. **Niger:** C.F.A.O. Niger, B.P. 675, Niaway. **Nigeria:** R.T. Briscoe (Nigeria) Ltd, 21 Creek Rd, Apapa, Lagos. **Pakistan:** Awami Autos Ltd, Westwharf, Karachi; National Motors Ltd, Hab Chauki Rd, S.I.T.E. Mauripur. **Panama:** Picardo Perez S.A., Apdo 25-B, David, Chiriqui. **Paraguay:** Toyotoshi S.A., Mariscal Lopez, P.O.B. 769, Asuncion. **Peru:** Toyota Del Perù S.A., Las Begonias 441, 11 Piso San Isdro, Lima. **Philippines:** Delta Motor Corp., 7785 Pasong Tamo, Makati, Metro Manila. **Portugal:** Salvator Caetano IMVT S.A.R.L., Apdo 51, 4401, Vila Nova de Gaia Codex. **Sierra Leone:** Baydoun & Abess, 38 Kissy Bye Pass Rd, Kissy Freetown. **Singapore:** Borneo Motors (Singapore) Pty Ltd, 33 Leng Kee Rd, Singapore 3. **South Africa:** Toyota Marketing Co. (Pty) Ltd, Stand 1, Wesco Park Sandton, Johannesburg. **Sri Lanka:** Freudeberg & Co. Ltd, Lloyd Bldg, Sir Baron Jayatileke Mawatha, Colombo. **Sultanate of Oman:** Suhail & Saud Bahwan, P.O.B. 169, Muscat. **Thailand:** Toyota Motor Thailand Co. Ltd, 180 Suriwongse Rd, Bangkok. **Togo:** C.I.C.A. Togo, 5 Ave du Marechal Foch, Lomè. **Trinidad Tobago:** Amar Auto Supplies Ltd, 177 Tragarete Rd, Port of Spain. **Venezuela:** Compania Anonima Tocars, Edificio Cars, Avda Los Illustres, Los Chaguamos, Caracas, Apdo C. 10, 503 Caracas. **Western Samoa:** Burns Philp (South Sea) Co. Ltd, P.O.B. 188, Apia. **Zaire:** Agence Africaine de Distribution de Materiel (Africa), Kinshasa, B.P. 1499, Lubumbashi.

TRABANT - see VEB SACHSENRING AUTOMOBILWERKE ZWICKAU

TRIUMPH - see BL Ltd

TVR ENGINEERING Ltd — **Great Britain**

Established in 1954 as Grantura Engineering Ltd. Present title since 1966. Chairman: A. Lilley. Managing Director: M.A. Lilley. Director: S. Halstead. Head office, press office and works: Bristol Ave, Blackpool, Lancs. 116 employees. About 400 cars produced in 1978. Most important models: Mk I (1954-60); Mk II (1960); Mk II A (1962); Mk III (1963-64); Mk III 1800 (1963); Griffith series 200 (1964); Griffith 400 (1965); 200 V8 (1966); Tuscan SE, Vixen 1600 (1967); Vixen S2 (1968); Tuscan V6 (1969); 1600 M (1972-73); 2500 (1970-73); 2500 M, 3000 M (1972); Turbo (1975); Taimar (1976); Convertible (1978). Entries and wins in numerous competitions. Outright winners of 1970, 1971 and 1972 Modsports Championships. 1976 win in class B production sports cars.

UAZ - ULIANOVSKY AVTOMOBILNY ZAVOD — **USSR**

Press office: Avtoexport, Ul. Volkhonka 14. Moscow 119902 Works: Ullanovsk.

URDAN INDUSTRIES Ltd — **Israel**
ROM CARMEL INDUSTRIES

Founded in 1958 as private company by L. Schneller and Y. Shubinski. From 1966 to 1971 partnership with Standard-Triumph Motor Co. From 1974 Rom Carmel Industries, member of CLAL group. Since October 1977 amalgamated with Urdan Industries Ltd. President: M. Tamari. Vice-President: I. Schnabel. General Manager: N. Nemirovsky. Head office, press office and works: P.O.B. 444, Haifa-Tirat Carmel. 400 employees. 1,080 cars produced in 1978. Most important models: Sussita, Carmel, Gilboa, Rom 1300, Rom 1301. All with bodywork in fiberglass reinforced polyester.

VANDEN PLAS - see BL Ltd

VAUXHALL MOTORS Ltd — **Great Britain**

First Vauxhall car produced in 1903. Transferred from Vauxhall district of London to Luton in 1905. Present title since 1907. Taken over by General Motors Corp. in 1925. President and Managing Director: F.P.J Beickler. Chairman, G.E. Moore. Directors, E.D. Fountain, D. Savage, J.P. McCormack, S.T. Weber, D.T. Young and A.J. Elred. Head office, press office and works: Kimpton Road, Luton, Beds. 31,000 employees. 144,579 Vauxhall cars produced in 1978. Most important models: 30/98 (1913), Cadet (1930), Velox (1949), Cresta (1954), Victor (1957), Viva (1963), Chevette (1975), Cavalier (1975), Carlton, Royale (1978). Numerous successes on track and hill-climbs (1909 to 1924).

ASSEMBLY IN OTHER COUNTRIES — **New Zealand:** General Motors New Zealand Ltd (associated company), Wellington.

Portugal: General Motors de Portugal Ltda (associated company), CP 2484, Av. Marechal Gomes de Costa, Lisbon 6.

VAZ - VOLZHSKY AVTOMOBILNY ZAVOD **USSR**

(Make: Lada)

Press office: Avtoexport, Ul. Volkhonka 14, Moscow 119902. Works: Togliatti. 75,000 employees. 726,000 cars produced in 1977.

VEB AUTOMOBILWERK EISENACH **German Democratic Republic**

(Make: Wartburg)

Head office and press office: Rennhahn 8, 59 Eisenach. 53,970 cars produced in 1977.

VEB SACHSENRING AUTOMOBILWERKE ZWICKAU **German Democratic Republic**

(Make: Trabant)

Founded in 1904 under the name of A. Horch Motorwagenwerke AG Zwickau, became Audi-Mobilwagenwerke AG Zwickau in 1909, merged with Auto Union in 1932, nationalized in 1946. Present title since 1958. Head office and press office: W. Rathenau Strasse, 95 Zwickau. 9,000 employees. Over 110,000 cars produced in 1978. Most important models: world record 600 hp 16-cyl-rear-engined car (1937-38); DKW 3.5-5 l, F2, F3, F4, F5, F6, F7, F8, (two-stroke front drive engine up to 1945); F8 (1949-52); P70, S 240 (1955-59); Trabant P50 (1958-62); 600 (1962-63); 601 (1964). Entries in numerous competitions Munich-Vienna-Budapest, Semperit, Thousand Lakes, Tulip, Monte Carlo, Vlatava, Pneumat (D.D.R.) Akropolis Rallies, Tour de Belgique.

VOLKSWAGEN (Mexico) - see VOLKSWAGENWERK AG

VOLKSWAGEN (Nigeria) - see VOLKSWAGENWERK AG

VOLKSWAGENWERK AG **Germany (Federal Republic)**

Founded in 1937 under name of Gesellschaft zur Vorbereitung des Deutschen Volkswagen mbH, became Volkswagenwerk GmbH in 1938. Present title since 1960. For volume of production is foremost German motor manufacturer. President: T. Schmücker. Directors: K.H. Briam, G. Hartwich, H. Münzner, F. Thomée, P. Frerk, E. Fiala, W.P. Schmidt. Head office and press office: 3100 Wolfsburg. Works: as above, Braunschweig, Emden, Hannover, Kassel, Salzgitter. 116,338 employees. 1,208,000 cars produced in 1978. Most important models: Limousine 1200 (1945); 1200 Convertible (1959); 1200 Karmann-Ghia Coupé (1955); 1200 Karmann-Ghia Convertible (1957); 1500 and 1500 Karmann-Ghia Coupé (1961); 1500 N Limousine, 1500 S Limousine, 1500 S Karmann-Ghia Coupé (1963); 1600 TL (1965); 411 (1968); 411 E, 411 LE (1969); (302, 1302 S, K 70 (1970)); 1303 (1972). Passat, Passat Variant (1973); Golf, Scirocco (1974); Polo (1975); Derby (1977); Golf Cabriolet, Jetta (1979).

MANUFACTURE AND ASSEMBLY IN OTHER COUNTRIES — **Belgium:** Volkswagen Bruxelles, S.A., Brussels (Passat). **Indonesia:** P.T. Garuda Mataram Motor Co., Djakarta (1200, 181, Golf, Passat). **Mexico:** Volkswagen de México S.A. de C.V. (associated company), Mexico City (1200, 181, Brasilia, Golf). **Nigeria:** Volkswagen of Nigeria (associated company), Lagos-Badagry Highway, km 18, Lagos (manuf. 1200, Igala, Passat). **South Africa:** Volkswagen of South Africa Ltd (associated company). Uitenhage (assem. 1200, Passat, Golf). **Yugoslavia:** TAS Tvornica Automobila Sarajevo, Sarajevo (Golf). 820,000 cars produced outside Federal Republic in 1978, including VW do Brasil and VW of America.

VOLKSWAGEN DO BRASIL S.A. **Brazil**

Founded in 1953. Chairman: W.F.J. Sauer. Head office, press office and works: v. Anchieta km 23.5, São Paulo. CEP 09700. 42,910 employees. 518,603 cars produced in 1978.

VOLKSWAGEN OF AMERICA Inc. **USA**

Volkswagen Manufacturing Corporation of America merged with Volkswagen of America on July 31, 1978. Volkswagen of America, Inc. (VWoA) was founded in October 1955. Chairman: T. Schmuecker. President and C.E.O.: J.W. McLernon. Executive Vice-Presidents: I.M. Anderson, N. Phillips. Group Vice-President: R.E. Dauch. Vice-Presidents: E.F. Beuler, A.E. Breckwoldt, U. Fahrun, J.T. Gresh, G. Grimm, J.E. Kerr, J.E. Masterson, J. Metz, D.F. Miller, R.L. Mugg, G. Reinecke, M.A. Ryan, F.J. Short. Head office: 27621 Parkview Blvd, Warren, Mich. 48092. Works: VW Westmoreland, East Huntingdon Township, Pennsylvania. 4,500 employees. 40,194 cars assembled in 1978. Assembly of VW Rabbit begun in 1978.

VOLVO AB **Sweden**

Founded in 1926. President and General Manager: P.G. Gyllenhammer. Head office, press office and works: S-405 08, Göteborg. About 62,000 employees. 197,000 cars produced in 1978. Most important models: P4 (1927); 53-56 (1939); PV 50 (1944); PV 444 (1947); P 1900 (1954-57); 122S Amazon (1956); P 544 (1958-62); P 1800 (1961); 144 (1966); 164 (1968); 240 (1975); 343 (1976).

ASSEMBLY IN OTHER COUNTRIES — **Australia:** Volvo Australia Pty Ltd, Melbourne (Liverpool). **Belgium:** Volvo Europa N.V. (subsidiary), P.B. 237, Ghent. **Canada:** Volvo (Canada) Ltd, Willowdale. **Holland:** Volvo Car B.V. Steenonvenweg, Helmond. **Malaysia:** Swedish Motor Assemblies Sdn Bhd (subsidiary), Batu Tiga, Industrial Estate, Selangor.

VOLVO CAR B.V. **Holland**

Founded in 1928 by Hub and Wim van Doorne, assumed title Van Doorne's Automobielfabrieken in 1958. In 1975 A.B. Volvo obtained a controlling interest of 75% in Van Doorne's Automobielfabrieken B.V. which became Volvo Car B.V. a member of the Volvo Group. The Company designes and manufactures the compact medium-sized Volvo cars. Managing Directors: A. van der Padt, A. de Bruin, O. Wibaut. Head office and press office: Steenovenweg, Helmond. Works: Born, Oss. About 6,000 employees. 65,500 cars produced in 1978.

WARTBURG - see VEB AUTOMOBILWERK EISENACH

YLN - YUE LOONG MOTOR COMPANY Ltd **Taiwan**

Founded in 1953 as Yue Loong Engineering Co. Ltd. Present title since 1960. President: T.L. Yen. Executive Vice-President: V. Wu. Special Assistant to Chairman and President: C.C. Yen. Managing Director: V.Z. Faung. Head office and press office: 150 Nanking East Road, Sec II, Taipei. Works: Hsin Tien Taipei. 2,300 employees. 39,867 cars produced in 1978. Under licence of Nissan Motor Co. and American Motors Corp. manufactures various types of sedans and jeeps, including YK-1 and YL-2. Models: 709, 803, 302, 902.

ZAZ - ZAPOROZHSKY AVTOMOBILNY ZAVOD **USSR**

Press office: Avtoexport, Ul. Volkhonka 14, Moscow 119902 Works: Zaporozhje. About 146,000 cars in 1977.

ZAVODI CRVENA ZASTAVA **Yugoslavia**

(Make: ZCZ)

Directors: M. Bojanic, R. Micic. Head office, press office and works: Apanskih boraca 2, 34000 Kragujevac. 30,000 employees. 243,659 cars produced in 1978.

ZIL **USSR**

Press office: Avtoexport, Ul. Volkhonka 14, Moscow 119902. Works: Moscow.

COACHBUILDERS

ARCADIPANE DESING Ltd **Austria**

Founded in 1977. Has produced four major prototypes, fourteen design studies; provides concept studies to manufactures. General Manager: P. Arcadipane. Head office, press office and works: 148 Northern Rd, West Heidelberg, 3081 Victoria.

BERTONE (Carrozzeria) S.p.A. **Italy**

Founded in 1912. Produces small and medium series of car bodles; bespoke production for car manufacturing firms and construction of prototypes. President and Managing Director: N. Bertone. Head office: c.so Peschiera 223, Turin. Press office and works: c.so Canonico Allamano 40-46, 10095 Grugliasco, Turin.

BITTER-AUTOMOBILE GmbH & Co. KG **Germany (Federal Republic)**

Head office and press office: Berliner Str. 57, 5830 Schwelm.

CARROSSERIE DUCHATELET S.A. **Belgium**

Founded in 1966. Manager: F. Duchatelet. Head office, press office and works: 144, quai du Roi Albert, 4020 Liège.

CHRIS HUMBERSTONE DESIGN Ltd **Great Britain**

Head office and press office: 4 Monument Rd, Woking, Surrey GU21 5LS.

CLENET COACHWORKS Inc.

Estabilished in 1976. President: A.J.M. Clénet. Vice-President and General Manager: T.L. Cadle. Vice-President: J.W. Whitman. Head office, press office and works: 495 South Fairview Ave, Santa Barbara. Cal. 93017.

COLEMAN-MILNE Ltd **Great Britain**

Founded in 1953. Specialist in the manufacture of Grosvenor, Dorchester and Minster limouisines. Chairman and Joint Managing Director: R.S.C. Milne. Joint Managing Director: D.H. Hackett. Head office: Colmil Works, Wigan Rd, Hart Common, Westhoughton, Bolton, BL5 2EE.

CRAYFORD AUTO DEVELOPMENT Ltd **Great Britain**

Founded in 1960, specialising in convertibles, estate cars and cross country vehicles. Directors: G.D. McMullan, J.J. Smith. Head office: High Street, Westerham, Kent.

DeLOREAN MOTOR COMPANY **USA**

Head office and press office: 280 Park Avenue, New York, N.Y. 10017.

DOME COMPANY Ltd **Japan**

President; M. Hayashi. Head office and press office: 310-2, Shimozaichi, Iwakura, Sakyo-ku, Kyoto.

PIETRO FRUA (Carrozzerie Speciali) **Italy**

Proprietor: P. Frua. Head office, press office and works: v. Papa Giovanni XXIII 13, 10047 Borgo San Pietro - Moncalieri, Turin.

GHIA S.p.A. **Italy**

Founded in 1915. Produces car bodles. Head office: v. A. da Montefeltro 5, 10134 Turin.

GRANDEUR MOTOR CAR CORPORATION **USA**

Founded in 1976 by C.R. Northey and C.W. Philips. President: C.R. Northey. Head office, press office and works: 1405 S.W. 8th St., Pompano Beach, Florida 33060.

GUANCI AUTOMOBILES Inc. **USA**

Founded in 1978. President: J.J. Guanci, Jr. Head office and works: 220 North Madison St, Woodstock, Illinois 60098. Public Relations: D. Emanuel, 17981-L Skypark Circle, Irvine, California 97714.

S.A. LOUIS HEULIEZ **France**

Founded in 1923. President and General Manager: G. Queveau. Head office and press office: rue L. Heuliez, 79140 Cerizay. Works: Cerizay, Le Pin, Brou, Broug en Bresse.

ITAL DESIGN SIRP S.p.A. **Italy**

Founded in 1968. Styling and design of cars in small, medium and large series; construction of models and prototypes. Directors: L. Bosio, G. Giugiaro, A. Mantovani. Head office and press office: v. A. Grandi 11, 10024 Moncalieri, Turin.

KAROSSERIE BAUR GmbH **Germany (Federal Republic)**

Directors: K. Baur, H. Baur. Head office, press office and works: Poststr. 40-62, 7 Stuttgart 1 - Berg.

LE VICOMTE CLASSIC COACHBUILDERS Inc. **Canada**

Head office and press office: P.O.B. 430, St. Sauveur des Monts, Quebec, JOR 1RO.

MINICARS Inc. **USA**

Head office and press office: 55 Depot Rd, Santa Barbara, California 93017.

OGLE DESIGN Ltd — **Great Britain**

Founded in 1954 as design group by late David Ogle. Car production began in 1960. Present Head: Tom Kare. Designs include Mini-based Ogle 2-seater, Reliant Scimitar GTE, Bond Bug and Sotheby Special. Head office, press office and works: Birds Hill, Letchworth, Herts SG6 1JA.

NEWPORT COACHWORKS Inc. — **USA**

President: J.A. Rowland. Head office, press office and works: 2909 Croddy Way, Santa Ana, California 92704.

PACIFIC COACHWORKS — **USA**

Established as a division of Minicars, Inc., in 1978. General Manager: Meg Di Napoli. Head office and works: 55 Depot Rd, Goleta, California.

PHAETON COACH CORPORATION — **USA**

Founded in 1969 as Eagle Coach Company. Present title since 1974. President and General Manager: R.J. Harris. Products include custom limousines, sport cars and utility vehicles. General offices and works: 2339 Inwood Rd, Dallas, Texas 75235.

PININFARINA (Carrozzeria) S.p.A. — **Italy**

Founded in 1930. Produces special and de luxe bodies. President: S. Pininfarina, Managing Director: R. Carli, Member of Board: E. Carbonato. Head office: c. Stati Uniti 61, Turin. Works: v. Lesna 78-80, 10095 Grugliasco, Turin.

SBARRO - SOCIETÉ DE FABRICATION D'AUTOMOBILES SBARRO S.a.r.l. — **Switzerland**

Founded in 1973. Proprietor: F. Sbarro. Head office, press office and works: ACA Atelier, 1411 Les Tuileries de Grandson, Yverdon, Lausanne.

SPARKS COACHBUILDERS Inc. — **USA**

Head office, press office and works: 935 Bailey Court, San Marcos, California 92069.

TAFCO DESIGN & ENGINEERING — **UISA**

Designer: Baron Samuel Tafoya. 2640 Woodside Drive, Dearborn, Michigan 48124.

THE PHANTOM VEHICLE COMPANY — **USA**

Founded in 1976 by a small group of designers, engineers and craftsmen. The first prototype is the turbocharged 3-wheel Turbo Phantom. President: R.J. Will. Head office: 630 Center St, Costa Mesa, California 92627. Press office: Box 1704, Newport Beach, California 92663. Works: 779 West 16th St, Costa Mesa, California 92627.

VEHICLE DESIGN FORCE — **USA**

Founded in 1976. President: G. Wiegert. Head office and press office: 1101 West Washington Blvd, Venice, California 90291.

ZAGATO (Carrozzeria) S.p.A. — **Italy**

Founded in 1919. Produces car bodies. President: E. Zagato. Managing Director: G. Zagato. Press office and works: v. Arese, 20017 Terrazzano di Rho, Milan.

ELECTRIC CAR BUILDERS

B&Z ELECTRIC CAR — **USA**

Address: 3346 Olive Avenue, Signal Hill, California 90807.

BRIGGS & STRATTON CORPORATION — **USA**

Address: 3300 North 124th St, Wauwatosa, Wisconsin 53222.

C.E.D.R.E. - SEVE — **France**

Address: 09230 Merigon, S.te Croix-Volvestre.

COMMUTER VEHICLES Inc. — **USA**

Address: Sebring Air Terminal, P.O.B. 1479, Sebring, Florida 33870.

COPPER DEVELOPMENT ASSOCIATION Inc. — **USA**

Address: 405 Lexington Avenue, New York, New York 10017.

DAIHATSU KOGYO COMPANY Ltd — **Japan**

Address: 1-1 Daihatsu-cho, Ikeda-city, Osaka 563.

DIE MESH CORPORATION — **USA**

Address: 629 Fifth Avenue, Pelham, New York 10803.

EAC - ELECTRIC AUTO CORPORATION — **USA**

Address: 2237 Elliott Avenue, Troy, Michigan 48084.

(US) ELECTRICAR CORPORATION — **USA**

Address: 2342 Main Street. Athol, Massachusetts 01331.

EVA - ELECTRIC VEHICLE ASSOCIATES Inc. — **Usa**

Address: 9100 Bank Street, Cleveland, Ohio 44125.

EVELEC S.A. — **Belgium**

Address: 41 rue de la Pépinière, 1000 Brussels.

FIAT AUTO S.p.A. — **Italy**

Address: corso Matteotti 26, 10121 Turin.

FLINDERS UNIVERSITY — **Australia**

Address: Stuart Road, Bedford Park, Adelaide, SA.

GARRETT - AIRESEARCH MANUFACTURING COMPANY of CALIFORNIA — **USA**

A division of The Garrett Corp. Address: 2525 West 190th Street, Torrance, California 90509.

GE - GENERAL ELECTRIC — **USA**

Address: Research and Development Center, P.O. Box 8, Schenectady, New York 12301.

GENERAL MOTORS CORPORATION — **USA**

Address: Chevrolet Division, 3044 West Grand Boulevard, Detroit, Michigan 48202.

GLOBE-UNION Inc. — **USA**

Address: 5757 North Green Bay Avenue, Milwaukee, Wisconsin 53201.

GURGEL S.A. INDUSTRIA E COMERCIO DE VEICULOS — **Brazil**

Addresss: Rodovia Washington Luiz, km 171, 13,500 Rio Claro, SP.

H-M VEHICLES Inc. — **USA**

Address: 1116 East Highway 13, Burnsville, Minnesota 55337.

HYBRICON Inc. — **USA**

Address: 11489 Chandler Boulevard, North Hollywood, California 91601.

JMJ ELECTRONICS CORPORATION — **USA**

Address: P.O. Box 25971, Oklahoma City, Oklahoma 73125.

MARATHON VEHICLES Inc. — **USA**

Address: 9190 Christopher Street, Fairfax, Virginia 22031.

MAZDA - TOYO KOGYO COMPANY Ltd — **Japan**

Address: 3-1 Fuchu-machi, Aki-gun, Hiroshima-ken.

McKEE ENGINEERING CORPORATION — **USA**

Address: 411 West Colfax Street, Palatine, Illinois 60067.

PGE - PROGETTI GESTIONI ECOLOGICHE — **Italy**

Address: via Rossellini 1, 20124 Milan.

PININFARINA (Carrozzeria) S.p.A. — **Italy**

Address: via Lesna 78-80, 10095 Grugliasco, Turin.

QUINCY-LYNN ENTERPRISES Inc. — **USA**

Address: 2231 W. Shangri-La Road, Unit W, Phoenix, Arizona 85029.

SBARRO - SOCIETÉ DE FABRICATION D'AUTOMOBILES SBARRO S.a.r.l. — **Switzerland**

Address: ACA Atelier, 1411 Les Tuileries de Grandson, Yverdon, Lausanne.

SEARS ROEBUCK & COMPANY — **USA**

Address: Sears Tower, Chicago, Illinois 60684.

SHERWOOD OVERSEAS COMPANY Pty Ltd — **Australia**

Address: 20 Hazelhurst Street, Kewdale, Western Australia 6106.

SOUTH COAST TECHNOLOGY Inc. — **USA**

Address: P.O. Box 3265, Santa Barbara, California 93105.

SUZUKI MOTOR COMPANY — **Japan**

Address: 300 Takatsuka, Kami-mura, Hamana-gun, Shizuoka-ken.

TEILHOL VOITURE ELECTRIQUE — **France**

Address; Zone Industrielle La Masse, 63600 Ambert.

TP LABORATORIES Inc. — **USA**

Address: P.O. Box 73, La Porte, Indiana 46350.

VOLVO AB — **Sweden**

Address: Car Division, Advanced Engineering Projects, Departement 56500, S-405 08 Göteborg.

WESTERN RESEARCH INDUSTRIES Inc. — **USA**

Address: 3013 West Sahara, Las Vegas, Nevada 89102.

(ROBERT STEVEN) WITKOFF DESIGN INNOVATIONS — **USA**

Address: 46 Kirkwood Drive, Glen Cove, New York 11542.

ZAGATO (Carrozzeria) S.p.A. — **Italy**

Address: v. Arese, 20017 Terrazzano di Rho, Milan.

Indexes

Name of car

Maximum speed

Makes, models and prices

NAME OF CAR

Cars called by names (in alphabetical order)

Model	Make
ACADIAN	PONTIAC (CDN)
ACCORD	HONDA
ALFA 6	ALFA ROMEO
ALFA ROMEO	FIAT (BR)
ALFASUD	ALFA ROMEO
ALFETTA	ALFA ROMEO
ALLEGRO	AUSTIN
ALPINE	TALBOT (GB)
ALTO	SUZUKI
AMBASSADOR	HINDUSTAN
AMERICAN TURBO	AMERICAN CUSTOM INDUSTRIES
ANADOL	OTOSAN
ASCONA	CHEVROLET (ZA), OPEL
ASPEN	DODGE (USA)
ASTRA	VAUXHALL
AUBURN PHAETON	TOMORROWS CLASSIC
AUSTER	NISSAN-DATSUN
AUSTIN-HEALEY	LENHAM
AVANTI II	AVANTI
AVENGER	TALBOT (GB)
BADAL	SUNRISE
BEARCAT	BLAKELY, STUTZ
BEL AIR	CHEVROLET (CDN)
BENTLEY DONINGTON	JOHNARD VINTAGE CAR
BETA	LANCIA, SEAT
BLACKHAWK	STUTZ
BLOWER PHAETON	CLASSIC CAR
BLUEBIRD	NISSAN-DATSUN
BOBCAT	MERCURY (CDN, USA)
BONNEVILLE	PONTIAC (USA)
BORA	MASERATI
BRASILIA	VOLKSWAGEN (BR)
BRAVA	FIAT (I)
BRISA	KIA
BUGATTI	CLASSIC CAR, LEDL, STIMULA
CAMARGUE	ROLLS-ROYCE
CAMARO	CHEVROLET (USA)
CAMPAGNOLA	FIAT (I)
CAPELLA	MAZDA
CAPRI	FORD (D, GB), MERCURY (USA)
CAPRICE CLASSIC	CHEVROLET (USA)
CARINA	TOYOTA
CARLTON	VAUXHALL
CATALINA	PONTIAC (CDN, USA)
CAVALIER	VAUXHALL
CAVALO DE FERRO	FORD (BR)
CEDRIC	NISSAN-DATSUN
CELESTE	MITSUBISHI
CELICA	TOYOTA
CENTURY	TOYOTA
CERVO	SUZUKI
CHAIKA	GAZ
CHARADE	DAIHATSU
CHARGER	DODGE (BR)
CHARMANT	DAIHATSU
CHASER	TOYOTA
CHEROKEE	JEEP CORPORATION
CHEVAIR	CHEVROLET (ZA)
CHEVETTE	CHEVROLET (BR, USA), VAUXHALL
CITATION	CHEVROLET (USA)
CIVIC	HONDA
CLUBMAN	MINI
COMMODORE	CHEVROLET (ZA), HOLDEN, OPEL
COMODORO	CHEVROLET (BR)
CONCORD	AMERICAN MOTORS
CONTINENTAL	LINCOLN
CORCEL	FORD (BR)
CORDOBA	CHRYSLER (USA)
CORNICHE	BENTLEY, ROLLS-ROYCE
COROLLA	TOYOTA
CORONA	TOYOTA
CORSA	TOYOTA
CORTINA	FORD (AUS, GB, ZA)
CORVETTE	CHEVROLET (USA)
COSMO	MAZDA
COUGAR	MERCURY (CDN, USA)
COUNTACH	LAMBORGHINI
CROWN	TOYOTA

Model	Make
CUSTOM CRUISER	OLDSMOBILE
CUTLASS	OLDSMOBILE
DART	DODGE (BR)
DEAUVILLE	DE TOMASO
DEBONAIR	MITSUBISHI
DELTA	DAIHATSU, LANCIA, OLDSMOBILE
DERBY	VOLKSWAGEN (D)
DE VILLE	CADILLAC, PANTHER
DINO	FERRARI
DIPLOMAT	DODGE (USA)
DIPLOMATA	CHEVROLET (BR)
DOLOMITE	TRIUMPH
DOUBLE-SIX	DAIMLER
DUAL COWL	AUBURN
DYANE	CITROËN
EAGLE	AMERICAN MOTORS
ECLAT	LOTUS
ELECTRA	BUICK
ELEGANTÉ	ELEGANT MOTORS
ELITE	LOTUS
ESCORT	FORD (AUS, D, GB, ZA)
ESPADA	LAMBORGHINI
ESPRIT	LOTUS
EXCELLENCE	FELBER
FAIRLADY	NISSAN-DATSUN
FAIRLANE	FORD (AUS, RA)
FAIRMONT	FORD (AUS, USA)
FALCON	FORD (AUS, RA)
FAMILIA	MAZDA
FIESTA	FORD (D, GB)
FIREBIRD	PONTIAC (USA)
FLEETWOOD	CADILLAC
FLORIAN	ISUZU
FORD «B»	TOTAL REPLICA
FORD V8	TIMMIS
FRAZER NASH	ANTIQUE & CLASSIC AUTOMOTIVE
FRONTE	SUZUKI
GALANT	MITSUBISHI
GALAXIE	FORD (BR)
GAMMA	LANCIA
GAZEL	STANDARD
GAZELLE	NISSAN-DATSUN
GEMINI	HOLDEN, ISUZU
GEPARD	CLASSIC CAR
GIULIETTA	ALFA ROMEO
GLORIA	NISSAN-DATSUN
GOLF	VOLKSWAGEN (D)
GRANADA	FORD (D, GB, USA, ZA)
GRAND AM	PONTIAC (USA)
GRAND LE MANS	PONTIAC (USA)
GRAND MARQUIS	MERCURY (USA)
GRAND PRIX	PONTIAC (USA)
GRAN FURY	PLYMOUTH
HARDTOP	REPLICARS
HI BOY	TOTAL REPLICA
HORIZON	PLYMOUTH, TALBOT (GB)
HURRYCANE	CUSTOCA
IGALA	VOLKSWAGEN (WAN)
ILTIS	VOLKSWAGEN (D)
IMPALA	CHEVROLET (USA)
JAGUAR	ANTIQUE & CLASSIC AUTOMOTIVE
JEEP	JEEP CORPORATION, MITSUBISHI
JETTA	VOLKSWAGEN (D)
JIMNY	SUZUKI
KADETT	OPEL
KHAMSIN	MASERATI
KITTEN	RELIANT
KYALAMI	MASERATI
LA CROSSE	AUTOMOBILI INTERMECCANICA
LADA	VAZ
LAGONDA	ASTON MARTIN
LANCER	MITSUBISHI
LANCIA BETA	SEAT
LANDCRUISER	TOYOTA
LASER	ELITE

Model	Make
LAUREL	NISSAN-DATSUN
LAURENTIAN	PONTIAC (CDN)
LE BARON	CHRYSLER (USA), DODGE (BR)
LE MANS	PONTIAC (USA)
LEONE	SUBARU
LE SABRE	BUICK
LIMA	PANTHER
LIMOUSINE	DAIMLER, HONGQI
LONGCHAMP	DE TOMASO
LUCE	MAZDA
MAGNUM	DODGE (BR)
MALIBU	CHEVROLET (USA)
MANTA	OPEL
MARATHON	CHECKER
MARINA	MORRIS
MARK II	TOYOTA
MARQUIS	MERCURY (CDN, USA)
MATRA	TALBOT (F)
MAX CUORE	DAIHATSU
MAXI	AUSTIN
MEHARI	CITROËN
MERAK	MASERATI
MERCEDES	LEDL
MIDGET	MG
MIGI	DAYTONA
MINI	NUOVA INNOCENTI
MINICA	MITSUBISHI
MINI-MOKE	LEYLAND
MIRADA	DODGE (USA)
MIRAGE	MITSUBISHI
MONARCH	MERCURY (USA)
MONTE CARLO	CHEVROLET (USA), LANCIA
MONZA	CHEVROLET (USA), OPEL
MOSKVICH	AZLK
MURAT	TOFAS
MUSTANG	FORD (USA)
NASR	EL NASR
NEWPORT	CHRYSLER (USA)
NEW YORKER	CHRYSLER (USA)
NINETY-EIGHT	OLDSMOBILE
OASIS	FELBER
OMEGA	OLDSMOBILE
OMNI	DODGE (USA)
OPALA	CHEVROLET (BR)
PACER	AMERICAN MOTORS
PADMINI	PREMIER
PANDA	FIAT (I)
PANTERA	DE TOMASO
PARISIENNE	PONTIAC (CDN)
PASSAT	VOLKSWAGEN (D, BR)
PATROL	NISSAN-DATSUN
PHAETON	DUTTON, REPLICARS
PHANTOM	ROLLS-ROYCE
PHOENIX	PONTIAC (USA)
PINTO	FORD (USA)
POLARA	DODGE (BR)
POLO	VOLKSWAGEN (D)
POLONEZ	POLSKI-FIAT
PONY	HYUNDAI
PRELUDE	HONDA
PRESIDENT	NISSAN-DATSUN
PULSAR	NISSAN-DATSUN
QUADRAPORTE	RAPPORT
QUATTROPORTE	MASERATI
RABBIT	VOLKSWAGEN (USA)
RANGE ROVER	LAND ROVER
REGAL	BUICK
REKORD	CHEVROLET (ZA), OPEL
REX	SUBARU
RITMO	FIAT (I), GIANNINI, SEAT
RIVIERA	BUICK
ROADSTER	REPLICARS
ROBIN	RELIANT
RODEO	RENAULT (F)
ROM	ROM CARMEL
ROYALE	STUTZ, VAUXHALL
SAFARI	MONTEVERDI
SAHARA	MONTEVERDI
SAVANNA	MAZDA
SCIMITAR	RELIANT
SCIROCCO	VOLKSWAGEN (D)

Model	Make
SCOUT	INTERNATIONAL HARVESTER
SEDAN	SHANGHAI
SENATOR	CHEVROLET (ZA), OPEL
SERIES III	EXCALIBUR
SEVILLE	CADILLAC
SHERPA	FIBERFAB
SIERRA	MONTEVERDI
SIGMA	CHRYSLER (AUS)
SILHOUETTE	LAMBORGHINI
SILVER SHADOW	ROLLS-ROYCE
SILVER WRAITH	ROLLS-ROYCE
SILVIA	NISSAN-DATSUN
SIMCA	TALBOT (E, F)
SKYHAWK	BUICK
SKYLARK	BUICK
SKYLINE	NISSAN-DATSUN
SOVEREIGN	DAIMLER
SPEEDSTER	AUBURN, AUTOMOBILI INTERMECCANICA
SPIRIT	AMERICAN MOTORS
SPITFIRE	TRIUMPH
SPORTS	NOVA, SPARTAN CARS
SPRINTER	TOYOTA
STANZA	NISSAN-DATSUN
STARFIRE	OLDSMOBILE
STARLET	TOYOTA
STASH	SBARRO
STRADA	FIAT (I)
STRATO	CUSTOCA
ST. REGIS	DODGE (USA)
SUNBEAM	TALBOT (GB)
SUNBIRD	HOLDEN, PONTIAC (USA)
SUNNY	NISSAN-DATSUN
SUPER	CATERHAM CARS
TAFT	DAIHATSU
TAIMAR	TVR
TALON	GP
TANGA	LEDL
TASMIN	TVR
TAUNUS	FORD (D, RA)
TERCEL	TOYOTA
THUNDERBIRD	FORD (USA)
TORINO	RENAULT (RA)
TORONADO	OLDSMOBILE
TRIMUTER	QUINCY-LYNN
TURBO	ARGYLL, PORSCHE, TVR
URRACO	LAMBORGHINI
VALIANT	CHRYSLER (AUS)
VANDEN PLAS	DAIMLER
VARIANT	VOLKSWAGEN (BR)
VERANEIO	CHEVROLET (BR)
VERSAILLES	LINCOLN
VIOLET	NISSAN-DATSUN
VISA	CITROËN
VOLARE'	PLYMOUTH
VOLGA	GAZ
WAGONEER	JEEP CORPORATION
WINDHOUND	SBARRO
ZASTAVA	ZCZ
ZEPHIR	MERCURY (USA)

Cars called by letters (in alphabetical order)

Model	Make
A4 CITY	LAWIL
A 11	AVALLONE
A 112	AUTOBIANCHI
A 310 V6	ALPINE RENAULT
AMX	AMERICAN MOTORS
BB	FERRARI
BJ 212	PEKING
CX	CITROËN
D TYPE	LYNX
G23	GINETTA
GS	CITROËN
GSA	CITROËN
GT	KELMARK
GTB	PUMA
GTE	PUMA
GTM	MARQUEZ
GTS	PUMA
HZ	HOLDEN
J 72	PANTHER
LL	LAFER
LNA	CITROËN
LTD	FORD (AUS, CDN, USA)
M 1	BMW (D)
MGB	MG
MK 2	SYD LAWRENCE
MP	LAFER
PLUS 8	MORGAN
S3 VARZINA	LAWIL
S 110 R	ŠKODA
SM 4.1	Sta MATILDE
SS	ARKLEY
T2	BENTLEY
T 613	TATRA
TI	LAFER
TR 7	TRIUMPH
TX-S	FAIRTHORPE
TX TRIPPER	TECHNICAL EXPONENTS
V8	ASTON MARTIN
X1/9	FIAT (I)
X-12	GURGEL
XJ	JAGUAR
XJ-S	JAGUAR

Cars called by numbers (in alphabetical order)

Model	Make
2 CV 6	CITROËN
4	FASA-RENAULT, RENAULT (F, RA)
IV PORTE	STUTZ
4/4 1600	MORGAN
5	FASA-RENAULT, RENAULT (F)
6	FASA-RENAULT, PANTHER, RENAULT (F, RA)
6.6 S	SCEPTRE
12	FASA-RENAULT, RENAULT (RA)
14	RENAULT (F)
16	RENAULT (F)
18	RENAULT (F)
20	RENAULT (F)
30	RENAULT (F)
66	VOLVO (NL)
88	LAND ROVER
90	ENVEMO
96	SAAB
99	SAAB
100	ARO
101	ARO
103	ARO
104	ARO, PEUGEOT
105	ŠKODA, SYRENA
109	LAND ROVER
114	ZIL
117	ISUZU, ZIL
120	ŠKODA
124	FIAT (I), SEAT
125	FIAT (RA)
125 P	POLSKI-FIAT
126	FIAT (I), GIANNINI
126 P	POLSKI-FIAT
127	FIAT (I), GIANNINI, SEAT
128	FIAT (I, RA)
131	FIAT (I), SEAT
132	FIAT (I), SEAT
133	FIAT (RA), SEAT
147	FIAT (BR)
150	TALBOT (E)
180	TALBOT (E)
181	VOLKSWAGEN (MEX)
200	MERCEDES-BENZ
230	MERCEDES-BENZ
240	ARO, MERCEDES-BENZ
241	ARO
242	ARO, VOLVO (S)
243	ARO
244	ARO, VOLVO (S)
245	VOLVO (S)
250	MERCEDES-BENZ, PORTARO
262	VOLVO (S)
264	VOLVO (S)
265	VOLVO (S)
280	MERCEDES-BENZ
300	MERCEDES-BENZ
302	YLN
304	PEUGEOT
305	PEUGEOT
308	FERRARI
316	BMW (D)
318	BMW (D)
320	BMW (D)
323	BMW (D)
343	VOLVO (NL)
345	VOLVO (NL)
350	MERCEDES-BENZ
353	WARTBURG
380	MERCEDES-BENZ
400	FERRARI
412	BRISTOL
450	MERCEDES-BENZ
469 B	UAZ
500	MERCEDES-BENZ
504	PEUGEOT
505	PEUGEOT
518	BMW (D, ZA)
520	BMW (D, ZA)
525	BMW (D)
528	BMW (D, ZA)
530	BMW (ZA)
600	MERCEDES-BENZ
600 S	FIAT (RA, U)
601	TRABANT
603	BRISTOL
604	PEUGEOT
626	MAZDA
628	BMW (D)
633	BMW (D)
635	BMW (D)
728	BMW (D, ZA)
730	BMW (ZA)
732	BMW (D)
733	BMW (ZA)
735	BMW (D)
745	BMW (D)
803	YLN
805	YLN
850	MINI
856	ELEGANT MOTORS
898	ELEGANT MOTORS
900	SAAB
902	YLN
911	PORSCHE
924	PORSCHE
928	PORSCHE
968-A	ZAZ
969-A	ZAZ
1000	MINI
1200	VOLKSWAGEN (D, MEX, WAN)
1275	MINI
1300	DACIA, FIAT (RA), TORO, VOLKSWAGEN (BR)
1301	DACIA
1500	DODGE (RA), VANDEN PLAS
1600	VOLKSWAGEN (BR)
1700	PRINCESS
1927 BUGATTI	ANTIQUE & CLASSIC AUTOMOTIVE
1930 BLOWER PHAETON	ANTIQUE & CLASSIC AUTOMOTIVE
1931 ALFA ROMEO	ANTIQUE & CLASSIC AUTOMOTIVE
1953 CORVETTE ROADSTER	TOMORROWS CLASSIC
2000	ALFA ROMEO, PRINCESS
2200	PRINCESS
2300	ROVER
2600	ROVER
3000	AC, TVR
3500	ROVER

MAXIMUM SPEED

Up to 65 mph

	mph
DAIHATSU Max Cuore Series	31
LAWIL S3 Varzina / A4 City	39
SUNRISE Badal	47
SUZUKI Jimny 55 Series (26 hp) / Jimny 8 Series (26 hp)	55
ZAZ 969-A 4x4	56
QUINCY-LYNN Trimuter G	60
STANDARD Gazel	60
SUZUKI Jimny 55 Series (41 hp) / Jimny 8 Series (41 hp)	60
PEKING BJ 212	61
CITROËN Mehari 4x4 / Mehari 2+2	62
TRABANT 601 Limousine / 601 Univeral	62
ARO 240 / 241 / 242 / 243 / 244 (68 hp, diesel)	65
DAIHATSU Taft Series (75 hp, diesel)	65
FIAT (I) 126 Berlina Base / 126 Personal	65
POLSKI-FIAT 126 P / 126 P 650	65
SUBARU Rex 550 SEEC-T Series (28 and 31 hp)	65
SUZUKI Cervo Series (28 hp)	65

From 66 mph to 100 mph

	mph
LAND ROVER 88" Regular / 109"	66
ARO 100 / 101 / 103 / 104	68
CITROËN 2 CV 6 Spécial / 2 CV 6 Club	68
FIAT (I) Campagnola Lunga / Campagnola Diesel Lunga	68
FIAT (RA) 600 S	68
FIAT (U) 600 S	68
MITSUBISHI Minica Ami 55 Series	68
NISSAN-DATSUN Cedric Series (60 hp, diesel) / Gloria Series (60 hp, diesel)	68
RENAULT (F) 4 Break Series (27 hp) / Rodeo 4	68
SUZUKI Fronte Series (28 and 31 hp) / Alto Hatchback	68
ZCZ Zastava 750 LC / Zastava 750 M	68
PORTARO 250	70
ARO 240 / 241 / 242 / 243 / 244 (83 hp)	71
DAIHATSU Taft Series (80 hp)	71
FASA-RENAULT 4 / 4 TL	71
FIAT (I) Panda 30 / Campagnola Diesel	71
LEDL Bugatti 35 B	71
UAZ 469 B	71
VOLKSWAGEN (D) 1200 L	71
VOLKSWAGEN (MEX) 1200 L / 181	71
VOLKSWAGEN (WAN) 1200	71
FIBERFAB Sherpa	73
GURGEL X-12 / X-12 TR	73
LAND ROVER 109" V8	73
MINI 850 City / 850 Super	73
HINDUSTAN Ambassador Mark 4	74
AZLK Moskvich 2138 / Moskvich 2136	75
CITROËN Dyane 6	75
EL NASR Nasr 133	75
FIAT (I) Campagnola	75
GIANNINI Fiat Giannini 126 Series (29 hp)	75
MERCEDES-BENZ 240 GD	75
MITSUBISHI Jeep Series (100 and 110 hp, 80 hp diesel)	75
PREMIER Padmini	75
RENAULT (RA) 4 S	75
SEAT 133 Lujo	75
SYRENA 105	75
TOYOTA Landcruiser K-BJ41V-KCY	75
VOLKSWAGEN (BR) 1300 / 1300 L	75
ZCZ Zastava 750 SC	75
FIAT (RA) 133 B	76
MERCEDES-BENZ 300 GD	76
RENAULT (F) 5 Berline Series (36 hp)	76
CITROËN LNA / Visa Spécial / Visa Club	77
FORD (GB) Escort Series (41 hp, economy)	77
MINI 1000 Super	77
JEEP CORPORATION Jeep Series (90 hp)	78
LEDL Mercedes SS 29	78
NISSAN-DATSUN Patrol 4WD	78
PEUGEOT 504 Break Series (59 hp, diesel)	78
RENAULT (F) 4 Break Series (34 hp, 845 cc)	78
RENAULT (RA) 6 GTL	78
SEAT 131 Diesel Perkins 5 Puertas	78
WARTBURG 353 W Tourist / 353 W De Luxe	78
YLN 803 DL	78
ZAZ 968-A	78
AMERICAN MOTORS Eagle Series	79
CLASSIC CAR Blower Phaeton	79
INTERNATIONAL HARVESTER Scout Series (76.5 hp, 101 hp diesel)	80
PREMIER Padmini De Luxe	80
RELIANT Kitten DL Saloon / Kitten DL Estate Car Robin 850 / Robin 850 Super	80
TALBOT (GB) Sunbeam Series (42 hp)	80
FIAT (RA) 133 L	81
FORD (D) Fiesta Series (40 hp) / Escort Series (46 hp)	81
FORD (GB) Fiesta Series (40 hp)	81
ISUZU Florian S11 Series (62 hp, diesel) / 117 Series (73 hp, diesel)	81
LEYLAND Mini-Moke Californian	81
MERCEDES-BENZ 230 G	81
MINI Clubman Saloon / Clubman Estate Car	81
NISSAN-DATSUN Laurel Series (60 hp, diesel)	81
PEUGEOT 504 Break Series (70 hp, diesel)	81
RENAULT (F) Rodeo 6	81
SHANGHAI Sedan	81
ŠKODA 105 S / 105 L	81
TALBOT (E) 180 Series (60 hp, diesel)	81
TOYOTA Crown Series (72 hp, diesel)	81
VOLKSWAGEN (D) Iltis	81
WARTBURG 353 W	81
CLASSIC CAR Gepard SS 100	82
VAZ Lada Niva 2121 4×4	82
FASA-RENAULT 6 TL / 7 TL	83
AUTOBIANCHI A 112 Junior	84
AZLK Moskvich 2137 / Moskvich 2140 Combi IZh	84
CLASSIC CAR Bugatti 35 B / Bugatti 55	84
DAIHATSU Charade Series (55 hp)	84
FIAT (I) Panda 45 / 127 Series (45 hp) / 132 Diesel 2000	84
FIAT (RA) 133 T	84
FORD (GB) Granada Series (63 hp, diesel)	84
GAZ Volga 24 Indenor diesel	84
JEEP CORPORATION Jeep Series (126 hp)	84
MERCEDES-BENZ 200 Limousine Series (60 hp, diesel)	84
NISSAN-DATSUN Cedric Series (91 hp, diesel) / Gloria Series (91 hp, diesel)	84
OPEL Rekord Series (65 hp, diesel)	84
PEUGEOT 104 Series (45 hp) / 304 Break Series (50 hp, diesel) / 305 Berline Series (50 hp, diesel) / 504 Berline Series (65 hp, diesel)	84
RENAULT (F) 6 TL	84
SEAT 127 Series (43 hp) / 132 Diesel 2200 / 132 Diesel 2200 Lujo	84
VOLKSWAGEN (D) Polo Series (40 hp) / Derby Series (40 hp)	84
ZCZ Zastava 101 B / Zastava 101 B Comfort / Zastava 101 Mediteran	84
AMERICAN MOTORS Spirit Series (82 hp) / Concord Series (82 hp)	85
AUSTIN Maxi Series (68 hp)	85
CHEVROLET (USA) Impala Series (105 hp, diesel) / Caprice Classic Series (105 hp, diesel)	85
FIAT (BR) 147 Series (57 hp)	85
FORD (D) Granada Series (63 hp, diesel)	85
GP Talon	85
OLDSMOBILE Delta 88 Series (105 hp, diesel) / Ninety Eight Series (105 hp, diesel) / Custom Cruiser Series (105 hp, diesel)	85
OPEL Ascona Series (58 hp, diesel)	85
PONTIAC (CDN) Catalina Series (105 hp, diesel) / Laurentian Series (105 hp, diesel) / Parisienne Series (105 hp, diesel)	85
TRIUMPH Dolomite Series (58 hp)	85
VOLVO (NL) 66 L / 66 L	85
CHEVROLET (ZA) Ascona Series (54 hp)	86
FASA-RENAULT 5 Series (50 hp)	86
FORD (D) Taunus Series (59 hp)	86
LAFER MP / TI	86
MAZDA Familia (USA) Series (52 hp)	86
MORRIS Marina Series (57 hp)	86
TALBOT (E) Simca 1200 Series (50 hp)	86
VOLKSWAGEN (BR) 1600 Limousine / Brasilia 2-dr / Brasilia 4-dr / Brasilia LS / Variant II	86
VOLKSWAGEN (WAN) Igala	86
AUSTIN Allegro 3 Series (45 hp)	87
AUTOBIANCHI A 112 Elegant / A 112 Elite	87
CHEVROLET (BR) Opala Caravan / Comodoro Caravan	87
CHEVROLET (USA) Citation Series (90 hp)	87
CHEVROLET (ZA) Ascona Series (57 hp)	87
DAIHATSU Charade Series (60 hp) / Delta Series	87
EL NASR Nasr 128	87
FASA-RENAULT 12 Series (57 hp)	87
FIAT (I) 128 CL 1100 / 128 Panorama Base 1100 / Ritmo Series (55 hp, diesel) / 131 Series (60 hp, diesel)	87
FIAT (RA) 128 C	87
FORD (GB) Cortina Series (60 hp)	87
GIANNINI Fiat Giannini 126 Series (41.4 hp)	87
HONDA Civic Van / Wagon Series	87
KIA Brisa 1000	87
MINI 1275 GT	87
NUOVA INNOCENTI Mini 90 N / Mini 90 SL	87
OLDSMOBILE Omega Series (90 hp)	87
OPEL Kadett Series (53 hp)	87
OTOSAN Anadol SL	87
PONTIAC (USA) Phoenix Series (90 hp)	87
RENAULT (F) 16 Berline Series (55 hp)	87
RENAULT (RA) 12 TL	87
ŠKODA 120 L	87
TALBOT (F) Simca 1100 Series (50 hp)	87
TOYOTA Mark II and Chaser Series (72 hp, diesel) Landcruiser FJ56V-K	87
VAZ Lada Series (60 hp)	87
VOLKSWAGEN (D) Golf Series (50 hp) / Golf Diesel Series	87
VOLKSWAGEN (USA) Rabbit Series (48 hp, diesel)	87
CHEVROLET (BR) Chevette Series	88
FORD (BR) Corcel II Base / Corcel II L / Corcel II LDO Corcel II Belina Base / Corcel II Belina L / Corcel II Belina LDO / Corcel II GT	88
FORD (ZA) Escort Series (57 hp) / Cortina Series (57 hp)	88
PEUGEOT 505 Berlina Series (70 hp, diesel)	88
VOLKSWAGEN (D) Passat Diesel Series	88
CITROËN Visa Super	89
FIAT (I) Strada Series	89
MERCEDES-BENZ 240 Limousine Series	89
RENAULT (F) 14 Berline Series (57 hp)	89
TALBOT (GB) Avenger Series (59 hp)	89
AMERICAN MOTORS Spirit Series (108 hp) / AMX Concord Series (108 hp) / Pacer Series	90
ANTIQUE & CLASSIC AUTOMOTIVE 1927 Bugatti 37B / 1931 Alfa Romeo / Frazer Nash TT Interceptor / Jaguar SS 100 / 1930 Blower Phaeton	90
AUDI Audi 80 Limousine Series (55 hp)	90
AVALLONE A 11	90
CHECKER Marathon Series (115 hp)	90
CHEVROLET (BR) Veraneio Series	90
CHEVROLET (USA) Chevette Series (70 hp)	90
CHRYSLER (USA) Le Baron Series (90 hp) / Cordoba (90 hp)	90

	mph
DACIA 1300 / 1301 Saloon / 1300 Break	90
DAYTONA Migi	90
DODGE (RA) 1500	90
DODGE (USA) Aspen Series (90 hp) / Diplomat Series (90 hp) / Mirada (90 hp)	90
FIAT (I) Ritmo Series (60 hp, 1,049 cc)	90
FIAT (RA) 128 CL / 128 CLF	90
GAZ Volga 24 / Volga 24-02	90
INTERNATIONAL HARVESTER Scout Series (148 hp)	90
ISUZU Gemini Series (61 hp, diesel)	90
JEEP CORPORATION Cherokee Series (114 hp) / Wagoneer Series (114 hp)	90
MAZDA Familia AP Series (70 hp)	90
NISSAN-DATSUN Pulsar Series (70 hp) / Sunny Series (70 hp)	90
OPEL Ascona Series (60 hp)	90
OTOSAN Anadol SV-1600	90
PLYMOUTH Volaré Series (90 hp)	90
POLSKI-FIAT 125 P 1300 / 125 P 1300 Estate	90
PONTIAC (CDN) Acadian Series (70 hp)	90
ROM CARMEL Rom 1301	90
SEAT 133 Lujo (52 hp)	90
ŠKODA S 110 R Coupé	90
TALBOT (F) Matra Rancho / Matra Rancho Grand Raid	90
VANDEN PLAS 1500	90
VOLKSWAGEN (BR) Passat Limousine Series (65 hp)	90
VOLVO (NL) 66 GL / 340 Series	90
YLN 302 DX	90
ZCZ Zastava 101 SC	90
CHEVROLET (CDN) Bel Air Series (105 hp, diesel)	91
CITROËN GS Spécial Break / CX 2500 Diesel Series	91
DODGE (USA) Omni Series	91
FORD (D) Granada Series (71 hp)	91
FORD (GB) Capri II Coupé Series (57 hp)	91
OPEL Rekord Series (60 hp)	91
PEUGEOT 305 Berline Series (65 hp) / 504 Break Series (73 hp)	91
PLYMOUTH Horizon Series	91
RENAULT (F) 20 TD / 20 GTD	91
TALBOT (F) Simca 1100 Series (58 hp)	91
VAUXHALL Chevette Series (56.6 hp)	91
CADILLAC De Ville Series (105 hp, diesel) / Fleetwood Series (105 hp, diesel)	92
CHRYSLER (AUS) Sigma GE Series (74 hp)	92
CITROËN GSA Club C Matic / GSA Pallas C Matic	92
FASA-RENAULT 12 Series (70 hp)	92
LINCOLN Continental Series (129 hp) / Continental Mark VI	92
MERCEDES-BENZ 300 Series (80 hp)	92
TALBOT (F) Simca Horizon Series (59 hp)	92
TALBOT (GB) Horizon Series (58 hp)	92
VAUXHALL Cavalier Series (56.6 hp)	92
VOLKSWAGEN (D) Jetta Series (60 hp)	92
VOLVO (S) 244 GL D6 / 245 GL D6	92
ALFA ROMEO Alfasud Series (63 hp)	93
AUDI Audi 100 Limousine Series (70 hp, diesel) / Audi 100 Avant Limousine Series (70 hp, diesel)	93
AZLK Moskvich 2140 / Moskvich 2140 IZh	93
BUICK Skylark Series (90 hp)	93
CADILLAC Seville (105 hp, diesel) / Fleetwood Eldorado (105 hp, diesel)	93
CHEVROLET (BR) Opala Sedan / Opala Coupé / Opala SS-4 Coupé / Opala SS-4 Caravan / Diplomata Sedan / Diplomata Coupé	93
CHEVROLET (USA) Chevette Series (74 hp)	93
CHRYSLER (USA) Newport (90 hp) / New Yorker (90 hp)	93
CITROËN GS Spécial Berline / GSA Club Break	93
DAIHATSU Charmant Series (72 hp)	93
DODGE (RA) 1500 M 1.8 / 1500 M 1.8 Rural	93
DODGE (USA) St. Regis (90 hp)	93
EL NASR Nasr 125 / Nasr 131 CL	93
FIAT (BR) 147 Series (72 hp)	93
FIAT (I) 131 Series (65 hp, 72 hp diesel) / 132 Diesel 2500	93
FORD (USA) Granada Series (97 hp)	93
GIANNINI Fiat Giannini 127 Series	93
HONDA Civic CVCC Series (68 hp) / Accord 1800 Series	93
KIA Brisa 1300	93
MARQUEZ GTM	93
MAZDA Familia AP Series (80 hp)	93
MERCEDES-BENZ 280 GE	93
MERCURY (USA) Monarch Series (97 hp)	93
MITSUBISHI Mirage Series (72 hp) / Lancer EX Series (80 hp)	93
MONTEVERDI Safari	93
NISSAN-DATSUN Violet Series (80 hp) / Auster Series (80 hp) / Stanza Series (80 hp)	93
OPEL Manta Series (60 hp)	93
PEUGEOT 304 Break Series (65 hp) / 604 Berline Series (80 hp, diesel)	93
PLYMOUTH Gran Fury Series (90 hp)	93
POLSKI-FIAT Polonez	93
PONTIAC (CDN) Acadian Series (74 hp) / Le Mans Series (115 hp) / Catalina Series (115 hp) / Laurentian Series (115 hp)	93
PONTIAC (USA) Le Mans Series (115 hp) / Grand Le Mans (115 hp) / Grand Am Series (115 hp) / Firebird Series (115 hp) / Bonneville Series (115 hp) / Catalina Series (115 hp)	93
SEAT Ritmo Series (64 hp) / 124-D / 124-D LS / 131 CL 1430 5 Puertas / 131 Diesel Perkins / 131 Diesel Perkins Supermirafiori	93
ŠKODA 120 LS	93
SUBARU Leone Series (72 hp)	93
TOFAS Murat 131	93
VOLKSWAGEN (D) Passat Series (55 hp)	93
VOLKSWAGEN (USA) Rabbit Series (62 and 76 hp)	93
AUSTIN Allegro 3 Series (90 hp)	94
HOLDEN VB Commodore Series (85 hp)	94
OLDSMOBILE Cutlass Series (105 hp, diesel) / Toronado (105 hp, diesel)	94
RENAULT (RA) 12 TS Break	94
TALBOT (F) Simca 1510 Series (68 hp)	94
TALBOT (GB) Alpine Series (68 hp)	94
DOGE (BR) Polara / Polara Gran Luxo	95
FORD (RA) Taunus L 2000 Sedan / Taunus GXL Sedan / Falcon Sedan Standard / Falcon Sedan De Luxe / Falcon Station Wagon Standard / Falcon Station Wagon De Luxe	95
MG Midget	95
MORRIS Marina Series (78 hp)	95
OLDSMOBILE Delta 88 Series (110 hp) / Ninety Eight Series (110 hp) / Custom Cruiser Series (110 hp)	95
PEUGEOT 305 Berline Series (74 hp)	95
RENAULT (F) 18 Series (64 hp)	95
ALFA ROMEO Alfetta 2000 Turbo D	96
AUSTIN Maxi Series (91 hp)	96
CHECKER Marathon Series (125 hp, diesel)	96
CHEVROLET (BR) Comodoro Sedan / Comodoro Coupé	96
CHEVROLET (USA) Monza Series (86 hp)	96
CUSTOCA Hurrycane / Strato ES	96
FORD (AUS) XD Falcon Series (110 hp) / Fairmont Series (110 hp)	96
FORD (D) Capri II Series (68 hp)	96
FORD (RA) Fairlane LTD 3600 Sedan	96
FORD (USA) Pinto Series / Mustang Series (88 hp) / Fairmont Series (88 hp)	96
GIANNINI Fiat Giannini Ritmo Series (72 hp)	96
HOLDEN Gemini TD Series / HZ Series (110 hp)	96
HYUNDAI Pony 2+1-dr Sedan / Pony 4-dr Sedan	96
LANCIA Delta Berlina 1300 (4 gears) / Delta Berlina 1300 (5 gears)	96
LAND ROVER Range Rover	96
MAZDA Familia (USA) Series (65 hp) / Luce Series (100 hp)	96
MERCURY (CDN) Bobcat Series / Marquis Meteor Series	96
MERCURY (USA) Bobcat Series (88 and 89 hp) / Zephyr Series (88 hp) / Capri Series (88 hp) / Marquis Series (130 hp) / Grand Marquis Series (130 hp)	96
MITSUBISHI Lancer EX Series (86 hp) / Celeste Series (80 hp) / Galant Sigma Series (86 hp) / Galant Lambda Series (86 hp) / Debonair Series	96
NISSAN-DATSUN Skyline Series (95 hp)	96
NUOVA INNOCENTI Mini 120 SL	96
OLDSMOBILE Starfire Series (86 hp)	96
PEUGEOT 504 Berline Series (79 hp)	96
POLSKI-FIAT 125 P 1500 / 125 P 1500 Estate	96
PONTIAC (USA) Sunbird Series (86 hp) / Grand Prix Series (115 hp) / Bonneville Series (125 hp, diesel) / Catalina Series (125 hp, diesel)	96
RENAULT (F) 14 Berline Series (69 hp)	96
RENAULT (RA) 12 TS	96
SEAT 124-D Especial / 131 1430 / 131 1430 Supermirafiori	96
TORO 1300	96
VAZ Lada Series (78 hp)	96
VOLKSWAGEN (D) Polo Series (60 hp) / Derby Series (60 hp) / Scirocco Series (60 hp)	96
FORD (RA) Falcon Sedan Futura	97
FORD (USA) Thunderbird (115 hp)	97
TOYOTA Corolla Series (72 hp) / Sprinter Series (72 hp)	97
ZCZ Zastava 101 Special	97
BUICK Century Series (110 hp) / Regal Series (110 hp)	98
CITROËN GSA Club / GSA Pallas / GSA X3	98
FORD (D) Fiesta Series (66 hp)	98
FORD (GB) Fiesta Series (66 hp)	98
LINCOLN Continental Series (140 hp) / Continental Mark VI	98
OPEL Kadett Series (75 hp) / Kadett SR Series	98
PEUGEOT 104 Series (72 hp)	98
VAUXHALL Astra Series	98
AUDI Audi 100 Limousine Series (85 hp) / Audi 100 Avant Limousine Series (85 hp)	99
AUTOBIANCHI A 112 Abarth	99
BMW (D) 316 / 518	99
BMW (ZA) 518	99
BUICK Skyhawk Series	99
CHEVROLET (CDN) Bel Air Series (115 hp)	99
CHEVROLET (USA) Impala Series (110 hp) / Caprice Classic Series (110 hp)	99
DAIHATSU Charmant Series (88 hp)	99
DODGE (USA) St. Regis (130 hp)	99
FIAT (I) 127 Series (70 hp) / Ritmo Series (75 hp) / Brava Series (80 hp) / 132 1600 Berlina	99
FIAT (RA) 128 1300 TV Iava	99
FORD (AUS) ZJ Fairlane Series (126 hp) / FC LTD Series (126 hp)	99
HOLDEN Sunbird Series	99
HONDA Civic CVCC Series (85 hp)	99
HONGQI 9-pass. Limousine	99
HYUNDAI Pony Station Wagon	99
ISUZU Florian SII Series	99
JEEP CORPORATION Cherokee Series (129 hp) / Wagoneer Series (129 hp)	99
LANCIA Delta Berlina 1500	99
MAZDA Capella Series (90 and 110 hp)	99
MERCEDES-BENZ 200 Limousine Series (94 hp)	99
MITSUBISHI Mirage Series (88 hp)	99
NISSAN-DATSUN Pulsar Series (92 hp) / Sunny Series (92 hp) / Bluebird Series (95 hp) / Laurel Series (105 hp)	99
NUOVA INNOCENTI Mini De Tomaso	99

	mph
OLDSMOBILE Cutlass Series (110 hp)	99
PONTIAC (USA) Grand Prix Series (155 hp) / Bonneville Series (140 hp) / Catalina Series (140 hp)	99
PRINCESS 1700 Series (87 hp) / 2000 Series (87 hp) 2200 Series (87 hp)	99
SEAT Ritmo Series (77) hp / 131 CL 1600 5 Puertas	99
TOYOTA Corsa Series (74 and 83 hp) / Tercel Series (74 and 83 hp) / Crown Series (110 hp)	99
VOLKSWAGEN (BR) Passat Limousine Series (80 hp)	99
BLAKELY Bearcat "S"	100
CHEVROLET (USA) Malibu Series (110 hp) / Montecarlo Series (110 hp)	100
ELITE Laser 917	100
FORD (CDN) LTD 2-dr Sedan	100
FORD (USA) Thunderbird (131 hp) / LTD Series (130 hp)	100
MERCURY (USA) Zephyr Series (119 hp) / Capri Series (118 hp)	100
TALBOT (F) Simca Horizon Series (83 hp)	100
TALBOT (GB) Avenger Series (80 hp) / Horizon Series (82 hp)	100
TIMMIS Ford V8 Roadster	100
TOTAL REPLICA Hi Boy / Ford "B" Phaeton	100
TRIUMPH Spitfire 1500	100

From 101 mph to 120 mph

	mph
FORD (AUS) Escort Series (98 hp) / Cortina TE Series (126 hp)	101
RENAULT (F) 18 Series (79 hp)	101
DODGE (BR) Dart Series	102
FORD (ZA) Granada Series (99 hp)	102
MITSUBISHI Celeste Series (105 hp) / Galant Sigma Series (105 hp)	102
PEUGEOT 504 Break Series (96 hp) / 505 Berline Series (96 hp)	102
SAAB 99 Series (100 hp) / 900 Series (100 hp)	102
TALBOT (E) 150 Series (75 hp)	102
TOMORROWS CLASSIC 1953 Corvette Roadster Replica (110 hp)	102
ALFA ROMEO Giulietta 1.3	103
BMW (D) 318	103
CHEVROLET (USA) Monza Series (110 hp)	103
CHEVROLET (ZA) Chevair Series / Rekord Series / Commodore Series (120 and 132 hp)	103
CHRYSLER (USA) Newport (155 hp) / New Yorker (155 hp)	103
DODGE (USA) Aspen Series (155 hp)	103
ENVEMO 90 Super Coupé / 90 Super Cabriolet	103
FORD (AUS) Cortina TE Series (109 hp)	103
FORD (BR) Galaxie 500 / Galaxie LTD / Galaxie Landau	103
FORD (GB) Granada Series (101 hp)	103
FORD (USA) Granada Series (134 hp)	103
ISUZU Gemini Series (100 hp)	103
LANCIA Beta Coupé 1300	103
MERCEDES-BENZ 300 Series (110 hp)	103
MERCURY (USA) Monarch Series (134 hp) / Marquis Series (140 hp) / Grand Marquis Series (140 hp)	103
MITSUBISHI Galant Lambda Series (120 hp)	103
NISSAN-DATSUN Cedric and Gloria Series (115 hp)	103
OLDSMOBILE Starfire Series (110 hp)	103
PLYMOUTH Volaré Series (155 hp)	103
PONTIAC (USA) Sunbird Series (110 hp)	103
RENAULT (F) 20 TL / 20 GTL / 20 TS Automatic	103
SEAT 131 Supermirafiori 1600	103
TALBOT (E) 150 Series (88 hp)	103
TOYOTA Starlet Series / Carina Series (88 hp) / Celica Series (88 hp) / Corona Series (88 hp) / Mark II Series (95 and 140 hp) / Chaser Series (95 and 140 hp)	103
VOLVO (S) 240 Series (97 hp)	103
YLN 902 SD	103
CHRYSLER (USA) Le Baron Series (155 hp)	104
CITROËN CX Reflex Break	104
DODGE (USA) Diplomat Series (155 hp)	104
AUTOMOBILI INTERMECCANICA Speedster	105
CHEVROLET (USA) Malibu Series (155 hp)	105
FAIRTHORPE TX-S 1500	105
FIAT (I) Brava Series (102 hp) / 124 Sport Spider 2000 132 2000 Berlina	105
MORGAN 4/4 1600 2-seater / 4/4 1600 4-seater	105
OLDSMOBILE Cutlass Series (155 hp)	105
PONTIAC (CDN) Le Mans Series (155 hp)	105
AUTOMOBILI INTERMECCANICA La Crosse	106
CHECKER Marathon Series (155 hp)	106
CHEVROLET (USA) Citation Series (115 hp) / Camaro Series (110 hp)	106
CHRYSLER (AUS) Valiant CM Series (163 hp)	106
FASA-RENAULT 5 Series (93 hp)	106
FELBER Oasis	106
FIAT (BR) Alfa Romeo 2300 B	106
FIAT (RA) 125 BN / 125 T / 125 S / 125 SL / 125 SF	106
FORD (RA) Taunus GXL 2300 Sedan / Taunus GT Coupé / Taunus GT Coupé SP	106
FORD (USA) LTD Series (140 hp)	106
HONDA Prelude Series	106
LANCIA Beta Berlina 1600	106
MAZDA 626 Series (for Europe)	106
MERCEDES-BENZ 230 Series	106
MONTEVERDI Sahara	106
NISSAN-DATSUN Bluebird Series (120 hp) / Silvia Series (105 hp) / Gazelle Series (105 hp)	106
OLDSMOBILE Omega Series (115 hp)	106
PONTIAC (USA) Phoenix Series (115 hp) / Le Mans Series (155 hp) / Grand Le Mans Series (155 hp) / Gran Am Series (155 hp)	106
PRINCESS 1700 Series (110 hp) / 2000 Series (110 hp) 2200 Series (110 hp)	106
RENAULT (F) 16 Berline Series (90 hp) / 20 TS	106
REPLICARS Phaeton / Roadster / Hardtop	106
SEAT 132 2000 Lujo	106
STUTZ IV Porte Sedan	106
SUBARU Leone Series (100 hp)	106
TALBOT (E) Simca 1200 Series (83 hp) / 180 Series (100 hp)	106
TALBOT (F) Simca 1510 Series (88 hp) / Simca 2 L Automatique	106
TALBOT (GB) Alpine Series (87 hp)	106
VOLVO (S) 260 Series (125 hp)	106
YLN 805 SD	106
BUICK Le Sabre Series (105 hp, diesel)	107
FIAT (I) 124 Sport Sider 2000i	107
MG MGB GT / MGB Sports	107
VAUXHALL Carlton 2000 Saloon / Carlton 2000 Estate Car	107
CHEVROLET (CDN) Bel Air Series (155 hp)	108
CHEVROLET (USA) Impala Series (155 hp) / Caprice Classic Series (155 hp)	108
CITROËN CX Reflex / CX Athena / CX 2400 Series	108
LANCIA Beta HPE 1600	108
PONTIAC (CDN) Catalina Series (155 hp) / Laurentian Series (155 hp) / Parisienne Series (155 hp)	108
RAPPORT Quadraporte	108
SPARTAN CARS 2-seater Sports / 2+2-seater Sports	108
TECHNICAL EXPONENTS TX Tripper 1500 / TX Tripper 1500 De Luxe	108
ALFA ROMEO Alfasud Series (95 hp) / Giulietta 1.6 Alfetta 1.6	109
BMW (ZA) 520	109
CHEVROLET (BR) Opala SS-6 Coupé / Opala SS-6 Caravan	109
CHEVROLET (USA) Camaro Series (190 hp)	109
CHRYSLER (AUS) Valiant CM Series (155 hp)	109
FIAT (BR) Alfa Romeo 2300 TI	109
FIAT (I) 132 2000i Berlina	109
FORD (D) Taunus Series (114 hp)	109
FORD (GB) Cortina Series (114 hp)	109
FORD (RA) Fairlane LTD-V8 Sedan	109
FORD (USA) Mustang Series (150 hp) / Fairmont Series (150 hp)	109
GIANNINI Fiat Giannini Ritmo Series (80 hp)	109
ISUZU 117 Series (110 hp)	109
LINCOLN Versailles	109
MAZDA Luce Series (140 hp)	109
NISSAN-DATSUN Violet Series (115 hp) / Auster Series (115 hp) / Stanza Series (115 hp) / Skyline Series (130 hp)	109
OPEL Ascona Series (100 hp)	109
PEUGEOT 505 Berline Series (110 hp)	109
PLYMOUTH Gran Fury Series (130 hp)	109
RENAULT (F) 5 Berline Series (93 hp)	109
RENAULT (RA) 12 Alpine	109
SEAT Lancia Beta HPE 2000	109
TALBOT (F) Simca 1610	109
TOYOTA Sprinter Series (115 hp) / Celica (USA) Series / Crown Series (145 hp)	109
VAUXHALL Cavalier Series (100 hp)	109
VOLVO (S) 260 Series (148 hp)	109
ARKLEY SS	110
BUICK Skylark Series (115 hp)	110
EXCALIBUR Series III	110
FORD (AUS) Escort Series (112 hp)	110
FORD (GB) Escort Series (110 hp)	110
MAZDA Cosmo Series (110 hp)	110
NOVA Sports	110
OLDSMOBILE Delta 88 Series (160 hp) / Ninety Eight Series (160 hp) / Custom Cruiser Series (160 hp)	110
PANTHER Lima	110
RENAULT (F) 30 TS Automatic	110
TOYOTA Corolla Series (115 hp)	110
LANCIA Beta Coupé 1600	111
LEDL Tanga	111
OPEL Rekord Series (110 hp)	111
PEUGEOT 504 Cabriolet / 504 Coupé	111
VOLKSWAGEN (D) Jetta Series (110 hp)	111
ALFA ROMEO Giulietta 1.8 / Alfetta GT 1.6 / Alfetta 1.8	112
AUDI Audi 80 Limousine Series (110 hp)	112
BMW (D) 320 / 520	112
CATERHAM CARS Super 7	112
CITROËN CX 2400 Pallas Injection C Matic	112
DODGE (BR) Le Baron / Charger R/T / Magnum	112
FIAT (I) X1/9 five speed / 131 Series (115 hp)	112
FORD (D) Escort Series (110 hp)	112
FORD (RA) Falcon Sedan Sprint	112
FORD (ZA) Escort Series (110 hp)	112
GAZ Chaika	112
HONGQI 6-pass. Limousine	112
ISUZU Gemini Series (130 hp) / 117 Series (135 hp)	112
LANCIA Beta Berlina 2000 / Beta HPE 2000	112
MAZDA Cosmo Series (140 hp) / Savanna RX7 Series	112
MERCEDES-BENZ 250 Limousine Series	112
NISSAN-DATSUN Laurel Series (140 hp) / Fairlady Series (130 and 145 hp) / President Series / Silvia Series (120 hp) / Gazelle Series (120 hp) / Cedric Series (145 hp, turbo) / Gloria Series (145 hp, turbo)	112
OLDSMOBILE Toronado (150 hp)	112
OPEL Commodore Series	112
ROLLS-ROYCE Phantom VI	112
SBARRO Replica BMW 328 Standard	112
SEAT 124 Especial 2000 / 131 Supermirafiori 2000	112
STUTZ Royale Limousine	11
TOYOTA Carina Series (135 hp) / Celica Series (140 hp) / Corona Series (135 hp) / Century Series	11
CHEVROLET (USA) Montecarlo Series (170 hp)	11
PEUGEOT 604 Berline Series (136 hp)	11
PUMA GTE 1600 Coupé / GTS 1600 Sport	11
RENAULT (F) 30 TX Automatic	11
VAUXHALL Royale Saloon	11

	mph
VOLKSWAGEN (D) Golf Series (110 hp)	113
FORD (ZA) Cortina Series (138 hp) / Granada Series (159 hp)	114
PANTHER J 72 4.2-litre	114
RENAULT (F) 30 TS	114
ROVER 2300	114
SEAT Lancia Beta Coupé 2000	114
TRIUMPH TR 7	114
VOLKSWAGEN (D) Passat Series (110 hp)	114
ALFA ROMEO Alfetta 2000 L	115
CADILLAC Seville (145 hp) / Fleetwood Eldorado (145 hp)	115
CHRYSLER (USA) Cordoba (185 hp)	115
DAIMLER Limousine	115
DODGE (USA) Mirada (185 hp)	115
HOLDEN VB Commodore Series (152 hp) / HZ Series (216 hp)	115
JAGUAR XJ 3.4	115
LANCIA Gamma Berlina 2000 / Gamma Coupé 2000	115
PEUGEOT 604 Berline Series (144 hp)	115
RENAULT (RA) Torino Grand Routier GR	115
TALBOT (F) Matra Bagheera	115
VAUXHALL Chevette Series (135 hp) / Royale Coupé	115
VOLKSWAGEN Scirocco Series (110 hp)	115
VOLVO (S) 240 Series (140 hp)	115
BUICK Century Series (170 hp) / Regal Series (170 hp)	116
OLDSMOBILE Toronado (160 hp)	116
OPEL Manta Series (110 hp)	116
TATRA T 613	116
TRIUMPH Dolomite Series (127 hp)	116
AUDI Audi 200 Limousine Series (136 hp)	117
BUICK Riviera Series (170 hp)	117
CITROËN CX 2400 GTI	117
LANCIA Beta Coupé 2000	117
PEUGEOT 504 V6 Coupé	117
RENAULT (F) 30 TX	117
AUDI Audi 100 Limousine Series (136 hp) / Audi 100 Avant Limousine Series (136 hp)	118
BENTLEY T2 Saloon / Corniche Saloon / Corniche Convertible	118
BMW (D) 323 i	118
BMW (ZA) 528 i	118
CADILLAC De Ville Series (150 hp) / Fleetwood Series (150 hp)	118
CHEVROLET (ZA) Senator	118
CITROËN CX Prestige	118
DAIMLER Sovereign 4.2 / Vanden Plas 4.2	118
FAIRTHORPE TX-S 2000	118
FELBER Excellence Coupé / Excellence Roadster	118
FORD (AUS) XD Falcon Series (200 hp) / Fairmont Series (200 hp)	118
JAGUAR XJ 4.2	118
LANCIA Montecarlo	118
MERCEDES-BENZ 280 Series (156 hp)	118
MERCURY (USA) Cougar XR-7 (115 hp)	118
OPEL Senator Series (140 hp)	118
PONTIAC (USA) Firebird Series (210 hp, turbo)	118
ROLLS-ROYCE Silver Shadow II / Silver Wraith II / Silver Wraith II with division / Corniche Saloon / Corniche Convertible / Camargue	118
SBARRO Windhound 4×4	118
STUTZ Blackhawk VI / Bearcat	118

	mph
TALBOT (F) Matra Bagheera X	118
BMW (ZA) 728	119
BUICK Electra Series (105 hp, diesel)	119
PORSCHE 924 (USA)	119
ROVER 2600	119
BMW (D) 525	120
BUICK Le Sabre Series (110 hp) / Electra Series (125 hp)	120
FORD (D) Granada Series (160 hp)	120
FORD (GB) Granada Series (160 hp)	120
K.M.B. GTM Mk 1-3	120
LENHAM Austin-Healey 3000	120
TALBOT (GB) Sunbeam Series (150 hp)	120

Over 120 mph

	mph
ALFA ROMEO Alfetta GTV 2000 L / 2000 Spider Veloce / Alfa 6	121
BMW (ZA) 730	121
LANCIA Gamma Berlina 2500 / Gamma Coupé 2500	121
MERCURY (USA) Cougar XR-7 (131 hp)	121
OPEL Monza Series (140 hp)	121
SAAB 99 Series (145 hp) / 900 Series (145 hp)	121
BMW (D) 728 i	122
FORD (D) Capri II Series (138 hp)	122
BMW (ZA) 733 i	123
PUMA GTB S2	123
AVANTI Avanti II	124
BMW (ZA) 530	124
CHEVROLET (USA) Corvette Coupé (190 hp)	124
FORD (GB) Capri II Coupé Series (138 hp)	124
MERCEDES-BENZ 280 Series (185 hp)	124
MONTEVERDI Sierra	124
PORSCHE 924	124
RENAULT (RA) Torino ZX Coupé	124
Sta **MATILDE** SM 4.1	124
STIMULA Bugatti 55	124
ZIL 114 Limousine / 117 Limousine	124
AC 3000 ME	125
AUDI Audi 200 Limousine Series (170 hp)	125
CADILLAC Seville (160 hp) / Fleetwood Eldorado (160 hp)	125
KELMARK GT	125
LOTUS Elite	125
SCEPTRE 6.6 S	125
TECHNICAL EXPONENTS TX Tripper 2000 Sprint	125
BUICK Le Sabre Series (170 hp)	126
ROVER 3500	126
ALFA ROMEO Alfetta GTV 2000 Turbodelta	127
BMW (D) 732 i	127
LAMBORGHINI Urraco P 200	127
MERCEDES-BENZ 350 Series (205 hp) / 600 Series	127
GINETTA G23	128
PANTHER De Ville Saloon / De Ville Convertible	128
BMW (D) 528 i	129
AMERICAN CUSTOM INDUSTRIES American Turbo	130
ASTON MARTIN V8 Volante	130
BMW (D) 628 CSi	130
BUICK Riviera Series (160 hp)	130
LOTUS Eclat 520	130

	mph
MERCEDES-BENZ 350 Series (195 hp) / 450 Series (217 and 225 hp)	130
MONTEVERDI Sierra Cabriolet	130
OPEL Senator Series (180 hp)	130
CHEVROLET (USA) Corvette Coupé (230 hp)	131
BMW (D) 735 i	132
BRISTOL 603 S2 / 412 S2	132
BUICK Electra Series (160 hp)	132
FERRARI Dino 208 GT 4	132
LOTUS Eclat 521 / Eclat 522 / Eclat 523 / Eclat 524	132
SBARRO Replica BMW 328 America	132
TVR Tasmin / 3000 Series (142 hp) / Turbo Series (142 hp) / Taimar Series (142 hp)	133
BMW (D) 633 CSi	134
MERCEDES-BENZ 380 Limousine Series	134
OPEL Monza Series (180 hp)	134
ALPINE-RENAULT A 310 V6	137
BMW (D) 745 i	137
LAFER LL	137
MASERATI Merak	137
BMW (D) 635 CSi	138
LOTUS Esprit S2	138
ASTON MARTIN Lagonda	140
DAIMLER Double-Six 5.3 / Double-Six Vanden Plas 5.3	140
JAGUAR XJ 5.3	140
JOHNARD VINTAGE CAR Bentley Donington	140
MERCEDES-BENZ 500 Limousine Series / 450 Series (240 and 286 hp)	140
PORSCHE 924 Turbo / 911 SC Coupé / 911 SC Coupé (USA) / 911 SC Targa	140
TVR 3000 Series (230 hp) / Turbo Series (230 hp) / Taimar Series (230 hp)	140
DE TOMASO Deauville	143
MASERATI Quattroporte	143
PORSCHE 928	143
FERRARI Dino 308 GT 4	148
DE TOMASO Longchamp 2+2	149
LAMBORGHINI Urraco P 250	149
SBARRO Stash HS Cabriolet	149
ARGYLL Turbo GT	150
ELEGANT MOTORS 898 Eleganté / 898 Phaeton / 856 Speedster / Eleganté Sports Brougham	150
JAGUAR XJ-S	150
LYNX D Type	150
MORGAN Plus 8	150
FERRARI 308 GTB / 308 GTS / 400 Automatic i	152
MASERATI Kyalami	152
LAMBORGHINI Silhouette / Espada 400 GT	155
MASERATI Merak SS	155
PORSCHE Turbo Coupé (USA) / 928 S	155
DE TOMASO Pantera L	158
ASTON MARTIN V8	160
PORSCHE Turbo Coupé	162
BMW (D) M 1	163
LAMBORGHINI Urraco P 300	165
FERRARI BB 512	169
ASTON MARTIN V8 Vantage	170
MASERATI Khamsin	171
DE TOMASO Pantera GTS	174
MASERATI Bora	174
LAMBORGHINI Countach "S"	196

ABBREVIATIONS FOR COUNTRIES

ARGENTINA	**RA**	GERMANY FR	**D**	SPAIN	**E**
AUSTRALIA	**AUS**	GREAT BRITAIN	**GB**	SOUTH AFRICA	**ZA**
BRAZIL	**BR**	ITALY	**I**	SWEDEN	**S**
CANADA	**CDN**	MEXICO	**MEX**	URUGUAY	**U**
FRANCE	**F**	NIGERIA	**WAN**	USA	**USA**

MAKES, MODELS AND PRICES

Page	MAKE AND MODEL	Price in GB £	Price in USA $	Price ex Works
	AC (Great Britain)			
142	3000 ME			13,238*
	ALFA ROMEO (Italy)			
191	Alfasud 1.2 4-dr Berlina (4 gears)			4,944,000*
191	Alfasud 1.2 4-dr Super Berlina (5 gears)			5,735,000*
191	Alfasud 1.3 4-dr Super Berlina	3,900*		6,030,000*
191	Alfasud 1.3 2+1-dr Giardinetta			6,443,000*
191	Alfasud 1.3 ti 2-dr Berlina			6,396,000*
191	Alfasud 1.3 2-dr Sprint Veloce Coupé			7,835,000*
191	Alfasud 1.5 4-dr Super Berlina	4,100*		6,337,000*
191	Alfasud 1.5 ti 2-dr Berlina	4,300*		6,702,000*
191	Alfasud 1.5 2-dr Sprint Veloce Coupé	5,420*		8,142,000*
192	Giulietta 1.3			8,921,000*
192	Giulietta 1.6	5,100*		9,499,000*
192	Giulietta 1.8	5,400*		10,030,000*
193	Alfetta 1.6			9,475,000*
193	Alfetta GT 1.6			10,006,000*
193	Alfetta 1.8			10,006,000*
193	Alfetta 2000 L	6,000*	10,595*	11,847,000*
193	Alfetta GTV 2000 L	6,800*	10,995*	11,930,000*
194	Alfetta GTV 2000 Turbodelta			17,098,000*
194	Alfetta 2000 Turbo D			—
194	2000 Spider Veloce		12,415*	11,493,000*
195	Alfa 6			20,453,000*
	ALPINE RENAULT (France)			
77	A 310 V6			94,000◊
	AMERICAN CUSTOM INDUSTRIES (USA)			
273	American Turbo			32,000
	AMERICAN MOTORS (USA)			
273	Spirit Sedan			4,193
273	Spirit Liftback			4,293
273	AMX			5,653
274	Concord 2-dr Sedan			4,753
274	Concord 4-dr Sedan			4,878
274	Concord 4+1-dr St. Wagon			5,078
274	Pacer 2-dr Hatchback			5,407
274	Pacer 2+1-dr St. Wagon			5,558
275	Eagle 2-dr Sedan			6,999
275	Eagle 4-dr Sedan			7,249
275	Eagle 4+1-dr St. Wagon			7,549
	ANTIQUE & CLASSIC AUTOMOTIVE (USA)			
275	1927 Bugatti 37 B			7,500
276	1931 Alfa Romeo			7,500
276	Frazer Nash TT Interceptor			10,550
276	Jaguar SS 100			12,995
277	1930 Blower Phaeton			11,500
	ARGYLL (Great Britain)			
142	Turbo GT (V8 engine)			12,500
142	Turbo GT (4-cylinder engine)			10,700

Page	MAKE AND MODEL	Price in GB £	Price in USA $	Price ex Works
	ARKLEY (Great Britain)			
143	SS			4,950*
	ARO (Romania)			
220	100			—
220	101			—
220	103			—
220	104			—
221	240			—
221	241			—
221	242			—
221	243			—
221	244			—
	ASTON MARTIN (Great Britain)			
143	V8		65,000*	29,998*
143	V8 Vantage			32,499*
143	V8 Volante		95,000*	37,999*
144	Lagonda			49,933*
	AUBURN (USA)			
277	Speedster			28,650
277	Dual Cowl Phaeton			60,000
	AUDI (Germany FR)			
101	Audi 80 2-dr Limousine			12,884*
101	Audi 80 4-dr Limousine			13,474*
101	Audi 80 L 2-dr Limousine			13,787*
101	Audi 80 L 4-dr Limousine			14,377*
101	Audi 80 S 2-dr Limousine			13,454*
101	Audi 80 S 4-dr Limousine			14,044*
101	Audi 80 LS 2-dr Limousine			14,357*
101	Audi 80 LS 4-dr Limousine	5,388*		14,947*
101	Audi 80 GL 4-dr Limousine			14,745*
101	Audi 80 GL 4-dr Limousine			15,335*
101	Audi 80 GLS 2-dr Limousine			15,315*
101	Audi 80 GLS 4-dr Limousine	5,887*		15,905*
101	Audi 80 LS 2-dr Limousine			14,685*
101	Audi 80 LS 4-dr Limousine			15,275*
101	Audi 80 GLS 2-dr Limousine		7,495*	15,643*
101	Audi 80 GLS 4-dr Limousine		7,685*	16,233*
101	Audi 80 GLE 2-dr Limousine			17,081*
101	Audi 80 GLE 4-dr Limousine	7,095*		17,671*
102	Audi 100 2-dr Limousine			16,435*
102	Audi 100 4-dr Limousine			17,065*
102	Audi 100 L 2-dr Limousine			17,375*
102	Audi 100 L 4-dr Limousine			18,005*
102	Audi 100 GL 4-dr Limousine			19,425*
102	Audi 100 5S 2-dr Limousine			17,475*
102	Audi 100 5S 4-dr Limousine			18,105*
102	Audi 100 L5S 2-dr Limousine			18,415*
102	Audi 100 L5S 4-dr Limousine	6,690*		19,045*
102	Audi 100 GL5S 4-dr Limousine	7,444*		20,465*
102	Audi 100 CD5S 4-dr Limousine			24,160*
102	Audi 100 5E 2-dr Limousine			18,617*
102	Audi 100 5E 4-dr Limousine			19,247*
102	Audi 100 L5E 2-dr Limousine			19,557*
102	Audi 100 L5E 4-dr Limousine			20,187*
102	Audi 100 GL5E 4-dr Limousine	7,849*	10,300*	21,390*
102	Audi 100 CD5E 4-dr Limousine	9,861*		24,875*
102	Audi 100 5D 2-dr Limousine			19,010*

The prices refer to all models listed in the volume. The first column shows the prices of cars imported into the United Kingdom; the second, the prices of cars imported into the United States of America; and the third, the prices of cars in the country of origin. Prices in the USA do not include US transportation fees, state and local taxes.

* *Prices including VAT and its equivalent in European countries and also SCT in Great Britain; prices of cars imported into the United States (East Coast) including ocean freight, US excise tax and import duty.*

◊ *Prices ex-showroom in European countries.*

 Due to the international monetary situation, all the prices shown are subject to confirmation.

Page	MAKE AND MODEL	Price in GB £	Price in USA $	Price ex Works
102	Audi 100 5D 4-dr Limousine			19,640*
102	Audi 100 L5D 2-dr Limousine			19,950*
102	Audi 100 L5D 4-dr Limousine			20,580*
102	Audi 100 GL5D 4-dr Limousine		11,100*	22,000*
102	Audi 100 CD5D 4-dr Limousine			25,490*
104	Audi 100 Avant L Limousine	6,186*		18,655*
104	Audi 100 Avant GL Limousine			20,075*
104	Audi 100 Avant L5S Limousine			19,695*
104	Audi 100 Avant GL5S Limousine	7,631*		21,115*
104	Audi 100 Avant CD5S Limousine			24,810*
104	Audi 100 Avant L5E Limousine			20,837*
104	Audi 100 Avant GL5E Limousine			22,040*
104	Audi 100 Avant CD5E Limousine	10,328*		25,525*
104	Audi 100 Avant L5D Limousine	7,504*		21,230*
104	Audi 100 Avant GL5D Limousine			22,650*
104	Audi 100 Avant CD5D Limousine			26,140*
105	Audi 200 5E Limousine			27,875*
105	Audi 200 5T Limousine			30,550*
	AUSTIN (Great Britain)			
144	Allegro 3 1.1 2-dr Saloon			3,220*
144	Allegro 3 1.3 2-dr Saloon			3,346*
144	Allegro 3 1.3 4-dr Saloon			3,476*
144	Allegro 3 1.3 2+1-dr Estate Car			3,724*
144	Allegro 3 1.3 L 2-dr Saloon			3,623*
144	Allegro 3 1.3 L 4-dr Saloon			3,752*
144	Allegro 3 1.3 L 2+1-dr Estate Car			4,000*
144	Allegro 3 1.3 HL 4-dr Saloon			4,191*
144	Allegro 3 1.5 L 4-dr Saloon			3,926*
144	Allegro 3 1.5 L 2+1-dr Estate Car			4,174*
144	Allegro 3 1.5 HL 4-dr Saloon			4,364*
144	Allegro 3 1.7 L 4-dr Saloon			4,367*
144	Allegro 3 1.7 L 2+1-dr Estate Car			4,615*
144	Allegro 3 1.7 HL 4-dr Saloon			4,530*
145	Maxi 1500 Saloon			4,093*
145	Maxi 1750 Saloon			4,411*
145	Maxi 1750 HL Saloon			4,671*
145	Maxi 1750 HLS Saloon			4,801*
	AUTOBIANCHI (Italy)			
195	A 112 Junior			4,596,000◊
195	A 112 Elegant			4,962,000◊
195	A 112 Elite			5,446,000◊
195	A 112 Abarth			5,717,000◊
	AUTOMOBILI INTERMECCANICA (USA)			
278	Speedster			17,900
278	La Crosse			44,900
	AVALLONE (Brazil)			
252	A 11			—
	AVANTI (USA)			
278	Avanti II			19,500
	AZLK (USSR)			
238	Moskvich 2138			—
239	Moskvich 2136			—
239	Moskvich 2140			—
239	Moskvich 2140 IZh			—
239	Moskvich 2137			—
239	Moskvich 2140 Combi IZh			—
	BENTLEY (Great Britain)			
146	T2 Saloon		77,150*	39,219*
146	Corniche Saloon		130,990*	58,392*
147	Corniche Convertible		139,500*	62,018*

Page	MAKE AND MODEL	Price in GB £	Price in USA $	Price ex Works
	BLAKELY (USA)			
279	Bearcat "S"			9,250
	BMW (Germany FR)			
105	316	5,100*		16,250*
106	318	—		17,350*
106	320	6,469*		19,850*
106	323 i	7,550*		22,500*
106	518	6,654*		19,550*
107	520	7,772*		22,300*
107	525	8,890*		24,950*
107	528 i	10,115*		29,150*
107	728 i	11,845*		33,700*
108	732 i	13,643*		37,700*
108	735 i	15,395*		43,750*
108	745 i	—		52,000*
108	628 CSi	—		46,000*
109	633 CSi	17,462*	31,870*	48,700*
109	635 CSi	18,740*		51,900*
109	M 1	—		—
	BMW (South Africa)			
339	518			8,890
340	520			10,850
340	528 i			13,390
340	530			15,350
340	728			15,900
340	730			19,690
341	733 i			23,500
	BRISTOL (Great Britain)			
147	603 S2			39,219*
147	412 S2			32,719*
	BUICK (USA)			
279	Skyhawk "S" Hatchback Coupé			4,993
279	Skyhawk Hatchback Coupé			5,211
280	Skylark 4-dr Sedan			5,306
280	Skylark 2-dr Coupé			5,160
280	Skylark Limited 4-dr Sedan			5,725
280	Skylark Limited 2-dr Coupé			5,579
280	Skylark Sport 4-dr Sedan			5,920
280	Skylark Sport 2-dr Coupé			5,774
281	Century Notch 4-dr Sedan			5,646
281	Century Aero 2-dr Coupé			5,546
281	Century Limited Notch 4-dr Sedan			6,132
281	Century 4+1-dr St. Wagon			5,922
281	Century 4+1-dr Estate Wagon			6,220
281	Century Sport Turbo 2-dr Coupé			6,063
282	Regal Coupé			6,305
282	Regal Limited Coupé			6,724
282	Regal Sport Coupé			6,952
282	Le Sabre Thin Pillar 4-dr Sedan			6,769
282	Le Sabre 2-dr Hardtop Coupé			6,674
282	Le Sabre Limited Thin Pillar 4-dr Sedan			7,071
282	Le Sabre Limited 2-dr Hardtop Coupé			6,929
282	Le Sabre Sport 2-dr Coupé			7,782
282	Le Sabre 4+1-dr Estate Wagon			7,673
284	Electra Limited 4-dr Sedan			9,287
284	Electra Limited 2-dr Coupé			9,132
284	Electra Park Avenue 4-dr Sedan			10,383
284	Electra Park Avenue 2-dr Coupé			10,244
284	Electra 4+1-dr Estate Wagon			10,513
285	Riviera Coupé			11,492
285	Riviera Sport Coupé			11,823
	CADILLAC (USA)			
285	Seville	15,859*		19,662

Page	MAKE AND MODEL	Price in GB £	Price in USA $	Price ex Works
286	Fleetwood Eldorado	15,739*		15,509
287	De Ville 2-dr Coupé			12,401
287	De Ville 4-dr Sedan			12,770
287	Fleetwood 4-dr Brougham			14,927
287	Fleetwood 4-dr Limousine			22,586
287	Fleetwood 4-dr Formal Limousine			23,388
	CATERHAM CARS (Great Britain)			
147	Super 7			5,416*
	CHECKER (USA)			
288	Marathon A 12			7,986
288	Marathon A 12 E De Luxe			9,060
	CHEVROLET (Brazil)			
253	Chevette STD 2-dr Sedan			147,000
253	Chevette L 2-dr Sedan			152,000
253	Chevette SL 2-dr Sedan			166,000
253	Chevette STD 4-dr Sedan			165,000
253	Chevette SL 4-dr Sedan			184,000
253	Chevette STD 2+1-dr Hatchback			164,000
253	Chevette SL 2+1-dr Hatchback			185,000
253	Opala 4-dr Sedan			207,000
253	Opala 2-dr Coupé			208,000
254	Opala Caravan			231,000
254	Opala SS-4 Coupé			253,000
254	Opala SS-4 Caravan			274,000
254	Opala SS-6 Coupé			276,000
254	Opala SS-6 Caravan			299,000
255	Diplomata 4-dr Sedan			343,000
255	Diplomata 2-dr Coupé			342,000
255	Comodoro 4-dr Sedan			230,000
255	Comodoro 2-dr Coupé			228,000
256	Comodoro Caravan			249,000
256	Veraneio Standard 4+1-dr St. Wagon			281,000
256	Veraneio De Luxo 4+1-dr St. Wagon			294,000
256	Veraneio Super Luxo 4+1-dr St. Wagon			342,000
	CHEVROLET (Canada)			
266	Bel Air 4-dr Sedan			7,384
266	Bel Air 2-dr Coupé			7,335
266	Bel Air 4+1-dr 6-pass. St. Wagon			8,083
266	Bel Air 4+1-dr 9-pass. St. Wagon			8,253
	CHEVROLET (South Africa)			
341	Ascona 4-dr Sedan			4,760
341	Ascona "S" 4-dr Sedan			5,145
341	Chevair De Luxe 4-dr Sedan			5,665
341	Chevair GL 4-dr Sedan			6,165
341	Chevair Automatic Berlina 4-dr Sedan			6,925
342	Rekord 4-dr Sedan			6,585
342	Rekord Automatic 4-dr Sedan			6,895
342	Rekord GL 4-dr Sedan			6,925
342	Rekord Automatic GL 4-dr Sedan			7,170
342	Rekord 4+1-dr St. Wagon			6,950
342	Rekord 4+1-dr Automatic St. Wagon			7,165
342	Commodore 4-dr Sedan			6,985
342	Commodore Automatic 4-dr Sedan			7,395
342	Commodore GL 4-dr Sedan			7,750
342	Commodore GL Automatic 4+1-dr St. Wagon			8,470
342	Commodore GL Automatic 4-dr Sedan			8,695
343	Senator			14,000
	CHEVROLET (USA)			
288	Chevette 4+1-dr Hatchback Sedan			4,417
288	Chevette 2+1-dr Scooter Hatchback Coupé			3,781
288	Chevette 2+1-dr Hatchback Coupé			4,288
289	Monza 2-dr Coupé			4,184

Page	MAKE AND MODEL	Price in GB £	Price in USA $	Price ex Works
289	Monza 2+1-dr Hatchback Coupé			4,497
289	Monza 2+1-dr Sport Hatchback Coupé			4,921
290	Citation 4+1-dr Hatchback Sedan			5,153
290	Citation 2-dr Coupé			4,491
290	Citation 2-dr Club Coupé			4,905
290	Citation 2+1-dr Hatchback Coupé			5,032
290	Camaro Sport Coupé			5,498
290	Camaro Rally Sport Coupé			5,915
290	Camaro Berlinetta Coupé			6,261
290	Camaro Z28 Sport Coupé			7,121
292	Malibu 4-dr Sedan			5,246
292	Malibu 2-dr Sport Coupé			5,133
292	Malibu 4+1-dr St. Wagon			5,401
292	Malibu Classic 4-dr Sedan			5,567
292	Malibu Classic 2-dr Sport Coupé			5,439
292	Malibu Classic 2-dr Landau Coupé			5,688
292	Malibu Classic 4+1-dr St. Wagon			5,653
292	Monte Carlo Sport Coupé			6,123
292	Monte Carlo Landau Coupé			6,411
293	Impala 4-dr Sedan			6,289
293	Impala 2-dr Coupé			6,180
293	Impala 4+1-dr 6-pass. St. Wagon			6,780
293	Impala 4+1-dr 9-pass. St. Wagon			6,925
293	Caprice Classic 4-dr Sedan			6,710
293	Caprice Classic 2-dr Sport Coupé			6,579
293	Caprice Classic 2-dr Landau Coupé			7,029
293	Caprice Classic 4+1-dr 6-pass. St. Wagon			7,099
293	Caprice Classic 4+1-dr 9-pass. St. Wagon			7,266
295	Corvette Coupé	12,098*		13,140
	CHRYSLER (Australia)			
393	Sigma GE Galant 4-dr Sedan			5,762
393	Sigma GE Galant 4+1-dr Wagon			6,419
393	Sigma GE GL 4-dr Sedan			6,314
393	Sigma GE GL 4+1-dr Wagon			6,862
393	Sigma GE SE 4-dr Sedan			7,113
393	Sigma GE SE 4+1-dr Wagon			7,663
393	Valiant CM 4-dr Sedan			7,021
393	Valiant CM 4+1-dr St. Wagon			7,389
393	Valiant CM Regal 4-dr Sedan			8,751
393	Valiant CM Regal 4+1-dr St. Wagon			9,069
393	Valiant CM Regal SE 4-dr Sedan			12,302
393	Valiant CM GLX Special 4-dr Sedan			8,067
	CHRYSLER (USA)			
295	Le Baron 4-dr Sedan			6,103
295	Le Baron 2-dr Coupé			5,948
295	Le Baron 4+1-dr Town and Country St. Wagon			6,894
295	Le Baron 4-dr Salon Sedan			6,348
295	Le Baron 2-dr Salon Coupé			6,229
295	Le Baron 4+1-dr Salon St. Wagon			6,305
295	Le Baron 4-dr Medallion Sedan			6,888
295	Le Baron 2-dr Medallion Coupé			6,783
296	Cordoba			6,601
297	Newport Pillared Hardtop			6,849
297	New Yorker Pillared Hardtop			10,459
	CITROËN (France)			
77	2 CV 6 Spécial	2,185*		18,500◊
77	2 CV 6 Club	—		20,900◊
78	Mehari 4x4	—		—
78	Mehari 2+2	—		24,000◊
78	Dyane 6	2,416*		22,200◊
79	LNA	—		24,900◊
79	Visa Spécial	—		25,000◊
79	Visa Club	3,112*		26,700◊
79	Visa Super	3,429*		29,000◊
80	GS Spécial Berline	3,500*		31,000◊
80	GS Spécial Break	3,766*		32,500◊

Page	MAKE AND MODEL	Price in GB £	Price in USA $	Price ex Works
80	GSA Club	4,060*		35,000◊
80	GSA Pallas	4,399*		37,600◊
80	GSA Club C Matic	4,215*		35,300◊
80	GSA Pallas C Matic	4,554*		37,600◊
80	GSA X 3	—		37,200◊
81	GSA Club Break	4,273*		36,300◊
81	CX Reflex	6,000*		46,100◊
81	CX Athena	6,578*		52,800◊
81	CX Reflex Break	—		52,300◊
81	CX 2400 Break Super	—		59,800◊
81	CX 2400 Familiale Super	7,151*		61,500◊
81	CX 2400 Pallas Berline	7,524*		56,700◊
82	CX 2400 GTI	8,204*		65,000◊
82	CX 2400 Pallas Injection C Matic	8,227*		65,500◊
82	CX Prestige	10,990*		83,600◊
82	CX 2500 Diesel Confort Berline	7,102*		53,700◊
82	CX 2500 Diesel Break Confort	7,167*		58,000◊
82	CX 2500 Diesel Super Berline	—		58,900◊
82	CX 2500 Diesel Break Super	—		65,100◊
82	CX 2500 Diesel Familiale Super	7,552*		66,800◊
82	CX 2500 Diesel Pallas Berline	7,724*		62,000◊
	CLASSIC CAR (Germany FR)			
110	Bugatti 35 B			21,500*
110	Bugatti 55			23,100*
110	Blower Phaeton			25,500*
110	Gepard SS 100			25,000*
	CUSTOCA (Austria)			
74	Hurrycane			125,000
74	Strato ES			130,000
	DACIA (Romania)			
221	1300 Saloon			—
221	1301 Saloon			—
222	1300 Break			—
	DAIHATSU (Japan)			
351	Max Cuore Standard 2-dr Sedan			572,000
351	Max Cuore DX 2-dr Sedan			628,000
351	Max Cuore Hi Custom 2-dr Sedan			681,000
351	Max Cuore DX 4-dr Sedan			648,000
351	Max Cuore Custom 4-dr Sedan			675,000
351	Max Cuore Hi Custom 4-dr Sedan			699,000
351	Max Cuore Hi Custom EX 4-dr Sedan			727,000
351	Charade XO 4+1-dr Sedan			653,000
351	Charade XG 4+1-dr Sedan	2,989*		698,000
351	Charade XT 4+1-dr Sedan			748,000
351	Charade XGE 4+1-dr Sedan			777,000
351	Charade XTE 4+1-dr Sedan			815,000
351	Charade XG 2+1-dr Coupé			704,000
351	Charade XT 2+1-dr Coupé			764,000
351	Charade XTE 2+1-dr Coupé	3,359*		830,000
352	Charmant 1300 De Luxe 4-dr Sedan			819,000
352	Charmant 1300 Custom 4-dr Sedan			857,000
352	Charmant 1300 Hi Custom 4-dr Sedan			891,000
352	Charmant 1300 LC 4-dr Sedan			921,000
352	Charmant 1600 Custom 4-dr Sedan			927,000
352	Charmant 1600 Hi Custom 4-dr Sedan			961,000
352	Charmant 1600 SC 4-dr Sedan			977,000
352	Charmant 1600 GC 4-dr Sedan			1,011,000
352	Delta Standard Wagon			—
352	Delta De Luxe Wagon			—
352	Delta Custom Wagon			—
352	Delta Custom EX Wagon			—
353	Taft Gran 1600 H-F20S (canvas doors)			—
353	Taft Gran 1600 H-F20SK (steel doors)			—
353	Taft Gran 1600 H-F20J (6-pass., canvas doors)			—
353	Taft Gran 1600 H-F20JK (6-pass., steel doors)			—

Page	MAKE AND MODEL	Price in GB £	Price in USA $	Price ex Works
353	Taft Gran 1600 H-F20V (4-pass., steel body)			—
353	Taft Diesel F50S (canvas doors)			—
353	Taft Diesel F50SK (steel doors)			—
353	Taft Diesel F50J (6-pass., canvas doors)			—
353	Taft Diesel F50JK (6-pass., steel doors)			—
353	Taft Diesel F50V (4-pass., steel body)			—
	DAIMLER (Great Britain)			
148	Sovereign 4.2			16,333*
148	Vanden Plas 4.2			21,415*
148	Double-Six 5.3			19,145*
149	Double-Six Vanden Plas 5.3			24,995*
149	Limousine			23,546*
	DAYTONA (USA)			
298	Migi			8,500
	DE TOMASO (Italy)			
196	Pantera L	—		26,850,000◊
196	Pantera GTS	19,061*		27,900,000◊
196	Deauville	24,418*		34,600,000◊
197	Longchamp 2+2	21,285*		32,500,000◊
	DODGE (Argentina)			
246	1500			14,100
246	1500 M 1.8			16,000
246	1500 M 1.8 Rural			17,500
	DODGE (Brazil)			
256	Polara			—
256	Polara Gran Luxo			—
257	Dart De Luxo 4-dr Sedan			—
257	Dart De Luxo 2-dr Coupé			—
257	Dart Gran 4-dr Sedan			—
257	Le Baron			—
257	Charger R/T			—
257	Magnum			—
	DODGE (USA)			
298	Omni 4+1-dr Hatchback			4,925
298	Omni 024 2+1-dr Hatchback			5,271
299	Aspen 4-dr Sedan			4,859
299	Aspen 2-dr Coupé			4,742
299	Aspen 4-dr Sedan Special			4,994
299	Aspen 2-dr Coupé Special			4,977
299	Aspen 4+1-dr St. Wagon			5,101
300	Diplomat 4-dr Sedan			5,832
300	Diplomat 2-dr Coupé			5,681
300	Diplomat 4+1-dr St. Wagon			5,971
300	Diplomat Salon 4-dr Sedan			6,119
300	Diplomat Salon 2-dr Coupé			5,997
300	Diplomat Salon 4+1-dr St. Wagon			6,661
300	Diplomat Medallion 4-dr Sedan			6,698
300	Diplomat Medallion 2-dr Coupé			6,551
300	Mirada			6,364
301	St. Regis			6,724
	DUTTON (Great Britain)			
149	Phaeton			—
	ELEGANT MOTORS (USA)			
302	898 Elegante			60,000
302	898 Phaeton			50,000
302	856 Speedster			40,000
302	Elegante Sports Brougham			60,000

Page	MAKE AND MODEL	Price in GB £	Price in USA $	Price ex Works
	ELITE (USA)			
302	Laser 917			7,500
	EL NASR (Egypt)			
337	Nasr 133			1,950
337	Nasr 128			3,603
338	Nasr 125			3,995
338	Nasr 131 CL			5,069
	ENVEMO (Brazil)			
258	90 Super Coupé			—
258	90 Super Cabriolet			—
	EXCALIBUR (USA)			
303	Series III SS Roadster			28,800
303	Series III SS Phaeton			28,800
	FAIRTHORPE (Great Britain)			
150	TX-S 1500			5,965*
150	TX-S 2000			—
	FASA-RENAULT (Spain)			
222	4			313,000
222	4 TL			353,000
222	5 GTL			448,000
222	5 Copa			682,000
222	6 TL			430,000
223	7 TL			437,000
223	12 TL			513,000
223	12 TL Familiar			544,000
223	12 TS			569,000
223	12 TS Familiar			595,000
	FELBER (Switzerland)			
235	Excellence Coupé			53,000
235	Excellence Roadster			57,000
235	Oasis			46,500
	FERRARI (Italy)			
197	Dino 208 GT 4			24,308,000*
197	Dino 308 GT 4	17,534*	38,460*	29,633,000*
197	308 GTB	18,973*	39,015*	31,860,000*
198	308 GTS	19,901*	43,185*	33,413,000*
198	400 Automatic i	31,809*		51,975,000*
198	BB 512	33,081*		55,755,000*
	FIAT (Argentina)			
246	600 S			—
247	133 B			—
247	133 L			—
247	133 T			—
247	128 C			—
248	128 CL			—
248	128 1300 TV Java			—
248	128 CLF			—
248	125 BN			—
248	125 T			—
248	125 S			—
249	125 SL			—
249	125 SF			—
	FIAT (Brazil)			
258	147 2+1-dr Sedan			131,000
258	147 L 2+1-dr Sedan			136,100
258	147 GL 2+1-dr Sedan			147,700
258	147 GLS 2+1-dr Sedan			157,400

Page	MAKE AND MODEL	Price in GB £	Price in USA $	Price ex Works
258	147 Rallye 2+1-dr Sedan			163,200
259	Alfa Romeo 2300 B			367,500
259	Alfa Romeo 2300 TI			469,200
	FIAT (Italy)			
199	126 Berlina Base	2,071*		2,932,000◊
199	126 Personal	2,289*		3,180,000◊
199	Panda 30			3,970,000◊
200	Panda 45			4,702,000◊
200	127 L 2-dr Berlina	2,849*		4,254,000◊
200	127 L 2+1-dr Berlina	3,049*		4,366,000◊
200	127 C 2-dr Berlina			4,738,000◊
200	127 C 2+1-dr Berlina			4,850,000◊
200	127 CL 2-dr Berlina			4,962,000◊
200	127 CL 2+1-dr Berlina	3,262*		5,074,000◊
200	127 Sport 2+1-dr Berlina	3,620*		5,735,000◊
201	128 CL 1100			5,782,000◊
201	128 Panorama Base 1100			5,511,000◊
201	Ritmo 60 L 2+1-dr Berlina			5,334,000◊
201	Ritmo 60 L 4+1-dr Berlina			5,581,000◊
201	Ritmo 60 CL 2+1-dr Berlina			5,876,000◊
201	Ritmo 60 CL 4+1-dr Berlina			6,124,000◊
201	Ritmo 65 L 4+1-dr Berlina	3,476*		5,717,000◊
201	Ritmo 65 CL 2+1-dr Berlina	3,643*		6,012,000◊
201	Ritmo 65 CL 4+1-dr Berlina	3,779*		6,260,000◊
201	Ritmo 75 CL 2+1-dr Berlina	4,078*		6,679,000◊
201	Ritmo 75 CL 4+1-dr Berlina	4,198*		6,927,000◊
201	Ritmo Diesel L 4+1-dr Berlina			6,915,000◊
201	Ritmo Diesel CL 4+1-dr Berlina			7,564,000◊
202	Strada 2+1-dr Sedan		4,496*	—
202	Strada 2+1-dr Custom Sedan		4,952*	—
202	Strada 4+1-dr Custom Sedan		5,102*	—
202	X1/9 five speed	5,533*	7,379*	7,877,000◊
203	131 Mirafiori 1300 L 4-dr Berlina			6,230,000◊
203	131 Mirafiori 1300 L 4+1-dr Panorama			6,738,000◊
203	131 Mirafiori 1300 CL 2-dr Berlina	3,825*		6,803,000◊
203	131 Mirafiori 1300 CL 4-dr Berlina	3,954*		7,127,000◊
203	131 Mirafiori 1600 CL 4-dr Berlina	4,349*		7,281,000◊
203	131 Mirafiori 1600 CL 4+1-dr Panorama	4,600*		7,788,000◊
203	131 Supermirafiori 1300 4-dr Berlina			8,177,000◊
203	131 Supermirafiori 1600 4-dr Berlina	5,201*		8,331,000◊
203	131 Supermirafiori 1600 4+1-dr Panorama	5,058*		8,962,000◊
203	131 Racing 2000 2-dr Berlina			8,897,000◊
203	131 Diesel 2000 L 4-dr Berlina			8,201,000◊
203	131 Diesel 2000 CL 4-dr Berlina			8,891,000◊
203	131 Diesel 2000 CL 4+1-dr Panorama			9,393,000◊
203	131 Diesel 2500 Super 4-dr Berlina			9,936,000◊
203	131 Diesel 2500 4+1-dr Panorama Super			10,508,000◊
205	Brava 2-dr Sedan		6,495*	—
205	Brava 4-dr Sedan		6,695*	—
205	Brava 4+1-dr St. Wagon			—
205	124 Sport Spider 2000		8,795*	—
206	124 Sport Spider 2000 i			—
206	132 1600 Berlina			8,921,000◊
206	132 2000 Berlina	5,742*		9,871,000◊
206	132 2000 i Berlina			10,655,000◊
207	132 Diesel 2000			10,768,000◊
207	132 Diesel 2500			11,281,000◊
207	Campagnola			12,248,000*
207	Campagnola Lunga			12,602,000*
207	Campagnola Diesel			14,018,000*
208	Campagnola Diesel Lunga			14,372,000*
	FIAT (Uruguay)			
272	600 S			47,500
	FIBERFAB (Germany FR)			
111	Sherpa			13,400*

Page	MAKE AND MODEL	Price in GB £	Price in USA $	Price ex Works
	FORD (Argentina)			
249	Taunus L 2000 Sedan			14,100
249	Taunus GXL Sedan			—
249	Taunus GXL 2300 Sedan			17,600
249	Taunus GT Coupé			20,100
249	Taunus GT Coupé SP			—
249	Fairlane LTD 3600 Sedan			—
250	Fairlane LTD-V8 Sedan			24,300
250	Falcon Sedan Standard			15,700
250	Falcon Sedan De Luxe			18,100
250	Falcon St. Wagon Standard			17,900
250	Falcon St. Wagon De Luxe			22,300
250	Falcon Sedan Futura			21,600
250	Falcon Sedan Sprint			23,100
	FORD (Australia)			
394	Escort L 2-dr Sedan			5,143
394	Escort L 4-dr Sedan			5,284
394	Escort GL 2-dr Sedan			5,471
394	Escort GL 4-dr Sedan			5,613
394	Escort Ghia 4-dr Sedan			6,543
394	Escort RS 2000 2-dr Sedan			6,568
394	Escort RS 2000 4-dr Sedan			6,709
395	Cortina TE L 4-dr Sedan			5,984
395	Cortina TE L 4+1-dr St. Wagon			6,616
395	Cortina TE GL 4-dr Sedan			6,454
395	Cortina TE GL 4+1-dr St. Wagon			7,136
395	Cortina TE Ghia 4-dr Sedan			7,139
395	Cortina TE Ghia 4+1-dr St. Wagon			7,821
395	XD Falcon GL 4-dr Sedan			7,116
395	XD Falcon GL 4+1-dr St. Wagon			7,565
395	Fairmont 4-dr Sedan			8,964
395	Fairmont 4+1-dr St. Wagon			9,607
395	Fairmont 4-dr Ghia Sedan			10,307
396	ZJ Fairlane Sedan			11,831
397	FC LTD 4-dr Sedan			17,093
397	FC LTD Cartier 4-dr Sedan			19,093
	FORD (Brazil)			
260	Corcel II Base 2-dr Sedan			157,300
260	Corcel II L 2-dr Sedan			175,100
260	Corcel II LDO 2-dr Sedan			209,000
260	Corcel II Berlina Base 2+1-dr St. Wagon			182,500
260	Corcel II Berlina L 2+1-dr St. Wagon			195,900
260	Corcel II Berlina LDO 2+1-dr St. Wagon			218,400
260	Corcel II GT			202,300
261	Galaxie 500 4-dr Sedan			399,300
261	Galaxie LTD 4-dr Sedan			447,500
261	Galaxie Landau 4-dr Sedan			510,800
261	Cavalo de Ferro			—
	FORD (Canada)			
267	LTD 2-dr Sedan			7,797
	FORD (Germany FR)			
111	Fiesta Limousine			9,605*
111	Fiesta L Limousine			10,231*
111	Fiesta S Limousine			11,615*
111	Fiesta Ghia Limousine			12,369*
113	Escort 2-dr Limousine			10,372*
113	Escort 4-dr Limousine			10,937*
113	Escort 2+1-dr Turnier			11,134*
113	Escort L 2-dr Limousine			10,917*
113	Escort L 4-dr Limousine			11,482*
113	Escort L 2+1-dr Turnier			11,729*
113	Escort GL 2-dr Limousine			12,047*
113	Escort GL 4-dr Limousine			12,612*
113	Escort GL 2+1-dr Turnier			12,350*
113	Escort Ghia 2-dr Limousine			14,236*
113	Escort Ghia 4-dr Limousine			14,801*
113	Escort Sport 2-dr Limousine			12,440*
113	Escort Sport 4-dr Limousine			13,005*
113	Escort RS 2000 2-dr Limousine			15,931*
114	Taunus 2-dr Limousine			12,295*
114	Taunus 4-dr Limousine			12,880*
114	Taunus 4+1-dr Turnier			13,505*
114	Taunus L 2-dr Limousine			13,540*
114	Taunus L 4-dr Limousine			14,125*
114	Taunus L 4+1-dr Turnier			14,750*
114	Taunus GL 2-dr Limousine			14,605*
114	Taunus GL 4-dr Limousine			15,190*
114	Taunus GL 4+1-dr Turnier			15,815*
114	Taunus Ghia 2-dr Limousine			16,545*
114	Taunus Ghia 4-dr Limousine			17,130*
115	Capri II L Coupé			13,691*
115	Capri II GL Coupé			15,305*
115	Capri II S Coupé			17,757*
115	Capri II Ghia Coupé			20,814*
117	Granada 2-dr Limousine			—
117	Granada 4-dr Limousine			—
117	Granada 4+1-dr Turnier			—
117	Granada L 2-dr Limousine			—
117	Granada L 4-dr Limousine			—
117	Granada L 4+1-dr Turnier			—
117	Granada GL 4-dr Limousine			—
117	Granada GL 4+1-dr Turnier			—
117	Granada Ghia 4-dr Limousine			—
117	Granada Ghia 4+1-dr Turnier			—
	FORD (Great Britain)			
150	Fiesta Saloon			2,840*
150	Fiesta L Saloon			3,148*
150	Fiesta S Saloon			3,648*
150	Fiesta Ghia Saloon			3,971*
151	Escort Popular 1100 2-dr Saloon			2,876*
151	Escort Popular 1100 Plus 2-dr Saloon			2,963*
151	Escort Popular 1100 4-dr Saloon			3,088*
151	Escort 1100 2+1-dr Estate Car			3,174*
151	Escort 1100 L 2-dr Saloon			3,193*
151	Escort 1100 L 4-dr Saloon			3,318*
151	Escort Popular 1300 2-dr Saloon			3,003*
151	Escort Popular 1300 Plus 2-dr Saloon			3,091*
151	Escort Popular 1300 Plus 4-dr Saloon			3,214*
151	Escort 1300 2+1-dr Estate Car			3,346*
151	Escort 1300 L 2-dr Saloon			3,287*
151	Escort 1300 L 4-dr Saloon			3,412*
151	Escort 1300 L 2+1-dr Estate Car			3,662*
151	Escort 1300 GL 2-dr Saloon			3,573*
151	Escort 1300 GL 4-dr Saloon			3,700*
151	Escort 1300 GL 2+1-dr Estate Car			4,023*
151	Escort 1300 Sport 2-dr Saloon			3,873*
151	Escort 1300 Ghia 2-dr Saloon			4,111*
151	Escort 1300 Ghia 4-dr Saloon			4,242*
151	Escort 1600 Sport 2-dr Saloon			3,985*
151	Escort 1600 Ghia 4-dr Saloon			4,353*
151	Escort RS 2000 2-dr Saloon			4,762*
151	Escort RS 2000 Custom 2-dr Saloon			5,386*
153	Cortina 1300 2-dr Saloon			3,503*
153	Cortina 1300 4-dr Saloon			3,638*
153	Cortina 1300 L 2-dr Saloon			3,849*
153	Cortina 1300 L 4-dr Saloon			3,985*
153	Cortina 1600 4-dr Saloon			3,848*
153	Cortina 1600 4+1-dr Estate Car			4,274*
153	Cortina 1600 L 4-dr Saloon			4,195*
153	Cortina 1600 L 4+1-dr Estate Car			4,661*
153	Cortina 1600 GL 4-dr Saloon			4,588*
153	Cortina 1600 GL 4+1-dr Estate Car			5,054*
153	Cortina 1600 Ghia 4-dr Saloon			5,422*
153	Cortina 1600 Ghia 4+1-dr Estate Car			5,888*
153	Cortina 2000 GL 4-dr Saloon			4,839*
153	Cortina 2000 GL 4+1-dr Estate Car			5,305*

Page	MAKE AND MODEL	Price in GB £	Price in USA $	Price ex Works
153	Cortina 2000 GLS 4-dr Saloon			4,991*
153	Cortina 2000 Ghia 4-dr Saloon			5,579*
153	Cortina 2000 Ghia 4+1-dr Estate Car			6,045*
153	Cortina 2300 GL 4-dr Saloon			5,474*
153	Cortina 2300 GL 4+1-dr Estate Car			5,941*
153	Cortina 2300 GLS 4-dr Saloon			5,627*
153	Cortina 2300 Ghia 4-dr Saloon			6,215*
153	Cortina 2300 Ghia 4+1-dr Estate Car			6,681*
154	Capri II 1300 L Coupé			3,867*
154	Capri II 1600 L Coupé			4,083*
154	Capri II 1600 GL Coupé			4,400*
154	Capri II 1600 S Coupé			4,970*
154	Capri II 2000 GL Coupé			4,673*
154	Capri II 2000 S Coupé			5,185*
154	Capri II 2000 Ghia Coupé			5,934*
154	Capri II 3000 S Coupé			5,574*
154	Capri II 3000 Ghia Coupé			6,704*
155	Granada 2000 L Saloon			5,499*
155	Granada 2000 L Estate Car			6,086*
155	Granada 2100 Diesel Saloon			5,943*
155	Granada 2300 L Saloon			6,101*
155	Granada 2300 L Estate Car			6,688*
155	Granada 2300 GL Saloon			7,240*
155	Granada 2800 GL Saloon (automatic)			7,733*
155	Granada 2800 GL Estate Car (automatic)			8,057*
155	Granada 2800i GLS Saloon			8,325*
155	Granada 2800i GLS Estate Car			8,649*
155	Granada 2800 Ghia Saloon (automatic)			9,173*
155	Granada 2800 Ghia Estate Car (automatic)			9,510*
155	Granada 2800i Ghia Saloon			9,595*
155	Granada 2800i Ghia Estate Car			9,931*
	FORD (South Africa)			
343	Escort 1300 L 4-dr Sedan			4,565*
343	Escort 1600 GL 4-dr Sedan			5,150*
343	Escort 1600 Sport 4-dr Sedan			4,615*
343	Escort 2000 RS 2-dr Sedan			6,390*
344	Cortina 1300 L 4-dr Sedan			5,445*
344	Cortina 1600 L 4-dr Sedan			5,670*
344	Cortina 1600 L 4+1-dr St. Wagon			6,050*
344	Cortina 2000 GL 4-dr Sedan			6,170*
344	Cortina 2000 GL 4+1-dr St. Wagon			6,600*
344	Cortina 3000 GL 4-dr Sedan			6,920*
344	Cortina 3000 GL 4+1-dr St. Wagon			6,920*
344	Cortina 3000 S 4-dr Sedan			7,305*
344	Cortina 3000 Ghia 4-dr Sedan			8,355*
344	Cortina 3000 Ghia 4+1-dr .St. Wagon			8,945*
345	Granada 2000 GL 4-dr Sedan			7,255*
345	Granada 3000 GL 4-dr Sedan			8,700*
345	Granada 3000 Ghia 4-dr Sedan			13,370*
	FORD (USA)			
303	Pinto 2-dr Sedan			4,999
303	Pinto 2+1-dr Runabout			5,156
303	Pinto 2+1-dr St. Wagon			5,570
304	Mustang 2-dr Sedan			5,961
304	Mustang 2+1-dr Sedan			6,151
304	Mustang Ghia 2-dr Sedan			6,446
304	Mustang Ghia 2+1-dr Sedan			6,514
305	Fairmont 2-dr Sedan			5,467
305	Fairmont 4-dr Sedan			5,634
305	Fairmont 4+1-dr St. Wagon			5,828
305	Fairmont Futura 2-dr Coupé			5,784
305	Fairmont Ghia 2-dr Sedan			5,953
305	Fairmont Ghia 4-dr Sedan			6,120
305	Fairmont Ghia Futura 2-dr Coupé			6,012
306	Granada 2-dr Sedan			6,001
306	Granada 4-dr Sedan			6,155
306	Granada Ghia 2-dr Sedan			6,452

Page	MAKE AND MODEL	Price in GB £	Price in USA $	Price ex Works
306	Granada Ghia 4-dr Sedan			6,606
306	Granada ESS 2-dr Sedan			6,597
306	Granada ESS 4-dr Sedan			6,750
306	Thunderbird Sedan			8,069
307	LTD S 2-dr Sedan			7,797
307	LTD S 4-dr Sedan			7,846
307	LTD 2-dr Sedan			7,998
307	LTD 4-dr Sedan			8,107
307	LTD Crown Victoria 2-dr Sedan			8,659
307	LTD Crown Victoria 4-dr Sedan			8,794
307	LTD S 4+1-dr St. Wagon			8,322
307	LTD 4+1-dr St. Wagon			8,487
307	LTD Country Squire 4+1-dr St. Wagon			9,169
	GAZ (USSR)			
239	Volga 24			—
240	Volga 24-02			—
240	Volga 24 Indenor Diesel			—
240	Chaika			—
	GIANNINI (Italy)			
208	Fiat Giannini 126 GP Base			3,135,000*
208	Fiat Giannini 126 GP Personal			3,370,000*
208	Fiat Giannini 126 GP Serie Speciale			3,685,000*
208	Fiat Giannini 126 GPS Base			3,310,000*
208	Fiat Giannini 126 GPS Personal			3,545,000*
208	Fiat Giannini 126 GPS Serie Speciale			3,860,000*
208	Fiat Giannini 126 Sport Base DC			3,505,000*
208	Fiat Giannini 126 Sport Personal DC			3,765,000*
208	Fiat Giannini 126 Sport Serie Speciale DC			4,060,000*
208	Fiat Giannini 126 GPA Base			3,555,000*
208	Fiat Giannini 126 GPA Personal			3,805,000*
208	Fiat Giannini 126 GPA Serie Speciale			4,110,000*
208	Fiat Giannini 126 Sport Base DC			3,805,000*
208	Fiat Giannini 126 Sport Personal DC			4,035,000*
208	Fiat Giannini 126 Sport Serie Speciale DC			4,350,000*
208	Fiat Giannini 127 NP 2-dr Berlina Base			4,575,000*
208	Fiat Giannini 127 NP 2+1-dr Berlina Base			4,695,000*
208	Fiat Giannini 127 NP 2-dr Berlina Confort			5,075,000*
208	Fiat Giannini 127 NP 2+1-dr Berlina Confort			5,195,000*
209	Fiat Giannini Ritmo Veloce 2+1-dr Confort 60 CL			6,220,000*
209	Fiat Giannini Ritmo Veloce 4+1-dr Confort 60 CL			6,520,000*
209	Fiat Giannini Ritmo Autostrada 2+1-dr Confort 60 CL			6,630,000*
209	Fiat Giannini Ritmo Autostrada 4+1-dr Confort 60 CL			6,920,000*
	GINETTA (Great Britain)			
157	G23			8,995*
	GP (Great Britain)			
157	Talon			3,900*
	GURGEL (Brazil)			
262	X-12			196,000
262	X-12 TR			196,000
	HINDUSTAN (India)			
346	Ambassador Mark 4			—

Page	MAKE AND MODEL	Price in GB £	Price in USA $	Price ex Works
	HOLDEN (Australia)			
398	Gemini TD 4-dr Sedan			5,324
398	Gemini TD SL 4-dr Sedan			5,574
398	Gemini TD SL X 4-dr Sedan			5,943
398	Gemini TD 4+1-dr St. Wagon			6,118
398	Sunbird 4-dr Sedan			5,995
398	Sunbird De Luxe 4-dr Sedan			6,161
398	Sunbird SL 4-dr Sedan			6,439
398	Sunbird SL/E 4-dr Sedan			7,096
398	VB Commodore 4-dr Sedan			7,192
398	VB Commodore S 4+1-dr St. Wagon			7,558
398	VB Commodore SL 4-dr Sedan			8,623
398	VB Commodore SL 4+1-dr St. Wagon			9,227
398	VB Commodore SL/E 4-dr Sedan			11,717
399	HZ Kingswood SL 4-dr Sedan			7,219
399	HZ Kingswood SL 4+1-dr St. Wagon			7,544
399	HZ Premier 4-dr Sedan			9,412
399	HZ Premier 4+1-dr St. Wagon			9,734
399	HZ Statesman De Ville 4-dr Sedan			12,372
399	HZ Statesman Caprice 4-dr Sedan			17,768
399	HZ Statesman SL/E 4-dr Sedan			14,205
	HONDA (Japan)			
353	Civic CVCC 1300 SE 2+1-dr Sedan	2,990*	3,699*	721,000
353	Civic CVCC 1300 GL 2+1-dr Sedan			807,000
353	Civic CVCC 1300 LX 2+1-dr Sedan		4,175*	855,000
353	Civic CVCC 1300 SE 4+1-dr Sedan	3,190*		764,000
353	Civic CVCC 1300 GF 4+1-dr Sedan			845,000
353	Civic CVCC 1300 LX 4+1-dr Sedan			885,000
353	Civic CVCC 1500 SE 2+1-dr Sedan		4,049*	781,000
353	Civic CVCC 1500 CE 2+1-dr Sedan		4,599*	877,000
353	Civic CVCC 1500 SE 4+1-dr Sedan			816,000
353	Civic CVCC 1500 CF 4+1-dr Sedan			912,000
353	Civic CVCC 1500 CX 4+1-dr Sedan			957,000
354	Accord 1800 GL 2+1-dr Hatchback	4,160*	5,799*	1,033,000
354	Accord 1800 LX 2+1-dr Hatchback		6,799*	1,093,000
354	Accord 1800 EX 2+1-dr Hatchback			1,200,000
354	Accord 1800 EX-L 2+1-dr Hatchback			1,340,000
354	Accord 1800 SL 4-dr Sedan	4,350*	6,365*	998,000
354	Accord 1800 GF 4-dr Sedan			1,108,000
354	Accord 1800 EX 4-dr Sedan			1,225,000
354	Accord 1800 EX-L 4-dr Sedan			1,385,000
355	Prelude XT 2-dr Coupé	4,950*		1,160,000
355	Prelude E 2-dr Coupé			1,260,000
355	Prelude XE 2-dr Coupé			1,400,000
355	Prelude XR 2-dr Coupé		6,445*	1,380,000
	HONGQI China (People's Republic)			
347	6-pass. Limousine			—
347	9-pass. Limousine			—
	HYUNDAI (Korea)			
349	Pony 2+1-dr Sedan			—
349	Pony 4-dr Sedan			—
349	Pony Station Wagon			—
	INTERNATIONAL HARVESTER (USA)			
308	Scout II 4x4			7,748
308	Scout II 4x4 Diesel			9,861
308	Scout Traveler 4x4			8,783
308	Scout Traveler 4x4 Diesel			10,378
	ISUZU (Japan)			
355	Gemini 1600 LD 4-dr Sedan			924,000
355	Gemini 1600 LD 2-dr Coupé			954,000
355	Gemini 1600 LT 4-dr Sedan			968,000
355	Gemini 1600 LT 2-dr Coupé			998,000
355	Gemini 1600 LS 4-dr Sedan			1,048,000
355	Gemini 1600 LS 2-dr Coupé			1,105,000
355	Gemini 1600 Minx 4-dr Sedan			1,040,000
355	Gemini 1600 Minx 2-dr Coupé			1,070,000
355	Gemini 1800 LT 4-dr Sedan			1,023,000
355	Gemini 1800 LT 2-dr Coupé			1,053,000
355	Gemini 1800 LS 4-dr Sedan			1,088,000
355	Gemini 1800 LS 2-dr Coupé			1,135,000
355	Gemini 1800 Minx 4-dr Sedan			1,095,000
355	Gemini 1800 LS/G 2-dr Coupé			1,210,000
355	Gemini LD 4-dr Sedan			1,045,000
355	Gemini LT 4-dr Sedan			1,129,000
355	Gemini Minx 4-dr Sedan			1,201,000
355	Gemini LT Coupé			1,159,000
355	Gemini Minx 2-dr Coupé			1,231,000
355	Gemini ZZR 4-dr Sedan			1,482,000
355	Gemini ZZT 4-dr Sedan			1,612,000
355	Gemini ZZR 2-dr Coupé			1,512,000
355	Gemini ZZT 2-dr Coupé			1,652,000
356	Florian SII 1800 De Luxe 4-dr Sedan			1,252,000
356	Florian SII 1800 Super De Luxe 4-dr Sedan			1,424,000
356	Florian SII Diesel 2000 Semi-De Luxe 4-dr Sedan			1,263,000
356	Florian SII Diesel 2000 De Luxe 4-dr Sedan			1,308,000
356	Florian SII Diesel 2000 Super De Luxe 4-dr Sedan			1,480,000
357	117 XT 1800 2-dr Coupé			1,527,000
357	117 XT 1950 2-dr Coupé			—
357	117 XTL 1950 2-dr Coupé			—
357	117 XC 1950 2-dr Coupé			1,765,000
357	117 XCJ 1950 2-dr Coupé			—
357	117 Giugiaro 2-dr Coupé			1,983,000
357	117 XG 2-dr Coupé			2,096,000
357	117 XE 2-dr Coupé			—
357	117 XD 2-dr Coupé			1,855,000
357	117 XDL 2-dr Coupé			1,990,000
	JAGUAR (Great Britain)			
158	XJ 3.4			13,998*
158	XJ 4.2		23,200*	15,339*
159	XJ 5.3		25,200*	18,156*
159	XJ-S		26,000*	19,187*
	JEEP CORPORATION (USA)			
308	Jeep CJ-5 Roadster			6,095
308	Jeep CJ-7 Roadster			6,295
309	Cherokee 2+1-dr Wagon			7,730
309	Cherokee Wide Wheel 2+1-dr Wagon			8,298
309	Cherokee 4+1-dr Wagon	9,454*		7,842
310	Wagoneer Standard			9,356
310	Wagoneer Limited			13,240
	JOHNARD VINTAGE CAR (Great Britain)			
160	Bentley Donington			25,875*
	KELMARK (USA)			
310	GT			11,400
	KIA (Korea)			
349	Brisa 1000			—
350	Brisa 1300			—
	K.M.B. (Great Britain)			
161	GTM Mk 1-3			—
	LAFER (Brazil)			
262	MP			277,900
262	TI			300,400
263	LL			567,900

Page	MAKE AND MODEL	Price in GB £	Price in USA $	Price ex Works
	LAMBORGHINI (Italy)			
209	Urraco P 200			20,532,000*
210	Urraco P 250			23,490,000*
210	Urraco P 300			25,650,000*
210	Silhouette			31,050,000*
210	Espada 400 GT			41,175,000*
211	Countach «S»			83,700,000*
	LANCIA (Italy)			
211	Delta Berlina 1300 (4 gears)			7,534,000◊
212	Delta Berlina 1300 (5 gears)			7,947,000◊
212	Delta Berlina 1500			8,419,000◊
212	Beta Berlina 1600	5,084*		9,186,000◊
212	Beta Coupé 1300	5,051*		9,139,000◊
213	Beta Coupé 1600	5,766*		10,036,000◊
213	Beta HPE 1600	6,514*		10,036,000◊
213	Beta Berlina 2000	5,377*	8,551*	9,812,000◊
213	Beta Coupé 2000	6,242*	9,500*	10,909,000◊
213	Beta HPE 2000	7,046*	9,985*	10,909,000◊
214	Montecarlo			9,635,000◊
214	Gamma Berlina 2000	7,950*		13,092,000◊
214	Gamma Coupé 2000			16,656,000◊
214	Gamma Berlina 2500			15,721,000◊
215	Gamma Coupé 2500			19,784,000◊
	LAND ROVER (Great Britain)			
161	88" Regular			—
161	109"			—
162	109" V8			—
162	Range Rover			12,396*
	LAWIL (Italy)			
215	S3 Varzina			2,950,000*
215	A4 City			2,950,000*
	LEDL (Austria)			
74	Bugatti 35 B			89,060
74	Mercedes SS 29			94,840
75	Tanga			185,000
	LENHAM (Great Britain)			
162	Austin-Healey 3000			7,100*
	LEYLAND (Australia)			
400	Mini-Moke Californian			3,775
	LINCOLN (USA)			
310	Versailles			14,674
311	Continental 4-dr Sedan			12,884
311	Continental 2-dr Coupé			12,555
311	Continental Mark VI 4-dr Sedan			15,824
311	Continental Mark VI 2-dr Coupé			15,424
	LOTUS (Great Britain)			
163	Elite 501			14,676*
163	Elite 502			15,641*
163	Elite 503		37,200*	16,227*
163	Elite 504		37,900*	16,445*
163	Eclat 520			12,974*
163	Eclat 521			14,002*
163	Eclat 522			14,999*
163	Eclat 523		36,100*	15,559*
163	Eclat 524		36,650*	15,808*
164	Esprit S2		35,600*	14,870*
	LYNX (Great Britain)			
164	D Type			24,000*

Page	MAKE AND MODEL	Price in GB £	Price in USA $	Price ex Works
	MARQUEZ (Brazil)			
263	GTM			—
	MASERATI (Italy)			
215	Merak	18,096*		25,150,000*
216	Merak SS	—	35,120*	30,200,000*
216	Quattroporte	28,900*		43,400,000*
216	Kyalami	25,540*		41,790,000*
216	Khamsin	28,031*	44,990*	42,750,000*
216	Bora	—		42,750,000*
	MAZDA (Japan)			
358	Familia AP 1300 Standard 2+1-dr Sedan			645,000
358	Familia AP 1300 XC 2+1-dr Sedan			685,000
358	Familia AP 1300 XT 2+1-dr Sedan			790,000
358	Familia AP 1300 XL 2+1-dr Sedan			830,000
358	Familia AP 1300 XC 4+1-dr Sedan			720,000
358	Familia AP 1300 XT 4+1-dr Sedan			825,000
358	Familia AP 1300 XL 4+1-dr Sedan			865,000
358	Familia AP 1400 XG 2+1-dr Sedan			898,000
358	Familia AP 1400 XE 4+1-dr Sedan			948,000
358	Familia (USA) GLC Regular 2+1-dr Sedan		3,695*	—
358	Familia (USA) GLC De Luxe 2+1-dr Sedan		3,995*	—
358	Familia (USA) GLC De Luxe 4+1-dr Sedan		4,145*	—
358	Familia (USA) GLC De Luxe 4+1-dr St. Wagon		4,445*	—
359	Capella 1600 Standard Sedan			850,000
359	Capella 1600 De Luxe Sedan			910,000
359	Capella 1600 GL Sedan			960,000
359	Capella 1600 Super Custom Sedan			1,030,000
359	Capella 1600 De Luxe Hardtop			945,000
359	Capella 1600 GL Hardtop			995,000
359	Capella 1600 Super Custom Hardtop			1,080,000
359	Capella 1800 GL Sedan			1,040,000
359	Capella 1800 GL Hardtop			1,100,000
359	Capella 1800 Super Custom Sedan			1,110,000
359	Capella 1800 Super Custom Hardtop			1,170,000
359	Capella 2000 Limited Sedan			1,295,000
359	Capella 2000 Limited Hardtop			1,330,000
360	626 4-dr Sedan		5,495*	—
360	626 2-dr Hardtop Coupé		5,795*	—
360	Luce 1800 DX Sedan			1,023,000
360	Luce 1800 GL Sedan			1,138,000
360	Luce 1800 SG Sedan			1,258,000
360	Luce 2000 ST Sedan			1,203,000
360	Luce 2000 SG Sedan			1,323,000
360	Luce 2000 SGX Sedan			1,428,000
360	Luce 2000 ST Hardtop			1,268,000
360	Luce 2000 SG Hardtop			1,388,000
360	Luce 2000 SGX Hardtop			1,493,000
360	Luce RE GT Hardtop			1,493,000
360	Luce RE SE-GT Hardtop			1,703,000
360	Luce RE Limited Hardtop			2,058,000
360	Cosmo 2000 ST Coupé			1,218,000
360	Cosmo 2000 SG Coupé			1,353,000
360	Cosmo 2000 SGX Coupé			1,533,000
360	Cosmo L 2000 SG Coupé			1,413,000
360	Cosmo L 2000 SGX Coupé			1,648,000
360	Cosmo RE GT Coupé			1,498,000
360	Cosmo RE SE-GT Coupé			1,648,000
360	Cosmo RE SE-Limited Coupé			1,848,000
360	Cosmo L RE SE-GT Coupé			1,763,000
360	Cosmo L RE SE-Limited Coupé			1,908,000
361	Savanna RX7 Custom 2+1-dr Coupé		7,195*	1,250,000
361	Savanna RX7 Super Custom 2+1-dr Coupé		7,995*	1,380,000
361	Savanna RX7 GT 2+1-dr Coupé			1,420,000
361	Savanna RX7 Limited 2+1-dr Coupé			1,730,000

Page	MAKE AND MODEL	Price in GB £	Price in USA $	Price ex Works
361	Savanna RX7 SE GT 2+1-dr Coupé			1,590,000
361	Savanna RX7 SE Limited 2+1-dr Coupé			2,130,000
	MERCEDES-BENZ (Germany FR)			
119	200 4-dr Limousine	7,823*		21,050*
119	200 D 4-dr Limousine	7,999*		22,159*
119	230 4-dr Limousine	8,965*		22,227*
119	230 C 2-dr Coupé	10,952*		27,751*
119	230 T 4+1-dr Limousine			26,465*
120	250 4-dr Limousine	10,334*		26,024*
120	250 Long Wheelbase 4-dr Limousine	14,043*		38,669*
120	250 T 4+1-dr Limousine	11,708*		30,261*
120	240 D 4-dr Limousine	8,981*	17,533*	23,674*
120	240 D Long Wheelbase 4-dr Limousine	14,043*		37,154*
120	240 TD 4+1-dr Limousine	10,430*		27,911*
121	300 D 4-dr Limousine	11,146*	24,536*	26,150*
121	300 D Long Wheelbase 4-dr Limousine			38,900*
121	300 TD 4+1-dr Limousine		28,056*	30,385*
121	300 SD Turbodiesel 4-dr Limousine		30,632*	—
122	280 4-dr Limousine			28,894*
122	280 2-dr Coupé			33,007*
122	280 S 4-dr Limousine			34,160*
122	280 E 4-dr Limousine	12,351*	26,193*	31,075*
122	280 CE 2-dr Coupé	13,425*	29,289*	35,188*
122	280 TE 4+1-dr Limousine	13,837*		35,256*
122	280 SE 4-dr Limousine	14,458*	30,503*	36,533*
122	280 SEL 4-dr Limousine			38,895*
122	280 SL 2-dr Roadster			38,996*
122	280 SLC 2-dr Coupé			45,934*
122	350 SE 4-dr Limousine	16,840*		40,680*
122	350 SEL 4-dr Limousine			43,042*
122	350 SL 2-dr Roadster	16,669*		43,143*
122	350 SLC 2-dr Coupé			50,082*
123	380 SE 4-dr Limousine			46,669*
123	380 SEL 4-dr Limousine			49,042*
124	500 SE 4-dr Limousine			50,680*
124	500 SEL 4-dr Limousine			56,161*
124	450 SE 4-dr Limousine	18,139*		45,629*
124	450 SEL 4-dr Limousine	19,161*	38,288*	51,087*
124	450 SL 2-dr Roadster	17,820*	35,839*	48,093*
124	450 SLC 2-dr Coupé	20,987*	42,592*	55,031*
124	450 SLC 5.0 2-dr Coupé			65,517*
124	450 SEL 6.9 4-dr Limousine	30,476*		81,247*
125	230 G			30,000*
125	280 GE			36,220*
125	240 GD			31,470*
126	300 GD			33,278*
	MERCURY (Canada)			
268	Bobcat 2-dr Special Sedan			5,039
268	Bobcat 2+1-dr Special Runabout			5,196
268	Bobcat 2+1-dr Special St. Wagon			5,611
268	Marquis Meteor 2-dr Sedan			7,836
268	Marquis Meteor 4-dr Sedan			7,886
	MERCURY USA)			
312	Bobcat 2+1-dr Runabout			5,196
312	Bobcat 2+1-dr St. Wagon			5,611
312	Bobcat Villager 2+1-dr St. Wagon			5,911
312	Zephyr 2-dr Sedan			5,676
312	Zephyr 4-dr Sedan			5,843
312	Zephyr 4+1-dr St. Wagon			6,037
312	Zephyr Z-7 2-dr Sports Coupé			5,818
313	Capri 2+1-dr Coupé			6,220
313	Capri Ghia 2+1-dr Coupé			6,577
314	Monarch 2-dr Sedan			6,071
314	Monarch 4-dr Sedan			6,224
315	Cougar XR-7			8,089
315	Marquis 2-dr Sedan			8,171
315	Marquis 4-dr Sedan			8,307
315	Marquis Meteor 2-dr Sedan			7,836

Page	MAKE AND MODEL	Price in GB £	Price in USA $	Price ex Works
315	Marquis Meteor 4-dr Sedan			7,886
315	Marquis Brougham 2-dr Sedan			8,984
315	Marquis Brougham 4-dr Sedan			9,189
315	Marquis 4+1-dr St. Wagon			8,712
315	Marquis Meteor 4+1-dr St. Wagon			8,444
315	Marquis Colony Park 4+1-dr St. Wagon			9,754
315	Grand Marquis 2-dr Sedan			9,746
315	Grand Marquis 4-dr Sedan			9,934
	MG (Great Britain)			
165	Midget			3,821*
165	MGB GT		7,950*	5,893*
166	MGB Sports			5,164*
	MINI (Great Britain)			
166	850 City			2,499*
166	850 Super			2,757*
166	1000 Super			2,829*
167	Clubman Saloon			3,135*
167	Clubman Estate Car			3,414*
167	1275 GT			3,524*
	MITSUBISHI (Japan)			
362	Minica Ami 55 Hi De Luxe 2-dr Sedan			563,000
362	Minica Ami 55 Super De Luxe 2-dr Sedan			629,000
362	Minica Ami 55 Gl 2-dr Sedan			653,000
362	Minica Ami 55 XL 2-dr Sedan			681,000
362	Mirage 1200 EL 2-dr Sedan			728,000
362	Mirage 1200 EL 4-dr Sedan			766,000
362	Mirage 1200 TL 4-dr Sedan			826,000
362	Mirage 1200 GL 2-dr Sedan			828,000
362	Mirage 1200 GL 4-dr Sedan			871,000
362	Mirage 1400 GL 2-dr Sedan			865,000
362	Mirage 1400 GL 4-dr Sedan			913,000
362	Mirage 1400 GLX 2-dr Sedan			922,000
362	Mirage 1400 GLX 4-dr Sedan			965,000
362	Mirage 1400 GLS 2-dr Sedan			1,030,000
362	Mirage 1600 GT 2-dr Sedan			982,000
362	Mirage 1600 GT 4-dr Sedan			1,025,000
363	Lancer EX 1400 EL 4-dr Sedan			858,000
363	Lancer EX 1400 GL 4-dr Sedan			930,000
363	Lancer EX 1400 SL 4-dr Sedan			995,000
363	Lancer EX 1600 GL 4-dr Sedan			985,000
363	Lancer EX 1600 XL 4-dr Sedan			1,041,000
363	Lancer EX 1600 XL-5 4-dr Sedan			1,066,000
363	Lancer EX 1600 GT 4-dr Sedan			1,080,000
363	Celeste 1400 SR 2+1-dr Coupé			935,000
363	Celeste 1400 GL 2+1-dr Coupé			975,000
363	Celeste 1400 GSL 2+1-dr Coupé			1,031,000
363	Celeste 1600 GL 2+1-dr Coupé			1,117,000
363	Celeste 1600 XL 2+1-dr Coupé			1,115,000
363	Celeste 1600 GT 2+1-dr Coupé			1,117,000
363	Celeste 2000 GT 2+1-dr Coupé			1,355,000
364	Galant Sigma 1600 L 4-dr Sedan			1,012,000
364	Galant Sigma 1600 GL 4-dr Sedan			1,087,000
364	Galant Sigma 1600 SL 4-dr Sedan			1,132,000
364	Galant Sigma 1600 SL Super 4-dr Sedan			1,222,000
364	Galant Sigma Eterna 1600 GL 4-dr Sedan			1,077,000
364	Galant Sigma Eterna 1600 SL Super 4-dr Sedan			1,202,000
364	Galant Sigma 2000 GL 4-dr Sedan			1,210,000
364	Galant Sigma 2000 GSL 4-dr Sedan			1,329,000
364	Galant Sigma 2000 GSL Super 4-dr Sedan			1,415,000
364	Galant Sigma Eterna 2000 GSL 4-dr Sedan			1,309,000
364	Galant Sigma Eterna 2000 GSL Super 4-dr Sedan			1,395,000
364	Galant Sigma 2000 Super Saloon			

Page	MAKE AND MODEL	Price in GB £	Price in USA $	Price ex Works
	4-dr Sedan			1,540,000
365	Galant Lambda 1600 SL 2-dr Coupé			1,195,000
365	Galant Lambda 1600 SL Super 2-dr Coupé			1,275,000
365	Galant Lambda Eterna 1600 SR 2-dr Coupé			1,225,000
365	Galant Lambda 2000 GL 2-dr Coupé			1,277,000
365	Galant Lambda 2000 GSL 2-dr Coupé			1,376,000
365	Galant Lambda 2000 GSL Super 2-dr Coupé			1,475,000
365	Galant Lambda 2000 Super Touring 2-dr Coupé			1,641,000
365	Galant Lambda Eterna 2000 XL 2-dr Coupé			1,460,000
365	Galant Lambda 2600 Super Touring 2-dr Coupé			1,839,000
365	Debonair De Luxe 4-dr Sedan			2,280,000
365	Debonair Super De Luxe 4-dr Sedan			2,440,000
365	Debonair Executive SE 5-pass. 4-dr Sedan			2,500,000
365	Jeep H-J58 (canvas top, 4-pass.)			1,285,000
365	Jeep H-J56 (canvas top, 4-pass.)			1,325,000
365	Jeep H-J26H (metal top, 5-pass.)			1,460,000
365	Jeep H-J46 (canvas top, 9-pass.)			1,410,000
365	Jeep J38 Wagon (6-pass.)			1,630,000
365	Jeep J54 Diesel (canvas top, 4-pass.)			1,470,000
365	Jeep J24 Diesel (canvas top, 7-pass.)			1,530,000
365	Jeep J24H Diesel (metal top, 5-pass.)			1,625,000
365	Jeep J44 Diesel (canvas top, 9-pass.)			1,578,000
365	Jeep J36 Diesel Wagon (6-pass.)			1,795,000
	MONTEVERDI (Switzerland)			
235	Sierra			62,900
235	Sierra Cabriolet			89,000
236	Sahara			39,700
236	Safari			59,500
	MORGAN (Great Britain)			
167	4/4 1600 2-seater			5,669*
168	4/4 1600 4-seater			6,260*
168	Plus 8			8,191*
	MORRIS (Great Britain)			
168	Marina 1300 2-dr Coupé			3,440*
168	Marina 1300 4-dr Saloon			3,582*
168	Marina 1300 4+1-dr Estate Car			4,066*
168	Marina 1300 L 2-dr Coupé			3,721*
168	Marina 1300 L 4-dr Saloon			3,825*
168	Marina 1300 HL 4-dr Saloon			4,232*
168	Marina 1700 4-dr Saloon			3,851*
168	Marina 1700 4+1-dr Estate Car			4,317*
168	Marina 1700 L 4-dr Saloon			4,094*
168	Marina 1700 L 4+1-dr Estate Car			4,559*
168	Marina 1700 HL 4-dr Saloon			4,531*
168	Marina 1700 HL 4+1-dr Estate Car			4,957*
	NISSAN-DATSUN (Japan)			
366	Pulsar 1200 Custom 4+1-dr Sedan			774,000
366	Pulsar 1200 Custom D 4+1-dr Sedan			804,000
366	Pulsar 1200 TS 4+1-dr Sedan			870,000
366	Pulsar 1200 TS Coupé			918,000
366	Pulsar 1200 Standard Hatchback			740,000
366	Pulsar 1200 Custom Hatchback			766,000
366	Pulsar 1200 Custom D Hatchback			796,000
366	Pulsar 1200 TS Hatchback			860,000
366	Pulsar 1400 TS 4+1-dr Sedan			945,000
366	Pulsar 1400 TS-G 4+1-dr Sedan			1,013,000
366	Pulsar 1400 TS Coupé			993,000
366	Pulsar 1400 TS Hatchback			925,000
366	Pulsar 1400 TS-X Hatchback			1,010,000
366	Pulsar 1400 TS-GE 4+1-dr Sedan			1,108,000

Page	MAKE AND MODEL	Price in GB £	Price in USA $	Price ex Works
366	Pulsar 1400 TS-XE 4+1-dr Sedan			1,090,000
366	Pulsar 1400 TS-XE Coupé			1,106,000
366	Pulsar 1400 TS-XE Hatchback			1,080,000
367	Sunny 1200 CT 2-dr Sedan			737,000
367	Sunny 1200 CT 4-dr Sedan			757,000
367	Sunny 1200 City De Luxe 2-dr Sedan			760,000
367	Sunny 1200 City De Luxe 4-dr Sedan			780,000
367	Sunny 1200 S Coupé			838,000
367	Sunny 1200 GL 2-dr Sedan	3,256*		850,000
367	Sunny 1200 GL 4-dr Sedan	3,363*		870,000
367	Sunny 1200 GS Coupé			910,000
367	Sunny 1400 De Luxe 2-dr Sedan			833,000
367	Sunny 1400 De Luxe 4-dr Sedan			853,000
367	Sunny 1400 ES Coupé			883,000
367	Sunny 1400 GL 2-dr Sedan	3,728*	3,749*	902,000
367	Sunny 1400 GL 4-dr Sedan	3,825*		917,000
367	Sunny 1400 GS Coupé	3,697*		947,000
367	Sunny 1400 SGL 4-dr Sedan			975,000
367	Sunny 1400 GX 4-dr Sedan		4,739*	962,000
367	Sunny 1400 GX Coupé		4,899*	1,001,000
367	Sunny 1400 SGX 4-dr Sedan			1,020,000
367	Sunny 1400 SGX Coupé			1,089,000
367	Sunny 1400 California 4+1-dr DX Sedan			934,000
367	Sunny 1400 California 4+1-dr GL Sedan			982,000
367	Sunny 1400 California 4+1-dr SGL Sedan			1,058,000
367	Sunny 1400 California 4+1-dr GX Sedan			1,035,000
367	Sunny 1400 GX-E 4-dr Sedan			1,032,000
367	Sunny 1400 RS-E Coupé			999,000
367	Sunny 1400 SGX-E 4-dr Sedan			1,090,000
367	Sunny 1400 SGX-E Coupé			1,134,000
368	Violet 1400 Standard Sedan	3,691*		858,000
368	Violet 1400 De Luxe Sedan			926,000
368	Violet 1400 De Luxe Hatchback Coupé			956,000
368	Violet 1400 GL Sedan			969,000
368	Violet 1400 GL Hatchback Coupé			999,000
368	Violet 1600 De Luxe Sedan	3,774*		951,000
368	Auster 1600 Custom Sedan			981,000
368	Violet 1600 GL Sedan			999,000
368	Violet 1600 GL Hatchback Coupé			1,029,000
368	Violet 1600 GL-L Sedan			1,063,000
368	Auster 1600 CS Sedan			1,042,000
368	Auster 1600 CS Hatchback Coupé			1,072,000
368	Violet 1600 GX Sedan			1,055,000
368	Violet 1600 GX Hatchback Coupé			1,085,000
368	Auster 1600 CS-L Sedan			1,105,000
368	Auster 1600 CS-L Hatchback Coupé			1,150,000
368	Stanza 1600 Luxury Sedan			976,000
368	Stanza 1600 Extra Sedan			1,032,000
368	Stanza 1600 Maxima Sedan			1,130,000
368	Stanza 1600 Resort 4+1-dr Sedan			1,026,000
368	Stanza 1600 Resort 4+1-dr L Sedan			1,082,000
368	Stanza 1600 Resort 4+1-dr G Sedan			1,192,000
368	Violet 1600 SGX-E Sedan			1,255,000
368	Violet 1600 SGX-E Hatchback Coupé			1,300,000
368	Auster 1600 CS-EL Sedan			1,179,000
368	Auster 1600 CS-EL Hatchback Coupé			1,224,000
368	Stanza 1600 GT-E Sedan			1,172,000
368	Stanza 1600 Maxima GT-E Sedan			1,230,000
368	Stanza 1800 Extra Sedan			1,080,000
368	Stanza 1800 Maxima Sedan			1,161,000
368	Stanza 1800 Resort 4+1-dr Sedan			1,140,000
368	Stanza 1800 Resort 4+1-dr G Sedan			1,226,000
368	Stanza 1800 Maxima X-E Sedan			1,353,000
368	Stanza 1800 Maxima GT-E Sedan			1,301,000
368	Stanza 1800 Resort 4+1-dr X-E Sedan			1,341,000
368	Auster 1800 GT Sedan			1,196,000
368	Auster 1800 GT Hatchback Coupé			1,226,000
369	Bluebird 1600 4-dr CT Sedan	3,990*		949,000
369	Bluebird 1600 4-dr DX Sedan			989,000
369	Bluebird 1600 4-dr GL Sedan			1,046,000
369	Bluebird 1600 4-dr GF Sedan			1,203,000
369	Bluebird 1600 2-dr GL Hardtop			1,081,000
369	Bluebird 1600 2-dr GF Hardtop			1,238,000
369	Bluebird 1800 4-dr GL Sedan	4,098*		1,127,000

Page	MAKE AND MODEL	Price in GB £	Price in USA $	Price ex Works
369	Bluebird 1800 4-dr GF Sedan			1,294,000
369	Bluebird 1800 4-dr SSS Sedan			1,208,000
369	Bluebird 1800 2-dr GF Hardtop			1,329,000
369	Bluebird 1800 2-dr SSS Hardtop			1,243,000
369	Bluebird 1800 4-dr SSS-E Sedan			1,326,000
369	Bluebird 1800 2-dr SSS-E Hardtop			1,361,000
369	Bluebird 2000 4-dr SSS-EL Sedan		8,129*	1,412,000
369	Bluebird 2000 4-dr SSS-EX Sedan			1,603,000
369	Bluebird 2000 4-dr SSS-EXG Sedan			1,698,000
369	Bluebird 2000 4-dr SSS-ES Sedan			1,473,000
369	Bluebird 2000 2-dr SSS-EL Hardtop		8,279*	1,447,000
369	Bluebird 2000 2-dr SSS-EX Hardtop			1,638,000
369	Bluebird 2000 2-dr SSS-EXG Hardtop			1,733,000
369	Bluebird 2000 2-dr SSS-ES Hardtop			1,508,000
370	Skyline 1600 TI Sedan			1,021,000
370	Skyline 1600 TI-L Sedan			1,110,000
370	Skyline 1600 TI-L Hardtop			1,145,000
370	Skyline 1800 TI Sedan			1,076,000
370	Skyline 1800 TI-L Sedan			1,199,000
370	Skyline 1800 TI-L Hardtop			1,234,000
370	Skyline 1800 TI-EL Sedan			1,301,000
370	Skyline 1800 TI-EL Hardtop			1,332,000
370	Skyline 1800 TI-EX Sedan			1,396,000
370	Skyline 1800 TI-EX Hardtop			1,428,000
370	Skyline 1800 TI-ES Sedan			1,414,000
370	Skyline 1800 TI-ES Hardtop			1,449,000
370	Skyline 2000 GT Sedan			1,289,000
370	Skyline 2000 GT Hardtop			1,334,000
370	Skyline 2000 GT-L Sedan			1,360,000
370	Skyline 2000 GT-L Hardtop			1,405,000
370	Skyline 2000 GT-E Sedan			1,408,000
370	Skyline 2000 GT-E Hardtop			1,451,000
370	Skyline 2000 GT-EL Sedan			1,465,000
370	Skyline 2000 GT-EL Hardtop			1,508,000
370	Skyline 2000 GT-EX Sedan			1,654,000
370	Skyline 2000 GT-EX Hardtop			1,698,000
370	Skyline 2000 GT-ES Sedan			1,657,000
370	Skyline 2000 GT-ES Hardtop			1,702,000
371	Laurel 1800 Standard 4-dr Sedan			1,098,000
371	Laurel 1800 Custom 4-dr Sedan			1,138,000
371	Laurel 1800 GL 4-dr Sedan			1,212,000
371	Laurel 1800 GL 2-dr Hardtop			1,241,000
371	Laurel 1800 GL 4-dr Hardtop			1,289,000
371	Laurel 1800 SGL 4-dr Sedan			1,344,000
371	Laurel 2000 Diesel Standard 4-dr Sedan			1,190,000
371	Laurel 2000 Diesel De Luxe 4-dr Sedan			1,284,000
371	Laurel 2000 Diesel GL 4-dr Sedan			1,406,000
371	Laurel 2000 Custom 6 4-dr Sedan			1,263,000
371	Laurel 2000 GL 6 4-dr Sedan	5,496*		1,390,000
371	Laurel 2000 GL 6 2-dr Hardtop			1,448,000
371	Laurel 2000 GL 6 4-dr Hardtop			1,512,000
371	Laurel 2000 SGL 4-dr Sedan			1,498,000
371	Laurel 2000 SGL-E 4-dr Sedan			1,603,000
371	Laurel 2000 SGL-E 2-dr Hardtop			1,659,000
371	Laurel 2000 SGL-E 4-dr Hardtop			1,717,000
371	Laurel 2000 GL 6-E 4-dr Hardtop			1,617,000
371	Laurel 2000 Medalist 4-dr Sedan			1,888,000
371	Laurel 2000 Medalist 2-dr Hardtop			1,965,000
371	Laurel 2000 Medalist 4-dr Hardtop			2,032,000
371	Laurel 2800 Medalist 4-dr Sedan			2,011,000
371	Laurel 2800 Medalist 2-dr Hardtop			2,063,000
371	Laurel 2800 Medalist 4-dr Hardtop			2,138,000
372	Fairlady Z Sports			1,460,000
372	Fairlady ZL Sports			1,625,000
372	Fairlady ZT Sports			1,795,000
372	Fairlady Z 2+2 Sports			1,598,000
372	Fairlady ZL 2+2 Sports			1,793,000
372	Fairlady ZT 2+2 Sports			1,988,000
372	Fairlady 280 ZL Sports			1,800,000
372	Fairlady 280 ZT Sports			2,155,000
372	Fairlady 280 ZL 2+2 Sports			1,965,000
372	Fairlady 280 ZT 2+2 Sports			2,373,000
373	President C 4-dr Sedan			3,846,000
373	President D 4-dr Sedan			4,238,000

Page	MAKE AND MODEL	Price in GB £	Price in USA $	Price ex Works
373	President Sovereign 4-dr Sedan			4,627,000
373	Silvia 1800 LS 2-dr Coupé			1,085,000
373	Silvia 1800 LS-L 2-dr Coupé			1,160,000
373	Silvia 1800 LS-X 2-dr Coupé			1,260,000
373	Silvia 1800 2+1-dr Hatchback LS-L			1,240,000
373	Silvia 1800 2+2-dr Hatchback LS-X			1,340,000
373	Gazelle 1800 2-dr T-I Coupé			1,165,000
373	Gazelle 1800 2-dr T-II Coupé			1,265,000
373	Gazelle 1800 2+1-dr Hatchback T-I			1,245,000
373	Gazelle 1800 2+1-dr Hatchback T-II			1,345,000
373	Silvia 1800 LSE-L 2-dr Coupé			1,255,000
373	Silvia 1800 LSE-X 2-dr Coupé			1,370,000
373	Silvia 1800 LSE-L 2+1-dr Hatchback			1,335,000
373	Silvia 1800 LSE-X 2+1-dr Hatchback			1,450,000
373	Gazelle 1800 TE-I 2-dr Coupé			1,260,000
373	Gazelle 1800 TE-II 2-dr Coupé			1,375,000
373	Gazelle 2+1-dr Hatchback TE-I			1,390,000
373	Gazelle 2+1-dr Hatchback TE-II			1,595,000
373	Silvia 2000 ZSE-L 2-dr Coupé		6,289*	1,385,000
373	Silvia 2000 ZSE-X 2-dr Coupé		7,039*	1,585,000
373	Silvia 2000 2+1-dr Hatchback ZSE-L		6,489*	1,465,000
373	Silvia 2000 2+1-dr Hatchback ZSE-X		7,289*	1,665,000
373	Gazelle 2000 XE-I 2-dr Coupé			1,390,000
373	Gazelle 2000 XE-II 2-dr Coupé			1,595,000
373	Gazelle 2000 2+1-dr Hatchback XE-I			1,470,000
373	Gazelle 2000 2+1-dr Hatchback XE-II			1,675,000
374	Cedric 200 Standard Sedan			1,324,000
374	Cedric 200 De Luxe Sedan			1,457,000
374	Cedric 200 Custom De Luxe Sedan			1,583,000
374	Cedric 200 GL Sedan			1,789,000
374	Cedric 200 Custom S Hardtop			1,730,000
374	Cedric 200 GL Hardtop			1,958,000
374	Cedric 200 E De Luxe Sedan			1,567,000
374	Cedric 200 E Custom De Luxe Sedan			1,723,000
374	Cedric 200 E GL Sedan			1,869,000
374	Cedric 200 E SGL Sedan			2,231,000
374	Cedric 200 E SGL Extra Sedan			2,315,000
374	Cedric 200 E Custom S Hardtop			1,810,000
374	Cedric 200 E GL Hardtop			2,038,000
374	Cedric 200 E SGL Hardtop			2,408,000
374	Cedric 200 E SGL Extra Hardtop			2,492,000
374	Gloria 280 E Brougham Sedan			2,721,000
374	Gloria 280 E Brougham Hardtop			2,850,000
374	Cedric 2000 Turbo SGL Extra Sedan			2,465,000
374	Cedric 2000 Turbo S Hardtop			2,263,000
374	Cedric 2000 Turbo SGL Extra Hardtop			2,642,000
374	Gloria 200 D Standard Sedan			1,359,000
374	Gloria 220 D Standard Sedan			1,304,000
374	Gloria 220 D DX Sedan			1,562,000
374	Gloria 220 D GL Sedan			1,852,000
374	Gloria 2800 D VO-6 Sedan			1,635,000
374	Gloria 2800 D VL-6 Sedan			1,962,000
374	Gloria 2800 D VX-6 Sedan			2,405,000
374	Gloria 2800 D VS-6 Hardtop			1,903,000
374	Gloria 2800 D UL-6 Hardtop			2,131,000
374	Gloria 2800 D VX-6 Hardtop			2,582,000
375	Patrol 4WD			1,337,000
	NOVA (Great Britain)			
169	Sports			5,200*
	NUOVA INNOCENTI (Italy)			
217	Mini 90 N			3,840,000*
217	Mini 90 SL			4,400,000*
218	Mini 120 SL			4,630,000*
218	Mini De Tomaso			5,145,000*
	OLDSMOBILE (USA)			
316	Starfire Coupé			4,750
316	Starfire SX Coupé			4,950
317	Omega 4-dr Sedan			5,266
317	Omega 2-dr Coupé			5,100

Page	MAKE AND MODEL	Price in GB £	Price in USA $	Price ex Works
317	Omega 4-dr Brougham Sedan			5,530
317	Omega 2-dr Brougham Coupé			5,380
318	Cutlass 4-dr Sedan			5,532
318	Cutlass 2-dr Salon Coupé			5,372
318	Cutlass 2-dr Salon Brougham Coupé			5,662
318	Cutlass 4-dr Luxury Supreme Sedan			6,353
318	Cutlass 2-dr Supreme Coupé			6,252
318	Cutlass 4-dr Brougham Sedan			6,776
318	Cutlass 2-dr Supreme Brougham Coupé			6,691
318	Cutlass 2-dr Calais Coupé			6,716
318	Cutlass 4+1-dr Cruiser St. Wagon			5,978
318	Cutlass 4+1-dr Cruiser Brougham Wagon			6,377
319	Delta 88 4-dr Sedan			6,552
319	Delta 88 2-dr Coupé			6,457
319	Delta 88 Royale 4-dr Sedan			6,864
319	Delta 88 Royale 2-dr Coupé			6,716
319	Delta 88 Royale Brougham 4-dr Sedan			7,160
319	Delta 88 Royale Brougham 2-dr Coupé			7,080
319	Ninety Eight 4-dr Luxury Sedan			9,112
319	Ninety Eight 4-dr Regency Sedan			9,741
319	Ninety Eight 2-dr Regency Coupé			9,619
319	Custom Cruiser 4+1-dr St. Wagon			7,443
320	Toronado			11,361
	OPEL (Germany FR)			
126	Kadett 2-dr Limousine			10,745*
126	Kadett 4-dr Limousine			11,315*
126	Kadett 2+1-dr Limousine			10,980*
126	Kadett 4+1-dr Limousine			11,550*
126	Kadett Luxus 2-dr Limousine	3,330*		11,420*
126	Kadett Luxus 4-dr Limousine	3,470*		11,990*
126	Kadett Luxus 2+1-dr Limousine			11,705*
126	Kadett Luxus 4+1-dr Limousine			12,275*
126	Kadett Berlina 2-dr Limousine			12,270*
126	Kadett Berlina 4-dr Limousine	4,593*		12,840*
126	Kadett Berlina 2+1-dr Limousine			12,555*
126	Kadett Berlina 4+1-dr Limousine	4,694*		13,125*
126	Kadett 2+1-dr Caravan			11,945*
126	Kadett 4+1-dr Caravan			12,515*
126	Kadett Luxus 2+1-dr Caravan	3,733*		12,620*
126	Kadett Luxus 4+1-dr Caravan			13,190*
127	Kadett SR 2-dr Limousine	4,495*		14,220*
127	Kadett SR 2+1-dr Limousine			14,560*
127	Ascona 2-dr Limousine			12,545*
127	Ascona 4-dr Limousine	3,934*		13,125*
127	Ascona Luxus 2-dr Limousine			13,465*
127	Ascona Luxus 4-dr Limousine	4,324*		14,045*
127	Ascona Berlina 2-dr Limousine			14,241*
127	Ascona Berlina 4-dr Limousine			14,664*
128	Manta 2-dr Coupé			13,765*
128	Manta Luxus 2-dr Coupé			14,685*
128	Manta Berlinetta 2-dr Coupé	5,661*		15,461*
128	Manta CC 2+1-dr Hatchback Coupé			14,180*
128	Manta CC Luxus 2+1-dr Hatchback Coupé	5,794*		15,100*
128	Manta CC Berlinetta 2+1-dr Hatchback Coupé			15,876*
128	Manta GT/E 2-dr Coupé			17,168*
128	Manta E Luxus 2-dr Coupé			17,229*
128	Manta E Berlinetta 2-dr Coupé			17,970*
128	Manta CC GT/E 2+1-dr Hatchback Coupé			17,583*
128	Manta CC E Luxus 2+1-dr Hatchback Coupé			17,644*
128	Manta CC E Berlinetta 2+1-dr Hatchback Coupé			18,385*
130	Rekord 2-dr Limousine			14,935*
130	Rekord 4-dr Limousine	5,469*		15,550*
130	Rekord Luxus 2-dr Limousine			15,785*
130	Rekord Luxus 4-dr Limousine			16,235*
130	Rekord Berlina 2-dr Limousine			16,575*
130	Rekord Berlina 4-dr Limousine	5,761*		17,025*

Page	MAKE AND MODEL	Price in GB £	Price in USA $	Price ex Works
130	Rekord 2+1-dr Caravan			15,540*
130	Rekord 4+1-dr Caravan			16,155*
130	Rekord Luxus 4+1-dr Caravan	6,210*		17,000*
131	Commodore 2-dr Limousine			17,895*
131	Commodore 4-dr Limousine			18,350*
131	Commodore Berlina 2-dr Limousine			18,575*
131	Commodore Berlina 4-dr Limousine			19,030*
132	Senator 4-dr Limousine	8,627*		24,415*
132	Senator C 4-dr Limousine			26,454*
132	Senator CD Automatic 4-dr Limousine			38,925*
132	Monza Hatchback Coupé	11,675*		26,430*
132	Monza C Hatchback Coupé			27,434*
	OTOSAN (Turkey)			
336	Anadol SL			—
336	Anadol SV-1600			—
	PANTHER (Great Britain)			
169	Lima			8,250*
170	J 72 4.2-litre			23,995*
170	De Ville Saloon			58,250*
171	De Ville Convertible			72,215*
171	6			—
	PEKING China (People's Republic)			
348	BJ 212			—
	PEUGEOT (France)			
83	104 GL 4+1-dr Berline	3,120*		26,100◊
83	104 ZA 2+1-dr Coupé	2,999*		—
83	104 GR 4+1-dr Berline	3,450*		28,800◊
83	104 ZR 2+1-dr Coupé	3,329*		27,700◊
83	104 ZR Grand Confort 2+1-dr Coupé	—		29,800◊
83	104 SR 4+1-dr Berline	3,599*		30,300◊
83	104 SR Grand Confort 4+1-dr Berline	—		33,000◊
83	104 S 4+1-dr Berline	4,059*		32,800◊
83	104 ZS 2+1-dr Coupé	3,939*		31,700◊
84	304 GL Break	3,751*		31,600◊
84	304 SL Break	4,048*		34,000◊
84	304 GLD Break	—		36,900◊
84	305 GL Berline	3,899*		33,200◊
84	305 GR Berline	4,248*		35,700◊
84	305 SR Berline	4,666*		38,800◊
84	305 SR Grand Confort Berline	—		41,600◊
84	305 GRD Berline	4,943*		41,000◊
84	305 GRD Grand Confort Berline	—		43,300◊
85	504 GR Berline	4,754*		38,000◊
85	504 SR Berline	—		41,100◊
85	504 GRD Diesel Berline	—		44,100◊
85	504 SRD Diesel Berline	—	9,598*	47,200◊
86	504 Break Essence	5,299*		40,300◊
86	504 GR Break	6,000*		44,100◊
86	504 Familial Break	6,311*		45,922◊
86	504 Break Diesel	5,971*		46,400◊
86	504 Familial Diesel Break	7,102*	10,198*	52,378◊
87	504 Cabriolet	—		66,700◊
87	504 Coupé	—		66,700◊
87	504 V6 Coupé	—		79,000◊
87	505 GR Berline	5,969*		44,900◊
87	505 SR Berline	6,453*		49,500◊
87	505 TI Berline	6,557*		50,400◊
87	505 STI Berline	7,041*		55,000◊
87	505 GRD Diesel Berline	6,744*		51,700◊
87	505 SRD Diesel Berline	7,228*		56,300◊
88	604 SL Berline	8,442*	13,998*	58,000◊
88	604 TI Berline	9,813*		64,570◊

Page	MAKE AND MODEL	Price in GB £	Price in USA $	Price ex Works
88	604 TI Grand Confort Berline	—		71,000◊
88	604 D Turbo Berline	9,508*		66,900◊
88	604 D Turbo Grand Confort Berline	—		72,600◊
	PLYMOUTH (USA)			
321	Horizon 4-dr Hatchback			4,925
321	Horizon TC3 2-dr Hatchback			5,271
322	Volaré 4-dr Sedan			4,847
322	Volaré 2-dr Coupé			4,730
322	Volaré 4-dr Sedan Special			4,994
322	Volaré 2-dr Coupé Special			4,977
322	Volaré 4+1-dr St. Wagon			5,089
322	Gran Fury Pillared Hardtop			6,280
322	Gran Fury Salon Pillared Hardtop			6,711
	POLSKI-FIAT (Poland)			
218	126 P			—
218	126 P 650			—
218	125 P 1300			—
219	125 P 1300 Estate			—
219	125 P 1500	2,373*		—
219	125 P 1500 Estate	2,736*		—
219	Polonez	3,194*		—
	PONTIAC (Canada)			
269	Acadian 4+1-dr Hatchback Sedan			5,081
269	Acadian 2+1-dr S Hatchback Coupé			4,345
269	Acadian 2+1-dr Hatchback Coupé			4,929
269	Le Mans 4-dr Sedan			—
269	Le Mans 2-dr Coupé			—
269	Le Mans 4+1-dr St. Wagon			—
270	Catalina 4-dr Sedan			—
270	Catalina 2-dr Coupé			—
270	Catalina 4+1-dr Safari St. Wagon			—
270	Laurentian 4-dr Sedan			7,531
270	Laurentian 2-dr Coupé			7,482
270	Laurentian 4+1-dr Safari St. Wagon			8,208
270	Parisienne 4-dr Sedan			8,250
270	Parisienne 2-dr Coupé			8,116
270	Parisienne 4+1-dr Safari St. Wagon			9,207
	PONTIAC (USA)			
324	Sunbird 2-dr Coupé			4,371
324	Sunbird 2-dr Sport Coupé			4,620
324	Sunbird 2+1-dr Sport Hatchback Coupé			4,731
325	Phoenix 4+1-dr Hatchback Sedan			5,250
325	Phoenix 2-dr Coupé			5,067
325	Phoenix LJ 4+1-dr Hatchback Sedan			5,704
325	Phoenix LJ 2-dr Coupé			5,520
326	Le Mans 4-dr Sedan			5,377
326	Le Mans 2-dr Coupé			5,274
326	Le Mans 4+1-dr Safari St. Wagon			5,861
326	Grand Le Mans 4-dr Sedan			5,728
326	Grand Le Mans 2-dr Coupé			5,560
326	Grand Le Mans 4+1-dr Safari St. Wagon			6,273
326	Grand Am 2-dr Coupé			7,299
327	Firebird 2-dr Hardtop Coupé			5,604
327	Firebird Esprit 2-dr Hardtop Coupé			5,967
327	Firebird Formula 2-dr Hardtop Coupé			6,954
327	Firebird Trans Am 2-dr Hardtop Coupé	9,734*		7,178
328	Grand Prix 2-dr Hardtop Coupé			6,219
328	Grand Prix 2-dr LJ Hardtop Coupé			6,598
328	Grand Prix 2-dr SJ Hardtop Coupé			7,044
329	Catalina 4-dr Sedan			6,397
329	Catalina 2-dr Coupé			6,341
329	Catalina 4+1-dr Safari St. Wagon			7,044

Page	MAKE AND MODEL	Price in GB £	Price in USA $	Price ex Works
329	Bonneville 4-dr Sedan			6,792
329	Bonneville 2-dr Coupé			6,666
329	Bonneville Brougham 4-dr Sedan			7,885
329	Bonneville Brougham 2-dr Coupé			7,696
329	Bonneville 4+1-dr Safari St. Wagon			7,625
	PORSCHE (Germany FR)			
133	924	9,103*	—	27,980*
133	924 (USA)	—	15,970*	—
133	924 Turbo	13,629*	—	39,980*
133	911 SC Coupé	16,109*	—	46,950*
134	911 SC Coupé (USA)	—	25,900*	—
134	911 SC Targa	16,109*	27,250*	49,950*
134	Turbo Coupé	27,950*	—	82,950*
134	Turbo Coupé (USA)	—	19,880*	—
134	928	21,827*	35,450*	56,900*
135	928 S	25,251*	—	72,900*
	PORTARO (Portugal)			
220	250			—
	PREMIER (India)			
346	Padmini			43,176
346	Padmini De Luxe			50,922
	PRINCESS (Great Britain)			
171	1700 L Saloon			4,458*
171	1700 HL Saloon			4,895*
171	1700 HLS Saloon			5,378*
171	2000 HL Saloon			5,170*
171	2000 HLS Saloon			5,651*
171	2200 HL Saloon			5,352*
171	2200 HLS Saloon			6,151*
	PUMA (Brazil)			
264	GTE 1600 Coupé			—
264	GTS 1600 Sport			—
264	GTB S2			—
	QUINCY-LYNN (USA)			
330	Trimuter G			4,995
	RAPPORT (Great Britain)			
172	Quadraporte			19,250*
	RELIANT (Great Britain)			
172	Kitten DL 2-dr Saloon			3,091*
172	Kitten DL 2+1-dr Estate Car			3,339*
173	Robin 850 2-dr Saloon			2,444*
173	Robin 850 2+1-dr Estate Car			2,681*
173	Robin 850 Super 2-dr Saloon			2,836*
173	Robin 850 Super 2+1-dr Estate Car			3,004*
174	Scimitar GTE			9,343*
174	Scimitar GTC			—
	RENAULT (Argentina)			
251	4 S			—

Page	MAKE AND MODEL	Price in GB £	Price in USA $	Price ex Works
251	6			—
251	6 GTL			—
251	12 TL			—
251	12 TS			—
252	12 TS Break			—
252	12 Alpine			—
252	Torino Grand Routier GR			—
252	Torino ZX Coupé			—
	RENAULT (France)			
89	4 Break	—		20,400◊
89	4 Export Break	2,624*		—
89	4 TL Break	—		22,500◊
89	4 TL Export Break	2,848*		—
89	4 GTL Break	—		24,300◊
89	Rodeo 4	—		24,402◊
90	Rodeo 6	—		39,396◊
90	5 2+1-dr Berline	2,841*		24,000◊
90	5 4+1-dr Berline	—		25,500◊
90	5 TL 2+1-dr Berline	3,218*		27,000◊
90	5 TL 4+1-dr Berline	—		28,500◊
90	5 GTL 2+1-dr Berline	3,397*		29,000◊
90	5 GTL 4+1-dr Berline	3,551*		30,500◊
90	5 Automatic 2+1-dr Berline	3,868*		32,500◊
90	5 TS 2+1-dr Berline	3,794*		32,000◊
90	5 Alpine 2+1-dr Berline	4,881*		42,800◊
91	6 TL	3,282*		27,400◊
92	14 TL Berline	3,640*		30,900◊
92	14 GTL Berline	3,771*		32,900◊
92	14 TS Berline	4,246*		36,100◊
92	16 TL Berline	4,238*		36,800◊
92	16 TX Berline	5,165*		43,100◊
92	16 TX Automatic Berline	5,532*		45,600◊
93	18 4-dr Berline	—		32,200◊
93	18 TL 4-dr Berline	3,887*		35,000◊
93	18 GTL 4-dr Berline	4,500*		38,400◊
93	18 4+1-dr Break	—		35,200◊
93	18 TL 4+1-dr Break	4,261*		38,000◊
93	18 TS 4-dr Berline	4,287*		38,700◊
93	18 GTS 4-dr Berline	4,952*		42,200◊
93	18 Automatic 4-dr Berline	4,990*		41,800◊
93	18 TS 4+1-dr Break	4,691*		41,700◊
93	18 TS 4+1-dr Break Automatic	5,016*		45,100◊
93	20 TL	5,292*		43,200◊
93	20 GTL	—		46,700◊
94	20 TS	6,414*		48,400◊
94	20 TS Automatic	6,739*		51,800◊
94	20 TD	—		49,700◊
94	20 GTD	—		53,800◊
94	30 TS	7,692*		53,800◊
95	30 TS Automatic	8,017*		57,200◊
95	30 TX	9,105*		62,800◊
95	30 TX Automatic	9,430*		65,200◊
	REPLICARS (USA)			
330	Phaeton			15,950
330	Roadster			16,450
330	Hardtop			18,450
	ROLLS-ROYCE (Great Britain)			
174	Silver Shadow II		77,600*	39,219*
175	Silver Wraith II		91,000*	46,208*
175	Silver Wraith II with division		—	48,725*
175	Corniche Saloon		131,300*	58,392*
175	Corniche Convertible		140,000*	62,018*
175	Phantom VI		—	—
175	Camargue		136,500*	71,137*

Page	MAKE AND MODEL	Price in GB £	Price in USA $	Price ex Works
	ROM CARMEL (Israel)			
337	Rom 1301			—
	ROVER (Great Britain)			
176	3500			9,675*
176	2600			7,699*
177	2300			6,576*
	SAAB (Sweden)			
230	99 GL 2-dr Sedan	5,165*	7,995*	—
230	99 GL 4-dr Sedan	5,635*		—
230	99 Turbo 2-dr Sport Sedan	7,750*		—
231	900 GL 2+1-dr Hatchback Sedan	6,350*		—
231	900 GL 4+1-dr Hatchback Sedan	—		—
231	900 GLS 2+1-dr Hatchback Sedan	6,640*		—
231	900 GLS 4+1-dr Hatchback Sedan	6,920*		—
231	900 GLi 2+1-dr Hatchback Sedan	—	9,295*	—
231	900 GLi 4+1-dr Hatchback Sedan	—		—
231	900 EMS 2+1-dr Hatchback Sedan	7,720*		—
231	900 GLE 4+1-dr Hatchback Sedan	8,555*	10,295*	—
231	900 Turbo 2+1-dr Hatchback Sedan	9,910*	12,595*	—
231	900 Turbo 4+1-dr Hatchback Sedan	10,310*	13,695*	—
	SBARRO (Switzerland)			
237	Replica BMW 328 Standard			35,000
237	Replica BMW 328 America			44,000
238	Stash HS Cabriolet			100,000
238	Windhound 4x4			65,000
	SCEPTRE (USA)			
331	6.6 S			50,000
	SEAT (Spain)			
223	133 Lujo			249,000*
224	127 900 2 Puertas			285,000*
224	127 900 2+1 Puertas			296,000*
224	127 900 4 Puertas			299,000*
224	127 900 2 Puertas Confort Lujo			315,000*
224	127 900 2+1 Puertas Confort Lujo			328,000*
224	127 900 4 Puertas Confort Lujo			332,000*
224	127 1000 2 Puertas Especial Confort Lujo			323,000*
224	127 1000 2+1 Puertas Especial Confort Lujo			335,000*
224	127 1000 4 Puertas Especial Confort Lujo			338,000*
224	Ritmo 65 CL			—
224	Ritmo 75 CL			—
225	124-D			378,000*
225	124-D LS			417,000*
225	124-D Especial			435,000*
225	124 Especial 2000			465,000*
225	131 1430			469,000*
225	131 Supermirafiori 1430			511,000*
226	131 CL 1430 5 Puertas			534,000*
226	131 Supermirafiori 1600			550,000*
226	131 CL 1600 5 Puertas			574,000*
226	131 Supermirafiori 2000			637,000*
227	131 Diesel Perkins			607,000*
227	131 Diesel Perkins Supermirafiori			662,000*
227	131 Diesel Perkins 5 Puertas			625,000*
227	132 2000 Lujo			664,000*
227	132 Diesel 2200			715,000*
227	132 Diesel 2200 Lujo			765,000*
227	Lancia Beta Coupé 2000			—
228	Lancia Beta HPE 2000			—

Page	MAKE AND MODEL	Price in GB £	Price in USA $	Price ex Works
	SHANGHAI (China People's Republic)			
348	Sedan			—
	ŠKODA (Czechoslovakia)			
75	105 S	1,970*		—
76	105 L	2,076*		—
76	120 L	2,183*		—
76	120 LS	2,448*		—
76	S 110 R Coupé	2,129*		—
	SPARTAN CARS (Great Britain)			
177	2-seater Sports			4,680*
177	2+2-seater Sports			5,035*
	Sta MATILDE (Brazil)			
264	SM 4.1			—
	STANDARD (India)			
347	Gazel			—
	STIMULA (France)			
95	Bugatti 55			138,000
	STUTZ (USA)			
331	IV Porte Sedan			74,765
331	Blackhawk VI 2-dr Coupé			69,500
331	Bearcat 2-dr Convertible			129,000
332	Royale Limousine			235,000
	SUBARU (Japan)			
376	Rex 550 SEEC-T B 2-dr Sedan			561,000
376	Rex 550 SEEC-T AI 2-dr Sedan			618,000
376	Rex 550 SEEC-T AI 4-dr Sedan			643,000
376	Rex 550 SEEC-T AII 4-dr Sedan			682,000
376	Rex 550 SEEC-T AIIG 4-dr Sedan			709,000
376	Rex 550 SEEC-T Swingback AI			638,000
376	Rex 550 SEEC-T Swingback AII			677,000
376	Rex 550 SEEC-T Swingback AIIG			704,000
376	Rex 550 SEEC-T Family			480,000
376	Leone 1300 E Swingback			730,000
376	Leone 1300 LE Swingback			825,000
376	Leone 1600 GLF Swingback			954,000
376	Leone 1600 GLS Swingback			1,045,000
376	Leone 1600 SRX Swingback			1,198,000
376	Leone 1600 L 4-dr Sedan	3,326*	4,998*	880,000
376	Leone 1600 LF 4-dr Sedan		5,348*	935,000
376	Leone 1600 GLF 4-dr Sedan	3,987*		1,010,000
376	Leone 1600 GLS 4-dr Sedan			1,120,000
376	Leone 1600 GLF Hardtop	3,725*	5,548*	1,042,000
376	Leone 1600 Swingback 4WD		5,998*	1,210,000
376	Leone 1600 Estate 4WD		6,248*	1,102,000
376	Leone 1800 GTL 4-dr Sedan			1,195,000
376	Leone 1800 GTS 4-dr Sedan			1,355,000
376	Leone 1800 GTL Hardtop			1,245,000
376	Leone 1800 GTS Hardtop			1,380,000
376	Leone 1800 4-dr Sedan 4WD			1,446,000
376	Leone 1800 Swingback 4WD			1,336,000
376	Leone 1800 Estate 4WD	4,983*		1,247,000
	SUNRISE (India)			
347	Badal			21,100*
	SUZUKI (Japan)			
378	Fronte FX 4+1-dr Hatchback			568,000
378	Fronte FXL 4+1-dr Hatchback			638,000
378	Fronte FXC 4+1-dr Hatchback			678,000
378	Fronte FXG 4+1-dr Hatchback			718,000
378	Fronte FS 4+1-dr Hatchback			589,000
378	Fronte FSL 4+1-dr Hatchback			638,000
378	Fronte FSC 4+1-dr Hatchback			678,000
378	Fronte FSG 4+1-dr Hatchback			718,000
378	Cervo CX Coupé			608,000
378	Cervo CXB Coupé			608,000
378	Cervo CXL Coupé			639,000
378	Cervo CXG Coupé			698,000
378	Cervo SC 100 Coupé	2,400*		—
378	Alto Hatchback			470,000
379	Jimny 55 SJ10F			748,000
379	Jimny 55 SJ10FM			768,000
379	Jimny 55 SJ10V			787,000
379	Jimny 55 SJ10VM			797,000
379	Jimny 8 SJ20F			889,000
379	Jimny 8 SJ20VM			908,000
379	Jimny 8 SJ20FM			879,000
	SYRENA (Poland)			
219	105			—
	TALBOT (France)			
96	Matra Rancho	6,316*		47,000◊
96	Matra Rancho Grand Raid			56,100◊
96	Matra Bagheera			47,600◊
96	Matra Bagheera X			55,100◊
97	Simca 1100 LE 2+1-dr Berline			23,700◊
97	Simca 1100 LE 4+1-dr Berline			25,700◊
97	Simca 1100 LE 4+1-dr Break			28,600◊
97	Simca 1100 GLS 4+1-dr Berline			29,200◊
97	Simca 1100 GLS 4+1-dr Break			30,950◊
97	Simca Horizon LS	3,320*		29,400◊
97	Simca Horizon GL	3,958*		32,800◊
97	Simca Horizon GLS			35,800◊
97	Simca Horizon SX			30,950◊
98	Simca 1510 LS			34,950◊
98	Simca 1510 GL			38,350◊
98	Simca 1510 GLS			41,850◊
98	Simca 1510 SX			47,300◊
99	Simca 1610			39,600◊
100	Simca 2 L Automatique	5,305*		43,100◊
	TALBOT (Great Britain)			
178	Sunbeam 1.0 LS			2,953*
178	Sunbeam 1.0 GL			3,235*
178	Sunbeam 1.3 LS			3,193*
178	Sunbeam 1.3 GL			3,476*
178	Sunbeam 1.6 GL			3,623*
178	Sunbeam 1.6 GLS			4,136*
178	Sunbeam 1.6 TI			4,433*
178	Sunbeam Lotus			6,995*
179	Avenger 1.3 LS Saloon			3,324*
179	Avenger 1.3 LS Estate Car			3,713*
179	Avenger 1.3 GL Saloon			3,794*
179	Avenger 1.3 GL Estate Car			4,207*
179	Avenger 1.6 LS Saloon			3,456*
179	Avenger 1.6 LS Estate Car			3,845*
179	Avenger 1.6 GL Saloon			3,926*
179	Avenger 1.6 GL Estate Car			4,339*
179	Avenger 1.6 GLS Saloon			4,298*
180	Horizon 1.1 LS			3,320*
180	Horizon 1.1 GL			3,801*
180	Horizon 1.3 LS			3,477*
180	Horizon 1.3 GL			3,958*
180	Horizon 1.3 GLS			4,350*
180	Horizon 1.5 SX Automatic			4,950*
181	Alpine 1.3 LS			4,027*
181	Alpine 1.3 GL			4,288*
181	Alpine 1.5 LS			4,218*
181	Alpine 1.5 GL			4,740*
181	Alpine 1.5 GLS			5,442*
181	Alpine 1.6 SX			6,495*

Page	MAKE AND MODEL	Price in GB £	Price in USA $	Price ex Works
	TALBOT (Spain)			
228	Simca 1200 L 2+1-dr			339,600*
228	Simca 1200 LS 4+1-dr			356,700*
228	Simca 1200 LX 2+1-dr			371,600*
228	Simca 1200 GLS 4+1-dr			383,300*
228	Simca 1200 GLS Confort 4+1-dr			399,800*
228	Simca 1200 GLS 4+1-dr Break			394,900*
228	Simca 1200 GLS Confort 4+1-dr Break			411,300*
229	150 LS			479,200*
229	150 S			509,600*
229	150 GT			543,000*
229	150 SX			645,500*
229	180			604,700*
229	180 Automatico			654,300*
229	180 Diesel			668,900*
229	180 Diesel De Luxe			705,100*
	TATRA (Czechoslovakia)			
76	T 613			—
	TECHNICAL EXPONENTS (Great Britain)			
182	TX Tripper 1500			4,243*
182	TX Tripper 1500 De Luxe			—
183	TX Tripper 2000 Sprint			4,895*
	TIMMIS (Canada)			
271	Ford V8 Roadster			30,000
	TOFAS (Turkey)			
336	Murat 131			—
	TOMORROWS CLASSIC (USA)			
333	1953 Corvette Roadster Replica			14,500
334	Auburn Phaeton			35,000
	TORO (Philippines)			
392	1300			—
	TOTAL REPLICA (USA)			
333	Hi Boy			15,500
333	Ford «B» Phaeton			22,500
	TOYOTA (Japan)			
379	Starlet DX 2+1-dr Sedan	3,044*		710,000
379	Starlet DX 4+1-dr Sedan	3,141*		735,000
379	Starlet XL 2+1-dr Sedan	3,273*		755,000
379	Starlet XL 4+1-dr Sedan	3,375*		780,000
379	Starlet S 2+1-dr Sedan			808,000*
379	Starlet S 4+1-dr Sedan			833,000
379	Starlet SE 2+1-dr Sedan			828,000
379	Starlet SE 4+1-dr Sedan			853,000
380	Tercel 1300 2-dr Standard Sedan		3,698*	694,000
380	Tercel 1300 2-dr De Luxe Sedan		4,148*	753,000
380	Tercel 1300 2+1-dr De Luxe Sedan		4,298*	773,000
380	Tercel 1300 2+1-dr Hi De Luxe Sedan			819,000
380	Tercel 1300 4-dr De Luxe Sedan			778,000
380	Tercel 1300 4-dr Hi De Luxe Sedan			824,000
380	Corsa 1300 2-dr Standard Sedan			700,000
380	Corsa 1300 2-dr De Luxe Sedan			759,000
380	Corsa 1300 2+1-dr De Luxe Sedan			779,000
380	Corsa 1300 4-dr De Luxe Sedan			784,000
380	Corsa 1300 4-dr GL Sedan			836,000
380	Tercel 1500 2+1-dr De Luxe Sedan			808,000
380	Tercel 1500 2+1-dr Hi De Luxe Sedan			854,000
380	Tercel 1500 S 2+1-dr Sedan			928,000
380	Tercel 1500 SE 2+1-dr Sedan			942,000
380	Tercel 1500 De Luxe 4-dr Sedan			819,000
380	Tercel 1500 Hi De Luxe 4-dr Sedan			859,000

Page	MAKE AND MODEL	Price in GB £	Price in USA $	Price ex Works
380	Tercel 1500 SE 4-dr Sedan			947,000
380	Corsa 1500 2+1-dr De Luxe Sedan			814,000
380	Corsa 1500 2+1-dr GL Sedan			869,000
380	Corsa 1500 2+1-dr S Sedan			936,000
380	Corsa 1500 GSL 2+1-dr Sedan			950,000
380	Corsa 1500 De Luxe 4-dr Sedan			819,000
380	Corsa 1500 GL 4-dr Sedan			871,000
380	Corsa 1500 GSL 4-dr Sedan			955,000
380	Corolla 1300 2-dr Standard Sedan		4,098*	718,000
380	Corolla 1300 2-dr DX Sedan		4,638*	773,000
380	Corolla 1300 2-dr GL Sedan			829,000
380	Corolla 1300 4-dr Standard Sedan			743,000
380	Corolla 1300 4-dr Custom De Luxe Sedan		4,758*	771,000
380	Corolla 1300 4-dr DX Sedan			798,000
380	Corolla 1300 4-dr GL Sedan			854,000
380	Corolla 1300 Hardtop DX			834,000
380	Corolla 1300 Hardtop GL			882,000
380	Corolla 1300 Coupé DX		5,048*	844,000
381	Corolla 1300 Coupé GL			904,000
381	Corolla 1300 Liftback DX		4,998*	854,000
381	Corolla 1300 Liftback GL			914,000
381	Corolla 1500 4-dr DX Sedan			844,000
381	Corolla 1500 4-dr GL Sedan			899,000
381	Corolla 1500 4-dr SE Sedan			977,000
381	Corolla 1500 Hardtop GL			927,000
381	Corolla 1500 Hardtop SE			1,008,000
381	Corolla 1500 Coupé SL			949,000
381	Corolla 1500 Coupé SR			1,043,000
381	Corolla 1500 Liftback GL			959,000
381	Corolla 1500 Liftback SE			1,045,000
381	Corolla 1600 4-dr GT Sedan			1,285,000
381	Corolla 1600 Hardtop GT			1,326,000
381	Corolla 1600 Coupé Levin			1,343,000
381	Corolla 1600 Liftback GT	3,780*		1,360,000
381	Corolla 1800 4-dr GL Sedan			970,000
381	Corolla 1800 4-dr SE Sedan			1,051,000
381	Corolla 1800 Hardtop GL			998,000
381	Corolla 1800 Hardtop SE			1,082,000
381	Corolla 1800 Coupé SL			1,020,000
381	Corolla 1800 Coupé SR			1,152,000
381	Corolla 1800 Liftback GL			1,030,000
381	Corolla 1800 Liftback SE			1,119,000
382	Sprinter 1300 4-dr Sedan DX			813,000
382	Sprinter 1300 4-dr Sedan XL			869,000
382	Sprinter 1300 Hardtop DX			849,000
382	Sprinter 1300 Hardtop XL			897,000
382	Sprinter 1300 Coupé DX			859,000
382	Sprinter 1300 Coupé ST			919,000
382	Sprinter 1300 Liftback DX			869,000
382	Sprinter 1300 Liftback XL			929,000
382	Sprinter 1500 4-dr Sedan DX			859,000
382	Sprinter 1500 4-dr Sedan XL			914,000
382	Sprinter 1500 4-dr Sedan SE			992,000
382	Sprinter 1500 Hardtop XL			942,000
382	Sprinter 1500 Hardtop SE			1,023,000
382	Sprinter 1500 Coupé ST			964,000
382	Sprinter 1500 Coupé SR			1,058,000
382	Sprinter 1500 Liftback XL			974,000
382	Sprinter 1500 Liftback SE			1,060,000
382	Sprinter 1600 GT 4-dr Sedan			1,300,000
382	Sprinter 1600 GT Hardtop			1,341,000
382	Sprinter 1600 Coupé Trueno			1,358,000
382	Sprinter 1600 GT Liftback			1,375,000
382	Sprinter 1800 4-dr Sedan XL			985,000
382	Sprinter 1800 4-dr Sedan SE			1,066,000
382	Sprinter 1800 Hardtop XL			1,013,000
382	Sprinter 1800 Hardtop SE			1,097,000
382	Sprinter 1800 Coupé ST			1,035,000
382	Sprinter 1800 Coupé SR			1,167,000
382	Sprinter 1800 Liftback XL			1,045,000
382	Sprinter 1800 Liftback SE			1,134,000
383	Carina 1600 Standard 2-dr Sedan			855,000
383	Carina 1600 Standard 4-dr Sedan			875,000

Page	MAKE AND MODEL	Price in GB £	Price in USA $	Price ex Works
383	Carina 1600 De Luxe 2-dr Sedan			922,000
383	Carina 1600 De Luxe 4-dr Sedan	3,841*		942,000
383	Carina 1600 De Luxe Hardtop			977,000
383	Carina 1600 Super De Luxe 4-dr Sedan			971,000
383	Carina 1600 Super De Luxe Hardtop			1,006,000
383	Carina 1600 ST 4-dr Sedan			1,046,000
383	Carina 1600 ST Hardtop			1,096,000
383	Carina 1600 SR Hardtop			1,091,000
383	Carina 1600 GT 4-dr Sedan			1,391,000
383	Carina 1600 GT Hardtop			1,426,000
383	Carina 1800 De Luxe 4-dr Sedan			999,000
383	Carina 1800 De Luxe Hardtop			1,097,000
383	Carina 1800 Super De Luxe 4-dr Sedan			1,133,000
383	Carina 1800 Super De Luxe Hardtop			1,183,000
383	Carina 1800 ST 4-dr Sedan			1,194,000
383	Carina 1800 ST Hardtop			1,238,000
383	Carina 1800 SE 4-dr Sedan			1,182,000
383	Carina 1800 SE Hardtop			1,193,000
383	Carina 1800 SR Hardtop			1,243,000
383	Carina 1800 EFI ST 4-dr Sedan			1,232,000
383	Carina 1800 EFI ST Hardtop			1,212,000
383	Carina 1800 EFI SR Hardtop			1,253,000
383	Carina 2000 SE 4-dr Sedan			1,296,000
383	Carina 2000 SE Hardtop			1,259,000
383	Carina 2000 GT 4-dr Sedan			1,501,000
383	Carina 2000 GT Hardtop			1,536,000
384	Celica 1600 ET Coupé			985,000
384	Celica 1600 LT Coupé			1,045,000
384	Celica 1600 LT Liftback			1,125,000
384	Celica 1600 ST Coupé	4,333*		1,095,000
384	Celica 1600 ST Liftback			1,175,000
384	Celica 1600 XT Coupé			1,130,000
384	Celica 1600 XT Liftback			1,226,000
384	Celica 1600 GT Coupé			1,467,000
384	Celica 1600 GT Liftback			1,563,000
384	Celica 1800 ST Coupé			1,125,000
384	Celica 1800 ST Liftback			1,205,000
384	Celica 1800 XT Coupé			1,160,000
384	Celica 1800 XT Liftback			1,256,000
385	Celica 1800 SE Coupé			1,284,000
385	Celica 1800 SE Liftback			1,380,000
385	Celica 1800 EFI ST Coupé			1,208,000
385	Celica 1800 EFI ST Liftback			1,288,000
385	Celica 2000 XT Coupé	5,463*		1,213,000
385	Celica 2000 XT Liftback			1,309,000
385	Celica 2000 SE Coupé			1,314,000
385	Celica 2000 SE Liftback	4,723*		1,410,000
385	Celica 2000 XX-L Liftback			1,466,000
385	Celica 2000 XX-S Liftback			1,576,000
385	Celica 2000 XX-G Liftback			1,696,000
385	Celica 2000 GT Rally Coupé			1,440,000
385	Celica 2000 GT Rally Liftback			1,536,000
385	Celica 2000 GT Coupé	5,768*		1,577,000
385	Celica 2000 GT Liftback			1,673,000
385	Celica 2600 XX-S Liftback			1,713,000
385	Celica 2600 XX-G Liftback			1,839,000
386	Celica Supra ST Hardtop		5,899*	—
386	Celica Supra GT Hardtop		6,429*	—
386	Celica Supra GT Liftback		6,659*	—
386	Corona 1600 Standard 4-dr Sedan			897,000
386	Corona 1600 De Luxe 4-dr Sedan		5,719*	989,000
386	Corona 1600 De Luxe Hardtop			1,024,000
386	Corona 1600 De Luxe Liftback			1,039,000
386	Corona 1600 GL 4-dr Sedan			1,046,000
386	Corona 1600 GL Hardtop			1,081,000
386	Corona 1600 GL Liftback			1,096,000
386	Corona 1600 SL 4-dr Sedan			1,107,000
386	Corona 1600 SL Hardtop			1,145,000
386	Corona 1600 SL Liftback			1,157,000
386	Corona 1800 De Luxe 4-dr Sedan			1,022,000
386	Corona 1800 De Luxe Hardtop			1,057,000
386	Corona 1800 De Luxe Liftback	5,269*		1,072,000
386	Corona 1800 GL 4-dr Sedan			1,107,000
386	Corona 1800 GL Hardtop			1,142,000
386	Corona 1800 GL Liftback			1,169,000
386	Corona 1800 SL 4-dr Sedan			1,169,000
386	Corona 1800 SL Hardtop			1,207,000
386	Corona 1800 SL Liftback			1,231,000
386	Corona 1800 SL Touring 4-dr Sedan			1,291,000
386	Corona 1800 SL Touring Hardtop			1,329,000
386	Corona 1800 SL Touring Liftback			1,355,000
386	Corona 2000 GL 4-dr Sedan			1,162,000
386	Corona 2000 GL Hardtop			1,197,000
386	Corona 2000 GL Liftback			1,224,000
386	Corona 2000 SL 4-dr Sedan			1,219,000
386	Corona 2000 SL Hardtop			1,257,000
386	Corona 2000 SL Liftback			1,281,000
386	Corona 2000 CX 4-dr Sedan			1,307,000
386	Corona 2000 CX Hardtop			1,342,000
386	Corona 2000 CX Liftback			1,371,000
386	Corona 2000 GT 4-dr Sedan			1,528,000
386	Corona 2000 GT Hardtop			1,571,000
386	Corona 2000 GT Liftback			1,592,000
388	Mark II 1800 Standard 4-dr Sedan			990,000
388	Mark II 1800 De Luxe 4-dr Sedan			1,066,000
388	Mark II 1800 De Luxe 2-dr Hardtop			1,107,000
388	Chaser 1800 De Luxe 4-dr Sedan			1,072,000
388	Chaser 1800 De Luxe 2-dr Hardtop			1,113,000
388	Mark II 1800 GL 4-dr Sedan			1,127,000
388	Mark II 1800 GL 2-dr Hardtop			1,169,000
388	Chaser 1800 XL 4-dr Sedan			1,133,000
388	Chaser 1800 XL 2-dr Hardtop			1,174,000
388	Mark II 2000 De Luxe 4-dr Sedan			1,096,000
388	Mark II 2000 De Luxe 2-dr Hardtop			1,137,000
388	Chaser 2000 De Luxe 4-dr Sedan			1,102,000
388	Chaser 2000 De Luxe 4-dr Hardtop			1,143,000
388	Mark II 2000 GL 4-dr Sedan			1,157,000
388	Mark II 2000 GL 2-dr Hardtop			1,198,000
388	Chaser 2000 XL 4-dr Sedan			1,163,000
388	Chaser 2000 XL 4-dr Hardtop			1,204,000
388	Chaser 2000 GS 4-dr Sedan			1,284,000
388	Chaser 2000 GS 4-dr Hardtop			1,362,000
388	Mark II 2000 GSL 4-dr Sedan			1,278,000
388	Mark II 2000 GSL 2-dr Hardtop			1,354,000
388	Chaser 2000 SXL 4-dr Sedan			1,366,000
388	Chaser 2000 SXL 2-dr Hardtop			1,438,000
388	Mark II 2000 LG 4-dr Sedan			1,459,000
388	Mark II 2000 LG 2-dr Hardtop			1,531,000
388	Chaser 2000 SGS 4-dr Sedan			1,482,000
388	Chaser 2000 SGS 2-dr Hardtop			1,554,000
388	Mark II 2000 LG Touring 4-dr Sedan			1,516,000
388	Mark II 2000 LG Touring 2-dr Hardtop			1,588,000
388	Chaser 2000 SG Touring 4-dr Sedan			1,608,000
388	Chaser 2000 SG Touring 2-dr Hardtop			1,645,000
388	Mark II 2000 Grande 4-dr Sedan			1,835,000
388	Mark II 2000 Grande 2-dr Hardtop			1,872,000
388	Mark II 2600 Grande 4-dr Sedan			—
388	Mark II 2600 Grande 2-dr Hardtop			2,092,000
388	Mark II Diesel DX 4-dr Sedan			1,243,000
388	Mark II Diesel GL 4-dr Sedan			1,304,000
388	Mark II Diesel GL-Extra 4-dr Sedan			1,404,000
390	Century D 4-dr Sedan			4,276,000
390	Century C 4-dr Sedan			3,876,000
390	Landcruiser FJ56V-K		8,998*	—
391	Landcruiser K-BJ41V-KCY		7,768*	—
391	Crown 2000 Standard Sedan			1,313,000
391	Crown 2000 De Luxe A Sedan			1,423,000
391	Crown 2000 De Luxe Sedan			1,554,000
391	Crown 2000 Super De Luxe Sedan			1,740,000
391	Crown 2000 De Luxe 4-dr Hardtop			1,544,000
391	Crown 2000 EFI Super De Luxe Sedan			1,833,000
391	Crown 2000 EFI Super Saloon Sedan			2,080,000
391	Crown 2000 EFI Super ED 2-dr Hardtop			1,961,000
391	Crown 2000 EFI Super Saloon 2-dr Hardtop			2,197,000

Page	MAKE AND MODEL	Price in GB £	Price in USA $	Price ex Works
391	Crown 2000 EFI Custom ED 4-dr Hardtop			1,808,000
391	Crown 2000 EFI Super ED 4-dr Hardtop			1,998,000
391	Crown 2000 EFI Super Saloon 4-dr Hardtop			2,224,000
391	Crown 2800 Super Saloon Sedan			2,360,000
391	Crown 2800 Royal Saloon Sedan			2,702,000
391	Crown 2800 Super Saloon 4-dr Hardtop			2,489,000
391	Crown 2800 Royal Saloon 4-dr Hardtop			2,724,000
391	Crown 2800 Royal Saloon 2-dr Hardtop			2,745,000
391	Crown 2200 Diesel Standard Sedan			1,407,000
391	Crown 2200 Diesel De Luxe A Sedan			1,521,000
391	Crown 2200 Diesel De Luxe Sedan			1,651,000
391	Crown 2200 Diesel Super De Luxe Sedan			1,833,000
391	Crown 2200 Diesel Custom ED 4-dr Hardtop			1,760,000
	TRABANT (Germany DDR)			
100	601 Limousine			—
100	601 Universal			—
	TRIUMPH (Great Britain)			
183	Dolomite 1300			3,997*
183	Dolomite 1500			4,299*
183	Dolomite 1500 HL			4,799*
183	Dolomite 1850 HL			5,365*
183	Dolomite Sprint			6,539*
184	Spitfire 1500		7,365*	4,308*
184	TR 7		8,465*	5,755*
	TVR (Great Britain)			
185	Tasmin			12,800*
185	3000 M Coupé			7,995*
185	Convertible 3000 S			8,730*
185	Turbo Coupé			11,995*
185	Convertible Turbo			12,730*
185	Taimar Hatchback Coupé			8,984*
185	Taimar Turbo Hatchback Coupé			12,984*
	VAZ (USSR)			
240	469 B			—
	VANDEN PLAS (Great Britain)			
186	1500			5,265*
	VAUXHALL (Great Britain)			
187	Chevette E 2-dr Saloon			2,921*
187	Chevette E 4-dr Saloon			3,047*
187	Chevette E 2+1-dr Hatchback			2,969*
187	Chevette L 2-dr Saloon			3,209*
187	Chevette L 4-dr Saloon			3,335*
187	Chevette L 2+1-dr Hatchback			3,257*
187	Chevette L 4+1-dr Estate Car			3,645*
187	Chevette GL 4-dr Saloon			3,705*
187	Chevette GL 2+1-dr Hatchback			3,627*
187	Chevette 2300 HS 2+1-dr Hatchback			5,939*
187	Cavalier 1300 L 2-dr Saloon			3,657*
187	Cavalier 1300 L 4-dr Saloon			3,782*
187	Cavalier 1600 L 2-dr Saloon			3,863*
187	Cavalier 1600 L 4-dr Saloon			3,989*
187	Cavalier 1600 GL 4-dr Saloon			4,451*
187	Cavalier 1600 GL 2+1-dr Sports Hatchback			4,768*
187	Cavalier 1600 GLS 2+1-dr Sports Hatchback			5,230*

Page	MAKE AND MODEL	Price in GB £	Price in USA $	Price ex Works
187	Cavalier 2000 GL 4-dr Saloon			4,694*
187	Cavalier 2000 GLS 4-dr Saloon			5,157*
187	Cavalier 2000 GLS 2+1-dr Sports Hatchback			5,473*
188	Astra GL Hatchback			4,602*
188	Astra L Estate Car			4,373*
189	Carlton 2000 Saloon			5,627*
189	Carlton 2000 Estate Car			6,197*
189	Royale Saloon			9,711*
190	Royale Coupé			10,069*
	VAZ (USSR)			
241	Lada 1200 4-dr Sedan	2,280*		—
241	Lada 1200 4+1-dr Combi	2,591*		—
241	Lada 1300 ES 4-dr Sedan	2,678*		—
241	Lada 1500 4-dr Sedan	—		—
241	Lada 1500 4+1-dr Combi	2,735*		—
241	Lada 1500 ES 4+1-dr Combi	3,099*		—
241	Lada 1600 4-dr Sedan	2,950*		—
241	Lada 1600 ES 4-dr Sedan	3,350*		—
242	Lada Niva 2121 4x4	4,273*		—
	VOLKSWAGEN (Brazil)			
265	1300			102,000
265	1300 L			106,000
265	1600 Limousine			110,000
265	Passat Surf 2-dr Limousine			164,000
265	Passat LS 2-dr Limousine			178,000
265	Passat LS 2+1-dr Limousine			184,000
265	Passat LS 4-dr Limousine			184,000
265	Passat TS 2-dr Limousine			199,000
265	Passat LSE 4-dr Limousine			214,000
266	Brasilia 2-dr Limousine			133,000
266	Brasilia 4-dr Limousine			134,000
266	Brasilia LS Limousine			144,000
266	Variant II			169,000
	VOLKSWAGEN (Germany FR)			
135	Polo Limousine	3,115*		9,403*
135	Polo L Limousine	3,439*		10,079*
135	Polo GL Limousine			10,886*
135	Polo S Limousine			9,736*
135	Polo LS Limousine			10,412*
135	Polo GLS Limousine	3,800*		11,219*
135	Polo GT Limousine			—
136	Derby Limousine			9,797*
136	Derby L Limousine			10,473*
136	Derby GL Limousine			11,103*
136	Derby S Limousine	3,301*		10,130*
136	Derby LS Limousine	3,650*		10,809*
136	Derby GLS Limousine	4,005*		11,436*
136	Derby CL Limousine			—
136	Derby CLS Limousine			—
136	Golf 2+1-dr Limousine	3,451*		10,463*
136	Golf 4+1-dr Limousine			11,043*
136	Golf 2+1-dr L Limousine			11,229*
136	Golf 4+1-dr L Limousine	3,918*		11,809*
136	Golf 2+1-dr GL Limousine			12,082*
136	Golf 4+1-dr GL Limousine			12,662*
136	Golf 2+1-dr S Limousine			11,144*
136	Golf 4+1-dr S Limousine			11,724*
136	Golf 2+1-dr LS Limousine	4,105*		11,910*
136	Golf 4+1-dr LS Limousine			12,490*
136	Golf 2+1-dr GLS Limousine			12,763*
136	Golf 4+1-dr GLS Limousine	4,572*		13,343*
136	Golf 2+1-dr GTI Limousine	5,444*		16,133*
136	Golf 2-dr GLS Cabriolet		8,895*	17,389*
136	Golf 2-dr GLI Cabriolet			20,052*
137	Golf Diesel 2+1-dr D Limousine			12,027*

Page	MAKE AND MODEL	Price in GB £	Price in USA $	Price ex Works
137	Golf Diesel 4+1-dr D Limousine			12,607*
137	Golf Diesel 2+1-dr LD Limousine			12,793*
137	Golf Diesel 4+1-dr LD Limousine	4,734*		13,374*
137	Golf Diesel 2+1-dr GLD Limousine			13,646*
137	Golf Diesel 4+1-dr GLD Limousine			14,226*
138	1200 L			8,505*
138	Scirocco Coupé			13,610*
138	Scirocco L Coupé			14,674*
138	Scirocco S Coupé			14,185*
138	Scirocco LS Coupé			15,249*
138	Scirocco GT Coupé			15,789*
138	Scirocco GL Coupé		7,745*	16,566*
138	Scirocco GTI Coupé			18,690*
138	Scirocco GLI Coupé	6,680*		19,467*
139	Jetta 2-dr Limousine			11,395*
139	Jetta 4-dr Limousine			11,975*
139	Jetta 2-dr L Limousine			12,190*
139	Jetta 4-dr L Limousine			12,770*
139	Jetta 2-dr GL Limousine			13,170*
139	Jetta 4-dr GL Limousine			13,750*
139	Jetta 2-dr S Limousine			12,070*
139	Jetta 4-dr S Limousine			12,650*
139	Jetta 2-dr LS Limousine			12,865*
139	Jetta 4-dr LS Limousine			13,445*
139	Jetta 2-dr GLS Limousine			13,845*
139	Jetta 4-dr GLS Limousine			14,425*
139	Jetta 2-dr LI Limousine			14,855*
139	Jetta 4-dr LI Limousine			15,435*
139	Jetta 2-dr GLI Limousine			15,835*
139	Jetta 4-dr GLI Limousine			16,415*
140	Passat 2+1-dr Limousine			12,258*
140	Passat 4+1-dr Limousine			12,849*
140	Passat 4+1-dr Variant	5,370*		13,247*
140	Passat 2+1-dr L Limousine			13,076*
140	Passat 4+1-dr L Limousine			13,666*
140	Passat 4+1-dr L Variant			14,064*
140	Passat 2+1-dr GL Limousine			14,064*
140	Passat 4+1-dr GL Limousine			14,655*
140	Passat 4+1-dr GL Variant			15,053*
140	Passat 2+1-dr S Limousine			12,778*
140	Passat 4+1-dr S Limousine			13,369*
140	Passat 4+1-dr S Variant			13,767*
140	Passat 2+1-dr LS Limousine	5,071*	7,590*	13,596*
140	Passat 4+1-dr LS Limousine		7,790*	14,186*
140	Passat 4+1-dr LS Variant		8,070*	14,584*
140	Passat 2+1-dr GLS Limousine	5,500*		14,584*
140	Passat 4+1-dr GLS Limousine			15,175*
140	Passat 4+1-dr GLS Variant	5,862*		15,573*
140	Passat 2+1-dr GLI Limousine			16,506*
140	Passat 4+1-dr GLI Limousine			17,098*
140	Passat 4+1-dr GLI Variant			17,495*
141	Passat Diesel 2+1-dr D Limousine			13,918*
141	Passat Diesel 4+1-dr D Limousine			14,509*
141	Passat 4+1-dr D Variant			14,907*
141	Passat 2+1-dr LD Limousine		8,110*	14,737*
141	Passat 4+1-dr LD Limousine		8,310*	15,326*
141	Passat 4+1-dr LD Variant	5,784*	8,590*	15,724*
141	Passat 2+1-dr GLD Limousine			15,724*
141	Passat 4+1-dr GLD Limousine			16,315*
141	Passat 4+1-dr GLD Variant			16,713*
141	Iltis			—
	VOLKSWAGEN (Mexico)			
271	1200 L			—
272	181			—
	VOLKSWAGEN (Nigeria)			
338	1200			—
339	Igala			—

Page	MAKE AND MODEL	Price in GB £	Price in USA $	Price ex Works
	VOLKSWAGEN (USA)			
334	Rabbit 2+1-dr Hatchback			4,995
334	Rabbit 2+1-dr Custom Hatchback			5,475
334	Rabbit 4+1-dr Custom Hatchback			5,650
334	Rabbit 2+1-dr De Luxe Hatchback			5,875
334	Rabbit 4+1-dr De Luxe Hatchback			6,050
	VOLVO (Holland)			
190	66 L			13,700*
190	66 DL			14,770*
190	66 GL			15,540
190	343 L			16,690
190	343 DL (manual)	4,151*		17,890
190	343 DL (automatic)	4,375*		19,090
190	343 GL			19,090
190	345 L			17,590
190	345 DL	4,450*		18,790
190	345 GL			19,990
	VOLVO (Sweden)			
233	244 DL 4-dr Sedan	5,995*	7,970*	—
233	244 GL 4-dr Sedan	7,379*	11,385*	—
233	244 GL "S" 4-dr Sedan	—	—	—
233	244 GLE 4-dr Sedan	7,996*	12,985*	—
233	244 GLT 4-dr Sedan	—	—	—
233	245 DL 4+1-dr St. Wagon	6,736*	8,565*	—
233	245 GL 4+1-dr St. Wagon	7,450*	—	—
233	245 GLE 4+1-dr St. Wagon	8,110*	12,985*	—
233	242 GT 2-dr Sedan	—	9,800*	—
233	244 GL D6 4-dr Sedan	—	—	—
233	245 GL D6 4+1-dr St. Wagon	—	—	—
234	264 GL 4-dr Sedan	8,556*	—	—
234	264 GLE 4-dr Sedan	9,706*	—	—
234	265 GL 4+1-dr St. Wagon	8,713*	—	—
234	265 GLE 4+1-dr St. Wagon	9,509*	—	—
234	262 C 2-dr Coupé	14,287*	17,345*	—
	WARTBURG (Germany DDR)			
100	353 W			—
101	353 W Tourist			—
101	353 De Luxe			—
	YLN (Taiwan)			
350	902 SD			—
350	803 DL			—
350	302 DX			—
350	805 SD			—
	ZAZ (USSR)			
242	968-A			—
242	969-A 4x4			—
	ZCZ (Yugoslavia)			
243	Zastava 750 LC			—
243	Zastava 750 M			—
244	Zastava 750 SC			—
244	Zastava 101 B			—
244	Zastava 101 Comfort			—
244	Zastava 101 SC			—
244	Zastava 101 Mediteran			—
244	Zastava 101 Special			—
	ZIL (USSR)			
243	114 Limousine			—
243	117 Limousine			—